ST. JAMES GUIDE TO
FANTASY WRITERS

Twentieth-Century Writers Series
(now St. James Guide to Writers Series)

Twentieth-Century Children's Writers
Twentieth-Century Crime and Mystery Writers
Twentieth-Century Romance and Historical Writers
Twentieth-Century Western Writers
Twentieth-Century Young Adult Writers

St. James Guide to Fantasy Writers
St. James Guide to Science Fiction Writers

ST. JAMES GUIDE TO
FANTASY WRITERS

FIRST EDITION

EDITOR
DAVID PRINGLE

ST. JAMES PRESS
An ITP Information/Reference Group Company

I(T)P
Changing the Way the World Learns

NEW YORK • LONDON • BONN • BOSTON • DETROIT • MADRID
MELBOURNE • MEXICO CITY • PARIS • SINGAPORE • TOKYO
TORONTO • WASHINGTON • ALBANY NY • BELMONT CA • CINCINNATI OH

David Pringle, *Editor*
Mike Ashley, Brian Stableford, *Contributing Editors*

ST. JAMES PRESS STAFF

David Collins, *Project Editor*

Margaret Mazurkiewicz, Michael J. Tyrkus, *Associate Editors*
Laura Standley Berger, Joann Cerrito, Nicolet V. Elert, Miranda H. Ferrara, Janice Jorgensen, *Contributing Editors*

Peter M. Gareffa, *Managing Editor*

Mary Beth Trimper, *Production Director*
Shanna Heilveil, *Production Assistant*
Cynthia Baldwin, *Art Director*

Victoria B. Cariappa, *Research Manager*
Barbara McNeil, *Research Specialist*

♾️ This book is printed on acid-free paper that meets the minimum requirements of American National Standard for Information Sciences—Permanence Paper for Printed Library Materials, ANSI Z39.48-1984.

ISBN 1-55862-205-5
Printed in the United States of America

I(T)P™   Gale Research Inc., an International Thomson Publishing Company.
ITP logo is a trademark under license.

10 9 8 7 6 5 4 3 2 1

CONTENTS

EDITOR'S NOTE

This work was conceived as the first of a two-volume set, the second to be entitled the *St. James Guide to Horror, Ghost, and Gothic Writers*. Hence the omission from the present volume of certain writers who, in the view of some readers, might have been expected to be included. Edgar Allan Poe, Algernon Blackwood, H. P. Lovecraft, Ray Bradbury, Stephen King and several hundred others, many of whom have written at least some fantasy fiction, will be covered in the forthcoming volume.

So this book endeavours to avoid comment on horror and gothic fiction (even though some overlaps of coverage are inevitable), concentrating instead on those types of fiction which may be regarded as "pure" fantasy: tales of magic, heroic fantasy, sword and sorcery, humorous fantasy, adult fairy tales, animal fantasy, timeslip romances, Arabian-Nights tales and chinoiserie, fantastic allegories, and fabulations. Although the emphasis is mainly on adult fiction, many children's fantasists who remain popular with adults are also included.

Of course, there is no such as thing as "purity" in the matter of literary genres, least of all in a field as protean as fantasy. Nevertheless, fantasy as a perceived type of modern fiction, regarded by most readers as quite distinct from horror and science fiction, is here to stay. Indeed, fantasy is one of the fastest-growing and most popular of present-day publishers' categories. Its origins may be traced back through the 17th, 18th, and 19th centuries—to Charles Perrault, the Brothers Grimm, Hans Christian Andersen, Lewis Carroll, William Morris, and many others—but it is only since the huge success of J.R.R. Tolkien's *The Lord of the Rings* and Robert E. Howard's "Conan" adventures, in their paperback editions of the 1960s, that fantasy has become a widely recognized genre. Since then, it has produced a large number of highly-praised (and in some cases bestselling) practitioners, most of whom have entries herein.

Following the established St. James Press style, each entry consists of a brief biography (where the facts have been available), a complete list of works, and a signed critical essay. In addition, many of the living authors were invited to comment on their own work. Original British and United States editions of all books have been listed (where known), and series titles/characters/locations have been indicated for fantasy publications. Entries include notations of film adaptations, and of critical studies; other critical materials are noted in the separate Reading List of secondary works on fantasy.

ACKNOWLEDGEMENTS

I should like to thank everyone who contributed to this book, from Jack Adrian to Jessica Yates, and not forgetting many of the entrants themselves who took time to provide facts and to write short statements about their work. But in particular I should like to give thanks to my two advisers, Mike Ashley and Brian Stableford. Each has a prodigious knowledge of the field, and each has added greatly to this volume; neither, however, should be blamed for any errors or omissions—those, alas, are the editor's responsibility.

ADVISERS

Mike Ashley   Brian Stableford

CONTRIBUTORS

Jack Adrian
Graham Andrews
Mike Ashley
K.V. Bailey
David V. Barrett
Steve Behrends
Wendy Bradley
Sandra Brandenburg
Paul Brazier
Mary Corran
Ian Covell
Mat Coward
Pete Crowther
Shira Daemon
Don D'Ammassa
Janice M. Eisen
Paul Di Filippo
Peter T. Garratt
Chris Gilmore
John Grant
Debora Hill
Liz Holliday
Robert Irwin

Edward James
Ben Jeapes
Neil Jones
S.T. Joshi
Cosette Kies
Paul Kincaid
David Langford
Rob Latham
Paul J. McAuley
Sally-Ann Melia
Chris Morgan
Pauline Morgan
Kim Newman
Stan Nicholls
Andy Sawyer
Darrell Schweitzer
Maureen Speller
Brian Stableford
Lucya Szachnowski
Lisa Tuttle
Gary Westfahl
Martin Morse Wooster
Jessica Yates

ST. JAMES GUIDE TO
FANTASY WRITERS

Donald Aamodt
Lynn Abbey
Achmed Abdullah
Dafydd ab Hugh
Gilbert Adair
Richard Adams
Patrick H. Adkins
Joan Aiken
Lloyd Alexander
Marc Alexander
Poul Anderson
F. Anstey
Piers Anthony
Eleanor Arnason
Edwin L. Arnold
David Arscott and David J. Marl
Constance Ash
Robert Asprin

Richard Bach
Robin Bailey
Frank Baker
John Kendrick Bangs
J.M. Barrie
John Barth
Donald Barthelme
Gael Baudino
L. Frank Baum
Peter S. Beagle
Helen Beauclerk
H. Bedford-Jones
Max Beerbohm
Clare Bell
John Bellairs
Stella Benson
Nancy Varian Berberick
Thomas Berger
Terry Bisson
James P. Blaylock
Hannes Bok
L.M. Boston
Elizabeth H. Boyer
Steven R. Boyett
Marion Zimmer Bradley
Gillian Bradshaw
Ernest Bramah
Richard Brautigan
Mayer Alan Brenner
K.M. Briggs
Terry Brooks
Mary Brown
Mildred Downey Broxon
Steven Brust
Emma Bull
Gerald Bullett
Richard Burns
Edgar Rice Burroughs
Linda E. Bushyager

James Branch Cabell
Moyra Caldecott

Orson Scott Card
Jonathan Carroll
Lewis Carroll
Angela Carter
Lin Carter
Joy Chant
Vera Chapman
Robert N. Charrette
C.J. Cherryh
G.K. Chesterton
Grace Chetwin
Lucie M. Chin
Molly Cochran
Adrian Cole
Allan Cole and Chris Bunch
John Collier
Glen Cook
Hugh Cook
Louise Cooper
Susan Cooper
W.J. Corbett
Marie Corelli
Mary Corran
Juanita Coulson
John Crowley

Kara Dalkey
Annie Dalton
W.A. Darlington
Avram Davidson
Grania Davis
Pamela Dean
L. Sprague de Camp
John DeChancie
Tom De Haven
Tom Deitz
Samuel R. Delany
Charles de Lint
Ian Dennis
Susan Dexter
Graham Diamond
Gordon R. Dickson
Stephen R. Donaldson
Carole Nelson Douglas
Wayland Drew
Diane Duane
Dave Duncan
Lord Dunsany
James Francis Dwyer

Edward Eager
M. Coleman Easton
David Eddings
E.R. Eddison
Teresa Edgerton
Claudia J. Edwards
Graham Edwards
Phyllis Eisenstein
Ru Emerson
Carol Emshwiller
John Erskine

Lloyd Arthur Eshbach
Rose Estes

Penelope Farmer
Raymond E. Feist
Bruce Fergusson
Timothy Findley
Charles G. Finney
Jack Finney
Pauline Fisk
Kenneth C. Flint
John M. Ford
Alan Dean Foster
Gardner F. Fox
Ronald Fraser
Michael Frayn
Esther M. Friesner
Nigel Frith
Maggie Furey

Paul Gallico
R. Garcia y Robertson
Craig Shaw Gardner
John Gardner
Alan Garner
David Garnett
Richard Garnett
Randall Garrett
Jane Gaskell
Patricia Geary
David A. Gemmell
Mary Gentle
Keren Gilfoyle
Alexis A. Gilliland
Sheila Gilluly
Parke Godwin
William Goldman
Lisa Goldstein
Terry Goodkind
Deborah Grabien
Kenneth Grahame
Joan Grant
John Grant
Roland J. Green
Sharon Green
Simon R. Green
Colin Greenland
Joyce Ballou Gregorian
Ken Grimwood
Stephan Grundy
Neil M. Gunn
Gary Gygax

H. Rider Haggard
Ann Halam
Barbara Hambly
Niel Hancock
Lyndon Hardy
Andrew Harman
Geraldine Harris
MacDonald Harris

Michael Harrison
M. John Harrison
Simon Hawke
Paul Hazel
Ben Hecht
Mark Helprin
James Hilton
Russell Hoban
Martin Hocke
P.C. Hodgell
Robert Holdstock
Tom Holt
William Horwood
Laurence Housman
Robert E. Howard
L. Ron Hubbard
Tanya Huff
Barry Hughart

Jean Ingelow
Margaret Irwin
Robert Irwin

Brian Jacques
John Jakes
John James
Mike Jefferies
Diana Wynne Jones
Jenny Jones
Robert Jordan
Norton Juster

Phyllis Ann Karr
Guy Gavriel Kay
Paul Kearney
Patrician Kennealy-Morrison
Susan Alice Kerby
Katharine Kerr
Garry Kilworth
Bernard King
Charles Kingsley
W.P. Kinsella
Rudyard Kipling
Richard A. Knaak
William Kotzwinkle
Katherine Kurtz
Ellen Kushner
Henry Kuttner

Mercedes Lackey
Andrew Lang
Noel Langley
Stephen R. Lawhead
John Lee
Tanith Lee
Ursula K. Le Guin
Fritz Leiber
C.S. Lewis
Wyndham Lewis
Megan Lindholm
David Lindsay

Holly Lisle
Penelope Lively
Morgan Llewelyn
A.R. Lloyd
Hugh Lofting
Nicholas Luard
Eric Lustbader
Elizabeth A. Lynn

R.A. MacAvoy
George MacDonald
Margaret Mahy
Laurie J. Marks
Stephen Marley
Graham Dunstan Martin
John Masefield
Norman H. Matson
Julian May
William Mayne
Dan McGirt
Patricia A. McKillip
Robin McKinley
A. Merritt
Faren Miller
Steven Millhauser
A.A. Milne
Hope Mirrlees
L.E. Modesitt, Jr.
Richard Monaco
Elizabeth Moon
Michael Moorcock
Brian Moore
C.L. Moore
John Morressy
Janet E. Morris
Jean Morris
Kenneth Morris
William Morris
James Morrow
Peter Morwood
Talbot Mundy
J. Warner Munn
Pat Murphy
Shirley Rousseau Murphy
Dwina Murphy-Gibb
John Myers Myers

Robert Nathan
E. Nesbit
Ruth Nichols
Douglas Niles
Jenny Nimmo
John Norman
Andrew Norton
Mary Norton
Alfred Noyes
Robert Nye

Flann O'Brien
Pat O'Shea
Andrew J. Offutt

Frank Owen

Norvell W. Page
Barry Pain
Diana L. Paxson
Mervyn Peake
Philippa Pearce
Steve Perry
Eden Phillpotts
Meredith Ann Pierce
Daniel Manus Pinkwater
Rachel Pollack
Tim Powers
John Cowper Powys
T.F. Powys
Terry Pratchett
Fletcher Pratt
E. Hoffmann Price

Alis A. Rasmussen
Melanie Rawn
Michael Reaves
Mickey Zucker Reichert
Jennifer Roberson
John Maddox Roberts
Michaela Roessner
Michael Scott Rohan
Kristine Kathryn Rusch
Salman Rushdie
Geoff Ryman

Fred Saberhagen
Jessica Amanda Salmonson
R.A. Salvatore
Fay Sampson
Charles R. Saunders
Elizabeth Ann Scarborough
Darrell Schweitzer
Allan Scott
George Selden
Carol Severance
Michael Shea
Delia Sherman
Will Shetterly
Susan Shwartz
James R. Silke
Andrew Sinclair
Clark Ashton Smith
Julie Dean Smith
Thorne Smith
Midori Snyder
Spedding
Nancy Springer
Mary Stanton
Christopher Stasheff
James Stephens
Francis Stevens
Caroline Stevermer
Mary Stewart
Brad Strickland
Thomas Burnett Swann

Antony Swithin

Judith Tarr
Roger Taylor
Sheri S. Tepper
James Thurber
Peter Valentine Timlett
J.R.R. Tolkien
Nikolai Tolstoy
Harry Turtledove
Mark Twain

Jack Vance
Robert E. Vardeman
George Sylvester Viereck
E. Charles Vivian
Paula Volsky

Karl Edward Wagner
Mervyn Wall
Evangeline Walton
Walter Wangerin, Jr.
Sylvia Townsend Warner
Freda Warrington
Lawrence Watt-Evans
Collin Webber
Margaret Weis
Manly Wade Wellman
Angus Wells

Martha Wells
Robert Westall
John Whitbourn
E.B. White
T.H. White
Oscar Wilde
Cherry Wilder
Vaughan Wilkins
Nancy Willard
Elizabeth Willey
Charles Williams
Michael Williams
Tad Williams
Philip G. Williamson
Connie Willis
David Henry Wilson
Jeanette Winterson
Gene Wolfe
Bridget Wood
Patricia C. Wrede
Patricia Wrightson
Janny Wurts
Jonathan Wylie

Jack Yeovil
Laurence Yep
Jane Yolen

Roger Zelazny
Paul Edwin Zimmer

FOREIGN-LANGUAGE AUTHORS

Hans Christian Andersen
Jorge Luis Borge
Italo Calvino
Madame D'Aulnoy
Michael Ende
Friedrich de la Motte Fouqué

Anatole France
Sylvie Germain
Jakob and Wilhelm Grimm
Gabriel García Márquez
Charles Perrault

AAMODT, Donald

Nationality: American.

FANTASY PUBLICATIONS

Novels

A Name to Conjure With. New York, Avon, 1989.
A Troubling Along the Border. New York, AvoNova, 1991.

*   *   *

A simultaneous strength and weakness of much genre fantasy fiction in recent years has been its predictability. On the one hand, readers can feel reasonable confidence about what they will find between the covers by reading the blurbs, sometimes just by examining the artwork. While the quality of the writing may vary, the story-line, characterization, and conventions of heroic fantasy are largely unchanged from one author to another. Unfortunately, the adverse side of this situation is that it is much more difficult to create a work that satisfies those reader expectations but also stands out enough to mark one author as significantly more interesting than another.

Donald Aamodt introduced Sandy MacGregor in *A Name to Conjure With,* his first published fiction. MacGregor is a bit of a loner who speculates about the nature of reality just in time to be abducted through a magical doorway into Zarathandra, a world of sorcery and personal combat, heroes and monsters. He has been brought there by the wizard Zhadnoboth, who expected to conjure a powerful demon with which he could assail his enemies.

This is an old, familiar, but still effective device in fantasy. The use of an Outsider as protagonist simplifies the task of explaining facets of the setting because they are new to the character as well as the reader, and the plight of someone from our own world thrown into a reality where the rules are very different has been an enduring theme in science-fiction and fantasy literature for as long as either has been written. The basic plot has been used for everything from serious high fantasy to low humour, and Aamodt attempts a bit of both here.

MacGregor is, as you might expect, a considerable disappointment to the sorcerer who pulled him across the border between worlds, but there's another level of manipulation, a master player behind the wizard. The goddess watching omnisciently from outside the action is pleased because she senses great potential in MacGregor and suspects that he will prove a powerful tool in her battle with a rival god. With three companions, MacGregor sets out on a dual quest to discover the nature of this strange new world, and to avoid death at the hands of the Zalkrings, followers of an evil god. The other members of the party are the usual array, comic-book characters one and all, an ineffectual sorcerer whose spells often go astray, a likable giant, and a mute.

What follows is a series of traditional encounters, battles and escapes, during which MacGregor gradually gains ascendancy over his companions and becomes their unofficial leader. The metaphor of the major characters as pieces in an elaborate chess game is reinforced several times, and when the evil power is finally destroyed, the goddess reveals herself. To MacGregor's dismay, she has an arrogant and petulant personality, condemns her own champion when he expresses his unhappiness with her manipulation of his life and those of his friends, although she subsequently forgives him and sets up the situation for the sequel.

Aamodt appears to have had some difficulty deciding upon the proper tone for the novel. On the one hand we have mildly humorous situations and a list of character names that seem designed to make us chuckle. On the other, we have several rather brutal killings, sometimes rather explicitly bloody, and the less than appealing nature of both sides of the major plot conflict, all of which generates a rather sombre mood. The inconsistent voices are distracting most of the time and occasionally quite jarring.

MacGregor returns in *A Troubling Along the Border,* which takes up where the first volume left off. The goddess has mellowed somewhat, apparently in an attempt to more clearly define good and evil. MacGregor leads a small band of soldiers patrolling the border of the chosen country of the goddess and that of the Rithian Empire, a powerful rival dominated by a villainous ruling elite. As is the case with most transplanted heroes, MacGregor has proven himself a skilful warrior and a fearless leader and requires only a slight nudge to embark on a new quest.

Early in this new adventure, he rescues Anala, a beautiful young woman with an unfortunate disposition, a sort of priestess of the goddess and every bit as egotistical. Zhadnoboth, the bumbling sorcerer, shows up as well for another series of mishaps and menaces, this time involving a mission to provide a charismatic leader to several disorganized border tribes who might be willing to rise up against the bellicose Rithian aristocracy under the right circumstances and with some covert aid from the goddess. She, of course, is bound by some vaguely defined rules that prohibit her from intervening personally to save her allies, a clumsy but necessary plot device.

As the protagonist and his friends confront, and overcome, werebeasts, bandits, and other dangers, Analae grows more tolerant and likable but in such a predictable fashion that there's no real sense of personality in the character. Indeed, it is in his characterization that Aamodt shows only limited improvement in his second novel, which otherwise has a tighter and more interesting plot, a disconcertingly large but more interesting cast of villains, and seems overall a much more controlled and effective work. The scenes in which MacGregor wanders through Zarathandra's version of hell are the high point of the novel.

No third adventure has yet appeared although the series is clearly designed to be open-ended. Barring the appearance of further, more original work, Sandy MacGregor will remain a two-dimensional character in a two-dimensional world. His adventures are entertaining but hardly memorable, and there is nothing to distinguish Zarathandra from scores of other fantasy worlds.

—Don D'Ammassa

ABBEY, Lynn

Nationality: American. **Born:** Marilyn Lorraine Abbey, 1948. **Family:** Married to novelist Robert Asprin, q.v.

FANTASY PUBLICATIONS

Novels (series: Elfquest; Rifkind Saga; Thieves' World; Ultima Saga; Unicorn Saga)

Daughter of the Bright Moon (Rifkind). New York, Ace, 1979.
The Black Flame (Rifkind). New York, Ace, 1980.
The Guardians. New York, Ace, 1982.
Unicorn & Dragon. New York, Avon, 1987; London, Headline, 1988.
Conquest (Unicorn). New York, Avon, 1988; as *The Green Man,* London, Headline, 1989.
The Forge of Virtue (Ultima). New York, Warner, 1991.
The Wooden Sword. New York, Ace, 1991.
Catwoman, with Robert Asprin. New York, Warner, 1992; as *Catwoman: Tiger Hunt,* London, Millennium, 1992.
The Temper of Wisdom (Ultima). New York, Warner, 1992.

Other

Editor, with Robert Asprin. *The Face of Chaos* (Thieves' World). New York, Ace, 1983; London, Titan, 1989.
Editor, with Robert Asprin. *Wings of Omen* (Thieves' World). New York, Ace, 1984; London, Titan, 1989.
Editor, with Robert Asprin. *Cross-Currents* (omnibus; includes *Storm Season* [edited by Asprin alone], *The Face of Chaos, Wings of Omen*). New York, Nelson Doubleday, 1984.
Editor, with Robert Asprin. *The Dead of Winter* (Thieves' World). New York, Ace, 1985; London, Titan, 1989.
Editor, with Robert Asprin. *Soul of the City* (Thieves' World). New York, Ace, 1986; London, Titan, 1989.
Editor, with Richard Pini and Robert Asprin, *The Blood of Ten Chiefs* (Elfquest). New York, Tor, 1986.
Editor, with Robert Asprin. *Blood Ties* (Thieves' World). New York, Ace, 1986; London, Titan, 1990.
Editor, with Robert Asprin. *The Shattered Sphere* (omnibus; includes *The Dead of Winter, Soul of the City, Blood Ties*). New York, Nelson Doubleday, 1986.
Editor, with Robert Asprin. *Aftermath* (Thieves' World). New York, Ace, 1987; London, Titan, 1990.
Editor, with Robert Asprin. *Uneasy Alliances* (Thieves' World). New York, Ace, 1988; London, Titan, 1990.
Editor, with Richard Pini and Robert Asprin, *Wolfsong: The Blood of Ten Chiefs* (Elfquest). New York, Tor, 1988.
Editor, with Robert Asprin. *Stealer's Sky* (Thieves' World). New York, Ace, 1989.
Editor, with Robert Asprin. *The Price of Victory* (omnibus; includes *Aftermath, Uneasy Alliances, Stealer's Sky*). New York, Nelson Doubleday, 1990.

*   *   *

Lynn Abbey's fantasy fiction is wide-ranging, much of her best-known shorter work being written jointly with her husband, Rob-

ert Asprin. Together, they have been responsible for the widely influential shared-world concept of the Thieves' World series, which has drawn in other well-known writers to create characters and plots for the imaginary town of Sanctuary in which the tales are based.

Abbey's solo novels cover several different worlds, from that of Rifkind, heroine of *Daughter of the Bright Moon* and *The Black Flame*—warrior, priestess, healer and witch, who first discovers her destiny and then fulfils it in these two novels in settings of desert, castle, and the dangerous untracked swamps of the Felmargue—to Britannia, land of the Ultima Saga, a more conventionally near-medieval background.

The settings of her novels, highly complex in detail, are important in providing a mood all her books share in common: whether the plot involves a quest, or a conflict of good versus evil, each world displays dirt and squalor and constant perils, both human and magical. These settings are designed to repel, not appeal to, the senses, and the major characters are similarly contrived to lack attractive or sympathetic qualities; Rifkind, a strong and all-powerful heroine, alone possesses the power and knowledge necessary to defeat the evil gods. Yet although she becomes pregnant by her doomed lover, Domnhall, and returns to her own people in the guise of a healer once the battle is won, she is still a woman apart, to be respected but never loved.

Some of the same themes are evident in *Unicorn & Dragon,* set in a manor in medieval England at the time of the Norman invasion, when wolves howl and bandits prowl the roads. Two sisters, Alison and Wildecent, are caught up in the political chaos of war between Saxon and Norman, which extends to a war of magic between Saxon *wicca* and the eastern sorcery of the Norman Ambrose, and a battle between the sisters for the affections of Stephen, the young stranger who arrives at the manor. The background details are superb, creating a vivid image of the style of living and social mores of the period; yet they are hardly appealing. None of the characters attracts sympathy, except perhaps Wildecent, whose past is shrouded in mystery; there is always a dark unpleasantness waiting in the wings in Abbey's novels.

The Wooden Sword, set in Walensor's world, shares the same characteristics. The heroine, Berika, believes she has summoned up a fetch in her efforts to prove herself a strong sorceress and escape an arranged marriage to the brutish Hirmin. Again, the setting is one of mud and medieval squalor, both in Berika's village and in Relamain, the town to which she and the fetch—in reality a nobleman who has lost both memory and 20 years of his life—escape. The details of the world and its magic are complex, ingenious, but unpleasant; Dart, the hero, is noble, but lacks the humanity which would engender empathy.

This deliberate creation of unlovable characters continues in the Ultima Saga. The five leading characters in both novels are all intentionally lacking in the high moral nature more common in fantasy. The first volume involves a quest by Jordan, a young noble, his brother Squirt, Drum, a blacksmith, and Althea, an orphan, to seek out Althea's missing magician brother, Balthan, a quest more important than they at first perceive. The evil they uncover in their search, during which Jordan is temporarily blinded, must be fought in the second tome by force and by magic.

The flaws in all five characters are made plain: Squirt is possessed by a demon which creates ungovernable and undesirable impulses; Jordan is self-centred and self-pitying; Althea is too malleable; Drum is self-satisfied and Balthan is essentially amoral. Their victory over the evil Inquisitor is accomplished despite these flaws, rather than by force of virtue. The background of the Ultima Saga is as dark and joyless as the characters, with a full complement of dirt, trolls and banditry. Again, it is a superbly conceived and delineated world, but not one to which a visit would seem desirable in real life.

Lynn Abbey's talent is unmistakable, most particularly in the creation of cheerless terrains peopled by sinister creatures of every type. She has constructed her own type of fantasy, where the endings are not always happy nor the heroes and heroines noble or fulfilled by their quests. She has a tendency—perhaps a realistic one given the settings—to make her female characters retreat into domesticity; for example, Althea, in *The Temper of Wisdom*, refuses to study sorcery and wants to marry Drum, and Berika in *The Wooden Sword* betrays Dart and accepts the protection of another nobleman, giving up other ambitions. Abbey's worlds invariably—and logically, in their settings—contain societies where perceived gender differences are rigidly enforced, perhaps a rare and realistic acceptance that in worlds where physical strength is a ruling force, women are naturally at a disadvantage.

Abbey possesses the ability to create dark nightmares, where motives for valour are more complex than simple virtue. Her characters reflect the worlds they inhabit, filled with unsettling, malign emotions. The dismal settings may occasionally irritate; but they are very well drawn, and filled with a rare depth of detail which is formidably imagined.

—Mary Corran

ABDULLAH, Achmed

Pseudonym for Alexander Nicholayevitch Romanoff (whose adopted Muslim name was Achmed Abdullah Nadir Khan el-Durani el Iddrissyeh). **Other Pseudonyms:** A. A. Nadir; John Hamilton. **Nationality:** British (of mixed Russian-Afghan descent). **Born:** Yalta, Crimea, 12 May 1881. **Education:** Indian School, Darjeeling; College Louis le Grand, France; Eton School; Oxford University; University of Paris. **Military Service:** British Army: captain. **Family:** Married 1) Jean Wick, literary agent (died 1939); 2) Rosemary A. Dolan in 1940. **Career:** Magazine writer and occasional screenwriter. Settled in the USA. **Died:** 12 May 1945.

FANTASY PUBLICATIONS

Novels (series: God of the Invincibly Strong Arms)

The Red Stain (Strong Arms). New York, Hearst's International Library, 1915; London, Simpkin Marshall, 1916.
The Blue-Eyed Manchu (Strong Arms). New York, Shores, 1917; London, Hutchinson, 1923.
The Mating of the Blades. New York, McCann, 1920; London, Hutchinson, 1921.
The Thief of Bagdad (novelization of screenplay). New York, Fly, 1924; London, Hutchinson, 1924.
The Flower of the Gods, with Anthony Abbot (Fulton Oursler). New York, Green Circle Books, 1936.

Short Stories

Wings: Tales of the Psychic. New York, McCann, 1920.

Alien Souls. New York, McCann, 1922; London, Hutchinson, 1923.
Mysteries of Asia. London, Philip Allan, 1935.

OTHER PUBLICATIONS

Novels

Bucking the Tiger. New York, Shores, 1917.
The Man on Horseback. New York, McCann, 1919.
The Trail of the Beast. New York, McCann, 1919; London, Hutchinson, 1921.
Night Drums. New York, McCann, 1921; London, Hutchinson, 1922.
A Buccaneer in Spats. London, Hutchinson, 1924.
Shackled. New York, Brentano's, 1924; London, Hutchinson, 1925.
The Remittance Woman. New York, Garden City, 1924.
The Wild Goose of Limerick. New York, Brentano's, 1926; London, Hutchinson, 1926.
The Year of the Wood-Dragon. New York, Brentano's, 1926.
Ruth's Rebellion, with Faith Baldwin. New York, Doran, 1927; as *Ruth and Peter,* London, Hutchinson, 1927.
Broadway Interlude, with Faith Baldwin. New York, Payson and Clarke, 1929; London, Selwyn and Blount, 1930.
They Were So Young. New York, Payson and Clarke, 1929; as *To an Eastern Throne,* London, Hutchinson, 1929.
The Veiled Woman. New York, Liveright, 1931; as *The Lady in the Veil,* London, Hurst and Blackett, 1931.
The Bungalow on the Roof. New York, Mystery League, 1931.
A Romantic Young Man. New York, Farrar, 1932; London, Hurst and Blackett, 1932.
Girl on the Make, with Faith Baldwin. New York, Long and Smith, 1932; London, Selwyn and Blount, 1932.
Fighting Through: The Story of a Pathan Chieftain. London, Frederick Warne, 1933.
Love Comes to Sally. New York, Burt, 1933.
Never Without You. New York, Farrar, 1934; London, Hurst and Blackett, 1934.
Deliver Us From Evil. New York, Putnam, 1939.
The Shadow of the Master, with Anthony Abbot (Fulton Oursler). London, Hurst and Blackett, 1940.

Short Stories

The Honourable Gentleman and Others. New York, Putnam, 1919.
The Benefactor's Club. London, Lloyd, 1921.
The Swinging Caravan. New York, Brentano's, 1925.
Steel and Jade. New York, Doran, 1927.

Plays

Toto, with Leo Ditrichstein (produced, New York, 1920).
The Grand Duke, with Lionel Atwill (produced, New York, 1921).
Black Tents. New York, Liveright, 1930.

Screenplay: *The Lives of a Bengal Lancer,* with Waldemar Young and others, 1934.

Poetry

Chanson Coleur Puce. Privately published, 1900.

Translator, *Lute and Scimitar: Poems and Ballads of Central Asia.* New York, Payson and Clarke, 1928.

Other

A Grammar of Little Known Bantu Dialects. Privately published, 1902.
Dreamers of Empire, with T. Compton Pakenham. New York, Stokes, 1929; London, Harrap, 1930.
The Cat Had Nine Lives (autobiography). New York, Farrar, 1933; as *My Nine Lives,* London, Hurst and Blackett, 1934.
For Men Only, with John Kenny (cookbook). New York, Putnam, 1937.
Arabian Hypnotism. New York, IPA Service, 1959 (reproduced from typewriting).

Editor, *Fifty Enthralling Stories of the Middle East.* London, Odhams, 1937.

*

Critical Study: "The Cat Had Nine Lives," *Wilson Library Bulletin,* October 1929.

*   *   *

If Achmed Abdullah's contribution to fantastic fiction is remembered at all (and that is rare) it is because of his book *The Thief of Bagdad,* even though it was the least original of Abdullah's prolific output. It was a novelization of the noted silent movie (1924) which had been conceived by Douglas Fairbanks, Sr., based on stories in the *Arabian Nights,* with a scenario written by Elton Thomas (Fairbanks) and Lotta Woods. Abdullah was able to take what was apparently a fairly loose script and adapt it into a lively and enthusiastic novel, conveying to the reader much of the verve and excitement of Fairbanks's own portrayal on the screen.

To most modern audiences, *The Thief of Bagdad* is better known in the Alexander Korda remake (1940) which had a completely new script by Lajos Biro. The original film tells of a quest: Ahmed, the eponymous thief, falls in love with the Caliph's daughter. Disguised as the Prince of the Isles he bids for her hand along with other rival princes. They are set a challenge to find the most remarkable gift to please the princess. Ahmed's quest leads him far and wide and ends with a race against time on a magic stallion to win the hand of the princess and defeat the Mongols who have captured Bagdad.

It is a vibrant and enjoyable novel, shallow on characterization but full of local colour and Oriental splendour. Abdullah was the ideal choice to adapt the film, as his own character in many ways reflected that of Ahmed the thief. His life was as colourful and mysterious as his characters, and he had travelled the world, enabling him to bring an authentic atmosphere to his settings. We may never know just how much of his writings were fictionalized autobiography. Abdullah retained an aura of mystery about his personal life. Even his autobiography, *The Cat Had Nine Lives,* reads like an adventure novel, and Abdullah quite probably used his literary licence to embellish some of the episodes. It is a vivid series of reminiscences of his travels and exploits from Russia to Tibet and from Afghanistan to Africa. In Africa he encountered the inexplicable, where he believed he may have shot a were-leopard. The book says little about his writing or his private life, but reveals a larger-than-life traveller and adventurer who thrived on the thrill of the hunt and recounting his adventures to the pearls of American society. His stories are much the same.

Even his birth is intriguing. He was the son of the Grand Duke Nicholas Romanoff, and was second cousin to the last Tsar of Russia. His mother was an Afghan princess and after his parents' divorce, Abdullah, who had been christened Alexander Romanoff, was raised as a Moslem (though he later became a devout Roman Catholic). He was educated at a number of private schools, including Eton, where he apparently arrived wearing a turban and earrings with a dagger tucked into his boot. He entered the British Army in 1900 and saw service in India, China, Tibet, the Middle East, France and Africa before he settled in the United States to pursue a writing career. This background provided the plots and episodes for nearly 30 novels and plays plus several hundred short stories published in the leading British and American magazines and pulps.

Abdullah's early passion was for poetry. He produced a collection of verse while still at college, *Chanson Coleur Puce,* and in later years gathered together a selection of poems from across central Asia which he translated as *Lute and Scimitar.* This may ultimately prove to be his most important work, capturing the essence of the Tartar and Mongol cultures.

His writing began as a more serious venture just before the outbreak of the World War I. The earliest stories are little more than episodes reflecting aspects of eastern life or culture such as "The Strength of the Little Thin Thread" (*Collier's,* 1912) which demonstrates how a man cannot deny or escape the caste into which he was born. Many of these early stories were collected as *Alien Souls.* The fantasy elements are small, but there is an all-pervading mystique of the Orient, with its belief in reincarnation and the power and omniscience of alien gods.

The more overtly fantastic stories were later collected as *Wings,* which is Abdullah's best collection with some of his most effective writing. They show a natural development from the stories in *Alien Souls,* with the mystical beliefs of the Orient having come to the fore, particularly in respect of man's psychic abilities. The title story (*All-Story Weekly,* 1918) develops the issue of caste by depicting a rajah who fears to leave India and so travels to England by astral projection. His out-of-body experience lasts too long and he dies, the narrator hearing the sound of invisible wings as the soul departs. "To Be Accounted For" (*Novel,* 1920) built upon the post-war interest in spiritualism. It tells of a soldier, expelled from his unit, who projects his astral body to the front to save the lives of his colleagues. "The Haunting Thing" (*All-Story Weekly,* 1917) is perhaps Abdullah's most effective fantasy short story. It deals with a woman who is haunted by the manifestation of her own evil. The scenes where the entity laughs are most atmospheric.

Only one other of Abdullah's collections contains stories of the fantastic, *Mysteries of Asia.* These are later stories and are far less well handled. They read like rejections from magazines brought hastily together for book publication. The stories build upon the mystique of the Orient, but lack the style and atmosphere more apparent in *Wings.* The most effective is "The Haunted Carpet," where the goddess Kali wreaks revenge through an enchanted carpet.

Abdullah's novels are generally less fantastic than his shorter fiction. His early work retained some of the Oriental mystique, particularly a sequence of stories in *All-Story Weekly* which ran between 1915 and 1916 under the general title of "The God of the Invincibly Strong Arms." It deals with an Oriental cult of the goddess Kali which, by secret machinations, seeks to pit East against

West. Written at the height of the First World War it found an interested readership, though seems little more than sensationalist fiction today. Only two parts of the series were printed in book form, *The Blue-Eyed Manchu* and *The Red Stain.* The style and plotting is reminiscent of Sax Rohmer's Dr. Fu Manchu stories, although Abdullah's local colour is more authentic.

After the war Abdullah's novels developed more as romantic mysteries with the fantastic element minimal if present at all. He became one of the leading writers of romantic adventure during the 1920s, able to conjure the exotic wonder of the orient to fascinate the growing number of women readers. Abdullah himself sought to encourage this approach, rather like a former-day Omar Sharif. He lived in opulent splendour in a New York apartment and sported a monocle and cane. He loved the high life, particularly on Broadway, and became involved in a number of stage productions as well as in work for the growing movie industry. His romantic adventure *A Buccaneer in Spats* could easily be a self-portrayal.

Only two of Abdullah's later works are remotely fantastic. Both *The Mating of the Blades* and *The Flower of the Gods* use the themes of astral projection and reincarnation in their portrayal of fated love.

Abdullah was a writer of his day. None of his work is sophisticated, but it has a superficial verve and excitement that invokes the wonder and mystery of the Orient. When spiced with romantic intrigue his work was able to captivate an audience thrilling for the escapism represented by foreign princes and climes. When it was spiced with the occult he was able to create dark and sinister visions of unknown cultures. Both of these came together in *The Thief of Bagdad,* the only book by Abdullah to remain in print and his most lasting legacy to the fantasy field.

—Mike Ashley

ab HUGH, Dafydd

Legally adopted name. **Nationality:** American. **Born:** 1960. **Education:** University of California, Los Angeles and Santa Cruz, M.A. in mathematics. **Military Service:** United States Navy. **Address:** c/o Pocket Books, 1230 Avenue of the Americas, New York, NY 10020, USA.

FANTASY PUBLICATIONS

Novels (series: Jiana in both books)

Heroing. New York, Baen, 1987.
Warriorwards. New York, Baen, 1990.

OTHER PUBLICATIONS

Novels

Arthur War Lord. New York, AvoNova, 1994.
Fallen Heroes. New York, Pocket, 1994.
Balance of Power. New York, Pocket, 1994.

*　　*　　*

Dafydd ab Hugh clearly writes in the sword-and-sorcery sub-genre, and his first two books, *Heroing* and *Warriorwards,* can be read as simple adventure stories. To do so, however, is to miss the point about what ab Hugh is doing: his novels enter into a dialogue with sword and sorcery, questioning its very premises, getting to the root of what it means to be a warrior, a slave, a hero.

The heroine of the books is Jiana Analena, a swordswoman with strong magical powers. She is a very contemporary sort of heroine: almost Hamlet-like in her tendency to self-absorbed reflection and analysis, she was, apparently, a sexually abused child who may or may not have killed the father who abused her. Her situation is somewhat ambiguous because, as is often the case in real life, Jiana's memories are variable and uncertain. As a result of her traumatic experiences, Jiana suffers from low self-esteem and may be a split personality; then again, her alter ego may in fact be a magical intrusion from another dimension. It appears that ab Hugh's ambiguity is deliberate.

The first book, *Heroing,* takes the apparent form of a quest novel. Jiana seeks to join the party of Prince Alanai of Bay Bay in his quest for the World's Dream, a magical artefact with the power to grant one wish, even if that wish means remaking the world. Jiana is turned down because she is a woman, with instructions to go home to her husband or father. But she is determined to join the quest in search of "foreverness," in search of a name. As she says: "I've fought creatures that would make Alanai's hair straighten! And I've won and lost enough treasure to buy a ladyship and a nice manor house on the coast somewhere. But who the hell's ever heard of *me?* When I'm dead, who's going to remember my name? I want to live forever—on tongues, if not in time! I want immortality."

Jiana begins following Prince Alanai's party, hoping to do some grand deed that will compel the Prince to allow her to join him. Along the way, though, she sees the aftermath of heroes, the death and devastation they leave behind them. Though she still defines herself as one—"It was not fear, or excitement, or the adventure of the hunt [that drove her on]. She was a Hero. That was her job"—she is beginning to wonder whether heroes aren't more trouble to the world than they're worth, and eventually she redefines her quest's purpose: to stop Prince Alanai from attaining the World's Dream and remaking the world. She does succeed in sneaking it out from under his nose, but then is uncertain what to do with it; she has learned not to trust the desire for power, not to try to remake the world because of her fear of unintended consequences.

Along the way she has attracted an admirer and apprentice: the innocent farm-boy Dida; she learns the consequences of taking responsibility for someone. Already unhappy at his love being spurned, Dida is captured by Prince Alanai's forces. The next time they meet, Dida has willingly joined with the Prince on his quest. At the end of the quest, as soldiers filled with the rage of battle destroy the ancient city where the World's Dream has been hidden, Dida rapes a young girl and is driven to near madness with self-loathing. Jiana finds him and, when Dida expresses his inability to live with what he's done, gives him a knife. Somewhat to her surprise, he kills himself. Full of grief, rage, and guilt, blaming herself for having caused Dida to go wrong, Jiana uses the World's Dream to bring him back to life.

Alanai is, naturally, enraged at this "waste." "WE COULD HAVE BEEN GODS!" he screams at her. To which she replies, "I know I'm a true warrior. I held the world in my palm—literally!—and I put it down again. Can you say the same?" The Prince, defeated, leaves, Jiana makes plans to go off with Dida, and the book is over with this apparently happy ending.

It is not long into *Warriorwards* before we learn that things did not turn out well and we see the long-term results of Jiana's heroism. Four years later, Dida has become an arrogant member of the ruling house's soldiery. Jiana has her name and the fame she desired, yet she feels like a failure, primarily because of how Dida turned out. Inspired by a vision given to her by a seer, she determines to take another apprentice, but to do it right this time. Her choice, or rather her destiny, is a girl with a crippled arm named Radience (sic), a slave in the caravan of a Caliph of Tool.

Jiana will not simply rescue Radience, though, for that would teach her nothing, and because, according to ab Hugh, slavery is of the mind more than of the body. Therefore, in order to show Radience how to free herself, Jiana has herself sold into slavery among the Toolians. Here ab Hugh takes the opportunity to examine the nature of slavery. It is easy to be a slave, despite the work and beatings: easy because you can go through life asleep, never having to decide anything, never having to take responsibility. Ab Hugh does not just tell us so, he illustrates it: Jiana almost falls into the trap, losing her original self in the timeless mindlessness of being a slave. Eventually, Jiana plans an escape, and Radience betrays her, but by taking responsibility for what she has done she demonstrates that she is no longer a slave. The physical escape is secondary, except that once again Jiana is taught a lesson about unintended consequences.

The rest of *Warriorwards* is devoted, as one might guess from the title, to Radience's training as a warrior. Jiana acts as a classic drill sergeant, teaching Radience not just technique, but to think and act as a warrior. This examination of slavery and warriordom does not hold together as well as the deconstruction of heroism of *Heroing*, but the two books work together as they trace Jiana's growth, enlightenment, and self-acceptance. A third book was promised at the end of *Warriorwards*, but it has not yet been published.

Jiana is something unusual in sword and sorcery: a truly self-aware hero. Ab Hugh makes us think about the conventions we take for granted, about what goes on down at the hero's feet and in his or her wake. The books emphasize responsibility and the consciousness of the consequences of one's acts. Jiana may not find the final answer to what it means to be a Hero, but it continues to be her true quest, as well as ab Hugh's and the reader's.

—Janice M. Eisen

ADAIR, Gilbert

Nationality: British. **Career:** Journalist, broadcaster, and film critic.

FANTASY PUBLICATIONS

Novels

Alice Through the Needle's Eye. London, Macmillan, 1984.
Peter Pan and the Only Children. London, Macmillan, 1987.
The Death of the Author. London, Heinemann, 1992.

OTHER PUBLICATIONS

Novels

The Holy Innocents. London, Heinemann, 1988.
Love and Death on Long Island. London, Heinemann, 1990.

Poetry

The Rape of the Cock. London, 1990.

Other

Hollywood's Vietnam: From The Green Berets to Apocalypse Now. London, Proteus, 1981; revised edition, London, Heinemann, 1989.
Myths & Memories. London, Fontana, 1986.
The Postmodernist Always Rings Twice: Reflections on Culture in the 90s. London, Fourth Estate, 1992.
Flickers. London, Faber, 1995.

Translator, *Correspondence, 1945-1984* by Francois Truffaut, edited by Gilles Jacob and Claude De Givray. New York, Farrar Straus and Giroux, 1990.
Translator, *A Void* by Georges Perec. London, Harvill, 1994.

*   *   *

For a writer who made his first reputation as a film critic, Gilbert Adair's fiction is remarkably unvisual. Even though, in *The Holy Innocents,* he wrote knowingly about cinephiles in Paris, there are no cinematic moments, no wide-screen dramas or telling descriptions. Instead his books are full of meditation and word-play, intense examinations of emotional drives that are barely understood even by his highly articulate characters. And the clear influences behind his books lie not in film but in other works of literature. His first two books, written for children, are sequels to established children's fantasy classics which successfully capture the tone and the style of their familiar forebears. His later works, written in a more self-consciously literary style, re-examine themes from other books. *Love and Death on Long Island* is a reworking of Thomas Mann's *Death in Venice,* in which an elderly mandarin writer develops an unexpected homosexual passion for a young actor glimpsed in a trashy film. Film also plays a key role in *The Holy Innocents,* in which a trio of teenagers use film as the trigger for acting out their sexual fantasies, unaware of the political turmoil gathering around them in the Paris of 1968. Both these books concern the tragedy of sexual fantasy intruding into real life, though neither of them could in any other sense be called fantasies (although *Love and Death on Long Island* does contain the telling remark: "only by aspiration to and concourse with some form of the super-natural . . . was the writer able to create out of the humility that is, or should be, his natural state and essence").

The Death of the Author, however, is an intricate literary fantasy in the manner of Vladimir Nabokov. The plot, which has certain striking similarities with the case of Paul Le Man, concerns a respected American scholar attempting to hide his past as a Nazi collaborator in Paris during the war. The collaborator is a proponent of a literary theory which claims that any work of literature has no true meaning, only the meaning given to it by the reader of the moment. He gives new meaning to his life by re-writing his own history. As different facts are revealed at different times, Adair is able to repeat the same scene in the same words three times, yet each time reveal something slightly different as the context changes (in the same way that Borges's Pierre Menard writes a *Quixote* in the same words as Cervantes but which is open to vastly different interpretation). Adair further compounds the complexity of viewpoint and interpretation in this novel by having his narrator continue the story after his own death to provide yet another twist in the tale.

It is Adair's first two novels, though, which are the most overtly fantastical of his books. A literary chameleon, he is able to capture the tone and manner of the original *Alice in Wonderland* and *Peter Pan* with remarkable verisimilitude—though it is *Alice* which gives him most scope for the puns, intellectual puzzles and word-games which run throughout his work. He recreates the style of Lewis Carroll's curious logic and nonsense poems so well that the book does read as if it belongs in the original canon, rather than being a clever pastiche. Alice's fall through the eye of a needle takes her to a land in which her adventures follow the letters of the alphabet, from the As of the 'aystack in which she lands to the ZZZ of sleep from which she wakes as she had previously woken beside the rabbit hole and looking glass. As in the return to J. M. Barrie's Never-Never Land, characters recur from the original books, in this case the Red Queen and White Queen whom Alice finds in an endless Q, and others are obvious analogues of characters from the other books. The Grampus and Italian Hairdresser (whose words have to be translated out of italic) are similar to the Walrus and the Carpenter, and the Welsh Rabbit (with its toasted cheese and Worcestershire sauce) is clearly a reincarnation of the White Rabbit; but other characters, the emu, the siamese cats joined at the tale, are original enough to make the book feel like a fresh development rather than a retread.

Nevertheless, for all the exuberance of *Alice* and *Peter Pan,* the lasting impression is of the cleverness of the author rather than the magic of his creation. Gilbert Adair is not a natural fantasist, except in so far as he recreates in all his fiction the magic worlds of other books and other writers.

—Paul Kincaid

ADAMS, Richard (George)

Nationality: British. **Born:** Newbury, Berkshire, 9 May 1920. **Education:** Bradfield College, Berkshire, 1933-38; Worcester College, Oxford, 1938-39, 1946-48; B.A. in modern history, 1948; M.A. 1953. **Military Service:** British Army, 1940-46. **Family:** Married Barbara Elizabeth Acland in 1949; two daughters. **Career:** Worked in the Ministry of Housing and Local Government, London, 1948-68; Assistant Secretary, Department of the Environment, London, 1968-74; writer-in-residence, University of Florida, Gainesville, 1975, and Hollins College, Virginia, 1976. **Awards:** Library Association Carnegie medal, 1972; *Guardian* award, 1973. **Member:** Fellow, Royal Society of Literature, 1975; President, Royal Society for the Prevention of Cruelty to Animals, 1980-82 (resigned). **Agent:** David Higham Associates Ltd., 5-8 Lower John Street, London W1R 4HA. **Address:** 26 Church Street, Whitchurch, Hampshire, Hampshire RG28 7AR, England.

FANTASY PUBLICATIONS

Novels

Watership Down. London, Collings, 1972; New York, Macmillan, 1974.
Shardik. London, Allen Lane/Collings, 1974; New York, Simon and Schuster, 1975.
The Plague Dogs. London, Allen Lane/Collings, 1977; New York, Knopf, 1978.
The Girl in a Swing. London, Allen Lane, and New York, Knopf, 1980.
Maia. London, Viking, 1984; New York, Knopf, 1985.
Traveller. New York, Knopf, 1988; London, Hutchinson, 1989.

Short Stories

The Iron Wolf and Other Stories (folktales). London, Allen Lane, 1980; as *The Unbroken Web,* New York, Crown, 1980.
The Bureaucats (for children). London, Viking Kestrel, 1985.

Poetry

The Tiger Voyage, illustrated by Nicola Bayley. London, Cape, and New York, Knopf, 1976.
The Ship's Cat, illustrated by Alan Aldridge. London, Cape, and New York Knopf, 1977.
The Legend of Te Tuna. Los Angeles, Sylvester and Orphanos, 1982; London, Sidgwick and Jackson, 1986.

Other

Editor, *Grimm's Fairy Tales.* London, Routledge, 1981.

OTHER PUBLICATIONS

Nature Through the Seasons, with Max Hooper and David A. Goddard. London, Kestrel, and New York, Simon and Schuster, 1975.
Nature Day and Night, with Max Hooper and David A. Goddard. London, Kestrel, and New York, Viking, 1978.
Voyage Through the Antarctic, with Ronald Lockley. London, Allen Lane, 1982; New York, Knopf, 1983.
A Nature Diary. London, Viking, 1985; New York, Viking, 1986.
The Day Gone By: An Autobiography. London, Hutchinson, 1990; New York, Knopf, 1991.

Editor, *Richard Adams's Favourite Animal Stories.* London, Octopus, 1981.
Editor, *The Best of Ernest Thompson Seton.* London, Fontana, 1982.
Editor, *Occasional Poets: An Anthology.* London, Viking, 1986.

*

Film Adaptations: *Watership Down,* 1978; *The Plague Dogs,* 1982.

* * *

Richard Adams's approach to fantasy writing is both experimental and didactic: every book expresses, sometimes explicitly, sometimes implicitly but always forcefully, an aspect of his moral standpoint; and every book seeks to do so in a striking or unusual manner. Predictably, his oeuvre has aroused very varied reactions to both manner and matter, but of his six novels to date, those which deal principally with animals (*Watership Down, The Plague Dogs, Traveller*) are more successful than the ones about people (*Shardik, The Girl in a Swing, Maia*).

The first, *Watership Down,* was an instant and overwhelming success, as much through its novelty as for any of its other virtues. Who would have contemplated writing an allegorical exposition of the feudal ideal of kingship in terms of the migration of a band of rabbits? Yet this is what is done, and no aspect is neglected. The journey begins at Sandleford Warren, where the Chief Rabbit (King) has grown old and soft, neglecting his responsibilities. In their search for a permanent home the fugitives encounter successively a warren with no chief, where the rabbits are melancholic, apathetic and demoralized, and Efrafa, where the Chief (Woundwort) has degenerated into a tyrant. The two principal characters, Hazel and Bigwig, represent the young man who finds greatness thrust upon him, and proves equal to it, and the natural lieutenant, who at first aspires to kingship but ultimately renounces his ambition, to lay his metaphorical sword at the true king's feet. Hazel, the Good King, lives long and rules wisely, before dying with dignity and ascending (presumably) to Rabbit Heaven.

The two "Plague Dogs" of the next animal tale escape from Lakeland-based Animal Research (Scientific and Experimental), a place very like C. S. Lewis's National Institute for Coordinated Experiments (note the acronyms, on which neither author comments). Their anabasis also has a happy, if somewhat contrived, outcome; but since it involves one of them being reunited with his owner, much of the action takes place perforce in the human world. We therefore have animals and humans who are equally capable of engaging in metaphysical speculation; intellectually the dogs are no less human than any of our own preliterate ancestors. The two modes of being interact, but to accept both simultaneously requires suspension of disbelief of a kind which many readers will find impossible. This is entirely a matter of temperament; for those who can take Grahame's *The Wind in the Willows* and Masefield's *The Midnight Folk* in their stride, *The Plague Dogs* should present no problems; for those who can't, no exposition of its literary merits will dispel the unease which permeates its assumptions.

In *Traveller* the problem is exacerbated. Here Adams adopts Anna Sewell's conceit in *Black Beauty,* that horses can not only talk among themselves but understand human speech as well. *Traveller* himself is an historical character, the warhorse of Robert E. Lee, who in retirement reviews his life and involvement with the Civil War for the benefit of a stable cat. It is therefore more a non-sexual love story than any other kind, for the bond of sympathy and respect between man and beast is forged early and deepens with time. Regrettably, Adams's occasional lapses into archness have become more pronounced: in particular, Traveller partakes in many bloody battles, but never comes to associate them with the term "war," which he hears often but conceives as some vague but desirable place, since all the people he knows are so keen to get there.

Adams's thought contains certain patterns which become more insistent as one reads him, most notably the concept of honourable obligation. It is central to feudal kingship, and is instinctively accepted by both Traveller and his master. Most pathetically, the dog Rowf is by his nature bonded to one of the scientists at ARSE, who does not, of course, accept that to be a dog's master and re-

ceive his love is to shoulder the burden of his vulnerability. Adams's overt belief that a truly moral social order must resemble the medieval model, with its emphasis on service, patriarchy and the payment of dues, will not find favour in all quarters; nor will his parallel assumption that it should be symbiotically involved with a metaphysical, teleological and prophetic religion. This last reappears in the debased form of a vague and arbitrary belief in clairvoyance; there is always someone with "powers" of indeterminate source, which he can neither control nor cultivate, and which exist mainly to emphasize Adams's belief in the Unseen World. But in the three animal books, with their overwhelmingly male *dramatis personae,* he keeps his sentimentality within bounds well enough to give full scope to his strengths. In the books about people, and sexual relationships thereamong, the strain begins to show.

Shardik takes place in a context best described as Sword sans Sorcery, more like Jane Gaskell's world than any other, and is generally regarded as a typically disappointing second novel. The great bear of the title is never more than a pawn in the hands of contending factions, who with varying degrees of cynicism use him as a religious symbol to further political ends. Unlike the animal books, *Shardik* is not linked to any real terrain, so Adams's favoured technique of underpinning the fantasy of his narrative with the truth of physical geography is unable to operate. The principal interest of the book is Adams's rather whimsical decision to stud the narrative with epic similes in the Homeric mode. They read neither more nor less oddly than those deployed by Milton in *Paradise Lost,* but it must be said that neither set has established a vogue.

The Girl in a Swing combines the supernatural horror story and the love story. Its basic premise is that Karin, a woman of spectacular beauty, will commit a grossly unnatural crime in order to secure (after very brief acquaintance) marriage to Alan Desland, the viewpoint character—who just happens to be an ugly, timid, virginal, dull mother's boy with the soul of a shopkeeper (not inappropriate, as Shaw might have observed, to one who keeps a shop). He is the most vividly realized of all Adams's characters, so that the book's principal interest is as an extended psychological portrait, nor is he without his (typically medieval) virtues of kindliness, courtesy, humility and a gritty, undemonstrative courage; but the question why such a woman should court the love of such a man is never addressed. This displays a curious weakness on Adams's part, since he emphasizes that Karin is an acknowledged beauty. The story would gain both pathos and credibility if she was in fact quite plain, but beautiful in his eyes alone.

Maia returns to the world of *Shardik,* but this time Adams has chosen for his central character an innocent young girl, newly come into womanhood. He immediately falls lickerishly in love with her, and arranges for her bodice to be well and variously ripped by admirers of both sexes. A humorous writer might have successfully combined erotic hokum and perils-of-Pauline with comedy, but Adams's cast of mind is solemn; the result is rather as if Melvyn Bragg had encountered Nabokov's *Ada,* and decided to go one better. The longest of his books, *Maia* contains the least.

—Chris Gilmore

ADKINS, Patrick H.

Nationality: American. **Born:** 1948. **Address:** c/o Ace Books, 200 Madison Avenue, New York, NY 10016, USA.

FANTASY PUBLICATIONS

Novels (series: Titans in all books)

Lord of the Crooked Paths. New York, Ace, 1987; London, Futura, 1990.
Master of the Fearful Depths. New York, Ace, 1989.
Sons of the Titans. New York, Ace, 1990.

*   *   *

Although Norse and Welsh mythology has long held a prominent place in modern fantasy, either directly or in thinly disguised costumes, the Greek and Roman gods have for the most part been ignored, perhaps because their exploits have been so thoroughly chronicled already. One portion of that mythos has been almost entirely neglected, however—the early life of the gods of Olympus, the time of Kronos and the creation of the human race, before Zeus and his followers came to power. Patrick Adkins has made a serious, scholarly, and entertaining attempt to bring together some of the disjointed and fragmentary stories of that period, creating fresh material to fill in the gaps.

Adkins's three published novels take place within a coherent chronology whose overall theme is the quest for absolute power over others, gods and human. His first novel, *Lord of the Crooked Paths,* opens just as the human race has appeared on the scene, diminutive creatures in the shape of the gods themselves, amusing playthings but of no real consequence to the denizens of Mount Olympus.

Kronos is king of the gods but his rule is not undisputed. There are rivals and conspiracies all around, and the recent discovery of a dead nymph proves that even the gods are mortal. To preserve his rule, Kronos kills his own children as they are born, but he is tricked into sparing the life of Zeus, his sixth child, who will eventually kill and replace his father—although Adkins has not extended his history to include that event. Kronos is also involved in arcane research into the nature of immortality, assisted by the rather repugant god Thanatos, research which he carefully conceals from public scrutiny. One of the most dangerous of his enemies is Proteus, the Shapechanger, who seeks to end Kronos' despotic rule. Proteus' lover, the nympha Nalassa, is also a kinder soul than most of her fellow gods, and it is through her intervention that humankind is freed to populate the Earth, although the gods can't resist the temptation to meddle in their affairs. The gods remain preoccupied with their own problems, and Adkins devotes little time to his few human characters.

It would have been all too easy for Adkins to have presented the gods simply as their familiar stereotypes, but he infuses each character with realistic motives and feelings, strengths and weaknesses. They may be gigantic in size, capable of controlling the elements or changing their physical bodies, but they remain people, prey to anger and grief and moments of joy. It's this quality that raises Adkins' work from interesting speculation to skilful fiction that draws its readers into the lives of the characters.

Nalassa escapes from Mount Olympus in *Master of the Fearful Depths,* but you're never really beyond the reach of the king of the gods. Proteus appeals to Oceanos, brother to Kronos, whose legions are prepared for the Greek equivalent of Ragnarok. Events proceed quickly and, unlike most second volumes in a series, this is a fascinating and complete tale in itself, a much better paced and presented story than its predecessor. The mortality of the gods, which results from their consumption of mortal food, gives Kronos a secret weapon against his enemies, resolved in a climactic scene in which he and his allies attempt to sway the rest of the gods to unite and destroy his enemies. The discovery of Nalassa, slain through Kronos' machinations, and some quick thinking by Proteus deny him the victory and leave him largely abandoned.

Adkins treads a delicate path here, superimposing entirely human ambitions and personality traits on literally larger than life characters with transcendent powers. Humankind plays little direct part in the proceedings, although it is already clear that the gods are beginning to be preoccupied with the lives of mortal creatures. His dialogue is crisp and intelligent throughout and the final confrontation is gripping even though the reader can anticipate the outcome well in advance.

The third, and apparently final, instalment in the series is *Sons of the Titans*; although an author's note indicated his intention to continue his mythological history, it seems unlikely at this late date that any such will appear. Zeus, saved from Kronos' usual habit of eating his newborn offspring alive, is now a young adult, still learning to master his supernatural abilities. Kronos continues to rule Olympus but the Titans have largely switched their allegiance to Mount Othrys and the Council of Titans. Unrest besets the Council, however, and plotters are already seeking a way to restore the monarchy by force and subterfuge.

Newly arrived among the Titans, Zeus is naive and a perfect tool for the conspirators. Or at least so it seems. His determination and strength of character disconcert those who thought to use him for their purposes, and he emerges as a potential player rather than a simple pawn in the game to come. His identity as the son of Kronos has been carefully concealed, even from the young god himself, but Rhea, his mother, eventually reveals that she tricked Kronos at his birth. But Zeus makes powerful enemies among the Titans after becoming involved with a pair of goddesses. Angered that the game is not going as they expected, they plot to eliminate Zeus by trapping him into an unwelcome liaison.

Presumably further volumes would have chronicled Zeus' defeat of his father and the return to Mt Olympus. Adkins has been compared to Thomas Burnett Swann, but the similarities are only superficial. Where Swann wrote intelligent stories in a dramatic, mythlike manner, Adkins writes about dramatic myths in an intelligent, thoughtful manner.

—Don D'Ammassa

AIKEN, Joan (Delano)

Nationality: British. **Born:** Rye, Sussex, 4 September 1924; daughter of the writer Conrad Aiken. **Education:** Wychwood School, Oxford, 1936-40. **Family:** Married 1) Ronald George Brown in 1945 (died 1955), one son and one daughter; 2) Julius Goldstein in 1976. **Career:** Worked for the BBC, 1942-43; information officer, then librarian, United Nations Information Centre, London, 1943-49; subeditor and features editor, *Argosy,* London, 1955-60; copywriter, J. Walter Thompson, London, 1960-61. **Awards:** *Guardian* award for children's literature, 1969; Mystery Writers of America Edgar Allan Poe award, 1972. **Agent:** A. M. Health, 79 St. Martin's Lane, London, WC2N 4AA; or, Brandt and Brandt, 1501 Broadway, New York, New York 10036, USA. **Address:**

The Hermitage, East Street, Petworth, West Sussex GU28 0AB, England.

Fantasy Publications

Novels (series: James III)

The Kingdom and the Cave. London, Abelard Schuman, 1960; New York, Doubleday, 1974.

The Wolves of Willoughby Chase (James III). London, Cape, 1962; New York, Doubleday, 1963.

Black Hearts in Battersea (James III). New York, Doubleday, 1964; London, Cape, 1965.

Nightbirds on Nantucket (James III). London, Cape, and New York, Doubleday, 1966.

The Whispering Mountain (James III). London, Cape, 1968; New York, Doubleday, 1969.

The Cuckoo Tree (James III). London, Cape, and New York, Doubleday, 1971.

Midnight Is a Place (James III). London, Cape, and New York, Viking Press, 1974.

The Shadow Guests. London, Cape, and New York, Delacorte Press, 1980.

The Stolen Lake (James III). London, Cape, and New York, Delacorte Press, 1981.

Dido and Pa (James III). London, Cape, and New York, Delacorte Press, 1986.

The Moon's Revenge. London, Cape, and New York, Knopf, 1987.

The Erl King's Daughter. London, Heinemann, 1988.

Voices. London, Hippo, 1988; as *Return to Harken House,* New York, Delacorte Press, 1988.

Is (James III). London, Cape, and New York, Delacorte Press, 1992.

The Haunting of Lamb House. London, Cape, 1991; New York, St. Martin's Press, 1993.

The Winter Sleepwalker. London, Cape, 1994.

Short Stories

All You've Ever Wanted and Other Stories. London, Cape, 1953.

More Than You Bargained For and Other Stories. London, Cape, 1955; New York, Abelard Schuman, 1957.

A Necklace of Raindrops and Other Stories. London, Cape, and New York, Doubleday, 1968.

A Small Pinch of Weather and Other Stories. London, Cape, 1969.

The Windscreen Weepers and Other Tales of Horror and Suspense. London, Gollancz, 1969.

Armitage, Armitage, Fly Away Home. New York, Doubleday, 1968.

Smoke from Cromwell's Time and Other Stories. New York, Doubleday, 1970.

All and More (omnibus; includes *All You've Ever Wanted, More Than You Bargained For*). London, Cape, 1971.

The Green Flash and Other Tales of Horror, Suspense, and Fantasy. New York, Holt Rinehart, 1971.

The Kingdom under the Sea and Other Stories (retellings). London, Cape, 1971.

A Harp of Fishbones and Other Stories. London, Cape, 1972.

All But a Few. London, Penguin, 1974.

Not What You Expected: A Collection of Short Stories. New York, Doubleday, 1974.

A Bundle of Nerves: Stories of Horror, Suspense, and Fantasy. London, Gollancz, 1976.

The Faithless Lollybird and Other Stories. London, Cape, 1977; New York, Doubleday, 1978.

The Far Forests: Tales of Romance, Fantasy, and Suspense. New York, Viking Press, 1977.

Tale of a One-Way Street and Other Stories. London, Cape, 1978; New York, Doubleday, 1979.

A Touch of Chill: Stories of Horror, Suspense, and Fantasy. London, Gollancz, 1979; New York, Delacorte Press, 1980.

A Whisper in the Night: Stories of Horror, Suspense, and Fantasy. London, Gollancz, 1982; New York, Delacorte Press, 1984.

Up the Chimney Down, and Other Stories. London, Cape, and New York, Harper, 1984.

The Last Slice of Rainbow and Other Stories. London, Cape, 1985; New York, Harper, 1988.

Past Eight O'Clock: Goodnight Stories. London, Cape, 1986.

A Goose on Your Grave. London, Gollancz, 1987.

A Foot in the Grave, with Jan Pienkowski. London, Cape, 1989; New York, Viking, 1991.

Give Yourself a Fright: Thirteen Tales of the Supernatural. New York, Delacorte Press, 1989.

A Fit of Shivers. London, Gollancz, 1990.

Other Publications

Novels

The Silence of Herondale. New York, Doubleday, 1964; London, Gollancz, 1965.

The Fortune Hunters. New York, Doubleday, 1965.

Trouble with Product X. London, Gollancz, 1966; as *Beware of the Banquet,* New York, Doubleday, 1966.

Hate Begins at Home. London, Gollancz, 1967; as *Dark Interval,* New York, Doubleday, 1967.

The Ribs of Death. London, Gollancz, 1967; as *The Crystal Crow,* New York, Doubleday, 1968.

The Embroidered Sunset. London, Gollancz, and New York, Doubleday, 1970.

Died on a Rainy Sunday. London, Gollancz, and New York, Holt Rinehart, 1972.

The Butterfly Picnic. London, Gollancz, 1972; as *A Cluster of Separate Sparks,* New York, Doubleday, 1972.

Voices in an Empty House. London, Gollancz, and New York, Doubleday, 1975.

Castle Barebane. London, Gollancz, and New York, Viking Press, 1976.

Last Movement. London, Gollancz, and New York, Doubleday, 1977.

The Five-Minute Marriage. London, Gollancz, 1977; New York, Doubleday, 1978.

The Smile of the Stranger. London, Gollancz, and New York, Doubleday, 1978.

The Lightning Tree. London, Gollancz, 1980; as *The Weeping Ash,* New York, Doubleday, 1980.

The Young Lady from Paris. London, Gollancz, 1982; as *The Girl from Paris,* New York, Doubleday, 1982.

Foul Matter. London, Gollancz, and New York, Doubleday, 1983.

Mansfield Revisited (sequel to *Mansfield Park* by Jane Austen). London, Gollancz, 1984; New York, Doubleday, 1985.

Deception. London, Gollancz, 1987; as *If I Were You,* New York,
    Doubleday, 1987.
Blackground. London, Gollancz, and New York, Doubleday, 1989.
Jane Fairfax (sequel to *Emma* by Jane Austen). London, Gollancz,
    and New York, St. Martin's Press, 1990.
Morningquest. London, Gollancz, 1992; New York, St. Martin's
    Press, 1993.
Eliza's Daughter (sequel to *Sense and Sensibility* by Jane Austen).
    London, Gollancz, and New York, St. Martin's Press, 1994.

Fiction (for children)

Night Fall. London, Macmillan, 1969; New York, Holt Rinehart, 1971.
Arabel's Raven. London, BBC Publications, 1972.
The Escaped Black Mamba. London, BBC Publications, 1973.
The Bread Bin. London, BBC Publications, 1974.
Tales of Arabel's Raven. London, BBC Publications, 1972; as
    Arabel's Raven, New York, Doubleday, 1974.
Mortimer's Tie. London, BBC Publications, 1976.
Go Saddle the Sea. New York, Doubleday, 1977; London, Cape,
    1978.
Mice and Mendelson, music by John Sebastian Brown. London,
    Cape, 1978.
Mortimer and the Sword Excalibur. London, BBC Publications,
    1979.
The Spiral Stair. London, BBC Publications, 1979.
Arabel and Mortimer (omnibus; includes *Mortimer's Tie, The Spiral
    Stair, Mortimer and the Sword Excalibur).* London, Cape, 1980;
    New York, Doubleday, 1981.
Mortimer's Portrait on Glass. London, Hodder and Stoughton, 1981.
The Mystery of Mr. Jones's Disappearing Taxi. London, Hodder
    and Stoughton, 1982.
Bridle the Wind. London, Cape, and New York, Delacorte Press, 1983.
Mortimer's Cross. London, Cape, 1983; New York, Harper, 1984.
The Kitchen Warriors. London, BBC Publications, 1983.
Fog Hounds, Wind Cat, Sea Mice. London, Macmillan, 1984.
Mortimer Says Nothing and Other Stories. London, Cape, 1985;
    New York, Harper, 1987.
The Teeth of the Gale. London, Cape, and New York, Harper,
    1988.
The Shoemaker's Boy. New York, Simon and Schuster, 1991.
The Midnight Moropus. New York, Simon and Schuster, 1993.
Hatching Trouble. London, BBC Publications, 1993.
A Creepy Company. London, Gollancz, 1993.

Plays

Winterthing, music by John Sebastian Brown (produced Albany,
    New York, 1977). New York, Holt Rinehart, 1972; included in
    Winterthing, and The Mooncusser's Daughter, 1973.
Winterthing, and The Mooncusser's Daughter, music by John
    Sebastian Brown. London, Cape, 1973; *The Mooncusser's
    Daughter* published separately, New York, Viking Press, 1974.
Street, music by John Sebastian Brown (produced London, 1977).
    New York, Viking Press, 1978.
Moon Mill (produced London, 1982).

Television Plays: *The Dark Streets of Kimballs Green,* 1976; *The
    Apple of Trouble,* 1977; *Midnight Is a Place* (serial), from her
    own story, 1977; *The Rose of Puddle Fratrum,* 1978; *Armitage,
    Armitage, Fly Away Home,* from her own story, 1978.

Poetry

The Skin Spinners. New York, Viking Press, 1976.

Other

The Way to Write for Children. London, Elm Tree, 1982; New
    York, St. Martin's Press, 1983.

Translator, *The Angel Inn,* by Contessa de Segur. London, Cape,
    1976; Owings Mills, Maryland, Stemmer House, 1978.

*

Film Adaptations: *The Wolves of Willoughby Chase,* 1989.

Joan Aiken comments:

I first began producing fantasy in the form of stories told to my
younger brother when he was about three and I was about ten. At
the age of 17 I began writing down these stories and they formed
the nucleus of my first collection, *All You've Ever Wanted* (dedicated to my brother). I then discovered that some of these stories
were saleable to adult magazines, and through the 1950s and 1960s
I wrote a large number of such part-adult part-juvenile fantasies
which were sold to magazines such as the English *Argosy* and later
incorporated into story-collections, either sold in the children's market by Cape (such as *A Small Pinch of Weather*) or in the adult
market by Gollancz as ghost/horror stories (such as *A Bundle of
Nerves* and *A Touch of Chill*). For fantasy, I prefer the short-story
length. However my children's novels occasionally contain a supernatural element. *The Stolen Lake* is one such example, in which
reincarnations of Arthur and Guinevere are found in a South American country. But the main fantasy element (if fantasy it can be
called) is in my James III series of alternate-historical novels for
children.

*   *   *

Aiken started as a writer of short stories, most of them being
fantasy of one kind or another; as a short-story writer she is probably unsurpassed in English-language children's literature. The fantasy stories can be divided into three types: fairy stories of traditional style, stories of "magical realism," in which magic appears
as an accepted part of daily life, and ghost stories. The "magical
realism" stories are perhaps her most distinctive contribution to fantasy literature: they are characterized by an acute and humorous
observation of real life, and an appreciation of the surrealistic possibilities of inserting magic into the lives of ordinary families in
20th-century Britain. A number of the stories feature the Armitage
family, whose children, Mark and Harriet, learn the basics of magic
at school and who have rather exaggerated ideas about their own
ability to control it.

Aiken is best known, however, for the series which started with
her second children's novel, *The Wolves of Willoughby Chase,* and
which is now published as the James III series. These exuberant
adventures can be counted as marginal fantasy through their use of
the device of alternative history (more usually adopted by writers
of science fiction than of fantasy); however, more traditional elements of the fantastic appear in later novels in the series, above all
in *The Stolen Lake*. The books are set in the 1830s, featuring characters who grew up in a world in which the Stuart line survives

and in which the Hanoverians are thus never brought to the English throne. While in our world there were a number of Jacobite attempts on the English throne, in Aiken's world it is the Hanoverians who scheme against the throne, providing plots and subplots for several of the novels.

> Bonnie Prince Georgie lies over the water;
> *He don't rule over this land though he oughter.*

The Hanoverian schemes are dastardly indeed, involving blowing up Battersea Castle during a royal visit (in *Black Hearts in Battersea*), shelling St. James's Palace with a giant cannon placed on the east coast of America (*Nightbirds on Nantucket*), rolling St. Paul's Cathedral into the Thames during the coronation of Richard IV (*The Cuckoo Tree*) or kidnapping the king under the Thames during the royal opening of the Rotherhithe Tunnel (*Dido and Pa*). Aiken almost manages to make these comic-book capers plausible, and always milks them for the maximum suspense and the most satisfying resolution.

The details of Aiken's world are only revealed, or invented, gradually. At the beginning of *The Wolves of Willoughby Chase*, an unsubtle "Note" explains that the action takes place in 1832, under Good King James III, and that the Channel Tunnel, recently completed, had allowed many starving wolves to cross from France. *The Wolves* remains Aiken's best-known book, and it achieved wider currency through the film of 1989. The film captures some of the menace of the book, but, thanks to spectacular miscasting, loses much of the subtlety of characterization. Even so, *The Wolves* does not have the fun and colour of the later books, nor their complexity of plot. As Aiken progresses through the series, she seems to find the confidence to become more outrageous and fantastical. She also allows herself the leisure to fill out the detail of her imaginary world—its history, its slang, its popular songs—and she does so by sly hints rather than blatant "Notes." Only seldom does she strike a jarring note, such as the anachronistic reference to an aged Queen Victoria in *The Stolen Lake*.

In *The Wolves of Willoughby Chase* the lives of young Bonnie Green and her cousin Sylvia are taken over by their sinister governess, Miss Slighcarp. They are saved thanks to Bonnie's courage and the resourceful young Simon, who lives mysteriously in a cave on the estate. At the beginning of *Black Hearts in Battersea* Simon, an apprentice painter in London, lodges with the Twites, and is befriended by the brat of the family, Dido. Finding Dido's father to be a Hanoverian, plotting against the king, he attempts to foil the plot and is kidnapped, along with Sophie (the Duchess of Battersea's maid) and Dido, but returns from a shipwreck in a gloriously over-the-top conclusion, to save the king and to discover that he is the lost son of the Duke of Battersea. Dido is lost at sea. In *Nightbirds on Nantucket* we learn that Dido has been picked up by a New England whaler. Its captain, Captain Casket, is obsessively seeking a pink whale, Rosie: a friend, not a potential target. Miss Slighcarp reappears, leading a Hanoverian plot, which is foiled by Dido. *The Stolen Lake* is linked more than the other novels to traditional elements of the fantasy tale, combining Arthurian characters with the lost-race story so beloved of writers of popular fiction in the late 19th and early 20th century. New Cumbria is a remote kingdom founded by the Romano-British who fled from the Anglo-Saxons in the fifth century; its queen is Ginevra—Guinevere—who has become a sinister demented figure during the 1,300 years in which she has waited the return of her husband. Dido Twite, on her way back to England on board *HMS Thrush*,

is crucial to the discovery that Captain Hughes' steward, Holystone, is Arthur himself.

Dido returns to England with Captain Hughes in *The Cuckoo Tree,* to find herself enmeshed in another Hanoverian plot. At the end, as she carries the train of King Richard IV at his coronation, her old friend Simon, now Duke of Battersea, spots her from a distance. But they do not meet again until *Dido and Pa.* In this novel we get to know Pa Twite better: a talented musician, a gifted composer of music and of little ditties, and an inveterate Hanoverian. He is inveigled by the sinister Margrave of Bad-Nordmarck into another plot; its unmasking ends in his death, and a reconciliation between his three children, Penny, Dido and Is (short for Isabett). In the final novel, *Is,* the attention turns to Dido's younger sister, who sets off to investigate rumours of a children's paradise, Playland, in the north of England, which has declared itself an independent kingdom. It turns out that Gold Kingy, the tyrannical monarch of the north, is Is's uncle Roy Twite and is fuelling his industrial revolution by enticing children north to form a pool of slave labour. Is reaches Roy's industrial stronghold at Blastburn, and, after establishing telepathic contact with many of the oppressed children, manages to lead them to safety and sees Roy's kingdom collapse. The royal heir, however, is one of the many children who died·in the factories, and King Richard dies of grief: his cousin, Simon, Duke of Battersea, succeeds him.

There are two other books set in the same world, which do not fit in the sequence: *The Whispering Mountain,* following the adventures of the son of the Captain Hughes encountered in *The Stolen Lake,* and *Midnight Is a Place,* in which the frightening world of child exploitation in Blastburn is seen from a different point of view. *The Shadow Guests* is not in the series at all; it is a sophisticated children's ghost story. *The Haunting of Lamb House,* set in the literary environs of Rye, Sussex, is an equally sophisticated adult ghost story.

—Edward James

ALEXANDER, Lloyd (Chudley)

Nationality: American. **Born:** Philadelphia, Pennsylvania, 30 January 1924. **Education:** Upper Darby Senior High School, Pennsylvania, graduated 1940; West Chester State College, Pennsylvania, 1942; Lafayette College, Easton, Pennsylvania, 1943; the Sorbonne, Paris, 1946. **Military Service:** Served in the United States Army Combat Intelligence and Counter-Intelligence corps, 1942-46: Staff Sergeant. **Family:** Married Janine Denni in 1946; one stepdaughter. **Career:** Cartoonist, layout artist, copywriter, and trade magazine editor, 1947-70. Author-in-residence, schools in Springfield, Pennsylvania, 1967-68, and Temple University, Philadelphia, 1970-74. Since 1970 director, Carpenter Lane Chamber Music Society, Philadelphia; since 1973 member of the Editorial Advisory Board, *Cricket* magazine, La Salle, Illinois. **Awards:** Jewish Book Council Isaac Siegel Memorial award, 1959; American Library Association Newbery Medal, 1969; National Book Award, 1971; Silver Pencil award (Netherlands), 1981; American Book Award, 1982; Children's Book Award (Austria), 1984; Golden Cat award (Sweden), 1984; Catholic Library Association Regina medal, 1986; Children's Book Award (Norway), 1987; Church and Synagogue Library Association Ott Award, 1987; Carolyn W. Field Award, 1987; Parents' Choice Award, 1991, 1992; Otter award, 1993; *Boston Globe*-Horn Book Award, 1993. **Agent:** Brandt and Brandt, 1501 Broadway, New York, New York 10036, USA. **Address:** 1005 Drexel Avenue, Drexel Hill, Pennsylvania 19026, USA.

FANTASY PUBLICATIONS

Novels (series: Prydain; Vesper Holly; Westmark)

Time Cat: The Remarkable Journeys of Jason and Gareth, illustrated by Bill Sokol. New York, Holt Rinehart, 1963; as *Nine Lives,* London, Cassell, 1963.
The Book of Three (Prydain). New York, Holt Rinehart, 1964; London, Heinemann, 1966.
The Black Cauldron (Prydain). New York, Holt Rinehart, 1965; London, Heinemann, 1967.
The Castle of Llyr (Prydain). New York, Holt Rinehart, 1966; London, Heinemann, 1968.
Taran Wanderer (Prydain). New York, Holt Rinehart, 1967; London, Fontana, 1979.
The High King (Prydain). New York, Holt Rinehart, 1968; London, Fontana, 1979.
Coll and His White Pig, illustrated by Evaline Ness (Prydain). New York, Holt Rinehart, 1965.
The Truthful Harp, illustrated by Evaline Ness (Prydain). New York, Holt Rinehart, 1967.
The Marvelous Misadventures of Sebastian. New York, Dutton, 1970.
The Cat Who Wished to Be a Man. New York, Dutton, 1973.
The Wizard in the Tree, illustrated by Laszlo Kubinyi. New York, Dutton, 1975.
The First Two Lives of Lukas-Kasha. New York, Dutton, 1978.
Westmark. New York, Dutton, 1981.
The Kestrel (Westmark). New York, Dutton, 1982.
The Beggar Queen (Westmark). New York, Dutton, 1984.
The Illyrian Adventure (Vesper Holly). New York, Dutton, 1986.
The El Dorado Adventure (Vesper Holly). New York, Dutton, 1987.
The Drackenberg Adventure (Vesper Holly). New York, Dutton, 1988.
The Jedera Adventure (Vesper Holly). New York, Dutton, 1989.
The Philadelphia Adventure (Vesper Holly). New York, Dutton, 1990.
The Remarkable Journey of Prince Jen. New York, Dutton, 1991.

Short Stories

The Foundling and Other Tales of Prydain, illustrated by Margot Zemach. New York, Holt Rinehart, 1973.
The Town Cats and Other Tales, illustrated by Laszlo Kubinyi. New York, Dutton, 1977.

OTHER PUBLICATIONS

Novel

And Let the Credit Go. New York, Crowell, 1955.

Fiction (for children)

The King's Fountain, illustrated by Ezra Jack Keats. New York, Dutton, 1971.
The Four Donkeys, illustrated by Lester Abrams. New York, Holt Rinehart, 1972; Kingswood, Surrey, World's Work, 1974.
The Fortune-Tellers, illustrated by Trina Schart Hyman. New York, Dutton, 1992.

Other

My Five Tigers. New York, Crowell, and London, Cassell, 1956.
Border Hawk: August Bondi, illustrated by Bernard Krigstein. New York, Farrar Straus, 1958.
Janine Is French. New York, Crowell, 1958; London, Cassell, 1960.
The Flagship Hope: Aaron Lopez, illustrated by Bernard Krigstein. Philadelphia, Jewish Publication Society, 1960.
My Love Affair with Music. New York, Crowell, 1960; London, Cassell, 1961.
Park Avenue Vet, with Louis J. Camuti. New York, Holt Rinehart, and London, Deutsch, 1962.
Fifty Years in the Doghouse. New York, Putnam, 1964; as *Send for Ryan!,* London, W. H. Allen, 1965.

Translator, *The Wall and Other Stories,* by Jean-Paul Sartre. New York, New Directions, 1948; as *Intimacy and Other Stories,* London, Nevill, 1949.
Translator, *Nausea,* by Jean-Paul Sartre. New York, New Directions, 1949; London, Hamish Hamilton, 1962; as *The Diary of Antoine Roquentin,* London, Lehmann, 1949.
Translator, *Selected Writings,* by Paul Eluard. New York, New Directions, 1951; London, Routledge, 1952; as *Uninterrupted Poetry: Selected Writings,* New Directions, 1975.
Translator, *The Sea Rose,* by Paul Vialar. London and New York, Nevill, 1952.

*

Film Adaptation: *The Black Cauldron,* 1985.

Bibliography: *Lloyd Alexander, Evangeline Walton Ensley, Kenneth Morris: A Primary and Secondary Bibliography* by Kenneth J. Zahorski, Boston, Hall, 1981; *Lloyd Alexander: A Bio-Bibliography* by James S. Jacobs and Michael O. Tunnell, Westport, Connecticut, Greenwood Press, 1991.

Manuscript Collection: Free Library of Philadelphia.

Critical Studies: *A Tribute to Lloyd Alexander* by Myra Cohn Livingston, Philadelphia, Drexel Institute, 1976; *Lloyd Alexander: A Critical Biography* by James S. Jacobs, unpublished dissertation, University of Georgia, 1978; *The Prydain Companion* by Michael O. Tunnell, Westport, Connecticut, Greenwood Press, 1989; *Lloyd Alexander* by Jill P. May, Boston, Twayne, 1991.

Lloyd Alexander comments:

After writing some dozen years for adults, writing for young people was the most creative and liberating experience of my life. In books for young people I was able to express my own deepest feelings far more than I could ever do in writing for adults. Though most of my books have been in the form of fantasy, I believe that is merely one of the many ways to express attitudes about real human relationships and problems.

*   *   *

As has happened before (Tolkien is the obvious example), Lloyd Alexander's Chronicles of Prydain began as a fantasy sequence for younger readers but grew tougher, more mature, more resonant as it continued. The common setting is the Old Wales of legend, owing more to the *Mabinogion* than to any Welsh history or geography. However, despite a general Welshness the connections are glancing. It feels almost a coincidence that both Wales and Prydain have an Isle of Mona (Anglesey), while Prydain's impeccably heroic warrior-mage Gwydion resembles his amoral namesake from the Fourth Branch of the *Mabinogion* only in a few sleights—for example, both magically disguise themselves as shoemakers. Alexander admitted that his version of Arawn, King of Annuvin (i.e. Annwfn or Annwn, the underworld), is altogether more villainous than the oddly honourable original found in the *Mabinogion*'s First Branch.

The mythic elements provide a backdrop for Alexander's original creations like Taran, the boy without lineage who is the continuing hero and clearly fated to grow into someone of importance—but is always hurrying this process along, over-extending himself and using more high-flown language than appropriate to his role as Assistant Pig-Keeper (of Hen Wen, the magic oracular sow who might derive distantly from the newly imported swine that Gwydion steals from Pryderi in the *Mabinogion*). Chief among those who slap him down again is Eilonwy, a royal young lady with a temper and a fondness for eccentric similes: "Listening to you is more confusing than trying to count your fingers and toes at the same time!" Also generally in attendance are Gurgi, a hairy, greedy, smelly and loyal creature of indeterminate species; Fflewddur Fflam, wandering bard and part-time king whose unfortunately magical harp snaps its strings whenever he utters an entirely pardonable exaggeration; and Doli, an irascible dwarf who is extremely allergic to his own talent of invisibility.

The Book of Three pits Taran, Gwydion and the other companions against a slightly routine villain called the Horned King, one of Arawn's many puppets. It's an exciting adventure, but there is never any real doubt that things will turn out for the best. In *The Black Cauldron,* though, matters become darker. Likeable characters can die; conventional Good Guys turn their coats; high prices are paid for dubious gains; victory requires a real sacrifice. Taran's excess of inverted snobbery (he's ashamed of not being "noble") is matched by the satanic pride of his supposed ally Ellidyr, who despite royal blood has an even huger chip on his own shoulder. The Black Crochan or Cauldron itself, which cooks dead bodies back into malevolent unlife as "Cauldron-Born" warriors, is borrowed from the strange, poisoned Second Branch of the *Mabinogion*; so is the only possible means of its destruction, the need for someone to enter it living and die. Using a comic-relief technique reminiscent of T. H. White's in *The Sword in the Stone,* Alexander has the Crochan guarded by Orddu, Orwen and Orgoch, cheerfully sinister hags who drive hard bargains and betray an ill-concealed enthusiasm for turning people into toads. They are not, however, merely three conventional witches.

Book three, *The Castle of Llyr,* is less dramatic but has its more thoughtful aspects. Rehabilitating a near-villain like Ellidyr in *The Black Cauldron* is an altogether easier literary task than this book's development of the amiable and accident-prone wimp Prince Rhun

into someone very nearly worthy of respect. There is also an interestingly pitiable minor menace in Glew, the self-made and self-centred giant whose potions of gigantism have left him as small-minded as ever, and who exhibits fussy resentment when Taran and company won't co-operate with his reasonable request to kill just one of the party. At the climax, it's Eilonwy's turn to make an important renunciation despite being bedazzled and ensorcelled by the devious Queen Achren.

The way grows harder again in *Taran Wanderer,* which sees our hero looking for his own pedigree (and convinced for one tragic interval that he's found it) among the Free Commots—the little kingdoms of the day being subdivided into cantrefs or hundreds, and the cantrefs into commots. These are the people for whom high fantasy does not traditionally show much concern: scavengers, farmers, potters, weavers, the folk whose common trades can, astonishingly, be as hard to learn as battle and kingship. After serving a succession of hard apprenticeships, Taran emerges as a passable jack-of-all-trades whose real forte is, after all, leading and organizing . . . as shown when he rallies the smallest commot of all to beat off a vicious gang of raiders.

Darker still, *The High King* ends with Taran in the title role after a protracted series of betrayals, defeats, doomed rearguard actions and deaths of too many characters we have come to know and often like. Ultimately, all the more "noble" and magical companions sail off like Tolkien's elves to the Summer Country and immortality. Taran and Eilonwy are invited, but popularly acclaimed High Kings and their consorts have responsibilities to the war-blasted land of Prydain: a last choice has to be made.

The series is impressive, atmospheric and, despite a few slightly too convenient short cuts of plotting (Taran's one stroke at a Cauldron-Born with the enchanted sword Dyrnwyn causes the whole undead army to fall over), avoids all options of easy wish-fulfilment. *The High King* won the Newbery Medal. Related Prydain titles, outside the central strand of Taran's growing-up, are *Coll and His White Pig* (Coll, an ex-Hero, is Taran's first tutor and keeper of the pig Hen Wen), *The Truthful Harp* and *The Foundling and Other Tales of Prydain.*

Alexander has written other series: the Westmark sequence of Graustarkian adventures, the Vesper Holly young-adult works set in an alternate Victorian era, and further children's fantasies. The Prydain books show him at his best and are constantly reprinted.

—David Langford

ALEXANDER, Marc (Elward)

Pseudonym: Mark Ronson. **Nationality:** New Zealander. **Born:** 1929.

Fantasy Publications

Novels (series: The Wells of Ythan in all books)

Ancient Dreams. London, Headline, 1988.
Magic Casements. London, Headline, 1989.
Shadow Realm. London, Headline, 1991.
Enchantment's End. London, Headline, 1992.

Short Stories

Not After Midnight: Thirteen Stories to Haunt Your Dreams (for children). London, Viking, 1985.

OTHER PUBLICATIONS

Novels as Mark Ronson

Bloodthirst. London, Hamlyn, 1979; as *Blood-Thirst,* New York, Lorevan, 1986.
Ghoul. London, Hamlyn, 1980; New York, Lorevan, 1987.
Ogre. London, Hamlyn, 1980; New York, Lorevan, 1987.
Plague Pit. London, Hamlyn, 1981; New York, Lorevan, 1987.
The Dark Domain. London, Century, 1984.
Whispering Corner. London, Arrow, 1989.

Short Stories as Mark Ronson

Grimalkin's Tales: Strange and Wonderful Cat Stories, with Stella Whitelaw and Judy Gardiner. London, Hamlyn, 1983.

*   *   *

A full evaluation of Marc Alexander's work will depend on the discovery of what else he has written. According to a publisher's blurb, he is "an established author of horror novels under a pseudonym" (Mark Ronson), but not much else is generally known about him. As far as the fantasy genre is concerned, the Alexander name appears on the Wells of Ythan tetralogy, a long narrative whose plot—though it becomes more complex with each book—can be stated quite simply: the quest to wake Sleeping Beauty.

Princess Livia of Ythan is kidnapped almost a century before the first book begins. After her father dies of a broken heart, the country suffers under the rule of a series of tyrannical Regents, backed by the merciless Guild of Witchfinders. Legends say the kidnapped Princess lies under an Enchantment: that she is alive, but asleep, only to wake if bathed in water from the Wells of Ythan. Naturally, a new age of prosperity and peace will begin if she does wake. Those who undertake the quest to waken her (many have tried, and died) must overcome some difficulties: the legends might not be true—nobody knows where the princess sleeps, nor where the Wells of Ythan can be found—and the Regent is aided by black magic, with informants everywhere ready to betray questers to imprisonment and death.

Ancient Dreams sets the scene: two youths embark on the quest. One is Krispin Tammasson, an apprentice toymaker who with his sister, Jennet, were the only survivors of the village of Toyheim after its destruction by the Wolf Horde. The other youth is Alwald, son of Grimwald—a Lord of the River March murdered soon after the book begins. Grimwald was a follower of the Pilgrim Path, a group who wear the Disk of Livia and secretly work towards her waking. Another follower is the Lady Eloira, Reeve of the High Wald, who gives sanctuary to Krispin and Jennet.

It is Eloira who sends the two men on the quest after discerning unexpected abilities in the young toymaker. She wins Krispin's agreement by vowing to care for Jennet (mentally regressed to childhood by the traumatic massacre) and to find out whether they are really brother and sister at all. For Jennet and Krispin were found as children, wandering in the forest; neither can remember before

that time. Tammas the Toymaker, the man who took them in, assumed they were brother and sister—but a sexual attraction has grown between them, and they are hoping it is not unnatural. Alwald is fighting his own sexual attraction to Demara, an attractive young woman who happens to be his stepmother. Only recently married to his father, Demara is now pregnant, but has been kidnapped.

Alwald and Krispin begin their adventures by rescuing Demara from the Wolf King; on their way back, they unexpectedly pause at the City of Blight where Krispin (responding to instructions given under hypnosis) retrieves The Esav, a magical jewel which—it turns out—is the *only* object that may persuade the Mage, the *only* person who knows where Livia sleeps, to tell them where she is. They travel to another city, to meet another Follower of the Pilgrim Path. Arrested, and thrown into a dungeon, they fortuitously meet Ognam, a jester imprisoned for mocking the Regent. Ognam is yet another Follower of the Path, and becomes an important member of the quest.

They all escape, and are then guided towards the heretical city of Thaarn, the *only* place to hold out against the rule of the Regents. It is now the *only* place that may hold information on the location of The Mage. Unknown to them, the Regent has been poisoned by a manikin conjured by his alchemist; the *only* remedy to this poison—now slowly transforming him to an homunculus—is water from the Wells of Ythan . . . and *only* Thaarn may have maps showing where the Wells are. The Regent's army is about to march on Thaarn, using heresy as an excuse . . . and so on.

Ancient Dreams moves forward by a series of cliff-hanging chances and coincidences. Fortuitous meetings, last-minute rescues, and secret identities abound. This pattern recurs through the entire series, becoming increasingly at odds with Alexander's developing interest in his characters. By the last book, the plot is switching almost wildly from scene to scene, trying to impart information on dozens of characters yet still keeping its momentum towards a final battle. It doesn't succeed, and the seeds of the failure are sown in the first book.

Obviously, Alexander planned little more than the underlying rationale and some of the major characters. As the series proceeded, new characters and ideas emerged and took over. This is evident in folk such as The Hump and Silvermane: the one a reviled hunchback, the other a beautiful woman who never shows her legs. Each is the *only* representative of unhuman races: Alexander vaguely suggests that they are aliens from distant lands, but really they are just fantastic freaks, included because Alexander liked the idea of them. They are mentioned in later books, but mainly sidelined because their powers might move the quest forward too rapidly. When finally found, the Mage also refuses to help to shorten the quest. There is an explanation for this too, but many readers may find it a poor excuse after the many cruel deaths that could have been avoided.

In fact, the whole quest is slowed only because it depends on a frustrating chain of unique chances—the only City; the only map; the only Mage; the only way to an island; the only talisman; the only water; the only cure. There's no doubt the author knows how improbable this seems, and while there are many touches of brutal reality, Alexander also excuses the outrageous coincidences by having characters suggest they are living out old folk tales, or that their story will be remembered as a fairy tale.

Fairy tales underlie the whole plot—not only the obvious "Sleeping Beauty" and "Beauty and the Beast," but "Hansel and Gretel," "Babes in the Wood," "The Ugly Duckling," "Bluebeard" and more. If Alexander had plotted in such a way that these stories reinforced each other, the series would be both impressive and memorable.

Since they remain unconnected, and hence lack resonance, most of the tales could be discarded without harming the overall plot. The plot could also be abbreviated without any loss to the real story; it is often vague, unfocused, and random. The characters act coherently, but the outcome of events, that is the *quest* itself, is not dependent on those particular actions. Heroes and villains alike react to accidents rather than using any real strategy.

The series has many strengths: characters with astonishingly complex and troubled emotions; the revelation of why there is no great magic left in the world and few powerful Mages; why the fortunate resemblance between Jennet and Livia (which impels much of the later plot) is neither fortunate nor coincidental; and the excellent Magic Casements—windows showing the past which not only may be looked through, but can be stepped through (their effect is carefully limited to ensure nothing important to the plot is revealed in advance). There is a cheerily controversial view of religion: the Regents' tyranny establishes its control, and justifies its terror tactics, by demonizing the former religion of the All Father. Since that entity created the whole of time in an instant, he cannot be implored to change anyone's fate. The tyranny replaces this with worship of his daughter, the Serene Mother, who *can* be persuaded to forgive sin . . . for a price. Suppression of the former religion is handled by the Guild of Witchfinders, who simultaneously destroy records of the past and crush current opposition under the guise of heresy.

The greatest strength of all is the final inversion of the entire series when the Enchantment's true genesis and purpose are revealed, to the astonishment (one presumes) of every reader and the author himself. One suspects the series began as a parody which turned more serious as Alexander wrote more of it: the heroes include a toymaker, a jester, and a comedian; every character turns out to have a secret identity; and many of the names are simple anagrams (e.g. Esav is Save). Yet this underlying humour and general romanticism is jarred by the eruptions of cruelty, torture and death, of plagues and blood sacrifice—and the vicious ending. Perhaps we should bear in mind that Marc Alexander is also a writer of horror fiction.

—Ian Covell

ANDERSON, Poul (William)

Nationality: American. **Born:** Bristol, Pennsylvania, 25 November 1926. **Education:** University of Minnesota, Minneapolis; B.S., 1948. **Family:** Married Karen Kruse in 1953; one daughter. **Career:** Freelance writer. President, Science Fiction Writers of America, 1972-73. **Awards:** Hugo award, 1961, 1964, 1969, 1972, 1973, 1979, 1982; Nebula award, 1971, 1972, 1982; Tolkien Memorial award, 1978; Guest of Honor, World Science Fiction Convention, 1959. **Agent:** Scovil-Chichak-Galen Literary Agency, 381 Park Avenue South, New York, New York 10016, USA. **Address:** 3 Las Palomas, Orinda, California 94563, USA.

Fantasy Publications

Novels (series: Holger Danske; The King of Ys)

The Broken Sword. New York, Abelard Schuman, 1954; revised edition, New York, Ballantine, 1971; London, Sphere, 1973.

Three Hearts and Three Lions (Holger Danske). New York, Doubleday, 1961; London, Sphere, 1974.
Operation Chaos. New York, Doubleday, 1971.
Hrolf Kraki's Saga. New York, Ballantine, 1973.
A Midsummer Tempest (Holger Danske). New York, Doubleday, 1974; London, Futura, 1975.
The Merman's Children. New York, Berkley, 1979; London, Sidgwick and Jackson, 1981.
The Demon of Scattery, with Mildred Downey Broxon. New York, Ace, 1979.
Conan the Rebel. New York, Bantam, 1980; London, Hale, 1984.
The King of Ys, with Karen Anderson (omnibus). New York, SF Book Club, 2 vols., 1988.
   Roma Mater, with Karen Anderson. New York, Baen, 1986; London, Grafton, 1988.
   Gallicenae, with Karen Anderson. New York, Baen, 1987; London, Grafton, 1988.
   Dahut, with Karen Anderson. New York, Baen, 1988; London, Grafton, 1989.
   The Dog and the Wolf, with Karen Anderson. New York, Baen, 1988; London, Grafton, 1989.

Short Stories

Fantasy. New York, Tor, 1981.
The Unicorn Trade, with Karen Anderson. New York, Tor, 1984.
Loser's Night (story). Eugene, Oregon, Pulphouse, 1991.
The Armies of Elfland. New York, Tor, 1992.

Other

Editor, *The Night Fantastic,* with Karen Anderson. New York, DAW, 1991.

Translator, *The Fox, the Dog, and the Griffin: A Folk Tale Adapted from the Danish of C. Molbech.* New York, Doubleday, 1966.

Other Publications

Novels

Vault of the Ages (for children). Philadelphia, Winston, 1952.
Brain Wave. New York, Ballantine, 1954; London, Heinemann, 1955.
No World of Their Own. New York, Ace, 1955; as *The Long Way Home,* London, Panther, 1975; New York, Ace, 1978.
Planet of No Return. New York, Ace, 1956; London, Dobson, 1966; as *Question and Answer,* New York, Ace, 1978.
Star Ways. New York, Avalon, 1956; as *The Peregrine,* New York, Ace, 1978.
The Snows of Ganymede. New York, Ace, 1958.
War of the Wing-Men. New York, Ace, 1958; London, Sphere, 1976; as *The Man Who Counts,* New York, Ace, 1978.
The Enemy Stars. Philadelphia, Lippincott, 1959; London, Coronet, 1973.
Perish by the Sword. New York, Macmillan, 1959.
Virgin Planet. New York, Avalon, 1959; London, Mayflower, 1966.
The War of Two Worlds. New York, Ace, 1959; London, Dobson, 1970.
We Claim These Stars. New York, Ace, 1959; London, Dobson, 1976.

Earthman, Go Home! New York, Ace, 1960.
The Golden Slave. New York, Avon, 1960.
The High Crusade. New York, Doubleday, 1960; London, Corgi, 1981.
Murder in Black Letter. New York, Macmillan, 1960.
Mayday Orbit. New York, Ace, 1961.
Rogue Sword. New York, Avon, 1960.
Twilight World. New York, Torquil, 1961; London, Gollancz, 1962.
After Doomsday. New York, Ballantine, 1962; London, Gollancz, 1963.
The Makeshift Rocket. New York, Ace, 1962; London, Dobson, 1969.
Murder Bound. New York, Macmillan, 1962.
Let the Spaceman Beware! New York, Ace, 1963; London, Dobson, 1969; as *The Night Face,* New York, Ace, 1978.
Shield. New York, Berkley, 1963; London, Dobson, 1965.
Three Worlds to Conquer. New York, Pyramid, 1964; London, Mayflower, 1966.
The Corridors of Time. New York, Doubleday, 1965; London, Gollancz, 1966.
Ensign Flandry. Philadelphia, Chilton, 1966; London, Coronet, 1976.
World Without Stars. New York, Ace, 1966; London, Dobson, 1975.
The Rebel Worlds. New York, NAL, 1969; London, Coronet, 1972; as *Commander Flandry,* London, Severn House, 1978.
Satan's World. New York, Doubleday, 1969; London, Gollancz, 1970.
A Circus of Hells. New York, NAL, 1970; London, Sphere, 1978.
Tau Zero. New York, Doubleday, 1970; London, Gollancz, 1971.
The Byworlder. New York, NAL, 1971; London, Gollancz, 1972.
The Dancer from Atlantis. New York, NAL, 1971; London, Sphere, 1977.
There Will Be Time. New York, Doubleday, 1972; London, Sphere, 1979.
The People of the Wind. New York, NAL, 1973; London, Sphere, 1977.
The Day of Their Return. New York, Doubleday, 1974; London, Corgi, 1978.
Inheritors of Earth, with Gordon Eklund. Radnor, Pennsylvania, Chilton, 1974.
Fire Time. New York, Doubleday, 1974; London, Panther, 1977.
A Knight of Ghosts and Shadows (Flandry). New York, Doubleday, 1974; London, Sphere, 1978; as *Knight Flandry,* London, Severn House, 1980.
The Worlds of Poul Anderson (omnibus; includes *Planet of No Return, The War of Two Worlds, World Without Stars*). New York, Ace, 1974.
Star Prince Charlie, with Gordon R. Dickson. New York, Putnam, 1975.
The Winter of the World. New York, Doubleday, 1976; London, Panther, 1980.
Mirkheim. New York, Berkley, 1977; London, Sphere, 1978.
The Avatar. New York, Berkley, 1978; London, Sidgwick & Jackson, 1980.
Two Worlds (omnibus; includes *World Without Stars, Planet of No Return*). Boston, Gregg Press, 1978.
A Stone in Heaven. New York, Ace, 1979.
The Devil's Game. New York, Pocket, 1980.
The Last Viking:
    The Golden Horn. New York, Zebra, 1980.
    The Road of the Sea Horse. New York, Zebra, 1980.
    The Sign of the Raven. New York, Zebra, 1981.

Orion Shall Rise. New York, Timescape, 1983; London, Sphere, 1984.
Annals of the Time Patrol (omnibus; includes *Guardians of Time, Time Patrolman*). New York, SF Book Club, 1984.
The Game of Empire. New York, Baen, 1985.
The Year of the Ransom. New York, Walker, 1988.
The Boat of a Million Years. New York, Tor, 1989; London, Sphere, 1990.
No Truce with Kings, with *Ship of Shadows* by Fritz Leiber. New York, Tor, 1989.
The Saturn Game, with *Iceborn* by Gregory Benford and Paul A. Carter. New York, Tor, 1989.
The Shield of Time. New York, Tor, 1990.
The Time Patrol (omnibus; includes *Guardians of Time, Time Patrolman, The Year of the Ransom* and other stories). New York, Tor, 1991.
The Longest Voyage, with *Slow Lightning* by Steven Popkes. New York, Tor, 1991.
Harvest of Stars. New York, Tor, 1993.

Short Stories

Earthman's Burden, with Gordon R. Dickson. New York, Gnome Press, 1957.
Guardians of Time. New York, Ballantine, 1960; London, Gollancz, 1961; augmented edition, New York, Tor, 1981.
Strangers from Earth. New York, Ballantine, 1961; London, Mayflower, 1964.
Orbit Unlimited. New York, Pyramid, 1961; London, Sidgwick & Jackson, 1974.
Un-Man and Other Novellas. New York, Ace, 1962; London, Dobson, 1972.
Time and Stars. New York, Doubleday, 1964; London, Gollancz, 1964.
Trader to the Stars. New York, Doubleday, 1964; London, Gollancz, 1965.
Agent of the Terran Empire. Philadelphia, Chilton, 1965; London, Coronet, 1977.
Flandry of Terra. Philadelphia, Chilton, 1965; London, Coronet, 1966.
The Star Fox. New York, Doubleday, 1965; London, Gollancz, 1966.
The Trouble Twisters. New York, Doubleday, 1966; London, Gollancz, 1967.
The Horn of Time. New York, NAL, 1968; London, Corgi, 1981.
Beyond the Beyond. New York, NAL, 1969; London, Gollancz, 1970.
Seven Conquests. New York, Macmillan, and London, Collier Macmillan, 1969; as *Conquests,* London, Granada, 1981.
Tales of the Flying Mountains. New York, Macmillan, 1970.
The Queen of Air and Darkness and Other Stories. New York, NAL, 1973; London, NEL, 1977.
The Many Worlds of Poul Anderson. Radnor, Pennsylvania, Chilton, 1974; as *The Book of Poul Anderson,* New York, DAW, 1975.
Homeward and Beyond. New York, Doubleday, 1975.
Homebrew. Cambridge, Massachusetts, NESFA Press, 1976.
The Best of Poul Anderson. New York, Pocket, 1976.
The Earth Book of Stormgate. New York, Berkley, 1978; London, NEL, 3 vols., 1981.
The Night Face and Other Stories. Boston, Gregg Press, 1979.

The Dark Between the Stars. New York, Berkley, 1981.
Explorations. New York, Tor, 1981.
The Psychotechnic League. New York, Tor, 1981.
Winners. New York, Tor, 1981.
Cold Victory. New York, Tor, 1982.
The Gods Laughed. New York, Tor, 1982.
Mauri and Kith. New York, Tor, 1982.
New America. New York, Tor, 1982.
Starship. New York, Tor, 1982.
Conflict. New York, Tor, 1983.
Hoka!, with Gordon R. Dickson. New York, Simon & Schuster, 1983.
The Long Night. New York, Tor, 1983; London, Sphere, 1985.
Time Patrolman. New York, Tor, 1983; London, Sphere, 1986.
Past Times. New York, Tor, 1984; London, Sphere, 1987.
Dialogue with Darkness. New York, Tor, 1985.
Space Folk. New York, Baen, 1989.
Inconstant Star. New York, Baen, 1990.
Alight in the Void. New York, Tor, 1991.
Kinship with the Stars. New York, Tor, 1991.

Other

Is There Life on Other Worlds? New York, Crowell Collier, and London, Collier Macmillan, 1963.
Thermonuclear Warfare. Derby, Connecticut, Monarch, 1963.
The Infinite Voyage: Man's Future in Space. New York, Crowell Collier, and London, Collier Macmillan, 1969.

Editor, *West By One and By One.* Privately printed, 1965.
Editor, *Nebula Award Stories 4.* New York, Doubleday, 1969.
Editor, *Mercenaries of Tomorrow,* with Martin H. Greenberg and Charles G. Waugh. New York, Lorevan, 1985.
Editor, *Terrorists of Tomorrow,* with Martin H. Greenberg and Charles G. Waugh. New York, Lorevan, 1986.
Editor, *Time Wars,* with Charles G. Waugh and Martin H. Greenberg. New York, Tor, 1986.
Editor, *Space Wars,* with Charles G. Waugh and Martin H. Greenberg. New York, Tor, 1988.

*

Bibliography: *Poul Anderson: Myth-Master and Wonder-Weaver— A Working Bibliography* by Phil Stephensen-Payne and Gordon Benson, Jr., 2 Vols.: Part 1—*Fiction;* Part 2—*Non-Fiction,* 5th edition, Leeds, Yorkshire, Galactic Central Publications, 1989.

Manuscript Collection: University of Southern Mississippi, Hattiesburg.

Critical Study: *Against Time's Arrow: The High Crusade of Poul Anderson* by Sandra Miesel. San Bernardino, California, Borgo Press, 1978.

*   *   *

One of the major American fantasy writers (also well known for his copious science fiction), Poul Anderson has an extensive knowledge of history which he has used to good effect throughout a career that now spans more than 40 years. *The Broken Sword,* a full-blooded heroic fantasy about the Elfland of Old Norse legend, was first published at a time when fantasy novels of any type were rare commodities in the United States. It remained out of print for a

decade and a half before being revived (and revised) for Ballantine Books in 1971. Despite its early neglect it has been an influential work, thanks to the enthusiasm of Michael Moorcock and a few other latter-day practitioners of Sword and Sorcery.

The Broken Sword is the tragic story of changeling half-brothers, the human-born Skafloc and the elf-born Valgard. Identical in appearance, and at first ignorant of each other's existence, they have very different natures: both are excellent warriors, though Skafloc is chivalrous and loving where Valgard is bloodthirsty and cruel. Skafloc, though human, gains all manner of skills from his elvish guardians:

> He learned the songs which could raise or lay storms, bring good or bad harvests . . . He learned the use of the cloak of darkness, and of the skins he could don to take the form of a beast. Near the end of his training he learned the mighty runes and songs and charms which could raise the dead, read the future, and compel the gods . . .

Meanwhile the evil and un-human Valgard slays most of his adoptive family, kidnaps his half-sister Freda, and flees from the lands of men, taking service with the Troll-King. There is war between the elves and the trolls, a savage conflict in the realm of Faerie which remains invisible to human beings, and Skafloc and Valgard emerge as the champions of either side. Inevitably, they meet and fight, time and again. Their sister Freda becomes a prize in the battle. Skafloc falls in love with her, not realizing that she is kin to him, and she returns his love. Their sinful union leads to Skafloc's doom, though not before Valgard too has been destroyed. It is a grim, blood-soaked tale of parricide, fratricide and incest, frequently absurd and full of excess, but narrated with a lyrical fury which is astonishing in its emotional force. The prose is often purple with alliteration and assonance, but appropriately so:

> The wind skirled and bit at them. Sleet and spindrift blew off the waters in stinging sheets, white under the flying fitful moon. The sea bellowed inward from a wild horizon, bursting onto skerries and strand . . . The night was gale and sleet and surging waves, a racket that rang to the riven driven clouds.

This is a darkly magical story, as few modern fantasies are. The author may have embroidered his material; nevertheless he remains true to the essential spirit of those Old Norse sagas which have inspired his remarkable novel.

Anderson's second fantasy, *Three Hearts and Three Lions,* is a very enjoyable tale in a rather different vein from *The Broken Sword* (although it was written soon after the other, having been serialized in *The Magazine of Fantasy and Science Fiction* in 1953). The light-hearted story of a modern man who is plunged into a world of medieval romance, it has much in common with L. Sprague de Camp and Fletcher Pratt's tales of Harold Shea, the "incomplete enchanter". The hero, Holger Carlsen, is an American-educated Dane who returns to his homeland in order to join the underground struggle against the Nazi occupiers during World War II. He is knocked unconscious during a desperate hand-to-hand fight—and awakes to find himself in a different universe.

By mysterious means, Holger has been transported to a land of Carolingian myth, a world of bold knights, beautiful damsels, foul witches and fire-breathing dragons. Charlemagne's empire still stands, with the Saracens to the south, and the realms of Faerie to the east. It seems that Holger has been brought here according to some deliberate plan: he is alone in a wood, but a fine steed awaits him, together with weapons and a suit of perfectly-fitting armour. When he removes the canvas cover from his shield, he sees that it bears "a design of three golden lions alternating with three red hearts on a blue background". He has little choice but to take up these accoutrements, mount the horse, and ride off in search of information. A friendly witch gives him shelter for the night and advises him to seek his fortune in the land of Faerie. She also introduces him to an unlikely guide—a three-foot dwarf named Hugi.

Holger and Hugi ride into the enchanted land of Faerie, where many adventures await them. On the way, they meet a lovely young swan-maiden who becomes their travelling companion. The perils come thick and fast: Duke Alfric of Faerie attempts to trick Holger into a hundred-year snooze beneath a hill; Morgan le Fay, who has "a body with more curves than a scenic highway", tries to seduce him; a dragon attacks them, but Holger defeats it by casting water down its gullet ("a little thermodynamics is all", he explains casually. "Caused a small boiler explosion"); they have run-ins with giants, trolls, and other tricky creatures—but, with Hugi's and the swan-maid's help, Holger wins through. The purpose of his quest becomes clear: he has been brought to this world to help the forces of Law defeat those of Chaos. He is Holger Danske, or Ogier le Danois, fabled in the Carolingian chronicles as a champion who is fated to return again and again.

Three Hearts and Three Lions is an entertaining tale of a type which has become exceedingly familiar in the past couple of decades but has rarely been done so well. The humour, romance and derring-do are all nicely balanced, the invention is profuse, and the whole is neatly wrapped up in just 160 pages. It is a pity that most of the multi-volume fantasy epics of recent years cannot show a comparable degree of wit and economy.

Anderson's third fantasy novel, *Operation Chaos*, was cobbled together from stories first published between 1956 and 1969. It has a sympathetically-portrayed werewolf hero in a contemporary world where magic works. His earlier adventures tend to be light and amusing; the lengthy last episode, however, involves a trip to Hell and embodies some serious theological and political speculation. The implicit identification of the late-1960s radical student movement with extremist Christian cults earned Anderson some criticism for his "reactionary" views (a criticism which has also been levelled at some of his space-operatic science fiction).

Later Anderson fantasies deal with such subjects as the heroes of Icelandic legend (*Hrolf Kraki's Saga*); Shakespeare's supernatural entities (*A Midsummer Tempest,* in which characters from *A Midsummer Night's Dream* meet those from *The Tempest,* and the hero Holger Danske also makes a return appearance); mer-folk in a late medieval Europe (*The Merman's Children*); Robert E. Howard's oft-revived sword-swinging barbarian hero (*Conan the Rebel*); and a mythical Dark Age kingdom (the over-long King of Ys tetralogy, written in collaboration with his wife, Karen Anderson). None of these has had quite the same impact as his first two fantasy novels, but all are highly professional.

In addition to his vast body of sf and a few crime-fiction titles, Anderson has also written a number of historical adventure novels which are not out-and-out fantasies but nevertheless have much in common with sword and sorcery; they include such fugitive early books as *The Golden Slave* and *Rogue Sword* as well as his later Last Viking trilogy.

—David Pringle

ANSTEY, F.

Pseudonym for Thomas Anstey Guthrie. **Nationality:** British. **Born:** London, 8 August 1856. **Education:** King's College School, London; Trinity Hall, Cambridge. **Career:** Called to the bar, 1880; worked briefly as a barrister. Regular contributor to *Punch,* London. **Died:** 10 March 1934.

FANTASY PUBLICATIONS

Novels

Vice Versa, or A Lesson to Fathers. London, Smith Elder, 1882.
The Tinted Venus. Bristol, Arrowsmith, 1885.
A Fallen Idol. London, Smith Elder, 1886.
Tourmalin's Time Cheques. Bristol, Arrowsmith, 1891.
The Brass Bottle. London, Smith Elder, 1900.
Only Toys! (for children). London, Grant Richards, 1903.
In Brief Authority. London, Smith Elder, 1915.
Humour and Fantasy (omnibus; includes *Vice Versa, The Tinted Venus, A Fallen Idol, The Brass Bottle* and short stories). London, Murray, 1931.

Short Stories

The Black Poodle and Other Tales. London, Longmans, 1884.
The Talking Horse and Other Tales. London, Smith Elder, 1892.
Paleface and Redskin and Other Stories (for children). London, Grant Richards, 1898.

OTHER PUBLICATIONS

Novels

The Giant's Robe. London, Smith Elder, 1884.
The Pariah. London, Smith Elder, 1889.
The Statement of Stella Maberley. London, Unwin, 1896.
Puppets at Large (for children). London, Bradbury Agnew, 1897.
Love Among the Lions. London, Dent, 1898.

Short Stories

The Travelling Companions. London, Longmans, 1892.
Baboo Jaberjee, B.A. London, Dent, 1897.
A Bayard from Bengal. London, Methuen, 1902.
Salted Almonds. London, Smith Elder, 1906.
Winnie: An Everyday Story. London, Murray, 1909.
Percy and Others. London, Methuen, 1915.
The Last Load. London, Methuen, 1925.

Play

The Imaginary Invalid, adaptation of *La Malade imaginaire* by Molière. London, Hodder and Stoughton, 1929.

Poetry

Mr. Punch's Model Music-Hall Songs and Dramas. London, Bradbury Agnew, 1892.

Other

Burglar Bill and Other Pieces. London, Bradbury Agnew, 1888.
Voces Populi. First and Second Series, London, Longmans, 1890 and 1892.
Mr. Punch's Pocket Ibsen. London, Heinemann, 1893.
The Man from Blankley's and Other Sketches. London, Longmans, 1893.
Under the Rose. London, Bradbury Agnew, 1894.
Lyre and Lancet. London, Smith Elder, 1895.
A Long Retrospect (autobiography). Oxford, Oxford University Press, 1936.

*

Film adaptations: *Vice Versa,* 1947, 1988; *The Brass Bottle,* 1964; *Goddess of Love* (TV movie), 1988, from the novel *The Tinted Venus* (uncredited).

*   *   *

F. Anstey's comic fantasies in which the ultra-conventional and pretension-bound world of the Victorian middle classes is disrupted by anarchic and amoral magical forces are the archetypes of a sub-genre of fantasy which is sometimes labelled "Ansteyan fantasy" in recognition of his example. He moved swiftly from such broad parodies of the Victorian ghost story as "The Wraith of Barnjum" (1879) and "The Curse of the Catafalques" (1882) to the classic personality-exchange novel *Vice Versa,* whose runaway success was the foundation-stone of his long career as a popular humorist. At times he seems to have thought this an unfortunate circumstance—like many celebrated comedians he yearned to be taken more seriously—but he took the abject failure of his more earnest works in reasonably good part.

Vice Versa is subtitled "A Lesson to Fathers," and strives with might and main to expose the hollowness of the delusion—allegedly common among adults—that a boy's schooldays are the happiest of his life. The pompous businessman who finds himself locked in his son's body has a thoroughly miserable time labouring under the many oppressions of boyhood, but is not in the end forced to suffer too much. While Anstey was always prepared to poke fun at the pretensions of the Victorian bourgeoisie he never lost sight of the fact that a bourgeois Victorian was exactly what Thomas Anstey Guthrie was, and that he had not the slightest interest in being anything else. By virtue of this admission, Anstey's fantasies retained an essential unthreatening amiability which allowed them to be thoroughly enjoyed even by the targets of their satire.

The Tinted Venus is one of several modern fantasies based on a Classical tale by Philostratus about a statue of the goddess of love which comes to life after a ring is placed on its finger in mock-betrothal. Anstey's hairdresser hero inevitably finds the attentions of the statue embarrassing, but the element of subtle threat is not fully worked out and the story stutters to a premature conclusion by virtue of having to be shoehorned into the slim standard format favoured by the publisher who commissioned it, J. W. Arrowsmith. *A Fallen Idol* makes up for this faint-heartedness in no uncertain terms, and there are moments of authentic horror as well as black-edged comedy in its account of a young painter who falls under the spell of a malevolent spirit preserved in a Jain idol. *A Fallen Idol* is perhaps the best of Anstey's early novels, although it was by no means the best-loved in its own day.

In 1887 Anstey became a full-time member of the staff of the humorous weekly *Punch,* and held that position for ten years (after which his contributions became irregular). This work absorbed the bulk of his humorous efforts, and he wrote only one comic fantasy novel, *Tourmalin's Time Cheques,* during that period. The hero of the novel is persuaded to deposit the time spent on a long sea cruise in a "time bank" from which he later reclaims it by the hour whenever he needs a respite from the stresses of life in London, but the hours are not redeemed in chronological order, thus generating a mounting crescendo of confusions which reach a climax when he finds the interest paid into his account duplicating hours through which he has already lived. The novel's premise was highly original—it is the first significant example of the "time paradox" sub-genre which was later to become a favourite with science-fiction writers—but the only available means to resolve the chronological tangle was, alas, the weakest of all narrative escape clauses.

Once his duties at *Punch* had become less arduous Anstey was able to produce his second bestseller, *The Brass Bottle,* in which a jinnee from the *Arabian Nights* becomes frustrated by the ungracious way in which his liberator reacts to his attempts to demonstrate his gratitude. The luckless hero desires only to retreat into comfortable and inconspicuous middle-class respectability with his beloved, and the munificence of the jinnee's generosity is a continual embarrassment to him. The jinnee eventually makes grander plans, forcing the young hero to apply considerable ingenuity to the problem of putting his power under severe restraint.

Anstey's fantasy for children, *Only Toys,* was condemned to virtual oblivion when the publisher went bankrupt on the eve of publication, but it is in any case an uneasy story whose allegorical representation of the adult world as a riot of avarice and aggression which no sensible child would want to enter ahead of time may have revealed more about the author's private dissatisfactions than he realized. His last full-length fantasy, *In Brief Authority,* also met with marketing misfortune by virtue of drawing on specifically Germanic folklore; by the time it was published England and Germany were at war. *In Brief Authority* is the sharpest of Anstey's satires, reversing his normal formula by dispatching a snobbish Victorian matriarch and her family into the *märchenland* of the Brothers Grimm, where she is mistakenly installed as the rightful queen. Her attempts to bring respectability to the semi-barbaric realm are not appreciated, and the sinister side of traditional folklore becomes increasingly evident before disaster is averted in the nick of time.

In his autobiography Anstey lamented that his kind of humour had gone out of fashion after the turn of the century, and he was partly right; it was the rigidity of Victorian social conventions and the exacting pressure of Victorian morality which made the anarchic thrust of pagan magic so absurdly effective a form of opposition. Even so, his work enjoyed something of a revival when John Murray published the omnibus *Humour and Fantasy,* and adaptations of *Vice Versa* for stage and screen have continued to enjoy success into the present day. Such British imitators of the Ansteyan method as W. A. Darlington and Susan Alice Kerby contrived to use his method to good effect in later periods, while the American humorist Thorne Smith found the formula highly effective in assaulting the moral repressions of the Prohibitionist era. The essential amiability and deft charm of Anstey's best work allows it to be read with pleasure today, and the lessons which he modestly sought to offer still have some pertinence to a modern world which harbours—at least in certain quarters—a foolish nostalgia for Victorian moral certainties.

—Brian Stableford

ANTHONY, Piers

Pseudonym for Piers Anthony Dillingham Jacob. **Nationality:** American. **Born:** Oxford, England, 6 August 1934; became United States citizen, 1958. **Education:** Goddard College, Plainfield, Vermont, B.A. 1956; University of South Florida, Tampa, teaching certificate 1964. **Military Service:** Served in the United States Army, 1957-59. **Family:** Married Carol Marble in 1956; one daughter. **Career:** Technical writer, Electronic Communications Inc., St. Petersburg, Florida, 1959-62; English teacher, Admiral Farragut Academy, St. Petersburg, 1965-66. Since 1966 freelance writer. **Awards:** Pyramid Fantasy and Science Fiction award, 1967; August Derleth award, 1977. **Address:** c/o Valet Publishing Co., P.O. Box 1990, Clayton, Georgia 30525, USA.

FANTASY PUBLICATIONS

Novels (series: Apprentice Adept; Incarnations of Immortality; Kelvin Rud; Mode; Xanth)

Hasan. San Bernardino, California, Borgo Press, 1977.
A Spell for Chameleon (Xanth). New York, Ballantine, 1977; London, Macdonald, 1984.
Pretender, with Frances Hall. San Bernardino, California, Borgo Press, 1979.
The Source of Magic (Xanth). New York, Ballantine, 1979; London, Macdonald, 1984.
Castle Roogna (Xanth). New York, Ballantine, 1979; London, Macdonald, 1984.
Split Infinity (Apprentice Adept). New York, Ballantine, 1980; London, Granada, 1983.
Blue Adept (Apprentice Adept). New York, Ballantine, 1981; London, Granada, 1983.
Centaur Aisle (Xanth). New York, Ballantine, 1982; London, Macdonald, 1984.
Ogre, Ogre (Xanth). New York, Ballantine, 1982; London, Futura, 1984.
Juxtaposition (Apprentice Adept). New York, Ballantine, 1982; London, Granada, 1983.
Night Mare (Xanth). New York, Ballantine, 1983; London, Futura, 1984.
Dragon on a Pedestal (Xanth). New York, Ballantine, 1983; London, Futura, 1984.
On a Pale Horse (Immortality). New York, Ballantine, 1984; London, Panther, 1985.
Bearing an Hourglass (Immortality). New York, Ballantine, and London, Severn House, 1984.
Crewel Lye: A Caustic Yarn (Xanth). New York, Ballantine, 1985; London, Futura, 1986.
With a Tangled Skein (Immortality). New York, Ballantine, 1985; London, Panther, 1986.
Golem in the Gears (Xanth). New York, Ballantine, and London, Futura, 1986.
Wielding a Red Sword (Immortality). New York, Ballantine, 1986; London, Grafton, 1987.
Out of Phaze (Apprentice Adept). New York, Putnam, 1987; London, New English Library, 1989.
Being a Green Mother (Immortality). New York, Ballantine, 1987; London, Grafton, 1988.

Dragon's Gold, with Robert E. Margroff (Kelvin Rud). New York, Tor, 1987; London, Grafton, 1991.
Vale of the Vole (Xanth). New York, Avon, 1987; London, New English Library, 1988.
For Love of Evil (Immortality). New York, Morrow, 1988; London, Grafton, 1989.
Heaven Cent (Xanth). New York, Avon, 1988; London, New English Library, 1989.
Robot Adept (Apprentice Adept). New York, Putnam, 1988; London, New English Library, 1989.
Serpent's Silver, with Robert E. Margroff (Kelvin Rud). New York, Tor, 1988; London, Grafton, 1991.
Pornucopia. Houston, Tafford, 1989.
Unicorn Point (Apprentice Adept). New York, Putnam, 1989; London, New English Library, 1990.
Man from Mundania (Xanth). New York, Avon, 1989; London, New English Library, 1990.
Chimaera's Copper, with Robert E. Margroff (Kelvin Rud). New York, Tor, 1990; London, Grafton, 1992.
And Eternity (Immortality). New York, Morrow, and London, Severn House, 1990.
Isle of View (Xanth). New York, Morrow, 1990; London, New English Library, 1991.
Orc's Opal, with Robert E. Margroff (Kelvin Rud). New York, Tor, 1990; London, HarperCollins, 1993.
Phaze Doubt (Apprentice Adept). New York, Putnam, 1990; London, New English Library, 1991.
Question Quest (Xanth). New York, Morrow, 1991; London, New English Library, 1992.
The Tatham Mound. New York, Morrow, 1991.
Virtual Mode. New York, Putnam, and London, HarperCollins, 1991.
The Colour of Her Panties (Xanth). New York, Morrow, and London, New English Library, 1992.
Fractal Mode. New York, Putnam, and London, HarperCollins, 1992.
Mouvar's Magic, with Robert E. Margroff (Kelvin Rud). New York, Tor, 1992.
Demons Don't Dream (Xanth). New York, Tor, and London, New English Library, 1993.
Chaos Mode. New York, Putnam, and London, HarperCollins, 1994.
Harpy Thyme (Xanth). New York, Tor, and London, New English Library, 1994.
Geis of the Gargoyle (Xanth). New York, Tor, 1995.

Novels with Roberto Fuentes (series: Jason Striker in all books)

Kiai! New York, Berkley, 1974.
Mistress of Death. New York, Berkley, 1974.
Bamboo Bloodbath. New York, Berkley, 1975.
Ninja's Revenge. New York, Berkley, 1975.
Amazon Slaughter. New York, Berkley, 1976.

OTHER PUBLICATIONS

Novels

Chthon. New York, Ballantine, 1967; London, Macdonald, 1970.
Of Man and Mantra: A Trilogy. London, Corgi, 1986.
   Omnivore. New York, Ballantine, 1968; London, Faber, 1969.
   Orn. New York, Avon, 1971; London, Corgi, 1977.
   Ox. New York, Avon, 1976; London, Corgi, 1977.

The Ring, with Robert E. Margroff. New York, Ace, 1968; London, Macdonald, 1969.

Battle Circle. New York, Avon, 1978; London, Corgi, 1984.

    Sos the Rope. New York, Pyramid, 1968; London, Faber, 1970.

    Var the Stick. London, Faber, 1972; New York, Bantam, 1973.

    Neq the Sword. London, Corgi, 1975.

Macroscope. New York, Avon, 1969; revised edition, London, Sphere, 1972.

The E.S.P. Worm, with Robert E. Margroff. New York, Paperback Library, 1970.

Race Against Time (for children). New York, Hawthorn, 1973.

Rings of Ice. New York, Avon, 1974; London, Millington, 1975.

Triple Détente. New York, DAW, 1974; London, Sphere, 1975.

Phthor. New York, Berkley, 1975; London, Panther, 1978.

But What of Earth?, with Robert Coulson. Toronto, Laser, 1976; revised edition, New York, Tor, 1989.

Steppe. London, Millington, 1976; New York, Tor, 1985.

Cluster. New York, Avon, 1977; London, Millington, 1978; as *Vicinity Cluster,* London, Panther, 1979.

Chaining the Lady. New York, Avon, and London, Millington, 1978.

Kirlian Quest. New York, Avon, and London, Millington, 1978.

Tarot. New York, Ace, and London, Grafton, 1987.

    God of Tarot. New York, Jove, 1979.

    Vision of Tarot. New York, Berkley, 1980.

    Faith of Tarot. New York, Berkley, 1980.

Thousandstar. New York, Avon, 1980; London, Panther, 1984.

Mute. New York, Avon, 1981; London, New English Library, 1984.

Viscous Circle. New York, Avon, 1982; London, Panther, 1984.

Refugee. New York, Avon, 1983; London, Panther, 1984.

Mercenary. New York, Avon, 1984; London, Panther, 1985.

Politician. New York, Avon, and London, Grafton, 1985.

Executive. New York, Avon, 1985; London, Grafton, 1986.

Shade of the Tree. New York, St. Martin's Press, 1986; London, Grafton, 1987.

Ghost. New York, Tor, 1986; London, Grafton, 1988.

Statesman. New York, Avon, and London, Grafton, 1986.

Through the Ice (completion of work by Robert Kornwise). Lancaster, Pennsylvania, Underwood Miller, 1989.

Total Recall (novelization of screenplay). New York, Morrow, 1989; London, Legend, 1990.

Balook. Lancaster, Pennsylvania, Underwood Miller, 1990.

Dead Morn, with Roberto Fuentes. Houston, Texas, Tafford, 1990.

Firefly. New York, Morrow, 1990.

Hard Sell. Houston, Texas, Tafford, 1990.

Mer-Cycle. Houston, Texas, Tafford, 1991; London, Grafton, 1993.

Isle of Woman: Geodyssey, Volume 1. New York, Tor, 1993.

Kilobyte. New York, Putnam, 1993.

Shame of Man: Geodyssey, Volume 2. New York, Tor, 1994.

Short Stories

Prostho Plus. London, Gollancz, 1971; New York, Bantam, 1973.

Anthonology. New York, Tor, 1985; London, Grafton, 1986.

Alien Plot. New York, Tor, 1992.

Other

Biography of an Ogre: The Autobiography of Piers Anthony to Age 50. New York, Ace, 1988.

Piers Anthony's Visual Guide to Xanth, with Jody Lynn Nye, illustrated by Todd Cameron Hamilton and James Clouse. New York, Avon, 1989.

Editor, with Barry N. Malzberg, Martin H. Greenberg, and Charles G. Waugh, *Uncollected Stars.* New York, Avon, 1986.

Editor, with Richard Gilliam, *Tales from the Great Turtle.* New York, Tor, 1994.

*

Bibliography: *Piers Anthony: Biblio of an Ogre—A Working Bibliography* by Phil Stephensen-Payne, Leeds, Galactic Central Publications, 1990.

Manuscript Collection: Syracuse University, New York.

Critical Study: *Piers Anthony* by Michael R. Collings, Mercer Island, Washington, Starmont House, 1983.

*   *   *

Attention to Piers Anthony's work usually focuses on the rich scatter of ideas in his early science fiction. His large body of fantasy is viewed (together with his growing propensity for "series" novels) as a surrender to commercial pressures and fashionable trends. To some extent this may be so, although this judgment would neglect the part played by Anthony's own writings in creating the market for a particular form of fantasy. In fact, he has created a fiercely loyal readership (whom he frequently addresses directly in lengthy afterwords to his novels) and much of this loyalty is due to his provision of a type of escapism which embodies an easily grasped symbolism.

Anthony's fantasies are marked by love of wordplay and by considered use of the genre as moral allegory. The first appears to great effect in the Xanth series, where puns (often supplied by readers) form the scenic background to his magical world: shoe-trees are literally trees on which shoes are grown; a particularly loathsome form of tick is called a cri-tic. This emblematic punning forms the roots of his second quality, plots which are often either lightly-disguised pantomimes of moral awakening (*A Spell for Chameleon*) or intensive but sugar-coated examinations of metaphysics.

A Spell for Chameleon opened the Xanth series and won a deserved award. It introduced the Florida-shaped land of Xanth which is appended to neighbouring Mundania—i.e. the everyday world in which most of us, especially the parents of Anthony's readers and the critics who review his books, belong. In magic Xanth, everyone has a specific talent: except, it seems, for young Bink, who must find exactly what his magical ability is or risk exile to the "normal" world. Entertaining, yet less dependent on puns than many of its sequels, it is a light fantasy focusing on the moral ambiguities of an "Evil Magician" who is essentially decent and honourable, and on the maturing of a sympathetically naive young hero. Anthony's most popular locale, Xanth often features (as in *Castle Roogna, Heaven Cent,* and *Isle of View*) children on the verge of puberty receiving their first understanding of the "adult conspiracy" of sex. This has resulted in considerable embarrassment to adult critics who tackle Anthony's books. It is certainly hard to take seriously at any level titles like *The Colour of Her Panties,* which follows through a long-running sub-theme to a plot in which the colour of Mela the Mermaid's underwear is vital to the outcome of the story. Nevertheless this also offers a clue, and indeed even a wholesome one, to Anthony's popularity.

Anthony makes it clear, through his copious "Author's Notes," that he writes for a young audience. While he offers little in the way of technical sex education, he does present a humorous way of dealing with the complexities of the new awarenesses his readers are encountering. The archness of his approach to the subject of the "adult conspiracy" to keep young children unaware of the Facts of Life is itself a conspiratorial beckoning to readers who have only just become aware of what these nods and winks are all about and to whom Anthony's facetious allegories are a part of their recent past. The increasing problem with the Xanth series not so much that Anthony is doing this but that he is doing little else. The exuberance of early instalments has declined into sub-metafictional games with his readers (one volume, *Question Quest*, is largely concerned with recounting the plots of the previous 13 and summarizing the next) and a mixture of "cuteness" and prurience in the prose which only emphasizes the juvenile level of engagement. Yet even in *Harpy Thyme*, the 17th Xanth novel, there are stories-within-stories—an observation of the life of Van Gogh; the story of "Veleno the Nymphomaniac" (a man, incidentally)—which are genuinely poignant vignettes, capable of surprising any reader locked into expectations of unchallenging entertainment.

More ambitious territory is charted in the Incarnations of Immortality series, where personifications of metaphysical qualities—Death, Nature, Time, Fate, God and Satan—insert fundamental moral conflicts into fictions of genre fantasy. The "universe" of the Incarnations series is (as typical with Anthony) one in which science and magic co-exist and complement one another: people travel by aeroplane or magic carpet, even by flying saucer or within the fish which swallowed Jonah. It is essentially a fairy-tale world for immature readers. However, although the series also suffers from the bland characterization and coy games with sexuality which are so much part of Anthony's fiction, it is also above average in both the mundane level of plotting and the allegorical qualities which arise naturally out of the storyline. There is humour (Death drives a limousine called with the bumper-sticker, "Death is Nature's way of telling you to slow down"), use of motif (Anthony uses musical themes, for example the folk song "Young and Growing" upon which he bases the opening chapters of *With a Tangled Skein*) and an effective reflection of his symbolic characters in plots which involve games, mazes or puzzles. Above all there is an open examination of moral questions such as sin, the functions of death, good and evil, which is rare in any sort of fiction for young people.

It is common in such genre fantasy for a series to decline in quality as it progresses, but Incarnations is an effective exception to this rule. The sixth and seventh books, covering the questions of Evil and Good, are among Anthony's best. He joins the pantheon of writers whose art is enlivened by a focus upon Satan. Hardly Miltonic, perhaps, but Satan in *For Love of Evil*—a 12th-century French sorcerer/monk who is corrupted by the then Evil One and takes his place only to question the ground-rules which condemn people to Hell—is still a character who embodies real debate on the issues. The following and final book, *And Eternity*, offers a genuine conclusion to the symbolic conflict by seeking for the qualities of engagement and compassion which appear to be missing in an Incarnation of God who is neglecting his duty. One admires the way the generic "solving of tasks" plot is both a red herring and a reflection of the moral progression within the story. Flawed though the series may be, it is an attempt to deal with some extraordinarily difficult issues in a way which is accessible to a readership hooked on genre fantasy.

The fusion/alternation of sf and fantasy modes continues through the Apprentice Adept series, set on a world containing both "Fantasy" and "Science" frames into which certain people like the hero Stile can cross. Significantly, he finds himself most fulfilled in the fantasy frame roamed by magical unicorns and werewolves. There is a plot involving conspiracy and (as often) self-knowledge, but the main attraction appears to be the lengthy descriptions of the various game-events by which the serfs of "Scientific" Proton can achieve citizen status. The conflict lacks tension because the "Science" frame—confined to generic stereotypes like voluptuous robots, self-willed machines and a wish-fulfilment social system of rich Citizens and naked Serfs—is scientific only in its vocabulary. When science is a form of magic, then opposing it with fairy-tale fantasy can lead to bathos rather than tension.

Other series, such as the Kelvin Rud sequence (in collaboration with Robert E. Margroff), contain the recognizable features of mildly titillating sex, juvenile characters, and indistinguishable science and fantasy "frames" within standard plots about prophecies and evil magicians. The knowing pedestrianism of the idea that people drink "coftee" or "pepacola," or sentences like "'Gasp, gasp, gasp,' Kelvin gasped," suggest that these books are deliberately unchallenging substitutes for production-line cartoons or the more anodyne school primers. However, the Mode books are closer to the "serious" fantasies of the Incarnations series, with a darker side to them in that the heroine is a suicidal 14-year-old with an active sexual nature. The use of the more imagistic territory of mathematical theory, such as Fractals, as pegs for Anthony's narrative structure shifts these books closer to the "sense of wonder" of science fiction.

Occasional singletons, such as *Hasan*, an Arabian-Nights fantasy, show more variety. The eponymous hero is tricked, like Aladdin, by a wicked magician, but survives to fall in love with a princess whom he possesses by stealing her cloak of feathers. Amusing touches of parody make it more than a retelling of a standard folk-tale. *Hasan* is an early work and such stand-alones are increasingly rare. While several series have come to an end, Anthony's bias still seems to be towards trilogies-and-more where much fancy is expended upon keeping the storyline going with a corresponding decline in the genuine vein of imagination which sparked the concept in the first place.

—Andy Sawyer

ARNASON, Eleanor (Atwood)

Nationality: American. **Born:** New York, 28 December 1942. **Education:** Swarthmore College, Pennsylvania, B.A., 1964; University of Minnesota, 1964-67. **Family:** Partner Patrick Arden Wood. **Awards:** James Tiptree, Jr. Award, 1991; Mythopoeic Society award, 1991. **Agent:** Virginia Kidd, PO Box 278, Milford, PA 18337, USA. **Address:** c/o National Writers Union, Local #13, PO Box 80026, Minneapolis, MN 55408, USA.

FANTASY PUBLICATIONS

Novels

The Sword Smith. New York, Condor, 1978.

Daughter of the Bear King. New York, Avon, and London, Headline, 1987.

OTHER PUBLICATIONS

Novels

To the Resurrection Station. New York, Avon, 1983.
A Woman of the Iron People. New York, Morrow, 1991.
Ring of Swords. New York, Tor, 1993.

*

Eleanor Arnason comments:

I consider myself primarily a science-fiction writer, with a strong interest in myth, folklore and other non-modern, non-western forms of knowledge. Most of my work is on the line between sf and fantasy. *Daughter of the Bear King* has an intelligent computer as well as magic. *The Sword Smith* has no magic, and dragons which are clearly intelligent theropod dinosaurs. *A Woman of the Iron People* got third place for the John W. Campbell award, given by the Center for the Study of Science Fiction at the University of Kansas to the best science-fiction novel of the year, *and* received the Mythopoeic Society's award for the best adult fantasy of the year. In both genres I strive for intellectual rigour, self-consistency and respect for fact. Fantasy should not be a refuge for people too lazy to do research or think.

*   *   *

Eleanor Arnason has never hesitated to subvert genre conventions. Her first novel, *The Sword Smith,* while ostensibly a charming fantasy, soon reveals itself as something that does not entirely conform to expectations. Unlike most fantasy novels the reader does not begin with a clear idea of what the characters are undertaking by way of a quest but is instead presented with the hasty, ill-planned flight of Limper, a smith on the run from his royal master because he is dissatisfied with making frivolous toys rather being able to use his skills properly. Accompanied by Nargri, a very young dragon for whom he is caring, Limper moves from one misadventure to another, coping with all eventualities ineptly but sufficiently to ensure his continued freedom. It's a far cry from the certainties of so many fantasy novels and suggests that Arnason is less interested in heroic posturing and more concerned with how people would most typically cope with such adventures.

Other themes are laid out in this novel, to appear again in her other work. Arnason's characters lay a great emphasis on travelling in order to learn and discover. Nargri wants to travel in order to gain knowledge; she is unusual among dragons in her restless desire for travel, although like her aunt, who perhaps not coincidentally, taught Limper his skills as a smith. Limper himself is on a journey of a more metaphysical nature, coming to terms with his smithing craft. A later companion, Coalbrow, turns out to be a girl in disguise, escaping from the stultifying life offered by her conservative family, providing Arnason with a chance to explore the way in which women are confined by certain gender expectations, even in a novel. All three are misfits but Arnason does not resolve their lives neatly. The novel draws to a close before they can be shown to have settled down to a new life. The reader is left to speculate on what might happen to them, with no reassurance at all. Life, Arnason suggests, can't be tidily reduced to a happy ending.

Arnason's second novel, *To the Resurrection Station,* although overtly science fiction exhibits strong traces of the Gothic and the fantastic throughout. The novel's opening is purely Gothic, with the young heroine suddenly revealed to be the last scion of an important house on New Hope, the Hernshaws, who founded the colony. Imprisoned in a remote house at the mercy of her apparently insane uncle, Belinda finds that she is part-native and due to be married to an unknown bridegroom at any moment. That Belinda is saved from this dubious fate by a fantastic string of coincidences which, according to her reluctant groom, she has herself generated smacks even more of the fantastic.

Much of the novel is devoted, like *The Sword Smith,* to a string of picaresque adventures during which Belinda learns more about the different patterns which shape the Cosmos and the conflicting views of the people she encounters. Arnason touches swiftly on issues which will appear again in her later books and the novel culminates in a return to Earth, to the eponymous resurrection station, where the personality of the Hernshaws' robot is downloaded, alas for its original male character, to a female body. Again, the novel ends unexpectedly, almost abruptly, as if demonstrating that life cannot be tidily compartmentalized.

Daughter of the Bear King is Arnason's finest work of fantasy. Although she settles for a more conventional structure to the story, leading the reader more gently into the action, Arnason also brings a much greater complexity and depth to her work without eschewing the quirkiness and sly wit which had, by this point, become a trademark of her fiction.

Esperance Olson, at 40, with two children raised and a husband absorbed in his work, is bored, and also experiencing strange, inexplicable dreams. A household accident transports her into the world she has been dreaming of, where they have been awaiting her and, disconcertingly, well aware of what she has been doing while she has been in our world. Esperance is, apparently, a daughter of the bear king, part of an elaborate scheme to defend the other world from a perceived threat which is characterized by a slipping of standards, shoddy workmanship, a sense of threatening decay. However, threatened by enemies within that world, Esperance's bearish nature asserts itself and she flees from the city as a bear.

The book charts her transformations between bear and woman, and her journeys between the two worlds. It is implied, but never confirmed, that the situation is nothing more than a nervous breakdown, the second world being a dream she has retreated into. The monsters assume the shapes of her husband and her (male) therapist and it is surely significant that her allies are both female, Ayra and her own daughter Jennifer. Ayra, accidentally transported to Earth, shows herself to be endlessly adaptable and settles into her new situation with equanimity while Esperance, shuttling between two worlds, gradually rediscovers her own strength of character, enabling her finally to make a choice as to which world she remains in.

Underlying the theme of Esperance's rediscovery of her independence is one of Arnason's greater themes, that of the Pattern which underlies the universe. Throughout the novel, the assumption has been that the Pattern must be undisturbed, must remain static. Nevertheless, Arnason suggests that the Pattern can and sometimes must be broken. The results may be destructive in the short term but in the long term something new and more significant may arise. Apart from which, no Pattern can be entirely static.

This is shown even more clearly in Arnason's *A Woman of the Iron People,* recipient of the James Tiptree Award. Although primarily a science-fiction novel, it has much to interest fantasy readers. A large portion of the book is devoted to Lixia's wanderings with Nia, an outcast from the Iron People. The men and women of her race live separate lives, coming together only to mate. For men and women to live together is unheard of and Nia's own banishment resulted from her living with a man away from the community of women. As the world is explored, it becomes apparent that although the natural laws require men and women to live apart, there are those who manage to live as they wish. The rigidity of the myths which bind the peoples are being constantly challenged, the Pattern altering constantly but subtly.

Eleanor Arnason continues to challenge our assumptions about the nature of genres, happily blending science fiction and fantasy to great effect. Likewise, in her hands the fantasy genre is not a secure refuge but yet anther means of challenging gender assumptions and exploring the cosmological implications of our own world.

—Maureen Speller

ARNOLD, Edwin L(ester Linden)

Nationality: British. **Born:** Swanscombe, Kent, 14 May 1857; son of the writer Sir Edwin Arnold. **Education:** Cheltenham College. **Family:** Married 1) Constance Boyce, one daughter; 2) Jessie Brighton in 1919. **Career:** Cattle breeder in Scotland, then worked in forestry in Travancore, India in late 1870s; staff member, *Daily Telegraph,* London, until 1908. **Died:** 1 March 1935.

FANTASY PUBLICATIONS

Novels

The Wonderful Adventures of Phra the Phoenician. London, Chatto and Windus, 3 vols., and New York, Harper, 1 vol., 1890.
Lepidus the Centurion: A Roman of To-day. London, Cassell, 1901; New York, Crowell, 1902.
Lieut. Gullivar Jones: His Vacation. London, Brown Langham, 1905; New York, Arno Press, 1975; as *Gulliver of Mars,* New York, Ace, 1964.

Short Stories

The Story of Ulla and Other Tales. London and New York, Longman, 1895.

OTHER PUBLICATIONS

Novel

The Constable of St. Nicholas. London, Chatto and Windus, 1894.

Other

A Summer Holiday in Scandinavia. London, Sampson Low, 1877.
On the Indian Hills; or, Coffee-Planting in Southern India. London, Sampson Low, 2 vols., 1881.
Coffee: Its Cultivation and Profit. London, Whittingham, 1886.

Bird Life in England. London, Chatto and Windus, 1887.
England as She Seems, Being Selections from the Notes of an Arab Hadji. London, Warne, 1888.
The Soul of the Beast. London, P.R. Macmillan, 1960.

Editor, *The Opium Question Solved, by Anglo-Indian.* London, Partridge, 1882.

*   *   *

From his father, who made an extensive study of Eastern religion and culture, Edwin Lester Arnold obtained a strong interest in the idea of reincarnation and the notion of karma (the doctrine that every living being is heir to the accumulated effects of the souls actions during previous incarnations). His principal literary model was H. Rider Haggard, who developed similar interests and expressed them in a sequence of exotic romances of history begun with *She* (1887).

Arnold's first karmic romance was *The Wonderful Adventures of Phra the Phoenician,* whose eponymous hero recalls a series of past "awakenings" in different eras of British history. His memories of youth are vague but he remembers having come to Britain as a merchant-adventurer, having bought a native bride named Blodwen from pirates. He is subsequently offered as a human sacrifice by Druids when the Romans invade, but a magical tattoo given to him by his witch-wife enables him to return periodically to serve as a soldier of fortune in various defences of right and the realm. He witnesses the ultimate withdrawal of the Romans, is involved in opposition to the Norman invasion of 1066, fights at the Battle of Crécy and befriends an Elizabethan scientist who is trying to build a steam engine.

In the course of these various reincarnations Phra meets several women highly reminiscent of his beloved, her spirit seemingly being inextricably linked to his. As the novel ends he is attempting to secure a more permanent reunion with her beyond the earth. The florid mock-archaic style in which the story is told has relegated the novel to the status of a period-piece, but it was widely read and enjoyed in its own day, when its central motif enjoyed considerable fashionability. George Griffith's *Valdar the Oft-Born* (1895) is a very close imitation of it, and there is a strong possibility that Arnold was himself heavily influenced by Edgar Lee's Haggard-inspired romance of serial revivification *Pharaoh's Daughter* (1889).

The short story "Rutherford the Twice-Born," which first appeared in *The Idler* in 1892, is similar in style to *Phra,* but makes rather more of the notion of karma. It recounts the tribulations of a man who comes into a tainted inheritance, but is absolved from guilt by a convenient vision which reveals that the passage of time has belatedly repaired the injustice by which his fortune was diverted from its true heirs generations before.

Lepidus the Centurion: A Roman of To-day is the story of a young Englishman who discovers a Roman tomb in which Lepidus, a nephew of the emperor Vespasian, has long lain in suspended animation. The story has comic elements concerned with the virile Roman's adaptation to Victorian life, but it is primarily a psychological melodrama. The two main characters are fragmentary aspects of a single soul, which come into conflict over the love of a woman. Like Phra, Lepidus commits suicide when he seems to have lost the prize, but his death somehow allows the hero to become complete for the first time, much as Rutherford becomes complete following the dream-revelation that he was descended from the true heir to his fortune as well as the false claimant.

Arnold's final fantasy novel, *Lieut. Gullivar Jones: His Vacation,* has attracted a good deal of interest from some modern readers by virtue of its intriguing similarities to the Martian fantasies of Edgar Rice Burroughs, although these are more likely to be due to the common influence of Haggard's *She* than to any direct imitation. Arnold must also have been famliar with Camille Flammarion's best-selling *Urania* (1890) which developed the author's thesis that souls were capable of serial reincarnation on different worlds in a Martian setting, and may well have read Hugh MacColl's Martian romance *Mr. Stranger's Sealed Packet* (1889) with which both *Lieut. Gullivar Jones* and Burroughs's interplanetary fantasies also have a good deal in common.

In Arnold's swashbuckling traveller's tale, Gullivar Jones—an American naval officer temporarily frustrated in his desire to marry by virtue of his lack of means—is whisked away to Mars by magic carpet and sides with the decadent inheritors of an ancient civilization, who are trying to defend the remnants of their culture against marauding barbarians. He saves the life of a princess of their race and then embarks on a quest to rescue her when she is given as a tribute to the barbarian king. He encounters many natural marvels before rescuing the princess, but his eventual success in this mission is inadequate to turn the tide of Martian history. The implacability of this fate is revealed in a final unfortunate confrontation with the prophetic globe of destiny, whose judgment is sufficiently dire to force Jones's return to earth, where he is reunited with his prosaic fiancée.

All three of Arnold's full-length fantasies are essentially playful, employing their philosophical devices as props to support amusing flights of romantic fancy. The novels are not weighed down by the ponderous weight of sincere belief, as Rider Haggard's later romances of reincarnation sometimes were. Perhaps by the same token, they lack the remarkable imaginative intensity which Haggard was able to bring to bear in his best works. In spite of their fundamental playfulness, however, Arnold's subdued erotic fantasies repeatedly strike a particular emotional chord, echoing a restless sense of frustration and dissatisfaction which might well have been something the author felt rather keenly.

As with many writers of fantastic fiction, it is when his imagination reached out to its furthest limits that Arnold's own sentiments seemed to be laid bare. Those modern readers who are able to sympathize with these sentiments and prepared to acclimatize themselves to Arnold's stylistic affectations and eccentricities will find that his work remains both amusing and intriguing.

—Brian Stableford

ARSCOTT, David, and MARL, David J.

Nationality: British.

Fantasy Publications

Novels

The Frozen City. London, Allen and Unwin, 1984.
A Flight of Bright Birds. London, Allen and Unwin, 1985.

*   *   *

David Arscott's and David J. Marl's two linked novels cast a slightly cold eye on the politics of genre fantasy. We are too accustomed to the simple polarization of Good and Evil tending to a final struggle followed by the restoration of a True King. Arscott and Marl laudably try to complicate the issues a little, but ultimately achieve a muddy effect rather than any new clarity. In both books they suggest alternative paths which are not followed up.

The Frozen City is heavy with intimations of parable and allegory. Its young protagonist Tom comes to the nameless city in a bad winter, but the place is frozen in various other senses. Politically there is a near-deadlock between some ineffectual-seeming good guys and the highly unpleasant organization of the Red Blade (whose beliefs seem more or less confined to the conviction that a stable rule entails being extremely nasty to the ruled). Geographically, there is a freeze on movement which is built into the city structure: whole sections are closed mazes which can be entered or left only by secret, guarded routes through the high buildings, or by dangerous roof-climbing. Ideologically, the nicer-seeming folk whose symbol is the Eye have a frozen set of aspirations involving a secret Other City, a literal underground to which art and beauty have been exiled (and which is both underpopulated and stagnant); meanwhile, the Red Blade operates by rigid and self-perpetuating codes.

The writing is adequate; the plot consists largely of young Tom doing a great deal of uncertain wandering around and learning all the above, while himself beset by sometimes too-didactically expressed problems of honesty and mercy *versus* practical politics. There is a good *frisson* when the nature of the Red Blade's leadership or non-leadership finally emerges with something of the philosophical brutality in Orwell's famous line: "The object of power is power." *The Frozen City* ends with the promise of imminent change, a warm plea against hereditary rule (lack of which is apparently the Red Blade's sole virtue), and Tom's vaguely anticlimactic reunion with the father he's been tepidly seeking all along. It seems to require a sequel.

A Flight of Bright Birds connects with the first story from an oblique angle and after some lapse of time. The original indeterminate setting is abandoned in favour of perhaps unwise references to Odysseus, Shakespeare, Columbus, Australia and railways. In separate narrative strands, two young, mysteriously linked heroes travel to the exotic city of O— (not the frozen city). One hangs out with actors, another with artists and a lovely deaf-and-dumb dancer. All this provides colour, but largely irrelevant colour; the dancer in particular seems fraught with significance which leads nowhere. Eventually the boys prove to be the twin sons of Tom and learn that the Eye and Blade are fighting again, and that it's up to them to act nobly. A manipulator who distrusts Noble Saviours pressures them to renounce all claim to leadership in the frozen city; the book ends as, by simple trickery, they avoid committing themselves in any way.

A third title did not follow.

—David Langford

ASH, Constance (Lee)

Nationality: American. **Born:** 1950. **Family:** Married to the musician Ned Sublette. **Address:** c/o Ace Books, 200 Madison Avenue, New York, NY 10016, USA.

FANTASY PUBLICATIONS

Novels

The Horsegirl. New York, Ace, 1988.
The Stalking Horse. New York, Ace, 1990.
The Stallion Queen. New York, Ace, 1992.

*   *   *

According to the many-worlds theory of Quantum Physics, there are numerous parallel dimensions surrounding us in every direction. Each choice we make in life, every time we go one way rather than another, a dimension is created in which an alternate self chose the other path. In her fantasy novels about Glennys the Stallion Queen, Constance Ash has created a dimension fairly close to ours, but far enough away to make it a little peculiar to our sensibilities. In volume one, *The Horsegirl,* Glennys is a child of eleven, living in a community of hideously warped farmers who vaguely resemble a cross between the Amish, Mormons and Islamites. The religion of her world is divided; the wealthy and sophisticated worship Eve, the First Mother, the Mother of Creation, who found her first baby in the wilderness with the assistance of a horse. Glennys's people, The Alaminites, worship Alam, the first man, who doesn't seem to have done much of anything except teach men to keep women as chattel and abuse them as often as possible without killing them (though this isn't frowned upon, and is indeed encouraged by the church elders in the case of women who refuse to obey men implicitly).

Glennys is doomed from the beginning not to fit into this world. Though she doesn't know this, she is really the bastard of the local Baron, who apprentices her to his stablemaster when his son discovers her "horse sense," a power some women possess to communicate psychically with horses.

This is a civilization that loves horses immensely, except for the crazy Alaminites, who believe horses are ministers of evil. From the time Glennys leaves her farm for a better life in the Baron's house, her own people hate her. They hate the Baron and anyone who doesn't follow their own warped beliefs, and before the book finishes they manage to murder him. His plantation is destroyed, and Glennys goes to the city of St. Lucien to make her way on her own. Her mother wants her to return to the farm (her father also dies during the book, though pretty much everyone considers this a blessing), but Glennys knows she can never live within the twisted community of her birth.

While it is a well-written and entertaining (if somewhat disheartening and gory) tale, *The Horsegirl* is really a social commentary on our own world and the destructive nature of conservative religion. In volume two, *The Stalking Horse,* Glennys starts a new life in St. Lucien, where she is training to be a ballet dancer. In a culture on the verge of technology, dancers and female performers of any kind are still considered concubines, and in this world they are classified as King's Daughters, allowed to contract their sexual services to a protector. But Glennys has never taken a lover since she became the Baron's concubine back at his plantation, before either of them knew they were father and daughter.

Glennys is hired by the Queen's Theatre to train horses for the ballet, and she is joined in St. Lucien by another Alaminite girl, Thea, who is a healer. In the course of the book Glennys falls in love with Jonathan, a court musician, and becomes embroiled in a war between the King of Nolan and some nobles who want his

throne for his inept brother. They finally kill the king, and the Alaminites go to war against the nobles, led by a truly crazy "Messiah" figure named Hans, who wants to marry Thea. She keeps running from him, and fortunately he never gets her.

Glennys puts herself under the protection of one of the nobles who is not involved in the conspiracy, Duke Albany. He buys her a lot of land out in the Saquave desert, where the horses are bred. By the end of the book the kingdom is in such chaos that Glennys, Thea, her half-brother Hengst, her mother Stella, two sisters and a large group of followers head into the desert to found Albany City.

By the opening of volume three, *The Stallion Queen,* 20 years have passed. Albany City (also known as Hometown to the residents) is a thriving if poor settlement, and Glennys, the acknowledged Stallion Queen, has made an alliance with most of the desert tribes. Nolan is in chaos under the rule of the useless King Roald, and one day the real king, Leon II, now a man, shows up in Albany looking for refuge. Glennys takes him in, but the Hometowners are confronted with a terrible evil lurking near them in the mountains: the Alaminites following Hans Rigg have built a town called Silver City, surrounded by stone walls, and they are systematically decimating the soil through mining and strip-logging, stealing women from Hometown and the tribes, and attempting to destroy the whole desert.

When Glennys's adopted daughter Cameron is kidnapped and given to two Alaminite brothers as a wife, it triggers a war for control of the desert and, ultimately, all of Nolan. Right triumphs but not until after much bloodshed and destruction, caused by the Alaminites and the nobles from Nolan who don't want Leon on the throne.

This is a thoughtful series, one which will give the reader new insight into the meaning of freedom, choice, and belief systems as well as entertaining mightily.

—Debora Hill

ASPRIN, Robert (Lynn)

Nationality: American. **Born:** St. Johns, Michigan, in 1946. **Education:** University of Michigan, Ann Arbor, 1964-65. **Military Service:** United States Army, 1965-66. **Family:** Married 1) Anne Brett, one daughter and one son; 2) Lynn Abbey, q.v. **Career:** Accounts clerk, 1966-70, payroll analyst, 1970-74, and cost accountant, 1974-78, University Microfilm, Ann Arbor. Since 1978 freelance writer. **Awards:** *Locus* award, for editing, 1982. **Address:** c/o Ace Books, 200 Madison Avenue, New York, NY 10016, USA.

FANTASY PUBLICATIONS

Novels (series: Elfquest; Myth; Thieves' World)

Another Fine Myth. Norfolk, Virginia, Donning, 1978; London, Legend, 1988.
Myth Conceptions. Norfolk, Virginia, Donning, 1980; London, Legend, 1990.
Myth Directions. Norfolk, Virginia, Donning, 1982; London, Legend, 1990.
Hit or Myth. Norfolk, Virginia, Donning, 1983; London, Legend, 1990.

Myth-ing Persons. Norfolk, Virginia, Donning, 1984; London, Legend, 1990.

Little Myth Marker. Norfolk, Virginia, Donning, 1985; London, Legend, 1991.

Myth Adventures (omnibus; includes *Another Fine Myth, Myth Conceptions, Myth Directions, Hit or Myth*). New York, Nelson Doubleday, 1984.

M.Y.T.H. Inc. Link. Norfolk, Virginia, Donning, 1986; London, Legend, 1991.

Myth Alliances (omnibus; includes *Myth-ing Persons, Little Myth Marker, M.Y.T.H. Inc. Link*). New York, Nelson Doubleday, 1987.

Myth-Nomers and Im-pervections. Norfolk, Virginia, Donning, 1987; London, Legend, 1991.

M.Y.T.H. Inc. in Action. Norfolk, Virginia, Donning, 1990; London, Legend, 1991.

Catwoman, with Lynn Abbey. New York, Warner, 1992; as *Catwoman: Tiger Hunt,* London, Millennium, 1992.

The Myth-ing Omnibus (includes *Another Fine Myth, Myth Conceptions, Myth Directions*). London, Legend, 1992.

The Second Myth-ing Omnibus (includes *Hit or Myth, Myth-ing Persons, Little Myth Marker*). London, Legend, 1992.

Sweet Myth-tery of Life. Norfolk, Virginia, Donning, 1994.

Other

Editor, *Thieves' World* (Thieves' World). New York, Ace, 1979; London, Titan, 1988.

Editor, *Tales from the Vulgar Unicorn* (Thieves' World). New York, Ace, 1980; London, Titan, 1988.

Editor, *Shadows of Sanctuary* (Thieves' World). New York, Ace, 1981; London, Titan, 1988.

Editor, *Sanctuary* (omnibus; includes *Thieves' World, Tales from the Vulgar Unicorn, Shadows of Sanctuary*). New York, Nelson Doubleday, 1982.

Editor, *Storm Season* (Thieves' World). New York, Ace, 1982; London, Titan, 1988.

Editor, with Lynn Abbey. *The Face of Chaos* (Thieves' World). New York, Ace, 1983; London, Titan, 1989.

Editor, with Lynn Abbey. *Wings of Omen* (Thieves' World). New York, Ace, 1984; London, Titan, 1989.

Editor, with Lynn Abbey. *Cross-Currents* (omnibus; includes *Storm Season* [edited by Asprin alone], *The Face of Chaos, Wings of Omen*). New York, Nelson Doubleday, 1984.

Editor, with Lynn Abbey. *The Dead of Winter* (Thieves' World). New York, Ace, 1985; London, Titan, 1989.

Editor, with Lynn Abbey. *Soul of the City* (Thieves' World). New York, Ace, 1986; London, Titan, 1989.

Editor, with Richard Pini and Lynn Abbey, *The Blood of Ten Chiefs* (Elfquest). New York, Tor, 1986.

Editor, with Lynn Abbey. *Blood Ties* (Thieves' World). New York, Ace, 1986; London, Titan, 1990.

Editor, with Lynn Abbey. *The Shattered Sphere* (omnibus; includes *The Dead of Winter, Soul of the City, Blood Ties*). New York, Nelson Doubleday, 1986.

Editor, with Lynn Abbey. *Aftermath* (Thieves' World). New York, Ace, 1987; London, Titan, 1990.

Editor, with Lynn Abbey. *Uneasy Alliances* (Thieves' World). New York, Ace, 1988; London, Titan, 1990.

Editor, with Richard Pini and Lynn Abbey, *Wolfsong: The Blood of Ten Chiefs* (Elfquest). New York, Tor, 1988.

Editor, with Lynn Abbey. *Stealer's Sky* (Thieves' World). New York, Ace, 1989.

Editor, with Lynn Abbey. *The Price of Victory* (omnibus; includes *Aftermath, Uneasy Alliances, Stealer's Sky*). New York, Nelson Doubleday, 1990.

Graphic Novels (series: Duncan and Mallory in all books)

Duncan and Mallory, with Mel White. Norfolk, Virginia, Donning, 1986.

The Bar-None Ranch, with Mel White. Norfolk, Virginia, Donning, 1987.

The Raiders, with Mel White. Norfolk, Virginia, Donning, 1988.

Other Publications

Novels

The Cold Cash War. New York, St. Martin's Press, and London, New English Library, 1977.

The Bug Wars. New York, St. Martin's Press, 1979; London, New English Library, 1980.

Tambu. New York, Ace, 1979.

Mirror Friend, Mirror Foe, with George Takei. Chicago, Playboy Press, 1979.

Cold Cash Warrior, with Bill Fawcett. New York, Ace, 1989.

Phule's Company. New York, Ace, 1990; London, Legend, 1991.

Phule's Paradise. New York, Ace, and London, Legend, 1992.

*   *   *

Robert Asprin's contribution to fantasy embraces the roles of author and editor. As a novelist he is best known for his Myth series of humorous fantasies; with wife Lynn Abbey he instigated and co-edited the Thieves' World anthology sequence.

His debut novel, *The Cold Cash War,* is a science-fiction satire in which huge conglomerates settle disagreements by employing mercenary armies to engage in simulated warfare. Written while Asprin was a Xerox Corporation employee, it is partly his response to what he saw as misguided speculation about the growing power of big business. The book also targeted the then embryonic gaming industry and the strain of militaristic sf embodied by Asprin's mentor Gordon R. Dickson. *The Cold Cash War* is important in respect of the author's subsequent work in establishing, at least initially, a reactive, occasionally iconoclastic tone.

Convinced that heroic fantasy in particular had become too overblown and pretentious by the end of the 1970s, Asprin planned *Another Fine Myth* as a rebuttal. But he has said the strongest influence on it was the Bob Hope and Bing Crosby *Road to . . .* movies (1940-1961), thus acknowledging that he approached the task from a broader comedic tradition than that to be found within the confines of fantasy. The Road films' input is to some extent apparent in the novel's vaguely Hollywoodish *Arabian Nights* setting, the kingdom of Possiltum, and most specifically in its two protagonists, Skeeve and Aahz. The former an incompetent aspiring magician, the latter a fearsome-looking but ineffectual demon, it takes no great imaginative leap to detect echoes of Hope and Crosby in their wise-cracking and the scrapes they get themselves into. In truth, the book's basically thin plot, dressed with plenty of gags and pratfalls, does little more than establish its cast and locale. However the utilization of various fantasy conventions for humorous purposes, and mild subversion of some of them, meant *Another Fine Myth* could lay claim to a lineage that includes *Unknown* magazine of the 1940s and in particular L. Sprague de Camp and Fletcher Pratt's series about the incomplete enchanter, Harold Shea.

Intended as a one-off, the novel was commercially successful enough to warrant a sequel, *Myth Conceptions*. Another light plot, concerning Skeeve and Aahz's part in repelling a barbarian invasion of Possiltum, confirmed the impression that the Myth stories would be largely character-driven. But *Myth Conceptions* and the third volume, *Myth Directions,* were still tilting at the windmills of fantasy's orthodoxies with sufficient vigour to keep the fans interested. *Myth Directions* parodies the fantasy quest. Skeeve, now sorcerer to the court of King Roderick, is beguiled by an attractive young woman, Tanda, into an odyssey through parallel dimensions in search of a magic relic. *Myth Directions* accentuated an aspect present from the outset, and which has remained virtually unchanged throughout the series—the depiction of women as either gorgeous babes or dreadful harridans, and often duplicitous. Only the saving grace of an essentially good-natured humorous ethos has prevented this element veering into the offensive.

Book four, *Hit or Myth,* saw the beginnings of a more rigidly formulaic structure. A structure further solidified when Skeeve, Aahz and others set up an all-purpose trouble-shooting agency (M.Y.T.H. Inc). This had the advantage of giving the characters a *raison d'etre,* but also introduced the danger that they need do no more than react to circumstances. From *Hit and Myth* onwards, the number of regular characters took a tangible leap and the humour started to rely more on self-referential assumptions of how they would behave in a given situation. They were being welded into an ensemble, similar to that in television sitcoms where the actors' idiosyncrasies become so familiar that most of the comedy can be generated by knowing nods and winks in the audience's direction. There is nothing inherently wrong with this. But in order to do it the succeeding volumes in the series have tended to sacrifice the satiric impulses that fuelled the earlier books. The Myth novels functioned best, and were at their funniest, when kicking at something. Latterly, the deflationery satire has given way to farce.

Asprin's recent return to the series with the tenth book, *Sweet Myth-tery of Life,* following several years of what was said to be writer's block, offers the recipe as before. A cast of unwieldy proportions, minimal plot developments and the almost complete absence of references to the genre in which it is embedded and supposedly commenting upon, hint that the series may be reaching the end of the road in its present form. Nevertheless, the books have sold in excess of one million copies in America by the early 1990s, and were making respectable inroads into the British and European markets.

The Thieves' World anthologies are generally acknowledged as instigating the whole shared-world phenomenon—stories by various writers set in the same universe and ultimately comprising one long interrelated narrative, or mega-novel. When Asprin and his spouse, the writer Lynn Abbey, conceived the sequence they were borrowing an idea long-used by TV. In exactly the same way as a series like *Star Trek* required its writers to respect the parameters of the universe in which it takes place, and not to violate the integrity of its characters, Asprin and Abbey laid down a framework for their contributors. They even had a manual (a "bible" in television parlance) outlining the rules. One of the attractions for many of the writers involved was that the environment, magical systems and other elements were a given, leaving them to concentrate on foreground events. The flexibility of the concept was such that over the 12 volumes published up to 1989 (containing between six and a dozen stories each), different writers got to handle the same characters, and in some cases the same situations, from divergent viewpoints. Thus Thieves' World could accommodate writers with styles as diverse as C. J. Cherryh and A. E. van Vogt while still retaining its internal consistency. It was also possible to submit a story that wasn't entirely resolved and have it completed, perhaps by another hand, in a later volume.

The catholic mix of contributors produced some fine additions to the Thieves' World mythos, excepting a few submissions that failed to gel, but the series is regarded as a milestone more for its innovative concept than for any individual stories, not least because it was owned and controlled by its creators. In effect, the editors acted as packagers. They commissioned the volumes' contents, sought an appropriate publisher and negotiated separately for sublicensing and merchandising rights. This offered the potential of increased income for the writers and democratized the balance of power between publisher and creators. At this time of writing, Thieves' World is dormant.

In 1990 Asprin began a new series, with *Phule's Company,* in which he appears to be attempting to transfer the Myth blueprint to science fiction. The two extant volumes at time of going to press portray a group of shambolic and eccentric military types loose in a space-opera scenario. It remains to be seen whether the Phule comedies will capture as dedicated an audience as the Myth books.

Asprin can take some credit for helping to move humorous fantasy away from the short form in which it was more usually found and making it acceptable at novel length. Sales as large as his suggest a readership extending far beyond fantasy enthusiasts, so it would be fair to assume he has contributed to the process of bringing the sub-genre to general attention. But his joint editorship of the Thieves' World anthologies will probably be judged his most substantial and enduring gift to the field.

—Stan Nicholls

B

BACH, Richard (David)

Nationality: American. **Born:** Oak Park, Illinois, 23 June 1936; direct descendant of Johann Sebastian Bach. **Education:** One year at California State University, Long Beach. **Military Service:** United States Air Force, 1956-59, 1961-62: Captain. **Family:** Married 1) Betty Jeanne Franks in 1957 (divorced 1971), three sons and three daughters; 2) Leslie Parrish in 1977. **Career:** Associate editor, West Coast editor, *Flying* magazine, 1961-64; charter pilot, flight instructor, aviation mechanic and barnstormer in Iowa and the American Midwest, 1965-70. **Agent:** Kenneth Littauer, Littauer & Wilkinson, 500 Fifth Avenue, New York, New York 10036, USA.

FANTASY PUBLICATIONS

Novels

Jonathan Livingston Seagull: A Story, photographs by Russell Munson. New York, Macmillan, 1970; London, Turnstone Press, 1972.
Illusions: The Adventures of a Reluctant Messiah. New York, Delacorte, and London, Heinemann, 1977.
There's No Such Place as Far Away, illustrated by Ronald Wagen. New York, Delacorte, 1979; London, Granada, 1980.
The Bridge Across Forever: A Lovestory (published as non-fiction). New York, Morrow, 1984.
One: A Novel. New York, Morrow, 1988.

Short Stories

A Gift of Wings (stories and essays), illustrated by K. O. Eckland. New York, Delacorte, 1974.

OTHER PUBLICATIONS

Other

Stranger to the Ground. New York, Harper and Row, 1963; London, Cassell, 1964.
Biplane. New York, Harper and Row, 1966; London, Collier Macmillan, 1984.
Nothing by Chance: A Gypsy Pilot's Adventures in Modern America, photographs by Paul E. Hansen. New York, Harper and Row, 1969; London, Collier Macmillan, 1984.

*

Film Adaptation: *Jonathan Livingston Seagull,* 1973.

Biography: *Above the Clouds: A Reunion of Father and Son* (includes letters and afterword by Bach), by Jonathan Bach. New York: Morrow, 1993.

*   *   *

Only the inflexible logic of literary taxonomy places Richard Bach in the category of fantasy: that is, if all narratives are either "realistic" or "fantastic," and since his novels are clearly not realistic, Bach must be a fantasy writer. However, appropriately enough for a writer whose central theme is the magic and excitement of flying as a perfect expression and symbol of human aspirations and freedom, Bach is difficult to pigeonhole in this fashion, for two reasons: first, while most modern fantasies derive from the rich and colourful materials of myths and legends, Bach works within two different, more austere traditions: fables, tales of talking animals to provide moral lessons for children; and parables, similarly motivated tales of people for adults. Second, while other fantasies are consciously created falsehoods, the assertions that underlie Bach's novels—that the material world is an illusion, that individuals can by will-power manipulate and alter that illusory world, that all people have lived and will live a multiplicity of different lives—apparently represent Bach's sincere beliefs. If Bach writes stories simply to present an accurate picture of the world as he believes it is, then, there is justice in Bach's own description of his work as "non-fiction".

In Bach's first fantasy, "Cat" (1962; collected in *A Gift of Wings*) inexperienced squadron pilots sometimes observe a Persian cat watching their planes; each time, they are then reminded of an important factor that saves their lives. The cat symbolizes the alertness and attention to detail necessary in aviation. In *There's No Such Place as Far Away,* the narrator undertakes to attend a girl's birthday party by means of a spiritual odyssey with several birds, who all offer a lesson about the true meaning of life; he finally offers the girl a magical ring which will let her make similar journeys. The overall effect is tendentious and cloying, like an over-extended Hallmark Card. Harder to dismiss is the better-known *Jonathan Livingston Seagull,* a book written for children that became an adult bestseller. Bach undeniably struck a chord with his story of a seagull, determined to fly as high and as well as he can, who ultimately soars to a higher spiritual plane and returns to inspire other seagulls to follow his example. A live-action film version, with songs by Neil Diamond, proved unpleasant for both Bach and filmgoers.

Despite *Jonathan*'s success, Bach's reputation as a writer must rest on what might be termed (by pigeonholers) his fantasy trilogy for adults: *Illusions: The Adventures of a Reluctant Messiah, The Bridge Across Forever* and *One.* The second appeared as an autobiography, but the books flow together: *Bridge* has an early reference to Donald Shimoda, the fictional messiah of *Illusions,* and *One* derives from speculations about alternate lives near the end of *Bridge.* Building on the theme of *Jonathan, Illusions* confronts the dilemma of the enlightened person who can draw crowds with apparent miracles but cannot get them to accept the deeper truths the miracles are designed to convey. Using the character of Shimoda, a one-time Messiah who gave up the job because of such frustrations, Bach concludes that all individuals must concentrate on their own spiritual quests, allowing others to attain (or not attain) enlightenment in their own ways. The novel effectively combines tidbits of oracular wisdom with Bach's real-life experiences as a barnstormer (recounted without embellishment in *Nothing by Chance*). *Bridge* focuses on one essential aspect of that spiritual quest—the need to find and accompany a "soulmate"—and describes how Bach met and achieved a relationship with actress Leslie Parrish; the story is largely factual because, one suspects, Bach felt that in illustrating this message he could not improve upon the truth.

In his most impressive work, *One,* Bach offers a cosmic vision of the vast universe that might be perceived by truly enlightened people—an endless array of their alternate lives in the past, present and future, each a response to different environments or different decisions. Flying in an airplane (of course), Bach and his wife magically find themselves above a vast shallow ocean, and every time they land, they encounter various versions of themselves—including Attila the Hun and the overseer of a dead future Earth—gaining insights into their own character and world in the process. Returning to their present-day reality brings a plane crash and Leslie's apparent death, until Bach realizes that he can refuse to accept the illusory world around him and thus bring Leslie back to life. Here, the scope of Bach's vision is truly breathtaking; the only disappointment is that the book is necessarily incomplete in developing its innumerable possibilities. It is a story one wishes were longer, and one that might spawn a worthwhile sequel.

In early non-fiction, Bach's writing featured long descriptive sentences, laden with metaphorical and emotional language, in the manner of Ray Bradbury (who wrote the "Prelude" to *Biplane*). Later, perhaps responding to Shimoda's advice that Messiahs should "Keep it simple," Bach's prose style became more straightforward and unadorned, without any striving for effect. As indicated, his mostly autobiographical fiction lacks the traditional accoutrements of fantasy, though there are moments of brilliant creativity: while walking on water has long been a traditional attribute of Messiahs, *Illusions* notes that a true Messiah should also be able to swim in the ground; and *One* includes a delightful scene with Tink, the "idea fairy," who supervises the manufacture of gigantic crystals sparkling with the interactions of various ideas.

As is the case with writers who claim to present the One Truth, Bach's fiction evokes wildly differing reactions, some seeing him as a true Messiah for our times, others as a purveyor of sentimental mystical hokum. Certainly, one might wish for a Richard Bach who was a little less focused on himself, a little less sure of his own wisdom, and a little more inclined to be entertaining instead of inspirational. However, as unenlightened readers without access to his alternate lives, we must accept and appreciate the Richard Bach that we have.

—Gary Westfahl

BAILEY, Robin W(ayne)

Nationality: American. **Born:** Robert Wayne Bailey, in Kansas City, Missouri, 2 August 1952. **Education:** Northwest Missouri State University; B.S. in English, 1974, M.A. 1976. **Family:** Married Diana Jean Piper in 1974. **Agent:** Richard Curtis, 171 East 74th Street, New York, NY 10021, USA. **Address:** 808 West 39th Terrace, Kansas City, MO 64111-4002, USA.

FANTASY PUBLICATIONS

Novels (series: Dragon; Frost)

Frost. New York, Pocket, 1983; London, Allen and Unwin, 1984.
Skull Gate (Frost). New York, Tor, 1985.

Bloodsongs (Frost). New York, Tor, 1986.
Enchanter. New York, Avon, 1989.
The Lake of Fire. New York, Bantam, 1989.
Nightwatch. Lake Geneva, Wisconsin, TSR, 1990.
The Lost City of Zork. New York, Avon, 1991.
Brothers of the Dragon. London, NEL, 1992; New York, Roc, 1993.
Straight on Till Mourning. London, NEL, 1993; as *Flames of the Dragon,* New York, Roc, 1994.
Triumph of the Dragon. New York, Roc, 1994.

*

Robin W. Bailey comments:

In my novels and short stories I like to use fantasy fiction to explore modern issues, such as growing old, abortion and unwanted children, homosexuality, abuse and violence. Even in my humorous fantasies such concerns take centre stage. My characters are people who "don't fit in" with their worlds or cultures, frequently caught between a desperate desire to fit in and a stubborn pride in the fact that they don't.

*   *   *

Robin Bailey's work is firmly in the tradition of quest fantasy. His first book, *Frost,* and its sequels follow the adventures of the eponymous heroine, a woman warrior who has lost her magical powers and been exiled because of a curse. The plot, which uses the standard apparatus of this type of fantasy—magical items, spells, the quest—is enlivened by Frost's feisty personality, and by more moral ambiguity than might be expected from a story which revolves around a war between light and darkness.

Bailey's more recent books, *Brothers of the Dragon* and *Straight on Till Mourning,* are the first two parts of a new quest fantasy series. The action concerns the attempts of two brothers from this world, Eric and Robert Podlowsky, to defend Palenoc—an alternate, magical kingdom—from the ravages of both Shandal Karg, the Queen of the Dark Lands, and Keris Chaterit, the Lord of the Kingdoms of Night. This situation will be familiar to most readers of genre fantasy, a familiarity increased by the presence of dragons and unicorns—especially since the unicorns are evil, the creations of Shandal Karg, and were once the spirits of her 12 most important generals: an almost direct transliteration of the Nazguls from Tolkien's *The Lord of the Rings*.

However, the quest which faces Robert and Eric is much less direct than the one set for Frodo. The brothers are both martial-arts experts, though Scott is also a successful horror novelist, while Eric is an alcoholic mailman who considers himself a failure. Initially, they stumble into Palenoc, apparently by accident. Then it seems that Robert's friend Scott is somehow involved, even though Robert saw him die in New York. This involvement is kept pretty much in the background; but there is a hint that he and Robert may have been lovers. Despite much of the book being told from Robert's point of view, this is never clarified; certainly Robert is also attracted to Alanna, one of the female dragon riders. However, Robert's main aim in Palenoc is to find Scott, whom he is convinced is still alive and in the power of Shandal Karg.

The first book is mostly concerned with setting up the situation; then the brothers go off to free some villagers who have been captured. It soon becomes clear that Robert looks like the Shae'aluth, the incarnation of Or-dhamu—the organizing principle of the universe—that the people of Palenoc are expecting to redeem them. It is also clear to the reader, though never explicitly stated, that Scott would also fit this description. At the end of the novel one of their new allies kills Keris Chaterit. Robert returns to this world while Eric stays in Palenoc. In the second book, Robert has been accused of Eric's murder. This is a promising development, since it allows us to see the relationship between Robert with his parents and the mundane world, where it soon becomes apparent that he is not that much more successful than Eric. The problem is swiftly dealt with, however, once he sends an old girlfriend, Katy, to retrieve Eric. Katy also elects to stay in Palenoc. The rest of this volume has a somewhat stronger, if still somewhat stock, plot, in which the protagonists go off to plant a gem in a plain in the centre of Chol-Hecate, one of the Dark Lands. They succeed, but only just, and at the end of the novel they have been split up, with each fearing the others dead. Clearly, there is at least one more book to come.

The Dragon series has some innovative ideas, including the possible bisexuality of one of its protagonists, and the fact that murder is almost impossible because the victim's ghost will come back to revenge itself on its murderer. Unfortunately, the plot underpinning them is rather diffuse, and based on somewhat overused fantasy concepts. For instance, considering that Bailey goes to some lengths to establish the real-world credentials of Robert, Katy and Eric, it is astonishing how quickly they adapt to Palenoc and come to call it home. This may, of course, be a plot element that will be addressed later in the series, but so far it hasn't even been remarked upon by anyone. Then again, early on it seems that things in Palenoc are based on elements of Robert's books. This could have been fascinating, perhaps allowing Bailey to explore the nature of the creative process itself. Unfortunately, it has apparently already been resolved into the much less interesting idea that Robert had once visited Palenoc and then forgotten about it—though this may yet turn out to be a red herring.

The magic also seems rather *ad hoc,* as if Bailey were simply making up anything he needed as he went along. For instance, there are the ghosts and people who can communicate with them, even to channelling their anger; but in one place Salyt, a councilwoman, tells Katy that all Palenoc magic is worked through crystals, even though at the time they are standing within a protective magic circle, which uses no stones. Add to this astral projection, and the fact that the dragon-riders call their mounts with music. None of this would matter if the characterization were strong enough to make us care about the characters. The opening of the first volume is certainly vivid enough to make one hope this will be the case, and Katy, in particular, is quite well drawn. However, there are also passages where it is difficult to tell Robert and Eric apart.

As it stands, then, *Brothers of the Dragon* and its sequel are a competent, if hardly revolutionary, addition to the quest fantasy genre. It would be intriguing to see what would result if, in future volumes, Bailey made more of Robert's sexuality and the personal nature of his quest, and rather less of the stock save-the-magic-kingdom side of the plot.

—Liz Holliday

BAKER, Frank (Edgar)

Nationality: British. **Born:** London, 22 May 1908. **Education:** Winchester Cathedral School. **Family:** Married Kathleen Lloyd, an actress, in 1943; two sons and one daughter. **Career:** Clerk in the Underwriting Room of the London Assurance for five years before undertaking secretarial work at a college for church musicians; wrote for stage, radio and television as well as book publication; composed music; accompanist at the Players Theatre, Albemarle Street, London. **Died:** 1982.

FANTASY PUBLICATIONS

Novels

The Twisted Tree. London, Davies, 1935.
The Birds. London, Davies, 1936.
Miss Hargreaves: A Fantasy. London, Eyre and Spottiswoode, 1940; New York, Coward McCann, 1941.
Sweet Chariot. London, Eyre and Spottiswoode, 1942; New York, Coward-McCann, 1943.
Mr. Allenby Loses the Way. New York, Coward McCann, 1945; London, Boardman, 1946.
Before I Go Hence: Fantasia on a Novel. London, Dakers, 1946; New York, Coward McCann, 1947.
Embers: A Winter Tale. New York, Coward McCann, 1946; London, Dakers, 1947.
The Downs So Free. London, Dakers, 1948.
Talk of the Devil. London, Angus and Robertson, 1956.

Short Stories

Blessed Are They: Eight Stories. London, Society of St. Paul, 1953.
Stories of the Strange and Sinister. London, Kimber, 1983.

OTHER PUBLICATIONS

Novels

Allanayr. London, Eyre and Spottiswoode, 1941; as *Full Score,* New York, Coward-McCann, 1942.
My Friend the Enemy. London, Boardman, 1948; New York, Coward-McCann, 1948.
The Road Was Free. London, Boardman, 1948.
Teresa: A Journey Out of Time. London, Davies, 1960.

Plays

Playing with Punch: A New Play (The Tragical Comedy of Punch and Judy). London, Boardman, 1944.

Other

I Follow But Myself (autobiography). London, Davies, 1968.
The Call of Cornwall. London, Hale, 1976.

*   *   *

Fantasies or near-fantasies by Frank Baker include *The Twisted Tree* (dark Cornish tragedy), *Sweet Chariot* (guardian-angel heavenly fantasy), *Before I Go Hence* (metaphysical time travel), *Embers: A Winter Tale* (the terrible beauty of death), *Mr. Allenby Loses the Way* (Thorne Smith-type whimsy) and *The Downs So Free* (more metaphysics). But Baker's now-uncertain literary reputation rests upon two occasionally reprinted novels—*The Birds* and *Miss Hargreaves*.

The Birds is one of those awful-warnings-to-us-all that appeared in the 1930s—Wells's *The Shape of Things to Come,* Huxley's *Brave New World,* Stapledon's *Odd John,* Rex Warner's *The Aerodrome,* and Balmer and Wylie's *When Worlds Collide* are other examples. Heroine Anna hears about the Days Before the Birds Came from her (anonymous) dying father. Fifty years before, Daddy saw the first mass bird-attack on human beings, in Trafalgar Square, London, and he "felt in everything a dread sense of the mock-world we had set up in place of the real world which was our heritage."

In the course of the novel Baker delivers unorthodox opinions on advertising, insurance, monarchy, blood sports, Christianity, music, cinema, homosexuality (greatly daring for those "mock-world" days) and public schools (team spirit/ sportsmanship). Spot the dictator in this satirical detail: "a small bird flew over his head, casting his load with a gentle plop on to the carefully brushed black hair." The author's introduction to the Panther paperback edition shows that Baker had mellowed with the passing years, but not by a great deal:

> [The world of 1935] differs little from ours of today, except that now there are many more people and the rat-race is swifter. But the birds are too swift. If they came today they would, I hope, be even more alert to the horrors which devil our present society . . . Let it be remembered, though, that the birds are our friends—if we can live up to them.

The reasons behind this avian terrorism are taken to be unknowable or at any rate beyond human knowledge. Not surprising, really: the changes come so thick, fast and cataclysmic that the very idea of rational investigation gets lost in the scuffle. Active resistance proves worse-than-useless, and the moral is "blessed are the meek." Racial survival depends upon dumb acceptance bordering on the neurasthenic—anticipating J. G. Ballard's terminal beachcombers by 30-odd years: "the men of my time had accustomed themselves to the habit of unconscious experience . . . 'My subconscious mind', they would say, 'led me to this or that action' . . . They did not seem to realize that 'subconscious' was but a label they themselves attached to a conscious Soul which, through lack of proper union with the physical body, had partially decayed."

The Birds is a basically plotless, idea-as-hero novel about ecological catastrophe (from humanity's point of view). Characterization barely rises above the "Very Young Man" level employed by H. G. Wells in *The Time Machine.* Also, Baker gives the story a decidedly Anglo-centric slant: "Of what went on in other parts of the world I can tell you no more than what I gathered from a study of the newspapers, from listening to wireless reports, or from hurrying to and from Lloyd's underwriting-room . . ."

The novel received mixed reviews: "Tediously unconvincing" (*Daily News*); "A vividly imaginative tour de force" (*Illustrated London News*). It sold neither widely nor too well, and Baker ran for cover as an itinerant church organist. Daphne du Maurier's famous short story of the same title and theme (about "Nature, abused . . .")

appeared in her collection *The Apple Tree* (Gollancz, 1952; published in the USA as *Kiss Me Again, Stranger,* Doubleday, 1953). These two fine works differ so much from each other that comparisons are more than usually odious. Hitchcock bought the du Maurier name for his 1963 film, but the screenplay (by Evan Hunter) bore little resemblance to her story—or to Baker's novel.

Four years after *The Birds* came *Miss Hargreaves.* Written as a joke, the novel was rejected by nine publishers: "But I persisted, because I liked it" (author's statement in *Twentieth Century Authors: First Supplement,* 1955). *Miss Hargreaves* does indeed start off as a graveyard-humour joke (almost literally). The narrator, Norman Huntley, is an oddly imaginative young man who works in his father's cathedral-town ("Cornford") bookshop. "Always be careful, my boy, what you make up. Life's more full of things made up on the Spur of the Moment than most people realize. Beware of the Spur of the Moment. It may turn and rend you."

Norman's best friend is the equally youthful Henry Beddow, who also works in the family business (a High Street garage). "The real link between Henry and me is that we both have a pretty fanciful imagination. We like to use it, too." Some months before the story opens, Norman and Henry take a holiday in the sleepy Ulster village of Lusk. Norman (especially) and Henry are provoked into frantic creativity by Squint, the unctuous sexton of Lusk's "bad enough to be reasonably beautiful" church. They claim special knowledge of the late Reverend Archer through a mutual friend, the imaginary Miss Constance ("Connie") Hargreaves. Made-up details multiply: she is almost 90 years old, a published poet, afflicted by rheumatoid arthritis, niece to the Duke of Grosvenor, and lives at Sable Lodge, Oakham, Rutlandshire. Even much later, on the Belfast-Liverpool ferry, the demonic duo can't leave well enough alone; according to them, Miss Hargreaves winters in the South of France, keeps a cockatoo named Dr. Pepusch, and is presently attending the Three Choirs Festival at Hereford. Henry suggests that Norman contact the old dear, care of the Manor Court Hotel, Hereford, inviting her to stay in Cornford. The letter is duly sent—and the hitherto non-existent Miss Hargreaves duly arrives in Cornford. "'Creative thought creates' (from the postcard by A.F.W.)" is Baker's apt choice of epigraph for the novel. Connie Hargreaves has brought her cockatoo, dog, harp and long-stay luggage—including the bath given to her by Reverend Archer 60 years before. But these farcical elements are soon given the authorial heave-ho. Norman, as prime creator, must come to terms with a spur-of-the-moment phantasm that just won't go away. He toys with possible causes (escaped lunatic, practical joke, coincidence, mass hallucination) before deciding that his invented person has actually materialized. The whole thing becomes an object lesson in what G. K. Chesterton called the Ethics of Elfland.

Miss Hargreaves is a better novel than *The Birds,* the characters of which are little more than Awful-Warning symbols. The eponymous spinster evokes sympathy for the plight in which she has been so involuntarily placed, much like Frankenstein's misnamed monster. "I have since adapted her for television, for sound-radio, for the theatre; and in each version Miss Hargreaves was played by Margaret Rutherford . . . England's leading comedy actress" (author's statement). Baker is long overdue for critical and popular rediscovery: some canny publisher (following the late, lamented Panther Books) should take up his work once more.

—Graham Andrews

BANCROFT, Laura. *See* BAUM, L(yman) Frank.

BANGS, John Kendrick

Pseudonyms: Roger Camerden, Gaston V. Drake, Horace Dodd Gastit, Blakeney Gray, Wilberforce Jenkins, John Kendrick, A. Sufferan Mann, Arthur Spencer Morley, Periwinkle Podmore, T. Carlyle Smith. **Nationality:** American. **Born:** Yonkers, New York, 27 May 1862. **Education:** Columbia College, New York, Ph.B., 1883. **Family:** Married Agnes Lawson Hyde in 1886. **Career:** Associate editor, *Life,* 1884-88; on editorial staff of *Harper's Monthly,* 1888-99; editor, *Harper's Weekly,* 1899-1901; editor, *Puck,* 1904-05. Writer, editor and humorist. **Died:** 21 January 1922.

FANTASY PUBLICATIONS

Novels (series: House-boat on the Styx)

Roger Camerden: A Strange Story (published anonymously). New York, Coombes, 1887.
Mephistopheles: A Profanation. New York, Gilliss, 1889.
Toppleton's Client, or A Spirit in Exile. New York, Webster, and London, Osgood McIlvaine, 1893.
Mr. Bonaparte of Corsica (published anonymously). New York and London, Harper, 1895.
A House-boat on the Styx. New York, Harper, 1895; London, Osgood McIlvaine, 1896.
A Rebellious Heroine. New York, Harper, 1896.
The Pursuit of the House-boat. New York, Harper, and London, Osgood McIlvaine, 1897.
The Enchanted Type-writer (House-boat). New York and London, Harper, 1899.
Olympian Nights. New York and London, Harper, 1902.
Alice in Blunderland. New York, Doubleday Page, 1907.
The Autobiography of Methuselah. New York, Dodge, 1909.

Short Stories

New Waggings of Old Tales (with Frank Dempster Sherman, as Two Wags). Boston, Ticknor, 1888.
The Water Ghost, and Others. New York and London, Harper, 1894.
Ghosts I Have Met, and Some Others. New York and London, Harper, 1898.
Over the Plum-pudding. New York, Harper, 1901.
Mr. Munchausen. Boston, Noyes Platt, 1901; London, Richards, 1903.
Bikey the Skicycle, and Other Tales of Jimmie-boy. New York, Riggs, 1902.
Jack and the Check-book. New York, Harper, 1911.
Shylock Homes: His Posthumous Memoirs. Arlington, Virginia, Dispatch-Box Press, 1973.

OTHER PUBLICATIONS

Novels

Lorgnette, with S. W. Van Schaik. New York, Coombes, 1886.
Katharine: A Travesty. New York, privately published, 1888.
Emblemland (for children). New York, Harper, 1902.
Mollie and the Unwiseman. Philadelphia, Coates, 1902.
The Whole Family, with others. New York, Harper, 1908.
Mollie and the Unwiseman Abroad. Philadelphia, Lippincott, 1910.

Short Stories

Tiddledywink Tales. New York, DeWitt, 1891; London, Griffith Farran, 1892.
In Camp With a Tin Soldier. New York, Russell, 1892.
Coffee and Repartee. New York and London, Harper, 1893.
Half-Hours with Jimmieboy. New York, Russell, 1893.
Mantel-piece Minstrels, and Other Stories. New York, Russell, 1896.
Past Jewels; Being Seven Tales of Domestic Woe. New York and London, Harper, 1897.
The Dreamers, a Club. New York, Harper, 1899.
The Booming of Acre Hill, and Other Reminiscences of Urban and Sub-urban Life. New York and London, Harper, 1900.
The Inventions of the Idiot. New York, Harper, 1904.
Mrs. Raffles. New York, Harper, 1905.
R. Holmes & Co. New York, Harper, and London, Bird, 1906.
Andiron Tales. New York, Winston, 1906.
Jimmieboy's Tool Chest. New York, Harper, 1907.
Potted Fiction. New York, Doubleday Page, 1908.
A Little Book of Christmas. Boston, Little Brown, 1912.
Santa Claus and Little Billie. New York, Browne and Howell, 1914.

Poetry

Carmen: The Song of the Toreador (adapted from the libretto by Bizet to accompany artwork by Frank M. Gregory). London, Dean, 1891.
The Flower Song and the Spinning Song (adapted to accompany artwork by Frank M. Gregory). London, Dean, 1891.
Lohengrin (adapted to accompany artwork by Frank M. Gregory). London, Dean, 1891.
Tiddledywink's Poetry Book. New York, Russell, 1892.
A Prophecy and a Plea. New York, privately published, 1897.
To the Rough Riders. New York, privately published, 1899.
Songs of Cheer. Boston, Sherman French, 1910.
Eight Brand New Bits of Christmas Cheer. New York, Leighton and Valentine, 1911.
Echoes of Cheer. Boston, Sherman French, 1912.
Line o' Cheer for Each Day of the Year. Boston, Little Brown, 1913.
The Foothills of Parnassus. New York and London, Macmillan, 1914.
Quest for Song. Boston, Little Brown, 1915.
The Cheery Way. New York, Harper, 1919.

Plays

The Bicyclers and Three Other Farces. New York and London, Harper, 1896.
Proposal Under Difficulties. New York, Harper, 1905.

The Worsted Man (musical). New York and London, Harper, 1905.
The Real Thing and Three Other Farces. New York and London, Harper, 1909.
Young Folk's Minstrels. New York, Harper, 1913.
The Chafing-Dish Party. New York, Harper, 1913.
A Dramatic Evening. New York, Harper, 1913.
The Fatal Message. New York, Harper, 1913.

Other

Three Weeks in Politics. New York and London, Harper, 1894.
The Idiot. New York and London, Harper, 1895.
Peeps at People. New York and London, Harper, 1899.
Cobwebs From a Library Corner. New York, Harper, 1899.
Uncle Sam Trustee: Cuba of Today. New York and London, Harper, 1902.
The Genial Idiot: His Views and Reviews. New York and London, Harper, 1908.
From Pillar to Post. New York, Century, 1916.
Half Hours With the Idiot. New York, Harper, 1917.

*

Critical Study: *John Kendrick Bangs, Humorist of the Nineties* by Francis Hyde Bangs, New York, Knopf, 1941.

*   *   *

John Kendrick Bangs was one of the foremost humorists of his day. Humour seldom dates well, and some of Bangs's gift fails to work today. Contemporaries claim that Bangs was even funnier in person than in his writing, and he was in great demand on the lecture circuit. Otherwise his humour poured out in hundreds of stories and essays, written for the magazines he edited, with most of them collected in almost 50 books, in addition to his poetry and plays. Remarkably for a humorist, Bangs used the supernatural in much of his writing. Mostly it was as a vehicle for social comment, but occasionally it rose to greater heights. Today he is remembered primarily for one or two ghost stories, the clever novel *A House-boat on the Styx* and his contributions to the canon of Sherlock Holmes.

A House-boat on the Styx, upon which Bangs's reputation was based, resurrects the shades of characters real and fictional throughout history at an exclusive Club they have established in Hades, on the Styx, having paid off Charon, the boatman, as a janitor with Saturdays off. The book is a succession of episodes spoofing not only issues of the day, but also matters of significance to the characters. There is, for instance, much discussion about the authorship of Shakespeare's plays, with various characters owning up to various plays. As with many of his contemporaries, Bangs had an ingenious mind for quirky inventions, such as a way of conveying tobacco smoke to the Club's smoking room so as to allow the shades to smoke without the inconvenience of cigars.

While the ghosts are off watching a fight between Samson and Hercules, a group of feminists who are excluded from the Club take over—just at the same time that the house-boat is stolen by Captain Kidd. In the sequel, *The Pursuit of the House-boat,* Bangs introduces the ghost of Sherlock Holmes (at that time still believed to have died at the Reichenbach Falls) to help track down the boat. This volume concentrates more on the women in the boat and their

plans to overthrow Captain Kidd. The added action, and the interplay between men and women, make the sequel even more enjoyable. Bangs later wrote a third volume, *The Enchanted Type-writer,* where the narrator is able to communicate with Boswell in Hades via an old typewriter, but the more static narrative makes this volume far less successful. The House-boat volumes have lost some of their humour in the intervening century, but because Bangs was parodying issues from throughout history most of the jokes are equally meaningful today. The inclusion of Sherlock Holmes has also guaranteed the books a lasting reputation.

Bangs had struck on the vein of parodying real and fictional characters from his earliest published works. *Katharine,* written in 1887, was a "travesty" of *The Taming of the Shrew,* whilst *Mephistopheles,* one of his earliest fantasies, was a parody of *Faust.* He continued the idea in a series of short stories, *New Waggings of Old Tales,* written with architect and poet Frank Dempster Sherman. Other books that fit into this vein include *Mr. Bonaparte of Corsica, The Dreamers, Mr. Munchhausen, Alice in Blunderland* and *The Autobiography of Methuselah.* He also wrote a series of pastiches of Sherlock Holmes featuring one Shylock Homes, which ran in various newspapers during 1903 but was not collected in book form until the 1970s as *Shylock Homes: His Posthumous Memoirs.* Also in this vein is *Olympian Nights,* which parodies American social mores in terms of the legendary Greek gods. Apart from the Holmes pastiches, most of these books lack the ingenuity and acceptability of the House-boat series and remain more as literary curios than as valued reading.

Bangs was clearly interested in weird and supernatural fiction and wrote many more fantasies, including some straight ghost stories. "The Water Ghost of Harrowby Hall" (*Harper's Weekly,* 1891) is among the most reprinted of all ghost stories. It tells of the ghost of a young female suicide who returns for an hour every Christmas Eve and thoroughly soaks the rooms at Harrowby Hall. The new owner seeks to exorcise her by freezing her solid. The humour of the story, which is mostly in the banter between the owner and the ghost, is dated and grates today, but the ingenious concept of a frozen ghost is one that could have been developed further. The story is collected in *The Water Ghost and Others.* Most of the remaining stories are weak jokes, such as "The Spectre Cook of Bangletop," about a ghostly cook who will only cease her haunting if her back-wages are paid. "The Literary Remains of Thomas Bragdon," however, is more substantial, and is an example of the puzzle story that Bangs enjoyed. Here the reader is left to decide whether two friends have succeeded in making contact after one has died, or whether it is solely the wish of the survivor.

Bangs had employed this type of story from the start, with *Roger Camerden: A Strange Story,* which was published pseudonymously as by the narrator. The reader is left with the puzzle as to whether the narrator is really dead or not. Bangs used this to best effect in "Thurlow's Christmas Story" (*Harper's Weekly,* 1894), which may have provided inspiration for Cleveland Moffett's "The Mysterious Card" (*Black Cat,* 1896). In an opening that strikes of autobiography we learn that the narrator, Thurlow, has lost his creative drive and is unable to deliver a Christmas story to his editor. He is increasingly plagued by his own ghost which taunts him like an evil doppelgänger. A mysterious visitor leaves Thurlow with the manuscript of a brilliant story, and Thurlow's ghost tempts Thurlow to sell the story as his own. Thurlow acquiesces, and copies out the story while destroying the original, but when he submits it the editor is furious at receiving a set of blank pages. Devoid of humour, this remains Bangs's most powerful ghost story.

Bangs wrote many more ghost stories, most of them humorous and most of them for Christmas issues of his magazines. They are collected in *Ghosts I Have Met* and *Over the Plum-pudding*. Apart from "Thurlow's Christmas Story," the most effective is another about doppelgängers, "Carleton Baker, First and Second," which considers the effect upon one when the other is hanged. Of his humorous ghost stories, "The Dampmere Mystery" is almost slapstick, but "The Flunking of Watkins's Ghost" is a clever consideration of how education had improved during the last century when a hundred-year-old ghost fails a modern exam.

Although Bangs was predominantly a product of his day, he was able to use the fantastic to step back from his era and parody life on a wider scale, and it was that ability which has assured his work a longer life than that of many of his contemporaries.

—Mike Ashley

BARRIE, (Sir) J(ames) M(atthew)

Nationality: British. **Born:** Kirriemuir, Forfarshire (now Angus), Scotland, 9 May 1860. **Education:** Misses Adam School, Kirriemuir; Glasgow Academy, 1868-70; Forfar Academy, 1870-72; Dumfries Academy, 1873-78; University of Edinburgh, 1878-82, M.A. 1882. **Family:** Married the actress Mary Ansell in 1894 (divorced 1909). **Career:** Drama and book critic, Edinburgh *Courant,* 1879-82; leader writer, Nottingham *Journal,* 1883-84. Lived in London after 1885: journalist, contributing to the *St. James's Gazette* and *British Weekly,* 1885-90. President, Society of Authors, 1928-37, and Dramatists' Club, 1934-37. **Awards:** LL.D.: University of St. Andrews, 1898; University of Edinburgh, 1909; D.Litt.: Oxford University, 1926; Cambridge University, 1930. Rector, University of St. Andrews, 1919-22; Chancellor, University of Edinburgh, 1930-37. Created Baronet, 1913; Order of Merit, 1922. **Died:** 19 June 1937.

FANTASY PUBLICATIONS

Novels

The Little White Bird. London, Hodder and Stoughton, 1902; as *The Little White Bird; or, Adventures in Kensington Gardens,* New York, Scribner, 1902; revised material for children, as *Peter Pan in Kensington Gardens,* illustrated by Arthur Rackham, 1906.
Peter and Wendy, illustrated by F. D. Bedford. London, Hodder and Stoughton, and New York, Scribner, 1911; as *Peter Pan and Wendy,* London, Hodder and Stoughton, 1921.
Farewell Miss Julie Logan: A Wintry Tale. London, Hodder and Stoughton, and New York, Scribner, 1932.

Plays

Peter Pan; or, The Boy Who Would Not Grow Up (produced London, 1904; Washington, D.C., and New York, 1905; revised version, produced London, 1905). Included in *Plays,* 1928.
When Wendy Grew Up: An Afterthought (produced London, 1908). London, Nelson, 1957; New York, Dutton, 1958.

Dear Brutus (produced London, 1917; New York, 1918). London, Hodder and Stoughton, and New York, Scribner, 1922.
Mary Rose (produced London and New York, 1920). London, Hodder and Stoughton, and New York, Scribner, 1924.

OTHER PUBLICATIONS

Novels

Better Dead. London, Swan Sonnenschein Lowrey, 1887; Chicago, Rand McNally, 1891.
When a Man's Single: A Tale of Literary Life. London, Hodder and Stoughton, 1888; New York, Lovell, 1892.
The Little Minister. London, Cassell, 3 vols., 1891; New York, Lovell, 1891.
Sentimental Tommy: The Story of His Boyhood. London, Cassell, and New York, Scribner, 1896.
Tommy and Grizel. London, Cassell, and New York, Scribner, 1900.
The Boy Castaways of Black Lake Island (for children). Privately printed, 1901.

Short Stories

Two of Them. New York, Lovell, 1893.
A Tillyloss Scandal. New York, Lovell, 1893.

Plays

Bandolero, The Bandit (produced Dumfries, 1877).
Caught Napping. Privately printed, 1883.
Richard Savage, with H. B. Marriott Watson (produced London, 1890). Privately printed, 1891.
Ibsen's Ghost; or, Toole Up-to-Date (produced London, 1891). Privately printed, 1939; edited by Penelope Griffin, London, Woolf, 1975.
Walker, London (produced London, 1892). London and New York, French, 1907.
The Professor's Love Story (produced New York, 1892; London, 1894). Included in *Plays,* 1942.
Becky Sharp, adaptation of the novel *Vanity Fair* by W. M. Thackeray (produced London, 1893).
Jane Annie; or, The Good Conduct Prize, with Arthur Conan Doyle, music by Ernest Ford (produced London, 1893). London, Chappell, and New York, Novello Ewer, 1893.
The Little Minister, adaptation of his own novel (produced Washington, D.C., New York, and London, 1897; as *Little Mary,* produced London, 1903). Included in *Plays,* 1942.
A Platonic Friendship (produced London, 1898).
The Wedding Guest (produced London, 1900). London, Fortnightly Review, and New York, Scribner, 1900.
Quality Street (produced London, 1902; New York, 1903). London, Hodder and Stoughton, 1913; New York, Scribner, 1918.
The Admirable Crichton (produced London, 1902; New York, 1903). London, Hodder and Stoughton, 1914; New York, Scribner, 1918.
Pantaloon (produced London, 1905). Included in *Half Hours,* 1914.
Alice Sit-by-the-Fire (produced London and New York, 1905). London, Hodder and Stoughton, and New York, Scribner, 1919.
Josephine (produced London, 1906).
Punch (produced London, 1906).

What Every Woman Knows (produced London, Atlantic City, New Jersey, and New York, 1908). London, Hodder and Stoughton, and New York, Scribner, 1918.

Old Friends (produced London, 1910; New York, 1917). Included in *Plays*, 1928.

A Slice of Life (produced London, 1910; New York, 1912).

The Twelve-Pound Look (produced London, 1910; New York, 1911). Included in *Half Hours*, 1914.

Rosalind (produced London, 1912; New York, 1915). Included in *Half Hours*, 1914.

The Dramatists Get What They Want (produced London, 1912; as *The Censor and the Dramatists,* produced New York, 1913).

The Will (produced London and New York, 1913). Included in *Half Hours*, 1914.

The Adored One: A Legend of the Old Bailey (produced London, 1913; as *The Legend of Leonora,* produced New York, 1914; shortened version, as *Seven Women,* produced London, 1917). *Seven Women* included in *Plays*, 1928.

Half an Hour (produced London and New York, 1913). Included in *Plays*, 1928.

Half Hours (includes *Pantaloon, The Twelve-Pound Look, Rosalind, The Will.* London, Hodder and Stoughton, and New York, Scribner, 1914.

Der Tag (produced London, 1914; as *Der Tag; or, The Tragic Man,* produced New York, 1914). London, Hodder and Stoughton, and New York, Scribner, 1914.

Rosy Rapture, The Pride of the Beauty Chorus, music by H. Darewski and Jerome Kern (produced London, 1915).

The Fatal Typist (produced London, 1915).

The New Word (produced London, 1915; New York, 1917). Included in *Echoes of the War,* 1918.

The Real Thing at Last (produced London, 1916).

Irene Vanbrugh's Pantomime (produced London, 1916).

Shakespeare's Legacy (produced London, 1916). Privately printed, 1916.

A Kiss for Cinderella (produced London and New York, 1916). London, Hodder and Stoughton, and New York, Scribner, 1920.

The Old Lady Shows Her Medals (produced London and New York, 1917). Included in *Echoes of the War,* 1918.

Reconstructing the Crime (produced London, 1917).

La Politesse (produced London, 1918).

A Well-Remembered Voice (produced London, 1918). Included in *Echoes of the War,* 1918.

Echoes of the War (includes *The Old Lady Shows Her Medals, The New Word, Barbara's Wedding, A Well-Remembered Voice).* London, Hodder and Stoughton, and New York, Scribner, 1918.

Barbara's Wedding (produced London, 1927; New York, 1931). Included in *Echoes of the War,* 1918.

The Truth about the Russian Dancers (ballet), music by Arnold Bax (produced London, 1920). New York, Dance Perspectives, 1962.

Shall We Join the Ladies? (produced London, 1921; New York, 1925). Included in *Plays*, 1928.

Neil and Tintinnabulum. Privately printed, 1925.

Representative Plays (includes *Quality Street, The Admirable Crichton, What Every Woman Knows, Dear Brutus, The Twelve-Pound Look, The Old Lady Shows Her Medals),* edited by W. L. Phelps. New York, Scribner, 1926.

The Plays of J. M. Barrie (includes *Peter Pan, The Admirable Crichton, Alice Sit-by-the-Fire, What Every Woman Knows, A Kiss for Cinderella, Dear Brutus, Mary Rose, Pantaloon, Half an Hour, Seven Women, Old Friends, Rosalind, The Twelve-Pound Look, The New Word, A Well-Remembered Voice, Barbara's Wedding, The Old Lady Shows Her Medals, Shall We Join the Ladies?).* London, Hodder and Stoughton, 1928; New York, Scribner, 1929; augmented edition, edited by A. E. Wilson (includes *Walker, London; The Professor's Love Story; The Little Minister; The Wedding Guest; The Boy David),* Hodder and Stoughton, 1942.

The Boy David (produced Edinburgh and London, 1936; New York, 1941). London, Davies, and New York, Scribner, 1938.

Screenplays: *The Little Minister,* 1915; *The Real Thing at Last,* 1916; *As You Like It,* with Robert Cullen, 1936.

Poetry

Scotland's Lament: A Poem on the Death of Robert Louis Stevenson. Privately printed, 1895.

Other

The New Amphion. Edinburgh, David Douglas, 1886.

Auld Licht Idylls. London, Hodder and Stoughton, 1888; New York, Cassell, 1891.

A Window in Thrums. London, Hodder and Stoughton, 1889; New York, Waverly, 1891.

An Edinburgh Eleven: Pencil Portraits from College Life. London, Office of the British Weekly, 1889; New York, Lovell, 1892.

My Lady Nicotine. London, Hodder and Stoughton, 1890; New York, Cassell, 1891.

A Holiday in Bed and Other Sketches. New York, New York Publishing Company, 1892.

A Lady's Shoe. New York, Brentano, 1893.

An Auld Licht Manse and Other Sketches. New York, Knox, 1893.

Allahakbarries C.C. (on cricket). Privately printed, 1893.

Margaret Ogilvy, by Her Son. New York, Scribner, and London, Hodder and Stoughton, 1896.

The Allahakbarrie Book of Broadway Cricket for 1899. Privately printed, 1899.

George Meredith 1909. London, Constable, 1909; as *Neither Dorking Nor the Abbey,* Chicago, Browne's Bookstore, 1910.

The Works (Kirriemuir Edition). London, Hodder and Stoughton, 10 vols., 1913.

Charles Frohman: A Tribute. Privately printed, 1915.

Who Was Sarah Findley? by Mark Twain, with a Suggested Solution of the Mystery. Privately printed, 1917.

The Works of J. M. Barrie. New York, Scribner, 10 vols., 1918.

Courage: The Rectorial Address Delivered at St. Andrews University, May 3rd 1922. London, Hodder and Stoughton, and New York, Scribner, 1922.

The Ladies' Shakespeare (lecture). Privately printed, 1925.

The Works (Peter Pan Edition). New York, Scribner, 14 vols., 1929-31.

The Entrancing Life (address). London, Hodder and Stoughton, and New York, Scribner, 1930.

The Greenwood Hat, Being a Memoir of James Anon 1885-1887. Privately printed, 1930; revised edition, London, Davies, and New York, Scribner, 1937.

M'Connachie and J.M.B.: Speeches. London, Davies, 1938; New York, Scribner, 1939.

Letters of J. M. Barrie, edited by Viola Meynell. London, Davies, 1942; New York, Scribner, 1947.

Plays and Stories, edited by Roger Lancelyn Green. London, Dent, 1962.

*

Film Adaptations: *The Little Minister,* 1915, 1921, 1934; *The Real Thing at Last,* 1916; *What Every Woman Knows,* 1917, 1921, 1934; *The Admirable Crichton,* 1918, 1957; *Sentimental Tommy,* 1921; *Peter Pan,* 1924, 1953, 1976 (TV movie), 1991 (as *Hook*); *A Kiss for Cinderella,* 1925; *Quality Street,* 1927, 1937.

Bibliography: *Sir James M. Barrie: A Bibliography* by B. D. Cutler, New York, Greenberg, 1931.

Manuscript Collections: Beinecke Library, Yale University, New Haven, Connecticut; Lilly Library, Indiana University, Bloomington.

Critical Studies (selection): *J. M. Barrie* by F. J. Harvey Darton, London, Nisbet, 1929; *The Story of J.M.B. (Sir James Barrie)* by Denis Mackail, London, Davies, and New York, Scribner, 1941; *Fifty Years of Peter Pan,* London, Davies, 1954, and *J. M. Barrie,* London, Bodley Head, 1960, New York, Walck, 1961, both by Roger Lancelyn Green; *J. M. Barrie: The Man Behind the Image* by Janet Dunbar, London, Collins, and Boston, Houghton Mifflin, 1970; *Sir James Barrie* by Harry M. Geduld, New York, Twayne, 1971; *J. M. Barrie and the Lost Boys* by Andrew Birkin, London, Constable, and New York, Potter, 1979; *The Case of Peter Pan, or, The Impossibility of Children's Fiction* by Jacqueline Rose, London, Macmillan, 1984; *J. M. Barrie* by Leonee Ormond, Edinburgh, Scottish Academic Press, 1987.

*   *   *

It was while walking his St. Bernard dog in Kensington Gardens that J. M. Barrie—already established as a novelist and playwright—first met the children of lawyer Arthur Llewellyn Davies, with whom he entered into a curious collaboration, spinning endless fantasies for their amusement. When the boys' father died Barrie assumed responsibility for them and their mother. Out of this experience arose the novel *The Little White Bird,* the story of a man who befriends a child in Kensington Gardens and becomes the benefactor of his family and a collaborator in the spinning of elaborate fantasies—one of which features a strange being named Peter Pan, who flew away from home when he was seven days old, thus becoming a "Betwixt-and-Between" who never grows older.

Most of Barrie's work in this particular phase of his career consisted of imaginatively-transfigured autobiography, and the story of Peter Pan is no exception. Barrie had stopped growing when he reached five feet in height, and apparently remained sexually impotent throughout his life, caught betwixt and between the worlds of childhood and adulthood. Peter Pan does try, on one occasion, to fly back home again, but he finds the nursery window barred; through it he sees his mother suckling another child. Barrie's own mother preferred his elder brother, David, who was killed when James was only six, never thereafter growing any older while retaining his stranglehold on her affections.

Peter Pan went on to become the leading character in Barrie's most famous fantasy, the play named for him; the work also exists in a novel version as *Peter and Wendy,* which contains a crucial extra scene. The play established Peter Pan as one of the most celebrated 20th-century myth-figures; his is one of those names which

everyone can recognize. The play also added Wendy to the repertoire of English forenames; it had not been so used before. In the new story Peter Pan lives in the Never Land with the Lost Boys and his fairy friend Tinker Bell, enjoying a neverending riot of adventures with wild animals, "redskins" and pirates. His ambivalent feelings regarding mothers—stemming from a lockout episode similar to that described in the earlier work—causes him to lure away the three children of the Darling family, but he is eventually forced to surrender them to their own destiny. The shape of this destiny is not spelled out in the play, but the novel's epilogue—in which Peter visits a grown-up Wendy—makes it abundantly clear.

The play includes many memorable lines, but there is one particular moment whose unprecedented theatricality is astonishing: the scene in which Tinker Bell drinks poison left for Peter by Captain Hook and Peter requests the audience to clap their hands in order to revive her. Barrie was so uncertain as to the likely success of this ploy that he ordered the orchestra to supply the necessary applause if the first-night audience failed to oblige, but the response turned out to be thunderous—thus demonstrating the remarkable fact that people can be moved very deeply by the plight of a character who is played by a spotlight.

Barrie went on to write two more classic fantasy plays. *Dear Brutus* has echoes of *A Midsummer Night's Dream,* describing the adventures of a group of people who enter a magic wood where they are transformed into the people they might have become had they made different choices. They have all been prey to the melancholy illusion that they would have been infinitely better off had they made different choices, but the experience proves otherwise to most of them. Only one character is left with a deeper sense of regret, when he loses the beloved daughter that his alter ego had. The astonishing emotional force that Barrie was able to incorporate into such scenes as this is displayed to more extended advantage in the harrowing timeslip romance *Mary Rose,* whose eponymous heroine makes the mistake of returning to a desolate islet where she once disappeared, quite unaccountably, for 20 days. The second time she is gone for many years, leaving behind a baby son who is grown up by the time she returns. Unable to adapt to her situation she languishes and dies, but remains on earth as a ghost until she achieves a sadly futile reunion with the child she can no longer recognize. All ghosts, Barrie once proposed, must be mothers searching for lost children, because no other motive could possibly be strong enough to keep souls back from the gates of Paradise. By the time he wrote *Mary Rose* Barrie had lost the Llewellyn Davies boys, at least in the sense that they had grown up (one of them had already been killed in action during the Great War).

Barrie published one more fantasy, the novella *Farewell Miss Julie Logan,* which first appeared as a Christmas supplement to *The Times* in memory of the Golden Age of Dickens' Christmas fantasies. It has much in common with his earliest literary works, which drew extensively on the legacy of his Scottish upbringing, but lacks the conviction and intensity which gave that early work its strength. It offers an account of the brief relationship between a young minister and a lovely female ghost, whose eventual exorcism is absurdly abrupt.

Barrie owed his popularity to a peculiar alloy of raw, unashamed sentimentality and haunting bitterness, which eventually allowed him to become the voice and imagination of a world which was slowly and inexorably losing faith in Victorian myths about the sanctity of motherhood and the innocence of childhood. The fact that *Peter Pan* and *Peter and Wendy* are nowadays regarded as works written for children (Barrie did not regard the play in that light) reflects a certain unwillingness by adults to recognize that their underlying message is profoundly bleak. Rewriting the story as a pantomime or a Disney cartoon—or as a nostalgic sequel, after the fashion of the Spielberg film *Hook*—does serve to deflect attention from the bitter heart of the myth, but it could not be nearly so powerful without its tragic quality. As the novel version takes care to emphasize, no happy ending is possible for boys like Peter, while girls like Wendy must firmly close the window to keep him out if they are to lead a full and rewarding life.

—Brian Stableford

BARTH, John (Simmons)

Nationality: American. **Born:** Cambridge, Maryland, 27 May 1930. **Education:** The Juilliard School of Music, New York; Johns Hopkins University, Baltimore, A.B. 1951, M.A. 1952. **Family:** Married 1) Ann Strickland in 1950 (divorced 1969), one daughter and two sons; 2) Shelly Rosenberg in 1970. **Career:** Junior instructor in English, Johns Hopkins University, 1951-53; instructor, 1953-56, assistant professor, 1957-60, and associate professor of English, 1960-65, Pennsylvania State University, University Park; professor of English, 1965-71, and Butler Professor, 1971-73, State University of New York, Buffalo. Since 1973 Centennial Professor of English and Creative Writing, Johns Hopkins University; now emeritus. **Awards:** Brandeis University Creative Arts award, 1965; Rockefeller grant, 1965; American Academy grant, 1966; National Book award, 1973. Litt. D.: University of Maryland, College Park, 1969. **Member:** American Academy, 1977, and American Academy of Arts and Sciences, 1977. **Agent:** Wylie Aitken and Stone, 250 West 57th Street, New York, New York 10107. **Address:** c/o Writing Seminars, Johns Hopkins University, Baltimore, Maryland 21218, USA.

FANTASY PUBLICATIONS

Novels

The Floating Opera. New York, Appleton Century Crofts, 1956; revised edition, New York, Doubleday, 1967; London, Secker and Warburg, 1968.
The End of the Road. New York, Doubleday, 1958; London, Secker and Warburg, 1962; revised edition, Doubleday, 1967.
The Sot-Weed Factor. New York, Doubleday, 1960; London, Secker and Warburg, 1961; revised edition, Doubleday, 1967.
Giles Goat-Boy; or, The Revised New Syllabus. New York, Doubleday, 1966; London, Secker and Warburg, 1967.
LETTERS. New York, Putnam, 1979; London, Secker and Warburg, 1980.
Sabbatical: A Romance. New York, Putnam, and London, Secker and Warburg, 1982.
The Last Voyage of Somebody the Sailor. Boston, Little Brown, 1991.
Once Upon a Time: A Floating Opera. Boston, Little Brown, 1994.

Short Stories

Lost in the Funhouse: Fiction for Print, Tape, Live Voice. New York, Doubleday, 1968; London, Secker and Warburg, 1969.

Chimera. New York, Random House, 1972; London, Deutsch, 1974.
The Tidewater Tales. New York, Putnam, 1987; London, Methuen, 1988.

OTHER PUBLICATIONS

The Literature of Exhaustion, and The Literature of Replenishment (essays). Northridge, California, Lord John Press, 1982.
The Friday Book: Essays and Other Nonfiction. New York, Putnam, 1984.
Don't Count on It: A Note on the Number of the 1001 Nights. Northridge, California, Lord John Press, 1984.
Further Fridays: Essays, Lectures, and Other Nonfiction, 1984-1994. Boston, Little Brown, 1995.

*

Bibliography: *John Barth: A Descriptive Primary and Annotated Secondary Bibliography* by Josephy Weixlmann, New York, Garland, 1976; *John Barth: An Annotated Bibliography* by Richard Allan Vine, Metuchen, New Jersey, Scarecrow Press, 1977; *John Barth, Jerzy Kosinski, and Thomas Pynchon: A Reference Guide* by Thomas P. Walsh and Cameron Northouse, Boston, Hall, 1977.

Manuscript Collection: Library of Congress, Washington, D.C.

Critical Studies: *John Barth* by Gerhard Joseph, Minneapolis, University of Minnesota Press, 1970; *John Barth: The Comic Sublimity of Paradox* by Jac Tharpe, Carbondale, Southern Illinois University Press, 1974; *The Literature of Exhaustion: Borges, Nabokov, and Barth* by John O. Stark, Durham, North Carolina, Duke University Press, 1974; *John Barth: An Introduction* by David Morrell, University Park, Pennsylvania State University Press, 1976; *Critical Essays on John Barth* edited by Joseph J. Waldmeir, Boston, Hall, 1980; *Passionate Virtuosity: The Fiction of John Barth* by Charles B. Harris, Urbana, University of Illinois Press, 1983; *John Barth* by Heide Ziegler, London, Methuen, 1987; *Understanding John Barth* by Stan Fogel and Gordon Slethaug, Columbia, University of South Carolina Press, 1990; *A Reader's Guide to John Barth* by Zack Bowen, Westport, Connecticut, Greenwood Press, 1994.

*   *   *

"A story with nothing fantastic in it lacks something essential," declares Fenwick Turner, the author figure from John Barth's *Sabbatical,* to his young wife Susan Seckler, as they navigate the familiar and beguiling—yet treacherous—reaches of Barth's beloved Chesapeake Bay (a locale which figures in nearly all his books, much in the manner of Faulkner's Yoknapatawpha County) in their small craft named *Story.* Becoming vehement, Turner continues: "Realism is your keel and ballast of your effing Ship of Story, and a good plot is your mast and sails. But magic is your wind, Suse. Your literally marvelous is your mother-effing wind."

True to this sentiment, all of Barth's own books have been touched by the literally marvelous to a greater or lesser degree, earning him a place in modern fantasy's pantheon at least as secure and impressive as that which he occupies in the larger postmodernist canon (a canon certain of his essays early on actually helped to define). Propelled by an unswerving concern with sex, language, the nature of narrative and curious ontological predicaments, his books range from the slim to the Garagantuan; journey from intimately detailed historical venues to contemporary bedrooms and on to uncharted parallel universes (or Universities); and play fast and loose with traditional fictional structures and conventions, while at the same time remaining true to Story's older attractions.

A twin himself—the motif of twins runs like a constant thread through his work—Barth has declared that his books can be profitably viewed in pairs, and objective consideration supports this view. Originally, Barth intended his first book, *The Floating Opera,* to be cast entirely in the form of a minstrel show. Excepting a few typographical oddities and a short scene aboard the riverboat of the title, little of this original innovative and typically adventurous scheme remains in the published book, which is the story of the *menage-a-trois* between Harrison and Jane Mack and the coldly affectless Todd Andrews, culminating in the latter's near-suicide in the year 1937. This is the least fantastic of Barth's books, although the image of an eccentric pre-Howard-Hughes millionaire bottling his excrement in rows of preserve jars (Barth loves the scatological) surely merits some notice.

Opera's twin is *The End of the Road,* an author-disowned film version of which was released in 1967. Jacob Horner, an ontological vacuum, is Todd Andrews's even more diseased counterpart. Dispossessed of any emotions or motivations, subject to immobilizing fugues, Horner is programmed for a partial humanity by a mysterious black man known only as the Doctor, who runs the Remobilization Farm, an unlicensed therapy centre highly predictive of several of the more shady New Age movements. Sent to teach at Wicomico College (the first usage of academia in the work of Barth, who himself has made teaching his second career), Horner becomes involved with Joe Morgan and his wife Rennie, eventually precipitating a life-or-death crisis through his blunderings.

Both of these early books share a first-person point-of-view which would prove congenial to Barth, and which he would frequently employ. And the young author's careful attention to fresh language—convoluted and startling just enough to draw attention to its own construction without interfering with the texts' considerable narrative powers—hinted at what was to come.

The Sot-Weed Factor, along with its twin, *Giles Goat-Boy,* are the massive pillars upon which Barth's reputation still firmly rests. These encyclopedic, energetic, relentless masterpieces share the themes of innocence besmirched and classical heroes betrayed, not least of all by their own misconceptions. Radically different in their venues and stylistic garbs, they are indisputably twins. And after the grim and somewhat half-hearted existentialism of the early books, the wild black humour of Books Three and Four clearly establishes Barth's mature form.

Set in a meticulously recreated 17th-century London and Maryland, *Sot-Weed* is a proto-steampunk work whose erudition and tone call to mind that of Avram Davidson. The hapless virgin and aspiring Poet Laureate of Maryland, Ebenezer Cooke, his twin Anna, along with their Pan-like tutor Henry Burlingame and a cast of hundreds, undergo innumerable insulting trials and hilarious misadventures, as Ebenezer attempts to claim his heritage and estate. The diddling of textbook History, complete with recondite conspiracies, spurious journals and erotic Magic Aubergines, forms the fantastic subtext to the picaresque surface narrative.

In his collection of essays, *The Friday Book,* which contains many fascinating insights into Barth's own work, as well as literature in general, Barth tells how, after the publication of *Sot-Weed,* he was complimented for his clever incorporation of the Universal Hero motifs into the book—a fact which had escaped his conscious

intentions! Intrigued, he made a study of the works of Joseph Campbell and others, and consciously set out in his next book to utilize them.

Elaborately supported by fake documents, *Giles Goat-Boy* is ostensibly "The Revised New Syllabus," the New Testament account of a parallel-world saviour. Giles's world is a fun-house mirror reflection of our own, caught in all its mid-1960s madness. The paradigm of all existence is the University, where West Campus is opposed by East Campus in the Quiet Riot (read Cold War). Into this satiric milieu is born the Goat-Boy, conceived by WESCAC, a horny computer, upon a suitable virgin. Assuming the mantle of Grand Tutor, Giles sets out from the goat farm where he was raised Tarzan-like by the herd and his foster father, Max. Encountering disbelief and treachery on all sides—not the least from a False Tutor named Harold Bray, whose initials and philosophy link him with *Sot-Weed*'s Henry Burlingame—Giles causes more harm than good, until finally discerning his true nature and mission. *Giles* shares the concerns and flavours of work from two of Barth's generational peers, Robert Coover and Kurt Vonnegut, as exemplified by the former's *The Origin of the Brunists* (1965) and the latter's *Cat's Cradle* (1963).

After two such prodigious novels, Barth switched for the time to collating and creating shorter work. *Lost in the Funhouse* collects all his short fiction to date, including many formal experiments. (However, in an essay titled "Writer's Choice," Barth plainly states that "I have no use for merely formalist tours de force," and in another, "More Troll than Cabbage," he sides with the forces who seek to dramatize "human life, its happiness and misery," over those who blindly play literary games, arguing that the best compromise is one of "passionate virtuosity.") Notable in this volume are "Night-Sea Journey," with its famous spermatic point-of-view, and the linked tales that introduce Ambrose Mensch, one of Barth's partially autobiographical author stand-ins.

Twin to *Funhouse* is *Chimera,* winner of the National Book Award. The opening piece in this assemblage of three interlocking fabulative novellas, "Dunyazadiad," makes explicit for the first time Barth's love for and indebtedness to the *Arabian Nights,* and to their teller, Scheherazade, whose neck a time-travelling Barth saves. A talismanic figure for Barth, emblematic of all writers and their dilemma of holding an audience and dredging up new stories, she will recur like a tutelary deity in his later books.

Breaking the pattern of paired books with his culminating seventh, *LETTERS,* Barth—like a mainstream Heinlein or Asimov—chose to consolidate all his previous books into one fictional universe. *LETTERS* features characters from all six earlier works—as well as the Author Himself—interacting in a vast recomplicated plot whose highlights are campus intrigue, the conspiratorial revisionism of American history, the filming of an avant-garde movie, and the attempt by Jerome Bray—descendent of Harold and a very large insect, visitor to our universe, programmer of the mysterious LILYVAC computer—to inseminate human females with his buzzing brood.

LETTERS is also a turning point in that Barth eschews his considerable talent for creating conversations among—and distinctive voices for—his characters. There is no actual dialogue in this epistolary novel, all talk being *recounted.* The two (again paired) books that follow will also employ this distancing technique, to their own diminution.

Sabbatical takes its husband and wife protagonists on a soul-searching cruise of the Chesapeake Bay at a crucial juncture in their lives. Susan Seckler's request to her husband for a sailing story suitable for a "four-thousand-year tradition" becomes the key that loosens his narrative blockage. And the fantastic element that Turner's own aesthetic demands is the appearance of Chessie, the Bay's own legendary monster.

The Tidewater Tales, a phrase that appeared as far back as *Chimera*'s "Bellerophoniad," is a literal sequel to *Sabbatical.* Peter Sagamore and wife Katherine reprise the voyage of the earlier couple, whom they soon meet in the flesh. What makes *Tidewater* a more vibrant and fantastic work is the actual appearance on the modern Bay of Odysseus, Don Quixote, and Scheherazade, who enliven the action considerably. *Tidewater* also contains a complete play entitled "Sex Education," which is the feminist flipside to "Night-Sea Journey."

In *The Last Voyage of Somebody the Sailor,* Barth returns to his love for tales within tales, specifically the milieu of *A Thousand Nights and a Night.* Dying in his hospital (or possibly asylum) bed, writer Simon Behler (whose last name is pronounced "Baylor," to evoke Sailor, and who shares Barth's middle and last initials) is visited by Death, the Destroyer of Delights, to whom he begins to tell a story about an aged Scheherazade, who is in her turn being visited by Death, to whom she begins to tell a story about Sindband the Sailor, who is entertaining a guest named Somebody who begins his own tale, which turns out to be—the life story of Simon Behler! The modernist narrative of Behler—beautifully evocative and nostalgic and funny—fails to suit the Baghdadians, who comment wryly on its unlikelihood. But as the many tales spiral around each other and eventually converge, the reader learns that Behler has slipped through time and space literally back into Haroun al-Rashid's era, where he undergoes almost as many darkly exotic adventures as Ebenezer Cooke, learning truths about himself—and the Job-like Sindbad—that the modern world could not teach.

Completing the duet with *Somebody* is *Once Upon a Time,* "a memoir bottled in a novel." The protagonist this time is no author stand-in, but "John Barth" himself. Cruising his beloved Bay waters in a fictional 1992 (projected from the vantage of a "real" 1990), "Barth" and his wife encounter a storm which mires them in a marsh. Probing for a way out, the narrator becomes separated from his wife. Encountering a drowned childhood friend and the simulacrum of his own twin sister, Barth is given a magic pen which functions as a time-travel device, allowing him to wander a "verbal hyperspace," recapitulating and re-orchestrating his life story to date, thereby gaining the requisite understanding to continue with both his literary career and quotidian life. The author calls this his "Last Book," in the sense that "it's meant to wrap up riffs that I've been noodling for forty years." One does indeed sense a kind of culmination of many familiar themes, opening the door for something bolder than and different from the rather circumscribed fiction of Barth's most recent quartet.

Brilliantly pursuing a program of "aesthetic irrealism" for four decades, faithful to "fantasy, a mode of literature as old as the narrative imagination," John Barth has piled up real treasures for us all against the Destroyer of Delights.

—Paul Di Filippo

BARTHELME, Donald

Nationality: American. **Born:** 7 April 1931 in Philadelphia, Pennsylvania. **Education:** Attended the University of Houston. **Fam-**ily: Married twice; one daughter. **Career:** Reporter, *Houston Post,* 1951, 1955-56; worked on public relations and news service staff and founding editor of university literary magazine *Forum,* University of Houston, 1956-59; director, Contemporary Arts Museum, Houston, 1961-62; managing editor, *Location* magazine, New York, 1962-64; visiting professor, State University of New York, Buffalo, 1972, and Boston University, 1973; visiting professor, City College of New York, 1974-89. **Military Service:** United States Army, 1953-55. **Awards:** Guggenheim Fellowship, 1966; National Book Award, 1972; American Academy Morton Dauwen Zabel Award, 1972. **Died:** 1989.

FANTASY PUBLICATIONS

Novels

Snow White. New York, Atheneum, 1967; London, Cape, 1968.
The Slightly Irregular Fire Engine or *The Thithering Dithering Djinn* (for children). New York, Farrar Straus, 1971.
The Dead Father. New York, Farrar Straus, 1975; London, Routledge, 1977.
The King. New York, Harper & Row, 1990.

Short Stories

Come Back, Dr. Caligari. Boston, Little Brown, 1964; London, Eyre & Spottiswoode, 1966.
Unspeakable Practices, Unnatural Acts. New York, Farrar Straus, 1968; London, Cape, 1969.
City Life. New York, Farrar Straus, 1970; London, Cape, 1971.
Sadness. New York, Farrar Straus, 1972; London, Cape, 1973.
Amateurs. New York, Farrar Straus, 1976; London, Routledge, 1977.
Great Days. New York, Farrar Straus, 1979; London, Routledge, 1979.
Sixty Stories. New York, Putnam, 1981.
Overnight to Many Distant Cities. New York, Putnam, 1983.
Forty Stories. New York, Putnam, 1987.

OTHER PUBLICATIONS

Novel

Paradise. New York, Putnam, 1986.

Uncollected Short Stories

"Basil from Her Garden," *New Yorker,* 21 October 1985.
"Tickets," *New Yorker,* 6 March 1989.

Other

Guilty Pleasures. New York, Farrar Straus, 1974.
The Teachings of Don B., The Satires, Parodies, Fables, Illustrated Stories, and Plays of Donald Barthelme, edited by Kim Herzinger. New York, Random House, 1992.

*   *   *

Donald Barthelme's wittily skewed, humorously melancholic and dementedly wise fictional worlds encompass killer pianos, souls captured on film, gigantic mythic fathers, mysterious cities and academies, famous literary personages granted absurd new existences, remote-controlled fleets of mothballed ships, and King Arthur fighting Nazis, among a myriad, myriad other marvellous impossibilities and resonant juxtapositions. A fantasist and fabulist of the first water whose career was conducted (and reputation made) entirely outside genre walls, he was a pivotal figure in a clear-cut lineage. Among his literary ancestors can clearly be placed Franz Kafka, S. J. Perelman, Max Ernst, Harold Pinter, and Luigi Pirandello, as well as a host of Dadaists and Surrealists. Peers who shared his concerns and techniques would include Ishmael Reed, Edward Gorey, Woody Allen, Samuel Beckett, Eugene Ionesco, Robert Coover—and the *Monty Python* comedy troupe. And his legacy extends to writers as diverse as Kathy Acker, Mark Leyner, Don Webb, R. A. Lafferty, Barry Malzberg, and James Sallis.

Barthelme's forte and preferred mode was the short—sometimes extremely short—story. Out of his 15 books for adults (there was one children's book, *The Slightly Irregular Fire Engine*), only four were novels. In the many collections—where fantasies mixed with mimetic pieces (mimetic, that is, by Barthelme's loose standards; even his most straightforward fiction seemed to conceal trapdoors to other worlds)—certain motifs and concerns were recombined and incremented. Music, art, divorce, fathers, cities, money, secret societies, communication breakdowns, women, artifacts of pop culture—all went into the unique Barthelme soup.

And while Barthelme was an innovator and experimenter with forms (his pictorial collage stories are perhaps his most famous contribution) he never lost sight of the power of sheer narration. Events in his stories are always clearly presented, and drama, even suspense, abounds. The mystery never inheres in *what* is happening, but *why*.

A final technique of Barthelme's which must be mentioned is that of the list or litany. As if to exhaust the real world, Barthelme would frequently include whimsical catalogues in his work. A partial list of his lists follows: furnishings, Italian novelists, princes, parts of the ear, musical forms, cathedral workers, books on the self, methods of decay, the things which nothing is not, the muscles of the leg, synonyms for surprise, practical jokes, animals and tools.

Come Back, Dr. Caligari established Barthelme's unique voice from the outset—a voice frequently built out of perfect-pitch transcription of the distinctive voices of his varied characters. This collection includes such fantasies as "Hiding Man" and "Me and Miss Mandible," the latter of which features an adult narrator mysteriously displaced to a elementary-school classroom, and is rife with the odd sexual tension that came to be a hallmark of the author's work. One of Barthelme's main artistic goals, as seen in "Up, Aloft in the Air," was to transfigure or perhaps strip aside the bland facade of American culture, revealing the true weirdness lurking underneath.

In 1967, Barthelme published *Snow White*, a subversion of the famous fairy tale in which the seven dwarfs—Clem, Bill, Hubert, Henry, Edward, Kevin, and Dan—are involved with the manufacture of Chinese baby food, Prince Paul is a dithering poseur, evil Queen Jane is in sexual thrall to her henchman, Hogo, and Snow White herself is something of a dreamy proto-feminist, as well as a slut. The anachronistic minglings found here continue throughout Barthelme's work.

Unspeakable Practices, Unnatural Acts contains marvellous stories ranging from the cyberpunkish "Report" to the Ballardian "Robert Kennedy Saved from Drowning." Also cropping up in this volume is Barthelme's determinedly anti-war stance, especially against the then-current Vietnam War. Oblique critiques such as "The President," in which the country's leader is a malignant dwarf, are typically found throughout the author's later work. Here also clues to Barthelme's aesthetic can be found, in such sentences as "Strings of language extend in every direction to bind the world into a rushing, ribald whole," and "Fragments are the only forms I trust."

City Life is notable for "Views of my Father Weeping," which foreshadows Barthelme's second novel, and for "On Angels," whose opening sentence reveals how deftly Barthelme was able to plunge the reader directly into his enigmatic scenarios: "The death of God left the angels in a strange position." "The City of Churches," to be found in Barthelme's next collection, *Sadness*, exemplifies Barthelme's unique blend of satire and gnosticism.

The publication of *Guilty Pleasures* in 1974 marked the gathering of Barthelme's ostensible "non-fiction." Although as editor Kim Herzinger remarked in his introduction to the posthumously assembled *The Teachings of Don B.* (which reprints much of *Guilty Pleasures*), it is often quite hard to distinguish between Barthelme's stories, parodies, and satires, and such entries as "The Angry Young Man" could easily be included in any of the short story collections.

The Dead Father is perhaps Barthelme's strongest work. A masterfully sustained meditation on the mythic and political meanings of patriarchy, structured as a traditional quest, it is by turns hilarious and tearful. Included within is another complete book, "A Manual for Sons," a medieval parody "translated from the English." With this book, in the chapter-long dialogues between the two main female characters, Barthelme invented a new kind of off-kilter, at-odds duet of speech, a technique he would employ notably in several stories collected in *Great Days*. Intervening between those two books, however, was *Amateurs*, notable for "Some of Us Had Been Threatening Our Friend Colby," in which a man willingly helps arrange his own public hanging for trivial reasons.

As a summation of his career to date, *Sixty Stories* and *Forty Stories* represent the best of the earlier books. Original to the former is the wonderful "The Emerald," a lunatic escapade involving a sentient gemstone. The latter also collects new pieces, among which "Sindbad" and "Bluebeard" illustrate Barthelme's delight in reworking old myths. The final collection published during the author's life is *Overnight to Many Distant Cities*, whose standout fantasy is "The Palace at Four A.M.," in which a repentant, yet vain king writes to his supernatural lover in an attempt to lure her back.

Barthelme's third novel, *Paradise*, is his most mimetic, packed with brand-names and other contemporary touchstones, and tells the story of 53-year-old Simon the architect who finds himself leery caretaker of three nubile young women. The only fantasy elements are sexual ones. *The King* conflates the standard Arthurian cast of characters with World War Two, and gives Barthelme a chance to mock medieval story-telling conventions and language.

Faced with the miraculous irreducibility of Barthelme's fictions, one is cast back on the words of the Dead Father. When asked what one of his puzzling yet glorious speeches means, he replies, "It meant I made a speech."

—Paul Di Filippo

BAUDINO, Gael

Nationality: American. **Born:** 1955 (?). Raised in Los Angeles; lives in Denver, Colorado.

FANTASY PUBLICATIONS

Novels (series: Dragonsword; Strands of Starlight)

Dragonsword. New York, Lynx Omega, 1988.
Strands of Starlight. New York, Signet, 1989; London, Orbit, 1990.
Gossamer Axe. New York, Roc, 1990.
Duel of Dragons (Dragonsword). New York, Roc, 1991.
Dragon Death (Dragonsword). New York, Roc, 1992.
Maze of Moonlight (Starlight). New York, Roc, 1993; London, Orbit, 1994.
Shroud of Shadow (Starlight). New York, Roc, 1993; London, Orbit, 1994.

*   *   *

Issues of sex and gender are central to Gael Baudino's books. Other important themes in her work are the necessity of change, even when not all the changes are positive, and the healing power of love. The first of these is particularly unusual among all the stagnant worlds of fantasy, but changelessness, according to Baudino, leads to death. One weakness is her treatment of evil and sexism as Siamese twins: if you meet a character who expresses sexist attitudes, you know he will turn out to be a villain, and if you meet a man who treats women as equals, you know he is a good guy.

The Dragonsword books could have been clichéd wish-fulfilment fantasies, as the ineffective and unhappy heroine is transformed into a heroic, sword-wielding Amazon in the fantasy world of Gryylth. What takes *Dragonsword* (the first book) beyond simple wish-fulfilment is that Gryylth is not the fantasy of Suzanne Helling, the heroine, but rather that of the annoying Solomon Braithwaite. She is a swordswoman who is reluctant to kill, though she overcomes her pacifism as the book progresses. Solomon is the weakest character, a completely unlikeable, sexist, self-centred bully; the sudden discovery of good qualities in him at the end of the book as he sacrifices himself for Gryylth is not credible.

The second and third Dragonsword books, *Duel of Dragons* and *Dragon Death,* form one story. If in the first book Suzanne had to explore Solomon's subconscious, in these she must dig into her own, confronting her own hippie attitudes in the ineffective people of Vaylle, who won't even defend themselves, and her nightmares of Vietnam in the brutal Grayfaces. The Grayfaces allow Suzanne to completely discard her unwillingness to kill, as they are not even fully human; this dehumanization of the enemy, in contrast to the first book, is a weakness. The other major weakness of the second two books is the loss of the tension between the reluctant heroine and the world into which she is forced, as Suzanne has accepted being part of Gryylth. At times, the books degenerate into generic hack-and-slash. There is much of interest in the Dragonsword novels, as Baudino explores a mind and a country permanently scarred by the Vietnam conflict, abroad and at home, but they are neither as ambitious nor as sophisticated as her other work.

Gossamer Axe brings together two worlds that might seem to have little in common: Celtic fantasy and heavy-metal music. Christa is a harper who was born in sixth-century Ireland and captured by the Sidh. She escaped with the help of a magical Sidh harp and has been trying for centuries to free her lover Judith, but has been unable to best the Sidh musician Orfide. In 1980s Denver she discovers the key: "the violence and passion of heavy metal" will break down the walls between the worlds and defeat Orfide.

The changeless, deadly world of the Sidh is symbolized by the use of present tense in scenes taking place there. The newness and difference of rock and roll is one of Christa's weapons, though it's sometimes hard to separate magical power from sheer volume. Central to the book is the idea of music as magic. It has power to kill or to heal in the right hands, and one needn't be Sidh to wield it. Even heavy metal has that power, especially today, as Christa acknowledges when she trades in her harps for an electric guitar of great power.

There are sexists to fight as well: those who would make Christa into a centrefold instead of a musician, those who dismiss the all-female band she forms as "a titty band," the abusive ex-lover of the lead singer, the incestuous father of the keyboardist, and the club owner who would use and then throw away the bass player. Christa fights them all with determination and self-possession supposedly gained from growing up in the egalitarian world of the ancient Irish, before the coming of the Christians. At times Baudino's agenda gets heavy-handed, particularly in her depiction of a heartless Catholic priest who contributes to the destruction of a family. Generally, paganism contributes its spirit to the novel but does not dominate it.

The series beginning with *Strands of Starlight* is set in an imaginary country, Adria, in the real medieval Europe, and tells the story of the decline and, in the forthcoming *Strands of Sunlight,* rebirth of the Elves. These Elves, though immortal, are not like the Sidh of *Gossamer Axe:* they feel, they grow, they make mistakes. They are like humans but better, wanting only to help and heal. It seems that they die out, not because humans don't need them any more, but because humans are not worthy of them. Why the Elves should then be reborn in 1980 will perhaps be made clear in the book to come.

The transition from 1500 (the approximate year of *Shroud of Shadow*) to 1980 is jarring, and it seems that it would have been more satisfying for Baudino to have let the last of the Elves die, though with the knowledge that there was still Elven blood among humans. However, without having read the (presumably) last book, it is unclear whether she has a greater purpose in mind to justify violating that sense of rightness.

The evils of the established Catholic Church, particularly the Inquisition, are depicted, and the goddess-worship of the Elves is shown as a clearly superior alternative to Christianity. Nevertheless, Baudino does not make the ideologue's mistake, but shows us good, decent Christians, lay and clergy alike; the point is made that the evil clergy are violating the tenets of their own religion. Love, help, and healing should be the centre of any religion, Baudino believes.

Gael Baudino takes familiar themes in fantasy and makes them her own. She deals with gender issues without preaching and conveys a message of love and acceptance.

—Janice M. Eisen

BAUM, L(yman) Frank

Pseudonyms: Floyd Akers; Laura Bancroft; John Estes Cooke; Captain Hugh Fitzgerald; Suzanne Metcalf; Schuyler Staunton; Edith Van Dyne. **Nationality:** American. **Born:** Chittenango, New York, 15 May 1856. **Education:** Schools in Syracuse and New York, and Peekskill Military Academy, New York, 1868-69. **Family:** Married Maud Gage in 1882; four sons. **Career:** Co-editor and co-publisher (with Harry Baum), amateur newspaper *The Rose Lawn Home Journal*, 1870-72; reporter, *New York World*, 1873-75; founding editor, *New Era*, Bradford, Pennsylvania, 1876; poultry farmer with B. W. Baum and Son; editor, *Poultry Record*, Syracuse, and columnist, *New York Farmer and Dairyman*, 1880; actor (as George Brooks) with May Roberts and the Sterling Comedy Company, New York, 1881; owner (as Louis F. Baum), Baum's Opera House, Richburg, New York, 1881-82; toured with own repertory company, 1882-83; salesman, Baum's Ever-Ready Castorine axle grease, 1883-88; owner, Baum's Bazaar general store, Aberdeen, Dakota Territory, 1888-90; editor, *Aberdeen Saturday Pioneer*, 1890-91; reporter, Chicago *Post*, 1891; buyer, Siegel Cooper and Company, Chicago, 1891; salesman, Pitkin and Brooks crockery firm, Chicago, 1891-97; founder, National Association of Window Trimmers, 1897, and founding editor and publisher, *Show Window: A Magazine for Merchants*, Chicago, 1897-1902; founding director, Oz Film Manufacturing Company (later Dramatic Features Company), Los Angeles, 1914-15. **Died:** 6 May 1919.

Fantasy Publications

Novels (series: Oz; Trot and Cap'n Bill)

A New Wonderland, illustrated by Frank Berbeck. New York, Russell, 1900; revised as *The Surprising Adventures of The Magical Monarch of Mo*, Indianapolis, Bobbs Merrill, 1903.
The Wonderful Wizard of Oz, illustrated by W. W. Denslow. Chicago and New York, Hill, 1900; London, Hodder and Stoughton, 1906; as *The New Wizard of Oz*, Bobbs Merrill, 1903.
Dot and Tot of Merryland, illustrated by W. W. Denslow. Chicago and New York, Hill, 1901.
The Master Key: An Electrical Fairy Tale, illustrated by Fanny Y. Cory. Indianapolis, Bowen Merrill, 1901; London, Stevens and Brown, 1902.
The Life and Adventures of Santa Claus, illustrated by Mary Cowles Clark. Indianapolis, Bowen Merrill, and London, Stevens and Brown, 1902.
The Enchanted Island of Yew, illustrated by Fanny Y. Cory. Indianapolis, Bobbs Merrill, 1903.
The Marvelous Land of Oz: A Sequel to The Wizard of Oz, illustrated by John R. Neill. Chicago, Reilly and Britton, and London, Revell, 1904.
Queen Zixi of Ix; or the Story of the Magic Cloak, illustrated by Frederick Richardson. New York, Century, 1905; London, Hodder and Stoughton, 1906.
The Woggle-Bug Book (Oz), illustrated by Ike Morgan. Chicago, Reilly and Britton, 1905.
John Dough and the Cherub, illustrated by John R. Neill. Chicago, Reilly and Britton, 1906; London, Constable, 1974.
Ozma of Oz, illustrated by John R. Neill. Chicago, Reilly and Britton, 1907; as *Princess Ozma of Oz*, London, Hutchinson, 1942.
Policeman Bluejay (as Laura Bancroft), illustrated by Maginel Wright Enright. Chicago, Reilly and Britton, 1907; as *Babes in Birdland*, Reilly and Britton, 1911; as L. Frank Baum, Reilly and Britton, 1917.
Dorothy and the Wizard in Oz, illustrated by John R. Neill. Chicago, Reilly and Britton, 1908.
The Last Egyptian: A Romance of the Nile (published anonymously), illustrated by Francis P. Wightman. Philadelphia, Stern, and London, Sisley, 1908.

The Road to Oz, illustrated by John R. Neill. Chicago, Reilly and Britton, 1909.
The Emerald City of Oz, illustrated by John R. Neill. Chicago, Reilly and Britton, 1910.
The Sea Fairies (Trot and Cap'n Bill), illustrated by John R. Neill. Chicago, Reilly and Britton, 1911.
Sky Island: Being the Further Exciting Adventures of Trot and Cap'n Bill, illustrated by John R. Neill. Chicago, Reilly and Britton, 1912.
The Patchwork Girl of Oz, illustrated by John R. Neill. Chicago, Reilly and Britton, 1913.
Tik-Tok of Oz, illustrated by John R. Neill. Chicago, Reilly and Britton, 1914.
The Scarecrow of Oz (Oz, Trot and Cap'n Bill), illustrated by John R. Neill. Chicago, Reilly and Britton, 1915.
Rinkitink in Oz, illustrated by John R. Neill. Chicago, Reilly and Britton, 1916.
The Lost Princess of Oz, illustrated by John R. Neill. Chicago, Reilly and Britton, 1917.
The Tin Woodman of Oz, illustrated by John R. Neill. Chicago, Reilly and Britton, 1918.
The Magic of Oz (Oz, Trot and Cap'n Bill), illustrated by John R. Neill. Chicago, Reilly and Britton, 1919.
Glinda of Oz, illustrated by John R. Neill. Chicago, Reilly and Lee, 1920.
Jaglon and the Tiger Fairies, illustrated by Dale Ulrey. Chicago, Reilly and Lee, 1953.
The Visitors from Oz (adapted from a comic strip by Baum, 1904-05), illustrated by Dick Martin. Chicago, Reilly and Lee, 1960.
A Kidnapped Santa Claus, illustrated by Richard Rosenbloom. Indianapolis and New York, Bobbs Merrill, 1969.

Short Stories

Mother Goose in Prose, illustrated by Maxfield Parrish. Chicago, Way and Williams, 1897; London, Duckworth, 1899.
American Fairy Tales, illustrated by Ike Morgan, Harry Kennedy and N. P. Hall. Chicago and New York, Hill, 1901; London, Constable, 1978; expanded as *Baum's American Fairy Tales*, illustrated by George Kerr, Indianapolis, Bobbs Merrill, 1908.
Twinkle and Chubbins: Their Astonishing Adventures in Nature-Fairyland (as Laura Bancroft), illustrated by Maginel Wright Enright. Chicago, Reilly and Britton, 1911.
Little Wizard Stories of Oz, illustrated by John R. Neill. Chicago, Reilly and Britton, 1914.
Little Bun Rabbit and Other Stories, illustrated by John R. Neill. Chicago, Reilly and Britton, 1916.
Once Upon a Time and Other Stories, illustrated by John R. Neill. Chicago, Reilly and Britton, 1916.
The Yellow Hen and Other Stories, illustrated by John R. Neill. Chicago, Reilly and Britton, 1916.
The Magic Cloak and Other Stories, illustrated by John R. Neill. Chicago, Reilly and Britton, 1916.
The Ginger-Bread Man, illustrated by John R. Neill. Chicago, Reilly and Britton, 1917.
Jack Pumpkinhead, illustrated by John R. Neill. Chicago, Reilly and Britton, 1917.
Animal Fairy Tales, illustrated by Dick Martin. Chicago, International Wizard of Oz Club, 1969.
The Purple Dragon and Other Fantasies, illustrated by Tim Kirk, edited by David L. Greene. Lakemont, Georgia, Fictioneer Books, 1976.

Plays

The Wizard of Oz, music by Paul Tietjens, lyrics by Baum, adaptation of the novel by Baum (produced Chicago, 1902; revised version, as *There Is Something New Under the Sun,* produced New York, 1903).

The Woggle-Bug, music by Frederic Chapin, adaptation of the novel *The Marvelous Land of Oz* by Baum (produced Chicago, 1905).

The Tik-Tok Man of Oz, music by Louis F. Gottschalk, adaptation of the novel *Ozma of Oz* by Baum (produced Los Angeles, 1913).

The Musical Fantasies of L. Frank Baum (includes *The Maid of Athens, The King of Gee-Whiz, The Pipes O' Pan*), illustrated by Dick Martin. Chicago, Wizard Press, 1958.

Screenplays: *The Fairylogue and Radio-Plays,* 1908; *The Patchwork Girl of Oz,* 1914; *The New Wizard of Oz,* 1914; *The Magic Cloak of Oz,* 1914; *The Last Egyptian,* 1914; *Violet's Dreams,* 1914.

Poetry

By the Candelabra's Glare: Some Verse, illustrated by W. W. Denslow and others. Chicago, privately printed, 1898.

Father Goose, His Book, illustrated by W. W. Denslow. Chicago, Hill, 1899.

The Army Alphabet, illustrated by Harry Kennedy. Chicago and New York, Hill, 1900.

The Navy Alphabet, illustrated by Harry Kennedy. Chicago and New York, Hill, 1900.

The Songs of Father Goose for The Kindergarten, The Nursery and The Home, music by Alberta N. Hall, illustrated by W. W. Denslow. Chicago and New York, Hill, 1900.

Father Goose's Year Book; Quaint Quacks and Feathered Shafts for Mature Children, illustrated by Walter J. Enright. Chicago, Reilly and Britton, 1907.

L. Frank Baum's Juvenile Speaker, Readings and Recitations in Prose and Verse, Humorous and Otherwise, illustrated by John R. Neill and Maginel Wright Enright. Chicago, Reilly and Britton, 1910; as *Baum's Own Book for Children,* Reilly and Britton, 1912.

Songs of Spring. Los Angeles, privately printed, 1916.

OTHER PUBLICATIONS

Novels

The Fate of a Crown (as Schuyler Staunton). Chicago, Reilly and Britton, and London, Revell, 1905.

Annabel: A Novel for Young Folks (as Suzanne Metcalf), illustrated by H. Putnam Hall. Chicago, Reilly and Britton, 1906.

Daughters of Destiny (as Schuyler Staunton). Chicago, Reilly and Britton, 1906.

Sam Steele's Adventures on Land and Sea (as Hugh Fitzgerald). Chicago, Reilly and Britton, 1906; as *The Boy Fortune Hunters in Alaska* (as Floyd Akers), 1908.

Sam Steele's Adventures in Panama (as Hugh Fitzgerald). Chicago, Reilly and Britton, 1907; as *The Boy Fortune Hunters in Panama* (as Floyd Akers), 1908.

Tamawaca Folks: A Summer Comedy (as John Estes Cooke). Macatawa, Michigan, Tamawaca Press, 1907.

The Boy Fortune Hunters in Egypt (as Floyd Akers). Chicago, Reilly and Britton, 1908.

The Boy Fortune Hunters in China (as Floyd Akers). Chicago, Reilly and Britton, 1909.

The Boy Fortune Hunters in Yucatan (as Floyd Akers). Chicago, Reilly and Britton, 1910.

The Boy Fortune Hunters in the South Seas (as Floyd Akers). Chicago, Reilly and Britton, 1911.

The Daring Twins: A Story for Young Folk, illustrated by Pauline M. Batchelder. Chicago, Reilly and Britton, 1911.

Phoebe Daring: A Story for Young Folk, illustrated by Joseph Pierre Nuyttens. Chicago, Reilly and Britton, 1912.

Novels as Edith Van Dyne

Aunt Jane's Nieces, illustrated by Emile A. Nelson. Chicago, Reilly and Britton, 1906.

Aunt Jane's Nieces Abroad, illustrated by Emile A. Nelson. Chicago, Reilly and Britton, 1906.

Aunt Jane's Nieces at Millville, illustrated by Emile A. Nelson. Chicago, Reilly and Britton, 1908.

Aunt Jane's Nieces at Work, illustrated by Emile A. Nelson. Chicago, Reilly and Britton, 1909.

Aunt Jane's Nieces in Society, illustrated by Emile A. Nelson. Chicago, Reilly and Britton, 1910.

Aunt Jane's Nieces and Uncle John, illustrated by Emile A. Nelson. Chicago, Reilly and Britton, 1911.

The Flying Girl, illustrated by Joseph Pierre Nuyttens. Chicago, Reilly and Britton, 1912.

Aunt Jane's Nieces on Vacation, illustrated by Emile A. Nelson. Chicago, Reilly and Britton, 1912.

The Flying Girl and Her Chum, illustrated by Joseph Pierre Nuyttens. Chicago, Reilly and Britton, 1912.

Aunt Jane's Nieces on the Ranch, illustrator anonymous. Chicago, Reilly and Britton, 1913.

Aunt Jane's Nieces Out West, illustrated by James McCracken. Chicago, Reilly and Britton, 1914.

Aunt Jane's Nieces in the Red Cross, illustrated by Norman P. Hall. Chicago, Reilly and Britton, 1915.

Mary Louise, illustrated by J. Allen St. John. Chicago, Reilly and Britton, 1916.

Mary Louise in the Country, illustrated by J. Allen St. John. Chicago, Reilly and Britton, 1916.

Mary Louise Solves a Mystery, illustrated by Anna B. Mueller. Chicago, Reilly and Britton, 1917.

Mary Louise and the Liberty Girls, illustrated by Alice Carsey. Chicago, Reilly and Britton, 1918.

Mary Louise Adopts a Soldier, illustrated by Joseph W. Wyckoff. Chicago, Reilly and Lee, 1919.

Plays

The Maid of Arran, music and lyrics by Baum, adaptation of the novel *A Princess of Thule* by William Black (also director; produced Syracuse and New York City, 1882).

Matches (produced Richburg, New York, 1882).

Kilmourne, or O'Connor's Dream (produced Syracuse, 1888).

Stagecraft, The Adventures of a Strictly Moral Man, music by Louis F. Gottschalk (produced Santa Barbara, California, 1914).

The Uplift of Lucifer, or Raising Hell, music by Louis F. Gottschalk (produced Santa Barbara, California, 1915). Edited by Manuel Weltman, privately printed, 1963.

The Uplifters' Minstrels, music by Byron Gay (produced Del Mar, California, 1916).
The Orpheus Road Company, music by Louis F. Gottschalk (produced Coronado Beach, California, 1917).

Poetry

The High-Jinks of L. Frank Baum. Chicago, Wizard Press, 1959.

Other

The Book of the Hamburgs: A Brief Treatise upon the Mating, Rearing and Management of the Different Varieties of Hamburgs. Hartford, Stoddard, 1886.
The Art of Decorating Dry Goods Windows and Interiors. Chicago, Show Window Publishing, 1900.
L. Frank Baum's "Our Landlady" (columns from the *Aberdeen Saturday Pioneer*). Mitchell, South Dakota, Friends of the Middle Border, 1941.

*

Film Adaptations: *The Patchwork Girl of Oz,* 1914, *The Wizard of Oz,* 1925, 1939, *The Wiz,* 1978, all from the novel *The Wonderful Wizard of Oz*; *The Wonderful Land of Oz,* 1969, *Journey Back to Oz,* 1974, *Return to Oz,* 1985, all from the novels *The Marvelous Land of Oz* and *Ozma of Oz.*

Bibliography: *L. Frank Baum: An Exhibition of His Published Writings, in Commemoration of the Centenary of His Birth, May 15, 1856* edited by Joan Baum and Roland Baughman, Columbia University Libraries, 1956; *The Annotated Wizard of Oz* edited by Michael Patrick Hearn, New York, Potter, 1973.

Manuscript Collection: Columbia University, New York.

Critical Studies: *Utopia Americana* by Edward Wagenknecht, Seattle, University of Washington Book Store, 1929; *The Wizard of Oz and Who He Was* edited by Russel Nye and Martin Gardner, East Lansing, Michigan State University Press, 1957; *To Please a Child: A Biography of L. Frank Baum* by Frank Joslyn Baum and Russell P. MacFall, Chicago, Reilly and Lee, 1961; *Wonderful Wizard, Marvelous Land* by Raylyn Moore, Bowling Green, Ohio, Popular Press, 1974; *The Wizard of Oz* edited by Michael Patrick Hearn (text and critical essays), New York, Schocken, 1983.

*   *   *

L. Frank Baum wrote, in an introduction to his best-known book: "The old-time fairy tale, having served for generations, may now be classed as 'historical' in the children's library; for the time has come for a series of newer 'wonder tales' in which the stereotyped genie, dwarf, and fairy are eliminated, together with all the horrible and blood-curdling incident devised by their authors to point a fearsome moral to each tale. Modern education includes morality; therefore the modern child seeks only entertainment in its wonder-tales and gladly dispenses with all disagreeable incident. Having this thought in mind, the story of *The Wonderful Wizard of Oz* was written solely to pleasure children of today. It aspires to being a modernized fairy tale, in which the wonderment and joy are retained and the heart-aches and nightmares are left out."

Long shunned by librarians, and neglected by scholars of children's literature, L. Frank Baum should be embraced and celebrated by fantasy readers and critics; for *The Wizard of Oz* is surely the most famous American fantasy ever written, and Oz, though limited by an intended audience of children, remains one of its most memorable and fully developed fantasy worlds.

Since he lived in several cities and worked as a travelling salesman, Baum undoubtedly spent some time studying maps, and he seemed to realize that fantasy could be effectively grounded on a firm and consistent geography. From the beginning, Oz was very much a mapped land—Munchkins in the east, Winkies in the west, Quadlings in the south, the Emerald City in the centre, the whole land surrounded by impassable deserts—and later books maintained the picture while adding various realms within and outside of Oz. It was only logical that Baum created a "Map of the Marvelous Land of Oz" for *Tik-Tok of Oz* and later Oz books; and while not the first fantasy writer to include a map of his imagined world, he certainly popularized the idea, and modern fantasy novels with pages of introductory maps owe him a debt.

In later stories, Baum also strived to impose a sense of consistency and logic on his Oz. Unlike countries of our world, Oz and its environs are "fairy lands" with magical properties: animals who visit Oz gain the ability to talk, for example, and inhabitants cannot die a natural death (though they can be killed or dismembered). Largely free of unpleasantness and strife, Oz became a true utopia (as argued in the first study of Baum, Edward Wagenknecht's *Utopia Americana*). Later books address and resolve apparent inconsistencies from earlier books: Toto had the ability to talk in Oz but chose to remain silent; and since the magic of Oz should have made the dismembered parts of the Tin Woodman's body remain alive, *The Tin Woodman of Oz* reveals that his body parts, with those of another dismembered man, were assembled to create a new person, Chopfyt.

Along with his commitment to consistency, Baum's other major characteristic is the fecundity and breadth of his creativity. Baum did not always avoid "stereotyped" European models: *Mother Goose in Prose* shows Baum working comfortably with European settings and themes, and Oz books include traditional characters like witches, griffins, giants, dragons and gnomes (defiantly spelled "nomes"). Neither did he wholly eliminate the "horrible and blood-curdling," as seen in the various unpleasant beings of *The Emerald City of Oz.* For an image of Baum's creative methods, consider the "Thing" of *The Marvelous Land of Oz*: the mounted head of a "Gump" (half-goat, half-elk), attached to two sofas, with two large palm leaves as wings on either side and a broom as a rudder in the back, all animated by a magical Powder of Life. Here are elements of real and imaginary nature, human artifice and traditional magic, all combined with Yankee ingenuity. Baum recognized no real distinctions between nature and magic, or magic and machines; all were equally wonderful, and all were a part of Oz. *Ozma of Oz* introduced both the mechanical Tik-Tok Man and the talking chicken Billina, and in *Glinda of Oz,* a submerged city is raised and lowered by a machine with gigantic gears powered by magic. Modern critics should not single out the engaging *The Master Key* as an early example of "science fiction" because its wonders are electrically powered; rather, the fact that a boy receives these devices from the "Demon of Electricity" shows Baum effortlessly blending magical and mechanical marvels.

While admiring his indefatigable imagination, one can fault Baum's narrative drive and world-view. Introducing Princess Ozma, who takes over Oz in the second book, was a major mistake, for this unfailingly sweet and good-hearted girl never comes to life as a character, and with her watchful magical eye on her friends she becomes a dreary *dea ex machina,* always ready to rescue anyone in danger. Despite Baum's professed commitment to "entertainment," there are several intrusive morals in later Oz books, and Baum's desire to avoid "nightmares" evolved into a desire to avoid conflict altogether, as villains became minor annoyances in stories that were meandering travelogues. Such generalizations do not always hold, and some later books, like *The Patchwork Girl of Oz* and *The Scarecrow of Oz,* are involving narratives; overall, though, general neglect of later Oz books is not unjustified. Certainly, no sequel has the thematic unity and evocative power of *The Wizard of Oz,* which has inspired fanciful allegorical readings (such as the notion that Dorothy's trip in silver shoes on the Yellow Brick Road [read gold] to the Emerald City [of prosperity] represents Baum's argument for bimetallism).

While readers naturally focus on his Oz books, Baum wrote other fantasies which deserve notice, especially *The Master Key* and *Queen Zixi of Ix,* generally regarded as his best non-Oz books. Also meritorious is *The Life and Adventures of Santa Claus,* which revises and secularizes the Christmas saint as a kindly man granted immortality for his good deeds by a council of magical beings. Of a very different character is his adult fantasy novel *The Last Egyptian,* a Haggardian tale of the descendant of an ancient Egyptian ruler who plots against Britishers who wronged his mother, with the minor fantasy element of a colour-changing jewel bearing an ancient curse; a routine effort, the book nevertheless suggests Baum had talents that were under-utilized in his children's books. There is, for example, an unusually adult sense of poignancy in his "The Dummy That Lived" (reprinted in *The Purple Dragon*), about a department-store mannequin, mischievously brought to life by a spirit, who vainly struggles to live the life of a real woman. Complaints about Baum's pedestrian prose style seem besides the point: as others note, fantastic creations are often well served by plain prose.

Baum is often compared—logically—to Lewis Carroll. While Baum lacked Carroll's mathematical mind and flair for literary parody, and Carroll could not match Baum's unbridled creativity, both men shared a fascination with young girls (most children in the Oz books are girls, and Russel B. Nye described Oz as "a little girl's dream"), a delight in puns and wordplay, and (especially in later works) a weakness for episodic plotting and sentimentality. Chauvinistic contrasts between the American Dorothy's assertiveness and the British Alice's passivity derive largely from film adaptations; in their books, Dorothy's desire to go home is not much stronger than Alice's, and both girls have moments of compliance and moments of defiance.

As a final sign of Baum's success, Oz has been profitably revisited by other creators: in the early 1900s, Baum's former illustrator W. W. Denslow produced stories with Oz characters, and after Baum's death, others wrote Oz books, prominently including Ruth Plumly Thompson, Oz illustrator John R. Neill, Jack Snow, and, most recently, Baum's great-grandson Roger Baum. Oz has been visited by Robert A. Heinlein (in *The Number of the Beast,* 1980) and Philip José Farmer (in *A Barnstormer in Oz,* 1982); and of course, there were two extraordinary film adaptations: *The Wizard of Oz* (1939), the definitive version of the first book, and *Return to Oz* (1985), a masterful blend of the second and third books. Both films tighten Baum's narrative and darken his vision, making Dorothy's life in Kansas genuinely grim and elevating the Wicked Witch of the West and the Nome King into embodiments of pure evil; they demonstrate, despite Baum's protestations, the genuine artistic power of "nightmares."

—Gary Westfahl

BEAGLE, Peter S(owyer)

Nationality: American. **Born:** New York City, 20 April 1939. **Education:** University of Pittsburgh, B.A. 1959; Stanford University, creative writing fellowship, 1960-61. **Family:** Married 1) Enid Elaine Nordeen in 1964 (divorced 1980); 2) Padma Hejmadi in 1988; two daughters and one son. **Awards:** Scholastic writing scholarship, 1955; Wallace Stegner Writing Fellowship, 1960-1961; Guggenheim Foundation award, 1972-73; NEA grant, 1977-78; Mythopoeic Fantasy award, 1987. **Agent:** McIntosh and Otis, Inc., 319 Madison Avenue, New York, NY 10017, USA. **Address:** 2135 Humboldt Avenue, Davis, California 95616, USA.

FANTASY PUBLICATIONS

Novels

A Fine and Private Place. New York, Viking, 1960; London, Muller, 1961.
The Last Unicorn. New York, Viking, and London, Bodley Head, 1968.
Lila the Werewolf (novella). Santa Barbara, California, Capra Press, 1974; revised edition, 1976.
The Fantasy Worlds of Peter S. Beagle (omnibus). New York, Viking, 1978; London, Souvenir Press, 1980.
The Folk of the Air. New York, Del Rey, 1986; London, Headline, 1987.
The Innkeeper's Song. New York, Roc, 1993.

Plays

The Last Unicorn, adaptation of his own novel (produced Seattle, Washington, 1988).

Screenplays: *The Lord of the Rings,* with Chris Conkling, 1978; *The Last Unicorn,* 1982.

OTHER PUBLICATIONS

Plays

The Midnight Angel (opera libretto; produced St. Louis, 1993).

Screenplay: *The Dove,* with Adam Kennedy, 1974.

Other

I See By My Outfit. New York, Viking, 1965.
The California Feeling, illustrated by Michael Bry and Ansel Adams. New York, Doubleday, 1969.
American Denim: A New Folk Art. New York, Abrams Warner, 1975.

The Lady and Her Tiger, with Pat Derby. New York, Dutton, 1976.
The Garden of Earthly Delights. New York, Viking, 1981.

*

Film Adaptations: *The Last Unicorn,* 1982.

Critical Study: *Peter S. Beagle* by Kenneth J. Zahorski, Mercer Island, Washington, Starmont House, 1988.

Peter S. Beagle comments:

I write what I would love to read if someone else had written it. But no one else quite does what I do, so I have to. That's really all the statement I can honestly make.

* * *

The extraordinary durability of Peter Beagle's early works cannot be accounted a mere accident of timing, a matter of fantasy reaching a starved audience when little was available. The flood of generic formula fantasies came later, and the popularity of *A Fine and Private Place* and *The Last Unicorn* survived intact. As was clear from Beagle's first novel, published when the author was 21, this is an extraordinary writer. *A Fine and Private Place* is a funny, romantic, sometimes sentimental novel in the manner of Beagle's mentor, Robert Nathan, from whose *One More Spring* (1933), Beagle acknowledged in a recent interview, it is, "if not a dead steal, a direct descendant" (interview by Darrell Schweitzer, *Marion Zimmer Bradley's Fantasy Magazine,* Spring 1994). It's about a misanthropic man who lives in a New York cemetery, fed by a talking raven akin to the one who served Elijah in the Bible. The protagonist becomes involved with ghosts (and ghostly romance) and is finally persuaded to return to the living world. His departure from the cemetery comes in a particularly exhilarating sequence.

Showing such exceptional promise at an early age, Beagle began near the top. He was first befriended by the poet Louis Untermeyer, who passed him on (at 17) to the literary agent Elizabeth Otis (who was also John Steinbeck's agent), who sold Beagle's first novel to one of the most prestigious American publishers. The career doors that opened to him were not those of genre publishing, but of mainstream.

The Last Unicorn remains the book for which Beagle will always be known and to which all his later work will be compared. Again acknowledging Nathan, he seems resigned to this, even as the older writer was resigned to *Portrait of Jennie* completely overshadowing one of the longest careers in the history of American literature. *The Last Unicorn* is what is loosely described as a Tolkien-type fantasy, although Beagle's influences were more Lord Dunsany, James Thurber, James Stephens, Charles Finney and Dorothy Lathrop (a children's fairy-tale writer and illustrator). It is the story of a unicorn's quest for her fellows, and is a metaphorically complex mixture of comedy and sometimes darker wonder (Beagle's ability to shift tone without destroying the unity of the whole reminds one of John Bellairs's *The Face in the Frost*), replete with (in addition to a vast amount of erudite unicorn lore) an inept magician named Schmendrick who remains immortal until he can become competent, a Robin Hood analogue who (like many of the characters) is fully aware that he exists in a legendary context and hopes to have songs of himself catalogued and numbered (with variants) by the famed Scottish folklorist James Francis Child, an ineffectual prince, a witch named Molly Grue, Momma Fortuna's Midnight Carnival (which could appear on a double-bill with the

Circus of Dr. Lao), a diseased king of the Waste Land, and ultimate, the demoniacal Red Bull, which the unicorn must confront. More than a fairy-tale, even one for adults, *The Last Unicorn* is a meditation on maturity, responsibility, and the assumption of expected roles. The magician learns to become a real magician. The prince becomes a proper hero. The king is healed. And the unicorn becomes a lovely lady, so that she may understand mortality, before returning to her original state. Thematically, the work returns to ideas from Dunsany, whose *The King of Elfland's Daughter* (1924) not only has much to do with unicorns but deals with characters emerging from the innocence of Elfland into the waking/adult world with its "tyranny of time."

But of course *The Last Unicorn* is far more than an sum of its disparate elements. Beagle welds them together with singular grace and charm. It is one of the enduring classics of American fantasy. It was successfully made into an animated film in 1982, from a screenplay by Beagle, whose other Hollywood projects have included co-authorship of the screenplay for Ralph Bakshi's considerably less successful adaptation of Tolkien's *The Lord of the Rings.*

After *The Last Unicorn,* though he worked in other fields, Beagle published no fantasy (other than a work-in-progress excerpt), until 1986, which had given a whole generation time to grow up treasuring his first two books, wondering if there would ever be any more, and building up impossible expectations for more of the same. *The Folk of the Air* was an event nearly as anticipated as Tolkien's *The Silmarillion,* and as such unfairly disappointing. The book does have its flaws, notably excessive length and a certain lack of organization which perhaps betrays its having been written over so long a period, but it is an able redemption of a fantasy cliche: suppose the pretend-wars and other activities medievalist groups like the Society for Creative Anachronism suddenly became magically real, complete with real bloodshed and death? It is also about duelling magicians and an evil magic which must be put down, with much description of what might be called the technical methodology of magic. The Berkeley, California, setting is particularly effective. The Berkeley of the late 1960s and early 70s, a hotbed of radicalism, social experimentation, and frequent departures from reality, is exactly where one would expect this sort of thing to happen.

While Beagle's wit still manifests itself in *The Folk of the Air,* the tone is ultimately darker than in his earlier books. *The Innkeeper's Song* is darker still. The novel grew out of a song (Beagle, who is a singer, has written many) about three mysterious women who arrive at an inn one night, one black, one brown (she keeps a pet fox), and one pale white. They overwhelm the innkeeper, nearly wreck the place, and make off with the stableboy. In the novel version, the black and brown women (the latter not really a woman) are students of a failing magician now hounded to death and beyond by another student, who has himself died and been reborn. The pale woman drowns in the first chapter, and is reanimated by the other two. The stableboy doesn't leave with the three at the end, although he, like all the other characters, cannot return to his previously innocent state.

As the three women descend upon the inn, followed by their dying and virtually powerless mentor, magical war breaks out. The errant student has gained a powerful (but ultimately empty) magic on the other side of death, which can only be countered by the pale woman, who has been there too. The story culminates in loss and transformation. What the (now twice-dead) pale woman cannot recover is her love for her boyfriend, who has followed her madly throughout the book. This is a long way from the multiple happy endings of *A Fine and Private Place.*

That Beagle's writing should continue to grow and change is to be applauded. One can only hope that the shorter interval between his third and fourth novels indicate a more prolific future for him.

—Darrell Schweitzer

BEAUCLERK, Helen (de Vere)

Pseudonym for Helen Mary Dorothea Bellingham. **Nationality:** British. **Born:** Cambridge, 20 September 1892. **Education:** Studied music in Paris. **Career:** Translator and secretary in London, 1914-18; staff member, London *Evening Standard* and Birmingham *Post*. **Died:** 1969.

FANTASY PUBLICATIONS

Novels

The Green Lacquer Pavilion. London, Collins, and New York, Doran, 1926.
The Love of the Foolish Angel. London, Collins, and New York, Cosmopolitan, 1929.

OTHER PUBLICATIONS

Novels

The Mountain and the Tree. London, Collins, 1935; New York, Coward McCann, 1936.
So Frail a Thing: Love Scenes of the Twentieth Century. London, Gollancz, 1940.
Shadows on a Wall. London, Gollancz, 1941.
Where the Treasure Is. London, Gollancz, 1944.
There Were Three Men. London, Gollancz, 1949.

Other

Translator, *The Tale of Igor.* London, Beaumont, 1918.
Translator, *War Nursing,* by Charles Richet. London, Heinemann, 1918.
Translator, with Nadia Evrenov, *Thamar Karsavina,* by Valerien Svetlov. London, Beaumont, 1922.
Translator, with Violet Macdonald, *Journey Through Life,* by Amedee Ozenfant. London, Gollancz, 1939.
Translator, *The Beggars,* by L R. des Forets. London, Dobson, 1949.
Translator, *Philippine,* by Danielle Hunebelle. London, Secker and Warburg, 1955.
Translator, *My Apprenticeships,* by Colette. London, Secker and Warburg, 1957.
Translator, *Honeymoon Round the World,* by Dominique Lapierre. London, Secker and Warburg, 1957.
Translator, *Earthly Paradise,* by Colette. London, Secker and Warburg, 1966.

*   *   *

Helen Beauclerk lived in France for much of her life and translated several novels from the French. It is not surprising, therefore, that the principal influences on her own literary work were French. Her two fantasy novels might be regarded as attempts to transpose materials derived from the rich tradition of French fantastic fiction into an English mode. *The Green Lacquer Pavilion* celebrates, albeit in slightly tongue-in-cheek fashion, the enduring French fascination with various facets of the legendary Orient. *The Love of the Foolish Angel* is a distillation of the spirit of the heretical fantasies of Anatole France, carefully ameliorated so as to avoid explicit literary Satanism.

In *The Green Lacquer Pavilion* an Oriental screen becomes a magical doorway by means of which eight people gathered for an English country house-party in 1710 are conveyed into a vividly ornate fantasy-world. The party is divided when six of its members are carried off by the polite but mercurial pirate Scarcabomba, and further divided when he delivers three of them to the Arabesque kingdom of Zapangore and maroons the other three on the South Sea island of Patakoko. In Zapangore the love-starved Lady Taveridge is reunited with an avatar of the young man she rejected in order to marry for wealth and position, while the ineffectual Lord Bedlow is possessed by the spirit of a cunning vizier after taking magical snuff. On Patakoko the dilettante magician Gilvry exerts his (very limited) powers to save his companions from being eaten by cannibals, covertly abetted by the ingenious common sense of Lady Bedlow. Meanwhile, surrounded by the gorgeous Chinoiserie of the eponymous pavilion's surroundings, the romantic aspirations of Valentine Clare are put to a severe test when the cunningly lustful Mrs. Wynton attempts to subvert his love-affair with the Princess Amarantha, while the phoenix-like Feng tries to protect him. All three adventures end misfortunately, leaving the participants little or none the wiser, although Lord Bedlow's political views are slightly modified. The probability that the assiduously romantic Mr. Clare will prove more deserving of the affections of his new beloved than he was of the love of Amarantha seems very slender indeed.

The style of *The Green Lacquer Pavilion* is as calculatedly lovely and as deftly ironic as its settings, contriving a marvellous alloy of French lushness and English delicacy. It probably owes its primary inspiration to the pre-revolutionary fantasies of writers like Bibiena and Crebillon *fils,* but the cynical and strangely melancholy undercurrent is closer in spirit to the work of those late 19th-century writers who became dissenters from and deriders of the excesses of Rousseauesque Romanticism and its associated cult of *sensibilité.* After the amiable comedy of the second section and the delightful decorativeness of the third, the author's ultimate refusal to pander to the sentimental delusions of Lady Taveridge or the hypocrisies of Valentine Clare provides the story with a distinctly bittersweet moral.

The Love of the Foolish Angel combines the themes of Anatole France's classic novels *Thaïs* (1890) and *La Révolte des anges* (1914), but softens their moral lessons. Its hero, Tamael, unwittingly attaches himself to the cause of rebellious Lucifer, and becomes a fallen angel by mistake. (Divine omniscience seemingly does not extend to the recognition of such errors nor divine omnipotence to their ready rectification; here—as in almost all fantasies based in the Christian Mythos—God and His Son are conspicuous by their absence.) In Hell Tamael is a blatant misfit, so he is dispatched to earth in order that he may tempt human beings to sin. Under the half-hearted tutelage of his fellow fallen angel Barshamoth he is appointed to be the tempter of a lovely girl named

Basilea, but promptly falls in love with her and elects to become her protector instead. This proves difficult, all the more so when he is bound to obedience by the conjurations of a sorcerer acting on behalf of a rich merchant enthusiastic to seduce Basilea. Tamael is eventually freed from his bondage by a holy man named Cyriacus and flees to Ctesiphon, where he voluntarily becomes the lackey of the dilettante sorceress Princess Shamyris. He observes her decadent lifestyle with indifference until Basilea—who has turned away from the path of virtue after thinking herself deserted by the one decent man she ever met—comes within her sphere of influence. Once again Tamael must exert his ingenuity to save her from the lustful merchant. This time Cyriacus is persuaded to work a more ambitious miracle in order to bring the lovers together, after which they proceed to their inevitable destiny with what may seem to some readers to be unseemly haste.

Beauclerk's Cyriacus is a much more sympathetic figure than Anatole France's Paphnuce, on whom he is clearly based, and Tamael is a good deal more weak-kneed than Arcade, France's rebel guardian angel. Shamyris is but a pale shadow of such gorgeous femmes fatales of French Decadent Romanticism as Gautier's Mademoiselle de Maupin and Arria Marcella and Octave Mirbeau's Clara (there is one passage in *The Love of the Foolish Angel* which indicates that Beauclerk had certainly read Mirbeau's *Le jardin des supplices,* and she surely had Clara in mind as well as Gautier's heroines when designing Shamyris' career of corruption). This kind of toning down is only to be expected in a novel published in English by a female author, but the resultant delicacy is not to the disadvantage of the tale, whose subtle challenge to the puritanical aspects of Christianity becomes all the more insidious by virtue of its careful understatement and insouciant charm.

Both these novels are among the most impressive products of the remarkable flowering of British fantasy which took place in the 1920s. They invite close comparison with such near-contemporary novels as Gerald Bullett's *Mr. Godly Beside Himself* (1924), Margaret Irwin's *These Mortals* (1925) and Ronald Fraser's *Flower Phantoms* (1926), each of which features a differently-compounded but fundamentally similar amalgam of visionary vigour and ironic disillusionment. Beauclerk's later novel *The Mountain and the Tree,* which charts the changing role of women in early human society with the aid of theories drawn from J. G. Frazer's *The Golden Bough,* might be considered marginally fantastic by virtue of its an opening sequence set in the Stone Age.

—Brian Stableford

BEDFORD-JONES, H(enry James O'Brien)

Pseudonyms: Donald F. Bedford; Montague Brisard; Cleveland B. Chase; George Souli Demourant; Paul Ferval; Captain Bedford Foran; Michael Gallister; Allan Hawkwood; Gordon Keyne; M. Lassez; Lucian Pemjean; Margaret Love Sangerson; David Seabrooke; Charles George Souli; Torquay Trevison; John Wycliffe. **Nationality:** American. **Born:** Napanee, Ontario, Canada, 29 April 1887. **Family:** Married 1) Helen Swing Williamson in 1914 (divorced); 2) Mary McNally Bernardin. **Career:** Full-time writer from 1908. **Died:** 16 May 1949.

FANTASY PUBLICATIONS

Novels (series: John Solomon)

Solomon's Quest (as Allan Hawkwood). London, Hurst and Blackett, 1924.
John Solomon, Supercargo (as Allan Hawkwood). London, Hurst and Blackett, 1924.
The Seal of John Solomon (as Allan Hawkwood). London, Hurst and Blackett, 1924.
Solomon's Carpet (as Allan Hawkwood). London, Hurst and Blackett, 1925.
John Solomon, Incognito (as Allan Hawkwood). London, Hurst and Blackett, 1925.
Gentleman Solomon (as Allan Hawkwood). London, Hurst and Blackett, 1925.
The Star Woman. New York, Dodd, Mead, 1924; London, Hurst and Blackett, 1925.
The Shawl of Solomon (as Allan Hawkwood). London, Hurst and Blackett, 1925.
The Wizard of the Atlas (as Allan Hawkwood). London, Hurst and Blackett, 1928.
The Temple of the Ten, with W. C. Robertson. West Kingston, Rhode Island, Grant, 1973.

OTHER PUBLICATIONS

Novels

The Cross and the Hammer. New York, Cook, 1912.
Flamehair the Skald. Chicago, McClurg, 1913.
Conquest. New York, Cook, 1914.
Under Fire. New York, Howell, 1915.
The Mesa Trail. New York, Doubleday, 1920; London, Hurst and Blackett, 1923.
The Mardi-Gras Mystery. New York, Doubleday, 1921.
Against the Tide (as John Wycliffe). New York, Dodd Mead, 1924.
The Hazards of Smith. London, Hurst and Blackett, 1924.
The Kasbah Gate. London, Hurst and Blackett, 1924.
Splendour of the Gods. London, Hurst and Blackett, 1924.
Blood of the Peacock. London, Hurst and Blackett, 1924.
The Cruise of the Pelican. London, Hurst and Blackett, 1924.
The Trail of the Shadow. London, Hurst and Blackett, 1924.
Viking Love (as Allan Hawkwood). London, Hurst and Blackett, 1924.
Afoul of Destiny. London, Hurst and Blackett, 1925.
Loot! London, Hurst and Blackett, 1925.
The Wilderness Trail. London, Hurst and Blackett, 1925.
Far Horizons. London, Hurst and Blackett, 1925.
Son of the Cincinnati (as Montague Brisard). Boston, Small Maynard, 1925.
Arizona Argonauts. New York, Garden City Press, 1925.
Mormon Valley. New York, Garden City Press, 1925.
Outlaw of Rattlesnake Gap. New York, Garden City Press, 1925.
The Second Mate. New York, Garden City Press, 1925.
The Sheriff of Pecos. New York, Garden City Press, 1925.
Rodomont. London, Hurst and Blackett, 1926.
Saint Michael's Gold. New York, Putnam, 1926.
The Black Bull. New York, Putnam, 1927.

D'Artagnan. New York, Covici, 1928.

The King's Passport. New York, Putnam, 1928; London, Stanley Paul, 1928.

Cyrano. New York, Putnam, 1930.

The Shadow. New York, Fiction League, 1930.

D'Artagnan's Letter, with Mary Bedford-Jones. New York, Covici, 1931.

Drums of Dambala. New York, Covici, 1932; London, Long, 1932.

The King's Pardon. New York, Covici, 1933.

The Mission and the Man. Pasadena, San Pasqual, 1939.

John Berry, with Donald Friede and Kenneth Fearing (as Donald F. Bedford). New York, Creative Age, 1947.

The California Trail. New York, Phoenix Press, 1948; London, Wright and Brown, 1952.

Poetry

Fruit Before Summer. Long Beach, privately published, 1915.

Translator, *The Breeze in the Moonlight,* by Haou k'ew chuan. New York, Putnam, 1926.

Translator, *From Centaur to Cross* by G. M. de Guérin. New York, Covici, 1929.

Translator, *Passion of Yang Kwei-fei,* from ancient Chinese texts by Georges Souli. New York, Covici, 1928.

Play

Radio Play: *Abe Lincoln's Story,* with Carl Haverlin. Mutual Broadcasting System, 2 January 1944.

Other

L'Arbre Croche Mission. Santa Barbara, privately published, 1917.

The Myth Wawatam, or Alex Henry Refuted. Santa Barbara, privately published, 1917.

The Story of Misión San Juan Capistrano. Santa Barbara, privately published, 1918.

This Fiction Business. Denver, Student-Writer Press, 1922; revised edition, New York, Covici, 1929.

Graduate Fictioneer. Denver, Author and Journalist, 1932.

*

Critical Studies: "H. Bedford-Jones in *Blue Book*" by William J. Clark, *Xenophile* 22, March-April 1976; "H. Bedford-Jones in *People's*" by William J. Clark, *Xenophile* 30, March 1977; *Post Mortem: H. Bedford-Jones* edited by Michael Murphy, St. Louis, Missouri, Norfolk Hall, 1980; "The Improbable Cockney" by Robert Sampson, in *Yesterday's Faces, Volume 6: Violent Lives,* Bowling Green State University Popular Press, 1993.

*   *   *

H. Bedford-Jones was one of the most prolific writers for the American pulp magazines. His total output is known to be in excess of 1,200 stories including over 100 novels. At his peak he was appearing with eight or nine stories per month, and it was not uncommon for his output to average a story a week plus a novel or

two a month for several years. Such production rarely equates to quality, yet at the same time Bedford-Jones was producing finely crafted translations of French and Chinese verse, and writing authoritatively upon his many special interests. He was a master wordsmith, appearing in most of the general fiction pulps, in particular *Argosy, Adventure, Blue Book* and *Short Stories.* He made the rare appearance in the slick magazines *Collier's Weekly, Liberty* and *Saturday Evening Post,* and had work adapted for the cinema, but he was primarily a creature of the pulps, and was one of their most popular writers.

A college drop-out, Bedford-Jones worked first as a typesetter and then as a stenographer before he was able to turn to full-time writing. His early passion had been for poetry, and he sold verse to local newspapers, but through his friend William Wallace Cook (1867-1933), Bedford-Jones began writing boys' books and dime novels. Mostly ghost-written for other authors, these books remain unidentified. He had taught himself to type and was capable of producing up to 25,000 words a day; together with his fertile imagination, this made him a natural for the pulps. He began to sell regularly from 1912 and by 1914 was a "name" writer. He settled first in Michigan, moving to Chicago, California and later France, before ending his days in Beverly Hills. Whilst in France he served as foreign correspondent for the *Boston Globe.* Pulp publisher Harold Hersey visited him in Paris in the 1920s and found him writing two novels simultaneously on two typewriters.

Bedford-Jones's forte was the historical adventure. His early novels, *The Cross and the Hammer* and *Flamehair the Skald,* were set in the days of the Vikings, but later works, such as *Cyrano* and *The King's Pardon,* concentrated on 16th- and 17th- century France. Bedford-Jones was almost the pulp equivalent of Alexandre Dumas. From fragments left by Dumas he completed *D'Artagnan,* a sequel to *The Three Musketeers,* whilst *Rodomont* has all the hallmarks of *The Count of Monte Cristo.* Although Bedford-Jones never rivalled the popularity of his contemporary historical romancer Rafael Sabatini, he was his equal in imagination and verve. Historical fiction comprises most of his best work, but it accounts for only a part of his output which included detective stories, westerns, sea stories, spy stories and foreign intrigue. Fantasy and weird adventure accounted for about ten percent of his work, or just over a hundred stories and novels.

His early fantastic work falls into the category of the lost-race adventure. In 1914 Bedford-Jones had created the character of John Solomon, a Bulldog Drummond-like English cockney who fights crime on an international scale. Not all of the adventures are fantastic, though there are always hints of darker powers. "The Seal of John Solomon" (*Argosy,* 1915), is a bona fide lost-race novel, featuring descendants of the Crusaders surviving in a castle built within a volcano deep in the Arabian desert, guarding a secret from the days of Mohammed. The series, which ran intermittently till 1931, has other occasional fantastic elements (such as rays conferring longevity, and ancient angelic guardians) sufficient to interest most fans of the genre. They are representative of much of Bedford-Jones's work where the fantastic bubbles quietly under the surface, suggestive of much but seldom overt. Other lost-world adventures from this period are "Khmer the Mysterious" and "The Golden Woman of Khmer" (both *People's,* 1919) under the Allan Hawkwood name, "The Brazen Peacock" (*Blue Book,* 1920), *Splendour of the Gods* (1924) and "The Temple of the Ten" (*Adventure,* 1921), written with W. C. Robertson (this last is the only Bedford-Jones novel-length fantasy to be reprinted in recent years).

During the 1920s Bedford-Jones concentrated on historical adventures and international intrigue, but the fantastic element began to creep back into his stories in the late 1930s, particularly in the pages of *Blue Book* where he had cornered the market in story series, often having three or four running simultaneously. These usually took a particular theme and followed its development through history, such as the "Arms and Men" series which started with man's discovery of weapons in "The Spear of Gleaming Willow" (1935), and the "Ships and Men" series which featured an episode on "The Flying Dutchman" (1938). His series about the Foreign Legion, "Warriors in Exile," included one story with a supernatural theme, "The Little Black God" (1938); but his main fantasy output began with the series "Trumpets from Oblivion" (1938-39).

This series is technically science fiction. It opens with Norman Fletcher of the Inventors' Club having perfected a device using ultrasonic sound to capture images of the past. But this serves only as a prelude for the Inventors' Club to view, via a three-dimensional screen, the facts behind ancient myths and legends. The series began with an exploration of the Sargasso Sea in "The Stagnant Death," but became increasingly more fantastic covering "The Singing Sands of Prester John," "Amazon Woman," "The Lady and the Unicorn," "The Lady of the Evil Eye," "The Wolf Woman," "The Heavenly Bird," "The Woman of the Sea" and "The Serpent People".

Bedford-Jones had a short series in *Weird Tales*, "The Adventures of a Professional Corpse" (1940-41), about a man who could feign death. The stories are low-quality work and borderline fantasy, but indicate a shift in the author's writing to more unusual themes. His best work continued to appear in *Blue Book*. "From Out the Dark Water" (1940, as by Michael Gallister) turns to his Irish heritage and has the Little People help repel a Nazi submarine landing. Under his Gordon Keyne alias he wrote the "Freedom's Coalition" series (1943), showing the post-war world state, and the "Quest, Inc." series (1943) which has a futuristic Bureau of Missing Persons. Under his own name, the ten-part "Counterclockwise" series (1943-44) used another time-viewing device to explore the secrets of the past.

"The Treasure Seekers," another series in *Blue Book* (1945-46), allowed Bedford-Jones the chance to return to the wild corners of the world in search of fabled treasure. The series has some of the elements of Rider Haggard's Allan Quatermain novels. This fascination for the lure of treasure and the influence of accursed gems extended to other stories. During 1940-41 he wrote a series for *Argosy* following the affect of jewels around the world. It started with "The Emerald of Isis" and continued with "The Ruby of France," "The Angry Amethyst," "The Sinister Sapphire," "Jeopardy's Jewel" and "The Perilous Pearl." He returned to this theme in *Blue Book* with a longer and more fascinating series, "The Sphinx Emerald" (1946-47), following the effect of this gem down through key periods of history.

This was Bedford-Jones's last main venture into fantasy. His writing output in the late 1940s declined to a merely human rate following a heart attack, but his fertile imagination never waned. It is possible that a full bibliographical assessment may identify Bedford-Jones as one of the most prolific of all writers. His quota of fantastic fiction on that scale is minimal and not significant, but had a zest to it which has kept it fresh over the years. It is certainly worthy of reconsideration. More may yet be hidden under forgotten and unknown pseudonyms.

—Mike Ashley

BEERBOHM, (Henry) Max(imilian)

Nationality: British. **Born:** London, 24 August 1872; half-brother of actor-manager Sir Herbert Beerbohm-Tree. **Education:** Charterhouse School; Merton College, Oxford. **Family:** Married Florence Kahn in 1910 (died 1951). **Career:** Contributor, *Yellow Book* and other periodicals; drama critic, *Saturday Review*; caricaturist, essayist, fiction writer. **Awards:** Honorary LL.D., Edinburgh University; knighthood, 1939. Lived in Italy in his later years. **Died:** 20 May 1956.

FANTASY PUBLICATIONS

Novel

Zuleika Dobson; or, An Oxford Love Story. London, Heinemann, and New York, Boni and Liveright, 1911.

Short Stories

The Happy Hypocrite: A Fairy Tale for Tired Men. New York and London, Lane, 1897.
A Christmas Garland, Woven by Max Beerbohm. London, Heinemann, and New York, Dutton, 1912; enlarged edition, London, Heinemann, 1950.
Seven Men. London, Heinemann, 1919; New York, Knopf, 1920; enlarged edition, as *Seven Men and Two Others,* London, Heinemann, 1950.
The Dreadful Dragon of Hay Hill. London, Heinemann, 1928.

OTHER PUBLICATIONS

Poetry

Max in Verse: Rhymes and Parodies, edited by J. G. Riewald. Brattleboro, Vermont, Greene Press, 1963; London, Heinemann, 1964.

Other

The Works of Max Beerbohm, with a Bibliography by John Lane. London, Lane, and New York, Scribner 1896.
Caricatures of Twenty-Five Gentlemen. London, Smithers, 1896.
More. New York and London, Lane, 1899.
Cartoons: 'The Second Childhood of John Bull'. London, Swift, 1901.
The Poets' Corner. London, Heinemann, and New York, Dodd Mead, 1904.
A Book of Caricatures. London, Methuen, 1907.
Yet Again. London, Chapman and Hall, 1909; New York, Lane, 1910.
Fifty Caricatures. London, Heinemann, and New York, Dutton, 1913.
A Note on 'Patience'. London, Miles, 1918.
And Even Now. London, Heinemann, 1920; New York, Dutton, 1921.
A Survey. London, Heinemann, and New York, Doubleday Page, 1921.

Rossetti and His Circle. London, Heinemann, 1922.

The Works of Max Beerbohm. London, Heinemann, 10 vols., 1922-28.

A Peep Into the Past. London and New York, privately printed, 1923.

Things Old and New. London, Heinemann, 1923.

Around Theatre. London, Heinemann, 2 vols., 1924; New York, Knopf, 1930.

The Guerdon. New York, privately printed, 1925.

Observations. London, Heinemann, 1925.

Leaves from the Garland. New York, privately printed, 1926.

A Variety of Things. London, Heinemann, and New York, Knopf, 1928.

Lytton Strachey. Cambridge, Cambridge University Press, 1943.

William Rothenstein: An Address. London, privately printed, 1945.

The Mote in the Middle Distance: A Parody of Henry James. Berkeley, California, Hart Press, 1946.

A Luncheon. Oxford, 1946.

Mainly on the Air. London, Heinemann, 1946; New York, Knopf, 1947.

Sherlockiana: A Reminiscence of Sherlock Holmes. Tempe, Arizona, Hill, 1948.

Dickens and Christmas, as George Moore Might Well Have Described Them. Berkeley, California, Hart Press, 1955.

Caricatures by Max, from the Collection of the Ashmolean Museum. Oxford, Oxford University Press, 1958.

Max's Nineties: Drawings 1892-1899. London, Hart Davis, and Philadelphia, Lippincott, 1958.

The Incomparable Max. London, Heinemann, and New York, Dodd Mead, 1962.

Max Beerbohm's Letters to Reggie Turner, edited by Rupert Hart-Davis. London, Hart Davis, 1964; New York, Lippincott, 1965.

More Theatres 1898-1903. London, Hart Davis, and New York, Taplinger, 1969.

The Bodley Head Max Beerbohm, edited by David Cecil. London, Bodley Head, 1970.

Last Theatres 1904-1910. London, Hart Davis, and New York, Taplinger, 1970.

Selected Prose, edited by David Cecil. Boston, Little Brown, 1971.

A Peep Into the Past and Other Prose Pieces, edited by Rupert Hart-Davis. London, Heinemann, and Brattleboro, Vermont, Greene Press, 1972.

Max & Will: Max Beerbohm and William Rothenstein, Their Friendship and Letters, 1893-1945, edited by Mary M. Lago and Karl Beckson. London, Murray, and Cambridge, Massachusetts, Harvard University Press, 1975.

Beerbohm's Literary Caricatures: From Homer to Huxley, edited by J. G. Riewald. Hamden, Connecticut, Archon, and London, Lane, 1977.

Letters of Max Beerbohm 1892-1956, edited by Rupert Hart-Davis. London, Murray, 1988.

Editor, *Herbert Beerbohm Tree: Some Memories of Him and His Art.* New York, Dutton, 1917; London, Hutchinson, 1920.

*

Bibliography: *Sir Max Beerbohm: Bibliographical Notes* by A. E. Gallatin, Cambridge, Massachusetts, Harvard University Press, 1944; *A Bibliography of the Works of Max Beerbohm* by A. E. Gallatin and L. M. Oliver, Cambridge, Massachusetts, Harvard University Press, 1952.

Critical studies (selection): *Sir Max Beerbohm, Man and Writer: A Critical Analysis with a Brief Life and a Bibliography* by J. G. Riewald, The Hague, Netherlands, Nijhoff, 1953; *Portrait of Max: An Intimate Memoir of Sir Max Beerbohm* by S. N. Behrman, New York, Random House, 1960; *Max: A Biography* by David Cecil, London, Constable, 1964; *Max Beerbohm* by Bruce R. McElderry, New York, Twayne, 1972; *The Lies of Art: Max Beerbohm's Parody & Caricature* by John Felstiner, London, Gollancz, 1973; *The Surprise of Excellence: Modern Essays on Max Beerbohm* edited by J. G. Riewald, Hamden, Connecticut, Archon, 1974; *Max Beerbohm, or The Dandy Dante* by Robert Vicusi, Baltimore, Johns Hopkins University Press, 1986; *Max Beerbohm and the Act of Writing* by Lawrence Danson, Oxford, Clarendon Press, 1989.

*   *   *

Max Beerbohm worked in an era before the hardening of genre boundaries, and his work kept straying almost imperceptibly into fantasy as he played his favourite literary games of parody and pastiche. It's useful to remember that he was a skilled cartoon-caricaturist of literary and other notables; there is a celebrated, subtly deflatory drawing of W. B. Yeats presenting Irish novelist George Moore to the Queen of the Fairies.

The Happy Hypocrite, for example, delicately caricatures Oscar Wilde's fairy tales (with a sideswipe at *The Picture of Dorian Gray*). In summary it seems straightforward. A very, very wicked nobleman falls in love with a pure young actress who rejects him because his depravity is so visible in his face. He therefore commissions a saintly wax mask to be worn for the rest of his life, and in this new guise woos and wins his Jenny. The idyll is threatened by a jealous ex-mistress, who tears off the mask . . . but by this time, virtuous living has made his real face as handsome as the false one.

All this is skewed by Beerbohm's telling, sending up the High Twee of the Wilde tales. The hero is called Lord George Hell, a cad and bounder notorious for staying up "until long after bedtime"; Cupid makes cameo appearances; the lovers marry "according to the simple rites of a dear little registry-office in Covent Garden"; virtue mainly consists of living on wholesome food Lord George has never before encountered, such as currant buns.

Beerbohm's overt literary parodies are collected in *A Christmas Garland*: two have some fantasy interest. "P.C. X, 36" imitates Kipling at his worst, with the first-person narrator fawning over a brutal policeman whose triumph is to arrest Santa Claus while "Kipling" eagerly shrieks, "Frog's-march him!" And "A Sequelula to 'The Dynasts'" gently spoofs Thomas Hardy's use of overseeing spirits (not to mention his diction) in his novel-poem of the Napoleonic wars.

In *Zuleika Dobson,* Beerbohm's peculiar process of pastiche and distortion is brought to bear on the already half-fantastic town and university of Oxford. The essence of the plot is that the beautiful but vapid Zuleika descends on Oxford and breaks the hearts of the entire undergraduate population, leading to mass suicide (with one craven exception) at the height of the Eights Week boat races. Later the Fellows of Judas College are seen dining happily at High Table, oblivious of the empty undergraduate benches—all oddly prophetic of college life a few years later, ravaged by the First World War.

Fantasy threads are woven through the book. Beerbohm cheekily explain that his auctorial omniscience is a special dispensation from

Clio, Muse of History . . . who has always been jealous that novelists, unlike historians, can read thoughts, and abuses Max like a fishwife for giving a character one hour of privacy. The stone heads of the Roman Emperors outside the Sheldonian Theatre sweat and tremble at the doom approaching Oxford. Pearls in Zuleika's earrings and her chief suitor the Duke of Dorset's shirt-studs turn ominously black and back again as emotions swing. When telegraphic news of an ancestral portent arrives from his butler, the Duke knows his fate:

> "Deeply regret inform your grace last night two black owls came and perched on battlements remained there through night hooting at dawn flew away none knows whither awaiting instructions Jellings."

What can he do but reply "Prepare vault for funeral Monday," don his full robes as a Knight of the Garter, and stride forth to the river Isis? Zuleika, meanwhile, soon dries her tears to consult the timetable of trains for Cambridge.

As a novel, *Zuleika Dobson* is a weird mix of preposterous humour, fantastic whimsy, nostalgia for bygone Oxford, and often affectedly fine writing. Fiercely defended by some critics, dismissed by others for failing to sustain its humorous promise, it occupies an indeterminate position between "cult classic" and genuine classic. It's the quintessential Oxford fantasy.

The collection *Seven Men* contains Beerbohm's finest fiction, including perhaps the best deal-with-the-devil story ever: "Enoch Soames". Soames is a dim figure orbiting the richly evoked 1890s literary scene—Wilde, absinthe, the Café Royal, the *Yellow Book*—who never quite makes it. His awful poems and pretensions are shown in pitilessly funny detail. He confides in Beerbohm (a character in all the stories, and the seventh man of the title) that he'd sell his soul to visit the British Museum Reading Room a century hence and find what posterity makes of him. The Devil, passing by, takes him at his word. Soames returns deeply embittered, having puzzled through the phonetic spelling of 1997 literary history to find himself recorded only as a character in a "sumwot labud sattire" by Max Beerbohm.

Other fantasies in *Seven Men* are "Hilary Maltby and Stephen Braxton," an offbeat tale of psychic projection (indeed, intimidation) resulting from literary envy, and "A. V. Laider"—sometimes reprinted in supernatural anthologies as a story of awful predestination, but in fact given a characteristic Beerbohm twist into what is both a joke and a character study of the eponymous Laider with his compulsive story-telling.

A bare footnote goes to *The Dreadful Dragon of Hay Hill,* the author's least successful fiction. Conceived during the 1914-18 war, it allegorically tells how an English tribe *circa* 39,000 BC is menaced by a fire-breathing dragon and is all the happier for it, unified by adversity, until a hero makes the error of defeating the menace. There is almost no wit beyond anachronistic description of geography in terms of where modern London's streets will be.

Beerbohm has often been written off as too precious, too much of a miniaturist, to retain a readership. But 1994 saw the centenary of his first professional appearance, with *Zuleika Dobson* and *Seven Men* (at least) still being reprinted regularly. Beerbohm is tougher than he looks.

—David Langford

BELL, Clare (Louise)

Pseudonym: Clare Coleman. **Nationality:** American. **Born:** Britain, 1952; emigrated to the USA, 1957. **Career:** Engineer for computer company, 1978-90. **Awards:** PEN Los Angeles award, 1983; International Reading Association's Children's Book award, 1984.

FANTASY PUBLICATIONS

Novels (series: Ratha)

Ratha's Creature. New York, Atheneum, 1983.
Clan Ground (Ratha). New York, Atheneum, 1984.
Ratha and Thistle-Chaser. New York, McElderry, 1990.
The Jaguar Princess. New York, Tor, 1993.
Ratha's Challenge. New York, McElderry, 1995.

OTHER PUBLICATIONS

Novels

Tomorrow's Sphinx. New York, McElderry, 1986.
People of the Sky. New York, Tor, 1989.
Daughter of the Reef (as Clare Coleman, with M. Coleman Easton). New York, Jove, 1992.
Child of the Dawn (as Clare Coleman, with M. Coleman Easton). New York, Jove, 1994.

* * *

Written for young adults, Clare Bell's novels *Ratha's Creature, Clan Ground* and *Ratha and Thistle-Chaser* form a series about sentient cats. The cats have evolved, somehow, from their feline neighbours and can both speak and use tools in a limited fashion. Since these are the qualifiers scientists often have used to identify and separate mankind from "lesser" creatures, the cats can best be described as "people." The books are very well written, and show the growth of the cave-dwelling cats' society as they learn about their environment. Ratha, a very young female in the first book, discovers fire and brings it back to her clan, who call themselves the Named. The elders do not want to listen to her arguments for the benefits of fire and a moral struggle ensues.

Another interesting lesson is brought to the reader's attention. It is obvious that the clan can breed with the less intelligent cats of the area, but it makes every attempt to keep itself separate. The clan is a herding society, keeping deer-like creatures for food purposes. As one would expect, when hunting becomes difficult, the wild cats in the area come seeking the easier prey of the Named's herds.

These are not the only foes, for there are large boars who make occasional ravages through clan grounds. These animals behave in a manner that is foreign to the nature of cats. They come in a group and viciously attack, stealing the herd beasts, of course, but also treating the cats as prey. The Named are a bare few generations from being simple cats and are really just developing their society. Mere existence is still a struggle, even genetic existence. For, sometimes, cubs are born who don't have "light in their eyes." Mating is still subject to instinct, by and large, and Ratha mates with one of two brothers whose connections to the wild cats are closer than some. If nothing else, this is a salutary lesson in breeding lines, and gives a good reason why we should be grateful that, as humans, we don't go into heat. The Named do and the results, for Ratha, are less than wonderful. She actually cared about the cat she mated with, Bonechewer—and the sight of her poor unintelligent cubs breaks her heart.

Nonetheless, she wins through when it comes to the matter of fire. The Named accept it and begin to use it in many ways. No longer is everyone a herder and/or a hunter. A new profession has been introduced. Some are firekeepers and they begin to do a new dance at the beginning of clan gatherings. The dance celebrates fire and its uses in defence.

By the time of the second volume, *Clan Ground,* Ratha is Queen due to her status as fire bringer. The older females are all called queens, but in her case she has become official head of the clan. Bonechewer's brother, Thakur, is now the herding teacher for the cubs and he has chosen not to mate. He fears that he will produce more cubs like his brother's, and does not want to look into the eyes of his own cubs and not see the light. When it comes to mating time, he takes off into the woods until the time has passed. Ratha is sterile; she has not conceived since her first litter.

The firekeepers have begun to treat their work almost as a religion, and their opening dances are becoming increasingly ritualized. Into this scene comes Orange-eyes. He is intelligent and bears a strong resemblance to a sabre-toothed tiger. The test Ratha imposes is one of bravery, the test of fire. He passes and is allowed to stay and hunt with the clan. The queens all find him attractive and he gains a mate during the appropriate season.

During this time Thakur has been off hunting, and keeping himself separate from the others, lest instinct take over and he should mate only to produce sub-standard cubs. He meets, and takes as a pet, a small lemur-like "treeling." The treeling has appendages similar to hands and proves to be clever if not exactly intelligent by clan standards, and Thakur starts training it to be of use in managing fire. One of the problems that has plagued the clan is their inability to easily pick up burning brands.

Orange-eye's cubs turn out to have no light in their eyes. Their mother, Fessran, sorrowfully abandons them and he takes over their raising. When Ratha finally takes them away from him, she does not kill them, merely leaves them for the wild cats to take in; but she does not tell Orange-eyes of this. He becomes angry, and ambitious, and succeeds in subverting the firekeepers into a cult who take payment from the other clan members. They set up a sort of a temple in a cave, with a centre fire that others have to pay tribute in order to see. The benefit of this cave-fire is that rains cannot douse it, and there is always a fire and a supply of wood from which to build defence fires. The firekeepers do not approve of the use of the treeling in keeping the fires going. They become very strict about the treelings, and take over the clan to the detriment of all. Ratha, Thakur and Fessran dig a system of ditches that flood the cave and put out the fire. In this way, the Named return to a system similar to the one they had known, but continue to associate with the treelings.

In *Ratha and Thistle-Chaser,* the queen's long-lost daughter comes to light. Thakur discovers her while he is hunting for new grounds for the Named. Their own lands have become drought-ridden, and they are in danger of starvation. It seems that Ratha's daughter, and some of the other cubs, might have been very intelligent indeed. But, perhaps, their intelligence took longer to manifest itself. The final question is whether or not they are the next

step in evolution. The Named take longer to grow up than the wild cats. These cubs take longer to grow up than the Named.

Ratha's Creature deservedly won a PEN Los Angeles award for the best writing for young people, and an International Reading Association's Children's Book award. I am sure intelligent young people over the age of 14 will enjoy this series, although the books may seem to be a bit violent. A very sensitive youngster should wait until a later age to read them. However, this series is *not* for youngsters only; there is a great deal to recommend the novels to the adult reader. I found them very enjoyable, and I am somewhat past my teenage years. These fantasies are Bell's best works, surpassing her science fiction.

—Sandra Brandenburg

BELLAIRS, John (Anthony)

Nationality: American. **Born:** Marshall, Michigan, 1938. **Education:** Notre Dame University, B.A. in English, 1959; University of Chicago, graduate study. **Family:** Married; one son. **Career:** Teacher, St. Teresa College, Minnesota; Shimer College, Illinois. **Died:** 8 March 1991.

FANTASY PUBLICATIONS

Novels (series: Anthony Monday; Johnny Dixon; Lewis Barnavelt)

The Pedant and the Shuffly. New York, Macmillan, 1968.
The Face in the Frost. New York, Macmillan, 1969.
The House With a Clock in Its Walls (Lewis Barnavelt). New York, Dial, 1973.
The Figure in the Shadows (Lewis Barnavelt). New York, Dial, 1975.
The Letter, the Witch, and the Ring (Lewis Barnavelt). New York, Dial, 1976.
The Treasure of Alpheus Winterborn (Anthony Monday). New York, Harcourt Brace Jovanovich, 1978.
The Curse of the Blue Figurine (Johnny Dixon). New York, Dial, 1983.
The Mummy, the Will, and the Crypt (Johnny Dixon). New York, Dial, 1983.
The Dark Secret of Weatherend (Anthony Monday). New York, Dial, 1984.
The Spell of the Sorcerer's Skull (Johnny Dixon). New York, Dial, 1984.
The Revenge of the Wizard's Ghost (Johnny Dixon). New York, Dial, 1985.
The Eyes of the Killer Robot (Johnny Dixon). New York, Dial, 1986.
The Lamp from the Warlock's Tomb (Anthony Monday). New York, Dial, 1988.
The Chessmen of Doom (Johnny Dixon). New York, Dial, 1989.
The Trolley to Yesterday (Johnny Dixon). New York, Dial, 1989.
The Secret of the Underground Room (Johnny Dixon). New York, Dial, 1990.
The Mansion in the Mist (Anthony Monday). New York, Dial, 1992.
The Ghost in the Mirror, with Brad Strickland (Lewis Barnavelt). New York, Dial, 1993.

The Vengeance of the Witch-Finder, with Brad Strickland. New York, Dial, 1993.

The Drum, the Doll, and the Zombie, with Brad Strickland. New York, Dial, 1994.

OTHER PUBLICATIONS

Short Stories

St. Fidgeta and Other Parodies. New York, Macmillan, 1966.

*

Film Adaptations: *The House With a Clock in Its Walls* (TV movie); *The Treasure of Alpheus Winterborn.*

* * *

A brief descriptive term for John Bellairs's books for children and adults might well be "magical mysteries." Clues abound, as well as danger and fearful occult happenings. The reader must follow the twists of the plot as dauntless, but all too human, protagonists solve the mystery, thwart dastardly villains and save the world once again. Throughout all of his books Bellairs demonstrates his love of adventure, and in his case, the adventures are generally involved with the supernatural.

A number of critics of fantasy literature praise Bellairs for his early work for adults, especially *The Face in the Frost.* This tale describes the quest of two old wizards, Prospero and Roger Bacon, as they seek the right magic to destroy the evil black magician Melichus who is out to control everything he can. Prospero and Roger must survive against just about every magical spell known in order to finally triumph. Humour abounds in this as in all of Bellairs's books, everything from subtle Latin puns to a description of the kitschy painting in a 20th-century antique/junk store of the infamous "Dogs Playing Poker." The action takes place during a vaguely Renaissance time-period in the fantasy lands of the North and South Kingdoms. Time-slips occur, however, and conjured settings appear, making for a very satisfying tale of magical derring-do.

In spite of his early success with adult fantasy, Bellairs obviously preferred to devote his energies to writing children's books. Most of these are illustrated by Edward Gorey, whose macabre and eerie black-and-white drawings supply a suitably spooky visual effect. There are three main series for the children's titles: the Johnny Dixon series with eight books, Anthony Monday four, and Lewis Barnavelt also with four. It would appear that Johnny Dixon was Bellairs's favourite, but he admitted in presentations that Lewis was something of an *alter ego* for the author as he really was as a child. Perhaps Johnny Dixon was created as the child Bellairs would like to have been, since they share the same first name. Also, it should be noted that Anthony Monday's first name is Bellairs's middle name. It would seem that there is something of Bellairs in all three of his main child protagonists.

But much of the appeal of the children's books for adult readers lies with Bellairs's adult characters. In the Johnny Dixon books, Johnny is involved in wonderful adventures by his neighbour, the fascinating Professor Roderick Childermass, described by Bellairs as being "short and elderly and crabby-looking, with wildly sprouting muttonchop whiskers, gold-rimmed glasses, and a nose that looked like an overripe strawberry." Mrs. Zimmermann, Lewis's neighbour, is a genuine witch. The favourite of Bellairs's adult characters for librarians is naturally the clumsy, yet fearless, Miss Eells who gets involved in supernatural mysteries in and out of the library with her young friend and employee, Anthony.

In all these stories, the young heroes are caught up in adventures which usually turn out to have magic of some sort involved, often the black magic of foul villains up to no good. In order to defeat the villains, the young protagonists and their adult friends must unravel mysterious clues often finding themselves in considerable danger. A typical villain is the one depicted in *The Dark Secret of Weatherend,* the late J. K. Borkman, who is using his occult powers even after death to destroy the world with his nefarious scheme of creating devastating weather.

Miss Eells calls on her brother, Emerson, who "was a rich lawyer who lived in St. Cloud [Minnesota] and he always dressed very well." Miss Eells, however, deciphers the clues involved, and with Anthony and Emerson manages to stop the weird weather. In this title, Bellairs created a villain with a soft side, for Borkman has left the clues himself to give whoever is struggling against him a fighting chance.

Part of the appeal in Bellairs's work lies with the personalities of the young characters in his stories. Like most kids, they worry a lot. They are youngsters who feel powerless about solving family problems, yet when they become involved in exciting adventures they act bravely. They have good basic instincts and always want to do the right thing. In Bellairs's tales of fantasy, the decency of the young heroes, coupled with the assistance of their adult friends, results in success every time. Conditioned Bellairs readers know that good will ultimately triumph over evil, but the author's rip-snorting plot twists keeps the suspense alive until the end. Bellairs's talent for writing humorous, mysterious, adventurous fantasies for all ages is evident in all of his writing.

—Cosette Kies

BENSON, Stella

Nationality: British. **Born:** Much Wenlock, Shropshire, 6 January 1892. **Family:** Married John O'Gorman Anderson in 1921. **Career:** Worked for Charity Organization Society, and ran a shop in Hoxton, London, 1913-17; involved in women's suffrage campaign from 1914; worked in Berkeley, California, 1918-20; travelled to China and India, 1920-21, and lived in China 1921-33. **Awards:** Royal Society of Literature Benson medal, 1932; Femina Vie Heureuse prize, 1932. **Died:** 6 December 1933.

FANTASY PUBLICATIONS

Novel

Living Alone. London, Macmillan, 1919.

Short Stories

The Awakening: A Fantasy. San Francisco, Lantern Press, 1925.
The Man Who Missed the 'Bus. London, Elkin Matthews & Marrot, 1928.

Christmas Formula and Other Stories. London, Furnival Books, 1932.
Collected Short Stories. London, Macmillan, 1936.

Play

Kwan-Yin. 1922.

<small>OTHER PUBLICATIONS</small>

Novels

I Pose. 1915.
This is the End. 1917.
The Poor Man. 1922.
Pipers and a Dancer. 1924.
Goodbye, Stranger. 1926.
The Far-Away Bride. 1930; as *Tobit Transplanted,* 1931.
Mundos: An Unfinished Novel. 1935.

Short Stories

Hope Against Hope and Other Stories. 1931.

Poetry

Twenty. 1918.
Poems. 1935.

Other

The Little World. 1925.
Worlds Within Worlds. 1928.
Some Letters 1928-1933, edited by Cecil Clarabut. 1978.

Editor, *Come to Eleuthera; or, New Lands for Old.* 1929(?).
Editor, *Pull Devil Pull Baker,* by Nicolas de Toulouse Lautrec de Savine. 1933.

*

Bibliography: In *Ten Contemporaries* by John Gawsworth, 1933.

Critical Studies: *Benson* by Phyllis Bottome, 1934; *Portrait of Benson* by R. Ellis Roberts, 1939; *Benson* by R. Meredith Bedell, 1983; *Benson: A Biography* by Joy Grant, 1987.

*   *   *

The Great War decisively interrupted the history of British scientific romance, whose stream dwindled to a trickle throughout the 1920s, but this dearth was compensated by a remarkable flow of first-rate fantasy novels, the first of which was Stella Benson's *Living Alone,* expanded from a brief sketch which originally appeared in the *Athenaeum.* The story is set during the war years, and describes the transformation of a young woman's tediously oppressive everyday life by a healthily chaotic infusion of magic.

Living Alone begins with the disruption of an unbearably prosaic committee meeting by a mysterious stranger who turns out to be a witch. Her intervention is unappreciated by the majority of the committee members but is welcomed by the novel's heroine, Sarah Brown, who follows the witch to the exotic "House of Living Alone," where she meets other magically-talented individuals. Her life is decisively changed, and in the wake of a series of strange encounters and vivid adventures—including an aerial combat involving two broomstick-riding witches and an air raid whose bombs provoke a few of the dead to rise from their graves in deluded expectation of the Last Judgement—she sets sail for a new life in America.

The manner and style of *Living Alone* are quirky to the point of surreality, and its eccentric sense of humour is likely to seem much more familiar to modern readers than it could possibly have been to its contemporary audience. Although Stella Benson once wrote (in John Gawsworth's *Ten Contemporaries*) that it was the first of her books which was "in some measure . . . about other people" it is still a deeply personal book—so deeply personal that the allegorical significance of its plot-twists and witty asides is sometimes frustratingly obscure—but in common with many other fantastically transfigured spiritual autobiographies it has a considerable power to move those readers who are capable of empathizing with the existential plight of its heroine. It is a glorious celebration of the power of the imagination, an unashamed apology for private escapism (which, as Tolkien famously remarked, ought to be reckoned the escape of a prisoner rather than the desertion of a soldier). The romantic subplot which concerns the magically-talented Richard Higgins and his imp-tormented lover Peony endorses conventional notions of the life-enhancing power of sexual communion, but the main narrative seeks a more self-sufficient destiny for the heroine, who must ultimately find her way to a House of Living Alone which has not so many supportive phantoms in it.

In following this narrative trajectory, the fantasy element in *Living Alone* proves—as in all great works of fantasy—to be ultimately self-destructive, recommending its elaborations and embroideries of everyday life as a means and not an end. However lovers of fantasy fiction might lament it, there is a certain propriety in the fact that the author never wrote another book like this—although she might have done so late in life had she not died unreasonably young, in self-imposed exile in China. The residual spirit of *Living Alone* is easily detectable in her most famous novel, *Tobit Transplanted,* but its fantastic embellishments are damped down into a far quieter and resolutely non-supernatural mode.

Further evidence of the striking originality of Stella Benson's world-view is provided by her briefer fantasies, all but one of which—the dramatic sketch *Kwan-Yin*—can be found in her posthumous volume of *Collected Short Stories,* although most of them had earlier appeared as independent pamphlets issued by various private presses. *The Awakening* is a not-entirely-irreverent allegory of divine underachievement akin to those of Laurence Housman, in which a narrator who might or might not be God offers an explanation of sorts for the dismal failure of the present Creation. *The Man Who Missed the 'Bus* is a darkly surreal and nightmarish story diametrically opposed in tone and content to *Living Alone.* "Christmas Formula" is a satirical extrapolation of the "gospel of commercial intimacy" which Benson found to be universally preached by the new advertising-supported magazines of the day. "A Dream" is an allegorical visionary fantasy in which one Mrs. Wander discovers an unpalatable truth about the order of things.

Stella Benson represented her progress as a writer as a journey from the intense self-absorption of the frankly-titled *I Pose* to a distanced and objective viewpoint manifest in *Tobit Transplanted.* It is not particularly unusual that such a journey should have passed through a vividly fantasized phase, nor that the fantasies involved should so resolutely mix the personal and the universal into an idiosyncratic alloy, but the remarkable stylization of the works in question remains unique, and they remain a valuable contribution to the tradition of fantasy literature.

—Brian Stableford

BERBERICK, Nancy Varian

Nationality: American. **Born:** 23 July 1951. **Education:** Pascack Hills High School, Montvale, New Jersey, 1965-69; Bergen Community College, Paramus, New Jersey, 1969-72. **Family:** Married Bruce A. Berberick in 1973. **Agent:** Maria Carvainis Agency, 235 West End Avenue, New York, NY 10024, USA. **Address:** 1911 Kenwood Avenue, Charlotte, NC 28205, USA.

FANTASY PUBLICATIONS

Novels (series: Elvish; Garroc)

Stormblade: Dragonlance Saga Heroes Volume Two. Lake Geneva, Wisconsin, TSR, 1988; London, Penguin, 1989.
The Jewels of Elvish. Lake Geneva, Wisconsin, TSR, 1989.
Shadow of the Seventh Moon (Garroc). New York, Ace, 1991.
A Child of Elvish. New York, Ace, 1992.
The Panther's Hoard (Garroc). New York, Ace, 1994.

*

Nancy Varian Berberick comments:

My work in the fantasy genre reflects my love of history and mythology. In my earlier work I wrote within a created fantasy world. But in two later novels, *Shadow of the Seventh Moon* and *The Panther's Hoard,* I wrote from a framework of British history with an ancient mythology as the heart, or perhaps the driving soul, of each tale. I believe that the best stories, in any genre, are about *people*: how one uses the magic, faces the ordeal, comports oneself on the adventure—this is where the real story lies. The rest is fireworks, lovely but soon over.

*   *   *

Nancy Varian Berberick is one of several fantasy writers who got their start by writing for the gaming company TSR and then moved on into other areas. Her first novel, *Stormblade,* is a traditional fantasy adventure story set within the Dragonlance series, which like all shared universes imposes rules that often make it difficult for writers to demonstrate their own abilities. A dwarf sets out on a quest to find a magic sword and perseveres despite the fact that the odds are stacked heavily against his succeeding. Her next book for TSR, *The Jewels of Elvish,* was completely original, although the Twin Kingdoms bear strong resemblance to many another fantasy world. One of the kingdoms is human, or mannish, the other elvish. Although the two sides have long been rivals sharing the same island, they are forced to unite against a common enemy. Barbarian raiders from the Northlands are raiding

coastal cities, apparently aided by dark sorcery. To seal the bond, the daughter of the Elvish king, Nikia, is married to a Mannish prince. Shortly after her marriage, Nikia's family heirloom, an ancient jewel, is stolen at the behest of the mistress of an evil sorcerer. Unless it is recovered, old magic may be turned against the alliance and the invaders may conquer both kingdoms.

A traditional set of adventures ensues: dusty dungeons, slave ships, pitched battles and an intricate web of dark intrigues. It's a straightforward plot without pretension or stylistic complexity, and as such it's an entertaining if rather familiar story. Berberick liked the setting well enough to return to it some years later, and for another publisher, with *A Child of Elvish,* a considerably more polished work set only a short time after the events of its predecessor.

Two warriors, one mannish, one elvish, are recruited by the ghost of a long dead queen to fulfil a quest. The Twin Kingdoms have been devastated by sorcery, the land infertile, the people lacking hope in the future, their leadership divided and prone to petty quarrels and rivalries. The only way to restore the land's vigour is by finding certain jewels of power which were scattered at the ghost queen's request long before, and then by performing a magical ceremony. This ritual requires the presence of a newborn child, specifically that of Nikia, whose parents represent both races. Her recruits have misgivings about her intentions, but are eventually prevailed upon to do her bidding. Adding to the tension is the potential danger if prince Garth were to learn that he is not in fact the child's father. Nikia has a human lover, so the deception has held, but if the secret were revealed the repercussions could destroy the uneasy peace that has so far held between the two peoples. The various conflicts are resolved more through political than physical measures this time; the prince dies and his putative daughter becomes heir apparent to the throne under the guardianship of a regent.

Berberick has clearly devoted much more attention this time to the characters, how they interact, how the society she created might be shaped to work as a single unit, and spends less time on battles and adventure, although there's enough of both to keep the plot moving quickly. It's not a major work, but shows signs of significant growth in her ability to create a credible world whose politics and characters act credibly.

A second series of novels was inaugurated with *Shadow of the Seventh Moon.* The setting is the British Isles, shortly after the fall of Arthur's Camelot, during the Dark Ages. Wotan, or Odin, has decided that mankind is to inherit the Earth and the Firstborn race, the dwarves, must vanish from the world. To this end, no new dwarves are born and war and accident contribute to their rapidly dwindling numbers. Garroc is the last of his race, a wanderer with a lifespan three times that of a human, who has captured the history of his people within his mind. But his life is also drawing toward a close, and in order to prevent the memory of the Firstborn race from vanishing entirely, he tells some of his stories to a human woman. This is the framework in which this and, to date, one follow-up novel are set.

The first tale is of his time as a warrior, when men and dwarves waged nearly constant war across the ruins of Arthur's kingdom, avenging blood debts, struggling for power, or just fighting because that's what they've always done. The leaders are often barely in control of their berserker followers, soldiers grieving for their losses and driven to crazed periods of murderous rage. It's also a tale of dark magic, uncertain pacts made with dark sorcery to return the dead to the land of the living. Despite the heavy doses of fantasy, the setting is the real world in actual historical times, and Berberick has made considerable effort to remain faithful to those fragments of history that have survived from that period.

Berberick's most recent novel is the second tale of Garroc, *The Panther's Hoard*. The battle lines continue to be uncertain and prone to sudden change as humans and dwarves struggle to fill the power vacuum caused by the fall of Camelot. Garroc is back, this time involved with headstrong human princes and a friend who unwisely makes an enemy of a powerful and mean-spirited member of the royal family. Treachery has become a way of life for human and dwarf alike, and some claimants to the throne are ruthless in pursuit of their ambitions, even if blood relatives stand in the way. There's a treasure to be found, battles to be won, and scoundrels to be outwitted.

Although Berberick has yet to write a novel that might propel her into prominence, she continues to turn out creditable, imaginative works with strong historical backgrounds and complex settings. More significantly, there has been steady improvement in the ambition and quality of her work from volume to volume, rather than a cautious unwillingness to try anything new.

—Don D'Ammassa

BERGER, Thomas (Louis)

Nationality: American. **Born:** Cincinnati, Ohio, 20 July 1924. **Education:** University of Cincinnati, B.A. 1948; Columbia University, New York, 1950-51. **Military Service:** United States Army, 1943-46. **Family:** Married Jeanne Redpath in 1950. **Career:** Librarian, Rand School of Social Science, New York, 1948-51; staff member, *New York Times Index,* 1951-52; associate editor, *Popular Science Monthly,* New York, 1952-54; film critic, *Esquire,* New York, 1972-73; writer-in-residence, University of Kansas, Lawrence, 1974; Distinguished Visiting Professor, Southampton College, New York, 1975-76; visiting lecturer, Yale University, New Haven, Connecticut, 1981-82; Regents' Lecturer, University of California, Davis, 1982. **Awards:** Dial fellowship, 1962; Western Heritage award, 1965; Rosenthal award, 1965. Litt.D.: Long Island University, Greenvale, New York, 1986. **Agent:** Don Congdon Associates, 156 Fifth Avenue, Suite 625, New York, New York 10010, USA.

Fantasy Publications

Novels

Regiment of Women. New York, Simon and Schuster, 1973; London, Eyre Methuen, 1974.
Arthur Rex: A Legendary Novel. New York, Delacorte Press, 1978; London, Methuen, 1979.
Nowhere. New York, Delacorte Press, 1985; London, Methuen, 1986.
Being Invisible. Boston, Little Brown, 1987; London, Methuen, 1988.
Changing the Past. Boston, Little Brown, 1989; London, Weidenfeld and Nicolson, 1990.

Other Publications

Novels

Crazy in Berlin. New York, Scribner, 1958.
Reinhart in Love. New York, Scribner, 1962; London, Eyre and Spottiswoode, 1963.
Little Big Man. New York, Dial Press, 1964; London, Eyre and Spottiswoode, 1965.
Killing Time. New York, Dial Press, 1967; London Eyre and Spottiswoode, 1968.
Vital Parts. New York, Baron, 1970; London, Eyre and Spottiswoode, 1971.
Sneaky People. New York, Simon and Schuster, 1975; London, Methuen, 1980.
Who Is Teddy Villanova? New York, Delacorte Press, and London, Eyre Methuen, 1977.
Neighbors. New York, Delacorte Press, 1980; London, Methuen, 1981.
Reinhart's Women. New York, Delacorte Press, 1981; London, Methuen, 1982.
The Feud. New York, Delacorte Press, 1983; London, Methuen, 1984.
The Houseguest. Boston, Little Brown, 1988; London, Weidenfeld and Nicolson, 1989.
Orrie's Story. Boston, Little Brown, 1990.
Meeting Evil. Boston, Little Brown, 1992.

Short Stories

Granted Wishes. Northridge, California, Lord John Press, 1984.

Play

Other People (produced Stockbridge, Massachusetts, 1970).

*

Film Adaptations: *Little Big Man,* 1970; *Neighbors,* 1981; *The Feud,* 1989.

Bibliography: In "Thomas Berger Issue" of *Studies in American Humor* (San Marcos, Texas), Spring and Fall 1983.

Manuscript Collection: Boston University Library.

Critical Study: *Thomas Berger* by Brooks Landon, Boston, Twayne, 1989.

*   *   *

Thomas Berger is a satirist who combines, in a typically American fashion, a cynical suspicion that human beings are incapable of getting things right with a sentimental appreciation of the tragedy inherent in that realization. His novels chronicling the life and times of Carlo Reinhart constitute a witty running commentary on the deceptive lures of the American Dream and he delights in turning a sceptical eye on the myths and suppositions of the favourite genres of American popular fiction—the Western in *Little Big Man,* the hard-boiled private eye novel in *Who is Teddy Villanova?*—in such a manner as to generate perfervid black comedies. His ventures into fantasy are similar in method but are sometimes surprisingly sober in outcome, their comic element usually tending more to subtle sarcasm than to ebullient farce.

The first of Berger's fantasies, *Regiment of Women,* is perhaps the sharpest of the many literary accounts of societies in which the roles and attitudes of males and females are reversed. Although it is notionally set in the future it is not a science-fiction novel, and could easily have distributed its imagery in some other convenient imaginary space. In contrast to the authors of most literary accounts of female social domination, Berger insists that the logic of sexual relationships is anchored in the act of copulation itself, and thus supposes that in a world where woman ruled sexual intercourse would perforce take place rather differently. The novel thus becomes a languorous but conscientious extrapolation of a fundamental inversion of commonplace sexual technique which initially seems quite shocking. The development of this central motif adds a brutal edge to the dark reflection of the sexual politics of the world we live in, while providing ample opportunity for comically transfigured discussions and situations.

Arthur Rex is a more relaxed and straightforwardly bawdy fantasy, one of many modern re-tellings of Malory's *Morte d'Arthur.* Although it is much wittier than the earnestly ponderous accounts which have come to dominate this sub-genre it gives the key characters a human dimension which they so often lack, drawing a better connection between the modern and the mock-Medieval than the common run of such novels. It has not the vaulting ambition of such neo-Arthurian epics as T. H. White's *The Once and Future King,* but it cleverly calls into ironic question the covert implications of a former American president's comparison of his establishment to Camelot.

Nowhere has the same protagonist as *Who is Teddy Villanova?* but it is no hard-boiled thriller. As its title suggests, it is a Utopian romance of sorts, set in the Ruritanian kingdom of San Sebastian where everyday life is lived according to a highly idiosyncratic pattern. Although Butler's *Erewhon* seems to be one of the novel's models, *Nowhere* never remotely approaches the sharpness of Butler's satirical edge, and the inventiveness of his account of San Sebastian quickly decays into casual whimsy, perhaps due to a crucial failure of conviction on the part of the author. It was quickly followed, though, by the much stronger *Being Invisible,* which extrapolates at novel length a cunning conflation of the literal and metaphorical notions of invisibility which had earlier been deployed in a number of notable short stories by various writers—perhaps most memorably in Charles Beaumont's "The Vanishing American." Berger's insignificant protagonist is condemned to writing advertising copy for the worst kinds of mail-order novelties while his ex-wife has taken up with a flashy hoodlum named Siv Zirko; thus tipped over the edge of desperation, he sets out to take command of his talent for remaining unnoticed so that he might use it for his own good—and, eventually, for the benefit of all mankind. Naturally enough, this project proves to be not quite as easy as it appeared to be at the planning stage, but it seems in the end that facultative transparency really does provide a window of opportunity through which a man might pass.

The idea of being able to make oneself invisible is one of the commonest of daydream fantasies; *Changing the Past* develops the one which is probably the commonest of all. Like the characters in J. M. Barrie's play *Dear Brutus,* Walter Hunsicker gets the chance to explore some of the possibilities aborted by his past choices—and like them he finds that the results are by no means as delightful as his profound sense of self-dissatisfaction has led him to suppose. He finds that had he set his sights on wealth and power he would have made terrifying enemies, that had he given himself over to hedonism he would have ended up a wreck, and that cultivation of artistic creativity would have made him all-too-painfully aware of his solitude. He takes as much comfort from these revelations as he can, although he realizes that it is not really a comforting thought to know that one lives in the mediocre best of possible worlds. The conviction that fate would have found a way to louse things up for him no matter how he might have tried to evade its penalties does indeed make him more appreciative of what he has, but it cannot endear him to the business of living.

In all Berger's works *angst* is always hovering overhead, as it tends to do in real life, obscuring the brightest rays of hope to the extent that their radiance becomes distinctly wan. A writer who consistently punctures myths and daydreams in this manner, however good-humouredly, always takes a risk; people are always likely to take against those messengers who bring them bad news. On the other hand, given that we all know, deep down, that our myths and daydreams are essentially hollow, such a writer can be appreciated for his honesty. Berger is a writer who gives the impression of being uncommonly honest, and to this he adds the contrasting gifts of blackly comic wit and open-hearted charm. It is a powerful combination when it works to full effect.

—Brian Stableford

BISSON, Terry (Ballantine)

Nationality: American. **Born:** Kentucky, 12 February 1942. **Education:** University of Louisville, 1960-64, BA in English. **Family:** several marriages; six children. **Career:** Automobile mechanic for many years; writer of comics, advertising copy, etc. **Awards:** Hugo, Nebula and Theodore Sturgeon awards, 1991; Phoenix award, 1993. **Agent:** Susan Ann Protter, 110 West 40th Street, New York, NY 10018, USA. **Address:** Box 416, Van Brunt Station, Brooklyn, NY 11215, USA.

FANTASY PUBLICATIONS

Novels

Wyrldmaker. New York, Pocket, 1981; London, Headline, 1988.
Talking Man. New York, Arbor House, 1986; London, Headline, 1987.

Short Stories

Bears Discover Fire and Other Stories. New York, Tor, 1993.

OTHER PUBLICATIONS

Novels

Fire on the Mountain. New York, Morrow, 1988.
Voyage to the Red Planet. New York, Morrow, 1990; London, Pan, 1992.

Plays

Two Guys from the Future, They're Made Out of Meat, Next, Are There Any Questions?, Partial People, The Toxic Donut, all produced West Bank Theatre, New York, 1992-93.

Other

Nat Turner: Slave Revolt Leader. New York, Chelsea House, 1988.
Car Talk with Click and Clack, with Tom and Ray Magliozzi. New York, Dell, 1990.

* * *

There are two predominantly rural schools in American fiction, the Southern writers following in the wake of William Faulkner and the more mid-western science fiction of writers like Clifford D. Simak. Terry Bisson is where these two schools come together. If his stories aren't set in the South (as *Talking Man* and *Fire on the Mountain* are) then his protagonists are likely to come from there (Bass, the spaceship pilot in *Voyage to the Red Planet*). Time and again his narrative voice is slow and discursive, and even in his out-and-out science fiction the greatest technological interest is liable to be in an old car engine. (Both the Southern fantasy *Talking Man* and the homage to old-fashioned sf adventure *Voyage to the Red Planet* contain a joke about oil not being past its sell-by date because it was already a million years old before it was put in the can.) That his work belongs to such readily identifiable literary traditions yet is still as uncategorizable, as *sui generis* as, for instance, the writings of R. A. Lafferty or Howard Waldrop, shows how skilfully he bends the tradition to suit his own off-beat imagination and generally comic end.

The importance to Bisson of working, even subversively, within a tradition is shown by his first and weakest novel, *Wyrldmaker.* There is nothing of the rural South, none of the lapel-grabbing conversational manner in this book. Instead we get an heroic fantasy plot with a hard science-fictional pay-off, in which a warrior figure must carry a magical sword through a series of bloody adventures in increasingly bizarre "wyrlds" until the sword is revealed to be a vital instrument in a planet-seeding enterprise which owes something to James Blish's *The Seedling Stars.* The plotting is staccato, the denouement perfunctory, the book fails to gel.

It is hard to recognize that the author of *Wyrldmaker* is the same person who went on to write *Talking Man,* a fluent and elegiac novel with none of the formula elements and clumsy structure of its predecessor. But in *Talking Man* Bisson had found his milieu, and the voice to go with it. This is a novel rich in the atmosphere of the American South, with that curious sense of nostalgia and what might have been which seems to characterize the best Southern writing. The eponymous Talking Man (who does not actually say a word throughout the novel) is a wizard from the end of time who has found a home tending old cars in a remote garage outside a little country town. When a timeless battle with his sister is renewed to disrupt the idyll, his daughter and a customer at the garage are swept into a quest that takes them across an ever-changing America to a resolution at a transformed North Pole. But however far the quest might take them, at the heart of the novel is a sense of the South as home (and home plays a very important part in much of Bisson's fiction) and as refuge, which is reclaimed at the end of the novel.

His next novel, *Fire on the Mountain,* depends even more literally on that sense of what the South was and what it might be-

come. It is an alternative history which examines what might have happened if John Brown's raid on Harper's Ferry had succeeded. The failure of the raid was one of the key turning-points in the events leading to the American Civil War, but in Bisson's history the raid sparks a slave revolt. (Bisson has also written a non-fiction book for children about Nat Turner who led a slave revolt in Virginia in 1831.) The success of this revolt eventually leads to the establishment of a Black Republic in the lands of the old Confederacy. The account of the revolt is stronger and more vivid than the utopian image of Nova Africa, perhaps because it gets closer to the heart of the South.

It was only after he had published these three novels that Bisson turned to writing short stories, with considerable success. Once more the gentle fantasies which form most of his short stories return again and again to a Southern setting or a countryman's voice. In "Bears Discover Fire", for instance, the sudden evolutionary advance of the bears is only incidental to the story of a family coming to terms with death. "Over Flat Mountain" imagines the Appalachians thrown up so high that the top of the range is outside the atmosphere, but the story of truckers who make the perilous journey across the mountain is really about running away from home and coming to terms with who you are. The South also appears in "The Two Janets", a comedy about famous writers suddenly and inexplicably moving to Bisson's own hometown, Owensboro, Kentucky; and in "The Coon Suit", a more disturbing story about good ol' boys out hunting. And it is surely the South's attitude to race which lies behind the bitter comedy of "Next".

Not that all his stories revolve around rural Kentucky or Virginia. Two of his most effective are "Canción Auténtica de Old Earth", a haunting tale of mysterious visitors watching without understanding an ancient ritual in the ruins of Earth, and "England Underway", in which Britain inexplicably sets sail across the Atlantic. But in both these stories the notion of home as a refuge and a magnet is strong. The visitors to Old Earth are in some way connecting with their ancestry, while Mr. Fox of Brighton is taking the certainties and comforts of home with him when he makes, unwittingly, a journey to visit American relatives he has long been afraid to make.

Most of Bisson's work is fantasy rather than science fiction not because his stories involve magic (it occurs fitfully in *Talking Man* but nowhere else) but because they eschew explanation. It isn't necessary to know how a child grows wings in "George", how bears discover fire, what makes England cast itself loose from its moorings. These are given to allow Bisson to explore the wonder of what comes next. But in two of his most recent works he pays overt homage to the traditions of science fiction also, though again only to subvert those traditions. *Voyage to the Red Planet* conveys all the old outward-bound spirit of adventure suggested by a trip to Mars, but here the ramshackle expedition is masterminded by a fly-by-night Hollywood film company, while the satirical view of Earth left behind includes a flight controller eventually reduced to calling the voyagers from a pay phone. "The Shadow Knows" takes another sf tradition, first encounter with an alien, but here the alien is as insubstantial as a shadow and the message it finally transmits to all mankind is no more than "a wave from a passing ship". It is this awareness of traditions brought to the service of a very individual imagination, which makes Terry Bisson one of the most distinctive fantasy authors writing today.

—Paul Kincaid

BLAYLOCK, James P(aul)

Nationality: American. **Born:** Long Beach, California, 20 September 1950. **Education:** California State University, Fullerton, B.A. 1972; M.A. 1974. **Family:** Married Viki Lynn Martin in 1972; two sons. **Career:** Pet-food store clerk, Garden Grove, California, 1967-72; construction worker, Placentia, California, 1972-80; part-time instructor, Fullerton Community College, 1976-89; part-time instructor of English, California State University, Fullerton, 1980-87. **Awards:** Philip K. Dick award, 1986; World Fantasy award, 1986. **Agent:** Merrilee Heifetz, Writers House, 21 West 26th Street, New York, NY 10016, USA. **Address:** 157 North Pine Street, Orange, CA 92666, USA.

FANTASY PUBLICATIONS

Novels (series: Elfin Ship; Langdon St. Ives)

The Elfin Ship. New York, Del Rey, 1982; London, Grafton, 1988.
The Disappearing Dwarf (Elfin Ship). New York, Del Rey, 1983; London, Grafton, 1989.
The Digging Leviathan. New York, Ace, 1984; Bath, Morrigan, 1988.
Homunculus (St. Ives). New York, Ace, 1986; Bath, Morrigan, 1988.
Land of Dreams. New York, Arbor House, 1987; London, Grafton, 1988.
The Last Coin. New York, Ace, 1988; London, Grafton, 1989.
The Stone Giant (Elfin Ship). New York, Ace, 1989; London, Grafton, 1990.
Lord Kelvin's Machine (St. Ives). Sauk City, Wisconsin, Arkham House, 1991; London, Grafton, 1993.
The Magic Spectacles (for children). Bath, Morrigan, 1991.
The Paper Grail. New York, Ace, 1991; London, Grafton, 1993.
Night Relics. New York, Ace, and London, HarperCollins, 1994.

Short Stories

Paper Dragons. Seattle, Washington, Axolotl Press, 1986.
The Pink of Fading Neon. Seattle, Washington, Axolotl Press, 1986.
The Shadow on the Doorstep, with Edward Bryant. Seattle, Washington, Axolotl Press, 1987.
Two Views of a Cave Painting; and The Idol's Eye. Seattle, Washington, Axolotl Press, 1987.
Doughnuts. Mission Viejo, California, A.S.A.P., 1994.

* * *

James Blaylock is perhaps the most singular fantasy writer to emerge in the 1980s. Although his eccentric fabulations tend to utilize fantasy tropes to ornament rather than drive their sometimes ramshackle but entertaining plots, nevertheless they are illuminated by a deep and affectionate knowledge of the genre.

His novels can be roughly divided into three loosely connected series. The first, *The Elfin Ship* and *The Disappearing Dwarf,* together with the later *The Stone Giant,* are adventures across what at first glance seems a fairly standard rural fantasy landscape, peopled with goblins, dwarfs, elves and reclusive magicians. However, the ambience of the novels and the sensibilities of their characters are 19th-century rather than medieval, and there are rich reso-

nances with Blaylock's admitted literary influences, Laurence Sterne and Robert Louis Stevenson. Within the framework of a picaresque journey, events are thrown together, like the devices of the singular inventors of Blaylock's later books, with seeming carelessness. But despite the relaxed, amiable treatment of even the most black-hearted of his characters, and the apparently casual planting of plot devices, Blaylock manages to draw everything together in set-pieces resonant with ridiculous coincidences, where all the elements he has thrown into the air briefly shape transcendent and very funny moments of revelation.

A second loose trilogy consists of science fantasies concerned with inventors and their fabulous machines. In *The Digging Leviathan,* set in 1950s Southern California, a cast of eccentrics discover a vast sea beneath Los Angeles through which may lie a route to the centre of a hollow Earth. Blaylock gleefully invokes Edgar Rice Burroughs's Pellucidar novels, the Dean drives of pulp science fiction, and the manic inventors and wonderful machines of Victorian scientific romances in a baggy plot that is concerned not so much with adventure as the fondly observed antics of a bunch of obsessives. The Victorian age of invention is evoked more explicitly in *Homunculus* (which won the Philip K. Dick Award) and *Lord Kelvin's Machine.* These are definitive steampunk fictions, a genre invented by Blaylock and fellow Californians Tim Powers and K.W. Jeter which is characterized by a romantic vision of Victorian London as it should have been, a playground for new technologies and sinister occult conspiracies grown from a fusion of the sensibilities of Wells and Dickens.

In *Homunculus,* Langdon St. Ives, gentleman adventurer, and other members of the Trismegustus Club, must thwart the scheme of the evil Ignacio Narbondo to reanimate corpses with essence of carp. Stirred into the plot are zombies, a dirigible piloted by a skeleton, an alien starship and a gloriously eccentric toymaker, and a search for the apparently immortal homunculus. The sequel, *Lord Kelvin's Machine,* is a successful, tightly-plotted homage to H.G. Wells which opens with the murder of St. Ives's wife by Narbondo. In the three-part story that follows, St. Ives uses the electromagnetic accumulator invented by Lord Kelvin to thwart Narbondo's plan to draw a comet down upon the Earth, then retrieves the stolen device, with which Narbondo is holding the British government to ransom, and finally uses it as the heart of a time-machine with which St. Ives plans his ultimate revenge on Narbondo and finally puts the world to rights.

The third triplet of Blaylock's novels is located, with increasing specificity, in various parts of California. *Land of Dreams* is set at an earlier time in the same Northern Californian coastal town as Blaylock's short story "Paper Dragons." The short story demonstrates Blaylock's fine eye for scrying the marvellous in the mundane; the novel folds together time travel and a sinister solstice carnival reminiscent of Ray Bradbury's *Something Wicked This Way Comes.* The complex yet satisfyingly resolved plot belies the charge that Blaylock is a writer of mere picaresque adventures.

The Last Coin and *The Paper Grail* are both contemporary fantasies. In the first, Andrew Vanbergen wants nothing more than to open his own café, but is drawn into a plot involving the Wandering Jew and the sinister Pennyman, who is pursuing the silver coins paid to Judas Iscariot. It cheerfully mixes domestic complications with symbols of a burgeoning apocalypse and, yet again, the life-enhancing properties of carp. The theme of irruption of unlooked for adventure into cosy domesticity and the uncovering by the hero of his own family's complex back-story are constants in Blaylock's work. Both are woven into what is perhaps his best novel to date,

The Paper Grail. Set in contemporary Northern California, its hero, Howard Barton, returns to the small coastal town in which he was brought up in search of a woodcut print rumoured to be the work of the legendary Japanese artist Hoku-sai. Swiftly, he becomes involved in a plot involving the fisher king and the Paper Grail itself; aided by his Uncle Roy, a kind of backwoods Disney, and Mr. Jimmers, who has invented a machine to raise the spirits of the dead, Barton must find the grail and keep it from the clutches of the witchy Mrs. Lamey and her yuppie cabal.

Barton is yet another innocent dreamer, escaping from a dead-end job as museum curator, but unlike many of Blaylock's characters, he is more active than acted upon. At one point he uses knowledge drawn from an anarchist manual to make a home-made bomb to enable him to escape from Mrs. Lamey's clutches, and he is involved in a romance whose outcome is satisfyingly integrated with that of the main plot, turning on the secret history of Barton's family. While *The Paper Grail* bears all the hallmarks of Blaylock's fictions, it is anchored to a specific contemporary locale, and there's less of the whimsy that like kudzu sometimes threaten to overwhelm his earlier novels. Its steely plot and realistic, touching portrayal of human hopes and fallibilities perhaps reveals a new direction for this highly individual writer.

—Paul J. McAuley

BOK, Hannes (Vajn)

Nationality: American. **Born:** Wayne Woodard (adopted the name Hannes Vajn Bok), Kansas City, Missouri, 2 July 1914. **Education:** Duluth high school, Minnesota. **Career:** Magazine illustrator. **Awards:** Hugo award for cover art, 1953. **Died:** 11 April 1964.

FANTASY PUBLICATIONS

Novels

The Fox Woman and the Blue Pagoda, with A. Merritt. New York, New Collectors' Group, 1946.
The Black Wheel, with A. Merritt. New York, New Collectors' Group, 1947.
The Sorcerer's Ship. New York, Ballantine, 1969.
Beyond the Golden Stair. New York, Ballantine, 1970.
The Fox Woman and the Blue Pagoda, and The Black Wheel, with A. Merritt (omnibus). New York, Arno Press, 1976.

Other

The Hannes Bok Memorial Showcase of Fantasy Art, edited by Emil Petaja. San Francisco, SISU, 1974.
A Hannes Bok Sketchbook, edited by Gerry de la Ree and Gene Nigra. Saddle River, New Jersey, de la Ree, 1976.
Beauty and the Beasts: The Art of Hannes Bok, edited by Gerry de la Ree. Saddle River, New Jersey, de la Ree, 1978.
A Hannes Bok Treasury, edited by Stephen D. Korshak. Lancaster, Pennsylvania, Underwood Miller, 1993.

*

Critical Studies: *And Flights of Angels: The Life and Legend of Hannes Bok* by Emil Petaja, San Francisco, SISU, 1968; *Bok* edited by Gerry de la Ree, n.p., de la Ree, 1974.

*   *   *

Hannes Bok is primarily remembered as a painter and illustrator, a prolific contributor to the pulp magazines of the 1940s and the fan specialty-press book field of the 1950s. He did his best work for *Weird Tales, Famous Fantastic Mysteries,* Shasta Press and Arkham House. A self-taught artist, he so admired the work of the great Maxfield Parrish that he often referred to himself as a "student" of that artist, although he did not actually study with Parrish. (According to his lifelong friend Emil Petaja, Bok corresponded with Parrish and later met him. They became friends. While there was no formal apprenticeship, Parrish's work was the major formative influence on Bok.)

Bok befriended science-fiction fans in high school, changing his name about this time for reasons that aren't certain, possibly because "Hannes Bok" merely sounded more exotic. Ray Bradbury introduced his work to Farnsworth Wright, editor of *Weird Tales,* and began Bok's professional career. By all accounts brilliant, quixotic, temperamental, often unwilling to compromise his work or knuckle under to art directors, Bok did most of his work for the marginal markets and achieved no great success in his lifetime, although he was a beloved figure in fandom and incontestably one of the greatest fantasy illustrators of his time. He withdrew from the fantasy field late in life, trying to break into fine art, disgusted by insensitive art directors and the shabby treatment he had received from the fan presses, which often paid poorly or not at all.

Bok's writing career is of secondary interest and confined to the 1940s. As a youth, he had so idolized the works of A. Merritt that in those pre-photocopier, pre-paperback days, so the story goes, he once transcribed *The Ship of Ishtar* longhand, merely so he could own a copy. His two novels, and one major novella show a heavy Merritt influence, but also Merritt's failings, including a tendency to drift off into vague clouds of deeply purple prose.

In all three major Bok fictions, the hero, an unheroic or ineffectual young man, makes an abrupt, involuntary transition into another world, where he rapidly becomes involved in sorcerous intrigue, beautiful women, magic mechanisms, etc., although the "magic" always has a thin veneer of pseudo-science. In *The Sorcerer's Ship* (originally published in *Unknown* in 1942), the hero swims too far from Coney Island and awakens on a raft in another world. The usual adventures ensue, though in an almost comical reverse of the tragic ending of *The Ship of Ishtar,* this time the hero, having rescued the Princess, invoked a god to defeat his foes, etc., gets himself and his lady-love ejected from the happily ever after when he suggests that the country become a democracy—which of course has no room for princesses.

In *Beyond the Golden Stair* (originally abridged at half-length, as "The Blue Flamingo" in *Startling Stories,* 1948), the hero and several villainous companions, on the run in the Florida Everglades after having been sprung from the penitentiary against his will by his cellmate, passes through an other-dimensional gate before the expected goings-on occur. His criminal companions meet suitable fates. The hero must leave his true love behind and depart the land of Khoire at the end, but hopes to find a token which will enable him to return.

The editor of *Science Fiction Quarterly* tried to pass "Starstone World" off as a book-length novel in the Summer 1942 issue, but it is not, one factor which may explain why it has never been reprinted. This time the hero gets hit by a car and awakens in the other world, in another body, the victim of the surgical operations of two rival sorcerers, who snatch minds across time and space to place in the bodies of recalcitrant slaves. He is sent on a quest to steal a jewel from an even more powerful sorceress, resulting in the expected adventures, intrigue, romance, and yet another attempt at a bittersweet ending.

While all three of these works have occasional imaginative touches and descriptions which would have made fine paintings, Bok's prose seldom rose above the pulp minimum. Disappointingly, an artist capable of such wonderfully delicate graphic work wrote leadenly, unable to hear the false note when an enchantress in an ethereal world promises to rectify something "in a jiffy."

Bok's shorter fiction, including six stories in *Weird Tales* between 1942 and 1944, one in *Unknown,* and a few in the lesser science-fiction magazines of the early 1940s are competent, but routine. He also collaborated (posthumously) with his idol Merritt, completing two Merritt fragments, providing magnificent illustrations, and becoming a partner in New Collector's Group, which published the results as *The Fox Woman and the Blue Pagoda* and *The Black Wheel.* Bok's written contributions do not measure up to the illustrations, and shady business practices by some of the partners in New Collector's Group helped sour him toward the fantasy field. (The statements of print-run limitations were not adhered to; Bok was cheated out of royalties on the extra copies.)

The appearance of his two longest works, including first publication of the full manuscript of *Beyond the Golden Stair,* in the Ballantine Adult Fantasy Series seems to have been an act of nostalgia on the part of editor Lin Carter. It has not led to any sustained revival of Bok's writing. But his art lives on, most recently collected in *A Hannes Bok Treasury.*

—Darrell Schweitzer

BOSTON, L(ucy) M(aria Wood)

Nationality: British. **Born:** Southport, Lancashire, 10 December 1892. **Education:** Downs School, Seaford, Sussex; Somerville College, Oxford. **Family:** Married in 1917 (marriage dissolved 1935); one son. **Career:** Trained as a nurse before going to France to treat the wounded in World War I; travelled in Europe, 1935-39; began the restoration of a manor house at Hemingford Grey, which later served as a background for her books; commenced her literary career at the age of 62. **Awards:** Carnegie Medal, 1961; Spring Book Festival award, 1967; Lewis Carroll Shelf award, 1969. **Died:** 25 May 1990.

FANTASY PUBLICATIONS

Novels

The Children of Green Knowe. London, Faber, 1954; New York, Harcourt, 1955.
The Chimneys of Green Knowe. London, Faber, 1958; as *Treasure of Green Knowe,* New York, Harcourt, 1958.

The River at Green Knowe. London, Faber, and New York, Harcourt, 1959.
A Stranger at Green Knowe. London, Faber, and New York, Harcourt, 1961.
An Enemy at Green Knowe. London, Faber, and New York, Harcourt, 1964.
The Stones of Green Knowe. London, Bodley Head, and New York, Atheneum, 1976.

Novels (for children)

The Castle of Yew. London, Bodley Head, and New York, Harcourt, 1965.
The Sea Egg. London, Faber, and New York, Harcourt, 1967.
The House that Grew. London, Faber, 1969.
Nothing Said. London, Faber, and New York, Harcourt, 1971.
The Guardians of the House. London, Bodley Head, 1974; New York, Atheneum, 1975.
The Fossil Snake. London, Bodley Head, 1975; New York, Atheneum, 1976.

OTHER PUBLICATIONS

Novels

Yew Hall. London, Faber, 1954.
Persephone. London, Collins, 1969; as *Strongholds,* New York, Harcourt, 1969.

Play

The Horned Man; or, Whom Will You Send to Fetch Her Away? London, Faber, 1970.

Other

Memory in a House (autobiography). London, Bodley Head, 1973; New York, Macmillan, 1974.
Perverse and Foolish: A Memoir of Childhood and Youth. London, Bodley Head, and New York, Atheneum, 1979.

*

Critical study: *Lucy Boston* by Jasper A. Rose, London, Bodley Head, 1965; New York, Walck, 1966.

*   *   *

On an impulse she likened to falling in love, in 1938 Lucy Boston bought the Manor House at Hemingford Grey in Cambridgeshire. The house was crumbling, practically uninhabitable, and as she worked to restore it she discovered that within a shoddy, crumbling shell were the still sturdy walls of a Norman hall, built circa 1120; later, she would suggest that hers might be the oldest continually inhabited house in England.

Nearly 15 years later, by then in her 60s, Lucy Boston embarked on a new career as a writer. Previously she had been a nurse, wife, mother, student and painter, but had only ever written some poetry for her own pleasure. But since settling down in the old manor house—and it quickly became a home she never wanted to leave—a relationship had developed which could be likened to a marriage, or to the inspirational love between painter and muse. The house was her muse and her greatest subject. It appears, scarcely altered, as Yew Hall, in her first novel, and, more memorably, as Green Knowe in the fantasy series which is her best known work.

In her memoir *Memory in a House* Mrs. Boston wrote that it was her restoration of the house and garden at Hemingford Grey which would be considered her work of art, but to her readers her books, especially the Green Knowe series, are her great achievement by which she will be remembered.

Although other atmospheric time fantasies have been written (Alison Uttley's *A Traveller in Time* and Philippa Pearce's *Tom's Midnight Garden* spring to mind), there is nothing in children's literature quite like the Green Knowe books. At the centre stands the house, more like a character in its own right than simply a setting, but also providing plot and theme. Frequently the house is spoken of as a living being, but it is also something more powerful than that: it is Time made manifest, a place where past and future overlap and where the lonely and dispossessed, if they are sensitive to its magic, may find a permanent home. The house is full of ghosts, but it is haunted only in the most benign sense: evil, when it appears, comes from the outside, from the activities of greedy or ignorant people incapable of responding to the natural, healing magic of the place. All of her books are deeply moral, without ever being moralistic or preaching.

The Children of Green Knowe begins the series with young Tolly (based on the author's son Peter who illustrated nearly all of her books) going to live with his great grandmother, Mrs. Oldknow, in her ancient house. She tells him stories about Linnet, Toby and Alexander—her ancestors, the children in a 17th-century painting hanging over the fireplace—and as he gradually becomes aware of their continuing presence in the house, they become his friends. The plot of this episodic novel matters far less than the sensitive, richly atmospheric writing and the development of the theme of the constant living presence of the past, and the interconnectedness of all life. *The Chimneys of Green Knowe* (also known as *The Treasure of Green Knowe*) returns Tolly to Green Knowe where, aided by the ghosts of Susan, a blind girl, and her young black servant Jacob, he searches for the jewels of Maria Oldknow, lost in 1798, and learns more about the history of the house.

In the next two books in the series, other children come to Green Knowe; Tolly and Mrs. Oldknow are away. In *The River at Green Knowe* two refugee boys, Ping and Oskar, and an English girl Ida spend a summer discovering the countryside around the house and having magical adventures; in *A Stranger at Green Knowe* Ping tries to help a gorilla who escapes from the zoo. This book, with its movingly portrayed relationship between boy and beast, gives expression not only to Boston's life-long love of the natural world, but also to her fear that everything she held precious was being destroyed by humanity's greed and increasing alienation from nature. This fear also comes to the fore in *An Enemy at Green Knowe* in which an evil witch is determined to destroy the house, but the author was able to convincingly imagine the means by which Tolly, Ping, and Mrs. Oldknow defeat her plans and preserve Green Knowe from harm. By the last book of the series, however, lacking any real faith in the future, Boston could only celebrate the past. *The Stones of Green Knowe* tells the story of how the Norman manor house came to be built, in 1120, through the eyes of Roger d'Aulneaux, the first boy to live there. On the edge of the nearby forest he discovers two ancient stones with the power to grant his wish to see the future of his house. He meets all "the others" met by Tolly in the earlier books—going forward to 1660 to meet Lin-

net, Toby and Alexander and then to 1800 where he meets Susan and Jacob. There have been changes, but nothing he cannot understand, until he goes forward to meet Tolly in 1970, where he is terrified by fighter jets roaring overhead, baffled by the many signs of civilization and absence of people, and desolated by the lack of the rich, unpolluted, living world he had known. Although he is glad to see that his home has been preserved and is still inhabited and cared for, he witnesses the removal—"To the local museum, where old things are kept"—of the ancient, magical stones. They still stand in his day; there is still magic in his day; but our modern world has been impoverished, and Tolly will not see him again.

A slighter story, not exactly part of the series and written for younger children, is *The Castle of Yew* about two children who shrink in size in order to play inside a yew clipped into the shape of a castle (the garden at Green Knowe, like its real-life counterpart in Hemingford Grey, contains fanciful topiary shapes) and then must ward off attacks by a cat, a bird and a squirrel as they struggle to survive.

Lucy Boston also wrote a few juvenile fantasies which were not set at Green Knowe, and it is one of these which she declared to be her own favourite: *The Sea Egg,* is about two little boys who find an egg on a beach, from which hatches a triton, or mer-baby, who plays with them and reveals some of the mysteries of the sea to them, was written after a visit to Cornwall and reflects the author's deep, almost mystical love for the sea.

—Lisa Tuttle

BOYER, Elizabeth H.

Nationality: American. **Education:** Brigham Young University, Provo, Utah; B.A. in English. **Family:** Married; two daughters. **Address:** c/o Ballantine/Del Rey, 201 East 50th Street, New York, NY 10022, USA.

FANTASY PUBLICATIONS

Novels (series: Alfar in all books)

The Sword and the Satchel. New York, Del Rey, 1980; London, Corgi, 1986.
The Elves and the Otterskin. New York, Del Rey, 1981; London, Corgi, 1986.
The Thrall and the Dragon's Heart. New York, Del Rey, 1982; London, Corgi, 1986.
The Wizard and the Warlord. New York, Del Rey, 1983; London, Corgi, 1987.
The Troll's Grindstone. New York, Del Rey, 1986; London, Corgi, 1987.
The Curse of Slagfid. New York, Del Rey, 1989; London, Corgi, 1990.
The Dragon's Carbuncle. New York, Del Rey, 1990.
The Lord of Chaos. New York, Del Rey, 1991.
The Clan of the Warlord. New York, Del Rey, 1992.
The Black Lynx. New York, Del Rey, 1993.
Keeper of Cats. New York, Del Rey, 1995.

*   *   *

Elizabeth Boyer has been a steady but non-prolific author of conventional fantasy adventure novels for well over a decade. Her first novel, *The Sword and the Satchel,* drew from Tolkien, Scandinavian and Arthurian sources to chronicle the adventures of Kilgore, a dreamer who marks himself as a warrior by proving himself fit to hold an enchanted sword. His quest is to defeat the evil sorcerer Surt, who has bested all previous challengers, and he is assisted by a grumpy wizard through a series of encounters that culminates with the destruction of Surt's power. It was a competent but largely undistinguished debut that set the pattern for subsequent, and much better, stories.

Boyer's second novel, *The Elves and the Otterskin,* showed considerable improvement in plot and pace, although most of the characterizations remain flat. Once again, she employs standard fantasy motifs, the slaying of a dragon, warring elves, an evil magician, magic swords, and the innocent man trapped into a heroic role. Ivarr is a more appealing protagonist, however, and his individual adventures are better shaped and resolved.

Brak is a very similar character whose adventures are chronicled in Boyer's third novel of the world of Alfar, *The Thrall and the Dragon's Heart.* He's from another realm, magically transported when he tries to intervene on behalf of an elf enslaved by an evil witch. In Alfar he discovers that yet another evil sorcerer is planning the subjugation of the world, this time by raising armies of the dead to do his bidding. This is a credible adventure story despite a penchant for unpronounceable proper names.

The last book in Boyer's first cycle of novels is *The Wizard and the Warlord,* one of her best efforts. Sigurd is a young man uncertain of his own potential, living in a village threatened by malevolent trolls. For mysterious reasons not revealed until late in the novel, he is abducted and brought to Alfar, where war has erupted between the two elvish kingdoms, one good, one evil. He spends most of the story escaping monsters and trying to figure out why so many powerful forces are interested in him, eventually gaining the maturity to take a hand in things himself. Boyer seemed to have settled into a comfortable pattern with this book, playing variations on her original theme and making no effort to break new ground. The strength of much modern fantasy is its predictability, but it is also in some ways its greatest weakness.

The next four novels of Alfar are known collectively as "The Wizard's War," and for the first time Boyer uses a continuing character as her protagonist. Leifr is introduced in *The Troll's Grindstone,* as he flees from his enemies by impersonating a citizen of Alfar. Unfortunately, he appears in the guise of a very unpopular traitor whose old enemies are quite pleased at another chance for vengeance. Another quest follows as Leifr obtains a magical sword and then sets out to find the enchanted grindstone that will restore its power and perhaps enable him to restore his original appearance.

Leifr's adventures continue through the next three books, each of which involves another instalment of his search for Ljosa, the woman he loves. Accompanied by his good friend Thurid, a minor magician, he fights and wanders his way through *The Curse of Slagfid, The Dragon's Carbuncle,* and *The Lord of Chaos.* In the first of these, the two friends are tricked into the classic fairy-tale role of performing a task for a wizard on penalty of eternal slavery if they fail. An old enemy returns from the dead in the second to steal Ljosa away, while Thurid has been seized by the wizard's guild and faces execution for violating their rules. Leifr is left to struggle with his own conflicting emotions as well as the physical dangers of Alfar. The continuing story is brought to a close with

the rescue of Ljosa and the thwarting of a sorcerous plot to plunge the world into a supernatural winter amidst which only the forces of evil could thrive. As a whole, the cycle is quite entertaining but the individual volumes solve only the immediate problems and not the central quest, and are therefore dramatically unbalanced.

Boyer inaugurated a new cycle of stories with *The Clan of the Warlord,* set once again in the world of the dark and light elves. This time the protagonist is female, Skyla, a disinherited priestess in a kingdom that has been overrun by the dark elves, raised by an elderly magician with weak and unreliable powers. Skyla discovers that she has magical abilities of her own, including shapechanging, and sets out to reclaim a lost treasure, a quest continued in *The Black Lynx* and presumably to be concluded in volumes to come. Skyla is by far the most interesting of Boyer's heroes although this new cycle suffers from the same truncation of the overall story into individual episodes. Her determination to regain her birthright makes her a stronger and more sympathetic character than Boyer's earlier heroes.

Boyer's infrequent short stories have to date been unmemorable, but her novels clearly have a wide and continuing readership. There's no effort to experiment with the form; Boyer is content to stay with demonstrably successful plots and devices. Her storytelling ability has improved in steady increments to date although it is unlikely that she will break out into a wider readership unless she abandons what has already proven to be a successful strategy.

—Don D'Ammassa

BOYETT, Steven R.

Nationality: American. **Born:** Atlanta, Georgia, 1960.

FANTASY PUBLICATIONS

Novels

Ariel: A Book of the Change. New York, Ace, 1983.
The Architect of Sleep. New York, Ace, 1986.
The Gnole, with Alan Aldridge. London, Heinemann, 1991.

* * *

Steven R. Boyett is a difficult writer to categorize. Both his solo novels were published in the Ace Fantasy line, yet they feature substantial science-fiction elements, especially in their evocations of context: *Ariel: A Book of the Change* is a quest fantasy set in a fragmented post-holocaust America, while *The Architect of Sleep* is a through-the-looking-glass tale set in a coherently extrapolated parallel world. Boyett's (as yet uncollected) short fiction has been equally schizophrenic, ranging from science fiction to fantasy to horror. The author's inability—or unwillingness—to conform to the conventions of any single genre has made his career a problematic one: it is rumoured that sequels to his second novel have had trouble finding a publisher. Certainly, in terms of longer work, he has been largely silent for almost a decade, during a time when it might be expected that a writer just entering his 30s would be starting to hit his stride. This silence—broken only by the publication of *The Gnole,* an environmental fantasy written in collaboration with well-known artist Alan Aldridge (and possibly more Aldridge's project than Boyett's)—is unfortunate, given the promise of his first two novels.

Both *Ariel* and *The Architect of Sleep* are essentially talking-animal fantasies, the former a bit twee in its portrait of a wise-cracking, foul-mouthed unicorn, the latter shrewd and hard-edged in its depiction of intelligent racoons. The novels differ, too, in their respective rationalizations of these fantastic creatures: in *Ariel,* an unexplained "Change" overtakes our world, suspending scientific laws and unleashing mythic entities, while in *Architect,* a mysterious warp in space permits access to a parallel earth of divergent evolutionary history. In both cases, the passage to otherness is more or less explicitly fantastic, but once this border has been crossed, *Architect* makes a more consistent effort than does *Ariel* to extrapolate the changed environment and its denizens.

Still, as remarked above, *Ariel* is not exactly a conventional quest fantasy either. Like the fiction of Tom Deitz which it resembles (and perhaps inspired), *Ariel* is set not in an autonomous secondary world, but in our world transformed by an irruption of faery. The cryptic Change, which not only ushered in unicorns, griffins, dragons, and other mythic beasties but also rendered all electrically-powered machines and any weapon more sophisticated than the crossbow magically inoperative, has produced a post-holocaust landscape familiar to science-fiction readers: sparsely populated, politically fragmented, and filled with the detritus of an archaic modernity.

The story opens five years after the advent of this strange new world, with Pete Garey, our hero, meeting and bonding with a wounded unicorn he names Ariel. They wander aimlessly for a bit, learning each other's ways and growing together (in scenes of an often painful cuteness), until they realize, following a bloody battle in Atlanta, that a powerful necromancer seeks Ariel's horn for its magical properties—which include the overcoming of death itself. Preceded by friend Malachi, a martial-arts guru who has taught Pete the art of swordplay, the pair set off for New York to confront and defeat this evil wizard. Once there, Ariel is promptly captured, while Pete escapes, joining up again with Malachi to aid a Washington D.C. collective who have been planning an offensive against the necromancer and his minions. The consequent assault, which features a breathless hang-glider dive-bombing of the Empire State Building (the wizard's H.Q.), is excitingly narrated, displaying Boyett's skill at scenes of violent action. Needless to say, Ariel is liberated, and the necromancer destroyed.

The plot, then, is standard-issue quest fantasy fare, but the tale is enlivened not only by its unusual setting but also by its arresting reflexive awareness of its positioning within that genre. Since Pete was himself an avid reader of fantasy prior to the Change, as well as a member of the Society for Creative Anachronism, he is both equipped with a battery of allusions to the relevant literary sources—especially Tolkien—and also uniquely well-prepared for the return of a magical feudalism. Another intriguing element is Boyett's foregrounding of the sexual sub-texts of his story: Pete's relationship with Ariel is frankly eroticized, and he is ultimately forced to choose between her and a young woman, Shaughnessy, to whom he at last surrenders his virginity—and thus his ability to commune with the unicorn. The painful departure of Ariel at the end represents Pete's loss of naive innocence, and thus remarks, perhaps, a self-reflexive comment on the limitations of fantasy's wish-fulfilment of adolescent desires.

The Architect of Sleep is an altogether more accomplished performance, but it is tragically marred by the fact that it is clearly the first volume of a projected series the later instalments of which have yet to materialize. It is thus a frustrating read, as the story abruptly cuts off just as it is gathering momentum.

James Bentley, a slightly more grown-up version of Pete from *Ariel,* passes through a mysterious portal while on a spelunking expedition and finds himself in a world of highly evolved racoons. The first one he meets, a female he names Truck, turns out to be one of the eponymous Architects of Sleep—political leaders gifted with the power of prophetic dreaming—who was deposed in a shadowy coup led by her "Stripes," eugenically engineered racoon warriors, and who is seeking to build a coalition to regain her throne. Bentley, along with various sharply individualized racoons (for example, Zorba, a bibulous, curmudgeonly physician), come together to aid Truck in her quest, but the novel ends before any real action has commenced. *Architect* sets up an involving world peopled with a meticulously extrapolated form of life (lacking vocal cords, the racoons communicate via a complex sign language; since horses were never introduced to North America, they use llamas as pack animals, etc.), but then crashes to a halt before the reader gets a chance to explore it.

It is difficult to project Boyett's future career from the evidence of these two novels. On the one hand, he displays a particular strength for picaresque characterization, his "heroes" being convincingly mundane, brainy sorts thrown into scenarios wildly over their heads—a strength which shows especially well at novel length. On the other hand, he appears to have abandoned the writing of novels entirely. One of his recent short stories—"Emerald City Blues," in Jessica Horsting and James Van Hise's 1992 anthology *Midnight Graffiti*—even suggests an *envoi* to quest fantasy in favour of horror, with its hilariously gruesome depiction of a lost-in-space bomber pilot nuking the eponymous capital of Oz. One awaits Boyett's fresh work, whatever it might be, with a sense of eager bafflement.

—Rob Latham

BRADLEY, Marion Zimmer

Pseudonyms: Lee Chapman; John Dexter; Miriam Gardner; Valerie Graves; Morgan Ives; John J. Wells. **Nationality:** American. **Born:** Albany, New York, 3 June 1930. **Education:** New York State College for Teachers, 1946-48; Hardin-Simmons University, Abilene, Texas, B.A. 1964; University of California, Berkeley. **Family:** Married 1) Robert A. Bradley in 1949 (divorced 1963), one son; 2) Walter Henry Breen in 1964 (divorced 1990), one son and one daughter. **Career:** Singer and writer; editor, *Marion Zimmer Bradley's Fantasy Magazine,* since 1988. **Awards:** *Locus* award, 1984. **Agent:** Scovil Chichak Galen Literary Agency, 381 Park Avenue South, New York, NY 10016, USA. **Address:** c/o Friends of Darkover, P.O. Box 72, Berkeley, California 94701, USA.

FANTASY PUBLICATIONS

Novels

The Mists of Avalon. New York, Knopf, 1982; London, Joseph, 1983.

Web of Light. Norfolk, Virginia, Donning, 1983.
Web of Darkness. Norfolk, Virginia, Donning, 1983.
Web of Darkness (omnibus; includes *Web of Light, Web of Darkness*). Glasgow, Drew, 1985; as *The Fall of Atlantis,* New York, Baen, 1987.
Night's Daughter. New York, Ballantine, and London, Inner Circle, 1985.
The Firebrand. New York, Simon and Schuster, 1987; London, Joseph, 1988.
Black Trillium, with Julian May and Andre Norton. New York, Doubleday, 1990; London, Grafton, 1991.
The Forest House. London, Joseph, 1993; New York, Viking, 1994.

Short Stories

Lythande (with one story by Vonda N. McIntyre). New York, DAW, 1986; London, Sphere, 1988.

Other

Editor, *Greyhaven: An Anthology of Fantasy.* New York, DAW, 1983.
Editor, *Sword and Sorceress 1-10.* New York, DAW, 1984-93; vols. 1-5 published London, Headline, 1988-90.
Editor, *The Spells of Wonder.* New York, DAW, 1989.

<small>OTHER PUBLICATIONS</small>

Novels

The Door Through Space. New York, Ace, 1961; London, Arrow, 1979.
Seven from the Stars. New York, Ace, 1962.
The Planet Savers, The Sword of Aldones. New York, Ace, 1962; London, Arrow, 2 vols., 1979.
I Am a Lesbian (as Lee Chapman). Derby, Connecticut, Monarch, 1962.
The Strange Women (as Miriam Gardner). Derby, Connecticut, Monarch, 1962.
The Colors of Space (for children). Derby, Connecticut, Monarch, 1963; revised edition, Norfolk, Virginia, Donning, 1983; London, Hodder, 1989.
My Sister, My Love (as Miriam Gardner). Derby, Connecticut, Monarch, 1963.
Spare Her Heaven (as Morgan Ives). Derby, Connecticut, Monarch, 1963; abridged edition, as *Anything Goes,* Sydney, Stag, 1964.
The Bloody Sun. New York, Ace, 1964; London, Arrow, 1978; revised edition, New York, Ace, 1979.
Falcons of Narabedla. New York, Ace, 1964; London, Arrow, 1984.
Twilight Lovers (as Miriam Gardner). Derby, Connecticut, Monarch, 1964.
Star of Danger. New York, Ace, 1965; London, Arrow, 1978.
Castle Terror. New York, Lancer, 1965.
Knives of Desire (as Morgan Ives). San Diego, Corinth, 1966.
No Adam for Eve (as John Dexter). San Diego, Corinth, 1966.
Souvenir of Monique. New York, Ace, 1967.
Bluebeard's Daughter. New York, Lancer, 1968.
The Brass Dragon. New York, Ace, 1969; London, Methuen, 1978.
The Winds of Darkover. New York, Ace, 1970; London, Arrow, 1978.

The World Wreckers. New York, Ace, 1971; London, Arrow, 1979.
Darkover Landfall. New York, DAW, 1972; London, Arrow, 1978.
Witch Hill (as Valerie Graves). San Diego, Greenleaf, 1972.
Dark Satanic. New York, Berkley, 1972.
In the Steps of the Master (novelization of television play). New York, Grosset and Dunlap, 1973.
Hunters of the Red Moon. New York, DAW, 1973; London, Arrow, 1979.
The Spell Sword. New York, DAW, 1974; London, Arrow, 1978.
Endless Voyage. New York, Ace, 1975; revised edition, as *Endless Universe,* 1979.
The Heritage of Hastur. New York, DAW, 1975; London, Arrow, 1979.
Can Ellen Be Saved? (novelization of television play). New York, Grosset and Dunlap, 1975.
Drums of Darkness. New York, Ballantine, 1976.
The Shattered Chain. New York, DAW, 1976; London, Arrow, 1978.
The Forbidden Tower. New York, DAW, 1977; London, Prior, 1979.
Stormqueen. New York, DAW, 1978; London, Arrow, 1980.
The Ruins of Isis. Norfolk, Virginia, Donning, 1978; London, Arrow, 1980.
The Survivors, with Paul Edwin Zimmer. New York, DAW, 1979; London, Arrow, 1985.
The Catch Trap. New York, Ballantine, 1979; London, Sphere, 1986.
The House Between the Worlds. New York, Doubleday, 1980; revised edition, New York, Del Rey, 1981.
Two to Conquer. New York, DAW, 1980; London, Arrow, 1982.
Survey Ship. New York, Ace, 1980.
Sharra's Exile. New York, DAW, 1981; London, Arrow, 1983.
Hawkmistress. New York, DAW, 1982; London, Arrow, 1985.
Thendara House. New York, DAW, 1983; London, Arrow, 1985.
The Inheritor. New York, Tor, 1984.
City of Sorcery. New York, DAW, 1984; London, Arrow, 1986.
Warrior Woman. New York, DAW, 1985; London, Arrow, 1987.
The Heirs of Hammerfell. New York, DAW, 1989; London, Legend, 1991.
Rediscovery: A Darkover Novel, with Mercedes Lackey. New York, DAW, 1993.

Short Stories

The Dark Intruder and Other Stories. New York, Ace, 1964.
The Jewel of Arwen. Baltimore, T-K Graphics, 1974.
The Parting of Arwen. Baltimore, T-K Graphics, 1974.
The Best of Marion Zimmer Bradley, edited by Martin H. Greenberg. Chicago, Academy Chicago, 1985; London, Sphere, 1990; revised edition, as *Jamie and Other Stories: The Best of Marion Zimmer Bradley,* Chicago, Academy Chicago, 1993.

Other

The Rivendell Suite. Privately printed, 1959.
A Complete, Cumulative Checklist of Lesbian, Variant, and Homosexual Fiction. Privately printed, 1960.
Men, Halflings, and Hero-Worship. Baltimore, T-K Graphics, 1973.
The Necessity for Beauty: Robert W. Chambers and the Romantic Tradition. Baltimore, T-K Graphics, 1974.

Editor, with the Friends of Darkover, *The Keeper's Price.* New York, DAW, 1980.

Editor, with the Friends of Darkover, *Sword of Chaos*. New York, DAW, 1982.

Editor, with the Friends of Darkover, *Free Amazons of Darkover*. New York, DAW, 1985.

Editor, with the Friends of Darkover, *The Other Side of the Mirror*. New York, DAW, 1987.

Editor, with the Friends of Darkover, *Red Sun of Darkover*. New York, DAW, 1987.

Editor, with the Friends of Darkover, *Four Moons of Darkover*. New York, DAW, 1988.

Editor, with the Friends of Darkover, *Domains of Darkover*. New York, DAW, 1990.

Editor, with the Friends of Darkover, *Renunciates of Darkover*. New York, DAW, 1991.

Editor, with the Friends of Darkover, *Leroni of Darkover*. New York, DAW, 1991.

Editor, with the Friends of Darkover, *Towers of Darkover*. New York, DAW, 1993.

Editor, with the Friends of Darkover, *Snows of Darkover*. New York, DAW, 1994.

Translator, *El Villano in su Rincon,* by Lope de Vega. Privately printed, 1971.

*

Bibliographies: *Leigh Brackett, Marion Zimmer Bradley, Anne McCaffrey: A Primary and Secondary Bibliography* by Rosemarie Arbur, Boston, Hall, 1982; *Marion Zimmer Bradley, Mistress of Magic: A Working Bibliography* by Phil Stephensen-Payne and Gordon Benson, Jr., Leeds, Yorkshire, Galactic Central, 1991.

Manuscript Collection: Boston University.

Critical Studies: *The Darkover Concordance: A Reader's Guide* by Walter Breen, Berkeley, California, Pennyfarthing Press, 1979; *Marion Zimmer Bradley* by Rosemarie Arbur, Mercer Island, Washington, Starmont House, 1985.

*   *   *

Although Bradley is now best known for her novel *The Mists of Avalon,* her reputation among fantasy readers rests primarily upon her Darkover novels—which arguably are not fantasy at all. The Darkover series is, indeed, a test case for definitions of the two genres. "The series could almost be read as science fiction," states the entry in Frank N. Magill's *Survey of Modern Fantasy Literature* (1983, vol. 1, p. 342); but the books "violate the commitment to logical extrapolation characteristic of pure science fiction". So do many other science-fiction novels: the Darkover books are in fact technically sf, but not "pure" sf. They belong to a sub-genre of sf which has been called "planetary romance," going back in a direct line to some of Bradley's earliest inspirations, pioneer women writers of science fantasy such as C. L. Moore and Leigh Brackett as well as writers of exotic adventure such as Rider Haggard and Anthony Hope. The Darkover series has a science-fictional rationale, but much of it has a fantasy feel. The action takes place on Darkover, a planet settled by humans and later rediscovered by the Terran Empire, but we have many of the familiar trappings of fantasy—a pseudo-medieval society, swordplay, sorcery, an elf-like race called the *chieri*. The novels are frequently about questing or com-

ing of age, as in fantasy, and not problem-solving, which is more common to science fiction.

If read in order of internal chronology the first novel is *Darkover Landfall,* which tells how humans crashland on an alien planet, meet the elf-like inhabitants, and experience the telepathic-inducing effects of the local flora. Thereafter several novels, such as *Stormqueen* and *Hawkmistress* explore the pseudo-medieval world of Darkover six centuries and more after the initial settlement: these are the novels that are closest to heroic fantasy. *Two to Conquer* is about the Compact, which ends the wars of the Ages of Chaos and outlaws the use of psychic weapons. Three centuries later comes the return of the Terrans, and several novels concerning the struggle between Darkovans and Terrans.

Different impressions of Darkover emerge if one reads the series in the order of writing rather than in the internal chronological order. The earliest published novels, beginning with *The Sword of Aldones* and *The Planet Savers* (both published in book form in 1962, but going back to drafts written while Bradley was 15), were told from the point of view of the Terran Empire. The protagonists were either earthmen who were living in the recently established colony, or else people whose allegiance was split between the technologically oriented earthmen and the more "primitive" descendants of the first earth colonists, with their strong concepts of honour and duty. A major theme of these early novels is questioning of such concepts as "progress" and "civilization." Even in the first novel, however, the fantasy trappings were evident: as in so many modern fantasy novels, two swords with supernormal powers are at the heart of the plot. Although the matrix jewel, a crystal with the power to concentrate psychic power, is amenable to scientific explanation—and the development of "matrix technology" is discussed in a number of the later novels—it is essentially an object surrounded with all the mystique associated with magical objects in works of fantasy.

Initially Bradley did not think in terms of writing a series, and she paid very little attention to internal consistency. Only when the books became popular, and the publisher Donald Wollheim began pressing her for more, did she begin constructing Darkover and its various societies with care. Eventually she rewrote the earliest book totally to fit in with her developed ideas: *The Sword of Aldones* became *Sharra's Exile.* The turning point was the early 1970s. Bradley had become alienated from the type of science fiction then being written, but intrigued by the possibilities of fantasy, which was then becoming a popular genre, and particularly pseudo-medievalist fantasy (she herself had become closely involved with the Society of Creative Anachronism). Wollheim also allowed her to write much longer novels (beginning with *The Heritage of Hastur*); the novels themselves became much more complex in terms of plot and psychological depth.

The other developments of the early 1970s which influenced the development of Darkover were the growth of feminism and an increasing openness about sex. Even as early as *The Sword of Aldones* Bradley had a strong female who was called an Amazon; in *The World Wreckers* she tentatively introduced a male homosexual relationship. But later in the 1970s and 1980s Bradley developed and strengthened her female characters, explored both gay and lesbian relationships, and investigated the question of women's freedom and independence, above all in *The Shattered Chain* where she not only has a society of women chained by men, but also a society of women who have sworn an Oath of Renunciation, the Renunciates or Free Amazons. Although attacked by conservative men and radical women, these novels did much to establish her popularity, particularly among women. Darkover had changed from being a series of colourful adventure novels into a means of writing, tangentially, about some of the most fundamental aspects of human relationships.

The Darkover series has attracted a devoted following, just like the television series *Star Trek,* complete with its fanzines, Darkover conventions and so on. As with *Star Trek,* most of the fans (the Friends of Darkover) are women; as with *Star Trek,* devotion frequently takes the form of amateur fiction set in the same universe. Much of this fiction is published in fanzines; it is significant that a large proportion of them choose to feature Free Amazons. (Bradley has noted, with some bemusement, that some of her fans have legally changed their names to those of Free Amazons.) Bradley herself has published a number of anthologies of Darkover stories written by other people.

Bradley has written other works involving fantasy, although some of them could be regarded as historical novels, notably a number of retellings of well-known tales. *Night's Daughter* is a spirited retelling of the story of Mozart's *Magic Flute,* with rather more internal logic than the original story. *The Forest House* continues her operatic interests, being an expanded version of Bellini's *Norma,* set in ancient Britain at the time of the Roman conquest. *The Firebrand* is the Trojan War seen from the viewpoint of Kassandra, with the Bradleian addition of a struggle between the ancient worship of the Earth Mother and a more recent patriarchal pantheon of gods. This was a formula which had already served Bradley well: her best-selling book, *The Mists of Avalon,* sees the Arthurian legend from the viewpoint of Guinevere and the other women of the story, and places Arthur against the background of the conflict between the matriarchal and more "natural" paganism of the Celts and the patriarchal and repressive new religion of the Christians.

Other fantasies by Bradley include two novels about the magic of ancient Atlantis, *Web of Light* and *Web of Darkness* (apparently based on unpublished juvenilia from the 1940s); and *Black Trillium,* with Julian May and Andre Norton, a standard quest-fantasy which opens a series, the other volumes of which to date have been written by May and Norton.

—Edward James

BRADSHAW, Gillian (Marucha)

Nationality: American. **Born:** Virginia, 14 May 1956. **Education:** University of Michigan, Ann Arbor (Hopwood award, 1977), B.A. (honors) 1977; Newnham College, Cambridge, M.A. 1979. **Family:** Married Robin Christopher Ball in 1981. **Address:** c/o Houghton Mifflin Company, 2 Park Street, Boston, MA 02108, USA.

FANTASY PUBLICATIONS

Novels (series: Arthurian Cycle)

Hawk of May (Arthurian Cycle). New York, Simon and Schuster, 1980; London, Eyre Methuen, 1981.

Kingdom of Summer (Arthurian Cycle). New York, Simon and Schuster, and London, Eyre Methuen, 1981.
In Winter's Shadow (Arthurian Cycle). New York, Simon and Schuster, and London, Methuen, 1982.
Down the Long Wind: The Magical Trilogy of Arthurian Britain (omnibus; includes *Hawk of May, Kingdom of Summer, In Winter's Shadow*). London, Methuen, 1988.
Horses of Heaven. New York, Doubleday, 1991.
The Dragon and the Thief. New York, Greenwillow, 1991.
The Land of Gold. New York, Greenwillow, 1992.
Beyond the North Wind. New York, Greenwillow, 1993.

OTHER PUBLICATIONS

Novels

The Beacon at Alexandria. Boston, Houghton Mifflin, 1986; London, Methuen, 1987.
The Bearkeeper's Daughter. Boston, Houghton Mifflin, 1987; London, Methuen, 1988.
Imperial Purple. Boston, Houghton Mifflin, 1989; as *The Colour of Power,* London, Methuen, 1989.

*   *   *

The story of Arthur and the Matter of Britain has proved remarkably attractive to fantasy writers in the last 20 years. In particular, it has become increasingly popular to tell the story from a viewpoint which does not appear in the legends. Gillian Bradshaw chose Gawain as the focus for her trilogy, although only the first book of the three is told directly from his point of view.

In *Hawk of May,* Bradshaw tells Gawain's, or Gwalchmai's, own story. As a child, he is a disappointment to his warrior father, Lot of Orkney, preferring the gentler arts of music and poetry. His mother, Morgause, is in this version of the story Uther's legitimate daughter and determined to be revenged on Arthur for taking Uther's kingdom. She is a witch with deep-laid plans and has already committed incest with the unwitting Arthur to produce Medraut. She attempts to bind Gwalchmai to her by teaching him to read and write, and initiating him into the magical black arts.

Gwalchmai finally turns against his mother and is taken magically to the Island of the Blessed where he meets Lugh, the Sun God, and pledges himself to the service of the Light, which Arthur also serves. Arthur, however, refuses to take Gwalchmai into his warband, the Family, and much of the book is taken up with Gwalchmai trying desperately to rid himself of the rumours of magic which surround him. Threading through the book is a complex discussion of battle between Light and Darkness, showing that the way of Light is not only the province of the Christian church in Arthur's Britain.

The Britain portrayed by Bradshaw is less the shifting allegorical landscape of the medieval writers, more the product of historical research; the Romans have fled from the country but many inhabitants still look back to this time of order and prosperity with nostalgia. Arthur is a warleader, sometimes styled Emperor in the old Roman way, although he is but one among many kings in a complex and constantly shifting series of political alignments.

The second volume of the trilogy, *The Kingdom of Summer,* is told through the eyes of Rhys ap Sion, a farmer who follows Gwalchmai to Camlann and becomes his body servant. From him we hear the story of Gwalchmai's search for a woman he has wronged in the past, a story with no precedent in medieval sources. Bradshaw's Gwalchmai is an earnest and conscientious man, a scholar and diplomat, a characterization at odds with some medieval sources, and she presents him as genuinely contrite for the wrongs he did Elidan by slaying her brother.

As Gwalchmai searches for Elidan he encounters once again his mother, Morgause, and his young half-brother Medraut, who has become a sorcerer and is already scheming to topple Arthur. As Champion of Light he challenges and defeats the Queen of Air and Darkness. Morgause is slain by Agravain, Gwalchmai's older brother, and one is left to assume that the threat to the kingdom has been removed. Gwalchmai is finally reunited with Elidan but she cannot forgive him.

The emphasis has shifted, by this time, from the battle between Dark and Light as abstract powers embodied in Gwalchmai, Arthur and Morgause, to the more familiar ground of the battle for supremacy between Arthur and his son and nephew Medraut, and as the title of the third book, *In Winter's Shadow,* suggests, it is concerned with the destruction of Arthur's hard-won kingdom.

Gwynhwyfar tells this portion of the story. Bradshaw portrays her as a strong and capable woman who runs Arthur's kingdom while he leads the army, and suggests that it is her private tragedies which precipitate the final downfall of the kingdom. Harried by her family, which wants preferment because of her status, haunted by her inability to have children, and well aware of The mischief being wrought by Medraut, she tries to poison him but is detected in the effort. Medraut in turn accuses her, rightly, of adultery with Bedwyr and the kingdom quickly divides into factions. Bedwyr, banished from the kingdom, carries out an ill-fated rescue attempt, killing Gwalchmai's recently discovered son, Gwyn, and taking Gwynhwyfar to Brittany, from whence she escapes to Arthur.In the final battle, Medraut dies, but Arthur's body is never found; thus Bradshaw tacitly acknowledges the idea of Arthur as the once and future king without compromising her attempt to treat the story more historically than some writers have favoured. Among the many modern versions of the Arthurian legends, Bradshaw's novels stand out for their sensitive exploration of well-known themes, and a genuine attempt to bring something fresh to the telling. Her stories are gripping and plausible, worthy additions to the modern canon.

Several of Bradshaw's subsequent books, such as *The Beacon at Alexandria,* are "straight" historical novels based on the recorded facts of Graeco-Roman or early medieval times. However, she has returned to historical fantasy more recently with the magical young-adult tales *The Dragon and the Thief,* set in ancient Egypt, and *Beyond the North Wind,* set in the ancient Greek world. The adult novel *Horses of Heaven,* which takes place in Afghanistan around 150 BC, also has fantasy elements.

—Maureen Speller

BRAMAH, Ernest

Pseudonym of Ernest Bramah Smith. **Nationality:** British. **Born:** near Manchester, Lancashire, 20 March 1868. **Education:** Manchester Grammar School. **Family:** Married Lucie Maisie Barker in 1897. **Career:** Farmer for three years; worked on a provincial newspaper, then secretary to Jerome K. Jerome, and staff member on Jerome's magazine *To-day*; editor, *The Minster,* London, 1895-96. **Died:** 27 June 1942.

FANTASY PUBLICATIONS

Novels (series: Kai Lung in all books)

Kai Lung's Golden Hours. London, Grant Richards, 1922; New York, Doran, 1923.
Kai Lung Unrolls His Mat. London, Richards Press, and New York, Doubleday, 1928.
The Moon of Much Gladness. London, Cassell, 1932; as *The Return of Kai Lung,* New York, Sheridan, 1938.

Short Stories

The Wallet of Kai Lung. London, Grant Richards, and Boston, Page, 1900.
The Story of Wan and the Remarkable Shrub and The Story of Ching-Kwei and the Destinies. New York, Doubleday, 1927; in *Kai Lung Unrolls His Mat,* 1928.
Kai Lung Beneath the Mulberry Tree. London, Richards Press, 1940.
Kai Lung: Six. Tacoma, Washington, Non-Profit Press, 1974.

OTHER PUBLICATIONS

Novels

What Might Have Been: The Story of a Social War. London, Murray, 1907; as *The Secret of the League,* London, Nelson, 1909.
The Bravo of London. London, Cassell, 1934.

Short Stories

The Mirror of Kong Ho. London, Chapman and Hall, 1905; New York, Doubleday, 1930.
Max Carrados. London, Methuen, 1914; Westport, Connecticut, Hyperion, 1975.
The Eyes of Max Carrados. London, Grant Richards, 1923; New York, Doran, 1924.
The Specimen Case. London, Hodder and Stoughton, 1924; New York, Doran, 1925.
Max Carrados Mysteries. London, Hodder and Stoughton, 1927; Baltimore, Penguin, 1964.
A Little Flutter. London, Cassell, 1930.
Best Max Carrados Detective Stories, edited by E. F. Bleiler. New York, Dover, 1972.

Other

English Farming and Why I Turned It Up. London, Leadenhall, 1894.
A Guide to the Varieties and Rarity of English Regal Copper Coins: Charles II-Victoria, 1671-1860. London, Methuen, 1929.

*

Bibliography: "Some Uncollected Authors," in *Book Collector 13* (London), 1964, and "A Bramah Biographer's Dilemma," in *American Book Collector 15* (Chicago), 1964, both by William White.

Manuscript Collections: Humanities Research Center, University of Texas, Austin; University of Illinois Library.

*   *   *

Ernest Bramah's fantasies are set in the definitive version of that ancient China that we all know but which never existed, replete with dragons, enchanters, spirits, corrupt mandarins, magical transformations and unfailing conversational politesse even in the most extreme situations. (After a mishap in a dark dungeon: "If it is not altogether necessary for your refined convenience that you stand on this one's face, he for his part would willingly forego the esteemed honour.")

The polished, professional storyteller Kai Lung relates each Oriental tale and also figures in framing narratives which make it possible to call *Kai Lung's Golden Hours* and *Kai Lung Unrolls His Mat* novels with inset stories, rather than collections. *The Moon of Much Gladness,* a genuine novel spoofing contemporary Western detective fiction in the old-Chinese setting, is unusual in that Kai Lung does not appear; the title page claims the whole book to be one of his narrations.

Bramah's comic method is founded on the trite-seeming fact that the flowery phrases of traditional Chinese etiquette sound irresistibly silly when translated into literal English equivalents. Even murderous brigands are apt to introduce themselves with great self-deprecation: "I am indeed Lin Yi . . . It is a dignified position to occupy, and one for which I am quite incompetent."

This seems a simple trick for a paragraph or two, but to maintain the unwavering artificial syntax and diction for a whole story—let alone a novel—requires impressive resources of vocabulary, circumlocution and euphemism. Bramah/Kai Lung can always find another and more ludicrous way of putting a commonplace sentiment; repeated phrases are quite rare. He is also a good coiner of quotable aphorisms (". . . there are few situations in life that cannot be honourably settled, and without loss of time, either by suicide, a bag of gold, or by thrusting a despised antagonist over the edge of a precipice on a dark night") and underhand ironies: ". . . the elder and less attractive of the maidens fled, uttering loud and continuous cries of apprehension in order to conceal the direction of her flight."

Kai Lung himself lives by the rules of our natural world; excepting some ambiguous prophecies, fantasy and the supernatural are relegated to the stories he tells. In *The Wallet,* "The Transmutation of Ling" offers a tricky variant of the Philosopher's Stone, a potion which the hero finds too late has converted his flesh to latent gold: when hairs or fingernails are cut off and "die," they transmute into pure gold. Trying to raise money on the prospect of becoming, posthumously, a large mass of treasure, Ling lets a shady entrepreneur float him on the market as The Ling (After Death) Without Much Risk Assembly, and the plot thickens. . . . In the same book, "The Vision of Yin" allows its hero a dubiously inspirational encounter with all China's past emperors.

In *Golden Hours,* "Ning, the Captive God, and the Dreams that Mark His Race" shows celestial *Realpolitik* and how a minor god may come to grief among mortals owing to wine, women and carelessness. "Lao Ting and the Luminous Insect" features a struggling student who can't afford a lamp to study after dark and is assisted by kindly fireflies. (The intricate Chinese system of competitive examinations for public posts is a recurring comic theme.) "Chang Tao, Melodious Vision and the Dragon" turns on Chinese dragons' ability to take human form; Chang Tao is challenged to detect whether the dragon Pe-lung's beautiful daughter is truly dragon-ish, and does so by an undisclosed investigation involving the fact that even when human-shaped all dragons possess a vestigial tail . . . Pe-lung seems fraught by doubts as to exactly how, during a long dark night, Chang Tao reached his correct decision.

In *Kai Lung Unrolls His Mat,* "Lin Ho and the Treasure of Fang-tso" reworks the popular theme of identity exchange, as unmuscular Lin Ho accidentally swaps bodies for a time with a huge and fearsome criminal who is himself pursued by a huger and more fearsome one. "Kin Weng and the Miraculous Tusk" has derring-do in a craft competition where an envious rival changes the exhibit labels to take credit for the perfect white bird carved from the tusk, only for Kin Weng's magically assisted carving to prove so lifelike that it takes flight before the judging. "The Great Sky Lantern" goes back to the early, chaotic days of the world, and a rash undertaking to bring back a piece of the Moon to make a lady's comb. Ruthless training is necessary, with our hero shackled to giant rocks and taunted with food just out of reach—until he develops the strength to uproot the rocks and drag them after him, even up precipices: thus trained, he finds that one leap without the hindering rocks can take him to the skies. . . .

Other, less overtly fantastic tales disclose surprising origins for willow-pattern plates, bamboo, chess, and the "remarkable shrub" whose dried leaves yield tea. Anachronistic jokes often appear, like the satire on trade unions in "Wong Ts'in and the Willow Plate Embellishment." Occasionally the good-humoured irony turns savage, and a few stories are (without abandoning Oriental polish) disconcertingly tragic or bitter.

Ernest Bramah also wrote in a different and very English vein about the blind detective Max Carrados. In the classic mystery tradition, Carrados's exploits are for the most part strictly rational—with exceptions, like the odd case where sinister emanations from a plague pit travel along the power-lines to emerge from a wall socket and trouble a child's dreams, or where a good-luck charm that actually seems to work is delicately identified by the expert numismatist Carrados as a nail from the True Cross.

Other authors could feasibly have written the detective stories; Kai Lung remains a unique and enduring creation.

—David Langford

BRAUTIGAN, Richard

Nationality: American. **Born:** 30 January 1933 in Tacoma, Washington. **Died:** 1984.

FANTASY PUBLICATIONS

Novels

In Watermelon Sugar. San Francisco, Four Seasons, 1964; London, Cape, 1970.

The Abortion: An Historical Romance 1966. New York, Simon and Schuster, 1971; London, Cape, 1973.

The Hawkline Monster: A Gothic Western. New York, Simon and Schuster, 1974; London, Cape, 1975.

Willard and His Bowling Trophies: A Perverse Mystery. New York, Simon and Schuster, 1976; London, Cape, 1976.

Sombrero Fallout: A Japanese Novel. New York, Simon and Schuster, 1976; London, Cape, 1977.

Dreaming of Babylon: A Private Eye Novel 1942. New York, Delacorte, 1977; London, Cape, 1978.

The Tokyo-Montana Express. New York, Delacorte, 1980; London, Cape, 1981.

OTHER PUBLICATIONS

Novels

A Confederate General from Big Sur. New York, Grove Press, 1965; London, Cape, 1970.

Trout Fishing in America. San Francisco, Four Seasons, 1967; London, Cape, 1970.

Short Stories

Revenge of the Lawn: Stories 1962-1970. New York, Simon and Schuster, 1971; London, Cape, 1972.

Uncollected Short Stories

"Football," in *Tri-Quarterly,* Winter, 1976.

"Great Golden Telescope," in *Redbook,* August, 1979.

Poetry

The Return of the Rivers. San Francisco, Inferno Press, 1957.

The Galilee Hitch-Hiker. San Francisco, White Rabbit Press, 1958.

Lay the Marble Tea: Twenty-Four Poems. San Francisco, Carp Press, 1959.

The Octopus Frontier. San Francisco, Carp Press, 1960.

All Watched Over by Machines of Loving Grace. San Francisco, Communication, 1967.

Please Plant This Book. San Francisco, MacKintosh, 1968.

The Pill Versus the Springhill Mine Disaster (Poems 1957-1968). San Francisco, Four Seasons, 1968; London, Cape, 1970.

The San Francisco Weather Report. Goleta, California, Unicorn, 1969.

Rommel Drives on Deep into Egypt. New York, Delacorte, 1970.

Loading Mercury with a Pitchfork. New York, Simon and Schuster, 1975.

June 30th, June 30th. New York, Delacorte, 1978.

*

Critical Studies: *Richard Brautigan,* by Terence Malley, New York, Warner, 1972.

*   *   *

Richard Brautigan's delightful, whimsical tales have much in common (simple vocabulary, repetitions) with traditional oral storytelling. And like traditional stories, they drift in and out of fantasy without really noticing there is anything different in what they do.

In the 1960s and early 70s, Brautigan combined postmodernist techniques with a hippy ethic. His first books were gentle comedies about contemporary America such as *A Confederate General from Big Sur* and *Trout Fishing in America,* but even in these books there is a distinct air of unreality, for instance in the curious hut which is too small to stand up in and which has one wall missing, which the narrator and his companions occupy in *A Confederate General from Big Sur.* And as the narrator imagines the Civil War adventures of his friend's ancestor, culminating in the arrival of a brigade of Indians from Big Sur to aid Lee at the Battle of the Wilderness, the novel drifts towards fantasy.

Later, Brautigan's technique tended towards putting incompatible styles together. *The Hawkline Monster,* for instance, is as its subtitle suggests a combination of Gothic novel and Western. As such it has distinct fantastical elements. Greer and Cameron, two gunmen, are lured by an Indian girl, Magic Child, to a remote house in Oregon. Their job is to kill an unspecified monster which lurks in ice caverns beneath the house. But strange things happen. Despite the heat of summer, Hawkline Manor is surrounded by permafrost and freezing cold. Magic Child changes into the exact twin of Miss Hawkline who runs the house. The giant butler dies and is transmogrified into a dwarf. The gunmen learn that the monster is the result of experiments with "The Chemicals" carried out by Professor Hawkline, who has since disappeared. But they manage to identify the villain as an animated and malicious point of light. By destroying the light they resurrect the Professor and the butler.

The Hawkline Monster is the most weird of Brautigan's novels, easily living up to its Gothic tag, but the character of the Western gunmen, the sense that this is the remote West in 1902, is sustained throughout the book. Though his books are playful, often comic, he did tend to maintain a core of reality running through them, the fantasy coming in a drift away from this reality. *Dreaming of Babylon,* for instance, is a typical private-eye story set in 1942. The narrator has had no client for months, and is so poor that he cannot afford bullets for his gun. When a beautiful woman hires him he thinks his luck has turned, but he finds himself caught in complex plot involving stealing a body from the morgue while gangsters try to steal the body from him. It is a clever pastiche of *film noir,* but the downfall of the detective, Card, is due to his dreaming of Babylon. The novel is punctuated with Card's fantasies involving baseball teams, villainous scientists, and private detectives in the Babylon of Nebuchadnezzar.

Brautigan's most overt fantasy, however, is also his weakest book. *In Watermelon Sugar* is set in a presumably post-holocaust world—there are hints of a lost civilization, and the setting for most of the story is called iDEATH, but nothing definite is said about what has happened. It is a largely plotless book, a series of glimpses of life in this idyllic rural world where practically everyone is nice, friendly and as sickly-sweet as the title. It is an attempt to present the hippy ideal and like that ideal did not long survive its era.

Brautigan's fall from popularity eventually led to his suicide in 1984. But his better books—*The Hawkline Monster, A Confederate General from Big Sur*—have a lasting appeal, and their influence can be seen in the work of a new generation of postmodernist writers such as Mark Amerika and William Vollman. But his lasting memorial is perhaps his most attractive fantasy, the library of unpublished books which he contemplated in *The Abortion* has been turned into reality in the Mayonnaise Library in a small town in New England.

—Paul Kincaid

BRENNER, Mayer Alan

Pseudonym: Rick North. **Nationality:** American. **Born:** Los Angeles, 3 May 1956. **Education:** University of California, Los Angeles, 1974-78, B.S. Engineering, Summa Cum Laude; UCLA Medical School, 1978-82, M.D. **Family:** Married Sandra Gail Daye in 1983; one daughter. **Career:** Designer, computer software and systems for health care. **Agent:** Joshua Bilmes, Scott Meredith Literary Agency, 845 Third Avenue, New York, NY 10022, USA. **Address:** 1815 Westholme Avenue, #4, Los Angeles, California 90025, USA.

FANTASY PUBLICATIONS

Novels (series: Dance of the Gods in all books)

Catastrophe's Spell. New York, DAW, 1989.
Spell of Intrigue. New York, DAW, 1990.
Spell of Fate. New York, DAW, 1992.
Spell of Apocalypse. New York, DAW, 1994.

OTHER PUBLICATIONS

Novels

Space Pioneers (as Rick North). New York, Zebra, 1991.

*

Mayer Alan Brenner comments:

In writing the Dance of the Gods sequence, my purpose was to comment on certain conventions of modern fantasy in particular and genre fiction in general: What makes magic "good" and technology "bad" (and then gives magic the typical colours of black and white)? Why are good and evil so easy to determine in fantasy fiction and so hard in real life? Why is genre fiction so neat and circumscribed, with conflicts ending in clear closure and characters resolving all doubts and achieving catharsis? What about the conflict between the inherent polytheism of having explicit gods hanging around and the monotheism our own world holds in high regard? Of course, no commentary is worth a jot if it isn't delivered through interesting characters and engrossing activities, so I've done my best to provide those as well.

Accordingly, the Dance of the Gods is set in what appears at the outset to be a standard pseudo-medieval setting with drifts of feudalism around the edges; the discipline and economic role of magic replaces that of technology in our own milieu, and the gods are incarnate actors on the human stage. Against this background, an array of typical and not-so-typical characters act out their intrigue-laden action-adventure plots. It gradually becomes apparent that none of them are heroes or villains, exactly, but regardless of that it is much safer to be somewhere else whenever any of them are around. As their increasingly grandiose stratagems collide against each other, the question of whether anyone really knows what they are doing—and whether any of it is at all a good idea—looms much larger than the matter of good guys and bad, anyway.

Their attitude toward magic, too, is that of user to tool. They may be impressed by it, especially when something flashy and new is involved, but they don't tend to think of it as something, well, "magical." After all, how many people in our own world are in awe of their toaster, especially after it's been around for a while and has gotten a bit bashed around the edges, with the cord perhaps too dangerously frayed? Since magic occupies the same ecological niche in these novels as technology in ours, it would make sense to say the same point of view applies. After all, people are still people, whether the beach where they find themselves washed up is ours or that of fantasy.

*   *   *

Funny fantasy has become a very popular subset of the genre in recent years, attracting writers of varying skills, and resulting in work that ranges from the sublime to the absurd. At the opposite end of the spectrum from outright farce is the humorous adventure story, a particularly difficult form because authors must find the right balance between the two contending elements. Too much humour and the reader no longer worries about the protagonist. Too little and the occasional jokes become little more than a distraction from the major plot. Few writers have the ability of Terry Pratchett or Esther Friesner to sustain a comedic mood over works of novel length, and those who do frequently end up repeating the same jokes.

Mayer Alan Brenner is one of those who has found the delicate path between the two extremes, and whose humour seems fresh and original throughout. *Catastrophe's Spell,* part of the ongoing series that makes up the body of the author's published work, is the first adventure of Maximilian the Vaguely Disreputable, an unlikely hero who is drawn into a maze of problems when several of his friends fall prey to a battle among sorcerous powers. Max sets off to rescue them, a serious character in the midst of some definitely non-serious situations—including a castle that moves of its own volition and at the most inopportune moments, a wizard who gets violently ill whenever he casts a spell, a supernatural sword with unusual properties, and the wayward spells cast by a brace of inept magicians. Max maintains his demeanour throughout, and the absurd situations are rendered just credibly enough to hold up the serious side of the tale.

The Dance of the Gods series continued with *Spell of Intrigue.* Max is headed back to the peaceful town of Oolsmouth after rescuing his friends, but right in the way of a new carload of trouble. Some human or inhuman power has been manipulating the commerce of the town, and now they have seized control of a prominent businessman's holdings and launched magical attacks against his shipping. Max and his allies all travel their separate ways back to Oolsmouth, and each must overcome wacky obstacles to get there.

The power behind the scenes is an unruly god, we learn in due course, secretly violating the rules of godhood to interfere in earthly matters for his own aggrandizement. Ultimately he is discovered through the good offices of Max and his cohorts, and sentenced to mortality by his peers. Dollops of genuinely funny humour enliven the book, although overall it has a much more serious tone than its predecessor, a light-hearted adventure story that moves rapidly from character to character, drawing the reader through a series of merry chases and battles.

Spell of Fate, the longest title in the series and the first not to be a complete story in itself, pursues the same theme. Max and his friends are now interested in overthrowing the gods entirely so that they will be forever free of their erratic interference. To do so, they must learn a new kind of magic that will give them the power to influence the realm of the gods. They are aided in their quest by the constant quarrelling among the gods, which prevents them from paying a great deal of attention to the plans of mere mortals.

The planned crowning of a new emperor becomes the focal point for the struggle. Brenner uses an interesting device to provide us the villain's point of view; the narrator is possessed by the chief villain, so we get to see much of the story through the eyes of Max's most deadly enemy. The third volume concludes with only a limited success for our heroes, as the story resumes immediately in *Spell of Apocalypse*.

The Great Karlini, Max's sorcerous ally, is one of the major players in the struggle for power among mortals and gods in the imperial city of Peridol. Max also must decide whether the secrets of magic should be reserved for the few who have plumbed its depths or provided to the populace at large. Unfortunately, spells in the hands of the untrained often have unpleasant, though extremely humorous, consequences. Once again, Brenner strikes a balance between tension and laughter, as the various contending forces gather their resources for the ultimate battle.

To date, Brenner has remained content to write within the single universe of Max and his friends, and he has done so with considerable success. His clear style and highly inventive humour provide otherwise conventional adventure stories with a depth of detail and originality that separates them from the great mass of modern fantasy novels. Brenner has a definite gift for thinking up absurd situations and making them seem plausible. Further adventures are probably on the way, and there's little doubt that there's an active, eager audience waiting for them.

—Don D'Ammassa

BRIGGS, K(atharine) M(ary)

Nationality: British. **Born:** London, 8 November 1898. **Education:** Lansdowne House; Lady Margaret Hall, Oxford, M.A. 1923; Ph.D. 1952. **Military Service:** Women's Auxiliary Air Force, 1941-45. **Career:** Freelance writer and folklorist; headed an amateur theatrical touring company for 15 years; visiting professor, University of Pennsylvania, Philadelphia, 1970, and University of California, Berkeley, 1973. President, Folklore Society of London, 1967-70. **Awards:** D.Litt.: Oxford University, 1969. **Died:** 15 October 1980.

FANTASY PUBLICATIONS

Novels

Hobberdy Dick. London, Eyre and Spottiswoode, 1955; New York, Greenwillow, 1977.
Kate Crackernuts. Oxford, Alden Press, 1963; revised edition, London, Kestrel, and New York, Greenwillow, 1979.

Fiction for Children

The Legend of Maiden-Hair. London, Stockwell, 1915.
The Witches' Ride, illustrated by Winifred Briggs. Dunkeld, Perthshire, Capricornus, 1937.

The Prince, the Fox, and the Dragon, illustrated by Winifred Briggs. Dunkeld, Perthshire, Capricornus, 1938.

Plays

Stories Arranged for Mime (The Golden Goose; Whuppity Stories; Jesper, Who Herded Hares). Dunkeld, Perthshire, Capricornus, 3 vols., 1937.

Other

The Personnel of Fairyland: A Short Account of the Fairy People of Great Britain for Those Who Tell Stories to Children. Oxford, Alden Press, 1953; Cambridge, Massachusetts, Bentley, 1954.
The Anatomy of Puck: An Examination of Fairy Beliefs among Shakespeare's Contemporaries and Successors. London, Routledge, 1959; New York, Arno Press, 1977.
Pale Hecate's Team: An Examination of the Beliefs on Witchcraft and Magic among Shakespeare's Contemporaries and His Immediate Successors. London, Routledge, and New York, Humanities Press, 1962.
The Fairies in Tradition and Literature. London, Routledge, 1967; as *The Fairies in English Tradition and Literature,* Chicago, University of Chicago Press, 1967.
A Dictionary of British Folk-tales in the English Language: Folk Narratives. London, Routledge, 2 vols., 1970; as *Folktales.* Bloomington, Indiana University Press, 2 vols., 1970.
Folk Legends. London, Routledge, and Bloomington, Indiana University Press, 2 vols., 1971.
A Dictionary of Fairies: Hobgoblins, Brownies, Bogies and Other Supernatural Creatures. London, Allen Lane, 1976; as *An Encyclopedia of Fairies,* New York, Pantheon, 1976.
A Sampler of British Folk-tales (selection from A Dictionary of British Folk-tales). London, Routledge, 1977; as *British Folktales,* New York, Pantheon, 1977.
The Vanishing People: A Study of Traditional Fairy Beliefs. London, Batsford, and New York, Pantheon, 1977.
Abbey Lubbers, Banshees and Boggarts: A Who's Who of Fairies, illustrated by Yvonne Gilbert. London, Kestrel, and New York, Pantheon, 1979.

OTHER PUBLICATIONS

Novels

The Lisles of Ellingham. Oxford, Alden Press, 1935.
The Castilians. Oxford, Alden Press, 1950.

Plays

The Garrulous Lady. London, Golden Vista Press, 1931.
The Peacemaker (produced Murthly, Perthshire, 1933). Dunkeld, Perthshire, Capricornus, 1938.
The Fugitive. Dunkeld, Perthshire, Capricornus, 1938.
The Lady in the Dark. Dunkeld, Perthshire, Capricornus, 1949.

Poetry

Whispers: An Experiment in Lino Cuts, with Elspeth Briggs, illustrated by the authors and Winifred Briggs. Dunkeld, Perthshire, Capricornus, 1940.

The Twelve Days of Christmas, with others, illustrated by Winifred Briggs. Dunkeld, Perthshire, Capricornus, 1952.

Other

A History of 75 Years. Privately printed, 1935.
Mime for Guides and Brownies. London, Girl Guides Association, 1955.
Dunkeld and Birman Guide. Oxford, Alden Press, 1956.
The Folklore of the Cotswolds. London, Batsford, and Totowa, New Jersey, Rowman and Littlefield, 1974.
Nine Lives: Cats in Folklore. London, Routledge, and New York, Pantheon, 1980.

Editor, with Ruth Lyndall Tongue, *Folktales of England.* London, Routledge, and Chicago, University of Chicago Press, 1965.
Editor, *Somerset Folk-lore* by Ruth Lyndall Tongue. London, Folk-lore Society, 1965.
Editor, *The Last of the Astrologers: Mr. William Lilly's History of His Life and Times from the Year 1602 to 1681.* London, Folk-lore Society, 1974.

*

Critical Study: *Katharine Briggs: Story-Teller* by H. Ellis Davidson, Cambridge, Lutterworth Press, 1986.

* * *

To read of the life and work of K. M. Briggs is to open a window on the past in two senses. Her study was folklore, the oral traditions of the people, fast vanishing throughout the 20th century; and it was made possible by private means and a family home, which enable her to write without the need for employment. Growing up during and after World War I, she never married; her close bonds with her two sisters, however, provided companionship, and from childhood she and her sisters invented a cycle of stories in the Bronte manner. This led to private publishing on their own press and to amateur dramatics, including plays by Briggs herself, in their Scottish home and new family home in Burford, Oxfordshire.

Thus it is that her two fantasy novels, *Hobberdy Dick* and *Kate Crackernuts,* represent the tip of the iceberg, both as fictions, when her life's work was the academic study of folklore, and as high-quality writing, when she had written much else that did not receive commercial publication. Indeed, we owe to the publishing house of Penguin-Puffin, in the 1970s, the rescue of her two fantasies from the obscure fate of the out-of-print book, as well as the commission of her great *Dictionary of Fairies.*

K. M. Briggs the folklorist cannot be separated from the fantasist, because the circumstantial detail of her fantasies is rooted in traditional folklore beliefs. As scholar she helped to rehabilitate the folk tale as suitable reading for children and adults, and to reestablish fantasy as a proper mode for children's reading, instead of being considered inferior to realism. Other scholars and creative writers in the post-World War II movement included J. R. R. Tolkien, C. S. Lewis and Roger Lancelyn Green (all Oxfordians, as was K. M. Briggs—and as was the first of the modern generation of folklore fantasists for children, Alan Garner).

After war service and achieving her Oxford D.Phil. on 17th-century folklore in 1952, K. M. Briggs was able to choose her own projects, and first set about publishing a book of folk tales, *The Personnel of Fairyland,* using Oxford's Alden Press. In humility she subtitled it "for those who tell stories to children," i.e. to be used as a sourcebook for other storytellers; and in scholarship she added a brief "Dictionary of Fairies" and list of sources. The book includes stories from Ireland, Scotland and Wales as well as England, and is prefaced by Briggs's heart-felt warnings against current fashions in fairy stories: "Weakened and sugary fairies of very remote folk origin." Briggs was herself a gifted story-teller from memory.

By now *Kate Crackernuts* had been finished, though it remained unpublished until 1963; she had better luck with *Hobberdy Dick,* which was taken by a commercial publisher. Meanwhile Routledge commissioned material from her doctorate thesis to become three scholarly but readable books, and agreed to publish her *Dictionary of British Folk-Tales.*

Briggs's other major contribution to scholarship is her *Dictionary of Fairies,* with entries not only for types of fairy and their characteristics, such as "Virtues esteemed by the fairies," but also for folktale collectors and for creative writers such as Kipling and Tolkien. Some classic tales are transcribed, others summarized. The book even includes the possible source of the term "hobbit," as a type of hobgoblin, turning up in the list of fairies compiled by the folklorist Michael Denham.

Briggs's works of scholarship have a strong narrative content; and her two historical fantasies grew from her research. In *Hobberdy Dick* a Puritan family buys an Oxfordshire manor house and thus inherits the family spirit, a brownie or lob called Hobberdy Dick. Naturally the Puritan master of the house, Mr. Widdison, will have nothing to do with the superstitions practised by the servants and taught to the younger children, such as Easter egg-rolling and the Christmas customs banned by the Puritan government. The reader, however, is swiftly brought to see the events from Dick's point of view, to believe in the old customs and reject the Puritan stance. There are two main episodes to the plot: the witch Mother Darke's plan to capture young Martha Widdison and use her to work spells, combatted by Dick and his fellow lobs; and Joel the eldest son's love for Anne—his stepmother's waiting woman, descended from an old Oxfordshire family come down in the world.

The power of Christianity is crucial, feared and honoured by Dick, who persuades the Christian characters to deal with evil too strong for him: laying a wicked ghost and releasing Martha from the witch's spell by reading the Bible. According to folklore, a freed brownie may join the fairies; Briggs improves on this by offering Dick a soul so that he may go to heaven.

Kate Crackernuts is a novelization for an older readership of the folktale from Joseph Jacobs's *English Fairy Tales.* A wicked stepmother favours her own daughter Kate over her new husband's daughter, and employs a witch to cast a spell over the other girl, to replace her head by a sheep's head. The two girls run away and take lodging with a family whose son is also under a spell—bewitched by the fairies to go and dance under the hill every night. Kate goes with him and finds out how to cure him and her sister; and the son and Kate are married. Briggs sets her tale in Scotland and Yorkshire in the 1650s, against the background of Cromwell's wars with the young King Charles. The characters speak authentic Scots with a period flavour. Briggs, who grew up in Scotland, is authoritative on the socioeconomic conditions of the time, such as the daily round of duties performed by the servants and the distinctions of rank between them and their masters. She takes a different approach to the supernatural in this book, from that in

Hobberdy Dick, where the magic was unquestionably real. In *Kate Crackernuts,* although the characters believe in magic, everything might be explained rationally. Witches inherited a centuries-old tradition, were real, and often evil, and worked their "magic" by suggestion, hypnosis, drugs and poisons. "Fairies" were the aboriginal survivors of an earlier race.

Thus in *Kate Crackernuts* the sheep's head is the product of suggestion: Katherine is sure she wears it, but Kate cannot see it, and to remove it, Kate must convince Katharine of the virtue of a charm she gets from the fairies. The fairy revels are also real: orgiastic dancing in a series of caverns inhabited by the "fairies," to which the local witches and gipsies repair. Yet, since the existence of witches and fairies in historical times is still a matter of supposition, the book remains a fantasy. What drew Briggs to this tale above all others, and what breathes so strongly through it, is her identification with the tomboy Kate, so protective of her beloved stepsister; this gives the tale the extra depth of a novel. Briggs's view of Kate's mother, a power among the witches, is also noteworthy.

After tasting the perfection of these two folklore-based fantasies, we are bound to regret that there were no more; yet maybe she only had two such stories in her. Consider how far, in *Hobberdy Dick,* the folklore drives the plot, as each episode illustrates the truth of a particular superstition; the witch's kidnap of Martha echoes the enchantment in *Comus;* and most significantly, the theme of the master's son in love with a servant-girl was itself the lovestory of K. M. Briggs's *own* father and mother! This same motif, of course, forms the conclusion to *Kate Crackernuts.* If, however, a percipient publisher had detected the virtues of these books in the 1950s and commissioned further such novels, might we not also have had a *Tam Lin* and *Childe Rowland* from her pen?

—Jessica Yates

BROOKS, Terry

Nationality: American. **Born:** Terence Dean Brooks, Sterling, Illinois, 8 January 1944. **Education:** Hamilton College, Clinton, New York, B.A. 1966; Washington and Lee University, Lexington, Virginia, LL.B. 1969. **Family:** Married Judine Elaine Alba in 1987; one daughter and one son from a previous marriage. **Career:** Partner, Besse, Frue, Arnold, Brooks and Miller, Attorneys at Law, Sterling, Illinois, 1969-86; writer from 1977. **Address:** c/o Ballantine/Del Rey, 201 East 50th Street, New York, NY 10022, USA.

Fantasy Publications

Novels (series: Magic Kingdom of Landover; Shannara)

The Sword of Shannara. New York, Random House, 1977; London, Futura, 1981.
The Elfstones of Shannara. New York, Del Rey, and London, Futura, 1982.
The Wishsong of Shannara. New York, Del Rey, and London, Futura, 1985.
Magic Kingdom For Sale/Sold! (Landover). New York, Del Rey, 1986; London, Futura, 1987.

The Black Unicorn (Landover). New York, Del Rey, 1987; London, Futura, 1988.
Wizard at Large (Landover). New York, Del Rey, and London, Futura, 1988.
The Scions of Shannara. New York, Del Rey, and London, Orbit, 1990.
The Druid of Shannara. New York, Del Rey, and London, Orbit, 1991.
Hook (novelization of screenplay). London, Arrow, and New York, Fawcett, 1992.
The Elf-Queen of Shannara. New York, Del Rey, and London, Legend, 1992.
The Talismans of Shannara. New York, Del Rey, and London, Legend, 1993.
The Tangle Box (Landover). New York, Del Rey, and London, Legend, 1994.

*   *   *

If Tolkien constructed the bandwagon for epic fantasy, it was Brooks who set it in motion. The "original" Shannara trilogy (*Sword . . . , Elfstones . . .* and *Wishsong of Shannara*) had all the set elements of an epic fantasy quest—a multitude of magical, humanoid races; good and bad wizards; and some vital mission that only a singularly unheroic, ill-equipped innocent from the back of beyond can perform. *The Sword of Shannara,* indeed, lifts plot and characters straight out of *Lord of the Rings* on a one-to-one basis: Frodo, Sam, Gandalf, Wormtongue, the Nazgul and the Mines of Moria, to name but a few, are all there and easy to recognize.

That said, Brooks also invested his own imagination in the Shannara world. It has a firmer rationale than Middle-Earth (it is a post-holocaust world of some description)—the implication is that it comes long after the age of Man, not long before as Middle-Earth does. Allanon, the Gandalf-analogue, begins as an enigmatic Gandalf-clone but grows in character and history as the series continues. The Ohmsford family, from which all the heroes are drawn, develops its own past and identity. The general impression is that *Sword . . .* was written to break into the market: with that out of the way, Brooks could get on with developing his world in his own fashion.

Some years after *Wishsong . . . ,* Brooks released a new Shannara series. In between, he started on the Landover series. The premise of the Landover books (beginning with *Magical Kingdom for Sale/ Sold!* and *The Black Unicorn*) lies uneasily with the tone in which Brooks tells the stories. Landover is a magical realm whose throne is offered for sale in the Christmas wishbook of a New York department store, for a trifling $1,000,000. The buyer is a disaffected, widowed Chicago lawyer named Ben Holiday. On getting to Landover, Holiday finds that his two closest companions are an incompetent wizard and a talking dog who used to be human, and the sale of the throne is part of a scam by the wizard's half-brother and the rightful heir to the kingdom.

So far, so jokey, and the jokes keep coming: the cowardly, dog-eating gnomes; Holiday's beloved, who keeps turning into a tree; the love-hate bantering between the wizard and the dog. Mixed in, however, are far more serious elements: the witch Nightshade conveys a genuine sense of menace; one never knows quite what to make of the dragon Strabo; and there is the very real depression that grips Holiday at the start of the series and makes him splash out $1,000,000 on what he still half believes to be a joke. Brooks lacks the ability to convey serious messages in a jokey voice and so has to switch visibly between the two tones. The reader gets disoriented while reading, and at the end is not quite sure what to make of the experience.

Nor is Landover as well-realized as the world of Shannara. It is clearly much smaller, and that presents no problem, but it appears to have a population of about 30. Only occasionally do we get the idea that this is a well-populated place. Though there have been four Landover novels to date, a goodly number for a series, there is nothing about *The Tangle Box* to indicate that it will necessarily the last. So far, the Landover stories have been a valiant break from the Shannara cycle and Brooks deserves credit for taking an established fantasy theme (someone from our own world rising to power in another) and producing a new idea (having that someone buy their way in). Brooks' misfortune is that—so far—he has never really found the right pitch for his delivery.

After commencing Landover, Brooks returned to Shannara with the "Heritage of Shannara" series. One of the strengths of the original three Shannaras was that, although interrelated, they were clearly written in isolation from one another. Each one has a different hero and deals with a specific adventure, giving it a beginning, a middle and an end. They can be read separately and the reader will not necessarily have to know of the other books in the trilogy. The Heritage of Shannara, however, is one long adventure, divided into four volumes (*Scions . . . , Druid . . . , Elf-Queen . . .* and *Talismans of Shannara*). This is not a new device in fantasy writing (*vide* the various fantasy series of David Eddings) but it tends to have a universal effect when deployed: the reader gets the impression of a vast, sprawling epic that could upon reflection have been cut by at least a quarter, at no one's loss save those who get their money from publishing as many books as possible.

Again, Brooks shows that he can take an old idea and give it a novel slant. There is—naturally, in this genre—an epic quest to be undertaken, but whereas this is normally (and was in the original three) something magical getting out of control, here it is to restore magic to the world. Again, it is members of the Ohmsford clan who must do the various tasks; instead of having one per volume, we have the simultaneous adventures of three Ohmsford descendants. It isn't like Brooks to give three characters equal weighting and he must be applauded for the attempt.

So what is one to make of Terry Brooks? He is a writer able to invest time and energy in his books, and the insertion of the early Landover novels between the two sets of Shannara chronicles shows that he is capable of diversity as well. The elements of his stories are familiar but the writing is sufficiently good to make the reader want to finish them. There is evidence for two suppositions: Terry Brooks is an original writer who uses familiar tropes because they are there, or he is a competent writer not afraid to exploit bandwagons. The weight of the evidence just tips in favour of the former.

—Ben Jeapes

BROWN, Mary

Nationality: British. **Born:** 1929.

FANTASY PUBLICATIONS

Novels

The Unlikely Ones. London, Century Hutchinson, and New York, McGraw Hill, 1986.

Pigs Don't Fly. New York, Baen, 1994.

OTHER PUBLICATIONS

Novels

Playing the Jack. London, Hutchinson, 1984; New York, Simon and Schuster, 1985.

*　　*　　*

Mary Brown is a minor novelist of somewhat limited imagination, whose two fantasies and one historical romance are all remarkably similar in many of their larger and smaller details of character, plot and setting.

The fantasies are two separate novels, involving different sets of characters, so that neither is in any sense a prequel or sequel. Both are talking-animal fantasies, in that one or more humans is able to converse with a range of animals via magic. Each has a teenage female narrator, a leading male in his twenties and a group of five disparate animals as its main characters. And both have quest plots including a great deal of cross-country travelling and a miscellany of melodramatic adventures, with a romantic sub-plot.

In *The Unlikely Ones,* the teenage narrator is called Thing. She is a Cinderella figure, badly treated by a wicked witch. Apart from being made to work hard, she is physically doubled up and in constant pain from a ruby which has been magically attached to her navel. Her only comfort is that she is not alone in her torment. The witch has similarly enslaved four animals: Corby the crow, Puddy the toad, Pisky the carp and Moglet the kitten, each being crippled by a different precious stone. The stones are the most important part of a dragon's hoard, stolen and hidden by the witch. After the witch's death, Thing and the animals flee (from the wrath of local villagers). Very soon they meet up with a hornless unicorn, Snowy, and a handsome young knight, Conn, who has been cursed by the same witch. This group of seven (a kind of gestalt, almost) goes off on a long and linked series of quests for a magician who will remove their various curses.

In *Pigs Don't Fly,* the teenage narrator, called Summer, has been a servant for her mother, the village whore. When her mother dies, Summer is told to leave by the villagers, so she does, burning down the hut she has lived in, and taking with her a legacy of gold coins and a magic ring (which, she discovers, enables her to communicate with animals). Gradually, Summer meets up with other unfortunates: a mongrel dog she names Growch, a neglected horse (Mistral), a handsome young knight (Sir Gilman, shortened to Gill) who has been attacked, robbed and left with a head wound that has removed both his memory and his sight, a courier pigeon with a broken wing (Traveler), a starving tortoise (Basher), and a very strange little pig with wings (the Wimperling), which is being maltreated in a carnival. Thus Brown has created another group of seven, who go on a rather rambling quest to seek out the proper homes of Gill and of some of the animals.

Both narrators have extremely poor self-images. Thing is sure that she is extremely ugly; she even wears a cloth mask over her face. Often she poses as a boy, though in her heart she adores Conn, her rusty knight. Summer starts off as a very plump girl, with spots, certain that no man could ever love her, though she adores Gill. And much later on, once she has slimmed down, she too poses as a boy. Of course, both narrators are eventually proved wrong, blossoming from ugly ducklings into beautiful swans, for Brown writes novels with determinedly happy endings. The only difference between the two is that, while Thing finds true love and happiness with Conn, Summer rejects Gill (and another man, a generous merchant who wants to marry her) in favour of the lure of foreign travel and a possible sequel or two.

While both narrators are strong personalities, well developed and changing over the course of the novels, most other characters are two-dimensional. Evil characters are wholly evil, good ones are wholly good, and most of the animals have one or two individual traits which are repeated many times over. For example, Snowy the unicorn is strong and comforting, always seeming to know a little more than the others, while Growch the dog complains a lot and is interested only in food and sex. The presence of all these animals lends both novels an air of tweeness.

Each novel contains one other character of note. In *The Unlikely Ones* this is The Ancient, a magician who is at first reluctant to help the seven, then sends them off on a wild goose chase around the country which, if it does anything other than lengthening the book, allows the seven to cast off some of their doubts and become better people (in the manner of *The Wizard of Oz*), before taking them along to the dragon and helping them renew themselves. He is an enigmatic, all-knowing character. And in *Pigs Don't Fly* there is the Wimperling, who gradually develops from being a small winged piglet into being a large winged pig capable of flying with Summer on his back, and at last into an enormous dragon capable of adopting human male shape.

The main plot elements are neatly (perhaps too neatly) resolved. In *The Unlikely Ones,* the five jewels are returned to a delighted dragon, the animals find suitable homes among their own kind and Thing and Conn fall contentedly into each other's arms. In *Pigs Don't Fly,* Gill is restored to his family (miraculously recovering his sight and memory at the most convenient moment due to another bang on the head), and the horse, pigeon, tortoise and pig rejoin their own kind; Summer has discovered herself, finding her real name, Talitha, accepting the fact of her beauty and losing her virginity in a deliberate and joyful manner to a most unexpected male—the Wimperling, after he has metamorphosed into a dragon.

But the bulk of each book consists of minor plot elements, random adventures along the way, which always threaten great disaster yet are in the end easily coped with, leaving the septet neither better nor worse off. Too much of Brown's plotting is accomplished through coincidence or contrivance; few of the adventures are at all tense or exciting. In part this is due to Brown's insistence on keeping each group of seven alive; the reader is never in any doubt that the dangers of physical attack or enchantment will be overcome without harm.

The setting for *The Unlikely Ones* is Britain, soon after the end of Roman occupation. *Pigs Don't Fly* has a similar setting, though the exact time and place are less certain. Both backgrounds are rural, with much lush description of the flora, fauna and climate of woods and moorlands. In *The Unlikely Ones* there is too much description, which tends to slow down the plot.

A few words are necessary concerning *Playing the Jack.* Despite being an historical romance set in England in 1785, it has many ingredients in common with the two fantasies. Its narrator is a teenage girl posing as a boy. She, too, is an orphan with a self-image problem, and she journeys the length and breadth of England (with a travelling carnival show) on a kind of quest for somebody to look after her and in order to discover her own personal-

ity. Here, too, there is one other strong character, Jack the owner and leader of the show, with whom she falls in love. The other members of the show are grotesques—"the world's fattest woman," a troupe of dwarfs, a man who has an almost magical control over his performing horse—which are analogous to the talking animals of the other two books. Here, too, the plot consists of many small, improbable adventures (often resolved by coincidence or contrivance), and there is an excess of description of the countryside and of the hardships involved in crossing it.

If Brown does decide to write a sequel to *Pigs Don't Fly* it seems likely that she will adhere to this same formula.

—Chris Morgan

BROXON, Mildred Downey

Pseudonym: Sigfridur Skaldaspillir. **Nationality:** American. **Born:** Atlanta, Georgia, 7 June 1944; grew up in Brazil. **Education:** Seattle University, B.A. in psychology 1965; B.S. in nursing 1970. **Family:** Married 1) G. D. Torgerson in 1965 (divorced 1969); 2) William D. Broxon in 1969 (died 1981). **Career:** Teacher's aide, Rainier State School, Buckley, Washington, 1966-67; psychiatric nurse, Harborview Medical Center, Seattle, 1970-72. Vice-president, Science Fiction Writers of America, 1975-77. **Agent:** Jarvis Braff Ltd., 260 Willard Avenue, Staten Island, NY 10314, USA. **Address:** 7337 22nd Avenue N.W., Seattle, WA 98117, USA.

FANTASY PUBLICATIONS

Novels

The Demon of Scattery, with Poul Anderson. New York, Ace, 1979.
Eric Brighteyes No. 2: A Witch's Welcome (as Sigfridur Skaldaspillir). New York, Zebra, 1979.
Too Long a Sacrifice. New York, Dell, 1981; London, Futura, 1983.

*　　*　　*

Although nearly all of Broxon's couple of dozen published short stories are science fiction, her three novels are historically-based fantasies involving Celtic or Norse warriors. *Too Long a Sacrifice* is her best known work and is highly regarded despite being seriously flawed. It is a plot-driven novel which takes a husband and wife from sixth-century pagan Ireland and sets them down, separately, in the war-torn Northern Ireland of 1980. Broxon's clear intent is to comment upon the bloody struggle between Catholics and Protestants, including the feelings of her protagonists, who do not, of course, know what Catholics and Protestants are. In order to achieve her aim, Broxon makes use of a whole series of conveniences and contrivances which tend to destroy any semblance of credibility and make the novel acceptable only as a work of allegory.

In order to get her protagonists through time, Broxon has them stay enchanted in the royal court of the Sidhe beneath Lough Neagh. Tadhg is a fine harper and singer who is enticed down below the waters, a changeling being left in his place; and Maire, a healer by profession, is his loving wife who pursues him and, finding that he cannot leave, drinks faerie wine deliberately, to stay with him. After 1,400 years they are released by the King and Queen of the Sidhe because the land above is bleeding and magic is dying. But before they leave, Tadhg and Maire are granted the magic powers of Sight (to see and understand hidden things), of Speech (so as to avoid any communication problems) and of invisibility (to be invisible whenever they choose).

To complicate matters, Maire is possessed by Maeve, the old goddess of summer, while Tadgh is possessed not only by the Hunter, the old god of winter, but also by the hate-beast, an unexplained supernatural force which makes him kill people and which, it is revealed, has been singlehandedly responsible for causing and maintaining the Troubles. Tadgh and Maire each believes that the other is dead. Tadgh is quickly involved with the IRA, helping to lead bloodthirsty revenge attacks. Maire discovers that she has amazing powers of healing, and she uses them selectively to help injured people. The way in which each realizes that the other is still alive but they keep on missing each other is farcical, and their presence at the same Belfast peace march, only seeing each other later on television, is extremely contrived. A final confrontation (on the historically important Hill of Tara) between good and evil, past and present, humans and gods is very artificial, especially in the way it sorts out and ties up all the strands of the plot.

If the plot lacks everything except pace, this is made up for by the backgrounds. Both the sixth century and the present are very well described. In particular, Broxon presents a remarkably honest and even-handed picture of recent Belfast. Characterization is minimal, with all characters fulfilling functions rather than coming across as people. Even Tadgh and Maire are undeveloped, though this could be claimed as a natural consequence of being possessed by gods. It is a pity that the gift of Sight could not have helped more to explain the 20th century to them, then the reader might have been spared their painful stranger-in-a-strange-land mistakes. Because all character interaction is abbreviated, it often appears trite or awkward; this is a novel which could have benefited from greater length.

The opposite is true of *The Demon of Scattery,* which is a novelette inflated into a short novel and further padded out by the addition of many interior illustrations. It is a rather slender tale of vikings attacking Ireland in the ninth century A.D. and being eventually discouraged (two of their three ships are destroyed and many men killed) by the conjuring up of a vengeful dragon, the eponymous demon.

The story is worth telling and often well told. Brigit is a young Christian nun, captured and repeatedly raped by Ranulf and his men. During the capture of Scattery Island (in the Shannon estuary on the west coast of Ireland) Ranulf sustains a life-threatening head wound. His father, Halldor, is the leader of this group of vikings. Brigit, a trained healer, feels it her Christian duty to try and save Ranulf's life. Halldor threatens her with death if she is not successful, and he takes her into his bed and rapes her anyway.

Thus we have a strange triangle. Halldor is a brutal man, a follower of Thor, contemptuous of all women, but especially of captives and Christians, yet he loves his only remaining son more than anything in the world. Perhaps it is believable that he should feel gratitude towards the woman who saves his son's life via a bit of brain surgery and a lot of careful nursing, and that he should respond positively to her Christian attitudes and her use of Ranulf as a bargaining counter. For her part, Brigit is in a state of considerable agitation. Can she maintain her faith when it seems that God is unwilling to prevent the slaughter of His followers? Due to being the sole survivor of her own religious community, she has no

place to go, especially when she finds herself pregnant. She is reviled by other Irish captives, accused of collaboration with the enemy. In a fit of pique she turns to the old gods of Ireland and through them curses Halldor and his followers, hence the dragon appears. At the apex of this triangle is Ranulf, gradually recovering and becoming converted to Christianity.

Less believable is the fact that Brigit should so quickly find love and sexual fulfilment with Halldor and also the fact that he should so easily forgive her for causing the destruction of so many of his comrades. The suggestion at the end of the book is that Brigit accompanies Halldor back to Norway, living a long and happy life as his *spaewife,* or concubine, while Ranulf eventually becomes a Christian monk.

The actual dragon attack scene is well handled, with it sinking two ships and then pursuing men onto the land. The only problem is that such a scene has been telegraphed all through, by the title, by the book cover, by many references, so that it comes as no surprise. In fact, most aspects of the book are well handled. The background detail gives an excellent sense of place without being intrusive. The two main characters are skilfully developed through the use of both viewpoints (though the rest of the vikings remain indistinguishable and indistinct, just a pack of wolves snarling in the background). This is an historical romance with just a small amount of fantasy in the form of the curse.

It seems, from the authors' afterwords, that the idea for the book was Broxon's, and that Anderson's contributions were the viking detail and, most probably, the overall polish. Broxon's only other fantasy novel, *Eric Brighteyes No. 2: A Witch's Welcome,* is a sequel to H. Rider Haggard's *Eric Brighteyes.* The setting is tenth-century Iceland, against which a dramatic romance is played out, in the style of the old Icelandic sagas, full of action, love, death and witchcraft.

—Chris Morgan

BRUST, Steven (Karl Zoltan)

Nationality: American. **Born:** 23 November 1955. **Address:** c/o Tor Books, 175 Fifth Avenue, New York, NY 10010, USA.

FANTASY PUBLICATIONS

Novels (series: Vlad Taltos; Phoenix Guards)

Jhereg (Taltos). New York, Ace, 1983.
To Reign in Hell. Minneapolis, Minnesota, Steel-Dragon Press, 1984.
Yendi (Taltos). New York, Ace, 1984.
Brokedown Palace. New York, Ace, 1986; London, Pan, 1991.
Teckla (Taltos). New York, Ace, 1987.
The Sun, the Moon, and the Stars. New York, Ace, 1987.
Taltos. New York, Ace, 1988; as *Taltos and the Paths of the Dead,* London, Pan, 1991.
Phoenix (Taltos). New York, Ace, 1990.
The Phoenix Guards. New York, Tor, 1991.
Taltos the Assassin (omnibus; includes *Jhereg, Yendi, Teckla*). London, Pan, 1991.
Gypsy, with Megan Lindholm. New York, Tor, 1992.

Agyar. New York, Tor, 1993.
Athyra (Taltos). New York, Ace, 1993.
Five Hundred Years After (Phoenix Guards). New York, Tor, 1994.

OTHER PUBLICATIONS

Novel

Cowboy Feng's Space Bar and Grille. New York, Ace, 1990.

* * *

Much of Stephen Brust's fantasy oeuvre is set in the two worlds of Fenario, home of Prince Miklos, and Dragaera, home of the assassin Vlad Taltos, the latter world being more technologically advanced than the former, which contains elements of the traditional Hungarian fairy tale. The universes are connected in a very tenuous fashion, which hints that they may be fragments of an exceedingly large design perhaps as yet only partly realized even by the author, though he drops certain teasing hints. Why, in the Vlad Taltos books, are humans referred to as Easterners? How did they get to Dragaera in the first place? Why doesn't anyone know why a period of 14 days (one day less than three five-day weeks) is called a fortnight? Specific invented fauna are common to both worlds, and Miklos is accompanied for much of *Brokedown Palace* by a talking taltos horse.

The surface story of *Brokedown Palace* is simple enough. Four royal brothers live together in the palace of the title, bachelors by choice rather than necessity, though all have their (somewhat arbitrarily chosen) peculiarities. Miklos, the youngest and least odd, falls foul of the eldest and oddest, King Laszlo of Fenario, and finds it necessary to hide himself in Faerie for a couple of years, whence he returns with the horse and a smattering of Power.

Taltos is an undefined term, not least for Miklos, and Brust hints at deeper levels of motivation than are strictly necessary to keep the action credible. The effect is somewhat as if Roger Zelazny (who admires Brust) had written his Amber books in the spirit of "The Man Who Loved the Faioli." There is skilful use of symbolism, as when a stone carving shows: "a man on a wild bull, holding a sword at his side as the animal reared . . . the way the rider's cloak was rippled by the wind, only a bit, made him catch his breath anew. Who was it? Where? What battle? Why a bull? Certainly it was a taltos bull, but there were no legends that quite fit what was depicted." Inevitably, Miklos learns the story (from a drunken coachman) later on. Meanwhile the parallel with Zelazny becomes more pronounced as a supernatural tree grows where the royal blood has been shed in anger on the palace floor. Can it (should it?) be eradicated?

Most of *Brokedown Palace* is given to exploring the relationships between the four brothers, the court wizard, Laszlo's mistress, Laszlo's fiancee and the Guard Captain Viktor, who may perhaps be a pretender. Brust wisely allows them time to gel, mainly from Miklos's viewpoint, against the growing menace of the tree and the enigmatic Greek chorus of the horse, so that this fairy tale for children doubles as a light novel for adults, who may perceive it as an allegory of renewal. Such allegories are notoriously prone to archness, mawkishness or both; Brust has very little of either. Their other principal danger is flat characterization, but the groundwork laid in the first half allows the people to become more real in the concluding *tour de force,* heavily stylized though it is. Less

wisely, Brust includes some short "interludes" consisting of further, even more traditional, short fairy tales, written in a homelier style, and hinting parabolically at how the book will develop. These impede the action, and in so far as they illumine it, the illumination is unwelcome.

The theme of continuing development is just as marked in the Vlad Taltos books, beginning with *Jhereg, Yendi* and *Teckla,* which are written in a fluent, cheerful, but slightly wordy style which arouses immediate interest and sympathy for the first-person protagonist, and sustains it, even through some very flat "realistic" dialogue in the strategic planning scenes.

The setting is Dragaera, a standard sort of pre-industrial-technology/magic-as-science world wherein Vlad, aided by his faithful, telepathic, venomous pet monster (hand-reared from the egg) carries on the business of racketeer and professional assassin. There are many agreeable flourishes: a quasi-immortal dominant race, among whom mere humans must tread carefully; a refreshingly uncomplicated sex-life for Vlad; and an interestingly complex code of honour based on the fact that most fatal injuries can be cured (at a price) by magic. The favoured means of long-distance travel is teleportation, which always leaves Vlad feeling nauseous. Some readers may find the overt criminality distasteful, especially as certain procedures destroy the soul as well as the body, but it's written in a spirit of good clean fun, reminiscent of Fritz Leiber's Gray Mouser fantasies or Damon Runyon's short stories.

There is little depth of characterization, which is not at first important; the first two books are strictly for entertainment. In the third Brust goes a little deeper. Draghaera has a brutally repressive social order based on institutionalized caste and race prejudice, as if the worst features of *apartheid* South Africa had been superimposed on a sanitized vision of India. Vlad, who has clawed his way out of the mire, can live with it, but his wife becomes involved in liberation politics. Much against his will Vlad must now involve himself, to preserve her from the consequences of what he perceives as her folly. The tension from this converts the third book into a forceful and original parable of social mobility. The side-effect is to make the first two books seem like mere preludes to the third, which is unfortunate as they do not constitute a three-decker novel, and they were not originally written in that spirit. The increasing compassion and idealism of Vlad's character, and even his delicately portrayed love for his wife (who started the relationship by killing him; the revival spell worked), sit uneasily with what has gone before.

Brust tries to square the circle by having Vlad wrestle cogently, if inarticulately, with his conscience, but it's never completely convincing. To take an example, Vlad is a loan-shark and owns a number of brothels, but there are no brothel scenes, for the good reason that if they were played light, the result would be low farce or soft porn; whereas, if they were played serious, the feelings of girls working there to clear debts would become such a factor as to make Vlad's character untenable. But there's plenty of mileage left in both Vlad and Dragaera, and the series has continued with *Taltos, Phoenix* and *Athyra,* with more volumes likely to come. One can look forward to the eventual resolution of their mysteries.

The author's other fantasy works include *The Phoenix Guards,* a loosely-linked "prequel" to the Vlad Taltos series, and its follow-up *Five Hundred Years After*—both novels displaying a rather obvious debt to the swashbuckling historical yarns of Alexandre Dumas and Rafael Sabatini. With Megan Lindholm, he has also written *Gypsy,* which is by contrast a contemporary or so-called "urban" fantasy and has been described by its publishers as "a gorgeous, myth-saturated novel of fantasy *noir.*" Brust's unusual, low-key vampire novel *Agyar* could also be classed as modern-day urban fantasy.

—Chris Gilmore

BULL, Emma

Nationality: American. **Born:** 1954. **Family:** Married fantasy writer Will Shetterly, *q.v.* **Address:** c/o Tor Books, 175 Fifth Avenue, New York, NY 10010, USA.

FANTASY PUBLICATIONS

Novels

War for the Oaks. New York, Ace, 1987.
Finder. New York, Tor, 1994.
The Princess and the Lord of Night (for children). New York, Harcourt Brace, 1994.

Short Stories

Double Feature, with Will Shetterly. Framingham, Massachusetts, NESFA Press, 1994.

Other (series: Liavek in all books)

Editor, with Will Shetterly, *Liavek.* New York, Ace, 1985.
Editor, with Will Shetterly, *The Players of Luck.* New York, Ace, 1986.
Editor, with Will Shetterly, *Wizard's Row.* New York, Ace, 1987.
Editor, with Will Shetterly, *Spells of Binding.* New York, Ace, 1988.
Editor, with Will Shetterly, *Festival Week.* New York, Ace, 1990.

OTHER PUBLICATIONS

Novels

Falcon. New York, Ace, 1989.
Bone Dance: A Fantasy for Technophiles. New York, Ace, 1991.

*   *   *

Often the fantasy tales that make the deepest impression with readers are those which find a new way to treat familiar subjects, either by placing them in a different context, or changing a single element that provides a novel perspective or a fresh variation on an old theme. Fantasy also has an inherent problem with verisimilitude, since the presence of magic introduces infinite possibilities and, in the hands of a lazy writer, an easy way to resolve conflicts by pulling a metaphorical rabbit out of the hat. Only the best writers are able to strike a consistent balance between reality and unreality, and Emma Bull is certainly one of the major names in the field, even though the body of her work is not particularly large.

Bull made a powerful debut *War for the Oaks,* a witty, amusing, and sometimes frightening story of the intrusion of an ancient magical battle into the modern world. Set in the American midwest, the novel assumes the existence of a secret world active within our own, but hidden from most mortal eyes. But now the war between the Seelie and the Unseelie, two rival nations of fairy folk, has spilled over into the life of Eddi, a frustrated rock musician whose life is transformed by an encounter in a deserted shopping mall. A haughty water spirit and a phouka—sometimes a man, sometimes a dog—inform her that she has the power to tip the balance of the conflict in either direction and an obligation to choose properly.

Eddi is understandably reluctant to accept her new role, particularly when the phouka follows her home in human form, thus alienating her boyfriend and complicating her life in other ways. Although she makes several attempts to discourage him from acting as her bodyguard, her attitude changes when agents of the other side make an attempt on her life. Eddi is drawn deeper into the struggle, convinced that her life cannot return to normal until the conflict has been resolved. Their continuing relationship changes both human and phouka, and theirs is one of the best stories of an evolving friendship to appear in modern fantasy. Bull handles the interface between reality and faerie with remarkable skill, so that even the most bizarre and wondrous events remain credible and even appropriate for the setting.

Bull's subsequent novels have all been well received, but they were science fiction rather than fantasy until the appearance of *Finder.* This time the setting is Bordertown, a shared world used by several authors, a kind of murky, gritty shadow land that lies between the real world and the realm of magic. It is home to all those who don't quite fit into the society on either side of the interface, and has evolved its own societal structure, which contains elements of both, and others unique to itself.

Orient is a young human living in exile there, guilty of some mysterious past crime in the real world. In Bordertown, he has his own unique talent, the ability to find missing objects instinctively, and with absolute certainty. This unlikely ability appeals to the local equivalent of the police when one of the less admirable residents is murdered, and Orient is blackmailed into helping track down the killer. From the outset, he is reluctant to become involved, even more so when his investigation uncovers a hidden battle between magical enemies, the presence of a new drug, and the onset of a puzzling plague that menaces human and inhuman alike.

Finder is also one of the more successful of several recent attempts to blend fantasy with elements of the traditional detective story, although Orient is not a stereotypical private eye. There's a strong cast of characters against whose presence the reader slowly discovers the truth about the protagonist while he is uncovering the truth about the murder. *Finder* is an odd contrast to *War for the Oaks* because the mood is so different, grim and relentlessly realistic at times, even though both use the contrast of magic and the real world.

The Princess and the Lord of Night is a children's book, a fairy tale in fact. A young princess has been cursed that, should she ever fail to obtain what she wants, the lives of her parents are forfeit. One day she realizes that what she wants most of all is to be free of the curse, and sets out to discover a way to outsmart the Lord of Night and save her family.

Bull is an infrequent writer of short fiction, although with Will Shetterly she edited five shared-world fantasy anthologies, *Liavek, The Players of Luck, Wizard's Row, Spells of Binding* and *Festival Week,* and contributed the lead story, "Badu's Luck," to the first of these. Her "Silver or Gold" appeared in the Tolkien memorial anthology, *After the King* (1992). In this last, a young village spell caster sets out on a journey to find her teacher, who was supposed to stay in touch by means of a magical drum but who appears to have fallen into some danger. She subsequently finds herself in a kingdom, where a prince has been ensorcelled and is presumed dead, and learns the terrible truth about the unwise choice his parents made in the matter. It's a Sleeping Beauty variant that comments on the assumption of personal responsibility unobtrusively under a facade of traditional fantasy.

One of the marks of a major writing talent is the willingness to attempt something new with each book rather than stick to what has proven successful in the past. Bull's novels and short stories share common elements, but each is a distinct creation with more points of difference than similarities. That quality makes it difficult to predict the future course of her work, but it also suggests that she will continue to surprise and entertain her readers as she explores the limits of her talent.

—Don D'Ammassa

BULLETT, Gerald (William)

Pseudonym: Sebastian Fox. **Nationality:** British. **Born:** London, 30 December 1893. **Education:** Private (left school at 16); Jesus College, Cambridge, 1918-21 (on ex-serviceman's grant), B.A. in English. **Military Service:** Royal Flying Corps, 1914-18. **Family:** Married Rosalind Gould in 1921; one daughter. **Career:** Bank clerk, 1909-14; later a journalist and freelance writer; worked for the British Broadcasting Corporation during World War II. **Died:** 3 January 1958.

FANTASY PUBLICATIONS

Novels

Mr. Godly Beside Himself: An Adventure in Two Days. London, Lane, 1924; New York, Boni & Liveright, 1925.
Marden Fee. London, Heinemann, 1931; New York, Knopf, 1931.

Short Stories

The Street of the Eye and Nine Other Tales. London, Lane, 1923; reprinted by Books for Libraries Press, Freeport, N.Y., 1971.
The Baker's Cart and Other Tales. London, Lane, 1925; reprinted by Books for Libraries Press, Freeport, N.Y., 1970.
The World in Bud and Other Tales. London, Heinemann, 1928.
Helen's Lovers and Other Tales. London, Heinemann, 1932.
Ten-Minute Tales and Some Others. London, Dent, 1959.

OTHER PUBLICATIONS

Novels

The Progress of Kay. 1916.
The Panther. 1926.

The Spanish Caravel (for children). 1927.
The History of Egg Pandervil. 1928.
Nicky Son of Egg. 1929.
Remember Mrs. Munch (for children). 1931.
I'll Tell You Everything, with J. B. Priestley. New York, Macmillan, 1932; London, Heinemann, 1933.
The Quick and the Dead. 1933.
Eden River. 1934.
The Jury. 1935.
The Happy Mariners (for children). 1935.
The Snare of the Fowler. 1936.
The Bending Sickle. 1938.
A Man of Forty. 1939.
When the Cat's Away. 1940.
The Elderbrook Brothers. 1943.
Judgment in Suspense. 1946.
Men at High Table. 1948.
The House of Strangers. 1948.
Cricket in Heaven. 1949.
The Trouble at Number Seven. London, Michael Joseph, 1952.
The Alderman's Son. London, Michael Joseph, 1954.
The Daughters of Mrs. Peacock. London, Dent, 1957.
The Peacock Brides. London, Dent, 1958.
Odd Woman Out, as Sebastian Fox. London, Dent, 1958.

Short Stories

Twenty-Four Tales. 1938.

Poetry

The Bubble. 1934.
Poems in Pencil. 1937.
The Golden Year of Fan Cheng-ta. 1946.
Poems. 1949.
News from the Village. Cambridge, Cambridge University Press, 1952.
Windows on a Vanished Time. London, Michael Joseph, 1955; Washington, Transatlantic Press, 1956.
Collected Poems. London, Dent, 1959.

Other

The Innocence of G. K. Chesterton. 1923.
Walt Whitman. 1924.
Modern English Fiction. 1926.
Germany. 1930.
The Story of English Literature. 1935.
Problems of Religion. 1938.
George Eliot. 1947.
The English Mystics. London, Michael Joseph, 1950.
Sydney Smith: A Biography and Selection. London, Michael Joseph, 1951.
Dreaming. 19??.

Editor, *The Testament of Light.* 1932.
Editor, *The English Galaxy of Shorter Poems.* 1933.
Editor, *The Testament of Light, Second Series.* 1934.
Editor, *The Jackdaw's Nest.* 1939.
Editor, *Readings in English Literature.* 19??.
Editor, *Silver Poets of the Sixteenth Century.* London, Dent, 1955.

Editor, *The Poems of John Keats*. London, Dent, 1957.

* * *

The decade following the end of the Great War saw a remarkable flowering of British fantasy, expressed principally in a group of novels in which characters whose real lives have become stale and enervated are rescued from the spiritual doldrums by an inoculation of life-enhancing fantasy. Gerald Bullett's *Mr. Godly Beside Himself* is one of the most striking of these novels, and might perhaps be appointed to serve as their archetype.

Mr. Godly is a businessman whose work and marriage have lost all their flavour. He becomes fascinated with his new secretary, with whom he hopes to start an affair, but his involvement with her introduces him to some strange characters and surreal situations, culminating in his entry into the Fairyland from which she hails. In order to go there, however, he must exchange places with his fairy *doppelgänger* Godelik. Godly finds that Fairyland is in a state of political turmoil by virtue of a backlash by traditionalists against the progressive force of reason and is distressed to realise that a revolution is imminent; meanwhile, the naïve Godelik finds problems adapting to the complicated demands and conventions of modern life. Neither partner in the exchange can find much comfort in the environment into which he has been transplanted, and Godly quickly becomes prey to an urgent sense of threat. His very survival is at stake, but he rises to the challenge as best he can, and he eventually comes back to earth a wiser and fitter man.

Like Stella Benson's *Living Alone* (1919) and Hope Mirrlees' *Lud-in-the-Mist* (1926), *Mr. Godly Beside Himself* pleads for a healthy reconciliation of reason and imagination—without which, the author argues, modern human life might easily become arid. Like all the best fantasy, it respects the forces of reason, but has grave reservations about the narrow-minded materialism to which an excessive regard for rationalism is sometimes parent. Like Benson's earlier novel, it develops this theme in a robustly quirky manner, shunning the traditional delicacy of sentimental fantasy in favour of a thoroughly modern surrealism.

Bullett was by no means incapable of delicacy, as is evidenced by his gentle timeslip romance "Helen's Lovers," but the constant surreal element in his work gives much of his fantasy a nightmarish edge. A brief preparatory sketch of the story which was to be elaborated into *Mr. Godly Beside Himself* is contained in "The Enchanted Moment" in *The Street of the Eye and Nine Other Tales,* in which a similar protagonist is more abruptly snatched into a parallel world where the drunken and dwarfish godling Dionysius contemptuously cuts him down to a much smaller size. The title story of the volume is a curious metaphysical fantasy whose paranoid central character finds it uncomfortably easy to support the suspicion that he is being closely monitored by an unkind deity. Also included is the subtle theriomorphic fantasy "Dearth's Farm," a tale of a married man whose spirit is ultimately displaced into a horse, which may be seen as an ironic echo of David Garnett's *Lady into Fox.*

In the supernatural stories in *The Baker's Cart and Other Tales* this surreal element is further exaggerated, usually to horrific effect. The grotesque tale of "The Dark House" and the posthumous fantasies "Queer's Rival" and "Last Days of Binnacle" are among the darkest of Bullett's fantasies, the last two items standing in sharp contrast to his gentle and sentimental posthumous fantasy "The Grasshopper," which can be found in *The World in Bud and Other Tales.*

The majority of the fantasies in *Helen's Lovers and Other Tales* are relatively gentle in their inclination. "Fiddler's Luck" and "Tangent in Trouble" develop in a conscientiously ironic manner the same kind of sexual subtext implied by Mr. Godly's fascination with the mysterious Maia, presenting a traditional folkloristic motif involving human males with supernatural females in a suitably sarcastic modern context. On the other hand, "Three Men at Thark" is a strangely disturbing tale of an over-explained poltergeist, while the ghostly *conte cruel* "The Elder" is perhaps the best of Bullett's horror stories.

The brief fantasies included among the previously-unreprinted stories in *Ten-Minute Tales* are inevitably slight, by virtue of having been written to a precise length, but the best of them—"Here be My Bones" and "Company for Prynne"—are elegant variations on a standard theme. Like several other British writers of this period, Bullett wrote some tales of this kind for the BBC, thus making a significant contribution to a rich tradition of broadcast weird fiction.

Although Bullett never wrote another fully-fledged fantasy novel after *Mr. Godly Beside Himself*—presumably feeling that he had made his point and did not need to repeat it—some of his later work does have elements of metaphysical speculation, and he wrote a notable essay on *Dreaming. Marden Fee* is one of several notable novels (of which the best-known is perhaps Alan Garner's *Red Shift*) which juxtapose eras of prehistory and history in order to construct melancholy romances of eternal recurrence. Bullett's version has three novellas whose cumulative effect is to inform us that we are joined to our ancestors "not by metaphor but by an unbreakable physical continuity. . . ." and that "[We] are no more than cells in a vast multiple organism . . . lives generating from one immortal sperm". Here the repeated pattern of events has a more sinister central motif than that featured in "Helen's Lovers," where the trick played by time, although more convoluted, is decidedly less brutal. *Cricket in Heaven* is not dissimilar in its implications, and uses another familiar method of marginal fantasy, reworking in a modern setting, with considerable elegance, the Classical story of Alcestis.

Bullett is an under-rated writer whose supernatural stories would certainly benefit from collection into a single volume; *Mr. Godly Beside Himself* fully deserves to be recognized as one of the classics of English fantasy.

—Brian Stableford

———

BUNCH, Christopher. *See* **COLE, Allan and Christopher BUNCH.**

———

BURNS, Richard

Nationality: British. **Born:** Sheffield, Yorkshire, 1 September 1958. **Education:** Sheffield and Lancaster universities. **Family:** Married Tina Davy in 1990; two children. **Career:** Part-time lecturer, book reviewer, poet and freelance writer. **Died:** 31 August 1992.

FANTASY PUBLICATIONS

Novels

Khalindaine. London, Allen and Unwin, 1986.
Troubadour. London, Unwin, 1988.

OTHER PUBLICATIONS

Novels

A Dance for the Moon. London, Cape, 1986.
The Panda Hunt. London, Cape, 1987.
Why Diamond Had to Die. London, Bloomsbury?, 198?.
Fond and Foolish Lovers. London, Bloomsbury, 1990.
Sandro and Simonetta. London, Bloomsbury, 1992.

*   *   *

Richard Burns was a restless writer who tried his hand at a variety of forms. He was an award-winning poet, he wrote two out-and-out genre fantasies, two psychological novels set in the 1920s, a thriller and an historical novel. But it was only with his second-to-last novel, a teasing and tender book which combines elements of all his previous work and which was published two years before his suicide, that he finally found a distinctive voice.

His first novel, *A Dance for the Moon,* tells of the men who were shell-shocked during the First World War. All the characters are psychologically damaged, cut adrift from their world. Even the psychologist who runs the private sanatorium where the book is set is an American who does not understand the ways of England. *The Panda Hunt* also tells of an outsider, a Chinese-American who cannot become part of the expatriate community in 1920s Paris, and who is hired as a guide for a panda hunt in China where he is just as much a stranger.

Burns's two fantasies written at about the same time, *Khalindaine* and its sequel *Troubadour,* may seem strange companions to these novels, but they share some of the same interests. They are concerned as much with the psychology of the characters as with their actions, and the leading characters are always cut adrift from their world. Three of the central figures in *Khalindaine* were all adopted at birth and feel uncomfortable within their proper milieu. Streetpoet, the most important character linking both books is actually a wandering minstrel unable to settle down.

Khalindaine is an isolated empire wrested from the non-human Agaskan by a now almost mythical hero. Since then the rulers of Khalindaine have been avatars of the hero who show their right to rule by stabbing themselves in the heart every Endyear and then being magically cured. But the current empress is dying and ambitious lords are plotting to seize power. Before they can do so, however, they must discover and eliminate her illegitimate son, the true heir, who is rumoured to be hidden somewhere in the remote Northreach. Meanwhile, the Agaskan are rising again and only the reborn hero can save the empire.

The setting is formulaic, as is the plot (largely driven by coincidence, as are all of Burns's plots). A mismatched group of companions—Ormaas the fur trader who might be the heir, his cousin Lara, the legless ex-warrior Khayrik, Streetpoet another adoptee and the young lord Consatine who might also be heir—set out from Northreach for the capital. Along the way they have various adventures including a hair-raising escape from the Agaskan army, Ormaas is killed by the plotters but Consatine reveals himself the true heir by saving the day in the great pitched battle which finally drives off the Agaskan.

The sequel is similarly routine in format. Consatine, now emperor, has been driven mad by the avatar of the hero. Meanwhile a fanatical puritanical religious movement who believe Ormaas was the true hero are on the verge of declaring civil war. Streetpoet sets out to find Lara in the hope that she will restore the emperor to his senses and so save the day.

However, though the settings, the clash of swords, the heroic quests, hair's-breadth escapades, and final climactic restoration of the true old order are all predictable elements of any genre fantasy, Burns does have an interestingly fresh approach. There can be few heroic fantasies, for instance, where the villain is driven not by evil but by the mental degeneration caused by syphilis, or equally where the economic effects of population growth form part of the overall picture.

Nevertheless, such refreshing and unusual perspectives apart, his two books do not ring many changes on the usual nature of genre fantasy. His world-building is familiar, and the accoutrements of castles, armour, medieval titles and magic don't stray an inch from the normal genre pattern. He is good at writing conversation—which can often be very witty—and particularly the muttering of many voices in a crowd scene, and all his books are decorated (not surprisingly) with pastiche verse which is often good, and always better than the doggerel usually found in formula fantasy. But his descriptive writing is slow and stately, rich in images but not always well suited to the bursts of dramatic action which carry the story forward.

It was only really in *Fond and Foolish Lovers* when his literary skills and interests combined in a book that was fully successful. Set between the death and the funeral of an elderly female academic in the North of England, it tells a complex tale of family conflicts and literary investigation. Extracts from the dead woman's works of literary criticism inform the search by her lover for clues about her past in her letters, while her family, colleagues and publishers weave together in intricate relationships. As with all of Burns's books, there is a large cast of characters and the novel's viewpoint shifts between them constantly, often in mid-sentence. But in this book there are curious passages of first-person narrative where the "I" might be the dead woman, or Burns, or the whole book could be a novel she was contemplating before her death. In the end it turns out to be some curious combination of all three, but it makes *Fond and Foolish Lovers* into a fascinating meditation on the nature of fantasy and reality.

—Paul Kincaid

BURROUGHS, Edgar Rice

Nationality: American. **Born:** Chicago, Illinois, 1 September 1875. **Education:** Harvard School, Chicago, 1888-91; Phillips Academy, Andover, Massachusetts, 1891-92; Michigan Military Academy, Orchard Lake, 1892-95. **Miliary Service:** United States 7th Cavalry, 1896-97; Illinois Reserve Militia, 1918-19. **Family:** Married 1) Emma Centennia Hulbert in 1900 (divorced 1934), two sons and one daughter; 2) Florence Dearholt in 1935 (divorced 1942).

Career: Instructor and Assistant Commandant, Michigan Military Academy, 1895-96; owner of a stationery store, Pocatello, Idaho, 1898; worked in his father's American Battery Company, Chicago, 1899-1903; joined his brother's Sweetser-Burroughs Mining Company, Idaho, 1903-04; railroad policeman, Oregon Short Line Railroad Company, Salt Lake City, 1904; manager of the stenographic department, Sears Roebuck and Company, Chicago, 1906-08; partner, Burroughs and Dentzer, advertising contractors, Chicago, 1908-09; office manager, Physicians Co-operative Association, Chicago, 1909; partner, State-Burroughs Company, salesmanship firm, Chicago, 1909; worked for Champlain Yardley Company, stationers, Chicago, 1910-11; manager, System Service Bureau, Chicago, 1912-13; freelance writer after 1913; formed Edgar Rice Burroughs, Inc., publishers, 1913, Burroughs-Tarzan Enterprises, 1934-39, and Burroughs-Tarzan Pictures, 1934-37; lived in California after 1919; mayor of Malibu Beach, 1933; also United Press Correspondent in the Pacific during World War II, and columnist ("Laugh it Off"), *Honolulu Advertiser,* 1941-42, 1945. **Died:** 19 March 1950.

FANTASY PUBLICATIONS

Novels (series: Pellucidar; Tarzan)

Tarzan of the Apes. Chicago, McClurg, 1914; London, Methuen, 1917.

The Return of Tarzan. Chicago, McClurg, 1915; London, Methuen, 1918.

The Beasts of Tarzan. Chicago, McClurg, 1916; London, Methuen, 1918.

The Son of Tarzan. Chicago, McClurg, 1917; London, Methuen, 1919.

Tarzan and the Jewels of Opar. Chicago, McClurg, 1918; London, Methuen, 1919.

Tarzan the Untamed. Chicago, McClurg, and London, Methuen, 1920.

Tarzan the Terrible. Chicago, McClurg, and London, Methuen, 1921.

At the Earth's Core (Pellucidar). Chicago, McClurg, 1922; London, Methuen, 1923.

Pellucidar. Chicago, McClurg, 1923; London, Methuen, 1924.

Tarzan and the Golden Lion. Chicago, McClurg, 1923; London, Methuen, 1924.

Tarzan and the Ant Men. Chicago, McClurg, 1924; London, Methuen, 1925.

The Cave Girl. Chicago, McClurg, 1925; London, Methuen, 1927.

The Eternal Lover. Chicago, McClurg, 1925; London, Methuen, 1927; as *The Eternal Savage,* New York, Ace, 1963.

The Tarzan Twins (for children). Joliet, Illinois, Volland, 1927; London, Collins, 1930.

Tarzan, Lord of the Jungle. Chicago, McClurg, and London, Cassell, 1928.

Tarzan and the Lost Empire. New York, Metropolitan, 1929; London, Cassell, 1931.

Tanar of Pellucidar. New York, Metropolitan, 1930; London, Methuen, 1939.

Tarzan at the Earth's Core (Pellucidar). New York, Metropolitan, 1930; London, Methuen, 1938.

Tarzan the Invincible. Tarzana, California, Burroughs, 1931; London, Lane, 1933.

Jungle Girl. Tarzana, California, Burroughs, 1932; London, Odhams, 1933; as *The Land of Hidden Men,* New York, Ace, 1963.

Tarzan Triumphant. Tarzana, California, Burroughs, 1932; London, Lane, 1933.

Tarzan and the City of Gold. Tarzana, California, Burroughs, 1933; London, Lane, 1936.

Tarzan and the Lion-Man. Tarzana, California, Burroughs, 1934; London, W. H. Allen, 1950.

Tarzan and the Leopard Men. Tarzana, California, Burroughs, 1935; London, Lane, 1936.

Tarzan and the Tarzan Twins, with Jad-Bal-Ja, the Golden Lion (for children). Racine, Wisconsin, Whitman, 1936.

Tarzan's Quest. Tarzana, California, Burroughs, 1936; London, Methuen, 1938.

Back to the Stone Age (Pellucidar). Tarzana, California, Burroughs, 1937.

The Lad and the Lion. Tarzana, California, Burroughs, 1938.

Tarzan and the Forbidden City. Tarzana, California, Burroughs, 1938; London, W. H. Allen, 1950.

Tarzan the Magnificent. Tarzana, California, Burroughs, 1939; London, Methuen, 1940.

Land of Terror (Pellucidar). Tarzana, California, Burroughs, 1944.

Tarzan and the "Foreign Legion". Tarzana, California, Burroughs, 1947; London, W. H. Allen, 1949.

Savage Pellucidar. New York, Canaveral Press, 1963.

Tarzan and the Tarzan Twins (omnibus; includes *The Tarzan Twins, Tarzan and the Tarzan Twins, with Jad-Bal-Ja, the Golden Lion*). New York, Canaveral Press, 1963.

Tarzan and the Madman. New York, Canaveral Press, 1964; London, New English Library, 1966.

Short Stories

Jungle Tales of Tarzan. Chicago, McClurg, and London, Methuen, 1919; as *Tarzan's Jungle Tales,* London, Four Square, 1961.

Tarzan and the Castaways. New York, Canaveral Press, 1964; London, New English Library, 1966.

OTHER PUBLICATIONS

Novels

A Princess of Mars. Chicago, McClurg, 1917; London, Methuen, 1919.

The Gods of Mars. Chicago, McClurg, 1918; London, Methuen, 1920.

The Warlord of Mars. Chicago, McClurg, 1919; London, Methuen, 1920.

Thuvia, Maid of Mars. Chicago, McClurg, 1920; London, Methuen, 1921.

The Mucker. Chicago, McClurg, 1921; as *The Mucker* and *The Man Without a Soul,* London, Methuen, 2 vols., 1921-22.

The Chessmen of Mars. Chicago, McClurg, 1922; London, Methuen, 1923.

The Girl from Hollywood. New York, Macaulay, 1923; London, Methuen, 1924.

The Land That Time Forgot. Chicago, McClurg, 1924; London, Methuen, 1925; in 3 vols., as *The Land That Time Forgot, The People That Time Forgot* and *Out of Time's Abyss,* New York, Ace, 1963.

The Bandit of Hell's Bend. Chicago, McClurg, 1925; London, Methuen, 1926.

The Mad King. Chicago, McClurg, 1926.

The Moon Maid. Chicago, McClurg, 1926; London, Stacey, 1972; in 2 vols., as *The Moon Maid* and *The Moon Men,* New York, Ace, 1962.

The Outlaw of Torn. Chicago, McClurg, and London, Methuen, 1927.

The War Chief. Chicago, McClurg, 1927; London, Methuen, 1928.

The Master Mind of Mars. Chicago, McClurg, 1928; London, Methuen, 1939.

The Monster Men. Chicago, McClurg, 1929.

A Fighting Man of Mars. New York, Metropolitan, 1931; London, Lane, 1932.

Apache Devil. Tarzana, California, Burroughs, 1933.

Pirates of Venus. Tarzana, California, Burroughs, 1934; London, Lane, 1935.

Lost on Venus. Tarzana, California, Burroughs, 1935; London, Methuen, 1937.

Swords of Mars. Tarzana, California, Burroughs, 1936; London, New English Library, 1966.

The Oakdale Affair; The Rider. Tarzana, California, Burroughs, 1937.

Carson of Venus. Tarzana, California, Burroughs, 1939; London, Goulden, 1950.

The Deputy Sheriff of Comanche County. Tarzana, California, Burroughs, 1940.

Synthetic Men of Mars. Tarzana, California, Burroughs, 1940; London, Methuen, 1941.

Escape on Venus. Tarzana, California, Burroughs, 1946; London, New English Library, 1966.

Llana of Gathol. Tarzana, California, Burroughs, 1948; London, New English Library, 1967.

Beyond Thirty. Privately printed, 1957; as *The Lost Continent,* New York, Ace, 1963.

The Man-Eater. Privately printed, 1957.

Beyond the Farthest Star. New York, Ace, 1963.

The Girl from Farris's. Kansas City, Missouri, House of Greystoke, 1965.

The Efficiency Expert. Kansas City, Missouri, House of Greystoke, 1966.

I Am a Barbarian. Tarzana, California, Burroughs, 1967.

Pirate Blood. New York, Ace, 1970.

Short Stories

John Carter of Mars. New York, Canaveral Press, 1964.
Tales of Three Planets. New York, Canaveral Press, 1964.
The Wizard of Venus. New York, Ace, 1970.

Other

Official Guide to the Tarzan Clans of America. Privately printed, 1939.

*

Film Adaptations: *Tarzan of the Apes,* 1918, *Tarzan the Ape Man,* 1932, 1959, 1981, *Greystoke: The Legend of Tarzan, Lord of the Apes,* 1984, all from the novel *Tarzan of the Apes; The Land That Time Forgot,* 1975; *At the Earth's Core,* 1976; *The People That Time Forgot,* 1977.

Bibliography: *A Golden Anniversary Bibliography of Edgar Rice Burroughs* by Henry Hardy Heins, Rhode Island, Grant, 1964; *Price and Reference Guide to Books Written by Edgar Rice Burroughs* by James A. Bergen, Jr., Beaverton, Oregon, Golden Lion, 1992.

Critical Studies: *Edgar Rice Burroughs: Master of Adventure* by Richard A. Lupoff, New York, Canaveral Press, 1965, revised edition, New York, Ace, 1968; *The Big Swingers* by Robert W. Fenton, New York, Prentice Hall, 1967; *Tarzan Alive: A Definitive Biography of Lord Greystoke* by Philip Jose Farmer, New York, Doubleday, 1972, London, Panther, 1974; "Tarzan Revisited" by Gore Vidal, in *Collected Essays, 1952-72,* London, Heinemann, 1974; *Edgar Rice Burroughs: The Man Who Created Tarzan* by Irwin Porges, Provo, Utah, Brigham Young University Press, 1975; *Barsoom: Edgar Rice Burroughs and the Martian Vision* by Richard A. Lupoff, Baltimore, Mirage Press, 1976; *A Guide to Barsoom* by John Flint Roy, New York, Ballantine, 1976; *The Burroughs Bestiary: An Encyclopedia of Monsters and Imaginary Beings Created by Edgar Rice Burroughs* by David Day, London, New English Library, 1978; *Tarzan and Tradition: Classical Myth in Popular Literature* by Erling B. Holtsmark, Westport, Connecticut, Greenwood Press, 1981; *Edgar Rice Burroughs* by Erling B. Holtsmark, Boston, Twayne, 1986; *Kings of the Jungle: An Illustrated Reference to "Tarzan" on Screen and Television* by David Fury, Jefferson, North Carolina, McFarland, 1994.

*   *   *

Burroughs poses problems of classification. Not infrequently he is referred to, very loosely, as a fantasy writer—and indeed it can be demonstrated that his work had a huge influence on later sword-and-sorcery writers such as Robert E. Howard, Fritz Leiber, Michael Moorcock and Lin Carter. But he is also regarded as a science fiction author, his Mars and Venus novels being among the pioneering examples of what is now termed the "planetary romance" (a colourful adventure story set on an alien planet)—which category is one of the two basic templates of popular American science fiction (the other being the "space opera" sub-genre initiated by E. E. "Doc" Smith). And yet, in his lifetime, Burroughs's fiction was regarded by his widest public as belonging neither to fantasy nor to science fiction but to the genre of the outdoor adventure story—in particular, to the tale of African or Indian adventure associated in that public's mind with H. Rider Haggard's *King Solomon's Mines* and Rudyard Kipling's *Jungle Books.* It was, of course, his Tarzan series which earned Burroughs this reputation, and these books remain by far and away his best-known works, the inspiration of countless films, comic strips, radio shows and television series.

Despite the fact that they contain few overt supernatural elements, and despite their adoption of many of the "realistic" conventions of safari romances, a strong case can be made for the Tarzan novels as fantasy. Young Lord Greystoke is reared by intelligent "great apes" of a nonexistent species. (In his *Tarzan Alive,* Philip Jose Farmer has attempted to science-fictionalize this anomaly by describing the apes as relict hominids, but Burroughs himself provides no such rationale). Tarzan not only learns to speak apish, but he is able to converse with all the other animals of the African forest. Once he reaches adulthood and uncovers the truth of his own paternity, he embarks on a long series of adventures which are fantastic in the extreme—he discovers the forgotten city of Opar, founded by survivors of sunken Atlantis; he stumbles upon the lost world of Pal-ul-Don, where men have tails and dinosaurs still roam; he encounters a race of matriarchal "giants" and an elf-like race of "ant-men" (who, by inadequately explained means, proceed to shrink Tarzan down to 18 inches in height for the duration of the adventure in question); he visits, by airship through a polar opening, the land of Pellucidar which lies at the Earth's core; he finds other lost cities, lost races and lost worlds galore (so many, in fact, that trying to find likely locations for them all on a map of Africa is a difficult task). In a handful of unashamedly supernatural episodes, he has brushes with witch-doctors, magicians, high priestesses and magical jewels (see, for example, *Tarzan the Magnificent*); and, as a result of one of those encounters, he enjoys the boon of eternal youth (see the discussion of longevity which occurs in the last apeman novel Burroughs published in his lifetime, *Tarzan and the "Foreign Legion"*).

Above all, though, the Tarzan series seems to me to be essentially fantasy because it is a clear example of what one might call the Fiction of the Heart's Desire: it portrays a world of endless pleasure and gratification (admittedly pre-pubertal). Tarzan himself is a mixture of many opposites—simultaneously a sophisticated English aristocrat and a naked beast-man of the wild; at one and the same time an embodiment of some kind of law and morality ("Lord of the Jungle") and a totally free avenger, a killer without the law; exemplifying the Noble Savage, Rousseau's ideal, and yet also a post-Darwinian invention, living as an "ape," eating his food raw, etc. Tarzan encapsulates in one figure the whole idea of evolution, for though he is a beast-man he is also a British lord, a highly intelligent autodidact, a master of many languages, and so on; Tarzan "collapses" the process of biological evolution—he is at once the brutish ancestor and the refined end-product. He allows readers to have their imaginative cake and eat it: he is a personification of both body and mind, flesh and intellect, Hercules and Odysseus. When he is functioning at his best there is no conflict between these "halves" of Tarzan's make-up; the opposites are in perfect harmony within him (he is sometimes thrown out of balance, as by the knock on the head in *Jewels of Opar*, and the action of the novel then centres on his regaining of the perfect equilibrium). Tarzan is simultaneously an aristocratic Dr. Jekyll and a benign Mr. Hyde; he is a healing amalgam, a daydream figure of perfect unity in all things.

One could go on in this vein. Tarzan personifies limitless phallic-aggressive gratification. He can kill anything, virtually with bare hands. He is an absolutely dominant figure, redeemed only by his happy indifference to the rest of humanity. He could be the ultimate Nazi *ubermensch*, were it not for the fact that he does not particularly wish to bend the rest of humanity to his will; he wants only his own total freedom (and that of those he loves). His general distaste for humanity usually prevents him from taking sides in human society's squabbles. Tarzan's political cause, if he has one, is individualistic and anarchistic; he is profoundly asocial, at his most characteristic when he is on his own in the jungle, a solitary hunter-gatherer. Apart from feeding himself, Tarzan does not *work*; his is very much a life of pastoral leisure, and he is often depicted by Burroughs as lazing on the back of Tantor the elephant. He is the dream self of the average American male, circa 1910-1940; he represents the liberation of the male ego, and, as Gore Vidal says in his witty essay on Tarzan, he *prevails*.

By and large, a few supernatural touches apart, Burroughs's Tarzan books belong to the type of fantasy which R. D. Mullen has termed *pseudo-natural*. In Mullen's review of Diana Waggoner's book *The Hills of Faraway* (*Science-Fiction Studies*

number 16, November 1978) he states: "Pseudonatural marvels include talking animals, talking toys, fabulous hybrids, quasi-human species, superhuman individuals of the Tarzan or Conan type; in sum, all unnatural things with merely natural powers however much exaggerated." Mullen adds that in superhero series, although some "may be sufficiently concerned with magic to count as Supernatural Fantasy, the Tarzan series is not. The point to be made here is that in all such stories the hegemonic marvel and hence pseudonatural hero himself is the superhuman and hence pseudonatural hero himself is the superhuman, so that these stories are quite properly called Heroic Fantasy."

Nevertheless, as I began by saying, Burroughs's *oeuvre* still poses problems of classification. His tales, whether set in the forests of Africa or on the dead sea-bottoms of Mars, are much of a muchness. Almost all of them feature heroic action, romantic derring-do, imaginary creatures and pseudo-natural fantastic events. To split his works between "fantasy" and "science fiction" (plus a few mundane novels, such as *The Girl from Hollywood*) is an unrewarding task but one which had to be undertaken for the sake of the above bibliography. For the reasons argued here, I regard the Tarzan series as fantasy. Because they are ancestral to modern-day planetary romance, I regard the Mars and Venus novels as science fiction. The Pellucidar series, about a scientifically impossible world at the earth's core, is harder to place. Clearly it draws, as do the Tarzan novels, on the tradition of "lost race" fiction, much of which (in examples by Rider Haggard, A. Merritt, etc) is classifiable as fantasy; yet these Burroughs books are regarded by many readers as science fiction. But since their status is at least debateable, and since there is a specific overlap between the Tarzan and Pellucidar series (*Tarzan at the Earth's Core*), I have chosen to categorize the hollow-world novels as fantasy for present purposes. There are also a few singletons, such as *The Cave Girl, The Eternal Lover* and *Jungle Girl,* which are more-or-less in the Tarzan vein and therefore are listed as fantasy. It should be borne in mind, though, that all Burroughs's adventure novels, in all their wonderful and dream-like settings, provide much the same sorts of pleasures.

There is a final, historical, point to be made about the importance of Burroughs to fantasy fiction. Prior to the late 1960s, there was no consciousness on the part of publishers, critics and the reading public of "fantasy" as a mass-market paperback publishing category. It could be said that the great fantasy boom began in the summer of 1965 with the release by Ace Books of their "pirate" paperback edition of Tolkien's *The Lord of the Rings* (see Humphrey Carpenter's biography of Tolkien for more details). Some months later, Ballantine Books issued an official edition of Tolkien's masterpiece, and by the end of 1966 a million copies of the latter edition had been sold (plus 100,000 of the Ace edition, which was then withdrawn from the market). In the present context, the interesting aspect of this well-publicized disagreement between two leading paperback houses is that the whole tussle had been prefigured in 1962-63 by a similar dispute over the paperback rights to Edgar Rice Burroughs's novels. Discovering that certain Burroughs titles were technically out of copyright, Ace rushed out editions of *At the Earth's Core* and other books in late 1962; as in the later Tolkien case, their rivals Ballantine came up with "official" editions, beginning in 1963 and including the whole of the Tarzan series (see Richard Lupoff's *Edgar Rice Burroughs: Master of Adventure* for more details). In the several years following, at least 50 million copies of Edgar Rice Burroughs's books were issued in U.S. paperback editions, and helped, along with Tolkien, to form the tastes of a new generation of readers. And, no doubt inspired by both the Burroughs and the Tolkien booms, Lancer Books began reissuing the works of Robert E. Howard (as edited by L. Sprague de Camp) in 1966. The rest is history: fantasy, particularly "heroic fantasy," had finally arrived as a high-profile, best-selling, non-juvenile publishing category. Edgar Rice Burroughs, one may claim, was the great initiator.

—David Pringle

BUSHYAGER, Linda E(yster)

Nationality: American. **Born:** 1947.

FANTASY PUBLICATIONS

Novels

Master of Hawks. New York, Dell, 1979.
The Spellstone of Shaltus. New York, Dell, 1980.

*   *   *

The resurgence of fantasy fiction in recent decades was given impetus by the immense though delayed popularity of the works of J. R. R. Tolkien. While the genre has continued to evolve ever since as new writers enter the fold, the influence of *The Lord of the Rings* remains a powerful one. It is sometimes easy to forget that there were other influential fantasy writers active at the time, and that some writers preferred to explore the possibilities suggested by Marion Zimmer Bradley, Andre Norton, and others.

Linda Bushyager was one such, although her only two novels appeared within a year of each other and there has been no fiction from her since. The protagonist of *Master of Hawks* is Hawk, a young man who can communicate telepathically with animals. The ability to see through the eyes of a bird comes in particularly handy when the Kingdom of York is embroiled in a war with the adjoining Empire, whose forces are probing for weaknesses in York's defences.

A possible key to winning the war is the Sylvan, a reticent forest folk who have stubbornly remained neutral even though it seems likely that they would be the Empire's next target. Each army is assisted by sorcerers as well as telepaths, but sometimes magic can be averted through the influence of enchanted stones. The result is an uneasy balance of power that can be tipped in any direction by a single miscalculation. Hawk is dispatched on a mission to convince the Sylvan to take an active part in the battle after a renegade governor makes an abortive attempt to attack them. Despite capture by the Empire, he succeeds in his mission, returning in time to thwart treachery within the Yorkish forces as well.

Master of Hawks is an unpretentious adventure story written in a crisp, clear prose style that is all too rare in most fantasy fiction.

Bushyager makes no real effort to explore the intricacies of her characters and the political and social structure of her world is sketchy, but she is more concerned with providing a fast-moving, entertaining story and the details that are necessary to make the action convincing are in place.

Although set in the same fantasy world, *The Spellstone of Shaltus* does not involve the same characters. Leah Carlton is a half-human, half-Sylvan sorceress who senses one day that something menacing has entered the castle where she lives with the Carlton clan. It reminds her of the evil sorcerer Shaltus, who was banished from the world some time before but who may have found a way to return from the land of the dead. In the past, Shaltus had created a blight that threatened to destroy the entire countryside, and Leah's father had been one of those who sought to destroy the intruder. Now it appears that he is back for revenge, having implanted his personality in a magical stone as a focus for his ghost.

Shortly after her family is alerted to the danger, evidence is found linking Leah to the Sylvans, whose relations with humans are still very ambiguous. She is accused of collaborating with the forces of darkness and condemned despite her protestations of innocence, but escapes with the assistance of a friend. The Sylvan take her in, but Leah discovers trouble there as well, a leader dying of poisoning and rivals struggling to take his place.

In short order we learn that a small group of conspirators among the Sylvan are responsible for everything, the poisoning of their leader, the incriminating spellstone found in Leah's belongings, and the renewed power of Shaltus. They hope to precipitate a war that will wipe out the human race entirely and leave them to rule the world, or what's left of it. Fortunately, they underestimate Leah's resourcefulness, and her determination to get to the bottom of the mystery and safeguard the ones she loves.

The Spellstone of Shaltus is particularly interesting in its use of a strong female lead character who isn't simply a feminine equivalent to Conan. Leah takes decisive action when needed, but she also takes the time to analyze the situations into which she is thrust. Characterization is much stronger here than in *Master of Hawks,* which is very reminiscent of Andre Norton's early novels, the plot is more complex, and there is considerable concern with what is happening to the minds of the characters as well as the bodies. The novel could almost have been set in Marion Zimmer Bradley's Darkover series, which often straddles the border between fantasy and science fiction. Bushyager's use of telepathy and precognition contribute to a very similar atmosphere.

Neither of these books can be described as a major fantasy novel, although they both hold up well compared to much of the standard fare being published today. Bushyager never loses sight of the fact that the first obligation of the writer is to tell an entertaining story, and she avoids archaic speech patterns and word use that many writers employ as a shortcut to creating a genuinely otherworldly texture. Had she continued to write, it would have been interesting to see if she had developed her own, original voice.

—Don D'Ammassa

C

CABELL, James Branch

Nationality: American. **Born:** Richmond, Virginia, 14 April 1879. **Education:** College of William and Mary, Williamsburg, Virginia, 1894-98, A.B. 1898. **Family:** Married 1) Priscilla Bradley Shepherd in 1913 (died 1949), one son; 2) Margaret Waller Freeman in 1950. **Career:** Instructor in Greek and French at the College of William and Mary while an undergraduate, 1896-97; staff member, Richmond *Times*, 1898, New York *Herald*, 1899-1901, and Richmond *News*, 1901; genealogical researcher in America and Europe, 1901-11; office worker at coal mine in West Virginia, 1911-13; genealogist, Virginia Society of Colonial Wars, 1916-28, and Virginia Sons of the American Revolution, 1917-24; editor, Virginia War History Commission, 1919-26; silent editor, *Reviewer*, Richmond, 1921; an editor, *American Spectator*, 1932-35. President, Virginia Writers Association, 1918-21. **Member:** American Academy. **Died:** 5 May 1958.

FANTASY PUBLICATIONS

Novels (series: The Biography of the Life of Manuel; The Nightmare Has Triplets)

The Soul of Melicent (Manuel). New York, Stokes, 1913; revised edition, as *Domnei*, New York, McBride, 1920; London, Lane, 1927.
The Cream of the Jest (Manuel). New York, McBride, 1917; London, Lane, 1923.
Jurgen (Manuel). New York, McBride, 1919; London, Lane, 1921.
Figures of Earth (Manuel). New York, McBride, 1921; London, Lane, 1922.
The High Place (Manuel). New York, McBride, and London, Lane, 1923.
The Silver Stallion (Manuel). New York, McBride, and London, Lane, 1926.
Something about Eve (Manuel). New York, McBride, and London, Lane, 1927.
The Works (Storisende Edition; includes "The Biography of the Life of Manuel": revised editions of earlier works, plus new material). New York, McBride, 18 vols., 1927-30.
The Way of Ecben (Manuel). New York, McBride, and London, Lane, 1929.
Smirt: An Urbane Nightmare (Triplets). New York, McBride, 1934.
Smith: A Sylvan Interlude (Triplets). New York, McBride, 1935.
Smire: An Acceptance in the Third Person (Triplets). New York, Doubleday, 1937.
Hamlet Had an Uncle. New York, Farrar and Rinehart, and London, Lane, 1940.
There Were Two Pirates. New York, Farrar Straus, 1946; London, Lane, 1947.
The Devil's Own Dear Son. New York, Farrar Straus, 1949; London, Lane, 1950.

Short Stories

The Music from Behind the Moon (Manuel). New York, Day, 1926.

The White Robe (Manuel). New York, McBride, and London, Lane, 1928.
The Witch-Woman (omnibus; includes revised versions of *The Music from Behind the Moon, The Way of Ecben, The White Robe*). New York, Farrar Straus, 1948.

OTHER PUBLICATIONS

Novels

The Eagle's Shadow. New York, Doubleday, and London, Heinemann, 1904; revised edition, New York, McBride, 1923.
The Cords of Vanity. New York, Doubleday, and London, Hutchinson, 1909; revised edition, New York, McBride, 1920; London, Lane, 1925.
The Rivet in Grandfather's Neck. New York, McBride, and London, McBride Nast, 1915.
Beyond Life. New York, McBride, 1919; London, Lane, 1925.
The King Was in His Counting House. New York, Farrar and Rinehart, 1938; London, Lane, 1939.
The First Gentleman of America. New York, Farrar and Rinehart, 1942; as *The First American Gentleman*, London, Lane, 1942.

Short Stories

The Line of Love. New York, Harper, 1905; revised edition, New York, McBride, 1921; London, Lane, 1929.
Gallantry. New York, Harper, 1907; revised edition, New York, McBride, 1922; London, Lane, 1928.
Chivalry. New York, Harper, 1909; revised edition, New York, McBride, 1921; London, Lane, 1928.
The Certain Hour. New York, McBride, 1916; London, McBride Nast, 1917.

Play

The Jewel Merchants (produced Richmond, 1921). New York, McBride, 1921.

Poetry

From the Hidden Way. New York, McBride, 1916; revised edition, 1924.
Ballades from the Hidden Way. New York, Crosby Gaige, 1928.
Sonnets from Antan. New York, Fountain Press, 1929.

Other

Branchiana (genealogy). Privately printed, 1907.
Branch of Abingdon. Privately printed, 1911.
The Majors and Their Marriages. Richmond, Hill, 1915.
The Judging of Jurgen. Chicago, Bookfellows, 1920.
Jurgen and the Censor. Privately printed, 1920.
Taboo: A Legend Retold from the Dirghic of Saevius Nicanor. New York, McBride, 1921.
Joseph Hergesheimer. Chicago, Bookfellows, 1921.
The Lineage of Lichfield: An Essay in Eugenics. New York, McBride, 1922.

Straws and Prayer-Books. New York, McBride, 1924; London, Lane, 1926.

Some of Us: An Essay in Epitaphs. New York, McBride, and London, Lane, 1930.

Townsend of Lichfield. New York, McBride, 1930.

Between Dawn and Sunrise: Selections, edited by John Macy. New York, McBride, and London, Lane, 1930.

These Restless Heads: A Trilogy of Romantics. New York, McBride, 1932.

Special Delivery: A Packet of Replies. New York, McBride, 1933; London, Philip Allan, 1934.

Ladies and Gentlemen: A Parcel of Reconsiderations. New York, McBride, 1934.

Preface to the Past. New York, McBride, 1936.

The Nightmare Has Triplets: An Author's Note on Smire. New York, Doubleday, 1937.

Of Ellen Glasgow: An Inscribed Portrait. New York, Maverick Press, 1938.

The St. John's: A Parade of Diversities, with A. J. Hanna. New York, Farrar and Rinehart, 1943.

Let Me Lie. New York, Farrar Straus, 1947.

Quiet, Please. Gainesville, University of Florida Press, 1952.

As I Remember It: Some Epilogues in Recollection. New York, McBride, 1955.

Between Friends: Letters of James Branch Cabell and Others, edited by Padraic Colum and Margaret Freeman Cabell. New York, Harcourt Brace, 1962.

The Letters of James Branch Cabell, edited by Edward Wagenknecht. Norman, University of Oklahoma Press, 1975.

*

Bibliography: *James Branch Cabell: A Complete Bibliography* by James N. Hall, New York, Revisionist Press, 1974; *James Branch Cabell: A Reference Guide* by Maurice Duke, Boston, Hall, and London, Prior, 1979.

Manuscript Collection: University of Virginia Library, Charlottesville.

Critical Studies: *No Place on Earth: Ellen Glasgow, James Branch Cabell, and Richmond-in-Virginia* by Louis D. Rubin, Jr., Austin, University of Texas Press, 1959; *James Branch Cabell* by Joe Lee Davis, New York, Twayne, 1962; *Jesting Moses: A Study in Cabellian Comedy* by Arvin R. Wells, Gainesville, University of Florida Press, 1962; *Cabell: The Dream and the Reality* by Desmond Tarrant, Norman, University of Oklahoma Press, 1967; *James Branch Cabell: Three Essays* by Carl Van Doren, H. L. Mencken, and Hugh Walpole, Port Washington, New York, Kennikat Press, 1967; *Cabell under Fire: Four Essays* by Geoffrey Morley-Mower, New York, Revisionist Press, 1975; *James Branch Cabell: The Richmond Iconoclast* by Dorothy B. Schlegel, New York, Revisionist Press, 1975; *In Quest of Cabell: Five Exploratory Essays* by William Leigh Godshalk, New York, Revisionist Press, 1976; *James Branch Cabell: Centennial Essays* edited by M. Thomas Inge and Edgar E. MacDonald, Baton Rouge, Louisiana State University Press, 1983; *From Satire to Subversion: The Fantasies of James Branch Cabell* by James D. Riemer, New York, Greenwood Press, 1989.

*   *   *

Ignored by the public for two decades of the century, a *cause celebre* in the 1920s, an established titan of American literature in the 1930s, and later only partially rescued from obscurity by fantasy enthusiasts and Southern regionalist academics, James Branch Cabell had a career almost as ironic as any of his fictional heroes. Cabell was the product of the often impoverished aristocracy of the post-Civil War South and grew up increasingly aware that the antebellum society his elders so passionately idealized never actually existed. Not surprisingly, his earliest fictions, social comedies or historical comedy-romances, tend to deflate ideals, although at first timidly. It is only in the 1929 revision of *The Line of Love* that the Demoiselle Melite, finding that the knight Adhelmar has given up all for her and died at her feet, realizes that: "She was now conscious of no emotion whatever. It seemed to her that she ought to be more greatly moved." Nevertheless, illustrator Howard Pyle found even the early Cabell unwholesome and soon had him dropped from the lists of the publisher, Harper and Brothers.

With *The Cream of the Jest,* Cabell came into his own, although still without commercial success. We discover that what seems to be the opening of a medieval romance is part of a novel written by the protagonist, who ranges through time, space and dreams in search of the ideal woman, Ettarre. But finally he learns that his own dying wife is the true Ettarre, and that the object of his search was with him all along.

In *Jurgen,* Cabell's most famous novel, this basic pattern is expanded further. A medieval (and middle-aged) pawnbroker, Jurgen, regains his youth. After a long series of fantastic adventures in Heaven, Hell and various imaginary lands, wooing legendary beauties, Jurgen, too, desires cosy domesticity and returns to his shrewish Dame Lisa. What made this book so famous was its allegedly salacious content, extremely mild by late-20th-century standards but in 1919 sufficient to bring down the wrath of the New York Society for the Suppression of Vice. The book was withdrawn from sale while the case was pending and prominent literary figures rallied to Cabell's defence. Before James Joyce's *Ulysses,* this was the most celebrated literary censorship case in American law. The book was exonerated, whereupon Cabell became a bestseller. With characteristic irony, he later thanked the New York Society for the Suppression of Vice for their invaluable help in invigorating his career.

But this new-found notoriety was hardly an unmixed blessing. Now Cabell was expected to be risque, and he was read for the wrong reasons. For all that some of his later works (especially *Something about Eve*) show conscious effort to live up to his own image, Cabell could only disappoint "naughty" readers. His work remained as elegantly complex as ever, probably little understood by most who read him because it was fashionable to do so.

The core of his work is the mythology of Dom Manuel and of the imaginary French province of Poictesme, which was to the 1920s what Middle-earth was to be to the 60s, complete with framed wall-maps issued by the publisher. Dom Manuel is a dull but ambitious swineherd who, through a series of often decidedly unheroic adventures, manages to drive out the Norsemen, and become known to legend as Dom Manuel the Redeemer. *The Silver Stallion* tells the not always edifying tales of Manuel's followers, supposedly heroic paladins. *The High Place, Something about Eve* and several others (including some of Cabell's mainstream novels) deal with various descendants of Manuel. Cabell, who was fond of genealogy, managed to incorporate virtually all his characters into one vast family tree, publishing the result as *The Lineage of Lichfield.* He also went back to rewrite his earlier, less successful works and attempted to tie often non-fantastic material into the Poictesme Mythos.

At his best, Cabell could be a witty, wise, sly writer, capable of both great irony and great beauty. Passages in his books are strangely moving, expressing regret that the ideals neither Cabell nor his characters believe in cannot exist in the real world. The typical Cabell novel is episodic, drags in spots, but features brilliant sequences. His style is filled with verbal trickery: anagrams of allegorical significance, metered poems set as prose, and abounding mythological and scholarly allusions. (But beware: Cabell often makes erudite references to nonexistent authorities.) Not surprisingly, one journal of Cabell scholarship, *Kalki,* devoted a great deal of space to exegesis.

After the Poictesme series, there was considerable question about what Cabell would do next. The introduction to *The Way of Ecben* was widely misinterpreted to the effect that Cabell was through with writing, when what he actually meant was that he would use a different byline, "Branch Cabell," to distinguish later books from what was now known as *The Biography of Manuel,* an 18-volume work issued in the uniform Storisende Edition. With the onset of the Great Depression, Cabell's career collapsed. Literary fashions changed radically, and Cabell was unable to change his manner. A possibly apocryphal critical remark sums up: "James Branch Cabell has something important to say. He has said it many times."

Later works sold badly. Of the Nightmare Has Triplets trilogy, *Smirt, Smith* and *Smire,* only the first volume even managed a second printing. Nevertheless, late Cabell has its attractions. The trilogy is an extended dream, allegedly "an attempt to extend the naturalism of Lewis Carroll." It is self-conscious, often autobiographical (complete with auctorial complaints about the public's inability to appreciate him), but inventive and strange, regarded by some as Cabell's best work. *There Were Two Pirates* is a charming novella about a historical pirate, who pillaged the Florida coasts in the 18th century. In Cabell's version, the pirate manages to separate himself from his shadow. The shadow then goes on with buccaneering and is eventually slain, while the pirate himself settles down to completely unearned moral respectability. A semi-sequel, *The Devil's Own Dear Son,* is about a man who learns that he is the son of a demon. But, like most Cabell heroes, he desires the comforts of home and rejects numerous magical possibilities offered by his increasingly exasperated father. In this last novel, Cabell's mannerisms, particularly the long, ironic, and innuendo-filled speeches between father and son, serve only to remind the reader that the possibly apocryphal critic may have been right after all. It is a tired book.

Cabell remains an important figure, though he is unlikely ever to be greatly popular again. He was incapable of escapism, for all he (and his characters) might yearn for it. *Jurgen,* at least, will survive.

—Darrell Schweitzer

CALDECOTT, Moyra

Nationality: British. **Born:** South Africa, 1 June 1927. **Education:** Girls' High School, Pietermaritzburg, Natal, South Africa; Natal University, B.A. in English and Philosophy, 1948; M.A. in English Literature, 1949. **Family:** Married Oliver Zerffi Stratford Caldecott in 1951 (died 1989); three children. Moved to Britain in 1951. **Address:** 52 Southdown Road, Bath BA2 1JQ, England.

FANTASY PUBLICATIONS

Novels (series: Ancient Egypt; Tall Stones)

The Tall Stones. London, Rex Collings, 1977; New York, Hill and Wang, 1978.
The Temple of the Sun (Tall Stones). London, Rex Collings, 1977; New York, Hill and Wang, 1978.
Shadow on the Stones (Tall Stones). London, Rex Collings, and New York, Hill and Wang, 1978.
Guardians of the Tall Stones (omnibus; includes *The Tall Stones, The Temple of the Sun, Shadow on the Stones*). London, Arrow, and Berkeley, California, Celestial Arts, 1986.
The Silver Vortex (Tall Stones). London, Arrow, 1987.
The Lily and the Bull. London, Rex Collings, 1979; New York, Hill and Wang, 1980.
Child of the Dark Star. Frome, Somerset, Bran's Head, 1984.
The Tower and the Emerald. London, Hamlyn, 1985.
Son of the Sun (Ancient Egypt). London Allison and Busby, 1986.
Daughter of Amun (Ancient Egypt). London, Arrow, 1989.
Daughter of Ra (Ancient Egypt). London, Arrow, 1990.
The Winged Man. London, Headline, 1993.

Short Stories

Adventures by Leaflight (for children). California, Green Tiger Press, 1978.
Women in Celtic Myth. London, Arrow, 1988; Rochester, Vermont, Destiny Books, 1992.
Crystal Legends. London, Aquarian Press, 1990.
Myths of the Sacred Tree. Rochester, Vermont, Destiny Books, 1993.

OTHER PUBLICATIONS

Novel

Etheldreda. London, Arkana, 1987.

Play

A Tibetan Wake (produced in Backwell, Somerset, 1990).

Other

Weapons of the Wolfhound. London, Rex Collings, 1976.
Twins of the Tylwyth Teg. Frome, Somerset, Bran's Head, 1983.
Taliesin and Avagddu. Frome, Somerset, Bran's Head, 1984.
Bran, Son of Llyr. Frome, Somerset, Bran's Head, 1985.
The Green Lady and the King of Shadows. Glastonbury, Gothic Image, 1989.

*

Moyra Caldecott comments:

I write novels as a way of exploring life. Most of my fantasy novels are set in ancient times, well researched as to time and place, the imaginative story making use of material from myth and legend, and drawing on what feel like reincarnational memories and sometimes on personal experiences of the paranormal. Only one is set in the future, *Child of the Dark Star*—on a planet colonized by humans and ruled by astrologers who have created a rigid caste system against which the hero rebels.

Guardians of the Tall Stones was originally three separate novels, followed by a fourth, *The Silver Vortex*. The story is set in Bronze Age Britain at a time when the great Neolithic stone circles were already ancient but still being used. *The Tower and the Emerald* is set in Dark Ages Britain and presupposes that the myth of the emerald, falling from the crown of Lucifer as he falls from heaven, is true. An Ancient Egyptian trilogy, set in the magnificent 18th Dynasty, comprises: *Daughter of Amun,* the story of the female pharaoh Hatshepsut; *The Son of the Sun,* the story of Akhenaten, the "heretic" pharaoh; and *Daughter of Ra,* the story of Tutankhamun and his wife, Ankhesenamun. I also write non-novels, i.e. collections of myths and legends around a central theme but from around the world (e.g. *Myths of the Sacred Tree* and *Crystal Legends*) and after each tale I give a commentary on what the story means esoterically.

*   *   *

Much of Moyra Caldecott's work shows a fascination with ancient peoples and their beliefs, be it the cultures of Minoan Crete or Bronze Age Britain. These are familiar territories for those fantasy writers who favour a historical setting with ample scope for speculation, though archaeologists would doubtless raise eyebrows at Caldecott's sanitized, almost Utopian Bronze Age, the setting for her first three books, and at her understanding of the function of stone circles in this archaic society.

A constant theme in fantasy novels of this nature is the conflict between the old and new, particularly in religious beliefs, and Caldecott is no exception to this. Her Tall Stones trilogy portrays a series of struggles between the Lords of the Sun, a shadowy organization of men and women who worship within the stone circles with which each village is associated, and a series of enemies who have embraced a darker religion. In the first two books, the threat is a renegade priest, Wardyke, who overthrows the priest in Kyra and Karne's village and imposes his own oppressive brand of religion on the people, as well as bringing his followers to the village. Caldecott contrasts their slovenly ways and lack of understanding of the relationship between man and his resources with the idealized lives of the original villagers. Similarly, she contrasts the harsh, demanding religion of sacrifice with the childlike, unquestioning attitude of the villagers who previously believed implicitly in the power of their priest. Although the villagers are forced to recognize that priests are not necessarily infallible and some of them are able to see beyond the confines of village life, little actually changes. The newcomers are absorbed into the village and adapt their ways but seem to bring nothing of value from their own lives, and the utopian dream remains undisturbed.

This view seems to be very much in keeping with Caldecott's philosophy of an underlying pattern to existence. In the second volume of the trilogy, Kyra and Karne leave their village for the Sacred Circle in the south of the country, because Kyra is to be trained as a priest. They come to recognize that spiritual development is at a different stage for each individual, thus marking a metaphysical break with the beliefs of their parents, much as their journey marks a physical break with the old ways. Nevertheless, they believe firmly in the Pattern which shapes the Universe and, furthermore, that escape is almost impossible.

This is reflected in another important theme in all of Caldecott's writing, namely reincarnation and the re-enacting, through the ages, of certain events. Karne and Kyra experience this when Karne's adopted son, Isar, becomes embroiled in an age-old tragedy of betrayal involving his natural father, Wardyke, as well as Kyra and her teacher at the Sacred Circle. Revenge has been sought, again and again, throughout the years, and the pattern has to be broken in order to avert further tragedy. Caldecott seems to visualize a constant recapitulation of wrongs which must be righted, even if it literally takes aeons, even as she seems to argue for the maintenance of the pattern within the world.

In *The Lily and the Bull,* Caldecott turns to Minoan Crete, using characters who were peripherally mentioned in the trilogy when encountered by Kyra in her spirit travels. Here, Quilla is the representative of the Goddess on Earth, although apparently a mortal woman, resisting the threat of the masculine Cult of the Bull. Caldecott paints a picture of a society with a relaxed attitude to religion—espousing the cult of the Goddess or the Bull as it suits each individual—until it is obliged take up the one on the orders of the corrupt Queen who is flouting society's rules in order to achieve greater power.

The Tower and the Emerald most clearly addresses the matter of reincarnation as Idoc, a sorcerer, is released from imprisonment by Viviane, after recognizing her as the reincarnation of the woman whose love he had lost—and her followers as the reincarnation of his own friends. Through them he proposes to assuage his need for vengeance. The setting is vaguely Arthurian, with names drawn from the chronicles and medieval stories, but this has little to do with the Matter of Britain.

Caldecott's work is repetitive and heavily reliant on a few well-worn themes and settings which have been more effectively dealt with by other writers in the genre. Neither is she well served by a simplistic writing style, bordering on the naive, in which all is told and nothing is shown. While she is undoubtedly sincere in her belief that ancient peoples possessed a mystic faith which was safeguarded by a caste of priests, Caldecott's ability to communicate this vision to her readers is limited.

—Maureen Speller

CAMERDEN, Roger. *See* **BANGS, John Kendrick.**

CARD, Orson Scott

Pseudonym: Brian Green. **Nationality:** American. **Born:** Richland, Washington, 24 August 1951. **Education:** Brigham Young University, Provo, Utah, B.A. in theatre 1975; University of Utah, Salt Lake City, M.A. in English 1981. **Family:** Married Kristine Allen in 1977; three sons and one daughter. **Career:** Volunteer Mormon missionary in Brazil, 1971-73; operated repertory theatre, Provo, 1974-75; proofreader, 1974, and editor, 1974-76, Brigham Young University Press; assistant editor, *Ensign* magazine, Salt Lake City, 1976-78; senior editor, Compute! Books, Greensboro, North Carolina, 1983; taught at the University of Utah, 1979-80, 1981,

Brigham Young University, 1981, Notre Dame University, Indiana, 1981-82, and Clarion Writers Workshop, East Lansing, Michigan, 1982. Local Democratic precinct election judge and Utah State Democratic Convention delegate. **Awards:** John W. Campbell award, 1978; Nebula award, for novel, 1985, 1986; Hugo award, for novel, 1985, 1986, 1987; World Fantasy award, for novelette, 1987; *Locus* award, for novel, 1988, 1989; Mythopoeic Fantasy award, 1988; Hugo award, for nonfiction, 1990. **Agent:** Barbara Bova, 207 Sedgwick Road, West Hartford, CT 06107, USA.

Fantasy Publications

Novels (series: Alvin Maker)

Hart's Hope. New York, Berkley, 1983; London, Unwin, 1986.
Seventh Son (Alvin). New York, Tor, 1987; London, Legend, 1988.
Red Prophet (Alvin). New York, Tor, 1988; London, Legend, 1989.
Prentice Alvin. New York, Tor, and London, Legend, 1989.
Hatrack River: The Tales of Alvin Maker (omnibus; includes *Seventh Son, Red Prophet, Prentice Alvin*). New York, Guild America, 1989.

Other

Editor, *Dragons of Light.* New York, Ace, 1980.
Editor, *Dragons of Darkness.* New York, Ace, 1981.

Other Publications

Novels

Hot Sleep. New York, Baronet, 1979; London, Futura, 1980.
A Planet Called Treason. New York, St. Martin's Press, 1979; London, Pan, 1981; revised as *Treason,* New York, St. Martin's Press, 1988.
Songmaster. New York, Dial Press, 1980; London, Futura, 1981.
The Worthing Chronicle. New York, Ace, 1983.
A Woman of Destiny. New York, Berkley, 1984; as *Saints,* New York, Tor, 1988.
Ender's Game. New York, Tor, and London, Unwin, 1985.
Speaker for the Dead. New York, Tor, 1986; London, Century, 1987.
Ender's War (omnibus; includes *Ender's Game, Speaker for the Dead*). New York: Nelson Doubleday, 1986.
Wyrms. New York, Arbor House, 1987; London, Legend, 1988.
The Abyss (novelization of screenplay). New York, Pocket, and London, Century, 1989.
Eye for Eye, with *The Tunesmith* by Lloyd Biggle, Jr. New York, Tor, 1990.
The Worthing Saga (omnibus; includes *The Worthing Chronicle* and short stories). New York, Tor, 1990; London, Legend, 1991.
Xenocide. New York, Tor, and London, Legend, 1991.
Lost Boys. New York and London, HarperCollins, 1992.
The Memory of Earth. New York, Tor, and London, Legend, 1992.
The Call of Earth. New York, Tor, and London, Legend, 1993.
Lovelock, with Kathryn H. Kidd. New York, Tor, 1994.
The Ships of Earth. New York, Tor, and London, Legend, 1994.
Earthfall. New York, Tor, 1995.

Short Stories

Capitol: The Worthing Chronicle. New York, Ace, 1979.
Unaccompanied Sonata & Other Stories. New York, Dial Press, 1980.
Cardography. Eugene, Oregon, Hypatia Press, 1987.
The Folk of the Fringe. West Bloomfield, Michigan, Phantasia Press, 1989; London, Legend, 1990.
Maps in a Mirror: The Short Fiction of Orson Scott Card. New York, Tor, 1990; London, Legend, 1991; in 2 vols., London, Legend, 1992; in 4 vols., as *The Changed Man, Flux, Cruel Miracles* and *Monkey Sonatas,* New York, Tor, 1992-93.

Plays

Tell Me That You Love Me, Junie Moon, adaptation of a work by Majorie Kellogg (also director: produced Provo, Utah, 1969).
The Apostate (produced Provo, Utah, 1970).
In Flight (produced Provo, Utah, 1970).
Across Five Summers (produced Provo, Utah, 1971).
Of Gideon (produced Provo, Utah, 1971).
Stone Tables (produced Provo, Utah, 1973).
A Christmas Carol, adaptation of the story by Dickens (also director: produced Provo, Utah, 1974).
Father, Mother, Mother, and Mom (produced Provo, Utah, 1974). Published in *Sunstone,* 1978.
Liberty Jail (produced Provo, Utah, 1975).
Rag Mission (as Brian Green), in *Ensign* (Salt Lake City), July 1977.
Fresh Courage Take (also director: produced, 1978).
Elders and Sisters (produced, 1979).
Wings (produced, 1982).

Other

Listen, Mom and Dad. Salt Lake City, Bookcraft, 1978.
Saintspeak. Berkeley, California, Signature, 1981.
Ainge. Midvale, Utah, Signature, 1982.
Compute's Guide to IBM PCjr Sound and Graphics. Greensboro, North Carolina, Compute, 1984.
Cardography. Eugene, Oregon, Hypatia Press, 1987.
Characters and Viewpoint. Cincinnati, Ohio, Writer's Digest, 1988; London, Robinson, 1989.
How To Write Science Fiction and Fantasy. Cincinnati, Ohio, Writer's Digest, 1990.

Editor, *Future on Fire.* New York, Tor, 1991.

*

Manuscript Collection: Brigham Young University, Provo, Utah.

Critical Study: *In the Image of God: Theme, Characterization, and Landscape in the Fiction of Orson Scott Card* by Michael R. Collings, Westport, Connecticut, Greenwood Press, 1990.

*   *   *

Card was one of the two or three most successful new science fiction authors of the 1980s. His first published story, "Ender's Game" (1977), was nominated for a Hugo Award. *Ender's Game,* the novel-length version, and its sequel, *Speaker for the Dead,* both won the two major sf awards for best novel of the year, the Hugo and the Nebula. But he is a science fiction writer with an interest in the mythopoeic: his sf frequently draws on elements from myth, fairy tale and other forms of fantasy.

His early novel *Hart's Hope* was a straight fantasy (though not a very accomplished one), with a protagonist whose magical talent was the negation of magic. Some of his science fiction novels would probably interest the reader of fantasy more. Much of *Songmaster,* for instance, could have been transformed into fantasy by a few minor changes, such as making the despot Mikal the ruler of a terrestrial rather than a galactic empire. It is the story of a boy trained as a Songbird, a singer whose improvised songs can control all his listeners' emotions; he grows up close to the sources of political power, and uses his powers to achieve the Empire for himself. Similarly, *Wyrms* is the quest of a young woman for her rightful throne, and for knowledge; it has the feel of a fairy tale, set as it is in a semi-medieval world populated not only by humans but by races called dwelfs, geblings and gaunts (reminiscent of the denizens of traditional fairy tale, such as dwarfs, elves and giants). Yet it is set on a colonized planet, and has a fully science-fictional rationale.

Card is a compelling storyteller, with a powerful, relentless and at times brutal imagination. Card himself has said that the two most powerful influences on his writing have been Shakespeare and Joseph Smith. Card was brought up, and remains, a committed member of the Church of the Latter-Day Saints, and the writings of Joseph Smith, and *The Book of Mormon,* are reflected, in complex ways, in his own work. Card's fascination with Messiah-figures who have the power to redeem others is one probable consequence of his Mormonism. Ender Wiggin is one of the best-known of Card's Messiahs; the last chapter of *Wyrms* is even called "The Return of Kristos". But for fantasy readers the most interesting will be Alvin Maker.

So far three novels of the Tales of Alvin Maker have appeared: *Seventh Son, Red Prophet* and *Prentice Alvin.* Card has said that *Alvin Journeyman* and *Master Alvin* will follow. With the Alvin series, Card has done for the fantasy of the Old World what the Church of the Latter-Day Saints has done for Christianity: he has brought it to America and integrated it into American history and geography. He has done it in part by manipulating American history: he uses the device, familiar to science fiction writers, of alternative history. The series is set in the early 19th century, in a North America some of whose history can be deduced from a map at the beginning of *Seventh Son*: Canada is French, but the Spanish still hold parts of the South; the rest of the Southern states are still Crown Colonies; New England is independent; and a new United States is expanding westwards, creating the state of Appalachee and various territories. Soon we learn that Oliver Cromwell had lived to a ripe old age, and that there is still a Lord Protector in England. Some of the same personages from our world make their appearances, but in very different circumstances. Napoleon Bonaparte is a French general posted to Canada; William Blake has become a wandering visionary in America, calling himself Taleswapper and playing a crucial part in the development of Alvin's talents.

What makes the Tales of Alvin Maker fantasy rather than science fiction—and fantasy of an unusual kind—is that magic is a common and accepted part of life. As in "our" America, farmers put hexes up on barns or doors as a protection against evil. In Alvin's America, hexes are effective and necessary, and there are those who are expert at creating them, as others have talents at precognition, fire-starting, or calming people's tempers. Most people accept these talents as part of everyday life; but churchmen, particularly those who have come over from Britain, can hardly bring themselves to admit that they exist. One character explains it thus: witches have been persecuted out of existence in Europe and have emigrated to North America in large numbers, bringing their talents with them.

The three published volumes take the life of Alvin from birth to the age of twenty. Alvin is the seventh son of a seventh son. He comes from a whole family of magically talented people, but it is clear from the outset that Alvin himself is going to exceed their powers. We know that he will be a Maker, and that there has not been a Maker for at least a thousand years. As yet it is not certain what a Maker is. It is, however, clear that a Maker has the power to create, and that because of his creative powers he is close to God, and opposed to the Unmaker, the supernatural force for evil and destruction. Alvin is a seer, and a prophet, and a powerful force for good; he is an analogue, perhaps, of Joseph Smith. Through the three books the Unmaker attempts to destroy Alvin, both directly and through servants such as the Reverend Philadelphia Thrower (who is convinced he is the agent of God rather than the Unmaker). Alvin matures, and learns more about his own powers and the powers of the Unmaker, who appears to be a more elemental and powerful figure than Satan. He also learns the skills to cope with the evils of the world: in *Red Prophet* with the land-hungry white settlers and their hatred of the Native Americans, and in *Prentice Alvin* with the slave-owners of the South. Even if Card never finishes the series (which is a possibility), it will be judged as one of the most important contributions to American fantasy-writing of recent years.

Card is also a writer of powerful and effective short stories, most of which have been collected in *Maps in a Mirror.* Many are science fiction, but of the fantasy stories the most significant are the fables in fairy-tale form, such as "Kingsmeat," and what is probably his most controversial story, "Lost Boys," which purports to be autobiographical, and tells a ghost story about his own family in part, as he realized afterwards, to exorcise his own feelings about his handicapped son. The latter has since been expanded into a full-length horror novel.

—Edward James

CARLSEN, Chris. *See* **HOLDSTOCK, Robert.**

CARROLL, Jonathan (Samuel)

Nationality: American. **Born:** New York(?), 1949; son of television playwright and screenwriter Sidney Carroll. **Family:** Married; one son. **Career:** Journalist, teacher, novelist and screenwriter. Has lived in Vienna, Austria, for many years. **Awards:** World Fantasy award, 1988; British Fantasy award, 1991. **Agent:** David Higham Associates, 5-8 Lower John Street, Golden Square, London, W1R 4HA, England.

FANTASY PUBLICATIONS

Novels

The Land of Laughs. New York, Viking Press, 1980; London, Hamlyn, 1982.

Voice of Our Shadow. New York, Viking Press, 1983; London, Arrow, 1984.

Bones of the Moon. London, Century, 1987; New York, Arbor House, 1988.

Sleeping in Flame. London, Legend, 1988; New York, Doubleday, 1989.

A Child Across the Sky. London, Legend, 1989; New York, Doubleday, 1990.

Black Cocktail (novella). London, Legend, 1990; New York, St. Martin's Press, 1991.

Outside the Dog Museum. London, Macdonald, 1991; New York Doubleday, 1992.

After Silence. London, Macdonald, 1992; New York Doubleday, 1993.

From the Teeth of Angels. London, HarperCollins, and New York Doubleday, 1994.

Short Stories

The Panic Hand (originally published in German as *Die Panische Hand,* circa 1989). London, HarperCollins, 1995.

OTHER PUBLICATIONS

Plays

Screenplays: *The Joker,* date unknown; plus others, not divulged.

*   *   *

The novels of Jonathan Carroll sit uncomfortably on the shelf next to those of, say, Stephen King or Guy Gavriel Kay. Despite *Twilight Zone* elements like talking dogs, personalized Deaths, serial killers, parallel worlds and evil angels, Carroll rarely fits easily into genre fantasy. However, he does spin off novels from developments within genre, skilfully inventing the fictional books and films which recur in his developing private world: the children's novels of Marshall France which sustain the life of a small town in *The Land of Laughs,* the Oz-like land of Rondua which the heroine of *Bones of the Moon* visits and writes about in a bestseller, the fairy tales which explain the life of an actor-turned screenwriter in *Sleeping in Flame,* the Midnight series of slasher films central to *A Child Across the Sky,* the "Paper Clip" cartoon strip drawn by the narrator of *After Silence,* or the Finky Linky children's television show which stars the protagonist of *From the Teeth of Angels.* There are almost subliminal echoes as influence seeps in, if only as inspiration for characters Carroll makes his own: a villain in *Outside the Dog Museum* is called Cthulu (altering Lovecraft's spelling), Bloodstone of the Midnight films and Finky Linky are echoes of Freddy Krueger and Froggy the Gremlin, and *After Silence* features a detective named Mary Poe.

Carroll's books are populated by modest but creative people: his gradually enlarging cast recurs, so each distinct new book is seen through a prism of character and incident with which devoted readers are familiar. Many Carroll protagonists are writers (Thomas Abbey of *The Land of Laughs,* Joe Lennox of *Voice of Our Shadow,* Cullen James of *Bones of the Moon,* Walker Easterling of *Sleeping in Flame*) but he also spotlights film director Weber Gregston and actor Philip Strayhorn (*A Child Across the Sky*), architect Harry Radcliffe (*Outside the Dog Museum*), cartoonist Max Fischer (*After Silence*), radio talkshow host Ingram York (*Black Cocktail*), or children's television personality Wyatt Leonard and movie star Arlen Ford (*From the Teeth of Angels*). The creativity of the characters is vital to the approach of an author who always chooses protagonists whose explorations of a world of pain and magic and mystery are as much the visions of an artist as the investigations of a detective. The double-edged pleasures of Carroll's novels rest with his fantastical visions and deft descriptions of tiny wonders (few writers can describe a snack as perfectly), but their seriousness is invested in character. The crossovers from book to book can be deceptive, as each individual work is coloured by its narrator (some have several). Max Fischer, caught up in a paranoid suspense plot that admits no magic, perceives a world very different from the continuum-tripping Cullen James, and their books present subtly irreconcilable events.

Typically, Carroll opens with a careful, loving account of the sunny lives of decent, productive people who glimpse a darkness at the edge of their vision and are gradually lured into a fantastical world inhabited by demigods of almost unimaginable malevolence (the worst of them is the Death of *From the Teeth of Angels*). Through *The Land of Laughs* and *A Child Across the Sky,* Carroll addresses the question of the responsibility of the creators of dark fantasies, but through the journeys of his protagonists, he explores a world in which any daydreaming, no matter how charming or innocent, must eventually tap into despair and horror. The makers of Midnight Kills are not simply irresponsible but unconsciously embodying deep truths through pop culture artefacts. Thomas Abbey realizes the community he has come to explore is the fading creation of an absent and all too-human God, addressing metaphysical issues through an examination of the process of creation, while the obsessive Max Fischer's investigation into the past of his new wife and her son reveals a tapestry of crime and madness which never veers into the outright impossible but conveys exactly the same sense of a reality that only exists through a fragile consensus which any person can deny at any moment. Carroll's books are full of perfect loves which congeal into lifelong battles but there are genuine relationships which withstand revelations of perfidy. Though the authorial voice tends to be clear-eyed and humane, there is a tendency for the leading characters to be flawed by a pompousness or shallowness for which Carroll often overcompensates with extreme punishments.

The Land of Laughs is such a strong debut (it remains the most perfectly-plotted of the novels and comes closest to having what Hollywood calls a "high concept" until *After Silence*) that it took three or four further novels for a greater pattern to emerge. While each book is complete in itself, and the early novels tend to have last-page twists which propel the reader out of the text with undue force and are usually revoked by references in later books, Carroll's *oeuvre* is stronger for the interrelationships between the stories he tells. Books like *A Child Across the Sky* or *From the Teeth of Angels,* which reintroduce supporting players from earlier novels as leading characters, can seem less rigorously plotted than they are simply because Carroll's narrative strategies are so unorthodox and insidious. He will advance the purpose of a book with thumbnail sketches of a restaurant or an art gallery, an anecdote told by a walk-on character, a letter from a relative of a major character or a digression on a character's unusual hobby (Abbey collects masks while his girlfriend is interested in puppetry) or profession (enlarging the theme, in *From the Teeth of Angels,* a mask shop owner compares the sales of his successful masks of Brezhnev and Gorbachev with dead-loss masks of Andropov and Chernenko).

Carroll is as much a novelist of social observation as a fantasist and has no little skill as a chronicler of the lives of almost-artists, but he is irresistibly drawn to explorations of the marvellous and the terrifying. If one side of his work inclines towards the literary mainstream (writing cheerfully of love affairs and mixed-up parents and terminal illness), another aspect is unable to forsake the devils and angels and monsters whose presence illuminate and almost make sense of human foibles and the half-glimpsed Oz-like workings of the universe. Revelations, when they come, are liable to be as brutal as the hint delivered by Death in *From the Teeth of Angels,* in the shape of a scary Los Angeles cop, when he says "sometimes it's better to learn through shock than persuasion." Carroll, it has to be said, is a master of both methods of instruction.

—Kim Newman

CARROLL, Lewis

Pseudonym for Charles Lutwidge Dodgson. **Nationality:** British. **Born:** Daresbury, Cheshire, 27 January 1832. **Education:** Attended school in Richmond, Surrey, 1844-46; Rugby School, Warwickshire, 1846-49; Christ Church, Oxford (Boultor scholar, 1851), B.A. (honours) in mathematics 1854, M.A. 1857. **Career:** Fellow, and Master of the House, 1855, sub-librarian, 1855, Bostock Scholar, 1855, Lecturer in Mathematics, 1856-81, and Curator of the Common Room, 1882-92, Christ Church, Oxford. Ordained, 1861. **Died:** 14 January 1898.

Fantasy Publications

Novels

Alice's Adventures in Wonderland, illustrated by John Tenniel. London, Macmillan, 1865; New York, Appleton, 1866; revised editions, 1886, 1897.
Through the Looking-Glass, and What Alice Found There, illustrated by John Tenniel. London, Macmillan, 1871; revised edition, 1897; Boston, Lee & Sheppard/ New York, Lee, Sheppard & Dillingham, 1972.
Alice's Adventures Underground. London, Macmillan, 1886; New York, Macmillan, 1886.
Sylvie and Bruno. London and New York, Macmillan, 1889.
Sylvie and Bruno Concluded. London and New York, Macmillan, 1893.

Short Story

Lewis Carroll, The Wasp in a Wig: The "Suppressed" Episode of Through the Looking Glass. Lewis Carroll Society, 1977.

Poetry

The Hunting of the Snark: An Agony in Eight Fits. London, Macmillan, 1867.
Phantasmagoria and Other Poems. London, Macmillan, 1869.
Rhyme? and Reason? London, Macmillan, 1883.
Three Sunsets and Other Poems. 1898.
The Collected Verse of Lewis Carroll. Dutton, 1929
For the Train: Five Poems and a Tale. London, Archer, 1932.
The Jabberwocky and Other Frabjour Nonsense. Crown, 1964.
The Poems of Lewis Carroll. Crowell, 1973.

*

Film Adaptations (selection): *Alice in Wonderland,* 1910, 1915, 1927, 1931, 1933, 1950, 1951, 1966 (TV movie), 1972, 1985 (TV movie), 1986 (TV serial), all based on the novels *Alice's Adventures in Wonderland* and *Through the Looking-Glass, and What Alice Found There.*

Bibliography: *Lewis Carroll: An Annotated International Bibliography, 1960-77* by Edward Guiliano, University Press of Virginia, 1980.

Critical Studies: *The Annotated Alice: Alice's Adventures in Wonderland and Through the Looking Glass* by Martin Gardner, New York, Potter, 1960; *Lewis Carroll* by Derek Hudson, Greenwood, 1972; *The Alice Concordance: A Concordance to Lewis Carroll's "Alice in Wonderland" and "Through the Looking Glass"* by Daryl Colquhoun, University of Adelaide Press, 1986; *Lewis Carroll* by Richard Michael Kelly, Twayne, 1990.

*   *   *

Lewis Carroll's two books about the dream-adventures of Alice have made a copious contribution to the common heritage of literary reference; almost everyone understands a conversational reference to a Mad Hatter's Tea-Party, or the import of such quotations as "Curiouser and curiouser," "Sentence first—verdict afterwards" and "Jam yesterday and jam tomorrow—but never jam today". The continuing popularity of the Alice books has run in parallel with considerable academic industry, whose bulk and variety far outstrips the academic interest taken in any other children's books. Martin Gardner's *The Annotated Alice* (1960) gives the original versions of all the rhymes which Carroll parodied, unfolds the conundrums and verbal tricks which pepper the narratives, and explains the ways in which Alice's encounters touch on authentic philosophical problems (elementary problems in logic crop up in the conversation of most of the characters in the first volume, while more abstruse questions about the significance of names and the status of general terms are obliquely raised in the second volume). Much additional commentary has been engendered by post-Freudian suspicions about the Reverend Dodgson's relationships with the children he befriended; such speculations have coloured the image of the books in spite of the fact that there is little material in the texts that lends itself to Freudian decoding.

The Reverend Dodgson invented "Lewis Carroll" for use on a poem published in *The Train* in 1856, a month before he first made the acquaintance of the four-year-old Alice Liddell, one of the five daughters of the newly-appointed Dean of Christ Church. In 1862 Dodgson presented Alice with a manuscript version of a story he had made up during a picnic, entitled "Alice's Adventures Under

Ground," which he eventually expanded into the familiar *Alice in Wonderland.* In the wake of its success Dodgson wrote *Through the Looking Glass,* presumably drawing on the same accumulated fund of anecdotes and whimsies, but adding a stronger and more complicated narrative frame by virtue of which the story symbolically recapitulates the moves in a game of chess. (The illustrator, John Tenniel, caused one chapter to be omitted; the missing episode was published more than a hundred years later as *The Wasp in a Wig.*)

Alice in Wonderland was a watershed in the history of children's literature whose significance can hardly be overstated. Earlier writers of fantasies for children had taken it for granted that part of their task was to produce moral fables which might play a significant role in their "civilization"; the idea that stories might be written for children which would entertain them without moralizing was both original and daring, and the idea that calculated nonsense was an appropriate form of entertainment was doubly so. *Alice in Wonderland* is not without moral sensibility, but the general tenor of its rhetoric is that it is both sensible and appropriate for children to take an occasional rest from the demands of duty. Alice is initially put to sleep by a tediously instructive text, and her valiant determination to use the time she spends in free fall productively reciting her lessons is soon put into proper perspective by the time-killing madness of the Mad Hatter's Tea-Party and by delightful parodic versions of some popular moralistic rhymes. Isaac Watt's sententiously worthy "How doth the little busy bee / Improve each shining hour" is neatly transmuted into "How doth the little crocodile / Improve his shining tail."

Although it is conspicuously light at heart, Carroll's brand of nonsense is conscientious in holding almost nothing sacred. This is not because the Reverend Dodgson was in any sense a radical—he was a devout supporter of Victorian morality, so ardent an upholder of theatrical censorship that he thought Thomas Bowdler's version of Shakespeare too liberal—but because he considered the Alice books to be a realm apart from the world where the rule of Moral Order was absolute: an utterly innocent imaginary space where such issues were quite irrelevant. When, late in life, Dodgson decided to write another children's fantasy—one which he intended to be of higher literary ambition and quality—he undertook the task in a very different spirit. *Sylvie and Bruno* and *Sylvie and Bruno Concluded* are not without ingenuity, but they are constructed on a firm moral-allegorical base which so comprehensively wrecks their imaginative ambitions that they seem to be the work of another and much less interesting man. The fact that they take aboard some of the mystical and spiritualistic claptrap which came to fascinate Dodgson late in life is also severely to their disadvantage.

As the title of the second volume suggests, the Alice books hold up a mirror to the world of Victorian rationalism in which everything is comprehensively skewed. The dream-fantasies end, scrupulously enough, with the restoration of all that was disturbed, but at the end of *Through the Looking-Glass* the reader is explicitly instructed to consider carefully the question of whose dream it has been (the Red King has, of course, laid claim to it in the text). The sentimental poem appended to the text, which celebrates the memory of the "golden afternoon" of the picnic on the river-bank, represents childhood itself as a mental Wonderland from whose dream children are unfortunately doomed to wake, and then suggests that the stream of Life down which we are all condemned to drift can also be regarded as a kind of dream. The pessimism implicit in this attitude remains covert in the Alice books but is more evident in the magnificent mock-epic poem *The Hunting of the Snark,* in which

a Victorian Ship of Fools is steered by reckless heroism, according to the advice of a blank map, to a fatal culminating encounter with the monstrous Boojum.

When Alice tells Humpty Dumpty that "One can't help getting older" Humpty Dumpty's reply is that "One can't, perhaps, but two can. With proper assistance, you might have left off at seven." Alice is, however, quite right. One can't help getting older, and one can't preserve the golden afternoon of childhood, even by the most determined efforts of social intercourse and communication. The carefully-shaped nonsense, by means of which the Reverend Dodgson sought to build a bridge into a realm which he and Alice could innocently and delightedly share, was a perilously fragile structure, and the Wonderland into which it led was not really what it appeared to be. Although it was the most fantastic realm imaginable by one of the most ingenious minds of its era, there was, in the end, far too much of the mature in it. The Alice books constitute one of the most heroic attempts ever made to get away from the stifling straitjacket of the here and now, but they were bound to fail. That failure is, in fact, a uniquely marvellous example of the dictum that although truth is certainly stranger than fiction, fiction is—according to its fashion—truer.

—Brian Stableford

CARTER, Angela (Olive)

Nationality: British. **Born:** Angela Olive Stalker. Eastbourne, Sussex, 7 May 1940. **Education:** University of Bristol, 1962-65, B.A. in English 1965. **Family:** Married Paul Carter in 1960 (divorced 1972); one son by later partner Mark Pearce. **Career:** Journalist, Croydon, Surrey, 1958-61. Arts Council Fellow in Creative Writing, University of Sheffield, 1976-78; visiting professor of Creative Writing, Brown University, Providence, Rhode Island, 1980-81; writer-in-residence, University of Adelaide, 1984. **Awards:** Rhys Memorial prize, 1968; Maugham award, 1969; Cheltenham Festival prize, 1979; Kurt Maschler award, for children's book, 1982; James Tait Black Memorial prize, 1985. **Died:** 16 February 1992.

FANTASY PUBLICATIONS

Novels

Heroes and Villains. London, Heinemann, 1969; New York, Simon and Schuster, 1970.
The Infernal Desire Machines of Doctor Hoffman. London, Hart Davis, 1972; as *The War of Dreams,* New York, Harcourt Brace, 1974.
The Passion of New Eve. London, Gollancz, and New York, Harcourt Brace, 1977.
Nights at the Circus. London, Chatto and Windus, 1984; New York, Viking Press, 1985.

Short Stories

Fireworks: Nine Profane Pieces. London, Quartet, 1974; New York, Harper, 1981; revised edition, London, Chatto and Windus, 1987.

The Bloody Chamber and Other Stories. London, Gollancz, 1979; New York, Harper, 1980.
Black Venus's Tale. London, Next Editions-Faber, 1980.
Black Venus. London, Chatto and Windus, 1985; as *Saints and Strangers,* New York, Viking, 1986.
American Ghosts and Old World Wonders. London, Chatto and Windus, 1993.

Plays

Vampirella (broadcast 1976; produced London, 1986). Included in *Come Unto These Yellow Sands,* 1984.
Come Unto These Yellow Sands (radio plays; includes *The Company of Wolves, Vampirella, Puss in Boots*). Newcastle-upon-Tyne, Bloodaxe, 1984.

Other

Editor, *The Virago Book of Fairy Tales.* London, Virago Press, 1990; as *The Old Wives' Fairy Tale Book,* New York, Pantheon, 1990.
Editor, *The Second Virago Book of Fairy Tales* (introduction completed by Marina Warner). London, Virago Press, 1992.

Translator, *Sleeping Beauty and Other Favourite Fairy Tales.* London, Gollancz, 1982; New York, Schocken, 1984.
Translator, *The Fairy Tales of Charles Perrault.* London, Gollancz, 1977; New York, Avon, 1978.

OTHER PUBLICATIONS

Novels

Shadow Dance. London, Heinemann, 1966; as *Honeybuzzard,* New York, Simon and Schuster, 1967.
The Magic Toyshop. London, Heinemann, 1967; New York, Simon and Schuster, 1968.
Several Perceptions. London, Heinemann, 1968; New York, Simon and Schuster, 1969.
Love. London, Hart Davis, 1971; revised edition, London, Chatto and Windus, 1987; New York, Penguin, 1988.
Wise Children. London, Chatto and Windus, 1991.

Plays

Screenplays: *The Company of Wolves,* with Neil Jordan, 1984; *The Magic Toyshop,* 1987.

Radio Plays: *Vampirella,* 1976; *Come Unto These Yellow Sands,* 1979; *The Company of Wolves,* from her own story, 1980; *Puss in Boots,* 1982; *A Self-Made Man* (on Ronald Firbank), 1984.

Poetry

Unicorn. Leeds, Location Press, 1966.

Other

Miss Z, The Dark Young Lady (for children). London, Heinemann, and New York, Simon and Schuster, 1970.
The Donkey Prince (for children). New York, Simon and Schuster, 1970.

Comic and Curious Cats, illustrated by Martin Leman. London, Gollancz, and New York, Crown, 1979.
The Sadeian Woman: An Exercise in Cultural History. London, Virago, 1979; as *The Sadeian Woman and the Ideology of Pornography,* New York, Pantheon, 1979.
Nothing Sacred: Selected Writings. London, Virago, 1982.
Moonshadow (for children). London, Gollancz, 1982.
Expletives Deleted: Selected Writings. London, Chatto and Windus, 1992.

Editor, *Wayward Girls and Wicked Women: An Anthology of Stories.* London, Virago Press, 1986; New York, Penguin, 1989.

*

Film Adaptations: *The Company of Wolves,* 1984; *The Magic Toyshop,* 1987.

*   *   *

By the time of her sadly premature death Angela Carter had already become a favourite contemporary object of literary study in British schools and universities, reflecting the fact that she warrants study under many currently fashionable rubrics—as a feminist, a fabulist and a postmodernist—as well as being a writer of the very highest calibre.

Although Carter's earliest novels are not fantasies per se they do have surreal, neo-Gothic and fabular elements, which are most extensively displayed in *The Magic Toyshop,* an allegory of female maturation and eventual empowerment. Her first formal fantasy was the futuristic *Heroes and Villains,* which imagines a post-holocaust world in which the ruined cities are inhabited by Professors protected by Soldiers, while forests metamorphosed by mutation and inhabited by Barbarians are gradually reclaiming the earth. The heroine is the daughter of a Professor who runs away to the wilderness in search of an enlightenment and a fulfilment which cost her dear in terms of pain and privation.

This kind of journey—from a decadent Order on the brink of ruination to an unprettified Chaos whose brutalities, mysteries and confusions nevertheless hold the elusive promise of the only kind of liberation there is—was to be the fundamental movement of all Carter's work. One of the epigraphs to *Heroes and Villains* quotes Leslie Fiedler's study of *Love and Death in the American Novel* to the effect that "The Gothic mode is essentially a form of parody, a way of assailing clichés by exaggerating them to the limit of grotesqueness," and this was to be the method of Carter's fantasies, extrapolated with a calculated garishness and deliberate perversity which no other writer has matched.

The Infernal Desire Machines of Doctor Hoffman takes its protagonist on a bizarre quest to rescue the world from the eponymous devices—whose purpose is nothing less than the annihilation of reason and reality—across a phantasmagoric landscape whose symbolism supposedly reflects the most secret and most cherished impulses of the human heart, including the most shameful. The imagery owes something to the Marquis de Sade (of whose works Carter carried out an extensive feminist analysis in *The Sadeian Woman*) and something to the Decadent Romanticism of Baudelaire, but its hallucinatory vividness is quite without parallel. Its ambition and intensity entitle it to be considered one of the masterpieces of modern fantasy. *The Passion of New Eve* is a more restrained but no less vivid work whose imaginary landscape is a symbolically transfigured America. Its protagonist is a young Englishman who lives for a while in a New York on the verge of social collapse before heading westwards. The ingenuous pioneer undergoes an enforced sex-change after falling into the hands of a self-appointed Earth Mother. He is then imprisoned by the crippled and inarticulate "poet" Zero, who believes that he has been psychologically castrated by the mysterious screen goddess Tristessa St. Ange, to whose ambiguous Adam Evelyn must become an equally ambiguous Eve when the Final War breaks out.

The Passion of New Eve is a more intimate and more tightly-focused work than *The Infernal Desire Machines of Doctor Hoffman,* and deals for the most part with more modern legends: the iconography of the mass media and contemporary political movements. It was the first of a series of steps by means of which Carter brought the subject matter of the earlier novel down to earth again, gradually reweaving its lurid imagery into the fabric of everyday life, so that dreams are once again reduced to the status of dreams although their secret meanings and significations have now been teased out, understood and—to the extent that they can be—accommodated. So far as novels are concerned, this trend continued in the picaresque and mock-Dickensian *Nights at the Circus,* which tells the life story of the amorous cockney angel Fevvers, who progresses from prostitution to circus stardom, and culminated in the more restrained theatricality of *Wise Children.* It also continued, however, in the remarkable series of short stories which—thanks to the adaptation of several of them into Neil Jordan's film *The Company of Wolves*—are perhaps her most widely known works.

The core of this series is constituted by the ideologically-transfigured fairy tales collected in *The Bloody Chamber and Other Stories,* which rework the covert sexual counselling implicit in the traditional tales so that the new versions exhort girls to grasp the nettle of their sexuality instead of perverting it to the service of male power-fantasies. Some earlier stories from *Fireworks*—notably the gorgeous extended prose-poems "Penetrating to the Heart of the Forest" and "Master"—helped prepare the ground for *The Bloody Chamber and Other Stories,* while some of those in *Black Venus*—notably "The Kiss" and "Peter and the Wolf"—are addenda to it, but the central works of this particular canon are the multiple versions of "Beauty and the Beast" and "Little Red Riding Hood" contained in the second collection and the four radio plays collected in *Come Unto These Yellow Sands.* "Come Unto These Yellow Sands" also has in common with some of the stories in *Black Venus*—notably "Black Venus" and "The Cabinet of Edgar Allan Poe"—a deep and insightful interest in the process by which the substance of dreams and unfathomable experiences is sometimes transmuted into great art.

Had she not been slain by cancer Angela Carter would undoubtedly have carried the various threads of her work further. What she did contrive to produce, however, is a monument to one of the most powerful imaginations of the century. There is a certain irony in the fact that she is so widely studied in schools, given that she is perhaps the most subversive—and certainly the most outspoken—proponent of a modern neo-Gothic Movement which recklessly celebrates that which the traditional Gothic found so frightening: the imminent and absolute collapse of traditional notions of Order and Nature. In Carter's work the substance of the unconscious, having advanced to be recognized, is given leave to pass into the castle of self-awareness as a welcome guest instead of being repelled as an enemy, in spite of the fact that the consequences of such a welcome might be the blasting apart of the ancient walls.

As the world gradually comes to recognize the inevitability of this spiritual evolution her reputation will grow even further. She was the most important English fantasist of her generation.

—Brian Stableford

CARTER, Lin(wood Vrooman)

Nationality: American. **Born:** St. Petersburg, Florida, 9 June 1930. **Education:** Columbia University, New York, 1953-54. **Military Service:** United States Army Infantry, 1951-53. **Family:** Married 1) Judith McQuown (divorced); 2) Noel Vreeland in 1964 (divorced). **Career:** Advertising and publishers' copy-writer, 1957-69; editorial consultant, Ballantine Books Adult Fantasy, 1969-73. **Awards:** Nova award, 1972. **Died:** 7 February 1988.

FANTASY PUBLICATIONS

Novels (series: Callisto; Conan; Green Star; Kylix; Terra Magica; Thongor; World's End; Zanthodon)

The Wizard of Lemuria. New York, Ace, 1965; London, Tandem, 1970; revised edition, as *Thongor and the Wizard of Lemuria,* New York, Berkley, 1969.

Thongor of Lemuria. New York, Ace, 1966; London, Tandem, 1970; revised edition, as *Thongor and the Dragon City,* New York, Berkley, 1970.

The Flame of Iridar. New York, Belmont, 1967.

Thongor Against the Gods. New York, Paperback Library, 1967; London, Tandem, 1970.

Conan of the Isles, with L. Sprague de Camp. New York, Lancer, 1968.

Thongor in the City of Magicians. New York, Paperback Library, 1968; London, Tandem, 1970.

Thongor at the End of Time. New York, Paperback Library, 1968; London, Tandem, 1971.

Giant of World's End. New York, Belmont, 1969.

Lost World of Time. New York, New American Library, 1969.

Thongor Fights the Pirates of Tarakus. New York, Berkley, 1970; as *Thongor and the Pirates of Tarakus,* London, Tandem, 1971.

The Quest of Kadji (Kylix). New York, Belmont, 1971.

Under the Green Star. New York, DAW, 1972.

Jandar of Callisto. New York, Dell, 1972; London, Futura, 1974.

Black Legion of Callisto. New York, Dell, 1972; London, Futura, 1975.

Sky Pirates of Callisto. New York, Dell, 1973; London, Futura, 1975.

The Black Star. New York, Dell, 1973.

When the Green Star Calls. New York, DAW, 1973.

By the Light of the Green Star. New York, DAW, 1974.

The Warrior of World's End. New York, DAW, 1974.

As the Green Star Rises. New York, DAW, 1975.

Mad Empress of Callisto. New York, Dell, 1975.

Mind Wizards of Callisto. New York, Dell, 1975.

The Enchantress of World's End. New York, DAW, 1975.

Lankar of Callisto. New York, Dell, 1975.

In the Green Star's Glow. New York, DAW, 1976.

The Immortal of World's End. New York, DAW, 1976.
The Barbarian of World's End. New York, DAW, 1977.
Ylana of Callisto. New York, Dell, 1977.
The Wizard of Zao (Kylix). New York, DAW, 1978.
Renegade of Callisto. New York, Dell, 1978.
The Pirate of World's End. New York, DAW, 1978.
Conan the Liberator, with L. Sprague de Camp. New York, Bantam, 1979; London, Sphere, 1980.
Tara of the Twilight. New York, Zebra, 1979.
Journey to the Underground World (Zanthodon). New York, DAW, 1979.
Zanthodon. New York, DAW, 1980.
Hurok of the Stone Age (Zanthodon). New York, DAW, 1981.
Darya of the Bronze Age (Zanthodon). New York, DAW, 1981.
Conan the Barbarian (novelization of screenplay), with L. Sprague de Camp. New York, Bantam, and London, Sphere, 1982.
Eric of Zanthodon. New York, DAW, 1982.
Kesrick (Magica). New York, DAW, 1982.
Kellory the Warlock (Kylix). New York, Doubleday, 1984.
Dragonrouge (Magica). New York, DAW, 1984.
Found Wanting. New York, DAW, 1985.
Mandricardo (Magica). New York, DAW, 1987.
Callipygia (Magica). New York, DAW, 1988.

Short Stories

King Kull, with Robert E. Howard. New York, Lancer, 1967; London, Sphere, 1974.
Conan, with Robert E. Howard and L. Sprague de Camp. New York, Lancer, 1967; London, Sphere, 1974.
Conan the Wanderer, with Robert E. Howard and L. Sprague de Camp. New York, Lancer, 1968; London, Sphere, 1974.
Beyond the Gates of Dream. New York, Belmont, 1969.
Conan of Cimmeria, with Robert E. Howard and L. Sprague de Camp, New York, Lancer, 1969; London, Sphere, 1974.
Conan of Aquilonia, with L. Sprague de Camp. New York, Lancer, 1971.
Conan the Buccaneer, with L. Sprague de Camp. New York, Lancer, 1971.
Conan the Swordsman, with L. Sprague de Camp and Björn Nyberg. New York, Bantam, 1978; London, Sphere, 1979.
Lost Worlds. New York, DAW, 1980.
The Conan Chronicles (omnibus), with Robert E. Howard and L. Sprague de Camp. London, Orbit, 2 vols., 1989-90.

Poetry

Dreams from R'lyeh. Sauk City, Wisconsin, Arkham House, 1975.

Other

Tolkien: A Look Behind "The Lord of the Rings". New York, Ballantine, 1969.
Lovecraft: A Look Behind the "Cthulhu Mythos". New York, Ballantine, 1972; London, Panther, 1975.
Imaginary Worlds: The Art of Fantasy. New York, Ballantine, 1973.
Middle-Earth: The World of Tolkien, illustrated by David Wenzel. New York, Centaur, 1977.

Editor, *Dragons, Elves, and Heroes.* New York, Ballantine, 1969.
Editor, *The Young Magicians.* New York, Ballantine, 1969.

Editor, *At the Edge of the World,* by Lord Dunsany. New York, Ballantine, 1970.
Editor, *The Dream-Quest of Unknown Kadath,* by H. P. Lovecraft. New York, Ballantine, 1970.
Editor, *Zothique,* by Clark Ashton Smith. New York, Ballantine, 1970.
Editor, *Golden Cities, Far.* New York, Ballantine, 1970.
Editor, *The Magic of Atlantis.* New York, Lancer, 1970.
Editor, *The Doom That Came to Sarnath,* by H. P. Lovecraft. New York, Ballantine, 1971.
Editor, *Hyperborea,* by Clark Ashton Smith. New York, Ballantine, 1971.
Editor, *New Worlds for Old.* New York, Ballantine, 1971.
Editor, *The Spawn of Cthulhu.* New York, Ballantine, 1971.
Editor, *Xiccarph,* by Clark Ashton Smith. New York, Ballantine, 1972.
Editor, *Discoveries in Fantasy.* New York, Ballantine, 1972; London, Pan, 1974.
Editor, *Beyond the Fields We Know,* by Lord Dunsany. New York, Ballantine, and London, Pan, 1972.
Editor, *Great Short Novels of Adult Fantasy 1-2.* New York, Ballantine, 2 vols., 1972-73.
Editor, *Evenor,* by George MacDonald. New York, Ballantine, 1972.
Editor, *Poseidonis,* by Clark Ashton Smith. New York, Ballantine, 1973.
Editor, *Flashing Swords! 1-5.* New York, Doubleday, 3 vols., 1973-77; New York, Dell, 2 vols., 1976-81.
Editor, *Over the Hills and Far Away,* by Lord Dunsany. New York, Ballantine, 1974.
Editor, *The Year's Best Fantasy Stories 1-6.* New York, DAW, 6 vols., 1975-80.
Editor, *Kingdoms of Sorcery.* New York, Doubleday, 1976.
Editor, *Realms of Wizardry.* New York, Doubleday, 1976.
Editor, *Weird Tales 1-4.* New York, Zebra, 1981-83.

OTHER PUBLICATIONS

Novels

The Star Magicians. New York, Ace, 1966.
The Man Without a Planet. New York, Ace, 1966.
Destination: Saturn, with David Grinnell. New York, Avalon, 1967.
The Thief of Thoth. New York, Belmont, 1968.
Tower of the Edge of Time. New York, Belmont, 1968.
The Purloined Planet. New York, Belmont, 1969.
Tower of the Medusa. New York, Ace, 1969.
Star Rogue. New York, Lancer, 1970.
Outworlder. New York, Lancer, 1971.
The Man Who Loved Mars. New York, Fawcett, and London, White Lion, 1973.
Time War. New York, Dell, 1974.
The Valley Where Time Stood Still. New York, Doubleday, 1974.
The Nemesis of Evil. New York, Doubleday, 1975.
Invisible Death. New York, Doubleday, 1975.
The Volcano Ogre. New York, Doubleday, 1976.
The City Outside the World. New York, Berkley, 1977.
The Earth-Shaker. New York, Doubleday, 1982.
Down to a Sunless Sea. New York, DAW, 1984.
Horror Wears Blue. New York, Doubleday, 1987.

*

Critical Study: *Lin Carter: A Look Behind His Imaginary Worlds*
by Robert M. Price, Mercer Island, Washington, Starmont House,
1991.

*   *   *

Lin Carter had three ambitions for his work: to make others aware
of the marvels he had found, the beauty, terror and glamour of fantasy in all its forms; to add to those marvels by way of collaboration and pastiche; and to create at least one piece of uniquely memorable fiction which might, in later years, stimulate a completely new
sub-genre of fantasy. Although there is some crossover, many Carter
books are straight emulations of his favourite authors: whole series are based on Edgar Rice Burroughs, Robert E. Howard and
Leigh Brackett. His short stories include homages to, and posthumous collaborations with, those same authors, plus Clark Ashton
Smith, H. P. Lovecraft, Lord Dunsany and so on.

A prevalent view of Carter is that he turned out endless copies
of Conan the Barbarian, but in fact this was a minor phase of his
work. His first novel was *The Wizard of Lemuria,* which he offered to L. Sprague de Camp for comment in the early 1960s. De
Camp suggested it bore overly heavy echoes of Tolkien, Howard
and Burroughs; admitting the influences, Carter said he had included
them to attract readers. The nomenclature and some of the background are taken from Burroughs' Barsoom, but the action and
development are almost totally Howardian: generic sword and sorcery—by Carter's definition, "an action tale, derived from the traditions of the pulp magazine adventure story, set in a land, age, or
world of the author's invention—a milieu in which magic actually
works and the gods are real . . . which pits a stalwart warrior in
direct conflict with the forces of supernatural evil". Carter's warrior is Thongor, his setting the lost continent of Lemuria half a
million years ago; the principal evil is a pre-human race called the
Dragon Kings, driven into exile millennia before, but scheming to
re-conquer the Earth. As the six-book series progresses, Thongor
rescues, courts and marries a princess; he battles wizardry, inhuman science and magical beasts; and after these books (so the reader
learns from chronicles quoted throughout the text) Thongor will
go on to found the Empire of the Golden Sun, which will hold
sway over the entire known world.

After the second Thongor book, Carter was asked to work on
several incomplete stories by Robert E. Howard. Competently finished, they were used in the book *King Kull.* Following this, it is
not surprising that L. Sprague de Camp turned to Carter for help in
fleshing out the Conan stories for republication. The eventual 12-
volume series folds the original Howard texts into a biography of
Conan from birth almost to death. There were complaints about
how much this altered Howard's original character (to the extent
that the original Howard texts were eventually published as separate collections—just as *King Kull* would be republished with all
Carter's changes removed), yet there is no doubt that the de Camp/
Carter Conan books were the main occasion for the popular revival of the barbarian hero, leading to many similar series by other
authors. Although the last of those 12 Conan titles appeared in 1977,
it had been completed some years before, and was delayed for legal reasons; Carter had little to do with the final Conan books which
bore his name, seeming only to write the first draft of one, and
contributing a few ideas to the others. Aside from these, the only
other works of his which are imitative of Conan are some short
stories about Thongor (in which he acquired a sex life), the excellent *Quest of Kadji,* and his single worst novel, *Lost World of Time.*

Edgar Rice Burroughs was a stronger influence, specifically the
John Carter of Mars, or Barsoom, series, about an extraordinary
hero transported to another planet which has inhabitants human
enough for romance, with bizarre monsters to be fought and alien
races to be befriended. Under strangely coloured skies, in lush
jungles or exotic deserts, these are adventures full of coincidence,
mistaken identities, and defeat piled on seeming victories, leading
to cliff-hanging ends in all the books except the last. Manuscripts
get written and find their way to the author, who denies authorship. Carter's Green Star and Callisto series began at much the same
time. The unnamed narrator of *Under the Green Star* is a cripple
from childhood, whose studies finally allow him to release his astral body to roam space until it launches itself towards the Green
Star. In *Jandar of Callisto,* Jonathan Dark (later renamed Jandar)
is a helicopter pilot who crashes in Cambodia and discovers a hidden city with a beam of light pointing upwards. The results are the
same: both heroes land on a distant planet, are captured or enslaved,
escape, fall in love with a princess (or the equivalent), do battle
constantly—and witness their princess carried off on the last page,
apparently never to be seen again. This prompts the manuscript,
suitably edited by Carter, that we have just read. The later volumes
follow the same pattern, with the hero gaining more respect, power
and companions in every book, until he is acknowledged as warlord or king or even emperor—and finally reunited with his true
love. The secret of such tales is that everything keeps moving: motion replaces emotion, character is defined by action.

The Callisto series breaks with tradition in its sixth book. Many
authors had received mysterious manuscripts, or met friends of heroes lost in other lands; Carter goes beyond. Finally allowed to
travel with his wife to Cambodia, to meet those investigating the
hidden city, the author gets too close to the beam of light and . . .
Lin Carter of Earth becomes Lankar of Callisto. Rapidly drawn
into the deadly events, Carter personally meets all those he has been
reading about, and becomes involved in the rescue of Jandar. This
breathtakingly conceited plot bears many parodic elements, and it
is no coincidence that Carter was also at this time writing the
World's End series, an even clearer lampoon of the genre. The last
Callisto books appeared after a long gap: *Ylana* is undistinguished
but reasonable, *Renegade* exists only to exhibit Darza, a game invented by Carter.

The Zanthodon books emulate Burroughs's Pellucidar series. Eric
Carstairs, adventurer *extraordinaire,* is persuaded to help a scientist prove that an anti-matter meteorite flashed down a volcano millions of years ago, and that the resultant explosion formed a massive cavern which gave rise to legends of an underground world.
Carstairs and the professor quickly find an entrance, and are soon
embroiled with dinosaurs, Neanderthals, Cro-Magnons, Atlanteans,
pirates and the like: whole populations have filtered down over millennia to settle in proximity, but not harmony, in Zanthodon. The
series is a spoof which gets wilder with every book, achieving a
mad kind of romantic grandeur in the last. Leigh Brackett's Martian tales prompted a number of Carter's books—some set on the
Red Planet, others on similar planets where space-age technology
can mingle with the remnants of ancient empires, and antique gods
can still be roused to omnipotent action. *The Star Magicians, Tower
at the Edge of Time, The Man Without a Planet* and *Outworlder,*
among others, are all space opera by courtesy—but they're also
fantasies. The last-named especially is a splendid tale of a swordsman fighting evil forces—it scarcely matters those forces turn out
to be "scientific". Carter later claimed these Martian books were
"disguised lost race romances," a revivification of a genre which

flourished in the late 19th century. They include some of his best work—limpid, considered, colourful, charming, with clever rationales and some neat humour, they pit their heroes against moral dilemmas of pride and greed and anger and vengeance. Their general quality is far above much of what Carter wrote, with *The City Outside the World* (opening with an echo of Moore's "Shambleau") edging out the others to be the best.

It took Carter a long time to find his own voice. His own suggestions for true "Carterian" series—those begun with *Lost World of Time*, *The Black Star* and *The Giant of World's End*—each ended after one book, though the last inspired a bizarre, desperately unfunny series re-telling the early life of *Giant*'s hero (it was stopped by the publisher after five of the planned ten books). Carter hoped his reputation would be made by "Khymyrium," an unpublished epic of many volumes which would recast the definition of fantasy fiction. In his studies of the genre, he isolated two basic plots: the Quest and the War. Tolkien had intertwined both, embedding them in a strongly structured other world with its own history, language, fauna and flora. Carter hoped to go one further, to create an entire world "from the magma up" and then write "non-fiction" about the thousand-year history of one city, Khymyrium. Supposedly ten years and more in the planning, only three short excerpts were ever published and the "dense and complex narrative" turned out to be ordinary, turgid and amazingly dull.

In his final years, Carter seemed to lose direction: his World's End series is a painful farce, showing just how unfunny Carter could be. *Tara of the Twilight* is a sexually explicit odyssey, as if trying to redress the many years in which he denied his characters even lustful thoughts. *Kellory the Warlock* is a stripped-down tale of brutality and revenge that comes to a harsh, scarcely romantic end, without even a hint of a sequel. Then, amazingly (by now he was ill and racked by pain) Carter began to produce books which nobody else could have written: the Terra Magica series, beginning with *Kesrick*. It was as though he had finally relaxed, as if the illness had burned away all the personae he tried to assume, to leave only wonder—a writer in love with fantasy. Terra Magica is so vast and magical that it contains all the fantastic lands, creatures and heroes from our legends; it has a real wind from the stars, and an actual stone bridge arcing into the sky for the spirits of the dead to walk upward. The books don't have plots as such, but the stories wander pleasantly from incident from incident, allowing the various heroes and heroines to meet mermaids, hippogriffs, dragons and the like, in lands from ancient myth as well as those invented by Cabell, Dunsany, Clark Ashton Smith, Ariosto and everyone else Carter had read. Amusing, romantic, gentle and seemingly effortless, the four novels exhibit qualities Carter had only promised hitherto.

Carter's extensive knowledge of fantasy and myth was used in different ways earlier in his career, as background to the studies he wrote, the anthologies he edited, and the Ballantine Adult Fantasy series. Almost the first extended study of a fantasy author, *Tolkien: A Look Behind the Lord of the Rings* was a bestselling insight into the myth-cycles that underlay, to greater and lesser extents, Tolkien's own world-myth. Intensely readable and informative (though of course it had to make guesses about information only revealed in Tolkien's *The Silmarillion* and later books), it traced Tolkien's progenitors back thousands of years through some fairly arcane and rare texts. *Imaginary Worlds: The Art of Fantasy* examines the evolution of fantasy from William Morris to the present day. Carter had already proved to his own satisfaction, in essays and introductions scattered through anthologies and collections, that the devel-

opment of fantasy could be traced through history—from the myths of Greece, Rome, Egypt, and so on, to Beowulf, Siegfried, and St. George, to the courtly excesses of the middle ages and their lampoon by Cervantes, after which they fell into disrepute until the late-19th century. By then, most of the real world had been explored and could scarcely sustain the idea of magical lost lands and unknown beasts; so writers had three choices—to set stories in the distant past (Atlantis, Mu), on other planets (Mars, the Moon), or to invent totally imaginary worlds. William Morris first invented those imaginary worlds. Carter suggested that after Morris, fantasy developed by influences—one author read another, then emulated or developed elements they liked, after which they too were copied or improved on. This view resulted in some strange comments (e.g. his suggestion that Lovecraft wrote Dunsanian fantasy before he'd read Dunsany because, Carter guessed, Lovecraft had read pre-Dunsanian fantasy by Edgar Allan Poe) and leaves the suspicion that Carter massaged some facts to prove his thesis.

Imaginary Worlds was the only non-fiction book to appear in the Ballantine Adult Fantasy series, a line of novels frequently acknowledged as the purest, strongest and most enjoyable fantasy series ever published. Given the freedom to select fantasy novels and books of short stories for revival, Carter made a varied choice, ranging from ancient myth to original fiction, to humour, occasional horror and the bizarre. It was an eclectic yet somehow unified selection, a single vision which was reinforced by the useful and informative introductions Carter wrote for every volume, placing each work in context and attempting to give some insight into its author or authors. The series reintroduced many readers to Morris, Dunsany, Cabell, Bramah and dozens of others, prompting a revival of fantasy fiction which did not come to an end because of the sudden curtailment of the series when Ballantine was purchased by another company.

Lin Carter was in love with fantasy; he disliked very few writers or works (perhaps Bradbury and Poe, and certainly Terry Brooks's *The Sword of Shannara*); he was unashamedly derivative, but only because he thought his work was the equal of what he imitated. His greatest failing was in knowing what to write but not how to write it, yet in the end he did find his own voice and was able to produce quality work. He had an inability to admit mistakes, and a bad habit of including his own stories in any anthology he compiled (a volume showing the chronological development of fantasy had a penultimate story by Tolkien and a final piece demonstrating "the sort of fiction we might expect to enjoy 'after Tolkien'"—Carter's first Khymyrium story).

Nevertheless, he was probably the single most important influence on fantasy in the 1970s and it was his misfortune to die with his estate in disarray, leaving little chance for his work to be reprinted. Perhaps some future editor of another "Adult Fantasy" series will revive the very best of it to allow readers a fuller appreciation of his work.

—Ian Covell

CHANT, (Eileen) Joy

Nationality: British. **Born:** London, 1945. **Education:** Romford County high school, Essex; College of Librarianship, Wales; University of Sussex. **Family:** Married Peter Rutter in 1981, 2 sons.

Career: Children's and schools' librarian, Romford, Essex; lecturer, School of Librarianship, Loughborough, Leicestershire; freelance writer; librarian, Southend-on-Sea, Essex. **Address:** 80 Oakleigh Park Drive, Leigh-on-Sea, Essex SS9 1RS, England.

FANTASY PUBLICATIONS

Novels (series: Vandarei in all books)

Red Moon and Black Mountain: The End of the House of Kendreth. London, Allen and Unwin, and New York, Doubleday, 1970.
The Grey Mane of Morning. London, Allen and Unwin, 1977; New York, Bantam, 1980.
When Voiha Wakes. London, Allen and Unwin, 1983; New York, Bantam, 1984.

Other

The High Kings (retellings). London, Allen and Unwin, and New York, Bantam, 1983.

*

Joy Chant comments:

I have always attributed my writing of fantasy to the fact that I learned to read extremely young (at two) and so had a reading skill and speed, and to a certain extent intellectual development, much in advance of my emotional age; so my reading in childhood was dominated by myth, legend, saints, wanderers, and history. I never read literary fantasy (not even C. S. Lewis) until I had been writing it for some time—in fact, until I first worked in a children's library.

Vandarei dominates my work. It originated in a childhood playworld, but soon was converted to a consciously organized setting: by my 20s I had established so much "fact" about it that arbitrary invention was no longer possible; new knowledge had to fit into the pattern imposed by the old, so that it could often feel quite easily like "discovering" a connection, or the story of a blank period, rather than invention. The books so far written represent a small fraction of what I know. My ambition is to complete *The Song of the King's Emerald,* the main Harani story: but even that only covers the long war with Lelarik, or the story of Halilak . . . My other imaginative passion to result in a book was the "Matter of Britain"; the figure of Arthur, the complexity, the ambivalence, the resonance of the story from the *Mabinogion* to Malory—I wanted to try!

*   *   *

Joy Chant is a pivotal figure in the development of heroic fantasy since Tolkien. She took the conventional "Narnian" framework—youngsters snatched into a fantasy world at divine bidding—and produced an epic fantasy for all ages, *Red Moon and Black Mountain,* where her treatment of near-forbidden and unrequited love marked it especially for adolescent readers. She also blended the high-fantasy, Elven-Arthurian style of Tolkien with the barbaric-heroic style of Bronze and Dark-Age heroic fantasy. Her importing of Earth's nomad cultures into her own fantasy world of Khendiol is a feature which other fantasy writers have followed. In *Red Moon and Black Mountain* Penelope Nicholas and teenage brother Oliver are piped into Khendiol by a god, one of the Six who govern the world under the One who created it. Penelope and Nicholas are catapulted onto a mountainside where they encounter the Princess In'serinna, enchantress of the Star Magic, on her way to witness a unique ritual, the battle of black and white eagles. Meanwhile Oliver is sent to the plains, to be adopted into a tribe of nomads under the name of Li'vanh, and furnished with his own unicorn to ride.

Tolkienian parallels are easy to find, not only in style—"At Danamol, at the fording of the river, there will they strike, and the Swan-king of Rennath has need of his friends"—but also in situation. The theme is war against the Black Enchanter, perverter of the Star Magic and servant of the Fallen One (i.e. the Lucifer of this world). Princess In'serinna chooses to give up her Star Magic and wed a Khentor huntsman and king's heir clad in green; like Tolkien's Arwen, then, but playing a larger part in the action. There are also, however, the nomads or Khentorei, their culture drawn from Asian Mongols, their heroic code of honour recalling Native Americans, and their rituals, such as horse-sacrifice and even the royal sacrifice, and their tricks of speech from the historical novels of Mary Renault. Sometimes the High and the Celtic traditions are blended in a short space: for example, "Deep have they delved indeed, to wake the earth magic." The meat of the story is Oliver's experience, fated to duel with Fendarl the Enchanter, and to make the royal sacrifice.

The Grey Mane of Morning is set centuries before, at a time of change for the Khentorei tribes. Culturally it is all-of-a-piece; Tolkienian style is banished. The Khentorei shift their camps according to the instinct of the Sacred King horse who leads them, and if they come too near the mountain; at the edge of the plains, the town-dwellers exact tribute. When a Chief's daughter and Priestess of the tribe is snatched as part of the tribute, her brother Mor'anh receives a vision from the god Kem'nanh to quicken him to action: to train his huntsmen into warriors and end the tribute. It is also a triangular love story. Mor'anh is loved by Manui, who is his lover but cannot keep him from pursuing selfish Runi, who rebels against the strict gender-roles of the tribes, and thus cannot take a lover because she has not chosen to take on womanhood. In order to get swords for the tribe Mor'anh makes an epic journey south to the City of Jemaluth, and established trade—or "civilized"—culture is seen through the plainsman's eyes: there is luxury, but also slavery and beggary; they are on the way to decadence. Returning, Mor'anh trains and leads his warriors to victory, but he is struck by sadness at the destruction of the enemy town by fire, and by grief at the death of Runi, who disobeyed custom and rode to the battle. But before that, he had given her up and wedded Manui according to tribal ritual; Manui's patience and wonderful joy when Mor'anh finally chooses her greatly please readers of romantic fantasy.

In the early 1980s Chant's career was relaunched with the republication of *Red Moon and Black Mountain* in the Unicorn series designed by Allen and Unwin to combine B-format Tolkien paperback editions with fantasies by his predecessors and modern authors. It was good to have "The Coming of the Starborn" anthologized (in *Lands of Never* edited by Maxim Jakubowski, 1983), expanding a passage in *Red Moon . . .* to narrate in epic style how nine Star-beings are to be wed nine mortals in order to beget a race of Starborn who will master the Star Magic. The novel *When Voiha Wakes* makes a complete shift in location and ethos. It is a young-adult fantasy set in the realm of Halilak in south-western Vandarei (the northern continent of Khendiol). The people of Halilak have no contact with the peoples we have already met; the story is contemporary with "The Coming of the Starborn." It is a feminist fantasy, with a flavour of Le Guin's *Always Coming Home.* Women dominate and organize cooperatively, and men live in their own town, in craft lodges. With no war and hardly any crime, men's main activity is craftwork in stone, wood, metal or textiles; women farm, hunt and negotiate with other cities. Local rulers are elected for life by their fellow-women; literacy is for women, forbidden to men. Women take men as lovers but do not set up house with them; a child would not know his or her father's identity. Rahike, recently elected to the post of Young Mistress, to succeed as local governor when the Old Mistress retires, takes a lover. True love, not lustful dalliance, it becomes a city-wide scandal, especially as the man is driven by the urge to compose music, which is not a legitimate craft, and is unlikely to qualify as a craftsman. If he becomes an itinerant musician, as he believes his god demands, the lovers will be parted forever.

Chant's published work ended with *The High Kings,* an illustrated gift-book retelling of the story of Arthur and his predecessors, drawn from Geoffrey of Monmouth and the *Mabinogion*—an unusual, if not unique, combination of sources. Since then her pen has been silent, but she may return to Khendiol one day.

—Jessica Yates

CHAPMAN, Vera (Ivy May)

Nationality: British. **Born:** Vera Fogerty, Bournemouth, Hampshire, 7 May 1898. **Education:** Oxford University, 1918-1921. **Family:** Married Rev. Charles Sydney Chapman in 1924 (died). **Career:** Housewife for many years; Student Welfare Officer, Colonial Office, 1945-1963; became a published author very late in life. Founded the Tolkien Society, 1969.

FANTASY PUBLICATIONS

Novels (series: The Three Damosels)

The Green Knight (Three Damosels). London, Rex Collings, 1975; New York, Avon, 1978.
The King's Damosel (Three Damosels). London, Rex Collings, 1976; New York, Avon, 1978.
King Arthur's Daughter (Three Damosels). London, Rex Collings, 1976; New York, Avon, 1978.
The Wife of Bath. London, Rex Collings, 1978; New York, Avon, 1979.
Blaedud the Birdman. London, Rex Collings, 1978; New York, Avon, 1980.
The Three Damosels (omnibus; includes *The Green Knight, The King's Damosel, King Arthur's Daughter*). London, Magnum, 1978.

Short Stories

The Notorious Abbess. Chicago, Academy Chicago, 1993.

OTHER PUBLICATIONS

Fiction for Children

Judy and Julia. London, Rex Collings, 1977.
Miranty and the Alchemist. New York, Avon, 1983; London, Deutsch, 1987.

*   *   *

Vera Chapman came late to publishing. She was in her 70s before her first book appeared. Before that, though, she had led a busy life as wife of a country vicar, living initially out in Portuguese East Africa (now Mozambique) and later in a succession of English country vicarages. She was also for a period a practising Druid. Her love of classic British myth, legend and literature led to her discovery of the works of J. R. R. Tolkien and she was instrumental in the founding of the British Tolkien Society in 1969, where she was always known by the soubriquet of Belladonna Took.

Her profile in the Tolkien Society and the revival of interest in fantasy fiction allowed her to indulge in her writing, and this attracted the interest of Rex Collings, the publisher of Richard Adams's *Watership Down.* Mrs. Chapman's work has concentrated mostly on British mythology, particularly that captured in the writings of Geoffrey of Monmouth, and inevitably this meant the Arthurian legend. Her first published works were the novels which make up trilogy *The Three Damosels.* Here she looked at the Arthurian world through the eyes and actions of three key women: Vivian, the grand-niece of Morgan le Fay, who must face the sorcery of Morgan through her love for Sir Gawain; Lynette, a fast-tempered girl, who becomes a messenger for King Arthur and must face the perils of an unchivalrous world; and Ursulet, the daughter of King Arthur, who battles against Sir Mordred over the British throne.

In each of the short novels Mrs. Chapman brought not simply a feminist view to Arthurian fiction, but a humanist one. Being related through the eyes of young girls, the books were marketed as children's fiction, but the coming-of-age traumas that the damosels face are also symbolic of the loss of innocence of ancient Britain as knightly chivalry is beset by Dark Age barbarity. The stories are much deeper than their labelling as children's books might suggest. Vera Chapman has a sharpness of vision and an awareness of character that brings the Arthurian age alive and shows its parallels to today's world. In recognition of this, the National Book League included *The Green Knight* among its list of Children's Books of the Year.

Vera Chapman completed a fourth Arthurian novel, *The Enchantresses,* which remains unpublished, although an extract appeared in the anthology *The Camelot Chronicles* (edited by Mike Ashley, 1992). This novel is the story of Arthur's elder half-sisters, Vivian, Morgan and Morgause, and how their lives interweave with the fate of Arthur's.

Mrs. Chapman turned to another of Geoffrey of Monmouth's legends for *Blaedud the Birdman.* Blaedud was a legendary king of Britain, the father of King Lear, who founded the city of Bath, practised magic, and attempted to fly. Mrs. Chapman's novel explores his life, particularly his attempts at flight, and brings to life ancient pre-Christian Britain with her knowledge of Druidical beliefs. *The Wife of Bath* is not a fantasy but incorporates one or two supernatural visions. It retells the life of Alison, the Wife of Bath in Chaucer's *Canterbury Tales,* and of her pilgrimage to Canterbury. It's a lively tale with some Chaucerian bawdiness, but generally it is tame and wholesome and it works well as a recreation of 15th-century England with a tinge of enchantment. Eventually published in 1993, though completed a decade earlier, was *The Notorious Abbess,* about the Abbess of Shaston, a series of stories about a rather unconventional nun with psychic powers who lived at the time of the Crusades. Mrs. Chapman's other published books, *Judy and Julia* and *Miranty and the Alchemist,* are written specifically for children.

Two further completed novels remain unpublished. *The Jerusalem Talisman* concerns a wife who, with her children, accompanies her husband on the Crusades. It includes a search for the Jerusalem Talisman, a rosary with each bead containing a hair from the head of Mary Magdalene, which when brought together will allow the Christians to take Jerusalem. An extract, "Crusader Damosel," was published in *The Fantastic Imagination II* (1978). *So Sweet a Changeling* is Vera Chapman's version of *A Midsummer Night's Dream* and tells the tale of the little Indian boy who Titania refuses to hand over to Oberon. All of Mrs. Chapman's work, published and unpublished, adds up to a select body of fiction which explores the depths of British legend and history, and shows how the one blurs into the other.

—Mike Ashley

CHARRETTE, Robert N.

Nationality: American. **Career:** Role-playing games designer.

FANTASY PUBLICATIONS

Novels (series: Shadowrun)

Never Deal With a Dragon (Shadowrun). New York, Roc, 1990; London, Roc, 1991.
Choose Your Enemies Carefully (Shadowrun). New York and London, Roc, 1991.
Find Your Own Truth (Shadowrun). New York, Roc, 1991; London, Roc, 1992.
Never Trust an Elf (Shadowrun). New York, Roc, 1992; London, Roc, 1993.
A Prince Among Men. New York, Warner, 1994.
A King Beneath the Mountain. New York, Warner, 1995.

OTHER PUBLICATIONS

Novels

Heir to the Dragon. Delavan, Wisconsin, FASA, 1989.
Wolves on the Border. Delavan, Wisconsin, FASA, 1989.
Wolf Pack. New York and London, Roc 1992.

*   *   *

Until recently, Robert Charrette wrote novels based on role-playing systems. It is now common practice for manufacturers to pub-

lish series of novels to complement their games, but Charrette is unusual in that he also designs the games his novels are based on. These games have extremely detailed backgrounds which explain everything from the geography of the countryside, through the politics of the day, to the belief systems of the imaginary world's inhabitants. They also provide a consistent, rigid framework of rules that limits what players can do and how powerful they can become. In particular, the rules codify the way magic and religion work. This has two effects on the novels. First, it should make them more consistent, at least in theory, since the background is so thoroughly developed before the books are written. Second, it means that many of the readers will be using the books either as inspiration for their own games or to clarify rules. Hence, an issue such as how a particular spell should be cast, or how much of an effect it can have, assumes great—perhaps disproportionate—significance to the core consumers of these fictions.

Though Charrette has worked on various games, Shadowrun is the only one that is even partially fantasy. The distinguishing feature of the game—and hence the novels—is its odd blend of cyberpunk science fiction and magic. The future Charrette gives us is a fairly standard, down-and-dirty corporate-controlled one, such as is common in the science fiction of Bruce Sterling, Pat Cadigan and William Gibson, among many others. What sets it apart is the addition of various magical beings—and so on, plus magic and shamanism that both work. Depending on your point of view, this is either a potent mixture or a bit of a mess.

For instance, there are computer hackers and cyborged humans that could almost have walked straight out of Gibson's *Neuromancer*; but there are also Native American shamans rubbing shoulders with the traditions of hermetic and sympathetic magic, real-world religions such as Christianity, *and* all the standard beings and creatures of Northern European mythology, such as elves, trolls, dwarves, orks (sic) and so on—all set within the northwest seaboard of the USA. This is almost certainly a response—at the game-design stage, not the novel-writing one—to the perceived desires of the games-players for role-playing the standard fantasy creatures. Since the games company and its primary market are American, and America is the natural home of cyberpunk, the game had to be set there, regardless of the inconsistency of some parts of the background. However, some of the action of Charrette's books takes place in Great Britain and Australia: at least here the magic is more closely tied to the mythology of the areas.

The Shadowrun novels themselves are fast-moving, action-based stories. They follow the progress of hero Sam Verner as he develops from corporate employee to shadowrunning (i.e. more or less illegal) shaman. His goal is to rescue his sister, who is slowly turning into the legendary North American monster, the Wendigo. Along the way he becomes involved with too many other shadowrunners, such as Dodger the elf and the female street-samurai Gray Otter, to count; he also makes an enemy of the elvish nation Tir Tairngire. Mixed in with this are subplots about his relationship with Hart, a female shadowrunner of dubious morality, and a mysterious artificial intelligence that inhabits the computer Matrix.

Even this sample barely hints at the complexities of a plot of labyrinthine deviousness. The problem is that, though Charrette is a competent writer, the characterization is not quite vivid enough to lift all the different protagonists off the page and into the reader's memory. It is hard to remember who did what to whom and when. However, the problem is eased by the fact that most of the characters spend a fair amount of time holding inner debates with themselves about whether they should trust the others, thus allowing readers to refresh their memories. Considering this, it is perhaps surprising that Charrette manages to bring his first three Shadowrun books, known as the Secrets of Power Trilogy, to a satisfactory and rather moving end, in which most if not all of the loose ends are tied up.

Since completing his Shadowrun sequence with the pendant novel *Never Trust an Elf,* Charrette has begun a quite independent series of "Arthurian" fantasy novels, commencing with *A Prince Among Men.* It remains to be seen whether these will succeed in establishing a wider reputation for him in the fantasy field.

—Liz Holliday

CHERRYH, C(arolyn) J(anice)

Nationality: American. **Born:** Carolyn Janice Cherry, in St. Louis, Missouri, 1 September 1942. **Education:** University of Oklahoma, Norman, 1960-64, B.A. in Latin 1964 (Phi Beta Kappa); Johns Hopkins University, Baltimore (Woodrow Wilson Fellow, 1965-66), M.A. in classics 1965. **Career:** Taught Latin and ancient history in Oklahoma City public schools, 1965-76. **Awards:** John W. Campbell award, 1977; Hugo award, 1979, 1982, 1989; Balrog award, 1982. **Agent:** Curtis Brown Ltd., 10 Astor Place, New York, NY 10003, USA. **Address:** Tau Ceti, Inc., 10413 Ski Drive, Oklahoma City, OK 73162, USA.

Fantasy Publications

Novels (series: Ealdwood; Hell; Morgaine; Rusalka; Sword of Knowledge)

Gate of Ivrel (Morgaine). New York, DAW, 1976; London, Futura, 1977.
Well of Shiuan (Morgaine). New York, DAW, 1978; London, Magnum, 1981.
Fires of Azeroth (Morgaine). New York, DAW, 1979; London, Methuen, 1982.
The Book of Morgaine (omnibus; includes *Gate of Ivrel, Well of Shiuan, Fires of Azeroth*). New York, Doubleday, 1979; as *The Chronicles of Morgaine,* London, Methuen, 1985.
The Dreamstone (Ealdwood). New York, DAW, 1983; London, Gollancz, 1987.
The Tree of Swords and Jewels (Ealdwood). New York, DAW, 1983; London, Gollancz, 1988.
The Gates of Hell, with Janet Morris. New York, Baen, 1986.
Kings in Hell, with Janet Morris. New York, Baen, 1987.
Legions of Hell. New York, Baen, 1987.
Exile's Gate (Morgaine). New York, DAW, 1988; London, Methuen, 1989.
The Paladin. New York, Baen, 1988; London, Mandarin, 1990.
A Dirge for Sabis, with Leslie Fish (Sword of Knowledge). New York, Baen, 1989.
Wizard Spawn, with Nancy Asire (Sword of Knowledge). New York, Baen, 1989.
Reap The Whirlwind, with Mercedes Lackey (Sword of Knowledge). New York, Baen, 1989.
Rusalka. New York, Del Rey, 1989; London, Methuen, 1990.

Chernevog (Rusalka). New York, Del Rey, 1990; London, Mandarin, 1991.
Ealdwood (omnibus; includes *The Dreamstone, The Tree of Swords and Jewels*). London, Gollancz, 1991.
Yvgenie (Rusalka). New York, Del Rey, 1991; London, Mandarin, 1992.
The Goblin Mirror. New York, Del Rey, and London, Legend, 1992.
Faery in Shadow. London, Legend, 1993; New York, Del Rey, 1994.

Short Stories

Soul of the City, with Janet Morris and Lynn Abbey. New York, Ace, 1986.

Other Publications

Novels

Brothers of Earth. New York, DAW, 1976; London, Futura, 1977.
Hunter of Worlds. New York, DAW, 1976; London, Futura, 1977.
The Faded Sun: Kesrith. New York, DAW, 1978.
The Faded Sun: Shon'Jir. New York, DAW, 1979.
The Faded Sun: Kutath. New York, DAW, 1980.
Hestia. New York, DAW, 1979; London, Gollancz, 1988.
Serpent's Reach. New York, DAW, 1980; London, Macdonald, 1981.
Wave Without a Shore. New York, DAW, 1981; London, Gollancz, 1988.
Downbelow Station. New York, DAW, 1981; London, Methuen, 1983.
The Pride of Chanur. New York, DAW, 1982; London, Methuen, 1983.
Merchanter's Luck. New York, DAW, 1982; London, Methuen, 1984.
Port Eternity. New York, DAW 1982; London, Gollancz, 1989.
Forty Thousand in Gehenna. Huntington Woods, Michigan, Phantasia Press, 1983; London, Methuen, 1986.
Voyager in Night. New York, DAW, 1984; London, Methuen, 1985.
Chanur's Venture. Huntington Woods, Michigan, Phantasia Press, 1984; London, Methuen, 1986.
Cuckoo's Egg. Huntington Woods, Michigan, Phantasia Press, 1985; London, Methuen, 1987.
The Kif Strike Back. Huntington Woods, Michigan, Phantasia Press, 1985; London, Methuen, 1987.
Angel with the Sword. New York, DAW, 1985; London, Methuen, 1987.
Chanur's Homecoming. New York, DAW, 1986; London, Methuen, 1988.
Glass and Amber. Cambridge, Massachusetts, NESFA Press, 1987.
The Faded Sun Trilogy (omnibus). London, Methuen, 1987.
Cyteen. New York, Warner, 1988; London, New English Library, 1989; in three volumes as *The Betrayal, The Rebirth* and *The Vindication,* New York, Popular Library, 1989.
Smuggler's Gold. New York, DAW, 1988.
Rimrunners. New York, Warner, 1989; London, New English Library, 1990.
Heavy Time. New York, Warner, and London, New English Library, 1991.
Hellburner. New York, Warner, and London, New English Library, 1992.
Chanur's Legacy. New York, DAW, 1992.

Foreigner. New York, DAW, and London, Legend, 1994.
Tripoint. New York, Warner, 1994.

Short Stories

Sunfall. New York, DAW, 1981; London, Mandarin, 1990.
Visible Light. West Bloomfield, Michigan, Phantasia Press, 1986;
  London, Methuen, 1988.
Festival Moon. New York, DAW, 1987.
Troubled Waters. New York, DAW, 1988.

Other

Editor, *Merovingen Nights.* New York, DAW, 1987.
Editor, *Fever Season.* New York, DAW, 1987.
Editor, *Divine Right.* New York, DAW, 1989.
Editor, *Flood Tide.* New York, DAW, 1990.

Translator, *The Green Gods,* by Charles and Nathalie Henneberg.
  New York, DAW, 1980.
Translator, *Star Crusade,* by Pierre Barbet. New York, DAW, 1980.
Translator, *The Book of Shai,* by Daniel Walther. New York, DAW,
  1984.

*

Bibliography: *C. J. Cherryh: Citizen of the Universe—A Working Bibliography* by Phil Stephensen-Payne, Leeds, West Yorkshire, Galactic Central, 1992.

C. J. Cherryh comments:

   While fantasy is fine, recall that I'm an archaeologist, and that I don't believe in unicorns or elves except as an expression of bronze-age civilizations and as useful markers in pre- and proto-literate ethnographies . . . all of which means that people who get me on fantasy panels usually discover my interest in the ancient world and in elves is pretty abstruse and amazingly hard-tech: archaeology is, after all, a science.

*   *   *

   C. J. Cherryh's writing stretches from high fantasy to hard science fiction, and her first published novel, *Gate of Ivrel,* the first in the (so far) four-book Morgaine series, straddles the two genres to some extent. However, although the background has a science-fictional underpinning, the series belongs firmly in the fantasy domain. Morgaine is the last survivor of a band, once a hundred strong, that has come down through the ages, from world to world, always moving futurewards, through the "Gates" that make such travel possible, sealing each Gate behind them. The human-seeming qhal eventually brought devastation to the Gate-linked time and space once before when one of their number used them to go back into the past and thus warp reality. Qhal still lurk in the ruins of the worlds they once ruled and, as long as the Gates continue to exist, the worlds remain in danger of another catastrophe. Morgaine's mission is to destroy every last Gate before this can happen.

   In this opening volume of the series, it is Nhi Vanye's ill-luck to stumble across the legendary Morgaine just as she appears a hundred or so years after she had last passed through his world. An outcast from his clan, the Nhi, Vanye is on the run and desperate, having killed one half-brother and maimed another when the two

attacked him. Morgaine is a demonic figure to Vanye, held responsible as she is for the ruin of the land when she last appeared. Nevertheless, she is able to claim Vanye as her vassal and sets out on a second and even more desperate attempt to destroy the Gate at Ivrel. Despite Vanye's deep distrust of Morgaine and his fear of what will happen to him, his sense of honour forces him to accompany her back to the lands he has only just escaped from, where among the many dangers they must face is his surviving half-brother.

   Vanye, like many of Cherryh's protagonists to one degree or another, whether in fantasy or science fiction, is an outsider. When we first meet him he is desperate, pushed to the edge and, during the course of the book, he is to be pushed even further. He is also typical in that both common sense and simple self-preservation pull him in one direction while other feelings, not wholly rational, urge him in another—in his case it is his stubborn adherence to his warrior code and also a grudging respect for and attachment to Morgaine. Another feature here that is typical of Cherryh's work is her use of what she calls the "intense" viewpoint: apart from the exposition in the introduction, all that we learn of the world and the events of the story comes to us through Vanye's own perceptions. Where the reader is likely to quickly bracket Morgaine as a heroine and Vanye's natural ally, he distrusts her from the first. Cherryh is particularly strong on her ability to exploit this inner world of suspicions, fears and tensions that can divide her protagonist from potential allies. Nevertheless, Vanye remains loyal to Morgaine, even refusing the chance to have his outlawing lifted. And, when Morgaine enters the Gate, futurewards, still intent on her mission, he follows her, leaving his own world and time irretrievably behind him.

   The sequel, *Well of Shiuan,* takes them to the drowning land of Shiuan, in pursuit of their enemy, Roh, an ancient qhal who has taken over the body of Vanye's own cousin. Despite the relationship forged in the first book, the tension between Vanye and Morgaine continues as fresh events unfold, highlighting their different priorities and goals, and, as with many a Cherryh series, distrust reappears from time to time. Nevertheless, they continue moving from world to world together in the further sequels, *Fires of Azeroth* and *Exile's Gate.*

   Another major strand of Cherryh's fantasy is shown in her sombre and effective evocation of the old Celtic world both in her stories concerning the elflady, Arafel, and also in non-Arafel short stories and a novel. In *The Dreamstone,* Arafel, the sole elf left in the world in the dwindling magical forest of Ealdwood and no natural ally of any human, befriends first Niall Cearbhallain, an ageing warrior on the run from his enemies, and then later the young Ciaran Ciulean when the forces of the rightful king and the usurpers clash over the now-dead Niall's fortress. Ciaran has elvish ancestry that is brought disturbingly to the fore through his dealings with Arafel, and particularly by his possession of a vanished elf-lord's dreamstone. This sets him apart from his fellow humans, including his own family. Again, as is typical of Cherryh's series, Ciaran's double-edged victory at the end of the first book only yields an interlude for peace and happiness before events turn threatening again. In the second book, *The Tree of Sword and Jewels,* Arafel must again ask Ciaran to bear the dreamstone in the struggle against an even greater menace—which is in league with Ciaran's own brother. These two books together rank among Cherryh's finest fantasy.

   Also drawing on the same Celtic background material, although with no obvious connection to the Ealdwood sequence, is the powerful and moving short story, "The Brothers," and its sequel, the novel *Faery in Shadow*. The young warrior Caith sets out to rescue the younger brother he has never met and to kill his uncle, Sliabhin, who he believes has killed their father. But in this dark world, where the Sidhe are abroad and curses have real power, kinslaying can only bring tragedy and all is not quite as Caith believes it to be. In *Faery in Shadow* we find Caith leading the wretched life of a wanderer and outcast, his only companion the tricksy phooka, Dubhain. The two become embroiled with a fey pair, brother and sister, and a witch who is using them all as pawns in a plot aimed to snare Caith's master, Nuallan, the Sidhe lord. Unfortunately, although the climax is well-wrought and exciting, the book is too slow-moving, especially at novel length, and so determinedly cheerless, even by Cherryh's standards, as to make it unnecessarily heavy-going.

In *Rusalka,* the opening of another series, Cherryh has drawn her inspiration from a less familiar mythology, that of early Russia, and the stories are set in an approximation of that time and place where magic and magical creatures are very real indeed—and she is particularly successful here at taking a fresh look at both. The reckless Pyetr, and his young friend, Sacha, become involved with a wizard, Uulamets, and the deadly rusalka who is the ghost of his murdered daughter. By the time they encounter Kavi Chernevog, the rival wizard who killed the girl, Pyotr has fallen in love with the rusalka and Sasha is just beginning to discover his own talent for magic. Again, just when Cherryh's main characters might feel they have reached firm ground, their story continues in *Chernevog* and *Yvgenie*.

Not directly related to the Rusalka sequence, but having something of the same Eastern European feel, is *The Goblin Queen,* which tells of brothers sent off over mountain to find the source of the danger that threatens their homeland. Again, as in the Rusalka books, magic is an integral part of the story, and Tamas, one of the brothers, becomes involved with a young witch who holds something that can be used in the magical conflict to come—a shard from the Goblin Queen's mirror. Interestingly, despite their uncomely appearance, Cherryh's lordly goblins seem to have more in common with the elves of standard fantasy than the low-brow orcs.

In contrast, magic plays no part in *The Paladin,* a singleton which is one of her most satisfying works to date, set in a time and place strongly reminiscent of ancient China and with overtones of samurai Japan. The nobleman Shoka was once the peerless master-warrior of the Empire of Chiyaden, but was forced to flee for his life when the foolish young Emperor ascended the throne. Now he lives a hermit's existence, with only his horse for company, in a hut on the mountainside on the very edge of the Empire. Years have passed; he has almost given up expecting assassins, when to his hill comes Taizu, a young, scarred girl who wants Shoka to teach her her warrior skills so that she can return to the Empire and kill the lord who butchered her family and neighbours. Shoka is willing to teach no-one, least of all a peasant girl. But Taizu is unusually determined and, against his better judgement, finds himself with an apprentice. Taizu proves an apt pupil, the relationship between master and student grows, until Shoka realizes both how deeply he has come to care for this revenge-driven peasant girl and how he himself has become embittered and purposeless in exile.

Inevitably, all too soon, the day comes when Taizu decides she is ready to set out on her assassination attempt. The experienced Shoka knows the chances of her succeeding are slim, let alone those of her returning to the cabin alive, but he knows too that he cannot stop her and so instead goes with her. Then events take an unlooked-

for turn as word spreads that the fabled master-warrior has left his mountaintop retreat and is returning to Chiyaden, bringing justice with him. A spontaneous uprising of the oppressed population puts Shoka at the head of rebellion, facing the overwhelming forces of the Empire. It is a familiar predicament for a Cherryh protagonist, caught in a situation where his common sense tell him things are utterly hopeless, and pulled in different directions by his respect and affection for Taizu and his sense of responsibility towards the rebels. With Taizu and a handful of the best rebel warriors, he heads for the centre of the Empire, determined to do what he can, making everything up as he goes along. The characterization of both Shoka and Taizu is particularly effective here, and the story is continuously involving, both in the first, relationship-centred half of the book and in the action-driven second half. We also get an absorbing and convincing awareness of what it might really mean to be such a warrior as Shoka in such a time and place as Chiyaden, the demands and hardship outweighing the glory. It is also strong on two other Cherryh trademarks: sustained tension, and a brief, sharp, furious climax. *The Paladin* is perhaps her most accessible fantasy novel and thus the best introduction to Cherryh's fantasy.

In addition to her major works, Cherryh also plotted the Sword of Knowledge series, set in a world that crosses gunpowder with a quasi-Roman empire—although the three books were then largely written by her three collaborators. She has also written a number of tales set in Robert Asprin and Lynn Abbey's Thieves' World shared universe, and in Janet Morris's Hell series of afterlife fantasies, plus several other shorter works. Finally, although her more recent science fiction is generally regarded as hard sf, some of her earlier sf works share a common feeling with her fantasy and might also be of interest to fantasy readers, particularly *Brothers of Earth* and *The Faded Sun* trilogy. Also, there is *Angel with the Sword,* the opening novel in Cherryh's own shared-world science-fiction series, Merovingen Nights, which is set on an isolated colony-planet that provides a Venice-like background for what is basically a fantasy adventure.

—Neil Jones

CHESTERTON, G(ilbert) K(eith)

Nationality: British. **Born:** London, 29 May 1874. **Education:** Colet Court School, London; St. Paul's School, London (editor, *The Debater,* 1891-93), 1887-92; drawing school, St. John's Wood, London, 1892; Slade School of Art, London, 1893-96. **Family:** Married Frances Alice Blogg in 1901. **Career:** Worked for the London publishers Redway, 1896, and T. Fisher Unwin, 1896-1902; contributor, *Daily News,* London, 1901-13, and the *Illustrated London News,* 1905-36; co-editor, *Eye Witness,* London, 1911-12, and editor, *New Witness,* 1916-23; regular contributor to the *Daily Herald,* London, 1913-14; leader of the Distributist movement after the war, and subsequently President of the Distributist League; convert to Roman Catholicism, 1922; editor, with H. Jackson and R. B. Johnson, Readers' Classics series, 1922; editor, *G. K.'s Weekly,* 1925-36; lecturer, Notre Dame University, Indiana, 1930; radio broadcaster, BBC, 1930s. Also an illustrator; illustrated some of his own works and books by Hilaire Belloc and E. C. Bentley. President, Detection Club, 1928. Honorary degrees: Edinburgh, Dublin and Notre Dame universities; Fellow, Royal Society of Literature. Knight Commander with Star, Order of St. Gregory the Great, 1934. **Died:** 14 June 1936.

FANTASY PUBLICATIONS

Novels

The Man Who Was Thursday: A Nightmare. London, Arrowsmith, and New York, Dodd Mead, 1908.
The Ball and the Cross. New York, Lane, 1909; London, Wells Gardner, 1910.
Manalive. London, Nelson, and New York, Lane, 1912.

Short Stories

The Coloured Lands, edited by Maisie Ward. London and New York, Sheed and Ward, 1938.
Daylight and Nightmare: Uncollected Stories and Fables, edited by Marie Smith. London, Xanadu, and New York, Dodd Mead, 1986.

Plays

Magic: A Fantastic Comedy. London, Secker, and New York, Putnam, 1913.
The Surprise. London, Sheed and Ward, 1953.

Poetry

Greybeards at Play: Literature and Art for Old Gentlemen. London, Brimley Johnson, 1900.
The Ballad of the White Horse. London, Methuen, and New York, Lane, 1911.

OTHER PUBLICATIONS

Novels

The Napoleon of Notting Hill. London, and New York, Lane, 1904.
The Flying Inn. London, Methuen, and New York, Lane, 1914.
The Return of Don Quixote. London, Chatto and Windus, and New York, Dodd Mead, 1927.

Short Stories

The Tremendous Adventures of Major Brown. London, Shurmer Sibthorp, 1903.
The Club of Queer Trades. London and New York, Harper, 1905.
The Innocence of Father Brown. London, Cassell, and New York, Lane, 1911; as *The Annotated Innocence of Father Brown,* edited by Martin Gardner, New York, Oxford University Press, 1987.
The Perishing of the Pendragons. New York, Paget, 1914.
The Wisdom of Father Brown. London, Cassell, 1914; New York, Lane, 1915.
The Man Who Knew Too Much and Other Stories. London, Cassell, and New York, Harper, 1922.
Tales of the Long Bow. London, Cassell, and New York, Dodd Mead, 1925.

The Incredulity of Father Brown. London, Cassell, and New York, Dodd Mead, 1926.
The Secret of Father Brown. London, Cassell, and New York, Harper, 1927.
The Sword of Wood. London, Elkin Matthews, 1928.
Stories. London, Harrap, 1928.
The Poet and the Lunatic: Episodes in the Life of Gabriel Gale. London, Cassell, and New York, Dodd Mead, 1929.
The Moderate Murderer, and the Honest Quack. New York, Dodd Mead, 1929.
The Ecstatic Thief. New York, Dodd Mead, 1930.
Four Faultless Felons. London, Cassell, and New York, Dodd Mead, 1930.
The Floating Admiral, with others. London, Hodder and Stoughton, 1931; New York, Doubleday, 1932.
The Scandal of Father Brown. London, Cassell, and New York, Dodd Mead, 1935.
The Paradoxes of Mr. Pond. London, Cassell, 1936; New York, Dodd Mead, 1937.
The Vampire of the Village. Privately printed, 1947.
Father Brown: Selected Stories, edited by Ronald Knox. London, Oxford University Press, 1955.
The Father Brown Omnibus. New York, Dodd Mead, 1983.
Thirteen Detectives: Classic Mystery Stories, edited by Marie Smith. London, Xanadu, 1987.
The Best of Father Brown, edited by H. R. F. Keating. London, Dent, 1987.

Play

The Judgment of Dr. Johnson. London, Sheed and Ward, 1927; New York, Putnam, 1928.

Poetry

The Wild Knight and Other Poems. London, Richards, 1900; revised edition, London, Dent, and New York, Dutton, 1914.
Poems. London, Burne Oates, 1915; New York, Lane, 1916.
Wine, Water, and Song. London, Methuen, 1915.
A Poem. Privately printed, 1915.
Old King Cole. Privately printed, 1920.
The Ballad of St. Barbara and Other Verses. London, Palmer, 1922; New York, Putnam, 1923.
(Poems). London, Benn, and New York, Stokes, 1925.
The Queen of Seven Swords. London, Sheed and Ward, 1926.
The Collected Poems of G. K. Chesterton. London, Palmer, 1927; revised edition, New York, Dodd Mead, 1932.
Gloria in Profundis. London, Faber and Gwyer, and New York, Rudge, 1927.
Ubi Ecclesia. London, Faber, 1929.
The Grave of Arthur. London, Faber, 1930.
Greybeards at Play and Other Comic Verse, edited by John Sullivan. London, Elek, 1974.
Collected Nonsense and Other Light Verse, edited by Marie Smith. London, Xanadu, and New York, Dodd Mead, 1987.

Other

The Defendant. London, Brimley Johnson, 1901; New York, Dodd Mead, 1902.

Twelve Types. London, Humphreys, 1902; augmented edition, as *Varied Types,* New York, Dodd Mead, 1903; selections as *Five Types,* Humphreys, 1910; New York, Holt, 1911; and as *Simplicity and Tolstoy,* Humphreys, 1912.

Thomas Carlyle. London, Hodder and Stoughton, 1902; New York, Pott, n.d.

Robert Louis Stevenson, with W. Robertson Nicoll. London, Hodder and Stoughton, and New York, Pott, 1903.

Leo Tolstoy, with G. H. Perris and Edward Garnett. London, Hodder and Stoughton, and New York, Pott, 1903.

Charles Dickens, with F. G. Kitton. London, Hodder and Stoughton, and New York, Pott, 1903.

Robert Browning. London and New York, Macmillan, 1903.

Tennyson, with Richard Garnett. London, Hodder and Stoughton, 1903; New York, Pott, n.d.

Thackeray, with Lewis Melville. London, Hodder and Stoughton, and New York, Pott, 1903.

G. F. Watts. London, Duckworth, and New York, Dutton, 1904.

Heretics. London and New York, Lane, 1905.

Charles Dickens. London, Methuen, and New York, Dodd Mead, 1906.

All Things Considered. London, Methuen, and New York, Lane, 1908.

Orthodoxy. London and New York, Lane, 1908.

George Bernard Shaw. London and New York, Lane, 1909; revised edition, London, Lane, 1935.

Tremendous Trifles. London, Methuen, and New York, Dodd Mead, 1909.

What's Wrong with the World. London, Cassell, and New York, Dodd Mead, 1910.

Alarms and Discursions. London, Methuen, 1910; New York, Dodd Mead, 1911.

William Blake. London, Duckworth, and New York, Dutton, 1910.

The Ultimate Lie. Privately printed, 1910.

A Chesterton Calendar. London, Kegan Paul, 1911; as *Wit and Wisdom of G. K. Chesterton,* New York, Dodd Mead, 1911; as *Chesterton Day by Day,* Kegan Paul, 1912.

Appreciations and Criticisms of the Works of Charles Dickens. London, Dent, and New York, Dutton, 1911.

A Defence of Nonsense and Other Essays. New York, Dodd Mead, 1911.

The Future of Religion: Mr. G. K. Chesterton's Reply to Mr. Bernard Shaw. Privately printed, 1911.

The Conversion of an Anarchist. New York, Paget, 1912.

A Miscellany of Men. London, Methuen, 1910; New York, Dodd Mead, 1912.

The Victorian Age in Literature. London, Williams and Norgate, and New York, Holt, 1913.

Thoughts from Chesterton, edited by Elsie E. Morton. London, Harrap, 1913.

The Barbarism of Berlin. London, Cassell, 1914.

London, photographs by Alvin Langdon Coburn. Privately printed, 1914.

Prussian Versus Belgian Culture. Edinburgh, Belgian Relief and Reconstruction Fund, 1914.

Letters to an Old Garibaldian. London, Methuen, 1915; with *The Barbarism of Berlin,* as *The Appetite of Tyranny,* New York, Dodd Mead, 1915.

The So-Called Belgian Bargain. London, National War Aims Committee, 1915.

The Crimes of England. London, Palmer and Hayward, 1915; New York, Lane, 1916.

Divorce Versus Democracy. London, Society of SS. Peter and Paul, 1916.

Temperance and the Great Alliance. London, True Temperance Association, 1916.

The G. K. Chesterton Calendar, edited by H. Cecil Palmer. London, Palmer and Hayward, 1916.

A Shilling for My Thoughts, edited by E. V. Lucas. London, Methuen, 1916.

Lord Kitchener. Privately printed, 1917.

A Short History of England. London, Chatto and Windus, and New York, Lane, 1917.

Utopia of Usurers and Other Essays. New York, Boni and Liveright, 1917.

How to Help Annexation. London, Hayman Christy and Lilly, 1918.

Irish Impressions. London, Collins, and New York, Lane, 1920.

The Superstition of Divorce. London, Chatto and Windus, and New York, Lane, 1920.

Charles Dickens Fifty Years After. Privately printed, 1920.

The Uses of Diversity: A Book of Essays. London, Methuen, 1920; New York, Dodd Mead, 1921.

The New Jerusalem. London, Hodder and Stoughton, 1920; New York, Doran, 1921.

Eugenics and Other Evils. London, Cassell, 1922; New York, Dodd Mead, 1927.

What I Saw in America. London, Hodder and Stoughton, and New York, Dodd Mead, 1922.

Fancies Versus Fads. London, Methuen, and New York, Dodd Mead, 1923.

St. Francis of Assisi. London, Hodder and Stoughton, 1923; New York, Dodd Mead, 1924.

The End of the Roman Road: A Pageant of Wayfarers. London, Classic Press, 1924.

The Superstitions of the Sceptic (lecture). Cambridge, Heffer, and St. Louis, Herder, 1925.

The Everlasting Man. London, Hodder and Stoughton, and New York, Dodd Mead, 1925.

William Cobbett. London, Hodder and Stoughton, 1925; New York, Dodd Mead, 1926.

The Outline of Sanity. London, Methuen, 1926; New York, Dodd Mead, 1927.

The Catholic Church and Conversion. New York, Macmillan, 1926; London, Burns Oates, 1927.

Selected Works (Minerva edition). London, Methuen, 9 vols., 1926.

A Gleaming Cohort, Being Selections from the Works of G. K. Chesterton, edited by E. V. Lucas. London, Methuen, 1926.

Social Reform Versus Birth Control. London, Simpkin Marshall, 1927.

Culture and the Coming Peril (lecture). London, University of London Press, 1927.

Robert Louis Stevenson. London, Hodder and Stoughton, 1927; New York, Dodd Mead, 1928.

Generally Speaking: A Book of Essays. London, Methuen, and New York, Dodd Mead, 1928.

(Essays). London, Harrap, 1928.

Do We Agree? A Debate, with G. B. Shaw. London, Palmer, and Hartford, Connecticut, Mitchell, 1928.

A Chesterton Catholic Anthology, edited by Patrick Braybrooke. London, Burns Oates, and New York, Kenedy, 1928.

The Thing (essays). London, Sheed and Ward, 1929.

G.K.C. a M.C., Being a Collection of Thirty-Seven Introductions, edited by J. P. de Fonseka. London, Methuen, 1929.

The Resurrection of Rome. London, Hodder and Stoughton, and New York, Dodd Mead, 1930.

Come to Think of It: A Book of Essays. London, Methuen, 1930; New York, Dodd Mead, 1931.

The Turkey and the Turk. Ditchling, Sussex, St. Dominic's Press, 1930.

At the Sign of the World's End. Palo Alto, California, Harvest Press, 1930.

Is There a Return to Religion? with E. Haldeman-Julius. Girard, Kansas, Haldeman Julius, 1931.

All is Grist: A Book of Essays. London, Methuen, 1931; New York, Dodd Mead, 1932.

Chaucer. London, Faber, and New York, Farrar Rinehart, 1932.

Sidelights on New London and Newer York and Other Essays. London, Sheed and Ward, and New York, Dodd Mead, 1932.

Christendom in Dublin. London, Sheed and Ward, 1932; New York, Sheed and Ward, 1933.

All I Survey: A Book of Essays. London, Methuen, and New York, Dodd Mead, 1933.

St. Thomas Aquinas. London, Hodder and Stoughton, and New York, Sheed and Ward, 1933.

G. K. Chesterton (selected humour), edited by E. V. Knox. London, Methuen, 1933; as *Running After One's Hat and Other Whimsies,* New York, McBride, 1933.

Avowals and Denials: A Book of Essays. London, Methuen, 1934; New York, Dodd Mead, 1935.

The Well and the Shallows. London and New York, Sheed and Ward, 1935.

Explaining the English. London, British Council, 1935.

Stories, Essays and Poems. London, Dent, 1935.

As I Was Saying: A Book of Essays. London, Methuen, and New York, Dodd Mead, 1936.

Autobiography. London, Hutchinson, and New York, Sheed and Ward, 1936.

The Man Who Was Chesterton, edited by Raymond T. Bond. New York, Dodd Mead, 1937.

Essays, edited by John Guest. London, Collins, 1939.

The End of the Armistice, edited by F. J. Sheed. London and New York, Sheed and Ward, 1940.

Selected Essays, edited by Dorothy Collins. London, Methuen, 1949.

The Common Man. London and New York, Sheed and Ward, 1950.

Essays, edited by K. E. Whitehorn. London, Methuen, 1953.

A Handful of Authors: Essays on Books and Writers, edited by Dorothy Collins. London and New York, Sheed and Ward, 1953.

The Glass Walking-Stick and Other Essays from the Illustrated London News 1905-1936, edited by Dorothy Collins. London, Methuen, 1955.

G. K. Chesterton: An Anthology, edited by D. B. Wyndham Lewis. London and New York, Oxford University Press, 1957.

Essays and Poems, edited by Wilfrid Sheed. London, Penguin, 1958.

Lunacy and Letters (essays), edited by Dorothy Collins. London and New York, Sheed and Ward, 1958.

Where All Roads Lead. London, Catholic Truth Society, 1961.

The Man Who Was Orthodox: A Selection from the Uncollected Writings of G. K. Chesterton, edited by A. L. Maycock. London, Dobson, 1963.

The Spice of Life and Other Essays, edited by Dorothy Collins. Beaconsfield, Buckinghamshire, Finlayson, 1964; Chester Springs, Pennsylvania, Dufour, 1966.

G. K. Chesterton: A Selection from His Non-Fictional Prose, edited by W. H. Auden. London, Faber, 1970.

Chesterton on Shakespeare, edited by Dorothy Collins. Henley on Thames, Oxfordshire, and Chester Springs, Pennsylvania, Dufour, 1971.

The Apostle and the Wild Ducks, and Other Essays, edited by Dorothy Collins. London, Elek, 1975.

The Spirit of Christmas: Stories, Poems, Essays, edited by Marie Smith. London, Xanadu, 1984; New York, Dodd Mead, 1985.

As I Was Saying: A Chesterton Reader, edited by Robert Knille. Grand Rapids, Michigan, Eerdmans, and Exeter, Paternoster, 1985.

The Bodley Head G. K. Chesterton, edited by P. J. Kavanagh. London, Bodley Head, 1985; as *The Essential Chesterton,* Oxford, Oxford University Press, 1987.

Collected Works, edited by Denis J. Conlon. Harrison, New York, Ignatius Press, 1986-87; San Francisco, Ignatius Press, 1989.

Editor, *Thackeray* (selections). London, Bell, 1909.

Editor, with Alice Meynell, *Samuel Johnson* (selections). London, Herbert and Daniel, 1911.

Editor, *Essays by Divers Hands 6.* London, Oxford University Press, 1926.

Editor, *G. K.'s* (miscellany from *G. K.'s Weekly*). London, Rich and Cowan, 1934.

*

Film Adaptations: *Father Brown, Detective,* 1935, *Father Brown,* 1954, *Father Brown, Detective,* 1974 (TV movie), and *Sanctuary of Fear,* 1979 (TV movie), all from his Father Brown stories.

Bibliography: *Chesterton: A Bibliography* by John Sullivan, London, University of London Press, 1958, supplement, 1968, and *Chesterton 3: A Bibliographical Postscript,* Bedford, Vintage, 1980.

Manuscript Collections: Humanities Research Center, University of Texas, Austin; John Carroll University Library, Cleveland, Ohio.

Critical Studies: *Paradox in Chesterton* by Hugh Kenner, New York, Sheed and Ward, 1947; *Chesterton: Man and Mask* by Garry Wills, New York, Sheed and Ward, 1961; *G. K. Chesterton* by Lawrence J. Clipper, New York, Twayne, 1974; *Chesterton: A Centennial Appraisal* edited by John Sullivan, New York, Barnes and Noble, 1974; *The Novels of G. K. Chesterton: A Study in Art and Propaganda* by Ian Boyd, New York, Barnes and Noble, and London, Elek, 1975; *Chesterton: The Critical Judgments 1900-1937,* edited by D. J. Conlon, 1976; *Chesterton: Explorations in Allegory* by Lynette Hunter, London, Macmillan, 1979; *The Outline of Sanity: A Biography of G. K. Chesterton* by Alzina Stone Dale, Grand Rapids, Michigan, Eerdmans, 1982; *G. K. Chesterton* by Michael Ffinch, London, Weidenfeld and Nicolson, 1986; *G. K. Chesterton: A Critical Study* by K. Dwarakanath, New Delhi, Classical, 1986; *G. K. Chesterton: A Half Century of Views* edited by D. J. Conlon, Oxford and New York, Oxford University Press, 1987; *Gilbert: The Man Who Was G. K. Chesterton* by Michael Coren, London, Cape, 1989, New York, Paragon House, 1990.

* * *

The flamboyance and heightened colours of G. K. Chesterton's fiction make it harder than usual to draw the line where fantasy begins. Or indeed where fiction ends: thanks to his characteristic tools of parable and eccentric imagery, several of his countless newspaper essays read like stories. Even the famous Father Brown detective tales, which follow the rules of the Detection Club and strictly exclude the supernatural, often contain a clear allegory—the mystery standing for a Mystery.

In one sense all his fiction is fantastic, but several of the novels are better regarded as sociological science fiction. *The Napoleon of Notting Hill*, with its study of fierce local nationalism, of individual London boroughs fighting with swords and halberds, seems more prophetic in the 1990s than ever before. *The Flying Inn*'s vision of the future has dated badly, though its drinking songs are still lively and the government's closing of all the pubs in England (partly as a gesture of Islamic solidarity) is not wholly remote from present-day fears of too much State interference for our own good. *The Return of Don Quixote* shows a crusade to give English politics a new image of medieval pageantry, only for flabby politicians who thought this a convenient PR exercise to fail when judged by the accompanying medieval standards.

Chesterton's fantasy masterpiece is *The Man Who Was Thursday*: a lurid comic melodrama, a theological shocker. Following an extravagant drawing-room argument about terrorism (in those days, "anarchism"), the detective hero Gabriel Syme shortly finds himself trapped amid bomb-happy anarchists at a crucial meeting deep underground, where through bravura rhetoric he contrives to be elected to the post of Thursday on the Central Anarchist Council whose dread members are named for the weekdays.

This happens in a fairy-tale London of luminous sunsets and dawns, where even the stones of the Embankment seem ominously like "the colossal steps of some Egyptian palace" and the Council—found at breakfast in a balcony overlooking Leicester Square—are figures from childhood nightmare. Monday's twisted smile, Friday's hateful physical decrepitude verging on corruption, Saturday's eyes hidden because (Syme fears) they may be too frightful to see; all these horrors are dwarfed by the gigantic President, Sunday.

Soon Syme is grotesquely chased across London by an impossible goblin pursuer; confronts the more intellectual terror of those feared, hidden eyes; crosses duelling-swords with the apparently invulnerable Wednesday; flees desperately across a France where every friend turns foe and the whole Earth seems to be with Sunday against Syme's pitifully few allies. . . . Underlying the repeated shocks, reversals, happy surprises and outright jokes there's a constant trickle of philosophical and theological speculation as the six weekdays of the Council—now all unmasked as detectives—struggle to understand their topsy-turvy world, and Sunday, and themselves. The melodrama is also metaphysical, as in the novels of Charles Williams; the romping physical action is thin ice over deep waters.

When the mask is pulled from Sunday himself, the trickster who is the great enemy but also the man in the dark room who recruited Syme and his companions into the police force . . . the book has to stop. An allegorical charge has been building up. Sunday isn't God—Chesterton once tentatively identified him as Nature—but whatever lies behind Sunday is too large to see. The ending reminds us gently that the subtitle was "A Nightmare."

The Ball and the Cross is less elusive. The cross is of course the Cross; the complementary ball is both the world and the dome of St. Paul's where, in a bizarre opening, Professor Lucifer pauses his flying machine to eject the ancient monk Michael, whom he has kidnapped for amusement. Michael is whisked off to an asylum and lost to sight.

Below in grey London, the worldly Turnbull is the last man who still thinks it worth preaching blasphemy and atheism. He's confronted by McIan, the last devout man who objects: only these two still believe religion worth fighting over, and they agree to a fight to the death. Society objects, and the pair are harried round the country as they seek a place to duel undisturbed, still hotly (and brilliantly) debating but forced into something like friendship. Their final refuge is a trap: a vast lunatic asylum run by Lucifer into which society's oddments are swept by a definition of insanity covering not only those wishing to fight over religion but anyone who helped, hindered, or even witnessed Turnbull's and McIan's impermissible adventures.

Of course Lucifer is not merely a professor, and soon he's tempting his prisoners with flawed utopias which distortedly reflect their own inner dreams. McIan is offered a theocratic fascism, full of heraldry, spectacle and good times except for the oppressed peasants. The socialist Turnbull naturally sees the glorious revolution, with unemployables being disposed of in a vast blaze of slums. Each rejects the offer and is thrown into a "hygienic" oubliette whose inhuman, irrational proportions clearly foreshadow the Objective Room of *That Hideous Strength*. (Michael, the last holy man, is in the deepest cell of all.) Like C. S. Lewis's book, *The Ball and the Cross* ends in cleansing fire . . . though not from Heaven.

Although Chesterton's religious bias is evident, his fantasies are less concerned to push a particular Catholic world-view than to insist that the world is worth viewing, and is constantly surprising when seen with unbored eyes. This theme recurs again and again, reaching an extreme in *Manalive* . . . a novel which has been called the acid test of a Chesterton fan and is most likely to repel the unsympathetic. Its hero Innocent Smith commits apparent crimes which are reaffirmations of the world—burgling what proves to be his own house, eloping with his own wife, or shooting at professed pessimists not to kill but to shock them out of claiming life isn't worth living.

The Ballad of the White Horse is Chesterton's verse epic about King Alfred, mentioned here for its vision of the Virgin Mary encouraging Alfred to greater efforts by refusing to encourage him ("I tell you naught for your comfort, / Yea, naught for your desire, / Save that the sky grows darker yet, / And the sea rises higher"). Some of his nonsense verse strays towards fantasy, notably in his first published book *Greybeards at Play,* while his serious poetry has many exotic outbreaks—as in the famous "Lepanto" with its glimpse of the Prophet himself urging on the Islamic forces: "And his voice through all the garden is a thunder sent to bring / Black Azrael and Ariel and Ammon on the wing. / Giants and the Genii, / Multiplex of wing and eye, / Whose strong obedience broke the sky / When Solomon was king."

The Coloured Lands is a posthumous collection of fragments and drawings, mostly fantastic juvenilia with dragons, nightmares and the seed of *Manalive* . . . The recent *Daylight and Nightmare* reprints some of this material, plus essays and squibs like the satirical "How I Found the Superman" which can plausibly be called fantasies.

Two Chesterton plays also use fantastic devices. *Magic* turns on a simple conjuring trick which is inexplicable because real magic has been used: the magician finally saves a tortured sceptic from insanity by devising a false explanation of how it was done. In the posthumous *The Surprise,* a life-sized puppet-play runs flawlessly and mechanically—and is then played again with the figures magically given free will, hurling the plot into chaos. To make the allegory unmistakable, the play's enraged Author finally appears on high: "Drop it! Stop! I am coming down."

The energy, fun and aggressive sanity of Chesterton's best writing, with its lurid colours, free-association of clever ideas, alliteration, polemic, puns and paradox, can only be conveyed by extended quotation. Much of his later output is weary—he wrote far too much journalism—and there's some truth in the occasional charge of anti-semitism (Chesterton reflected contemporary prejudices, though good-heartedly and never with the virulence of his friend and disastrous influence Hilaire Belloc). But *The Man Who Was Thursday* in particular has established itself as a genuine classic, and looks set to stay in print well into the next century.

—David Langford

CHETWIN, Grace

Nationality: British. **Born:** Nottingham; emigrated to the United States in 1964. **Education:** University of Southampton, Highfield, B.A. in philosophy. **Family:** Married Arthur G. Roberts; two daughters. **Career:** High school English and French teacher, Auckland, New Zealand, 1958-62; high school English teacher and department head, Devon, England, 1962-63; director, Group '72-'76 (drama group), Auckland, 1972-76; dance company director in New Zealand for four years; produced operas at the amateur level; writer since 1983. **Agent:** Jean V. Naggar Literary Agency, 216 East 75th Street, New York, NY 10021, USA. **Address:** 37 Hitching Post Lane, Glen Cove, NY 11542, USA.

FANTASY PUBLICATIONS

Novels (series: Tales of Gom)

On All Hallows' Eve. New York, Lothrop, 1984.
Out of the Dark World. New York, Lothrop, 1985.
Gom on Windy Mountain. New York, Lothrop, 1986.
The Riddle and the Rune (Gom). New York, Lothrop, 1987.
The Crystal Stair (Gom). New York, Bradbury, 1988.
The Starstone (Gom). New York, Bradbury, 1989.
Child of the Air. New York, Bradbury, 1991.
Friends in Time. New York, Bradbury, 1992.
The Chimes of Alyafaleyn. New York, Bradbury, 1993.
Jason's Seven Magnificent Night Rides. New York, Bradbury, 1994.

OTHER PUBLICATIONS

Novels

The Atheling. New York, Bluejay, 1987; London, Corgi, 1990.
Collidescope. New York, Bradbury, 1990.

Fiction for Children

Mr. Meredith and the Truly Remarkable Stone, illustrated by Catherine Stock. New York, Bradbury, 1989.

Box and Cox, illustrated by David Small. New York, Bradbury, 1990.

* * *

Best known for her tetralogy about the young wizard, Gom, Grace Chetwin has produced a dozen fantasy and science-fiction novels for teenagers and two books for younger children. Her Gom series has been praised for its judicious blend of Germanic legends and fantasy invention, but her other works have been criticized for flaws of integration and sometimes unsympathetic central female characters. Elements of science fiction in some of the stories provide a modern touch, and Chetwin's ability to write spirited dialogue and create interesting fantasy worlds are noteworthy.

Gom on Windy Mountain, the first book in her series about Gom, tells of Gom's birth and boyhood. The tenth child of Stig, the Woodcutter, and Wife, Gom is deserted by his mother on the day of his birth because his father had wanted no more children. It is clear from the beginning that Gom is different from his nine older siblings and has inherited psychic talents from his mother. Gom eventually learns that his mother is a wizard, Harga the Brown, and when Gom's father dies near the end of the book, Gom leaves on a quest to find his mother. In the three subsequent books of the series, Gom seeks his destiny with many adventures called the Legends of Ulm. Chetwin is successful in this series with maintaining the spirit of German fairy tales, and particularly in creating an appealing hero, Gom. There is use of familiar details, such as forests, woodcutters, and magically-endowed characters. Some scenes set in deep, mysterious caves are reminiscent of George MacDonald's *The Princess and the Goblin.* Chetwin has been able to strike exactly the right story-telling tone for her fairytale-like creations. This, coupled with the appeal of Gom, explains the success of this series.

In contrast, Chetwin's new series, which started with *The Chimes of Alyafaleyn,* featuring a female protagonist, appears to be off to a rockier start than the Gom books. It centres on a girl, Caidrun, who, like Gom, possesses psychic powers. In her technological society, Caidrun must wear a special helmet which blocks her extraordinary abilities. Caidrun, a rather disagreeable youngster, has only one friend, Tamborel. Caidrun rebelliously destroys the balance of *heymin,* delicate balls that maintain harmony, and as a result nearly brings about the end of her world. Tamborel helps her discover the source of *heymin* and disaster is averted. Caidrun is typical of many of Chetwin's petulant female characters. Readers of her books might well wonder if Chetwin likes boys better than girls, since it is primarily girls who must learn lessons about being nicer people.

For example, in *On All Hallows' Eve,* Chetwin's first published work, the sixth-grade heroine is sulking because of a forced move from England to the United States. Her perpetual pouting is cured only after she is transported into Otherworld, where she must struggle with a witch queen in order to save her sister and two boys who have been teasing Meg. Meg accepts her task unwillingly, but succeeds and comes to recognize her own snobbishness. The sequel, *Out of the Dark World,* deals with a technological threat; her cousin has been trapped in a computer of the future. This second book about Meg is illustrative of Chetwin's other failing: her lengthy explanations about New Age philosophies and computers get in the way of the plot, encouraging impatient readers to skip long paragraphs of details.

In the science-fiction novel *Collidescope,* time travel is introduced as a plot device. A modern teenage girl and an 18th-century Native

American boy come into contact with an alien from outer space. All three become involved in thwarting the villain, an adversary of the spaceman. Again, the female character is less attractive than the male. She is self-centred and, although not as unsympathetic as some of Chetwin's other young female protagonists, she comes across as far less decent than the boy. In *Child of the Air* Chetwin creates one of her few sympathetic female characters, Mylanfyndra, who must deal with evil much like the dark and seamy Victorian world portrayed by Charles Dickens. Since she lives in an alternative world, Mylanfyndra and her brother find they can fly and are able to escape from the drudgery of the workhouse. This imaginative flight is more immediately liberating than that of Oliver Twist.

Examination of Chetwin's work to date emphasizes the superior qualities she exhibited as author of the Gom series. Her other books have some good qualities, but do not measure up to Chetwin's stories of the young wizard.

—Cosette Kies

CHIN, M. Lucie

Nationality: American.

Fantasy Publications

Novel

The Fairy of Ku-She. New York, Ace, 1988; London, Fontana, 1991.

*   *   *

The Fairy of Ku-She was the first (and so far only) novel by M. Lucie Chin. The writer's intention appears to be to marry modern narrative techniques to the traditional fairy-story mode, though in a legendary Chinese setting rather than a western one. The amalgam is an interesting one, if not wholly successful. The atmosphere of ancient China, and especially the lives of the upper classes, are vividly evoked. One particularly striking example is the way in which the marriage of two wives to one husband is shown to be possible without rancour or jealousy. Another is the relationship of the bonded servants to their owners.

The narrative scope of the book is, at once, both very wide and extremely limited. The limitations arise from the writer's preoccupations with the domestic detail of day to day life. There is very little action, and this leads to occasional longueurs, especially to readers more used to the fast pacing of much modern fantasy. Yet the scale is also almost epic, in the sense that it covers 20 or so years spent by the Fairy of Ku-She as a mortal woman. She has been banished from Heaven for her slowness in recovering her magical golden chopsticks, which have been stolen; their loss means that no snow can fall on Earth, resulting in widespread drought. In her attempt to recover her property, she marries a mortal and falls in love with him. The son she bears him is the eventual agent of the Jade Emperor's true punishment. The child, himself immortal, is tested and taken into Heaven when he is twelve, against his parents wishes. They are powerless to do anything about this. The action then moves on several years, and we see the son, now an

embittered and powerful young man, laying waste to both Heaven and earth. The remainder of the book deals with Ku-She's attempts to deal with this situation.

The attempt to cover such a long period of time results in a lack of focus to the novel. Though the story is definitely Ku-She's, it is hard to say whether it is really about her relationship with her husband, or about her fall from grace and subsequent restoration, or about her battle with her child. This problem is exacerbated by the attempt to remain in the story-telling mode—external, omniscient, non-realistic—while at the same time ascribing realistic motivations to the characters. Had the mode been strictly realistic, there would have been no doubt that it was an exploration of character; had it been strictly that of the story-teller, the emphasis would have shifted to the mythic elements of the story—first the quest for the chopsticks, then the fight against the son. But it is hard to believe that that mode could have been sustained at novel length.

Nowhere is this more problematic than in the development of the son. Within a space of a few pages Chin shows him changing from a likeable, hardworking little boy—albeit an occasionally hot-tempered one—into a grotesquely angry, almost psychopathic figure, capable of the most outrageous acts of needless cruelty. We are told this happens, and we are told why. Yet we are not shown—but since we *have* been shown his childhood, it is very hard to believe the transformation. There are clues, but they are very subtle. The same technique is used on a smaller scale with other characters, when the consequences of some actions are shown, rather than the actions themselves. This appears to be the case particularly when anything especially violent occurs, such as the deaths of several of the major characters towards the end of the narrative.

In some ways, the most interesting aspect of the book is its total lack of any redemptive quality. In the last third of the novel, the son is shown to be a classic fantasy villain—the embodiment of pure evil. There is never a moment when his plight touches us—never a moment when we think he might be saved from the anger that has consumed him.

The Jade Emperor, and his relationship with Ku-She, fit neatly into this world view. He is cruel and unbending, worshipped because he is powerful, not because he is good. When Ku-She is first punished, it is as much because she will not give the Jade Emperor some information he wants as for any other reason. In some ways, the whole point of the book seems to be that by its end she has learned that this was foolish. Yet there is nothing of redemption here, nothing of the gaining of wisdom, except in the most basic sense that it is unwise to anger those more powerful than oneself. This is offered as a coda, almost in the manner of the moral that accompanies some fairy tales.

Overall, this novel is interesting rather than an overwhelming success. Yet it is an honourable attempt to break free of the straitjacket of most modern fantasy, and it doesn't seem unreasonable to hope that if the author wishes to do so she will find a way to combine the two different schools of fantasy more completely.

—Liz Holliday

COCHRAN, Molly

Nationality: American. **Family:** Married novelist and screenwriter Warren B. Murphy in 1984; one son. **Career:** Writer (all her fiction has been published under Murphy's name or in acknowledged collaboration with him and others; her name has preceded his on their joint works). **Awards:** Mystery Writers of America Edgar Allan Poe award, 1985. Lives in Bethlehem, Pennsylvania.

FANTASY PUBLICATIONS

Novels

Grandmaster, with Warren Murphy. New York, Pinnacle, 1984; London, Macdonald, 1985.
High Priest, with Warren Murphy. New York, New American Library, 1987.
The Hand of Lazarus, with Warren Murphy. New York, Pinnacle, 1988.
The Forever King, with Warren Murphy. New York, Tor, and London, Millennium, 1992.

OTHER PUBLICATIONS

Novels

Balance of Power, with Richard Sapir and Warren Murphy. New York, Pinnacle, 1981.
Spoils of War (as Warren Murphy). New York, Pinnacle, 1981.
Next of Kin (as Warren Murphy). New York, Pinnacle, 1981.
Dying Space (as Warren Murphy). New York, Pinnacle, 1982.
Skin Deep (as Warren Murphy). New York, Pinnacle, 1982.
Killing Time (as Warren Murphy). New York, Pinnacle, 1982.
Shock Value (as Warren Murphy). New York, Pinnacle, 1983.
Last Drop (as Warren Murphy). New York, Pinnacle, 1983.
Time Trial (as Warren Murphy). New York, Pinnacle, 1983.
Master's Challenge, with Richard Sapir and Warren Murphy. New York, Pinnacle, 1984.
Date with Death (as Warren Murphy), with Warren Murphy and Ed Hunsburger. New York, Pinnacle, 1984.
The Eleventh Hour, with Warren Murphy and Will Murray. New York, Pinnacle, 1987.
The Temple Dogs, with Warren Murphy. New York, New American Library, 1989.

Other

Dressing Thin. N.p., n.d.

*   *   *

Molly Cochran joined the Warren B. Murphy/Richard Ben Sapir "fiction factory" anonymously in the early 1980s, and subsequently married Murphy as well as becoming his leading collaborator on fiction after Sapir's death in 1987 (for further details of these authors see the entry under Murphy's name in *Twentieth-Century Crime and Mystery Writers,* 3rd edition). Cochran wrote, or cowrote with Murphy and others, a number of the immensely long Destroyer series of fantasy-tinged contemporary thrillers before cowriting her first acknowledged fantasy, *Grandmaster.* It is not surprising, therefore, that this Edgar award-winning novel should be an unusual work, one which combines the fantastic with elements of espionage, cold-war theatrics and international murder.

It is the story of two men, very old enemies reincarnated, who are destined to battle one another until both are dead—and they are very hard to kill. The narrative begins with a woman, the true villainess of the piece: she is thousands of years old, kept alive by magic, and believes herself to be a goddess. She has summoned to her the man who will be her champion, the Prince of Death. Since much of the background of the book involves chess masters (hence the title), he is known as the Black King. His true identity isn't revealed until later in the story—that of a highly-placed Russian official, head of an organization so secret it answers to no one, not even the KGB. At first, it is difficult to tell whether Alexander Zharkov is indeed the Black King, or whether that honour goes to Justin Gilead, the Grandmaster. Gilead is a chess champion at the age of 11 when his father is murdered; he bests Zharkov in an international match. Of course, this is before either of them knows his destiny.

After the death of Gilead's father he is spirited away into the mountains of Tibet to a monastery called Amne Xachim. There the monks have been waiting for him, for he is the Patanjali, or reincarnation of Brahma. They raise Gilead, teaching him martial arts, survival skills and giving him a classical education. By the time he is ready to join the CIA he can speak 12 languages. He has already met Varja, the self-styled "goddess" who attempts to murder him for the gold snake-amulet he wears and who steals away Duma, Gilead's first love. Varja is the head of a strange cult in the mountains of either Nepal or Burma (the book is a little vague here) and heads an abbey of "nuns" she uses as prostitutes.

During the course of the book, Zharkov believes he has killed Gilead on three separate occasions. But Gilead is superhuman, as is Zharkov, and neither can die without the other. They leave an impressive trail of bodies in their wake, however—although Gilead would prefer not to kill people, it always comes down to him or them. By the end of the novel, he thinks he has finally killed Zharkov, then realizes that if he is alive, his enemy must also be. It's a strange and unusual fantasy adventure, full of intrigue and interesting side-plots, well-written and with good characterization.

A couple of subsequent novels, *High Priest* and *The Hand of Lazarus,* are also thrillers with strong fantastic elements; but the first "classic" fantasy by Cochran and Murphy (and the only such to date) is *The Forever King,* a wonderful urban time-travel story about King Arthur. Some readers might be wearied at the thought of yet another tale about Camelot, but this one is different from run-of-the-mill Arthuriana. It takes place in modern-day England, and features Merlin, who has been alive and waiting for his king to be reincarnated all this time, the reborn king himself, and Sir Galahad, who has also been reborn as a burned-out alcoholic ex-FBI agent. Arthur is now Arthur Blessing, a young boy without parents who is being raised by his aunt Emily. Emily is a brilliant scientist who has little time for children in her life, who does her best by Arthur but longs to be alone with her research. Arthur befriends an old man in their apartment house, Mr. Goldberg (one of the many disguises Merlin uses to be near and to protect Arthur), and one day he finds a strange, bronze cup rolling in the gutter.

What would a classic fantasy be without a villain? *The Forever King* has a terrific one in Saladin, the Saracen who has been alive much longer than Merlin, thanks to once owning the bronze cup. The cup itself, which came to be known as the Holy Grail, was originally an alien artefact that found its way to Earth long before recorded history. Originally found by a wandering hill-man, the cup fell into Saladin's hands when the man took him in. This was when he was 15 years old, and had escaped from slavery in Kish.

Born as a prince in Elam, he was captured when the city was overrun by soldiers from Kish. He escaped when Kish had a earthquake. Once he killed the hill-man, who was thousands of years old due to the healing properties of the cup, Saladin was also able to live forever.

He lost the cup once during the life of Christ, when it was coated with mud and found its way to the Last Supper table. He recovered it after ten years (he was now 25, though he had lived for centuries) only to lose it again in modern-day England. Incarcerated in an insane asylum for serial murders, Saladin must escape in order to retrieve the cup. He does so by burning the place down, aided by his own descendants, over whom he has a strange kind of psychic control. When he discovers that Arthur Blessing has the cup, he sends assassins to kill him. They shoot Emily, but Arthur inadvertently heals her with the cup, and they decide they must flee. Arthur has received a telegram telling him he has inherited a castle and some land in the south of England, so they decide to go there.

In another disguise, that of a tourist named Taliesin, Merlin sets the scene for Galahad, now Hal Woczniak, also to come to England. This involves his winning the trip on a television game show that no one ever wins; it is fortunate that Hal's hobby is British history of the Dark Ages. When he arrives in London, wondering what he is doing there, he is caught up in a strange journey that takes him to the Camelot of fifth-century England and the now-ruined Camelot of today, where Arthur's sword resides in a block of ancient masonry. The battle between the good, the evil and the disillusioned rages through the British countryside. The result is a tremendous story, crying out for a sequel.

—Debora Hill

COLE, Adrian (Christopher Synnot)

Nationality: British. **Born:** Plymouth, Devon, 22 July 1949. **Education:** Callington Grammar School, Cornwall. **Family:** Married in 1977; two children. **Career:** Librarian, Birmingham Public Libraries, 1967-76; local government officer, Devon County Council, 1977-91; school administrator, Bideford College, Devon, since 1991. **Agent:** Abner Stein, 10 Roland Gardens, London SW7 3PH, England. **Address:** The Old Forge, 35 Meddon Street, Bideford, Devon EX39 2EF, England.

FANTASY PUBLICATIONS

Novels (series: Dream Lords; Omara; Star Requiem)

A Plague of Nightmares (Dream Lords). New York, Zebra, 1975.
Lord of Nightmares (Dream Lords). New York, Zebra, 1975.
Bane of Nightmares (Dream Lords). New York, Zebra, 1976.
Moorstones. Barnstaple, Devon, Spindlewood, 1982.
The Sleep of Giants. Barnstaple, Devon, Spindlewood, 1983.
A Place Among the Fallen (Omara). London, Allen & Unwin, 1986; New York, Avon, 1990.
Throne of Fools (Omara). London, Unwin Hyman, 1987; New York, Avon, 1990.

The King of Light and Shadows (Omara). London, Unwin Hyman, 1988; New York, Avon, 1990.
The Gods in Anger (Omara). London, Unwin Hyman, 1988; New York, Avon, 1991.
Mother of Storms (Star Requiem). London, Unwin Hyman, 1989; New York, Avon, 1992.
Thief of Dreams (Star Requiem). London, Unwin Hyman, 1989; New York, Avon, 1993.
Warlord of Heaven (Star Requiem). London, Unwin Hyman, 1990; New York, Avon, 1993.
Labyrinth of Worlds (Star Requiem). London, Unwin Hyman, 1990; New York, Avon, 1993.
Blood Red Angel. New York, Avon, 1993.

Short Stories

The Coming of the Voidal. Burton-on-Trent, Staffordshire, Spectre Press, 1977.
Longborn the Inexhaustible. Dagenham, Essex, British Fantasy Society, 1978.

OTHER PUBLICATIONS

Novels

Madness Emerging. London, Hale, 1976.
Paths in Darkness. London, Hale, 1977.
The LUCIFER Experiment. London, Hale, 1981.
Wargods of Ludorbis. London, Hale, 1981.

*

Adrian Cole comments:

My work is predominantly action-based fantasy, horror and pulp adventure, evolving as it does from the classic fantasy and adventure writers such as Rider Haggard, Edgar Rice Burroughs, Robert E. Howard, H. P. Lovecraft, and J. R. R. Tolkien. I began writing very much in the sword-and-sorcery vein, and in early works such as the Dream Lords trilogy the influences of pulp writers are very evident.

Moorstones and *The Sleep of Giants,* written as much for younger readers as for adults, saw a marked change of style as I used the very real landscapes of Dartmoor and the southwest of England. Elements of *The Lord of the Rings* and Stephen R. Donaldson's Thomas Covenant books are visible in the Omaran Saga, a heroic-fantasy quartet which further develops my recurring theme of power and its abuse—and introduces Simon Wargallow, perhaps my most interesting character to date. I further explored the fusion of genres in the Star Requiem quartet, which mixes fantasy, science fiction and horror, and demonstrates my fascination for bio-technology. My most recent novel is *Blood Red Angel,* a particularly dark and sombre fantasy, with images grim and forbidding, on the harder edge of current genre fiction.

*   *   *

The big problem with Adrian Cole's work is deciding how to classify it. Superficially, most of it appears to be fantasy but often elements of horror or science fiction creep in.

The Dream Lords trilogy is clearly the early work of a writer who still had to learn his trade. It is distinguished only by its ungainly and unconvincing mixture of genres. Its post-holocaust setting is upon various planets of our solar system, mostly Earth, now called Ur, and planet five, now called Zurjah. The action is heroic fantasy with hi-tech trimmings and some horror elements. The hero is Galad Sarian, a young man of noble birth, who is undergoing Dream Lord training on Zurjah. His love for Taria, a nobleman's daughter, and the enmity of his dastardly cousin, Rava Taxak, result in Galad's adventures, including his imprisonment in the dreadful city of Karresh on Ur. Although the Dream Lords possess spaceships for interplanetary travel and hoverdiscs for shorter distances, there are primitive barbarians to be fought, and most fighting is done with bows and swords. The three books form one story, with a happy ending only to volume three.

While *Moorstones* and *The Sleep of Giants* are both illustrated fantasy novels aimed at the juvenile reader, the former has an adult protagonist (Kelvin, deaf and dumb since a childhood incident) and the latter features the holiday adventures of early teenagers Roddy and Donna. Both novels are at least partly set on Dartmoor.

The Omaran Saga purports to be the first of Cole's work to have been written specifically for an adult audience and the four volumes that comprise it are probably the only ones to date that can be described purely as fantasy. Omara is a world where the people have no belief in magical power—indeed, a group known as the Deliverers, lead by Simon Wargallow, go round killing those who might be tempted to believe. Into the first volume, *A Place Among the Fallen*, enters Korbillian, a man who has Power, with a tale of mindless evil growing like a cancer in the east. He draws to him those who might help him in his bid to destroy it. They go reluctantly at first, but gradually are won to his cause. This is a good-versus-evil quest fantasy with a lot of familiar elements such as underground races, bad lands, hostile vegetation. These elements recur in later volumes. The second book, *Throne of Fools,* sees the survivors of the previous quest, lead now by Wargallow, heading westwards. Their purpose is two-fold; to win a throne for Guile, the rightful heir to the Remoon Empire, and to put a stop to the evil machinations of the Sorcerer King. More familiar themes occur; outlaws prove to be valuable allies, an evil army surges from underground, a simpleton conceals sharp intelligence.

The Star Requiem series is a little harder to classify. Innasmorn has all the hallmarks of a fantasy world. The inhabitants have a relatively primitive society and do not use metal. There are god-like powers at large which some are able to channel, but into Innasmorn comes a group of humans fleeing from genocide. They use bio-technology and have come from another world. The way to cross between worlds belongs to fantasy—a passage is opened and the tunnel is guarded by beings that can be appeased only by blood. All four volumes in the series constitute one complete story. It ranges the Innasmornians against the invading human population which is endangered from both sides, the natives, and the pursuing Csendook who possess a bloodthirsty militaristic culture.

Cole's strengths lie in his ability to tell a pacey, action-packed story even though the elements of it may be borrowed from elsewhere. He has also developed the knack of creating unusual races—he is not tempted to populate the place with elf or dwarf look-alikes. The Csendook are much nastier than that and are probably more closely related to *Tyrannosaurus rex* than any primate-descended humanoid. There is originality in Cole's writing, particularly in the denouement of the Star Requiem series although, as with the Omaran Saga, there are too many standard fantasy elements to circumnavigate before it is reached. His latest novel, *Blood Red Angel,* while again suffering from an identity crisis—it is either a highly unusual fantasy setting, or an extremely far-future scenario—contains some of his most elaborate creations. Most striking is the apparent hierarchical structure of society which turns out to be a complex metamorphosis between races at each stratum.

Cole's greatest weakness is his poor stylistic development. In his earlier books this is understandable as he is still learning his trade, but they are still present in *Blood Red Angel*. Most prominent is his wandering point of view, drifting in turn to each character involved in a particular scene or piece of action. The Star Requiem series also has another problem to contend with. This is length. It has a very convoluted plot, many elements of which give the appearance of being time-wasters. Characters vanish for volumes at a time while other, formerly minor ones, take centre stage. *Blood Red Angel* is complete in one volume, more compact, and works better, partly because there are fewer focal characters. These are less predictable than those in earlier novels who seem to follow courses of action along well worn grooves.

—Pauline Morgan

COLE, Allan and Chris(topher R.) BUNCH

Nationality: American. **Born:** 1943 (both writers). **Careers:** Television scriptwriters, for *The Rockford Files, Quincy, Magnum P.I.* and other series. Both authors live in Washington State, and all their novels have been written in collaboration.

FANTASY PUBLICATIONS

Novels (series: Anteros in all books)

The Far Kingdoms. New York, Del Rey, and London, Legend, 1994.
The Warrior's Tale. New York, Del Rey, and London, Legend, 1994.
Kingdoms of the Night. New York, Del Rey, and London, Legend, 1995.

OTHER PUBLICATIONS

Novels

Sten. New York, Del Rey, 1982.
The Wolf Worlds. New York, Del Rey, 1984.
The Court of a Thousand Suns. New York, Del Rey, 1986.
A Reckoning for Kings. Atheneum, 1987.
Fleet of the Damned. New York, Del Rey, 1988.
Revenge of the Damned. New York, Del Rey, 1989.
The Return of the Emperor. New York, Del Rey, 1990.
Vortex. New York, Del Rey, 1992?
Empire's End. New York, Del Rey, 1993?
A Daughter of Liberty. Ballantine, 1993.

*   *   *

The first two fantasy novels of experienced writers Allan Cole and Chris Bunch, *The Far Kingdoms* and *The Warrior's Tale,* are based on a very standard milieu: Orissa, a city-state near the sea, with late-medieval technology and magic that works. There the first-person hero of the first book, the red-haired, hot-blooded Amalric Antero, makes a fool of himself over an expensive and dishonest prostitute, and finds that a period of absence would be diplomatic and would help to restore himself in his own eyes no less than those of his aged father and good-sort lesbian sister. What better than to go on a quest?

For a quest you need a companion or two, and it is Antero's good fortune to fall in with Janos Greycloak, a top professional soldier with a long and bloody past, a smattering of illegal magic and a compulsion to go on a quest of his own, which might just lie in the same direction—to seek the Far Kingdoms of the title, somewhere to the mysterious east. In between lie hostile primitives, hostile sophisticates, harsh deserts, wanton women, treacherous allies, inclement weather and all the ingredients of a rattling good yarn in the style of Fritz Leiber.

This is all very agreeable, in a non-cerebral way, with virtues and vices typical of the genre. The writing is often vivid, the grammar is only occasionally uncertain, the construction is of necessity episodic, with rather a lot of *deus ex machina* in the later development, but not disjointed. While the likeable Amalric is the only character of any depth, this is not billed as a work of deep psychological import, and achieves what at first appear to be very limited ambitions.

But as the book progresses the tone becomes gradually darker. Janos is a good friend and has saved Antero's life on several occasions, but he is a man driven by an obsession, which gradually saps his morals and his sanity *pari passu*. There are hints of this from about midway, but they are put on hold while the pair do battle with the corrupt and venal theocracy which rules Orissa, coming to a head when, after vast tribulation, hair's-breadth escapes, etc., they make it to Irayas, capital of the Far Kingdoms. There they find a polity very similar to Ursula Le Guin's Omelas and ruled by King Domas, whose character presents the first serious weakness in the book: he's supposed to be virtuous and loveable, but comes over as a blustering and boring old fool. All cannot be well in such a place, nor is it, though the grim secret is in no way allegorical.

Having got there, it's necessary to get back again and meet the welcome of the theocrats, but the pair have demons of their own to lay first. It makes for a sombre ending to a tale with more complexity than depth, but the authors keep the themes of friendship, justice and responsibility in focus so that it works well enough.

The Warrior's Tale is another first-person story, and set a few years later. This time the narrator is Rali, Amalric's lesbian sister, by now risen to command of the Maranonian Guard, a female elite corps roughly equivalent to the Sacred Band of Thebes. She and her warriors are at the forefront of a war against Lycanth, Orissa's ancient hereditary enemy, and having taken the last citadel (with great verve and at great cost) are despatched in pursuit of the surviving Archon, a great and evil wizard, who has fled across uncharted seas, but may well come back to wreak vengeance unless hunted down and killed.

This is the signal for another long, episodic fantasy with plenty of bloodshed, treachery, capture, escape, conjuration, sea-battles and night-time forays against defended positions. It works less well for three reasons.

The first is that Rali, being a woman and therefore only semi-literate (she can read but not write), must impart her story to a "scribe," whom she occasionally teases or berates for no obvious reason, and who, possibly in revenge, preserves all the contractions of her speech. The narrative therefore bristles with that'd, it'd, would've and all the other tedious demoticisms that are only acceptable in the direct speech of low characters, and rapidly tire eye and ear alike. Moreover, to achieve contrast the really low characters have to use a dialect even more replete with apostrophes, which is more wearing still and makes them harder to take seriously.

The second reason is Rali's lesbianism. Very few writers can tackle this subject, especially in the first person, without descending into pornography, preciosity or both. Cole and Bunch mainly dodge the issue on the reasonable grounds that Rali has quarrelled with her last lover and is too busy fighting to seek another. But to fill the void they insert occasional diatribes against the unfairness of life in sexist Orissa. In the latter part of the book the authors try to give the lesbianism more of a role. When Rali meets the beautiful and exotic princess Xia, for example, and it's love at first sight, the authors try their hands at some sex-writing, but the description of what goes on is repetitive and unconvincing.

The third reason is a general air of haste in the construction. Near the beginning the Archon invades one of Rali's dreams and wounds her sufficiently to draw blood on her waking body. As sympathetic and contagious magic have a large role, a sequel to this episode is clearly called for but none is forthcoming. Everyone, including the authors, seems to forget about it. In the same spirit, Rali visits two islands called Tristan and Isolde, but as there is no resonance with that legend the names have all the look of a foolish whim.

As in *The Far Kingdoms,* the book ends on a rather downbeat note, and with a strong hint that the Antero family will be back on their travels in due course.

—Chris Gilmore

COLLIER, John (Henry Noyes)

Nationality: British. **Born:** London, 3 May 1901. **Education:** private. **Family:** Married 1) Shirley Lee Palmer in 1936 (divorced 1943); Margaret Elizabeth Eke in 1945. **Career:** Poetry editor, *Time and Tide,* London, in the 1920s and 1930s; screenwriter in the United States. **Awards:** Mystery Writers of America Edgar Allan Poe award, 1952; International Fantasy award, 1952. **Died:** 6 April 1980.

FANTASY PUBLICATIONS

Novels

His Monkey Wife; or, Married to a Chimp. London, Davies, 1930; New York, Appleton, 1931.
Defy the Foul Fiend; or, The Misadventures of a Heart. London, Macmillan, and New York, Knopf, 1934.

Short Stories

Green Thoughts. London, Joiner and Steele, 1932.
The Devil and All. London, Nonesuch Press, 1934.

Variation on a Theme. London, Grayson, 1935.
Witch's Money. New York, Viking Press, 1940.
Presenting Moonshine: Stories. London, Macmillan, and New York, Viking Press, 1941.
Green Thoughts and Other Strange Tales. New York, Editions for the Armed Services, 1943.
The Touch of Nutmeg and More Unlikely Stories. New York, Readers Club, 1943.
Fancies and Goodnights. New York, Doubleday, 1951; abridged version as *Of Demons and Darkness,* London, Corgi, 1965.
Pictures in the Fire. London, Hart Davis, 1958.
The John Collier Reader. New York, Knopf; London, Souvenir Press, 1975.

OTHER PUBLICATIONS

Novels

Tom's a-Cold. London, Macmillan, 1933; as *Full Circle,* New York, Appleton Century, 1933.

Short Stories

No Traveller Returns. London, White Owl Press, 1931.
An Epistle to a Friend. London, Ulysses Bookshop, 1931.

Plays

Wet Saturday (produced New York). New York, One-Act, n.d.
His Monkey Wife, music by Sandy Wilson, adaptation of the novel by Collier (produced London, 1971).
Milton's "Paradise Lost": Screenplay for Cinema of the Mind. New York, Knopf, 1973.

Screenplays: *Sylvia Scarlett,* with Gladys Unger and Mortimer Offner, 1936; *Elephant Boy,* with Akos Tolnay and Marcia de Sylva, 1937; *Her Cardboard Lover,* with Anthony Veiller and William H. Wright, 1942; *Deception,* with Joseph Than, 1946; *Roseanna McCoy,* 1949; *The Story of Three Loves,* with others, 1953; *I Am a Camera,* 1955; *The War Lord,* with Millard Kaufman, 1965.

Poetry

Gemini: Poems. London, Ulysses Bookshop, 1931.

Other

Just the Other Day: An Informal History of Britain Since the War, with Iain Lang. London, Hamilton, and New York, Harper, 1932.

Editor, *The Scandal and Credulities of John Aubrey.* London, Davies, and New York, Appleton, 1931.

*   *   *

John Collier's output was not large. The fantastic novels, *His Monkey Wife* and *Defy the Foul Fiend,* have worn badly, although his science-fiction novel *Tom's a-Cold* and novella *No Traveller Returns* still have their admirers. The best of his work is to be found in the short-story collections *The Devil and All, Fancies and Goodnights, Presenting Moonshine* and others. One British collection appeared under the title *Of Demons and Darkness*; but that title is ill chosen, since although demons are plentiful, the tone is generally sunny when they are present. There is more darkness in his tales of infidelity and domestic murder, though even in "Bird of Prey," the darkest story of all, he never invokes the crudely horrific.

Linking him to the tradition, critics have tended to invoke Poe, Bierce, O. Henry and especially Saki, though in truth his humour and his approach to deeds of darkness have as much in common with De Maupassant, Lord Dunsany, Frank Stockton, P. G. Wodehouse and Gerald Kersh in his lighter vein. Most specifically, the misogyny and latent sadism of Saki are wholly absent. Collier is a writer of tall stories, which may or may not include supernatural elements, and with his essentially humane outlook, worldly urbanity of tone and occasional choice of a French setting, he recalls his contemporary, Marcel Ayme, and looks forward to Roger Zelazny—most notably when one compares the stories "Evening Primrose" and "Museum Piece".

In both a young man finds that the effort of earning a living has become unconscionably irksome, and decides to take up residence where living is free, a department store and a museum respectively. There the protagonists graze on the refreshments provided, disguising themselves at need as tailors' dummies and statues. Both find love in their new abodes, but both arouse the hostility of others who have had the same idea before them.

Like all the best fantasists, Collier informs his worlds with strict logic. In "Squirrels Have Bright Eyes" another young man, despairing of the love of a female big-game hunter, purports to have killed himself and had himself stuffed so as to acquire a permanent niche in her studio. The question then becomes, how to profit from her remorse at his death, when to do so must, by definition, demonstrate his continued animation?

"Variation on a Theme" uses the device of a gorilla who, released from Regent's Park Zoo, sets about the task of captivating the London literary world. But alas! The gorilla is a vulgar and dishonest individual whose preferred strategy is to plagiarize. He succeeds at first, but in due course his sins find him out—though not through anything so obvious as exposure. How a fully articulate and marginally literate gorilla should find himself in a cage in the first place is not, of course, a proper question. To Collier the cage is the best place for him, and that is enough.

Similar logic informs "Gavin O'Leary," the tale of a flea who becomes a film star. Collier's premise is that fleas imbibe personality and preoccupations along with the blood of their hosts, and here is the scene where several partake of a besotted film fan:

> The crazy drinkers were free to take their perilous fill, and the scene was worse than any opium den. Some wept and moaned their lives away in corners; some, dirty, unkempt, lost to the world, lay abandoned in feverish reverie; others sprang from the window, drowned themselves in the slop-pail or took Keatings . . . Gavin, though he sipped and sipped till the potent liquor entered into the very tissues of his being, was made of sterner stuff.

It's not surprising that such a style-driven writer should be at his best when handling that most stylized of themes, the deal with the devil. Of the 36 stories making up *Of Demons and Darkness,* six involve something on those lines, though the traditional Faustian bargain doesn't tend to figure. More typically Satan or one of his cohorts will approach a gentleman in a temporarily embarrassed position (e.g., having just embarked on suicide for no better reason than sundry debts to tradesmen) whereupon the battle of wits begins. But win or lose, the Devil wisecracks for the amusement of the reader. In "The Devil, George and Rosie" he warns his new undermanager of the protocols governing the new annexe to Hell:

> "This is," he said, "little better than mandated territory. We have built up, step by step, and with incredible ingenuity, a system under which we may live very tolerably, but we have only done it by sailing devilishly near the metaphysical wind. One single step beyond the strict legal limits, and I am back on my red-hot throne, in that pit whose bottomlessness I shall heartily envy. As for you—"

That incomplete threat is enough to assure the reader that George and Rosie will defeat the Devil, though it does nothing to anticipate the delicious *double entendre* which concludes that tale. Collier, if not invariably on the side of the angels, inclines to those who, though they may live by their wit and their wits, do so to a code which may be flexible but is ultimately a code of honour—and as such, fit for ladies and gents. John Collier never wrote for anyone else.

—Chris Gilmore

COOK, Glen (Charles)

Pseudonym: Greg Stevens. **Nationality:** American. **Born:** New York City, 9 July 1944. **Education:** Roseville Joint Union High School, California; University of Missouri, Columbia, 1962-65. **Military Service:** 8 years in the United States Navy and Navy Reserve. **Family:** Married Carol Ann Fritz in 1971; three sons. **Career:** Since 1965, various manufacturing jobs (assembly, inspection, material control, and supervisor) for General Motors, St. Louis. **Agent:** Russell Galen, Scovil-Chichak-Galen Literary Agency, 381 Park Avenue South, Suite 1112, New York, NY 10016, USA. **Address:** 4106 Flora Place, St. Louis, MO 63110, USA.

Fantasy Publications

Novels (series: Black Company; Dread Empire; Garrett)

A Shadow of All Night Falling (Dread Empire). New York, Berkley, 1979.
October's Baby (Dread Empire). New York, Berkley, 1980.
All Darkness Met (Dread Empire). New York, Berkley, 1980.
The Swordbearer. New York, Pocket, 1982.
The Fire in His Hands (Dread Empire). New York, Pocket, 1984.
The Black Company (Black Company). New York, Tor, 1984; London, Roc, 1992.
Shadows Linger (Black Company). New York, Tor, 1984; London, Roc, 1992.
With Mercy Toward None (Dread Empire). New York, Baen, 1985.
The White Rose (Black Company). New York, Tor, 1985.

Annals of the Black Company (omnibus; includes *The Black Company, Shadows Linger, The White Rose*). New York, Nelson Doubleday, 1986.
Sweet Silver Blues (Garrett). New York, New American Library, 1987.
Reap the East Wind (Dread Empire). New York, Tor, 1987.
All Ill Fate Marshalling (Dread Empire). New York, Tor, 1988.
Cold Copper Tears (Garrett). New York, New American Library, 1988.
Bitter Gold Hearts (Garrett). New York, New American Library, 1988.
Old Tin Sorrows (Garrett). New York, New American Library, 1989.
The Tower of Fear. New York, Tor, 1989; London, Grafton, 1991.
Shadow Games (Black Company). New York, Tor, 1989.
The Silver Spike (Black Company). New York, Tor, 1989.
Dreams of Steel (Black Company). New York, Tor, 1990.
Dread Brass Shadows (Garrett). New York, Roc, 1990.
Red Iron Nights (Garrett). New York, Roc, 1991.
Deadly Quicksilver Lies (Garrett). New York, Roc, 1993.

Other Publications

Novels

The Swap Academy (as Greg Stevens). San Diego, Publisher's Export Corp., 1970.
The Heirs of Babylon. New York, Signet, 1972.
Shadowline. New York, Warner, 1982.
Starfishers. New York, Warner, 1982.
Star's End. New York, Warner, 1982.
A Matter of Time. New York, Ace, 1985.
Passage at Arms. New York, Popular Library, 1985.
Doomstalker. New York, Warner, 1985.
Warlock. New York, Warner, 1985.
Ceremony. New York, Warner, 1986.
The Dragon Never Sleeps. New York, Warner, 1988.
Sung in Blood. Cambridge, Massachusetts, NESFA Press, 1990.

*   *   *

As someone who spent his life working in a General Motors factory, Glen Cook can appropriately be considered the working man's fantasy writer, sympathetic more to the peasants and footsoldiers of his fantasy worlds than to their kings and nobles. In his best singleton, *The Tower of Fear,* Cook effectively focuses on the plight of a humble carpenter who is caught up against his will in dangerous intrigue involving efforts to revive a dead wizard and remove the foreigners occupying his city; his most noteworthy creation, private eye Garrett, presents himself as a common man helping other common people cope with problems caused by cruel and indifferent rulers; the soldiers of the Black Company unhappily function as bound mercenaries in wars between wizards and rebels; and even the princes and wizards of the Dread Empire novels are usually Poor Boys Made Good—children of peasants or pig farmers who rise by merit to high positions—not persons To The Manor Born.

Cook first attracted attention for the Dread Empire series, initially a trilogy, with four more books added later. Part soap opera, part narrativized logistics game, the first three novels chronicle the wars, romances and schemes of a handful of characters in a fantasy realm roughly analogous to the ancient Old World, with regions corresponding to Europe, the Middle East and China (the Dread Empire). In later novels, Cook seems to lose interest in his original cast and tries with limited success to shift attention to new characters; the last novel, *An Ill Fate Marshalling,* maddeningly devotes two-thirds of its space to retelling the story of *Reap the East Wind* from the viewpoint of a different character—a sure sign of an exhausted series.

The Swordbearer seems like routine fantasy in the Dread Empire mould—with mighty battles of kings and wizards involving a minor nobleman who wields a sword with a murderous mind of its own—but Cook's protagonists come to realize they are only pawns being controlled by selfish gods. Interestingly, Cook grows sympathetic to his high-born heroes only by recasting them as unwilling servants.

Cook's second major series, the Black Company, was initially a trilogy concerning a band of brutal adventurers, first bound to serve the mysterious and evil Lady, but later fighting for her opponent. Befitting its title, the mood in this series is brutal and dark: the heroes routinely slaughter other men, while the villains routinely slaughter women and children as well. Yet Cook is clearly more comfortable dealing with the manipulated underlings of wars and intrigues, not their manipulators; and the Company physician Croaker, outwardly as cruel as his comrades but inwardly troubled by their activities, is an effective and involving narrator. Particularly interesting in these novels are a variegated group of wizards serving the Lady collectively known as the Taken. Three later novels are not as successful, in part because Croaker first becomes, in *Shadow Games,* the Captain of the Black Company (a role he does not seem suited for), does not appear in *The Silver Spike* (which focuses on other characters), and is shifted to the sidelines in *Dreams of Steel.*

Cook's third fantasy series, the Garrett novels, should be regarded as his crowning achievement, though the books at first glance are little more than mindless entertainment. The hero is a Philip Marlowe-like private detective named Garrett living in the city of TunFaire, where he solves mysteries involving dwarfs, elves, wizards and other typical denizens of fantasy; a major supporting character is the Dead Man, a dead creature called a Loghyr who remains sentient and telepathic, though immobile, to serve as Garrett's Nero Wolfe-like partner. Considering this premise, one might dismiss the books as little more than humorous incongruity, a combination of divergent forms—fantasy and detective fiction—for satiric effect. However, despite a light tone reminiscent of Raymond Chandler, Cook tells these stories with both lively imagination and surprising conviction, and the apparently disparate elements blend together with remarkable success. On reflection, this is perhaps not surprising: after all, Chandler's Marlowe was always a knight-errant in disguise, and his shadowy and mysterious Los Angeles was always a displaced fantasy world. Better than a critical argument, then, the Garrett novels demonstrate a fundamental similarity between fantasy and detective fiction.

If the Garrett books serve as an interesting commentary on detective fiction, they are even more powerful as a commentary on modern fantasy. While Garrett solves murders and tracks down magical artefacts, the rulers of TunFaire have waged destructive war against a neighbouring country and also seek to crush a rebel leader named Glory Mooncalled who improbably keeps avoiding capture. This is exactly the sort of saga that was the focus of Cook's previous series—and, of course, of most modern fantasies. But here, these battles and campaigns are only a peripheral subplot, of little concern to Garrett and his friends struggling to cope with immedi-

ate problems; and Garrett offers many bitter remarks about incompetent nobles who send conscripted citizens to be slaughtered in senseless wars, corrupt wealthy merchants and their frivolous children, and leaders of Humans-First campaigns who wrongly blame elves, dwarfs, centaurs and other nonhuman refugees fleeing to TunFaire for the city's gradual descent into chaos. Cook thus suggests that modern fantasy is fundamentally misdirected, celebrating and glamorizing the wealthy and powerful while ignoring the plights of the poor and powerless, who regard the supposedly important exploits of their masters only as troubling disturbances in their daily struggle for existence. And, in chronicling Garrett's adventures, Cook seems to find his true voice; while his other series gradually declined, the most recent Garrett novel, *Deadly Quicksilver Lies,* is just as lively and imaginative as the series's first instalment.

None of this should suggest that the Garrett novels are ponderous or polemical; for they serve primarily—and well—as light-hearted diversions. Nevertheless, Cook's Garrett series demands attention as an important—and, in its way, quite serious—contribution to modern fantasy.

—Gary Westfahl

COOK, Hugh (Walter Gilbert)

Nationality: New Zealander. **Born:** Billericay, Essex, England, 9 August 1956. **Agent:** Colin Smythe Ltd., P.O. Box 6, Gerrards Cross, Buckinghamshire SL9 8XA, England.

FANTASY PUBLICATIONS

Novels (series: Chronicles of an Age of Darkness in all books)

The Wizards and the Warriors. Gerrards Cross, Buckinghamshire, Smythe, 1986; as *Wizard War,* New York, Popular Library, 1987.
The Wordsmiths and the Warguild. Gerrards Cross, Buckinghamshire, Smythe, 1987; in 2 vols. as *The Questing Hero* and *The Hero's Return,* New York, Popular Library, 1987-88.
The Women and the Warlords. London, Corgi, 1987; as *The Oracle,* New York, Popular Library, 1989.
The Walrus and the Warwolf. London, Corgi, 1988; abridged as *Lords of the Sword,* New York, Roc, 1991.
The Wicked and the Witless. London, Corgi, 1989.
The Wishstone and the Wonderworkers. London, Corgi, 1990.
The Wazir and the Witch. London, Corgi, 1990.
The Werewolf and the Wormlord. London, Corgi, 1991.
The Worshippers and the Way. London, Corgi, 1992.
The Witchlord and the Weaponmaster. London, Corgi, 1992.

OTHER PUBLICATIONS

Novels

Plague Summer. London, Hale, 1980.
The Shift. London, Cape, 1986; New York, Vintage, 1987.

*

Hugh Cook comments:

The ten volumes of the Chronicles deal with power struggles in an age of warlords. The plots interweave and overlap; they can be read in any order, the major characters of one book frequently appearing as minor characters in another, and vice versa. They are bloody ("the thigh was prodigiously bruised and swollen with blood, and Morsh Bataar was crying from the pain"—*The Witchlord and the Weaponmaster*), visceral ("Yen Olass touched the silvery blue umbilical cord, and started as she felt it pulsing"—*The Women and the Warlords*), unromantic ("preservation of traditional royal prerogatives by way of rape, torture, looting arson, sundry oppressions of peasants"—*The Wizards and the Warriors*), and unrestrained in the use of such fantasy devices as dragons, walking mountains, death-stones, bottles (very much) larger inside than out, wizards, demons, dorgis, shabble and the Hermit Crab. Warning: skipping will rapidly render these closely-written books unintelligible; read with care, or not at all.

*   *   *

Hugh Cook's lengthy fantasy series, the Chronicles of an Age of Darkness (known in the United States, for its first few volumes at any rate, as the Wizard War Chronicles) is an inventive but uneasily humorous and often quite unpleasant saga. It is sometimes difficult to determine what Cook is trying to do in these books. The whole series (which, it was claimed originally, would run to 20 volumes but seems to have ceased with ten) is set in one place and time, with different characters and interconnecting plots and settings; but straightforward entertainment and good cheer, which one might expect from the conventional way in which the novels are packaged by their publishers, are not always easy to find. One is uncertain whether Cook is attempting to write high fantasy, a satire on high fantasy, or "low" comic fantasy.

In the first volume, *The Wizards and the Warriors,* we meet three wizards who are on a quest to vanquish an evil fellow practitioner. Only one of these wizards comes close to being likeable; two of them are downright revolting. The exception is Miphon, a younger wizard who does most of the work and has all the positive attributes. The first villain is pretty standard fare, the evil wizard who wants to rule the world: named Heenmor, he has stolen the "death stone," a forbidden artefact he believes will enable him to carry out his mission of dominance.

Part of the problem with Cook's writing is that so many of his characters, even the peripheral ones, are unpleasant in the extreme. Once the reader knows this is a dark-age world, it seems unfair for the author to keep throwing disgusting images and metaphors at her by the barrel-full. The first novel is stuffed full with every magical device, possibility and problem known to fantasy—to the point, sometimes, of confusion. The wizards join up with two warriors (hence the book's title) who hail from a culture that hates wizards and has vowed to destroy them all. It is finally revealed that there are three legitimate heroes in the book: the wizard Miphon, the warrior Morgan Hearst and the forestman Blackwood. These three set out to defeat one villain (who conveniently dies before they reach him) and are then confronted with a series of other people who turn villain under the spell of the "death stone," which enables them to bring stone to life or turn living matter into stone. There are some good plot-turns and fantastic devices in this tale and it has a splendid high-fantasy ending. However, some readers may doubt that it was worth reading the whole volume to get there.

The second novel, *The Wordsmiths and the Warguild,* isn't as cluttered but is not much of an improvement as far as the characters go. The story takes place in Sung, neighbouring kingdom to Estar, the place where the first volume began. The hero, Togura, leaves his family rather than marry the princess Slerma, a horrible creation if ever there was one. He is inducted into the Wordsmiths, who show him a machine called the Odex. The Odex, a magical linguistic tool, has begun to spew out mythical and now real monsters. Togura kills one, thereby establishing himself as a hero, and when the machine swallows his beloved, Day, he goes on a quest to find the Index, a guide to the Odex. His is a strange and picaresque journey through a disquieting world—some of it under-explained and relatively obscure to the reader. He is twice captured and made a slave, the first time by a group of marsh-dwellers who live in a ruined city with a huge tower in the centre. In the tower is a torture machine which the old men who rule the city use as a tool for political power, and eventually they throw Togura into the machine. What is never explained is why these people live this way; since Togura can't speak their language, he can't talk to his captors, and the reader is left in the dark as well. The machine is rationalized as an artefact from "before the Days of Wrath." There is no further explanation of why there was technology back then that has been lost to this culture, but Cook refers frequently to other machines and technological wonders that nobody knows how to fix or maintain any longer.

Togura eventually completes his quest, and, surprisingly, this novel has a terrific ending too. But again, one questions whether it was worth it. It has become clear by now that Hugh Cook is trying to be enormously funny and clever, a fully paid-up member of the Robert Asprin/Esther Friesner/Terry Pratchett school of jokey fantasy, but for this reader he rarely succeeds.

By volume three, however, Cook shows remarkable improvement in that he manages to keep the disgusting images to a dull roar. *The Women and the Warlords* is basically the story of Yen Olass, an oracle in the city of Gendormargensis. This is the first glimpse of any kind of civilization that Cook has provided so far in the series, and several of the people who inhabit it are even likeable. There are some repeating characters who appear during Yen's journey across the ocean to participate in the invasion of Estar; she eventually winds up in the company of Morgan Hearst, from the first volume. Yen Olass becomes a hero by the end of the tale even if she seems an unlikely one at the beginning; there were hints, however, that she was more of a human character than the men in the story. There are more women in this book than the others (which is appropriate, given its title), and Yen Olass is a fascinating character who endures much, as all Cook's heroes do, before finding a happy ending.

Volume four, *The Walrus and the Warwolf,* reunites many of the characters from the earlier novels. Miphon, Hearst, the pirates, and Alish (the villain who obtains the "death stone" and tries to rule the world) all figure at one time or another in the story. This one is about Drake, sword-maker's apprentice on the island of Stokos. He runs away after stealing a sword belonging to his master, Gouda Muck, a most despicable old man who invents a new religion. Drake's adventures lead him to join the pirates, battle monsters of the Swarm (this is never fully explained, but the Swarm is an army of monsters who flood out of the south and attack everyone they can) and generally make a nuisance of himself. He does this very well, since he is only 17 when the book starts and a real pain in the neck. He chases his true love, who doesn't want to have anything to do with him throughout most of the book, and when she finally falls in love with him she finds she has contracted a disgusting venereal disease, called Blue Leprosy, which he got from sleeping with his sister, a temple prostitute. Drake may save her if he can convey her to a strange island where the inhabitants have powers left over from the ancient age of technology. Those islanders made Drake immune to all diseases and practically immortal, so that he never contracted Blue Leprosy himself; now he must get them to save Zanya if he can.

There isn't room to describe all the volumes here, for there are many of them and they are of considerable bulk: the tenth and perhaps final novel, *The Witchlord and the Weaponmaster,* runs to over 700 pages of smallish print. Before reaching the last of those pages some readers may well tire of this epic—with its characters popping in and out of each other's books and never getting much further along in time—though each rumbustious volume succeeds in adding another aspect to the wizard war.

—Debora Hill

COOPER, Louise

Nationality: British. **Born:** Hertfordshire, 29 May 1952. **Education:** St. Albans High School for Girls, 1963-67. **Family:** Married Gary Cooper in 1970. **Career:** Various secretarial jobs, St. Albans, 1967-75; blurbwriter, copyeditor, and proofreader for various publishing houses, London, 1975-84; freelance writer from 1984. **Agent:** Charles Walker, Peters, Fraser and Dunlop Group Ltd, 503-504 The Chambers, Chelsea Harbour, Lots Road, London SW10 0XF, England.

FANTASY PUBLICATIONS

Novels (series: Chaos Gate; Indigo; Star Shadow; Time Master)

The Book of Paradox. New York, Delacorte Press, 1973; London, Futura, 1975.
Lord of No Time. London, Sphere, 1977.
The Initiate (Time Master). New York, Tor, 1985; London, Allen and Unwin, 1986.
The Outcast (Time Master). New York, Tor, and London, Unwin Hyman, 1986.
The Master (Time Master). New York, Tor, and London, Unwin Hyman, 1987.
Mirage. London, Unwin Hyman, 1987; New York, Tor, 1988.
Nemesis (Indigo). London, Unwin Hyman, 1988; New York, Tor, 1989.
Inferno (Indigo). London, Unwin Hyman, 1988; New York, Tor, 1989.
The Thorn Key (for children). London, Orchard, 1988.
Inferno (Indigo). London, Unwin Hyman, 1989; New York, Tor, 1990.
Nocturne (Indigo). London, Unwin Hyman, 1989; New York, Tor, 1990.
The Sleep of Stone. New York, Atheneum, 1991.
Troika (Indigo). London, Grafton, and New York, Tor, 1991.
Avatar (Indigo). London, Grafton, 1991; New York, Tor, 1992.
The Deceiver (Chaos Gate). New York, Bantam, 1991; London, HarperCollins, 1993.

The Pretender (Chaos Gate). New York, Bantam, 1991; London, HarperCollins, 1993.
The Avenger (Chaos Gate). New York, Bantam, 1992; London, HarperCollins, 1993.
Revenant (Indigo). London, HarperCollins, 1992; New York, Tor, 1993.
Aisling (Indigo). London, HarperCollins, 1993; New York, Tor, 1994.
Star Ascendant (Star Shadow). London, HarperCollins, 1994; New York, Tor, 1995.
Eclipse (Star Shadow). London, HarperCollins, 1994.
Moonset (Star Shadow). London, HarperCollins, 1995.

OTHER PUBLICATIONS

Novels

Blood Summer. London, New English Library, 1976.
In Memory of Sarah Bailey. London, New English Library, 1977.
Crown of Horn. London, Hamlyn, 1981.
The Blacksmith. London, Hamlyn, 1982.

*

Louise Cooper comments:

You won't find sweeping epics of kingdoms, great battles and noble heroes in my books; nor will you find any elves, dragons or wise old sages. What you *will* find is stories that focus very strongly and closely on a small number of distinctive, complex and often ambiguously-motivated characters, in whose worlds sorcery and the supernatural are everyday realities. And there's usually a twist or two along the way.

Thus far most of my work has been concentrated in just two settings: the alternative earth of Indigo, the princess who opened a grim Pandora's box and let seven demons loose; and the more starkly occult world of the Time Master, Chaos Gate and Star Shadow trilogies, where humans are often used as pawns in the eternal, vicious conflict between the gods of Chaos and Order. I'm now branching out into new dimensions, but though settings and characters might change, the dark and uneasy (some have said nightmarish!) atmosphere of my books certainly won't.

I set out to achieve two aims. One, and of prime importance, to entertain by telling absorbing, well-plotted, and well-paced stories. And two, to explore the nature of good and evil and other concepts which are often taken as absolutes, and how easy—or otherwise—they really are to define. I don't claim to have all the answers; but I like to think I pose a few interesting questions.

*   *   *

Louise Cooper began writing very young, and produced, in *The Book of Paradox,* what critic Mike Ashley has referred to as "a most impressive first novel . . . a compelling fantasy of another world with the hero in search of his dead beloved, aided by the book of the title" (*Who's Who in Horror and Fantasy Fiction,* 1977). Several of her subsequent titles, such as *Blood Summer,* were horror novels; but she returned to pure fantasy in the mid-1980s with the Time Master trilogy.

This is set in a world ruled by the forces of Order and their seven gods, where the counter-balancing power, Chaos, has been banished and its gods considered demons. One of the gods of Chaos is born as a young man, Tarod, and the trilogy ostensibly deals with his growing up, ignorant of his background, to become a senior member of the Circle of Initiates, priest-sorcerers of Order. However his love for a wholly human woman, Cyllan, and their relationship, complicated by both parties having been brought up firmly to believe beings of Chaos are inherently evil, overshadows the wider story as the trilogy develops. The attempt of the gods of Chaos to return to the world and establish equilibrium, while reasonably interesting of itself, is not fully worked out, and much of the time the plot is sidetracked by some tiresome attempts to destroy Tarod by using his affection for Cyllan as a lever against him. The resolution by which equilibrium is attained is particularly unconvincing and the gods of Order, here and in the books which follow, are sufficiently arrogant, spiteful and petty-minded for it to be incredible that anyone should consider them worthy of worship.

In Cooper's return to this milieu, in her Chaos Gate trilogy, there is an attempt to destroy equilibrium by a minor demon who obtains the soul stone in which resides the essence of one of the Chaos lords. His half-human daughter, Ygorla, uses her demonic powers to set herself up as empress of all she surveys and the gods are helpless to intervene, Chaos because of the soul stone which effectively renders one of their number hostage, and Order because, conveniently, their powers cannot act on chaotic beings. Although the resolution to this trilogy is livelier than the first, Ygorla is an uninventive villainess whose idea of exercising supreme power is to have people tell her she's marvellous. The human characters who have to try to thwart her are rather more interesting: Karuth, the sister of the High Initiate, calls Tarod back into the world in spite of the rest of the Circle deciding to abandon equilibrium because of Ygorla and pledge themselves once more solely to Order. Karuth's lover Strann is crucial to the plot as an intimate of Ygorla but, again, his concern that people will think him a traitor hardly rings true in circumstances where everyone has, in one way or another, to bow the knee to Ygorla's magic powers. Overall, the interesting world created is marred by cardboard characters.

Strangely, Cooper's other substantial work, the Indigo saga, has more rounded and interesting characters but only something of a cardboard world for them to act in. In the first, *Nemesis,* a sparky, trousered princess accidentally unleashes seven demons and then has to go and re-leash them, assisted only by a telepathic wolf. She doesn't get very far, but then this is only the first volume in a series of eight. In *Troika,* book five, things start to fall apart: the McGuffin for Indigo's pursuit of the demons was that her lover Fenran was being held in some purgatorial other dimension and would be released when she won through. This plot token is devalued when Indigo meets Fenran's descendant and double Veness and forms a liaison with him. Indeed "lover" seems to be an inaccurate description of Fenran since we are told that Indigo loses her virginity to Veness. However as we reach volume eight, *Aisling,* the entire edifice begins to crumble and the plot—search out and destroy each of seven demons—unravels with the revelation that the major characters, the imp Nemesis and the emissary of the Earth Mother who laid the quest on Indigo, are themselves aspects of Indigo's own personality, as are the demons. This is so self-referential as to vanish in a puff of logic if you think about it for two consecutive seconds, and is a waste of some intriguing characters.

Cooper is a prolific and pleasant writer who perhaps has yet to find her talent's center: if one day she can marry together the intriguing world-picture of the Chaos Gate trilogy with the lively and appealing characters of the Indigo saga she may produce something of the first rank.

—Wendy Bradley

COOPER, Susan (Mary)

Nationality: British. **Born:** Burnham, Buckinghamshire, 23 May 1935. **Education:** Slough High School, Buckinghamshire; Somerville College, Oxford, 1953-56, M.A. 1956. **Family:** Married Nicholas J. Grant in 1963 (divorced 1982); one son, one daughter, three stepchildren. **Career:** Reporter and feature writer, *Sunday Times,* London, 1956-63; moved to the United States in 1963; US columnist, Cardiff *Western Mail,* 1963-72. **Awards:** Boston *Globe-Horn Book* award, 1973; American Library Association Newbery Medal, 1976; Welsh Arts Council Tir na n'Og award, 1976, 1978; B'nai B'rith Janusz Korczak award, 1984; Humanitas prize, 1984; Christopher award, 1984. **Address:** c/o Margaret K. McElderry Books, 866 Third Avenue, New York, NY 10022, USA.

FANTASY PUBLICATIONS

Novels (series: The Dark Is Rising)

Over Sea, Under Stone, illustrated by Margery Gill (Dark Is Rising). London, Cape, 1965; New York, Harcourt Brace, 1966.
Dawn of Fear, illustrated by Margery Gill. New York, Harcourt Brace, 1970; London, Chatto and Windus, 1972.
The Dark Is Rising, illustrated by Alan Cober. London, Chatto and Windus, and New York, Atheneum, 1973.
Greenwitch (Dark Is Rising). London, Chatto and Windus, and New York, Atheneum, 1974.
The Grey King, illustrated by Michael Heslop (Dark Is Rising). London, Chatto and Windus, and New York, Atheneum, 1975.
Silver on the Tree (Dark Is Rising). London, Chatto and Windus, and New York, Atheneum, 1977.
Seaward. New York, Atheneum, and London, Bodley Head, 1983.
The Boggart. New York, McElderry, 1993.

Fiction for Children

Jethro and the Jumbie, illustrated by Ashley Bryan. New York, Atheneum, 1979; London, Chatto and Windus, 1980.
The Silver Cow: A Welsh Tale, illustrated by Warwick Hutton. New York, Atheneum, and London, Chatto and Windus, 1983.
The Selkie Girl, illustrated by Warwick Hutton. New York, McElderry, 1986; London, Hodder and Stoughton, 1987.
Matthew's Dragon, illustrated by Joseph A. Smith. New York, McElderry, 1991.
Tam Lin, illustrated by Warwick Hutton. New York, McElderry, 1991.
Danny and the Kings, illustrated by Joseph A. Smith. New York, McElderry, 1993.

Other Publications

Novel

Mandrake. London, Hodder and Stoughton, 1964.

Plays

Foxfire, with Hume Cronyn, music by Jonathan Holtzman (produced Stratford, Ontario, 1980; Minneapolis and New York, 1982). New York and London, French, 1983.

Television Plays: *Dark Encounter,* 1976; *The Dollmaker,* with Hume Cronyn, from the novel by Harriette Arnow, 1983; *Foxfire,* 1987; *A Promise to Keep,* 1990; *To Dance with the White Dog,* 1993.

Other

Behind the Golden Curtain: A View of the USA. London, Hodder and Stoughton, 1965; New York, Scribner, 1966.
J. B. Priestley: Portrait of an Author. London, Heinemann, 1970; New York, Harper, 1971.

Editor, *Essays of Five Decades,* by J. B. Priestley. Boston, Little Brown, 1968; London, Heinemann, 1969.

*

Manuscript Collection: Osborne Collection, Toronto Public Library.

*   *   *

Susan Cooper's well-known Dark is Rising sequence is an epic fantasy, drawing heavily on Celtic and Anglo-Saxon legend to provide weaponry for the good and evil sides in opposition throughout the novels. Her backgrounds are equally the stuff of legend: Cornwall, North Wales and the Chilterns, but also outside time, on a lost island, and in the interior of a Welsh mountain.

The Dark is Rising comprises five novels concerned with the ultimate battle between good and evil, the Light and the Dark, in which immortal Old Ones and Dark Lords as well as mortals play their part. *Over Sea, Under Stone,* the first, deals with the search for the grail by three children, Simon, Jane, and Barney Drew, on holiday in Cornwall with their adoptive uncle Merriman Lyon (Merlin). The Arthurian overtones are plain, with the three pursuing their quest by means of an ancient map, opposed by creatures of the Dark who desire the grail for their own ends.

In *The Dark is Rising,* Merriman Lyon appears once more, this time in Buckinghamshire as teacher and Old One, tutoring Will Stanton, the seventh son of a seventh son, who wakes on his eleventh birthday to discover he, too, is one of the immortals on the side of the Light. As he seeks the six signs which will defeat the Dark when it rises at the turn of the year, he learns his own powers and their part in the long-fought war, where magic is bound by strict rules except for Wild Magic, which stands beyond any constraint.

The search for weapons for the Light—a harp, six sleepers, and the raven boy—continues in *Greenwitch* and *The Grey King,* where Cooper expands the complexities of Wild Magic and the difficulty of relations between mortals and immortals. The Greenwitch, an offering made to Tethys, the sea, by the women and girls of Trewissick in the same Cornish setting as *Over Sea, Under Stone,* holds a secret desired by both Light and Dark. Jane Drew, who helped in its making, is instrumental in winning this secret for the Light, proving mortals play a role in the war.

Conversely, in *The Grey King,* it is human emotions which are the danger—jealousy, anger and hate, which open mortal minds to the invasion of the Dark. The fourth book is strongly Arthurian in content. Will Stanton is sent to the mountains in North Wales to continue his work for the Light; here he meets Bran, the raven boy, unknown to himself the son of Arthur Pendragon, brought forward in time by Guinevere with Merriman's assistance, and whose coming triggers a sequence of events which prove nearly fatal to the Light.

Silver on the Tree is the culmination of the conflict, where humans as well as Old Ones play a decisive part in the final battle. The three Drews, Will, Merriman, and Bran are involved in the last quest for the crystal sword with which the Dark will be defeated, Wild and Old Magic driving away the Dark which has entered the hearts of humankind.

Cooper's scholarly knowledge of legend, and skill in drawing together all the complexities of the five books into a triumphant finale, produce an epic of great power. There are differences in quality in the novels—*Greenwitch,* except for that creation, is perhaps the weakest, and *The Dark is Rising* and *The Grey King* the strongest; *Silver on the Tree,* while suitably life-affirming in its conclusion, is slightly preachy, but that is a natural hazard of the subject matter. Cooper deals with the innate antagonism between mortals and immortals impressively, and in *The Grey King* reaches great heights as she mingles the worlds and peoples of legend and the present day. The sequence is a remarkable achievement, and Cooper's gifts for description and characterization provide additional pleasure to novels already replete with intellectual enjoyment.

Seaward is a natural successor to the sequence. A boy and girl, Westerly and Cally, struck by personal tragedy, pass from their own world into a hostile land ruled by the enchantment of the cruel Taranis and the kindly Lugan. All Westerly and Cally know is that they must go seaward, where they will find their loved ones. The land is inhabited by fantastic creatures, from the cold Stonecutter who wishes to keep Cally a prisoner forever, to the insect-like Peth, who gives his life for the children.

The story is about the circle of life and death, and again the ending emphasizes that while to choose life (and thus the future) is more difficult, since it is unknown and must end in death, to choose to live in the past, that is death, is to allow nothing to change for better or worse.

Ending on a note of hope is also apparent in *The Boggart,* a less serious book about the collision of technology with the Boggart, a mischievous spirit living in a castle in the Scottish Highlands. Cooper's solution to the problem of the Boggart, lost near the end in a computer game in Canada and lonely for its old home, is both ingenious and highly appealing.

Cooper's books are intensely satisfying for readers of all ages. She succeeds in producing the most desirable aspect of books for children—the subversive element where children are more aware of the subtext than adults—while discussing issues of extreme complexity.

Would that there were more of them.

—Mary Corran

CORBETT, W(illiam) J(esse)

Nationality: British. **Born:** Birmingham, Warwickshire, 21 February 1938. **Education:** Billesley Secondary School, Birmingham, 1942-53. **Military Service:** Physical training instructor in the British Army. **Career:** Has worked as a merchant seaman, baker's assistant, furniture removal man, slaughterman, and builder. **Awards:** Whitbread award, 1983. **Agent:** Murray Pollinger, 4 Garrick Street, London WC2B 9BH, England. **Address:** 6 Selborne Grove, Billesley, Birmingham, England.

FANTASY PUBLICATIONS

Novels (series: Pentecost in all books)

The Song of Pentecost, illustrated by Martin Ursell. London, Methuen, 1982; New York, Dutton, 1984.
Pentecost and the Chosen One, illustrated by Martin Ursell. London, Methuen, 1984; New York, Delacorte Press, 1987.
Pentecost of Lickey Top, illustrated by Martin Ursell. London, Methuen, 1987.

OTHER PUBLICATIONS

Fiction for Children

The End of the Tale and Other Stories, illustrated by Tony Ross. London, Methuen, 1985.
The Bear Who Stood on His Head, illustrated by Martin Ursell. London, Methuen, 1988.
Dear Grumble. London, Methuen, 1989.
Toby's Iceberg. London, Methuen, 1990.
Little Elephant. London, Methuen, 1991(?).
Duck Soup Farm. London, Methuen, 1992(?).
The Grandson Boy. London, Methuen, 1993.

*   *   *

W. J. Corbett came to sudden prominence in 1982 with the publication of *The Song of Pentecost,* which took the Whitbread Prize as best children's book of the year. An animal story which skirts between the two poles of the genre, imaginative realism and allegorical whimsy, it is similar to *Watership Down* in aspects of its plot and to *The Wind in the Willows* in its sense of pantheistic melancholy, but altogether original in its ironic humour. A naive snake tricked out of his ancestral pond, a family of harvest mice searching for a home away from City overspill, a poetic fox, a mendacious frog, an insane owl haunted by the memory of a terrible crime, and an insect playing both ends against the middle are just some of the characters of a complex but accessible tale which weaves in and out of mercurial shifts of personality. The story begins and ends with death while in between is enough double-dealing to fill a Jacobean tragedy, most but not all of it the result of the manipulations of Corbett's particular Trickster, a seven-legged bug called a "cockle-snorkle". Over and above this there is a dramatic clarity and a sense of hope which creates a feeling of allegory without collapsing into the soft mysticism of so many "adult" animal fantasies.

Pentecost, the harvest-mouse leader, brings his charges safely to Lickey Top by means of a subsidiary quest to regain the pond of a dim-witted but treacherous snake who has been swindled out of his inheritance. Corbett's surface-naive delight in catch-phrase, colloquialism and alliterative cadences only illuminates more sharply his mastery of comic effect—the boastful "Uncle" mouse is both Kenneth Grahame's "Toad" and triumphantly his own character in his chorus-like subversion of communal values—and his ability to evoke light and shade. There are chilling undercurrents in the story of Owl's "crime" and the light-hearted betrayal which stored guilt upon guilt, while the elegiac ending is beautifully written. Corbett's animal characters are less animal-fantasy than the beast-fable of traditional folk tale, clear landmarks of the human moral landscape: the unselfish leadership of the Pentecost mouse, the malicious cockle-snorkle, delighting in discord, the proudly individualistic but kind fox, all allow a meaningful morality-play to unfold.

Pentecost and the Chosen One sees the successor to the first "Pentecost" failing to come to terms with his own feeling of inadequacy in contrast with his predecessor's heroism. The words of a prophecy take him to the city and a tribe of urban mice under a tyrant's yoke. There, he finds the "Chosen One," an identical mouse who has received the mirror-image of Pentecost's prophecy and is revelling in the ambiguous status this favour of Fate gives him. Their change of place gives each mouse the chance to grow and discover what leadership really means. Growth means having to undergo the humiliation of apparent failure. Even the amoral cockle-snorkle, who brings misrule to this microcosm, is tested.

The final part of the trilogy, *Pentecost of Lickey Top,* introduces another character in the overbearing Otter whose bullying ways threaten the Lickey Top community with chaos when he shoulders his way into it. At last there is a genuine problem for Pentecost to tackle, although the solution is present all the time in the Old Sett, where the badgers recount their Golden Treasury to while away the years spent hiding from the threats invented by the malicious cockle-snorkle. Change, however, is the half-understood common factor. Not only is the peace of the country winter disrupted by Otter's belligerence, there is more fundamental change to the order of things. After winter comes spring, and we can see the forerunner of further change in the three-legged mouse and the dissatisfied cub who become the younger analogues of Pentecost and Fox and who literally stumble upon the solution. The badgers must regain contact with the outside world and Pentecost and Fox must take into account the desire of the younger generation for independence. The cockle-snorkle must fend off a rival, while the reclusive Owl is in search of a mate. Change and continuity are, however, part of the same process. By accepting that he will one day hand over to the three-legged mouse, Pentecost displays the wisdom so conspicuously lacking in Uncle's conceit.

Following the "Pentecost" trilogy, Corbett has tended to concentrate on stories for younger children. Many still use animal characters, as in the collection of fables *The End of the Tale* or the delightful young whale in *Toby's Iceberg. The Grandson Boy* re-approaches his concern for relationships and community from the more realistic viewpoint of an old lady, her grandson, and the village "delinquents," saved from cosiness by the wit and wry characterization which shot through *Pentecost.*

Corbett's achievement as a major author for the young, and one who can be read rewardingly by adults, centres, however, upon the Pentecost books. Their allegorical features become clearer, perhaps, to adults. There are clues in the fact that each successive leader-mouse is designated "Pentecost" and the cockle-snorkle is referred to as "the Devil garbed in pleasing guise." But those whose tastes do not run to allegory can be reassured that these are stories in which the melodramatic qualities of the characters, rather than an insistent author, portray whatever message there is to be portrayed.

—Andy Sawyer

CORELLI, Marie

Nationality: British. **Born:** Mary Mackay, London, 1 May 1855. **Education:** Privately educated; studied music and made debut as a pianist, London, 1884. **Career:** Writer from 1885; settled in Stratford-upon-Avon, 1901. **Died:** 21 April 1924.

FANTASY PUBLICATIONS

Novels

A Romance of Two Worlds. London, Bentley, 2 vols., 1886; New York, Ivers, 1 vol., n.d.
Ardath: The Story of a Dead Self. London, Bentley, 3 vols., 1889; New York, Ivers, 1 vol., n.d.
The Soul of Lilith. London, Bentley, 3 vols., 1892; New York, Lovell, 1 vol., 1892.
The Sorrows of Satan; or, The Strange Experiences of One Geoffrey Tempest, Millionaire: A Romance. London, Methuen, 3 vols., 1895; Philadelphia, Lippincott, 1 vol., 1896.
Ziska. Bristol, Arrowsmith, and Chicago, Stone and Kimball, 1897.
The Strange Visitation of Josiah McNason: A Christmas Ghost Story. London, Newnes, 1904; as *The Strange Visitation,* London, Hodder and Stoughton, 1912.
The Young Diana: An Experience of the Future. London, Hutchinson, and New York, Doran, 1918.
The Secret Power. London, Methuen, and New York, Doubleday, 1921.

OTHER PUBLICATIONS

Novels

Vendetta; or, The Story of One Forgotten. London, Bentley, 3 vols., 1886; New York, Ivers, 1 vol., n.d.
Thelma: A Society Novel. London, Bentley, 3 vols., 1887; New York, Ivers, 1 vol., n.d.
My Wonderful Wife: A Study in Smoke. London, White, 1889; New York, Ivers, 1890.
Wormwood: A Drama of Paris. London, Bentley, 3 vols., 1890; New York, Munro, 1 vol., 1890.
Barabbas: A Dream of the World's Tragedy. London, Methuen, 3 vols., 1893; Philadelphia, Lippincott, 1 vol., 1892.
Silence of the Maharajah. New York, Merriam, 1895.
The Distant Voices, A Fact or Fancy. Philadelphia, Lippincott, 1896.
The Murder of Delicia. London, Skeffington, and Philadelphia, Lippincott, 1896; as *Delicia,* London, Constable, 1917.
The Mighty Atom. London, Hutchinson, and Philadelphia, Lippincott, 1896.

Jane: A Social Incident. London, Hutchinson, and Philadelphia, Lippincott, 1897.
Boy. London, Hutchinson, and Philadelphia, Lippincott, 1900.
The Master-Christian. London, Methuen, and New York, Dodd Mead, 1900.
Angel's Wickedness: A True Story. New York, Beers, 1900.
Temporal Power: A Study in Supremacy. London, Methuen, and New York, Dodd Mead, 1902.
God's Good Man: A Simple Love Story. London, Methuen, and New York, Dodd Mead, 1904.
The Treasure of Heaven: A Romance of Riches. London, Constable, and New York, Dodd Mead, 1906.
Holy Orders. London, Methuen, and New York, Stokes, 1908.
The Devil's Motor. London, Hodder and Stoughton, and New York, Doran, 1910.
The Life Everlasting: A Reality of Romance. London, Methuen, and New York, Doran, 1911.
The Philosopher and the Sentimentalist. New York, Paget, 1911.
Innocent: Her Fancy and His Fact. London, Hodder and Stoughton, and New York, Doran, 1914.
My "Little Bit." London, Collins, and New York, Doran, 1919.
Love—and the Philosopher: A Study in Sentiment. London, Methuen, and New York, Doran, 1923.

Short Stories

The Hired Baby and Other Stories and Social Sketches. Leipzig, Tauchnitz, 1891; New York, Optimus, 1894.
Three Wise Men of Gotham. Philadelphia, Lippincott, 1896.
Cameos. London, Hutchinson, and Philadelphia, Lippincott, 1896.
The Song of Miriam and Other Stories. New York, Munro, 1898.
The Love of Long Ago and Other Stories. London, Methuen, 1920; New York, Doubleday, 1921.

Poetry

Poems, edited by Bertha Vyver, London, Hutchinson, and New York, Doran, 1926.

Other

The Silver Domino; or, Side-Whispers, Social and Literary. London, Lamley, 1892.
Patriotism or Self-Advertisement? A Social Note on the War. London, Greening, and Philadelphia, Lippincott, 1900.
The Greatest Queen in the World: A tribute to the Majesty of England 1837-1900. London, Skeffington, 1900.
An Open Letter to His Eminence Cardinal Vaughan. London, Lamley, 1900.
A Christmas Greeting of Various Thoughts, Verses and Fancies. London, Methuen, 1901; New York, Dodd Mead, 1902.
The Passing of the Great Queen. London, Methuen, and New York, Dodd Mead, 1901.
The Vanishing Gift: An Address on the Decay of the Imagination. Edinburgh, Philosophical Institution, 1902.
The Plain Truth of the Stratford-upon-Avon Controversy. London, Methuen, 1903.
Free Opinions Freely Expressed on Certain Phases of Modern Social Life and Conduct. London, Constable, and New York, Dodd Mead, 1905.

Faith Versus Flunkeyism: A Word on the Spanish Royal Marriage. London, Rapid Review, 1906.

Woman or Suffragette? A Question of National Choice. London, Pearson, 1907.

America's Possession in Shakespeare's Town. Edinburgh, Morrison and Gibb, 1909.

Is All Well with England? London, Jarrolds, 1917.

Eyes of the Sea (on the Grand Fleet). London, Marshall, 1917.

Mistaken Both Ways. New York, Paget, 1922.

Praise and Prayer: A Simple Home Service. London, Methuen, 1923.

Open Confession to a Man from a Woman. London, Hutchinson, 1924; New York, Doran, 1925.

Harvard House Guide Book, with Percy S. Brentnall and Bertha Vyver. Privately printed, 1931.

*

Film Adaptations: *The Sorrows of Satan,* 1917, 1926; *The Treasure of Heaven,* 1917; *Thelma,* 1918.

Bibliography: By Richard L. Kowdczyk, in *Bulletin of Bibliography* (Boston), 1973.

Critical Studies: *The Writings of Marie Corelli* by S. Boswin, Bombay, Examiner Press, 1907; *Marie Corelli: The Life and Death of a Best-Seller* by George Bullock, London, Constable, 1940; *Marie Corelli: The Woman and the Legend* by Eileen Bigland, London, Jarrolds, 1953; *Marie Corelli: The Story of a Friendship* by William Stuart Scott, London, Hutchinson, 1955; *Now Barabbas Was a Rotter: The Extraordinary Life of Marie Corelli* by Brian Masters, London, Hamish Hamilton, 1978.

*   *   *

For ten or fifteen years around the turn of the last century Marie Corelli was the most popular writer in the English language, although no one—least of all the contemporary critics and reviewers, who despised and derided her work—could figure out why. She evidently touched some hidden chord in her readers, and gave them something which was exactly right to fill a void inside them, but no one out of tune with her peculiar world-view can find anything rewarding in her works.

"Marie Corelli" fantasized her life as fervently as she fantasized her books, lying about her name, age and origins so insistently that her true history remains clouded to this day, but there is no doubt that her adoptive (and perhaps true) father, Charles Mackay, doted on her. He encouraged her to believe that she was unusually gifted, so successfully that she became utterly incapable of doubting her own genius. Her *alter ego* was invented in 1884, the name first being applied to poems which she submitted to various literary magazines. She claimed that it was her true name, embellishing her letters of submission with extravagant stories about her imagined Italian origins. Her first full-length book, *A Romance of Two Worlds,* is set in 1884 and features as its unnamed heroine exactly the kind of person that Marie Corelli was supposed by her inventor to be: gifted, exotic, sensitive, but as yet unable to fulfil her abundant promise because of an unfortunate weakness of body and spirit and because other people are too crass to appreciate her true worth.

A Romance of Two Worlds is a first-person account of an amazing religious revelation, full of forceful essays in theology and morality. The unorthodoxy of the former—a strange hybrid of pious Christianity and then-fashionable pseudo-science—is excused by the rigorous conventionality of the latter. The narrative's fundamental purpose is to rescue a religious faith in decline by recruiting the language of science to "prove" its essential truth. The hidden potential of the heroine is first recognized by the painter Raffaello Cellini, who can produce realistic images of the angels by virtue of his acquaintance with the Chaldean mystic Casimir Heliobas. Heliobas infuses her with the human electricity that is the substance of which souls are made, renewing her physical and spiritual strength. Thus equipped with boundless self-confidence, she becomes fit company for the angels, and goes with one of them on a conducted tour of the universe. She learns that the inhabitants of all other worlds are much happier than the men and women of earth, because no other planet is so deeply steeped in sin and its consequent miseries. Eventually, she is allowed to see God in His true form, as a "Great Circle of Electric Fire."

Heliobas returns in *Ardath* to work miracles on behalf of a male protagonist, who is similarly recruited to the company of the angels. After falling in love with one he is despatched through time to the city of Al-Kyris, 5,000 years before Christ, where he meets an earlier incarnation of himself and eventually proves himself worthy of his ideal. Never one for half-measures, the author permits the man and the angel to undergo an actual wedding ceremony in one of Europe's great cathedrals.

The Soul of Lilith is narrower in scope than the earlier novels, featuring a far less noble occultist whose less worthy ambitions are ultimately frustrated by fate, but it was soon followed—although the best-selling historical romance *Barabbas* came in between—by a more extravagant ground-breaking fantasy, *The Sorrows of Satan,* which revealed that even the arch-enemy of mankind was secretly on the side of the angels, having repented his rebellion. Corelli's Satan longs for the day when mankind will begin to resist the temptations which he lays before them, at which time even he might be forgiven and redeemed, but Geoffrey Tempest—the male protagonist of the novel—is far too easily recruited to the cause of his own damnation to give him any shred of hope. While attending to Tempest's corruption, however, Satan is fortunate enough to meet the saintly novelist Mavis Clare, with whose indomitable incorruptibility he inevitably falls in love.

It was in *The Sorrows of Satan* that Marie Corelli reached the pinnacle of her unique literary achievement. As delusions of grandeur and expressions of devout wish-fulfilment go, the fascination of the Devil was an unsurpassable masterstroke. She continued to churn out pious bestsellers, but there was no further boundary to surpass, and it was all mere repetition; her later novels became increasingly tired and lacklustre. *Ziska* is a karmic romance with far less to recommend it than Haggard's *She,* which presumably inspired it. *The Strange Visitation of Josiah McNason,* a Christmas fantasy written in such slavish imitation of Dickens' *A Christmas Carol* as to constitute a virtual plagiarism, is equally weak. Her fantasy of magical rejuvenation, *The Young Diana*—which was written when the author was much older than she pretended to be—is undermined by the fact that even she had lost faith in the achievability of her most ardent desires. Her last fantasy novel, *The Secret Power,* tends towards science fiction in its use of advanced aircraft and atomic super-science, but fails miserably to recapitulate the naïve excitement of *A Romance of Two Worlds* while introducing a rather jaundiced heroine to a hopelessly confused "revelation" of the true nature of God—whose attributes now include radioactivity as well as electric power.

The enervation of Corelli's later novels was mirrored by disappointments in real life, which added to the burden of growing old. After the death of Charles Mackay she moved to Stratford-upon-Avon, where she became besotted with the painter Arthur Severn (much to his embarrassment), recruiting his talents to the illustration of her feverishly eccentric novelette *The Devil's Motor.*

Marie Corelli presumably owed her success to the fact that she was prepared to expose to the world the silly sophistry by which she tried to shore up her religious faith with borrowed jargon, supplemented by her narcissistic fantasies of being more suited for the company of angels than mere men. Unabashed by the savage derision of more sensible folk, she heroically took this crusade into an imaginative *terra incognita* which no one else has ever dared explore. The astonishing, if temporary, success of her works demonstrates that her expression of her own delusions and aspirations were capable of soothing, at least in some small measure, the distress of millions of her contemporaries.

—Brian Stableford

CORRAN, Mary

Nationality: British. **Born:** Mary Waterhouse, Birmingham, England, 18 August 1953. **Education:** Roedean School, Brighton, Sussex; Lady Margaret Hall, Oxford University, 1977-80, M.A. in modern history. **Family:** Married Thomas H. Corran in 1977. **Career:** Trainee system analyst, Reading, Berkshire, 1980-82; oil analyst, various stockbroking companies, banks and financial institutions, City of London, 1982-92. **Agent:** Michael Thomas, A. M. Heath, 79 St. Martin's Lane, London, WC2N 4AA, England. **Address:** 13 Sutton Place, Hackney, London E9 6EH, England.

FANTASY PUBLICATIONS

Novels

Imperial Light. London, Millennium, 1994.
Fate. London, Millennium, 1995.

*

Mary Corran comments:

The worlds of *Imperial Light* and *Fate* are entirely separate, as are the themes which are to be developed in their successors. In *Imperial Light* there is a strand of science fantasy, for the world in which the book is set does not exist in isolation; it exists for itself, but also for some greater purpose of which its citizens are essentially unaware. A battle rages over and about the people, unseen but not unfelt, touching the lives of individuals who are caught up by their natures on either side, good or evil—unless neither side can be identified as "good." The book is about different kinds of power, about responsibility, about the nature of divinity and the misuse of pious belief by an organized religion.

Fate, by contrast, is set in a more fragmented world where luck rules each person and each nation from the moment of birth. The series that it opens takes place in an arena where superstitions come true, where there is only so much good luck in the entire world,

and if one nation or person seizes too much, others must lose it. The theme of the first book is whether humans have fixed fate or free will; whether it is possible to read the future, or whether predestination and fortune-telling are only possibilities, not definite. In this context, the series hopes to explore what is innate and what is only socialized in human nature, and to try to laugh at the more ludicrous efforts of humanity to bind itself with chains of custom and tradition.

* * *

Both Mary Corran's novels to date are set in a standard heroic-fantasy context and are political in character, being concerned with the attempts of the principals to restore the fortunes of their respective countries, both of which have fallen to tyranny and poverty, with women bearing the brunt of both evils. Both books make use of an over-arching symbol (light and fate, respectively); they employ alternating male and female viewpoints, the female being more important, with a hint that the two may find love with each other; and both present the author's moral and political views with (considering their liberal and orthodox character) unnecessary vehemence.

Of the two, *Imperial Light,* written from the viewpoints of Kyria, a young girl from a fishing village, and Hilarion, heir to the local empire, is the less successful. The villains of the piece, a malevolent priesthood called the Order of Light and led by the unrelievedly evil Querdon, have no obvious motivation for the evil they do; they engage in torture, murder, deception and extortion in the manner traditional to evil priests, but without apparent enjoyment, and without the benefit of an evil theology to lend credibility to these dour activities, a lack which extends to the plotting. Kyria's variation on the standard fantasy quest is a mission to carry "lightstones" across the country, but though the priests and their minions capture her and throw her into dungeons and torture chambers on several occasions, they never think to strip-search her—either for business or pleasure, despite making lickerish remarks about her appearance. They can't, for if they did they would find the lightstones and her mission would surely fail.

The ending is weak as well, a literal *deus ex machina,* when the Good Gods belatedly get their collective finger out and strike the tower of the False Gods with divine lightning. Kyria perceives this problem and wrestles with it, but she reaches no good conclusion; instead she and her surviving allies engage in an orgy of self-congratulation as they divide the fruits of victory. The gods offer more visions than assistance until the climax, but Kyria and we remain as ignorant of their nature and intentions as she was at the outset.

Fate works better at every level, starting with the over-arching symbol which gives the book its rather melodramatic title. The people of Darrian are obsessed with oracles, prophecies, divinations and fortune-telling, to the dismay of Asher, a young woman of forceful personality and logical mind, to whom the explicit determinism and implicit denial of free will are equally hateful. Indeed, much of the book is concerned with the many things Asher finds hateful, together with her determination not to be overwhelmed by them, and to thwart them so far as she can.

As a woman in a patriarchal society her capacity is circumscribed, but Asher is resourceful; she escapes her loveless marriage to live in Venture with a group of like-minded women, where she uses her position as a treasury clerk to embezzle modest sums which help finance an "underground railway" for runaway slaves. Asher is the only major viewpoint, and Corran has obviously devoted some care to delineating her character. While the effect is not entirely believable in the context—her worldview is much like that of a Fabian suffragette and pioneer of the Secular Society, circa 1910—Asher is coherent and attractive enough to arouse and sustain interest.

Her dislike of prophecies, etc., derives partly from being the survivor of twins, her brother (confusingly referred to as "identical") having died at birth. To the people of Darrian this marks her as special, having the luck of two, and enjoying partial immunity from Fate. If so minded one can therefore account for some of her character, and especially her various rebellions, in terms of a Freudian guilt complex, the socially acceptable view being that a male survivor would have been preferable. It certainly adds to the tension when she is summoned to the temple and told that her own fate is intimately bound up with that of the ruling house of Darrian, currently very much in eclipse.

For Darrian has been conquered and reduced to client status by the Kamiri, an unpleasant, grey-skinned race who have re-introduced chattel-slavery and who are bleeding the country white with demands for tribute. The word of the oracle is that only Vallis, last surviving princess of the ruling line, can save the country; but she has disappeared, and it is Asher's destiny to go in search of her, accompanied by Mallory, a childhood friend who re-enters her life in a manner which seems entirely too pat not to be fated in some sense. Given these postulates the story flows logically enough; despite the surface similarities, *Fate* succeeds by avoiding the crudity of its predecessor at almost every level.

Although there's still a tendency to preach to the reader, there's less of the pious hectoring which so marred the previous book, and (quite as important) none of its idiot-plotting. This is most notable in the character of the principal villain, Avorian, whose motivation is entirely comprehensible. He had not originally been a bad man, but he has been corrupted by a combination of ambition, vanity and his whole-hearted acceptance of the fatalistic philosophy which Asher finds so repulsive. He has also suffered from mumps as a young man, and been rendered sterile by it, an affliction he refuses to acknowledge. It's an unusual but valid plot mechanism; the difference between Avorian and Querdon symbolizes the very considerable advance between Mary Corran's first and second novels. Character-driven heroic fantasy is rare, and here we have a successful example.

—Chris Gilmore

COULSON, Juanita (Ruth)

Nationality: American. **Born:** Juanita Ruth Wellons, Anderson, Indiana, 12 February 1933. **Education:** Ball State University, Muncie, Indiana, B.S. 1954, M.A. 1961. **Family:** Married the writer Robert Coulson in 1954; one son. **Career:** Elementary school teacher, Huntington, Indiana, 1954-55; collator, Heckman Book Bindery, North Manchester, Indiana, 1955-57; publisher, *SFWA Forum,* two years. Since 1953 editor, with Robert Coulson, *Yandro* fan magazine; since 1963 freelance writer. **Awards:** Hugo award, for editing, 1965. Guest of Honour, World Science Fiction Convention, 1972. **Agent:** James Allen, Box 278, Milford, PA 18337, USA. **Address:** 2677W-500N, Hartford City, Indiana 47348, USA.

FANTASY PUBLICATIONS

Novels

The Web of Wizardry. New York, Ballantine, 1978.
The Death God's Citadel. New York, Ballantine, 1980.

OTHER PUBLICATIONS

Novels

Crisis on Cheiron. New York, Ace, 1967.
The Singing Stones. New York, Ace, 1968.
The Secret of Seven Oaks. New York, Berkley, 1972.
Door into Terror. New York, Berkley, 1972.
Stone of Blood. New York, Ballantine, 1975.
Unto the Last Generation. Toronto, Laser, 1975.
Fear Stalks the Bayou. New York, Ballantine, and Skirden, Lancashire, Magna, 1976.
Space Trap. Toronto, Laser, 1976.
Dark Priestess. New York, Ballantine, 1977.
Fire of the Andes. New York, Ballantine, 1979.
Tomorrow's Heritage. New York, Ballantine, 1981.
Outward Bound. New York, Ballantine, 1982.
Legacy of Earth. New York, Ballantine, 1989.
The Past of Forever. New York, Ballantine, 1989.
Star Sister. New York, Ballantine, 1990.

*   *   *

Juanita Coulson was too young, or not yet ready, to have written for *Planet Stories* in the 1940s, and she only just made it into the Golden Age of Ace Doubles. Her debut science-fiction story was "Another Rib" (*Fantasy & Science Fiction,* June 1963), a pseudonymous collaboration—as "John Jay Wells"—with Marion Zimmer Bradley. But Coulson soon found her true literary vocation as a pulp novelist. Ace published *Crisis on Cheiron* (doubled with *The Winds of Gath* by E. C. Tubb) in 1967 and *The Singing Stones* (backed with Tubb's *Derai*) the very next year.

Crisis on Cheiron might have run as a two-part serial in *Analog Science Fact/Science Fiction* without rattling any slide rules among that magazine's broadly technophilic readership. Carl Race must troubleshoot a commingled eco-disaster and trade war on developing/exploited Cheiron, where—as the name suggests—Centaur-like beings are the dominant life form. And the Ethnic Protection Division stands ready to punish any infringement of Abo (i.e., native Cheironian) rights. The background is furnished in early Darkover. Nevertheless, Coulson's use of science goes far beyond the psionic piffle that Bradley made her own: "Without insects, a terrene-type world would die . . . Cheiron's principal flora were fruits and legumes, all insect-pollinated; when the forage crops went, it would be more and more difficult to feed the planet's domesticated animals . . ." It could be said that Coulson anticipated *The Swarm*— but quietly.

Her rather different second book, *The Singing Stones,* might almost have been snapped up by *Planet Stories* for a lead novel. It's the same Terran Federation/Ethnic Protection Division/dependent aboriginals sort of tale, but the Darkovan decor is now well-and-truly foregrounded. This time, the galactic troubleshooter is Geoff Latimer. He becomes embroiled in the conflict between Deliyas ("entrepreneur to the idle rich of a dozen stellar systems") and its fiefdom sister planet, Pa-Liina ("Here There Be Dragons"). Coulson spends most of *The Singing Stones* in science-fantasy overdrive. The Pa-Liinan Stones of Song are quasi-telepathic, intoxicating minerals: "A tremendous sensation welled within his brain, bringing with it an overwhelming impression of peace and well being. No euphoric mist or alcoholic or drug could remotely compete with the reaction." Behind them is a Talbot Mundy-type "Goddess" out of no known mythology.

The next two Coulson science-fiction novels, *Unto the Last Generation* and *Space Trap*, rework familiar themes: population control and first contact. They are models of logical structure allied with common sense, despite being restricted by Laser Books' word-length straitjacket and moral slant.

Logical structure and common sense are the hallmarks of Coulson's first full-blooded (no idle adjective) fantasy novel, *The Web of Wizardry*, published in 1978. The dedication reads "For Marion Zimmer Bradley"—as well it might, considering the heavy emphasis placed upon psionics-as-a-form-of-magic. Krantin, where the action takes place, had already been featured in two short stories, "Wizard of Death" and "The Dragon of Tor-Nali." From first page of the novel to last, Coulson seldom relaxes the narrative drive for introspection and/or mushy love stuff. "Enchanters at war—as an empire hangs in the balance" (front-cover blurb) gives the basic situation in a nutshell. There isn't much in the way of plot and counterplot, let alone conceptual breakthroughs, but genre expectations are amply fulfilled (and then some, for the perceptive reader).

Warriors from expansionist Markuand invade Krantin, backed up by the seemingly all-powerful spells of a nameless Master Wizard. The least-forlorn hope for rescue is an alliance with "Destre (or Destre-Y) the plainspeople of Krantin" (Glossary). In fact, things depend upon the synergistic Web of Wizardry, mind-spun by "sorkras" like Uloduvol and Lady Lira Nalu. Destre-born-but-citified Danaer ("of the clan of Tlusai") figures largely in this war to end all warlocks. Fellow fantasist C. J. Cherryh hailed *The Web of Wizardry* as "a richly detailed construction of fantasy" (back-cover blurb). True—yet *Web* could easily have been a science-fantasy, à la Darkover or Jack Vance's *The Dragon Masters,* with some deft *Astounding/Analog* psi-babble. For example: "It is a peculiar skill— enabling me to transport people and objects instantly across the space it might take a rider many . . . candle-marks to travel." This translates into pure Rhine-land teleportation.

As with other adept fantasy authors, Coulson has a penchant for the naming of names (see above). But even adept fantasy authors can nod off when new-wording mundane items, and Coulson is no exception. The horse-like beasts of Krantin are called: (a) blacks, ". . . a very sturdy animal, useful in mines and on farms"; (b) roans, ". . . a hardy breed well adapted to survival in grassland or desert" (quotations taken from Glossary).

Coulson brought back Krantin in *The Death God's Citadel* (obviously she resisted the possible title of *Destre-Y Rides Again*). It's the mixture-much-as-before, but seasoned with quirky humour, as when a were-spell cast on one of the major characters results in some deeply embarrassing moments as he transforms, without warning, into a cat. It should be noted that the Krantin novels are entire unto themselves, not episodes in an unfinished trilogy.

For the first 20-odd years of her writing life, Coulson was over-influenced by Marion Zimmer Bradley (much as the young Robert Bloch took after H. P. Lovecraft). *Unto the Last Generation* began to look more and more like a flash in the brain-pan. Then she veered away from psionic whimsy to the hard stuff, with the Children of the Stars science-fiction tetralogy: *Tomorrow's Heritage, Outward Bound, Legacy of Earth,* and *The Past of Forever.* Although Coulson has proved herself expert at building aerial castles, it's clear that she won't take up residence in one of them. Mighty-thewed psychopaths—male or Amazonian—are treated with indifference, at best. As Damon Knight said of Robert E. Howard's Conan, "the human race . . . never could produce such a man, and sane writers know it" (*In Search of Wonder,* 1967). The sane writers he referred to might well have included Juanita Coulson.

—Graham Andrews

———

CRAIG, Randolph. *See* **PAGE, Norvell.**

———

CRAY, Roberta. *See* **EMERSON, Ru.**

———

CROWLEY, John (William)

Nationality: American. **Born:** Presque Isle, Maine, 1 December 1942. **Education:** Indiana University, Bloomington, B.A. 1964. **Family:** Married Laurie Block in 1984; two daughters. **Career:** Freelance photographer and commercial artist, 1964-67. Since 1967, freelance writer of documentary and television films. **Awards:** World Fantasy award, 1982, 1990; American Institute of Arts and Letters award, 1989. **Agent:** Ralph Vicinanza, 111 Eighth Avenue, New York, NY 10011, USA. **Address:** c/o Bantam Books, 1540 Broadway, New York, NY 10036, USA.

Fantasy Publications

Novels (series: Aegypt)

Little, Big. New York, Bantam, 1981; London, Gollancz, 1982.
Aegypt. New York, Bantam, and London, Gollancz, 1987.
Love & Sleep (Aegypt). New York, Bantam, 1994.

Short Stories

Novelty. New York, Doubleday, 1989.
Antiquities: Seven Stories. Seattle, Washington, Incunabula, 1993.

Other Publications

Novels

The Deep. New York, Doubleday, 1975; London, New English Library, 1977.

Beasts. New York, Doubleday, 1976; London, Futura, 1978.
Engine Summer. New York, Doubleday, 1979; London, Gollancz, 1980.
Great Work of Time (novella). New York, Bantam, 1991.

Plays

Screenplays (selection of many documentaries): *World of Tomorrow,* 1989; *Fit: Episodes in the History of the Body,* 1990.

Other

Editor, with Howard Kerr and Charles L. Crow, *The Haunted Dusk: American Supernatural Fiction, 1820-1920.* Athens, Georgia, University of Georgia Press, 1983.

*

Manuscript Collection: University of Texas, Austin.

John Crowley comments:

I don't regard my work as entirely characterizable by genre, although I have delighted in using the themes and devices of genre (both science fiction and fantasy) in unusual ways. *Little, Big* used the most standard imagery of fairies and fairyland for somewhat non-standard fictional effects. I am currently working on a four-volume novel using magic, astrology, alchemy, etc., in similar ways.

*   *   *

"I believe there is a Story which appears in countless different forms—fairy tales, myths, and so on—and which has a physiological meaning that is incontrovertible." With this bold assertion (made in an interview conducted by Thomas Disch and printed in *Science Fiction Digest,* January/February 1982), the American author John Crowley firmly plants the roots of his own fantastic work in the deep and fertile soil cultivated by such figures as Carl Jung and Joseph Campbell, George MacDonald, C. S. Lewis, J. R. R. Tolkien, E. R. Eddison and Charles Williams. No mere colonial Inkling clone, however, Crowley has brilliantly cloaked his archetypical concerns in ingenious, indigenous forms which reveal that modern, even futuristic settings and characters are fully capable of embodying the "manifestation of the holy" which lies at the heart of his work.

Crowley's first two novels—*The Deep* and *Beasts,* both perhaps definable as "science fantasies"—while accomplished achievements in their own right, can best be seen as fledgling efforts toward the unique fusion of the supernal and the quotidian which he was fully to win in his next three books: *Engine Summer, Little, Big* and *Aegypt.*

The Deep is a genre-straddling book typical of Crowley's expectation-confounding impulses. The seemingly artificial disc-on-a-pillar-world of the novel, watched over by an enigmatic being known as Leviathan and his android servant, the Visitor, bears affinities to such classic science-fiction venues as Christopher Priest's *Inverted World* (1974) and even Larry Niven's *Ringworld* (1970). (Geography is a strong presence in all of Crowley's books.) Yet the action which occupies the foreground is eminently medieval, a chaotic tale of treachery, ambition and war between the Blacks and the Reds, cast at times in Shakespearean diction. Also notable in this initial offering are several features which will appear more fully

in later works. A concern with secret societies operating parallel to overt centres of power appears in the organization of assassins known as the Just. Esoteric systems for embodying almost ineffable knowledge can be seen in the array of cryptic gods worshipped by the Reds and the Blacks, and also in the Fifty-Nine Tarot-like Cards of the Just (precursor of Nora Cloud's deck in *Little, Big*). Finally, the paradoxical role of humans—at once minuscule and infinite, meaningless and godlike, intermediaries between heaven and earth—is shadowed forth.

Beasts seems at first to be indisputably science fiction: the tale of a waning United States where self-sufficient arcologies sprout and animal-human hybrids roam (one such chimera, the caustic Reynard the Fox, serves as political advisor to a satrap, and will play a pivotal role in the destinies of the main characters), and this entropic scenario, which seems more like a collectively mythic Fisher-King failure of will and energy than any actual *real-politik* prognostication, will reappear in the latter portions of *Little, Big.* But the sly identification of the "leo" known as Painter with solar and Christian myths (consider also Lewis's Aslan), and the late-breaking revelation that the tutor Loren Casaubon has been playing Merlin to his young student's Arthur, lofts the novel out of the simply realistic and into the emblematic.

Neither of these two books quite prepares the reader for the third, *Engine Summer.* Reminiscent on the surface level of such uncomplicated post-apocalyptic Arcadian picaresques as Edgar Pangborn's *Davy* (1964), the angel-informed *Engine Summer* is in reality a deeply touching, exquisitely written meditation on memory and loss, identity and simulation, and the limits of love. The story of Rush that Speaks, who lives in a community of Truthful Speakers, told (inescapably and inevitably, as it turns out) in his utterly believable and charming voice, *Engine Summer* boasts the kind of rich texture associated with such thickly descriptive books as Ursula Le Guin's *The Left Hand of Darkness* (1969). Amid a welter of discards and misunderstood history evocative of Jack Vance's *The Dying Earth* (1950), Rush travels from innocent childhood to scarred maturity, becoming both more and less than human, perhaps the "saint" he once sought to be.

Occurring for the first time in this novel is a favourite image of Crowley's: the Filing System is a set of antique slides used by the Truthful Speakers for divination. Projected one atop another, the image they cast becomes both more information-packed, yet harder to read. This symbol will crop up again in his next two books as an example of how enigmas may persist in the face of details. (Or, as Auberon Barnable learns in *Little, Big,* mystery may endure despite "a vast superfluity of ambiguous evidence.")

In the aforementioned interview, Crowley consents with certain reservations to Disch's suggestion that *Little, Big* may be the best book Crowley will ever write. It is indeed hard to imagine a more satisfying work, both on an artistic and an emotional level. Composed from 1969 through 1978, it is the kind of definitive masterwork which seems to contain everything the author thought or felt during the period of composition. Yet the book remains an integral organic whole constrained by an elaborate, over-arching mythos and symbolic architecture based on ancient notions of Faerie.

At its heart a love story, the romance between Daily Alice Drinkwater and Smoky Barnable, the book is also an elucidation of the simple secret hinges of the natural world, a multi-generational family saga, a *bildungsroman,* a conspiracy thriller and an alternate cosmology, among other things. Packed with allusions to classic fairy tales and children's fantasies (Crowley has a predilection for making "books out of other books," a possibly sterile trap for those less talented, which he escapes with a generous infusion of his own hard-won observations), *Little, Big* managed to inaugurate a sub-genre that has come to be known as "urban fantasy," although nothing in this vein written by anyone else has come close to the elegant textures and soulful resonance Crowley achieved.

The Renaissance scholar, mystic and Memory Artist Giordano Bruno makes a brief off-stage appearance in *Little, Big*, presaging his central role in Crowley's next book, *Aegypt*. Ostensibly the plain tale of untenured history professor Pierce Moffett, a 1960s survivor trying to find a new footing in a changing world by relocating to the idyllic Faraway Hills (and on this level, the book tastes very much like Thomas Pynchon's *Vineland*, 1990), *Aegypt* soon reveals itself to be something quite other: a Gnostic explication of the world and its historical sea-changes—one of which is currently (that is, in the book's 1976 setting) underway—its action organized around the twelve houses of the Zodiac (three are traversed in this opening volume of the series).

Pierce is eventually revealed to be an incarnation of both Grailhunting Percival and possibly also a literal fallen angel, echoing the plight of the Visitor in *The Deep*. The main narrative is supplemented by excerpts from the historical novels of fictional author Fellowes Kraft, which feature such wizardly figures as Bruno, Doctor Dee and Shakespeare, conspirators all. At novel's end, Pierce is seemingly poised for a romance with one Rosie Rasmussen, whose first name evokes the promise of Rosicrucian mysteries yet to unfold.

Aegypt's direct sequel, *Love & Sleep*, comprising another three Zodiacal houses, does not immediately pick up the labyrinth-spanning thread so circuitously laid down, but instead starts with a vivid recapitulation of Pierce's Kentucky childhood, in which his foot was first planted on the trail of arcane mysteries. Meanwhile, in Kraft's intertwined historical excerpts, Dee and Bruno cross paths, the Philosopher's Stone is created, and an empire-shattering wind (felt all the way into Pierce's present) is raised.

When the Faraway Hills setting is regained, new characters are introduced—notably a mysterious and powerful Christian evangelist named Honeybeare—and the pressure of Pierce's quest for the secret history of our world(s) pushes him into a hazy land close to insanity, in which a mysterious phantom son who wears the likeness of an alchemical archetype appears. Falling in love not with Rosie Rasmussen but with her dark twin, Rose Mucho, whose desertion is the final blow in his unhinging, Pierce at novel's end is poised "to lose everything, mind as well as heart, occupation too," as the change-winds strip him down, perhaps in necessary preparation for eventual transcendence.

Crowley's relatively scarce short fiction—collected in *Novelty* and *Antiquities*—while less majestic than his novels, repays reading, both as separate entities and for the light the stories shed on the longer works. "In Blue" can be seen as taking place in the future of *Beasts*, whose arcology cadres also dressed all in blue. "The Nightingale Sings At Night" features Dame Kind, whom we are told Daily Alice eventually became. "Snow" deals with the same issues of memory and simulation as does *Engine Summer*. "Novelty" takes place in the identical Seventh Saint Bar and Grill which Auberon Barnable frequents.

One intriguing facet of Crowley's work which is seldom if ever mentioned is the empathy and centrality he bestows on gay characters. In *The Deep*, the Red King is gay, with a male consort. In *Beasts*, Loren Casaubon nurses an unrequited love for his boy student, Sten. In *Little, Big* Auberon has a desperate fling with the brother of his lost love, Sylvie. In *Aegypt*, novelist Kraft is perpetually seeking for the euphemistic "Ideal Friend". Hare, the confused protagonist of "In Blue," is bisexual. In the fantasy field, such candour and sympathy toward homosexual characters are all too rare.

Perhaps it is most useful to conclude by letting Crowley—always a keen and perceptive and conscious artist—summarize his own subject and methodology, through the musings of two of his fictional authors. From "Novelty": "He had really only the one subject, if subject was the word for it, this idea of a notion or a holy thing growing clear in the stream of time, being made manifest in unexpected ways to an assortment of people." And from Aegypt: ". . . what grants meaning in folktales and legendary narratives . . . is not logical development so much as thematic repetition, the same ideas or events or even the same objects recurring in different circumstances, or different objects contained in similar circumstances."

—Paul Di Filippo

D

DALKEY, Kara (Mia)

Nationality: American. **Born:** 1953.

FANTASY PUBLICATIONS

Novels (series: Sagamore)

The Curse of Sagamore. New York, Ace, 1986.
The Nightingale. New York, Ace, 1988.
Euryale. New York, Ace, 1988.
The Sword of Sagamore. New York, Ace, 1989.

*   *   *

Kara Dalkey's byline first appeared above a series of short stories she wrote for the short-lived but high-quality shared-universe sequence, *Liavek,* each of which involved a prominent art critic and his adventures in that city. Sorcerous attacks are at the core of "Before the Print Is Dry" and "Portrait of Vengeance," both of which involve a mystery which must be resolved to free the protagonist from a magical curse. The shortest and most impressive of the set was "The World in the Rock," a quietly effective story of a young girl and the visions she sees in a lump of stone.

Other short tales of note include "Nightwail," set in another shared universe, the Borderlands. The world of magic and contemporary America overlap in the shadowy regions where the story is set. A mysterious and frightening banshee sings mournfully for the dead, and some wonder if she's responsible for hastening their demise. Dalkey spins two different threads here, one the mystery of a freshly discovered corpse, the other an amusing use of the banshee, whose nature is communicable, carrying with it a great talent for singing. "The Peony Lantern" is even more serious and chilling, a very unusual and effective variation of a traditional ghost story set in historical Japan, a backdrop she uses to great effect in *The Nightingale.*

Dalkey's first novel was *The Curse of Sagamore.* Abderian is prince and heir apparent to his father's throne as ruler of the Kingdom of Euthymia. His family gained the monarchy through happenstance; a former king was so unhappy with his progeny that he abdicated in favour of the court jester, from whose line Abderian springs. Abderian himself is uninterested in the job and would far rather defer the honour to his brother Cyprian, but he bears the mark of the Curse of Sagamore and is thus fated to so rule. This upsets his father, who believes Abderian is plotting an overthrow, as well as a number of other contenders, some of whom are aided by magic, and all of whom seem determined to cut Abderian's life short.

Not without reason, he decides to flee the castle, but as you might expect, he quickly falls into bad company and worse straits. In due course he approaches a fabled wizard who might be able to remove the curse, but there are more surprises ahead for Abderian as well as the reader. The novel is humorous fantasy, although it avoids farce and has its more serious moments, a good example of middle-of-the-road fantasy adventure as it has evolved in recent years, as is its sequel. *The Sword of Sagamore* carries the story along in very much the same fashion, although both the prose and the plot seem more polished. Cyprian is a competent if uninspiring king but utter catastrophe hangs on the horizon as the mark of the Curse of Sagamore disappears from the arm of Abderian. Could another wizard have found a way to remove the curse, or are his old enemies the Lizard priests plotting once more?

A quest is obviously what is called for, but Abderian has less than great luck assembling a group of companions, most notable of which is the animated skeleton of the original jester king, Sagamore, whose greatest skill is an ability to make a wisecrack at the least provocation. The mark of the curse has moved magically to an infant, a child half-human and half-demon and now capable of causing absolute destruction to the world. In order to save everything he holds dear, Abderian has to master his own magical abilities and channel those of others, even assume the body of a dragon in his quest to track down the dark powers plotting against Euthymia. The humour this time around is less overwhelming despite some genuinely funny situations, and Dalkey provides an underlying adventure story of considerable merit in itself.

It is not, however, simply in her short fiction that Dalkey writes in a more serious tone. *The Nightingale* is based on the Hans Christian Andersen fairy tale, although it is cognizant of the fact that Andersen was writing for adults rather than children. The Nightingale of the title is a young woman with an incredible talent for song. But all gifts have their price, and hers is the dark legacy of an ancestor whose evil spirit has not yet relinquished its grip on the world. Set in ancient Japan, it is presented in a series of very short scenes, cumulatively revealing an emperor's court filled with convoluted conspiracies. Chinese ghosts are considerably more substantial than those of the west, and sometimes indistinguishable from the living, and Katte's quest for vengeance is the underlying thread that ties everything together. Without question this is Dalkey's finest novel to date.

But almost as satisfying is *Euryale,* set in the days of the Roman Empire. Euryale is a woman who has come to Rome to seek a magical or miraculous means by which stone can be turned to flesh, and perhaps a release from the curse which has destroyed her life. For she has been transformed into a gorgon along with her sister, and anyone who meets her gaze is immediately turned to stone, including the one man whom she truly loved.

Unfortunately, fate has more tricks in store for her as she seeks an answer to her problem within the capital city of an increasingly corrupt and faltering Roman Empire. When she finally does restore the life of her lover, Euryale discovers that the feelings between them have changed, that she is still a monster in his eyes even though he loves her. The novel is an effective, inventive new look at the gorgon myth and even as we know Euryale is doomed to fail, we retain the hope that she will find some solace in her condition.

Kara Dalkey has proven herself capable of writing superior fantasy, both serious and humorous, and it is this flexibility that will probably ensure that her byline continues to find an audience, regardless of the direction her muse may next take her.

—Don D'Ammassa

DALTON, Annie

Nationality: British. **Born:** 5 December 1948 in London, England. **Education:** Attended Camberwell School of Arts and Crafts and Hornsey School of Art. **Family:** Married Andrew F. Stimson (a zoologist), 29 June 1979; one son. **Agent:** Laura Cecil, 27 Alwyne Villas, London N1 2HG, England. **Address:** 18 Brenda Rd., London S.W. 17(7DB), England.

FANTASY PUBLICATIONS

Novels

Out of the Ordinary. London, Methuen, 1988.
Night Maze. London, Methuen, 1989.
The Afterdark Princess. London, Methuen, 1990.
The Witch Rose. London, Methuen, 1990.
The Alpha Box. London, Methuen, 1991.
Demon-Spawn. London, Blackie, 1991.
Naming the Dark. London, Methuen, 1992.
Swan Sister. London, Methuen, 1992.
The Real Tilly Beany. London, Methuen, 1993.
Tilly Beany and the Best Friend Machine. London, Methuen, 1993.

*   *   *

Annie Dalton is one of a new generation of children's fantasy writers who seem set to become the heirs to crossover writers like Susan Cooper who have developed a strong adult following. In several of her books, Dalton has taken the traditional motif of having a young protagonist as the descendent or incarnation of the "powers of light" (as Cooper has Will in her Dark is Rising series) and taken it a step further. It has become commonplace that fantasy in children's literature is a way of expressing the (often) inexpressible. Dalton has written strong fantasies for a wide variety of age-groups, with vivid depictions of magic which bring the undercurrents of childhood confusion and adolescent longing closer to the surface.

Her first novel, *Out of the Ordinary,* was a strongly imaginative fantasy for teenagers which stuck close to the standard format of having a young person in our world become a saviour of a magical parallel country, but it possessed a vigorous and sometimes ironic undercurrent. Molly is a dreamer who can sometimes sense places which are not "there," and at the age of 15 is attempting to reconcile the ordinariness of her life and appearance with the inexplicable longings which used to send her dashing hopefully in and out of cupboards in vain attempts to find Narnia. A scribbled attempt at an advertisement for a part-time job starts "good with children and animals" and ends up "quests undertaken . . . enchantments broken". In mysterious circumstances, the mute Floris is left to be fostered by Molly's mother Maureen and it is clear that Molly's task is to protect him from harm. The world that he comes from becomes clearer but the nature of the curse which has apparently been laid upon him is opaque until, with the help of her new friend Icarus, Molly confronts the Magus. The plot demands too much help from Icarus's aunt, a modern-day witch, but the novel possesses the strength of much fantasy for young people as opposed to the "adult" genre: simply, that the fantasy is contrasted with real people in real situations: Maureen struggling to make ends meet, slowly developing a life of her own after years spent looking after

waifs and strays, Molly balancing the fate of a world with the tedium of school, even Molly's self-centred but not altogether dreadful brothers.

Dalton then made an extraordinary leap forward with *Night Maze.* Gerard Noone is "reclaimed" from a children's home by his wealthy family and goes to live with them in Owlcote, their Elizabethan house. There, from his sister Harriet and from what he pieces together from his own observations and memories, he learns of the curse of emotional and creative sterility on the Noones stemming from the neglect by the alchemist Thomas Noone of his daughter Alice in his obsessive quest for gold. In each generation, a Noone has the chance to resolve this curse. Gerard—brought in from outside yet so physically part of the family—is the catalyst by which healing takes place, although it is Harriet, even more of an outsider, adopted by Avery and Caroline Noone before the birth of their own children, who is able to raise and lay the powers inside the Night Maze.

Night Maze is about emotional involvement: Thomas Noone's chasing the illusion of perfect alchemical gold and the subsequent crippling of his descendants: embittered Old Harriet, blustering but emotionally infantile Avery, his brother Will extinguishing his poetic gifts. Dalton works with traditional imagery: the old riddle about "Earth, Water, Fire and Air," alchemy, and mazes are focuses for turbulent magic which storms within and around her characters. Beyond "official reality" is another, more elemental sort "that's much bigger and every now and then it breaks out into the official sort and shakes it up a bit". Or, in realistic terms, the book is about how people who, as Gerard puts it, "live in totally different continents," can learn to communicate. The wildness and richness of Dalton's imagery creates a perfect metaphor for the turbulence of adolescent years, but readers other than adolescents will appreciate the way in which "official" and "unofficial" realities are made to be two sides of the same coin.

The Afterdark Princess and *The Witch Rose,* for younger children, are perfect examples of how fantasy deals with the deepest realities. The former tells of the transformation of spoiled, cowardly Joe in the hands of Alice the perfect baby-sitter. Joe's journey through Afterdark and its quest-epic dangers enables him to confront his everyday fears. The book's tone is light enough to amuse the reader but never slackens into self-parody: Joe's lack of self-confidence is real and the monsters and marvels are concrete despite their analogues in the "daylight" world. *The Witch Rose* presents a little girl's view of a rift and reconciliation between parents as Laurel and her mother try to keep one step ahead of magic, but this is hardly "really" or "merely" an excuse for a touching ending, and an adult reader would discern a story whose emotional depths are only emphasized by being cloaked by the lightest and most revealing of fantastic imagery.

The Alpha Box, in contrast, demands and repays work from the reader in the way that it combines several different threads of the fantastic. Joss and Asha are both remote from their peers, Asha because of her absent parents, Joss because of his mother's sudden split from her husband, and his dreams of writing songs. But they, and a few friends, are among the few who do not get caught up with The Hoarsemen, the local rock group whose music speaks to alienated youth in a way that goes beyond mere cultism. The box which Asha finds on her birthday may be the box which goes with her name (which means "Hope") but Joss's blue guitar, which comes to him from the same mysterious source, is also symbolic. Behind the tentative attempts at a relationship between the two teenagers there is also the background of the apocalyptic progress of The Hoarsemen from cult rock band to something altogether more sinister, whose ascetic followers are eager for transcendence as they await the opening of a channel to another realm.

The climax of *The Alpha Box* makes oblique reference to the ending of the film *Close Encounters of the Third Kind*, and *Naming the Dark* also uses science fiction and fantasy as touchstones for teenage longing for connection and meaning as it extends a basic theme of *Night Maze*. Owen Fisher discovers that there is more to Kevin Moody's drivelling about lost Atlantis that there seems. Kevin, the school loser, believes that he and Owen were once heroes and the town of Loxley, where the blighted talents of its sons stultify in boredom, is camouflage for something which has been hidden for centuries. Kevin reads too many fantasy books. But Kevin could be right. And reluctantly, Owen receives proof enough that he is right. *Naming the Dark* is a complex fantasy of the relationships between men and women, success and failure. Owen's adversary is, in the end, nothing out of the conventional fantasy gamebook, despite the Arthurian echoes in the story, but the potential darkness within people, the sterility which awakens when people are afraid to live up to their abilities.

Swan Sister perhaps rivals *Night Maze* as Dalton's tour de force. As a fantasy, it touches upon folk tales involving changelings, the power of names, and folk who transform into swans. As a "realistic" story it is about a family damaged by social and personal negligence. Ellen's pregnant mother finds her dream-home in Suffolk. The sadness Ellen feels as the swans fly over is somehow linked with the locality. When the baby is born, Ellen is cast as her sister's protector but is unable to defend her against the influence of the swans who have lost their cygnets in the growing pollution of the environment. Lily grows up strange and withdrawn. Ellen's father is overwhelmed by his problems at work, which turn out to be intimately connected with the pollution. Lily is finally taken by the swans. Her disappearance precipitates a crisis which is resolved only by Ellen and her father coming to terms with the numinous sense of place which has been almost destroyed by human lack of care.

Atmospheric, lucid on the surface but with enigmatic undercurrents, *Swan Sister* combines realism with the deeper magical logic of folk tale. It is stories like this, in fact, which raise the point about where and for whom a true British tradition of "magical realism" exists. Certainly, the pat distinctions of "fantasy" and "reality" are not enough to describe the way Dalton manipulates both modes in a manner which is natural to the conventions of children's writing but which has in her work been expressed with a particular brilliance.

—Andy Sawyer

DARLINGTON, W(illiam) A(ubrey Cecil)

Nationality: British. **Born:** Taunton, Somerset, 20 February 1890. **Education:** Cambridge University, 1912. **Family:** Married Marjorie Sheppard in 1918 (died 1973). **Career:** Schoolmaster, 1913-14; drama critic, 1920-68. **Died:** 1979.

FANTASY PUBLICATIONS

Novels (series: Alf)

Alf's Button. London, Herbert Jenkins, 1919; New York, Stokes, 1920.

Wishes Limited. London, Herbert Jenkins, 1922.
Egbert. London, Herbert Jenkins, 1924.
Alf's Carpet. London, Herbert Jenkins, 1928.
Alf's New Button. London, Herbert Jenkins, 1940.

Plays

Alf's Button (based on his novel). London, Herbert Jenkins, 1925.

Screenplays: *Alf's Button*, 1920, 1930.

OTHER PUBLICATIONS

Novels

Mr. Cronk's Cases. London, Herbert Jenkins, 1933.

Plays

Carpet Slippers. London, Deane, 1937.
The Key of the House. London, Deane, 1950.

Other

Through the Fourth Wall (essays). London, Chapman and Hall, 1922; New York, Brentano's, 1922.
Literature in the Theatre (essays). London, Chapman and Hall, 1925; New York, Holt, 1925.
Sheridan. London, Duckworth, 1933; New York, Macmillan, 1933.
J. M. Barrie. London and Glasgow, Blackie, 1938.
I Do What I Like (autobiography). London, Macdonald, 1947.
The Actor and His Audience. London, Phoenix House, 1949; New York, Dent, 1949.
The World of Gilbert and Sullivan. New York, Crowell, 1950; London, Peter Nevill, 1951.
Sheridan, 1751-1816. London, National Book League, 1951.
Six Thousand and One Nights: 40 Years a Critic. London, Harrap, 1960.
Laurence Olivier. London, Morgan Grampian, 1968.

*

Film Adaptations: *Alf's Button*, 1920, 1930, 1938 (as *Alf's Button Afloat*, 1938), all from the novel *Alf's Button*.

*   *   *

When Thomas Anstey Guthrie came to write his autobiography he lamented that the kind of humorous fantasy which he had written as F. Anstey had had its day. The rigid conventions of Victorian society had decayed rapidly after the turn of the century, and this liberalization had reduced the metaphorical impact of imaginary disruptions of the world of the Victorian bourgeoisie by anarchic magic. There is, however, more than one kind of social rigidity, and the Great War introduced vast numbers of ordinary Britons to the kind associated with military life, thus creating the opportunity for W. A. Darlington to take over where Anstey had left off.

The hero of the sketches which Darlington wrote for the magazine *Passing Show* before developing them into *Alf's Button* is a far cry from the uptight protagonists of Anstey's novels, being a working-class cockney highly reminiscent of the parodic characters featured in many of Anstey's comic dialogues for *Punch.* Alf became astonishingly popular in spite of the open contempt with which he was treated by his patronising creator. *Alf's Button* sold a quarter of a million copies in ten years—a record for a first novel, according to the publisher Herbert Jenkins. Jenkins was inspired by the success of the novel to publish many more humorous fantasies in its wake, desperately trying to repeat the coup; P. G. Wodehouse's *Laughing Gas* and J. Storer Clouston's *Button Brains* are the most notable. It was in pursuit of this quest that Jenkins played the leading role in maintaining the tradition of Ansteyan fantasy through the 1920s and 1930s.

The premise of *Alf's Button* is that Aladdin's lamp was disinterred when metals became scarce during the war and melted down to make uniform buttons, the captive djinn remaining associated with one of those on Alf Higgins's battle-dress. Like the jinnee in Anstey's *The Brass Bottle* the djinn which Alf christens Eustace is way behind the times, and his own ignorance is compounded by the awful stupidity of Alf and his companion-in-arms Bill Grant. They do manage to get through a lot of beer and enjoy one particularly sumptuous leave, but accomplish little else before Bill's belated resolution to steal the button and put a stop to the war is abruptly frustrated by its accidental loss in battle.

Rather confusingly, *Alf's Carpet* is a sequel to the film version of *Alf's Button* rather than the book, the film having evolved from a successful stage play, completing a gradual metamorphosis of the plot. At the end of the film version, the button is given to the djinn—so that he might be liberated from his servitude—at the request of Alf's better half, Liz, who knows well enough what a degrading business domestic service is. (Liz does not appear in the book at all.) The new story tells how Alf and Bill come into possession of a magic carpet whose potential they fail to exploit as miserably as they failed to capitalize on the button. After some preliminary adventures the carpet is cut up and reshaped into a pair of slippers, which cause much confusion in the household of the vicar who comes into possession of them. On a happier note, however, the carpet's magic lends assistance to the love-life of Alf's and Bill's old captain, Jimmy Donaldson.

Alf's Button was still in print when World War II broke out, although its sales had slowed to a trickle, and the temptation to follow it up with more of the same was irresistible. The liberated Eustace expresses his gratitude in *Alf's New Button,* which grants Alf six wishes. Although this is twice the usual ration Alf is far less than half as adept as most literary heroes who receive such gifts, and he wastes them profligately (with a little climactic help from Liz) in his now-customary fashion. The war remains peripheral to the action, and the story seems remarkably obstinate in refusing to step out of a deep rut of triviality; the book's abject failure to repeat its predecessor's coup is not at all surprising.

Although they never came remotely close to duplicating the success of *Alf's Button,* the two comic fantasies which Darlington wrote in between that book and its first sequel are rather better, mainly because their central characters belong to the stratum of society with which Darlington was familiar, and are drawn with greater sympathy as well as a higher degree of conviction. The hero of *Wishes Limited* is a would-be novelist fortunate enough to find favour with the fairy Folinelle, whose attempts to grant his wishes are unfortunately somewhat restricted by rules imposed by the Trades Unions which have revolutionized fairyland. Although his first novel, completed with supernatural aid, is a great success, its unexpectedly risqué content lands him in trouble with his peers—particularly with

his fiancée. Although it does not reach the standards of its model this remains the most readable of Darlington's Ansteyan pastiches.

Egbert, the story of a rising young barrister who offends a wizard and is consequently turned into a rhinoceros, is less adventurous than *Wishes Limited* but also less confused. The hero of the story is a friend of the luckless metamorph; his trials and tribulations while looking after the rhinoceros are by no means trivial but he never has the opportunity to make such a complete idiot of himself as Darlington's other protagonists and therefore comes out of the story fairly well. There is never any doubt about the fact that he is far more worthy than Egbert to marry the girl with whom both of them are in love, and his eventual victory in that contest is a foregone conclusion.

It must be said that in his fantasy novels Darlington did not come remotely close to making good use of his undeniable ability as a writer (he was a very successful journalist and a drama critic of some importance). Like Richard Marsh and "R. Andom" before him, he demonstrated that Ansteyan fantasy is remarkably easy to do badly, and thereby paid an ironic compliment to the very few authors who have managed to do it well. The runaway commercial success of *Alf's Button* was, however, a significant event in the history of British fantasy fiction, which helped to clear the way for the reprinting of Anstey's works and the first publication of many others in a similar vein, almost all of them better than *Alf's Button* itself.

—Brian Stableford

DAVIDSON, Avram (James)

Nationality: American. **Born:** Yonkers, New York, 23 April 1923. **Education:** New York University, 1940-42; Yeshiva University, New York, 1947-48; Pierce College, Canoga Park, California, 1950-51. **Military Service:** United States Navy, 1942-46; served in the Israeli Army in the Arab-Israeli war, 1948-49. **Family:** Married Grania Kaiman (divorced); one son. **Career:** Editor, *The Magazine of Fantasy and Science Fiction,* New York, 1962-64. From 1964, freelance writer. **Awards:** Hugo award, 1958; Hugo award for editing, 1963; Ellery Queen award, 1958; Mystery Writers of America Edgar Allan Poe award, 1961; World Fantasy award, 1976, 1979; World Fantasy life achievement award, 1986. **Died:** 8 May 1993.

FANTASY PUBLICATIONS

Novels (series: Peregrine; Vergil Magus)

The Island Under the Earth. New York, Ace, 1969; London, Mayflower, 1975.
The Phoenix and the Mirror; or, the Enigmatic Speculum (Vergil). New York, Doubleday, 1969; London, Mayflower, 1975.
Peregrine: Primus. New York, Walker, 1971.
Ursus of Ultima Thule. New York, Avon, 1973.
Peregrine: Secundus. New York, Berkley, 1981.
Vergil in Averno. New York, Doubleday, 1987.
Marco Polo and the Sleeping Beauty, with Grania Davis. New York, Baen, 1988.

Short Stories

Or All the Seas with Oysters. New York, Berkley, 1962; London, White Lion, 1976.
What Strange Stars and Skies. New York, Ace, 1965.
Strange Seas and Shores. New York, Doubleday, 1971.
The Enquiries of Dr. Eszterhazy. New York, Warner, 1975; expanded as *The Adventures of Dr. Eszterhazy,* Philadelphia, Owlswick Press, 1991.
Polly Charms the Sleeping Woman. Williamsburg, Virginia, College of William and Mary, 1977.
The Redward Edward Papers. New York, Doubleday, 1978.
The Best of Avram Davidson, edited by Michael Kurland. New York, Doubleday, 1979.
Collected Fantasies of Avram Davidson, edited by John Silbersack. New York, Berkley, 1982.
And Don't Forget the One Red Rose. Seattle, Washington, Dryad Press, 1986.

Other

Editor, *Best from Fantasy and Science Fiction 12-14.* New York, Doubleday, 3 vols., 1963-65; London Gollancz, 2 vols., 1966; Panther, 1 vol., 1967.
Editor, *Magic for Sale.* New York, Ace, 1983.

OTHER PUBLICATIONS

Novels

Joyleg, with Ward Moore. New York, Pyramid, 1962.
And on the Eighth Day (as Ellery Queen). New York, Random House, 1964.
Mutiny in Space. New York, Pyramid, 1964; London, White Lion, 1973.
The Fourth Side of the Triangle (as Ellery Queen). New York, Random House, 1965.
Rogue Dragon. New York, Ace, 1965.
Rork! New York, Berkley, 1965; London, Rapp and Whiting, 1968.
Masters of the Maze. New York Pyramid, 1965; London, White Lion, 1974.
The Enemy of My Enemy. New York, Berkley, 1966.
Clash of Star-Kings. New York, Ace, 1966.
The Kar-Chee Reign. New York, Ace, 1966.

Other

Crimes and Chaos (essays). Evanston, Illinois, Regency, 1962.
Adventures in Unhistory. Philadelphia, Owlswick Press, 1993.

*

Bibliography: "A Bibliography of Avram Davidson" by Richard Grant, in *Megavore 9* (Calgary, Alberta), June 1980.

Manuscript Collections: California State University, Fullerton; Texas A&M University, College Station.

*   *   *

Wit, ironic charm and erudition rather than passion characterize the fiction of Avram Davidson, for all, in real life, he held convictions passionately. An Orthodox Jew who could not forget the Holocaust, he refused to allow any of his works ever to be translated into German, even after his death. But he was also the most bookish of fantasists, in the best sense, capable of creating startling vistas from esoteric sources.

The most celebrated of his fantasy novels, *The Phoenix and the Mirror,* is set in ancient Rome and features Vergil, the author of the *Aeneid,* as its hero; but Davidson's Rome and Vergil are not those of history. In the Middle Ages, there arose the legend that the first-century poet had actually been a powerful sorcerer who had performed numerous miraculous feats. Davidson wrote the legend, making his setting the Classical world as viewed through the imagination of the medieval romancers, thus twice removed from the 20th-century reader's reality. The two Peregrine books are likewise set in an alternate Dark Age Europe, filled with odd characters and odder allusions. The Triune Monarchy of Scythia-Pannonia-Transbalkania, setting for the Dr. Eszterhazy stories, is a similar historical-literary construct, a genteel caricature of the 19th-century Austro-Hungarian Empire. It borders on Graustark, and, if hints in the second Peregrine book are to be followed, it grew out of the Middle Roman Empire. Of course there wasn't a Middle Roman Empire. Davidson, however, can persuasively argue that there should have been, citing numerous authorities, spitting off endless, charming anecdotes about those authorities, piling historical in-joke upon in-joke. When he read a fragment from an ancient Greek writer about a world existing underneath the one we know, Davidson had to set a novel there (*The Island Under the Earth*). *Ursus of Ultima Thule* likewise envisions a classic, imaginary realm, the primal northern land of ancient myth.

It was Davidson's strength that he could take legends, of which most readers have never even heard, and make them the subject of entertaining stories. His weakness was that he could also get lost in the apparatus, heaping on just one more nugget of neat stuff until he'd confused much of his audience.

The result was disaster in the commercial marketplace. Publishers truly didn't know what to do with a Davidson novel, as evidenced by Avon's packaging of *Ursus of Ultima Thule* as sword-and-sorcery, completely with a muscular, skin-clad hero on the cover. Davidson's mannered, convoluted style appealed to very few Conan or Thongor fans, one imagines. Though his work was highly respected by critics, colleagues and hard-core fans, it never sold. Many of his planned series never came to fruition because he couldn't get the sequels published. Because he couldn't sell the sequels, he didn't always write them. *The Island Under the Earth* is the opening of a never-completed trilogy.

But even his most sympathetic admirers must admit that he was better as a short story writer than novelist, precisely because, in short length, he didn't lose storyline and characters in a mass of detail. Even in the Eszterhazy stories, which range from short story to novella, are better in shorter length.

Damon Knight once suggested that Avram Davidson was, at his best, the finest short story writer in English since John Collier. Davidson's collections bear this out. Such stories as "The Golem," "Great is Diana," "The King's Evil," "Or the Grasses Grow," "Or All the Seas With Oysters," are deftly crafted, subtle, even sly, and make optimum use of Davidson's scholarship, particularly his grasp of period detail. "The King's Evil," for example, superbly recreates the language, colour, and texture of 18th-century London. Only very slowly, almost in retrospect, do we recognize that the portly, eccentric fellow who was hurried off by some soldiers must have been King George III during one of his lapses into madness. The stranger's touch cured scrofula. The breast-fetishist travelling in Asia Minor may have touched a deformed woman, or perhaps it was the Goddess of the Ephesians, now fallen on hard times. In any case, he certainly proved fertile afterward. "Or All the Seas With Oysters" is the ultimate story of the paranoia aroused by inanimate objects. When someone discovers that paperclips breed, become coat-hangers, then evolve into bicycles, he seems crazy—but he comes to a convincingly bad end.

Davidson's best stories have been compared to Collier, Saki, Lord Dunsany (in his Jorkens mode), and to R. A. Lafferty, but his effects are, not surprisingly, uniquely his own. Of his novels, the two Vergil books are the richest and most satisfying. A fragmentary third awaits in manuscript and may see publication. Any collection of his short stories makes splendid reading. *The Adventures of Dr. Eszterhazy* assembles a major cycle, about a scholarly, vaguely Sherlockian investigator, whose startling encounters range from gigantic, animate gingerbread men to the last archaeopteryx (which gets accidentally served for supper in the sole uncollected adventure, "The Odd Old Bird"). The "Limekiller" series, set largely in the Caribbean, still uncollected, is less humorous, somewhat darker in tone.

Davidson may be always doomed to be underappreciated, but he remains a true original, and, in his own subtle way, one of the greats.

—Darrell Schweitzer

DAVIS, Grania (Eve)

Nationality: American. **Born:** Wisconsin, 17 July 1943. **Education:** Sonoma State University, B.A. in literature and history 1977; University of Hawaii, B.A. in Asian studies 1977, International Business Certificate 1990. **Family:** Married 1) the writer Avram Davidson (q.v.) in 1960 (divorced), one son; 2) Stephen Davis in 1968, one son. **Career:** Numerous short-term jobs in travel consultancy and teaching, from 1967; published author, editor, translator and journalist from 1972. **Agent:** Pamela Buckmaster, Carnell Literary Agency, Danescroft, Goose Lane, Little Hallingbury, Bishops Stortford, Herts. CM22 7RG, England. **Address:** 557 Whitewood Drive, San Rafael, CA 94903, USA.

FANTASY PUBLICATIONS

Novels

The Rainbow Annals. New York, Avon, 1980.
Moonbird. New York, Doubleday, 1986.
Marco Polo and the Sleeping Beauty, with Avram Davidson. New York, Baen, 1988.

Short Stories

The King and the Mangoes. California, Dharma Press, 1975.
The Proud Peacock and the Mallard. California, Dharma Press, 1976.

OTHER PUBLICATIONS

Novels

Doctor Grass. New York, Avon, 1978.
The Great Perpendicular Path. New York, Avon, 1980.

*

Grania Davis comments:

I have lived around a lot. I have dwelled in a mountain village in Mexico, on a primitive sandbar in Belize, and on a beach in Hawaii. I have taught in Tibetan refugee settlements in India, and worked as a military historian in neon-lit Tokyo. I have travelled extensively in North America, Europe, and Asia/Pacifica.

My travels have inspired a series of fantasy novels based on the interwoven myths of the orient. *The Rainbow Annals* is based on Tibetan legends. *Moonbird* uses Balinese myths. *Marco Polo and the Sleeping Beauty,* written in collaboration with Avram Davidson (who was himself a legend), is set in China. I am currently working on *Ghost Town Jamboree,* a fantasy set in old California, which links the cross-cultural currents of Eurasia. My short stories reflect my sojourns abroad.

I have settled down recently, dividing my time with my family in Marin County, California, and on the north shore of Oahu, Hawaii. I enjoy playing with time and space, but rarely write about other planets—this one is too interesting.

*   *   *

One of the most elusive of fantasists, Grania Davis has published only four solo novels and one in collaboration with her ex-husband, the late Avram Davidson; all are now out of print. Her short fiction, some also co-written with Davidson, has likewise been sparse, amounting to less than two dozen tales in over two decades of work (her first story was published in 1972); despite their limpid intelligence and eccentric charm, these stories remain uncollected. Davis's obscurity is unfortunate given the singular quality of her work; readers who make the effort to locate her novels will certainly be rewarded.

In the mid-1970s Davis provided the text for two saddle-stapled booklets, *The King and the Mangoes* and *The Proud Peacock and the Mallard,* published by a Northern California specialty press; instalments in a series, designed for children, briefly narrating episodes from the "Jataka Tales"—which chronicle the prehuman incarnations of the Buddha—the stories function both as pointed moral allegories and as quaint animal fantasies (the Bodhisattva manifests as a monkey and a duck, respectively). Though slight works done on commission, they clearly prefigured major themes in Davis's subsequent career, especially her absorption in the richness of Asian cultural history and her commitment to translating this folkloric material into genre terms. (Davis lived in Japan between 1979 and 1982, working with a translators' group; see her foreword to *Best Japanese Science Fiction Stories,* 1989, an anthology edited by John L. Apostolou and Martin H. Greenberg.) She is thus a significant precursor, though unrenowned, of a trend toward "Oriental" themes in contemporary fantasy literature, crystallized in the more celebrated recent work of Barry Hughart and Jeanne Larsen.

Davis's first two novels, *Doctor Grass* and *The Great Perpendicular Path,* showed her ambivalent immersion in the concerns of the American counterculture, especially its yearning fascination for non-Western spiritual practices; the latter book is a deft portrait, at once satirical and sympathetic, of a handful of middle-class California couples who travel to a secluded Mexican resort to learn tantric yoga and sexual liberation. Neither novel is explicitly fantastic, but both effectively limn the social context in which Davis's later activations of Asian mythology find their place and meaning.

With *The Rainbow Annals,* Davis moves her narrative directly into this mythic realm, producing a novel-length version of her religious-allegorical juveniles. The foreground story chronicles the cyclic incarnations of a Monkey-God and his demoness lover against the backdrop of the rise and diffusion of Buddhism in Asia; it is a fanciful tale, by turns dark and sparkling, rich in weird incident and earthy detail. Among the more striking elements are its various incarnations of evil: Black Shen, a sallow-faced, blood-swilling demon flying about with his screeching pack of crows; the Black Emperor, a dire sorcerer able to summon an army of rotting zombies to do his bidding; and the Black Duke of Lang, a cynical conspirator adept at tactics of mind control. These villains are confronted by the Monkey-God's avatars in a series of battles that grow progressively less fantastic in form, indicating the decline of mythic and the rise of historical time. Despite its essentially whimsical nature, the novel has a strong thematic undercurrent—the inculcation of an Eastern ethic of compassionate acceptance: "Form is emptiness, emptiness is form. There is no suffering, cause of suffering or cessation of suffering. There is only mind." *The Rainbow Annals* is one of the rare successful translations of Asian spiritual values in the canon of American fantasy literature.

Her next novel is another; *Moonbird* also makes use of non-Western myths, this time the polytheistic syncretism of the islanders of the Malay Archipelago. Set on an island near Bali, the story focuses on Madai, a native youth gifted with the ability to summon and command the god Garuda, who manifests as a giant seabird made of moonstone. Together the pair explore a bizarre undersea kingdom, travel to the moon, and eventually devote themselves to healing the island's sick and infirm; this project earns Madai a reputation as a powerful shaman, which soon attracts a trio of Californians—an anthropologist, a psychologist, and a physician—in the employ of a wealthy woman dying of cancer who is seeking a miraculous cure. Madai finds himself torn between the opposed forces of Vishnu, the Preserver (represented by the Moonbird), and Siva, the Destroyer (whose agent in the story is an eerie witch-spirit named Rangda): should he intervene to save the rich American or permit nature to take its degenerating course?

Moonbird is Davis's best novel, combining a shrewdly judged perspective on the collision of Eastern and Western cultures (less satirically pointed than in *The Great Perpendicular Path*) with a meticulously detailed evocation of an exotic world, from its daily cuisine to its shadowy deities. As in *The Rainbow Annals,* the figures of evil are the most memorable, especially the vile Rangda, with her matted hair, curving tusks and protruding eyeballs, who revels in human corruptibility. Throughout, Davis's narration manages to fuse sensuous immediacy with ethereal sweetness, an extraordinary accomplishment.

Aside from some scattered short fiction (much of it published in *The Magazine of Fantasy and Science Fiction*), Davis has fallen silent since *Moonbird.* Her collaborative novel, *Marco Polo and the Sleeping Beauty,* seems to owe more to Davidson's wry obsession with the curious collusion of historical and legendary sources; though a diverting enough entertainment, it does not satisfy the ap-

petite for another of Davis's heartfelt explorations of the human dimensions of myth. One can only wonder when a fresh fantasy will emerge from her sparkling if sporadic pen.

—Rob Latham

DEAN, Pamela

Form of her name used by Pamela Collins Dean Dyer-Bennett. **Nationality:** American. **Born:** 1953. **Address:** c/o Tor Books, 175 Fifth Avenue, New York, NY 10010, USA.

FANTASY PUBLICATIONS

Novel (series: Secret Country)

The Secret Country. New York, Ace, 1985.
The Hidden Land (Secret Country). New York, Ace, 1986.
The Whim of the Dragon (Secret Country). New York, Ace, 1989.
Tam Lin. New York, Tor, 1991.
The Dubious Hills. New York, Tor, 1994.

*   *   *

Too often, hopeful fantasy writers draw so heavily from what has already proven popular that they fail to provide anything to distinguish themselves from the crowd. Trolls and elves, evil magicians and robust or reluctant heroes, beautiful princesses and hideous monsters have become the staples of most modern fantasy. The quieter or less conventional novels that occasionally appear are frequently lost in the onrushing tide of Tolkien clones. Pamela Dean has consistently avoided this trap, and even those stories that are superficially conventional are actually very different in content.

Dean's very impressive first published fantasy, *The Secret Country,* was packaged somewhat misleadingly. Although there are in fact unicorns in the book, they're almost incidental, and I suspect some readers may have been quite surprised by the story itself. Fortunately, there is an audience for intelligently written fantasy, and Dean's subsequent books have attracted a loyal following. *The Secret Country* has much of the feel of a classic fairy tale, using children as its main characters, but aimed nonetheless at adult readers. A group of children fond of fantasy role-playing find themselves caught up in the real thing when they discover a magical sword lying under a hedge, the key to the Secret Country.

They find themselves in the very same fantasy world that they created in their fantasy game, so close in detail that they are accepted as the children of the local king and precipitated into situations which they have played out in the past. Although this enables them to anticipate problems some of the time, they hadn't explored every possibility of their fantasy world, and some of the events yet to come are ones they would prefer not to experience. There are also disturbing indications that they may be in considerable danger if they don't make the right guesses, that some aspects of the world are mutable. Even though some of them believe it to be just an hallucination, the substance of the fantasy world is so intense that they feel compelled to act as though it were real.

The Hidden Land continues directly where its predecessor leaves off, the children still arguing whether or not they are experiencing real events. The king is doomed to die and war lurks on the horizon, they know, but the longer they stay, they less they can anticipate the details of what is to come. And with the loss of their one advantage, their continued existence in the Secret Country becomes extremely perilous, so much so that they ultimately seek to escape.

The story ends with *The Whim of the Dragon*. A mysterious message lures the children back to the Secret Country, which has now progressed past the point where they feel confident about predicting the course of future events. Nor do they believe it simply an illusion but rather a real world with real people whose lives have been altered by their interference. In its entirety, the trilogy proves that even within the limits of an admittedly much overused setting, a skilful writer can create something fresh and original. Dean's prose is crisp and intelligent, her characters well differentiated and deftly drawn, and the background and politics of her fantasy world is complex and credible.

Dean's next novel, *Tam Lin*, is complete unto itself and makes use of a contemporary setting. Based on the Scottish folk song, it was one of a series of novels by various hands designed to illustrate the fact that fairy tales were not intended to be stories for children, but rather reflected in dramatic form some of the complex forces that affect human existence. The novel is a remarkable work, focused on a bright young woman's arrival and experiences at a small college, filled with romantic notions, exploring the world of literature and ideas, learning to discover who she really is. The fantasy is in fact incidental to the story itself, although the atmosphere is reminiscent of William Morris at times.

Dean's most recent novel is *The Dubious Hills*. Unlike most fantasy writers, Dean is not content to write the same story over and over. The Dubious Hills are located adjacent to the Secret Country, but they're a far different place and this is a very different kind of story. Magic is considerably less predictable here, and most people lose the talent in the process of maturing. When a young girl befriends an injured wolf, she changes the course of her life, because the wolf is a shapeshifter, and he returns to his human form. In that shape, he announces his intention to teach her that which she needs to know, but the most important question is whether or not she can trust him in the first place. *The Dubious Hills* is a pastoral fantasy, free of clashing armies, evil sorcerers, and the other devices of mainline genre fantasy. It is instead the story of self-discovery, thoughtful, witty, humorous at times, with a richly developed setting and a cast of believable characters.

Although Dean is an infrequent writer of shorter tales, "Owlswater" (in *Xanadu*, edited by Jane Yolen, 1993) is of particular interest. An apprentice magician is travelling to the place where all dreams become real, accompanied by several animal friends. Along the way he discovers the body of a dead knight, and thoughts of mortality and immortality alter the nature of his journey. Set in the fringes of the Hidden Lands, "Owlswater" is particularly effective in its description of the protagonist's change of personality in response to his experiences.

It is difficult to predict in advance which stories will survive and which will disappear once out of print, but original voices tend to have a better chance than those who simply repeat the lyrics of others. Pamela Dean is not a member of the chorus, and I would not be surprised if one day her stories of the Hidden Country were mentioned in the same breath as Narnia and Oz.

—Don D'Ammassa

de CAMP, L(yon) Sprague

Nationality: American. **Born:** New York City, 27 November 1907. **Education:** Trinity School, New York; Snyder School, North Carolina; California Institute of Technology, Pasadena, B.S. in aeronautical engineering 1930; Massachusetts Institute of Technology, Cambridge, summer 1932; Stevens Institute of Technology, Hoboken, New Jersey, M.S. 1933. **Military Service:** United States Naval Reserve, 1942-45: Lieutenant Commander. **Family:** Married Catherine A. Crook in 1939; two sons. **Career:** Instructor, Inventors Foundation Inc., New York, 1933-36; principal of School of Inventing and Patenting, International Correspondence Schools, Scranton, Pennsylvania, 1936-37; editor, Fowler-Becker Publishing Company, New York, 1937-38, and American Society of Mechanical Engineers, New York, 1938; assistant mechanical engineer, Naval Aircraft Factory, Philadelphia, 1942; radio scriptwriter, *Voice of America* series, 1948-56; publicity writer, Gray and Rogers, Philadelphia, 1956. Freelance writer. Member of the Advisory Board, Society for the History of Technology. **Recipient:** International Fantasy award, 1953; Gandalf award, 1976; Grand Master Nebula award, 1978; World Fantasy Life Achievement award, 1984. **Address:** 3453 Hearst Castle Way, Plano, TX 75025-3605, USA.

FANTASY PUBLICATIONS

Novels (series: Conan; Harold Shea; Incorporated Knight; Jorian)

The Incomplete Enchanter, with Fletcher Pratt (Harold Shea). New York, Holt, 1941; London, Sphere, 1979.
Land of Unreason, with Fletcher Pratt. New York, Holt, 1942.
The Carnelian Cube, with Fletcher Pratt. New York, Gnome Press, 1948.
The Castle of Iron, with Fletcher Pratt (Harold Shea). New York, Gnome Press, 1950.
The Undesired Princess. Los Angeles, Fantasy, 1951.
The Return of Conan, with Björn Nyberg. New York, Gnome Press, 1957; as *Conan the Avenger,* New York, Lancer, 1968; London, Sphere, 1974.
Wall of Serpents, with Fletcher Pratt (Harold Shea). New York, Avalon, 1960; as *The Enchanter Compleated,* London, Sphere, 1980.
Conan of the Isles, with Lin Carter. New York, Lancer, 1968; London, Sphere, 1974.
The Goblin Tower (Jorian). New York, Pyramid, 1968; London, Sphere, 1979.
The Clocks of Iraz (Jorian). New York, Pyramid, 1971.
Conan the Buccaneer, with Lin Carter. New York, Lancer, 1971.
The Fallible Fiend. New York, New American Library, 1973; London, Remploy, 1974.
The Compleat Enchanter: The Magical Misadventures of Harold Shea (omnibus; includes *The Incomplete Enchanter, The Castle of Iron*), with Fletcher Pratt. New York, Nelson Doubleday, 1975; London, Sphere, 1979.
Conan the Liberator, with Lin Carter. New York, Bantam, 1979; London, Sphere, 1980.
Conan and the Spider God. New York, Bantam, 1980; London, Hale, 1984.
The Treasure of Tranicos, with Robert E. Howard (Conan). New York, Ace, 1980.

Conan the Barbarian (novelization of screenplay), with Lin Carter. New York, Bantam, and London, Sphere, 1982.

The Unbeheaded King (Jorian). New York, Del Rey, 1983.

The Reluctant King (omnibus; includes *The Goblin Tower, The Clocks of Iraz, The Unbeheaded King*). New York, Nelson Doubleday, 1985.

The Incorporated Knight, with Catherine Crook de Camp. West Bloomfield, Michigan, Phantasia Press, 1987.

Intrepid Enchanter: The Complete Magical Misadventures of Harold Shea (omnibus; includes *The Incomplete Enchanter, The Castle of Iron, Wall of Serpents*), with Fletcher Pratt. London, Sphere, 1988; as *The Complete Compleat Enchanter,* New York, Baen, 1989.

The Honorable Barbarian (Jorian). New York, Del Rey, 1989.

The Undesired Princess, and The Enchanted Bunny, with David A. Drake. New York, Baen, 1990.

The Pixilated Peeress, with Catherine Crook de Camp (Incorporated Knight). New York, Del Rey, 1991.

Sir Harold and the Gnome King (Harold Shea). Newark, New Jersey, Wildside Press, 1991.

The Enchanter Reborn, with Christopher Stasheff (Harold Shea). New York, Baen, 1992.

Short Stories

Tales from Gavagan's Bar, with Fletcher Pratt. New York, Twayne, 1953; expanded edition, Philadelphia, Owlswick Press, 1978.

The Tritonian Ring and Other Pusadian Tales. New York, Twayne, 1953; London, Sphere, 1978.

Tales of Conan, with Robert E. Howard. New York, Gnome Press, 1955; as *Conan: The Flame Knife,* New York, Ace, 1981.

Conan the Adventurer, with Robert E. Howard. New York, Lancer, 1966; London, Sphere, 1974.

Conan, with Robert E. Howard and Lin Carter. New York, Lancer, 1967; London, Sphere, 1974.

Conan the Usurper, with Robert E. Howard. New York, Lancer, 1967; London, Sphere, 1974.

Conan the Freebooter, with Robert E. Howard. New York, Lancer, 1968; London, Sphere, 1974.

Conan the Wanderer, with Robert E. Howard and Lin Carter. New York, Lancer, 1968; London, Sphere, 1974.

Conan of Cimmeria, with Robert E. Howard and Lin Carter. New York, Lancer, 1969; London, Sphere, 1974.

The Reluctant Shaman and Other Fantastic Tales. New York, Pyramid, 1970.

Conan of Aquilonia, with Lin Carter. New York, Lancer, 1971; London, Sphere, 1977.

Conan the Swordsman, with Lin Carter and Björn Nyberg. New York, Bantam, 1978; London, Sphere, 1979.

The Purple Pterodactyls: The Adventures of W. Wilson Newbury, Ensorcelled Financier. Huntington Woods, Michigan, Phantasia Press, 1979.

The Conan Chronicles, with Robert E. Howard and Lin Carter (omnibus; includes *Conan, Conan of Cimmeria, Conan the Freebooter*). London, Orbit, 1989.

The Conan Chronicles 2, with Robert E. Howard and Lin Carter (omnibus; includes *Conan the Wanderer, Conan the Adventurer, Conan the Buccaneer*). London, Orbit, 1990.

Other

Editor, *Swords and Sorcery.* New York, Pyramid, 1963.

Editor, *The Spell of Seven.* New York, Pyramid, 1965.

Editor, *Conan the Conqueror* by Robert E. Howard. New York, Lancer, 1967; London, Sphere, 1974.

Editor, *Conan the Warrior* by Robert E. Howard. New York, Lancer, 1967; London, Sphere, 1974.

Editor, *The Fantastic Swordsmen.* New York, Pyramid, 1967.

Editor, *Warlocks and Warriors.* New York, Putnam, 1970.

OTHER PUBLICATIONS

Novels

Lest Darkness Fall. New York, Holt, 1941; London, Heinemann, 1955.

Genus Homo, with P. Schuyler Miller. Reading, Pennsylvania, Fantasy Press, 1950.

Rogue Queen. New York, Doubleday, 1951; London, Pinnacle, 1954.

Cosmic Manhunt. New York, Ace, 1954; as *A Planet Called Krishna,* London, Compact, 1966; as *The Queen of Zamba,* New York, Davis, 1977.

Solomon's Stone. New York, Avalon, 1957.

An Elephant for Aristotle. New York, Doubleday, 1958; London, Dobson, 1966.

The Tower of Zanid. New York, Avalon, 1958.

The Bronze God of Rhodes. New York, Doubleday, 1960.

The Glory That Was. New York, Avalon, 1960.

The Dragon of the Ishtar Gate. New York, Doubleday, 1961.

The Search for Zei. New York, Avalon, 1962; as *The Floating Continent,* London, Compact, 1966.

The Hand of Zei. New York, Avalon, 1963.

The Arrows of Hercules. New York, Doubleday, 1965.

The Golden Wind. New York, Doubleday, 1969.

The Hostage of Zir. New York, Berkley, 1977.

The Great Fetish. New York, Doubleday, 1978.

The Prisoner of Zhamanak. Huntington Woods, Michigan, Phantasia Press, 1982.

The Bones of Zora, with Catherine Crook de Camp. Huntington Woods, Michigan, Phantasia Press, 1983.

The Stones of Nomuru, with Catherine Crook de Camp. Norfolk, Virginia, Donning, 1988.

Divide and Rule, with *The Sword of Rhiannon* by Leigh Brackett. New York, Tor, 1990.

The Wheels of If, with *The Pugnacious Peacemaker* by Harry Turtledove. New York, Tor, 1990.

The Swords of Zinjabar, with Catherine Crook de Camp. New York, Baen, 1991.

The Venom Trees of Sunga. New York, Del Rey, 1992.

Short Stories

Divide and Rule. Reading, Pennsylvania, Fantasy Press, 1948.

The Wheels of If. Chicago, Shasta, 1948.

The Continent Makers and Other Tales of the Viagens. New York, Twayne, 1953.

Sprague de Camp's New Anthology of Science Fiction. London, Panther, 1953.

A Gun for Dinosaur and Other Imaginative Tales. New York, Doubleday, 1963.

The Virgin and the Wheels. New York, Popular Library, 1976.

The Best of L. Sprague de Camp. New York, Nelson Doubleday, 1978.

The Virgin of Zesh, and The Tower of Zanid. New York, Ace, 1983.

Rivers of Time. New York, Baen, 1993.

Poetry

Demons and Dinosaurs. Sauk City, Wisconsin, Arkham House, 1970.

Phantoms and Fancies. Baltimore, Mirage Press, 1972.

Heroes and Hobgoblins. West Kingston, Rhode Island, Grant, 1978.

Other

Inventions and Their Management, with Alf K. Berle. Scranton, Pennsylvania, International Textbook Company, 1937; revised edition, as *Inventions, Patents, and Their Management,* Princeton, New Jersey, Van Nostrand, 1959.

The Evolution of Naval Weapons. Washington, D.C., Department of the Navy, 1947.

Lands Beyond, with Willy Ley. New York, Rinehart, 1952. *Science-Fiction Handbook: The Writing of Imaginative Fiction.* New York, Hermitage House, 1953; revised edition, with Catherine Crook de Camp, Philadelphia, Owlswick Press, 1975.

Lost Continents: The Atlantis Theme in History, Science, and Literature. New York, Gnome Press, 1954.

Engines (for children). New York, Golden Press, 1959; revised edition, 1961, 1969.

The Heroic Age of American Invention. New York, Doubleday, 1961.

Man and Power (for children). New York, Golden Press, 1961.

Energy and Power (for children). New York, Golden Press, 1962.

The Ancient Engineers. New York, Doubleday, and London, Souvenir Press, 1963.

Ancient Ruins and Archaeology, with Catherine Crook de Camp. New York, Doubleday, 1964; London, Souvenir Press, 1965; as *Citadels of Mystery,* London, Fontana, 1972.

Elephant. New York, Pyramid, 1964.

Spirits, Stars, and Spells: The Profits and Perils of Magic, with Catherine Crook de Camp. New York, Canaveral Press, 1966.

The Story of Science in America, with Catherine Crook de Camp. New York, Scribner, 1967.

The Great Monkey Trial. New York, Doubleday, 1968.

The Conan Reader. Baltimore, Mirage Press, 1968.

The Day of the Dinosaur, with Catherine Crook de Camp. New York, Doubleday, 1968.

Darwin and His Great Discovery (for children), with Catherine Crook de Camp. New York, Macmillan, 1972.

Scribblings. Cambridge, Massachusetts, NESFA Press, 1972.

Great Cities of the Ancient World. New York, Doubleday, 1972.

The Miscast Barbarian: A Biography of Robert E. Howard (1906-1936). Saddle River, New Jersey, de la Ree, 1975.

Blond Barbarians and Noble Savages (essays). Baltimore, T-K Graphics, 1975.

Lovecraft: A Biography. New York, Doubleday, 1975; London, New English Library, 1976.

Literary Swordsmen and Sorcerers: The Makers of Heroic Fantasy. Sauk City, Wisconsin, Arkham House, 1976.

The Ragged Edge of Science. Philadelphia, Owlswick Press, 1980.

Dark Valley Destiny: The Life of Robert E. Howard, with Catherine Crook de Camp and Jane Whittington Griffin. New York, Bluejay, 1983.

The Fringe of the Unknown. Buffalo, Prometheus, 1983.

Editor, *The Wolf Leader,* by Alexander Dumas. Philadelphia, Prime Press, 1950.

Editor, with George H. Scithers, *The Conan Swordbook.* Baltimore, Mirage Press, 1969.

Editor, with George H. Scithers, *The Conan Grimoire.* Baltimore, Mirage Press, 1972.

Editor, with Catherine Crook de Camp, *3000 Years of Fantasy and Science Fiction.* New York, Lothrop, 1972.

Editor, with Catherine Crook de Camp, *Tales Beyond Time.* New York, Lothrop, 1973.

Editor, *To Quebec and the Stars,* by H.P. Lovecraft. West Kingston, Rhode Island, Donald M. Grant, 1976.

Editor, *The Blade of Conan* (articles). New York, Ace, 1979.

Editor, *The Spell of Conan* (articles). New York, Ace, 1980.

Editor, with others, *Footprints on Sand: A Literary Sampler.* Chicago, Advent, 1981.

*

Bibliography: *De Camp: An L. Sprague de Camp Bibliography* by Charlotte Laughlin and Daniel J. H. Levack, Columbia, Pennsylvania, Underwood Miller, 1983.

Manuscript Collections: Mugar Memorial Library, Boston University; Harry Ransom Humanities Center, University of Texas, Austin.

*   *   *

L. Sprague de Camp began writing fiction for John W. Campbell Jr's *Astounding Science Fiction,* but did not get into his literary stride until Campbell founded a fantasy companion, *Unknown.* The new magazine was ideally suited to de Camp's idiosyncratic imagination, which combined a talent for logical extrapolation with a whimsical sense of humour. It was de Camp, alone and in collaboration, who set the characteristic tone of the new magazine, which became justly celebrated for works in which a science-fictional kind of rational argument was applied to premises borrowed from traditional fantasy, with results which extended from the quirkily menacing to the farcically absurd.

De Camp's first long stories for *Unknown* were more sf than fantasy. In "Divide and Rule" Earth has been invaded by alien "hoppers" who have reinstituted the chivalric code as part of their quasi-feudal programme of social control. In the classic timeslip romance *Lest Darkness Fall* a hero displaced into the sixth century contrives to avert the Dark Ages by means of his humble inventions in communication tehnology. In early collaborative stories, however, de Camp allowed his imagination freer rein. "None But Lucifer," written with Horace L. Gold, is an audacious exercise in literary Satanism in which a young American applies for a job in the Satanic hierarchy and deploys his ingenuity to such good effect that he climbs rapidly through the ranks. Then, in 1940, de Camp formed a long-standing literary partnership with Fletcher Pratt which was launched with the first of the Harold Shea stories, "The Roaring Trumpet."

In this series, Shea's scientist mentor Reed Chalmers has contrived to formalize the mathematics of magic, manipulation of whose equations is capable of opening doorways into any and all imaginary worlds. Fine-tuning the process proves, however, annoyingly difficult, and Chalmers initially translocates himself and his companions into the wrong worlds. In the first two novellas, collected as *The Incomplete Enchanter,* Shea visits the world of Norse mythology and the world of Spenser's *Faerie Queene.* In *The Castle of Iron* he is snatched out of his own world into that of Ariosto's *Orlando Furioso,* where much confusion results from the similiarity between it and the derivative Spenserian world in which he has found his ideal woman. De Camp and Pratt wrote two more novels with *Unknown* in mind, but only *The Land of Unreason*—in which an American visiting Ireland is mistaken for a changeling by drunken little people and borne away to King Oberon's fairyland—actually appeared there. *The Carnelian Cube,* a rather less inspiring odyssey through several absurd alternative worlds, ultimately appeared in book form some years after the demise of the magazine.

The solo work which de Camp wrote for *Unknown* in parallel with his collaborations with Pratt is similar in method and tone. The early alternative-history story "The Wheels of If" retains a strong science-fictional element, but *The Undesired Princess* and *Solomon's Stone* are outright fantasies. The former describes the adventures of a discreetly ingenious hero in a fairy tale world where subtle shades of colour and meaning are conspicuous by their absence. The latter examines the predicament of an accountant displaced from his body by a demon, who is forced thereby to survive on an astral plane inhabited by the dream-projections of ordinary men, where he is manifest as a dashing cavalier. All of these stories consist of series of exotic encounters strung together like beads on a necklace, which are often (but not always) very amusing but tend to be a little disapointing *en masse* by virtue of the virtual absence of any framing plot. This tendency to use simple linear plots—which give the impression of being made up as they progress—is a handicap which de Camp has never fully overcome, although it is a fault which is less damaging to works in the fantasy genre than most others.

Although the de Camp/Pratt partnership was reformed after several years of war-induced separation it never quite reached its former heights. The two Harold Shea novellas collected in *Wall of Serpents,* which take the hero into the world of the *Kalevala* and the realm of Irish mythology, are lacklustre by comparison with the earlier stories in the series, but the collaborators found a richer vein of humour in the series of fantastic tall tales whose early examples were collected as *Tales from Gavagan's Bar.* De Camp was to carry forward both these lines of work after Pratt's death, in the Harold Shea novella *Sir Harold and the Gnome King* and the anecdotes collected in *The Purple Pterodactyls,* but the sparkle was missing. It seems that de Camp requires a collaborator as a foil to make the best of his comic talents, and has recently appointed his wife, Catherine Crook de Camp, to this position with productive results; their combined talents (previously displayed in some excellent non-fictional works) are turned to this purpose in *The Incorporated Knight* and *The Pixilated Peeress.*

In the 1950s de Camp became increasingly involved with the "sword and sorcery" sub-genre pioneered by Robert E. Howard, which he helped to popularize with a series of eclectic representative anthologies. *The Tritonian Ring* is a relatively light-hearted exercise in this vein and he wrote several short stories set in the same imaginary prehistoric era. When Gnome Press collected the Conan stories, de Camp completed a few unfinished stories, adapted a few more of Howard's unpublished manuscripts, and revised a pastiche written by Bjorn Nyberg. When the series was reprinted in paperback in the 1960s and 1970s, de Camp and Lin Carter expanded it further, and de Camp again began producing heroic fantasies of his own. The Jorian series, begun with *The Goblin Tower,* are ac-

complished exercises in this vein. Although de Camp is incapable of taking this kind of subject-matter as seriously as Howard did, and is deeply committed to the principles of decency and civilization rather than the supposed ideals of virile barbarism, the gloss of urbanity and sophistication which his own sword-and-sorcery novels consequently acquire is not at all to their disadvantage. The Jorian series draws productively on the experience which de Camp had gained in writing a number of excellent historical novels set in and around the Classical world (*An Elephant for Aristotle, The Bronze God of Rhodes, The Dragon of the Ishtar Gate,* etc, none of which are actually fantasies). The later Jorian books, *The Clocks of Iraz, The Unbeheaded King* and *The Honorable Barbarian* easily maintained the standard set by the first volume. *The Fallible Fiend,* which is set in the same quasi-Hellenistic milieu and features a demonic hero named Zdim, is equally delightful.

De Camp's historical study of *Literary Swordsmen and Sorcerors* is an excellent survey of the authors whose work was ultimately drawn together to constitute a "history" of the nascent genre of heroic fantasy.

—Brian Stableford

DeCHANCIE, John

Nationality: American. **Born:** 3 August 1946 in Pittsburgh, Pennsylvania. **Education:** University of Pittsburgh, B.A., 1968. **Family:** Married Holly Marie Seliy (a nurse) 31 July 1976; two children. **Career:** Engineer, WQED Public Television, Pittsburgh, Pennsylvania, 1970-75; self-employed film and videotape producer and director, 1975-84; field representative, Broadcast Music, Inc., New York, New York, 1984-86; writer, 1986—.

FANTASY PUBLICATIONS

Novels (series: Castle Perilous)

Castle Perilous. New York, Ace, 1988.
Castle for Rent. New York, Ace, 1989.
Castle Kidnapped. New York, Ace, 1989.
Castle War! New York, Ace, 1990.
Castle Murders. New York, Ace, 1991.
Castle Dreams. New York, Ace, 1992.
Castle Spellbound. New York, Ace, 1992.
Magicnet. New York, AvoNova, 1994.

OTHER PUBLICATIONS

Novels

Starrigger. New York, Ace, 1983.
Red limit Freeway. New York, Ace, 1984.
Paradox Alley. New York, Ace, 1986.
Crooked House, with Thomas F. Monteleone. New York, Tor, 1987.
Dr. Dimension: Master of Spacetime, with David Bischoff. New York, Roc, 1994.

Other

Peron. New York, Chelsea House, 1987.
Nasser. New York, Chelsea House, 1987.

*   *   *

Humour has always been an important part of fantasy fiction, perhaps most notably during the period when *Unknown* was publishing L. Sprague de Camp, Fletcher Pratt and others, although its popularity goes through periodic up-and-down swings. Farcical fantasy has virtually become a sub-genre of its own recently, and its leading practitioners include Esther Friesner, Craig Shaw Gardner and John DeChancie.

After writing an excellent trilogy of innovative and amusing science-fiction novels, DeChancie turned to fantasy with *Castle Perilous.* The eponymous castle is a vast edifice with 144,000 doors, each of which leads to another world or time, and almost as many enemies, a kind of lightweight Gormenghast with a motley crew of residents and Guests, the latter people who have stepped through a Portal between worlds, either intentionally or otherwise. Gene Ferraro is a recent college graduate with a philosophy major who finds himself transported to this setting when he drives into the basement of a parking garage and finds the only exit leads to another universe. With a furry accomplice named Snowclaw, a beautiful witch named Linda, and determined to find his way home, Gene wanders through the Escher-like corridors of the castle while a besieging army pounds away at the outer walls and the owner, Lord Incarnadine, plots his strategy.

The setting is ideal for a series, since the castle can drift around in time and space and contains what is for all practical purposes an infinite number of rooms and possibilities. DeChancie strikes a good balance between humour and adventure, traditional fantasy motifs and new twists, and the result was a novel that almost demanded a sequel. So it was no surprise when *Castle For Rent* appeared the following year.

DeChancie turns up the humour this time. The castle has been invaded by a host of not particularly bright demons and its original inhabitants have been scattered throughout the various universes. Gene Ferraro and his friends are back, determined to find the Portal through which the nasties are coming and close it down. They solve the mystery after several zany encounters and uncover a traitor in Lord Incarnadine's family, exchanging wisecracks at the least provocation throughout.

Something goes wrong with the castle itself in *Castle Kidnapped* and many of its residents are dumped into unlikely alternate universes where dinosaurs play golf, men are sex toys, and other scenarios, each seemingly designed to afford the victim the greatest possible inconvenience. There's little pretence of serious adventure this time, although the plot is lively and full of action. Gene, now a champion swordsman, tracks down the man responsible, along with his demonic henchman, but not before he has de-stabilized the entire web of universes, whose individual realities we now learn are dependent upon the castle itself.

The imbalance carries over into the fourth instalment, *Castle War!* A duplicate Castle Perilous appears, but it's a mirror image, and the two conflicting realities prepare for battle in the ultimate Evil Twin story. What follows is a series of farcical encounters as no one on either side can be truly certain who's who and what's what. It was far more successfully funny than its predecessors and is still the best episode.

Castle Murders spoofs the traditional murder mystery as well as fantasy when a corpse is discovered after a party and our regular cast of characters compete with each other to solve the case. The humour is more restrained this time, but it's back in full force in *Castle Dreams.* Lord Incarnadine is dead, although that doesn't prevent him from being a continuing character, and his relatives and others are all anxious to grab as much power as they can. Complete with footnotes, a "surprise" ending, and with study notes appended, this is so far the most bizarre entry in the series. The most recent title is *Castle Spellbound,* which has its funny moments but lacks the clever plots that enlivened the earlier volumes. Something has gone wrong with the web of magic under which the castle operates; time and space are not acting as they should. The scenes set in an alternate universe where there is space travel of a sort are fun, but otherwise the book repeats older themes and situations.

DeChancie's next and most recent fantasy is not part of the series and is far from traditional. *MagicNet* involves the intersection of our own universe with another. The protagonist, Skye King, listens to the murder of Grant, computer-hacker friend, while talking to him on the telephone, and arrives on the scene in time to be menaced by what is clearly a demon. Naturally he can't tell the police exactly what happened, but neither is he willing to just walk away from the situation. Before his death, Grant implanted his personality in a computer program that was written by a combination of science and magic, and which holds the key to the survival of the entire universe. But King is computer-illiterate, sceptical of the situation, and not entirely easy with the prospect of signing up to do battle with hideous demons.

Nevertheless, at the urging of his friend, King enlists the aid of a friendly and attractive witch and sets out to thwart Merlin, an evil genius living in Los Angeles, or at least a variant of that city, this one filled with Boschian architecture and creatures out of legends. DeChancie mixes technology, virtual reality, dreamscapes, and traditional fantasy themes and images with wild abandon, leavened with some dry humour, and propelled by a clever and fast-moving plot. The mixture of contemporary reality and magical otherness is carefully balanced and effectively presented. Despite a comparatively light tone, there's considerably more meat here than is found in the Castle books, a clear indication that he is potentially a writer who can break out into a wider readership.

—Don D'Ammassa

De HAVEN, Tom

Nationality: American. **Born:** Bayonne, New Jersey, 1 May 1949. **Education:** Rutgers University, B.A., 1971; Bowling Green University, M.F.A., 1973. **Family:** Married Santa Sergio in 1971; two daughters. **Career:** Managing editor, Magazine Associates, New York, 1973-76; freelance editor, 1977-80; adjunct professor of creative writing, Hofstra University, Hempstead, New York, 1981-87; assistant professor of American Studies, Rutgers University, New Brunswick, New Jersey, 1987-90; associate professor of American Studies, Virginia Commonwealth University, Richmond, from 1990. **Awards:** National Endowment for the Arts fellowship, 1979, 1986. **Agent:** Charles Verrill, Liz Darhansoff Agency, 1220 Park Avenue, New York, NY 10128, USA.

FANTASY PUBLICATIONS

Novels (series: Chronicles of the King's Tramp)

Funny Papers. New York, Harper and Row, 1985.
Joe Gosh (for children). New York, Walker, 1988.
Walker of Worlds (King's Tramp). New York, Doubleday, 1990; London, Roc, 1991.
The-End-of-Everything-Man (King's Tramp). New York, Doubleday, 1991; London, Roc, 1993.
The Last Human (King's Tramp). New York, Bantam, 1992; London, Roc, 1995.

Short Stories

Sunburn Lake: A Trilogy. New York, Viking, 1988; London, Penguin, 1990.

OTHER PUBLICATIONS

Novels

Freaks' Amour. New York, Morrow, 1979; London, Penguin, 1986.
Jersey Luck. New York, Harper and Row, 1980.
U.S.S.A. Book 1. New York, Avon, 1987.

Short Stories

Pixie Meat. N.p., Water Row Press, 1990.

Other

Neuromancer: The Graphic Novel, Volume 1, illustrated by Bruce Jensen (adaptation of William Gibson's novel *Neuromancer*). N.p., Epic Comics, 1989.

* * *

Tom De Haven is among those writers who are bringing to fantasy an intelligently hard-edged approach similar to that which was injected into science fiction by the cyberpunks a decade ago (it is no coincidence, perhaps, that De Haven has scripted a graphic-novel version of William Gibson's cyberpunk classic *Neuromancer*). To say that his well-received trilogy "Chronicles of the King's Tramp" is a fantasy about characters from our world finding themselves in another—trying to prevent the walls between worlds from being breached and the resulting chaos which would ensue—would be true; but such a summary would not highlight the magnificently quirky nature of the story. It is told partly from the view of the characters from the realm of Lostwithal—Jack, a Walker, Squintik, a Mage—and partly from the view of a group of 20th-century Americans including Jere Lee, a bag lady, Herb, the chauffeur to a pharmaceuticals billionaire who has some very nasty skeletons in his cupboard, Money Campbell, the billionaire's mistress, and Geebo, whom we first meet cleaning car windows after having his memory erased.

De Haven's staccato writing style sometimes strains too far for a hardboiled effect, but generally it works effectively to underscore the imagistic revelation of his strange series of cosmoses where animals can suddenly be invested with human consciousness and a

veritable bureaucracy of magic exists. Lostwithal is the human world of the Moment of Iss, just as our Earth is the human world of the Moment of Kemolo. (There is an "earlier" Moment, Feerce.) Its inhabitants operate a rigorous form of magic, underpinned by a philosophical system called Perfect Order. Walkers, for example, ramble the worlds and act as a combination of information-gatherers and detectives. As is traditionally the case, the very survival of the cosmos is at stake in the attempts of the Mage of Four, Mage of Luck to summon the Epicene which will tear into the legendary Fourth Moment, Bulcease, and open up all four Moments to its evil inhabitants, the Last Humans.

While many fantasies set up their world and moral conflict in the first three chapters, by the end of *Walker of Worlds* both characters and reader are still confused about how all this jigsaw fits together. But this is not the confusion of an ill-planned or shoddily-told story, rather the bewilderment of encountering a world which makes perfect sense—in its own terms. The cliffhanger De Haven leaves us with—as all writers in their first volume of a trilogy must do—is the feeling that billionaire Eugene Bowman, though sad, stupid, weak and guilty, is not exactly the human villain of the piece and that his adversary Peter Musik (an investigative journalist) may not yet be the hero. The climax of the second book is what in less imaginative hands would have closed the third.

While much of the appeal of fantasy is in the way the author creates an imaginary world, many creators are content to build from a relatively limited set of materials. De Haven's Lostwithal, in contrast, is as alien a world as anything packaged as science fiction. Its "Perfect Order" is as founded as any of our particular ideologies (and not without its controversies and "progressive/conservative" debates), but furthermore De Haven remembers that a hegemonic system is not necessarily explainable by all who live within it or understandable by all who come across it. What the human characters hear when Lostwithalian terms are spoken are phrases which are evocative—"The Book of True and Cruel"—but only partly explainable in terms of concepts they are familiar with. They deal with this as best they can—Peter Musik in desperate attempts to record and analyze, Bowman spending much of the second book in a fugue viewing imaginary TV shows—and their confusion adds to the verisimilitude of De Haven's imaginative invention. Some customs and terminologies, surreally incomprehensible on their initial glimpse, are revealed more fully on a later occasion. Others remain enigmatic, but by a word here, a laconic sentence there, a reflection of pattern and climax, a picture is revealed.

Meanwhile, those elements of the story told from the viewpoint of the Lostwithalians open their world's nature up to the reader without losing any shred of its ambiguous brilliance. The plot converges upon the Isle of Mites, where Perfect Order is weakest, to culminate in a climax which at once takes us towards the third volume. Several new characters, human and Lostwithalian, are introduced: the Art-Prince, Frank Luks the mercenary, the Anglophile Lostwithalian Ukrops with his souvenirs, and one who appears to be alien to both realms but whose concerns and nature we so far cannot guess. Along the way, Jack, a Walker, and his former lover Didge, a Dispeller, are given histories as real and as vivid as any of the Earthly ones, and their motives are similar but not identical to those which could be imagined for human characters.

De Haven knows that good fantasy lingers in the mind long after the book is finished. Even by the end of the third volume, *The Last Human,* there is much to puzzle over, and more new characters. The Chronicles of the King's Tramp may become known as one of the particular small excellences of the fantasy field. It uses the common features of the genre as its readers and writers have shaped it—the small group of characters fighting against a mysterious threat, the carefully imagined world, even the trilogy structure itself—and sharpens and polishes them. De Haven's characters are complex and varied, his non-humans arising as naturally out of their world as do those from environments we recognize: not the least delightful and skilful part of his craft is the way we suddenly begin to perceive Lostwithalians not as imaginary exotics but as "ordinary": the infinite ordinariness of real people. The author's story-telling is carefully shaped and gripping, with moments of terror and humour propelling the quest for self-knowledge which is the unacknowledged heart of each of the character's roles in the larger play. At times scarcely recognizable as genre fantasy, this sequence is one of the diamonds which lie at its heart.

—Andy Sawyer

DEITZ, Tom

Form of his name used by Thomas Franklin Deitz. **Nationality:** American. **Born:** 1952.

FANTASY PUBLICATIONS

Novels (series: David Sullivan; Soulsmith)

Windmaster's Bane (Sullivan). New York, Avon, 1986; London, Orbit, 1988.
Fireshaper's Doom (Sullivan). New York, Avon, 1987; London, Orbit, 1989.
Darkthunder's Way (Sullivan). New York, Avon, 1989.
The Gryphon King. New York, Avon, 1989.
Sunshaker's War (Sullivan). New York, Avon, 1990.
Stoneskin's Revenge (Sullivan). New York, Avon, 1991.
Soulsmith. New York, AvoNova, 1991.
Dreambuilder (Soulsmith). New York, AvoNova, 1992.
Wordwright (Soulsmith). New York, AvoNova, 1993.

*   *   *

Tom Deitz writes very convincingly (as far as his settings are concerned) about contemporary rural Georgia, USA, where he was brought up and still lives. In all his novels he is merely fictionalizing the name of the county. His David Sullivan books are set in Enotah County, his Soulsmith trilogy in Welch County. He brings fantasy into the lives of the inhabitants through the visits of figures of fantasy or through inherited special powers. Obviously, such an approach to a fantasy setting is intended to provide credibility and, to a certain extent, it succeeds.

What is unclear is whether Deitz is writing for an adult or a young-adult market. His characters are mostly teenagers. They live ordinary teenage lives—attending High School, driving their own cars, dating, worrying about their relationships with parents and with those they are or would like to be dating, skinny-dipping in lakes and rivers. To a certain extent this is plausible but banal. Clearly, too, it is intended as a convincingly normal bulwark to the fantasy elements. Yet it brings with it two distinct problems. The

first is that it is boring for the adult reader. The second is that it is all a little old-fashioned; surely this is a rose-tinted view of the Georgia of 20 or so years ago, when Deitz was growing up there, although it purports to be the present day. Where are the crime, the drug problems, the pregnancies, the almost ubiquitous sex, that are so much a part of today's real teenage culture?

Each of Deitz's books contains fresh, exciting elements (mostly fantasy-connected) and clumsy or over-familiar elements (mostly as part of the plot). Thus, there is a true thrill for any reader when, fairly early on in *Windmaster's Bane,* 16-year-old David Sullivan goes out at night and sees a large group of the Sidhe (immortal Irish faery-folk, human-sized or taller) riding across his father's farm—they are using a Straight Track, a kind of magical short-cut. Deitz's description of the Sidhe is full of fine detail. It is a moment of wish-fulfilment, for one can imagine that this is what the young Deitz (or, indeed, any of his readers) would like to have seen at a similar age. It is also an unbelievable coincidence, since David has just been reading about the Sidhe (and is therefore familiar with their personalities and bargaining rituals) and since he has just discovered that he possesses some supernatural powers, including the ability to see such creatures of magic. And it is a plot contrivance too, since if he had watched the Sidhe without saying anything or from a greater distance, none of the events in the series of novels would have come to pass.

The flaws of coincidence, contrivance and cliche run deeply throughout all of Deitz's plots—which also tend be over-complex. It is difficult for the careful reader to avoid the conclusion that the author is forever making his characters act in particular ways (often stupidly or out of character) purely in order to further the plot. A few examples are necessary. Too often David Sullivan is the only one (out of all members of humanity and faery) who can save the situation. Too often characters are kidnapped. Too often David Sullivan is present when exciting events occur. And in each of the David Sullivan books more humans learn the "secret" of the existence of faery and its magic.

Later books in the David Sullivan series make use of Cherokee and other Native American mythology, sometimes in conjunction with Celtic myth (a war in the lands of faery adversely affects the Indian spirit world, for example), though the awkwardnesses of complexity remain. With few exceptions, the scenes set in these fantasy worlds do not work well and are lacking in credibility.

Similar problems inflict *Soulsmith* and its sequels. Here we have Ronny Dillon, a 17-year-old who finds he has special powers just when he needs them. The plot is excessively complex, requiring much pulling of strings by the author and much explanation of details by one character to another. Coincidence again plays too large a part, with one less-than-credible twist following close on another in places. The central idea here is similar to that in Roger Zelazny's "Amber" series—all members of a family inherit thought-reading and other powers. While only the head of the family, the Master of Cardalba, will normally exercise these powers to their fullest, there are squabbles over who should be his heir apparent, with an illegitimate claimant and an unrevealed pair of twins (of whom Ronny is one and his "friend" Lewis is the other) causing complications.

The parallels between Deitz's two series are considerable. In each the teenage protagonist has a strong male friend and a tentative relationship with a teenage female, who is taken away from him. In each he develops some supernatural powers and must use them to defend himself against the greater powers of his enemies.

There is a tendency for Deitz's characters to be underdeveloped. For example, Ailill, who is David Sullivan's chief adversary in *Windmaster's Bane* and *Fireshaper's Doom,* is presented as wholly bad, with no redeeming features; he has no good reason to be vindictive against David and his family. Similarly, Matthew Welch, the Master of Cardalba, is a living testament to the old saying that power corrupts; he has insufficient reason to be as unpleasant towards Ronny and Lewis as he is. And the girlfriends of both David (Liz) and Ronny (Winnie) are nothing more than pretty faces who need to be rescued.

A notable exception to the last point is the Road Man, an enigmatic, earthy character whose inconsistencies and unconventional ways are the finest and most original ingredient in *Soulsmith.* He begins to teach Ronny about metal-smithing and life, stealing each scene in which he (as one of his strange alter egos, the Day Man, the Night Man or the Sunset Man) appears.

And an exception to most of the foregoing is *The Gryphon King,* in which the characters are mainly college students at the University of Georgia. One, Jason Madison, has to deal with an ensorcelled sword and a mummer's play which can raise the Devil, as well as with a rival half-brother. Although some of the plot elements are familiar, the greater maturity of the characters and the well-described college setting make this a more entertaining book for the adult reader.

To sum up, Deitz is a writer of some promise, whose novels possess unusual features and occasional elements of great originality. While his characters are mostly young adults, he tells a deeper and more complex story than one might expect for that readership.

—Chris Morgan

DELANY, Samuel R(ay)

Nationality: American. **Born:** New York, 1 April 1942. **Education:** Dalton School and Bronx High School of Science, both New York; City College of New York (Poetry Editor, *The Promethean*), 1960, 1962-63. **Family:** Married Marilyn Hacker in 1961 (divorced 1980); one daughter. **Career:** Writer from 1962; Butler Professor of English, State University of New York, Buffalo, 1975; fellow, Center for Twentieth-Century Studies, University of Wisconsin, Milwaukee, 1977; fellow, Society for the Humanities, Cornell University, New York, 1987; from 1988, professor of comparative literature, University of Massachusetts, Amherst. **Awards:** Nebula award, 1966, 1967 (twice), 1969; Hugo award, 1970, 1989. **Agent:** Henry Morrison Agency, PO Box 235, Bedford Hills, NY 10507, USA.

FANTASY PUBLICATIONS

Novels (series: Nevèrÿon)

Nevèrÿona; or, The Tale of Signs and Cities. New York, Bantam, 1983; London, Grafton, 1989.

Short Stories

Tales of Nevèrÿon. New York, Bantam, 1979; London, Grafton, 1988.

Flight from Nevèrÿon. New York, Bantam, 1985; revised edition, London, Grafton, 1989.
The Bridge of Lost Desire. New York, Arbor House, 1987; revised as *Return to Nevèrÿon,* London, Grafton, 1989.

OTHER PUBLICATIONS

Novels

The Jewels of Aptor. New York, Ace, 1962; revised edition, Ace, and London, Gollancz, 1968.
Captives of the Flame. New York, Ace, 1963; revised edition, as *Out of the Dead City,* London, Sphere, 1968; Ace, 1977.
The Towers of Toron. New York, Ace, 1964; revised edition, London, Sphere, 1968.
City of a Thousand Suns. New York, Ace, 1965; revised edition, London, Sphere, 1969.
The Ballad of Beta-2. New York, Ace, 1965.
Empire Star. New York, Ace, 1966.
Babel-17. New York, Ace, 1966; London, Gollancz, 1967; revised edition, London, Sphere, 1969; Boston, Gregg Press, 1976.
The Einstein Intersection. New York, Ace, 1967; London, Gollancz, 1968.
Nova. New York, Doubleday, 1968; London, Gollancz, 1969.
The Fall of the Towers (omnibus; revised texts; includes *Out of the Dead City, The Towers of Toron, City of a Thousand Suns*). New York, Ace, 1970; London, Sphere, 1971.
The Tides of Lust. New York, Lancer, 1973; Manchester, Savoy, 1979; revised as *Equinox,* New York, Masquerade, 1994.
Dahlgren. New York, Bantam, 1975; revised edition, New York, Gregg Press, 1977; London, Grafton, 1992.
Triton. New York, Bantam, 1976; London, Corgi, 1977.
The Ballad of Beta-2, and Empire Star. New York, Ace, 1975; London, Sphere, 1977.
Empire: A Visual Novel, illustrated by Howard V. Chaykin. New York, Berkley, 1978.
Stars in My Pocket Like Grains of Sand. New York, Bantam, 1984; London, Grafton, 1986.
The Star Pit, with *Tango Charles and Foxtrot Romeo* by John Varley. New York, Tor, 1989.
We, in Some Strange Power's Employ, Move on a Rigorous Line, with *Home is the Hangman* by Roger Zelazny. New York, Tor, 1990.
They Fly at Ciron. Seattle, Washington, Incunabula, 1992.
The Mad Man. New York, Richard Kasak, 1994.
Atlantis: Model 1924. Seattle, Washington, Incunabula, 1995.

Short Stories

Driftglass: 10 Tales of Speculative Fiction. New York, Doubleday, 1971; London, Gollancz, 1978; expanded as *Driftglass/ Starshards,* London, Grafton, 1993.
Distant Stars. New York, Bantam, 1981.
The Complete Nebula Award-winning Fiction of Samuel R. Delany. New York, Bantam, 1986.

Play

Wagner/Artaud: A Play of 19th and 20th Century Critical Fictions. New York, Ansatz Press, 1988.

Other

The Jewel-Hinged Jaw: Notes on the Language of Science Fiction.
New York, Dragon Press, 1977.
The American Shore: Meditations on a Tale by Thomas M. Disch—
"Angouleme". Elizabethtown, New York, Dragon Press, 1978.
Heavenly Breakfast: An Essay on the Winter of Love (memoir).
New York, Bantam, 1979.
Starboard Wine: More Notes on the Language of Science Fiction.
Pleasantville, New York, Dragon Press, 1984.
The Motion of Light on Water: Sex and Science Fiction Writing in
the East Village 1957-1965. New York, Arbor House, 1988; ex-
panded as *The Motion of Light on Water: East Village Sex and*
Science Fiction Writing 1960-1965, with The Column at the
Market's Edge, London, Paladin, 1990.
The Straits of Messina. Seattle, Washington, Serconia Press, 1989.
Silent Interviews: On Language, Race, Sex, Science Fiction, and
Some Comics. Hanover, New Hampshire, Wesleyan University
Press, 1994.

Editor, with Marilyn Hacker, *Quark 1-4.* New York, Paperback
Library, 4 vols., 1970-71.
Editor, *Nebula Award Winners 13.* New York, Harper, 1980.

*

Bibliography: *Samuel R. Delany: A Primary and Secondary Bib-*
liography by M. W. Peplov and R. S. Bravard, Boston, Hall, 1980.

Critical Studies: *The Delany Intersection* by George Edgar Slusser,
San Bernardino, California, Borgo Press, 1978; *Worlds Out of*
Words: The SF Novels of Samuel R. Delany by Douglas Barbour,
Frome, Somerset, Bran's Head, 1979; *Samuel R. Delany* by Jane
Branaham Weedman, Mercer Island, Washington, Starmont House,
1982; *Samuel R. Delany* by Seth McEvoy, New York, Ungar,
1985.

*   *   *

In a genre known for the youth of its practitioners, Delany published his first novel, *The Jewels of Aptor,* at the age of only 20.
Although containing some fantasy elements, *The Jewels of Aptor*
is post-apocalypse science fiction, sharing the same far future as
the more overtly science-fictional trilogy *The Fall of the Towers.*
Notable for deeply embedded mythological elements and colourful,
carefully worked-out backgrounds depicted with brilliantly concise
clarity, Delany's later science-fiction tales won both Nebula and
Hugo awards, but before the 1980s his only published works which
are unambiguously fantasy consisted of two short stories,
"Prismatica" and "Ruins" (both collected in *Distant Stars*), and a
pornographic novel with fantastic elements, *The Tides of Lust* (a
second pornographic novel, *Hogg,* remains unpublished). However,
beginning with a collection of linked stories, *Tales of Nevèrÿon,*
much of Delany's work in the 1980s was devoted to the Nevèrÿon
fantasy series, which also includes the novel *Neveryóna* and two
further collections, *Flight from Nevèrÿon* and *The Bridge of Lost*
Desires.
The series is ostensibly sword-and-sorcery fantasy set in a richly
detailed barbaric milieu and re-deploying tropes drawn from Robert E. Howard, John Norman, Fritz Leiber, Joanna Russ and others. Although consisting for the most part of linked stories, told

from several often conflicting viewpoints, nonetheless there is a
strong narrative thread. Untangled, it follows the enslavement of
Gorgik, his education and eventual liberty from slavery, and his
leadership of a rebellion to overthrow slavery which, after reversals and betrayal by his barbarian lover, at last wins him the title
Liberator. However, the main events of this central story often occur off-stage or exist only as allusions to past events or rumours
embedded in tales tangential to the main story. Delany is as much
concerned with showing how fact turns into legend as with narrative; one of the many threads that weave the series together is the
gradual revelation of the true story of particularly bloody political
intrigue amongst the ruling family of Nevèrÿon—on which is based
a rhyme chanted by children as they bounce rubber balls.
Thus, although the series draws deeply from and often playfully
alludes to its pulp antecedents, it is not concerned with the one-
dimensional heroics of those early sword-and-sorcery quest plots.
Although there are quests within several of the tales, none are
straightforward, and all are illuminated (some would claim obscured) by a searching self-critical light. "The Tale of Potters and
Dragons" starts out as the quest of two rivals, a potter's boy and
the young female secretary of a wealthy woman, for the source of
the rubber balls popular with children of the city; the tale ends,
amidst the ruined orchards falsely believed to supply the sap which
makes the balls, with the off-stage murder of the boy and the enlightenment of the secretary by a barbarian woman. For the secretary, the story is not a quest at all, but a rite-of-passage. The tale's
subversive irony is compounded by the commercial alliance struck
up by the potter and the wealthy woman at the ending.
Both the first story in *Tales of Nevèrÿon,* "The Tale of Gorgik,"
and the novel *Nevèrÿona,* are also rites-of-passage. In the first, the
mine-slave Gorgik attains redemption and liberty through palace
intrigue; in the second, a young girl learns just how hard it is for a
woman to escape from her original social context, but finally succeeds in doing so by the only acceptable route, which is to say,
Art. Just as the quests are inconclusive, or diverted to other ends,
so the lessons of rites-of-passage are as much internalized as applied to the world. Similarly, such quests as there are in the series
are inconclusive, or are diverted into other tales.
If the series is not straightforward narrative fantasy, nor is it,
despite the morass of details (often brilliantly evocative, but equally
often maddeningly stilted and deliberately artificial), primarily concerned with a fictive recreation—albeit with Nameless Gods and a
breed of flying, fireless dragons near extinction lurking at its borders—of a fabled prehistoric Eurasian/African civilization. Instead,
Delany is here at play, examining the origins of the multivalent emblematic signs through which meanings filter from one system to
another. In his critical works, Delany has stated his intense interest
in the science of signs, or semiotics, as it is applied to the themes
of sf. In the Nevèrÿon series, his intentions are underlined by the
essays and appendices which book-end the tales (some under nom-
de-plume K. Leslie Steiner, which Delany uses to critique his own
fiction) and which explicate (not always reliably) the extensive
meditations on the signs and signifiers of slave-collars, bouncing
rubber balls, barbarian swords, dragons and other iconographic
tropes embedded in the narrative.
The Nevèrÿon series can be read as an extended criticism not
only of the entire system of signs deployed within the fantasy genre,
but also of itself. It is a semiotic fantasy about the evolution of
ideas, their effect on society and the individual, and the mutative
flux of symbols and signs within that evolving system, set in a
time when the emblems of modern society were freshly minted—

money, markets, prostitution, corridors, fountains, slavery, paved roads, writing (which one of the characters transforms from a system of signs standing for *things,* to signs standing for *words,* and, by extension, *ideas*), and much more. An iron collar is not only the general sign for slavery, but, for Gorgik, and its closure around his neck, or around the neck of his lover, is the manifest sign of desire: in bondage, eroticism and economics are shown be inextricably mixed.

Much of that desire is homosexual, an important element of ancient cultures not much addressed by the fantasy field. Delany has given a searingly honest account of his bisexuality in *The Motion of Light on Water.* In the last part of *Flight from Nevèrÿon,* he contrasts the reactions of the inhabitants of Nevèrÿon to a sexually transmitted plague with his own reactions and those of the New York gay community to the first onset of AIDS. This intertwining of fantasy and documentary is the most affecting part of a complex and intellectually challenging metafiction.

The Nevèrÿon series has not changed the basic grammar of fantasy, nor is it likely to. Nevertheless, it is a bold experiment and an exhilarating although sometimes exhausting (and exhaustive) reading experience. It has defined a cutting edge which for the most part has yet to be colonized and extended by others.

—Paul J. McAuley

de LINT, Charles (Henri Diederick Hoefsmit)

Pseudonym: Samuel M. Key. **Nationality:** Canadian. **Born:** Bussum, Netherlands, 22 December 1951. **Family:** Married MaryAnn Harris in 1980. **Career:** Worked in retail records, Ottawa, Ontario, 1971-83; musician in Wickentree (Celtic band), Ottawa, 1970-85, and Jump at the Sun, 1990-92. Full-time writer and musician. Publisher/editor, Triskell Press. **Awards:** Small Press and Artists Organization award, 1982; William L. Crawford award, 1984; Canadian SF/Fantasy award, 1988; Readercon Small Press award, 1989; Homer award, 1992. **Agent:** Richard Curtis Associates, 171 East 74th Street, New York, NY 10021, USA. **Address:** P.O. Box 9480, Ottawa, Ontario K1G 3V2, Canada.

FANTASY PUBLICATIONS

Novels (series: Borderland; Brian Froud's Faerielands; Philip Jose Farmer's Dungeon; Moonheart; Urban Faerie)

The Riddle of the Wren. New York, Ace, 1984.
Moonheart: A Romance. New York, Ace, 1984; London, Pan, 1990.
The Harp of the Grey Rose. Norfolk, Virginia, Donning, 1985.
Mulengro: A Romany Tale. New York, Ace, 1985.
Yarrow: An Autumn Tale. New York, Ace, 1986; London, Pan, 1992.
Ascian in Rose (novella; Moonheart). Seattle, Washington, Axolotl Press, 1987.
Jack, the Giant-Killer: A Novel of Urban Faerie. New York, Ace, 1987.
Greenmantle. New York, Ace, 1988; London, Pan, 1991.
Wolf Moon. New York, New American Library, 1988.

Westlin Wind (novella; Moonheart). Eugene, Oregon, Axolotl Press, 1989.
The Valley of Thunder (Philip Jose Farmer's Dungeon). New York, Bantam, 1989.
The Hidden City (Philip Jose Farmer's Dungeon). New York, Bantam, 1990.
The Fair in Emain Macha (novella), with *Ill Met in Lankhmar* by Fritz Leiber. New York, Tor, 1990.
Drink Down the Moon: A Novel of Urban Faerie. New York, Ace, 1990.
The Dreaming Place. New York, Atheneum, 1990.
Ghostwood (Moonheart). Eugene, Oregon, Axolotl Press, 1990.
The Little Country. New York, Morrow, 1991; London, Pan, 1993.
Our Lady of the Harbour (novella). Eugene, Oregon, Axolotl Press, 1991.
Spiritwalk (Moonheart omnibus; includes *Ascian in Rose, Westlin Wind, Ghostwood*). New York, Tor, 1992; London, Macmillan, 1994.
Into the Green. New York, Tor, 1993.
The Wild Wood (Brian Froud's Faerielands). New York, Bantam, 1994.
Memory and Dream. New York, Tor, 1994.

Short Stories

The Oak King's Daughter: A Tale of Cerin Songweaver. Ottawa, Ontario, Triskell Press, 1979.
The Moon Is a Meadow: A Tale of Tam Tinkern. Ottawa, Ontario, Triskell Press, 1980.
A Pattern of Silver Strings: A Tale of Cerin Songweaver. Ottawa, Ontario, Triskell Press, 1981.
Glass Eyes and Cotton Strings: A Tale of Cerin Songweaver. Ottawa, Ontario, Triskell Press, 1982.
In Mask and Motley: A Tale of Cerin Songweaver. Ottawa, Ontario, Triskell Press, 1983.
The Calendar of the Trees. Ottawa, Ontario, Triskell Press, 1984.
Laughter in the Leaves: A Tale of Cerin Songweaver. Ottawa, Ontario, Triskell Press, 1984.
The Badger in the Bag: A Tale of Cerin Songweaver. Ottawa, Ontario, Triskell Press, 1985.
Three Plushketeers and the Garden Slugs. Ottawa, Ontario, Triskell Press, 1985.
The Rafters Were Ringing: A Tale of Cerin Songweaver. Ottawa, Ontario, Triskell Press, 1986.
The Lark in the Morning: A Tale of Cerin Songweaver. Ottawa, Ontario, Triskell Press, 1987.
The Drowned Man's Reel. Ottawa, Ontario, Triskell Press, 1988.
Berlin. Ottawa, Ontario, Fourth Avenue Press, 1989.
The Stone Drum. Ottawa, Ontario, Triskell Press, 1989.
Ghosts of Wind and Shadow. Ottawa, Ontario, Triskell Press, 1990.
Cafe Purgatorium, with Dana Anderson and Ray Garton. New York, Tor, 1991.
Hedgework and Guessery. Eugene, Oregon, Pulphouse, 1991.
Paperjack. Cheap Street, 1991.
Uncle Dobbin's Parrot Fair. Eugene, Oregon, Pulphouse, 1991.
Merlin Dreams in the Moondream Wood. Eugene, Oregon, Pulphouse, 1992.
Dreams Underfoot: The Newford Collection. New York, Tor, 1993.
The Wishing Well. Eugene, Oregon, Axolotl Press, 1993.
The Ivory and the Horn: A Newford Collection. New York, Tor, 1995.

OTHER PUBLICATIONS

Novels

Svaha. New York, Ace, 1989.
Angel of Darkness (as Samuel M. Key). New York, Berkley, 1990.
From a Whisper to a Scream (as Samuel M. Key). New York, Berkley, 1992.
I'll Be Watching You (as Samuel M. Key). New York, Jove, 1994.

Short Stories

De Grijze Roos (The Grey Rose). Antwerp, Een Exa Uitgave, 1983.

Other

Editor, *World Fantasy Convention, 1984.* Ottawa, Ontario, Triskell Press, 1984.

*   *   *

Unlike many authors whose output may be sectioned off under various headings—just one of which might be the catch-all "fantasy"—Charles de Lint's burgeoning body of work cannot be easily sub-categorized. Everything he produces bears a vague scent of the unreal and the other-worldly, whether it's a novel or a short story, and whether it's set in his baroque fictional small town of Newford, the carefully undeveloped (and thus quintessentially English) backwater Cornish village of Mousehole, or even a futuristic America in which the West Coast and Florida are underwater. Each setting bears the same delicate balance of the fantastic and the commonplace. And with each story, the reader gets the impression that this other reality does exist and, given the right circumstances, is within reach.

In 1991, de Lint—then already highly regarded for a string of novels, most notably the loosely-connected quartet comprising *Moonheart* and its successors *Ascian in Rose, Westlin Wind* and *Ghostwood*—produced *The Little Country,* building on and echoing many of the themes in *Moonheart,* and, in so doing, developing them considerably.

The Little Country tells the story of Janey Little, a successful singer who has returned to her family home in the small southern England village of Mousehole. Aside from her musical inspirations, Janey's life has been greatly influenced by two books written by her grandfather's friend, Billy Dunthorn, and she is delighted to discover, on rooting through the attic, a third book by Dunthorn, in manuscript form, entitled *The Little Country.* Janey begins to read the manuscript—which tells of the adventures of Jodi and her friend, Denzil Gossip, who live in the fictional town of Bodbury—and, as she does so, her world begins to change, subtly at first but building the further she gets into the book. Parallels soon show themselves, coming to a head with the introduction of the Manhattan-based Order of the Grey Dove, a secret society dedicated to the pursuance of Darkness and presided over by the Svengali-like John Madden.

Madden must have the book, at all costs. Enter Michael Bett who, posing as a *Rolling Stone* reporter, arrives at Mousehole to do an interview with Janey—Bett is, however, somewhat well-versed in the art of murder, and he takes every opportunity to hone his craft still further. Like Jonathan Carroll's *Bones of the Moon* (1987), *The Little Country* progresses by interspersing the events

in the two stories—Mousehole and Bodbury—and filling the proceedings with charm, excitement and, above all, complete believability. But there, all resemblance to Carroll ends. Indeed, it is the author's unerring knack of concentrating on his characters and filling them out, making them so real, that places his work at the forefront of the field.

In her introduction to his story "Timeskip" in *Year's Best Fantasy and Horror,* co-editor Terri Windling calls de Lint a pioneer of "urban fantasy": the description is so accurate that any attempt to paraphrase it would be pointless. Perhaps the most representative example of this approach of melding the mundane and the magical into an almost seamless whole is not a novel but a collection of inter-related short stories. *Dreams Underfoot* (subtitled "The Newford Collection") is the most engaging and consistently entertaining of his short-story collections, with each tale taking place in and around Newford, a fictional town built on the ruins of Old City, which now lies deep underground as a result of the Great 'Quake of the 1800s.

There was some talk of renovating the ruins of Old City as a tourist attraction—as had been done with the old, sunken town of Seattle—but the project proved to be unrealistic. Thus the labyrinthine streets, alleys and sewers of Old Town missed their opportunity to be yet another theme park and, instead, provide shelter for the inevitable motley collection of human flotsam and jetsam who make their fragile homes in the darkness and the damp. But there are entities other than bag ladies and drunks that inhabit the depths of Old Town, beings with their own rules and their own attitudes. And they have a habit of surfacing every now and again into Newford, where their comings and goings—and their own myths and legends—are recorded courtesy of local author/anthropologist/mystic Christy Riddell in his books *Underhill and Deeper Still* and *How to Make the Wind Blow.* More books-within-books!

As a palette from which to create word pictures, this home-grown mythology may sound "old hat" but it's actually extraordinarily innovative and refreshing. In Newford, de Lint gives us a microcosm of life and of American society, but he does it against a bizarre backdrop which co-exists with the everyday. Thus the town becomes a veritable beachhead between normality and abnormality. Blending H. P. Lovecraft's imagery, Lord Dunsany's poetry, Jonathan Carroll's surrealism and Alice Hoffman's small-town strangeness, de Lint's Newford stories are a haunting mixture of human warmth and cold inevitability, of lessons learned and prices to be paid. These elements are de Lint's stock-in-trade.

Lost in these fictional streets are a tweed-suited ghost who walks the same route every time it rains; a young boy with wire-cutters whose sole mission in life is to free chained-up bicycles; a race of elf-like troglodytes whose king must appear every full-moon in order to retain his throne; a woman whose belief is physically translated to a crow imprisoned within her chest; and a local variant on the Yeti who makes occasional forays into the back-alleys scavenging for food in the trashcans.

Amidst literary doffs-of-the-cap to Tolkien, Chesterton and Twain, and both contemporary and traditional musical references—including occasional mentions of the fictional band No Nuns Here—the participants assemble: faerie folk, magicians, hustlers and shucksters . . . painters, wizards, Earth Mothers, fiddlers and even ordinary people. They gather along the streets of Newford, standing well back from streetlights and sunshine alike, nestling in disused doorways and boarded-up subway entrances. And from there they steal reality, leaving in its wake a mixture of benign otherworldiness and dark apprehension . . . coupled with a lingering aftertaste of the indomitable strength of the human spirit.

—Peter Crowther

DENNIS, Ian

Nationality: Canadian. **Born:** Kingston, Ontario, 10 August 1952. **Education:** University of Toronto, B.A. 1975; M.A. in English, 1976 (editor, various student magazines). **Career:** Computer operator and supervisor, Ministry of Government Services, Toronto, Ontario, 1977-86; freelance computer consultant from 1986. **Awards:** Norma Epstein Literary award, 1976. **Agent:** Bella Pomer Agency, 22 Shallmar Boulevard, Penthouse 2, Toronto, Ontario M5N 2Z8, Canada.

FANTASY PUBLICATIONS

Novels

Bagdad. Toronto, Macmillan Canada, 1985; London, Allen and Unwin, 1986.
The Prince of Stars. Toronto, Macmillan Canada, and London, Unwin, 1987.
The Prince of Stars in the Cavern of Time (omnibus; contains *Bagdad* and *The Prince of Stars*). New York, Viking Overlook, 1989.

*   *   *

Ian Dennis's *Bagdad* and *The Prince of Stars* are highly unusual novels. Set in the *Arabian Nights* world of old Persia and Iraq, they tell the tale of the overthrow of the Caliph of Bagdad (sic) by the Ripe Fruit Party, and the subsequent troubles of the rump of the Royal Party. And it is a tale, told in a tale-teller's overblown declamatory style, full of action, incident, innuendo and arch asides.

> . . . the courtyard. Filling its grand squareness was a veritable liquid rainbow of people, soft yet bright, a surface that swelled and undulated on the stone floors with the motion of oceanic waters at dawn or dusk, or the tops of trees in the wind, seen from the crest of a high promontory . . .
>
> "How vividly the people smell!" remarked he aloud to himself. "They rise in your nostrils quite unlike attargul or incense or any other exotic fragrance . . ."

The style, though perfect for the story, is off-putting to the reader used to normal fantasy novels, and takes a long time to get used to. It is, eventually, worth the effort, because Dennis tells a good tale with the authentic ring of the mysterious east.

Zardin al-Adigrab, leader of the Ripe Fruit Party, breaks into the Caliph's impregnable palace through an impossibly dangerous underwater route, and single-handedly slaughters everyone he encounters, including the Caliph—or rather, three identical men who it turns out have taken it in turns to perform the tedious duties of being Caliph. A small group escape: the Caliph's chief concubine, who is the self-styled Empress, with her lovely lithe lover Amina, her son, the self-centred and utterly useless Prince of Stars, the Grand Vizier, the Captain of the Guard and a bodyguard, a couple of world-weary eunuchs and a boy—these last three classic Wise Fool figures who provide deep philosophical musings and light entertainment to the reader. This group heads off along the River Tigris towards Basrah, with Zardin al-Adigrab and a few followers in hot pursuit.

That is the entire plot of the first book, though not its entire content, because every time the characters pause for five minutes they tell tales to each other, and these—classic stories of princes and princesses and heroes and ordinary men having extraordinary adventures—are the real heart of the book.

The second book, a straight continuation of the first (it begins with Chapter Nine), relates the adventures of the two parties, the pursued and the pursuers, as they travel through the Rub al Khali, the Empty Quarter, and then cross the sea to Abyssinia—still telling wondrous tales all along the way. They are made captives, they escape, they meet fearsome desert Arabs and a strong but peaceful tribe of women led by the wise Younger Sister of Ramlat Ghafah. The Prince of Stars and the delightful Amina fall in love, but never get around to consummating it. In a strange setting of mountain slopes and valleys that exactly mirror each other, the two parties are mysteriously completely annihilated except for Zardin, and the Prince and Amina. Each thinking that the other party has slaughtered their own, the Prince and Zardin (who are revealed now to be physically identical) fight to the death. In the final chapter the Prince is back in Bagdad, installed as the new Caliph; but he leaves all the government to his new Grand Vizieress, Amina, and the Younger Sister, who becomes Special Guest Under-Vizier Responsible for Social Improvement and the Army—while he writes "optimistic history books which glorified the past and minimized current difficulties and were used in schools to train the children of the newly literate populace to read."

Has everything changed, or does all remain the same? Still in the Caliphal Palace are the two wives of the former Captain of the Guard, who flirt with young men and tell each other tales and muse on what has been and what is. The second book ends with this beautifully understated summary of the whole work:

> "Some people died," said Hind, "some people stayed alive."
> "Some virginities were lost," said Su'ad, and then pointedly added. "But new ones were created."
> "Some things changed, some things continued," went on Hind, banally.
> "There were great historical events!" cried Su'ad.
> "That Which Was Within was brought forth!"
> "That Which Was Without was hidden under the hill, too."
> "Were you under the impression that something happened?" Hind asked again.

This could perhaps be interpreted as: when all of life's events are but a story, what is reality? As with *The Canterbury Tales* and *The Decameron,* the true heart of these two books are the many tales related in them. As with Samuel R. Delany's Nevèr on books, several of the tales are about characters in the outer story, illustrating the process of the creation of myth and legend.

It is difficult to assess these works in comparison with standard fantasy novels, simply because they are so utterly different in both content and literary style. Judged purely on their own merits, however, they are unusual little gems.

—David V. Barrett

DEXTER, Susan (Elizabeth)

Nationality: American. **Born:** Greenville, Pennsylvania, 20 July 1955. **Education:** Lawrence County Area Vocational-Technical School, 1971-73. **Career:** Fashion layout artist, Fishers Big Wheel, Inc., New Castle, Pennsylvania, 1974-92. **Address:** 1510 Delaware Avenue, New Castle, PA 16105, USA.

Fantasy Publications

Novels (series: The Warhorse of Esdragon; The Winter King's War)

The Ring of Allaire (Winter King). New York, Del Rey, 1981; London, Fontana, 1987.
The Sword of Calandra (Winter King). New York, Del Rey, 1985; London, Fontana, 1987.
The Mountains of Channadran (Winter King). New York, Del Rey, 1986; London, Fontana, 1987.
The Wizard's Shadow. New York, Del Rey, 1993.
The Prince of Ill Luck (Warhorse). New York, Del Rey, 1994.
The Wind-Witch (Warhorse). New York, Del Rey, 1994.

*

Susan Dexter comments:

A wizard whose magic doesn't work. A sarcastic cat. A foundling unicorn. A pig-keeper's son. A blue-eyed dog. A cursed prince. A horse sired by the wind. A farmer's widow who can whistle the wind. The peddler who's had his shadow stolen . . . These are my companions when I sit down at my desk, or when I'm walking down the street—they've been in my head, squabbling and discussing and adventuring for years. Such a relief to get them onto paper at last, before it gets too crowded in there!

*   *   *

Susan Dexter works as a fashion illustrator and freelance artist, and moonlights as a fantasy novelist. This probably explains her relatively small output, though what she has produced is delightful classic fantasy. Her first novel, *The Ring of Allaire,* was the beginning of a trilogy, The Winter King's War. It was funny, touching, and human—qualities often lacking in high fantasy. Set in an imaginary medieval world, it is the story of Tristan, apprentice wizard who can't quite get it right. While this is a relatively commonplace theme, there are many twists and turns to the story, which also contains a delightful heroine, a number of well-drawn secondary characters, and a villain who is never seen but exerts enormous influence.

One day Tristan, 19 years old, is late coming home after gathering herbs and magic rocks. He is caught in what seems to be a storm, but when he arrives at the cottage he shares with his master, Blais, it is to discover the place in chaos and Blais dead. The wizard has managed to transfer his essence into a small incense burner, and leaves final instructions for Tristan to set out on a quest—a quest to find three things that will save the world from Nimir, the Winter King. First, Tristan must cross a dimensional barrier into our world and rescue Valadan, the warrior-stallion, from where he has been imprisoned in a run-down carousel. He must then find the Princess Allaire, guardian of the nine rings, where she is imprisoned in a magic sleep within Darkenkeep, Nimir's fortress. Then he must find the tenth ring, which will release Allaire's powers so she may wed the prince of Calandra, enabling him to become the king and defeat Nimir.

A formidable task for one young, inept wizard. Accompanying him on his quest is Thomas, a psychic cat and Minstral, a bird with magic in his song. After rescuing the horse Valadan (who is also psychic, and can converse with Thomas as well as Tristan), the apprentice wizard joins forces with Polassar, and they set out for Darkenkeep. Hundreds of other wizards have failed in finding Allaire, so Tristan is amazed when it is relatively easy for him. He is discovering, however, that he may be the most powerful wizard of them all—if he can just learn to control his magic.

Princess Allaire is awakened, and falls in love with her prince, Polassar. Tristan feels somewhat left out, and wonders if perhaps Allaire is not too bright, despite her sweetness and beauty; how can she possibly wield the power to defeat Nimir, even if they find the third ring? The solution to this puzzle is found when they are joined by Elisena, a mysterious witch they meet in the castle of an enemy lord who wants to steal Allaire from Polassar. Elisena helps them escape and then reveals that she is the real Allaire, disguised for hundreds of years in different bodies while her hand-maiden slept as the captive princess. Now all they need is the last ring, for which they must return to Darkenkeep. By the end of volume one, Tristan has fallen in love with Elisena, she has found her ring, and it has been discovered that Tristan, a foundling, is the real King of Calandra. Now all he has to do is convince his people . . .

In volume two, *The Sword of Calandra,* Tristan is married to Elisena, Polassar to Allaire, and they are living in a crumbling castle that contains a throne on which the King of Calandra must sit in order to be crowned. Unfortunately, without the king's magic sword it is death to sit on the throne, so Tristan and Polassar are off again, on a search for the sword that leads them to Koverlir, city of the mages, a down-on-her-luck Tarot card reader, and a master sword-forger who has foresworn his art. There Tristan is imprisoned, beaten up countless times, and finally has a new sword forged only to return home and discover the real one has been there all along, in the possession of a boy who wants to be a warrior. The newly-crowned King of Calandra and his queen manage to turn back the creeping winter that has overtaken Calandra and banished the other seasons, but now they face the task of uniting a country that has been without a king for about a century.

In volume three, *The Mountains of Channadran,* Tristan and Elisena discover that they have been unsuccessful in stopping the continuous winter forever. They travel north with Polassar and Reynaud, another wizard, in order to confront Nimir in his stronghold of Channadran. Thomas, Valadan and Minstrel go along, too, but at one point Valadan and the other horses are sent home, since they cannot brave the high mountains. This conclusion to the series is a disappointing one: Tristan seems to behave like a fool on far too many occasions, and like a sulky child on many others. Part of this is due to the fact that he detests the other wizard,

Reynaud, who proves himself to be a loyal friend at the end (which costs him his life—this is disappointing, too, since Reynaud is one of the most likeable characters in the book).

There is a good passage when the travellers stop at a white stone tower in order to ask the assistance of a man named Royston Ambere, lord of the birds. He helps them in their trek through the mountains, and his birds bring shipments of food to the travellers. Royston's daughter, Welslin Fateweaver, chooses Tristan as her hero (I think Reynaud would have been a better choice), giving him a small crystal which she tells him is her heart. When Tristan finally comes face-to-face with Nimir, who is definitely not human and barely qualifies as alive, it is Welslin's "heart" and his magic sword that save him and rid the world of the constant winter.

In a later novel, *The Wizard's Shadow,* Dexter progresses far in both technique, style and characterization. Set within the same world as the Winter King's War trilogy, this book is about a Peddler named Crocken who makes a bargain with the shadow of what he believes to have been a wizard. He agrees to accompany the shadow to the far away kingdom of Armyn in order that the shadow may be avenged on his murderers.

Once in Armyn, Crocken accidentally rescues a princess from being savaged by a wild boar, and is instantly proclaimed a hero. All is not right within the palace of Axe-Edge, however, with a prince whose bite is deadly, a visiting princess (from the kingdom of Calandra) who has taken a vow of silence until she makes him a betrothal shirt, and her lady-in-waiting, who has some strange and wonderful powers herself. Crocken, the reader discovers near the end of the book, is the sister of Crewzel, who was an adult when he was born—he hasn't seen her since. This book is a complete and satisfying tale in itself, but Dexter has since commenced another series, the Warhorse of Esdragon, opening with *The Prince of Ill Luck.* We have much to look forward to.

—Debora Hill

DIAMOND, Graham (R.)

Nationality: American. **Born:** 18 August 1945 in Manchester, England; came to United States in 1948; naturalized citizen, 1953; **Education:** Attended State University of New York, 1964-65. **Family:** Married Miriam Disman, 25 March 1967; two daughters. **Career:** Designer, Macmillan Publishing Company, Inc., New York, New York, 1968-69; editorial artist, *New York Times,* 1969—. **Agent:** Nat Sobel, 128 E. 56th St., New York, New York 10017, USA. **Address:** c\o *New York Times,* 229 W. 43rd St., New York, New York 10036, USA.

FANTASY PUBLICATIONS

Novels (series: Haven; Marrakesh; Samarkand)

The Haven. New York, Playboy Press, 1977.
Lady of the Haven. New York, Playboy Press, 1978.
Dungeons of Kuba (Haven). New York, Playboy Press, 1979.
The Thief of Kalimar. New York, Gold Medal, 1979.
Captain Sinbad. New York, Gold Medal, 1980.
The Falcons of Eden (Haven). New York, Playboy Press, 1980.

Samarkand. New York, Playboy Press, 1980.
The Beasts of Hades (Haven). New York, Playboy Press, 1981.
Samarkand Dawn. New York, Playboy Press, 1981.
Marrakesh. New York, Gold Medal, 1981.
Marrakesh Nights. New York, Gold Medal, 1984.
Cinnabar. New York, Gold Medal, 1985.
Forest Wars (Haven). New York, Lion Press, 1994.

*   *   *

Graham Diamond's first-published novel was *The Haven,* volume one of a Haven trilogy that segued—from the second book—into the still-open-ended Adventures of the Empire Princess series. The first Haven book is a besieged-enclave science-fantasy yarn, in the manner of *The House on the Borderland* (Hodgson), *Earth's Last Citadel* (Kuttner and Moore) and *The Last Castle* (Vance). This time, the Redoubt of All Humanity is menaced by sentient animals led by a lupine demadogue—as some wag (probably Baird Searles) once put it.

For the most part, these bioengineered/mutant woodland creatures become friends to what is left of Man. Diamond tries hard (in *The Haven* and beyond), but his pathetic-fallacy wolves lack the mythic grandeur of Jack London's Buck/White Fang. They talk human, act human, are human—with incongruous names like Cicero, Garth, Casca, and Hector.

The siege of Haven is duly lifted. Volume two, *Lady of the Haven,* concentrates on the eponymous princess-cum-wolf-leader, Anastasia (Stacy, for short), also known as Khalea ("bridge between sun and moon"), also known as AnaFara ("daughter of Fara—the Fate that guides all forest Dwellers"). Her saga continues in *Dungeons of Kuba, The Falcons of Eden, The Beasts of Hades* and, after a considerable hiatus, *Forest Wars.*

There is a faintly comic tinge to the name Stacy (recalling Alvin in Arthur C. Clarke's *The City and the Stars*). Other contemporary-sounding monikers—Trevor, Nigel, Desmond—also seem jarring in this far-future epic. Likewise place names like Aberdeen, Rhonnda, and Newfoundland. A sprinkling of more exotic nomenclature would not have gone amiss. But the whole is greater than the often jerry-built parts. Fellow-author Andre Norton called the Haven/Empire Princess series a "superb creation . . . I have been recommending it to all"—and quite right, too.

While the Haven books were still appearing, Diamond produced his first out-and-out fantasy novel, *The Thief of Kalimar.* The setting, as front-paper mapped by Edward Meehan, might be a parallel-world Earth, with land masses resembling Europe (Brittany, Aran, etc) and Africa (Land of the Baboons). Kalimar is a "vast land" located in north-west Africa (or wherever). Ramagar, the thief of the novel's title, acquires the "glittering scimitar" Blue Fire that rightfully belongs to a beggar who turns out to be more than he seems.

Diamond manages two memorable set-pieces, both displaying his affinity with the sea: an almost-descent-into-the-maelstrom; the Calling of the Sirens. And Mariana, the Thiefess of Kalimar, is no mere lust-interest bimbo. Andre Norton liked it: "An excellent story . . . absorbing . . . keeps one reading on eagerly" (back-cover endorsement).

Samarkand takes place in or near that very city, "where West met East at the crossroad of the world, the city through which all caravans must pass, home of a thousand trade routes from Damascus in the West to Cathay in the East." Kazir chieftain Tariq is the male protagonist: "The Kazirs were Samarkand, and Samarkand was them—even in the depths of their exile." In reality Samarkand (now called Zarafsha; population 481,000) was once the capital of Mongol-hordeing Tamerlane. However, Diamond didn't attempt some Harold Lamb-type (Genghis Khan/Sulieman the Magnificent/Tamerlane himself) fictional biography: his fantasized Samarkand comes under attack from the hitherto unknown-to-history Kabul the Hun and his great army. Magic *per se* is limited to the clairvoyant "Golden Rocks of Babylon" (pages 39-40). The novel-stealing female protagonist is Sharon (another faintly comic name, at least in the British Isles), "she who bears the mark . . . the one for which [Samarkand has] all reason to hope. With her there shall be a new glory"—and a sequel: *Samarkand Dawn.*

Marrakesh is another Arabian-Nights city that Diamond has made his revisionist own. Daniel, apprentice goldsmith and two-fisted poet, rescues the alluring Siana, whose grandfather turns out to be Ali (Forty Thieves) Baba. The poet Omar Khayyam pops in an out of the action, rather like Obi-wan Kenobi in the *Star Wars* films. "How Samiah, the dustman's beautiful daughter, joined the struggle to destroy the Assassins is unfolded [in *Marrakesh Nights*]. It all began when she met young Gideon, who wasn't really a rent collector after all" (blurb).

With *Captain Sinbad,* Diamond took the picaroon *Arabian Nights* hero, made famous once more by Ray Harryhausen special-effect movies, and turned him into a credible human being. An earlier film, Douglas Fairbanks Jr's *Sinbad the Sailor* (1947), is the nearest cinematic equivalent as far as the characterization is concerned—minus the body linguistics and demented grin. From the novel's introduction:

> "Nearly two centuries before Marco Polo began his wondrous travels to Cathay, at a time of history when the new religion of Islam was sweeping the world from Persia to the peninsula of Iberia, there lived in the fabled city of Baghdad a merchant by the name of Sinbad . . .
>
> "The tale told in these pages is nothing like those told by the lovely Scheherazade in *The Thousand and One Nights*. It is a new and accurate account of Sinbad the man, whose true exploits have never before been recounted . . .
>
> "This story reveals him as he actually was—hero and daring adventurer, yes—but no less a man, and thus as fallible and vulnerable as we all are. None of these facts was ever told by Scheherazade; indeed, the beautiful princess would surely have been dismayed to hear of them . . ."

Anyone expecting some oft-told tales about (say) the Roc of Ages will be disappointed—perhaps even bitterly so. Sinbad flees Baghdad after Schahriar the Caliph has taken (almost) unto himself Scheherazade, his betrothed. To help reclaim "Sherry" (her pet name), the captain goes looking for the Red Dahlia: "it was reliably reported that the owner of such a flower might have any wish granted . . . no matter how strange or difficult." Or so claims Don Giovanni, the talking bullfrog . . .

Sir Richard (*Arabian Nights*) Burton is probably laughing in his grave. And Sherry would have looked askance at Sinbad's enforced sojourn on the Greek isle of Phalos, where female pirates use him with the utmost barbarity. As ever, sword predominates over sorcery and common sense over both: Diamond prefers the natural-super to the supernatural. Even the Red Dahlia, once found, doesn't "work" in conventional Faerie fashion.

Graham Diamond has written several undeservedly neglected novels. Apart from the generous Andre Norton, few people have

taken him seriously as a fantasy author—yet he is better than, or at any rate no worse than, some writers who are now dragonhold names. *The Haven* and its sequels, and *Captain Sinbad,* provide more than enough justification for wider popularity.

—Graham Andrews

DICKSON, Gordon R(upert)

Nationality: American. **Born:** Edmonton, Alberta, Canada, 1 November 1923; emigrated to the United States at age 13. **Education:** University of Minnesota, Minneapolis, B.A. 1948, and graduate study, 1948-50. **Military Service:** United States Army, 1943-46. **Career:** Freelance writer, 1950—. **Awards:** Hugo award, 1965, 1981 (twice); Nebula award, 1966; Skylark award, 1975; Derleth award, 1977; Jupiter award, 1977. President, Science Fiction Writers of America, 1969-71. **Agent:** Kirby McCauley, 155 East 77th Street, New York, NY 10021, USA.

FANTASY PUBLICATIONS

Novels (series: Jim Eckert; Jamie the Red)

The Dragon and the George (Jim Eckert). New York, Doubleday, 1976; London, Grafton, 1992.
Jamie the Red, with Roland Green. New York, Ace, 1984.
Beyond the Dar al-Harb (Jamie the Red). New York, Tor, 1985.
The Dragon Knight (Jim Eckert). New York, Tor, 1990; London, Grafton, 1992.
The Dragon on the Border (Jim Eckert). New York, Ace, 1992; London, Grafton, 1993.
The Dragon at War (Jim Eckert). New York, Ace, 1993; London, HarperCollins, 1993.
The Dragon, the Earl, and the Troll (Jim Eckert). New York, Ace, 1994.

Short Stories

The Last Dream. New York, Baen, 1986.

OTHER PUBLICATIONS

Novels

Alien from Arcturus. New York, Ace, 1956; revised as *Arcturus Landing,* 1978.
Mankind on the Run. New York, Ace, 1956; as *On the Run,* 1979.
The Genetic General, Time to Teleport. New York, Ace, 1960; *The Genetic General* published separately, London, Digit, 1961; expanded edition of *The Genetic General,* as *Dorsai!,* New York, DAW, and London, Sphere, 1976.
Secret under the Sea (for children). New York, Holt Rinehart, 1960; London, Hutchinson, 1962.
Naked to the Stars. New York, Pyramid, 1961; London, Sphere, 1978.

Delusion World, Spacial Delivery. New York, Ace, 1961. *Necromancer.* New York, Doubleday, 1962; London, Mayflower, 1963; as *No Room for Man,* New York, Macfadden, 1963.

Secret Under Antarctica (for children). New York, Holt Rinehart, 1963.

Secret Under the Caribbean (for children). New York, Holt Rinehart, 1964.

Space Winners (for children). New York, Holt Rinehart, 1965; London, Faber, 1967.

The Alien Way. New York, Bantam, 1965; London, Corgi, 1973.

Mission to Universe. New York, Berkley, 1965; revised edition, New York, Ballantine, 1977; London, Sphere, 1978.

Planet Run, with Keith Laumer. New York, Doubleday, 1967; London, Hale, 1977.

The Space Swimmers. New York, Berkley, 1967; London, Sidgwick and Jackson, 1968.

Soldier, Ask Not. New York, Dell, 1967; London, Sphere, 1975.

None But Man. New York, Doubleday, 1969; London, Macdonald, 1970.

Wolfling. New York, Dell, 1969.

Spacepaw (for children). New York, Putnam, 1969.

Hour of the Horde. New York, Putnam, 1970.

The Tactics of Mistake. New York, Doubleday, 1971; London, Sphere, 1975.

Sleepwalker's World. Philadelphia, Lippincott, 1971; London, Hale, 1973.

The Outposter. Philadelphia, Lippincott, 1972; London, Hale, 1973.

The Pritcher Mass. New York, Doubleday, 1972.

Alien Art. New York, Dutton, 1973; London, Hale, 1974.

The R-Master. Philadelphia, Lippincott, 1973; London, Hale, 1975; revised as *The Last Master,* New York, Tor, 1984.

Gremlins, Go Home! (for children), with Ben Bova. New York, St. Martin's Press, 1974.

Star Prince Charlie (for children), with Poul Anderson. New York, Putnam, 1975.

Three to Dorsai! (omnibus). New York, Doubleday, 1975.

The Lifeship, with Harry Harrison. New York, Harper, 1976; as *Lifeboat,* London, Dobson, 1978.

Time Storm. New York, St. Martin's Press, 1977; London, Sphere, 1978.

The Far Call. New York, Dial Press, and London, Sidgwick and Jackson, 1978.

Home from the Shore. New York, Sunridge Press, 1978.

Pro. New York, Ace, 1978.

Masters of Everon. New York, Ace, 1980; London, Sphere, 198?.

Love Not Human. New York, Ace, 1981.

The Final Encyclopedia. New York, Tor, 1984; London, Sphere, 1985.

The Forever Man. New York, Ace, 1986; London, Sphere, 1987.

Way of the Pilgrim. New York, Ace, 1987; London, Sphere, 1988.

The Chantry Guild. New York, Ace, 1988; London, Sphere, 1989.

The Earth Lords. New York, Ace, 1988; London, Sphere, 1989.

Dorsai's Command, with Troy Denning and Cory Glaberson. New York, Ace, 1989.

Wolf and Iron. New York, Tor, 1990; London, Orbit, 1991.

Young Bleys. New York, Tor, 1991; London, Orbit, 1993.

Other. New York, Tor, 1994.

Short Stories

Earthman's Burden, with Poul Anderson. New York, Gnome Press, 1957.

Danger—Human. New York, Doubleday, 1970; as *The Book of Gordon Dickson,* New York, DAW, 1973.

Mutants. New York, Macmillan, 1970.

The Star Road. New York, Doubleday, 1973; London, Hale, 1975.

Ancient, My Enemy. New York, Doubleday, 1974; London, Sphere, 1978.

Gordon R. Dickson's SF Best, edited by James R. Frenkel. New York, Dell, 1978; revised as *In the Bone: The Best Science Fiction of Gordon R. Dickson,* New York, Ace, 1987.

The Spirit of Dorsai. New York, Ace, 1979.

In Iron Years. New York, Doubleday, 1980.

Lost Dorsai. New York, Ace, 1980.

Hoka!, with Poul Anderson. New York, Simon and Schuster, 1983.

Dickson! Boston: NESFA, 1984; revised as *Steel Brother,* New York, Tor, 1985.

Survival! New York, Pocket Books, 1984.

Forward!, edited by Sandra Miesel. New York, Baen, 1985.

Invaders!, edited by Sandra Miesel. New York, Baen, 1985.

The Dorsai Companion. New York, Ace, 1986.

The Man the Worlds Rejected. New York, Tor, 1986.

Mindspan, edited by Sandra Miesel. New York, Baen, 1986.

Stranger. New York, Tor, 1987.

Beginnings. New York, Baen, 1988.

Ends. New York, Baen, 1988.

Guided Tour. New York, Baen, 1988.

Other

Editor, *Rod Serling's Triple W: Witches, Warlocks and Werewolves.* New York, Bantam, 1963.

Editor, *Rod Serling's Devils and Demons.* New York, Bantam, 1967.

Editor, with Poul Anderson and Robert Silverberg, *The Day the Sun Stood Still.* Nashville, Nelson, 1972.

Editor, *Combat SF.* New York, Doubleday, 1975.

Editor, *Nebula Winners 12.* New York, Harper, 1978.

Editor, *The Harriers.* New York, Baen, 1991.

Editor, with Martin G. Greenberg and Charles G. Waugh, *Robot Warriors.* New York, Ace, 1991.

*

Bibliography: *Gordon R. Dickson: A Primary and Secondary Bibliography* by Raymond H. Thompson, Boston, Hall, 1983.

*   *   *

It once seemed that Gordon Dickson would never start writing fantasy. In the 1950s (one of his most prolific periods) he wrote stories based on almost any premise: humour, philosophy, a trick of logic. These apprentice pieces included westerns and radio plays, but the majority were solid science fiction. Only in the very late 1950s did he produce a small number of short fantasies, many of which segued into horror with demons and devils, cruel transformations, bitterness and death. There were rare comedies—"The Girl Who Played Wolf," "Ballad of the Shoshonu," "St. Dragon and the George"—but even these possessed a sharp note (e.g. the Shoshonu woman's human spouse learns she will turn into a dragon on their wedding night) and overly blatant moral lessons.

Then—apart from some occasional rewrites of fairy tales ("Operation P-Button"; "3-Part Puzzle")—Dickson seemed simply to stop writing fantasy until 1976. So it appeared. Yet examination of his science-fiction work reveals very strong fantasy elements: a changeling in *Wolfling*, a child of the gods who makes his final home among humans; the underground world of "The Seats of Hell" (1960; expanded as *The Earth Lords*) where dwarfish Lords and Ladies keep human slaves; the humorous *Gremlins Go Home* explains the Little People as an alien race marooned on Earth, still looking for a way home. In *Sleepwalker's World,* a power broadcast system has the side-effect of putting the entire world to sleep; the Old Man—the lord of shadows, immortal and secret ruler of our world—is using the power to oppose humanity's move into space. Rafe Harald, a modern Ulysses, returns from the moon to the dark tower of Earth, and the narrative becomes a straight battle between ultimate good and total evil.

Dickson's fiction continually utilizes *the* prime theme of myth and fantasy—the marvellous hero who must oppose a menace to his society or race. Courageous, dedicated and humble, he fights even though it means his loss or exile, or death; for heroes are temporary, created by the race to overcome an obstacle to our evolution, and thereafter expendable. Dickson's heroes may be self-willed and self-centred: movers and shapers, who can shape their own destruction or find a victory has turned to ashes, yet they remain true heroes—committed to the human race. Selfishness and cowardice are explored but never rewarded in a Dickson story.

Although he is often seen as a militarist, most Dickson narratives are actually about tolerance, imbued with respect for different belief systems. Should those beliefs prove inimical to life, or to human potential, then they can be opposed and destroyed; but in almost all stories, the human and the alien (or creature) finally form a partnership, based on the resemblances they find between their beliefs. In Dickson's realistic works, this bond is made between man and dolphin, or dog, or wolf; science fiction allows humanity to commune with aliens whose appearance is monstrous (or even worse, not quite human) yet whose inner souls are ethical, honourable, heroic or just.

The splendid Dilbians of *Spacial Delivery* and *Spacepaw* are ten feet tall, and resemble slim Kodiak bears on their hind legs; primitive, touchy and insular, they are also exceptionally moral, romantic, and quick-witted. The Hoka of *Earthman's Burden, Star Prince Charlie* and *Hoka!* are also ursine: looking like giant teddy bears, they not only appreciate human fantasies, they live them out—as cowboys, pirates, foreign legionnaires, or operatic spear-carriers, their absolute belief in human fictions and fables is naturally funny, and amazingly affecting.

Dickson's main endeavour, the "Childe Cycle"—to which his energies have been devoted for over 30 years—is designed to portray the evolution of "the responsible man." Dickson suggests that, since the Middle Ages, the human race has been evolving ethically: that we are gaining the powers of gods, allied with an increasing sense of empathy (rather than sympathy) that enables us to respond to the mistreatment of others by imagining ourselves in their place, and understanding their outlook. Empathy underlies those science-fiction plots of humans communing with aliens; often, the hero possesses the same mental outlook as the alien. In fantasy, this human-alien bond reaches the extreme: the human becomes the creature.

In his earliest fantasies, this was an inconsequential or cruel process, but in the comedies it became desirable and necessary to explore the resemblances and correspondences between species. Transformation is the basis of his most sustained fantasy creation, the series opening with *The Dragon and the George*. Dickson's first full-length fantasy novel begins with a college history teacher pur-

suing his vanished girlfriend—and waking inside the body of a dragon. Desperately trying to adapt to his new body, and to the complex circumstances, while continually misunderstanding what's happening, he finally has to battle an ultimate evil. The original novella (1957) is a pacey, brief sketch of the novel, but at its close the hero had only been transformed so he could learn a moral lesson which enabled him to face his employer. The novel is much more: one of the best fantasies ever written.

Dickson says it should be seen as alternate-world science fiction derived from his researches into the 14th century (research which is planned to be the basis of the historical Childe novels on the life of Sir John Hawkwood). Dickson walks an impossibly thin line between showing medieval life as it really was (short, dangerous, hard on peasants) and a gloriously romantic vision of noble deeds done for noble reasons. He shows the harsh physical effort really needed to carry a sword or lance for longer than a minute; and yet he has the direst evil defeated by the strength of a loving heart. His magical laws are developed with logic and rigour; characters remain ordinary humans even when imbued with mythic status; and there are sudden insights that jar the reader like a blow. The book's main joke "is the overall difficulty of a 20th-century person having with difficulty to adjust to medieval ways" and the comedy is splendidly sustained from first page to last.

Yet after this first brilliant Jim Eckert novel, Dickson left fantasy again—devoting his energies to the massively complex Childe Cycle. It was almost a decade before the collaborative *Jamie the Red*: a muscular fantasy on a large canvas, this tale of a wilful Scottish prince exiled to France, to meet fate, fortune and sorcery, is curiously flat and uninvolving. Clearly intended as the first of a series, there is only one sequel, written by Dickson alone: this short novel (*Beyond the Dar al Harb*) makes no mention of the original novel, and is a dense, *Arabian Nights*-type tale of revenge and treachery. Stylish, colourful, highly emotional, it is a pity no more were written.

The majority of Dickson's early short fantasies were compiled in *The Last Dream,* one of a flurry of books collecting all his brief works. Finally, a decade and a half after *The Dragon and the George,* Dickson wrote its sequel; or rather, three sequels in a mere three years. *The Dragon Knight, The Dragon on the Border* and *The Dragon at War* do not dilute the impact or power of the first book, but attention from fans has been less marked, probably because fantasy—especially comic fantasy—has exploded in popularity in the interim, and it is sometimes hard to pick the originals from the clones.

Jim Eckert of *The Dragon and the George* has chosen to live on that other world. Dubbed a Knight, and with the talent to transform himself occasionally into a dragon, the comedy that develops round Eckert is based (as Dickson rightfully says) on the fact Eckert "can't be a knight to save his life, even though he bears the name, because he wasn't trained from boyhood to be one. This is *Unknown*-type fiction." Eckert's skills in mathematics, logic, and history, solve many problems—but his inability to stop his medieval companions from thinking in medieval ways (rather than listening to his 20th-century Reason) causes arguments and misunderstandings. The light tone of the books hovers close to tragedy as readers are continually shown how these parfait knights and their ladies are also arrogant, snobbish, and narrow-minded; obeying restrictive and deadly social rules, they are quite capable of killing someone on principle if that someone happens to oppose anyone of a higher rank. The knights are chivalric, but only towards an ideal: real peasants and lesser mortals (such as cowards and foreigners) are of no actual concern or consequence. This brutish and insular approach, this lack of empathy, is common to all the characters, and continually shocks Eckert and the reader.

In these later books, Eckert is caught up in a magical war between England and France. England uses good men and true, plus magic, but France (it seems) is backed by Dark Forces which can (in *The Dragon on the Border*) animate murderous spirits of the dead, or ally with sea serpents in *The Dragon at War*. Yet in each novel, the real enemy is not what it appears—and the central concerns are not battles or tactics, but emotions: devotion, fortitude, courage, humility, commitment, cooperation and love.

Dickson may never produce the promised historical novels in the "Childe" sequence, but these fine books are history as we wish it had been, and fantasy as it should be written: funny, charming, satirical, melancholic and generous.

—Ian Covell

DONALDSON, Stephen R(eeder)

Pseudonym: Reed Stephens. **Nationality:** American. **Born:** Cleveland, Ohio, 1947; son of a medical missionary; lived in India, 1950-63. **Education:** College of Wooster, Ohio, B.A. in English 1968; Kent State University, Kent, Ohio, M.A. in English 1971. **Career:** Assistant dispatcher, Akron City Hospital, Ohio, 1968-70; teaching fellow, Kent State University, 1971; acquisitions editor, Tapp-Gentz Associates, West Chester, Pennsylvania, 1973; associate instructor, Ghost Ranch Writers Workshops, New Mexico, 1973-75. **Awards:** British Fantasy award, 1979; John W. Campbell award, 1979; Balrog Fantasy award, 1981, 1983, 1985; Saturn award, 1983; Science Fiction Book Club award, 1988, 1989; College of Wooster Distinguished Alumni award, 1989; Julia Verlanger award, France, 1990; Atlanta Fantasy Fair award, 1992. Litt.D. (honorary): College of Wooster, Ohio, 1993. Lives in New Mexico. **Agent:** Howard Morhaim, Room 709, 175 Fifth Avenue, New York, NY 10010, USA.

FANTASY PUBLICATIONS

Novels (series: Chronicles of Thomas Covenant; Mordant's Need)

Lord Foul's Bane (Covenant). New York, Holt Rinehart and Winston, 1977; London, Fontana, 1978.
The Illearth War (Covenant). New York, Holt Rinehart and Winston, 1977; London, Fontana, 1978.
The Power That Preserves (Covenant). New York, Holt Rinehart and Winston, 1977; London, Fontana, 1978.
The Wounded Land (Covenant). New York, Del Rey, and London, Collins, 1980.
Gilden-Fire (novella). Columbia, Pennsylvania, Underwood Miller, 1981.
The One Tree (Covenant). New York, Del Rey, and London, Collins, 1982.
White Gold Wielder (Covenant). New York, Del Rey, and London, Collins, 1983.
Daughter of Regals (novella). West Kingston, Rhode Island, Grant, 1984.

The Mirror of Her Dreams (Mordant's Need). London, Collins, and New York, Del Rey, 1986.
A Man Rides Through (Mordant's Need). New York, Del Rey, and London, Collins, 1987.

Short Stories

Daughter of Regals and Other Tales. New York, Del Rey, 1984; expanded edition, London, Fontana, 1987.

Other

Editor, *Strange Dreams: Unforgettable Fantasy Stories.* New York, Bantam, 1993; London, HarperCollins, 1994.

OTHER PUBLICATIONS

Novels

The Man Who Killed His Brother (as Reed Stephens). New York, Ballantine, 1980.
The Man Who Risked His Partner (as Reed Stephens). New York, Ballantine, 1984.
The Man Who Tried to Get Away (as Reed Stephens). New York, Ballantine, and London, Collins, 1990.
The Gap Into Conflict: The Real Story. London, Collins, 1990; New York, Bantam, 1991.
The Gap Into Vision: Forbidden Knowledge. New York, Bantam, and London, HarperCollins, 1991.
The Gap Into Power: A Dark and Hungry God Arises. New York, Bantam, and London, HarperCollins, 1992.
The Gap Into Madness: Chaos and Order. New York, Bantam, and London, HarperCollins, 1994.

Other

Epic Fantasy in the Modern World: A Few Observations. Kent, Ohio, Kent State University Libraries, 1986.

*

Critical Studies: *The Atlas of The Land* by Karen Wynn Fonstad, New York, Del Rey, 1985.

Manuscript Collection: Kent State University Libraries, Kent, Ohio.

Stephen R. Donaldson comments:

I consider myself a student of the relationship/tension between epic vision and mundane reality. Epic vision deals with heroism and glory, mystery and transcendence. Mundane reality deals in—to use Sartre's phrase—"futile passion". Most of us are able to dream "epic vision," but we live "mundane reality." We probably wouldn't be human without both, and yet we're lost in the apparent conflict between them. In one way or another, this conundrum seems to be the essential theme of all my work.

*   *   *

Stephen R. Donaldson's is one of the most remarkable literary success stories. He spent years labouring on the first trilogy of the

Chronicles of Thomas Covenant, while it was rejected by 47 publishers on the grounds that the central character's predicament would make it unacceptable to readers—but when it was finally bought and published the trilogy became a huge spontaneous bestseller. It is interesting to know that the editorial staff of so many publishers can be utterly and unanimously wrong in their considered judgment of what the reading public will like and respond to.

The editors who rejected the books could not believe that readers would be willing to identify with a leper; they were not only wrong but spectacularly wrong. *Lord Foul's Bane, The Illearth War* and *The Power That Preserves*—which add up to a three-decker novel rather than a trilogy in the conventional sense, although the first two volumes dutifully bring the hero back from the Secondary World in order to provide appropriate textual breaks—and their similarly-structured follow-up threesome, *The Wounded Land, The One Tree* and *White Gold Wielder,* demonstrated that vast numbers of readers were not only prepared to immerse themselves in the plight of a man with a particularly horrible disease, but were avid to do so. They were prepared to be absolutely fascinated by that character's translocation into a secondary world whose history, geography and metaphysics reflected that predicament, so that his struggle for survival as a social being became inextricably entwined with the demand that he play saviour to an entire world. They were enthusiastic to participate in his quest, which was explicitly stated to be a hard battle against his own unbelief, primarily directed against an enemy which personified the determination of others to despise him. In making Covenant's adversary—his satan, in the literal meaning of the term—a Despiser, Donaldson seemingly got down to the nitty-gritty of everyday experience of anxiety in a new way, so that the Chronicles seemed to many of its readers to be a revelation.

An important aspect of the runaway success of the Chronicles was that it caught the imagination of many female readers. There is a definite propriety, if not a certain inevitability, about the fact that the real protagonist of the Second Chronicles of Thomas Covenant is Linden Avery. When Donaldson began to experiment with a very different narrative voice in the novella *Daughter of Regals*—which might be regarded as a preliminary sketch for the two-part novel *Mordant's Need*—he used a female protagonist again. Females have more than a head start in the everyday routines of being despised, feeling guilty and taking blame, and these characteristics can be easily attached to female characters in stories. Terisa Morgan, the female hero of *The Mirror of Her Dreams* and *A Man Rides Through* (*Mordant's Need*), does not need to be diseased, nor to commit some evil act (Covenant commits a rape while still convinced that he is dreaming) in order that the reader may believe in her utter lack of self-esteem. The picaresque space opera contained in the "Gap" series of science-fiction novels also deploys a female character, Morn Hyland, as its one and only innocent.

Much heroic fantasy is masculine in character, celebrating the joys of machismo and the values of lusty barbarism or chivalrous nobility against supposedly-corrupt civility or mundane amiability, but Donaldson's work is very different. The heroism of his protagonists is fundamentally patient and resilient, becoming active and assertive only occasionally and with great difficulty. Whatever physical power Donaldson's characters have is not only magical, but locked up within them, mysteriously beyond the reach of conscious control; they usually do not believe that they have it, and sometimes—as in *Daughter of Regals*—have powerful, if misleading, reasons to believe that they do not have it. Nor, for the most part, do his male and female heroes compensate for their lack of physical power with exceptional cleverness; although they are no

fools they always lack the information necessary to help them reason their way through their predicaments.

The fact that Thomas Covenant cannot consciously command his own magical power seems to make him incapable of moral action—he must often stand by, raging helplessly, while evil is done which he does not know how to prevent, and when power finally does erupt from his ring he is as helpless to direct it as those who suffer its wrath—but this serves to make his plight all the more interesting. This deeply-felt uncertainty about the propriety of any and every action brings a quality of exaggerated suspense to the Second Chronicles which very few fantasy novels have, creating the space for an unexpected and unusual conclusion.

Although he is the son of a missionary Donaldson is not much given to preaching—his dissent from the message of traditional preachers is made abundantly clear by the chapter of the Chronicles ironically entitled "The Danger of Dreams" and by the novella "Ser Visal's Tale"—but he is steadfastly aligned on the side of the angels. The moral import of his fantasies is their very heart and soul; few other writers in the genre are capable of reaching such a terrible pitch of indignation and horror at the contemplation of the human capacity for abusing others. Coolly clinical critics sometimes complain about the purple effect this has on his literary style, but it undoubtedly touches a chord in his readers. This intensity is also conducive to extreme long-windedness—the two volumes of *Mordant's Need* maintain a narrative of considerable intricacy, set in a single location for nearly three-quarters of its total length (which is well over half a million words)—but that too is something which many fantasy readers like.

Donaldson's pseudonymous mystery stories have not enjoyed the same success as his other works, and it remains to be seen whether his venture into science fiction will be as successful as his fantasies, but he remains a unique and very interesting writer. The awesome rhetorical passion of his work may occasionally carry him into unproductive territory—as it seems to do in some passages in the middle volume of the Second Chronicles and the peripatetic sequence of *Mordant's Need*—but it is also responsible for the powerful driving force of his narratives and their undoubted climactic triumphs, and it is worthy of admiration.

—Brian Stableford

DOUGLAS, Carole Nelson

Nationality: American. **Born:** Carole Nelson, Everett, Washington, 5 November 1944. **Education:** College of St. Catherine, St. Paul, Minnesota, 1962-66, B.A. in speech and theatre and English Literature. **Family:** Married Sam Scott Douglas in 1967. **Career:** Reporter and feature writer, St. Paul *Dispatch* and *Pioneer Press,* 1967-83; columnist for various magazines; freelance writer from 1984. **Agent:** Howard Morhaim Literary Agency, 175 Fifth Avenue, Room 709, New York, NY 10010-7848, USA. **Address:** 3920 Singleleaf Lane, Fort Worth, TX 76133-6821, USA.

FANTASY PUBLICATIONS

Novels (series: Sword & Circlet; Taliswoman)

Six of Swords (Sword & Circlet). New York, Del Rey, 1982; London, Corgi, 1985.

Exiles of the Rynth (Sword & Circlet). New York, Del Rey, 1984; London, Corgi, 1986.

Keepers of Edanvant (Sword & Circlet). New York, Tor, 1987; London, Corgi, 1988.

Heir of Rengarth (Sword & Circlet). New York, Tor, 1988; London, Corgi, 1989.

Seven of Swords (Sword & Circlet). New York, Tor, 1989; London, Corgi, 1990.

Cup of Clay (Taliswoman). New York, Tor, 1991.

Seed Upon the Wind (Taliswoman). New York, Tor, 1992.

OTHER PUBLICATIONS

Novels

Amberleigh. New York, Jove, 1980.

Fair Wind, Fiery Star. New York, Jove, 1981; revised edition, New York, Tor, 1993.

Her Own Person. New York, Ballantine, 1982.

In Her Prime. New York, Ballantine, 1982.

The Best Man. New York, Ballantine, 1983.

Lady Rogue. New York, Ballantine, 1983.

Azure Days, Quicksilver Nights. New York, Bantam, 1985.

Probe. New York, Tor, 1985.

The Exclusive. New York, Ballantine, 1986.

Counterprobe. New York, Tor, 1988.

Crystal Days. New York, Bantam, 1990.

Crystal Nights. New York, Bantam, 1990.

Good Night, Mr. Holmes. New York, Tor, 1990.

Good Morning, Irene. New York, Tor, 1991.

Irene at Large. New York, Tor, 1992.

Catnap. New York, Tor, 1992.

Pussyfoot. New York, Tor, 1993.

Irene's Last Waltz. New York, Tor, 1994.

Cat on a Blue Monday. New York, Tor, 1994.

Cat in a Crimson Haze. New York, Tor, 1995.

*

Carole Nelson Douglas comments:

I had already sold publishers two long historical novels, one a post-feminist Gothic set in 1893 Ireland and the other a female swashbuckler and coming-of-age tale with a fantasy element set during the English Civil War in the 1640s, when I decided to write a fantasy proper. Looking back, I see that a fantasy element often touches my writing. My current Midnight Louie mystery series stars a detective cat that narrates his own chapters in his own voice. My other mystery series, about the only woman to outwit Sherlock Holmes, Irene Adler, features an appearance by the Golem of Prague in its fourth instalment, *Irene's Last Waltz.* I've also written a novella in which Irene Adler meets Bram Stoker's Dracula.

What intrigued me when I began my first fantasy novel, *Six of Swords,* was the challenge of world-building: creating credible but extravagant new worlds for my characters to explore and inhabit. I soon discovered that fantasy writing draws on the deepest subconscious themes. My "made-up" worlds—and the creatures and objects with which I populated them—quickly revealed themselves as metaphors for the personal and psychological issues my characters faced. Although I've also written novels published as science fiction, historical and contemporary romance, and mystery, I find

fantasy the most difficult genre to write. Fantasy requires both writer and reader to dig most deeply into the substrata of the human psyche.

*   *   *

The most obvious aspect of Carole Nelson Douglas's writing is its sheer variety. She has written mystery and romance, historical novels, science fiction and fantasy; and yet there are common threads through them all. Her work seldom manages to avoid just a touch of outrageous fantasy. The Midnight Louis mystery series has an overweight cat (19.8 pounds of puss) as one of its protagonists. He shares the honours with high-heel-loving female denizen of Las Vegas, Ms Temple Barr. Ms Barr is merely trying to go about her life, and her job as a publicist, in a normal fashion—but bodies keep getting in the way. Midnight Louis himself is interested in food, in satisfying his curiosity, and in "little dolls"; in this age of feminism, only a cat could get away with referring to women, feline or otherwise, as "little dolls". His voice is that of a modern-day private eye in the Mike Hammer tradition.

Douglas's other mystery series, the Irene Adler adventures, also makes forays into the world of fantasy. Irene is *"the* woman" in Sherlock Holmes's life—not a romantic interest, of course, she merely intrigues him with her brilliance. She sets out to solve mysteries with a liberated husband, and a female Watson of her own. She has occasion to bump up against Holmes now and then, and sometimes bests him. No social barriers are able to constrain her; and in the gaslit era of Sherlock Holmes that must count as fantasy of a sort.

In *Cup of Clay,* book one of the Taliswoman series, a newspaper reporter named Alison Carver is somehow transported from her family's woodland retreat to a land of fantasy and rigid structures, known as Veil. As is usually the case, this world's ways of life are not to the benefit of women. Many women are treated well, in harem-like quarters, but they have no opinions or public thoughts, for none are allowed. This is a land of contrasts: there is kindness, but only for the perfect; there is honour, but only in proscribed ways. The first children Carver meets are the Littlelost; those who have been abandoned and exiled by their parents because of "deformities," such as crossed eyes or stuttering, and who experience things in common with most uncherished children of our world. They are used by vicious men known as takers, to help them harvest Etherion, a highly prized plant product.

This is a hellish environment for a feature writer who has just done a piece on the conviction of brutal child abusers, and who has unresolved issues from the accidental death of her own sister, not to mention her relationship with her less-than-wonderful brother. She also meets Rowan, a man who has been trained to be a hero from birth, and finds that she shares the scarring on her neck (from a childhood accident) with him. He believes her to be a man despite all evidence to the contrary. She is dressed as a man and therefore is one, in his opinion. Rowan is on a quest to become the guardian of the Cup of Earth, and all hell breaks loose when Carver is chose instead. Rowan has been taught to be one-dimensional, and that dimension is himself and his quest. Alison Carver befriends the children, breaks the rules of womanhood in this strange place, and even begins to make Rowan see sense. This is helped by the fact that one of the Littlelost is Rowan's sibling. He begins to question the right and wrong of abandoning those who are less than perfect. When she returns to her woodland home in our world, the cup comes with her.

By the second book in the series, *Seed Upon the Wind,* the absence of the cup has taken its toll upon the parallel land of Veil. Without the Cup of Earth and its protective powers, Veil has succumbed to a number of ills. Carver and Rowan fight together to rid the lands of its unwanted new dangers, and Rowan, self-centered though he might still be, is committed to helping the Littlelost. The sense of strong personal involvement in these novels is admirable: they approach real and everyday problems with a new eye. No senseless wars here; when these characters fight, they have a real reason to do so.

In *Keepers of Endanvant* book one of Sword and Circlet, the Torloc and the humans are at odds. It is up to one Torloc female, a seeress named Irissa and her human lover, Kendric, the Wrathman, who has gained magical powers through bed-bond with Irissa, to brings matters to a better pass. Theirs is the unenviable job of battling the wizard Geronfrey. They end up as exiles, unable to travel through the Gates between worlds, and forever on guard against Geronfrey. By the third book in the series, *Seven of Swords,* 18 years have passed and they have two children, a daughter, Javelle, and a son, Thane. Thane is blessed with magical powers, but Javelle is not, and when their father needs help it is his skill and talents that must prevail. The story of how they do so is exciting and well-crafted.

Carole Nelson Douglas is a writer of talent and imagination, who has a knack of keeping a story interesting through many volumes. One way she has of doing this is to keep changing the story, and to make each book complete and whole in itself. It doesn't really matter where you start in any of her series; you will understand what is happening and enjoy the discoveries she has created for you.

—Sandra Brandenburg

DREW, Wayland

Nationality: Canadian. **Born:** Oshawa, 12 September 1932. **Education:** Oshawa Collegiate and Vocational Institute; University of Toronto. **Family:** Married Gwendolyn Drew in 1957; one son, three daughters. **Agent:** Amanda Urban, International Creative Management, 40 West 57th Street, New York, NY 10019, USA.

Fantasy Publications

Novels

Dragonslayer (novelization of screenplay). London, Fontana, and New York, Del Rey, 1981.
Willow (novelization of screenplay). New York, Del Rey, and London, Sphere, 1988.

Other Publications

Novels

The Wabeno Feast. Toronto, Anasi, 1973.

The Erthring Cycle. New York, Nelson Doubleday, 1986.
   The Memoirs of Alcheringia. New York, Del Rey, 1984.
The Gaian Expedient. New York, Del Rey, 1985.
The Master of Norriya. New York, Del Rey, 1986.
Batteries Not Included (novelization of screenplay). New York, Berkley, 1987.
Halfway Man. Ottawa, Ontario, Oberon Press, 1989.

Other

Superior: The Haunted Shore, with Bruce Littlejohn. Toronto, Gage, and New York, Beaufort, 1975.
Brown's Weir (travel), with Gwendolyn Drew. Ottawa, Ontario, Oberon Press, 1983.
A Sea Within: The Gulf of St. Lawrence (travel), with Bruce Littlejohn. Toronto, McClelland and Stewart, 1984.

*   *   *

It is difficult to write a novelization of a movie screenplay and create something worthwhile in its own right. The author is hampered by the limitations of a plot that cannot be altered, and the amount of embellishment is often strictly limited. Wayland Drew's fantasy novels are both film novelizations, although he has written original fiction of his own, including a science-fiction trilogy that has much of the feel of traditional fantasy. It is interesting to note, however, that in both cases, the books were subsequently reprinted in editions that deleted from the cover all mention of the original inspiration, that both were expected to sell on their own merits.

Dragonslayer is based on the screenplay by Hal Barwood and Matthew Robbins from the very popular Disney film. Galen is a young man apprenticed to Ulrich, an aging sorcerer. When Valerian and a group of representatives from a distant village appeal for help against a rampaging dragon, Ulrich proves too feeble to undertake the journey. Full of himself, Galen convinces the delegation that he can undertake the task in his master's place, but his subsequent attempt to imprison the dragon in its mountain cave only makes the situation worse. He has also discovered that Valerian is actually a young woman, disguised as a man to escape the lottery system that periodically sacrifices young women to appease the dragon.

Intrigue follows as the king reacts angrily to Galen's interference, preferring to avoid risking the dragon's displeasure by continuing the lottery, which has been rigged to exclude his own daughter. She discovers what her father has done and exposes the fraud, subsequently losing her life despite Galen's attempt to save her. Galen remains determined to correct his past mistakes, however, and penetrates into the dragon's lair for the first in a series of climactic scenes that are nearly as effective in the novel as they were in the film. Ulrich returns for the final battle in a plot twist that verges on the implausible, and the dragon is finally defeated. Credit for the victory is claimed by more than one party, however, and Galen and Valerian are repulsed enough by the circumstances to seek a new life elsewhere.

Drew has done an excellent job of translating the film to words, adding considerable amounts of dialogue and descriptive text that help bring the fantasy world to life. There's some additional material on the origin and nature of dragons, the king is fleshed out considerably, and the satire involving the self-styled religious leader who claims responsibility for the death of Vermithrax is much better than in the filmed version. It's still the book of the movie, but it's also an interesting novel in its own right.

Willow is a very different story. Based on a screenplay by Bob Dolman and the original story by George Lucas, it pulls together a number of conventions from literary and cinematic fantasies. Willow Ulfgood discovers a Daikini child floating in the river, and that event changes his life forever. The child has been set adrift to save her from the sorceress Bavmorda, who fears a prophecy that such a child will someday end her rule.

Willow is a would-be magician from Nelwyn, although his magic doesn't quite work. When Death Dogs from the sorceress come in search of the child, he is entrusted with her safety and ordered to lead the pursuers away from Nelwyn and find her a proper home among her own kind. The early stages of the journey are enlivened with a campfire story which appears to be original to the book.

Eventually they encounter Madmartigan, a Daikini, and a bit of a rogue. Reluctantly, Willow turns over the child, but his doubt is well founded. In an attempt to correct his mistake, Willow and his companions are captured by the Brownies, and after a series of captures and escapes reclaim the child and fall in with Madmartigan once again. The plot proceeds at breakneck pace from there onward, with battles, monsters, and chases until the final confrontation, when Madmartigan proves himself honorable and a hero after all, and Willow proves himself as well. Bavmorda is thwarted in her efforts to destroy the child and perishes along with her evil empire.

There was less room in this novelization for Drew to improvise. The plot is complex and involves so much physical action that much of the story is merely a transcription of the film. There is a brief epilogue and a pair of original tales embedded in the text, as well as a better development of Willow as a person, although the rest of the characters remain fairly flat. It's a competently done work, but remains the sketch of a novel with little value separate from the film, where *Dragonslayer* is interesting in itself.

Although Drew has proven himself capable of writing original works of interest, none of these have as yet been fantasy. It remains to be seen whether he will return to that genre with original work.

—Don D'Ammassa

DUANE, Diane (Elizabeth)

Nationality: American. **Born:** New York City, 18 May 1952. **Education:** Roosevelt High School, New York; Dowling College, Oakdale, New York, 1970-71; Pilgrim State Hospital School of Nursing, Brentwood, New York, 1971-74, R.N., specializing in psychiatry, 1974. **Family:** Married the writer Peter Morwood (*q.v.*) in 1987; they reside in Ireland. **Career:** Staff nurse, Payne Whitney Clinic, New York, 1974-76; assistant to writer David Gerrold, 1976-79; freelance writer from 1979. **Agent:** Donald A. Maas, 157 West 57th Street, Suite 1003, New York, NY 10019, USA. **Address:** c/o Pocket Books, Simon and Schuster Building, 1230 Avenue of the Americas, New York, NY 10020, USA.

FANTASY PUBLICATIONS

Novels (series: Tale of the Five; Wizardry)

The Door into Fire (Tale of the Five). New York, Dell, 1979; London, Magnum, 1981.

So You Want to Be a Wizard? (Wizardry). New York, Delacorte Press, 1983; London, Corgi, 1991.
The Door into Shadow (Tale of the Five). New York, Bluejay, 1984; London, Corgi, 1991.
Deep Wizardry. New York, Delacorte Press, 1985; London, Corgi, 1991.
Keeper of the City, with Peter Morwood. New York, Bantam, 1989.
High Wizardry. New York, Delacorte Press, 1990; London, Corgi, 1991.
Support Your Local Wizard (omnibus; includes *So You Want to Be a Wizard?, Deep Wizardry, High Wizardry*). New York, Guild American, 1990.
The Door into Sunset (Tale of the Five). London, Corgi, 1992; New York, Tor, 1993.
A Wizard Abroad (Wizardry). London, Corgi, 1993.

OTHER PUBLICATIONS

Novels

The Wounded Sky. New York, Pocket, 1983; London, Titan, 1988.
My Enemy, My Ally. New York, Pocket, 1984; London, Titan, 1989.
The Romulan Way, with Peter Morwood. New York, Pocket, 1987; London, Titan, 1989.
Spock's World. New York, Pocket, 1988; London, Pan, 1990.
Doctor's Orders. New York, Pocket, and London, Titan, 1990.
Space Cops: Mindblast, with Peter Morwood. New York, Avon, 1991.
Space Cops: Kill Station, with Peter Morwood. New York, AvonNova, 1992.
Space Cops: High Moon, with Peter Morwood. New York, AvonNova, 1992.
Dark Mirror. New York and London, Pocket, 1993.
SeaQuest DSV, with Peter Morwood (novelization of television script). New York, Ace, and London, Millennium, 1993.
Spider Man: The Venom Factor. New York, Putnam, 1994.

Plays

Television Plays: various episodes, *Scooby-Doo, Captain Caveman, Space Ghost, Fonz and the Happy Days Gang, Laverne and Shirley in the Army, Biskitts, Glofriends, Transformers, My Little Pony, Star Trek: The Next Generation, Dinosaucers, Batman,* 1979-94.

*

Diane Duane comments:

It strikes me as a chancy business to be making statements about my own work, since by this time next year my assessment of it may have shifted completely—and Heaven only knows what other people's assessments will have done. But never mind . . .

There are certain tendencies in my writing so obvious that even *I* notice them. One is a tendency to mix genres, peppering fantasy as liberally with hard science as possible (so that some people look at some of my works, like the "Wizard" group, and consider them to be science fiction), and salting what should otherwise be hard science fiction with metaphysical questions. Another thing that keeps popping up is a considerable affection for alien creatures, the odder the better—possibly based on memories of a rather isolated childhood in which I was mostly treated by my agemates as if I *was* from another planet.

The only generalization past the above that I feel I can safely make is that there is a certain—I have to use the buzz-word, for it's exact—"life-affirming" quality about my fiction. Over the time I spent learning nursing, and practising it, I saw a lot of death, and came to the conclusion that, about 90% of the time, life is preferable . . . but that, depending on how you interact with it, death can be defeated even in the act of it happening. If my characters have little patience for people killing one another or making others' lives wretched (or their own), and if death sometimes seems imperманent or ineffectual in the face of other Powers, those tendencies can correctly be seen as a function of the way the author sees life. One constant reader, whose opinion I trust, has summed up the whole attitude (at least partly mockingly) as "irreversible niceness." I plead guilty, and hope to keep living up to the accusation.

*   *   *

Diane Duane writes mainly in the science-fiction and fantasy fields, often in worlds created by others and sometimes in collaboration with her husband Peter Morwood. The more important volumes of her output over the last 15 years are those fantasy series which are original to her. They consist of two series, one for adults, the other for teenagers.

Her first published book was volume one of what came to be known as the Tale of Five series, *The Door Into Fire*. This is swords-and-sorcery and begins with Herewiss, Prince of Brightwood, receiving a message from his loved, Freelorn. Freelorn is the exiled heir to the throne of Arlen and is being besieged in a tower by the usurper. Herewiss is a sorcerer, and on his way single-handedly to rescue Freelorn he saves the life of a fire elemental and hears of a hold, in the wastelands where no one normally goes, which might contain the answers to some of his problems. In some respects this is a quest novel but Herewiss's quest is as much spiritual as physical. While many of the women of this world possess a Fire which can be focused to produce real magic, as opposed to sorcery which is all spell-construction and largely illusion, no man has been born for a thousand years with enough Fire to focus it to greater effect. Herewiss has the Fire but he cannot find anything strong enough to act as a focus—the women use rods but these shatter when Herewiss tries to use them. He hopes that the hold in the wastelands may help him solve his problems. Freelorn, though, thinks that regaining his own kingdom has priority.

Although this series is called the Tale of the Five, it is not clear from the first volume who the Five are. In fact, the fifth member of the group does not appear until the second volume, *The Door Into Shadow*. This part is told from Segnbora's point of view. She is a warrior in a world where men and women have equality and so her choice of profession is not unusual. She, like Herewiss, has been unable to find a strong enough focus for her Fire, but unlike him has given up trying. Until she meets a dying dragon. When a dragon dies it goes *mdahaih*. Its entire personality takes up residence within the mind of another of its kind. In this case, Segnbora finds she is suddenly the recipient, not just of one dragon, Hasai, but of all his predecessors as well, all waiting in her mind to give her the benefit of their advice. So while Herewiss is using his new-found powers to move mountains and drive the invading Reavers from the land, Segnbora has to cope with her new situation and to face up to the reasons in her past which have so far prevented her from being able to focus her own power.

The Five, then, are Herewiss, Sunspark the fire elemental, Freelorn, Segnbora and the dead dragon Hasai. Volume three is largely Freelorn's story in which he comes into his own kind of power, that of one-ness with the land of which he believes he should be king. Of all the characters he has had the most maturing to do, but as the story heads towards a climax each of the others has a significant part to play. At the end of *The Door into Sunset* everything seems to have been neatly resolved, but we are told that the tale will be concluded in a projected fourth volume, *The Door Into Starlight*.

Duane's second series was written specifically for young adults and is largely contemporary in setting. *So You Want To Be a Wizard*, begins when 13-year-old Nita Callahan finds a book in the library which turns out to be a wizard's manual, full of information and spells. Because of it she meets Kit Rodrigez, and the two fledgling wizards have to battle against the perennial evil entity known as the Lone Power. This adventure takes them to an alternative Manhattan where machines are sentient and predatory. *Deep Wizardry* sees Nita and Kit joining forces with a dolphin wizard and facing the Lone Power in the seas off the California coast. In *High Wizardry*, it is the turn of Nita's obnoxious sister Dairine to become the newest wizard. Her manual is in the form of a portable computer. Nita and Kit chase her across the universe to be present at the birth of a new race and Dairine's confrontation with the Lone Power. *A Wizard Abroad* is set in Ireland, where the author now lives, and although Nita and Kit are still important players in the story they form part of a company of older and more experienced wizards, including Nita's Aunt Annie.

Throughout the series, both Nita and Kit are maturing, and we see their behaviour change accordingly. The books work well for young people as the two young wizards are forced to rely on their own abilities and, though there may be guidance from adults, there is little interference.

The series were written concurrently, and it is inevitable that there is some leakage of ideas between the two. In the Tale of the Five, there is a mythology of the Goddess, who has a triple aspect and can appear as Maiden, Mother, and Crone. As Maiden she created the world, but when she finished it she accidentally sealed Death into her creation, who appears as the Dark or Shadow in the novels and is the principal opponent of the Five. The Lone Power of the Wizardry series is a very similar entity though more recognizable as Lucifer, the fallen Angel, of Christian mythology. He invented entropy, which will eventually destroy the universe; so in both there is the inevitable prospect of a final Death, but in both the opposing powers struggle to hold this at bay for as long as possible.

Another similarity concerns the powers of the sorcerers and wizards. Herewiss and Segnbora are both at their most powerful immediately after first focusing their Fire. This time is called Breakthrough, and after the initial surge they can expect their powers to decline. In fact, the use of Fire actively shortens their life-span. Nita, Kit, and Dairine as children are more powerful than the older wizards but they too expect their abilities to wane as they age. At one point Nita consciously constructs a spell knowing that she is using up part of her life to do so.

Spells in all books are for the most part constructed by words, the final one of which locks everything into place and makes it happen. And the strongest magic can be worked only if there is an element of self-sacrifice. Herewiss, Segnbora and Freelorn in turn offer their lives, as do Nita and Dairine. The sacrifice is not always accepted, but it has to be made. Other common factors in the two series are the way that the characters develop maturity, and the readability of all volumes.

Duane's other fantasy writing is a collaboration with Peter Morwood. *Keeper of the City* is the second volume of a sword-and-sorcery series created by Bill Fawcett, the others of which are written by different authors. All the books are set in the same landscape where the *liskask* (reptilians) are attempting to conquer the *mrem* (feline hominoids). Some characters appear in more than one volume. This one, by Duane and Morwood, is the most competently written of the first four.

Duane has also written half a dozen Star Trek novels on her own and one in collaboration with Morwood. They also collaborated on the first *SeaQuest* novelization, based on the TV series, and three of the *Starcops* novels. In addition, she has written copiously for children's animated television.

—Pauline Morgan

DUNCAN, Dave

Nationality: Canadian. **Born:** Newport on Tay, Scotland, 30 June 1933. **Education:** Dundee High School; University of St. Andrews, Fife: B.Sc. in chemistry and geology, 1955. **Family:** Married Janet Hopwell; one son, two daughters. **Career:** Petroleum geologist, 1955-66; geological consultant, 1967-86. Has lived in Calgary, Alberta, since 1955. **Awards:** Canadian Science Fiction and Fantasy award, 1990. **Agent:** Richard Curtis Associates, 171 East 74th Street, New York, NY 10021, USA.

FANTASY PUBLICATIONS

Novels (series: Seventh Sword; A Man of His Word; A Handful of Men)

A Rose-Red City. New York, Del Rey, 1987; London, Legend, 1989.
The Reluctant Swordsman (Seventh Sword). New York, Del Rey, 1988; London, Legend, 1990.
The Coming of Wisdom (Seventh Sword). New York, Del Rey, 1988; London, Legend, 1990.
The Destiny of the Sword (Seventh Sword). New York, Del Rey, 1988; London, Legend, 1991.
Magic Casement (Man of His Word). New York, Del Rey, 1990.
Faery Lands Forlorn (Man of His Word). New York, Del Rey, 1991.
Perilous Seas (Man of His Word). New York, Del Rey, 1991.
Emperor and Clown (Man of His Word). New York, Del Rey, 1992.
The Reaver Road. New York, Del Rey, 1992.
The Cutting Edge (A Handful of Men). New York, Del Rey, 1992; London, Raven, 1994.
Upland Outlaws (A Handful of Men). New York, Del Rey, 1993.
The Stricken Field (A Handful of Men). New York, Del Rey, 1993.
The Living God (A Handful of Men). New York, Del Rey, 1994.
The Hunter's Haunt. New York, Del Rey, 1995.
The Cursed. New York, Del Rey, 1995.

OTHER PUBLICATIONS

Novels

Shadow. New York, Del Rey, 1987; London, Legend, 1989.

West of January. New York, Del Rey, 1989.
Strings. New York, Del Rey, 1990.
Hero! New York, Del Rey, 1991.

*

Dave Duncan comments:

Speculative fiction begins by assuming at least one impossible thing, which in my case often concerns the nature of magic. I enjoy inventing worlds or universes whose laws are unfamiliar to us and yet self-consistent. My ambition is to be Advisor to God, next time around.

* * *

Scots-Canadian writer Dave Duncan should not be confused with American science-fiction novelist and screenwriter David Duncan (born 1913). Launching a writing career when most people contemplate retirement, Duncan first published *A Rose-Red City,* which features a timeless city called Mera governed by a mysterious Oracle who periodically "recruits" people from various eras of Earth's history to enjoy lives of eternal happiness. Two citizens, the ineffectual Jerry Howard and combative Achilles, are sent to recruit a divorced woman who has just kidnapped her children from her ex-husband; but the house they stay in during their mission is unexpectedly assaulted by an army of demons in a long and suspenseful sequence. Then, after some rather illogical plot developments, Jerry and the woman are sent to ancient Crete, where they must re-enact Theseus's slaying of the Minotaur, and when she decides to remain in Mera, Achilles is revealed as her missing son. Not entirely successful, the novel does distinguish itself for its brief but haunting glimpses of an attractive Shangri-La; one wishes Duncan had spent more time there.

Next came Duncan's first major achievement in fantasy: the Seventh Sword trilogy, set in a world of variable geography where an all-encompassing River connects all cities and unpredictably transports sailors from one city to another. A man from Earth is reborn in the body of a mighty Swordsman, and an enigmatic god assigns him to unite other Swordsmen and their allies against the sinister "Sorcerers" who are threatening the world. However, his unique background enables him to deduce that the Sorcerers are really primitive scientists with benevolent motives, so he forges an alliance between them and the Swordsmen. An effective unifying motif is that Duncan's hero seems to make one blunder after another, but in retrospect it always emerges that the apparent error was in fact the correct step; and the trilogy ends unexpectedly but satisfyingly when he realizes that he must turn over his sword and his power to his former protégé.

The Reaver Road is a charming singleton about an amusingly duplicitous "Trader of Tales" named Omar who is sent by the gods to observe a besieged city traditionally rescued by the reappearance of its protector god to personally lead the city's army to victory. He learns that the city priests are plotting, as they apparently did in former times, to find an ordinary human to impersonate the god; but a merchant's son suddenly seems to become the god, and Omar is then regarded as an accompanying god. The ambiguity Duncan does not resolve is whether the triumphant hero was actually taken over by the god's spirit or whether he simply displayed personal initiative—an ambiguity heightened by the unreliability of narrator Omar, who tells several conflicting stories about his background during the novel.

Decidedly less successful was Duncan's first tetralogy, *A Man of His Word*, focused on two people in the land of Pandemia (presumably meaning "land of all people," not "land of widespread disease"): Princess Inos of Kranegar, a small isolated kingdom in the north, and Rap, a stableboy who, during a long separation from Inos, gradually develops great magical powers which he employs to overcome a villainous warlock, and who then settles down with Inos as (together) King and Queen of Kranegar. As always, Duncan's story is energetic and imaginative; the most memorable supporting characters are five men—a scholar, a thief, a minstrel, a charming rogue, and a brutal killer—who sequentially occupy the same body. However, there are conspicuous weaknesses in these novels. While Rap is a typically likable Duncan hero, he largely lacks the charm and good humour of his predecessors; and Inos, though Duncan works very hard on her character development, still seems more like a compendium of romance-novel clichés than a real person. Titles taken from a John Keats poem, and quotations at the end of each chapter, introduce a new and unwelcome air of pretentiousness to Duncan's narrative; and reading the second and third novels, *Faery Lands Forlorn* and *Perilous Seas,* one gets the feeling that Duncan is killing time, arbitrarily moving Rap and Inos from one dangerous situation to another simply to prolong the story and fill four volumes.

Although his previous novels employed overt magic only sparingly, this series is sated with fantastic effects, and his extended attention to the feuds and schemes of Pandemia's sorcerers, instead of his protagonists's fates, becomes tiresome. Perhaps most troubling is Duncan's obsession with describing the various differences in appearance and personality of the different human races of Pandemia—named jotunns, imps, fauns, goblins and djinns—which gives the tetralogy an atmosphere of racism. For example, goblins are roughly analogous to American Indians—with names like Little Chicken and Bright Water—and are described as sadistic and gleeful torturers; when a sorceress suggests that Inos should marry a goblin, she reacts with horror and revulsion, and readers are supposed to share and endorse her displeasure. Actual American Indians might feel differently.

However, Duncan did considerably better with his second Pandemia tetralogy, *A Handful of Men*, where the defeated warlock returns to seize control of the empire and cause havoc throughout the land, while Rap joins the new emperor and a few companions in an extended effort to overthrow him; the warlock is finally destroyed by divine intervention, and Rap briefly serves as a warlock himself to help establish a new era of peace and justice in Pandemia. These four novels benefit from a faster pace and greater sense of purpose, as the events seem less contrived, more genuinely important, and Duncan effectively introduces some interesting new characters, including Shandie, the exiled emperor; Ylo, his ambitious aide who becomes a hero in spite of himself; and Rap's son Gath, who has the ability to see two hours into the future. There are some problems—more superfluous quotations, weak female characters, and a *deux ex machina* sort of conclusion—but it remains an enjoyable experience which deserved its success as Duncan's breakthrough into hardcover publication. Still, Duncan would be better advised to return to the River or the Reaver Road before revisiting Pandemia.

—Gary Westfahl

DUNSANY, Lord

Edward John Moreton Drax Plunkett, 18th Baron Dunsany. **Nationality:** Irish. **Born:** London, 24 July 1878; succeeded to the barony, 1899. **Education:** Cheam School, Surrey; Eton College, Berkshire; then privately tutored; Royal Military Academy, Sandhurst, Surrey. **Military Service:** 2nd lieutenant in the Coldstream Guards in Gibraltar and in the Boer War, 1899-1902; captain in the Royal Inniskilling Fusiliers during World War I; wounded in the Dublin Easter Rebellion, 1916; served in the Home Guard during World War II. **Family:** Married Lady Beatrice Child-Villiers in 1904; one son. Lived at Dunstall Priory, Kent, and Dunsany Castle, County Meath. **Career:** Byron professor of English literature, University of Athens, 1940-41. D.Litt.: University of Dublin, 1939. Fellow, Royal Society of Literature, and Royal Geographical Society; member, Irish Academy of Letters. **Died:** 25 October 1957.

FANTASY PUBLICATIONS

Novels

The Chronicles of Rodriguez. London, Putnam, 1922; as *Don Rodriguez: Chronicles of Shadow Valley,* New York, Putnam, 1922.
The King of Elfland's Daughter. London and New York, Putnam, 1924.
The Charwoman's Shadow. London and New York, Putnam, 1924.
The Blessings of Pan. London and New York, Putnam, 1926.
The Curse of the Wise Woman. London, Heinemann, and New York, Longman, 1933.
The Strange Journeys of Colonel Polders. London, Jarrolds, 1950.

Short Stories (series: Jorkens)

The Gods of Pegana. London, Elkin Matthews, 1905; Boston, Luce, 1916.
Time and the Gods. London, Heinemann, 1906; Boston, Luce, 1913.
The Sword of Welleran and other Stories. London, G. Allen, 1908; Boston, Luce, 1916.
A Dreamer's Tales. London, G. Allen, and Boston, Luce, 1910.
The Book of Wonder: A Chronicle of Little Adventures at the Edge of the World. London, Heinemann, 1912; Boston, Luce, 1913.
Fifty-One Tales. London, Elkin Matthews, and New York, Kennerley, 1915; as *The Food of Death,* Hollywood, California, Newcastle, 1974.
Tales of Wonder. London, Elkin Matthews, 1916; as *The Last Book of Wonder,* Boston, Luce, 1916.
Tales of Three Hemispheres. Boston, Luce, 1919; London, Fisher Unwin, 1920.
The Travel Tales of Mr. Joseph Jorkens. London and New York, Putnam, 1931.
Jorkens Remembers Africa. New York, Longman, 1934; as *Mr. Jorkens Remembers Africa,* London, Heinemann, 1934.
Jorkens Has a Large Whiskey. London, Putnam, 1940.
The Fourth Book of Jorkens. London, Jarrolds, and Sauk City, Wisconsin, Arkham House, 1948.
The Man Who Ate the Phoenix. London, Jarrolds, 1949.
Jorkens Borrows Another Whiskey. London, M. Joseph, 1954.

At the Edge of the World, edited by Lin Carter. New York, Ballantine, 1970.

Beyond the Fields We Know, edited by Lin Carter. New York and London, Ballantine, 1972.

Gods, Men, and Ghosts: The Best Supernatural Fiction of Dunsany, edited by E. F. Bleiler. New York, Dover, 1972.

Over the Hills and Far Away, edited by Lin Carter. New York, Ballantine, 1974.

The Ghosts of the Heaviside Layer, and Other Fantasms, edited by Darrell Schweitzer. Philadelphia, Owlswick Press, 1980.

OTHER PUBLICATIONS

Novels

Up in the Hills. London, Heinemann, and New York, Putnam, 1936.

Rory and Bran. London, Heinemann, and New York, Putnam, 1937.

The Story of Mona Sheehy. London, Heinemann, 1939; New York, Harper, 1940.

Guerrilla. London, Heinemann, and New York, Bobbs Merrill, 1944.

The Last Revolution. London and New York, Jarrolds, 1951.

His Fellow Men. London, Jarrolds, 1952.

Short Stories

Tales of War. London and New York, Putnam, 1918.

The Little Tales of Smethers and Other Stories. London, Jarrolds, 1952.

Plays

The Sphinx at Gizeh, in *Tripod,* May 1912.

Five Plays [includes *The Glittering Gate* (produced 1909), *The Gods of the Mountain* (produced 1911), *King Argimines and the Unknown Warrior* (produced 1911), *The Golden Doom* (produced 1912), *The Lost Silk Hat* (produced 1913)]. Boston, Little Brown, and London, Grant Richards, 1914.

Plays of Gods and Men [includes *The Tents of the Arabs* (produced 1914), *The Queen's Enemies* (produced 1916), *The Laughter of the Gods* (produced 1919)]. London, Fisher Unwin, and New York, Luce, 1917.

A Night at an Inn (produced 1916).

The Murderers (produced 1919).

The Prince of Stamboul (produced 1919?).

If (produced 1921). London and New York, Putnam, 1921.

Cheezo (produced 1921). London and New York, Putnam, 1921.

Plays of Near and Far [includes *The Compromise of the King of the Golden Isles, The Flight of the Queen, Cheezo, A Good Bargain, If Shakespeare Lived Today, Fame and the Poet* (produced 1924)]. London and New York, Putnam, 1922.

Lord Adrian (produced 1923). Waltham Saint Lawrence, Berkshire, Golden Cockerel Press, 1933.

If Shakespeare Lived Today. London and New York, Putnam, 1923.

Alexander and Three Small Plays (includes *The Old King's Tale, The Evil Kettle, The Amusements of Khan Kharuda*). London and New York, Putnam, 1925.

Alexander (produced 1938). London and New York, Putnam, 1925.

Mr. Faithful (produced 1927). New York, French, 1935.

Seven Modern Comedies [includes *Atalanta in Wimbledon, The Raffle, The Journey of the Soul, In Holy Russia, His Sainted Grandmother* (produced 1926), *The Hopeless Passion of Mr. Bunyon, The Jest of Hahalaba* (produced 1927)]. London and New York, Putnam, 1928.

The Old Folk of the Centuries. London, Elkin Matthews, 1930.

Plays for Earth and Air [includes *Fame Comes Late, A Matter of Honour, Mr. Sliggen's Hour, The Pumpkin, The Use of Man, The Bureau de Change, The Seventh Symphony, Golden Dragon City, Time's Joke, Atmospherics*]. London, Heinemann, 1937.

The Strange Lover (produced 1939).

Poetry

Fifty Poems. London and New York, Putnam, 1929.

Mirage Water. London, Putnam, 1938; Philadelphia, Dorrance, 1939.

War Poems. London, Hutchinson, 1941.

A Journey. London, Macdonald, 1943.

Wandering Songs. London, Hutchinson, 1943.

The Year. London, Jarrolds, 1946.

To Awaken Pegasus and Other Poems. Oxford, Ronald, 1949.

Other

Selections. Churchtown, Dundrum, Cuala Press, 1912; Boston, Little Brown, 1916.

Nowadays. Boston, Four Seas, 1918.

Unhappy Far-Off Things. London, Elkin Matthews, and Boston, Little Brown, 1919.

If I Were Dictator: The Pronouncements of the Grand Macaroni. London, Methuen, 1934.

My Talks with Dean Spanley. London, Heinemann, and New York, Putnam, 1936.

My Ireland. London, Jarrolds, and New York, Funk and Wagnalls, 1937.

Patches of Sunlight (autobiography). London, Heinemann, and New York, Reynal and Hitchcock, 1938.

While the Sirens Slept (autobiography). London, Jarrolds, 1944.

The Donellan Lectures 1943. London, Heinemann, 1945.

A Glimpse from a Watchtower: A Series of Essays. London, Jarrolds, 1946.

The Sirens Wake (autobiography). London, Jarrolds, 1945.

Editor, *Modern Anglo-Irish Verse.* N.p., 1914.

Editor, *Last Song* by Francis Ledwidge. London, Herbert Jenkins, 1918.

*

Bibliography: *Lord Dunsany: A Bibliography* by S. T. Joshi and Darrell Schweitzer, Metuchen, New Jersey, Scarecrow Press, 1993.

Critical Studies: *Dunsany the Dramatist* by Edward Hale Bierstadt, Boston, Little Brown, 1917; revised edition, 1919; *Dunsany, King of Dreams: A Personal Portrait* by Hazel Smith, London, Weidenfeld and Nicolson, and New York, Exposition Press, 1959; *Pathways to Elfland: The Writings of Lord Dunsany* by Darrell Schweitzer, Philadelphia, Owlswick Press, 1989; *Lord Dunsany, Anglo-Irish Writer* by S. T. Joshi, Westport, Connecticut, Greenwood Press, 1995.

*   *   *

Between 1905 and 1919 Lord Dunsany produced one of the most remarkable bodies of work in the history of fantasy literature. Because he was an unknown writer, he had to pay for the publication of his first book, *The Gods of Pegana*; but its unexpected critical success, as well as that of its successors—the story collections *Time and the Gods, The Sword of Welleran, A Dreamer's Tales, The Book of Wonder, Fifty-one Tales, The Last Book of Wonder* and *Tales of Three Hemispheres*; and the play collections *Five Plays* and *Plays of Gods and Men*—established Dunsany as a distinctive voice in English and Irish literature.

These volumes are, however, by no means monolithic in their contents or their quality. The first two volumes (and these alone) create an entire cosmogony of gods out of whole cloth, with their own demigods, priests and worshippers. The "real" world makes no appearance, and the realm of Pegana *is* the real world in Dunsany's imagination. But this gesture is not merely an escapist fantasy. The creation of a "new" and ersatz religion implies some dissatisfaction with the religion (Christianity) in which Dunsany was nominally raised. Dunsany was very likely an atheist, and his creation of the Gods of Pegana—with the remote Mana-Yood-Sushai as Yahweh, and the rest of the universe consisting merely of his dreams as he is lulled to sleep by the rhythmical drumming of Skarl the Drummer—underscores several principal tenets in Dunsany's philosophy, chiefly the need for reunification with the natural world by a repudiation of industrial civilization. This, indeed, may be the central theme in all Dunsany's work. His gods are created in a spirit of what might be called *aesthetic animism*: they represent the forces of the natural world, and thereby reestablish that bond between human beings and Nature which modern civilization has been inexorably loosening.

There are, of course, many other subsidiary themes in Dunsany's early work—removal of humanity from centre stage in the universe (what H. P. Lovecraft would call "cosmicism"); anti-clericalism (several early fables are satires on the duplicity of priests); the awesome figure of Time (which can slay even the gods) and the power of art to defeat or restrain it; and imagination as a refuge from the prosiness of ordinary existence. Dunsany's early plays—which were spectacularly successful in Ireland, England and America—speak in tones reminiscent only of Greek tragedy of the hand of Destiny overwhelming hapless mortals (see *The Gods of the Mountain* and *The Golden Doom*), but also of those same mortals asserting their dignity and self-worth when they have been laid low (*King Argimenes and the Unknown Warrior*) or avenging their foes hideously (*The Queen's Enemies*). Many of these plays are set in an imaginary world, but some are set in the historical past (Egypt in *The Queen's Enemies*, Greece in *Alexander*), although Dunsany's intentional liberties with the historical record make these realms seem more fantastic than real. *If*, Dunsany's last great theatrical success, is a compelling meditation on the role of time: a man is offered the chance to change a single incident in his past; he naively picks a very insignificant episode, believing that it could not have had much of an effect upon the future, but of course he learns differently.

But with *The Book of Wonder* a change is detectable in Dunsany's attitude toward the fantastic. Not only does the "real" world make increasing incursions into his work, but fantasy is increasingly made the butt of jest or self-parody. The stories in *The Book of Wonder* (as well as some of those in *The Last Book of Wonder*) were based upon illustrations by S. H. Sime; and in many of them a certain poverty of imagination is evident. It is as if the *Gods of Pegana* style were running dry, so that all Dunsany could do was to poke fun at it. Now, instead of cosmic struggles between gods and humans, we have petty thieves given their comeuppance or equally petty demigods squabbling with one another.

Nevertheless, this early work is inexhaustibly rich in philosophical depth and in beauty of prose. The secret of Dunsany's prose lies, in fact, in its simplicity (he modelled it consciously on the King James Bible) and in its daring use of metaphor: in "The Raft-Builders" (in *Fifty-one Tales*) he compares writing to rafts, most of which are "unseaworthy"; but he then concludes: "There goes the raft that Homer made for Helen."

Dunsany admitted that he turned to writing novels because he was disappointed with the reception of his short stories. In the early 1920s he wrote four in quick succession: *The Chronicles of Rodriguez, The King of Elfland's Daughter, The Charwoman's Shadow* and *The Blessing of Pan*. The first is a charming picaresque novel set in Renaissance Spain; the third, also set in Spain, is the delightful if insubstantial story of a charwoman who unwisely gives up her shadow to a wizard to gain immortality and the attempt of a young man to restore it to her. *The King of Elfland's Daughter* is a much more significant proposition. Superficially this novel represents a remarkable return to the prose style of the early tales, but thematically it is quite different. What appears to be a contrast between the timeless realm of Elfland and the "real" world represented by the land of Erl dissolves upon analysis: "Erl" is German for "elf," so that the distinctions between fantasy and reality become problematical. As in some tales in *The Last Book of Wonder*, fantasy becomes a matter of perspective: the creatures of Elfland look upon the land of Erl with as much amazement as the people of Erl regard Elfland. There is eventual harmony between the two worlds as Alveric, prince of Erl, marries Lirazel, the daughter of the king of Elfland. *The Blessing of Pan* restricts the realm of faery even further: this novel, set entirely in a small village in England, tells of the entrancing tune that a boy plays on a set of Pan-pipes he has made, and of the harried but ultimately unsuccessful attempts of a well-meaning clergyman to fight against its seductive power. This is a conflict both of Nature and civilization and of paganism and Christianity; and Dunsany's clear preference for the first of these dichotomies is very evident.

Later works utilize what might be called *the nonhuman perspective* to convey Dunsany's overriding nature-versus-humanity theme. Several plays focus on this theme: *The Old Folk of the Centuries* is about a boy turned into a butterfly; *Mr. Faithful* hilariously deals with a young man who, desperate for a job, becomes a watchdog; *The Use of Man* (in *Plays for Earth and Air*) is a tart satire in which a man is called up in front of the spirits of all the other animals and is asked what the "use" of man is, just as we might ask what use badgers or mosquitoes are to us. The non-fantastic novel *Rory and Bran* is a long joke in which it is never made clear that Bran is a dog accompanying the boy Rory to market. This topos reaches its culmination in *My Talks with Dean Spanley* (in which a staid clergyman, under the influence of wine, speaks of his belief that in a past life he was a dog) and *The Strange Journeys of Colonel Polders*, a forgotten masterpiece of comic fantasy in which a retired colonel offends an Indian swami and is forced to occupy an endless succession of animal bodies (dog, cat, eel, sparrow, Barbary sheep, etc.), and actually likes the experience because animals are so much closer to Nature and have natural comforts that human beings find very difficult to attain.

Dunsany's five volumes of tales involving the clubman Joseph Jorkens are a unique subset of his work. Written over a thirty year span, they tread the very borderline of the supernatural in their accounts of fantastic inventions, improbable trips to outer space, and strange journeys to remote corners of the world. Although the reader can never quite believe Jorkens's narratives, there is no single point at which they can be proven definitively false. These stories were enormously popular in Dunsany's day and appeared in the best-paying magazines in America and England.

The fantasy quotient steadily decreases over the course of Dunsany's career, although one of the most delightful aspects of his writing is his ability to infuse an air of strangeness in works that, in their incidents, are purely mainstream. Consider *Atalanta in Wimbledon* (in *Seven Modern Comedies*), one of his best later plays. Here a young woman takes out an ad in the paper saying that she will marry any man who can defeat her in ping-pong, but if her opponent loses he must die by the sword. This outrageous parody of medieval custom (the woman comes by this idea after reading William Morris) creates a sense of bizarrerie in spite of the general buffoonery of the action. In other works there is doubt whether the supernatural enters at all. *The Curse of the Wise Woman,* perhaps his best novel and his first work to deal explicitly with Ireland, is the poignant story of a development company that seeks to drain a bog and the efforts of a witch or wise woman to stop it; in the end a titanic storm (perhaps summoned by the wise woman's curses, perhaps caused by the powers of the bog, or perhaps a mere coincidence) destroys the development company's equipment and saves the bog. But Dunsany does something very different in *The Story of Mona Sheehy*: here a young girl thinks she is the child of the fairies when in fact she is merely the result of an illicit union between a noblewoman and a farmer. The novel is based in part on a very early tale ("The Kith of the Elf-Folk," in *The Sword of Welleran*) where an actual child of the fairies is made to dwell amongst human beings; but here the climax is Mona Sheehy's realization that she is in fact human and that her life as a simple country girl is far superior to her imagined status as a fairy.

It is difficult in a small compass to convey the richness and variety of Lord Dunsany's work, which runs the gamut from imaginary-world fantasy to pungent satire (*Cheezo*) to science fiction (*The Last Revolution*) to delicate and pensive tales about Ireland (*Up in the Hills, His Fellow Men*). The first of his autobiographies, *Patches of Sunlight,* is also a delightful exposition of his childhood and his beginnings as a writer. His early stories and plays are so distinctive that they have given birth to the adjective "Dunsanian"; but his later work, which tends to be ignored and scorned even by his supporters, is full of a very different sort of substance. The vigour that Dunsany retained over a fifty year writing career is nearly unparalleled in fantasy literature, and all his work, early and late, deserves resurrection.

—S. T. Joshi

DWYER, James Francis

Nationality: Australian. **Born:** Camden, New South Wales, 22 April 1874. **Career:** Traveller and writer. **Died:** 11 November 1952.

FANTASY PUBLICATIONS

Novels (series: Spillane)

The White Waterfall. New York, Doubleday, 1912; London, Cassell, 1913.

The Spotted Panther. New York, Doubleday, 1913; London, Melrose, 1914.
Evelyn: Something More Than a Story. New York, Vanguard Press, 1929; London, Sampson Low, 1931.
The Lady with Feet of Gold (Spillane). London, Jenkins, 1937.
The City of Cobras (Spillane). London, Jenkins, 1938.

Short Stories

Breath of the Jungle. Chicago, McClurg, 1915.

OTHER PUBLICATIONS

Novels

The Green Half-Moon. Chicago, McClurg, 1915; London, Hodder and Stoughton, 1917.
O Splendid Sorcery. New York, Vanguard Press, 1930; London, Sampson Low, 1930.
The Romantic Quest of Peter Lamonte. London, Sampson Low, 1932.
Cold-Eyes. London, Methuen, 1934.
Hespamora. London, Methuen, 1935.

Short Stories

The Bust of Lincoln. New York, Doubleday, 1912.

Other

Leg Iron on Wings. New York, Georgian House, 1949.

* * *

James F. Dwyer was a writer of exotic adventure stories usually with settings in the Far East, an area with which he was very familiar. He was born in Australia and imbued with a love of travel and of the fantastic by his father, a noted local teller of tall tales. This may have initially led Dwyer astray. In his early career, working in the post office, he was found guilty of forgery and imprisoned for seven years. It was while in prison that he began writing. Released after three years, he had the urge to escape all confinement and became a compulsive traveller, earning his keep by writing. After gold-prospecting in Australia, he travelled throughout the Far East, the East Indies and Africa.

All of Dwyer's stories, fantastic or otherwise, reflect this love of adventure. They are written in the style of the traveller's tale, often stretching the truth, and finding fascination and wonder in all parts of the globe. His stories are also imbued with a strong sense of humour. One could well imagine Dwyer sitting back in some bar in an outpost of Empire, enthralling his audience with his latest exuberant yarn. They have a touch of Rider Haggard about them, though they are more down-to-earth than that writer's romances.

Dwyer's earliest stories are his most fantastic. He wrote prolifically both for the leading slick magazines, like *Collier's Weekly* and *Sunset,* and for the leading pulps, especially *Argosy, Adventure* and *Blue Book.* His only collection of stories, *Breath of the Jungle,* exemplifies the traveller's tale. It includes several stories narrated by a naturalist in the East Indies and they all reflect the power of the jungle over civilized man. This is best exemplified by

"The Soul Trapper" (*Collier's Weekly,* 1911) where a man is driven mad by the jungle but is saved from total mental degradation by the singing of a beautiful native woman. "Jungle Graduate" (*Harper's Weekly,* 1910) is a particularly vicious story of a man who seeks to train an orangutan by terrifying him into submission. The ape learns quickly and soon turns the tables on his master. Years later Alfred Hitchcock anthologized this as one of his *Stories They Wouldn't Let Me Do on TV.*

All of Dwyer's early short stories convey powerful messages, reinforced by his experiences in the wild. He brought to jungle fiction what Algernon Blackwood was bringing to the forests and mountainous regions of Europe in portraying the interplay between man and nature. Dwyer's later short fiction became more light-hearted and romantic. He found a particular niche in women's magazines, especially *Woman's Home Companion,* where he was able to picture some of his more romantic adventures around the world. At the same time in *Blue Book* he was writing boisterous adventure yarns. It is a shame that no further collections of his stories have been made. There are sufficient for another fantasy volume, including the lost civilization adventure "The City of the Unseen" (*Argosy,* 1913), "City of Pleasure" (*Liberty,* 1933), about a dream paradise not unlike Shangri-La, and "The Cave of the Invisible" (*Blue Book,* 1939), an effective story about ghosts of the past created from the trapped atmosphere in a cave.

Dwyer's novels followed a similar pattern of development. His early work was more fantastic, developing the wonder of lost worlds and strange cults. *The White Waterfall* is essentially a love story but it is set against the fascinating backcloth of a strange lost civilization in a remote Pacific island. It was originally serialized in *Cavalier* and may have had some slight influence upon Abraham Merritt who, a few years later, would use a similar setting for *The Moon Pool.* Fantasy historian Sam Moskowitz has called Dwyer's novel "easily one of the best adventure novels *The Cavalier* was to publish".

The Spotted Panther takes its basis from the work of Rider Haggard and develops it into what could be regarded almost as a blueprint for the "Indiana Jones" movie adventures. Three explorers, led by Red Templeton, are seeking a legendary sword, lost for four centuries in Borneo. If it falls into the wrong hands it might enable the Orient to overpower the West. The fantasy element is minimal but remains fundamental to the belief in the story. Its sequel, "The Treasure of Vanished Men," apparently has not been published in book form.

Dwyer wrote few novels after the First World War, but returned to the fantasy mould with *Evelyn: Something More Than a Story.* A dying woman finds that she can communicate with the dead and by this means she can help others. The story suffers slightly from the sentimental overtones only too prevalent in the postwar spiritualist boom, but is nevertheless an originally plotted and ingenious work.

Toward the end of his writing career Dwyer increased the fantasy content of his adventure stories again, including a popular series in *Blue Book.* Two of these, *The Lady with Feet of Gold* and *The City of Cobras* (originally "Caravan Treasure") were published in book form and showed that Dwyer had lost none of his skill in the quarter-century since *The White Waterfall.* Exotic locales, ancient civilizations and the power of the wild were Dwyer's stock in trade. *The City of Cobras,* which involves a search for the secret of longevity, was inspired by a trek Dwyer undertook across the Sahara when he was 60. One potentially misleading title is *O Splendid Sorcery,* which is not a work of fantasy but a tale of love between a man and a blind Irish girl.

The Second World War limited Dwyer's travelling but, more than that, it took the final mystery out of the hidden corners of the world. No one who had fought the Japanese in the jungles of Burma would thrill again to the exotic wonder of lost temples. Dwyer continued to write for the pulps, but his output dwindled. He settled in the south of France after the War.

Dwyer's work is perhaps too closely associated with the overused lost-civilization theme, and the originality, humour and above all intensity of his writing is overlooked. He was a good writer who produced some intelligent work, and there is probably much more tucked away in old magazines that is worth resurrecting.

—Mike Ashley

E

EAGER, Edward (McMaken)

Nationality: American. **Born:** Toledo, Ohio, in 1911. **Education:** Harvard University, Cambridge, Massachusetts. **Family:** Married Jane Eberly in 1938; one son. **Died:** 23 October 1964.

FANTASY PUBLICATIONS

Novels (series: Half Magic)

Half Magic, illustrated by N. M. Bodecker. New York, Harcourt Brace, and London, Macmillan, 1954.
Knight's Castle, illustrated by N. M. Bodecker (Half Magic). New York, Harcourt Brace, and London, Macmillan, 1956.
Magic by the Lake, illustrated by N. M. Bodecker (Half Magic). New York, Harcourt Brace, and London, Macmillan, 1957.
The Time Garden, illustrated by N. M. Bodecker (Half Magic). New York, Harcourt Brace, 1958; London, Macmillan, 1959.
Magic or Not?, illustrated by N. M. Bodecker. New York, Harcourt Brace, and London, Macmillan, 1959.
The Well-Wishers, illustrated by N. M. Bodecker. New York, Harcourt Brace, 1960; London, Macmillan, 1961.
Seven-Day Magic, illustrated by N. M. Bodecker. New York, Harcourt Brace, 1962; London, Macmillan, 1963.

OTHER PUBLICATIONS

Novels (for children)

Mouse Manor, illustrated by Beryl Bailey-Jones. New York, Farrar Straus, 1952.
Playing Possum, illustrated by Paul Galdone. New York, Putnam, 1955.

Poetry

Red Head, illustrated by Louis Slobodkin. Boston, Houghton Mifflin, 1951.

Plays

Pudding Full of Plums (produced Cambridge, Massachusetts).
Dream with Music (lyrics only), book by Sidney Sheldon, Dorothy Kilgallen, and Ben Roberts, music by Clay Warnick (produced New York, 1944).
The Liar, with Alfred Drake, music by John Mundy, lyrics by Eager, adaptation of a play by Goldoni (produced New York, 1950).
The Gambler, with Alfred Drake, adaptation of a play by Ugo Betti (produced New York, 1952).
The Adventures of Marco Polo: A Musical Fantasy (lyrics only), book by William Friedberg and Neil Simon, music by Clay Warnick and Mel Pahl (televised, 1956). New York, French, 1959.
Call It Virtue, adaptation of a play by Luigi Pirandello (produced New York, 1963).
Gentlemen, Be Seated, with Jerome Moross, music by Moross, lyrics by Eager (produced New York, 1963).
Rugantino (lyrics only), book by Alfred Drake, music by Armando Trovaioli, adaptation of a play by Pietro Garinei, Sandro Giovanini, Festa Campanile, and Franciosa (produced New York, 1964).
The Happy Hypocrite, music by James Bredt, adaptation of the story by Max Beerbohm (produced New York, 1968).

Television Plays: *The Marriage of Figaro,* from the libretto by Lorenzo da Ponte, music by Mozart, 1954; *The Adventures of Marco Polo* (lyrics only), 1956.

* * *

Edward Eager's fantasy novels for children openly admit the author's admiration for the earlier English writer, E. Nesbit. Eager's spirited American characters are often to be found reading and referring to various Nesbit books. The American children then discover Nesbit-style magic themselves but find out that magic is an unpredictable gift and cannot be easily controlled. It is in part this lack of certainty that helps create some of the ever-present humour in the books.

The four connected fantasies, sometimes called the Half Magic series, are solidly-based tales involving slightly quirky magic that must be figured out in order to be used effectively. Two titles not connected to the Half Magic books, *Magic or Not?* and *The Well-Wishers,* tantalize the reader by never revealing whether magic, or just happy coincidence, is taking place.

The Half Magic series centres on an extended family living in Toledo in the 1920s and later in the 1950s. In the first title, *Half Magic,* four brother and sisters—Mark, Jane, Katharine and Martha—discover a magic talisman which grants wishes, but only in half quantity. A thoughtlessly expressed desire for the excitement of a fire provides a fire as requested, but only a children's playhouse burns down rather than a full-sized house. In wishing human speech for their pet cat, the children discover that the indignant cat is only able to say partially English words combined with proper cat talk. When the children try to return the cat to normalcy, Jane tells the charm to let the cat say nothing in the future except "music." (Since they must request doubled wishes to make them turn out right, Jane has reasoned that the cat would say only the first syllable of the word, "mew.") Alas, the unfortunate cat can now say only, "Sic, Sic, Sic."

In the next title, *Knight's Castle,* the children of the original four become the protagonists. Roger and Ann, Martha's children, must go to Baltimore with their parents where they stay with Katharine's family, including her two children, Jack and Eliza. The two city cousins are a bit snobbish to the younger and less sophisticated Roger and Ann, but when Roger discovers magic by building a model city for his old toy knight, the four children take part in medieval adventures set in Roger's more contemporary urban setting. There is a toy castle, but there are also toy cars for the knights and their ladies to use. The magical adventure of the children in their fantasy world is based on the story of Sir Walter Scott's *Ivanhoe.*

In *Magic by the Lake* the series returns to the original brother and sisters on vacation. They capture a wish-granting turtle but, as usual in Eager's fantasies, things don't always work out as the wishers intended. For example, Jane and Katharine wish to be 16, but the resulting confusion at a dance—with Mark and Martha appearing as their original ages—illustrates to the children once again that magic wishes don't necessarily make dreams come true. In this book there is a brief scene involving four other children named Roger, Ann, Jack and Eliza. This is a hint of the next book to come in the series, *The Time Garden,* which focuses on the cousins of *Knight's Castle*. Rather than finding magical adventures in a world of their creation, the four cousins discover a magical thyme plant in the garden which permits time travel. On one trip to the past they meet four children named Mark, Jane, Katharine and Martha.

One book by Eager which is separate, *Seven-Day Magic,* involves a new set of characters. Five children find a wonderful book at the library that writes itself—as magic provides exciting adventures and even helps adults important to the children. As with the other Eager novels, the magic is tricky and must come to an end when the time comes to return the book to the library. In *Seven-Day Magic* Eager depicts, as always, kind and loving sibling relationships.

The two maybe-magic books by Eager, *Magic or Not?* and *The Well-Wishers,* are less satisfying than the Half Magic series. This is due not only to the ambivalence regarding the existence of magic at work or not, but also to the somewhat heavy-handed approach to social issues of the 1960s, such as racial integration. The sequel, *The Well-Wishers,* is even a bit more disappointing in having chapters written by each of the five children involved in the story, a device which doesn't work well in this case and seems gimmicky.

In viewing Eager's seven fantasy novels, there are certain elements that provide lasting charm and appeal. The humour generally holds up, providing chuckles for today's children as well as those contemporary to the books' publication. The obvious relish of Eager for children, and children's books about magic, provide a freshness in the stories. All in all, Eager is never nasty about any of the people in his books; the bad citizens usually see the error of their ways and reform, providing happy endings. The rewriting of *Ivanhoe* in *Knight's Castle* is such a case: for many, if not most, young readers of Scott's classic really want Ivanhoe to end up with Rebecca rather than Rowena. For readers, adults and children who are reading Eager for the first time, there are many references to other works of fantasy, such as L. Frank Baum's Oz books, as well as the aforementioned E. Nesbit. Eager also refers to other books of his own, probably as a guide to readers who want the story to keep going rather than as self-promotion. All of Eager's fantasies are illustrated by N. M. Bodecker, whose decorative and humorous black-and-white pictures complement the text nicely.

—Cosette Kies

EASTON, M(alcolm) Coleman

Nationality: American. **Born:** 1942. **Career:** Has worked in computer science and engineering research.

FANTASY PUBLICATIONS

Novels (series: Kyala)

Masters of Glass (Kyala). New York, Popular Library, 1985.

Iskiir. New York, Popular Library, 1986.
The Fisherman's Curse (Kyala). New York, Popular Library, 1987.
Spirits of Cavern and Hearth. New York, St. Martin's Press, 1988.

OTHER PUBLICATIONS

Novels

Swimmers Beneath the Bright. New York, Popular Library, 1987.
Daughter of the Reef (as Clare Coleman, with Clare Bell). New York, Jove, 1992.
Child of the Dawn (as Clare Coleman, with Clare Bell). New York, Jove, 1994.

*   *   *

Despite following three routine fantasy novels with an exceptional one, Easton has made little impact upon the genre so far. *Masters of Glass* and its sequel, *The Fisherman's Curse,* are set in a simple European-medieval type of society, familiar from so many other fantasy novels. There are farmers, fishermen, innkeepers and peddlers; a non-intrusive pantheistic religion holds sway; nasty creatures dwell in the forest and beneath the sea.

The sole item of originality is provided by the Vigens, who are makers of glass beads. They are rare and skilled craftsmen, who possess the ability to cast glass in the exact colour shades of the eyes of various animals, and they are also magicians, since the bead gives power over the animal. (It is a fascinating variation on the "evil eye" tradition.) This seems to be the only manifestation of magic in Easton's world and, as is sometimes the fate of magicians in fantasy novels, the Vigens are pariahs, seldom respected and often mistrusted.

In *Masters of Glass,* a village is menaced by Lame Ones (giant trolls), and Vigen Watnojat's eye talismans prove ineffective because of the lack of a mineral (astablak) necessary in their manufacture. Watnojat's apprentice is killed and his father, a fisherman called Pelask, curses any other men's sons whom Watnojat might take as apprentices. But Watnojat (an old man) appoints a girl apprentice, Kyala, and they go off on a quest for astablak. After some frustrations, they obtain supplies of the mineral from another Vigen, Untmur, who uses his powers to control people (a despicable crime). In the end it is Kyala who is the driving force in their escape from Untmur, in casting new beads and in killing off the Lame Ones; indeed, Watnojat is mortally wounded in this battle.

The Fisherman's Curse, which follows straight on, shows how Pelask's curse affects Kyala. In a series of unconvincing plot developments, she is blamed (by the inhabitants of her home village) for Pelask's fishing boat being wrecked and Pelask lost, and for the appearance of a sea monster in the area. Only help from the local woodcarver, Bremig (who is ironically a relative of Pelask's and who becomes Kyala's lover) saves her from serious harm. After considerable rushing around, Kyala identifies the monster as a giant squid, crab and snake, operating together; she casts beads in the colours of each pair of eyes and manages to defeat them.

While *Masters of Glass* is relatively slow-moving, *The Fisherman's Curse* has a plot that is brisker yet less credible. Each book contains a few impressively successful scenes. Often these are magical applications of the beads—in conjunction with extreme heat or blood. Many plot elements are fairly traditional: quests, the defeat of an evil sorcerer, the discovery of one's hidden talents at a time of crisis, calling up the dead for advice, the youngster whose knowledge and advice are ignored by older people. Easton's characterization is shallow in both books. The reader is barred from too many of the thoughts or intentions of Kyala and Bremig (both viewpoints are used, though to no great effect).

There is a spiritual aspect to these novels. In times of her greatest need, Kyala is helped (augmented is perhaps the right word) by the power of Ormek, the sun god. And there is a suggestion that she cannot call on this power while she loves Bremig. All this is in pointed contrast to the pomposity of the established church. It is in small areas like this that Easton shows hints of an original voice at work, though the lack of proper development of such originality also denotes a lack of confidence.

Iskiir, which was Easton's second book to be published, in between the last two dealt with, is an Arabian fantasy. It, too, suffers from plot elements that are unconvincing, and this time there is no good original idea as a counterbalance. The eponymous hero is a young goatherd, one of the few to survive when his home village in the mountains is attacked and crushed by stone monoliths. He flees to a city to live with his cousin, Yeniski, who pretends to be a magician, and there he falls in love with the beautiful Adeh. But the monoliths appear, threatening the city, and the three have to seek help from a real magician who lives in the desert. Iskiir discovers that not only does he possess a useful magical ability, but that his girlfriend has a complementary power: they are the only ones who can defeat the monoliths and save the city. The revelation about the monoliths being created out of dates by a fanatical religious cult is somewhat less than satisfying.

In *Spirits of Cavern and Hearth,* Easton displays great sharpness of characterization and firmness of plotting to produce a memorable and satisfying piece of work. Here, his fantasy world contains two inimical groups of people, the settled, land-owning Hakhan and the more nomadic Chirudak, who compete for space. But the differences between them—and their conflicts—are shown by Easton in terms of their differing spiritual beliefs. The Hakhan are too materialistic to bother with true spirituality, generally believing that gods are a worthless superstition, though they maintain a formalized religion. By contrast, the Chirudak do not feel the need for permanent ownership of land (or most other possessions), yet they have retained a strong spirituality.

The plot concerns Yarkoi Dolmi, a Hakhan physician, who becomes "god-stricken," that is, suffering from a strange disease which not only rejuvenates his body but also lays his mind open to direct contact with the playful (and occasionally malevolent) spirits of cavern and hearth. He can see these tiny creatures. But Hakhan society casts him out; he is forced to travel north and live with the Chirudak—who revere such god-stricken individuals. Yarkoi is a fine character, who changes and develops through the novel, becoming a bridge between the two cultures.

The harsh lands of the Chirudak are well described. There, Yarkoi has to adapt to an alien (to him) way of life and of thinking. He is helped by a woman called Etoudoori, and through her he meets shamans and also Kag, the god-stricken leader of the Chirudak. There is considerable originality here, as well as a more successful treatment of Easton's favourite setting (modest pre-industrial) and theme (personal feelings about magic, religion and the relationship between them).

—Chris Morgan

EDDINGS, David

Nationality: American. **Born:** Spokane, Washington, 7 July 1931. **Education:** Reed College, Portland, Oregon, B.A. in literature 1954; University of Washington, Seattle, M.A. in English 1961. **Military Service:** United States Army, 1954-56. **Family:** Married Judith Lee Schall in 1962. **Agent:** Eleanor Wood, Blasingame, McCauley, and Wood, 111 Eighth Avenue, Suite 1501, New York, NY 10011, USA.

FANTASY PUBLICATIONS

Novels (series: The Belgariad; The Elenium; The Malloreon; The Tamuli)

Pawn of Prophecy (Belgariad). New York, Del Rey, 1982; London, Century, 1983.
Queen of Sorcery (Belgariad). New York, Del Rey, 1982; London, Century, 1983.
Magician's Gambit (Belgariad). New York, Del Rey, 1983; London, Century, 1984.
Castle of Wizardry (Belgariad). New York, Del Rey, and London, Century, 1984.
Enchanter's Endgame (Belgariad). New York, Del Rey, 1984; London, Century, 1985.
Guardians of the West (Malloreon). New York, Del Rey, and London, Bantam Press, 1987.
King of the Murgos (Malloreon). New York, Del Rey, and London, Bantam Press, 1988.
Demon Lord of Karanda (Malloreon). New York, Del Rey, and London, Bantam Press, 1988.
Sorceress of Darshiva (Malloreon). New York, Del Rey, and London, Bantam Press, 1989.
The Diamond Throne (Elenium). New York, Del Rey, and London, Grafton, 1989.
The Ruby Knight (Elenium). London, Grafton, 1990; New York, Del Rey, 1991.
The Seeress of Kell (Malloreon). New York, Del Rey, and London, Bantam Press, 1991.
The Sapphire Rose (Elenium). London, HarperCollins, 1991; New York, Del Rey, 1992.
Domes of Fire (Tamuli). London, HarperCollins, 1992; New York, Del Rey, 1993.
The Shining Ones (Tamuli). London, HarperCollins, and New York, Del Rey, 1993.
The Hidden City (Tamuli). London, HarperCollins, and New York, Del Rey, 1994.

OTHER PUBLICATIONS

Novels

High Hunt. New York, Putnam, 1973; London, HarperCollins, 1993.
The Losers. New York, Ballantine, 1992; London, Grafton, 1993.

*   *   *

Although J. R. R. Tolkien's *The Lord of the Rings* is considered to have influenced the form of the modern epic fantasy, the epic is probably the oldest narrative form in oral and written literature alike. Thus, while modern commentators may criticize fantasy epics for their slavish fidelity to Tolkien's seminal masterpiece, they overlook the fact that the epic form has been honed over many thousands of years and that certain plot components will inevitably appear. Modern writers of fantasy epics are therefore always seeking to present these components in new and attractive arrangements. David Eddings has succeeded more than most. Though comparisons with Tolkien's work are inevitably made, there is no doubt that Eddings has lent his own distinctive touch to the epic form through several epic series. The first of these is the Belgariad.

The child who is unaware of his own identity and destiny is a plot device which goes back to classical times. Eddings' hero, Garion, grows up in very simple circumstances; his friends are farm boys, a vagrant story-teller he calls Mr. Wolf, and his own beloved Aunt Pol, housekeeper on the farm where he lives and works. His destiny begins to work itself out when, as a teenager, enquiries are made about him by mysterious strangers, forcing him to flee with Pol, Mr. Wolf and Durnik, the farm's blacksmith and Pol's earnest admirer.

Thus begins Garion's quest. The form will be familiar to readers. Garion acquires a band of companions who will become his friends and advisers, each with peculiar but necessary skills which will save the day, time and again. Pol and Mr. Wolf, in particular, turn out to be wizards, capable of great feats of magic, as is Garion himself, as the son of wizards. We witness his assumption of these skills and his gradual maturing into adulthood. We also learn more about his destiny, which is nothing more or less than to save the world—threatened because a powerful talisman has been stolen by representatives of Torak, the maimed god of the dark. Garion must fulfil the Prophecy by retrieving this artefact, slaying Torak and taking his rightful place as the King of Riva.

In contrast with *The Lord of the Rings,* Eddings' epic tale is a gentler and altogether more domestic affair. The characters are rarely separated from one another for more than a few hours and escape easily from any danger which might befall them. None of the main characters is seriously injured, let alone dies, and from the outset there is an all-pervading sense of certainty that they will succeed in their quest, but simultaneously no sense of urgency to complete it as the characters tour the various kingdoms of the West. Eddings' characters are uniformly attractive and his villains are inexplicably likeable, even some of the Murgos, who are reviled by all the characters and routinely slaughtered whenever encountered. This emotional monotone gives the series an unfortunate cosiness and security. One reads for comfort rather than to be swept up by the enormity of events and to receive an emotional charge.

Nevertheless, Eddings' writing in the series shows an attractive humour which is certainly lacking in Tolkien's writing. The dialogue is often very sharp and witty, and conveys a strong sense of the nature of the individual characters as well as suggesting a tight-knit group committed to a cause, which may possibly explain the great popularity of the series.

Likewise, Eddings' kings and queens are refreshingly ordinary in many ways, with very human faults. However, it might be argued that we, as readers, are privileged to see them in this fashion. Typically of fantasy epics, we see little of the life of ordinary inhabitants of this world, except for occasional allusions to their comparative treatment as serfs or freeborn peasants in different countries. As readers, we are part of a privileged club. Similarly, while Eddings, unlike Tolkien, does admit that women exist in his world, he shows an irritating tendency, which borders on mania, to marry everyone off tidily at the end of each series and to ensure that the

women are all pregnant. Although Garion's wife-to-be, Ce'nedra is allowed to raise an army on his behalf, and the other wives of rulers assume authority while their husbands are at war, Eddings' attitude comes across as very patronising towards the "little women."

The Belgariad established a successful formula which Eddings immediately reused in the Malloreon series, using the same cast of characters. On this occasion, Garion's son is in danger as he has been chosen by the forces of Darkness to become the new Child of Dark. Garion and his companions once again expend much time and energy in chasing across the kingdoms of the West before the child is retrieved. Once again, everything is neatly resolved as the double series is brought to a close with the creation of a new God, and hence a new cycle of events. However, the very familiarity of the characters and the repetitious nature of the plot weakened the attraction of this series compared to the first.

His more recent work, in the Elenium and Tamuli series, has confirmed this tendency to work over familiar ground. The two series focus on the relationship between the royal family of Elenia and the House of Sparhawk. In each generation Sparhawk is the Royal Champion and, as the series opens, the current Sparhawk is pledged to undertake a quest for a mysterious stone in order to save the life of his Queen, who is seriously ill. Thus, Eddings' protagonist is once more enabled to explore his world on behalf of the readers.

Nevertheless, the Belgariad, and to a lesser extent the Malloreon, have created a new style of epic fantasy, where interplay between the characters carries as much weight as the heroic deeds undertaken, and where protganists are seen to have a more fully-developed life within the novels. It is to be regretted that Eddings cannot step far beyond this tried and tested formula but he has undoubtedly made an important contribution to the development of the fantasy epic.

—Maureen Speller

EDDISON, E(ric) R(ucker)

Nationality: British. **Born:** Adel, Yorkshire, 24 November 1882. **Education:** Public schools; Oxford University. **Family:** Married Winifred Grace Henderson in 1909; one daughter. **Career:** Civil servant, Board of Trade, from 1906; deputy comptroller-general, Department of Overseas Trade, 1930-37. **Awards:** Knight Commander of the Order of St. Michael and St. George, 1924; Companion of the Order of the Bath, 1929. **Died:** 18 August 1945.

FANTASY PUBLICATIONS

Novels (series: Zimiamvia)

The Worm Ouroboros: A Romance. Edinburgh, Clark, 1922; New York, Dutton, 1926.
Mistress of Mistresses: A Vision of Zimiamvia. London, Faber, and New York, Dutton, 1935.
A Fish Dinner in Memison (Zimiamvia). New York, Dutton, 1941; London, Pan Ballantine, 1972.
The Mezentian Gate (Zimiamvia). London, Curwen Press, 1958; New York, Ballantine, 1969.

OTHER PUBLICATIONS

Novel

Styrbiorn the Strong. London, Cape, and New York, Boni, 1926.

Other

Editor, *Poems, Letters, and Memories of Philip Sydney Nairn.* Privately printed, 1916.

Editor and translator (from Icelandic), *Egil's Saga* by Snorri Sturlson. Cambridge, University Press, 1930; New York, Greenwood Press, 1968.

*

Critical Study: "Superman in a Bowler: E. R. Eddison" in *Literary Swordsmen and Sorcerers: The Makers of Heroic Fantasy* by L. Sprague de Camp, Sauk City, Wisconsin, Arkham House, 1976.

*   *   *

To modern fantasy, Eddison is somewhat like Olaf Stapledon to modern science fiction: a writer of philosophical epics that owe little to the purely genre concerns of what crystallized afterwards but without which later essays in the form would have been far less ambitious. His archaic and "poetic" styles have perhaps divorced him from mass appeal. He was, however, influential upon fellow novelists: Fritz Leiber cites two of his characters as sources of his sword-and-sorcery heroes Fafhrd and the Gray Mouser. If "heroic fantasy" has any meaning beyond the sword-and-sorcery mould it is in the works of this writer in the English tradition of "imaginary worlds" from the Brontes' *Gondal* to Tolkien's *Silmarillion.* His work may not be dissimilar at root to the fascination with the "natural aristocrat" which fuelled the writing of Robert E. Howard and his imitators, but where Howard fantasized an iconoclastically barbarian hero, Eddison, an English civil servant, rejoiced in lineage, literary cultivation, and feudal ties.

In *The Worm Ourobouros* Eddison created a magnificent plot involving necromancy, a quest and base treachery all wrapped up in High Renaissance decoration; a baroque delight in cadences and description which balances equally baroque characters and themes. Lessingham, an aristocrat whose ancestors were Lake District Vikings, is asleep in the uncanny "Lotus Room" of his country house. In a dream, he is transported to the planet Mercury to become the invisible observer of a titanic war between two of its nations. (Indeed, so "invisible" is Lessingham that after 26 pages he vanishes from the text).

This Mercury of "Demons" and "Witches" is a world built from fictions and aspirations of the Heroic Ages. Eddison plays homage to his sources by including in his text poems from our own Classic and Renaissance writers which arise naturally from the barbarically sophisticated world he describes, where chivalrous Honour wars with crafty Policy. The circular ending denies a sequel, and after *The Worm* Eddison wrote a historical novel (*Styrbiorn the Strong*) and produced a translation of *Egil's Saga.* He then returned, but obliquely, to the world of *The Worm* for a projected trilogy which would express more fully his ideas of the relationships between Art, Religion and Existence. *Mistress of Mistresses, A Fish Dinner in Memison* and *The Mezentian Gate* offer another tragic conflict, darker and more metaphysically complex,

with our own world playing a not too glamorous part in the scheme of things. More supple in prose style than *The Worm,* they are also more ornately plotted, taking an imaginative leap into a multileveled cosmology to work backwards through the sequence with each successive telling illuminating the previous books. (Only a third of the final volume was complete by Eddison's death, although the rest survived in summary.)

Lessingham now is a central character, taking part in several guises in the action, although the beginning of *The Worm* is echoed by starting *Mistress of Mistresses* with Lessingham's death in our world and following him resurrected in Zimiamvia, an afterworld of *The Worm*'s "Mercury," as an aristocrat of aristocrats who is nevertheless fighting on the wrong side in the war of Succession of the late King Mezentius. We have another scenario of conflict between "Honour" (the King's descendants) and "Policy" (the scheming Horius Parry) which also involves Duke Barganax, the bastard son of Mezentius, and the chivalric Lessingham whose family loyalty and love of adventure causes him to support his despicable cousin Parry. There are echoes of Lessingham's earthly life as a 20th-century scholar-soldier who has written a History comparable to Gibbon, has conquered Paraguay, and has carved out his own personal fiefdom in the Arctic.

More supple and varied than *The Worm,* the Zimiamvia sequence continues its use of High Literature—Sappho, Homer, Shakespeare, Webster—as touchstones, while the prose itself ranges from descriptive narrative to languorous prose-poems. Built upon a foundation of echoes, correspondences, half-remembered dreams and snatches of poetry as characters recall in various stages of dimness or clarity incarnations in other worlds, Eddison's novels reveal a fascinating theme of transmutation of identity and dark erotic symbolism: a pagan philosophy of a male/female creative dualism whose "love" infuses the universe. All that is, is this "love" expressed in various ways through the juxtaposition of key characters and inter-related cosmologies which becomes clearer as the Zimiamvian trilogy progresses.

A Fish Dinner in Memison and *The Mezentian Gate* show us the "earlier" life of Lessingham and his wife, the history of Zimiamvia leading up to the death of Mezentius, and the connections between the two. They also make clearer how Eddison's multidimensional cosmos formed and continued through the relationship of the Divine pair of whom most of the leading characters are "dresses." This is expressed variously through the relationships of Mezentius and the Duchess of Memison, the Lessinghams, and Barganax and his mistress Fiorinda (who also may "be" both the earthly Lessingham's wife and the mistress who promises "I will perform" over his bier). It is commented on at various points by the wandering philosopher Doctor Vandermast. In *A Fish Dinner* the suggested theme of Zimiamvia as a domain created for earthly heroes is turned on its head as the novel shows something of the political situation preceding the action of *Mistress* and more of the implications of that important scene near the end of the book where, in an almost casual aside to illustrate a dinner-table question about what worlds they would create were they gods, Mezentius forms a universe bound by "clockwork" laws of cause and effect, into which the couples around that dinner table enter to experience a created cosmos.

Eddison uses his literary sources to distil Renaissance values as we see them or understand Renaissance figures themselves to have seen them, which enables him to praise aristocratic and heroic virtues without examining their darker sides too closely. It is certainly possible, however, to read the sequence knowing full well that the "real" Lessingham, in the context of the 20th century, can be described as nothing more than a fascist adventurer. When we see the Lessinghams in their "modern" lives, we see people for whom society is nothing more than an elite served by a mass of spear-carriers. Zimiamvia is the literal description of this apotheosis of privilege, where even a classic literary figure of "Discontent" such as Parry's weaselly secretary Gabriel Flores is trapped forever in his role as grovelling underdog. It seems that Zimiamvia, as well as being an artistic creation built on foundations of High Culture, is both a heightened aspect of our world and a preexistent superior model in which deities amuse themselves. Our universe eventually expires at the point of a pin, and Eddison's gloriously heroic creation, full of some of the most unforgettable scenes and characters in fantasy, collapses uneasily on the supposition that our world is a nothing, most of us are probably not even real in any significant sense, and only a few supermen like Lessingham are worth bothering about.

One can suggest that Eddison's heroes seem to be a fictional way of suggesting that the world was made for cultivated ex-public-schoolboys in which to play. Certainly, there are parallels between the fictional Lessingham and Eddison's friend Philip Sydney Nairn, whose poems and letters Eddison edited after his early death in 1914 and who was known by at least one female acquaintance as "The Viking." But any "explanation" of Zimiamvia must be as strongly rooted in the cultural resonance with an earlier age of glorious chivalry and vivid drama which is suggested by Nairn's forenames as in any correspondence between real or fictional English country gentlemen who died with much promise to be fulfilled. In any case, the complex relationship between the Human and the Divine can suggest a reverse reading. The Zimiamvian books as a whole are a wonderful exercise in building a fantasy cosmos to explore the aspirations and motives of characters in such a world "were it real." Which cosmos this sentence refers to, though, may be part of the metaphysical ambiguity of the work.

—Andy Sawyer

EDGERTON, Teresa (Ann)

Nationality: American. **Born:** 1949. **Address:** c/o Ace Books, 200 Madison Avenue, New York, NY 10016, USA.

FANTASY PUBLICATIONS

Novels (series: Chronicles of Celydonn; Green Lion; Goblin)

Child of Saturn (Green Lion). New York, Ace, 1989.
The Moon in Hiding (Green Lion). New York, Ace, 1989.
The Work of the Sun (Green Lion). New York, Ace, 1990.
Goblin Moon. New York, Ace, 1991.
The Gnome's Engine (Goblin). New York, Ace, 1991.
The Castle of the Silver Wheel (Celydonn). New York, Ace, 1993.
The Grail and the Ring (Celydonn). New York, Ace, 1994.

*   *   *

If anyone knows how to write a medieval fantasy, it is Teresa Edgerton. But her knowledge comes only partially through research.

The reason the Green Lion trilogy, her first published work, was so accurate as to the details of medieval life and culture is because for 15 years of her life that is where she lived. As a Tarot Card reader for the California Renaissance Faire, Edgerton grew up, met her husband, and raised her children steeped in the atmosphere and nostalgia of the Middle Ages.

The first volume of the Green Lion trilogy, *Child of Saturn,* is the story of Teleri, an apprentice Wizard, and Ceilyn, a young knight. The theme of the female wizard is a favourite one in recent years, among traditional fantasy authors both male and female. Teleri and Ceilyn are both sympathetic characters, surrounded on all sides by those older but not necessarily wiser than they, and villains whom they aren't quite equipped to vanquish. An unusual aspect of these books (*Child of Saturn* was followed by *The Moon in Hiding* and *The Work of the Sun*) is that they are Christian fantasy. Unlike most created worlds, Celydonn is a Christian kingdom that somehow reconciles (not too successfully) the magic that is a part of its characters' lives. As in much classic fantasy, male wizards are more accepted than female ones, who are often thought of as witches, and this makes Teleri's task even more difficult, particularly as at the beginning of the first book she is extremely shy and practically invisible at the glittering court of the king. While she is convinced she likes it this way, Ceilyn and the need to confront the evil threatening them convince her otherwise, and by the end of the trilogy she is a beautiful, self-contained woman with great power and great love.

Edgerton has continued to write about Celydonn, the world of the Green Lion trilogy, in her later books, *The Castle of the Silver Wheel* and *The Grail and the Ring.* These novels feature as heroine Gwenlliant, one of the secondary characters of the first trilogy. Gwenlliant, younger sister of the knight Garanwyn, was one of the handmaidens to Queen Sidonwy. A natural psychic, Gwenlliant was untrained when a black magician attempted to draw her onto the dark path. Rescued by Teleri, Gwenlliant is thrown into a prolonged sleep by her proximity to black magic. Upon awakening, she is well again.

As an adult in the new books, Gwenlliant is married to Prince Tryffin of Tir Gwengelli, deputy consul to the land of Mochdreff. An adept of earth magic, Gwenlliant can communicate with the earth itself, but dark magic again attacks her and throws her and her baby son into a shadow realm, from which she must escape. She is the only one who can save the land of Celydonn from a monster created by the dark magic.

As enjoyable as the Green Lion trilogy and the subsequent volumes about Celydonn are, I consider Edgerton's best works so far to be the two books she wrote following the trilogy. The first, *Goblin Moon,* takes place on an alternative earth during what would be our 18th century. This world is magical, and in the city of Thornburg on the river Lunn elves, dwarfs, and men live in harmony together; but they can't live in harmony with the goblins who prey on them all. The world of Thornburg is one dimension over from ours—which is how Edgerton explains our belief in goblins and dwarfs: things we don't have but because that world is so close to ours the ideas seep back and forth across the dimensional barrier.

The story begins when a strangely preserved body is discovered in a river, sealed in a box with a lot of antique books. The body and books are taken to Jenks, owner of a used bookshop. Unfortunately, Jenks is also a would-be alchemist, and the "body" is in reality an ensorcelled sorcerer, not of the benevolent sort. There are several layers to the story, and the second consists of Jenks's niece Sera, companion to a wealthy young woman. The rich residents of Thornburg are bizarre, much as in our own dimension during the 18th century—one of their favourite entertainments is to hold funerals for people still alive; indeed, the "dead" person honoured usually attends. These occasions are accompanied by a picnic.

Elsie, Sera's employer, is pursued by a strange nobleman named Jarl Skogsra. Some of the characters in the book are difficult to determine as to motive; they turn out to be villains when they appear to be friends. This makes the fantasy suspenseful; there are many outright villains as well, against which the heroine, Sera, and the hero, Francis Love Skelbrooke, are pitted to the death. So Edgerton combines fantasy, period romance and suspense novel in a cunningly interwoven fashion.

Not only is the world of *Goblin Moon* fascinating, but the characters are beguiling. The hero, Lord Skelbrooke, is based on the best traditions of Georgette Heyer and Baroness Orczy, but with a twist: he's certainly a handsome swashbuckler who can be counted on to save a maiden in distress and battle ten men in order to do it, but he's also a junkie, addicted to a drug called "sleep dust." And in order to win the hand of his beloved he has to kick the habit (something he doesn't do until the sequel, *The Gnome's Engine*). That beloved isn't the usual romantic heroine, either—Edgerton specializes in female characters who aren't exactly what they seem, and Sera, who starts out as a mousy paid companion, progresses by the end of the story to a pioneering heroine who helps to save the world. But Francis Skelbrooke is the most fascinating character in the books, at least to female readers:

"I had intended for him to be a traditional romantic hero, and the turning point in his development came when the High Priest of the Satanic cult (the Knights of Mezztopholeez) was about to mutilate and murder the girl, and Skelbrooke tells him, 'Stop or I'll shoot'. The High Priest stops, but Skelbrooke shoots him anyway. In all the stories I've read the hero always has the villain at his mercy, but he never shoots." (From "Interview With Teresa Edgerton" in *Marion Zimmer Bradley's Fantasy Magazine,* Fall 1991.)

In *The Gnome's Engine,* the contrasts between the decadent residents of the continent of Euterpe and the New World are striking; it is in this new land that Skelbrooke joins with Mr. Jonas, gnome-scientist, in creating his marvellous scientific engine. And only in an alternative reality as crazy as this one could that engine be a tremendous combination of magic and science. The world is saved (again) from the dark forces, Skelbrooke kicks the habit, Sera finally gets her hero and finds fulfilment (though her escape from the Jarl and her crazy mother was probably enough of that to last a lifetime). Edgerton is a talented fantasy writer, both in her Celtic and medieval modes, and one hopes there will be more novels about Skelbrooke and Sera and their adventures in the New World.

—Debora Hill

EDWARDS, Claudia J(ane)

Nationality: American. **Born:** 13 July 1943 in Monterey, California. **Education:** University of Texas, B.A., 1965. **Career:** Peace Corps volunteer, Palau, Micronesia, 1966-68; elementary school teacher, Joseph City Public School, Arizona, 1969-70, Sierra Vista Public Schools, 1970—. **Address:** Route 1, Box 100C, Hereford, Arizona 85615, USA.

FANTASY PUBLICATIONS

Novels (series: Forest King)

Taming the Forest King. New York, Popular Library, 1986; London, Headline, 1987.
A Horsewoman in Godsland (Forest King). New York, Popular Library, 1987; London, Headline, 1988.
Bright and Shining Tiger (Forest King). New York, Popular Library, and London, Headline, 1988.
Eldrie the Healer. New York, Pageant, 1989.

*   *   *

Claudia Edwards's first three fantasy novels are all set in the same world, although otherwise unrelated to one another. They attracted little critical attention at the time of publication, which is to be regretted—for each, in its way, challenged some assumptions made about fantasy writing. Although fantasy fiction often makes use of strong female protagonists, their roles are generally limited to that of healer, witch or royalty in jeopardy, women who have been thrust temporarily into a controlling position and who are only too happy to retreat to a more conservative role as soon as circumstances allow. By contrast, Edwards's female characters are shown to have actively made a choice and to have deliberately eschewed a conventional female role.

In her first novel, *Taming the Forest King,* Edwards's protagonist, Tevra, is colonel of a troop of light cavalry, sent to a distant province on the orders of the king to act as his representative. This commission has been earned entirely on merit and is accepted entirely without question by almost everyone within the military environment. The conservative Forest Lords regard the king's choice as bizarre but quickly come to recognize that Tevra is a soldier and a diplomat. Her sex is incidental. The feminist message is blunt but mostly well-handled. Tevra is a likeable and competent character who worries about the fact that for years she has concealed her love for her second-in-command, Hetwith. Admittedly, the revelation that Hetwith also loves her, providing a neat resolution of their dilemma, is handled in an overly sentimental fashion but it does not spoil the overall portrait of a woman who is firmly in charge of her own destiny and who is clearly capable of carrying out the difficult task of sorting out the corruption and rebellion in a distant province.

A Horsewoman in Godsland begins in an equally uncompromising fashion. Adelinda is a misfit in her own society, which offers only marriage as a respectable employment for women. Adelinda's desire to go into business as a horse-breeder disturbs her family, who would much rather see her married off as soon as possible. Adelinda is considered too old for marriage by her own society's standards, and has a reputation for promiscuity which deters men of her own class, while the one man she did love had been of too low a class to make a suitable match. The chance to introduce horses into another kingdom, and to train people in handling them, is therefore not to be missed, representing good commercial sense and a chance to escape her family.

Godsland, however, is very different from Adelinda's own country. Women are nothing more than slaves, to be distributed to men in marriage as the village priests see fit. Adelinda's employer is a bishop in the Church of the Quadrate God who is appalled by this threat to everything he believes in and sets himself the task of subjugating Adelinda to his will. It is an attempt doomed to failure, not least because Edwards is simply not equal to the task of exploring the complex human emotions at play. Bishop An-Shai's need to subdue Adelinda to his will clearly stems from more than the fact that she represents a threat to his authority, but while it is no surprise that by the end of the book Adelinda will become his wife, and for reasons which are as much to do with politics as because of any genuine affection between them, the process by which this is achieved is crudely and predictably laid out in comparison to the earlier novel, although the earlier sentimentality is mercifully absent. Nevertheless, Edwards' strong interest in a woman's right to control of her own life persists in this novel and Adelinda is a worthy opponent to An-shai. Interesting too is her portrayal of a religious system which is entirely cynical in that it is intended exclusively to keep the peasants under control; indeed the higher clerics are viewed with suspicion by their superiors if they do believe in the Quadrate God, and Edwards' presentation of An-Shai's struggle between belief and practicality is more strongly drawn than his battle with Adelinda.

In her third novel, *Bright and Shining Tiger,* Edwards strays into seemingly more conventional territory. Her protagonist, Runa, is a witch, exiled by those who fear her powers. In her travels she comes across a deserted fortress guarded by a supernatural cat who acknowledges her as the castle's rightful guardian, more or less forcing her to take control of the castle and the tiller folk who expect her to provide protection for her. More worryingly, the castle should be ruled by a Margrave as well as the Mantic whose role she has assumed, and Runa is forced to consider that she will be expected to marry this man and surrender her freedom, although she has no intention of doing so.

It is disappointing that Runa does accept Taharka as her Margrave as comparatively easily as she does, even if Edwards does portray her as a virgin, scared to consummate the relationship; an unusual twist this, in a genre where women are either celibate, compliant or to be raped, and rarely shown to consider sex in an ambivalent way. Nevertheless, Runa does seek to maintain her personal freedom by not assuming the traditional role of the Mantic, guarding her fortress, her lord and her people by magical means, but does actively participate in improving the economy of her lands and outwitting the other Margraves and Mantics.

Claudia Edwards' novels, although at times uneven in their exploration of male-female relationships, nevertheless provide a welcome contrast to the more conventional perceptions of women in fantastic writing.

—Maureen Speller

EDWARDS, Graham

Nationality: British. **Born:** Shepton Mallett, Somerset, 1965. **Education:** Art school, London. **Family:** Married; two children. **Career:** Designer. **Address:** c/o HarperCollins, 77-85 Fulham Palace Road, London W6 8JB, England.

FANTASY PUBLICATIONS

Novel

Dragoncharm. London, HarperCollins, 1995.

*   *   *

Among all the talking-animal fantasy novels which have followed in the wake of Richard Adams's rabbits in *Watership Down,* there have been societies of moles, owls, eagles, weasels, horses, hares, foxes, wolves and divers other creatures but, until now as far as this critic knows, not dragons on their own.

It is obvious that *Dragoncharm* is Graham Edwards's first novel, since it is imbued throughout with the *gosh-wow!* enthusiasm of naivete, which no professional author can hope to achieve through artifice. The over-the-top style of writing, the hugely melodramatic plot which succeeds in sidestepping credibility, and the characters—every one of them acting like a schoolboy—conspire to produce a pacey adventure that, except for a few literary pretensions, might have been well suited to the typical teenage reader.

The setting is an Earthlike world inhabited by dragons. Trolls have lived there but are long since extinct, and a single basilisk still exists, though it has slept for centuries. Faeries are there, too, though they play only a minute role. The dragons are of two distinct kinds: the Charmed, who possess magical skills, and the Naturals, who do not. For decades they have lived side by side, without strife, for the most part ignoring each other. Both kinds are intelligent and articulate, politically aware, and often subject to military training and discipline. Whether they possess technological abilities of any kind, or whether the castles, towers and tunnels used from time to time by both kinds have been magically produced by the charm possessed by Charmed dragons is never made clear.

For some reason an idyllic period comes to an end. This may be due to the ruthless nature of one dragon, Wraith (also known as the Black Dragon and the Master), or it may be due to Edwards's oft-repeated phrase "the world is turning." Whichever is responsible, Naturals and Charmed are soon engaging in war, though there are enough factions to ensure that the members of each side are fighting among themselves. Many thousands of dragons are killed for no good reason.

Against this peace and war background, certain young dragons seem destined to survive and to be instrumental in bringing about significant change to the whole of dragon society. One is Fortune, a Natural; the other is his friend and companion in adventure Cumber, a Charmed. They escape from a massacre of dragons at South Point, where they both formerly lived, flying to Aether's Cross (to find that strife has been there ahead of them) and finally to Covamere, where they hope to alert Halcyon, the chief of the council of dragons, to the problems.

In the end, in a contrived and overlong finale, Fortune is the one who travels down into the maze below Covamere and symbolically seizes (and offers to give away) the Seed of Charm, defeating Wraith and bringing about not only peace but the end of all magical powers. The reason for Fortune being the chosen one is simple: his father did a similar thing decades earlier and history has to repeat itself.

Accompanying the major plot is a romantic strand of questionable credibility. Fortune meets a young female Natural, Gossamer, at Aether's Cross, and at once they fall in love with each other. A little later, they all meet up with another young female Natural, Velvet, at Covamere, and she and Cumber fall in love. Of course, the young lovers are separated and worry about each other's safety for a while, but the course of true love runs very smoothly indeed, adding to the artificially happy ending.

While Fortune is clearly the novel's hero, he is not greatly developed as a character, remaining a shallow and shadowy figure throughout. This is because Edwards chooses to use almost all his characters, and there are many of them, as viewpoint characters. Thus the reader learns the thoughts of almost 20 different dragons, though these thoughts are for the most part unsurprising, with all characters falling into stock moulds. For example, Wraith is wholly evil with no compensating traits, while Cumber is loyal and practical but shy of emotion.

Of course, while Edwards calls his characters dragons, they are in fact just shallow and simplified representations of humans, complete with human emotions and sensibilities. It is difficult for the reader to take them seriously as dragons when their behaviour is so human. More precisely, their behaviour is always slightly boisterous, slightly naive, slightly self-conscious, just as if they were all about 13 years old. This is not to suggest that the novel has been written for or would be enjoyed by readers of that age, since too much time is taken up with dragons thinking to themselves instead of doing things.

Dragoncharm attempts to deliver messages, albeit simple ones, to its readers. From the beginning it is clear that the Naturals and Charmed are going to stop ignoring each other and then stop fighting each other, and will learn to live in peace, because Fortune learns to accept a Charmed as a friend. It is obvious that good will triumph over evil (so there is no tension in the defeat of Wraith), but the sacrifice necessary by Fortune so that good can win is, of course, Christian. At the end, Fortune, Gossamer, Cumber and Velvet all go to live on the idyllic island of Haven, which is clearly meant to be taken as Heaven.

It is, perhaps, a considerable achievement to have written a lengthy novel about a dragon society without deviating from any of the dragon cliches which have grown up within the fantasy genre, though it is not necessarily one to be proud of.

—Chris Morgan

EGREMONT, Michael. *See* **HARRISON, Michael.**

EISENSTEIN, Phyllis

Nationality: American. **Born:** Phyllis Kleinstein, Chicago, Illinois, 26 February 1946. **Education:** University of Chicago, 1963-66; University of Illinois, Chicago, 1978-81, B.A. in anthropology 1981. **Family:** Married Alex Eisenstein in 1966. **Career:** Co-founder and director, Windy City SF Writers Conference, Chicago, 1972-77; anthology trustee, Science Fiction Writers of America, 1976-81; since 1989, has taught science-fiction writing at Columbia College, Chicago. **Awards:** Balrog award, 1978. **Address:** 6208 North Campbell, Chicago, IL 60659, USA.

FANTASY PUBLICATIONS

Novels (series: Alaric the Minstrel; Cray Ormeru)

Born to Exile (Alaric). Sauk City, Wisconsin, Arkham House, 1978; London, HarperCollins, 1992.
Sorcerer's Son (Cray). New York, Del Rey, 1979; London, Grafton, 1990.
The Crystal Palace (Cray). New York, Signet, 1988; London, Grafton, 1991.
In the Red Lord's Reach (Alaric). New York, Signet, 1989; London, HarperCollins, 1992.

OTHER PUBLICATIONS

Novels

Shadow of Earth. New York, Dell, 1979.
In the Hands of Glory. New York, Pocket, 1981.

*

Phyllis Eisenstein comments:

I never intended to be a fantasy writer. Rather, my goal, from the age of eight, was to be a science-fiction writer, thereby writing in the genre I loved best. But I always enjoyed fantasy. Some of my earliest reading was of the Andrew Lang colour-coded fairy-tale books, which led me on to Grimm, Perrault, and others. And by the time I was ten or eleven, I had read most of Edgar Allan Poe's fiction, which made for an interesting balance. I was reading the science-fiction magazines and the Groff Conklin anthologies by then, and it was becoming clear to me that science fiction and fantasy were a continuum—a spectrum, with sf at the violet end, fantasy at the red end, and a whole array of hard-to-categorize stories in the middle.

When the old *Twilight Zone* TV show came on the air, I saw that it spanned that spectrum, and it confirmed my feeling that there were no hard and fast barriers, that I could write in any color of the spectrum and still be in the same universe. One result of that feeling is that some of my stories are those hard-to-categorize creatures, those in-betweeners that might be science fiction or might be fantasy. But some are solidly in the fantasy end of the spectrum. With all that material from the Western European folkloric tradition absorbed in my formative reading years, it was almost inevitable that some fantasy ideas would leap out of my imagination and demand to be put down on paper. Important human questions were explored in that folkloric tradition—including questions of morality, identity, loyalty, compulsion—and they remain worth exploring, whether in a traditional, a modern, or a futuristic context.

My own work in the fantasy arena tends to focus on the problems of individuals rather than on world-spanning events. I am interested in the outsider, the alienated, the reluctant sorcerer, the seeker for a lost heritage—people searching for their places in the scheme of things, and for whatever happiness they can snatch from an indifferent universe. My stories also frequently concern the lust for power, and the sense of responsibility that must contend with it, the perils of obsessive hatred, and the emptiness of revenge. At least, these things can be found in my work. All of these aspects of the human condition speak to me much more strongly than any supposed struggle between abstract Good and Evil, so I leave that "larger canvas" to others.

*   *   *

The relative sparsity of Eisenstein's output—six novels and about 30 short stories and novellas spread over nearly 25 years—means that her contribution to fantasy fiction could easily be overlooked, were it not that her creations are so memorable. For in some of her fiction, especially *Sorcerer's Son,* she has combined convincing characterization with well developed story-lines steeped solidly in myth and magic, resulting in a body of work that is rare but impressive.

Some of her stories, especially those written with her husband Alex, are science fiction. She first entered the realms of fantasy with "Born to Exile" (*Fantasy & Science Fiction,* 1971), which introduced us to the character of Alaric, a minstrel with powers of teleportation. Alaric was a character Eisenstein had dabbled with in her fiction since she was 15, and it is interesting that when we first meet Alaric he is also 15 and seeking to recover something of his lost past. Alaric had been found on a hillside as a new-born babe with a severed hand clutching his ankle. He was believed to be a witch-child and though loved by his foster mother was reviled and whipped by his foster-father. It was while being whipped that he sought escape and discovered his power of teleportation, though the superstitious society in which he had been raised caused him to fear it as much as his fellows. The stories that were revised to make the first Alaric novel are an exploration of alienation and loneliness in conflicting societies, as Alaric strives to discover himself, and ultimately realizes his past is no better than the rest of the world he has come to know. The sequel, *In the Red Lord's Reach,* sees Alaric endeavouring to come to terms with his past, and to accept what he is for its own sake.

This same melancholia pervades Eisenstein's other fantasy novel sequence, although *Sorcerer's Son* is more hopeful and positive. Whereas the world of Alaric is essentially mundane, with the fantastic represented by the freakish powers of Alaric's family, the world of Cray Ormeru is one of clearly defined logical magic. Cray believes he is the son of a wandering knight, briefly a lover to his mother, Delivev, a sorceress with power over all web-weaving creatures. In fact the knight, Gildrum, was a demon controlled by the evil reclusive sorcerer Rezhyk, who wished to impregnate Delivev in order that she will be unable to spy on him. Cray, like Alaric, sets out to discover his father, and in the process comes under the power of Rezhyk. This novel has all the atmosphere and enchantment of fairy tale, along with a striking development of a believable magical world. The characters, though moulded by their world, create the story, which is intense and absorbing. This same intensity continues in the novel's sequel, *The Crystal Palace,* which Eisenstein had not originally planned, but which grew out of her fascination with the world and characters she had created. It is that all-pervasive believability, structured within a world straight from fairy tale, that makes these two novels so enchanting and enjoyable.

Eisenstein's one other novel bordering on fantasy is *Shadow of Earth,* though it is usually categorized as science fiction because it presents an alternative Earth where the Spanish Armada was victorious and the savagery of the Inquisition dominates. It is essen-

tially a portrayal of an alien culture where scientific advance is anathema. Celia, via a scientific device, finds herself transported to this world, where she is enslaved and raped. A resourceful and determined woman, however, Celia fights back and at length escapes the world. This novel was originally written in 1971 and as such is a forerunner of much later feminist fiction. It creaks slightly in its opening chapters, but the alternative world is fully developed and convincingly portrayed.

Eisenstein's shorter fiction is long overdue for collection. She succeeds in blending the mood of horror and fantasy with the trappings of science fiction to create many fascinating concepts. Often these stories are imbued with a haunting longing for the unattainable, either a man long dead as in "In the Western Tradition" (*F & SF,* 1981) or a man of your dreams, as in "Nightlife" (*F & SF,* 1982). Eisenstein's most pointed dark fantasy is "Dark Wings" (*Shadows 5,* 1982) in which a girl is haunted by the vision and sound of a large bird. She tries to capture it in her paintings and, just as she feels she has mastered it, the bird comes to claim her. Eisenstein has written two other overt fantasies set in medieval magical worlds, "The Demon Queen" (*Amazing Stories,* 1984) and "The Amethyst Phial" (*F & SF,* 1984). These continue her earlier themes of alienation and betrayal.

Although Phyllis Eisenstein may never be prolific, this is compensated for by the quality and intensity of her works, which make them all the more memorable.

—Mike Ashley

———

ELLIOTT, Kate. *See* **RASMUSSEN, Alis A.**

———

EMERSON, Ru

Pseudonym: Roberta Cray. **Nationality:** American. **Born:** Monterey, California, 15 December 1944. **Education:** University of Montana, Missoula, 1963-66. **Career:** Legal secretary in Los Angeles, 1966-83, and in Salem, Oregon, 1984-85. **Agent:** Richard Curtis Associates, 171 East 74th Street, New York, NY 10021, USA. **Address:** 2600 Reuben-Boise Road, Dallas, OR 97338, USA.

FANTASY PUBLICATIONS

Novels (series: Nedao; Night-Threads)

The Princess of Flames. New York, Berkley, 1986; London, Unwin, 1987.
To the Haunted Mountains (Nedao). New York, Berkley, 1987.
In the Caves of Exile (Nedao). New York, Berkley, and London, Headline, 1988.
On the Seas of Destiny (Nedao). New York, Berkley, and London, Headline, 1989.
Beauty and the Beast: Masques (novelization of television script). New York, Avon, 1990.

Spell Bound. New York, Ace, 1990.
The Calling of the Three (Night-Threads). New York, Ace, 1990.
The Two in Hiding (Night-Threads). New York, Ace, 1991.
One Land, One Duke (Night-Threads). New York, Ace, 1992.
The Craft of Light (Night-Threads). New York, Ace, 1993.
The Bard's Tale: Fortress of Frost and Fire, with Mercedes Lackey.
   New York, Baen, 1993.
The Sword and the Lion, as Roberta Cray. New York, DAW, 1993.
The Art of the Sword (Night-Threads). New York, Ace, 1994.

*   *   *

Most of Ru Emerson's work is sword-and-sorcery fantasy. The main exceptions are *Spell Bound,* which is a historical alternate-world fantasy, and *Masques* which is a tie-in to the *Beauty and the Beast* television series.

Her first novel, *The Princess of Flames,* was well received, an excellent debut for a fresh, enthusiastic writer. The title refers to a tarot card as well as to the main protagonist, Elfrid. Elfrid is the illegitimate daughter of King Alster of Darion. When he is deposed by his eldest son, Sedry, she goes into exile with him. The rest of the novel relates how the usurper is eventually dethroned. There are Shakespearean elements to the plot, showing the influence of the Bard on Emerson's work. Elfrid and Alster's flight into exile has parallels with that of King Lear and Cordelia, the old man having been unhinged by the events leading up to their banishment. And Elfrid travels disguised as a boy partly because women are not supposed to use weapons though many do have some skill. The magic in this world is taken for granted—it is part of the characters' way of life. Elfrid, herself, is able to use magic and the way the Tarot cards fall influences the actions of the participants. Throughout there is a great sense of pace.

The promise of this first novel did not blossom in the Nedao trilogy. Although each book is rounded enough to complete the particular tale being told in a volume, it is difficult to understand the next without being familiar with the earlier ones. In *To the Haunted Mountains,* Ylia, heir to the throne of Nedao, is forced to flee after the Tehlatt invade and her parents are killed. Guided by Nisana, a magical cat who is also the narrator, Ylia crosses some nasty mountains. On the way she has to become self-sufficient and learn to use the magic she has inherited from her mother, and develop the weapons skills she will need to survive. In *In the Caves of Exile* Ylia has to lead the remnants of her people, not just in building a new life but against all the unpleasant things her relatives, on her mother's side, throw at her. Even with help, she is too much of a super-woman to be entirely credible. In *On the Seas of Destiny* Ylia's people are again under attack as her cousin Vess plots his revenge by first attacking her children and then by kidnapping her. Many standard elements occur within the trilogy and although there is a lot of action, the prose style makes it a slow read.

The Night-Threads sequence has a lot more to offer. The first three volumes constitute a parallel-world sword-and-sorcery novel in three parts. In *The Calling of the Three* we are introduced first to the stubborn, arrogant sin-Duchess Lialla and her crippled brother Aletto. Their uncle, Jadek, should have handed over the rule of the duchy to Aletto several years ago but has found excuses not to. When Jadek insists Lialla marries the man of his choice, she and Aletto flee. We then meet characters from our own world: Jennifer, an ambitious lawyer, her sister, Robyn, who is an ageing hippy, and her son Chris. Although they each have their own problems they are drawn between worlds to help Lialla and Aletto. What makes this trilogy different from the Nedao series is the care with which the characters, particularly those from contemporary California, are portrayed. Only Chris, who is familiar with fantasy gaming, has any sympathy with the situation in which they find themselves. Though youthfully naive, he has to mediate between the others—both of whom are suffering considerable culture shock. Lialla is put out not only because she cannot see how these three, one of whom is a peacenik, can help her brother oust her uncle but also because Jennifer shows a natural talent for manipulating Thread, the kind of magic Lialla desires to master, when she has had to struggle to reach only a lowly degree of competence. To some extent the trilogy follows familiar and predictable patterns, and some of the themes are repeated in later volumes but it has far more tension and immediacy and the characters are more credible—they have rough edges and real fears, more so than in the Nedao trilogy.

The Craft of Light and *The Art of the Sword,* though billed as parts of the Night-Threads series, are quite separate volumes from the initial trilogy but continue to follow the adventures of the three characters from contemporary America.

Spell Bound is altogether a different type of fantasy novel. It is set in an alternate Europe of the 17th century, a time when Germany was a number of small kingdoms. Within the boundaries of Saxe-Baden, the Cinderella tale is played out, but the fairy godmother is actually a witch seeking revenge for the death of her mother. In this world there are two kinds of magic—Green Magic for the village witches, Gold for the alchemical sorcerers. Ilse dabbles in both and she was the intended victim of the error that cost her mother her life. Even though the setting has some historical credibility—Prince Conrad (Charming) misspent his youth in Paris—it also has the feel of a traditional fairy tale. This might be because the plot becomes fairly predictable from very early on or because it lacks the depth of characterization achieved in *The Calling of the Three.* Perhaps it is because much of the time the protagonists are isolated in virgin woodland, or because some elements of real life at that time are missing; for example there is hardly any mention of religion at a time when it would play an important part in the lives of ordinary people as well as nobility.

Emerson's strength is her ability to tell an action-packed story, but the degree of her competence is extremely variable. She can be very good with character development but does not always take the trouble. Similarly, her magic systems are often highly original but her plots are predictable. Her principal characters from the fantasy worlds tend to be scions of royal or noble houses, get themselves exiled and spend the bulk of the story trying to recover their inheritance. Perhaps more irritating is the way her writing style sometimes lets her down. In particular her point of view tends to wander. This is less noticeable in later novels, but when it occurs it reduces the natural tension of the confrontations her characters find themselves in, which are otherwise well handled.

Emerson has also collaborated with Mercedes Lackey on the shared-world fantasy novel *Fortress of Frost and Fire.*

—Pauline Morgan

EMSHWILLER, Carol

Nationality: American. **Born:** Carol Fries, Ann Arbor, Michigan, 12 April 1921. **Education:** University of Michigan, B.A. in music and design, 1949; Ecole Nationale Superieure des Beaux-Arts, Paris

(Fulbright Fellow), 1949-50. **Family:** Married the film-maker Ed Emshwiller in 1949; two daughters and one son. **Career:** Since 1978, member of the Continuing Education Faculty, New York University; organized workshops for Science Fiction Bookstore, New York, 1975, 1976, and Clarion Science Fiction Workshop, 1978, 1979; guest teacher, Sarah Lawrence College, Bronxville, New York, 1983. **Awards:** MacDowell fellowship, 1971; Creative Artists Public Service grant, 1975; National Endowment grant, 1979; New York State grant, 1988; New York University award for teaching excellence, 1989; World Fantasy award, 1991. **Address:** 210 East 15th Street, Apartment 12E, New York, NY 10003, USA.

FANTASY PUBLICATIONS

Novel

Carmen Dog. London, Women's Press, 1988; San Francisco, Mercury House, 1989.

Short Stories

Joy in Our Cause. New York, Harper and Row, 1974.
Verging on the Pertinent: Stories. Minneapolis, Minnesota, Coffee House Press, 1989.
The Start of the End of It All, and Other Stories. London, Women's Press, 1990; revised edition, San Francisco, Mercury House, 1991.
Venus Rising. Cambridge, Massachusetts, Edgewood Press, 1992.

OTHER PUBLICATIONS

Plays

Television Plays: *Pilobolis and Joan,* 1974; *Family Focus,* 1977.

*   *   *

Carol Emshwiller's work was first published in the pulp magazines of the 1950s, but the witty, stylish, often satirical short stories she is best known for are grounded in the New Wave science-fiction movement of the 1960s. Much of her work—including her only novel to date, *Carmen Dog*—is fantasy, or, loosely speaking, magical realism. Even her science-fiction stories have an odd surrealist feel to them, so that they seem to sit at the juncture of the two genres. The title story of her collection *The Start of the End of it All* is an example of this. Here, a woman is collaborating with alien invaders. It is a stock science-fictional situation, yet Emshwiller imbues it with such strangeness—from the little silver fish the woman gives birth to, to the aliens' demand that she choose between them and her cats, and the cultural terrorism they initiate— that it is difficult to see it as anything *but* fantasy.

Most of her stories concern the relationship between the sexes. Though she considers herself a feminist, her work does present certain difficulties when regarded in that context. In particular, her fiction tends to assert that some traits—such as loyalty and nurturing—are intrinsically female, and therefore immutable. Furthermore, many of the women in Emshwiller's work seem to regret the situations they find themselves in, without finding a way to escape from them—at least not without paying a great price.

The short story "Fledged" is a case in point. It is told from the point of view of a man whose life is disrupted by the arrival of a woman who is changing into a huge bird. Eventually, he realizes that she is his ex-wife, Julia. At first he simply finds her an embarrassment and an annoyance, but at the end of the story, when she flies away, he envies her wings. Only then can he admit to even such a small emotion as loving his cat. The message of the story— if there is one—seems double-edged. Julia has gained her freedom, but at the expense of almost everything that marks her out as human. Her husband has lost his false security, but seems to have gained some kind of emotional insight.

This theme of animals transforming into humans and vice versa is a recurring one in Emshwiller's work. It is the central conceit of her novel, *Carmen Dog,* but here it affects only women. Pooch, a golden setter, is slowly becoming a woman. The novel follows her adventures after she runs away with the human baby of her household (because its mother is turning into a snapping turtle), is used as an experimental laboratory animal, and eventually becomes part of a revolution. Along the way she fulfils an ambition to become an opera singer and falls in love with a human man who is also a singer.

Politically—and, given Emshwiller's stated position, it is difficult to ignore this aspect of the work—there are a couple of problems here. The first is the way that animals that are turning into humans retain the qualities traditionally associated with them; meanwhile, women turn into the animals that best embody their personalities. The underlying assumption seems to be that personalities and talents are inborn—that they cannot be changed simply by breaking social condition. Most noticeably, even right at the end of the book, Pooch's values remain "loyalty, unselfishness and a modicum of modesty." These extend even to those men who have mistreated her the most. Secondly, science is seen wholly as something men do, as completely against women's interests—and, in fact, as completely against everyone's interests, because it seeks to control "motherhood" and thus the continuation of the species. When the rebellion comes, it does so by overthrowing the scientists or subverting some of them to the female cause. The only sympathetic men in the book are artists or those who reject science. Finally, the epilogue makes it clear that though Pooch eventually succeeds in her ambition to become an opera singer, she only finds true fulfilment through her marriage and her children.

—Liz Holliday

ERSKINE, John

Nationality: American. **Born:** New York City, 5 October 1879. **Education:** Columbia University, New York, B.A. 1900, M.A. 1901, Ph.D. 1903. **Family:** Married 1) Pauline Ives in 1915 (divorced 1945); 2) Helen Worden, two children. **Career:** Lecturer, Amherst College, Massachusetts, 1903-09; Columbia University, 1909-23; pianist, New York Symphony Orchestra; president, Juilliard School of Music, New York, 1928-37. **Died:** 2 June 1951.

FANTASY PUBLICATIONS

Novels

The Private Life of Helen of Troy. Indianapolis, Bobbs Merrill, 1925; London, Nash and Grayson, 1926.

Galahad: Enough of His Life to Explain His Reputation. Indianapolis, Bobbs Merrill, and London, Nash and Grayson, 1926.
Adam and Eve: Though He Knew Better. Indianapolis, Bobbs Merrill, 1927; London, Nash and Grayson, 1928.
Penelope's Man: The Homing Instinct. Indianapolis, Bobbs Merrill, 1928; London, Nash and Grayson, 1929.
Tristan and Isolde: Restoring Palamede. Indianapolis, Bobbs Merrill, 1932; London, Lane, 1933.
Venus, The Lonely Goddess. New York, Morrow, 1949; London, Wingate, 1950.

Short Stories

Cinderella's Daughter and Other Sequels and Consequences. Indianapolis, Bobbs Merrill, 1930.

OTHER PUBLICATIONS

Novels

Sincerity: A Story of Our Time. Indianapolis, Bobbs Merrill, 1929; as *Experiment in Sincerity,* London, Putnam, 1930.
Uncle Sam in the Eyes of His Family. Indianapolis, Bobbs Merrill, 1930.
Unfinished Business. Indianapolis, Bobbs Merrill, 1931.
Bachelor-of-Arts. Indianapolis, Bobbs Merrill, 1934.
Forget If You Can. Indianapolis, Bobbs Merrill, 1935.
Solomon, My Son! Indianapolis, Bobbs Merrill, 1935; London, Joseph, 1936.
The Brief Hour of Francois Villon. Indianapolis, Bobbs Merrill, 1937; London, Joseph, 1938.
The Start of the Road. New York, Stokes, 1938.
Give Me Liberty. New York, Stokes, 1940.
Casanova's Women: Eleven Months of a Year. New York, Stokes, 1941.
Mrs. Doratt. New York, Stokes, 1941.
The Voyage of Captain Bart. Philadelphia, Lippincott, 1943.

Short Stories

Peter Kills the Bear. London, Mathews and Marrot, 1930.
Young Love: Variations on a Theme. Indianapolis, Bobbs Merrill, 1936.
The Memory of Certain Persons. Philadelphia, Lippincott, 1947.

Plays

A Pageant of the Thirteenth Century for the Seven Hundredth Anniversary of Roger Bacon. New York, Columbia University, 1914.
Hearts Enduring: A Play in One Scene. New York, Duffield, 1920.
Jack and the Beanstalk, music by Louis Gruenberg (produced New York, 1931). Indianapolis, Bobbs Merrill, 1931.
Helen Retires (opera libretto). Indianapolis, Bobbs Merrill, 1934.

Poetry

Actaeon and Other Poems. New York, Lane, 1907.
The Shadowed Hour. New York, Lyric, 1917.
Collected Poems 1907-22. New York, Duffield, 1922.
Sonata and Other Poems. New York, Duffield, 1925.

Other

The Elizabethan Lyric. New York, Macmillan, 1903.
Leading American Novelists. New York, Holt, 1910.
Written English: A Guide to the Rules of Composition, with Helen Erskine. New York, Century, 1910; revised edition, 1913, 1917.
The Moral Obligation to Be Intelligent and Other Essays. New York, Duffield, 1915; revised edition, London, Davies, 1921.
Democracy and Ideals. New York, Doran, 1920.
The Kinds of Poetry and Other Essays. New York, Duffield, 1920; London, Nash and Grayson, 1927.
The Literary Discipline. New York, Duffield, 1923; London, Nash and Grayson, 1927.
American Character and Other Essays. New York, Chautauqua Press, 1927.
Prohibition and Christianity, and Other Paradoxes of the American Spirit. Indianapolis, Bobbs Merrill, and London, Nash and Grayson, 1927.
The Delight of Great Books. Indianapolis, Bobbs Merrill, and London, Nash and Grayson, 1928.
The Influence of Women and Its Cure. Indianapolis, Bobbs Merrill, 1936.
Song Without Words: The Story of Felix Mendelssohn (biography). New York, Messner, 1941.
The Complete Life. New York, Messner, 1943; London, Melrose, 1945.
The Philharmonic Symphony Society of New York: Its First Hundred Years. New York, Macmillan, 1943.
What Is Music? Philadelphia, Lippincott, 1944.
The Human Life of Jesus (biography). New York, Morrow, 1945.
My Life as a Teacher. Philadelphia, Lippincott, 1948.
My Life in Music. New York, Morrow, 1950.

Editor, *Selections from Spenser's The Faerie Queen.* New York, Longman, 1905.
Editor, *Selections from Tennyson's Idylls of the King.* New York, Holt, 1912.
Editor, with W. P. Trent, *Great Writers of America.* New York, Holt, and London, Williams and Norgate, 1912.
Editor, *Interpretations of Literature,* by Lafcadio Hearn. New York, Dodd Mead, 1915.
Editor, *Appreciations of Poetry,* by Lafcadio Hearn. New York, Dodd Mead, 1916; London, Heinemann, 1919.
Editor, *Life and Literature,* by Lafcadio Hearn. New York, Dodd Mead, 1917.
Editor, with others, *The Cambridge History of American Literature.* New York, Putnam, 4 vols., 1917-21; as *A History of American Literature,* Cambridge, Cambridge University Press, 4 vols., 1918-21.
Editor, *Talks with Writers,* by Lafcadio Hearn. New York, Dodd Mead, 1920.
Editor, *Books and Habits,* by Lafcadio Hearn. New York, Dodd Mead, 1921; London, Heinemann, 1922.
Editor, *Pre-Raphaelite and Other Poets,* by Lafcadio Hearn. New York, Dodd Mead, 1922; London, Heinemann, 1923.
Editor, *A Musical Companion: A Guide to the Understanding and Enjoyment of Music.* New York, Knopf, 1935.

*

Film Adaptations: *The Private Life of Helen of Troy,* 1927; *A Lady Surrenders,* 1930, from his novel *Sincerity.*

Critical Studies: "John Erskine: Enough of His Mind to Explain His Art" by William S. Knickerbocker, in *Sewanee Review 35* (Tennessee), 1927; "John Erskine" by Annie R. Marble, in *A Study of the Modern Novel: British and American Since 1900,* New York, Appleton, 1928.

*　　*　　*

John Erskine developed in his prose works an idiosyncratic form of fantasy, the potential of which he explored assiduously in half a dozen novels and a collection of short stories. The form has remained virtually untouched by other writers and is considered by some critics to be so marginal as hardly to belong to the genre of fantasy at all, although it cannot sensibly be excluded. Erskine's work belongs to the "de-supernaturalizing" school of fantasy favoured by writers such as Henry Treece, whereby well-known myths and legends are reinterpreted in such a fashion that their supernatural components are reduced to mere mundanity; unlike most writers of that school, however, Erskine does not perform such operations with the intention of reconstructing a "lost" historical reality whose events might have provided the seed of the myth, but rather with the satirical purpose of reducing the supposedly-arcane motives and preoccupations of mythical characters to the petty operations typical of the psychology of contemporary Americans. It is this allegorical quality which requires that the work be regarded as a species of fantasy.

The Private Life of Helen of Troy describes Helen's readjustment to family life following the fall of Troy, when she becomes once again the linch-pin and driving force of Menelaos' household. After a few laconic passages in the first few chapters the story is told entirely in dialogue, so that matters of historical setting simply do not arise; there are occasional conversational references to such matters as human sacrifice, but these are as marginally relevant to Helen as many of the unpleasantnesses of contemporary global politics and religion were to U.S. housewives of the 1920s. This narrative method also confers a curious objectivity on the story; characters can only be judged by what they say, and readers must judge for themselves whether the fact that Helen is infinitely more glib than those around her really entitles her to sympathy and heroic status. The one supernatural force credited by her is love, to whose supposedly irresistible agency she responds (in her own eyes, at least) with a superb frankness and honesty. This was to remain a constant theme in Erskine's work; a preoccupation with the supposed hypocrisies and dishonesties by which many individuals betray or pervert the ideal of love is so constant in his prose fiction as almost to qualify as an obsession.

In general, Erskine does not consider males of the species capable of honest love. Helen's Menelaos is a bumbling fool. The protagonist of *Galahad* is an unbearable prig. Adam in *Adam and Eve* is a hapless victim of manipulation. Odysseus in *Penelope's Man* is a pusillanimous hypocrite and charlatan who persistently falls for his own self-justifying patter. Many females of the species are, however, little or no better. *Adam and Eve* is really the story of Lilith and Eve, two alternative ideals of femininity which tempt the weak-willed Adam, and it is inevitable throughout that the cretin will eventually forsake the independent, frank and free-spirited Lilith for the wheedling, over-demanding, censorious emotional blackmailer Eve. *Adam and Eve* is the most vicious of Erskine's satires, and the most convoluted of his allegories, partly because he is forced to pay more attention to setting in designing his (rather peculiar) alternative Eden. Lilith and Eve have contrasting attitudes to "nature" as well as contrasting social strategies, but

Erskine becomes uneasy whenever his characters turn their attention to larger matters than intimate personal relationships. Like most fantasies based in the Biblical mythos this one features God the Absentee Landlord rather than God the Almighty, but Lilith's cleverness is severely tested by her attempts to reconcile Adam to the essential iniquities of His Creation.

Penelope's Man is the funniest of Erskine's satires, in that it must take aboard a whole series of exemplary females with whom Odysseus involves himself while ostensibly going home, and has to feature a few actual events in order to keep him moving. It is also the most jaundiced of them; none of the females is very nice, and one or two of them are every bit as pathetic as Odysseus is. For a while afterwards Erskine's work became more directly involved with the modern, the fantastic element being virtually eliminated, although *Uncle Sam*—an allegorical extension of an interest in the "American Character" developed literally in the essay of that title—does concern itself with myths of a kind.

The stories in *Cinderella's Daughter and Other Sequels and Consequences* re-work the motifs of classic fairy tales in such a way as to contemplate different social issues—the generation gap in the title story, domestic economics in "Beanstalk," organized religion in "Conversion"—but Erskine remains most comfortable when casually overturning the assumptions of traditional tales of love and marriage, as in "The Patience of Griselda," "Sleeping Beauty" and the cynically effective "Beauty and the Beast." These may be compared and contrasted with recent feminist re-castings of similar traditional tales, serving to remind would-be decoders that there is more than one way to turn an ideology on its head.

It was perhaps inevitable that Erskine should eventually return almost to his starting-point, and *Venus, The Lonely Goddess* may be regarded as a kind of reappraisal of the argument set out in *The Private Life of Helen of Troy.* It is by far the most abstruse of his allegorical *contes philosophiques,* and perhaps the only one which is blatantly and unequivocally a fantasy. It concerns itself with gods rather than men, and although the gods in question—like the original Olympians on which they are modelled—are replete with human attributes they do also function as abstract ideas made incarnate. Venus, unlike Helen or Lilith, is love itself rather than merely a frank and self-confident lover; the reader does not have the option of doubting her self-assessment, and there is no alternative but to share her confused insouciance as she attempts analysis of what it actually is that she stands for. In his earlier books the author was able to retain a supposedly objective stance, posing as a neutral observer even-handedly submitting the evidence to the reader, but the method of *Venus, The Lonely Goddess* requires him for the first time to reach some kind of conclusion—that is to say, to have Venus make some kind of discovery about herself, however tiny or tentative. This is one of the merits of outright fantasy: it makes prevarication more difficult. Erskine's Venus does, in the end, make a discovery about herself, and although it may seem to some readers to be a small enough triumph, it is not negligible.

—Brian Stableford

ESHBACH, Lloyd Arthur

Nationality: American. **Born:** Palm, Pennsylvania, 20 June 1910. **Education:** Attended school to the tenth grade; Charles Morris Price School of Advertising and Journalism, Philadelphia. **Family:** Married Helen Margaret Richards in 1931 (died 1978); two sons. **Career:** Worked for department stores, 1925-41; advertising copywriter, Glidden Paint Company, Reading, Pennsylvania, 1941-50; publisher, Fantasy Press, Reading, 1950-58, and Church Center Press, Myerstown, Pennsylvania, 1958-63; advertising manager, 1963-68, and sales representative, 1968-75, Moody Press, Chicago; clergyman for three small churches in eastern Pennsylvania, 1975-78. **Awards:** Milford award, 1988; Collectors' Award, 1991. **Agent:** James Allen, Virginia Kidd, Box 278, Milford, PA 18337. **Address:** 220 South Railroad Street, Myerstown, Pennsylvania 17067, USA.

FANTASY PUBLICATIONS

Novels (series: Gates of Lucifer in all books)

The Land Beyond the Gate. New York, Ballantine, 1984.
The Armlet of the Gods. New York, Ballantine, 1986.
The Sorceress of Seath. New York, Ballantine, 1988.
The Scroll of Lucifer. New York, Ballantine, 1990.

Short Stories

The Elfin Lights. Everett, Pennsylvania, Crawford, 1934.
The Tyrant of Time. Reading, Pennsylvania, Fantasy Press, 1955.

OTHER PUBLICATIONS

Novels

Subspace Encounter (completion of novel by E. E. Smith). New York, Berkley, 1983; London, Panther, 1984.

Plays

Radio Series, with H. Donald Spatz: *The Crimson Phantom, The Bronze Buddha, Tales of the Crystal, Cupid's Capers, The Pennington Saga, The Doings of the Dinwiddies,* and *Tales of Tomorrow,* 1933-35.

Other

Over My Shoulder: Reflections on a Science Fiction Era. Philadelphia, Train, 1983.

Editor, *Of Worlds Beyond: The Science of Science-Fiction Writing.* Reading, Pennsylvania, Fantasy Press, 1947; London, Dobson, 1965.
Editor, *Alicia in Blunderland,* by P. Schuyler Miller. Philadelphia, Train, 1983.

*

Manuscript Collection: Temple University, Philadelphia.

*   *   *

Eshbach's main writing career was in the early 1930s as one of the pioneer contributors to the science-fiction magazines. Like many of his contemporaries' works, Eshbach's stories were strong on ideas and vision but weak on characters and plotting, though he had a better feel for a story-line than some. His early story, "The Valley of the Titans" (*Amazing Stories,* 1931) was heavily influenced by the work of Abraham Merritt (Eshbach even copied some passages with little editing), and that balance of the fantastic alongside scientific development remained in much of Eshbach's writings.

He was, nevertheless, predominantly a science-fiction writer, and apart from a few stories in *Weird Tales* and *Strange Stories,* and a short radio series, *Tales of the Crystal,* which explored the fantastic and mysterious, Eshbach did not venture into fantasy fiction until after he retired and returned to writing in the 1980s. A couple of his short fantasies are included in his collection *The Tyrant of Time.* It should be noted here, though, that during his period as publisher of Fantasy Press, one of the first and probably most influential specialist publishers of science fiction, Eshbach did bring into hardcover some early classics of fantastic fiction, including *Darker Than You Think* by Jack Williamson, *The Bridge of Light* by A. Hyatt Verrill and *Beyond Infinity* by Robert Spencer Carr.

When Eshbach returned to writing it was to fantasy, a medium he found more exciting than science fiction. He began with *The Land Beyond the Gate,* the first in the four-volume Gates of Lucifer sequence. In each volume the main protagonist, Alan MacDougal, enters a different alternate-world of mythology through the space-time portals, and is pitted against Lucifer, who is attempting to take over those worlds. The first two volumes focus more on Celtic mythology, but the third introduces Babylonian legend and the final volume takes us into the very grip of Hell itself.

The concept and writing are heavily influenced by the work of Merritt, which further emphasizes the impact that writer had on the young minds of the 1920s. In one sense the series is a blending of the imagery of Merritt with the approach of de Camp and Pratt in their adventures featuring Harold Shea in various mythical worlds. Unfortunately Eshbach's series lacks the indefinable otherworldliness of Merritt and the inventiveness and humour of de Camp and Pratt, and all of its characters are stereotypes of good and evil. The series' strengths are in the excitement and vivacity of the plotting, which bowls the reader along, and Eshbach's ability for creating new and more evil enemies. The first volume is the best and the remainder, despite their different settings, become repetitive. The series is a good introduction for new readers to the escapist value of fantastic fiction, and the fascination of ancient mythology, but it adds little to the enrichment of the field overall.

Eshbach's contribution to the fantasy field was of far more importance as an architect behind the scenes, and this is brought vividly to life in his fine set of memoirs, *Over My Shoulder.*

—Mike Ashley

ESTES, Rose

Nationality: American. **Born:** Chicago, Illinois. **Career:** Former employee of TSR, Inc.

FANTASY PUBLICATIONS

Novels (series: Endless Quest; Find Your Fate; Greyhawk; The Hunter; Saga of Lost Lands; Troll)

Dungeon of Dread (Endless Quest). Lake Geneva, Wisconsin, TSR, 1982.

Mountain of Mirrors (Endless Quest). Lake Geneva, Wisconsin, TSR, 1982.

Pillars of Pentegarn (Endless Quest). Lake Geneva, Wisconsin, TSR, 1982.

Return to Brookmere (Endless Quest). Lake Geneva, Wisconsin, TSR, 1982.

Circus of Fear (Endless Quest). Lake Geneva, Wisconsin, TSR, 1983.

Dragon of Doom (Endless Quest). Lake Geneva, Wisconsin, TSR, 1983.

Hero of Washington Square (Endless Quest). Lake Geneva, Wisconsin, TSR, 1983.

Revenge of the Rainbow Dragons (Endless Quest). Lake Geneva, Wisconsin, TSR, 1983.

Revolt of the Dwarves (Endless Quest). Lake Geneva, Wisconsin, TSR, 1983.

Indiana Jones and the Lost Treasure of Sheba (Find Your Fate). New York, Ballantine, 1984.

Case of the Dancing Dinosaur. New York, Random House, 1985.

The Children of the Dragon (Find Your Fate). New York, Random House, 1985.

The Trail of Death (Find Your Fate). New York, Random House, 1985.

The Mystery of the Turkish Tattoo (Find Your Fate). New York, Random House, 1986.

Blood of the Tiger (Lost Lands). New York, Bantam, 1987; London, Bantam, 1989.

Master Wolf (Greyhawk). Lake Geneva, Wisconsin, TSR, 1987; London, Penguin, 1988.

The Price of Power (Greyhawk). Lake Geneva, Wisconsin, TSR, 1987; London, Penguin, 1988.

Brother to the Lion (Lost Lands). New York, Bantam, 1988.

The Demon Hand (Greyhawk). Lake Geneva, Wisconsin, TSR, and London, Penguin, 1988.

The Name of the Game (Greyhawk). Lake Geneva, Wisconsin, TSR, 1988.

Spirit of the Hawk (Lost Lands). New York, Bantam, 1988.

The Eyes Have It (Greyhawk). Lake Geneva, Wisconsin, TSR, 1989.

The Hunter. New York, Warner, 1990.

Skryling's Blade, with Tom Wham. New York, Ace, 1990.

The Hunter on Arena. New York, Warner, 1991.

The Hunter Victorious. New York, Warner, 1992.

Elfwood. New York, Ace, 1992.

The Stone of Time. New York, Ace, 1992.

Mountains and Madness. New York, Baen, 1993.

Troll-Taken. New York, Ace, 1993.

Troll-Quest. New York, Ace, 1995.

*   *   *

In the early 1980s a new publishing format became popular, spin-off novels from role-playing games which involve players taking the parts of wizards, trolls and other fantasy characters. The major publisher of the original games and books, TSR (Tactical Studies Rules), Inc., had been producing the game accoutrements and rule books since the early 1970s, but the increased popularity of the original game Dungeons & Dragons eventually led to the development of other games, accompanying magazines and toy figurines. The novels, based on the idea of already existing Choose-Your-Own-Adventures for children, were proposed by Rose Estes as a natural extension of the fantasy experience. Already an employee of TSR, Estes developed the early Endless Quest titles for salary rather than royalties.

The tight format of these books requires terse, precise writing. Illustrations are an important part of the books, helping to create the atmosphere of magical kingdoms and fantastic adventures. Although the word-count in these books was strictly limited, Estes was able to create enchanted lands with sharply defined characters. In one of the earliest novels, *Return to Brookmere,* she quickly sets the mood by describing the main character Brion as a five-foot-tall elf with elvensight, clever and smart. This description is one that the young teens and pre-teens, primary marketing targets for the books, would be happy to adopt. In another early title, *Dungeon of Dread,* "you," the hero, are described as a human fighter, "5'9" tall and weigh[ing] about 150 pounds. You are smart and have survived many adventures using little more than your wits. You are well schooled in the use of weapons and are a powerful opponent." Many teenage boys would like to imagine themselves in this persona.

Estes has written for other reader's-choice series, such as the Find Your Fate line. In spite of the rigid formulae involved in series books like these, Estes has a particular talent for creating sympathetic characters and exciting plot twists which invite the reader-participant to use logic in making selections for plot development.

The plot-choice books waned somewhat in popularity by the early 1990s, probably due to the increased availability of computer games for the same market, although there are still devotees of the games and game books. In the meantime, Estes was writing other works in more conventional formats, such as children's adventures, but still using the fantasy motif. She has continued to be involved with game books, such as *Mountains and Madness* in the Iron Dragons series intended as enrichment for players of Iron Dragons from Mayfair Games. But probably her best known and most popular game-related books are the titles in the Greyhawk series.

Adult fantasy series were a natural avenue for Estes, who has contributed titles to existing series and those she had created, such as Saga of Lost Lands and The Hunter. Both of these series use vaguely prehistoric times as a setting for fantasy. The Lost Lands series is similar in tone to Ice-Age novels by other authors. Estes puts more emphasis on the world that has been created by means of details of a harsh primitive life and the importance of the belief in magic. The rich descriptions of this world and her clearly delineated characters who inhabit these lands show Estes' skill in creating an imaginary setting. Her dialogue, however, is shaky. For example, in *Blood of the Tiger,* the first book in the Saga of Lost Lands series, the hero, Emri, explains the current political situation in his tribe to Hawk, a youngster from a rival clan. Emri uses appropriately stilted words, but his young companion replies in a colloquial style, "It sounds like you've got enough problems without dragging me into camp." This anachronistic slip may have been used deliberately to emphasize the age difference between Emri and Hawk, but it is still a jarring note.

In the other vaguely prehistoric series, the Hunter, a heroic chieftain reminiscent of Robert E. Howard's Conan, must battle high-tech magic and trickery. The writing here is less descriptive and places more emphasis on the heroic deeds of the brutal protagonist.

In most of her books, both children's and adult, Estes focuses on male characters. In a few cases, however, she uses female protagonists. Her conventional children's fantasy, *Children of the Dragon,* tells about Lydia, the eleven-year-old daughter of the Dragonlord who tends Tecla. The people of the country are alarmed when Tecla, now an old dragon, lays eggs, for they fear that a dragon population boom will cause chaos in their well-ordered land. Lydia and her two brothers must save Tecla's heir, a newly-hatched dragon. The three children demonstrate their various strengths and weaknesses, save the baby dragon and learn the importance of team effort. In the end, however, Lydia does not become the new dragonlord; one of her brothers does. In a recent Estes adult fantasy, *Troll-Taken,* a mother must rescue her baby from the evil trolls who have stolen the human infant and left a changeling in its place. The mother exhibits fierce determination to get her child back, but this aggressiveness is never suggested to be inappropriate for a traditional female role. Estes is willing to give her female characters ability and intelligence, but she does not espouse feminist revisionism in her stories of fantasy and magic.

In addition to her skills of tight writing and vivid characters, Estes also uses colourful descriptions to enhance the fantasy settings of her stories. For example, in *Children of the Dragon,* a neighbouring territory is described simply and effectively: "To the west were the unknown lands, a place of mystery which few people entered and from which no one ever returned." It is obvious, too, that although Estes may use short descriptions, she has given much thought to the characters, as the appendix in *Troll-Taken* illustrates. Here is an elaborate history of the development of the Under Dwellers (trolls) beneath the city of Chicago. Estes does not do well with humour. For example, in *Elfwood,* a medieval-magic book, the overall style is a bit reflective of Piers Anthony and Terry Pratchett, but she does not write subtle, or even ribald, humour convincingly. Overall, however, Estes has created credible fantasy works distinctive for their carefully constructed worlds and characters.

—Cosette Kies

F

FARMER, Penelope (Jane)

Nationality: British. **Born:** Westerham, Kent, 14 June 1939. **Education:** Private, 1945-56; St. Anne's College, Oxford, 1957-60, B.A. (honours) in history 1960; Bedford College, University of London, diploma in social studies 1962; doctoral study at Keele University, since 1988. **Family:** Married 1) Michael John Mockridge in 1962 (divorced 1977), one daughter and one son; 2) Simon Shorvon in 1984. **Career:** Teacher, London County Council Education Department, 1961-63; sociological researcher, 1985-90. **Awards:** American Library Association notable book, 1962; Carnegie Medal commendation, 1963. **Agent:** Deborah Owen, 78 Narrow Street, London E14 8BP, England. **Address:** 30 Ravenscourt Road, London W6 0UG, England.

FANTASY PUBLICATIONS

Novels

The Summer Birds, illustrated by James Spanfeller. London, Chatto and Windus, and New York, Harcourt Brace, 1962; revised edition, London, Bodley Head, 1985.
The Magic Stone, illustrated by John Kaufmann. New York, Harcourt Brace, 1964; London, Chatto and Windus, 1965.
Emma in Winter, illustrated by Laszlo Acs. London, Chatto and Windus, and New York, Harcourt Brace, 1966.
Charlotte Sometimes, illustrated by Chris Connor. London, Chatto and Windus, and New York, Harcourt Brace, 1969.
A Castle of Bone. London, Chatto and Windus, and New York, Atheneum, 1972.
William and Mary. London, Chatto and Windus, and New York, Atheneum, 1974.
Year King. London, Chatto and Windus, and New York, Atheneum, 1977.
Eve: Her Story. London, Gollancz, 1985; San Francisco, Mercury House, 1988.
Thicker Than Water. London and New York, Walker, 1989.
Stone Croc. London and New York, Walker, 1991.

Other (retellings of myth for children)

Daedalus and Icarus, illustrated by Chris Connor. London, Collins, and New York, Harcourt Brace, 1971.
The Serpent's Teeth: The Story of Cadmus, illustrated by Chris Connor. London, Collins, 1971; New York, Harcourt Brace, 1972.
The Story of Persephone, illustrated by Graham McCallum. London, Collins, 1972; New York, Morrow, 1973.
Heracles, illustrated by Graham McCallum. London, Collins, 1975.

OTHER PUBLICATIONS

Novels

Standing in the Shadow. London, Gollancz, 1984.

Away from Home: A Novel in Ten Episodes. London, Gollancz, 1987.
Glasshouses. London, Gollancz, 1988; North Pomfret, Vermont, Trafalgar Square, 1989.
Snakes and Ladders. London, Little Brown, 1993.

Fiction for Children

The China People, illustrated by Pearl Falconer. London, Hutchinson, 1960.
The Saturday Shillings, illustrated by Prudence Seward. London, Hamish Hamilton, 1965; as *Saturday by Seven,* London, Penguin, 1978.
The Seagull, illustrated by Ian Ribbons. London, Hamish Hamilton, 1965; New York, Harcourt Brace, 1966.
Dragonfly Summer, illustrated by Tessa Jordan. London, Hamish Hamilton, 1971; New York, Scholastic, 1974.
August the Fourth, illustrated by Jael Jordan. London, Heinemann, 1975; Los Angeles, Parnassus Press, 1976.
The Coal Train, illustrated by William Bird. London, Heinemann, 1977.
The Runaway Train, illustrated by William Bird. London, Heinemann, 1980.

Play

Television Play: *The Suburb Cuckoo,* 1961.

Other

Editor, *Beginnings: Creation Myths of the World,* illustrated by Antonio Frasconi. London, Chatto and Windus, 1978; New York, Atheneum, 1979.

Translator, with Amos Oz, *Soumchi,* by Oz, illustrated by William Papas. London, Chatto and Windus, 1980; New York, Harper, 1981.

*   *   *

Although most are published for children, the fantasies of Penelope Farmer are subtle, ambiguous, evocative works which reward the more mature reader. Plot, particularly in her earlier books, tends to be slight and of minimal importance. What matters is atmosphere, the vivid evocation of sensations, whether of magical experience or everyday life, and delineation of character.

In *The Summer Birds,* Charlotte and Emma Makepeace meet a strange boy who teaches them, and then the other ten children in their small country school, to fly. They spend an unforgettable summer enjoying the power and freedom of flight, all the more precious because they know it will end with the summer when the boy goes away. On the last day he tries to lure them away to somewhere unknown; the others are eager for any adventure, but Charlotte, suspicious, will not go—and forbids the others—unless he tells them the truth. At last he tells them he is a rare bird who has been given human form for the summer as a gift from the birdlord, his only chance to find others to join him. Otherwise, his species will perish. If they go with him, they will become birds on a far-away island and never return to human life.

Two of the children, solid girls who "could not imagine or want another life as birds on a strange island far away," refuse, but the others are wildly tempted, including Charlotte, a lonely girl who is obviously as drawn to the boy as she is to the experience of flight. Yet even as she is tempted, she knows it would be wrong. Her attempt to dissuade the others lacks the vigour of their arguments for it (as one boy, from a large, poor family exclaims, "Don't you think it'd be better to spend our lives flyin' than growin' up and goin' to work at eight o'clock every day?") yet it touches the bird-boy, who abruptly forbids them to come with him, saying, "I should be a thief stealing lives." His misery is obvious, and one little girl, nicknamed Maggot, announces that she will go with him so that his kind will not die.

The book's weakness is most evident in the climactic scene. Charlotte is the viewpoint character, and the story is always hers; that she should lose the boy, and his gift of flight, after only one magical summer is inevitable, foreshadowed even in the title. Yet there is no real conflict or growth for her. She seems from the beginning to have known the magic will be temporary and does not fight to keep it. Why going away with the boy should be wrong for Charlotte but not for Maggot is particularly unclear. The other children all have families who would miss them, whereas Maggot lives with an uncle who takes little notice of her—but Charlotte and Emma live with an eccentric grandfather who likes girls only when they're demure, and love for him is certainly not her reason for feeling she must remain at home. The strengths of *The Summer Birds* remain—the elegiac tone and the utterly convincing descriptions of flight.

Two more stories about Charlotte and Emma follow. *Emma in Winter* focuses on the younger sister, who meets one of her schoolmates in her dreams at night, while *Charlotte Sometimes* is perhaps Farmer's most popular and successful book. When Charlotte goes away to boarding school, she finds herself slipping back in time on alternate days, from 1963 to 1918, where she is taken for a girl called Clare. Life at a new school would be hard enough, but to be there only half the time, while learning on other days to acquire a different personality, is particularly difficult, and often disturbing. When on one of her visits to the past, Charlotte/Clare is forced to leave the school; she almost despairs of ever getting back to her own time, but does finally return. This is a satisfying, convincing and well-worked-out time fantasy which raises interesting questions about the boundaries of personality and its continuity throughout one human lifetime.

A Castle of Bone is the most complex and ambiguous of Farmer's fantasies, although much of its richness and meaning is buried deeply enough for the unsophisticated reader to miss entirely. Hugh has just acquired a cupboard from a junk-shop—an ugly, shoddy thing he nevertheless felt compelled to buy. Yet once it is installed in his room he doesn't want to use it, and finds it impossible to visualize when he's not actually looking at it. That night he finds himself wandering through an unknown country towards a strange castle—he realizes this is more than a dream when he wakes cold and with his feet wet with snow. The next day Anna from next door places Hugh's pigskin wallet inside, and moments later a live pig rushes squealing out. They discover that the cupboard has the power to regress whatever is put into it to an earlier form, but their light-hearted investigations are brought to a halt when Penn—Anna's brother and Hugh's best friend—is turned into a baby. Anna, Hugh, and Hugh's sister Jean find it a struggle looking after the baby, and Hugh's perception of himself and his best friend (who always used to tell him what to do) is permanently changed. They track

down the shop where the cupboard came from, and the old shop-keeper, although infuriatingly obscure, does finally say that they must all go into the cupboard together, by their own will rather than waiting to be drawn, and go into the castle and there, seeing the choices clearly, try to decide. The cupboard takes them all into Hugh's "dream" landscape, but in separate pairs. Hugh and Jean find Anna with Penn in the castle's great hall, where there is an apple tree and a great stone basin full of fire. As Anna lifts the baby towards the flames they realize she's about to put Penn into the fire. Hugh knows this is his moment to act, but he cannot decide between "Stop Anna" and "let her." He is frozen until Jean stabs him with the pin of her brooch. Then, without thought, as if at random, he chooses, saying, "Stop Anna." Released by his words, Jean takes the baby from Anna; the four walk into a void together and then emerge from the cupboard into Hugh's bedroom, with Penn his real age again. Hugh feels walls enclosing him, imprisoning him in "a castle of bone" which is himself. Penn has no memory of what has happened to him and refuses to believe it, and when Anna puts her broken sandal in the cupboard, nothing happens. It's over; Hugh feels the loss of magic, yet at the same time can scarcely believe it ever happened.

A brief conversation between Hugh and Anna connects their experience with the ancient religion behind Greek myths in which the death-goddess must choose herself a consort, whom she first makes immortal by putting him in a fire. Odysseus didn't want that immortality, preferring life, and ran away from the Goddess several times. (Readers of Robert Graves's *The White Goddess* will recognize his interpretation here, and also the connection between the many trees mentioned in the text and the ancient Celtic tree alphabet.) Yet, as Anna points out, fastening on her symbolic broken sandal, Penn didn't run away—Hugh stopped him. And whether or not this was the "right" thing to do is a question that cannot be answered, can scarcely be asked. On this note of ambiguity, a choice made, a turning away from incest, from undifferentiated personalities and magical thinking towards a more solitary, prosaic, individuality, the book ends, almost demanding another reading.

Penelope Farmer's many other fantasies range from juvenile retellings of Greek myth to the adult reworking of the Garden of Eden narrative in *Eve: Her Story*. However, *A Castle of Bone* seems likely to remain the high point of her career as a fantasist.

—Lisa Tuttle

FEIST, Raymond E(lias)

Nationality: American. **Born:** Southern California, 1945. **Education:** University of California, San Diego. **Family:** Married novelist Kathlyn Starbuck; one daughter. **Address:** c/o Doubleday, 666 Fifth Avenue, New York, NY 10103, USA.

FANTASY PUBLICATIONS

Novels (series: Empire; Riftwar)

Magician (Riftwar). New York, Doubleday, 1982; London, Granada, 1983; in two vols. as *Magician: Apprentice* and *Magician: Master,* New York, Bantam, 1986; revised edition, New York, Doubleday, and London, HarperCollins, 1992.

Silverthorn (Riftwar). New York, Doubleday, and London, Granada, 1985.

A Darkness at Sethanon (Riftwar). New York, Doubleday, and London, Grafton, 1986.

Daughter of the Empire, with Janny Wurts. New York, Doubleday, and London, Grafton, 1987.

Faerie Tale. New York, Doubleday, and London, Grafton, 1988.

Prince of the Blood (Riftwar). New York, Doubleday, and London, Grafton, 1989.

Servant of the Empire, with Janny Wurts. New York, Doubleday, and London, Grafton, 1990.

The King's Buccaneer (Riftwar). New York, Doubleday, and London, HarperCollins, 1992.

Mistress of the Empire, with Janny Wurts. New York, Doubleday, and London, HarperCollins, 1992.

Shadow of a Dark Queen (Riftwar). New York, Doubleday, and London, HarperCollins, 1994.

* * *

In his early novels Raymond Feist drew extensively on his experience of fantasy role-playing games. He had been a game designer and was thus capable of working at a deeper theoretical level than those writers who simply tried to turn the "scripts" of their games into stories. *Magician* deploys several motifs which have become part of the staple diet of such game-scenarios in an ingenious but fairly conventional manner. The central characters, Pug and Tomas, are on the threshold of adulthood and their initial status is low, but there are opportunities in their immediate environment which facilitate rapid advancement. Pug, aided by his unparalleled but latent talents, is gradually schooled as a magician; he is powerful enough to be equal to any situation but has to win control of his power by slow degrees. Tomas sets out to be a warrior, and is likewise granted uncontrolled but potentially infinite greatness when he stumbles across a friendly dragon which gives him a miraculous suit of armour. The plot features the various kinds of non-human races that game designers borrowed from J. R. R. Tolkien—elves, dwarfs, etc.—and such stock characters as the enigmatic magician who puts in an occasional appearance in order to supply useful (but cryptic) explanations or to move the plot along. The rifts which allow characters to move between the two worlds of Midkemia and Kelewan are likewise deployed in games-masterish fashion to move the wheels of the plot (and also to provide a suitably extravagant *deus ex machina* by way of eventual conclusion).

As *Magician* progresses, however, Feist gradually moves away from game-like concerns, becoming more interested in the moral dilemmas of his royal characters and with the thorny question of the political legitimacy of their authority. This was to become something of a preoccupation, requiring him to be careful lest its discussion impede the pace of his narratives—although *Magician,* like most modern fantasy novels, is very long and its plot is occasionally able to languish for a while so that background information can be filled out or updated. The substantially revised edition of 1992 is even longer than the original, but does smooth the pace of the narrative somewhat and also discards certain fringe-elements which became irrelevant in the light of the later development of the series.

Feist, like others before him, submitted to publishing convention by dividing the equally long sequel to *Magician* into two parts—*Silverthorn* and *A Darkness at Sethanon*—in order that they might be represented as the second and third parts of a trilogy, but the division is artificial. The story told therein is essentially a re-

prise of *Magician,* although its inheritance of characters from the first novel reduces its dependence on the rags-to-responsibility career-building motif, here represented in the subplot which follows the exploits of the reformed thief Jimmy the Hand. The carrying over of characters like Prince Arutha and Pug shifts the emphasis of the main plot-line towards the preservation of that which has already been earned.

The eventual climax of *A Darkness at Sethanon* is a more fully developed near-apocalypse than the one featured in the first novel, and though it is resolved by an equally straightforward *deus ex machina* it is the kind of device which does not bear frequent repetition. For this reason, if for no other, it is not surprising that the subsequent extrapolation of the series has seen a conspicuous narrowing of scope. The more recent novels in the series jettison most of the borrowed apparatus of *Magician* so that the author can concentrate on more idiosyncratic devices. A measure of epic sweep is retained in the collaborative novels written with Janny Wurts—*Daughter of the Empire, Servant of the Empire* and *Mistress of the Empire,* which are set on Kelewan—but Feist's new series of Midkemian novels, begun with *Prince of the Blood* and *The King's Buccaneer,* are action-adventure novels in a lower key. These solo novels offer further repetitions of the standard motif of princely reconciliation to mature responsibility by virtue of displacement into picaresque adventures; they tend to reduce the role of magic to a more-or-less arbitrary bag of tricks whose contents can be evoked when necessary to move plots which are little more than neo-Ruritanian romances.

The "dark fantasy" *Faerie Tale* is perhaps better regarded as a horror story than as a fantasy, but it does make interesting use of imaginative materials more familiar in a fantasy context. Like many modern horror novels it follows the fortunes of a contemporary American family whose newly-acquired house proves to be the focal point of a menacing crescendo of supernatural intrusions. In its later phases, however, *Faerie Tale* strays from this formula to take the form of a curious quest fantasy, in which the eight-year-old hero must go into the Land of Faerie to rescue his twin, who has been swapped for an extraordinarily loathsome changeling. This climactic part of the story makes extravagant use of the common fairy-tale motif whereby success in an enterprise is dependent on following apparently arbitrary rules very scrupulously, and thus concentrates its attention on that part of folklore which most closely reflects and anticipates the methodology of role-playing games. Because *Faerie Tale* has the temporal and spatial limitations of a horror novel it cannot reproduce the career-building and long-distance journeying which are characteristic of heroic fantasy, but it nevertheless remains a rite-of-passage story in which a powerless innocent is enabled to make his way safely through a difficult and dangerous adventure by carefully making use of the resources provided for him. *Faerie Tale* remains the most interesting of Feist's works, but given that he is still not far removed from the beginning of his career it is probable that he has other experiments still to try.

—Brian Stableford

FERGUSSON, Bruce (Chandler)

Nationality: American. **Born:** Bridgeport, Connecticut, 7 March 1951. **Education:** Wesleyan University. **Career:** Reporter and photographer, Hartford *Times*; worked briefly in advertising.

FANTASY PUBLICATIONS

Novels (series: Six Kingdoms in all books)

The Shadow of His Wings. New York, Arbor House, 1987; London, Grafton, 1988.
The Mace of Souls. New York, Morrow, 1989; London, Grafton, 1990.

*   *   *

Bruce Fergusson writes gritty fantasies set in an unpleasant, dangerous, pseudo-medieval world. His heroes resemble nothing so much as hard-boiled detectives, walking the mean streets of the Six Kingdoms on their respective quests. Yet there is little of the cliché to be found in his work, and his writing never rings false; to use Ursula Le Guin's metaphor, we never leave Elfland and find ourselves in Poughkeepsie.

The Shadow of His Wings is an unusual quest novel. Lukan, the hero, is an honourable man in a dishonourable world who learns that he must follow no rules but his own in order to survive. His sense of honour never leaves him, though, whether he is refusing to betray the immortal Erseiyr, a strangely pathetic winged being, or declining to take the throne for fear of his own potential abuse of power. He ends up on his quest almost by accident, as he pursues a woman who has gone to seek the Erseiyr with a coin stolen from Lukan, but once on it he keeps always on the path of honour.

The Mace of Souls is also a quest novel, but its protagonist, Falca, begins as the inverse of Lukan. Also victim of a tragic home life, he has little honour, making his money through robbery and extortion. The antihero is redeemed, though, by falling in love with the wealthy woman he has selected as a mark. The woman, Amala, also plans to use Falca, in her case to break away from her possessive twin brother, but falls in love with him as well. When her soul is taken by the cult of the Spirit-Lifters, Falca, like Lukan, pursues what has been stolen from him, surprisingly enough finding himself on the path of honour as well. He too must resist temptation at the end, in his case that of joining the Spirit-Lifters and experiencing the many souls they have stolen.

Unhealthy sibling relationships are central to both novels. Lukan's brother, Vearus, hates and resents him deeply, despite having been his father's favourite, because he knows that Lukan is a better person than he. His discovery of magic and the evil uses to which he puts it bring him power, which he uses to destroy Lukan's life; ironically, it is this that eventually drives Lukan onto the quest that brings him fame and power beyond Vearus's dreams.

Amala's relationship with her twin, Alatheus, is the mirror image of that of Lukan and Vearus, warped by too much love. The love is psychological, though apparently not physically, incestuous. Alatheus cannot let Amala go, nor can he allow her to have too close a relationship with anyone or anything else; as a child, he steals and hides the instrument she is learning to play beautifully, and as an adult, he attempts to kill Falca for becoming her lover. He has enough self-awareness to realize that part of him is pleased at the theft of Amala's soul, because now he can care for her forever and she can never rebel or leave. Falca eventually slays him in self-defense, and that is the only way to cut the cords that entwine the twins.

Both books also feature the redemptive power of love; unfortunately, here is where Fergusson falls into cliché. Lukan's honour

and love redeem the amoral thief Rui Ravenstone, who previously has wanted only wealth and power. As stated above, the love of Amala reforms Falca, turning him from antihero to man of courage and honour.

The Mace of Souls explores one aspect of the Six Kingdoms that is merely mentioned in passing in *The Shadow of His Wings*: the plight of the aboriginal races displaced by the humans who settled the Six Kingdoms. In particular, the book focuses on the Timberlimbs, a tree-dwelling race considered barely more than animals by the humans, who are being killed and forced from their woods into the cities. There is a tinge of the noble savage to the Timberlimbs; we see them degraded at the beginning of the novel, and later learn the beauty of their culture and the devotion of which they are capable.

The Timberlimbs provide *The Mace of Souls* with an ending much different from the pastoral happy ending of *The Shadow of His Wings*. Amala's soul has been restored, the lovers are reunited, and the shadow cast by Alatheus has been removed; nonetheless, things are not happy and there is much to do, as Falca and Amala plan to go to the Timberlimbs and try to help them fight the soldiers who are routing them.

The Shadow of His Wings and *The Mace of Souls* are very similar in structure, as a reluctant hero goes through adventures, has something precious stolen from him, and sets out on a quest to get it. Yet *The Mace of Souls* is much darker, from the character of Falca to the horrific nature of the Spirit-Lifters' soul-thieving to the unresolved ending. It is also a more mature work, although it doesn't have the power of the first book to sweep the reader away from the first paragraphs. It is to be hoped that the long silence since the publication of *The Mace of Souls* is merely a hiatus, and that Fergusson will resume his writing career.

—Janice M. Eisen

———

FIELD, Gans T. *See* **WELLMAN, Manly Wade.**

———

FINDLEY, Timothy

Nationality: Canadian. **Born:** Toronto, Ontario, 30 October 1930. **Education:** Rosedale Public School, Toronto; St. Andrews College, Aurora, Ontario; Jarvis Collegiate, Toronto; Royal Conservatory of Music, Toronto, 1950-53; Central School of Speech and Drama, London. **Career:** Stage, television, and radio actor, 1951-62; charter member, Stratford Shakespearean Festival, Ontario, 1953; contract player with H. M. Tennent, London, 1953-56; toured U.S. in *The Matchmaker,* 1956-57; studio writer, CBS, Hollywood, 1957-58; copywriter, CFGM Radio, Richmond Hill, Ontario. Playwright-in-residence, National Arts Centre, Ottawa, 1974-75; writer-in-residence, University of Toronto, 1979-80, Trent University, Peterborough, Ontario, 1984, and University of Winnipeg, 1985. Chairman, Writers Union of Canada, 1977-78. **Awards:** Canada Council award, 1968, 1978; Armstrong award, for radio writing,

1971; ACTRA award, for television documentary, 1975; Toronto Book award, 1977; Governor General's award, 1977; Anik award, for television writing, 1980; Canadian Authors Association prize, 1985. D.Litt.: Trent University, 1982; University of Guelph, Ontario, 1984. Officer, Order of Canada, 1986. **Agent:** Virginia Barber Literary Agency, 353 West 21st Street, New York, NY 10011, USA. **Address:** Box 419, Cannington, Ontario L0E 1EO, Canada.

FANTASY PUBLICATIONS

Novels

Not Wanted on the Voyage. Toronto, Viking, 1984; New York, Delacorte Press, and London, Macmillan, 1985.
Headhunter. Toronto, HarperCollins, 1993; New York, Crown, 1994.

OTHER PUBLICATIONS

Novels

The Last of the Crazy People. New York, Meredith Press, and London, Macdonald, 1967.
The Butterfly Plague. New York, Viking Press, 1969; London, Deutsch, 1970.
The Wars. Toronto, Clarke Irwin, 1977; New York, Delacorte Press, and London, Macmillan, 1978.
Famous Last Words. Toronto, Clarke Irwin, and New York, Delacorte Press, 1981; London, Macmillan, 1987.
The Telling of Lies. Toronto, Penguin, 1986; London, Macmillan, and New York, Dell, 1988.

Short Stories

Dinner Along the Amazon. Toronto and London, Penguin, 1984; New York, Penguin, 1985.
Stones. Toronto, Penguin, 1986; New York, Dell, 1988.

Plays

The Paper People (televised 1968). Published in *Canadian Drama* (Toronto), vol. 9, no. 1, 1983.
The Journey (broadcast 1971). Published in *Canadian Drama* (Toronto), vol. 10, no. 1, 1984.
Can You See Me Yet? (produced Ottawa, 1976). Vancouver, Talonbooks, 1977.
John A., Himself, music by Berthold Carriere (produced London, Ontario, 1979).
Strangers at the Door (radio script), in *Quarry* (Kingston, Ontario), 1982.
Daybreak at Pisa: 1945, in *Tamarack Review* (Toronto), Winter 1982.

Screenplays: *Don't Let the Angels Fall,* 1970; *The Wars,* 1983.
Radio Plays and Documentaries: *The Learning Stage* and *Ideas* series, 1963-73; *Adrift,* 1968; *Matinee* series, 1970-71; *The Journey,* 1971; *Missionaries,* 1973.

Television Plays and Documentaries: *Umbrella* series, 1964-66; *Who Crucified Christ?,* 1966; *The Paper People,* 1968; *The Whiteoaks of Jalna* (7 episodes), from books by Mazo de la Roche, 1971-72; *The National Dream* series (8 episodes), with William Whitehead, 1974; *The Garden and the Cage,* with William Whitehead, 1977; *1832* and *1911 (The Newcomers* series), 1978-79; *Dieppe 1942,* with William Whitehead, 1979; *Other People's Children,* 1981; *Islands in the Sun* and *Turn the World Around (Belafonte Sings* series), with William Whitehead, 1983.

Other

Imaginings, with Janis Rapaport, illustrated by Heather Cooper. Toronto, Ethos, 1982.

*

Critical Studies: "Timothy Findley Issue" of *Canadian Literature* (Vancouver), Winter 1981; *Timothy Findley* by Wilfred Cude, Toronto, Dundurn Press, 1982.

*   *   *

Although most of Timothy Findley's work is mainstream fiction, he has made a significant contribution to that small sub-genre perhaps best described as rewritings of Noah's Flood, with his novel *Not Wanted on the Voyage.*

There is much that is not wanted on the voyage, certainly not by Noah Noyes—Mrs. Noyes, for instance, and Lucy, the mysterious wife taken by his son Ham in the days just prior to the Flood. But Jaweh's edict is clear, that Noah will take his wife and his sons and their three wives, and this he must obey. Findley's Noah is no kindly patriarch or lover of animals. His Noah is part-scientist, part-magician, and experiments happily on animals in order to gain his knowledge, and exercises a brutal tyranny over his family, most particularly over his wife, through whose eyes we see much of the story unfold.

By the same token, Jaweh, the Old Testament God, is a tired man, weary of the world he has created and the way in which it is abused. He seems not to realize that his friend Noah is as bad as all the rest, and when, having seen Noah's Masque of Creation, he decides to wipe clean the slate and start again, he cannot realize that the seeds of corruption will be sown afresh in the new world by the very man who is supposed to lead the animals and people safely to that world. There is much about Noah that is questionable, including his relationship with his daughter-in-law, Hannah, and in the close confinement of the Ark, this madness spreads. Down in the hold, Mrs. Noah and her few supporters, including her blind cat Mottyl, strive to uphold all that was best in the pre-diluvian world but her efforts can at best be only partially successful, even with the help of Lucy, the fallen angel.

Findley's tale is bitter, very unlike, for example, Jeanette Winterson's *Boating For Beginners.* He dwells upon the stink and the noise of the Ark, on the need for survival, on Noah's brutality, presenting the Ark as the microcosm for all that is bad in the world as well as all that is good, implying perhaps that there can never be an escape, for all that there will be moments of respite.

Certain of Findley's other novels are fantastic in a postmodernist, fabulist or "metafictional" manner. *Famous Last Words* utilizes Ezra

Pound's fictitious Hugh Selwyn Mauberley as a character; and, in a similar fashion, *Headhunter* plays with revivifed characters and themes from Joseph Conrad's *Heart of Darkness* and other famous works of the past.

—Maureen Speller

FINNEY, Charles G(randison)

Nationality: American. **Born:** Sedalia Missouri, 1 December 1905. **Education:** Missouri University, 1925. **Military Service:** United States Army; served in Tientsin, China, 1927-30. **Family:** Married Marie Doyle in 1939; two daughters. **Career:** Various posts, Arizona *Daily Star,* Tucson, until 1970; contributor to magazines, including the *New Yorker* and *Harper's.* **Awards:** American Booksellers Association Award for most original novel of the year, 1935. **Died:** 16 April 1984.

FANTASY PUBLICATIONS

Novels

The Circus of Dr. Lao, illustrated by Boris Artzybasheff. New York, Viking Press, 1935; London, Grey Walls Press, 1948.
The Unholy City. New York, Vanguard Press, 1937; London, Panther, 1976.
The Magician Out of Manchuria (omnibus; includes *The Unholy City, The Magician Out of Manchuria*). New York, Pyramid, 1968; abridged edition, containing *The Magician Out of Manchuria* only, London, Panther, 1976.

Short Stories

The Ghosts of Manacle. New York, Pyramid, 1964.

OTHER PUBLICATIONS

Novels

Past the End of the Pavement. N.p., 1939.

Other

The Old China Hands. N.p, n.d.

*

Film Adaptation: *The Seven Faces of Dr. Lao,* 1963, from his novel *The Circus of Dr. Lao.*

*   *   *

Despite a modest-sized output, Charles G. Finney remains as much a one-book author as Bram Stoker. *The Circus of Dr. Lao* is famous. Everything else is "by the author of *The Circus of Dr. Lao*". Both the author's army experiences in the Orient (the book

was begun in China in 1929) and his newspaper work are obvious influences on this classic, absurdist short novel in which a mysterious Chinese brings a fantastic circus into an Arizona town, replete with mythical beasts and genuine demigods, all to the discomfiture of the town's smug inhabitants. The wondrous attractions are summarized in an effusive advertisement the venerable Doctor places in the town's newspaper. What follows fulfils the ad's seemingly impossible promises exactly, up to and including a vision of the destruction of the hitherto unknown lost city of Woldercan. The narrative is an amazing display of wit and invention, the incidents strung together according to the announcement, with no other plot or structure, a sheer *tour de force*. The Doctor remains inscrutable to the end. Truly, this is one of the few books in which the inevitable is continually surprising. The main text is followed by a long appendix, elucidating what has gone before, often slyly hinting at more than was stated. The novel was filmed in 1963, much trivialized, as *The Seven Faces of Dr. Lao,* with a juvenile lead and a conventional plot (about shady realestate dealings) added. That any of Finney's substance survived is all but miraculous, yet some of it did, along with the interesting suggestion (not at all strong in the book) that the Doctor and his exhibits are one and the same; hence the Seven Faces, all of them portrayed by Tony Randall, with special effects by George Pal.

Dr. Lao proved such a unique book that even the author couldn't equal it. *The Unholy City,* ostensibly set in Asia, rapidly turns into a broad caricature of American society, as the hero finds a large cache of money and goes through a series of hectic adventures until the loot runs out. The satire is freewheeling, topical and ultimately formless, the book's social attitudes now badly dated.

The collection *The Ghosts of Manacle* is far less ghostly than the book's packaging suggests. Some of the contents are fantasies and odd fables, ranging from a tale of shape-changing ("The Black Retriever") to the life and death of a rattlesnake, told from the snake's point of view; but its centerpiece is another short novel, "The End of the Rainbow," a comic tall tale about treasure-hunting in Arizona, not actually fantastic at all, although reminiscent of Avram Davidson in his most exaggerated mode. A final fantasy short novel, *The Magician Out of Manchuria,* is again rambling, witty and strongly erotic, if slight, concerning a wandering Chinese magician in a rapidly modernizing China which has little use for him.

One associational item, *Past the End of the Pavement,* is a mainstream novel about childhood. *The Circus of Dr. Lao* was showcased again in Ray Bradbury's 1956 anthology, *The Circus of Dr. Lao and Other Improbable Stories,* and has been reprinted numerous times since, often with the brilliant Boris Artzybasheff illustrations which graced the original edition. This one story seems as fresh as ever, only dated by a now politically-incorrect racial caricature (Mumbo Jumbo, King of Congo) which is very much of a piece with all the other caricatures in the book.

Perhaps it is the central image, of the enchanted circus filled with supernatural exhibits, which resonates so powerfully. Certainly we have seen many traces of it since, most obviously in Ray Bradbury's "Black Ferris" (1948) and *Something Wicked This Way Comes* (1962). It could also be claimed that Finney's stylistic manner prefigures those of R. A. Lafferty, Avram Davidson, and perhaps even Daniel Manus Pinkwater.

—Darrell Schweitzer

FINNEY, Jack

Nationality: American. **Born:** Walter Braden Finney, Milwaukee, Wisconsin, 1911. **Education:** Knox College, Galesburg, Illinois. **Family:** Married Marguerite Guest; one daughter and one son. **Career:** Self-employed writer. **Awards:** World Fantasy life achievement award, 1987. **Agent:** Don Congdon Associates, 156 Fifth Avenue, Suite 625, New York, NY 10010, USA.

FANTASY PUBLICATIONS

Novels

The Woodrow Wilson Dime. New York, Simon and Schuster, 1968.
Time and Again. New York, Simon and Schuster, 1970; London, Weidenfeld and Nicolson, 1980.
Marion's Wall. New York, Simon and Schuster, 1973.
From Time to Time. New York, Simon and Schuster, 1995.

Short Stories

The Third Level. New York, Rinehart, 1957; as *The Clock of Time,* London, Eyre and Spottiswoode, 1958.
I Love Galesburg in the Springtime: Fantasy and Time Stories. New York, Simon and Schuster, 1963; London, Eyre and Spottiswoode, 1965.
Forgotten News: The Crime of the Century and Other Lost Stories. New York, Doubleday, 1983.
About Time: Twelve Stories. New York, Simon and Schuster, 1986.

OTHER PUBLICATIONS

Novels

Five Against the House. New York, Doubleday, and London, Eyre and Spottiswoode, 1954.
The Body Snatchers. New York, Dell, and London, Eyre and Spottiswoode, 1955; as *Invasion of the Body Snatchers,* Dell, 1961; London, Sphere, 1978.
The House of Numbers. New York, Dell, and London, Eyre and Spottiswoode, 1957.
Assault on a Queen. New York, Simon and Schuster, 1959; London, Eyre and Spottiswoode, 1960.
Good Neighbor Sam. New York, Simon and Schuster, and London, Eyre and Spottiswoode, 1963.
The Night People. New York, Doubleday, 1977.

Play

Telephone Roulette, adaptation of his story "Take a Number." Chicago, Dramatic Publishing Company, 1956.

*

Film Adaptations: *Five Against the House,* 1955; *Invasion of the Body Snatchers,* 1956, 1978, 1994, all from his novel *The Body Snatchers; Good Neighbor Sam,* 1964; *Assault on a Queen,* 1966; *Maxie,* 1985, from his novel *Marion's Wall.*

*   *   *

A significant contributor to several commercial genres, Jack Finney is best known as author of the thrice-filmed science-fiction horror novel *The Body Snatchers,* often republished under the movie title *Invasion of the Body Snatchers.* His other novels (most of which have been filmed) range from smart, urban comedy (*Good Neighbor Sam*) through heist thrillers (*Assault on a Queen, Five Against the House*) to nightmarish, urban comedy (*The Night People*). In his ease with genre-hopping, he is part of a distinguished American lineage that stretches from Edgar Allan Poe to Michael Crichton: his best works, which have their own distinctive themes, are not hampered by his preference for a slick-magazine style over the pulpiness of many of his contemporaries.

A fantasist by default, his best-known works are notionally science fiction but skimp on the detail that would mark a Hugo Gernsback-John W. Campbell-authorized practitioner of the field. *The Body Snatchers* has an alien invasion, but unlike Robert Heinlein's comparable *The Puppet Masters* (1951) could as easily be about demonic possession for the story and its social-psychological implications to work. *Time and Again,* a romantic mystery with a modern-day hero who thinks himself back into a richly reimagined turn-of-the-century New York, is framed by a government time-travel project but descends from Twain's *A Connecticut Yankee in King Arthur's Court* rather than Wells's *The Time Machine.* (A belated sequel, *From Time to Time,* was published in 1995.) Similarly, *The Woodrow Wilson Dime* is a parallel-world story which gets through its Einsteinian time-stream explanation ("The Funhouse Mirror Theory of the Universe") before concentrating on farcical, neurotic marital romance.

Marion's Wall, filmed as *Maxie* with Glenn Close, is a rare outright fantasy in the vein of Thorne Smith, with the hero's wife possessed by the spirit of a flapper who died before she could become a silent-film star. Essentially farcical (the hero is presented with the problem of deciding whether it is adultery to sleep with his wife if another mind is in her body), *Marion's Wall* is as concerned with evoking the minutiae (and slang) of the past as *Time and Again* with a strong undercurrent of dissatisfaction with a plasticized present. Finney reveals a strong streak of film-buffery in the inclusion of a film collector who resembles exactly Lon Chaney as the Phantom of the Opera and has vaults containing such literally fabulous rarities as a complete *Greed* and a silent *Great Gatsby* with Valentino and Gloria Swanson as Gatsby and Daisy.

Finney's interests recur throughout his cross-genre work: in *The Woodrow Wilson Dime, Marion's Wall* and the non-fantastic *Good Neighbor Sam* (aptly filmed as a Jack Lemmon vehicle), extraordinary circumstances revitalize a slumping marriage. His short stories of the 1950s define the area that Rod Serling, whose teleplay "Walking Distance" is a pastiche of Finney's "The Third Level," would call the Twilight Zone. His recurrent theme is of a lost past or alternate now where life and love are somehow better than in his tartly-characterized, body-snatched American present. Perhaps the best expressions of this yearning are the perfect short stories "The Third Level," "Second Chance" and "The Love Letter," in which by-ways into the past are found via an extra level of New York's Grand Central Station, a 1920s car and a secret drawer in an old desk. *Time and Again* and *The Woodrow Wilson Dime* are vastly more complex versions of the theme, with the former standing as perhaps Finney's most substantial, important novel. His influence is considerable: he is cited by Stephen King (whose *conte cruel* "The Ledge" is a homage to Finney's unforgettable "Contents of the Dead Man's Pocket") and Richard Matheson (whose *Bid Time Return* is a conscious variation on *Time and Again*) as a model.

—Kim Newman

FISK, Pauline

Nationality: British. **Born:** 27 September, 1948 in London, England. **Education:** Attended Wimbledon County School for Girls, 1959-66. **Family:** Married David Davies (an architect), 12 February, 1972; one son and four daughters. **Career:** Writer. **Awards:** Smarties prize, 1990. **Address:** Cecil Ware Literary Agents, John Spencer Square, Canonbury, London N1 2L3, England.

FANTASY PUBLICATIONS

Novel

Midnight Blue. Oxford, England, and Batavia, Illinois, Lion, 1990.

OTHER PUBLICATIONS

Short Stories

The Southern Hill. Oxford, England, Lion, 1972.

Novel

Telling the Sea. Oxford, England, and Batavia, Illinois, Lion, 1992.

*   *   *

Towards the end of Pauline Fisk's *Midnight Blue* the young heroine, Bonnie, after attempting to resolve the threat to her adopted family by a melodramatic leap from a window, and contacting the chthonic deity Wild Edric in a thunderstorm or in deep underground tunnels, finds that the only real option is "this boring, quite ridiculous act of self-sacrifice". We are required to look under the hallucinatory, brilliant surface of this story.

Bonnie and her mother Maybelle are trying to make a home together, but Maybelle's domineering mother, who has brought Bonnie up from babyhood, cannot let go of either of them. Escaping from "Grandbag," Bonnie discovers Michael's balloon, set to take him to "the land beyond the sky". She climbs into the balloon's gondola and, with the help of the mysterious "Shadowboy," passes through the sky as if through a mirror, to a world which is almost but not quite identical to hers.

This world beyond the sky is inhabited by people who are analogues of the people she knows, including Bonnie herself, here called "Arabella." Arabella is as lonely as she, but for different reasons. Bonnie is accepted into the family but still feels estranged: the Shadowboy, unwilling to take human feelings upon himself, remains for the moment on the Hill. The situation is unresolved until Bonnie discovers that "Grandbag" also has her analogue in the evil "Grandmother Marvell" who appears to be able to do liter-

ally the soul-withering which "Grandbag" does metaphorically. Bonnie comes through her first temptation successfully, and her relationship with Arabella is settled but there is still Grandmother Marvell to deal with. Can the presences of the ancient Lord and Lady of the Hill—who appear to be the old gods Edric and Godda—help Bonnie?

Midnight Blue is clearly a novel about dysfunctional family relationships; a theme which is also present in the non-fantasy *Telling the Sea* where 13-year-old Nona has to be the "adult" in her relationship with her victimized mother and in which the subsidiary characters also have family difficulties to resolve. But it (and *Telling the Sea*) is a novel of healing rather than wounding. Even the attempted suicides in both novels (which have disturbed some adult readers of books packaged for teenagers) are cathartic, clearing the way for understanding. For Bonnie, indeed, to throw herself from the window is self-sacrifice, the only way she can see to prevent Grandmother Marvell from entering the house. Nevertheless, these emotional undercurrents add depth and complexity to the stories, and as a fantasy, where Fisk is also dealing with symbolism and metaphor, the result in *Midnight Blue* is a somewhat elusive richness.

The deep blue of the sky, for instance, reflected in the "midnight blue" of the balloon, which tears apart to let Bonnie through, has at once a powerful beauty as an image and a sense of almost catatonic emptiness. The Shadowboy, a kind of inexplicable genie called up by the attempt to cross worlds, gains substance and a name, but is an eerie invention ("'What are you?'/'I don't know'"). The other-world itself, with its easy acceptance of people who fall out of the sky and its hints of underlying wild magic coupled with its prosaic ordinariness, is seen as if through a shimmering heat-haze. Like all major fantasies, there is a sense of something stronger, stranger than what is described.

Fisk's narratives are both visually striking and driving in their physical and emotional suspense. There are gaps in *Midnight Blue*—we know, for instance, that Bonnie has found out more about how the other-world can be reached than we have—but the obliqueness this creates only adds to the shimmering, half-understood quality of the book. Fisk has not written enough fantasy to suggest that she is a permanent exponent of the field, but *Midnight Blue,* which won the "Smarties" Book Prize in 1990 and was nominated for two other major children's awards, is worth any number of lesser novels.

—Andy Sawyer

———

FLETCHER, George U. *See* **PRATT, (Murray) Fletcher.**

———

FLINT, Kenneth C(ovey)

Pseudonym: Casey Flynn. **Nationality:** American. **Born:** 23 June, 1947 in Omaha, Nebraska. **Education:** University of Nebraska at Omaha, B.A., 1970, M.A., 1972. **Family:** Married Judith

McCormick (a museum instructor and program developer), 9 January, 1971; two sons. **Career:** University of Nebraska at Omaha, instructor in humanities, 1972-78; Plattsmouth Community Schools, Plattsmouth, Nebraska, English teacher and department head, 1979-87; freelance writer, 1987—; instructor at writing seminars for schools and community groups; volunteer, Omaha Western Heritage Museum. **Agent:** Russell, Galen, Scott Meredith Literary Agency, Inc., 845 Third Ave., New York, New York 10022, U.S.A. **Address:** 11353 Jones St, Omaha, Nebraska 68154, USA.

FANTASY PUBLICATIONS

Novels (series: Finn MacCumhal; Gods of Ireland; Sidhe)

A Storm Upon Ulster (Sidhe). New York, Bantam, 1981; as *The Hound of Culain,* London, Bantam, 1986.

Riders of the Sidhe. New York, Bantam, 1984; London, Bantam, 1986.

Champions of the Sidhe. New York, Bantam, 1984; London, Bantam, 1987.

Master of the Sidhe. New York, Bantam, 1985; London, Bantam, 1987.

Challenge of the Clans (Finn MacCumhal). New York, Bantam, 1986; London, Bantam, 1987.

Storm Shield (Finn MacCumhal). New York, Bantam, 1986; London, Bantam, 1988.

The Dark Druid (Finn MacCumhal). New York, Bantam, 1987; London, Bantam, 1988.

Isle of Destiny: A Novel of Ancient Ireland. New York, Bantam, 1988; London, Bantam, 1990.

Cromm. New York, Doubleday, 1990.

Most Ancient Song (Gods of Ireland; as Casey Flynn). New York, Bantam, 1991.

The Enchanted Isles (Gods of Ireland; as Casey Flynn). New York, Bantam, 1991.

Otherworld. New York, Bantam, 1992.

Legends Reborn. New York, Bantam, 1992.

Star Wars: The Heart of the Jedi. 1993.

*   *   *

Kenneth C. Flint has based all his novels to date (with the exception of *Otherworld*) on Irish Celtic mythology, though they range from retellings of ancient legend to stories involving contemporary settings and characters.

Celtic myth consists of a number of myth-cycles and legends, of which one of the better known is the story of Cuculain and the Red Branch. Flint retells his story in his first novel, *The Hound of Culain.* Cuculain is the champion of Conchobar, King of Ulster, and the novel principally concerns the rivalry between the king and Meave, queen of Connacht.

The next three books in the series form a trilogy, which, although making one complete story can also be read as separate volumes. They concern the adventures of Lugh Lamfada. He was one of the very early Irish heroes, thus setting these books before *The Hound of Culain* chronologically. The Tuatha de Danann (the Children of Danu) have come to Ireland, winning the country from the indigenous Firbolgs. However, their tenancy has been challenged by the Fomor, a race of whom many members show horrific deformities. Bres, the high-king of the de Dananns, has kept the Fomor at bay by paying a tribute which has drained the strength and resources of his people. Any rebels, or those skilled with magic who might upset the arrangement, have been banished to the Mountains of Morne. Lugh is a youth who has been reared on an island and has no idea of the situation in Eire. When the Fomor attack and destroy his home he is first sent to the isle of Manannan, the Sea-god. Manannan sends him on to Eire where he raises a rebellion and Bres is deposed. In the second of these volumes, *Champions of the Sidhe,* Bres returns with a Fomor army. The de Dananns are weakened by their years of deprivation under his rule so their only chance is for Lugh and his companions to return the Manannan's isle and bring back the magical cauldron which will restore the strength of anyone who eats from it. In the final part, *Master of the Sidhe,* the battle is taken to the Fomor in their base, which is an island surmounted by a tower of glass.

The basic plots for these books have been lifted straight from Irish mythology but the trimmings are Flint's own interpretation. The Fomor, led by Balor One-Eye, are the decadent remnants of a race who enjoyed a high level of technology. Their civilization collapsed, with the majority of the survivors being affected by genetic damage that produces hideous mutants. Only the undeformed are able to remain in the Tower, the rest being exiled to Eire. The Tower itself is kept working by an ancient technology which provides electricity for lifts, refrigeration plants, lighting, heating, etc. Balor himself appears to be a robotic being with one eye which when opened releases a devastating infra-red beam.

The next three books, again forming a trilogy within which each volume tells a separate tale, use a different myth-cycle as their source. The de Dananns have been long defeated by the invading Milesians. They have retreated to underground Sids, visible only to the outsider as grassy mounds, and are now virtually immortal. Their magic is still around but is less evident. These books tell the tale of Finn, leader of the Fianna, an army of warriors specially picked to protect Ireland from invasion. *Challenge of the Clans* tells of Finn's birth and childhood and the way he has to prove himself in order to avenge his father's death, win the chieftainship of his clan and take his rightful place as captain of the Fianna— remarkable feats for a youth of around 17. In *Storm Shield,* Ireland is invaded by the Fomor king, Daire Donn, who wears invincible armour. To counter this threat, Finn has to win the sword and shield that the ancient de Dananns forged from the metal that formed Balor's head. In *The Dark Druid,* Finn falls in love with Sabd a woman who is obsessively desired by the druid Fear Doirche, who steals her from Finn and turns her into a fawn. Finn neglects his duties in his search for Sabd, wandering the countryside in a state of madness before the resolution is reached.

The de Dananns (Sidhe) are in evidence throughout these books, Finn himself is half Sidhe, but the people are very suspicious of them and in most cases Sidhe magic is the cause of their problems. This is still the case in *Isle of Destiny.* Here Flint returns to his original hero, Cuculain. This is almost a prequel to *The Hound of Culain* in that it deals with Cuculain's early life before he was given that sobriquet. He goes through this book as Sentata. The principal tale is that of Conaire Mor, the High-king of Ireland, and his desire to bring peace to the country. Woven around this is the story of Meave. She begins as the reluctant wife of Conchobar, King of Ulster, but when he divorces her Mor sends her as an emissary to Aileel, King of Connacht, in an attempt to persuade him to agree to Conaire Mor's peace. She succeeds by helping Aileel settle his own war with the Firbolgs and marrying him, thus setting the scene for the rivalry between Connacht and Ulster in *The Hound of Culain.*

Flint's more recent books still use Celtic mythology as a base but with contemporary elements. In *Cromm,* Colin is an advertising artist who dreams about ancient Ireland in which his *alter ego* (also called Colin) is battling the evil of Cromm Cruaich who demands blood sacrifices. In the modern Ireland, Colin finds that Cromm lives again and he has to defeat him. This book links past and present, but *Legends Reborn* brings the Sidhe into modern New York. A Sidhe woman follows Michael Kean from Ireland to America but is followed by one of Ireland's legendary heroes, who believes her to have been kidnapped.

Because Flint is drawing on extant material for his plots there are few surprises. His characters are superheroes of the past. They are expected to triumph and to show extraordinary talents. The writing itself is stylistically poor. Flint tends to take an omniscient viewpoint, dipping into the various characters' thoughts almost at random. This makes the characters remote and prevents them developing beyond the two-dimensional. He also has the irritating habit of trying to find alternative words to "said" when attributing speech. Occasionally he attempts to write the dialogue with Irish speech patterns but this is inconsistent and ultimately all the characters speak English or American. All his characters tend to be good or evil, with no gradations between them, and many of the villains are deformed as well. There is however plenty of action and considerable pace in the writing.

Otherworld is different from the rest, being a dark fantasy. Set in the present day it has a government agent as its protagonist and is centred on murder by supernatural forces.

—Pauline Morgan

———

FLYNN, Casey. *See* **FLINT, Kenneth C(ovey).**

———

FORD, John M.

Pseudonym: Michael J. Dodge. **Nationality:** American. **Born:** 1957. **Awards:** World Fantasy award, 1984. **Address:** c/o Tor Books, 175 Fifth Avenue, New York, NY, 10010, USA.

FANTASY PUBLICATIONS

Novels

The Dragon Waiting: A Masque of History. New York, Timescape, 1983; London, Corgi, 1985.

Short Stories

Casting Fortune. New York, Tor, 1989.

OTHER PUBLICATIONS

Novels

Web of Angels. New York, Pocket, 1980.
The Princes of Air. New York, Pocket, 1982.
Star Trek: Voyage to Adventure (for children; as Michael J. Dodge). New York, Pocket, 1984; London, Carousel, 1985.
The Final Reflection. New York, Pocket, 1984; Bath, Firecrest, 1985.
How Much for Just the Planet? New York, Pocket, 1987.
The Scholars of Night. New York, Tor, 1988.
Fugue State, with *The Death of Doctor Island,* by Gene Wolfe. New York, Tor, 1990.
Growing Up Weightless. New York, Bantam, 1993.

Other

On Writing Science Fiction, with George H. Scithers and Darrell Schweitzer. Philadelphia, Owlswick Press, 1981.

*   *   *

John M. Ford is a many-sided author, having written in a variety of fields but without a large output in any of them. His fantasy publications are restricted to two volumes though he has produced a number of short stories.

The most important of his books is *The Dragon Waiting,* for which he won the 1984 World Fantasy Award. It is set in an alternate 15th century. The great power is Byzantium, which is gradually conquering the rest of the world, sometimes by force, sometimes by stealth. It is a world where there is no dominant religion, Christianity is just another of the many cults that have their adherents and exist alongside each other in reasonable tolerance. There are wizards, and vampirism is a communicable disease.

The four main characters are well drawn. Three of them are introduced in each of the first three long chapters. As a boy, Hywel Peredur unwittingly helped a captive wizard escape as he was being taken to his death through Wales. Discovering that he had the potential to become a wizard himself, he followed the escapee into exile as his apprentice. Dimitrius Ducas was initiated into the cult of Mithras as a child. His father was the Byzantine governor of Gaul—France having been divided into three, England controlling part with a buffer state ruled by the old French Royal Family in between. Dimitrius is forced to flee when he is coerced into being the figurehead of a rebellion which goes wrong. Cynthia Ricci is Lorenzo di Medici's doctor. He persuades her to flee when Florence is under great threat from the Byzantium-backed Duke of Milan and his armies. Hywel, Dimitri and Cynthia meet up in an inn in a snowstorm along with Gregory von Bayern, a vampire and military scientist. The only thing they have in common, initially, is their hatred of Byzantium, and in order to do something to thwart the empire they travel together via France to England. This England is ruled by Edward IV, who is soon to be struck down by magic. Having sown the seeds, Ford provides another reason why Richard, Duke of Gloucester killed the princes in the Tower.

In making a few simple changes to the structure of the world (vampirism and magic), Ford has thought through the consequences. An historian of the period would undoubtedly pick up more of the ramifications, but there is much that a reader with a general knowledge of 15th-century European history will recognize. Ford has taken the accepted version of events and added his own twists to them. This is extremely cleverly done, making the reader feel knowledgable—nothing is forced and overstressed. The result is that Ford's version seems correct for the duration of the book. It does have flaws. There is a very large cast, many of which had real counterparts in our history and it is difficult, not only to keep track of them but also value their roles. The lesser characters are often very sketchily portrayed, which becomes irritating when events turn on the actions of these, especially if they have actual historical provenance. It is also difficult to keep track of time. In some instances years may have passed between chapters, or even paragraphs, and this can cause momentary confusions. The plot is complex and has many twists and turns before a climax is reached but even this is played down. As with many real political events, the significance of the pointers is not always apparent until the denouement. With this fiction, however, an enhancement of the undercurrents would have greatly clarified the situation.

Ford's other fantasy book, *Casting Fortune,* is a collection of three stories set in a common world. The first two, "A Cup of Worrynot Tea" and "Green is the Colour," both appeared in volumes of the *Liavek* shared-world series edited by Will Shetterly and Emma Bull. In this world, wizards are people who have been able to "invest their luck" to use as a power source. They can only do this on their birthday each year, and the amount of time they have to do it in, which is proportional to the amount of luck they can invest and therefore their power as a wizard, depends on the length of time their mothers were in labour. The technological level of this world is probably early Victorian. The two reprinted stories are cleverly constructed detective stories. In both cases, though, the endings are compressed and confusing. The third story, "The Illusionist," is a short novel. It concerns the playwright, Virson ola Vivar who, after producing seven successful tragedies, declares his intention of making his next play a comedy. He chooses four unknown performers to take all the roles and although much of the plot is taken up with schooling them towards the first night there is still room for intrigue, murder and magic. The story can easily be read alone, both without the others in the book and without having any knowledge of the original shared world. As in *The Dragon Waiting,* there are many twists and turns in the narrative—the obvious is unlikely to be the truth—but again, the whole would have been strengthened by more attention to the minor characters whose roles are, as in the play, small but significant.

Ford has also written science-fiction novels, including several *Star Trek* spinoffs, and a spy novel set in the near future, as well as a number of short stories.

—Pauline Morgan

FOSTER, Alan Dean

Pseudonym: George Lucas. **Nationality:** American. **Born:** New York City, 18 November 1946. **Education:** University of California, Los Angeles, B.A. in political science 1968; M.F.A. in film 1969. **Military Service:** United States Army Reserve, 1969-75. **Family:** Married JoAnn Oxley in 1975. **Career:** Head copywriter, Headlines Ink Agency, Studio City, California, 1970-71; instructor in English and film, University of California, Los Angeles, intermittently since 1971, and Los Angeles City College, 1972-76.

Awards: Galaxy award, 1979; Southwest Book award, 1990. **Agent:** Virginia Kidd, Box 278, Milford, PA 18337, USA. **Address:** Box 12757, Prescott, AZ 86304, USA.

FANTASY PUBLICATIONS

Novels (series: Spellsinger)

Luana (novelization of screenplay). New York, Ballantine, 1974.
Clash of the Titans (novelization of screenplay). New York, Warner, and London, Macdonald, 1981.
Spellsinger at the Gate. Huntington Woods, Michigan, Phantasia Press, 1983; in 2 vols. as *Spellsinger,* New York, Warner, 1983, and London, Futura, 1984; and *The Hour of the Gate,* New York, Warner, and London, Futura, 1984.
Krull (novelization of screenplay). New York, Warner, and London, Corgi, 1983.
The Day of the Dissonance (Spellsinger). Huntington Woods, Michigan, Phantasia Press, 1984; London, Futura, 1985.
The Moment of the Magician (Spellsinger). Huntington Woods, Michigan, Phantasia Press, 1984; London, Macdonald, 1985.
Shadowkeep. New York, Warner, 1984; London, W. H. Allen, 1985.
Pale Rider (novelization of screenplay). New York, Warner, and London, Arrow, 1985.
The Paths of the Perambulator (Spellsinger). West Bloomfield, Michigan, Phantasia Press, 1985; London, Macdonald, 1986.
Season of the Spellsong (omnibus; includes *Spellsinger, The Hour of the Gate, The Day of the Dissonance*). New York, Nelson Doubleday, 1985.
The Time of the Transference (Spellsinger). West Bloomfield, Michigan, Phantasia Press, 1986; London, Futura, 1987.
Spellsinger's Scherzo (omnibus; includes *The Moment of the Magician, The Paths of the Perambulator, The Time of the Transference*). New York, Nelson Doubleday, 1987.
Son of Spellsinger. New York, Warner, and London, Orbit, 1993.
Chorus Skating (Spellsinger). New York, Warner, 1994; London, Orbit, 1995.

OTHER PUBLICATIONS

Novels

The Tar-Aiym Krang. New York, Ballantine, 1972; London, New English Library, 1979.
Bloodhype. New York, Ballantine, 1973; London, New English Library, 1979.
Icerigger. New York, Ballantine, 1974; London, New English Library, 1976.
Dark Star (novelization of screenplay). New York, Ballantine, 1974; London, Futura, 1979.
Star Trek Log One-Ten (novelizations of TV scripts). New York, Ballantine, 10 vols., 1974-78; in 3 vols., New York, Pocket, 1993; London, Pocket, 1995.
Midworld. New York, Doubleday, 1975; London, Macdonald and Jane's 1977.
Star Wars (as George Lucas; novelization of screenplay). New York, Ballantine, 1976.
Orphan Star. New York, Del Rey, 1977; London, New English Library, 1979.

The End of the Matter. New York, Del Rey, 1977; London, New English Library, 1979.

Splinter of the Mind's Eye. New York, Del Rey, and London, Sphere, 1978.

Mission to Moulokin. New York, Del Rey, and London, New English Library, 1979.

Alien (novelization of screenplay). New York, Del Rey, and London, Macdonald and Jane's, 1979.

The Black Hole (novelization of screenplay). New York, Del Rey, 1979.

Cachalot. New York, Del Rey, 1980.

Outland (novelization of screenplay). New York, Warner, and London, Sphere, 1981.

The Thing (novelization of screenplay). New York, Bantam, and London, Corgi, 1982.

Nor Crystal Tears. New York, Del Rey, 1982.

For Love of Mother-Not. New York, Del Rey, 1983; London, New English Library, 1984.

The Man Who Used the Universe. New York, Warner, 1983; London, Futura, 1984.

The I Inside. New York, Warner, 1984; London, Futura, 1985.

The Last Starfighter (novelization of screenplay). New York, Berkley, and London, W.H. Allen, 1984.

Slipt. New York, Berkley, 1984.

Starman (novelization of screenplay). New York, Warner, 1984; London, Corgi, 1985.

Voyage to the City of the Dead. New York, Del Rey, 1984; London, New English Library, 1986.

Sentenced to Prism. New York, Del Rey, 1985; London, New English Library, 1988.

Aliens (novelization of screenplay). New York, Warner, and London, Futura, 1986.

Into the Out Of. New York, Warner, 1986; London, New English Library, 1987.

The Deluge Drivers. New York, Del Rey, 1987; London, New English Library, 1988.

Glory Lane. New York, Ace, 1987; London, New English Library, 1989.

Flinx in Flux. New York, Del Rey, 1988; London, New English Library, 1989.

Alien Nation (novelization of screenplay). New York, Warner, and London, Grafton, 1988.

To the Vanishing Point. New York, Warner, 1988; London, Sphere, 1989.

Maori. New York, Berkley, 1988.

Quozl. New York, Ace, 1989.

Cyber Way. New York, Ace, 1990; London, Orbit, 1992.

A Call to Arms. New York, Del Rey, 1991.

Cat-a-Lyst. New York, Ace, 1991; London, Orbit, 1992.

Alien 3 (novelization of screenplay). New York and London, Warner, 1992.

Codgerspace. New York, Ace, 1992, and London, Orbit, 1993.

The False Mirror. New York, Del Rey, 1992.

The Complete Alien Omnibus (omnibus of the three *Alien* screenplay novelizations). New York and London, Warner, 1993.

The Spoils of War. New York, Del Rey, 1993.

Greenthieves. New York, Ace, 1994; London, Orbit, 1994.

Ascending Whine. New York, Ace, 1995.

Design for Great Day, with Eric Frank Russell. New York, Tor, 1995.

Short Stories

With Friends Like These . . . New York, Del Rey, 1977.

The Horror on the Beach: A Tale in the Chthulhu Mythos. San Diego, California, Valcour and Krueger, 1978.

. . . Who Needs Enemies? New York, Del Rey, 1984.

The Metrognome and Other Stories. New York, Del Rey, 1990.

Play

Screen treatment: *Star Trek: The Motion Picture,* 1979.

Other

Editor, *The Best of Eric Frank Russell.* New York, Del Rey, 1978.

Editor, *Animated Features and Silly Symphonies.* New York, Abbeville, 1980.

Editor, with Martin H. Greenberg, *Smart Dragons, Foolish Elves.* New York, Ace, 1991.

Editor, with Martin H. Greenberg, *Betcha Can't Read Just One.* New York, Ace, 1993.

*   *   *

The work of Alan Dean Foster may be divided into two broad categories: his novelizations of films, and his original novels both science fiction and fantasy. Over a period of 20 years, he has produced a large *oeuvre,* though no outstanding works.

Among Foster's earliest original science-fiction novels, two of the best are *Mission to Moulokin* and *The Tar-Aiym Krang,* and it could be argued that they have strong fantasy elements. *Mission to Moulokin* tells the story of Ethan Frome Fortune and his companion Skua September. Ethan is the brains, Skua the muscle, and the two make a living as interplanetary salesmen. They set off from the ice-planet of Tran-Ky-Ky to the trading post of Brass Monkey. They are distracted from this goal by a call from help from the Tran, who are being exploited by off-planet profiteers. So Ethan and Skua set off on their heroic mission to Moulokin to bring relief to the gentle Tran. Their adventures involve skimming down ice-canyons and over ice rivers. So Ethan and Skan, instead of escaping the ice planet, have to brave even greater frozen wastelands as a "rite of passage" to their final and triumphant departure for their home.

The Tar-Aiym Krang is the story of Flinx, "an ethical thief who steals only from the crooked." Flinx is also a telepath and soothsayer who makes a living by divining personal details of passing shoppers. One day, he is asked to locate a red-headed man, among all the population of Drallar. As fate would have it, the man is standing right there in the crowd at the foot of Finx's platform or stage. After a chase both hunters and their red-headed prey are left dead in a dark alley. Flinx then steals the map at the cause of the quarrel and so is set on a journey to discover the legendary Krang, vanished artifact of the long dead Tar-Aiym.

These early works are set in a future human society and mix science with supernatural powers, telepathy, and other forms of magic. But in more recent years Foster has written a series of novels that can be described as "pure" fantasy. The eight-part *Spellsinger* series follows the adventures of Buncam Spellsinger and his son Jon Tom. Friends of otters and giant sloths, Buncam and Jon Tom become involved in adventures-quests where they face attacks from hounds, thieves, and vicious hares. To muster his magic powers,

Buncam Spellsinger invents spellsongs using old rock lyrics, while his son Jon Tom uses rap. With their elements of magic, talking to animals, and medieval settings, these novels are standard fantasy fare, amusingly done, and they will certainly appeal to young adults.

In contrast, *Cat-a-Lyst* and *Cyber Way* are science-fantasy novels with one foot in the contemporary world. *Cat-a-Lyst* is the story of film star Jason Carter who come across a computer disk which turns out to contain archaeological files and a map leading to a mysterious Inca treasure horde. He sets off with his cat to discover this treasure. His South American guide also has a cat, as has the guardian of the Inca site. Cats are the common thread and the key to the solution of this quest, which concerns tabloid journalists, soccer hooligans, and ancient Incas. *Cyber Way* is another treasure hunt: this time a priceless Navaho sand painting is destroyed, and the computer-buff detective Vernon Moody sets off to discover why. In his quest for the truth, he runs foul of Navaho magical powers which will set against him giant snakes, snowstorms, and killer coyotes.

Perhaps the best-known and most visible part of Foster's work consists of the movie novelizations. He has built a strong reputation with his readable book versions of blockbuster science-fiction films such as George Lucas's *Star Wars* and the horror/sf trilogy *Alien*, *Aliens*, and *Alien 3*. The secret to Foster's success in this field is his conscientious approach. In an interview in *Interzone* magazine (February 1994), he says: "I think if you don't put at least 40 to 60 percent original material into the book, then you are cheating the reader. Anybody can sit down and simply transcribe a screenplay into prose form. I don't look on it as a work of transcription, I look on it as a collaboration, and I approach it in that way." He also speaks of improving the sense of situation and deepening the characterization. Others of his novelizations which fall into the fantasy rather than the science-fiction area include *Luana* (a jungle-woman adventure based on a little-known Italian movie), *Clash of the Titans* (based on Greek myth), *Krull* (a sword-and-sorcery/science-fiction crossover), and the interesting fantasy-western from a Clint Eastwood film, *Pale Rider*.

Whatever the genre, Alan Dean Foster writes colourful action adventures. He has tackled a wide variety of characters and backdrops, from far-future science fiction to fantastic animal quests to contemporary thrillers. Almost all his work has a magical, supernatural element. Though the stories often revolve around a simple "quest for treasure" or "journey to save the oppressed" formula, these tales are good solid fare, with little sex and violence. With their changing backdrops and concerns, Foster's books can be said to reflect the fantasy genre as a whole over the last two decades.

—Sally Ann Melia

FOX, Gardner F(rancis)

Pseudonyms: Jefferson Cooper; Lynna Cooper; Jeffrey Gardner; James Kendricks; Simon Majors; Kevin Matthews; John Medford Morgan; Bart Somers. **Nationality:** American. **Born:** Brooklyn, New York, 20 May 1911. **Education:** St. John's University, Jamaica, New York, B.A. 1932, LL.B. 1935. **Family:** Married Lynda J. Negrini in 1937; one son and one daughter. **Career:** Lawyer; from 1937, comic-book writer (*Batman*, *Superman*, *The Flash*, *Green Lantern* and others). **Died:** 24 December 1986.

FANTASY PUBLICATIONS

Novels (series: Kothar; Kyrik; Llarn)

Warrior of Llarn. New York, Ace, 1964.
The Druid Stone (as Simon Majors). New York, Paperback Library, 1965.
Thief of Llarn. New York, Ace, 1966.
Kothar—Barbarian Swordsman. New York, Belmont, 1969.
Kothar of the Magic Sword! New York, Belmont, 1969.
Kothar and the Demon Queen. New York, Belmont, 1969.
Kothar and the Conjurer's Curse. New York, Belmont, 1970.
Kothar and the Wizard Slayer. New York, Belmont, 1970.
Kyrik: Warlock Warrior. New York, Nordon, 1975; London, Flamingo, n.d.
Kyrik Fights the Demon World. New York, Nordon, 1975; London, Jenkins, 1976.
Kyrik and the Wizard's Sword. New York, Nordon, 1976.
Kyrik and the Lost Queen. New York, Nordon, 1976.

OTHER PUBLICATIONS

Novels

The Borgia Blade. New York, Fawcett, 1953; London, Fawcett, 1954.
Madame Buccaneer. New York, Fawcett, 1953; London, Fawcett, 1954.
Woman of Kali. New York, Fawcett, 1954; London, Muller, 1960.
The Gentleman Rogue. New York, Fawcett, 1954; London, Red Seal, 1959.
Rebel Wench. New York, Fawcett, 1955; London, Fawcett, 1958.
Queen of Sheba. New York, Fawcett, 1956.
One Sword for Love. London, Fawcett, 1956.
The Conquering Prince. New York, Fawcett, 1957; London, Eclipse, n.d.
Terror Over London. New York, Fawcett, 1957.
Creole Woman. New York, Fawcett, 1959.
Iron Lover. New York, Avon, 1959.
The Roman and the Slave Girl (as John Medford Morgan). New York, New American Library, 1959.
Witness This Woman. New York, Fawcett, 1959; London, Muller, 1961.
Bastard of Orleans. New York, Avon, 1960.
Scandal in Suburbia. New York, Hill, 1960.
Barbary Devil (as Jeffrey Gardner). New York, Pyramid, 1961.
Ivan the Terrible. New York, Avon, 1961.
Cleopatra (as Jeffrey Gardner). New York, Pyramid, 1962.
Five Weeks in a Balloon (novelization of screenplay). New York, Pyramid, 1962.
Tom Blood, Highwayman. New York, Avon, 1962.
One Wife's Ways. New York, Fawcett, and London, Muller, 1963.
Escape Across the Cosmos. New York, Paperback Library, 1964.
The Arsenal of Miracles. New York, Ace, 1964.
The Hunter out of Time. New York, Ace, 1965.
Beyond the Black Enigma (as Bart Somers). New York, Paperback Library, 1965.
Lion of Lucca. New York, Avon, 1966.
Abandon Galaxy! (as Bart Somers). New York, Paperback Library, 1967.

The Stonehedge Slaves [sic]. New York, Belmont, 1969.
Conehead. New York, Ace, 1973.
Carty. New York, Doubleday, 1977; London, Hale, 1979.
The Bold Ones. New York, Nordon, 1976.
The Liberty Sword. New York, Nordon, 1976.
Hurricane. New York, Nordon, 1976.
Savage Passage. New York, Belmont, 1978.
Blood Trail. New York, Belmont, 1979.

Novels as Jefferson Cooper

Arrow in the Hill. New York, Dodd Mead, 1955.
The Bloody Sevens. New York, Permabooks, 1956.
The Swordsman. New York, Pocket Books, 1957.
The Questing Sword. New York, Permabooks, 1958; London, Consul, 1960.
Captain Seadog. New York, Pocket Books, 1959.
Veronica's Veil. New York, Permabooks, 1959.
Delilah. New York, Paperback Library, 1962.
Jezebel. New York, Paperback Library, 1963.
Slave of the Roman Sword. New York, Paperback Library, 1965.
Sappho of Lesbos. New York, Paperback Library, 1966.
This Sword for Hire. New York, Paperback Library, 1966.

Novels as Kevin Matthews

Barbary Slaves. New York, Popular Library, 1956.
Tory Mistress. New York, Popular Library, 1956.
Woman of Egypt. New York, Popular Library, 1958; London, Panther, 1961.
The Devil Sword. New York, Hillman, 1960.
Cardboard Lover. New York, Hillman, 1961.
Catherine the Great. New York, Tower, 1964.
The Pagan Empress. New York, Tower, 1964.
Helen of Troy. New York, Tower, 1965.

Novels as James Kendricks

Beyond Our Pleasure. Derby, Connecticut, Monarch, 1959.
Sword of Casanova. Derby, Connecticut, Monarch, 1959.
The Adulterers. Derby, Connecticut, Monarch, 1960.
She Wouldn't Surrender. Derby, Connecticut, Monarch, 1960.
The Wicked, Wicked Women. Derby, Connecticut, Monarch, 1961.
Love Me Tonight. Derby, Connecticut, Monarch, 1963.

Novels as Lynna Cooper

An Offer of Marriage. New York, New American Library, 1976.
Substitute Bride. New York, New American Library, 1976.
Her Heart's Desire. New York, New American Library, 1976.
The Hired Wife. New York, New American Library, 1978.
Forgotten Love. New York, New American Library, 1979.
Hearts in the Highlands. New York, New American Library, 1980.
Inherit My Heart. New York, New American Library, 1981.

*   *   *

Any ten-best list of authors who gained proficiency, and appalling prolificacy, in nearly every pulp-fiction genre would have to include the name of Gardner F. Fox—arguably near or at the top. He wrote fantasy novels, science fiction, historical swashbucklers,

romance, westerns, soft pornography and just about everything else. (In addition to all the titles listed in the above bibliography, he is said to have written as Rod Gray the "Lady from L.U.S.T." and as Glen Chase the "Cherry Delight of N.Y.M.P.H.O." series of paperback originals.) Moreover, from 1937 until the late 1960s, Fox was a stalwart of the National Periodicals/*Superman* DC comic-book writing team. In comics, he helped create, develop or revive many superheroes, including Batman, the Flash, Green Lantern, the Atom, Zatara, Hawkman, the Spectre, and the Justice Society—later the Justice League—of America; and his Robert E. Howard-esque hero, Crom the Barbarian, graced the comic-strip section bound in with *Out of This World Adventures* pulp magazine.

Although beginning in comics, Fox soon made his mark in the all-reading department of popular fiction. "The Weirds of the Woodcarver" appeared, aptly enough, in *Weird Tales* (September 1944). However, Fox's most characteristic work found its way into the slam-bang *Planet Stories* (1945 onwards), including "Man Nth" and "Tonight the Stars Revolt!," which Brian W. Aldiss reprinted in his *Galactic Empires* science-fiction anthology. Fox mixed well the firewater cocktail of three-parts fantasy to one-part science (of a sort): pure space opera, of a type "justly recalling the horse-opera which, under a skin of molecular thinness, it so much resembles," in the words of Kingsley Amis (*New Maps of Hell,* 1960).

In 1953, Fox cracked the lucrative paperback-original market. *The Borgia Blade* was the first of many print-the-legend historical novels. *Woman of Kali* borders on fantasy; *One Sword for Love* deals intelligently with the mythical Prester John. At the same time, he remained faithful to DC Comics, creating series such as Star Hawkins, Space Museum, and the Star Rovers for *Strange Adventures* and *Mystery in Space.* (There was even *Strange Sports Stories,* an exotic hybrid that didn't take.) Adam Strange (*Showcase* 17-19; *Mystery in Space* 53-100, 102) was Fox's most viable brainchild in superhero-space-opera-fantasy mode. Strange, a two-fisted archaeologist become "Earth's first spaceman," is irregularly teleported by "Zeta-Beam" to the planet Rann of star-sun Alpha Centauri, where he meets up with Alanna, his "interplanetary sweetheart". The super-scientific but recovering-from-atomic-war Rann suffers more alien invasions than St. Mary Mead does murders; see, for example, "The Mechanical Masters of Rann" (*Mystery in Space* 65, February 1961).

Fox adapted the Adam Strange comic-book scenario for use in the novel *Warrior of Llarn,* which reads like a continuation of *Planet Stories* by other means. Compare-and-contrast with Henry Kuttner's *The Dark World* (*Startling Stories,* Summer 1946; Ace Books, 1965): "Come to me, man of Earth! I call! I call!" (Fox); "Ganelon! I call you, Ganelon! By the seal in your blood—hear me!" (Kuttner). Alan Morgan, keep-fit offspring of a prosperous Middle West lawyer, duly answers the call—to find himself on the planet Llarn, out near Canopus. Like Kuttner's call-hero, Edward Bond, Morgan gets tangled up in a power struggle beyond his immediate comprehension. But Fox plays several fly variations on the familiar theme.

"Llarn was a world of uncharted deserts where cities of incredible age lay broken and empty, destroyed long ago in the great War . . . before long (Alan Morgan) had met the lovely Tuarra, princess of Kharthol . . . he would fight his way across the entire planet to win her . . . even against the immortal radiation-being which had brought him here for its own unfathomable purpose" (in the words of Donald A. Wollheim, Ace blurbmeister). *Thief of Llarn* appeared two years later. Alan Morgan plays a cross-time chess game to win the ". . . incredible jewel of Zaxeron, held in an impenetrable light shaft guarded by all-destroying fires" (blurb). The two Llarn novels represent Fox's best extended science-fantasy work: Alan Morgan is John Carter of Mars with a three-digit intelligence quotient.

Fox didn't produce an echt sword-and-sorcery novel until the red-dagger year of 1969: *Kothar—Barbarian Swordsman*; *Kothar of the Magic Sword!* (exclamation mark optional); *Kothar and the Demon Queen.* The inaugural volume was actually a collection, containing "The Sword of the Sorcerer," "The Treasure in the Labyrinth" and "The Woman in the Witch-Wood." From the introduction by Donald MacIvers, Ph.D., who might even have been real:

"From out of the deepest, most violent recesses of mankind's dark, collective memory, Kothar the gigantic barbarian strides, the enchanted sword Frostfire glittering in his mighty hand. Lusty, hot-blooded, masterful, unafraid of things real or unreal, Kothar dominates the misty, bloody world created for him, and for us, by the distinguished American writer Gardner F. Fox, and though Kothar's world existed in another age, another dimension, it comes vividly to life."

Reference is also made to the work of Alfred Kremnitz, a German philosopher ("no longer widely read"): "The Industrial Revolution, the Age of Materialism, will almost certainly drive people back to mysticism rather than away from it." Not to worry: Fox is soon off and spinning yarns about the "sellsword" (he had a way with neologisms . . .) Cumberian (. . . most of the time). Over the five-book sprint, Kothar developed into an affable Conan the Humanitarian—but tough with it. And the "tease-body" witch, Red Lori, makes for a fine arch-foeperson: "I shall be with you . . . stirring up trouble where you rest your golden head. You shall pay, barbarian—you shall pay!" (*Kothar—Barbarian Swordsman*).

The late Lin Carter didn't think much of (a) Fox—"indifferent talents and slender skills"; or (b) Kothar—"jolly fun, if a bit routine" (*Imaginary Worlds,* Ballantine, 1973). Point (a) must be taken as opinion, not fact. Point (b) is a palpable hit—but too many heroic fantasies fall down badly in the jolly-fun department.

In 1975, Fox let loose upon the world *Kyrik: Warlock Warrior,* the first of four novels about Kyrik—of the Victories. From the author's Introduction (no Donald MacIvers, Ph.D., this time):

"Kyrik was a king and a barbarian, as well as warlock and warrior . . . much is to be told of Kyrik and his world, of the men he fought and the women he loved, of the mysteries and wonders of the lands where he rode his black stallion, and wielded his sword, Bluefang. You will find mention also of Illis, that lovely demon-goddess whom he loved and worshipped, and who took a very personal interest in his affairs."

Deja vu?—well, not quite. The differences between Kyrik and Kothar loom larger than the obvious similarities. One: the Kyrik novels are better written and thought-out, perhaps enough to have satisfied Lin Carter. Two: the narrative tone lacks the grey humour that leavened Kothar's equally doom-laden shenanigans. "Always his sword swung or darted, and where it touched, blood flowed" (*Kyrik and the Lost Queen*) is no isolated example.

Fox's singleton fantasy, *The Druid Stone* (as by "Simon Majors"), is a jolly-fun novel if ever there was one. Soldier-of-misfortune Brian Creoghan encounters Moira ("her voice danced in his ears") MacArt and her warlock brother, Ugony. Creoghan turns into Kalgorrn of High Mayence, from Dis—where the titular slab

has wafted him. He comes upon Red ("straining him to her flesh") Fann. Enter a "monster out of hell" yclept Sthloo. And there are the wonky dimensio-spheres to worry about . . .

We're on much firmer ground with *Five Weeks in a Balloon* (novelization of the 1962 film inspired by Jules Verne's *voyage extraordinaire*) and *Terror Over London* (which offers an ingenious theory about "the man who might have been Jack the Ripper").

If justice rules the sevagram, Gardner F. Fox will soon get all of the (sadly posthumous) credit he deserves as a reliable fictioneer. Fox's minimalist fantasy-can-be-fun novels show up the dour trilogy merchants who never use one phrase when something can be elongated to five chapters—at least.

—Graham Andrews

FRASER, (Sir Arthur) Ronald

Nationality: British. **Born:** 3 November 1888. **Education:** St. Paul's School, London. **Military Service:** Served in World War I. **Family:** Married Sylvia Blanche Powell in 1915; two sons. **Career:** Civil servant: general secretary during Anglo-American negotiations, 1933; Board of Trade representative to the British Ambassador, Buenos Aires, 1933; commercial minister, British Embassy, Paris, 1944-49; resident government director, Suez Canal company. President, Caledonian Society of France, 1946-53. **Awards:** M.B.E. (Member, Order of the British Empire), 1930; C.M.G. (Companion, Order of St. Michael and St. George), 1934; K.B.E. (Knight Commander, Order of the British Empire), 1949; Companion, Order of Orange (Nassau). **Died:** 12 September 1974.

FANTASY PUBLICATIONS

Novels (series: Venus)

The Flying Draper. London, Unwin, 1924; New York, Smith, 1931; revised edition, London, Cape, 1940.
Landscape with Figures. London, Unwin, 1925; New York, Boni and Liveright, 1926; revised edition, London, Cape, 1952.
Flower Phantoms. London, Cape, 1926; New York, Boni and Liveright, 1927.
Miss Lucifer. London, Cape, 1939.
The Fiery Gate. London, Cape, 1943.
Sun in Scorpio. London, Cape, 1949.
Beetle's Career. London, Cape, 1951.
A Visit from Venus. London, Cape, 1958.
Jupiter in the Chair (Venus). London, Cape, 1958.
Trout's Testament (Venus). London, Cape, 1960.
City of the Sun (Venus). London, Cape, 1961.
A Work of the Imagination: The Pen, the Brush, the Well. Gerrards Cross, Buckinghamshire, Smythe, 1973.

OTHER PUBLICATIONS

Novels

The Vista. London, Cape, 1928.

Rose Anstey. London, Cape, 1930.
Marriage in Heaven. London, Cape, 1932; New York, Scribners, 1933.
Tropical Results. London, Cape, 1933.
The Ninth of July. London, Cape, 1934.
Surprising Results. London, Cape, 1935.
A House in the Park. London, Cape, 1937.
Bird Under Glass. London, Cape, 1938.
Financial Times. London, Cape, 1942.
Circular Tour. London, Cape, 1946.
Maia. London, Cape, 1948.
Glimpses of the Sun. London, Cape, 1952.
Bell From a Distant Temple. London, Cape, 1954.
Flight of Wild Geese. London, Cape, 1955.
Lord of the East. London, Cape, 1956.
The Wine of Illusion. London, Cape, 1957.

Other

Latin America: A Personal Survey. London, Hutchinson, 1953.

Translator, *Her-Bak, Egyptian Initiate* by Isha Schwaller de Lubicz. London, Hodder and Stoughton, 1967.
Translator, *The Mysteries of Chartres Cathedral,* by Louis Charpentier. London, Research into Lost Knowledge Organisation, 1972.

*   *   *

Ronald Fraser was a highly idiosyncratic writer who made use of a variety of fantasy motifs in the course of his long career, but always to the same metaphorical effect—which was to insist that the seeming limitations of mundane existence were to some degree arbitrary, and to hope that some measure of transcendence might be accomplished if only a way could be found. The tacit optimism of this quest was, however, perennially undercut by his assumption that any such way would be open only to the few, permanently beyond the reach of the many amongst whom the few must nevertheless dwell.

Fraser's first novel, *The Flying Draper,* was called "Wellsian" by many reviewers, as much because of the career of its central character (who has risen from humble origins to become a professor of biology and unorthodox social philosopher) as its imaginative quality; it is, however, much more ethereal in tone and much vaguer in implication than H. G. Wells's fantasies. Albert Codling is a superman with a perfect memory and the ability to fly, but he has achieved this state by spiritual means, according to his own original theories of human nature—which are, of course, mystical and heretical in nature. He is initially pained by the adverse reaction of his fellow men to his triumphs, but comes to realize in the end that his destiny lies outside the scope of ordinary human affairs. Codling's effect on the relationship between Sir Philip Wokingham and his wife-to-be is stressful; this was the first in a long series of relationships strained almost to breaking point by spiritual differences, which became the principal thread of continuity connecting all of Fraser's fantasies and his many novels devoid of supernatural content.

Landscape with Figures is a rather effete Oriental fantasy which seeks "to reproduce, in words, experiences that have come in contemplating the landscapes, flowers and figures in Chinese pictures". Like many of Fraser's novels it juxtaposes an aging aristocrat whose

quest for wisdom is already coloured by defeatism, Lord Sombrewater, with a romantically-inclined young man who retains more hope despite having fewer intellectual resources, Ambrose Herbert. Fraser was to dabble in Eastern mysticism again, most notably in *The Wine of Illusion,* but he was never totally comfortable with any borrowed philosophy and was capable of much greater intensity when developing metaphorical and metaphysical systems of his own. His first *tour de force* of this kind was *Flower Phantoms,* a uniquely bizarre and brilliant work in which the progress to maturity of a young woman requires the supernatural intervention of the plants at Kew Gardens. She is contentedly engaged to be married but is unexcited by her fiancée and is decidedly at odds with the materialistic values of modern society, which are all-too-solidly incarnate in her brother Hubert. She is more "in tune" with the imagined spirits of the hothouse flowers with which she works, and she develops an empathy that eventually allows her to spend a night of awesome passion with a giant orchid: an experience whose stored-up bounty serves to reconcile her—to the limited extent that she can ever be reconciled—to the sadly mundane future which awaits her.

Fraser seemed reconciled to more mundane materials himself for some years after publishing *Flower Phantoms,* but eventually produced a similarly ambitious account of a young woman's spiritual career in *Miss Lucifer,* whose heroine is able to perceive a much greater and finer reality than those around her. Her dreams and occasional waking visions inform her as to the former incarnations of her soul and the metaphysical context in which such reincarnations occur, one of whose consequences is a moral consciousness significantly at odds with that possessed by other people, including the man she consents to marry. This is the most earnest of all of Fraser's fantasies, and might be reckoned the best by those who can take their philosophical pretensions seriously, although sceptics have every reason to prefer the marvellous exoticism of *Flower Phantoms. The Fiery Gate* is a more muted marginal fantasy of superhumanity with a male protagonist.

Beetle's Career comes close to science fiction in its account of the eponymous scientist's experiments in nuclear physics, which lead to the development of an ultimate weapon whose happier spin-off devices include new medical treatments and a device for photographing the soul. Fraser went on to deploy more science-fictional devices in the four-book series begun with *A Visit from Venus.* Here the conflict between the mystical world-view favoured by Fraser and the positivism of science is developed as a dialogue between General Sir Brian Hungerford and Sir James Outright, assisted by the newspaper magnate Lord Undertone and various others—notably the writer Septimus Shandy. Their discussions, provoked by discoveries made with the aid of a far-seeing mechanical Eye which exploits the mysteries of "hyperphysical light," are carefully observed by the butler Troutbeck (Trout for short). The benevolent and superior "planetary spirits"—more akin to the Classical deities than science-fictional aliens—are content simply to make their voice heard in the first volume, but *Jupiter in the Chair* transplants the ongoing discussion to the stage of an interplanetary conference. The researches of the characters continue in the Eastern kingdom of Jellabad in *Trout's Testament,* and are further extended in *The City of the Sun* in a strange odyssey in the Bolivian rain forest, which eventually brings Undertone and Shandy to a curious final enlightenment. The essential lesson to be learned is little different from that contained in *Miss Lucifer,* and hardly less bitter in its judgment of the limited resources of everyday life and conventional human relationships, but these late works take care to wrap their message in several layers of humorous and whimsical sugar-coating. Given that Fraser was in his 70s when he wrote them it is not surprising that they embody a tolerant complacency which his younger self would have found hard to accommodate.

—Brian Stableford

FRAYN, Michael

Nationality: British. **Born:** London, 8 September 1933. **Education:** Kingston Grammar School, Surrey; Emmanuel College, Cambridge, B.A. 1957. **Military Service:** Royal Artillery and Intelligence Corps, 1952-54. **Family:** Married Gillian Palmer in 1960; three daughters. **Career:** Reporter, 1957-59, and columnist, 1959-62, *The Guardian,* Manchester and London; columnist, *The Observer,* London, 1962-68. **Awards:** Maugham award, 1966; Hawthornden prize, 1967; National Press award, 1970; *Standard* award for play, 1976, 1981, 1983, 1985; Society of West End Theatre award, 1977, 1982; British Theatre Association award, 1981, 1983; Olivier award, 1985. **Agent:** Elaine Greene Ltd., 31 Newington Green, London N16 9PU, England.

FANTASY PUBLICATIONS

Novel

Sweet Dreams. London, Collins, 1973; New York, Viking Press, 1974.

OTHER PUBLICATIONS

Novels

The Tin Men. London, Collins, 1965; Boston, Little Brown, 1966.
The Russian Interpreter. London, Collins, and New York, Viking Press, 1966.
Towards the End of the Morning. London, Collins, 1967; as *Against Entropy,* New York, Viking Press, 1967.
A Very Private Life. London, Collins, and New York, Viking Press, 1968.
The Trick of It. London and New York, Viking Press, 1990.
A Landing on the Sun. London, Viking, 1991; New York, Viking Press, 1992.
Now You Know. London, Viking, 1992; New York, Viking Press, 1993.

Plays

Zounds!, with John Edwards, music by Keith Statham (produced Cambridge, 1957).
The Two of Us (includes *Black and Silver, The New Quixote, Mr. Foot, Chinamen*) (produced London, 1970; Ogunquit, Maine, 1975; *Chinamen* produced New York, 1979). London, Fontana, 1970; *Chinamen* published in *The Best Short Plays 1973,* edited by Stanley Richards, Radnor, Pennsylvania, Chilton, 1973; revised version of *The New Quixote* (produced Chichester and London, 1980).

The Sandboy (produced London, 1971).
Alphabetical Order (produced London, 1975; New Haven, Connecticut, 1976). Included in *Alphabetical Order and Donkeys' Years,* 1977.
Donkeys' Years (produced London, 1976). Included in *Alphabetical Order and Donkeys' Years,* 1977.
Clouds (produced London, 1976). London, Eyre Methuen, 1977.
Alphabetical Order and Donkeys' Years. London, Eyre Methuen, 1977.
The Cherry Orchard, adaptation of a play by Chekhov (produced London, 1978). London, Eyre Methuen, 1978.
Balmoral (produced Guildford, Surrey, 1978; revised version, as *Liberty Hall,* produced London, 1980). London, Methuen, 1987.
The Fruits of Enlightenment, adaptation of a play by Tolstoy (produced London, 1979). London, Eyre Methuen, 1979.
Make and Break (produced London, 1980; Washington, D.C., 1983). London, Eyre Methuen, 1980.
Noises Off (produced London, 1981; New York, 1983). London, Methuen, 1982; New York, French, 1985.
Three Sisters, adaptation of a play by Chekhov (produced Manchester, 1985; London, 1987). London, Methuen, 1983.
Benefactors (produced London, 1984). London, Methuen, 1984.
  Wild Honey, adaptation of a play by Chekhov (produced London, 1984; New York, 1986-87). London, Methuen, 1984.
Number One, adaptation of a play by Jean Anouilh (produced London, 1984).
Plays 1 (includes *Alphabetical Order, Donkey's Years, Clouds, Make and Break, Noises Off*). London and New York, Methuen, 1985.
Clockwise (screenplay). London, Methuen, 1986.
The Seagull, adaptation of a play by Chekhov (produced Watford, Hertfordshire, 1986). London, Methuen, 1986.
Uncle Vanya, adaptation of a play by Chekhov. London, Methuen, 1987.
Look, Look. London, Methuen, 1990.
Audience: A Play in One Act. New York, French, 1991.
Plays: Two (includes *Benefactors, Balmoral, Wild Honey*). London, Methuen, 1992.
Here. London, Methuen, 1993.

Television Plays and Documentaries: *Second City Reports,* with John Bird, 1964; *Jamie, On a Flying Visit,* 1968; *One Pair of Eyes,* 1968; *Birthday,* 1969; *Beyond a Joke* series, with John Bird and Eleanor Bron, 1972; *Laurence Sterne Lived Here* (*Writers' Houses* series), 1973; *Imagine a City Called Berlin,* 1975; *Making Faces,* 1975; *Vienna: The Mask of Gold,* 1977; *Three Streets in the Country,* 1979; *The Long Straight* (*Great Railway Journeys of the World* series), 1980; *Jerusalem,* 1984; *First and Last,* 1989; *Heaven* (*Listen to This* series), 1990; *Magic Lantern: Prague,* 1993.

Other

The Day of the Dog (*Guardian* columns). London, Collins, 1962; New York, Doubleday, 1963.
The Book of Fub (*Guardian* columns). London, Collins, 1963; as *Never Put Off to Gomorrah,* New York, Pantheon, 1964.
On the Outskirts (*Observer* columns). London, Collins, 1964.
At Bay in Gear Street (*Observer* columns). London, Fontana, 1967.
Constructions (philosophy). London, Wildwood House, 1974.
Great Railway Journeys of the World, with others. London, BBC Publications, 1981.

*The Original Michael Frayn: Columns from the Guardian and The
Observer.* Edinburgh, Salamander Press, 1983.
Listen to This: Sketches and Monologues. London, Methuen, and
New York, French, 1990.

Editor, *The Best of Beachcomber,* by J. B. Morton. London,
Heinemann, 1963.

Translator, *Plays,* by Anton Chekhov. London, Methuen, 1988.
Translator, *The Sneeze: Plays and Stories by Anton Chekhov.* Lon-
don, Methuen, and New York, French, 1989.
Translator, *Exchange,* by Yuri Trifonov. London, Methuen, 1990.

*   *   *

Michael Frayn is that rare phenomenon, an "outsider" from the
"mainstream" (to use the agoraphobic language of genre) who
moves in science fiction and fantasy without embarrassment—his
or ours. This is achieved through precise, witty writing, honed by
years as a humorous/satirical newspaper columnist and, later, a playwright.

Two of his novels are science fiction. *The Tin Men* is a hilarious
romp about a shambolic artificial-intelligence project whose efforts
cast wicked reflections on the supposed human intelligence that's
being simulated. For example, the presentation of a mechanical (not
even electronic) text generator which composes flawlessly pompous newspaper editorials has a certain moral for writers—and readers. *A Very Private Life* offers an ambiguous utopia or dystopia of
crowded, sanitary solitude, somewhere between Forster's *The Machine
Stops* and a virtual-reality scenario. The light narration, distanced by
present and future tenses ("Once upon a time there will be a little girl
called Uncumber"), has a deceptively gentle satirical edge.

Frayn's true fantasy novel is *Sweet Dreams,* a clever contribution to the "afterlife" sub-genre, which shows Heaven as offering
all you most want. For the young architect Howard Baker—who
in a tasteful discontinuity drives straight through a red light in London on to the ten-lane expressway entering Heaven City—eternal
bliss naturally entails cosy suburban life with all his friends and a
constant round of dinner parties whose menu is always taramasalata,
gigot aux haricots and apple crumble. One can fly and do miracles
too, but that's rather gauche.

Although there are apparent humiliations in Heaven, they are
marvellously funny ones ideal for recounting to laughing companions. There is marriage and (because this is Heaven) a pleasantly
enigmatic mistress on the side. Even work continues: Baker can
show his architectural mettle when, joining the design team doing
the specifications for the Alps, he lands the plum job of creating
the trademark image for the whole project: "In just six and a half
hours he has produced the Matterhorn."

Slyly concealed here is a gesture (perhaps two-fingered) to that
view of God as seeing all secular time simultaneously yet being
eternally surprised by the vagaries of free will. While flattered to
be used as the original model for several important facial tics in
another new heavenly project called "Man," Baker is horrified when
he finds that this life business will entail death and that indeed many
people will die on his own beloved Matterhorn . . . until at last his
memory of actual mortal life is jogged. But ahead lies the prospect
of going into partnership with God and reforming everything with
the *right people* (taramasalata, *gigots aux haricots,* apple crumble)
in charge; though somehow things, including death, stay just the
same.

Finally, having like James Branch Cabell's Jurgen achieved absolutely everything possible to a rising executive in the hierarchy
of Heaven, he drives through another red light and. . . . *Sweet
Dreams* is a highly amusing parable of human desires and limitations: short, astringent and producing many an embarrassed smile
of self-recognition.

Theology, that ancient sub-genre of fantasy, is occasionally
touched on in Frayn's essays and sketches. Two examples: "The
Monolithic View of Mirrors" (*At Bay in Gear Street,* 1967), sym-
pathizes with the "Carthaginian Monolithic" believers who are painfully tempted to avoid accidents through use of the car rear-view
mirrors prohibited by their clergy—who do not themselves drive.
And the TV sketch "Heaven" (*Listen to This,* 1990) returns to *Sweet
Dreams* territory as a divine executive charged with arranging a
death objects not to the killing but to the difficulty of having the
chap hit, as aesthetically decreed, by an avalanche in Norfolk.

Michael Frayn continues to write distinguished novels and may
yet turn to fantasy again.

—David Langford

FRIESNER(-STUTZMAN), Esther M(ona)

Nationality: American. **Born:** 16 July 1951. **Education:** Vassar
College, B.A. in Spanish and Drama, 1972; Yale University, M.A.
in Spanish, 1975, Ph.D. in Spanish, 1977. **Family:** Married Walter
Stutzman in 1974; one son, one daughter. **Awards:** *Romantic Times*
Outstanding New Fantasy Writer, 1986; Voice of Youth Advocates
Best Science Fiction/Fantasy citation, 1988; Skylark Award, 1994.
Agent: Richard Curtis Associates, 171 East 74th Street, New York,
NY 10021, USA. **Address:** 53 Mendingwall Circle, Madison, CT
06443, USA.

FANTASY PUBLICATIONS

Novels (series: Chronicles of the Twelve Kingdoms; Demons; Tim
Desmond; Majyk)

Mustapha and His Wise Dog (Twelve Kingdoms). New York,
Avon, 1985.
Spells of Mortal Weaving (Twelve Kingdoms). New York, Avon,
1986.
Harlot's Ruse. New York, Warner, 1986.
New York by Knight. New York, Signet, 1986; London, Headline,
1987.
The Silver Mountain. New York, Warner, 1986.
The Witchwood Cradle (Twelve Kingdoms). New York, Avon,
1987.
Elf Defense. New York, Signet, 1988; London, Headline, 1989.
Druid's Blood. New York, Signet, 1988; London, Headline, 1989.
Here Be Demons. New York, Ace, 1988; London, Orbit, 1990.
The Water King's Laughter (Twelve Kingdoms). New York, Avon,
1989.
Demon Blues (Demons). New York, Ace, 1989; London, Orbit, 1991.
Sphynxes Wild. New York, Signet, 1989.

Hooray for Hellywood (Demons). New York, Ace, 1990; London, Orbit, 1992.
Gnome Man's Land (Tim Desmond). New York, Ace, 1991.
Harpy High (Tim Desmond). New York, Ace, 1991.
Unicorn U (Tim Desmond). New York, Ace, 1992.
Yesterday We Saw Mermaids. New York, Tor, 1992.
Split Heirs, with Lawrence Watt-Evans. New York, Tor, 1993.
Wishing Season (for children). New York, Macmillan, 1993.
Majyk by Accident. New York, Ace, 1993.
Majyk by Hook or Crook. New York, Ace, 1994.
The Sherwood Game. New York, Baen, 1995.

Short Stories

Ecce Hominid. Eugene, Oregon, Pulphouse, 1991.
It's Been Fun. Eugene, Oregon, Pulphouse, 1991.

Other

Editor, with Martin H. Greenberg, *Alien Pregnant by Elvis and Other Tabloid Tales.* New York, DAW, 1994.
Editor, with Martin H. Greenberg, *Chicks in Chainmail.* New York, Baen, 1995.

*   *   *

Esther M. Friesner brings to her writing an impressive knowledge of fantasy lore, a wild imagination, and a lively sense of humour. However, she is not always successful in sustaining her inventive premises—creating problems most notable in her multivolume works—and her recent works unfortunately emphasize humour of the most adolescent kind.

Friesner's career began auspiciously with *Mustapha and His Wise Dog,* a charming, though insubstantial, story, told to children at an Arabian bazaar, about a likable young man and his dog, who can both speak and change into human form. In the second Chronicles of the Twelve Kingdoms novel, *Spells of Mortal Weaving,* however, the special voice of the storyteller is gone, replaced by flat prose; Mustapha is reduced to cameo appearances as Friesner features other, less interesting characters—a young prince seeking to claim his throne and his friends; and the story is a classic example of the Idiot Plot, as intelligent characters make senseless decisions and people with awesome magical powers are suddenly rendered helpless—all to keep the plot in motion. Somewhat better is the third book, *The Witchwood Cradle,* about a wizard's magical sister and her efforts to protect her nephew, though the novel ends strangely with the heroine's inexplicable decision to marry the archvillain Morgeld. Having discovered that she could be funny, Friesner added one more book to the series, *The Water King's Laughter,* in her new style, introducing the first of her inept adolescent heroes—a tone-deaf would-be minstrel who is really the lost king of the Waterfolk—and training the denizens of the Twelve Kingdoms to speak in fluent wisecrack. On this incongruous note, the projected 12-volume series apparently came to a premature end.

Here Be Demons, the first book in the Demons trilogy, begins well with ancient demons in the North African desert who face the intriguing challenge of tempting some modern mortals to surrender their souls. However, after taking some potshots at American academics and reporters, Friesner finds the premise is not going anywhere, so she whisks her characters off on a dull underworld journey. The second and best Demons book, *Demon Blues,* features

Noel Cardiff, the son of a now-reformed demon and a television commentator, who learns of his true nature while attending Yale University—where a magically preserved Richard the Lion-Hearted later engages in a memorable battle supported by members of the Society for Creative Anachronism. However, the final book, *Hooray for Hellywood,* is a mess, as Friesner quickly abandons her story of a demon disguised as a television evangelist who goes to Hollywood to make a movie and instead plunges into another redundant underworld travelogue.

Although her Tim Desmond trilogy offered a promising scenario—a hole in the Leeside lets minor household sprites, then major gods and heroes, come to modern New York to complicate the life of hapless young student Tim Desmond, implausibly chosen as their champion—the entire series becomes more irritating than amusing, as Friesner seems determined to put a joke on every page, no matter what the cost to the credibility or atmosphere of her narrative. Particularly dire is the third book, *Unicorn U,* which fails to provide the story implied by the title—the humorous adventures of magical and folkloric creatures at a modern college—but rather sends its characters on a pointless, one-liner-laden tour of various mythical underworlds.

Based on its first volume, her new Majyk series seems doomed to the same terminal silliness, as Tim Desmond is renamed Kendar Gangle and cast as an incompetent apprentice wizard accidentally given vast magical powers that he can barely control. To exemplify its level of humour, Friesner presents a village named Cheeseburgh—so its residents can be called Cheeseburghers—and a publishing company favoured by the king is named Full Court Press.

Friesner's singletons are generally more rewarding, although some suffer from problems seen in her series: *Elf Defense,* for example, has a wonderful comic idea—an elf king who wishes to reclaim his mortal bride, hiding in Connecticut, is confronted by a determined divorce lawyer—but Friesner cannot develop the concept, so her characters abruptly journey to the elf's magical kingdom, giving her story a jarring and unpleasant conclusion; and *Split Heirs,* written with Lawrence Watt-Evans, is best described as an extended homage to Abbott and Costello, filled with tiresome banter interrupting a contrived plot about royal triplets separated at birth. However, among her earlier novels, *New York by Knight* stands out as an evocative and well-structured story about St. George and the dragon appearing in New York to prepare for their final battle while recruiting unlikely allies from the citizenry; the conclusion, though, lacks the power that the novel deserves.

Druid's Blood, perhaps the strangest Sherlock Holmes pastiche of them all, features Holmes and Watson clones in a 19th-century England ruled by ancient Druid magic, where spells protect the nation's shores, and where Queen Victoria annually and publicly engages in a pagan mating ritual. Instead of exploiting this scenario for cheap jokes, Friesner develops her premise seriously and carefully, and makes her novel a shrewd commentary on the Holmes canon by making the Watson figure the true hero of the story, a man of suppressed magical talents inappropriately inclined to rely on others' help when he should take matters into his own hands. Even more impressive is *Yesterday We Saw Mermaids,* the atmospheric first-person narrative of another sea voyage in 1492 that takes an odd assortment of characters to a land of endangered mythical creatures governed by Prester John (here described as one of the Wise Men who was too proud to accept the humbly born Jesus as the true Messiah); the possible birth of a second Saviour is thwarted by a villainous priest. Like David Lindsay's *A Voyage to*

Arcturus, Yesterday We Saw Mermaids takes the form of allegory without conveying a clear single meaning in its story; it is a book that rewards rereading, and one that might someday generate long critical analyses.

Measured by raw talent alone, Friesner must be counted as a major figure in contemporary fantasy, though she now seems to be wasting her skills on raucous humour. If we are lucky, she will continue to pause between comedy routines to produce more memorable works like *Druid's Blood* and *Yesterday We Saw Mermaids*.

—Gary Westfahl

FRITH, Nigel (Andrew Silver)

Nationality: British. **Born:** Kettering, Northamptonshire, 30 November 1941. **Education:** Windsor School, Hamm, Germany, 1953-59; St. Catherine's College, Oxford University, 1960-63, B.A., and 1969-72, M.Litt. **Career:** Directed street theatre company, Stratford, England, 1964; actor, Ravinia Festival, Chicago, 1964; resident tutor, Harlech College, Wales, 1965-68; part-time lecturer, Oxford Polytechnic, 1971-78; tutor, Centre for Medieval and Renaissance Studies, Oxford, from 1979. **Agent:** Carolyn Whitaker, London Independent Books, 1A Montagu Mews North, London W1H 1AJ, England.

FANTASY PUBLICATIONS

Novels

The Legend of Krishna. London, Sheldon Press, 1975; New York, Schocken, 1976; as *Krishna,* London, Unwin, 1985.
The Spear of Mistletoe: An Epic. London, Routledge and Kegan Paul, 1977; as *Asgard,* London, Unwin, 1982.
Jormundgand. London, Unwin, 1986.
Dragon. London, Unwin Hyman, 1987.
Olympiad. London, Unwin Hyman, 1988.
Snow. London, Breese Books, 1993.

OTHER PUBLICATIONS

Plays

Commedia (performed Oxford, 1987).
Magic (performed Oxford, 1989).
Hesod (performed Oxford, 1994).

Poetry

The Lover's Annual. London, Phoenix House, 1965.

*

Nigel Frith comments:

I believe that artistic forms are never outmoded. My first published book, *The Lover's Annual,* was written in the troubadour tradition of love poetry. My next, *Krishna,* was structured on the

Homeric epic model, and my third, *Asgard,* was in full Homeric style as well as form. Three other epics followed: *Jormundgand, Dragon,* and *Olympiad.* In 1987 I used not just the literary form but the old acting style and set-design for my *commedia dell'arte* comedy, *Commedia.* I then used the poetic form of historical tragedy for my next directed-and-designed production, *Magic.* On a trip to Japan in 1992 and subsequently I studied Noh play techniques, and directed my own Noh play, *Hesod,* in private performance in 1994. I believe that in the 21st century art will be the dominant concern of life. All my work is aimed towards founding a style rich and powerful enough to support this. It will come from the merging of the old and the new, and the Eastern and Western traditions.

*   *   *

Nigel Frith specializes in epic tales of myth and legend, and his first five novels fit into that mould, relying on extant tales for much of their content. The sixth, *Snow,* is different in that it draws on his own experiences in Oxford academic circles for its background (he is a university tutor).

The earliest of the books, *The Legend of Krishna,* uses a segment of Hindu mythology as its basis. Krishna was the superhero of his day, being capable of great feats of strength and endurance. He appears as a blue-skinned cowherd in the region of Braj. He is seen by his fellows as an idler and a prankster but he is adored by the women, Radha in particular. During the story Krishna battles against demons and tyrants, and visits the gods in their palaces. He also goes through a period of rebirth and self-discovery. The book ignores totally Krishna's later life (or incarnation) as friend and advisor to Ajuna, as set out in the *Bhagavad Gita.*

The Spear of Mistletoe, later retitled *Asgard,* retells the story of Balder, the Norse god of light. This is an extremely well-known story, telling of how, when it is prophesied that Balder will die, all things are asked to take an oath that they will never harm him. Only the mistletoe is not asked, and Loki, the devious god of fire, uses this against him. In this there is a parallel with *Krishna,* where the hero's main antagonist is the jealous fire god Agni who, like Loki, works for Krishna's downfall. In *Asgard,* Frith does not stick strictly to the traditional tale but manipulates his characters to provide a plot that is more coherent that the original. This is also the case in his next novel, *Jormundgand.* Again taken from Norse mythology, this chronicles the adventures of the field-god Frey and his attempts to win and woo the ice-maiden Hron. Hron actually seems to be a fictional invention of Frith, as most sources give Gerd as Frey's passion, and although some of the wooing is recognizable, there are significant differences, as if Frith is beginning to feel the constraints of the format he has chosen.

Dragon is drawn from Chinese myth. When the Weaver-girl elopes with the Cowherd, her father, the Jade Emperor and chief of the Chinese pantheon, persuades the Celestial Dragon to go to Earth in search of them. This is despite the Dragon's warning that, because of his nature, chaos will inevitably result. Intertwined is the story of the feckless poet, Nai, and his wooing of the sleeve-dancer Xiang. To complicate matters, the philosophers Confucius and Lao zi, now gods in their own right, have taken an interest in the poet. This secondary story is again an invention of Frith's.

The final volume, *Olympiad,* was published in the year of the Seoul olympics. Tired of the bloodshed between warring factions in classical Greece—each vying for the favours and assistance of immortals, the gods plan the Games as a method of deciding who is best without unnecessary killing. Organized by the hero Heracles, these Games become a focus for the retelling of several Greek myths, including that of Atalanta and the golden apples.

Frith himself describes these novels as a Pangaia, calling *Krishna, Asgard* and *Olympiad* the Pangaia series, but *Jormundgand* and *Dragon* the Pangaia sequence. In all of these books he has attempted to adopt an epic style of storytelling similar to that of his original source material. The biggest problem with this is that it leads to a stilted and ungainly style which allows no room for character development. This is partly because the original epics, whatever their source, would have been created as bardic stories. Spoken, the continual thrust of the action would have entertained the audience, but the written word requires a different approach to keep the interest of the reader. Frith's most recent novel, *Snow,* could at first glance be dismissed as a ghost story since it revolves around strange happenings connected to the house of a long-dead professor and the encounters that O'Ryan, an undergraduate at his college, has there. In fact it has a mythological theme, with the Muses as the cause of the mysterious visions. O'Ryan is somewhat old-fashioned in outlook and writes lyric love poetry, and at one point is equated to Arion the bard, who was thrown overboard from the ship he was travelling in and was rescued by dolphins. In the hands of another this might have been a vivid story; however, the style here is dry and the characterization almost nonexistent but without the excuse the earlier books have. The dons tend to lecture each other about English literature, which slows up the story considerably. The book also contains black-and-white illustrations executed by Frith himself.

—Pauline Morgan

FUREY, Maggie

Nationality: British. **Address:** c/o Legend Books, Random House, 20 Vauxhall Bridge Road, London SW1V 2SA.

FANTASY PUBLICATIONS

Novels (series: Artefacts of Power in all books)

Aurian. London, Legend, and New York, Bantam, 1994.
Harp of Winds. London, Legend, 1994; New York, Bantam, 1995.
The Sword of Flame. London, Legend, 1995.

*   *   *

Maggie Furey's debut novel *Aurian: Book One of the Artefacts of Power* is written largely but not exclusively from the viewpoint of her eponymous heroine. Aurian's world is a standard sword-and-sorcery environment, and Aurian's principal distinction among female protagonists is that she is a "mage"—potentially immortal and with what used to be called psi talents. Here magic is contingent on the cultivation and discipline of immanent powers rather than ritual, powerful artefacts or control of spirits, though all of these come into play as the book develops.

As it opens she is approaching adolescence and showing signs of major potential; but even more importantly, she will in due course

become fertile and has not yet been spoken for, which gives her rarity value above and beyond her magical and personal attributes. Mages can breed with mortals, and breed true as often as not, so there ought to be plenty of them, but no; female mages lose their powers during pregnancy, which deters them from breeding. How about the males, then? They have normal appetites, and their powers give them plenty of clout, but they have prejudices against that sort of thing; consequently, by the time the book opens their total number is into single figures. Where did all the immortals go? *Taedium vitae* (plus the odd misfortune) seems to have done for the lot.

The extreme contrivance of this situation begins immediately to detract from the story, which is a pity because the fantasy *bildungsroman* is rather well done. Aurian is taken to the mages' academy, there to develop her powers, grow to womanhood and in her spare time become formidable with her sword. Predictably enough she also arouses the sexual interest of most of the men she meets, especially Forral, the great swordsman who trains her, and Miathan, the Archmage and villain of the piece.

Here we have more evidence of structural weakness. Miathan is represented as a cold-blooded, highly manipulative individual of great experience and cunning, accustomed to planning over decades; yet he not only allows the vision of eventually seducing and siring a son on Aurian to distort every aspect of his political judgement, but shows a complete lack of psychological insight in all his dealings with her. He has also secretly fathered a bastard on a mortal woman, which suggests that he might be prepared to restore the mages' numbers by some applied eugenics, but this idea never occurs to him, even to be rejected. The impression given is that Furey is lying about her own creation, and her writing becomes uneasy in consequence. She attempts to remedy matters with preachy little asides to the reader, but they only draw attention to the fundamental inconsistencies:

> Miathan wrestled with the possibilities, falling into the classic trap of those who spend their lives plotting and scheming against others. He was convinced that the others, in their turn, were plotting to overthrow him.

Aurian never even considers Miathan as a possible suitor, and falls into Forral's arms, for all that he's old enough to be her father, drinking heavily, and enough over the hill to lose to her in a set-piece duel.

And so the book lurches along, through individual scenes that generally work well enough. Furey's eye for detail, especially faces and postures, is good, and her ear for the language lets her down only when she ventures out of her depth: when (as often happens) people start cursing and swearing we're told it turns the air blue, but the only examples are the likes of "Great Gods!" and "Damn!" She makes good use of alternating viewpoints, maintains a cracking pace and even finds room for some broad but effective humour—which fails to compensate for crudely ineffective plot mechanisms. Forral, allegedly the best swordsman in the world, exercises against the 14-year-old Aurian with fully honed weapons and nearly kills her—to buy a pair of blunted swords would be too much trouble. Miathan, wishing to bring in an unpopular measure, knows perfectly well that his two fellow councillors disapprove, but is still shocked when they vote him down. One wonders how such a political imbecile came to hold his position.

The fundamental defect would seem to be that during composition the story evolved away from the writer's initial concept, something for which she was not prepared and which she handled badly.

She started with a fairly detailed outline of her story; having created her characters, she was able to bring them to life, as many aspiring writers fail to do; their interaction might well have made a very good book, but because it wasn't the book she originally intended she felt it necessary to drag them back into line, to the detriment of the credibility, and thus the interest, of the whole.

It's fair to say that as the novel progresses and becomes more episodic the structural weaknesses tend to recede; the alternating viewpoints diverge into subplots but the unity is strong enough to take the strain. But as the faults are most prominent near the beginning and it's over 600 pages long, one suspects that many readers will give up before reaching the best parts, let alone venturing upon the sequel, *Harp of Winds.*

That book stands to *Aurian* much as Tolkien's *The Two Towers* stands to *The Fellowship of the Ring,* being told in parallel from a number of different viewpoints, including those of Aurian, her scattered companions, her mother, her enemies, and other, newly introduced characters, all contending on the physical and magical planes in varying degrees of confusion as to what is going on. It has the earlier book's virtues of colour, action, and suspense, with plenty of changes of locale, and a sense that all the disparate elements will come together in due course is never absent; but although Furey keeps a lot of balls in the air without losing track, there are rather too many of them, too close together, and at the same time too ignorant of each other, to avoid a cluttered effect. The forthcoming third volume may well produce an effective climax, but will need to clear a lot of air first.

—Chris Gilmore

G

GALLICO, Paul (William)

Nationality: American. **Born:** New York City, 26 July 1897. **Education:** De Witt Clinton High School, and Columbia University, New York, B.S. 1921. **Military Service:** U.S. Navy, 1918. **Family:** Married 1) Alva Thoits Taylor in 1921 (divorced); 2) Elaine St. John in 1935 (divorced 1936); 3) Pauline Gariboldi in 1939 (divorced 1954); 4) Baroness Virginia von Falz-Fein in 1963; two children by first marriage. **Career:** Review secretary, National Board of Motion Picture Review, New York, 1921; assistant managing editor and columnist, New York *Daily News*, 1922-1936; instructor in short-story writing, Columbia University, 1939, 1944. Lived mainly in Europe after 1936. War correspondent, *Cosmopolitan*, 1944-45. **Died:** July 1976.

FANTASY PUBLICATIONS

Novels

The Abandoned. New York, Knopf, 1950; as *Jennie,* London, Joseph, 1950.
Thomasina: The Cat Who Thought She Was God. New York, Doubleday, 1957; as *Thomasina,* London, Joseph, 1957.
Too Many Ghosts. New York, Doubleday, 1959; London, Joseph, 1961.
The Hand of Mary Constable. New York, Doubleday, and London, Heinemann, 1964.
The Man Who Was Magic: A Fable of Innocence. New York, Doubleday, and London, Heinemann, 1966.
Manxmouse (for children). New York, Coward McCann, and London, Heinemann, 1968.
The House That Wouldn't Go Away. London, Heinemann, 1979.

Short Stories

The Small Miracle. London, Joseph, 1951; New York, Doubleday, 1952.
The Best of Paul Gallico. London, Joseph, 1988.

OTHER PUBLICATIONS

Novels

Trial by Terror. New York, Knopf, and London, Joseph, 1952.
The Foolish Immortals. New York, Doubleday, and London, Joseph, 1953.
The Love of Seven Dolls. New York, Doubleday, and London, Joseph, 1954.
Mrs. 'Arris Goes to Paris. New York, Doubleday, 1958; as *Flowers for Mrs. Harris,* London, Joseph, 1958.
Mrs. 'Arris Goes to New York. New York, Doubleday, 1960; as *Mrs. Harris Goes to New York,* London, Joseph, 1960.
Scruffy: A Diversion. New York, Doubleday, and London, Joseph, 1962.

Coronation. New York, Doubleday, and London, Heinemann, 1962.
The Day the Guinea Pig Talked (for children). London, Heinemann, 1963; New York, Doubleday, 1964.
Love, Let Me Not Hunger. New York, Doubleday, and London, Heinemann, 1963.
The Day Jean-Pierre Was Pignapped (for children). London, Heinemann, 1964; New York, Doubleday, 1965.
The Day Jean-Pierre Went Round the World (for children). London, Heinemann, 1965; New York, Doubleday, 1966.
Mrs. 'Arris Goes to Parliament. New York, Doubleday, 1965; as *Mrs. Harris, M.P.,* London, Heinemann, 1965.
The Day Jean-Pierre Joined the Circus (for children). London, Heinemann, 1969; New York, Doubleday, 1970.
The Poseidon Adventure. New York, Coward McCann, and London, Heinemann, 1969.
The Matilda. New York, Coward McCann, and London, Heinemann, 1970.
The Zoo Gang. New York, Coward McCann, and London, Heinemann, 1971.
The Boy Who Invented the Bubble Gun: An Odyssey of Innocence. New York, Delacorte Press, and London, Heinemann, 1974.
Mrs. Harris Goes to Moscow. London, Heinemann, 1974; as *Mrs. 'Arris Goes to Moscow,* New York, Delacorte Press, 1975.
Beyond the Poseidon Adventure. New York and London, ?, 1978.

Short Stories

The Adventures of Hiram Holliday. New York, Knopf, and London, Joseph, 1939.
The Secret Front. New York, Knopf, 1940.
The Snow Goose. New York, Knopf, and London, Joseph, 1941.
Confessions of a Story Writer. New York, Knopf, 1946; as *Confessions of a Story-Teller,* London, Joseph, 1961.
The Lonely. London, Joseph, 1947; New York, Knopf, 1949.
Snowflake. London, Joseph, 1952; New York, Doubleday, 1953.
Ludmila: A Story of Liechtenstein. London, Joseph, 1955; as *Ludmila,* New York, Doubleday, 1959.
Further Confessions of a Story Writer: Stories Old and New. New York, Doubleday, 1961.
The Snow Goose, and The Small Miracle. London, Penguin, 196?.
Ludmila, and The Lonely. London, Penguin, 1967.
Miracle in the Wilderness: A Christmas Story of Colonial America. New York, Delacorte Press, 1975.

Plays

Screenplays: *No Time to Marry,* 1937; *Joe Smith, American,* 1942; *The Pride of the Yankees,* 1942; *The Clock,* 1945; *Never Take No for an Answer,* 1951; *Lili,* 1953 (from his own story *Love of Seven Dolls*); *Merry Andrew,* 1957; *Big Operator,* 1959; *The Three Lives of Thomasina,* 1964.

Other

Farewell to Sport. New York, Knopf, 1938.
Golf is a Friendly Game. New York, Knopf, 1942.
Lou Gehrig: Pride of the Yankees. New York, Grosset, 1942.

The Steadfast Man: A Biography of St. Patrick. New York, Doubleday, and London, Joseph, 1958.

The Hurricane Story. New York, Doubleday, 1960.

The Silent Miaow: A Manual for Kittens, Strays, and Homeless Cats, photographs by Suzanne Szasz. New York, Crown, and London, Heinemann, 1964.

The Golden People. New York, Doubleday, 1965.

The Story of Silent Night. New York, Crown, and London, Heinemann, 1967.

The Revealing Eye: Personalities of the 1920s. New York, Atheneum, 1967.

Honourable Cat. New York, Crown, and London, Heinemann, 1972.

*

Film Adaptations: *Lili,* 1953 (from *Love of Seven Dolls*); *The Three Lives of Thomasina,* 1964 (from *Thomasina*); *The Poseidon Adventure,* 1972; *Beyond the Poseidon Adventure,* 1979.

*   *   *

Paul Gallico was a prolific writer, with a mass of journalism and over 40 books to his credit by the time he died. Although few remain in print, in their heyday his novels were extremely popular and a number were adapted as films. He enjoyed several reputations as an author: in the 1930s, he was "the highest-paid sports writer in New York"; in the 1940s, he was acclaimed for his wartime fable of the Dunkirk evacuation, *The Snow Goose,* and for his amusing stories about the unlikely adventurer Hiram Holliday (which later formed the basis of a popular television series); in the 1950s, he emerged as a writer of fantasies about animals and children, among other "fairy tales in modern dress"—a label, bestowed by his British publisher, which in fact applies to almost all his novels, to the comedies about the cockney charlady Mrs. 'Arris just as much as to the cat books and to such gossamer-light novellas as *Snowflake* (which is, as its title suggests, the tale of a flake of snow).

The fantasy for which Gallico became best known was *The Abandoned* (perhaps more widely familiar as *Jennie,* which seems to have been the author's favoured title). Markedly sentimental, as are most of his novels, it tells the story of a small boy named Peter who is transformed into a white cat after a near-fatal road accident. The book amounts to a closely observed description of feline habits and manners (written by an author who at one stage in his life owned 23 cats).

The eponymous Jennie is the cat, abandoned by her people, who rescues Peter from ignorance and teaches him the ways of feline behaviour: how to wash, when and how to catch mice and fight other tomcats, and how to deal with humans. Peter, who has adored cats only from a distance since his socialite mother, his absent military father, and his adoring nanny have all forbidden him to own one, is taken by Jennie Baldrin on a tour of exploration from the feline view: to Mr. Grims, who feeds them and wants them to live with him; from London to Glasgow by means of a cargo boat on which they earn their passage by catching mice; back to London and Peter's home, where his family has gone but they find Jennie's people. Although reunited with her own, Jennie stays with Peter, only for him to betray her by going away with a seductive Siamese. The end comes when he finds Jennie once more, but faces the prospect of losing her when Dempsey, the vicious alley cat, claims her, and Peter must fight or lose his only friend. Although Peter wins,

he is mortally wounded, only to wake to find himself become a boy once more in a hospital bed.

The story is Gallico's view of humankind translated to the feline world. Peter is as abandoned as Jennie, seeing little of his parents; he dreams of his mother's love, which is Jennie's love, all-forgiving and devotional. In the end he must fight to achieve what he wants most, which is also his battle against dying from the injuries he sustained in the road accident. It is an extraordinary book, wonderful in its imagination and detail of feline behaviour, but at the same time flawed by Gallico's belief in fundamental characteristics of gender. Jennie, as a female, must be loving and forgiving, willing to sacrifice herself for Peter, whereas he, a boy and thus selfish, must own her, he dominant, she submissive.

Gallico made use of his knowledge of felines to good effect in many of his books, including *Thomasina,* about a cat belonging to a lonely girl named Mary. Her sour veterinarian father refuses treatment when Thomasina falls ill and apparently dies, then comes back to life at the hands of a wild healer woman, the cat now believing herself to be an Egyptian goddess. In this tale, as the father is tamed and made gentle by association with the healer Lori, so Thomasina is healed and returns home to Mary, who is close to death because she feels betrayed by Thomasina's death and her father's cruelty.

Gallico can also be surprisingly sharp. In *Too Many Ghosts* and *The Hand of Mary Constable* he creates a leading character— Alexander Hero—who investigates psychic phenomena, seeking proof of such episodes but mostly failing to find it. Hero is an unusual character, flawed (in his own admission) by a tendency to fall in love with any attractive woman who crosses his path; yet he is also a realist, and his condemnation of the people with whom he mixes is based on their capacity for evil, not their morals.

One of the themes in both these novels, expanded in *The Man Who Was Magic,* is the desire to distinguish what is false from what is true, and the fear as well as longing which comes from an encounter with truth. *The Man Who Was Magic* concerns a man who can perform real magic in a city of conjurers, and the terror he arouses by his ability. Magic tricks clearly interested Gallico, who explains the workings of many common stage tricks—and more ingenious effects—in his books; yet this interest comes across as a desire for belief in God, which must depend on faith and is not open to proof. True magic, as in *The Small Miracle,* where a boy appeals to St. Francis to heal his donkey, is effectively a gift of God and beyond human understanding. Alexander Hero wants to believe in ghosts, but finds human contrivance instead.

Despite their sentimental nature, Paul Gallico's novels and shorter tales possess qualities which place them apart from most of their time; he made use of strong female protagonists when it was by no means popular to do so, and he is sympathetic to the human condition rather than condemnatory, forgiving of weakness and willing to find a capacity for good in most. His fascination with animals and their relationships with humans offers food for thought, while allowing him to pull at the heart-strings of his readers in a fashion which is almost Victorian.

—Mary Corran

GARCIA y ROBERTSON, R(odrigo)

Nationality: American. **Born:** 1949.

FANTASY PUBLICATIONS

Novel

The Spiral Dance. New York, Morrow, 1991.

* * *

Rod Garcia is a qualified historian who taught the history of science, technology and the future before turning to full-time writing. His knowledge not only of mankind's history, but of the development and idiosyncrasies of its cultures, is evident in his fiction and is central to the development of his themes. Much of his work is only arbitrarily science fiction or fantasy because he has deliberately endeavoured to fuse both fields by recognizing that magic and science may only be two different viewpoints of the same thing.

This was noticeable from his first published story, "The Flying Mountain" (*Amazing,* 1987). Set in Turkey at the time of the advancing Mongol Empire, it portrays an alternative civilization where the Mongols have discovered the secret of ballooning. Basically science fiction, it is written as a fantasy with the Turks fearing the magic of the Mongols.

Garcia's knowledge and understanding of the history and myths of other nations is profound. "Three Heads for the High Kings" (*Weird Tales,* 1989) is an Arthurian story but set in the very real world of the distant north at the start of the Dark Ages. "The Wagon God's Wife" (*Asimov's,* 1989) retells an incident from a Norse saga featuring the clash of cultures between the old religion and Christianity. "The Great Fear" (*Weird Tales,* 1990) is a tale of witchcraft in medieval France, while "Gypsy Trade," which has been optioned as a movie, is a remarkable study of witchcraft in western Europe at the time of the great migration of gypsies.

Garcia's exploration of old and ancient cultures has required detailed development, making his work usually of novelette or novella length. This has allowed him to expand them more readily into novels. His first, *The Spiral Dance,* draws upon two stories in *The Magazine of Fantasy and Science Fiction* which are set in Scotland and northern England during the reign of Elizabeth I. As in "The Wagon God's Wife," Garcia again explores a clash of cultures and religion, here the struggle between Catholics and Protestants, but brings into play the power of the more ancient religion of elder Britain. Countess Anne of Northumberland discovers the power of witchcraft and, in league with a Scottish werewolf, endeavours to win back the English throne. Garcia has completed a sequel to this novel which awaits publication.

The fantastic elements in Garcia's work may be fundamental but they are often hidden below the surface, manipulating the events but not always directly visible. This is especially true in "Four Kings and an Ace," where the fantasy is subtle and almost non-existent. It tells of a young Chinese girl who comes to late 19th-century San Francisco and uses her latent powers to escape from prostitution and establish herself.

Garcia has written few overt science-fiction stories, though his sequence of stories in *Asimov's SF Magazine* making up the as-yet unpublished novel *Virgin and the Dinosaur,* are the most evident. These follow the adventures of a newly married couple who have established a time-travel agency to aid research. This allows Garcia to explore a wide range of historical periods, and the fantasy feel is strongest in the prehistoric sequence of the title novella (1992), where the couple are on honeymoon in the Mesozoic.

Another forthcoming novel, *American Woman,* considers the history and myth of the American Indians. "The Other Magpie" (*Asimov's,* 1993) is a profound story set at the time of General Custer. Again the fantasy element is slight but significant.

Garcia's ability to recreate past cultures and beliefs is excellent, and in mixing myth and technology he is adding a depth of understanding frequently missing from historical fantasies.

—Mike Ashley

GARDNER, Craig Shaw

Nationality: American. **Born:** Rochester, New York, 2 July 1949. **Education:** Boston University. President, Horror Writers of America, since 1990. **Agent:** Merrilee Heifetz, Writers House, 21 West 26th Street, New York, NY 10010, USA. **Address:** P.O. Box 458, Cambridge, MA 02238, USA.

FANTASY PUBLICATIONS

Novels (series: Arabian Nights; Cineverse; Dragon Circle; Ebenezum; Wuntvor)

A Malady of Magicks (Ebenezum). New York, Ace, 1986; London, Headline, 1988.
A Multitude of Monsters (Ebenezum). New York, Ace, 1986; London, Headline, 1988.
A Night in the Netherhells (Ebenezum). New York, Ace, 1987; London, Headline, 1989.
The Exploits of Ebenezum (omnibus; includes *A Malady of Magicks, A Multitude of Monsters, A Night in the Netherhells*). New York, Nelson Doubleday, 1987.
A Difficulty with Dwarves (Wuntvor). New York, Ace, 1987; London, Headline, 1989.
An Excess of Enchantments (Wuntvor). New York, Ace, 1988; London, Headline, 1989.
Wishbringer (novelization of a computer game). New York, Avon, 1988.
A Disagreement with Death (Wuntvor). New York, Ace, and London, Headline, 1989.
The Wanderings of Wuntvor (omnibus; includes *A Difficulty with Dwarves, An Excess of Enchantments, A Disagreement with Death*). New York, Nelson Doubleday, 1989.
Slaves of the Volcano God (Cineverse). New York, Ace, and London, Headline, 1989.
Bride of the Slime Monster (Cineverse). New York, Ace, and London, Headline, 1990.
Revenge of the Fluffy Bunnies (Cineverse). New York, Ace, and London, Headline, 1990.
The Cineverse Cycle (omnibus; includes *Slaves of the Volcano God, Bride of the Slime Monster, Revenge of the Fluffy Bunnies*). New York, Guild America, 1991.
The Other Sinbad (Arabian Nights). London, Headline, and New York, Ace, 1991.
A Bad Day for Ali Baba (Arabian Nights). London, Headline, 1991; New York, Ace, 1992.
Scheherazade's Night Out (Arabian Nights). London, Headline, and New York, Ace, 1992.

Raven Walking (Dragon Circle). London, Heinemann, 1994; as *Dragon Sleeping,* New York, Ace, 1994.

Dragon Waking (Dragon Circle). London, Heinemann, and New York, Ace, 1995.

OTHER PUBLICATIONS

Novels

The Lost Boys (novelization of screenplay). New York, Berkley, 1987.

Back to the Future Part II (novelization of screenplay). New York, Berkley, and London, Headline, 1989.

Batman (novelization of screenplay). New York, Warner, and London, Futura, 1989.

Back to the Future Part III (novelization of screenplay). New York, Berkley, and London, Headline, 1990.

The Batman Murders. New York, Warner, 1990; London, Penguin, 1991.

Batman Returns (novelization of screenplay). New York, Warner, and London, Mandarin, 1992.

*   *   *

There are two main strands to Craig Shaw Gardner's professional writing career: movie novelizations and other ties on the one hand, and comic fantasy on the other.

It was in the latter field that he began, publishing the various short stories that later contributed to his first novel, *A Malady of Magicks* (although, paradoxically, his first-published story, "A Malady of Magicks" in 1978, was not among these). That novel initiated his Ebenezum trilogy, which follows the adventures through a generic Fantasyland, as related by the apprentice Wuntvor, of the wizard Ebenezum, who has been made allergic to magic by the arch-demon Guxx Unfufadoo and quests to the fabled city of Vushta in search of a cure. Their enemies send against them demons, monsters, assassins, etc., but the plucky pair—aided by various gathered companions—press on doughtily. At last the forces of darkness carry off Vushta to the Netherhells, safely out of even a wizard's reach; but Ebenezum and Wuntvor quest even there to save the day.

The Ballad of Wuntvor trilogy is a continuation, with Ebenezum less central and the focus now on Wuntvor, who—to the wrath of an impatient Death—seems to be turning into the Eternal Apprentice, and thus becoming immortal. Both series contain occasional delights—very occasional—but are essentially Terry Pratchett without the wit or imaginative scope; the writing is slapdash and the humour clumsy and weak.

It was refreshing when Gardner looked to his own imagination for a new trilogy: the Cineverse cycle. Delores, statuesque girlfriend of PR-man Roger, is seized by the sinister Dr. Dread and transported to the Cineverse, a set of parallel universes in which all the B-movies take place—and from which, it emerges, Delores originally came. With the aid of a Captain Crusader Decoder Ring left over from his childhood, Roger pursues her, discovering that the villains have created and are fostering the Change, whereby Movie Magic—in which the good guys always win—is being wiped off the face of all the universes. Once again the humour is somewhat leaden, but this time the frequent flashes of wild inventiveness are sufficient to carry the reader along.

Gardner's next trilogy, beginning with *The Other Sinbad,* is a considerably more ambitious and more successful work of com-

edy, amounting to a subversively alternate version of the heart-matter of *The 1001 Nights.* The original Sinbad has left the sea and is living in complacent retirement. A *djinni,* Ozzie, threatens him with great and terrible vengeance for an unspecified crime, but is confused by the presence of another Sinbad, a humble porter; Ozzie reappears periodically to repeat the same threat and suffer the same confusion. Sinbad the Sailor is bankrupt again, and so together the pair undertake skewed versions of the seven voyages, and seem to have absolved themselves when Sinbad the Porter is seized by a lustful Fatima, Queen of the Apes—a cliff-hanger to impel us into volume two, *A Bad Day for Ali Baba.* Here Ali discovers a sentient treasure-filled cave and helps himself; his brother-in-law attempts to do likewise, but is cut to (undead) pieces. Returning to the cave, Ali is recruited by the Forty Thieves, whose thieving can be successful only when there are exactly 40 of them. Also in the cave are Aladdin, Sinbad the Porter and, isolated by the greedy cave in its Palace of Beautiful Women, plenty of . . . beautiful women. The men free the women but also Ozzie, who decrees a storytelling contest whose prize is *not* dying horribly. Sinbad, Ali and Scheherazade are forced to take part; the stories of the first two constitute the books we have just read, while the third proceeds to tell the trilogy's concluding volume, *Scheherazade's Night Out.* This takes the form of an extremely complicated tales-within-tales-within-tales narrative, recording how Scheherazade eventually ran out of stories to tell her murderous husband and, in search of more, eventually came by magic carpet to the cave, where she has since been incarcerated. As her tale ends, her enemies arrive in pursuit; in the ensuing tussle all the heroes escape to live happily ever after. Interestingly, in this concluding sequence, Scheherazade's creative imagination is seen as being itself a potent, usable magical force.

Gardner's novelizations are among the better of their kind, making up for any deficiencies of execution by a refreshing lack of perfunctoriness: they read like books someone has enjoyed writing rather than—as so often in this sub-genre—mere financial exercises. Of much more note is his singleton novel *The Batman Murders,* an adventure featuring the comics rather than the movie characters. As part of yet another madcap plot the Joker is brainwashing Gothamites into believing they are Batman, so that the climax of each of his crimes can be the killing of his old adversary. This is not a profound work, but it is good entertainment, and the wry humour Gardner displays here—as opposed to the knockabout variety he deploys elsewhere—is surprisingly funny.

—Jane Barnett and John Grant

GARDNER, John (Champlin, Jr.)

Nationality: American. **Born:** Batavia, New York, 21 July 1933. **Education:** De Pauw University, Greencastle, Indiana, 1951-53; Washington University, St. Louis, A.B. 1955; State University of Iowa (Woodrow Wilson Fellow, 1955-56), M.A. 1956, Ph.D. 1958. **Family:** Married 1) Joan Louise Patterson in 1953, two children; 2) Liz Rosenberg in 1980. **Career:** Taught at Oberlin College, Ohio, 1958-59; California State University, Chico, 1959-62, and San Francisco, 1962-65; Southern Illinois University, Carbondale, 1965-74; Bennington College, Vermont, 1974-76; Williams College, Williamstown, Massachusetts, and Skidmore College, Saratoga Springs, New York, 1976-77; George Mason University, Fairfax,

Virginia, 1977-78; State University of New York, Binghamton, 1978-82. Visiting professor, University of Detroit, 1970-71, and Northwestern University, Evanston, Illinois, 1973. Editor, *MSS,* and Southern Illinois University Press Literary Structures series. **Awards:** Danforth fellowship, 1970; National Endowment for the Arts grant, 1972; American Academy award, 1975; National Book Critic's Circle award, 1976. **Died:** 4 September 1982.

FANTASY PUBLICATIONS

Novels

Grendel. New York, Knopf, 1971; London, Deutsch, 1972.
In the Suicide Mountains. New York, Knopf, 1977.
Freddy's Book. New York, Knopf, 1980; London, Secker and Warburg, 1981.
Vlemk the Box-Painter. Northridge, California, Lord John Press, 1980.
Mickelsson's Ghosts. New York, Knopf, and London, Secker and Warburg, 1982.

Short Stories

The King's Indian: Stories and Tales. New York, Knopf, 1974; London, Cape, 1975.
Dragon, Dragon and Other Timeless Tales (for children). New York, Knopf, 1975.
Gudgekin the Thistle Girl and Other Tales (for children). New York, Knopf, 1976.
The King of the Hummingbirds and Other Tales (for children). New York, Knopf, 1977.
The Art of Living, and Other Stories. New York, Knopf, 1981; London, Secker and Warburg, 1983.

OTHER PUBLICATIONS

Novels

The Resurrection. New York, New American Library, 1966.
The Wreckage of Agathon. New York, Harper, 1970.
The Sunlight Dialogues. New York, Knopf, 1971; London, Cape, 1973.
Jason and Medeia (novel in verse). New York, Knopf, 1973.
Nickel Mountain: A Pastoral Novel. New York, Knopf, 1973; London, Cape, 1974.
October Light. New York, Knopf, 1976; London, Cape, 1977.

Plays

William Wilson (libretto). Dallas, New London Press, 1978.
Three Libretti (includes *William Wilson, Frankenstein, Rumpelstiltskin*). Dallas, New London Press, 1979.

Poetry

Poems. Northridge, California, Lord John Press, 1978.

Other

The Gawain-Poet. Lincoln, Nebraska, Cliff's Notes, 1967.

Le Morte D'Arthur. Lincoln, Nebraska, Cliff's Notes, 1967.
The Construction of the Wakefield Cycle. Carbondale, Southern Illinois University Press, 1974.
The Construction of Christian Poetry in Old English. Carbondale, Southern Illinois University Press, 1975.
A Child's Bestiary (for children). New York, Knopf, 1977.
The Poetry of Chaucer. Carbondale, Southern Illinois University Press, 1977.
The Life and Times of Chaucer. New York, Knopf, and London, Cape, 1977.
On Moral Fiction. New York, Basic Books, 1978.
On Becoming a Novelist. New York, Harper, 1983.
The Art of Fiction: Notes on Craft for Young Writers. New York, Knopf, 1984.

Editor, with Lennis Dunlap. *The Forms of Fiction.* New York, Random House, 1962.
Editor, *The Complete Works of the Gawain-Poet in a Modern English Version with a Critical Introduction.* Chicago, University of Chicago Press, 1965.
Editor, with Nicholas Joost, *Papers on the Art and Age of Geoffrey Chaucer.* Edwardsville, Southern Illinois University Press, 1967.
Editor, *The Alliterative Morte Arthure, The Owl and the Nightingale, and Five Other Middle English Poems, in a Modernized Version, with Comments on the Poems, and Notes.* Carbondale, Southern Illinois University Press, 1971.
Editor, with Shannon Ravenel, *The Best American Short Stories 1982.* Boston, Houghton Mifflin, 1982.

Translator, with Nobuku Tsukui, *Tengu Child,* by Kikuo Itaya. Carbondale, Southern Illinois University Press, 1983.
Translator, with John Maier, *Gilgamesh.* New York, Knopf, 1984.

*

Bibliography: *John Gardner: A Bibliographical Profile* by John M. Howell, Carbondale, Southern Illinois University Press, 1980; *John Gardner: An Annotated Secondary Bibliography* by Robert A. Morace, New York, Garland, 1984.

Critical Studies: *John Gardner: Critical Perspectives* edited by Robert A. Morace and Kathryn VanSpanckeren, Carbondale, Southern Illinois University Press, 1982; *Arches and Light: The Fiction of John Gardner* by David Cowart, Carbondale, Southern Illinois University Press, 1983; *A World of Order and Light: The Fiction of John Gardner* by Gregory L. Morris, Athens, University of Georgia Press, 1984.

*   *   *

By the time of his death in a motorcycle accident, John Gardner had gored so many sacred cows of the mainstream establishment (in his 1978 treatise, *On Moral Fiction* and elsewhere) and made sufficiently pretentious public statements about his own philosophical depth that, quite possibly, his place in literature may not be finally established until everyone who knew him as a contemporary is dead. He was certainly a controversial figure, a fearful snob, and an ideologue of what he considered to be traditional storytelling—rejecting postmodernist word games and nihilism, his own work rooted in classics as old as *The Epic of Gilgamesh* (which he helped translate) and in medieval romance (a field where, again, he made substantial contributions as biographer of Chaucer and as translator of *The Alliterative Morte Arthure*), but only gravitating toward fantasy reluctantly. He gored a few cows in the fantasy field too, and is venomously caricatured (though with his name misspelled) in Stephen King and Peter Straub's *The Talisman*.

Ironically, his permanent place in literature may well prove to be that of a fantasist of the second rank. Several of his mainstream novels are well-regarded, particularly *The Sunlight Dialogues* and *October Light,* but he is foremost the author of *Grendel,* a retelling of the *Beowulf* epic from the viewpoint of the monster, a creature curiously addicted to the same sort of verbal play and nihilism which Gardner himself denounced. *Grendel* is an angry book for rebellious readers looking to thumb their noses at the world, critically compared to (but never as popular as) J. D. Salinger's *The Catcher in the Rye* and Vonnegut's *Cat's Cradle.* It is all spite and spleen, the monster (who narrates) railing at the folly of human heroism and the meaninglessness of his own existence, finding a purpose only in his own evil—as something for heroes to react against. As a novel, it has an interesting voice, but lacks dramatic incident, and is flawed by uncontrolled anachronisms, as if Grendel is somehow aware he is a character in 20th-century fiction.

The dragon in the story, by contrast, transcends time and has a deliberately anachronistic viewpoint reminiscent of T. H. White's Merlin. But Gardner, not quite in control of his material, is unable to use this device to its maximum effect.

Ursula Le Guin, in reviewing *Vlemk the Box-Painter,* precisely defined Gardner's weakness as a fantasist, quoting from *On Moral Fiction,* in which Gardner says, "truth is useful in realistic art but is much less necessary in the fabulous." For this reason, Gardner seldom took the trouble to make the "mere" fantastic convincing, and would not have cared that the various characters in *Grendel* use phrases and espouse ideas unlikely for their time and place, any more than he would have eliminated references to "funk" and "biological constraints" from his posthumous "Julius Caesar and the Werewolf" (published in *Playboy,* September 1984) had he lived to revise it. Gardner's *Grendel* is no more a Dark Age monster than his Julius Caesar is an ancient Roman. They are both merely made-up, part of what is, for Gardner, a less serious type of fiction.

This profound misapprehension of the whole nature of fantasy keeps Gardner out of the front rank. Otherwise, he was, at times, nearly as good (and even as profound) a writer as he thought he was. His very best fantastic work, *Freddy's Book,* is a brilliantly bizarre post-medieval allegory of a knight sent to kill the Devil. It rings true on all levels, but as a tale-within-a-tale, "written," not by John Gardner, but by the reclusive, neurotic giant, Freddy, who tries to explain his world through fantasy in ways realistic novelist John Gardner would never allow himself. It is a work which demands close re-reading. As far as verisimilitude goes, it would seem that Freddy had a much greater emotional need to get the details right than did Gardner. Freddy, the character, takes fantasy seriously.

Otherwise much of the best of Gardner's fantasy may be found in his fairy tales for children (*Gudgekin the Thistle Girl,* etc.), and in such crossover books as *Into the Suicide Mountains.* Some fantastic fiction occurs in his adult collections, including the curious Poe-parody, "The Ravages of Spring" in *The King's Indian. Mickelsson's Ghosts* has supernatural touches, but the thrust of the narrative is largely in other directions. The uncollected "Julius Caesar and the Werewolf" is formless and unsatisfactory, but left in a draft state and so may not represent the author's final intentions.

At the furthest remove—his mainstream novels and their merits considered quite separately—Gardner the fantasist may prove to be a two-book writer: remembered for *Grendel,* a curiosity, and *Freddy's Book,* a small masterpiece.

—Darrell Schweitzer

GARNER, Alan

Nationality: British. **Born:** Congleton, Cheshire, 17 October 1934. **Education:** Alderley Edge Primary School, Cheshire; Manchester Grammar School; Magdalen College, Oxford. **Military Service:** Royal Artillery: Second Lieutenant. **Family:** Married 1) Ann Cook in 1956 (marriage dissolved), one son and two daughters; 2) Griselda Greaves in 1972, one son and one daughter. **Awards:** Library Association Carnegie Medal, 1968; *Guardian* award, 1968; Chicago International Film Festival prize, 1981; Mother Goose award, 1987. **Address:** "Toad Hall," Blackden, Holmes Chapel, Crewe, Cheshire CW4 8BY, England.

FANTASY PUBLICATIONS

Novels

The Weirdstone of Brisingamen: A Tale of Alderley. London, Collins, 1960; as *The Weirdstone,* New York, Watts, 1961; revised edition, London, Penguin, 1963; New York, Walck, 1969.
The Moon of Gomrath. London, Collins, 1963; New York, Walck, 1967.
Elidor, illustrated by Charles Keeping. London, Collins, 1965; New York, Walck, 1967.
The Owl Service. London, Collins, 1967; New York, Walck, 1968.
Red Shift. London, Collins, and New York, Macmillan, 1973.

Short Stories

Fairy Tales of Gold (The Girl of the Golden Gate, The Golden Brothers, The Princess and the Golden Mane, The Three Golden Heads of the Well), illustrated by Michael Foreman. London, Collins, 4 vols., 1979; 1 vol. edition, Collins, and New York, Philomel, 1980.
Book of British Fairy Tales (retellings), illustrated by Derek Collard. London, Collins, 1984; New York, Delacorte, 1985.

OTHER PUBLICATIONS

Fiction for Children

The Old Man of Mow, photographs by Roger Hill. London, Collins, 1967; New York, Doubleday, 1970.
The Breadhorse, illustrated by Albin Trowski. London, Collins, 1975.
The Stone Book Quartet, illustrated by Michael Foreman. London, Collins, 1983; New York, Dell, 1988.
The Stone Book. London, Collins, 1976; New York, Collins World, 1978.

Tom Fobble's Day. London, Collins, 1977; New York, Collins World, 1979.

Granny Reardun. London, Collins, 1977; New York, Collins World, 1978.

The Aimer Gate. London, Collins, 1978; New York, Collins World, 1979.

The Lad of the Gad (folktales). London, Collins, 1980; New York, Philomel, 1981.

Jack and the Beanstalk, illustrated by Julek Heller. London, Collins, 1985; New York, Delacorte, 1992.

A Bag of Moonshine (folktales), illustrated by Patrick James Lynch. London, Collins, and New York, Delacorte, 1986.

Plays

Holly from the Bongs: A Nativity Play, music by William Mayne, photographs by Roger Hill (produced Goostrey, Cheshire, 1965). London, Collins, 1966; revised version, music by Gordon Crosse (produced London, 1974), published in *Labrys 7* (Frome, Somerset), 1981.

The Belly Bag, music by Richard Morris (produced London, 1971).

Potter Thompson, music by Gordon Crosse (produced London, 1975). London, Oxford University Press, 1975.

To Kill a King (televised, 1980). Published in *Labrys 7* (Frome, Somerset), 1981.

The Green Mist, in *Labrys 7* (Frome, Somerset), 1981.

Screenplays: *Places and Things,* 1978; *Images,* 1981.

Radio Plays: *Have You Met Our Tame Author?,* 1962; *Elidor,* 1962; *The Weirdstone of Brisingamen,* from his own story, 1963; *Thor and the Giants,* 1965, revised version, 1979; *Idun and the Apples of Life,* 1965, revised version, as *Loki and the Storm Giant,* 1979; *Baldur the Bright,* 1965, revised version, 1979; *The Stone Book, Granny Reardun, Tom Fobble's Day* and *The Aimer Gate,* from his own stories, 1980.

Television Plays: *The Owl Service,* from his own story, 1969; *Red Shift,* from his own story, 1978; *Lamaload,* 1979; *To Kill a King* (*Leap in the Dark* series), 1980; *The Keeper,* 1982.

Other

Editor, *The Hamish Hamilton Book of Goblins: An Anthology of Folklore,* illustrated by Krystyna Turska. London, Hamish Hamilton, 1969; as *A Cavalcade of Goblins,* New York, Walck, 1969; as *A Book of Goblins,* London, Penguin, 1972.

Compiler, *The Guizer: A Book of Fools.* London, Hamish Hamilton, 1975; New York, Greenwillow, 1976.

*

Manuscript Collection: Brigham Young University, Provo, Utah.

Critical Studies: *A Fine Anger: A Critical Introduction to the Work of Alan Garner* by Neil Philip, London, Collins, and New York, Philomel, 1981; *Alan Garner Issue* of *Labrys 7* (Frome, Somerset), 1981.

* * *

Alan Garner's earliest novels, written specifically for children, are of his works the most unequivocally fantasies, and thus claim particular attention here. Though for children, the sophisticated deployment of trans-dimensionality and "inner time" gives them a wider than juvenile appeal. In the sequence *The Weirdstone of Brisingamen* and *The Moon of Gomrath* he explores a large fund of mythopoeic material, adapting it to the requirements of his stories and shaping his narratives to exhibit the deep structures of Norse and Celtic myth. In each novel two children wandering a perilous scene are caught up in magical experiences, their protector on the mundane side of the divide being a blunt Cheshire farmer, Gowther Mossock, and on the mythic side the wizard Cadellin. The theme of *The Weirdstone of Brisingamen* is that of the Knights sleeping under the Hill who must only be wakened at a duly critical time. The girl, Susan, unknowingly holds the key, the Weirdstone, of which goblin-like witch-commanded creatures strive to gain control. The vividly depicted arena of contest is Alderley Edge, that forested sandstone ridge rising from the Cheshire Plain. In *The Moon of Gomrath* Susan allows her magic bracelet to leave her possession and is only preserved from annihilation by her brother's following a ley line to the Pennine Hills to fetch a restoring herb. In doing this he awakens the dangerous Old Magic. When the children light a fire at the Celtic festival of Gomrath, there are more manifestations of the Old Magic in the form of the Wild Hunt. It is these horsemen, however, summoned by horn blast, who come to Susan's aid when, after saving her brother from the evil Morrigan she is herself again in peril.

Garner later tended to be dismissive of these books. The melange of borrowings, re-tellings and transfusions from such a variety of sources—the *Mabinogion,* Carmichael's *Carmina Gadelica,* etc.—while vehicle for much exciting action is often overwhelming, the children seeming almost pawn-like protagonists. A prominent and entirely convincing "character" is Alderley Edge and all of Garner's "home ground" between it and the Goyt Valley. This remains true of most of his later work, as does the persistence of themes related to the "Matter of Britain" and to the magic object as key to transition between worlds, planes of being or spans of time.

Elidor is a better-ordered fantasy. While still eclectically pursuing mythic (chiefly Celtic) themes, Garner brings them to a finer point of concentration in this essentially Platonic story. Neil Philip has proposed comparisons between Elidor, a country beyond and underlying the mundane world, and C. S. Lewis's Narnia. It is a just comparison in that neither land is an ultimate perfection: both are subject to the "fallen" condition of the wasteland; and both offer doors to and from the mundane world—this being in *Elidor* suburban Alderley and inner-city Manchester. It is in the latter environment that young protagonist Roland finds unlooked-for entry to Elidor, a *Tir na nOc* become waste, with its crippled King and symbolic treasures, in the guardianship of which lie possibilities for renewal. The half-demolished Manchester church and the Dark Tower to which Roland (or Childe Roland) and his siblings come are one and the same. The children return home with artefacts from the broken church, symbolic of (or sharing essence with) the Grail objects. There follow continual trauma-producing manifestations of Elidor's penetration of their urban/suburban world. The climax is enacted before the crumbling church which, at the death of Findhorn, the hunted and sacrificial unicorn, is made radiant with promise, this through the momentary glory of a supernaturally restored window, before the drabness of dereliction reasserts itself.

The role of artefacts as "conductors" of experience, merging different existences and temporalities, persists in two distinguished novels in which fantasy counterpoints realism, while performing in a subtler key. The main protagonists of *The Owl Service* and *Red Shift* are not children but adolescents. The mundane concerns are more adult and involve the protagonists more autonomously in the stories' myth-impregnated complexities. *The Owl Service*'s Welsh valley is, like *Elidor*'s Manchester, a world of imperfection. Garner, in the introduction to *The Guizer,* his collection of "Trickster" folk tales and legends, writes of "harmonics of the great theme" traceable in a multiplicity of secondary or derivative stories. So it is in *The Owl Service,* where, from the Fourth Branch of the Mabinogi, the myth of the faithless woman made from flowers is re-enacted (or reborn) in a story of contemporary Welsh/English ethnic, class and family tensions. The owl/flower decorated plates of the title act as the "mediumistic" artefact, creating a timeless identity with the legendary past. Again, in *Red Shift,* the artefact there being a Neolithic axe-head, a traditional story is thematic. On the stage of historic Cheshire, happenings of the Roman occupation, of the English Civil War and of the 20th-century suburban "wasteland" are seen as being virtually synchronous. At every phase the insight of a woman is a supportive or modifying factor in the crises suffered by the hero (or anti-hero), who is throughout psycho-physically impaired. Thematically, as Garner himself avers, the novel is a reprise of the Scottish ballad "Tam Lin." Both this novel and *The Owl Service* are substantially narrated through a sparse, muscular, sometimes elliptical dialogue, a prose style which is the hallmark of this period of Garner's writing. It is consonant with his interest in and scripting for film, radio and television.

Garner's main works of the 1970s are the four short novels *The Stone Book, Granny Reardun, The Aimer Gate* and *Tom Fobble's Day,* together comprising *The Stone Book Quartet.* This is a generation novel, reflective of the author's own family history from mid-19th century to World War II. The Cheshire scene, the Cheshire dialect, Garner's taut, direct narration, do not here point in the direction of fantasy, yet in the relationships of successive craftsmen to materials and traditions of their craft can be discerned a complex web of correspondences echoing those of the earlier novels. Children grow, rebel, mature, or fail, and in that progress undergo archetypally resonant experiences which are keys to a unity encompassing all that exists between an ancient handprint deep in a mine and horizons which stretch to the sea when viewed from the summit of church steeples. Diverse as Alan Garner's fictions are, there is just such an underlying unity suffusing and binding all of them.

—K. V. Bailey

GARNETT, David

Pseudonym: Leda Burke. **Nationality:** British. **Born:** Brighton, Sussex, 9 March 1892; son of the writer Edward Garnett and the translator Constance Garnett. **Education:** University College School, London, 1906-08; Imperial College of Science and Technology, London, 1910-15, A.R.C.S. 1913, D.I.C. 1915. **Military Service:** Conscientious objector in World War I; served in the Royal Air Force Volunteer Reserve, 1939-40: Flight Lieutenant; planning officer and historian, Political Warfare Executive, 1941-46. **Family:** Married 1) Rachel Alice Marshall in 1921 (died 1940), two

sons; 2) Angelica Bell in 1942, four daughters. **Career:** Partner, Birrell and Garnett, booksellers, London, 1920-24; partner, Nonesuch Press, London, 1923-35; literary editor, *New Statesman and Nation,* London, 1932-34; director, Rupert Hart-Davis Ltd., publishers, London, 1946-52. **Awards:** Hawthornden prize, 1923; James Tait Black Memorial prize, 1923. Fellow, Imperial College of Science and Technology, 1956; fellow, and Companion of Literature, 1977, Royal Society of Literature. D.Litt.: University of Birmingham, 1977. C.B.E. (Commander, Order of the British Empire), 1952. **Died:** 17 February 1981.

FANTASY PUBLICATIONS

Novels

Lady into Fox. London, Chatto and Windus, 1922; New York, Knopf, 1923.
A Man in the Zoo. London, Chatto and Windus, and New York, Knopf, 1924.
Two by Two: A Story of Survival. London, Longman, 1963; New York, Atheneum, 1964.

OTHER PUBLICATIONS

Novels

Dope-Darling (as Leda Burke). London, Laurie, 1919.
The Sailor's Return. London, Chatto and Windus, and New York, Knopf, 1925.
Go She Must! London, Chatto and Windus, and New York, Knopf, 1927.
No Love. London, Chatto and Windus, and New York, Knopf, 1929.
The Grasshoppers Come. London, Chatto and Windus, and New York, Brewer Warren and Putnam, 1931.
Pocahontas; or, The Nonpareil of Virginia. London, Chatto and Windus, and New York, Harcourt Brace, 1933.
Beany-Eye. London, Chatto and Windus, and New York, Harcourt Brace, 1935.
Aspects of Love. London, Chatto and Windus, 1955; New York, Harcourt Brace, 1956.
A Shot in the Dark. London, Longman, 1958; Boston, Little Brown, 1959.
A Net for Venus. London, Longman, 1959.
Ulterior Motives. London, Longman, 1966; New York, Harcourt Brace, 1967.
A Clean Slate. London, Hamish Hamilton, 1971.
The Sons of the Falcon. London, Macmillan, 1972.
Plough over the Bones. London, Macmillan, 1973.
Up She Rises. London, Macmillan, 1977; New York, St. Martin's Press, 1978.

Short Stories

The Old Dovecote and Other Stories. London, Mathews and Marrot, 1928.
A Terrible Day. London, Joiner and Steele, 1932.
An Old Master and Other Stories. Tokyo, Yamaguchi Shoten, 1967.
Purl and Plain and Other Stories. London, Macmillan, 1973.

Other

Never Be a Bookseller. London, Chatto and Windus, and New York, Knopf, 1929.

A Rabbit in the Air: Notes from a Diary Kept While Learning to Handle an Aeroplane. London, Chatto and Windus, and New York, Brewer Warren and Putnam, 1932.

War in the Air September 1939-May 1941. London, Chatto and Windus, and New York, Doubleday, 1941.

The Campaign in Greece and Crete. London, His Majesty's Stationery Office, 1942.

The Golden Echo (autobiography). London, Chatto and Windus, 1953; New York, Harcourt Brace, 1954.

The Flowers of the Forest. London, Chatto and Windus, 1955; New York, Harcourt Brace, 1956.

The Familiar Faces. London, Chatto and Windus, 1962; New York, Harcourt Brace, 1963.

The White-Garnett Letters (correspondence with T. H. White), edited by Garnett. London, Cape, and New York, Viking Press, 1968.

First "Hippy" Revolution. Cerrillos, New Mexico, San Marcos Press, 1970.

The Master Cat: The True and Unexpurgated Story of Puss in Boots (for children). London, Macmillan, 1974.

Sir Geoffrey Keynes: A Tribute. Privately printed, 1978.

Great Friends: Portraits of Seventeen Writers. London, Macmillan, 1979; New York, Atheneum, 1980.

Editor, with others, *The Week-End Book.* London, Nonesuch Press, and New York, Dial Press, 1924.

Editor, *The Letters of T. E. Lawrence.* London, Cape, 1938; New York, Doubleday, 1939.

Editor, *The Battle of Britain,* H. A. St. George Saunders. London, Air Ministry, 1941.

Editor, *Fourteen Stories,* by Henry James. London, Hart Davis, 1946.

Editor, *The Novels of Thomas Love Peacock.* London, Hart Davis, 1948.

Editor, *The Essential T. E. Lawrence.* London, Cape, and New York, Dutton, 1951.

Editor, *The Selected Letters of T. E. Lawrence.* London, Cape, 1952; Westport, Connecticut, Hyperion Press, 1979.

Editor, *Carrington: Letters and Extracts from Her Diaries.* London, Cape, 1970; New York, Holt Rinehart, 1971.

Translator, *The Kitchen Garden and Its Management,* by V. A. Gressent. London, Selwyn and Blount, 1919.

Translator, *A Voyage to the Island of the Articoles,* by Andre Maurois. London, Cape, 1928; New York, Appleton, 1929.

Translator, *338171 T. E. (Lawrence of Arabia),* by Victoria Ocampo. London, Gollancz, and New York, Dutton, 1963.

*

Film Adaptation: *The Sailor's Return,* 1978.

Manuscript Collection: University of Texas, Austin.

*   *   *

David Garnett was the grandson of Richard Garnett, author of the classic fantasy collection *Twilight of the Gods,* and the son of Edward and Constance Garnett—the former one of the leading publishers' readers of the days, the latter a prolific translator who introduced the classics of Russian literature to English readers. With the benefit of such prestigious antecedents and his close association with the Bloomsbury group—the self-elected leaders of literary and moral fashionability in the England of the 1920s—it is hardly surprising that his first major literary work should be calculated to make a splash by virtue of its originality, urbanity and cool irony. The novella *Lady into Fox* duly won the James Tait Black Memorial Prize and the Hawthornden Prize, and became the most successful and widely-read English fantasy of a decade in which such works flourished as never before.

The story is set in the 19th century but its mannered style is more reminiscent of the 18th. It is the tale of an Oxfordshire gentleman, Richard Tebrick, who falls in love with a girl named Silvia Fox. Their marriage is happy, but founders on a seemingly trivial difference of outlook, when he attempts to force her to watch the progress of a hunt even though she has a profound distaste for such sport; she undergoes an instantaneous metamorphosis and becomes a fox. He makes valiant attempts to preserve the marriage—and its essential decorum—in spite of this awkward circumstance, but the task becomes increasingly difficult as Silvia's residual human traits are slowly but inexorably eroded. He remains faithful to her even after her escape from the family home and the delivery of a litter of cubs, but with an awful inevitability the hunting season comes around again, and she runs back to his loving arms only to be torn therefrom by the savage hounds. He goes mad, but the last lines of the text reveal, in typically laconic fashion, that he eventually "recovered his reason and lived to a great age, for that matter he is still alive."

The precise meaning of this seeming-parable eluded many contemporary readers and has exercised critics ever since. A simple and relatively straightforward decoding process reveals the message that in spite of the pretensions of Victorian ideology, women are essentially vixens for whom the respectability of marriage and the expectations of dutiful husbands constitute terms of imprisonment; if and when the contradictory requirements of their role become too much, their unfolding fate is to be seduced, pitied, debauched, forgiven, and ultimately ripped to pieces. Such a fate is, of course, horrific in its way, but it is fatal only for them, not for their lamenting menfolk, who will in time recover. The main problem with this decoding is, of course, the blatant conflict of its leaden earnestness with the inescapable awareness that the story is, after all, a calculatedly quaint and lighthearted joke. One of the great virtues of fantasy as a literary form is that its motifs, being nonrealistic and hence apparently nonserious, can be employed to transform black tragedy into gilded comedy, thus adding an extra deft turn to the glittery screw of irony.

Lady into Fox was so successful in its demonstration of this moral sleight-of-hand that it spawned a fascinating series of supposed parodies which are really homages, faithfully—but more absurdly—reproducing its calculated confusion of message and mockery. In Laurence Housman's "Lady into George Fox" a clergyman's wife metamorphoses into her Quaker ancestor, thus taking respectability to an awkward and self-defeating extreme. In Christopher Ward's *Gentleman into Goose* (1924) a wife whose ineffectual husband reverts to his symbolic type finds the situation far less tolerable than the doggedly noble Richard Tebrick (Ward was, of course, an American). Less directly imitative but nevertheless clearly Garnett-influenced is John Collier's *His Monkey Wife,* which amiably satirizes Bloomsbury mores by suggesting that any sane man would be far better off married to a loyal chimpanzee than an advanced "new woman." *Sylva* (1961), by the French novelist Vercors, is a charming inversion of Garnett's story in which a vixen metamorphoses into a woman.

Garnett never wrote another wholehearted fantasy, but his next novella, *A Man in the Zoo* (which is frequently reprinted in harness with *Lady into Fox*) offers a similarly oblique parable—a sequel of sorts, in which the roles have been reversed. John Cromartie, disappointed by the non-exclusivity of his beloved's affection for him, volunteers himself as a specimen of *Homo sapiens* for display at Regent's Park Zoo. There he forms a relationship with a caracal lynx, which saves him from a potentially fatal encounter with a jealous orangutan and provides a certain perverse consolation until his beloved finally gives way to moral pressure and agrees that she will "share a cage" with him for life, if that is the price she must pay for his company. The curator, unwilling to place such an exhibition as this before the public, turns the two of them out to join the crowd in the main body of the park—which is of course, "chiefly composed of couples like themselves."

Both these novellas were enhanced in their early editions by wood engravings produced by Garnett's first wife, "Ray" Marshall, who died in 1940; he subsequently married the daughter of Vanessa Bell—a central figure of the Bloomsbury group who lived with Duncan Grant, the dedicatee of *Lady into Fox*. Much of Garnett's later work is historical fiction, ranging from *Pocahontas*, a retelling of the well-known American tale, to *The Sons of the Falcon,* a story of the 19th-century Caucasus. One late "historical" novel which may be claimed as fantasy is *Two by Two,* a recension of the Biblical narrative of Noah's Ark.

—Brian Stableford

GARNETT, Richard

Nationality: British. **Born:** 1835. **Career:** Superintendent of the British Museum reading room; cataloguer and bibliographer. **Died:** 1906.

FANTASY PUBLICATIONS

Short Stories

The Twilight of the Gods. London, Unwin, 1888; expanded edition, London, Lane, 1903.

OTHER PUBLICATIONS

Poetry

Poems. London, Elkin Mathews & John Lane, 1893; Boston, Copeland & Day, 1893.
The Queen and Other Poems. London and New York, John Lane the Bodley Head, 1901.

Other

Io in Egypt, and Other Poems. London, Bell and Daldy, 1859.

Idylls and Epigrams. London, Macmillan, 1869.
A Chaplet from the Greek Anthology. New York, Stokes.
Life of Thomas Carlyle. London, W. Scott, 1887; (reprinted) New York, AMS Press, 1979.
Life of Ralph Waldo Emerson. London, W. Scott and New York, T. Whittaker, 1888; (reprinted) Folcroft, Pennsylvania, Folcroft Library Editions, 1974.
Life of John Milton. London, 1890; (reprinted) New York, AMS Press, 1970.
The Age of Dryden. London, 1895; (reprinted) Freeport, New York, Books for Libraries Press, 1971.
William Blake, Painter and Poet. London, Seeley, 1895; (reprinted) Folcroft, Pennsylvania, Folcroft Library Editions, 1973.
A History of Italian Literature. London, 1898; (reprinted) Port Washington, New York, Kennikat Press, 1970.
Essays in Librarianship and Bibliography. London, 1899; (reprinted) New York, Franklin, 1970.
Essays of an Ex-Librarian. London, 1901; (reprinted) Freeport, New York, Books for Libraries Press, 1970.
Tennyson (with G.K. Chesterton). London, Hodder & Stoughton, 1903; (reprinted) Philadelphia, R. West, 1978.
Coleridge. London, Bell, 1904; (reprinted) Folcroft, Pennsylvania, Folcroft Library Editions, 1972.
Letters about Shelley, Interchanged by Three Friends (with Edward Dowden and Wm. Michael Rossetti. London, 1917; (reprinted) New York, AMS Press, 1971.

Editor, *Tales and Stories* by Mary Shelley. London, Paterson, 1891.
Editor, *Nelson's Literature Readers.* London, Edinburgh, and New York, Thomas Nelson & Sons, 1904.

*

Critical Studies: *Richard Garnett: The Scholar as Librarian* by Barbara McCrimmon, Chicago, American Library Association, 1989.

*   *   *

Richard Garnett followed in the footsteps of his similarly-named father (1789-1850) in working for the library of the British Museum. From 1875 to 1884 he presided over the reading room, placing his legendary erudition at the disposal of visiting scholars; he eventually became the editor of the great catalogue which remains the foundation-stone of English bibliography. He edited many works for publication and produced several biographies and volumes of verse, as well as assembling the marvellous short stories and satirical fables which he wrote as *jeux d'esprits* in a vividly brilliant collection, *The Twilight of the Gods,* which is quite without compare in the annals of English fantasy. The 12 stories added to the second edition (making 28 in all) include only a handful written after publication of the first volume, and are mostly inferior to the original selection, although "Alexander the Ratcatcher"—which was first published in the *Yellow Book* in 1897—is a striking exception and there is no item in the expanded collection which does not fully deserve its preservation.

The stories in *The Twilight of the Gods* may be seen as an extrapolation into English literature of an extraordinarily rich tradition of French fantasy fiction which had then extended from the *contes philosophiques* of Voltaire and the satires of Jacques Cazotte through the *contes* and *nouvelles* of Charles Nodier and Théophile Gautier to the sophisticated pagan fantasies of Anatole France and the *contes cruels* of Villiers de l'Isle Adam. Garnett's tales borrow motifs from Classical fantasy and the ideologically mythologized history of Christianity, deploying them in ironic fables which champion Epicurean humanism against Puritan intolerance with sarcastic wit, unrepentant whimsicality, calculated bizarrerie and consummate charm. Nothing similar had been attempted in English since the tragic curtailment of John Sterling's promising career half a century earlier, although Garnett's example presumably helped to inspire his near-contemporary Vernon Lee to produce those of her fantasies which are of a similar ilk.

The title-story of the collection sets the mood by describing the career of Prometheus following his liberation from the terrible fate to which he was condemned by the tyrannical Olympians, whose authority has collapsed. He takes up residence with the last priestess of Apollo, taking on the protective coloration of a superficial Christianity while preserving a more tolerant philosophy of life. A similar elegiac tone is found in "The Dumb Oracle," in which Apollo stands in for one of his priests who cannot tolerate the use of deception in the management of an oracle, and in the fable "Pan's Wand". Apollo also takes a hand in the ironic tale of "The Poet of Panopolis," in which he opposes a demon in trying to establish a candidate for a vacant bishopric.

It is not only Christianity which is criticized in *The Twilight of the Gods* as a source of intolerance; the perils of apostolic responsibility are also examined in "Abdallah the Adite" and "Ananda the Miracle-Worker," and extremist tendencies in secular philosophy are scathingly exposed in a hilarious account of an attempt by Plotinus to found a Platonic republic in "The City of the Philosophers". It is, however, the more colourful aspects of Christian mythology which provide Garnett with his most striking materials. "The Demon Pope" is an amusing development of one of several Medieval tales of devil-led popes. "The Bell of St. Euschemon" is a delightful tale in which a saint becomes friendly with the demon inhabiting a miraculous church-bell. "The Claw" is an ironically ghoulish tale of an unusual diabolical pact. "Alexander the Ratcatcher" is a baroque account of the Borgia pope returning to Rome to buy absolution from one of his successors with a promise to alleviate a plague of rats. "Madam Lucifer" reveals the true power behind the throne of Hell.

Insofar as they are allegorical, the most consistent theme of Garnett's tales is to do with the vanity of human wishes. In "The Elixir of Life" the sage Aboniel offers his students a gamble against death, in which the elixir of immortality is contained in one of seven phials whose counterparts contain deadly poisons. "Pan's Wand" and "The Firefly" are both tales in which serial metamorphoses fail to deliver a satisfactory state of being. "The Poison Maid" is an acknowledged but accidental recapitulation of Nathaniel Hawthorne's "Rappaccini's Daughter". The early fable "A Page from the Book of Folly," the visionary fantasy "The Talismans," and the formal allegories "Truth and her Companions" and "The Three Palaces" all take some trouble to celebrate the dubious advantages of illusion. This tendency is extrapolated to scaldingly sarcastic limits in such dark-edged parables as "The Wisdom of the Indians" and "Duke Virgil." Like all the best fantasy, therefore, Garnett's work is cautionary as well as celebratory; it warns against the myriad inappropriate employments of the human imagination while stoutly insisting on the life-enhancing necessity of its proper exercise.

The Twilight of the Gods is a book for connoisseurs of fantasy. It exhibits the aesthetics of exoticism to finer advantage than any other single volume. Its influence can be clearly seen in the work of numerous later fantasists, perhaps most significantly in the short stories of Lord Dunsany, the Epicurean fantasies of Eden Phillpotts

and the delicate fabulations of Kenneth Morris, but none of these later writers manifested quite the same precious alloy of erudition, wit and literary elegance. The Bodley Head edition of 1924, illustrated by Henry Keen, is an extraordinarily handsome volume, more prized as a collectors' item than any of the earlier editions.

—Brian Stableford

GARRETT, (Gordon) Randall

Pseudonyms: Darrell T. Langart; Mark Phillips; Robert Randall. **Nationality:** American. **Born:** Lexington, Missouri, 16 December 1927. **Education:** Texas Tech University, Lubbock, B.S. **Military Service:** United States Marine Corps during World War II: Corporal. **Family:** Married Vicki Ann Heydron. **Career:** Industrial chemist, Battle Creek, Michigan, and Peoria, Illinois: then freelance writer. **Died:** 31 December 1987.

FANTASY PUBLICATIONS

Novels (series: Lord Darcy)

Pagan Passions, with Larry M. Harris. New York, Beacon, 1959.
Too Many Magicians (Darcy). New York, Doubleday, 1967; London, Macdonald, 1968.

Novels with Vicki Ann Heydron (series: Gandalara in all books)

The Steel of Raithskar. New York, Bantam, 1981.
The Glass of Dyskornis. New York, Bantam, 1982.
The Bronze of Eddarta. New York, Bantam, 1983.
The Well of Darkness. New York, Bantam, 1983.
The Search For Kä. New York, Bantam, 1984.
Return to Eddarta. New York, Bantam, 1985.
The River Wall. New York, Bantam, 1986.
The Gandalara Cycle: Volume 1 (omnibus; includes *The Steel of Raithskar, The Glass of Dyskornis, The Bronze of Eddarta*). New York, Bantam, 1986.
The Gandalara Cycle: Volume 2 (omnibus; includes *The Well of Darkness, The Search For Kä, Return to Eddarta*). New York, Bantam, 1986.

Short Stories (series: Lord Darcy)

Takeoff! Virginia Beach, Donning, 1979.
Murder and Magic (Darcy). New York, Ace, 1979.
Lord Darcy Investigates (Darcy). New York, Ace, 1981.
Lord Darcy (omnibus; includes *Too Many Magicians, Murder and Magic, Lord Darcy Investigates*). New York, Nelson Doubleday, 1983.
Takeoff Too. Virginia Beach, Donning, 1987.

OTHER PUBLICATIONS

Novels

The Shrouded Planet (as Robert Randall, with Robert Silverberg). New York, Gnome Press, 1957.

The Dawning Light (as Robert Randall, with Robert Silverberg). New York, Gnome Press, 1959.
Brain Twister (as Mark Phillips, with Laurence M. Janifer). New York, Pyramid, 1962.
Unwise Child. New York, Doubleday, 1962; London, Mayflower, 1963; as *Starship Death,* New York, Leisure, 1982.
Anything You Can Do . . . (as Darrell T. Langart). New York, Doubleday, and London, Mayflower, 1963; as *Earth Invader,* New York, Leisure, 1983.
The Impossibles (as Mark Phillips, with Laurence M. Janifer). New York, Pyramid, 1963.
Supermind (as Mark Phillips, with Laurence M. Janifer). New York, Pyramid, 1963.

Short Stories

The Best of Randall Garrett, edited by Robert Silverberg. New York, Pocket Books, 1982.

Other

Pope John XXIII, Pastoral Prince. Derby, Connecticut, Monarch, 1962
A Gallery of the Saints. Derby, Connecticut, Monarch, 1963.

*   *   *

Although a prolific writer, with several hundred stories to his credit, many under pseudonyms, Garrett is probably best remembered for his series of stories about Lord Darcy. Darcy is the Investigator-in-Chief for the Court of King John in an alternate England where Richard the Lion-Hearted did not die in 1199 but went on to establish a mighty Angevin Empire which has lasted to the present day. In this alternate world magic is a science, and its rules are codified, but the full laws of physics have yet to be established. Darcy works with his forensic sorcerer Sean O Lochlainn, who uses scientific means (within the rules of his world) to solve crimes.

The Lord Darcy series was the first to combine successfully fantasy, science fiction and mystery. Indeed all of the stories are primarily mysteries set in an alternate science-fantasy world, and they are all intensely satisfying: the novel *Too Many Magicians* is regarded by many as one of the best locked-room mysteries ever written. Intriguingly, but perhaps appropriately, the series began in that most stoic of science fiction magazines, *Analog,* whose editor, John W. Campbell, Jr., had almost single-handedly created modern science fiction in the 1940s. Campbell had a predilection for stories involving psychic powers, and Garrett was one of his most prolific contributors using that theme. Campbell thus encouraged Garrett to explore a magical world on a scientific premise. "Magic," Campbell proclaimed, "approached as a logical, laws-of-nature system, is not fantasy—it's science fiction." Yet this series, a child of science fiction, sired by mystery, is at its heart fantasy.

The series began with "The Eyes Have It" (*Analog,* January 1964), in which a murder is committed by black magic, and ran intermittently through to "The Napoli Express" (*Isaac Asimov's SF Magazine,* April 1979). Throughout, Garrett, who was one of fantasy's best parodists, would mirror well-known mystery characters or plots, particularly those of Agatha Christie, Rex Stout, Dorothy L. Sayers, John Dickson Carr and, of course, Arthur Conan Doyle. But Garrett didn't simply borrow ideas, he would heavily embroider them and, with remarkable finesse, adapt them seamlessly to his alternate world. His irrepressible humour and ability to pun was never far away, and the later stories in the series are rather more

shamelessly imitative, though they are also arguably the better written. After Garrett's death the series was continued by Michael Kurland: these stories are clever, but lack Garrett's sparkle and panache.

Garrett had sold his first story in 1944, though did not begin writing regularly until 1952. Because only a small percentage of his short fiction has been reprinted (and that mostly his humorous parodies in the two *Takeoff!* volumes) his writing is more closely linked with science fiction. Yet some of his earliest stories appeared in *Fantasy Magazine, Mystic* and *Beyond,* and during the 1950s and early 1960s he regularly contributed to *Fantastic,* often in collaboration with Robert Silverberg. Most of this was admittedly hackwork, but Garrett's inventiveness usually made the stories bright and readable, as in "The Mummy Takes a Wife" (*Fantastic,* December 1956, as Clyde Mitchell, with Robert Silverberg) in which a mummy comes back to life on board ship, and "The Trouble With Magic" (*Fantastic,* March 1959) in which a girl summons a demon to help her solve a crime. This latter story was an early example of Garrett developing his treatment of magic as a science. Unfortunately it also includes the howler of referring to Alistair Cooke in mistake for Aleister Crowley. It is to this same period that *Pagan Passions,* written with Larry M. Harris, belongs. This is an erotic fantasy in which the Greek gods return to a high-tech future.

Garrett's best story from this period is the unfairly neglected "A Fortnight of Miracles" (*Fantastic,* February 1965). Set in a medieval fantasy world, and told in good humour, it concerns a knight accursed with invisibility and a sorcerer who helps him return to normal. Later fantasies of note are "Something Rich and Strange" with Avram Davidson (*F & SF,* June 1961) about a mermaid; the charming Celtic fantasy "The Final Fighting of Fion Mac Cumhaill" (*F & SF,* September 1975); and "The Horror Out of Time" (*F & SF,* March 1978), a spoof on H. P. Lovecraft's "Dagon" which succeeds in being chilling on its own merits.

It was a tragedy that Garrett, who had a phenomenal memory and a sharp wit, contracted meningitis in 1979, resulting in a near complete loss of memory and a slow and debilitating death. He had married his third wife, Vicki Ann Heydron, in 1978 and together they had plotted the Gandalara science-fantasy series, though it was Heydron who did the writing. The series, which was well received, is in the style of Edgar Rice Burroughs, and features a university professor who finds himself transferred into an alien body on the desert-world of Gandalara. They may contain some of Garrett's ideas but the books are essentially Heydron's.

—Mike Ashley

GASKELL, Jane

Nationality: British. **Born:** Grange-over-Sands, Lancashire, 7 July 1941. **Family:** Married Gerald Lynch in 1963 (divorced 1968); one daughter. **Career:** Feature writer for the *Daily Mail,* London, 1965-84. **Awards:** Somerset Maugham prize, 1971. **Agent:** Sharland Organization, 9 Marlborough Crescent, London W4 1HE, England.

FANTASY PUBLICATIONS

Novels (series: Atlan)

Strange Evil. London, Hutchinson, 1957; New York, Dutton, 1958.

King's Daughter. London, Hutchinson, 1958; New York, Pocket, 1979.
The Serpent (Atlan). London, Hodder and Stoughton, 1963; New York, Paperback Library, 1968; in two vols. as *The Serpent* and *The Dragon,* New York, St. Martin's Press, 1977; London, Futura, 1985.
The Shiny Narrow Grin. London, Hodder and Stoughton, 1964.
Atlan. London, Hodder and Stoughton, 1965; New York, Paperback Library, 1968.
The City (Atlan). London, Hodder and Stoughton, and New York, St. Martin's Press, 1966.
A Sweet, Sweet Summer. London, Hodder and Stoughton, 1969; New York, St. Martin's Press, 1972.
Some Summer Lands (Atlan). London, Hodder and Stoughton, 1977; New York, St. Martin's Press, 1979.

OTHER PUBLICATIONS

Novels

Attic Summer. London, Hodder and Stoughton, 1963; New York, Paperback Library, 1966.
The Fabulous Heroine. London, Hodder and Stoughton, 1965.
All Neat in Black Stockings. London, Hodder and Stoughton, 1966.
Summer Coming. London, Hodder and Stoughton, 1972.
Sun Bubble. London, Weidenfeld and Nicolson, 1990.

Plays

Screenplay: *All Neat in Black Stockings,* with Hugh Whitemore, 1969.

*

Film Adaptation: *All Neat in Black Stockings,* 1969.

Jane Gaskell comments:

Fantasy is a special part of life as well as of literature. Fairy tale is, apparently, necessary to us as a species.

*   *   *

Jane Gaskell's writing career started at its peak: her first novel, *Strange Evil,* is a remarkable work. Judith, perhaps in her early 20s, is startled when her unknown cousin Dorinda, daughter of an estranged aunt, suddenly arrives in London with a fiancé in tow. Immediately it is clear that Dorinda and Zameis are somehow otherworldly, and soon Judith realizes they and various other "people" she encounters in their company are fairies—although neither the twee pixies of Victorian children's books nor the darker entities of tradition. They take her to fairyland, an alternate world contiguous with but mutually invisible to ours, accessible *via* various points of overlapping between the two worlds—the one they use is at the apex of Notre Dame's dome. Travelling *via* a moving silver belt across the fairy world's sky, they reach the Mountain, Dorinda's and Zameis's home. Outside the Mountain, banished by its occupants as adherents of an outmoded religion, "lesser" races are in terminal decline because they have been barred from the Mountain's life-giving heart. Inside, there is a sex-based culture—a sort of promiscuitocracy—and a religion centred on a reified god,

Baby; Judith finds also Demmimodica, evil genius of the Mountain folk, and Enaj, who, against the trend, wishes the external communities to be permitted access to the fount of life. Plots and battles ensue, Judith winning the day and a life of love with Enaj by destroying Baby—who is tantrumishly tyrannous, like any baby, but vast—through ridiculing him rather than, as everyone else, revering him.

The vividness of *Strange Evil* is hard to describe: though the book is full of flaws, it has the feel—like, say George MacDonald's *Lilith* (1895) or David Lindsay's *A Voyage to Arcturus* (1920)—of being at the head of a new tradition of fantasy writing. There are countless flashes of brilliance in both writing (". . . ten or twelve trees which awed her as nothing had done before. It took her three looks to see the top of them") and realization (Demmimodica's hall is of impossible opulence when he is there but a cesspool of decay in his absence; among the fairy world's denizens are wraithish entities that gain sexual gratification through feeding on the nonsexual emotions of "mortals"). But the publisher's decision to focus on Gaskell's age (14 at time of writing, 16 by publication), commercially shrewd in 1957, has effectively erased this major work of the fantastic imagination from histories of the genre.

King's Daughter, a swift successor, is far more consciously *written,* and at the same time less original—as if Charlotte Brontë had taken over from Emily. About 200,000 years ago, when the world has lost its first moon but not yet gained its current one, Bulinga, daughter of a (deceased) Atlantean princess and the brutish king of backwater Grood (somewhere in today's Indochina), flees for the haven of her mother's homeland. She has picaresque adventures, many concerned with the preservation of her eagerly contested virtue; the tale can be regarded as one of mental sexual awakening, as her emotional fixations shift from pretty youths to interesting men. She dies having failed to attain both Atlan (Atlantis) and sexual initiation.

Despite its setting, the novel contains little fantastication aside from the presence of technological debris from a lost, even earlier age. The same glittery perceptiveness that permeated *Strange Evil* persists: ". . . the filth [did not] transfer itself to his elegant garments. . . . There was always a distance between him and what he was near."

Gaskell then wrote several sex comedies, of which her next fantasy, *The Shiny Narrow Grin,* is one: heroine is picked up by handsome vampire; lots of trendy promiscuity ensues. Her serious return to the genre came with the Atlan Saga—so-called not because it is set in Atlan (less than one-quarter is) but because Atlan represents, as for Bulinga in *King's Daughter,* an unattainable *idée fixe*: outsiders can conquer and colonize Atlan, but cannot *reach* it. (The saga is set in Bulinga's world and age, but on the far side of the Pacific; an artist called Scridol from *King's Daughter* appears in *Some Summer Lands.*)

The first three volumes are narrated by the incarnate goddess Cija, daughter of the Dictatress of an obscure South American nation and its supposedly celibate High Priest. Her birth ill-omened, she was secreted in a bleak tower. Now that she is 17, though, her mother releases her to seduce and murder the half-reptile General Zerd, who is bloodily carving his way towards the mighty, vacuum-shielded continent of Atlan. Cija eventually seduces him but cannot kill him, for she loves as well as hates him. Whenever estranged or distanced from Zerd, she engages in another love-hate union—with her half-brother, Smahil. Her sex life throughout is further complicated by rapes, one-night stands and, much later, expedient marriage to a psychopath.

The Serpent sees her progress, in parallel with but rarely together with Zerd, across South America and finally to Atlan, where she arrives to bring warning of his conquering intentions only to find he has already taken control. In *Atlan,* now married to Zerd, she is installed as Empress, but soon—Sedili, his amazonian first wife, having arrived with her own horde—exiled to a remote castle (whose attics are occupied by a former-day Frankenstein complete, in due course, with lumbering Monster), whence her further downfall—complete with obligatory rape—is inevitable. She, like all outlanders, is rejected by Atlan—not just by its heartland aboriginals, collectively called Ancient Atlan, but by the land ("'You would love it [the landscape] if it let you,' Nal muttered"). Yet her elder child Nal is accepted—as its new, true Emperor—because, fathered by Smahil, he represents an incestuous union of god-lines. *The City* finds Cija, with toddler daughter Seka (fathered by Zerd), back in her mother's dictatorship. She works her way up from squalid anonymity, but is seized by cannibalistic apemen, with one of whom, Ung-g, she finds true, if inarticulate, love. "Rescued," she alone knows she is pregnant by Ung-g.

It was an odd ending for a trilogy. The series' 1977 reissue (with *The Serpent* split as *The Serpent* and *The Dragon*) saw the publication of an addendum, *Some Summer Lands.* Focus and narrator are now Seka, Cija's daughter; earlier Seka vacillated oddly between babyhood and toddlerhood, but here she is a precocious little girl. She and Cija undergo diverse adventures before being rescued to a now-welcoming Atlan by the charismatic Juzd, representative of Ancient Atlan. Large tracts of this fascinatingly bad book are suffused with a bizarre school-playground sex-obsession, orgasms and genitalia lurking everywhere ("Sedili rolled herself a cheroot and tamped it hard on her clitoris, which stood up ready to be of use")—as if Gaskell were aiming for pornography but balking at eroticism. Nauseatingly, child-molesting is treated as if rather jolly. Yet there are also sections in which Gaskell seems at last to have become *interested* in her Atlantean epic: in a lengthy central anti-pastoral she weaves traditional threads (an idiot savant fisherman who hates the sea and his catch; a psychopath and his grandmother who lure guests and then despatch them *via* a trick bed) to produce tale-telling of a vibrancy unattained since *Strange Evil.*

All four volumes share preoccupations: the relationship between people and their surrounding, sentient landscape; the need for heroines ceaselessly to escape frying-pans and fall into fires; a suckling-fixation. Strongest is the regard for animals: prized above horses for riding are giant, often vicious, birds; Cija finds her only true, unforced love with an ape; in *The Serpent* a mysterious white puma figures occasionally, its appearances clearly having colossal impact on Cija (and presumably on her creator) yet none on the plot; in *Atlan* the Yulven (wolves) combine primeval savagery with psychic sophistication and thus embody Ancient Atlan. And, of course, there is the half-animal Zerd himself, together with his more animal brothers: Zerd's beastness contributes greatly to his portrayed sexual magnetism, right down to reptilian loin-prongs that hold females in place during coition.

The close of *Some Summer Lands* indicates more to follow, but Gaskell has since eschewed fantasy (a later novel, *Sun Bubble,* contains a few paranormal events but is remorselessly realist). Riches are buried in all her books, but often too deeply. Perhaps, had *Strange Evil* been published as a novel rather than a freak, her literary career might have been gloriously more rewarding.

—John Grant

GEARY, Patricia (Carol)

Nationality: American. **Born:** Vista, California, 19 April 1951. **Education:** Vassar College, B.A.; University of California, Irvine, M.F.A. **Family:** Married Sherwood Armitage Hunter. **Career:** Instructor, Orange Coast Community College, Costa Mesa, California, 1976-78; instructor, Irvine Valley College, Irvine, California, 1978-81; assistant professor, Louisiana State University, Baton Rouge, 1981-87; assistant professor, University of Redlands, California, from 1987. **Awards:** Philip K. Dick award, 1988. **Agent:** Virginia Barber Literary Agency, 353 West 21st Street, New York, NY 10011, USA.

FANTASY PUBLICATIONS

Novels

Living in Ether. New York, Harper, 1982.
Strange Toys. New York, Bantam, 1987; London, Corgi, 1990.

*   *   *

Patricia Geary's two fantasy novels are based in the mysticism of New Age philosophies and earlier occult belief systems. If the books by Geary are to be classified with any earlier fantasy works, they would probably best be considered part of the spiritually inclined writings of authors such as Marie Corelli who explored occult mysteries to help explain the meaning of life. Comparisons are also possible with more contemporary books, including the New Age nonfiction of actress Shirley MacLaine. Geary's work, however, does not try to explain so much as illustrate the investigation of such metaphysical matters by the characters in her books.

Living in Ether, Geary's first published work, received considerable critical attention. Its plot and theme seem to typify the California-mellow lifestyle of recent decades. The heroine, Deirdre Gage, is a psychic with a troubled past who broods about the suicide of her brother Robert some years earlier. Didi's relationship with her parents was odd, and at the start of the book she appears to be alone in the world. But the spirit of Robert communicates with her, and her spiritual contacts hint obliquely that Didi must come to terms with her past. A new psychic client, Brandon, exerts a powerful attraction for Didi, and she agrees to contact the spirit of the Japanese writer Yukio Mishima (a real person) who committed ritual suicide with his lover. Told in the first person, Didi's somewhat reluctant search for self is composed of memories, mysterious messages from the spirit world, dreams and some action on her own. A visit to another psychic provides faint clues, as does a trip to her estranged mother. It is revealed that Didi and Robert had been incestuous lovers as well as close friends and ballet partners. In the final scene, Didi agrees to re-enact Mishima's suicide with her client, now lover, Brandon. But although readers are led to believe the suicide will be for real, it is merely playacting that Brandon wants.

Geary's second book, *Strange Toys,* is something of a variation on *Living in Ether.* In this story, the protagonist, Pet, also is the narrator. The scene focuses more on New Orleans than California as a setting, and on voodoo rather than psychic messages as a device, but the overall theme is very similar to Geary's first book. Divided roughly into three parts, the novel tells about Pet as a child, then as a teenager, and finally as an adult. Pet's family is as dysfunctional as Didi's, with the strangest member being her oldest sister, Deane, who dabbles in voodoo and specializes in being a thoroughly bad teenager. The first part of novel deals with the family's unsuccessful search for runaway Deane. In the second part, Pet, the only survivor of her family's car accident, leaves her new home in California to look for Deane. In the final section, Pet, now an adult, finally discovers her sister as a melting shadow in a voodoo rite in the swamps.

Both novels have heavy overtones of mysticism and symbolism. They both contain humour as well, for the two female protagonists offer many wry comments on events. The details provided are sharp and good, such as Pet's obsession with her toy poodle collection as a child, and Didi's concern for "rightness" in all aspects of her daily life, such as the exact organization of her clothes' closet. Yet some of these details are overused, such as slimy snail tracks and Emeraude perfume. Obviously, these details have certain associations for the author, but with only two novels to examine, it's not easy to come up with any symbolism involved.

The books are permeated with an air of distance and off-centred personal relationships. Family dynamics are all-important, especially in *Strange Toys*. Friends are only a minor part of Pet's life even after her parents and sister June are killed. Didi seems removed from most living people, other than Brandon, and concentrates more on her communications with the spirits of the dead. Children's relationships with parents are unconventional; both sets of children call their parents by their first names, and the siblings have very close associations with each other. The personalities of the different characters are distinct, although the narrative tone of the two books seem oddly similar in style and purpose.

The female protagonists are both consumed with finding out certain things. Didi still broods about Robert until it appears that Brandon may take the place of her dead brother. Pet cannot forget her love-hate relationship with Deane. Pet also becomes a fanatic bodybuilder and weight lifter, but she finds physical strength alone cannot help her erase Deane's memory.

Writers are sometimes called "one-book authors" and it is possible that Geary is such an author with two versions of a single theme. Even so, these two works stand out because of their message and unusual approach.

—Cosette Kies

GEMMELL, David A(ndrew)

Pseudonym: Ross Harding. **Nationality:** British. **Born:** London, 1 August 1948. **Education:** Faraday Comprehensive School. **Family:** Married Valerie Gemmell; one son, one daughter. **Career:** Worked for Pepsi Cola, London, 1965; reporter and editor, *Westminster Press,* London, 1966-72; editor, *Hastings Observer,* 1976; editor, *Folkestone Herald,* 1984. Since 1986, full-time writer. **Address:** 180 Mill Lane, Hastings TN35 5EU, England.

Fantasy Publications

Novels (series: Drenai; Macedon; Sipstrassi)

Legend (Drenai). London, Century, 1984; as *Against the Horde,* Delavan, Wisconsin, New Infinities, 1988.

The King Beyond the Gate (Drenai). London, Century, 1985; Delavan, Wisconsin, New Infinities, 1988.
Waylander (Drenai). London, Century, 1986; Delavan, Wisconsin, New Infinities, 1988.
Wolf in Shadow (Sipstrassi). London, Century, 1987; as *The Jerusalem Man,* New York, Baen, 1988.
Ghost King (Sipstrassi). London, Century, 1988.
Last Sword of Power (Sipstrassi). London, Legend, 1988.
Knights of Dark Renown. London, Legend, 1989.
The Last Guardian (Sipstrassi). London, Legend, 1989.
The Lost Crown (for children). London, Hutchinson Children's, 1989.
Lion of Macedon. London, Legend, 1990; New York, Del Rey, 1992.
Quest for Lost Heroes (Drenai). London, Legend, 1990.
The Dark Prince (Macedon). London, Legend, 1991.
Drenai Tales (omnibus; includes *Waylander, Legend, King Beyond the Gate* and an original short story). London, Legend, 1991.
Morningstar. London, Legend, 1992.
Stones of Power (omnibus; includes *Wolf in Shadow, Ghost King, Last Sword of Power* and *The Last Guardian*). London, Legend, 1992.
Waylander II: In the Realm of the Wolf. London, Legend, 1992.
Bloodstone (Sipstrassi). London, Legend, 1994.
Ironhand's Daughter. London, Legend, 1995.

Short Stories

The First Chronicles of Druss the Legend. London, Legend, 1993.
The Second Chronicles of Druss the Legend: Druss the Axeman. London, Legend, 1995.

Graphic Novels

Legend, adapted by Stan Nicholls, illustrated by Fangorn. London, Legend, 1993.
Wolf in Shadow, adapted by Stan Nicholls, illustrated by Fangorn. London, Legend, 1994.

Other Publications

Novel

White Knight, Black Swan (as Ross Harding). London, Arrow, 1993.

*   *   *

David Gemmell's first novel, *Legend,* coincided with a revival of interest in heroic fantasy at the beginning of the 1980s. The substantial readership it attracted has been built upon by 16 subsequent books (at time of writing), making him one of the UK's most popular authors in the genre.

Probably his best known, and consistently strongest-selling title, *Legend* has acquired the status of a contemporary classic in the fantasy adventure field, and it established themes that continue to influence his work. It is set in the dying days of the mighty Drenai empire, whose rulers, steeped in complacency and incompetence, fail to respond decisively when the northern warrior tribes of the Nadir unite against them. In seeking to appease charismatic Nadir leader Ulric, the Drenai succeed only in conveying their weakness and encouraging his ambitions. It reaches the point where all that stands between the Nadir hordes and the heart of empire is Delnoch

Pass. This is protected by a massive dros (fortress), but its vastly out-numbered defenders are plagued by hopelessness and poor leadership. It's left to a disparate assembly of individuals, not all immediately recognizable as heroic, to hold the pass and deny Chaos its triumph.

The novel's extensive cast embraces a broad range of types, mostly youthful or at least in their prime. But the principal player, Druss the Axeman, is nearing the end of his active life. A legendary figure (the book's title partly refers to him), he bears an awesome martial reputation. Now in his sixties, and subject to the ailments encroaching age brings, he has to put as much effort into mustering his own declining powers as mounting the defence. For him, time is as big an enemy as the Nadir. His internal contradictions—patriarchal, decent, stubborn, homicidal by turn—and the onset of his physical frailties, makes Druss considerably more rounded and believable than the average fantasy hero.

There is an audacity in presenting an old man as central to this kind of story. It breaks the rules. But it works perfectly in engaging the reader's sympathy. However Druss is so dominant it's easy to overlook the fact that the other characters are equally well drawn. Ulric, for example, is far from being a stereotypical villain. Like everyone else in the book, his personality is neither black nor white, but an amalgam of greys. He is certainly driven, but that doesn't necessarily make him evil. And he is allowed his nobility.

The depiction of its protagonists is one of *Legend's* major achievements, revealing a flair for characterization that has recurred in all Gemmell's succeeding novels. *Legend* also originated several motifs that remain pivotal to his work—the lone hero, often tortured by loss or doubt; the battle against advancing age; redemption found in pursuing seemingly lost causes; complex villains, and elite, usually mystical, groups. Likewise, the author's knowledge of military strategy, and ability to depict authentic one-on-one combat, first found expression in *Legend*.

The King Beyond the Gate continues the Drenai Saga begun by *Legend*. It takes place a century later and features Tenaka Khan, an outcast due to his mixed Drenai and Nadir parentage. As with *Legend*, we have the concept of strength in unity, an interesting villain in mad Emperor Ceska, and several mystical groups, including one whose members are past their prime (the tyranny of time again). There is also the implication that fate is as strong a motivating factor as free will. *King Beyond the Gate* definitely has value but lacks the raw power of its predecessor. *Waylander*, third in the Drenai Saga, is more satisfying. Following the assassination of the Drenai king, only Waylander the Slayer can prevent genocide at the hands of invading Vagrians. To do this he has to venture into Nadir territory to retrieve the fabled Armour of Bronze. Ironically, killer-for-hire Waylander was the man who murdered the king.

Waylander marked the point when all the themes touched upon in *Legend* started to come together in a totally coherent way. Deftly spaced climaxes, naturalistic dialogue and well-ordered pace add polish to a compelling narrative. But the following novel, *Wolf in Shadow*, provided a complete unity of content and style. The first in the Sipstrassi Tales series, it introduced the character Jon Shannow. Obsessed with finding Jerusalem, and his own salvation, he melancholically wanders the chaotic landscape of a world where civilization was destroyed 300 years before, when the Earth tilted on its axis. His woman taken for sacrifice, Shannow is pitted against immortal satanist Abaddon and his Hellborn army. Sipstrassi stones, fragments of meteorites conferring regenerative and magical powers on their possessors, act as an ingenious McGuffin. *Wolf in Shadow* is a terrifically entertaining adventure yarn.

Ghost King, the second Sipstrassi tale, takes place during the Roman occupation. In a reversal of *Legend*, the hero is a boy,

Thurso, caught in the machinations of an evil witch. His relationship with elderly wise man Culain recalls that between Arthur and Merlin, and there is an Excalibur-like Sword of Power. *Ghost King* reworks the Arthurian myth in a genuinely inventive way. The third Sipstrassi title, *Last Sword of Power*, is set against the Roman Empire's decline. Britannia faces a new threat from Goth chieftain Wotan's dark magic, and Roman-born Uther's alliance of tribes is the only opposition. But, true to form, Uther is an old man, struggling to hold together his fragmenting kingdom.

Knights of Dark Renown is a non-series novel. When a brotherhood of warriors, the Knights of the Gabala, enter a portal to a parallel world, one, Manannan, stays behind. Derided as the Coward Knight, he expunges his shame in a battle with evil. *The Last Guardian* returns to the Sipstrassi and brings back Jon Shannow, a particular favourite with Gemmell's readers. In a succession of superb action sequences Shannow faces a reptilian army admitted to his present via a gateway from the past. The fourth in the Drenai Saga, *Quest for Lost Heroes* has farm boy Kiall and Chareos the Blademaster lead a colourful company of fighters to free peasant slave girl Ravenna.

The two-volume Macedon series, *Lion of Macedon* and *Dark Prince*, are arguably Gemmell's most elegant and accomplished offerings to date. Presenting an alternative version of Ancient Greece, they tell of military genius Parmenion and protege the young Alexander, future architect of the world's greatest empire, who is possessed by a dark spirit that feeds on death and destruction. Cleverly melding real historical characters and events with imaginative extrapolation, and conveying a marvellous sense of period, the Macedon novels are among the finest heroic fantasies of recent years.

Non-series *Morningstar* is nearer to standard sword and sorcery, although its heroes, bandit Jarek Mace and bard Owen Odell, are impressive creations. Latterly, Gemmell has added to the mythos of *Waylander*, with *In the Realm of the Wolf*, and to the continuing adventures of Jon Shannow, with *Bloodstone*; while *Ironhand's Daughter* introduces a new series, the Pallides Saga. And the author has begun to relate the early adventures of his most remarkable and fondly regarded character in *The First* and *Second Chronicles of Druss the Legend*.

David Gemmell's facility with characters and ability to inject the stories with a truly mythic quality, his accessible prose and emphasis on universal concerns, have earned him an audience well beyond the confines of the genre. As a constructor of rousing fantasy adventures he has few peers.

—Stan Nicholls

GENTLE, Mary

Nationality: British. **Born:** Eastbourne, Sussex, 29 March 1956. **Education:** Attended high school in Hastings, Sussex. **Career:** Has worked as movie projectionist, clerk, and civil servant. **Address:** 29 Sish Lane, Stevenage, Hertfordshire SG1 3LS, England.

FANTASY PUBLICATIONS

Novels (series: White Crow)

A Hawk in Silver (for children). London, Gollancz, 1977; New York, Lothrop Lee, 1985.

Rats and Gargoyles (White Crow). London, Bantam Press, and New York, Roc, 1990.
The Architecture of Desire (White Crow). London, Bantam Press, 1991.
Grunts! London, Bantam Press, 1992.

Short Stories

Scholars and Soldiers. London, Macdonald, 1989.
Left to His Own Devices (White Crow). London, Orbit, 1994.

OTHER PUBLICATIONS

Novels

Golden Witchbreed. London, Gollancz, 1983; New York, Morrow, 1984.
Ancient Light. London, Gollancz, 1987; New York, New American Library, 1989.

Other

Editor, with Roz Kaveney. *The Weerde.* London, Roc, 1992.
Editor, with Roz Kaveney. *Villains!* London, Roc, 1992.
Editor, with Roz Kaveney. *The Weerde, Book 2.* London, Roc, 1993.

*   *   *

Although she had published a little-noticed juvenile fantasy in the late 1970s, what brought Mary Gentle to prominence during the 1980s was the two-novel sequence *Golden Witchbreed* and *Ancient Light.* These were essentially science fiction, telling of lost technologies on a "medieval" planet (Orthe) and of problems of cultural change and intrusive exploitation accompanying the revival of those technologies and the introduction of new ones.

The move from science fiction back to fantasy comes in the 1989 collection of stories, *Scholars and Soldiers.* Some of these are set on Orthe or on a comparable planet; but two of them, "Beggars in Satin" and "The Knot Garden," which between them fill almost half the book, break quite new ground, and in fact represent the beginning of Gentle's White Crow sequence of stories and novels.

In acknowledgments prefacing this collection Mary Gentle waves a hand in the direction of Ben Jonson, so indicating a debt to Jacobean drama and the masque, but starts by thanking George Hay "for telling me I ought to read Frances Yates' *The Art of Memory* and thus getting me hooked on Early Modern Science and things Hermetic". Those two stories introduce "things Hermetic," that is to say things pertaining to what throughout subsequent novels she terms *magia,* and to the symbolisms of ancient occult beliefs and practices. The vehicle for these is the "Invisible College," representative of renaissance Rosicrucianism. Of this the itinerant young woman Valentine (the White Crow) is a scholarly instrument, but is also a soldier, the two roles being incompatible only on the surface. She comes to the City where the gross and gigantic Lord Architect Casaubon builds, high above the slum River Quarter, his marble facades and plans his Miracle Garden of parterres, mazes and statues. This he creates, although himself untidy and gross of personal habit, as a perfection of ordered harmony. Nevertheless, it and the City are afflicted by plague, blight, earthquake and flood.

In "Beggars in Satin" it is the presence of the Invisible College and the magic of music of the common people, patterning macrocosm into microcosm, which arrests Chaos. In "The Knot Garden," it is Valentine (now the Lord Architect's Lady) who, after being translated to the sphere of the Star Demons, the Lords of the Shining Path, returns to a City overtaken by the crisis of revolution with the secret of celestial correspondences. She is thus able to bring humans and Star Lords into an accord as those gods materialize on Earth at the time of the Grand Conjunction of planets and of the Sun's eclipse. All of these arcane happenings are narrated in the oath-sprinkled style of Renaissance melodrama and are set in that City of marble facades, fountains, mud and squalor—from which Casaubon and Valentine finally depart, leaving it to the people.

To consider now a novel outside of the chronology of its writing, *The Architecture of Desire* is in certain of its themes a reprise of "The Knot Garden". In other respects it is a comparatively realistic story, still centred on a City, in this case a "skewed" 17th-century London, where Whitehall lies south of the River Thamys, opposite to the alleys of Northbankside. It is a London where a deposed Queen Carola maintains court, though within the regime of the female Protector, Olivia. Valentine and Lord-Architect Casaubon travel from their country house to London, he having been summoned by the Protector to attend to the rebuilding of the Cathedral of St. Sophia, which at every stage has been arrested by a blight on its stones and structure. A metaphysical freeze and snowfall was one of the symbolic "Knot Garden" manifestations; and the action of *The Architecture of Desire* is also affected by the physicality of an icy winter. It is a bleak novel, involving the expiations of three rapes, for one of which the White Crow incurs a guilt which her *magia,* practised vainly beneath the dome of the unfinished cathedral, cannot turn aside. A journeying escape, as at the end of "The Knot Garden," is the chosen way out.

Between "The Knot Garden" and *The Architecture of Desire* came *Rats and Gargoyles,* a huge, sprawling fantasy mixing gothic horror with Renaissance Neoplatonism. In it Casaubon and Valentine are again protagonists and a city is its setting. This city, at the heart of the world, has 36 districts in each of which there is a temple or Fane to its Decan—each Decan a ruler of ten degrees of the Great Zodiacal Circle. The earthly presence of the Decan is an amalgam of the organic and the stony inorganic, the gargoylish demons of chaos being their slaves and acolytes. The counter-principle is the New Temple of humanistic harmony, the conception of which is Casaubon's. The episodic structuring of the novel together with a style of dialogue sometimes difficult to disentangle, calls for concentrated reading, but its rewards lie in splendidly sustained imaginings such as Valentine's metamorphosis into White Crow as literal, if metaphysical, bird; the transformation of maggots into flower petals with the breaking of the domination of the Decans: and the description of the planned garden for the New Temple, identifying correspondences of macrocosm and microcosm in terms of proportion. (A "documentary" engraving, one of several, shows Heidelberg Castle's 17th-century gardens as a model.)

Mary Gentle's later humorous novel, *Grunts!,* could have been expected in the light of her continual preoccupation with things military and the martial arts. Less foreseeable was this uncompromising plunge into a fantasy of the Last Battle between Good and Evil, with sympathies weighted on the side of the evil orcs, fortuitously equipped with all the paraphernalia of the U.S. Marines—which is not to say that spells, and curses are not essential armour. It is parodic comic-book stuff, by turns grim and amusing.

War, the Thirty Years War, is the setting for "What God Abandoned," one of Mary Gentle's more recent short stories. It first appeared in *The Weerde,* one of a number of shared theme anthologies (another is *Villains!*) which she has co-edited, and is reprinted in *Left to His Own Devices.* In it a shape- and sex-changing long-life androgyne meets the young Descartes and Michael Maer in the siege-ruined city of Prague. This story epitomizes Mary Gentle's imaginative concentration on the man/woman soldier, on the splendours and miseries of combat, and on the construction of great palaces and gardens and the mysteries of which their forms may be symbolic—all consistent components of her major works of fantasy.

—K. V. Bailey

GILFOYLE, Keren

Nationality: British.

Fantasy Publications

Novels

A Shadow on the Skin. London, Headline, 1993.

*   *   *

Keren Gilfoyle's published fiction to date consists of one novel entitled *A Shadow on the Skin,* which, for a debut novel, was received with a good deal of acclaim.

The setting has a flavour of Renaissance Europe but is less important than the characters that live in it. The thrust of the story concerns the machinations of the Desaighnes family. In their heyday they had strong mental powers and could control others by the force of their will. They are tyrannical and wealthy. Now their abilities are waning due to inbreeding, and Halenne, the last of the Great Ones, recognizes that the future of the family lies with the half-breeds which have normally been killed at birth. Although members of the family still have the power, or Inheritance as it is called, it is blocked and cannot be freed—a factor that was useful at the start as it prevented untrained children from accidentally killing themselves and others. However, three of the children of Princess Guliey Varinss, a younger daughter of the Ordombriyen ruling house, and Sedriaan Desaighnes, still survive. Nikleis and Bekhet have been brought up and corrupted by the Family but the youngest, Tobias, has been raised by his mother to deny his Inheritance. Factors outside Halenne's control conspire to cause Tobias to flee with his mother back to her home country of Aparissa. Thus begins the chase that continues for most of the book, during which Tobias's powers are awakened by an encounter with an energy creature called a litchfire which fuses with him for its own survival.

The theme that runs throughout this book is Power. Halenne has it and can wield it, but despite what the Family is—and she is aware of all their depravities—she wishes the Desaighnes to continue to have that power when she is gone. Thus she wants Tobias, to train him and teach him to take on her mantle. Tobias however does not want power in any form. He has seen its corrupting influences, not least in his brother and sister. Both Nikleis and Bekhet see themselves as Halenne's successors though she recognises that they are too selfish to bring the Family back to its former glory—Nikleis is cruel for the sake of it and Bekhet uses her Inheritance to satisfy her personal lusts.

The power of faith is also important. Tobias's mother has always believed in the power of the Redeemer, a Christ-like figure who is the focus of religious belief in Aparissa, but whose religion has been outlawed in Desaighnes-controlled territory. During his flight, Tobias falls in with a priest and discovers that faith is not dead but conveys a different sort of power to its adherents—one that is universal and forward-looking rather than selfish and immediate.

Tobias has power thrust upon him and he has to learn that it is not all corrupting and that it is the wielder who must shape what power does. For much of the book he is running away from himself and from his power until he discovers that there is nowhere left to go. His power comes partly from his Inheritance and partly from the litchfire that has melded with him, thus giving him a greater potential than anyone else.

In the fens around Rysjek, where Tobias often fled in his childhood to escape his brother's bullying, lurks another power. This exists as a delicate balance between the people who dwell there and the old litchfire that guides them and protects the fens from invasion in return for food. The people are poor and have only a subsistence living but there is harmony. It is this that Tobias thinks he wants until he is driven out of the fens.

In this book, Keren Gilfoyle has managed to avoid many of the pitfalls that beset the paths of first novels. She had created a plausible world and sustains a credible plot, even though the chase goes on rather longer than necessary. Her characterisation is good, at its best when dealing with the stronger personalities within the Desaighnes family, less so with weaker ones such as Guliey Varinss. Tobias himself, though the focus of the novel, is much more of a blank sheet on which the picture is being drawn during the duration of the book as his romantic ideas of escaping into the fens, and then taking his mother home to a joyous reunion with her kin are shattered and from his sheltered naivety he has to build a new world picture.

One thing this novel lacks is the spontaneity that tends to come to longer established writers who have deadlines to meet. This has the feel of having been worked on long and lovingly and the result is definitely well crafted.

Gilfoyle's next novel (as yet unscheduled) will be a very different approach to fantasy. It is set partly in contemporary Britain, and partly in the fantasy world of Ambard. Laura, the principal character, was a child actress who starred in the film made from the book in which Ambard was first created. When they start talking of re-releasing the film, strange things begin to happen to Laura, including the disappearance of her daughter.

This is an author whose progress will be interesting to chart.

—Pauline Morgan

GILLILAND, Alexis A(rnaldus)

Nationality: American. **Born:** Bangor, Maine, 10 May 1931. **Education:** Purdue University, West Lafayette, Indiana, B.S. 1953;

George Washington University, Washington, D.C., M.S. 1963. **Military Service:** United States Army Presidential Honor Guard, 1954-56. **Family:** Married 1) Dorothea Cohle in 1959 (died 1991); two sons; 2) Elisabeth S. Uba in 1993. **Career:** Thermochemist, National Bureau of Standards, 1956-67, and chemist and specification writer, Federal Supply Service, 1967-82, both in Washington, D.C. Since 1982, freelance writer. Also a cartoonist. **Awards:** Hugo award, for art, 1980, 1983, 1984, 1985; John W. Campbell award, 1982. **Address:** 4030 Eighth Street South, Arlington, VA 22204, USA.

FANTASY PUBLICATIONS

Novels (series: Wizenbeak in all books)

Wizenbeak, illustrated by Tim Kirk. New York, Bluejay, 1986.
The Shadow Shaia. New York, Del Rey, 1990.
Lord of the Troll-Bats. New York, Del Rey, 1992.

OTHER PUBLICATIONS

Novels

The Revolution from Rosinante. New York, Del Rey, 1981.
Long Shot for Rosinante. New York, Del Rey, 1981.
The Pirates of Rosinante. New York, Del Rey, 1982.
The End of the Empire. New York, Del Rey, 1983.

Other (cartoons)

The Iron Law of Bureaucracy. Port Townsend, Washington, Loompanics, 1979.
Who Says Paranoia Isn't "In" Any More? Port Townsend, Washington, Loompanics, 1984.
The Waltzing Wizard. Mercer Island, Washington, Starmont, 1989.

*   *   *

Alexis Gilliland writes humorous fantasies about serious subjects, treating issues of governance with an ironic touch. Sometimes his light tone clashes with his material, but he generally provides a clear-eyed view of what really goes on behind palace walls.

His fantasies are a series about Wizenbeak, a character who originally appeared in cartoon form. He is a magician and mountebank whose "specialties are water wizardry and card tricks." In fact, Wizenbeak performs little actual magic in the three books, leaving most of the work to his familiars, the troll-bats, who use power produced by others to perform amazing feats. What magic there is in the Wizenbeak books is carefully, almost scientifically, controlled; this is magic as designed by a science fiction writer.

The dissonance between Gilliland's humorous tone—humour supported by apparent anachronisms, with allusions to real-world figures from William Shakespeare to Spiro Agnew—and his subject matter is at its strongest in *Wizenbeak,* which deals with witch-burning and civil war, neither of which is a subject lending itself to a light touch. The conflict relaxes in *The Shadow Shaia* and *Lord of the Troll-Bats*; while both involve continued civil war and death, in neither is the material so unremittingly grim.

Gilliland is at his best writing of plots and counterplots and of the substance of ruling a kingdom. His books are truly political, not in the sense that they preach a point of view, but rather in that they are steeped in politics as a way of life. His humorous but clear explanations succeed in making even land reform an interesting subject, and his description of the ways the Church has gained and kept wealth and temporal power is both amusing and believable.

Wizenbeak goes through many changes in his life: starting as an obscure provincial water wizard and troll-bat handler at the beginning of *Wizenbeak,* he becomes head of a colonizing expedition, leads a civil war, and by the end of *The Shadow Shaia* is both Patriarch of the Syncretist Church and King of Guhland. Yet he changes little, except for adopting the royal "we": he remains a basically good person who chafes at the demands of politics yet knows he cannot ignore them, a reluctant leader bored by the details of policy.

The other characters tend to be undeveloped. The most baffling is that of Eilena Jankura, alias Janko. She goes from being a poor provincial maiden, to apprentice to Wizenbeak, to impersonator of the Witch-Queen Shaia, to troll-bat trainer, to avatar of Lady Alanji of the Flowers, but her inner self, if she has one, never comes clear. She seems to make all the changes effortlessly. The other characters tend to have one motivation each: Shaia's is to secure the throne for her son; Pardus Murado's is to preserve the church-soldiery called the Tarelian Order; Patriarch Gorabani's is to unseat Shaia, and then Wizenbeak, and thus increase the power of the Syncretist Church.

The troll-bats are a seemingly minor piece of window-dressing in the early part of the trilogy, but it gradually becomes clear that their importance has been underestimated by all, Wizenbeak especially. In *Lord of the Troll-Bats* we learn that these animals are in fact highly intelligent, at least in large enough groups, and that they have their own civilization on the other side of a mountain range where humans are kept as domestic animals and bred for docility and stupidity. This inversion of the accepted order is nothing new in the science fiction genre, but Gilliland interests us, not so much in the troll-bats themselves, as in the culture developed by the humans living under troll-bat domination. There is also a great irony, in that the humans were originally led to an accommodation with the troll-bats by a woman who sought an end to male domination.

For apparently light fantasies, the Wizenbeak books are remarkably cynical. Everyone in them, heroes and villains, at least sometimes follows the path of expediency, even killing for political reasons (though Wizenbeak himself usually kills only the villainous and feels bad about it afterward). Both church and state are corrupt to the core; the populace is easily roused to mob violence and happy to support the burning of witches and to denounce relatives and neighbours. It is only Gilliland's humour and the way in which Wizenbeak manages to steer things in the right direction that keep the books from being bleak.

In short, Alexis Gilliland writes light fantasy with a dark undertone—sometimes too dark. His books are cynical, and the endings are not unadulteratedly happy; the ending of *Lord of the Troll-Bats* is remarkably ambiguous. He writes of politics and the workings of government with a sense both of the real and of the ridiculous.

—Janice M. Eisen

GILLULY, Sheila

Nationality: American.

Fantasy Publications

Novels (series: Book of the Painter; Greenbriar Queen)

Greenbriar Queen. New York, Signet, 1988; London, Headline, 1989.
The Crystal Keep (Greenbriar Queen). New York, Signet, 1988; London, Headline, 1989.
Ritnym's Daughter (Greenbriar Queen). New York, Signet, 1989; London, Headline, 1990.
The Boy from the Burren (Painter). New York, Roc, 1990; London, Headline, 1991.
The Giant of Inishkerry (Painter). New York, Roc, and London, Headline, 1992.
The Emperor of Earth-Above (Painter). New York, Roc, and London, Headline, 1993.

*   *   *

Sheila Gilluly's first six novels are magical heroic fantasy, set in a world that is not only pseudo-medieval but also very familiar because most of its names and other details have been used by other fantasy writers (Tolkien in particular) or are taken directly from ancient Celtic society. She has tried to compensate for this lack of originality by a fast pace and the frequent introduction of new characters, details and dangers. Unfortunately, the results have been shallowness and reduced credibility.

The six books are all connected, in two trilogies. The Greenbriar Queen trilogy covers events ranging over almost 40 years in the kingdom of Ilyria. The Painter trilogy (written and published later though set some centuries earlier) details a handful of years of the early life of Aengus the Painter, a semi-mythic figure supposedly responsible for some of the magical artefacts appearing in the other trilogy.

Plot elements are almost entirely routine. Characters are kidnapped in almost every book; there are frequent quests by land or sea in search of kidnap victims or magical artefacts; there are frequent attacks upon individuals or groups of good characters especially by an evil god, Tydranth (using both supernatural and human agents). In all volumes the plots are advanced through alternating pieces of good and bad fortune and through revelations; all of these come too thick and fast to be believable.

There is far too much plot in the six books for it all to be recounted here. In brief, *Greenbriar Queen* tells of the deposing of the evil King Dendron of Ilyria and his powerful wizard Rasullis 20 years after they have seized the throne. Dendron's niece, Ariadne, raised as a farm girl and long thought dead, is enthroned. The restoration is accomplished mainly by a small group of the First Watch (troops still loyal to the old king, Ariadne's father). These include Captain Tristan, Peewit the Littleman, Kursh the dwarf and Imris who is both a minstrel and a Yoriandir (a green-skinned tribe who have power over trees). They form a kind of composite hero. There are two particularly memorable set-piece scenes. One is where Ariadne discovers that as the true heir to the Greenbriar throne her blood is able to react with a particular crystal to produce a magical

and instantly-growing briar rose with blue flowers, the hips of which can be distilled into an elixir to heal any ills. The other is where Ariadne visits the underworld, home of the gods (here known as Powers).

The Crystal Keep is set five years on, when Tydranth the evil Power tries to destabilize Ilyria by inciting the wolf-god Beldis to kill people, by breaking through the firmament that roofs the world and by causing the dwarf Kursh to attack Ariadne's consort Ka-Salin with an axe, killing him and wounding her toddler son, Gerrit. Ariadne is determined to have Kursh executed, but Peewit understands that Kursh was being controlled by a Power and helps him to escape to his (Kursh's) homeland of Jarlshof, where his family is famous for blowing glass crystal. In order to save her kingdom, Ariadne decides to travel to the Crystal Keep, the mythical abode on Earth of the Power Aashis, in the hope of renewing her magic crystal. She is accompanied by Alphonse, a young wizard who is in love with her. The over-dramatic ending is inconclusive, and this volume does not stand on its own.

Ritnym's Daughter is an even more complex re-run of *The Crystal Keep* another 13 years on, with Tydranth causing the neighbouring kingdom of Shimarrat to threaten invasion. Assassins are sent into Ilyria and plans are made to steal the magic crystal. But the loyal (though banished) Kursh returns to Ilyria as the ambassador from Jarlshof on the occasion of Gerrit's coming-of-age, and he brings Peewit with him. The crystal is stolen and both Kursh and Peewit are reinstated. Tydranth sends Shadows to kill people and Skinwalkers to impersonate them (notably Alphonse). After Ilyria seems lost—caught in permanent winter and affected by an incurable plague—all is eventually saved. Even Ariadne dies and is brought back to life. In a welter of fast plotting, with each twist or revelation less credible than the last, a happy ending is reached by the end of the book, with Gerrit King of Shimarrat and Ariadne still Queen of Ilyria.

One of Gilluly's major errors in this trilogy is that she uses the viewpoints of a couple of dozen or so characters, indiscriminately, paragraph by paragraph. The results are that the reader is often unsure whose thoughts are being used, none of the characters is properly developed, and there is a jerkiness in the flow of the story. There are several strong human-interest stories in this trilogy, yet Gilluly fails to present any of them properly because she chooses not to stay with the character most centrally involved. An entire novel could have been written about Kursh or Peewit or Ariadne or Alphonse or Gerrit.

In her other trilogy, Gilluly sensibly uses Aengus the Painter as her narrator throughout, though this does not prevent the books from being less satisfactory overall. *The Boy from the Burren* begins well, with Aengus as a deprived but streetwise 14-year-old being bought from his father by Bruchan, the leader of a sect of the Brothers of the Wolf, a peaceful commune inhabiting the island of Skellig Inishbuffin. Aengus has a talent as a painter, which means the illustrating of a storyteller's story as it is told, normally using coloured sands. But revelations come in bunches. Aengus is Bruchan's grandson and has a great destiny to fulfil, and everybody seems to know this. In particular, the evil Jorem, head of another group of Brothers of the Wolf, is so determined to kill or control Aengus that he attacks Skellig Inishbuffin. Only Aengus escapes.

The Giant of Inishkerry is set about four years later. Aengus is now a successful pirate, working with Timbertoe and his crew of dwarves. As the only person of normal height aboard the ship, the Inishkerry Gem, Aengus is known as "the giant of Inishkerry." The overcomplex plot is concerned with wise women (*siochlas*) and a vital ceremony of renewal. The most senior siochla or Maid of the Vale is kidnapped by Jorem, and Aengus and the pirates rescue her. The novel is hackneyed swords-and-sorcery fantasy with no development of Aengus towards the talented figure he is to become.

The Emperor of Earth-Above purports to continue the story of Aengus, yet it has little connection with anything that has gone before. Presumed dead, Aengus is sent off in a funeral boat, arrives at a tropical paradise without his memory and helps the locals to fight against their enemies. There is much long-winded mysticism, perhaps suggesting that Aengus is the reincarnation of an ancient hero, Colin the Mariner. Clearly this is not the end of the story of Aengus.

The settings and details throughout Gilluly's novels nearly all seem to have been borrowed. Names and countrysides are often recognizably Irish or Scottish. She has made some use, too, of fairy tales. Although there are good scenes and clever magical effects, either they are insufficiently developed (like the Yoriandir with their power over trees, or the rare and semi-mythical Littlemen) or they are rather too familiar.

Gilluly is a very competent descriptive writer, yet her ability to provide the right amount of information at the right time is poorly developed; time and again she makes some elements too obvious while leaving others unclear. Also, she has a tendency to call each of her characters by several different names or forms of address, making the reader's task unnecessarily difficult. Another problem is the tone of these novels. Much of *Greenbriar Queen* comes across to the reader as faintly comic because it concerns the bumbling attempts of ageing dwarves to play at being soldiers and heroes—as in the film *Time Bandits*. Elsewhere Gilluly has twee scenes featuring a talking cat and more than one talking mouse; such scenes are out of place in otherwise grim novels.

—Chris Morgan

GODWIN, Parke

Nationality: American. **Born:** 1929. **Awards:** World Fantasy award, 1982.

FANTASY PUBLICATIONS

Novels (series: Roman Britain; Robin Hood)

Firelord (Roman Britain). New York, Doubleday, 1980; London, Futura, 1985.
A Cold Blue Light, with Marvin Kaye. New York, Charter, 1983.
Beloved Exile (Roman Britain). New York, Bantam, 1984; London, Bantam, 1986.
The Last Rainbow (Roman Britain). New York, Bantam, 1985; London, Bantam, 1986.
A Truce With Time. New York, Bantam, 1988.
Sherwood (Robin Hood). New York, Morrow, 1991.
Robin and the King (Robin Hood). New York, Morrow, 1993.

Short Stories

The Fire When It Comes. New York, Doubleday, 1984.

Other

Editor, *Invitation to Camelot: An Arthurian Anthology of Short Stories.* New York, Ace, 1988.

OTHER PUBLICATIONS

Novels

Darker Places. New York, Popular Library, 1971.
A Memory of Lions. New York, Popular Library, 1976.
The Masters of Solitude, with Marvin Kaye. New York, Doubleday, 1978; London, Magnum, 1979.
Wintermind, with Marvin Kaye. New York, Doubleday, 1982; London, Futura, 1987.
Waiting for the Galactic Bus. New York, Doubleday, 1988; London, Bantam, 1989.
The Snake Oil Wars. New York, Doubleday, 1989.

*   *   *

Not to be confused with his 19th-century namesake, the current Parke Godwin is an actor and playwright who has contributed to the fields of mystery, fantasy, historical, supernatural and science fiction. Spreading his talent across all of these genres, and allowing for his fairly small output, it is easy for his work to be overlooked, but Godwin has not only established himself as a noted author of Arthurian novels, but also won the World Fantasy Award for his ghost story "The Fire When It Comes".

Although his first published work was the murder mystery *Darker Places,* Godwin rapidly became more associated with fantasies. This originated with a few stories in *Fantastic,* starting with "The Lady of Finnegan's Hearth" (1977). Here Isolde, of legend, is seen as a high-spirited Irish girl who died before her time and yearns to leave heaven. Consigned to hell she escapes and seeks love and excitement at the home of luckless widower Marty Finnegan. It's a lively story with the right level of humour. Godwin's next, "The Last Rainbow" (1978)—not to be confused with the later novel—is set in medieval England and tells of a young girl's encounter with two fairies. Both stories have a light touch about them, fantasies in the fairytale mode rather than dark suspense.

This lighter mood changed dramatically with the start of Godwin's trilogy set in the final days of Roman Britain. *Firelord* is the story of King Arthur, told by himself. It preceded Marion Bradley's *The Mists of Avalon* by two years, but in telling Arthur's story from his viewpoint rather than a female one, it allows us to experience more deeply his motives and dilemmas. What we see is a pragmatic Arthur living in the real world of Britain under threat from the Saxons. Although the whole of the legend from Malory is retold here, we have no chivalrous knights or quests. Instead we have Britain on the verge of collapsing under the Saxon onslaught, and Arthur seeking the realistic solution. It remains one of the most readable and logical of all Arthurian novels. It was a finalist for the 1981 World Fantasy Award.

It was followed by *Beloved Exile,* which picks up the narrative after Arthur's death, from the viewpoint of Guinevere. This novel, which clearly relies less on legend, has a stronger Celtic feel, probably as a result of a closer attachment to the period by Godwin following his painstaking research. We see Guinevere and the remnant knights struggling for identity in a world now dominated by the Saxons, seeking to hold the old kingdom together until betrayal sends Guinevere into bondage.

The final novel in this series is *The Last Rainbow,* which is not Arthurian, and is set several decades earlier. It tells of the early days of St. Patrick, or Padrec as Godwin calls him, before his mission to Ireland. Padrec is sent to convert the Picts in northern Britain and there encounters Dorelei, the Queen of Faerie. There is an even stronger Celtic atmosphere in this novel, as Godwin again explores the relationship between Christianity and paganism. He also uses the theme, in an afterword, to explore the parallels between the ancient Picts and the American Indians, both struggling to survive in a world that was now dancing to another tune.

Godwin brought the same understanding of loss of identity to his next series, featuring Robin Hood. Godwin had earlier written a novel set in Norman England, *A Memory of Lions,* and he returned to the period with *Sherwood* and *Robin and the King.* We are now in a world where the Saxon culture has been displaced by the Norman, and the old values have been overthrown. Robin struggles to live by the old code but has to recognize that the world has moved on. The fantasy element in these books, as in *Firelord* and *Beloved Exile,* is minimal but provides an undercurrent of otherworldliness to emphasize the change in cultures. Godwin's strength is in recreating these worlds and bringing the characters and their values to life.

Godwin's science fiction also has a fantastic basis: *Waiting for the Galactic Bus* and *The Snake Oil Wars* are developed from the concept that aliens have planted life on Earth, and reviewing it millennia later are dissatisfied with the outcome. Although the novels are undeniably science fiction, Godwin brings to them the almost Fortean feel that we are all but pawns in a cosmic game, and have no idea of the rules.

Godwin also has a talent for ghost stories. "The Fire When it Comes" (*Fantasy and Science Fiction,* 1981), which gave its title to Godwin's only collection of short fiction, is a powerful story about an actress who has committed suicide, but is brought back to an understanding of the world by a new inmate to her apartment who is sensitive to her presence. Godwin looked at the concept from another angle in "Influencing the Hell Out of Time and Teresa Golowitz" (*Twilight Zone,* 1982), in which a spirit is re-embodied and sent back in time to save the life of a suicide. As with long-lost cultures, Godwin also explores the theme of alienation with humans.

Godwin collaborated on a ghost novel with Marvin Kaye, *A Cold Blue Light,* about a haunted house and the influence of the spirit upon a range of characters. Godwin probably brought a more sensitive hand to this novel, strengthening the relationships between the people and the spirit. The sequel, *Ghosts of Night and Morning* (1987), is solely by Kaye and is far more violent.

Godwin has written one other ghost novel, *A Truce With Time,* labelled a contemporary love story. It has the same sensitivities as "The Fire When It Comes," and marks Godwin as an authentic writer of the supernatural as distinct from horror fiction.

—Mike Ashley

GOLDMAN, William

Pseudonym: Harry Longbaugh. **Nationality:** American. **Born:** Chicago, Illinois, 12 August 1931; brother of the writer James Goldman. **Education:** Highland Park High School; Oberlin College, Ohio, 1948-52, B.A. in English 1952; Columbia University, New York, 1954-56, M.A. in English 1956. **Family:** Married Ilene Jones in 1961 (divorced); two daughters. **Military Service:** Served in the United States Army, 1952-54: Corporal. **Awards:** Academy Award for screenplay, 1970, 1977. **Address:** 50 East 77th Street, New York, New York 10021, USA.

FANTASY PUBLICATIONS

Novels

The Princess Bride. New York, Harcourt Brace Jovanovich, 1973; London, Futura, 1988.
The Silent Gondoliers. New York, Ballantine, 1984.

OTHER PUBLICATIONS

Novels

The Temple of Gold. New York, Knopf, 1957.
Your Turn to Curtsy, My Turn to Bow. New York, Doubleday, 1958.
Soldier in the Rain. New York, Atheneum, and London, Eyre and Spottiswoode, 1960.
Boys and Girls Together. New York, Atheneum, 1964; London, Joseph, 1965.
No Way To Treat a Lady (as Harry Longbaugh). New York, Fawcett, and London, Muller, 1964; as William Goldman, New York, Harcourt Brace, and London, Coronet, 1968.
The Thing of It Is. . . . New York, Harcourt Brace, and London, Joseph, 1967.
Father's Day. New York, Harcourt Brace, and London, Joseph, 1971.
Marathon Man. New York, Delacorte Press, 1974; London, Macmillan, 1975.
Magic. New York, Delacorte Press, and London, Macmillan, 1976.
Tinsel. New York, Delacorte Press, and London, Macmillan, 1979.
Control. New York, Delacorte Press, and London, Hodder and Stoughton, 1982.
The Color of Light. New York, Warner, and London, Granada, 1984.
Heat. New York, Warner, 1985; as *Edged Weapons,* London, Granada, 1985.
Brothers. New York, Warner, and London, Grafton, 1986.

Uncollected Short Stories

"Something Blue," in *Rogue* (New York), 1958.
"Da Vinci," in *New World Writing 17.* Philadelphia, Lippincott, 1960.
"Till the Right Girls Come Along," in *Transatlantic Review 8* (London), Winter 1961.
"The Ice Cream Eat," in *Stories from the Transatlantic Review,* edited by Joseph F. McCrindle. New York, Holt Rinehart, 1970.

Plays

Blood, Sweat and Stanley Poole, with James Goldman (produced New York, 1961). New York, Dramatists Play Service, 1962.
A Family Affair, with James Goldman, music by John Kander (produced New York, 1962).
Butch Cassidy and the Sundance Kid (screenplay). New York, Bantam, and London, Corgi, 1969.
The Great Waldo Pepper (screenplay). New York, Dell, 1975.

Screenplays: *Masquerade,* with Michael Relph, 1964; *Harare (The Moving Target)*, 1966; *Butch Cassidy and the Sundance Kid*, 1969; *The Hot Rock (How to Steal a Diamond in Four Uneasy Lessons)*, 1972; *The Stepford Wives,* 1974; *The Great Waldo Pepper*, 1975; *All the President's Men*, 1976; *Marathon Man*, 1976; *A Bridge Too Far*, 1977; *Magic*, 1978; *The Princess Bride*, 1987; *Heat*, 1987; *Misery*, 1990; *Memoirs of an Invisible Man*, with Robert Collector and Dana Bodner, 1992.

Television Film: *Mr. Horn,* 1979.

Other

The Season: *A Candid Look at Broadway.* New York, Harcourt Brace, 1969; revised edition, New York, Limelight, 1984.
Wigger (for children). New York, Harcourt Brace, 1974.
The Story of "A Bridge Too Far." New York, Dell, 1977.
Adventures in the Screen Trade: *A Personal View of Hollywood and Screenwriting.* New York, Warner, 1983; London, Macdonald, 1984.
Wait Till Next Year: *The Story of a Season When What Should've Happened Didn't and What Could've Gone Wrong Did,* with Mike Lupica. New York, Bantam, 1988.
Hype and Glory. New York, Villard, and London, Macdonald, 1990.

*

Critical Study: *William Goldman* by Richard Andersen, Boston, Twayne, 1979.

*   *   *

Though William Goldman is best known as a mainstream novelist and screenwriter, he has written one delightful work which may be claimed as a fantasy novel, *The Princess Bride* (jokingly subtitled "S. Morgenstern's Classic Tale of True Love and High Adventure . . . The 'good parts' version abridged by William Goldman"). He has also written a sequel, or companion novel, to that work, entitled *The Silent Gondoliers*, and has contributed another novel, *Magic,* to the horror genre. He has also adapted notable works of fantasy and the macabre by other writers (Ira Levin, Steven King) to the big screen.

The words "rollicking" and "swashbuckling" might have been invented to describe *The Princess Bride,* yet in it Goldman also manages to satirize New York life, the publishing industry, critics, and the whole fantasy genre. Along the way he pulls off a feat of alienation that would have made Bertolt Brecht proud. He does this by pretending that he is presenting the "good parts" version of an older book—*The Princess Bride* by S. Morgenstern—based on the true story of Buttercup and Westley, two citizens of the ancient mid-European country of Florin. This version, he tells us in an extended introduction that also purports to explain how he became a writer, is an abridgment he has made to get rid of the longueurs in which Morgenstern satirized Florinese society. Goldman "replaces" them with bridging sections that speak directly to the reader, if not in Goldman's own voice, then surely in one close to it. Without these bridging passages, *The Princess Bride* would have been merely excellent. With them, it is a *tour de force.* Cynical and bitter in places, at times they are also at least as funny as anything in the story proper.

Ostensibly, their purpose is to allow Goldman to condense some of the narrative, while commenting on it at the same time. In a round-about way, this has the same effect as Morgenstern's original version would have had, if it had ever existed—it lets us know what the writer thinks of a hidebound, class-ridden society. For instance, Goldman spends a page explaining that he has cut out 56 pages of Morgenstern's descriptions of various noble ladies packing and unpacking. Whether Goldman intended it or not, these passages also act as little tutorials on the art of narrative pacing and plotting that would repay study by any aspiring writers in his audience. His comments on publishing are even more illuminating.

Though there are fewer of them, the most powerful bridging sections are the ones that show us the author's relationship with his father, and with his own work. The sections where Goldman describes how his father read to him as a child are especially moving. To what extent they have been fictionalized is unclear: they are described with unrelenting naturalism, but Goldman Senior is presented as a Florinese expatriate. Their power comes, at least in part, from Goldman's refusal to sentimentalize or idealize, while at the same time commenting from an adult perspective on his own behaviour and that of his father.

None of this would count for much if the story it supported wasn't so strong. In fact, even taken alone it is an immensely enjoyable romp. Essentially it's the one about the beautiful common girl forced into a marriage with a wicked prince until she is rescued by her one true love, a farm boy. Along the way, he first has to defeat the mercenaries who have kidnapped her, then turn them into allies. Only with their help is he finally able to defeat the evil prince who is the true enemy. Within this framework, Goldman manages to move seamlessly from high farce—for instance, most of Fezzik's scenes, or those with Max the Miracle Man—to true pathos, as when Buttercup finally realizes how she has been tricked by Humperdinck. In passing he manages some moments of true tension: the fight on the Cliffs of Insanity, for instance, and the scene where Buttercup agrees to marry Humperdinck as long as he promises not to harm Westley—the tension here deriving from the difference between what Buttercup assumes and the reader suspects. And as for the torture scenes, they may not be graphic but they are nevertheless chilling.

As with all the best fairy tales, the characters are cardboard cut-outs—but Goldman pulls off a real trick by making us care for them all. He does this without exploring their motivation in any great detail. If anything, the sub-plot characters, Fezzik and Montoya, are treated somewhat more realistically than Buttercup and Westley. For Goldman, action seems to be everything—as he tells us in the bridging sections.

Even so, the characters are not completely without their complexities. Take Buttercup: Goldman could easily have made her into a simple spoilt brat—but she isn't. She's a pragmatist, albeit not a very bright one. She twice chooses marriage to Prince Humperdinck, both times to avoid death. The second time, she's not only trying to save her own life but also that of Westley, her true love—but in so doing she inadvertently hands him over to be tortured. Westley, on the other hand, is ridiculously competent—strong, brave, and intelligent. Coming from a lesser writer, this might seem a bit offensive, especially since Buttercup is the only woman of note in the book. With Goldman, it comes across as a comment on the tradition he is working in.

Finally, *The Princess Bride* has one of the most effective closing scenes of any novel, in any genre. It would be quite unfair to reveal it.

—Liz Holliday

GOLDSTEIN, Lisa

Nationality: American. **Born:** Los Angeles, California, 21 November 1953. **Education:** University of California, Los Angeles, B.A. 1975. **Family:** Married Douglas Asherman in 1986. **Career:** Co-owner, Dark Carnival Bookstore, Berkeley, California, 1976-82. **Awards:** American Book award, 1983. **Agent:** Lynn Seligman, 400 Highland Avenue, Upper Montclair, NJ 07043, USA.

FANTASY PUBLICATIONS

Novels

The Red Magician. New York, Pocket, 1982; London, Unwin, 1987.
The Dream Years. New York, Bantam, 1985; London, Unwin, 1986.
A Mask for the General. New York, Bantam, 1987; London, Legend, 1989.
Tourists. New York, Simon and Schuster, 1989.
Strange Devices of the Sun and Moon. New York, Tor, 1993.
Summer King, Winter Fool. New York, Tor, 1994.

Short Stories

Daily Voices. Eugene, Oregon, Pulphouse, 1989.
Travelers in Magic. New York, Tor, 1994.

*   *   *

In Lisa Goldstein's short story "Death is Different" a visitor arrives in a strange country. In the taxi from the airport she thinks she sees auto lights flying in the air, but realizes they are just reflections in the car window. "She bent closer to the window, put her hands around her eyes, but she could see nothing real outside, only the flying lights, the phantom buildings."

This moment, in which a fantastical map is overlaid on the mundane world, is typical of Goldstein's fantasy. Shifting landscapes and uncertain borders continually leave her protagonists uncertain of the world they inhabit. In *The Red Magician,* Kicsi's hometown is near borders which "ebbed and flowed around it like tides". In *The Dream Years,* Robert St. Onge is transported through time when the familiar streets of Paris are stretched and distorted. Like St. Onge, Tom Nashe in *Strange Devices of the Sun and Moon* has a thorough knowledge of the geography of his city, but when he chases fairies he finds himself in an unknown and subtly different place. This device is made concrete in the novel *Tourists,* and in the short stories "Death is Different" and "Tourists," which are all set in a city where the layout of the streets is unstable, ever liable to shift into new configurations.

The moment of fantasy in Goldstein's work is the moment in which her characters move from one geography to another, real or imagined. (In fact, in novels like *The Dream Years* and *Strange Devices* she is insistent that there is no difference between reality and imagination.) But this shift does not take us into entire other worlds, as we might pass through C. S. Lewis's magical wardrobe. In *Strange Devices* the land of faerie is coextensive with Elizabethan England: Alice sees the fairy dance just beyond Moorgate, and the final confrontation between the white queen and red king is in St. Paul's Churchyard. When St. Onge steps through time he is still in Paris, time has made the world different but it has not

made it a different world. And this fantastical device, mapping realities and perceptions one upon another, works as a metaphor throughout her work though the import of the metaphor has shifted as her novels have grown progressively more complex in theme and execution.

Her first novel, *The Red Magician,* which won the American Book Award in 1983, is a sometimes awkward blend of magic and the horror of the Nazi holocaust. Kicsi is a teenage girl in a small Jewish village in Central Europe. The village rabbi is challenged by a stranger, Vörös, the red-haired magician of the title, who warns of terrible dangers approaching. In their magical battles, in which Vörös barely holds his own, the rabbi represents tradition, fear of the unknown causing him to see Vörös's urgings to flee as a direct challenge to his own authority and security. Their battles appear to split the world, but when the world really does turn upside down and the villagers are taken to concentration camps, the magic stops. Only after the war, when Vörös rescues Kicsi does the magic return, and it is here that the novel is most successful. For Kicsi is weighed down with the guilt of survival, and it is Vörös's magic, and his renewed battle with the rabbi, which returns her to life.

Lisa Goldstein's second novel, *The Dream Years,* again blends history and fantasy, but in this case the mix is more integral to the novel. The book is an overt homage to the Surrealists, whose work has clearly influenced much of what Goldstein has written. Other influences—the ethics and aspirations of 1960s youth culture, and the blues—are also represented here. The story of Robert Johnson being taught to play the guitar by the devil at a crossroads features in an important episode in the novel and is also mentioned in Goldstein's introduction to her short-story collection, *Daily Voices.* Such modern myths clearly play a large part in the formulation of her own ideas.

Robert St. Onge is a typical Goldstein protagonist: like Vörös, like Mary in *A Mask for the General,* like Casey in *Tourists,* he is not quite at home in the milieu in which he finds himself. This makes the geographical disruption of Goldstein's fantasy all the more resonant. St. Onge is a member of André Breton's circle in 1920s Paris who is at one point exiled from the group for writing a realist novel about the city. He becomes obsessed with a girl and finds himself pursuing her across time to revolutionary Paris of 1968. The contrast between surrealists and student revolutionaries makes for a vivid and intriguing novel, though it takes an intrusion from further in the future to drive the plot to a climax. St. Onge finds himself having to lead the surrealists in a pitched battle against the forces of conformity; like the pitched battles which end *The Red Magician* or *Strange Devices,* the actual outcome is almost irrelevant to the protagonists beyond teaching them to be true to their own individuality.

A Mask for the General, Goldstein's third and weakest novel, is a transitional work. It moves from the relatively clear-cut conflicts of *The Red Magician* and *The Dream Years* to the murkier and more complex conspiracies of *Tourists* and *Strange Devices.* The only one of her books to be set, other than peripherally, in the future and in America, it also retreads much of the ground already covered in *The Dream Years.* Again we get the 60s counter-culture opposing, rather ineffectually, the dictatorial conformism of the General. But where a mask was worn by the conformist in *The Dream Years,* in *A Mask for the General* it is the badge of the Tribes. The mask somehow reflects and releases the wearer's true identity, and it is a mask which, in a not entirely convincing conclusion, works a magical transformation on the world.

Goldstein seems much more sure as a writer when she distances herself from her native culture. She satirized American cultural blindness in two effective short stories, "Death is Different" and "Tourists," where American certainties were useless in a land where streets changed their layout and the people learned their news from mysterious playing cards distributed every day. She returned to Amaz for her fourth and, in some respects, most powerful novel, *Tourists.* The cultural relativity of Amaz beguiles and entraps the American visitors. Dr. Mitchell Parmenter is a visiting academic whose safe enquiry into the myth of the Jewel King's Sword is mystifyingly transformed into a quest for something real and politically important. His wife finds her way through the shifting streets to liquor shops. One daughter, Casey, embraces the local culture only to find herself a pawn in a vast, multi-sided conspiracy revolving around the rediscovery of the Sword. While the other daughter, Angie, withdraws more and more into her own fantasy world which surprisingly reveals the key to the whole mystery. The disintegration of a conventional American family, the contrast between fantasy and reality, past and present, the way that neither the physical nor the psychological geography of Amaz is fixed, make this her most resonant, complex and satisfying novel to date.

Lisa Goldstein's fifth novel, *Strange Devices of the Sun and Moon,* may, at first sight, appear to be a more conventional fantasy than any she has written to date. It involves, for instance, the interaction between humans and fairies. Yet in its overlaying of history and fantasy it harks back to *The Dream Years,* and in the multi-layered plot it is every bit as complex and intriguing as *Tourists.* The setting is the London of Elizabeth I, a time when plots and conspiracies flourished, and the novel reflects this. Christopher Marlowe, playwright and spy, uncovers plots against the Queen. Curious conspirators plot to make the mysterious Arthur king. Bookseller George schemes to marry Alice Wood and finds himself caught up in the magical plans of alchemist Hogg. And behind it all is the war between the white queen and red king which will decide whether the fairy folk remain within the realm of man. The lives of Marlowe and his fellow writers, Thomas Nashe and Tom Kyd; the beliefs current in Elizabethan England; even life in the court and in the streets of the plague-ridden city are all skilfully interwoven in a magical plot. And after the final battle, as the roads between England and Faerie fade in the same way that the avenues of time closed in *The Dream Years,* Alice like all Goldstein protagonists must be true to her own individuality. It is the only way to make sense of a reality that is never as stable as it might appear.

—Paul Kincaid

GOODKIND, Terry

Nationality: American. **Address:** c/o Tor Books, 175 Fifth Avenue, New York, NY 10010, USA.

FANTASY PUBLICATIONS

Novels (series: The Sword of Truth in all books)

Wizard's First Rule. New York, Tor, and London, Millennium, 1994.
Stone of Tears. New York, Tor, and London, Millennium, 1995.

*   *   *

Terry Goodkind's debut novel, *Wizard's First Rule,* is an heroic fantasy of very considerable pretension and with strong echoes of Guy Gavriel Kay's *Tigana.* There are also parallels with Tolkien, but these lie principally in some close analogues among the secondary characters (Zedd = Gandalf, Samuel = Gollum, Scarlet = Smaug), and in the central plotline, which is a standard sort of quest.

Richard Cypher, the hero, is selected for the role of Seeker, which is ill defined but requires self-control and self-sacrifice on an heroic scale, at a point when the Forces of Good seem likely to be overwhelmed by the local Dark Lord, a magician of great power rather ineptly named Darken Rahl. Rahl is in search of a magic box, which will allow him to enslave or destroy the world, and will die unless he finds it before winter. Richard must find it first, prevent Rahl from getting it and if possible survive himself, but that has a low priority.

The tone is darker than usual for heroic fantasy and is defined from the outset when the quest is triggered by the appearance of a mysterious lady called Kahlan in Richard's country of Hartland. She has escaped from the Midlands, where the box must be, through a magical boundary. To get her out took the efforts of five magicians, who then killed themselves lest the details be wrung from them by torture—a sacrifice worth making, if it will bring her into contact with Richard, who may (perhaps) be persuaded to return with her, for together they can (perhaps) do what neither can separately.

Like Guy Gavriel Kay, Goodkind is at pains to build up a strong cast of characters, so that we care how both they and their quest fare; like Kay he presents scenes from within the heart of the enemy citadel, though Darken Rahl succeeds as a villain in a very different mode from Brandin the Tyrant; even more than Kay, he stresses throughout the concept of sacrifice. With the whole universe at stake, Richard and his comrades cannot and must not flinch from laying down their own, their friends', and each other's lives if it means a marginally better chance (there's never a really good chance) of victory for their cause, but there's never any certainty for anyone that they themselves will remain on the same side—their minds may be enslaved, so that it would be better that they were dead. Moreover, sundry prophecies suggest that may well happen.

The themes of sacrifice and teamwork recur constantly. Richard, Kahlan, and Zedd all possess secrets which they would like to share with the others but must not, and Kahlan's also precludes her from a sexual relationship with Richard, though it's what they both desire. By contrast (and this is a book full of parallels and balanced contrasts), Richard is at one point captured by Denna, a sorceress with whom, over nearly 60 pages of sado-masochism, he falls in love, and whom he (inevitably) kills. Such a *tour de force* is structurally impossible to justify: *inter alia,* it makes the ending look hasty. But the quality of writing sustains the interest of what in other hands would be monotonous, distasteful and incredible.

The climax consists of the usual confrontation between rival magics, though done rather better than usual; but in parallel it has all the major characters, good and evil, forced into confrontation with their own natures. Only those who can recognize themselves for what they are will achieve self-mastery and through that mastery of Fate.

All this makes for a violet-hued book, and for such books extreme dignity of language is vital. This is where Goodkind falls down, rarely but glaringly, when he introduces a third major viewpoint.

A child called Rachel comes into possession of the magic box. Rachel is supposed to be intelligent, naturally good and brave enough to have been neither broken nor corrupted by a life full of arbitrary ill-treatment. To ensure there's no mistake, she is contrasted with Princess Violet, a child of preternatural viciousness. Such a character can work only if the reader is allowed to react to her essential dignity and the pathos of her situation. Unfortunately, Goodkind systematically robs her of both by loading her with a vocabulary of nauseating cuteness. For Rachel nothing is good or small or false; only the "bestest," the "littlest" and "pretend" will do, while the only pejorative adjective she knows is "mean." As such diction peppers her thoughts no less than her conversation, she ruins the atmosphere whenever she appears, whether solo or accompanied. Meanwhile, Violet's words are simple and unaffected, however vile their import.

There are few such lapses, and in another context they would matter less, but a book which depends on creating and sustaining an atmosphere of tragic grandeur cannot afford such infantilism. The reader is forced to recreate the mood each time Rachel comes to ruin it, which is wearing on the imagination and detracts from the many merits of Goodkind's writing. Nevertheless, this is just the beginning of what may prove to be a big career: a second volume, *Stone of Tears,* in what is now being described as the Sword of Truth series, has been announced for publication later in 1995.

—Chris Gilmore

GRABIEN, Deborah

Nationality: British.

FANTASY PUBLICATIONS

Novels

Woman of Fire. London, Piatkus, 1988; as *Eyes in the Fire,* New York, St. Martin's Press, 1989.
Fire Queen. New York, Bantam, 1990.
Plainsong: A Fable for the Millennium. New York, St. Martin's Press, 1990; London, Pan, 1992.
And Then Put Out the Light. London, Pan, 1993.

*   *   *

Many women write fantasy for adults, but they divide overwhelmingly into three groups: those whose gender is irrelevant to their style and preoccupations; those whose gender is relevant to style, content or both, but not to approach; and the feminists. Deborah Grabien is unusual in that her writing is indisputably fantasy, but has all the hallmarks of what is disparagingly called "women's fiction." This is not to condemn it, but to observe that the women she uses as viewpoint characters are not notably forceful or frighteningly talented; their backgrounds and values are middle-class, they desire domestic tranquillity, and the situations which perplex and threaten them are none of their choosing.

The tone is set by her first novel, *Woman of Fire,* which uses two major viewpoints. Marian is the wife of a successful English businessman, living in an attractive house on Dartmoor: Lunica is a young woman of the Dumnonii, an iron-age tribe which had lived

nearby some two millennia before. For no obvious reason their lives begin to resonate, so that they can occasionally perceive each other. The consequences are distressing for both, since Marian has no idea what is going on, while Lunica's ideas are forthright but wrong. Lunica is also in danger from the local Chief Druid, who, feeling threatened by the power he recognizes in her, wants nothing more than to burn her alive in a wicker basket.

The book is static in structure; its tension is generated by the questions of what will happen to Lunica, and to what extent her fate will affect Marian's, but neither has much ability to affect events. The strong feeling of approaching catastrophe compensates for lack of action on the way, and is only slightly marred by a careless approach to background detail: *pace* Grabien, a titmouse is not a mammal, and there are no abandoned iron-age villages standing on Dartmoor. When the climax comes it's violent enough for anyone, but provides no rationale.

Plainsong: A Fable for the Millennium presents an unusual combination: a sexless rural idyll and some fairly heavy blasphemy. As the story opens, almost the whole human race has died from a plague which attacks most severely those who live stressful lives. The few survivors include a number of children, an illiterate moron and Julia, a pregnant poetess. This being a fable, there are also animals who converse rationally with the humans and among themselves. Many of them, for reasons never explained, have adopted the speech patterns attributed to the deserving poor in English novels of the 1930s, though an occasional Americanism slips through, or halfway through—a character who can't give "a flying damn" must be some kind of first.

So far, so idyllic; but some of the beasts have been around for many millennia, as have some of the humans who also gradually coalesce around Julia, awaiting her Time. These include the nymph Calypso, one-time companion of Odysseus, and Max, also known as Ahasuerus, the Wandering Jew. Max would surely not have survived the plague had he not been cursed with immortality, for he tends to favour such stressful activities as getting Julia with child during a one-night stand in Bloomsbury. He also has frequent converse with Jesus, whose character has taken a turn for the worse over the centuries. He, too, is awaiting the Time, but more in the spirit of Herod than the Redeemer. He suspects the child is set to usurp his Godhead, and is disinclined to move over.

This is the only source of tension in a short but slow-moving book, yet against all reason, not to mention all prejudice, *Plainsong* works, mainly through maintaining an extremely even tone. The only conventional excitement comes at the end, when various subsidiary characters converge to be in at the birth, but although everyone pretends to be in a tearing hurry, it clearly matters not a jot whether they arrive together or in time, as the conflict fizzles out in the milk of human kindness. Grabien is clearly too fond of her characters to let anything dreadful happen to them.

The book's principal defect as a fable is that the general divorce of cause and effect leads to a total lack of a moral framework. Grabien doesn't merely disdain to answer such questions as why Calypso and sundry beasts are immortal, why Julia's little fling should precipitate the plague, or how the new polity should be ordered; she is patently unaware that such questions get asked.

Emily Moon-Bourne, heroine of Grabien's later novel *And Then Put Out the Light,* is a large lady, never beautiful and now pushing 40, who decides in the wake of a profitable but wounding divorce to visit Europe, in vague but obvious search of adventure. Once she gets to Italy it is her uncomfortable experience to meet the Man of her Dreams—literally. A classic Latin lover (except that he's English), he has haunted her imagination since adolescence; and here he suddenly is, known only as Martin and typecast as Lucifer in a piece of traditional street theatre. Emily so forgets herself as to go looking for him, but no luck. Instead of trying to find where the troupe will play next she visits England and France, her holiday proceeding in sightseeing, conversation with women she meets on the way, and internal monologue disguised as dialogue with her inner self.

With the book three parts over the only hints of the supernatural are two almost-meetings with Martin (is he following her? if so, how?) and two encounters with unseasonable wasps. Otherwise it's a fictionalized travelogue. Then, in the last quarter, Martin, having finally let her catch up with him, trifles with Emily's affections to their mutual gratification before abruptly and permanently vanishing. And does it end happily? No chance! Except that it does, in a quite outrageous fashion.

Grabien's is not an influential voice; she's too far from the main stream of genre fantasy, and too close to women's-magazine writing. Even so, she deserves attention for her carefully wrought prose and her believably low-key characterization. Above all, she comes as a refreshing change after the thud-and-blunder of so much sword and sorcery.

—Chris Gilmore

GRAHAME, Kenneth

Nationality: British. **Born:** Edinburgh, 8 March 1859. **Education:** St. Edward's School, Oxford, 1868-75. **Family:** Married Elspeth Thomson in 1899; one son (died 1920). **Career:** Worked for Grahame Currie and Spens, parliamentary agent's office, London, 1875-79; from 1879 gentleman-clerk, and secretary, 1898-1907, Bank of England, London. Secretary of the New Shakespeare Society, London, 1877-91. **Died:** 6 July 1932.

Fantasy Publications

Novel

The Wind in the Willows, illustrated by Graham Robertson. London, Methuen, and New York, Scribner, 1908.

Short Stories

The Golden Age. London, Lane, and Chicago, Stone and Kimball, 1895.
Dream Days. London and New York, Lane, 1898; revised edition, 1899.
The Headswoman. London and New York, Lane, 1898.
First Whisper of The Wind in the Willows, edited by Elspeth Grahame. London, Methuen, 1944; Philadelphia, Lippincott, 1945.

Other Publications

Other

Pagan Papers. London, Elkin Mathews and Lane, 1893; Chicago, Stone and Kimball, 1894.

Fun o' the Fair. London, Dent, 1929.
The Kenneth Grahame Day Book, edited by Margery Coleman. London, Methuen, 1937.
Paths to the River Bank: The Origins of The Wind in the Willows, edited by Peter Haining. London, Souvenir Press, 1983.
My Dearest Mouse: The Wind in the Willows Letters. London, Pavilion, 1988.

Editor, *Lullaby-Land: Songs of Childhood,* by Eugene Field, illustrated by John Lawrence. New York, Scribner, 1897; London, Lane, 1898.
Editor, *The Cambridge Book of Poetry for Children.* London, Cambridge University Press, 2 vols., and New York, Putnam, 1916.

*

Film Adaptations: *The Wind in the Willows,* 1949, 1983 (TV movie), 1984 (TV movie).

Critical Studies: *Kenneth Grahame: Life, Letters, and Unpublished Work* by Patrick R. Chalmers, London, Methuen, 1933; *Kenneth Grahame 1859-1932: A Study of His Life, Work, and Times,* London, Murray, 1959, as *Kenneth Grahame: A Biography,* Cleveland, World, 1959, abridged as *Beyond the Wild Wood: The World of Kenneth Grahame,* Exeter, Devon, Webb and Bower, 1982, and New York, Facts on File, 1983, by Peter Green; *Kenneth Grahame* by Eleanor Graham, London, Bodley Head, and New York, Walck, 1963; *Kenneth Grahame: An Innocent in the Wild Wood* by Alison Prince, London, Allison and Busby, 1994.

* * *

There is a certain irony in the fact that a Scot—Kenneth Grahame, whose claret-loving father could (and, in his cups, often did) substantiate a direct familial line back to Robert the Bruce—wrote that perfect paradigm of the English (not British) pastoral idyll, *The Wind in the Willows.* More poignantly, this best-loved of all anthropomorphic classics was inspired not simply by intense feelings for nature and the English countryside (although these are there) but by deeper, darker and far more complex emotions, of yearning and unhappiness and regret. Perhaps even more melancholic is the thought that had its author been a happier man *The Wind in the Willows* would never have been written.

Grahame is perceived to be a fantasist on the strength of two works: *The Wind in the Willows* and the short story "The Reluctant Dragon". Yet in truth most of his *oeuvre* is more or less fantastic in tone and substance; all of it inspired by "the country of the mind," that fabulous terrain much inhabited by Grahame as a refuge from the real world. Indeed, a knowledge of his life is crucial even to the most basic understanding of his work, since just about everything he wrote (even early, neo-pagan essays as one of editor and critic W. E. Henley's "clever young men") demonstrates a harking back to, and an intense evocation of, a world not precisely of childhood but of a kind of earthly paradise lost that, paradoxically, had never quite been experienced.

Grahame led two lives: one he disliked, one he feared. As a Wellsian quill-driver toiling in the oppressive maw of the Bank of England he reached surprising—indeed Wellsian—heights, becoming at length Secretary. As a *belles-lettrist* he mixed with essayists, aesthetes, bluestockings, "New Women": in short those who tended to flout conventions. His fellow scribes (such as the poet, critic and sensation-writer Coulson Kernahan, the journalist Sidney Ward, the novelists Beatrice Harraden and George Moore, the essayist Andrew Lang, and so on) viewed his "day job" with wry but entirely uncensorious amusement; colleagues in Threadneedle Street, however, were aghast not only at his literary proclivities (the Bank's consultant physician wrote in horror, "They tell me he *writes tales*") but at the company he kept. Working at the Bank, even on the most rarefied echelons, was so stultifying an experience that Grahame fictionalized it into a minor terror tale, "Long Odds" (*The Yellow Book,* July 1895), during the course of which a senior City clerk meets on a tube-train Death, who is gleefully ticking off names in a notebook. The clerk jumps off the train before his own name is reached, resigns from his office and flees to Venice (a favourite haunt of Grahame's)—yet in real life he could never bring himself to break free of the "Old Lady" and plunge wholeheartedly into the dangerous, yet invigorating, waters of Bohemianism.

Grahame wrote superbly about childhood, perhaps because his experience of the state had by no means been a happy one: due to the alcoholism of his father he was brought up, miserably, by elderly relatives. His writing was thus a response to the various stresses and strains experienced during childhood and adulthood; his neo-pagan paeans to the Bohemian life an escape from the drudgery of the Bank; his enormously complex stories of childhood (by no means "children's stories") in many ways a revenge for his own unhappy pre-adult years and against "grown-ups," elderly relatives, the stifling and mean-spirited *bourgeoisie*—generally speaking, all those in authority. Them, in a moment of demonic genius, he labelled "Olympians".

These acute, not cute, stories gathered into *The Golden Age* (favourite bedtime reading of Kaiser Wilhelm II) and *Dream Days,* are shot through with fantasy of the richest kind: vivid, adventure-filled daydreams in which the natural barriers between imagination and hard reality become blurred then disappear altogether, the anonymous I-hero/narrator (Grahame himself) shifting from persona to persona at will—pirate chief, knight-at-arms, haughty Crusader, Indian brave—the rest of the world now seen as real, now as fantasy (cows in a farmer's field becoming a herd of stampeding bison on the prairie). The delightful "A Saga of the Seas" (*Dream Days*) is a full-blown, no-nonsense fantasy in which virtually all that is related is the I-hero's fearsome voyage as freelance swashbuckler in the South Seas, cutting pirates' throats with reckless abandon, plundering treasure-ships, rescuing beauteous princesses: all a tribute to the power of the imagination (although the geography goes awry at times).

On occasion a chill wind whips up from nowhere, clouds pass across the sun. In "The Argonauts" (*The Golden Age*) the children borrow a boat and launch themselves onto the wine-dark sea (actually the local brook) to seek the crazed sorceress Medea. Landing on "some rough and trammell'd strand," they naturally (as though, indeed, it is the most natural occurrence in the world, such is the supreme self-confidence and self-absorption of the child) find her . . . have running games with her . . . play hide-and-seek with her . . . but do not quite realize (as the reader perfectly realizes) that this "Medea" is indeed mad, that an emotional catastrophe has mildly unhinged her. Here are all kinds of resonances, all kinds of shadings; beneath a veneer of nostalgia for childhood scrapes and delights, the multi-level narrative is a masterpiece of obliquity, realism, sophistication.

A masterpiece, too, of juggling with reality and with his own—as creator, writer, hero, subject, Chorus—personas. While constantly existing on two quite disparate and distinct levels—as re-worker

of reality (the writer) and as experiencer of fantasy (the story's subject)—more often than not he adds other clubs to the ones he seems effortlessly to be keeping in the air. In the nearly sublime "The Roman Road" (*The Golden Age*), the I-hero/narrator meets an artist and they discuss, yearningly, "the Golden City," that embodiment of all our hearts's desires. Here Grahame is not only the writer and the undisillusioned I-hero/boy but also the disenchanted adult, whose sense of loss and regret is set down as dispassionately by Grahame as is the untroubled optimism of the child. It is a breathtaking achievement.

Grahame's most famous short story, "The Reluctant Dragon" (*Dream Days*), also has its fair share of metaphor and multi-level narrative: for here Grahame is not only the children listening to the tale as told by the "circus-man" (yet another persona and one he positively revelled in when he wrote the nostalgia-drenched introduction to "Lord" George Sanger's *Seventy Years a Showman* in 1926) but the three central characters—the Dragon (irresponsible Bohemianism), St. George (public service), and the Boy (the optimistic, uncorrupted, essentially wise child)—as well. All the Dragon wants is to be left alone, but the villagers (not Grahame, for once, but the prodnoses, the ravening Philistines: in short, the Establishment) want it dead. In the end, thanks to the clear-eyed ingenuity of the Boy, there is a faked battle and he, Dragon and St. George stroll off arm-in-arm into the sunset (or, to be more precise, the moonrise).

There is a measure of tranquillity in that finale, with all the disparate and warring elements in Grahame's psyche for the moment at rest (soon after the story was published its author was elected to the Secretaryship of the Bank, an elevation he would certainly have known about while writing it). And rather more than a measure in his masterpiece *The Wind in the Willows* (which remains much of the book's charm)—although, too, a good deal more than a measure of transformed though sublimated anxiety and misery.

This, on the face of it, simple tale of anthropomorphic adventures in fact has almost limitless depths. It is above all a hymn to the late-Victorian and Edwardian squirearchy, as well as a protest against not-so-creeping urbanization and encroachment in general, by outsiders (the Wild Wooders) and alien tides: modernity, gadgets, insolence and bouts of *jacquerie* from the lower orders (ironically Grahame the near-Bohemian has become Grahame the arch-reactionary). As well, the book is a more or less direct response to his disastrous marriage to Elspeth Thomson, not only a ferocious snob but fantastical and fey—precisely what Grahame himself was not. He dealt in altogether harder currency.

Even so, while certainly not fey *The Wind in the Willows* is essentially a clubman's paradise, virtually free of women and guilt—"clean," as Grahame himself, in a somewhat giveaway phrase, wrote for the book's original dust-jacket blurb, "of the clash of sex." And while this pre-lapsarian cosiness is made to seem enormously attractive, it just as skilfully serves to hide a fundamental flaw at the book's heart, a flaw which in other hands might well have destroyed the idyll utterly. The braggadocio Toad, wonderful conflation of Oscar Wilde and Horatio Bottomley (the overweening aesthete and the thumping crook), who can drive a car, smoke a cigar and pass himself off as a washerwoman, is merely the most conspicuous instance of the massive breakdown in the story's internal logic. For the principal animals all speak and indulge in a variety of social intercourse—but also eat meat (cured hams hang from the rafters in Badger's kitchen). Other animals are simply . . . animals. The horse that tows the barge Toad cadges a lift on is a beast of burden, nothing more; and sheep are farmed by humans, cats caressed.

Yet such is the force of Grahame's imagination, the skill with which he delineates his world, that even the bizarre collection of artefacts and accessories in Mole End—busts of Garibaldi and Queen Victoria, a gold-fish pond, a sardine-opener—is really no more extraordinary than a bunch of field-mice singing of the Infant Jesus. Accept one, you accept all.

Other creators of anthropomorphic epics—Richard Adams, William Horwood, Aeron Clement, *et al.*—strive desperately for the grand effect, the stupendous adventure, filling their canvases with deadening detail, all more or less missing the point. William Horwood's sequel *The Willows in Winter* (1993) concentrates on Toad as airman, as though Toad as motorist was the crucial motif of the original. Nor do Grahame's followers (lucky for them) have their mentor's emotional problems, failures and crises to fuel their compositions, or his pessimism (it should be recalled that Badger's rambling home is burrowed out in earth *above* the ruins of a once-thriving city: a clear indication as to Grahame's views on the permanence of humankind).

Even so *The Wind in the Willows* breaks every rule of story-making, with its sloppy construction (a plot which jumps about all over the shop), its redundancies (two of the finest chapters, "The Piper at the Gates of Dawn" and "Wayfarers All," have no business in the book at all), and its lack of an identifiable hero (if Mole and Rat are the central characters, why concentrate on Toad?; if Toad, he is surely the most egregious in literature). Yet in all this confusion lies much of the book's strength, as well as in its essential reality: the reality of myth—far more vigorous than mere "real life."

—Jack Adrian

GRANT, Joan

Nationality: British. **Born:** Joan Marshall, London, 12 April 1907. **Education:** Private. **Family:** Married 1) Leslie Grant in 1927, one daughter; 2) Charles Beatty in 1940; 3) Denys Kelsey in 1960. **Died:** 3 February 1989.

FANTASY PUBLICATIONS

Novels

Winged Pharaoh. London, Barker, 1937; New York, Harper, 1938.
Life as Carola. London, Methuen, 1939; New York, Harper, 1940.
Eyes of Horus. London, Methuen, 1942.
Lord of the Horizon. London, Methuen, 1943.
Scarlet Feather. London, Methuen, 1945.
Return to Elysium. London, Methuen, 1947.
The Laird and the Lady. London, Methuen, 1949.
So Moses Was Born. London, Methuen, 1952.

Short Stories

The Scarlet Fish and Other Stories. London, Methuen, 1942.
Redskin Morning and Other Stories. London, Methuen, 1944.

OTHER PUBLICATIONS

Other

Vague Vacation (travel). London, Barker, 1947.
Time Out of Mind (autobiography). London, Barker, 1956; as *Far Memory,* New York, Harper, 1956.
A Lot to Remember, with Denys Kelsey. London, Hale, 1962.
Many Lifetimes, with Denys Kelsey. New York, Doubleday, 1967; London, Gollancz, 1969.
The Complete Works of Joan Grant. New York, Arno Press, 12 vols., 1980.

*   *   *

Winged Pharaoh, Joan Grant's first book, was reviewed enthusiastically on its appearance in 1937 for its vivid picture of ancient Egypt. Technically a historical novel rather than a fantasy, much of its appeal nevertheless lay in its occult trappings and the author's claim that it was dictated in "direct communication with the Powers of Light," taken down by Grant's husband Leslie, whom she subsequently left for the occultist Charles Beatty, who himself transcribed later novels.

Grant's early life was marked by her mother's psychic experiences which she inherited, developing the psychometric ability to sense from an object the experiences and feelings of people who had handled it in the past. This turned her towards writing books which she claimed were not historical novels but "far memories" of past lives. It was from an Egyptian scarab that she felt sensations which became *Winged Pharaoh,* a description of the life of Sekeeta, a Princess of First Dynasty Egypt who comes to rule with her brother as a "Winged Pharaoh"—one who is also an initiated Priestess. Behind the plot, a straightforward first-person birth-to-death narrative, is a doctrine heavily influenced by Theosophical interpretations of Eastern religions. Egypt—which can trace itself back to Atlantis (called here Athlanta)—is in touch with the Powers of Light and its priests are adepts of healing, astral travel, and communication. Much of the book consists of conversations where Sekeeta is instructed in the truth behind the mysteries of life and death, most importantly the cycle of rebirth and how our actions in this life influence our fates in the future. Although the word itself is never used, this is a version of the Eastern doctrine of "karma".

Apart from an ill-starred love affair with a Cretan architect, some visits abroad, and a few astral and physical battles, most of the action is interior: the explication, directly or through parable and poetry, of the philosophy that what happens in this life is unimportant compared to the wider scope of our "life" in Eternity. While something like this is at the heart of most if not all major religions, in *Winged Pharaoh* it buttresses a quiet conservatism which manifests itself as if life is some sort of Supernatural Curriculum overseen by kindly but patronizing middle-class aunts and uncles. There are opposing forces to be overcome: not only the outright evil pre-Babylonians, who are on a much lower karmic plane and are controlled by demonic forces, but also "younger" races such as the Cretans. Dio, Sekeeta's lover, argues against the pantheon of gods interpreted by the Egyptian priesthood and prefers to entertain ideas which prefigure 20th-century rationalism. While persuasively argued, the irony is that Sekeeta, with her superior insight, "knows" that he is wrong.

There has always been a section of the reading public thirsty for anything which condemns modern humanism. *Winged Pharaoh* was greeted with enthusiasm not only by romantic feudalists like Dennis Wheatley, whose "black magic" novels were profoundly influenced by it, but by novelists of lower-class life such as Howard Spring. The series of books which followed charted the "transmigrations" of the author's soul. *Life as Carola,* was set in 16th-Century Italy, but Grant returned to Egypt with *Eyes of Horus* and its sequel *Lord of the Horizon* to tell the story of the resistance movement against a corrupt Pharaoh at the end of the XIth Dynasty, two thousand years later than the events of *Winged Pharaoh.* Her last novel, *So Moses Was Born,* is in form much more of a conventional historical novel and is difficult to see as written from any concept of "far memory," being told from a variety of stances and incorporating in the narrative events seen from the viewpoints of characters other than the protagonist Nebunefer. There is less overt supernaturalism, but the novel can be read as suggesting that the spiritual torch is about to be handed over to the Hebrews and their strange singular god, and (by extension) the Christians.

Other novels show other cultures. *Return to Elysium* is the story of a Greek girl of the 2nd century AD, herself with the gift of "far memory." Most interestingly, *Scarlet Feather* makes the point that the soul is neither male nor female, by having its female North American Indian protagonist wear the red feather of initiation as a warrior brave.

Grant's readers focused upon the almost hallucinatory clarity, the "eyewitness account" of her descriptions. There is considerable detail, of everyday life, events, feelings, objects (though rarely places) which gives the reader the feeling that these inhabitants of a distant time and place were just like us—down to a three-year-old Egyptian princess who will not go to bed until given a cosy account of the pleasures of astral travel. Grant describes detailed surgical operations in *Winged Pharaoh*; and the nightmarish scenes viewed by Sekeeta in her initiation evince a Dantean fascination for the punishment of sinners after death—a "Peruvian" priest, for instance, constantly relives the experience of having his heart torn from his body. In *Eyes of Horus,* Ra-ab witnesses what everyone reading a book about Ancient Egypt wants to know—how a corpse actually is embalmed and mummified.

Despite her claims, there seems little in Grant's novels which a competent knowledge of ancient history gleaned from archaeological experience—and Grant spent time excavating in the Middle East—could not have provided. There are problems of chronology, and the psychology of Grant's characters is mundanely 20th-century. Judged as historical novels, her works are flawed by the sentimentality of much popular writing of the time. As supernatural fantasies they offered not only a reassurance that the Forces of Light had everything under control but a concrete and detailed descriptiveness which offered "evidence" for her visions.

Although Grant's novels have achieved enough of a vogue among "New Age" readers to be reprinted, their main influence in post-War years has been in their effect on Dennis Wheatley. It would seem that *Winged Pharaoh* might have suggested to Dennis Wheatley a framework or rationale for his own "occult" novels. His first black magic novel was published in 1935, two years before he first met Grant, but when characters in his later books discourse on the combat between Light and Darkness, they mirror and acknowledge Joan Grant's ideas. Grant's novels therefore form an important strand in modern fantastic fiction. While standing too close to the borderline between historical novels and fantasies to appeal wholeheartedly to modern readers of both, they are fascinating records of the manifestations of early 20th-century occultism.

—Andy Sawyer

GRANT, John

Pseudonym for Paul Barnett. **Other Pseudonyms:** Eve Devereux; Freddie Duff-Ware; Armytage Ware. **Nationality:** British. **Born:** Aberdeen, 22 November 1949. **Education:** Robert Gordon's College, Aberdeen, 1955-63; Strathallan School, 1963-67; King's and University Colleges, London, 1967-68. **Family:** Married Catherine Sarah Campbell Stewart in 1974; one daughter. **Career:** Editorial assistant, rising to editorial director, Frederick Muller, London, 1969-75; science editor, Elsevier International Projects, Oxford, 1976-77; sponsoring editor, David and Charles/Westbridge, Newton Abbot, Devon, 1978-80; commissioning editor, Webb and Bower, Exeter, 1980; freelance writer and editor from 1980. **Agent:** Robert Kirby, Sheil Land Associates Ltd., 43 Doughty Street, London WC1N 2LF, England. **Address:** 17 Polsloe Road, Exeter, Devon EX1 2HL, England.

FANTASY PUBLICATIONS

Novels

Albion. London, Headline, 1991.
The World. London, Headline, 1992.

Novels with Joe Dever (series: Lone Wolf in all books)

Eclipse of the Kai. London, Beaver, 1989; New York, Berkley, 1990.
The Dark Door Opens. London, Beaver, 1989; New York, Berkley, 1990.
The Sword of the Sun. London, Beaver, 1989; in 2 vols., as *The Tides of Treachery* and *The Sword of the Sun,* New York, Berkley, 1990.
Hunting Wolf. London, Beaver, 1990; New York, Berkley, 1991.
The Claws of Helgedad. London, Red Fox, 1991.
The Sacrifice of Ruanon. London, Red Fox, 1991.
The Birthplace. London, Red Fox, 1992.
The Book of the Magnakai. London, Red Fox, 1992.
Legends of the Lone Wolf Omnibus (omnibus; includes *Eclipse of the Kai, The Dark Door Opens*). London, Red Fox, 1992.
The Lorestone of Varetta. London, Red Fox, 1993.
The Secret of Kazan-Oud. London, Red Fox, 1994.
The Rotting Land. London, Red Fox, 1994.

Short Stories with Joe Dever

The Tellings (Lone Wolf). London, Red Fox, 1993.

OTHER PUBLICATIONS

Novels

The Truth About the Flaming Ghoulies. London, Muller, Blond and White, 1983.
Sex Secrets of Ancient Atlantis. London, Grafton, 1985.
Earthdoom, with David Langford. London, Grafton, 1987.
The Hundredfold Problem. London, Virgin, 1994.

Other

A Directory of Discarded Ideas. Sevenoaks, Kent, Ashgrove, and Englewood Cliffs, New Jersey, Salem Press, 1981.

A Book of Numbers. Sevenoaks, Kent, Ashgrove, and Englewood Cliffs, New Jersey, Salem Press, 1982.

Dreamers: A Geography of Dreamland. Bath, Avon, Ashgrove, and Englewood Cliffs, New Jersey, Salem Press, 1983.

The Depths of Cricket. London, Grafton, 1986.

Encyclopedia of Walt Disney's Animated Characters. London, Hamlyn, 1987; Harper and Row, 1987; revised edition, New York, Hyperion, 1993.

The Advanced Trivia Quizbook. London, Arrow, 1987.

Great Mysteries. London, Apple, 1988.

An Introduction to Viking Mythology. London, Apple, 1989.

The Great Unsolved Mysteries of Science. London, Apple, and Edison, New Jersey, Chartwell, 1989.

Unexplained Mysteries of the World (omnibus; includes *Great Mysteries, Great Unsolved Mysteries of Science*). London, Apple, 1991.

Book of World Flags (as Eve Devereux). London, Apple, 1992; as *Flags of the World,* Avenel, New Jersey, Crescent, 1992.

Monsters. London, Apple, 1992; as *Monster Mysteries,* Edison, New Jersey, Chartwell.

Parlour Games, with Ron Tiner (as Armytage Ware). London, Letts, and Boston, Bulfinch, 1992.

Conjuring Tricks, with Ron Tiner (as Armytage Ware). London, Letts/Bulfinch, 1992.

Juggling and Feats of Dexterity, with Ron Tiner (as Armytage Ware). London, Letts, and Boston, Bulfinch, 1992.

Card Games, with Ron Tiner (as Armytage Ware). Boston, Bulfinch, Bulfinch, 1992.

Practical Jokes, with Ron Tiner (as Freddie Duff-Ware). London, Letts, and Boston, Bulfinch, 1993.

The Ultimate Card Trick Book (as Eve Devereux). London, Apple, and Edison, New Jersey, Chartwell, 1994.

Editor, *Aries 1.* Newton Abbot, Devon, David and Charles, 1979.

Editor, with Colin Wilson, *The Book of Time.* Newton Abbot, Devon, Westbridge, 1980.

Editor, with Colin Wilson, *The Directory of Possibilities.* Exeter, Devon, Webb and Bower, 1981.

Technical editor, *The Encyclopedia of Science Fiction,* 2nd edition, edited by John Clute and Peter Nicholls. London, Orbit, 1993.

Other (as Paul Barnett)

Editor, with A. Hallam and Peter Hutchinson, *Planet Earth: An Encyclopedia of Geology.* London, Phaidon, 1977.

Editor, with John-David Yule, *Phaidon Concise Encyclopedia of Science and Technology.* London, Phaidon, 1978.

Translator, *Electric Children: Roots and Branches of Modern Folk-Rock.* London, Muller, and New York, Taplinger, 1976.

*

John Grant comments:

I find generic categorizations—indeed, the whole notion of classifying imaginative fiction except for purposes of loosely-worded expedience—restrictive, and most of my fictions are mongrelizations of more than one perceived genre. As a result I no longer feel easy with descriptions of my fiction as "fantasy" or (much more rarely applied) "science fiction"; rather, I prefer to think of my books as novels set to a greater or lesser extent in fantasy, sf, or other *venues,* but dealing with matters that seem to me legitimate preoccupations for *any* novelist. This is as true of most of my Lone Wolf quasi-novelizations (notably from *The Sacrifice of Ruanon* onwards, although that book itself was ferociously mutilated by the publisher) as it is of my "more serious" work, both published and forthcoming.

Those preoccupations themselves vary over time, but tend to be fairly fundamental ones that are to my mind more neglected than they should be in late-20th-century English-language fiction: discovering and coming to terms with the truth (or otherwise) about origins; the relationships between different forms of reality (coloured by my strictly amateur personal interest in quantum physics); the mysteries of the creation (coloured by my less amateur interest in cosmology) and the reconciliation of different perceptions of the nature and purposes (if any) of creation; the nature of godhood, and the interactions between deities and mortals; and so forth. In order to tackle such themes I am progressively creating/exploring through my fictions a physical/mental structure of interrelated realities which I call the "polycosmos" (Michael Moorcock having already bagged the term "multiverse" for his own somewhat different uses); my major exposition of the polycosmos published to date is in *The World*—the only book of mine that comes close to fully satisfying me—although there is much relevant material also in *The Birthplace* and *The Rotting Land,* with significant further exploration scheduled for the three novels I plan to write after completing work on *The Encyclopedia of Fantasy* (scheduled for 1996).

All in all, my main purpose in writing fiction is to stop me getting bored.

*   *   *

At a time when fantasy relies heavily on the formulaic and superficial, John Grant's writing comes as an exhilarating antidote to the conventional trappings of the genre. This is typified by his two major fantasy novels, *Albion* and *The World.*

Albion opens with the washing ashore of a shipwrecked sailor, Terman. He has landed on the beach of Albion, a land rumoured to exist but impossible to locate. Terman speculates that it exists only sometimes. Incredibly, this proves to be true. The inhabitants of Albion have a span of memory only as long as what they call a "waking period". After each "sleeping period," they retain no memory of their previous existence, the land may have changed entirely, and they exist in an wholly instinctive fashion.

As Terman is to discover, his presence in Albion has an odd effect on those around him. He names people and as he does so they acquire memory and a life based on that memory. But even with Terman's presence, the people can do nothing against the Ellonia, who use the peasants to farm the land and to supply whores. But Terman's son, Lian, will be able to lead the people; he does not have his father's reservations and he has inherited his gift of memory.

If *Albion* was a conventional fantasy novel, Lian's task would be accomplished with depressing inevitability, and all would live happily ever after, but Grant is not an author who takes the conventional route. Instead, we follow the motley band of peasants through setbacks and victories to apparently final defeat. Although the peasants enjoy a brief freedom, one Despot is replaced by another. And yet, much as our own period clings to the myth of Arthur the Once and Future King, Grant also offers a hope which is fulfilled, in a way, in *The World*.

The World provides many more clues as to what is going on in Grant's Albion and World. Whereas *Albion* showed what it was like to live in a world that was constantly reinvented and renewed, with the implication that there was not necessarily one plane of existence, one universe, but maybe more than one overlapping, *The World* ventures into those overlapping worlds, culminating in an extraordinary chase across the multiplicity of worlds, some close to our own, others far beyond anything we might imagine.

At the same time, *The World* points up the cyclical nature of existence even more strongly than did *Albion*. In that novel, the ever-renewing cycle was made concrete in the constant renewal of the land itself but also in the constant vying among the Ellonians for promotion through elaborate and savage ritual contests. In *The World* we see Anya, daughter of Lian, work her way through another cycle of existence, as she fights the Ellonian repressors, from idealist to savage despot in her own right, corrupted by the power she sought to resist.

Grant further pursues this vision of interlocking worlds through the presence of Alyss, "a sort of goddess." Alyss's powers seem limitless but her own capricious nature means that her interventions within the world of Albion aren't always what one might expect or indeed what our heroes and heroines might look for. With Alyss, Grant neatly subverts all genre expectations of omnipotent beings; her unexpectedness catches despots and tyrants off-guard and infuriates those who feel they might reasonably expect her to be on their side. As with much else in these novels, nothing can be guaranteed or relied upon.

In the end, the reader is left with nothing but uncertainty, and a world which constantly shifts. Consequently, we may not have seen what we thought we saw, much as Albion, when Terman first saw it, changed with the blink of an eye. The very stability of the fantasy genre, reliable, predictable, formulaic, is undermined by Grant's quantum approach to fantasy. The *status quo* must continually be challenged, and this Grant has done very successfully with these remarkable novels.

—Maureen Speller

GREEN, Roland J(ames)

Pseudonym: Jeffrey Lord. **Nationality:** American. **Born:** 2 September 1944 in Bradford, Pennsylvania. **Education:** Oberlin College, Oberlin, Ohio, B.A., 1966, M.A., 1968; doctorate studies, University of Chicago. **Family:** Married Frieda A. Murray. **Agent:** Lurton Blassingame. **Address:** 629 W. Oakdale, Chicago, Illinois 60657, USA.

FANTASY PUBLICATIONS

Novels (series: Conan; Wandor)

Wandor's Ride. New York, Avon, 1973.

Wandor's Journey. New York, Avon, 1975.
Wandor's Voyage. New York, Avon, 1979.
Wandor's Flight. New York, Avon, 1981.
Jamie the Red, with Gordon R. Dickson. New York, Ace, 1984.
Throne of Sherran: The Book of Kantela, with Frieda A. Murray. New York, Tor, 1985.
Conan the Valiant. New York, Tor, 1988.
Conan the Guardian. New York, Tor, 1991.
Conan the Relentless. New York, Tor, 1992.
Conan and the Gods of the Mountain. New York, Tor, 1993.
Conan at the Demon's Gate. New York, Tor, 1994.
Conan and the Mists of Doom. New York, Tor, 1995.

Novels as Jeffrey Lord (series: Richard Blade)

Kingdom of Royth (Blade 9). New York, Pinnacle, 1974.
Ice Dragon (Blade 10). New York, Pinnacle, 1974.
Dimension of Dreams (Blade 11). New York, Pinnacle, 1974.
King of Zunga (Blade 12). New York, Pinnacle, 1975.
The Golden Steed (Blade 13). New York, Pinnacle, 1975.
The Temples of Ayocan (Blade 14). New York, Pinnacle, 1975.
The Towers of Melnon (Blade 15). New York, Pinnacle, 1975.
The Crystal Seas (Blade 16). New York, Pinnacle, 1975.
The Mountains of Brega (Blade 17). New York, Pinnacle, 1976.
Warlords of Gaikon (Blade 18). New York, Pinnacle, 1976.
Looters of Tharn (Blade 19). New York, Pinnacle, 1976.
Guardians of the Coral Throne (Blade 20). New York, Pinnacle, 1976.
Champion of the Gods (Blade 21). New York, Pinnacle, 1976.
The Forests of Gleor (Blade 22). New York, Pinnacle, 1977.
Empire of Blood (Blade 23). New York, Pinnacle, 1977.
The Dragons of Englor (Blade 24). New York, Pinnacle, 1977.
The Torian Pearls (Blade 25). New York, Pinnacle, 1977.
City of the Living Dead (Blade 26). New York, Pinnacle, 1978.
Master of the Hashomi (Blade 27). New York, Pinnacle, 1978.
Wizard of Rentoro (Blade 28). New York, Pinnacle, 1978.
Treasure of the Stars (Blade 29). New York, Pinnacle, 1978.
Gladiators of Hapanu (Blade 31). New York, Pinnacle, 1979.
Pirates of Gohar (Blade 32). New York, Pinnacle, 1979.
Killer Plants of Binaark (Blade 33). New York, Pinnacle, 1980.
The Ruins of Kaldac (Blade 34). New York, Pinnacle, 1981.
The Lords of the Crimson River (Blade 35). New York, Pinnacle, 1981.
Return to Kaldac (Blade 36). New York, Pinnacle, 1983.
Warriors of Latan (Blade 37). New York, Pinnacle, 1984.

OTHER PUBLICATIONS

Novels

Janissaries 2: Clan and Crown, with Jerry Pournelle. New York, Ace, 1982.
Starship Sapphire, with Andrew J. Offutt (as John Cleve). New York, Berkley, 1984.
Great King's War, with John F. Carr. New York, Ace, 1985.
Peace Company. New York, Ace, 1985.
Janissaries 3: Storms of Victory, with Jerry Pournelle. New York, Ace, 1987.
Peace Company 2: These Green Foreign Hills. New York, Ace, 1987.

Starcruiser Shenandoah 1: Squadron Alert. New York, Signet, 1989.
Peace Company 3: The Mountain Walks. New York, Ace, 1989.
Starcruiser Shenandoah 2: Division of the Spoils. New York, Roc, 1990.
Starcruiser Shenandoah 3: The Sum of Things. New York, Roc, 1991.
Starcruiser Shenandoah 4: Vain Command. New York, Roc, 1992.
Starcruiser Shenandoah 5: The Painful Field. New York, Roc, 1993.
Starcruiser Shenandoah 6: Warriors for the Working Day. New York, Roc, 1994.

Other

Editor, *The Burning Eye,* with Jerry Pournelle and John F. Carr. New York: Baen, 1988.
Editor, *Death's Head Rebellion,* with Jerry Pournelle and John F. Carr. New York: Baen, 1990.

*   *   *

Roland Green was a bestselling author before most readers knew his name. Under the house pseudonym Jeffrey Lord, he was writing the Blade series from its ninth volume, and wrote all but one of the remaining volumes before the series ended in 1984 with number 37 (Ray Nelson had written number 30). Conceived by book packager Lyle Kenyon Engel, Blade was one of many paperback-original series begun in the late 1960s (in 1969, to be precise) which pits a lone hero against everything from the Mafia to aliens. Richard Blade is a special agent for a secret intelligence unit, a human guinea-pig repeatedly sent into "Dimension X"—a realm where time and space are so confused that Blade might find himself in a historical setting, in the future, in an alternative reality, or in a world where magic is real.

These are very basic science fantasies, their plots focused on action, on Blade's strength and his warrior skills. After Roland Green took over with book nine, *Kingdom of Royth,* the series began to improve in coherence and humour. However, the books remained limited—not so much because they were written quickly (in about six weeks each) but because editorial control deliberately kept each self-contained. Their template plots (journey to Dimension X, confront a menace, overcome a menace, return to Earth) gave no opportunity to develop character or storyline through several books. Green's involvement was kept secret until 1982, when there were plans for a massive format change; but the plans fell through, and the final books limped onto the market, to vanish quietly. By then, Green was busy on more personal and powerful projects.

His first novel under his own name was the splendid *Wandor's Ride,* in which Bertan Wandor, a foundling grown to become House Master of the Order of Duelists, learns he might be the prophesied future King of the Five Crowns who will bring peace to five warring kingdoms. To prove his merit, Wandor has to gather a number of allies and accomplish a series of tasks. Green could have imitated the approach of other series—send Wandor on one quest per book, to find the next magical object—but this sequence was different from the start: Wandor is no mere swashbuckler, bemoaning his lost loves as he heads towards the next adventure, surrounded by two-dimensional allies and opposed by paper enemies; he is a deep, complex and contrary hero, shaped by his experiences, realistically attaining the wisdom that comes from marriage and respon-

sibility. The growing complexity of each book was matched by an increase in their length, and while there is a small amount of repetition (the heroine, Gwynna, is kidnapped several times) they are carefully crafted and entertaining works, to which Green devoted considerable effort. As Green was writing the last Blade book in 1982, he was scheduled to write the climactic fifth Wandor novel, projected to be called *Wandor's Battle,* and had even roughed out plans for a follow-up trilogy. Yet these and any other Wandor books were never written; the series simply stopped, and it is probable that no more will be published.

Green had written more than 30 fantasy novels, most of them badly distributed, the majority under a pseudonym, but everything was about to change for him. He had met Jerry Pournelle, who liked the Wandor books; they found a shared interest in military history and the work of H. Beam Piper. Pournelle's science-fiction novel *Janissaries* (1979), featured American mercenaries transported to a planet whose society was pre-technological and feudal; this obvious homage to earlier works such as Piper's *Lord Kalvan of Otherwhen* (1965) attracted fans of both fantasy and high-tech sf, and many demanded a follow-up. In 1981, Pournelle asked Green to collaborate on the sequel, with Green producing the first draft from an outline; the resulting *Janissaries 2: Clan and Crown* was even stronger than its original—deeper, more emotionally complex, possessing greater charm and humanity. For various reasons, Green's name was not on the cover, but this was to become the first in a run of successful collaborations, several of them sf rather than fantasy.

The fantasy *Jamie the Red* was co-written with Gordon R. Dickson. Its eponymous hero, a manipulative and arrogant prince, is exiled from Scotland to seek his fortune in a magic-imbued Europe. Though well drawn and excitingly presented, the hero is perhaps too angry, too cold, and this intended first in a series has had only one sequel—the beautiful short novel *Beyond the Dar al Harb* (1985) which was written by Dickson alone, and made no reference at all to the events of the preceding novel.

Green also co-wrote *The Book of Kantela,* first of the proposed Throne of Sherran trilogy, with his wife Frieda Murray. A young widowed Queen, Kantela, finds herself under siege by warring factions conspiring to usurp her throne. With the aid of her soldier-lover, she quickly learns to wield power and to play the complex political/military games. Though there are overtones of Piper-esque "Lord Kalvan"-type tactics and characters, *The Book of Kantela* has the romantic aura that suffused the early Wandor novels but became less noticeable in later books. This series also stopped after a single book. Green collaborated once more with Jerry Pournelle on the sf novel *Janissaries 3: Storms of Victory,* but his subsequent works have been written solo, and most have been straight science fiction. He has alternated production of these books with contributions to the heroic-fantasy Conan saga, beginning with *Conan the Valiant* which has been followed by several more.

Green is an entertaining author of muscular fantasy; he can create distinct and attractive adult characters (especially women) who often possess an understated and charming humour. Unfortunately, market needs have shifted his science-fantasy adventures firmly into the arena of military science fiction, and his fantasy now seems restricted to re-runs of a series (Robert E. Howard's Conan) long past its best days.

—Ian Covell

GREEN, Sharon

Nationality: American. **Born:** 6 July, 1942 in Brooklyn, New York. **Education:** New York University, B.A., 1963. **Family:** Divorced; three sons. **Career:** American Telephone and Telegraph Co., shareowner correspondent, 1964-66; homemaker, 1966-79; Kurt Orban Co., Inc. (steel importers), North Brunswick, New Jersey, assistant sales manager, 1979-84; writer, 1984—. **Agent:** Cherry Weiner, 28 Kipling Way, Manalapan, New Jersey 07726, USA. **Address:** Highland Park, New Jersey.

FANTASY PUBLICATIONS

Novels (series: Far Side of Forever; Jalav, Terrilian)

The Warrior Within (Terrilian). New York, DAW, 1982.
The Crystals of Mida (Jalav). New York, DAW, 1982.
The Warrior Enchained (Terrilian). New York, DAW, 1983.
An Oath to Mida (Jalav). New York, DAW, 1983.
The Warrior Rearmed (Terrilian). New York, DAW, 1984.
Chosen of Mida (Jalav). New York, DAW, 1984.
The Will of the Gods (Jalav). New York, DAW, 1985.
To Battle the Gods (Jalav). New York, DAW, 1986.
The Warrior Challenged (Terrilian). New York, DAW, 1986.
The Rebel Prince. New York, DAW, 1987.
The Far Side of Forever. New York, DAW, 1987.
Lady Blade, Lord Fighter. New York, DAW, 1987.
The Warrior Victorious (Terrilian). New York, DAW, 1988.
Mists of the Ages. New York, DAW, 1988.
Hellhound Magic (Forever). New York, DAW, 1989.
Dawn Song. New York, Avon, 1990.
Silver Princess, Golden Knight. New York, Avon, 1992.
The Hidden Realms. New York, Avon, 1993.
Dark Mirror, Dark Dreams. New York, Avon, 1994.

OTHER PUBLICATIONS

Novels

Mind Guest: A Diana Santee Spaceways Novel. New York, DAW, 1984.
Gateway to Xanadu: A Diana Santee Spaceways Novel. New York, DAW, 1985.
Haunted House. Toronto, Harlequin, 1990.

*   *   *

Sharon Green is a writer whose work has been compared to that of science-fantasist John Norman. This has done her no favours with a public beyond Norman's specialized fetishistic following, though the comparison was at first encouraged by her own publishers. Although much of her early work can be claimed as science fiction of the "planetary romance" type, it tends to be regarded as fantasy, perhaps because of the ubiquity in it of muscular barbarians; but there are few supernatural elements, and some effort is made to differentiate her imaginary planets from the off-the-peg clones of the medieval Earth where such characters usually ply their swords.

Green's reputation was shaped by her first novel, *The Warrior Within*. She has written little that is more powerful than the opening chapters. Terrilian, the viewpoint character, is a diplomat living on a civilized world much like the modern USA. She has vaguely-defined special powers, which lead to her being treated with exaggerated respect, though few of her colleagues seem to like her, as she is bad-tempered.

At the start of the novel she is raped by Tammad, a visitor from a far more primitive planet. It rapidly becomes apparent that her colleagues are conspiring to put her entirely under Tammad's control, at least until she has helped him complete some obscure diplomatic business which suits their purpose. Terrilian is entirely helpless: she is told that if she does not agree to go to his planet and become his possession for a set period, at the end of which he has agreed to release her, she will be kidnapped and sent anyway. If this happens, there is no guarantee she will ever be released.

After the first few chapters, this ceases to be a realistic account of the brutal abuse of a woman: nor is it in any meaningful sense a plea for the kind of consensual sado-masochism which has recently dared to speak its name. Once they reach Tammad's world, he both seeks and respects Terrilian's advice, but never allows her any autonomy at all. He has the ability to tell when she will be aroused by a forceful approach, and always ignores her feeble protests that she would prefer to be asked. She can be punished for behaving immodestly in front of others, though when he feels like it he commands her to sleep with his retainers. She is expected to act in a slave-like capacity, though Tammad makes it clear that she is not, in his view, a true slave, being free to walk away into the jungle if she wishes. If, however, she decides to do this, she may take nothing with her, not even clothing. The rest of his tribe are at least as misogynistic as he, and the other tribes of the planet even worse, so she stays. Tammad's favoured method of discipline is to strip Terrilian and beat her with a stick on the "hips and thighs."

Terrilian shows no overtly masochistic enjoyment of this treatment, but nevertheless falls in love with Tammad, and tries to compromise with him. Though at times he shows her a begrudging and bewildered respect, at others he treats her even worse, and his reasons for punishing her become more trivial. At the end of the novel, Tammad keeps his word, and returns Terrilian to her own people. She is upset that he appears not to be distressed by the need to do this, and seeks comfort from her father, who we now learn is the bureaucrat responsible for her plight in the first place. (This is not made clear at the beginning, when the characters are introduced; the fact that the novel is dedicated to Green's own father is interesting, but I do not know if it has any significance.)

At the start of the next book in the series, *The Warrior Enchained,* Terrilian is again leading an independent and effective life on her own world. However, as soon as Tammad appears and demands that she return with him, she agrees. He soon starts to mistreat her again, she rebels, and before long her plight is even worse than it has been.

Published in parallel with these novels was a similar series featuring Jalav, an Amazon warrior. In the first, *The Crystals of Mida,* the eponymous sacred crystals are stolen and the Amazons go in search of them. Before long they are seized and brutalized by "males" whom they themselves have previously captured and treated in much the same way. Jalav is not a clone of Terrilian; she is more like a female version of the male Tammad, proud and totally inflexible in attitude. The books lack some of the disturbing feel of the Terrilian novels: the Amazons have no difficulty coping with their planet whenever, as often happens, they arm themselves and escape their captors. Though described as a "slip of a girl" and easy to overcome in unarmed combat, Jalav is resourceful and deadlier than the males with her sword. The story thus becomes a stylized fetishistic ritual of escape and punishment. Its main strengths lie in its resolutely uncolloquial style, which seems stiff at first, but gradually grows on the ear as the way dignified barbarians might speak, and the similarly consistent development, or rather lack of it, in Jalav's world-view. For her there is no easy conversion to the attitudes of her (in some ways) more civilized captors.

Green's more recent work seems to be moving away from her roots in sado-masochistic Norman conquests and into high fantasy proper. In *Dawn Song,* for instance, most of the usual elements of her 1980s books are missing. There is a more imaginative fantasy background, in which the Princess of a Moon Kingdom sets out to recover a stolen sacred flame. Though resourceful and adept at interesting magics (she can talk to trees and has delightful conversations with spiders), she is thoroughly spoiled, as stubborn as Jalav, and constantly denigrates the ability of her male companions to help her. These are veritable New Men compared to their predecessors in Green's fiction, for which relief they don't get much thanks. There is one torture scene, glossed over and not sexually charged, and the story ends without anyone being forced to do anything sexual against their will.

—Peter T. Garratt

GREEN, Simon R(ichard)

Nationality: British. **Born:** Bradford-on-Avon, Wiltshire, 25 August 1955. **Education:** Fitzmaurice Grammar School; Thames Polytechnic, 1973-76, B.A. in humanities; Leicester University, 1977-78, M.A. in modern English and American literature. **Career:** Shop assistant; stage and television actor; freelance writer. **Agent:** Joshua Bilmes, Scott Meredith Literary Agency, 845 Third Avenue, New York, NY 10022, USA. **Address:** 37 St. Laurence Road, Bradford-on-Avon, Wilts. BA15 1JQ, England.

FANTASY PUBLICATIONS

Novels (series: Blue Moon Rising; Hawk and Fisher)

Hawk and Fisher. New York, Ace, 1990; as *No Haven for the Guilty,* London, Headline, 1990.
Winner Takes All (Hawk and Fisher). New York, Ace, 1991; as *Devil Take the Hindmost,* London, Headline, 1991.
The God Killer (Hawk and Fisher). New York, Ace, and London, Headline, 1991.
Blue Moon Rising. New York, Roc, and London, Gollancz, 1991.
Wolf in the Fold (Hawk and Fisher). New York, Ace, 1991; as *Vengeance for a Lonely Man,* London, Headline, 1992.
Guard Against Dishonor (Hawk and Fisher). New York, Ace, 1991; London, Headline, 1992.
Blood and Honour (Blue Moon). London, Gollancz, 1992; New York, Roc, 1993.
The Bones of Haven (Hawk and Fisher). New York, Ace, 1992; as *Two Kings in Haven,* London, Headline, 1992.

Down Among the Dead Men (Blue Moon). London, Gollancz, and New York, Roc, 1993.
Shadows Fall. London, Gollancz, and New York, Roc, 1994.

OTHER PUBLICATIONS

Novels

Robin Hood: Prince of Thieves (novelization of screenplay). New York, Berkley, and London, Fantail, 1991.
Mistworld. New York, Ace, and London, Gollancz, 1992.
Ghostworld. New York, Ace, and London, Gollancz, 1993.
Hellworld. New York, Ace, 1993; London, Gollancz, 1995.
Deathstalker. London, Gollancz, and New York, Roc, 1995.

*

Simon R. Green comments:

My fantasy work has always had a firm emphasis on verisimilitude, on giving a real feeling of what it would actually be like to live in a fantasy world. There are dragons, unicorns and demons, princesses and sorcerers, but none of them are at all what you'd expect. My six Hawk and Fisher books have been described as *Hill Street Blues* in a fantasy setting. There are battles and wonders and political intrigues in my work, along with a general willingness to go tearing off in any direction that looks like fun. I am also prone to spooky moments, and the occasional sudden descent into heart-stopping terror. My books take no prisoners, and not all my characters get out alive.

*   *   *

Simon R. Green first came to prominence in the USA with his Hawk and Fisher series of novels. Subsequently, these were published in the UK by Headline. Meanwhile, Gollancz published *Blue Moon Rising* and *Blood and Honour* as by "Simon Green" (perhaps they thought the "R" was unnecessary). These are pure straight-down-the-line heroic fantasy, while the "Simon R. Green" novels—the Hawk and Fisher series and later novels such as *Mistworld* and *Ghostworld*—stand in stark contrast, with their sprawling mish-mash crossover of genre tropes from science fiction, fantasy, horror, and television cops shows, soap operas and comedies.

Green's first pure fantasy, *Blue Moon Rising,* displays all his trademarks. First and foremost is the sense that medieval-type fantasy worlds are far from comfortable, noble, or romantic. On the first page, we see the hero, Prince Rupert, in full armour chasing and failing to catch a flea inside his breastplate, and suffering the trickle of rain down the back of his neck from a leaky helmet. He has been sent out to kill a dragon in the safe expectation he will be killed in the process—he is the second son of the king, and thus perceived as a threat to the first son who wants to inherit the crown. Almost immediately, we discover the second of Green's trademarks—his wry sense of humour. Rupert is riding a unicorn, and the implication about his sexual activity, confirmed later in the book, is thoroughly counter-heroic. The unicorn is no dumb cypher, however. It talks, and indeed engages in some rather barbed banter with Rupert, and this is undoubtedly Green's third trademark: the overturning of stereotyped expectations. This overturning continues as he encounters a dragon with the usual hoarded treasure—but this one doesn't collect gold, it collects butterflies—and Princess Julia, who has been abandoned as a sacrifice to the dragon but has set up home with it instead. This team of four then set off on a tortuous adventure that culminates in the final battle between good and evil where, as usual in such things, evil almost triumphs but is beaten back, as per the formula, by a combination of selflessness, loyalty, raw courage and faith in the power of good.

Green has other trademarks that are less commendable. He has a propensity for battle scenes that appear to be little more than accounts of computer games where wave after wave of aliens throw themselves at the defences to be annihilated and where every single one has to be killed before the next level can be attained. Of course, it could be argued that such computer games emulate high fantasy instead of the other way round, but in these books the sudden waves and silences become too formulaic. Formulaic, too, are some of the plots. Green's second high fantasy, *Blood and Honour,* set in the same world as *Blue Moon Rising* but somewhat later in time, is a simple double-replaces-highly-placed-but-incapacitated-man plot, one previous example of which is Heinlein's *Double Star* (after Anthony Hope's *The Prisoner of Zenda*). Despite this, *Blood and Honour* is actually a very good book indeed, with Green's by-now familiar overturning of expectations and wry humour in full flow. Alas, the same cannot be said for the third book in the series, *Down Among the Dead Men.* Again set in the fantasy world of *Blue Moon Rising,* only a few years after the final battle of that story, the plot this time is lifted whole from *Ghostworld,* one of Simon R. Green's crossover science-fiction/fantasy novels. Peculiarly, both books were published in the same year by the same publisher, and most confusingly, *Down Among the Dead Men* is also published as by "Simon R. Green, author of *Blue Moon Rising.*"

Fundamentally, in both stories a small group of people is sent to investigate why an isolated but fortified emplacement of great value has suddenly ceased communicating; in one it is a fort in the forest, in the other a mine, Base 13 (Green never misses an obvious opportunity to load names with meaning), on an alien planet. First they have to break in against their own fortifications, then they have to descend into the bowels beneath the fort/base to find and destroy the previously unsuspected ancient evil on top of which the places were built. Considered as locked-room mysteries, the science-fiction version is by far the better, because where evil-magic-can-be-defeated-by-a-brave-and-good-heart explains all in *Down Among the Dead Men,* in *Ghostworld* the team have to actually solve the mystery to the reader's satisfaction as well.

Solving mysteries is also the stock in trade of Hawk and Fisher, the husband-and-wife team of Captains of the Guard in the city of Haven, "by popular acclaim the vilest and most corrupt city in the Low Kingdoms" (this last is quoted from the first page of *Guard Against Dishonour,* but can be found almost verbatim in all six Hawk and Fisher books, as can many other stock descriptions. Indeed, they become so familiar it is almost as if you were reading Homer, with his "wine dark, fish-infested seas"). Green's Hawk and Fisher stories at first seem little more than standard buddy-cop-procedural stories set in a fantasy city where sword and sorcery is the everyday currency. However, in these books, awash with cliche, Green actually presents some of his most startling and original thinking (my particular favourite is *The God Killer,* where Hawk and Fisher have to solve a serial-killer mystery where the victims are all superannuated gods whose supernatural powers have become severely attenuated by the fact that almost no one believes in them any more). It is not even the ideas *per se* that are so startling, but the effortless way Green harnesses so many of them into

an often whimsical story—it is here more than anywhere that the influence of American television shows is so evident.

Of course the one thing you can't do in a television show is kill off one of the partners. And Green, while the eternal iconoclast, knows which side his bread is buttered, so he would never do this to Hawk and Fisher. Nevertheless, he explores precisely this line in *Mistworld,* where he plunders the characters from Hawk and Fisher shamelessly to create Sergeants Topaz and Michael Gunn of the city watchmen (Green never calls his cops "policemen"). The setting is the same science-fictional universe as *Ghostworld,* where the Empire has nearly wiped out the rebels—if this sounds familiar, it must have become clear by now that Green uses second-hand material quite shamelessly, but it is never a problem because he always makes it over into something new. In this universe we have starships and blasters and personal force-shields, which means that the only way to kill someone who is wearing one is with a slow moving weapon such as a sword blade. On Mistworld, few people can afford energy weapons anyway, so everyone goes armed with swords. After a couple of scene-setting chapters, Topaz's husband Michael is killed in mistake for her. The bulk of the story is taken up with her not only pursuing the assassin, but also finding out the overarching plot behind the assassination.

Most recently, Green has produced a very fat book within each stream of his oeuvre. *Shadows Fall* is a 20th-century fantasy (and thus slightly resembles John Crowley's *Little, Big* in its charm and whimsy). Shadows Fall is a town on the edge of reality where all dreams, legends and heroes that anyone has ever believed in go when their popularity starts to wane. Here they become real, and then slowly fade away until they are called to go through the Forever Door. There are several plots hatched to take over Shadows Fall, and the upshot is yet another abattoir-like final battle very similar to that in *Blue Moon Rising* in that all the good guys are killed and the reverse to good triumphing over evil comes very late indeed. Green's creativity is in full flow, however. He does plunder fantastic characters from the world we know, but he changes their names—thus Sean Morrison is a famous rock singer, and the juvenile atomic terrapins get a passing mention—and the wit and humour is there to the last as well.

The other fat book, *Deathstalker,* is set firmly in the science-fictional universe of *Mistworld* and *Ghostworld.* But whereas those novels tell simple stories of specific incidents, *Deathstalker* is a sprawling galaxy-spanning space opera of the first water, with plots, counterplots, subplots, and lots and lots of inscrutable aliens, space ships, space pirates, and space battles. The empire is no longer a back-drop to the action; it is centre stage. There are plots against the evil empress, richly drawn scenes within the court, and far-flung acts of treachery both against her and by her against her subjects. It defies description, except to say that Green never once loses his hold on the reader; everything, no matter how outrageous, inventive, or horrifying is eminently believable, and the story grips to the last page.

Simon R. Green encompasses the whole gamut of fantastic genre fiction, and it would be unfair to confine him to only one. Indeed, if it is true that in any sufficiently advanced science fiction the science is indistinguishable from magic, then there is no fundamental difference between his sf and fantasy. However, the important thing to remember is that he is master of all these genres, and whatever he takes it upon himself to do he does with great skill. It is only to be regretted that he spends so much time on formulaic battles. Of course, he has produced some 15 books over the past five years, so perhaps he can be forgiven some hack work. One can't help feeling, however, that if he spent a little less time simply producing, and a little more time looking at all the details of his stories, then he would have the potential to be one of our best living fantasists.

—Paul Brazier

GREENLAND, Colin

Nationality: British. **Born:** Dover, Kent, 17 May 1954. **Education:** St. Lawrence College, Ramsgate, Kent, 1964-72; Pembroke College, Oxford, 1972-79, B.A. in English literature and language (honors) 1975; D.Phil. in English literature 1981. **Career:** Fellow in creative writing, Science Fiction Foundation, North East London Polytechnic, 1980-82; co-editor, *Interzone* magazine, London, 1982-85; UK coordinator, Eaton Conference on Science Fiction, University of California, Riverside/North East London Polytechnic, 1983-84; part-time tutor, University of London Extramural Department, 1985-90; chair, Science Fiction Writers' Conference, Milford, Hampshire, 1986. Since 1989, reviews editor, *Foundation* magazine, London. **Awards:** J. Lloyd Eaton award, for criticism, 1985; Arthur C. Clarke award, 1991; British Science Fiction Association award, 1991. **Agent:** Maggie Noach, 21 Redan Street, London W14 0AB, England; or, Martha Millard, 204 Park Avenue, Madison, NJ, 07940, USA. **Address:** 2A Ortygia House, 6 Lower Road, Harrow, Middlesex HA2 0DA, England.

FANTASY PUBLICATIONS

Novels

Daybreak on a Different Mountain. London, Allen and Unwin, 1984.
The Hour of the Thin Ox. London, Allen and Unwin, 1987.
Other Voices. London, Unwin Hyman, 1988.
Harm's Way. London, HarperCollins, and New York, AvoNova, 1993.

OTHER PUBLICATIONS

Novels

Take Back Plenty. London, Unwin Hyman, 1990; New York, Avon, 1991.
Seasons of Plenty. London, HarperCollins, 1995.

Other

The Entropy Exhibition: Michael Moorcock and the British 'New Wave' in Science Fiction. London and Boston, Routledge, 1983.
Magnetic Storm: The Work of Roger and Martyn Dean. London, Dragon's World, 1984.
The Freelance Writer's Handbook, with Paul Kerton. London, Ebury, 1986.

Editor, with John Clute and David Pringle, *Interzone*: The First Anthology. London, Dent, 1985; New York, St. Martin's Press, 1986.

Editor, *Michael Moorcock: Death is No Obstacle* (interviews). Manchester, Savoy, 1992.

*

Colin Greenland comments:

My fiction is richly and definitively fantastic, whether it takes the accents of otherworld fantasy, science fiction, horror or whatthehell-was-that? It tends to be about real people in imaginary worlds, people who are, like you and I, trying to live satisfactory lives under unsatisfactory, unpredictable conditions where other people are in charge, violence may ensue at any minute, and all the plethora of instruction manuals are untrustworthy, contradictory, and in any case have been ineptly translated from some obscure foreign language. Lewis Carroll's Alice meets Mervyn Peake's Titus Groan in M. John Harrison's Viriconium. Expect exotic locations, alien entities, bizarre mysteries, one or two words you don't know and three or four others you haven't seen for a while and didn't expect to see here.

*   *   *

Greenland's first published book, *The Entropy Exhibition,* was an expansion of his Oxford University Ph.D. thesis on Michael Moorcock and the New Wave in science fiction; and his early fantasies are very much products of that era of British sf and fantasy—an era that was by this time essentially over. His more recent novels have demonstrated almost a backlash against these formative influences, although still retaining the careful, crafted, style-conscious "voice" of his earlier work.

His first three novels deploy standard high-fantasy tropes in an attempt to redefine the concerns of the sub-genre. In *Daybreak on a Different Mountain* two members of the ruling class, the Aigu, depart the walled city of Thryn on a quest to discover the Cirnex, the prophet of Thryn's official religion, which is worship of the god Gomath. The stimulus for their quest is interestingly chosen—the religion's earthly leader has decreed that one of the two errants is in fact the mysterious Cirnex, and their mission is to prove this is not the case—but the tale itself soon dissolves into a series of picaresque adventures, illuminated not frequently enough by some sprightly ideas and images. After their return, their quest enigmatically successful, one of the questers develops miraculous powers and takes over the rôle of Gomath in the reconstituted religion; the other becomes, in effect, the Cirnex, just as he was originally accused. There is a timorousness, a coyness, about both telling and tale that renders it ultimately unsatisfying: one has the feeling that the tyro writer lacked the courage simply to slap together the raw materials and enjoy the cake, instead covering his confection in a superfluity of tasteful, and concealing, decoration.

The same strictures apply to *The Hour of the Thin Ox* and *Other Voices*—set in different parts of the same world—but by now Greenland had learned to deploy his not inconsiderable wit: both tales are still styled rather than told, and both have baroque plots leading to inconclusive conclusions, yet their humour saves them from inconsequentiality. In the former novel two disparate characters from different sides in a war in a primitive province far from both their homes are forced by circumstances to question the nature of their loyalties and indeed what they truly desire from their lives. For long enough their loyalty is to each other, but in the ultimate—once baddies have been slain and conquerors defeated (in a last hurrah for the golden hordes of the New Wave, the victory comes about through the influence of a hallucinogenic plant)—the two discover their loyalties are, individually, to themselves; the lovers part to pursue their own careers. In *Other Voices*, Greenland's masterpiece of style over content, the titular princess of a subject country discovers that she must side with the rebellious outcast tribes in order to oust the conquerors and regain her kingdom for not just herself but her subjects. The book is highly entertaining, passing the time prettily; but little more. Its title could, cynically, be taken as a comment on these first three novels.

As early as 1985 Greenland had been talking of the need for "real" science-fiction writers to recapture from the movie-makers the field of space opera—long regarded as the black sheep of sf's family—to show that from seemingly unpromising materials good tales could be wrought. He seemed a maverick choice for self-nomination, but the product of his endeavours, *Take Back Plenty*, was hugely successful, scooping all three of the UK awards for best science-fiction novel. Oddly, Greenland has shown little interest in attempts by others to perform a similar exercise with the tropes of pulp fantasy.

His next novel is certainly his most significant, and most readable, piece of fantasy. *Harm's Way* conjures a universe in which spaceflight is feasible by sailing-ship, tacking through the aether from one inhabited planet to the next. Set in a distant analogue of our 19th century, the tale concerns Sophie Farthing, daughter of a murdered London whore, as she quests to discover her father, who proves to be the implacably ruthless Lord Lychworthy, Earl of Io and all-powerful Master of the Most Exalted Hierarchy and Worshipful Guild of Aether Pilots. Aided by her beloved, the assassin who could not bear to kill her, she at last despatches her father to attain interworldly prestige and the promise of marital bliss. Occasionally the sickly tweeness that marred some of Greenland's earlier work raises its head here (of the Earl's home, in third-person narrative: "Who could have ordered such a mansion built here, beyond all prospect of company? Only one who prefers to keep the trappings of civilization but dispense with the annoyance of neighbours. Already we suspect he must be the most confirmed misanthrope"), but for the most part the cod-Dickensian narration works well, being a part of the telling of the tale rather than an end in itself.

Greenland's return to fantasy with *Harm's Way* might more profitably be thought of as a fresh beginning, his status that of enormously promising newcomer rather than practised hand. He seems, finally, to have shaken off the dead, emulatory weight of the New Wave—to have acquired the confidence to stop speaking with other people's voices.

—John Grant

GREGORIAN, Joyce Ballou

Nationality: American. **Born:** Boston, Massachusetts, 1946. **Education:** Radcliffe College. **Family:** Married John B. Hampshire. **Career:** Worked in the family rug business; lectured on Armenian and Middle-Eastern topics; compiled museum catalogues on the subject of oriental rugs; also a horse-breeder, and composer and performer. **Died:** May 1991.

FANTASY PUBLICATIONS

Novels (series: Tredana in all books)

The Broken Citadel. New York, Atheneum, 1975; London, Orbit, 1989.
Castledown. New York, Atheneum, 1977; London, Orbit, 1989.
The Great Wheel. New York, Ace, 1987; London, Orbit, 1990.

*   *   *

Few high fantasies since *The Lord of the Rings* have been as detailed and intricate as Joyce Ballou Gregorian's trilogy, though the first volume, on its own, leaves the reader unsure whether or not it is aimed at a juvenile audience. Sibby Barron, an 11-year-old schoolgirl from contemporary Massachusetts, is transported by accident (she is trespassing in an old, deserted house near her home) to another world. The world of Tredana and Treclere, two competing city-states, is at perhaps a Renaissance level of technology and includes a number of different national or tribal groups with a mainly Middle-Eastern flavour. Sibby is not simply a spectator; she is also an important catalyst in the politics and turbulent events that link the two cities and their fortunes over two decades.

Apart from the complexity of background, the trilogy is marked out by its romantic content and brisk plot. There is romance here in every sense of the word. Each volume includes some love interest, toned down in *The Broken Citadel* due to Sibby's age. In *Castledown* she marries one of her leading men and has a daughter by another. In *The Great Wheel*, aged about 30, she renews liaisons with both of them. In another sense of romance, the trilogy is full of emotion. Also, it is full of descriptions of beautiful women, handsome men, exotic landscapes and colourful minor characters. The trilogy is plot-driven, there being few pages in which exciting events are not occurring; reversals of fortune happen very frequently. None of these elements is at all original, yet they are so fluently combined that the reader accepts them.

Such bulging plots are difficult to precis. In *The Broken Citadel*, Sibby finds herself on a coastal stretch of the fantasy world. She joins a small group from Tredana, including young Prince Leron (heir to the throne) and Dansen (a scholar) who are en route to rescue Dastra, the imprisoned daughter of the goddess-queen Simirimia of Treclere. They succeed, but a tidal wave scatters them and Sibby, together with Dansen and Dastra (a spoilt brat) travel to Tredana via a desert tribe, the Karabdu, whose leader is the young and handsome Ajjibawr. The Karabdu are tent-dwelling nomads who breed horses and carry curved swords; but for their fair hair and blue eyes they might be Arabs.

Sibby gets to Tredana to find that Leron is presumed dead and that his aged father, Mathon, is handing over the throne to Ddiskeard, Leron's cousin. She goes to Treclere to help free Leron and, eventually, to unseat Queen Simirimia (who is, by some strange means, Sibby's mother). Back in Tredana, Sibby, Leron and Dansen help Mathon to escape from Ddiskeard and they all go off into exile. Just as Leron decides that Sibby is old enough for physical love, she is snatched back to the Massachusetts moment from which she had departed.

In *Castledown*, Sibby is six years older and at college; eight years have passed in Tredana. An ouija board session transports her this time; she has forgotten all about her previous visit. Leron, Mathon and Dansen are still in exile, and Ajjibawr is deposed, presumed dead. Sibby joins a group of travelling players, is kidnapped, rescued by Ajjibawr, has a brief affair with him, is shipwrecked at Tredana, helps Leron regain his kingdom, then marries him. But she is kidnapped again, this time by Michael, her loutish boyfriend from our own world, who has followed her through. At length she escapes, rejoins Leron and has Ajjibawr's baby. Once again she returns involuntarily to our world, to marry Michael.

The Great Wheel is set about 12 years later, just after Sibby has divorced Michael. Tredana is threatened by the invasion of the aged Tibir Agan, whose enormous Angul horde has moved across the continent. Sibby, now thirty, finds herself the sword-bearer of Tibir, saving his life. A rebel Angul, Tammush, captures Sibby, who finds that Ajjibawr is aiding Tammush. Her memories of him return only gradually and they become lovers again. Later Sibby encounters Leron and is forced (by Tibir) to marry him. Then Leron and Ajjibawr return to Tredana, with Leron as Tibir's vassal lord. Sibby uses her healing powers on Tibir, who is taken to an underworld and forced to play a game of castledown, for his life and empire, against Vazdz, chief of the gods. Sibby follows and sees Tibir win the game (Vazdz cheats) and his battle. Tibir brings Sibby and Ajjibawr together by generous gifts, then he dies. His world empire, only three weeks in existence, begins to break up. This time Sibby is not transported back to our world.

While Gregorian's major characters are well drawn and considerably detailed, such multitudes of minor characters are involved that many are no more than ciphers. As is often the case in high fantasy, the dialogue here is sometimes comically formal and stilted, though in general the writing style is smooth and assured, with plot elements blending together more convincingly than one would suppose. There is a cleverness of presentation in each book, with *The Broken Citadel*'s sections being based upon a set of tarot-like cards, *Castledown*'s sections being named after the stages in the chess-like game of that name, and *The Great Wheel* being divided into world ages, adding up to a metaphysical great wheel.

Throughout the trilogy there is great and loving use made of horses—not surprising if one knows that Gregorian was an expert breeder of Arabian horses. The complexity of names, relationships and events means that the trilogy repays re-reading, and this has led to its minor cult status. While the books are actually less deep than they at first appear, everything in them holds together well, and there is never a dull moment.

—Chris Morgan

GRIMWOOD, Ken(neth)

Nationality: American. **Born:** 1945(?). **Career:** News director, KFWB radio, Los Angeles, California. **Awards:** World Fantasy award, 1987.

FANTASY PUBLICATIONS

Novels

Replay. New York, Arbor House, 1986; London, Grafton, 1987.
Into the Deep. New York, Morrow, 1995.

OTHER PUBLICATIONS

Novels

Breakthrough. New York, Doubleday, 1976; London, Allen, 1977.
Elise. New York, Doubleday, 1977.
The Voice Outside. New York, Doubleday, 1982.

*   *   *

Ken Grimwood, with three non-genre novels to his credit, came to the attention of fantasy readers with *Replay,* which won the World Fantasy Award in competition against several better-known candidates. *Replay* is the story of a 43-year-old man trapped in a dead-end job and a dull marriage, who suddenly dies of a heart attack and wakes up in his 18-year-old body, back in 1963, with his memories of the "future" intact. He does the obvious things, betting on sporting events and the like to make himself rich and powerful. He tries to prevent the assassination of John Kennedy, but finds that he cannot alter large-scale events. He does, however, manage a better marriage (to someone other than his first wife), begets a child, and generally achieves a better life, only to have all these gains (including the child's existence) wiped out by another "death" at age 43. His life is caught in a loop. Every time he dies, he is back in 1963. Every time a specific moment approaches in 1988, he will die again, no matter what precautions he takes. Eventually he makes contact with other such time-looped "repeaters."

Replay is smoothly written and deftly observed, making excellent use of cultural and period detail. Though the characterizations are somewhat shallow, the novel builds interest as the protagonist lives his life again, and ultimately becomes an intriguing meditation on questions of free will and the nature of time.

The later novel, *Into the Deep,* hovers right on the edge of science fiction in the same way that Arthur C. Clarke's *Childhood's End* does. The subject matter is ultimately mystical, but it is given a strong scientific gloss, without openly admitted supernaturalism. The story is one of transformation, as various humans make telepathic contact with dolphins, only to discover that a vaster, planetary "Source-Mind" has been reaching out to mankind for millennia. Now humans, dolphins, and whales must work together to avert global ecological catastrophe. This averted, a utopia ensues, with mankind once more in harmony with nature, the equal (if not superior) intelligence of the cetaceans fully recognized, and vast wisdom and knowledge gained (by the humans) as folks meld with the Source-Mind. (Not surprisingly, persons from non-Western, "primitive" cultures are far more adept at this than insensitive, sceptical Westerners.) There are hints that this planetary mind is in touch with other group-intelligences throughout the universe, and that such a melding represents, as it does in *Childhood's End,* a higher stage of human evolution.

Depending on one's perspective, *Into the Deep* is either fantasy or New Age science fiction. It is far trendier than *Replay,* virtually a catalogue of current pop-mystical ideas, and therefore more likely to date and less likely to have lasting impact. But Ken Grimwood remains a very capable writer, whose future career could be interesting.

—Darrell Schweitzer

GRUNDY, Stephan

Nationality: American. **Born:** New York City, 28 June 1967. **Education:** Southern Methodist University, B.A. in English and German studies; currently completing a Ph.D. thesis at Cambridge University, England.

FANTASY PUBLICATIONS

Novel

Rhinegold. New York, Bantam, and London, Michael Joseph, 1994.

*

Stephan Grundy comments:

My work is based on the legends of the early Germanic peoples (Anglo-Saxons, Germans, Scandinavians). *Rhinegold* retells the tale of the Volsungs and Nibelungs from which Wagner drew the plot of his Ring Cycle and Tolkien got many of the elements he used in his histories of Middle-Earth—the sword broken and re-forged, the dragon guarding the hoard, the cursed ring of power. The tales of the North are the largely unrecognized cultural inheritance of the English-speaking peoples; it is the purpose of my writing to bring these stories, and the knowledge of the culture and gods that shaped them, into the light of day again. Much of modern fantasy is based second- or third-hand on the myths and folklore of the Northern peoples; *Rhinegold* returns to the source from which the fathers of the genre got the greatest part of their inspiration.

*   *   *

Rhinegold, the only fantasy novel so far by Stephan Grundy, is a substantial book, retelling the story of the Ring of the Nibelungs (best known from Wagner's *Ring* and *The Nibelungenlied*) at great length and dead straight. It is dedicated to Wagner and Tolkien, which defines the standards by which it requires to be judged. It first appeared in the German language in 1992, and was published to much acclaim in the English-speaking world two years later.

Grundy adopts an elevated style full of rich descriptive passages and including some archaic Nordic words, of which the least familiar, like "wod" and "orlog," work best, implying a cast of mind significantly removed from the modern; others, like "ween" and "steed" just look affected. He also uses some unfamiliar variants—Wodan rather than Woden or Wotan, Sigifrith for Siegfried, walkurja for valkyrie—apparently to serve some overall linguistic consistency, and to enhance an overwhelmingly serious-minded effect, so that the reader's reaction will depend very much on how seriously he is willing to take the story. Just as the original audience to Aeschylus's trilogy knew what evils would befall the Atreides, many who buy the book will already know it in outline, so the sense of gathering doom, which appears from the moment Loki kills the were-otter, is entirely appropriate. This is high tragedy in the grandest Germanic manner, and is presented as such from the outset.

That aside, there are striking parallels to Greek tragedy, especially in the character of Sigilind, whose husband has treacherously murdered her father and brothers. She must remain true to her marriage vows, but she must also avenge them if she can. She therefore binds her sons to avenge their uncles and grandfather—against

their father. The parallel with Orestes could hardly be closer, and the outcome is just as gruesome in detail, though quite different in essence. A similar tragedy befalls Gundrun, whose brothers murder her husband and marry her to Attila the Hun, who subsequently betrays and murders them. Her vengeance on all these wrongs provides the book's climax.

There's a metaphysical difficulty with the role of the gods. Wodan manipulates the development of the story, not entirely creditably, and to an end which hardly justifies the means. The Aesir are not the Olympians, and their motivations are far more opaque. They are also more circumscribed, both by Fate (which also bound the Olympians, though less closely) and by obligations to blood-kin (which the Olympians tended to ignore). That obligation cuts both ways: if you have been wronged by someone, you are required to take what revenge you can against all his kith and kin, no matter how innocent, though the degree of vengeance may vary. Thus, Sigifrith hacks the living heart out of Ingwe, who has treacherously murdered his father, and doesn't lift a finger to interfere when one of his followers is violating a woman of Ingwe's people in a mud puddle; neither the act nor the omission in any way compromises his status as hero. In other contexts the book sanctions cold-blooded murder on several occasions as well as glorifying raiding (i.e., hot-blooded murder in pursuit of gain) throughout.

But the chief psychological difficulty lies in the Germanic conception of the afterlife, which is fundamental to the actions of all the principal characters: they rejected the concept of honourable retirement. An ageing warrior, whose reflexes had slowed and whose joints had stiffened, could not sit back in the reflection that he had won through where others had succumbed and devote his declining years to imparting lore to the young—far from it. He was in danger of the worst fate of all, to die from natural causes. Only those who met death in battle would be summoned to join the gods at Asgard, there to feast and joust until Ragnarok. Hence the practice (not confined to the old) of fighting "berserk" (i.e., in the front line and without armour) to compel an invitation. That this bleak philosophy influenced real behaviour is certain—there's plenty of historic evidence for it—the only question is how far it permeated daily life. In the context of an heroic myth it is never questioned.

So the tale unfolds, the scenes of rape, mayhem, witchcraft, murder, incest, conspiracy, frenzy and torture interspersed with tenderness, hunting, domesticity, skilled craftsmanship and feasting. The variations in mood and pace help to sustain interest in the Matter of the Walsings, which is the first great family saga of the post-Dark Age tradition. At over 700 close-printed pages Grundy has plenty of room for incident—far more than Wagner could fit into *The Ring,* for instance—but Grundy never becomes discursive; every incident enriches the principal theme. Even his essays in alliterative verse come off better than most, including those of Lewis and Tolkien. Altogether, *Rhinegold* would be an extraordinary achievement from a novelist with a string of awards covering decades; for a first novel it's breathtaking.

Finally, no new book can be completely divorced from the context of its time. This one has qualities which demand that it be taken as seriously as the author could hope for, but it also has resonances with the *Germanen Order,* the *Kraft durch Freude* movement and all the iconography of renascent Nazism, down to the latest backstreet hate-sheet from Leipzig or Birmingham. These must be faced, and faced down, for it is a genuine classic, written to define and make accessible one of the great cycles of legend. As such, it stands above the moral and political preoccupations of a particular decade or century. Many will find it unpalatable, for which they can hardly be condemned, but those who can stomach it have something enduring to enjoy.

—Chris Gilmore

GUNN, Neil M(iller)

Nationality: British. **Born:** Caithness, Scotland, 8 November 1891. **Education:** The Highland School, and privately. **Family:** Married Jessie Dallas Frew in 1921. **Career:** Civil servant until 1937; customs and excise officer; freelance writer. **Awards:** James Tait Black Memorial prize, 1938. LL.D.: Edinburgh University. **Died:** 15 January 1973.

FANTASY PUBLICATIONS

Novels

The Green Isle of the Great Deep. London, Faber, 1944.

Short Stories

Hidden Doors. Edinburgh, Porpoise Press, 1929.

OTHER PUBLICATIONS

Novels

The Grey Coast. London, Cape, and Boston, Little Brown, 1926.
Morning Tide. Edinburgh, Porpoise Press, and New York, Harcourt Brace, 1931.
The Lost Glen. Edinburgh, Porpoise Press, 1932.
Sun Circle. Edinburgh, Porpoise Press, 1933.
Butcher's Broom. Edinburgh, Porpoise Press, 1934; as *Highland Night,* New York, Harcourt Brace, 1935.
Highland River. Edinburgh, Porpoise Press, and Philadelphia, Lippincott, 1937.
Wild Geese Overhead. London, Faber, 1939.
Second Sight. London, Faber, 1940.
The Silver Darlings. London, Faber, 1941; New York, Stewart, 1945.
Young Art and Old Hector. London, Faber, 1942; New York, Stewart, 1944.
The Serpent. London, Faber, 1943; as *Man Goes Alone,* New York, Stewart, 1944.
The Key of the Chest. London, Faber, 1945; New York, Stewart, 1946.
The Drinking Well. London, Faber, 1946; New York, Stewart, 1947.
The Shadow. London, Faber, 1948.
The Silver Bough. London, Faber, 1948.
The Lost Chart. London, Faber, 1949.
The Well at the World's End. London, Faber, 1951.
Blood Hunt. London, Faber, 1952.
The Other Landscape. London, Faber, 1954.

Short Stories

The White Hour and Other Stories. London, Faber, 1950.

Plays

Back Home. Glasgow, Wilson, 1932.
The Ancient Fire (produced by the Scottish National Players, in the 1930s).
Choosing a Play: A Comedy of Community Drama. Edinburgh, Porpoise Press, 1938.
Old Music. London, Nelson, 1939.
Net Results. London, Nelson, 1939.

Other

Whisky and Scotland: A Practical and Spiritual Survey. London, Routledge, 1935.
Off in a Boat (travel). London, Faber, 1938.
Storm and Precipice and Other Pieces. London, Faber, 1942.
Highland Pack (travel). London, Faber, 1949.
The Atom of Delight (autobiography). London, Faber, 1956.

*

Critical Studies: *The Scottish Tradition in Literature* by Kurt Wittig, Edinburgh, Oliver and Boyd, 1956; *Essays on Neil M. Gunn* edited by David Morrison, Thurso, Caithness Books, 1971; *Neil M. Gunn: The Man and the Writer* edited by Alexander Scott and Douglas Gifford, Edinburgh, Blackwood, 1973; *The Novels of Neil M. Gunn: A Critical Study* by Margery McCulloch, Edinburgh, Scottish Academic Press, 1987.

*   *   *

"Whatever my writing may look like," Neil Gunn once wrote in a letter to Naomi Mitchison, "I'm just a hard-bitten realist". It was true; Gunn's writing often had a hallucinatory intensity, especially when it dealt with dreams and visions, but he was always determined that—unlike the schoolmaster in his short story "Half-Light"—he would never fall prey to the "Celtic Twilight hallucinations" of Fiona MacLeod (William Sharp). His early short story "Visioning," first published in 1923, eloquently proposes that the proper exercise of the imagination is to bring the real into better focus. Gunn lamented the decline of Highland life and folkways just as passionately as William Sharp's *alter ego* did, but he saw no point in trying to breathe new literary life into old legends. In addition to the above-mentioned examples several other stories in the collection *Hidden Doors* feature visions, but only the title story and "Such Stuff as Dreams" can be classed as marginal fantasies, by virtue of allowing dreams to presage or determine moments of death. Nor can the historical novel *Sun Circle* be reckoned a fantasy, even though its depiction of Druid belief and ritual is (inevitably) wholly imaginary. Perhaps ironically, it was not until Gunn made a conscientious attempt to cast off the downbeat fatalism of his early novels, determining instead to isolate and celebrate that which was positive and worthwhile in the experience of Highland life, that he was drawn to write his only true fantasy.

The Green Isle of the Great Deep is a sequel to *Young Art and Old Hector,* which further developed a stratagem used in *The Silver Darlings,* by which the quietly heroic endeavours of certain characters are made to echo the exploits of legendary figures. The folkloristic tales which the aged Hector MacDonald communicates to the boy Art Macrae in the earlier book remain exemplary tales, but in the second volume the two are allowed to pass through the magic doorway of a salmon pool to experience an elaborate and sustained vision of the eponymous green isle, which is the land of the dead (also known in Celtic legend as Tir nan Og). They find that the modern condition of the legendary land mirrors the predicament of the actual Highlands in that it has been taken over by alien administrators whose claim to superior wisdom is very dubious. These well-intentioned usurpers have rendered the fruit of the tree of knowledge inedible and forbidden its consumption. Their chief agent, a master of sophistry known as the Questioner, has convinced everyone of the folly of trying to go over their heads with any direct appeal to God—everyone, that is, except the irrepressible Art and the querulous but stubborn Hector, who succeed in bringing the Almighty out of retirement to set things right.

Art and Hector both speak, each after his particular fashion, for a certain kind of freedom which Highland life—in spite of its narrow parochiality—still preserves (in Gunn's eyes) although contemporary urban civilization has quite lost sight of it. All of Gunn's subsequent works involved themselves, in one way or another, with the attempt to analyse and characterize, in the spiritual autobiography that was his last book, as *The Atom of Delight*. Although he broadened the terms of his discussion to include political arguments inspired by contemporary debates about socialism and fascism and mystical ideas of the kind made briefly fashionable by P. D. Ouspensky, sometimes enlivening his plots with elements borrowed from the thriller genre in order to maintain reader interest, he was continually drawn back to the Highland settings with which he felt uniquely comfortable.

Several of Gunn's later novels stray into the borderlands of fantasy while in dogged pursuit of philosophical questions, but none fully crosses the boundary. *Second Sight* comes closest, not only by virtue of its depiction of the young chemist Geoffrey's ironic failure to disprove the precognitive vision of the old ghillie Alick, but also in its use of the symbolic hunt for the stag King Brude as the arena in which the vision ultimately comes true. *The Silver Bough* and *The Well at the World's End* both take their titles from legendary motifs which play considerable symbolic significance within the plots. Each features a quest by philosophically sophisticated protagonists in search of a magical illumination, but that which awaits the characters at the end of their quests is a recognition of the magicality of the mundane. *The Other Landscape* is a similar quest story, which forsakes the imagery of Celtic folklore for the ideologies of Eastern mysticism which came to fascinate Gunn late in life. Although *The Other Landscape* has strong affinities with such outright metaphysical fantasies as Gerald Warre Cornish's *Beneath the Surface* (1918), a typically Scottish parsimony constrains its dabbling with mysticism.

Even the adventure described in *The Green Isle of the Great Deep* is ultimately rationalized as a dream, but while Art and Hector were on the far side of the salmon pool Neil Gunn's imagination was briefly set free, in an atypical but altogether healthy fashion. The book is all the more interesting because Gunn's determined antipathy to the nostalgic fantasizing of MacLeod and other mournful celebrants of the Celtic Twilight caused him to present a thoroughly modernized land of the dead, which has more in common with such "futuristic" allegories as Ruthven Todd's *The Lost Traveller* (1943) and George Orwell's *Nineteen Eighty-Four* (1949)

than the conventional apparatus of Celtic fantasy. *The Green Isle of the Great Deep* is a fine illustration of the fact that some of the best fantasies are the work of hardened realists.

—Brian Stableford

GYGAX, (Ernest) Gary

Nationality: American. **Born:** 27 July, 1938 in Chicago, Illinois. **Family:** First marriage ended in divorce; two sons; second marriage: married Gail Carpenter, 15 August, 1987; one son, three daughters. **Career:** Co-creator of the *Dungeons & Dragons* role-playing game and co-founder of the games-publishing company TSR, Inc., from 1974. **Address:** P.O. Box 388, Lake Geneva, Wisconsin 53147, USA.

FANTASY PUBLICATIONS

Novels (series: Dangerous Journeys; Gord the Rogue; Greyhawk Adventures; Sagard the Barbarian)

The Ice Dragon, with Flint Dille (Sagard). New York, Pocket, 1985.
The Green Hydra, with Flint Dille (Sagard). New York, Pocket, 1985.
The Crimson Sea, with Flint Dille (Sagard). New York, Pocket, 1985.
Saga of Old City (Greyhawk). Lake Geneva, Wisconsin, TSR, 1985.
The Temple of Elemental Evil, with Frank Mentzer. Lake Geneva, Wisconsin, TSR, 1985.
Artifact of Evil (Greyhawk). Lake Geneva, Wisconsin, TSR, 1986.
The Fire Demon, with Flint Dille (Sagard). New York, Pocket, 1986.
Sea of Death (Gord). Lake Geneva, Wisconsin, New Infinities, 1987.
City of Hawks (Gord). Lake Geneva, Wisconsin, New Infinities, 1987.
Come Endless Darkness (Gord). Delavan, Wisconsin, New Infinities, 1988.
Dance of Demons (Gord). Delavan, Wisconsin, New Infinities, 1988.
The Anubis Murders (Dangerous Journeys). New York and London, Roc, 1992.
The Samarkand Solution (Dangerous Journeys). New York and London, Roc, 1993.
Death in Delhi (Dangerous Journeys). New York and London, Roc, 1993.

Short Stories

Night Arrant (Gord). Lake Geneva, Wisconsin, New Infinities, 1987.

OTHER PUBLICATIONS

Other

Advanced Dungeons & Dragons: Monster Manual. Lake Geneva, Wisconsin, TSR, 1977.

Advanced Dungeons & Dragons: Players Handbook. Lake Geneva, Wisconsin, TSR, 1978.

Advanced Dungeons & Dragons: Dungeon Masters Guide. Lake Geneva, Wisconsin, TSR, 1979; 2nd edition, 1989.

Advanced Dungeons & Dragons: Monster Manual II. Lake Geneva, Wisconsin, TSR, 1983.

Official Advanced Dungeons & Dragons Unearthed Arcana. Lake Geneva, Wisconsin, TSR, 1985.

Oriental Adventures, with David Cook and Francois Marcela-Froideval. Lake Geneva, Wisconsin, TSR, 1985.

Role-Playing Mastery. New York, Perigee, 1987.

Master of the Game. New York, Perigee, 1989.

*   *   *

As a games designer and entrepreneur, Gary Gygax was one of the prime movers behind the immense boom in fantasy role-playing games that began in the 1970s. In the mid-1980s he turned to writing novels, most of them based on games scenarios. These include the Sagard the Barbarian series (in collaboration with Flint Dille) commencing with *The Ice Dragon,* and the Gord the Rogue series beginning with *Sea of Death*—routine fantasy adventures of a type which tends to attract little attention from critics but is nevertheless pleasing to role-playing gamers. (See the entry on Gygax's colleague Rose Estes for more about this kind of novel.) After a hiatus as far as fiction is concerned, the most recent series to carry Gygax's name is the game-tied Dangerous Journeys, beginning with *The Anubis Murders,* set in a fantasy world which draws heavily on the ancient Egyptian civilization of pharaohs and pyramids.

The Anubis Murders introduces Magister and great AEgyptian wizard-priest Setne Inhetep. He is less than thrilled when three high mages tell him of the dreadful spate of murders spreading through the elite circles of the distant Avillonia. The only connection between these horrible acts of violent magic is a statuette of the ancient god Anubis. So Setne Inhetep and his beautiful bodyguard, Rachelle, are torn from their holiday in Iberian to investigate a series of gruesome murders. Though Setne Inhetep suspects the followers of the god Anubis, somebody is trying to set up Setne and Rachelle themselves. As the murders increase across all the kingdoms of Avillonia, riots break out and the good name of Setne Inhetep and the Pharaoh he represents, are jeopardized. Setne and his assistant are looking for the truth, yet every move seems to incriminate them. Without giving too much away, I can say there is a successful outcome. Magister Setne is taking a well-earned rest when the demands of the sequel encroach on his leisure time.

The sequel is *The Samarkand Solution,* which begins with a gathering of wizard-priests. This start separates Setne from his beloved warrior-companion Rachelle. During the following adventure, Setne will not only be vulnerable to violent attack but also prey to female advances. Leaving the conference, Setne spots in a crowd a master assassin, Yakeem, and trails him through the market to the river.

This is the site of two of Setne's magical tricks. He first transforms himself into a water spider to skim the water's surface to reach a fishing boat, then he calls a giant fish from the river depths to propel the boat at speed through the waters. So it is that he spots the assassin entering the nearby city of On, a place of murder, thievery and treason. Shortly afterwards the Prince Ram-f-amsu dies in magical and horrific circumstances. To investigate this murder, Setne has to dig deep into the lifestyle of Prince Ram-f-amsu. This includes freeing a beautiful slave girl the Prince kept imprisoned in his villa and uncovering a plot to overthrow the pharaoh. As Setne gets closer to solving the mysteries so more and more people die, each mysterious death part of *The Samarkand Solution.* The denouement involves poisonous spiders and a huge cover-up, the Pharaoh having preferred one of his princes to die by suicide than for his people to know of a plot to replace him.

The final book in the trilogy sees Setne and Rachelle in action against *The Dance of Death.* Here a plague is sweeping through the palaces and temples of lower AEgypt. Magister Setne Inhetep has to trace the evil to its source, and if he fails the Triple Kingdom may be plunged into darkness from which there is no escape. These three fantasies are also detective stories which follow in the footsteps of Conan Doyle. Though Setne Inhetep has no loyal Watson at his side, at each stage of the investigation there is always some less-well-informed person to whom Setne Inhetep explains the situation. The novels also borrow from Agatha Christie: the last chapter inevitably has Setne sitting down and explaining to a third party what the entire story has been and how he came to his clever and lucid conclusion.

Detective stories set against a fantasy backdrop face two problems unknown to both Sherlock Holmes and Hercule Poirot. First, for the reader to be interested, he or she has to have a real feel for the world that the detective and criminal inhabit. Unfortunately, in Gygax's novels we have but a sketchy idea of AEgyptian society; there is little sense of place, no exotic strangeness. AEgypt seems to be a mishmash of Ancient Egyptian locations and society, with a gloss of 20th-century America applied. This formula does little justice to the greatness of Ancient Egyptian civilization and makes a nonsense of important tenets of a free and democratic society. Second, for a fantasy story to work, the mystery itself has to be one that could not happen in "normal" society. Though Gary Gygax makes much use of Setne Inhetep's magical powers, this is not enough to make the investigations strong and original in their own right. Finally, most detective stories succeed or fail on the strength of the central character. Here Gary Gygax's Dangerous Journeys are badly let down by Setne Inhetep's treatment of women. While in his speech Setne Inhetep deplores the condition of women in AEgyptian society, in his acts and thoughts he is patronising and oppressive, shoring up by his deeds values he professes to abhor.

—Sally Ann Melia

H

HAGGARD, (Sir) H(enry) Rider

Nationality: British. **Born:** Bradenham, Norfolk, 22 June 1856. **Education:** Ipswich Grammar School, Suffolk; Lincoln's Inn, London, 1881-85; called to the Bar, 1885. **Family:** Married Louisa Mariana Margitson in 1880; one son and three daughters. **Career:** Secretary to Sir Henry Bulwer, Lieutenant-Governor of Natal, South Africa, 1875-77; member of the staff of Sir Theophilus Shepstone, Special Commissioner in the Transvaal, 1877; Master and Registrar of the High Court of the Transvaal, 1877-79; returned to England, 1879; managed his wife's estate in Norfolk, from 1880; worked in chambers of Henry Bargave Deana, 1885-87; co-editor, *African Review*, 1898; travelled throughout England investigating condition of agriculture and the rural population, 1901-02; British Government Special Commissioner to report on Salvation Army settlements in the United States, 1905; chairman, Reclamation and Unemployed Labour Committee, Royal Commission on Coast Erosion and Afforestation, 1906-11; member of Dominions Royal Commission, 1912-17. Conservative Parliamentary candidate for East Norfolk, 1895; Chairman of the Committee, Society of Authors, 1896-98; vice-president, Royal Colonial Institute, 1917; founder, Liberty League, 1920. **Awards:** Knighted, 1912; K.B.E. (Knight Commander, Order of the British Empire), 1919. **Died:** 14 May 1925.

FANTASY PUBLICATIONS

Novels (series: Allan Quatermain; Ayesha)

King Solomon's Mines (Quatermain). London and New York, Cassell, 1885.
She: A History of Adventure (Ayesha). New York, Harper, 1886; London, Longman, 1887; as *The Annotated She: A Critical Edition of H. Rider Haggard's Victorian Romance,* edited by Norman Etherington, Bloomington, Indiana University Press, 1991.
Allan Quatermain (Quatermain). London, Longman, and New York, Harper, 1887.
Maiwa's Revenge (Quatermain). New York, Harper, and London, Longman, 1888.
Cleopatra. London, Longman, and New York, Harper, 1889.
The World's Desire, with Andrew Lang. London, Longman, and New York, Harper, 1890.
Eric Brighteyes. London, Longman, and New York, United States Book Company, 1891; as *The Saga of Eric Brighteyes,* Hollywood, Newcastle Publishing, 1974.
Nada the Lily. New York and London, Longman, 1892.
Montezuma's Daughter. New York and London, Longman, 1893.
The People of the Mist. London and New York, Longman, 1894.
Heart of the World. New York, Longman, 1895; London, Longman, 1896.
Stella Fregelius: A Tale of Three Destinies. London and New York, Longman, 1904.
Ayesha: The Return of She. London, Ward Lock, and New York, Doubleday, 1905.

Benita: An African Romance. London, Cassell, 1906; as *The Spirit of Bambatse,* New York, Longman, 1906.
The Ghost Kings. London, Cassell, 1908; as *The Lady of the Heavens,* New York, Authors and Newspapers Association, 1908.
The Yellow God: An Idol of Africa. New York, Cupples and Leon, 1908; London, Cassell, 1909.
Morning Star. London, Cassell, and New York, Longman, 1910.
Queen Sheba's Ring. London, Nash, and New York, Doubleday, 1910.
Red Eve. London, Hodder and Stoughton, and New York, Doubleday, 1911.
The Mahatma and the Hare: A Dream Story. London, Longman, and New York, Holt, 1911.
Marie (Quatermain). London, Cassell, and New York, Longman, 1912.
Child of Storm (Quatermain). London, Cassell, and New York, Longman, 1913.
The Wanderer's Necklace. London, Cassell, and New York, Longman, 1914.
The Holy Flower (Quatermain). London, Ward Lock, 1915; as *Allan and the Holy Flower,* New York, Longman, 1915.
The Ivory Child (Quatermain). London, Cassell, and New York, Longman, 1916.
Finished (Quatermain). London, Ward Lock, and New York, Longman, 1916.
Love Eternal. London, Cassell, and New York, Longman, 1918.
When the World Shook: Being an Account of the Great Adventure of Bastin, Bickley, and Arbuthnot. London, Cassell, and New York, Longman, 1919.
The Ancient Allan (Quatermain). London, Cassell, and New York, Longman, 1920.
She and Allan (Quatermain; Ayesha). New York, Longman, and London, Hutchinson, 1921.
The Virgin of the Sun. London, Cassell, and New York, Doubleday, 1922.
Wisdom's Daughter: The Life and Love Story of She-Who-Must-Be-Obeyed (Ayesha). London, Hutchinson, and New York, Doubleday, 1923.
Heu-Heu, or The Monster (Quatermain). London, Hutchinson, and New York, Doubleday, 1924.
Queen of the Dawn: A Love Tale of Old Egypt. New York, Doubleday, and London, Hutchinson, 1925.
The Treasure of the Lake (Quatermain). New York, Doubleday, and London, Hutchinson, 1926.
Allan and the Ice Gods: A Tale of Beginnings (Quatermain). London, Hutchinson, and New York, Doubleday, 1927.
Belshazzar. London, Paul, and New York, Doubleday, 1930.

Short Stories

A Tale of Three Lions, and On Going Back (Quatermain). New York, Lovell, 1887.
Allan's Wife and Other Tales (Quatermain). London, Blackett, and New York, Harper, 1889.
Black Heart and White Heart, and Other Stories. London, Longman, 1900; as *Elissa, the Doom of Zimbabwe, and Black Heart and White Heart,* New York, Longman, 1900.

Smith and the Pharaohs and Other Tales. Bristol, Arrowsmith, 1920; New York, Longman, 1921.

The Best Short Stories of Rider Haggard, edited by Peter Haining. London, Joseph, 1981.

OTHER PUBLICATIONS

Novels

Dawn. London, Hurst and Blackett, 3 vols., 1884; New York, Appleton, 1 vol., 1887.

The Witch's Head. London, Hurst and Blackett, 3 vols., 1884; New York, Appleton, 1 vol., 1885.

Jess. London, Smith Elder, and New York, Harper, 1887.

Mr. Meeson's Will. New York, Harper, and London, Blackett, 1888.

Colonel Quaritch, V.C. New York, Lovell, 1888; London, Longman, 3 vols., 1888.

Beatrice. London, Longman, and New York, Harper, 1890.

Joan Haste. London and New York, Longman, 1895.

Doctor Therne. London and New York, Longman, 1898.

Swallow: A Tale of the Great Trek. New York and London, Longman, 1899.

Lysbeth: A Tale of the Dutch. New York and London, Longman, 1901.

Pearl-Maiden: A Tale of the Fall of Jerusalem. London and New York, Longman, 1903.

The Brethren. London, Cassell, and New York, Doubleday, 1904.

The Way of the Spirit. London, Hutchinson, 1906.

Fair Margaret. London, Hutchinson, 1907; as *Margaret,* New York, Longman, 1907.

The Lady of Blossholme. London, Hodder and Stoughton, 1909.

Moon of Israel: A Tale of the Exodus. London, Murray, and New York, Longman, 1918.

Mary of Marion Isle. London, Hutchinson, 1929; as *Marion Isle,* Garden City, Doubleday, 1929.

Other

Cetywayo and His White Neighbours; or, Remarks on Recent Events in Zululand, Natal, and the Transvaal. London, Trübner, 1882; revised edition, 1888; reprinted in part as *The Last Boer War,* London, Kegan Paul, 1899; as *A History of the Transvaal,* New York, New Amsterdam, 1899.

My Fellow Laborer. New York, Munro, 1888.

An Heroic Effort. Frome, Somerset, Butler and Tanner, 1893.

Church and the State: An Appeal to the Laity. Privately printed, 1895.

East Norfolk Representation. Privately printed, 1895.

Lord Kimberly in Norfolk. Privately printed, 1895.

Speeches of the Earl of Iddesleigh and Mr. Rider Haggard, with the Earl of Iddesleigh. London, Kegan Paul, 1895.

A Visit to the Victoria Hospital. Privately printed, 1897.

A Farmer's Year, Being His Commonplace Book for 1898. London and New York, Longman, 1899.

A Winter Pilgrimage. London and New York, Longman, 1901.

Rural England. London and New York, Longman, 2 vols., 1902.

Rural England (speech). Privately printed, 1903.

A Gardener's Year. London and New York, Longman, 1905.

Report on the Salvation Army Colonies. London, His Majesty's Stationery Office, 1905; as *The Poor and the Land,* London and New York, Longman, 1905.

The Wedding Gift, Harry Furniss's Christmas Annual for 1905. London, Furniss, 1905.

The Real Wealth of England. London, W.L., 1908.

Regeneration, Being an Account of the Social Work of the Salvation Army in Great Britain. London, Longman, 1910; New York, Longman, 1911.

Rural Denmark and Its Lessons. New York and London, Longman, 1911.

A Call to Arms to the Men of East Anglia. Privately printed, 1914.

The After-War Settlement and the Employment of Ex-Servicemen in the Overseas Dominions. London, Saint Catherine Press, 1916.

The Salvation Army. Privately printed, 1920.

The Days of My Life: An Autobiography, edited by C. J. Longman. London and New York, Longman, 2 vols., 1926; one chapter separately printed as *A Note on Religion,* London, Longman, 1927.

The Private Diaries of Sir H. Rider Haggard 1914-1925, edited by D. S. Higgins. London, Cassell, and New York, Stein and Day, 1980.

*

Film Adaptations: *She,* 1916, 1919, 1925, 1935, 1965, 1985; *Cleopatra,* 1917; *Dawn,* 1917; *King Solomon's Mines,* 1919, 1937, 1950, 1985; *Allan Quatermain,* 1919, *King Solomon's Treasure,* 1977, *Allan Quatermain and the Lost City of Gold,* 1987, all from the novel *Allan Quatermain*; *Beatrice,* 1921; *Stella Fregelius,* 1921; *Moon of Israel,* 1924.

Bibliographies: *A Bibliography of the Writings of Sir Henry Rider Haggard* by J. E. Scott, London, Elkin Mathews, 1947; *H. Rider Haggard: A Bibliography* by D. E. Whatmore, London, Mansell, 1987; *The Haggard Guide: A Simplified and Revised Bibliography of the Major Works of H. Rider Haggard* by Roger T. Allen, Peoria, Illinois, Spoon River Press, 1987.

Manuscript Collection: Norfolk Record Office, Norwich, England.

Critical Studies: *The Cloak That I Left* (biography) by Lilias Rider Haggard, London, Hodder and Stoughton, 1951; *Rider Haggard: His Life and Works* by Morton N. Cohen, London, Hutchinson, 1960, New York, Walker, 1961, revised edition, London, Macmillan, 1968; *H. Rider Haggard: A Voice from the Infinite* by Peter Berresford Ellis, London, Routledge, 1978; *Rider Haggard, The Great Storyteller* by D. S. Higgins, London, Cassell, 1981, as *Rider Haggard: A Biography,* New York, Stein and Day, 1983; *Rider Haggard* by Norman Etherington, Boston, Twayne Publishers, 1984; *Rider Haggard and the Fiction of Empire: A Critical Study of British Imperial Fiction* by Wendy R. Katz, Cambridge, Cambridge University Press, 1987; *The Critical Reception of Sir Henry Rider Haggard: An Annotated Bibliography* by Lloyd Siemens and Roger Neufeld, Greensboro, University of North Carolina at Greensboro Press, 1991; *Rider Haggard and the Lost Empire* by Tom Pocock, London, Weidenfeld and Nicolson, 1993.

*   *   *

If you stripped away the veneers placed on man by modern civilization, H. Rider Haggard came to believe, you would find a powerful, primal savage (he personally thought himself to be the reincarnation of a Zulu warrior). Similarly, to fully understand the magic and mystery of Haggard's fantasies, one must first strip away a century of critical misperceptions.

Some of these can be impatiently brushed aside by anyone familiar with his work. Though not immune to the political prejudices of their day, Haggard's novels hardly constitute briefs for British imperialism; instead, Haggard could display remarkable admiration for the civilized qualities of indigenous peoples and their capacity for self-government—seen most clearly, no doubt, in the sympathetic and respectful portrait of Allan Quatermain's Zulu companion Umslopogaas and his people in *Nada the Lily*. And while modern feminists have chastised Haggard's Ayesha, She Who Must Be Obeyed, as an unflattering and stereotypical portrait from a man horrified by the Power of Women, his novels actually feature a wide variety of female characters, including some who share Ayesha's intelligence and resourcefulness without her aura of manipulative evil—such as the native girl Ustane in *She*. However, some positive characterizations must be challenged as well. Haggard has been lauded for the authenticity of his African adventures and the travels which provided background for other romances; but he was never interested in obtaining more than a few touches of local colour for his stories and, even when describing people and places he knew well, he sometimes made up more than he remembered. Also, critics unwilling to praise Haggard for other reasons have conceded he was a "master storyteller"; in fact, Haggard's stories could seem awkward and meandering whenever he departed from the simple pattern of the journey into the unknown. It is the evocative power of Haggard's stories, not the artistry of their construction, that commands attention.

Haggard was a man who deeply disliked and mistrusted what he saw as the contrivances and artificiality of modern civilization; and unable to persuasively articulate his concerns directly in novels set in modern England (like the feeble *Colonel Quaritch, V.C.*), he crafted his lost worlds as attractive antitheses of European culture: often dominated by women, not men, their power derived from ancient magic, not modern laws and customs, and their disputes settled by direct combat, not legalistic manoeuvrings. Yet both Haggard and his aristocratic heroes also enjoyed and appreciated life in contemporary Europe, and despite the magnetic appeal of the lost lands they discover, they always want to return to their own civilized worlds.

It is these contradictory impulses that energize Haggard's first and finest romances, *King Solomon's Mines* and *She*; it is by no means absurd to compare these works, as some critics have, to Joseph Conrad's "Heart of Darkness" as complex symbolic tales of a gradual descent from civilization to savagery. If *She* seems the stronger of the two works, it is because what Leo Vincey finds as his African heart of darkness—a beautiful yet demonic immortal woman—is a more compelling and fascinating figure than the lost treasures Allan Quatermain unearths in *King Solomon's Mines*. Indeed, rather than narrowly regarding Ayesha as Haggard's opinion of women, one could more usefully see her as emblematic of the simultaneous attractiveness and repulsiveness of the primitive impulse within the human spirit—something overwhelmingly appealing that must, nevertheless, finally wither away and die like Ayesha herself in order for humanity to progress. Eventually, Haggard resolved this conflict through his growing interest in spiritualism and reincarnation, so he could calmly accept himself as a unified English gentleman with a savage soul, and his heroes could confront ancient worlds without feeling any threat to their identity. Thus, his later novels can seem pallid not only because they recycle elements from previous novels, but because they are not as powerfully driven by opposing desires to embrace and reject the exotic worlds they depict.

Readers who wish to move beyond *King Solomon's Mines* and *She* may wish to read the other adventures of Quatermain and Ayesha, though they will find that those characters and their adventures both grow progressively less involving. Others may seek out later works like *When the World Shook* and *Allan and the Ice Gods* because some critics have labelled them pioneering works of "science fiction." A better policy would be to the read the ten romances Haggard produced in his first decade as a successful writer. It is an impressive list: in addition to *King Solomon's Mines, She* and *Nada the Lily,* there are *Allan Quatermain* and *Maiwa's Revenge,* the earliest—and best—sequels to *King Solomon's Mines* (actually, since Quatermain died at the end of *Allan Quatermain, Maiwa's Revenge* is technically the first of many "prequels" to the original two novels); two atmospheric historical romances, *Cleopatra* and *Montezuma's Daughter*; and Haggard's best African singleton, *The People of the Mist,* which effectively engages a reader's attention though it is little more than a cautious revision of *King Solomon's Mines.*

The other two novels may be of special interest to modern fantasy readers. *The World's Desire,* written with Andrew Lang, is a sequel to Homer's *Odyssey*: after Ithaca is destroyed by plague, Aphrodite sends Odysseus to Egypt, where he is embroiled in a lethal triangle involving the Pharaoh's wife Meriamum, who vainly loves him, and Helen of Troy, now enshrined as a local goddess, whom he really loves; the Biblical story of the Jewish Exodus from Egypt serves as a surprising subplot. Remarks about the three people's destiny to meet again in future lives have led some to view the novel as a prequel to *She*. A not entirely successful blend of disparate elements, *The World's Desire* remains an intriguing commentary on Homer, recasting Odysseus's travels as a search for Love and seeing that desire as his fatal weakness. *Eric Brighteyes* features the Icelandic hero Eric the Unlucky, who earns the mighty sword Whitefire and wins several battles but is ultimately doomed by the witch Swanhild, who jealously keeps him away from his true love Gudruda and finally brings about his death; again, Christianity briefly appears when Eric talks of a new god, the White Christ, who hates bloodshed. With a story rather similar to *The World's Desire*—and other Haggard novels—*Eric Brighteyes* is distinguished by its well-sustained epic prose style, which refutes another common misperception of Haggard—that he lacked ability as a writer. (The recurring problem is not that Haggard was a poor writer, but that he was a hasty writer, usually rushing to finish a novel in six weeks.)

Among the many later novels, perhaps the most interesting are the so-called Zulu trilogy—*Marie, Child of Storm* and *Finished*—and *The Ancient Allan,* which describes Quatermain's previous life in Babylon. Standing out from the other romances are two fantastic curiosities: *Stella Fregelius,* the cautionary tale of a scientist who first invents a form of radio but later destroys himself with obsessive efforts to contact a dead woman's spirit; and *The Mahatma and the Hare,* a polemic against hunting conveyed by a man's dream dialogue with a dead hare, who describes his tormented life of being hunted by men and finally torn apart by their dogs.

The extent of Haggard's influence on modern fantasy is almost incalculable. Many fantasies, from Victorian fairy tales to modern homages to J. R. R. Tolkien, can seem Eurocentric, domesticated and comforting; Haggard insisted on fantasies that were more exotic, unfamiliar and disturbing. All that later writers had to do was to replace his stodgy English protagonists with heroes who were more attuned to their wild environments: thus, Edgar Rice Burroughs marvellously revisited Haggard's Africa with the character of Tarzan and transplanted his romances to Mars with the equally vigorous John Carter, while Robert E. Howard vigorously explored Haggard's past worlds with the brutal Conan the Barbarian. All the numerous writers who have followed in Burroughs's and Howard's footsteps are also, in a real sense, the children of H. Rider Haggard.

—Gary Westfahl

HALAM, Ann

Pseudonym of Gwyneth Ann Jones. **Nationality:** British. **Born:** Manchester, 14 February 1952. **Education:** Notre Dame Convent, Manchester; University of Sussex, Brighton, 1970-73, B.A. in history of ideas with Latin. **Family:** Married Peter Wilson Gwilliam in 1976; one son. **Career:** Executive officer, Manpower Services Commission, Hove, East Sussex, 1975-77; lived and worked in Singapore, 1977-80. **Awards:** James Tiptree, Jr., award, 1991. **Agent:** Herta Ryder, Toby Eady Associates, 18 Park Walk, London SW10 0AQ, England. **Address:** 30 Roundhill Crescent, Brighton, East Sussex BN2 3FR, England.

FANTASY PUBLICATIONS

Novels (series: Inland)

Water in the Air (as Gwyneth Jones). London, Macmillan, 1977.
The Influence of Ironwood (as Gwyneth Jones). London, Macmillan, 1978.
Dear Hill (as Gwyneth Jones). London, Macmillan, 1980.
Ally, Ally Aster. London, Allen and Unwin, 1981.
The Alder Tree. London, Allen and Unwin, 1982.
King Death's Garden (as Gwyneth Jones). London, Orchard, 1986.
The Daymaker (Inland). London, Orchard, 1987.
The Hidden Ones. London, Women's Press, 1988.
Transformations (Inland). London, Orchard, 1988.
The Skybreaker (Inland). London, Orchard, 1990.
Dinosaur Junction. London, Orchard, 1992.
The Haunting of Jessica Raven. London, Orion, 1994.

OTHER PUBLICATIONS

Novels as Gwyneth Jones

The Exchange. London, Macmillan, 1979.
Divine Endurance. London, Allen and Unwin, 1984; New York, Tor, 1989.
Escape Plans. London, Allen and Unwin, 1986.
Kairos. London, Unwin Hyman, 1988.
White Queen. London, Gollancz, 1991; New York, Tor, 1993.
Flowerdust. London, Headline, 1993; New York, Tor, 1995.
North Wind. London, Gollancz, 1994.

Short Stories as Gwyneth Jones

Identifying the Object. Austin, Texas, Swan Press, 1993.

*

Ann Halam comments:

Genre critics often describe my work as unusually complex and demanding. It could be that I try to bring the values, in characterization and depth of detail, of a literary novelist to genre forms. This in turn could be because of my grounding in fantasy written for older children—in the world of children's books the adult distinction between "genre" and "mainstream" writing styles is (or was) almost non-existent. The fantastic enters my novels in many forms: Utopian world-building (the Inland series); hard science exposition (*Escape Plans, The Hidden Ones*); near-future extrapolation (*White Queen*); yuppie urban nightmare (*Kairos*); science fantasy and ghost story respectively in the best-loved of my books, *Divine Endurance* and *King Death's Garden*. I've only once written a book that's entirely realist narrative (*The Exchange*). Fiction without any non-real element seems to me tainted with a deeply-buried absurdity. Fiction happens in the mind of the reader and the writer, not in the material world—and in the mind, as in fantastic fiction, the apparently immutable rules of the physical world are constantly broken. It would seem that "magical realism," the acceptable non-realist genre of the mainstream, should attract me, but I find this isn't so. So far, I prefer the popular form: the contemporary folk tales of our culture—a fiction that tells the truth about the world and human nature, by means of candid and obvious make-believe.

*   *   *

Writing as Ann Halam, Gwyneth Jones is best known for her Inland trilogy, but even before that she had produced several unusual fantasy novels for young readers. *Ally, Ally Aster* concerned children confronted by an ancient family secret which required them to overcome an ice elemental, while *The Alder Tree* turned on a confrontation between a young girl and an oriental dragon in human guise. Although unusual in their choice of subject matter, it was *King Death's Garden,* described as "A Ghost Story," which took Halam into realms of greater complexity, setting the story of Maurice's discovery in the cemetery alongside the unhappiness of his daily life. Maurice is a self-confessed wimp, subject to asthmatic attacks and demanding. When his parents and young sister go abroad for his father's work, he feels he has been abandoned in Britain with his great-aunt. Sadly, Maurice can't see how he has become too absorbed in his own condition to accept help and friendship from others. Instead, he becomes obsessed with the supernatural researches of the professor for whom his great-aunt formerly kept house, and spends much of his time in the cemetery where the Professor conducted his research. There he meets Moth, a strange young girl in rags. We are never entirely sure whether Moth is simply an imaginary friend conjured by Maurice or indeed a genuine spirit awakened by the Professor; this ambiguity and uncertainty is what gives the novel much of its power, as we observe Maurice retreating increasingly into the world he has created for himself, rejecting the outside world.

The Inland trilogy, beginning with *The Daymaker,* presents a startling contrast. In this, we are propelled into an imaginary world which, as the books unfold, is seen to be possibly our own world, or one much like it, in the far future. There are few clues as to what has actually happened—all that is clear is that at some point there has been a rejection of the use of complex technology, and machinery is now regarded with fear and suspicion. In compensation, as it were, magic exists within this world, but it is organized under strict conditions, known as the Covenant. This operates on the understanding that a balance has to be maintained within the world, and magic can be wielded only by common consent of the people, each community being represented by a Covener. Magic is primarily the prerogative of women, although some men are capable of wielding a genuine magic rather than the art of illusion.

Into this world is born Zanne of Garth, a girl who is eventually revealed to have a remarkable magical talent, to which the feared technology responds. The Coveners view Zanne as a tool through which the technology can be put to rest but Zanne, with her empathy for the machinery and her perception of what it could mean, fights against this notion before reaching a reconciliation within herself. Thus she travels first to disable the Daymaker, a power station, and then, in *Transformations,* is obliged to confront what, to contemporary eyes, appears to be a mine containing radioactive material, although in Inland, it prompts people to become werebeasts. In the last of the series, *The Skybreaker,* Zanne and her companion, Holne, travel to Magia, a neighbouring land, where rumour has it that there is a Skybreaker, or rocket. This last novel provides Halam with an opportunity to discuss the different ways in which magic, or the Covenant, is regarded. In the second novel, set right on the borders of Inland, although the Covenant remained intact, it nevertheless had become subtly corrupted by the Minithers' harsh life, which looked for retribution from the world if anything went wrong, and what should have been an easy binding became a rigorous law. In Magia, the magic has become ritualized and corrupt because power effectively resides in one person, the Lady Monkshood, the Great Mage. Although superficially similar to the magic with which Zanne is familiar, when she observes Magia's practices, Zanne realizes that magic is not only used in a more profligate fashion than she is accustomed to, but that it is also used entirely at the Mage's discretion, and that her belief that she can foretell the future and change the world without consulting others will destroy the world.

Halam's socialist vision of a magic which affects the balance of the world and which should be operated only by common consent is very much at odds with the more traditional view of magic as a power which resides in the few and is used at their discretion, without consultation. The series is all the more refreshing for that. She captures very well Zanne's dilemma in that she loves the bygone technology and recognizes how it might help her people but simultaneously understands that this moment is not right for its use, when the cost is too terrible, and there is no disappointment in Zanne's eventual agreement to use her skills for the general good of the community, even though she is personally in disagreement with it.

—Maureen Speller

HAMBLY, Barbara (Joan)

Nationality: American. **Born:** San Diego, California, 1951. **Education:** University of California at Riverside, M.A. in medieval history. **Career:** Research assistant, high-school teacher, and other occupations before becoming a freelance writer. A black belt in karate, has competed in national tournaments; lives in Los Angeles. **Address:** c/o Del Rey Books, 201 East 50th Street, New York, NY 10022, USA.

FANTASY PUBLICATIONS

Novels (series: Darwath; Sun Wolf and Starhawk; Sun-Cross; Windrose)

The Time of the Dark (Darwath). New York, Del Rey, 1982; London, Unwin, 1985.
The Walls of Air (Darwath). New York, Del Rey, 1983; London, Unwin, 1985.
The Armies of Daylight (Darwath). New York, Del Rey, 1983; London, Unwin, 1985.
The Ladies of Mandrigyn (Sun Wolf). New York, Del Rey, 1984; London, Unwin, 1986.
Dragonsbane. New York, Del Rey, and London, Unwin, 1986.
The Silent Tower (Windrose). New York, Del Rey, 1986; London, Unwin, 1987.
The Witches of Wenshar (Sun Wolf). New York, Del Rey, and London, Unwin, 1987.
The Unschooled Wizard (omnibus; includes *The Ladies of Mandrigyn, The Witches of Wenshar*). New York, Nelson Doubleday, 1987.
The Silicon Mage (Windrose). London, Unwin, and New York, Del Rey, 1988.
Darkmage (omnibus; includes *The Silent Tower, The Silicon Mage*). New York, Nelson Doubleday, 1988.
Those Who Hunt the Night. New York, Del Rey, 1988; as *Immortal Blood,* London, Unwin, 1988.
The Dark Hand of Magic (Sun Wolf). New York, Del Rey, and London, Unwin, 1990.
The Rainbow Abyss (Sun-Cross). London, Grafton, and New York, Del Rey, 1991.
Magicians of the Night (Sun-Cross). London, Grafton, and New York, Del Rey, 1992.
Sun-Cross (omnibus; includes *The Rainbow Abyss, Magicians of the Night*). New York, Guild America, 1992.
Dog Wizard (Windrose). New York, Del Rey, and London, HarperCollins, 1993.
Stranger at the Wedding. New York, Del Rey, 1994; as *Sorcerer's Ward,* London, HarperCollins, 1994.
Bride of the Rat God. New York, Del Rey, 1994; London, Raven, 1995.
Travelling with the Dead. London, Voyager, and New York, Del Rey, 1995.

OTHER PUBLICATIONS

Novels

The Quirinal Hill Affair. New York, St. Martin's Press, 1983; as *Search the Seven Hills,* New York, Ballantine, 1987.
Ishmael: A Star Trek Novel. New York, Pocket, 1985; London, Titan, 1989.
Beauty and the Beast (novelization of TV script). New York, Avon, 1989; London, Unwin, 1990.

Beauty and the Beast: Song of Orpheus. New York, Avon, 1990.
Star Trek: Ghost Walker. New York, Pocket, and London, Titan, 1991.
Children of the Jedi. New York, Bantam, and London, Bantam Press, 1995.

*   *   *

Barbara Hambly has a special talent for reclaiming and reworking familiar themes of fantasy, making them over into a seamless gestalt which is very much her own. Usually a vein of tough-minded "dirty realism" runs through the plot, countering the over-romantic or wish-fulfilment aspects of magic and lending conviction to the whole. Far from commanding respect, magicians in Hambly's fantasy worlds are invariably distrusted and generally persecuted by Church and/or State.

In her initial venture, the Darwath trilogy, this technique is still being perfected and some of the source material is visible. The name of wizard Ingold Inglorion vaguely recalls Tolkien's elf-lord Gildor Inglorion; the wizardly betrayal of volume two, *The Walls of Air,* reeks of Saruman's treachery in *The Lord of the Rings*; the menacing creatures called the Dark who threaten to burst through from the other side of reality are all too reminiscent of Lovecraftian horrors. But the story moves along well from its conventional starting-point with two people from our own world transferred into the threatened fantasy realm and helping, not very effectively, to repel the Dark. Ultimately, a somewhat unexpected (in fantasy if not in sf) solution is reached: when the objectives of the seemingly mindless and inimical Dark are understood, an alternative solution can be offered.

Hambly's most popular sequence must be the open-ended series of novels about the unbrutal mercenary Sun Wolf and his hard-bitten lady second-in-command Starhawk. *The Ladies of Mandrigyn* sees Sun Wolf abducted by the eponymous women, who demand to be trained in martial skills. Their aim is to overthrow the nasty Wizard King Altiokis who has conquered the city of Mandrigyn and condemned its men to slave labour.

The slightly unexpected outcome carries a certain wry conviction, with the successful Sun Wolf being banished from Mandrigyn as a scapegoat—blamed for the way the women's victory has wrecked a once male-dominated social order. But the book's most effective frisson comes from the *nuuwa,* hideous eyeless humanoids which at first seem like routine "encounter monsters" but prove to be former humans. Their debasement results from entities conjured by Altiokis, magical flame-motes which burn through the eyeball, eat the brain and warp the body. It is a considerable jolt when Sun Wolf, who "ought" to be an indestructible warrior-hero, is infected by such a mote and can survive only by paying Odin's price.

In the course of this crowded book he has been through a painful initiation into magical powers, and *The Witches of Wenshar* sees him trying to bring them under control at a deeply flawed school of witchery. Instead, a string of apparently supernatural murders confuses the issue and the book becomes a sort of detective thriller. Next comes *Dark Hand of Magic,* in which the dirty-realism strain is at its most effective. Sun Wolf's grimy gang of mercenaries are conducting a routine city-siege which refuses to go as it should owing to a literal curse of bad luck. Again there is a mystery element (who is the opposing wizard? exactly how has his mysteriously dispersed and self-renewing hex been laid?) and an ongoing magical struggle, but it's the convincing grubbiness, smell, and itch

of the beleaguered encampment that sticks in the mind. Every so often the reader has the overwhelming urge to take a shower. . . .

The fine stand-alone novel *Dragonsbane* is a lighter-hearted work opening with some gleeful subversion of heroic dragon-slaying quests. Its bespectacled hero is a practical man whose one previous success (famed in story and song) was achieved by fighting dirty, extensively aided by his mistress, the witch Jenny—who is the strongest character here. When a dangerous new dragon needs to be eliminated, the path to this straightforward-seeming objective is beset with tangles of politics and clouded by the fact that the dragon is by no means the prime menace: such complication and recomplication of expected fantasy goals is another Hambly hallmark.

A different reversal of expectation drives the Sun-Cross diptych. In fantasy, representatives of our real world are called with tedious frequency to solve the problems of imaginary lands: this time, would-be wizards struggling in a world almost devoid of magic (that is, our own) summon a genuine if low-powered mage from Fantasyland . . . the jolting realization being that the summoners are the occult fringe of the Nazi SS, desperately researching magical weaponry to counter the imminent Allied invasion. The sun-cross, a icon of magic power, is the swastika . . . and, as David Brin hinted in his short story "Thor Meets Captain America," the link between death camps and necromancy is almost too convincing not to be true.

But the division of this narrative into two volumes is not wholly fortunate. *The Rainbow Abyss* is a mildly entertaining and episodic tour of the fantasy world, reeking of delaying actions: by auctorial decree, the interworld portal called a Dark Well functions only at solstices and equinoxes! Its far more ambitious follow-up *Magicians of the Night* opens with the apprentice mage Rhion's arrival in embattled Germany, whereupon the real story begins . . . a little too belatedly. All the otherworld detail of the first book is in the end partly justified by the dark illumination thrown back from World War II on to the fantasy realm's squabbles (Rhion comes to acknowledge that there are worse things than lack of magic), but by this time it seems almost an afterthought.

Other works include the Antryg Windrose sequence beginning with the complete two-volume story in *The Silent Tower* and *The Silicon Mage.* There are portal crossings between our modern Silicon Valley and a standard (for Hambly) fantasy realm where magicians, church, state, and the possibly mad wizard Windrose are all at odds. Joanna, a Californian computer systems designer, is drawn into this mess: her expertise and Antryg's secret knowledge combine to unravel what's happening behind the scenes, with a Dark Mage (thought long dead) stalking the plot in disguise and indeed providing much false or slanted information to the reader during *The Silent Tower.* This potent mage's plan for immortality rather implausibly involves being coded into a supercomputer magically powered by a toll on all the lives of two universes. After much tension and sacrifice, matters are sorted out, although a very nearly literal *deus ex machina* is needed to save Antryg for new life as a Californian bartender. This really concludes the story, but *Dog Wizard* sees Antryg returned to his fantasy home to confront certain loose ends such as being under sentence of death there—even if this sentence was actually carried out in *The Silicon Mage*! *Stranger at the Wedding* is an unrelated book set in the same general world.

The very different *Immortal Blood* (also known as *Those Who Hunt the Night*) is a ripping melodrama of vampires by gaslight, the expected deviation from stereotype being that the mortal hero—

a don and retired spy—is not hunting vampires but commissioned by them to track down the unknown hunter who *is* destroying valued members of the vampire community. It's an enjoyably rattling yarn despite occasional lapses in the British background (Lewis Carroll never became "Professor Dodgson") and in the rational hero's rationalism (knowing that sunlight kills vampires, he nevertheless invests in silver charms rather than experiment with magnesium flares or electrical discharge tubes).

Barbara Hambly never gives her likeable characters an easy ride—the price of success tends to be harrowing. She can be relied on to question the insidious default assumptions which make so much genre fantasy so depressingly generic; she prefers good slangy dialogue to the airy nothings of High Fantasy diction. Further novels are awaited with keen interest.

—David Langford

HANCOCK, Niel (Anderson)

Nationality: American. **Born:** 8 January, 1941 in New Mexico. **Career:** Writer. **Military Service:** U.S. Army, 1966-68; served in Vietnam. **Agent:** Collier Associates, 875 Avenue of the Americas, Suite 1003, New York, New York 10001, USA. **Address:** Austin, Texas.

Fantasy Publications

Novels (series: Circle of Light; Wilderness of Four; Windameir Circle)

Greyfax Grimwald (Circle of Light). New York, Popular Library, 1977.
Faragon Fairingay (Circle of Light). New York, Popular Library, 1977.
Calix Stay (Circle of Light). New York, Popular Library, 1977.
Squaring the Circle (Circle of Light). New York, Popular Library, 1977.
Dragon Winter. New York, Popular Library, 1978.
Across the Far Mountain (Wilderness of Four). New York, Popular Library, 1982.
The Plains of the Sea (Wilderness of Four). New York, Popular Library, 1982.
On the Boundaries of Darkness (Wilderness of Four). New York, Popular Library, 1982.
The Road to the Middle Islands (Wilderness of Four). New York, Warner, 1983.
The Fires of Windameir (Windameir Circle). New York, Popular Library, 1985.
The Sea of Silence (Windameir Circle). New York, Popular Library, 1987.
A Wanderer's Return (Windameir Circle). New York, Popular Library, 1988.
The Bridge of Dawn (Windameir Circle). New York, Popular Library, 1991.

*　　*　　*

Niel Hancock's three linked tetralogies of novels (and one singleton) explore territory familiar to any habitual reader of fantasy literature. Titanic struggles between the forces of Dark and Light sprawl across many strange lands, involving kings and queens, and the least important of animals. The tales are set primarily in the World Before Time, Atlanton Earth. The geography of this world, or in fact series of worlds, is complex and never entirely explained, being multi-layered and multi-named. The Upper Worlds are the province of magicians and other powerful beings for whom time, as perceived by the inhabitants of the Lower Worlds, moves scarcely at all. At the heart of these upper worlds is Cypher, the home of Lorini, Lady of Light. Her sister Dorini is the Lady of Dark who seeks to subjugate the lower worlds of Windameir and wear the High Crown of Windameir herself.

The resonances with Tolkien's *The Lord of the Rings* are unavoidable throughout but Hancock works hard to establish his own signature on the story, taking familiar elements and attempting to twist them into new and pleasing shapes. Thus, the Circle of Light series focuses on the activities of three characters, Bear, Otter and Dwarf who, having dwelt in a mysterious world beyond Atlanton Earth, are obliged to return to Earth as guardians of the Arkenchest, one of five artefacts destined to save Atlanton Earth from Dorini's rule.

Guided by the magicians Greyfax Grimwald and Faragon Fairingay, they journey through this new world, acquiring an assortment of human friends, participating in battles, until Lorini and her world of Cypher are finally saved from Dorini's dark forces and the pattern, the Circle, is completed. It is implied throughout the series that the creatures are following a vast circular pattern which has ensured that they were in the right place at the right moment but Hancock seems never to fully realize his worlds' philosophy.

Nevertheless, he does create some memorable characters in Bear, Otter and Dwarf who, in particular, are very different from their Hobbit counterparts in *The Lord of the Rings*. Hancock's wizards are more unpredictable than Tolkien's and less easily understood. At times they seem to be serious and earnest, as befits the familiar perceptions of magicians, but at other times they seem as light-hearted as Otter, and their involvement with the fate of Atlanton Earth seems almost to be on a whim. As an antidote to the high epic style of the more familiar tales of Middle-earth, Hancock's novels provided a very welcome and whimsical contrast.

After completing this unusual epic, Hancock produced *Dragon Winter,* a novel about a group of animals, featuring bears, badgers and otters threatened by dark forces. Although apparently unrelated to the Atlanton Earth novels, it nevertheless encompasses many of Hancock's preoccupations, including the use of particular animals and a mystical belief in multi-layered worlds, with no character lost or dead so much as moved to another level of being.

Hancock then moved back to Atlanton Earth, to delve into its early history. Sadly, with the Wilderness of Four series, the lighter touch of the earlier tetralogy seemed to elude him. The Wilderness of Four novels are a complex vision of the early history of Atlanton Earth, telling the stories of characters mentioned in the Circle of Light books, most particularly Brian Brandigore, Olthar Othlinden and Lord Borim, respectively dwarf, otter and bear, and Trianion, husband of Lorini. Each volume follows the story of one creature and how it comes to realize its role in the story of Atlanton Earth. In the early volumes, it seems clear that the intention is for all the creatures to meet at the edge of the Roaring Sea and in some way act together, but this intent is never entirely fulfilled. Indeed, it is only in the most recent cycle of Hancock's novels, beginning with *The Fires of Windameir,* that it is even confirmed that the creatures, the Keepers as they become known, ever met.

It is tempting to speculate that Hancock perhaps became bored with his concept. In the first two volumes of the second tetralogy, *Across the Far Mountain* and *The Plains of the Sea,* the narrative quickly settles into a familiar pattern of a creature discovering its true destiny, being suddenly thrust into a position of power and then having to act upon this without any clear indication of what it is supposed to be doing. In *On the Boundaries of Darkness,* the pattern is warped somewhat by the discovery that the boy Trianion is in fact a member of the Circle of Elders, spending time on Atlanton Earth for reasons that again are not made entirely clear, but in volume four, *The Road to the Middle Islands,* the pattern is restored as we learn about the life of Olthar Othlinden, the otter. Hancock seems to think that the tetralogy reaches a conclusion, but for the reader it is less clear. Throughout the series, important action is relegated to a brief epilogue but the sequence's greatest problem is the reader's knowledge that the battle between Light and Dark is not to be resolved for aeons yet to come.

The third tetralogy, the Windameir Circle, begins with hints at a shift in Hancock's interest. The first novel concentrates on Owen Helwin, son of two characters who featured in *The Road to the Middle Islands,* and it is indirectly from them that we learn of the characters' meeting at all. Owen has his own problem—his mother has been enchanted by a brooch which, we learn, was made by her estranged brother, long believed dead. Although Famhart sets out to find a cure, it is up to Owen and Darek to discover the true cure which they manage to do, revealing in the process that Darek is in fact a young woman, the Lady Deros. Once again set against a background of violence and upheaval in a previously secure world, the focus is much more on the activities of humans. There are two comedic talking horses, and two mysterious characters, Wallach and Gillerman, who are not unlike Greyfax and Faragon, but the implication is that Hancock is moving towards something new, although characters from previous books still appear.

The Atlanton Earth novels have not achieved cult status in the same way as Tolkien's novels. Although it is hinted that there is a rich history lurking behind the first set of stories, Hancock's attempts to explore this became too repetitive to maintain the reader's interest, and indeed one has the impression that the task was finally beyond him. Nevertheless, among the many imitators of *The Lord of the Rings,* Niel Hancock ranks among the more innovative.

—Maureen Speller

HARDY, Lyndon (Maurice)

Nationality: American. **Born:** Los Angeles, 16 April 1941. **Education:** California Institute of Technology, 1958-62, B.S. in physics; University of California, 1962-66, Ph.D. in high-energy physics. **Family:** Married Joan Taresh in 1966; two children. **Career:** Engineer, TRW Systems, Redondo Beach, California, from 1966. **Address:** 19616 Redbeam Avenue, Torrance, CA 90503, USA.

FANTASY PUBLICATIONS

Novels (series: Arcadia in all books)

Master of the Five Magics. New York, Del Rey, 1980; London, Corgi, 1985.
Secret of the Sixth Magic. New York, Del Rey, 1984; London, Corgi, 1986.
Riddle of the Seven Realms. New York, Del Rey, 1988; London, Corgi, 1989.

*

Lyndon Hardy comments:

My magical universe is one in which the laws of magic are rigorously defined, rather than omnipotent powers that have no bounds.

*   *   *

The sudden upsurge in the popularity of fantasy fiction during the past two decades revealed some developmental problems that trap less-talented writers into constant rewrites of all too familiar plots. For the most part, fantasy readers tend to expect familiar settings, usually a pre-industrial society, almost always European in structure, and authors who stray too widely must invest considerable effort in fleshing out their world and making it seem consistent, credible, and interesting. An even greater problem is the element of magic, because when all things become possible, the "little black bag" syndrome creeps in. It is difficult to feel any real suspense when our hero is in danger if we know he or one of his companions can whip out a convenient spell or call upon some supernatural force to deliver himself from peril.

Several authors have addressed the magic problem by drawing up very specific rules and compelling their characters to abide by them. Jack Vance's Dying Earth series limited the spells an individual could remember at any one time to a very small number. Larry Niven suggested that magic might be confined to specific geographical areas. Lyndon Hardy uses a similar approach in the three published novels of his Arcadia series, starting with *Master of the Five Magics.* For this novel he devised a very specific code of magic, and then superimposed it on a world that contains diverse though familiar aspects, European, Arabic and Asian.

Hardy's fantastic realm is governed by five different magical systems, thaumaturgy, alchemy, magic, sorcery and wizardry, each of which is codified by a set of clearly defined rules. Thaumaturgy, for example, operates through the principles of sympathy and contagion, like produces like and two substances, once joined, are never completely separate again. Alodar is a young apprentice thaumaturge whose career-changes during the course of the novel provide a guided tour of the various schools of magic.

During the siege of a frontier castle, Alodar makes two decisions. First, he acknowledges that he loves Queen Vendora despite his low social standing, and second, concludes that thaumaturgy is not the branch of magic he wishes to master. In his quest to gain the respect to which he feels entitled, Alodar moves from one master to another, seeking knowledge from alchemists, magicians, sorcerers, before finally deciding to become a wizard and master the art of controlling demons. As he passes from one stage to another Alodar matures and realizes that the true quest was to discover in himself the makings of an Archimage, master of all five of the magical arts. His evolution as a character altered by his experiences is a refreshing reminder that even fantasies need to be about believable people.

Hardy introduced an extraneous force in the sequel, *Secret of the Sixth Magic*. Melizar is a strange being whose presence seems to negate the natural functioning of normal magic. Jemidon is a grown man, too old to be apprenticed in the normal fashion, but determined to become a sorcerer. Melizar's advent coincides with a mysterious failure of the art of sorcery, after which the other forms of magic become progressively less viable as well. After various adventures, Jemidon recognizes the connection with Melizar, a creature of a cold alternative universe who is aided by a host of imps.

In order to save the world, Jemidon is forced to enter the universe which is Melizar's home, a bizarre place where an entirely new form of magic, metamagic, governs the laws of nature. Armed with this knowledge, Jemidon returns to restore order to his own world. As was the case with Alodar, who makes a brief appearance in the waning chapters of this book, Jemidon is also on a journey of self-discovery, and emerges a stronger and more complete person after accepting the role fate has cast for him.

The third and to date last book from Hardy is *Riddle of the Seven Realms*, set in the same universe as its two predecessors. This time we have a different kind of hero, a rogue whose own misdeeds catapult him into a series of adventures that will shape the future course of not only his own life but of the entire world. Kestrel attempts to swindle a witch, but in the process opens a gateway between the universes and lets in a djinn, who is desperately searching for magical aid for his master. Concerned only about his own objectives, Kestrel uses the djinn to hoodwink several wizards, but they discover his perfidy and chase him across the border into the domain where Alodar serves as Archimage.

Alodar sends Kestrel and his djinn companion on a wild journey through several universes, each with its own laws. Once again, Hardy's ability to superimpose a system of logic on patterns of magic is the high point of the book, which is diversely inventive and filled with remarkable ideas and exotic settings. Both the human and the inhuman protagonist discover their true natures this time, a reprise of Hardy's recurring theme: "Once a person has accepted herself, everything else will follow."

Never the most prolific of writers, Hardy has been silent in the fantasy world for several years now. The three published novels are probably not substantial enough in themselves to establish his reputation, although they are certainly superior to much of the work produced by more active and popular fantasy writers. If more fantasists emulated Hardy's careful codification of the principles of magic, they might find that their own work became more coherent and appealing.

—Don D'Ammassa

HARMAN, Andrew

Nationality: British. **Address:** c/o Legend Books, Random House, 20 Vauxhall Bridge Road, London SW1V 2SA.

FANTASY PUBLICATIONS

Novels

The Sorcerer's Appendix. London, Legend, 1993.
The Frogs of War. London, Legend, 1994.
The Tome Tunnel. London, Legend, 1994.
101 Damnations. London, Legend, 1995.
Fahrenheit 666. London, Legend, 1995.

*　　*　　*

Humorous fantasy has become very popular over the last decade, with series of novels from, in particular, Robert Asprin and Craig Shaw Gardner in the USA, and Terry Pratchett and Tom Holt in the UK. Andrew Harman is one of the latest recruits to this subgenre, using plots which are extremely involved though essentially silly (reminiscent of Holt) and frequent bad puns (even worse than those of Piers Anthony).

Harman's first four novels, published in rapid succession, have the same setting, the kingdoms of Rhyngill and Cranachan, separated by the Talpa Mountains, with some scenes in various other contiguous countries. Some characters appear in two or three of the books, though none in all four. This is a familiar pseudo-medieval setting, with kings, castles, magicians, dragons, stupid men-at-arms, dwarfs and an oppressed rural majority. But because Harman is determined to amuse the reader he adds many British 1990s references, however anachronistic they may be, most in the form of puns. It would not be right to class this as satire, which is altogether a higher form of humour than Harman aspires to. On the other hand, it does seem that these novels lurch from one contrived joke to the next rather than being planned in the normal manner. Credibility and any kind of verisimilitude are sacrificed to the ideal of including as many silly names and punning references as possible. The result of this is that the novels are a slow read, a condition exacerbated by the large numbers of characters and the frequent changes of scene and viewpoint.

In *The Sorcerer's Appendix* (a title which bears no relation to its contents) the competing kingdoms of Rhyngill and Cranachan are introduced. The former is agriculturally bountiful, but its people are starving because King Klayth takes 74 per cent of the food in tax, supposedly to fill his warehouses. In fact the food is no sooner gathered than it is secretly shipped across the mountains to Cranachan, because Klayth's chief advisor is a Cranachan, and in this book the Cranachans are the evil ones. This is easily ascertained because their king shouts and threatens a lot, and because their Head of Security and Wars is called Khah Nij. In fact, the Cranachans need all this stolen food to feed the Rhyngill army, which they captured in a very brief war some 13 years earlier.

Caught up in the middle are starving peasants, such as Firkin and Hogshead, two youths determined to put things right by going to see King Klayth and possibly overthrowing him. Their journey and their problems of finding the king in a vast and almost deserted castle occupy quite a bit of the book. But there are various subplots, one involving a vampire named Vlad and a rerun of the Hansel and Gretel fairy tale, and a much more entertaining diversion, set 15 years earlier, involving the harvesting of lemming pelts, which led to the war between the kingdoms. Lemming jokes abound: lemming mousse is a great delicacy, while lemming-skin purses seem to leap from pockets and handbags off shoulders. In the end, Firkin and Hogshead, aided by the wizard Merlot and the castle chef's daughter, Courgette, but hindered by the over-enthusiastic Prince Chandon, do get to see King Klayth. The false advisor is unmasked and all live happily ever after—until the next adventure.

Firkin, Hogshead, Courgette and Merlot also feature in *The Frogs of War* and in *The Tome Tunnel,* along with too many other characters. Each of these books contains so many characters that none are properly developed, while it is always unclear which character, if any, is meant to be a hero. Firkin, for example, is neither brave nor clever, achieving good results by accident.

101 Damnations does not involve Firkin and his chums, though it does involve a group of researchers at Losa Llamas (= Los Alamos) who were introduced in *The Frogs of War* and who are using magic rather than science. These are Thurgia, Wat, Phlim and Practz, all relatively indistinguishable. The protagonist of the novel is, arguably, Cheiro Mancini (= cheiromancer), a Virtual Ecology Technician or VET, who creates magical replicas (via Projected Empathic Taxidermy) of pet animals.

In an exceedingly convoluted plot, Mancini becomes Court Livestock Image Consultant to the bloodthirsty despot Empress Tau, so that he can steal one of her 101 pet damnations (which resemble dalmatians but are supernatural and very dangerous). He uses it in an attempt to tap into a natural thaumafer (like an aquifer, except that this is magic rather than water), which may give him unlimited power. He is aided by seven dwarfs, digging for the thaumafer, and opposed by the Losa Llamas researchers, by Empress Tau's guards, and by a group of animal-rights protestors who believe that he is going to harm a dragon. Once again, everything such as sense and characterization is subservient to the making of jokes and puns.

Many of Harman's jokes are silly names. Sir Taindeth is a vermin exterminator. Lake Hellarwyl (= like hell I will) is a place on the map. Fhet Ucheeni (= fetucchini) is a drug dealer. Mancini drives a Fraree Sports Cart (= Ferrari). A route through the Talpa Mountains is called Foh Pass (= faux pas). Instead of Bedouins, Harman has D'vanouins. The most British and most convoluted pun concerns prostitutes in the town of Fort Knumm, who are known as Fort Knumm Hand Maidens (= Fortnum & Mason's, a famous top-people's grocery store in London). He tries to create more humour through the use of frequent footnotes (in the manner of Terry Pratchett), though this does not always succeed.

Thus, what Harman is doing is sometimes clever and occasionally very amusing, but it consists mainly of jokes for the sake of jokes and is a little way removed from the conventional fantasy novel.

—Chris Morgan

HARRIS, Geraldine (Rachel)

Nationality: British. **Born:** 17 October 1951. **Education:** King's College, Cambridge, 1973-77, B.A. (honours) 1977, M.A. 1980; Wadham College, Oxford, 1977-84, D.Phil. in Egyptology 1985. **Family:** Married Richard G. E. Pinch in 1978. **Career:** Freelance Egyptologist and writer.

FANTASY PUBLICATIONS

Novels (series: Seven Citadels)

White Cranes Castle, illustrated by Lisa Jensen. London, Macmillan, 1979.
Prince of the Godborn (Seven Citadels). London, Macmillan, and New York, Greenwillow, 1982.
The Children of the Wind (Seven Citadels). London, Macmillan, and New York, Greenwillow, 1982.
The Dead Kingdom (Seven Citadels). London, Macmillan, and New York, Greenwillow, 1983.
The Seventh Gate (Seven Citadels). London, Macmillan, and New York, Greenwillow, 1983.

OTHER PUBLICATIONS

Other

Gods and Pharaohs from Egyptian Mythology, illustrated by John Sibbick and David O'Connor. London, Lowe, 1982; New York, Schocken, 1983.
The Junior Atlas of Ancient Egypt. London, Lionheart, 1989.
New Kingdom Votive Offerings to Hathor. Oxford, Griffith Institute, 1989.

*   *   *

Geraldine Harris's first novel was the juvenile *White Cranes Castle.* It is set in a slightly mythologized feudal Japan where magic works and monsters are real, though both are rare. The story concerns the life story of Akari, the son of a Japanese noble who committed suicide; his mother goes into a monastery as a (Buddhist) nun, and Akari is taken into the household of his maternal uncle, the Damiyo, the regional governor. Here, he grows up beside Mikoto, the Damiyo's son. The two are very different: Mikoto is a warrior—an ambiguous prophecy made at the time of his birth foretold that he would regain a lost, magical sword; but Akari is a scholar, and he is taken under the wing of Naginoki, the greatest monk of the area. As the story progresses, we learn that Akari's father killed himself because he did not dare to fulfil his desire to strike the Bell of Saneyori. Doing so would summon the dragon that sleeps in the lake in the grounds of the family house. Akari dedicates his life to doing this in his father's stead, and finally does so when a drought sears the land; he finds that the creature is a seven-headed great dragon. By this time, it has been discovered that the sword is being held by the dragon. Mikoto is sent to get it, the assumption being that he will fight for it. But Akari has already spoken to the dragon, and kept their interest: bore the dragon and it will kill you. When Mikoto's courage fails, Akari riddles the dragons and wins the sword. He triumphs, yet the outcome is that he has lost Mikoto's trust, and, ultimately, his friendship—Mikoto cannot believe that Akari will tell no one, thereby preserving Mikoto's honour. In the end, Akari is forced to retire to a monastery, but even there he may not be safe from Mikoto.

The narrative is deftly woven, and Harris pulls off a very difficult trick by showing us how different—and unacceptable to most modern readers—their sexist and class-ridden society is, without once going outside the viewpoint of her characters. However, there are problems not so much with the book as with the readership it is aimed at. The outcome of the prophecy is never in doubt, an

Akari's role in its fulfilment is obvious to a sophisticated reader, at least in outline, from the beginning. This would seem to show that the book is aimed at a juvenile audience. Yet Akari's riddling with the dragons is so surreal, and so devious, that it is hard to see more than a few children understanding it, and perhaps fewer still having the patience to wrestle with it. Added to this is the ambiguity of the ending, which seems to indicate a deeper meaning to the book than is readily apparent on the surface.

This ambiguity is also evident in Harris's other work, the four-volume Seven Citadels sequence. These were also marketed initially as juvenile titles, though they are definitely adult in theme and tone. They feature one of those convoluted genealogies so prevalent in genre fantasy, together with a fairly standard quest-centred plot.

Prince Kerish-lo-Taan, a son of the Emperor of Galkis by a slave girl, is one of the Godborn, the elite rulers of the Galkian Empire. He is sent to find and free the Saviour who can rescue the Empire from both its internal strife and the various enemies that assail its borders. To do this, he must acquire the keys to the seven gates of the Saviour's prison. Each of these is currently held by a different, ultra-powerful sorcerer. For a sorcerer to give up a key means the loss of immortality. Nevertheless, Kerish sets out with his half-brother Forollkin. The four books chronicle the adventures the two have on their quest, the companions they acquire, and the people they meet, including Gwerath, whom both the brothers grow to love.

Some parts of the narrative are more successful than others: the game Kerish plays with the sorcerer Ellandellore, who has been trapped by the possession of his key into a mad eternal childhood, is genuinely frightening. To this is added a fairly sophisticated exposition of politics, societies and people ("The worst of tyrants may be gentlest of men to those they love," says Kerish at one point), and some gratifyingly strong people. However, some of the names—the Ultimate Mountains, for example—are almost parodic, and the books occasionally slip over into sentimentality, particularly in the handling of Lilahnee the marsh cat.

The main strength of the sequence comes with Harris's handling of character. She is afraid neither to show her protagonists as complex and faulty heroes at best, nor to allow them to grow as their quest—which takes many years—proceeds. Nor does she give them easy choices. Nowhere is this more apparent than in the climax of the sequence. To free the saviour Kerish must go through the final gate: the gate of death. There, he finds that the Saviour he seeks is his own self. The choice he is offered is far from simple. He watches his country fall to the invaders in accelerated time. He is also shown all those he has ever loved: they will be waiting for him, here on the far side of death's gate. His choice is whether to be reborn into the world (whether as a baby or as himself is not made clear) and become the Saviour, a hope for his scattered people; he will be able not only to rebuild the Empire, but to make it a more equal society. Or, he can remain dead, where he is promised peace. He chooses the former, with all its pain and suffering.

—Liz Holliday

HARRIS, MacDonald

Pseudonym for Donald William Heiney. **Nationality:** American. **Born:** 1921. **Died:** 1993.

FANTASY PUBLICATIONS

Novels

The Balloonist. New York, Farrar Straus and Giroux, 1976.
Herma. New York, Athenaeum, 1981; London, Gollancz, 1982.
Screenplay. New York, Athenaeum, 1982.
The Little People. New York, Morrow, 1985.

OTHER PUBLICATIONS

Novels

Private Demons. Boston, Houghton Mifflin, 1961.
Mortal Leap. New York, Norton, 1964.
Trepleff. London, Gollancz, 1968; New York, Holt Rinehart, and Winston, 1969.
Bull Fire. New York, Random House, and London, Gollancz, 1973.
Yukiko. New York, Farrar Straus and Giroux, 1977; London, Gollancz, 1978.
Pandora's Galley. New York, Harcourt Brace Jovanovich, 1979.
The Treasure of Sainte Foy. New York, Atheneum, 1980.
Tenth. New York, Atheneum, 1984.
Glowstone. New York, Morrow, 1987.
Hemingway's Suitcase. New York, Simon and Schuster, 1990.
A Portrait of My Desire. New York, Simon and Schuster, 1993.

Short Stories

The Cathay Stories and Other Fictions. Santa Cruz, California, Story Line Press, 1988.
Glad Rags. Brownsville, Oregon, Story Line Press, 1991.

Other

They Sailed Alone: The Story of the Single-Handers. Boston, Houghton Mifflin, 1972.

Other (as Donald W. Heiney)

Essentials of Contemporary Literature. Great Neck, New York, Barron, 1955.
America in Modern Italian Literature. New Brunswick, New Jersey, Rutgers University Press, 1964.
Barron's Simplified Approach to Ernest Hemingway. Woodbury, New York, Barron, 1965; revised edition, 1967.
Barron's Simplified Approach to Thomas Mann. Woodbury, New York, Barron, 1966.
Three Italian Novelists: Moravia, Pavese, Vittorini. Ann Arbor, Michigan, University of Michigan Press, 1968.
Essentials of Contemporary Literature of the Western World: Recent American Literature to 1930, with Lenthiel W. Downs. Woodbury, New York, Barron, 1973.
Essentials of Contemporary Literature of the Western World: Continental European, with Lenthiel W. Downs. Woodbury, New York, Barron, 1973.
Essentials of Contemporary Literature of the Western World: British, with Lenthiel W. Downs. Woodbury, New York, Barron, 1973; revised as *English Literature: 1900 to the Present,* with Lenthiel W. Downs and Arthur H. Bell, Hauppauge, New York, Barron, 1994.

Essentials of Contemporary Literature of the Western World: Recent American Literature After 1930, with Lenthiel W. Downs. Woodbury, New York, Barron, 1973; revised as *American Literature: 1930 to the Present,* with Lenthiel W. Downs and Arthur H. Bell, Hauppauge, New York, Barron, 1994.

*   *   *

MacDonald Harris is a neglected writer whose works deserve more attention. In many ways, he is the American equivalent of Canadian novelist Robertson Davies. Like Davies, Harris was a writer whose works border fantasy fiction, and, on four occasions, cross over. Like Davies, Harris was fascinated by the Victorian and Edwardian eras. Like Davies, Harris is a novelist of ideas and esoteric knowledge; his readers learn a great deal about art, culture and linguistics. And like Davies, Harris was a novelist who did not begin to hit his stride until he was in his mid-50s.

Harris's works are also hard to classify. *Glowstone,* for example, is a historical novel whose protagonist strongly resembles Marie Curie in that she is a French scientist obsessed with a corrosive, radioactive substance that closely resembles radium. Because the substance is given an imaginary name, some critics have declared that *Glowstone* is a science-fiction novel, when it is in fact a historical novel with no fantastic elements. In *Bull Fire,* characters in a contemporary family drama act in ways that resemble the myth of the Minotaur, though the novel is not a fantasy.

And even in Harris's fantasies, the fantastic elements are quite subdued. *Screenplay* is a bittersweet time-travel romance similar to Richard Matheson's *Bid Time Return* or Jack Finney's *Time and Again.* But unlike Matheson or Finney, Harris never explains why his characters are able to pass through a magic movie screen and enter the silent-movie era.

Harris's first fantasy novel, *The Balloonist,* was the first of his books to receive national attention, winning a nomination for the National Book Award for best novel. Dedicated to Jules Verne, the novel is a pastiche of a Verne adventure novel. Set in 1897, *The Balloonist*'s hero is a Swedish explorer who is obsessed with being the first person to fly over the North Pole in a balloon. This imaginary voyage is vivid, exciting, richly detailed, and periodically interrupted by reveries where the dying explorer, marooned on the Arctic icepack, reminisces about his romance with a Portuguese-American opera-singer who delights in teaching the virile hero the pleasures of cross-dressing and other gender-bending exercises. The result is an odd and not always successful amalgam, as if Verne had collaborated with one of the decadent French novelists of the 1890s.

Harris's next fantasy, *Herma,* is, at over 250,000 words, his longest and perhaps his best novel. Herma is a girl growing up in a small Southern California town shortly after the turn of the century. When she is 16, Herma discovers two truths about herself—she has a world-class voice and, by staring in a mirror and concentrating intently, she can transform her genitals and switch genders. This trick enables Harris to tell two parallel stories. Herma (who has no other name) rises in the world of opera, moving first to San Francisco, then to Paris. Puccini composes *The Girl of the Golden West* for her, and she ultimately triumphs at the Paris Opera by playing all three female leads in *The Tales of Hoffmann.* But periodically Herma transforms herself into "Fred Hite," whose income from "his" living as Herma's manager enables him to fly airplanes, a skill that ultimately qualifies him for the Lafayette Escadrille during the First World War. Only Marcel Proust guesses that Herma and Fred Hite are the same person.

Herma is an intricate, well-constructed work. Harris did a great deal of research for the novel, which ensures that the worlds he describes, from the rehearsals at the Paris Opera to World War I dogfights, are vividly and memorably described. The scenes of Herma surviving the San Francisco earthquake of 1906 are particularly powerful. But at its heart *Herma* is a fantasy where, as in Harris's other novels, the fantastic elements are given little weight; the author finds the techniques of Edwardian voice coaches far more interesting than Herma's gender-switching powers.

Harris's next novel, *Screenplay,* is his most conventional fantasy. It begins in contemporary Los Angeles, where Alys, a bored under-sexed aesthete, lives on a trust fund, his only delights being watching silent movies and driving some 1920s-era cars that he has inherited. But then Alys rents a room to an aged eccentric who calls himself Julius Nesselrode and who claims to be a famous Hollywood director. Alys discovers that several valuable family heirlooms are missing—and that they very much resemble props that appear in the silent films Alys is watching. This clue enables Alys to discover that Nesselrode is using a fading movie screen in a long-closed theatre to leap through time.

Alys spends most of *Screenplay* in the 1920s, wooing Moira, an ingenue, and energetically taking part in several movies. Once again, Harris is strongest at describing the background of his book; he's best at showing the bewildering speed with which silent-film directors cranked out two-reeler after two-reeler. One day Alys is an extra in a film about the assassination of Abraham Lincoln; the next, he's spending hours marching across burning Southern California beaches pretending to be an Arab sheik. *Screenplay* is a first-rank fantasy, solidly constructed and very plausible. Of all of Harris's books, it's the one that fantasy readers would find most appealing.

Harris's last fantasy, *The Little People,* is less important and less interesting than his earlier works. In it, a literature professor from America, on sabbatical, ends up in a small town in Cornwall, where he rents a room from an ancient Cornish family in the hopes that he will have enough leisure to finish a monograph on medieval English literature. He quickly finds that most of the members of the Cornish family are mad, wicked, eccentric, and possibly inbred. The home's woods are rife with fairies, and our dazed hero adds to his delusions by periodically sleepwalking into the woods, where the fairies taunt him with ancient and esoteric rituals.

The Little People is an unsuccessful novel because it violates a rule first proposed by Damon Knight—to have strange people do strange things in a book is one strangeness too many. While Harris's earlier novels featured normal characters in unusual situations, *The Little People* is little more than a contrived parade of grotesque characters unleavened by wit or comedy. The fantasy elements in the novel are very slight; the fairies not only do nothing more than dance and taunt the hero, but their removal would not alter the plot.

While *The Little People* is a not particularly admirable failure, Harris's best fantasies—*The Balloonist, Herma* and *Screenplay*—are important, neglected, and enjoyable works that ought to be better known.

—Martin Morse Wooster

HARRISON, Michael

Pseudonyms: Quentin Downes, Michael Egremont. **Nationality:** British. **Born:** Milton, Kent, England, 25 April 1907. **Education:**

Attended King's College and the School of Oriental and African Studies, University of London. **Family:** Married Maryvonne Aubertin, 1950 (died 1977); two step daughters. **Career:** Editor of publications including *The British Ink Maker*; market research executive and industrial and technical consultant; creative director of advertising agency. **Agent:** Jonathan Clowes Ltd., 22 Prince Albert Rd., London NW1 7ST, England. **Died:** 1991.

FANTASY PUBLICATIONS

Novels

The Bride of Frankenstein (as Michael Egremont). London, Reader's Library, 1936.
Higher Things. London, Macdonald, 1945.
The Brain. London, Cassell, 1953.

Short Stories

Transit of Venus. London, Transit Press, 1936.

OTHER PUBLICATIONS

Novels

Weep for Lycidas. London, Barker, 1934.
Spring in Tartarus: An Arabesque. London, Barker, 1935.
All the Trees Were Green. London, Barker, 1936.
What Are We Waiting For? London, Rich and Cowan, 1939.
Vernal Equinox. London, Collins, 1939.
Battered Caravanserai. London, Rich and Cowan, 1942.
Reported Safe Arrival: The Journal of a Voyage to Port X. London, Rich and Cowan, 1943.
So Linked Together. London, Macdonald, 1944.
The House in Fishergate. London, Macdonald, 1946.
Treadmill. London, Langdon Press, 1947.
Sinecure. London, Laurie, 1948.
There's Glory for You! London, Laurie, 1949.
Thing Less Noble: A Modern Love Story. London, Laurie, 1950.
Long Vacation. London, Laurie, 1951.
The Dividing Stone. London, Cassell, 1954.
A Hansom to St. James's. London, Cassell, 1954.

Uncollected Short Stories

"The Vanished Treasure," in *Ellery Queen's Crime Carousel.* New York, New American Library, 1966.
"Wit's End," in *Best Detective Stories of the Year 1971,* edited by Allen J. Hubin. New York, Dutton, 1971.
"Whatever Happened to Young Russell?" in *Ellery Queen's Headliners.* Cleveland, World, 1971; London, Gollancz, 1972.
"The Facts in the Case of the Missing Diplomat," in *Ellery Queen's Mystery Anthology.* New York, Davis, 1973.
"The Jewel of Childeric," in *Ellery Queen's Faces of Mystery.* New York, Davis, 1977.
"The Murder in the Rue St. Andre des Arts," in *50 Classics of Crime Fiction 1950-75: Classic Short Stories of Crime Detection,* edited by Jacques Barzun and Wendell Hertig Taylor. New York, Garland, 1983.

"Sherlock Holmes and the Woman," in *The New Adventures of Sherlock Holmes.* New York, Carroll and Graf, 1987.
"Some Very Odd Happenings at Kibblesham Manor House," in *Eternal City,* edited by David Drake. New York, Baen, 1990.

Other

Dawn Express: There and Back. London, Collins, 1938.
Gambler's Glory: The Story of John Law of Lauriston. London, Rich and Cowan, 1940.
Count Cagliostro, Nature's Unfortunate Child. London, Rich and Cowan, 1942.
They Would Be King. London, Somers, 1947.
Post Office, Mauritius 1847: The Tale of Two Stamps. London, Stamp Collecting, 1947.
The Story of Christmas: Its Growth and Development from Earliest Times. London, Odhams Press, 1951; revised edition as *Saturnalia,* London, Skoob Books, 1990.
Airborne at Kitty Hawk: The Story of the First Heavier-than-Air Flight Made by the Wright Brothers. London, Cassell, 1953.
Charles Dickens: A Sentimental Journey in Search of an Unvarnished Portrait. London, Cassell, 1953; New York, Haskell House, 1976.
A New Approach to Stamp Collecting, with Douglas Armstrong. London, Batsford, 1953; New York, Hanover Press, 1954.
Beer Cookery: 101 Traditional Recipes. London, Spearman Calder, 1954.
Peter Cheyney, Prince of Hokum: A Biography. London, Spearman, 1954.
In the Footsteps of Sherlock Holmes. London, Cassell, 1958; New York, Fell, 1960; revised edition, Newton Abbot, Devon, David and Charles, 1971; New York, Drake, 1972.
The History of the Hat. London, Jenkins, 1960; New York, Berkeley, 1974.
London Beneath the Pavement. London, Davies, 1961; revised edition, 1971.
Rosa (biography of Rosa Lewis). London, Davies, 1962.
Painful Details: Twelve Victorian Scandals. London, Parrish, 1962.
London by Gaslight 1861-1911. London, Davies, 1963.
London Growing: The Development of a Metropolis. London, Hutchinson, 1965.
Mulberry: The Return in Triumph. London, W.H. Allen, 1965.
Lord of London: A Biography of the Second Duke of Westminster. London, W.H. Allen, 1966.
Technical and Industrial Publicity. London, Business Publications, 1968.
The London That Was Rome: The Imperial City Recreated by the New Archaeology. London, Allen and Unwin, 1971.
Fanfare of Strumpets. London, W.H. Allen, 1971.
Clarence: The Life of H.R.H. the Duke of Clarence and Avondale 1864-1892. London, W.H. Allen, 1972; as *Clarence: Was He Jack the Ripper?,* New York, Drake, 1974.
The London of Sherlock Holmes. Newton Abbot, Devon, David and Charles, and New York, Drake, 1972.
The Roots of Witchcraft. London, Muller, 1973; Secaucus, New Jersey, Citadel Press, 1974; revised edition, London, Skoob Books, 1990.
The World of Sherlock Holmes. London, Muller, 1973; New York, Dutton, 1975.
Theatrical Mr. Holmes: The World's Greatest Consulting Detective, Considered Against the Background of the Contemporary Theatre. London, Convent Garden Press, 1974.

Fire from Heaven; or, How Safe Are You from Burning? (on spontaneous combustion). London, Sidgwick and Jackson, 1976; revised edition, London, Pan, 1977; London, Skoob Books, 1990. New York, Methuen, 1978.
I, Sherlock Holmes. New York, Dutton, 1977.
Vanishings. London, New English Library, 1981.
Immortal Sleuth: Sherlockian Musings and Memories. Dubuque, Iowa, Gasogene Press, 1983.
A Study in Surmise: The Making of Sherlock Holmes. Bloomington, Indiana, Gaslight, 1984.
A Sheaf of Sherlock. Dubuque, Iowa, Gasogene Press, 1990.

Editor, *Under Thirty* (anthology of short stories). London, Rich and Cowan, 1939.
Editor, *Beyond Baker Street: A Sherlockian Anthology.* Indianapolis, Bobbs Merrill, 1976.

*

Manuscript Collections: Mugar Memorial Library, Boston University.

*   *   *

After writing two mundane novels while supporting himself as a newspaper gossip columnist (with occasional forays into writing thrillers for the boys' papers) Michael Harrison was hired to write a volume in one of the pioneering series of film novelizations then being issued—sometimes in huge editions—by the Reader's Library; it happened to be *The Bride of Frankenstein,* the 1935 sequel to James Whale's 1931 version of Mary Shelley's novel. As with most such projects, the result was a hastily written piece of hackwork, issued under a pseudonym, which largely ignored the script and embroidered the basic storyline with dialogue and commentary of the novelizer's invention. It benefited, however, from the fact that *The Bride of Frankenstein* was one of the best monster movies of its period, and Harrison brought a certain casual zest and stylishness to the project; the book can certainly stand comparison with the 1958 novelization of Jimmy Sangster's script for *The Revenge of Frankenstein* (which bears Sangster's name on the cover, although the title page suggests that the novelization process was carried out by one Hurford Janes).

Several fantasies in Harrison's own idiosyncratic manner can be found in the short-story collection, *Transit of Venus,* although the title novella—a baroque and strikingly misogynistic Robinsonade—does not quite qualify as one of them. "Mother Earth" is an intriguing account of a child who has an unnatural affinity with the earth. "Where Thy Heart Is" (the only story to have appeared previously) is a deft weird tale featuring a vampiric book. "The K'ang Hsi Vase" is an earnest tale of metempsychosis. "The Legend of Brother Content" is a humorous tale in which an indolent monk borrows the devil's horse and must then suffer the temptations of Satanic gratitude.

Harrison's most important fantasy novel was *Higher Things,* which was written before the outbreak of World War II although it was not published until the war was reaching its climax. This work is a late addition to what had by then become a robust English tradition of stories about men who discover that they have the power of levitation, following on the heels of Ronald Fraser's *The Flying Draper* (1924), Neil Bell's "The Facts About Benjamin Crede" (1935), and Eric Knight's "The Flying Yorkshireman" (1938). Like

The Flying Draper, Harrison's *Higher Things* is a consciously Wellsian fantasy embodying and gently parodying H. G. Wells's ideals of personal and evolutionary progress. Like many a Wellsian hero the narrator of the story, James Faraday, is a young man of humble station (he is a bank clerk) who dreams of far better things for himself and for the world. At first he employs his new-found talent as a means of trivial escapism, but moves on to grander plans. Like Wells himself he goes to confront the dictator whose ambitions pose a threat to the World Order, but fails to talk sense into him and decides instead that he must escape the world's toils and travails altogether with the aid of a will-powered spaceship aimed at Mars. As we have only the narrator's word for all this, of course, it remains possible—perhaps altogether likely—that the whole thing is mere delusion; this is why the story is clearly a fantasy despite its thematic links with the tradition of British scientific romance. The mannered comedy is subtle and charming, and the serious themes which underlie it are addressed with all due intelligence; it is one of the finest fantasies of the 1940s.

Higher Things was the first of a group of four novels which Harrison lumped together as "The Rowcester Novels"; the others are not fantasies, although the mystery story *The Darkened Room* includes a minor science-fictional motif in the form of a cat whose life is artificially prolonged with the aid of an artificial heart—an idea first displayed in one of the stories in *Transit of Venus,* "For Ever and Ever."

Harrison's third fantasy novel, *The Brain,* was inspired by the manner in which World War II was finally brought to a close. It is one of a group of novels written in horrified reaction to the advent of the atom bomb; its immediate British predecessors include F. Horace Rose's *The Maniac's Dream* (1946) and H. de Vere Stacpoole's *The Story of My Village* (1947). Most novels in this group are, of course, scientific romances, but Harrison again followed an example set by Ronald Fraser (in *Beetle's Career,* 1951) by extrapolating his story into the realms of surreal symbolism. In *The Brain* the "mushroom cloud" of a test explosion mysteriously duplicates the shape of a human brain, mirroring that of the narrator, Royal Eberhardt (whose testimony is far more reliable than that of James Faraday). The giant Brain quickly achieves a power and maturity appropriate to its size, assuming godlike capabilities. It then offers a Faustian bargain to its human counterpart, promising him access to unlimited knowledge and power over his contemporaries—but Eberhardt only finds the status of demi-god appealing while it is unbalanced by a better moral influence, which eventually enters the plot in the shape of the priest Father Merlozzo. As is commonplace in such fantasies—and common even in science-fiction stories which have a licence to be bolder—the author contents himself in the end with reiterating the ancient and cowardly adage that there are Things Man Was Not Meant To Know, thus adding yet another item to the interminable list of sub-Frankensteinian parables. The novel suffers from the absence of the leavening wit which made *Higher Things* exceptional.

Although Harrison wrote no more fantasy novels after *The Brain,* it is perhaps appropriate to mention his contribution to one of the most popular and most pernicious scholarly fantasies of the 20th century. His book on *The Roots of Witchcraft* is an elaboration of the altogether unwarranted "theories" of Margaret Murray; it is far more fantastic, and much sillier, than any of his acknowledged fictions.

—Brian Stableford

HARRISON, M(ichael) John

Pseudonym: Ron Fawcett. **Nationality:** British. **Born:** Warwickshire, 26 July 1945. **Education:** At schools in England. **Career:** Groom, Atherstone Hunt, Warwickshire, 1963; student teacher, Warwickshire, 1963-65; clerk, Royal Masonic Charity Institute, London, 1966; literary editor and reviewer, *New Worlds,* 1968-75; regular contributor, *New Manchester Review,* 1978-79. **Agent:** Anthony Sheil Associates, 43 Doughty Street, London WCIN 2LF, England.

FANTASY PUBLICATIONS

Novels (series: Viriconium)

The Pastel City (Viriconium). London, New English Library, 1971; New York, Doubleday, 1972.
A Storm of Wings (Viriconium). London, Sphere, and New York, Doubleday, 1980.
In Viriconium. London, Gollancz, 1982; as *The Floating Gods,* New York, Pocket Books, 1983.
The Course of the Heart. London, Gollancz, 1992.

Graphic Novel

The Luck in the Head, illustrated by Ian Miller. London, Gollancz, 1993.

Short Stories

The Ice Monkey and Other Stories. London, Gollancz, 1983.
Viriconium Nights. New York, Ace, 1984; revised edition, London, Gollancz, 1985.

OTHER PUBLICATIONS

Novels

The Committed Men. London, Hutchinson, and New York, Doubleday, 1971.
The Centauri Device. New York, Doubleday, 1974; London, Panther, 1975.
Climbers. London, Gollancz, 1989.

Short Stories

The Machine in Shaft Ten and Other Stories. London, Panther, 1975.

Other

Fawcett on Rock (ghost-written as by Ron Fawcett). N.p., 1987.

*   *   *

M. John Harrison first found his voice as a critic and short story writer in *New Worlds* magazine, in the late 1960s and early 1970s. Although his fictions were notable from the beginning for their finely worked surfaces, Harrison's precise evocations of the quid-dity of the world should not blind us to the strong narrative structures underpinning them. His first novel was post-holocaust science fiction, but with his second he defined an arena in which he was able to experiment with, and reify, the escapist imagery and childish refusal to confront the world (as he sees it) of much contemporary fantasy. *The Pastel City* is far-future science fantasy in which the Earth is littered with the decayed relics of an advanced interstellar culture. Viriconium is the city at the end of time whose inhabitants use and appease these remnants as if they are magical, although the nominal hero of the book, tegus-Cromis, is armed with nothing more than an ordinary sword and a steel ring which signifies that he is the Queen of Viriconium's champion. The sword is soon broken; the ring is lost; tegus-Cromis tetchily abandons the final confrontation. These sarcasms on the traditional role of the hero in fantasy, and a scrupulous particularity in attending to the ruined landscapes in which tegus-Cromis confronts Viriconium's enemies, enliven a simple plot in which Viriconium is off-handedly saved from treachery and conquest by what are basically brain-eating robots, and repopulated by Reborn men from a past era.

The sequel to *The Pastel City, A Storm of Wings,* is notable for a heightening of the attention which Harrison pays to the particularity of the world of Viriconium and the internal lives of its inhabitants (not always separable). An invasion of giant insects, more metaphysical than otherwise, is thwarted by a single act of self-sacrifice; the interest lies not in the plot, but in Harrison's depiction of characters so paralysed by their past that they fail to confront the present.

This paralysis, an implicit criticism of fantasy fiction itself, is made explicit in *In Viriconium,* in which a plague of despair creeps across the city. The Reborn men have vanished into the past, leaving behind the Barley Brothers, gods of the city who have taken on human form as a degraded version of Midland yobs (Harrison is at his most lively and funny in his depictions of the Barley Brothers' blundering burlesque). Ashlyme, a portrait painter who possesses a degraded version of the signs of tegus-Cromis's heroic status (he has a sword he keeps in a cupboard, and a steel ring he has only been told is valuable, but not why), tries and fails to rescue another painter, Audsley King (who is in some sense the Fisher King). His failure is a failure of inaction or commitment; in all the novel, only The Grand Cairo, an evil dwarf who is the instrument of the Barley Brothers' governance, has the will to act. The Grand Cairo's will lends impetus to Ashlyme's impotent scheme to rescue Audsley King, but his bad temper results in its failure, when he casually kills a woman. Finally, Ashlyme assumes the role of priest and kills one of the corn-god Barley Brothers (who address him throughout the novel as vicar); the city is redeemed; Audsley King feverishly produces paintings concerned not with rural fantasies, but the world itself.

The stories collected in *Viriconium Nights,* and the associated graphic novel *The Luck in the Head,* make quite plain Harrison's view of the relationship between fantasy and the world, and his disdain for those decadent forms of high fantasy which imitate and heighten only selected aspects of the world. Viriconium—or Uruconium, or Vira Co—is an arena in which the poorly remembered versions of the past are played over and over. "The world is so old that the substance of reality no longer knows quite what it ought to be. The original template is hopelessly blurred. History repeats over and again this one city and a few frightful events . . ." In the central story "Viriconium Knights," a thuggish swordsman, a crude echo of tegus-Cromis, is given visions of what he (and Viriconium) might be, fails to grasp the chance of change, and passes into a different version of Viriconium, becoming only what he was before. By the final story, "A Young Man's Journey to Viriconium," Viriconium has become only an ideal to be sought for in this world, a way of escape that is not easily grasped.

Climbers, emphatically not fantasy, is also crammed with the desperation of those who need to escape their mundane lives—in this case by rock climbing. Only by paying scrupulous attention to the surface of the world can they succeed; otherwise they will, literally, fall. "Egnaro," collected in *The Ice Monkey,* echoes this theme of the desperate necessity of escape, while several of the other stories prefigure Harrison's best fantasy novel, *The Course of the Heart.*

In this last, three Cambridge undergraduates enact a magical ritual under the guidance of a shabby mage, Yaxley. The novel lays bare the consequences of the climax of that ritual, a visualization of the neoPlatonic Pleroma, which none can quite remember. Two, Pam and Lucas, marry, but are haunted by the demons which they have brought back with their glimpse of the Pleroma: for Pam a white couple endlessly making love; for Lucas a destructive dwarf. Their marriage fails, but they are still bound to each other by the complex shared fiction of the Coeur, an imaginary country, a buffer between this world and the Pleroma, woven from a Gnostic secret history. This gains increasing importance as Pam becomes fatally ill, and becomes by metonymy the country of their love for each other (in a related short story, "The Gift," a couple find an undiscovered city within themselves, and are allowed to inhabit it). The third participant in the ritual, the unnamed narrator, fails to understand this binding: Lucas's assertion that Pam is the descendant of the rulers of the Coeur seems to him to be woundingly delusive, and he mistakes Lucas's manuscript of the secret history for a novel.

The narrator seems the least affected by Yaxley's ritual, haunted by nothing more than the scent of roses. He prospers, perhaps because he has not severed his relationship with Yaxley; he participates in a macabre ritual (called by Yaxley an infolding, a deliberate echo of the shabby urban magics, whose degraded signs are also an echo of Viriconium's blurred myths, of the story "The Incalling") in which a Thatcherite businessman despoils his own daughter for worldly gain. Although the narrator condemns the ritual, he fails to save the girl or stop the ritual, which ends in catastrophe. In the end, he also loses the sign of the goodness which he has gained from the world, when his wife is killed in a road accident. He is left alone, still not understanding, because he has, by inaction, failed to connect with anything.

The Course of the Heart utilizes the associative narrative technique developed in *Climbers* to powerful affect: it is a rich tapestry of echoes, just as the Coeur is a neo-Platonist echo of real history. One feels that Harrison, in full control of a sheaf of carefully honed techniques, has placed himself in a unique position between the mainstream fiction of the World and the Pleroma of ideal fantasy. Although his regard can be scourging, we miss his fierce lessons on reading the real and the fantastic at our peril.

—Paul J. McAuley

HAWKWOOD, Allan. *See* **BEDFORD-JONES, H(enry James O'Brien).**

HAWKE, Simon

Pseudonyms: S. L. Hunter; J. D. Masters. **Nationality:** American. **Born:** Nicholas Valentin Yermakov, New York City, 30 September 1951. **Education:** Valley Forge Military Academy, Pennsylvania; American University, Washington, D.C.; Hofstra University, Hempstead, New York, B.A. in English and communications 1974. **Career:** Has worked as musician, broadcaster, journalist, salesman, bartender, and factory worker. **Agent:** Adele Leone Agency, 26 Nantucket Place, Scarsdale, NY 10583, USA.

FANTASY PUBLICATIONS

Novels (series: Marvin Brewster; The Wizard)

The Wizard of 4th Street. New York, Popular Library, 1987.
The Wizard of Whitechapel. New York, Popular Library, 1988.
The Wizard of Sunset Strip. New York, Popular Library, 1989.
The Wizard of Rue Morgue. New York, Popular Library, 1990.
The Samurai Wizard. New York, Warner, 1991.
The Nine Lives of Catseye Gomez. Arvada, Colorado, Roadkill Press, 1991.
The Wizard of Santa Fe. New York, Warner, 1991
The Reluctant Sorcerer (Brewster). New York, Warner, 1992.
The Wizard of Camelot. New York, Warner, 1993.
The Inadequate Adept (Brewster). New York, Warner, 1993.
The Wizard of Lovecraft's Cafe. New York, Warner, 1993.

OTHER PUBLICATIONS

Novels

The Ivanhoe Gambit. New York, Ace, 1984; London, Headline, 1987.
The Timekeeper Conspiracy. New York, Ace, 1984; London, Headline, 1987.
The Pimpernel Plot. New York, Ace, 1984; London, Headline, 1988.
Timewars. New York, Berkley, 1984; London, Headline, 1988.
The Zenda Vendetta. New York, Ace, 1985; London, Headline, 1988.
The Nautilus Sanction. New York, Ace, 1985; London, Headline, 1988.
The Khyber Connection. New York, Berkley, 1986; London, Headline, 1989.
Psychodrome. New York, Ace, 1987.
The Argonaut Affair. New York, Berkley, 1987; London, Headline, 1989.
Friday the 13th (novelization of screenplay). New York, New American Library, 1987.
The Dracula Caper. New York, Berkley, 1988; London, Headline, 1989.
Friday the 13th, Part II (novelization of screenplay). New York, New American Library, 1988.
Friday the 13th, Part III (novelization of screenplay). New York, New American Library, 1988.
Jason Lives: Friday the 13th, Part VI (novelization of screenplay) New York, New American Library, 1988.
The Shapechanger Scenario: Pyschodrome 2. New York, Ace, 1988.

The Lilliput Legion. New York, Ace, 1989.
The Cleopatra Crisis. New York, Berkley, 1990.
The Hellfire Rebellion. New York, Ace, 1990.
Predator 2 (novelization of screenplay). New York, Berkley, 1990.
Batman: To Stalk a Specter. New York, Warner, and London, Roc, 1991.
The Six-Gun Solution. New York, Ace, 1991.
Dark Sun: The Outcast. Lake Geneva, Wisconsin, TSR, 1993.
The Romulan Prize. New York, Pocket, and London, Titan, 1993.
The Patrian Transgression. New York, Pocket, and London, Titan, 1994.
Dark Sun: The Seeker. Lake Geneva, Wisconsin, TSR, 1994.
Blaze of Glory. New York, Pocket, 1995.

Novels as Nicholas Yermakov

Journey from Flesh. New York, Berkley, 1981.
Last Communion. New York, New American Library, 1981.
Fall into Darkness. New York, Berkley, 1982.
Clique. New York, Berkley, 1982.
Epiphany. New York, New American Library, 1982.
Battlestar Galactica 6: The Living Legend (novelization of screenplay), with Glen A. Larson. New York, Berkley, 1982.
Battlestar Galactica 7: War of the Gods (novelization of screenplay), with Glen A. Larson. New York, Berkley, 1982.
Jehad. New York, New American Library, 1984.

Novels as J. D. Masters

Steele. New York, Charter, 1989.
Cold Steele. New York, Charter, 1989.
Killer Steele. New York, Charter, 1990.
Jagged Steele. New York, Charter, 1990.
Renegade Steele. New York, Charter, 1990.
Target Steele. New York, Charter, 1990.
Fugitive Steele (as S. L. Hunter). New York, Charter, 1991.

*   *   *

Much of Simon Hawke's writing can be regarded as science fiction to some degree. But the novels under consideration here also contain magic, and so can be regarded as fantasy. Although belonging to two main series, each book can be read in isolation despite having common backgrounds and common characters. Anything important from previous books in the series is recapped in some form to enable the reader to understand the story.

The Wizard series is set in the 23rd century, in a future where magic has been reborn. Towards the end of the previous century the technological age collapsed from a combination of factors including depletion of resources such as fuels, pollution and overpopulation. When civilization was at its lowest ebb, the ancient sorcerer, Merlin, was released from the enchantment placed on him by Morgana and Nimue back in King Arthur's time. He brought a revival of magic. *The Wizard of Camelot,* although not the first written, tells this story. By the time *The Wizard of 4th Street* begins, magic has taken over the role that science has in present society. Even the cabs are operated by adepts chanting spells of impulsion and levitation. This book sets the scene for the rest of the series. An adept, Wyrdrune, who was thrown out of college for unauthorized use of magic, decides to steal three runestones of un-

known magical properties from an auction room in front of the world's most prominent wizards. Cat-burglar Kira also has the same idea. Thrown together at the moment of committing the act, they try to fence the jewels, only to find they keep coming back. With a hired killer on their trail, Wyrdrune asks his old teacher, Merlin, for help. It seems that these runestones have been the guardians of a prison for the Dark Ones, the remnants of a race of Mages of immense power who gain energy from killing. Stolen from their warding place, thus releasing the Dark Ones into the world, the stones adopt Wyrdrune, Kira and their potential assassin, who is King Arthur's son Modred, giving them the power to vanquish the Dark Ones.

This sets up the premise for a series of books wherein the three seek out and destroy the world's enemies. Fortunately, everything is not straightforward. In London (*The Wizard of Whitechapel*), they discover that Merlin's spirit has taken possession of a street urchin, Billy Slade. In Japan (*The Samurai Wizard*), Modred is killed and his runestone and spirit fuses with Wyrdrune giving him a double personality. In New Mexico (*The Wizard of Santa Fe*) Billy, Merlin and the ancient sorcerer Gorlois (the father of Morgana in Arthurian legend) fuse to form a complex, powerful but unique individual, blending the best features of each personality. In *The Wizard of Lovecraft's Cafe,* the group are attacked at the instigation of one of the Dark Ones working through the Bureau of Thaumaturgy (the equivalent of the FBI) and Modred's spirit is transferred to the cop John Angelo but, weak and traumatized, Angelo/Modred cannot remember who or what he is.

The Nine Lives of Catseye Gomez is an offshoot of the Wizard series. Gomez is a thaumagene, a magically and genetically enhanced cat with the ability to reason and communicate on a human level. He was introduced in *The Wizard of Santa Fe* as a feline friend of the adept Paul Ramirez. When Paul dies, Gomez is invited to Denver by one of Paul's old friends, commissioner of police, Jay Solo. The cat is an aficionado of 20th-century crime fiction, the novels of Spillane, Chandler and Hammett, so is quite happy to help in the investigation of the murder of a radio personality outside Solo's block. Basically it is an old-fashioned crime novel set in a magically enhanced future.

All these novels stand alone, partly because large chunks at the start are devoted to recapping all that has happened in the previous books. It is difficult to know if these are intended as comedy—there are decided humorous elements, such as the besom that, as in Disney's *Fantasia,* has been magically animated. This broom, however, has the personality of a caricature of a Jewish mother. There are elements of farce in the events portrayed but the humour is not sustained, partly because it is also a good-versus-evil scenario and partly because of the sometimes plodding writing style. When action is taking place and the plot is moving forward the pace is smooth and fast and a lot of the content is imaginative.

The series that begins with *The Reluctant Sorcerer* also has science fiction elements. Marvin Brewster invents a time machine. When it fails to return he builds another but this time goes with it. Instead of travelling in time in our world, he arrives in a fantasy world, his machine destroying itself on landing. Stranded in a world where magic works, he is mistaken for a powerful sorcerer. Being well-read, he relies on the premise that "any science sufficiently advanced will appear to be magic," and amazes his new friends with such things as soap. Meanwhile he knows that the only way home is to locate the rogue time machine. This has fallen into to hands of the evil sorcerer, Warrick the White, who finds it useful for making people disappear.

As in the Wizard series, the books stand alone because of the exposition provided in each one, but this series is definitely intended as humorous although most of the effects come across as silly rather than comic and the good jokes are drawn out so long that they become irritating. There are good ideas, even humorous ones, as when Warrick, by means of a magic spell, is able to converse with the narrator and interrupt the flow of the story to the point of getting information not otherwise accessible to him, or a dragon is plagued with copulating fairies in the same way that a horse would be bothered by blowflies. The second volume, *The Inadequate Adept,* does not further the narrative overmuch, playing on farcical situations for its effect. It has too many narrative strands, including some in the contemporary world. Brewster's fiancee tries to locate him, and a disreputable reporter looking for a good story pursues the victims that Warrick has sent through the time machine (if it can really be regarded as such) to our world with a compulsion on them to return to him in Pittsburgh (not Pittsburgh, USA, but the capital of the kingdom of Pitt). It only leads to confusion and distraction.

Hawke has a mind full of original ideas, but he is such a prolific writer that he rarely develops them to the depths that they deserve.

—Pauline Morgan

HAZEL, (E.) Paul

Nationality: American. **Born:** 1 July, 1944 in Bridgeport, Connecticut. **Education:** Yale University, B.A., 1966, M.A.T., 1967. **Family:** Married Karen Murov, 18 June, 1966; one daughter, one son. **Career:** English teacher, New Haven, Connecticut, 1967-72, Ridgefield, Connecticut, 1972-73; director of personnel for Ridgefield public schools, 1973—; writer. **Address:** 14 Lewis Dr., Ridgefield, Connecticut 06877, USA.

Fantasy Publications

Novels (series: Finnbranch)

Yearwood (Finnbranch). Boston, Atlantic Monthly Press, 1980.
Undersea (Finnbranch). Boston, Atlantic Monthly Press, 1982.
Winterking (Finnbranch). Boston, Atlantic Monthly Press, 1985.
The Finnbranch (omnibus; includes *Yearwood, Undersea, Winterking*). London, Sphere, 1986.
The Wealdwife's Tale. New York, AvonNova, 1993.

*   *   *

One of the greatest failings of much modern fantasy writing has been its homogeneity. With a few exceptions, most new titles are variations of old themes, imitations of previously successful novels, often painfully lacking in any single feature that would distinguish one from another. The witty inventiveness of a James Branch Cabell, the rich metaphor of C. S. Lewis, the complex societies of E. R. Eddison, the wry, and the original humour of Ernest Bramah are largely ignored in favour of countless reiterations of Tolkien and Howard, or elaborations of Norse or Mediterranean myth.

While many of these works are entertaining, few are likely to make a significant enough impression to obtain any permanent importance in the development of fantasy fiction.

One exception to this general rule is Paul Hazel, whose infrequent but highly regarded novels blend authentic legend with a creative imagination, expressed in a sophisticated style and through the use of subtle devices of plot and character rather than belabouring the reader with tedious accounts of trivial matters. Hazel is not concerned with a blow-by-blow description of a battle, the length of a monster's fangs, or endless sequences of capture and escape. His books deal with the psychology of the characters, and with the magical realm in which they live.

The Finnbranch trilogy, published over a five-year period, recounts the life of Finn, bastard son of a witch and a king.

Finn's passage to manhood is the subject of *Yearwood,* and it's a convoluted passage. After discovering his father's identity, Finn decides to claim the throne, but he is diverted for a time to the world of the dead. Upon his return, he is tricked into sleeping with his sister and later killing his own father, maneuvered in part by his mother's desire to shape the nature of her grandchildren. Finn's adventures are filled with wonder and often macabre experiences, but he never abandons his ambition to rule his father's domain.

The story continues in *Undersea.* Finn recovers from his wounds among his mother's people and hears a prophecy of his own death, or rather his deaths. From there he returns by a roundabout route to the undersea kingdom of the selkies, the sealmen. There his right to lead is challenged, but Finn's adventures have transformed him into a mature man capable of dealing with his enemies, both through words and deeds. We are also introduced to Llugh, Finn's son by his sister, known as the Shining One. Hazel shows us all this through Finn's narration, and the world is shaped by the character's perceptions, a magical, not quite in focus realm of magic, intrigue, and predestination.

The concluding volume, *Winterking,* is unexpectedly set in modern times, though in a world close to but not entirely congruent with our own. The new world has been settled by Europeans, for example, but it is most certainly not America as we know it. There's a nobility and the place names are different, although otherwise it bears a strong resemblance to our reality.

Wykeham is a college student who drops out of school to confront a squatter on the family estate, but he is also Wyck, a character from the previous book, who is ageless and lives in a world that is part reality, part imagination. Wyck's encounters frequently take place on two levels, the ostensible real world as fashioned in the novel, and an underlying one in which immortals still engage in enigmatic dealings with one another.

The local Duke has taken an unusual interest in Wykeham, and questions his teacher, revealing that there is something subtly wrong with their reality, that the place names make no sense, that perhaps the universe isn't quite what it seems to be. The possibility that everything is an illusion, that the world exists only as an act of Wyck's imagination, gives the entire story a dreamlike atmosphere that is at once disturbing and intriguing.

Hazel's most recent novel is *The Wealdwife's Tale,* not directly related to the Finnbranch trilogy but sharing much of the same approach toward the world of myth. The Duke of West Redding has been grieving ever since the death of his wife, neglecting his children and his duties, and devoting most of his time to the creation of a flying machine with which he hopes to penetrate the magical woods nearby and bring back the soul of his wife, which he believes now dwells there.

In due course and after inevitable mishaps, he does in fact find the image of his Elva, but it's not at all clear that she's the same woman, and in fact several other characters he encounters have names that are anagrams of hers. And when he brings his "wife" back to his home, he has actually brought a curse down upon his family. It's a grim version of an old fairy tale, infused with a sense of mystery and dread, and with unusually compelling characters that help make the created world seem almost as real as our own.

Hazel's short stories are even rarer than his novels, but one that deserves recognition here is "Cerridwen and the Quern of Time." Cerridwen, who also appears briefly in *Undersea,* has a brief encounter with a god and is forever changed. As with the novels, it is infused with magic and wonder.

Although Hazel's work does not have the broad general appeal that has made lesser writers into bestsellers, his work has attracted a loyal readership and considerable serious critical attention. It is likely that when all of the imitation hobbits and neo-Arthurian look-a-likes have been relegated to the status of collectors' items, Hazel's work will still be read and appreciated by ensuing generations of readers.

—Don D'Ammassa

HECHT, Ben

Nationality: American. **Born:** New York City, 28 February 1893. **Education:** Racine High School, Wisconsin; a violin prodigy, he gave a concert at the age of 10. **Family:** Married: 1) Marie Armstrong in 1915 (divorced 1925), one daughter; 2) Rose Caylor in 1925, one daughter. **Career:** Journalist from the age of 16, Chicago *Journal,* 1914-18; Chicago *News,* 1918-23; contributor, *Little Review, Smart Set* and other periodicals; founder editor, Chicago *Literary Times,* 1923-25; thereafter, freelance playwright, journalist, novelist, short-story writer and Hollywood's highest-paid and most prolific screenwriter (also occasional film producer and director). Active in the cause of Israel, 1940s. **Awards:** Academy Award, 1928, 1935; Writers Guild Laurel Award, 1980. **Died:** 18 April 1964.

FANTASY PUBLICATIONS

Novels

Fantazius Mallare: A Mysterious Oath. Chicago, Covici McGee, 1922.
The Kingdom of Evil: A Continuation of the Journal of Fantazius Mallare. Chicago, Covici, 1924.
Miracle in the Rain. New York, Knopf, 1943.

Short Stories

A Book of Miracles. New York, Viking Press, 1939; London, Nicolson and Watson, 1940.
The Collected Short Stories of Ben Hecht. New York, Crown, 1945; London, Hammond, 1950.

OTHER PUBLICATIONS

Novels

Erik Dorn. New York, Putnam, 1921.
Gargoyles. New York, Boni and Liveright, 1922.
The Florentine Dagger: A Novel for Amateur Detectives. New York, Boni and Liveright, 1923; London, Heinemann, 1924.
Humpty Dumpty. New York, Boni and Liveright, 1924.
Count Bruga. New York, Boni and Liveright, 1926.
A Jew in Love. New York, Covici Friede, 1931.
I Hate Actors! New York, Crown, 1944; as *Hollywood Mystery!,* 1946.
The Cat That Jumped Out of the Story (for children). Philadelphia, Pennsylvania, 1947.
The Sensualists. New York, Messner, 1959; London, Blond, 1960.

Short Stories

Broken Necks and Other Stories. Girard, Kansas, Haldeman Julius, 1924; revised edition, as *Broken Necks,* Chicago, Covici, 1926.
Tales of Chicago Streets. Girard, Kansas, Haldeman Julius, 1924.
Infatuation and Other Stories of Love's Misfits. Girard, Kansas, Haldeman Julius, 1927.
Jazz and Other Stories of Young Love. Girard, Kansas, Haldeman Julius, 1927.
The Policewoman's Love-Hungry Daughter and Other Stories of Chicago Life. Girard, Kansas, Haldeman Julius, 1927.
The Sinister Sex and Other Stories. Girard, Kansas, Haldeman Julius, 1927.
The Unlovely Sin and Other Stories. Girard, Kansas, Haldeman Julius, 1927.
The Champion from Far Away. New York, Covici Friede, 1931.
Actor's Blood. New York, Covici Friede, 1936.
Concerning a Woman of Sin and Other Stories. New York, 1947.

Plays

The Master Poisoner, with Maxwell Bodenheim. New York, 1918.
The Wonder Hat, with Kenneth S. Goodmam. New York, Shay, 1920.
The Hero of Santa Maria, with Kenneth S. Goodmam. New York, Shay, 1920.
The Hand of Siva, with Kenneth S. Goodmam. New York, 1920.
The Egotist. 1923.
The Wonder Hat and Other One-Act Plays, with Kenneth S. Goodmam. New York and London, Appleton, 1925.
Christmas Eve. New York, Covici Friede, 1928.
The Front Page, with Charles MacArthur. New York, Covici Friede, 1928; London, Richards and Toulmin, 1929.
The Great Magoo, with Gene Fowler. New York, Covici Friede, 1931.
Twentieth Century, with Charles MacArthur. New York, 1932.
Jumbo, with Charles MacArthur. New York, 1935.
To Quito and Back. New York, Covici Friede, 1937.
Fun To Be Free: Patriotic Pageant, with Charles MacArthur. New York, Dramatists Play Service, 1941.
Ladies and Gentlemen, with Charles MacArthur. New York, Los Angeles and London, French, 1941.
We Will Never Die. New York, 1943.
A Flag is Born. New York, American League for a Free Palestine, 1946.

Hazel Flagg. New York, 1953.
Winkelberg. New York, 1958.

Screenplays (selection): *Underworld,* 1927; *Scarface,* 1932; *Hallelujah, I'm a Bum,* 1932; *Design for Living,* 1932; *Twentieth Century,* 1934; *The Scoundrel,* 1935; *Barbary Coast,* 1935; *Nothing Sacred,* 1938; *It's a Wonderful World,* 1939; *Gunga Din,* 1939; *Wuthering Heights,* 1939; *Angels Over Broadway,* 1940; *Comrade X,* 1940; *China Girl,* 1942; *Spellbound,* 1945; *Notorious,* 1946; *The Specter of the Rose,* 1946; *Kiss of Death,* 1947; *The Miracle of the Bells,* 1948; *Where the Sidewalk Ends,* 1950; *Monkey Business,* 1952; *Ulysses,* 1955; *Miracle in the Rain,* 1956; *A Farewell to Arms,* 1957; *Hello Charlie,* 1959.

Other

1001 Afternoons in Chicago. Chicago, Covici McGee, 1922.
Cutie: A Warm Mama, with Maxwell Bodenheim. Chicago, Hechtshaw, 1924.
1001 Afternoons in New York. New York, Viking, 1941.
A Guide for the Bedevilled. New York, Scribner, 1944.
A Child of the Century (autobiography). New York, Simon and Schuster, 1954.
Charlie: The Improbable Life and Times of Charles MacArthur. New York, Harper, 1957.
Perfidy. New York, Messner, 1961.
Gaily, Gaily (autobiography). New York, Doubleday, 1963; London, Elek, 1964.
Letters from Bohemia. New York, Doubleday, 1964.

*

Film Adaptations: *The Front Page,* 1930, 1940 (as *His Girl Friday*), 1974, 1988 (as *Switching Channels*); *Twentieth Century,* 1934; *Miracle in the Rain,* 1956; *Gaily, Gaily,* 1969; *Je hais les acteurs,* 1986.

Critical Studies: *The Five Lives of Ben Hecht* by Doug Fetherling, Toronto, 1977; *Ben Hecht, Hollywood Screenwriter* by Jeffrey Brown Martin, Ann Arbor, Michigan, 1985.

*   *   *

Ben Hecht's career as a writer was as diverse as it is possible to be in a world of specialist journeymen. He first made his name as a cavalier reporter for the Chicago daily *News,* and drew upon that experience in writing his early novels and plays—most famously in the oft-filmed play *The Front Page,* which he wrote with his most frequent collaborator Charles MacArthur. He went on to enjoy a productive career as a screenwriter in Hollywood, where he presumably laboured under a pressure to conform to established norms which was even greater than that he had experienced as a reporter. He was always a fervent radical in every respect, however, and his resistance against the pressure to meet and satisfy the expectations of his various audiences frequently boiled over, occasioning the production of a series of scaldingly sarcastic fictions, whose best and most extreme examples are vivid fantasies.

By far the most striking of these reactive fantasies is the self-consciously Decadent, Huysmans-inspired *Fantazius Mallare,* which offers an account of the eponymous artist's descent into madness. Mallare's hope that he has transcended the desires of the flesh is challenged by the tempting presence of a girl named Rita, bought from gypsies upon a whim; after suffering a hallucination while strangling a beggar he is convinced that he has murdered her, and regards her continued presence as a haunting. Scorned by his rejection of her advances, Rita exacts a cunning revenge by offering herself to the hunchbacked black dwarf who is his servant—sight of which consummation breaks the dam holding Mallare's emotions in check and shatters his intellectual composure. As if the story were not shocking enough in itself, Hecht prefaced it with a long sentence "affectionately" dedicating the "dark and wayward book" to his enemies, whose various categories he elaborates at extraordinary length. The marvellously evocative illustrations by Wallace Smith were considered sufficiently obscene to get the book banned.

The sequel to *Fantazius Mallare, The Kingdom of Evil*—the only one of Hecht's fantasies which is almost long enough to qualify as a proper novel—is a phantasmagoria populated by the disparate fragments of Mallare's shattered personality, who are busy preparing a temple in anticipation of the advent of a god, Synthemus. Synthemus does indeed arrive to take possession of his shrine, but he is no redeemer intent on repair and salvation; in this world sanity has no power to resist the all-powerful forces of Chaos. Unfortunately, the illustrations for the sequel, executed by Anthony Angarola, are not in the same league as Wallace Smith's. Hecht's interest in split personalities is further reflected in his baroque mystery story *The Florentine Dagger,* which was allegedly written on a bet to prove that he could write an entire novel in 24 hours; this too had striking illustrations by Wallace Smith in its first edition.

The stories in *A Book of Miracles*—most but not quite all of which were reprinted in *The Collected Short Stories of Ben Hecht*—include several skittish comedies, including "The Heavenly Choir," in which the spirits of the dead break in on radio broadcasts to ludicrous effect, and the novella "The Adventures of Professor Emmett," in which the eponymous neurotic scientist is transformed into a stone-eating termite with a mission to warn the president of the menace to mankind posed by his nascent species. Far more powerful, however, are two earnest moralistic novellas based in religious folklore. "Death of Eleazer" is about the supernaturally-diverted trial of an American Nazi, who may or may not be a demon in disguise, for the murder of a saintly rabbi (Hecht became an outspoken Zionist in the 1940s). The excellent but slightly over-sentimentalized "Remember Thy Creator" echoes Anatole France's classic *The Revolt of the Angels* in explaining how the Archangel Michael, sent to earth to bring men closer to God, realizes that they have little to gain from such closeness and becomes a dignified renegade.

All Hecht's short stories are written in a deliberately mannered style, which was calculated to provide him with some relief from the terse tone required of his reportage (*The Collected Short Stories* includes an oddly defensive justificatory preface which confirms that this was the case). They contrast strongly with the sickly sentimental *Miracle in the Rain,* which probably began life as a treatment for the film which it eventually became; it has affinities with the elegiac romantic fantasies of Robert Nathan, but lacks their elegance—and, one suspects, their sincerity. Hecht's other work for the movies included scripts for several tales of psychological delusion—including the famous Alfred Hitchcock film *Spellbound,* whose dream-sequence was designed by Salvador Dali, and his self-directed tale of an insane ballet dancer, *The Specter of the Rose*—but rarely ventured into outright fantasy; one minor exception was a supernaturally-framed melodrama of redemption written in collaboration with Noel Coward, *The Scoundrel.*

Fantasy was never more than a self-indulgent sideline for Hecht, and he has never been reckoned an important contributor to the genre, but his best work displays a powerful and idiosyncratic imagination which was occasionally moved by deeply-felt emotions to brilliant effect. *Fantazius Mallare* remains the one truly outstanding product of the otherwise rather etiolated American Decadent Movement.

—Brian Stableford

HELPRIN, Mark

Nationality: American. **Born:** New York, 28 June 1947. **Education:** Harvard College, A.B. 1969, A.M. 1972; Magdalen College, Oxford, postgraduate study, 1976-77. **Military Service:** Israeli Infantry and Air Corps, border guard, 1972-73. **Family:** Married Lisa Kennedy in 1980; two daughters. **Career:** Briefly merchant seaman; instructor at Harvard University; contributor, *New Yorker* and other magazines. **Awards:** PEN/Faulkner award, National Jewish Book award, American Academy and Institute of Arts and Letters award, Prix de Rome, all 1982.

FANTASY PUBLICATIONS

Novels

Refiner's Fire: The Life and Adventures of Marshall Pearl, a Foundling. New York, Knopf, 1977.
Winter's Tale. New York, Harcourt, and London, Weidenfeld and Nicolson, 1983.
Swan Lake (for children). Boston, Houghton, 1989.

Short Stories

A Dove of the East and Other Stories. New York, Knopf, 1975.
Ellis Island and Other Stories. New York, Seymour Lawrence/Delacorte, 1981.

OTHER PUBLICATIONS

Novel

A Soldier of the Great War. 1991.

Other

Editor, with Shannon Ravenel, *The Best American Short Stories.* Boston, Houghton, 1988.

*   *   *

The first story in Mark Helprin's first book, *A Dove of the East and Other Stories,* is indisputably a fantasy. "A Jew of Persia" is the tale of an immigrant from Iran, now living in Tel Aviv, who has been pursued for most of his life by a minor yet formidable devil in human form who is bent on revenging the protagonist's effron-

tery in resisting him once in the mountains of his old home. In miniature, this early story contains nearly all the elements that will come to distinguish Helprin's work: an unfaltering, unconcealed strong narrator's voice at once mythic yet prosaic, old-fashioned yet postmodern; the struggle between good and evil, duty and abdication; the grim necessities imposed on every individual by the simple act of existence; the centrality of family; heritage (most often Jewish; Helprin's mother was descended from Jews once resident in China) as the governor of identity. All modulated by a sense that surface existence is both merely a scrim over a deeper reality, and simultaneously all we can ever really know and cherish.

Yet perhaps because Helprin is so adept at depicting the quotidian—his visual descriptions, rich in metaphor, of mountains, cities, countryside, people are instantly evocative and crisply cinematic, his appreciation for the miracle of daily life and its appurtenances so keen—the underlying strata of the fantastic which crops up everywhere in his work has been generally ignored.

Readers searching only for further overt fantasy would be generally disappointed by the rest of the stories in *Dove,* none of which feature supernaturalism. Many are slight mood pieces, some as short as three pages, worthy apprentice efforts. Quite a few, such as "Lightning North of Paris," evoke the pitiless ambience of Hemingway in his prime, an obvious model (within limits) for Helprin, as is Melville. But the cumulative effect of the volume is one that establishes Helprin's view of life as a fairy tale. Entries such as "Elizabeth Ridinoure" and "Katherine Comes to Yellow Sky" succeed in transforming such simple yet pivotal events as falling in love and relocating to a strange place into archetypical moments full of grace and promise, wherein every woman is a princess and every man a knight.

Helprin's first novel, *Refiner's Fire,* is best capsulized by its unabashedly romantic subtitle: "The life and adventures of Marshall Pearl, a foundling." From the semi-autobiographical protagonist's stormy birth (he shares Helprin's actual birthday and some of his *curriculum vitae*) in the midst of a naval battle (his given name is a pun on "martial"), through adolescent run-ins with Jamaican terrorists, to his climactic blooding in the Yom Kippur War, Helprin leads the reader on an odyssey of maturation and self-discovery, as Pearl continually pushes himself to his limits and beyond (as do most of Helprin's sympathetic characters). Early in the book, Helprin signals his intention to mix realism with fantasy: "He could not restrain himself from consideration of that which was feasible mainly in the magical world, and, strangely enough, sometime in this one." From Pearl's arcane home-town—6,000 inhabitants obsessively sustain 30 fire-fighting regiments; a history professor makes an annual biplane flight to squelch Communism—to a surreal abattoir where time stops, to the mysteries hidden in New York's sewers, Helprin makes seamless transitions between achingly beautiful mimetic passages and wild-eyed flights of fancy, placing him firmly in the magical-realist camp.

Another tradition which can easily encompass Helprin is that of the quintessentially American Tall Tale. Vast improbabilities told with a straight face (Helprin once seriously confided to a reporter that he had been raised by a dog) amuse Helprin, whose sense of humour can best be described as mordant and droll, and he strews them liberally throughout his books. *Ellis Island and Other Stories* contains four stories of particular note. "The Schreuderspitze" is notable both for its mountain setting (Helprin is a retired climber), which will recur often, and for its notion of redemption through sacrifice and flights of the spirit. "Letters from the *Samantha*" is an enigmatic parable about a mysterious ape found adrift, very reminiscent of William Hope Hodgson's sea stories. Finally, both

"A Vermont Tale," with its portrayal of a mythic winter, and "Ellis Island," the farcical misadventures of an immigrant in turn-of-the-century New York, point directly to Helprin's next book, the monumental *Winter's Tale*.

Helprin is a maximalist writer, and *Winter's Tale* is richly stuffed with indelible incidents and impulsively melodramatic characters. His work manages to be both formally and aesthetically challenging, while remaining the cliched "good read." Set mainly in a city whose contours and history both overlap and diverge radically from the mundane New York we are all familiar with, *Winter's Tale* is split into two portions, the first and shorter detailing the Gilded Era exploits of one Peter Lake (like Marshall Pearl, a foundling), master thief and mechanic, lucky "owner" of the magical white horse Athansor, as he manoeuvres through a landscape dotted with magical Adirondack towns, insane and orgulous bandits, opulent oyster- and whorehouses, Utopian newspapers and semi-savage Baymen, among a thousand other lavishly and lovingly described impossibilities. The second portion concerns itself with the descendants of many of the early characters, along with several new ones and not a few revenants (including Lake himself, who gradually assumes the role of Fisher King), as they strive to avert or hasten the arrival of "the truly just city" which New York has the potential to become as our century cataclysmically slides into the next.

Unswervingly propulsive, sustainedly symbolic, gaudily illustrative of love, death and renewal, *Winter's Tale* must rank as one of the finest fantasy novels of the modern era, and the linchpin of Helprin's career to date. One character's passing observation could easily stand as the book's motto: "Magic . . . was all about time, and could stop it and hold it for the inquisitive eye to look through as if through cold and splendid ice."

Swan Lake, beautifully illustrated by award-winning children's book artist Chris Van Allsburg, is a novelette concerned once again with Helprin's core themes of duty and devotion as exemplified by the tale of treachery and misapprehension in a Ruritanian setting. It suffers a bit from being narrated one remove from the long-past action, and its climactic revelation of identity is easily guessed in advance. *A Soldier of the Great War* details the incredible sufferings and eventual transcendence of one Alessandro Giuliani, light-intoxicated peacetime student of aesthetics, later soldier, deserter, Alpinist, prisoner, and escapee during World War I. Helprin eschews fantasy almost totally in this nonetheless Homeric and affecting work, save for one central conceit: the entire Italian military effort is secretly under the control of a mad dwarf named Orfeo, head scribe at the Ministry of War, who is wont to rave of "the blessed sap" that flows through the universe, and to perform such arbitrary miracles as shipping the army's entire supply of cinnamon—several thousand tons—to one unlucky camp.

Jackson Mead, the Lucifer of *Winter's Tale*, undoubtedly speaking for Helprin, summarizes Helprin's work: "Everything in the world . . . comes down to love or a fight, which, when they are hot enough to be flame, rise and combine . . . [pushing] a human soul to the highest state of grace . . ."

—Paul Di Filippo

HILTON, James

Pseudonym: Glen Trevor. **Nationality:** British. **Born:** Leigh, Lancashire, 9 September 1900. **Education:** The Leys, Cambridge, 1915-18; Christ's College, Cambridge, BA in history and English, 1921. **Family:** Married 1) Alice Brown (divorced 1937); 2) Galina Kopineck (divorced 1945). **Career:** Part-time college instructor and journalist; freelance novelist, screenwriter and radio writer from 1933. **Awards:** Hawthornden prize for fiction, 1933; Academy award for screenwriting, 1943. **Member:** Governing board, Academy of Motion Picture Arts and Sciences; vice-president, Screen Writers Guild. Became an American citizen, 1948. **Died:** 20 December 1954.

Fantasy Publications

Novel

Lost Horizon. London: Macmillan, and New York, Morrow, 1933.

Other Publications

Novels

Catherine Herself. London, Unwin, 1920.
Storm Passage. London, Unwin, 1922.
The Passionate Year. London, Butterworth, 1923; Boston, Little Brown, 1924.
The Dawn of Reckoning. London, Butterworth, 1925.
The Meadows of the Moon. London, Butterworth, 1926; Boston, Small Maynard, 1927.
Terry. London, Butterworth, 1927.
The Silver Flame. London, Butterworth, 1928.
And Now Goodbye. London, Benn, 1931; New York, Morrow, 1932.
Murder at School, as Glen Trevor. London, Benn, 1931; as *Was It Murder?* by James Hilton, New York, Harper, 1933.
Contango. London, Benn, 1932; as *Ill Wind,* New York, Morrow, 1932.
Rage in Heaven. New York, King, 1932.
Knight Without Armour. London, Macmillan, 1933; as *Without Armour,* New York, Morrow, 1934.
Goodbye, Mr. Chips. London, Macmillan, and Boston, Little Brown, 1934.
We Are Not Alone. London, Macmillan, and Boston, Little Brown, 1937.
Random Harvest. London, Macmillan, and Boston, Little Brown, 1941.
The Story of Dr. Wassell. Boston, Little Brown, 1943; London, Macmillan, 1944.
So Well Remembered. Boston, Little Brown, 1945; London, Macmillan, 1947.
Nothing So Strange. Boston, Little Brown, 1947; London, Macmillan, 1948.
Morning Journey. London, Macmillan, and Boston, Little Brown, 1951.
Time and Time Again. London, Macmillan, and Boston, Little Brown, 1953.

Short Stories

To You, Mr. Chips. London, Hodder and Stoughton, 1938.

Play

To You, Mr. Chips: A Play, with Barbara Burnham. London, Hodder and Stoughton, 1938.

Screenplays: Camille, with Zoe Akins and Frances Marion, 1936; We Are Not Alone, with Milton Krims, 1939; Foreign Correspondent, with Charles Bennett, Joan Harrison and Robert Benchley, 1940; The Tuttles of Tahiti, with S. Lewis Meltzer and Robert Carson, 1942; Mrs. Miniver, with Arthur Wimperis, George Froeschel and Claudine West, 1942; Forever and a Day, with others, 1944; The Story of Dr. Wassell, with Alan le May and Charles Bennett, 1944.

Other

Twilight of the Wise. London, St. Hugh's Press, 1949.
H.R.H.: The Story of Philip, Duke of Edinburgh. London, Muller, and Boston, Little Brown, 1956.

*

Film Adaptations: Knight Without Armour, 1937; Lost Horizon, 1937, 1973; Goodbye, Mr. Chips, 1939, 1969; We Are Not Alone, 1939; Rage in Heaven, 1941; Random Harvest, 1942; The Story of Dr. Wassell, 1944; So Well Remembered, 1947.

*　　*　　*

James Hilton's Lost Horizon is one of those rare books which have added a new concept to the English language. The name of Shangri-La, the Tibetan lamasery situated above a preternaturally fertile mountain-rimmed valley, whose inhabitants enjoy a long-extended youth, has come to be used with reference to any remote and idyllic retreat from the hostile and confusing world; it has become a modern equivalent of such ancient imaginary lands as Tir-na-noc or the Isles of the Blest.

Lost Horizon was a remarkably timely work, in that it offered a delicious escapist glimpse of a haven in which the ominous troubles of the Great Depression and the rise of Fascism in Europe were utterly irrelevant, but it also tapped a deeper and more enduring vein of feeling which connected it to some of our oldest and most cherished myths. It became the basis of one of the most celebrated Hollywood films of the 1930s, directed by Frank Capra and starring Ronald Colman.

The focal point of the novel is the dilemma which faces its hero, Hugh Conway, when he must decide whether to remain in the magical haven of Shangri-La as the High Lama's spiritual heir or return to the hurly-burly of a world which seems to be lurching towards its end. Conway has built a reputation for courage by virtue of his exploits in the consular service, but his imperturbability under pressure is actually a kind of spiritual anaesthesia, which has possessed him ever since the Great War. The world has come to seem meaningless and Conway perceives himself as one who stands apart from the main stream of human history, incapable of any true moral commitment. When the critical point in the plot arrives, Conway does not dare to believe in the reality of Shangri-La, but he discovers the requisite courage once he finds himself back in the dark and troubled outer world, and belatedly commits himself to the recovery of the mistakenly-forsaken ideal.

There can be little doubt that Lost Horizon was a deeply personal book—as intimately personal, in its own way, as Hilton's other best-seller, Goodbye, Mr. Chips. That curious nostalgia which informs so many Englishmen that their schooldays were the happiest days of their lives, which saturates Goodbye, Mr. Chips, is by no means absent from Lost Horizon; when Conway is asked whether there is anything in the outer world remotely like Shangri-La he confesses that it reminds him, just a little, of Oxford. In spite of their considerable differences at the surface level, Hilton's two most famous books have the same story buried within them, defining the forceful pattern of their emotional charge: the story of a heart-sick man who miraculously finds his heart's desire in a most unexpected place while far from home, and then proceeds to lose it again. The schoolmaster who loses his wife to unkind death has no means of literal recovery—even one as potentially hard-won as Conway's—but he does have the legacy of a personal transformation, which carries him forward regardless and grants him a kind of salvation.

We do not know enough about James Hilton's personal history to account for the more intimate meanings which these themes had for him, but the spiritual state attributed to Hugh Conway was closely akin to that of many people who had lived through the Great War. Whether they had actually fought in the trenches, or served in some non-combatant capacity on the battlefields of northern France, or simply suffered the tribulations and deprivations of life in wartime England, many Britons felt that a vision of the future had been vouchsafed to them during the Big Pushes and the Zeppelin raids: a vision of civilization teetering on the brink of annihilation by fleets of bombers which would one day rain high explosives, incendiary bombs and poison gas upon towns and cities, factories and homes. It was easy enough for those readers who were sensitive enough to have understood what a foul and wretched war the Great War had been to believe wholeheartedly in Hugh Conway's spiritual anaesthesia and to sympathize, at least to some degree, with his relief in the temporary abandonment of all moral commitment. It was also easy enough for such people to accept that the call of duty which was poured like poison into Conway's ear by his cowardly aide Mallinson was a treacherous temptation, and fervently to wish that he might hear the voice of true sanity and turn back, forsaking the evil world for the lovely dream. As the Depression tightened its grip on Europe and America alike, it was easy enough to think that the world was doomed, and not so very difficult to feel, in self-consciously perverse fashion, that it thoroughly deserved its doom. To this state of mind, intoxicating news of a safe—albeit illusory—haven where the world-weary might surrender their souls to eternal bliss was very welcome.

Hilton's other work was occasionally rather outré, but consistently refused to dabble in the stuff of dreams. His only other near-fantasy was "The Bat-King" (1936), written not long after his emigration to America to work in the movies. In this story an explorer in the Carlsbad caverns discovers a man who has been lost there for many years; the unlucky individual, whose sense of sight has atrophied, claims that he has been kept alive by bats which have fed him and appointed him their king. Once brought back to the light he makes a half-hearted stab at picking up the threads of his former life but finds that his wife, believing him dead, has remarried—leaving him no recourse but to do the decent thing and tender his resignation from existence. The story may be regarded as a bitter and ruthlessly disillusioned counterpart to Lost Horizon.

Leslie Halliwell's reverent but somewhat lacklustre novel Return to Shangri-La (1987) is, of course, a sequel to Capra's film rather than Hilton's book.

—Brian Stableford

HOBAN, Russell (Conwell)

Nationality: American. **Born:** Lansdale, Pennsylvania, 4 February 1925. **Education:** Lansdale High School; Philadelphia Museum School of Industrial Art, 1941-43. **Military Service:** United States Army Infantry, 1943-45: Bronze Star. **Family:** Married 1) Lillian Aberman (i.e., the illustrator Lillian Hoban) in 1944 (divorced 1975), one son and three daughters; 2) Gundula Ahl in 1975, three sons. **Career:** Magazine and advertising agency artist and illustrator; story board artist, Fletcher Smith Film Studio, New York, 1951; television art director, Batten Barton Durstine and Osborn, 1951-56, and J. Walter Thompson, 1956, both in New York; advertising copywriter, Doyle Dane Bernbach, New York, 1965-67. Since 1967, full-time writer; since 1969 has lived in London. **Awards:** Christopher award, for children's book, 1972; Whitbread award, for children's book, 1974; George G. Stone Center for Children's Books award, 1982; Ditmar award (Australia), 1982; John W. Campbell Memorial award, 1982. **Agent:** David Higham Associates Ltd., 5-8 Lower John Street, London W1R 4HA, England.

FANTASY PUBLICATIONS

Novels

The Mouse and His Child. New York, Harper, 1967; London, Faber, 1969.
The Lion of Boaz-Jachin and Jachin-Boaz. New York, Stein and Day, and London, Cape, 1973.
Kleinzeit. London, Cape, and New York, Viking Press, 1974.
Pilgermann. London, Cape, and New York, Summit, 1983.
The Medusa Frequency. London, Cape, and New York, Atlantic Monthly Press, 1987.

Short Stories

The Moment Under the Moment (includes essays). London: Cape, 1992.

OTHER PUBLICATIONS

Novels

Turtle Diary. London, Cape, 1975; New York, Random House, 1976.
Riddley Walker. London, Cape, and New York, Summit, 1980.

Fiction for Children

Bedtime for Frances. New York, Harper, 1960; London, Faber, 1963.
Herman the Loser. New York, Harper, 1961; Kingswood, Surrey, World's Work, 1972.
The Song in My Drum. New York, Harper, 1962.
London Men and English Men. New York, Harper, 1962.
Some Snow Said Hello. New York, Harper, 1963.
The Sorely Trying Day. New York, Harper, 1964; Kingswood, Surrey, World's Work, 1965.
A Baby Sister for Frances. New York, Harper, 1964; London, Faber, 1965.

Bread and Jam for Frances. New York, Harper, 1964; London, Faber, 1966.
Nothing to Do. New York, Harper, 1964.
Tom and the Two Handles. New York, Harper, 1965; Kingswood, Surrey, World's Work, 1969.
The Story of Hester Mouse Who Became a Writer. New York, Norton, 1965; Kingswood, Surrey, World's Work, 1969.
What Happened When Jack and Daisy Tried to Fool the Tooth Fairies. New York, Four Winds Press, 1965.
Henry and the Monstrous Din. New York, Harper, 1966; Kingswood, Surrey, World's Work, 1967.
The Little Brute Family. New York, Macmillan, 1966.
Save My Place. New York, Norton, 1967.
Charlie the Tramp. New York, Four Winds Press, 1967.
A Birthday for Frances. New York, Harper, 1968; London, Faber, 1970.
The Stone Doll of Sister Brute. New York, Macmillan, and London, Collier Macmillan, 1968.
Harvey's Hideout. New York, Parents' Magazine Press, 1969; London, Cape, 1973.
Best Friends for Frances. New York, Harper, 1969; London, Faber, 1971.
The Mole Family's Christmas. New York, Parents' Magazine Press, 1969; London, Cape, 1973.
Ugly Bird. New York, Macmillan, 1969.
A Bargain for Frances. New York, Harper, 1970; Kingswood, Surrey, World's Work, 1971.
Emmet Otter's Jug-Band Christmas. New York, Parents' Magazine Press, and Kingswood, Surrey, World's Work, 1971.
The Sea-Thing Child. New York, Harper, and London, Gollancz, 1972.
Letitia Rabbit's String Song. New York, Coward McCann, 1973.
How Tom Beat Captain Najork and His Hired Sportsmen. New York, Atheneum, and London, Cape, 1974.
Ten What? A Mystery Counting Book. London, Cape, 1974; New York, Scribner, 1975.
Dinner at Alberta's. New York, Crowell, 1975; London, Cape, 1977.
Crocodile and Pierrot, with Sylvie Selig. London, Cape, 1975; New York, Scribner, 1977.
A Near Thing for Captain Najork. London, Cape, 1975; New York, Atheneum, 1976.
Arthur's New Power. New York, Crowell, 1978; London, Gollancz, 1980.
The Twenty-Elephant Restaurant. New York, Atheneum, 1978; London, Cape, 1980.
The Dancing Tigers. London, Cape, 1979.
La Corona and the Tin Frog. London, Cape, 1979.
Flat Cat. London, Methuen, and New York, Philomel, 1980.
Ace Dragon Ltd. London, Cape, 1980.
The Serpent Tower. London, Methuen, 1981.
The Great Fruit Gum Robbery. London, Methuen, 1981; as *The Great Gumdrop Robbery.* New York, Philomel, 1982.
They Came from Aargh! London, Methuen, and New York, Philomel, 1981.
The Battle of Zormla. London, Methuen, and New York, Philomel, 1982.
The Flight of Bembel Rudzuk. London, Methuen, and New York, Philomel, 1982.
Ponders (Jim Frog, Big John Turkle, Charlie Meadows, Lavinia Bat). London, Walker, and New York, Holt Rinehart, 4 vols., 1983-84.

The Rain Door. London, Gollancz, 1986; New York, Crowell, 1987.
The Marzipan Pig. London, Cape, 1986; New York, Farrar Straus, 1987.
Monsters. New York, Scholastic, and London, Gollancz, 1989.
Jim Hedgehog's Supernatural Christmas. London, Hamilton, 1989; New York, Clarion Books, 1992.
Jim Hedgehog and the Lonesome Tower. London, Hamilton, 1990; New York, Clarion Books, 1992.

Plays

The Carrier Frequency, with Impact Theatre Co-operative (produced London, 1984).
Riddley Walker, adaptation of his own novel (produced Manchester, 1986).

Television Play: *Come and Find Me,* 1980.

Poetry (for children)

Goodnight. New York, Norton, 1966; Kingswood, Surrey, World's Work, 1969.
The Pedaling Man and Other Poems. New York, Norton, 1968; Kingswood, Surrey, World's Work, 1969.
Egg Thoughts and Other Frances Songs. New York, Harper, 1972; London, Faber, 1973.

Other (for children)

What Does It Do and How Does It Work? Power Shovel, Dump Truck, and Other Heavy Machines. New York, Harper, 1959.
The Atomic Submarine: A Practice Combat Patrol under the Sea. New York, Harper, 1960.

*   *   *

The Mouse and His Child has been acclaimed as a classic of children's literature. However, Hoban did not specifically write it for children and it can be and is read by adults. Indeed, while the story makes sense at a child's level of understanding, many of the book's themes, paradoxes and parodies will go over the head of even the most sophisticated child. The clockwork tin mouse-father and child constitute a single toy seemingly doomed to dance round in circles. When the story opens, they are in a toyshop together with a large doll's house, a toy elephant and a toy seal. The mouse-father and -son, however, are bought by a family and years later, when their clockwork mechanism breaks down, they are discarded. The rest of the story then concerns their quest for the paradise they lost when they were purchased. They also seek the means to become self-winding. Their quest is simultaneously a flight as Manny Rat seeks to use them as slave labour in the chain-gang of tin toys that are employed on the scrapheaps on which the rats feed. In the end, father and child are reunited with the elephant and the seal in the doll's house and an artificial family is reconstituted in the refurbished doll's house. However, despite the cosy ending, the overall stress of this bleak yet comic book has been on such matters as the predatory ruthlessness of society, the pressures of commerce, the phoneyness of much academic discourse and the problems posed by the nature of infinity.

Father-son relations are the heart of *The Mouse and His Child.* They also figure largely in Hoban's first novel to be written overtly for adults, *The Lion of Boaz-Jachin and Jachin-Boaz.* In this novel,

the father and son live in a world which closely parallels our own, but one in which lions are extinct. The father, who has been earning a decent living by making rather strange maps, suddenly abandons his wife and son to go in quest of a nonexistent lion. His deserted and resentful son conjures up a lion from an ancient stone relief which pursues and haunts the father. The picaresque and bizarrely satirical quests of the two men are concluded when the son rescues the father from the leaping lion.

In *Kleinzeit,* an extraordinary linguistic fantasia, Hoban fools around with the possibilities of words and presents his readers with a universe that is not only animated, but also hip and highly articulate. Hoban gives new life to the ephemera of advertisements, graffiti, jargon and cliches. Kleinzeit, the not very heroic hero of this novel, loses his job and finds himself in hospital, suffering from, among other things, trouble with his asymptotes, dissonance in his diapason, a skewed hypotenuse and 12 percent polarity. He has verbally enriched, picaresque encounters with God, the Word, his mirror, a tramp called Redbeard and the Hospital. The mysticism already detectable in *The Mouse and His Child* is here to the fore. "'What does it all mean?' said Kleinzeit. 'How can there be a meaning?' said Hospital. 'Meaning is a limit. There are no limits.'"

Turtle Diary is Hoban's most accessible novel (even more so than *The Mouse and His Child*). It chronicles the attempt of two eccentric and lonely diary-keeping people to release the turtles from the London Zoo and deliver them back to the sea. It is quirky rather than strictly fantastic. *Riddley Walker,* which belongs more to science fiction than to fantasy, is an epistemological fable cast in the form of what is effectively a prose poem. "On my naming day when I come 12 I gone front spear and kilt a wyld boar he parbly ben the las wyld pig on the Bundel Downs anyhow there hadnt ben none for a long time befor him nor I aint looking to see none agen." This is the opening sentence of the novel which is set in a Britain (more specifically in Kent) which has reverted to barbarism after the nuclear holocaust. In the 2,000 and more years which have passed since then, only folk memories of the "Littl Shynin Man the Addom" have been preserved. The story of the catastrophe is recorded in legendary form in one of their sacred books, the Eusa Story. It opens with the words, "Wen Mr. Clevver wuz Big Man of Inland they had evere thing clevver. They had boats in the ayr & picters on the win & evere thing lyk that." Twentieth-century technology has become the stuff of myth. The priestly Riddley Walker, a "connexion man", interprets the government's puppet shows which reenact the legendary past. There is a plot concerning the feud between the Pry Mincer and the Ardship of Cambry and the rediscovery of gunpowder, but the real subjects of the book are language and the power of certain primal stories and legends. "Why is Punch crookit? Why will he always kill the babby if he can?" This novel, like *Kleinzeit,* bursts out of the straitjacket of standard English and is astonishing in its verbal inventiveness and meaningful punning. Riddley is the Caedmon of the barbarism to come.

Pilgermann has a Jewish protagonist as its eponymous hero. He is caught up in the events of the First Crusade in the 1090s. However, this is hardly a standard historical novel. (One of its themes is the horribleness of history.) Rather, it is an enquiry into the nature of existence, an enquiry which strains towards and even beyond the bounds of what is sayable. After sex with Sophia, who is both an incarnation of Gnosis and the wife of a German tax collector, Pilgermann is castrated. He then sets off towards Jerusalem and on his way has many bizarre and sometimes anachronistic encounters. He meets a bear-dancer who thinks his bear is God, a randy Death who copulates with all and sundry, Bodwild the Sow and Udo the relic-collector. Jerusalem is not attainable and Pilgermann's journey terminates in Antioch where he is commissioned to design a vast tiled pattern which conceals within it a hidden lion. This design is the focal image of the whole book—the embodiment of a vision of an individual's existence as a pattern of waves and particles. The novel, which is loosely structured, does not yield up its meanings easily. "I can't tell this as a story because it isn't a story; a story is what remains when you leave out all of the action."

The Medusa Frequency, despite its penchant for puns and all kinds of jokes, is also a difficult and extremely serious novel. In part, it is a meditation on the author's involvement with his word-processor (an Apple II) and on his strategies to avoid writer's block (superstitiously referred to in this book as "blighter's rock"). As the novelist Herman Orff struggles with his machine, a Kraken stirs somewhere in the depths of the machine's Undermind and cryptic messages appear on the screen. Orff (Orpheus), who also writes the storylines for Classic Comics, soon finds himself involved in a partial reenactment of classic myths as he quests for his lost love Luise (Eurydice) and has encounters with Melanie Falsepercy (Persephone).

The Moment Under the Moment is a collection of short stories (mostly fantastic) and essays. On the dustjacket, Hoban has concisely summed up the story-structures and themes which pervade his novels in a complex meshwork of recurring enquiries and allusions: "I'm interested in the strangeness of things, the strangeness of human consciousness; the strangeness of life and death; the strangeness of what the living and the dead are to each other; the strangeness of ideas (Orpheus and Eurydice, for example; King Kong and Fay Wray) that seem to have been with us long before the stories of them happened." As early as 1983 Victoria Glendenning, reviewing *Pilgermann,* wrote that Hoban's "integrity has won him a devoted if increasingly tested following to which I belong." A difficult but rewarding writer who offers something more substantial than mere entertainment.

—Robert Irwin

HOBB, Robin. *See* **LINDHOLM, Megan.**

HOCKE, Martin

Nationality: British. **Born:** Cologne, Germany, 6 September 1938. **Education:** Magdalen College, Brackley, Northamptonshire, 1950-55; Royal Academy of Dramatic Art, London, 1955-57. **Family:** Married 1) Luise Eilers in 1960 (divorced), one daughter; 2) Pauline Sunley in 1975. **Career:** English teacher, Berlitz School and others, in Germany, Italy and Britain; briefly location manager for Paramount Pictures; actor and broadcaster, Italian radio; translator from Italian into English; freelance writer from 1988. **Agent:** Dialogue Business Services, 5 Hillcrest, Broadway Road, Evesham, Worcestershire CV32 5HR.

FANTASY PUBLICATIONS

Novels

The Ancient Solitary Reign. London, Grafton, 1989.
The Lost Domain. London, HarperCollins, 1993.

*   *   *

Martin Hocke's two novels published in English are talking-animal fantasies. They are concerned with owls, principally with three species—the Barn owl, the Tawny owl and the Little owl—in English countryside areas during and just after World War II. In fact, the two novels cover the same events from two different points of view; the differences between them are so slight, with so little being added to the picture, that it is questionable whether the second novel was worth writing.

The owls lack the charming naivete of Richard Adams's rabbits in *Watership Down.* Too intelligent and sophisticated to be credible as mere owls, they are instead human types, as were William Horwood's moles in *Duncton Wood* and its sequels. Yet only sporadically does Hocke achieve the epic qualities of Horwood's work, due to a much smaller cast list and a general lack of audacity.

It is unfortunate that *The Ancient Solitary Reign* begins not only with the fledglinghood of Hunter, its Barn owl protagonist, but in the style of a twee children's book. The cosy picture of Hunter and his slightly younger sister, Dawn Raptor, and brother, Quaver, being taught the rights and wrongs of owl life by their parents is enough to put off any adult reader. Only after several chapters does the plot kick into gear, with Hunter flying off on his own to stay with and be instructed by an older owl, Beak Poke. But Beak Poke has been killed by a car and instead Hunter meets the two owls who will be most important in his life, Yoller and Alba.

Yoller is a young Tawny owl from an aristocratic family and is rather laid-back in his behaviour. Despite the millennia of antipathy between their two species, Hunter and Yoller quickly form a lasting friendship. Together they help to defeat an outside threat and go on a long and dangerous journey. Alba is a female Little owl, slightly older than Hunter, but unmated. She and Hunter fall in love (anthropomorphism is endemic in both novels), save each other's life and live together for some time, though they cannot of course mate.

While none of these three is particularly prejudiced, the attitudes of others (especially parents) to their friendships form the main theme of the novels: inter-species intolerance based on tradition and territory. The bottom line is food supply. Although they all feed principally on small mammals, the Tawny owls prefer woodland habitats, the Barn owls prefer farmland and the Little owls, being immigrants from mainland Europe only about a century ago (fifty years before the plot begins), are forced into pockets of poorer land between the others. Both of the other species look down upon the Little owls, calling them "immigrants" and "foreigners." Generally, each family group of owls has its own territory, which will be defended to the death against any other species that tries to hunt there. Hocke has laid down rules of etiquette for his owls, including the procedure for overflying another owl's territory and a prohibition against hunting in the territory even of another member of the same species unless invited.

Apart from the ongoing minutiae of owl life, the plot has four main strands. One is the presence in the middle of the setting of the Lost Domain, a mostly wooded private estate which has formerly been patrolled by "men with firesticks" (gamekeepers with shotguns) so that no owls have lived there for a century or so. But during the war the estate is abandoned and just after the war it is colonized by Little owls but is still the subject of territorial claims by others.

A second strand is the outside threat. This is an Eagle owl which escapes from a zoo (during a wartime bombing raid) and flies north, for some unexplained reason killing all the owls it comes across. It is a giant by comparison to the Tawny and Barn owls, being faster and more powerful as well as having several times the wingspan. While some owls prefer to hide rather than to fight, Yoller and Hunter are chief amongst the warriors, bringing their species together for a while at least. Even Alba joins in the battle. The result is a splendid set-piece scene, with several owls (including Hunter's father) being killed before the monster is brought down. Both Hunter and Yoller are badly injured and are, to a certain extent, revered as war heroes. Alba nurses Hunter back to health, but she realizes that she loves him too much and that they should both have a chance at breeding, so she leaves him and goes off to join her own kind in the Lost Domain—and is later killed there when men with firesticks return.

The third strand is a quest. Yoller has to fetch his own promised mate, May Blossom, from the city, six nights' flying time to the south. He invites Hunter to join him, and because Alba is dead Hunter accepts. *En route* they come across another Barn owl, Holly, who lives with her dying mother, and there is mutual attraction between Hunter and Holly. In the city the two rural owls detest the noise, the bright lights all night and the monotonous diet of pigeon. Yoller gets trapped by some wire netting whilst feeding on the ground and only escapes by sacrificing a talon. Hunter is hit by a motor vehicle and taken away by its occupants. He wakes up in the zoo (or prison, as it is known to the owls). He is incarcerated with another male Barn owl, Humanoid, who has been raised by a human female and is fixated upon human females, wanting to mate with them. After quite a few months there, Hunter seizes his opportunity to escape when Humanoid tries to pop an item of food into their female keeper's mouth (as a gift before attempting to mate).

The fourth strand is political. The very conservative hierarchy of the Barn owls has been changed during Hunter's absence by the election to power of Winger, an owl from the south who fled during the Eagle owl episode. He tries to impose his New Apostasy upon all Barn owls and has radical ideas about breeding methods, proposing to breed with three females (owls are normally monogamous). At the same time, while Yoller is supposedly the leader of the local Tawny owls (succeeding his father) his mate May Blossom has very quickly come to be the decision-maker. She intends to make war on the Barn owls for territorial reasons. Only Hunter can save owlkind from a disastrous war. After a brief but bloody battle he exposes and banishes Winger, refusing any official position but being content to go off and mate with Holly. In an unnecessary final episode, Hunter is shot dead by a man with a firestick while protecting his family.

All these plot elements occur in both books. The difference is that while *The Ancient Solitary Reign* is meant to be the third-person story of Hunter, adapted from the epic poem composed by his brother Quaver, *The Lost Domain* is Yoller's first-person account, told in his dotage to the wind as he waits for other Tawny owls to come and kill him (for his belief in inter-species harmony). Yoller, knowing Quaver's version, makes much of the differences between the two, but these are generally insignificant.

Hocke's owl societies hover uncomfortably between reality and fantasy. He seems to have researched his species, yet he chooses to overlook important factors. For example, in reality all three of these species breed each year, producing several eggs each time, and Barn owls often produce two broods a year, yet nowhere in either book is there any acknowledgement of this; both Hunter's and Yoller's parents seem to breed once, have one clutch of eggs and never breed again. The lack of fantasy elements is equally strange—and disappointing. Apart from talking, these owls do nothing else with their great intelligence. They have no machines or written records and have never succeeded in communicating with humans. There is an acceptance, by the owls, that mankind is encroaching upon their wild territory year by year, yet they do nothing about this.

Martin Hocke, who worked for a good deal of his adult life in Italy before becoming a full-time author, has written a third owl fantasy which has been published in the Italian language but has not as yet appeared in English. Apparently, the three books are conceived as a trilogy.

—Chris Morgan

HODGELL, P(atricia) C(hristine)

Nationality: American. **Born:** Des Moines, Iowa, 16 March 1951. **Education:** Eckend College, B.A., 1973; University of Minnesota, M.A., 1976, Ph.D. in 19th-century English literature, 1987. **Career:** English lecturer, University of Wisconsin, Oshkosh, from 1981. **Agent:** Donald A. Maass, 157 West 57th Street, Suite 1003, New York, NY 10019, USA. **Address:** 1237 Liberty Street, Oshkosh, WI 54901, USA.

FANTASY PUBLICATIONS

Novels (series: the Kencyrath in all books)

God Stalk. New York, Atheneum, 1982.
Dark of the Moon. New York, Atheneum, 1985.
Chronicles of the Kencyrath (omnibus; includes *God Stalk, Dark of the Moon*). London, New English Library, 1988.
Seeker's Mask. Eugene, Oregon, Hypatia Press, 1994.

Short Stories

Bones. Eugene, Oregon, Hypatia Press, 1993.
Child of Darkness. Eugene, Oregon, Hypatia Press, 1993.

OTHER PUBLICATIONS

Other

Modern Science Fiction and Fantasy: A Study Guide, with Michael M. Levy. Minneapolis, Minnesota, University of Minnesota Extension, 1981.

*

P. C. Hodgell comments:

My fantasies are part of a daydream cycle which I began as a lonely child, growing up in my grandmother's house. They tell the story of Jame, chosen daughter of a race and not very happy about it. Neither are her people, either about the thankless role which their god has given them as his champions against a world-devouring enemy, or about Jame as a nascent aspect of that god, specifically That-Which-Destroys. The action takes place primarily on a secondary world, Rathillien, although a whole chain of parallel universes connected by overlapping threshold worlds is involved. Down this chain of creation comes Perimal Darkling, the ancient enemy, overwhelming each universe in turn. Jame's people, the Kencyrath, are supposed to stop this deadly progression, but are beginning to question the code of honour which binds them to their seemingly hopeless task. On the other hand, only honour keeps Jame balanced between her god-tainted blood and her training as a cast-out child in Perimal Darkling itself. Now, returning to Rathillien, she must save not only herself but her people, from enemies without and within.

*   *   *

P. C. Hodgell's elaborate, moody fantasy fiction all takes place in the world of Rathillien and focuses on Jame of the people known as the Kencyrath. In the books thus far published, we follow Jame from exile without a past to sister and heir of the Highlord of the Kencyrath. Hodgell's writing is dense and visual, and she displays a truly original imagination, even when tackling familiar areas of fantasy.

For 30 millennia, the Three-Faced God has been opposing the chaotic entity Perimal Darkling, which seeks to overwhelm the connecting worlds of the Chain of Creation. To fight this entity, the god created the Kencyrath out of three different races to be his champions, then, apparently, abandoned them. Over and over the Kencyrath have been defeated, retreating from world to world before Perimal Darkling. Three thousand years before the opening of *God Stalk*, Gerridon Highlord betrayed his people to Perimal Darkling in return for immortality. The remnants of the Kencyrath fled to Rathillien, shorn of some of the magical objects they needed for their fight, betrayed, abandoned, and obsessed with honour. Over time, the Highborn, who rule the Kencyrath, fell to quarrelling with each other, and at the time we enter the story are just coming out of a period of near-anarchy.

The three novels, though all part of the same story, are very different from one another. *God Stalk* takes place in over a year of time in one city, *Dark of the Moon* in less than a month over much of a continent, and *Seeker's Mask* within a week in scattered places. The focus of each book is also different. The first centres on Jame's self-discovery as she figures out who she is, and her quest to reconcile the many gods of Tai-tastigon with her people's monotheism. The second is a more usual epic fantasy novel, with its broad scale and two intersecting plot lines, its intrigues and battles. The third has the feel of a transitional novel; its plot is diffuse and uncertain.

God Stalk is a truly remarkable first novel. As it opens, a wounded Jame is fleeing from the dangerous Haunted Lands and the burned-out Keep that was once her home to the god-ridden city of Tai-tastigon. Her goal is to somehow reach the twin brother she remembers from childhood and bring him their father's ring and sword. In the course of her stay in Tai-tastigon, she becomes involved in an undeclared but vicious trade war, joins the Thieves'

Guild, incurs the enmity of a renegade Kencyr priest, commits theocide and then revives the god, and engages in any number of minor adventures. All the while she is gradually learning more about her talents and identity as pieces of her missing past return. While all the characters are interesting and well-delineated, the most fascinating character is the city of Tai-tastigon itself, with its mazes and gods, its festivals and tribes. Jame's self-discovery and quest for the truth about the gods are the book's focus; what plot there is works subtly, almost in the background.

By contrast, *Dark of the Moon,* which follows Jame from the time she leaves Tai-tastigon to her final reunion with her brother Torisen, who turns out to be Highlord, is all plot. It is also full of wonders, though in this case the wonders of the world Rathillien, which predate the coming of the Kencyrath: the *imus* of the old religion, the *rathorns* who die of their own ivory armour and who may well have destroyed the mysterious race known as the Builders, the remarkably civilized werewolves known as Wolvers. Hodgell also gives us some glimpses into her version of chaos, the mixture of animate and inanimate that is the notable feature of worlds overtaken by Perimal Darkling. This provides ambiguity to the magical artefacts used by the Kencyrath, such as the Book Bound in Pale Leather, which are also both animate and inanimate.

The title of *Seeker's Mask* refers to the blindfold in a version of Blind Man's Bluff, and this provides a good metaphor for the novel. Jame blunders throughout from episode to episode, never sure where she is going or what her ultimate goal is, other than survival. As a result, the book is less satisfying and compelling than the first two in the series. Once again, though, Hodgell opens up new worlds of wonder, in this case the world of the cloistered Highborn women and that of the Merikit, a people native to Rathillien.

Hodgell's writing is some of the most vivid in fantasy fiction. The first chapter of *God Stalk* is absolutely brilliant. As Jame enters Tai-tastigon during the Feast of Dead Gods, the eerie terror grows and grows, and we share Jame's confusion and fear. The cities, the forests, the creatures of Rathillien all live in our minds.

Hodgell's worst flaw is too much complexity. Fantasy novels should not need appendices, yet without those Hodgell includes it's almost impossible to sort out the Thieves' Guild or the organization of the Kencyrath. The multiplicity of characters, factions, religions and motives becomes too much to juggle. Yet Hodgell does a good job of gradually revealing information such as the history of the Kencyrath.

Nearly all of Hodgell's characters are ambiguous: Jame has a Darkling soul but is unfallen, Torisen is basically good but highly flawed, Tubain the innkeeper and Kirien the Jaran heir are sexually ambiguous, Kindrie the healer both is and is not one of the priests. The weakest character in the books is Caldane, Lord Caineron because he lacks this ambiguity, being an unadulterated villain. It is laughable when he lures and crushes an innocent mouse; he might as well be twirling his moustache and snickering evilly. This is an uncharacteristic failure on Hodgell's part. Even Gerridon, who is clearly evil—how else can you describe someone who sacrifices two-thirds of his people to win immortality for himself—is not such a sneering, cliched villain.

Jame is a traditional fantasy heroine in that she survives against impossible odds. The Kencyrath are supposed to be hard to kill, but in Jame's case it gets ridiculous, particularly in *Dark of the Moon.* For the most part, though, the action sweeps the reader along and prevents thinking too hard about the improbabilities.

Hodgell is a highly successful, imaginative stylist who creates worlds and characters well worth exploring. Plotting is not her greatest strength, but weaknesses often pass unnoticed in the face of her compelling writing. Her books are deep, rich, and philosophical.

—Janice M. Eisen

HOLDSTOCK, Robert (Paul)

Pseudonyms: Robert Black; Ken Blake; Chris Carlsen; Robert Faulcon; Richard Kirk. **Nationality:** British. **Born:** Hythe, Kent, 2 August 1948. **Education:** University College of North Wales, Bangor, 1967-70, B.Sc. (honours) in applied zoology 1970; London School of Hygiene and Tropical Medicine, 1970-71, M.Sc. in medical zoology 1971. **Career:** Research student, Medical Research Council, London, 1971-74. Since 1974, freelance writer. **Awards:** British Science Fiction Association award, 1985; World Fantasy award, 1985, 1993. **Address:** 54 Raleigh Road, London N8 0HY, England.

FANTASY PUBLICATIONS

Novels (series: Berserker; Mythago; Raven)

Shadow of the Wolf (Berserker; as Chris Carlsen). London, Sphere, 1977.
Swordsmistress of Chaos (Raven; with Angus Wells, as Richard Kirk). London, Corgi, 1978.
A Time of Ghosts (Raven; as Richard Kirk). London, Corgi, 1978.
The Bull Chief (Berserker; as Chris Carlsen). London, Sphere, 1979.
The Horned Warrior (Berserker; as Chris Carlsen). London, Sphere, 1979.
Lords of the Shadows (Raven; as Richard Kirk). London, Corgi, 1979.
Mythago Wood. London, Gollancz, 1984; New York, Arbor House, 1985.
Lavondyss: Journey to an Unknown Region (Mythago). London, Gollancz, 1988; New York, Morrow, 1989.
The Hollowing (Mythago). London, HarperCollins, 1993.
Merlin's Wood, or The Vision of Magic (Mythago). London, HarperCollins, 1994.

Short Stories

The Bone Forest (Mythago). London, Grafton, 1991.

Other

Magician, with Malcolm Edwards. Limpsfield, Surrey, Dragon's World, 1982.
Realms of Fantasy, with Malcolm Edwards. Limpsfield, Surrey, Dragon's World, 1983.
Lost Realms, with Malcolm Edwards. Limpsfield, Surrey, Dragon's World, 1985.

OTHER PUBLICATIONS

Novels

Eye Among the Blind. London, Faber, 1976; New York, Doubleday, 1977.

Legend of the Werewolf (novelization of screenplay; as Robert Black). London, Sphere, 1976.
Earthwind. London, Faber, 1977; New York, Pocket Books, 1978.
The Satanists (novelization of screenplay; as Robert Black). London, Futura, 1978.
Necromancer. London, Futura, 1978; New York, Avon, 1980.
Cry Wolf (novelization of television script; as Ken Blake). 1981.
Where Time Winds Blow. London, Faber, 1981, and New York, Pocket Books, 1982.
The Untouchables (novelization of television script; as Ken Blake). 1982.
Operation Susie (novelization of television script; as Ken Blake). 1982.
You'll Be All Right (novelization of television script; as Ken Blake). 1982.
Bulman (novelization of television script). London, Futura, 1984.
The Emerald Forest (novelization of screenplay). New York, Zoetrope, and London, Penguin, 1985.
One of Our Pigeons Is Missing (novelization of television script). London, Futura, 1985.
The Fetch. London, Orbit, 1991.

Novels as Robert Faulcon

Night Hunter. London, Arrow, 1983; New York, Charter, 1987.
The Talisman. London, Arrow, 1983; New York, Charter, 1987.
The Ghost Dance. London, Arrow, 1984; New York, Charter, 1987.
The Shrine. London, Arrow, 1984; New York, Charter, 1988.
The Hexing. London, Arrow, 1984; New York, Charter, 1988.
The Labyrinth. London, Arrow, 1987; New York, Charter, 1988.
The Stalking (omnibus; includes *Night Hunter, The Talisman*). London, Arrow, 1987.
The Ghost Dance (omnibus; includes *The Ghost Dance, The Shrine*). London, Arrow, 1987.
The Hexing and The Labyrinth (omnibus). London, Legend, 1989.

Short Stories

In the Valley of the Statues. London, Faber, 1982.

Other

Alien Landscapes, with Malcolm Edwards. London, Pierrot, 1979.
Tour of the Universe, with Malcolm Edwards. London, Pierrot, and New York, Mayflower, 1980.

Editor, with Christopher Priest, *Stars of Albion.* London, Pan, 1979.
Editor, with Christopher Evans, *Other Edens.* London, Unwin Hyman, 3 vols., 1987-89.

*   *   *

Before producing the *Mythago Wood* cycle, his major fantasy work, Robert Holdstock was a prolific professional author of various fictions, including dark-hued but fairly standard heroic fantasy under the names Chris Carlsen (the Berserker series) and Richard Kirk (with Angus Wells, the Raven series). More indicative of deeper concerns are early science fiction novels (*Eye Among the Blind, Earthwind, Where Time Winds Blow*), which touch on primal matters and the scientific process, and a run of imaginative parapsychological horror novels including *Necromancer,* the Night

Hunter series (written as Robert Faulcon) and the more mature *The Fetch*. The Mythago cycle germinates in the novella "Mythago Wood" (1982), which aptly sprouted into the novel of the same name, and develops in the novels *Lavondyss, The Hollowing* and *Merlin's Wood* and the novella "The Bone Forest." Shadows of the cycle spread over much, if not most, of Holdstock's other work, especially *The Labyrinth,* climactic novel of the Night Hunter series, and the stories collected in *In the Valley of the Statues* and *The Bone Forest,* even informing his novelization of John Boorman's film *The Emerald Forest.*

Set in Gloucestershire just after World War Two, *Mythago Wood* explores a tract of primal forest inhabited by mythagos, imagined-into-reality archetypes of old tales, songs and traditions, compelled to live out over and over their legends. A boldly original premise, worked through with enough thoroughness to suggest the all-pervasive importance of myth without damaging the essential mystery, *Mythago Wood* is a shamelessly enjoyable adventure novel. Young Steven Huxley follows his vanished brother Christian into haunted Ryhope Wood, vaguely guided by the jottings of his scientist father George (who first tracked the wood and invented the "mythago" concept) and encountering perils, a breathtaking pagan princess and a pig-monster of William Hope Hodgson proportions. Stirred in with the adventure is a serious and mind-stretching meditation on the nature of collective imagination, bristling with so many ideas that a series was not only inevitable but—a rare thing—necessary.

While replete with quests, magic, folklore and comings-of-age, the Mythago cycle is by no means a conventional fantasy series. Each new component adds to the tapestry rather than simply extends the commercial life of the property. *Lavondyss* is no simple Tome Two in the Towering Trilogy, but a major novel in its own right, returning to Ryhope Wood for a deeper, darker, chillier journey into the source of all legendry. Tallis Keeton, 13-year-old sister of one of the adventurers from the first book, lives on the outskirts of the wood, and becomes aware of the magic around her. She is inspired to carve masks and tell stories, and attracts the attention of no less a personage than the composer Ralph Vaughan Williams, who guest-appears collecting tunes. Tallis has had a vision of the death of Scathach, a noble young warrior to whom she speaks from an oak, and is given an assortment of other clues as to the nature of her destiny and her mission. Inevitably, she is drawn into the woods in pursuit of her lost brother and finds herself travelling back through folk history to Lavondyss, the source of all myths, an edenic paradise that may also be an ice age wilderness.

Considerably less straightforward than *Mythago Wood, Lavondyss* subverts quests with dallyings and side-stories, is sometimes maddeningly difficult to follow. It soon loses its appealing innocence of tone as Tallis experiences the brutal, bloody, messy realities of Iron Age living and (in an astonishing section) is torn from her body and becomes a tree, witness to unspeakable depravities, and a female version of the Green Man of pub-sign and ghost-story fame. The imbecile smugness of much folkloric fantasy is nowhere to be found, and Holdstock marvellously evokes a physical environment as harsh and cruel as it is magical and beautiful. His theme is the reality at the heart of the myth, and he writes of the stinks and atrocities behind the heroic images, even has he reaffirms and recreates their beauty.

"The Bone Forest" returns to George Huxley and his family, already showing the tensions that will break them up in *Mythago Wood.* The Holdstockian obsession with taking different paths to the centre of the labyrinth (the central theme, fittingly, of *The Laby-rinth,* a cross-over between his two main fantasy strands) expands into an almost Borgesian notion of shifting alternate realities, with George arguing through his diary with a doppelganger version of himself, and never quite sure if the world he returns to after his trips into the wood is the same as the one he has left. *The Hollowing* again changes mood subtly, with Richard Bradley (another of the relay team of protagonists who probe the wood) embarking on a quest to reclaim his son Alex, who has gone feral in the wood and is providing a new impetus to the creation of more ferocious, corrupt and corrupting mythagoes. Like *The Fetch, The Hollowing* is at heart the story of a tangled father-son relationship, complicated by paranormal powers, but it takes a series of powerful by-paths, exploring variants on myths as powerful as the Tower of Babel and the Old Age of Jason. Sundered families and quests to reunite lost kinsmen are central to much of Holdstock's fiction, as if one of his primal myths were John Ford's film of *The Searchers*: the relatively simple, if neurotic, drive of the protagonist of the Night Hunter books to rescue his kidnapped wife and son grows into the far stranger searches and reunions of the Mythago cycle and *The Fetch.*

Though wrapped up in an earthy take on the Matter of Britain, the Mythago series (developing themes from *Necromancer* and the Night Hunter horror novels) also reflect Holdstock's science fiction background and scientific training, extending the parapsychological concerns of Nigel Kneale's television work (*Quatermass and the Pit, The Road, The Stone Tapes*). A succession of blinkered but visionary scientists attempt to understand the processes they may have, in part, created, allowing Holdstock another, superficially more rational, way into the trackless wilderness that can only really be penetrated by the obsessed and heartbroken. Collectively, the Mythago series starts to feel like a life's work and shows the development of a good writer painfully metamorphosing into a genuinely important fantasist.

—Kim Newman

HOLT, Tom

Nationality: British. **Born:** London, 13 September 1961. **Education:** Westminster School, 1974-79; Wadham College, Oxford University, 1979-86; College of Law, London, 1986-88. **Family:** Married Kim Nicola Foster in 1988; one child. **Career:** Lawyer. **Agent:** James Hale, 47 Peckham Rye, London SE15 3SX, England.

FANTASY PUBLICATIONS

Novels

Expecting Someone Taller. London, Macmillan, 1987; New York, St. Martin's Press, 1988.
Who's Afraid of Beowulf? London, Macmillan, and New York, St. Martin's Press, 1988.
Flying Dutch. London, Orbit, 1991; New York, St. Martin's Press, 1992.
Ye Gods! London, Orbit, 1992; New York, St. Martin's Press, 1993.
Overtime. London, Orbit, 1993.
Here Comes the Sun. London, Orbit, 1993.

Grailblazers. London, Orbit, 1994.
Faust Among Equals. London, Orbit, 1994.

OTHER PUBLICATIONS

Novels

Lucia in Wartime. London, Macmillan, 1985; New York, Harper and Row, 1986.
Lucia Triumphant. London, Macmillan, 1986; New York, Harper and Row, 1988.
Goatsong. London, Macmillan, 1989; New York, St. Martin's Press, 1990.
The Walled Orchard. London, Macmillan, 1990; New York, St. Martin's Press, 1991.

Poetry

Poems by Tom Holt. London, Michael Joseph, 1973.

Other

I, Margaret (humour). London, Macmillan, 1989.

*

Tom Holt comments:

I tend to write between midnight and 3 a.m.; and keen students of the genre should be able to tell which bits were written when I've fallen asleep and the machine goes on typing on its own. Most of my heroes are me in disguise, and nearly all my heroines are called Jane.

*   *   *

Tom Holt's farcical fantasies incline to quasi-realistic backgrounds—usually today's reliably ordinary Britain. This base reality suffers assaults from myth and legend, from elsewhere and elsewhen.

Expecting Someone Taller, for example, presumes the historical accuracy of Wagner's *Ring* cycle. The initially downtrodden and inept hero Malcolm runs his car over a badger who is a disguised Giant of legend, and who before dying crossly hands over his burden: the Tarnhelm and the Nibelungs' Ring. Despite the efforts of Alberich, Loge, the all-powerful but henpecked (by his eight remaining Valkyrie daughters) Wotan, Huginn and Muninn, the Rhine Maidens, and sundry lesser deities, Malcolm continues to wield the world-controlling Ring and bring to it the quality unknown in any former bearer: a slightly wimpish niceness. Thus all the world goes better except for matters irretrievably accursed by fate, such as England's test-match scores. The interleaving of mythic and mundane is generally very funny. Only the finale, with Wotan finally maddened into all-out attack and the entire might of Asgard going rapidly *phut* when opposed by the Ring, seems a little weak.

Its successor *Who's Afraid of Beowulf* is funnier still, with King Hrolf and his longship crew of Norsemen awakening from a 1,200 years' enchanted slumber to deal with the sorcerer-king who has been running Britain for all those centuries. Good points include the revenants' lack of awe at modern technology (they had all that stuff; they just called it magic), set-pieces like their interpretation

of the London Underground map as a genealogical chart, and a running gag about the portmanteau game Goblin's Teeth played by the chthonic spirits Zxerp and Prexz ("Double Rune Score. I think I'll have another longhouse on Uppsala."). The sorcerer-king having been a little too easily dealt with, the Norsemen restore normality by rowing off to Valhalla, where the catering is awful—and whence Hrolf sends a final postcard to the young female archaeologist entangled in their adventures, ending "See you in about sixty years."

The emphasis of Holt's comic fantasies is on hilarious incidental invention and off-the-wall ideas rather than plot, but the regular basic structure tends to go: (a) misplaced figures of history and legend impinge on the 20th century; (b) the running of the world is revealed as involving bizarre and inefficient conspiracies (one recurring character is a BBC chap whose dream is to link Kennedy's assassination with the Milk Marketing Board); (c) a major upheaval, like the erasure of Asgard's forces or the sorcerer-king's removal, leaves matters in a slightly more rational state. The story will feature many anachronistic gags.

Thus in *Flying Dutch* it's Vanderdecken the Flying Dutchman and his immortal crew who emerge from history (their eternal exile being because the elixir of life has the side effect of body odour on a scale to boggle skunks), the world economy having come to pivot on an ancient insurance policy taken out by Vanderdecken and bloated by compound interest. This is duly sorted out. *Ye Gods!* introduces a Hercules-like Hero into a suburban home (absentee father: Jupiter), leading to a childhood and adolescence complicated by tasks like serpent-strangling, dragon-slaying, and generally heroing around . . . all part of a Promethean plot to neutralize the Greek pantheon and end their meddling with human affairs.

Overtime sees Blondel of Richard Lionheart fame promoted at rock gigs scattered throughout history, courtesy of a daft time-travel premise whereby all official doors labelled NO ENTRY (in every era) are secretly linked by the corridors of bureaucratic time. Antichrist, antipopes and various murderous henchmen appear, and ultimately God is prevailed on to rearrange the structure of time more sensibly. An amusing *and* dramatically effective moment comes when Blondel's song is finally answered by the imprisoned Richard in the dread Chastel des Larmes Chaudes, appearing in its temporary aspect of a "bouncy castle."

Here Comes the Sun offers a *reductio ad absurdum* of interventionalist theology, with the massed efforts of a vast, inefficient and under-budgeted spiritual bureaucracy required for such chores as, each day, starting up the obsolescent Sun and coaxing it across the sky. An efficient young mortal lady is recruited, and progresses from being an effective new broom to the rank of Holy Roman Empress (the secret empire being this book's Hidden Conspiracy) with the power to abolish, retrospectively, the entire ant's-nest of celestial functionaries and substitute natural law—and thus, a Sun that works by itself.

More farcical yet, *Grailblazers* shows the Grail Knights in modern England, pursuing such noble quests as pizza delivery. But a knight who has spent many centuries in enchanted sleep returns to urge a revival of the Quest, which leads to Australia (being where the unicorns went), Atlantis (a offshore company accessible only by faxing oneself) and the brooding castle of diabolical Santa Claus (formerly Wotan). It's good fun, but the knights are such buffoons and their quest so absurd that there's no plot tension, nor any sense of revelation or closure when the quest proves to be a set-up. A similar mad inconsequentiality afflicts *Faust Among Equals,* with

Hell's board of directors constructing a "EuroBosch" Musical Hell theme park in the wake of their management buyout, super-sorcerer Faust on the run (with sidekick Helen of Troy) after his unprecedented escape from Hell PLC, the ultimate bounty hunter in pursuit, etc. Eventually God, here depicted as an old-fashioned repairman, is persuaded to rearrange history.

Holt's comedy has become steadily more polished, and his flow of weird ideas continues unchecked. One worries that the "real world" settings are increasingly a mere stage backdrop for farce—a paper-thin world that isn't worth the saving—while the latest two books lack the former reality anchor of an ordinary 20th-century character in a leading role. Nevertheless, Holt entertains.

—David Langford

HORWOOD, William

Nationality: British. **Born:** Oxford, England, 1944. **Education:** Bristol University; degree in geography. **Career:** Journalist, *Campaign* magazine and *Marketing* journal; features editor, *Daily Mail,* London, 1971-78. **Awards:** London Academy of Music and Dramatic Art, Gold Medal in public speaking. Council member, Society of Authors. **Address:** P.O. Box 446, Oxford OX1 2SS, England.

FANTASY PUBLICATIONS

Novels (series: Duncton Chronicles)

Duncton Wood. Richmond, Surrey, Country Life, 1980.
The Stonor Eagles. Richmond, Surrey, Country Life, 1982.
Callanish. London, Allen Lane, 1984.
Skallagrigg. London, Viking, 1987.
Duncton Quest. London, Century, 1988.
Duncton Found. London, Century, 1989.
Duncton Tales. London, HarperCollins, 1991.
Duncton Rising. London, HarperCollins, 1992.
Duncton Stone. London, HarperCollins, 1993.
The Willows in Winter (sequel to *The Wind in the Willows* by Kenneth Grahame). London, HarperCollins, 1993; New York, St. Martin's Press, 1994.
Journeys to the Heartland. London, HarperCollins, 1995.

*

Film Adaptation: *Skallagrigg,* 1994 (television movie).

*   *   *

William Horwood's major work—in terms of both size and popularity—is a talking-animal fantasy series concerning moles. In six fat volumes, this epic saga of mole life in a present-day English woodland has achieved bestseller status in Britain. The original setting, Duncton Wood itself, is based on a wood very close to Oxford, but some of the moles from there journey to other mole sites—only 20 miles to Uffington, the centre of the mole church, and much

farther into Wales and northern England. (A mile is a great distance to a creature less than six inches long.) The reasons for these travels are most often religious, the seeking out of lost relics known as Books and Stillstones.

The six volumes, commencing with the author's debut novel *Duncton Wood,* are all heavily plotted and full of characters, drama and emotion—far too complex to allow summarization here. It is enough to say that several generations of Duncton moles try to improve the spiritual and political lot of the Duncton tunnel system (and, by extension, of moles everywhere) by fighting for democracy against despotism and for good against evil, though the good-versus-evil struggle becomes muddied when, in the second trilogy, a religious sect called the Newborns arises.

These are moles with, more or less, a human level of intelligence. They have philosophies, institutions, artefacts and written records. If one draws a comparison with the rabbits in *Watership Down* by Richard Adams (the archetype within this sub-genre), Adams's rabbits are simple creatures, behaving as the reader expects rabbits to, while Horwood's moles are sentient aliens living in our midst. It is hard to accept either that such intelligent creatures can exist at all, or that if they do exist they have not made contact with mankind.

What saves the credibility of these intelligent moles is that they are at the same time wild animals, whose society is dominated by violence and sex. Every spring they feel an irresistible urge to mate, and males will fight to the death to mate with their chosen female. At any time both males and females will fight for territory. Such fights, with teeth and claws, are described by Horwood quite often and in great detail. This violence, together with the seasonal mating (where love plays no part and promiscuity is the norm) means that the Duncton books are not aimed at children—another factor which sets them apart from *Watership Down.*

The characters of Horwood's moles are often complex and well rounded, though exaggerated for the sake of the plots. Even minor characters are reasonably well drawn. All are firmly based on humans, though sometimes one has the feeling that they are inconsistent enough (in their behaviour) to be groups of children. The mole religion is not Christianity but has many elements in common with it. It is highly evolved, involving the worship of standing stones (or Stones, as Horwood calls them). Religion and the continuing struggle between good and evil are strands which run right through the six books. Much of the plot has religious connotations and many of the journeys are "Holy Grail" quests.

There is also a strand of mysticism in the books, sometimes separate from the religious one. Various instances of telepathy, clairvoyance and precognition are important to the plot. More frequently referred to is the power of the healer in mole society: subtle magic is used in the picking and preparation of herbal remedies, while psychic healing is often resorted to in serious cases, with the healer apparently passing some of her (healers are most often female) lifeforce to her patient.

Horwood's rural settings are authentic and attractively described. He has visited the places he makes use of, in addition to researching their flora, fauna and climate. In general, Horwood's writing style is a straightforward one, not overly complicated. His Duncton books are too full of emotion (overdone for the sake of entertainment) to achieve subtlety. These are populist adventure novels and have succeeded as such.

The Stonor Eagles is mostly about the mythology and struggle for survival of the sea-eagle or white-tailed eagle (*Haliaetus albicilla*), a species resident in Scandinavia and Iceland, formerly present in the Western Isles off Scotland and now being re-introduced there. The plot is split between eagles and humans. Cuillin, the last sea-eagle in Scotland, flies across the North Sea to join others of her kind in Norway, and has dreams of a return to the Isle of Skye, though it is Cuillin's daughter, Mourne, who does return there. The novel also covers the life of James Stonor, an artist specializing in pictures and sculpture of sea-eagles, whose father has originated much of their mythology.

The eagles (as with Horwood's moles) are shown to possess good communications skills, talking with each other and with different species. For example, Cuillin consults the Raven of Storr (which is, in fact, a group of ravens living on Storr Cliff on Skye, who act as a great fount of knowledge) and they converse with a human fluency upon abstract subjects. Cuillin has more trouble understanding Norwegian sea-eagles, who speak a different language. Although no technology or written language is ascribed to these eagles (as it is to the moles) they have sophisticated customs (including intricate ritual flights, a kind of three-dimensional dance), beliefs and myths. They all believe in Haforn, the first sea-eagle. They are intelligent enough to realize that their species is dying out (due to persecution and pollution by men) and that they must breed successfully to survive.

If *The Stonor Eagles* is propaganda for the conservation of sea-eagles, *Callanish* is propaganda for the freeing of eagles from zoo cages. Its plot concerns Creggan, a golden eagle (*Aquila chrysaetos*) captured in Scotland and brought to London Zoo. He escapes, but returns to help other eagles escape from the zoo. There is no direct connection between this novel and *The Stonor Eagles,* though the eagles think and talk to each other here, too, in the same intelligent manner. The title is the name of a place on Lewis, in the Western Isles, where one of the other eagles comes from and which is held sacred by golden eagles.

Skallagrigg is mostly a grand saga about physically and mentally handicapped people and the injustices they have suffered. Although it is narrated in the year 2019, it is not science fiction; it looks back over about a century but concerns itself mainly with Esther, a spastic growing up in Britain from the 1960s to the 1980s. At the novel's core is a fantasy element that is both slight and important. The Skallagrigg itself is a modern mythic figure—a saviour who will come to the aid of handicapped people when they most need him, and about whom stories are told (by patients) in institutions for the handicapped all over Britain. Horwood (whose daughter suffers from cerebral palsy, a fact which has caused him to become a partisan for the rights of the disabled) demystifies things with a non-supernatural explanation, yet he only manages this by asserting another fantasy element—telepathy between twins. Whatever the basis of the myth of the Skallagrigg, it provides a spiritual uplift for most or perhaps all of the novel's handicapped characters at one time or another.

Recently, Horwood has commenced two new series in the talking-animal vein which has proved so successful for him in the past. *The Willows in Winter,* a bestseller in Britain during 1993, has been announced as the first of a number of sequels to Kenneth Grahame's masterpiece *The Wind in the Willows* (1908); and *Journeys to the Heartland* is the opening volume of a trilogy of large novels about intelligent wolves which will be given the overall title *The Wolves of Time.*

—Chris Morgan

HOUSMAN, Laurence

Nationality: British. **Born:** Bromsgrove, Worcestershire, 18 July 1865; younger brother of the poet A. E. Housman and the writer Clemence Housman. **Education:** Bromsgrove School; National Art Training School, South Kensington. **Career:** Book designer and illustrator, from late 1880s; art critic, *Manchester Guardian,* until 1907; novelist, poet, and playwright. **Died:** 20 February 1959.

Fantasy Publications

Novel

Gods and Their Makers. London, John Lane, 1897.

Short Stories

A Farm in Fairyland. London, Kegan Paul, 1894.
The House of Joy. London, Kegan Paul, 1895.
All-Fellows: Seven Legends of Lower Redemption. London, Kegan Paul, 1896.
The Field of Clover. London, Kegan Paul, 1898.
The Blue Moon. London, Murray, 1904.
The Cloak of Friendship. London, Murray, 1905.
Gods and Their Makers, and Other Stories. London, Allen and Unwin, 1920.
A Doorway in Fairyland. London, Cape, 1922.
Moonshine & Clover. London, Cape, 1922.
All-Fellows and The Cloak of Friendship. London, Cape, 1923.
Ironical Tales. London, Cape, 1926.
Turn Again Tales. New York, Holt, 1930.
What Next?: Provocative Tales of Faith and Morals. London, Cape, 1938.
Strange Ends and Discoveries: Tales of This World and the Next. London, Cape, 1948.
The Kind and the Foolish: Short Tales of Myth, Magic and Miracle. London, Cape, 1952.

Other Publications

Novels

An Englishwoman's Love-Letters. London, Murray, and New York, Doubleday Page, 1900.
A Modern Antaeus. London, Murray, 1901; New York, Doubleday Page, 1904.
John of Jingalo. London, Chapman and Hall, and New York, Holt, 1912.
The Royal Runaway and Jingalo in Revolution. London, Chapman and Hall, 1914.
Trimblerigg: A Book of Revelation. London, Cape, 1924.
The Life of H.R.H. the Duke of Flamborough. London, Cape, 1928.

Short Stories

Odd Pairs. 1925.

Plays

Bethlehem. London and New York, Macmillan, 1902.
Prunella, or Love in a Dutch Garden, with Harley Granville Barker. London, Bullen, and New York, Brentano, 1906; revised edition, London, Sidgwick and Jackson, 1930.
The Vicar of Wakefield. London, Johnson, 1906.
Oxford Historical Pageant. Oxford, Oxford Pageant Company, 1907.
The Chinese Lantern. London, Sidgwick, and New York, Brentano, 1908.
The Wheel (includes *Apollo in Hades, Death of Alcestis, The Doom of Admetus*). London, Sidgwick and Jackson, 1910; New York, French, 1920.
Alice in Ganderland. London, Woman's Press, 1911.
Lysistrata. London, Woman's Press, 1911.
The Lord of the Harvest. New York, French, 1916.
Nazareth. New York, French, 1916.
The Death of Orpheus: A Drama in Verse. London, Sidgwick and Jackson, 1921.
Little Plays of St. Francis. London, Sidgwick and Jackson, 1922; Boston, Small Maynard, 1923.
The Followers of St. Francis. London, Sidgwick and Jackson, and Boston, Small Maynard, 1923.
Palace Plays. London, Cape, 1930.
Victoria Regina. London, Cape, 1934; New York, Scribner, 1935.
Palestine Plays. London, Cape, 1942; New York, Scribner, 1943; as *Old Testament Plays,* Cape, 1950.
The Family Honour. London, Cape, 1950.

Poetry

Green Arras. London, John Lane, 1896.
Spikenard: A Book of Devotional Love Poems. London, Grant Richards, 1898.
Rue. London, Unicorn, 1899.

Other

Articles of Faith in the Freedom of Women. London, Woman's Press, 1910.
Echo de Paris: A Study from Life. London, Cape, 1923; New York, Appleton, 1924.
The Unexpected Years: Autobiography. London, Cape, and Indianapolis, Bobbs Merrill, 1936.
A. E. H.: A Memoir. London, Cape, 1937; New York, Scribner, 1938.
What Can We Believe?, with H. R. L. Sheppard. London, Cape, 1939.

*

Bibliographies: *Laurence Housman, 1865-1959* by Ivor Kemp, Street, Somerset County Library, 1967; *Catalogue of the Ian Kenyur-Hodgkins Collection of Laurence Housman,* Oxford, Warrack Perkins, 1978.

Critical Studies: *Laurence Housman 1865-1959, Clemence Housman 1861-1955, Alfred Edward Housman 1859-1936* by I. G. Kenyur-Hodgkins, London, National Book League, 1975.

*   *   *

"The main aim of these tales is to show how easily faith may become a bad substitute for morals," Laurence Housman wrote in the preface to *What Next?* He went on in that same preface to coin the dictum that "Miracles make good fairy-tales but bad theology." These two observations encapsulate the underlying philosophy of all his fantastic fiction, which does indeed deal extensively—but always ironically—with miracles, and which persistently argues that faith is a thoroughly bad thing when used—as it so often is—to justify cruelty, selfishness, arrogance, and wilful blindness to reality.

Housman's early tales for children, first assembled in four collections and later recombined in the two Cape collections of 1922, are whimsical and rather rambling but they are conscientiously subversive of many of the moral attitudes implicit in the moralistic reformulations of traditional tales popularized by Perrault and the Brothers Grimm. They do not come close to matching the standard set by their primary model—the oeuvre assembled in Oscar Wilde's collections *The Happy Prince* and *A House of Pomegranates*—but they remain notable for their occasional reversals of sex-roles, as in "The Prince with the Nine Sorrows" and "Japonel". Housman was an enthusiastic champion of women's rights, which cause is featured in several of his essays and plays a prominent part in his utopian satires *John of Jingalo* and *The Royal Runaway*. His other extended satire, *Trimblerigg*, also carries over certain themes and elements of method from his moralistic fantasies.

The Christian fantasies featured in *All-Fellows* and *The Cloak of Friendship* (also reprinted, with one extra tale, by Cape) are considerably more powerful than the children's tales, usually offering heart-rending accounts of virtuous individuals subject to all manner of evil circumstances, unaided until it is too late by supernatural intervention. The models for these tales are to be found in French fiction, among the works of Anatole France, Marcel Schwob, and other writers who found traditional tales of the lives of the saints unreasonably masochistic and life-denying. "Damien, the Worshipper" and "The Troubling of the Waters" are among the best English examples of this reluctantly heretical kind of fiction.

Housman's later work in this vein suffered a dramatic loss of force because the author had by then begun to find it far easier to be sarcastic and irreverent; this casualness robs later tales of the tragic dimension which feature so poignantly in the earlier collections. "The Real Temptation of St. Anthony" in *Ironical Tales* is sharply satirical but lacks a certain dignity, while "The Man Who Did Not Pray" in *What Next?* retains its power as a parable only by being transposed into a safely non-Christian context. Housman did, however, retain sufficient strength of feeling after finishing *The Cloak of Friendship* to produce one more very striking parable, albeit of a non-religious sort, in the horrifically intense "Man and Dog," which was written in 1909 and reprinted in the otherwise non-fantastic *Odd Pairs*. The two tales told to Housman by Oscar Wilde, which he recorded in his respectful and revealing memoir *Echo de Paris,* are idiosyncratic parables in this same dark vein, which Housman seems to have taken to heart for a while.

Housman's only long fantasy, *Gods and Their Makers,* is an extended *conte philosophique* examining the relationship between men and their imagined gods. Its protagonist belongs to a tribe whose custom requires every member to design and manufacture a personal deity. Tragic folly leads him to be banished to an island where these gods enjoy a strange afterlife following the death of their inventors. They are so hungry for worshippers that he becomes the focal point of their existence, but this curious empire is by nature precarious and cannot long endure. The novella was reprinted in 1920 together with two brief allegories of a type which is also further represented in later collections. In these brief, essay-like tales various gods and their various makers fall prey to the hazards of underachievement by virtue of ignorance and incomprehension. The briefer *contes philosophiques* grouped as "Philosophical Romances" in *Ironical Tales* are as calculatedly trivial as most of Housman's later work, but they exhibit a similar independence of spirit. *Ironical Tales* also includes a parody of David Garnett's *Lady into Fox,* "Lady into George Fox," which is one of the most amusing of Housman's comedies even if it is read in ignorance of its model.

Housman's literary career was so dogged by controversy that he was wont to refer to himself as "England's most censored playwright." He was constantly at loggerheads with the Lord Chamberlain over his alleged disrespect for the Christian God and the English royal family. These conflicts, together with the fact that his abilities were compared very unfavourably to those of his elder brother, seemed gradually to sap his self-confidence; he ended his career a far more dispirited writer than he had been at its beginning. His early work nevertheless remains a highly significant contribution to modern religious fantasy; among British writers he is perhaps surpassed only by T. F. Powys and Charles Williams (although it is entirely understandable that the stubbornly devout prefer the works of C. S. Lewis).

—Brian Stableford

HOWARD, Robert E(rvin)

Nationality: American. **Born:** Peaster, Texas, 24 January 1906. **Education:** Attended schools in Bagwell, Cross Cut, Burkett, Cross Plains and Brownwood, Texas; Howard Payne College, Brownwood. **Career:** Various minor jobs, then full-time writer from 1925. **Died:** 11 June 1936.

FANTASY PUBLICATIONS

Novels (series: Conan; Solomon Kane; Kull)

Conan the Conqueror. New York, Gnome Press, 1950; London, Boardman, 1954; revised by L. Sprague de Camp, New York, Lancer, 1967; as *Conan: The Hour of the Dragon,* edited by Karl Edward Wagner, New York, Putnam, 1977.
Almuric. New York, Ace, 1964; London, New English Library, 1971.
The Return of Skull-Face, with Richard A. Lupoff. West Linn, Oregon, Fax, 1977.
The Treasure of Tranicos, with L. Sprague de Camp (Conan). New York, Ace, 1980.

Short Stories

Skull-Face and Others. Sauk City, Wisconsin, Arkham House, 1946; as *Skull-Face Omnibus,* London, Spearman, 1974; in 2 vols. as *Skull-Face and Others* and *The Valley of the Worms and Others,* London, Panther, 1976.
The Sword of Conan. New York, Gnome Press, 1952.
The Coming of Conan. New York, Gnome Press, 1953.

King Conan. New York, Gnome Press, 1953.
Conan the Barbarian. New York, Gnome Press, 1955.
Tales of Conan, with L. Sprague de Camp (contains non-Conan stories rewritten by de Camp to feature Conan). New York, Gnome Press, 1955; as *Conan: The Flame Knife,* New York, Ace, 1981.
The Dark Man and Others. Sauk City, Wisconsin, Arkham House, 1963; London, Panther, 2 vols., 1978-79.
Conan the Adventurer, with L. Sprague de Camp. New York, Lancer, 1966; London, Sphere, 1973.
Conan the Warrior, with L. Sprague de Camp. New York, Lancer, 1967; London, Sphere, 1973.
Conan the Usurper, with L. Sprague de Camp. New York, Lancer, 1967; London, Sphere, 1974.
King Kull, with Lin Carter. New York, Lancer, 1967; London, Sphere, 1974.
Conan, with L. Sprague de Camp and Lin Carter. New York, Lancer, 1967; London, Sphere, 1974.
Wolfshead. New York, Lancer, 1968.
Conan the Freebooter, with L. Sprague de Camp. New York, Lancer, 1968; London, Sphere, 1974.
Conan the Wanderer, with L. Sprague de Camp and Lin Carter. New York, Lancer, 1968; London, Sphere, 1974.
Red Shadows (Solomon Kane). West Kingston, Rhode Island, Grant, 1968; in 3 vols. as *The Moon of Skulls, The Hand of Kane, Solomon Kane,* n.p., Centaur Press, 1969-71.
Bran Mak Morn. New York, Dell, 1969.
Conan of Cimmeria, with L. Sprague de Camp and Lin Carter. New York, Lancer, 1969; London, Sphere, 1974.
Red Blades of Black Cathay, with Tevis Clyde Smith. West Kingston, Rhode Island, Grant, 1971.
Marchers of Valhalla. West Kingston, Rhode Island, Grant, 1972; revised ed., Grant, 1977; London, Sphere, 1977.
The Sowers of the Thunder. West Kingston, Rhode Island, Grant, 1973; London, Sphere, 1977.
The Lost Valley of Iskander. West Linn, Oregon, Fax, 1974; London, Futura, 1976.
The People of the Black Circle (Conan). West Kingston, Rhode Island, Grant, 1974; revised edition, New York, Berkley, 1977.
Worms of the Earth. West Kingston, Rhode Island, Grant, 1974; London, Futura, 1976.
The Grey God Passes. Columbia, Pennsylvania, Miller, 1975.
Valley of the Lost. Columbia, Pennsylvania, Miller, 1975.
A Witch Shall Be Born (Conan). West Kingston, Rhode Island, Grant, 1975.
Red Nails (Conan). West Kingston, Rhode Island, Grant, 1975; revised edition, New York, Berkley, 1979.
The Tower of the Elephant (Conan). West Kingston, Rhode Island, Grant, 1975.
The Book of Robert E. Howard, edited by Glenn Lord. New York, Zebra, 1976.
The Devil in Iron (Conan). West Kingston, Rhode Island, Grant, 1976.
The Grim Land and Others. Lamoni, Indiana, Stygian Isle Press, 1976.
Pigeons from Hell. New York, Zebra, 1976.
Rogues in the House (Conan). West Kingston, Rhode Island, Grant, 1976.
The Second Book of Robert Howard, edited by Glenn Lord. New York, Zebra, 1976.
Swords of Shahrazar. West Linn, Oregon, Fax, 1976; London, Futura, 1976.

Conan of Aquilonia, with L. Sprague de Camp and Lin Carter. New York, Prestige, 1977.
Conan: The People of the Black Circle. New York, Berkley, 1977.
The Illustrated Gods of the North. West Warwick, Rhode Island, Necronomicon Press, 1977.
The Robert E. Howard Omnibus. London, Futura, 1977.
Son of the White Wolf. West Linn, Oregon, Fax, 1977.
Sword Woman. 1977.
Black Canaan. New York, Berkley, 1978.
Queen of the Black Coast (Conan). West Kingston, Rhode Island, Grant, 1978.
Skulls in the Stars (Solomon Kane). New York, Bantam, 1978.
Black Colossus. West Kingston, Rhode Island, Grant, 1979.
The Gods of Bel-Sagoth. New York, Ace, 1979.
Hawks of Outremer. West Kingston, Rhode Island, Grant, 1979.
The Hills of the Dead (Solomon Kane). New York, Bantam, 1979.
Jewels of Gwahlur. West Kingston, Rhode Island, Grant, 1979.
The Road of Azrael. West Kingston, Rhode Island, Grant, 1979.
Lord of the Dead. West Kingston, Rhode Island, Grant, 1981.
Robert E. Howard's Kull. West Kingston, Rhode Island, Grant, 1985.
The Pool of the Black One (Conan). West Kingston, Rhode Island, Grant, 1986.
Cthulhu: The Mythos and Kindred Horrors, edited by David Drake. New York, Baen, 1987.
The Conan Chronicles, with L. Sprague de Camp and Lin Carter (omnibus; includes *Conan, Conan of Cimmeria, Conan the Freebooter*). London, Orbit, 1989.
Robert E. Howard's World of Heroes, edited by Mike Ashley. London, Robinson, 1989.
The Conan Chronicles 2, with L. Sprague de Camp and Lin Carter (omnibus; includes *Conan the Wanderer, Conan the Adventurer, Conan the Buccaneer,* the last by de Camp and Carter alone). London, Orbit, 1990.

OTHER PUBLICATIONS

Novel

Three-Bladed Doom. New York, Zebra, 1977.

Short Stories

A Gent from Bear Creek. London, Jenkins, 1937; West Kingston, Rhode Island, Grant, 1965; selection, as *The Pride of Bear Creek,* Grant, 1966.
The Vultures; Showdown at Hell's Canyon. Lakemont, Georgia, Fictioneer, 1973.
The Incredible Adventures of Dennis Dorgan. West Linn, Oregon, Fax, 1974.
Tigers of the Sea. West Kingston, Rhode Island, Grant, 1974.
Black Vulmea's Revenge and Other Tales of Pirates. West Kingston, Rhode Island, Grant, 1976.
Vultures of Whapeton. New York, Zebra, 1976.
The Last Ride. New York, Berkley, 1978.
The Iron Man, & Other Tales of the Ring. West Kingston, Rhode Island, Grant, 1979.
Mayhem on Bear Creek. West Linn, Oregon, Fax, 1979.
The Adventures of Lal Singh. Mount Olive, North Carolina, Cryptic, 1985.

Post Oaks and Sand Roughs. West Kingston, Rhode Island, Grant, 1990.

Poetry

Always Comes Evening: The Collected Poems of Robert E. Howard. Sauk City, Wisconsin, Arkham House, 1958.
Etchings in Ivory: Poems in Prose. Pasadena, California, Glenn Lord, 1968.
Singers in the Shadows. West Kingston, Rhode Island, Grant, 1970.
Echoes from an Iron Harp. West Kingston, Rhode Island, Grant, 1972.
A Song of the Naked Lands. N.p., Squires, 1973.
The Gold and the Grey. N.p., Squires, 1974.
Shadows of Dreams. West Kingston, Rhode Island, Grant, 1989.

Other

The Last Cat Book. New York, Dodd, Mead, 1984.
Robert E. Howard: Selected Letters, 1923-1930, edited by Glenn Lord, Rusty Burke and S. T. Joshi. West Warwick, Rhode Island, Necronomicon Press, 1990.
Robert E. Howard: Selected Letters, 1931-1936, edited by Glenn Lord. West Warwick, Rhode Island, Necronomicon Press, 1991.

*

Film Adaptations: *Conan the Barbarian,* 1981, *Conan the Destroyer,* 1984, *Red Sonja,* 1985, all inspired by Howard's stories although not based on specific books.

Bibliography: *The Last Celt: A Bio-Bibliography of Robert E. Howard* by Glenn Lord, West Kingston, Rhode Island, Grant, 1976.

Critical Studies (selection): *Conan's World and Robert E. Howard* by Darrell Schweitzer, San Bernardino, California, Borgo Press, 1979; *Dark Valley Destiny: The Life of Robert E. Howard* by L. Sprague de Camp, Catherine Crook de Camp and Jane Whittington Griffin, New York, Bluejay, 1983; *The Dark Barbarian—The Writings of Robert E. Howard: A Critical Anthology* edited by Don Herron, Westport, Connecticut, Greenwood Press, 1984; *One Who Walked Alone: Robert E. Howard, The Final Years* by Novalyne Price Ellis, West Kingston, Rhode Island, Grant, 1986; *Robert E. Howard* by Marc A. Cerasini and Charles Hoffman, Mercer Island, Washington, Starmont House, 1987.

*   *   *

That Robert E. Howard was neither a well-adjusted nor psychologically healthy individual is clear enough from the facts of his life: a brilliant young man with considerable literary ability, stifled in a backwater milieu, dominated by a stern father and an overwhelming mother, he expressed his pent-up rage in luridly violent pulp fantasies, then, as he had long planned to do, shot himself through the brain when his mother's death was imminent. It would be easy, then, to dismiss Howard as a neurotic, of perhaps clinical interest only, were his fiction not so massively popular for so long after his death. Hundreds of thousands, if not millions of copies of his books have been sold. Countless comic-book adaptations of his work (particularly the Conan series) persist. Three films, two of them starring Arnold Schwarzenegger as Conan and one starring Brigitte Nielsen as Red Sonja, have enjoyed commercial, if not critical, success. Howard is very nearly a major cultural figure. His influence on 20th-century fantasy is simply inescapable. While he may have had his antecedents, he effectively created and defined the sword-and-sorcery story. His barbarian hero is a pop archetype, as instantly recognizable as Tarzan or Sherlock Holmes.

H. P. Lovecraft commended his "description of vast megalithic cities of the elder world, around whose dark towers and labyrinthine nether vaults lingers an aura of pre-human fear and necromancy no other writer could duplicate." His vivid historical imagination—and his ability to identify emotionally with characters in the remote past—could just as readily be applied to the supernatural and non-historical. Thus, he wrote as intensely about British barbarians heroically resisting Roman invaders (in the Bran Mak Morn series) as he did about King Kull of Atlantis resisting the serpent-men of Valusia.

Gore certainly flowed across Howard's pages, to the extent that August Derleth facetiously suggested in the introduction to *Skull-Face and Others* that a collected Conan series would have to be printed on blood-red paper with accompanying thunderclaps; but there was far more to Howard, at least to the best of Howard, than sheer violence for its own sake. Howard romanticized the primitive, his ideas on the subject coming to their fullest fruition in the Conan series. Conan is a wild savage from the frozen wastes of Cimmeria—an analogue to a Viking or a barbarian Goth in Howard's pseudo-historical Hyborian Age—who has virtues and strengths lost to civilized men. With them, not to mention a strong arm, sheer ruthlessness and considerably more intelligence than is discoverable in most of his imitators, he is able to make himself king of Aquilonia, the chief civilized country of the day.

As Howard wrote the series, the stories come in random order, as if the great barbarian were standing by the author's side, relating his exploits as he chose to recall them. Later editing has neatly arranged them in chronological order, following the hero's career from his teens into his mid-40s, with pastiches and fragments completed by other writers (often to the dismay of purists). A purist re-editing, or de-editing, by Karl Edward Wagner for Berkley-Putnam, the first to restore the original title (and minor internal inconsistencies) to *The Hour of the Dragon,* ran for three volumes but was aborted before completion. The standard text therefore remains that edited by L. Sprague de Camp, pastiches and all. (But de Camp must be given credit for assembling and selling the series in paperback; without him, there would have been no Howard explosion in the 1960s, and all arguments would be moot.)

The strength of Howard's writing was its emotional intensity, coupled with an often poetic prose style that could reach great heights of descriptive vividness. (Not surprisingly, he was a poet of considerable ability.) His weakness was an inability to grasp reality, an immature attitude toward life that comes through in his characters, and often, due to limited education and cultural opportunities, blunders of ignorance and a certain narrowness of outlook, which caused him to adopt then-popular "Aryan" racial ideas uncritically, although without much of what the later 20th century would call racism. If blacks were incurably barbaric, that wasn't necessarily a bad thing in Howard's book.

Howard could be terribly sloppy, as when Conan is described as wearing three different kinds of helmet in a single chapter of *Conan the Conqueror* because Howard thought the three terms for them were synonyms, or when a character in a historical tale shoots Tamerlane with a pistol centuries before pistols were invented. The setting of the Conan series often seems like a series of movie sets:

the pirate movie, the thieves' quarter from *The Hunchback of Notre Dame,* the D. W. Griffith spectacle, etc. Anachronisms abound, leaving the reader to wonder why the Aquilonians, with their 14th-century plate armour and heavy cavalry, don't just trample over some of the surrounding peoples, whose technological level seems to be that of classical antiquity, or even before.

Understandably, Howard was far less successful writing stories set in the real world, although he sold many, to middle-level pulps, always falling short of the best markets, notably *Adventure* which was a life-long goal. Had he lived, he certainly would have matured as a writer, and probably moved more into historical and mainstream writing. He spoke of wanting to write a great epic of the American southwest. Instead, he is remembered almost entirely as a fantasist, for the Conan series most of all, but also for several other cycles, those of King Kull (a Conan prototype), Bran Mak Morn, and Solomon Kane (a 16th-century Puritan adventurer); along with a vast body of miscellaneous work ranging from a poor Edgar Rice Burroughs-imitation interplanetary novel (*Almuric*) to masterful Southern regional horror ("Pigeons from Hell").

—Darrell Schweitzer

HUBBARD, L(aFayette) Ron(ald)

Nationality: American. **Born:** Tilden, Nebraska, 13 March 1911. **Education:** George Washington University, Washington, D.C., B.S. in civil engineering 1934; Princeton University, New Jersey, 1945; Sequoia University, Ph.D. 1950. **Family:** Married Mary Sue Whipp; two daughters and two sons. **Career:** Wrote travel and aviation articles in the 1930s; explorer: Commander, Caribbean Motion Picture Expedition, 1931, West Indies Mineral Survey Expedition, 1932, and Alaskan Radio-Experimental Expedition, 1940. Director, Hubbard Foundation; founding director, Church of Scientology, 1952; director, Dianetics and Scientology, 1952-66; resigned all directorships, 1966. **Died:** 29 January 1986.

FANTASY PUBLICATIONS

Novels

Death's Deputy. Los Angeles, Fantasy, 1948.
Slaves of Sleep. Chicago, Shasta, 1948.
Triton, and Battle of Wizards. Los Angeles, Fantasy, 1949.
The Kingslayer (omnibus; includes "The Beast" and "The Invaders"). Los Angeles, Fantasy, 1949; as *Seven Steps to the Arbiter,* Chatsworth, California, Major, 1975.
Fear, and Typewriter in the Sky. New York, Gnome Press, 1951; London, Cherry Tree, 1952.
From Death to the Stars (omnibus; includes *Death's Deputy* and *The Kingslayer*). Los Angeles, Fantasy, 1953.
Fear, and The Ultimate Adventure. New York, Berkley, 1970.
The Case of the Friendly Corpse. Los Angeles, Bridge, 1991.

Short Stories

Lives You Wished to Lead But Never Dared, edited by V. S. Wilhite. Clearwater, Florida, Theta Press, 1978.

OTHER PUBLICATIONS

Novels

Buckskin Brigades. New York, Macaulay, 1937; London, Wright and Brown, 1938.

Final Blackout. Providence, Rhode Island, Hadley, 1948.

Return to Tomorrow. New York, Ace, 1954; London, Panther, 1957.

Battlefield Earth: A Saga of the Year 3000. New York, St. Martin's Press, 1982; London, Quadrant, 1984.

The Invaders Plan. Los Angeles, Bridge, 1985; London, New Era, 1986.

Black Genesis. Los Angeles, Bridge, and London, New Era, 1986.

The Enemy Within. Los Angeles, Bridge, and London, New Era, 1986.

An Alien Affair. Los Angeles, Bridge, 1986; London, New Era, 1987.

Fortune of Fear. Los Angeles, Bridge, 1986; London, New Era, 1987.

Death Quest. Los Angeles, Bridge, and London, New Era 1987.

Voyage of Vengeance. Los Angeles, Bridge, 1987; London, New Era, 1988.

Disaster. Los Angeles, Bridge, 1987; London, New Era, 1988.

Villainy Victorious. Los Angeles, Bridge, 1987; London, New Era, 1988.

The Doomed Planet. Los Angeles, Bridge, 1987; London, New Era, 1988.

Short Stories

Ole Doc Methuselah. Austin, Texas, Theta Press, 1970; London, New Era, 1993.

Poetry

Hymn of Asia: An Eastern Poem. Los Angeles, Church of Scientology, 1974.

Other

Dianetics: The Modern Science of Mental Health. New York, Hermitage House, 1950; London, Ridgway, 1951.

Science of Survival. Wichita and East Grinstead, Sussex, Hubbard, 1951.

Self Analysis. Wichita, International Library of Arts and Science, 1951.

Dianetics: The Original Thesis. Wichita, Wichita Publishing, 1951.

Handbook for Preclears. Wichita, Scientic Press, 1951.

Notes on the Lectures of L. Ron Hubbard. Wichita, Hubbard, 1951.

Advanced Procedure and Axioms. Wichita, Hubbard, 1951.

Scientology 8-80. Phoenix, Hubbard, and East Grinstead, Sussex, Scientology, 1952.

A Key to the Unconscious. Phoenix, Scientic Press, 1952.

Dianetics: The Evolution of a Science. London, Hubbard, 1953; Phoenix, Hubbard, 1955.

Scientology: A History of Man. London, Hubbard, 1953.

How to Live Though an Executive. Phoenix, Hubbard, 1953.

Self-Analysis in Dianetics. London, Ridgway, 1953.

Scientology 8-8008. London, Hubbard, 1953.

Dianetics 1955! Phoenix, Hubbard, 1954.

The Creation of Human Ability: A Handbook for Scientologists. Phoenix, Hubbard, and London, Scientology, 1955.

This Is Scientology: The Science of Certainty. London, Hubbard, 1955.

The Key to Tomorrow (selections), edited by U. Keith Gerry. Johannesburg, Hubbard, 1955.

Scientology: The Fundamentals of Thought. London, Hubbard, 1956.

Problems of Work. Johannesburg, Hubbard, 1957.

Fortress in the Sky (on the moon). Washington, D.C., Hubbard, 1957.

Have You Lived Before This Life? London, Hubbard, 1958; New York, Vantage, 1960.

Self-Analysis in Scientology. London, Hubbard, 1959.

Scientology: Plan for World Peace. East Grinstead, Sussex, Scientology, 1964.

Scientology Abridged Dictionary. East Grinstead, Sussex, Hubbard, 1965.

A Student Comes to Saint Hill. Bedford, Sidney Press, 1965.

Scientology: A New Slant on Life. London, Hubbard, 1965.

East Grinstead. East Grinstead, Sussex, Hubbard, 1966.

Introduction to Scientology Ethics. Edinburgh, Scientology, 1968; Los Angeles, Bridge, 1985.

The Phoenix Lectures. Edinburgh, Scientology, 1968.

How to Save Your Marriage. Copenhagen, Scientology, 1969.

When in Doubt, Communicate: Quotations from the Work of L. Ron Hubbard, edited by Ruth Minshull and Edward M. Lefshon. Ann Arbor, Michigan, Scientology, 1969.

Scientology 0-8. Copenhagen, Scientology, 1970.

Mission into Time. Copenhagen, Scientology, 1973.

The Management Series 1970-1974. Los Angeles, American Saint Hill Organization, 1974.

The Organization Executive Course. Los Angeles, American Saint Hill Organization, 8 vols., 1974.

Dianetics Today. Los Angeles, Scientology, 1975.

Dianetics and Scientology Technical Dictionary. Los Angeles, Scientology, 1975.

The Technical Bulletins of Dianetics and Scientology. Los Angeles, Scientology, 1976-86.

The Volunteer Minister's Handbook. Los Angeles, Scientology, 1976.

Axioms and Logics. Los Angeles, Scientology, 1976.

A Summary of Scientology for Churches. Los Angeles, Scientology, 1977.

The Book of Case Remedies. Los Angeles, Scientology, 1977.

What Is Scientology. Los Angeles, Scientology, 1978.

The Research and Discovery Series. Los Angeles, Scientology, 1980-86.

The Second Dynamic (selection), edited by Cass Pool. Portland, Oregon, Heron, 1981.

Self-Analysis. Los Angeles, Bridge, 1982.

Scientology: Fundamentals of Thought. Los Angeles, Bridge, 1983.

Dianetics: The Evolution of a Science. Los Angeles, Bridge, 1983.

The Problems of Work. Los Angeles, Bridge, 1983.

The Dynamics of Life. Los Angeles, Bridge, 1983.

The Way to Happiness. Los Angeles, Bridge, 1984.

Purification: An Illustrated Answer to Drugs. Los Angeles, Bridge, 1984.

The Learning Book. Copenhagen, New Era, 1984.

Child Dianetics. Los Angeles, Bridge, 1989.

Other texts and pamphlets published.

*

Bibliography: *The Fiction of L. Ron Hubbard* by William J. Widder, Los Angeles, Bridge, 1994.

Critical Studies: *Bare-Faced Messiah: The True Story of L. Ron Hubbard* by Russell Miller, London, Joseph, 1987; New York, Holt, 1988; *A Piece of Blue Sky: Scientology, Dianetics, and L. Ron Hubbard Exposed* by Jon Atack, London, Lyle Stuart, and New York, Carol, 1990.

*   *   *

For much of his pre-War career L. Ron Hubbard was primarily an adventure-story and western writer whose touches of offbeat human interest, knack for pithy characterization, and an at times by no means conventional approach to many of the genres he worked in (his western *Buckskin Brigades* is an unusual, and unusually fine, pro-Indian tale) elevated him out of the general pulp-fiction ruck. Yet like all pulp writers he played the field, and although most reference books note his entry into the fantasy market in 1938, when John W. Campbell recruited him into the *Astounding* stable, he had written in the genre before—notably "The Death Flyer" (*Mystery Novels Magazine,* April 1936), an excellent ghost story set in a lonely loggers' camp in northern Maine, which chillingly utilizes the recurring-fate motif (each year lost souls on a wrecked train must live again their final moments), and "Nine Lives," an hilarious tale about a seemingly death-proof cat, written for *Argosy* as part of a series of "hazardous occupations" stories (all later gathered into the first-rate collection *Lives You Wished to Lead But Never Dared*).

These two quite different modes point up a duality in Hubbard's general approach to story-telling; indeed, both in his imaginative fiction and in life there were, in essence, two quite distinct L. Ron Hubbards. There was the snook-cocker whose fantasy tales are a delight: full of swaggering derring-do, Rabelaisian jests, rollicking action, sword-fights and epic battles, all demonstrating much the same raffish charm as their creator. The other Hubbard was undoubtedly a tougher and in many ways less agreeable proposition, whose fantasy exhibits an altogether bleaker aspect of his muse. This dichotomy can be seen at the very start of his fantasy career, perhaps fuelled by John W. Campbell himself. Hubbard's first story for *Astounding,* "The Dangerous Dimension" (July 1938), is an out-and-out romp, farcically detailing the misadventures of the absent-minded and put-upon (his colleagues insult him, his housekeeper bullies him) boffin Dr. Henry Mudge, who cannot stop his wishes from coming true.

"The Tramp" (a three-part novella, *Astounding,* September-November 1938) revealed Hubbard's other persona. The story is built around the notion of the "evil eye," personified in the unfortunate hobo Doughface Jack, whose eyes have the dreadful power to cure or kill. There are few laughs; and even fewer in *Death's Deputy,* in which "Destruction" claims the soul of the hero, Clay McLean, transforming him into a living jinx whose very existence invites death to all around him. Only love can redeem him but, in an ironic climax, when it finally comes McLean dies, the curse transferring to his wife. Another curse is featured in the eerie oater "Shadows From Boothill" (*Wild West Weekly,* June 1940), which turns Chamisso's "shadowless man" idea upside down: Brazos, the half-breed killer fleeing Texan justice, has too many shadows, since he's also pursued, closely, by those of his victims.

Hubbard's notorious paean to Nietzschean values, the eternal-war science-fiction novel *Final Blackout,* is even grimmer, although its author, now, is shown to be a poor prophet, merely transporting an exaggerated version of World War One Flanders devastation a couple of hundred years into the future (there is some mention of "pneumatic rifles" but in the main the protagonists pitch into each other with .45 automatics, trench mortars, and planes whose motion and velocity are still, bizarrely, determined by propellers). Once lauded as a powerful piece of anti-war propaganda (chiefly, to be sure, by Hubbard himself), *Final Blackout* has lost its sting, its chief character, the (typically) nameless "Lieutenant," merely an ice-hearted and really rather tiresome *ubermensch* (Hubbard was fond of the type: Alan Corday in the excellent Einsteinian time-dilation tale *Return to Tomorrow* is cut from much the same cloth, but is an altogether more rounded, and thus sympathetic, figure).

Apart from the use of 1940s artefacts and slang, Hubbard's lighter fantasies (mainly for Campbell's matchless magazine *Unknown*) have not dated nearly so much; most are characterized by some ingenious plot-premises and twists (one or two of which were swiped from friends, colleagues, and even, possibly as a deadline hurtled towards him, himself). There is a mild obsession with *The Arabian Nights.*

In "The Ghoul" (*Unknown,* August 1939), a 50,000-word novella which really should have been book-formed by now, "Irish," the accident-prone (due to hyper-inquisitiveness) bellhop, unwittingly saves a group of invisible lost souls from the clutches of a sorcerer, then spends all his time fending said, and revenge-filled, sorcerer off. In what is probably Hubbard's most famous light fantasy, *Slaves of Sleep,* Jan Palmer is cursed by an enraged djinn to exist in two worlds: this one, and the parallel plane of sleep, in which he's a roistering buccaneer. In each world he just about sorts out besetting problems, including accusations of murder and the ministrations of a sinister psychiatrist. Hubbard's loathing of psychiatry (and communism) pretty well sabotages the never-reprinted post-War sequel, "The Masters of Sleep" (*Fantastic Adventures,* October 1950), which otherwise contains some splendid sea battles. But even exciting and actionful set-pieces cannot excuse ludicrous caricatures such as the crazed lobotomist Dr. Felix Dyhard ("insanity comes from thinking") of Balmy Springs.

Stevie Jebson, in *The Ultimate Adventure,* is electric-chaired by another mad scientist into a story by Scheherazade ("The City of Brass"), has a run-in with distinctly unfriendly ghouls (they eat people's heads), but, like many of Hubbard's heroes, finds the fantasy world he's trapped in more to his taste than reality, and becomes its ruler. Jules Riley in *The Case of the Friendly Corpse* similarly ends his days as king, in his case of a hellish dimension which Hubbard based on a cod prospectus for an infernal university dreamed up by two science-fiction fans (who both appear in the story). One of the best (of many) comic conceits in the novel concerns Riley's personal imp who makes a hash of resuscitating a corpse, mixing up the revival formula with the spell for winning friends and influencing people: the only partially re-animated corpse is powerfully attracted to Riley (hence the title). Alas, the ending is seriously flawed, Hubbard, perhaps at a loss for a denouement, bringing on Sir Launcelot (sic), King Arthur and the "true cross" to rout the villains. There is a similar "with-one-bound-he-was-free" absurdity in the climax to "Danger in the Dark" (*Unknown,* May 1939), in which the hero airily destroys the indestructible shark-god Tadamona with mere magnesium flares.

Hubbard never had the discipline or, indeed, tolerance for research of his fellow Campbell-protege L. Sprague de Camp, who, around this time, rescued a Hubbard short-story idea (ferocious Far Eastern jollop causes its drinker, like Alice, to become gigantic or micro-sized) in "The Last Drop" (*Astonishing Stories,* November 1941). No polymath (despite all protestations to the contrary by his Scientology adherents), Hubbard often needed his science sharpening up and de Camp obliged, supplying facts and figures as well as his usual overlay of irony. Though published in late 1941 the tale was written much earlier; perhaps in revenge Hubbard had de Camp's and Fletcher Pratt's hero Harold Shea gobbled up by a serpent in *The Case of the Friendly Corpse* (Pratt got his own back some years later by inserting a blow-by-blow account of an embarrassing incident in Hubbard's past—he'd been trapped aboard a yacht off the Alaskan coast by an enraged bear—into his own superb political fantasy *The Well of the Unicorn,* 1948).

Two other short stories needed no honing at all: "The Crossroads" (*Unknown,* February 1941), in which a farmer stumbles across an inter-temporal highway-intersection and trades off his fruit and vegetables for gold and nectar and weapons that haven't yet been invented; and his last tale for *Unknown,* the perfect, even elegiac, "The Room" (April 1942), in which the den of a wise old boonies' doc conceals a gateway, and an escape, to other dimensions.

One last rollicking fantasy is *Typewriter in the Sky,* in which the hero Mike de Wolf is hurled into his friend Horace Hackett's pulp pirate yarn "Blood and Loot" via a massive jolt of electricity. In the story, Mike has to battle the careless anachronisms Hackett (much like Hubbard himself, on occasion) throws into the action, knowing, too, that as he is the villain, Miguel de Lobo, at some stage he has to die. This is all good fun—made even funnier when one discovers that part of the actual story Hubbard sold Campbell was self-plagiarized from his own yarn "Under the Black Ensign," published five years earlier.

And finally there is *Fear,* Hubbard's masterpiece: a novel of perfectly controlled tension and terror in which Hubbard does not put a foot wrong. Everything that occurs to the unfortunate James Lowry (by no means a Nietzschean superman) in his search for his missing four hours, and his hat, in the otherwise comfortable groves of academe (the perfect setting for nightmare) is utterly, relentlessly, logical. And, what is worse, the horror throughout is entirely explicable. *Fear* is truly one of the outstanding dark-fantasy novels of the 20th century, written by, certainly, one of its more fascinating storytellers.

—Jack Adrian

HUFF, Tanya (Sue)

Nationality: Canadian. **Born:** 1957. **Education:** Ryerson Polytechnic Institute, B.A.A. in radio and television arts. **Career:** Bookstore owner, Toronto. **Address:** c/o DAW Books, 375 Hudson Street, 3rd Floor, New York, NY 10014-3658, USA.

Fᴀɴᴛᴀsʏ Pᴜʙʟɪᴄᴀᴛɪᴏɴs

Novels (series: The Novels of Crystal; Victory Nelson)

Child of the Grove (Crystal). New York, DAW, 1988.
The Last Wizard (Crystal). New York, DAW, 1989.
Gate of Darkness, Circle of Light. New York, DAW, 1989.
The Fire's Stone. New York, DAW, 1990.

Blood Price (Nelson). New York, DAW, 1991.
Blood Trail (Nelson). New York, DAW, 1992.
Blood Lines (Nelson). New York, DAW, 1993.
Blood Pact (Nelson). New York, DAW, 1993.
Sing the Four Quarters. New York, DAW, 1994.
Fifth Quarter. New York, DAW, 1995.

*   *   *

There is evidence that Tanya Huff did not plan a career as a writer. She graduated from Ryerson Polytechnical Institute with a degree in Radio and Television Arts. It was probably the bookstore she opened in Toronto (and still runs today), Bakka, that changed her mind. Her first fantasy, *Child of the Grove,* was followed by a sequel, *The Last Wizard,* and collectively they are known as the Novels of Crystal, after the wizard heroine of the story. *Child of the Grove* introduces Crystal, the next-to-last wizard of Ardhan, a little girl who has been bred specifically to save a world from the evil sorcerer Kraydak. As she grows into a woman, Crystal reconciles her position as princess with that of wizard, not always successfully. At the end of the book Kraydak is destroyed, and Crystal becomes the last wizard. In the second volume she discovers it isn't enough to destroy Kraydak, since he left behind some of his power. His stronghold must also be destroyed. Though she feels that she is alone in the world, Crystal finds friends by chance; the only friend she has ever had is the mysterious Lord Death, an immortal who fulfils his job with a great deal of compassion. He is in love with Crystal, though he hasn't admitted it. Through the chance saving of a wanderer named Jago, Crystal finds two friends in him and his brother, Raulin, who also falls in love with her. When she becomes Raulin's lover in fact as well as thought, Lord Death becomes immensely jealous and depressed, with the result that this immortal behaves in a humorously adolescent manner. These books were an impressive debut, and make highly entertaining reading.

They were followed by *Gate of Darkness, Circle of Light,* an urban fantasy about modern-day Toronto (where Huff lives). It is the story of Evan, an adept of the light, and his fight against an adept of the dark. In this he is assisted by a street musician, a young girl, a bag lady, a social worker, and a cat. This novel intersperses city living with the fantastic and was the precursor to Huff's later work about modern-day Toronto.

The Fire's Stone is more in the classic fantasy mould. This could be called a quest for the dysfunctional and involves three heroes, none older than 25, who must save their country from wizardly destruction. While the book has all the usual ingredients of fantasy, Huff's magic lies in her characters, and she surpasses herself here. Aaron, a clan heir from a country so bleak and a people so barbaric he has abandoned his life and legacy in order to become a master thief, arrives in the city of Ischia a few weeks before catastrophe is about to strike. By a strange quirk of fate and the friendship of an old woman who was once a master gem-cutter, Aaron is captured and rescued by Darvish, third prince of Ischia. Darvish is an impressive fighter, as tall, dark, and handsome as a prince should be. He is also a dissipated drunk, who will sleep with anyone, male or female, who comes his way. Darvish is particularly downhearted at present, because he has been ordered to marry a 17-year-old princess he has never met in order to cement an alliance between their countries. When the princess, also a powerful wizard, arrives at his palace to talk him out of marrying her, they are plunged into the quest. This is a humorous, hugely entertaining book with a good helping of tongue-in-cheek and a slap of feminism.

The quest itself involves the Fire Stone, stolen from its place above Darvish's city by a wizard who wants its power. He is too smart to touch the stone himself, however, and when the heroes find the actual thieves they discover them dead, burned up by the stone. There is a traitor in Ischia, who is collaborating with the wizard in order to find his own power. The entire kingdom will be destroyed by flooding, however, if the stone isn't recovered in time. The quest is enjoyable in itself, and the perils of the heroes are entertaining, but it is the interaction between the three—and their final, bizarre solution to their threesome—that is the best element of the story.

For the last few years, Huff has been working on a modern-day vampire series, set in Toronto. The first book, *Blood Price,* began the story of Victory Nelson, private detective, Michael Celluci, police sergeant, and Henry Fitzroy, bastard son of Henry VIII, romance writer and . . . vampire. Henry is the vampire-as-hero, the one every woman would like to meet. Handsome, dashing, vulnerable and a superhero, Henry leaves little to be desired except his daily disappearances. He doesn't kill for blood and still considers himself to be a good Catholic boy. Vicki Nelson is an ex-police detective cashiered due to failing eyesight caused by a deteriorating nerve disease that will eventually render her blind. Celluci is her sometime lover, and in this first volume Henry becomes her other love interest. This continues throughout the series, with Henry and Michael finally becoming allies and grudging friends. In *Blood Price,* a demon called up from Hell by a nerdish, vengeful, and psychopathic college student rages its way through the city on a killing spree. It is this demon that brings Vicki and Henry together; she has been selected as a sacrifice to it, and he can smell it and sense its evil presence long before he finds it.

The second volume *Blood Trail,* is the most delightful of the group and the least gory. Henry asks Vicki for her assistance when some friends of his are being murdered—friends who just happen to be werewolves. They live on a big sheep ranch in the Canadian countryside, and someone is picking them off with a long-range rifle while they run in wolf's clothing. The villains of this book are fundamentalist Christians who seek to rid the world of "demons," and nearly succeed until Henry, Vicki, and Mike save the werewolf family and bring down the psychos.

In *Blood Lines,* an Egyptian mummy unearthed in England is transported to a museum in Canada. Unknown to the museum curator there is an ancient curse and a warning to keep it in its sarcophagus—it is the remains of an evil wizard, and the soul is still trapped inside. When that soul is unwittingly released and takes possession of a human body, all Hades breaks loose in Toronto until Henry, Vicki, and Mike save the city. They must bring down the rejuvenated Anwar Tawfik before he takes over the Canadian government and turns the country into his version of a "paradise"— slaves at his beck and call, lots of babies and children to devour for their life-force, and many people ready to suffer horribly for the glory of the nasty, little god he serves.

The fourth book is *Blood Pact,* and it is the goriest and least enjoyable of the series. This one involves the supposed death by heart attack of Vicki's mother, who comes to discover her mother was actually murdered and has been reanimated as a zombie. The zombies are being made by the doctor who was Marjorie's boss at a large hospital, and by two graduate students—all crazy as loons. By the time Marjorie is finally laid to rest, Vicki has been mortally wounded and must be made into a vampire herself. Though this cures her nerve disease and restores her eyesight, it means she and Henry must live in different cities. She and Mike remain in Toronto,

after Vicki spends a year-in-training with Henry in Ontario, where she goes to live. A sad ending for this glorious threesome, but hopefully not the end of these wonderful novels.

—Debora Hill

HUGHART, Barry

Nationality: American. **Born:** Peoria, Illinois, 13 March 1934. **Education:** Columbia University, New York, B.A. in English 1956. **Military Service:** United States Air Force, 1956-60. **Career:** Technical representative, 1960-63, and vice president, 1963-65, Techtop Weapons; manager, Lenox Hill Bookshop, New York City, 1965-70. Since 1970, freelance writer. **Awards:** World Fantasy award, 1985. **Agent:** Martha Millard, 204 Park Avenue, Madison, NJ 07940, USA. **Address:** 2928 North Beverly Avenue, Tucson, AZ 85712, USA.

FANTASY PUBLICATIONS

Novels (series: Master Li and Number Ten Ox in all books)

Bridge of Birds. New York, St. Martin's Press, and London, Century, 1984.
The Story of the Stone. New York, Doubleday, 1988; London, Bantam, 1989.
Eight Skilled Gentlemen. New York, Doubleday, and London, Bantam, 1991.

*   *   *

Barry Hughart's three novels to date, *Bridge of Birds, The Story of the Stone* and *Eight Skilled Gentlemen,* are strongly reminiscent of Ernest Bramah's *Kai-Lung* books. They too are set in what is best described as a vision of China as it appeared to bemused westerners—a land crammed with bizarre superstitions and no less bizarre religious observances, enriched with a cuisine of extraordinary delicacy, and no less extraordinary ingredients; with a civil service where advancement depended exclusively on familiarity with the classics and corruption was not merely rife but institutionalized; with plastic and graphic arts of staggering beauty, coexisting with official torture of appalling barbarity; the land of a people as beautiful, cheerful and ingenious as any on Earth.

Hughart, whose approach is if anything even more erudite than Bramah's, has evoked this vision in a series of comedy mysteries wherein the Master Li Kao adopts a role not wholly unlike that of Sherlock Holmes, and his adventures are recounted by his Dr. Watson-style amanuensis and supplier of muscle, Number Ten Ox (though Watson was never expected to carry Holmes piggyback). The parallel with Conan Doyle is deliberate, and extends even to Li having a "slight flaw in is character" (bouts of uncontrollable drunkenness) quite as disastrous as Holmes's cocaine addiction, but the humour comes straight from Brahmah.

The books are difficult to quote from, as the effects generally depend on flights of fancy sustained beyond what would seem to be their utmost range. Consider this passage from Li's account of the human kidneys (of which there are four):

"The season of the kidneys is winter, and their orientation is north, and their element is water; their smell is putrid, their taste is salty, and their colour is black; their animal is the tortoise, their mountain is Hang-shan, and their deity is Hsuan-ming; their virtue is wisdom, their emotion is fear, and they make the low moaning sound yu; the emperor of the kidneys is Chuan-hsu, they take the spirit form Hsuan Yen—the two-headed stag commonly called Black Darkness—and of all body parts they are the most unforgiving. What have you been doing to these great and dangerous organs?"

And so on, for two splendid pages. No less brilliant is the occasion from *The Story of the Stone* when Li Kao invents a rocket-powered helicopter from first principles, and has Number Ten Ox build it from readily available local materials.

The success of the stories themselves is all the more remarkable as the combination of fantasy (or science fiction) and the mystery genre is notoriously difficult to handle: Alfred Bester managed it in *The Demolished Man,* but only by making the story hinge, not on *whodunnit?* but on *whydidhe?* Jack Vance failed with the Magnus Ridolph stories, and though *Araminta Station* is a marvellous book, the murder mystery is its weakest aspect. Hughart succeeds brilliantly.

The stories are far too complex and full of surprises for summaries to be practicable. They need not be taken seriously, only admired for their glorious scope and elan and the skill with which they are put together, but they have their depths, even so. The key lies in the unsurpassed urbanity of Hughart's style. This allows him, in *Bridge of Birds,* to begin a section with an account of the Chinese sword dance so beguiling as almost to compel belief; this modulates into a description of how an unquiet soul is laid to rest; from there to a very necessary murder in cold blood. All this is done in ten pages, and without the least sense of incongruity. Later, in among the fantasy and bawdry, a dying man offers a most dignified and touching prayer for his dead daughter, again with no sense that decorum has been broken and wholly without mawkishness.

The Story of the Stone includes a visit to Hell, a catamite of incomparable beauty, and a new variation on the old cliche about the man who is found dead without a mark on him, but with an expression of total horror on his face. All good clean fun; yet at its heart lies a beautiful little allegory about the redemptive power of love—Hughart's most favoured theme.

Eight Skilled Gentlemen (a traditional description of a boat-crew—the cox was deemed to be a player) begins with a grave robbing and involves a fraud in which rascally mandarins and palace eunuchs adulterate tea as never before. Ancient forgotten demigods are revived, and all strands are gathered together in a marvellous account of a boat race between mixed crews of natural and supernatural powers, but quite as much pleasure lies in the ornamentation. This includes as a minor character the murderer Sixth-degree Hosteler Tu, whose knowledge of Chinese cuisine is encyclopedic, and who cannot resist imparting it even when killing; a bedroom farce of baroque lubricity realized as a shadow play; what must be the most mouth-watering account of cannibal cookery in any literature; and for the scholarly a very rude in-joke about Horace's "Journey to Brundisium."

The background colour of cod chinoiserie is sustained at the highest level throughout, enlivened with sly jokes at the expense of western culture. Even the poetry (whether it owes more to Hughart's scholarship or his imagination) looks like a faithful translation of something that must have been magnificent in the original.

—Chris Gilmore

I

INGELOW, Jean

Nationality: British. **Born:** Boston, Lincolnshire, 17 March 1820.
Career: Poet, writer and editor; editor, *Youth's Magazine*. **Died:**
20 July 1897.

FANTASY PUBLICATIONS

Novels

Mopsa the Fairy. London, Longmans Green, and Boston, Roberts,
1869.

Short Stories

The Little Wonder-Horn. London, King, 1872.
The Little Wonder-Box. London, Griffith Farran, 1887.

OTHER PUBLICATIONS

Novels

Allerton and Dreux; or, the War of Opinion. London, Wertheim
and MacIntosh, 1857; New York, Garland, 1975.
Off the Skelligs. London, King, and Boston, Roberts, 1872.
Fated to be Free. London, Sampson Low, and Boston, Roberts,
1875.
Sarah De Berenger. London, 1879; Boston, Roberts, 1879.
Don John. London, Sampson Low, and Boston, Roberts, 1881.
John Jerome: His Thoughts and Ways. London, Sampson Low,
and Boston, Roberts, 1886.
A Motto Changed. New York, Harper, 1894.
Laura Richmond. London, Wells Gardner, 1901.

Short Stories

Tales of Orris. Bath, Binns, 1860; omitting one story, as *Stories
Told to a Child,* London, Routledge, 1865; Boston, Roberts,
1866.
Studies for Stories from Girls' Lives. London, Routledge, and Bos-
ton, Roberts, 1864.
Poor Matt; or, the Clouded Intellect. Boston, Roberts, 1866.
Deborah's Book and the Lonely Rock. 1867.
The Golden Opportunity. 1867.
The Grandmother's Shoe. 1867.
Little Rie and the Rosebuds, and Can and Could. 1867.
The Minnows With Silver Tails, and Two Ways of Telling a Story.
1867.
The Moorish Gold, and the One-Eyed Servant. 1867.
The Suspicious Jackdaw and the Life of John Smith. London, 1867.
The Wild-Duck Shooter, and I Have a Right. 1867.
A Sister's Bye-Hours. London, Routledge, and Boston, Roberts,
1868.

Very Young, and Quite Another Story. London, Longmans, and New
York, Munro, 1890.
The Black Polyanthus and Widow Maclean. London, Wells Gardner,
1903.

Poetry

A Rhyming Chronicle of Incidents and Feelings, edited by Edward
Harston. London, Longman, 1850.
Poems. London, Longman, and Boston, Roberts, 1863.
Home Thoughts and Home Scenes, with others. London, Routledge,
and Boston, Tilton, 1865.
Songs of Seven. Boston, Roberts, 1866.
A Story of Doom, and Other Poems. London, Longmans Green,
and Boston, Roberts, 1867; as *Poems: Second Series,* London,
Longmans, 1874.
Monitions of the Unseen: Poems of Love and Childhood. Boston,
Roberts, 1870.
The Shepherd Lady and Other Poems. Boston, Roberts, 1876.
One Hundred Holy Songs, Carols and Sacred Ballads. London,
Longmans Green, 1878.
Poems (revised editions of *Poems,* 1863, and *A Story of Doom and
Other Poems,* 1867). New York, 1880; London, 1893.
The High Tide on the East Coast of Lincolnshire. Boston, Rob-
erts, 1883.
Poems of the Old Days and the New. London, Longman, and Bos-
ton, Roberts, 1885.
Lyrical and Other Poems. London, Longmans, 1886.
The Old Man's Prayer. London, 1895.

*

Critical Studies: *Some Recollections of Jean Ingelow and Her Early
Friends,* London, Gardner Darton, 1901; *An Appreciation of Jean
Ingelow* by E. A. Stedman, London, 1935; *Jean Ingelow: Victo-
rian Poetess* by Maureen Peters, Ipswich, Boydell Press, 1972;
Forbidden Journeys by Nina Auerbach and U. C. Knoepflmacher,
Chicago, University of Chicago Press, 1992.

*   *   *

In her day, Jean Ingelow was regarded as one of the finest women
poets, so good in fact that her admirers petitioned for her to be
made Poet Laureate following the death of Lord Tennyson. Today
though, apart from "The High Tide on the Coast of Lincolnshire,
1571," which still appears in anthologies, her verse has been forgotten, and she is now best remembered for a long and complex
fairy story, *Mopsa the Fairy.*
    Ingelow was born and reared in Lincolnshire, the eldest of nine
children. Despite her father's early fortunes as a banker, later financial straits forced the family to move to London in 1863. Ingelow
had already begun to make a reputation for her poetry and short
stories, which had started to appear in 1850. Her collection of *Poems* issued in 1863 was an immense success, going through more
than 20 editions and selling around a quarter of a million copies.

She was respected in literary circles, especially by the Pre-Raphaelites, and was later termed the "lost Pre-Raphaelite". Millais illustrated her *Studies for Stories.* She shared with William Morris an intense passion for nature and the simple life away from industrial London, and this love of the countryside pervades her writing. She was also a devout Christian. An early novel, *Allerton and Dreux,* considered the clash of religious opinion, while a popular narrative poem, "A Story of Doom," considered the innocence of the world before the Flood.

Despite her early moralistic tales for children nothing quite prepared her readers for the sudden depth of *Mopsa the Fairy.* The title masks a deep and multi-layered novel which can be enjoyed superficially as a work for children, but also appreciated as a study of emerging relationships between adolescent boys and girls. It clearly owes its inspiration to Lewis Carroll's *Alice in Wonderland,* though is more akin to the work of George Macdonald, especially *At the Back of the North Wind.* All of these books were products of that remarkably fertile decade, the 1860s, which also saw publication of Charles Kingsley's *The Water-Babies.*

In *Mopsa the Fairy,* Jack discovers a nest of fairies and with the aid of an albatross seeks to return them to Fairyland via the wonderful river. The journey is filled with hazards and adventures. The fairies grow at a different rate than Jack and are thus rapidly full-grown. Jack learns something of the nature of Fairyland, which is our world but far back in history outside Time. About half-way through the novel Mopsa, one of the rescued fairies, suddenly matures and her presence begins to dominate the story. The novel becomes increasingly a tale of lost innocence, and explores the demands upon women to look after men who cling to their boyhood fantasies. Much of this is reflective of Ingelow's own childhood, having to help support the growing family, and perhaps also of a failed romance. She never married, but there are suggestions in her writings of loves lost. All of this makes *Mopsa the Fairy* more than just a quaint fairy tale; it can be seen as a subjective exploration of the pressures of adolescence on children. It could lay claim to being the first feminist fairy story.

Ingelow clung to the magic of *Mopsa* for one further collection of stories, *The Little Wonder-Horn,* which retains the same dream-like quality of that treasured glimpse of wonder soon to be lost and never repeated. The stories in this volume were later reprinted individually and reissued as booklets within a box called *The Little Wonder-Box,* a much valued item for Victorian children and highly collectible today.

After this flirtation with fantasy, Ingelow returned to more melodramatic fare, much of which is still respectable and unfortunately overlooked. *Off the Skelligs* is a tale of romance and strife in southwest Ireland, which saw a sequel, *Fated to be Free. Sarah De Berenger* is about a mother shamed by her convict husband. *Don John* considers the plight of two children exchanged at birth. In all of these works, as in *Mopsa,* Ingelow draws strong female characters and considers in depth the hardships of the world plagued upon women.

Ingelow continued to write poetry and stories until her death. By then the world had moved on and already her fiction was being overtaken by the gathering demands of the new century. But she always steadfastly believed that mankind's true happiness came from an appreciation of beauty, which she strove to paint in her writings.

—Mike Ashley

IRWIN, Margaret (Emma Faith)

Nationality: British. **Born:** London, 1889. **Education:** Clifto School, Bristol; Oxford University. **Family:** Married the artist Joh Robert Monsell in 1929. **Died:** 11 December 1967.

FANTASY PUBLICATIONS

Novels

Still She Wished for Company. London, Heinemann, 1924.
These Mortals. London, Heinemann, 1925.

Short Stories

Madame Fears the Dark: Seven Stories and a Play. London: Chatt & Windus, 1935.

OTHER PUBLICATIONS

Novels

How Many Miles to Babylon? London, Constable, 1913.
Come Out to Play. London, Constable, 1914; New York, Doran, 191£
Out of the House. London, Constable, and New York, Doran, 191€
Who Will Remember? New York, Seltzer, 1924.
Knock Four Times. London, Heineman, and New York, Harcour Brace, 1927.
Fire Down Below. London, Heineman, and New York, Harcour Brace, 1928.
None So Pretty. London, Chatto & Windus, and New York, Harcour Brace, 1930.
Royal Flush: The Story of Minette. London, Chatto & Windus, an New York, Harcourt Brace, 1932.
The Proud Servant: The Story of Montrose. London, Chatto & Windus, and New York, Harcourt Brace, 1934.
The Stranger Prince: The Story of Rupert of the Rhine. Londor Chatto & Windus, and New York, Harcourt Brace, 1937.
The Bride: The Story of Louise and Montrose. London, Chatto & Windus, and New York, Harcourt Brace, 1939.
The Gay Galliard: The Love Story of Mary Queen of Scots. Lon don, Chatto & Windus, 1941; New York, Harcourt Brace, 1942
Young Bess. London, Chatto & Windus, 1944; New York, Harcour Brace, 1945.
Elizabeth, Captive Princess. London, Chatto & Windus, and Nev York, Harcourt Brace, 1948.
Elizabeth and the Prince of Spain. London, Chatto & Windus, an New York, Harcourt Brace, 1953.

Short Stories

Mrs. Oliver Cromwell and Other Stories. London, Chatto & Windus 1940.
Bloodstock and Other Stories. London, Chatto & Windus, 1953 New York, Harcourt Brace, 1954.

Other

South Molton Street. London, Mate, 1927.

The Great Lucifer: A Portrait of Sir Walter Raleigh. London, Chatto & Windus, 1936; New York, Harcourt Brace, 1960.

* * *

Once Margaret Irwin had achieved her considerable literary success as a writer of historical novels she not unnaturally elected to specialize in that genre. Unfortunately, this decision robbed the fantasy genre of one of its most promising recruits; two of her early novels had been highly significant contributions to the remarkable flowering of British fantasy which took place in the decade following the end of the Great War, and the stories collected in *Madame Fears the Dark* also made elegant use of fantastic motifs in the construction of subtle black comedies.

Still She Wished for Company might be reckoned the archetype of a fascinating sub-species of fantastic fiction which exists in the borderlands of fantasy and historical romance: the timeslip romance. The story carefully interweaves the lives of two women living in different periods of time: Juliana Clare in 1779 and Jan Challard in the present. Each woman is initially perceived in the other's world as a phantom, but the barrier of time is further weakened by the occult experiments of Juliana's brother Lucian, in which she is used as a medium in order to obtain a more profound contact with Jan, who has haunted him since childhood.

In most stories of this kind the agent that cracks the barrier of time or otherwise renders it permeable is erotic attraction, construed as the kind of irresistible supernatural force which it sometimes seems to be to those who suffer its upheavals, but the situation is more complicated here. Insofar as Jan can be regarded as a literal or metaphorical "reincarnation" of one of the characters from the past, it is Lucian rather than Juliana to whom she is intimately linked, and the end-point towards which the narrative moves is not a transcendental union but rather a liberation which will free both Juliana and Jan from Lucian's unfortunate and life-threatening influence. The ending, although happy in its fashion and possessed of an undeniable moral propriety, is a curiously bittersweet one whose subtlety and originality are bound to make connoisseurs of fantasy regret that the author never returned to such themes as a more mature stylist. The two darkly ironic timeslip romances in *Madame Fears the Dark,* "The Earlier Service" and "The Curate and the Rake," were presumably written not long afterwards.

These Mortals is equally original and equally powerful, but is so little-known—in spite of being reprinted, along with its predecessor, in a uniform edition of Irwin's works issued in the 1950s—that it qualifies as one of the lost classics of English fantasy. It tells the story of Melusine, daughter of the enchanter Aldebaran, who is brought up in isolation in a lovely palace because he has long since tired of interfering in the lives of men. To her, the world of mortals is a place of legend which she longs to explore, and she cannot be satisfied with his summary judgment to the effect that "All the intricacies of their laws, their societies, their towns, their nations amount only to this: that each individual human being dreads solitude and tries to circumvent it". She must find this out for herself, and she does. A magic boat conveys her to a nation ruled by Eminondas and Adelisa, who welcome her with open arms when they see that her shoes are studded with diamonds, hopeful that she will be a good influence on their daughter Blanchelys and a suitable bride for their son Pharamond.

Melusine's ability to turn herself into a moonbeam helps her to penetrate the polite appearances of the court to discover the sad truth which underlies all the hypocrisies and illusions of its members. She evades the amorous pursuit of the gentlemen of the court but falls in love with the infinitely more virile Garth, a barbarian king entombed by Eminondas in a deep dungeon for refusing to marry Blanchelys. Unfortunately Blanchelys makes use of a magic spell unwisely entrusted to her by Melusine to fascinate and marry Garth, forcing Melusine to resort to a peculiarly convoluted strategy in order to win him back—which she succeeds in doing only with the greatest difficulty. Although the ending duplicates that of more conventional romances it carries the same unsettling and bittersweet undertones as the ending of *Still She Wished for Company* because the rhetoric of the story will not allow love to be any kind of all-encompassing solution for human ills. Aldebaran's dismissive judgment to the effect that love is merely "a prolonged struggle to find the happiness we desire in another because we have not found it in ourselves" is never contradicted, even though Melusine, in the end, cannot withstand its magical power. The vividly sardonic short story "Monsieur Seeks a Wife," which recounts the history of a hapless man's marriage to a witch-wife from the more familiar male point of view, retains a shadow of the same ambiguity.

After careful study of these two novels one can hardly help but suspect that Margaret Irwin might have had more than her fair share of disappointments in love before turning to literary work and might initially have been drawn to such endeavours as a way of working through her own intense but awkwardly mixed feelings. If so, it is intriguing to observe that her allegorical introspection achieved results quite different from those attained by other similarly inspired writers. In particular, these two novels may fascinatingly be compared to and contrasted with two early fantasies (one of them a timeslip romance) by another writer who likewise deserted fantasy in order to write highly successful historical novels: *The City Lies Four-Square* (1939) and *By Firelight* (1948) by Edith Pargeter—who is nowadays better known as "Ellis Peters." Whatever the experiential source of their emotional intensity and idiosyncratic philosophy, however, Margaret Irwin's fantasies are works of great distinction which are amply capable of rewarding the attention of modern readers.

—Brian Stableford

IRWIN, Robert (Graham)

Nationality: British. **Born:** Guildford, England, 23 August 1946. **Education:** Epsom College, Surrey; Oxford University, 1964-67; B.A. and M.A. in history. **Family:** Married Helen Elizabeth Taylor in 1972; one child. **Career:** Researcher at the School of Oriental and African Studies, London, 1967-72; lecturer in history at St. Andrews University, 1972-77, and part-time lecturer at other institutions in the years following. Fellow, Royal Asiatic Society, and Society of Antiquaries. **Agent:** Juri Gabriel, 35 Camberwell Grove, London SE5 8JA, England. **Address:** 39 Harleyford Road, London SE11 5AX, England.

FANTASY PUBLICATIONS

Novels

The Arabian Nightmare. Sawtry, Cambridgeshire, Dedalus, 1983; revised edition, London and New York, Viking, 1987.
The Limits of Vision. London and New York, Viking, 1986.

OTHER PUBLICATIONS

Novels

The Mysteries of Algiers. London and New York, Viking, 1988.
Exquisite Corpse. Sawtry, Cambridgeshire, Dedalus, 1995.

Other

The Middle East in the Middle Ages: The Early Mamluk Sultanate, 1250-1382. London, Croom Helm, and Carbondale, Southern Illinois University Press, 1986.
The Arabian Nights: A Companion. London, Allen Lane, and New York, Viking, 1994.

*

Robert Irwin comments:

A statement on my own work would be so portentous. A useful statement would assist the general reader in seeing through my work, thereby bringing the game to a premature end. However, to be portentous, all my novels are autobiographical and the first the most so. The three novels that are in print so far are dreams, tiny details and political disagreements can be seen (at least I see them that way) as parts of a single novel which should be completed in another two parts.

None of my novels fit comfortably in genre categories (alas, perhaps) and, superficially at least, I do not think that they resemble one another. In the end though I think that they are concerned with the powers of the imagination. But, whatever I think, I do not regard myself as the proprietor of the meaning of my work.

*   *   *

The Arabian Nightmare is a thoroughly modern fantasy cast in a classical mould. Its literary antecedents are *The Thousand and One Nights,* which first came to Europe in the French edition issued between 1704 and 1717 (on which Irwin has written the definitive critical commentary), and *The Saragossa Manuscript,* supposedly written by the Polish count Jan Potocki and allegedly first published in French in 1804. Each of these earlier works makes use of a discursive and convoluted narrative structure in which tales are embedded within other tales. The first displayed for fascinated Europeans an exotic, mysterious and highly intriguing Eastern world; the second has a most effective recurrent motif in that its hero, who goes to sleep beneath a gallows-tree, is victim of a terrible dream from which he continually awakes only to find that his awakenings are illusory moments of relief in a nightmare which will never let him go. Robert Irwin takes up this theme, of a man lost in a dream so tortuous he can never be certain that he has awakened, or ever will awake, and populates the dream in question with the phantasmagoria of that mythical Orient which so obsessed the French Romantic writers of the 19th century. Irwin brings to this task a remarkable freshness of outlook; he enlivens his consideration of the nature of dreams with ideas drawn from modern psychological inquiry, and he fills out his marvellous descriptions of 15th-century Cairo and its dream-analogue with details drawn from the illuminating perspective of modern historical studies. (He had previously built a considerable reputation as a scholar in the fields of Arabic Studies and Middle Eastern history.)

It is typical of the kind of deceptive scheme featured in *The Arabian Nightmare* that it can never become clear whether the dream into which the protagonist, Balian of Norwich, delivers himself really is the eponymous condition. That is a nightmare which, by definition, can never be remembered—and so, every time Balian thinks he awakes, he feels entitled to reassure himself that he has not, after all, suffered that dread fate . . . but while he only thinks that he awakes, he might indeed be its victim. In much the same way, the reader is invited to wonder who, within the tale, is its true teller . . . and every time a conclusion is there to be drawn it is quickly confounded. The text is thus engaged in a constant game of self-deconstruction which links it to the fancies of the latest generation of French Romantics, the Barthesian mythologists and Derrida-esque post-structuralists.

There never was another tale as self-conscious in its convolutions as this one, and never one which brought the unease of the dream-state into such seductively sinister intercourse with the intelligence of the reader. *The Arabian Nightmare* is a tale which reminds us, unremittingly, of the precariousness of our identity in the face of a world whose solidity and predictability might at any moment dissolve, and abandon us to be rent upon the rack of our anxieties. And yet, even while he taunts and undermines his readers with this cognitive vertigo, Irwin writes with great charm and suave wit, and almost compels us to believe that in nightmares—even though they be horrid—there is such wonder and such plenitude as would make a fool of any man who preferred jejune reality. There is no greater achievement towards which the literary fantasist might aim, and no modern writer has come closer than Irwin to realizing that achievement; in view of this it is rather extraordinary that the book first had to be issued by a small private press, and was only reprinted by a commercial publisher when it received a series of rave reviews.

The Limits of Vision makes a stark and frankly absurd contrast with *The Arabian Nightmare* in contracting its imaginative horizons to the paranoid fantasies of Marcia, a housewife engaged in a continuous war against the household dirt which—according to her arcane understanding—is actually the empire of the incarnate spirit of evil, Mucor. *The Limits of Vision* is a calculatedly silly book whose packaging is replete with warnings against the awful dangers to health and hygiene posed by "dirty books," and it is very funny, but it really is about "the limits of vision" and the unlimitedness of the human imagination. Marcia's imaginary dialogues with all manner of intellectual giants, and such parallel activities as the planning of a corrective sequel to *The Brothers Karamazov,* are certainly not without philosophical depth or existential bravery. The denouement's timely reminder that anyone who isn't paranoid in today's world must be stark raving mad makes the novel—potentially, at least—a considerable force for moral rearmament in the life of any person who finds housework intellectually and spiritually stultifying. (The only people who don't are, of course, the people who don't do it.)

Although Irwin's third novel, *The Mysteries of Algiers,* is a thoroughly satisfactory political melodrama, his return to more fantastic themes is eagerly awaited by those who believe that he has the potential to become the finest English fabulist of the *fin de siècle* period. Two fine short stories contained in the Dedalus anthologies *Tales of the Wandering Jew* (1991) and *The Dedalus Book of Femmes Fatales* (1992), "Waiting for the Zaddik" and "Singing

Underwater," demonstrate that he is capable of effective work in an altogether earnest vein. The former is a brilliantly bleak *conte philosophique*: a stark meditation upon the historical significance of the Holocaust.

—Brian Stableford

————

IVERSON, Eric. *See* **TURTLEDOVE, Harry Norman.**

————

JACQUES, Brian

Nationality: British. **Born:** Liverpool, 15 June 1939. **Education:** Attended Roman Catholic school in Liverpool. **Career:** Seaman, 1954-57; railway fireman, 1957-60; longshoreman, 1960-65; long-distance truck driver, 1965-75; docks representative, 1975-80; freelance radio broadcaster from 1980. Broadcasts for BBC Radio Merseyside include the music programmes "Jakestown" and "Saturday with Brian Jacques" and documentaries "We All Went Down the Docks," "Gangland Anthology," "The Eternal Christmas," "Centenary of Liverpool," "An Eyeful of Easter," "A Lifetime Habit," and "The Hollywood Musicals," a six-part series. Broadcaster for BBC Radio 1 and Radio 2; member of BBC Northwest Television Advisory Council. Presents humorous lectures at schools and universities. Patron of Royal Wavertree School for the Blind. **Awards:** National Light Entertainment award for Radio from Sony Company, 1982; Rediffusion award for Best Light Entertainment Programme on Local Radio, 1982; Parents' Choice Honour Book for Literature award, 1987; Children's Book of the Year award, Lancashire County Library, 1988; W.A. Young Readers Book award, 1991.

FANTASY PUBLICATIONS

Novels (series: Redwall in all books)

Redwall. London, Hutchinson, 1986; New York, Philomel, 1987.
Mossflower. London, Hutchinson, and New York, Philomel, 1988.
Mattimeo. London, Hutchinson, 1989; New York, Philomel, 1990.
Mariel of Redwall. London, Hutchinson, 1991; New York, Philomel, 1992.
Salamandastron. London, Hutchinson, 1992; New York, Philomel, 1993.
Martin the Warrior. London, Hutchinson, 1993; New York, Philomel, 1994.
The Bellmaker. London, Hutchinson, 1994.

Short Stories

Seven Strange & Ghostly Tales. London, Hutchinson, and New York, Philomel, 1991.

*   *   *

Well-known locally on his native Merseyside as a radio broadcaster, playwright and chronicler of native "Scouser" life, Brian Jacques achieved international prominence as a novelist thanks to his Redwall books. Aimed specifically at children, they feature an animal community centred around the mice of Redwall Abbey, with the ever-popular formula of quests, villains, slapstick humour and above all plenty to eat and drink. Their ready acceptance by children has been no real surprise. They mix excitement and comedy, are long enough for the satisfaction of expert readers while being episodic enough to keep reluctant readers interested, and above all provide that valuable bridge between the domestic adventures of the Enid Blyton school and the country of the imagination explored by the practitioners of the post-Tolkien role-playing-game novel. What is, perhaps, more unusual is that they have apparently been taken up by a somewhat older audience in the United States. It would seem that standard fantasy-adventure novels do not necessarily have to have human characters.

The world of Redwall is one centred upon the peace-loving but heroic mice and their allies: badgers, otters, hedgehogs and moles. Opposed are the more traditionally "verminous" woodland beasts: weasels, stoats, and above all rats. The books are animal fantasy partly in the Kenneth Grahame mould (these creatures wear clothes, wield weapons and act like humans). We have mice battling with wildcats and hedgehogs attacking foxes without any overt incongruity in size: this is an imaginative adventure sequence, not an exercise in realism. *Redwall* tells how the callow, clumsy Matthias saves the Abbey from the hordes of Cluny the Scourge by untangling a series of cryptic clues and turning out to be the appointed successor of the legendary Martin the Warrior. *Mossflower* provides the series with a history by telling the story of how Martin came from the north to save Mossflower from the tyranny of the wildcat rulers and was thus instrumental in the founding of Redwall Abbey. *Martin the Warrior* adds to our knowledge of the early life of the hero-mouse. *Mattimeo* reflects the plot of the first novel by having the son of Matthias kidnapped by a slave-trading fox and eventually proving himself also to be a true successor of Martin. *Mariel of Redwall* is set some generations between the times of Martin and Mattimeo and is about a warrior mousemaid who helps the mice and their allies to rid the seas of the piratical Searats led by the insane Gabool. Finally, *Salamandastron* combines three separate epics into one: the siege of the eponymous mountain by the treacherous Ferahgo the weasel, the theft of Martin's sword by one of the weasel's followers, and the quest to find a cure for the fatal sickness which comes to Redwall.

These stories are told in a narrative which mixes the character-cliche of children's comics with traditional Liverpudlian hearty sentimentality. The creatures of Redwall are, essentially, dramatic types. In *Redwall*, we have Basil Stag Hare, an indomitable, silly military type whose character is defined by his first name: that is, he uses expressions like "blighter," "what-what" and "m'dear feller." His comic speech and his greed when faced with a plate or three of delicacies are only equalled by his bravery: he is matched by the Hon. Rosie in *Mariel of Redwall* with her horsey guffaw. Moles speak in thick rustic dialect and are frequently deferential to the "gennelbeasts." Badgers are motherly and/or unbeatable warriors. There are also the infants: Baby Rollo in *Redwall* (a vole), Dumble in *Salamandastron* (a dormouse), and Baby Grubb in *Mariel of Redwall* (a mole) are indefatigably naughty, cheek their elders with innocent wisecracks, steal food and in general are lovable tornadoes of trouble. The general impression is of a juvenile carnival. Much play is made of the excellent cuisine on offer at Redwall, and fond descriptions of the characters' enjoyment of cakes and puddings (as well as the "October ale") take up a considerable amount of the text and allow opportunity for (literal) slapstick humour and good-natured barracking of each other's capacity to eat and drink.

Complementing this is a more melodramatic, even darker strand. While their spear-carriers are merely brutishly stupid, it is harder to laugh at Jacques's main villains, who are savage and cunning. Vermin are vermin: there can be no such thing as a good weasel or a sympathetic fox (though birds of prey such as eagles and falcons tend to be noble beasts). The disruption they threaten to the happy bucolic paradise is real. The action and fighting is the same as in any similar novel for an older readership. Redwall's inhabitants, for all their comic clownishness at the dinner-table, feel fear and experience danger. Characters whom the reader has come to find sympathetic and amusing are killed. When the stern badger Urthstripe confronts Farran, the poisoner-fox in *Salamandastron,* the tension is such that Jacques wisely leaves Urthstripe's retribution off-stage: we are at a different level from the humorous gothic and *Beano*-ish whackings offered by Samkim and Arula to their foes. To take the implications present here to their full extent would be to cross the line into fully adult violence.

While the plots are predictable, their twists and turns are enjoyable and Jacques milks them successfully for all the suspense he can. When eating and playing tricks his characters are children; when battling we are in young adult fighting-fantasy territory. Throughout (and elsewhere: in the stories in *Seven Strange and Ghostly Tales,* for example), a good-humoured but by no means unindulgent moral line is taken. In each of the "supernatural" stories a young miscreant gets his or her come-uppance as hinted at in the preceding doggerel rhymes. The Redwall stories offer a similar defence of traditional values of good behaviour, though one may look suspiciously at the species-specificity of evil, and the way the outsider "vermin" are punished for what in the Redwall infants is "high spirits" and "healthy naughtiness."

The success of these novels, then, is no surprise, nor is it undeserved. The hearty gusto of the epic is one which inspires enough suspension of disbelief to join in the game and genuinely enjoy the experience. In both the writing and the themes of the stories there is a nostalgia for a kind of innocently old-fashioned storytelling which creates an atmosphere of Greyfriars School meeting H. Rider Haggard. Only rarely does this nostalgia undercut the sense of knockabout adventure fantasy. Children's literature needs this kind of lengthy, involving, clear-cut read—and there is no shame in bringing adults along for the ride as well.

—Andy Sawyer

JAKES, John (William)

Pseudonyms: William Ard; Alan Payne; Jay Scotland. **Nationality:** American. **Born:** Chicago, Illinois, 31 March 1932. **Education:** DePauw University, Greencastle, Indiana, A.B. 1953; Ohio State University, Columbus, M.A. in American Literature 1954. **Family:** Married Rachel Ann Payne in 1951; three daughters and one son. **Career:** Copywriter, later promotion manager, Abbott Laboratories, North Chicago, 1954-60; copywriter, Rumrill Company, Rochester, New York, 1960-61; freelance writer, 1960-65; copywriter, Kircher Helton and Collett, Dayton, Ohio, 1965-68; copy chief, later vice-president, Oppenheim Herminghausen and Clarke, Dayton, 1970-71; creative director, Dancer Fitzgerald Sample Company, Dayton, 1969-70. Since 1971, freelance writer. Writer-in-residence, DePauw University, 1979; Research Fellow, Department of History, University of South Carolina, 1989. **Awards:** Ohio Governor's award, 1977, 1989. LLD., Wright State

University, Dayton, 1965; D.Litt., DePauw University, 1977; L.H.D., Winthrop College, 1985; L.H.D., University of South Carolina, 1993. **Address:** c/o Rembar and Curtis, Attorneys, 19 West 44th Street, New York, NY 10036, USA.

FANTASY PUBLICATIONS

Novels (series: Brak the Barbarian; Gavin Black)

Brak the Barbarian Versus the Sorceress. New York, Paperback Library, 1969; as *Brak the Barbarian—The Sorceress,* London, Tandem, 1970.
Brak the Barbarian Versus the Mark of the Demon. New York, Paperback Library, 1969; as *Brak the Barbarian—The Mark of the Demons,* London, Tandem, 1970.
The Last Magicians. New York, New American Library, 1969.
Masters of the Dark Gate (Gavin Black). New York, Lancer, 1970.
Mention My Name in Atlantis. New York, DAW, 1972.
Witch of the Dark Gate (Gavin Black). New York, Lancer, 1972.
Brak: When the Idols Walked. New York, Pocket Books, 1978.

Short Stories

Brak the Barbarian. New York, Avon, 1968; London, Tandem, 1970.
The Fortunes of Brak. New York, Dell, 1980.

OTHER PUBLICATIONS

Novels

The Texans Ride North (for children). Philadelphia, Winston, 1952.
Wear a Fast Gun. New York, Arcadia House, 1956; London, Ward Lock, 1957.
A Night for Treason. New York, Bouregy, 1956.
The Devil Has Four Faces. New York, Bouregy, 1958.
This'll Slay You (as Alan Payne). New York, Ace, 1958.
The Impostor. New York, Bouregy, 1959.
Johnny Havoc. New York, Belmont, 1960; London, Severn, 1990.
Make Mine Mavis (as William Ard). Derby, Connecticut, Monarch, 1961.
And So to Bed (as William Ard). Derby, Connecticut, Monarch, 1962.
Give Me This Woman (as William Ard). Derby, Connecticut, Monarch, 1962.
Johnny Havoc Meets Zelda. New York, Belmont, 1962; as *Havoc for Sale,* New York, Armchair Detective Library, 1990.
Johnny Havoc and the Doll Who Had "It". New York, Belmont, 1963; as *Holiday for Havoc,* New York, Armchair Detective Library, 1991.
G. I. Girls. Derby, Connecticut, Monarch, 1963.
When the Star Kings Die. New York, Ace, 1967.
Making It Big. New York, Belmont, 1968; as *Johnny Havoc and the Siren in Red,* New York, Armchair Detective Library, 1991.
The Asylum World. New York, Paperback Library, 1969; London, New English Library, 1978.
The Hybrid. New York, Paperback Library, 1969.
The Planet Wizard. New York, Ace, 1969.
Secrets of Stardeep (for children). Philadelphia, Westminster Press, 1969.

Tonight We Steal the Stars. New York, Ace, 1969.
Black in Time. New York, Paperback Library, 1970.
Mask of Chaos. New York, Ace, 1970.
Monte Cristo #99. New York, Curtis, 1970.
Six-Gun Planet. New York, Paperback Library, 1970; London, New
English Library, 1978.
Time Gate (for children). Philadelphia, Westminster Press, 1972.
On Wheels. New York, Paperback Library, 1973.
The Bastard. New York, Pyramid, 1974; as *Fortune's Whirlwind*
and *To an Unknown Shore,* London, Corgi, 2 vols., 1975.
Conquest of the Planet of the Apes (novelization of film script).
New York, Award, 1974.
The Rebels. New York, Pyramid, 1975; London, Corgi, 1979.
The Seekers. New York, Pyramid, 1975; London, Corgi, 1979.
The Furies. New York, Pyramid, 1976; London, Corgi, 1979.
The Titans. New York, Pyramid, 1976; London, Corgi, 1979.
The Patriots (omnibus; includes *The Bastard, The Rebels*). Day-
ton, Ohio, Landfall Press, 1976.
The Warriors. New York, Pyramid, 1977; London, Corgi, 1979.
The Pioneers (omnibus; includes *The Seekers, The Furies*). Day-
ton, Ohio, Landfall Press, 1977.
The Lawless. New York, Jove, 1978; London, Corgi, 1979.
The Americans. New York, Jove, 1980; London, Fontana, 1989.
The Bastard Photostory (with photos from television movie based
on *The Bastard*). New York, Jove, 1980.
Excalibur! (with Gil Kane). New York, Dell, 1980.
North and South. New York, Harcourt Brace, and London, Collins,
1982.
Secrets of Stardeep, and Time Gate (omnibus). New York, New
American Library, 1982.
Love and War. New York, Harcourt Brace, 1984; London, Collins,
1985.
Heaven and Hell. New York, Harcourt Brace, 1987; London,
Collins, 1988.
California Gold. New York, Random House, 1989; London, Collins,
1990.
Homeland. Garden City, Doubleday, and London, Little Brown,
1993.

Novels as Jay Scotland

The Seventh Man. New York, Bouregy, 1958.
I, Barbarian. New York, Avon, 1959; revised edition (as John
Jakes), New York, Pinnacle, 1976.
Strike the Black Flag. New York, Ace, 1961.
Sir Scoundrel. New York, Ace, 1962; revised edition, as *King's
Crusader,* New York, Pinnacle, 1977.
The Veils of Salome. New York, Avon, 1962.
Arena. New York, Ace, 1963.
Traitors' Legion. New York, Ace, 1963; revised edition, as *The
Man from Cannae,* New York, Pinnacle, 1977.

Short Stories

The Best of John Jakes, edited by Martin H. Greenberg and Jo-
seph D. Olander. New York, DAW, 1977.
The Best Western Stories of John Jakes, edited by Martin H.
Greenberg and Bill Pronzini. Athens, Ohio University Press,
1991; as *In the Big Country: The Best Western Stories of John
Jakes,* New York, Hall, 1993.

Plays

Dracula, Baby (lyrics only). Chicago, Dramatic Publishing Com-
pany, 1970.
Wind in the Willows, adaptation of the novel by Kenneth Grahame.
Elgin, Illinois, Performance, 1972.
A Spell of Evil. Chicago, Dramatic Publishing Company, 1972.
Violence. Elgin, Illinois, Performance, 1972.
Stranger with Roses, adaptation of his own story. Chicago, Dra-
matic Publishing Company, 1972.
For I Am a Jealous People, adaptation of the story by Lester del
Rey. Elgin, Illinois, Performance, 1972.
Gaslight Girl, music by Claire Strauch, book and lyrics by John
Jakes. Chicago, Dramatic Publishing Company, 1973.
Pardon Me, Is This Planet Taken? Chicago, Dramatic Publishing
Company, 1973.
Doctor, Doctor!, music by Gilbert M. Martin, adaptation of a play
by Molière. New York, McAfee Music, 1973.
Shepherd Song. New York, McAfee Music, 1974.
A Christmas Carol, adaptation of the novel by Dickens (produced,
1989-93).

Other

Tiros: Weather Eye in Space. New York, Messner, 1966.
Famous Firsts in Sports. New York, Putnam, 1967.
Great War Correspondents. New York, Putnam, 1968.
Great Women Reporters. New York, Putnam, 1969.
Mohawk: The Life of Joseph Brant, illustrated by Roger Hane. New
York, Crowell Collier Press, 1969.
Susanna of the Alamo: A True Story (for children), designed and
illustrated by Paul Bacon. San Diego, Gulliver Books, 1986.

Editor, *New Trails.* New York, Doubleday, 1994.

*

Film Adaptations (all TV mini-series): *The Bastard,* 1978; *The
Rebels,* 1979; *North and South,* 1985; *North and South: Book II,*
1986, from the novel *Love and War; Heaven and Hell—North and
South: Book III,* 1994.

Bibliography: in *The Best Western Stories of John Jakes,* edited
by Martin H. Greenberg and Bill Pronzini, Athens, Ohio University Press, 1991.

Manuscript Collections: University of Wyoming, Laramie; Thomas Cooper Library, University of South Carolina, Columbia.

Critical Study: *The Kent Family Chronicles Encyclopedia,* edited
by Robert Hawkins, New York, Bantam, 1979.

*   *   *

Today, John Jakes is a thoroughly respectable author who writes
articles for *Parade* magazine extolling the virtues of libraries and
who, as a kind of all-American James A. Michener, generates vast
historical epics glamorizing and mythologizing America's past by
describing fictional families whose members conveniently happen
to meet the legends of American history or conveniently happen to
participate in its major events. One could argue such novels are

fantasies in spirit, perhaps not entirely unrelated to Jakes's earlier careers in the netherworlds of popular fiction; it is amusing to speculate, for example, that the name Kent was chosen so that an imagined conclusion to the Kent Family Chronicles could describe Jonathan and Martha Kent adopting the alien child who would become the greatest American hero of them all, Superman.

But the focus here must be on Jakes's pure fantasy works, beginning with the most prominent skeleton in his closet—Brak the Barbarian. Though obviously inspired by Robert E. Howard's Conan, Brak is in every way a pale imitation, lacking Conan's distinctive manner of speech, eagerness for battle, or lust for beautiful women. Instead, all the calm and phlegmatic Brak ever wants to do is to continue travelling south, where, he believes for some reason, he will find his "destiny". Unfortunately, there is always a loathsome monster or sinister sorceress blocking his path; or, more often, a conniving individual will somehow coerce, cajole, or bribe Brak into fighting some supernatural evil. At times, Brak can defeat his enemy with only his broadsword and brute strength; at other times, when his opponent serves the evil god Yob-Haggoth, Brak may require timely assistance from priests of the Christian-like "Nameless God". Of Brak's ten stories and three novels, "The Barge of Souls" is perhaps the best: Brak is forced to take the place of both the body and soul of a dead prince, ritualistically riding in a boat with the wife's corpse down to a deadly waterfall. He is saved when the wife's ghost finally locates her late husband's true spirit in the blood on the sword of the treacherous companion who killed him and destroyed his body. Here, Brak himself is as uninvolving as ever, but his plight is unusually imaginative and evocative. (In 1969 Jakes declared that he had already plotted—and reserved for later publication—a final Brak adventure where he finally reaches the south; if so, fans of Jakes's historical novels may someday be in for a big surprise.)

The singleton *Mention My Name in Atlantis* is subtitled in full: "Being, at Last, the True Account of the Calamitous Destruction of the Great Island Kingdom, Together with a Narrative of Its Wondrous Intercourses with a Superior Race of Other-Worldlings, as Transcribed from the Manuscript of a Survivor, Hoptor the Vintner, for the Enlightenment of a Dubious Prosperity". It offers a more colourful and lively Conan figure, Conax the Chimerical, who shares the original's florid speech and brutal passions; but the character is gently satirized as the unwelcome and disruptive companion of the narrator, Hoptor the "Vintner"—actually a procurer, who calls his women his "vintages"—as he struggles to stay alive in the corrupt and decadent capital of Atlantis. This is undoubtedly Jakes's most enjoyable fantasy, highlighted by Hoptor's amusingly defensive accounts of his own indefensible actions. However, the novel's science-fictional elements—aliens who visit Earth searching for the "Fluid of Life," which turns out to be wine, and finally take the Atlanteans back to their world and destroy the continent—are rather less successful. *The Last Magicians,* another singleton, is the muddled tale of Cham, one of the two remaining Red Magicians now displaced by the more benevolent Blue Magicians, who is unwillingly recruited to battle the other Red Magician now raising armies of zombies in a desperate effort to avoid defeat; with the help of a little Blue Magic, he finally though illogically succeeds. And the short story "Machine" (in *The Best of John Jakes*) is an early—and routine—horror tale about a man who believes that his toaster, like other machines, is inhabited by an evil spirit; when he tries to destroy the toaster, its spirit then takes over his body.

Jakes's second fantasy series, featuring a soldier turned newsman named Gavin Black, began infelicitously with *Master of the Dark Gate.* Bronwyn, the untrustworthy resident of a parallel world, enlists Black to destroy the "Gate" linking our world to another parallel Earth where evil rulers conspire to destroy and repopulate our Earth; a few passages of pseudo-scientific explanations can be ignored as strictly perfunctory. The novel exemplifies what James Blish called the idiot plot, kept in motion only because everyone involved is an idiot. For example, from the very beginning Black's enemy, the despicable and effeminate Tarn, knows that Black is carrying a sword and explosive device inside his artificial leg; yet when he captures Black, Tarn allows him to keep those weapons. Later, after Tarn finally musters the common sense to take them away, he sportingly decides to give them back, ultimately enabling Black, of course, to achieve victory. Only marginally better is the sequel, *Witch of the Dark Gate,* where Bronwyn manipulates Black into visiting another parallel world in a supposed effort to locate Black's lost love and Bronwyn's missing daughter; cruelly abandoned by Bronwyn, Black is left to assist residents against an invasion force from Tarn's world. The novel ends with Black worried about a coming final confrontation with residents of the other Earth, obviously preparing readers for a third volume that never appeared—due, one suspects, to the absence of popular demand.

Since his characteristic fantasy plot features a reluctant hero tricked by disreputable people into doing good deeds, one is tempted to interpret these works autobiographically—Jakes picturing himself as a reluctant writer tricked by disreputable editors and publishers into writing fantasies. Certainly, while his fantasies can have interesting and creative moments, only *Mention My Name in Atlantis* seems to have been written with any genuine enthusiasm for the task. Therefore, while Brak always sought to go south, Jakes has undoubtedly benefited, both financially and aesthetically, from his decision to go west.

—Gary Westfahl

JAMES, John

Nationality: British. **Born:** 1924(?) in Wales. **Education:** Selwyn College, Cambridge, M.A., 1950. **Family:** Married Helen Mary Norman; one son, one daughter. **Career:** Civil servant, England, 1949—; writer. **Died:** 1993.

FANTASY PUBLICATIONS

Novels

Votan. London, Cassell, 1966.
Not For All the Gold in Ireland. London, Cassell, 1968.

OTHER PUBLICATIONS

Novels

Men Went to Cattraeth. London, Cassell, 1969.
Seventeen of Leyden. London, Cassell, 1970.
The Lords of Loone. London, Cassell, 1972.

The Bridge of Sand. London, Hutchinson, 1976.
Talleyman. London, Gollancz, 1986.
Talleyman in the Ice. London, Futura, 1987(?).

Other

The Paladins (social history of the Royal Air Force). London,
Futura 1991.

* * *

With some exceptions, there's a very fuzzy dividing line between,
say, a Celtic fantasy novel and a Celtic historical novel. The exceptions include the far too many fantasy novels which, historically,
are rubbish; and those historical novels which eschew the supernatural, and are often the duller for it. And then, in a category of
his own, there's John James.

John James wrote both straight historical novels and humorous
rewrites of legends. His attitude to magic and the supernatural was
straightforward: the people of the time believed in it, therefore (for
them at least) it existed; religion was as much a vital but commonplace marvel of their daily lives as electric light and the telephone
are of ours. He's been quoted as saying, "Roman religion is about
giving the god his dinner on time, with all the proper words and
ceremonial, in case he starts an earthquake. Greek religion is about
saying, 'This place feels creepy; there must be a god about. Let's
think up a story as to why this should be.'"

Even in his least fantastic early historical novel, the tragic *Men
Went to Cattraeth,* the post-Romano-British army setting out around
500 AD to destroy the invading Saxon "savages" look for omens
in the clouds, and the poet Aneirin, the narrator, accepts as fact that
the Roman Wall dividing England from Scotland "was raised in
one night, complete from sea to sea, by the magician Vergil, at the
bidding of King Hadrian."

The Bridge of Sand is ostensibly a straight story, of the soldier-
poet Juvenal, under orders from Agrippa in 80 AD, taking his troupe
of cavalry and infantry to find the supposed land bridge between
Britain and Ireland, the land of gold. On the way, though, Juvenal
meets first a goddess, then a whole bunch of gods, and accepts
them as a normal part of his adventure, no different from hunting
deer or having a battle. The author doesn't attempt to put forward
any "rational" explanation—tricks of the light, drugged food, the
effects of alcohol—which might occur to the sceptical 20th-cen-
tury reader. James is relating the narrator's experience; Juvenal believes he meets gods so, so far as James is concerned, he does
meet gods.

John James's best-known novels are humorous retellings of myth,
featuring a Romanized Greek adventurer, Photinus. *Votan* begins:

Well, if you really want to know how it was I came to
be chained to an oak tree, half-way up in the middle of
nowhere, with wolves trying to eat me out of it, I'll tell
you . . . go down to any of the taverns around the Praetorian
barracks and listen to what the soldiers sing . . .

High the Allfather
Hung in the hornbeam;
Nine days and no drinking,
Nine nights and no nurture . . .

or:

Alfege the Earl, Odin-born,
Great in guile, wise in war . . .

I often go down there and listen. It never crosses their
minds that it was only me all the time. Half the songs are
about me; the other half I made up myself, anyway.

Photinus, a doctor, leaves Vindabonum to wander through Europe, blending into legends and leaving them behind him. Eventually he reaches the Aser (Æsir) in the Halls of Asgard, where he
makes an enemy of Loki and, at some point, loses an eye; he goes
on to Britain, where he meets Taliesin, the last of the bards; he
returns to Asgard, and gets involved in adventures and schemes
and wars, culminating in the fall of the Halls of Asgard. Photinus
becomes Votan, Woden, Odin.

Votan is a humorous novel, but it makes some serious points. It
shows how myths are made; how Votan, who believes in and meets
the Allfather, but knows himself to be but a man, sometimes finds
it convenient to let people believe he's more than that; how people
see what they expect to see, and believe what they want to believe,
with a little encouragement; how a little trickery can go a long way.
But primarily the novel is fun, an irreverent romp through Germanic mythology.

Not For All the Gold in Ireland is closer to other writers' Celtic
fantasy novels in that it is based on *The Mabinogion.* Like most
sequels it has to live in the shadow of its forerunner; if it suffers at
all, it's only because of the brilliance of *Votan.* Photinus the Greek,
fresh from his travels through Europe as Votan, the Germanic/Norse
god, takes the name Mannanan as he travels through Britain and
Ireland in his quest to gain a monopoly on the gold trade with Ireland.

In a story loosely based on one of the tales of *The Mabinogion,*
Mannanan makes shoddy shoes, shields and saddles with his companion Pryderi, sups merrily with both Roman soldiers and British
fighters, matches wits several times with Gwawl, sees the God,
the Muse, the Awen come upon his scruffy mate Taliesin the Druid,
meets and marries Rhiannon . . . and all this and more before he
even sets foot on the Island of the Blessed—where things don't go
quite according to plan . . .

Like *Votan,* this book is a humorous recasting of, in this case,
second-century AD history and legend, and where one starts and
the other leaves off, or where the author casts both aside and lets
his imagination run wild, is never easy to spot and doesn't matter a
fig anyway. John James knows his period, and knows how to have
fun with it. It is a shame that, because of poor sales, publishers
have not taken up his unpublished works, which apparently include a humorous Arthurian novel, *The Fourth Gwenevere,* and two
more Photinus books, one telling the story of "what really happened at Pompeii," and the other having Photinus journey to Africa
and China. Sadly, we're unlikely ever to have the pleasure of reading these.

—David V. Barrett

JEFFERIES, Mike

Nationality: British. **Born:** Farnborough, Kent, 11 September
1943; raised partly in Australia. **Education:** Hurstmere Secondary

School, Sidcup, Kent, 1954-59; University of London, Goldsmiths School of Art, 1961-65; diploma in illustration. **Career:** Illustrator, medical artist, graphic designer, art teacher; rider in international equestrian competitions. **Family:** Married Sheila Elizabeth Billings in 1981; three step-children. **Agent:** Howard Morhaim Literary Agency, 175 Fifth Avenue, New York, NY 10010, USA. **Address:** The Old Swan, Great Massingham, Norfolk PE32 2JA, England.

FANTASY PUBLICATIONS

Novels (series: Loremasters of Elundium; Heirs to Gnarlsmyre)

The Road to Underfall (Elundium). London, Fontana, 1986; New York, Harper and Row, 1990.
Palace of Kings (Elundium). London, Collins, 1987; New York, Harper and Row, 1990.
Shadowlight (Elundium). London, Fontana, 1988; New York, Harper and Row, 1990.
Glitterspike Hall (Gnarlsmyre). London, Fontana, 1989; New York, Harper, 1991.
Hall of Whispers (Gnarlsmyre). London, Fontana, 1990; New York, Harper, 1992.
Shadows in the Watchgate (Gnarlsmyre). London, Grafton, 1991; New York, Harper, 1992.
Hidden Echoes. London, Grafton, 1992; New York, Harper, 1993.
Stone Angels. London, HarperCollins, 1993; New York, HarperCollins, 1994.
Children of the Flame. London, HarperCollins, 1994.

*   *   *

Despite the publication of nine novels, Mike Jefferies is one of the least able of contemporary British fantasy writers. His main shortcoming is the lack of credibility in his characters and plots, though this is closely followed by his penchant for melodrama and his inability to write natural dialogue.

Loremasters of Elundium is an awkward and unrewarding trilogy of heroic high fantasy, with some magic used on both sides. A weak king, Holbian, fails to deal decisively with the armies of darkness, so a new hero (and king-in-waiting) is required. This is Thane, a 15-year-old boy who is at first ridiculed and tormented as a kind of Cinderella figure. He is addressed as "child" by most adults. Yet he is given the chance to take a message from King Holbian to an outlying fortress, and this becomes a rite-of-passage journey during which Thane learns to be a warrior. Within a year, it seems, this boy has done many great deeds and succeeded Holbian. Yet he still has the final battle to fight, against Kruel, the magically created and swift-growing champion of evil.

Throughout, everything is plot-driven, with almost no space devoted to character development. Thus the large numbers of characters remain simply as names, one batch blandly good and the other batch wholly evil. Jefferies makes the mistake of using everybody's viewpoint, often changing viewpoints several times within a page; he even uses the viewpoints of horses and owls. Indeed, the first volume of the trilogy is very horse-oriented, with as much regard being given to them as to the humans.

Dialogue is a problem area here; the author tries to put too much information into dialogue and ends up with characters declaiming pompous and overlong speeches at each other, even in the heat of battle.

The two Heirs to Gnarlsmyre volumes are somewhat dismal in mood. The plot of *Glitterspike Hall* revolves around a succession problem, with Lord Miresnare's eldest daughter, Marrimian, wanting to succeed him and to rule over the city of Glor and the unpleasant marshes of Gnarlsmyre. But such a feminist desire is heresy, and almost everyone is opposed to Marrimian, including most of those living in the castle (Glitterspike Hall itself), in Glor, and on the marshes. Marrimian's nasty sister Pinvey supports the marshman Mertzork in his bid for the throne.

At the end of the book Marrimian does, indeed, seize the throne and Miresnare is killed. Then, in *Hall of Whispers,* her problem becomes one of feeding everybody and at the same time of convincing people to support her against Mertzork and Pinvey. Of course, Marrimian triumphs easily in the end against her evil antagonists. An awkwardness is that Marrimian is helped by Krann, the reincarnated good aspect of Kruel, who caused so much trouble in Elundium towards the end of the previous trilogy. He has wandered away from Elundium to sort out his thoughts and has come across Gnarlsmyre by chance. It is plot developments such as this which rob Jefferies' books of credibility.

Although there are occasional good ideas here, they are all spoilt. Excitement is marred by melodramatic presentation; a feminist theme is unfortunately lost. *Glitterspike Hall* fails to be a frightening place because it contains too many bloodthirsty animals to be credible. *Hall of Whispers,* in particular, is too predictable, with too many characters and viewpoints, too much aimless rushing around. It is notable only for the development of a trend towards horror in Jefferies' novels. Even in his fantasy he tends to dwell upon killings, tortures, rapes and disagreeable sights (for example the opening up of a room in which three of Marrimian's sisters have starved to death).

Jefferies' other four novels are all separate, with contemporary settings. It is easier to think of them all as fantasy, though *Hidden Echoes* contains science-fiction elements while the other three all have supernatural horror themes and *Stone Angels* in particular could be described as horror rather than fantasy. *Shadows in the Watchgate* is set mostly in present-day Norwich in the county of Norfolk. A mad taxidermist named Ludo Strewth gets his spells wrong, causing his collection of stuffed animals to come to life and claw people to death in one of the oldest parts of Norwich. Then Strewth spots Tuppence Trilby, an American photographic model who has just bought an old house in Norwich, and he is determined to stuff her, as part of his collection. She is aided by troops of cavalry from displays in a local museum, brought back to life by that same wayward magic. Caught in a museum fire started by Strewth, Tuppence is rescued by the soldiers and by Dec Winner, a part-time fireman who is really a handsome, unmarried chemical engineer, capable of producing a powder to kill the various resurrected beasts. Alas, Tuppence shoots Strewth dead.

The hero of *Hidden Echoes* is Denso Alburton, a fantasy writer. Together with a publisher from New York, Harry Murmers, and an attractive female scientist, Mya Capthorne, Alburton is taken forcibly into another world, full of clocks, where time is stored. To avoid the risk of this being thought of as a science-fiction novel, Jefferies opens up various cracks in reality so that all manner of nasty mythical monsters can slip through and threaten Earth. As ever, a happy ending is contrived at the last minute.

There is no doubt that Jefferies does have good ideas. *Stone Angels* could potentially have been an above-average horror novel. The idea that Norwich Cathedral could have two life-size carvings of angels capable of coming to life, a dark angel trying to please the devil by killing people as a blood sacrifice and a white angel trying to stop him, is worthy of development. It is such a pity that Jefferies chose a pair of totally unsympathetic main characters and then, perhaps realizing this, added a totally implausible one to complement them. Jarvin Mandrake, a young man not yet recovered from a nervous breakdown and whose favourite pastime is getting drunk, is appointed as resident archaeologist at Norwich Cathedral (because his uncle is a bishop). With the help of Joni, a young female vagrant, he uncovers the activities of the dark angel, Abaddon, and discovers why the white angel, Shateiel, is incapable of controlling him. Everybody is against Jarvin except Martyn Burr, the local doctor, who provides money, accommodation, laboratory testing facilities and even a pistol, just when they are required. The whole plot is full of conveniences like this, right to the end, where it is discovered that Abaddon's host of demons can be killed by being splashed with water from a holy spring. The author tries, somewhat unsuccessfully, to make the reader side with Jarvin and Joni and against various authority figures connected with the cathedral.

It would be nice to report that the historical scenes in *Children of the Flame* are similarly worth reading, since there are quite a number of them. Unfortunately, they are not. The complex plot centres around a curse cast in France in 1347 upon the two children of Lord Cerventis, the local nobleman, for his treatment of two young sisters found trespassing on his land. The one sister, Aglia, calls up the witch Hecate from hell, who casts the curse. Some protection from the curse is obtained, but each time these two souls are reincarnated they are threatened with eternal damnation by the ghostly presences of the two sisters and Cerberus (the three-headed dog). A British woman and an American pilot were threatened in 1942 and discovered or remembered enough of the curse to be able to avoid it. But the current couple to be reincarnated (Joel and May, born in 1972) are trying to find out how to fight off their ghostly adversaries. Eventually they find out enough to be able to cancel the curse entirely.

The main problems here are two-fold: the hauntings are standard, predictable stuff, and the reader knows all the answers while Joel and May do not, which removes much of the suspense. The plot is held together by coincidences of time and place which help to destroy credibility. Also, while the reader's sympathies are meant to be with Joel and May, they are in fact with Aglia and her sister Harlonis, so badly treated for such a minor transgression.

Mike Jefferies, who is art college-trained, has illustrated his own books and is probably more talented as an artist than as a novelist.

—Chris Morgan

JONES, Diana Wynne

Nationality: British. **Born:** London, 16 August 1934. **Education:** Friends' School, Saffron Walden, Essex, 1946-53; St. Anne's College, Oxford, 1953-56, B.A. 1956. **Family:** Married J.A. Burrow in 1956; three sons. **Awards:** *Guardian* award, 1978; Boston *Globe-Horn Book* Honor Book award, 1984, 1986. **Agent:** Laura Cecil, 17 Alwyne Villas, London N1 2HG. **Address:** 9 The Polygon, Clifton, Bristol BS8 4PW, England.

FANTASY PUBLICATIONS

Novels (series: Chrestomanci; Dalemark; Howl)

Wilkins' Tooth, illustrated by Julia Rodber. London, Macmillan, 1973; as *Witch's Business,* New York, Dutton, 1974.
The Ogre Downstairs. London, Macmillan, 1974; New York, Dutton, 1975.
Eight Days of Luke. London, Macmillan, 1975; New York, Greenwillow, 1988.
Cart & Cwidder (Dalemark). London, Macmillan, 1975; New York, Atheneum, 1977.
Dogsbody. London, Macmillan, 1975; New York, Greenwillow, 1977.
Power of Three. London, Macmillan, 1976; New York, Greenwillow, 1977.
Charmed Life (Chrestomanci). London, Macmillan, and New York, Greenwillow, 1977.
Drowned Ammet (Dalemark). London, Macmillan, 1977; New York, Atheneum, 1978.
The Spellcoats (Dalemark). London, Macmillan, and New York, Atheneum, 1979.
The Magicians of Caprona (Chrestomanci). London, Macmillan, and New York, Greenwillow, 1980.
The Homeward Bounders. London, Macmillan, and New York, Greenwillow, 1981.
The Time of the Ghost. London, Macmillan, 1981.
Witch Week (Chrestomanci). London, Macmillan, and New York, Greenwillow, 1982.
Archer's Goon. London, Methuen, and New York, Greenwillow, 1984.
Fire and Hemlock. New York, Greenwillow, 1984; London, Methuen, 1985.
Howl's Moving Castle. London, Methuen, and New York, Greenwillow, 1986.
The Lives of Christopher Chant (Chrestomanci). London, Methuen, and New York, Greenwillow, 1988.
Castle in the Air (Howl). London, Methuen, 1990; New York, Greenwillow, 1991.
Black Maria. London, Methuen, 1991; as *Aunt Maria,* New York, Greenwillow, 1991.
A Sudden Wild Magic. New York, Morrow, 1992.
The Crown of Dalemark (Dalemark). London, Mandarin, 1993.
Hexwood. London, Methuen, 1993; New York, Morrow, 1994.

Short Stories

Who Got Rid of Angus Flint?, illustrated by John Sewell. London, Evans, 1978.
The Four Grannies, illustrated by Thelma Lambert. London, Hamish Hamilton, 1980.
Warlock at the Wheel and Other Stories. London, Macmillan, and New York, Greenwillow, 1984.
Chair Person, illustrated by Glenys Ambrus. London, Hamish Hamilton, 1989.
Wild Robert, illustrated by Emma C. Clark. London, Methuen, 1989; Boston, Hall, 1992.
Yes, Dear, illustrated by Graham Philpot. London, Collins; New York, Greenwillow, 1992.
Stopping for a Spell, illustrated by Joseph A. Smith. New York, Greenwillow, 1993.

Other

Editor, *Hidden Turnings: A Collection of Stories Through Time and Space.* London, Methuen, 1989.

OTHER PUBLICATIONS

Novels

Changeover. London, Macmillan, 1970.
A Tale of Time City. New York, Greenwillow, and London, Methuen, 1987.

Plays

The Batterpool Business (produced London, 1967).
The King's Things (produced London, 1969).
The Terrible Fisk Machine (produced London, 1970).

Other

The Skiver's Guide, illustrated by Chris Winn. London, Knight, 1984.

*

Film Adaptations: *Archer's Goon,* 1992 (TV serial).

*   *   *

Possibly the best British children's fantasy writer, Diana Wynne Jones's novels are possessed of an exuberance that enchants. Aimed primarily at readers between 10 and 14 years old, the books hold a fascination for the adult reader too, in part because of the author's willingness to tackle adult issues, in part because of the complex characterization and richly plotted background. As with Joan Aiken, Jones's most outstanding skill, evident in the Chrestomanci series (*Charmed Life, The Magicians of Caprona, Witch Week* and *The Lives of Christopher Chant*), is her ability to make magic and the fantastic seem normal. This was first seen in her earlier novel, *The Ogre Downstairs,* a relatively simple story of step-siblings forced to deal with each other when their new chemistry sets prove more interesting than expected, and has reached new levels of complexity and sophistication with her more recent work, such as *Howl's Moving Castle* and *Castle in the Air.*

Whilst many writers attempt to tackle large issues in ways children will understand, Jones is adept at making these issues the context of the plot rather than weighing the novel down with pedagogic intent. *Dogsbody,* the story of a star sent down to earth as a dog to recover a lost tool, manages to tackle the issues of racial prejudice, loneliness in many different forms, and terrorism, all with great humour and sympathy, and without forgetting the humanity of those on the wrong side or distracting from the adventure mystery which is the meat of the novel. *Archer's Goon* manipulates sibling rivalry, adult fallibility and the complexities of town management with a bubbling humour which surprisingly compliments the novel's tension. This ability to combine humour and threat is a hallmark of Jones' writing which has become a stronger thread in her later novels as her intended readership appears to have become slightly older. *Black Maria,* a tale of witchcraft, baby werewolves and sleeping heroes in an otherwise innocent-seeming fishing village, is suffused with underlying threat, whilst the running scarecrow in *Howl's Moving Castle* is both amusing and terrifying.

In addition to the single novels, Jones has written two sequences, the Chrestomanci sequence and the Dalemark series. The Chrestomanci sequence is set in a alternative world where magic works and is legal. Logically, therefore, the government has to be involved in regulating magic and Chrestomanci, the off-stage hero in the first three of these novels, is the principal civil servant responsible. That Jones manages to make civil servants interesting to the younger reader is a testimony to her skill; that she does this by boring her young heroes and heroines reinforces this. The main action in all four novels revolves around a range of young people learning the scope of their own talents and adapting to the responsibilities talent implies, from Cat (*Charmed Life*), who must learn not to rely on his sister, to Tonino and Angelica (*The Magicians of Caprona*), who find that doing things differently may be an advantage, to the children in *Witch Week* whose irresponsibility threatens their own lives and those of their teachers. The Dalemark sequence is very different, being more conventional other-world fantasy, with quests, lost princes, a magical musical instrument and a number of gods. Although the four novels, *Cart & Cwidder, Drowned Ammett, The Spellcoats,* and *The Crown of Dalemark* are linked, all but the last of these can be read independently. *Cart & Cwidder* is perhaps the lightest in tone, centred on a family of travelling musicians making their way through the repressive South of Dalemark. *Drowned Ammet,* which details the escape of three very different children from the South, is a confusing book, full of moral uncertainties but retaining the strong sense of adventure and tension. *The Spellcoats,* a story of prehistoric Dalemark, is the most sinister and frightening, with none of the humour which a fan of Diana Wynne Jones has come to expect.

Similarly lacking in humour is Jones' *Fire and Hemlock,* aimed at an older, perhaps later teenage audience. Inspired by the ballad of Tam Lin, *Fire and Hemlock* is more than just a retelling in modern dress, but the book still feels constrained by the need to retell an already told story. One nice touch, however, are the books which Polly, the heroine, receives from Tom Lynn over the years, "the things they told me in the bookshop that nobody should grow up without reading." Whether they spark off beloved memories or send you scurrying to the bookshop or library, a fair number of them should be found elsewhere referenced in this volume.

Jones' recent novel, *A Sudden Wild Magic,* returns to the idea of alternative worlds existing side by side and to that exuberant humour which characterizes much of her work. A secret coven of witches, in a very ordinary Britain, protects the country from invasion and all things perilous. However, the coven has discovered that the world is threatened by an outside power, Arth, which is inflicting various stresses on the planet, most notably global warming. Earth, it seems, is being used for experimentation by the mages who run Arth: the problems faced by Arth are being duplicated on Earth, so that the mages can learn from the solutions which Earth comes up with. It is all justified in the name of science and the belief that Earth is not as "real" as Arth. To combat this, the coven sends through a crack team of women to break the resolve of the all-male mages. To add to the ensuing chaos, the team inadvertently take with them a stowaway, the sister of one of the coven leaders, a single parent with her toddler in tow. The novel is chaotic, its form fitting the magic which the plot lets loose, and, as with Jones' earlier novels, effortlessly feminist.

—Farah Mendlesohn

JONES, Gwyneth. *See* HALAM, Ann.

JONES, Jenny

Nationality: British. **Born:** Essex, 1954. **Address:** c/o Gollancz, The Cassell Group, Wellington House, 125 Strand, London WC2R 0BB, England.

FANTASY PUBLICATIONS

Novels (series: Flight Over Fire)

Fly by Night (Flight Over Fire). London, Headline, 1990.
The Edge of Vengeance (Flight Over Fire). London, Headline, 1991.
Lies and Flames (Flight Over Fire). London, Headline, 1992.
The Webbed Hand. London, Point Fantasy, 1994.
The Blue Manor. London, Gollancz, 1995.

*   *   *

Jenny Jones's earliest books consisted of the trilogy collectively entitled Flight Over Fire. The three volumes, *Fly by Night, The Edge of Vengeance,* and *Lies and Flames,* add up to one long novel.

Eleanor Knight, female yuppie, finds herself transported to Chorolon, a world remote in space and time, where she becomes embroiled in the conflict of the Cavers (followers of Asret, the Moon, driven from their homes to live in a cave-system on a desolate island where it is always dusk and never stops raining) and the Peraldonians (followers of Lycias, the Sun, and very much in control). The Sun and Moon entities are allegorical but also personal creations: people can engage them in conversation, though at considerable risk; the Gods lie.

Eleanor is there only because a Caver magical ritual has gone wrong, but the fact of being brought over in such a way has invested her with a Lunar power which she is unable to control. Altogether, Eleanor is a well-conceived heroine: sufficiently selfish, lazy, petulant, and vain for most readers to find some community of spirit and to afford plenty of scope for improvement through adversity.

So far, so conventional; but though the plot is simple in essence, Jones uses a complex approach. Sun and Moon have at one time lived in harmony, but the balance has been destroyed by Lucian Lefevre, solar high priest but also an evil magician, who has trapped the Bird of Time, creating Stasis. Physical laws have given place to magic, somewhat in the manner of Roger Zelazny's *Jack of Shadows;* now no one ages or dies from natural causes, but very few are born and all creativity has been leached from the world.

For those who are young and handsome and not especially creative or imaginative, this state of affairs has much to offer; the conflict is by no means a straight fight between Good and Evil. Moreover, even among the Cavers and those others who wish to break the Stasis, the unnatural character of their lives has worked a subtle deformation; because they cannot age or bear children, they can no longer love as once they did, yet they still feel the lack. To delineate this, Jones switches viewpoint among many subsidiary characters, a strategy which pays off handsomely, especially in the case

of Lady Nerissa, a woman for whom religious observance has become an end in itself, obscuring the purpose which once it served.

Eleanor's story is counterpointed with that of Phinian Blythe, a soldier of the Peraldonians, whose wife is treacherously murdered by Lefevre in order to maintain the Stasis. She is pregnant but the Stasis is fragile and could be broken by the introduction of too much new life. Blythe changes sides, and both main characters become embroiled in a series of bloody skirmishes as Eleanor embarks, most unwillingly, on the quest which she has been set—to release the Bird of Time, and so destroy the Stasis.

Jenny Jones is good at scenes of violence and torture (the novel has a high body-count), but there is nothing thud-and-blunder about the writing, and she concentrates on the mental anguish which torture entails. She's good on all the less happy emotions, especially those deriving from guilt, remorse, and betrayal, and has a fine line in natural and supernatural monsters, the creations of Lefevre. These include Skarrak (who shifts form between spider-mantis and an unnaturally beautiful woman clothed in golden light), and the Fosca, an earthier variant on Tolkien's winged Nasghul, balanced by the Arrarat, intelligent, telepathic, giant hawks allied with the Cavers. After one or two longueurs in the first 50, the book sustains a cracking pace for 1100 pages.

This is not achieved without cost; Jones tailors her locales to her characters' mental states, so that the symbolism of stormy cliff-top, echoing dead city or scent-steeped boarding-house bedroom becomes the mood of the action and engulfs the players. The writing gains vividness, but the novel tends to fragment into scenes; despite Jones's great skill as she shuttles back and forth between scattered groups, their obsessions exist against the background, rather than in the context, of the attempts first to break, then to reimpose the Stasis. No major character fails to come under a curse or into the grip of an obsession, but the great variety and vivacity of the writing tends to obscure the unifying factors for characters and reader alike. Though all the elements come together in a suitably gory climax, the convergence does look a trifle forced.

The same could be said of *War and Peace,* but Jones also loses some credibility in her social organization. Even in the near timelessness of her world, the durability of the contending factions (including many people already old when the Stasis began), without natural replenishment, is hard to swallow. One gets a sense that they have been preserved to make the conflict more interesting. The author also has a habit of declaring that a character has only been slightly wounded after we've seen what looks like a clear enough account of his murder. In Jones's world it's unwise to bet on anyone's death if you haven't dismembered the corpse yourself—and even that doesn't always work.

Despite its occasional failures of integration, Flight Over Fire is an extraordinary achievement for a first novel, demonstrating a vivid imagination, an assured command of the language and a broad emotional range. Jenny Jones's potential is formidable, and we look forward to its realization.

—Chris Gilmore

JORDAN, Robert

Pseudonym of James Oliver Rigney, Jr. **Nationality:** American. **Born:** Charleston, South Carolina, 1948. **Education:** Military College, South Carolina, degree in physics. **Military Service:** United States Army, 1968-70; served in Vietnam, awarded Distinguished Flying Cross and Bronze Star. **Career:** Freelance writer since 1977. **Address:** c/o Tor Books, 175 Fifth Avenue, New York, NY 10010, USA.

FANTASY PUBLICATIONS

Novels (series: Conan; The Wheel of Time)

Conan the Invincible. New York, Tor, 1982; London, Sphere, 1984.
Conan the Defender. New York, Tor, 1982; London, Sphere, 1984.
Conan the Unconquered. New York, Tor, 1983; London, Sphere, 1985.
Conan the Triumphant. New York, Tor, 1983; London, Sphere, 1985.
Conan the Magnificent. New York, Tor, 1984; London, Sphere, 1986.
Conan the Destroyer (novelization of screenplay). New York, Tor, 1984; London, Sphere, 1985.
Conan the Victorious. New York, Tor, 1984; London, Sphere, 1987.
The Eye of the World (Wheel of Time). New York, Tor, and London, Orbit, 1990.
The Great Hunt (Wheel of Time). New York, Tor, 1990; London, Orbit, 1991.
The Dragon Reborn (Wheel of Time). New York, Tor, 1991; London, Orbit, 1992.
The Shadow Rising (Wheel of Time). New York, Tor, and London, Orbit, 1992.
The Fires of Heaven (Wheel of Time). New York, Tor, and London, Orbit, 1993.
Lord of Chaos (Wheel of Time). New York, Tor, and London, Orbit, 1994.
The Conan Chronicles (omnibus; includes *Conan the Invincible, Conan the Defender, Conan the Unconquered*). New York, Tor, 1995.

*   *   *

"Nobody alive writes Conan better than Robert Jordan," pronounced L. Sprague de Camp, keeper of the flame as far as Robert E. Howard's barbarian swordsman is concerned, and obviously one who should be a good judge of sequels by other hands. For years, Robert Jordan was known only as a Howard/Conan pasticheur, and it was a task he performed with undoubted relish. His additions to the best-known of all sword-and-sorcery sagas are vigorous, lusty, and full of excellent scene setting.

Jordan's original series, the open-ended sequence of Wheel of Time books, is an absorbing and solid epic set in a world where magical power comes from two complementary, equal but separate sources, *saidin* and *saidar,* male and female. However in the previous age there was a titanic struggle against personified evil, who was imprisoned by the male power-wielders, and the backlash of the struggle tainted the male half of the source so that now only female magicians can operate safely: the male ones find their powers warped and they are driven into madness. A sect of female magicians devote themselves to finding and "gentling" such men, cutting them off from their powers forever.

Jordan's protagonist, Rand, is very much the typical questing hero: from a small village with small horizons, he is ambivalent about leaving home and facing the world. He has a mysterious secret, that his father isn't his father (but then what hero's is?) and a knack of being rescued from life-threatening situations by handy flashes of lighting which make it pretty clear from day one that he is going to turn out to be a male magic-wielder and more than likely the Dragon Reborn, the messianic figure of legend.

In *The Eye of the World,* the first of the series, Rand, his two friends Perrin and Mat, his feisty girlfriend Egwene and the village wisewoman Nynaeve, leave home with Moraine, a female mage, and her bodyguard Lan (who is so Aragon-like it is no surprise at all when he is revealed as an uncrowned king). Both women turn out to have an inborn ability to tap into the female power and Mat has the luck of the devil and Perrin a wild talent with wolves: this is no ordinary group. They flee various forms of nastiness all intent on the three boys who are the centre of the pattern, the weave of history—this refrain is repeated so often you begin to think the only reason they are so important is that every power source in the world is determined to recruit, destroy, or otherwise acquire them. They find the source of the power, the eponymous Eye, and defeat their particular devil with surprising ease. Loose ends abound ready for the many sequels.

In the second book, *The Great Hunt,* the emphasis is on the youthful lead characters continuing with their various kinds of esoteric training. The women manage to fall for a pretty obvious trap when they are captured by invaders from over the sea who have a device which enables them to enslave magic-wielders by use of a restraining leash. However, having fallen for it, they get matter-of-factly on with rescuing each other—and continue to believe that they are far more capable of rescuing their menfolk than vice versa.

The Dragon Reborn, volume three, has a pantomime ending in which Rand, Mat, Moraine, the other women and Rand's desert-dwelling followers the Aiel (in the real world) and Perrin, his dead wolf-friend and his new girlfriend (in the equivalent area of the dream world) *all* arrive coincidentally, separately, and simultaneously at the site of the final battle. Jordan almost pulls it off by using Rand's ability to act as a sort of distorting influence on history to create coincidences elsewhere in the plot—but not quite. He seems to have lost control of his plot somewhat in this volume, so its weave is beginning to show holes, principally the gaping hole at the centre that he creates by letting Rand wander off with no one to share his thoughts.

In *The Shadow Rising,* the length of time it is taking to get to the resolution of the plot begins to become irksome. Rand is both the promised saviour and destroyer of his society, the man prophesied to work magic and take on the forces of evil which are about to escape from imprisonment. However his coming is also therefore the starting signal for the battle between good and evil and so for the world to change irrevocably. In previous volumes Rand has been developing and testing his powers and acquiring various plot tokens which proclaim his legitimacy and enhance his powers. He is also allegedly destined to go mad as a result of the "taint" on the male source of magic, and his own and his followers' apprehensions stemming from this have been worth reading. In this book, however, he has also developed a "bubbles of evil" side effect, which means that there are a couple of flashy special-effects scenes with very little connection to anything else that has happened.

The Fires of Heaven is a stronger and more focused volume, largely because Jordan omits Perrin and his entourage of characters altogether and concentrates on Rand on the one hand and Nynaeve and Elayne on the other. Finally a major character (Moraine) dies, although the death is signalled for miles and the aftermath (Lan bonding to Nynaeve) is, by this time, predictable. Jordan's cast list continues to grow, and his strength is in how he juggles with the multiple and multiplying field of characters without losing any of the depth of characterization or pace of plotting. He is particularly strong on the integrity of minor characters caught up on the edges of horrific events over which they appear to have neither influence nor control. He is also strong in creating differentiated women characters and describing their uneasy relationships with their menfolk, although there are occasions when the observation that the genders speak different languages is reduced to a tedious round of the women conniving with each other to infantilize the men and the men conniving with each other to find the women inscrutable. His continuous harping on domestic chores as the foundation of training for women characters following any kind of mystic discipline may irritate those to whom is seems unlikely that you would bother to run away from home to become a wielder of esoteric mental powers if it meant you still wound up doing laundry.

On the whole, however, this saga is turning into a really impressive piece of work, albeit one which makes the reader long for it to be over so that the finished work can be tested to see whether the whole is as good as the sum of its parts.

—Wendy Bradley

JUSTER, Norton

Nationality: American. **Born:** Brooklyn, New York, 2 June 1929. **Education:** University of Pennsylvania, Philadelphia, B. Arch. 1952; University of Liverpool (Fulbright scholar), 1952-53. **Military Service:** United States Naval Reserve Civil Engineer Corps, 1954-57. **Family:** Married Jeanne Ray in 1964. **Career:** Architect, Juster and Gugliotta, New York, 1960-68; instructor in environmental design, Pratt Institute, New York, 1960-70. Since 1969 architect, Juster-Pope-Frazier Associates, Shelburne Falls, Massachusetts, and since 1970 Professor of Design, Hampshire College, Amherst, Massachusetts (retired: Emeritus). **Awards:** Ford grant, 1960; George G. Stone Center for Children's Books award, 1971. **Agent:** Mildred Marmur Associates, 310 Madison Avenue, New York, NY 10017, USA. **Address:** 259 Lincoln Avenue, Amherst, MA 01002, USA.

FANTASY PUBLICATIONS

Novel

The Phantom Tollbooth, illustrated by Jules Feiffer. New York, Epstein and Carroll, 1961; London, Collins, 1962.

OTHER PUBLICATIONS

Fiction for Children

The Dot and the Line: A Romance in Lower Mathematics. New York, Random House, 1963; London, Nelson, 1964.
Alberic the Wise and Other Journeys, illustrated by Domenico Gnoli. New York, Pantheon, 1965; London, Nelson, 1966.

Otter Nonsense, illustrated by Eric Carle. New York, Philomel, 1982; London, Faber, 1983.

Poetry

As: A Surfeit of Similes, illustrated by David Small. New York, Morrow, 1989.

Other

Stark Naked: A Paranomastic Odyssey, illustrated by Arnold Roth. New York, Random House, 1969.
So Sweet to Labor: Rural Women in America 1865-1895. New York, Viking Press, 1979.

*

Film Adaptations: *The Dot and the Line,* 1965; *The Phantom Tollbooth,* 1969.

* * *

In a review, Naomi Lewis described *The Phantom Tollbooth* as "one of the most brilliant pieces of nonsense written in our time, and not so nonsensical either," a description which well sums up this extraordinary book. Part extended joke, part moral fable, part fairy story, there is little with which one can compare it except perhaps John Bunyan's *Pilgrim's Progress.* It is almost entirely *sui generis.*

The story centres on Milo, an aimless boy who, though he has everything a child might hope for, is nevertheless bored. The Phantom Tollbooth of the title mysteriously appears in his room one day and, having assembled it, he sets off in his little electric car to see what adventures might befall him on the way to his chosen destination, Dictionopolis.

His miniature odyssey takes him through what can only be termed an allegorical landscape, as he meets, among many others the Whether Man, in the land of Expectations—"we certainly don't get many travellers these days"—and the Lethargians, who cannot bear to think. Befriended by the Watchdog, portrayed by illustrator Jules Feiffer as a large and thoughtful mongrel with a watch on its side, Milo is guided through the increasingly complex world of words and numbers as he meets first King Azaz in Dictionopolis and the Mathemagician in Digitopolis and learns about their respective subjects.

This would perhaps seem dull and didactic except that Juster has the wit to combine these lessons with a gentle fairy story, the quest to rescue Princesses Rhyme and Reason, without whom the kingdom is falling apart. Only Milo can do this and only after he has completed his task does he learn that it was really impossible.

Juster's flair for combining wit and knowledge makes this charming story far more than a moralistic tale, exhorting people to read and learn. At the end, Milo's new-found enthusiasm for reading, and his realization that knowledge can provide him with all the excitement and adventures he could want proves very infectious, and the serious message is further leavened by Jules Feiffer's amusing illustrations.

—Maureen Speller

K

KARR, Phyllis Ann

Nationality: American. **Born:** Oakland, California, 25 July 1944. **Education:** Colorado State University, 1962-66, A.B. in modern languages; Indiana University at Bloomington, M.L.S., 1971. **Family:** Married Clifton Alfred Hoyt in 1990. **Career:** Branch librarian, East Chicago Public Library, Indiana, 1967-1970; library cataloguer, University of Louisville, Kentucky 1971-76. Writer from 1977. **Agent:** Owlswick Literary Agency, 113 Deepdale Road, Strafford, PA 19087, USA. **Address:** HCR 61, Box 6050, Barnes, WI 54873, USA.

FANTASY PUBLICATIONS

Novels (series: Frostflower)

Frostflower and Thorn. New York, Berkley Books, 1980.
Frostflower and Windbourne. New York, Berkley Books, 1982.
The Idylls of the Queen. New York, Ace Books, 1982.
Wildraith's Last Battle. New York, Ace Books, 1982.
At Amberleaf Fair. New York, Ace Books, 1986.

OTHER PUBLICATIONS

Novels

Lady Susan (completion of story by Jane Austen). New York, Everest House, 1980; London, Corgi, 1984.
My Lady Quixote. New York, Fawcett, 1980.
Meadow Sons. New York, Fawcett, 1981.
Perola. New York, Fawcett, 1982.
The Elopement. New York, Fawcett, 1982.
The Gardener's Boy . . . Albuquerque, New Mexico, Buckethead Enterprises, 1988.

Other

The King Arthur Companion. Reston, Virginia, Reston, 1983.

*

Manuscript Collection: Special Collections, University of Oregon.

Phyllis Ann Karr comments:

My general aim has been either to treat the fantastic as everyday, or to limit the fantasy elements in my work in order to emphasize them, or both. I use a variety of styles (e.g. *Wildraith's Last Battle* is very bloody, while *At Amberleaf Fair* does not even use any words for "fight" or "struggle," with the single exception of "brawl"). Two sides of human nature seem perpetually to recur in most of my works, whether I plan it or not. I call them Sir Kay and Sir Ruthven, after King Arthur's seneschal and the Gilbert & Sullivan character, two of my own literary favourites since childhood. Kay is hardbitten and practical, Ruthven gentle and dreamy.

To see them very clearly, read *Frostflower and Thorn.* Sir Kay himself, in his own name, tells the story in *The Idylls of the Queen,* while an alternate-world version of Ruthven is a major character in *At Amberleaf Fair.* If you're looking for an author's recommendation of "which of my books to start with," I'd say one of those two, if you can get hold of a copy, or else *Lady Susan.* I like to think, however, that my works are too different one from another for any one to serve as a truly representative sample of the whole schmear.

*   *   *

Phyllis Ann Karr is probably best known to fantasy readers for her stories about the sorceress Frostflower and swordswoman Thorn, though she is also an Arthurian scholar, having completed a study of Arthurian literature in *The King Arthur Companion,* as well as being a writer of historical mysteries and historical romances.

Her first professional stories were historical mysteries in *Ellery Queen's Mystery Magazine* in 1974, but she had already had several short stories in the fantasy small press featuring Torin the Toymaker. These stories reflect very much the quiet mid-West American life of Karr in Indiana and Wisconsin. Although set in a fantasy world they are devoid of the usual trappings of sword-and-sorcery but feature the everyday lives of rural folk who live in a world of magic. Torin is a magician who has given up travelling to make toys and puzzles for children. The Torin stories are scattered through various small-press magazines and anthologies and would make a good collection. Fortunately Karr has also written a Torin novel, *At Amberleaf Fair,* which combines her talents for fantasy and mystery. Visiting the fair to sell his games, Torin finds himself involved in theft, near-murder and intrigue. Amberleaf could almost be the fantasy equivalent of Miss Marple's St. Mary-in-the-Mead, it is so homely, but the magic of the world gives it an added dimension.

Fantasy and mystery are no strangers to Karr. Perhaps her most endearing novel is *The Idylls of the Queen.* Taking a cue from Malory's *Morte D'Arthur,* Karr develops a murder mystery from the death of Sir Patrise at a banquet organized by Guinevere and in full view of King Arthur and the Knights of the Round Table. This gave Karr a chance to explore the motives and lives of the knights from a new angle, making it one of the most refreshing of recent Arthurian novels.

Karr's first fantasy novel was *Frostflower and Thorn,* which revealed a new side to her otherwise tranquil fantasies. In this world men are farmer priests and women are warriors. Thorn, a young warrior, becomes pregnant, and seeks the aid of the sorceress Thorn to quicken time and deliver the baby within a day. For this outrage they are banished, and the novel explores their travels. Thorn is a true warrior, violent and amoral, whilst Frostflower seeks to operate within her own code. The two thus clash, and it is the interplay between these ill-mixed characters that is the strength of the series. A second book, *Frostflower and Windbourne,* adds the extra element of mystery as Frostflower and Thorn seek to help another sorceress, Windbourne, who is accused of murdering a farmer-priest. Other stories in the series have appeared in anthologies and magazines, in particular the first two volumes of Marion Zimmer Bradley's *Sword and Sorceress* series, and *Marion Zimmer*

Bradley's Fantasy Magazine. The short stories are less violent and more reflective but have continued to develop the characters.

Wildwraith's Last Battle is a non-series novel which continues to explore clashes of character between two strong individuals. In this case Wildwraith, a goddess punished for her cruelty to become human, and Ylsa, a mercenary who, as a result of an accidental death, is set on a path of collision with Wildwraith.

Karr has also written a series of romantic historical novels (including completing an unfinished work by Jane Austen), and although that softer side is always evident in her fantasies, especially the Torin stories, it is clear she saves her fantasies for her more extravagant considerations. This makes them continually unpredictable and exciting.

—Mike Ashley

KAY, Guy Gavriel

Nationality: Canadian. **Born:** 7 November 1954. **Education:** University of Manitoba, B.A. in philosophy, 1975; University of Toronto, Ll.B., 1978. **Family:** Married Laura Beth Cohen in 1984; one son. **Career:** Associate producer and principal writer, "The Scales of Justice," CBC, Canada, 1982-89. **Awards:** Casper award, 1987; Aurora award, 1991. **Agent:** Sterling Lord (Canada), 10 St. Mary Street, Suite 510, Toronto, Ontario M4Y 1P9, Canada.

Fantasy Publications

Novels (series: The Fionavar Tapestry)

The Summer Tree (Fionavar). Toronto, McClelland and Stewart, and New York, Arbor House, 1984; London, Allen and Unwin, 1985.
The Wandering Fire (Fionavar). Toronto, Collins, New York, Arbor House, and London, Allen and Unwin, 1986.
The Darkest Road (Fionavar). Toronto, Collins, and New York, Arbor House, 1986; London, Unwin Hyman, 1987.
Tigana. Toronto, Viking Canada, New York, Roc, and London, Viking, 1990.
A Song For Arbonne. Toronto, Viking Canada, and London, HarperCollins, 1992; New York, Crown, 1993.
The Lions of Al-Rassan. London, HarperCollins, 1995.

*

Manuscript Collection: Merrill Collection, Toronto Public Library.

*   *   *

Guy Gavriel Kay's Fionavar Tapestry trilogy appeared at a time when large fantasy works, and Kay's was clearly one work in three volumes, inevitably invited comparison with J. R. R. Tolkien's *The Lord of the Rings.* The comparison was made but lent extra weight by the fact that Kay had actually worked in the 1970s as assistant to Christopher Tolkien, Tolkien's son and literary executor, preparing *The Silmarillion* for publication.

Equally inevitable is that most trilogies of that period drew on Tolkien's work for inspiration, some more slavishly than others, and it has not perhaps been as clearly acknowledged as it should have been that Kay's trilogy, while it had resonances of *The Lord of the Rings,* was nevertheless a work of great originality.

The story opens in modern America, as an ill-assorted group of students are brought together through the machinations of a man they know as Lorenzo Marcus, an academic and recluse. Having brought them together, he claims to be from another world and to be a magician called Loren Silvercloak. He has been sent from his own world, Fionavar, to bring back five people for two weeks as a gift to celebrate the long reign of King Ailell, "Red Indians to the Court of King James" as one character describes it. However, as later becomes apparent, there is much more behind Silvercloak's mission, as the five students, Kevin, Paul, Jennifer, Kim and Dave, become involved in Fionavar's destiny.

Fionavar is the world of worlds, a Platonic form perhaps. Kay describes it thus: "There are many worlds, caught in the loops and whorls of time. Seldom do they intersect, and so for the most part they are unknown to each other. Only in Fionavar, the prime creation, which all the others imperfectly reflect, is the lore gathered and preserved that tells of how to bridge the worlds." In practice, this means that the myths and legends of different portions of the United Kingdom and Norse myths are mixed together, apparently haphazardly, underpinned by conflict between the patriarchy of the Council of Mages and the matriarchal priestesses of the Goddess. Indeed, this mish-mash has earned a good deal of scorn from some critics, unfairly I think, because Fionavar's position as the prime world means that there is no reason why they shouldn't co-exist. More appropriate would be to criticize the absence of other world mythologies.

Despite this criticism, Kay does produce an absorbing fantasy. His characters travel into Fionavar, each with troubles and dark secrets. Dave is at odds with his father, who favours his brother over him, and is lacking in self-worth. Paul is haunted by the death of his girlfriend in an accident, and Kevin is aware that for all his popularity, there is much about his life that is superficial. Jennifer is recovering from the disintegration of a relationship. Only Kim seems to be aloof. Within Fionavar, they all, eventually, find healing and reconciliation and purpose as they become involved in the familiar story of a realm threatened by a dark force which is unleashed upon the world once again. Nevertheless, Kay does his best to stamp his own personality upon the story and includes new elements. He does not hesitate to kill off attractive characters such as Kevin, and Diarmuid, one of Ailell's sons; and Jennifer's rape by Rakoth Maugrim, the fallen god, is one of the more shocking episodes in the fantasy. The reader's emotions are frequently racked by the story, an experience similarly reported by the more devoted readers of *The Lord of the Rings.* Like Tolkien, Kay recognizes that there must be sacrifice as well as a happy ending and the Fionavar trilogy is more successful than most modern fantasies for acknowledging this.

Since then, Kay has published several other ambitious novels. The first, *Tigana,* was promoted and presented in a style more suited to a family saga, but was nevertheless a novel of some substance. Tigana, the eponymous province, has been deliberately wiped out by Brandin the Tyrant, to assuage his grief after his son's fall in battle. As a sorcerer, Brandin is able to cast a spell which means that no one can hear the name when spoken, and he obliterates all physical traces of the province. Nevertheless, there are survivors who remember their home, and the novel is an intricate web of plotting as a number of these people gradually come together around Alessan, the lost prince of Tigana, and seek to restore it—among them Devin, a troubadour, who travels in Alessan's company, and Dianora, now one of Brandin's courtesans, who has plotted a long and complicated course of action in order to gain access to Brandin.

Perhaps the biggest problem with *Tigana* is that all the characters, villains excluded, are too attractive for their own good, and one might almost surmise that Kay has unwisely fallen too much in love with his creations. The restoration of Tigana, when it finally but inevitably comes, is almost an anti-climax as Brandin is defeated in a battle he actually surrenders, though his motives are unclear.

However, many of the preoccupations of the Fionavar Tapestry remain, including, on Brandin's part, an awareness of the existence of other worlds, and a symbiotic relationship between him as magician and his fool as source, much as existed between Loren Silvercloak and his assistant Matt Soren. There is a sense that this novel was intended to be much more closely related to the Fionavar trilogy than it now is.

By contrast, *A Song for Arbonne* seems to have no relationship at all to Fionavar, although Kay's interest in troubadours seems to have increased, and there is a continuing fascination with matriarchal and patriarchal religion vying for supremacy. Although set in a mythical land, this novel is clearly based on Provence, during the time of the troubadours and the Court of Love, which provides a dilute background for a tale which is, it must be confessed, somewhat humdrum. The story eventually settles down to focus on Blaise, the younger son of Galbert, the unscrupulous adviser to King Ademar. Blaise has rejected all his father's schemes for him and travels Arbonne as a mercenary. After he hires himself to Bertran de Talair, Blaise is obliged to recognize that he must confront his father and challenge the weak and corrupt Ademar for the throne of Gorhaut, which he duly does. The novel is strong on background flavour, and many of its characters are as attractive as those in *Tigana,* but the plot might easily have been accomplished in half the pages.

Kay remains among the foremost modern fantasy writers on the strength of the Fionavar Tapestry which, while it acknowledged the debt to Tolkien's work, nevertheless set a new standard in what could be achieved in original fantasy writing.

—Maureen Speller

KEARNEY, Paul

Nationality: British. **Born:** Ballymena, County Antrim, 14 February 1967. **Education:** St. Louis Grammar School, Ballymena, 1978-85; Lincoln College, Oxford, 1985-88, B.A. in English literature. **Military Service:** Royal Irish Rangers, British Army, from 1988; still serving: lieutenant. **Agent:** Campbell, Thomson and McLaughlin, 1 King's Mews, London WC1N 2JA, England.

Fantasy Publications

Novels

The Way to Babylon. London, Gollancz, 1992.

A Different Kingdom. London, Gollancz, 1993.
Riding the Unicorn. London, Gollancz, 1994.

*

Paul Kearney comments:

My books are fantasy; they have monsters, magic and mayhem by the bucketful, but they also have a very strong strain of what is "real" running through them. I prefer fantasy which has a firm grounding in the possible, the explicable, even the mundane. And my heroes, as a result, tend to be practical and hard-headed, not to say cynical. My books have divided critics into two camps: those who prefer the "fantasy" aspect, and those who like the "real" elements in them. For me, both elements are necessary, and the most fascinating part of a novel is the conflict, the tension between the mundane and the fantastical. It is the fault-line where the pair meet that produces the sparks. I need those sparks to keep my own interest high, and, I hope, that of the readers.

*   *   *

His first novel, *The Way to Babylon,* establishes Paul Kearney's riveting *modus operandi*—a much-troubled man of this world crosses over into a fantasy world where he undergoes severe physical and mental trials, and finally returns to this world much changed, but having come to terms with his problems, to find that practically no time has passed. In this first novel, Michael Riven, an ex-soldier turned writer of fantasy novels, is recuperating from a severe climbing accident in which his wife was killed, when he begins to see fantastic figures in the landscape around his London nursing home. When he is well enough, he returns to the bothy in the Scottish highlands from where he and his wife used to go climbing together. Here he meets a traveller who conducts him up into the mountains where he crosses over into the fictional land of his novels to seek his dead wife, and has various adventures before returning to his Scottish bothy a sadder and a wiser man.

In *A Different Kingdom,* the second novel, eight-year-old Michael Fay lives on a farm in a remote part of Northern Ireland. He encounters Rose, an older cousin, with whom he forms a powerful bond, but who is certainly also conducting an adult affair. Rose becomes pregnant from this affair, and is spirited away one night. Michael is told later that she has died. In the meantime, he becomes aware that there is a magical hollow on the farm where savage strangers can be seen at certain times. He also becomes convinced that Rose's affair was with one of these people and that she has not died, but rather has gone to live in this different kingdom. Finally, five years later, he crosses over into the fantasy world to search for her. He never finds her, but instead is accepted into the world of the wolf-people who live there, and grows to maturity as a warrior and a lover, with his partner Cat. Again after various adventures he returns to the real world to find that no time has passed and that he has to carry on as a 13-year-old schoolboy with the mind and heart of a warrior. However, there is a twist, in that this sudden maturity means that he does not fit into his world any more, and throws a strange light onto his gradual decay into slobbish young adulthood.

Kearney's third book, *Riding the Unicorn,* follows the same pattern: Willoby, a hulking prison officer and all-round unpleasant man, is having a life crisis, with his wife and his adolescent daughter finding him more and more difficult to live with. He begins to hear voices, and thinks he is going mad. He is relieved of duty at the prison, but he only gets worse, as he is gradually drawn into a sword-and-sorcery fantasy world where his life is given meaning again by the more primeval type of struggle he encounters there. He returns to this world more than once, each time bearing the wounds he has suffered in the other, but each time with hardly any time having passed here (and thus he baffles the medical staff who are trying to treat him), until finally he takes positive action in the fantasy world and returns to this one nearly dead, but at last at peace with himself.

It would be easy to assume from the above that Paul Kearney is just another fantasist in love with the trappings of an earlier way of life who has found a neat if rather cliched way to justify the adolescent day-dreams of contemporary men. But this would do Kearney an injustice. He treads a very fine line between the present-day real and the fantasy world for large parts of these books, when it is obvious that it would have been much easier for him to abandon the link with modern Britain and write undiluted quasi-medieval fantasy wholeheartedly. Strangely, though, Kearney actually writes much better about modern Britain than he does about warrior kings or forests full of dire-wolves and magic.

It becomes clear that the link with the here-and-now is not gratuitous. Far from being merely a justification for the existence of the story, it is in fact almost the whole reason for the telling of the story. Certainly, the problems Kearney gives his protagonists are horribly intractable, and this is probably one of the sources of his power in writing about them. Whether it is a man who cannot accept the death of his wife from his own carelessness, an eight-year-old boy who has formed a powerful and sexual bond with a woman much too old for him, or a prison officer who is more of a prisoner in the claustrophobic confines of the prison than any old lag, what we see are modern men confronted with insurmountable problems. The two grown men are both ex-soldiers, while the boy becomes a warrior in his fantasy, and thus Kearney displays the ineffable but overly simplistic attraction of solving a problem with the sword in your hand. Of course, this is not a viable solution to these men's modern problems, and each of the characters has to come to terms both with their fraught lives and this atavistic desire to face down adversity by force of arms.

Kearney's fictions are thus much more than mere sword-and-sorcery fantasy; they are allegories of mental anguish, where the protagonist's only escape is into fantasies where problems are solvable by force, and of the real-world healing that can result from this escape. The reason Kearney writes reality better than fantasy is that he is more involved with it. While fantasy can have an important role to play, the real world is always there at the end of the story. Finally, what sets these books apart from most run-of-the-mill fantasy is that, while being heroes in their fantasy worlds, his characters have to learn to face up to their real-life problems as well.

—Paul Brazier

KENNEALY-MORRISON, Patricia

All books published under the name Patricia Kennealy until 1993. **Nationality:** American. **Born:** New York, 4 March 1946. **Education:** Saint Bonaventure University, Olean, New York, 1963-65; Harpur College, Binghamton, New York, 1965-67; B.A. in English

Literature. **Family:** Married James Douglas Morrison in 1970 (died 1971). **Career:** Lexicographer, Macmillan Company, New York, 1967-68; editorial assistant, then editor in chief, *Jazz and Pop* magazine, 1968-71; senior copywriter, RCA Records, 1971-73; copy director, CBS Records, 1973-79; copy director, the New School, 1979-81; freelance from 1981. **Agent:** Henry Morrison Agency, PO Box 235, Bedford Hills, NY 10507, USA. **Address:** c/o Lizard Queen Productions, Inc., 151 First Avenue, Suite 120, New York, NY 10003, USA.

FANTASY PUBLICATIONS

Novels (series: Keltiad)

The Copper Crown. New York, Bluejay, 1984; London, Grafton, 1986.
The Throne of Scone. New York, Bluejay, 1986; London, Grafton, 1987.
The Silver Branch. New York, New American Library, 1988; London, Grafton, 1991.
The Hawk's Grey Feather. New York, Roc, 1990; London, Grafton, 1992.
The Oak Above the Kings. New York, Roc, and London, HarperCollins, 1994.

OTHER PUBLICATIONS

Other

Strange Days: My Life With and Without Jim Morrison. New York, Dutton, and London, HarperCollins, 1992.

*

Patricia Kennealy-Morrison comments:
My series of books known collectively as "The Keltiad" is science fantasy rather than science fiction, blending Celtic mythology, space-age technology and high fantasy to create a unique and, it is to be hoped, harmonious blend. There are to be 18 books in all, five trilogies and three one-offs—perhaps more if warranted. The basic premise is that the Tuatha De Danaan, the magical pre-Celtic race of ancient Ireland, left Earth for outer space in the year 453 AD. St. Patrick was too close behind them, and magic was being replaced by the invading Christianity, so, using secrets of Atlantis, the Danaans took Celtic culture and civilization to distant stars, founding a vast interstellar empire known as Keltia, where all that was best and most enlightened in that great culture flourished as one likes to think it might have done here on Earth had not Christianity, secularism and cultural imperialism (Romans, Saxons, Normans) so brutally and finally intervened.

The first trilogy, "The Tales of Aeron", though published first is in fact next-to-last in chronology; I wrote these books first because in them the Kelts are making themselves known to the Earthfolk from whom they have been sundered for 3,000 years, and it seemed easiest and least confusing to introduce them to the readers at the same time. (Also it was my consort Jim Morrison's advice to write these first, and he was quite correct to suggest it.) "The Tales of Arthur", the second trilogy published, is of course the Arthurian legends in outer space; I make extensive use of many traditional Arthurian motifs, but I have significantly altered the tale to fit my own and third-millennium sensibilities. Future trilogies will cover other aspects of the Celtic mythological canon (including the story of St. Brendan, here the Astrogator, not the Navigator) as well as original plotlines, with a timeframe of 10,000 BC to 3,500 AD. It may sound strange at first—Celtic legends in outer space—but the more I read in the original sourcebooks, the more it sounded as if I were actually writing non-fiction, not science fantasy. Some of what may seem the most outrageous inventions or liberties aren't anything of the sort: I found them, I didn't have to invent them at all—flaming swords that could cut through any substance (the god Lugh's sword, or a *Star Wars* lightsabre?); boats that can sail over land as well as water (faerie vessels, or antigravity helms?). But "The Keltiad" is also a loving evocation of the best and worthiest of ancient Celtic society, and readers seem to find in it resonances for their own lives, as well as simple enjoyment of the fantasy.

*   *   *

For a time in the early 1990s, Patricia Kennealy-Morrison was perhaps best known for her non-fiction book *Strange Days,* and for the depiction of a certain part of her early life in a well-publicized Hollywood movie. She describes her book, and the film, thus: "This is a memoir of my time with my late husband, Jim Morrison of the U.S. rock group The Doors. We exchanged wedding vows in a private religious ceremony on 24 June 1970, and he died in Paris of an accidental heroin overdose on 3 July 1971. In 1990, I worked with film director Oliver Stone on his production of *The Doors,* in the capacity of technical advisor and consultant. I also appeared in a speaking part (a cameo as the priestess who performed the wedding ceremony between the onscreen "Jim Morrison" and "Patricia Kennealy") and I was myself portrayed in the film by American actress Kathleen Quinlan. The film opened in 1991 to almost universal disdain, including mine." For the best part of a decade prior to her published autobiography, however, she was known to fantasy readers as the author of an ambitious series of novels published under her maiden name of Patricia Kennealy (although all reprints now carry the Kennealy-Morrison byline).

The *Mabinogion,* the Irish legends and the Matter of Britain loom large in fantasy writing as some kind of literary gold mine, with countless writers working at the seam but very few achieving any notable success. Original work can be created within the constraints of the legends but too often writers settle for a straightforward retelling of old, familiar stories, and it takes a rare talent to bring anything new to them. Patricia Kennealy-Morrison lit upon the idea of sending St. Brendan the Navigator into space rather than to America, thus becoming St. Brendan the Astrogator, and having him and his followers create a vast galactic empire, Keltia. To explore this new universe, Kennealy-Morrison has created a vast series, the Keltiad, to comprise at least 18 volumes, of which five have so far appeared.

"The Tales of Aeron," covered in *The Silver Branch, The Copper Crown* and *The Throne of Scone,* appeared first and provide an introduction to the world of the Keltiad. For thousands of years, Keltia remains hidden from its traditional enemies, who have also travelled into space, and contact is lost with Earth until a probe ship from Earth accidentally arrives in Keltic space. The High Queen Aeron sees this as an opportunity to re-establish friendly relations with the home world, but not everyone agrees with her. Inevitably this leads to war between the Kelts, the Fomori and Cabiri Imperium, and when Aeron loses her throne, she sets off on a quest to find Arthur and the lost treasures of Keltia.

There is no denying that this is a pretty conceit, but does it offer us a new angle on the traditional stories? The answer, regrettably, has to be no. Most fantasy sagas utilize a combination of familiar ingredients—unsuitable love affairs, marriages born out of statecraft rather than love, wilful young people who are determined to shape their own destiny, rulers with empire-expanding ambitions, quests for lost treasures, political intrigue. In these respects, Kennealy-Morrison's Keltiad novels differ very little from the norm. We have the usual rich mixture of royalty in elaborate costumes, plotting and intriguing, for good or for ill, spiced with magic and, in this instance, fused with more traditional science-fictional elements as well. Yet there is no real feeling that this world is uniquely, specifically Keltic. The names might be changed, the setting shifted, and the story would be as familiar and as forgettable as it is here.

Possibly, the fault lies with Kennealy-Morrison being more interested in writing *within* the world she has created than attempting to achieve a rationale *for* that world, a distinction which perhaps is one reason for a perceived difference between science-fiction and fantasy writing. Certainly, so far at least, Kennealy-Morrison shows no signs of explaining how Brendan and his descendants settled in space, although the Keltiad is to include a section entitled "The Tales of Brendan" which may provide further details of this. In the meantime, there are the first two volumes of "The Tales of Arthur," *The Hawk's Grey Feather* and *The Oak Above the Kings,* with a further volume, *The Hedge of Mist,* to come. This latter series tends to confirm the notion that Kennealy-Morrison is intending to transfer the various British legends to a new galactic setting.

The attraction of Kennealy-Morrison's work undoubtedly lies in the wealth of detail, derived from her extensive knowledge of mythology and druidic practice, but I would argue that this is, however fascinating, insufficient to support familiar plots and a sense of having seen it all before. The combination of space ships and magic simply isn't enough to rescue the novels.

—Maureen Speller

KERBY, Susan Alice

Pseudonym for Alice Elizabeth Burton. **Nationality:** British. **Born:** Cairo, Egypt, 4 October 1908. **Family:** Married John Theodore Aitken (divorced). **Career:** Worked in journalism, radio and advertising. **Died.**

FANTASY PUBLICATIONS

Novels

Miss Carter and the Ifrit. London, Hutchinson, 1945.
Mr. Kronion. London, Werner Laurie, 1949.

OTHER PUBLICATIONS

Novels

Cling to Her, Waiting (as Elizabeth Burton). London, Dakers, 1939.
Fortnight in Frascati. London, Dakers, 1940.

Many Strange Birds. London, Hutchinson, 1947; as *Fortune's Gift,* New York, Dodd, 1947.

Gone to Grass. London, Hutchinson, 1948; as *The Roaring Dove,* New York, Dodd, 1948.

Other (as Elizabeth Burton)

The Elizabethans at Home: On Everyday Life in the Time of Elizabeth 1. London, Secker and Warburg, 1958; as *The Pageant of Elizabethan England,* New York, Scribner, 1959.

The Jacobeans at Home. London, Secker and Warburg, 1962; as *The Pageant of Jacobean England,* New York, Scribner, 1962.

Here Is England. New York, Farrar Straus, 1965.

The Georgians at Home, 1714-1830. London, Longmans Green, 1967; as *The Pageant of Georgian England,* New York, Scribner, 1968.

The Early Victorians at Home. London, Longman, 1972; as *The Pageant of Early Victorian England, 1837-1861,* New York, Scribner, 1972.

Elizabethans, Georgians and Early Victorians. London, Arrow, 1973.

Victorians. London, Readers Union, 1974.

The Early Tudors at Home. London, Alan Lane, 1976; as *The Pageant of Early Victorian England, 1485-1558,* New York, Scribner, 1976.

*   *   *

The kind of fantasy associated with the work of F. Anstey, in which the everyday world is temporarily disrupted by the intervention of some magical refugee from some ancient mythology, to considerable comic effect, works best when the anarchic magic can be opposed to a particularly rigid and stifling set of social norms. It is not surprising that the sub-genre should have fallen into disuse in adult fantasy (though not, of course, in children's fiction) when the Victorian era came to an end, but nor is it surprising that it should have been fruitfully resurrected whenever historical circumstances were unusually conducive. Just as the deprivations of World War I produced W. A. Darlington's *Alf's Button,* so the rigours of life on the home front of World War II produced Susan Alice Kerby's *Miss Carter and the Ifrit.* Perhaps Miss Kerby, who had spent the greater part of her life in Canada, found wartime London especially dismal once the worst of the Blitz was over and the effects of rationing became acute and routine. The original model for the story is Anstey's *The Brass Bottle,* but it is highly likely that the success of Darlington's book and the film based on it inspired Kerby to try to reproduce that runaway success (as Darlington did himself in *Alf's New Button*). Unfortunately, *Miss Carter and the Ifrit* falls between two stools; it has neither the casual sweep and elegance of Anstey's original nor the conscientiously down-market synthetic chirpiness of Darlington's.

The heroine of Kerby's novel is a spinster who is every bit as respectable, in her own way, as Anstey's hero, but her respectability is of that colourless and essentially unobtrusive kind which British spinsters have made their own. Unlike Sylvia Townsend Warner in the classic *Lolly Willowes,* Kerby is relatively restrained in painting the picture of her heroine's martyrdom, and the character's eventual redemption is far less savagely ironic than that gifted to Warner's heroine. The Ifrit released from a burning log is as over-enthusiastic as his two predecessors, but because he is intent on reform from the beginning he lacks the dangerous edge which

Anstey's djinn had. His relationship with Miss Carter is fatally cosy from the outset, and the help he gives her in overcoming the restrictions of rationing and repairing her damaged love-life is too unproblematic to work up any real pitch of narrative vigour.

Kerby's second Ansteyan romance, *Mr. Kronion,* follows the formula less slavishly, and is a more interesting book in consequence. It tells the story of a mysterious visitor who takes up brief residence in the aptly-named Oxfordshire village of Festering Mere (Alice Elizabeth Burton spent the latter part of her life at Grass Ground Farm near Witney in Oxfordshire). For a while his presence is obliquely disruptive; various strange events occur which offer hints as to his true identity. As the plot proceeds, however, it becomes clear that he is a staunch defender of the values for which the village stands: values which are imperilled by the rapid social changes of the post-war decade. The quintessentially English rural ideal of which the village is a symbol is, of course, doomed to pass into historical oblivion, just as the Classical Olympus to which Mr. Kronion once belonged has retreated into the mists of legend, and there is a certain propriety in the manner in which they join forces for one last-ditch attempt to turn back the tide of time. Like the Ifrit, the magical visitor is not as anarchic a force as he once was—the unbridled sexual appetites which he once represented and embodied have been calmed by urban sophistication—but this mellowing allows the author to develop a particular mood of nostalgic sentimentality which is new to the sub-genre and not to its disadvantage.

Mr. Kronion takes aboard some ideas which Kerby had considered in her previous comic novel, *Gone to Grass* (known in the US as *The Roaring Dove*), which is not fantasy although it is set in a hypothetical Utopian community. The nature of the earlier story required her to address certain questions about how people really ought to live which had never come into focus in *Miss Carter and the Ifrit* (whose concerns are entirely bound up with how people ought not to have to live), and the redeployment of such notions in *Mr. Kronion* helps to make its elusive central character far more interesting as a reformed deity-of-old than the Ifrit could ever have been. Mr. Kronion's philosophical discussions with the eccentrically-named human hero, Palladio Boquera, are thoughtful without ever becoming oppressive, and this is the hallmark of good light fantasy. British fantasy did not enjoy the same kind of dramatic resurgence in the decade following World War II as it had in the decade following the end of World War I, but this is one of the works of the period which may be profitably compared and contrasted, in terms of its outlook and ideology, with the parallel works of the early 1920s.

—Brian Stableford

KERR, Katharine

Nationality: American. **Born:** Cleveland, Ohio, 3 October 1944. **Education:** Stanford University, 1962-63. **Family:** Married 1) Loren Means in 1964 (marriage dissolved); 2) Howard Kerr in 1973. **Career:** Fantasy game designer for TSR, Inc., and contributing editor, *Dragon* magazine, early 1980s; freelance author since mid-1980s. **Agent:** Elizabeth Pomada, 1029 Jones St., San Francisco, CA 94109, USA. **Address:** 51 Sweeny, San Francisco, CA 94134, USA.

FANTASY PUBLICATIONS

Novels (series: Deverry in all books)

Daggerspell. New York, Doubleday, 1986; London, Grafton, 1988; revised edition, New York, Bantam, and London, HarperCollins, 1993.

Darkspell. New York, Doubleday, 1987; London, Grafton, 1988; revised edition, New York, Bantam, and London, HarperCollins, 1994.

The Bristling Wood. New York, Doubleday, 1989; as *Dawnspell: The Bristling Wood,* London, Grafton, 1989.

The Dragon Revenant. New York, Doubleday, 1990; as *Dragonspell: The Southern Sea,* London, Grafton, 1990.

A Time of Exile: A Novel of the Westlands. New York, Doubleday, and London, Grafton, 1991.

A Time of Omens: A Novel of the Westlands. London, HarperCollins, and New York, Bantam, 1992.

A Time of War: Days of Blood and Fire. London, HarperCollins, 1993; as *Days of Blood and Fire: A Novel of the Westlands,* New York, Bantam, 1993.

A Time of Justice: Days of Air and Darkness. London, HarperCollins, 1994; as *Days of Air and Darkness: A Novel of the Westlands,* New York, Bantam, 1994.

OTHER PUBLICATIONS

Novels

Polar City Blues. New York, Bantam, and London, Grafton, 1991.
Resurrection. Eugene, Oregon, Pulphouse, 1992.
Freezeframes. London, HarperCollins, and New York, Tor, 1995.

*

Manuscript Collection: Williamson Collection, Eastern New Mexico University, Portales.

*   *   *

Katharine Kerr has achieved a surprising feat: she has taken the tired and clichéd world of Celtic myth and she has set all eight of her fantasy novels against the same background, using essentially the same characters, and yet these novels have for the most part been fresh, surprising and entertaining—a popular and a critical success.

Most of Tolkien is there in her work. Her Kingdom of Deverry might be Wales or Cornwall or Brittany, but is carefully none of these, just as Tolkien's Middle-earth is not quite the English Midlands. Otherwise, their pseudo-medieval settings are similar. Kerr writes romantic stories of feuding humans who live in castles, go on quests, make alliances and occasionally go to war. She allows some of her characters to employ magic, which she calls *dweomer,* partly a hereditary talent and partly developed through long study. She makes use of gnomes (mostly referred to as Wildfolk; small, ugly but cute creatures who offer help and mute warnings to those humans whom they favour), of elves (the Elcyion Lacar, a human-sized sub-race mostly hated by humans yet capable of interbreeding), and of dwarfs (very short, stocky metal-workers, who are accepted as human). The later books in the series even bring in dragons.

Kerr concerns herself almost entirely with the nobility, or with those who have been or will be noble, since reversals of fortune are one of her most frequently used plot devices. Her one significant divergence from Tolkien, indeed, from nearly all other writers of this kind of heroic fantasy, is that she makes great use of reincarnation. She postulates that certain key characters will be reborn time after time within the same society; their names and families will be different yet their personalities (and perhaps even their appearances) will remain fairly constant between reincarnations.

The plots of these novels are far too involved to allow any sort of detailed resume. There is one main story which continues through each book; this is accompanied, sometimes counterpointed, by stories of some of the same characters (in different incarnations) in earlier centuries. The three most significant characters in the main story are Jill, Rhodry and Nevyn. Jill is common-born in this incarnation, the daughter of a disgraced master-swordsman, Cullyn the silver dagger. The significance of being a silver dagger is that one is a mercenary soldier, hired to help guard caravans or fight battles, but is disliked by all. Jill becomes a silver dagger, too, before falling in love with Rhodry, brother of a local lord. But Rhodry is banished by his brother and is forced to work as a silver dagger himself. Later, Rhodry succeeds his brother, but Jill leaves him and trains her powers of *dweomer;* she is always a strong, independent character. When Rhodry's half-elvish blood keeps him youthful for too many decades, he fakes his own death and lives simply again, eventually using the power of an elvish ring to enslave a dragon, Arzosah, and use her to win a great battle and save his people.

Nevyn is the most powerful exponent of *dweomer.* A banished prince, he has lived a single long life for over 400 years, hoping to meet up with the reincarnation of Brangwen, the great love of his early life. Jill is that reincarnation (though not the first one), and although she does not fall in love with him, he is able to train her in the *dweomer,* only then allowing himself to die. His name is a self-deprecating pun; it means no-one. Yet it is he who first sees Jill's great talent for *dweomer* and Rhodry's vital importance to the future of Deverry. In fact, Nevyn is skilfully used by Kerr as an important viewpoint character in order to put across the existence of reincarnation, since only he is in a position to recognize the returning personalities as people he knew or was even related to in centuries past.

Some of the lesser stories, from past eras, are extremely entertaining, with memorable plots and characters. Perhaps the strongest, set 300 years before the main action, shows Jill's former incarnation, Gweniver, as a warrior priestess who has sworn a vow of chastity and to revenge the death of her family. She becomes terrifying when she is taken over by the Goddess, whom she serves, and then goes into a berserker state in battle. Gweniver has a chaste love for Ricyn (who will later be reborn as Rhodry), and they are happy to die together in battle.

As with any big series of novels, there are some contrived plot elements and poorly developed characters in places. The worst of this occurs in *Darkspell,* where the main plot revolves around the evil scheming of adherents to the dark *dweomer* (or black magicians). Like B-movie villains, they are lacking in intelligence and fight amongst themselves. In order to show how unrelievedly evil they are, Kerr depicts them as gay rapists! (Thus the book seems to contain a strong anti-gay message.) Another example of contrived plotting is when Rhodry is kidnapped and enslaved on an island far to the south and has to be rescued by his elvish half-brother.

Because of the plot complexity and all the different eras involved, the individual volumes in the series are difficult to read in isolation. Kerr is not so inconsiderate of the reader as to finish a volume on a cliffhanger (as some fantasy authors do), and she does attempt to offer an explanation of some of what has gone before during the early parts of each book; even so, it is recommended that the books be read in the proper order. (This still leaves gaps in the overall story; Nevyn's death, for example, is never shown, only reported, and Jill's character seems to change suddenly with her development of *dweomer.*) Kerr has rewritten *Daggerspell* and *Darkspell* fairly recently to eliminate discrepancies, yet some few problems of this nature remain.

Two important aspects of Kerr's world are honour and wyrd. Personal honour is so highly regarded that even the slightest suggestion of dishonour in a member of the nobility will bring about a duel to the death or a feud or a suicide. One of the greatest acts of dishonour in the books is a case of incest between brother and sister, resulting in a child. Wyrd means personal destiny, something which is fixed from birth; it can be foreseen but not avoided.

These are all highly emotional novels, full of conflicts of loyalty, blood feuds and, above all, highly romantic love affairs. Nor must this be taken as a criticism; Kerr's work is always entertaining, and if its emotional level is slightly over the top that is in keeping with the plot events and with the overall writing style. This is in many ways a romanticized and sanitized version of early medieval life and is more readable for that reason. But Kerr is also a clever writer, subtle for the most part in her characterization and plot development, capable of surprising the reader more often than most of her contemporaries, and occasionally very lyrical in her descriptive passages.

—Chris Morgan

KILWORTH, Garry (Douglas)

Pseudonym: Garry Douglas. **Nationality:** British. **Born:** York, 5 July 1941. **Education:** Khomaksar School, Aden, 1952-54; Royal Air Force Bridgenorth School, 1954-56, and Cosford Cadet School, 1956-58; H.N.C. in business studies 1974; King's College, London University, 1983-86, B.A. (honours) in English. **Military Service:** Royal Air Force, Signals Master, 1958-74; G.S.M. Aden Campaign Medal. **Family:** Married Annette Jill Bailey in 1962; one son and one daughter. **Career:** Senior executive, Cable and Wireless, London and Caribbean, 1974-82. Since 1982, freelance writer. **Awards:** Gollancz-*Sunday Times* science-fiction competition prize, 1974; World Fantasy award, 1993. **Agent:** Maggie Noach, 21 Redan Street, London W14 0AB, England. **Address:** Wychwater, The Chase, Ashingdon, Essex SS4 3JE, England.

FANTASY PUBLICATIONS

Novels

Spiral Winds. London, Bodley Head, 1987.
Hunter's Moon: A Story of Foxes. London, Unwin Hyman, 1989; as *The Foxes of First Dark,* New York, Doubleday, 1990.
Midnight's Sun: A Story of Wolves. London, Unwin Hyman, 1990.

Frost Dancers. London, HarperCollins, 1992.

Short Stories

The Songbirds of Pain: Stories from the Inscape. London, Gollancz, 1984.
In the Hollow of the Deep Sea Wave. London, Bodley Head, 1989.
Dark Hills, Hollow Clocks: Stories from the Otherworld (for children). London, Methuen, 1990.
Hogfoot Right and Bird-Hands. Cambridge, Massachusetts, Edgewood Press, 1993.
In the Country of Tattooed Men. London, Grafton, 1993.

OTHER PUBLICATIONS

Novels

In Solitary. London, Faber, 1977; New York, Avon, 1979.
The Night of Kadar. London, Faber, 1978; New York, Avon, 1980.
Split Second. London and Boston, Faber, 1979.
Gemini God. London and Boston, Faber, 1981.
A Theatre of Timesmiths. London, Gollancz, 1984; New York, Warner, 1986.
Highlander (novelization of screenplay), as Garry Douglas. London, Grafton, 1986.
Witchwater Country. London, Bodley Head, 1986.
The Wizard of Woodworld (for children). London, Dragon, 1987.
Abandonati. London, Unwin Hyman, 1988.
Cloudrock. London, Unwin Hyman, 1988.
The Street, as Garry Douglas. London, Grafton, 1988.
The Voyage of the Vigilance (for children). London, Armada, 1988.
The Rain Ghost (for children). London, Hippo, 1989; New York, Scholastic, 1990.
The Drowners (for children). London, Methuen, 1991.
The Third Dragon (for children). London, Hippo, 1991.
Standing on Shamsan. London, HarperCollins, 1992.
Billy Pink's Private Detective Agency (for children). London, Methuen, 1993.
Angel. London, Gollancz, 1993.
Archangel. London, Gollancz, 1994.
The Electric Kid (for children). London, Corgi, 1994.
The Phantom Piper (for children). London, Methuen, 1994.

Poetry

Tree Messiah. Newport, Envoi Poets, 1985.

*

Garry Kilworth comments:

The kind of fantasy I write tends to be bizarre rather than epic, apart from my animal fantasy, which to date owes much to Rudyard Kipling. I enjoy writing fantasy because I love secret worlds: entering them, exploring them, discovering their histories and mythologies. I enjoy getting lost in dark mountains and woods, and finding such creatures there which never graced the mundane world of the motor car and aeroplane. Those who wish to accompany me are welcome companions.

*   *   *

One of the most versatile writers in his field, Kilworth is best known to a mass readership as the author of a series of animal stories in which the lives of foxes, wolves and most recently hares are dramatized in a way which recalls such earlier classics of the "animal" tale as *Ring of Bright Water* as well as *Watership Down*. His stories and novels range from science fiction to horror to magical realism. Recently, after a shaky start with some formulaic sf, he has begun to write for children: *The Drowners,* a historical ghost story, was short-listed for the Carnegie award and the collection *Dark Hills, Hollow Clocks* revisits the territories of both European and Asian folktale to original effect.

In whatever genre he writes, Kilworth skirts the borderlands of convention to come up with stories which are never less than gripping and readable for the way they strive to eschew the obvious. The science-fictional "explanation" of *Abandonati,* for example, a quest among the tramps and street people who have been left behind when the rich leave the planet, is less important than the bewilderment of the characters themselves, with the result that the novel is a vividly mysterious fable. *Spiral Winds* approaches magical realism from a different direction, beginning as a "mainstream" novel involving the British withdrawal from Aden witnessed by two friends who as boys were involved in a motorcycle accident which killed an adventurer famous for his exploits in the Middle East. The ambiguity of Alan and Jim's experiences in the desert allows for a naturalistic reading, but also for a complex layering of time and geography. The original short story of the same title (republished as "Spiral Sands") presents the same ambiguity of pursuers and pursed in the same environment, but with different characters.

Like many fantasy writers, Kilworth evokes an almost literal spirit of place, but in his case, the locations are rich and varied: the deserts of Arabia and the Essex estuaries are both parts of his personal landscapes. The novel *Witchwater Country*, although itself a realistic novel of childhood, has as part of its symbolic background the dark folklore of the Essex marshes. The short story "The Thunder of the Captains" brings these tales of black magic more closely to the fore, while the children's novel *Billy Pink's Private Detective Agency* weaves legends of spirits which follow the lost traveller into a more amusing tale, into which is woven homage to a more celebrated fictional detective. Yet, in common with so many of the best fantasy writers, Kilworth is as eclectic as he is particular. Other short stories, such as "The Sculptor," are set in definitely other worlds. With its Italian-Renaissance characters, the story explores more than just analogues of the already-noted settings of desert and water. Its Tower is that of Babel: its confrontation of the High Priest da Vinci and the sculptor Niccolo reflects one of Kilworth's preoccupations, the canker at the heart of a perfect work of art, the illusory danger of perfection. Another such "fusion" is "The Ragthorn" (with Robert Holdstock), which follows a search for the literal Tree of Life through clues handed down in literary texts since earliest times. Its pastiches of *The Iliad* and *Hamlet* are effective and to the point, and the coda which rounds it off chillingly ironic, but its importance as a story is underlined by the fact that it is a collaboration with Holdstock, whose own explorations of English mythology and "place" are among the pinnacles of current fantasy writing. The 1993 World Fantasy award the story won recognizes its subtle integration of each contributor's style and themes.

Kilworth has written, in the introduction to *The Songbirds of Pain,* of his desire that "each story can be viewed from more than one perspective," and the unsettling effect of many of his stories is because he can eschew the conventions of fantasy and science fic-

tion while reminding the reader of their whereabouts somewhere in the background. In cases such as the novella "In the Hollow of the Deep Sea Wave," what is in part a science fictional or fantasy extrapolation, the nature of a society where an individual official is responsible for the actions of his predecessors in the role, is set not in another world but in the here and now (albeit a remote island in the Indian Ocean). With this carefully built sociology to the fore, the second element of the fantastic in the story (concerning an item of the islanders' mythology) is carefully delineated to be either "within" the story itself or within the mind of the character involved.

The nearest Kilworth comes to specifically genre work is in his animal stories, which fuse "realistic" accounts of the lives of foxes (*Hunter's Moon*), wolves (*Midnight's Sun*) and hares (*Frost Dancers*) with myth and folklore. Kilworth's animal stories are among the best in this sub-genre. His beasts have their specific cultures: the conformist, pragmatic wolves, the individualistic if ritual-bound foxes, and the spontaneous, superstitious hares. In each book, a change of environment and circumstance allows the animal protagonists dimly to glimpse a level of existence beyond that to which they are bound, and to gain the resources to overcome danger. There is an epic quality to these fictions, taken as a whole (the England of *Hunter's Moon* and the Canada of *Midnight's Sun* are linked because of their canid culture, while *Hunter's Moon* and *Frost Dancers* share secondary characters such as a naturalist and his dog). Above all, however, they are deeply-felt responses to nature and landscape. Skelter, in *Frost Dancers,* is a mountain hare transported from the Scottish mountains to the flat estuary lands so much a feature of many of Kilworth's other novels: both environments are skilfully visualized, and Skelter's sense of being in a strange and alien environment is sympathetically contrasted with the native beasts' comfortable sense of place.

Kilworth's animal societies are credible versions of what can be seen in the wild, given the added capacities of communication, reason, and their own culture based on a series of creation-myths. While a certain degree of anthropomorphism is necessary (his animal protagonists are given strongly recognizable personalities and face similar moral choices to those which we as humans must decide upon) Kilworth creates a world which is both natural and alien. The myths and legends of his canids and lagomorphs, for instance, are reworkings of human stories into other viewpoints, enabling Kilworth to explore the nature of religious myth and hero-story, but central to them is the conflict between humanity and the natural world. To the beasts, it is the human race which is alien in its motivations. This enables Kilworth to tell several stories at once to great effect, as in *Midnight's Sun* where wolf and man journey together across the tundra after a plane crash, or (again) *Frost Dancers,* where the hares witness without understanding a human domestic tragedy and where (more ironically) we revisit at second-hand and in summary form the plot of *Watership Down*.

Fortunately for his readers, Kilworth is not a writer whose progress can be neatly charted. His animal stories and to some extent his "marsh" locations aside, he is a writer for whom the pleasure of reading lies in the excellence of his writing and the quality of his imaginings instead of any familiarity of settings or theme. In particular, he is one of the most accomplished of short-story writers. The subtitle of his collection *The Songbirds of Pain: Stories from the Inscape* offers a clue to his ability: quite simply, the capacity to visualize the concentrated essence of a scenario (analogous to Gerard Manley Hopkins's term "inscape") and allow the rules which govern the situation to be inferred by the reader—and, in many cases, by the story's protagonist. If Kilworth's plots in novel or short story were not so gripping, far more attention might be given to his mastery of technique, but as it is he has the balance between the crafts of storytelling and the process of "literary" writing as near perfect as it is possible to come.

—Andy Sawyer

KING, Bernard

Pseudonym: Aubrey Melech. **Nationality:** British. **Born:** 1946.

FANTASY PUBLICATIONS

Novels (series: Chronicles of the Keeper; Starkadder)

Starkadder. London, New English Library, 1985.
Vargr-Moon (Starkadder). London, New English Library, 1986.
The Destroying Angel (Keeper). London, Sphere, 1987.
Time-Fighters (Keeper). London, Sphere, 1987.
Death-Blinder (Starkadder). London, New English Library, 1988.
Skyfire (Keeper). London, Sphere, 1988.

OTHER PUBLICATIONS

Novels

Witch Beast. London, Sphere, 1989.
Blood Circle. London, Sphere, 1990.

Other

Missa Niger: La Messe Noire, as by Aubrey Melech. Northampton, Sut Anubis Books, 1985.
Ultima Thule: The Vanished Northern Homeland. London, Asatru Folk Runic Workshop and Rune Gild, 1992.

Translator, *The Grimoire of Pope Honorius III.* Northampton, Sut Anubis Books, 1984.

*   *   *

In more than one way, the published fiction of Bernard King represents only the tip of the iceberg. His first novel, *Starkadder,* has the feel of continuation about it: there are references to major, shaping events preceding the novel's start, as if it were the third volume of a trilogy; yet at story's end we sense that the curtains have not long opened, that preliminary scenes have been performed but the bulk of the play is yet to come. In fact, King wrote some 15 unpublished novels before *Starkadder* (and earlier had published two limited-edition chapbooks on Black Magic), but to take this as more than a part-explanation for the book's sequelish aspects would be to mislead through oversimplification. Indeed, in any analysis of King's corpus of work there is a constant danger of oversimplification.

Starkadder is a bloody tale of Viking slaughter and magic in late-Dark-Age Sweden. On the throne is King Oli, a late member of the Yngling Dynasty said to have been founded by Odin himself. Oli is mad, as even Odin admits; yet the Allfather is reluctant to see the overthrow of the king for fear it would spell also the end of the Yngling Dynasty, and with it the eclipse of the old gods by the new, southern god: the white Christ. The Norns, by contrast, ache for the tranquillity of extinction: Skuld, as their representative, games with Odin in order, against the god's will, to bring about the downfall of the Ynglings.

Into this complex game comes the embodiment of the doomed Norse ways: Starkadder, child of the rape of a mortal virgin by a giant. Odin, recognizing the infant's potential greatness, endowed him with three lifespans; Thor, recalling the crime whereby the child had been conceived, decreed that each lifespan would end in Starkadder committing an act of betrayal, and suffering all the dishonour the act incurred. By the time we meet him, Starkadder has already committed two betrayals. Now in the twilight of his lives, he is the most feared man in the kingdom, bound to Oli by honour, even though the king knows Starkadder must one day betray him. Yet Starkadder resists his destiny, understanding the gods cannot be thwarted yet trying to thwart them nonetheless.

Despite the Stella Gibbons connotations, the name Starkadder is drawn from the *Gesta Danorum* of Saxo Grammaticus (circa 1140-1206), as is the nature of the curse—although King modifies the personality considerably. Most of the other characters have a similar rooting in "history." Principal among them is Hather Lambisson, tutored by the old warrior; while this novel is about Starkadder and Hather, its two successor novels—*Vargr-Moon* and *Death-Blinder*—are about Hather and, to only a slightly lesser extent, the sword Tyrfing, stolen from the Dwarfs and cursed to kill any mortal who claims its ownership. *Starkadder* concerns itself with the grooming of Hather for greatness, and ends with Starkadder killing Oli and inadvertently Hather's father Lambi, and allowing himself to be killed for honour by Hather. In *Vargr-Moon* Hather's first wife Astrid aims to transform herself into a *vargr*—a sort of super-werewolf—through eating 13 living human hearts, the 13th of which must be that of her own and Hather's son. In this she is covertly abetted by King Omund, Oli's son, himself now growing mad on the throne and paranoid about Hather's political power. Aided by Saeunna, who will become his third wife, Hather saves the lad and the kingdom. King has described *Vargr-Moon* as a "spaghetti Northern." In *Death-Blinder* a Lappish sorcerer has blasphemously taken one of Odin's names for himself and plans, in effect, world domination; again Omund secretly aids evil, and again Hather and Saeunna save the day, but this time at fatal cost. Odin and Skuld, their meddling growing wearisome to them, declare a truce until Ragnarok.

All three books contain much gratuitous gore and are so clumsily written as to be difficult to read (*Death-Blinder* is somewhat smoother), yet it is evident that a far keener intellect is speaking than the standard hack-and-slash material will allow to be heard. This clumsiness—notably frequent confusion of viewpoints—has never left King. It is perhaps significant that the most professionally written of his novels, *Blood Circle,* is the least interesting in terms of ideas, being a fairly conventional—and rather nastily sadistic—Black Magic horror yarn. His other full-scale venture into the horror genre, *Witch Beast,* concerns itself with the attempt by the evil spirit Black Shuck to establish itself as a canine god in succession to our "human" one. As with the Viking series, the ideas are more intriguing than a synopsis suggests. And again there is the sense that there is more to the story than is being told.

King's major work is the Chronicles of the Keeper trilogy, an outstanding construction that is that rarest of things: not just three sequentially related novels and not just a single long novel in three volumes, but a work that could exist only as a trilogy. Its primary thesis is that, after the Creation, lesser gods were permitted to rule the Earth, over which they established the Thulean Empire—the Thule of legend being not so much a place as an idea, having physical existence only in "alterjective" reality. In human Neanderthal times there emerged among the Thuleans a faction that wished to suppress and destroy humanity; the benign majority, to counter this, implanted religion in the human mind—so that never again would mortals seek to revere the Thuleans—and withdrew from physical existence. They appointed a human being as the "Keeper" of, in effect, the balance between good and evil; in nearly 65,500 years since the appointment of the first, there have been only 129 Keepers, each playing a secret rôle in the cultural evolution of the human species while also countering attempts by agents of the anti-human Thuleans to establish a new Thulean Empire. The current incumbent, Pythonius Meeres—alias Johannes Faust—is nearing the end of his self-allotted span. He chooses as his successor a police officer, Bob Ferrow, who despite extended incredulity is drawn deeper and deeper into Thulean machinations, especially the separate attempts of immortal (but not invulnerable) cat's-paws Rufus Williamson and Erzebet von Bamberg to rip the fabric between our reality and alterjective reality, and thereby to permit the triumphant irruption of one or other vile Thulean deity. In the end, of course, Ferrow is safely installed and the worst of the evil avoided.

Touching many bases—magic mushrooms, UFOs, conspiracies, secret masters, witchcraft, familiars (depicted as an intelligent, deliberately hidden species of bloodsuckers) and much else—the work builds up immensely complicated patterns of cross-connections, some rooted in history and others, indistinguishably, with origins that are entirely fanciful. The writing is generally journeyman at best (*The Destroying Angel* was written before *Starkadder*), uncertain of its voice (sometimes wallowing in sub-Priestleyan orotundity, sometimes plunging into schlock horror) and littered with infelicities ("Her English accent would have cut glass, even [here] in the Highlands where pewter or pottery was more traditional"—from *Time-Fighters*), yet the structuring of the trilogy is as impressive as it is unconventional. And still there is the feeling that much remains unrevealed. A long explanatory prequel, *Monkey Dance*, is unpublished.

King has published no fiction since 1990. Of his non-fiction work since then, the limited-edition chapbook *Ultima Thule: The Vanished Northern Homeland* is of particular interest in that it sets out more rigorously some of the underpinning of the Chronicles of the Keeper trilogy. Despite King's seemingly incurable clumsiness of writing, it would be a pity if this highly individualistic voice remained silent.

—John Grant

KINGSLEY, Charles

Nationality: British. **Born:** Holne, Devon, 12 June 1819; brother of the novelist Henry Kingsley. **Education:** Helston Grammar School, Cornwall, 1833-35; King's College, London, 1835-38; Magdalene College, Cambridge, 1838-42, B.A. in classics, 1842, M.A., 1860. **Family:** Married Frances Grenfell in 1844; two sons, two daughters; his daughter Mary became a novelist under the name Lucas Malet. **Career:** Curate, 1842-44, and rector, 1844-75, Eversley, Hampshire; contributor, *Politics for the People,* 1848, and *The Christian Socialist,* 1850-51; professor of English Literature, Queen's College, London, 1848; Regius Professor of Modern History, Cambridge, 1860-69; history tutor to the Prince of Wales, 1861; Canon of Chester, 1869-73; Canon of Westminster and chaplain to the Queen, 1873-75. **Died:** 23 January 1875.

FANTASY PUBLICATIONS

Novels

The Water-Babies: A Fairy Tale for a Land-Baby. London, Macmillan, 1863; Boston, Burnham, 1864.

Short Stories

The Heroes, or Greek Fairy Tales for My Children (retellings). Cambridge, Macmillan, and Boston, Ticknor and Fields, 1856.

OTHER PUBLICATIONS

Novels

Alton Locke, Tailor and Poet: An Autobiography. London, Chapman and Hall, 2 vols., 1850; New York, Harper, 1 vol., 1850.
Yeast: A Problem. London, Parker, and New York, Harper, 1851.
Hypatia, or New Foes with an Old Face. London, Parker, 2 vols., 1853; New York, Lowell, 1 vol., 1853.
Westward Ho! Cambridge, Macmillan, 3 vols., 1855; Boston, Ticknor and Fields, 1 vol., 1855.
Two Years Ago. Cambridge, Macmillan, 3 vols., 1857; Boston, Ticknor and Fields, 1 vol., 1857.
Hereward the Wake: "Last of the English". London, Macmillan, 2 vols., 1866; Boston, Ticknor and Fields, 1 vol., 1866.
The Tutor's Story: An Unpublished Novel, completed by Lucas Malet. London, Smith Elder, and New York, Dodd, 1916.

Poetry

The Saint's Tragedy, or The True Story of Elizabeth of Hungary. London, Parker, 1848; New York, International Book Company, 1855.
Andromeda and Other Poems. London, Parker, and Boston, Ticknor and Fields, 1858.

Other

Twenty-Five Village Sermons. London, Parker, 1849; Philadelphia, Hooker, 1855.
Cheap Clothes and Nasty (as Parson Lot). Cambridge, Macmillan, 1850.
Phaeton, or Loose Thoughts for Loose Thinkers. Cambridge, Macmillan, 1852; Philadelphia, Hooker, 1854.
Alexandria and Her Schools. Cambridge, Macmillan, 1854.
Brave Words for Brave Soldiers and Sailors. Cambridge, Macmillan, 1855.

Glaucus, or The Wonders of the Shore. Cambridge, Macmillan, and Boston, Ticknor and Fields, 1855; revised edition, Macmillan, 1873.

Miscellanies. London, Parker, 2 vols., 1859.

The Limits of Exact Science as Applied to History: An Inaugural Lecture. Cambridge, Macmillan, 1860.

Speech of Lord Dundreary in Section D on Friday Last, on the Great Hippocampus Question. Cambridge and London, Macmillan, 1862.

Mr. Kingsley and Mr. Newman: A Correspondence. London, Longmans Green, 1864.

"What, Then, Does Dr. Newman Mean?": A Reply. London, Macmillan, 1864.

The Roman and the Teuton. Cambridge and London, Macmillan, 1864.

The Irrationale of Speech, by a Minute Philosopher. London, Longmans, 1864.

The Hermits. London, Macmillan, and Philadelphia, Lippincott, 1868.

Madam How and Lady Why, or First Lessons in Earth Lore for Children. London, Bell and Daldy, 1870; New York, Macmillan, 1885.

At Last: A Christmas in the West Indies. London, Macmillan, and New York, Harper, 1871.

Town Geology. London, Strahan, 1872; New York, Appleton, 1873.

Plays and Puritans, and Other Historical Essays. London, Macmillan, 1873.

Prose Idylls, New and Old. London, Macmillan, 1873.

Health and Education. London, Isbister, and New York, Appleton, 1874.

Lectures Delivered in America in 1874. London, Longmans, and Philadelphia, Coates, 1875.

Charles Kingsley, His Letters and Memories of His Life, edited by Frances E. Kingsley. London, Kegan Paul, 2 vols., 1876.

The Works of Charles Kingsley. London, Macmillan, 28 vols., 1880-89.

American Notes: Letters from a Lecture Tour, 1874, edited by R. B. Martin. Princeton, New Jersey, Princeton University Library, 1958.

*

Film Adaptations: *Hereward the Wake,* 1965 (TV serial); *The Water Babies,* 1978.

Bibliography: *Charles Kingsley: A Reference Guide* by Styron Harris, Boston, Hall, 1981.

Manuscript Collections: British Library; Cambridge University Library; Stapleton and Parrish collections, Princeton University.

Critical Studies (selection): *Charles Kingsley, 1819-1875* by Margaret F. Thorp, Princeton University Press, 1937; *Charles Kingsley and His Ideas* by Guy Kendall, London and New York, Hutchinson, 1947; *Canon Charles Kingsley: A Biography* by Una Pope-Hennessy, London, Chatto and Windus, 1948; *The Dust of Combat: A Life of Charles Kingsley* by Robert B. Martin, London, Faber, 1959; *The Kingsleys: A Biographical Anthology* edited by Elspeth Huxley, London, Allen and Unwin, 1973; *The Beast and

the Monk: A Life of Charles Kingsley* by Susan Chitty, London, Hodder and Stoughton, 1975; *Charles Kingsley* by Brenda Collom, London, Constable, 1975; *The Novels of Charles Kingsley: A Christian Social Interpretation* by Allan J. Hartley, Folkestone, Kent, Hour-Glass Press, 1977; *Charles Kingsley* by Larry K. Uffelman, Boston, Twayne, 1979.

*   *   *

There is a certain dichotomy in the mood and modes of Charles Kingsley's writing. He was a realistic novelist, whether the realism was in the service of such socially conscious, didactic fiction as *Two Years Ago* and *Yeast;* or whether it gave colour to historical romances like *Hereward the Wake* and *Westward Ho!* But he was also a teller of tales which either drew on the myths and legends of mankind, as in *The Heroes* and his long narrative poem "Andromeda," or invoked an original vein of fantasy, as in *The Water-Babies.*

Although Kingsley's literary reputation was founded mainly on his sociologically oriented novels, now readable chiefly as documents of his age, it is only in *The Heroes* and *The Water-Babies,* both written for children, that he finds any popular readership today. Before considering these, however, it is worth looking at certain of the major novels from the point of view specific to this appraisal. Sir Leslie Stephen wrote of Kingsley that he "called himself a Platonist in philosophy and had a taste for the mysteries, liking to recognize a divine symbolism in nature". This attribute favoured a constant breaking through of the fantastic into even his most realistic fiction. In *Yeast,* for example, a novel that was pro-Christian Socialist and anti-Benthamite propagandist, background and dialogue are prosaically realistic, yet Kingsley's perception that "consciousness is a dim candle—over a deep mine," is time after time realized in dream, reverie and metaphor. The gigantic gamekeeper, Tregarva, lamenting his plebian status, says that "he feels sometimes as if he was enchanted, pent up, like folks in fairy tales, in the body of some poor dumb beast". Animal metamorphosis is the central image in the heroine Agemone's dream, following her reading of her own (and Kingsley's) sensuous poem "Sappho"; and her dying delirious reverie (she contracts typhus in the Manchester slums) of the cleansing and transforming power of water, which is "to babble and gurgle and trickle and foam for ever and ever," anticipates a dominant motif in *The Water-Babies.*

In *Hypatia,* vividly set in fifth-century Alexandria, a melting pot of Greek, Egyptian, Jewish and (intrusive) Northern "Gothic" cultures, Kingsley, while able to rehearse many of his philosophic and moralistic concerns, is given much scope for excursions into the fantastic. These are, however, usually integral to the plot. Thus Hypatia's lyrical revelation to the renegade monk, Philammon, of the mystic ramifications of the Flower of Isis, is critical to their relationship. At the other cultural extreme, the essential nature of the "Gothic" ethos, so significant for the melodramatic climax of the novel, is perfectly brought out through the fantasizing of the Asgard-seeking northerners. Their boasting, their telling of tales of fabulous beasts, of "ghosts, ogres, and fire-drakes, and nicors," culminates in a chanting of the saga of Odin and the Alruna wives, which, Kingsley's footnote says, he wrote after the style of "the earlier Eddaic poems".

Certainly in his poetry of myth and legend Kingsley was technically adept: ballad quatrains for "The Song of the Little Baltung," tetrametric couplets for "The Swan Neck," above all a virtuoso use of unrhymed hexameter in his finest poem, "Andromeda". A few lines, in the scene where Medusa is unveiled, serve to show his mastery there of the imagery of fantasy:

Thus fell the boy on the beast; thus rolled up the beast in his horror,
Once, as the dead eyes glared into his; then his sides, death-sharpened,
Stiffened and stood, brown rock, in the wash of the wandering water.

The same mastery appears in the prose of Kingsley's retelling of that legend, and of those of the Argonauts and of Theseus in *The Heroes, or Greek Fairy Tales for My Children.* The stories are a little simplified and sanitized, but do not lose their mythic force. Here is the end of Aietes' "serpents' teeth" warriors: "Then the magic furrows opened, and the kind earth took them home into her breast; and the grass grew up all green again above them, and Jason's work was done."

The Water-Babies: A Fairy Tale for a Land Baby is, along with "Andromeda," the work in which Kingsley most nearly approached genius. In strange respects it mirrors elements of his 13-years earlier novel, *Alton Locke,* a starkly realistic first-person story of the pilgrimage of a Chartist manqué towards an envisioned New World paradise, via working-class struggle, rick-burning involvement, prison, and eventually a redeeming love. At its crisis-point the narrative switches from realism to the fantasy of Alton's long brainstorm dream, where he undergoes metamorphoses (coral, crab, fish, antelope, giant sloth and ape) in evolutionary sequence, and then experiences a recapitulation of human history, which is in danger either of arrest or of a retrogressive devolution unless altruism prevails. Throughout all this, enemies and loves of Alton's own life-history appear in confusing, yet challenging or guiding, animal guises. Such a scenario is also, in essence, that of *The Water Babies.* The story opens amid industrial grime and deprivation, with Tom, the boy sweep, lost in a labyrinth of soot. Through traumatic misadventure he comes to the cleansing river which runs "clear and cool," and then "strong and free . . . away to the sea." After his metamorphosis into a newt-like (or foetal) underwater manikin, Tom empathizes with sea and river creatures, is led by protean fairies and feminine incarnations from his past (Ellie, the Irishwoman) through a spiritually/bodily transforming pilgrimage, in which stagnation and degeneration are overcome, to achieve, after his kindness to Grimes (his purgatorially imprisoned old taskmaster), the Atlantean paradise of St. Brendan's Isle.

In abridged versions read by children the pleasure lies mainly in Tom's adventuring with creatures of stream and tide—the caddisworm, the otter, the lobster, the old whale. These Kingsley succeeds in anthropomorphizing without falsifying their nature. For adult readers, the platonic allegories and Dante-esque nuances, the Rabelaisian word-lists and satires, the idiosyncratic tilting at fads and theories, largely compensate for some naive moralizing. Just as in Kingsley's realistic novels the realism is suffused with and highlighted by fantasy, so in *The Water-Babies,* his most enduring fantasy, the mid-Victorian scene, and in a timeless sense our own world, are explored and observed in estranging, and thereby sharpening, fairy-tale perspectives.

—K. V. Bailey

KINSELLA, W(illiam) P(atrick)

Nationality: Canadian. **Born:** Edmondton, Alberta, 25 May 1935. **Education:** University of Victoria, B.A. 1974; University of Iowa, M.F.A., 1978. **Family:** Married 1) Myrna Salls in 1957, two daughters; 2) Mildred Clay-Heming in 1965 (divorced 1978), one daughter; 3) Ilene Ann Knight in 1978. **Career:** Clerk, Government of Alberta, Edmonton, 1954-56; manager, Retail Credit Co., Edmonton, Alberta, 1956-61; owner, Caesar's Italian Village (restaurant), 1967-72; editor, *Martlet,* 1973-74; cab driver, Victoria, British Columbia, 1974-76; instructor, Creative Writing and English, University of Calgary, 1978-83; since 1983, full-time writer. **Awards:** Edmonton *Journal* prize, 1966; Canadian Fiction award, 1976; Houghton Mifflin Literary Fellowship, 1982; Books in Canada First Novel Award, 1982; Canadian Authors Association prize for fiction, 1982; Writer's Guild of Alberta award for fiction, 1982, 1983; Writer's Guild of Alberta O'Hagan novel medal, 1984; Vancouver award for writing, 1987; Canadian Booksellers Association Author of the Year, 1987; Leacock Medal for Humour, 1987; Order of Canada, 1994. D.Litt.: Laurentian University, Sudbury, Ontario, 1990. **Agent:** Nancy Colbert, 55 Avenue Road, Toronto, Ontario, M5R 3L2, Canada. **Address:** 15325 19a Avenue, White Rock, British Columbia, V4B 5G3, Canada.

FANTASY PUBLICATIONS

Novels

Shoeless Joe. Boston, Houghton Mifflin, 1982; London, Allison and Busby, 1988.
The Iowa Baseball Confederacy. Boston, Houghton Mifflin, 1986.

Short Stories

Shoeless Joe Jackson Comes to Iowa. Ottawa, Oberon Press, 1980; Dallas, Southern Methodist University Press, 1993.
The Thrill of the Grass. Toronto, Penguin, 1984; New York, Penguin, 1985.
Red Wolf, Red Wolf. Toronto, Collins, 1987; Dallas, Southern Methodist University Press, 1990.
The Further Adventures of Slugger McBatt: Baseball Stories. Boston, Houghton Mifflin, and Toronto, Collins, 1988.

OTHER PUBLICATIONS

Novel

Box Socials: A Novel. Toronto, HarperCollins, 1991; New York, Ballantine, 1992.

Short Stories

Dance Me Outside. Ottawa, Oberon Press, 1977; as *Dance Me Outside: More Tales from the Ermineskin Reserve,* Boston, Godine, 1986.
Scars: Stories. Ottawa, Oberon Press, 1978.
Born Indian. Ottawa, Oberon Press, 1981.
The Ballad of the Public Trustee. Vancouver, William Hoffer, 1982.

The Moccasin Telegraph and Other Stories. Toronto, Penguin, 1983; as *The Moccasin Telegraph and Other Indian Tales,* Boston, Godine, 1984.
The Fencepost Chronicles. Don Mills, Ontario, Totem Press, 1986; Boston, Houghton Mifflin, 1987.
Chapter One of a Work in Progress. Vancouver, William Hoffer, 1988.
The Miss Hobbema Pageant. Toronto, Collins, 1989; New York, Harper, 1990.
The First and Last Annual Six Towns Area Old Timers' Baseball Game. Minneapolis, Coffee House Press, 1991.
The Dixon Cornbelt League. Toronto, HarperCollins, 1993.

Poetry

Rainbow Warehouse, with Ann Knight. Porter's Lake, Nova Scotia, Pottersfield Press, 1989.

Other

Two Spirits Soar: The Art of Allen Sapp. New York, Stoddard, 1990.
A Series for the World: Baseball's First International Fall Classic, with others. San Francisco, Woodford, 1992.

*

Film Adaptation: *Field of Dreams,* 1989, from the novel *Shoeless Joe.*

Bibliography: *W. P. Kinsella: A Partially-Annotated Bibliographical Checklist* by Ann Knight, Iowa City, A-Cross Publications, 1983.

Manuscript Collection: National Library of Canada, Ottawa.

Critical Study: *The Fiction of W. P. Kinsella: Tall Tales in Various Voices* by Don Murray, Fredericton, New Brunswick, York Press, 1987.

W. P. Kinsella comments:

They say that an author writes in cycles. When you start out writing at an early age you produce fantastical stories because you have no life experiences to write about. And then, as you get this experience, you write about it (or your perceptions of it); later on, you return to the fantastical. I think I've gone that route because I started out writing science fiction. I was a science fiction and fantasy buff—especially the latter—during my teenage years. I was influenced a lot by Ray Bradbury, especially his early works, which I think are just fantastically good. I'm referring to such works as *The Golden Apples of the Sun, The Martian Chronicles,* and *The Illustrated Man.* I read the magazines *Fantasy and Science Fiction* and *Galaxy,* the major ones of that ilk which were available back in the 1950s. (From "Interview with Bill Kinsella: On the Other Short Fictions," in *The Fiction of W. P. Kinsella: Tall Tales in Various Voices,* 1987, page 30.)

*   *   *

After producing some well-received realistic stories, many about American Indians in the Ermineskin Reserve, W. P. Kinsella drifted into writing idiosyncratic fantasy stories that often express his unalloyed enthusiasm for the game of baseball, which Kinsella argues is an absolutely perfect experience for players and spectators, a panacea for all human problems. Undoubtedly, Kinsella's devotion to baseball has inspired his best work; but his focus on the game may limit his appeal. Consider "The Thrill of the Grass," which takes place during the baseball strike of 1981. A disconsolate fan, who numbly goes to the stadium with nothing to do, finds a mysterious door that lets him walk onto the field. He then silently recruits other fans to rip up the field of artificial turf, square foot by square foot, and replace it with square feet of sod with real grass. To someone who sees a baseball strike as a true tragedy and regards artificial turf as a sacrilege blighting the game, the story will be powerful and evocative; to someone who thinks baseball is only a game, the story may seem overwrought, even silly.

Kinsella's first and best novel, *Shoeless Joe,* concerns an Iowa farmer who, in response to a strange disembodied voice, builds a baseball field on his farm, where Shoeless Joe Jackson—a player banished from baseball after a famous scandal—and other dead players come to play baseball. Another mysterious message leads him to find the reclusive writer J. D. Salinger, who confessed in a fictional interview that his lifelong dream was to play baseball; they attend a game, then respond to a third message by seeking out an obscure player named Moonlight Graham who played one inning in the major leagues as a defensive replacement. They find he has died, but Graham then reappears as a young man and joins the other players on the field. The final chapter, "The Apotheosis of J. D. Salinger," has Salinger happily going off with the players into whatever realm they occupy when not playing baseball. In this haunting novel, the baseball field is a wonderful world where people get a second chance in life: Ray's father can finally play major league baseball, the disgraced Shoeless Joe can finally return to the game, Graham can finally fulfil his dream of facing major league pitching, and Salinger can finally find happiness. The memorable film version, *Field of Dreams,* captured the novel's atmosphere and charm, effectively replaced Salinger with a fictitious writer, and deservedly won wide popularity.

Kinsella's second novel, *The Iowa Baseball Confederacy,* concerns a man obsessed with proving the existence of an Iowa minor league in the early 1900s, and his friend, an aging minor-leaguer still dreaming of making it to the big leagues. They are mystically transported back to 1906 to witness and participate in an exhibition game between the Iowa Baseball Confederacy All-Stars and the famed Chicago Cubs of Tinkers, Evers and Chance. Amazingly, the game remains tied and extends over a thousand innings during forty days and nights of rain. Though imaginative and entertaining, the novel is not as effective, in part because, by this time, some critic had told Kinsella he was writing "magic realism," and the novel gradually lapses into a gaudy surrealism that contrasts unfavorably with the subtle magic of *Shoeless Joe.* Theodore Roosevelt appears to take a turn at bat; Leonardo da Vinci flies over in a balloon, announcing he invented the game; a statue comes to life and plays right field; and an Indian who believes an Iowa victory will reunite him with a lost sweetheart finally wins the game as a pinch-hitter. Moreover, while *Shoeless Joe* had a timeless idyllic aura, there is a haunted, apocalyptic mood to *The Iowa Baseball Confederacy,* as the men realize that once the game is over they will be returned to the present and the entire experience of the Confederacy and its All-Star game will be wiped forever from human memory; so there is little feeling of triumph in the victory of the minor-leaguers.

Readers who enjoyed *Shoeless Joe* and *The Iowa Baseball Confederacy* will be disappointed by Kinsella's third novel, *Box Socials,* about a Canadian who bats against pitcher Bob Feller in an exhibition game briefly described after numerous digressions about other residents of his rural area; it is neither a fantasy nor, really, a story about baseball, and some may dislike its deliberately convoluted and repetitive prose style.

While most of Kinsella's stories are fantastical only in that events or characters may seem improbable or surrealistic, some stories, like the following examples, can be regarded as fantasies proper. In "The Battery," a homage to magic realism, two twins demonstrate even before birth that they are destined to become a major league pitcher and catcher who can only be effective when working together; the pitcher reappears in "Butterfly Winter," making love to a beautiful native girl while covered with butterflies. In "The Last Pennant Before Armageddon," the manager of the Chicago Cubs, incredibly in first place near the end of the season, learns that the world will be destroyed when the Cubs finally win another pennant, so he altruistically mis-manages his team to defeat. "Distances," a "prequel" to *The Iowa Baseball Confederacy,* shows that novel's protagonists as young men playing in a con-man's exhibition game. "Reports Concerning the Death of the Seattle Albatross Are Somewhat Exaggerated" concerns a bird-like alien who, while on a surveillance mission on Earth, works as a baseball mascot. And "Searching for Freddy" describes an ex-major leaguer who secretly travels across the country, helping young players become effective base-stealers, before he finally fades away, his spirit reborn in a young ballplayer. Fantasies not involving baseball include "Red Wolf, Red Wolf," where one of Flannery O'Connor's fictional characters magically appears and comes to live with her; "Sister Ann of the Cornfields," a prophetess who appears in an Iowa field and gets a hostile reception; and "The History of Peanut Butter," a farcical account of the power and virtues of that food throughout human history. Kinsella's short stories are always entertaining, often imaginative, and at times brilliant; it is unfortunate that, in today's critical climate, his talents will be evaluated solely by his novels.

—Gary Westfahl

KIPLING, (Joseph) Rudyard

Nationality: British. **Born:** Bombay, India, 30 December 1865, of English parents; moved to England, 1872. **Education:** United Services College, Devon, 1878-82. **Family:** Married Caroline Starr Balestier in 1892; two daughters and one son. **Career:** Assistant editor, *Civil and Military Gazette,* Lahore, 1882-87; assistant editor and overseas correspondent, *Pioneer,* Allahabad, 1887-89; full-time writer from 1889; lived in London, 1889-92, and Brattleboro, Vermont, 1892-96, then returned to England; settled in Burwash, Sussex, 1902. Rector, University of St. Andrews, 1922-25. **Awards:** Nobel Prize for Literature, 1907; Royal Society of Literature Gold Medal, 1926. LL.D.: McGill University, Montreal, 1907; D.Litt.: University of Durham, 1907; Oxford University, 1907; Cambridge University, 1907; University of Edinburgh, 1920; the Sorbonne, Paris, 1921; University of Strasbourg, 1921; D.Phil.: University of Athens, 1924. Honorary Fellow, Magdalene College, Cambridge, 1932. Associate member, Académie des Sciences Mo-

rales et Politiques, 1933. Refused the Poet Laureateship, 1895, and the Order of Merit. **Died:** 18 January 1936.

FANTASY PUBLICATIONS

Short Stories

The Jungle Book, illustrated by J. Lockwood Kipling and others. London, Macmillan, and New York, Century, 1894.
The Second Jungle Book, illustrated by J. Lockwood Kipling. London, Macmillan, and New York, Century, 1895; revised edition, Macmillan, 1895.
Just So Stories for Little Children, illustrated by the author. London, Macmillan, and New York, Doubleday, 1902.
Puck of Pook's Hill, illustrated by H. R. Millar. London, Macmillan, and New York, Doubleday, 1906.
Rewards and Fairies, illustrated by Frank Craig. London, Macmillan, and New York, Doubleday, 1910.
Thy Servant a Dog, Told by Boots. London, Macmillan, and New York, Doubleday, 1930; revised edition, as *Thy Servant a Dog and Other Dog Stories,* Macmillan, 1938.
All the Mowgli Stories. London, Macmillan, 1933; New York, Doubleday, 1936.
Phantoms and Fantasies: 20 Tales. New York, Doubleday, 1965.
The Complete Supernatural Stories of Rudyard Kipling, edited by Peter Haining. London, Allen, 1987.
Kipling's Fantasy, edited by John Brunner. New York, Tor, 1992.

OTHER PUBLICATIONS

Novels

The Light That Failed. New York, United States Book Company, 1890; London, Macmillan, 1891.
"Captains Courageous": A Story of the Grand Banks, illustrated by I. W. Taber. London, Macmillan, and New York, Century, 1897.
Kim, illustrated by J. Lockwood Kipling. New York, Doubleday, and London, Macmillan, 1901.

Short Stories

Plain Tales from the Hills. Calcutta, Thacker Spink, 1888; New York, Lovell, and London, Macmillan, 1890.
Soldiers Three: A Collection of Stories. Allahabad, Wheeler, 1888; London, Sampson Low, 1890.
The Stories of the Gadsbys: A Tale Without a Plot. Allahabad, Wheeler, 1888; London, Sampson Low, and New York, Lovell, 1890.
In Black and White. Allahabad, Wheeler, 1888; London, Sampson Low, and New York, Lovell, 1890.
Under the Deodars. Allahabad, Wheeler, 1888; revised edition, London, Sampson Low, 1890.
The Phantom 'Rickshaw and Other Tales. Allahabad, Wheeler, 1888; revised edition, London, Sampson Low, 1890.
Wee Willie Winkie and Other Child Stories. Allahabad, Wheeler, 1888; revised edition, London, Sampson Low, and Chicago, Rand McNally, 1890.
Soldiers Three, and Under the Deodars. New York, Lovell, 1890.

The Phantom 'Rickshaw, and Wee Willie Winkie. New York, Lovell, 1890.

The Courting of Dinah Shadd and Other Stories. New York, Harper, and London, Macmillan, 1890.

Mine Own People. New York, United States Book Company, 1891.

Life's Handicap, Being Stories from Mine Own People. New York and London, Macmillan, 1891.

The Naulahka: A Story of West and East, with Wolcott Balestier. London, Heinemann, and New York, Macmillan, 1892.

Many Inventions. London, Macmillan, and New York, Appleton, 1893.

Soldier Tales. London, Macmillan, 1896; as *Soldier Stories,* New York, Macmillan, 1896.

The Day's Work. New York, Doubleday, and London, Macmillan, 1898.

Stalky & Co. London, Macmillan, and New York, Doubleday, 1899; revised edition, as *The Complete Stalky & Co.,* Macmillan, 1929, Doubleday, 1930.

The Kipling Reader. London, Macmillan, 1900; as *Selected Stories,* 1925.

Traffics and Discoveries. London, Macmillan, and New York, Doubleday, 1904.

Abaft the Funnel. New York, Dodge, 1909.

Actions and Reactions. London, Macmillan, and New York, Doubleday, 1909.

Kipling Stories and Poems Every Child Should Know, edited by Mary E. Burt and W. T. Chapin, illustrated by Charles Livingston Bull and others. New York, Doubleday, 1909.

A Diversity of Creatures. London, Macmillan, and New York, Doubleday, 1917.

Selected Stories, edited by William Lyon Phelps. New York, Doubleday, 1921.

Land and Sea Tales for Scouts and Guides. London, Macmillan, and New York, Doubleday, 1923.

Debits and Credits. London, Macmillan, and New York, Doubleday, 1926.

Selected Stories. London, Macmillan, 1929.

Humorous Tales. London, Macmillan, and New York, Doubleday, 1931.

Animal Stories. London, Macmillan, 1932; New York, Doubleday, 1938.

Limits and Renewals. London, Macmillan, and New York, Doubleday, 1932.

Collected Dog Stories. London, Macmillan, and New York, Doubleday, 1934.

Ham and the Porcupine. New York, Doubleday, 1935.

More Selected Stories. London, Macmillan, 1940.

Twenty-One Tales. London, Reprint Society, 1946.

Ten Stories. London, Pan, 1947.

A Choice of Kipling's Prose, edited by W. Somerset Maugham. London, Macmillan, 1952; as *Maugham's Choice of Kipling's Best: Sixteen Stories,* New York, Doubleday, 1953.

A Treasury of Short Stories. New York, Bantam, 1957.

(Short Stories), edited by Edward Parone. New York, Dell, 1960.

Kipling Stories: Twenty-Eight Exciting Tales. New York, Platt and Munk, 1960.

The Best Short Stories, edited by Randall Jarrell. New York, Hanover House, 1961; as *In the Vernacular: The English in India and The English in England,* New York, Doubleday, 2 vols., 1963. *Famous Tales of India,* edited by B. W. Shir-Cliff. New York, Ballantine, 1962.

Short Stories, edited by Andrew Rutherford. London, Penguin, 2 vols., 1971-76.

Twenty-One Tales, edited by Tim Wilkinson. London, Folio Society, 1972.

Tales of East and West, edited by Bernard Bergonzi. Avon, Connecticut, Limited Editions Club, 1973.

Kipling's Kingdom: Twenty-Five of Kipling's Best Indian Stories, Known and Unknown, edited by Charles Allen. London, Joseph, 1987.

Kipling's Science Fiction, edited by John Brunner. New York, Tor, 1992.

Play

The Harbour Watch (produced London, 1913; revised version, as *Gow's Watch,* produced London, 1924).

Verse

Schoolboy Lyrics. Privately printed, 1881.

Echoes (published anonymously), with Alice Kipling. Privately printed, 1884.

Departmental Ditties and Other Verses. Lahore, Civil and Military Gazette Press, 1886; London, Thacker Spink, 1890.

Departmental Ditties, Barrack-Room Ballads, and Other Verse. New York, United States Book Company, 1890.

Barrack-Room Ballads and Other Verses. London, Methuen, and New York, Macmillan, 1892.

Ballads and Barrack-Room Ballads. New York, Macmillan, 1893.

The Seven Seas. New York, Appleton, and London, Methuen, 1896.

Recessional. Privately printed, 1897.

An Almanac of Twelve Sports, illustrated by William Nicholson. London, Heinemann, and New York, Russell, 1898.

Poems, edited by Wallace Rice. Chicago, Star, 1899.

Recessional and Other Poems. Privately printed, 1899.

The Absent-Minded Beggar. Privately printed, 1899.

With Number Three, Surgical and Medical, and New Poems. Santiago, Chile, Hume, 1900.

Occasional Poems. Boston, Bartlett, 1900.

The Five Nations. London, Methuen, and New York, Doubleday, 1903. *The Muse Among the Motors.* New York, Doubleday, 1904.

A Collected Verse. New York, Doubleday, 1907; London, Hodder and Stoughton, 1912.

A History of England (verse only), with C. R. L. Fletcher. London, Oxford University Press-Hodder and Stoughton, and New York, Doubleday, 1911; revised edition, 1930.

Songs from Books. New York, Doubleday, 1912; London, Macmillan, 1913.

Twenty Poems. London, Methuen, 1918.

The Years Between. London, Methuen, and New York, Doubleday, 1919.

Verse: Inclusive Edition 1885-1918. London, Hodder and Stoughton, and New York, Doubleday, 3 vols., 1919; revised edition, 1921, 1927, 1933.

A Kipling Anthology: Verse. London, Methuen, and New York, Doubleday, 1922.

Songs for Youth, from Collected Verse. London, Hodder and Stoughton, 1924; New York, Doubleday, 1925.

A Choice of Songs. London, Methuen, 1925.

Sea and Sussex. London, Macmillan, and New York, Doubleday, 1926.

St. Andrews, with Walter de la Mare. London, A. and C. Black, 1926.

Songs of the Sea. London, Macmillan, and New York, Doubleday, 1927.

Poems 1886-1929. London, Macmillan, 3 vols., 1929; New York, Doubleday, 3 vols., 1930.

Selected Poems. London, Methuen, 1931.

East of Suez, Being a Selection of Eastern Verses. London, Macmillan, 1931.

Sixty Poems. London, Hodder and Stoughton, 1939.

Verse: Definitive Edition. London, Hodder and Stoughton, and New York, Doubleday, 1940.

So Shall Ye Reap: Poems for These Days. London, Hodder and Stoughton, 1941.

A Choice of Kipling's Verse, edited by T. S. Eliot. London, Faber, 1941; New York, Scribner, 1943.

Sixty Poems. London, Hodder and Stoughton, 1957.

A Kipling Anthology, edited by W. G. Bebbington. London, Methuen, 1964.

The Complete Barrack-Room Ballads, edited by Charles Carrington. London, Methuen, 1973.

Kipling's English History: Poems, edited by Marghanita Laski. London, BBC Publications, 1974.

Kipling: A Selection, edited by James Cochrane. London, Penguin, 1977.

Early Verse by Rudyard Kipling 1879-89, edited by Andrew Rutherford. Oxford, Clarendon Press, and New York, Oxford University Press, 1986.

Other

Quarette, with others. Lahore, Civil and Military Gazette Press, 1885.

The City of Dreadful Night and Other Sketches. Allahabad, Wheeler, 1890.

The City of Dreadful Night and Other Places. Allahabad, Wheeler, and London, Sampson Low, 1891.

The Smith Administration. Allahabad, Wheeler, 1891.

Letters of Marque. Allahabad, Wheeler, and London, Sampson Low, 1891.

American Notes, with *The Bottle Imp* by Robert Louis Stevenson. New York, Ivers, 1891.

Out of India: Things I Saw, and Failed to See, in Certain Days and Nights at Jeypore and Elsewhere. New York, Dillingham, 1895.

The Kipling Birthday Book, edited by Joseph Finn. London, Macmillan, 1896; New York, Doubleday, 1899.

A Fleet in Being: Notes of Two Trips with the Channel Squadron. London, Macmillan, 1898.

From Sea to Sea: Letters of Travel. New York, Doubleday, 1899; as *From Sea to Sea and Other Sketches,* London, Macmillan, 1900. *Works* (Swastika Edition). New York, Doubleday, Appleton, and Century, 15 vols., 1899.

Letters to the Family (Notes on a Recent Trip to Canada). Toronto, Macmillan, 1908.

The Kipling Reader (not same as 1900 collection of short stories). New York, Appleton, 1912.

The New Army in Training. London, Macmillan, 1915.

France at War. London, Macmillan, and New York, Doubleday, 1915.

The Fringes of the Fleet. London, Macmillan, and New York, Doubleday, 1915.

Tales of "The Trade". Privately printed, 1916.

Sea Warfare. London, Macmillan, and New York, Doubleday, 1916.

The War in the Mountains. New York, Doubleday, 1917.

To Fighting Americans (speeches). Privately printed, 1918.

The Eyes of Asia. New York, Doubleday, 1918.

The Graves of the Fallen. London, Imperial War Graves Commission, 1919.

Letters of Travel (1892-1913). London, Macmillan, and New York, Doubleday, 1920.

A Kipling Anthology: Prose. London, Macmillan, and New York, Doubleday, 1922.

Works (Mandalay Edition). New York, Doubleday, 26 vols., 1925-26.

A Book of Words: Selections from Speeches and Addresses Delivered Between 1906 and 1927. London, Macmillan, and New York, Doubleday, 1928.

The One Volume Kipling. New York, Doubleday, 1928.

Souvenirs of France. London, Macmillan, 1933.

A Kipling Pageant. New York, Doubleday, 1935.

Something of Myself for My Friends Known and Unknown. London, Macmillan, and New York, Doubleday, 1937.

Complete Works (Sussex Edition) London, Macmillan, 35 vols., 1937-39; as *Collected Works* (Burwash Edition), New York, Doubleday, 28 vols., 1941 (includes revised versions of some previously published works).

A Kipling Treasury: Stories and Poems. London, Macmillan, 1940.

Kipling: A Selection of His Stories and Poems, edited by John Beecroft. New York, Doubleday, 2 vols., 1956.

The Kipling Sampler, edited by Alexander Greendale. New York, Fawcett, 1962.

Letters from Japan, edited by Donald Richie and Yoshimori Harashima. Tokyo, Kenkyusha, 1962.

Pearls from Kipling, edited by C. Donald Plomer. New Britain, Connecticut, Elihu Burritt Library, 1963.

Rudyard Kipling to Rider Haggard: The Record of a Friendship, edited by Morton Cohen. London, Hutchinson, 1965; Rutherford, New Jersey, Fairleigh Dickinson University Press, 1968.

The Best of Kipling. New York, Doubleday, 1968.

Stories and Poems, edited by Roger Lancelyn Green. London, Dent, 1970.

Kipling's Horace, edited by Charles Carrington. London, Methuen, 1978.

American Notes: Rudyard Kipling's West, edited by Arrell M. Gibson. Norman, University of Oklahoma Press, 1981.

The Portable Kipling, edited by Irving Howe. New York, Viking Press, 1982.

"O Beloved Kids": Rudyard Kipling's Letters to His Children, edited by Elliot L. Gilbert. London, Weidenfeld and Nicolson, 1983; New York, Harcourt Brace, 1984.

Kipling's India: Uncollected Sketches 1884-1888, edited by Thomas Pinney. London, Macmillan, and New York, Schocken, 1985.

The Illustrated Kipling, edited by Neil Philip. London, Collins, 1987.

A Choice of Kipling's Prose, edited by Craig Raine. London, Faber, 1987.

Kipling's Japan, edited by Hugh Cortazzi and George Webb. London, Athlone Press, 1988.

Editor, *The Irish Guards in the Great War.* London, Macmillan, and New York, Doubleday, 2 vols., 1923.

*

Film Adaptations: *Captains Courageous,* 1937, 1977 (TV movie); *Wee Willie Winkie,* 1937; *Gunga Din,* 1939, from the poem in *Barrack-Room Ballads*; *Soldiers Three,* 1951; *The Light That Failed,* 1939; *The Jungle Book,* 1942, 1967, 1994; *Kim,* 1951, 1984 (TV movie); *Stalky and Co.,* 1982 (TV serial).

Bibliography: *Rudyard Kipling: A Bibliography Catalogue* by James McG. Stewart, edited by A. W. Keats, Toronto, Dalhousie University-University of Toronto Press, 1959, London, Oxford University Press, 1960; "Kipling: An Annotated Bibliography of Writings about Him" by H. E. Gerber and E. Lauterbach, in *English Fiction in Transition 3* (Tempe, Arizona), 1960, and 8, 1965.

Manuscript Collections: Cornell University Library, Ithaca, New York; Library of Congress, Washington, D.C.; Houghton Library, Harvard University, Cambridge, Massachusetts; Pierpont Morgan Library, New York.

Critical Studies (selection): *Rudyard Kipling: His Life and Work* by Charles Carrington, London, Macmillan, 1955, revised edition, 1978, as *The Life of Rudyard Kipling,* New York, Doubleday, 1955; *Rudyard Kipling* by Rosemary Sutcliff, London, Bodley Head, 1960, New York, Walck, 1961; *The Readers' Guide to Rudyard Kipling's Work,* Canterbury, Gibbs, 1961; *Kipling: The Critical Heritage,* London, Routledge, and New York, Barnes and Noble, 1971, both edited by Roger Lancelyn Green; *Kipling and the Children* by Green, London, Elek, 1965; *Kipling's Mind and Art* edited by Andrew Rutherford, Edinburgh, Oliver and Boyd, and Stanford, California, Stanford University Press, 1964; *Rudyard Kipling* by J. I. M. Stewart, London, Gollancz, and New York, Dodd Mead, 1966; *Rudyard Kipling: Realist and Fabulist* by Bonamy Dobrée, London and New York, Oxford University Press, 1967; *Kipling and His World* by Kingsley Amis, London, Thames and Hudson, 1975, New York, Scribner, 1976; *The Strange Ride of Rudyard Kipling: His Life and Works* by Angus Wilson, London, Secker and Warburg, 1977, New York, Viking Press, 1978; *Rudyard Kipling* by Lord Birkenhead, London, Weidenfeld and Nicholson, 1978; *Rudyard Kipling* by James Harrison, Boston, Twayne, 1982; *Rudyard Kipling and the Fiction of Adolescence* by Robert F. Moss, New York, St. Martin's Press, and London, Macmillan, 1982; *Kipling: Interviews and Recollections* edited by Harold Orel, London, Macmillan, 2 vols., 1983, New York, Barnes and Noble, 2 vols., 1984; *A Kipling Companion* by Norman Page, London, Macmillan, 1984; *Kipling and Orientalism* by B. J. Moore-Gilbert, London, Croom Helm, 1986; *Kipling's Hidden Narratives* by Sandra Kemp, Oxford, Blackwell, 1988; *Rudyard Kipling* by Martin Seymour-Smith, London, Macdonald, 1989.

*   *   *

Rudyard Kipling is best remembered as the writer and poet of the British Empire in India: but within and outside this milieu, he wrote many remarkable science-fiction, fantasy and supernatural stories. These are scattered through his numerous story collections—though recent volumes have assembled this material. Kipling's great skill and literary craftsmanship can be overpowering, especially when showing off his remarkable ability with dialect and now-dead slang, or in the complex, bitter, allusive tales of his later years.

From the earliest he was adept at framing and distancing supernatural themes: "In the House of Suddhoo" and "The Gate of the Hundred Sorrows" (*Plain Tales from the Hills*) have a fantastic flavour "legitimized" by devices of magical fakery—repeated in the sinisterly comic "The Sending of Dana Da" (*Soldiers Three*), whose victim suffers a plague of tiny, injured white cats—and opium dreams. "The Phantom Rickshaw" (*Wee Willie Winkie*) is a conventional haunting, lent power by its intensity and the exotic Indian setting of these early works; "The Strange Ride of Morrowbie Jukes" (same collection) enters nightmare territory as the eponymous Briton finds himself trapped in a Village of the Dead where Indians who prove too lively when sent to the burning ghats are exiled.

In later ghost stories, ambiguity increases. We never learn what shocking image was photographed from the dead man's retina in "At the End of the Passage" (*Life's Handicap*), while the possession in "The Mark of the Beast" (same collection) might *possibly* have been suggestion or illness. A phantom army moves almost imperceptibly through the Afghan military action in "The Lost Legion" (*Many Inventions*): English troops think they may hear something, while the enemy is stricken with terror. The ghostly lost children haunting a blind woman's estate in the over-sentimental "They" (*Traffics and Discoveries*) are invisible and elusive, as is precisely why the protagonist must never revisit that seemingly idyllic place. One of the cruellest tales, "Swept and Garnished" (*A Diversity of Creatures*), confronts a well-off Berlin woman with five children fresh from current World War I shelling: they and the blood they leave on the floor may be purely subjective. Particularly oblique is the late, dark "The Wish House" (*Debits and Credits*), whose heroine believes in a supernatural deal whereby (for no longer requited love) she accepts whatever her man might otherwise have suffered—in the form of a physical and malign ulcer. Atypically, "A Madonna of the Trenches" (same collection) has an undeniable apparition of the dead near the front line, but is less about a ghost than the shattering spiritual implications for those who see it. "The House Surgeon" (*Actions and Reactions*) unravels a complex haunting in which the fearful shadow of one living person's obsession troubles a whole household . . . including its dead.

Strange dreams and time-dislocated perceptions recur in the best fantasies. "The Finest Story in the World" (*Many Inventions*) features an unimportant man who relates vivid, tantalizing glimpses of past lives—but to Kipling the narrator's frustration he rejects ancient mysteries for the throes of young love. In "The Bridge-Builders" (*The Day's Work*) a new Ganges bridge is threatened by both floods and old Hindi gods, who argue its fate while the English engineer and builder overhears them in a haze of opium. "The Brushwood Boy" (same collection) contains one of literature's few successful depictions of a dream country with the skewed logic, geography and menace of dreams: the perfect (indeed, too good to be true) young soldier who has dreamt all his life of this landscape eventually finds in reality the woman he repeatedly met there. "Wireless" (*Traffics and Discoveries*) hints at a resonance across time mediated by nearby amateur radio experiments, as a tipsy chemist's assistant, dying like John Keats from TB, tries to write poetry for his girlfriend (named, like Keats's, Fanny) and, drafting and redrafting, converges unknowingly on famous lines from "The Eve of St. Agnes" and "Kubla Khan". Two people's recurring fits of horrors in "In the Same Boat" (*A Diversity of Creatures*) are finally vanquished when traced to shocks experienced by the victims' pregnant mothers (shades of Dianetics!).

Kipling's best-known vein of fantasy is the anthropomorphic, with speaking beasts or inanimate objects. The tales of Mowgli (in

The Jungle Book and *The Second Jungle Book,* rearranged in *All the Mowgli Stories*), the child adopted by wolves and grown into a more convincingly complex Jungle Lord than Tarzan, have the raw force of myth. Many scenes are unforgettable: the ransoming of the infant Mowgli from the tiger who claims him; his assertion of dominance over the wolf-council by wielding the "Red Flower," fire; the terrible dance of Kaa the python that hypnotizes monkeys into his jaws, while Mowgli's eyes see only an old snake wriggling ("Kaa's Hunting"); the bloodless yet devastating erasure of the village that mistreated Mowgli's adoptive parents ("Letting in the Jungle"); the ancient cobra guarding forgotten treasure in the Cold Lairs, and the brutal parable of greed and murder that follows when one item strays from this hoard ("The King's Ankus"); the campaign against a huge pack of the feared dhole-dogs, culminating in bloodbath ("Red Dog"). The Disney movie travesty conveys little of these stories' intensity.

The tall tales and whimsical fables of *Just So Stories* contrast strongly with the *Jungle Books'* careful realism—offering exuberantly daft "origin myths" for the whale's narrow throat, the camel's hump, the rhinoceros' skin, the leopard's spots, the elephant's trunk, etc. They should be read aloud. Other chatty-animal stories include "Rikki-Tikki-Tavi" (*The Jungle Book*) with its epic battle between cobras and the eponymous mongoose hero; "The Undertakers" (*The Second Jungle Book*), a professional dialogue amongst scavengers (jackal, adjutant-crane and crocodile) with a grisly conclusion; and "A Walking Delegate" (*The Day's Work*) and "The Mother Hive" (*Actions and Reactions*), political parables where dissidents are pictured respectively as a seditious horse preaching democracy rather than obedience to human Law, and an infestation of wax-moth destroying the hive whose weak bees listen to liberal sentiments.

The Law is always important: the harsh Jungle Law or Army discipline (cf. "The Army of a Dream," in *Traffics and Discoveries,* that dire wish-fulfilment fantasy of a perfect national army in militarized England), or the kindlier but now politically unacceptable administration of the Raj which in many stories treats Indian natives as unruly children. The Law is also co-operation, as discovered by the myriad individualized components of "The Ship That Found Herself" (*The Day's Work*), which learn to work together during a rough maiden voyage. Another inanimate fantasy in the same collection, ".007," features railway engines: .007 isn't accepted by his fellow-steamers until a heroic rescue mission. . . .

Some tales deal in myth or eschatology, like the astrological fable of fate and death "The Children of the Zodiac" (*Many Inventions*), the Arabesque Adam-and-Eve variant "The Enemies To Each Other" (*Debits and Credits*), "The Gardener" (same collection) with its near-subliminal hint of Christ's presence, and two linked stories of the celestial Civil Service—"On the Gate" (same collection) and "Uncovenanted Mercies" (*Limits and Renewals*)—showing Heaven and Hell as bureaucracies whose officials (including Death, St. Peter, Gabriel and Satan) do their best for human souls by juggling with the letter of biblical Law.

Puck of Pook's Hill and *Rewards and Fairies* comprise lively historical vignettes, framed by the device of Puck conjuring figures from the past to entertain children. Some are fantasies: "Dymchurch Flit" (*Puck . . .*) definitively relates the departure of the Fair Folk, "Cold Iron" (*Rewards . . .*) shows the dreams of elves wrecked by the work of a smith-god, and "The Knife and the Naked Chalk" (*Rewards . . .*) depicts myth in the making as the prehistoric man who paid a fearful price for the secret of iron must become a god, separated by divinity from his people and intended

woman. The late *Thy Servant a Dog,* an obsessively twee narration from the canine viewpoint, is not highly regarded.

Kipling's science fiction also deserves attention, notably the airship sequence "With the Night Mail" (*Actions and Reactions*) and "As Easy As A.B.C." (*A Diversity of Creatures*). The borderline story, "A Matter of Fact" (*Many Inventions*) describes the sighting of fantastic sea monsters with intense realism; another, "A Doctor of Medicine" (*Rewards and Fairies*) is a *tour de force* of astrological reasoning which by wild luck indicates that the Black Death can be countered by killing rats.

Although his stories need closer attention from us than from his contemporaries, Kipling's range and power remain deeply impressive. In 1907 he was the first Briton to receive the Nobel Prize for Literature.

—David Langford

KIRK, Richard. *See* **HOLDSTOCK, Robert (Paul).**

KIRK, Richard. *See* **WELLS, Angus.**

KNAAK, Richard A(llen)

Nationality: American. **Born:** Chicago, Illinois, 28 May 1961. **Education:** University of Illinois at Urbana-Champaign, B.A. 1984. **Career:** Warehouseman, Motorola, 1984-85, Schaumburg, Illinois; resumé writer, Allen & Associates, 1986; office clerk, Sears Mortgage, 1986-88; freelance writer from 1988. **Agent:** Peekner Literary Agency, 3121 Portage Road, Bethlehem, PA 18017, USA. **Address:** PO Box 8158, Bartlett, IL 60103, USA.

<small>FANTASY PUBLICATIONS</small>

Novels (series: DragonLance Heroes; Dragonrealm)

The Legend of Huma (DragonLance Heroes). Lake Geneva, Wisconsin, TSR, 1988; London, Penguin, 1989.
Firedrake (Dragonrealm). New York, Warner, 1989; London, Orbit, 1990.
Icedragon (Dragonrealm). New York, Warner, 1989; London, Orbit, 1990.
Kaz the Minotaur (DragonLance Heroes). Lake Geneva, Wisconsin, TSR, and London, Penguin, 1990.
Wolfhelm (Dragonrealm). New York, Warner, 1990; London, Orbit, 1991.

Shadow Steed (Dragonrealm). New York, Warner, 1990; London, Orbit, 1991.
The Shrouded Realm (Dragonrealm). New York, Warner, 1991.
Children of the Drake (Dragonrealm). New York, Warner, 1991.
Dragon Tome (Dragonrealm). New York, Warner, 1992.
The Crystal Dragon (Dragonrealm). New York, Warner, 1993.
King of the Grey. New York, Warner, 1993.
The Dragon Crown (Dragonrealm). New York, Warner, 1994.
Frostwing. New York, Warner, 1995.

*

Richard A. Knaak comments:

First and foremost, I have always tried to entertain my readers. I do not go out and try to write the "Great Novel," preferring to work on something enjoyable to both myself and others. Yet, while I am a story-teller first, if one reads carefully, one will see the other points I am trying to get across. My main characters are generally the "Everyman," the regular person, perhaps with abilities he does not yet understand, who becomes caught up in impossible situations that *he* must solve. The heroes of my Dragonrealm novels and of *King of the Grey* are prime examples. Whatever one gets out of reading one of my works, I hope that they have at least been entertained for a time. That means I've done my job.

* * *

Richard Knaak's first fantasy novel, *The Legend of Huma,* is a prequel to the original DragonLance books by Margaret Weis and Tracy Hickman, set in the imaginary world of Krynn. The DragonLance saga, like most of TSR's fantasy novels, is designed to be compatible with their "Advanced Dungeons and Dragons" role-playing game, though sales of the novels outstrip those of the game. Huma is mentioned in the original books as a legendary hero who discovered the magical Dragonlances, and *The Legend of Huma* is his story.

Knaak's book is set against a background of plague, famine and war between good and evil. The lances—weapons enchanted against dragons—are eventually used to tip the balance in titanic battles between mighty airborne cavalry. Huma begins as a relatively lowly Knight of Solamnia, belonging to the Order of the Rose who venerate wisdom and justice. The story is essentially a traditional knightly quest, where success comes from upholding the tenets of the Order as much as from fighting evil. Huma's wisdom and justice are demonstrated early in the book when he rescues a prisoner who turns out to be a minotaur—traditionally a race inimical to humans. The minotaur, Kaz, declares that he owes Huma a debt for saving his life and spends the rest of the book following Huma around, giving the Knight the opportunity to repeat the act of chivalry on numerous occasions.

A silver dragon notices Huma's noble actions and takes an interest in the Knight. Later, when Huma is wounded in battle, a beautiful, silver-haired girl nurses him. She, it turns out, is the dragon in human form. They fall in love, but she does not tell him she is a dragon and Huma does not realize it until the eve of the final battle. No tale of chivalry would be complete without a little unrequited love. After the kind of long and hazardous journey which is traditional in quests, Huma finds an ancient building hidden in the mountains, where he undergoes three tests in order to gain the DragonLances. First, he must kill an ancient dragon—which he

does, using a powerful, sentient sword from the dragon's hoard. A magical mirror then transports Huma back to the Knights' stronghold, Vingaard Keep, where the Grand Master, Trake, has died of the plague and the second-in-command is seriously ill. Huma uncovers and defeats a traitor responsible for spreading the disease among their ranks. The renegade's identity comes as a surprise and provides one of the best-handled scenes in the book. Finally, Huma finds himself back in the dragon's treasure cavern where his last test is to resist being possessed by the magic sword he found there. The sentient and evil weapon promises him power if he kills an innocent priest but, after a struggle of will, Huma's sense of virtue wins through.

Having proved his worth, Huma is granted the DragonLances. However, the forces of evil, under Galen Dracos, have almost defeated the knights by the time Huma reaches Vingaard Keep with his prize. Huma and his silver dragon decide to raid Galen Dracos' fortress and meet their enemy face to face. Galen Dracos captures Huma and, being a typical evil tyrant, gloats over him before killing him. The mage has a magical green globe capable of allowing his patron, the malevolent deity Takhisis, entry to the world of Krynn. Galen's downfall is that he tries to double-cross the goddess and steal the globe's power for himself at the last minute. Takhisis defeats her traitorous servant but Huma snatches the opportunity to smash the globe. The goddess is weakened, but not defeated, and the end of the story would not be complete without Huma battling Takhisis using a Dragonlance. He wins, despite being mortally wounded, and in true knightly tradition offers the goddess an honourable surrender if she willingly leaves Krynn taking her evil dragons with her.

Kaz survives as a witness and the knights honour his actions. Knaak's second DragonLance novel, *Kaz the Minotaur,* shows Kaz trying to follow in Huma's footsteps after the Knight's death. Although these books are well-constructed tales of knightly quests, they are not overly original. There are just too many clichés such as mad, evil mages whose fortresses crumble when they are defeated. What Knaak is good at, however, is describing dragons; and he has the opportunity to do quite a lot of that in his next series, the Dragonrealm novels.

The Dragonrealm books are set in a land ruled by different coloured dragons—red, gold, green, silver, etc. The colours reflect different spheres of interest, magical ability and temperament as well as the type of land the creatures command. For instance, the Green dragon rules the forests and the Red dragon lives in the volcanic Hellplains. The series involves plots and power-struggles between dragons and humans, dragons and dragons, humans and each other and various ancient races, powerful elemental creatures, witches and warlocks and even a sole-surviving alien from a long-destroyed planet. Battles rage, lands are devastated and the various factions change sides faster than you can turn the pages. The hero, Cabe Bedlam, is of the Luke Skywalker type—a young lad with untrained powers who eventually learns that his father is an evil warlock who has dabbled too much with the dark side.

By the end of the first volume, *Firedrake,* it is easy to sympathize with the survivors' view that "the tragic part in their minds was that so many had died fighting over a thing that few could even understand." The later books are less confusing, but Knaak's tendency to rescue characters from by trouble using a *deus ex machina* palls after a while.

—Lucya Szachnowski

KOTZWINKLE, William

Nationality: American. **Born:** Scranton, Pennsylvania, 22 November 1938. **Education:** Rider College, Lawrenceville, New Jersey; Pennsylvania State University, University Park. **Family:** Married Elizabeth Gundy in 1970. **Career:** Cook, Le Figaro Cafe, New York City, 1963; wrote for tabloid newspaper, mid-1960s. Lived in New York 1957-70, New Brunswick, Canada, 1970-83, and Maine since 1983. **Awards:** Bread Loaf Conference scholarship; World Fantasy award, 1977. **Agent:** Henry Dunow, Harold Ober Associates, 425 Madison Avenue, New York, NY 10017, USA.

FANTASY PUBLICATIONS

Novels

Doctor Rat. New York, Knopf, and Henley-on-Thames, Oxfordshire, Ellis, 1976.
Fata Morgana. New York, Knopf, and London, Hutchinson, 1977.
Herr Nightingale and the Satin Woman (novella), illustrated by Joe Servello. New York, Knopf, 1978; London, Hutchinson, 1979.
The Exile. New York, Seymour Lawrence, and London, Bodley Head, 1987.

Short Stories

Hearts of Wood and Other Timeless Tales. Boston, Godine, 1986.
The Hot Jazz Trio, illustrated by Joe Servello. Boston, Houghton Mifflin, 1989.

OTHER PUBLICATIONS

Novels

Hermes 3000. New York, Pantheon, 1972.
The Fan Man. New York, Avon, and Henley-on-Thames, Oxfordshire, Ellis, 1974.
Night-Book. New York, Avon, 1974.
Swimmer in the Secret Sea. New York, Avon, 1975; Henley-on-Thames, Oxfordshire, Ellis, 1976.
Jack in the Box. New York, Putnam, 1980; London, Abacus, 1981; as *Book of Love,* Boston, Houghton Mifflin, 1990.
Christmas at Fontaine's. New York, Putnam, 1982; London, Deutsch, 1983.
E.T.: The Extra-Terrestrial (novelization of screenplay). New York, Putnam, and London, Barker, 1982.
Superman III (novelization of screenplay). New York, Warner, and London, Arrow, 1983.
Queen of Swords. New York, Putnam, and London, Deutsch, 1984.
E.T.: The Book of the Green Planet. New York, Berkley, 1985.
The Midnight Examiner. Boston, Houghton Mifflin, 1989.
The Game of Thirty. Boston, Houghton Mifflin, 1994.

Short Stories

Elephant Bangs Train. New York, Pantheon, and London, Faber, 1971.
Jewel of the Moon. New York, Putnam, 1985.

Play

Screenplay: *Book of Love,* 1991.

Other (for children)

The Fireman. New York, Pantheon, 1969.
The Ship That Came Down the Gutter. New York, Pantheon, 1970; Kingswood, Surrey, World's Work, 1976.
Elephant Boy: A Story of the Stone Age. New York, Farrar Straus, 1970.
The Day the Gang Got Rich. New York, Viking Press, 1970.
The Oldest Man and Other Timeless Stories. New York, Pantheon, 1971.
Return of Crazy Horse. New York, Farrar Straus, 1971.
The Supreme, Superb, Exalted, and Delightful, One and Only Magic Building. New York, Farrar Straus, 1973.
Up the Alley with Jack and Joe. New York, Macmillan, 1974.
The Leopard's Tooth. Boston, Houghton Mifflin, 1976.
The Ant Who Took Away Time. New York, Doubleday, 1978.
Dream of Dark Harbor. New York, Doubleday, 1979.
The Nap Master. New York, Harcourt Brace, 1979.
The Extra Terrestrial Storybook. New York, Putnam, 1982.
Great World Circus. New York, Putnam, 1983.
Trouble in Bugland: A Collection of Inspector Mantis Mysteries. Boston, Godine, 1983.
The World Is Big and I'm So Small. New York, Crown, 1986.
The Empty Notebook. Boston, Godine, 1990.

*

Film Adaptation: *Book of Love,* 1991, from his novel *Jack in the Box.*

Manuscript Collection: Seymour Lawrence Room, University of Mississippi.

*   *   *

A Fata Morgana is a particular kind of mirage—tricky, magical and difficult to take hold of. Not only did Kotzwinkle use it as the title of the most sparkling of his fantasy novels, but it serves well as a metaphor for all of his work. He is an exceedingly clever and innovative writer who has always operated on the borderlands of the genre, yet his themes and treatments have been so different from book to book that he is difficult to generalize about or to categorize.

Fata Morgana appears to be an historical detective story. It is set mainly in the Paris of 1861, following the fortunes of Inspector Picard of the Paris police as he investigates the life and crimes of Ric Lazare, a young fortune-teller who preys on Parisian high society. But the book is well titled, for nothing is what it seems. Lazare is revealed to be wise and talented beyond his apparent years—a trapeze artist, an expert toy-maker, a black magician, who is perhaps centuries old. It is clear that Lazare is in control of Picard, either allowing him to travel across central Europe in search of Lazare's roots and earlier crimes, or maybe implanting this journey in Picard's mind to warn him off. Does Lazare control time itself? Does he kill and resurrect Picard? Kotzwinkle presents these as possibilities, yet refrains from committing himself.

This is, above all, a light and entertaining novel. It paints a rich and fascinating picture of Paris and especially of the solitary, middle-aged Picard, who is too fond of good food and plump prostitutes. He is a sad figure, posing unsuccessfully as Monsieur Sanjoy ("without joy?"), a dealer in pearls, and lusting after the ample charms of Lazare's wife (up to the moment when she offers herself to him).

By contrast with the solidity of background and protagonist, the plot is dream-like, verging on the surreal. Kotzwinkle makes much use of the symbolism of tarot cards, mirrors and toys, creating one illusion on top of another.

While Kotzwinkle does always break new ground in each of his novels, it is dangerous to generalize even here, since *Herr Nightingale and the Satin Woman* has some strong parallels with *Fata Morgana*. Here again, is a middle-aged policeman investigating international crime. But Inspector Bagg is from Scotland Yard, the date is probably the early 1930s and this is a book heavily illustrated by Joe Servello with a text of only novella length.

Herr Nightingale and the Satin Woman is subtly (sometimes obscurely) presented in brief impressionistic passages which omit many basic details. It is clear only that Bagg is chasing Herr Nightingale (a German veteran of World War I) and the enigmatic Satin Woman (his beautiful accomplice) as they travel in Europe, to China, and back to Cairo and Istanbul, buying and selling machine-guns. As the fortunes of each side suffer frequent reversals, Bagg is corrupted by wealth.

What Kotzwinkle is doing is not only satirizing the romantic crime-adventure novels of the inter-bellum period (and earlier) but adding a surrealistic side to everything, which blurs the reality. Hence, Bagg deals with a talking mole. The Satin Woman buys a cricket in a cage, but the cricket plays the piano and has a sexual relationship with her. Later, Bagg acquires a golden caterpillar, a magical creature which purloins gold and other precious trinkets, storing them inside Bagg's head. Even when Bagg returns to London, the caterpillar continues its thieving, while "Bagg fights down the urge to arrest himself." Like Picard in *Fata Morgana,* Bagg is a loveable character with a strong past.

As different as any novel could possibly be from the foregoing is *Doctor Rat,* which is political propaganda against the treatment of animals by humans, whether through experimentation, as a food resource or in zoos. It is an astonishing *tour de force,* by turns satirical, comic, disgustingly unpleasant and overly sentimental; it won a World Fantasy Award.

To tell his story, Kotzwinkle uses multiple animal narrators. Principal among these is the eponymous (and self-styled) Doctor Rat, the oldest and cleverest rat in a large laboratory. He claims medical training and great authority, boasting that he has written scientific papers, songs and poetry. He is an extreme reactionary, an apologist for all the dreadful experiments carried out in the laboratory, which have resulted in the torturing, maiming and killing of innumerable rats, dogs and so on.

The other rats rebel, but Doctor Rat defies them, escaping capture and undergoing a series of bizarre adventures (all within the lab itself, which seems to expand, *Tardis*-like, in order to accommodate it all). He meets oriental rats, a nymphomaniac rat (what a pity he has been castrated early in his life) and a gay rat, and he is dosed with cocaine. Of course, rat behaviour is being heavily anthropomorphized, but with great comic effect.

Alternating with the rat episodes (and paralleling them in a way that seems too contrived) are even briefer chapters narrated (re-

spectively) by a dog, a pig, a hyaena, a snake, a whale, and so on, as all the animals of the world congregate together—one huge mass of them on each continent. They are friendly towards each other and communicate freely (though wordlessly). The purpose which drives them is to merge their thought streams and achieve unity, so that mankind will recognize their intelligence and stop killing them.

There is some repetition as each species of animal begins its migration to the assembly zone (though in general the novel is remarkably well sustained). And Kotzwinkle is guilty of a blatant and rather maudlin attempt to make animals seem noble, attractive and in all ways better than humans.

If humans had assembled to meet the animals on their own terms, unity might have been achieved, but the human reaction is, as usual, to assert control. So the military attacks the animal assemblies, mainly with machine guns, then burns the bodies (an action notably reminiscent of the Holocaust).

At the end, only Doctor Rat is left alive. This is not intended as a realistic narrative, and it combines allegory with the satire. It is a book which cannot be read without considerable emotional reaction.

The Exile is very different again. It concerns David Caspian, a rich and successful Hollywood film star, now aged 45. He is relatively happily married, relatively stable in his profession, relatively sane. Then he begins to experience shifts into the body of Felix Falkenhayn, a black-marketeer in Nazi Germany towards the end of World War II. Each shift lasts minutes or hours. Felix is obviously not Caspian, but some of the Germans look exactly like friends and colleagues of Caspian's. He has no control over these shifts, and is merely an observer while Felix is in charge of the body. Meanwhile, his own body seems to behave as normal during his "missing" periods; on the film-set he gives superlative performances without having any memory of them.

After each occasion, Caspian describes his experiences to his analyst, and both of them try to invent explanations, mostly psychological. Felix, who is dishonest, but not an amoral man, discovers the existence of concentration camps and is horrified; he tries to help one particular Jewish girl. At length he is captured and tortured. His mind escapes from his body, leaving Caspian trapped. Back in contemporary Los Angeles, in Caspian's body, Felix reveals all this to the analyst—who does not believe him.

Most striking about the novel is the restrained yet chilling tone of the writing. There is a terrifyingly dark and brooding quality throughout, with some wit but (deliberately) no humour. Both settings are very convincing. This is arguably Kotzwinkle's masterwork.

The three stories in *The Hot Jazz Trio* are best described as surreal fantasies, one set in 1920s Paris (where a magician's assistant is kidnapped by a magic box), one in ancient Egypt and one amongst hoboes who are trying, literally, to evade Death by riding trains through different dimensions. All three are humorously playful. The five stories in *Hearts of Wood & Other Timeless Tales* are mainly adult fairy tales. In addition, four of the 15 stories in *Jewel of the Moon* are fantasies.

Several others of Kotzwinkle's novels (including *Swimmer in the Secret Sea, Christmas at Fontaine's* and *Queen of Swords*) have been described as fabulations, for example by John Clute and Peter Nicholls in *The Encyclopedia of Science Fiction,* but none of these has any true fantasy elements.

—Chris Morgan

KURTZ, Katherine

Nationality: American. **Born:** Coral Gables, Florida, 18 October 1944. **Education:** University of Miami, Coral Gables, B.S. in chemistry 1966; University of California, Los Angeles, M.A. in history 1971. **Family:** Married Scott Roderick MacMillan in 1983; one son. **Career:** Senior training technician, Los Angeles Police Department, 1969-81. Since 1981, full-time writer. **Agent:** Russell Galen, Scovil Chichak Galen Literary Agency, 381 Park Avenue South, New York, NY 10016, USA. **Address:** Holybrooke Hall, Bray, County Wicklow, Ireland.

FANTASY PUBLICATIONS

Novels (series: The Adept; Chronicles of the Deryni; Heirs of Saint Camber; Histories of King Kelson; Legends of Saint Camber)

Deryni Rising. New York, Ballantine, 1970; London, Pan Ballantine, 1973.
Deryni Checkmate. New York, Ballantine, 1972; London, Pan Ballantine, 1973.
High Deryni. New York, Ballantine, 1973; London, Century, 1985.
The Chronicles of the Deryni (omnibus; includes *Deryni Rising, Deryni Checkmate, High Deryni*). New York, Nelson Doubleday, 1985.
Camber of Culdi (Legends of Saint Camber). New York, Ballantine, 1976; London, Century, 1985.
Saint Camber (Legends of Saint Camber). New York, Del Rey, 1978; London, Century, 1985.
Camber the Heretic (Legends of Saint Camber). New York, Del Rey, 1981; London, Century, 1987.
Lammas Night. New York, Ballantine, 1983; London, Severn House, 1986.
The Bishop's Heir (King Kelson). New York, Del Rey, and London, Century, 1984.
The King's Justice (King Kelson). New York, Del Rey, 1985; London, Arrow, 1986.
The Quest for Saint Camber (King Kelson). New York, Del Rey, 1986; London, Century, 1987.
The Harrowing of Gwynedd (Heirs of Saint Camber). New York, Del Rey, and London, Century, 1989.
The Adept, with Deborah Turner Harris. New York, Ace, 1991; Wallington, Surrey, Severn House, 1992.
King Javan's Year (Heirs of Saint Camber). New York, Del Rey, 1992.
The Lodge of the Lynx, with Deborah Turner Harris (Adept). New York, Ace, 1992; Sutton, Surrey, Severn House, 1993.
The Templar Treasure, with Deborah Turner Harris (Adept). New York, Ace, 1993; Sutton, Surrey, Severn House, 1994.
The Bastard Prince (Heirs of Saint Camber). New York, Del Rey, 1994.
Dagger Magic, with Deborah Turner Harris (Adept). New York, Ace, 1994.

Short Stories

The Deryni Archives. New York, Ballantine, 1986.

Other

Deryni Magic: A Grimoire. New York, Ballantine, 1990.

OTHER PUBLICATIONS

Novel

The Legacy of Lehr. New York, Walker, 1986; London, Century, 1988.

*

Bibliography: *The Work of Katherine Kurtz: An Annotated Bibliography and Guide* by Boden Clarke and Mary A. Burgess, San Bernardino, Borgo Press, 1993.

*   *   *

At the end of the 1960s Lin Carter edited the Ballantine Adult Fantasy series, which capitalized upon the success of J. R. R. Tolkien in the United States and was a significant factor in the fantasy boom and in the growth of fantasy as a separate marketing category. The earliest books in the series were all well-established classics: reprints of Lord Dunsany and William Morris, for instance. The first new author that he published was Katherine Kurtz, with her novel *Deryni Rising.* A quarter of a century later, although Kurtz has begun to branch out into other areas of fantasy, she is still publishing the Deryni books, and it is for those that she is likely to remain best known. They have achieved something of a cult following, like Marion Zimmer Bradley's Darkover books.

The Deryni novels chronicle the affairs of one kingdom, so far over some 250 years or thereabouts, and were not written in order of internal chronology. They have so far appeared grouped in a number of trilogies; the exception is *The Deryni Archives,* which collects a number of short stories spread over the whole chronological extent of the series. The trilogies run as follows in internal chronological order: the Legends of Camber of Culdi (*Camber of Culdi, Saint Camber* and *Camber the Heretic*); the Heirs of Saint Camber (*The Harrowing of Gwynedd, King Javan's Year* and *The Bastard Prince*); the Chronicles of the Deryni (*Deryni Rising, Deryni Checkmate* and *High Deryni*); and the Histories of King Kelson (*The Bishop's Heir, The King's Justice,* and *The Quest for Saint Camber*). In 1991, Kurtz announced that there would be a "Childe Morgan" trilogy, set immediately before the Chronicles of the Deryni, and a single volume about King Kelson's bride. *Deryni Magic: A Grimoire* is a "non-fiction" book describing the Deryni and their magical rituals, and providing a certain amount of background information about the cycle as a whole.

Like Tolkien, Kurtz had training in medieval studies; like Tolkien she has provided maps, family-trees and indices in order to help readers understand and feel part of her world. Unlike him, she has failed to invent a world with any cultural depth or internal logic; its linguistic incoherence, in particular, would have made Tolkien weep. All that we know of the "Deryni universe," as Kurtz calls it, consists of a territory apparently on the western edge of an ocean, which can hardly be larger than the British Isles in size. At its western edge are territories reminiscent of Ireland, such as "The Connait" (in our world Connacht or Connaught), but also one reminiscent of Anglo-Saxon England: "Howicce" (in our world Hwicce, a kingdom in the English West Midlands). There is no sea separating these "Irish" territories from the Welsh kingdoms, the most important of which, where most of the action of the novels takes place, is Gwynedd (in our world the name of the most important kingdom of Dark Age Wales). Not far away is the kingdom of Torenth, which has a Moorish, Islamic, duke. Although the "Deryni universe" thus has a totally different geography from our own, aspects of its history are surprisingly very similar. The events take place between the ninth and eleventh centuries AD, against the background of a social and religious system very like that of the ninth to eleventh centuries of our own world, with a warrior aristocracy with its power based on land, and a church using Latin as its language of learning and ritual. The language of laymen and of ordinary speech is unclear: those with Irish, Welsh and English names seem to have no problems understanding each other, and we might well assume they are (implausibly) speaking English.

Apart from the geographical and linguistic differences from our world, there is the fact of the Deryni: a race of beings with magical powers who live side-by-side with humans. They have the ability to read and control minds, to summon up illusions, to move objects, to teleport themselves, with the help of portals, from one part of the land to another. The rituals involved are described in the novels lovingly and at length, and they are fully explained in *Deryni Magic*. Deryni can obviously use their magic to obtain power over humans; just as easily, they become hated and feared by the majority human population. The series begins with the removal of the hated Deryni kings of Gwynedd by Camber MacRorie. He installs a king from the Haldane dynasty: a human, but with some magical powers himself. Camber is a secret Deryni himself, but he realizes that unrestricted and irresponsible use of magical power will bring destruction to his race. The Legends of Camber of Culdi trace the career of Camber himself, until his disappearance from the scene, and his proclamation as heretic by the established church. The Heirs of Saint Camber takes up the story, and records the beginning of a violent reaction of humans against their former Deryni lords. By the Chronicles of the Deryni (the earliest published, and the most tightly written), the Deryni are ready to make a cautious come-back, with the help of the idealistic young King Kelson, himself a half-Deryni. The Histories of King Kelson chronicles the last struggle between Kelson and the intolerant bishops.

The imagined world is flawed: a conflict between magic and the Church might better have been elaborated within an alternative history, as in Randall Garrett's Lord Darcy stories, or in John Whitbourn's *A Dangerous Energy* (1992). But the magic is well-realized, the characters much better drawn than in most modern fantasies, and, for anyone with a romantic interest in the Middle Ages, the saga will inevitably have a great deal of fascination.

Kurtz has made a few other ventures into fantasy of a different type. The singleton *Lammas Night* is an occult adventure story set in modern times, a work of "soft" dark fantasy rather than out-and-out horror. Similarly, *The Adept*, with Deborah Turner Harris, is the start of a new series, now up to four volumes in extent, in which Sir Adam Sinclair (an aristocratic figure with hints of John Buchan and Dorothy Sayers) is a magician with the task of defending late 20th-century Britain from its occult enemies.

—Edward James

KUSHNER, Ellen (Ruth)

Nationality: American. **Born:** Washington, DC, 6 October 1955. **Education:** Bryn Mawr College, Pennsylvania, 1973-75; Columbia University, New York, 1975-77, A.B. 1977. **Career:** Editorial assistant, Ace Books, 1977-79; associate editor, Pocket Books, 1979-80; freelance copywriter, reviewer, artists' representative, 1980-87; producer/announcer, WGBH Radio, Boston, from 1987. **Awards:** World Fantasy award, 1991; Mythopoeic award, 1991. **Agent:** Julie Fallowfield, McIntosh and Otis, 310 Madison Avenue, New York, NY 10017, USA.

FANTASY PUBLICATIONS

Novels

Swordspoint: A Melodrama of Manners. London, Allen and Unwin, and New York, Arbor House, 1987.
Thomas the Rhymer. New York, Morrow, 1990; London, Gollancz, 1991.
St. Nicholas and the Valley Beyond. New York, Viking Studio, 1994.

Other

Editor, *Basilisk*. New York, Ace, 1980.

OTHER PUBLICATIONS

Novels for children (adventure game-books)

Outlaws of Sherwood Forest. New York, Bantam, and London, Corgi, 1985.
The Enchanted Kingdom. New York, Bantam, and London, Corgi, 1986.
Statue of Liberty Adventure. New York, Bantam, and London, Corgi, 1986.
The Mystery of the Secret Room. New York, Bantam, and London, Corgi, 1986.
Knights of the Round Table. New York, Bantam, and London, Corgi, 1988.

Plays

Radio Plays: Co-author, *Which Way's Witch: A June Foray Halloween Spell*, 1991; *Festival of Liberation: The Passover Story in World Music*, 1992; *A Door is Opened: A Jewish High Holiday Meditation*, 1992; *Beyond 1492: 500 Years of Jewish Song and Legend*, 1992 (also producer, director and narrator of the last three items).

*   *   *

Ellen Kushner is an elegant writer whose first adult novel, *Swordspoint*, captured a dramatic ambience of decadent swashbuckling. Set largely in Riverside, the seedy district of an unnamed city in a nameless country analogous to the world of the Jacobean playwrights, it features concentric circles of conspiracy centred upon a concept of honour which allows the city's aristocracy to settle quarrels by proxy. Riverside's own aristocracy, and the district's link with the powerful lords who rule the country since the fall of the monarchy, are the swordsmen, half-entertainers, half-assassins who can be hired to challenge and kill by a prescribed ritual. The greatest living swordsman is St. Vier who can be hired for stylish killings but who "doesn't do weddings." Among the aristocracy, Lord Halliday is heading for re-election as Crescent Chancellor, the most powerful position in the Council. Lord Ferris is conspiring against him, and is trying to hire St. Vier to assassinate him. Meanwhile Lord Horn, spurned in his love for the young Michael Godwin, is also trying to get St. Vier to challenge him. Horn blackmails St. Vier into accepting his assignment by kidnapping his lover Alec, a half-insane student of mysterious but possibly noble origins. Godwin has ambitions of becoming a swordsman also, and his instructor, in accordance with the choices offered by ritual and custom, accepts the challenge himself. The victorious St. Vier returns for a cruel revenge on Lord Horn which results in his arrest and trial, where further layers of conspiracy are revealed.

The sinister delicacy of the story partly focuses upon the character of Alec; nervously feral, forever testing limits, baiting people to see them loose control and watch them die at St. Vier's hands. His part in the story suggests further levels of personal and political intrigue: his own tale is only half-told by the end, his motives only half-explained. Although there is something unsatisfactory about the way Michael disappears from the story to belie his apparent significance, this is counterbalanced by the elegant cynicism of the trial scene, with Ferris carefully manipulating the shape of his own downfall.

Kushner returned to this world in a short story, "The Swordsman Whose Name Was Not Death" (*Fantasy and Science Fiction,* September 1991). St. Vier is approached by a young boy seeking instruction, and is later asked for help by a noble heiress escaping an arranged marriage. Although this hackneyed scenario is wittily reversed by the confrontation between St. Vier and Alex and the girl, with its commentary on how the alleged trash-romance of the eponymous novel of an aristocratic girl who becomes the lover of a swordsman is a real metaphor for the possibilities for women to create realities out of their fantasies, the early, crude street-dialogue estranges the reader from the carefully-crafted world which has been Riverside and its surroundings up until now. A more representative short story is the earlier "Unicorn Masque" (in the anthology *Elsewhere,* edited by Terri Windling and Mark Alan Arnold): a particularly Elizabethan/Jacobean fantasy in which the main character's relationship to his Masters is more than the normal bonds of patronage. Like many such characters, he is a tool in his Masters' hands, but here this is perhaps more than a metaphor. Nevertheless, in keeping with the English Renaissance's preoccupation with the Self, even a tool can exercise responsibility.

Kushner's second adult novel, *Thomas the Rhymer,* slips more into "real" history by exploring the life and psyche of the title character who was at once both a historical Scottish poet and the subject of a ballad in which he was for seven years the lover of the Queen of Elfhame. Nevertheless, this is fantasy of the classic kind, capturing the uncanny shifting between middle-earth and faerie which is characteristic of the border ballads. Thomas's years in Elfhame are splendid and perilous; he returns changed, bearing the Elf-Queen's gift of truth-speaking and having to pick up the pieces of his relationships with Meg and Gavin, the peasant couple who sheltered him before his abduction, and with Elspeth, whom he marries. Each major character (except the Elf-Queen) narrates a part of the story, with Thomas himself narrating his own sojourn in the land of the Faeries from which many of the tales he has sung about have come, and his own conflict with the Elf-lord known as Hunter, from whose riddle Thomas both lays a soul to rest and creates one of his own most dramatic ballads. Changes of viewpoint allow Kushner to vary her stances towards her source material and allow it to be filtered through markedly different characters, although in general her prose is simpler, less oblique than in *Swordspoint.* Still

beautifully written, the first-person narration allows the directness of the ballad-form full rein. The glamour—faerie "glamour" in the terrifyingly hypnotic sense of the word—of the elvish world is heightened both by the superstitious references to it in earlier episodes and by the irony of Meg's down-to-earth initial disbelief of Thomas's tale on his return. The circular tragedy of "True Thomas" is seen more clearly by Elspeth as his gift is used to show that true answers to questions may not result in what the questioner has in mind.

Elfhame had already been obliquely visited by means of Kushner's contributions to Terri Windling's shared-world Borderlands series of anthologies, which imagines the return of Faerie to urban America. In "Charis" (*Borderlands,* 1986) the ballad of "Tam Lin" is alluded to, although the story is one of Machiavellian politics. "Charis" is one of the stories in the series which successfully captures the mixture of other-worldly wildness and streetwise seediness which is its *raison d'etre.* Hinted at in it are the dangerous, amoral motives and inexplicable magics of the plane Thomas explores in *Thomas the Rhymer.*

Kushner's work covers a narrow compass so far, but, like the ballads and dramas which find echoes in her fiction, its emotional undercurrents are deep. Unlike many American fantasy writers who interpret British folklore and literary history, she is never sentimentally cosy. The hard edge to her approach is sharpened by the life and originality of her characters and her stylish ability to create worlds which are not mere reflections of her sources but alternates in their own right. By adding just the right amount of hints and unfollowed-up asides to her descriptions of Riverside or Elfhame, she makes more of them than a first reading can satisfy. Her characters move in these worlds as much (or as little) at home as we do in ours, and the differences in dialogue and narrative styles between *Swordspoint* and *Thomas the Rhymer* suggest a writer already fully aware that how you tell a story affects what you are telling.

—Andy Sawyer

KUTTNER, Henry

Pseudonyms: Lawrence O'Donnell (with C. L. Moore); Lewis Padgett (with C. L. Moore). **Nationality:** American. **Born:** Los Angeles, California, 7 April 1915 (also reported as 1914). **Education:** University of Southern California, 1950-1958; B.A., English major, Psychology minor, 1954; M.A. in English not completed. **Military Service:** United States Army Medical Corps during World War II. **Family:** Married Catherine Lucille Moore, q.v., in 1940. **Career:** Worked for a literary agency, Los Angeles, in the 1930s; full-time writer, 1939-58; edited *Air Trails* magazine in the 1950s. All his fiction after 1940 was to some extent in collaboration with C. L. Moore, although this was not always acknowledged. **Died:** 3 February 1958.

Fantasy Publications

Novels

Well of the Worlds (as Lewis Padgett, with C. L. Moore). New York, Galaxy, 1953.

Beyond Earth's Gate (as Lewis Padgett, with C. L. Moore). New York, Ace, 1954.
Valley of the Flame, with C. L. Moore. New York, Ace, 1964.
The Dark World, with C. L. Moore. New York, Ace, 1965; London, Mayflower, 1966.
The Mask of Circe, with C. L. Moore. New York, Ace, 1971.
The Startling Worlds of Henry Kuttner, with C. L. Moore (omnibus; includes *Beyond Earth's Gate* [under its original title, "The Portal in the Picture"], *Valley of the Flame, The Dark World*). New York, Warner, 1987.

Short Stories

A Gnome There Was, and Other Tales of Science Fiction and Fantasy (as Lewis Padgett, with C. L. Moore). New York, Simon and Schuster, 1950.
Ahead of Time: Ten Stories of Science Fiction and Fantasy. New York, Ballantine, 1953; London, Weidenfeld and Nicolson, 1954.
Line to Tomorrow (as Lewis Padgett, with C. L. Moore). New York, Bantam, 1954.
Remember Tomorrow. Sydney, American Science Fiction, 1954.
Way of the Gods. Sydney, American Science Fiction, 1954.
No Boundaries, with C. L. Moore. New York, Ballantine, 1955; London, Consul, 1961.
Bypass to Otherness. New York, Ballantine, 1961.
Return to Otherness. New York, Ballantine, 1962.
The Best of Kuttner, Volume 1. London, Mayflower, 1965.
The Best of Kuttner, Volume 2. London, Mayflower, 1966.
Dr. Cyclops, with Edmond Hamilton and Bryce Walton. New York, Popular Library, 1967.
The Best of Henry Kuttner. New York, Doubleday, 1975.
Clash by Night and Other Stories, with C. L. Moore, edited by Peter Pinto. London, Hamlyn, 1980.
Chessboard Planet and Other Stories, with C. L. Moore. London, Hamlyn, 1983.
Elak of Atlantis. New York, Gryphon Press, 1985.
Prince Raynor, illustrated by Gary Lovisi. New York, Gryphon Press, 1987; San Bernardino, California, Borgo Press, 1989.
Secret of the Earth Star and Others, compiled and introduced by Sheldon Jaffery. Mercer Island, Washington, Starmont House, 1991.

Other Publications

Novels

The Brass Ring (as Lewis Padgett, with C. L. Moore). New York, Duell, Sloan and Pearce, 1947; London, Sampson Low, 1947; as *Murder in Brass,* New York, Bantam, 1947.
The Day He Died (as Lewis Padgett, with C. L. Moore). New York, Duell, Sloan and Pearce, 1947.
Fury (as Lawrence O'Donnell, with C. L. Moore). New York, Grosset and Dunlap, 1950; London, Dobson, 1954; as *Destination Infinity,* New York, Avon, 1958.
Tomorrow and Tomorrow and The Fairy Chessmen (as Lewis Padgett, with C. L. Moore). New York, Gnome Press, 1951; as *Tomorrow and Tomorrow* and *The Far Reality,* London, Consul, 2 vols., 1963; *The Fairy Chessmen* published separately as *Chessboard Planet,* New York, Galaxy, 1956.
Man Drowning. New York, Harper, 1952; London, New English Library, 1961.

The Murder of Ann Avery. New York, Permabooks, 1956.
The Murder of Eleanor Pope. New York, Permabooks, 1956.
Murder of a Mistress. New York, Permabooks, 1957.
Murder of a Wife. New York, Permabooks 1958.
Earth's Last Citadel, with C. L. Moore. New York, Ace, 1964.
The Time Axis, with C. L. Moore. New York, Ace, 1965.
The Creature From Beyond Infinity. New York, Popular Library, 1968.

Short Stories

Robots Have No Tails (as Lewis Padgett). New York, Gnome Press, 1952; as *The Proud Robot: The Complete Galloway Gallegher Stories* (as Henry Kuttner), London, Hamlyn, 1983.
Mutant (as Lewis Padgett, with C. L. Moore). New York, Gnome Press, 1953; London, Weidenfeld and Nicolson, 1954.
Clash by Night, with *The Jungle* by David Drake. New York, Tor, 1991.

*

Bibliography: by Donald H. Tuck, in *Henry Kuttner: A Memorial Symposium* edited by Karen Anderson, Berkeley, California, Sevagram, 1958; *Catherine Lucille Moore & Henry Kuttner: A Marriage of Souls and Talent—A Working Bibliography, 3rd Edition* by Virgil S. Utter and Gordon Benson, Jr., Leeds, West Yorkshire, Galactic Central Publications, 1989.

Henry Kuttner commented:

As for the science-fiction field itself, I believe I am interested in it because it is the imaginative fiction of today. If I'd lived in the 19th century I'd probably have been interested in the Gothic. In fact, my first published fiction was Gothic, in the old *Weird Tales* magazine of the twenties, when Farnsworth Wright was editor. Its masthead said, "Tales of the Bizarre and the Unusual," and my wife and I, years before we met, had both moved straight from a juvenile addiction for the Oz books and the Burroughs Mars books into writing and selling "weird fiction" to *Weird Tales.* We met, incidentally, through writing for the same magazine. It was the only outlet in those days for the imaginative sort of stories we both enjoyed writing.

At that time there was a group of magazines specializing in weird-stories-with-logical-explanations, and I found these easy to write too. From there I moved into historical adventure pulps, and then modern adventure. Then one of the editors I wrote for asked me to try some science fiction. (From "About the Author" in *Ahead of Time,* 1953, pages 178-79.)

*   *   *

As Henry Kuttner described his life, he wrote horror and fantasy stories as a sort of youthful indulgence before settling into his mature career as a science-fiction writer; and by purist standards, Kuttner's fantasy output is rather limited. However, in the 1940s and 1950s, Kuttner mastered the form known as science fantasy, stories that combine the structure and mood of fantasy with fig leaves of scientific or pseudo-scientific explanation; and his works in that category which veer toward fantasy might be properly and honourably annexed to the field.

Noticeably unimpressive are Kuttner's early stories about Elak of Atlantis. Among the earliest—and dullest—imitations of Robert

E. Howard's Conan, they include "Thunder in the Dawn," "The Spawn of Dagon," "Beyond the Phoenix" and "Dragon Moon." Heir to the throne of an Atlantean kingdom, Elak yields his claim to a younger brother and lives as a wanderer because he killed his stepfather in a dispute; after battles with occult evils and his brother's death, Elak returns to become king. Obviously the works of an apprentice writer, the Elak stories are almost pure plot, displaying little thought, atmosphere, or character development; Elak's companion, who lives only to get drunk at every conceivable opportunity, is thuddingly unsuccessful as comic relief. Perhaps most unsatisfying is Elak's helplessness facing opposition; while all heroes sometimes require human or divine assistance, Elak invariably requires it. Since it is hard to imagine that Kuttner deliberately sought to depict an incompetent hero, one must assume these stories reflect a beginner's difficulty in plotting fantastic tales, and they have predictably received little attention—as is also true of his stories about Prince Raynor, another sword-and-sorcery hero.

A decade or so later, whether due to the assistance of wife C. L. Moore or his own maturation as a writer, Kuttner proved a better storyteller, as evidenced by the novels in *The Startling Worlds of Henry Kuttner. Beyond Earth's Gate* is a compelling, intoxicating adventure involving a New York man who, after hearing from his late uncle about a marvellous land named Melasco, is transported to that realm, a parallel Earth where an ancient cult has dominated the world since Roman times, keeping the populace oppressed and maintaining all scientific advances as priestly secrets. With his girl friend—who also travelled to Melasco—as a new spokeswoman, the priests incongruously depict New York as the Paradise people reach if they lead a virtuous life; but the hero follows his uncle's example and leads a revolt against the priests. Like A. E. van Vogt's science-fiction novel *The World of Null-A, Beyond Earth's Gate* has the logic of a dream, inviting not rational analysis but awestruck fascination.

More sedate and Lovecraftian in tone, *Valley of the Flame* describes an energy source called the Flame that landed on Earth long ago to create a strange land where creatures evolved and lived at fantastically rapid rates, so hundreds of lifetimes might pass in one day. One intelligent race flourished before the Flame made them degenerate into horrible monsters; a successor race descended from cats enlists the help of two men from our world to harness the power of the Flame to prevent their own degeneration. *The Dark World* again features a parallel Earth, this one imbued with superscience that seems like magic, where powerful people known as the Coven—counterparts to mythical beings like gorgons, vampires, and werewolves—struggle to maintain control over their Dark World against a rebel leader from our world named Edward Bond. Ingeniously, the story is told from the perspective of an unsympathetic character, Coven member and Bond's Dark World counterpart Ganelon, who first seems benignly influenced by memories implanted in his mind when he took Bond's place, but later displays his true sinister motives before being defeated.

A possible problem in such stories is that the fast and furious plot can grow overly complicated, demanding lengthy and implausible explanations—as seen in two other Kuttner novels. *Well of the Worlds* describes a gateway from a uranium mine to another world dominated by evil immortals, with all events justified by explanations involving atomic theory that would have been dismissed as ludicrous years before the story was written. Briefly, Kuttner makes this world seem fascinating, a hollow world with an upper shell, a lower shell, and floating islands in between serving as stepping-stones; but after presenting this picture, Kuttner unfortunately rushes back to his convoluted tale of treachery and rebellion against the immortals. In *The Mask of Circe,* Kuttner rationalizes the Greek gods as advanced beings from another time-stream; a modern man, in a peculiar way a reincarnation of Jason, sails to their realm in a ghostly *Argo* and finally fulfils Jason's broken promise to Circe by using the Golden Fleece—actually a super-scientific weapon—to destroy the evil and artificially created god Apollo. In these novels, as he tries to explain and justify every event in extreme detail, Kuttner has little time left to provide involving adventures.

Kuttner was often at his best in writing short fiction, so it is unsurprising that, in a reversal of the normal pattern, his stories have remained in print more than his novels. Among his more memorable fantasy stories are "Call Him Demon," a story about a boy who outwits a cannibalistic monster convincingly told from a child's point of view; "Masquerade," which plays with horror-story conventions by having the guests at the lonely mansion, not the hosts, turn out to be the monsters; "A Gnome There Was," where a man lost in a mine is transformed into a gnome, apparently condemned to an endless routine of mining and brawling with other gnomes, until he effects an ultimately disastrous escape; "The Misguided Halo," concerning an ordinary man accidentally given a halo by an errant angel; "By These Presents," where a man tries to outwit the Devil by selling his soul in exchange for an immortality he soon regrets; and "Housing Problem," the delightful story of a man who builds a beautiful little house to attract pixies as tenants—who pay the rent in good luck instead of money.

Compared to modern fantasy writers, Kuttner can seem crude and unpolished, and he may never again enjoy a wide audience; however, those who can overlook occasional infelicities will be richly rewarded by the astounding energy and creativity of his works. One hopes there will always be a few readers around to appreciate Henry Kuttner's special magic.

—Gary Westfahl

L

LACKEY, Mercedes (Ritchie)

Nationality: American. **Born:** Chicago, Illinois, 24 June 1950.
Education: Purdue University, West Lafayette, Indiana, B.S. 1972.
Family: Married 1) Anthony Lackey in 1972 (divorced 1990); 2)
the artist Larry Dixon in 1990. **Career:** Artist's model, South Bend,
Indiana, 1975-81; computer programmer, Associates Data Process-
ing, South Bend, 1979-82, and American Airlines, Tulsa, Oklahoma,
1982-90; freelance writer from 1990. **Agent:** Russell Galen, Scovil-
Chichak-Galen Literary Agency, 381 Park Avenue South, Suite
1112, New York, NY 10016, USA. **Address:** PO Box 8309, Tulsa,
OK 74101-8309, USA.

FANTASY PUBLICATIONS

Novels (series: Bard's Tale; Bardic Voices; Diana Tregarde;
Halfblood Chronicles; Heralds of Valdemar; Last Herald-Mage;
Mage Storms; Mage Wars; Mage Winds; Serrated Edge; Vows
and Honor)

Arrows of the Queen (Heralds of Valdemar). New York, DAW,
1987; London, Legend, 1988.
Arrow's Flight (Heralds of Valdemar). New York, DAW, 1987;
London, Legend, 1989.
Arrow's Fall (Heralds of Valdemar). New York, DAW, 1988; Lon-
don, Legend, 1989.
The Oathbound (Vows and Honor). New York, DAW, 1988.
Burning Water (Tregarde). New York, Tor, 1989.
Magic's Pawn (Last Herald-Mage). New York, DAW, 1989; Lon-
don, Roc, 1992.
Oathbreakers (Vows and Honor). New York, DAW, 1989.
Reap the Whirlwind, with C. J. Cherryh. New York, Baen, 1989.
Children of the Night (Tregarde). New York, Tor, 1990.
Magic's Promise (Last Herald-Mage). New York, DAW, 1990; Lon-
don, Roc, 1992.
Magic's Price (Last Herald-Mage). New York, DAW, 1990; Lon-
don, Roc, 1992.
Knight of Ghosts and Shadows, with Ellen Guon. New York, Baen,
1990.
The Last Herald-Mage (omnibus; includes *Magic's Pawn, Magic's
Promise, Magic's Price*). New York, Guild America, 1990.
By the Sword. New York, DAW, 1991.
The Elvenbane, with Andre Norton (Halfblood Chronicles). New
York, Tor, 1991; London, Grafton, 1993.
Jinx High (Tregarde). New York, Tor, 1991.
Born to Run, with Larry Dixon (Serrated Edge). New York, Baen,
1992.
Castle of Deception, with Josepha Sherman (Bard's Tale). New
York, Baen, 1992.
The Lark and the Wren (Bardic Voices). New York, Baen, 1992.
Summoned to Tourney, with Ellen Guon. New York, Baen, 1992.
Wheels of Fire, with Mark Shepherd (Serrated Edge). New York,
Baen, 1992.
Winds of Fate (Mage Winds). New York, DAW, 1992.
Winds of Change (Mage Winds). New York, DAW, 1992.

Fortress of Frost and Fire, with Ru Emerson (Bard's Tale). New
York, Baen, 1993.
Prison of Souls, with Mark Shepherd (Bard's Tale). New York,
Baen, 1993.
The Robin and the Kestrel (Bardic Voices). New York, Baen, 1993.
When the Bough Breaks, with Holly Lisle (Serrated Edge). New
York, Baen, 1993.
Winds of Fury (Mage Winds). New York, DAW, 1993.
The Black Gryphon, with Larry Dixon (Mage Wars). New York,
DAW, and London, Millennium, 1994.
A Cast of Corbies, with Josepha Sherman (Bardic Choices). New
York, Baen, 1994.
Sacred Ground. New York, Tor, 1994; London, Voyager, 1995.
Storm Warning (Mage Storms). New York, DAW, and London,
Millennium, 1994.
Vows and Honor (omnibus; includes *The Oathbound,
Oathbreakers*). New York, Guild America, 1994.
Elvenblood, with Andre Norton (Halfblood Chronicles). New York,
Tor, and London, HarperCollins, 1995.
Storm Rising (Mage Storms). New York, DAW, 1995.
The White Gryphon, with Larry Dixon (Mage Wars). New York,
DAW, and London, Millennium, 1995.

OTHER PUBLICATIONS

Novels

Wing Commander: Freedom Flight, with Ellen Guon. New York,
Baen, 1992.
Rediscovery: A Darkover Novel, with Marion Zimmer Bradley. New
York, DAW, 1993.
If I Pay Thee Not in Gold, with Piers Anthony. New York, Baen,
1993.
The Ship Who Searched, with Anne McCaffrey. New York, Baen,
1993; London, Orbit, 1994.

*   *   *

Mercedes Lackey must surely win a prize for being the most
prolific writer in the fantasy field over the past eight years. Whether
individually or in collaboration, she has produced an astonishing
number of novels since the appearance of *Arrows of the Queen* in
1987 and is widely regarded as one of the successes of the past
decade.

The majority of her own works (some in collaboration with her
husband, Larry Dixon) take place within the world of Valdemar
over a 600-year timescale, encompassing Valdemar (a Scandinavian name meaning "famous ruler") and its surrounding states; the
Heralds of Valdemar, the protectors of that land, are chosen for
their innate goodness by their bonded Companions, horses which
are both telepathic and godlike in nature. Each set of novels explores further geographic territory within the world, and by the Mage
Winds trilogy, set at the same period as the best-selling Heralds
series, Lackey incorporates characters, weapons and races from earlier novels—such as the Hawkbrother Adepts from the Last Herald-Mage trilogy; and the Shin'a'in from *The Oathbound* and

Oathbreakers, along with Need, the magic sword from the same novels, which appears also in *By the Sword.*

Lackey's world is filled with magical persons and animals, from the equine Companions to bondbirds and gryphons, and each form of magic has detailed rules; she is highly adept at creating complex fantasy structures and combining these with a powerful talent for story-telling. She draws on a wide range of knowledge of different cultures, both oriental and occidental, for her invention of empathetic characters whose personal conflicts are often as important to her plots as the wider issues of good and evil. Vanyel, the hero of the Last Herald-Mage trilogy, is a tormented character driven by two prime factors: the loss of his male Herald lover, and the foreknowledge of his own death. Tarma, the Shin'a'in swordswoman in *The Oathbound* and *Oathbreakers,* is driven by the need to recreate her destroyed clan. These inner conflicts are one of the main attractions of the earlier novels, even if they are less compelling in Lackey's later works.

The two Bardic Voices novels, which fall outside the Valdemar setting, are concerned with music, one of Lackey's great interests. Rune, the heroine of *The Lark and the Wren,* has ambitions to become a Guild musician, despite her humble background. The novel details her training (a Lackey speciality) and struggles, and her failure and success with an alternative group of bards, with whom she discovers a gift for magic in her music. The novels are enjoyable, and Lackey's knowledge of her subject detailed, but there is a curious confusion at the end of *The Lark and the Wren,* as if a need to add scope was discovered, so that the final rescue and restoration of the lost King of Birnam comes as an afterthought rather than part of the main plot.

Also well outside the Valdemar setting are the tales in the author's Diana Tregarde series, an effective blend of horror, fantasy and private investigation. Lackey's large number of collaborative novels cover a still wider field, with varying degrees of success. The science-fiction novel *Rediscovery,* with Marion Zimmer Bradley, although as well written as might be expected, is surprisingly deficient in emotive quality; *Freedom Flight,* with Ellen Guon, is a fast-moving story, but no more. Although anyone as prodigiously prolific as Lackey must produce novels of varying quality, and while her enviable skills as a writer can always ensure pace and readability, some of her earlier works possess a greater depth of characterization than the later novels, although this is hardly surprising when the sheer scale of her work since 1987 is taken into consideration.

These are, however, relatively minor criticisms of a writer with an outstanding gift for story-telling and a computer keyboard that must sometimes smoke from the speed with which she composes her latest tome. We could wish for more individual works and fewer collaborations, but no doubt Lackey will somehow manage to produce both.

—Mary Corran

LANG, Andrew

Pseudonym: A. Huge Longway. **Nationality:** British. **Born:** Selkirk, Scotland, 31 March 1844. **Education:** St. Andrews University, 1861-63; University of Glasgow, 1863-64; Balliol College, Oxford, B.A. 1866. **Family:** Married Leonora Blanche Alleyne in 1875. **Career:** Fellow, Merton College, Oxford, 1868-75; journal-ist from 1875; co-founder of *St. Leonard's Magazine*; Gifford Lecturer, St. Andrews University, 1888; Ford Lecturer, Oxford University, 1904. **Awards:** Open fellowship, Merton College, 1868. LL.D.: St. Andrews University, 1888, and Oxford University, 1904. **Died:** 20 July 1912.

FANTASY PUBLICATIONS

Novels

That Very Mab, with May Kendall (pseudonym of Leonora Alleyne, Mrs. Andrew Lang). London, Longmans Green, 1885.
He, with W. H. Pollock. N.p., 1887.
The Gold of Fairnilee. Bristol, Arrowsmith, 1888.
Prince Prigio. Bristol, Arrowsmith, 1889.
The World's Desire, with H. Rider Haggard. London, Longmans Green, and New York, Harper, 1890.
Prince Ricardo of Pantouflia: Being the Adventures of Prince Prigio's Son. London, Longmans Green, 1893.
The Chronicles of Pantouflia (omnibus; includes *Prince Prigio, Prince Ricardo of Pantouflia*). 1943; New York, Dutton, 1961.

Short Stories

The Princess Nobody: A Tale of Fairy Land. London, Longmans Green, 1884.
In the Wrong Paradise and Other Stories. London, Kegan Paul Trench, 1886.
My Own Fairy Book. London, Longmans Green, 1895.
Tales of a Fairy Court (Tales for the Children no. 1). London, Collins, 1907.

Other

Editor, *The Blue Fairy Book.* London, Longmans Green, 1889.
Editor, *The Red Fairy Book.* London, Longmans Green, 1890.
Editor, *The Green Fairy Book.* London, Longmans Green, 1892.
Editor, *The Yellow Fairy Book.* London, Longmans Green, 1894.
Editor, *The Pink Fairy Book.* London, Longmans Green, 1897.
Editor, *The Grey Fairy Book.* London, Longmans Green, 1900.
Editor, *The Violet Fairy Book.* London, Longmans Green, 1901.
Editor, *The Crimson Fairy Book.* London, Longmans Green, 1903.
Editor, *The Brown Fairy Book.* London, Longmans Green, 1904.
Editor, *The Orange Fairy Book.* London, Longmans Green, 1906.
Editor, *The Olive Fairy Book.* London, Longmans Green, 1907.
Editor, *The Lilac Fairy Book.* London, Longmans Green, 1910.

OTHER PUBLICATIONS

Novels

Much Darker Days, as A. Huge Longway. London, Longmans Green, 1884.
The Mark of Cain. Bristol, Arrowsmith, 1888.
A Monk of Fife: A Romance of the Days of Jeanne d'Arc. London, Longmans Green, 1895.
Parson Kelly, with A. E. W. Mason. London, Longmans Green, 1900.
The Disentanglers. London, Longmans Green, 1901.

Short Stories

Old Friends: Letters in Epistolary Parody. London, Longmans Green, 1890.

Poetry

Ballads and Lyrics of Old France, with Other Poems. London, Longmans Green, 1872.
XXII Ballades in Blue China. London, Kegan Paul, 1880.
XXII and X:XXXII Ballades in Blue China. London, Kegan Paul, 1881.
Helen of Troy. N.p., Bell, 1882.
Ballades and Verses Vain. New York, Scribner, 1884.
Rhymes a la Mode. London, Kegan Paul, 1885.
Grass of Parnassus: Rhymes Old and New. London, Longmans Green, 1888.
Ban and Arriere Ban: A Rally of Fugitive Rhymes. London, Longmans Green, 1894.
New Collected Poems. London, Longmans Green, 1905.

Other

The Library. London, n.p., 1876.
Letters on Literature. London, Longmans Green, 1880.
Letters to Dead Authors. New York, Scribner, 1886; London, Longmans Green, 1892.
Books and Bookmen. N.p., Coombes, 1886.
Lost Leaders. London, Longmans Green, 1889.
How to Fail in Literature. N.p., Field and Tuer, 1890.
Life, Letters and Diaries of Sir Stafford Northcote. Edinburgh, Blackwood, 1890.
Essays in Little. N.p., Henry, 1891.
Homer and the Epic. London, Longmans Green, 1893.
The Life and Letters of John Gibson Lockhart. New York, Scribner, 1897.
Prince Charles Edward. N.p., Goupil, 1900.
Alfred Tennyson. New York, Dodd, 1901.
Adventures Among Books. London, Longmans Green, 1905.
John Knox and the Reformation. London, Longmans Green, 1905.
The Puzzle of Dickens' Last Plot. London, Chapman and Hall, 1905.
Homer and His Age. London, Longmans Green, 1906.
Sir Walter Scott. New York, Scribner, 1906.
The Story of Joan of Arc (for children). New York, Dutton, 1906.
The Maid of France, Being the Story of the Life and Death of Jeanne d'Arc. London, Longmans Green, 1908.
La Jeanne d'Arc de M. Anatole France. Paris, n.p., 1909.
Sir George Mackenzie: King's Advocate of Rosehaugh. London, Longmans Green, 1909.
The World of Homer. London, Longmans Green, 1910.
Sir Walter Scott and the Border Minstrelsy. London, Longmans Green, 1911.
History of English Literature from Beowulf to Swinburne. London, Longmans Green, 1912.
Shakespeare, Bacon, and the Great Unknown. London, Longmans Green, 1912.

Editor, *English Worthies.* 9 vols. London, Longmans Green, 1885-87.
Editor, *Ballads of Books.* London, Longmans Green, 1888.

Translator, with S. H. Butcher, *The Odyssey,* by Homer. London, Macmillan, 1878.

*

Critical Studies: *Andrew Lang: A Critical Biography* by Roger Lancelyn Green, Leicester, Ward, 1946.

*   *   *

Andrew Lang's interest in mythology and folklore was developed long before he began writing fiction; his classic scholarly essay on "Mythology and Fairy Tales" (1873) demolished Max Müller's ridiculous but then-fashionable theory that myths and folktales arose as a "disease of language" by virtue of a failure of memory which gradually dissociated stories from the primal deities which had spawned them. Müller's fondness for explaining traditional tales as decayed solar myths was brilliantly lampooned in Lang's mock-essay on "The Great Gladstone Myth," which "proves" that the prime minister of England was an imaginary figure invented to embody such a solar myth. Lang's fondness for this kind of lampooning led him to the production of some notable literary parodies, including one of Hugh Conway's shilling shocker *Dark Days* (*Much Darker Days* by "A. Huge Longway") and one of Rider Haggard's *She* (the anonymously issued *He,* written in collaboration with Walter Herries Pollock). *He* is a kind of "anti-fantasy," substituting a crude swindle for the supernatural apparatus of Haggard's original. A more original satire is *That Very Mab,* in which Queen Mab, having relocated her fairy court on an island near Samoa when the Puritans came to power in England, is displaced again when missionaries arrive and returns to her homeland to investigate the present state of its affairs. After hearing the views of poets and professors on the origins and nature of religion and the views of a nihilist on politics she decides that England is still no place for an honest fairy.

Lang's interest in myth and folklore infected much of his early poetry, notably the fine fairy poem "The Fortunate Isles". He followed up his translation of *The Odyssey* (in collaboration with S. H. Butcher) with his own epic *Helen of Troy,* which appeared before his translation of *The Iliad,* but he did little more in this vein thereafter. His first original fairy tale, *The Princess Nobody,* was written as an alternative text to accompany the illustrations in Richard Doyle's *In Fairyland;* it is a determinedly non-serious effort in which one Prince Comical is eventually and rather fortuitously transformed into Prince Charming. *The Gold of Fairnilee,* which Lang's biographer Roger Lancelyn Green considered the finest thing he ever wrote, is in a much more earnest vein, combining memories of his boyhood (which was spent within a couple of miles of Fairnilee) with the legacy of his scholarly investigations in a fine story of the Land of Faerie as it is actually represented in Scottish folklore: a bleak underworld inhabited by soulless and unfeeling creatures. The story is set at the time of the Battle of Flodden (1513) and involves actual historical characters with fairies somewhat after the fashion of James Hogg's *The Brownie of Bodsbeck* (1818).

Like *Helen of Troy, The Gold of Fairnilee* was not a commercial success, and Lang was never tempted to repeat the experiment. His decision to forsake seriousness in favour of calculatedly trivial amusement was doubtless hardened when *Prince Prigio*—a lighter and much sillier story—sold very well. Apparently modelled on Thackeray's *The Rose and the Ring, Prince Prigio* tells the story of a prince cursed with too much intelligence, who alienates everyone with his insistent cleverness until such time as he subjects it to a proper discipline of humility. He then becomes able to perform heroic acts and undo the fatal consequences of his earlier mistakes. If Lang was talking (metaphorically, of course) about himself, there must be a covert black undercurrent to the seemingly off-hand comedy which gives the story its momentum. The fast-paced but rather plotless sequel, *Prince Ricardo of Pantouflia,* features a rather more conventional hero engaged in similarly silly exploits; it is combined with its predecessor in the omnibus *The Chronicles of Pantouflia. Tales of a Fairy Court* is also set in Pantouflia, but it is very minor work.

The stories assembled with "The Great Gladstone Myth" in *In the Wrong Paradise and Other Stories* are conscientiously lighthearted, although most have a satirical edge. The best of them is the novella "The End of Phaeacia," which develops Lang's anthropological interests in a tale of a bigoted missionary who unwittingly causes the destruction of an island where the glories of Classical civilization have been marvellously preserved. In the title story the hapless protagonist proceeds through a whole series of imagined afterlives in search of a suitable one, discovering that one man's idea of paradise is another's idea of hell, and concluding that the fervently devout ought perhaps to refrain from foisting their prejudices on those whose tastes and values are very different. The prehistoric fantasy "The Romance of the First Radical" displays, with similarly amiable irony, the inevitable fate of all who have the misfortune to be ahead of their time.

Lang's perennial fascination with Homer and Helen of Troy bore further imaginative fruit when he and his friend Henry Rider Haggard wrote *The World's Desire,* in which Odysseus finally returns to Ithaca only to find it depopulated by the plague and sets off in search of Helen, who is now worshipped as a goddess in Egypt. Like all of Haggard's heroes, however—and it could be argued that this version of Odysseus is their purest archetype—he is seduced from his divinely endorsed quest by another and infinitely less worthy woman. Lang's extensive contributions to the first draft of the book seem to have been submerged by the revisions carried out by his collaborator, reduced thereby to background coloration.

Lang was far better known in his own day—and is better remembered today—as an editor than as a writer, particularly for the series of anthologies begun with *The Blue Fairy Book.* These became so popular that he ran out of familiar colours long before the public's appetite was sated. The collections include traditional tales of all kinds, eclectically selected from a wide range of sources, but their compiler regarded them as hackwork (much of the actual work involved was done by his wife), and their success seems to have completed his disillusionment with the produce of his own literary labours.

Even Roger Lancelyn Green, his most ardent champion, describes Lang as a "sadly disappointing author" on the grounds that he failed to make any abundant use of his undoubted imaginative powers and literary talent. The evidence of *The Gold of Fairnilee* suggests that he might have been one of the greatest fantasy writers of all time had he only found the motivation to persist with work that embodied a degree of imaginative and intellectual maturity, but he could never see the point of doing that while there was no ready-made audience, so he didn't.

—Brian Stableford

LANGLEY, Noel

Nationality: British. **Born:** Durban, South Africa, 25 December 1911. Became US citizen in 1961. **Education:** University of Natal, B.A. **Military Service:** Canadian navy, 1943-45; lieutenant. **Family:** Married 1) Naomi Mary Legate in 1937 (divorced 1954), three sons, two daughters; 2) Pamela Deeming in 1959. **Career:** Playwright, screenwriter and novelist, mainly in Britain and the USA. **Awards:** Donaldson award, with Robert Morley, 1948. **Died:** 4 November 1980.

FANTASY PUBLICATIONS

Novel

The Tale of the Land of Green Ginger. New York, Morrow, 1937; revised as *The Land of Green Ginger,* London, Penguin, 1966.

Short Stories

Tales of Mystery and Revenge. London, Barker, 1950.

OTHER PUBLICATIONS

Novels

Cage Me a Peacock. London, Barker, 1935; New York, Morrow, 1937.
There's a Porpoise Close Behind Us. London, Barker, 1936; as *So Unlike the English,* New York, Morrow, 1937.
Hocus Pocus. London, Methuen, 1941.
The Music of the Heart. London, Barker, 1946.
The Cabbage Patch. London, Barker, 1947.
Nymph in Clover. London, Barker, 1948.
The Inconstant Moon. London, Barker, 1949.
Somebody's Rocking My Dreamboat, with Hazel Pynegar. London, Barker, 1949.
Cuckoo in the Dell, with Hazel Pynegar. London, Barker, 1951.
The Rift in the Lute. London, Barker, 1952.
Where Did Everybody Go? London, Barker, 1960.
The Loner. N.p., Triton, 1967.
A Dream of Dragonflies. London, Macmillan, 1970.

Plays

Three Plays: Farm of Three Echoes, For Ever, Friendly Relations. London, Miles, 1936.
Farm of Three Echoes. London, French, 1940.
Edward, My Son, with Robert Morley. London, French, 1948.
Little Lambs Eat Ivy: A Light Comedy in Three Acts. London, French, 1950.
An Elegance of Rebels: A Play in Three Acts. London, Barker, 1960.

Screenplays: *Maytime,* 1936; *The Wizard of Oz,* 1939; *Florian,* 1940; *Unexpected Uncle,* 1941; *They Made Me a Fugitive,* 1947; *Edward, My Son,* 1948; *Adam and Evelyne,* 1949; *Trio,* 1950; *Tom Brown's Schooldays,* 1951; *Scrooge,* 1951; *Ivanhoe,* 1952; *The Pickwick Papers,* 1952; *Knights of the Round Table,* 1953; *The Prisoner of Zenda,* 1953; *Our Girl Friday,* 1954; *Svengali,* 1954; *The Search for Bridey Murphy,* 1956; *The Vagabond King,* 1956; *The Vicious Circle,* 1957.

Other

Edgar Cayce on Reincarnation. N.p., Hawthorn, 1968.

Editor, *On the Death of My Son* by Jasper Swain. N.p., Turnstone, 1974.

*

Film Adaptations: *Edward, My Son,* 1948.

*   *   *

More or less forgotten these days, in his time Noel Langley was a successful author of delicately malicious satires such as *Cage Me a Peacock,* which gave the story of the Rape of Lucretia new depths. In this a peasant girl learns to make the best of both worlds as, torn from her pastoral idyll, she weaves a joyous web of bigamy and deception while she works her way through the ranks of the Roman Army. By contrast, *There's a Porpoise Close Behind Us* turns its attention to London theatre life, and *Hocus Pocus* satirizes the Hollywood film industry. The subject matter of the latter novels is not surprising, as Langley was also a prolific playwright, screenwriter and director, numbering among his many credits screenplays for the classic movie fantasy *The Wizard of Oz,* the Alastair Sims version of *Scrooge* (Dickens's *A Christmas Carol*), and the occult *The Search for Bridey Murphy* (which he also directed).

But Langley is now best remembered by fantasy readers for his children's novel, *The Tale of the Land of Green Ginger,* a comic continuation of the story of Aladdin. The story opens with the birth of Aladdin's son who, at a day old, describes his grandmother as looking like a button-nosed tortoise. Amazed at his son's virtuosity, Aladdin summons the genie, Abdul, for advice, and is told that Abu Ali has been chosen to rescue a magician. The magician had created for himself a floating land, the Land of Green Ginger, but in casting the spells, had inadvertently turned himself into a button-nosed tortoise and was awaiting liberation.

When Abu Ali reaches adulthood, he sets out on a dual quest to find a wife and also to rescue the magician. The two plots are closely-knit. Narrowly avoiding being boiled in oil by the wicked father of his chosen wife Silver Bud, Abu Ali is forced to compete with the two wicked princes Rubdub Ben Thud and Tintac Ping Foo, in a further quest to win the hand of Silver Bud. Aided by Boomalakkawee, son of Abdul, Omar Khayyam and an extremely sarcastic spinster mouse, Abu Ali naturally achieves the quest and wins the hand of Silver Bud.

Langley's theatrical interests show up particularly strongly in this novel, which is constructed much along the lines of a traditional pantomime, including traditional pantomime villains, and rescue from a nasty fate in the nick of time, not to mention a love of increasingly preposterous names. Langley is always conscious of his audience and frequently addresses them directly as he elucidates the action in classic pantomime style.

Some of the stories collected in *Tales of Mystery and Revenge* are ironic or sentimental fantasies, including an effective piece about a ghost revisiting his dying lover (and the volume also contains two African black-magic stories, of horror-fantasy interest). It is to be regretted that Langley's humour and satire, somewhere in style between Thorne Smith and Michael Arlen, have fallen so much out of fashion that only the one novel and a handful of short stories are now remembered—but it is perhaps understandable in that his works do belong so firmly to their period.

—Maureen Speller

LAWHEAD, Stephen R.

Nationality: American. **Born:** 1950. **Education:** Kearney State College, Nebraska, B.A.; attended Northern Baptist Theological Seminary, Illinois. **Family:** Married Alice Slaikeu; two sons. **Career:** Worked for *Campus Life* magazine for five years; writer.

Fantasy Publications

Novels (series: Dragon King; Pendragon Cycle; Song of Albion)

In the Hall of the Dragon King. Westchester, Illinois, Crossway, 1982; Oxford, Lion, 1982.
The Warlords of Nin (Dragon King). Westchester, Illinois, Crossway, 1983; Lion, 1983.
The Sword and the Flame (Dragon King). Westchester, Illinois, Crossway, 1984; Lion, 1984.
Taliesin (Pendragon Cycle). Westchester, Illinois, Crossway, 1987; Oxford, Lion, 1987.
Merlin (Pendragon Cycle). Westchester, Illinois, Crossway, 1988; Oxford, Lion, 1988.
Arthur (Pendragon Cycle). Westchester, Illinois, Crossway, 1989; Oxford, Lion, 1989.
The Paradise War (Song of Albion). Batavia, Illinois, and Oxford, Lion, 1991.
The Silver Hand (Song of Albion). Batavia, Illinois, and Oxford, Lion, 1992.
The Endless Knot (Song of Albion). Batavia, Illinois, and Oxford, Lion, 1993.
Pendragon. New York, Avon, and Oxford, Lion, 1994.

Other Publications

Novels

Dream Thief. Westchester, Illinois, Crossway, 1983.
The Search for Fierra. Westchester, Illinois, Crossway, 1985.
Howard Had a Spaceship (for children). 1986.
The Siege of Dome. Westchester, Illinois, Crossway, 1986.
Emphyrion (contains *The Search for Fierra* and *The Siege of Dome*). Oxford, Lion, 1990.

*   *   *

Stephen Lawhead is published by Lion, a house specializing in Christian-oriented fiction, and much, though not all, of his work reflects this. He first attracted attention with the Dragon King series, set in a typical modern-fantasy pastiche of the medieval world. Lawhead does not try to import Christianity directly into this setting, though the message is clear enough. Quentin, the central character, starts as an acolyte in a temple drifting towards materialism. He can only relate to the old High Priest, and seeks a better way of relating to the "Most High." Eventually he departs to embark on a more active career of saving his land from sorcerers and their minions. Later he falls in love with the daughter of the series-eponymous Dragon King. In the end he "fulfils the promise of the ages" by becoming Dragon King himself, but he is to be a Priest King.

The next series, the Pendragon Cycle, enters the more familiar, though still problematic, Christian territory of Arthur and the Dark Ages. It is only a few decades since the status of Arthur was rescued from that of a discredited legend by such writers as the Catholic crypto-historian Geoffrey Ashe, who clearly identified him as the Christian defender of a flickering candle of civilization against a pounding sea of heathen barbarism. Since then, however, paganism has unexpectedly revived and staked a claim, if not to Arthur himself, then to many elements of the legend. There are strong, ambiguous female figures on the pre-Christian tapestry to which the semi-historical figures have been tacked, and their presence has interested feminist writers.

Lawhead approaches this fertile and ever-stimulating soil with a new twist: he sets most of the early part of the first novel, *Taliesin,* in Atlantis. This is not the Atlantis whose engulfment by the sea had been described by Plato some 800 years before the earliest possible date for Arthur, but a section of the lost continent which had survived, unknown to the philosopher, and remained, unnoticed and unchanging, until it suffered exactly the same fate as its predecessor—presumably a case of geology repeating itself.

Princess Charis, the central figure of *Taliesin,* is a young woman who defies convention by entering the bull-dance, practised in the same way as on Crete (which spoil-sport historians have identified as the likeliest real source for the story of Atlantis). Distracted from this by the submersion of their rump continent, Charis and the other survivors head for Britain, where they land in the South-West, apparently unnoticed by the Roman or sub-Roman authorities. There, they become models for the more benign supernatural beings, such as the Lady of the Lake. The stage is then set for the series to proceed along the lines of muscular Christianity against the rest. Anyone expecting the rehabilitation of Morgan the Fey to be picked up by Lawhead will be disappointed. She appears here as a totally unredeemable monster, who sleeps, not with Arthur, but with her own son, to produce Mordred as another, incestuous, son, and the inevitable nemesis.

In his later series, Song of Albion, Lawhead takes a very different approach to the echoes of the Celtic world. The first novel *The Paradise War* begins in the modern world, at Oxford (where Lawhead had spent a year researching the Pendragon Cycle). Two eccentric postgraduates, an aristocratic British dilettante and an earnest American scholar, take it on themselves to investigate a series of anomalous occurrences they have read about. An aurochs has appeared in a field, dying from a blow by an Iron Age spear: wolves roam the streets; they themselves see a green man.

Before long the dilettante disappears, and the American redoubles his efforts. He meets an odd professor, who believes the strange happenings indicate disturbances in the Otherworld, the ideal echo of this one believed in by the Celts. Our hero passes through a gate between the two worlds which sometimes exists in an ancient cairn. To this point, the novel has represented the best of Lawhead, witty and amusing, but it rapidly goes flat. Lawhead's enthusiasm for things Celtic is infectious, but the Otherworld is not a concept which bears examining in the detail we are given in this type of novel. It comes over as a prettified version of the real Iron Age.

Our hero is trapped by orders of the king, who insists he spend several years learning to become a warrior. Luckily, he soon loses interest in going back, and anyway time is different in the Otherworld should he decide to. His friend, though, has become increasingly corrupt and addicted to the less desirable side of Otherworld life, and by the second book, *The Silver Hand,* he is very much part of the problem.

My own hope was that Lawhead would produce more amusing modern-scene material like the first half of *The Paradise War.* Instead, in his most recent work, he has returned to the Dark Ages and matters Arthurian. *Pendragon,* a belated fourth book in the Pendragon Cycle, is intended as the opening volume of a further trilogy, of which books two and three are projected to be entitled *Grail* and *Avalon.*

—Peter T. Garratt

———

LAWSON, Susan. *See* **WEIS, Margaret (Edith).**

———

LEE, John

Nationality: American.

FANTASY PUBLICATIONS

Novels (series: Unicorn in all books)

The Unicorn Quest. New York, Tor, 1986; London, Futura, 1987.
The Unicorn Dilemma. New York, Tor, 1988; London, Orbit, 1989.
The Unicorn Solution. New York, Tor, 1991.
The Unicorn Peace. New York, Tor, 1993.
The Unicorn War. New York, Tor, 1995.

*   *   *

The world of Strand is a magical collection of small kingdoms which has for ages defended itself successfully against invasions from the Poisoned Lands. The invaders use mechanical devices rather than magic as weapons, and each succeeding wave has employed more powerful armaments. Despite the clear progression to higher and higher technology, the people of Strand believe that they will continue to deny the invaders access to their lands. But then a prominent seer informs the governing council that he has found a way to rend the fabric of time and peer into the future, and the future that he sees includes the overwhelming of Strand's defences and the subjugation of its people.

So begins John Lee's epic Unicorn series, five volumes published to date and with more possibly to follow. To avert their fate, the rulers of Strand send two people on a quest to find the mythical unicorn, a beast known only through legend but whose ability to alter the course of time is revealed through a magical dream.

Jarrod is a young magician still uncertain of his abilities, and Marianna is a plucky young woman, daughter of King Darius. Even as Jarrod and Marianna prepare to leave on their quest, the defending army is routed and it appears they may be too late to avert doom. Nevertheless, after many adventures, they succeed in finding the unicorns and enlisting their magic in repelling the invaders, though at a cost so heavy to both sides that real peace seems a likely prospect at last.

It's a surprisingly strong first novel despite the overly familiar theme and occasional problems with pacing, particularly in the early chapters. Lee's fantasy realm is original enough to be interesting in its own right, and his characters are credible and sympathetic. The climactic reversal, in which we discover that Marianna has survived an earlier "death" scene is unfortunately predictable but not germane to the main plot.

The immediate sequel is *The Unicorn Dilemma*. It is in many ways a reprise of the first novel. A fresh attack is imminent along a different front and Darius, father of Marianna, journeys to a nearby kingdom to help the local ruler organize a defence. The battle scenes are longer and more complex, and the interplay among the characters is handled much more convincingly this time. Lee explores the consequences of a war between magic and science, and devises ingenious ways for his characters to disable tanks and other war machines.

Jarrod and Marianna are back with the unicorns, who communicate telepathically and swing the tide of battle favourably once again, although they express dismay at the human mindset as well as that of the invaders who, we learn, are actually gaseous creatures who can only interact with the material world by occupying and manipulating mechanical suits. It's a device that raises more questions than it answers, but Lee wisely keeps his villains at the edges of the stage, even in the heat of battle. All in all, a much better book than the first.

Next came *The Unicorn Solution*. Jarrod, who has greatly improved his grasp of magic, travels with one of the unicorns to a remote town near the borders of Strand. There Jarrod consults the Oracle, hoping to discover the secret of a spell that will banish the invaders permanently. The answer is as vague as oracular pronouncements usually are, but Jarrod learns as well that the unicorns are preparing to return to their own lands. Unless he can reach the Place of Power and find the magic he needs, the future of Strand may be in jeopardy once more.

Halfway through the novel, Lee throws in a few surprises, not all of which work. We learn of the Guardian, for example, a godlike figure who oversees the working of the universe, and who intends that the balance between the inhabitants of Strand and the invaders be maintained, although he inadvertently gives Jarrod the power to exterminate them completely. His existence is jarring, however, and distracts our attention from the other characters and the conflict that was central to the first two books. The prose itself is considerably more polished, and the early chapters are engrossing and convincing, but the second half seems uncontrolled and hastily done.

Lee's fourth entry in the series is *The Unicorn Peace*, set after the unicorns have left Strand and the invaders have ceased their relentless attacks. Freed of outside pressure, the humans have taken to feuding among themselves; as the unicorns had advised Jarrod a book or two previously, the species is drawn to combat by some undeniable inner force. Most of the struggle has been political as the surviving nobility attempts to partition the land now firmly under human control, but already some of the arguments are erupting

into threats and even overt attacks on outposts. And although magicians traditionally do not involve themselves in politics, Jarrod is determined to stop the violence before it evolves into open warfare.

What follows is primarily a series of political manoeuvres interspersed with short action scenes as internal order begins to disintegrate. Ultimately the unicorns reappear, but what seems to be a sign of hope has a darker side, as a faction of the unicorns—who seem to be an alien species from another planet—decides to emigrate to Strand and claim lands currently unused by humans. The clear implication that conflict between humans and unicorns is inevitable seems designed to set the stage for another book.

Lee shows a progressively better grasp of characters and situations from book to book, and in most ways *The Unicorn Peace* is the best of his novels. Jarrod has become a deeper and more interesting character, and the world of Strand is much better realized this time. The unsettling cliffhanger ending is a considerable letdown, however, and as a whole the novel seems to be moving away from the magic and wonder of the earlier volumes into a more conventional primitive fantasy world.

The series is uneven, though beguiling. Lee's use of incongruities is one of his major assets, and he demonstrates continuing improvement in his handling of characters and settings. Whether he will use these skills to produce original material or continue to reprise his own work remains to be seen.

—Don D'Ammassa

LEE, Tanith

Nationality: British. **Born:** London, 19 September 1947. **Education:** Prendergast Grammar School, Catford, London; and an art college, London. **Family:** Married John Kaiine in 1992. **Career:** Worked as a library assistant, London; freelance writer from 1975. **Awards:** August Derleth Award, 1980; World Fantasy Award, 1983. **Address:** c/o Hodder Headline, 338 Euston Road, London NW1 3BH, England.

FANTASY PUBLICATIONS

Novels (series: Birthgrave; Blood Opera; Secret Books of Paradys; Tales from the Flat Earth; Unicorn; Wars of Vis)

The Dragon Hoard, illustrated by Graham Oakley (for children). London, Macmillan, and New York, Farrar Straus, 1971.
Animal Castle, illustrated by Helen Craig (for children). London, Macmillan, and New York, Farrar Straus, 1972.
The Birthgrave. New York, DAW, 1975; London, Futura, 1977.
Companions on the Road (for children). London, Macmillan, 1975.
The Storm Lord (Wars of Vis). New York, DAW, 1976; London, Futura, 1977.
The Winter Players (for children). London, Macmillan, 1976.
Companions on the Road, and The Winter Players: Two Novellas (for children). New York, St. Martin's Press, 1977.
East of Midnight (for children). London, Macmillan, 1977; New York, St. Martin's Press, 1978.
Volkhavaar. New York, DAW, 1977; London, Hamlyn, 1981.

The Castle of Dark (for children). London, Macmillan, 1978.
Vazkor, Son of Vazkor (Birthgrave). New York, DAW, 1978; as *Shadowfire,* London, Futura, 1979.
Quest for the White Witch (Birthgrave). New York, DAW, 1978; London, Futura, 1979.
Night's Master (Flat Earth). New York, DAW, 1978; London, Hamlyn, 1981.
Death's Master (Flat Earth). New York, DAW, 1979; London, Hamlyn, 1982.
Shon the Taken (for children). London, Macmillan, 1979.
Sabella; or, The Blood Stone. New York, DAW, 1980; London, Unwin, 1987.
Kill the Dead. New York, DAW, 1980; London, Legend, 1990.
Day by Night. New York, DAW, 1980.
Delusion's Master (Flat Earth). New York, DAW, 1981.
Lycanthia, or The Children of Wolves. New York, DAW, 1981; London, Legend, 1990.
Sometimes, After Sunset (omnibus; includes *Sabella* and *Kill the Dead*). Garden City, New York, Nelson Doubleday, 1981.
Prince on a White Horse (for children). London, Macmillan, 1982.
Sung in Shadow. New York, DAW, 1983.
Anackire (Wars of Vis). New York, DAW, 1983; London, Futura, 1985.
The Wars of Vis (omnibus; includes *The Storm Lord* and *Anackire*). Garden City, New York, Nelson Doubleday, 1984.
Dark Castle, White Horse (omnibus; includes *The Castle of Dark* and *Prince on a White Horse*). New York, DAW, 1986.
Delirium's Mistress (Flat Earth). New York, DAW, 1986.
Tales from the Flat Earth: The Lords of Darkness (omnibus; includes *Night's Master, Death's Master* and *Delusion's Master*). Garden City, New York, Nelson Doubleday, 1987.
Tales from the Flat Earth: Night's Daughter (omnibus; includes *Delirium's Mistress* and *Night's Sorceries*). Garden City, New York, Nelson Doubleday, 1987.
The Book of the Beast (Paradys). London, Unwin, 1988; Woodstock, New York, Overlook Press, 1991.
Madame Two Swords (for children). New York, Donald M. Grant, 1988.
The White Serpent: A Novel of Vis. New York, DAW, 1988.
A Heroine of the World. New York, DAW, 1989; London, Headline, 1994.
The Blood of Roses. London, Century, 1990.
Black Unicorn. New York, Atheneum, 1991; London, Orbit, 1994.
The Book of the Dead (Paradys). Woodstock, New York, Overlook Press, 1991.
Dark Dance (Blood Opera). London, Macdonald, 1992.
The Book of the Mad (Paradys). Woodstock, New York, Overlook Press, 1993.
Heart-Beast. London, Headline, 1992; New York, Dell, 1993.
Elephantasm. London, Headline, 1993.
Personal Darkness (Blood Opera). London, Little, Brown, 1993.
Darkness, I (Blood Opera). London, Little, Brown, 1994.
Gold Unicorn. New York, Atheneum, 1994; London, Orbit, 1995.
Vivia. London, Little Brown, 1995.
Reigning Cats and Dogs. London, Headline, 1995.

Short Stories

The Betrothed. Sidcup, Kent, Slughorn Press, 1968.
Princess Hynchatti and Some Other Surprises, illustrated by Helen Craig (for children). London, Macmillan, 1972; New York, Farrar Straus, 1973.

Unsilent Night (miscellany). Cambridge, Massachusetts, NESFA Press, 1981.
Cyrion. New York, DAW, 1982.
Red as Blood; or, Tales from the Sisters Grimmer. New York, DAW, 1983.
The Beautiful Biting Machine. New Castle, Virginia, Cheap Street, 1984.
Tamastara; or, The Indian Nights. New York, DAW, 1984.
The Gorgon and Other Beastly Tales. New York, DAW, 1985.
Dreams of Dark and Light: The Great Short Fiction of Tanith Lee. Sauk City, Wisconsin, Arkham House, 1986.
Night's Sorceries (Flat Earth). New York, DAW, 1987; London, Legend, 1988.
The Book of the Damned (Paradys). London, Unwin, 1988; Woodstock, New York, Overlook Press, 1990.
Forests of the Night. London, Unwin, 1989.
Women as Demons: The Male Perception of Women Through Space and Time. London, Women's Press, 1989.
Into Gold. Eugene, Oregon, Pulphouse, 1991.
Nightshades: Thirteen Journeys into Shadow. London, Headline, 1993.

Other Publications

Novels

Don't Bite the Sun. New York, DAW, 1976.
Drinking Sapphire Wine. New York, DAW, 1977; published with *Don't Bite the Sun,* London, Hamlyn, 1979.
Electric Forest. New York, DAW, 1979.
The Silver Metal Lover. New York, DAW, 1982; London, Unwin, 1986.
Days of Grass. New York, DAW, 1985.
Eva Fairdeath. London, Headline, 1994.

Plays

Radio Plays: *Bitter Gate,* 1977; *Red Wine,* 1977; *Death Is King,* 1979; *The Silver Sky,* 1980.

Television Plays: *Sarcophagus,* 1980, and *Sand,* 1981, both for *Blake's Seven* series.

*

Bibliography: By Mike Ashley, in *Fantasy Macabre 4* (London), 1983.

*   *   *

Tanith Lee is one of the most prolific writers working in fantasy and science fiction. Over the course of more than 20 years she has produced a string of novels and short stories for adults and children, often at a rate of two or three books a year. As may be expected from such an output, the quality can be variable, but at her best she produces intense exercises in literary decadence that are replete with recurring images and symbols.

Most strikingly her books feature estranged heroines caught up in some subservient relationship with a man (captivity or enslavement are common). The heroine becomes erotically empowered, but the end result is as likely to be tragic as victorious. Thus in *A*

Heroine of the World, for instance, Aradia becomes in effect a spoil of war who loses not only her country but her name (she becomes at various points Ara, Aara and Ayaira) as she is taken from her homeland by the retreating Kronian army. A captive who also suffers the privations of her captors on a vividly described hunger-march in appalling conditions, Aradia's survival depends on her relationship with the men around her and her understanding of her goddess. Survival makes Aradia a heroine, but the men are far from being heroes, a pattern that has held true throughout Tanith Lee's career, from *The Birthgrave* to *Vivia.*

In *Vivia* the men are particularly brutal. Vivia's father, a petty lord who holds his entire court in fear, is first seen single-handedly carrying his dead warhorse into his castle. His mad grief for the horse allows plague into the castle. Vivia alone survives by sexual liaison with a "dark god" which turns her into a vampire. Zulgaris, another warlord, finds Vivia and takes her as his mistress, even providing a harem of young girls so that Vivia can drink their blood. His prisoner as much as his mistress, Vivia is used by Zulgaris in sexual experiments that form part of his tampering with magic and science. But as Vivia's personal and sexual power grow, Zulgaris's worldly, political power crumbles.

Though such scenarios suggest a strong feminist theme underlying Lee's work, and the Women's Press has published a collection of her stories with the telling subtitle: "The Male Perception of Women through Space and Time," the erotic empowerment of Lee's women comes at a high price. Death, and after death vampirism, feature again and again in her books. In *Sabella,* for instance, the title character becomes a vampire under the influence of a Martian necklace; in *The Blood of Roses* vampirism becomes a means of revenge from beyond the grave; while in the Blood Opera sequence it is a symbol of family loyalty and personal growth. In every instance, no matter what else vampirism might portray, it is a potent symbol for sex and has grown into an ever more dominant motif in her work.

But however much Lee might write about vampires (and though they are usually sympathetic, vampirism itself is inevitably associated with dark torments and an increasing distance from what we might consider the normal mores of society) they are not the only creatures from folklore that inhabit her work. One of the most interesting and often most effective features of her fiction is the reworking of traditional elements. This is perhaps best illustrated by the collection *Red as Blood,* which twists familiar fairy stories so that Snow White is revealed to be the villain of the piece and Sleeping Beauty is malignant not innocent. Traditional Indian stories comprise the basic material of her collection *Tamastara,* while the form the goddess takes in *Anackire* (a snake's tail, serpents for her hair, and eight arms) clearly owes something to Kali. Lee has even taken classical literature for her source: the story of Romulan and Iuletta in a parallel Renaissance Italy in *Sung in Shadow* doesn't do much to hide its Shakespearean inspiration.

After the vampire, however, the figure from folklore that probably suits Tanith Lee's fantasy best is the werewolf, which features in *Lycanthia.* The opportunity to delve into the darker side of her characters offered by shape-changing is analogous to the transformations wrought by death and vampirism.

This notion that reality is unreliable, that transformations might at any moment reveal the skull beneath the skin, upsetting our sense of self and moral precepts, is another consistent feature in her work. Thus in the Flat Earth sequence, Delirium, Madness and Delusion are the superhuman forces which shape the desires and ambitions of humankind. And again in the fourth book in the sequence,

Delirium's Mistress, it is the daughter of Night who fulfils the archetypal fate of a Tanith Lee heroine by becoming in turn mistress, fugitive, champion and goddess.

The threat and mystery of such transformations, and of death, even forms a part of her children's books, at a level of complexity unusual in the genre. In *Prince on a White Horse,* for instance, the central character, who may have died, wakes into a strange world where things have a habit of turning into something else. Lee's books for children, in fact, have a clarity and directness which make them among the very best of her works.

In her novels for adults, on the other hand, her writing can become arcane, idiosyncratic and often over-wrought, relying for its effect on a clotted style heavy on visual detail in which the same symbols appear again and again. Few colours appear in her novels, for instance, that are not white as bone, black as night or red as blood. Nevertheless, at her best Tanith Lee can lead her reader into a vivid, dramatic and utterly unique landscape of surreal and terrifying dreams.

—Maureen Speller

LE GUIN, Ursula K(roeber)

Nationality: American. **Born:** Berkeley, California, 21 October 1929; daughter of writer Theodora Kroeber and anthropologist Alfred L. Kroeber. **Education:** Radcliffe College, Cambridge, Massachusetts, A.B. 1951 (Phi Beta Kappa); Columbia University, New York (Faculty Fellow; Fulbright Fellow, 1953), M.A. 1952. **Family:** Married Charles A. Le Guin in 1953; two daughters and one son. **Career:** Instructor in French, Mercer University, Macon, Georgia, 1954, and University of Idaho, Moscow, 1956; department secretary, Emory University, Atlanta, 1955; has taught writing workshops at Pacific University, Forest Grove, Oregon, 1971, University of Washington, Seattle, 1971-73, Portland State University, Oregon, 1974, 1977, 1979, in Melbourne, Australia, 1975, at the University of Reading, England, 1976, Indiana Writers Conference, Bloomington, 1978, 1983, and University of California, San Diego, 1979. **Awards:** Boston *Globe-Horn Book* award, for children's book, 1969; Nebula award, 1969, 1974 (twice), 1991; Hugo award, 1970, 1973, 1974, 1975, 1988; National Book award for children's book, 1972; Jupiter award, 1974 (twice), 1976; Gandalf award, 1979; University of Oregon Distinguished Service award, 1981; *Locus* award (twice), 1983; Janet Heidinger Kafka award, 1986; Pushcart prize, 1991; Harold D. Vursell award, American Academy and Institute of Arts and Letters, 1991; OILA award, 1992. Guest of Honor, World Science Fiction Convention, 1975. D.Litt. Bucknell University, Lewisburg, Pennsylvania, 1978; Lawrence University, Appleton, Wisconsin; D.H.L.: Lewis and Clark College, Portland, 1983; Occidental College, Los Angeles, 1985. Lives in Portland, Oregon. **Agent:** Virginia Kidd, 538 East Harford Street, Milford, PA 18337, USA; dramatic agent: William Morris Agency, 1350 Avenue of the Americas, New York, NY 10019, USA.

Fantasy Publications

Novels (series: Earthsea; Orsinia)

A Wizard of Earthsea. Berkeley, California, Parnassus Press, 1968; London, Gollancz, 1971.

The Tombs of Atuan (Earthsea). New York, Atheneum, 1971, London, Gollancz, 1972.

The Farthest Shore (Earthsea). New York, Atheneum, 1972; London, Gollancz, 1973.

Earthsea (omnibus; includes *A Wizard of Earthsea, The Tombs of Atuan, The Farthest Shore*). London, Gollancz, 1977; as *The Earthsea Trilogy,* London, Penguin, 1979.

Malafrena (Orsinia). New York, Putnam, 1979; London, Gollancz, 1980.

The Beginning Place. New York, Harper, 1980; as *Threshold,* London, Gollancz, 1980.

Tehanu: The Last Book of Earthsea. New York, Atheneum, and London, Gollancz, 1990.

Short Stories

The Wind's Twelve Quarters. New York, Harper, 1975; London, Gollancz, 1976.

Orsinian Tales. New York, Harper, 1976; London, Gollancz, 1977.

The Compass Rose. New York, Harper, 1982; London, Gollancz, 1983.

Buffalo Gals and Other Animal Presences. Santa Barbara, California, Capra Press, 1987; as *Buffalo Gals,* London, Gollancz, 1990.

A Fisherman of the Inland Sea. New York, HarperPrism, 1994.

OTHER PUBLICATIONS

Novels

Rocannon's World. New York, Ace, 1966; London, Tandem, 1972.

Planet of Exile. New York, Ace, 1966; London, Tandem, 1972.

City of Illusions. New York, Ace, 1967; London, Gollancz, 1971.

The Left Hand of Darkness. New York, Ace, and London, Macdonald, 1969.

The Lathe of Heaven. New York, Scribner, 1971; London, Gollancz, 1972.

The Dispossessed: An Ambiguous Utopia. New York, Harper, and London, Gollancz, 1974.

Very Far Away from Anywhere Else. New York, Atheneum, 1976; as *A Very Long Way from Anywhere Else,* London, Gollancz, 1976.

The Word for World is Forest. New York, Putnam, 1976; London, Gollancz, 1977.

Three Hainish Novels (omnibus; includes *Rocannon's World, Planet of Exile, City of Illusions*). New York, Nelson Doubleday, 1978.

The Eye of the Heron. London, Gollancz, 1982; New York, Harper, 1983.

Always Coming Home, illustrated by Margaret Chodos. New York, Harper, 1985; London, Gollancz, 1986.

The New Atlantis, with *The Return from Rainbow Bridge* by Kim Stanley Robinson. New York, Tor, 1989.

The Eye of the Heron & The Word for World Is Forest (omnibus). London, Gollancz, 1991.

Short Stories

The Water Is Wide. Portland, Oregon, Pendragon Press, 1976.

Gwilan's Harp. Northridge, California, Lord John Press, 1981.

The Visionary: The Life Story of Flicker of the Serpentine of Telina-Na, with Wonders Hidden, by Scott Russell Sanders. Santa Barbara, California, Capra Press, 1984.

Searoad: Chronicles of Klatsand. New York, HarperCollins, 1991; London, Gollancz, 1992.

Fiction for Children

Leese Webster, illustrated by James Brunsman. New York, Atheneum, 1979; London, Gollancz, 1981.

The Adventure of Cobbler's Rune, illustrated by Alicia Austin. New Castle, Virginia, Cheap Street, 1982.

Solomon Leviathan's Nine Hundred and Thirty-First Trip Around the World, illustrated by Alicia Austin. New Castle, Virginia, Cheap Street, 1983.

A Visit from Dr. Katz, illustrated by Ann Barrow. New York, Atheneum, 1988; as *Dr. Katz,* London, Collins, 1988.

Catwings, illustrated by J. Schindler. New York, Orchard, 1988.

Catwings Return, illustrated by J. Schindler. New York, Orchard, 1989.

Fire and Stone, illustrated by Laura Marshall. New York, Atheneum, 1989.

Fish Soup, illustrated by Patrick Wynne. New York, Atheneum, 1992.

A Ride on the Red Mare's Back, illustrated by Julie Downing. New York, Orchard, 1992.

Wonderful Alexander and the Catwings, illustrated by J. Schindler. New York, Orchard, 1994.

Plays

No Use to Talk to Me, in *The Altered Eye,* edited by Lee Harding. Melbourne, Norstrilia Press, 1976; New York, Berkley, 1978.

King Dog (screenplay), with *Dostoevsky* by Raymond Carver and Tess Gallagher. Santa Barbara, California, Capra Press, 1985.

Hernes (produced Portland, Oregon, 1994).

Poetry

Wild Angels. Santa Barbara, California, Capra Press, 1975.

Tillai and Tylissos, with Theodora Kroeber. N.p., Red Bull Press, 1979.

Torrey Pines Reserve. Northridge, California, Lord John Press, 1980.

Gwilan's Harp. Northridge, California, Lord John Press, 1981.

Hard Words and Other Poems. New York, Harper and Row, 1981.

In the Red Zone, illustrated by Henk Pander. Northridge, California, Lord John Press, 1983.

Wild Oats and Fireweed. New York, Harper and Row, 1988.

No Boats. N.p., Ygor and Buntho, 1992.

Blue Moon Over Thurman Street, photographs by Roger Durband. N.p., NewSage, 1993.

Going Out with Peacocks. New York, HarperCollins, 1994.

Other

From Elfland to Poughkeepsie (lecture). Portland, Oregon, Pendragon Press, 1973.

Dreams Must Explain Themselves. New York, Algol Press, 1975.

The Language of the Night: Essays on Fantasy and Science Fiction, edited by Susan Wood. New York, Putnam, 1979; revised edition, edited by Ursula K. Le Guin, London, Women's Press, 1989.

Dancing at the Edge of the World: Thoughts on Words, Women, Places. New York, Grove Press, and London, Gollancz, 1989.
The Way of the Water's Going, photographs by Ernest Waugh and Alan Nicholson. New York, Harper and Row, 1989.
Myth and Archetype in Science Fiction. Eugene, Oregon, Pulphouse, 1991.
Talk About Writing. Eugene, Oregon, Pulphouse, 1991.
Findings. N.p., Ox Head, 1992.
The Art of Bunditsu. N.p., Ygor and Buntho, 1993.
Earthsea Revisioned (lecture). Cambridge, Massachusetts, Children's Literature New England, and Cambridge, England, Green Bay, 1993.

Editor, *Nebula Award Stories 11.* London, Gollancz, 1976; New York, Harper, 1977.
Editor, with Virginia Kidd, *Interfaces.* New York, Ace, 1980.
Editor, with Virginia Kidd, *Edges.* New York, Pocket Books, 1980.
Editor, with Brian Attebery, *The Norton Book of Science Fiction.* New York and London, Norton, 1993.

*

Film Adaptation: *The Lathe of Heaven,* 1982 (TV movie).

Bibliography: *Ursula K. Le Guin: A Primary and Secondary Bibliography* by Elizabeth Cummins Cogell, Boston, Hall, 1983.

Manuscript Collection: University of Oregon Library, Eugene.

Critical Studies: *The Farthest Shores of Ursula K. Le Guin* by George Edgar Slusser, San Bernardino, California, Borgo Press, 1976; "Ursula Le Guin Issue" of *Science-Fiction Studies* (Terre Haute, Indiana), March 1976; *Ursula Le Guin* by Joseph D. Olander and Martin H. Greenberg, New York, Taplinger, and Edinburgh, Harris, 1979; *Ursula K. Le Guin: Voyager to Inner Lands and to Outer Space* edited by Joseph W. De Bolt, Port Washington, New York, Kennikat Press, 1979; *Ursula K. Le Guin* by Barbara J. Bucknall, New York, Ungar, 1981; *Ursula K. Le Guin* by Charlotte Spivack, Boston, Twayne, 1984; *Approaches to the Fiction of Ursula K. Le Guin* by James Bittner, Ann Arbor, Michigan, UMI Research Press, and Epping, Essex, Bowker, 1984; *Understanding Ursula K. Le Guin* by Elizabeth Cummins, Columbia, University of South Carolina Press, 1990.

*   *   *

Ursula Le Guin is primarily known as a science-fiction writer, in which field she is one of the most distinguished living practitioners, whose reputation extends far beyond the confines of the genre itself. Her fantasy would seem a secondary aspect of her fiction, though in several essays she has argued that such distinctions mean little. The unifying interest in virtually all her work is a sense of another place, an imagined world existing either in outer space, or on a slightly different version of the Earth. From well before the beginning of her professional career, she showed an interest in utopias. The influence of Austin Tappan Wright, author of *Islandia* (1942), has always been strong, most overtly expressed in early stories and a novel, *Malafrena,* set in an imaginary Central European country called Orsinia. These, with one ambiguous exception in *Orsinian Tales,* include no explicitly fantastic or supernatural elements but may be regarded by some readers as marginal fantasy

of the Ruritanian sort. Many of her shorter stories are fables, the most famous of which, "The Ones Who Walk Away from Omelas," is now a classic of science fiction, but has occasioned (Le Guin would say, meaninglessly) arguments over whether it is science fiction at all. It is a deft, stark thought-experiment on the cost of the good life. (If one person must suffer hideously to make utopia possible for everybody else, is it worth it?) The setting is merely elsewhere, the technique, more description than narration, reminiscent of Borges.

Central to Le Guin's fantasy is the Earthsea series, for many years one of the most celebrated of trilogies, transformed belatedly into a tetralogy, although not (as Le Guin has testified, refuting claims printed elsewhere) due to feminist criticism of the first three volumes. The Earthsea books are best read in conjunction with Le Guin's ground-breaking essay, "From Elfland to Pougkeepsie" (reprinted in *The Language of the Night*). As examples of theory put into practice, they have few peers. The essay calls for a purity of style in fantastic writing, not obtrusive fake-archaism but a deeper magic of precisely the right phrase from precisely the right point of view. She discusses E. R. Eddison and Lord Dunsany in this context, along with the nearly forgotten Kenneth Morris, whose posthumous reputation she managed to revive in a few short paragraphs.

Language is the key to the Earthsea novels. They are set in an archipelago, and tell of the youth, education, and career of a great wizard, Ged. While there are some medieval or antique elements, this is not the standard, generic fantasy setting with 13th-century Europe sanitized and transplanted. Even the racial configurations are off-standard (a point overlooked by most illustrators). Most people in Earthsea are vaguely Polynesian, brown-skinned. The hero has a friend at college who is black. The wild barbarians from the fringe islands (a culture explored in *The Tombs of Atuan*) are white. The setting is made vividly real because the author has written her world from the inside, from the point of view of people who accept various supernatural assumptions which do not apply to our world. The power of myth manifests itself in a primal, stripped-down otherness, in which the most important things are (at least symbolically) in plain sight. Le Guin has compared this sort of imaginative exercise to dreaming.

But sense of otherness does not preclude the hard edges of life. The fourth volume presents a reverse image of the traditional fantasy novel of quests and power. Ged has grown old and helpless. The grim, ambiguous storyline concerns people who stayed home or remained in the background and didn't get noticed in the epics. It is about the subtle, pervasive power of women.

Le Guin's otherworlds tend to be utilitarian, not mere flights of fantasy. They teach, harkening back to the utopian tradition. In the Earthsea books (and two short Earthsea stories in *The Wind's Twelve Quarters*) the lessons are subtle and far below the surface. In some of her science fiction, particularly the novella *The Word for World is Forest,* didacticism can gain the upper hand.

In the non-Earthsea fantasy *The Beginning Place,* imagination and allegory strike an uneasy balance, as two young people, both of whom suffer drab, unsatisfactory lives in our world, find their way through a "gateway" into another realm, which is itself rather drab and unsatisfactory after a while: a quiet, medieval land of perpetual twilight, where one of the characters (the young woman) is a welcome guest but doesn't really belong and the other (the young man) is (to the heroine at least) an unwelcome intruder who disturbs the escapist value of the place. But he may also be the long-awaited hero who will save it. The two of them go on a brief and gritty quest, conquer fear, and find one another. But the setting is purely a device; its geography and inhabitants little more than names; far from the vivid, living Earthsea. For a Le Guin novel, *The Beginning Place* generated little excitement. It is a minor work.

The Earthsea books are central to 20th-century fantasy, probably more influential than anything other than *The Lord of the Rings,* often taken as models by other writers because they create a world as vivid as Tolkien's, but on a smaller, more intimate scale. Le Guin has turned Tolkien's epic into a novel of character, with a smaller, more sharply realized cast; and, for all the Earthsea books were published as ostensible juveniles, they are in every sense more adult, fully willing to admit that even beloved characters fade and die or come to nasty, abrupt ends, where Tolkien hedges mortality in endless appendices, reluctant to let go.

—Darrell Schweitzer

LEIBER, Fritz (Reuter, Jr.)

Nationality: American. **Born:** Chicago, Illinois, 24 December 1910. **Education:** University of Chicago, Ph.B. 1932; Episcopal General Theological Seminary, Washington, D.C. **Family:** Married (1) Jonquil Stephens in 1936 (died 1969); one son (the writer Justin Leiber); (2) Margo Skinner in 1991. **Career:** Episcopal minister at two churches in New Jersey, 1932-33; actor, 1934-36; editor, Consolidated Book Publishers, Chicago, 1937-41; instructor in Speech and Drama, Occidental College, Los Angeles, 1941-42; precision inspector, Douglas Aircraft, Santa Monica, California, 1942-44; associate editor, *Science Digest,* Chicago, 1944-56. Lecturer, Clarion State College, Pennsylvania, summers 1968-70. **Awards:** Hugo award, 1958, 1965, 1968, 1970, 1971, 1976; Nebula award, 1967, 1970, 1975, and Grand Master Nebula award, 1981; Ann Radcliffe award, 1970; Gandalf award, 1975; Derleth award, 1976; World Fantasy award, 1976, 1978; Locus award, 1985; Bram Stoker Lifetime Achievement award, 1988. Guest of Honor, World Science Fiction Convention, 1951, 1979. **Died:** 5 September 1992.

FANTASY PUBLICATIONS

Novels (series: Fafhrd and the Gray Mouser)

The Sinful Ones. New York, Universal, 1953; revised edition, New York: Pocket, 1980.
The Swords of Lankhmar (Fafhrd and Mouser). New York, Ace, 1968; London, Hart Davis, 1969.
Rime Isle (Fafhrd and Mouser; novella). Chapel Hill, North Carolina, Whispers Press, 1977.
Ill Met in Lankhmar (Fafhrd and Mouser; novella), published with *The Fair in Emain Macha* by Charles de Lint. New York, Tor, 1990.

Short Stories

Night's Black Agents. Sauk City, Wisconsin, Arkham House, 1947; London, Spearman, 1975.
Two Sought Adventure (Fafhrd and Mouser). New York, Gnome Press, 1957; revised and expanded as *Swords Against Death,* New York, Ace, 1970; London, New English Library, 1972.

The Secret Songs. London, Hart Davis, 1968.
Swords Against Wizardry (Fafhrd and Mouser). New York, Ace, 1968; London, Prior, 1977.
Swords in the Mist (Fafhrd and Mouser). New York, Ace, 1968; London, Prior, 1977.
Swords and Deviltry (Fafhrd and Mouser). New York, Ace, 1970; London, New English Library, 1971.
You're All Alone. New York, Ace, 1972.
Swords and Ice Magic (Fafhrd and Mouser). New York, Ace, and London, Prior, 1977.
Bazaar of the Bizarre (Fafhrd and Mouser). West Kingston, Rhode Island, Grant, 1978.
The Ghost Light (includes autobiographical essay). New York, Berkley, 1984.
The Knight and Knave of Swords (Fafhrd and Mouser). New York, Morrow, 1988; London, Grafton, 1990.
The Three of Swords (omnibus; includes *Swords and Deviltry, Swords Against Death, Swords in the Mist*). New York, Nelson Doubleday, 1989.
Swords' Masters (omnibus; includes *Swords Against Wizardry, Swords of Lankhmar, Swords and Ice Magic*). New York, Guild America, 1990.

OTHER PUBLICATIONS

Novels

Gather, Darkness! New York, Pellegrini and Cudahy, 1950; London, New English Library, 1966.
Conjure Wife. New York, Twayne, 1953; London, Penguin, 1969.
The Green Millennium. New York, Abelard Press, 1953; London Abelard Schuman, 1959.
Destiny Times Three. New York, Galaxy, 1957.
The Big Time. New York, Ace, 1961; London, New English Library, 1965.
The Silver Eggheads. New York, Ballantine, 1962; London, New English Library, 1966.
The Wanderer. New York, Ballantine, 1964; London, Dobson, 1967.
Tarzan and the Valley of Gold (novelization of screenplay). New York, Ballantine, 1966.
A Specter Is Haunting Texas. New York, Walker, and London, Gollancz, 1969.
Our Lady of Darkness. New York, Berkley, 1977; London, Millington, 1978.
Ship of Shadows (novella), published with *No Truce with Kings,* by Poul Anderson. New York, Tor, 1989.

Short Stories

The Mind Spider and Other Stories. New York, Ace, 1961.
Shadows with Eyes. New York, Ballantine, 1962.
A Pail of Air. New York, Ballantine, 1964.
Ships to the Stars. New York, Ace, 1964.
The Night of the Wolf. New York, Ballantine, 1966; London, Sphere, 1976.
Night Monsters. New York, Ace, 1969; revised edition, London, Gollancz, 1974.
The Best of Fritz Leiber, edited by Angus Wells. London, Sphere, and New York, Doubleday, 1974.
The Book of Fritz Leiber. New York, DAW, 1974.

The Second Book of Fritz Leiber. New York, DAW, 1975.

The Worlds of Fritz Leiber. New York, Ace, 1976.

The Change War. Boston, Gregg Press, 1978; revised edition, as *Changewar,* New York, Ace, 1983.

Heroes and Horrors, edited by Stuart David Schiff. Browns Mills, New Jersey, Whispers Press, 1978.

Ship of Shadows. London, Gollancz, 1979.

The Mystery of the Japanese Clock. Santa Monica, California, Montgolfier Press, 1982.

Riches and Power: A Story for Children. New Castle, Virginia, Cheap Street, 1982.

In the Beginning. New Castle, Virginia, Cheap Street, 1983.

Quicks Around the Zodiac: A Farce. New Castle, Virginia, Cheap Street, 1983.

The Leiber Chronicles: Fifty Years of Fritz Leiber, edited by Martin H. Greenberg. Arlington Heights, Illinois, Dark Harvest Press, 1990.

Poetry

The Demons of the Upper Air. Glendale, California, Squires, 1969.

Sonnets to Jonquil and All. Glendale, California, Squires, 1978.

Other

Fafhrd & Me, edited by John Gregory Betancourt. Newark, New Jersey, Wildside Press, 1990.

Editor, with Stuart David Schiff, *The World Fantasy Awards 2.* New York, Doubleday, 1980.

*

Bibliography: *Fritz Leiber: A Bibliography 1934-1979* by Chris Morgan, Birmingham, England, Morgenstern, 1979; *Fritz Leiber: Sardonic Swordsman—A Working Bibliography, 2nd ed.* by Phil Stephensen-Payne and Gordon Benson, Jr., Leeds, West Yorkshire, Galactic Central Publications, 1990.

Critical Studies: "Fritz Leiber Issue" of *Fantasy and Science Fiction* (New York), July 1969; *Fritz Leiber* by Jeff Frane, San Bernardino, California, Borgo Press, 1980; *Fritz Leiber* by Tom Staicar, New York, Ungar, 1983; *Witches of the Mind: A Critical Study of Fritz Leiber* by Bruce Byfield, West Warwick, Rhode Island, Necronomicon Press, 1991.

*   *   *

Fritz Leiber's work spans the entire spectrum of modern imaginative fiction, including science fiction, fantasy and horror. His fiction was much appreciated by discerning readers of all of these genres, winning numerous and varied awards. He made outstanding contributions to both horror and science fiction but his greatest literary monument is the long fantasy series chronicling the adventures of Fafhrd and the Gray Mouser, which demonstrated that the pulp sub-genre of "sword-and-sorcery" fiction created by Robert E. Howard was capable of artistic sophistication, in terms of both literary elegance and psychological depth.

It is fitting that Leiber's career began and ended with Fafhrd and the Mouser; the first significant story he wrote was the fine baroque novella "Adept's Gambit" (eventually published in *Night's Black Agents*), the first story he sold was the swashbuckling "Two Sought Adventure" (1939), and the last significant work of fiction he published was the erotic novel "The Mouser Goes Below," which makes up the final part of *The Knight and Knave of Swords.* Many of the other stories in the series (which eventually filled seven volumes) are among the finest heroic fantasies ever written; these include the brilliantly satirical "Lean Times in Lankhmar," the zestful adventure story *The Swords of Lankhmar,* and a group of stories written in grief-stricken response to the terminal illness and death in 1969 of his first wife, Jonquil Stephens, most notably the harrowing "Ill Met in Lankhmar" (1970).

Leiber based the character of the large-sized and big-hearted barbarian Fafhrd on himself and the character of the small and slyly ingenious Mouser on his friend Harry Otto Fischer, who actually invented them and wrote the first part of the novella which ultimately became "The Lords of Quarmall" (1964), one of the darkest fantasies in the series. As with many other Leiber characters their weaknesses are often more evident than their strengths—in an introduction to *The Swords of Lankhmar* the author observes that "they drink, they feast, they wench, they brawl, they steal, they gamble, and surely they hire out their swords to powers that are only a shade better, if that, than the villains"—but this insistent emphasis on their flawed humanity helps to illuminate the particular quality of their own heroism, and the nature of heroism in general. Fafhrd and the Mouser do not live in a world where Good and Evil are polarized and personified, but in a world where even the gods are wayward, quarrelsome, meddlesome and mean; they are frequently victimized by cruel circumstance and by their own black moods, but they are survivors avid to extract all the pleasures which life provides as compensation for its pains.

Leiber's ability to project his own emotions and personal struggles into his work is perhaps the key to its effectiveness. He was the son of an actor and had acting experience of his own, and many of his best stories give the impression that they are being intensely lived as well as deftly and fervently performed. He has the ability to inject a vivid realism into the most bizarre situations, whether they are developed with playful delight, gentle sentimentality or fierce intensity. The autobiographical writings which he produced in some profusion in his later years (most notably the long essay which concludes *The Ghost Light*) are remarkable for the calm reflectiveness of their self-analysis as well as their frankness about the recurrent alcoholism which periodically interrupted his career.

Leiber's other early work for the pulps included a number of stories which devise hauntings uniquely appropriate to contemporary urban landscapes, beginning with the brilliant "Smoke Ghost" (1941) and its classic description of a ghost fitted to the tenor of modern times: "A smoky composite face with the hungry anxiety of the unemployed, the neurotic restlessness of the person without purpose, the jerky tension of the high-pressure metropolitan worker, the uneasy resentment of the striker, the callous opportunism of the scab, the aggressive whine of the panhandler, the inhibited terror of the bombed civilian, and a thousand other twisted emotional patterns." This was to be the manifesto for almost all Leiber's horror stories, and also for a number of effective dark fantasies on the borderline between genres, whose impact is more subtly disturbing and often curiously sentimental. "Four Ghosts in Hamlet" (1965) is one such story, "Midnight by the Morphy Watch" (1974) another; it is no coincidence that the theme of each story is one of Leiber's passions: theatre in the first instance, chess in the second. Other stories in this eerily intimate vein include "The Girl with the Hungry Eyes" (1949), the quasi-autobiographical "The Button-

Molder" (1979) and "The Ghost Light" (1984). The novels *Conjure Wife* and *Our Lady of Darkness* are primarily horror stories, but the premises in which they are based are introduced in a relatively even-handed fashion. The former imagines that campus wives routinely assist their husbands' careers with the aid of witchcraft, and builds its horrific crescendo from quiet beginnings; the latter deploys "paramental entities" which are the demonic "souls" of modern cities in a story which has enough autobiographical elements as almost to qualify as a roman à clef.

Leiber also wrote a number of remarkable surreal fantasies. The first and most substantial of these was a novel intended for *Unknown Worlds* which was set aside when that magazine folded in 1943. It eventually appeared in abridged form as "You're All Alone" (1950) and in a full-length version as *The Sinful Ones,* but the latter was initially issued by a sleazy paperback publisher with several mildly pornographic passages inserted into the text, and it was not until 1980—by which time the short version had been reprinted more than once—that Leiber was able to produce a more satisfactory text. The premise of the story is that the vast majority of people are automata following a deterministic script, but that a few individuals can exercise sufficient free will to step outside their roles, becoming effectively invisible to everyone except others of their kind. Some of Leiber's shorter works in this vein are stories of alcohol-disrupted perception, most notably "The Secret Songs" (1962) and "The Winter Flies" (1967 as "The Inner Circles"). The brilliantly phantasmagoric "Gonna Roll the Bones" (1967) is launched from a similar platform, although it ranges much further.

Leiber never fitted comfortably into the marketplace into which his fiction was launched; for most of his life his work was mostly confined to its interstices, his awesome versatility and originality often seeming to constitute handicaps rather than assets. No other career has demonstrated so clearly the difficulties which 20th-century writers of fantastic fiction have faced in publishing new and unconventional work—but he did manage to publish, and thereby to expand the limits and ambitions of the genres in which he worked, much to the delight of the members of his audience who recognized him for what he was: one of the finest American short story writers of his generation.

—Brian Stableford

LEWIS, C(live) S(taples)

Pseudonyms: Clive Hamilton; N. W. Clerk. **Nationality:** British. **Born:** Belfast, Northern Ireland, 29 November 1898. **Education:** Wynyard House, Watford, Hertfordshire, 1908-10; Campbell College, Belfast, 1910; Cherbourg School, Malvern, Worcestershire, 1911-13, and Malvern College, 1913-14; privately, in Great Bookham, Surrey, 1914-17; University College, Oxford (scholar; Chancellor's English Essay prize, 1921), 1917, 1919-23, B.A. (honours) 1922. **Military Service:** Somerset Light Infantry, 1917-19: First Lieutenant. **Family:** Married Joy Davidman Gresham in 1956 (died 1960); two stepsons. **Career:** Philosophy tutor, 1924, and lecturer in English, 1924, University College, Oxford; fellow and tutor in English, Magdalen College, Oxford, 1925-54; professor of Medieval and Renaissance English, Cambridge University, 1954-63; lecturer, University College of North Wales, Bangor, 1941;

Riddell lecturer, University of Durham, 1943; Clark lecturer, Cambridge University, 1944. **Awards:** Gollancz prize, 1937; Library Association Carnegie Medal, 1957; D.D., University of St. Andrews, Fife, 1946; Docteur-ès-Lettres, Laval University, Quebec, 1952; D.Litt., University of Manchester, 1959; Hon.Dr., University of Dijon, 1962; University of Lyon, 1963; Honorary Fellow, Magdalen College, Oxford, 1955; University College, Oxford, 1958; Magdalene College, Cambridge, 1963; Fellow, Royal Society of Literature, 1948; Fellow, British Academy, 1955. **Died:** 22 November 1963.

FANTASY PUBLICATIONS

Novels (series: Narnia)

The Pilgrim's Regress: An Allegorical Apology for Christianity, Reason, and Romanticism. London, Dent, 1933; New York, Sheed and Ward, 1935; revised edition, London, Bles, 1943; Sheed and Ward, 1944.

The Space Trilogy. New York, Collier, 1986; as *The Cosmic Trilogy,* London, Bodley Head, 1990.
  Out of the Silent Planet. London, Lane, 1938; New York, Macmillan, 1943.
  Perelandra. London, Lane, 1943; New York, Macmillan, 1944; as *Voyage to Venus,* London, Pan, 1953.
  That Hideous Strength: A Modern Fairy-Tale for Grown-Ups. London, Lane, 1945; New York, Macmillan, 1946; abridged edition, as *The Tortured Planet,* New York, Avon, 1958.

The Screwtape Letters. London, Bles, 1942; New York, Macmillan, 1943; revised edition, as *The Screwtape Letters and Screwtape Proposes a Toast,* Bles, 1961; Macmillan, 1962.

The Great Divorce: A Dream. London, Bles, and New York, Macmillan, 1946.

The Lion, The Witch, and the Wardrobe (Narnia). London, Bles, and New York, Macmillan, 1950.

Prince Caspian: The Return to Narnia. London, Bles, and New York, Macmillan, 1951.

The Voyage of the "Dawn Treader" (Narnia). London, Bles, and New York, Macmillan, 1952.

The Silver Chair (Narnia). London, Bles, and New York, Macmillan, 1953.

The Horse and His Boy (Narnia). London, Bles, and New York, Macmillan, 1954.

The Magician's Nephew (Narnia). London, Lane, and New York, Macmillan, 1955.

The Last Battle (Narnia). London, Lane, and New York, Macmillan, 1956.

Till We Have Faces: A Myth Retold. London, Bles, 1956; New York, Harcourt Brace, 1957.

Short Stories

Of Other Worlds: Essays and Stories, edited by Walter Hooper. London, Bles, 1966; New York, Harcourt Brace, 1967.

The Dark Tower and Other Stories, edited by Walter Hooper. London, Collins, and New York, Harcourt Brace, 1977.

Boxen: The Imaginary World of the Young C. S. Lewis, edited by Walter Hooper. London, Collins, and San Diego, Harcourt Brace, 1985.

OTHER PUBLICATIONS

Poetry

Spirits in Bondage: A Cycle of Lyrics (as Clive Hamilton). London, Heinemann, 1919.

Dymer (as Clive Hamilton). London, Dent, and New York, Dutton, 1926.

Poems, edited by Walter Hooper. London, Bles, 1964; New York, Harcourt Brace, 1965.

Narrative Poems, edited by Walter Hooper. London, Bles, 1969; New York, Harcourt Brace, 1972.

Other

The Allegory of Love: A Study in Medieval Tradition. Oxford, Clarendon Press, and New York, Oxford University Press, 1936.

Rehabilitations and Other Essays. London and New York, Oxford University Press, 1939.

The Personal Heresy: A Controversy, with E. M. W. Tillyard. London and New York, Oxford University Press, 1939.

The Problem of Pain. London, Bles, 1940; New York, Macmillan, 1944.

The Weight of Glory. London, S.P.C.K., 1942.

Broadcast Talks: Right and Wrong: A Clue to the Meaning of the Universe, and What Christians Believe. London, Bles, 1942; as *The Case for Christianity,* New York, Macmillan, 1943.

A Preface to "Paradise Lost" (lectures). London and New York, Oxford University Press, 1942; revised edition, 1960.

Christian Behaviour: A Further Series of Broadcast Talks. London, Bles, and New York, Macmillan, 1943.

The Abolition of Man; or, Reflections on Education with Special Reference to the Teaching of English in the Upper Forms of Schools. London, Oxford University Press, 1943; New York, Macmillan, 1947.

Beyond Personality: The Christian Idea of God. London, Bles, 1944; New York, Macmillan, 1945.

Miracles: A Preliminary Study. London, Bles, and New York, Macmillan, 1947.

Vivisection. London, Anti-Vivisection Society, and Boston, New England Anti-Vivisection Society, 1947.

Transposition and Other Addresses. London, Bles, 1949; as *The Weight of Glory and Other Addresses,* New York, Macmillan, 1949.

The Literary Impact of the Authorized Version (lecture). London, Athlone Press, 1950; Philadelphia, Fortress Press, 1963.

Mere Christianity. London, Bles, and New York, Macmillan, 1952.

Hero and Leander (lecture). London, Oxford University Press, 1952.

English Literature in the Sixteenth Century, Excluding Drama. Oxford, Clarendon Press, 1954.

De Descriptione Temporum (lecture). London, Cambridge University Press, 1955.

Surprised by Joy: The Shape of My Early Life. London, Bles, 1955; New York, Harcourt Brace, 1956.

Reflections on the Psalms. London, Bles, and New York, Harcourt Brace, 1958.

Shall We Lose God in Outer Space? London, S.P.C.K., 1959.

The Four Loves. London, Bles, and New York, Harcourt Brace, 1960.

The World's Last Night and Other Essays. New York, Harcourt Brace, 1960.

Studies in Words. London, Cambridge University Press, 1960; revised edition, 1967; New York, Cambridge University Press, 1990.

An Experiment in Criticism. London, Cambridge University Press, 1961.

A Grief Observed (as N. W. Clerk; autobiography). London, Faber, 1961; Greenwich, Connecticut, Seabury Press, 1963.

They Asked for a Paper: Papers and Addresses. London, Bles, 1962.

Beyond the Bright Blur (letters). New York, Harcourt Brace, 1963.

Letters to Malcolm, Chiefly on Prayer. London, Bles, and New York, Harcourt Brace, 1964.

The Discarded Image: An Introduction to Medieval and Renaissance Literature. London, Cambridge University Press, 1964.

Screwtape Proposes a Toast and Other Pieces. London, Fontana, 1965.

Letters, edited by W. H. Lewis. London, Bles, and New York, Harcourt Brace, 1966; revised edition, edited by Walter Hooper, London, Collins, 1988.

Studies in Medieval and Renaissance Literature, edited by Walter Hooper. London, Cambridge University Press, 1966.

Spenser's Images of Life, edited by Alastair Fowler. London, Cambridge University Press, 1967.

Christian Reflections, edited by Walter Hooper. London, Bles, and Grand Rapids, Michigan, Eerdmans, 1967.

Letters to an American Lady, edited by Clyde S. Kilby. Grand Rapids, Michigan, Eerdmans, 1967; London, Hodder and Stoughton, 1969.

Mark vs. Tristram: Correspondence Between C. S. Lewis and Owen Barfield, edited by Walter Hooper. Cambridge, Massachusetts, Lowell House Printers, 1967.

A Mind Awake: An Anthology of C. S. Lewis, edited by Clyde S. Kilby. London, Bles, 1968; New York, Harcourt Brace, 1969.

Selected Literary Essays, edited by Walter Hooper. London, Cambridge University Press, 1969.

God in the Dock: Essays on Theology and Ethics, edited by Walter Hooper. Grand Rapids, Michigan, Eerdmans, 1970; as *Undeceptions: Essays on Theology and Ethics,* London, Bles, 1971.

The Humanitarian Theory of Punishment. Abingdon, Berkshire, Marcham Books Press, 1972.

Fern-Seed and Elephants and Other Essays on Christianity, edited by Walter Hooper. London, Fontana, 1975.

The Joyful Christian: 127 Readings, edited by William Griffin. New York, Macmillan, 1977.

They Stand Together: The Letters of C. S. Lewis to Arthur Greeves 1914-1963, edited by Walter Hooper. London, Collins, and New York, Macmillan, 1979.

C. S. Lewis at the Breakfast Table and Other Reminiscences, edited by James T. Como. New York, Macmillan, 1979; London, Collins, 1980.

The Visionary Christian: 131 Readings, edited by Chad Walsh. New York, Macmillan, 1981.

On Stories and Other Essays on Literature, edited by Walter Hooper. New York, Harcourt Brace, 1982.

Of This and Other Worlds, edited by Walter Hooper. London, Collins, 1982.

The Cretaceous Perambulator, with Owen Barfield, edited by Walter Hooper. Oxford, C. S. Lewis Society, 1983.

The Business of Heaven: Daily Readings from C. S. Lewis, edited by Walter Hooper. London, Fount, and New York, Harcourt Brace, 1984.

Letters to Children, edited by Lyle W. Dorsett and Marjorie Lamp Mead. New York, Macmillan, 1985.

First and Second Things: Essays on Theology and Ethics, edited by Walter Hooper. London, Collins, 1985.

Present Concerns, edited by Walter Hooper. London, Fount, and San Diego, Harcourt Brace, 1986.

Timeless at Heart: Essays on Theology, edited by Walter Hooper. London, Fount, 1987.

The Essential C. S. Lewis, edited by Lyle W. Dorsett. New York, Macmillan, 1988.

Letters: C. S. Lewis and Don Giovanni Calabria: A Study in Friendship, edited and translated by Martin Moynihan. London, Collins, and Ann Arbor, Michigan, Servant Books, 1988.

All My World Before Me: The Diary of C. S. Lewis 1922-27, edited by Walter Hooper. San Diego, Harcourt Brace, 1991.

Editor, *George MacDonald: An Anthology.* London, Bles, 1946; New York, Macmillan, 1947.

Editor, *Arthurian Torso, Containing the Posthumous Fragment of "The Figure of Arthur,"* by Charles Williams. London, and New York, Oxford University Press, 1948.

*

Film Adaptations: *The Lion, The Witch, and the Wardrobe,* 1979 (TV movie).

Bibliography: "A Bibliography of the Writings of C. S. Lewis" by Walter Hooper, in *Light on C. S. Lewis* edited by Jocelyn Gibb, London, Bles, 1965; *C. S. Lewis: An Annotated Checklist of Writings about Him and His Works* by Joe R. Christopher and Joan K. Ostling, Kent, Ohio, Kent State University Press, 1974.

Manuscript Collections: Bodleian Library, Oxford; Wheaton College, Illinois.

Critical Studies (selection): *C. S. Lewis* by Roger Lancelyn Green, London, Bodley Head, and New York, Walck, 1963, revised edition, in *Three Bodley Head Monographs,* Bodley Head, 1969; *C. S. Lewis: A Biography* by Green and Walter Hooper, London, Collins, and New York, Harcourt Brace, 1974, revised edition, 1988, and *Past Watchful Dragons: The Narnian Chronicles of C. S. Lewis,* New York, Macmillan, 1979, and *Through Joy and Beyond: A Pictorial Biography of C. S. Lewis,* New York, Macmillan, 1982, both by Hooper; *Light on C. S. Lewis* edited by Jocelyn Gibb, London, Bles, 1965; *The Lion of Judah in Never-Never Land: The Theology of C. S. Lewis Expressed in His Fantasies for Children,* Grand Rapids, Michigan, Eerdmans, 1973, and *The C. S. Lewis Hoax,* Portland, Oregon, Multinomah, 1988, both by Kathryn Ann Lindskoog; *The Secret Country of C. S. Lewis* by Anne Arnott, London, Hodder and Stoughton, 1974, Grand Rapids, Michigan, Eerdmans, 1975; *The Longing for Form: Essays on the Fiction of C. S. Lewis* edited by Peter J. Schakel, Kent, Ohio, Kent State University Press, 1977, and *Reading with the Heart: The Way into Narnia* by Schakel, Grand Rapids, Michigan, Eerdmans, 1979; *The Inklings: C. S. Lewis, J. R. R. Tolkien, Charles Williams and Their Friends* by Humphrey Carpenter, London, Allen and Unwin, 1978, Boston, Houghton Mifflin, 1979; *The Literary Legacy of C. S. Lewis* by Chad Walsh, New York, Harcourt Brace, and London, Sheldon Press, 1979; *A Guide Through Narnia* by Martha C. Sammons, Wheaton, Illinois, Shaw, and London, Hodder and

Stoughton, 1979; *Narnia Explored* by Paul A. Karkainen, Old Tappan, New Jersey, Revell, 1979; *Companion to Narnia* by Paul F. Ford, New York, Harper, 1980; *C. S. Lewis, Spinner of Tales: A Guide to His Fiction* by Evan K. Gibson, Grand Rapids, Michigan, Christian University Press, 1980; *C. S. Lewis* by Margaret Patterson Hannay, New York, Ungar, 1981; *C. S. Lewis: The Art of Enchantment* by Donald E. Glover, Athens, Ohio University Press, 1981; *C. S. Lewis* by Brian Murphy, Mercer Island, Washington, Starmont House, 1983; *The Politics of Fantasy: C. S. Lewis and J. R. R. Tolkien* by Lee D. Rossi, New York, and Epping, Essex, Bowker, 1984; *Clive Staples Lewis: The Drama of a Life* by William Griffin, New York, Harper, 1986; *C. S. Lewis: His Literary Achievement* by C. N. Manlove, London, Macmillan, 1987; *C. S. Lewis* by Joe R. Christopher, Boston, Twayne, 1987; *C. S. Lewis, Man of Letters: A Reading of His Fiction* by Thomas Howard, Worthing, Sussex, Churchman, 1987; *Jack: C. S. Lewis and His Times* by George Sayer, London, Macmillan, 1988; *C. S. Lewis and His World* by David Barratt, Grand Rapids, Michigan, Eerdmans, 1988; *The Taste of the Pineapple: Essays on C. S. Lewis as Reader, Critic, and Imaginative Writer* edited by Bruce L. Edwards, Bowling Green, Ohio, Bowling Green State University Press, 1988; *Owen Barfield on C. S. Lewis* edited by G. B. Tennyson, Middletown, Connecticut, Wesleyan University Press, 1989; *The Riddle of Joy: G. K. Chesterton and C. S. Lewis* edited by Michael H. Macdonald and Andrew A. Tadie, Grand Rapids, Michigan, Eerdmans, and London, Collins, 1989; *C. S. Lewis: A Biography* by A. N. Wilson, London, Collins, and New York, Norton, 1990; *The C. S. Lewis Handbook* by Colin Duriez, Eastbourne, Monarch, and Grand Rapids, Michigan, Baker, 1990; *The Magical World of the Inklings: J.R.R. Tolkien, C. S. Lewis, Charles Williams, Owen Barfield* by Gareth Knight, Shaftsbury, Element, 1990; *A Christian for All Christians: Essays in Honour of C. S. Lewis* edited by Andrew Walker and James Patrick, London, Hodder and Stoughton, 1990; *C. S. Lewis: A Biography* by A. N. Wilson, London, Collins, 1990; *Planets in Peril: A Critical Study of C. S. Lewis's Ransom Trilogy* by David C. Downing, Amherst, Massachusetts, University of Massachusetts Press, 1992; *Word and Story in C. S. Lewis* edited by Peter J. Schakel and Charles A. Huttar, Columbia, Missouri, University of Missouri Press, 1992.

*   *   *

Besides his scholarly work as an English don from 1925 to his death, C. S. Lewis had twin literary careers in fantasy and Christian apologetics—often shading into each other. Skipping the juvenilia (the *Boxen* animal fantasies, wisely unpublished in Lewis's lifetime), his first book-length fantasy was *The Pilgrim's Regress.* This allegory of his own path to religion takes place in a carefully mapped spiritual landscape full of vivid images (like the oppressive giant of Freudian analysis whose gaze makes one's skin transparent and shows the nasty mess within), but is frequently too personal, allusive and obscure—even in the revised edition with explanatory running heads.

Lewis's best-known work of apologetics is the epistolary *The Screwtape Letters,* an experienced demon's advice to an inept tempter. This is good reading even for non-Christians: it's entertaining, it offers between the lines a sinisterly grotesque picture of Hell's "Lowerarchy," and there is much shrewd character analysis. Lewis had a clear eye for the little lazinesses and snobberies which, whether or not you call them sins, do deaden and poison human relations. Such insight permeates the allegory *The Great Divorce,* where Hell is a suburb of infinite dreariness whose occupants are self-damned: even a day trip to Heaven persuades few of them to abandon their comforting character flaws.

The Cosmic Trilogy begins as science fiction in *Out of the Silent Planet,* an exhilarating story whose science is wonky but leads to unforgettable descriptions of Malacandra, an impossible and beautiful Mars with three intriguing "human" races. It is explored by Ransom, a philologist abducted there by the wicked scientist Weston. The book was written partly in response to H. G. Wells's repulsive Martians and to the scientism Lewis saw in Wells: a cruelly funny scene shows Weston explaining vaulting human ambitions for planetary conquest to Malacandra's tutelary "eldil"—but the rhetoric must be literally translated by Ransom, emerging as *reductio ad absurdum* pidgin.

In *Perelandra,* Ransom is wafted to a Venus which nods to science-fiction tradition by being mostly ocean, with floating vegetable islands whose disorienting beauty inspires Lewis's most evocative descriptive passages. The ambiguous mysticism of book one resolves into clear theology: eldils are not just energy beings but angels; the "silent planet" Earth is, uniquely, the domain of the fallen or "bent" eldil; Perelandra/ Venus is unfallen, with the loss of Eden still in the balance. Weston, now a puppet of evil in its most horridly banal form, tempts this world's green-skinned Eve to defy an arbitrary prohibition issued by Maleldil, or God. After many weary arguments, Ransom concludes (unflatteringly to the naive but intelligent lady) that the only way to save her is to fight and kill the tempter.

That Hideous Strength takes the story to Earth and presents evil in fearfully plausible form: the National Institute for Co-ordinated Experiments, supposedly a cutting-edge research organization given special powers as in some Soviet five-year plan. This takes over an English town via devious manipulations in academia, ensnaring recruits with the temptation Lewis identified as that of the Inner Ring—where getting into a coveted clique becomes more important than the morality of what the inner circle *does.* Further into NICE, the idea of scientific impartiality is warped into a dehumanizing process, involving the sinister irrationalities of the "Objective Room" that boils empathy out of its subjects. At the centre of the maze, a bodiless human head exists in a state of obscene pseudo-life (reacting to a notion in J. D. Bernal's 1929 futurological squib *The World, the Flesh and the Devil,* about trading our bodies for improved mechanical versions). The Head is animated by Earth's dark eldils, which the NICE scientific magicians cannot recognize as evil spirits but call "macrobes".

Against this almost hysterically hateful set-up, there is only Ransom (transfigured by Venusian experiences but also incurably wounded, and calling himself Mr. Fisher-King) with his household of good folk and animals, plus the new recruit Jane who in dreams is a reluctant seer. But Merlin lies sleeping nearby, and both factions hope for his assistance. Some fine scenes ensue, notably the NICE banquet on which the curse of Babel is laid, and the terrible ends of the institute and its leaders. There are also flashes of annoying unfairness, as when H. G. Wells (then dying) appears as a vulgar, uneducated Cockney, or when Jane is unanswerably told that by using contraception she has caused a great saviour of Britain not to be born—a put-down Lewis would hardly have tried on an equally childless virgin or nun. Overall, the novel's heartfelt strength outweighs the flaws.

The seven Narnia books have been highly popular since their first appearance, not only with the intended young audience. *The Lion, the Witch and the Wardrobe* introduces four children (through the wardrobe's portal) to the land of Narnia, locked in winter by the Witch's magic and peopled with fauns, giants and talking beasts. One child's betrayal is redeemed by the lion Aslan, who suffers a kind of crucifixion (and in later books is explicitly equated with Christ), followed by resurrection and the overthrow of evil. The children reign over Narnia for decades but ultimately return through the wardrobe, no older than before.

In *Prince Caspian* they are recalled to a Narnia long after their rule, to help Caspian and the country's magical creatures rise against a long tyranny of intolerant human invaders. Aslan is more elusive here. One of Narnia's best-loved characters is introduced: Reepicheep, a talking mouse whose spirit and magniloquence are far larger than his body. *The Voyage of the Dawn Treader* relates a marvellous sea-journey led by Caspian, to strange islands and ultimately the shores of "Aslan's country" itself. En route, a further unregenerate child from Earth is taught needed lessons by temporary and uncomfortable transformation into a dragon. *The Silver Chair* happens at the end of the now aged Caspian's reign: two earthly children travel beyond Narnia (ably assisted by Puddleglum, the enjoyably Eeyorish "Marsh-wiggle" whose pessimism conceals competence), seeking Caspian's magically abducted son, and suffer shocks and reversals as—usually in hindsight—they realize their failure to follow the *exact letter* of Aslan's instructions. *The Horse and His Boy* backtracks to the Golden Age of that long reign in book one, with the adventures of a fugitive Narnian talking horse and his boy companion in Calormene, a generic Arabia that has designs on Narnia to the north. Aslan keeps popping up to push along the plot and deal out punishments for small sins.

At the beginning of Narnia's chronology, when on Earth "Mr. Sherlock Holmes was still living in Baker Street," *The Magician's Nephew* accounts for various anomalies: the wardrobe, the street-lamp burning in the Narnian waste, the land's tradition of human rulers, and the parallel-world origin of the Witch. In one of Lewis's most numinous scenes, Aslan actually sings Narnia out of the void and into existence. Concluding the saga, *The Last Battle* deploys Narnian-scale versions of Antichrist's emergence, Armageddon, and the Last Judgement. Night falls on Narnia and the door is shut on it forever. After this intensely moving farewell, the sequel in heaven (which is also Narnia, England, and everywhere) seems anti-climactic, with non-believers perhaps finding it hard to swallow a happy ending where everybody dies.

As a whole the series is wildly uneven and inconsistent: but its combination of sheer imaginative exuberance and frequent sense of fun works well, and the high moments can still bring a suspicious prickling to the eyes of jaded adults.

Lewis's last adult novel, *Till We Have Faces,* is a highly competent and harrowing retelling of the Eros and Psyche myth from an unusual viewpoint, but somehow lacks magic—as do the oddments collected in *The Dark Tower,* whose title fragment is something of an embarrassment. The posthumously collected *Poems* feature several fantastic items, including a "Narnian Suite."

—David Langford

LEWIS, (Percy) Wyndham

Nationality: British and Canadian. **Born:** Amherst, Nova Scotia, 18 November 1882. **Education:** Rugby School, 1897-98; Slade

School of Art, London, 1898-1901. **Military Service:** Royal Artillery, 1916; War Artist, 1917-18. **Family:** Married Gladys Anne Hoskins in 1929. **Career:** Travelled in Europe, studying art in Paris and elsewhere, 1902-08; painter and art critic; founder, Vorticist group, 1913; co-founder, editor and contributor, various little magazines, including *Blast,* 1914-15, *The Tyro,* 1921-22, and *The Enemy,* 1927-29; lecturer, Assumption College, Windsor, Ontario, 1943-45; art critic, *The Listener,* 1946-50. **Awards:** Lit.D., University of Leeds, 1952. **Died:** 7 March 1957.

FANTASY PUBLICATIONS

Novels

The Human Age:
    The Childermass. London, Chatto and Windus, and New York, Covici Friede, 1928; revised edition, London, Methuen, 1956.
    Monstre Gai, Malign Fiesta. London, Methuen, 1955; separate editions, London, Jupiter, 1966.

Plays

Enemy of the Stars. London, Harmsworth, 1932.

Radio Plays: *The Childermass,* adaptation of his own novel, 1951; *Monstre Gai* and *Malign Fiesta,* with D. G. Bridson, adaptations of his own novels, 1955.

OTHER PUBLICATIONS

Novels

Tarr. London, Egoist, and New York, Knopf, 1918.
The Apes of God. London, Arthur, 1930; New York, McBride, 1932.
Snooty Baronet. London, Cassell, 1932; New York, Haskell House, 1971.
The Revenge for Love. London, Cassell, 1937; Chicago, Regnery, 1952.
The Vulgar Streak. London, Hale, 1941; New York, Jubilee, 1973.
Self Condemned. London, Methuen, 1954; Chicago, Regnery, 1955.
The Red Priest. London, Methuen, 1956.
The Roaring Queen, edited by Walter Allen. London, Secker and Warburg, and New York, Liveright, 1973.
Mrs. Duke's Million, edited by Frank Davey. Toronto, Coach House Press, 1977.

Short Stories

The Wild Body, A Soldier of Humour, and Other Stories. London, Chatto and Windus, 1927; New York, Harcourt Brace, 1928.
Rotting Hill. London, Methuen, 1951; Chicago, Regnery, 1952.
Unlucky for Pringle: Unpublished and Other Stories, edited by Fox and Robert Chapman. London, Vision, and New York, Lewis, 1973.

Plays

The Ideal Giant, The Code of a Herdsman, Cantleman's Springmate. London, Little Review, 1917.

Poetry

Engine-Fight Talk. N.p., 1933.
Collected Poems and Plays, edited by Alan Munton. Manchester, Carcanet, 1979.

Other

Harold Gilman: An Appreciation. London, Chatto and Windus, 1919.
The Caliph's Design: Architects! Where is Your Vortex? London, Egoist, 1919.
Fifteen Drawings. N.p., 1920.
The Art of Being Ruled. London, Chatto and Windus, and New York, Harper, 1926.
The Lion and the Fox: The Rule of Hero in the Plays of Shakespeare. London, Richards, and New York, Harper, 1927.
Time and Western Man. London, Chatto and Windus, and New York, Harcourt Brace, 1927.
Paleface: The Philosophy of the "Melting Pot." London, Chatto and Windus, 1929; New York, Haskell House, 1969.
Satire and Fiction. London, Chatto and Windus, 1930; Folcroft, Pennsylvania, Folcroft Library, 1975.
Hitler. London, Chatto and Windus, 1931; New York, Gordon, 1972.
The Diabolical Principle, and The Dithyrambic Spectator. London, Chatto and Windus, 1931; New York, Haskell House, 1971.
The Doom of Youth. New York, McBride, and London, Chatto and Windus, 1932.
Filibusters in Barbary. New York, National Travel Club, and London, Grayson, 1932.
Thirty Personalities and a Self-Portrait (drawings). N.p., 1932.
The Old Gang and the New Gang. London, Harmsworth, 1933; New York, Haskell House, 1972.
One-Way Song. London, Faber, 1933.
Snooty Baronet. London, Cassell, 1932; New York, Haskell House, 1971.
Men Without Art. London, Cassell, 1934; New York, Russell, 1964.
Left Wings Over Europe; or, How to Make a War About Nothing. London, Cape, 1936; New York, Gordon, 1972.
Count Your Dead: They Are Alive! or, A New War in the Making. London, Dickson, 1937; New York, Gordon, 1972.
Blasting and Bombardiering (autobiography). London, Eyre and Spottiswoode, 1937; Berkeley, University of California Press, 1967.
The Mysterious Mr. Bull. London, Hale, 1938.
The Jews, Are They Human? London, Allen and Unwin, 1939; New York, Gordon, 1972.
Wyndham Lewis the Artist: From "Blast" to Burlington House. London, Laidlaw, 1939; New York, Haskell House, 1971.
The Hitler Cult, and How It Will End. London, Dent, 1939; New York, Gordon, 1972.
America, I Presume. New York, Howell Soskin, 1940.
Anglosaxony: A League That Works. Toronto, Ryerson, 1941.
America and Cosmic Man. London, Nicholson and Watson, 1948; New York, Doubleday, 1949.
Rude Assignment: A Narrative of My Career Up-to-Date. London, Hutchinson, 1950.
The Writer and the Absolute. London, Methuen, 1952; Westport, Connecticut, Greenwood Press, 1975.
The Demon of Progress in the Arts. London, Methuen, 1954; Chicago, Regnery, 1955.

The Letters of Wyndham Lewis, edited by W. K. Rose. London, Methuen, 1963; Norfolk, Connecticut, New Directions, 1964.

A Soldier of Humor, edited by Raymond Rosenthal. New York, New American Library, and London, New English Library, 1966.

Wyndham Lewis on Art, edited by Walter Michel and C. J. Fox. London, Thames and Hudson, and New York, Funk and Wagnalls, 1969.

Wyndham Lewis: An Anthology of His Prose, edited by E. W. F. Tomlin. London, Methuen, 1969.

Enemy Salvoes: Selected Literary Criticism, edited by Fox. London, Vision, and New York, Barnes and Noble, 1976.

*

Bibliography: *A Bibliography of the Writings of Wyndham Lewis* by Bradford Morrow and Bernard Lafourcade, Santa Barbara, California, 1978.

Critical Studies (selection): *Wyndham Lewis* by Hugh Kenner, Norfolk, Connecticut, New Directions, 1954; *Wyndham Lewis: A Portrait of the Artist as Enemy* by Geoffrey Wagner, London Routledge and Kegan Paul, 1957; *Wyndham Lewis* by William Pritchard, New York, Twayne, 1968; *The Filibuster: A Study of the Political Ideas of Wyndham Lewis* by D. G. Bridson, London, Cassell, 1972; *The Enemy: A Biography of Wyndham Lewis* by Jeffrey Meyers, London Routledge and Kegan Paul, 1980; *Wyndham Lewis: A Revaluation* edited by Jeffrey Meyers, London, Athlone, 1980.

* * *

Wyndham Lewis was one of the most important Modernist critics of the early 20th century. He was co-editor with Ezra Pound of the celebrated periodical *Blast: Review of the Great English Vortex* (1914-15). Their new movement petered out after the Vorticist Exhibition of 1915 and Lewis's belated enlistment to fight in the Great War. He became increasingly isolated thereafter, initially by virtue of his scathing satirical attacks on his contemporaries—especially the Bloomsbury group—and later, more profoundly, as a result of his links with the British Fascist Movement. Lewis's exemplary Vorticist drama *Enemy of the Stars,* first published in *Blast* and later reprinted in book form, is a fantastic extravaganza whose surreally impractical stage-directions provide a context for the conflict between Hanp—symbolic of violent and dull-witted Mankind—and Arghol, the wise and rational spirit of intellectualism whose adventures can never quite escape the constraints imposed by his adversary. Arghol's refusal to be manifest in a false and debased self ultimately results in his murder by Hanp, but the murder is quickly followed by Hanp's suicide.

The Human Age—which was never completed, the projected fourth section, *The Trial of Man,* existing only as a series of synoptic notes appended to the third—is the oddest, most earnest and perhaps most important modern recapitulation of *The Divine Comedy.* The first part would have remained unsupplemented had it not been for the public reaction to a BBC radio dramatization of 1951, which prompted the Third Programme to commission the continuation. By then, alas, Lewis was blind and his wife had to read back his barely-legible longhand script for correction; it is not surprising, therefore, that the second and third parts are somewhat rough-hewn.

In *The Childermass* the Everyman figure Pullman and his ill-favoured companion Satterthwaite (who was once his fag at school and consequently insists on addressing him as "Pulley" while himself being diminished as "Satters") find themselves uncongenially reincarnated in an exotic and disturbing wasteland. Their form is a reversion to type occasioned by "psychic mummification." Ambitious for salvation, they are condemned to a period of purgatorial waiting while their destiny is decided, apparently by the enigmatic Bailiff with whom Satters comes face-to-face after trampling Tom Paine to death during a "time-hallucination." The Bailiff—who stands for all that Lewis abhorred—is one of the Princes of Time, who can determine entry into the Magnetic City, but his demands become increasingly incoherent and when he returns there Pullman and Satters do not follow him.

Lewis had originally intended to continue *The Human Age* in a second and concluding volume whose main focus would have been a surrealized political debate between the right-wing Hyperidiens and the left-wing raggle-taggle associated with the Bailiff, but his Fascist phase had run its course by the 1950s and he had become much more interested in more abstract matters of theological reconstruction. In *Monstre Gai* Pullman and Satters change direction, entering what is now referred to as Third City to find a "degenerate, chaotic outpost of Heaven" under the sway of a hyper-efficient but not very well-appointed Welfare State. Once a testing-ground for salvation, Third City has lost that function and is now under siege and bombardment by the Devil's artillery. The negligence of Third City's presiding angel has permitted the wayward Bailiff—the "gay monster" of the title—to establish a criminal Underworld which Pullman is tempted to join; he quickly rises through its ranks to become the Bailiff's right-hand man.

In *Malign Fiesta* Pullman joins the Bailiff in flight to Matapolis, a modernized Hell ruled by the affable but profoundly misogynistic Sammael. Pullman soon transfers his allegiance to this new master, who intends to remove the forces of Hell from their servitude to the Divine Plan, hoping to bring about an ultimate "annihilation of the Divine" by humanizing the angels. The "malign fiesta" of the title is a wild party at which the angels will be encouraged to consort with human *femmes fatales*; Pullman has high hopes for this fête but it turns out to be a horribly vulgar affair. God ultimately intervenes, threatening Pullman with eternal damnation if he will not mend his ways, and the righteous forces of Heaven launch an all-out assault on Matapolis.

The fourth part of the reschematized story was to have dealt with Pullman's exploits in Angeltown (i.e., Heaven), to which he is removed by God's soldiers at the end of *Malign Fiesta,* but Lewis—like many others who followed in the footsteps of Dante—found the problem of designing a God and a Heaven adequate to the demands of the modern imagination quite intractable (all those who have tried, including Wyndham Lewis's downmarket namesake C.S. Lewis in *The Great Divorce,* have produced images so pathetically ridiculous as to be embarrassing). Instead of continuing the work Lewis redirected his efforts into a comfortably realistic contemporary novel, *The Red Priest.*

Although they are conscientiously difficult books, and in spite of the fact that the second and third volumes develop the project in a fashion radically different from the author's original plan, the three volumes of *The Human Age* constitute the boldest and most extravagant posthumous fantasy written in the 20th century. Perhaps it is intrinsic to their nature that works of this quixotic kind can never be brought to sensible completion; were they not frustrated and frustrating they would fail ingloriously in their duty to remind us that there is, after all, no actual Heaven to restore and repair—

however belatedly—the moral order which is so conspicuously lacking in the world as it is. (Hell, of course, poses no difficulties even for relatively unimaginative writers.)

—Brian Stableford

LINDHOLM, Megan

Form of her name used by Margaret Astrid Lindholm Ogden. **Pseudonyms:** Robin Hobb. **Nationality:** American. **Born:** 1952. **Family:** Married; four children. Lives in Washington State.

FANTASY PUBLICATIONS

Novels (series: Reindeer People; Windsingers)

Harpy's Flight (Windsingers). New York, Ace, 1983.
The Windsingers. New York, Ace, 1984.
The Limbreth Gate (Windsingers). New York, Ace, 1984.
The Windsingers (omnibus; contains *Harpy's Flight, The Windsingers, The Limbreth Gate*). London, Corgi, 1986.
The Wizard of the Pigeons. New York, Ace, 1986; London, Corgi, 1987.
The Reindeer People. New York, Ace, 1988; London, Unwin, 1989.
Wolf's Brother (Reindeer People). New York, Ace, 1988; London, Unwin, 1990.
Luck of the Wheels (Windsingers). New York, Ace, 1989.
Cloven Hooves. New York, Bantam, 1991; London, HarperCollins, 1993.
Gypsy, with Steven Brust. New York, Tor, 1992.
The Farseer 1: The Assassin's Apprentice (as Robin Hobb). New York, Bantam, and London, HarperCollins, 1995.

Short Story

The Silver Lady and the Fortyish Man. Eugene, Oregon, Hypatia Press, 1994.

OTHER PUBLICATIONS

Novels

Alien Earth. New York, Bantam, 1992; London, Grafton, 1993.

*   *   *

Megan Lindholm's "urban" fantasy novel *The Wizard of the Pigeons* came as something of a revelation at time when the bookshop shelves were being swamped with formulaic quest-fantasies. It concerns a Vietnam veteran known only as Wizard, who lives among the street people of Seattle. He has some very limited powers, such as sometimes being able to tell people the truth, and having an affinity for pigeons and surviving effortlessly on the streets, so that most people don't even realize he is homeless. These powers may be magical in nature—his ability to speak the Truth, for instance, certainly involves knowing more than he possibly could. To maintain the powers, he has to keep to certain very stringent balancing points—rules—such as telling the truth, not touching women and carrying less than a dollar in change.

Wizard's existence is threatened by the coming of Mir, the greyness. He begins to forget how to survive, and begins to break his own rules, especially when he gets involved with Lynda, a "regular person." The breakdown which follows this affects not only him, but also his fellow street-people, some of whom also have similar powers. On a larger scale, it also has repercussions in the wider world. Eventually, Wizard's friend Cassie shows him that the rules he is supposed to follow are at least partly self-imposed, and unnecessary; the others are there to keep the balance, and keep those who have power from helping themselves. Only then is he able to find the power within himself to regain his magic and restore the world.

The achievement of the book lies in two areas. The first is the vivid, almost journalistic, description of the street-people's lives, which is nevertheless achieved with great economy. The second is the way in which Lindholm links Wizard's disintegration and regeneration less with obvious mythic archetypes such as the Fisher King—though they are there—than with his real world experiences in Vietnam, and the psychological truth of what is happening to him. Mir exists both within Wizard and in the external world: it cannot be beaten by anyone except Wizard, and then only if he can regain his internal balance by remembering who he is and what is important in his life. There is also a refreshing refusal to obey the usual tropes of fantasy fiction: Wizard is the centre of the book, and his ultimate victory over the greyness only comes about because Cassie lends him her power; yet it is Cassie herself who pays the price.

Lindholm's next two works, *The Reindeer People* and *Wolf's Brother* are, in effect, one book, since the second provides the resolution to the first. They concern Tillu, a primitive woman living sometime in pre-history, in a part of the world that may be Lapland or, perhaps, Alaska. Though she is the central viewpoint character, the books are really the story of her son Kerlew, and his attempts to find a place in the world. Physically different from the local tribespeople—he is Tillu's rape-child, his father any one of a group of travelling strangers, while Tillu herself is the product of a marriage of people from different areas—Kerlew is also mentally and emotionally off centre; he may be a little autistic, and certainly suffers from fits. He is therefore taken on as an apprentice by Carp, his tribe's Shaman, against Tillu's wishes, having already been perceived as having caused a plague with a curse he made.

Tillu escapes with him, and eventually they take up with a tribe of semi-nomadic hunter-gatherers, who welcome Tillu for her healing skills. She and Kerlew are more-or-less adopted by Heckram. Complications arise because she obtains evidence that Joboam, the herd-lord's favourite, attacked and killed Elsa, Heckram's betrothed. This comes to a head after Carp arrives to claim Kerlew, having tracked him down. Woven through all this are various encounters with the spirit beasts that guide the shamans, and, indeed, some of the ordinary tribes-people. In the end, Kerlew is able to save Tillu and Heckram from Joboam's plotting because he chooses Wolf for his spirit guide over Wolverine, who guides both Carp and Joboam. This allows him to turn his back on their greediness and lust for power, and to use his shamanic powers for the good of the tribe.

Although there is a clear mystical element to the narrative, this is more than balanced by Tillu's practical attitude to healing: she has skills and knowledge, and she knows how to use them, and that is all there is to it. However, if there is a problem with these books, this is where it lies. Tillu is simply too modern a heroine—too pragmatic, and too introspective—to be convincing as a primitive woman. At first glance, the tribe which she allies herself with seems idealized, also. The women have an unlikely amount of personal and economic freedom, without there being any clear matriarchal structure to the society. Even if this is anthropologically correct—and it may be—it still feels wrong. A closer look, however, reveals that, though the women appear free, their lives are circumscribed by the violence of the men; Lindholm shows us that how much real freedom they have depends on their ability to manage or deflect this.

Lindholm's later fantasy novel, *Cloven Hooves,* also deals with the relationships between the sexes. This time, it concerns Evelyn, who grew up in the Alaskan wilderness and was befriended by a faun. As a grown woman, she marries the beautiful but feckless Tom, whose family disapprove of her, and has a son. Matters come to a head when they pay an extended visit to his family, who try to take her son away: the women of the family are supposed to be in a feminine mould that Evelyn cannot conform to. The outcome of all this is to drive her home, back to the faun, by whom she has a child—*son* is possibly the wrong word. The meat of the novel concerns not so much which choices she makes, as the processes she goes through in order to make them, and what she decides to give up in order to gain what she really needs. The problem with the book—and this is very much a personal reaction—is that, in attempting to critique the way certain types of women live, Lindholm has to show us a great deal of them, and this is, at times, quite tedious.

The Assassin's Apprentice, published under Lindholm's pseudonym Robin Hobb, is an above-average book, being entertaining after a slow start, sporadically surprising, sometimes subtle and very occasionally brilliant. It is historically-based fiction, with relatively small amounts of fantasy, concerning a vaguely European-medieval maritime kingdom, the Six Duchies.

One of the more interesting aspects of the book is that some of its best features, namely telepathic communication, the mental conditioning by a band of invaders—the Red Ship Raiders—of their victims, and the alienness of other societies, are generally considered to be ingredients of science fiction rather than of fantasy. Stylistically, the novel is inconsistent, but occasionally Hobb (Lindholm) produces an exquisitely poetical phrase which says much of human nature in just a few words. In general, the book is more deliberate and less successful in its early chapters, and it flows better and with more depth later on.

The Assassin's Apprentice is only the first volume in a trilogy, and now that the author has developed her wonderful characters and complex backgrounds, she should be able to write two fine novels about the nature of the Red Ship Raiders, the various mental skills of her young protagonist and the political in-fighting of the nobility.

No summary of Lindholm's work would be complete without a mention of her short fiction, and in particular the prize-winning *The Silver Lady and the Fortyish Man.* This concerns a writer who has lost her inspiration. She meets a man who may not be a wizard, and may or may not be in danger from an ancient enemy. The woman helps him, without ever finding out the truth. She becomes attached to him, though the relationship is not resolved. The true resolution of the story is that by the end of the story the woman has regained her inspiration, has given up her dead-end job and has begun to write again.

—Liz Holliday and Chris Morgan

LINDSAY, David

Nationality: British. **Born:** Blackheath, London, 3 March 1876. **Education:** Lewisham Grammar School, London, and a secondary school in Jedburgh, Roxburgh. **Military Service:** Grenadier Guards, 1916-18. **Family:** Married Jacqueline Silver in 1916; two daughters. **Career:** Worked for Price Forbes, insurance brokers, 1894-1916; lived in Cornwall, 1919-29, and after 1929 in Sussex. **Died:** 16 July 1945.

FANTASY PUBLICATIONS

Novels

A Voyage to Arcturus. London, Methuen, 1920; New York, Macmillan, 1963.
The Haunted Woman. London, Methuen, 1922; Hollywood, Newcastle, 1975.
Sphinx. London, Long, 1923; New York, Carroll and Graf, 1988.
Devil's Tor. London, Putnam, 1932; New York, Arno Press, 1978.
The Violet Apple, and The Witch. Chicago, Chicago Review Press, 1976; London, Sidgwick and Jackson, 1978.

OTHER PUBLICATIONS

Novel

Adventures of Monsieur de Mailly. London, Melrose, 1926; as *A Blade for Sale,* New York, McBride, 1927.

*

Critical Studies: *The Strange Genius of David Lindsay* by J. B. Pick, Colin Wilson, and E. H. Visiak, London, Baker, 1970; as *The Haunted Man,* San Bernardino, California, Borgo Press, 1979; *The Life and Works of David Lindsay* by Bernard Sellin, translated by Kenneth Gunnell, Cambridge, University Press, 1981; *David Lindsay* by Gary K. Wolfe, Mercer Island, Washington, Starmont House, 1982; *David Lindsay's Vision* by David Power, Nottingham, Pauper's Press, 1991.

*   *   *

Isaac Asimov has remarked that the solar family of planets could be described as "Jupiter plus debris". The reputation of David Lindsay consists of *A Voyage to Arcturus* plus debris, of which only one item, *The Violet Apple,* contains fantasy elements of any great originality (although *Devil's Tor,* which is about the reuniting of two halves of an ancient stone and the founding of a new race by a chosen man and woman, has its admirers: the critic Gary K. Wolfe has described it as "a sprawling, slow-moving, and at times brilliant exposition of the myth of the Eternal Feminine").

Written in 1925-27, *The Violet Apple* was published posthumously in the 1970s, when it might have enjoyed a certain cult following as a literary grotesque had it been better written. It is primarily an insipid tale of *haut bourgeois* dalliance among four scions of the minor gentry, very much in the style of "light" novelist Dornford Yates, and with an explicit morality quite as unlikely and repulsive. At an early point one male enquires of another (who is already showing grey hairs) if he has any experience of women, the implication being that a man who is not a virgin has no business paying court to a woman who is (he is reassured). The interest in this gruesome exchange is that Lindsay obviously regarded the question and the assumption behind it as in no way impertinent, and the answer as credible.

The story revolves round an unusual McGuffin, a pip from the Biblical Tree of Knowledge, no less. This is germinated and nurtured by one of the characters, bears two tiny violet apples, and promptly dies. Unfortunately, although the scenes which follow the eating of the apples raise the standard considerably, and are the more interesting for having been composed so long before Aldous Huxley's *The Doors of Perception* (1954), they arrive too late to save the book. The author's message, spelt out in the final chapter, is crudely and explicitly anti-intellectual: the conversation of a yokel in a public house is to be preferred over the works of Homer, Sophocles, Dante, Shakespeare, Tolstoy—or David Lindsay, for that matter.

A Voyage to Arcturus, by contrast, has enjoyed cult status if no great following from its first publication in 1920. It is bears all the hallmarks of allegory, but the purport of the allegory remains opaque to the end. The viewpoint character, Maskull, is introduced as a man of mystery, accompanied by an equally mysterious "friend" called Nightspore. Neither Maskull's antecedents, nor the nature of their relationship, nor its duration is ever hinted at, but the pair of them accept with alacrity the invitation of a violent and sinister individual called Krag to visit Torrance, only planet of Arcturus, by means of a crystal pod. Once there they are to meet with Surtur, or "Crystalman," owner/controller/god of Torrance. Maskull sleeps through the journey, and awakes to find himself deserted. By way of compensation he has grown a handy telepathic organ on his head ("breve") and a long prehensile tentacle ("magn") extending from his chest.

Thus equipped he sets forth in search of Crystalman, enjoying and enduring sundry relationships and much gnomic conversation with Torrance's varied inhabitants, in every case physically alluring persons whose monolithic personalities illustrate conflicting extremes of post-World War I *Weltanschauung.* To Maskull's dismay, many of them die by violence or suicide during or shortly after their discussions. Whenever this happens the corpse takes on a "vulgar, leering expression" which is Crystalman's trademark. Maskull is also disturbed to learn that Krag is regarded as a demiurge opposed to Crystalman.

As he progresses his magn metamorphoses (to suit the company) into a third arm, which sloughs off later. His breve, likewise, is replaced by sundry other organs, though this never hinders his communication. Altogether, the symbolism is so crude as to read at times like a savage lampoon of Freud; an interpretation that, considering Lindsay's period and personal history, would have much to commend it were there the least scintilla of a suggestion that a single scene was being played any way but dead straight.

At the end of the book Maskull dies, to be replaced by Nightspore; the two have always been sundered aspects of the same individual, but what follows can hardly be called a reunification. Nightspore experiences a vision in which all dualities—the One and the Many, the Immanent and the Transcendent, Pleasure and Pain, Krag and Crystalman—are shown to derive from the breaking of a primeval pantheism, but the final question, "What do you mean to do?" remains forever unanswered.

The conclusion to be drawn is that the allegory of *A Voyage to Arcturus* presents a man of powerful libido and even more powerful repressions surveying the various moral standpoints available to him by means of an easily accessible symbolism of which he himself is unaware. It's a strained interpretation, but no other avoids contradiction by at least one feature of this extremely puzzling but supremely unselfconscious book. It is certainly quite unlike the didactic fantasies of the preceding era, and equally certain that nothing like it will ever appear again—least of all from those few writers, such as C. S. Lewis and Donald Suddaby, who appear to have been influenced by it.

—Chris Gilmore

LISLE, Holly

Nationality: American.

FANTASY PUBLICATIONS

Novels

Fire in the Mist. New York, Baen, 1992.
Bones of the Past. New York, Baen, 1993.
When the Bough Breaks, with Mercedes Lackey. New York, Baen, 1993.
Minerva Wakes. New York, Baen, 1994.

*   *   *

The role of female characters in fantasy fiction has generally been no better than in science fiction, mysteries, or any other genre. Most of the time they're a part of the plot rather than characters in themselves, either they're the fair maidens requiring rescue, an awkward and shallow romantic love interest, a beautiful companion the hero explains everything to, or relegated to some similar subservient position. There have been exceptions, of course, Robert E. Howard's Red Sonia, C. L. Moore's Jirel of Joiry, and some of Andre Norton's characters come to mind. But for the most part, even though the field is increasingly dominated by women writers, there's a marked tendency to feature male protagonists.

Holly Lisle is one of the pleasant exceptions. Her first published novel, *Fire in the Mist,* follows the adventures of Faia, a village girl who returns from a trading trip to discover her family, friends, and neighbours have all succumbed to a plague. Faia has always had a touch of magic, but on that occasion she briefly draws such power into herself that magicians leagues away feel the impact of her presence and the weather is altered for the entire land. Although Faia decides to renounce the use of magic, circumstances dictate otherwise. Her strength is so great that the organized magical guilds insist that she be trained so that she will not inadvertently cause another disaster. Reluctantly she agrees to submit to their care, but has difficulty fitting in because of her peasant background. At the same time, an evil entity is seeking a new body, that of a woman with magical abilities, a role for which Faia seems ideally suited.

Despite occasional awkwardness in the dialogue, this was an impressive first novel. Most of the story takes place in a university where various forms of magic make up the subject matter, and the setting is perfect for the mysterious conspiracy that drives the main story line. Nor is Faia a one-dimensional character leadenly performing the tasks laid out for her. She has doubts as well as certainties, and tries to stay aware of the way her environment shapes her personality.

Bones of the Past takes one of the characters from the first novel, Medwind Song, and sends her on a journey of research into the ruins of the fabled City of the First Folk. Medwind is afflicted with a serious problem. She is capable of speaking to the bones of the dead, and those departed spirits demand that she train someone to take her place after she herself dies. But Medwind appears incapable of bearing a child despite having taken nearly a dozen husbands in her attempts to become pregnant, and her attempt to find another child to fill that role has nearly disastrous results.

After rescuing the waking dead from a netherworld to which they are accidentally sent, Medwind is presented with an artefact of the First Folk, and the main plot is underway. The journey she and her companions make to that fabled city is fraught with dangers, physical and magical, and even their goal isn't quite what they expected. Rather than answering questions about human history, the city proves to have been the dwelling place of another race entirely. This is a longer and more polished novel than *Fires in the Mist,* and with a very different setting and mood despite the continuity of characters from one to the other. Lisle's dialogue is markedly improved and the plot is more clearly directed toward its resolution.

Her third solo novel is *Minerva Wakes.* This time Lisle contrasts the real and the fantastic. Minerva is a harried, insecure homemaker whose life goes awry when she spots a dragon buying Pop-Tarts at a local supermarket. That evening her three kids are kidnapped by monsters into a parallel universe. Minerva follows in a desperate rescue attempt, while her husband comes home to find a dragon sitting in the bedroom singing pornographic songs.

Eventually Minerva and her husband Darryl are pitted against a mysterious entity in that other realm, who must be defeated if their children are to be saved. The adventure is leavened with more than a little humour, although there's an undercurrent of seriousness throughout that provides a stronger focus than in most humorous fantasy. There's a message as well, because part of the problem besetting the couple arises from the fact that Darryl and Minerva have let their lives get away from them, have taken the road of expediency and expectation rather than make conscious decisions about important life choices. This is one of those rare cases where an author's humorous work is superior to her more serious efforts, because the humour serves to draw attention to the absurdities her characters accept as truth.

It is impossible to judge how much of the collaborative novel, *When the Bough Breaks* was written by Lisle. Set in Mercedes Lackey's "Serrated Edge" series, it involves the interaction of the real world and Faerie and blurs the lines distinguishing each such that we have elves in hot-rods and other anachronisms. It is however likely that her work on this book helped shape Lisle's approach to *Minerva Wakes,* as it too uses the contrast of reality and fantasy to good effect. Lisle has not written much short fiction, but her story "Knight and the Enemy" from *The Enchanter Reborn,* set in the world of the Incomplete Enchanter as created by L. Sprague de Camp and Fletcher Pratt, is an amusing adventure tale that shouldn't be overlooked. She is on the whole a writer displaying considerable early talent, and the potential to become much better as she practices her craft.

—Don D'Ammassa

LIVELY, Penelope (Margaret)

Nationality: British. **Born:** Penelope Margaret Low, Cairo, Egypt, 17 March 1933; came to England, 1945. **Education:** Boarding school in Sussex, 1945-51; St. Anne's College, Oxford, B.A. (honours) in modern history 1956. **Family:** Married Jack Lively in 1957; one daughter and one son. **Career:** Has been presenter for BBC Radio programme on children's literature; regular reviewer for newspapers and magazines in England. Fellow, Royal Society of Literature, 1985. **Awards:** Library Association Carnegie Medal, 1974; Whitbread award, 1976; Southern Arts Association prize, 1979; Arts Council National Book award, 1980; Booker prize, 1987. **Agent:** Murray Pollinger, 4 Garrick Street, London WC2E 9BH. **Address:** Duck End, Great Rollright, Chipping Norton, Oxfordshire OX7 5SB, England.

FANTASY PUBLICATIONS

Novels

Astercote, illustrated by Antony Maitland. London, Heinemann, 1970; New York, Dutton, 1971.
The Whispering Knights, illustrated by Gareth Floyd. London, Heinemann, 1971; New York, Dutton, 1976.
The Wild Hunt of Hagworthy, illustrated by Juliet Mozley. London, Heinemann, 1971; as *The Wild Hunt of the Ghost Hounds,* New York, Dutton, 1972.
The Driftway. London, Heinemann, 1972; New York, Dutton, 1973.
The Ghost of Thomas Kempe, illustrated by Antony Maitland. London, Heinemann, and New York, Dutton, 1973.
The House in Norham Gardens. London, Heinemann, and New York, Dutton, 1974.
A Stitch in Time. London, Heinemann, and New York, Dutton, 1976.
The Voyage of QV66, illustrated by Harold Jones. London, Heinemann, 1978; New York, Dutton, 1979.
The Revenge of Samuel Stokes. London, Heinemann, and New York, Dutton, 1981.
A House Inside Out, illustrated by David Parkins. London, Deutsch, 1987; New York, Dutton, 1988.

Short Stories

Uninvited Ghosts and Other Stories, illustrated by John Lawrence. London, Heinemann, 1984; New York, Dutton, 1985.

OTHER PUBLICATIONS

Novels

The Road to Lichfield. London, Heinemann, 1977.
Treasures of Time. London, Heinemann, and New York, Doubleday, 1979.
Judgement Day. London, Heinemann, 1980; New York, Doubleday, 1981.
Next to Nature, Art. London, Heinemann, 1982.
Perfect Happiness. London, Heinemann, 1983; New York, Dial Press, 1984.

According to Mark. London, Heinemann, 1984; New York, Beaufort, 1985.
Moon Tiger. London, Deutsch, 1987; New York, Grove Press, 1988.
Passing On. London, Deutsch, 1989.
City of the Mind. London, Deutsch, 1991.
Cleopatra's Sister. London, Viking and New York, Harper, 1993.

Short Stories

Nothing Missing But the Samovar and Other Stories. London, Heinemann, 1978.
Corruption and Other Stories. London, Heinemann, 1984.
Pack of Cards: Stories 1978-86. London, Heinemann, 1986; New York, Grove Press, 1989.

Fiction for Children

Going Back. London, Heinemann, and New York, Dutton, 1975.
Boy Without a Name, illustrated by Ann Dalton. London, Heinemann, and Berkeley, California, Parnassus Press, 1975.
The Stained Glass Window, illustrated by Michael Pollard. London, Abelard Schuman, 1976.
Fanny's Sister, illustrated by John Lawrence. London, Heinemann, 1976; New York, Dutton, 1980.
Fanny and the Monsters, illustrated by John Lawrence. London, Heinemann, 1979.
Fanny and the Battle of Potter's Piece, illustrated by John Lawrence. London, Heinemann, 1980.
Dragon Trouble, illustrated by Valerie Littlewood. London, Heinemann, 1984.
Debbie and the Little Devil, illustrated by Toni Goffe. London, Heinemann, 1987.
Judy and the Martian. London, Simon and Schuster, 1992.
The Cat, the Crow, and the Banyan Tree, illustrated by Terry Milne. London, Walker, and Cambridge, Massachusetts, Candlewick Press, 1994.
Good Night, Sleep Tight, illustrated by Adriano Gon. London, Walker, 1994.

Plays

Television Plays: *Boy Dominic* series (3 episodes), 1974; *Time Out of Mind,* 1976.

Other

The Presence of the Past: An Introduction to Landscape History. London, Collins, 1976.
Oleander, Jacaranda: A Memoir. New York, Harper, 1994.

*   *   *

As an adult novelist, Penelope Lively is firmly in the realist tradition, but she began her career as a writer for children, and in children's literature fantasy provides one of the most obvious and potent means of expressing the constant, living presence of the past. Time, memory, history and landscape have been important constants through all of Lively's work.

In her first book, *Astercote,* two children discover the ruins of a Cotswold village which vanished in the 14th century when its population was wiped out by the Black Death, and become involved in the search for a lost religious relic which local people believe can protect them from the return of the Plague, or from other evils. Somewhat confused, and disappointing in its resolution, this was nevertheless a promising debut.

The Wild Hunt of Hagworthy is considerably more effective, with a traditional supernatural return-of-the-repressed plot and vividly naturalistic writing which makes it quite convincing. The trendy new vicar in a Somerset village decides to beef up the tourist trade with a revival of a nearly forgotten horn-dance when he discovers the old masks with stag-horns. Older locals mutter darkly about unwanted consequences, but the younger ones are eager to join in the fun. Yet something strange happens to the young men when they don the masks, just as the placid summer day turns suddenly threatening and thundery when they dance. At night the village is disturbed by sounds, and glimpses, of mysterious huntsmen and their ghostly hounds. Will young Lucy, a visitor to the village, be able to save her new friend—an outcast among the village boys—and stop the return of an ancient evil?

The Driftway is an episodic and didactic tale which uses historical events to teach a lesson to an unhappy, runaway modern boy. Running away from home, Paul and his young sister are helped by a man in a horse-drawn cart who travels the ancient "driftway" between Banbury and Northampton. As they travel, Paul glimpses people from earlier times and hears their stories, which have something to say to him.

Lively's first few books, although well-written and entertaining, are in general fairly standard children's fare. With her fifth book, though, she made a triumphant leap into something wholly original and lasting. The special qualities of *The Ghost of Thomas Kempe* were immediately recognized—it was awarded the Carnegie Medal in 1973. Humour comes to the fore in the inspired portrait of ten-year-old James Harrison who discovers his house is haunted by the ghost of a 17th-century sorcerer. Thomas Kempe doesn't like the fact that people nowadays can receive weather forecasts from their television sets and medicine for their ills from the chemist—he wants back his old business of selling spells, potions and predictions to the local people, and is determined that James shall be his apprentice. Poor James gets it from both sides—punishments from Kempe and from his parents who believe in mischievous boys but not in malicious spirits. So the boy sets out bravely to find a way of exorcising his ghost. The blend of humour and magic works wonderfully, the characters are most vividly drawn and realized, and Lively manages to make some subtler points about the interplay of past and present in individuals, as James makes the imaginative recognition that older people were once children like himself.

This same point, and related ones about the importance of memory and its connection to both reality and imagination, are integral to the 1976 Whitbread winner, *A Stitch in Time,* which has a marginal fantasy element. Eleven-year-old Maria is a highly imaginative child who has conversations with cats and clocks and petrol pumps, loves to read and think, but doesn't relate very well to other people. During a summer vacation with her parents in Lyme Regis, she makes friends with a boy her age through their shared interest in fossil-collecting, and also feels a strange affinity with another little girl, Harriet, who lived in what is now a holiday house a hundred years before. She sees a sampler Harriet started, and wonders why it was finished by her sister. She suspects that perhaps the little girl didn't live to grow up, for her presence still seems to linger in the house. She often hears the sound of a small dog barking, and because no one else can hear it, concludes this was Harriet's dog. At times a sort of benign possession takes place, and she seems to be having Harriet's own long-ago experience, culminating in the terrifying re-experience of a landslide. But although the landslide was real, Harriet did not die in it; things did not happen quite as Maria at first believed. Whether there was anything supernatural involved in her experiences is left deliberately ambiguous; Maria herself is aware that she's exceptionally imaginative.

Since embarking on her increasingly successful career as a novelist for adults in 1977, Lively has written less often for children, and her approach to fantasy has changed. My impression is that she came to find the fantasy tradition in which she began (of magical intrusions into the lives of realistically portrayed people) increasingly difficult to accept. Most of her novels, for whatever age group they were written, reflect many of the same concerns, yet only in her earlier children's books does the past physically return—in her adult novels personal memory and intellectual knowledge are the only means by which the past may be apprehended; there are no actual hauntings, no magic that works. In her more recent books for children, fantasy is presented in a much more broadly humorous vein, which can be a distancing technique.

The Revenge of Samuel Stokes seems to be an attempt to recapture the success of *The Ghost of Thomas Kempe,* but it is a disappointment after the earlier book. The story of a modern housing estate plagued by intrusions from the past (brick walls, ornamental fountains, cooking smells and even a lake emerge inexplicably into the present) is perhaps too improbable; it lacks the tantalizing edge of ambiguity which applies when hauntings are kept closer to home and described through the experience of one believable, well-drawn character. It's a farce, of course, but lacking in the genuine wackiness which makes farce work. The humour seems forced, and the characters slightly formulaic.

The Voyage of QV66 is a talking-animal satire, set after another great Flood, when all the humans have left the earth to animals. An assortment of creatures set off in a flat-bottomed boat for London Zoo and have various adventures along the way. *A House Inside Out* is a series of interconnected stories which are fantasies only because the viewpoint characters are mice, a dog, and a wood-louse who share a house with a family of generally unaware human beings in Birmingham.

—Lisa Tuttle

LLOYD, A(lan) R(ichard)

Nationality: British. **Born:** London, 22 February 1927. **Education:** Kingston School of Art, Kingston upon Thames, Surrey. **Military Service:** British Army, Royal Fusiliers. **Family:** Married Daphne Chaffe; one son. **Career:** Journalist, *Jersey Evening Post,* then freelance magazine writer; full-time author from 1962. **Address:** c/o HarperCollins, 77-85 Fulham Palace Road, London W6 8JB, England.

Fantasy Publications

Novels (series: Kine in all books)

Kine. London, Hamlyn, and New York, St. Martin's Press, 1982; as *Marshworld,* London, Arrow, 1990.

Witchwood. London, Muller, 1989.
Dragonpond. London, Muller, 1990.

Other Publications

Novels

The Eighteenth Concubine (as Alan Lloyd). London, Hutchinson, 1972.
Trade Imperial (as Alan Lloyd). London, Cassell, and New York, Coward McCann and Geoghegan, 1979.
The Last Otter. London, Hutchinson, 1984; as *The Boy and the Otter,* New York, Holt Rinehart, 1985.
The Farm Dog. London, Century, 1986.
Wingfoot. London, Grafton, 1993.

Other (as Alan Lloyd)

The Drums of Kumasi. London, Longman, 1964.
The Year of the Conqueror. London, Longman, 1966; as *The Making of the King 1066,* New York, Holt Rinehart, 1966.
The Spanish Centuries. New York, Doubleday, 1968.
Franco. New York, Doubleday, 1969; London, Longman, 1970.
The King Who Lost America. New York, Doubleday, 1971; as *The Wickedest Age,* Newton Abbot, Devon, David and Charles, 1971.
The Maligned Monarch. New York, Doubleday, 1972; as *King John,* Newton Abbot, Devon, David and Charles, 1973.
Marathon. New York, Random House, 1973; London, Souvenir, 1974.
Destroy Carthage. London, Souvenir, 1977.
The Great Prize Fight. London, Cassell, and New York, Coward McCann and Geoghegan, 1977.

*

A. R. Lloyd comments:

While my trilogy of Kine stories can most obviously be described as fantasy fiction, all my animal novels contain fantastical/mystical elements, with a strong insistence on the affinity between Man, the land and wildlife—or, in the case of *Wingfoot* (set in the Hebrides), the coast and sea-life. About the furious adventures of Kine I have created the mythology of a kingdom on the one hand mysterious, on the other—at least to lovers of the English countryside—familiar in detail and atmosphere. Largely descriptive of the acres surrounding the Kentish farmhouse I occupied with my wife for twenty years, the Kine tales are told with an economical simplicity characteristic of a pretension-phobic writer whose books have appealed, in a variety of languages, not only to large numbers of adults but to older children. I write painfully slowly, achieve "effortlessness" by dogged rewriting, and have yet to produce the book which comes up to my expectations.

*   *   *

All the novels of A. R. Lloyd are closely linked with natural history. Some of them follow the pattern of set by Henry Williamson in his well-known novel *Tarka the Otter* (1927)—where, although the lives of the principal animal characters are described, their interactions with other creatures, and Man, are as observed by naturalists. Lloyd's Kine trilogy takes this approach one step further, into the realms of fantasy. Here the animals communicate with each other and are accorded human traits.

The first of the books introduces the weasel, Kine, and the valley he hunts in. Initially we see him living his normal life: mating, raising kits, hunting rabbits, fighting rats. Then word spreads that the valley has been invaded by a group of vicious mink. Kine's mate, Kia, and all but one of the kits are killed by mink. Kine seeks revenge, accompanied by all the weasels from the surrounding areas that have met and been charmed by Kia. Although none of the feats accomplished by the weasels is impossible for the small creatures, they are aided considerably by good fortune. All the animals can communicate with each other and Kine is helped by other species including an elderly rook, Watchman, a marsh frog, Bunda, and Scrat, a shrew that scuttles across the pages as a harbinger of doom.

In the second volume, *Witchwood,* Kine's enemies are warfarin-immune super-rats which have invaded the woods. Initially, his plans to fight the king rat, Rattun, are delayed when he is trapped inside a horsebox and taken some distance from home. Heading back to the valley, he has to overcome a number of perils but is aided by the elderly rook, Watchman, and two sparrows as well as his daughter, Wonder, and her kits. Old Scrat's grandson continues to wail doom throughout the valley.

The final volume, *Dragonpond,* finds an aging Kine taking only the second mate in his life, surprising since weasels are usually solitary animals, except during the mating season when they seek partners. Kine's enemy this time is a polecat which teams up with a rather nasty escaped jill ferret, and a bellicose little owl. Again Kine has his allies, the rook, the shrew (actually the great-great-grandson of the original Scrat but still wailing doom through the woods), neighbouring weasels, including his own daughter, Wonder, and her mate, and the pair of scatterbrained fight-loving sparrows from *Witchwood.*

In all three a human element is provided by the people who live in the valley—Poacher, Ploughman, Ploughman's daughter and in the later volumes, the girl's husband and child. These blend in with the countryside, not seeking to change it, and so take on a role similar to other animals in the story, noticed but not unduly affecting the lives of the wild creatures.

The pace in all the books is fast but the characters are over-anthropomorphized. Long memories are granted to them as are other emotions such as grief and hatred, and Kine is not only able to plan strategies for defeating his enemies but to direct his allies—the sparrows are sent to summon aid of Wonder in *Dragonpond,* and Scrat is persuaded to act as a spy.

Some of the stylistic problems in Lloyd's writing are more noticeable in his other books such as *The Last Otter.* This is the story of an otter struggling for survival against poachers, pollution and a runaway boy determined to protect it. The human side of the plot is unbelievable but the overwriting is very noticeable. The otters rarely swim, but rather travel, plunge, vector, breast, stroke, surge or cruise, and the heron that informs the world of the goings-on along the waterside seems to do everything except fly once it is airborne. Similarly, *Wingfoot* is about a seal, but also about the people who live on the island where Wingfoot spends the summer months. It is two stories that run parallel, of a young girl, Aggie, and her love for the seals, and of the life of a seal told in much the same way as the naturalist Simon King would do with a camera instead of prose.

Whereas in *The Last Otter* and *Wingfoot* a high proportion of the narrative follows the relevant animal from its perspective, *The Farm Dog* mainly sticks to the human side of events. It is set in the 1940s in rural England. Zac is a dog which appears mysteri-

ously, starved and bedraggled, but although essential to this particular plot, is only incidental to the lives of the characters trying to make sense of the war with Germany. The book is very readable but lacking in depth.

The issues addressed within Lloyd's books are very real, and at their best his novels do provide an entertaining way of putting them across to younger readers.

—Pauline Morgan

LLYWELYN, Morgan

Pseudonym: Shannon Lewis. **Nationality:** Irish. **Born:** In the United States, 3 December 1937. **Family:** Married Charles Llywelyn (died); one son. **Career:** Has worked as a horse trainer, model, dance teacher, and legal secretary. **Agent:** Abner Stein, 10 Roland Gardens, London SW7 3PH, England.

FANTASY PUBLICATIONS

Novels

Lion of Ireland: The Legend of Brian Boru. Boston, Houghton Mifflin, 1979; London, Bodley Head, 1980.
The Horse Goddess. Boston, Houghton Mifflin, 1982; London, Macdonald, 1983.
Bard: The Odyssey of the Irish. Boston, Houghton Mifflin, 1984; London, Sphere, 1985.
Red Branch. New York, Morrow, 1989; as *On Raven's Wing,* London, Heinemann, 1990.
The Isles of the Blest. New York, Ace, 1989.
Druids. New York, Morrow, 1991.
The Elementals. New York, Tor, 1993.

OTHER PUBLICATIONS

Novels

The Wind from Hastings. Boston, Houghton Mifflin, 1978; London, Hale, 1980.
Personal Habits (as Shannon Lewis). New York, Doubleday, 1982.
Grania: She-King of the Irish Seas. Boston, Houghton Mifflin, 1986; London, Sphere, 1987.
Finn MacCool. New York, Forge, and London, Heinemann, 1994.

Other

Xerxes. New York, Chelsea House, 1988.

*

Manuscript Collection: University of Maryland, College Park.

Morgan Llywelyn comments:
(1990) The entire body of my work comprises a look at the Celtic culture of Western Europe, from its emergence through its decline,

with special emphasis on Ireland. The Celts were the foundation stock of Europe, exerting a powerful influence on subsequent Western civilization that even their conquest by the Romans could not destroy. Celtic literature, music, concepts of individual freedom and acting in harmony with nature, are all relevant in today's world. Through my novels, I hope to reacquaint the modern descendants of this ancient people with the high level of their civilization. They have become the stuff of legend and fairy tale, spawning 10,000 fantasies from King Arthur to Druids in Outer Space, yet they were real people whose contribution to our own culture has never been sufficiently recognized or appreciated. Because they were so vigorous, so colourful, so passionate, their historical deeds are more exciting than fiction and will continue to inspire me, I hope, for many years to come.

*   *   *

The majority of Morgan Llywelyn's books may be regarded as fictional biographies. Each book takes a person, often historical or legendary, and relates the story of their life. Most of the novels with a fantasy connection rely heavily on Celtic mythology, particularly that of the Irish. Each book is complete in itself.

Her first book with elements of fantasy was *Lion of Ireland.* This is the story of Brian Boru, a documented historical character who was High King of Ireland at the start of the 11th century A.D. Through his efforts as a warrior and diplomat, Brian united most of the country and threw out the Viking invaders. Llywelyn has added much to the story, in particular concerning his private life and the women in it. The fantasy thread is slender and concerns Fiona, a woods-woman Brian meets in his youth and who follows his career. She is a druid, able to communicate with the spirits of the trees, and is always in the vicinity when Brian is in greatest need of help.

The fantasy is much stronger in *The Horse Goddess,* which tells of Epona, a woman of the keltoi people at the dawn of the Iron Age. Her tribe are salt miners in the Austrian Alps and their smith has developed a method of making iron strong enough for weaponry. It is this that draws the Scythian horsemen to the village. Epona has just discovered that she is *drui,* able to communicate with the spirits, but rejects training as she detests the chief priest, Kernunnos, preferring to run away with the Scythians. With them she learns horsemanship and eventually brings those skills back to her tribe. But not before Kernunnos has pursued her across the continent in the spirit form of a great white wolf. The events used here just predate the Celtic explosion across Europe, and Llywelyn has drawn on early Celtic mythology for her sources, many of the characters being the human counterparts that became the deities of these people. This book also gives an insight into the process of mythmaking.

For *Bard,* Llywelyn looks again to Irish mythology. The bard is Amergin, who is generally regarded as a probable historical character. Most of the book is set on the Iberian coast where Amergin's Gaelic tribe live by farming, trading and mining tin. The mines are almost exhausted and the Phoenician ships have stopped coming. Overpopulation, overgrazing and the arrival of a small fleet of weather-battered ships act as catalysts for a migration, to Ierne. Thus Amergin's people become the latest invaders of Ireland. The fantasy is in Ireland awaiting them, in the guise of the Tuatha de Dannan, an earlier wave of settlers. These people would prefer to live in peace and are gradually developing psychic powers—Shinann,

for example, does not speak but communicates as clearly as if she did. Others can control the weather. After the de Danann are defeated in battle they become Unbodied, infusing their spirits into the fabric of Ireland and leaving the country to the iron-wielding Gaels.

Red Branch (also known as *On Raven's Wing*) is the history of Cuchulain. The fantasy here is again limited. Mostly it occurs as passages which are an overview of events from the perspective of Morrigan, the Irish battle goddess, who watches over Cuchulain in the form of a raven. The hero also acquires a magic spear which used to belong to the vanished Tuatha de Danann and which has the properties of a heat-seeking missile—whatever it is thrown at, it will hit, however the quarry twists and turns.

In *The Isles of the Blest,* there is more fantasy. This time the story is the retelling of the tale of Connla, who is lured away to the Realm of Fairy by Blaithine who promises him a life of bliss. *Finn MacCool,* on the other hand, contains no fantasy even though the story has been drawn from the same well of legend and the Finn of myth had magical dealings with the sidhe. In Llywelyn's story all the events which have come down as fantastic are exaggerations or inventions of Finn's mind. Like *The Horse Goddess,* the book can be regarded as a story of mythmaking but with a different slant.

Because Llywelyn has used the wealth of Celtic material that is freely available, most of these novels tell stories that will either be familiar to the reader, or have been used as a basis for other fantasy novels, where the fantasy elements are much stronger. Since she has chosen to keep each life confined to one book, which can be a distinct advantage, and because she often covers a large span of time, her characters, with the exception of the principle one, are rarely developed in depth.

Of her other books, *The Elementals* is in four parts, each dealing with a cataclysm triggered by one of the elements, beginning with flood and the survivors who settle in Ireland. Spanning the ages, the fourth part is set in contemporary times and concerns the hole in the ozone layer. As such, this book can be regarded as fantasy. *Grania* isn't fantasy, being the history of an Elizabethan woman who makes her living as a pirate captain, but it has the same form, telling just the life story of the central character and with an Irish setting.

—Pauline Morgan

LOFTING, Hugh (John)

Nationality: American. **Born:** Maidenhead, Berkshire, 14 January 1886; emigrated to the United States, 1912; naturalized citizen. **Education:** Mount St. Mary's College, Chesterfield, Derbyshire; Massachusetts Institute of Technology, Cambridge, 1904-05; London Polytechnic, 1906-07. **Military Service:** Irish Guards in Flanders, 1916-17. **Family:** Married 1) Flora W. Small in 1912 (died 1927), one son and one daughter; 2) Katherine Harrower-Peters in 1928 (died 1928); 3) Josephine Fricker in 1935, one son. **Career:** Prospector and surveyor in Canada, 1908-09; civil engineer, Lagos Railway, West Africa, 1910-11, and United Railways, Havana, Cuba, 1912; worked for British Ministry of Information, New York, 1915. **Awards:** American Library Association Newbery Medal, 1923. **Died:** 27 September 1947.

FANTASY PUBLICATIONS

Novels (series: Dr. Dolittle; all illustrated by the author)

The Story of Dr. Dolittle, Being the History of His Peculiar Life and Astonishing Adventures in Foreign Parts. New York, Stokes, 1920; as *Doctor Dolittle,* London, Cape, 1922.
The Voyages of Dr. Dolittle. New York, Stokes, 1922; London, Cape, 1923.
Dr. Dolittle's Post Office. New York, Stokes, 1923; London, Cape, 1924.
Dr. Dolittle's Circus. New York, Stokes, 1924; London, Cape, 1925.
Dr. Dolittle's Zoo. New York, Stokes, 1925; London, Cape, 1926.
Dr. Dolittle's Caravan. New York, Stokes, 1926; London, Cape, 1927.
Dr. Dolittle's Garden. New York, Stokes, 1927; London, Cape, 1928.
Dr. Dolittle in the Moon. New York, Stokes, 1928; London, Cape, 1929.
The Twilight of Magic, illustrated by Lois Lenski. New York, Stokes, 1930; London, Cape, 1931.
Dr. Dolittle's Return. New York, Stokes, and London, Cape, 1933.
Dr. Dolittle and the Secret Lake. Philadelphia, Lippincott, 1948; London, Cape, 1949.
Dr. Dolittle and the Green Canary. Philadelphia, Lippincott, 1950; London, Cape, 1951.

Short Stories

Gub Gub's Book: An Encyclopedia of Food (Dr. Dolittle). New York, Stokes, and London, Cape, 1932.
Dr. Dolittle's Puddleby Adventures. Philadelphia, Lippincott, 1952; London, Cape, 1953.

OTHER PUBLICATIONS

Fiction for Children

The Story of Mrs. Tubbs. New York, Stokes, 1923; London, Cape, 1924.
Noisy Nora. New York, Stokes, and London, Cape, 1929.
Tommy, Tilly and Mrs. Tubbs. New York, Stokes, 1936; London, Cape, 1937.

Poetry

Porridge Poetry: Cooked, Ornamented, and Served by Hugh Lofting. New York, Stokes, 1924; London, Cape, 1925.
Victory for the Slain. London, Cape, 1942.

Other

Dr. Dolittle's Birthday Book. New York, Stokes, 1935.

*

Film Adaptation: *Doctor Dolittle,* 1967.

Critical Study: *Hugh Lofting* by Edward Blishen, in *Three Bodley Head Monographs,* London, Bodley Head, 1968.

*   *   *

The exploits of Dr. Dolittle are nowadays best known through the eponymous film starring Rex Harrison as the doctor who could talk to animals. The film, however, barely scratches the surface of Hugh Lofting's remarkable output, spanning some thirty years, and mostly concerning Dr. Dolittle, a man of medicine in early Victorian times. Dolittle begins as a doctor serving humans, but his habit of continually acquiring new pets drives away his wealthy patients and then his housekeeper sister (though she is to appear regularly, if fleetingly, through the series of stories about him). This is of little consequence to Dolittle as he much prefers animals anyway. It is by chance that he learns from his parrot Polynesia that animals have their own languages. Under her tuition, he gradually acquires these languages and sets up in business as a veterinarian. His fame spreads worldwide, and his gifts as an animal linguist precipitate him into ever more preposterous adventures. At various times in his career, he runs a circus and a zoo, organizes an animal pantomime, a canary opera, and a swallow Post Office, all with the assistance of his animal friends, most notably Polynesia the parrot, Jip the dog, Gub-Gub the pig, Dab-Dab the duck, Too-Too the owl and Chee-Chee the monkey.

Yet, beneath this whimsy, it is clear that Lofting intended his books to do more than simply entertain. His message, emphasized time and again, is that people should treat animals more kindly. Admittedly, in many of the stories, this is carried to absurd and preposterous lengths, such as the forming of Animal Town and its many animal clubs, but the various philanthropic exercises carried out by the animals and Dolittle himself resonate powerfully with concerns in the modern world and suggest also that Lofting was an early environmentalist. Dolittle is an indefatigable worker, very much the opposite of what his name would imply, and on several occasions in his travels stops to assist the natives in building a new and better society. In some respects, this smacks of a colonial paternalism which would no longer be tolerated, as do occasional references to "coons" and "niggers" but bearing in mind the time in which the stories are set, Dolittle's aspirations are very mild compared to those of other campaigners active during the 1830s, and the language is simply that which would have been used. One suspects that Lofting himself was very concerned with improving the lot of his fellow man as well as his fellow animal. Throughout the books, Dolittle's human concerns are with curing diseases and improving hygiene and sanitation, and it is universally agreed that as a doctor for humans or animals alike, there is none better.

Humanitarian messages apart, what makes these books so delightful some sixty years after they were first published is the verve with which Lofting describes his portly hero's adventures, and the delightful characters, mostly animal, that he creates. Lofting's imagination runs riot as he packs Dolittle off to search for floating islands, to visit African kingdoms, even to visit the moon. His world is filled with a mass of weird and wonderful creatures such as the pushmi-pullyu and the Great Glass Sea-Snail, as well as the more mundane animals such as the white mouse, the cockney sparrow and the irrepressible pig, Gub-Gub, and an ever-changing cast of plough horses and mongrel dogs. Lofting anthropomorphizes them shamelessly but nevertheless shows himself to have been an astute naturalist and observer, much like his character. One also cannot help but admire the way in which he sustains his inventiveness over many volumes of stories, rarely sounding repetitive.

Lofting briefly ventured into other areas, creating another animal-loving character for younger children, Mrs. Tubbs, and also publishing a full-length fairy story, *The Twilight of Magic,* which seems to owe a considerable debt to the fantasies of E. Nesbit (though a eulogistic introduction by Mary Treadgold overstates the case). Lofting's Dr. Dolittle stories are almost certainly unique in the sub-genre of animal fantasies. There is nothing else quite like them and after six decades they are still refreshingly entertaining and inventive.

—Maureen Speller

LORD, Jeffrey. *See* **GREEN, Roland J(ames).**

LUARD, Nicholas (Lambert)

Pseudonym: James McVean. **Nationality:** British. **Born:** London, 26 June 1937; childhood spent partly in Iran. **Education:** Winchester College, Hampshire, 1951-54; the Sorbonne, Paris, 1954-55; Cambridge University, M.A. 1960; University of Pennsylvania, Philadelphia, M.A. 1961. **Military Service:** Coldstream Guards, 1955-57: Lieutenant. **Family:** Married Elizabeth Baron Longmore in 1963; one son and three daughters. **Career:** Worked in theatre and publishing; co-founder, *Private Eye* magazine and the Establishment Club, Soho, London. **Agent:** Jonathan Clowes Ltd, 22 Prince Albert Road, London NW1 7ST.

FANTASY PUBLICATIONS

Novels

Gondar. London, Century Hutchinson, and New York, Simon and Schuster, 1988.
Kala. London, Century Hutchinson, 1990.
Himalaya. London, Century, 1992.
Sanctuary. London, Hodder & Stoughton, 1994.

OTHER PUBLICATIONS

Novels

The Warm and Golden War. London, Secker and Warburg, 1967; New York, Pantheon, 1968.
The Robespierre Serial. London, Weidenfeld, 1975; New York, Harcourt Brace, 1975.
Travelling Horseman. London, Weidenfeld, 1975.
The Orion Line. London, Secker and Warburg, 1976; as *Double Assignment,* New York, Harcourt Brace, 1977.
Bloodspoor (as James McVean). New York, Dial, 1977.
The Dirty Area. London, Hamish Hamilton, 1979; as *The Shadow Spy,* New York, Harcourt Brace, 1979.
Seabird Nine (as James McVean). New York, Coward, McCann & Geoghegan, 1981.
Titan (as James McVean). London, Macdonald, 1984.

Other

Refer to Drawer (with Dominick Elwes). 1964.
The Last Wilderness: A Journey Across the Great Kalahari Desert. London, Elm Tree, 1981.
Andulucia: A Portrait of Southern Spain. London, Century, 1984.
Wild Life Parks of Africa. London, Joseph, 1985.
Landscape in Spain, photographs by Michael Busselle. London, Pavilion, 1988.

*   *   *

Nicholas Luard is a man of parts. He was a precocious linguist, then a soldier ("trained as a NATO long-range patrol commander with a special sabotage and forward intelligence unit," according to his brief biography in Donald McCormick's *Spy Fiction: A Connoisseur's Guide,* 1990), then a "King of Satire" at Cambridge (close associate of the late comedian Peter Cook and comedian-writer-director Dr. Jonathan Miller), then a writer of espionage thrillers (and of environmentalist thrillers as "James McVean"), then an author of travel books such as *The Last Wilderness*—all this before turning his hand to a type of fantasy that draws on the myths of deepest, darkest Africa and is reminiscent of nothing so much as updated Rider Haggard adventure-romance. As such, he is one of a new breed of writers who emerged in the 1980s, producing great colourful epics drawing on the lore of distant places and times gone by.

His first bestseller in this vein was *Gondar.* This tells of Jamie Oran, a 19th-century Scottish explorer set on discovering the source of Africa's mightiest river, the Nile. On his travels he meets Rachel Ozoro, Gondar's rightful Queen, forced into exile by a power-hungry priest. Jamie and Rachel join forces to reconquer Gondar; however in seeking that success, they are also sowing the seeds for their inevitable separation. Their tale is told in the expansive style of the great escapist saga-novel.

Rachel Ozoro's downfall has come about because she was part of a royal dynasty whose powers draw on myths and magic: Rachel is supposed to be the daughter of the River God Nile and her virgin mother Esther. In fact a clean-limbed shepherd boy was selected by the high priest to join Esther in a remote cave on the waterside. When Esther was pregnant, the high priest discretely murdered the shepherd boy and announced to the population that the new infant was the child of the great River God. Having been party to both murder and deception to ensure Rachel's existence, the high priest finds it hard to forget her true origins. Thus in the fullness of time he takes control, and the remainder of the novel tells of Jamie's and Rachel struggle to overthrow the evil priest. They will be assisted by two beautiful twin Malindan tribesfolk, stolen as infants from their father's home by Arab traders and brought up as slaves within other African tribes. The tragedy of the lives of the sad and much abused brother and sister is a truthful tale of an ancient Africa, hostile to its own as well as to outsiders.

Gondar is beautifully written, with breathtaking landscapes and richly described towns and villages. Each of the four characters, Jamie, Rachel and the Malindan twins, is confidently drawn; their tales, all four, vital and interesting. When the novel was first released it was deservedly a bestseller, with rave reviews from the *Sunday Times* ("exotic, imaginative, gorgeously readable") and the *New York Times Review of Books* ("a fascinating feat of storytelling").

This achievement was followed by *Kala,* another epic fantasy out of Africa, also set in the 19th century but with echoes of antiquity, and featuring a classic "lost city." The eponymous Kala is the heroine who, Mowgli-fashion, has been raised by hyenas to become a magnificent, if mute, wild child of the savanna. She is stolen from her native lands by showmen who have no other concern than "to show a pair of naked titties on a London stage." So follow Dickensian images of Kala, the feral child raised in the savanna sun, caged and hounded in the worse possible conditions in a dusty, dirty London playhouse. Her salvation comes in the form of a crippled theatre carpenter, Ben, and Mary-Ellen, a self-taught anthropologist from South Africa. *Kala* has most of the qualities of *Gondar* but the plot is weaker. Both Mary Ellen and Ben have traumatic pasts, both aspire to better lives; the quest to save Kala will bring them together, and the book ends with Mary Ellen setting up her own centre to study wild-life in Africa with Ben at her side. Despite the upbeat ending, the novel is weakened by the fact that we cannot get inside the skin of Kala. As she is mute, we never hear her voice except in the form of lonely howls; animal-like, she seems to have no emotions other than reflexes. We can never hear her thoughts, although we are vouchsafed brief glimpses of Queen Cleopatra who, it is hinted, was Kala's ancestor. Mary Ellen and Ben both love Kala for her beauty and for what she represents. Yet like a caged jaguar or lioness, Kala returns no love to them—no affection, nor even loyalty.

The third fantasy by Nicholas Luard is *Himalaya*. Here, a female member of a party of explorers becomes lost while trekking in Nepal. Caught in an avalanche, she tumbles into an uncharted valley, a green strip of land far below the high peaks. In this isolated place of tranquillity lives a primitive people: the Yeti. The valley Yeti are split in two tribes, and young males fight amongst themselves in the shadow of an old and weakening leader. From an epic mountain quest, the story takes a sudden turn to something reminiscent of Jean Auel's prehistoric "loincloth-ripper" *Clan of the Cave Bear* (1980), and the narrative becomes rather too stereotyped. Although in many ways a fine adventure fantasy, *Himalaya* is the least successful of Luard's novels in this vein. With its remote mountain and valley setting, Luard has denied himself the grand vistas of the African plain or even the dingy darkness of Victorian Britain. There are compensations, though, in the descriptions of the high snow-capped peaks walling the valley. The sections where the mountaineers first espy the lush green land below them are wonderful. Where *Gondar* told the tales that hang like mists around the Mountains of the Moon, and *Kala* drew on the continent-wide African myth of children brought up by wild animals of the plain, *Himalaya* hinges on whether or not one can bring oneself to believe that the Yeti exist, whether in this century they may live on undiscovered in some distant Himalayan valley.

Given Nicholas Luard's diverse literary career to date, it may be that *Himalaya* is his last fantasy epic, which would be a pity. His works set a new standard, his undoubted story-telling talent combining the tradition of great tales with the colours of a very real Africa, and reviving forgotten myths.

—Sally Ann Melia

LUSTBADER, Eric (Van)

Nationality: American. **Born:** New York City, 24 December 1946. **Education:** Stuyvesant High School, New York, 1960-64; Columbia University, 1964-68, B.A. in sociology. **Family:** Married Victoria Schochet in 1982. **Career:** Teacher, Project Head Start and All-Day Neighborhood Schools, New York, 1967-69; editor, *Cash Box* magazine, New York, 1970-72; assistant to president for A&R, Elektra Records, New York, 1972-73; director of publicity and creative services, Dick James Music (USA), New York, 1973-76; manager of creative services, CBS Records, New York, 1977-79; freelance writer from 1980. **Agent:** Henry Morrison, Inc., PO Box 235, Bedford Hills, NY 10507, USA.

FANTASY PUBLICATIONS

Novels (series: Sunset Warrior in all books)

The Sunset Warrior. New York, Doubleday, 1977; London, Star, 1979.
Shallows of Night. New York, Doubleday, 1978; London, Star, 1979.
Dai-San. New York, Doubleday, 1978; London, Star, 1980.
Beneath an Opal Moon. New York, Doubleday, 1980.

OTHER PUBLICATIONS

Novels

The Ninja. New York, Evans, and London, Granada, 1980.
Sirens. New York, Evans, and London, Granada, 1981.
Black Heart. New York, Evans, and London, Granada, 1984.
The Miko. New York, Villard, and London, Granada, 1984.
Jian. New York, Villard, and London, Granada, 1985.
Zero. New York, Random House, and London, Grafton, 1986.
Shan. New York, Random House, and London, Grafton, 1987.
French Kiss. New York, Fawcett, and London, Grafton, 1988.
White Ninja. New York, Fawcett, and London, Grafton, 1990.
Angel Eyes. New York, Fawcett, and London, HarperCollins, 1991.
Black Blade. New York, Fawcett, and London, HarperCollins, 1992.
The Kaisho. New York, Pocket, and London, HarperCollins, 1993.
Floating City. New York, Pocket, and London, HarperCollins, 1994.
Second Skin. New York, Pocket, and London, HarperCollins, 1995.

* * *

Before he became a bestselling author with his particular brand of exotic thriller fiction, Eric Van Lustbader (who has since dropped the "Van" from his byline) wrote a fantasy trilogy. He is best known for adventure novels such as *The Ninja,* which feature martial-arts combat, sex, and strong oriental connections—all of which ingredients are to be found in his early fantasy novels too. Generally, his more recent bestsellers all contain a few fantasy elements, especially *White Ninja,* but it is only that early trilogy (his first published work) and a slightly later connected fantasy, *Beneath an Opal Moon,* which are sufficiently fantastic to be considered here.

The Sunset Warrior is the odd-one-out of these fantasies. For a start, it is actually science fiction, supposedly set in a post-holocaust future. It contains none of the oriental flavour and little of the magic to be found in later volumes. And it is more scrappily written, clearly the product of an inexperienced writer. Moreover, it seems as if the author changed his ideas during the writing of the trilogy, so that many of the details given in this first book are conveniently forgotten in later volumes.

The setting for *The Sunset Warrior* is a "Freehold," a self-contained community in a multilevel subterranean location. It is three kilometres below the surface and is said to be the last of its kind, the very last refuge for humanity following a holocaust which may or may not have left Earth's surface covered with ice. The Freehold is full of science-fiction cliches. It has an authoritarian regime with absolutely no personal freedom. The advanced technology which keeps the place habitable is gradually breaking down. The society is rigidly stratified, with Scholars, Workers, and Neers (the jargon for engineers) all following in their fathers' footsteps and with traditions being vitally important. In fact everything is collapsing, and political power groups are manoeuvring for control.

The hero, Ronin (most of the names in this volume are Germanic-sounding), gets caught up between the groups because he is affiliated to none of them. He is a champion Bladesman, highly skilled with a sword and other weapons, trained personally by the Salamander, the greatest combat expert in the Freehold. He comes into conflict with Security when he tries to help Borros the Magic Man (a misnomer; he is a scientist). Borros urges Ronin to go on a quest Downshaft to a strange empty city below the lowest level, where Ronin finds an important old scroll and a fighting gauntlet made from the hand of a deadly creature, the Makkon. Then he risks escaping Upshaft towards the surface.

The novel is marred by too much jargon, by too many revelations (for example, Ronin's girlfriend, K'reen, turns out to be his long-lost sister, trained secretly by the Salamander, but Ronin only discovers this after he has fought and killed her), and by the lack of an ending.

Shallows of Night continues the story, with Ronin escaping out into a frozen world. Surprisingly, Borros has also managed to escape, and they skim for days across a flat sea of ice in a small ship, including running through a gale. They are pursued by Freidal, the dreaded Security chief, but Ronin kills Freidal's men and apparently kills Freidal himself. Borros is killed by a sea monster, the ship is reaches clear water, is sunk, and Ronin is lucky to be picked up. He is taken to the great tropical port city of Sha'angh'sei.

It is at this point that Lustbader discovers the style and ingredients which have served him so well ever since, and at the same time he drops any pretence of a post-holocaust future. He describes the overcrowded, cosmopolitan Sha'angh'sei in vivid, sensual detail, stressing its oriental nature, its dangers, the universal carrying of swords, daggers, axes. And very soon he is increasing the sexual content, too. The resulting image is of a sort of 18th-century Hong Kong or Singapore.

Ronin's mission now is to get the scroll translated, but again he is caught between political factions—the Reds and the Greens. In between sword-fights, he is taken to the city's premier bordello, Tencho, where he has sex with Matsu, who is later killed by a Makkon, and with Kiri, who turns out to be the Empress of Sha'angh'sei. He saves a young woman, Moeru, whom he finds wounded on the street; she is mute but also very special and is able to help Ronin later.

Ronin and Kiri travel overland to Kamado, a great besieged citadel, where they participate in a bloody battle against non-human warriors. A temporary victory is secured, due in considerable measure to Ronin's fighting abilities with his sword and the Makkon gauntlet. Here are the first hints of his apotheosis into something more than a human being, partly through eating a mysterious root. It is more important than ever for the scroll to be translated, and Ronin is sent off with Moeru to sail to the fabled land of Ama-no-mori, where the lost race of men, the Bujun, are said to live. But on board, as first mate, is Freidal, who has miraculously survived and wants his revenge upon Ronin.

Dai-San carries on from that point, with Ronin's ship attacked by three ships of non-human creatures. These are too easily killed, but Freidal tries to take advantage of Ronin in the midst of the battle and proves a much more formidable opponent before Ronin rips him apart with the Makkon gauntlet. However, Moeru disappears onto one of the enemy ships. In yet another of the contrived plot occurrences which pepper Lustbader's fantasy novels, the ship is wrecked and all the crew are killed except for Ronin and the ship's navigator, Moichi. They cross a jungle and come across the great but almost deserted city of Xich Chih, centre of a former Aztec-type civilization. After sex with a priestess, Ronin has to fight and defeat five warriors. He does so, and a plumed serpent god flies off with him and Moichi, depositing the latter on a ship and Ronin on Ama-no-mori, which is very Japan-like.

Introduced to Ama-no-mori's high society by Okami, a Bujun warrior, Ronin is amazed to see Moeru. He steals her away from captivity, but discovers that her husband is the only man who can translate the scroll he carries. And when the husband, Nikumu, reads the scroll, his body is taken over by its long-dead author, who welcomes Ronin as "the champion of all men." After some mysticism, Ronin wakes to find himself changed; he knows he is the Sunset Warrior, with a great destiny to fulfil. He has an invincible pair of swords made for him by a female smith, then he travels back to Kamado to participate in the great battle which will settle the fate of mankind.

His mission now is to prevent the extermination of humanity by the invading non-human warriors and by the four Makkon beasts and their master, the dreaded Dolman. In an exceedingly bloody battle, the Sunset Warrior discovers that his old trainer the Salamander is not only a senior agent of the Dolman but, on the point of defeat, becomes the Dolman and tries to absorb the Sunset Warrior. In the end it is the Sunset Warrior who wins, absorbing others and becoming a new composite entity, the Dai-San.

Beneath an Opal Moon begins in Sha'angh'sei "six seasons" later. Its protagonist is Moichi, a friend of Ronin and his navigator on the voyage to Ama-no-mori. In fact this is a murder-mystery novel with lots of martial arts, lots of lush descriptions, and little fantasy. Moichi is called in to investigate a double murder—of the son of the leader of the Greens and of a foreigner. He gets tangled up with several beautiful women: with Aufeya whom he saves from a slave market, who comes from Dalucia and who is at the centre of the mystery; with Chiisai, warrior daughter of the Bujun leader, who helps him in his investigations; with Aufeya's mother, Tsuki, who first denies her daughter's existence, then attacks him, then beds him; and with Sardonyx, a dangerous sorceress who almost discovers how to control time.

Lustbader has complex and generally unconvincing plots. He covers over this flaw by much fast-moving action (usually hand-to-hand fighting) and by strong, slightly over-the-top descriptions. Sadism and sex feature ever more strongly. Overall, his fantasies are different and memorable.

—Chris Morgan

LYNN, Elizabeth A(nne)

Nationality: American. **Born:** New York City, 8 June 1946. **Education:** Case Western Reserve University, Cleveland, B.A. 1967; University of Chicago (Woodrow Wilson Fellow, 1967-68), M.A.

1968. **Career:** Public school teacher, Chicago, 1968-70; unit manager, St. Francis Hospital, Evanston, Illinois, 1970-72, and French Hospital, San Francisco, 1972-75; formerly teacher in the Women's Studies Program, San Francisco State University. **Awards:** World Fantasy Award, 1980.

Fantasy Publications

Novels (series: Chronicles of Tornor)

Watchtower (Tornor). New York, Berkley, 1979; London, Hamlyn, 1981.
The Dancers of Arun (Tornor). New York, Berkley, 1979; London, Hamlyn, 1982.
The Northern Girl (Tornor). New York, Berkley, 1980.
The Silver Horse. New York, Bluejay, 1984.

Short Stories

The Woman Who Loved the Moon, and Other Stories. New York, Berkley, 1981.
The Red Hawk. New Castle, Virginia, Cheap Street, 1983.
Tales from a Vanished Country. Eugene, Oregon, Pulphouse, 1990.

Other Publications

Novels

A Different Light. New York, Berkley, 1978; London, Gollancz, 1979.
The Sardonyx Net. New York, Berkley, 1981.

*   *   *

Elizabeth A. Lynn's first book was the science-fiction novel *A Different Light,* and she went on to write another, *The Sardonyx Net.* However, she has also written several fantasy works. Most notably among these is the Chronicles of Tornor trilogy, the first volume of which, *Watchtower,* won the 1980 World Fantasy Award for best novel.

Lynn describes the slow decline of the Tower of Tornor, a northern keep, by showing it at three separate times. In each case, she weaves together the stories of several inhabitants (or descendants of inhabitants), their friends and lovers. This gives the books a realistic feel—objectively, there are no heroes or villains, yet each person is the hero of their own story. Yet it also makes the narrative thread difficult to follow at times, particularly since some of the names Lynn has chosen are very similar (some are even anagrams of each other), and on occasion the pacing flags.

In *Watchtower,* Tornor is at the peak of its influence and strength: but at the start of the novel it is invaded by Col Istor, an outlaw. The major protagonist is Ryke, a watch commander. To save the life of Errel, the heir to Tornor, he reluctantly agrees to serve under Col Istor. This changes when Norres and Sorren, two members of the green clan of messengers, arrive. Such messengers are normally *ghya,* or genderless, but this pair are using that to disguise the fact that they are women. One of them, Sorren, is a bastard daughter of Athor, the old Lord of Tornor.

With the help of the two women, Ryke and Errel journey south to Vanima, the Valley of Van, whose people have invented a new style of weaponless dance-fighting that does not kill. Errel becomes a *cheari,* one of Van's dancers, and much later the pair return north. They raise an army from the other keeps, and the dancers infiltrate Tornor. Though they will not fight, they let the army into Tornor, and the invaders are slaughtered. The book ends with Errel leaving Tornor to remain with the dancers, and Sorren sacrificing something of her relationship with Norres in order to rule Tornor.

The overriding theme of this book appears to be survival, and the sacrifices necessary to make it possible. There is an interesting ambiguity in the moral position of the *chearis*—they will fight but not kill; they will not attack Col Istor, but they will enable the army from Cloud Keep to do so—but Lynn does not choose to foreground it in this book.

The middle volume of the trilogy, *The Dancers of Arun,* is set several generations after *Watchtower.* Again, the narrative begins in Tornor Keep, but it quickly moves away, and this time it does not return. Kerris is the nephew of Morven, the Lord of the Keep. He cannot fight, because his arm was amputated by outlaws when he was a child, and he has strange visions; therefore he is apprenticed to the Keep's scribe.

As the book opens, the Keep is visited by a band of *chearis,* among them Kel, Kerris's older brother. Kerris leaves the Keep with them, and the narrative follows his progress as he becomes Kel's lover, and comes to terms with his visions. These, it transpires, are signs that Kerris is a witch. Kel persuades him to go to Elath, where Sefer—Kel's other lover—runs a school. In a subplot that for many other writers would have been the main narrative thrust of the novel, barbarians lay siege to Elath. They want to be trained to use their mental powers, and although it looks at first as if Lynn will allow a too-easy solution—her characters do sometimes seem to suffer from being entirely too reasonable—in the end none is found and Sefer is killed. In the aftermath, Kerris realizes that he has not yet found his true home. He moves on, but the book ends on a hopeful note as the reader is brought to the realization that he will eventually come to understand and accept himself.

The last volume is *The Northern Girl.* This is jumps a few more generations. Unlike the other two books, it does not begin in Tornor. Instead it starts in Kendra-on-the-Delta, a major city only mentioned in the other novels. Like *The Dancers of Arun,* it is a rite of passage. This time the main subject is Sorren, an indentured servant to Arré Med, a member of the ruling council. Like Kel, Sorren has visions; she also owns a pack of fortune-telling cards. The implication is that these are the ones readers first saw in *Watchtower,* and that Sorren is Ryke's descendant. Her storyline concerns her desire to leave the city and find the place she can see in her visions—Tornor. Before she can do this, she becomes a bit-player in the her employer's story, for there is a conspiracy to destabilize the city, and this in turn leads to a plot to kill Arré Med. Once this is out of the way, Sorren is free to seek her destiny in Tornor. What she finds is nearly a ruin, almost unable to support even the few people who live there; but Sorren becomes an agent of hope, since she is able to suggest an alliance with Arré Med. Thus, even in this pessimistic ending there is a suggestion of renewal to come.

Again, the *chearis* are involved, because they have put a ban on the use of certain types of sword in the city, and the conspiracy involves the breaking of this ban. Lynn comes much closer to discussing the ethics and morality of the *chearis* in this book, despite the fact that they are never seen directly.

There are so many equally weighted themes in these novels that it can be difficult to see where to direct one's attention. However, it is clear that the philosophy of the *chea*—the idea that the balance of the world must be maintained—is central. For this reason it is a pity Lynn did not choose to explore it more explicitly. Yet the trilogy, taken as a whole, almost embodies the philosophy in itself: Tornor starts out at the peak of its fortunes, falls and rises, then falls again, yet with the hope of a further rise to come. The characters in the books struggle for survival and yet find survival is worth nothing without self-awareness and self-acceptance. Alone, each of these novels is a worthwhile read; taken together, they are much more than that.

—Liz Holliday

M

MacAVOY, R(oberta) A(nn)

Nationality: American. **Born:** Cleveland, Ohio, 13 December 1949.
Education: Case Western Reserve University, Cleveland, 1967-71, B.Sc. 1971. **Family:** Married Ronald Allen Cain in 1978. **Career:** Financial aid officer's assistant, Columbia College, New York, 1975-78; computer programmer, SRI International, Menlo Park, California, 1979-83. Since 1982, full-time writer. **Awards:** John W. Campbell Best New Writer award, 1984. **Agent:** Richard Curtis Associates, 171 East 74th Street, New York, New York 10021. **Address:** Underhill at Nelson Farm, 1669 Nelson Road, House 6, Scotts Valley, CA 95066, USA.

FANTASY PUBLICATIONS

Novels (series: Black Dragon; Damiano; Nazhuret of Sordaling)

Tea with the Black Dragon. New York and London, Bantam, 1983.
Damiano. New York, Bantam, 1984; London, Bantam, 1985.
Damiano's Lute. New York, Bantam, 1984; London, Bantam, 1985.
Raphael (Damiano). New York, Bantam, 1984; London, Bantam, 1985.
The Book of Kells. New York, Bantam, 1985.
A Trio for Lute (omnibus; includes *Damiano, Damiano's Lute, Raphael*). New York, Nelson Doubleday, 1985.
Twisting the Rope: Casadh an t'Sugain (Black Dragon). New York, Bantam, 1986.
The Grey Horse. New York, Bantam, 1987; London, Bantam, 1988.
Lens of the World (Nazhuret). New York, Morrow, 1990; London, Headline, 1991.
King of the Dead (Nazhuret). New York, Morrow, and London, Headline, 1991.
Winter of the Wolf (Nazhuret). London, Headline, 1993; as *The Belly of the Wolf,* New York, Morrow, 1993.

OTHER PUBLICATIONS

Novel

The Third Eagle: Lessons Along a Minor String. New York, Doubleday, 1989; London, Bantam, 1990.

*   *   *

With the exception of her science fiction tale *The Third Eagle* all MacAvoy's published novels have been fantasy in one form or another, but within them there is a great range. She is an author who constantly strives to achieve something new.

Her debut novel, *Tea with the Black Dragon,* won her the John W. Campbell Best New Writer Award in 1984. A contemporary fantasy set in California's Silicon Valley, it brings together Martha Macnamara, a middle-aged fiddler with an Irish-American Ceili band, and Mayland Long, an ancient Chinese Dragon in human form. Both are eccentrics. Martha has come to San Francisco at the be-hest of her daughter who has subsequently disappeared. In many ways this is a detective novel with a touch of fantasy, in which the principal characters are superbly portrayed. The sequel, *Twisting the Rope,* is a similar kind of book. By now, Long is the road manager of Martha's band. Eight weeks into their tour, one of the musicians is found hanging by a handmade Irish rope from a Santa Cruz pier, and Long determines to unravel the mystery of this death. Again the touches of fantasy are small, the magic is underlying, residing mainly in the fact that Long is not what everyone perceives him to be. The main characters are unusual because they are older than the norm and as such have a wealth of worldly experience to draw upon.

This is not the case with Damiano Delstrego. The hero of the Lute trilogy is young, inexperienced and naive. The setting is a parallel-world Renaissance Italy where magic is real. Damiano is the son of a wizard who has two friends, a talking dog and the archangel Raphael, who only he can see. When his city is attacked he seeks help, not altruistically for the sake of the people, but humanly for the woman he loves. In the process he meets Saara, a Finnish witch, and Gaspare, a street urchin. The first volume, *Damiano,* can almost stand alone. It is the skill of the writer, and the knowledge that there is more to be told that leads the reader to seek out the rest of the trilogy. By the end of this volume, Damiano has surrendered his magic to Saara and it is as an ordinary human that he sets off westwards with only his skill as a musician to pay his way. *Damiano's Lute* finds Damiano and Gaspare travelling through France, and they are in Avignon when plague strikes. In he third book, *Raphael,* Damiano is no longer the central character. This role has been taken over by Raphael, who has become human, tricked into the condition by his brother, Lucifer. The trilogy is a very ambitious project, combining a number of complex themes. For Damiano first, then Raphael, it is a voyage of self-discovery. Linked with this is a battle of good versus evil as both characters fight the traps set for them by Lucifer. The historical background is well researched, with the subtleties of having magic working against this background carefully calculated. In a situation where it would be easy to descend into cliche or sentimentality, MacAvoy manages to tread lightly and balance the many strands so that often the result is unexpected.

MacAvoy's next novel, *The Book of Kells,* is equally well researched. This time the period is Ireland a thousand years ago; a time when Vikings were causing much trouble, burning Christian settlements and raping the women. The fantasy element lies principally the way in which the two main characters, artist John Thorburn and historian Derval O'Keane, are transported back into the past. This approach provides the opportunity to compare outlooks of people and societies separated by a long span of time. In *The Grey Horse,* the setting is again Ireland, but this time in the late 19th century. The grey horse is a pooka. In human form he calls himself Ruairi MacEibhir and his purpose in the village is the courting of Maire NiStandun. The story of relationships within a small village community are convincingly handled.

The most recent trilogy, of which *Lens of the World* is the first volume, is different again. It is set in an imaginary world, but most of the trappings that are expected in fantasy are missing. There are no powerful sorcerers, magic swords or creeping evils. It is the story of Nazhuret of Sordaling and is written as the reminiscences of a forty year-old man looking back over his formative years. Nazhuret entered the Royal Sordaling School as a child with no memory of what had occurred before. He guesses that he must have some noble blood, as this is a requirement for entry, but knows nothing more of his past. He sees himself as a short, goblin-like figure but he is a survivor, learning all the skills of swordsmanship his masters can teach. When he finally has to leave he falls in with Powl who keeps him in an observatory on a hillside, trapped by his curiosity and the compelling personality of his mentor, who proceeds to teach him a range of strange skills, including lens grinding. This volume can easily stand alone but the second volume, *The King of the Dead,* continues the story from almost the point where the first finished. Nazhuret believes that he has settled to study in peace with his lover, Arlin, who is expecting their child. Suddenly they are attacked and although all the assassins perish, Arlin miscarries. Arising from this, the pair find themselves as ambassadors to the neighbouring country in an attempt to prevent a war that would be devastating for both sides.

Winter of the Wolf, although the third part of the trilogy, is also a separate novel. Nazhuret is now fifty-five and has a grown daughter whose passion is firearms. With the death of King Rudolf of Velonya, Nazhuret's longtime friend, father and daughter are forced to flee, finding themselves caught up in politics. Velonya is descending into civil war, with Rudolf's son on one side and a religious-based faction on the other. The source of their philosophy happens to be the narrative that forms the first two books in the trilogy. Nazhuret is an interesting and complex character. Although at the centre of events he sees himself as insignificant and wonders why others should be so intent on trying to kill him. Even at fifty-five, he has an innocence that others find impossible to believe in so he is constantly changing and developing.

In all her books, including the science fiction novel *The Third Eagle,* MacAvoy's emphasis is always upon the people, especially relationships between them and the way their perceptions change throughout the book, mirroring real life. She does not choose as her focus the kind of characters that more mundane fantasy authors might, thus avoiding the cliches of the genre. Many of them, like Martha Macnamara in *Tea with the Black Dragon,* are older—even grandparents. The fascination with them stems partly from their ordinariness and partly from the skill MacAvoy uses to portray them. Her extraordinary characters are those like Mayland Long (in *Tea with the Black Dragon*) Raphael (in the Lute trilogy) and Ruairi (in *The Grey Horse*) who are supernatural creatures—dragon, archangel and pooka—who have become human for various reasons. Above all, MacAvoy is able to tell a good story without wasting words—all her books are short compared with many being produced these days, and are more enjoyable because of it.

—Pauline Morgan

MacDONALD, George

Nationality: British. **Born:** Near Huntly, Aberdeenshire, 10 December 1824. **Education:** King's College, University of Aberdeen, 1840-45, M.A. 1845; Congregationalist Theological College, Highbury, London, 1848-50. **Family:** Married Louisa Powell in 1850 (died 1902); eleven children. **Career:** Private tutor in London, 1845-48; minister, Trinity Congregational Church, Arundel,

Sussex, 1850-53; lecturer and preacher in Manchester, 1855-56, Hastings, Sussex, 1857-59, and London, from 1859: taught at Bedford College; editor, with Norman MacLeod, *Good Words for the Young* magazine, 1870-72; lived partly in Bordighera, Italy from 1877. LL.D.: University of Aberdeen, 1868. Granted Civil List pension, 1877. **Died:** 18 September 1905.

FANTASY PUBLICATIONS

Novels

Phantastes: A Faerie Romance for Men and Women. London, Smith Elder, 1858; Boston, Loring, 1870.
Adela Cathcart (includes "The Light Princess" and others as interpolated stories). London, Hurst and Blackett, 3 vols., 1864; revised edition, excluding fantasy stories, New York, Munro, 1882.
The Portent: A Story of the Inner Vision of the Highlanders, Commonly Called the Second Sight. London, Smith Elder, 1864; New York, Munro, 1885; as *Lady of the Mansion,* n.p. (USA), 1983.
At the Back of the North Wind, illustrated by Arthur Hughes. London, Strahan, 1870; New York, Routledge, 1871.
The Princess and the Goblin, illustrated by Arthur Hughes. New York, Routledge, 1871; London, Strahan, 1872.
The Wise Woman: A Parable. London, Strahan, 1875; as *The Lost Princess: A Double Story,* New York, Dodd Mead, 1876; as *The Lost Princess,* London, Wells Gardner Darton, 1895.
The Princess and Curdie, illustrated by James Allen. Philadelphia, Lippincott, 1882; London, Chatto and Windus, 1883.
The Flight of the Shadow. London, Kegan Paul, and New York, Appleton, 1891.
Lilith: A Romance. London, Chatto and Windus, and New York, Dodd Mead, 1895.
Visionary Novels: Lilith, Phantastes. N.p. (USA), 1954; as *Phantastes, and Lilith,* London, Gollancz, 1962.
The Princess and the Goblin, and The Princess and Curdie, edited by Roderick McGillis. Oxford, Oxford University Press, 1990.

Short Stories

Dealings with the Fairies, illustrated by Arthur Hughes. London, Strahan, 1867; New York, Routledge, 1891.
Works of Fancy and Imagination. London, Strahan, 10 vols., 1871.
The Fairy Tales of George MacDonald, edited by Greville MacDonald. London, Fifield, 5 vols., 1904.
The Portent and Other Stories. N.p., 1909.
Fairy Tales. N.p., 1920.
The Light Princess and Other Tales of Fantasy, edited by Roger Lancelyn Green. London, Gollancz, 1961.
Evenor, edited by Lin Carter. New York, Ballantine, 1972.
The Gifts of the Child Christ and Other Tales. London, Sampson Low, 2 vols., 1882; as *Stephen Archer and Other Tales,* 1883; as *The Gifts of the Child Christ: Fairy Tales and Stories for the Childlike,* edited by Glenn Edward Sadler, Grand Rapids, Michigan, Eerdmans, and London, Mowbray, 1973.
The Complete Fairy Tales of George MacDonald. New York, Schocken, 1977.
The World of George MacDonald: Selections from His Works of Fiction. Wheaton, Illinois, Harold Shaw, 1978.
The Christmas Stories of George MacDonald, illustrated by Linda Hill Griffith. Elgin, Illinois, Cook, 1981.

OTHER PUBLICATIONS

Novels

David Elginbrod. London, Hurst and Blackett, 3 vols., 1863; New York, Munro, 1879.

Alec Forbes of Howglen. London, Hurst and Blackett, 3 vols., 1865; New York, Harper, 1872.

Annals of a Quiet Neighbourhood. London, Hurst and Blackett, 3 vols., 1867; New York, Harper, 1867.

Guild Court. London, Hurst and Blackett, 3 vols., 1867; New York, Harper, 1868.

Robert Falconer. London, Hurst and Blackett, 3 vols., 1868; Boston, Loring, n.d.

The Seaboard Parish. London, Tinsley, 3 vols., 1868; New York, Routledge, 1868.

Ranald Bannerman's Boyhood, illustrated by Arthur Hughes. London, Strahan, and New York, Routledge, 1871.

The Vicar's Daughter: An Autobiographical Story. Boston, Roberts, 1871; London, Tinsley, 3 vols., 1872.

Wilfrid Cumbermede. London, Hurst and Blackett, 3 vols., 1872; New York, Scribner, 1872.

Gutta-Percha Willie, The Working Genius, illustrated by Arthur Hughes. London, King, and Boston, Hoyt, 1873.

Malcolm. London, King, 3 vols., 1875; Philadelphia, Lippincott, 1875.

St. George and St. Michael. London, King, 3 vols., 1876; New York, Ford, 1876(?).

Thomas Wingfold, Curate. London, Hurst and Blackett, 3 vols., 1876; New York, Munro, 1879.

The Marquis of Lossie. London, Hurst and Blackett, 3 vols., 1877; Philadelphia, Lippincott, 1877.

Paul Faber, Surgeon. London, Hurst and Blackett, 3 vols., 1879; Philadelphia, Lippincott, 1879.

Sir Gibbie. London, Hurst and Blackett, 3 vols., 1879; Philadelphia, Lippincott, 1879.

Mary Marston. London, Sampson Low, 3 vols., 1881; Philadelphia, Lippincott, 1881.

Warlock o' Glen Warlock. New York, Harper, 1881; as *Castle Warlock: A Homely Romance,* London, Sampson Low, 3 vols., 1882.

Weighed and Wanting. London, Sampson Low, 3 vols., 1882; New York, Harper, 1882.

Donal Grant. London, Kegan Paul, 3 vols., 1883; New York, Harper, 1883.

What's Mine's Mine. London, Kegan Paul, 3 vols., 1886; New York, Harper, 1886.

Home Again. London, Kegan Paul, and New York, Appleton, 1887.

The Elect Lady. London, Kegan Paul, and New York, Munro, 1888.

A Rough Shaking, illustrated by W. Parkinson. New York, Routledge, 1890; London, Blackie, 1891.

There and Back. London, Kegan Paul, 3 vols., 1891: Boston, Lothrop, n.d.

Heather and Snow. London, Chatto and Windus, 2 vols., 1893; New York, Harper, 1893.

Salted with Fire. London, Hurst and Blackett, and New York, Dodd Mead, 1897.

Short Stories

Far above Rubies. New York, Dodd Mead, 1899.

Poetry

Within and Without: A Dramatic Poem. London, Longman, 1855; New York, Scribner, 1872.

Poems. London, Longman, 1857.

A Hidden Life and Other Poems. London, Longman, 1864; New York, Scribner, 1872.

The Disciple and Other Poems. London, Strahan, 1867.

Dramatic and Miscellaneous Poems. New York, Scribner, 2 vols., 1876.

A Book of Strife, in the Form of the Diary of an Old Soul. Privately printed, 1880.

A Threefold Cord: Poems by Three Friends, with John Hill MacDonald and Greville Matheson, edited by George MacDonald. Privately printed, 1883.

The Poetical Works of George MacDonald. London, Chatto and Windus, 2 vols., 1893.

Rampolli: Growths from a Long-Planted Root, Being Translations Chiefly from the German, Along with a "Year's Diary of an Old Soul." London, Longman, 1897.

Other

Unspoken Sermons. London, Strahan and Longman, 3 vols., 1867, 1886, 1889; New York, Routledge, n.d.

England's Antiphon. London, Macmillan, 1868; Philadelphia, Lippincott, n. d.

The Miracles of Our Lord. London, Strahan, and New York, Randolph, 1870.

Orts. London, Sampson Low, 1882; as *The Imagination and Other Essays,* Boston, Lothrop, 1883; revised edition, as *A Dish of Orts.* Sampson Low, 1893.

The Tragedie of Hamlet, Prince of Denmark: A Study of the Text of the Folio of 1623. London, Longman, 1885.

The Hope of the Gospel (sermons). London, Ward Lock, and New York, Appleton, 1892.

The Hope of the Universe. London, Victoria Street Society for the Protection of Animals from Vivisection, 1896.

George MacDonald: An Anthology, edited by C. S. Lewis. London, Bles, 1946; New York, Macmillan, 1947.

Editor, *A Cabinet of Gems, Cut and Polished by Sir Philip Sidney, Now for the More Radiance Presented Without Their Setting.* London, Elliot Stock, 1892.

Translator, *Twelve of the Spiritual Songs of Novalis.* Privately printed, 1851.

Translator, *Exotics: A Translation of the Spiritual Songs of Novalis, The Hymn Book of Luther, and Other Poems from the German and Italian.* London, Strahan, 1876.

*

Bibliography: *A Centennial Bibliography of George MacDonald* by John Malcolm Bullock, Aberdeen, University Press, 1925; *George MacDonald's Books for Children: A Bibliography of First Editions* by Raphael B. Shaberman, London, Cityprint Business Centres, 1979.

Critical Studies: *George MacDonald and His Wife* by Greville MacDonald, London, Allen and Unwin, 1924; *The Golden Key: A*

Study of the Fiction of George MacDonald by R. L. Wolfe, New Haven, Connecticut, Yale University Press, 1961; *The Harmony Within: The Spiritual Vision of George MacDonald* by Rolland Hein, Grand Rapids, Michigan, Christian University Press; *George MacDonald* by David S. Robb, Edinburgh, Scottish Academy, 1987; Eureka, California, Sunrise, 1989; *George MacDonald* by William Raeper, Tring, Hertfordshire, and Batavia, Illinois, Lion, 1987; *The Gold Thread: Essays on George MacDonald* edited by William Raeper, Edinburgh, Edinburgh University Press, 1990.

*   *   *

From the incredible tide of fantasy literature that washed over—or welled up from—Victorian England (a flood that includes such exceptional names as Carroll, Barrie, Kingsley, Lang, Haggard and Morris) it is hard to pick a fish more strange, and yet somehow completely representative of his peers, than George MacDonald, that involuntarily expatriate Scotsman who was both humble, selfless minister and well-paid, auditorium-filling showman; mystically devout Christian and (on some deeper level) earthy Celtic pagan; poor rural child and (relatively) prosperous cosmopolitan adult. And, as a testament to the power of his fantastic visions, out of the 52 books he compiled in his 42-year career, it is only his fairy tales for children and "faerie romances for men and women" which remain supremely alive today.

Losing his pulpit in 1852 for preaching what the congregation considered heresy (the notion that the souls of animals might end up in heaven along with those of humans), MacDonald turned more and more to writing and editing to support his growing family (eventually amounting to eleven children). Plagued all his long life by ill health and debts, he nevertheless remained unswerving to his new vocation, once turning down an offer of $20,000 per year (a fortune for the 19th century) to become the pastor of an American church.

Beginning as a poet, MacDonald experienced his first success with the publication of a book-length poem entitled *Within and Without*. He would continue to write poetry all his life—embedding many verses within both his books and his letters—but fantasy elements in *The Poetical Works of George MacDonald* are sparse. "The Golden Key" is a first working-out of the plot found in the vastly superior story of the same name. Ballads such as "The Unseen Model," "The Homeless Ghost" and "The Dead Hand" are Poe-like bits of macabre, possibly showing the influence of one of MacDonald's early favourites, E. T. A. Hoffmann. "The Sangreal" deals with Arthurian legend. Only the long "Somnium Mystici" captures bits of the same sense of dreamlike, sometimes unspeakably numinous revelations which form the backbone of his prose fantasies.

A man of wide-ranging interests (he once seriously considered becoming a chemist, was noted as a Shakespearean scholar, and was keenly interested in the burgeoning science of evolution, salting his works with metaphors involving extinction and the early fruits of creation), MacDonald was to produce many mimetic novels, some with autobiographical content. But for his first book-length fiction, he chose to work in the mode of dream romance—a mode which he would triumphantly return to at the end of his career.

Phantastes is the story of a youth named Anodos and his sojourn on another plane of existence fraught with allegorical marvels. The protagonist's name itself is possibly meant to evoke thoughts of "anodyne," but no precise mappings are suitable for most of MacDonald's allegories, which are slippery and elusive.

And from book to book, his symbols become multi-valued: as a single example, the good snake creature of *The Princess and Curdie* becomes the traditional evil snake of "The Light Princess". As critic Roger Lancelyn Green says, "[His] is a magic hard to explain: if we could explain the story it would not be there any more—just as if we tried to cut up a soap-bubble to see how the lovely colours were put into it."

The first two chapters of this novel are remarkable for how many of MacDonald's favourite and most resonant archetypes appear: dead, but not necessarily lost parents (MacDonald's birth-mother died when he was quite young); flowing streams and dark forests that overwhelm man-made creation; hidden doors; and, most importantly, the image of the Wise Woman, a deity both old and young, human and supernatural, often depicted with long flowing hair that trails off into mist, who is a combination of many Biblical figures (Eve, both Marys) as well as older vessels of wisdom.

Phantastes departs in several places from the main narrative to include ill-fitting independent stories and is flawed to that extent. But its remarkably odd, surprisingly non-Christian imagery is very potent. Anodos spends decades on the dream-plane, his consciousness finally experiencing a vivid death, burial and disintegration/reintegration, only to awake in his own land after an absence of a mere three weeks, forever transformed by the spiritual resurrection which, for MacDonald, was a necessary prelude to true life.

The Portent is MacDonald's next foray into the supernatural. This is the story of another sensitive youth, Duncan Campbell, who, taking the position of tutor at a cold-hearted estate, finds himself fated to love the eerie young woman who is the reincarnation of his lost soulmate, as he himself is the reincarnation of hers. Guided by the crone who raised him (this book's Wise Woman), and who possesses "the second sight," Campbell eventually wins through all obstacles to secure his bride, but not without cost.

Notable is the evocative description of the deserted and haunted half of the mansion where much of the book's action takes place. MacDonald's geographies are frequently projections of psychic landscapes, as is made explicit in "The Day Boy and the Night Girl," when one of the title characters wonders: "Was it outside of her, or something taking place in her head?" Also of interest is MacDonald's deliberate blending of good and evil: not only is Campbell the reincarnation of the ancient good lover, but he also appears at times to embody qualities and traits of his ancient rival, who rides through time forever on a horse with one clanking shoe.

MacDonald's next fantasy, *At the Back of the North Wind,* marks the beginning of his string of remarkable, uncondescending tales for children, many of the shorter of which were first told orally or written down for his own brood. The tale of a young boy named Diamond who has the beautiful but elementally harsh and Olympian North Wind as his secret friend (she can appear as a woman of any size, from sprite-like to gigantic), the book is divided into three unequal portions. In the first, Diamond experiences many adventures with the North Wind, including a visit to her kingdom, all of which transfigure his already gentle personality into something almost saintly. The middle portion of the book is the Dickensian depiction of Diamond's daily life and struggles, in which his earlier adventures stand him in good stead, though the North Wind is notably offstage. The two penultimate chapters of the book reintroduce the North Wind, who comes to claim Diamond as her own, transporting him to her titular realm which, in many ways, is a synonym for the land beyond death.

The Princess and the Goblin is a more traditional fairy tale, set in the requisite medieval kingdom, one menaced by burrowing goblins, more clumsy and ridiculous than nasty, precursors of the Nomes who continually threaten Oz. The child-princess in danger is rescued by the miner boy Curdie, who refuses an offer from her father the king to accompany them to court, preferring the simple life with his parents. The mystical power of the book lies entirely with the princess's great-great-grandmother, who dwells high in a tower not easily accessible to all, or at all times. A figure who changes age and appearance dramatically, who spins moonlight and refreshes souls in a fire of burning roses, she is the force of duty and necessity, a compelling voice out of the whirlwind whose tools are stubborn mortals whom she loves, but must often break before they are suitable for her hidden uses.

The sequel, *The Princess and Curdie,* is a much different book. Darker, richer, more poetic in its diction, it tells of Curdie's journey to the king's city under the direction of the princess's grandmother ("The Mistress of the Silver Moon") in order to rescue it from human treachery and accompanying decay. Curdie assumes Christ-like proportions ("I am come to set things right in this house"), and debased conspirators are righteously executed. The compressed ending of the book allots Curdie and his princess bride a happy and just reign, but the kingdom is eventually expunged from the face of the earth due to a resurgence of greed and indifference.

The Wise Woman relates the "prince-and-pauper" moral adventures of two bad girls, each spoiled in a different way, who receive a perhaps over-preachy chastisement from the title character, whose magic house is the most compelling item in the story. *The Flight of the Shadow* reads at first like a fantasy in the vein of *The Portent,* with mysterious ghostly riders appearing at symbolic moments in the life of a cloistered woman raised by her kind but tormented uncle much in the manner of *The Tempest*'s Prospero and Miranda. (Narrated convincingly in first-person by the niece, this book adds to MacDonald's reputation as an empathizer and worshiper of women.) However, all supernatural elements are explained away by the revelation of the uncle's long-lost twin, who was the spectre.

At age 71, MacDonald produced his last long fantasy, *Lilith.* Like the earlier *Phantastes,* it is the story of a young man's journey through a dimension which is essentially the reified battlefield of impulses warring within him and within every human heart. At first written almost automatically (the original manuscript ran from page to page with little punctuation or paragraphing), but later extensively revised, *Lilith* is more consistent in its narrative and symbolic thrust than *Phantastes* and is less weird. As Mr. Vane struggles to best the hideously wounded yet attractive Lilith, whom he both loves and hates, he is aided by an elvish tribe of Little Ones (whose method of speaking and thinking is convincingly *other*) and by the parents of the human race, a crotchety Adam and a rather underutilized Eve. As in MacDonald's first novel (with which it shares, across 40 years, an enigmatic epigram from Novalis: "Our life is no dream, but it should and will perhaps become one") the hero literally dies back into our world.

Throughout his career, MacDonald was also a prolific short-story writer, and many of his shorter works are fully as deep as his longer books. (Over the years, the stories have been mixed and matched in various reprint editions, making bibliographical notation difficult.) "The Carasoyn" is a brilliant depiction of the trouble inherent in dealing with fairies, evocative of the work of such latter-day writers as Jack Vance. "The Golden Key" is notable for its transcendant image of ghostly figures endlessly climbing a rainbow. "Cross Purposes" exhibits beautiful dream transitions akin to those in Lewis Carroll's books (the two men were friends). Both "The Gray Wolf" and "The Cruel Painter" share ties with *Lilith,* the former for its were-beast theme, the latter for its vampirish love-object named—Lilith.

A spiritual man, MacDonald always acknowledged earthly passions. In *Phantastes,* a subplot about a girl with a singing sphere which the hero breaks (she weeps, but later claims it was the best thing that ever happened to her), is remarkably sexual, as are the caresses of the Little Ones, which the narrator of *Lilith* enjoys. In so many of his books, characters long for a simple redemptive kiss, perhaps nowhere more tellingly than in the story "Birth, Dreaming, Death," in which a friendless miser receives from his old nurse "the last unction of a woman's kiss."

Literally wordless and frail for the final five years of his life, MacDonald was tended until death by his youngest daughter, who surely gave him that final kiss.

—Paul Di Filippo

MAHY, Margaret

Nationality: New Zealander. **Born:** Whakatane, 21 March 1936. **Education:** University of Auckland, B.A. 1957, Diploma of Librarianship 1958. **Family:** Has two daughters. **Career:** Assistant librarian, Petone Public Library, 1958-59; librarian, School Library Service, Christchurch, 1967-76; since 1976 children's librarian, Canterbury Public Library, Christchurch. **Awards:** New Zealand Library Association Esther Glen award, 1970, 1973, 1983, 1985; New Zealand Literary Fund grant, 1975; British Library Association Carnegie Medal, 1983, 1985; *Observer* prize, 1987. **Address:** R.D.1, Lyttelton, New Zealand.

FANTASY PUBLICATIONS

Novels

The Haunting. London, Dent, 1982; New York, Atheneum, 1983.
The Changeover: A Supernatural Romance. London, Dent, and New York, Atheneum, 1984.
The Catalogue of the Universe. London, Dent, 1985; New York, Atheneum, 1986.
Aliens in the Family. London, Methuen, and New York, Scholastic, 1986.
The Tricksters. London, Dent, 1986; New York, McElderry, 1987.
Memory. London, Dent, and New York, McElderry, 1987.

Fiction for Younger Children

The Dragon of an Ordinary Family, illustrated by Helen Oxenbury. New York, Watts, and London, Heinemann, 1969.
A Lion in the Meadow, illustrated by Jenny Williams. New York, Watts, and London, Dent, 1969; augmented edition, as *A Lion in the Meadow and Five Other Favourites,* Dent, 1976.
Mrs. Discombobulous, illustrated by Jan Brychta. New York, Watts, and London, Dent, 1969.
Pillycock's Shop, illustrated by Carol Barker. New York, Watts, and London, Dobson, 1969.

The Procession, illustrated by Charles Mozley. New York, Watts, and London, Dent, 1969.

The Little Witch, illustrated by Charles Mozley. New York, Watts, and London, Dent, 1970.

Sailor Jack and the 20 Orphans, illustrated by Robert Bartelt. New York, Watts, and London, Dent, 1970.

The Princess and the Clown, illustrated by Carol Barker. New York, Watts, and London, Dobson, 1971.

The Boy with Two Shadows, illustrated by Jenny Williams. New York, Watts, and London, Dent, 1971.

The Man Whose Mother Was a Pirate, illustrated by Brian Froud. London, Dent, 1972; New York, Atheneum, 1973.

The Railway Engine and the Hairy Brigands, illustrated by Brian Froud. London, Dent, 1973.

Rooms for Rent, illustrated by Jenny Williams. New York, Watts, 1974; as *Rooms to Let,* London, Dent, 1975.

The Witch in the Cherry Tree, illustrated by Jenny Williams. London, Dent, and New York, Parents' Magazine Press, 1974.

Clancy's Cabin, illustrated by Trevor Stubley. London, Dent, 1974.

The Rare Spotted Birthday Party, illustrated by Belinda Lyon. London, Watts, 1974.

Stepmother, illustrated by Terry Burton. London, Watts, 1974.

The Bus Under the Leaves, illustrated by Margery Gill. London, Dent, 1975.

Ultra-Violet Catastrophe! or, The Unexpected Walk with Great-Uncle Magnus Pringle, illustrated by Brian Froud. London, Dent, and New York, Parents' Magazine Press, 1975.

The Great Millionaire Kidnap, illustrated by Jan Brychta. London, Dent, 1975.

The Boy Who Was Followed Home, illustrated by Steven Kellogg. New York, Watts, 1975; London, Dent, 1977.

Leaf Magic, illustrated by Jenny Williams. London, Dent, 1976; New York, Parents' Magazine Press, 1977.

The Wind Between the Stars, illustrated by Brian Froud. London, Dent, 1976.

David's Witch Doctor, illustrated by Jim Russell. London, Watts, 1976.

The Pirate Uncle, illustrated by Mary Dinsdale. London, Dent, 1977.

Nonstop Nonsense, illustrated by Quentin Blake. London, Dent, 1977; New York, McElderry, 1989.

The Great Piratical Rumbustification, and The Librarian and the Robbers, illustrated by Quentin Blake. London, Dent, 1978; Boston, Godine, 1986.

Raging Robots and Unruly Uncles, illustrated by Peter Stevenson. London, Dent, 1981.

The Pirates' Mixed-Up Voyage, illustrated by Margaret Chamberlain. London, Dent, 1983; New York, Dial, 1993.

Jam: A True Story, illustrated by Helen Craig. London, Dent, 1985; Boston, Atlantic Monthly Press, 1986.

The Blood and Thunder Adventure on Hurricane Peak, illustrated by Wendy Smith. London, Dent, 1989.

Short Stories

The First, Second, Third Margaret Mahy Story Book: Stories and Poems, illustrated by Shirley Hughes. London, Dent, 3 vols., 1972-75.

The Great Chewing-Gum Rescue and Other Stories, illustrated by Jan Ormerod. London, Dent, 1982.

Leaf Magic and Five Other Favourites, illustrated by Margaret Chamberlain. London, Dent, 1984.

The Birthday Burglar, and A Very Wicked Headmistress, illustrated by Margaret Chamberlain. London, Dent, 1984; Boston, Godine, 1988.

The Downhill Crocodile Whizz and Other Stories, illustrated by Ian Newsham. London, Dent, 1986.

Mahy Magic, illustrated by Shirley Hughes. London, Dent, 3 vols., 1986.

The Horrible Story and Others, illustrated by Shirley Hughes. London, Dent, 1987.

The Door in the Air and Other Stories, illustrated by Diana Catchpole. London, Dent, 1988.

Plays

Television Scripts: *A Land Called Happy Woolly Valley*; *Once Upon a Story*; *The Margaret Mahy Story Book Theatre.*

Poetry

Seventeen Kings and Forty Two Elephants, illustrated by Charles Mozley. London, Dent, 1972; New York, Dial Press, 1987.

The Tin Can Band and Other Poems, illustrated by Honey de Lacey. London, Dent, 1989.

OTHER PUBLICATIONS

Other

New Zealand: Yesterday and Today. London, Watts, 1975.
Plus numerous brief readers for young children.

*   *   *

Margaret Mahy has produced many fantasies for children, but is probably best known for her two Carnegie Medal-winning novels, *The Haunting* and *The Changeover.* In most of her novels, Mahy selects a moment in time when the main character is going through a momentous period of change, often from child to adult.

In *The Changeover,* Laura Chant, a girl who foresees danger, is confronted with a series of difficult conflicts: her divorced mother is developing a new relationship; her small brother, Jacko, is dying after being stamped on the hand by the sinister Carmody Braque, his life being eaten away while Braque visibly rejuvenates; and Laura herself, who has always known that Sorensen Carlisle at her school is a witch, finds herself drawn into the sorcerous Carlisle household as the only hope of saving Jacko. The development of her relationship with Sorensen, hitherto an unspoken acknowledgement, progresses as Sorry learns to admit to human love after being deeply scarred by childhood experiences of abuse; and Laura, as she undergoes the changeover to become a full witch as the only means of rescuing Jacko, becomes adult, her growing closeness to Sorry mirroring the evolution of her mother's relationship to Chris, her new lover. The need for acceptance of the changes and for mother and daughter to understand that each must be allowed to make their own decisions, while Laura and Sorry also struggle to contain their own immediate desires—both sexual and witchly vengeful—make for conflicts which require (and receive) the most skilful and sensitive handling.

The Tricksters also deals with an alteration in the power-structure of a family, this time from the viewpoint of Harry Hamilton, the 17-year old middle daughter in a family of five dominated by the beautiful and arrogant Christobel. Gathering for Christmas in Carnival's Hide, their summer house in New Zealand, the family is disrupted by the addition of sinister visitors. The three Carnival brothers, apparently descendants of the Carnival who built the house, are accepted by the other Hamiltons at face value, but Harry believes that in some fashion the three are connected with the violent death of Teddy Carnival many years before, and even more closely with her own secret writing, in which her characters closely resemble the brothers. Even the house itself seems to know the Carnivals, reverting to an earlier decor overnight, and Harry's gradual understanding that the trio are in fact the three different natures of Teddy, each struggling for dominance, develops alongside her final revolt against Christobel and the secret which poisons her own family.

The Catalogue of the Universe is yet another treatment of growing up. *Memory,* too, deals with the concepts of maturing and responsibility, where Jonny, the hero, has to learn the difference between truth and his imagination in order to be able to grow into adulthood, doing so while caring for the chance-met Sophie, an elderly lady suffering from senile dementia. *Aliens in the Family* deals with another form of maturity, where children of divorced parents, one on a visit to her remarried father and her new stepbrother and sister, become involved with Bond, an alien boy who has come to earth to undergo a test for his school. In the process of overcoming Bond's enemies, the three discover what is actually important, as opposed to the faces they present to the world.

The Haunting deals with equally crucial issues in a story in which young Barney is being haunted by his uncle, one of the Scholar family magicians. It is unclear at first whether the haunting is with sinister intent or from loneliness, and the pursuit of a solution is confused by the family's circumstances—Barney's mother is dead, his father remarried, and his two sisters either too loquacious or deeply silent. It is plain being a magician is to be set apart, an unwelcome heritage which is fought rather than sought, and the dynamics of the whole family are altered by the conclusion, when it becomes known that not Barney but his silent sister, Troy, is the magician. Again, Mahy deals with the difference between expectations and reality, a subject she understands deeply, and in the process produces descriptive prose of an enviable quality.

Mahy always engenders hope in her work, so that change, no matter how unsettling, is always the prelude to something better. Using New Zealand for her settings, the fantasies she develops deal with difference rather than plain sorcery, most commonly within the context of family politics; they are compelling and immediate, and her characters possess great depth and sympathy as well as humour and charm. Mahy's output should be read by all age groups: her prose deserves respect, both for its directness and for powers of description outstanding even in a field renowned for good writing.

—Mary Corran

MAJORS, Simon. *See* **FOX, Gardner (Francis).**

MANN, Jack. *See* **VIVIAN, E. Charles.**

MARKS, Laurie J.

Nationality: American. **Born:** 27 March, 1957 in Newport Beach, California. **Education:** Attended Westmont College; Brown University, B.A., 1980. **Career:** Author. Farm manager of family-owned orange grove, Riverside, California, 1980-89; farmer in San Luis Obispo County, California, 1989—; Youth Service Center, Inc., secretary, 1985-87; Riverside County Coalition for Alternatives to Domestic Violence, program assistant, 1987-88; Rape Survivors' Support Group, Riverside Area Rape Crisis Center, volunteer facilitator, 1988-89; Children's Advocacy Council of Riverside, secretary/coordinator, 1988-89; San Luis Obispo Literary Council, administrative assistant, 1990-92, marketing consultant, 1992—. **Agent:** Valerie Smith, Route 44-55, R.D. Box 160, Modena, New York 12548, USA. **Address:** San Luis Obispo County, California.

FANTASY PUBLICATIONS

Novels (series: Children of Triad)

Delan the Mislaid (Triad). New York, DAW, 1989.
The Moonbane Mage (Triad). New York, DAW, 1990.
Ara's Field (Triad). New York, DAW, 1991.
The Watchmaker's Mask. New York, DAW, 1992.
Dancing Jack. New York, DAW, 1993.

*   *   *

One of the most difficult tasks in science fiction or fantasy is to write a story in which the protagonist is not a human being without making it difficult for the reader to identify with that character. Laurie J. Marks assumed that very task with her first novel, *Delan the Mislaid,* and proved equal to the demand. Delan is an apparently deformed being shunned by everyone he meets and cruelly treated by a sorcerer before he meets Eia, who recognizes him as one of her own kind and helps him through a metamorphosis into one of the Aeyrie, a race of beautiful winged creatures.

Delan finds a new home among a hermaphroditic people who have mastered a technology far in advance of the rest of this magical realm. Unfortunately, Delan is still under the sorcerous influence of the villainous Teksan, who hopes to use his thrall as a tool to steal the Aeyrie's secrets and destroy their influence in the world. Fortunately Delan overcomes the curse at a critical moment and the sorcerer is defeated.

Delan the Mislaid is the opening volume of Children of Triad, a genuine trilogy in that the individual books are separate tales and not just sections of a larger work. The follow-up, *The Moonbane Mage,* concentrates on Laril, another member of the Aeyrie, heir to the leadership position of that race. Unfortunately, Laril is headstrong and thoughtless and commits a crime for which exile is the only suitable punishment.

Laril is sent to another community but inadvertently winds up in a mysterious Aeyrie kingdom whose ruler has abandoned the race's usual disdain for power. Raulyn plans to use Aeyrie technology to become master of the world, and aims to use Laril as one of his weapons. With an army of Walkers, non-winged soldiers who dominate the lowlands, he sets out, opposed and eventually defeated by Delan and the rest of the Aeyrie. The sequel lacks some of the original novelty of the first, and the villain lacks real substance, but the rest of the characters are well delineated and the aerial duels are convincing and thrilling.

The final volume is *Ara's Field*. The world has been divided among the Aeyrie in the sky, the Walkers on the land, and the Mer on the sea for countless ages, and the rivalry among them has often been violent. Triad is a small settlement where representatives of all three races have found a way to live in uneasy but lasting harmony, and they wish to extend it throughout the world.

Unfortunately, in order to derail this plan, someone is systematically assassinating high-ranking members of two species, and blaming the crimes on the Mer. Delan leaves life as an artist once again to assist his people, this time by discovering the true identity of the killers, a secret which reveals the existence of a mysterious fourth race. The trilogy concludes on a hopeful note, although the world of the Aeyrie is rich enough that we may yet see the author return to this setting for further adventures.

Marks's next novel, *The Watcher's Mask,* has an altogether different and equally original setting. On the island of Callia dwell the many-souled people, a race whose leaders' bodies encompass a number of disparate personalities. A brutal and ambitious warlord decides to seize control of the entire island, and to ensure the continuity of his rule he has enslaved the many-souled and conditioned them to become his personal servants, using their multi-layered wisdom to defeat his enemies.

The protagonist is one of these people, a woman who in one persona or another has broken rebellions, exposed malcontents, and generally helped to maintain the status quo. Unfortunately, she is sometimes unable to remember what she did while another persona was in control and fears for her own sanity. In fact, another element of her multiple identities has overcome the ruler's conditioning and is actually undermining his reign, although some of her potential allies are ethically opposed to violence and refuse to help her plot the death of the emperor. Ultimately she discovers that violence isn't always the proper solution, and the novel ends unexpectedly with a limited reconciliation between the emperor and his subjects rather than the familiar rebellion.

Marks' most recent novel is *Dancing Jack,* another non-traditional fantasy. The setting bears some superficial resemblance to that of *The Watcher's Mask,* although it is a far more technologically advanced world, something akin to Earth in the 19th century. The protagonist is a woman who has retreated mentally and physically from the aftermath of a failed rebellion, hoping to live out her years tilling the fields of her now-dead family's holdings. Ash believes herself the last of her line until she hears rumours that one of her nephews may have survived, and may possess the hereditary magical abilities of her family. Ash abandons her farm to track him down, only to walk into fresh trouble when she finds him acting as part of yet another attempt to rebel against the authoritarian government of their world. This time there's no compromise, and her enemy dies before Ash can resume her life.

Although her plots are familiar ones, Marks embellishes them adroitly enough, and her settings are fully realized, inventive, and colourful. There's also a clear progression in ability through the novels, each more polished than the preceding ones. Marks seems on the verge of separating herself from the pack of competent fantasy writers and emerging as one of the more innovative and interesting ones. Time will tell us if that promise will be fulfilled.

—Don D'Ammassa

MARLEY, Stephen

Nationality: British. **Born:** 1946. **Address:** c/o Legend Books, Random House, 20 Vauxhall Bridge Road, London SW1V 2SA.

FANTASY PUBLICATIONS

Novels (series: Chia Black Dragon in all books)

Spirit Mirror. London, Collins, 1988.
Mortal Mask. London, Legend, 1991.
Shadow Sisters. London, Legend, 1993.

OTHER PUBLICATIONS

Novels

The Life of the Virgin Mary. Luton, Bedfordshire, Lennard, 1988.
Dreddlocked. London, Virgin, 1993.
Dread Dominion. London, Virgin, 1994.
Managra. London, Virgin, 1995.

*   *   *

All three of Marley's fantasy novels are set against a background of Ancient China, blending myth, magic and history, and although all of them involve the same principal character each can be read in isolation.

The first, *Spirit Mirror,* is poor in comparison with the two later novels but is important as it introduces the principle character, Chia the sorceress of Black Dragon Mountain. It begins on the Eve of the Feast of the Dead. On that night, Chia sees in a dream a former lover, Fu the Unlucky, being dragged into the ancient burial mound set atop Spirit Hill. From the nearby town of San Lung, people are disappearing. Other strange happenings, usually involving reflective surfaces, cause the abbot of the Buddhist temple in the vicinity to send for the sorcerer of Luminous Cloud Mountain. Chia, drawn by her visions, arrives before him and suspects that behind all the events is her old adversary, Nyak. Both Chia and Nyak are immortals, Chia is the daughter of a Celestial Being, Nyak the offspring of the last of the Thzan-tzai (shape-changing immortals) and a human woman—or so she believes. Chia's body undergoes regeneration roughly every three years and during this process some memory is lost. At the point at which this story is set, Chia is about to fall into the death sleep of renewal, and so her powers of concentration are not at their best and she makes mistakes. At the end of this book she discovers the truth, that she and Nyak are twins and that they killed their father in the tomb of Spirit Hill. While the more resilient Chia is able to cope with this knowledge, it destroys Nyak, literally.

Mortal Mask takes up the story two years later. Although Nyak's body has been destroyed, his spirit lives on, determined to revenge itself on Chia by merging with her to recreate the powerful hermaphrodite Thzan-tzai being that their father had been. Chia is drawn to Silver Music Bay after the death of her dogs leads her to suspect that Nyak may not be totally finished with her. Gradually, as she begins to remember, a picture of her true origins starts to emerge. The fact that things appear to be different from the original story told in *Spirit Mirror* are explained by Chia's faulty memory. This gives Marley the opportunity to flesh out the family history of Chia and Nyak and to make changes where the new facts don't match with his original conception.

Shadow Sisters continues Chia's story. It is set 400 years after the end of *Mortal Mask* and begins in seventh-century Rome where Chia is involved in an attempt to overthrow the Pope. As everything goes horribly wrong she flees back to China pursued by a group of zealots determined to destroy her. Back in China she discovers that she has become a cult figure, and a group of women, determined to destroy the current Emperor, act in her name. Once again she finds herself drawn to the San Lung area. The town has been long deserted, peopled now only by malicious ghosts, and the Buddhist Temple, abandoned at the end of *Spirit Mirror,* has become the sinister Shadow Hill, which attracts rocks and boulders towards it. Once again, Chia can only triumph by remembering things from her past that are deeply buried.

In many ways this series charts the evolution of a fictitious plot. In the beginning ideas are tentative, half-formed (as is Chia's background in *Spirit Mirror*), but as the characters establish their identities in the latter two novels, pieces fall into place, giving clarity to the whole. Things which are unknown to Chia at the start are unknown to the author also, so discovery and enlightenment are two-way. The writing itself shows the same kind of development between the first volume and its sequel; Marley has a much clearer, more positive style in both *Mortal Mask* and *Shadow Sisters* than in *Spirit Mirror.* He uses a blend of genre techniques, and although the main thrust is that of myth-based historical fantasy there are considerable leanings towards horror in some of the descriptions.

One thing that makes Marley's style stand out from others is the use of an introspective point of view. This is particularly noticeable in the first hundred pages of *Mortal Mask.* He uses a number of different characters to introduce and carry aspects of the plot that would be limited by a single point of view, but in most cases the individuals are on their own and where there is interaction there is still a feeling of isolation as though the incident is being reviewed rather than taking place in the immediate present. While some authors would ultimately produce a work of infinite boredom using this form, Marley makes a creditable job of using isolated characters to carry the action forward with pace, interest, and curiosity.

It would have been very easy to fall into the trap of making Chia an immensely powerful, infallible goddess. In fact, she is able to make mistakes and learn by them; for her, to be immortal is not to be omnipotent, more something to regret as the people she allows herself to love inevitably age and die. In the China she knows she has a reputation for evil. She is called Castrator, Assassin, Cannibal, Desecrator—names by which her imitators in *Shadow Sisters* identify themselves—and has to live with the effects that being a living legend entail, showing the process of myth-making. Her truth is not the same as that of those who live four centuries after the event. Chia is superhuman and immortal, but she is also human and fallible and this comes over clearly in the writing. Ultimately

she is the kind of character that it is easy to identify with and who will always have plenty of scope for development.

—Pauline Morgan

MARTIN, Graham Dunstan

Nationality: British. **Born:** Yorkshire, 1932. **Career:** Lecturer in French literature, Edinburgh University, from 1965.

FANTASY PUBLICATIONS

Novels

Giftwish (as Graham Martin). London, Allen and Unwin, 1980.
Catchfire (as Graham Martin). London, Allen and Unwin, 1981.
The Soul Master. London, Allen and Unwin, 1984.
Half a Glass of Moonshine. London, Unwin Hyman, 1988.

OTHER PUBLICATIONS

Novels

Time-Slip. London, Unwin Paperbacks, 1986.
The Dream Wall. London, Unwin Paperbacks, 1987.

Other

Language, Truth and Poetry: Notes Towards a Philosophy of Literature. Edinburgh, Edinburgh University Press, 1975.
The Architecture of Experience: The Role of Language and Literature in the Construction of the World. Edinburgh, Edinburgh University Press, 1981.
Shadows in the Cave: Mapping the Conscious Universe. London, Penguin Arkana, 1990.

Editor, *Anthology of Contemporary French Poetry.* Edinburgh, Edinburgh University Press, 1972.

Translator, various works of poetry by Paul Valéry, Jean-Claude Renard, Louis Labé and others.

*   *   *

Graham Dunstan Martin's first two novels were ostensibly for children, though the style of writing marks them more as teenage novels, and they stand up quite well to adult reading. *Giftwish,* set in a fairly typical fantasy realm in our own world's remote past, is the story of 16-year-old Ewan, a country lad who is picked by Feydom's evil wizard Hoodwill to be a living sacrifice to renew the spell which cuts off Feydom from the magic of next-door Kendark, so keeping the former Twin Kingdoms apart from each other. Ewan escapes, travels across the land, meets the young witch Catchfire, and with her help, and the power of the sword Giftwish, finally destroys the Necromancer, the evil wizard who runs Kendark. Ewan finds the Crown and becomes king of Kendark.

Catchfire continues the story. An earlier Necromancer had set up the magical barrier between the countries by sacrificing a nine-year-old girl; Ewan enters the Land of Sorrow's End, a paradise limbo-world, and brings the girl back to life, so breaking the spell. He and Catchfire eventually destroy Hoodwill. Catchfire and Princess Starfall, the king of Feydom's daughter, are two halves of the same whole, and merge into a composite person; the ineffectual king abdicates, and the Two Kingdoms are reunited under Ewan and Catchfire/Starfall.

These are well-plotted and well-written stories; magic in particular is extremely well-handled. Good and evil are too clearly delineated in the characterization—though Martin is clearly making the point, by the symbolism of both Catchfire/Starfall and Kendark/Feydom, that darkness and light need each other for balance and completeness.

The Soul Master, Martin's first adult novel, continues his exploration of good and evil by using the science-fictional device of mind-domination in a fantasy novel. Kosmion has discovered a way of taking over the bodies of as many people as he wishes, leaving their minds awake but impotent in their skulls. A young musician, Lithran, is enslaved, but manages eventually to overcome the control and leads a rebellion against Kosmion. Again, good and evil are a little too polarized. Almost until the end of the book, all the bad guys effectively are Kosmion, in their speech and actions if not in their thoughts; through the viewpoint of Lithran, however, we are able to see how it feels to be forced to perform evil acts against one's will. This is a very dark book which, in its concentration on authoritarianism and domination, prefigures *The Dream Wall.*

Martin's two science-fiction novels also deal with the subjects of religion and authority. *Time-Slip* is set in a 21st-century post-holocaust Scotland in which a new religion based on the infinite number of parallel worlds removes personal responsibility—and therefore sin—because in Ifwhere you didn't commit the action which you committed in Herenow, and in the infinity of parallel worlds, one of you had to do it anyway. *The Dream Wall* is about the religion of fundamentalist Marxism-in-action. It is unusual in that the same pair of characters, Sue and John, live in communist Britain of 2116 and in pre-communist Britain of 2007; each pair dreams the lives of the other pair. Which is the real, and which the dream couple? Martin's fascination with probability and branching world-lines surfaces again when the earlier Sue prevents a political assassination which had/would have triggered the world of the later Sue—while in the future world, scientists find a way of stopping the individuality of dreaming, and so bring an end to that world.

Half a Glass of Moonshine is both more assured and more complex than Martin's earlier novels. Again he delves into the nature of consciousness, time, and possible multiple realities. Kirsty, a research lecturer in parapsychology, knows that her husband Justin was killed in a plane crash two weeks ago—but her bank manager swears that Justin withdrew £2,000 from their joint account a couple of days ago. Did Justin fake his death, or is the person who withdrew the money an impostor, or has Justin lost his memory, or could the person in the bank be an apparition, a ghost-photograph of previous Justins withdrawing money? Further apparitions, or dreams, or inexplicable psychic phenomena occur, and Kirsty spends the book trying to make sense of it all. At one point she sees a very unhappy Justin speaking to her from beyond the grave— or is she instead projecting her own worries and fears? Perhaps, after all, "reality . . . must be created by people's minds. The other

world might be, then, a sort of collective hallucination, created and maintained by those who dreamed it." There are no clearcut explanations, but what is clear (as in several of Martin's other books) is that the author does not think much of rationalist, materialist, "scientific" thinking. *Half a Glass of Moonshine* is perhaps nearer to magic realism than to fantasy or science fiction; extraordinary things occur in a very ordinary world and are debated at length, and the only real conclusion to be drawn is that asking questions is ultimately more important than finding answers.

There is relatively little action in Martin's books, and there is usually a lot of deep discussion between the characters, trying to analyse or make sense of their situation. The authorial voice is often heard, though rarely in a way that appears intrusive; one gets the impression that Martin has written his novels not so much to propound his theories as to explore them himself, along with the reader. His style is often a little formal, almost old-fashioned (cf. early Fred Hoyle), but very readable and at times quite beautiful. Despite his Yorkshire birth Martin's later writing is distinctively Scottish, not just in his use of Scottish words and settings, but in the very speech patterns and personalities of many of his characters. His characterization is excellent, especially in his later books (his female lead characters Sue and Kirsty are particularly well drawn); allowing for a little dramatization, these are people whom we might meet at any time in real life, particularly as students or academics. His plotting is sound if not always very original, and he handles deep and dark subjects with at times a deft touch of humour. His half-dozen novels have a character all of their own, and each one leaves images and questions in the mind long after it is finished. His writing matures considerably through these six novels; it is to be hoped that he returns to writing fiction.

—David V. Barrett

MASEFIELD, John (Edward)

Nationality: British. **Born:** Ledbury, Herefordshire, 1 June 1878. **Education:** Warwick School, 1888-90; cadet on merchant training ship *Conway,* Liverpool, 1891-93. **Military Service:** With the British Red Cross in France and Gallipoli, 1915; commissioned by British government to observe and write on Battle of the Somme, 1916-17. **Family:** Married Constance de la Cherois Crommelin in 1903 (died 1960); one daughter and one son. **Career:** Apprentice on White Star barque *Gilcruix* on trip to Chile, 1894; sixth officer, White Star mail ship *Adriatic,* 1895; bartender, Columbian Hotel, New York, 1895; worked at Alexander Smith carpet factory, Yonkers, New York, 1895-97; worked in City of London, 1897; clerk, Capital and Counties Bank, London, 1898-1901; art exhibition secretary, Wolverhampton, 1902; sub-editor, *Speaker* magazine, London, 1903; staff member, Manchester *Guardian,* 1904-05, and feature writer from 1907. Lectured in the United States, 1916 and 1918, and for the British Council in many European countries. President, Society of Authors, 1937-67; First President, National Book League; member, British Council Books and Periodicals Committee. **Awards:** (For poetry) Royal Society of Literature Polignac prize, 1912; Shakespeare Prize (Hamburg), 1938; William Foyle prize, 1961; National Book League prize, 1964. D.Litt.: Yale University, New Haven, Connecticut, 1918; Harvard University, Cambridge,

Massachusetts, 1918; Oxford University, 1922; Cambridge University, 1931; LL.D.: University of Aberdeen, 1922; Honorary degrees: universities of Glasgow, 1923, Manchester, 1923, Liverpool, 1930, St. Andrews, 1930, and Wales, 1932. Honorary member, American Academy, 1930; named Poet Laureate, 1930; Order of Merit, 1935; Royal Society of Literature Companion of Literature, 1961. **Died:** 12 May 1967.

FANTASY PUBLICATIONS

Novels (series: Kay Harker in both books)

The Midnight Folk. London, Heinemann, and New York, Macmillan, 1927.
The Box of Delights; or, When the Wolves Were Running. London, Heinemann, and New York, Macmillan, 1935.

OTHER PUBLICATIONS

Novels

Captain Margaret: A Romance. London, Grant Richards, and Philadelphia, Lippincott, 1908.
Multitude and Solitude. London, Grant Richards, 1909; New York, Kennerley, 1910.
The Street of To-Day. London, Dent, and New York, Dutton, 1911.
Sard Harker. London, Heinemann, and New York, Macmillan, 1924.
Odtaa. London, Heinemann, and New York, Macmillan, 1926.
The Hawbucks. London, Heinemann, and New York, Macmillan, 1929.
The Bird of Dawning; or, The Fortune of the Sea. London, Heinemann, and New York, Macmillan, 1933.
The Taking of the Gry. London, Heinemann, and New York, Macmillan, 1934.
Victorious Troy!; or, The Hurrying Angel. London, Heinemann, and New York, Macmillan, 1935.
Eggs and Baker; or, The Days of Trial. London, Heinemann, and New York, Macmillan, 1936.
The Square Peg; or, The Gun Fella. London, Heinemann, and New York, Macmillan, 1937.
Dead Ned: The Autobiography of a Corpse. London, Heinemann, and New York, Macmillan, 1938.
Live and Kicking Ned. London, Heinemann, and New York, Macmillan, 1939.
Basilissa: A Tale of the Empress Theodora. London, Heinemann, and New York, Macmillan, 1940.
Conquer: A Tale of the Nika Rebellion in Byzantium. London, Heinemann, and New York, Macmillan, 1941.
Badon Parchments. London, Heinemann, 1947.

Short Stories

A Mainsail Haul. London, Elkin Mathews, 1905; revised edition, 1913; New York, Macmillan, 1913.
A Tarpaulin Muster. London, Grant Richards, 1907; New York, Dodge, 1908
The Taking of Helen. London, Heinemann, and New York, Macmillan, 1923.

Fiction for Children

A Book of Discoveries. London, Wells Gardner, and New York, Stokes, 1910.
Lost Endeavour. London, Nelson, 1910; New York, Macmillan, 1917.
Martin Hyde, The Duke's Messenger. London, Wells Gardner, and Boston, Little Brown, 1910.
Jim Davis; or, The Captive of the Smugglers. London, Wells Gardner, 1911; New York, Stokes, 1912.

Plays

The Campden Wonder (produced London, 1907). Included in *The Tragedy of Nan and Other Plays,* 1909.
The Tragedy of Nan (produced London, 1908). Included in *The Tragedy of Nan and Other Plays,* 1909.
The Tragedy of Nan and Other Plays (includes *The Campden Wonder* and *Mrs. Harrison*). London, Grant Richards, and New York, Kennerley, 1909.
The Tragedy of Pompey the Great (produced London, 1910). London, Sidgwick and Jackson, and Boston, Little Brown, 1910; revised version (produced Manchester, 1914), Sidgwick and Jackson, and New York, Macmillan, 1914.
The Witch, adaptation of a play by Hans Wiers-Jenssen (produced Glasgow, 1910; London, 1911). New York, Brentano's, 1926; as *Anne Pedersdotter,* Boston, Little Brown, 1917.
Philip the King (produced Bristol and London, 1914). Included in *Philip the King and Other Poems,* 1914.
The Faithful (produced Birmingham, 1915; London and New York, 1919). London, Heinemann, and New York, Macmillan, 1915.
Good Friday: A Dramatic Poem (produced London, 1917). New York, Macmillan, 1915; as *Good Friday: A Play in Verse,* Letchworth, Hertfordshire, Garden City Press, 1916.
The Sweeps of Ninety-Eight (produced Birmingham, 1916). With *The Locked Chest,* Letchworth, Hertfordshire, Garden City Press, and New York, Macmillan, 1916.
The Locked Chest (produced London, 1920). With *The Sweeps of Ninety-Eight,* Letchworth, Hertfordshire, Garden City Press, and New York, Macmillan, 1916.
Esther, adaptation of the play by Racine (produced Wootton, Berkshire, 1921). London, Heinemann, and New York, Macmillan, 1922.
Berenice, adaptation of the play by Racine (produced Oxford, 1921). London, Heinemann, and New York, Macmillan, 1922.
Melloney Holtspur (produced London, 1923). London, Heinemann, and New York, Macmillan, 1922.
A King's Daughter: A Tragedy in Verse (produced Oxford, 1923; London, 1928). London, Heinemann, and New York, Macmillan, 1923.
Tristan and Isolt: A Play in Verse (produced Oxford, 1923; London, 1927). London, Heinemann, and New York, Macmillan, 1927.
The Trial of Jesus (produced London, 1926). London, Heinemann, and New York, Macmillan, 1925.
Verse and *Prose Plays.* New York, Macmillan, 2 vols., 1925.
The Coming of Christ (produced Oxford, 1928). London, Heinemann, and New York, Macmillan, 1928.
Easter: A Play for Singers. London, Heinemann, and New York, Macmillan, 1929.
End and Beginning. London, Heinemann, and New York, Macmillan, 1933.

A Play of Saint George. London, Heinemann, and New York, Macmillan, 1948.

Poetry

Salt-Water Ballads. London, Grant Richards, 1902; New York, Macmillan, 1913.

Ballads. London, Elkin Mathews, 1903; revised edition, as *Ballads and Poems,* 1910.

The Everlasting Mercy. London, Sidgwick and Jackson, and Portland, Maine, Smith and Sale, 1911.

The Story of a Round-House and Other Poems. New York, Macmillan, 1912; revised edition, 1913.

The Widow in the Bye Street. London, Sidgwick and Jackson, 1912; with *The Everlasting Mercy,* New York, Macmillan, 1912.

Dauber. London, Heinemann, 1913; with *The Daffodil Fields,* New York, Macmillan, 1923.

The Daffodil Fields. London, Heinemann, and New York, Macmillan, 1913.

Philip the King and Other Poems. London, Heinemann, and New York, Macmillan, 1914.

Good Friday and Other Poems. New York, Macmillan, 1916.

Sonnets. New York, Macmillan, 1916.

Salt-Water Poems and Ballads. New York, Macmillan, 1916; revised edition, as *Poems,* 1929, 1935, 1953.

Sonnets and Poems. Letchworth, Hertfordshire, Garden City Press, 1916.

The Cold Cotswolds. Privately printed, 1917.

Poems of John Masefield. edited by Henry Seidel Canby and others. New York, Macmillan, 1917.

Lollingdon Downs and Other Poems. New York, Macmillan, and London, Heinemann, 1917.

Rosas. New York, Macmillan, 1918.

Reynard the Fox; or, The Ghost Heath Run. New York, Macmillan, and London, Heinemann, 1919.

Animula. London, Chiswick Press, 1920.

Enslaved. New York, Macmillan, 1920.

Enslaved and Other Poems. London, Heinemann, and New York, Macmillan, 1920.

Right Royal. New York, Macmillan, and London, Heinemann, 1920.

King Cole. London, Heinemann, and New York, Macmillan, 1921.

The Dream. London, Heinemann, and New York, Macmillan, 1922.

Selected Poems. London, Heinemann, 1922; New York, Macmillan, 1923; revised edition, 1938.

King Cole and Other Poems. London, Heinemann, 1923; as *King Cole, The Dream, and Other Poems,* New York, Macmillan, 1923.

The Dream and Other Poems. New York, Macmillan, 1923.

The Collected Poems of John Masefield. London, Heinemann, 1923; revised edition, 1932, 1938; as *Poems,* 1946.

Poems. New York, Macmillan, 2 vols., 1925.

Sonnets of Good Cheer to the Lena Ashwell Players . . . London, Mendip Press, 1926.

Midsummer Night and Other Tales in Verse. London, Heinemann, and New York, Macmillan, 1928.

South and East. London, Medici Society, and New York, Macmillan, 1929.

The Wanderer of Liverpool (verse and prose). London, Heinemann, and New York, Macmillan, 1930.

Poems of the Wanderer: The Ending. Privately printed, 1930.

Minnie Maylow's Story and Other Tales and Scenes. London, Heinemann, and New York, Macmillan, 1931.

A Tale of Troy. London, Heinemann, and New York, Macmillan, 1932.

A Letter from Pontus and Other Verse. London, Heinemann, and New York, Macmillan, 1936.

Lines on the Tercentenary of Harvard University. New York, Macmillan, 1936; London, Heinemann, 1937.

The Country Scene in Poems and Pictures, illustrated by Edward Seago. London, Collins, 1936; New York, Collins, 1938.

Tribute to Ballet in Poems and Pictures, illustrated by Edward Seago. London, Collins, and New York, Macmillan, 1938.

Some Verses to Some Germans. London, Heinemann, and New York, Macmillan, 1939.

Shopping in Oxford. London, Heinemann, 1941.

Gautama the Enlightened and Other Verse. London, Heinemann, and New York, Macmillan, 1941.

Natalie Maisie and Pavilastukay: Two Tales in Verse. London, Heinemann, and New York, Macmillan, 1942.

A Generation Risen. London, Collins, 1942; New York, Macmillan, 1943.

Land Workers. London, Heinemann, 1942; New York, Macmillan, 1943.

Wonderings: Between One and Six Years. London, Heinemann, and New York, Macmillan, 1943.

Reynard the Fox . . . with Selected Sonnets and Lyrics. London, Heinemann, 1946.

On the Hill. London, Heinemann, and New York, Macmillan, 1949.

Selected Poems (new selection). London, Heinemann, and New York, Macmillan, 1950.

In Praise of Nurses. London, Heinemann, 1950.

Bluebells and Other Verse. London, Heinemann, and New York, Macmillan, 1961.

Old Raiger and Other Verse. London, Heinemann, 1964; New York, Macmillan, 1965.

In Glad Thanksgiving. London, Heinemann, and New York, Macmillan, 1967.

The Sea Poems. London, Heinemann, 1978.

Selected Poems, edited by John Betjeman. London, Heinemann, and New York, Macmillan, 1978.

Selected Poems, edited by Donald E. Stanford. Manchester, Carcanet, 1984.

Other

Sea Life in Nelson's Time. London, Methuen, 1905; New York, Macmillan, 1925.

On the Spanish Main; or, Some English Forays on the Isthmus of Darien. . . . London, Methuen, and New York, Macmillan, 1906.

Chronicles of the Pilgrim Fathers. London, Dent, and New York, Dutton, 1910.

My Faith in Woman Suffrage. London, Woman's Press, 1910.

William Shakespeare. London, Williams and Norgate, and New York, Holt, 1911; revised edition, London, Heinemann, and New York, Macmillan, 1954.

John M. Synge: A Few Personal Recollections. . . . Churchtown, Ireland, Cuala Press, and New York, Macmillan, 1915.

Gallipoli. London, Heinemann, and New York, Macmillan, 1916.

The Old Front Line; or, The Beginning of the Battle of the Somme. London, Heinemann, and New York, Macmillan, 1917.

The War and the Future. New York, Macmillan, 1918; as *St. George and the Dragon,* London, Heinemann, 1919.

The Poems and Plays of John Masefield. New York, Macmillan, 2 vols., 1918.

The Battle of the Somme. London, Heinemann, 1919.

John Ruskin. Privately printed, 1920.

The Taking of Helen and Other Prose Selections. New York, Macmillan, 1924; as *Recent Prose,* London, Heinemann, 1924; revised edition, Heinemann, 1932; Macmillan, 1933.

Shakespeare and Spiritual Life (lecture). London and New York, Oxford University Press, 1924.

With the Living Voice (lecture). London, Heinemann, and New York, Macmillan, 1925.

Oxford Recitations. New York, Macmillan, 1928.

Chaucer (lecture). Cambridge, University Press, and New York, Macmillan, 1931.

Poetry (lecture). London, Heinemann, 1931; New York, Macmillan, 1932.

The Conway: From Her Foundation to the Present Day. London, Heinemann, and New York, Macmillan, 1933; revised edition, Heinemann, 1953; Macmillan, 1954.

Collected Works (Wanderer Edition). London, Heinemann, 5 vols., 1935-37.

Some Memories of W. B. Yeats (includes verse). Dublin, Cuala Press, and New York, Macmillan, 1940.

In the Mill (autobiography). London, Heinemann, and New York, Macmillan, 1941.

The Nine Days Wonder: The Operation Dynamo. London, Heinemann, and New York, Macmillan, 1941.

The Twenty Five Days. London, Heinemann, 1941.

I Want! I Want! London, National Book Council, 1944; New York, Macmillan, 1945.

New Chum (autobiography). London, Heinemann, 1944; New York, Macmillan, 1945.

A Macbeth Production. London, Heinemann, 1945; New York, Macmillan, 1946.

Thanks Before Going. . . . London, Heinemann, 1946; New York, Macmillan, 1947; revised edition, Heinemann, 1947.

A Book of Both Sorts: Selections from the Verse and Prose of John Masefield. London, Heinemann, 1947.

A Book of Prose Selections. London, Heinemann, and New York, Macmillan, 1950.

St. Katherine of Ledbury and Other Ledbury Papers. London, Heinemann, 1951.

So Long to Learn: Chapters of an Autobiography. London, Heinemann, and New York, Macmillan, 1952.

An Elizabethan Theatre in London. Privately printed, 1954.

The Story of Ossian. London, Heinemann, and New York, Macmillan, 1959.

Grace Before Ploughing: Fragments of Autobiography. London, Heinemann, and New York, Macmillan, 1966.

The Letters of John Masefield to Florence Lamont, edited by Corliss and Lansing Lamont. London, Macmillan, and New York, Columbia University Press, 1979.

Letters to Reyna, edited by William Buchan. London, Buchan and Enright, 1983.

Letters to Margaret Bridge, 1915-1919, edited by Donald E. Stanford. Manchester, Carcanet, 1984.

Letters from the Front 1915-17, edited by Peter Vansittart. London, Constable, 1984; New York, Watts, 1985.

Brangwen: The Poet and the Dancer (letters), edited by John Gregory. Lewes, Sussex, Book Guild, 1988.

Editor, with Constance Masefield, *Lyrists of the Restoration . . .* London, Grant Richards, 1905; New York, Stokes, n.d.

Editor, *The Poems of Robert Herrick.* London, Grant Richards, 1906.

Editor, *Dampier's Voyages . . .* London, Grant Richards, 2 vols., 1906; New York, Dutton, 1907.

Editor, *A Sailor's Garland.* London, Methuen, and New York, Macmillan, 1906.

Editor, *The Lyrics of Ben Jonson, Beaumont, and Fletcher.* London, Grant Richards, 1906.

Editor, with Constance Masefield, *Essays, Moral and Polite 1660-1714.* London, Grant Richards, 1906; Freeport, New York, Books for Libraries Press, 1971.

Editor, *An English Prose Miscellany.* London, Methuen, 1907.

Editor, *Defoe* (selections). London, Bell, and New York, Macmillan, 1909.

Editor, *The Loyal Subject,* in *The Works of Beaumont and Fletcher,* edited by A. H. Bullen. London, Bell, 1910.

Editor, *My Favourite English Poems.* London, Heinemann, and New York, Macmillan, 1950.

Translator, *Polyxena's Speech from the Hecuba of Euripides.* New York, Macmillan, 1928.

*

Film Adaptations: *The Box of Delights,* 1984 (TV serial).

Bibliography: *Bibliography of John Masefield* by C. H. Simmons, New York, Columbia University Press, 1930; London, Oxford University Press, 1931.

Critical Studies: *John Masefield* by L. A. G. Strong, London, Longman, 1952; *John Masefield* by Muriel Spark, London, Peter Nevill, 1953; *John Masefield* by Margery Fisher, London, Bodley Head, and New York, Walck, 1963; *Remembering John Masefield* by Corliss Lamont, Rutherford, New Jersey, Fairleigh Dickinson University Press, 1971, London, Kaye and Ward, 1972; *John Masefield* by Sanford Sternlicht, Boston, Twayne, 1977; *John Masefield: A Life* by Constance Babington Smith, London, Oxford University Press, and New York, Macmillan, 1978.

*   *   *

John Masefield may be best known among older adults for having been Poet Laureate and for such much-anthologized verse as "I must go down to the sea again," but by and large he belongs to that large number of pre-World War II poets and novelists whose work has been overshadowed by modernism. Among his novels, romantic historical quests, full of danger and disquiet, made him popular among adults and children: *Sard Harker* (listed as an adult novel but of a type which would have been read by older children) was one such. In more ways than one, his fantasies echo the characters and images found there.

Nowadays, the televised adaptation of his children's fantasy *The Box of Delights* has become one of the classic perennials of the Christmas period, and both *Box* and its predecessor *The Midnight Folk* are parts of any serious fantasy reader's library of influential works, still capable of appealing to all ages. *The Midnight Folk* reflects Masefield's rip-roaring sea stories with its plot involving a buried pirate treasure in the grounds of Young Kay Harker's home, "Seekings", and the race to find it between Kay (presumably a descendent of the eponymous "Sard"), aided by the midnight folk—a cat, an otter and various supernatural visitations—and his governess who in reality is a witch. The mysterious and wicked Abner Brown, whose ancestor was involved in the piracy, is also part of the conspiracy.

Like much British fantasy of the first half of the century, *The Midnight Folk* has a vein of darkness and melancholy. Kay is a sensitive, orphaned boy who has had his toys removed "because they will only remind him of the past". Like all small boys, he lives in the present; we do not experience him brooding on the loss of his parents, yet clearly the fantasy elements arise from this loss. One can, if necessary, suggest obvious psychological interpretations of Kay's search for a family treasure which has been taken from him, but more generally, he is the kind of child for whom the romantic escapism of Masefield's "realistic" adventures is tailor-made. His sojourns in the "midnight world" are frequently through the mediation of dream, but often reality and otherworldliness are intertwined, and Kay experiences rather than comprehends what is happening in the way of a small child for whom the unexpected is just another form of the everyday. His innocence protects him from the strangeness and terror of some of the episodes, but although Masefield is reticent about much of the witchcraft and humorous about other aspects, it is real Black Magic which threatens Kay: "There were some strange little woodcuts on the bookshelves. When he looked at these more closely, they frightened him, much as the discs had. Then there were some most strange playing-cards with Latin underneath their figures; he did not like the look of these . . . He began to be very much afraid." After adventures through time and space, Kay is victorious over the conspirators and finds a new guardian and surrogate parent in "Caroline Louisa, who loved your Mother" previously met as one of his midnight protectors riding a black mare with golden wings.

The Box of Delights gives us an older Kay, returning to Seekings from boarding school full of heartiness and proudly acquired slang, but still out of his depth when two villains dressed as curates enter his railway carriage. He also meets an old Punch-and-Judy man, whose cryptic warning that "the wolves are running" sends Kay fully into the story's plot. The old man, Cole Hawlings, is being pursued by the "curates" and, later, hands Kay his "Box of Delights," from which all manner of marvels appear and through which Kay can be both reduced to minuscule proportions and made to travel swiftly from place to place. By using the Box, he can also travel in time, and discovers that it was made in the Middle Ages by Arnold of Lodi and came into the possession of the philosopher Ramon Lully, who himself had formulated the Elixir of Life. Also seeking the Box is the leader of the "curates": Kay's old enemy Abner Brown, who, believing that Hawlings (or, as we discover him to be, Lully) had left the box in the keeping of the Bishop of Tatchester, kidnaps the Bishop and all his fellow ecclesiastics to intimidate them into giving up the secret of the Box.

There are magical scenes here too: shape-changing wolves, Herne the Hunter, visits to the times of Arthur and of Troy. But this, as we have seen, is an older Kay. Caroline Louisa has been removed from the scene by a combination of plot-device and kidnapping but the "real" world impinges more upon Kay, sometimes to the book's disadvantage. Kay is no longer alone, but part of a social network of friends, including the delightful Maria with her passion for pistols and her pride at having been expelled from three schools. This increasing realism strains the fantasy. Whereas in *The Midnight Folk* the tonal differences between a talking fox and a squire called Sir Hassle Gassle collapse into the supremely serious whimsy with which T. H. White was to triumph a decade later in *The Sword in*

the Stone, in *The Box of Delights* the differences between Abner Brown as a Black Magician living on the same plane as Herne the Hunter and an immortal philosopher on the one hand, and as a gang leader using futuristic silver vertical-landing aircraft and fast cars to "scrobble" clergymen called Canon Honeytongue and Isaiah Dogma, pull the story in different directions. In any case, however, Masefield resolves the contradictory plot elements in an ending which need hardly have been articulated but which, by the very fact that it is, undercuts the element of the fantastic in the story.

There are passages which are amusing, passages which are deeply imaginative, and passages which are capable of raising a chill feeling at the nape of one's neck, but they rarely come together. Nevertheless, both are books that can be enjoyed by adult fantasy readers, although (as is usually the case) not for the jokes which have been inserted to appeal to adults or give a "grown-up" air to the tales but for their accurate if sometimes unnerving picture of how the ordinary and the fantastic are not, to a child, the same categories an adult would use.

—Andy Sawyer

MATSON, Norman H(aghejm)

Nationality: American. **Born:** 1893. **Family:** Married the novelist Susan Glaspell in 1925 (divorced 1932). **Career:** Journalist; contributor of short stories to various magazines. Travelled widely. **Died:** 1965.

FANTASY PUBLICATIONS

Novels (series: The Passionate Witch)

Flecker's Magic. New York, Boni and Liveright, 1926; as *Enchanted Beggar.* Philadelphia, Lippincott, 1959.
Doctor Fogg. New York, Macmillan, 1929.
The Passionate Witch, with Thorne Smith. New York, Doubleday Doran, 1941; London, Barker, 1942.
Bats in the Belfry (Passionate Witch). New York, Doubleday Doran, 1943.

OTHER PUBLICATIONS

Novel

Day of Fortune. 1928.

Play

The Comic Artist, with Susan Glaspell (produced London, 1928). New York, Stokes, and London, Benn, 1927.

Other

The Log of the Coriolanus (travel). 1930.

*

Film Adaptation: *I Married a Witch,* 1942, from his novel *The Passionate Witch.*

*   *   *

Norman Matson's work is best-known today by virtue of its spin-off into other media. *The Passionate Witch,* which he completed from a fragment left behind by Thorne Smith after the latter's death, was filmed shortly after publication as *I Married a Witch,* and the film became the basis for the 1960s television series *Bewitched.* Directed in Hollywood by talented French film-maker Rene Clair, the movie is, however, one of the rare cinematic adaptations that improves upon its model; and the legacy which the television series owes to the book is very slight indeed.

Matson's first fantasy, *Flecker's Magic,* is a modern addition to the rich tradition of cautionary tales which suggest that if people were indeed able to have their wishes granted it would only cause trouble. The hero, an American art student in Paris, is so well aware of this principle that when a passing witch gives him a wishing-ring he is thrown into an agony of indecision, partly because he is unsure as to what he really wants out of life and partly because he is anxious about the effect that a reckless wish might have on the world around him. In the meantime he attempts to pursue a relationship with the pulchritudinous giver of the ring, who turns out to be fronting for a much less lovely and rather more sinister figure. His eventual decision, while not perhaps inappropriate in the context of the morals usually put forward by such stories, might strike some readers as an act of cowardice as well as a dramatic let-down.

The witch in *Flecker's Magic* is the last survivor of her kind, having been the only one to realize the supposed truth that the basis of modern science is no more "rational" than that of her magic. This dubious and not very coherent argument is extrapolated, after a fashion, in *Doctor Fogg,* which deploys science-fictional imagery in pursuit of a similarly hackneyed and pusillanimous moral (that there are things men would be better off not knowing). Flecker appears in a minor role, although centre stage is taken by the eponymous hero, whose experimental electromagnetic apparatus not only receives messages seemingly transmitted by another civilization but also a beautiful naked blonde, whose mysterious advent is quickly followed by the death of his wife. After much narrative shilly-shallying about the disruptive social effects of the information he receives from his interstellar correspondents, Fogg eventually blows his apparatus to kingdom come and sets up house with his enigmatic visitor—who is human enough to bear him a child, although it is far from clear that they are or ever can be soulmates.

Matson's awkward ambivalence regarding magical women is taken a step further in *The Passionate Witch.* The hero of the book is a typically pompous and morosely prudish Thorne Smith businessman, T. Wallace Wooly, Jr., who stands in dire need of loosening up. In Smith's distinctive brand of Americanized Ansteyan fantasy such loosening up is usually accomplished by lavish supplies of booze, sometimes—but not necessarily—aided and abetted by sexy women, and the effects are all to the good. Matson, however, takes a rather grimmer and more disapproving argumentative line. Wooly's witch-wife, Jennifer, is far more sinister than Smith's heroines; whereas their magic is mischievous without being truly malevolent, hers is downright nasty. She is summarily killed by a church cross which she has caused to fall, but Wooly is then forced to turn to drink because he needs it to insulate him from a curse she has placed on him, which renders him uncomfortably telepathic.

She is inconveniently reincarnated as a horse, but he eventually escapes her influence and marries his faithful secretary. In the movie, the part of the witch became a vehicle for Veronica Lake at her sultriest and most plaintively seductive, and the character was sympathetically softened in accordance. Thorne Smith probably intended that the character be more sympathetically treated when he set out to write the story, but he would have made her far more robust, and he would surely never have provided such a cosy and sober happy ending.

In *Bats in the Belfry,* his solo sequel to *The Passionate Witch,* Matson makes some amends for his near-betrayal of Smith's offbeat ideals. Married life with Betty the ex-secretary becomes ineffably tedious, and Wooly begins to hear Jennifer's voice, pleading for release from the grave. He consents, and she embarks upon a career of wholesale seduction, in a vein of which Smith would surely have approved. Betty is turned into a cat, but the terms on which Wooly and his wayward witch resume their relationship are peculiar and ultimately unsatisfying; in the end his "real" marriage is restored in all its inglorious tedium. To some extent this oddly-recomplicated ending reflects Matson's inability to embrace Thorne Smith's zestfully unorthodox morality, but comparison with his earlier fantasies implies that there is a deeper-lying uncertainty about Matson's own attitude to the mythology of romance and the possibility of ever living happily after marriage. Whether his superficial purpose is comic or moralistic, there is a bitter undercurrent in all Matson's fantasy fiction which is cynically suspicious of the glamour possessed by lovely young women and back-handedly contemptuous of the dullness of not-so-lovely wives. In this respect the books may be a little more revealing than their author intended, or might have wished.

—Brian Stableford

MAY, Julian

Pseudonyms: Lee N. Falconer; Ian Thorne. **Nationality:** American. **Born:** Chicago, Illinois, 10 July 1931. **Education:** Rosary College, River Forest, Illinois, 1949-53. **Family:** Married Thaddeus (Ted) E. Dikty in 1953 (died); two sons and one daughter. **Career:** Editor, Booz Allen & Hamilton, Chicago; editor, Consolidated Book Publishers, Chicago, 1954-57; founder, with Ted Dikty, Publication Associates, in Chicago, 1957-68, Naperville, Illinois, 1968-74, West Linn, Oregon, 1974-80, and 1980-92 in Mercer Island, Washington. Freelance writer: in addition to the books listed below, she has published almost 300 nonfiction works, mainly for children, and a series of brief (48-page) movie novelizations as "Ian Thorne". **Awards:** *Locus* award, 1982. **Address:** P.O. Box 851, Mercer Island, WA 98040, USA.

FANTASY PUBLICATIONS

Novels (series: Trillium)

Black Trillium, with Marion Zimmer Bradley and Andre Norton. New York, Doubleday, 1990; London, Grafton, 1991.
Blood Trillium. New York, Bantam, 1992; London, HarperCollins, 1992.

Other

A *Gazeteer of the Hyborian World of Conan* (as Lee N. Falconer). West Linn, Oregon, Starmont House, 1977.

OTHER PUBLICATIONS

Novels

The Many-Colored Land. Boston, Houghton Mifflin, 1981; London, Pan, 1982.
The Golden Torc. Boston, Houghton Mifflin, 1982; London, Pan, 1982.
The Nonborn King. Boston, Houghton Mifflin, and London, Pan, 1983.
The Adversary. Boston, Houghton Mifflin, and London, Pan, 1984.
Intervention: A Root Tale to the Galactic Milieu and a Vinculum Between It and the Saga of Pliocene Exile. Boston, Houghton Mifflin, and London, Collins, 1987; in 2 vols. as *The Surveillance* and *The Metaconcert,* New York, Del Rey, 1989.
Jack the Bodiless. New York, Knopf, and London, HarperCollins, 1992.
Diamond Mask. New York, Knopf, and London, HarperCollins, 1994.

Short Story

Brede's Tale. Mercer Island, Washington, Starmont House, 1982.

Other

A Pliocene Companion. Boston, Houghton Mifflin, 1984; London, Pan, 1985.

*

Bibliography: *The Work of Julian May: An Annotated Bibliography and Guide* by T. E. Dikty and R. Reginald, San Bernardino, California, Borgo Press, 1985.

*   *   *

Though early in her career Julian May produced a couple of magazine science-fiction stories and subsequently a variety of juvenile books, it was not until 1981 that her major skills as a blender of science fiction and fantasy emerged with the publication of *The Many-Colored Land.* That is what the continent of Europe was called by those of the dimorphic and metapsychically-endowed race transplanted from the Duat Galaxy to Earth at the time of the pre-glacial Pliocene. The reason for removal was the anachronistic practice of ritual warfare by these unpacifiable sections of the Tanu and Firvulag sub-races. They continued their battles and tourneys over the face of their new homeland. This first novel and its successors, *The Golden Torc, The Nonborn King* and *The Adversary* comprise the Saga of the Exiles. The "exiles" are not only the Duat peoples but, preeminently, human exiles from 21st and 22nd Century Earth, malcontents who jib at the authoritarian concord imposed on their planet as a result of an extraterrestrial "Great Intervention" (to be described here later). These exiles have entered the Pliocene through a one-way time portal. The Saga is the complex story of the inter-

action with Tanu and Firvulag of two groups: a small band of variously talented individualists and defeated activists of the Metapsychic Rebellion of 2083, members of the phenomenally psycho-operant Remillard family, who rear their exiled children on Ocala Island, the Pliocene site of present-day Florida.

The scenario thus far, if at the limits of science fiction, is recognizably within that genre, to which time travel, alien interventions, and psi powers are not unknown. Such genre credentials are reinforced by the author's manipulation of scientific terms and concepts. The time portal is more properly a "tau-field generator". Julian May's Pliocene Europe is well-researched (granted the odd Loch Ness-type monster). A key event at the end of *The Golden Torc* is the disruption of the Tanu/Firvulag "Grand Combat" by the breaking of the Gibraltar barrier to let in the Atlantic. An appendix discusses soberly the timing and tectonics of this historical happening, but the actual narrative takes license to identify the determinant factor as the telekinetic revenge act of a psychotic super-operant.

It is in terms of imagery, analogy, and metaphor that the Saga chiefly exerts its spell as fantasy. Such tropes are deployed to establish correspondences and resonances between the Many-Coloured Land and its peoples and those bodies of myth which share the same archetypes. Evocative nomenclature plays its part, as Julian May makes clear in one of her Appendices, where she writes of her "archetypal human characters" such as Aiken Drum, Felice Landry and Mercy Lambelle, as being "out of Celtica via Jung and Joseph Campbell among others."

The Tanu and the Firvulag share an anthem which is recognized by the human exiles as akin to that melody of mysterious origin, the "Londonderry Air". The Tanu wear golden torcs which enhance their psychic potential. The Firvulag are known as "The Little People" and their king's palace at High Vrazel lies under a mountain in the Vosges. He and his race are shape-shifters, appearance being changed by a single mental/magical gesture. Mutated Firvulag—the "Howlers"—are trolls and bogles. The Tanu, riding their chalicos (proto-horses) levitate when on the Flying Hunt, anticipating Teutonic myth; and there is an omnipresence of Wagnerian archetypes (Aiken Drum, after the flooding of the White Silver Plain, is described as "king of the ruins. A demigod in Gotterdammerung").

However far the Saga moves towards fantasy, a hold is always maintained on the science-fictional. The Howlers have mutated into their goblinesque forms because their home-ground is radioactive. Shape-shifting is sometimes illusionary, sometimes "higher forms of shape-shifting involve actual manipulation of the molecules and real physical change" (*A Pliocene Companion*). Nevertheless, the fictive conventions of far-sensing and shape-shifting operate most convincingly in the modes of fantastic play. There is a certain fairy tale, dreamlike quality pervading the Many-Colored Land experience. The young generation of Remillards as they grow up are strongly motivated to find a way back through the time portal to the "real" world of the Galactic Milieu, while avoiding turning (like fairy gold) to dust.

Intervention, the first of the novels to follow the Saga of the Exiles quartet, narrates events which predate exits to the Pliocene, tells of the rise of a metapsychically endowed section of the human race, centred on the Remillard family, and of the opposition of "normal" humanity to the metapsychics' unifying aims. During a critical confrontation in the year 2013 the telepaths call for extraterrestrial aid, and immediately, in the "Great Intervention," alien races, who in their starships had been monitoring the planet, descend to take control of Earth, readying it for integration into the "Galactic Milieu" of metapsychic minds and races and for the colonizing of many planets. The deliberations of the Lylmik (pseudocorporeal supervising aliens), and their appearances in human guise, produce a vein of high fantasy and near-farcical humour (humour, sly, sharp, or satirical, constantly sparkles in May's narrative).

Intervention is in part related, very humanly, through the reminiscences of long-lived, alcoholic, antiquarian bookseller, "Uncle" Rogi Remillard, a device used to even greater extent in *Jack the Bodiless,* the first published novel of the projected Galactic Milieu trilogy (the others are *Diamond Mask* and *Magnificat*), which prefaces and recounts the Metapsychic Rebellion of 2083. This rebellion against alien-originated constraints is headed by members of the very family that had invoked the Great Intervention, and it is as a result of their defeat that they incur exile to the Pliocene—which is where we came in. This chronologically reversed order of writing, the requirement to match Pliocene and 21st/22nd Century chronologies, together with the complexities of Remillard genealogy, might make for confusion were it not for the accompanying carefully constructed summaries, maps, family trees, etc. These have been supplemented by the author's *A Pliocene Companion,* a compilation which also makes explicit the many ideational influences, particularly those of Teilhard de Chardin's evolutionary and synthesizing concepts. Julian May adds speculative depth to entertaining fantasy.

Less significantly—in the area of "pure," or heroic, fantasy rather than science fantasy—May was the prime mover behind the Trillium series of novels co-authored with veteran writers Marion Zimmer Bradley and Andre Norton. These are entertaining quest-adventures which shuffle standard secondary-world ingredients.

—K. V. Bailey

MAYNE, William

Pseudonyms: Martin Cobalt; Dynley James; Charles Molin. **Nationality:** British. **Born:** 16 March 1928 in Kingston upon Hull, Yorkshire. **Education:** Attended the Cathedral Choir School, Canterbury, 1937-42. **Career:** Writer of children's books; lecturer, Deakin University, Geelong, Victoria, 1976-77; Fellow in Creative Writing, Rolle College, Exmouth, Devon, 1979-80. **Awards:** Carnegie Medal from British Library Association for best children's book of the year, 1957, for *A Grass Rope; Boston Globe-Horn Book* Honor award, 1989, for *Gideon Ahoy;* Phoenix award honor, 1991, for *A Game of Dark.* **Agent:** David Higham Associates Ltd., 5-8 Lower John St., Golden Square, London W1R 4HA, England.

FANTASY PUBLICATIONS

Novels

A Grass Rope, illustrated by Lynton Lamb. London, Oxford University Press, 1957; New York, Dutton, 1962.
The Glass Ball, illustrated by Janet Duchesne. London, Hamish Hamilton, 1961; New York, Dutton, 1962.
Earthfasts. London, Hamish Hamilton, 1966; New York, Dutton, 1967.

Over the Hills and Far Away. London, Hamish Hamilton, 10968; as *The Hill Road,* New York, Dutton, 1969.
A Game of Dark. London, Hamish Hamilton, and New York, Dutton, 1971.
The Jersey Shore. London, Hamish Hamilton, and New York, Dutton, 1973.
A Year and a Day, illustrated by Krystyna Turska. London, Hamish Hamilton, and New York, Dutton, 1976.
It. London, Hamish Hamilton, 1977; New York, Greenwillow, 1978.
Gideon Ahoy. London, Viking Kestrel, 1987; New York, Delacorte, 1989.
Antar and the Eagles. New York, Doubleday, 1989.

Short Stories

All the King's Men. London, Cape, 1982; New York, Delacorte, 1988.

PUBLICATIONS FOR YOUNG ADULTS

Novels

Follow the Footprints, illustrated by Shirley Hughes. London, Oxford University Press, 1953.
The World Upside Down, illustrated by Shirley Hughes. London, Oxford University Press, 1954.
A Swarm in May, illustrated by C. Walter Hodges. London, Oxford University Press, 1955; Indianapolis, Bobbs-Merrill, 1957.
Choristers' Cake, illustrated by C. Walter Hodges. London, Oxford University Press, 1956; Indianapolis, Bobbs-Merrill, 1958.
The Member of the Marsh, illustrated by Lynton Lamb. London, Oxford University Press, 1956.
The Blue Boat, illustrated by Geraldine Spence. London, Oxford University Press, 1957; New York, Dutton, 1960.
The Long Night, illustrated by D.J. Watkins-Pitchford. London, Blackwell, 1957.
Underground Alley, illustrated by Marcia Lane Foster. London, Oxford University Press, 1958; New York, Dutton, 1961.
The Gobbling Billy (as Dynely James), with R.D. Caesar. London, Gollancz, and New York, Dutton, 1959; by William Mayne and Dick Caesar, Leicester, Brockhampton Press, 1969.
The Thumbstick, illustrated by Tessa Theobald. London, Oxford University Press, 1959.
Cathedral Wednesday, illustrated by C. Walter Hodges. London, Oxford University Press, 1960.
The Fishing Party, illustrated by Christopher Brooker. London, Hamish Hamilton, 1960.
The Rolling Season, illustrated by Christopher Brooker. London, Oxford University Press, 1960.
Thirteen O'Clock, illustrated by D.J. Watkins-Pitchford. Oxford, Blackwell, 1960.
The Changeling, illustrated by Victor Adams. London, Oxford University Press, 1961; New York, Dutton, 1963.
Summer Visitors, illustrated by William Stobbs. London, Oxford University Press, 1961.
The Last Bus, illustrated by Margery Gill. London, Hamish Hamilton, 1962.
The Twelve Dancers, illustrated by Lynton Lamb. London, Hamish Hamilton, 1962.
The Man from the North Pole, illustrated by Prudence Seward. London, Hamish Hamilton, 1963.

On the Stepping Stones, illustrated by Prudence Seward. London, Hamish Hamilton, 1963.

A Parcel of Trees, illustrated by Margery Gill. London, Penguin, 1963.

Plot Night, illustrated by Janet Duchesne. London, Hamish Hamilton, 1963; New York, Dutton, 1968.

Words and Music, illustrated by Lynton Lamb. London, Hamish Hamilton, 1963.

A Day without Wind, illustrated by Margery Gill. London, Hamish Hamilton, and New York, Dutton, 1964.

Sand, illustrated by Margery Gill. London, Hamish Hamilton, 1964; New York, Dutton, 1965.

Water Boatman, illustrated by Anne Linton. London, Hamish Hamilton, 1964.

Whistling Rufus, illustrated by Raymond Briggs. London, Hamish Hamilton, 1964; New York, Dutton, 1965.

The Big Wheel and the Little Wheel, illustrated by Janet Duchesne. London, Hamish Hamilton, 1965.

Pig in the Middle, illustrated by Mary Russon. London, Hamish Hamilton, 1965; New York, Dutton, 1966.

Dormouse Tales (The Lost Thimble, The Steam Roller, The Picnic, The Football, The Tea Party) (as Charles Molin), illustrated by Leslie Wood. London, Hamish Hamilton, 5 vols., 1966.

The Old Zion, illustrated by Margery Gill. London, Hamish Hamilton, 1966; New York, Dutton, 1967.

Rooftops, illustrated by Mary Russon. London, Hamish Hamilton, 1966.

The Battlefield, illustrated by Mary Russon. London, Hamish Hamilton, and New York, Dutton, 1967.

The Big Egg, illustrated by Margery Gill. London, Hamish Hamilton, 1967.

The House on Fairmont, illustrated by Fritz Wegner. London, Hamish Hamilton, and New York, Dutton, 1968.

The Toffee Join, illustrated by Shirley Hughes. London, Hamish Hamilton, 1968.

The Yellow Aeroplane, illustrated by Trevor Stubley. London, Hamish Hamilton, 1968; Nashville, Nelson, 1974.

Ravensgill. London, Hamish Hamilton, and New York, Dutton, 1970.

Royal Harry. London, Hamish Hamilton, 1971; New York, Dutton, 1972.

The Incline. London, Hamish Hamilton, and New York, Dutton, 1972.

Skiffy, illustrated by Nicholas Fisk. London, Hamish Hamilton, 1972.

The Swallows (as Martin Cobalt). London, Heinemann, 1972; as *Pool of Swallows,* Nashville, Nelson, 1974.

Max's Dream, illustrated by Laszlo Acs. London, Hamish Hamilton, and New York, Greenwillow Books, 1977.

Party Pants, illustrated by Joanna Stubbs. London, Knight, 1977.

While the Bells Ring, illustrated by Janet Rawlins. London, Hamish Hamilton, 1979.

The Mouse and the Egg, illustrated by Krystyna Turska. London, MacRae, 1980; New York, Greenwillow Books, 1981.

Salt River Times, illustrated by Elizabeth Honey. Melbourne, Nelson, and London, Hamish Hamilton, 1980; New York, Greenwillow Books, 1980.

The Patchwork Cat, illustrated by Nicola Bayley. London, Cape, and New York, Knopf, 1981.

Skiffy and the Twin Planets. London, Hamish Hamilton, 1982.

Winter Quarters. London, Cape, 1982.

The Mouldy, illustrated by Nicola Bayley. London, Cape, and New York, Random House, 1983.

A Small Pudding for Wee Gowrie, illustrated by Martin Cottam. London, Macmillan, 1983.

Underground Creatures. London, Hamish Hamilton, 1983.

Drift. London, Cape, 1985; New York, Delacorte, 1986.

Animal Library (Come, Come to My Corner, Corbie, Tibber, Barnabas Walks, Lamb Shenkin, A House in Town, Leapfrog, Mousewing), illustrated by Kenneth Lilly, Peter Visscher, Martin Baynton, Jonathan Heale, Barbara Firth, and Sarah Fox-Davies. London, Walker, 8 vols., 1986-87; first 3 vols. published Englewood Cliffs, New Jersey, Prentice-Hall, 1987.

The Blemyahs, illustrated by Juan Wijngaard. London, Walker, 1987.

Kelpie. London, Cape, 1987.

Tiger's Railway, illustrated by Juan Wijngaard. London, Walker, 1987.

The Farm that Ran Out of Names. London, Cape, 1989.

Low Tide. New York, Delacorte, 1993.

Other

Editor, with Eleanor Farjeon, *The Hamish Hamilton Book of Kings,* illustrated by Victor Ambrus. London, Hamish Hamilton, 1964; as *A Cavalcade of Kings,* New York, Walck, 1965.

Editor, with Eleanor Farjeon, *The Hamish Hamilton Book of Queens,* illustrated by Victor Ambrus. London, Hamish Hamilton, 1964; as *A Cavalcade Queens,* New York, Walck, 1965.

Editor (as Charles Molin), *Ghosts, Spooks, Spectres.* London, Hamish Hamilton, 1967; New York, David White, 1968.

Editor, *The Hamish Hamilton Book of Heroes,* illustrated by Krystyna Turska. London, Hamish Hamilton, 1967; as *William Mayne's Book of Heroes,* New York, Dutton, 1968.

Editor, *The Hamish Hamilton Book of Giants,* illustrated by Raymond Briggs. London, Hamish Hamilton, 1968; as *William Mayne's Book of Giants,* New York, Dutton, 1969.

Editor, *Ghosts.* London, Hamish Hamilton, and New York, Nelson, 1971.

Composer, music for *Holly from the Bongs,* by Alan Garner, 1965.

PUBLICATIONS FOR CHILDREN

Fiction

No More School, illustrated by Peter Warner. London, Hamish Hamilton, 1965.

Robin's Real Engine, illustrated by Mary Dinsdale. London, Hamish Hamilton, 1972.

Hob Stories (Red Book, Green Book, Yellow Book, Blue Book), illustrated by Patrick Benson. London, Walker, and New York, Philomel, 4 vols., 1984.

*

Biography: Essay in *Something about the Author Autobiography Series,* Volume 11, Detroit, Gale, 1991; entry in *Third Book of Junior Authors,* New York, H.W. Wilson, 1972.

Critical Study: Entry in *Contemporary Literary Criticism,* Volume 12, Detroit, Gale, 1979.

*   *   *

William Mayne is a subtle, sophisticated author whose work (like Alan Garner's) is not always easily pigeonholed as being for children. Oblique strokes of fantasy run through his large output, sometimes almost invisible, sometimes rationalized away . . . there is a genuine creepiness in the noisy dragon of the 1956 *The Member for the Marsh,* which proves to be a pumping engine.

Earthfasts may be his finest tale of the supernatural, with its lovingly described Yorkshire countryside shadowed with increasing strangeness and disorientation as time goes out of joint. A regimental drummer boy emerges into the 1960s after what he experienced as a few minutes' underground treasure-hunt in 1742. With him comes a candle whose cold-burning flame is measuring a different time; this remains above ground after he has (quite soon) walked drumming back into a crevice seemingly only eight inches wide.

Earth is disturbed. Standing stones move. Giants, boggarts, and wild boar are abroad. Two engaging modern boys struggle to make sense of the upheaval with uncertain tools of logical and scientific thought—each inclined to scepticism, each half-resentful, half-glad that the other has also witnessed the incredible. One stares too long into the otherworld light of the candle and is taken by a strange calamity as a crack of "clear darkness, with the clearness . . . of bramble jelly" opens across earth and sky. Some harrowing while later, there's a satisfactory resolution.

Earthfasts succeeds through Mayne's sense of place, precise ear for conversation and dialect, and ability to describe the enigmatic with clarity while preserving its enigma.

More ambiguity is packed into the slim *A Game of Dark,* both an evocatively written fantasy performance and—conceivably—not fantasy but a tale of neurosis, of a boy finding hallucinated metaphors for issues he can't deal with. Donald phases between repressed family life in our world and a bleak medieval town besieged by the malevolent Worm. This icy-white, stinking, limbless monster seems a multiplex echo of Donald's crippled father (white-haired, white-faced, full of censorious godliness), his dislike for said father, and his guilt at feeling dislike. Other real-life characters are similarly refracted in the alternate world which Donald calls his "game of darkness."

The spare conclusion is fraught with possible readings. Donald's alter-ego slays the Worm, but not honourably; the restrictions on how knights may act prove as painful as those on what, between mother, father, and son, can be said. In reality, the father evidently dies. Having renounced fantasy, the son goes to sleep consoled . . . by having metaphorically killed his sire, by having learned to love him even too late, or merely because "the dreadful breathing" of sickness no longer sounds through the house? This whole dark game is not easily forgotten.

It is another notable supernatural performance, lighter-hearted and often funny despite M. R. James-like horror *frissons*: heroine Alice gropes for the buried foot of an old stone cross and feels a dry, rough hand take hers. Her story sympathetically shows the problems of a highly imaginative and thus "difficult" child. Against a modern ecclesiastical background the familiar of a centuries-dead witch is freed, leading to much bizarre poltergeist activity. Alice must either lay "IT" to rest or accept it as a companion and source of power, an uneasy decision made grimmer by the implication that she herself killed the witch through an accident of fractured time. The final choice of exorcism involves not bell, book, and candle but an amusing labyrinth of committee meetings as by filibustering and bribery Alice reorganizes the town's traditional St. Cuthbert Parade to take a route whose pattern can loose and bind.

These are fantasy highlights from a large, mixed output, all written with the same sure touch . . . the only niggle being that sometimes it seems oversubtle for the age groups Mayne is ostensibly addressing. But he never underestimates children's abilities and, perhaps, neither should we.

—David Langford

McGIRT, Dan(iel)

Nationality: American. **Born:** Sylvester, Georgia, 1967. **Career:** Lawyer.

FANTASY PUBLICATIONS

Novels (series: Jason Cosmo in all books)

Jason Cosmo. New York, Signet, 1989; London, Pan, 1990.
Royal Chaos. New York, Roc, and London, Pan, 1990.
Dirty Work. New York, Roc, and London, Pan, 1993.

*   *   *

Dan McGirt's novels mine a very well-explored vein of humorous fantasy . . . more in the tradition of Robert Asprin or Craig Shaw Gardner than Tom Holt or Terry Pratchett (despite a passing homage to the latter's Luggage, in the form of a chest made of "insipid wormwood" rather than "sapient pearwood").

In *Jason Cosmo* the eponymous hero, a quiet villager, is kicked into action by the discovery that bounty hunters are out to get him—since the unspeakable Dark Magic Society has for no apparent reason placed a large price on his head. Luckily befriended by the mirror-shaded wizard Mercury Boltblaster, he is prolongedly chased around a fairly standard fantasy land studded with droll names: Lower Hicksnittle, the Festering Wart Tavern, Offal, King Luggo, the Incredibly Dark Forest. It is found written on his aura that he is fated to be a Hero. A featherbrained solar goddess blesses him and grants him the strength of ten when standing in sunlight; he humorously acquires indestructible magic armour by filling out a questionnaire. One set-piece scene involves a SDI/laser-like magical defence system whose merry failure to function as intended is plonkingly signalled by its acronym AMOK.

There is an ultimate confrontation with the Dark Magic crew, and a happy ending. The jokes, alas, are not on average very good, while arbitrary irruptions of magic, anachronism and attempted punchlines hamper any build-up of narrative suspense.

Royal Chaos and *Dirty Work* are follow-up novels which offer, essentially, more of the same. Cosmo goes up against further unbeatable menaces, and (aided by numerous props, plot devices and *deus ex machina* interventions) beats them. The third book in particular leans heavily on repetition: numerous passages, for example, in which the principal humour seems to be that they *are* so obviously padded. That the Assassins & Cutthroats Labour Union should be the ACLU might be worth a smile in America, but this surely fades after more than two dozen further uses of the initials.

Most tiresome is an increasingly frequent use of the very old gag of "postmodern" self-referentiality, with characters forever discussing their own fictional development, the likely course of the plot ("Well obviously Solana is my new female lead, but I'm not supposed to realize that yet"), the "subtle foreshadowing" in what's just been said, etc. "Could you just get to the point?" "Not without a lot of buildup." This summarizes too much of McGirt's technique.

Occasional funny jokes can be found. Further volumes are unsubtly foreshadowed.

—David Langford

McKILLIP, Patricia A(nne)

Nationality: American. **Born:** Salem, Oregon, 29 February 1948. **Education:** San Jose State University, B.A. 1971, M.A. in English 1973. **Awards:** World Fantasy award, 1975. **Agent:** Howard Morhaim Literary Agency, 174 Fifth Avenue, Room 709, New York, NY 10010, USA. **Address:** 2661 California, No. 14, San Francisco, CA 94115, USA.

FANTASY PUBLICATIONS

Novels (series: Chronicles of Morgon; Cygnet)

The Forgotten Beasts of Eld. New York, Atheneum, 1974; London, Futura, 1987.
The Riddle-Master of Hed. New York, Atheneum, 1976; London, Sidgwick and Jackson, 1979.
Heir of Sea and Fire. New York, Atheneum, 1977; London, Sidgwick and Jackson, 1979.
Harpist in the Wind. New York, Atheneum, and London, Sidgwick and Jackson, 1979.
Riddle of Stars (omnibus; includes *The Riddle-Master of Hed, Heir of Sea and Fire, Harpist in the Wind*). New York, Nelson Doubleday, 1979; as *The Chronicles of Morgon, Prince of Hed,* London, Sidgwick and Jackson, 1981.
The Changeling Sea. New York, Atheneum, 1988.
The Sorceress and the Cygnet. New York, Ace, 1991; London, Pan, 1992.
The Cygnet and the Firebird. New York, Ace, 1993; London, Pan, 1994.
Something Rich and Strange. New York, Bantam, 1994.

OTHER PUBLICATIONS

Novels

Stepping from the Shadows. New York, Atheneum, 1982.
Moon-Flash. New York, Atheneum, 1984.
The Moon and the Face. New York, Atheneum, 1985.
Fool's Run. New York, Warner, and London, Macdonald, 1987.

Novels for Children

The House on Parchment Street, illustrated by Charles Robinson. New York, Atheneum, 1973.

The Throme of the Erril of Sherill, illustrated by Julie Noonan. New York, Atheneum, 1973; expanded edition, New York, Tempo, 1984.
The Night Gift, illustrated by Kathy McKillip. New York, Atheneum, 1976.

*   *   *

Despite her use of traditional fantasy elements, McKillip is one of the most innovative and highly regarded fantasy writers of the post-Tolkien period. A problem in assessing her work is that almost all of it has been aimed, at least partly, at a young adult audience. The half-dozen books dealt with here are her greatest achievements; although all of them make some concessions to the juvenile reader, they rise far above the young adult fantasy sub-genre and may be read with great enjoyment by adults. All six principal works share certain features. They are high fantasies, they are highly romantic (by which is meant that in each is a love-interest plotline of some importance), and they all deal with the accretion of power and with the corrupting effect which may accompany power.

The Forgotten Beasts of Eld is a deceptively simple novel, stylistically lyrical, often surprising, and wonderfully consistent. Presented as a fairy tale, though with great and involving emotion, it shows absolute power, the bitterness of revenge, great love and the search for a heart's desire. Sybel, the last of a line of wizards, lives on her own in a palace on Eld Mountain. She has power over animals and, in particular, controls an inherited collection of six legendary beasts: Ter the falcon, Cyrin the boar, Gules the lion, Moriah the cat, Gyld the dragon and the Black Swan of Tirlith. She communicates telepathically with them. And she is searching for one other legendary beast, the Liralen, a very special bird. When the action begins, she is just 16.

Then Coren of Sirle, a handsome young man, brings Tamlorn, a baby boy who is her cousin, for her to look after. She raises him as a mother for twelve years, before giving him to his father, King Drede, who is Coren's enemy. Both Coren and Drede fall in love with Sybel and want to marry her. Drede uses a wizard to summon and control Sybel (because he fears her powers) but she calls on the Blammor, a mist like creature that is fear made manifest; this kills the wizard. Sybel then decides to marry Coren, but she is determined to have her revenge upon Drede, to the extent of threatening her marriage. At last, when her plans for Drede's defeat (involving the use of her animals in battle) are nearly complete, she realises the wrongness of this revenge. She frees her beasts and returns to Eld, alone. But Drede is defeated and dies of fear, while Sybel is reunited with Coren and discovers that the Blammor is also the Liralen—her heart's desire. There is subtlety and symbolism here, as well as scenes of great power. For example, McKillip conjures up the excitement of flying through the night upon a dragon's back with an intensity unmatched by other writers.

McKillip's trilogy about Morgon of Hed contains many excellent ingredients yet is too quirky and inconsistent to be satisfying. Most of the action is internalized or is reported. In *The Riddle-Master of Hed,* Morgon first appears as a young man happy to accept his destiny as heir to the king of the tiny farming island of Hed (the smallest of six kingdoms on the eastern side of a continent). He has been an able student at college and has recently won a dangerous contest of logic ("riddling," the question and answer system upon which all knowledge is based in these lands) in which the prize was the hand in marriage of a king's daughter, Raederle. Before Morgon can claim his bride, circumstances draw him into a grand tour of the other kingdoms. Gradually he discovers that he is uniquely talented and has a great destiny to fulfil. This is symbolized by the mark of three stars on his forehead.

Morgon's travels quickly broaden his mind, allowing him to develop his enormous mental abilities. He learns how to change shape into a vesta (a kind of deer), into a tree and, later, into a crow; he learns how to give a magic shout and how to play a magic harp. In short, he discovers himself to be a superman (though not a heroic figure; throughout the trilogy he seems reluctant to use his powers to their fullness). He travels to a remote mountain to meet the High One (a kind of spiritual ruler over all these lands) but finds that a wizard, Ghisteslwchlohm, has usurped the position.

In *Heir of Sea and Fire,* Raederle goes on a separate but parallel trip, searching for Morgon, who is thought to be dead. After excessive to-ing and fro-ing, mainly by ship and in the company of a number of teenaged girls, she does find Morgon, alive, and like him she learns to develop and use her inherited powers of wizardry. Their relationship seems to blossom very quickly, though the pace of the narrative is slow and few questions are answered. Soon Morgon and Raederle are inseparable and are arguing like an old married couple. Despite this bit of naturalism, the more powerful they become, the less human they seem.

In *Harpist in the Wind,* the final volume, there is a grand battle with shape-changers, and Morgon is aided by some very elderly wizards. Here the action is less aimless than in previous volumes, as Morgon seems to be pushed towards maximizing his powers and visiting the high tower on Wind Plain. There he finds that the harpist Deth (who has both helped and betrayed him) and the blind wizard Yrth are not only the same person but are incarnations of the High One, who has been covertly training Morgon to succeed him.

Despite the confusing and elusive nature of some aspects of the trilogy, it has much originality and depth. Its structure as a nested series of riddles to be pondered over by the reader is deliberate (though this surely limits its effectiveness as a work for teenagers). There is a great deal of shape-changing symbolism: in order to beat the shape-changers both Morgon and Raederle must not only join them in the sense of changing their own shapes, but must learn to adapt mentally to the changing situation. Also, there is some symbolism of names (Deth and Yrth may be read as Death and Earth). And while Morgon learns to control earth and air by magical means, Raederle does the same with water and fire; thus magic's four elements are tamed by the new High One and his lady.

The Sorceress and the Cygnet and *The Cygnet and the Firebird* are the first two volumes in a new series of magical fantasy, where young but accomplished magicians come into conflict with godlike beings who are the subject of myth and are also constellations in the sky. Stylistically, these are the best of McKillip's work, being full of poetic description and subtlety. In terms of plot they are flawed, with the first volume possessing confusingly labyrinthine details and the second volume being too simple and predictable. Everything may be part of a great myth. As one of the characters remarks, "Sometimes it seems that all of the constellations exist in a strange, ancient tale that we only catch glimpses of, in our short lives, while they move slowly as centuries through it."

Characters are divided up into Wayfolk, who travel about (seasonally, at least), holders, who live in fortresses, and enigmatic gods, who seem to go wherever they please. Virtually all of the characters have magical powers, which may be either inherited or learned and do not seem be governed by rules. This leads inevitably to some unbelievable pieces of magic, such as the moving of the whole of the Ro house to the top of a mountain and back.

Corleu is a teenaged member of the Wayfolk (and an accomplished storyteller) who is tricked into a quest by the Gold King. He is helped by Nyx, an aberrant daughter of Ro Hold, who prefers to live alone and practice her magic in a strange magical house. She helps Corleu, though when it is clear that the object of his quest is in Ro Hold, which is being secretly infiltrated by the gods, she joins forces with her cousin, Meguet, to keep the hold safe. In fact, Meguet, whose inescapable destiny is to keep Ro Hold safe from intruders, is arguably the main character in both volumes; the fact that she does not appear until 75 pages into *The Sorceress and the Cygnet* and that the first third of that novel is told using Corleu as viewpoint character must be ascribed to McKillip's idiosyncrasy.

In *The Cygnet and the Firebird,* a sequel and a slightly easier novel to follow, Meguet and Nyx are magically transported to a far-off land (whose changing realities are most beautifully described) so that they can discover who is attacking Ro Hold and put a stop to it. Once again, it is the imagery which is most striking, and once again there is a romantic subplot as Meguet pursues her love affair with Hew, the Gatekeeper of Ro Hold.

To sum up, while *The Forgotten Beasts of Eld* is McKillip's most complete and successful work to date, her talents for innovation and descriptive writing are so great that she may yet produce a fantasy novel which is even greater.

—Chris Morgan

McKINLEY, (Jennifer Carolyn) Robin

Nationality: American. **Born:** Warren, Ohio, 16 November 1952. **Education:** Dickinson College, Carlisle, Pennsylvania, 1970-72; Bowdoin College, Brunswick, Maine, B.A. (summa cum laude) in English 1975. **Family:** Married Peter Dickinson, q.v., in 1992. **Career:** Editor and transcriber, Ward and Paul, Washington D.C., 1972-73; research assistant, Research Associates, Brunswick, 1976-77; bookstore clerk, Maine, 1978; teacher and counsellor in private secondary school, Natick, Massachusetts, 1978-79; editorial assistant, Little, Brown, Inc., Boston, Massachusetts, 1979-81; barn manager on horse farm, Holliston, Massachusetts, 1981-82; clerk, Books of Wonder, New York, 1983; freelance reader and editor, 1983-90. **Awards:** American Library Association Newbery Medal, 1985; World Fantasy award for best anthology, 1986; D.Let., Bowdoin College, 1986. **Agent:** Merrilee Heifetz, Writers House Inc., 21 West 26th Street, New York, NY 10010, USA. **Address:** Bramdean Lodge, Bramdean, Alresford, Hampshire SO24 0JN, England.

Fantasy Publications

Novels (series: Damar)

Beauty: A Retelling of the Story of Beauty and the Beast. New York, Harper, 1978; London, MacRae, 1983.
The Blue Sword (Damar). New York, Greenwillow, 1982; London, MacRae, 1983.
The Hero and the Crown (Damar). New York, Greenwillow, and London, MacRae, 1985.

The Outlaws of Sherwood. New York, Greenwillow, 1988.
Deerskin. New York, Ace, 1993.

Short Stories

The Door in the Hedge. New York, Greenwillow, 1981; London, MacRae, 1984.
A Knot in the Grain and Other Stories. New York, Greenwillow, 1994.

Other

Adapter, *Tales from The Jungle Book* by Rudyard Kipling. New York, Random House, 1985.
Adapter, *Black Beauty* by Anna Sewell. New York, Random House, 1986; London, Hamish Hamilton, 1987.
Adapter, *The Light Princess* by George MacDonald. San Diego, Harcourt, 1988.
Adapter, *The Little Mermaid* by Hans Christian Andersen. San Diego, Harcourt, 1989.

Editor, *Faery.* New York, Ace, 1985.
Editor, *Imaginary Lands.* New York, Greenwillow, 1985; London, MacRae, 1987.

OTHER PUBLICATIONS

Fiction for Children

My Father Is in the Navy. New York, Greenwillow, 1992.
Rowan. New York, Greenwillow, 1992.

* * *

A romance involving someone called Harry Crewe in a mountainous frontier-land bordering an Empire and a threat from the north, with soldiers fighting for the Queen and courageous hillfolk of who evoke the respect of the "old sweats," sounds for all the world like one of those post-*Kim* boys' adventures set on the Northwest Frontier. Even allowing for the fact that "Harry" is in fact Angharad, a spirited tomboy from a family whose blue blood has developed a slight taint over the years and who has been taken in by Sir Charles and his Lady on her father's death, and that the *kelar* of the Damar hillfolk is a gift which seems to enable certain psychic powers, in *The Blue Sword* we are still treading those imaginary valleys where the Wolf of Kabul gripped generations of young British story-paper readers. McKinley adds a touch of *The Sheik* as Harry is abducted by the hillfolk king Corlath, who is frustrated by the Homelanders' refusal of a pre-emptive alliance against the half-human Northerners. Harry becomes a warrior, trained for victory in the Trials, and finds her own gift of *kelar,* thanks partly to the mysterious sage Luthe. She eventually deserts her adopted hillfolk to answer the threat of the Northerners, holding off a narrow pass with a group of sympathetic Homelanders, bearing the Blue Sword Gonduran which once was wielded by the ancient queen Aerin.

If anything in the fantasy genre is a ripping yarn, this is. Its nearness to the romances of the British in India prevents it from being highly original in absolute terms, but gives it enough reference points to make it an exciting read in any mode, and its quasi-Victorianism is refreshingly different from the quasi-medievalism of most such fantasy.

The Hero and the Crown is a prequel which tells the story of Aerin, mentioned in *The Blue Sword.* If Aerin is, like Harry, a gangling orphaned tomboy adrift in a world with which she cannot quite come to terms, that, to some extent, is the point. Aerin's mother, the king's second wife, was from the North, and the Damarians mistrust her for this. After years of experimenting, Aerin succeeds in isolating the recipe for a flameproof ointment and embarks on an alternative career as a dragon-slayer: first the small vermin, increasing in the country because of a malign influence from the North, and then the Great Dragon Maur itself.

However, slaying Maur is for many only proof of Aerin's ambiguity, for surely nothing human could kill such a fearsome creature. The regard her cousin Tor holds her in is suspicious, for he is the king's heir and it appears as if history is repeating itself and a witchwoman is beguiling royalty. After meeting Luthe (the same Luthe Harry met in *The Blue Sword*) she sets herself against the mage Asgad, the source of all the tension in the land. Naturally she wins, but even a reader used to such fiction would find her adventures gripping. While Asgad himself speaks in conventional melodrama-ese ("No mortal can best me . . . it will avail you naught") Aerin's quests are skilfully and darkly written: we are spared the mechanical progression a simple plot summary gives of these events because she does not escape unscathed. After a lengthy recovery from the injuries inflicted by Maur, she sets out against Asgad knowing that he is as far above Maur in power as Maur was above the small dragons she originally fought. Further tension comes from the lightly sketched (but shadowy menaces are all the more sinister) presences of the almost-but-not-quite-human Northerners.

The Damar books are essentially fairy tales (in more senses than one: they have been published as fantasies for young people, although their British paperback publications have been under an "adult" imprint). So it is no surprise that earlier Mckinley had written more overtly in this mode. *Beauty,* emphatically a fantasy novel and not just a "retelling," is a version of the old tale of "Beauty and the Beast," in which McKinley provides motive and character without losing the eeriness which is at the heart of the story. Beauty is only the plain-though-clever narrator's nickname: her real name, in keeping with family custom, is the more austere "Honour" although both names are, in their fashion, appropriate as the story makes clear.

McKinley has also used fairy tales as the basis for the stories in *The Door in the Hedge,* a collection of four pieces introduced by "The Stolen Princess" which uses the Dunsanyish setting of a land bordering Faerieland haunted by its magic and peril and blessed by its dreams. The other stories, "The Princess and the Frog," "The Hunting of the Hind" and "The Twelve Dancing Princesses," have their roots in traditional collections but share something of the shimmering, ironic humour of Hans Christian Andersen. Like Andersen, McKinley dwells upon the surface of her stories, allowing setting to conquer plot because we know the basic plot of these stories anyway, but is able to suggest darker depths, like the music of "The Twelve Dancing Princesses" which is played against the suggestion of an empty splendour behind which is something less nameable than silence. The evil charisma of Alyander in "The Princess and the Frog," the spell under which the princesses dance like automata, the Hind's perilous enchantment, are counterpoint to the detailed mystery of the surface narrative. As McKinley captivates by her detail, so she is reminding her readers of the dangers of such captivation, and it is this sense of awareness which permeates her "fairy-tale" stories.

More recently, she has turned to other aspects of folk tale. *The Outlaws of Sherwood* is only fantasy in the sense that Robin Hood is a figure out of romance and legend, and McKinley's retelling is an attractive mixture of the "received" version of the tale and the necessary reinterpretations every age has added since the 14th century. Hence, McKinley's Robin is granted individuality through his actual mediocrity at bowmanship and his early suspicion of his symbolic role, while her Marion is joined by another female rebel to provide another of the author's action-adventure role-models.

—Andy Sawyer

MERRITT, A(braham)

Nationality: American. **Born:** Beverly, New Jersey, 20 January 1884. **Education:** Philadelphia High School. **Family:** Married 1) Eleanor Ratcliffe (died); 2) Eleanor Humphrey; one daughter. **Career:** Reporter, then night city editor, *Philadelphia Inquirer,* 1902-11; staff member from 1912, and editor, 1937-43, *American Weekly.* **Died:** 30 August 1943.

FANTASY PUBLICATIONS

Novels

The Moon Pool. New York and London, Putnam, 1919.
The Ship of Ishtar. New York and London, Putnam, 1926; original version, Los Angeles, Borden, 1949.
The Face in the Abyss. New York, Liveright, 1931; London, Futura, 1974.
Dwellers in the Mirage. New York, Liveright, 1932; London, Skeffington, 1933; original version, New York, Avon, 1944.
The Metal Monster. New York, Avon, 1946.
The Black Wheel, completed by Hannes Bok. New York, New Collectors' Group, 1947.

Short Stories

Thru the Dragon Glass. New York, ARRA, 1932.
Three Lines of Old French. Milheim, Pennsylvania, Bizarre Series, 1939.
The Fox Woman, and The Blue Pagoda, with Hannes Bok. New York, New Collectors' Group, 1946.
The Fox Woman and Other Stories, edited by Donald A. Wollheim. New York, Avon, 1949.
A. Merritt: Reflections in the Moon Pool, edited by Sam Moskowitz. Philadelphia, Train, 1985.

OTHER PUBLICATIONS

Novels

Seven Footprints to Satan. New York, Boni and Liveright, and London, Richards, 1928.
Burn, Witch, Burn! New York, Liveright, 1933; London, Methuen, 1934.

Creep, Shadow! New York, Doubleday, 1934; as *Creep, Shadow, Creep!,* London, Methuen, 1935.

Other

The Story Behind the Story. Privately printed, 1942.
The Challenge of Beyond. Privately printed, 1954.

*

Film Adaptations: *Seven Footprints to Satan,* 1929; *The Devil Doll,* 1936, from his novel *Burn, Witch, Burn!.*

Bibliography: *A. Merritt: A Bibliography of Fantastic Writings* by Walter James Wentz, Los Angeles, Bibby, 1965.

* * *

Abraham Merritt was a successful journalist, first as a city reporter with the *Philadelphia Inquirer* and later as the editor of William Randolph Hearst's *American Weekly.* His fiction took exotic escapism to previously unexplored extremes and may well have provided a welcome relief from the pressure of reporting the crimes and catastrophes of the real world. For his vivid fantasies Merritt devised a purple prose style which presumably contrasted strongly with the terseness required of his reportage. These works were among the most popular ever published in the pulp magazines; he became the leading light of the reprint magazines *Famous Fantastic Mysteries* and *Fantastic Novels* and was briefly afforded the honour of having a similar magazine named after him.

Merritt's odysseys in exotica began with the brief and rather tentative "Through the Dragon Glass" (1917) and "The People of the Pit" (1918), but he rapidly progressed to "The Moon Pool" (1918), a definitive study of the teasing allure of the exotic. In the novel-length sequel combined with it in the book version he explains what lay beyond the magic doorway described in the story. Although the plot of the novel is pure pulp cliché the lush setting is crowded with the gaudy imagery which was to become Merritt's hallmark. The first magazine version of *The Metal Monster,* published in 1920, borrows most of its imagery from science fiction, substituting an authentic alien life-form for the seemingly supernatural guiding entity of the earlier novel. Hugo Gernsback, who was to found the first specialist science fiction pulp six years later, was a great admirer of Merritt and reprinted much of his work, including a thoroughly rewritten version of *The Metal Monster* entitled "The Metal Emperor," but Merritt was never entirely happy with the story and it was not reprinted in book form during his lifetime, and then in an abridged version.

The Ship of Ishtar (serialized in 1924) more closely resembles modern heroic fantasy in its use of a parallel world and an ongoing struggle between Good and Evil, here personified as the gods Ishtar and Nergal. The victory ultimately won by Good, aided and abetted by a heroic archaeologist displaced from our world, is distinctly Pyrrhic; the happy ending is obviously contrived for propriety's sake. This downbeat tendency in Merritt's work became increasingly exaggerated despite the conscientious efforts made by his editors to thwart it. Merritt next tried his hand at a thriller in the vein of Sax Rohmer, *Seven Footprints to Satan,* which proved popular although it is by no means an artistic success.

The book version of *The Face in the Abyss* combines abridged versions of two novellas, the first of which had been published before *The Ship of Ishtar*: "The Face in the Abyss" (1923) and "The Snake-Mother" (1930). The book version is highly unsatisfactory, the impact of the earlier story being entirely lost (as, to some extent, the impact of "The Moon Pool" was when it was combined with its sequel). The original serials, however, display some of Merritt's finest work, deploying science-fictional imagery in a more effective fashion than *The Metal Monster* without losing any of the emotional impact of Merritt's passion for the exotic. Here that passion is fully revealed, in quasi-allegorical fashion, as a critique of the awful mundanity of human nature, ruled by the twin principles of Greed and Folly. A similar allegory is embedded in the notable short story "The Woman of the Wood" (1926), one of the most popular stories ever to appear in *Weird Tales*.

Dwellers in the Mirage is Merritt's most coherent and controlled work, and a highly significant contribution to the then-ailing tradition of "lost race" fiction. The hero, tormented by ancestral memories, is driven to a confrontation with destiny in a hidden world in Alaska, where the forces whose conflict rages in his psyche are incarnate in two females, one of them by far the best of Merritt's numerous *femmes fatales*: the witchwoman Lur. Unfortunately, Merritt was not allowed to resolve this conflict as he wished and thought appropriate; both the serial and book version carry a false ending grafted on by an editor. The real ending was not revealed until the novel was reprinted in *Fantastic Novels* in 1941, and some subsequent paperback editions still retain the false ending.

Merritt's subsequent work reverted to the thriller format, with supernatural embellishments. *Burn, Witch, Burn!* pits a doctor and a gangster against murderous dolls devised by a witch; its sequel *Creep, Shadow!* involves the same heroes with the plight of one of the doctor's friends, inheritor of an ancient curse relating to the destruction of the legendary city of Ys. (Merritt had earlier reworked the plot of Robert W. Chambers's classic "The Demoiselle d'Ys"—itself a pastiche of Theophile Gautier—in the touching "Three Lines of Old French," 1919.) The second novel is the more interesting of the two, largely because of its invocation of a sexy *femme fatale*, but the plots of both books are weakened by the fact that the heroes are mere observers whose actions make little contribution to the ultimate resolutions.

Merritt had by this time grown thoroughly dissatisfied with his literary work, having apparently convinced himself that he had lost the ability to weave the imagery which was his primary inspiration into coherent plots. Although he continued to function adequately in the office, he became increasingly neurotic, suffering from hypochondria and alcoholism as well as deafness. When he died he left behind a number of fragmentary works, two of which were used as the bases of novels by artist Hannes Bok. Both of the resultant collaborations are readable, but neither is entirely satisfactory and neither bears much resemblance to Merritt's own work.

It is easy enough to make fun of Merritt's idiosyncratic prose style, but there was a purpose and a philosophy behind it; like Clark Ashton Smith, Merritt used exotic language in order to convey a sense of the alien, to make every effort possible to distance the reader from mundanity. Merritt is by no means the only fantasy writer to have attempted to make escapism both a vocation and an artform, but he did so with an intensity which few others could match, and it is not surprising that readers who can attune themselves to his strategies still think of him as the best of all such writers.

—Brian Stableford

MILLER, Faren (Carol)

Nationality: American. **Born:** California, 3 September 1950. **Education:** University of California, Berkeley, B.A. in English; M.A.; Ph.D., 1978. **Career:** Editorial assistant, *Locus* magazine, from 1981; subsequently associate editor and regular book-review columnist. **Address:** c/o Locus Publications, PO Box 13305, Oakland, CA 94661, USA.

FANTASY PUBLICATIONS

Novel

The Illusionists. New York, Warner, 1991.

*   *   *

Faren Miller, a long-time editor and book reviewer for *Locus* magazine, has published one novel of her own, the moody fantasy *The Illusionists,* and is working on a second, non-related book. Her writing is intricate, lyrical, and somewhat obscure.

The Illusionists is set in the ancient desert city of Xalycis, divided into enclaves by tribes and money. Xalycis was once ruled by mages, who fell and disappeared under mysterious circumstances; in the ruins of their city, known as the Tumbles, minor magical artefacts known as relicts are often found and sold. At the beginning of the novel, someone stumbles across a true magical Artefact, which leaves a trail of blood and insanity through the book. Bought by the wealthy Aubric i-Arnix, it is stolen, and Aubric killed, by Hendor Ebrin, the Vinculine, a rising power in the city. A varied collection of people—including Moabet Shar, a gifted "percept" with an uncontrollable power of prophecy; her lover Stilpin, a merchant; Gherifan Arnix, prodigal son of the murdered man; and Lodvin Chityr, a renegade chemic—are out to retrieve the Artefact and stop Ebrin from using it to further his deadly ambitions.

The plot of *The Illusionists* often moves agonizingly slow; for chapter after chapter, nothing seems to advance. Miller spends her time instead creating a mood, which she does very successfully. The writing is lyrical without verging into the purple. The characters speak musically, beautifully, and this is so compelling that their occasional lapse into the vulgar vernacular is disconcerting.

The style, however lovely, does contribute to the book's frustrating opaqueness. It also sets up a barrier to empathizing with the characters. This is not just because we are not always provided with enough information, as for instance in understanding why Gherifan leaves home. The action might be happening on a stage, the reader is so distant from the characters. The book is thus less involving than it might have been, though the spell of the language keeps the reader going.

Towards the end of the novel, the plot finally begins to move quickly, perhaps too quickly. The final confrontation with the Artefact, in the eerie setting of the ruined Tumbles, with all the major characters brought together, should be dramatic, but it is instead confusing. The ending suffers from an unsatisfying lack of resolution; it is possible that Miller is leaving an opening for a sequel.

The centre of *The Illusionists,* as one might gather from the title, is illusion; few people, or things, are what they seem. Moabet learns to use scents to disguise people, to create "masks"—a fascinating idea, and almost believable as Miller depicts it. Gherifan plays roles within roles, going incognito as a gambling house's enforcer, and then, in that role, taking on another as the wealthy foreign owner of an inn in the rich enclave of Xalycis. The Vinculine, an apparently solid citizen, is in fact a thief and a murderer. The Artefact itself seems a thing of glowing power but is really an intelligent entity—or rather a combination of two entities—and is dangerously insane.

The setting of Xalycis is fascinating. There are tribal cultures: the Thrani, whose hermaphrodite prophet "reads" the bones of the dead, and the Shandar, a formerly nomadic people who worship horses and do the deadly knifedance. There is the world of the chemics, who produce illegal drugs and legal scents, who create portraits in aroma. There are the very wealthy, in their enclave of Wallwalk, who are thrust up against the rest of Xalycis only when they visit various disreputable inns for gambling, sex, and drugs. And there is the underworld, with its own strange initiation rituals.

There is also the variety of people to whom we are introduced: the merchants, chemics, actors and criminals. Moabet Shar is a particularly interesting creation. As a "percept," she learns and absorbs information very easily and draws useful and valuable conclusions. She is haunted by her "flaw," though, the uncontrollable bouts of prophecy that have more than once caused her difficulty. Those abilities turn out to be crucial, though, in the battle over the Artefact, once she learns to use them instead of being used by them.

Too often, however, Miller tells us that remarkable things are going on but fails to show us. Moabet is a prime example. "What must the life of a percept be," one character thinks, "with such fierce, immediate comprehension at her command? Like living in the centre of a fire, . . . all swiftness and terrifying energy." However, we never get any such feeling from Moabet as Miller portrays her. On a more global scale, we are told that the finding of the Artefact "set enormous forces in motion. . . . Greed, envy, ambition, intellectual fascination, faith in its crudest form, and joyous delight in miracles." Yet we catch barely a glimpse of the changes the Artefact's discovery is supposedly wreaking.

The Illusionists is more effective than its plotting and characterization warrant. Miller's use of language and setting cast a spell that keeps the reader going and creates images that linger in the mind. Plotting and characterization can be learned; that kind of writing ability is more difficult to come by. While flawed, *The Illusionists* shows real promise.

—Janice M. Eisen

MILLHAUSER, Steven

Nationality: American. **Born:** New York City, 3 August 1943. **Education:** Columbia College, New York, B.A. 1965; Brown University, graduate study, 1968-71. **Awards:** Prix Medicis Etranger, France, 1975; World Fantasy Award, 1990.

FANTASY PUBLICATIONS

Novels

From the Realm of Morpheus. New York, Morrow, 1986.

Short Stories

In the Penny Arcade. New York, Knopf, 1986.
The Barnum Museum. New York, Poseidon Press, 1990.
Little Kingdoms. New York, Poseidon Press, 1993.

OTHER PUBLICATIONS

Novels

Edwin Mullhouse: The Life and Death of an American Writer, 1943-1954, by Jeffrey Cartwright. New York, Knopf, 1972.
Portrait of a Romantic. New York, Knopf, 1977.

*   *   *

Steven Millhauser's first two novels, the trickily-titled *Edwin Mullhouse: The Life and Death of an American Writer, 1943-1954, by Jeffrey Cartwright,* and the more straightforward *Portrait of a Romantic,* were quasi-autobiographical studies of childhood and adolescence, respectively; though they skirted the borders of fantasy in their evocation of the hallucinatory dreamworlds of youth, they were essentially realistic novels. *Portrait* did, however, suggest the author's potentially divided allegiance between realism and romanticism, an aesthetic hesitation explicitly staged in the narrative in the protagonist's vacillating commitment to two male friends, one a hard-headed rationalist, the other a decadent aesthete. In Millhauser's subsequent work, romanticism has largely won out, often in the form of overtly fantastic themes rendered in a languid, lapidary prose that evokes the literature of Romantic decadence.

Like *Portrait, In the Penny Arcade,* Millhauser's first collection of stories, stages this conflict of artistic ideologies. The volume is divided into three sections: Part I consists of a brilliant novella, "August Eschenburg," which narrates the life of an obsessive 19th-century dollmaker whose creations, animated by intricate clockwork mechanisms, are almost supernaturally lifelike; Part II contains three slickly realistic tales of boring W.A.S.P.s and their tiny problems; and Part III features three exuberant fabulations that push beyond the borders of realism towards dreamy fantasy. Thus, Millhauser's own (rather barren) realistic stories are framed by a meditation on the historical origins of mimetic representation on the one hand, and by excursions beyond conventional mimesis on the other. Moreover, Millhauser presents realism as itself a kind of fantasy, a pathological compulsion to capture life in its precise particularity—a theme conveyed not only by the career of mad artificer Eschenburg, but also by the horde of small-town children in Part III's "Snowmen," who craft realistic ice sculptures with "a skill so excessive, an elaboration so painfully and exquisitely minute, that it could scarcely conceal a desperate restlessness." Significantly, in reaction to this crazed realism, other children begin to fashion gargoyles and trolls and other fantastic entities, and finally to push against the very limits of representation by moulding "ungraspable figures . . . direct expressions of shadowy inner realms." The book's finale, "Cathay," shows Millhauser similarly chafing against realistic constraint, with its fragmented, languorous images of an Orientalist dreamworld.

From the Realm of Morpheus, Millhauser's third novel, is literally set in a world of dreams, the eponymous domain of the god of sleep. In the very first scene the narrator, Carl Hausman, discovers, in a thicket near a small-town park, a passageway to the underworld, and the remainder of the novel relates his experiences amid the denizens of this subterranean wonderland. Shepherded by Morpheus, a bibulous ribald and indefatigable chatterbox, Carl wanders through a vast Borgesian library and a murmuring hall of mirrors; encounters Ignotus, a young man sprung to life from the canvas of a painting; falls in love with a giantess; is swallowed by a whale and dragged down to lost Atlantis; and travels to the moon on the back of a flying island. These pixilated adventures offer endless opportunities for tongue-in-cheek philosophizing, rendered in a high-flown mock-epic style with vaguely allegorical overtones; Millhauser's literary model would appear to be Herman Melville's weird fantasia *Mardi*. Like that precursor, *Morpheus* is an intriguing failure, a compendium of glittering incident and windy claptrap. Even the most bemused reader is likely to find the leisurely disconnection among the episodes wearying, and certainly can endure only so many mayhaps, forwhys, 'sdeaths, and suchlike anachronistic fustian. As an experiment in sustaining a lush, romantic reverie, *Morpheus* is obviously important for Millhauser's development as a writer, but it only confirms that the best expression of his talent for fantasy lies in shorter forms.

The Barnum Museum, a collection of ten stories, and *Little Kingdoms*, a gathering of three novellas, are the proof of this judgment. Barnum is a brilliantly cohesive harvest of daydreams, ranging from metafictional takes on classic works of fantasy ("The Eighth Voyage of Sinbad," "Alice, Falling") to brooding meditations on the puerile profundities and kitschy wonders of mass culture ("A Game of Clue," "The Barnum Museum") to renewed interrogations of the uncertain limits of realism ("The Invention of Robert Herendeen"). High points of the volume include "Klassik Komix #1," a narration—panel by panel—of a comic-book rendering of T. S. Eliot's "Prufrock," which shrewdly juggles the materials of high and low culture; "The Sepia Postcard," a disturbing horror story in which the eerily mutable title object insinuates itself into the narrator's disintegrating life; and "Eisenheim the Illusionist," which, in its luminous portrait of a 19th-century magician whose artistic mastery seems to make illusion "real," forms a kind of diptych with Penny Arcade's "August Eschenberg". "Eisenheim" won a World Fantasy Award in 1990 (under the alternative title "The Illusionist"), indicating that the mainstream Millhauser's fabulations have begun to reach a genre audience.

The novellas in *Little Kingdoms* add substance to Barnum's basic conceits while avoiding the attenuation of the maundering *Morpheus*. "The Little Kingdom of J. Franklin Payne" is an absorbing study of the gradual descent into a solipsistic dreamscape of the title character, a cartoonist whose work comes to supplant his life; it is Millhauser's most focused statement of the curious imbrication of realism and fantasy. Franklin's romantic "desire to release himself into the free, the fantastic, the deliberately impossible . . . stimulated in him an equal and opposite impulse toward the mundane and plausible, toward precise illusionistic effects". Millhauser cleverly deploys these effects to evoke a luxuriant fairytale world in "The Princess, the Dwarf, and the Dungeon". In "Catalogue of the Exhibition: The Art of Edmund Moorash (1810-1846)," another artist disappears into his creation; in this case, it is a Romantic painter whose dubious autobiography is read off his strange, tortured canvases. Like Moorash's weirdly distorted portraits, Millhauser strains against realism's "mimetic fetters" to achieve an almost mystical perception of human identity.

One of the most intriguing of contemporary mainstream fantasists, Steven Millhauser has consistently attempted to unravel the confusing clash and complicity—formal as well as ontologi-

cal—between realism and romanticism. As a result, his best work is both sensuously pleasurable and philosophically rich.

—Rob Latham

MILNE, A(lan) A(lexander)

Nationality: British. **Born:** London, 18 January 1882. **Education:** Westminster School, London (Queen's scholar), 1893-1900; Trinity College, Cambridge (editor, *Granta*, 1902), 1900-03, B.A. (honours) in mathematics 1903. **Military Service:** Royal Warwickshire Regiment, 1914-18. **Family:** Married Dorothy de Selincourt in 1913; one son, Christopher Robin Milne. **Career:** Freelance journalist, 1903-06; assistant editor, *Punch*, London, 1906-14. **Died:** 31 January 1956.

FANTASY PUBLICATIONS

Fiction

Once on a Time, illustrated by H. M. Brock. London, Hodder and Stoughton, 1917; New York, Putnam, 1922.
A Gallery of Children, illustrated by Saida. London, Stanley Paul, and Philadelphia, McKay, 1925.
Winnie-the-Pooh, illustrated by Ernest Shepard. London, Methuen, and New York, Dutton, 1926.
The House at Pooh Corner, illustrated by Ernest Shepard. London, Methuen, and New York, Dutton, 1928.
Prince Rabbit, and the Princess Who Could Not Laugh, illustrated by Mary Shepard. London, Ward, and New York, Dutton, 1966.

Plays

Make-Believe (includes *The Princess and the Woodcutter, Oliver's Island, Father Christmas and the Hubbard Family*), music by George Dorlay, lyrics by C. E. Burton (produced London, 1918). Included in *Second Plays*, 1921.
The Man in the Bowler Hat: A Terribly Exciting Affair (produced New York, 1924; London, 1925). London and New York, French, 1923.
King Hilary and the Beggarman (produced London, 1926).
The Ivory Door: A Legend (produced New York, 1927; London, 1929). New York, Putnam, 1928; London, Chatto and Windus, 1929.
Toad of Toad Hall, music by H. Fraser-Simson, adaptation of *The Wind in the Willows* by Kenneth Grahame (produced Liverpool, 1929; London, 1930). London, Methuen, and New York, Scribners, 1929.
The Ugly Duckling. London, French, 1941; in *Twenty-Four Favorite One-Act Plays*, edited by Bennett Cerf and Van H. Cartmell, New York, Doubleday, 1958.

Poetry (illustrated by Ernest Shepard)

When We Were Very Young. London, Methuen, and New York, Dutton, 1924.
Now We Are Six. London, Methuen, and New York, Dutton, 1927.

OTHER PUBLICATIONS

Novels

Lovers in London. London, Alston Rivers, 1905.
Mr. Pim. London, Hodder and Stoughton, 1921; New York, Doran, 1922; as *Mr. Pim Passes By,* London, Methuen, 1929.
The Red House Mystery. London, Methuen, and New York, Dutton, 1922.
Two People. London, Methuen, and New York, Dutton, 1931.
Four Days' Wonder. London, Methuen, and New York, Dutton, 1933.
One Year's Time. London, Methuen, 1942.
Chloe Marr. London, Methuen, and New York, Dutton, 1946.

Short Stories

The Secret and Other Stories. London, Methuen, and New York, Fountain Press, 1929.
Birthday Party and Other Stories. New York, Dutton, 1948; London, Methuen, 1949.
A Table Near the Band and Other Stories. London, Methuen, and New York, Dutton, 1950.

Plays

Wurzel-Flummery (produced London, 1917). London and New York, French, 1922; revised version, in *First Plays,* 1919.
Belinda: An April Folly (produced London and New York, 1918). Included in *First Plays,* 1919.
The Boy Comes Home (produced London, 1918). Included in *First Plays,* 1919.
First Plays (includes *Wurzel-Flummery, The Lucky One, The Boy Comes Home, Belinda, The Red Feathers*). London, Chatto and Windus, and New York, Knopf, 1919.
The Red Feathers (produced Leeds, 1920; London, 1921). Included in *First Plays,* 1919.
The Lucky One (produced New York, 1922; Cambridge, 1923; London, 1924). Included in *First Plays,* 1919; as *Let's All Talk about Gerald* (produced London, 1928).
The Camberley Triangle (produced London, 1919). Included in *Second Plays,* 1921.
Mr. Pim Passes By (produced Manchester, 1919; London, 1920; New York, 1921). Included in *Second Plays,* 1921.
The Romantic Age (produced London, 1920; New York, 1922). Included in *Second Plays,* 1921.
The Stepmother (produced London, 1920). Included in *Second Plays,* 1921.
Second Plays (includes *Make-Believe, Mr. Pim Passes By, The Camberley Triangle, The Romantic Age, The Stepmother*). London, Chatto and Windus, 1921; New York, Knopf, 1922.
The Great Broxopp: Four Chapters in Her Life (produced New York, 1921; London, 1923). Included in *Three Plays,* 1922.
The Truth About Blayds (produced London, 1921; New York, 1922). Included in *Three Plays,* 1922.
The Dover Road (produced New York, 1921; London, 1922). Included in *Three Plays,* 1922.
Three Plays (includes *The Dover Road, The Truth About Blayds, The Great Broxopp*). New York, Putnam, 1922; London, Chatto and Windus, 1923.
Berlud, Unlimited (produced London and New York, 1922).

Success (produced London, 1923; as *Give Me Yesterday,* produced New York, 1931). London, Chatto and Windus, 1923; New York, French, 1924.
The Artist: A Duologue. London and New York, French, 1923.
To Have the Honour (produced London, 1924; as *To Meet the Prince,* produced New York, 1929). London and New York, French, 1925.
Ariadne; or, Business First (produced New York and London, 1925). London and New York, French, 1925.
Portrait of a Gentleman in Slippers: A Fairy Tale (produced Liverpool, 1926; London, 1927). London and New York, French, 1926.
Four Plays (includes *To Have the Honour, Ariadne, Portrait of a Gentleman in Slippers, Success*). London, Chatto and Windus, 1926.
Miss Marlow at Play (produced London, 1927; New York, 1940). London and New York, French, 1936.
The Fourth Wall: A Detective Story (produced London, 1928; as *The Perfect Alibi,* produced New York, 1928). New York, French, 1929; London, French, 1930.
Michael and Mary (produced New York, 1929; London, 1930). London, Chatto and Windus, 1930; New York, French, 1932.
They Don't Mean Any Harm (produced London and New York, 1932).
Four Plays (includes *Michael and Mary, To Meet the Prince, The Perfect Alibi, Portrait of a Gentleman in Slippers*). New York, Putnam, 1932.
Other People's Lives (produced London, 1932). London and New York, French, 1935.
More Plays (includes *The Ivory Door, The Fourth Wall, Other People's Lives*). London, Chatto and Windus, 1935.
Miss Elizabeth Bennet, adaptation of the novel *Pride and Prejudice* by Jane Austen (produced London, 1938). London, Chatto and Windus, 1936.
Sarah Simple (produced London, 1937; New York, 1940). London, French, 1939.
Gentleman Unknown (produced London, 1938).
Before the Flood. London and New York, French, 1951.

Screenplays: *The Bump,* 1920; *Five Pounds Reward,* 1920; *Bookworms,* 1920; *Twice Two,* 1920; *Birds of Prey (The Perfect Alibi),* with Basil Dean, 1930.

Poetry

For the Luncheon Interval: Cricket and Other Verses. London, Methuen, and New York, Dutton, 1925.
Behind the Lines. London, Methuen, and New York, Dutton, 1940.
The Norman Church. London, Methuen, 1948.

Other

The Day's Play (*Punch* sketches). London, Methuen, 1910; New York, Dutton, 1925.
The Holiday Round (*Punch* sketches). London, Methuen, 1912; New York, Dutton, 1925.
Once a Week (*Punch* sketches). London, Methuen, 1914; New York, Dutton, 1925.
Happy Days (*Punch* sketches). New York, Doran, 1915.
Not That It Matters. London, Methuen, 1919; New York, Dutton, 1920.

If I May. London, Methuen, 1920; New York, Dutton, 1921.
The Sunny Side. London, Methuen, 1921; New York, Dutton, 1922.
Selected Works. London, Library Press, 7 vols., 1926.
The Ascent of Man. London, Benn, and New York, Dutton, 1928.
By Way of Introduction. London, Methuen, and New York, Dutton, 1929.
Those Were the Days: The Day's Play, The Holiday Round, Once a Week, The Sunny Side. London, Methuen, and New York, Dutton, 1929.
When I Was Very Young (autobiography). London, Methuen, and New York, Fountain Press, 1930.
A. A. Milne (selections). London, Methuen, 1933.
Peace with Honour: An Enquiry into the War Convention. London, Methuen, and New York, Dutton, 1934; revised edition, 1935.
It's Too Late Now: The Autobiography of a Writer. London, Methuen, 1939; as *Autobiography,* New York, Dutton, 1939.
War with Honour. London, Macmillan, 1940.
War Aims Unlimited. London, Methuen, 1941.
Going Abroad? London, Council for Education in World Citizenship, 1947.
Books for Children: A Reader's Guide. London, Cambridge University Press, 1948.
Year In, Year Out. London, Methuen, and New York, Dutton, 1952.

*

Film Adaptations: *Birds of Prey* (*The Perfect Alibi*), 1930; *Michael and Mary,* 1931; *Where Sinners Meet,* 1934, from his play *The Dover Road*; *Four Days' Wonder,* 1936; *Winnie the Pooh and the Honey Tree,* 1966; *Winnie the Pooh and the Blustery Day,* 1968; *Winnie the Pooh and Tigger Too,* 1974; *Winnie the Pooh and a Day for Eeyore,* 1983.

Bibliography: *A. A. Milne: A Handlist of His Writings for Children* by Brian Sibley, Chislehurst Common, Kent, Henry Pootle Press, 1976; *A. A. Milne: A Critical Bibliography* by Tori Haring-Smith, New York, Garland, 1982.

Manuscript Collection: Humanities Research Center, University of Texas, Austin.

Critical Studies: *A. A. Milne* by Thomas Burnett Swann, New York, Twayne, 1971; *The Enchanted Places* by Christopher Milne, London, Eyre Methuen, 1974, New York, Dutton, 1975; *The Pooh Perplex* by Frederick C. Crews, Milton Keynes, Buckinghamshire, Clark, 1979; *Winnie-the-Pooh, Capitalist Lackey?* by Simon Colverson, Andoversford, Gloucestershire, Whittington Press, n.d.; *The Tao of Pooh* by Benjamin Hoff, London, Methuen, 1982; *The Te of Piglet* by Benjamin Hoff, 1992.

*   *   *

In a world only slightly different from ours, A. A. Milne would be recalled today—if he were recalled at all—as a writer whose career began with throwaway humorous essays, and who graduated to scripting fashionable plays and producing well-crafted albeit unremarkable mimetic novels and short stories, the occasional detective fiction and volume of light verse, all of which now exude a slightly stale odour of either Edwardian drawing-rooms and clubs, post-Great War forced elation, or post-Hitlerian Era contraction of British frontiers.

But as matters do stand in this world, Milne's name is forever and inextricably linked with and upheld by just one of his literary creations, much as the reputation of his older contemporary, Arthur Conan Doyle, rests solely on Sherlock Holmes. That creation, of course, is Winnie-the-Pooh, the Bear of Little Brain.

Born to a struggling, mildly scatterbrained Victorian schoolmaster and his capable wife (the latter functioning as chef, bookkeeper and general factotum in a succession of more or less successful teaching establishments) Milne was to lead an idyllic if unexceptional childhood (narration of which takes up two-thirds of his *Autobiography*). This domain of beloved memories was to function throughout his life as a potent source of inspiration, most clearly in the four famous children's books which continue to attract a steady readership today: *When We Were Very Young, Winnie-the-Pooh, Now We Are Six* and *The House At Pooh Corner.* As Christopher Milne—son and real-life model for the book's Eternal Child, Christopher Robin—recounts in his own fascinating autobiography, *The Enchanted Places,* his father's personality was primarily a nostalgic one, always looking back toward a Golden Age of emotion, sentiment and everyday magics.

In his college years, Milne discovered that he and his beloved older brother Ken shared a talent for light verse. This led to professional sales and, eventually, an assistant editorship at the famous British humour magazine, *Punch.* Here, Milne, forced to write an essay a week (he tells the anecdote of desperately opening an encyclopedia at random as his deadline approached and composing an essay on the first topic he saw—goldfish, as it turned out), quickly honed his skills. In some of these early pieces (collected in *Once A Week*), Milne exhibits early traces of the genial, fantastical humour seasoned with gentle yet sardonic jabs that came to mark his best work, including *Pooh.* "Under Entirely New Management" and "A Farewell Tour" contain snatches of life as seen from a dog's point of view. "The King's Sons" is a kind of "fractured fairy tale" he would return to very soon.

Married by now, Milne was soon caught up in World War I. In uniform, but still at home, he was convinced by his wife Dorothy to write his first book, a fantasy for both children and adults entitled *Once On A Time.* This is an assured and hilarious send-up of the traditional fairy tale so many of Milne's contemporaries must have been reared on. King Merriwig of Euralia goes to war against his neighbour, the King of Barodia, irked by the latter's disturbing habit of continually overflying Euralia in his seven-league boots. Merriwig, leaving young Princess Hyacinth behind as regent, her guardian that nefarious charmer, the poetaster Countess Belvane, soon is farcically besieging Barodia. Meanwhile, Belvane sets out to bankrupt the kingdom, forcing Hyacinth to summon another neighbour, Prince Udo, who is unfortunately transformed en route by Belvane into a large chimera of rabbit, lion and sheep. After many amusing confusions and disasters, the war is won, all characters are married off, and everyone lives dimwittedly ever-after. The whole affair has the kind of charm James Thurber (whose career curiously parallels Milne's) was to exhibit later in such books as *The Wonderful O.*

It was also during this period that Milne began turning out plays, one of which bears mention. *The Ivory Door,* which Milne called "the best play which I have written," tells the story of another timeless kingdom. In this one, however, a grim realism pervades. In the throne room of King Perivale is a locked door through which one of his ancestors once vanished, and which is reputed to lead straight to hell, or worse. Fascinated by the door since childhood, Perivale determines at last to brave it. He soon discovers the startling truth: the Ivory Door leads only to a commonplace tunnel that surfaces beyond the palace walls. All glamour and romance vanish in a flash. However, complications remain. Returning to the palace, Perivale is hailed as a demonic impostor. In a farce of almost Kafkaesque dimensions, nobility and commoners alike cling to their legends, rather than face reality. In the end, Perivale and his new bride are forced to abdicate and flee. One wonders if the moral and theme of this play were portents of the personal dilemma Milne was soon to experience. For by this time, all of the books that would so come to dominate his career had appeared, to great acclaim and sales.

The rhymes in *When We Were Very Young* establish the ambience of the Pooh tales: a kind of crystalline Age of Innocent Wonder and Imagination, where the most commonplace object is inherently exotic, fleeting yet forever. In almost haiku-like poems such as "Summer Afternoon" and "Twinkletoes," to Yeatsian ones like "Water Lilies" and "The Mirror," Milne creates a world of charm and security, threatened only superficially by the menacing bears (of all creatures!) in "Lines and Squares." (Here full credit should be given to Milne's collaborative illustrator, Ernest H. Shepard, whose evocative drawings are such an integral part of all four books.)

Introduced in the poem "Teddy Bear," the famous Winnie—later to be Disney-animated, Latinized, sung-about and endlessly spun-off—makes his first appearance. The unforgettable personalities, incidents and atmosphere of Pooh's Forest are by now too well-known and repeatedly evoked to demand recounting. Inhabiting the same magical territory as Grahame's *The Wind in the Willows* (which Milne was to dramatize in his best-remembered play, *Toad of Toad Hall*), Beatrix Potter's *The Tale of Peter Rabbit* and Barrie's *Peter Pan*, Pooh lives a life full of mundane pleasures, imagined dangers and homey catastrophes. Carrollian nonsense dialogue and the morose hilarity of Eeyore the Donkey mitigate any saccharine moments, providing a full measure of pleasure for adult readers as well as for children.

What has not been generally remarked is the influence of the Pooh milieu on later writers. Surely the crisp geography of Richard Adams's *Watership Down* is Pooh-derived, as are the homey burrows and snack-obsessed character of Tolkien's hobbits. During the 1950s and 1960s, Pogo and the other animal inhabitants of Walt Kelly's Okefenokee Swamp occupied their time in a most Pooh-like fashion. More recently, the immensely popular U.S. comic strip by Bill Watterson, *Calvin and Hobbes,* contains the most obvious avatars of Christopher Robin and Pooh in modern times. Two authorized additions to the canon, at first seeming oddly incongruent with Milne's lifelong agnosticism (his famous poem, "Vespers," he once revealed to be about the inherent egotism of those who pray) are *The Tao of Pooh* and *The Te of Piglet* by Benjamin Hoff, explications of Taoist philosophy as hidden within and exampled by Milne's texts.

Attempting unsuccessfully to bid farewell to his creation in the elegiac last chapter of *The House At Pooh Corner,* Milne also turned his back on fantasy in general, as if feeling the mode was unable to coexist with adult concerns. Only toward the end of his life, in a few short stories that include "Before the Flood" (a Monty-Pythonesque life of Noah) and "The Balcony" (both 1950), did he give vent to his fantastic impulses. (The latter is a keenly disturbing narration of one man's afterlife experiences.)

But whether willingly or stubbornly, gratefully or resentfully, fairly or not, Milne had seen his large career distilled to a handful of children's fantasies permanently emblazoned on the minds of several generations, where "on the top of the Forest, a little boy and his Bear will always be playing."

—Paul Di Filippo

MIRRLEES, Hope

Nationality: British. **Born:** 1887. **Education:** Oxford University; student, and later lifelong friend, of the eminent classical scholar Jane Harrison. **Died:** 1 August 1978.

FANTASY PUBLICATIONS

Novel

Lud-in-the-Mist. London, Collins, 1926; New York, Ballantine, 1970.

Other

Editor and translator, with Jane Harrison, *The Book of the Bear: Being Twenty-One Tales Newly Translated from the Russian*. London, Nonesuch Press, 1926.

OTHER PUBLICATIONS

Novels

Madeleine, One of Love's Jansenists. London, Collins, 1919.
The Counterplot. London, Collins, 1924.

Poetry

Paris: A Poem. Richmond, Surrey, Hogarth Press, 1919.
Moods and Tensions: Seventeen Poems. Privately printed, n.d. (1920?).
Poems. Cape Town, South Africa, Gothic Printing, 1963.

Other

A Fly in Amber: Being an Extravagant Biography of the Romantic Antiquary Sir Robert Bruce Cotton. London, Faber, 1962.

Translator, with Jane Harrison, *The Life of the Archpriest Avvakum, by Himself*. London, Woolf, 1924.

*   *   *

Hope Mirrlees's one fantasy novel, *Lud-in-the-Mist,* is prefaced by a quotation from British classical scholar and "armchair anthropologist" Jane Harrison (1850-1938), author of *Prolegomena to the Study of Greek Religion* (1903) and other influential works: "The Sirens stand, as it would seem, to the ancient and the modern, for the impulses in life as yet immoralised, imperious longings, ecstasies, whether of love or art, or philosophy, magical voices calling to a man from his 'Land of Heart's Desire', and to which if he hearken it may be that he will return no more—voices, too, which, whether a man sail by or stay to hearken, still sing on." This statement (its exact source in Harrison's writings is not given), by a close friend and collaborator of Hope Mirrlees's, seems aptly chosen.

But *Lud-in-the-Mist* is built—like Christina Rossetti's poem "Goblin Market"—around the image, not of the Greek Sirens, but of forbidden fairy fruit. Here, though, the fruit's rejection by the staid burghers of Lud is an error. The nearby Fairyland doesn't stand for prohibited sexual pleasures but for that whole complex of yearning, dissatisfaction and desire for inaccessible beauty that supposedly provokes lyric poets and creative artists.

The Mayor of Lud, Nathaniel Chanticleer, has been troubled all his life by the attraction and repulsion of a certain plangent strain of melancholy which he calls the Note . . . at one stage he did badly at cards since he couldn't bear to hold the high-scoring Lyre of Bones. The Note is associated with the "vulgar" song "Columbine" whose chorus haunts the book ("With lily, germander and sops in wine / With sweet-briar / And bon-fire / And strawberry-wire / And columbine") and also with fairy fruit. But even to speak of the fruit is smutty talk in Lud—euphemisms are used, and the stuff has no existence in law (important throughout), so those who smuggle it must be amusingly prosecuted under the legal fiction that they imported contraband silk.

After his son is believed to have eaten the fruit, and his daughter is seduced away with her entire dancing class by fairy music, Chanticleer is stung into action against the fruit-smuggling operations of the sinister Dr. Endymion Leer . . . only to be outwitted, humiliated, framed by fruit planted in his own home, and legally declared dead. Nevertheless he persists.

His investigations uncover the secret of an old murder, duly leading to several hangings: this is not the twee fairy story indicated by the cover of its 1970 Ballantine Adult Fantasy reissue, but a tough-minded and witty as well as whimsical novel. (Several neat detective ploys appear: the sinister omen of blood oozing from a coffin is actually a clue to how forbidden, squashy fruits are being smuggled.) The point of the murder subplot is to hint that fairy fruit is not itself evil, the commerce in it having been tainted by this crime of the principal smugglers.

Ultimately, learning that his son has crossed the border into the Elfin Marches—thought in Lud to be wholly synonymous with death—Chanticleer follows on a lurid nightmare journey to the brink of a black abyss. He can only leap.

The eventual result is that he and his son return; the borders are opened; fairy fruit becomes acceptable again, and is indeed candied for export in boxes, "the painted lids of which showed that art was creeping back". Chanticleer is still not entirely satisfied—but rather than fearing it, longs to hear that Note again. With death, he may. It is a moving book, shifting unpredictably from drollery to menace to a high poignancy that sticks in the mind.

Mirrlees's other volume which may be classifed as fantasy is the anthology she co-translated and co-edited with Jane Harrison, *The Book of the Bear.* The collaborators seem to have taken a fairly free hand with these 21 Russian folk-tales and poems that feature "the Bear" in all its forms. While the Bear is obviously symbolic of the Russian state, it is also seen as a symbol of mankind (as distinct from womankind) and the book may be viewed as something of a statement about men. The stories are selected from the works of Tolstoy, Pushkin, Krylov, Remizov, Chemnitzer and others (and so are not specifically feminist in origin). Although the tales were written originally as adult fables, the translations are slanted more towards children and as a result lose some of their original charm.

Hope Mirrlees was an outspoken and single-minded individual who recognized that she was seen as something of an outcast from society (because of her relationship with another woman, Jane Harrison). This desire for distinction, almost notoriety, seems to have fuelled her social and writing activities. She was a friend of Virginia Woolf who, while respecting her abilities, regarded her as "over-dressed and over-elaborate . . . a little unrefined [and] vain but lacking self-confidence," a combination that resulted in a precocious but unstable personality. Some of this is noticeable in *Lud-in-the-Mist,* which goes out of its way to portray the potential for conflict between an old-fashioned and traditional Lud (or London) and the free-thinking but forbidden lands of Faery.

—David Langford and Mike Ashley

MODESITT, L(eland) E(xton), Jr.

Nationality: American. **Born:** Denver, Colorado, 19 October 1943. **Education:** Williams College, 1961-65, B.A. **Military Service:** U.S. Navy, 1965-70: Lieutenant, Naval Aviator. **Family:** Married 1) Virginia Dale Eschenburg in 1964 (divorced, 1976), four children; 2) Christina Alma Gribben in 1977 (divorced, 1991), two children; 3) Carol Ann Janes Hill, in 1992, two step-children. **Career:** Market research analyst, C. A. Norgren, Englewood, Colorado, 1970-71; real-estate agent, Koelbel & Co., Denver, Colorado, 1971-72; legislative assistant, U.S. Representative William Armstrong, Washington, D.C., 1973-78; staff director, U.S. Representative Ken Kramer, Washington, D.C., 1979-81; director, Office of Legislation and Congressional Relations, U.S. Environmental Protection Agency, Washington, D.C., 1981-85; senior manager, environmental projects, Multinational Business Services, Washington, D.C., 1985-91; adjunct instructor in literature and writing, Plymouth State College, New Hampshire, 1990-93; independent consultant and freelance writer from 1991. **Address:** 255 South Sunny View Road, Cedar City, UT 84720, USA.

FANTASY PUBLICATIONS

Novels (series: Recluce in all books)

The Magic of Recluce. New York, Tor, 1991; London, Orbit, 1994.
The Towers of the Sunset. New York, Tor, 1992; London, Orbit, 1994.
The Magic Engineer. New York, Tor, 1994; London, Orbit, 1995.
The Order War. New York, Tor, and London, Orbit, 1995.
The Death of Chaos. New York, Tor, 1995.

OTHER PUBLICATIONS

Novels

The Fires of Paratime. New York, Timescape, 1982; expanded as *The Timegod,* New York, Tor, 1993.
The Hammer of Darkness. New York, Avon, 1985.
The Ecologic Envoy. New York, Tor, 1986.

Dawn for a Distant Earth. New York, Tor, 1987.
The Silent Warrior. New York, Tor, 1987.
In Endless Twilight. New York, Tor, 1988.
The Ecolitan Operation. New York, Tor, 1989.
The Ecologic Secession. New York, Tor, 1990.
The Green Progression, with Bruce Scott Levinson. New York, Tor, 1991.
Timedivers' Dawn. New York, Tor, 1992.
Of Tangible Ghosts. New York, Tor, 1994.

*

L. E. Modesitt comments:

I got into writing fantasy as a result of a series of discussions with other writers. As a consultant and a former political staffer and economist, I have often been discouraged at the lack of consideration some writers give to the basics of human society, i.e. the reasons for its organizational structure and the economics of its operations. In my efforts to ask why a fantasy could not incorporate realistic economics, technology and functional social structures evolved from necessity—and still remain a fantasy, I ended up writing the books in the Recluce universe.

In *The Magic of Recluce,* for example, young Lerris has a problem common to many young people. He is bored with his life, primarily because he refuses to see why his society exists as it does. Solid attention to order in life does hold off chaos, but because the system works Lerris does not see its benefits until he experiences a more "chaotic" culture, at which point he finds himself in a great deal of difficulty. He also has to find a way to make a living, falling back on his wood-working skills.

In *The Towers of the Sunset,* one of the heroes, Creslin, finds that despite his prowess with the blade and the song, his life is not his to order as he pleases. He is literally linked by magic and necessity to a woman who is attracted to him but who dislikes his tendency to resort to force. Moreover, the cold requirements of economics and the imperatives of the climate of the island of Recluce bring him up short time after time—as do his tendencies to overreach himself magically and physically.

Because I also have what appears to be an old-fashioned belief that nothing of value is obtained without work and struggle, this is also reflected in my writing, although I try to recognize that what may be a cost to one individual has little or no value to another. Thus, in *The Magic Engineer,* the young warrior captain Brede can lift a blade with little impact on himself. Yet he is revolted by Dorrin's application of magic and technology to the battlefield, while Dorrin finds it impossible to used edged weapons, even as he is destroying thousands. In the end, however, both pay heavily.

*   *   *

L. E. Modesitt is an established science-fiction adventure-story writer, author of two mid-range sf trilogies and a few other books, who turned to heroic fantasy in the early 1990s. Although he is an author capable of giving much pleasure, the results have been mixed.

The Magic of Recluce is a splendid tale which grips from the first sentence. It is immediately accessible, engagingly written and does not suffer from that bane of so much would-be epic fantasy, "elevated language". The hero, Lerris, is a bored teenager from the perfect continent of Recluce. Because of his boredom with all the perfection which surrounds him, he is sent out into the world on "dangergeld"—a type of quest-cum-rite-of-passage used by his society to winnow out those who do not fit into its perfection. He finds that he is a "blackstaffer," that the staff his uncle gave him as a parting gift is useful for much more than mere hiking, and that he has an in-built power to act as a focus of Order and so to combat the white-clad Chaos-masters. The world he finds himself in is, roughly speaking, 18th-century in flavour—with coaches and horses, unreliable pistols and early steamships which are little used because of their potential for focusing Chaos.

As well as creating an interesting and likeable world, Modesitt develops the character of Lerris with considerable insight. The cry of "boring!" which comes from adolescents in the face of almost everything can be puzzling to adults, but in Modesitt's hands Lerris's boredom is rendered comprehensible. Another worthwhile feature of the book is the lightly handled consideration of feminism, as treated in the portrayals of the women warriors, the woman Ordermistress who is Lerris's counterpart, and Lerris's affection for the humble Deirdre, woodcrafter Destrin's daughter.

In *The Towers of the Sunset* we learn how Recluce, the land of Order-magic, came to be founded by Creslin and Megaera, unwanted spare royals linked together by a magic bond and pressurized from all sides until they are driven to colonize Recluce, a land so desolate no one else wants it. The problem with the book lies mainly in the setting: Creslin is a male who has grown up in a society swayed by the legend which states that a man should never be allowed to rule because it was men who got the angels thrown out of heaven. Fair enough, and Creslin's reaction to being eyed up by his mother's female warriors has an authentic ring to it. Megaera is also brought up in a land dominated by the same legend, and her first reaction to the enforced link to Creslin is horror at finding herself bound to a mere man. However, once they flee outside the legend-dominated territory, and encounter patriarchy, Megaera's resistance and Creslin's utter insensitivity to her feelings both ring false. Surely it would never occur to either of them that Creslin could dominate Megaera if they have been raised to believe there are many things that cannot be done by a mere man? No, once outside the legend-territory they should still have its indoctrination in their heads—but neither of them does.

Nevertheless the novel is a good read, and one might look forward to third, *The Magic Engineer.* Alas, this one turned out to be deeply irritating on account of being written in the present tense for no apparent reason and also because of its irksomely predictable plot. The new hero, Dorrin, is an apprentice healer, apprentice smith and aspiring engineer, and he is exiled from Recluce because he doesn't fit in. (One would expect Modesitt to explain how Recluce can function if it continually lobotomizes itself by exiling anyone with intelligence or angst.) Dorrin spends the required time at the charmingly named Recluce "Academy of Useless and Violent Knowledge" and then goes into exile—where he has to put together his own household and living circumstances in the face of implacable enmity from the white wizards of Chaos. The novel develops into yet another of those tales where the villain makes the classic mistake of pursuing a hero whose heroism develops precisely because of the opposition, and who would have been a happy nobody if he had been left in peace to practice fretwork and midwifery.

The by-no-means untalented Modesitt is developing into a very prolific writer, and has produced two more episodes in the Recluce series since this essay was drafted; it is to be hoped that these and future books will show a return to the freshness and strength of the first volume in the series.

—Wendy Bradley

MONACO, Richard

Nationality: American. **Born:** New York City, 23 April 1940. **Education:** Columbia University, New York, 1966-69. **Family:** Married 1) Judy Jacobs in 1968; 2) Adele Leone in 1983; one child. **Career:** Assistant to director, Group for Contemporary Music, Columbia University, 1966-70; curator of music, Columbia University, 1967-70; film and poetry editor, *University Review,* 1968-70; lecturer, New School for Social Research, New York, 1972-77; lecturer, Morley College, Westchester County, New York, 1973-77; talk-show host, WNYC-FM radio, New York, 1974-77; senior vice-president and president, Adele Leone Agency, New York, 1978-93; president, Wildstar Associates, Westchester County, from 1993. **Agent:** Adele Leone, Acton, Dystel, Leone and Jaffe, Inc., 79 Fifth Avenue, New York, NY. **Address:** 26 Nantucket Place, Scarsdale, NY 10583, USA

FANTASY PUBLICATIONS

Novels (series: Leitus; Parsival)

Parsival; or, A Knight's Tale. New York, Macmillan, 1977; London, Sphere, 1978.
The Grail War (Parsival). New York, Simon and Schuster, 1979; London, Sphere, 1980.
The Final Quest (Parsival). New York, Putnam, 1980; London, Sphere, 1982.
Runes (Leitus). New York, Ace, 1984.
Blood and Dreams (Parsival). New York, Berkley, 1985.
Broken Stone (Leitus). New York, Ace, 1985.
Journey to the Flame. New York, Bantam, 1985.

OTHER PUBLICATIONS

Novels

The Cult Candidate. London, Sphere, 1982.
Unto the Beast. New York, Bantam, 1987.

Plays

The Realities of the Business (produced New York, 1976).
Parsival (produced New York, 1977).

Other

The Logic of Poetry. New York, McGraw Hill, 1974.
Rubouts. New York, Avon, 1990.
Bizarre America. New York, Berkley, 1992.
The Dracula Syndrome, with Bill Burt. New York, Avon, 1993.

Editor, *New American Poetry.* New York, McGraw Hill, 1973.

*   *   *

Richard Monaco, a gifted writer of music, poetry, plays, fiction and non-fiction, attracted attention with his first fantasy novel, *Parsival,* based on the popular Arthurian legends. Monaco daringly avoided the prevalent and reverent approach to the legends by portraying a bawdy, rough and brutal tale of the Dark Ages. In fact, some reviewers have hinted that the sombre tone of the stories might belong to the horror rather than the fantasy genre. In spite of the prevailing mood of depression, the Parsival books are fantasy because of the tie to the Arthurian stories.

Often referred to as a trilogy, the publication of the last book in the series, *Blood and Dreams,* created a quartet with the original *Parsival* and its sequels, *The Grail War* and *The Final Quest.* The central character of the books is Parsival, at first a protected and naive young man who leaves the sheltering castle of his queen mother. He discovers a world of terror and magic, yet also imbued with hope and a little chivalry. Monaco's Britain is no Camelot; it is a brooding and sinful place where the reader is grateful for the occasional sunshine of happiness and morality. In some ways, the Monaco books might best be compared to the music of Wagner as used in the John Borman film *Excalibur,* rather than the cheerful tunes of the Broadway musical *Camelot.* Certainly, the Parsival saga is very different from other latter-day Arthurian stories, for example, those by Mary Stewart. Monaco can be credited with creating a different, more original Arthurian legend than before, but it has not been the preferred one of most readers. Selected bibliographies of various fictional accounts of the King Arthur stories often omit Monaco's version.

The basic plot has not been tampered with; Parsival yearns to join the famous knights of the round table where he is ultimately pronounced to be so pure in heart that he must be the one to seek the holy grail. In Monaco's hands, however, Parsival's purity is described as being the result of emotional disorders brought about because of his stifling upbringing. Such ironic touches are typical in the Monaco treatment; not only is chivalry dead, it probably never amounted to much in the first place. Much of this is due the terribly devastated landscape of the novels, for Arthur's kingdom has been laid waste by a dreadful war which has left the countryside bleak and harsh.

There is also the constant reminder of Parsival's growing cynicism. By the fourth book, *Blood and Dreams,* Parsival muses, "When I was seventeen I killed a man and took his gear. I learned chivalry. A blond boy full of dreams. Everyone agreed that I was like a giant nine-year-old. My mother had hated the world and kept me locked away from it as long as she could. Now, almost twenty years later, I wished she'd done an even better job." A sad commentary from a knight who is not only tired and discouraged, but disillusioned as well.

The dark tone of Monaco's Parsival books is not used in all his fantasy writing. Two books about the clash of Roman might and British druid magic are less dismal and more in the mainstream of the fantasy genre. *Runes* and its sequel, *Broken Stone,* are basically a love story between Leitus, a noble Roman, and Bita, a British druid. The lovers must battle evil with magic and courage throughout the ancient Roman empire. In this ancient world, magic is real and the ancient gods exist. Mortal men and women deal with this world as they did in the old classical legends, bravely and desperately, with no guarantee of success.

Others of Monaco's novels are apparently inspired by a general surge of interest in Nazi occultism popularized by the Indiana Jones movies. One, *Journey to the Flame,* is a tribute to the adventure writer H. Rider Haggard, who is a central character in the book. The plot describes an attempt by a bunch of budding Nazis just prior to World War II to locate the kingdom of Kor described by Haggard in his fictional works about Ayesha, better known as She-

Who-Must-be-Obeyed. The villains are after ancient occult secrets which they intend to employ to further their nefarious plan.

Another title, *Unto the Beast,* also uses Nazis as villains, but the theme of the book is an explanation of sorts about the origins of Nazi foulness, an ancient evil which has escaped from hell to earth. This last book, especially, is reminiscent of Dennis Wheatley's occult novels, but without Wheatley's careful use accurate details of black magic.

In recent years, Monaco has written more nonfiction than fiction, including titles such as *Bizarre America* and *The Dracula Syndrome* with Bill Burt. A case can certainly be made for the real horrors of today that are often much worse than the imagined terror of fictional fantasy and horror, but one cannot help but wonder if Monaco is no longer interested in creating worlds of fantasy in favour of tabloid commercialism.

—Cosette Kies

MOON, (Susan) Elizabeth (Norris)

Nationality: American. **Born:** McAllen, Texas, 17 March 1945. **Education:** Rice University, B.A. in history 1968; University of Texas at Austin, B.A. in biology 1975; graduate study at the University of Texas at Austin, 1975-77. **Military Service:** United States Marine Corps, 1968-71. **Family:** Married Richard S. Moon in 1969; one son. **Career:** Emergency Medical Service volunteer, 1979-84; member of Florence City Council, 1980-84. **Awards:** Compton Crook Award, 1988. Lives in Florence, Texas. **Agent:** Joshua Bilmes, Scott Meredith Literary Agency, Inc., 845 Third Avenue, New York, NY 10022, USA.

Fantasy Publications

Novels (series: Paksenarrion in all books)

Sheepfarmer's Daughter. New York, Baen, 1988.
Divided Allegiance. New York, Baen, 1988.
Oath of Gold. New York, Baen, 1989.
Surrender None: The Legacy of Gird. New York, Baen, 1990.
The Deed of Paksenarrion (omnibus; includes *Sheepfarmer's Daughter, Divided Allegiance, Oath of Gold*). New York, Baen, 1992.
Liar's Oath. New York, Baen, 1992.

Other Publications

Novels

Sassinak, with Anne McCaffrey. New York, Baen, 1990; London, Orbit, 1991.
Generation Warriors, with Anne McCaffrey. New York, Baen, and London, Orbit, 1992.
Hunting Party. New York, Baen, 1993.
The Planet Pirates, with Anne McCaffrey and Jody Lynn Nye (omnibus; includes *The Death of Sleep* by Anne McCaffrey and Jody Lynn Nye, *Sassinak, Generation Warriors*). New York, Baen, 1993.

Sporting Chance. New York, Baen, 1994.

Short Stories

Lunar Activity. New York, Baen, 1990.

* * *

Elizabeth Moon established herself as a major fantasy writer with her first trilogy, focused on the heroic adventures of a woman warrior named Paksenarrion. In many ways, the novels seem like standard fantasies, set in a faraway medieval land inhabited by humans, elves, dwarves, orcs, and various practitioners of good and evil magic. However, Moon actually builds her story on a quite different tradition of fantastic literature, one which regularly features female heroes: *The Lives of the Saints.*

The first book, *Sheepfarmer's Daughter,* describes the education of the eventual saint: Paksenarrion runs away from a marriage arranged by her father and enlists in a mercenary company, where she works hard to become a superb fighter, distinguishes herself in several battles and a desperate cross-country journey, displays a deep-rooted commitment to moral values, and begins to sense that she has special powers and a special mission in life. *Divided Allegiance* depicts the testing of the saint: Paksenarrion leaves her company, disgusted by the immorality of their recent actions; commits herself to the service of Gird, an ancient saint who once led a peasant revolt; and is accepted for training as a paladin, a warrior for Gird who will develop magical powers. Now fighting largely by herself, she must three times enter a dark underground chamber or cave to battle with evil forces; after the third encounter, she is magically tainted with evil, and the bungled process of expunging it takes away her courage, leaving her a pathetic wanderer. *Oath of Gold* displays the true emergence and final victory of the saint: her courage restored by a magical being called a Kuakgan, Paksenarrion is unmistakably chosen by the gods, as she spontaneously develops the powers of a paladin and embarks on a quest to restore the Duke of her former company to his proper position as the king of an elven kingdom. At one point, to rescue the Duke, she submits to five days of torture and humiliation at the hands of her enemies, but somehow lives through the ordeal to help lead the Duke to the country he will lead. Overall, then, Paksenarrion is far more similar to Joan of Arc than to Frodo Baggins; however, Moon departs from that pattern in one significant respect: lives of saints, like that of Joan, usually end with the death and triumphant martyrdom of the protagonists, but Moon allows her heroine to survive her final torments, possibly for practical reasons—to please editors who prefer happy endings, or to leave an opening for further sequels.

The Paksenarrion trilogy is impressive in many ways: the often-praised realism of her depiction of military life (surely derived from Moon's own experience in the Marine Corps); a narrative that is both episodic and subtly integrated; a carefully and thoughtfully developed background; and many interesting supporting characters. Its major flaw results from Moon's choice of generic model. Like most saints, Paksenarrion seems not quite real, too good to be true, almost incapable of doing an evil deed or thinking an evil thought. She professes no interest in sexual activity—as is appropriate in a literary tradition sanctioned by a church which celebrates female chastity—and implausibly maintains her virginity until her final humiliation. With monotonous regularity, the good characters that Paksenarrion encounters quickly recognize her extraordinary virtues and rush to assist and advise her. It is almost as if Moon consciously reached back to *The Lives of the Saints* to provide a modernized role model for young female readers, a woman who could outfight any man while maintaining higher moral standards in her adventures.

After the trilogy, Moon has returned to the world of Paksenarrion three times. A short appendage to the trilogy, "Those Who Wait in Darkness," describes how a young man who watched Paksenarrion's torments is then inspired by her courage to join the Girdsmen. In *Surrender None: The Legacy of Gird,* she goes back in time to tell the story of Gird and his rebellion. Again drawing on her military experience, Moon thoroughly and convincingly describes how a determined peasant might organize a guerrilla army to successfully overthrow evil nobleman; this may be the first fantasy novel to discuss the importance of digging proper latrines for travelling warriors, and there are also evocative portrayals of the rural peasant society that Gird emerged from and longs to rejoin. Despite a final miraculous event in which Gird, like Christ, magically purges the land of lingering bitterness by dying, he seems less like a saint than Paksenarrion, displaying a number of human weaknesses, including a fiery temper and a drinking problem. Other fantasy elements, like Gird's encounter with a Kuakgan and a visit to the gnomes, seem almost like intrusions in what might otherwise be an effective historical novel.

Compared to her other fantasies, *Liar's Oath* is disappointing, a dull and meandering novel mostly focused on Luap, former disciple of Gird, who handles problems during Gird's last years and after his death, rediscovers his own magical powers, leads others of his kind to live in a distant stronghold later visited by Paksenarrion, and is gradually tempted into evil and defeated by malevolent elves; in a final vision, he speaks with Paksenarrion, who promises that she will someday return to his stronghold and release his spirit. Breaking away from the structure of the saint's life to describe a less admirable character, Moon seems to flounder uncertainly; the only conceivable purposes of the novel are to better explain how Gird's world evolved into Paksenarrion's world and—perhaps—to lay the groundwork for another novel about Paksenarrion.

Still, given the strength of her first four fantasies, it is surprising that Moon has recently devoted her energies to two competent but unremarkable science-fiction series. Perhaps the market for saints' lives is not what it used to be.

—Gary Westfahl

MOORCOCK, Michael (John)

Pseudonyms: Bill Barclay; Edward P. Bradbury; James Colvin; Desmond Reid. **Nationality:** British. **Born:** Mitcham, Surrey, 18 December 1939. **Family:** Married 1) Hilary Bailey in 1962, two daughters and one son; 2) Jill Riches in 1978; 3) Linda Steel in 1983. **Career:** Editor, *Tarzan Adventures,* London, 1956-57, and *Sexton Blake Library,* Fleetway Publications, London, 1958-61; editor and writer for Liberal Party, 1962-63; editor from 1964 and publisher from 1967, *New Worlds,* London. From 1955, songwriter and member of various rock bands including Hawkwind and Deep Fix. **Awards:** British Science Fiction Association award, 1966; Nebula award 1967; Derleth award, 1972, 1974, 1975, 1976; *Guardian* Fiction prize, 1977; Campbell Memorial award, 1979;

World Fantasy award, 1979. Guest of Honour, World Fantasy Convention, New York, 1976. **Agent:** Sheil Land Associates Ltd., 43 Doughty Street, London WC1N 2LF, England; or, Howard Morhaim Literary Agency, 175 Fifth Avenue, Suite 709, New York, NY 10010, USA.

FANTASY PUBLICATIONS

Novels (series: Corum; Erekosë; Elric; Hawkmoon; Von Bek)

Stormbringer (Elric). London, Jenkins, 1965; New York, Lancer, 1967; revised edition, New York, DAW, 1977.
The Jewel in the Skull (Hawkmoon). New York, Lancer, 1967; London, Mayflower, 1969; revised edition, New York, DAW, 1977.
Sorcerer's Amulet (Hawkmoon). New York, Lancer, 1968; as *The Mad God's Amulet,* London, Mayflower, 1969; revised edition, New York, DAW, 1977.
The Sword of the Dawn (Hawkmoon). New York, Lancer, 1968; London, Mayflower, 1969; revised edition, New York, DAW, 1977.
The Secret of the Runestaff (Hawkmoon). New York, Lancer, 1969; as *The Runestaff,* London, Mayflower, 1969; revised edition, New York, DAW, 1977.
The Eternal Champion (Erekosë). London, Mayflower, and New York, Dell, 1970; revised edition, New York, Harper, 1978.
Phoenix in Obsidian (Erekosë). London, Mayflower, 1970; as *The Silver Warriors,* New York, Dell, 1973.
The Knight of the Swords (Corum). London, Mayflower, and New York, Berkley, 1971.
The Queen of the Swords (Corum). London, Mayflower, and New York, Berkley, 1971.
The King of the Swords (Corum). London, Mayflower, and New York, Berkley, 1971.
The Sleeping Sorceress (Elric). London, New English Library, 1971; New York, Lancer, 1972; revised edition, as *The Vanishing Tower,* New York, DAW, 1977; London, Panther, 1984.
Elric of Melniboné. London, Hutchinson, 1972; as *The Dreaming City,* New York, Lancer, 1972.
The Bull and the Spear (Corum). London, Allison and Busby, and New York, Berkley, 1973.
Count Brass (Hawkmoon). London, Mayflower, 1973; New York, Dell, 1976.
The Champion of Garathorm (Hawkmoon). London, Mayflower, 1973; New York, Berkley, 1985.
The Oak and the Ram (Corum). London, Allison and Busby, and New York, Berkley, 1973.
The Sword and the Stallion (Corum). London, Allison and Busby, and New York, Berkley, 1974.
The Quest for Tanelorn (Hawkmoon). London, Mayflower, 1975; New York, Dell, 1976.
The Sailor on the Seas of Fate (Elric). London, Quartet, and New York, DAW, 1976.
The Swords Trilogy (omnibus; includes *The Knight of the Swords, The Queen of the Swords, The King of the Swords*). New York, Berkley, 1977; as *The Swords of Corum,* London, Grafton, 1986; as *Corum,* London, Millennium, 1992.
The History of the Runestaff (omnibus; includes *The Jewel in the Skull, The Mad God's Amulet, The Sword of the Dawn, The Runestaff*). London, Hart Davis MacGibbon, 1979; as *Hawkmoon,* London, Millennium, 1992.

Gloriana; or, The Unfulfill'd Queen. London, Allison and Busby, 1978; New York, Avon, 1979; revised edition, London, Millennium, 1993.

The Golden Barge. Manchester, Savoy, 1979; New York, DAW, 1980.

The War Hound and the World's Pain (Von Bek). New York, Pocket Books, 1981; London, New English Library, 1982.

The Chronicles of Castle Brass (Hawkmoon; omnibus; includes *Count Brass, The Champion of Garathorm, The Quest for Tanelorn*). London, Granada, 1985; as *Count Brass,* London, Millennium, 1993.

The City in the Autumn Stars (Von Bek). London, Grafton, 1986; New York, Ace, 1987.

The Dragon in the Sword (Erekosë). New York, Ace, 1986; London, Grafton, 1987.

The Chronicles of Corum (omnibus; includes *The Bull and the Spear, The Oak and the Ram, The Sword and the Stallion*). London, Grafton, and New York, Ace, 1987; as *The Prince With the Silver Hand,* London, Millennium, 1993.

The Fortress of the Pearl (Elric). London, Gollancz, and New York, Ace, 1989.

The Revenge of the Rose (Elric). London, Grafton, and New York, Ace, 1991.

The Eternal Champion (Erekosë; omnibus; includes *The Eternal Champion, Phoenix in Obsidian, The Dragon in the Sword*). London, Millennium, 1992.

Von Bek (omnibus; includes *The Warhound and the World's Pain, The City in the Autumn Stars* and a short story). London, Millennium, 1992.

Elric of Melniboné (omnibus; includes *Elric of Melniboné, The Fortress of the Pearl, The Sailor on the Seas of Fate* and short stories). London, Millennium, 1993.

Stormbringer (Elric; omnibus; includes *Stormbringer, The Vanishing Tower, The Revenge of the Rose* and short stories). London, Millennium, 1993.

Earl Aubec (omnibus; includes *The Golden Barge* and short stories). London, Millennium, 1993.

Graphic Novels

Elric: The Return to Melniboné, illustrated by Philippe Druillet. Brighton, Unicorn Bookshop, 1973.

The Swords of Heaven, the Flowers of Hell, illustrated by Howard V. Chaykin. New York, 1979.

The Crystal and the Amulet, illustrated by James Cawthorn. London, Savoy, 1986.

Short Stories

The Stealer of Souls and Other Stories (Elric). London, Spearman, 1963; New York, Lancer, 1967.

The Singing Citadel (Elric). London, Mayflower, and New York, Berkley, 1970.

The Jade Man's Eyes (Elric). Brighton, Unicorn Bookshop, 1973.

Sojan (juvenilia; includes essays). Manchester, Savoy, 1977.

The Weird of the White Wolf (Elric). New York, DAW, 1977; London, Panther, 1984.

The Bane of the Black Sword (Elric). New York, DAW, 1977; London, Panther, 1984.

Elric at the End of Time: Fantasy Stories. London, New English Library, 1984; New York, DAW, 1985.

OTHER PUBLICATIONS

Novels

Caribbean Crisis (as Desmond Reid, with James Cawthorn). London, Fleetway, 1962.

The Sundered Worlds. London, Compact, 1965; New York, Paperback Library, 1966; as *The Blood Red Game,* London, Sphere, 1970.

The Fireclown. London, Compact, 1965; New York, Paperback Library, 1967; as *The Winds of Limbo,* Paperback Library, 1969.

Warriors of Mars (as Edward P. Bradbury). London, Compact, 1965; New York, Lancer, 1966; as *The City of the Beast* (as Michael Moorcock), Lancer, 1980.

Blades of Mars (as Edward P. Bradbury). London, Compact, 1965; New York, Lancer, 1966; as *The Lord of the Spiders* (as Michael Moorcock), Lancer, 1970.

The Barbarians of Mars (as Edward P. Bradbury). London, Compact, 1965; New York, Lancer, 1966; as *The Masters of the Pit* (as Michael Moorcock), Lancer, 1970.

The Twilight Man. London, Compact, 1966; New York, Berkley, 1970; as *The Shores of Death,* London, Sphere, 1970.

The LSD Dossier (ghosted for Roger Harris). London, Compact, 1966.

Printer's Devil (as Bill Barclay). London, Compact, 1966; revised edition, as *The Russian Intelligence* (as Michael Moorcock), Manchester, Savoy, 1980.

Somewhere in the Night (as Bill Barclay). London, Compact, 1966; revised edition, as *The Chinese Agent* (as Michael Moorcock), London, Hutchinson, and New York, Macmillan, 1970.

The Wrecks of Time. New York, Ace, 1967; revised edition, as *The Rituals of Infinity,* London, Arrow, 1971; New York, DAW, 1978.

The Final Programme. New York, Avon, 1968; London, Allison and Busby, 1969; revised edition, London, Fontana, 1979.

The Ice Schooner. London, Sphere, and New York, Berkley, 1969; revised edition, London, Harrap, 1985; New York, Berkley, 1987.

Behold the Man. London, Allison and Busby, 1969; New York, Avon, 1970.

The Black Corridor, with Hilary Bailey (uncredited). London, Mayflower, and New York, Ace, 1969.

A Cure for Cancer. London, Allison and Busby, and New York, Holt Rinehart, 1971; revised edition, London, Fontana, 1979.

The Warlord of the Air. London, New English Library, and New York, Ace, 1971.

An Alien Heat. London, MacGibbon and Kee, and New York, Harper, 1972.

Breakfast in the Ruins. London, New English Library, 1972; New York, Random House, 1974.

The English Assassin. London, Allison and Busby, and New York, Harper, 1972; revised edition, London, Fontana, 1979.

The Land Leviathan. London, Quartet, and New York, Doubleday, 1974.

The Hollow Lands. New York, Harper, 1974; London, Hart Davis MacGibbon, 1975.

The Distant Suns, with Philip James (i.e. James Cawthorn). Llanfynydd, Dyfed, Unicorn Bookshop, 1975.

The Adventures of Una Persson and Catherine Cornelius in the Twentieth Century. London, Quartet, 1976.

The End of All Songs. London, Hart Davis MacGibbon, and New York, Harper, 1976.

The Condition of Muzak. London, Allison and Busby, 1977; Boston, Gregg Press, 1978.

The Transformation of Miss Mavis Ming. London, W. H. Allen, 1977; as *A Messiah at the End of Time,* New York, DAW, 1978; as *Constant Fire* in *Behold the Man and Other Stories,* London, Phoenix House, 1994.

The Cornelius Chronicles (omnibus). New York, Avon, vol. 1, 1977, vol. 2, 1986, vol. 3, 1987.

The Entropy Tango. London, New English Library, 1981.

Warrior of Mars (omnibus; includes *Warriors of Mars, Blades of Mars, Barbarians of Mars*). London, New English Library, 1981.

The Steel Tsar. London, Mayflower, 1981; New York, DAW, 1982.

The Great Rock 'n' Roll Swindle (novelization of screenplay). London, Virgin, 1980; revised as *Gold Diggers of 1977* in *Casablanca,* London, Gollancz, 1989.

Byzantium Endures. London, Secker and Warburg, 1981; New York, Random House, 1982.

The Brothel in Rösenstrasse. London, New English Library, 1982; New York, Carroll and Graf, 1987.

The Dancers at the End of Time (omnibus; includes *An Alien Heat, The Hollow Lands, The End of All Songs*). London, Granada, 1983; revised edition, London, Millennium, 1993.

The Laughter of Carthage. London, Secker and Warburg, and New York, Random House, 1984.

The Nomad of Time (omnibus; includes *The Warlord of the Air, The Land Leviathan, The Steel Tsar*). London, Granada, 1984; revised as *A Nomad of the Time Streams,* London, Millennium, 1993.

Mother London. London, Secker and Warburg, 1988; New York, Harmony, 1989.

Jerusalem Commands. London, Cape, 1992.

Sailing to Utopia (omnibus; includes *The Ice Schooner, The Black Corridor, The Distant Suns* and a short story). London, Millennium, 1993.

The Cornelius Quartet (omnibus; includes *The Final Programme, A Cure for Cancer, The English Assassin, The Condition of Muzak*). London, Phoenix House, 1993.

A Cornelius Calendar (omnibus; includes *The Adventures of Una Persson and Catherine Cornelius in the Twentieth Century, The Entropy Tango, Gold Diggers of 1977* and a short story). London, Phoenix House, 1993.

Behold the Man and Other Stories (omnibus; includes *Behold the Man, Breakfast in the Ruins, Constant Fire*). London, Phoenix House, 1994.

Blood: A Southern Fantasy. London, Millennium, 1995.

Short Stories

The Deep Fix (as James Colvin). London, Compact, 1966.

The Time Dweller. London, Hart Davis, 1969; New York, Berkley, 1971.

Moorcock's Book of Martyrs. London, Quartet, 1976; as *Dying for Tomorrow.* New York, DAW, 1978.

The Lives and Times of Jerry Cornelius. London, Allison and Busby, 1976; New York, Dale, n.d.; revised edition, London, Grafton, 1987.

Legends From the End of Time. London, W. H. Allen, and New York, Harper, 1976; revised edition, London, Millennium, 1993.

My Experiences in the Third World War. Manchester, Savoy, 1980.

The Opium General and Other Stories. London, Harrap, 1984.

Casablanca (includes essays). London, Gollancz, 1989.

Plays

Screenplay: *The Land That Time Forgot,* with James Cawthorn, 1974.

Other

Epic Pooh. London, British Fantasy Society, 1978.

The Retreat from Liberty: The Erosion of Democracy in Today's Britain. London, Zomba, 1983.

Letters from Hollywood, illustrated by Michael Foreman. London, Harrap, 1986.

Wizardry and Wild Romance: A Study of Epic Fantasy. London, Gollancz, 1987; revised edition, London, Gollancz, 1988.

Fantasy: The 100 Best Books, with James Cawthorn. London, Xanadu, and New York, Carroll and Graf, 1988.

Michael Moorcock: Death is No Obstacle, with Colin Greenland (interviews). Manchester, Savoy, 1992.

Editor, *The Best of New Worlds.* London, Compact, 1965.

Editor, *Best SF Stories from New Worlds 1-8.* London, Panther, 8 vols., 1967-74; New York, Berkley, 6 vols., 1968-71.

Editor, *The Traps of Time.* London, Rapp and Whiting, 1968.

Editor (anonymously), *The Inner Landscape.* London, Allison and Busby, 1969.

Editor, *New Worlds Quarterly 1-5.* London, Sphere, 5 vols., 1971-73; New York, Berkley, 4 vols., 1971-73.

Editor, with Langdon Jones, *The Nature of the Catastrophe.* London, Hutchinson, 1971; revised as *The New Nature of the Catastrophe,* London, Millennium, 1993.

Editor, with Charles Platt, *New Worlds 6.* London, Sphere, 1973; as *New Worlds 5,* New York, Avon, 1974.

Editor, *Before Armageddon: An Anthology of Victorian and Edwardian Imaginative Fiction Published Before 1914.* London, W. H. Allen, 1975.

Editor, *England Invaded: A Collection of Fantasy Fiction.* London, W. H. Allen, and New York, Ultramarine, 1977.

Editor, *New Worlds: An Anthology.* London, Fontana, 1983.

*

Film Adaptation: *The Final Programme,* 1973.

Bibliography: *The Tanelorn Archives* by Richard Bilyeu, North Dakota, Pandora's Books, 1981; *Michael Moorcock: A Reader's Guide* by John Davey, London, Davey, 1992.

Manuscript Collections: Bodleian Library, Oxford University; Sterling Library, Texas A&M University, College Station.

Critical Study: *The Entropy Exhibition: Michael Moorcock and the British "New Wave" in Science Fiction* by Colin Greenland, London, Routledge, 1983.

*   *   *

Michael Moorcock is or at least has been a terrifyingly prolific author, who is pleased to make genre boundaries ooze and distort as in some painting by Dali. His mainstream work flows into his science fiction, the science fiction into the fantasy, generally within the context of all-encompassing jargon terms like the "multiverse" (a word the author was chagrined to learn was not his own coinage) or the Conjunction of the Million Spheres. The fantasy is not easily separated out.

Early "science fantasies" include the short stories of the warrior lord, Sojan, and the Michael Kane *Warrior of Mars* trilogy, both rather clearly in the vein of Edgar Rice Burroughs. Somewhat more successful were the fantasies of Erekosë, *The Eternal Champion*, doomed forever to be reincarnated and fight once more against evil. This immediately establishes the keynote of the typical Moorcock fantasy hero: being doomed.

His first novel *The Golden Barge* (written in 1958 though published much later) is an allegory much influenced by Mervyn Peake, in which the unlikable hero Jephraim Tallow successively rejects the lures of family, love, philosophy and power to follow the will-o'the'wisp Golden Barge which drifts downriver, always unattainable. The pursuit of the barge is disastrous; to reject the pursuit is worse.

Very soon a more durable doomed hero emerged: Elric of Melniboné, whose moody character is the best known in all the Moorcock multiverse. He lives in Byronic melancholy, tormented by his betrayals such as causing the downfall and diaspora of his own people. As a member of a vaguely elfin Elder Race in a world now human-dominated, he is an outsider. He owes too many debts to his patron demon Arioch. He is maimed, an albino forever lacking in strength, and thus exists in uneasy symbiosis with the black sword, Stormbringer, both hating and drawing power from its habit of feeding on opponents' souls to nourish its owner. The curse of the sword is that it is equally happy to gorge itself on allies, friends and lovers, and regularly claims all three. With it Elric travels through tainted, blasted or luridly surreal landscapes that throb with the pathetic fallacy. . . .

The end of this myth is told in the series' first-written novel *Stormbringer,* whose headlong questing culminates with an apocalyptic battle wherein Elric supports the Law gods against his nominal masters of Chaos. A better, paler, duller world is born, with one leavening of chaos and old night: Stormbringer itself, which finally turns on its guilt-ridden master ("Farewell, friend. I was a thousand times more evil than thou") and flies free, promising interesting times.

Many further tales of Elric were squeezed into his (retrospectively) crowded life, incidentally making the series bibliographically complex as the stories in the initial Elric collection *The Stealer of Souls* were incorporated along with later material into an emerging chronology. The smoky colours of the early tales are still striking, despite elements of the formulaic. For example, the amount of varied supernatural aid on which Elric is able to call does eventually become a little risible (and indeed certain over-the-top gestures and speeches are surely deliberately parodic . . . though only in *Elric at the End of Time,* a semi-farcical crossover with the science fiction *Dancers at the End of Time* sequence, does Moorcock openly laugh at the doomed lord). Likewise, Elric's emotional agonies over his recurring betrayals and Stormbringer's fated slayings take on the air of overly familiar landmarks.

But Moorcock's nasty inventiveness remains impressive. Just as E. E. Smith took the space-adventure formula far beyond its old boundaries by thinking on a galactic scale, so Moorcock escalated the action of sword-and-sorcery. Chaos does not wish merely to enslave some country but to transform the entire world into shifting, nightmare flux. Gods and demons plunge directly into the action, and like mortals can be killed or at least permanently expelled from this "plane". Again and again entire aspects of the multiverse hang in the balance . . . the Cosmic Balance, which is righted at the end of *Stormbringer* but soon goes awry elsewhere.

The Hawkmoon or Runestaff tetralogy is more of a standard good-versus-evil saga, lacking a character of Elric's stature but with flashes of that series' intensity. The hideous beast- and insect-masks worn by the wicked warlords of Granbretan (from which name we infer a far future) are an effective touch, as is the sinister mix of magic and technology. Thus hero Dorian Hawkmoon is maimed by the cybermagical "Machine of the Black Jewel," which implants the living jewel in his forehead in hope of subjecting him to Granbretan's control. . . . Many battles ensue and many plot devices besides the Jewel are invoked: the Mad God's Amulet, the Sword of the Dawn, the enigmatic Runestaff itself, etc. Following the initial sequence, three more Hawkmoon books put the hero through further unlikely hoops until a finale which, involving Elric, Corum, Erekosë, the Black Sword, the Jewel and (literally and physically) the Cosmic Balance, tries perhaps too hard for eschatological impact.

In the Swords trilogy there is more of Elric's grand manner. Here the hero is Corum, who indeed is suspiciously Elric-like: a doomed prince, apparently the last of his elfish race in a world now ruled by the despised human "Mabden," and maimed (of course) by the loss of his hand and eye. Acquiring a sorcerous eye and hand which let him see and reach into dark places for darker allies, he sets out against the Sword Rulers. These are three Chaos gods—already encountered in *Stormbringer*—who tyrannize his and adjacent worlds. The concluding *The King of the Swords* features some of Moorcock's most spectacular landscapes of chaos, and an agreeable reversal when the alien Lost Gods (owners and repossessors of those magical replacement organs) choose to help Corum by slaughtering the entire Chaos pantheon and, by way of fairness, the gods of Law as well. Let the Cosmic Balance swing as it will, they say: "Now you can make your own destiny."

Not forever: a second Corum trilogy set well into the future sees his world afflicted with a new batch of gods from another plane, the Fhoi Myore, diseased, pitiable and malevolent. They plan to introduce a permanent Fimbulwinter as the best climate for their health, and Corum with his allies must collect an impressive array of plot tokens (notably the bull, spear, oak, ram, sword and stallion of the books' titles) to defeat and oust them. There are certain signs of weariness here.

The conceits of the multiverse and the Champion run through most Moorcock fantasies. Everything connects; the timeless city of Tanelorn, still point of the turning world, is accessible in every plane; and—as John Daker alias Erekosë is perpetually aware—each doomed hero (also apparently each hero's sidekick, like Elric's Moonglum and in particular Corum's Jhary-a-Conel) is merely another incarnated aspect of the Eternal Champion. More than once, several of these incarnations meet and jointly clobber some menace beyond their individual powers. It is all something of a game. The author's grin is perhaps a little evident when the recurrence of names like Jerry Cornelius and Jherek Carnelian culminates in a temporary companion for Elric who mislays his own name: "I am something beginning with 'J' and something beginning with 'C'."

The effect of the Elric stories is cumulative, and several of the individual items don't bear examination. Such strictures do not apply to Moorcock's finest single fantasy performance *Gloriana; or, The Unfulfill'd Queen.* Its alternate Elizabethan London, capital of Albion and its empire, is full of shades and allusions: to history, to Spenser's *Faerie Queen,* and to Moorcock's own fiction. Here the self-reference is playful and ironic, avoiding "Gloriana meets Elric" plot turns but with Arioch's and other old gods' names dropped; with a cameo appearance of *The Golden Barge*'s Jephraim Tallow; with Dr. Dee speculating on the spheres of the multiverse. Above all, the labyrinthine and Gormenghastly palace setting offers a genuinely mature homage to Peake.

At the heart of its tortuous action is the awkward knot of six-foot-six Queen Gloriana's unfulfill'dness: innocent yet perverse, emphatically and repeatedly not a virgin, she yearns for true orgasm. All around are pageantry, diplomacy, intrigue, corruption, bloody melodrama spiced with wit. As though in a slowly turning crystal, characters gradually appear in new lights. Despite indomitable loyalty to the Queen, her Chancellor, grim Lord Montfallcon, ultimately stands for repression, stasis, death: he supports noble ends through tainted means, her unlamented father's old ways of blood and iron. On the more overtly villainous side, the chilly spymaster Captain Quire seems a mere thug; then a proud artist of covert activities; then the traitor who is to ruin and discredit Queen Gloriana; and ultimately, won over by her, he stands against Montfallcon on the side of life and love. The slow, alchemical transformation is most satisfying.

Gloriana was to have been Moorcock's farewell to fantasy, but further books followed. *The War Hound and the World's Pain* is a deceptively smooth-flowing Quest for the Grail, the Cure for the World's Pain (always in Capitals), undertaken by the eponymous Graf Ulrich von Bek—a 17th-century soldier and killer who proves more complex than expected. *The Dragon in the Sword* goes back to the first "Eternal Champion" and is rife with cross-referenced stories intersecting Erekosë's . . . finally giving that hero rest, if not for long. *The Fortress of the Pearl* and *The Revenge of the Rose,* elegant if sometimes enervated instalments of Elric's life, lack both the ungainliness and raw force of the older work. *Fortress,* for example, is largely set in a dreamworld which mutedly recalls the chaos landscapes of our hero's subsequent career, and in which he—stripped of Stormbringer for the duration—is noticeably ineffectual. (As though to compensate for this, the re-sworded Elric improbably takes on an entire city in a concluding bloodbath.)

Although nominally science fiction, the *Dancers at the End of Time* books use technologies that might as well be magic, with many fantasy trappings. At the end of time, a literal *fin de siècle,* a gaggle of characters like the protagonist Jherek Carnelian play extravagantly with their omnipotence and pursue strange sensations. And what could be more exotic than forgotten emotions like love and guilt? When Jherek decides to fall in love with the impeccably moral (and married) Mrs. Amelia Underwood, a temporary visitor from the past, and to pursue her home to 1896 . . . the result is richly and uniquely comic, thick with bizarre misunderstandings and extraordinary adventures.

The nonfiction *Wizardry and Wild Romance* is Moorcock's own idiosyncratic survey of fantasy: enjoyable when lambasting his dislikes (over-high style, sentimentality, right-wing and/or Christian tendencies: Adams, Lewis, Tolkien) but elsewhere tending merely to quote substantial chunks of approved authors and remark without analysis or explanation that this is good stuff.

His own body of fantasy includes many hastily or lazily written, page-turning potboilers . . . redeemed by extraordinary imagery, the lingering melancholy of Elric and others, the acid of irony always eating into romanticism, and the cheeky audacity of that multiverse concept (however overplayed). The books written with full attention and love, like *Gloriana* and the *Dancers at the End of Time* sequence, need no excuses.

—David Langford

MOORE, Brian

Pseudonyms: Michael Bryan; Bernard Mara. **Nationality:** Canadian. **Born:** Belfast, Northern Ireland, 25 August 1921; emigrated to Canada in 1948; moved to the United States in 1959. **Education:** St. Malachy's College, Belfast. **Military Service:** British Ministry of War Transport, in North Africa, Italy and France, 1943-45. **Family:** Married 1) Jacqueline Scully in 1951; 2) Jean Denney in 1966; one son. **Career:** Served with United Nations Relief and Rehabilitation Administration (UNRRA) mission to Poland, 1946-47; reporter, Montreal *Gazette,* 1948-52; Regents' Professor, 1974-75, and since 1976, Professor, University of California, Los Angeles. **Awards:** Authors Club of Great Britain award, 1956; Beta Sigma Phi award, 1956; Quebec literary prize, 1958; Guggenheim fellowship, 1959; Governor-General's award, 1961, 1975; American Academy grant, 1961; Canada Council fellowship, 1962; W. H. Smith literary award, 1973; National Catholic book award, 1973; James Tait Black Memorial prize, 1976; Scottish Arts Council senior fellowship, 1983; Royal Society of Literature Heinemann award, 1986; *Sunday Express* Book of the Year award, 1988; Hughes Irish Fiction award, 1988. **Agent:** Curtis Brown, 10 Astor Place, New York, NY 10003, USA. **Address:** 33958 Pacific Coast Highway, Malibu, CA 90265, USA.

FANTASY PUBLICATIONS

Novels

Fergus. New York, Holt Rinehart, 1970; London, Cape, 1971.
The Great Victorian Collection. New York, Farrar Straus, and London, Cape, 1975.
Cold Heaven. New York, Farrar Straus, and London, Cape, 1983.

OTHER PUBLICATIONS

Novels

Wreath for a Redhead. Toronto, Harlequin, 1951; as *Sailor's Leave,* New York, Pyramid, 1953.
The Executioners. Toronto, Harlequin, 1951.
French for Murder (as Bernard Mara). New York, Fawcett, 1954; London, L. Miller, 1956.
A Bullet for My Lady (as Bernard Mara). New York, Fawcett, 1955; London, Muller, 1956.
Judith Hearne. Toronto, Collins, and London, Deutsch, 1955; as *The Lonely Passion of Judith Hearne,* Boston, Little Brown, 1956.
This Gun for Gloria (as Bernard Mara). New York, Fawcett, 1956; London, Muller, 1957.
Intent to Kill (as Michael Bryan). New York, Dell, and London, Eyre and Spottiswoode, 1956.
Murder in Majorca (as Michael Bryan). New York, Dell, 1957; London, Eyre and Spottiswoode, 1958.
The Feast of Lupercal. Boston, Little Brown, 1957; London, Deutsch, 1958; as *A Moment of Love,* London, Panther, 1965.
The Luck of Ginger Coffey. Boston, Little Brown, and London, Deutsch, 1960.
An Answer from Limbo. Boston, Little Brown, 1962; London, Deutsch, 1963.

The Emperor of Ice-Cream. New York, Viking Press, 1965; London, Deutsch, 1966.

I Am Mary Dunne. New York, Viking Press, and London, Cape, 1968.

Catholics. London, Cape, 1972; New York, Harcourt Brace, 1973.

The Doctor's Wife. New York, Farrar Straus, and London, Cape, 1976.

The Mangan Inheritance. New York, Farrar Straus, and London, Cape, 1979.

The Temptation of Eileen Hughes. New York, Farrar Straus, and London, Cape, 1981.

Black Robe. New York, Dutton, and London, Cape, 1985.

The Colour of Blood. London, Cape, and New York, Dutton, 1987.

Lies of Silence. London, Bloomsbury, and New York, Doubleday, 1990.

No Other Life. London, Bloomsbury, and New York, Doubleday, 1993.

Short Stories

Two Stories. Northridge, California, Santa Susana Press, 1978.

Plays

Catholics, adaptation of his own novel (televised 1973; produced Seattle, 1980; Belfast, 1985).

Screenplays: *The Luck of Ginger Coffey,* 1964; *Torn Curtain,* 1966; *The Slave,* 1967; *Catholics,* 1973; *The Blood of Others,* 1984; *The Sight,* 1985; *Black Robe,* 1991.

Other

Canada, with the editors of *Life.* New York, Time, 1963; revised edition, 1968.

The Revolution Script. New York, Holt Rinehart, 1971; London, Cape, 1972.

*

Film Adaptations: *The Luck of Ginger Coffey,* 1964; *Catholics* (TV movie), 1973; *The Lonely Passion of Judith Hearne,* 1987; *The Temptation of Eileen Hughes* (TV movie), 1988; *Black Robe,* 1991; *Cold Heaven,* 1992.
Manuscript collection: Special Collections, University of Calgary, Alberta.

Critical Studies: *Brian Moore,* Toronto, Copp Clark, 1969, and *Brian Moore,* Boston, Twayne, 1981, both by Hallvard Dahlie; *Brian Moore* by Jeanne Flood, Lewisburg, Pennsylvania, Bucknall University Press, 1974; *Brian Moore: A Critical Study* by Jo O'Donoghue, Montreal, McGill-Queen's University Press, 1991.

*   *   *

Brian Moore is a realistic novelist of distinction, author of *The Luck of Ginger Coffey* and *The Doctor's Wife* among many other highly praised works. But he has also written several novels in a fantastic vein, the first being the very readable but minor *Fergus,* about a Hollywood screenwriter who is haunted by ghosts from his guilty Irish past. Moore's second fantasy, *The Great Victorian Collection,* is one of his finest books, an amusing and engrossing fable about the fate of the marvellous in our matter-of-fact society.

The protagonist, Anthony Maloney, is an assistant professor of history and an expert in all things Victorian, who checks into the Sea Winds Motel in Carmel, California. He has been attending a seminar at Berkeley, and intends to leave within a couple of days. However, his sojourn at the motel is destined to last many months, as a result of the remarkable event which takes place during his first night there. As he sleeps, he dreams that he awakes and looks through his window onto the motel's previously empty parking lot. What he sees there resembles a marketplace, "a maze of narrow lanes lined with stalls, some permanently roofed, some draped in green tarpaulin awnings." He dreams of opening his window, climbing out, and walking down the central aisle of the market, "an aisle dominated by a glittering crystal fountain, its columns of polished glass soaring to the height of a telegraph pole." Laid out on the stalls around him is "the most astonishing collection of Victorian artefacts, *objets d'art,* furniture, household appliances, paintings, jewellery, scientific instruments, toys, tapestries, sculpture, handicrafts, woollen and linen samples, industrial machinery, ceramics, silverware, books, furs, men's and women's clothing, musical instruments, a huge telescope mounted on a pedestal, a railway locomotive, marine equipment, small arms, looms, bric-a-brac, and curiosa."

Then Maloney really wakes up—only to look out the window and find that his dream has come true. The incredible collection of Victoriana is there, somehow conjured into existence by his sleeping mind. Maloney cannot believe his luck. Feverishly, he inspects the valuable objects—which are full of an inexpressible pathos when so far removed from their original time and place—but soon discovers that if he attempts to take any of them from the parking lot they immediately deteriorate and become "fakes". The collection must remain *in situ*: it must be covered, guarded, preserved, and eventually exploited. The remainder of the novel deals with the consequences of this miracle. We never learn why the exhibition materialized in the first place—it is simply a given, like Gregor Samsa's transformation into a beetle at the beginning of Kafka's "The Metamorphosis". Instead, the story describes, in logical, realistic, and frequently comical fashion, the reactions of all those who come in contact with Maloney and his glorious heap of Victoriana. It tells how the collection becomes a media sensation, a scientific conundrum, a seven-days-wonder, a sideshow, and at length an all-but-forgotten curiosity. It also tells how the great Victorian collection destroys its "creator". Interpret it how you will (and of course it is tempting to view it as an allegory of the novelist's fate in the modern world), Moore's book is an elegant, ironic, and touching parable.

Like *The Great Victorian Collection,* Moore's *Cold Heaven* is a tale of the miraculous in conflict with the mundane. The first three or four chapters are written with a driving intensity which keeps one turning the pages, avidly. Marie Davenport, a lapsed Catholic, is on holiday with her selfish husband, Alex, in the south of France. She is about to leave him for another man, but has not yet plucked up the courage to tell him the news. They paddle out to sea in a tiny boat; Alex plunges into the water for a swim, and Marie watches in horror as he is struck on the head by a passing motorboat. Alex is rushed to the hospital, unconscious. Marie accompanies him, fighting a rising sense of dread and guilt. She is instantly aware that she is being "punished" by supernatural powers—not so much for her adultery, but because she has chosen to ignore a strange event, possibly a divine message, which she experienced on the west coast of America exactly one year before. After long hours of anxious waiting in the foreign hospital, Marie is informed that her husband has died. However, it soon becomes apparent that he will refuse to rest in peace.

It would be wrong to recount more of the plot, for this is a novel which depends on its surprises. Like a good Alfred Hitchcock film (and Moore once wrote a script for Hitchcock), it keeps one in an eerie suspense. The reader enters a world of the uncanny where everyday details have taken on a preternatural significance. *Cold Heaven* is by no means a conventional "ghost story," nor a mere case study in religious delusion. Nor is it, in any literal sense, a tale of zombies and angels. In the main, it is the story of one modern woman's refusal to be cowed by the inexplicable, the ineffable; it is about a courageous *non serviam*. Although the narrative is told from Marie's point of view, it also evokes sympathy for the husband, Alex—self-obsessed, unimaginative, and materialistic as he is. Brian Moore's style is spare but cunningly crafted, and much of the burden of his novel rests on what remains unsaid.

Yet the book has imperfections. The earlier part seems to have been written at white heat, but towards the end the narrative drifts—after the characters have taken up residence in a motel near Carmel, California (very similar to the setting of *The Great Victorian Collection*). There is some unsatisfactory shifting of viewpoint in these later scenes, and the tension slackens. After reading the novel I looked up a newspaper interview with Brian Moore ("The Novelist Who Listens to Women" by Philip Oakes, *Sunday Times,* 4 October 1981) and was impressed by several points. Although he attended a Jesuit school in Ireland, Moore states: "I never had any faith. I could never forget that my grandfather was a Protestant lawyer who changed his religion to help his business." Midway through the writing of his first novel, in the 1950s, Moore "was seriously injured when, out swimming, he was struck on the head by a passing speed-boat and taken to hospital with his skull fractured in six places. 'Of course it was terrible at the time, but now I believe that a brush with death does wonders for a writer's energy.'" The emotional fuel which still flows from this incident obviously adds power to *Cold Heaven*. Moore also remarks in the interview: "I never know how the story will end. I change my mind along with the characters." This too is evident from a reading of the novel, but it remains a brilliantly written and moving book.

—David Pringle

MOORE, C(atherine) L(ucille)

Pseudonyms: Lawrence O'Donnell (with Henry Kuttner); Lewis Padgett (with Henry Kuttner). **Nationality:** American. **Born:** Indianapolis, Indiana, 24 January 1911. **Education:** University of Southern California, Los Angeles, B.S. 1956 (Phi Beta Kappa), M.A. 1964. **Family:** Married 1) Henry Kuttner, q.v., in 1940 (died 1958); 2) Thomas Reggie in 1963. **Career:** Staff member, later president, Fletcher Trust Company, Indianapolis, 1930-40; first professional fiction sale, November 1933; most of her work between 1940 and 1958 was written in collaboration with Henry Kuttner, though this was not always acknowledged; instructor in writing and literature, University of Southern California, 1958-61; television scriptwriter, 1958-63. **Died:** 1987.

FANTASY PUBLICATIONS

Novels

Well of the Worlds (as Lewis Padgett, with Henry Kuttner). New York, Galaxy, 1953.
Beyond Earth's Gate (as Lewis Padgett, with Henry Kuttner). New York, Ace, 1954.
Valley of the Flame, with Henry Kuttner. New York, Ace, 1964.
The Dark World, with Henry Kuttner. New York, Ace, 1965; London, Mayflower, 1966.
The Mask of Circe, with Henry Kuttner. New York, Ace, 1971.
The Startling Worlds of Henry Kuttner, with Henry Kuttner (omnibus; includes *Beyond Earth's Gate* [under its original title, "The Portal in the Picture"], *Valley of the Flame, The Dark World*). New York, Warner, 1987.

Short Stories

A Gnome There Was, and Other Tales of Science Fiction and Fantasy (as Lewis Padgett, with Henry Kuttner). New York, Simon and Schuster, 1950.
Shambleau and Others. New York, Gnome Press, 1953; abridged edition, London, Consul, 1961.
Line to Tomorrow (as by Lewis Padgett, with Henry Kuttner). New York, Bantam, 1954.
Northwest of Earth. New York, Gnome Press, 1954.
No Boundaries, with Henry Kuttner. New York, Ballantine, 1955; London, Consul, 1961.
Jirel of Joiry. New York, Paperback Library, 1969; as *Black God's Shadow,* West Kingston, Rhode Island, Grant, 1977.
The Best of C. L. Moore, edited by Lester del Rey. New York, Doubleday, 1975.
Clash by Night and Other Stories, with Henry Kuttner, edited by Peter Pinto. London, Hamlyn, 1980.
Scarlet Dream. West Kingston, Rhode Island, Grant, 1981; as *Northwest Smith,* New York, Ace, 1982.
Chessboard Planet and Other Stories, with Henry Kuttner. London, Hamlyn, 1983.

OTHER PUBLICATIONS

Novels

The Brass Ring (as Lewis Padgett, with Henry Kuttner). New York, Duell, 1964; London, Sampson Low, 1947; as *Murder in Brass,* New York, Bantam, 1947.
The Day He Died (as Lewis Padgett, with Henry Kuttner). New York, Duell, 1947.
Fury (as Lawrence O'Donnell, with Henry Kuttner). New York, Grosset and Dunlap, 1950; London, Dobson, 1954; as *Destination Infinity,* New York, Avon, 1958.
Tomorrow and Tomorrow, and The Fairy Chessmen (as Lewis Padgett, with Henry Kuttner). New York, Gnome Press, 1951; as *Tomorrow and Tomorrow* and *The Far Reality,* London, Consul, 2 vols., 1963; *The Fairy Chessmen* published as *Chessboard Planet,* New York, Galaxy, 1956.
Judgment Night (includes stories). New York, Gnome Press, 1952.

Doomsday Morning. New York, Doubleday, 1957; London, Consul, 1960.
Earth's Last Citadel, with Henry Kuttner. New York, Ace, 1964.
The Time Axis, with Henry Kuttner. New York, Ace, 1965.

Short Stories

Mutant (as Lewis Padgett, with Henry Kuttner). New York, Gnome Press, 1953; London, Weidenfeld and Nicolson, 1954.
Vintage Season, with *In Another Country* by Robert Silverberg. New York, Tor, 1990.

*

Manuscript Collection: Lovecraft Collection, Brown University Library, Providence, Rhode Island.

Bibliography: *Catherine Lucille Moore & Henry Kuttner: A Marriage of Souls and Talent—A Working Bibliography, 3rd Edition* by Virgil S. Utter and Gordon Benson, Jr., Leeds, West Yorkshire, Galactic Central Publications, 1989.

*   *   *

According to her own account, C. L. Moore began writing as a way of improving her typing skills while holding a job at a bank during the Great Depression. Her byline was not an attempt to conceal her gender, but to conceal from her boss at the bank that she had a second source of income. In *Weird Tales,* where her first story appeared, female bylines were relatively common. Moore's debut, "Shambleau," caused an immediate sensation. Editor Farnsworth Wright quit work early and declared it C. L. Moore Day. This story of a seductive, Martian medusa was one of the most spectacular slush-pile finds in the history of the field, and, apparently, the first story its author ever completed.

"Shambleau" began the adventures of Northwest Smith, hardbitten but romantic interplanetary adventurer, the archetype for all such all the way down to Han Solo in the *Star Wars* movies. His exploits take place on a conventional, Edgar Rice Burroughs-influenced Mars or Venus, but with fantastic elements which were, by *Weird Tales* standards, undeniably "weird" and very close to the supernatural. In "Scarlet Dream," a mystical Martian embroidery transports Smith into another dimension where a nameless Thing appears periodically to devour the victims stranded there. The snake-haired title character of "Shambleau" doesn't turn men to stone at a glance, but she is a kind of psychic vampire. The emphasis is on atmosphere, horror, and sensuality.

It was the nearly raw-sexual element of Moore's writing which made her so revolutionary in the pulps of the 1930s. Her early stories are structured like seductions, drawing the reader into an increasingly vivid web of emotional, lyrical prose, until a climax is reached in a burst of imagery rather than logical plotting or the clever solution to a puzzle. "Shambleau" is a literal seduction, which would have been the end of Northwest Smith but for a timely rescue by his Venusian sidekick, Yarol.

Shortly after beginning the Smith series, Moore branched out with the unambiguously fantastic tales of Jirel, warrior-woman of the imaginary medieval land of Joiry. Again, the emphasis is on the emotional, the romantic, and the overtly sexual. In the first story of the series, "The Black God's Kiss," Jirel ventures into another di-

mension to gain the kiss of a hideous idol, so she might use it to destroy a man who has betrayed her, but whom she still loves. Jirel is almost a female Conan the Barbarian. Certainly she would have won his respect: fearless, loyal, relentless in her revenge, willing to yield to no man. While such a character has precedents, particularly in the quasi-historical novels of Leslie Barringer, no other such series emerged in fantasy until the advent of explicitly feminist sword-and-sorcery decades later.

Moore's prose resembles Robert E. Howard's at its very best, vivid, poetic, economical. She is far less inclined to purple passages, though some of the rhetorical climaxes do seem to go on too long. While, arguably, virtually all of the Jirel and Northwest Smith stories have the same structure, and are best read in isolation, this repetition would have been regarded as a strength by a pulp editor. Since stories were rarely reprinted, writers were encouraged to sell what almost amounted to the same story to the same magazine, over and over, to give the magazine some continuity. But, unlike most pulp fiction, Moore's continues to hold up well. Unlike most pulp writers, she could actually write.

In 1937, she collaborated with Henry Kuttner on "The Quest of the Starstone," a *Weird Tales* novelette in which Northwest Smith and Jirel meet across the centuries; but it seems to have pleased neither author, and remains uncollected. After the end of the 1930s, very few stories appeared under the Moore byline, and of these, fewer still were fantasies, as both she and Kuttner moved into John W. Campbell's stable at *Astounding* and concentrated on science fiction. One striking, late fantasy is "Fruit of Knowledge," published in *Unknown* in 1940, which tells the story of the Biblical Lilith, presenting her as a jealous, supernatural seductress in the classic C. L. Moore mould. Remarkably, this is a Judeo-Christian fantasy which is neither satirical, sentimental nor silly. "Daemon" (in *Famous Fantastic Mysteries,* 1946) concerns a mentally-retarded man who lacks a soul himself, but can see the "daemons" (souls or guardian spirits) of each person, and thus learns of good and evil. He can also see the god Pan.

Otherwise, Moore's fantasy, along with her science fiction, blended with Kuttner's. After their marriage the two collaborated (often pseudonymously) so intimately that neither could be sure who had written what. Unfairly, Kuttner is often given sole credit for such works as the Merrittesque, quasi-fantasy *The Dark World* (in *Startling Stories,* 1946, book 1965), *The Mask of Circle* (*Startling Stories* 1948, book 1971), and many others, to which Moore made substantial contributions. For further discussion of these science-fantasy novels attributed in part to Moore, see the separate entry on Henry Kuttner. After Kuttner's early death in 1958, Moore gave up fiction writing, but continued working in television for a few years (with scripts for *77 Sunset Strip* and other series), then quit writing altogether. Her small body of solo work is, however, sufficient to keep her name alive.

—Darrell Schweitzer

———

MORAN, Daniel. *See* **VARDEMAN, Robert E(dward).**

———

MORRESSY, John

Nationality: American. **Born:** Brooklyn, New York, 8 December 1930. **Education:** St. John's University, New York, B.A. in English 1953; New York University, M.A. 1961. **Military Service:** United States Army, 1953-55. **Family:** Married Barbara Ann Turner in 1956. **Career:** Writer and reviewer, Equitable Life, New York, 1957-59; instructor, St. John's University, 1962-66; assistant professor, Monmouth College, West Long Branch, New Jersey, 1966-67; writer-in-residence, Worcester Consortium, Massachusetts, 1977; visiting writer and Elliott Professor of English, University of Maine, Orono, 1977-78; since 1968, associate professor, professor, and writer-in-residence, Franklin Pierce College, Rindge, New Hampshire. **Awards:** Bread Loaf Writers Conference Fellowship, 1968; University of Colorado Writers Conference Fellowship, 1970; Balrog award, 1984. **Agent:** William Morris Agency, Inc., 1350 Avenue of the Americas, New York, NY 10019, USA. **Address:** PO Box 33, Apple Hill Road, East Sullivan, NH 03445, USA.

FANTASY PUBLICATIONS

Novels (series: Kedrigern; Iron Angel)

Ironbrand (Iron Angel). Chicago, Playboy Press, 1980.
Graymantle (Iron Angel). New York, Playboy Press, 1981.
Kingsbane (Iron Angel). New York, Playboy Press, 1982.
The Time of the Annihilator (Iron Angel). New York, Ace, 1985.
A Voice for Princess (Kedrigern). New York, Ace, 1986.
The Questing of Kedrigern. New York, Ace, 1987.
Kedrigern in Wanderland. New York, Ace, 1988.
Kedrigern and the Charming Couple. New York, Ace, 1990.
A Remembrance for Kedrigern. New York, Ace, 1990.

OTHER PUBLICATIONS

Novels

The Blackboard Cavalier. New York, Doubleday, 1966; London, Gollancz, 1967.
The Addison Tradition. New York, Doubleday, 1968.
A Long Communion. New York, Walker, 1974; as *Displaced Persons,* New York, Popular Library, 1976.
Starbrat. New York, Walker, 1972; London, New English Library, 1979.
Nail Down the Stars. New York, Walker, 1973; London, New English Library, 1979; as *Stardrift,* New York, Popular Library, 1975.
The Humans of Ziax II (for children). New York, Walker, 1974.
Under a Calculating Star. New York, Doubleday, 1975; London, Sidgwick and Jackson, 1978.
The Windows of Forever (for children). New York, Walker, 1975.
A Law for the Stars. Toronto, Laser, 1976.
The Extraterritorial. Toronto, Laser, 1977.
Frostworld and Dreamfire. New York, Doubleday, 1977; London, Sidgwick and Jackson, 1979.
The Drought on Ziax II (for children). New York, Walker, 1978.
The Mansions of Space. New York, Ace, 1983.

Short Stories

Other Stories. Amherst, Massachusetts, Northern New England Review Press, 1983.

*

John Morressy comments:

Any writer of fiction who practises his craft long enough seems ineluctably to be drawn to try his hand at fantasy. That happened to me in 1980, when an editor enquired, "Have you ever thought of writing a fantasy novel?" I truthfully answered "No," and a few days later set to work on *Ironbrand,* which became the first book of a dark fantasy trilogy. When the trilogy was completed, I wrote a science-fiction novel, but then returned to fantasy to write a novel prefatory to the trilogy. Since then, I have written a series (five, so far) of light fantasy novels, and several stories, about a wizard, his wife, and their friends and clients.

I write fantasy chiefly because I enjoy it. I like to think of myself as following the tradition of the great old story-tellers (most of them unnamed and unknown to us) who gave us our myths and tales and legends, and whose work will still be delighting readers when works now more celebrated have long been forgotten. Fantasy is, after all, the oldest literary genre and still the basis of all fiction. However realistic, or even naturalistic, it claims to be, fiction consists of made-up stories about imaginary people; in other words, it is fantasy.

*   *   *

John Morressy's fantasy is all classifiable as sword and sorcery, but the two series so far exemplify such opposing poles in mood and characterization as to give a strong impression that the author is writing more to display his virtuosity than from any deep commitment. The subtle interlinkage which was such an admirable and unusual feature of his science-fictional Del Whitby series is missing, and the worlds of both series are stock worlds.

The success of television's *Star Trek* has shown that enthusiasm for soap opera can overlap enthusiasm for science fiction, but whether the marriage of sword and sorcery with situation comedy can achieve as much remains uncertain. The Kedrigern books, of which *A Voice for Princess* is the first, derive from sword and sorcery in the tradition of L. Sprague de Camp, with transformations, rhyming spells and a general air that nothing is to be taken very seriously; the sitcom is in the middle-class Jewish tradition, going back at least as far as *Life with the Lyons,* where strong-minded but affectionate women hen-peck their clever but impractical husbands into reasonable compliance with the social norms. The effect is thoroughly amiable, and their comparative lack of following is probably because the books have emerged unsupported by any television series.

Like all sitcoms, they depend for their effects on simple, two-dimensional characters, a single strong story-line with short-lived offshoots to lend it body, and (most of all) repeated jokes which become either tedious with repetition or cosy with familiarity according to taste. Kedrigern is a wizard of middle years (ageing from about 160 to 170 through the series) and formidable powers whose preferences are to dress so unpretentiously as to border on the shabby, to spend as much time as he can quietly in the country, and to uphold good against evil as long as it's not too hazardous. His wife, Princess, has lost all memory of her antecedents but gains a pair of functional wings; once she acquires a wand as well people tend to annoy her by mistaking her for a fairy godmother, while her husband annoys her by inopportune suggestions that she get some knitted wing-covers. His large black stallion belies its docility and sweet nature with its baleful red eyes, huge steel hoofs, and the long, twisty, silver horn protruding from its forehead (though it can take offence at being called a unicorn by the ignorant).

Since Kedrigern dislikes travelling the logic of sitcom ensures that he constantly finds himself required by honourable obligation or the importunities of Princess to undertake quests and missions, which form the principal plots of the books. On the way he meets characters even flatter than himself, such as Hamarak, a large, good-natured peasant whose only real ambition is to eat as much fresh bread as he can hold but finds kingship thrust upon him, and Belsheer, a fellow wizard who has been transformed into a bee and can only retain a grip on his humanity by the repetition of wise saws. Kedrigern Does Good all round (subject to occasional grumbles) and all ends happily until the next episode.

The running gags may get tedious, but the incidental jokes are generally much better. The entire series can be approached as a gentle send-up of the conventions of light fantasy, but within that mode Morressy, who is a more literary writer than surface reading would suggest, guys writers ranging from Spenser to Dostoevsky. At one point he attributes to Kedrigern the vitality of the whole corpus of European fairy tale—he meets a rather uninspired writer and, in his usual kindly fashion, gives him a few pointers about plot development.

The Iron Angel series is both more conventional and a lot heavier, and while it attempts something worthwhile, achieves only qualified success. Fantasy heroes tend to conform with greater or less precision to one of three two-dimensional archetypes: the unbendingly noble (David Gemmell's Druss), the playful, womanizing scaramouche (Fritz Leiber's Gray Mouser), or the flawed and angst-driven (Michael Moorcock's Elric). For Ironbrand, Morressy essayed something subtler. The three brothers Colberane, Ordred and Staver are admirable young men of royal blood, but they have been brought up for their own safety in a village in the back of beyond where they might have grown old and died as farmers, ignorant of their mighty antecedents, had not their hereditary enemy come in search of them with lethal magics. Greatness is thrust upon them, and they're off on an extremely dangerous quest, little comforted by ambiguous written prophecies and the patronage of an ancient prophetess.

So far, so conventional, but although the brothers are handsome, brave and far from stupid, it must be admitted that Colberane is a bit stodgy; Ordred is vain, careless and impatient with anything that requires prolonged thought; and Staver, the principal viewpoint character, who bears the Iron Angel sword of the title, also bears the psychological burden with which the other two have laid upon him—he suspects, and not without reason, that when joint ventures are planned their agenda includes lumbering him with the dirty end of the stick and the thin end of the carrot. There is scope for all three to grow up as the action proceeds, and so they do; but since there was little wrong with them to begin with, the effect is a flattening rather than a deepening of character. The psychology is even cruder in *Graymantle*; the hero, Ambescand, is a living epitome of every manly virtue virtually from birth, to which in old age he adds an inappropriate and unconvincing humility.

The writing is far from incompetent—the series is in every way superior to 90 percent of the sword and sorcery produced on both sides of the Atlantic, including much that has achieved far more commercial success—but it has a derivative and disengaged air—like a cocktail of three parts Tolkien to three of David Gemmell to one of water. There are moments when heroic fantasy requires a grandiloquent style, and while Morressy's essays avoid bathos, they lack conviction; one feels that the gentle humour of Kedrigern and the gritty pragmatism of Del Whitby suit him better. Much the same goes for the poetry which embellishes the series. It has infinitely more pretention than Kedrigern's doggerel spells, and is well enough done to pass for the work of (for instance) Alfred Noyes; but it doesn't stand comparison with his chosen epigraphs, which are famous passages from Chesterton. The conclusion is that Morressy would find more mileage if he concentrated on Del Whitby's universe, which is his own creation, while maintaining Kedrigern for light relief.

—Chris Gilmore

MORRIS, Janet E(llen)

Nationality: American. **Born:** Boston, Massachusetts, 25 May 1946. **Education:** Attended New York University, 1965-66. **Family:** Married Christopher C. Morris in 1971. **Career:** Lighting designer, Chip Monck Enterprises, New York, 1963-64; night manager, Christopher Morris Band, 1975, 1977; bass player, Christopher Morris Band, 1975, 1977; songwriter and recording artist; project director, U.S. Global Strategy Council, 1989. Since 1990, research director, Non-Lethal Programs; associate, Institute for Geopolitical Studies. Lives in West Hyannisport, Massachusetts. **Agent:** Perry Knowlton, Curtis Brown Agency, 10 Astor Place, New York, NY 10003, USA.

FANTASY PUBLICATIONS

Novels (series: Hell; Thieves' World)

Beyond Sanctuary (Thieves' World). New York, Baen, 1985.
Beyond the Veil (Thieves' World). New York, Baen, 1985.
Beyond Wizardwall (Thieves' World). New York, Baen, 1986.
The Gates of Hell, with C. J. Cherryh. New York, Baen, 1986.
Kings in Hell, with C. J. Cherryh. New York, Baen, 1987.
Tempus (Thieves' World). New York, Baen, 1987.
City at the Edge of Time, with Chris Morris (Thieves' World). New York, Baen, 1988.
The Little Helliad, with Chris Morris. New York, Baen, 1988.
Explorers in Hell, with David A. Drake. New York, Baen, 1989.
Tempus Unbound (Thieves' World). New York, Baen, 1989.
Storm Seed, with Chris Morris (Thieves' World). New York, Baen, 1990.

Other

Editor, *Heroes in Hell.* New York, Baen, 1986.
Editor, *Rebels in Hell.* New York, Baen, 1986.
Editor, *Crusaders in Hell.* New York, Baen, 1987.
Editor, *Angels in Hell.* New York, Baen, 1987.
Editor, *Masters in Hell.* New York, Baen, 1988.
Editor, *War in Hell.* New York, Baen, 1988

Editor, *Prophets in Hell.* New York, Baen, 1989.

OTHER PUBLICATIONS

Novels

High Couch of Silistra. New York, Bantam, 1977; revised edition, as *Returning Creation,* New York, Baen, 1984.
The Golden Sword. New York, Bantam, 1977.
Wind from the Abyss. New York, Bantam, 1978.
The Carnelian Throne. New York, Bantam, 1979.
Dream Dancer. New York, Putnam, and London, Fontana, 1980.
Cruiser Dreams. New York, Berkley, and London, Fontana, 1980.
I, the Sun. New York, Bantam, 1980.
Earth Dreams. New York, Berkley, 1982.
The 40-Minute War, with Chris Morris. New York, Baen, 1984.
Active Measures, with David A. Drake. New York, Baen, 1985.
MEDUSA, with Chris Morris. New York, Baen, 1986.
Kill Ratio, with David A. Drake. New York, Ace, 1987.
Warlord! New York, Pocket, 1987.
Outpassage, with Chris Morris. New York, Pageant, 1988; London, New English Library, 1990.
Target, with David A. Drake. New York, Ace, 1989.
Threshold, with Chris Morris. New York, Roc, 1990.
Trust Territory, with Chris Morris. New York, Roc, 1992.
The Stalk, with Chris Morris. New York, Roc, 1993.

Other

The Warrior's Edge, with John B. Alexander and Richard Groller. New York, Morrow, 1990.

Editor, *Afterwar.* New York, Baen, 1985.

*   *   *

Janet E. Morris is one of those authors who have had successful careers in both fantasy and science fiction, steadily maintaining her career in both genres for over a decade. During that time she has published more than 20 novels, including some collaborations with her husband, Chris Morris, and others. Her speciality, in both science fiction and fantasy, is military strategy and planning. She is a member of the Association for Electronic Defense, the New York Academy of Sciences, the National Space Society, the National Intelligence Center, and the U.S. Global Strategy Council (it seems amazing that she actually had the time to write all her books as well).

Morris is best known to fantasy readers for her work on the Thieves' World shared-world books, and for the creation of Tempus, her own ongoing hero in those books. Tempus is a complex, tormented anti-hero who is immortal and under the curse of a god who manipulates him at will. When the god takes over, Tempus must go out and rape women; in fact, there is no other way he can have sex with them, because part of his curse is that anyone who loves him (apart from his sister, Cime), will die. This is rather awkward for Tempus's friends, and he attempts not to have any. The sister, Cime, is also immortal, and under her own curse. She wears rods of diamond in her hair, and travels the world of the Rankan empire killing sorcerers by putting the rods through their brains.

A charming pair, the reader might say. In order to understand Tempus and Cime, it is necessary to comprehend the workings of the imaginary Sanctuary, a small, insignificant city at the edge of the empire. Sanctuary is a place dominated by the dregs of life, and ruled by a younger brother of the Emperor known for his incompetence. Thus it is a harsh and barbaric world these characters inhabit, and Thieves' World, probably the finest shared-universe series ever, produced many tormented characters like Tempus and Cime. Morris and Marion Zimmer Bradley were the only two contributors who went on to write entire novels about their characters. (Bradley's character, Lythande, was also a fascinating one: a wizard under a curse—they were popular in Thieves' World—who could never reveal to a man that she was a woman.)

Tempus first appears in Sanctuary as the head of the royal guards, a position that makes him unpopular with the dwellers of the city. Before the prince arrived, Sanctuary was in the unique position of being lawless, a city named for the thieves and outlaws it harbored. Ruled by gangsters and mob-bosses, it didn't welcome the intrusion of law-givers from a far-away capital city. A port town, Sanctuary was also in a desert, which added to the savage nature of its inhabitants. Women were, as is usual in a desert culture, considered chattels, and though there are some unusual and powerful female figures in both the Thieves' World books and Morris's novels, they must fight for every inch of freedom.

To date Morris has written eight novels about Tempus, making him and his friends the most fruitful of the Sanctuary crowd. Most of them take place outside the city of Sanctuary, exploring the rest of the world that was only hinted at in the original shared-universe series. I wondered, when I first encountered Tempus, whether Morris's fans mostly consisted of adolescent boys: her other work is bloody, weapons-and-war-oriented, and much of her science fiction consists of battles against governments, corporations, and outlaws. But I grew to commiserate with Tempus, even though he first repulsed me. Was there ever a more sympathetic murderer/rapist-as-anti-hero invented? When Tempus's god possesses him he becomes a savage sex-machine, who can only achieve satisfaction through rape. That, combined with his curse, make him a complicated and pathetic character indeed.

The strongest aspect of the original Thieves' World series (now a favourite of collectors and difficult to find) was the characters; and since Janet Morris produced an entire pantheon of supporting characters for her hero, she was well able to go on to all those Tempus novels. In addition to sister Cime, there were all Tempus's friends, the Stepsons. The Prince's guard was an elite group of "sacred banders": for readers unfamiliar with this concept, "sacred banders" have their place in the history of earth, usually in extreme patriarchal societies like Greece. Tempus's "Stepsons" were all bisexual, and their band-mates were their lovers. Since they also had a healthy interest in women, this made for many complications of a literary nature.

The first of the Tempus novels, *Beyond Sanctuary,* begins when the Stepsons are officially disbanded and Tempus leaves Sanctuary. Some of the Stepsons remain behind, but Tempus embarks on a long journey across the desert toward the capital city of Ranke. On the way he meets Jihad, the woman who will become his long-time lover and the mother of his son, Cyrus. These two remain together throughout the series, battling evil and rescuing various Stepsons from predicaments involving witches, sorcerers and general bad guys. In *Tempus Unbound,* our hero is finally released from his bondage to his god, only to be eventually taken over by an even more important deity, the Storm God.

In *The City at the Edge of Time* Nico, one of the Stepsons, marries a princess and remains in the legendary city in which no one ages. After Tempus rescues the city from where it is mired at the edge of time, Nico expects to remain there forever. Though he does become the King, he is recalled into service by Tempus, in the last book of the series. In this final novel, *Storm Seed,* Morris reunited all her characters: Tempus, finally released from his bondage to his god only to be possessed by another; the vampire-witch Roxanne, Tempus's nemesis and Stepson Nico's lover; Jihan, who is also immortal and not human, but a "Froth Daughter" and one of the children of Stormbringer; Kama (Tempus's daughter), the female warrior, and her beloved Stepson, Critias . . . a rich and varied pantheon of villains and heroes, well worth all those novels.

While writing the Tempus series, Morris also produced another shared-universe series which she edited and wrote much for. This series started with *Heroes in Hell* in 1986 and continued through ten more books (a twelfth, *Legions of Hell,* was written by C. J. Cherryh alone). It consists for the most part of interconnecting short stories peopled with historical characters and set in a common location (Hell, in this case, unsurprisingly). Various authors, most prominently Cherryh, participated in writing these highly diverting tales. Though the books are well written and the research involved was evidently considerable, the tales become somewhat tedious after one has read a few in each volume. History buffs should enjoy them, however, if only to discover the fates of their favorite heroes and heroines.

After completing these two series, Morris returned to science fiction, producing a number of vigorous novels with husband Chris and several other authors, including *Threshold* and *Trust Territory.* It is to be hoped that she returns to fantasy soon, with a major new series.

—Debora Hill

MORRIS, (Margaret) Jean

Pseudonym: Kenneth O'Hara. **Nationality:** British. **Born:** Sevenoaks, Kent, 15 January 1924. **Education:** Bromley High School, Kent; University of London, honours graduate. **Family:** Has one daughter. **Awards:** Arts Council bursary, for drama, 1955. **Address:** Flat 1, 56 Pevensey Road, Eastbourne, East Sussex BN21 3HT, England.

FANTASY PUBLICATIONS

Novels

The Path of the Dragons. London, Hutchinson, 1980.
The Donkey's Crusade. London, Bodley Head, 1983.
The Song under the Water. London, Bodley Head, 1985.
The Troy Game. London, Bodley Head, 1987.
The Paper Canoe. London, Bodley Head, 1988.
A New Magic. London, Bodley Head, 1990.
A New Calling. London, Bodley Head, 1992.

Short Stories

Twist of Eight, illustrated by Jolyne Knox. London, Chatto and Windus, 1981.

OTHER PUBLICATIONS

Novels

Man and Two Gods. London, Cassell, 1953; as *A Man and Two Gods,* New York, Viking Press, 1954.
Half of a Story. London, Cassell, 1957.
The Adversary. London, Cassell, 1959.
The Blackamoor's Urn. London, Cassell, 1962.
A Dream of Fair Children. London, Cassell, 1966.

Novels as Kenneth O'Hara

A View to a Death. London, Cassell, 1958.
Sleeping Dogs Lying. London, Cassell, 1960; New York, Macmillan, 1962.
Underhandover. London, Cassell, 1961; New York, Macmillan, 1963.
Double Cross Purposes. London, Cassell, 1962.
Unknown Man, Seen in Profile. London, Gollancz, 1967.
The Bird-Cage. London, Gollancz, 1968; New York, Random House, 1969.
The Company of St. George. London, Gollancz, 1972.
The Delta Knife. London, Gollancz, 1976.
The Ghost of Thomas Penry. London, Gollancz, 1977.
The Searchers of the Dead. London, Gollancz, 1979.
Nightmares' Nest. London, Gollancz, 1982.

Plays

Island of Gulls (produced Guildford, Surrey, 1956).
The Spongees, in *Eight Plays 1,* edited by Malcolm Stuart Fellows. London, Cassell, 1965.
Anne of Cleves (televised 1970). Published in *The Six Wives of Henry VIII,* edited by J. C. Trewin, London, Elek, 1972.

Radio Plays: *Safety of the City,* 1961; *The Heretic,* 1962; *Sonata Form of Words,* 1962; *Royal Hunt and Storm,* 1963; *The Mislaid Cause,* 1964; *The Singing Bird,* 1964; *Explosions,* 1965; *Travelling in Winter,* 1971; *The Road to Oxford,* 1976.

Television Play: *Anne of Cleves,* 1970.

Other

The Monarchs of England. New York, Charterhouse, 1975.

Translator, with Radost Pridham, *The Peach Thief and Other Bulgarian Stories.* London, Cassell, 1968.

* * *

Jean Morris did not turn to writing for children until her middle years, in response to her daughter's enthusiasm for reading. Her talent was soon recognized with the short-listing of *The Donkey's Crusade* for two children's book awards. Her first four fantasy novels are notable for their untypical settings: neither set in contemporary Britain nor in outright secondary worlds, they are historical fantasies. *The Path of the Dragons* is set in mythical Greece, more precisely on an island named Atlantis which must be Crete, where Atlantids from outer space have settled, in order to educate and civilize Earthlings. Dragons create paths in the air by their flight, which the Atlantids then use for their own air-transport. The story ends in a cataclysm, severing contact between the stranded Atlantids and their home planet. With its science-fictional "explanation" of the development of Mediterranean civilization, the book is more "science fantasy" than pure fantasy.

The Donkey's Crusade, set in the Middle East and Asia, and opening in Antioch, describes the quest of a monk, his novice guide, a street urchin and their donkey in search of Prester John, following up a supposed letter from the legendary emperor in the Vatican archives. The fantastic element lies in the donkey's intelligence and power of speech, warning his companions against danger; otherwise it is a sophisticated historical novel about the relations between Christians, Muslims, and Mongols in the 13th century A.D., and a plea for religious and social tolerance by reference to the brutal massacres and city sackings which are the consequence of war.

Jean Morris has also written, in *Twist of Eight,* eight revisionist fairy tales about heroes and heroines who reject the stereotype when it comes to re-enactment of the traditional stories. Here are new versions of "The Sleeping Beauty," "Cinderella," "Tam Lin" and "Swan Lake," among others.

The Troy Game is, in my opinion, her masterpiece. The setting and period are unspecified, though must be post-Roman Britain, and the theme was suggested by her daughter. Brannock, a chieftain's younger son, is sent by his village's priest to seek "the hall of my Order." The hall is enchanted, and to find it Brannock must trace a troy, or spiral maze, over miles of rough terrain, using a "bob"—a brooch on a thong which works like a divining rod. It is not a simple spiral, but doubles back on itself inside and outside before heading for the centre. Brannock is told "the Order built their hall here because of the troy"—and this resembles the belief that ley-lines predated their man-made markers.

On reaching the hall, Brannock finds the priests split between collaboration with the invading easterners—or invoking "the land" to take revenge. Thus Jean Morris joins the line of post-war children's fantasists who have employed the motif of the Wild Hunt—Garner, Cooper, Lively, Diana Wynne Jones, for example. *The Troy Game* stands above Morris's other fantasies because it is based on half-forgotten traditions, giving it a numinous air, whereas in her other books the magic is self-contrived.

In *The Paper Canoe* Morris shifted setting and age-group to the teenage problem novel, and here the fantasy is "all in the mind." Carly, awaiting her external examination results, is convinced that she has failed, and retreats into a vivid serial daydream where she is canoeing down a wide river in a fantasy version of Africa, where she grew up. Her starting-point is a small paper canoe which she uses to trigger off the daydream. Characters from the real world appears disguised, in the daydream, and it adds up to a most successful portrait of a teenage girl undergoing a temporary breakdown.

While Morris is admired by children's-book reviewers, she has not attained the popularity, even among well-read children, of Garner or Diana Wynne Jones. It could have been a deliberate attempt to reach a larger audiences when she chose a more typical form of children's fantasy for her two most recent books, and portrayed contemporary children facing and foiling evil magic. *A New Magic* and its sequel *A New Calling,* which combine magic with new technology, may also be termed "science fantasy."

In *A New Magic* four children are farmed out by their wealthy parents to have summer holiday coaching on a country estate. Their

tutor is also cataloguing the library prior to sale—as the estate is being converted to a health farm. However, she is really a witch—related to the family who used to own the estate, and conspiring with her brother to sabotage the conversion and take over the estate with the aid of a mainframe computer which casts spells when set to Reality Mode. The children discover the plot, being computer-literate, and defeat the witch, but she returns in *A New Calling* with a magical camcorder which traps people into a zombified or animal form as long as the spell is preserved on a videocassette. After getting rid of the children the witch plans to take over the county by videoing members of parliament and bank managers, and then, presumably, the whole country. These two fantasies are quite unlike her previous work, though the children's names—Aspasia, Leo, Gareth and Sophie—and their privileged backgrounds still distance the books from the modern child reader. The witch is as evil as a Disney villainess and meets a well-deserved and unpleasant end.

—Jessica Yates

MORRIS, Kenneth (Vennor)

Nationality: British. **Born:** Carmarthenshire, Wales, 31 July 1879. **Education:** Christ's Hospital, London, 1887-1895; graduated as Senior Deputy Grecian. **Career:** Joined the Theosophical Society in Dublin, Ireland, 1896; joined Cardiff Theosophical Lodge No. 1, Wales, 1899; staff member of Universal Brotherhood and Theosophical Society, Point Loma, California, 1908-1930; professor of History and Literature, Raja Yoga College, Point Loma, California, 1908-1930. President of Theosophical Society (Wales), 1930-1937. **Died:** 21 April 1937.

FANTASY PUBLICATIONS

Novels

The Fates of the Princes of Dyfed (as Cenydd Morus). Point Loma, California, Aryan Theosophical Press, 1914.
Book of the Three Dragons. New York, Longmans Green, 1930.
The Chalchiuhite Dragon: A Tale of Toltec Times. New York, Tor, 1992.

Short Stories

The Secret Mountain and Other Tales. London, Faber and Gwyer, 1926.
Through Dragon Eyes, edited by Helynn Hoffa. La Jolla, California, Ben Sen Press, 1980.
The Dragon Path: Collected Stories of Kenneth Morris, edited by Douglas A. Anderson. New York, Tor, 1995.

OTHER PUBLICATIONS

Other

On Verse, "Free Verse," and the Dual Nature of Man. Point Loma, California, Theosophical Publishing, 1924.

Golden Threads in the Tapestry of History. San Diego, California, Point Loma Publications, 1975.

*

Bibliography: *Lloyd Alexander, Evangeline Walton Ensley, Kenneth Morris* by Kenneth J. Zahorski and Robert H. Boyer, Boston, Hall, 1981.

* * *

"Someday I will be discovered," Kenneth Morris told one of his students during his long stay at the Theosophical utopian commune at Point Loma, California, "perhaps a hundred years after I am gone."

The numbers may be wrong, but otherwise the lifelong mystic would have been pleased to have known that he had actually made a prophetic utterance. Kenneth Morris is one of the finest stylists ever to write fantastic fiction and also one of the least known. It is virtually useless to speak of him as an influential writer. He is more of a lost ancestor, who could have ranked alongside Lord Dunsany and E. R. Eddison as one of the masters of "high" fantasy prose, had his work been widely enough available for subsequent generations to read it. Instead, most of his fiction, non-fiction and verse remained hidden in obscure Theosophical journals. Morris apparently never had any interest in publishing in commercial periodicals. His two book publications from major imprints, *The Secret Mountain* and *Book of the Three Dragons,* were brought about by the intercessions of others. In any case, the time was not right. Realism was dominant. Even the most successful fantasists of the 1920s and 1930s, such as Dunsany and James Branch Cabell, had to be rediscovered decades later.

The rediscovery (or, actually, initial discovery) of Morris began in 1969, when Lin Carter included in his anthology *Dragons, Elves, and Heroes* a brief excerpt from *Book of the Three Dragons*—a volume otherwise known only as a legendary collector's item. More important was a brief mention of Morris in Ursula Le Guin's seminal essay, "From Elfland to Poughkeepsie" (1973) which awakened critical interest. Le Guin had clout where Carter did not; she remains the only major fantasy figure to have acknowledged reading Morris. If he was an important influence on her, however, this is not immediately evident. Instead, Morris's influence and final position in the field will perhaps be determined a generation into the future.

Morris was a lifelong, entirely sincere Theosophist, who somehow managed to transform Madame Blavatsky's humbuggeries into a genuine philosophical system, which then infused his work as thoroughly as Christianity did that of C. S. Lewis. When Morris begins an essay, "The Epic of Wales," about the medieval *Mabinogion,* with the statement that Theosophy was the religion of ancient Wales, the sceptical reader may cringe, but the critic must read on to understand Morris's thought and method. In his novels *The Fates of the Princes of Dyfed* and *Book of the Three Dragons,* Morris employs magnificent, somewhat eccentric prose, to retell and amplify ancient Welsh tales, which he sees as an allegory of the development of the human soul. While Theosophy had influenced fantasy before, rather frivolously in the case of Edgar Rice Burroughs, more seriously with Talbot Mundy, Morris used it to give his works genuine depth.

Morris is often compared to Lord Dunsany, but there is a profound difference in outlook. Dunsany was a worldly-wise sceptic, who romantically longed for a purer, more natural mode of existence which he knew probably never was and certainly never would be again. In Dunsany, fate and the gods play tricks on mankind, whose works and aspirations are meaningless in a cosmic context. In Morris, the universe is essentially benevolent. Spiritual progress is possible, if only one can discover the inner light, which we all possess and which Theosophy reveals. In one of his short stories, "The Night of Al Kadr," a Spanish Christian warrior sneaks into a Moorish fortress, bent on slaughter, but instead ineffable peace prevails, because the aged Muslim lord of the place is a member of the secret Theosophical White Brotherhood which works for the betterment of mankind.

Such masters resemble the Taoist immortals, among whom the Chinese hero of "Red-Peach-Blossom Inlet" dwells for a time, but can never rediscover once he has departed their company. (Morris wrote three Chinese stories, all concerned with enlightenment and artistry; they are, incidentally, far, far superior to the much better-known pseudo-Chinese tales Frank Owen was publishing in *Weird Tales* about the same time.)

"The Secret Mountain," the title story of Morris's first collection, tells of Varglon Fflamlas, a slave in Babylon, who has three dreams. In the first, he has become a poet, inspired to chant a great song before the king. But in the middle of the performance, a stranger (one of the Brotherhood, no doubt) appears, whispers something to the poet, and the recital falters. The poet no longer cares about the king's rewards, having received a hint of a higher truth. In a subsequent dream, Fflamlas is a general leading troops into battle. The same thing happens. He leaves the battle, in search of the snow-capped Mountain of the Gods. And again, as a dream-king, he abandons kingship at the stranger's whisper and seeks the Gods.

Varglon Fflamlas, waking, then runs away, along the road that stretches from Babylon to Camelot (making clear, if it were not so already, but this is not set in the historical Babylon, but a never-never land as fabulous as Dunsany's "East"). He achieves enlightenment in the wilderness, finding within himself memories of his former life among the gods on the mountain. He returns to Babylon, is arrested and crucified. Dying, he beholds the snowy Secret Mountain of the Gods among the clouds. But he is not a deluded fool, dying for an illusion. Instead, he is a divine instrument, his purpose being to bring enlightenment to Babylon. ("In the night the city gates were opened from within, and the Gods entered Babylon; there to reign, it is said, for a thousand years or more.")

Here we see all of Morris's key themes: the secret Theosophical masters directing mankind toward truth, the discovery of that truth within oneself, and the final path to enlightenment through suffering. Not surprisingly, several of his stories deal with near-death or after-death experiences, in which divine or philosophical truth is unveiled.

The genuine achievement of Kenneth Morris is that he wrote such material, from such a viewpoint, without producing saccharine sermons for the Theosophical faithful. He never lost his artistry with language, his sense of myth, or his ability to make imaginative use of what he found in the legends and literatures of many cultures. His final novel, *The Chalchiuhite Dragon,* set in ancient Mexico and concerning the coming of the messiah Quetzalcoatl, is as fine and rich as anything he drew out of Welsh, Chinese, Persian or any other sources.

—Darrell Schweitzer

MORRIS, William

Nationality: British. **Born:** Walthamstow, Essex, 24 March 1834. **Education:** Preparatory school in Walthamstow, 1843-47; Marlborough College, Wiltshire, 1848-51; privately, 1852-53; Exeter College, Oxford, 1853-55, B.A. 1856, M.A. 1875. Served in the Artists Corps of Volunteers, 1859-61. **Family:** Married Jane Burden in 1859; two daughters. **Career:** Articled to G. E. Street's architectural firm, Oxford and London, 1856; founding editor, *Oxford and Cambridge Magazine,* 1856; practising painter, 1857-62; friend of Edward Burne-Jones, Dante Gabriel Rossetti, and other members of the Pre-Raphaelite Brotherhood; founder, with Burne-Jones, Rossetti, Ford Madox Brown, and others, Morris Marshall Faulkner & Co. design firm, London, 1861-74, subsequently Morris & Co., 1874-96; lived at Red House, Bexley, Kent, 1861-65, and in London from 1865 (at Kelmscott House, Hammersmith, from 1878); travelled in Iceland, 1871 and 1873; with Rossetti leased Kelmscott Manor, near Lechlade, Gloucestershire, 1871; public lecturer on art, architecture, and socialism, 1877-96; founder, Kelmscott Press, Hammersmith, 1890-96. Treasurer, National Liberal League, 1879; member, Democratic Federation, 1883, then the Socialist League, 1884; editor of its journal *Commonweal,* 1884-90, and League delegate to the International Socialist Working-Men's Congress, Paris, 1889; founding member, Hammersmith Socialist Society, 1890. Examiner, South Kensington School of Art, later Victoria and Albert Museum, London, 1876-96; founding member and secretary, Society for the Protection of Ancient Buildings, 1877; president, Birmingham Society of Arts, 1878-79; member, 1888, and master, 1892, Art Workers Guild: exhibited with the Arts and Crafts Exhibition Society. Honorary fellow, Exeter College, 1882. **Died:** 3 October 1896.

FANTASY PUBLICATIONS

Novels

A Tale of the House of the Wolfings and All the Kindreds of the Mark (prose and verse). London, Reeves and Turner, 1889; Boston, Roberts, 1890.
The Roots of the Mountains: Wherein Is Told Somewhat of the Lives of the Men of Burgdale. London, Reeves and Turner, 1890; New York, Longman, 1896.
The Story of the Glittering Plain Which Has Also Been Called the Land of Living Men, or the Acre of the Undying. Hammersmith, Middlesex, Kelmscott Press, and Boston, Roberts, 1891.
The Wood Beyond the World. Hammersmith, Middlesex, Kelmscott Press, 1894; Boston, Roberts, 1895.
Child Christopher and Goldilind the Fair. Hammersmith, Middlesex, Kelmscott Press, 2 vols., 1895; Portland, Maine, Mosher, 1900.
The Well at the World's End: A Tale. Hammersmith, Middlesex, Kelmscott Press, and New York, Longman, 1896.
The Water of the Wondrous Isles. London, and New York, Longman, 1897.
The Sundering Flood. Hammersmith, Middlesex, Kelmscott Press, and New York, Longman, 1897.

Short Stories

The Hollow Land and Other Contributions to the Oxford and Cambridge Magazine. London, Longman, 1903.

Golden Wings and Other Stories. Van Nuys, California, Newcastle, 1976.

OTHER PUBLICATIONS

Novels

A Dream of John Ball, and A King's Lesson. London, Reeves and Turner, 1888; East Aurora, New York, Roycroft, 1898.
News from Nowhere; or, An Epoch of Rest, Being Some Chapters from a Utopian Romance. Boston, Roberts, 1890; London, Longman, 1891.
The Novel on Blue Paper, edited by Penelope Fitzgerald. London, and West Nyack, New York, Journeyman Press, 1982.

Play

The Tables Turned; or Nupkins Awakened: A Socialist Interlude (produced 1887). London, Commonweal Office, 1887.

Poetry

The Defence of Guenevere and Other Poems, edited by Robert Steele. London, Bell and Daldy, 1858; Boston, Roberts, 1875.
The Life and Death of Jason: A Poem. London, Bell and Daldy, and Boston, Roberts, 1867; revised edition, London, Bell and Daldy, and Boston, Roberts, 1867, 1888.
The Earthly Paradise: A Poem. London, Ellis, 3 vols., 1868-70; Boston, Roberts, 1868-71; revised edition, New York, Longman, 1890.
The Story of Sigurd the Volsung and the Fall of the Niblungs. London, Ellis and White, 1876; Boston, Roberts, 1877.
The Pilgrims of Hope: A Poem in Thirteen Parts. London, Forman, 1886; Portland, Maine, Mosher, 1901.
Poems by the Way. Hammersmith, Middlesex, Kelmscott Press, 1891; Boston, Roberts, 1892.
A Book of Verse: A Facsimile of the Manuscript Written in 1870. London, Scolar Press, 1980.
The Juvenilia, with a Checklist and Unpublished Early Poems, edited by Florence S. Boos. London, and New York, William Morris Society, 1983.

Other

Love Is Enough; or, The Freeing of Pharamond: A Morality. London, Ellis and White, and Boston, Roberts, 1873.
Hopes and Fears for Art: Five Lectures Delivered in Birmingham, London, and Nottingham, 1878-1881. London, Ellis and White, and Boston, Roberts, 1882.
Lectures on Art. London, Macmillan, 1882.
A Summary of the Principles of Socialism Written for the Democratic Federation, with H. M. Hyndman. London, Modern Press, 1884.
Art and Socialism: A Lecture; and Watchman, What of the Night? The Aims and Ideals of the English Socialists of Today. London, Reeves, 1884.
Chants for Socialist: No. 1. The Day is Coming. London, Reeves, 1884.
The Voice of Toil, All for the Cause: Two Chants for Socialists. London, Justice Office, 1884.

The God of the Poor. London, Justice Office, 1884.

Chants for Socialists. London, Socialist League Office, 1885; New York, New Horizon Press, 1935.

The Manifesto of the Socialist League. London, Socialist League, 1885; revised edition, 1885.

The Socialist League: Constitution and Rules at the General Conference. London, Socialist League, 1885.

Address to Trades' Unions (The Socialist Platform - No. 1). London, Socialist League, 1885.

The Aims of Art. London, Commonweal Office, 1887.

Signs of Change: Seven Lectures. London, Reeves and Turner, 1888; New York, Longman, 1896.

Socialist Platform (collected pamphlets), with others. n.p., 1888; revised edition, 1890.

Statement of Principles of the Hammersmith Socialist Society. Hammersmith, Hammersmith Socialist Society, 1890.

Under an Elm-Tree: or, Thoughts in the Country-side. Aberdeen, Scotland, Leatham, 1891; Portland, Maine, Mosher, 1912.

Manifesto of English Socialists, with G. B. Shaw and H. M. Hyndman. London, Twentieth Century Press, 1893.

The Reward of Labour: A Dialogue. London, Hayman Christy, 1893.

Letters on Socialism. London, Wisel, 1894.

How I Became a Socialist. London, Twentieth Century Press, 1896.

Architecture, Industry, and Wealth: Collected Papers. London, and New York, Longman, 1902.

Collected Works, edited by May Morris. London, and New York, Longman, 24 vols., 1910-15; supplement, as *William Morris: Artist, Writer, Socialist,* Oxford, Blackwell, 2 vols., 1936.

Communism, a Lecture. London, Fabian Society, 1903.

The Letters of William Morris to His Family and Friends, edited by Philip Henderson. London, and New York, Longman, 1950.

Unpublished Letters, edited by R. P. Arnot. London, Labour Monthly, 1951.

Selected Writings and Designs, edited by Asa Briggs. Baltimore, Penguin, 1962.

The Unpublished Lectures of William Morris, edited by Eugene D. LeMire. Detroit, Michigan, Wayne State University Press, 1969.

Icelandic Journals. Fontwell, Centaur Press, 1969; New York, Praeger, 1970.

Early Romances in Prose and Verse, edited by Peter Faulkner. London, Dent, 1973; Van Nuys, California, Newcastle, 1976.

Socialist Diary, edited by Florence Boos. Iowa City, Iowa, Windhoven Press, 1981; London, History Workshop Journal, 1982.

The Ideal Book: Essays and Lectures on the Arts of the Book, edited by William S. Peterson. Berkeley, University of California Press, 1982.

Political Writings of William Morris, edited by A. L. Morton. London, Lawrence and Wishart, and New York, International, 1973.

The Collected Letters of William Morris, edited by Norman Kelvin. Princeton, Princeton University Press, 3 vols., 1984-87.

Morris by Himself: Designs and Writings, edited by Gillian Naylor. N.p., 1988.

Translator, with Eiríkr Magnússon, *Grettis Saga: The Story of Grettir the Strong.* London, Ellis, 1869; New York, Longman, 1901.

Translator, with Eiríkr Magnússon, *Völsunga Saga: The Story of the Volsungs and Niblungs with Certain Songs from the Elder Edda.* London, Ellis, 1870; edited by H. Sparling, London, and New York, Walter Scott, 1888.

Translator, with Eiríkr Magnússon, *Three Northern Love Stories and Other Tales.* London, Ellis, and New York, Longman, 1875.

Translator, *The Aeneid of Virgil Done Into English Verse.* Boston, Roberts, 1875; London, Ellis and White, 1876.

Translator, *The Odyssey of Homer Done into English Verse.* London, Reeves and Turner, 2 vols., 1887; New York, Longman, 1897.

Translator, with Eiríkr Magnússon, *The Saga Library.* London, Quaritch, 5 vols., 1891-1905.

Translator, with others, *The Order of Chivalry,* by Hugues de Tabarie. Hammersmith, Middlesex, Kelmscott Press, 1893.

Translator, *The Tale of King Florus and the Fair Jehane.* Hammersmith, Middlesex, Kelmscott Press, 1893; Portland, Maine, Mosher, 1898.

Translator, *Of the Friendship of Amis and Amile.* Hammersmith, Middlesex, Kelmscott Press, 1894.

Translator, *The Tale of the Emperor Coustans and of Over Sea.* Hammersmith Press, 1894; Portland, Maine, Mosher, 1899.

Translator, with A. J. Wyatt, *The Tale of Beowulf, Sometime King of the Fold of the Weder Geats.* Hammersmith, Middlesex, Kelmscott Press, 1895; New York, Longman, 1910.

Translator, *Old French Romances.* London, G. Allen, and New York, Scribner, 1896.

Translator, with Eiríkr Magnússon, *The Story of Kormak, the Son of Ogmund,* edited by Grace Calder. London, William Morris Society, 1970.

*

Bibliography: *A Bibliography of the Works of William Morris* by Temple Scott, London, G. Bell, 1897; *Handlist of the Public Addresses of William Morris* by R. C. H. Briggs, London, William Morris Society, 1961; *William Morris in Private Press and Limited Editions: A Descriptive Bibliography of Books by and about William Morris 1891-1981* by John J. Walsdorf, Phoenix, Arizona, Oryx, and London, Library Association, 1983; *A Bibliography of the Kelmscott Press* by William S. Peterson, Oxford, Clarendon, 1984; *William Morris: A Reference Guide* by Gary L. Aho, Boston, G.K. Hall, 1985.

Critical Studies (selection): *The Life of William Morris* by J. W. Mackail, London, and New York, Longman, 2 vols., 1899; *The Kelmscott Press and William Morris, Master Craftsman* by H. H. Sparling, London, Macmillan, 1924; *William Morris: Romantic to Revolutionary* by E. P. Thompson, London, Lawrence and Wishart, 1955, revised edition, New York, Pantheon, 1976, London, Merlin Press, 1977; *Against the Age: An Introduction to William Morris* by Peter Faulkner, London, Allen and Unwin, 1980; *William Morris: The Critical Heritage* edited by Peter Faulkner, London, and Boston, Routledge and Kegan Paul, 1973; *William Morris: The Man and the Myth* (includes letters) by R. P. Arnot, New York, Monthly Review Press, and London, Lawrence and Wishart, 1964; *The Work of William Morris* by Paul Thompson, London, Heinemann, and New York, Viking, 1967, revised edition, London, Quartet Books, 1977; *William Morris: His Life, Work, and Friends* by Philip Henderson, London, Thames and Hudson, and New York, McGraw-Hill, 1967; *William Morris: His Life and Work* by Jack Lindsay, London, Constable, 1975, New York, Taplinger, 1979; *William Morris: Aspects of the Man and His Work* edited by Peter Lewis, Loughborough, Loughborough Victorian Studies Group, 1978; *Worlds Beyond the World: The Fantastic Vision of William Morris* by Richard Mathews, San Bernardino, California,

Borgo Press, 1978; *A Pagan Prophet: William Morris* by Charlotte Oberg, Charlottesville, University Press of Virginia, 1978; *William Morris and His World* by Ian Bradley, New York, Scribners, and London, Thames and Hudson, 1978; *William Morris* by Frederick Kirchhoff, Boston, Twayne, 1979; *William Morris* by Peter Stansky, Oxford and New York, Oxford University Press, 1983; *William Morris: His Art, His Writings, and His Public Life: A Record* by Aymer Vallance, London, Studio Editions, 1986; *William Morris: His Life and Work* by Stephen Coote, London, Garamond, 1990.

* * *

William Morris is probably best known today for his wallpaper and fabric designs. Of his fictional work, it is only *News from Nowhere* which is still widely read. This work inspired generations of socialists and remains for many the most attractive of all utopian visions. But its prominence has obscured the fact that in other fictions Morris helped create the genre of high fantasy, celebrating heroism, honour, romance and magic in a pseudo-medieval world—a genre which, under Tolkien and his successors, came to dominate late-20th-century fantasy.

Morris brought a number of enthusiasms to his writing. He had read widely in medieval literature, and was particularly excited by the myths and legends of the North: he translated several Icelandic sagas into English for the first time. His love of crafts and of medieval art (which he shared with his friends in the Pre-Raphaelite Brotherhood) was in part aesthetic, but in large part also a reaction against the Industrial Revolution, which had flooded the world with cheap, standardized and soulless artefacts at the expense of the creativity of individual workers. His personal discovery of Karl Marx, and his subsequent deep involvement in the socialist movement, was crucial in his development as a writer.

Morris read Edward Bellamy's utopia *Looking Backward* when it appeared in 1888 and was appalled by its picture of industrial armies and consumerist socialism. His own *News from Nowhere* was a direct response. Bellamy's hero Julian West had travelled from 1887 to the Boston of 2000 by pseudo-scientific means; Morris's anonymous hero (presumably Morris himself) merely goes home to his shabby suburb after a stormy socialist meeting, and "wakes up" in the 21st century: both his characters and himself suspect he is in a dream, though at the end, when he fades away and wakes up in dingy Hammersmith, he argues that it was not so much a dream as a vision. Morris's vision is of an England after a violent revolution. Towns have been demolished: what had been London is now a collection of small villages, in the midst of which just a few old public buildings could still be found, such as the British Museum and the Houses of Parliament (the latter being a useful storage place for manure). Many familiar elements of earlier Utopias make their appearance: there is no private property, no money, no laws, no state coercion, no state. Morris's Marxism allows him to construct the economic and social bases of his communist future with care; his own interests makes that future appear very much like an idealized Middle Ages, its rural inhabitants guaranteed their happiness by the disappearance of the twin oppressors of feudalism and religion. Morris's unshakeable belief in the essential goodness of men and women makes the book seem unworldly to many in the late 20th century. However, Morris paints the beauty of the 21st century with charm and good humour, and his total distrust of the state and deep concern for the environment give the book considerable contemporary appeal.

Morris spent much of the time between the publication of *News from Nowhere* and his death in 1896 writing a series of romances or fantasies set in imagined worlds which recall the idealized Middle Ages of the classic fairy tale. Some have seen these fantasies as a betrayal by the old socialist of his former beliefs and as a retreat into an irrelevant and escapist other-world by someone who had been so concerned with the reform of this one. Others have been repelled by the artificially medieval language, well represented by the opening words of *The Water of the Wondrous Isles*: "Whilom, as tells the tale, was a walled cheaping-town hight Utterhay, which was builded in a bight of the land a little off the great highway which went from over the mountains to the sea." Yet these romances were the culmination of Morris's enthusiasm for medieval literature, which predated his socialism by many years; the language provides the necessary cultural distancing; and some of Morris's familiar social and political concerns are indeed to be found in his romances. At the end of the 20th century, we perhaps find these fantasies easier to appreciate than contemporaries did, attuned as we are to the concept of the other-world fantasy, thanks largely to the works of Morris's admirers, such as C. S. Lewis and J. R. R. Tolkien.

Apart from "The Hollow Land" and some early short stories, his first experiments in fantasy fiction were *A Tale of the House of the Wolfings* and *The Roots of the Mountains,* historical romances with magical elements. They were followed by *The Story of the Glittering Plain,* his first full-blown fantasy, written just after *News from Nowhere.* But three of the five books which then followed represent Morris' greatest achievement in this field, and are among the most lyrical and enchanting fantasies in the English language. He began the longest, *The Well at the World's End,* in 1892: he called it "the Interminable," and worked on it for two years, publishing it (at his own Kelmscott Press) only in the year of his death. Ralph, the youngest son of King Peter of Upmeads, secretly leaves on a quest, in which he finds love with the Lady of Abundance and loses it again when the Lady is killed by her husband; he eventually drinks of the Well with his new love Ursula, and returns home to find all wrongs righted. The parallels with the quest for the Holy Grail are clear, but the emphasis is deliberately different. Neither the Church, with its other-worldly approach, nor other male-dominated institutions, can offer the happiness in this world which Ralph desires; he achieves his quest through the love and wisdom of women.

The Water of the Wondrous Isles can be read as a comment on male and female sexuality, on the tension between female prudence and male lechery which sours relationships between the sexes. The child-woman Birdalone has grown up in a wood, knowing only a wicked witch and the fairy Habundia (another appearance of the figure Abundance from the medieval *Roman de la Rose*). But the book celebrates Birdalone's own awareness of her beautiful body (which Morris frequently mentions), and her desire to be loved; her quest is achieved, and she and her lover "lived without shame and died without fear." In *The Wood Beyond the World,* too, there is a quest: Golden Walter leaves his life of commercial prosperity in Langton (London?), in search of truth and moral improvement. In the Wood he finds a powerful and immortal Lady and a deformed dwarf: these two symbolize, perhaps, femininity and masculinity in their extreme undiluted forms. Walter himself, and the Lady's Maid, have personalities which represent balance and creativity. As in any true quest, Walter finds his personal and moral fulfilment: he marries the Maid and becomes a king. He has left Commerce and presides over a world of older, truer values.

In Morris's last fantasy, *The Sundering Flood,* finished on his deathbed, the social intent is even clearer. Two lovers are separated by a great river, in a forbidding landscape inspired by Iceland: the only crossing is at the City. Osberne travels to the city, and through social evolution at the same time: from his own simple communal village, through a feudal society (he rejects knighthood), and into the commercial City, which is itself on the brink of a revolution of the craftsmen against grasping capitalists. The narrator is a cleric, and the Church, for once, is on the side of morality and justice: a temporary lapse of Morris's Marxism, perhaps. All these fantasies nevertheless achieve the rare feat of forging a delicate beauty out of a profound social conscience. Few of his successors in pseudo-medieval fantasy have that same sense of commitment underlying their work.

—Edward James

MORROW, James (Kenneth)

Nationality: American. **Born:** Philadelphia, Pennsylvania, 17 March 1947. **Education:** University of Pennsylvania, Philadelphia, 1965-69, B.A. in creative writing; Harvard University Graduate School of Education, Cambridge, Massachusetts, 1969-70, M.A. in teaching 1970. **Family:** Married Jean Pierce Morrow in 1972; one daughter and one son. **Career:** English teacher, Cambridge Pilot School, Massachusetts, 1970-71; instructional materials specialist, Chelmsford Public Schools, Massachusetts, 1972-74; lecturer in instructional media, Tufts University, Medford, Massachusetts, 1977-79; contributing editor, *Media and Methods* magazine, 1978-80; co-director, Institute for Multimedia Learning, Westford, Massachusetts, 1978-84; science writer, *A Teacher's Guide to NOVA,* WGBH-TV, Boston, 1979-84; children's book author, Learningways Corporation, Cambridge, 1982-87; freelance fiction reviewer, *Philadelphia Inquirer,* 1986-90; visiting lecturer in fiction writing, Pennsylvania State University, University Park, 1990. Freelance fiction writer since 1980. **Awards:** Pennsylvania Council of the Arts fellowship, 1988; Nebula Award, 1988, 1992; World Fantasy Award, 1991. **Agent:** Writers House, 21 West 26th Street, New York, NY 10010, USA. **Address:** 810 North Thomas Street, State College, PA 16803, USA.

FANTASY PUBLICATIONS

Novels

This Is the Way the World Ends. New York, Holt, 1986; London, Gollancz, 1987.
Only Begotten Daughter. New York, Morrow, 1990; London, Century, 1991.
Towing Jehovah. New York, Harcourt Brace, and London, Arrow, 1994.

Short Stories

Swatting at the Cosmos. Eugene, Oregon, Pulphouse, 1990.
Bible Stories for Adults. New York, Harcourt Brace, 1995(?).

OTHER PUBLICATIONS

Novels

The Wine of Violence. New York, Holt Rinehart, 1981; London, Century, 1991.
The Continent of Lies. New York, Holt Rinehart, 1984; London, Gollancz, 1985.
City of Truth. London, Legend, 1991.

Fiction for Children

The Quasar Kids. Lexington, Massachusetts, Heath, 1987.
What Makes a Dinosaur Sore? Lexington, Massachusetts, Heath, 1987.
The Lima Bean Dream, with Marilyn Segal. Lexington, Massachusetts, Heath, 1987.
Not too Messy, Not too Neat, with Marilyn Segal. Lexington, Massachusetts, Heath, 1988.
The Best-Bubble Blower. Lexington, Massachusetts, Heath, 1988.

Play

Screenplay: *A Political Cartoon,* with Joe Adamson, 1973.

Other

Moviemaking Illustrated: The Comicbook Filmbook (textbook), with Murray Suid. Rochelle Park, New Jersey, Hayden, 1973.
Media and Kids (textbook), with Murray Suid. Rochelle Park, New Jersey, Hayden, 1977.
The Grammar of Media Kit (textbook), with Jean Morrow. Rochelle Park, New Jersey, Hayden, 1978.
The Creativity Catalogue (textbook), with Murray Suid. Belmont, California, Pitman Learning, 1982.
The Adventures of Smoke Bailey (novelization of computer game). Cambridge, Massachusetts, Spinnaker, 1983.
Ready to Read (textbook), with Lillian Lieberman and Murray Suid. Palo Alto, California, Monday Morning, 1986.
Start to Read (textbook), with Lillian Lieberman and Murray Suid. Palo Alto, California, Monday Morning, 1986.
Read and Write (textbook), with Lillian Lieberman and Murray Suid. Palo Alto, California, Monday Morning, 1986.

Editor, *Nebula Awards 27-29.* New York, Harcourt Brace, 3 vols., 1993-95.

*

James Morrow comments:

Love, music, and stories are the best things in life, and none of them comes easily. Shortly after arriving at the University of Pennsylvania in 1965, I attempted to develop my story-making abilities by taking creative writing courses. I didn't get far. Much to my bewilderment, the tacit message of a typical Penn fiction workshop seemed to be this: whatever you write, write small. Don't embarrass yourself. Abridge your ambitions. Report on small people doing small things. But suppose one doesn't care for small? Suppose one has no use for fiction in which the plot, as Ben Hecht once sarcastically remarked, is the opening of a door? Suppose one has a taste for gods, heroes, monsters, magic, ideas? "Don't swat at the Cosmos," my first writing teacher kept telling me. A solid image, to be sure—professors are skilled at such rhetoric—but not, I think, very good advice.

In the years following my formal education, I've grown increasingly convinced that among the beginning writer's most precious prerogatives is the right to make a fool of himself. The neophyte should not only be encouraged to write about the small things he knows; he should also be encouraged to write about the large things he can envision. As long as the typical college writing workshop caters to the cult of reality, as long as it is characterized by what Ray Bradbury calls "fear of the imagination," its products will be, on the whole, mere autobiographical confession, forever threatening to turn fiction into an eccentric branch of journalism.

The primacy of imagination in fantasy literature must not be taken as a rationale for laziness. When Bradbury asks us to consider the humble "dandelions" of the fiction world, he doesn't disparage its royal roses. A genre author is every bit as obligated to bleed for his craft as the mainstream writer. His primary duty is to torment himself, forever shouting in his own ear, "Make it better! Make it better! Make it better!"

*   *   *

"In Iran," wrote fellow author Michael Bishop of James Morrow in admiration, "this guy wouldn't last two sentences."

Inevitably, after publishing a novel about the incarnation of Jesus Christ's younger sister and another about a sea captain towing the corpse of God, not to mention several decidedly unorthodox revisions of Biblical episodes, James Morrow is nowadays compared to Salman Rushdie even more often than he is compared to Kurt Vonnegut. Neither is precisely accurate, though it seems unlikely Morrow will be published in Iran soon. He is primarily a satirist on ethical and religious matters, whose work wanders in and out of science fiction, depending on the presence or absence of overt supernaturalism. In context, such distinctions are not particularly important.

Two early novels, *The Wine of Violence* and *The Continent of Lies,* are social satires, set on other planets, though, in a tradition stretching back at least as far as Voltaire, Morrow's would-be ideal (and often absurd) societies could have just as readily been placed in remote or imaginary regions of the Earth. The novella *City of Truth* is likewise science fiction, about a society in which everyone is hard-wired to tell the literal truth all the time. Here we encounter his main theme: the need to outgrow dependency on dogma or irrational belief.

"Bible Stories for Adults, No. 31: The Covenant" states this most explicitly. A contribution to an alternate-history anthology (*What Might Have Been, Vol 1,* ed. Gregory Benford and Martin H. Greenberg), the story postulates that, after Moses cast down the tablets in wrath upon his return from Mount Sinai, God did *not* provide a backup copy. Therefore mankind has spent the intervening millennia trying to piece together the fragments. The robot/computer which has completed the task destroys itself and the text, after a savage critique of the Commandments, realizing that human beings must mature beyond the need for a divinity. We are to take responsibility for ourselves, Morrow tells us again and again.

His first novel to arguably cross from science fiction into overt fantasy, *This is the Way the World Ends,* not only demands human responsibility, but puts mankind on trial. After a nuclear war, the final survivors of the doomed human race are tried by revenants of generations never to be born. There is much polemicizing about disarmament, but in *This is the Way the World Ends* Morrow's great strengths appear. His comedy contains truth. It is funny and ultimately moving because it convinces. Humour is used to present material which, otherwise, might be too grim or too shrill to remain readable. The novel's nightmarish, despairing climax is only acceptable because the lively narrative has approached it by degrees of calculated absurdity. This is a difficult technique, achieved by few other writers, in fantasy or elsewhere. (Mark Twain, T. H. White and Mervyn Wall come to mind.)

Only Begotten Daughter, the first of Morrow's books which might have gotten him into serious trouble with ayatollahs, not to mention the American radical right, suggests that Christ's mission was a failure, and that when the younger sister of Jesus is born miraculously in a sperm bank, the best thing Julie Katz can do is conceal her divinity, or find some way to give it up entirely. Unfortunately the Devil, who inspires religious movements, tempts her into performing miracles. Upheavals result. A breakaway theocratic dictatorship comes to power in New Jersey, and, like Christ in the hands of Dostoevsky's Grand Inquisitor, Julie Katz is the very first person the religious authorities need to destroy. She undergoes a passion very similar to her brother's before ultimately renouncing godhood, for the benefit of humankind.

Synopsis only hints at the richness of this extraordinary novel. It is more than satire or farce. Morrow achieves real drama, with a level of emotional involvement impossible in, say, a satirical movie such as *Monty Python's Life of Brian.* The shabby crucifixion of Julie Katz is genuinely terrible. Once again, Morrow has used comedy to reveal his story's dark heart.

Towing Jehovah takes place after the death of God. The divine corpse has been found floating in the South Atlantic. A discredited oil-tanker captain, who seeks personal redemption for his role in an environmentally disastrous spill, is engaged by the Vatican and by the last survivors of the soon-to-be-extinct Heavenly Hosts to tow the body into the Arctic before it rots. Many adventures befall captain and crew along the way, as they battle moral breakdown and existential confusion. The mission is assaulted by rationalists, feminists, and ultimately the Catholic Church itself, who find the proven (former) existence of God, the maleness of God, and the removal of the authority of God to be threatening. This time, comedy prevails. While there is drama, the characters are convincing as individuals rather than types, and occasional dark moments occur, *Towing Jehovah* is more amusing than moving, its most obvious virtue being its awesomely deadpan, detailed elaboration of its absurd premise. Morrow reports that a sequel is planned: a few of God's brain cells are found to have survived after all.

As long as Morrow takes on the Almighty, he works in a distinguished tradition of satirical fantasy. Illustrious predecessors include Mark Twain (*The Mysterious Stranger, Letters from the Earth*), the playwright Elmer Rice (*The Adding Machine*), and James Branch Cabell. Heaven and Hell have long been the stuff of comedy, at least in the West, out of the reach of ayatollahs. Eventually, one assumes, Morrow will have to move on to other material, but meanwhile his delvings into sacred matters have yielded impressive results. By examining most cherished beliefs, Morrow calls on us to examine ourselves.

—Darrell Schweitzer

MORWOOD, Peter

Pseudonym of Robert Peter Smith. **Nationality:** British. **Born:** 1956. **Family:** Married fantasy writer Diane Duane in 1987. **Address:** c/o Legend Books, Random House UK Ltd., 20 Vauxhall Bridge Rd., London SW1V 2SA, England.

FANTASY PUBLICATIONS

Novels (series: Clan Wars; Horse Lords; Prince Ivan)

The Horse Lord. London, Century, 1983; New York, DAW, 1987.
The Demon Lord (Horse Lords). London, Century, 1984; New York, DAW, 1987.
The Dragon Lord (Horse Lords). London, Arrow, 1986; New York, DAW, 1987.
The Warlord's Domain (Horse Lords). London, Legend, 1989; New York, DAW, 1990.
Keeper of the City, with Diane Duane. New York, Bantam, 1989.
Prince Ivan. London, Legend, 1990.
Firebird (Prince Ivan). London, Legend, 1992.
The Golden Horde (Prince Ivan). London, Legend, 1993.
Greylady (Clan Wars). London, Legend, 1993.
Widowmaker (Clan Wars). London, Legend, 1994

OTHER PUBLICATIONS

Novels

The Romulan Way, with Diane Duane. New York, Pocket, 1987; London, Titan, 1989.
Rules of Engagement. New York, Pocket, 1990.
Space Cops: Mindblast, with Diane Duane. New York, Avon, 1991.
Space Cops: Kill Station, with Diane Duane. New York, AvonNova, 1992.
Space Cops: High Moon, with Diane Duane. New York, AvonNova, 1992.
SeaQuest DSV, with Diane Duane (novelization of television script). New York, Ace, and London, Millennium, 1993.

*   *   *

On the whole, Peter Morwood's novels are written to stand alone, although knowledge of previous volumes in a series is an advantage, while familiarity with earlier series can be a handicap. With the exception of *Keeper of the City,* written with Diane Duane, the books fall into two groups—those in which the island of Alba is a prominent feature, and those based on Russian mythology and history.

Morwood's first published book, *The Horse Lord,* introduces us to a society that is based largely on that of Japan complete with the strict honour codes that every warrior and noble is expected to adhere to. The internal illustrations by the author add to this belief. The book concerns a naive younger son, Aldric Talvalin, who unwittingly resurrects a long-dead sorcerer, Kalarr cu Ruruc. Before this becomes common knowledge, Aldric's entire family with the exception of the brother who hates him (who was away at court at the time) and Aldric (who was detained in a neighbouring town for

causing an affray) are slaughtered by the wizard Duergar Vathach, an enemy agent seeking to cause political instability in Alba. Befriended by the wizard, Gemmel, Aldric is trained and prepared for his task of slaying the evil ones. Romantic interest is provided by Kyrin, who tries to steal from him and who, just as he falls in love with her, returns home to marry her betrothed. Before the evil ones can be defeated, Aldric is given the sword, Isileth, and makes a side-trip to wrest a weapon from a firedrake's lair.

Although the plot is somewhat simplistic and there are numerous stylistic problems and occasional plot conveniences, the society in *The Horse Lord* is such that it is worth exploring further. Instead, in volume two (*The Demon Lord*) Aldric sets sail for the continent. He is now effectively head of Clan-Talvalin but feels obliged to take the mission offered by his king as a test of loyalty. His task is to destroy Lord Crisen Segharlen, who has been stealing King Rynert's gold. Again there are sorcerers for Aldric to defeat. At the start of *The Dragon Lord,* we are told that the king has betrayed Aldric to the Empire that is trying to overthrow Alba. The only difference this makes to the plot is to give an excuse for Gemmel and the king's champion, Dewan, to charge off to rescue him. From the rich tapestry of Alban society in *The Horse Lord,* these two books become no more than plain adventure with little to mark them out from the rest of the genre. The narrative is flat and the action seems clinical, partly because Morwood tends to switch viewpoint with great rapidity. *The Dragon Lord,* in particular, could have been related effectively in a third of the time, there being too much extraneous wordage, not just in the adjectival descriptions but also in self-indulgent passages which add nothing to the plot: for example, the discussion on dragons with a chance-met story-teller who bears a strong resemblance to Anne McCaffrey—there is even a drawing of her.

The War Lord's Domain is much the same kind of book. Aldric is now reunited with Kyrin, and they have to travel to the city of Drakkenborg to steal a jewel possessed by Voord, the sorcerer Aldric had so much trouble with in *The Dragon Lord.*

Greylady and *Widowmaker* are the first two volumes of a new series with the same setting as the Horse Lords books but taking place about 500 years earlier. They are the "true story" of how the Horse Lords came to Alba and settled it, as told by a bard 300 years after the events. The original Albans came as invaders but tended to be welcomed by the peasantry as less oppressive masters than the native nobility. The principal character is Bayrd ar'Talvlyn, a minor noble who discovers he is a sorcerer (as distinct from a wizard: the former is an innate talent, the latter has to be learned). When sorcery is used against the invaders, Bayrd is sent to look for a native wizard who will side with them. He finds Eskra, whom he later marries, and a ruined fortress which he wins (to the annoyance of his liege lord) and vows to rebuild. He also finds, hidden beneath the fortress, the sword Isileth. The Greylady of the title is not this sword but the name of the one Alban Overlord holds as his authority to rule and is mentioned about twice. Isileth is the Widowmaker. In the second volume, set some years after the first, the Albans face Kalarr cu Ruruc, a 20-year-old sorcerer planning the destruction of his country's invaders. Gemmel also makes his first appearance, as an itinerant wizard.

There are a number of major inconsistencies between the two series, a few of which can be explained by the rider that at intervals the history of the Albans is rewritten to make it more palatable to the listeners. This does not allow for other discrepancies, such as the age of cu Ruruc, his background and means of death, unless Morwood intends to write further books in which this sorcerer is resurrected for more than a few years, allowed to age and is defeated again. But since Gemmel was around at the time perhaps he should have said something; after all, he has somehow gained caretakership of one of Clan Talvalin's most important possessions. Although Morwood has clearly done a lot of research, especially for the Prince Ivan series, there are gaping holes in his experience. In *Greylady,* for example, the Albans experience a "Russian" winter, yet they are on an island the size of Britain in a similar geographic position.

The Prince Ivan series is on the surface a different type of fantasy, but common themes abound. This Russia is ruled by tzars who resemble the Alban Clan lords in almost everything except costume. They are insular, suspicious of magic and have a high regard for honour. *Prince Ivan,* however, does stick very much to the original folk tale. Ivan's three sisters have all made spectacular marriages to sorcerers, and it is now his turn to find a bride. All suggest that Mar'ya Morevna would be suitable. (Interestingly, there is a princess whom Aldric has to rescue in *The Dragon Lord* called Marya Marevna.) *Firebird* includes the eponymous mythical beast in its plot, but Ivan's Russia is now very much part of our world but set in the early 13th century when crusading knights, finding the Holy Land a bit too difficult, set their sights on the conquest of Russia. Magic is still an important element in the story but is more limited. By the final volume, *The Golden Horde,* the theme is mostly that of an historical novel with magical leanings. The ending is weak but does offer an explanation of why the exploits of Ivan and his family are folk tale rather than history, and why magic has disappeared.

The Keeper of the City, Morwood's collaboration with Diane Duane, is a far more competent piece of writing. It is the second volume of a series devised by Bill Fawcett, each of which is written by different authors. This is a reasonably complex thriller set in a fantasy world where all the main characters are feline *mrem.* Reswen is the chief constable with a network of spies (all Morwood's fantasy has a network of spies), one of which is the wizard Lorin (magic is a capital offence in this world). Reswen suspects that the delegation from the east, ostensibly sent to set up trade links, is more than it appears. Unfortunately he cannot prove it. Only Lorin begins to suspect that the liskash, the mrem's ancient enemy is plotting something. The writing here is much more tightly controlled than in any other of Morwood's books, indicating the superior influences of Duane.

—Pauline Morgan

MUNDY, Talbot

Pseudonym for William Lancaster Gribbon. **Other Pseudonym:** Walter Galt. **Nationality:** American (originally British; granted US citizenship, 1917). **Born:** London, 23 April 1879. **Education:** Rugby School, Warwickshire, 1893-95. **Family:** Married 1) Kathleen Steele in 1903 (divorced 1908); 2) Inez Craven in 1908 (divorced 1912); 3) Harriette Rosemary Strafer in 1913 (divorced 1924); 4) Sally Ames in 1924 (divorced 1931); 5) Mrs. Theda Allen (Dawn) Webber in 1931. **Career:** Spent time travelling and farming, 1896-99; undertook administrative duties in India, 1899-1902, and Africa, 1903-08 (where twice imprisoned); moved to New York, 1909; full-time writer from 1911. **Died:** 5 August 1940.

FANTASY PUBLICATIONS

Novels (series: Jimgrim/Ramsden; Tros; Ommony; King/Yasmini)

The Caves of Terror (King/Yasmini). New York, Garden City Publishing, 1924; London, Hutchinson, 1934.
The Nine Unknown (Jimgrim/Ramsden). Indianapolis, Bobbs Merrill, 1924; London, Hutchinson, 1924.
Om: The Secret of Ahbor Valley (Ommony). Indianapolis, Bobbs Merrill, 1924; London, Hutchinson, 1925.
The Devil's Guard (Jimgrim/Ramsden). Indianapolis, Bobbs Merrill, 1926; as *Ramsden,* London, Hutchinson, 1926.
Queen Cleopatra (Tros). Indianapolis, Bobbs Merrill, 1929; London, Hutchinson, 1929.
Black Light. Indianapolis, Bobbs Merrill, 1930; London, Hutchinson, 1930.
Jimgrim (Jimgrim/Ramsden). New York, Century, 1931; London, Hutchinson, 1931; as *Jimgrim Sahib,* New York, Royal, 1953.
The Mystery of Khufu's Tomb (Jimgrim/Ramsden). London, Hutchinson, 1933; New York, Appleton Century, 1935.
Tros of Samothrace. London, Hutchinson, 1934; New York, Appleton Century, 1934; divided as *Tros,* New York, Avon, 1967; London, Tandem, 1971; *Helma,* New York, Avon, 1967; London, Tandem, 1971; *Helene,* New York, Avon, 1967; London, Tandem, 1971; *Liafail,* New York, Avon, 1967; London, Tandem, 1971; re-divided as *Lud of Lunden,* New York, Zebra, 1976; *Avenging Liafail,* New York, Zebra, 1976; *The Praetor's Dungeon,* New York, Zebra, 1976.
Full Moon. New York, Appleton Century, 1935; as *There Was a Door,* London, Hutchinson, 1935.
Purple Pirate (Tros). New York, Appleton Century, 1935; London, Hutchinson, 1935.
The Thunder Dragon Gate. London, Hutchinson, 1937; New York, Appleton Century, 1937.
Old Ugly Face. New York, Appleton Century, 1940; London, Hutchinson, 1940.

OTHER PUBLICATIONS

Novels

Rung Ho! New York, Scribner, 1914; London, Cassell, 1914.
The Winds of the World. London, Cassell, 1916; Indianapolis, Bobbs Merrill, 1917.
King—of the Khyber Rifles. Indianapolis, Bobbs Merrill, 1916; London, Constable, 1917.
Hira Singh's Tale. London, Cassell, 1918; as *Hira Singh,* Indianapolis, Bobbs Merrill, 1918.
The Ivory Trail. Indianapolis, Bobbs Merrill, 1919; London, Constable, 1919; as *Trek East,* New York, Royal, 1953.
The Eye of Zeitoon. Indianapolis, Bobbs Merrill, 1920; London, Hutchinson, 1920.
Guns of the Gods. Indianapolis, Bobbs Merrill, 1921; London, Hutchinson, 1921.
Her Reputation. Indianapolis, Bobbs Merrill, 1923; as *The Bubble Reputation,* London, Hutchinson, 1923.
Cock o' the North. Indianapolis, Bobbs Merrill, 1929; as *Gup Bahadur,* London, Hutchinson, 1929.
The Hundred Days and The Woman Ayisha. New York, Century, 1930; in 2 vols as *The Hundred Days* and *The Woman Ayisha,* London, Hutchinson, 1930.

The Marriage of Meldrum Strange. London, Hutchinson, 1930.
W.H.: A Portion of the Record of Sir William Halifax. London, Hutchinson, 1931; as *The Queen's Warrant,* New York, Royal, 1953.
Jungle Jest. London, Hutchinson, 1931; New York, Century, 1932.
The Lost Trooper. London, Hutchinson, 1931.
When Trails Were New. London, Hutchinson, 1932.
C.I.D. London, Hutchinson, and New York, Century, 1932.
The Lion of Petra. London, Hutchinson, 1932; New York, Appleton Century, 1933.
The Gunga Sahib. London, Hutchinson, 1933; New York, Appleton Century, 1934.
The King in Check. London, Hutchinson, 1933; New York, Appleton Century, 1934; as *Affair in Araby,* New York, Royal, 1953.
All Four Winds (omnibus; includes *King—of the Khyber Rifles, Jimgrim, Black Light, Om*). London, Hutchinson, 1933.
Jimgrim and Allah's Peace. London, Hutchinson, 1933; New York, Appleton Century, 1936.
The Red Flame of Erinpura. London, Hutchinson, 1934.
Caesar Dies. London, Hutchinson, 1934; New York, Centaur, 1973.
The Seventeen Thieves of El-Kalil. London, Hutchinson, 1935.
East and West. New York, Appleton Century, 1937; as *Diamonds See in the Dark,* London, Hutchinson, 1937.

Short Stories

Told in the East. Indianapolis, Bobbs Merrill, 1920
The Soul of a Regiment. San Francisco, Alex Dulfer, 1924.
Romances of India (omnibus; includes *King—of the Khyber Rifles, Guns of the Gods, Told in the East*). New York, Burt, 1936.
The Valiant View. London, Hutchinson, 1939.

Other

I Say Sunrise. London, Dakers, 1947; Philadelphia, Wells, 1949.

*

Film Adaptations: *The Black Watch,* 1929, *King of the Khyber Rifles,* 1954, both from the novel *King—of the Khyber Rifles.*

Bibliography: *Talbot Mundy Biblio* by Bradford M. Day, New York, privately published, 1955.

Critical Studies: *Talbot Mundy: Messenger of Destiny* edited by Donald M. Grant, West Kingston, Rhode Island, Grant, 1983; *The Last Adventurer: The Life of Talbot Mundy,* by Peter Berresford Ellis, West Kingston, Rhode Island, Grant, 1984; "Talbot Mundy" by E. F. Bleiler in *Supernatural Fiction Writers,* Volume 2, edited by Bleiler, New York, Scribner, 1985; "Adventures of the Two Americans" and "Riders and Swordsmen," in *Yesterday's Faces, Volume 6: Violent Lives* by Robert Sampson, Bowling Green, Ohio, Popular Press, 1993.

*   *   *

Although little of his work remains in print, Talbot Mundy is still remembered as one of the great adventure-story writers for the pulp magazines, particularly *Adventure* (where his tales appeared sometimes long before book publication). His work has been favourably compared to that of Haggard and Kipling, and it is as a fusion of their work at its most mystical and most colourful that his best writing may be considered.

Mundy was a prolific writer and over half of his work falls outside the fantasy category, although it is almost all part of that rip-roaring larger-than-life derring-do escapism that so thrilled readers between the two World Wars. But his later works, especially after he became involved with the Theosophists in the early 1920s, became increasingly mystical. Mundy held the sincere belief that the supernatural was nothing more than the outward emanations of a forgotten ancient science, and this message imbues all of his later fantasies.

Mundy was a born storyteller: indeed he reinvented the first half of his life in order to hide a sordid period as a philanderer, confidence trickster and criminal. It was not until the diligent researches of Peter Berresford Ellis that Mundy's past as a rogue all across Southern Africa was revealed. Yet once Mundy had moved to America in 1909, and been nearly killed in a mugging, his personality changed to that of a reasonably honest and upright citizen (apart from his dealings with women) and he channelled his talent for deceit and fabrication into creating some of the most exciting fiction published in the pulps. His first story, "A Transaction in Diamonds," appeared in 1911, his first book, *Rung Ho!,* in 1914, and his fame came with the twice-filmed *King—of the Khyber Rifles* in 1916.

King—of the Khyber Rifles is a straightforward adventure novel with no fantastic undertones other than the hint of reincarnation. But it features two of Mundy's characters who would reappear in Mundy's first true fantasy novel, *Caves of Terror* (as "The Grey Mahatma," *Adventure,* 10 November 1922). These are Athelstan King of the Secret Service who is trying to stop a holy war on the North West Frontier, and Yasmini, a beautiful spy whose loyalties are never really revealed. A variety of characters weave their way in and out of Mundy's novels, sometimes having adventures of their own, not all fantastic. In *Caves of Terror* King, in partnership with American mining engineer Jeff Ramsden, seeks to stop Yasmini obtaining the occult secrets of a powerful holy man, the Grey Mahatma, one of the Nine Unknown, keepers of the Ancient Wisdom.

The sequel to *Caves of Terror* is *The Nine Unknown* (*Adventure,* 20 March-30 April 1923) which brings into the fray Mundy's other main character at this time, James Schuyler Grim or Jimgrim. The Jimgrim stories, which are narrated by Jeff Ramsden, began after Mundy's visit to Palestine in 1920 where he encountered an American agent who had joined the British Field Intelligence in Palestine during the War. Mundy used this character as the basis for Grim, an American Secret Service Agent working for the British. Jimgrim first appeared in the straightforward war story "The Adventure at El Kerak" (*Adventure,* 10 November 1921), and further adventures followed tracing Jimgrim's exploits throughout the Near East. With the oddly titled "Moses and Mrs. Aintree" (*Adventure,* 10 September 1922; no separate book publication) Grim, now a soldier-of-fortune employed by Meldrum Strange, one of the richest men in the world, discovers an occult sect in Egypt protecting an ancient likeness of Moses. This story and *The Mystery of Khufu's Tomb* (as "Khufu's Real Tomb," *Adventure,* 10 October 1922), added mysticism and the occult to the increasing public fascination for Egyptology following Carter's discovery of the tomb of Tutankhamen.

The Nine Unknown brought all these aspects together as Strange employs Jimgrim and Ramsden to discover what has happened to all of the world's gold. They find themselves caught in a fight between Good (represented by the mysterious Nine Unknown) and

Evil (a sect of Kali worshippers) both with supernatural powers. From here on the Jimgrim stories become more and more fantastic, with Grim taking on an increasingly superhuman role through *The Devil's Guard* (as "Ramsden," *Adventure,* 8 June-8 August 1926) and reaching messianic proportions in the final novel *Jimgrim* (as "King of the World," *Adventure,* 15 November 1930-15 February 1931) where Grim pits himself against the ultimate villain. The later Jimgrim books are compelling. Mundy's sincere belief in the teachings of Theosophy, along with his own convincing creativity, allows the reader to drift from the real to the unreal with easy acceptance. The characters are fully developed (and increasingly well known to the readers) and the writing is tight and powerful.

The 1920s saw Mundy at the top of his writing powers. Indian and Tibetan mysticism reappear in a few other non-series novels of which the best is *Om: The Secret of Ahbor Valley* (*Adventure,* 10 October-30 November 1924), where forester Cottswold Ommony enters the Ahbor Valley in search of his long lost sister and encounters a stone which reflects to men the truth of their own inner psyche. *Om* is not only a fascinating mystical novel but a beautiful portrayal of Indian life. Mundy's later novels in this vein lack the early power and vision, though *Full Moon* (*American Weekly,* 28 October 1934-27 January 1935), with its search for the entrance to the fourth dimension in caves beneath India, has the old flair and is reminiscent of some of A. Merritt's work.

Mundy's other great series features Tros of Samothrace. These are basically historical novels, set at the time of the Roman invasion of Britain, and the fantastic elements are minimal but essential, linking the ancient Greek mysteries to the knowledge and power of the Druids. The novels always hint at secrets darker than they ever reveal. The stories are convincing examples of Mundy's version of history. His own dislike of Julius Caesar results in that leader's portrayal initially as a villain, though a begrudging respect emerges in later books. Tros, on the other hand, is strongly depicted as a master sea captain, a man of irreproachable character, and an adventurer with desires to voyage around the world. Alas, Tros's full adventures were never completed, but the three original books, *Tros of Samothrace* (originally a series of novellas in *Adventure* during 1925/26), *Queen Cleopatra* and *Purple Pirate,* are a fascinating alternative portrayal of ancient Britain, Egypt and the last days of the Roman republic.

Mundy wrote for the leading pulp magazine *Adventure* at a time when it also featured the work of other respected adventure writers, including Harold Lamb, H. Bedford-Jones, Arthur Howden-Smith, J. Allan Dunn, Arthur O. Friel and Achmed Abdullah, but then, as now, there were few readers who did not regard the stories of Talbot Mundy as the most vivid and exciting of them all. For strength of character, vividness of setting, and sincerity of plotting, his Oriental fantasies remain among the best.

—Mike Ashley

MUNN, H(arold) Warner

Nationality: American. **Born:** Athol, Massachusetts, 5 November 1903. **Family:** Married Malvena Ruth Beaudoin in 1930 (died 1972); four sons. **Career:** Full-time writer, 1925-1930; afterwards held various jobs, ending as office manager of a heating company; retired 1968. **Died:** 10 January 1981.

FANTASY PUBLICATIONS

Novels (series: Gwalchmai in all books)

King of the World's Edge. New York, Ace, 1966.
The Ship from Atlantis. New York, Ace, 1967.
Merlin's Ring. New York, Ballantine, 1974; London, Futura, 1977.
Merlin's Godson (omnibus; includes *King of the World's Edge, The Ship from Atlantis*). New York, Ballantine, 1976.

Short Stories

The Werewolf of Ponkert. Providence, Rhode Island, Grandon, 1958.
The Affair of the Cuckolded Warlock. Tacoma, Washington, Lanthorne Press, 1975.
What Dreams May Come. Tacoma, Washington, Swan Press, 1978.
In the Hulks. Tacoma, Washington, Swan Press, 1979.
In Regard to the Opening of Doors. Tacoma, Washington, Swan Press, 1979.
The Transient. Tacoma, Washington, Swan Press, 1979.
The Baby Dryad. Tacoma, Washington, Folly Press, 1980.
Tales of the Werewolf Clan, Volume 1: In the Tomb of the Bishop. West Kingston, Rhode Island, Grant, 1979.
Tales of the Werewolf Clan, Volume 2: The Master Goes Home. West Kingston, Rhode Island, Grant, 1979.

OTHER PUBLICATIONS

Novels

The Lost Legion. New York, Doubleday, 1980.

Poetry

Christmas Comes to the Little Horse. Tacoma, Washington, privately printed, 1974.
Twenty-Five Poems. Tacoma, Washington, Folly Press, 1975.
The Banner of Joan. West Kingston, Rhode Island, Grant, 1975.
To All Amis. Tacoma, Washington, privately printed, 1976.
Season Greetings With Spooky Stuff. Tacoma, Washington, privately printed, 1976.
There Was a Man. Tacoma, Washington, privately printed, 1977.
The Pioneers. Tacoma, Washington, Swan Press, 1977.
Dawn Woman. Tacoma, Washington, Swan Press, 1979.
Fairy Gold. Tacoma, Washington, Swan Press, 1979.
Of Life and Love and Loneliness. Tacoma, Washington, privately printed, 1979.

*

Critical Studies: *Presenting Moonshine,* Tacoma, Washington, privately printed, 1975; "Warlock of Tacoma: An Appreciation" by Jessica Amanda Salmonson, *The Chicago Fantasy Newsletter,* February-May 1981; "H. Warner Munn: A Bibliography" by Mike Ashley, *Kadath,* July 1981.

*　　*　　*

H. Warner Munn is a name still closely linked to *Weird Tales,* even though he had only eleven stories in the magazine, and all but one of those within the years 1925 to 1933. Yet his total writing, which recommenced after his retirement in 1968, stretches to four novels, nearly 40 stories and almost 200 poems, almost all of it in the realms of the fantastic or occult.

Munn began writing through the encouragement of H. P. Lovecraft, who questioned why a werewolf story had not been told from the viewpoint of the werewolf. Munn took to the task and produced "The Werewolf of Ponkert" (*Weird Tales,* 1925). Brenryk is the afflicted human who, under the influence of the demonic Master, becomes a werewolf and is forced to kill his wife and sacrifice his daughter. He rebels against this state and prefers to suffer death rather than a life of damnation. Munn later extended the series by following a generation at a time, linking each new accursed werewolf with some catastrophe in history. These later stories were eventually collected in the two-volume *Tales of the Werewolf Clan.*

Munn's other short stories in *Weird Tales* were more horror than fantasy. His last appearance, though, pointed the way to the future. This was with the short novel *King of the World's Edge* (1939) which, when reprinted in paperback in the 1960s, regenerated his writing career. The novel fits within the Arthurian canon though it is unlike any other Arthurian adventure. It follows the flight of Merlin, or Myrddin Ambrosius, out of Britain with Gwalchmai (or Sir Gawain), and the Roman centurion Ventidius Varro, who narrates the story. They sail across to America, arriving in the land of the Aztecs, where Merlin is recognized as their god Quetzalcoatl. This situation was further developed in the sequel *The Ship from Atlantis,* when Varro despatches Gwalchmai back to Rome to encourage them to explore the new World. But Gwalchmai never reaches Rome. Trapped in the Sargasso Sea, he encounters a capsule bearing a survivor from Atlantis. This now sets the background for Munn's most adventurous novel, *Merlin's Ring.* This is a vast fantasy saga, following the love story of Gwalchmai and the Atlantean sorceress Corenice through the course of history from the fall of Atlantis to Joan of Arc. Munn's painstaking research, his love for historical detail, and his fascination for the occult, all contributed to giving this novel a depth and scope rare in historical fantasy.

Munn completed one other novel, *The Lost Legion,* a borderline fantasy about a Roman legion in the Far East. Although he was working on further novels, the remainder of his published work was short fiction, mostly in the small press. Plans were afoot for these to be collected in book form as *The Melldrum Box,* but that never came to pass. A few were issued as privately published chapbooks, including the charming Christmas fantasy "The Baby Dryad" about the dryad of a Scots Pine threatened by the North Wind. Amongst these later stories is "Deposition at Rouen" (*Weirdbook,* 1973) which shows Munn's growing interest in Joan of Arc, which also resulted in an epic narrative poem, *The Banner of Joan.* Most of Munn's later stories are quiet, reflective fantasies, but a few are bolder. "The Merlin Stone" (*Weirdbook,* 1977) tells of the discovery of an ancient race of Pictish fairies in Scotland. The story suggests Munn was working toward linking his Arthurian stories with Lovecraft's Cthulhu cycle, a concept he had started in the earlier-written but later-published "The Stairway to the Sea" (*Weirdbook,* 1978) and continued in "The Wanderers of the Waters" (*Weirdbook,* 1981).

Munn was one of the few writers from *Weird Tales*'s early days able to reestablish his reputation in the 1970s. That he did it with such singular effect is a mark of his originality and dedication.

—Mike Ashley

MURPHY, Pat(rice Anne)

Nationality: American. **Born:** 9 March 1955. **Education:** University of California at Santa Cruz, B.A. in biology and general science, 1976; participated in the University's Science Writing Program. **Career:** Author of numerous science articles for magazines and newspapers, 1976-82; Senior Research Writer, Educational Graphics Department, Sea World, Inc., 1978-82. Since 1982, editor and contributor, *Exploratorium Quarterly,* San Francisco. **Awards:** Nebula award for novel, 1987; Nebula award for novelette, 1987; Theodore Sturgeon Memorial award, 1987; Philip K. Dick award, 1990; World Fantasy award, 1991. **Agent:** Jean Naggar, 216 East 75th Street, New York, NY 10021, USA. **Address:** c/o Exploratorium, 3601 Lyon Street, San Francisco, CA 94123, USA.

FANTASY PUBLICATIONS

Novel

The Falling Woman. New York, Tor, 1986; London, Headline, 1988.

Short Stories

Points of Departure. New York, Bantam, 1990.
Letters from Home, with Pat Cadigan and Karen Joy Fowler. London, Women's Press, 1991.

OTHER PUBLICATIONS

Novels

The Shadow Hunter. New York, Popular Library, 1982; London, Headline, 1988.
The City, Not Long After. New York, Doubleday, 1989; London, Pan, 1990.
Pigasus (for children). New York, Dial, 1994.

Other

Tuna and Billfish—Fish without a Country, with James Joseph and Witold Klave, paintings by George Mattson. La Jolla, California, Inter-American Tropical Tuna Commission, 1979.
Explorabook: A Kid's Science Museum in a Book, with John Cassidy and Paul Doherty. N.p., Klutz Press, 1991.
By Nature's Design: Photography, photographs by William Neill. San Francisco, Chronicle Books, 1993.

Editor, *Bending Light: An Exploratorium Toolbook.* New York, Little Brown, 1993.

*

Pat Murphy comments:

Many of my stories deal with outsiders, people who are trapped in a world where they do not belong. Sam, the Neanderthal who has been yanked from his own time; the nameless alien woman who lingers in Mexico, unable to find her way home; Rachel, the chimp with the mind of a teenage girl—these are characters who have, in a sense, found that secret door I was always looking for. They've entered a new world filled with exotic things and strange people; it just happens to be the world in which we live every day . . . When I was a kid, I knew that fantastic things were waiting just around the corner, lingering in the shadows, lurking behind the rhododendron bush. Some were nice and some were horrible—like the witches under the bed or the monsters that hid in storm drains. I imagined their lives and they became real. Now that I'm a grown-up, I am doing what I wanted to do then: I am opening the secret doorway and letting them into our world; I am walking through the secret passage and visiting theirs. (From "Afterword—Why I Write" in *Points of Departure,* 1990, pages 315-16.)

*   *   *

With her background as a science writer, and long experience working at a uniquely interactive science museum, Pat Murphy apparently would be naturally inclined to write science fiction; however, while much of her fiction fits that category, she has also written remarkable fantasies. The chief example, of course, is *The Falling Woman,* alternately narrated by an archaeologist, Elizabeth Butler, who can see people from the past, and her estranged daughter Diane, who develops the same ability. While excavating Mayan ruins, Elizabeth is surprised when her daughter, upset by the death of her father, suddenly joins the expedition; then a Mayan priestess begins talking to her, explains that she once sacrificed her young daughter to please the gods and urges the archaeologist to kill Diane. While resisting this impulse, she is injured, but her daughter rescues her, and the women then seem to move towards a reconciliation.

In one respect, *The Falling Woman* is a ghost story with a common theme: the vengeful ghost who tries to make a living person adopt the ghost's personality and behaviour. However, with accurate accounts of Mayan civilization and a scientist as one protagonist, Murphy also gives the novel the flavor of science fiction, and it functions as a commentary on the mentality that drives both science and science fiction. The novel briefly presents one of Murphy's favourite themes: that scientists, like most humans, are obsessed with finding patterns in nature—an idea developed at greater length in *By Nature's Design.* However, Elizabeth's desire for patterns almost destroys her: she begins living by the Mayan calendar, expecting good or bad events on given days, thus succumbing to astrology; and she is tempted to kill her own daughter because that would mean following an old pattern. Murphy thus suggests that despite the emphasis on new discoveries and inventions in science, a quest for patterns may also lead to dangerous repetition of the past. In this way, Murphy changes the traditional ghost story, where the scientist plays the role of sceptic or rational analyst; here, the scientist falls into the role of victim.

Moreover, since Elizabeth observes not only one or two individual ghosts, but a panoply of people and images from all aspects of Mayan life, the novel is a fantasy, as the colourful Mayan civilization in effect becomes a second setting for the novel. And, as both a fantasy and commentary on fantasy, the novel analyzes the effects of an obsession with the past. Elizabeth is determined to avoid the future: an archaeologist who studies only past civilizations and ignores her own society, who attempted suicide and endangers her health by chain-smoking, and who wilfully abandons her own daughter. She literarlly lives in the past, and like the falling woman she sees on a pot, she is plunging towards death; her unhappiness graphically illustrates the dangers in the nostalgia that is often the basis of fantasy. The novel has no easy solutions to this problem; Elizabeth will keep working as an archaeologist, prob-

ing into the past, but her resolve to quit smoking and spend more time with her daughter suggests she is finally thinking about her future as well.

This rich, complex novel, to be sure, has other themes and concerns, including a feminist statement about the problems women face trying to succeed in a "man's world," as Elizabeth must make herself cold and childless to focus on her career; while men in the novel are either ineffectual, like Elizabeth's colleague Tony, or manipulative, like the man who seduces and abandons Diane. Remarks about the brutality of Mayan culture and religion are met by rebuttals about covert cruelties in our civilization, providing a warning against cultural chauvinism of any kind. Yet the novel never becomes a thesis and also is an entertaining story about the lives and interactions of some interesting people.

Some of Murphy's short stories, like *The Falling Woman,* are fantasies about the need to resist the dangerous allure of the past. In "Dead Men on TV," a woman compulsively watches her dead father's old movies on television and imagines he is calling her to join him in that realm; instead, she destroys her television and VCR. In "Don't Look Back," a woman who returns to her old college and jobs always finds a younger version of herself taking her place, strengthening her resolve to start a new career in New York. "In the Abode of the Snows" concerns a man who, while seeking to fulfil his late father's dream of finding a yeti, somehow becomes a yeti himself. Other stories juxtapose a dying fantasy world and emerging scientific world with sincere admiration for lost values and beliefs. In "Touch of the Bear," a Neanderthal taken by time travel to a natural preserve in the future maintains a belief in animal spirits, and the spirit of a dead bear takes possession of a friend's daughter. In "Bones," an eight-foot-tall Irishman gifted with magical powers to attract animals and heal people goes to London to lead Irish immigrants back to Ireland; after his quest fails and he dies, his skeleton, preserved by a surgeon intent on scientific research, eventually provides evidence linking the pituitary gland to human growth. Other fantasy stories include "In the Islands," about a scientist who discovers, but does not reveal, a race of merpeople; "With Four Lean Hounds," about a girl who rescues magical creatures—a giant, an undine, a dragon, and the four winds—from her tyrannical mother; "On the Dark Side of the Station Where the Train Never Stops," about a "fireborn" woman—one of the beings who secretly perform tasks like inventing ants and bringing starlight to Earth—who chooses to become the North Star; and "Sweetly the Waves Call to Me," about a lonely student who achieves a strange rapport with silkies.

Murphy's science fiction stories may resemble fantasies, like "On a Hot Summer Night in a Place Far Away," "Good-Bye, Cynthia," "A Falling Star Is a Rock from Outer Space" and "Recycling Strategies for the Inner City," all concerning aliens on Earth who seem derived from mythology, not exobiology. Murphy can make fantasy sound like sf, and sf sound like fantasy; it is difficult to fit her work into patterns.

—Gary Westfahl

MURPHY, Shirley Rousseau

Nationality: American. **Born:** Oakland, California, 20 May 1928. **Education:** California School of Fine Arts (now San Francisco

Art Institute), 1947-51, A.A. in fine art and commercial art 1951. **Family:** Married Patrick J. Murphy in 1951. **Career:** Packaging designer, Sam Kweller, Los Angeles, 1952-53; interior decorator, Bullock's Department Store, Los Angeles, 1953-55; teacher of mosaics, San Bernardino Valley College, California, 1953-61; documents assistant, Canal Zone Library Museum, Panama, 1964-67. Painter and sculptor. Individual shows: Jack Carr Gallery, South Pasadena, California, 1957; San Bernardino Valley College, and Whittier Art Association, California, both 1958; Ojai Valley Art Center, California, and Ash Grove Gallery, Los Angeles, both 1959; Cherry Gallery, San Bernardino, and Light House Gallery, Hermosa Beach, California, both 1960; Richmond Museum, California, 1963. Since 1963 freelance writer. **Agent:** Martha Millard, 204 Park Avenue, Madison, NJ 07940, USA. **Address:** 1977 Upper Grandview Road, Jasper, GA 30143, USA.

FANTASY PUBLICATIONS

Novels (series: Children of Ynell; Dragonbards)

The Grass Tower, illustrated by Charles Robinson. New York, Atheneum, 1976.

The Ring of Fire (Children of Ynell). New York, Atheneum, 1977.

Silver Woven in My Hair, illustrated by Alan Tiegreen. New York, Atheneum, 1977; London, Macdonald and Jane's, 1978.

Soonie and the Dragon, illustrated by Susan Vaeth. New York, Atheneum, 1979.

The Wolf Bell (Children of Ynell). New York, Atheneum, 1979.

The Castle of Hape (Children of Ynell). New York, Atheneum, 1980.

Caves of Fire and Ice (Children of Ynell). New York, Atheneum, 1980.

The Joining of the Stone (Children of Ynell). New York, Atheneum, 1981.

Valentine for a Dragon, illustrated by Kay Chorao. New York, Atheneum, 1984.

Nightpool (Dragonbards). New York, Harper, 1985.

The Ivory Lyre (Dragonbards). New York, Harper, 1987.

The Dragonbards. New York, Harper, 1988.

Medallion of the Black Hound, with Welsh Suggs. New York, Harper, 1989.

The Catswold Portal. New York, Roc, 1992.

OTHER PUBLICATIONS

Fiction for Children

The Sand Ponies, illustrated by Erika Weihs. New York, Viking Press, 1967.

White Ghost Summer, illustrated by Barbara McGee. New York, Viking Press, 1967.

Elmo Doolan and the Search for the Golden Mouse, illustrated by Fritz Kredel. New York, Viking Press, 1970.

Carlos Charles, with Patrick Murphy. New York, Viking Press, 1971.

Poor Jenny, Bright as a Penny. New York, Viking Press, 1974.

The Flight of the Fox, illustrated by Don Sibley. New York, Atheneum, 1978.

The Pig Who Could Conjure the Wind, illustrated by Mark Lefkowitz. New York, Atheneum, 1978.

Mrs. Tortino's Return to the Sun, with Patrick Murphy, illustrated by Susan Russo. New York, Lothrop, 1980.

Tattie's River Journey, illustrated by Tomie de Paola. New York, Dial Press, and London, Methuen, 1983.

The Song of the Christmas Mouse, illustrated by Donna Diamond. New York, HarperCollins, 1990.

Wind Child, illustrated by Leo and Diane Dillon. New York, HarperCollins, 1995.

*

Manuscript Collection: de Grummond Collection, University of Southern Mississippi, Hattiesburg.

Shirley Rousseau Murphy comments:

Speaking animals fill my fantasies. I find an honesty and directness among animals which is not always so apparent in humankind; I like the play of philosophies between human and animal. And I take great pleasure in my animals' wit, in their sharp indignation, their free spirits. In the trilogy which began with *Nightpool,* the otters and foxes and the singing dragons sprang totally alive in the first draft, beasts so full of themselves that they at once set the tone, directed the real texture of life among Tirror's island nations. Later, a stray cat sparked the first glimmer of story for *The Catswold Portal.* The little calico moved into our house, soon ruled it, would lie on my desk smiling up at me from a nest of clawed manuscript pages, so bright and intense that I began to see her green eyes lighting a human face—to see her as a young shapeshifter, and that was Melissa. I think that good fantasy springs from Joy, that it must create the sense of moving several inches above the earth. The light around you shifts, secrets are revealed, your deepest self is touched, maybe at first glance by darkness—by disillusionment, that darkest antagonist—but ultimately by what C. S. Lewis has named Joy, ultimate, unattainable, infinite, toward which human life forever seeks.

*   *   *

An accomplished prize-winning artist as well as an author, Shirley Rousseau Murphy has provided a number of sensitive and intricate fantasies for children and young adults. She has recently written a fantasy for adults, *The Catswold Portal,* which has been well received critically. Murphy is best known for two fantasy series for young adults, the Children of Ynell and Dragonbards. Both are high fantasy. The former is the set in an elaborate and complex imaginary world. The latter also creates a wonderful land, but it is one that invites comparison with Anne McCaffrey's Pern. Both series have the feeling of C. S. Lewis's Narnia books as well, because of the emphasis of the eternal struggle between good and evil.

The Children of Ynell quintet focuses on the central character of Ramad, a seer of Ynell, who possesses psychic abilities as well as magical secrets. He is the illegitimate son of young Tayba. A quest runs throughout the rather complicated storylines of the five books which involves locating and restoring a jade runestone with great mystical power. The power of the runestone is well known, and many people search for the nine pieces of the stone, both good and evil. Ramad battles powerful foes, such as Vinniver, his mother's paramour, and ruler of Burgdeeth. Vinnivir has created an oppressive religion for his country, and with his magical powers he has instituted a cruel regime. Another villain is the monster Hape, who is constructed along the lines of some monsters of Greek mythology, with three heads (an eel, a serpent and a horned man/cat). Other creatures in the books inspired by Greek mythology are winged horses and spirit wolves. In addition to the search for the runestone shards, a strong theme of the importance of fighting for freedom and human dignity is present in the series. A complicating factor in the stories is the ability of the characters to use time travel by means of three starfire stones. It is only by means of going into the past that the world is saved in the end.

Murphy has created a detailed alternative world for the Children of Ynell series. It is as closely and tightly woven as an elaborate tapestry. It is clear that she spent much time and gave careful attention to the many facets of this fantasy world. Yet it is that very care that makes the stories hard to follow for some young readers. In a sense, Murphy has created her own mythology from details of existing legends, but the intertwining tales are so different from better known sagas that a great deal of effort is required from readers to keep it all straight. The series might well have been more successful had it been written for adults rather than younger readers.

The Dragonbards trilogy also employs elements from various mythologies; Greek, Norse and a bit of influence from medieval romances. The storyline is less complex than the Children of Ynell series, which results in a more powerful narrative. Murphy creates a new fantasy land, one with dragons and talking otters, as well as magic. The hero of the Dragonbards books is Tebriel, the heir to the kingdom of Tirror who has been brought up by the talking otters. In *Nightpool,* the first book in the trilogy, Tebriel talks not only with his foster otter family, but foxes and dragons. He joins forces with his own singing dragon, Seastrider, who is also psychic. The singing dragons are also shapechangers. In the second book, *The Ivory Lyre,* Tebriel seeks the legendary minstrel (who is also Tebriel's mother), Meriden, and must battle evil beings who are determined to kill the singing dragons and talking animals. The scenes depicting gladiator contests are bizarre, reminding readers of the grotesque and savage games held in ancient Rome. Tebriel finds his long-lost sister, Camery, and discovers a powerful ivory lyre. *The Dragonbards* concludes the trilogy and allows the forces of good to triumph over evil, the Dark.

Murphy's first book to deal in fantasy was *The Grass Tower,* the story of a teenage telepathic girl. After completing her two high fantasy series, Murphy collaborated with a twelve-year-old boy, Welsh Suggs, on *Medallion of the Black Hound.* It is essentially a time-travel story, in which the son of a contemporary history teacher finds himself transported back to an ancient Celtic-like society where he encounters magic and mythologically-inspired beasts. Fortunately, the young hero has a magic medallion to help him defeat the powers of evil.

More recently, Murphy created a high fantasy for adults, *The Catswold Portal.* Again, she has constructed a fascinating fantasy world in which Melissa, the amnesiac Faerie Queen, must battle for her heritage with the evil Queen Siddonie. Siddonie is already ruler of many kingdoms, but she wants Melissa's as well. Some of the inhabitants of this world are Catswolders, shape-changers who can shift from human to cat form. There are other creatures in this world, both good and bad, such as the foul Black Dragon of the Hellpit. A gateway to our world is provided; a gate in a San Francisco garden which is surrounded by beautifully carved cats' heads. In the end, good and virtue triumph. The parallel story in the book about a burned-out artist with problems who lives near the Catswold portal is also resolved. As an adult fantasy, *The Catswold Portal* seems to present a more comfortable format for Murphy, whose fantasies for younger readers are sometimes overcomplicated and confusing.

—Cosette Kies

MURPHY-GIBB, Dwina

Nationality: Irish. **Family:** Married to singer Robin Gibb. **Address:** Residences in Britain and the United States.

FANTASY PUBLICATIONS

Novels (series: Cormac)

Cormac: The Seers. London, Pan, 1992.
Cormac: The King Making. London, Pan, 1994.

*   *   *

Dwina Murphy-Gibb's projected trilogy is mainly ancient historical romance, with small fantasy elements. The setting (not made clear in the books themselves) is Ireland in the later third century AD, and these first two volumes cover a fictionalization of the conception, birth and upbringing of Cormac mac Art, a real High King of Ireland who flourished circa AD 275.

The best element of the books is the setting. Murphy-Gibb's attention to detail, based on much research, is very convincing. One can easily believe in these cultured trappers and herders, living a simple, uncertain life, beset by natural disaster and occasional raiding by the warriors of a corrupt ruler. They have a well-developed feeling for the supernatural, with visions, prophecies and magic potions being part of their everyday existence. Small duns (fortified places of habitation) are described, together with crafts, celebrations and rituals. Only the occasional detail, such as where a character bags a brace of golden pheasants (an Asian species, not imported to Western Europe until recent times) is wrong.

Less sure is the plot, which moves at a snail's pace, making overmuch of the minutiae of life—the incidents which are commonplace and tend to obscure the main thrusts of the plot, especially in the early part of the first book. Information is repeated and too many pages are spent in detailing the setting and introducing a multitude of characters. The inference is that very little of Cormac's birth and early life is known, so that the author had to pad out the story to make it into a trilogy. Also, she has a tendency to obscure the exact passing of time, so that Cormac's age at particular junctures is not clear.

In essence, the plot is this: Achtan, a young and beautiful Druid's daughter, lies with (and is impregnated by) Art mac Conn, the High King of Ireland, shortly before he is killed by his usurping nephew Lugaid mac Conn. Changing her name to Grainne, Achtan travels to another dun to live and to have her baby. She is aided by Cromlach the seer (who first predicts that the child will be a future High King), by Mora a healing woman who is heavily into animal rights, and by Cred the smith (who loves her). Omens at the time of Cormac's birth alert Lugaid, who sends investigators and then goes himself to seek out this High King-to-be. Cormac is hidden by magic and moved to another dun by friends. As a boy of about eight he is sent off to be educated in the bearing of arms and other kingly duties by Goll mac Airt, a huge one-eyed warrior. At the age of twelve he is sent, under an assumed name, to Teamhair (better known as Tara) the seat of the High Kings. There he fools Lugaid but is identified by a Druid and is spirited away by his friends.

None of the characters is much more than a stock figure, devoid of individuality. This is due partly to the large number of characters, partly to the way in which not one of them is "on-stage" for more than half the time, and partly to the confusing way in which the author gives the thoughts of nearly all of them at one time or another, shifting viewpoint paragraph by paragraph. The result is that the reader learns a small amount about perhaps two dozen characters, all of whom remain shallow. Even Grainne, who is the protagonist of *The Seers,* never becomes a fully rounded and believable personality. Young Cormac, the protagonist of *The King Making,* speaks like a philosophy graduate from the age of six and is thus totally unbelievable. In fact, much of the dialogue consists of characters lecturing each other in over-formal language at too great a length.

Despite having achieved some success with her poetry, Murphy-Gibb is not a good prose stylist. She rarely manages to create tension or to surprise the reader, and her writing is sometimes clumsy and unclear. An excess of emotion blights some scenes. Greetings and farewells seem to be too long and too extreme, as do the celebrations of Cormac's birth. Indeed, there are some scenes (notably a reunion between Grainne and Cred at the end of *The Seers*) which could have come straight out of a romantic novel. And sentimentality is also a problem. A wolf cub, which becomes Cormac's inseparable companion, is frequently at the centre of some maudlin passages.

Some of the best scenes in the two volumes are connected with magic. While most of the magic is fairly mild, consisting of visions and prophecies, there is a clever episode where Cromlach conceals Grainne and the infant Cormac from Lugaid's search-party. Not only does he put Grainne into a coma and place a spell upon that part of a cave where she lies, so that it looks like a rock wall, but he also exchanges Cormac with a wolf cub to be doubly sure. Later, when Lugaid comes to do his own searching, he is fobbed off with the gift of a supposed magic mirror (in which he believes completely) in the only successful comic scene in the books.

Each of the two volumes has a glossary of Irish words used, with their meanings and pronunciations—a very useful extra for any reader.

—Chris Morgan

MYERS, John Myers

Nationality: American. **Born:** Northport, Long Island, New York, 11 January 1906. **Education:** St. Stephens College; Middlebury College, Vermont; University of New Mexico, Albuquerque. **Military Service:** United States Army during World War II. **Family:** Married Charlotte Shanahan in 1943; two daughters. **Career:** Various jobs including newspaperman, advertising copywriter, and hog farmer, 1925-40; special lecturer and writer's conference director, Arizona State University, Tempe, 1948-49; organized a collection of Western Americana for the Arizona State University Library. **Died:** 30 October 1988.

FANTASY PUBLICATIONS

Novels

The Harp and the Blade. New York, Dutton, 1941.
Silverlock. New York, Dutton, 1949.
The Moon's Fire-Eating Daughter, edited by Hank Stine, illustrated by Thomas Canty. Virginia Beach, Donning, 1981.

OTHER PUBLICATIONS

Novels

Out on Any Limb. New York, Dutton, 1942.
The Wild Yazoo. New York, Dutton, 1947; London, Macdonald, 1948.
Dead Warrior. Boston, Little Brown, 1956; London, Arrow, 1957.
I, Jack Swilling, Founder of Phoenix, Arizona. New York, Hastings House, 1961.

Poetry

Maverick Zone: Red Conner's Night in Ellsworth; The Sack of Calabasas; The Devil Paid in Angel's Camp. New York, Hastings House, 1961.
The Chaparral Cock, Crow I. Privately printed, 1967.
The Chaparral Cock, Crow II. Privately printed, 1968.

Other

The Alamo. New York, Dutton, 1948; Lincoln, University of Nebraska Press, 1973.
The Last Chance: Tombstone's Early Years. New York, Dutton, 1950; as *The Tombstone Story,* New York, Grosset and Dunlap, n.d.
Doc Holliday. Boston, Little Brown, 1955; London, Jarrolds, 1957.
The Deaths of the Bravos. Boston, Little Brown, 1962.
Pirate, Pawnee, and Mountain Man: The Saga of Hugh Glass. Boston, Little Brown, 1963; as *The Saga of Hugh Glass: Pirate, Pawnee, and Mountain Man,* Lincoln, University of Nebraska Press, 1976.
San Francisco's Reign of Terror. New York, Doubleday, 1966.
Print in a Wild Land. New York, Doubleday, 1967.
The Border Wardens. Englewood Cliffs, New Jersey, Prentice Hall, 1971.

Editor, *Building a State in Apache Land: The Story of Arizona's Founding Told by Arizona's Founder,* by Charles D. Poston, illustrated by Larry Toschik. Tempe, Arizona, Aztec Press, 1963.
Editor, *The Westerners: A Roundup of Pioneer Reminiscences.* Englewood Cliffs, New Jersey, Prentice Hall, 1969.

*

Critical Study: *A Silverlock Companion: The Life and Works of John Myers Myers* edited by Fred Lerner, Center Harbor, New Hampshire, Niekas, 1988.

*   *   *

Primarily noted for fiction and nonfiction about the American West, John Myers Myers made one major contribution to fantasy, his novel *Silverlock*. A man from our world, known as Shandon Silverlock, mysteriously travels to a magical land called the Commonwealth, a patchwork amalgam of places and characters from innumerable myths, legends and literary works. There, he experiences three quests: first, to reach the mainland of the Commonwealth and establish himself safely; second, to help a composite character called Lucius Gil Jones reclaim his sweetheart and proper place in society; and third, to go through various regions of Hell to reach the fountain of Hippocrene, where an oracle has told him to drink and gain wisdom. During his adventures, Silverlock meets and interacts with a bewildering variety of famous and obscure literary characters, including Circe from Homer's *Odyssey,* Robin Hood, Beowulf, the Green Knight from *Sir Gawain and the Green Knight,* Calidore from Edmund Spenser's *The Faerie Queene,* Shakespeare's Hamlet, Cervantes's Don Quixote and Sancho Panza, Piscator from Izaac Walton's *The Compleat Angler,* the Houyhnhnms from Swift's *Gulliver's Travels,* Natty Bumppo from James Fenimore Cooper's novels, and the Mad Hatter, March Hare, and Dormouse from Lewis Carroll's *Alice in Wonderland.* Other passages parallel episodes in works like Dante's *Inferno,* Defoe's *Robinson Crusoe* and Twain's *The Adventures of Huckleberry Finn* without introducing their protagonists. Such a listing is necessarily incomplete; even literate readers will be unable to identify all the characters and works that Myers refers to. Although only sporadically in print since its first publication, *Silverlock* has attained the status of a cult classic among science-fiction and fantasy fans—deservedly so, because the novel is consistently lively and entertaining, and because Myers is generally excellent at mimicking the voices of the writers he draws from; especially noteworthy, perhaps, are his homages to Walton and Carroll. Many readers have also appreciated the many song lyrics that Myers includes in the novel and have frequently set them to music.

Despite its many virtues, however, one can understand why *Silverlock* has not been widely popular. Like Swift's Gulliver, Silverlock is not really a consistent character, but rather changes in response to the situation he is in and the people he is around. It is difficult to care about his predicaments, and it is hard to see why, for example, Silverlock is good enough to warrant various kind gestures in the first two books or why he is bad enough to deserve a harrowing journey through Hell in the final book. Moreover, despite the introductory map included in modern editions, the Commonwealth is not a consistently realized fantasy world like Tolkien's Middle-earth; rather, it resembles Spenser's land of Faerie, where even a short walk may arbitrarily lead to a new and completely different environment. The book's major appeal is as a game of literary Trivial Pursuit: readers are pleased and proud when they recognize one of the characters and are depressed and irritated when they cannot. To put the point charitably, reading *Silverlock* is truly a pleasure, but not the sort of pleasure traditionally found in fantasy; an annotated edition, which identified and discussed all the references in the novel, might take all the fun out of reading it.

The Moon's Fire-Eating Daughter, incorrectly labelled a sequel to *Silverlock,* actually shares with that book only an abundance of literary allusions and a story-line involving a surreal journey through various factual and fictional realms. A college professor named George Puttenham—after the Renaissance author of *The Art of English Poesie*—is recruited by Babylonian gods to complete a survey of "the Road" (of literature). After preliminary journeys to Aldebaran and Mercury, George has various adventures—such as booking passage on Noah's Ark, journeying underwater in the form of various sea creatures, visiting El Dorado, and participating in a poetry contest at Troy—before returning home to court and marry a young woman who lives in his apartment building. Although there are some figures from myths and legends, like Apollo, Bacchus, and Merlin, most of the book involves brief encounters not with characters but with authors—including Homer, Aeschylus, Martial, Spenser, Cervantes, Molière, Swift, Goethe, Rousseau, Wordsworth, George Sand, Chekhov, Twain, and Henry James—and by means of his various experiences and discussions of poetry with these figures, George learns how to be a poet. Here, Myers makes no effort to emulate the styles of other writers; instead, the narrator and characters all speak in the same irritating and obfuscatory combination of pompous circumlocution and tough-guy slang (the line "where does poetry get off in considering itself separate from other writing?" is attributed to Ralph Waldo Emerson). The novel has a few inspired moments—like a television-style interview with Aphrodite after she first rises out of the sea foam—but overall, it will surely be a disappointment to readers of *Silverlock.*

Although Ace Books republished *The Harp and the Blade* as a fantasy, it might be better regarded as an historical novel about a tenth-century minstrel travelling through France who teams up with a noble warrior named Conan—who bears little resemblance to, and does not seem based on, Robert E. Howard's creation—so that they can defeat an evil chieftain and establish a peaceable kingdom. Early in the novel, the hero does have a night-time encounter with a group of trolls led by a Druid priest who curses him with a compulsion to do good deeds that apparently inspires his later actions; but these events could be easily attributed to poor night vision and the hero's natural altruism. Still, *The Harp and the Blade* is a charming and evocative depiction of the type of environment often seen in fantasy, and its sustained success indicates that Myers, had he not been so concerned with celebrating the works of other writers, could have produced a memorable fantasy that was entirely his own.

—Gary Westfahl

N-O

NATHAN, Robert (Gruntal)

Nationality: American. **Born:** New York, 2 January 1894. **Education:** Public School 6 and the Collegiate School, New York; Ethical Culture School, Geneva; Phillips Exeter Academy, New Hampshire, 1910-12; Harvard University, Cambridge, Massachusetts, 1912-15. **Family:** Married 1) Dorothy Michaels in 1915 (divorced, 1922); 2) Nancy Wilson in 1930 (divorced, 1936); 3) Lucy Lee Hall Skelding in 1936 (divorced, 1939); 4) Janet McMillen Bingham in 1940 (divorced, 1951); 5) Clara May Blum Burns in 1951 (divorced, 1955); 6) Shirley Kneeland in 1955 (died, 1969); 7) Joan Winnifrith in 1970; one child. **Career:** Advertising solicitor, New York, 1916-18; lecturer, New York University School of Journalism, 1924-25; screenwriter, Metro-Goldwyn-Mayer, Hollywood, 1943-49. Composer and illustrator. President, United States P.E.N., 1940-42; Chancellor, Academy of American Poets. **Member:** American Academy, 1935. **Died:** 18 May 1985.

FANTASY PUBLICATIONS

Novels

Jonah. New York, McBride, 1925; as *Son of Ammitai,* London, Heinemann, 1925.
The Bishop's Wife. Indianapolis, Bobbs Merrill, and London, Gollancz, 1928.
There is Another Heaven. Indianapolis, Bobbs Merrill, 1929.
Portrait of Jennie. New York, Knopf, and London, Heinemann, 1940.
But Gently Day. New York, Knopf, 1943.
The River Journey. New York, Knopf, 1949.
The Innocent Eve. New York, Knopf, 1951.
The Train in the Meadow. New York, Knopf, 1953.
So Love Returns. New York, Knopf, 1958; London, W. H. Allen, 1959.
The Wilderness-Stone. New York, Knopf, and London, W. H. Allen, 1961.
The Devil With Love. New York, Knopf, and London, W. H. Allen, 1963.
The Fair. New York, Knopf, 1964.
Mia. New York, Knopf, 1970; London, W. H. Allen, 1971.
The Elixir. New York, Knopf, 1971.
The Summer Meadows. New York, Delacorte Press, 1973.
Heaven and Hell and the Megas Factor. New York, Delacorte Press, 1975.

OTHER PUBLICATIONS

Novels

Peter Kindred. New York, Duffield, 1919.
Autumn. New York, McBride, 1921.
The Puppet Master. New York, McBride, 1923; London, Lane, 1924.
The Fiddler in Barly. New York, McBride, 1926; London, Heinemann, 1927.
The Woodcutter's House. Indianapolis, Bobbs Merrill, 1927; London, Matthews and Marrot, 1932.
The Orchid. Indianapolis, Bobbs Merrill, 1931; London, Matthews and Marrot, 1932.
One More Spring. New York, Knopf, and London, Cassell, 1933.
Road of Ages. New York, Knopf, and London, Constable, 1935.
The Enchanted Voyage. New York, Knopf, 1936; London, Constable, 1937.
The Barly Fields: A Collection of Five Novels (includes *The Fiddler in Barly, The Woodcutter's House, The Bishop's Wife, The Orchid, There is Another Heaven*). New York, Knopf, 1938; London, Constable, 1939.
Winter in April. New York, Knopf, and London, Constable, 1938.
Journey of Tapiola. New York, Knopf, and London, Constable, 1939.
They Went On Together. New York, Knopf, and London, Heinemann, 1941.
Tapiola's Brave Regiment. New York, Knopf, 1941.
The Sea-Gull Cry. New York, Knopf, 1942.
Mr. Whittle and the Morning Star. New York, Knopf, and London, Low, 1947.
Long After Summer. New York, Knopf, 1948; London, Low, 1949.
The Married Look. New York, Knopf, 1950; as *His Wife's Young Face,* London, Staples Press, 1951.
Nathan 3 (omnibus; includes *The Sea-Gull Cry, The Innocent Eve, The River Journey*). London, Staples Press, 1952.
Sir Henry. New York, Knopf, 1955; London, Barker, 1956.
The Rancho of the Little Loves. New York, Knopf, 1956.
The Color of Evening. New York, Knopf, and London, W. H. Allen, 1960.
A Star in the Wind. New York, Knopf, and London, W. H. Allen, 1962.
The Mallott Diaries. New York, Knopf, 1965.
Stonecliff. New York, Knopf, 1967.

Short Story

The Weans. New York, Knopf, 1960.

Plays

Music at Evening (produced White Plains, New York, 1937).
Jezebel's Husband, or Jonah in Zebulon (produced Mountainholm, Pennsylvania, 1952). Included in *Jezebel's Husband, and The Sleeping Beauty,* 1953.
Jezebel's Husband, and The Sleeping Beauty. New York, Knopf, 1953.
Juliet in Mantua. New York, Knopf, 1966.
Susan and the Stranger (produced Los Angeles, 1979).

Screenplays: *The White Cliffs of Dover,* with others, 1944; *Yolanda and the Thief,* with others, 1945; *The Clock,* with Joseph Schrank, 1945; *Pagan Love Song,* with Jerry Davis, 1950.

Poetry

Youth Grows Old. New York, McBride, 1922.

A Cedar Box. Indianapolis, Bobbs Merrill, 1929.
Selected Poems. New York, Knopf, 1935; London, Constable, 1936.
A Winter Tide: Sonnets and Poems. New York, Knopf, 1940.
Dunkirk: A Ballad. New York, Knopf, 1942.
Morning in Iowa. New York, Knopf, 1944.
The Darkening Meadows. New York, Knopf, 1945.
The Green Leaf: The Collected Poems. New York, Knopf, 1950.
The Married Man. New York, Knopf, 1962.
Evening Song: Selected Peoms 1950-1973. Santa Barbara, California, Capra Press, 1973.

Other

The Concert. New York, House of Books, 1940.
Journal for Josephine (memoirs). New York, Knopf, 1943.
The Snowflake and the Starfish (for children). New York, Knopf, 1959.
Tappy (for children). New York, Knopf, 1968.

*

Film Adaptations: *The Bishop's Wife,* 1947; *Portrait of Jennie,* 1949.

Bibliography: *Robert Nathan: A Bibliography* by Dan H. Laurence, New Haven, Connecticut, Yale University Press, 1960.

Manuscript Collection: Yale University, New Haven, Connecticut.

Critical Studies: *The Work of Robert Nathan* by Louis Bromfield, Indianapolis, Bobbs Merrill, 1927; *Robert Nathan* by Clarence Sandelin, New York, Twayne, 1969; "Portrait of Nathan" by Ben Indick, in *Exploring Fantasy Worlds: Essays on Fantastic Literature* edited by Darrell Schweitzer, San Bernardino, California, Borgo Press, 1985.

Robert Nathan commented:

(1982) I have tried—as far as I could—to be a comforter in the world . . . not through what I know, but what I don't—and cannot—know. I have tried to suggest the mystery and the magic.

*   *   *

At the beginning of a career of astonishing length, Robert Nathan thought that his first, grittily realistic, novel *Peter Kindred* had been completely overshadowed by F. Scott Fitzgerald's *This Side of Paradise* and immediately began casting around for a distinct literary vein of his own. *Autumn,* a quaint pastoral novel written in a calculatedly naïve style, began excavating that vein. Like its sequels similarly set in the village of Barly, *Autumn* has marginal fantasy elements, and most of Nathan's subsequent works have a wide-eyed innocence which readily accommodates peripheral wonders; it is not easy to draw a line separating his naturalistic works from his outright fantasies and some bibliographers consider that novels like *The Fiddler in Barly, The Orchid* and *The Rancho of the Little Loves* can be classified as fantasy even though their fantastic elements are not central and their "magical" agencies not necessarily supernatural.

The Old Testament fantasy *Jonah* was something of a departure for Nathan, as was a later novel exploring Jewish identity in the context of a hypothetical new diaspora, *Road of Ages.* Nathan claimed to have difficulty in distinguishing Judaism and Christian-

ity and tended to favour imagery which overlapped the two creeds. *The Bishop's Wife* is a reverently sentimental Christian fantasy in which the archangel Michael, dispatched in answer to the prayers of an overstretched bishop, falls in love with the clergyman's wife; when she rejects his overtures, the angel realizes that physically based human love is but a faint shadow of the ideal love natural to Heaven. Nathan must have believed very strongly in this principle, given the tenor of most of his later fantasies and the astonishing number of his marriages. *Another Heaven* continued the religious theme with an ironic exploration of the afterlife of a Jew who had converted to Protestant Christianity for appearances' sake.

Nathan's most famous fantasy—by far his most effective hymn of praise to spiritual love—is *Portrait of Jennie,* the tale of an artist whose ailing spirit and stalled career are redeemed by a series of visitations from a girl who is living according to a different and more rapid time-scheme. She first meets him as an infant, but after being surprised in his room on the threshold of puberty decides that she cannot come again until she is of an age to marry him. The makers of the Hollywood film based on the book obviously felt that Nathan's own ending is undesirably bleak, but in fact it is the only one possible; it is fundamental to his world-view that true love is supernatural, and that reduction to mere marriage diminishes it. For Nathan the most intense love is love that is about to be lost to death, or love that has already been lost to death. This intimate and intense interweaving of love and mortality extends through the posthumous fantasy *But Gently Day,* the allegorical *The River Journey*—whose personification of Death, Mr. Mortimer, strongly recalls the angel of *The Bishop's Wife*—and the sentimental romance *So Love Returns.* Although there is something rather suspect about the kind of sentiment expressed by these novels they are all beautifully executed and highly effective; they represent the perfect fusion of Nathan's delicate literary style and compelling emotional fervour.

The Innocent Eve is the first of Nathan's several flirtations with literary Satanism. Here Lucifer volunteers to take control of the atom bomb, in order that mankind might be saved from its ravages, but is ironically thwarted by the innocence of a film starlet. He is similarly frustrated in the offbeat Faustian tale *The Devil With Love,* in which he tries unsuccessfully to bargain for a few hearts after deciding that he has more than enough souls already. Nathan's concern with modern weapons of war was again displayed in the context of a religious parable in *Heaven and Hell and the Megas Factor,* in which an angel and a demon are forced to join forces in the desperate cause of human salvation.

The Train in the Meadow is a further posthumous fantasy, subtler and broader in its focus than its predecessors; *The Summer Meadows* returns to the same imaginative territory in a more elegiac vein. *The Wilderness-Stone* is a curious timeslip romance in which a man's recollections of a past friendship somehow envelop and absorb a young female neighbour; it is in some respects an inversion of *Portrait of Jennie* and is perhaps the most interesting of Nathan's later works. *Mia* is also a timeslip romance, more closely recapitulative of *Portrait of Jennie,* while *The Elixir* is a phantasmagoric extrapolation of the same theme, borrowing materials earlier deployed in the satirical comedy *Sir Henry* and the historical fantasy *The Fair* in order to compile a quirky collage of British history and myth. Such works as *The Mallott Diaries,* which features Neanderthal survivors in Arizona, and the brief "Digging the Weans" (1956; reprinted as *The Weans*) in which future archaeologists report their findings regarding the decline and fall of American civilization, are noteworthy ventures into satirical science fiction.

Nathan's work was never fashionable and much of it was never reprinted in paperback for the mass market. His deceptively simple style is perhaps something of an acquired taste, and his sentimentality hovers perpetually on the brink of mawkishness, but there is such a remarkable depth of feeling in his best works that they become disturbing for the best possible reasons. He deserves to be more widely read and more fully appreciated.

—Brian Stableford

NESBIT, E(dith)

Pseudonyms: E. Bland; Fabian Bland. **Nationality:** British. **Born:** London, 15 August 1858. **Education:** Attended an Ursuline convent in Dinan, France, 1869, and schools in Germany and Brighton. **Family:** Married 1) the writer Hubert Bland in 1880 (died 1914), two sons, one daughter, one adopted daughter, and one adopted son; 2) Thomas Terry Tucker in 1917. **Career:** Journalist, elocutionist, greeting cards decorator; poetry critic, *Athenaeum* magazine, London, 1890s; co-editor, *Neolith* magazine, London, 1907-08; general editor, Children's Bookcase series, Oxford University Press and Hodder and Stoughton, 1908-11. Founding member, 1884, and member of the Pamphlet Committee, Fabian Society. **Awards:** Granted a Civil List pension, 1915. **Died:** 4 May 1924.

Fantasy Publications

Novels

Five Children and It, illustrated by H. R. Millar. London, Unwin, 1902; New York, Dodd Mead, 1905.
The Phoenix and the Carpet, illustrated by H. R. Millar. London, Newnes, and New York, Macmillan, 1904.
The Story of the Amulet, illustrated by H. R. Millar. London, Unwin, 1906; New York, Dutton, 1907.
The Enchanted Castle, illustrated by H. R. Millar. London, Unwin, 1907; New York, Harper, 1908.
The House of Arden, illustrated by H. R. Millar. London, Unwin, 1908; New York, Dutton, 1909.
Harding's Luck, illustrated by H. R. Millar. London, Hodder and Stoughton, 1909; New York, Stokes, 1910.
The Magic City, illustrated by H. R. Millar. London, Macmillan, 1910; New York, Coward McCann, 1958.
The Wonderful Garden; or The Three C's, illustrated by H. R. Millar. London, Macmillan, 1911; New York, Coward McCann, 1935.
Wet Magic, illustrated by H. R. Millar. London, Laurie, 1913; New York, Coward McCann, 1937.

Short Stories

The Book of Dragons, illustrated by H. R. Millar. London and New York, Harper, 1900.
Nine Unlikely Tales for Children, illustrated by H. R. Millar and Claude Shepperson. London, Unwin, and New York, Dutton, 1901.
Fairy Stories, edited by Naomi Lewis, illustrated by Brian Robb. London, Benn, 1977.

Plays

Cinderella (produced London, 1892). London, Sidgwick and Jackson, 1909.
The Magician's Heart (produced London, 1907).

Other Publications

Novels

The Prophet's Mantle (as Fabian Bland, with Hubert Bland). London, Drane, 1885; Chicago, Belford Clarke, 1889.
The Secret of the Kyriels. London, Hurst and Blackett, and Philadelphia, Lippincott, 1899.
The Red House. London, Methuen, and New York, Harper, 1902.
The Incomplete Amorist. London, Constable, and New York, Doubleday, 1906.
Daphne in Fitzroy Street. London, George Allen, and New York, Doubleday, 1909.
Salome and the Head: A Modern Melodrama. London, Alston Rivers, 1909; as *The House with No Address,* New York, Doubleday, 1909.
Dormant. London, Methuen, 1911; as *Rose Royal,* New York, Dodd Mead, 1912.
The Incredible Honeymoon. New York, Harper, 1916; London, Hutchinson, 1921.
The Lark. London, Hutchinson, 1922.

Short Stories

Something Wrong. London, Innes, 1893.
Grim Tales. London, Innes, 1893.
The Butler in Bohemia, with Oswald Barron. London, Drane, 1894.
In Homespun. London, Lane, and Boston, Roberts, 1896.
Thirteen Ways Home. London, Treherne, 1901.
The Literary Sense. London, Methuen, and New York, Macmillan, 1903.
Man and Maid. London, Unwin, 1906.
These Little Ones. London, George Allen, 1909.
Fear. London, Stanley Paul, 1910.
To the Adventurous. London, Hutchinson, 1923.
Tales of Terror, edited by Hugh Lamb. London, Methuen, 1983.
In the Dark: Tales of Terror, edited by Hugh Lamb. Wellingborough, Northamptonshire, Thorsons, 1988.

Fiction for Children

Listen Long and Listen Well, with others. London, Tuck, 1893.
Sunny Tales for Snowy Days, with others. London, Tuck, 1893.
Told by Sunbeams and Me, with others. London, Tuck, 1893.
Fur and Feathers: Tales for All Weathers, with others. London, Tuck, 1894.
Lads and Lassies, with others. London, Tuck, 1894.
Tales That Are True, for Brown Eyes and Blue, with others, edited by Edric Vredenburg, illustrated by M. Goodman. London, Tuck, 1894.
Tales to Delight from Morning till Night, with others, edited by Edric Vredenburg, illustrated by M. Goodman. London, Tuck, 1894.
Hours in Many Lands: Stories and Poems, with others, edited by Edric Vredenburg, illustrated by Frances Brundage. London, Tuck, 1894.

Doggy Tales, illustrated by Lucy Kemp-Welch. London, Ward, 1895.

Pussy Tales, illustrated by Lucy Kemp-Welch. London, Ward, 1895.

Tales of the Clock, illustrated by Helen Jackson. London, Tuck, 1895.

Dulcie's Lantern and Other Stories, with Theo Gift and Mrs. Worthington Bliss. London, Griffith Farran, 1895.

Treasures from Storyland, with others. London, Tuck, 1895.

Tales Told in Twilight: A Volume of Very Short Stories. London, Nister, 1897.

Dog Tales, and Other Tales, with A. Guest and Emily R. Watson, edited by Edric Vredenburg, illustrated by R.K. Mounsey. London, Tuck, 1898.

Pussy and Doggy Tales, illustrated by Lucy Kemp-Welch. London, Dent, 1899; New York, Dutton, 1900.

The Story of the Treasure Seekers, Being the Adventures of the Bastable Children in Search of a Fortune, illustrated by Gordon Browne and Lewis Baumer. London, Unwin, and New York, Stokes, 1899.

The Wouldbegoods, Being the Further Adventures of the Treasure Seekers, illustrated by Arthur H. Buckland and John Hassell. London, Unwin, 1901; New York, Harper, 1902.

The Revolt of the Toys and What Comes of Quarrelling, illustrated by Ambrose Dudley. London, Nister, and New York, Dutton, 1902.

Playtime Stories. London, Tuck, 1903.

The Rainbow Queen and Other Stories. London, Tuck, 1903.

The Story of the Five Rebellious Dolls. London, Nister, 1904.

The New Treasure Seekers, illustrated by Gordon Browne and Lewis Baumer. London, Unwin, and New York, Stokes, 1904.

Cat Tales, with Rosamund Bland, illustrated by Isabel Watkin. London, Nister, and New York, Dutton, 1904.

Pug Peter: King of Mouseland, Marquis of Barkshire, D.O.G., P.C. 1906, Knight of the Order of the Gold Dog Collar, Author of Doggerel Lays and Days, illustrated by Harry Rountree. Leeds, Alf Cooke, 1905.

Oswald Bastable and Others, illustrated by C. E. Brock and H. R. Millar. London, Wells Gardner, 1905; New York, Coward McCann, 1960.

The Railway Children, illustrated by C. E. Brock. London, Wells Gardner, and New York, Macmillan, 1906.

The Magic World, illustrated by H. R. Millar and Spencer Pryse. London and New York, Macmillan, 1912.

Our New Story Book, with others, illustrated by Elsie Wood and Louis Wain. London, Nister, and New York, Dutton, 1913.

The New World Literary Series, Book Two, edited by Henry Cecil Wyld. London, Collins, 1921.

Five of Us—And Madeline, edited by Mrs. Clifford Sharp, illustrated by Nora S. Unwin. London, Unwin, 1925; New York, Adelphi, 1926.

Plays

A Family Novelette, with Oswald Barron (produced London, 1894).

The King's Highway (produced London, 1905).

The Philandrist; or, The Lady Fortune-Teller, with Dorothea Deakin (produced London, 1905).

Unexceptionable References (produced London, 1912).

Poetry

Lays and Legends. London and New York, Longman, 2 vols., 1886-92.

The Lily and the Cross. London, Griffith Farran, and New York, Dutton, 1887.

The Star of Bethlehem. London, Nister, 1887.

Leaves of Life. London and New York, Longman, 1888.

The Better Part and Other Poems. London, Drane, 1888.

Easter-Tide: Poems, with Caris Brooke. London, Drane, and New York, Dutton, 1888.

The Time of Roses, with Caris Brooke and others. London, Drane, 1888.

By Land and Sea. London, Drane, 1888.

Landscape and Song. London, Drane, and New York, Dutton, 1888.

The Message of the Dove: An Easter Poem. London, Drane, and New York, Dutton, 1888.

The Lilies Round the Cross: An Easter Memorial, with Helen J. Wood. London, Nister, and New York, Dutton, 1889.

Corals and Sea Songs. London, Nister, 1889.

Life's Sunny Side, with others. London, Nister, 1890.

Sweet Lavender. London, Nister, 1892.

Flowers I Bring and Songs I Sing (as E. Bland), with H. M. Burnside and A. Scanes. London, Tuck, 1893.

Holly and Mistletoe: A Book of Christmas Verse, with Norman Gale and Richard Le Gallienne. London, Ward, 1895.

A Pomander of Verse. London, Lane, and Chicago, McClurg, 1895.

Rose Leaves. London, Nister, 1895.

Songs of Love and Empire. London, Constable, 1898.

The Rainbow and the Rose. London and New York, Longman, 1905.

Ballads and Lyrics of Socialism 1883-1908. London, Fabian Society, 1908.

Jesus in London: A Poem. London, Fifield, 1908.

Ballads and Verses of the Spiritual Life. London, Elkin Mathews, 1911.

Garden Poems. London, Collins, 1912.

Many Voices. London, Hutchinson, 1922.

Poetry (for children)

Songs of Two Seasons, illustrated by J. MacIntyre. London, Tuck, 1890.

The Voyage of Columbus, 1492: The Discovery of America, illustrated by Will and Frances Brundage. London, Tuck, 1892.

Our Friends and All about Them. London, Tuck, 1893.

As Happy as a King, illustrated by S. Rosamund Praeger. London, Ward, 1896.

Dinna Forget, with G. C. Bingham. London, Nister, 1897; New York, Dutton, 1898.

To Wish You Every Joy. London, Tuck, 1901.

Other

Wings and the Child; or, The Building of Magic Cities. London, Hodder and Stoughton, and New York, Doran, 1913.

Editor, *Battle Songs.* London, Max Goschen, 1914.

Editor, *Essays,* by Hubert Bland. London, Max Goschen, 1914.

Other (for Children)

The Children's Shakespeare, edited by Edric Vredenburg, illustrated by Frances Brundage. London, Tuck, 1897; Philadelphia, Altemus, 1900.

Royal Children of English History, illustrated by Frances Brundage. London, Tuck, 1897.

Twenty Beautiful Stories from Shakespeare: A Home Study Course, edited by E. T. Roe, illustrated by Max Bihn. Chicago, Hertel and Jenkins, 1907.

The Old Nursery Stories, illustrated by W. H. Margetson. London, Oxford University Press-Hodder and Stoughton, 1908.

My Sea-Side Book, with George Manville Fenn. London, Nister, and New York, Dutton, 1911.

Children's Stories from Shakespeare, with *When Shakespeare Was a Boy,* by F.J. Furnivall. Philadelphia, McKay, 1912.

Children's Stories from English History, with Doris Ashley, edited by Edric Vredenburg, illustrated by John H. Bacon and Howard Davie. London, Tuck, 1914.

Long Ago When I Was Young, illustrated by Edward Ardizzone. London, Whiting and Wheaton, and New York, Watts, 1966.

Editor, with Robert Ellice Mack, *Spring [Summer, Autumn, Winter] Songs and Sketches.* London, Griffith Farran, and New York, Dutton, 4 vols., 1886.

Editor, with Robert Ellice Mack, *Eventide Songs and Sketches.* London, Griffith Farran, 1887; as *Night Songs and Sketches,* New York, Dutton, 1887.

Editor, with Robert Ellice Mack, *Morning Songs and Sketches.* London, Griffith Farran, 1887; as *Noon Songs and Sketches,* New York, Dutton, 1887.

Editor, with Robert Ellice Mack, *Lilies and Heartsease: Songs and Sketches.* New York, Dutton, 1888(?).

Editor, *The Girl's Own Birthday Book.* London, Drane, 1894.

Editor, *Poet's Whispers: A Birthday Book.* London, Drane, 1895.

Editor, *A Book of Dogs, Being a Discourse on Them, with Many Tales and Wonders,* illustrated by Winifred Austin. London, Dent, and New York, Dutton, 1898.

Editor, *Winter-Snow,* illustrated by H. Bellingham Smith. New York, Dutton, 1898(?).

*

Film Adaptations: *Five Children and It,* 1951, 1991 (television serials); *The Railway Children,* 1951 (television serial), 1968 (television serial), 1970; *The Story of the Treasure Seekers,* 1953, 1961, 1982 (television serials); *The Phoenix and the Carpet,* c. 1980s (television serial); *The Return of the Psammead,* 1993 (television serial), from the novel *The Story of the Amulet.*

Critical Studies: *E. Nesbit: A Biography* by Doris Langley Moore, London, Benn, 1933, revised edition, Philadelphia, Chilton, 1966, Benn, 1967; *Magic and the Magician: E. Nesbit and Her Children's Books* by Noel Streatfeild, London, Benn, and New York, Abelard Schuman, 1958; *E. Nesbit* by Anthea Bell, London, Bodley Head, 1960, New York, Walck, 1964; *A Woman of Passion: The Life of E. Nesbit* by Julia Briggs, London, Hutchinson, 1987.

*   *   *

Because they were written in the Edwardian era, the books of E. Nesbit have taken on the cosy, rosy glow of the period novel, yet beneath that it can be recognized that she was the first truly modern writer for children, and that she made an indelible impact on children's fantasy for decades to come. She was a professional writer, forced into the role of family breadwinner when her husband's business failed and he became ill, and she turned her hand to everything from greeting-card verse to mystery novels. Most of what she wrote was sentimental and not very good. Her novels and poetry are forgotten now, and with the exception of some short horror stories written for adults, only her children's books are still remembered and read.

Her first success came in 1897 when, after writing some childhood reminiscences for a girls' paper, she was moved to attempt a novel for children. The first instalment of what was to become *The Treasure Seekers* appeared in *The Illustrated London News* under a pseudonym, and was immediately recognized as something unique. Andrew Lang singled it out for special praise, and Nesbit was from then on much in demand. This first book, not a fantasy, was about the Bastable children—believable, individual and extremely well-drawn—who attempt to restore their family's fortunes and have a series of amusing and exciting adventures. Nesbit was not the only contemporary writer to write about "real" children with sufficient sympathy and wit to make them appealing to both young and older readers, but she was, with Rudyard Kipling and Kenneth Grahame, one of the first.

She went on to write more stories about the Bastable children, interspersed with some knowing and funny modern fairy tales collected as *The Book of Dragons* and *Nine Unlikely Tales for Children.* In 1902 her first full-length fantasy, *Five Children and It,* was published (first serialized as "The Psammead" in *The Strand Magazine*). "It" is the Psammead, or sand-fairy, which the children—Cyril, Robert, Anthea and Jane, sometimes unwillingly accompanied by their baby brother, always called "the Lamb"—discover in a sand-pit during their summer holidays. They befriend it—a not entirely rewarding experience, for it is a bad-tempered creature—and it grants them one wish a day. Somehow, none of their wishes—to be "as beautiful as the day," to become rich, to have wings—work out quite as they had hoped, but luckily they all end at sundown. The same children have more magical adventures in *The Phoenix and the Carpet,* this time carried to exotic locations on a magic carpet, with the not-always-reliable guidance of a phoenix which hatched from the egg they found rolled inside the carpet.

The five children make their final appearance in the book of Nesbit's I've always liked the best, *The Story of the Amulet.* Spending the summer with their nurse in Bloomsbury, the children discover the Psammead languishing in a pet shop, and in gratitude for being rescued, it tells them where to find half of an ancient amulet. This amulet takes them through time in search of its lost half: when they find it, it will grant their heart's desire. It seems likely that the author got the idea of writing about time-travel from her good friend H. G. Wells: *The Time Machine* had been published in 1895, and there is a sly tribute to him buried in the text, in the section where the children travel into a Fabian Utopian future. In "The Green and Burning Tree," her essay on children's time fantasy, Eleanor Cameron has suggested that Nesbit was the first to use the idea (previously found in folklore and fairy tale, and now quite common) that the time spent elsewhere in time will be found, on return to "reality" to have taken no time at all, and also that *The Story of the Amulet* was the first children's time fantasy ever written involving modern children. C. S. Lewis recalled it as being the book which "first opened my eyes to antiquity," and he, like Charles Williams, continued to re-read it with pleasure in adulthood.

Nesbit's richest, most complex, and, for many readers her best, fantasy is *The Enchanted Castle*. In this book the rules which so strictly governed the operation of magic in her earlier stories (one wish a day; wishes dissolve at sunset, etc.) are nowhere to be found, and "let's pretend" abruptly becomes real. The theme of the danger of granted wishes receives its strongest expression in this story, which begins with three children pretending a ring they have found is magic—only to discover that it really is. A ghost appears in response to an unspoken wish, stone dinosaurs come to life after dark, and, most terrifying of all, the Ugly-Wuglies, creatures assembled from old clothes, pillows, broomsticks and coat hangers, with painted masks for faces, to provide an audience for the children's play, take on a zombie-like life of their own. As in her adult horror stories, the fears and darker experiences of her childhood come to the fore in this one book.

After *The Enchanted Castle* came two closely interlinked time fantasies, *The House of Arden* and *Harding's Luck*. In the first, Edred and Elfrida meet the mouldiwarp, a magical white mole which takes them back in time to search for the lost treasure which will restore the fortunes of their family and Arden Castle (based on Hurstmonceaux on the Sussex downs). The second book, more a companion volume than a sequel, tells the story of Dickie Harding, a lame, slum-dwelling orphan who, also through the aid of the Mouldiwarp, travels back to Jacobean England, where he is Richard Arden, no longer crippled, and the true heir to the house of Arden—his cousins, Edred and Elfrida, belong to a younger branch of the family. Eventually everything is worked out for the best and everyone gets his or her heart's desire. The two books together make up E. Nesbit's most seriously intentioned fantasy, taking on the Fabian socialist issues only previously touched on in *The Story of the Amulet* and, although unable to come up with any solutions to modern social problems, bearing a strong moral message. They were the books she herself felt proudest to have written. Because of their moral seriousness, perhaps, her usual humour and lightness of touch are missing, but they are still among her most memorable books.

After that she wrote *The Magic City*, inspired by her own delight in constructing miniature cities from ordinary household objects, in which two children shrink in size and are able to enter the city they built. Edward Eager took the same starting point rather more successfully in his *Knight's Castle* (1956). Her last novel for children was *Wet Magic*, about some children who rescue a mermaid and enter her undersea world; probably her weakest fantasy, it still displays her unmistakable magic touch. The best of E. Nesbit's novels live on, not only in the affections of readers, but on BBC television, where a number of her stories have been produced as "classic serials" several times over in the course of the past 45 years. Along with Charles Dickens, the Brontës and Jane Austen, she is one of the authors whose works are most frequently adapted to that medium in Britain.

—Lisa Tuttle

NEWMAN, Kim. *See* **YEOVIL, Jack.**

NICHOLS, (Joanna) Ruth

Nationality: Canadian. **Born:** Toronto, Ontario, 4 March 1948. **Education:** University of British Columbia, Vancouver, B.A. (honours) 1969; McMaster University, Hamilton, Ontario (Woodrow Wilson fellow) M.A. 1972, Ph.D. 1977. **Family:** Married William Norman Houston in 1974. **Career:** Lecturer, Carleton University, Ottawa, 1974. **Awards:** Canada Council Fellowship, 1972, 1973, 1974; Canadian Library Association Award, 1973. **Agent:** Nancy Colbert, The Colbert Agency, 303 Davenport Road, Toronto, Ontario M5R 1K5, Canada.

FANTASY PUBLICATIONS

Novels

A Walk Out of the World, illustrated by Trina Schart Hyman. Toronto, Longman, and New York, Harcourt Brace, 1969.
The Marrow of the World, illustrated by Trina Schart Hyman. Toronto, Macmillan, and New York, Atheneum, 1972.
Song of the Pearl. Toronto, Macmillan, and New York, Atheneum, 1976.
The Left-Handed Spirit. Toronto, Macmillan, and New York, Atheneum, 1978.

OTHER PUBLICATIONS

Novel

Ceremony of Innocence. London, Faber, 1969.
The Burning of the Rose. New York, St. Martin's Press, 1989.

Other

Framework for Reading, with Joan Dean. London, Evans, 1974.

*

Manuscript Collection: Mills Memorial Library, McMaster University, Hamilton, Ontario.

*   *   *

Ruth Nichols's few fantasies were written mostly in her youth (her latter-day book, *The Burning of the Rose,* is a large historical novel with some fantastic elements). They follow the same conventional pattern: a child or young person passes into another world. Here they experience certain unthreatening adventures as a result of which they grow in self-knowledge and compassion before passing back safely through the barrier. These are not stories meant to shock or undermine our notions of reality but rather to soothe us with the reassurance that everything after all is right with the world. Reading her children's books in particular is like intruding on an old-fashioned teacher reading a soft-voiced story of conformity and duty to a class of infants. *A Walk Out of the World* even echoes a traditional fairy story in its opening words: "Once there were a brother and sister. . . ."

In this particular but typical story Judith and Tobit enter a wood near their Canadian home and emerge in another world. They are quickly taken in by the followers of the rightful king and find themselves playing an inevitable role in overcoming the usurper and putting the world to rights. There is little genuine danger despite the fact that they step right into a generations-long war, and in fact there are often longueurs in which nothing happens, as if Nichols hasn't quite worked out how to keep her plot moving. The children, as good little children should, seem to spend an inordinate amount of time worrying about what their parents will be thinking about back in the real world; but these thoughts are soothed by the old woman who is head of the clan and who takes on the role of mother to all the good characters in the story.

There is a similar old woman in *Song of the Pearl,* fulfilling much the same sort of role. Wise and comforting, the mother figure is clearly important in Nichols's view of the world. Although *Song of the Pearl* is actually a novel for young adults, there is little in it that differs from what she would write for children. True, there is a rape early in the book, but it is a curiously unviolent and undamaging rape: in Nichols's world, nothing can be really bad. Mary Margaret Redmond dies when she is 17, and is instantly transported to an afterlife where she meets Paul, her handsome guide to this new world who turns out to have been her husband in the first of their many existences.

There is some sense that Nichols is trying to impart a feminist message into her book, for during her journey Margaret finds herself briefly inhabiting the consciousness of an Elizabethan wife and an Amerindian slave. But though there is a taste of the hardships they suffered, these episodes are so short, so lacking in drama, and so suffused with the warm glow of knowing that everything will be all right in the end, that they end up having little impact. Most of the book takes place in an ancient Chinese household transplanted *en masse* to this strangely non-etherial afterlife. Here Margaret learns forgiveness and discovers who she has been in her former lives, before she and Paul are reborn once more as lovers.

Ruth Nichols writes well, and has a talent for describing attractive little watercolour scenes, but seems not to have the ability to put these at the service of a plot that does any more than recycle conventional elements.

—Maureen Speller

NILES, Douglas

Nationality: American. **Career:** Role-playing game scenarist. **Address:** c/o TSR Inc., P.O. Box 756, Lake Geneva, WI 53147, USA.

FANTASY PUBLICATIONS

Novels (series: DragonLance; Endless Quest; Forgotten Realms)

Escape from Castle Quarras (Endless Quest). Lake Geneva, Wisconsin, TSR, 1985.
Tarzan and the Well of Slaves (Endless Quest). Lake Geneva, Wisconsin, TSR, 1985.
Lords of Doom (DragonLance). Lake Geneva, Wisconsin, TSR, 1986.
Darkwalker on Moonshae (Forgotten Realms). Lake Geneva, Wisconsin, TSR, 1987; London, Penguin, 1988.

Black Wizards (Forgotten Realms). Lake Geneva, Wisconsin, TSR, and London, Penguin, 1988.
Darkwell (Forgotten Realms). Lake Geneva, Wisconsin, TSR, and London, Penguin, 1989.
Flint, the King, with Mary Kirchoff (DragonLance). Lake Geneva, Wisconsin, TSR, and London, Penguin, 1990.
Ironhelm (Forgotten Realms). Lake Geneva, Wisconsin, TSR, and London, Penguin, 1990.
Viperhand (Forgotten Realms). Lake Geneva, Wisconsin, TSR, and London, Penguin, 1990.
Feathered Dragon (Forgotten Realms). Lake Geneva, Wisconsin, TSR, and London, Penguin, 1991.
The Kinslayer Wars (DragonLance). Lake Geneva, Wisconsin, TSR, 1991.
Prophet of Moonshae (Forgotten Realms). Lake Geneva, Wisconsin, TSR, 1992.
The Coral Kingdom (Forgotten Realms). Lake Geneva, Wisconsin, TSR, 1992.
The Druid Queen (Forgotten Realms). Lake Geneva, Wisconsin, TSR, 1993.
First Quest: Pawns Prevail. Lake Geneva, Wisconsin, TSR, 1995.
A Breach in the Watershed. New York, Ace, 1995.

Short Story

Lankhmar, City of Adventure, with Bruce Nesmith and Ken Rolston. Lake Geneva, Wisconsin, TSR, 1985.

Other

Dungeoneer's Survival Guide: A Sourcebook for Advanced Dungeons & Dragons Game Adventures in the Unknown Depths of Underdark! Lake Geneva, Wisconsin, TSR, 1986.

*   *   *

Douglas Niles is one of TSR's more prolific fantasy authors. He has also designed numerous role-playing scenarios for Advanced Dungeons and Dragons as well as the AD&D Battle System. Niles certainly displays a clear understanding of military tactics, and describes battles realistically in all his novels. Following sundry contributions to the Endless Quest and DragonLance series, his principal three trilogies are set within TSR's Forgotten Realms background. The Moonshae and Druidhome books concern events in the Moonshae isles—a collection of islands with a Celtic, early-Arthurian atmosphere. The people of the isles, known as the Ffolk, worship the Earthmother rather than the pantheon of new gods revered elsewhere in the Realms.

In *Darkwalker on Moonshae* the Earthmother is threatened by an old enemy; the Beast. This creature has the ability to corrupt people through physical contact and assume the likeness of anyone it wishes. It uses this power to infiltrate the Earthmother's loyal druids, turn one of the king's guards into a werewolf and lead the Northmen, ancient enemies of the Ffolk, to war against them while in the guise of their king. The heroes of the trilogy are the young prince of Corwell, Tristan Kendrick, and his father's ward, a beautiful young druid called Robyn. They are first shown visiting a spring festival, the harmony of which is marred by a prophecy from the druids that "the shadow of mighty evil" falls across Tristan's path and threatens the Moonshaes and their goddess.

Unfortunately, the book's opening itself is marred by the implausible way in which one of the other major characters is introduced. A pickpocket, who admits he was trained as an assassin, steals Tristan's purse and attacks him when captured. For some inexplicable reason Tristan not only forgives the man but employs him as his bodyguard! The thief, called Daryth, proves his worth by saving the prince's life several times, but this doesn't negate the unlikely nature of the appointment. *Darkwalker on Moonshae* also fails to capitalize on the potential of the Beast's capability to corrupt people without their companions realizing it. The werewolf eventually runs off and leads a pack of wolves, the corrupted druid merely acts as an informer for the Northmen and the Beast, as the Northmen's king, leads them to war only to have his nature revealed before a decisive battle. Tristan eventually fights the Beast face to face and kills it.

The rest of the Moonshae trilogy, *Black Wizards* and *Darkwell*, and the follow-up Druidhome trilogy, consisting of *Prophet of Moonshae, The Coral Kingdom,* and *The Druid Queen,* follow similar patterns. In each, some powerful, evil being or deity seeks to gain control of the Moonshaes at the expense of the Earthmother; Tristan and Robyn fight against all odds to prevent it and eventually triumph. During the course of this Tristan is crowned king, marries Robyn and they have two daughters. In the latter series the youngest daughter, Dierdre, is jealous of her elder sibling, resents the lack of freedom her parents grant her, and is balked in her desired career to be a mage. These are surely things that teenagers could identify with, but Dierdre decides to take rebelliousness to its utmost limits and makes a pact with the new gods in exchange for power.

The theme of sibling jealousy and filial disagreement is used to keep suspense running throughout the trilogy. On several occasions Dierdre is tempted to side with her family's enemies but chooses to remain loyal to her kin. Only in the final book does she act against them but even then, although she has the power to kill them, explains that she will spare them if they agree to serve the new gods. She sees the Earthmother, and her own mother Robyn who serves the Earthmother, as the only enemy. She claims that the Earthmother prevents progress within the Moonshaes—she does not specifically state her feelings about Robyn at that point but it is easy to see how she feels thwarted by her. Nevertheless, the family stand united against Dierdre, she is killed by her sister Alicia, and everyone consoles each other that they did the right thing. However, it seems unsatisfying that Dierdre is dismissed as just a "monster", and the book would have been more interesting if her predicament had been better explored.

The Maztica trilogy, consisting of *Ironhelm, Viperhand,* and *Feathered Dragon,* also deals with a clash between the gods of the Forgotten Realms and those of another culture in a story that loosely parallels the conquest of the Aztecs by the Spanish. It has all the things one would expect: bloodthirsty gods who demand sacrifices of living hearts, warriors who can magically transform into jaguars and a legion of seasoned mercenaries, explorers, and priests destroying an ancient civilization in their greed for gold and in the name of their god.

The story in not a straightforward fight between good and evil. Both cultures have good and evil gods and both have a mixture of right and wrong on their sides. A love story involving a native slave girl and a renegade mercenary is intertwined with that of battles between Mazticans and the invading forces. Things become more complicated as the capital city is destroyed by volcano after an uneasy peace has been arranged. A second wave of mercenaries arrives, seeking to overthrow and steal the gold of the first legion. As in most Niles books, the machinations of gods become more important than the affairs of mortals and by book three we have epic fights between deities incarnate. Eventually, the humans realize they have been used as pawns and make a huge sacrifice to banish the gods involved to their immortal planes so that they can live in peace.

—Lucya Szachnowski

NIMMO, Jenny

Nationality: British. **Born:** Windsor, Berkshire, 15 January 1944. **Education:** Attended private boarding schools, 1950-60. **Family:** Married David Wynn Millward in 1974; two daughters and one son. **Career:** Actress and assistant stage manager, Theatre Southeast, Sussex and Kent, 1960-63; governess, Amalfi, Italy, 1963; photographic researcher, 1964-66, assistant floor manager, 1966-68 and 1971-74, and director and writer of children's programmes, 1970, all BBC Television, London. Since 1975 full-time writer. **Awards:** Smarties prize, 1986; Welsh Arts Council Tir na n'Og award, 1987. **Agent:** Murray Pollinger, 4 Garrick Street, London WC2E 9BH, England. **Address:** Henllan Mill, Llangynyw, Welshpool, Powys SY21 9EN, Wales.

FANTASY PUBLICATIONS

Novels

The Snow Spider, illustrated by Joanna Carey. London, Methuen, 1986; New York, Dutton, 1987.
Emlyn's Moon, illustrated by Joanna Carey. London, Methuen, 1987; as *Orchard of the Crescent Moon,* New York, Dutton, 1989.
The Chestnut Soldier. London, Methuen, 1989; New York, Dutton, 1991.
Ultramarine. London, Methuen, 1991; New York, Dutton, 1992.
Rainbow and Mr. Zed. London, Methuen, 1992; New York, Dutton, 1994.
The Snow Spider Trilogy (omnibus; includes *The Snow Spider, Emlyn's Moon, The Chestnut Soldier*). London, Mammoth, 1993.

OTHER PUBLICATIONS

Fiction for Children

The Bronze Trumpeter, illustrated by Caroline Scrace. London, Angus and Robertson, 1975.
Tatty Apple, illustrated by Priscilla Lamont. London, Methuen, 1984.
The Red Secret, illustrated by Maureen Bradley. London, Hamish Hamilton, 1989.
The Bears Will Get You, illustrated by Wendy Smith. London, Methuen, 1990.
Delilah and the Dogspell, illustrated by Emma Chichester-Clark. London, Methuen, 1991.
Jupiter Boots, illustrated by Paul Warren. London, Heinemann, 1991.

The Breadwitch, illustrated by Ben Cort. London, Heinemann, 1993.
Delilah and the Dogspell, illustrated by Ben Cort. London, Methuen, 1993.
The Starlight Cloak, illustrated by Justin Todd. London, Collins, and New York, Dial, 1993.
The Stone Manse, illustrated by Helen Craig. London, Walker, and New York, Carousel, 1993.
The Witches and the Singing Mice, illustrated by Angela Barrat. London, Collins, and New York, Dial, 1993.

*

Film Adaptations: *The Snow Spider,* 1988 (television serial); *Emlyn's Moon,* 1990 (television serial); *The Chestnut Soldier,* 1991 (television serial).

* * *

The Welsh legends of the *Mabinogion* have proved a rich mine for many fantasy writers, although most have been content to retell the stories with perhaps a slight gloss. Few writers truly incorporate the legends into new and original work. One thinks, naturally, of Alan Garner's *The Owl Service* and Susan Cooper's *The Dark is Rising* sequence, and also Lloyd Alexander's Prydain tales, but few writers can match them. One who has, however, is Jenny Nimmo, with her prize-winning Snow Spider trilogy.

The trilogy centres on Gwyn Griffiths, or Gwydion Gwyn as his grandmother, his Nain, calls him. Her great-great-grandmother was a witch, and Gwyn is the seventh generation after; she has little power herself and is eagerly awaiting what Gwyn may become. For his ninth birthday, Nain gives him five extremely strange presents—an ancient brooch, a pipe, a piece of seaweed, a broken figure of a horse and a scarf which once belonged to his sister, and urges him to see what he can do with them.

The brooch is given to the wind and in return he is given a silver spider, Arianwen, who will stay with him as a kind of familiar. In *The Snow Spider,* her function is to provide a means of contact between him and his lost sister Bethan. She vanished on the hills and, depending on how one wishes to view Gwyn's discovery of her whereabouts, she has disappeared in a spaceship or gone to a world where she will remain a child forever. Nevertheless, she returns briefly from time to time in other guises as Gwyn and Arianwen seek to heal the suffering of his family, and while Gwyn comes to terms with his own power.

While events in the first novel are centred on Gwyn's parents' farm, and other children play a peripheral role, in the second book, *Emlyn's Moon,* we follow the family of Gwyn's friend Alun Lloyd, as they move into town. Here, Nia, the middle child, the one everyone forgets the name of, discovers the Llewellyn family, Emlyn and his father Idris, and the wonderful chapel where they live and work—Idris is a painter. She also discovers that Emlyn and Gwyn are cousins but that there is some deep rift between the families, centring on the disappearance of Emlyn's mother. The story focuses on Nia as she begins to assert herself within her huge and rowdy family, discovering her talent as an artist, and also solving the mystery of Emlyn's mother's disappearance. She is also a friend to Gwyn, being the only one who takes his magical abilities entirely seriously. Gwyn himself, in this novel, is uneasy about his magical talents as he grows older, an unease which persists into the third and darkest of the three novels, *The Chestnut Soldier.*

Five years have passed since Gwyn first became aware of his magical powers. His unease with his magic has grown to the extent that he feels as though the magic is physically shrinking him. Only one gift remains unused, the mutilated horse which contains the demon that once was Efnisien, brother to Branwen. Gwyn is longing to set the prince free although he knows that he can't. The arrival of Evan Llyr, an obscure relation of the Lloyd family, precipitates a new crisis between the Lloyds, Griffiths and Llewellyns, and Gwyn prepares for a battle whose outcome he cannot predict. It is in this novel that Gwyn finally comes to terms with himself as magician and meets his illustrious and capricious ancestor, Gwydion the magician, who teaches him that even magicians can make mistakes.

In many respects, this third book is the most ambiguous of the three, in that one is not sure just how many of the incidents are brought about by magic and how much are the product of a psychological catastrophe. Is Evan Llyr the host of the frustrated and imprisoned Efnisien, or is he simply a man who is suffering as a result of his experiences as a soldier in Northern Ireland?

The three novels are undoubtedly a stunning achievement. Nimmo explores Gwyn's dual existence as ancient magician and young boy through five years, by turns showing his enthusiasm and weariness for his role as his awareness grows, and also his final acceptance of what he is. She also examines the complex and intertwined relationships of the three families, showing how their fates rest with one another. She captures the intensity of adolescence and contrasts it well against the intensity of Gwyn's magical existence. Her writing is powerful and as musical as the Welsh culture about which she is writing.

—Maureen Speller

NORMAN, John

Pseudonym for John (Frederick) Lange (Jr.). **Nationality:** American. **Born:** Chicago, Illinois, 3 June 1931. **Education:** University of Nebraska, Lincoln, B.A. 1953; University of Southern California, Los Angeles, M.A. 1957; Princeton University, New Jersey, Ph.D. 1963. **Military Service:** United States Army: Sergeant. **Family:** Married Bernice L. Green in 1956; two sons and one daughter. **Career:** Radio writer; story analyst, Warner Brothers; film writer, University of Nebraska; technical writer, Rocketdyne (North American Aviation); Instructor in Philosphy, Hamilton College, Clinton, New York, 1962-64. Since 1964, member of the department, and since 1974, Professor of Philosophy, Queens College, City University of New York. **Address:** Department of Philosophy, Queens College, Flushing, New York 11367, USA.

FANTASY PUBLICATIONS

Novels (series: Gor)

Tarnsman of Gor. New York, Ballantine, 1966; London, Sidgwick and Jackson, 1969.
Outlaw of Gor. New York, Ballantine, 1967; London, Sidgwick and Jackson, 1970.

Priest-Kings of Gor. New York, Ballantine, 1968; London, Sidgwick and Jackson, 1971.

Nomads of Gor. New York, Ballantine, 1969; London, Sidgwick and Jackson, 1971.

Assassin of Gor. New York, Ballantine, 1970; London, Sidgwick and Jackson, 1971.

Ghost Dance. New York, Ballantine, 1970; London, Sphere, 1972.

Raiders of Gor. New York, Ballantine, 1971; London, Tandem, 1973.

Captive of Gor. New York, Ballantine, 1972; London, Tandem, 1973.

The Gor Omnibus (includes *Tarnsman of Gor, Outlaw of Gor, Priest-Kings of Gor*). London, Sidgwick and Jackson, 1972.

Hunters of Gor. New York, DAW, 1974; London, Tandem, 1975.

Marauders of Gor. New York, DAW, 1975; London, Star, 1977.

Time Slave. New York, DAW, 1975; London, Star, 1981.

Tribesmen of Gor. New York, DAW, 1976.

Slave Girl of Gor. New York, DAW, 1977; London, Star, 1978.

Beasts of Gor. New York, DAW, 1978; London, Star, 1979.

Explorers of Gor. New York, DAW, 1979; London, Star, 1980.

Fighting Slave of Gor. New York, DAW, 1980; London, Star, 1981.

Guardsman of Gor. New York, DAW, 1981; London, Star, 1982.

Rogue of Gor. New York, DAW, 1981; London, Star, 1982.

Blood Brothers of Gor. New York, DAW, 1982; London, Star, 1983.

Savages of Gor. New York, DAW, and London, Star, 1982.

Kajira of Gor. New York, DAW, and London, Star, 1983.

Players of Gor. New York, DAW, and London, Star, 1984.

Mercenaries of Gor. New York, DAW, and London, Star, 1985.

Dancer of Gor. New York, DAW, 1985; London, Star, 1986.

Renegades of Gor. New York, DAW, and London, Star, 1986.

Vagabonds of Gor. New York, DAW, and London, Star, 1987.

Magicians of Gor. New York, DAW, 1988.

The Telnarian Histories: The Chieftain. New York, Warner, 1991.

OTHER PUBLICATIONS

Other

The Cognitivity Paradox: An Inquiry Concerning the Claims of Philosophy (as John Lange). Princeton, New Jersey, Princeton University Press, 1970.

Imaginative Sex. New York, DAW, 1975.

Editor (as John Lange), *Values and Imperatives: Studies in Ethics,* by Clarence I. Lewis. Stanford, California, Stanford University Press, 1969.

*

Film Adaptations: *Gor,* 1988, from the novel *Tarnsman of Gor; Outlaw of Gor,* 1989.

Critical Studies: "Negative Exempla: Lust Without Love on Counter-Earth Gor" by George Peek, *Extrapolation* vol. 25, no. 1, Spring 1984; "John Norman: The Literature of Difference" by L. J. Hurst, *Foundation* no. 33, Spring 1985.

*   *   *

John Norman is the pseudonym of John Frederick Lange, an academic principally engaged in teaching philosophy, most recently at Queens College, New York. Best known, and notorious, for his

Gor series, he has a claim to being the most reviled author in the history of fantasy fiction.

His premier novel, and first in the Gor sequence, *Tarnsman of Gor,* is a standard sword-and-sorcery adventure strongly reminiscent of Edgar Rice Burroughs's John Carter of Mars series. Its hero, Tarl Cabot, is transported with minimal explanation to the planet Gor, a world that has always shared Earth's orbit but is unknown to us because it sits on the other side of the Sun. Strictly speaking, this premise would place the series in the science fantasy category, were it not for its absurdity. The contemptuous disregard with which the author conveys the "scientific" rationale of such nonsense to his readers indicates, at best, a lack of even the most cursory research.

The society Tarl Cabot finds himself in is feudal, caste-stratified and curiously ignorant of the practical advantages afforded by wearing more than the absolute minimum of clothing. By chance a master swordsman, he spends most of the book slaughtering an assortment of villains and monsters on his way to rescuing beautiful if physically improbable female captives. This formula repeats with few variations in the four subsequent volumes. Indeed their plots, and those of all that followed, are interchangeable: typically, Cabot incurs the wrath of an evil warlord/magician, battles his way up a hierarchy of sub-villains, kills the leader and gains his female "prize." The early Gor novels can be summed up as routine, mostly anodyne, semi-juvenile romps.

However, with book six, *Raiders of Gor,* the plots began to take a more sinister turn. The background sexism apparent from the beginning moved centre stage and became overtly misogynistic. The women characters, hitherto portrayed as objects of desire, were now utilized as recipients of violent sadism and humiliation. Worse, they were depicted as willing participants in their own oppression, able to achieve sexual gratification only when subjected to physical abuse. From this point the series grew increasingly extreme in what can only be called its advocacy of abduction, enslavement, rape, disfigurement and dominance of women. By volume 12, *Beasts of Gor,* Norman was peppering the texts with long diatribes, usually delivered by Cabot, justifying this world-view. They always end with the female at whom they are directed surrendering her foolish notions of independence and embracing male supremacy. It may be no coincidence that the passion with which this "argument" was presented was in direct proportion to the rise of the women's movement.

Depressingly, the series was enormously popular; to such an extent that its publisher, DAW Books, saw fit to exploit the phenomenon by issuing Norman's nonfiction tome *Imaginative Sex* in 1974. An examination of this work reveals that "imaginative" equals female submissiveness and the sex manifests only as sadomasochism. It remains the sole departure from DAW's policy of publishing exclusively fantasy and science fiction. But, like Norman's non-Gor one-offs *Ghost Dance* and *Time Slave,* it achieved substantial sales. A couple of bad, low-budget, Italian-made, sword-and-sorcery movies have been based on the first two Gor novels, and in 1991 the author launched a new series, the Telnarian Histories, with *The Chieftain.*

The Gor sequence expired in 1988 and is unlikely to be resurrected by any respectable publisher. During its 22-year reign it drew outright condemnation from readers, fans, critics, fantasy authors who saw it as bringing the field into disrepute, educators and feminists. (On one of the rare occasions he sought to defend the series, Norman blamed the last-named for bringing about its cancellation.) As recently as 1993 a man accused of rape and sexual assault cited the books' influence as part of his defence during a High Court trial in London. He received a lengthy custodial sentence. It was not the first time a defendant in such a case had referred to the novels in mitigation for his behaviour. Whether they can be held responsible as contributing in any way to violent sexual crime remains unproven. But perhaps being brought forward in this context offers the perspective that they really have no place in the genre at all. Viewing them as aids to masturbatory male power fantasies, employing fantasy conventions as simple expediency, could reveal their true intent. Readers wishing to locate out-of-print volumes, for collecting or other purposes, might like to know that sightings of shrink-wrapped copies have been reported from pornographic bookshops as far afield as Amsterdam's red light district, London's Soho and New York's Times Square.

—Stan Nicholls

NORTON, Andre

Pseudonyms: Andrew North; Allen Weston. **Nationality:** American. **Born:** Alice Mary Norton, Cleveland, Ohio, 17 February 1912. **Education:** Western Reserve University, Cleveland, 1930-32. **Career:** Children's librarian, Cleveland Public Library, 1932-50; special librarian, Library of Congress, Washington, D.C., during World War II; editor, Gnome Press, New York, 1950-58. **Awards:** Grand Master of Fantasy award, 1977; Gandalf award, 1977; Fritz Leiber award, 1983; Lensman award, 1983, 1987; Grand Master Nebula award 1983; Jules Verne award, 1984; Daedalus award, 1986. **Agent:** Russell Galen, 3 Haverford Road, Cranbury, NJ 08512-9204, USA. **Address:** 1600 Spruce Avenue, Winter Park, FL 32789, USA.

FANTASY PUBLICATIONS

Novels (series: Magic; Moon Magic; Trillium; Witch World; Zero Stone)

Rogue Reynard. Boston, Houghton Mifflin, 1947.
Huon of the Horn. New York, Harcourt Brace, 1951.
Witch World. New York, Ace, 1963; London, Tandem, 1970.
Web of the Witch World. New York, Ace, 1964; London, Tandem, 1970.
Steel Magic. Cleveland, World, 1965; London, Hamish Hamilton, 1967; as *Gray Magic,* New York, Scholastic, 1967.
Three Against the Witch World. New York, Ace, 1965; London, Tandem, 1970.
Year of the Unicorn (Witch World). New York, Ace, 1965; London, Tandem, 1970.
Moon of Three Rings (Moon Magic). New York, Viking Press, 1966; London, Longman, 1969.
Octagon Magic. Cleveland, World, 1967; London, Hamish Hamilton, 1968.
Warlock of the Witch World. New York, Ace, 1967; London, Tandem, 1970.
Fur Magic. Cleveland, World, 1968; London, Hamish Hamilton, 1969.
Sorceress of the Witch World. New York, Ace, 1968; London, Tandem, 1970.

Dread Companion. New York, Harcourt Brace, 1970; London, Gollancz, 1972.
Exiles of the Stars (Moon Magic). New York, Viking Press, 1971; London, Longman, 1972.
The Crystal Gryphon (Witch World). New York, Atheneum, 1972; London, Gollancz, 1973.
Dragon Magic. New York, Crowell, 1972.
Forerunner Foray. New York, Viking Press, 1973; London, Longman, 1974.
Here Abide Monsters. New York, Atheneum, 1973.
The Jargoon Pard (Witch World). New York, Atheneum, 1974; London, Gollancz, 1975.
Lavender-Green Magic. New York, Crowell, 1974.
Red Hart Magic. New York, Crowell, 1976; London, Hamish Hamilton, 1977.
Wraiths of Time. New York, Atheneum, 1976; London, Gollancz, 1977.
Quag Keep. New York, Atheneum, 1978.
Yurth Burden. New York, DAW, 1978.
Zarsthor's Bane (Witch World). New York, Ace, 1978; London, Dobson, 1981.
Seven Spells to Sunday, with Phyllis Miller. New York, Atheneum, 1979.
Gryphon in Glory (Witch World). New York, Atheneum, 1981.
Horn Crown (Witch World). New York, DAW, 1981.
Moon Called. New York, Simon and Schuster, 1982.
'Ware Hawk (Witch World). New York, Atheneum, 1983; London, Gollancz, 1989.
Wheel of Stars. New York, Simon and Schuster, 1983.
House of Shadows, with Phyllis Miller. New York, Atheneum, 1984.
Gryphon's Eyrie, with A. C. Crispin (Witch World). New York, Tor, 1984.
Were-Wrath. New Castle, Virginia, Cheap Street, 1984.
Ride the Green Dragon, with Phyllis Miller. New York, Atheneum, 1985.
Flight in Yiktor (Moon Magic). New York, Tor, 1986; London, Methuen, 1988.
The Gate of the Cat (Witch World). New York, Ace, 1987.
The Magic Books (omnibus; includes *Fur Magic, Steel Magic, Octagon Magic*). New York, New American Library, 1988.
Imperial Lady: A Fantasy of Han China, with Susan Shwartz. New York, Tor, 1989.
Black Trillium, with Marion Zimmer Bradley and Julian May. New York, Doubleday, 1990; London, Grafton, 1991.
Dare to Go A-Hunting (Moon Magic). New York, Tor, 1990.
The Elvenbane, with Mercedes Lackey. New York, Tor, 1991; London, Grafton, 1993.
Storms of Victory, with P. M. Griffin (Witch World). New York, Tor, 1991.
The Mark of the Cat. New York, Ace, 1992; London, Legend, 1993.
Songsmith, with A. C. Crispin (Witch World). New York, Tor, 1992.
Empire of the Eagle, with Susan Shwartz. New York, Tor, 1993.
Golden Trillium. New York, Bantam, 1993.
The Hands of Llyr. New York, Morrow, 1994.

Short Stories

High Sorcery. New York, Ace, 1970.
Garan the Eternal. Alhambra, California, Fantasy, 1972.
Spell of the Witch World. New York, DAW, 1972; London, Prior, 1977.

Trey of Swords. New York, Grosset and Dunlap, 1977; London, Star, 1979.
Lore of the Witch World. New York, DAW, 1980.
Serpent's Tooth. Winter Park, Florida, Andre Norton Ltd., 1987.
Moon Mirror, edited by Ingrid Zierhut. New York, Tor, 1988.
Wizards' Worlds, edited by Ingrid Zierhut. New York, Tor, 1989.

Other

Editor, with Robert Adams, *Magic in Ithkar.* New York, Tor, 4 vols., 1985-87.
Editor, *Tales of the Witch World.* New York, Tor, 3 vols., 1987-90; London, Pan, 1989-90.
Editor, with Martin H. Greenberg, *Catfantastic.* New York, DAW, 3 vols., 1989-94.
Editor, *Four from the Witch World.* New York, Tor, 1989.
Editor, *Flight of Vengeance,* by Pauline Griffin and Mary Schaub (Witch World). New York, Tor, 1992.
Editor, *On Wings of Magic,* by Patricia Mathews and Sasha Miller (Witch World). New York, Tor, 1993.

OTHER PUBLICATIONS

Novels

The Prince Commands. New York, Appleton Century, 1934.
Ralestone Luck. New York, Appleton Century, 1938.
Follow the Drum. New York, Penn, 1942.
The Sword Is Drawn. Boston, Houghton Mifflin, 1944; London, Oxford University Press, 1946.
Scarface. New York, Harcourt Brace, 1948; London, Methuen, 1950.
Sword in Sheath. New York, Harcourt Brace, 1949; as *Island of the Lost,* London, Staples Press, 1953.
Star Man's Son, 2250 A.D. New York, Harcourt Brace, 1952; London, Staples Press, 1953; as *Daybreak, 2250 A.D.,* New York, Ace, 1954.
Star Rangers. New York, Harcourt Brace, 1953; London, Gollancz, 1968; as *The Last Planet,* New York, Ace, 1955.
At Swords' Point. New York, Harcourt Brace, 1954.
Murders for Sale (as Allen Weston, with Grace Allen Hogarth). London, Hammond, 1954; as *Sneeze on Sunday* (as Andre Norton), New York, Tor, 1991.
The Stars Are Ours! Cleveland, World, 1954.
Sargasso of Space (as Andrew North). New York, Gnome Press, 1955; as Andre Norton, London, Gollancz, 1970.
Star Guard. New York, Harcourt Brace, 1955; London, Gollancz, 1969.
Yankee Privateer. Cleveland, World, 1955.
The Crossroads of Time. New York, Ace, 1956; London, Gollancz, 1967.
Plague Ship (as Andrew North). New York, Gnome Press, 1956; as Andre Norton, London, Gollancz, 1971.
Stand to Horse. New York, Harcourt Brace, 1956.
Sea Siege. New York, Harcourt Brace, 1957.
Star Born. Cleveland, World, 1957; London, Gollancz, 1973.
Star Gate. New York, Harcourt Brace, 1958; London, Gollancz, 1970.
The Time Traders. Cleveland, World, 1958.
Secret of the Lost Race. New York, Ace, 1959; as *Wolfshead,* London, Hale, 1977.

The Beast Master. New York, Harcourt Brace, 1959; London, Gollancz, 1966.
Galactic Derelict. Cleveland, World, 1959.
Voodoo Planet (as Andrew North). New York, Ace, 1959.
Shadow Hawk. New York, Harcourt Brace, 1960; London, Gollancz, 1971.
Storm Over Warlock. Cleveland, World, 1960.
The Sioux Spaceman. New York, Ace, 1960; London, Hale, 1976.
Ride Proud, Rebel! Cleveland, World, 1961.
Star Hunter. New York, Ace, 1961.
Catseye. New York, Harcourt Brace, 1961; London, Gollancz, 1962.
Eye of the Monster. New York, Ace, 1962.
The Defiant Agents. Cleveland, World, 1962.
Lord of Thunder. New York, Harcourt Brace, 1962; London, Gollancz, 1966.
Rebel Spurs. Cleveland, World, 1962.
Key Out of Time. Cleveland, World, 1963.
Judgment on Janus. New York, Harcourt Brace, 1963; London, Gollancz, 1964.
Ordeal in Otherwhere. Cleveland, World, 1964.
Night of Masks. New York, Harcourt Brace, 1964; London, Gollancz, 1965.
The X Factor. New York, Harcourt Brace, 1965; London, Gollancz, 1967.
Quest Crosstime. New York, Viking Press, 1965; as *Crosstime Agent,* London, Gollancz, 1975.
Victory on Janus. New York, Harcourt Brace, 1966; London, Gollancz, 1967.
Operation Time Search. New York, Harcourt Brace, 1967.
Dark Piper. New York, Harcourt Brace, 1968; London, Gollancz, 1969.
The Zero Stone. New York, Viking Press, 1968; London, Gollancz, 1974.
Bertie and May, with Bertha Stemm Norton. Cleveland, World, 1969; London, Hamish Hamilton, 1971.
Postmarked the Stars. New York, Harcourt Brace, 1969; London, Gollancz, 1971.
Uncharted Stars. New York, Viking Press, 1969; London, Gollancz, 1974.
Ice Crown. New York, Viking Press, 1970; London, Longman, 1971.
Android at Arms. New York, Harcourt Brace, 1971; London, Gollancz, 1972.
Breed to Come. New York, Viking Press, 1972; London, Longman, 1973.
Iron Cage. New York, Viking Press, 1974; London, Kestrel, 1975.
Merlin's Mirror. New York, DAW, 1975; London, Sidgwick and Jackson, 1976.
Outside. New York, Walker, 1975; London, Blackie, 1976.
The Day of the Ness, with Michael Gilbert. New York, Walker, 1975.
Knave of Dreams. New York, Viking Press, 1975; London, Kestrel, 1976.
No Night Without Stars. New York, Atheneum, 1975; London, Gollancz, 1976.
The White Jade Fox. New York, Dutton, 1975; London, W. H. Allen, 1976.
Star Ka'at, with Dorothy Madlee. New York, Walker, 1976; London, Blackie, 1977.
The Opal-Eyed Fan. New York, Dutton, 1977.
Velvet Shadows. New York, Fawcett, 1977.
Star Ka'at World, with Dorothy Madlee. New York, Walker, 1978.

Snow Shadow. New York, Fawcett, 1979.
Star Ka'ats and the Plant People, with Dorothy Madlee. New York, Walker, 1979.
Star Ka'ats and the Winged Warriors. New York, Walker, 1981.
Ten Mile Treasure. New York, Pocket Books, 1981.
Voorloper. New York, Ace, 1981.
Forerunner. New York, Pinnacle, 1981.
Caroline, with Enid Cushing. New York, Pinnacle, 1982.
Stand and Deliver. New York, Dell, 1984.
Forerunner: The Second Venture. New York, Tor, 1985.
The Jekyll Legacy, with Robert Bloch. New York, Tor, 1990.
Brother to Shadows. New York, Avon, 1993.
Redline the Stars, with P. M. Griffin. New York, Tor, 1993.
Firehand, with P. M. Griffin. New York, Tor, 1994.

Short Stories

The Many Worlds of Andre Norton, edited by Roger Elwood. Radnor, Pennsylvania, Chilton, 1974; as *The Book of Andre Norton,* New York, DAW, 1975.
Perilous Dreams. New York, DAW, 1976.

Other

Editor, *Bullard of the Space Patrol,* by Malcolm Jameson. Cleveland, World, 1951.
Editor, *Space Service.* Cleveland, World, 1953.
Editor, *Space Pioneers.* Cleveland, World, 1954.
Editor, *Space Police.* Cleveland, World, 1956.
Editor, with Ernestine Donaldy, *Gates to Tomorrow: An Introduction to Science Fiction.* New York, Atheneum, 1973.
Editor, *Small Shadows Creep: Ghost Children.* New York, Dutton, 1974; London, Chatto and Windus, 1976.
Editor, *Baleful Beasts and Eerie Creatures.* Chicago, Rand McNally, 1976.
Editor, with Ingrid Zierhut, *Grand Masters' Choice.* Cambridge, Massachusetts, NESFA, 1989.

*

Film Adaptations: *The Beastmaster,* 1982, from the novel *The Beast Master.*

Bibliography: *Andre Norton: A Primary and Secondary Bibliography* by Roger C. Schlobin, Boston, Hall, 1980, revised edition by Roger C. Schlobin and Irene R. Harrison, Framingham, Massachusetts, NESFA Press, 1994; *Andre Norton: Grand Master of the Witch World—A Working Bibliography* by Phil Stephensen-Payne, Leeds, Yorkshire, Galactic Central, 1991.

Manuscript Collections: Andre Norton Ltd., Winter Park, Florida; George Arents Research Library, Syracuse University, New York.

*   *   *

In the 1950s and 1960s Andre Norton was one of the very few writers producing good science fiction for young readers, and unlike Robert A. Heinlein she wrote exclusively for the juvenile market. Her science fiction novels are mostly set in the same future: a Galaxy in which humans and aliens have both colonized worlds, and in which young men, the normal protagonists, can frequently find adventures in conflict with grasping merchants, conspiring criminals or sinister aliens. Two of her most popular sf novels, *The Beast Master* and *Catseye,* revolve around two elements which often crop up in her novels: humans who have telepathic or empathic communication with their animals (most frequently cats), and powerful and mysterious artefacts belonging to a vanished galactic race with high technology, the Forerunners. Unlike most writers of science fiction, Norton regards technology with suspicion. She celebrates simple and traditional lifestyles, like that of the Navaho protagonist of *The Beast Master,* and frequently has her protagonists trekking alone across the surface of alien planets without the protection of the high technology that brought them there in the first place. (Note that the entertaining 1982 movie based on *The Beast Master,* starring muscleman Marc Singer in a very Tarzan-like role, removes most science fiction elements and turns the story into heroic fantasy.)

Norton's juveniles introduced many young readers to sf, and to many of its most significant motifs and tropes. But in the early 1960s she embarked on a fantasy series which made her much more widely known, spreading her appeal more to a female readership, for instance, but also persuading her publishers to market her books to adults as well as teenagers. By the 1980s almost all her books were marketed as adult novels, including the reprints of her early juveniles: at the time of writing nearly 60 of her books are in print in the United States.

Some of her earliest novels, such as *Rogue Reynard* and *Huon of the Horn,* retellings of medieval fable and romance, are certainly classifiable as fantasies. But the series which made her name as a fantasy writer was "Witch World," currently running to almost 20 novels and collections. (There are now also several anthologies of stories edited by Norton and set on Witch World, written by A. C. Crispin, Mercedes Lackey, Elizabeth Scarborough and others.) The first novel, *Witch World,* was not intended as the start of a series, but as a one-off inspired by an episode in medieval history. It gives a science-fictional rationale to the series, although Norton much reduced this emphasis later in the series. The protagonist is an Englishman, Simon Tregarth, brought to Estcarp on the planet called Witch World through a Gate, an ancient stone in Cornwall with Arthurian associations. Tregarth defends Witch World from the invasion of the alien Kolder, whose superior technology includes machines which can take over the minds of their enemies. The magic of the witches of Estcarp itself depends on a kind of technology, mind-power enhanced by special jewels, recalling the powerful jewels and other objects with psychic powers to be found in Norton's science fiction novels. Indeed, for this reason it was possible at first for publishers to assume that the series was indeed sf: the first edition of *Spell of the Witch World* carried the blurb "The Long-Awaited New Book of Extra-Galactic Super-Science". But the alien Kolder disappear from the scene, and contacts with the outside world via the Gates rarely occur again. Only the mysterious Old Ones, with their own lingering magic/technology, recurring throughout the Witch World series, remind readers of science fiction precursors, notably the Forerunners of Norton's own earlier novels.

The Witch World novels and associated short stories do not tell one unbroken story. In *Horn Crown,* the earliest chronologically (although published only in 1981), we learn that Witch World had been deserted by the Old Ones, who left the Gates open for gradual human colonization. But *Horn Crown* stands on its own. The bulk of the novels, which are arranged in two or three groups, deal with a much later period in Witch World's history. The first few, all written during the 1960s (*Witch World, Web of the Witch World, Three Against the Witch World, Warlock of the Witch World* and *Sorceress of the Witch World*), deal with Estcarp and its matriarchal society, ruled by women with magical talents, the witches, and follow the adventures of Simon, his wife Jaelithe and their three children in Estcarp and neighbouring kingdoms. Another series, beginning with *The Crystal Gryphon* and continuing with *Gryphon in Glory* and *Gryphon's Eyrie,* takes place across the sea from Estcarp, in Arvon and High Halleck. The male protagonist Kerovan is hooved and amber-eyed, a throwback to the Old Ones; other novels set in the same part of Witch World also concern men who are part beast: *Year of the Unicorn* features the Wereriders, wolf-men, and *The Jargoon Pard* a hero, son of the shape-changing Wererider of the previous volume, who could change into a leopard. The importance of seeing beyond surface appearances, however horrible, to the true personality beneath, and thus the importance of battling against prejudice, is a message to be found in Norton's science fiction as well. The Witch World books offer other messages to the reader of fantasy. She describes a world similar to that of the standard sword-and-sorcery fantasy, with a low level of technology, a semifeudal society, and male sword-wielding warriors. Yet in this world physical violence seldom solves anything. The power to achieve and to resolve rests with women, who, with rare exceptions, possess a monopoly of magical powers. Magic, if used by individuals, however, frequently corrupts: magical success in these novels is achieved by means of cooperation. If, as Diana Waggoner claims (*The Hills of Faraway,* page 254), the series is "afflicted with wooden characters, overwritten prose, and disjointed plotting," there is nevertheless much colour, mystery and humanity, and a number of strong female characters: it is not surprising that they have won a large following.

Among Norton's copious output there are numerous other fantasies. In the late 1960s she produced the "Magic" series of books for younger children, each of which uses an object to propel the child protagonists into a magical world: in *Steel Magic* picnic utensils become talismans in an Arthurian world; in *Fur Magic* it is an Indian medicine bag; in *Octagon Magic* a doll's house; and in *Lavender-Green Magic* a maze, which takes the children back to Puritan New England. Other fantasies include *Here Abide Monsters,* in which a young couple discover a gateway (a Bermuda triangle) to a fairy world; *Moon Called,* resplendent with standard Jewels and Swords; and *Quag Keep,* a novel based on the fantasy role-playing game "Dungeons and Dragons." Norton's health in recent years has not allowed her to maintain her output of novels, but she has been active as a collaborator, writing fantasies together with A. C. Crispin and Mercedes Lackey, and a gothic-horror novel, *The Jekyll Legacy,* with Robert Bloch. With both Marion Zimmer Bradley and Julian May, she wrote *Black Trillium,* an overblown fairy story: it was followed by *Blood Trillium,* by May, and *Golden Trillium,* by Norton herself. She has been prolific as an editor too: not only her own *Tales of the Witch World,* but also, with Robert Adams, four volumes of *Magic in Ithkar* and, with Martin H. Greenberg, three volumes of fantasies about her favourite animals, *Catfantastic I, II* and *III.* Andre Norton remains one of America's most popular writers and an enduring phenomenon of the fantasy field.

—Edward James

NORTON, Mary

Nationality: British. **Born:** Mary Pearson, London, 10 December 1903. **Education:** St. Margaret's Convent, East Grinstead, Sussex. **Family:** Married 1) Robert C. Norton in 1926, two daughters and two sons; 2) Lionel Bonsey in 1970. **Career:** Actress, Old Vic Theatre Company, London, 1925-26; lived in Portugal, 1926-39; worked for the BBC, 1940, and the British Purchasing Company, New York, 1941; from 1942 actress in London. **Awards:** Library Association Carnegie Medal, 1953. **Died:** 29 August 1992.

FANTASY PUBLICATIONS

Novels (series: Borrowers)

The Magic Bed-Knob; or, How to Become a Witch in Ten Easy Lessons, illustrated by Waldo Peirce. New York, Hyperion Press, 1943; illustrated by Joan Kiddell-Monroe, London, Dent, 1945.
Bonfires and Broomsticks, illustrated by Mary Adshead. London, Dent, 1947.
The Borrowers, illustrated by Diana Stanley. London, Dent, 1952; New York, Harcourt Brace, 1953.
The Borrowers Afield, illustrated by Diana Stanley. London, Dent, and New York, Harcourt Brace, 1955.
Bedknob and Broomstick (revised versions of *The Magic Bed-Knob* and *Bonfires and Broomsticks*), illustrated by Erik Blegvad. London, Dent, and New York, Harcourt Brace, 1957.
The Borrowers Afloat, illustrated by Diana Stanley. London, Dent, and New York, Harcourt Brace, 1959.
The Borrowers Aloft, illustrated by Diana Stanley. London, Dent, and New York, Harcourt Brace, 1961.
The Borrowers Omnibus (includes *The Borrowers, The Borrowers Afield, The Borrowers Afloat, The Borrowers Aloft*). London, Dent, 1966.
Are All the Giants Dead?, illustrated by Brian Froud. London, Dent, and New York, Harcourt Brace, 1975.
The Borrowers Avenged, illustrated by Pauline Baynes. London, Kestrel, and New York, Harcourt Brace, 1982.

Short Stories

Poor Stainless, illustrated by Diana Stanley. London, Dent, and New York, Harcourt Brace, 1971.
Poor Stainless (collection), illustrated by Justin Todd. London, Viking, 1994.

*

Film Adaptations: *Bedknobs and Broomsticks,* 1971; *The Borrowers,* 1973 (TV movie); *The Borrowers,* 1992, 1993 (TV serials).

*   *   *

Mary Norton's "Borrowers" are perhaps midway between Jonathan Swift's Lilliputians and Terry Pratchett's "nomes" as examples of how the device of contrasting small folk against large can create amusing satire. The Borrowers are Norton's wonderful explanation of how the small items we leave about in our households—safety-pins, needles, matchboxes—can never be found when we want them. The race of minuscule humanoids who are at once so dependent on humans that they borrow their names (after a fashion) and so afraid of being seen, are a charming conceit, but Norton is too good a writer to rely on charm. The Borrower family we meet in the first book and follow throughout subsequent adventures—romantic Arriety Clock and her parents, dependable Pod and the harassed, conservative Homily—are skilfully drawn characters, and through Homily's narrative of the history of the previous Borrower families who have shared their house we perceive something of the melancholy nature of Borrower society: one of hand-me-down and improvisation. "Sometimes there were days and days when they lived on crumbs and water out of the flower-vases." Arriety's shock when she discovers that there are considerably more human beings in the world than Borrowers is the genuine chill of someone who has had their world-view overturned. A comparison with the later use of this same device by Terry Pratchett is inevitable, but Norton's humour is gentler, sadder. From the start, we are aware not of the differences between the large and small folk, but the similarities between them.

The last Borrowers in the house in which they live, the Clocks are forced to move after Arriety has befriended the boy who has come to stay. He is separated from his parents in India, recovering from an illness; she, with no company but that of her parents, is looking for friendship and adventure. But his interest in Arriety and her family leads to the threat of discovery by the other humans. They escape and, with the aid of the wild Spiller, find temporary refuge. Forced to move again, they end up in Mr. Potts's model village where the kindly Miss Menzies discovers their presence and the wicked Platters, owners of a rival model village, steal them. Escaping ingeniously by balloon, they find refuge away from humans (although *The Borrowers Avenged,* written over 20 years later, tells of a further attempt by the Platters to steal them).

Norton lets the implications of her story unfold through a mixture of tension and humour. Tied to the human race for subsistence, the Borrowers' greatest fear is of being discovered. Their attitude to humanity is therefore ambiguous; they flee away from it, but must always return to some form of symbiosis. Norton's prose reflects this ambiguity. There are moments of terror, as when the boy to whom Arriety has revealed the secret of the Borrowers' existence levers up the floorboards to reveal their home; finely-caught detail—in her panic, Arriety still notices the faint soap-scent of the boy's hand; and lyrically pastoral occasions when the Borrowers discover the countryside. They are symbolically children, small beings living off bigger ones in a world not built to scale for them, but while many writers have used this device Norton, though still writing for children, does not impose this view upon her audience. The Borrowers are the titular subjects of the saga, but there is a wider story being told. It is not accidental, for instance, that in many places the focus is upon the humans as much, if not more, as upon the Borrowers.

The first two books give us the story as told to or discovered by Kate, who stands for reader and author. When we read about Arriety and her family and their adventures, much of what we are reading is conjecture: a distancing effect which takes us into the imaginations of the viewpoint characters, first Kate and then (in *The Borrowers Aloft* and *The Borrowers Avenged*) Miss Menzies. Both latter books begin with several chapters in which she, rather than the small people she has "adopted," is the central character. These in many ways are among the most delightful parts of the series, with the gentle humour of Miss Menzies explaining to an only half-listening Mr. Potts about the Borrowers who have come to live in his model village, and the delicately tender scene where she is trying to report their disappearance to the village policeman, struggling against the realization that she is indeed giving the appearance of a deluded old maid.

This estrangement is particularly marked in the final Borrowers novel in which the Platters become more coldly sinister, Arriety and her family come to share their new quarters with three ghosts (who appear, but do not interact), and the happy ending suggested at the close of the previous book seems to have been undercut. Peagreen's final question about being safe ("Are we? Ever?") sums up the series. Despite its humour and ingenuity, the current of unease which runs through the series allows the reader to feel for its characters and their plight and make it truly a fantasy classic.

Poor Stainless is an independent Borrowers story narrated by Homily to Arrietty. Originally a birthday gift for the great children's writer Eleanor Farjeon, it offers a glimpse of the days when the house was full of Borrower families, and the social relationships between them. Norton's other books are more specifically "for children." *Bedknob and Broomstick* is a Nesbit-like story of a magic bed which transports children from place to place. Somewhat dated in style, it possesses an interestingly ambiguous witch. *Are All the Giants Dead?* is an amusing journey into fairy-tale territory by a young boy who actually prefers science fiction and does not realize until he is told that the characters he has met were Beauty and the Beast, Cinderella, and the Sleeping beauty. It is notable for the lucid dream-like quality of its introductory chapter, although it may also serve as an exasperated sigh that "the children of today" prefer to dream about cosmonauts rather than Jack the Giant-killer.

—Andy Sawyer

NOYES, Alfred

Nationality: British. **Born:** Wolverhampton, 16 September 1880. **Education:** Exeter College, Oxford. **Family:** Married 1) Garnett Daniels in 1907 (died 1926); 2) Mary Weld-Blundell in 1927, one son and two daughters. **Career:** Professional poet; contributor, *Blackwood's Magazine* and other periodicals; Lowell lecturer, Harvard, 1913; professor of English Literature, Princeton, 1914-23; guest lecturer at many other universities in later years. Converted to the Roman Catholic Church, 1925. Lived in the USA for some years during the 1940s; retired to the Isle of Wight, England. **Awards:** Companion of the British Empire, 1918; honorary degrees from Yale, Glasgow, Syracuse and California universities. **Died:** 28 June 1958.

FANTASY PUBLICATIONS

Novel

The Devil Takes a Holiday. London, Murray, 1955.

Short Stories

Walking Shadows: Sea Tales and Others. London, Cassell, and New York, Stokes, 1918.
Beyond the Desert: A Tale of Death Valley. New York, Stokes, 1920.
The Hidden Player. London, Hodder and Stoughton, and New York, Stokes, 1924.

Plays (in verse)

The Forest of Wild Thyme. Edinburgh and London, Blackwood, 1905.

Sherwood; or, Robin Hood and the Three Kings. New York, Stokes, 1911; revised as *Robin Hood,* Edinburgh and London, Blackwood, 1926.

Other

Editor, *The Magic Casement: An Anthology of Fairy Poetry.* London, Chapman and Hall, 1908; New York, Dutton, 1909.

OTHER PUBLICATIONS

Novels

The Wine-Press: A Tale of War. Edinburgh and London, Blackwood, and New York, Stokes, 1913.
Mystery Ships, Trapping the U Boat. London, Hodder and Stoughton, 1916.
The Return of the Scare-Crow. London, Cassell, 1929; as *The Sun Cure,* New York, Cosmopolitan, 1929.
The Last Man. London, Murray, 1940; as *No Other Man,* New York, Stokes, 1940.
The Secret of Pooduck Island (for children). New York, Stokes, 1943; London, Hutchinson, 1946.

Play

Rada. New York, Stokes, 1914; revised as *Rada: A Belgian Christmas Eve,* London, Methuen, and New York, Stokes, 1915.

Poetry

The Loom of Years. London, Richards, 1902.
The Flower of Old Japan. London, Richards, 1903.
Poems. Edinburgh and London, Blackwood, 1904.
Drake: An English Epic. Edinburgh and London, Blackwood, 2 vols., 1906-08.
The Flower of Old Japan and Other Poems. New York and London, Macmillan, 1907.
Forty Singing Seamen and Other Poems. Edinburgh and London, Blackwood, 1907; New York, Stokes, 1913.
The Golden Hynde and Other Poems. New York, Macmillan, 1908.
The Enchanted Island and Other Poems. Edinburgh and London, Blackwood, 1909; New York, Stokes, 1910.
Collected Poems. Edinburgh and London, Blackwood, 2 vols., 1910; New York, Stokes, 1913; vol. 3, Edinburgh and London, Blackwood, and New York, Stokes, 1920; enlarged edition, Edinburgh and London, Blackwood, 4 vols., 1927.
The Prayer for Peace. N.p., 1911.
The Carol of the Fir-Tree. London, Burns and Oates, 1912.
Tales of the Mermaid Tavern. Edinburgh and London, Blackwood, and New York, Stokes, 1913.
The Lord of Misrule and Other Poems. New York, Stokes, 1915.
A Salute from the Fleet and Other Poems. London, Methuen, 1915.
The New Morning: Poems. New York, Stokes, 1918.
The Elfin Artist and Other Poems. Edinburgh and London, Blackwood, and New York, Stokes, 1920.
Selected Verse. N.p., 1921.
The Victory-Ball. N.p., 1921.
The Watchers of the Sky. Edinburgh and London, Blackwood, and New York, Stokes, 1922.

Songs of Shadow-of-a-Leaf and Other Poems. Edinburgh and London, Blackwood, 1924.
The Book of the Earth. Edinburgh and London, Blackwood, and New York, Stokes, 1925.
Dick Turpin's Ride and Other Poems. New York, Stokes, 1927.
Ballads and Poems. Edinburgh and London, Blackwood, 1928.
The Strong City. N.p., 1928.
The Last Voyage. Edinburgh and London, Blackwood, and New York, Stokes, 1930.
Poems. N.p., 1931.
The Torch-Bearers (omnibus; includes *The Watchers of the Sky, The Book of the Earth, The Last Voyage*). Edinburgh and London, Blackwood, and New York, Stokes, 1937.
If Judgement Comes. New York, Stokes, 1941.
Shadows on the Down and Other Poems. New York, Stokes, 1941; London, Hutchinson, 1945.
Poems of the New World. Philadelphia, Lippincott, 1942.
Collected Poems. Philadelphia, Lippincott, 1947; London, Murray, 1950; enlarged edition, London, Murray, 1963; New York, McCutcheon, 1966.
Daddy Fell Into the Pond and Other Poems for Children. New York, Sheed and Ward, 1952.
A Letter to Lucian and Other Poems. London, Murray, 1956; Philadelphia, Lippincott, 1957.

Other

William Morris. London, Macmillan, 1908.
In Memory of Swinburne. Privately printed, 1909.
What is England Doing? N.p., 1916.
Some Aspects of Modern Poetry. London, Hodder and Stoughton, and New York, Stokes, 1924.
New Essays and American Impressions. New York, Holt, 1927.
The Opalescent Parrot. London, Sheed and Ward, 1929.
Tennyson. Edinburgh and London, Blackwood, 1932.
The Unknown God. London and New York, Sheed and Ward, 1934.
Voltaire. London and New York, Sheed and Ward, 1936.
Dynamic Religion, with others. N.p., 1938.
Orchard's Bay. London and New York, Sheed and Ward, 1939; as *The Incompleat Gardener,* London, Sheed and Ward, 1955.
Pageant of Letters. New York, Sheed and Ward, 1940.
The Edge of the Abyss. New York, Dutton, 1942; London, Murray, 1944.
Horace: A Portrait. New York, Sheed and Ward, 1947; as *Portrait of Horace,* London, Sheed and Ward, 1947.
Two Worlds for Memory (autobiography). London, Sheed and Ward, and Philadelphia, Lippincott, 1953.
The Accusing Ghost; or, Justice for Casement. London, Gollancz, 1957; as *The Accusing Ghost of Roger Casement,* New York, Citadel Press, 1957.

Editor, *The Golden Book of Catholic Poetry.* Philadelphia, Lippincott, 1946.

*

Critical Study: *Alfred Noyes* by Walter Copeland Jerrold, London, Shaylor, 1930.

*   *   *

Alfred Noyes published his first book of poetry in 1902, when he was hardly into his 20s, but his work remained firmly anchored in the traditions of the 19th century and he spent his entire literary life railing against the iniquities of the 20th. Whenever he dabbled in visionary prophecy, as he did in such poems as "Lucifer's Feast" and in his scientific romance *The Last Man,* he produced images of horror and doom, and the two World Wars through which he lived served to confirm his faith in the acuity of his imagination. His magnum opus, the verse trilogy *The Torch-Bearers,* set out to celebrate the triumphant progress of scientific discovery—the first volume deals with the wondrous revelations of astronomy and the second with the sciences of the earth, especially evolutionary theory—but his subsequent conversion to Roman Catholicism was correlated with an abrupt shift in outlook. In the third volume the march of science becomes a journey undertaken by a modern Ship of Fools, whose equipment with radio enables it to steer more accurately but threatens to deflect the attention of passengers and crew from the awareness that their ultimate destination lies beyond this world.

As might be expected of a determinedly anti-Modernist poet whose great hero was Tennyson, Noyes embarked upon numerous poetic journeys to the Land of Faerie, which is displayed in familiar guise in *The Forest of Wild Thyme* and in a rather bizarre Orientalized form in *The Flower of Old Japan.* The imaginary Medieval kingdom of Prester John is featured in one of his best-known ballads, "Forty Singing Seamen," while various English legends are used in his patriotic works, which routinely invoke the imagery of English fairy mythology. In *Drake: An English Epic* the links are metaphorical, but when dealing with figures of dubious historicity Noyes felt free to make them literal, as in the verse play *Sherwood; or, Robin Hood and the Three Kings,* which features a fairy *deus ex machina.* His early short stories, however, use fantastic motifs in a very different way; "The Lusitania Waits" and "The Log of the Evening Star" in *Walking Shadows* are orthodox and rather pedestrian ghost stories. The later collection *The Hidden Player* consists of evident hackwork feebly imitative of Conan Doyle, but the allegorical "Checkmate," which features a fateful game against an invisible player, and "The Immortal," which features a problematic elixir of life, are of some interest.

The Last Man made a notable contribution to the history of science fiction by virtue of its introduction of the "doomsday weapon"—an ultimate deterrent whose use obliterates aggressors and those under threat without discrimination—but it is firmly rooted in the morbid tradition of "last man" fiction and poetry which flourished in the early 19th century in the wake of Cousin de Grandville's *Le Dernier Homme* (1805; translated into English in 1806) and extended into the 20th by courtesy of M. P. Shiel's remarkable allegory of evolution (modelled on the Book of Job) *The Purple Cloud* (1901). Noyes' God—being infinitely more orthodox in his methods than Shiel's—has far less difficulty designing a concluding miracle, preserving not only the Last Man and the Last Woman but also a company of Tuscan peasants and a Benedictine Monastery, but not all readers will agree with Noyes' opinion that this situation qualifies as the best possible launching-pad for the rebirth of civilization.

The Devil Takes a Holiday, Noyes' only *bona fide* fantasy novel, takes its inspiration from the discovery and use of the atom bomb, which Noyes naturally construed as an authentic doomsday weapon. The advent of such a device seemed to him so horrific that it forced him to the remarkable imaginative extreme of having the Devil himself arrive on earth (in California, of course, in the guise of an international financier) to condemn it. The Devil's holiday is, of course, a comic affair but the comedy serves to underscore the dark insistence that scientific progress and human irresponsibility in deploying its technological harvest have brought unprecedented and nigh-unthinkable evils into the world. Noyes might have taken some inspiration from Robert Nathan's *The Innocent Eve* (1951), which similarly involves a sympathetic Satan with the atom bomb in a California setting, and it is possible that Nathan was aware of Noyes' novel when he produced his second disquisition on the same theme, *Heaven and Hell and the Megas Factor* (1975).

As a diehard enemy of Modernism, Noyes was doomed to plumb the depths of unfashionability long before he died, and he lived to see his once-popular poetry derided and damned by Leavisite critics. Even if it is regarded merely as a historical curiosity, however, his fairy poetry is a significant contribution to that quaint but not insignificant sub-genre, and *The Devil Takes a Holiday* is an interesting example of English Literary Satanism.

—Brian Stableford

NYE, Robert

Nationality: British. **Born:** London, 15 March 1939. **Education:** Dormans Land, Sussex; Hamlet Court, Westcliff, Essex; Southend High School, Essex. **Family:** Married 1) Judith Pratt in 1959 (divorced 1967), three sons; 2) Aileen Campbell in 1968, one daughter, one stepdaughter, and one stepson. **Career:** Since 1961 freelance writer; since 1967 poetry editor, *The Scotsman;* since 1971 poetry critic, *The Times.* Writer-in-residence, University of Edinburgh, 1976-77. **Awards:** Eric Gregory award, 1963; Scottish Arts Council bursary, 1970, 1973, and publication award, 1970, 1976; James Kennaway Memorial award, 1970; *Guardian* Fiction prize, 1976; Hawthornden prize, 1977. Fellow, Royal Society of Literature, 1977; Society of Authors travel scholarship, 1991. **Agent:** Sheil Land Associates, 43 Doughty Street, London WC1N 2LF, England; or, Wallace, Aitken, and Sheil Inc., 118 East 61st Street, New York, NY 10021, USA. **Address:** 2 Westbury Crescent, Wilton, Cork, Ireland.

FANTASY PUBLICATIONS

Novels

Merlin. London, Hamish Hamilton, 1978; New York, Putnam, 1979.
Faust. London, Hamish Hamilton, 1980; New York, Putnam, 1981.

Other (for children)

Taliesin. London, Faber, 1966; New York, Hill and Wang, 1967.
March Has Horse's Ears. London, Faber, 1966; New York, Hill and Wang, 1967.
Bee Hunter: Adventures of Beowulf. London, Faber, 1968; as *Beowulf: A New Telling,* New York, Hill and Wang, 1968; as *Beowulf, The Bee Hunter,* Faber, 1972.
Wishing Gold. London, Macmillan, 1970; New York, Hill and Wang, 1971.

Poor Pumpkin. London, Macmillan, 1971; as *The Mathematical Princess and Other Stories,* New York, Hill and Wang, 1972.

Cricket: Three Stories. Indianapolis, Bobbs Merrill, 1975; as *Once upon Three Times,* London, Benn, 1978.

Out of the World and Back Again. London, Collins, 1977; as *Out of This World and Back Again,* Indianapolis, Bobbs Merrill, 1978.

The Bird of the Golden Land. London, Hamish Hamilton, 1980.

Harry Pay the Pirate. London, Hamish Hamilton, 1981.

Three Tales (includes *Beowulf, Wishing Gold, Taliesin*). London, Hamish Hamilton, 1983.

Other Publications

Novels

Doubtfire. London, Calder and Boyars, and New York, Hill and Wang, 1968.

Falstaff. London, Hamish Hamilton, and Boston, Little Brown, 1976.

The Voyage of the Destiny. London, Hamish Hamilton, and New York, Putnam, 1982.

The Memoirs of Lord Byron. London, Hamish Hamilton, 1989.

The Life and Death of My Lord Gilles de Rais. London, Hamish Hamilton, 1990.

Mrs. Shakespeare: The Complete Works. London, Sinclair Stevenson, 1993.

Short Stories

Tales I Told My Mother. London, Calder and Boyars, 1969; New York, Hill and Wang, 1970.

Penguin Modern Stories 6, with others. London, Penguin, 1970.

The Facts of Life and Other Fictions. London, Hamish Hamilton, 1983.

Plays

Sawney Bean, with Bill Watson (produced Edinburgh, 1969; London, 1972; New York, 1982). London, Calder and Boyars, 1970.

Sisters (broadcast 1969; produced Edinburgh, 1973). Included in *Penthesilea, Fugue, and Sisters,* 1975.

Penthesilea, adaptation of the play by Heinrich von Kleist (broadcast 1971; produced London, 1983). Included in *Penthesilea, Fugue, and Sisters,* 1975.

The Seven Deadly Sins: A Mask, music by James Douglas (produced Stirling, 1973; Edinburgh, 1974). Rushden, Northamptonshire, Omphalos Press, 1974.

Mr. Poe (produced Edinburgh and London, 1974).

Penthesilea, Fugue, and Sisters. London, Calder and Boyars, 1975.

Radio Plays: *Sisters,* 1969; *A Bloody Stupit Hole,* 1970; *Reynolds, Reynolds,* 1971; *Penthesilea,* 1971; *The Devil's Jig,* with Humphrey Searle, from a work by Thomas Mann, 1980.

Poetry

Juvenilia 1. Northwood, Middlesex, Scorpion Press, 1961.

Juvenilia 2. Lowestoft, Suffolk, Scorpion Press, 1963.

Darker Ends. London, Calder and Boyars, and New York, Hill and Wang, 1969.

Agnus Dei. Rushden, Northamptonshire, Sceptre Press, 1973.

Two Prayers. Richmond, Surrey, Keepsake Press, 1974.

Five Dreams. Rushden, Northamptonshire, Sceptre Press, 1974.

Divisions on a Ground. Manchester, Carcanet, 1976.

A Collection of Poems 1955-1988. London, Hamish Hamilton, 1990.

Other

Editor, *A Choice of Sir Walter Ralegh's Verse.* London, Faber, 1972.

Editor, *William Barnes: A Selection of His Poems.* Oxford, Carcanet, 1972.

Editor, *A Choice of Swinburne's Verse.* London, Faber, 1973.

Editor, *The Faber Book of Sonnets.* London, Faber, 1976; as *A Book of Sonnets,* New York, Oxford University Press, 1976.

Editor, *The English Sermon 1750-1850.* Cheadle, Cheshire, Carcanet, 1976.

Editor, *PEN New Poetry.* London, Quartet, 1986.

Editor, with Elizabeth Friedmann and Alan J. Clark. *First Awakenings: The Early Poems of Laura Riding.* Manchester, Carcanet, and New York, Persea Press, 1992.

Editor, *A Selection of the Poems of Laura Riding.* Manchester, Carcanet, 1994.

*

Manuscript Collections: University of Edinburgh; University of Texas, Austin; Colgate University, Hamilton, New York; National Library of Scotland, Edinburgh.

*   *   *

There is a point when it is difficult to tell where historical fiction ends and historical fantasy begins. When that point is further confused by unsettling postmodern techniques—anachronisms, lists, the breaking down of the distinction between author, character and reader—it becomes even harder. It is this imprecise territory which Robert Nye occupies.

Typically he takes characters who are part historical, part literary, part mythical—Falstaff, Faust, Gilles de Rais—and presents either their autobiography or the memoirs of a close companion. The writing of the book becomes the key event within the novel. Thus, in *Merlin,* Merlin is apparently the narrator of his own life but suspects that the book is actually being written by the Devil his father, while the Devil believes he is writing the book but suspects that the shape of the narrative is slipping from his control. Similarly in *Faust,* Kit Wagner sets out secretly to write the story of the old magician but cannot avoid the suspicion that Faust is manipulating the story.

All the writers who occupy centre stage, in every one of Nye's adult novels from *Falstaff* on, proclaim that they are trying to pin the truth to the page. Wagner is perhaps the archetypal example, a man who believes nothing, trying to steer a middle course between Faust's conviction about his pact with the devil and Helen of Troy's devout and loudly proclaimed faith in the Catholic church. Wagner's account of the last 40 days before Faust's debt to the devil comes due is meant to give the lie to their belief, but he finds himself having to set down strange events which cannot be explained by his lack of belief. It is as if the act of writing in itself is an act of lying; Nye's subject is the impossibility of truth. As Nye himself has said: "The connection between fiction and lying interests me.

As a matter of fact I do not write short stories so much as tall stories, fibs, lies, whoppers."

It is such tall stories which make his central characters larger than life, as if, in other ways, the page cannot contain them. They are rumbustious, earthy figures, given to exaggeration and lechery. Falstaff begins his memoirs by claiming to have been "begotten on the giant of Cerne Abbas" and devotes an entire chapter to the art of farting. Faust is perpetually drunken and "so real you can smell him through oak doors five inches thick." Merlin is repeatedly involved, first as voyeur, later as participant, in sexual scenes which always follow the same significant pattern. Their historical milieu is gritty and carefully researched, yet this realism is always overlaid with legend. The historical John Fastolf still fits within his life the exploits of the Shakespearian braggart, often in variant forms as when the Battle of Gadshill is described three different ways. Merlin, witnessing his life from within the crystal cave, may write with a very modern sensibility and a string of scatological jokes, yet these postmodern games still contain a very straightforward account of the most familiar features of his legend. He stops Vortigern's tower destroying itself by releasing the dragons trapped under the hill, he brings Stonehenge from Ireland, he disguises Uther as the Duke of Cornwall so that Uther might lie with Ygraine and beget Arthur, he hides Arthur away in the forest until the boy is old enough to draw the sword from the stone, and he accompanies Arthur and his court on the quest for the Holy Grail. However real the tone, however clever the jokes and wordplay, the magic is not questioned. In the short story "Glendower" the portents which attend the birth of Owain Glendower are never given anything but a supernatural explanation. While his experimental early novelette, "The Same Old Story" contains as its centrepiece a fairly straight retelling of the traditional story of Reynardine. Even the sceptic Wagner, in *Faust,* must accept the evidence of his own eyes when, for instance, he, Faust and Helen are transported instantly from Germany to the wedding feast of Henry VIII.

Yet overlaying this overt magic is yet another magic, the magic of words, the way fiction creates its own realities. Mostly Nye uses this to upset our expectations: his story "The Whole Story," for instance, features Gertrude Stein, D. H. Lawrence, James Joyce, Kipling, Chesterton and Yeats, but in this story Stein is the heiress of Wuthering Heights, Lawrence is her fiancé, Kipling is a butler with a penchant for nudity, and Chesterton a detective investigating a scheme by Joyce and Yeats to usurp the Nobel Prize for Literature. In the novels these games with fictionality provide a third and distinct perspective on what is written. There is the truth the narrator is trying to tell; there is the legend which shapes the overall story; and there is the sudden conscious and self-referential fiction which breaks the frame for the reader. In *Merlin* there is the image of the devil smoking cigarettes and providing constant re-interpretations of events in previous chapters. Mrs. Shakespeare can make a casual aside which the reader will pick up as a knowing reference to Jane Austen. These dislocations, fictions within fictions— Merlin listing what is to come in his book before he has yet written it, Wagner becoming more and more uncertain of the truth as the scenes he describes undermine what he has previously said— leave the reader deliberately lost between worlds. By the time one has unravelled the layers of truth and fiction, lies and belief that form these complex, hilarious books, one can never be quite certain whether the narrator is consciously telling the truth or Nye is consciously creating a fiction.

—Paul Kincaid

O'BRIEN, Flann

Pseudonym for Brian O'Nolan (or O Nuilláin). **Other Pseudonym:** Myles na gCopaleen. **Nationality:** Irish. **Born:** Strabane, County Tyrone, 5 October 1911. **Education:** Synge Street School, Dublin; Blackrock College, Dublin; University College, Dublin, B.A. 1932, M.A. 1935. Travelling scholarship to Germany, 1933-34. **Family:** Married Evelyn MacDonnell in 1948. **Career:** Civil servant, Dublin, 1935-53, and columnist, *Irish Times,* 1940-66. **Awards:** AE Memorial Fund prize, 1939. **Died:** 1 April 1966.

FANTASY PUBLICATIONS

Novels

At Swim-Two-Birds. London, Longman, 1939; New York, Pantheon, 1951.
The Dalkey Archive. London, MacGibbon and Kee, 1964.
The Third Policeman. London, MacGibbon and Kee, 1967.

OTHER PUBLICATIONS

Novels

The Hard Life: An Exegesis of Squalor. London, MacGibbon and Kee, 1961.
An Béal Bocht (as Myles na gCopaleen; in Gaelic). Dublin, National Press, 1941; translated as *The Poor Mouth: A Bad Story About the Hard Life,* London, Hart Davis MacGibbon, 1973.

Short Stories

Stories and Plays. London, Hart Davis MacGibbon, 1973.
The Various Lives of Keats and Chapman, and The Brother, edited by Benedict Kiely. London, Hart Davis MacGibbon, 1976.

Plays

Thirst (sketch; produced 1942).
The Insect Play, from a play by Karel Capek (produced 1943).
Faustus Kelly (produced 1943). Dublin, Cahill, 1943.
Mairead Gillan, from a play by Brinsley McNamara (as Brian O Nuilláin; in Gaelic). Dublin, Oifig an tSoláthair, 1953.

Other

Cruiskeen Lawn (as Myles na gCopaleen). Dublin, *Irish Times,* 1943.
The Best of Myles: A Selection from Cruiskeen Lawn, edited by Kevin Nolan. London, Hart Davis MacGibbon, 1968.
Further Cuttings from Cruiskeen Lawn, edited by Kevin Nolan. London, Hart Davis MacGibbon, 1976.
The Hair of the Dogma: A Further Selection from Cruiskeen Lawn, edited by Kevin Nolan. London, Hart Davis MacGibbon, 1977.
A Flann O'Brien Reader, edited by Stephen Jones. New York, Viking, 1978.
The Other Myles, edited and translated by Patrick C. Power. N.p., 1978.

Myles Away from Dublin, edited by Martin Green. London, Granada, 1985.
Myles Before Myles, edited by John Wyse Jackson. London, Grafton, 1988.

*

Critical Studies: *Myles: Portraits of Brian O'Nolan* edited by Timothy O'Keefe, London, Brian and O'Keefe, 1973; *Flann O'Brien: A Critical Introduction* by Anne Clissman, Dublin, Gill and MacMillan, 1975; *Four Irish Legendary Figures in "At Swim Two Birds"* by Eva Wappling, Uppsala University, 1984; *Alive Alive O!: Flann O'Brien's "At Swim-Two-Birds"* edited by Rudiger Imhof, Dublin, Wolfhound Press, 1985; *Flann O'Brien: An Illustrated Biography* by Peter Costello and Peter van der Kamp, London, Bloomsbury, 1988; *No Laughing Matter: The Life and Times of Flann O'Brien* by Anthony Cronin, London, Grafton, 1989.

*   *   *

It is typical that Flann O'Brien's comic fantastic masterpiece should contain its own justificatory manifesto embedded within it. The novel's narrator (typically) in a pub argues that "a satisfactory novel should be a self-evident sham to which the reader could regulate at will the degree of his credulity. It was undemocratic to compel characters to be uniformly good or bad or poor or rich. Each should be allowed a private life . . . Characters should be interchangeable as between one book and another. The entire corpus of existing literature should be regarded as a limbo from which discerning authors could draw characters as required . . ." At the end of the narrator's discourse, his interlocutor, a Dublin student called Brinsley replies: "That is all my bum." *At Swim-Two-Birds* is one of the most famous modernist novels of the 20th century.

In this complexly structured, Shandyesque book not only are stories framed within stories, but the frame structure is unstable, so that characters in the framed stories may control events in the story which frames their own. An idle pub-crawling student is writing a novel about a novelist called Dermot Trellis. Trellis in turn is writing a novel about John Furriskey, a character he does not like and whom he has determined to present as depraved. However, Furriskey seizes the opportunity presented by Trellis's falling asleep to lead a virtuous life and later to torment his author by getting him written into a painful scene, in which he is tormented by the Pooka. The Pooka, like his rival the Good Fairy, is a creature from Irish folklore who has wandered into 20th-century Dublin. Similarly the legendary Irish hero Finn Mac Cool and mad king Sweeney have been borrowed from Ireland's heroic past. The novel brilliantly parodies a large range of Irish literary genres, from the high diction of ancient bards to contemporary Dublin journalism. It also invents a new genre, the Irish western, and features a rustling episode and a shootout between cowboys in the Dublin area. Much of the fun of *At Swim-Two-Birds* comes not so much from the ludicrously unstable narrative structure or from the certainly bizarre events, but from O'Brien's brilliance as a parodist. In this and others of his books he showed that he had a finely attuned ear for the stale cliches of advertising and journalism, the stately periphrases of the drunk, the would-be fine writing of amateurs and sheer Dublin blarney. The whole thing, free-wheeling, loose-limbed nonsense about nothing very much—unless it is the possibilities of fiction and language—reads as if it was composed in a pub.

The Hard Life is rich in eccentric characters and contains fantastic elements, such as the patent medicine that makes one of the char-

acters fall through a staircase, but it is not in essence a fantasy novel. However, *The Dalkey Archive,* although it is not one O'Brien's fantastic masterpieces, is certainly fantasy. Mick the protagonist encounters the crackpot philosopher-scientist De Selby, who has a scheme for abolishing time and thereby destroying the world. In order to foil De Selby's scheme, Mick goes in search of James Joyce, who has not died, but has gone into hiding in a remote part of Ireland. Joyce, when discovered, proves to be a keen Catholic, and the novel's wild plot provides lots of space for farcical theological debate, in which St. Augustine also participates.

The Third Policeman is a better book. It is a weird, comic, Irish blend of *Crime and Punishment* and Dante's *Inferno.* It begins: "Not everyone knows how I killed old Philip Mathers, smashing his jaw in with my spade; but first it is better to speak of my friendship with John Diviney because it is he who first knocked old Mathers down by giving him a great blow in the neck with a special bicycle-pump which he manufactured himself out of a hollow iron bar." Bicycles haunt this novel. The narrator, crazy kind of idiot-savant, after murdering Mathers for his money falls into the clutches of the local constabulary. The narrator, who does not realize that he is already dead, is promised that he will be hanged by the police. In the meantime, the policemen good-humouredly pass on instruction in all sorts of curious lore. One of their many pet theories is that bicycles and their riders take on each other's characteristics as their constituent atoms mingle over time. They also take the narrator to a strange sort of underworld where no time passes and where anything can be had for the asking, but none of it can be brought back above ground. Although an attempt by a band of one-legged men to rescue the (one-legged) narrator from his hanging fails to materialize, he subsequently effects what he thinks is his escape and, after some curious encounters, including one with the "third policeman," returns home, only to discover that he himself has been murdered by his friend Diviney years ago.

A special and relishable feature of the book is its footnotes, masterpieces of cod scholarship devoted to elucidating the philosophy and bibliography of De Selby. De Selby is a philosopher whose ideas are much more interesting than they are plausible. For example, De Selby held that photography demonstrates that motion is an illusion. Again, he argued, against the received wisdom, that the regular occurrence of nightfall is really due to accretions of "black air." There are many things to marvel over in de Selby's philosophy. Although there is comedy on every page, the overall impression left on the reader is unmistakably sinister. The message of O'Brien's courteous but avenging policemen is that in some way the torments of Hell and the problem of infinity are intimately linked.

—Robert Irwin

OFFUTT, Andrew J(efferson V.)

Pseudonyms: John Cleve, Jeff Douglas, J. X. Williams (house name). **Nationality:** American. **Born:** Louisville, Kentucky, 16 August 1937. **Education:** University of Louisville, B.A. in English 1955, M.A. in history, Ph.D. in psychology. **Family:** Married Mary Joe McCartney McCabe in 1958; two daughters and two sons. **Career:** Sales agent, Procter and Gamble, 1957-62; agency manager, Coastal States Life Insurance Company, Lexington, Kentucky, 1963-68; insurance agent, Andrew Offutt Associates, 1968-71; since 1971, full-time writer. Treasurer, 1973-76, and President, 1976-78, Science Fiction Writers of America. **Awards:** *If* prize, 1954. **Address:** Funny Farm, Haldeman, Kentucky 40329, USA.

FANTASY PUBLICATIONS

Novels (series: Cormac mac Art; War of the Wizards; Conan; War of the Gods on Earth; Thieves' World)

Sword of the Gael (Cormac mac Art). New York, Zebra, 1975.
The Black Sorcerer of the Black Castle. Aberdeen, Maryland, Hall Publications, 1976.
The Undying Wizard (Cormac mac Art). New York, Zebra, 1976.
Demon in the Mirror, with Richard K. Lyon (War of the Wizards). New York, Pocket Books, 1977.
The Mists of Doom (Cormac mac Art). New York, Zebra, 1977.
The Sign of the Moonbow (Cormac mac Art). New York, Zebra, 1977 (1980 Ace edition incorrectly credits Keith Taylor as co-author).
My Lord Barbarian. New York, Ballantine, 1977; London, Magnum, 1979.
Conan and the Sorcerer. New York, Grosset and Dunlap, 1978.
Conan, The Sword of Skelos. New York, Bantam, 1979.
The Iron Lords (War of the Gods). New York, Harcourt, Brace, 1979.
Shadows Out of Hell (War of the Gods). New York, Berkley, 1980.
Conan the Mercenary (incorporates *Conan and the Sorcerer*). London, Sphere, 1980; New York, Ace, 1981.
When Death Birds Fly, with Keith Taylor (Cormac mac Art). New York, Ace, 1980.
The Eyes of Sarsis, with Richard K. Lyon (War of the Wizards). New York, Pocket Books, 1980.
Web of the Spider, with Richard K. Lyon (War of the Wizards). New York, Pocket Books, 1981.
The Tower of Death, with Keith Taylor (Cormac mac Art). New York, Ace, 1982.
The Lady of the Snowmist (War of the Gods). New York, Ace, 1983.
Shadowspawn (Thieves' World). New York, Ace, 1987.
Deathknight. New York, Ace, 1990.
The Shadow of Sorcery. New York, Ace, 1993.

Other

Editor, *Swords Against Darkness 1-5.* New York, Zebra, 5 vols., 1977-79.

OTHER PUBLICATIONS

Novels

The Sex Pill (as J. X. Williams). San Diego, Phenix Publishers, 1968.
Evil Is Live Spelled Backwards. New York, Paperback Library, 1970.
The Balling Machine, with D. Bruce Berry (as Jeff Douglas). New York, Bee-Line Books, 1971.

The Great 24-Hour Thing. Los Angeles, Orpheus Press, 1971.
The Castle Keeps. New York, Berkley, 1972; London, Magnum, 1978.
Messenger of Zhuvastou. New York, Berkley, 1973, London, Magnum, 1977.
Ardor on Aros. New York, Dell, 1973.
The Galactic Rejects (for children). New York, Lothrop, 1973.
Operation: Super Ms. New York, Berkley, 1974.
The Genetic Bomb, with D. Bruce Berry. New York, Warner, 1975.
Chieftain of Andor. New York, Dell, 1976; as *Clansman of Andor,* London, Magnum, 1978.
King Dragon. New York, Ace, 1980.

Novels as John Cleve (co-authors uncredited)

Jodinareh. North Hollywood, Brandon House, 1970.
The Juice of Love. New York, Midwood Books, 1970.
Barbarana. North Hollywood, Brandon House, 1971.
Manlib! New York, Carlyle Communications, 1974.
The Sexorcist. New York, Carlyle Communications, 1974; as *Unholy Revelry,* New York, Carlyle Communications, 1976.
The Accursed Tower. New York, Grove Press, 1974.
The Passionate Princess. New York, Grove Press, 1974.
Julamer the Lioness. New York, Grove Press, 1975.
My Lady Queen. New York, Grove Press, 1975.
Of Alien Bondage. New York, Berkley, 1982.
Corundum's Woman. New York, Berkley, 1982.
Escape from Macho. New York, Berkley, 1982.
Satana Enslaved. New York, Berkley, 1982.
Master of Misfit. New York, Berkley, 1982.
Purrfect Plunder. New York, Berkley, 1982.
The Manhuntress, with Geo. W. Proctor. New York, Berkley, 1982.
Under Twin Suns. New York, Berkley, 1982.
In Quest of Qalara. New York, Berkley, 1983.
The Yoke of Shen, with Geo. W. Proctor. New York, Berkley, 1983.
The Iceworld Connection, with Jack C. Haldeman II and Vol Haldeman. New York, Berkley, 1983.
Star Slaver, with G. C. Edmondson. New York, Berkley, 1983.
Jonuta Rising, with Victor Koman. New York, Berkley, 1983.
Assignment: Hellhole, with Robin Kincaid. New York, Berkley, 1983.
Lady Beth, edited by John Cleve: A Victorian Classic. New York, Grove Press, 1984.
Starship Sapphire, with Roland Green. New York, Berkley, 1984.
The Planet Murderer, with Dwight V. Swain. New York, Berkley, 1984.
The Carnadyne Horde, with Victor Koman. New York, Berkley, 1984.
Race Across the Stars, with Robin Kincaid. New York, Berkley, 1984.
King of the Slavers. New York, Berkley, 1985.
Saladin's Spy. New York, Grove Press, 1986.

*　　　*　　　*

The career of Andrew J. Offutt could be used to exemplify the disastrous effects of the modern marketplace in fantasy and science fiction. By the early 1970s, Offutt had earned a modest reputation for writing offbeat, often humorous science fiction and fantasy—emphasized by the habit of not capitalizing his name. Then, after becoming a full-time writer, Offutt committed himself to churning out product, including novels about Robert E. Howard's Cormac mac Art and Conan, a dreadful science fiction series under a pseudonym, and several stories and a novel for the Thieves' World series. As a result, he is now virtually unknown and rarely publishes; one hopes he invested his money wisely.

To appreciate the unique talent Offutt once seemed to be, one must turn to early works: "Population Implosion" (in *World's Best Science Fiction 1968* edited by Donald A. Wollheim and Terry Carr, 1969), where a man learns that large numbers of inexplicable deaths are occurring because there are a finite number of souls—five billion—so that now, with the world's population at that level, every new birth demands a corresponding death; "For Value Received" (in *Again, Dangerous Visions* edited by Harlan Ellison, 1971), a surrealistic tale of a newborn child's parents who refuse to pay a disputed bill, leaving the girl to be raised to adulthood in the hospital; *Ardor on Aros,* an amusing tribute to Edgar Rice Burroughs's Mars novels; and *The Black Sorcerer of the Black Castle,* a brief and lively Conan parody where Kimon the Konerian uses his sword Goreater to defeat occult menaces but is double-crossed by the woman he was rescuing. Not exactly masterpieces, the stories do display a quirky imagination and humour rarely found in later works.

Still, Offutt's career as a writer-for-hire began rather well with *Sword of the Gael,* which merits recognition as one of the best homages to Howard ever written. Unjustly exiled from Ireland, Cormac mac Art rediscovers his lost love in a strange island castle, battles a monstrous snake, octopus and human enemies, and finally reaches Ireland, where he wins a competition to earn redemption. But an air of contrivance creeps into the next book, *The Undying Wizard,* where Cormac, now called the reincarnation of Howard's King Kull (thus diminishing his distinctive character), must confront Kull's old enemy, the unkillable wizard Thulsa Doom, discovered when Cormac returns to the castle. *Sword of the Gael,* about a disgraced hero who struggles to return home and regain a place in society, is a story that meant something; in *The Undying Wizard,* Offutt mechanically sets up an extended Punch-and-Judy show, with Doom as the perfect foil who can be butchered again and again by Cormac and still come back for another round. A similar emptiness permeates *The Mists of Doom,* where Doom transports his foes to another dimension and to more meaningless adventures.

Offutt might have redeemed himself when asked to write a new Conan novel, but *Conan and the Sorcerer* is a tepid tale that gives Howard's barbarian little chance to display his prowess or unique personality. The novel is also marred by shoddy plotting; at one point, the dead brother of Conan's foe describes three special devices that are the only ways to defeat the wizard, preparing readers for a later quest to obtain the devices; when Conan instead quickly kills the wizard with a dose of his own poison, readers have every right to feel cheated. While writing more Cormac mac Art and Conan novels, Offutt also earned some money from two trilogies: the War of the Wizards, which grandiosely recounts the far-ranging and convoluted struggle of two powerful wizards, prominently involving a resourceful heroine; and the War of the Gods on Earth, the saga of a hero given conflicting assignments by rival gods which is distinguished only by its unusually awful writing.

The few people who have actually read all his novels might endlessly debate which one represents the low point of Offutt's career; but one strong candidate for that dubious honour would be *Shadowspawn,* featuring the colourless master thief of the shared Thieves' World. In the novel, he and his girlfriend languidly travel from Sanctuary to a new city where they slowly become disturbed by a dull mystery involving magical coins and a vengeful wizard. *Shadowspawn* reads like a novelette padded out to become a novel; when a writer takes over a page to discuss various clothing styles in a city, summarizes all preceding adventures involving his hero, lavishes attention on minor characters, and describes in extreme detail lengthy negotiations to sell some horses, these are sure signs of a desperate struggle to achieve a certain word length. The excess verbiage might be excused if there were any signs that the underlying story was written for any reason other than to fulfil a contract; unfortunately, except for a very few flashes of the old Offutt wit, there is no such evidence here.

As if belatedly realizing that this derivative and lifeless work was ruining his reputation, Offutt then rallied his energies to produce the genuinely original—and worthwhile—*Deathknight.* Marketed as and maintaining the tone of fantasy, it gradually emerges as a science fiction novel about a far-future Earth devastated by global disaster that has renounced technology and large government in favour of a simple feudal society loosely united by an enigmatic group of warriors known as Deathknights. The Deathknight Falc and his unwanted companion, a stubborn young woman, discover and thwart a plot to discredit the Deathknights, reestablish an empire, and get back on the path of scientific progress. The novel succeeds because Offutt meticulously and convincingly develops his medieval world and makes his characters complex and involving; also, Offutt remarkably departs from the usual pattern of such novels by sympathizing with those who would still reject science, not those who would restore it. By this time, though, readers had no reason to expect a good novel from Offutt, so *Deathknight* did not receive the attention it deserved. For as Cormac mac Art learned, once you have lost your good name, it is hard to earn it back.

—Gary Westfahl

O'SHEA, (Catherine) Pat(ricia)

Nationality: Irish. **Born:** Patricia Shiels, in Galway, 22 January 1931. **Education:** Presentation Convent, 1935-44, and Convent of Mercy, 1945-47, both Galway. **Family:** Married J. J. O'Shea in 1953 (separated); one son. **Awards:** British Arts Council drama bursary, 1967. **Address:** 19 Chandos Road, Chorlton-cum-Hardy, Manchester M21 0SS, England.

FANTASY PUBLICATIONS

Novels

The Hounds of the Morrigan, illustrated by Stephen Lavis. Oxford, Oxford University Press, 1985; New York, Holiday House, 1986.
Finn MacCool and the Small Men of Deeds (retelling), illustrated by Stephen Lavis. Oxford, Oxford University Press, and New York, Holiday House, 1987.

*

Pat O'Shea comments:

To me, fantasy suggests the wonderful, the magical, the world of dreams. Magic, after all, is one of the oldest things. When the world was full of unexplainable wonders it existed before religion, and as religion before science, and as science before either of these things became systematic. And fantasy, from the Greek "phantazo," means to make visible, clear or manifest; whence phantasm, the word for a vision or dream. Coincidentally, *The Hounds of the Morrigan* began as a dream, that later became just a part of the story. And it was the liberation that fantasy brings to the imagination that I enjoyed most.

Previously, I had written for the theatre where one is always constricted by what is possible rather than what is imaginable, by the number of actors available or affordable and by the sets that could not be changed at the speed of thought. In my story there is no difficulty at all in having the Sergeant suddenly and surprisingly finding himself up the Amazon on a rubber duck one moment and back in the Garda Barracks sipping cocoa the next; an earwig who thinks he is Napoleon and leads his hordes into battle; the Morrigan blowing the half-moons off her fingernails to fly as sharp weapons, embedding themselves in the walls of a cave in a later battle; or the She-Warriors materializing from the dust-motes in a sunbeam and jumping down to earth. These would give the average stage director a few problems!

With fantasy it is easy to create a separate world where the imagination can run free. The only restriction is that world's own logic, which creates itself as the story is written; the one constraint is to keep within the logic of the world created. And fantasy is part of everyday life for all of us when we create scenarios about and around what is for us—the impossible or the hoped-for. The fantasy usually starts with, "What if. . . ." The dreams that follow cannot be described as other than fantasy—so it is not an alien or arcane property, the possession of a select few, but part of all of us; as children we practise it all the time. It seems to me that it is too much a part of us, and has been for too long a time, for it to be dismissed as escapist as sometimes happens, unless it is valid for other joys that lift us up from the mundane to be dismissed as well—like music, poetry, ceremonial happenings, drama and film.

*　　*　　*

Pat O'Shea's one full-length fantasy novel, *The Hounds of the Morrigan,* is a fat, colourful and satisfying tale of chases and quests through a modern Ireland interwoven with Faerie and thick with legend. Nominally written for young readers, it has wider appeal thanks to its inventiveness, breakneck pace, mythical erudition, exuberant humour and Celtic twilight shading occasionally into true darkness. Though not deep, it has great charm.

Young Pidge discovers the evil serpent Olc-Glas trapped in an old book by the binding words of St. Patrick, and the Morrigan's alarming but inept Hounds are soon in pursuit—though their initial strategy is a little transparent, consisting of badly lettered road signs: THIS IS A VERY SAFE ROAD. A BOY CAN CYCLE ON IT WITH HIS EYES SHUT . . . TRY IT TODAY.

The living image of Olc-Glas is cased in iron to be guarded by the Great Eel, who is nearly tempted from his duty by the Morrigan's deployment of that most attractive of all worms the (unwilling) Brandling Breac, only to be distracted by the malaprop frogs which Pidge and his much younger but redoubtably pig-headed sister Brigit have befriended by saving one from Macha and Bodhbe, the witches whose black-comedy rôles disguise their true

nature as other aspects of the three-in-one Morrigan, Queen of Destruction, who with Olc-Glas's power will become irresistible.

The pursuit of Pidge and Brigit across Ireland/Tir-na-nOg continues with this same breathless density: a talking ass carries them through a stone circle by secret paths to the railway station of Victorian Galway, where their next guide weaves through time and across water before being revealed as the legendary druid Cathbad, and the children continue by magical kite, flying swans, extinct Irish elk, and so on. Throughout, the creatures of the Dagda or Good Lord help them along, since the Dagda cannot directly intervene until the Morrigan raises her own hand against them. A wondrously daft sequence features militant earwigs led by their own Napoleon ("If I have to be loony to be great—adieu, sanity; ze cost is but a trifle") in a merciless nose-nipping assault on the Hounds. Cats, spiders, a weathervane, a fox, ducks, geese and a homing pigeon also assist, each with its own peculiar way of speech. Heroes of myth like Cuchulain and Queen Maeve and the gods themselves turn out to fight for the good cause. There is much effective blarney. (It may be a gentle homage to James Stephens's *The Crock of Gold* when a Sergeant of the Gardai is repeatedly bewitched and bewildered by the evil three . . . converted, for example, to a gold charm on the Morrigan's bracelet.)

After some hair-raising final twists and obstacles—like the immense, oily maze which is a single fingerprint placed by the Morrigan on her magical map—the children thwart the evil goddess's scheme. Olc-Glas is destroyed and the world saved. The one sour note comes when, in the subtly cruel tradition of much children's fantasy, Pidge's and Brigit's memories of their adventure are erased by the kindly god of love Angus Og. Often afterwards they meet their best companion the fox and don't understand why he's so tame and seems to know them. Otherwise it's an excellent romp, full of colour and sunlight.

—David Langford

OWEN, Frank

Pseudonym: Roswell Williams. **Nationality:** American. **Born:** 1893. **Died:** 13 October 1968.

FANTASY PUBLICATIONS

Novels (series: Scobee Trent)

The House Mother (Trent). New York, Lantern Press, 1929.
Rare Earth (Trent). New York, Lantern Press, 1931.
Loves of Lo-Foh (as Roswell Williams). New York, Kendall, 1936.

Short Stories

The Wind That Tramps the World: Splashes of Chinese Color. New York, Lantern Press, 1929.
The Purple Sea: More Splashes of Chinese Color. New York, Lantern Press, 1929.
Della-Wu, Chinese Courtesan, and Other Oriental Love Tales. New York, Lantern Press, 1931.
A Husband for Kutani. New York, Furman, 1938.
The Porcelain Magician. New York, Gnome Press, 1948.

OTHER PUBLICATIONS

Novels

The Professional Virgin. New York, Lantern Press, 1931.
Three in a Bed. New York, Godwin, 1932.
The Damned Lover. New York, Macaulay, 1933.
Woman Without Love. New York, Watt, 1933.
The Hand-Made Lady. New York, Carlyle, 1934.
Vagabond Lady. New York, Macaulay, 1934.
Madonna of the Damned. N.p., 1935.
Dark Destiny (as Roswell Williams). New York, Elliot, 1936.
Between the Covers. New York, Macaulay, 1938.
The Scarlet Hill. New York, Carlyle House, 1941.

Fiction for Children

Coat Tales from the Pockets of the Happy Giant, with Ethel Owen. N.p., Abingdon Press, 1927.
Dream Hills of Happy Country, with Ethel Owen. N.p., Abingdon Press, 1928.
Wind-Blown Stories, with Ethel Owen. N.p., Abingdon Press, 1930.
Blue Highway, with Ethel Owen. N.p., Abingdon Press, 1932.

Play

Christmas Rehearsal, with Ethel Owen. N.p., Abingdon Press, 1935.

Poetry

Pictureland. New York, Lantern Press, 1929.

Other

Editor, *Bedside Bonanza; or, a Lodestone of Love and laughter.* New York, Fell, 1944.
Editor, *Murder for the Millions.* New York, Fell, 1946.
Editor, *Teen-Age Companion.* New York, Lantern Press, 1946.
Editor, *Fireside Mystery Book.* New York, Lantern Press, 1947.
Editor, *Teen-Age Outdoor Stories.* New York, Lantern Press, 1947.
Editor, *Teen-Age Sports Stories.* New York, Lantern Press, 1947.
Editor, *Teen-Age Baseball Stories.* New York, Lantern Press, 1948.
Editor, *Teen-Age Football Stories.* New York, Lantern Press, 1948.
Editor, *Teen-Age Mystery Stories.* New York, Lantern Press, 1948; as *Mystery Stories,* New York, Pocket, 1964.
Editor, *Teen-Age Stories of Action.* New York, Lantern Press, 1948.
Editor, *Teen-Age Winter Sports Stories.* New York, Lantern Press, 1949.
Editor, *Teen-Age Victory Parade.* New York, Lantern Press, 1950.

*   *   *

Little biographical information is available on this author. Sources are even divided as to which byline was his real name. As Hung Long Tom he wrote poetry; as Roswell Williams he wrote what E. F. Bleiler describes as "soft erotica"; he is also believed to have used the pseudonym Richard Kent. But he is remembered for pseudo-Chinese stories and novels under what was probably his real name, Frank Owen, which appeared in a variety of adventure and Oriental pulp magazines in the 1920s and 1930s, in addition to *Weird Tales.* His last collection was the first book published by Gnome Press, which went on to become a significant science fiction and fantasy specialty house.

By no means an important, or even very skilled writer, Owen is of more interest as a representative of a cultural phenomenon. He was one of the practitioners of the so-called "Oriental tale," setting his stories in that timeless, placid, fairy-tale China created in the Western imagination during the past two centuries. Ironically, as he wrote, the real China was undergoing some of the greatest convulsions in its long and often violent history. Only toward the end of his career did Owen touch, barely, on reality. Stories of the early 1940s show subtle, ultimately inscrutable Chinese easily able to handle the Japanese invaders. Whether Owen had ever visited Asia is uncertain. From the lack of specific cultural details in his fiction, it seems unlikely.

Owen's stories attempt delicate effects, as were traditional in Western "Oriental" tales. The prose tries to be poetic, but the author's clumsiness betrays him. He may be compared to Lafcadio Hearn and especially to Ernest Bramah, but is far inferior to either. His prose style resembles the occasionally quaint primitivism of David H. Keller, but the author's ear can apparently detect nothing wrong with a sentence like, "But at last he succeeded in getting his cosmos readjusted" (seemingly a feat worthy of a super-science hero of the E. E. "Doc" Smith mould, but what Owen means is the character reoriented himself in a strange situation) or even "he sped off on his endless tramp which never ends." (Both from "The Wind That Tramps the World.") In one story ("The Blue City") an alleged Chinese "mystic" sage launches into a lecture, not about the Tao or some Buddhist concept, but animal perception and the nature of the spectrum, as if he had just attended an experiment in some Western university laboratory and picked up much of the jargon. Indeed, Owen showed a consistent inability to achieve an Asian mind-set.

His fantastic concepts, not particularly Chinese, were occasionally interesting. In "The Blue City," the hero passes into the sky to view a city paradise, complete with beautiful maiden ready to embrace him. But if he lingers until dawn, the sunrise will destroy him in a searing, ecstatic burst of indescribable beauty. In the end, it does, but he meets the maiden again in spirit form. "The Tinkle of the Camel's Bell" echoes Nathaniel Hawthorne's "Rappaccini's Daughter" as much as Seabury Quinn's "The Phantom Farmhouse" (which appeared in *Weird Tales* three years earlier) and involves an immortal woman living in a phantom house. Whatever she touches, dies. And a few stories feature memorably grotesque images, such as the title object in "The Fan." It's made from the lips of a courtesan's former lovers.

With the beginning of the Cold War and the rise of the Maoist regime, the imaginary, magical China with its quietly wise mandarins and fairy-tale maidens ceased to be any more convincing than the Mars of Edgar Rice Burroughs. Charles G. Finney actually wrote an effective swan-song to the vanishing Oriental tale in "The Magician Out of Manchuria" (published in 1968 but probably written much earlier). Owen wasn't so deft. He merely became obsolete and his writing career ended.

—Darrell Schweitzer

P

PADGETT, Lewis. *See* KUTTNER, Henry.

————

PADGETT, Lewis. *See* MOORE, C(atherine) L(ucille).

————

PAGE, Norvell W(ooten)

Pseudonyms: Randolph Craig; Grant Stockbridge. **Nationality:** American. **Born:** Richmond, Virginia, 1904. **Career:** Journalist, New York *Herald Tribune, Times* and *World-Telegram,* 1924-34; full-time writer 1934-43. President, American Fiction Guild, 1934-35. Government report writer, 1943-45, 1948-49 and 1954-55. Publicist with Atomic Energy Commission, 1950-61. **Died:** 1961.

FANTASY PUBLICATIONS

Novels (series: Prester John in both books)

Flame Winds. New York, Berkley, 1969.
Sons of the Bear-God. New York, Berkley, 1969.

Novels as Randolph Craig (series: Dr. Skull in both books)

The City Condemned to Hell. Oak Lawn, Illinois, Pulp Press, 1975.
Satan's Incubators. Oak Lawn, Illinois, Pulp Press, 1975.

Novels as Grant Stockbridge (series: The Spider in all books)

Wings of the Black Death. New York, Berkley, 1969.
City of Flaming Shadows. New York, Berkley, 1969.
Death Reign of the Vampire King. New York, Pocket, 1975.
Hordes of the Red Butcher. New York, Pocket, 1975.
The City Destroyer. New York, Pocket, 1975.
Death and the Spider. New York, Pocket, 1975.
Builder of the Black Empire. New York, Dimedia, 1980.
Master of the Death Madness. New York, Dimedia, 1980.
Overlord of the Damned. New York, Dimedia, 1980.
The Citadel of Hell. Greece, Hanos, 1983.
The Spider and Hell's Factory. Greece, Hanos, 1984.
Satan's Death Blast. New York, Dimedia, 1984.
Corpse Cargo. New York, Dimedia, 1985.
Prince of Evil. New York, Dimedia, 1985.
The Spider, Master of Men! (includes "Secret City of Crime," "The Spider and the Pain Master"). New York, Carroll and Graf, 1991.
The Spider, Master of Men! #2 (includes "Dictator of the Damned," "The Mill-Town Massacres," both by Emile C. Tepperman). New York, Carroll and Graf, 1991.

The Spider, Master of Men! #3 (includes "Death's Crimson Juggernaut," "The Red Death Rain"). New York, Carroll and Graf, 1992.
The Spider, Master of Men! #4 (includes "Death Reign of the Vampire King," "The Pain Emperor"). New York, Carroll and Graf, 1992.
The Spider, Master of Men! #5 (includes "Judgment of the Damned," "Master of the Flaming Horde"). New York, Carroll and Graf, 1993.
The Spider, Master of Men! #6 (includes "Slaves of the Laughing Death," "Satan's Murder Machines"). New York, Carroll and Graf, 1993.
The Spider, Master of Men! #7 (includes "King of the Red Killers," "Green Globes of Death"). New York, Carroll and Graf, 1993.
The Spider, Master of Men! #8 (includes "The Devil's Paymaster," "Legions of the Accursed Light"). New York, Carroll and Graf, 1993.

*

Critical Study: *Spider* by Robert Sampson, Bowling Green, Ohio, Popular Press, 1987.

* * *

Norvell W. Page was one of the most prolific writers for the hero and mystery pulp magazines. In a single period of ten years he wrote over 250 stories of which almost half were short-novel length. He is best remembered today for authoring most of the lead novels featuring the Spider, a remorseless crusader against crime whose adventures were chronicled monthly in *The Spider* magazine.

Formerly a reporter on various New York papers, Page became noted for his eye for a story and his speed of composition. He began to sell hard-boiled detective stories to the pulps in 1930, the earliest known being "The Devil Muscles In" (*Detective-Dragnet Magazine,* 1930) under the name N. Wooten Page. He soon became a regular, his stories becoming increasingly more gruesome and bizarre. He had the lead novel, "Dance of the Skeletons," in the October 1933 *Dime Mystery* magazine, regarded now as the first of the weird-menace pulp issues. Page's story of fraudsters who disappear linked to a sudden appearance of many nameless skeletons set the trend for the grotesque which dominated these pulps during the 1930s.

Page was a likeable, bluff, bearded man who rapidly earned a reputation for delivering editorial needs to tight deadlines. In October 1933 Popular Publications launched *The Spider* magazine in an attempt to cash in on the popularity of *The Shadow* at Street and Smith. The first two novels were written by R. T. Maitland Scott around characters and plots suggested by publisher Henry Steeger, but after two novels Scott quit, and Page was asked if he would continue the series, now penned under the house name of Grant Stockbridge. Page was only too keen to oblige. Scott's rather mild-mannered gentleman crook was transformed into a larger-than-life vigilante who, with his girlfriend Nita Van Sloan and a small cohort of aides, seeks to rid America of increasingly fearsome master criminals. The Spider was the alter-ego of millionaire socialite Richard Wentworth, who would transform himself into the cloaked, hunchbacked and fanged Spider to seek vengeance.

The crimes became increasingly fantastic, though in most cases the villains employed scientific horrors rather than supernatural to wreak terror. New York was threatened by plagues, rabid animals, a metal-eating virus, Neanderthal men, robots, and endless cults and madmen. The most fantastic story of the series was "Death and the Spider" (January 1942) in which a supernatural agency personifying Death kills its way relentlessly toward America's government.

Page wrote about 90 of the 118 Spider novels, sharing the others with Emile C. Tepperman and Wayne Rogers. The speed at which they were written allowed for no finesse. Page's skill was to launch straight into the action and not to stop for 40,000 words. The action was violent; women were not safe, with rape and violation abundant. Wentworth and his helpers were frequently hospitalized, but always triumphed in the end. Nevertheless Page was able to develop the characters of Wentworth and Van Sloan through the series and they became immensely influential on later pulp- and comic-book heroes. Perhaps the most fascinating aspect is how Wentworth and the Spider became increasingly dual personalities of the same man, almost like Jekyll and Hyde. This affected Page himself who apparently frequently cavorted around the editorial offices and his home in Florida in a cape and slouch hat.

Throughout his period of writing for *The Spider,* Page poured out scores of stories for other magazines, all typical garish pulp fare, including one of the classic pulp titles of all time, "How Green Are My Corpses!" (*Dime Mystery,* 1941). Although his stories were frequently weird and bizarre, and always over the top, few were fantastic, but the best were three short novels he wrote for *Unknown.* Two of these, "Flame Winds" (June 1939) and "Sons of the Bear-God" (November 1939), feature Wan Tengri (Page's version of Prester John) who is a mighty gladiator from first-century Alexandria, who escapes to Central Asia and finds himself fighting Mongol magic. Page's incessant capacity for action gives the novels a vibrancy and excitement that overcomes any routine hackwork.

Page's third Prester John novel was rejected as being too formulaic. He had one further novel in *Unknown,* "But Without Horns" (June 1940), which is more in line with his Spider adventures. The novel follows the effects of a mutant superman (who never appears in the story) who is systematically destroying inferior mankind. Its parallels with Hitler's pogrom against the Jews are obvious.

Page is also credited with authoring two other weird-menace novels as Randolph Craig: "The City Condemned to Hell" for *The Octopus* and "Satan's Incubator" for *The Scorpion* (both 1939). Here Jeffrey Fairchild, alias Dr. Skull, alias the Skull Killer, finds himself battling supernatural foes which are manifestations of Satan seeking to create a Hell on Earth. The novels are similar to the Spider adventures, although the action is even more hectic and exhilarating, and bear all the hallmarks of Page's work. Research by Robert Weinberg, however, reveals that payments for the stories went to the husband-and-wife team of Edith and Ejler Jacobson. It is likely that the Jacobsons rewrote the second novel to convert it for the newly titled magazine.

Page ceased writing for the pulps in 1943 and became involved in wartime work for the government. He never returned to writing fiction. His Spider novels have always remained popular among pulp enthusiasts, and a number have been reprinted in the last 20 years. They remain quintessential examples of pulp writing at its most flamboyant.

—Mike Ashley

PAIN, Barry (Eric Odell)

Nationality: British. **Born:** Cambridge, 28 September 1864. **Military Service:** Royal Naval Volunteer Reserve, 1915-17: chief petty-officer. **Education:** Sedbergh School; Corpus Christie College, Cambridge, B.A. 1886 (editor, *Granta*). **Family:** Married Amelia Nina Anna Lehmann in 1892 (died 1920); two daughters. **Career:** Army coach, Guildford, Surrey, for four years; journalist, London; contributor to the *Daily Chronicle, Black and White* and *Cornhill Magazine*; editor, *To-Day,* from 1897. **Died:** 5 May 1928.

FANTASY PUBLICATIONS

Novels

The One Before. London, Grant Richards, 1902.
Robinson Crusoe's Return. London, Hodder and Stoughton, 1906.
The Diary of a Baby: Being a Free Record of the Unconscious Thought of Rosalys Ysolde Smith Aged One Year. London, Eveleigh Nash, 1907.
An Exchange of Souls. London, Eveleigh Nash, 1911.
The Shadow of the Unseen, with James Blyth. London, Chapman and Hall, 1907.
Going Home: Being the Fantastic Romance of the Girl with Angel Eyes and the Man Who Had Wings. London, Werner Laurie, 1921.
Humorous Stories (omnibus). 1930.

Short Stories

Stories in the Dark. London, Grant Richards, 1901.
The New Gulliver and Other Stories. London, Werner Laurie, 1913.
Collected Tales: Volume One. London, Secker, 1916.

OTHER PUBLICATIONS

Novels

Graeme and Cyril. 1893.
Eliza. 1900.
Lindley Kays. 1904.
Wilhelmina in London. 1906.
Eliza's Husband. 1908.
The Luck of Norman Dale, with James Blyth. London, 1908.
The Gifted Family. 1909.
Proofs Before Pulping. London, Mills and Boon, 1909.
The Exiles of Faloo. 1910.
Eliza Getting On. 1911.
Exit Eliza. 1912.
Eliza's Son. 1913.

Mrs. Murphy. 1913.
Edwards: The Confessions of a Jobbing Gardener. 1915.
Me and Marris. 1916.
Confessions of Alphonse. 1917.
The Death of Maurice. 1920.
Marge Askinforit. 1920.
If Summer Don't. 1922.
The Charming Green Hat Fair. 1925.
Dumphry. 1927.
The Later Years. 1927.

Short Stories

In a Canadian Canoe. 1891.
Stories and Interludes. 1892.
Kindness of the Celestial and Other Stories. 1897.
The Octave of Claudius. 1897.
Wilmay and Other Stories of Women. 1898.
Three Fantasies. 1904.
Memoirs of Constantine Dix. 1905.
Here and Hereafter. 1911.
Stories in Grey. 1911.
Stories Without Tears. 1912.
One Kind and Another. 1914.
Futurist Fifteen. 1914.
Innocent Amusements. 1918.
The Problem Club. 1919.
Tamplin's Tales of His Family. 1924.
Short Stories of To-day and Yesterday. 1928.

Other

Playthings and Parodies. 1896.
The Romantic History of Robin Hood. 1898.
Nothing Serious. 1901.
Little Entertainments. 1903.
Why I Don't. 1903.
First Lessons in Story-Writing. 1907.
The Short Story. 1915.

* * *

Barry Pain began his publishing career—some time after his graduation—in the pages of the Cambridge University students' journal *Granta,* where he published sarcastic accounts of "The Celestial Grocery" and "The Girl and the Beetle" (the latter subtitled "A Story of Here and Hereafter"), both of which were reprinted in *In a Canadian Canoe.* He wrote humorous pieces for many of the popular periodicals founded in the boom years of the 1890s, occasionally dabbling in detective stories and supernatural fiction. Although he seems to have considered serious fiction his "real work" he rarely got around to writing any, apparently finding exercises in parody much more congenial. His first fantasy of any real note was "The Glass of Supreme Moments," in which a young man enabled by a *femme fatale* to look into the eponymous instrument finds that his own supreme moment (in striking contrast to the more worldly triumphs of his contemporaries) is the moment of death; this was reprinted in *Stories and Interludes,* which also contains "Exchange," an eccentric tale of metempsychosis.

The best of Pain's early supernatural fiction is reprinted in *Stories in the Dark,* which includes—among others—a curiously straight-faced study of paranoid delusions of grandeur, "The Diary of a God," and the widely-reprinted tale of "The Moon-Slave," in which a mildly rebellious princess dances to her doom on her wedding eve. Most of Pain's later collections contain a few fantasies but there has never been a book exclusively devoted to his fantastic fiction; *Three Fantasies* actually includes only one, and that very minor. *Collected Stories* is the only volume apart from *Stories in the Dark* to contain a majority of supernatural items. (Twelve Pain stories are reprinted in a 1989 book called *Stories in the Dark,* edited by Hugh Lamb, but the volume is filled out—for no apparent reason—with stories by Jerome K. Jerome and Robert Barr).

Pain's first fantasy novel, *The One Before,* is an Ansteyan comedy tracking the chaos caused by a ring which causes its wearers to fall prey to the emotional tendencies of its previous wearer; it is a cut above most such exercises in pastiche. His subsequent work leaned for a while towards the horrific; the novel he wrote in collaboration with Blyth is a rather rough-hewn horror story involving witchcraft, and *An Exchange of Souls* is a borderline scientific romance about an experiment in personality transplantation which goes tragically awry. The five supernatural stories in *Here and Hereafter* are relatively conventional stories of hauntings, although "Smeath," "Rose Rose" and "Linda" in *Stories in Grey* are less conventional and hence more interesting. "Rose Rose" is an effective tale of an artist's model who continues sitting for him after her death but whose image proves appropriately elusive. The fantasies in *Short Stories of To-day and Yesterday* are also unconventional, though a trifle weak; "The Tree of Death," set in an imaginary land and featuring a highly unusual life-form, is the best of them.

Robinson Crusoe's Return is a marginal fantasy in which Defoe's model of the 18th-century entrepreneurial spirit finds modern England not to his liking. The equally marginal *Diary of a Baby* is in a similar vein. Both are reprinted in the omnibus *Humorous Stories.* By far the best of Pain's stories of this kind is "The New Gulliver" a Utopian satire mocking the aspirations of science and technology, but this seems to be the first half of a novel which ran out of inspiration and was hastily redefined as an abruptly-curtailed novella.

The most interesting of Pain's longer works is the allegorical novella *Going Home,* in which the chronically dissatisfied Dora Muse meets the ebullient radical George Overman and is introduced to the winged man, Eagle, whom he has raised from boyhood in seclusion on his country estate. Dora and Eagle are, of course, made for one another, but the "home" to which they must go in order to be together is not of this earth; the child whose birth concludes the romance is born to Dora's one-time maid, now married to George (who has been knighted). Although considered silly by some commentators, the story offers a fascinating insight into the workings of Pain's quirky imagination and it has an abundance of charm for those sympathetic to its calculatedly naïve style and odd theme.

Pain always gave the impression of being capable of better work than he did; although he made his living from his writing he contrived to remain a mere dabbler, distracting himself with whimsies and never taking the risk of wholehearted commitment. His incapacity remains puzzling, the work he actually did remains tantalizing. Perhaps there was more foresight in "The Glass of Supreme Moments" than he realized at the time, or ever could have hoped.

—Brian Stableford

PAXSON, Diana L(ucile)

Nationality: American. **Born:** 1943. **Education:** Mills College; University of California, M.A. in comparative literature. **Family:** Married; two sons. **Address:** c/o William Morrow and Co., Inc., 1350 Avenue of the Americas, New York, NY 10019, USA.

FANTASY PUBLICATIONS

Novels (series: The Chronicles of Westria; Del Eden)

Lady of Light (Westria). New York, Timescape, 1982.
Lady of Darkness (Westria). New York, Timescape, 1983.
Brisingamen (Del Eden). New York, Berkley, 1984.
Silverhair the Wanderer (Westria). New York, Tor, 1986; London, New English Library, 1990.
White Mare, Red Stallion. New York, Berkley, 1986; London, New English Library, 1988.
The Earthstone (Westria). New York, Tor, 1987; London, New English Library, 1990.
The Paradise Tree (Del Eden). New York, Ace, 1987.
The Sea Star (Westria). New York, Tor, 1988; London, New English Library, 1991.
The White Raven. New York, Morrow, and London, New English Library, 1988.
Lady of Light, Lady of Darkness (omnibus). London, New English Library, 1990; as *Mistress of Jewels,* New York, Tor, 1991.
The Wind Crystal (Westria). New York, Tor, 1990; London, New English Library, 1992.
The Serpent's Tooth. New York, Morrow, 1991.
The Jewel of Fire (Westria). New York, Tor, 1992.
Master of Earth and Water, with Adrienne Martine-Barnes. New York, Morrow, 1993.
The Wolf and the Raven. New York, Morrow, 1993.
The Shield Between the Worlds, with Adrienne Martine-Barnes. New York, Morrow, 1994.

*   *   *

Diana L. Paxson has experimented with three kinds of fantasy: traditional sword-and-sorcery in the Westria Chronicles, contemporary fantasy in *Brisingamen* and its follow-up, and Celtic-historical in *The White Raven* and other books.

Her first published book was *Lady of Light,* the beginning of the Westria Chronicles. It is conventional sword-and-sorcery, the story of Faris, who becomes the wife of Jehan, King of Westria and Mistress of the Jewels. These Jewels, one for each of the sovereign elements—earth, air, fire, and water—are the power of the land, and through them, Faris will effectively rule it as Jehan will rule the people of Westria. The evil sorcerer, Caolin, is her opponent, and as she learns her powers she has to face him. *Silverhair the Wanderer* is the next volume and follows Farin, the twin brother of Faris, in his search for his sister who has disappeared after her final confrontation with Caolin. It is a series of episodes spanning 18 years, and it is only at the end of it when he has discovered that Caolin is still alive and is lusting after the domination of Westria again that he is told that his sister is dead but her son, Julian, is alive. The last four books in the series follow Julian's attempts to

find and master the four Jewels which disappeared at the same time as his mother. Without them he stands no chance of defeating Caolin, who attempts to stop him at every opportunity, or convincing the people that he is the true heir to Westria. The series is effectively one long book divided into digestible portions. However, they are very traditional forms of this fantasy sub-genre, containing many familiar elements and predictable plot elements. The rest of Paxson's output is much more exciting.

Brisingamen is a modern-day fantasy, set in contemporary California. Karen Ingold finds the beads of a necklace in the bottom of an old chest she is repairing. She restrings and wears them, little knowing that by doing so she is awakening the spirit of the Norse goddess, Freya, for whom she will become the earthly vessel. But if Freya is abroad so is her rival, Loki, who, as he did in the old tales, attempts to steal the necklace and bring about Ragnarok. This blend of legend in a modern world is extremely well handled and the characters and setting are well realized. Paxson did a similar thing in *The Paradise Tree.* The setting is still Berkeley, California, and Del Eden, who acted as Karen's guide and mentor in *Brisingamen,* is still an important character. The main characters are Ruth Racusak, a computer programmer, and David Mason, a genetic engineer. They are brought together by Joseph Roman, a charismatic guru who has charmed Ruth's friend Ariel. Ariel reacts badly to the hallucinogenic drug that Roman administers at a meeting and that David has manufactured. Whereas in *Brisingamen* Karen's interests led to the invocation of the Norse gods, Ruth's Jewish background is partially responsible for the powers involved here: they belong to the Judaeo-Christian pantheon and are angels rather than gods. Dark and Light angels are summoned, and battle to restore the equilibrium. The attention to detail is excellent in both books, and both are also romances, but *The Paradise Tree* is a little too cluttered with jargon and the climax does not have quite the same grandeur as *Brisingamen.*

The first of Paxson's historical fantasies, *White Mare, Red Stallion,* is set against a Celtic background in a period when the old magic was still practiced. The country is Alba (now Dumfriesshire, Scotland) and the date is about A.D. 196, when most of the Roman legions have been withdrawn to participate in the power struggle in Rome. Maira is the daughter of the chieftain of the White Horse Clan and has the misfortune to fall in love with a man from a neighboring tribe. When his vassal kills her father she swears vengeance. The war is both internal and external as she attempts to reconcile loyalty and love. There is also magic in the manifestations of the old gods and their lore. In some ways it is a scene setter for *The White Raven,* though there are no characters in common and the two tales are separated by distance and time. There is, however, a common belief structure even though in the sixth century Christianity was a recognized force for change and both have the illusion of historical reality.

The White Raven is a retelling of the story of Tristan and Iseult, here called Drustan and Esseilte. It is told from the point of view of Branwen (whose name means white raven), who is the cousin and servant of Esseilte and travels with her from Ireland for her marriage to Marc'h of Kernow, High King of Britain. Branwen is an intimate witness to the tragedy which unfolds. Both books are well researched and have a ring of authenticity, and both consider the well-being of the land to be linked with Earth Magic.

In her more recent work, Paxson has done the same thing for Germanic myth. *The Wolf and the Raven* is the first volume in a trilogy devoted to the story of Sigfrid and Brunahild. The plot uses the same sources as Wagner's *The Ring of the Nibelung,* but whereas some authors might be content with retelling the operatic version, Paxson has made sure that the historical setting of fifth-century Europe is as accurate as possible.

Paxson's writing is at its best and most confident when she is sure about her settings, such as in *Brisingamen,* where they are places she has experienced first-hand, or *The White Raven,* where she is building on a wealth of research. She also handles such matters as rituals and belief systems well. When she has to invent the whole of the culture, as in the Westria Chronicles, the writing is less stylish, the plots less original, and the characters more stereotyped.

—Pauline Morgan

PEAKE, Mervyn (Laurence)

Nationality: British. **Born:** Of missionary parents in Kuling, China, 9 July 1911. **Education:** Tientsin Grammar School; Eltham College, Kent, 1923-29; Croydon College of Art, Surrey, 1929; Royal Academy Schools, London, 1929-33. **Military Service:** British Army, 1941-43; military artist for the Ministry of Information, 1943-45. **Family:** Married Maeve Gilmore in 1937; two sons and one daughter. **Career:** Lived on Sark, Channel Islands, 1933-35 and 1945-49; teacher, Westminster School of Art, London, 1935-41, and Central School of Art, London, 1949-60. Book and magazine illustrator: one-man shows—Calman Gallery, London, 1943; Peter Jones Gallery, London, 1944; toured Europe as staff artist of the *Leader,* 1945; hospitalized for encephalitis, 1964-68. **Awards:** Royal Literary Fund bursary, 1948; Heinemann award, 1951. Fellow, Royal Society of Literature. **Died:** 18 November 1968.

FANTASY PUBLICATIONS

Novels (series: Titus)

Titus Groan. London, Eyre and Spottiswoode, and New York, Reynal and Hitchcock, 1946.
Gormenghast (Titus). London, Eyre and Spottiswoode, and New York, British Book Center, 1950.
Mr. Pye. London, Heinemann, 1953.
Titus Alone. London, Eyre and Spottiswoode, 1959; New York, Weybright and Talley, 1967; revised edition, revised by Langdon Jones, Eyre and Spottiswoode, 1970.
The Titus Books: Titus Groan, Gormenghast, Titus Alone. London, Penguin, 1983; as *The Gormenghast Trilogy,* New York, Viking Overlook, 1988.

Short Stories

Boy in Darkness, edited by Kenyon Calthrop. Exeter, Devon, Wheaton, 1976.
Peake's Progress: Selected Writings and Drawings of Mervyn Peake, edited by Maeve Gilmore. London, Allen Lane, 1978; revised edition, London, Penguin, and Woodstock, New York, Overlook Press, 1981.

OTHER PUBLICATIONS

Plays

The Connoisseurs (produced 1952).
The Wit to Woo (produced 1957).

Radio Writing: *The Artist's World,* 1947; *Book Illustrations,* 1947; *Alice and Tenniel and Me,* 1954; *Titus Groan,* from his own novel, 1956; *The Voice of One,* 1956; *For Mr. Pye—An Island,* from his own novel, 1957.

Poetry

Shapes and Sounds. London, Chatto and Windus, and New York, Transatlantic, 1941.
Rhymes Without Reason. London, Eyre and Spottiswoode, 1944.
The Glassblowers. London, Eyre and Spottiswoode, 1950.
The Rhyme of the Flying Bomb. London, Dent, 1962; New York, British Book Center, 1976.
Poems and Drawings. London, Keepsake, 1965.
A Reverie of Bone and Other Poems. London, Rota, 1967.
Selected Poems. London, Faber, 1972.
A Book of Nonsense. London, Owen, 1972; New York, Dufour, 1975.
Twelve Poems 1939-1960. Hayes, Middlesex, Bran's Head, 1975.

Other

Captain Slaughterboard Drops Anchor (for children). London, Country Life, 1939; revised edition, Country Life, 1945; New York, Macmillan, 1967.
The Craft of the Lead Pencil. London, Wingate, 1946.
Letters from a Lost Uncle (for children). London, Eyre and Spottiswoode, 1948.
Drawings by Mervyn Peake. London, Grey Walls, and New York, British Book Center, 1950.
Figures of Speech (drawings). London, Gollancz, 1954.
The Drawings of Mervyn Peake, text by Hilary Spurling. London, Davis Poynter, 1974.
Mervyn Peake: Writings and Drawings, edited by Maeve Gilmore and Shelagh Johnson. London, Academy Editions, 1974; New York, St. Martin's Press, 1974.
Sketches from Bleak House. London, Methuen, 1983.

*

Film Adaptation: *Mr. Pye,* 1986 (television serial).

Bibliography: "Peake in Print: A Bibliographical Checklist" by Dee Berkeley and G. Peter Winnington, in *Mervyn Peake Review,* Autumn 1981 and Spring 1982.

Manuscript Collections: D. M. S. Watson Library, University College, London; Imperial War Museum, London; Bodleian Library, Oxford; Berg Collection, New York Public Library.

Critical Studies: *A World Away: A Memoir of Mervyn Peake* by Maeve Gilmore, London, Gollancz, 1970; *Mervyn Peake: A Biographical and Critical Exploration* by John Batchelor, London, Duckworth, 1974; *Mervyn Peake* by John Watney, London, Michael

Joseph, 1976; *Mervyn Peake: A Personal Memoir* by Gordon Smith, London, Gollancz, 1984; *A Child of Bliss: Growing Up With Mervyn Peake* by Sebastian Peake, Luton, Lennard, 1989.

*   *   *

Despite his various volumes of comic and serious verse, his attempts to make a name for himself as a playwright and his exceptional ability as an illustrator, Mervyn Peake's real claim to lasting fame rests on his idiosyncratic and incomplete trilogy about Titus Groan, sometimes referred to as the Gormenghast Trilogy. "There would be tears and there would be strange laughter. Fierce births and deaths beneath umbrageous ceilings. And dreams, and violence, and disenchantment" (*Titus Groan*). Titus, 77th Earl of Groan and heir to the monstrous and sprawling ritual-ridden castle of Gormenghast, scarcely features in the first volume of the trilogy which bears his name, for he is only two years old when the book finishes. Instead the plot of the novel is chiefly concerned with the struggle for supremacy in the castle's hierarchy between the austere Flay and the fat and hedonistic cook Swelter—a struggle which will end in the triumph of neither, but which will assist the rise of *Gormenghast*'s chief protagonist, the crippled scullion Steerpike, a coldhearted and ambitious villain in the Shakespearean mode. In this and succeeding volumes the reader is introduced to a rich gallery of grotesques including the manic-depressive 76th earl Lord Sepulchrave who goes mad after the burning of the library and is eaten by owls; Barquentine, the Master of Ritual; Sourdust the librarian; Cora and Clarice Groan, the batty aunts; Rottcodd, curator of the Hall of Bright Carvings; Fuchsia, Titus's proud and sullen sister; the 18 Grey Scrubbers destined by birth and long tradition to do the washing-up; and the melancholy Muzzlehatch with his zoo.

It is not enough for Titus to be born into his inheritance; he has to fight for it. In *Gormenghast*, Titus grows towards rebellious manhood and comes into his own. He explores the castle and ventures beyond the walls where the "outer folk" live in poverty and produce carvings for the castle. Steerpike, who is perhaps in some sense Titus's alter ego and who has usurped the post of Master of Ritual after murdering Barquentine, is courting Fuschia and has plans to take over the castle. However, Titus has identified him as the murderer of his father, his aunts and the Keeper of the Rituals. Although Steerpike goes into hiding, floods force him into the upper regions of the castle where he is spotted, pursued and slain by Titus.

From volume to volume the pace accelerates and a great deal happens in the short and unfinished third volume, *Titus Alone*. Titus has escaped from the castle and its environs and explores the world outside. It is a strange futuristic world—stranger even than Gormenghast. Many of Titus's encounters are hostile and unfortunate. Titus's affair with Cheeta, the exquisitely sophisticated daughter of a scientist, proves particularly ill-fated. Cheeta has a marvellous face, but a warped brain and, denied Titus's love, she vengefully organizes a midnight party whose trappings and guests parody Titus's memories of owl-haunted Gormenghast. Most people Titus has encountered doubt the existence of Gormenghast, but Titus finds a way back to the castle. But then, just as he approaches a point from which he will be able to see it, he turns away "for he carried his Gormenghast within him."

The visual and linguistic qualities of the trilogy are particularly evident in Peake's evocations of the sprawling castle and dependent dwellings: "Over their irregular roofs would fall throughout the seasons, the shadows of time-eaten buttresses, of broken and lofty turrets, and, most enormous of all, the shadow of the Tower of Flints. This tower, patched unevenly with black ivy, arose like a mutilated finger from among the fists of knuckled masonry and pointed blasphemously at heaven, At night owls made of it an echoing throat; by day it stood voiceless and cast its long shadow." Peake possessed a remarkably strong visual sense married to an ability to translate his visions into words, and in the intensely realized castle of Gormenghast the heaviness of masonry is matched by the density of the prose which shapes that masonry. The trilogy is to a considerable extent a fantasy of topography and scale. The enclosed and ritual-driven Forbidden City of Peking may have served as a partial model for Peake's castle. (Peake spent much of his boyhood in China). The sombre ambience furnishes a curious setting for wild, satirical comedy at the expense of the castle's gloomy denizens. However, it also seems possible that the castle is an image of the labyrinth that is the human mind, with all its unexplored corridors and cellars. Towards the end of *Titus Alone*, Titus has the sensation that "the earth wandered through his skull . . . a cosmos in the bone; a universe lit by a hundred lights and thronged by shapes and shadows; alive with endless threads of circumstance . . . action and event. All futility: disordered; with no end and no beginning." A degenerative disease which affected the brain prevented Peake from producing a fully finished version of *Titus Alone*. However, it does not appear that he intended the story to end with this volume and a few pages have survived of a projected *Titus Awakes*. Although the trilogy can be characterized as "Gothic," it is not very much like anything else in that or any other genre.

Mr. Pye is by comparison a light-weight fantasy about a visitor to the island of Sark who finds himself growing angel's wings and his efforts to get rid of those embarrassing appendages. However, "Boy in Darkness," "Dance Macabre" and "Same Time, Same Place" are outstanding and distinctly sinister fantasy short stories. Peake also produced a small body of beguiling juvenile fantasy, including *Captain Slaughterboard Drops Anchor, Letters from a Lost Uncle* and *Rhymes Without Reason*.

—Robert Irwin

PEARCE, (Ann) Philippa

Nationality: British. **Born:** Great Shelford, Cambridgeshire. **Education:** Perse Girls' School, Cambridge, 1929-39; Girton College, Cambridge, B.A. (honours) in English and history 1942, M.A. **Family:** Married Martin Christie in 1963 (died 1965); one daughter. **Career:** Civil servant, 1942-45; scriptwriter and producer, 1945-58, and freelance producer, 1960-62, BBC Radio, London; assistant editor, Educational Department, Clarendon Press, Oxford, 1958-60; children's editor, Andre Deutsch Ltd., publishers, London, 1960-67. Freelance reviewer and lecturer. **Awards:** Library Association Carnegie Medal, 1959; Whitbread award, 1978. **Agent:** Laura Cecil, 17 Alwyne Villas, London N1 2HG, England.

FANTASY PUBLICATIONS

Novels

Tom's Midnight Garden, illustrated by Susan Einzig. London, Oxford University Press, and Philadelphia, Lippincott, 1958.

Short Stories

The Shadow-Cage and Other Tales of the Supernatural, illustrated by Janet Archer. London, Kestrel, and New York, Crowell, 1977.
Who's Afraid and Other Strange Stories, illustrated by Peter Melnyczuk. London, Viking Kestrel, 1986; New York, Greenwillow, 1987.

Other

Beauty and the Beast (retelling), illustrated by Alan Barrett. London, Longman, and New York, Crowell, 1972.

Editor, *Stories from Hans Christian Andersen,* illustrated by Pauline Baynes. London, Collins, 1972.

OTHER PUBLICATIONS

Fiction for Children

Minnow on the Say, illustrated by Edward Ardizzone. London, Oxford University Press, 1955; as *The Minnow Leads to Treasure,* Cleveland, World, 1958.
Still Jim and Silent Jim. Oxford, Blackwell, 1960.
Mrs. Cockle's Cat, illustrated by Antony Maitland. London, Constable, 1961; Philadelphia, Lippincott, 1962.
A Dog So Small, illustrated by Antony Maitland. London, Constable, 1962; Philadelphia, Lippincott, 1963.
The Strange Sunflower, illustrated by Kathleen Williams. London, Nelson, 1966.
The Children of the House, with Brian Fairfax-Lucy, illustrated by John Sergeant. London, Longman, and Philadelphia, Lippincott, 1968; as *The Children of Charlecote,* London, Gollancz, 1989.
The Elm Street Lot, illustrated by Mina Martinez. London, BBC Publications, 1969; augmented edition, London, Kestrel, 1979.
The Squirrel Wife, illustrated by Derek Collard. London, Longman, 1971; New York, Crowell, 1972.
What the Neighbours Did and Other Stories, illustrated by Faith Jaques. London, Longman, 1972; New York, Crowell, 1973.
The Battle of Bubble and Squeak, illustrated by Alan Baker. London, Deutsch, 1978.
The Way to Sattin Shore, illustrated by Charlotte Voake. London, Kestrel, and New York, Greenwillow, 1983.
Lion at School and Other Stories, illustrated by Caroline Sharpe. London, Viking Kestrel, 1985; New York, Greenwillow, 1986.
Emily's Own Elephant, illustrated by John Lawrence. London, MacRae, 1987; New York, Greenwillow, 1988.
The Tooth Ball, illustrated by Helen Ganly. London, Deutsch, 1987.
Freddy, illustrated by David Armitage. London, Deutsch, 1988.
Old Belle's Summer Holiday, illustrated by William Geldart. London, Deutsch, 1989.

Other

Wings of Courage (adaptation), by George Sand, illustrated by Hilary Abrahams. London, Kestrel, 1982.

*   *   *

Since its first publication in 1958, when it won the Carnegie Medal as the outstanding English children's book of the year, *Tom's Midnight Garden* by Philippa Pearce moved surely into the position of a classic. It belongs, with the Green Knowe books by L. M. Boston, in the sub-genre of time fantasy, and it is one of the best.

Young Tom Long is sent to stay with his childless aunt and uncle in their flat in an old house in Cambridgeshire. There's no one to play with and nothing to do, and Tom is miserable. But one night, hearing old Mrs. Bartholomew's clock in the hall striking thirteen, he goes down to investigate and discovers that everything has changed. The house is differently furnished and occupied by people who do not seem to see him, and outside the back door, instead of the small, paved area overlooked by the backs of other houses, there is a large, wonderful garden. Night after night, Tom returns to play in the garden, and there he meets Hattie, a little girl who, like himself, has been longing for someone to play with, and they become friends—even though each thinks the other must be a ghost. Time in the garden works differently from time in Tom's "real" life. No matter how many hours he spends playing there, when he returns to his bed no time has passed, and although he returns faithfully every night, Hattie comments sometimes on how long he has been away, and she is visibly growing up. One night, during a memorable storm, he sees a fir tree struck and felled by lightning; but the next night when he returns the garden is sunlit and the fir tree stands in its usual position. Although he is happy to accept the existence of Hattie and the garden and to play there by night, during the day Tom puzzles over the meaning of Time and relativity and what is happening. He wants to stay and play in the garden forever, but his parents have summoned him home. And something else is happening: his final visits to the past take place in winter, when the nearby river has frozen solid. After a memorable journey ice-skating down the river to Ely with Hattie, Tom is forced to recognize that his companion has outgrown him and become a young woman. On his last night in the flat Tom attempts to return to the garden and fails. In despair, he calls out for Hattie—and finds her again, along with the answer to some of his questions. His Hattie is old Mrs. Bartholomew at the top of the house, dreaming of her lonely childhood and of playing in the garden which had been attached to the house in the 1880s. She remembers Tom even as he recognizes her, and the book ends on a warm and thoroughly satisfactory note of their friendship affirmed.

Pearce's characters are well-drawn, rounded and believable, the narrative rich and compelling. The garden and countryside around it are so well-described, the sense of place is so powerful that it is not surprising to learn that Philippa Pearce grew up in the mill house on the upper reaches of the river Cam, and that the house and garden are based closely upon the actual house and garden as they were when her father was growing up. The fantasy is both intellectually and emotionally convincing, the events and their sequence as rigorously worked out and justified as a time paradox can ever be, and the author manages the difficult feat of balancing paranormal and psychological explanations without ever forfeiting the reader's comprehension or credulity.

None of Philippa Pearce's other book-length works are fantasies, although her third children's novel, *A Dog So Small,* approaches the subject of fantasy, with a warning of the dangers of trying to live in a world no one else can see, and the necessity of accepting what you are given for what it is, rather than yearning for the impossible. She has, however, also written a number of supernatural short stories, many of them dealing with the influence of past on present lives, and various types of haunting. Most are the fairly traditional type of ghost story, some are humorous, and some are unusual and chilling horror stories which, although published for younger readers, would also be of interest to adults.

—Lisa Tuttle

PERRY, Steve(n Carl)

Nationality: American. **Born:** Baton Rouge, Louisiana, 31 August 1947. **Family:** Married Dianne Waller; two children. **Career:** Numerous jobs, including swimming instructor, toy assembler, car-rental clerk, martial-arts instructor, private detective, licensed practical nurse, certified physician's assistant, and part-time writing instructor. Novelist and television writer. **Agent:** Jean V. Naggar Literary Agency, 216 East 75th Street, New York, NY 10021, USA.

FANTASY PUBLICATIONS

Novels (series: Conan)

Conan the Fearless. New York, Tor, 1986; London, Sphere, 1988.
Conan the Defiant. New York, Tor, 1987; London, Sphere, 1990.
Conan the Indomitable. New York, Tor, 1989.
Conan the Free Lance. New York, Tor, 1990
Conan the Formidable. New York, Tor, 1990.

OTHER PUBLICATIONS

Novels

The Tularemia Gambit. New York, Fawcett, 1981.
Sword of the Samurai, with Michael Reaves. New York, Bantam, 1984.
Civil War Secret Agent. New York, Bantam, 1984.
Hellstar, with Michael Reaves. New York, Berkley, 1984.
The Man Who Never Missed. New York, Ace, 1985; London, Sphere, 1989.
Matadora. New York, Ace, 1986; London, Sphere, 1989.
The Machiavelli Interface. New York, Ace, 1986; London, Sphere, 1990.
Dome, with Michael Reaves. New York, Berkley, 1987; London, Gollancz, 1988.
The Omega Cage, with Michael Reaves. New York, Ace, 1988.
The 97th Step. New York, Ace, 1989.
The Albino Knife. New York, Ace, 1991.
The Hero Curse. Portland, Oregon, DimeNovels, 1991.
Black Steel. New York, Ace, 1992.
Aliens: Earth Hive. New York, Bantam, 1992; London, Millennium, 1993.
Brother Death. New York, Ace, 1992.
Aliens: Nightmare Asylum. New York, Bantam, 1993; London, Millennium, 1994.
Aliens: The Female War, with Stephani Perry. New York, Bantam, 1993; London, Millennium, 1994.
Spindoc. New York, Ace, 1994.
Stellar Ranger. New York, AvoNova, 1994.
Aliens vs. Predator: Prey, with Stephani Perry. New York, Bantam, and London, Millennium, 1994.

Plays

Television Plays: Various episodes of animated series *Centurions, The Real Ghostbusters, Chuck Norris: Karate Commandos, The Spiral Zone, U.S. Starcom, Batman: The Animated Show, Conan and the Young Warriors* and *Gargoyles,* 1986-94.

Other

Workshops: The Minefields of Science Fiction. Eugene, Oregon, Pulphouse, 1991.

* * *

Steve Perry is probably best known for his science-fiction novels, which frequently involve professional assassins, adventurers and martial artists as their protagonists, and invariably use action-oriented plots. Some of those same elements appear in his fantasy novels, all five of which feature the famous Robert E. Howard hero, Conan of Cimmeria. Although the central character and setting are common to all those writers who have contributed to this ongoing series, there are certain differences in the details of Conan's personality from one author to another, and Perry's novels have a distinct flavour resulting from his use of subsidiary characters as an offset to the protagonist's fairly simplistic profile.

Conan the Fearless was his first title, and the only one to deal with a mature Conan. Perry's barbarian hero is not only a powerful and skilled fighter but keen of wit as well, a trait not generally attributed to the character. He goes back to sleep within moments of having killed a handful of assassins in his rented room, but is also adept at swapping metaphorical banter with a crafty crone in the town's market.

Conan faces a broad spectrum of dangers in this adventure, a device which Perry uses in all five novels. Shortly after arriving in Corinthia, he becomes protector of a young child with magical abilities who is being sought by an evil sorcerer and his pet demon. There are other interested parties as well, including a shape-changing corrupt local official and a beautiful but treacherous witch. He succeeds primarily through brute force, the brains being provided by Vitarius, a minor wizard who intervenes at opportune times, and as expected the villains all get their just deserts. Overall it is one of the better of the new Conan adventures, primarily because of the interesting array of villains and the careful interlacing of the various sub-plots.

Another evil sorcerer opens Perry's next in the series, *Conan the Defiant.* Neg the Malefic is aided by the zombies he has created in the bowels of his castle and the Men With No Eyes, a mysterious group of deadly figures, blind, but with other abilities that make them extremely dangerous. Conan befriends a member of a benign cult that practices the martial arts, then sets out for revenge when his friend is murdered during the theft of a magical stone. Neg is responsible, having discovered that the gem is the key to greatly increasing his sorcerous powers. Opposed to Neg is Tuanne, one of those undead servants who has escaped his domination. She also wants the stone, because it is the key to releasing her own spirit and those of her fellow zombies. This time it's a much younger Conan who must use his wits to penetrate Neg's fortified castle, racing against time as a newly wakened army of zombies is rising from the ground to complete a sinister plan of conquest. He also must deal with the presence of two female companions, although Perry doesn't stray from the tradition that keeps Conan's dalliances largely offstage and unemotional.

Conan the Indomitable chronicles events immediately following those of *Conan the Defiant*. Still accompanied by Elashi, a beautiful desert-dweller with a mind of her own, the barbarian stumbles into the world of the Black Caves, an underground realm where two magical powers are at war, a seductive witch and an ages old man, both of whom command legions of deformed creatures. This time Perry is closer to the spirit of the original Howard stories, which were less concerned with the character than with the exotic settings in which he found himself. The Black Caves are a complex world whose balance of power is upset by the presence of Conan and his companions. Perry uses the other characters extensively, at times upstaging Conan, and it is through their cooperative actions that the two villains are despatched and the denizens of the underworld set free.

Perry returned to his original formula for *Conan the Free Lance*, which also continues directly from its predecessor. Once again Conan is on his own, although he immediately gains a new companion, the woman Cheen, when he helps her fight off a pair of dragons. Despite his determination not to become involved in yet another local war, a multi-sided one this time, he is soon entangled with a sorcerer cursed to periods of insubstantiality, a changeling, and is even uncertain of the intentions of Cheen, who is determined to help her people even at the cost of Conan's life. This is at one time the best of Perry's fantasy novels and the one least true in feel to the original character. There's a complex mesh of conflicting interests, a well developed culture, and a nasty villain, but for much of the story Conan seems almost out of place in the setting, and it's only in the waning chapters that he takes control of the plot once again.

Perry's most recent Conan story to date is *Conan the Formidable*, a more traditional tale. After defeating a small group of bandits, Conan meets an attractive but oversized young woman who delivers him into the hands of her father, a warlord hoping to use magic and the force or arms to extend the borders of his rule. Raseri is a Jatte, one of a race of giants living in uneasy proximity to the Vargs, reptilian humanoids who inhabit a nearby swamp. Conan escapes from captivity only to find himself hunted by various parties, and without any friends to watch his back. He eludes his pursuers successfully, only to fall into the clutches of Dake, a sorcerer who collects people as exhibits in his travelling circus. Naturally, Conan helps to destroy Dake's power before returning to deal with his former captor as well. This is the most controlled of the five novels, and the best plotted and paced, nearly as good as *Conan the Indomitable*.

To date, Perry has produced no fantasy set in a world of his own creation, but his use of a strong cast of supporting characters, complex plots, and the development of original settings mark his Conan novels as well above average.

—Don D'Ammassa

PHILLPOTTS, Eden

Pseudonym: Harrington Hext. **Nationality:** British. **Born:** Mount Aboo, India, 4 November 1862. **Education:** Mannamead School, now Plymouth College. **Family:** Married 1) Emily Topham in 1892 (died 1928), one son and one daughter; 2) Lucy Robina Webb in 1929. **Career:** Clerk, Sun Fire Office, London, 1880-90; assistant editor, *Black and White*, London, for several years in the 1890s. Regular contributor to *The Idler*, London. Lived in Devon from 1898. **Died:** 29 December 1960.

FANTASY PUBLICATIONS

Novels

A Deal with the Devil. London, Bliss, 1895; New York, Warne, 1901.
The Flint Heart: A Fairy Story. London, Smith Elder, and New York, Dutton, 1910; revised edition, London, Chapman and Dodd, 1922.
Evander. London, Richards, and New York, Macmillan, 1919.
Pan and the Twins. London, Richards, and New York, Macmillan, 1922.
The Lavender Dragon. London, Richards, and New York, Macmillan, 1923.
The Treasures of Typhon. London, Richards, 1924; New York, Macmillan, 1925.
Circe's Island, and The Girl and the Faun. London, Richards, and New York, Macmillan, 1926.
The Miniature. London, Watts, 1926; New York, Macmillan, 1927.
Arachne. London, Faber and Gwyer, 1927; New York, Macmillan, 1928.
The Apes. London, Faber, and New York, Macmillan, 1929.
Alcyone: A Fairy Story. London, Benn, 1930.
The Owl of Athene. London, Hutchinson, 1936.
Golden Island: A Fairy Story. London, Everett, 1938.

Short Stories

Fancy Free. London, Methuen, 1901.
The Girl and the Faun. London, Palmer and Hayward, 1916; Philadelphia, Lippincott, 1917.

OTHER PUBLICATIONS

Novels

The End of a Life. Bristol, Arrowsmith, 1891.
Folly and Fresh Air. London, Trischler, 1891; New York, Harper, 1892; revised edition, London, Hurst and Blackett, 1899.
A Tiger's Cub. Bristol, Arrowsmith, 1892.
Some Every-Day Folks. London, Osgood, 3 vols., 1894; New York, Harper, 1895.
Lying Prophets. London, Innes, and New York, Stokes, 1896.
Children of the Mist. London, Innes, 1898; New York, Putnam, 1899.
The Human Boy. London, Methuen, 1899; New York, Harper, 1900.
Sons of Morning. London, Methuen, and New York, Putnam, 1900.
The Good Red Earth. Bristol, Arrowsmith, and New York, Doubleday, 1901; as *Johnny Fortnight*, Arrowsmith, 1904; revised edition, Arrowsmith, 1920.
The River. London, Methuen, and New York, Stokes, 1902.
The Golden Fetich. London, Harper, and New York, Dodd Mead, 1903.
The American Prisoner. London, Macmillan, 1903; London, Methuen, 1904.

The Farm of the Dagger. London, Newnes, and New York, Dodd Mead, 1904.

The Secret Woman. London, Methuen, and New York, Macmillan, 1905.

Doubloons, with Arnold Bennett. New York, McClure, 1906; as *The Sinews of War,* London, Laurie, 1906.

The Portreeve. London, Methuen, and New York, Macmillan, 1906.

The Poacher's Wife. London, Methuen, 1906; as *Daniel Sweetland,* New York, Authors and Newspapers Association, 1906.

The Virgin in Judgment. New York, Reynolds, 1907; London, Cassell, 1908; abridged edition, as *A Fight to the Finish,* Cassell, 1911.

The Whirlwind. London, Chapman and Hall, and New York, McClure, 1907.

The Human Boy Again. London, Chapman and Hall, 1908.

The Mother. London, Ward Lock, 1908; as *The Mother of the Man,* New York, Dodd Mead, 1908.

The Statue, with Arnold Bennett. London, Cassell, and New York, Moffat Yard, 1908.

The Three Brothers. London, Hutchinson, and New York, Macmillan, 1909.

The Haven. London, Murray, and New York, Lane, 1909.

The Thief of Virtue. London, Murray, and New York, Lane, 1910.

Demeter's Daughter. London, Methuen, and New York, Lane, 1911.

The Beacon. London, Unwin, and New York, Lane, 1911.

The Forest on the Hill. London, Murray, and New York, Lane, 1912.

From the Angle of Seventeen. London, Murray, 1912; Boston, Little Brown, 1914.

The Lovers: A Romance. London, Ward Lock, and Chicago, Rand McNally, 1912.

The Three Knaves. London, Macmillan, 1912.

Widecombe Fair. London, Murray, and Boston, Little Brown, 1913.

The Joy of Youth: A Comedy. London, Chapman and Hall, and Boston, Little Brown, 1913.

Faith Tresillion. New York, Macmillan, 1914; London, Ward Lock, 1916.

The Master of Merripit. London, Ward Lock, 1914.

Brunel's Tower. London, Heinemann, and New York, Macmillan, 1915.

Old Delabole. London, Heinemann, and New York, Macmillan, 1915.

The Green Alleys. London, Heinemann, and New York, Macmillan, 1916.

The Human Boy and the War. London, Methuen, and New York, Macmillan, 1916.

The Nursery (Banks of Colne). London, Heinemann, 1917; as *The Banks of Colne,* New York, Macmillan, 1917.

The Chronicles of St. Tid. London, Skeffington, 1917; New York, Macmillan, 1918.

The Spinners. London, Heinemann, and New York, Macmillan, 1918.

Storm in a Teacup. London, Heinemann, and New York, Macmillan, 1919.

Miser's Money. London, Heinemann, and New York, Macmillan, 1920.

Orphan Dinah. London, Heinemann, 1920; New York, Macmillan, 1921.

The Bronze Venus. London, Richards, 1921.

Eudocia. London, Heinemann, and New York, Macmillan, 1921.

The Grey Room. New York, Macmillan, and London, Hurst and Blackett, 1921.

Number 87 (as Harrington Hext). London, Butterworth, and New York, Macmillan, 1922.

The Red Redmaynes. New York, Macmillan, 1922; London, Hutchinson, 1923.

Children of Men. London, Heinemann, and New York, Macmillan, 1923.

The Thing at Their Heels (as Harrington Hext). London, Butterworth, and New York, Macmillan, 1923.

Cheat-the-Boys. London, Heinemann, and New York, Macmillan, 1924.

The Human Boy's Diary. London, Heinemann, and New York, Macmillan, 1924.

Redcliff. London, Hutchinson, and New York, Macmillan, 1924.

Who Killed Diana? (as Harrington Hext). London, Butterworth, 1924; as *Who Killed Cock Robin?,* New York, Macmillan, 1924.

George Westover. London, Hutchinson, 1925; New York, Macmillan, 1926.

The Monster (as Harrington Hext). New York, Macmillan, 1925.

A Voice from the Dark. London, Hutchinson, and New York, Macmillan, 1925.

A Cornish Droll. London, Hutchinson, 1926; New York, Macmillan, 1928.

The Marylebone Miser. London, Hutchinson, 1926; as *Jig-Saw,* New York, Macmillan, 1926.

Dartmoor Novels (Widecombe Edition: includes stories). New York, Macmillan, 20 vols., 1927-28.

The Jury. London, Hutchinson, and New York, Macmillan, 1927.

The Ring Fence. London, Hutchinson, and New York, Macmillan, 1928.

Tryphena. London, Hutchinson, and New York, Macmillan, 1929.

The Complete Human Boy (omnibus). London, Hutchinson, 1930.

The Three Maidens. London, Hutchinson, and New York, Smith, 1930.

"Found Drowned." London, Hutchinson, and New York, Macmillan, 1931.

Stormbury. London, Hutchinson, 1931; New York, Macmillan, 1932.

Bred in the Bone. London, Hutchinson, 1932; New York, Macmillan, 1933.

The Broom Squires. London, Benn, and New York, Macmillan, 1932.

A Clue from the Stars. London, Hutchinson, and New York, Macmillan, 1932.

The Captain's Curio. London, Hutchinson, and New York, Macmillan, 1933.

Nancy Owlett. London, Tuck, and New York, Macmillan, 1933.

Mr. Digweed and Mr. Lumb. London, Hutchinson, 1933; New York, Macmillan, 1934.

A Shadow Passes. London, Hutchinson, 1933; New York, Macmillan, 1934.

Witch's Cauldron. London, Hutchinson, and New York, Macmillan, 1933.

Minions of the Moon. London, Hutchinson, 1934; New York, Macmillan, 1935.

The Oldest Inhabitant: A Comedy. London, Hutchinson, and New York, Macmillan, 1934.

Portrait of a Gentleman. London, Hutchinson, 1934.

Ned of the Caribbees. London, Hutchinson, 1935.

Physician, Heal Thyself. London, Hutchinson, 1935; as *The Anniversary Murder,* New York, Dutton, 1936.

The Wife of Elias. London, Hutchinson, 1935; New York, Dutton, 1937.

The Book of Avis (omnibus). London, Hutchinson, 1936.
A Close Call. London, Hutchinson, and New York, Macmillan, 1936.
Wood-Nymph. London, Hutchinson, 1936; New York, Dutton, 1937.
Farce in Three Acts. London, Hutchinson, 1937.
Lycanthrope: The Mystery of Sir William Wolf. London, Butterworth, 1937; New York, Macmillan, 1938.
Dark Horses. London, Murray, 1938.
Portrait of a Scoundrel. London, Murray, and New York, Macmillan, 1938.
Saurus. London, Murray, 1938.
Monkshood. London, Methuen, and New York, Macmillan, 1939.
Tabletop. London, Macmillan, 1939.
Thorn in Her Flesh. London, Murray, 1939.
Awake Deborah! London, Methuen, 1940; New York, Macmillan, 1941.
Chorus of Clowns. London, Methuen, 1940.
Goldcross. London, Methuen, 1940.
A Deed Without a Name. London, Hutchinson, 1941; New York, Macmillan, 1942.
Ghostwater. London, Methuen, and New York, Macmillan, 1941.
Flower of the Gods. London, Hutchinson, 1942; New York, Macmillan, 1943.
Pilgrims of the Night. London, Hutchinson, 1942.
A Museum Piece. London, Hutchinson, 1943.
The Changeling. London, Hutchinson, 1944.
They Were Seven. London, Hutchinson, 1944; New York, Macmillan, 1945.
The Drums of Dombali. London, Hutchinson, 1945.
Quartet. London, Hutchinson, 1946.
There Was an Old Woman. London, Hutchinson, 1947.
Fall of the House of Heron. London, Hutchinson, 1948.
Address Unknown. London, Hutchinson, 1949.
Dilemma. London, Hutchinson, 1949.
The Waters of Walla. London, Hutchinson, 1950.
Through a Glass Darkly. London, Hutchinson, 1951.
George and Georgina. London, Hutchinson, 1952.
The Hidden Hand. London, Hutchinson, 1952.
His Brother's Keeper. London, Hutchinson, 1953.
The Widow Garland. London, Hutchinson, 1955.
Connie Woodland. London, Hutchinson, 1956.
Giglet Market. London, Hutchinson, 1957.
There Was an Old Man. London, Hutchinson, 1959.

Short Stories

My Adventure in the Flying Scotsman: A Romance of London and North-Western Railway Shares. London, Hogg, 1888; edited by Tom Schatz, Boulder, Colorado, Aspen Press, 1975.
Summer Clouds and Other Stories. London, Tuck, 1893.
Down Dartmoor Way. London, Osgood McIlvaine, 1895.
Loup-Garou! London, Sands, 1899.
The Striking Hours. London, Methuen, and New York, Stokes, 1901.
The Transit of the Red Dragon and Other Tales. Bristol, Arrowsmith, 1903.
Knock at a Venture. London, Methuen, and New York, Macmillan, 1905.
The Unlucky Number. London, Newnes, 1906.
The Folk Afield. London, Methuen, and New York, Putnam, 1907.
The Fun of the Fair. London, Murray, 1909.

Tales of the Tenements. London, Murray, and New York, Lane, 1910.
The Old Time Before Them. London, Murray, 1913; revised edition, as *Told at the Plume,* London, Hurst and Blackett, 1921.
The Judge's Chair. London, Murray, 1914.
Black, White, and Brindled. London, Richards, and New York, Macmillan, 1923.
Up Hill, Down Dale. London, Hutchinson, and New York, Macmillan, 1925.
Peacock House and Other Mysteries. London, Hutchinson, 1926; New York, Macmillan, 1927; selection, as *The End of Count Rollo and Other Stories,* London, Todd, 1946.
It Happened Like That. London, Hutchinson, and New York, Macmillan, 1928.
The Torch and Other Tales. London, Hutchinson, and New York, Macmillan, 1929.
(Selected Stories.) London, Harrap, 1929.
Cherry Gambol and Other Stories. London, Hutchinson, 1930.
They Could Do No Other. London, Hutchinson, and New York, Macmillan, 1933.
Once Upon a Time. London, Hutchinson, 1936.
The King of Kanga, and The Alliance. London, Todd, 1943.

Other

In Sugar-Cane Land. New York, McClure, 1893.
My Laughing Philosopher. London, Innes, 1896.
Little Silver Chronicles. Philadelphia, Biddle, 1900.
My Devon Year. London, Methuen, and New York, Macmillan, 1903.
My Garden. London, Country Life, and New York, Scribner, 1906.
The Mound by the Way. Philadelphia, Biddle, 1908.
Dance of the Months. London, Gowans and Gray, 1911.
My Shrubs. London and New York, Lane, 1915.
The Eden Phillpotts Calendar, edited by H. Cecil Palmer. London, Palmer and Hayward, 1915.
A Shadow Passes. London, Palmer and Hayward, 1918; New York, Macmillan, 1919.
One Hundred Pictures from Eden Phillpotts, edited by L. H. Brewitt. London, Methuen, 1919.
A West Country Pilgrimage. London, Parsons, and New York, Macmillan, 1920.
Thoughts in Prose and Verse. London, Watts, 1924.
A West Country Sketch Book. London, Hutchinson, 1928.
Essays in Little. London, Hutchinson, 1931.
A Year with Bisshe-Bantam. London, Blackie, 1934.
The White Camel (for children). London, Country Life, 1936; New York, Dutton, 1938.
A Mixed Grill. London, Watts, 1940.
From the Angle of 88 (autobiography). London, Hutchinson, 1951.
One Thing and Another. London, Hutchinson, 1954.
Selected Letters, edited by James Y. Dayanda. Lanham, Maryland, University Press of America, 1984.

*

Bibliography: *Eden Phillpotts: A Bibliography of First Editions* by Percival Hinton, Birmingham, George Worthington, 1931.

Critical Studies: *Eden Phillpotts: An Assessment and a Tribute* edited by Waveney Girvan, London, Hutchinson, 1953; *Eden*

Phillpotts on Dartmoor by K. F. Day, Newton Abbott, Devon, David and Charles, 1981.

*   *   *

The astoundingly prolific Eden Phillpotts, who lived to the age of 98 and wrote almost to the last, began his career as a fantasist with two brief comic fantasies in *The Idler*: "The Spectre's Dilemma" and "Friar Lawrence" (both 1892). He also wrote one full-length Ansteyan fantasy, *A Deal with the Devil*—in which the extra seven years earned by a dying man in consequence of the deal involve him in accelerated rejuvenation—and a curious philosophical tract in the form of a series of dialogues between the protagonist and a bronze bust, *My Laughing Philosopher,* before achieving moderate fame and establishing a reputation as the poor man's Thomas Hardy with his novels of life on Dartmoor.

Phillpotts published the first and best of his juvenile fantasies, *The Flint Heart,* in 1910 but did not turn his hand to adult fantasy until he wrote *The Girl and the Faun* for publication in a handsome edition illustrated by Frank Brangwyn in 1916. This touching tale of the ill-fated love of the immortal Coix for the mortal Ione adopts a sympathetic viewpoint akin to that of Anatole France's tales of satyrs. Phillpotts was subsequently to develop this vein of nostalgic sentimentality into a more robust championship of the Epicurean ideals upheld by France in a remarkable series of Classical fantasies.

In *Evander* two gods, Bacchus and Apollo, contend for the adoration of a woman whose husband worships the former. The eponymous disciple of Apollo wins her affection for a while, but she ultimately forsakes Apollonian austerity for Bacchic delights (Phillpotts clearly had in mind the conflict of Apollonian and Dionysian ideologies imagined by Nietzsche in *The Birth of Tragedy*). *Pan and the Twins* imagines a similar ideological conflict between two brothers, one a Christian and the other a follower of Pan; like France and Nietzsche, Phillpotts is critical of the life-denying asceticism of Christianity, advocating a warmer Epicureanism here symbolized by the altogether amiable Pan. In *The Treasures of Typhon* a distinctly half-hearted disciple of Epicurus embarks on a quest for a magical plant, aided by the ability to converse with trees—by which means he gradually learns how to be a better and truer Epicurean. In the fine novella *Circe's Island* a boy searches for his father—who has been turned into an animal by the sorceress—needing only to identify him to set him free; in the meantime, he is given good advice about the art of living well by Odysseus, a temporary resident of the island.

The Miniature, more of an essay than a story, takes the form of a commentary by the Classical gods on the philosophical evolution of mankind, who have much to say about the psychological utility of religion; it ends on a bleak note with mankind's annihilation in a nuclear holocaust—a possibility which came to preoccupy the author later in life. *Arachne,* by contrast (which might perhaps have been written earlier), is a very effective recapitulation of the Greek legend, which does not hesitate to alter the conclusion in order to establish a better moral than the original. *Alcyone* is misleadingly subtitled in the same way as the author's juvenile fantasies, perhaps as a desperate marketing ploy, but it chronicles the allegorical odyssey of the rather crass poet Euphranor in search of his destiny—a destiny which ultimately cannot accommodate the eponymous immortal lover. It is far the most sarcastic of the Classical fantasies, and one cannot help suspecting that it is to some degree painfully self-critical.

Alongside these Classical fantasies Phillpotts wrote two other fantasies using different backgrounds to the same effect. *The Lavender Dragon* is a charming tale in which a benevolent dragon steals lonely humans to populate a utopian community, whose tolerance and justice contrast sharply with the oppressive tyranny of Feudalism and its misguided knights errant. *The Apes* is an ironic allegory of evolution similar to *The Miniature,* in which simians gathered in conference boast of their discoveries but prove very reluctant to come to terms with the idea that they will ultimately be superseded by new and better species.

The Owl of Athene begins as a Classical fantasy in which a council of Olympians decides to put mankind to the test, but veers abruptly into the realms of scientific romance as the land surface of the earth is invaded by giant crabs. Phillpotts followed this up with the fine scientific romance *Saurus*—a far cry from his earlier pseudonymous foray into the genre, *Number 87*—and subsequently used that kind of imaginative framework for his more philosophically-inclined works. Science-fictional imagery also began to displace fantasy in his juvenile works, the amiable talking animals of *Golden Island* being replaced by giant spiders in the robust treasure-island story *Tabletop.*

This change of method was, in a sense, altogether fitting; Phillpotts was, after all a hardened rationalist. He issued a collection of *Thoughts in Prose and Verse* under the banner of the Rationalist Press Association—which is, ironically, the only one of his many collections apart from his first to include a significant quantity of fantasy—and he wrote two notable mystery stories in which characters who hold to supernatural explanations of seemingly-inexplicable are roundly criticized for their folly, *The Grey Room* and *Lycanthrope.* Phillpotts's fantasies, however, serve to remind us that fantasy too is at its best when it offers no insult to reason, using its imagery to the allegorical end of reminding us that life is what we make it and that we must therefore be very careful in making what we can of it. Pan, in *Pan and the Twins,* serves not only as an example of a saner moral outlook than that of Christ's fervent disciples but also as a philosopher of progress; religion, he opines, is a temporary necessity required so that "we shall not perish of to much truth," but one day men will be able to escape their "cages" of faith to confront the world in all its awful glory.

Phillpotts's fantasies were not commercially successful, and he evidently found it increasingly difficult to publish them once the brief post-war boom which British fantasy enjoyed in the 1920s was past, but they are excellent works in spite of an occasional tendency to prolixity and pomposity. There is no finer body of English fiction dedicated to the noble purpose of teaching us to be better Epicureans.

—Brian Stableford

PIERCE, Meredith Ann

Nationality: American. **Born:** Seattle, Washington, 5 July 1958. **Education:** University of Florida, Gainesville, 1975-80, B.A. in liberal arts 1978, M.A. in English 1980. **Career:** Teaching assistant, Office of Instructional Resources, 1978, and Department of English, 1978-80, University of Florida; bookseller, Bookland, 1981, and Waldenbooks, 1981-87, both Gainesville; since 1987 library assistant, Alachua County library district, Gainesville.

Awards: *Scholastic Magazine* prize, 1973; International Reading Association award, 1983; Bread Loaf Writers Conference Broughton fellowship, 1984; Special Award for Children's Literature, Florida Department of State, Division of Cultural Affairs, 1987. **Address:** 424-H Northeast Sixth Street, Gainesville, FL 32601, USA.

FANTASY PUBLICATIONS

Novels (series: Aeriel; Firebringer)

The Darkangel (Aeriel). Boston, Little Brown, 1982; London, Collins, 1983.
A Gathering of Gargoyles (Aeriel). Boston, Little Brown, 1984.
Birth of the Firebringer. New York, Four Winds Press, and London, Macmillan, 1985.
The Woman Who Loved Reindeer. Boston, Atlantic Monthly Press, 1985; London, Hodder and Stoughton, 1987.
Where the Wild Geese Go, illustrated by Jamichael Henterly. New York, Dutton, 1988.
The Pearl of the Soul of the World (Aeriel). Boston, Little Brown, 1990.
The Darkangel Trilogy (omnibus; includes *The Darkangel, A Gathering of Gargoyles, The Pearl of the Soul of the World*). New York, Guild America, 1990.
Dark Moon (Firebringer). Boston, Little Brown, 1992.

* * *

Meredith Ann Pierce came to prominence with the publication of her first novel, *The Darkangel,* remarkable partly because it was written when she was only 23, but also because it was an original work treated with mature skill. The plot is intriguing: Aeriel, a slave girl, sets out to rescue her friend and mistress Eoduin, who has been taken by the darkangel (vampyre/icarus) as his bride. The latter discovers her waiting for him on the mountain and takes her to his castle, to be servant to his twelve-and-one brides, now become indistinguishable wraiths. The brides tell Aeriel the darkangel is not yet a full vampyre, for although he has drunk their blood their souls lie in leaden vials on his belt, and it is only when he fills the fourteenth vial and takes them all to his mother, the lorelei, for her to drink, that he will lose his own soul. The wraiths urge Aeriel to kill the darkangel, but she cannot bring herself to do so, for she has looked into his eyes and seen him to be beautiful; she has told him tales and fed his vicious gargoyles, who keep her prisoner in the castle.

Talb, the troll-like magician *duarough,* hears Aeriel's dilemma and tells her a rhyme which might show the way to undo the icarus, explaining he is not in fact a son of the lorelei but a mortal child, stolen away at an early age. Aeriel is sent on her travels to find the strong-hoof of the starhorse, pursued by the darkangel who is filled with rage by one of the tales she has related to him, concerning the loss of the chieftain of the Tour-of-Kings' son, a boy named Irrylath. The darkangel wounds Aeriel, but she is saved by the intervention of the lion Pendarlon, one of the old wardens of the lands of the moon. With his help, she finds the strong-hoof and returns to the darkangel's castle, where he selects her for his fourteenth bride, but on their wedding night she makes him drink a special water of life, distilled from the strong-hoof, and poisons him.

Yet as he lies helpless, Aeriel cannot bring herself to kill him, and gives him her own human heart to save him. In return, as she

lies dying, the duarough strips off the lead that has covered the vampyre's own heart and places it in Aeriel's breast. The darkangel wakes to know himself the same Irrylath of Aeriel's tale. His wings fall from him, and he and Aeriel use their feathers to escape to Esternesse, where they must find the means to prevent the lorelei stealing another child, for once she has seven icari they will conquer the kingdoms of the moon. They must fight both the icari and the lorelei herself.

The story itself possesses a fairy-tale—even an *Arabian Nights*—quality, but that is to underrate the extraordinarily evocative nature of the work, rich with the power of myth. Beautifully written, the pace of *The Darkangel* is rapid, but without loss of empathy or atmosphere. The characters possess the unreality of mythical creatures, but that does not render them any less appealing.

A Gathering of Gargoyles, the second book, continues Aeriel's voyage of discovery, this time across the Sea-of-Dust and the lands beyond, where she pursues the understanding of the second part of the riddle of how to defeat the lorelei and her vampyre sons. In the process she also uncovers the secret of her own identity. This novel, too, is filled with magic invention, from the messenger heron to the gathering of the gargoyles loosed by Aeriel in *The Darkangel* from the vampyre's castle. The second book builds on the first with great skill, expanding characters, places and the scope of the plot, drawing in many threads from its predecessor. The lorelei searches for Aeriel as she seeks the lost *lons* in order to restore them for the battle to come when the starhorse, the Avarclon or warden of Avaric, is brought back to life in Esternesse. The same fairy-tale elements exist, the same imaginative invention in a tale both more rounded and more complex, which nonetheless loses nothing of the sense of time-and-place-suspended of *The Darkangel.*

The Woman Who Loved Reindeer, although different in theme and setting, contains the same mixture of myth and fantasy as Pierce's earlier work. Set in a mystic Lapp-type culture, it deals with Caribou, a seer, who has brought up a child she discovers to be a *trangyl,* half-human and half-reindeer and able to adopt either form. He seems incapable of human emotion and deserts her to run with the herd, but returns to rescue her and her people when Caribou's own land is threatened by the upheavals of the firelords. They escape across the burning lands, aided by sea-maidens in attaining their final destination. The details of the culture in the book are carefully drawn and completely convincing; Pierce succeeds in evoking the atmosphere of a vulnerable primitive people dependent on utilizing every resource offered them to survive. Nor is she averse to dealing with the positive and negative sides of human emotion, in which logic has a lesser part to play than fear or need or love.

The small quantity of Pierce's work is high in quality. There is a magic in the weaving of her tales which is deeply absorbing. The atmospheres she creates tend to linger in the mind, and there is a directness and lack of sentimentality about her characters which engender a powerful appeal.

—Mary Corran

PINKWATER, Daniel Manus

Nationality: American. **Born:** Memphis, Tennessee, 15 November 1941. **Education:** Bard College, Annandale-on-Hudson, New

York, B.A. 1964. **Family:** Married Jill Schutz in 1969. **Career:** Art instructor, Children's Aid Society, 1967-69, Lower West Side Visual Arts Center, 1969, and Henry Street Settlement, 1969, all New York, and Bonnie Brae Farm for Boys, Millington, New Jersey, 1969; assistant project director, Inner City Summer Arts Program, Hoboken, New Jersey, 1970. Regular commentator, *All Things Considered,* National Public Radio, from 1987. **Awards:** New Jersey Institute of Technology award, 1975; American Library Association Notable Book award, 1976; *New York Times* Outstanding Book, 1978; Children's Choice book award from the International Reading Association and the Children's Book Council, 1981; Parents' Choice award, 1982. **Address:** 111 Crum Elbow Road, Hyde Park, NY 12538, USA.

FANTASY PUBLICATIONS

Novels (series: Snarkout Boys)

Wizard Crystal. New York, Dodd Mead, 1973.
Magic Camera. New York, Dodd Mead, 1974.
Lizard Music. New York, Dodd Mead, 1976.
The Hoboken Chicken Emergency. Englewood Cliffs, New Jersey, Prentice Hall, 1977.
The Last Guru. New York, Dodd Mead, 1978.
Yobgorble: Mystery Monster of Lake Ontario. New York, Clarion, 1979.
The Worms of Kukumlima. New York, Dutton, 1981.
The Snarkout Boys and the Avocado of Death. New York, Lothrop, 1982.
The Snarkout Boys and the Baconburg Horror. New York, Lothrop, 1984.

OTHER PUBLICATIONS

Fiction for Children

The Terrible Roar (as Manus Pinkwater). New York, Knopf, 1970.
Bear's Picture (as Manus Pinkwater). New York, Holt Rinehart, 1972.
Fat Elliot and the Gorilla (as Manus Pinkwater). New York, Four Winds Press, 1974.
Blue Moose (as Manus Pinkwater). New York, Dodd Mead, 1975; London, Blackie, 1977.
Three Big Hogs (as Manus Pinkwater). New York, Seabury Press, 1975.
Wingman (as Manus Pinkwater). New York, Dodd Mead, 1975.
Around Fred's Bed (as Manus Pinkwater), illustrated by Robert Mertens. Englewood Cliffs, New Jersey, Prentice Hall, 1976.
The Big Orange Splot. New York, Hastings House, 1977.
The Blue Thing. Englewood Cliffs, New Jersey, Prentice Hall, 1977.
Fat Men from Space. New York, Dodd Mead, 1977.
Alan Mendelsohn: The Boy from Mars. New York, Dutton, 1979.
Pickle Creature. New York, Four Winds Press, 1979.
Return of the Moose. New York, Dodd Mead, 1979.
Java Jack, with Luqman Keele. New York, Crowell, 1980.
The Magic Moscow. New York, Four Winds Press, 1980.
The Wuggie Norple Story, illustrated by Tomie de Paola. New York, Four Winds Press, 1980.

Attila the Pun. New York, Four Winds Press, 1981.
Tooth-Gnasher Superflash. New York, Four Winds Press, 1981.
Roger's Umbrella, illustrated by James Marshall. New York, Dutton, 1982.
Slaves of Spiegel. New York, Four Winds Press, 1982.
Young Adult Novel. New York, Crowell, 1982.
I Was a Second Grade Werewolf. New York, Dutton, 1983.
Devil in the Drain. New York, Dutton, 1984.
Ducks! Boston, Little Brown, 1984.
The Frankenbagel Monster. New York, Dutton, 1986.
The Moosepire. Boston, Little Brown, 1986.
The Muffin Fiend. New York, Lothrop, 1986.
Aunt Lulu. New York, Macmillan, 1988.
Guys from Space. New York, Macmillan, 1989.
Uncle Melvin. New York, Macmillan, 1989.
Borgel. New York, Macmillan, 1990.
Doodle Flute. New York, Macmillan, 1991.
Wempires. New York, Macmillan, 1991.
The Phantom of the Lunch Wagon. New York, Macmillan, 1992.
Author's Day. New York, Macmillan, 1993.
Spaceburger. New York, Macmillan, 1993.

Other

Superpuppy: How to Choose, Raise, and Train the Best Possible Dog for You, with Jill Pinkwater. New York, Seabury Press, 1977.
Fish Whistle: Commentaries, Uncommentaries, and Vulgar Excesses. Reading, Massachusetts, Addison Wesley, 1989.
Chicago Days/Hoboken Nights. Reading, Massachusetts, Addison Wesley, 1991.

*

Film Adaptation: *The Great Hoboken Chicken Emergency* (TV movie), 1984.

*   *   *

One of the keys to appreciating Daniel Manus Pinkwater's many works for children lies with accepting nonsense and silliness as a valid part of humorous fantasy. Pinkwater's many books for children all include wild flights of fancy, sometimes magical, sometimes simply asking readers to suspend adherence to reality. This bold and direct approach to fantasy is enhanced by Pinkwater's illustrations, which are flat and simple, almost childlike.

An early Pinkwater title to attract attention was *Lizard Music.* In this story, young Victor is left home alone. Being resourceful he copes well enough, but naturally stays up late to watch television. After viewing *The Body Snatchers* he is amazed to see a band of life-sized lizards playing instruments on the screen. The following day he decides to go to Hogboro (Chicago, called Baconburg in other books) and he meets the Chicken Man, an elderly African American with a trained chicken, Claudia. Victor encounters other odd things in the city; some are hints to him that the television lizards are real. Eventually, Victor goes with the Chicken Man to the Invisible Island, home of the lizards. As in most good stories of magical adventuring, Victor finally goes home, barely beating the return of his parents and sister.

In some ways, *Lizard Music* has more structure and is more conventional than most of Pinkwater's work. Yet humour is present at all times and readers have no need to be frightened. Pinkwater can be counted on to tell his stories in such direct terms there is never concern that any of his tales will turn into horror at any point. His works might well be compared to Douglas Adams' humorous science-fiction novels for adults, and it should be noted that a number of Pinkwater's books involve space themes.

Pinkwater apparently finds chicken funny, since they are featured in a number of his stories. In *The Hoboken Chicken Emergency* young Arthur must find his family's Thanksgiving turkey. Alas, all he can locate is a 266-pound chicken named Henrietta. Henrietta escapes and terrorizes Hoboken, and a famous chicken catcher is hired to trap the large bird. Fortunately, Arthur is able to convince people that all Henrietta wants is love, then she will stop eating every potato in town. If Henrietta had been able to communicate as well as Claudia, she wouldn't have had such problems.

In the two Snarkout Boys books, a pair of adventurous lads find many strange things in Hogburg. They delight in sneaking out at night to go to the Snark (Clark) theatre to watch old movies on an ever-changing bill. Perhaps inspired by the infamous film, *The Attack of the Killer Tomatoes,* an evil and voracious avocado of death appears.

At first glance Pinkwater's work appears to be wildly implausible and based on as few facts as possible. However, he uses some reality in his stories. For example, the Chicken Man was based on a real person who used to ride the city buses of Chicago freely with his performing chicken. On the other hand, it is unlikely that a 266-pound chicken really roamed the streets of Hoboken, or an avocado of death ever horrified Chicagoans. Yet, sometimes with Pinkwater, it's not always a certain thing as to what is reality and what is fiction. This results in a surreal quality that is ever-present in Pinkwater's books.

Pinkwater seems to like weird creatures and uses them to the great delight of his young readership. In *Yobgorgle* readers are presented with a monster reminiscent of the Loch Ness monster, yet the idea of such a creature cavorting in Lake Ontario seems oddly out-of-place, and as a result, funny. But just when you think you have a handle on Pinkwater, he throws you off again. In *The Worms of Kukumlima,* readers are presented with one of the silliest adventures quests ever, a search for the chess-playing worms that can only be found in Africa.

In trying to analyse Pinkwater's work, one can discover a few probable influences, such as *The Rocky and Bullwinkle* television program first shown in the 1960s. Certainly, the moose in his stories for very young children bears a lot of resemblance to Bullwinkle. Also, movies play an important part in setting certain scenes and influencing plots. American popular culture is very evident in Pinkwater's books, and the author uses these details to great advantage. It is apparent that Pinkwater grabs anything he wants to create a laugh. His stories are wild trips into a fantasyland that is often ridiculous and just plain fun.

Pinkwater is almost mischievous in his blending of reality and fantasy. Sometimes a real setting is bent totally out of shape, and in other situations, fantasy becomes surprisingly real. In *The Last Guru,* for example, the astonishing guru turns out to be a fake, not a true mystic at all. Yet, in an odd way, this very unpredictable quality in Pinkwater has become a hallmark of his work, and one his fans like. In the end, it's hard to take Pinkwater seriously, but he's probably the last person who'd want you to do so.

—Cosette Kies

POLLACK, Rachel (Grace)

Nationality: American. **Born:** Richard A. Pollack, in Brooklyn, New York, 1945. **Career:** English teacher, State University of New York, Plattsburgh, early 1970s; published writer from 1971; lived, working part-time as a lecturer and Tarot reader, in the Netherlands, 1973-90. **Awards:** Arthur C. Clarke award, 1988. **Address:** c/o Orbit Books, Little, Brown and Company (UK), Brettenham House, Lancaster Place, London WC2E 7EN.

FANTASY PUBLICATIONS

Novels

Unquenchable Fire. London, Century, 1988; Woodstock, New York, Overlook Press, 1992.
Temporary Agency. London, Orbit, and New York, St. Martin's Press, 1994.

Other

Editor, with Caitlín Matthews, *Tarot Tales.* London, Legend, 1989.

OTHER PUBLICATIONS

Novels

Golden Vanity. New York, Berkley, 1980.
Alqua Dreams. New York, Watts, 1987; London, Legend, 1990.

Other

Seventy-Eight Degrees of Wisdom: A Book of Tarot. Wellington, Northamptonshire, Aquarian Press, 2 vols., 1980-83; San Bernardino, California, Borgo Press, 1986.
Salvador Dali's Tarot. Salem, New Hampshire, Salem House, and London, Rainbird, 1985.
A Practical Guide to Fortune Telling: Palmistry, the Crystal Ball, Runes, Tea Leaves, the Tarot. London, Sphere/Rainbird, 1986; as *Teach Yourself Fortune Telling,* New York, Holt, 1986.
Tarot: The Open Labyrinth. Wellingborough, Northamptonshire, Aquarian Press, 1986; San Bernardino, California, Borgo Press, 1989.
The New Tarot. Wellingborough, Northamptonshire, Aquarian Press, 1989; Woodstock, New York, Overlook Press, 1990.
Tarot Readings and Meditations. Wellingborough, Northamptonshire, Aquarian Press, 1990.

Editor, with Mary K. Greer, *New Thoughts on Tarot: Transcripts from the First International Newcastle Tarot Symposium.* North Hollywood, California, Newcastle, 1989.

*   *   *

Much of Rachel Pollack's fiction could be identified as science fiction rather than as fantasy; indeed, *Unquenchable Fire,* which deals with New Age mysticism and working magic—by most definitions fantasy themes—won the Arthur C. Clarke Award for the best science fiction novel published in the UK in its year. But it is very often at the fuzzy interface between genres that the most significant work appears (John Crowley's *Little, Big,* Mark Helprin's *Winter's Tale,* much of Michael Swanwick's work, etc.). Gene Wolfe and Sheri S. Tepper use fantasy tropes (and the better elements of fantasy writing style) in what are actually science fiction novels. At this level of quality—and this includes Rachel Pollack—genre borderlines become not so much troublesome as meaningless.

Rachel Pollack is best known as an authority on the esoteric, having written several serious studies on Tarot, including the companion volume to the controversial Salvador Dali pack, and the delightful and richly illustrated *The New Tarot,* which examines over 70 of the Tarot packs that have come on the market in the last two decades; she has also designed her own Tarot pack. Her largely fantasy anthology *Tarot Tales,* co-edited with Arthurian authority Caitlín Matthews, contains original stories inspired by Tarot spreads or individual cards, and its notable contributors include Scott Bradfield, M. John Harrison, Garry Kilworth and Michael Moorcock, among others.

Pollack's fascination with religion imbues her more recent fiction with a rare depth and complexity, making it perhaps a little difficult for the casual reader but tremendously rewarding for anyone prepared to put in some effort. Her fiction deals with the interplay of philosophical abstracts with the solid, the "real" world. She asks questions about the nature of reality, making the reader step slightly to one side, enabling us to examine and explore our own society—and ourselves—from a new, and often spiritual viewpoint.

This is seen most of all in *Unquenchable Fire* and *Temporary Agency.* But even in the early and neglected *Golden Vanity,* a seemingly traditional science fiction novel about the less pleasant aspects of Earth's first contact with extra-terrestrials, Pollack explores meditation exercises, visualization, and the self-deceptions of the kookier side of New Age religion. Her second science fiction novel, *Alqua Dreams,* contains mythological, religious, and deeply philosophical questions. The inhabitants of Planet Keela believe that they're all dead; their "life" is simply a delusion forced on them by the liar god Canumaira. The Terran trading negotiator is called an alqua: one suffering from the illusion that he is alive. He finds himself trying to convince the people that they are wrong, that they do exist, that they are real. The novel is a challenging study of two totally incompatible philosophical belief systems: the ancient debate between Platonic and Aristotelian life-views.

In *Unquenchable Fire,* a complex and moving—and challenging—tale of story telling and myth-creation set in an alternate present-day America, Pollack draws heavily on her knowledge of myth and religion. In the world she creates, a magical religion loosely based on shamanistic and some current New Age beliefs is an essential part of everyone's life, Tellers of mythic stories are revered, dreams are computer-analyzed for their meaning, and Woolworth's sells amulets. Personal miracles, while not commonplace, happen often enough to be greeted with joy rather than disbelief. Neighbours hold group meetings to raise each others' spiritual awareness.

It's as if the New Age Aquarians have taken over the materialistic America we know. But human nature, with all its jealousies and spites, is much the same; Pollack shows that changing the spiritual infrastructure has little effect in itself; the only meaningful revolution is the one inside. Jennifer Mazdan has to cope with becoming pregnant from a dream, and with the knowledge that her unborn child will be especially significant; but she also has to cope with

the pettiness of her neighbours. The stories told by the Tellers within the book are Pollack's own myths of creation and destruction, of power and love and betrayal; myths of a society quite different from our own—yet similar enough to draw parallels. It's by no means an easy book, but it is a very powerful and stimulating examination of the spiritual aspects of life.

Temporary Agency is a much simpler and far more accessible novel than *Unquenchable Fire,* in whose world it is set. It's less mystical, more hard-edged, and more straightforward, and the alternative reality is utterly believable—more so than in the previous book. A teenage girl becomes tangled up in the efforts of a Ferocious One (a malign spiritual being in human form) to entrap her adult cousin Paul who has fallen in love with the Ferocious One. As the story develops, Paul and others become possessed by unpleasant spiritual forces. Without in any way preaching, Pollack again uses fantasy to point up the darker side of esoteric religion. Neither book pretends that a New Age religious world will be all sweetness and light; people are still people, with all their failings, loves, jealousies, selfishness and ambitions.

Pollack is a writer well worth following, though her depth of thought requires her readers to work probably just that little bit too hard for her ever to become a "popular" author of fiction.

—David V. Barrett

POWERS, Tim(othy Thomas)

Pseudonym: William Ashbless. **Nationality:** American. **Born:** Buffalo, New York, 29 February 1952. **Education:** California State University. **Awards:** Philip K. Dick Memorial award, 1984, 1986; World Fantasy award, 1993. **Address:** c/o Ace Books, 200 Madison Avenue, New York, NY 10016, USA.

FANTASY PUBLICATIONS

Novels

The Drawing of the Dark. New York, Ballantine, 1979; London, Mayflower, 1981.
The Anubis Gates. New York, Ace, 1983; London, Chatto and Windus, 1985.
Dinner at Deviant's Palace. New York, Ace, 1985; London, Chatto and Windus, 1986.
On Stranger Tides. New York, Ace, 1987; London, Grafton, 1988.
The Stress of Her Regard. Lynbrook, New York, Charnel House, 1989; London, Grafton, 1991.
Last Call. New York, Morrow, 1992; London, HarperCollins, 1993.
Expiration Date. London, HarperCollins, 1995.

Short Stories

Night Moves. Seattle, Washington, Axolotl Press, 1986.
The Way Down the Hill. Seattle, Washington, Axolotl Press, 1986.

OTHER PUBLICATIONS

Novels

Epitaph in Rust. Toronto, Laser, 1976; restored text, as *An Epitaph in Rust,* Cambridge, Massachusetts, NESFA Press, 1989.
The Skies Discrowned. Toronto, Laser, 1976; revised as *Forsake the Sky,* New York, Tor, 1986.

Poetry

Twelve Hours of the Night (as William Ashbless, with James P. Blaylock). New Castle, Virginia, Cheap Street, 1985.
A Short Poem (as William Ashbless). Tacoma, Washington, Folly Press, 1987.

*

Bibliography: *A Checklist of Tim Powers* by Tom Joyce and Christopher P. Stephens. Hastings-on-Hudson, New York, Ultramarine, 1991.

* * *

Powers's not inconsiderable reputation in the field of fantasy has been established with only a half-dozen novels published over more than a decade. His breakthrough came with *The Anubis Gates,* a textbook example of Powers's ability to blend the iconography of science fiction and fantasy to deliver something which has all the atmosphere of fantasy but with the logic and invention of science fiction. The book's opening frame concerns time travel back to the London of Lord Byron, but once the protagonist is there and now implanted in the body of tragic poet William Ashbless, we are propelled into a grotesque harlequinade of an alternate London that becomes defiantly more believable as the action becomes more fantastic.

The novel was a turning point in Powers's career in more ways than one. It established Powers as a name to watch and developed a reputation that has never yet failed to deliver. It also won the Philip K. Dick Memorial Award for the year's best original paperback novel, a fitting accolade, as Powers was a close friend of Dick in his final years. He was strongly influenced by Dick's philosophy of the world we see being a facade for a hidden darker reality which may betray itself to those psychotically attuned.

His writing had started with a fairly traditional science fiction novel, *The Skies Discrowned.* It's a formulaic story of a young protagonist who seeks revenge and an opportunity to restore harmony in an interplanetary empire with failing technology. The novel was ruined by editorial butchery and is best read in its restored version, *Forsake the Sky.* A similar fate befell his second novel, *Epitaph in Rust,* though this did show a move away from the traditional, with perhaps a token nod to Walter M. Miller's *A Canticle for Leibowitz.* We follow the adventures of a young monk in a post-holocaust California who escapes from his rural retreat only to become embroiled in revolution. Although the plot is still formulaic, the characterization was developing and showing signs of Powers's later trademark of the fated hero.

It is rather interesting to contrast this early work with *Dinner at Deviant's Palace,* which Powers wrote nearly a decade later and which also won the Philip K. Dick Memorial Award. Powers returns to a post-holocaust California but one that is considerably more gothic and manic than in his earlier simplistic exploration, involving a trip to hell and a confrontation with the Dark Lord. Powers's first two novels met the fate meted out to most of the high-profile/poorly managed Laser Book series, and a lesser author may have buckled as a result. But Powers then came under the more masterly direction of Lester del Rey who helped shape the burgeoning talent in a rousingly picaresque novel, *The Drawing of the Dark.* This was Powers's first significant fantasy, and the first of an intended series in which the fated hero, as a reincarnation of King Arthur, returns to battle evil and save mankind. In this instance it is as Brian Duffy, soldier of fortune, who is sent to 16th-century Vienna to help protect the city from the Turks, and to allow the drawing of a brew which will recall the Fisher King.

Although it is primarily an adventure novel, Powers manages to interweave an intricate background of historical events and Arthurian legends, a blending of myth and reality which would become his trademark. The novel shows the influence upon Powers of the works of Rafael Sabatini, one of his favourite writers.

Lester del Rey decided not to continue the series, so Powers recast the next novel as *The Anubis Gates.* The result became the archetypical novel of the "steampunk" sub-genre, with Powers seen as the leader of a trio of Californian writers (the others being James P. Blaylock and K. W. Jeter) who were reshaping the face of fantasy. It was this that made *The Anubis Gates* such an original work, bringing to life the underworld of early-19th-century London with such clarity that it supersedes the historical original.

Powers further developed his fantastic recreations of history in *On Stranger Tides,* another Sabatini-style swashbuckler of piracy and the search for the Fountain of Youth. Immortality is a recurring theme in Powers's work, whether via the perpetuation of the body as in *On Stranger Tides,* or the immortality of the soul as in the Fisher King sequence. The theme was used most poignantly in one of his rare short stories, "The Way Down the Hill" (*Fantasy & Science Fiction,* December 1982; later issued as a chapbook), where a group of immortals regularly meet to decide where their souls shall live on.

The Stress of Her Regard is perhaps Powers's most accomplished novel to date, again exploring immortality, this time in the shape of a vampire and her impact on the nightmare world of Byron, Keats and Shelley. Powers again injects an sf concept with the idea that behind historical reality is an immortal non-carbon-based lifeform controlling destiny. With *Last Call* Powers moved from historical Europe to modern California, creating a supernatural backcloth not unlike that in the work of James Blaylock. In this novel a gambler, who won a game in exchange for his life, is faced with the consequences 21 years later. It is another in Powers's series that draws upon the Fisher King legend for its plot.

In these novels Powers has demonstrated a remarkable new angle of vision blended with skilled plotting and writing to develop one of the most original talents in fantasy of the 1980s.

—Mike Ashley

POWYS, John Cowper

Nationality: British. **Born:** Shirley, Derbyshire, 8 October 1872; brother of the writers T. F. and Llewelyn Powys. **Education:** Sherborne School, Dorset; Corpus Christi College, Cambridge,

M.A. 1894. **Family:** Married Margaret Alice Lyon in 1896 (died 1947); one son. **Career:** Teacher at a girls' school in England, 1894; lecturer on English literature in the United States, 1904-34: returned to England each summer, 1910-28; lived in New York and California, 1928-34; returned to Britain in 1934 and settled in North Wales. **Awards:** Foreign Book prize (France), 1966. D. Litt.: University of Wales, Cardiff, 1962. **Died:** 17 June 1963.

FANTASY PUBLICATIONS

Novels

A Glastonbury Romance. New York, Simon and Schuster, 1932; London, Lane, 1933.
Morwyn; or, The Vengeance of God. London, Cassell, 1937; New York, Arno Press, 1976.
Porius: A Romance of the Dark Ages. London, Macdonald, 1951; New York, Philosophical Library, 1952.
Atlantis. London, Macdonald, 1954.
The Brazen Head. London, Macdonald, and Hamilton, New York, Colgate University Press, 1956.
All or Nothing. London, Macdonald, 1960.

Short Stories

The Owl, The Duck, and—Miss Rowe! Miss Rowe! Chicago, Black Archer Press, 1930.
Up and Out (also includes "The Mountains of the Moon: A Lunar Love Story"). London, Macdonald, 1957.
Real Wraiths. London, Village Press, 1974.
Two and Two. London, Village Press, 1974.
You and Me. London, Village Press, 1975.
Three Fantasies. Manchester, Carcanet, 1985.

OTHER PUBLICATIONS

Novels

Wood and Stone: A Romance. New York, Shaw, 1915; London, Heinemann, 1917.
Rodmoor: A Romance. New York, Shaw, 1916; London, Macdonald, 1973.
Ducdame. New York, Doubleday, and London, Richards, 1925.
Wolf Solent. New York, Simon and Schuster, 2 vols., 1929; London, Cape, 1 vol., 1929.
Weymouth Sands. New York, Simon and Schuster, 1934; altered version, as *Jobber Skald,* London, Lane, 1935; original version, as *Weymouth Sands,* London, Macdonald, 1963.
Maiden Castle. New York, Simon and Schuster, 1936; London, Cassell, 1937.
Owen Glendower. New York, Simon and Schuster, 2 vols., 1940; London, Lane, 1941.
The Inmates. London, Macdonald, and New York, Philosophical Library, 1952.
After My Fashion. London, Pan, 1980.

Short Stories

Romer Mowl and Other Stories, edited by Bernard Jones. St. Peter Port, Guernsey, Toucan Press, 1974.

Plays

The Idiot, with Reginald Pole, adaptation of a novel by Dostoevsky (produced New York, 1922).
Paddock Calls. London, Greymitre, 1984.

Poetry

Odes and Other Poems. London, Rider, 1896.
Poems. London, Rider, 1899.
Wolf's Bane: Rhymes. New York, Shaw, and London, Rider, 1916.
Mandragora. New York, Shaw, 1917.
Samphire. New York, Seltzer, 1922.
Lucifer: A Poem. London, Macdonald, 1956.
John Cowper Powys: A Selection from His Poems, edited by Kenneth Hopkins. London, Macdonald, 1964; Hamilton, New York, Colgate University Press, 1965.
Horned Poppies: New Poems. North Walsham, Norfolk, Warren House, 1983.
Verses on the Sad Occasion of the Death of Tippoo Tib. N.p., Marks, 1988.

Other

The War and Culture: A Reply to Professor Munsterberg. New York, Shaw, 1914; as *The Menace of German Culture,* London, Rider, 1915.
Visions and Revisions: A Book of Literary Devotions. New York, Shaw, and London, Rider, 1915.
Confessions of Two Brothers, with Llewelyn Powys. Rochester, New York, Manas Press, 1916; London, Sinclair Browne, 1982.
One Hundred Best Books. New York, Shaw, 1916.
Suspended Judgments: Essays on Books and Sensations. New York, Shaw, 1916; London, Village Press, 1975.
The Complex Vision. New York, Dodd Mead, 1920.
The Art of Happiness. Girard, Kansas, Haldeman Julius, 1923.
Psychoanalysis and Morality. San Francisco, Colbert, 1923.
The Religion of a Sceptic. New York, Dodd Mead, 1925; London, Village Press, 1975.
The Secret of Self Development. Girard, Kansas, Haldeman Julius, 1926; London, Village Press, 1974.
The Art of Forgetting the Unpleasant. Girard, Kansas, Haldeman Julius, 1928.
The Meaning of Culture. New York, Norton, 1929; London, Cape, 1930; revised edition, Norton, 1939; Cape, 1940.
Debate: Is Modern Marriage a Failure? with Bertrand Russell. New York, Discussion Guild, 1930; edited by Margaret Moran, North Walsham, Norfolk, Warren House, 1983.
In Defence of Sensuality. New York, Simon and Schuster, and London, Gollancz, 1930.
Dorothy M. Richardson. London, Joiner and Steele, 1931.
A Philosophy of Solitude. New York, Simon and Schuster, and London, Cape, 1933.
Autobiography. New York, Simon and Schuster, and London, Lane, 1934.
The Art of Happiness (not same as 1923 book). New York, Simon and Schuster, and London, Lane, 1935.
The Enjoyment of Literature. New York, Simon and Schuster, 1938; revised edition, as *The Pleasures of Literature,* London, Cassell, 1938.
Mortal Strife. London, Cape, 1942.

The Art of Growing Old. London, Cape, 1944.

Pair Dadeni; or, The Cauldron of Rebirth. Carmarthen, Wales, Druid Press, 1946.

Dostoievsky. London, Lane, 1946.

Obstinate Cymric: Essays 1935-1947. Carmarthen, Wales, Druid Press, 1947.

Rabelais. London, Lane, 1948; New York, Philosophical Library, 1951.

In Spite Of: A Philosophy for Everyman. London, Macdonald, and New York, Philosophical Library, 1953.

Letters to Louis Wilkinson 1935-1956. London, Macdonald, and Hamilton, New York, Colgate University Press, 1958.

Homer and the Aether. London, Macdonald, 1959.

Letters to Glyn Hughes, edited by Bernard Jones. Stevenage, Hertfordshire, Ore, 1971.

Letters to Nicholas Ross, edited by Arthur Uphill. London, Rota, 1971.

Letters 1937-1954, edited by Iorweth C. Peate. Cardiff, University of Wales Press, 1974.

An Englishman Upstate. London, Village Press, 1974.

Letters to His Brother Llewelyn 1902-1925, edited by Malcolm Elwin. London, Village Press, 1975.

Letters to Henry Miller. London, Village Press, 1975.

Letters to C. Benson Roberts. London, Village Press, 1975.

Letters to Clifford Tolchard. London, Village Press, 1975.

Letters to G. R. Wilson Knight, edited by Robert Blackmore. London, Cecil Woolf, 1983.

Letters to Sven-Erik Tackmark, edited by Cedric Hentschel. London, Cecil Woolf, 1983.

The Diary 1930, edited by Frederick Davies. London, Greymitre, 1987.

*

Bibliography: *A Bibliography of the Writings of John Cowper Powys* by Thomas Dante, Mamaroneck, New York, Appel, 1975.

Manuscript Collections: Churchill College, Cambridge; Colgate University, Hamilton, New York; Humanities Research Center, University of Texas, Austin.

Critical Studies: *Welsh Ambassadors: Powys Lives and Letters* by Louis Marlow, London, Chapman and Hall, 1936, revised edition, Hamilton, New York, Colgate University Press, 1971; *The Powys Brothers* by R. C. Churchill, London, Longman, 1962; *The Saturnian Quest: A Chart of the Prose Works of John Cowper Powys* by G. Wilson Knight, London, Methuen, and New York, Barnes and Noble, 1964; *John Cowper Powys: Old Earth-Man* by H. P. Collins, London, Barrie and Rockliff, 1966; *The Powys Brothers: A Biographical Appreciation* by Kenneth Hopkins, London, Phoenix House, and Rutherford, New Jersey, Fairleigh Dickinson University Press, 1967; *Essays on John Cowper Powys* edited by Belinda Humfrey, Cardiff, University of Wales Press, 1972; *John Cowper Powys, Novelist* by Glen Cavaliero, Oxford, Clarendon Press, 1973; *The Demon Within: A Study of John Cowper Powys's Novels* by John A. Brebner, London, Macdonald, 1973; *John Cowper Powys* by Jeremy Hooker, Cardiff, University of Wales Press, 1973; *The Immortal Bard* by Henry Miller, London, Village Press, 1973; *John Cowper Powys and the Magical Quest* by Morine Krissdottir, London, Macdonald and Jane's, 1980; *John Cowper Powys: In Search of a Landscape* by C. A. Coates, London, Macmillan, 1982; *The Brothers Powys* by Richard Perceval Graves, London, Routledge, 1983; *The Ecstatic World of John Cowper Powys* by H. W. Fawkner, Rutherford, New Jersey, Fairleigh Dickinson University Press, 1986.

*   *   *

John Cowper Powys was the eldest son of a clergyman; he could hardly escape concern with matters of theology, nor could he help experiencing a painful tension when he eventually rejected his father's orthodox piety in favour of a very different metaphysics. This new and highly idiosyncratic metaphysical system was first outlined at some length as a kind of commentary accompanying the otherwise non-fantastic events of *A Glastonbury Romance,* the second of the novels making up the author's "Wessex quartet". In the first paragraph of this work we are introduced to "the divine-diabolical soul of the First Cause of all life" and the remarkable climactic passages constitute a hymn to the earth-mother Cybele; the grail-quest which organizes the plot conflates the Christian grail with a Druidic "pagan grail" supposedly linked to Cybele's worship. This calculated paganization of Powys's quasi-Manichean view of a universe in which good and evil are equal in power and intimately entangled may have been a diplomatic compromise; as early as 1906 he had expressed a much more direct challenge to religious orthodoxy in the epic poem he first called "The Death of God" and eventually published as *Lucifer,* which is one of the most striking works of English Literary Satanism.

A significant subsidiary theme in *A Glastonbury Romance* is the attempt by Owen Evans to exorcise his unholy obsession with sadistic imagery. Powys confessed in his *Autobiography* that he suffered, guiltily, from an exactly similar preoccupation. Powys's literary fantasies are essentially baroque elaborations of his personal fantasies and may be regarded as an attempt to explore and come to terms with them; it is, of course, easy enough for a man to construe disturbing dreams as quasi-supernatural visitations, even though he may be well aware of the absurdity of so doing. Powys's most extended attempt to use fantasy to examine his fascination with sadistic imagery was *Morwyn,* which represents itself as a tirade against vivisection. The narrator is thrust into a strange Underworld by a meteor, accompanied by his beloved dog and a young girl ("morwyn" is Welsh for "maiden"). The sector of Elysium in which they find themselves has been transformed into Hell by the passions of its sadistic inhabitants, but the Marquis de Sade appoints himself guide and guardian to the visitors, assisting them to flee from Torquemada and the narrator's scientist father, who have evil designs upon the girl and the dog. With the help of Taliesin they discover the navel of the universe, where Merlin sleeps alongside Cronos and other forgotten deities; there they participate in a show trial which tries to assess the degrees of guilt appropriate to different crimes of cruelty. It seems that "the System-of-Things" intends that there should be a gradual evolution in mankind of pity and sympathy, but that science has taken over from perverted religion in blocking this progress.

Powys was by this time in his sixties and had retired to Wales, whose mythology crops up repeatedly in other novels of the period. Merlin reappears as Myrddin Wyllt, a representative of "true" religion, in *Porius,* an eccentric historical novel which transfigures Arthurian legend. Another historical novel with fantasy elements, *The Brazen Head,* employs a popular legend in which either Roger Bacon or Albertus Magnus (in the novel they are collaborators) fashions a magical head to deliver oracles but misses the opportunity to hear them. *Atlantis,* a sequel to Homer's *Odyssey* (Powys was subsequently to "explain"—or transform—the meaning of the *Iliad* in his nonfictional account of *Homer and the Aether*) is much more nakedly fantastic, reintroducing into Powys's work a reckless and riotous animism which he had first displayed long before in the eccentric short story *The Owl, the Duck and—Miss Rowe! Miss Rowe!,* which featured the various "inhabitants" of a room his brother Llewellyn then occupied in New York. This bizarre exercise in surrealism was to provide a kind of template for the series of highly exotic fantasy novellas with which Powys (by then in his late eighties) concluded his career.

Only three of these lengthy fantasies were published while Powys was still alive, although the much shorter "Shillyshally" (1961) is a product of the same phase of his career; perhaps the wonder is that any were published at all, given that they are among the most eccentric works ever penned. They manifest a peculiar combination of vivid intensity and flagrantly absurdity; the names attached to the characters quickly decay into baby-talk (Powys called it "suckfist gibberish"). Powys did, however, remain in control of the work, unrepentantly and unapologetically conscious of its increasing silliness.

The most lucid of these last stories is "The Mountains Of the Moon," in which the moon is inhabited by the astral bodies of earthly dreamers, which have intuitive knowledge of metaphysical truths. Its relative gentleness contrasts with the aggressive thrust of "Up and Out: A Mystery Tale," in which four survivors of the world's explosion—including the monstrous Org and his inamorata Asm—float through the cosmos encountering various philosophers, deities and personified ideas. The prolix *All or Nothing* is similar, though earthbound. *You and Me* revisits the moon; *Real Wraiths* follows four ghosts through a series of encounters with various representatives of the Underworld; *Two and Two* allows the magician Wat Kums to journey through the cosmos on a titan's back. The final novellas in the series, collected in *Three Fantasies,* dissolve into near-dementia: "Topsy-Turvy" is a kind of replay of *The Owl, the Duck and—Miss Rowe! Miss Rowe!,* featuring the "inhabitants" of Powys's own room in Blaenau-Ffestiniog; "Cataclysm" is an apocalyptic fantasy thematically linked to *Morwyn*; "Abertackle" is a chaotic confusion of images plucked almost at random from the author's repertoire.

No other writer ever provided such a detailed account of his descent into mental incoherence, but it cannot be denied that Powys's account is of considerable interest and value precisely because it is unparalleled. There is a measure of real heroism in the desperate and obsessed groping for enlightenment and understanding which these stories represent.

—Brian Stableford

POWYS, T(heodore) F(rancis)

Nationality: British. **Born:** Shirley, Derbyshire, 20 December 1875; brother of John Cowper Powys, q.v., and the writer Llewelyn Powys. **Education:** Attended private schools, and at Dorchester Grammar School. **Family:** Married Violet Rosalie Bodds in 1905; two sons and one adopted daughter. Lived in Dorset for most of his life; writer from 1908. **Died:** 27 November 1953.

FANTASY PUBLICATIONS

Novels

Mockery Gap. London, Chatto and Windus, and New York, Knopf, 1925.
Mr. Weston's Good Wine. London, Chatto and Windus, 1927; New York, Viking, 1928.
Unclay. London, Chatto and Windus, 1931; New York, Viking, 1932.

Short Stories

The Left Leg. London, Chatto and Windus, and New York, Knopf, 1923.
Fables. London, Chatto and Windus, and New York, Viking, 1929; as *No Painted Plumage,* Chatto and Windus, 1934.
The Key of the Field. London, Jackson, 1930.
The Only Penitent. London, Chatto and Windus, 1931.
The Two Thieves. London, Chatto and Windus, 1932; New York, Viking, 1933.
Two Stories: Come and Dine, and Tadnol, edited by Peter Riley. Hastings, Sussex, Brimmell, 1967.

OTHER PUBLICATIONS

Novels

Black Bryony. London, Chatto and Windus, and New York, Knopf, 1923.
Mark Only. London, Chatto and Windus, and New York, Knopf, 1924.
Mr. Tasker's Gods. London, Chatto and Windus, and New York, Knopf, 1925.
Innocent Birds. London, Chatto and Windus, and New York, Knopf, 1926.
Kindness in a Corner. London, Chatto and Windus, and New York, Viking, 1930.
When Thou Wast Naked. London, Golden Cockerel, 1931.

Short Stories

A Stubborn Tree. London, Archer, 1926.
Feed My Swine. London, Archer, 1926.
A Strong Girl and the Bride. London, Archer, 1926.
What Lack I Yet? London, Archer, and San Francisco, Gelber Lilienthal, 1927.
The Rival Pastors. London, Archer, 1927.
The House with the Echo: Twenty-Six Stories. London, Chatto and Windus, and New York, Viking, 1928.
The Dewpond. London, Mathews and Marrot, 1928.
Christ in the Cupboard. London, Lahr, 1930.
The White Paternoster and Other Stories. London, Chatto and Windus, 1930; New York, Viking, 1931.
Uriah on the Hill. Cambridge, Minority Press, 1930.
Uncle Dottery: A Christmas Story. Bristol, Hill, 1930.
The Tithe Barn and The Dove and the Eagle. London, Bhat, 1932.
Captain Patch: Twenty-One Stories. London, Chatto and Windus, 1935.
Make Thyself Many. London, Grayson, 1935.

Goat Green, or The Better Gift. London, Golden Cockerel, 1937.
Bottle's Path and Other Stories. London, Chatto and Windus, 1946.
God's Eyes a-Twinkle: An Anthology of the Stories of T. F. Powys. London, Chatto and Windus, 1947.
Rosie Plum and Other Stories, edited by Francis Powys. London, Chatto and Windus, 1966.
The Scapegoat, edited by Peter Riley. Hastings, Sussex, Brimmell, 1966.
The Strong Wooer. London, Ward, 1970.
Three Short Stories. Loughton, Essex, Dud Norman Press, 1970.

Other

An Interpretation of Genesis. Privately printed, 1907; London, Chatto and Windus, and New York, Viking Press, 1929.
The Soliloquy of a Hermit. New York, Arnold Shaw, 1916; as *Soliloquies of a Hermit,* London, Melrose, 1918.

*

Bibliography: *A Bibliography of T. F. Powys* by Peter Riley. Hastings, Sussex, Brimmell, 1967.

Critical Studies: *The Novels and Stories of T. F. Powys* by William Hunter, Cambridge, Frazer, 1930; *T. F. Powys* by Henry Coombes, London, Barrie and Rockcliff, 1960; *The Powys Brothers* by R. C. Churchill, London, Longman, 1962; *Theodore: Essays on T. F. Powys* edited by Brocard Sewell, Aylesford, St. Albert's Press, 1964; *The Powys Brothers: A Biographical Appreciation* by Kenneth Hopkins, London, Phoenix House, and Rutherford, New Jersey, Fairleigh Dickinson University Press, 1967; *T. F. Powys* by J. Lawrence Mitchell, Minneapolis, University of Minnesota, 1982; *The Brothers Powys* by Richard Perceval Graves, London, Routledge, 1983.

*   *   *

Like his elder brother John, Theodore Powys found his father's orthodox theology difficult to reconcile with his experience of the world and of his own inner self, and like John he used fantastic fiction as a means of exploring alternatives. His quest was not as far-ranging; he was able to bring it to a conclusion much sooner and it did not take him into such exotic territory. Indeed, Theodore's fantasies, which are all set in a chain of tiny villages surrounding a hill in Dorset, seem positively claustrophobic by comparison with John's; whereas John eventually journeyed to the limits of the cosmos in search of deities appropriate to his moral philosophy, Theodore simply imported them into his own back yard. The idiosyncratic world-view which informed this process is laid out in Theodore's *Soliloquies of a Hermit,* which represents emotions like the black despair which periodically possessed him as supernatural forces—"the moods of God"—and imagines Christ (as an idea if not an actual presence) as a force appointed to interrupt and ameliorate these moods.

T. F. Powys's longer fantasies are painstakingly constructed allegories which feature a series of symbolic characters representing God and his agents. The most frequently deployed of these characters, first featured in the novella "The Left Leg," is Mr. Jar (Jehovah). Jar has long been absent from the village in which "The Left Leg" is set, leaving the vile Farmer Mew to exploit his fellows mercilessly, murdering and raping in pursuit of his lust to possess everything. When Jar returns, Mew—who is desperately afraid of Jar, though he does not know why—tries to destroy him, but is literally hoist by his own petard. *Mockery Gap* features a more kindly Christ-figure in the mute fisherman whose presence briefly illuminates the lives of those who are capable of love and tenderness. Their consequent victories are, however, small and hard-won; Powys was never able to muster any real confidence in the power of love to overcome the implacable forces of hatred, lust and greed.

In *Mr. Weston's Good Wine* a more fatherly God comes to the village of Folly Down in the form of a wine-salesman concerned to settle a few outstanding accounts, as reckoned by his faithful assistant Michael. Mr. Weston deals in two kinds of wine, one light and exhilarating, the other dark and deadly; in Powys' view, both are holy gifts and the latter is more devoutly to be desired by virtue of its reliability and its finality. The dark wine is not death in general but a specific sort of merciful death, which is contrasted with the more brutal deaths unceremoniously meted out the wicked. It is, however, far from clear exactly how the death of the wicked is worse than the death of the good, given that the devil is here only a roaring lion employed by Mr. Weston to throw a scare into people. The upshot of Mr. Weston's visit is that much evil is wiped out and some virtue rewarded, but the problematic weighing of good and evil is further confused by the dubiousness of the rewards that virtue achieves.

Fables is a series of surreal dialogues, some of them between men and agents of nature, others featuring nonhuman creatures and inanimate objects. "Darkness and Nathaniel" is yet another of the many stories in which Powys sings the praises of merciful death. A projected second volume never materialized, although a few items of this kind are scattered through Powys's other collections, along with some other supernatural stories. "Christ in the Cupboard" in *The White Paternoster* is an effective tale in which Jesus visits a virtuous family only to be put away when his charity imperils their wealth; when they finally have need of him he has metamorphosed into the devil.

The Key of the Field and *The Only Penitent* are fine allegorical novelettes, both of which were reprinted in the collection *Bottle's Path* and again in *God's Eyes a-Twinkle.* In the former Jar is a squire who lets a field to a good man; he is dispossessed of it by greedy neighbours but is ultimately saved from wretchedness when Jar lets him into his beautiful garden. In the latter a vicar opens a confessional which no one visits until Jar turns up to admit that he is responsible for "every terror in the earth," his only claim to absolution being that he also invented death. This message is extensively amplified in *Unclay,* which some critics consider to be Powys's masterpiece, although *Mr. Weston's Good Wine* is far better known. Death is here personified not as a scythe-wielding ancient but as a personable young man named John, who mislays the warrant instructing him to gather in certain souls, and must then observe the suffering which those he has been commanded to release undergo while he searches for it. The sadistic Farmer Mere, who buys the innocent Susie from her miserly father John Dawe in order that he may despoil her, is the most monstrous of all the villains featured in Powys's novels; some contemporary critics considered his fascination with such characters unhealthy.

In Powys's last long fantasy, the novella *The Two Thieves,* George Douse steals four bottles from the devil containing Greed, Pride, Anger and Cruelty. These liquors permit him to grow rich and powerful, but the devil warns him to beware of another thief, Jar—here called "Tinker Jar"—who might yet take back the gifts and their produce. As in *Unclay,* the climactic triumph of morality is rousing, but by no means consolatory. Powys seems to have found it an adequate conclusion, though, for he wrote virtually nothing more during the last 20 years of his life. Oddly enough, the most upbeat of all his allegories, "Come and Dine"—which features Mr. Weston in an uncommonly generous mood—was only published posthumously. A few minor stories featuring Mr. Jar also remained long unpublished, including "The Scapegoat" and "No Wine."

T. F. Powys was possessed by a peculiar kind of angst which he understood not as a fear of death but rather as an agony of self-loathing which no honest and moral man could escape except by death. Death, in his eyes, was good and merciful because it led to oblivion, and the only kind of happiness achievable on earth was a kind of blind drunkenness incapable of being long sustained. Few readers are able to identify wholeheartedly with the fantasies which rework this world-view in allegorical form, but it is not beyond the reach of understanding and the very horror of it lends a powerful impetus to the author's artistry. He remains the most impressive Christian fantasist of modern times.

—Brian Stableford

PRATCHETT, Terry (David John)

Nationality: British. **Born:** 1948. **Education:** Wycombe Technical High School, Buckinghamshire. **Family:** Married Lyn Pratchett; one daughter. **Career:** Journalist in Buckinghamshire, Bristol and Bath; press officer, Central Electricity Board Western Region, 1980-87. **Awards:** British Science Fiction award, 1990. **Agent:** Colin Smythe Ltd., P.O. Box 6, Gerrards Cross, Buckinghamshire SL9 8XA, England.

FANTASY PUBLICATIONS

Novels (series: Discworld; Johnny)

The Carpet People (for children). Gerrards Cross, Buckinghamshire, Smythe, 1971.
The Colour of Magic (Discworld). Gerrards Cross, Buckinghamshire, Smythe, and New York, St. Martin's Press, 1983.
The Light Fantastic (Discworld). Gerrard's Cross, Buckinghamshire, Smythe, 1986; New York, Signet, 1988.
Equal Rites (Discworld). London, Gollancz, 1987; New York, Signet, 1988.
Mort (Discworld). London, Gollancz, 1987; New York, Signet, 1989.
Sourcery (Discworld). London, Gollancz, 1988; New York, Signet, 1989.
Wyrd Sisters (Discworld). London, Gollancz, 1988; New York, Roc, 1990.
Pyramids (Discworld). London, Gollancz, 1989; New York, Roc, 1990.
Guards! Guards! (Discworld). London, Gollancz, 1989; New York, Roc, 1991.
Eric, illustrated by Joash Kirby (Discworld). London, Gollancz, 1990.

Good Omens: The Nice and Accurate Predictions of Agnes Nutter, Witch, with Neil Gaiman. London, Gollancz, and New York, Workman, 1990.
Moving Pictures (Discworld). London, Gollancz, 1990; New York, Roc, 1992.
Reaper Man (Discworld). London, Gollancz, 1991; New York, Roc, 1992.
Witches Abroad (Discworld). London, Gollancz, 1991; New York, Roc, 1993.
Only You Can Save Mankind (Johnny; for children). London, Doubleday, 1992.
Small Gods (Discworld). London, Gollancz, 1992; New York, HarperCollins, 1994.
Lords and Ladies (Discworld). London, Gollancz, 1992.
Johnny and the Dead (for children). London, Doubleday, 1993.
Men at Arms (Discworld). London, Gollancz, 1993.
Soul Music (Discworld). London, Gollancz, 1994; New York, HarperPrism, 1995.
Interesting Times (Discworld). London, Gollancz, 1994.

OTHER PUBLICATIONS

Novels

The Dark Side of the Sun. Gerrards Cross, Buckinghamshire, Smythe, 1976.
Strata. Gerrards Cross, Buckinghamshire, Smythe, and New York, St. Martin's Press, 1981.
Truckers (for children). London, Doubleday, 1989; New York, Delacorte, 1990.
Diggers (for children). London, Doubleday, and New York, Delacorte, 1990.
Wings (for children). London, Doubleday, 1990; New York, Delacorte, 1991.

Other

The Unadulterated Cat, with illustrations by Gray Jolliffe. London, Gollancz, 1989.
The Discworld Companion, with Stephen Briggs. London, Victor Gollancz, 1994.

*   *   *

Terry Pratchett's Discworld novels, with their lush Josh Kirby jacket paintings, offer the most recognizable brand image of funny fantasy in Britain today. Other publishers have been quick to package humorous or meant-to-be-humorous fantasies to look as much as possible like Pratchett's, but the actual contents of these "rival" works have always fallen short. (The Kirby covers do not appear on U.S. editions.)

Although Pratchett's humour had early roots in parody, he very soon grew beyond mere fiddling with others' preoccupations. The early science-fiction novel *The Dark Side of the Sun* tips its hat towards Larry Niven's Known Space books, with their motley aliens who provide a comedy-of-humours cast list since we interpret their alien ways as a single, overdeveloped human eccentricity. But those who have never read Niven can enjoy this book's entertaining interstellar chases and outrageous McGuffin. *Strata* is the only Pratchett novel which is diminished by lack of acquaintance with the sources which it tweaks (principally Niven's *Ringworld*). Its splendidly daft setting is a flat world where the stars are fixed in a crystal sphere and a fusion-reactor sun chugs in Ptolemaic orbit . . . the whole thing being an artifical construct inhabiting a larger universe much like our own. Soon the discoverers are talking about old myths of worlds that rest on elephants that stand on turtles. This was surely the seed of Discworld.

Pratchett's achievement in the Discworld series is slightly frightening: so many books since 1983, and so consistently funny with scarcely a wobble. *The Colour of Magic* started it all, a genial and shambolic assembly of four linked stories set on the Discworld, a vast fantasy gameboard supported by four elephants standing on the great turtle A'tuin who swims endlessly through space. All the series' most overt pastiche appears in this book, with allusions to Fritz Leiber's Fafhrd and the Gray Mouser, H. P. Lovecraft's tentacled abominations and (extensively) Anne McCaffrey's dragonriders. Then came *The Light Fantastic,* a long romp with a high density of jokes which made it clear that Pratchett could be continuously funny at novel length.

Once established, the astrophysics of Discworld receded into the background, fleetingly mentioned in later books as "series glue." Discworld is a place where any story can be told, and its geography is fluid. But (and this is another major strength) it is not just another of those realms where anything can happen. Events are governed by a steely common-sense which may only be overruled by the important need to insert another joke or demented footnote. When the chief city Ankh-Morpork goes up in flames, there is good reason: a tourist has introduced the delighted underworld to the concept of fire insurance. When an aged wizard seals himself in an impregnable casket to defeat Death, he soon and inevitably hears a grim voice next to him saying "DARK IN HERE, ISN'T IT?"— following from the author's logical comment that "he has not yet considered the important part that airholes must play in an enterprise of this kind."

Death always appears, mirthlessly grinning and speaking in HOLLOW CAPITALS. Other recurring characters include Rincewind the failed magician (seen in the first two books; in *Sourcery*; in *Eric,* a slim Faust rewrite produced chiefly as a vehicle for Kirby illustrations and later reissued without them; and in *Interesting Times*), the Luggage (a murderously implacable trunk which runs on countless little legs and eats the unwary) and the Librarian of the wizards' Unseen University—perhaps the only powerful, macho librarian role-model in fiction, since his inadvertent transformation into an orang-utan. *Equal Rites* introduced the most popular of them all, the witch with a personality like granite and a whim of chromium steel: Granny Weatherwax.

Rites was a slight wobble in the course of Discworld, with the fun not wholly meshing with some thoughtful material about magic ethics and balance that vaguely recalls the Earthsea books of Ursula Le Guin. But next came *Mort,* in which Pratchett could be seen perfecting his technique of seamlessly melding the grim and the funny, as Death takes an apprentice who thoroughly messes up his duties. Discworld was now unstoppable.

Sourcery brought the disc to the brink of apocalypse as magic gets out of hand and the old Mage Wars resume; the Four Horsemen are in evidence and we learn that Pestilence's favourite tipple is a small egg nog with a cherry in it. *Pyramids* returns to deathly matters with (after an account of schooling in Ankh-Morpork's Guild of Assassins, its final exam uncannily resembling a British driving test with extreme prejudice) a jaundiced evocation of life and afterlife in Discworld's wildly exaggerated version of Ancient Egypt, from time-distorting pyramids to the traditional embalmers' jokes: "Your name in lights. Get it?"

In *Wyrd Sisters,* Granny Weatherwax and her three-witch coven are embroiled in a Shakespearean melange, with special focus on *Macbeth. Guards! Guards!* was a ground-breaking Discworld novel, possibly the best to date, as Pratchett demonstrated that he could now take *any* old collection of genre trappings and give it a Discworld spin. This one is a warped police procedural, with the burnt-out City Guards of Ankh-Morpork up against a particularly uncute dragon which incinerates a number of people very thoroughly indeed. Down these mean streets, etc.

Moving Pictures, the most dotty and shambolic of them all, saw Hollywood fever sweeping Ankh-Morpork with the alchemists' invention of a (demon- and salamander-powered) movie technology. Then it was back to the darker side with *Reaper Man* (Death is prematurely retired for growing too involved with his charges, and all life breaks loose), *Witches Abroad* (Granny Weatherwax versus a monstrously *good* Fairy Godmother who has made Destiny an offer it can't refuse and believes in forcing stories to come out as they should, no matter what the unfortunate characters want), *Small Gods* (the grimmest of all, with inflexible religion and a torturing Inquisition . . . and somehow many a smile as well, as the Great God Om finds himself incarnated as a small tortoise sustained only by the faith of his one *real* believer; this is another contender for the Best Discworld Book trophy), *Lords and Ladies* (the elves of legend return to Discworld and prove to be a particularly vicious, unpleasant lot). . . .

Men at Arms directly continues the story of the Ankh-Morpork Watch from *Guards! Guards!,* with a sort of serial killer apparently on the rampage, armed with the world's one high-velocity rifle (invented by Renaissance genius Leonard of Quirm). *Soul Music* is both a third Death novel with his adopted grand-daughter Susan thrust temporarily into the dread role, and a reworking of the *Moving Pictures* insanity as the mega-decibel magic of rock music sweeps Ankh-Morpork. *Interesting Times* takes us and Rincewind to the Counterweight Continent on the far side of Discworld, which is "all the China you can remember": an empire whose insane tyrant rules an unthinkingly obedient populace, where elaborate competitive examinations in poetry and literature must be passed to become a nightsoil collector— all threatened by the geriatric Genghis Cohen and his Silver Horde of nonagenarians (seven in all). . . . There is some spectacular slaughter.

As Pratchett points out, "Not everything in a Discworld book is meant to be funny." The surface hilarity glitters all the more for having such solid, uncompromising bones: in the best of the series the silly footnotes and mirthful throwaway lines are ornaments on a structure of steel.

Away from the main stream of Discworld, *Good Omens* with Neil Gaiman spoofs the *Omen/Damien* movies with its notion of the Antichrist growing up as a pleasant kid, hauntingly and intentionally reminiscent of Richmal Crompton's William. Despite one scene (involving maggots) more macabre than he normally permits himself, the overall effect is very Pratchett-like. A version of Death appears, though not as a guest character: Death is at home anywhere. There is a closing anti-apocalypse.

For slightly younger readers, the science-fiction "Book of the Nomes" trilogy (*Truckers, Diggers* and *Wings*) stars tiny alien visitors long stranded on Earth, and is healthily subversive—as witness the chapter epigraphs from the nomes' religious teachings, based on the underfloor world of a large shop. "And Arnold Bros (est. 1905) divided the Store into Departments. . . ." *Only You Can Save Mankind* takes a wry look at video games when the young hero Johnny confronts the unthinkable: space invaders who surrender and want peace. In the fantasy sequel *Johnny and the Dead* he becomes the spokesman for the ghosts of all those buried in a graveyard threatened by property developers. The dead folks' gradual discovery that they needn't just hang around their graves (but with a little effort can monkey with telephones, radio, the world communications net . . .) is both funny and touching.

Meanwhile Discworld lurches on through space and UK bestseller charts. Pratchett knows that easy writing makes unfunny reading; the whole remarkable enterprise is fuelled not only by comic talent but by a vast capacity for hard work.

—David Langford

PRATT, (Murray) Fletcher

Pseudonym: George U. Fletcher. **Nationality:** American. **Born:** Buffalo, New York, 25 April 1897. **Education:** Hobart College, Geneva, New York, 1915-16; University of Paris, 1931-33. Served in the War Library Service during World War I. **Family:** Married Inga Marie Stephens. **Career:** Librarian, 1918-20; staff member, Buffalo *Courier Express,* 1920-23; freelance writer from 1923; regular contributor, *American Mercury* and *Saturday Review of Literature*; military advisor, *Time* and *New York Post* during World War II; staff member, Bread Loaf Writers Conference. President, Authors Club, 1941; co-founder, American Rocket Society. **Awards:** United States Navy award, 1957. **Died:** 10 June 1956.

FANTASY PUBLICATIONS

Novels

The Well of the Unicorn (as George U. Fletcher). New York, Sloane, 1948; as Fletcher Pratt, New York, Ballantine, 1967.
The Blue Star. New York, Ballantine, 1969.

Novels with L. Sprague de Camp (series: Harold Shea)

The Incomplete Enchanter (Harold Shea). New York, Holt, 1941; London, Sphere, 1979.
Land of Unreason. New York, Holt, 1942.
The Carnelian Cube. New York, Gnome Press, 1948.
The Castle of Iron (Harold Shea). New York, Gnome Press, 1950.
Wall of Serpents (Harold Shea). New York, Avalon, 1960; as *The Enchanter Compleated,* London, Sphere, 1980.
The Compleat Enchanter: The Magical Misadventures of Harold Shea (omnibus; includes *The Incomplete Enchanter, The Castle of Iron*). New York, Nelson Doubleday, 1975; London, Sphere, 1979.
Intrepid Enchanter: The Complete Magical Misadventures of Harold Shea (omnibus; includes *The Incomplete Enchanter, The Castle of Iron, Wall of Serpents*). London, Sphere, 1988; as *The Complete Compleat Enchanter,* New York, Baen, 1989.

Short Stories

Tales from Gavagan's Bar, with L. Sprague de Camp. New York, Twayne, 1953; expanded edition, Philadelphia, Owlswick Press, 1978.

Other

Editor, *Witches Three.* New York, Twayne, 1952.

OTHER PUBLICATIONS

Novels

Double in Space (*Project Excelsior, The Wanderer's Return*). New York, Doubleday, 1951.
Double Jeopardy. New York, Doubleday, 1952.
The Undying Fire. New York, Ballantine, 1953; as *The Conditioned Captain,* in *Double in Space,* 1954.
Double in Space (*Project Excelsior, The Conditioned Captain*). London, Boardman, 1954.
Invaders from Rigel. New York, Avalon, 1960.
Alien Planet. New York, Avalon, 1962.

Other

The Heroic Years: Fourteen Years of the Republic 1801-1815. New York, Smith and Haas, 1934.
The Cunning Mulatto and Other Cases of Ellis Parker, American Detective. New York, Smith and Haas, 1935; as *Detective No. 1,* London, Methuen, 1936.
Ordeal by Fire: An Informal History of the Civil War. New York, Smith and Haas, 1935; revised edition, New York, Sloane, 1948; London, Lane, 1950; as *A Short History of the Civil War,* New York, Bantam, n.d.
Hail, Caesar! New York, Smith and Haas, 1936; London, Williams and Norgate, 1938.
The Navy: A History. New York, Doubleday, 1938.
Road to Empire: The Life and Times of Bonaparte the General. New York, Doubleday, 1939.
Sea Power and Today's War. New York, Harrison Hilton, 1939; London, Methuen, 1940.
Secret and Urgent: The Story of Codes and Ciphers. Indianapolis, Bobbs Merrill, and London, Hale, 1939.
Fletcher Pratt's Naval War Game. New York, Harrison Hilton, 1940.
Fighting Ships of the U.S. Navy. New York, Garden City Publishing Company, 1941.
America and Total War. New York, Smith and Durrell, 1941.
The U.S. Army. Racine, Wisconsin, Whitman, 1942.
What the Citizen Should Know about Modern War. New York, Norton, 1942.
The Navy Has Wings. New York, Harper, 1943.
My Life to the Destroyers, with Captain L. A. Abercrombie. New York, Holt, 1944.
The Navy's War. New York, Harper, 1944.
A Short History of the Army and Navy. Washington, D.C., Infantry Journal, 1944.
Fleet Against Japan. New York, Harper, 1946.
Empire of the Sea. New York, Holt, 1946.
Night Work: The Story of Task Force 39. New York, Holt, 1946.
A Man and His Meals, with Robeson Bailey. New York, Holt, 1947.
The Empire and Glory: Napoleon Bonaparte 1800-1806. New York, Sloane, 1948.
The Marines' War. New York, Sloane, 1948.
Eleven Generals: Studies in American Command. New York, Sloane, 1949.

The Third King. New York, Sloane, 1950.

War for the World: A Chronicle of Our Fighting Forces in World War II. New Haven, Connecticut, Yale University Press, 1950.

Prebble's Boys: Commodore Prebble and the Birth of American Sea Power. New York, Sloane, 1950.

Rockets, Jets, Guided Missiles, and Space Ships. New York, Random House, 1951; London, Sidgwick and Jackson, 1952.

The Monitor and the Merrimac. New York, Random House, 1951.

By Space Ship to the Moon (for children). New York, Random House, 1952; London, Publicity Products, 1953.

Stanton, Lincoln's Secretary of War. New York, Norton, 1953.

All About Rockets and Jets. New York, Random House, 1955.

The Civil War. New York, Garden City Books, 1955.

Famous Inventors and Their Inventions. New York, Random House, 1955.

The Battles That Changed History. New York, Doubleday, 1956.

Civil War on Western Waters. New York, Holt, 1956.

The Compact History of the United States Navy. New York, Hawthorn, 1957.

Editor, *World of Wonder.* New York, Twayne, 1951.

Editor, *Civil War in Pictures.* New York, Garden City Books, 1951.

Editor, *The Petrified Planet.* New York, Twayne, 1952.

Editor, *My Diary, North and South,* by Sir William Howard Russell. New York, Harper, 1954.

Translator, *The Great American Parade,* by H. J. Duteil. New York, Twayne, 1953.

*   *   *

Fletcher Pratt was a prolific contributor to the Gernsback science fiction pulps, both as a translator and a writer. He liked to write in collaboration with others, and sometimes signed stories he wrote alone as if they were collaborations. The works of non-fiction which he wrote in the 1930s were entirely serious but he does not seem to have taken his early fiction at all seriously. When he teamed up with L. Sprague de Camp to write for *Unknown* they produced work of a much higher quality than Pratt had previously achieved, but it was comic fantasy of a determinedly frivolous kind.

By means of the arcane "mathematics of magic" elaborated but not quite mastered by scientist Reed Chalmers, the unheroic but resourceful Harold Shea was dispatched by Pratt and de Camp into a series of imaginary worlds based on various ancient mythologies. There he lived on his wits, matching his cleverness and practicality against the naïve magic of gods and men, with considerable success. *The Incomplete Enchanter* conflates two novellas: "The Roaring Trumpet" (1940) featuring the world of Norse mythology in the run-up to Ragnarök, and "The Mathematics of Magic" (1940) featuring the world of Spenser's *Faerie Queene. The Castle of Iron* expands a further novella (1941) in which the characters are drawn into the world of Ariosto's *Orlando Furioso* and are somewhat confused by the fact that it is inhabited by different versions of the characters which Spenser borrowed and reshaped to his own purposes. Shea's beloved, Belphebe, is embarrassingly absorbed into her *alter ego* Belphegor, setting Shea a problem which no literary hero had ever had to face before.

The Land of Unreason, similarly expanded from an *Unknown* novella (1941), is identical in spirit. Its protagonist is an American tourist in Britain who is carried off by little people drunk on whiskey, which he has inadvertently provided. King Oberon's fairyland

is as open to confusion and disruption by common sense and logic as the realms which Shea visited, and although the protagonist's attempts to come to terms with magic run far from smoothly he finally muddles through the quest which he is set. Even the revised version is unrepentantly slapdash. Pratt and de Camp wrote one more novel for *Unknown,* but the magazine folded before publishing it; it appeared belatedly in book form. *The Carnelian Cube* is the story of an archaeologist who finds a magic stone which allows him to wish himself into a series of alternate worlds in search of one which will suit him, but his Utopian quest is frustrated at every turn. The story is even more disorganized and half-hearted than its predecessor.

When the collaborators were reunited after the war they found a more congenial literary form in the anecdotal whimsies collected as *Tales from Gavagan's Bar.* These ultra-tall tales work rather better than the two slightly dispirited novellas which they added to the Harold Shea series: "The Wall of Serpents" (1953) and "The Green Magician" (1954). In the former Shea visits the world of the *Kalevala,* in the latter he explores the realm of Irish mythology. By this time, however, Pratt had written two solo fantasy novels of a very different kind.

In the 1950s "sword-and-sorcery" fiction was regarded as a minor sub-genre of pulp adventure fiction, following in the footsteps of Robert E. Howard's Conan stories. Although Fritz Leiber's early tales of Fafhrd and the Gray Mouser had brought a measure of literary sophistication into the form it had not yet been ennobled as "heroic fantasy." There was no ready market for tales set in such milieux which were painstaking in construction and earnest in tone, but Pratt did manage to find a publisher for *The Well of the Unicorn,* a pseudo-historical fantasy in which magic plays a marginal role and its use invariably causes more problems than it solves. The world in which the story is set is borrowed from Lord Dunsany's play *King Argimenes and the Unknown Warrior* (1911) but much elaborated; the story itself is a *bildungsroman* tracking the growth to maturity of the son of a dispossessed landowner bent on rebellion against the conquering Vulkings. Although it falters in its purpose and dissolves into anti-climax it was at the time of its publication the most concerted attempt by a modern American writer to produce serious work of this kind.

Pratt followed *The Well of the Unicorn* with *The Blue Star,* a more original and altogether more impressive work, but had to publish it himself in an anthology, *Witches Three,* which he put together for his then employer. The hero of the novel is instructed to seduce a witch in order to take possession of the talisman of the title for use by the revolutionary movement to which he belongs, but the plan quickly goes wrong. He and the witch meet again in a country ruled by an oppressive religious cult, where they build a new and better relationship before going into exile yet again. The hero's sentimental education is brought into sharp focus—with a degree of sexual frankness unusual at the time—and the political philosophy which serves as an ideological background is carefully considered. *The Blue Star* is one of the finest heroic fantasies of its period and it is a great pity that Pratt was forced to conclude that there was no point in attempting more fiction of this kind. Unfortunately, he did not live to see the boom in heroic fantasy started by the American paperback publication of Tolkien's *The Lord of the Rings,* which brought his two solo novels back into print and belatedly delivered them to the appreciative consideration of a much wider audience.

—Brian Stableford

PRICE, E(dgar) Hoffmann (Trooper)

Nationality: American. **Born:** Fowler, California, 3 July 1898. **Military Service:** United States Cavalry, 1917-23. **Career:** Engineer, 1923-32; full-time writer, 1932-52; microfilm technician and photographer, 1952-68; resumed writing in old age. **Family:** Married 1) Helen Price in 1928 (divorced 1931); 2) Wanda Price in 1934 (divorced 1945); 3) Loriena Price in 1959. **Awards:** World Fantasy Lifetime Achievement award, 1984. **Died:** 18 June 1988.

FANTASY PUBLICATIONS

Novels

The Devil Wives of Li Fong. New York, Del Rey, 1979.
The Jade Enchantress. New York, Del Rey, 1982.

Short Stories

Strange Gateways. Sauk City, Wisconsin, Arkham House, 1967.
Far Lands, Other Days. Chapel Hill, North Carolina, Carcosa, 1975.

OTHER PUBLICATIONS

Novels.

Grubstake. New York, Zebra, 1979.
Operation Misfit. New York, Del Rey, 1980.
Operation Longlife. New York, Del Rey, 1983.
Operation Exile. New York, Del Rey, 1986.
Operation Isis. New York, Del Rey, 1987.

*   *   *

E. Hoffmann Price had a writing career that stretched over 60 years, but most of it was crammed into a 20-year period in the 1930s and 1940s when he wrote about 500 stories for the pulp magazines. Some appeared under the pen name of Hamlin Daly; others remain untraced under various house names. His early sales, and those for which he is best remembered, were to *Weird Tales,* but when he turned to writing full-time in 1932, he expanded to more lucrative fields. These were initially the detective pulps, but Price later graduated to the more general adventure pulps, *Top-Notch, Argosy* and *Adventure.* Much of his writing was for the Spicy magazines, which peppered their fiction with lurid sex (by the standards of the day), but Price's passion always remained with the supernatural, and he sought to weave it into his stories whenever possible. The best of these are collected in two volumes, *Strange Gateways,* and the mammoth *Far Lands, Other Days,* which contains an enlightening introduction by Price about his writings.

Price's best stories are fantasies set in the Middle or Far East. These began with his first sale to *Weird Tales* of "The Rajah's Gift" (1925), a sardonic vignette about a rajah who bestows death upon his favourite rather than have him suffer the ravages that come with power. His next sale, "The Stranger from Kurdistan" (1925), caused a ripple of controversy in *Weird Tales* because it featured a manifestation of the devil disowning his worshippers and paying hom-

age to Christ. It remained one of the more popular stories from *Weird Tales*'s early years.

Price had a passion for collecting oriental carpets and these feature in several of his stories. In both "The Girl from Samarcand" (*Weird Tales,* 1929) and "Khosru's Garden" (*Weird Tales,* 1940), the carpets serve as an escape from the reality about us to a world of bliss and harmony. One of his best oriental fantasies is "Well of the Angels" (*Unknown,* 1940) set in Arabia, where an engineer attempts to rescue two angels trapped in a tower, in return for supernatural aid. It contains a good blend of Price's wry humour, down-to-earth philosophy, and knowledge of eastern wisdom.

In "The Word of Santiago" (*Weird Tales,* 1926), Price introduced the character of Pierre d'Artois, a French master swordsman, based on the author's own fencing teacher when he was in France in the early 1920s. D'Artois frequently finds himself facing supernatural foes, usually minions of the devil-worshipping cult of Malik Taus. Although Price regarded these as the worst of his stories, they have a style and panache that keep them alive. The longest of them is "Satan's Garden" (*Weird Tales,* 1934) in which he faces an evil Tibetan adept capable of reincarnating the dead.

But the D'Artois stories are not representative of Price at his best. His better stories reflect the colour and life of the world about him. A much travelled man, having spent his army days in France, the Philippines and Mexico, Price was able to portray these lands with passion and conviction. He was also a qualified astrologer, a student of Theosophy and a practising Buddhist, which enabled him to write with authority in these areas. His more considered stories, therefore, have a depth that is greater than standard pulp fare. Price was never afraid to speak his mind, and his stories contain much of his homespun philosophy. These aspects can be seen in "The Infidel's Daughter" (*Weird Tales,* 1927), a story combining black magic and astrology as well as Price's views about the Ku Klux Klan (here represented as the Knights of the Saffron Mask).

Apart from oriental fantasies, Price also wrote many stories for the western pulps, and occasionally blended the two, as in "Apprentice Magician" (*Weird Tales,* 1939) which brought Egyptian sorcery to the Californian outback. Price is also remembered as the only author to be jointly credited in collaboration with H. P. Lovecraft during that author's lifetime, with "Through the Gates of the Silver Key" (*Weird Tales,* 1934). Price travelled throughout the United States, and was the only author to meet all three of the legendary *Weird Tales* triumvirate, Lovecraft (who lived in Rhode Island), Robert E. Howard (Texas) and Clark Ashton Smith (Northern California), as well as many other authors and artists. His book of reminiscences about them (originally called *The Book of the Dead*) was never published but extracts in various magazines, especially "The Jade Pagoda" in *Witchcraft & Sorcery* (1971-74), make delightful reading. Price collaborated with other writers, most prominently Otis Adelbert Kline, with whom he wrote one of the worst serials ever to appear in *Argosy,* "Satans on Saturn" (1940).

After the pulp field faded away in the early 1950s, Price stopped writing fiction but was tempted back in 1971 by Gerald Page, editor of *Witchcraft & Sorcery.* Price wrote several new oriental fantasies including two novels. Both demonstrate his lifelong knowledge of Buddhism. *The Devil Wives of Li Fong,* set in ancient China, portrays a hapless apothecary who has married two wealthy ladies. But they turn out to be reincarnated spirits, punished for a crime in a past life, who must work out their karma in a new life. *The Jade Enchantress* is a wonderfully contrived adventure of spiritual and earthly entanglements which also shows Price's sense of humour.

Price also produced four science fiction novels starting with *Operation Misfit*. Basically space operas set in a dystopian future, Price used the series as vehicles for his trenchant anti-establishment views, and they are perhaps more valuable as an intelligent and experienced old man's view of society than they are as fiction. As entertainment they are not as good as his fantasies which are rare of their kind and will always be worthy of revisiting.

—Mike Ashley

R

RASMUSSEN, Alis A.

Pseudonym: Kate Elliott. **Nationality:** American. **Born:** Des Moines, Iowa, 27 July 1958. **Education:** University College of North Wales, Bangor, 1977-78; Mills College, Oakland, California, B.A. in English literature, 1980. **Family:** Married Jay Silverstein in 1985; three children. **Agent:** Russell Galen, Scovil-Chichak-Galen Literary Agency, 381 Park Avenue South, #1112, New York, NY 10016, USA.

FANTASY PUBLICATIONS

Novels (series: Highroad)

The Labyrinth Gate. New York, Baen, 1988.
A Passage of Stars (Highroad). New York, Bantam, 1990.
Revolution's Shore (Highroad). New York, Bantam, 1990.
The Price of Ransom (Highroad). New York, Bantam, 1990.

Novels as Kate Elliott (series: Jaran; The Sword of Heaven)

Jaran. New York, DAW, 1992; London, Pan, 1994.
An Earthly Crown (Sword of Heaven). New York, DAW, 1993.
His Conquering Sword (Sword of Heaven). New York, DAW, 1993.
The Law of Becoming (Jaran). New York, DAW, 1994.

*

Alis A. Rasmussen comments:

It is difficult for me to make a personal statement about my writing, since the novels themselves are my personal statement. They speak for me. I am interested in the evolution of cultures, in change over time, in the crossing of borders between cultures, whether they be states or genders, religions or "races," human or otherwise. My books focus on character, and on the interaction of characters with each other and their world. Mostly, I try to write the kind of book I would like to read: a world that the reader can become immersed in, can live in, a story in which the characters come alive, a novel that, when you finish it, you ask: "Is this all? Isn't there more?"

* * *

Alis A. Rasmussen, who also writes as Kate Elliott, has varied interests that include the study of Shotokan karate (in which she has received a brown belt) as well as the occasional broadsword practice session with the Society for Creative Anachronism. To readers of her novels, the accuracy of her depiction of sword-fights is notable, but there are other pleasures to be found there too.

Her first published fantasy was *The Labyrinth Gate,* which she has described as "a through-the-looking-glass novel where a couple that has just gotten married receives a deck of strange Tarot cards and is thrown into a fantasy world". The husband and wife find themselves journeying through a ruined city, which is also an ac-

tual labyrinth. In this book, as in her later works, Rasmussen has developed highly believable characters and a credible matrilineal society. One is struck by the depth of her people, even in this early work, although she has improved her art with the passage of time.

In her Highroad science-fantasy trilogy Rasmussen builds another alien society and explores the feelings of people who live in perilous times. She doesn't exclude women from the battle lines, and this lends a reality to her work. This series exhibits a rich panorama of changing societies, and a world where abrupt change is never easy. It poses the questions: How do you love when death is all around you? How do you do your duty with fear, reasonable fear, clogging your arteries? Rebellion, battle and change march in a complicated dance of death and progress.

Her second series (written as Kate Elliott) concerns the Jaran, who are a people who have been transplanted to a planet outside our solar system. Although all of Rasmussen's work under the Elliott name may qualify as science fiction, it seems to have the feel of fantasy. The novels are concerned with culture, how people live, and how their societies work, as well as the high adventure of discovering new pathways to take other than the scientific/technological. She includes women as central characters in all her novels—and not in traditional roles, when viewed by the standards of our western culture—without discounting their sexuality, or the genuine concerns of women in almost any society (reproduction is central to how a young woman leads her life, but it isn't the only factor). Her female characters often wield power that is theirs by virtue of their femininity, and the wonder of giving life is as real as the necessary ending of life. Rasmussen explores the day-to-day life of a matrilineal clan of nomadic horse-breeders. For good measure, she throws a rebellious human heir to a non-human dukedom into the pot, as well as exploring the question: "Do you want to live forever?"

The feature that qualifies her work as science fiction is the fact that the non-humans are space-travellers, as are some of the humans. However, this is science fiction of the "planetary romance" sub-genre, a type of story which has no emphasis on high technology and constantly borders on other-worldly fantasy. In these books, Rasmussen carries the reader to new heights of understanding and humanity in work of consistently high quality, amply displaying her true interest in cultures and the ways in which they evolve and function. A central theme for her is culture-clash: she delves into what happens when strikingly different cultures collide, and although much of what she reveals is familiar there are always interesting twists of fate and personality. One factor that is very important in her work is the existence of a character who is outside the central society. Rasmussen has a real talent for using such characters to explore the meanings of habits and customs that might otherwise be incomprehensible. While her characters often experience culture shock, she keeps her readers well informed as to the reasons behind particular behaviours. Some examples are: men who are swordsmen and warriors, but embroider designs on their own clothing and are shy and modest in the presence of females; and a slave who contradicts the patterns we have come to expect in a fantasy novel and does not want her freedom when it is offered.

The aliens in Rasmussen's "Kate Elliott" novels have what appears to be a separate-but-equal society in which their women are artists and artisans who live almost entirely outside the sphere of male influence. The stories are varied and rich without being tedious; despite all the carefully worked-out detail, the reader is moved along the plot-lines briskly.

Rasmussen's latest novel at this time of writing is a sequel to *Jaran* entitled *The Law of Becoming*. She describes it as a difficult book to write, and no doubt this is partially because she has been "reaching for new levels of craft," always a challenging goal. Rasmussen has also announced that she is working on a new epic fantasy trilogy that is, as yet, untitled.

—Sandra Brandenburg

RAWN, Melanie (Robin)

Nationality: American. **Born:** California, c.1953. **Education:** Scripps College, B.A. in history. **Career:** Teacher, editor, then full-time writer. Lives in Los Angeles. **Address:** c/o DAW Books, 375 Hudson Street, 3rd Floor, New York, NY 10014-3658, USA.

Fantasy Publications

Novels (series: Dragon Prince; Dragon Star)

Dragon Prince. New York, DAW, 1988; London, Sidgwick and Jackson, 1989.
The Star Scroll (Dragon Prince). New York, DAW, 1989; London, Pan, 1990.
Sunrunner's Fire (Dragon Prince). New York, DAW, 1990; London, Pan, 1991.
Stronghold (Dragon Star). New York, DAW, 1990; London, Pan, 1992.
The Dragon Token (Dragon Star). New York, DAW, 1992; London, Pan, 1993.
Skybowl (Dragon Star). New York, DAW, 1993; London, Macmillan, 1995.
The Ruins of Ambrai. New York, DAW, 1994.

Other Publications

Novel

Knights of the Morningstar (novelization of TV script). New York, Ace, and London, Boxtree, 1994.

*   *   *

Melanie Rawn has now written two trilogies of novels set in a land where dragons still fly, a world ruled by princes and overseen by a religious caste with powers of telepathy and telekinesis. The men prove themselves by their acts of bravery when faced with huge fire-breathing dragons, their womenfolk by their abilities as household managers and night-time companions. These are preposterous fantasies to weave at the end of this cynical 20th century, yet it would be too easy to denigrate the books. Melanie Rawn writes with unfailing conviction and absorbing confidence. The stories make compulsive reading, and in view of this Rawn may be declared one of the best writers of the popular fantasy genre.

The first, and perhaps strongest, book in the series is *Dragon Prince*. It tells the story of Prince Rohan, who comes to be king after his father is killed in one-to-one combat with a dragon. Rohan is the most unpromising candidate for prince: he has yet to kill a dragon; he has never been bloodied in battle. Worse, he is a scholar who spends too much of his time with the religious leader and telepath Lady Andrade. Chad, his brother-in-law, seems a much better bet. However if Chad has aspirations to be prince, these are instantly forgotten when the old prince dies. In fact, Chad and Rohan ride out together to slaughter the dragon that fatally injured the old prince.

Returning with the dragon's teeth slung around his neck, Rohan organizes his father's funeral pyre, and sets besides his corpse the dragon who killed him. Dragon and prince were equals in battle, and in death they should be equally honoured. This proves very controversial: since dragons are seen as pests, eating cattle and sheep, it is a prince's duty to take on the adult males in one-to-one combat, while every Lord and Baron enjoys taking part in the wholesale slaughter of dragons at the time of Hatching. Yet Rohan wants to set an "environmentally friendly" agenda; he is desperate to find good reason for his people to live in harmony with the dragons. In time, Prince Rohan will discover that the dragons' egg-shells when heated turn to gold. This will lead to a sea-change in the people's attitude to dragons.

In the first instance, however, the focus of *Dragon Prince* is Rohan's one true love Sioned, chosen for him, and he for her, by the Lady Andrade. Though it is love at first sight, and despite the need for an heir to secure Prince Rohan's position, the marriage is delayed. Prince Rohan has a plan: he intends to trick the evil high prince into agreeing to sign ever more generous treaties, by the dual charade of pretending to be stupid and hinting he will marry one of the high prince's 17 daughters. If one had expected the high prince to see through Rohan, or to fight back with some devilish scheme of his own, one would be disappointed. Prince Rohan procures all the treaties he wants, and in the confusion the high prince murders his mistress Palida, who looked set to be Prince Rohan's number-one enemy. After half a book of Rohan's plotting and scheming, this first defeat of the high prince is an anticlimax. The high prince has not lived up to his reputation, and Rohan seems to have won all to easily. In the second half of the book, the spurned Princess Ioanthe takes on the cloak of evil princess. Plague and recession spread across the lands. Dragon-shell gold keeps the Prince Rohan solvent; however, Sioned becomes ill, then infertile. Rohan's heir will in the end be provided by the hated Ioanthe.

Though well written, *Dragon Prince* seems to build up, then throw away, aspects of the plot-line. Why did brother-in-law Chad not want to usurp Prince Rohan? Why could the high prince not see through Rohan's charade when he courts his daughters? Why was there no opposition within Rohan's court, despite his well-known plan to "play the fool" with the high prince, and his intent to marry Sioned, the pauper telepath? Worse, the economics of the princedom are decidedly shaky. We are told it is an arid desert, yet there is an unlimited underground water supply. The wealth of the princedom is its agriculture, and to enhance production Rohan decrees that those who work the land *should own it*. Then, however, the prince forbids the slaughter of dragons. It is unclear how the growing dragon population, with their taste for cattle and sheep, will affect the increase in agricultural productivity.

Yet it seems unfair to point up these weaknesses when the focus of the novel is Prince Rohan and his lovely Sioned. Theirs is a wonderful story, well told. *Dragon Prince* has been followed by five sequels. These tell the ongoing saga of Rohan's son Pol and his own descendants as they fight to preserve their princely legacy. The roots of Melanie Rawn's craft feed on J. R. R. Tolkien's *Lord of the Rings*; however, her work rides firmly on Anne McCaffrey's coat-tails, whose science-fiction tales of men taming "dragons" to their own ends precede Melanie Rawn's by 20 years or more. As an introduction to the fantasy genre for a teenager or young reader, I would certainly recommend Melanie Rawn's books. For the more sophisticated reader, the novels are colorful feasts of words and images, but in the end are unsatisfying.

—Sally Ann Melia

REAVES, (James) Michael

Nationality: American. **Born:** 1950. **Career:** Has worked as a television scriptwriter. **Address:** c/o Tor Books, 49 West 24th Street, 9th Floor, New York, NY 10010, USA.

FANTASY PUBLICATIONS

Novels (series: Shattered World)

Dragonworld (as J. Michael Reaves), with Byron Preiss. New York, Bantam, 1979; London, Bantam, 1980; revised edition, New York, Bantam, 1983.
The Shattered World. New York, Timescape, 1984; London, Futura, 1986.
The Burning Realm (Shattered World). New York, Baen, and London, Futura, 1988.
Street Magic. New York, Tor, 1991.

Short Stories

Darkworld Detective (as J. Michael Reaves). New York, Bantam, 1982.

OTHER PUBLICATIONS

Novels

I—Alien. New York, Tempo, 1978.
Sword of the Samurai, with Steve Perry. New York, Bantam, 1984.
Hellstar, with Steve Perry. New York, Berkley, 1984.
Dome, with Steve Perry. New York, Berkley, 1987; London, Gollancz, 1988.
The Omega Cage, with Steve Perry. New York, Ace, 1988.

Plays

Television Plays: Various episodes of *The Twilight Zone* (1985-86 version) and the juvenile animated series *Centurions, The Real Ghostbusters, Chuck Norris: Karate Commandos, The Spiral Zone* and others.

*   *   *

Although Reaves is a competent and skilled writer, the bulk of his work has been produced to follow conventional formats, usually within shared-world projects developed by packaging agencies, especially that of Byron Preiss. As much of his work has also been in collaboration, Reaves's own voice is not always immediately apparent, and it is further masked by his ability to blend easily into formula fiction.

Most of Reaves's recent work has been science fiction, and even his early work, while packaged as fantasy and dealing with fantasy images is nevertheless rooted in science fiction. But the fantasy elements remain uppermost. In his first story, "The Breath of Dragons" (*Clarion III,* edited by Robin Scott Wilson, 1973), the dragon-theme is strongly fantastic, although the setting of the alien planet and the plot of hunting dragons for their fire-bladders is basic science fiction.

The same otherworldly atmosphere is developed in his series of stories about Kamus of Kadizhar, the only private detective on an alien planet. The settings are wholly fantastic, but the writing and plotting deliberately imitate classic writers of mystery fiction. "The Big Spell" was straight out of Raymond Chandler, whilst the origins for "The Maltese Vulcan," "Murder on the Galactic Express" and "The Man With the Golden Raygun" are clear from their titles. The first two stories appeared in the anthology series *Weird Heroes* in 1977 but the others are original to Reaves's first collection, *Darkworld Detective.* For reasons of his own Reaves decided not to continue the series and a second volume, *Kamus of Kadizhar,* was written by John Shirley.

Reaves's ability to emulate other writers is on a par with Randall Garrett's and Piers Anthony's, though he brings his own vibrancy to it which makes the stories more action-packed but less polished than Garrett's, and less contrived than Anthony's. Unfortunately it has made him a chameleon writer, easily blending into other writers' styles and not seeking his own voice. For this reason he has easily collaborated with Steve Perry on his own novels set in the Matador universe, and he has readily adapted to Byron Preiss's packaged works, especially with *Dragonworld,* a passable but highly formulaic fantasy adventure which sought to tie in to the post-Tolkien fantasy boom.

The same can be said for Reaves's Shattered World series. Again many of the fantasy formulae are present. A world has been sundered by a war of sorcery and the survivors endeavour to rebuild it. In many ways it is only a fantasy equivalent of a post-holocaust sf novel, but Reaves does manage to develop characters as individuals, especially the likeable rogue, Beorn, who has to pay the ultimate sacrifice.

Probably the closest Reaves has come to developing his own voice has been in his short fiction, where he can bring more polish to his adaptive abilities and develop basic ideas into powerful stories. His best have appeared in *Fantasy & Science Fiction* and *Rod Serling's The Twilight Zone Magazine.* "Shadetree" (*F&SF,* September 1977), a story about a strange little boy, is not unlike the work of Ray Bradbury, and was called by the editor, "one of the scariest stories we've ever published." Reaves's ability to pile on the horror relentlessly has resulted in several powerful horror stories, especially the haunted house story "The Tearing of Greymare House" (*F&SF,* March 1983), and the especially effective "Werewind" (*F&SF,* July 1981) about a sorceric wind that drives people to murder.

Reaves's most original work has been contemporary fantasy rather than high fantasy, which has been too imitative. In addition to his short fiction, there is the novel *Street Magic.* A runaway teenager, living on the San Francisco streets, is recognized by the fairies as a changeling with the power to unlock the gates back to their own world. Although the boy senses he is different, his suppressed and abused childhood suffocates his ability to tap into his hidden power. The novel becomes an infectious race against time.

Much of Reaves's work is lost in the ephemeral celluloid of children's short animation films, and although he has written other teleplays for such series as *The Twilight Zone*, where his adaptiveness allows him to build upon the styles of Rod Serling and Richard Matheson, none of these has yet been captured in print. It may be hoped that Reaves develops his abilities, particularly as a short-story writer, to produce works of more lasting quality and perhaps, in that process, reveal his own voice.

—Mike Ashley

REICHERT, Mickey Zucker

Full name Miriam Susan Zucker Reichert. **Nationality:** American. **Born:** 1962. **Career:** Medical doctor; later a freelance writer. **Address:** c/o DAW Books, 375 Hudson Street, 3rd Floor, New York, NY 10014-3658, USA.

Fantasy Publications

Novels (series: Bifrost Guardians; Renshai)

Godslayer (Bifrost). New York, DAW, 1987.
Shadow Climber (Bifrost). New York, DAW, 1988.
Dragonrank Master (Bifrost). New York, DAW, 1989.
Shadow's Realm (Bifrost). New York, DAW, 1990.
By Chaos Cursed (Bifrost). New York, DAW, 1991.
The Last of the Renshai. New York, DAW, 1992; London, Millennium, 1993.
The Western Wizard (Renshai). New York, DAW, 1992; London, Millennium, 1993.
Child of Thunder (Renshai). New York, DAW, 1993; London, Millennium, 1994.
The Legend of Nightfall. New York, DAW, 1993.

Other Publications

Novel

The Unknown Soldier. New York, DAW, 1994.

*   *   *

Mickey Zucker Reichert has two specialties in the fantasy field—thieves, and Norse legends. Her two fantasy series, the Bifrost Guardians and the Renshai trilogy, are based on old Norse tales, or rather, on Norse religious myths. Reichert grapples with the legend of Ragnarok, the day the world as we know it ends (the equivalent of Armageddon to Christians). In the Renshai trilogy the most noble and successful of the world's warriors are the eponymous Renshai. Men, women and children are all warriors in their society, although they do strive to protect their young children, as any society must for survival's stake. The race must survive but, it seems, there is no particular value in the survival of an individual. Traditionally, there is nothing honourable about dying of old age, in your bed: people who manage to do so are condemned to an eternity in Hell. Warriors, those who leave this life covered in battle glory and gore, spend eternity in Valhalla and are accounted as honourable beings.

In *The Last of the Renshai,* the first book, the Renshai settlement is attacked, in a base fashion, and all but one are killed. The reasoning behind the attack is that the Renshai are rumoured to routinely dismember those they kill in battle: a person cannot enter Valhalla unless they are physically whole; wounds are acceptable, but no parts can be missing. So, naturally, the other warriors in the land resent this practice. As is to be expected among a clan so interested in war, there were not many Renshai to start with. The one pitiful remaining child is forced to survive by his mother, and he watches her die. He would rather have gone out in the traditional Renshai manner.

The gods and the wizards (most of them, anyway) are trying busily to avoid the inevitability of Ragnarok. But, since no one is certain exactly how to do so, they often work at cross purposes. Loki, the mischief-maker (chaos-inspired), is only partially evil: he strikes one as more of a candidate for psychotherapy than as an inherently immoral personage. The issue in this series is a matter of balance, not good versus evil, but the necessity of having all things in one world in order to keep it together. This is the best of Reichert's two series. The plots have many twists and turns, and not a few surprising developments. These are excellent books for readers who are interested in battles, gods and magical turns of fate. Reichert is faithful to the legends, and treats her readers with respect.

The earlier Bifrost Guardians series also centers around Ragnarok. Volume one, *Godslayer,* begins in Vietnam. Larson, an American soldier, dies in the war there and is more than a little surprised to wake up as an elf in a period that is prehistoric in our time. He has been pulled back through time by a god who wants to stop Ragnarok, or the force of chaos, from taking control. His usefulness is mainly due to the fact that he has no natural barriers to keep the god at bay. During the magical heyday of the Norse, all people come naturally equipped with such barriers, and this makes it difficult for a god with ambition. The task he sets for Larson is the elimination of Loki. Reichert is playing with the same basic tenet of Odin-worshippers as she was to do in the second series: balance is what matters; good and evil are just two sides of the whole.

Larson picks up a number of companions and acquaintances during his continuous attempts at the heroic. There is a swordmaster (himself a fascinating character), a wizard or three, various gods, and one charming little thief. The thief, Shadow Climber, is the son of a famous warrior who was convicted as a traitor and hung. Needless to say, he was innocent, and the boy ended up watching his own father's execution. He was forced by his mother to aid in her suicide and, now a small and underage orphan, turned to thievery to survive. By the time he is an adult, Shadow Climber is the most competent of thieves; in fact, his major failing is the inability to shrug off the words "but that's impossible": the minute he hears such a challenge, he begins the heroic task of burgling. In his opinion, there is no place so well guarded that he cannot successfully get in and out. (This is almost, but not quite, true.) The little thief has the added charm of being a Robin Hood: he gives much of his "take" away to help children and other helpless people in the streets.

In fact it is this kind of morality that makes the characters in this series so enjoyable. Of particular note are the female characters, who are very much in evidence, very strong, and real movers of the story. There is a quality of morality and kindness to most of the lead characters that keeps one reading with pleasure. Unfortunately it is not quite enough: the series goes on too long, and I found myself wishing, in the last book or two, that the characters would all die and put an end to it—then we could know whether they end up in Hel, which is disgustingly but convincingly depicted, or succeed in going to Valhalla.

In her singleton *The Legend of Nightfall* Reichert once again tackles the idea of a master thief. This book is the kind of fantasy that spirits readers away and makes them wish they could lead a life as interesting as the one depicted (but only if survival is guaranteed). I think it's the best of her fantasy work. She abandons the Norse legends, with great benefit. Here we have a character, Nightfall, who wants to live. He, like Shadow Climber in the long series, is a compulsive thief; the thrill of the challenge takes him places a wiser man would pass by. Nightfall, although not actually known by face, is a thief of some reputation; it is this fact which gets him in trouble. He is wanted, of course, but in this case by more than just the usual guardians of the law; he is sought by an evil wizard because of his magical talent: his weight and mass, but not his size, can be shifted at will.

If he has his wits about him Nightfall cannot be shifted from a spot he chooses to hold, because he becomes too heavy for the strongest person to move. At another split thought, he becomes as light as a feather and can perform incredible jumps. In practice, it is possible for him to be light when he takes off for a jump, heavy when he wishes to descend, and light enough to land without jarring himself. Wizards gain extra powers by virtue of stealing them and the souls of their rightful owners, and the royal wizard has a plot which involves the youngest prince. He plans to gain Nightfall's talent, and rid himself of the extremely moral Prince Edward in one fell blow. So Edward, who appears to be a bumbling fool, is set the quest of getting himself "landed" within a year (younger princes are not automatically granted land or the right to rule anything). Nightfall must aid the prince, and if he should fail all will be forfeit.

Reichert has a special talent when it comes to thieves. She treats them playfully, and has a clear understanding of the "thrill" of thievery that can suck an unwary soul in.

—Sandra Brandenburg

ROBERSON, Jennifer

Pseudonyms: Jennifer O'Green; Jay Mitchell. **Nationality:** American. **Born:** Kansas City, Missouri, 26 October 1953. **Education:** Northern Arizona University, Flagstaff, B.S. in journalism; University of London, American Studies Program, 1982. **Family:** Married Mark O'Green (divorced). **Career:** Bookseller and advertising copywriter, Phoenix, Arizona; investigative reporter, Cheyenne, Wyoming; freelance writer from 1985. **Agent:** Russell Galen, Scovil-Chichak-Galen Literary Agency, 381 Park Avenue South, #1112, New York, NY 10016, USA. **Address:** c/o *Children of the Firstborn*, 610 North Alma School Road, Suite 18, Box 104, Chandler, Arizona 85224, USA.

FANTASY PUBLICATIONS

Novels (series: Chronicles of the Cheysuli; Sword-Dancer Cycle)

Shapechangers (Cheysuli). New York, DAW, 1984; London, Corgi, 1987.
The Song of Homana (Cheysuli). New York, DAW, 1985; London, Corgi, 1987.
Legacy of the Sword (Cheysuli). New York, DAW, 1986; London, Corgi, 1988.
Sword-Dancer. New York, DAW, 1987.
Track of the White Wolf (Cheysuli). New York, DAW, 1987; London, Corgi, 1988.
A Pride of Princes (Cheysuli). New York, DAW, 1988; London, Corgi, 1989.
Sword-Singer. New York, DAW, 1988.
Daughter of the Lion (Cheysuli). New York, DAW, 1989; London, Corgi, 1990.
Sword-Maker. New York, DAW, 1989.
Flight of the Raven (Cheysuli). New York, DAW, 1990.
Sword-Breaker. New York, DAW, 1991.
A Tapestry of Lions (Cheysuli). New York, DAW, 1992.

OTHER PUBLICATIONS

Novels

Smoketree. New York, Walker, 1985.
Kansas Blood (as Jay Mitchell). New York, Zebra Books, 1986.
Royal Captive (as Jennifer O'Green). New York, Dell, 1987.
Lady of the Forest. New York, Zebra, 1992.
Glen of Sorrows. New York, Bantam, 1995.

* * *

Jennifer Roberson's longest fantasy series to date has been the eight-volume Chronicles of the Cheysuli. It begins with *Shapechangers,* the story of a girl named Alix, a prince named Carillon and two brothers, Finn and Duncan. The brothers are also princes, of a tribe called the Cheysuli, an outlawed race of shapechangers. The Cheysuli have familiars, animals with whom they can communicate telepathically, and whatever their animal is, that is the shape they can become. Finn has a grey wolf for his familiar, and Duncan a hawk. But Alix, who is the daughter of a princess and a Cheysuli warrior, has more power than any of the tribe.

Through Alix, Carillon and the Cheysuli are reconciled, though it was his uncle who outlawed them when his wife Lindir (Alix's mother), ran away with his Cheysuli bodyguard. Alix marries Duncan, the ruler of the Cheysuli, and discovers her powers, which are extensive and include being able to take any animal form. When Carillon must fight for his right to the throne, Finn goes with him to become his bodyguard. The throne is being ruled by his uncle, assisted by a powerful wizard named Tynstar.

This is a multi-generational saga, continuing through seven more volumes. Finn marries Carillon's sister Tourmaline, and a war begins between the two peoples, and between Carillon and his uncle, for claim of the throne of Homana. Add to this equation the Ihlini sorcerers, lead by Tynstar, and the action is swift, constant and exciting.

Duncan and Alix have two children, Bronwyn and Donal. Carillon marries his cousin Electra and they have one child, Aislinn, who marries Donal. Electra is really in love with Tynstar, and has a son by him named Strahan. Donal has two children by a Cheysuli woman named Sorcha, Ian and Isolde. Donal and Aislinn (who is basically aligned with her mother and Tynstar) have Niall. In volume four, *Track of the White Wolf,* Niall is a prince who is accepted by neither his Homanan people nor the Cheysuli and is beleaguered by his cousin Strahan, a sorcerer like good old Dad. Niall marries Gisella (daughter of Bronwyn and husband Alaric) and they have four children, Brennan, Hart, Corin and Keely; then he has one child, Maeve, by a woman named Deirdre. Confusing? It's a great deal easier when you read the books.

By volume five, *A Pride of Princes,* Brennan, Hart and Corin are fighting for their lives and their throne (Brennan is actually the prince who will rule). Volume six, *Daughter of the Lion,* is about Keely, twin sister of Corin and the only one who has the same powers Alix had. She is destined to fight Strahan. Volume seven, *Flight of the Raven,* skips to another generation, that of Aidan, son of Brennan, and his queen Aileen. He is now the heir to the Lion Throne and is sent on a quest by ancestors from his own history, to fight Strahan's son Lochiel. He renounces his throne in favour of his own son, Kellin. In volume eight, *A Tapestry of Lions,* Kellin must father a child with an Ihlini woman in order to fulfil a hundred-year-old prophecy and unite all his people, but he doesn't want to.

In her second, and shorter, fantasy series, Roberson ventures further into the "savage world" genre, and a very different type of sword-and-sorcery. This four-book series, about the adventures of Tiger and Del, begins with *Sword-Dancer.* The narrator of the story is Tiger, a "sword-dancer" from the South. A sword-dancer is a mercenary for hire, trained in the art of fighting by masters, and master himself over a magic that resides within his sword. Tiger is better known as the Sandtiger, and has no other name; this derives from his killing of a sandtiger at the age of 15 and also from the four claw-mark scars that run down his face.

Tiger meets Delilah, a female sword-dancer from the North, when she hires him to accompany her across the Punja, or desert waste. She is searching for her brother, kidnapped four years earlier by a raiding party that raped her and killed her parents. Now 20, Delilah is an anomaly in a culture as stultifying as all desert cultures are, where women are a commodity to be bargained and are never allowed to own themselves.

Del is wanted by her teachers for killing her own sword-master. In the North, they believe that the first person (or animal) killed by a sword enters into the sword and becomes its soul; Del wanted her sword-master's soul in her sword, so she killed him. Now she must return home and fight for her honour, or be murdered by bounty-hunters. She won't return until she finds her brother, however. When she finally does, he has been castrated and had his tongue removed, rescued from his captors by a wandering desert tribe and adopted by them to care for their old chieftain. He refuses to leave them and go home with Del, so she and Tiger are forced to leave him in the desert. At the end of the book Tiger's sword Singlestroke is broken in a sword-dance with another Northern bounty-hunter, and he takes the man's Northern sword as his own.

In volume two, *Sword-Singer,* Tiger accompanies Del north to face her teachers. After many adventures, they are pursued by a pack of unreal, otherworldly dogs, which were sent, they believe, by Del's people. When they finally reach the island where the sword-masters live Tiger is tricked by them into fighting Del. At the end of the book Tiger leaves the island to chase down the hell-hounds, who have been killing people all over the North. He believes Del will die of her wounds, and he can't forgive himself.

In volume three, *Sword-Maker,* Del catches up with Tiger and they chase down the hounds to an imprisoned wizard in a cave fortress. He "absorbs" sword-dancers in order to obtain their power; soon he will have enough to escape. He wants Del, but Tiger "sings" his magic sword into power and "requenches" it in the wizard's blood, killing him but now imprisoning his soul in the sword. Now Tiger and Del must journey back to the south, to find the brother of the wizard, Shaka Obre. Only the good wizard can vanquish the bad. Before they can find the wizard they are drawn off into the ruined city of Iskandar, where a Prophet is supposedly going to tell the people about a Messiah who will teach them to turn the sand into grass.

The would-be Messiah is Del's rapist/raider, Aladar. The Prophet is her brother, Jamail, magically restored with a tongue. But it turns out Aladar isn't the Messiah, but Tiger is, though nobody realizes except Tiger and Jamail. Tiger kills Aladar, and he and Del are pursued into the Punja by a band of religious fanatics who put a price on his head.

In volume four, *Sword-Breaker,* the quest for Shaka Obre continues. They finally find him, Tiger loses his evil wizard, teaches the desert-dwellers the magic of irrigation (this is indeed a backward culture), and in the end he and Del sail off to find his homeland and start a new life as ex-sword-dancers. It adds up to a thoroughly enjoyable and well-written series, with pleasing characters and situations.

—Debora Hill

ROBERTS, John Maddox

Nationality: American. **Born:** 1947. **Address:** c/o Tor Books, 175 Fifth Avenue, New York, NY 10010, USA.

FANTASY PUBLICATIONS

Novels (series: Conan; Stormlands)

King of the Wood. New York, Doubleday, 1983.
Conan the Valorous. New York, Tor, 1985.
Conan the Champion. New York, Tor, 1987.
Conan the Marauder. New York, Tor, 1988.
Conan the Bold. New York, Tor, 1989.
The Islander (Stormlands). New York, Tor, 1990.
The Black Shields (Stormlands). New York, Tor, 1991.
Conan the Rogue. New York, Tor, 1991.
The Poisoned Lands (Stormlands). New York, Tor, 1992.
Conan and the Treasure of the Python. New York, Tor, 1993.
The Steel Kings (Stormlands). New York, Tor, 1994.
Conan and the Manhunters. New York, Tor, 1994.
Queens of Land and Sea. New York, Tor, 1994.
Conan and the Amazon. New York, Tor, 1995.

OTHER PUBLICATIONS

Novels

The Strayed Sheep of Charon. Garden City, New York: Doubleday, 1977; revised as *Cestus Dei,* New York, Tor, 1983.

Space Angel. New York, Del Rey, 1979.
The Cingulum. New York, Tor, 1985.
Act of God, with Eric Kotani. New York, Baen, 1985.
Cloak of Illusion. New York, Tor, 1985.
The Island Worlds, with Eric Kotani. New York, Baen, 1987.
Between the Stars, with Eric Kotani. New York, Baen, 1988.
The Sword, the Jewel, and the Mirror. New York, Tor, 1988.
Spacer: Window of the Mind. New York, Del Rey, 1988.
The Enigma Variations. New York, Tor, 1989.
Delta Pavonis, with Eric Kotani. New York, Baen, 1990.
SPQR. New York, Avon, 1990.
SPQR II: The Catiline Conspiracy. New York, Avon, 1991.
The Sacrilege: An SPQR Mystery. New York, Avon, 1992.
The Temple of the Muses: An SPQR Mystery. New York, Avon, 1992.

*   *   *

A prolific producer of all sorts of fiction, Roberts creates works that range from hard science-fiction adventure (as in his four novels with Eric Kotani [a pseudonym of Yoji Kondo]), comic space operas (*Space Angel*) and philosophical ruminations about Catholicism (*The Strayed Sheep of Charon/Cestus Dei*). At his best, Roberts is an energetic adventure novelist whose works display considerable knowledge of ancient and medieval history. This historical knowledge is not limited to Roberts's fantasies; *Cestus Dei,* for example, is a science-fiction novel set on a planet which combines Imperial Roman society with atomic weapons and a decadent Catholic church. The SPQR series (*SPQR, SPQR II, The Sacrilege, The Temple of the Muses*) are very entertaining police-procedural novels (with no fantastic elements) set in the last years of the Roman Republic; the hero, a minor Roman functionary, somehow knows most of the major politicians of the era.

Roberts's first fantasy novel, *King of the Wood,* is technically science fiction, since it takes place in an alternate world. The premise is an intriguing one: in the year 1000, scores of pagans flee Norway for America in order to escape Christianity. They are joined by Irish pagans defeated in the battle of Clontarf and by Christian Saxons escaping the Norman Conquest. In the 11th century, Spanish Muslims invade and conquer Florida; the Saxon, Irish, and Norwegian immigrants split into a Christian kingdom of Treeland in the North and a pagan kingdom of Thorsheim in the South.

Three centuries later, the hero of *King of the Wood* travels throughout Roberts's alternate America, engaging in various battles both with his fellow immigrants and with "Skraelings" (American Indians). His adventures enable Roberts to describe each of the societies he has created, climaxed with a fierce battle between Aztecs and Norse warriors. *King of the Wood* is told with a great deal of verve and wit, and is one of Roberts's best fantasies.

Roberts's next fantasies were a series of Conan novels that eventually stretched to seven volumes. Though Roberts has written more about Conan than most other writers, with the possible exception of Robert Jordan, the best that can be said about these books is that they are well-written adventure novels about a character who only occasionally resembles the hero created by Robert E. Howard. Roberts's Conan is less philosophical than L. Sprague de Camp's and Lin Carter's depictions and far less violent than he is portrayed in Howard's own stories. Roberts also avoids attempting any imitation of Howard's inimitable style.

Roberts's only series of fantasy novels that aren't pastiches is the Stormlands sequence (*The Islander, The Black Shields, The Poi-*

soned Lands, The Steel Kings). On a distant planet which, thousands of years before, had advanced technology, a young boy named Hael is brought up to be a king of a primitive tribe which periodically engages in protracted warfare with neighbouring tribes. In *The Islander,* Hael united the tribes in his region by discovering a mountain of iron which enable all the tribes to create a large number of steel weapons. Once installed as king of the People of the Plains, Hael must periodically defend his kingdom against other tribes who discover a technological advance (such as gunpowder) lost for millennia. The Stormlands sequence (still incomplete) is a sword-and-sorcery series for readers who like their fantasy violent and primitive; they are energetic novels, but not inventive.

—Martin Morse Wooster

ROESSNER, Michaela(-Marie)

Nationality: American. **Born:** San Francisco, California, 27 January 1950. **Education:** California College of Arts and Crafts, Oakland, B.F.A. in ceramics; Lone Mountain College, San Francisco, M.F.A. in painting. **Family:** Married Richard C. Herman. **Career:** Has worked as maskmaker, janitor, audio-visual technician, toy person for children's store, freelance office worker for arts and somatics organizations; and assistant editor, *Locus* magazine, 1980-81. **Awards:** Crawford award, 1989; John W. Campbell award, 1989. **Agent:** Merrilee Heifetz, Writers House, 21 West 26th Street, New York, NY 10010, USA.

FANTASY PUBLICATIONS

Novel

Walkabout Woman. New York, Bantam, 1988.

OTHER PUBLICATIONS

Novel

Vanishing Point. New York, Tor, 1993.

*   *   *

Michaela Roessner has published one fantasy novel, *Walkabout Woman,* which is based on the myths and magic of the Australian Aborigines. It is a notable first novel, a beautiful, original fantasy set in a world completely alien to most readers.

The novel begins in 1949, when Raba, a young Aborigine girl living in a camp by a missionary settlement, is six. Raba's clan-aunt, Djilbara, who is the camp *wuradilagu,* or healing-woman, recognizes that Raba possesses very strong magic—so strong that it must be hidden from the old men of the tribe, who would kill her as a threat to their power. With help from the spirits of the Land, Raba will be able to return her people to the Dreamtime. In the first part of the novel, which covers Raba's childhood, she must fight a sorcerer whose ambition and egotism would destroy the tribe's ties to the Dreamtime. All ends in tragedy. In the second part, Raba has become assimilated and is a professor of medieval history, having suppressed the memory of her past. It catches up with her, and with the help—and, eventually, hindrance—of a young Welsh witch named Gwyneth, Raba is able to return to her people and lead them to the Dreamtime, away from the crumbling "whitefella" world.

This critic has no way of verifying the authenticity of Roessner's portrait of Aborigines and their ways, but the verisimilitude never fails. Many science-fiction writers could take a lesson in the depiction of alien races from Roessner. Despite the utter foreignness of Aboriginal thought to Westerners, it isn't long before their ways begin to seem normal and the ways of the white missionaries an intrusion.

Roessner does fall a bit into the trap of depicting the noble savage against the soulless white race—not completely unfair, given the history of white treatment of the Aborigines. Not all whites are evil, but none understand the Aborigines, even those attempting to "help" them. White meddling causes or exacerbates many problems, particularly in the first part of the book. In the end, we learn that the white race has been doomed ever since it gave up hunting and gathering for agriculture, with each technological advance taking it irrevocably further away from its own Dreamtime. This complete rejection of what is usually called civilization may strike a sour note with many readers, but it fits with the book's complete steeping in Aboriginal thought.

Part I of the book, which is set almost completely among the Aborigines, with occasional departures into the mission school, is the more successful. The mythos and culture of the Aborigines is of great interest, and Roessner's rich descriptions of the setting make it vivid and beautiful. Part II, being shorter and set in the white world, lacks some of this richness and interest. As in Part I, Raba must fight a determined wielder of magic; however, her new foe never seems as frightening as her old, nor are we as caught up in her battle. Nonetheless, Part II brings the events of the book to a satisfying close.

It is hard to evaluate characterization when the characters are so alien to the reader's way of thinking. The most critical character, Raba, is also the most comprehensible and sympathetic. Her problems, her triumphs, and her tragedies all affect the reader deeply. One gets the sense—probably false—that one knows what it is like to grow up as a young Aborigine girl. When Raba's assimilation into the white world begins to fall apart, the reader is swept along with it.

The other characters are more difficult to understand, as Roessner does not delve as deeply into their heads. Djilbara's twin motivations of protecting Raba and the tribe's connection to the Dreamtime are understandable. The motives of Numada, the sorcerer who threatens Raba's and the tribe's existence, are less so; he seems inherently evil, rather than a flawed human being. Huroo, Raba's lover and part of the tragedy that takes place, is annoyingly weak, always being driven by others.

In the white world, there are only two characters of any consequence. Dorothy Landell is the schoolteacher who adopts Raba as a cause and sponsors her into the university. She is well-meaning but not always bright, endearingly fussy, sometimes frustratingly obtuse. She is more a caricature of a maiden schoolteacher than a true character. Gwyneth, the young Welsh witch who helps and then fights Raba, is more complex. She is manipulative but helpful, and the depths of her needs and desires, which we slowly come to recognize, turn out to be dangerous. Because we understand her needs, she is a more believable antagonist than is Numada, though she never seems as threatening.

Walkabout Woman is a fascinating novel and a successful attempt to bring the magic of the Australian Aborigines to life. Roessner is a highly gifted writer who handles an alien culture with seeming ease. Any future fantasy novels she writes (and, following her science-fiction novel *Vanishing Point,* she is said to be working on a new long fantasy) should amply repay reading.

—Janice M. Eisen

ROHAN, Michael Scott

Pseudonym: Michael Scot. **Nationality:** British. **Born:** Edinburgh, 22 January 1951. **Education:** Edinburgh Academy, 1956-69; St. Edmunds Hall, Oxford University, 1970-73, M.A. in jurisprudence. **Family:** Married Deborah Morris Hickenlooper in 1977. **Career:** Senior editor, encyclopedias and reference projects, Elsevier International, Oxford, 1973-78; reference book editor, Laurence Urdang, Aylesbury, Buckinghamshire, 1978-79; technical editor, ICL, Bracknell, Berkshire, 1980; partner and senior editor, Asgard Publishing Services, Leeds, West Yorkshire, from 1984. Contributor, *Opera Now, Music Magazine, Classic CD* and other magazines. **Awards:** International Association for the Fantastic in the Arts, William F. Crawford award, 1990. **Agent:** Maggie Noach, 21 Redan Street, London, W14 0AB, England.

FANTASY PUBLICATIONS

Novels (series: Spiral; The Winter of the World)

The Ice King, with Allan Scott. London, New English Library, 1986; as *Burial Rites,* New York, Berkley, 1987.
The Anvil of Ice (Winter of the World). London, Macdonald, and New York, Morrow, 1986.
The Forge in the Forest (Winter of the World). London, Macdonald, and New York, Morrow, 1987.
The Hammer of the Sun (Winter of the World). London, Macdonald, and New York, Morrow, 1988.
Chase the Morning (Spiral). London, Futura, and New York, Morrow, 1990.
The Gates of Noon (Spiral). London, Gollancz, 1992; New York, Morrow, 1993.
A Spell of Empire: The Horns of Tartarus, with Allan Scott. London, Orbit, 1992.
Cloud Castles (Spiral). London, Gollancz, 1993; New York, Morrow, 1994.
The Lord of Middle Air. London, Gollancz, 1994.

OTHER PUBLICATIONS

Novel

Run to the Stars. London, Arrow, 1982; New York, Ace, 1986.

Other

The Hammer and the Cross, with Allan Scott. Oxford, Alder Publishing, 1980.

The Classical Video Guide, with Jeremy Siepmann and Michael Oliver. London, Gollancz, 1994.

*

Michael Scott Rohan comments:

It's rarely easy to sum up one's own work; it's too liable to sound either over-simple or plain pretentious. This much I can say with certainty—all my life I've been a ravenous reader of all kinds of literature, but taking a special pleasure in science fiction and fantasy, and I try to write more of what I'd want to read myself. I don't think of them as separate genres; I believe the best of one is infused with the spirit of the other, and I'd like to write more of both.

I've written three main kinds of fantasy so far. The Winter of the World trilogy could be called heroic, Tolkienesque fantasy, set in a fairly closely imagined Ice Age in which the ice itself is the animate weapon and domain of older powers seeking to sterilize the world to restore the lifeless perfection they once knew. The embattled ancestors of humanity find a kind of magic in metalworking, and odd enemies and allies in an epic struggle to preserve their civilization. The tales of the Spiral, on the other hand, are firmly rooted in today's world, but see it surrounded by a whirlpool of constantly changing parallels that reflect its mysterious and magical archetypes, ranging from legendary places such as Huy Braseal to a certain film. Into this maelstrom of, legend is sucked a young businessman, Stephen Fisher, in danger of sacrificing his basic decency to his yuppie ambitions. Over the course of the books, at the cost of appalling dangers, he works out a better destiny both here and out on the Spiral. *Lord of Middle Air* is more heroic in style, based on the legends that surround a very remote ancestor and namesake of mine; I intend it to be the first of a series of Scottish tales. The Spell of Empire series, with my co-author Allan Scott, sets out to be a swashbuckling romp through a neoclassical Europe in which the Roman Empire fell rather differently and the old gods still hold sway; other titles are planned.

Above all I enjoy storytelling. I try to make my stories entertaining, but that needn't mean illiterate or mindless; there's sex and violence in them, as there is in human existence, but not just for cheap effect. There is love and heroism as well, because often they're inextricably mingled. Above all I aim for a sense of vision, of a wider world, of infinite possibilities and truths that myth and science together only reflect. I'm a great believer in escapism, the vital safety valve on an unendurable world. "As yourself," Tolkien once said, "who is most interested in preventing escape? Gaolers!" I hope I'm slipping the occasional cake through the bars. They have files in them—but I want the cakes to be enjoyed for their own sake, too.

*   *   *

Michael Scott Rohan's first novel, *Run to the Stars,* was science fiction; his debut fantasy (with a modern archaeological setting and horror overtones), *The Ice King,* was written with Allan Scott, and the Rohan/Scott collaborations are discussed in the essay on Scott.

The Winter of the World trilogy's seeming fantasy world is actually prehistoric Earth at the height of an ice age: the Wurm glaciation, an evil climate promoted by supernatural Ice powers. Other powers like the enigmatic Raven (Odin) help beleaguered humanity in their own ways, and there is a wise Elder Race of apparent neanderthals. The hero Elof survives the bloody sacking of his vil-

lage by sea-reavers in *The Anvil of Ice,* to become apprenticed to an Ice-serving Mastersmith under whose grudging tuition he emerges as a gifted maker of magical tools and weapons— like the "mindsword" which scatters opponents in terror. All this smithcraft is lovingly researched and described. The first book's closing confrontation between Elof and his former master has a neat magical twist . . . even if it's somewhat conventional for the hitherto irresistible evil army, once made leaderless, to disperse in a single paragraph.

Book two, *The Forge in the Forest,* succumbs a little to a middle volume's characteristic longueurs as our hero goes on immense journeys through terrific perils. There are still some strikingly enjoyable highlights of battle and smithy-work: for example, an early and consciously Wagnerian scene sees Elof using lightning to reforge an indestructible sword apparently reinforced with carbon fibre.

Such technological buttressing of fantasy tropes continues through *The Hammer of the Sun,* where even the Ice powers' main scheme proves to be based on a plausible altering of Earth's albedo. After straying from his path of heroism in a disastrous attempt to shackle the more-than-woman Klara whom he loves too possessively and who may not be bound, Mastersmith Elof falls on evil times and is made a slave, crippled by his own creations. He rises above this, literally; his stature has been growing until he now casts mythic shadows as a proto-Vulcan, while even his prentice work like the Tarnhelm will echo through human mythology. Now the tally of his creations increases almost outrageously: having already mastered electroplating and perfect energy accumulators, he adds Greek fire, distillation, napalm, powered flight and the solar furnace . . . while sly textual hints convey that the literal Hammer of the Sun with which Elof destroys the crucial redoubt of the Ice amounts to a tactical nuclear weapon.

While leaving much to inexplicable magic, this underpinning of practical physics adds considerable conviction—though sometimes its exposition sits oddly with outbreaks of "high fantasy" diction.

The Spiral trilogy uses the fantasy tradition of magical realms co-existing with ours, with importance given to borders, portals and crossings. Our known "real" world and its mindset comprise the Core: around it is the Spiral, a shifting between-region leading out to the spiritual ultimates of the Rim. Spiral time is negotiable, and mythic or historic places can be reached as easily as the real seaports where Spiral meets Core. Hence there's much fantasy action-adventure and piracy on literal high seas, since only ships can negotiate the Spiral (volume three extends this to zeppelins and even a helicopter). The first book, *Chase the Morning,* has a memorable scene when the unbelieving hero first sees an old-fashioned sailing vessel climbing from a dull English dock up through the cloudscapes of sunset.

This trilogy is set in the near future, each linked volume having a separate plot. *Chase the Morning* is an exhilarating pursuit of the not-quite-hero Steve Fisher's kidnapped secretary, sailing the Spiral with colourful and sometimes sinister allies to a climax of voodoo and possession in Haiti. Good set-pieces include the blazing appearance of a *dupiah* demon in a seafront warehouse, and techno-fantasy *frissons* like Fisher's early tracing of his new friend's ship *Iskander* in a CD-ROM Lloyd's Register: Reg. Huy Brazeal, 1868. The book's chief problem is that while we're repeatedly told that Fisher is a worthless "hollow man," with a crucial plot point depending on this, his first-person narration is engaging and he's constantly doing heroic things.

The Gates of Noon happens years later, with Fisher caught up in a multi-sided political and supernatural dispute over a new water system for (now) rainfall-starved Bali. His shipping company undertakes to transport the relevant computer gear, against strong opposition in Spiral and Core. Fisher rides guard on the container, which is gaudily protected by spray-can graffiti symbols thanks to a sorcerous ally. There's more neat crossover of magic and science when, beset by unpleasantness on the rail-freight stage of the container's journey, the magician complains there's no power to work with and Fisher points out the adjacent high-voltage wiring. Later our hero succumbs to the wiles of a death-goddess who is one of the opposing forces, and subsequently learns that, possessed, he climbed naked down 40 storeys from a Bangkok hotel room to steal his own shipment . . . More Spiral sea-chases ensue, including landfall on Skull Island of King Kong fame. There are vivid confrontations and unmaskings. When all the concerned Forces are revealed, Fisher settles matters with a fast-talking diplomatic compromise more science fiction than fantasy in tone.

Further years elapse before *Cloud Castles,* this time-discontinuity once again leaving Fisher free of his girlfriend from the previous book. Here the action is on a still more cosmic scale. When Fisher inadvertently steals the revered Spear associated with the holy Graal (later ingeniously concealing it in an automated container delivery system) one notes his name, his reiterated description as a hollow man, spiritually maimed, etc, and the fact that he's remotely descended from German royalty . . . Apotheosis looms, but not before a muster of the Graal knights from all of history for rousing struggle with adversaries old and new—the worst of the new being an entire malevolent mountain (the Brocken) seething with the degenerated bodies and souls of once-humans incorporated into its being. There is an interview with a godlike Rim entity who offers Fisher the business whizkid his ultimate career opportunity; and again he gets the girl, this time a female Graal knight.

These Spiral books are full of audacious ideas and scenes, not to mention a pleasant sense of fun. They effectively contrast the fantastic with the streetwise, business-canny depiction of the Core. Despite patches of sloppy or hasty writing, the trilogy reads well.

Like others before him, Rohan repeatedly and effectively mixes a toughening alloy of science-fictional techniques and logic into his fantasy narratives. A new sequence of books based on Scots myth and history is planned, beginning with *The Lord of Middle Air*— a story of the 13th-century Borders featuring the historical "wizard" Michael Scot, one of Rohan's own ancestors.

—David Langford

RUSCH, Kristine Kathryn

Pseudonym: Sandy Schofield. **Nationality:** American. **Born:** 1960. **Family:** Married Dean Wesley Smith. **Career:** Editor, *Pulphouse: The Hardback Magazine,* 1988-93; editor, *The Magazine of Fantasy and Science Fiction,* from 1991. **Awards:** John W. Campbell Award, 1990; Hugo Award, 1994.

Fantasy Publications

Novels

The White Mists of Power. New York, Roc, 1991; London, Millennium, 1992.

Heart Readers. London, Millennium, and New York, Roc, 1993.
Traitors. London, Millennium, 1993; New York, Roc, 1994.

Other Publications

Novels

Afterimage, with Kevin J. Anderson. New York, Roc, 1992.
Facade. New York, Abyss, 1993; London, Millennium, 1994.
The Big Game: Star Trek, Deep Space Nine #4, with Dean Wesley Smith (as Sandy Schofield). New York, Pocket, 1993.
Alien Influences. London, Millennium, 1994.
Sins of the Blood. New York, Dell, 1994; London, Millennium, 1995.
The Escape: Star Trek, Voyager #2, with Dean Wesley Smith. New York, Pocket, 1995.

Short Stories

The Gallery of His Dreams. Eugene, Oregon, Axolotl Press, 1991.

Other

Characterization. Eugene, Oregon, Pulphouse, 1990.
The Rules: A Short Course in the Basics. Eugene, Oregon, Pulphouse, 1990.
Setting. Eugene, Oregon, Pulphouse, 1990.

Editor, with Dean Wesley Smith, *Science Fiction Writers of America Handbook: The Professional Writer's Guide to Writing Professionally.* Eugene, Oregon, Writer's Notebook Press, 1990.
Editor, *The Best of Pulphouse: The Hardback Magazine.* New York, St. Martin's Press, 1991.
Editor, with Edward L. Ferman, *The Best from Fantasy & Science Fiction: A 45th Anniversary Anthology.* New York, St. Martin's Press, 1994.

*   *   *

Kristine Kathryn Rusch has an impressive *curriculum vitae*: editor of *Pulphouse: The Hardback Magazine,* and winner of a Hugo award for her editing, then editor of *The Magazine of Fantasy and Science Fiction,* she has also managed to produce many short stories and several chapbooks on how to write, and a handful of exceptional novels.

As there is no physical link—temporal or spatial—between any fantastic world and ours, and thus literally anything is possible, then the similarities that make it possible for readers in our world to comprehend the stories at all must be abstracts. Now, most abstracts—religion, science, philosophy, etc.—have a two-way relationship with their realities; they are both derived from reality and in turn used to try to control it. Morality alone exists independent of reality. It cannot be derived from behaviour, but is most surely seen as the only control of behaviour. If genres within fiction were defined solely by their concerns, then fantasy would thus have to be defined by its concern with morality, and the best fantasy would explore the subtleties and ramifications of moral behaviour in a way that would bring home its lessons most forcefully to its real-world readership. By this token all of Rusch's novels are first-class fantasy. Sadly, generic fiction is more usually defined—or at least described—by reference to the physical characteristics of the stories, and by this token Rusch's novels span the whole range of the fantastic.

The first two are best classified as fantasy, in that the worlds depicted are strangely amorphous—they have no real edges. *The White Mists of Power* and *Heart Readers* are straight—down-the-line American imaginings of a medieval European/Middle Eastern background with added magic, and as such might be easily dismissed as merely derivative. But Rusch is not that easy to dismiss. Where other such novels display little more than the recycling of cliches hinted at here, these books contain a depth of characterization and a subtlety of plotting unusual in modern fantasy. Oddly enough, *The White Mists of Power,* the first of her novels, is definitely the weakest; novelists usually produce a strong debut and then struggle to match it. *The White Mists of Power* has a central theme as nebulous as its title, and is redeemed only by its characterization.

Heart Readers is much stronger, in that the central theme is the characterization, this time of women oppressed by men, albeit in this pseudo-medieval setting—and it seizes the attention and refuses to let go. It appears to be a cross-over science-fiction novel, in that the "heart reading" of the title is a woman-only telepathic trait linked, believe it or not, to the women's sexual fidelity within a lesbian relationship, but the fact that this idea is peripheral to the real story of moral struggle combines with the exotically unreal setting (again, there seem to be no edges) to mark this firmly as a fantasy. There is a powerful evocation of the loyalties intimate emotions can generate in people and the stresses that these loyalties cause, so that the book is markedly superior to standard run-of-the-mill fantasy, and the depth of insight afforded the reader into the homosexual relationship is reminiscent of Samuel R. Delany at his best.

Traitors illuminates its theme of betrayal on several levels with such bewildering skill that it is sometimes hard to realize that this is the same author who wrote the rather unfocused *The White Mists of Power.* There is everything here, from sexual betrayal within a personal relationship to the paired ultimate betrayals of state and friendship via much abstruse political intrigue, but Rusch, ever more adventurous, is not content with merely depicting traitorism and what appear to be its causes, but rather is using it to investigate the higher-still rule of personal integrity and loyalty that is the cause of each betrayal in the book. Rusch makes us understand, and this is no mean achievement, that betrayal is merely the name given by the injured party to the acts of another that largely they have not understood. This novel moves closer to science fiction than the previous two in that its believably envisioned and complete setting is a world that has two separate kingdoms spread over an archipelago (reminiscent, surely on purpose, of Ursula Le Guin). It gives the reader the sense that this world is whole, it has edges, and that there must be other worlds out there too.

With *Facade* Rusch shows another side to her talent by setting a novel on Earth in, so to speak, a day-after-tomorrow here-and-now. Apparently a psychological thriller/serial killer hackwork following the then-current fashion for such books, only this story's denouement reveals what the reader has uncomfortably suspected all along, that this is an excellent novel of inner landscapes and personal crises and is in fact an extremely dark fantasy. It was published around the same time as Ursula Le Guin's *Searoad,* and again is strangely redolent of that masterwork, with its remote out-of-season seaside setting and its cast of strangely alien but comfortingly real characters.

Alien Influences completes the transition to science fiction promised by the earlier novels. But it also manages to include yet more generic influences—not only does it contain serial murders as in *Facade,* it also introduces detective-genre themes in following the story of the failure who is sent to solve the crimes and whose resentment of his previous vilification is at least in part the motor for his need to succeed this time. It is set partly on an alien planet that has been partly colonized by humans and partly in the space station of the pan-galactic human empire that colonized the planet. In finally exposing not only the criminals but the social decadence that both led to the crimes and led to the mystical alien natives being accused of the murders, Rusch displays a rare and growing mastery of her media, and an extraordinary insight into the society she lives in and how it might be changed.

Most recently, Rusch has taken on the biggest cliche of all, the vampire novel, and made it over in her own image. *Sins of the Blood,* despite having a black cover with a thoroughly evil-looking vampire on it, is listed as a science-fiction novel, and indeed uses all of Rusch's awesome power to depict a parallel-world present-day USA where vampires are a recognized European phenomenon and each state has its own laws and ways of dealing with the problem: Wisconsin eradicates them, while Oregon tries to rehabilitate them. As is usual with Rusch's novels, she does not merely repeat the cliches; she adds to them, draws them out, discovers new depths, all while providing the sucks for bucks the anticipated audience would expect, and while putting both Anne Rice and Poppy Z. Brite to shame for pure eroticism. And then she adds an entirely new dimension—vampires can have human children who can either turn into vampires when they mature, or possibly be rescued from their fate. Finally, behind the sex and the blood-sucking, this novel is concerned with the deep moral problems of finding ways to control a problem that is, after all, only natural.

Kristine Kathryn Rusch is a truly astonishing talent, and it is hard to imagine how she could better her work in the various genres without moving into the biggest genre, mainstream fiction. We can only hope she will produce more excellent genre works before being seduced away to the bright lights of mainstream success.

—Paul Brazier

RUSHDIE, (Ahmed) Salman

Nationality: British. **Born:** Bombay, India, 19 June 1947. **Education:** Cathedral School, Bombay; Rugby School, Warwickshire, 1961-65; King's College, Cambridge, 1965-68, M.A. (honours) in history 1968. **Family:** Married 1) Clarissa Luard in 1976 (divorced 1987); 2) the writer Marianne Wiggins in 1988 (separated). **Career:** Worked in television in Pakistan and as an actor in London, 1968-69; freelance advertising copywriter, London, 1970-81; council member, Institute of Contemporary Arts, London, from 1985. Sentenced to death for *The Satanic Verses* in a religious decree (*fatwa*) by Ayatollah Khomeini, and forced to go into hiding, February 1989. **Awards:** Booker prize, 1981; English-Speaking Union award, 1981; James Tait Black Memorial prize, 1982; Foreign Book prize (France), 1985; Whitbread prize, 1988. Fellow, Royal Society of Literature, 1983. **Agent:** Aitken and Stone Ltd., 29 Fernshaw Road, London SW10 0TG, England.

FANTASY PUBLICATIONS

Novels

Grimus. London, Gollancz, 1975; New York, Overlook Press, 1979.
Midnight's Children. London, Cape, and New York, Knopf, 1981.
Shame. London, Cape, and New York, Knopf, 1983.
The Satanic Verses. London, Viking, 1988; New York, Viking, 1989.
Haroun and the Sea of Stories. London, Granta, 1990; New York, Viking, 1991.
The Moor's Last Sigh. London, Cape, 1995.

Short Stories

East, West. London, Cape, 1994; New York, Pantheon, 1995.

OTHER PUBLICATIONS

Other

The Jaguar Smile: A Nicaraguan Journey. London, Pan, and New York, Viking, 1987.
Is Nothing Sacred? (lecture). London, Granta, 1990.
Imaginary Homelands: Essays and Criticism 1981-1991. London, Granta, and New York, Viking, 1991.
The Wizard of Oz. London, British Film Institute, 1992.

*

Critical Studies: *The Perforated Sheet: Essays on Salman Rushdie's Art* by Uma Parameswaran, New Delhi, Affiliated East West Press, 1988; *The Rushdie File* edited by Lisa Appignanesi and Sara Maitland, London, Fourth Estate, 1989, Syracuse, New York, Syracuse University Press, 1990; *Salman Rushdie and the Third World: Myths of the Nation* by Timothy Brennan, London, Macmillan, 1989; *A Satanic Affair: Salman Rushdie and the Rage of Islam* by Malise Ruthven, London, Chatto and Windus, 1990; *The Rushdie Affair: The Novel, the Ayatollah, and the West* by Daniel Pipes, New York, Birch Lane Press, 1990; *Salman Rushdie: Sentenced to Death* by W. J. Weatherby, New York, Carroll and Graf, 1990; *Distorted Imagination: Lessons from the Rushdie Affair* by Ziauddin Sardar and Merryl Wyn Davies, London, Grey Seal, 1990; *Salman Rushdie* by James Harrison, New York, Twayne, 1991.

*   *   *

Inadvertently propelled to bestsellerdom when the Ayatollah Khomeini of Iran condemned him to death for alleged blasphemies against Islam in *The Satanic Verses,* Rushdie remains perhaps the most controversial novelist of all time, and his book the most dangerous (if unread) fantasy novel ever written. The continued danger to Rushdie's life from Muslim fanatics and the overall failure of the civilized world to defend basic human rights in this instance have only drawn attention away from the book itself, as literature. Certainly most of those ready to kill or die over it have not read it, or even seen a copy, since it remains banned in most Muslim countries. Even in the West, Rushdie's fame far exceeds his readership.

An American newspaper survey concluded that only five percent of those who rush out to buy *The Satanic Verses* to defy the Ayatollah actually read it.

The Satanic Verses is a complex satire in a magic-realist mode, in which the fantastic elements occur incidentally among details of social realism, without any attempt to systematize them as would occur in a genre fantasy. Two Indian actors miraculously survive the terrorist bombing of a plane, falling 20,000 feet into England. One is transformed into a devil, the other an angel. But the "angel" is by far the less angelic, an egomaniac who lives out a series of outrageous scenarios, some caricaturing the early history of Islam. Most outrageously, he imagines himself as Mohammed's secretary, who discovers he can interpolate anything he wants into the *Koran.* But the fantasy fails, the undeceived Prophet erases the subversive material and righteousness seems to triumph. Or does it? Meanwhile a scurrilous poet, modelled on Rushdie himself, has gone into hiding in a brothel, disguised as a eunuch. When the ladies discover the truth, they "marry" him, taking the names of the Prophet's wives, setting up a bawdy parody of Mohammed's domestic life. They too suffer the wrath of the believers, but, again, not before they get a chance to enjoy themselves.

The effect is as if a crazed Christian fantasized himself into the life of Christ and rewrote some of the gospels, casting doubt on the whole, before getting caught. One recalls *Monty Python's Life of Brian,* which, the film is careful to explain, isn't about Jesus at all, but about the kid in the other manger down the street. However, the similarities are clear enough. The Islamic world, lacking Western traditions of satire, failed to get the joke. Additionally, one cannot help but note that Khomeini himself is venomously caricatured as a seedy fanatic living in a London flat, spewing hatred into tape cassettes while having sexual fantasies about the empress of Iran. So possibly the Ayatollah's wrath was as much personal as political or religious.

Another antireligious subplot concerns an Indian girl who leads her followers to the seashore, where, she prophesies, the waters will part, leaving a dry path to Mecca. The waters don't part, and everyone drowns. But religion is only a small part of the overall material of *The Satanic Verses,* a brilliant, Cabellesque satire which is difficult to summarize. The most easily identifiable thematic thread is that of the condition of Indians living in Britain, losing their culture, regaining harmony when they return to India. The condition of the world becomes progressively stranger—monsters abound, London turns tropical—until the two Indian actors are gone from Britain. How much of their experience is real, how much hallucinated or dreamed, is never made clear, nor is it a concern for Rushdie, who thus remains outside of the main tradition of fantasy fiction. Rushdie, unlike Tolkien or Robert E. Howard, or Ursula Le Guin (in her Earthsea books) is not writing a realistic novel in an imaginary setting, or even a novel in the *Unknown Worlds* mode in which one fantastic element intrudes into the familiar. *The Satanic Verses* is a fanciful, unrealistic story which never tries to convince on such a level. Such deliberate artificiality in narrative writing is as current as post-Modernism, but as old as Lucian of Samosata.

Rushdie's first novel, *Grimus,* is a surrealistic mix of satire and Native American myth, about a man who receives immortality and goes on a fantastic quest. In *Midnight's Children* all children born on the night of the partition between India and Pakistan find themselves possessed of miraculous powers; the complex narrative yields political allegory first, then myth. *Shame* likewise uses fantasy to illuminate Asian socio-political conflicts.

Haroun and the Sea of Stories, Rushdie's first fiction since the Ayatollah's death-threat forced him to go into hiding, is a fable of an imprisoned storyteller cut off from the sources of his inspiration. His son embarks on a fantastic quest to turn on the pipeline of Story once again. It is very self-referential, on the surface comic, sort of an Asian *Yellow Submarine,* but ultimately bitter. Rushdie, because of *The Satanic Verses,* will forever be isolated from the very experiences which he has previously transmogrified into fantasy.

Fantasy is but one of the techniques in the repertoire of the recent collection *East, West;* one of the stories even plays with *Star Trek* imagery in a broader cultural context. Some of the essays in *Imaginary Homelands* reflect on fantastic matters, on Kurt Vonnegut, on Terry Gilliam's film *Brazil,* and on the nature of fantasy itself; and Rushdie has also written a booklet about the fantasy film *The Wizard of Oz.*

—Darrell Schweitzer

RYMAN, Geoff(rey Charles)

Nationality: British. **Born:** Canada, 1951; lived in the USA for a decade, then moved to London in 1973. **Career:** Civil servant. **Awards:** British Science Fiction award, 1985, 1990; World Fantasy award, 1986; Arthur C. Clarke award, 1990; John W. Campbell Memorial award, 1991. **Agent:** Maggie Noach, 21 Redan Street, London, W14 0AB, England. **Address:** c/o HarperCollins Publishers, 77-85 Fulham Palace Road, London W6 8JB, England.

FANTASY PUBLICATIONS

Novels

The Warrior Who Carried Life. London, and Boston, Allen and Unwin, 1985.
The Unconquered Country: A Life History. London, and Boston, Allen and Unwin, 1986.
"Was . . ." London, HarperCollins, and New York, Knopf, 1992.

Other

Coming of Enkidu (play plus novel fragment). Birmingham, England, Birmingham SF Group, 1989.

OTHER PUBLICATIONS

Novels

The Child Garden, or A Low Comedy. London, Unwin Hyman, 1989; New York, St. Martin's Press, 1990.

Short Stories

Unconquered Countries: Four Novellas. New York, St. Martin's Press, 1994.

* * *

Unique among modern fantasists, Geoff Ryman takes as his subject the often dangerous but ultimately redemptive qualities of fantasy itself, addressing narratives to such established but shifting texts as the Epic of Gilgamesh (*The Warrior Who Carried Life*) and *The Wizard of Oz* (*"Was . . ."*). Intensely aware of the appeal and value of supposedly "escapist" fictions, Ryman consistently probes the pain and hurt which is at their root, creating novels whose spikiness and intensity cut against the grain of most contemporary fantasy.

The consensus worlds of the genre are prettified visions of medieval romance filtered through Tolkien or Western-style primal bloodbaths patterned after Robert E. Howard, but Ryman chose in "The Unconquered Country" (*Interzone* magazine, 1984), his first significant story, to extrapolate a magical land from the reality of recent history. A long novella slightly expanded into a short novel, *The Unconquered Country: A Life History* is set in a version of Cambodia during the Vietnam War where all human products (weapons, houses, even the War) are literally alive, suggesting a responsibility which the race is unwilling to shoulder. As if the setting were not far enough removed from the mainstream, Ryman chooses also to tell his story not through the viewpoint of one of the Western outsiders whose presence signals such disaster (the Big Men), but through Third Child, a peasant girl whose innocent lack of understanding forces the reader to decide what is "really" happening.

The miracle of *The Unconquered Country* is that it addresses sobering and serious matters with a light touch that is something of a Ryman characteristic, using a wry authorial voice not to make bearable the unbearable but to underline the essential humanity of the book's vision. Here, Third Child finds herself caught up in the evacuation of a hospital at the armed prompting of another of many interdependent but hostile factions, and Ryman displays a fine blend of humour and tragic grace:

> Third found herself suddenly in a line of marching things, all down around her knees, hunch-backed, bobbing, and all talking at once, very softly and clearly. "I am a delicate piece of life-saving equipment," said a little beige box on muscular, human legs. Another, armoured like a beehive, waddled ahead of it. "I can take over cerebral functions for all blood groups," it announced in a hushed voice. "Please treat me with care."

The Warrior Who Carried Life, Ryman's first novel, appeared between the magazine and book versions of *The Unconquered Country,* and is his closest approach to traditional fantasy, though his intention (signalled in the subtle oxymoron of the title) is a subversion and deconstruction of the brutal assumptions of the genre. With chapter titles ("The Wells of Vision," "The Wound Between the Worlds," "When the Dragon Wakes, We Will See Him Together, Each of You and Me") that evoke and parody the heavy tone of William Morris, *The Warrior Who Carried Life* deploys the furniture of sword and sorcery rigidly excluded from *The Unconquered Country*: swordsmen, monsters, quests, revelations, dragons, exotic perils. A character in *The Unconquered Country* offers to trade a fortune for a drink of Coca-Cola, but Cal Cara Kerig, the heroine of *The Warrior Who Carried Life,* is engaged on a quest which defies such trivialities as money or soft drinks. Like the Conan of John Milius's film and many another fantasy hero (Clint Eastwood's Josey Wales, for instance), Cara is orphaned by violence and becomes a warrior (even transforming into a man) and sets out on a quest for revenge. However, the thrust of the novel is that Cara can only overcome peril by turning away from violent revenge and redeeming her world by rediscovering her (female, pacifist, loving) self.

The Child Garden, a science-fiction novel, is similar in tone to *The Warrior Who Carried Life,* lovingly detailed in its imagined greenhouse future, and equally oppositional to the plot assumptions of its genre, following a vast project involving space travel which is not exploratory or commercial in intent but artistic. If *The Child Garden* is a putting-on-a-show musical, *"Was . . . ,"* Ryman's most impressive and important novel to date, takes the concept to extremes by having as its hero the story first told in *The Wonderful Wizard of Oz,* L. Frank Baum's 1900 novel, and then retold, with significant alterations, in the 1939 MGM film *The Wizard of Oz,* with Judy Garland as Dorothy Gale, the Kansas farm-girl transported by a twister to the Land of Oz, where the Yellow Brick Road leads to the Emerald City and each stretch of undergrowth contains a magical new friend or enemy. *The Child Garden* follows the creation and staging of a Dante-inspired show which is a literal space opera, while *"Was . . ."* tracks the evolution of a familiar tale as it is passed from hand to hand, from creator to consumer, from the specific to the general.

For Ryman, the story of Dorothy and Oz exists in a nebulous space clustered around but not limited to the book (and its many sequels) and the film (and its several less-known follow-ups), taking shape in the minds of readers and viewers, so that their impressions and memories—even if they are wrong—are as important and substantial a layer of the core text as the original material. Starting from the impressions of Jonathan, an HIV-positive actor (who has starred in a series of child-abuse slasher movies along the lines of the Freddy Krueger films, inviting comparison with Jonathan Carroll's *A Child Across the Sky*), who becomes obsessed enough with the film to visit Manhattan, Kansas, where he believes a real Dorothy might have lived, *"Was . . ."* travels through the layers of the story's existence, tracing back through Judy Garland's unhappy Hollywood career to Baum's brief spell as a teacher in the Midwest to reach Ryman's newly imagined core for the Oz story, the harsh childhood of a real Dorothy Gael (sic) on a Kansas farm in the 1880s. In this primal scene (where Ryman's Dorothy greatly resembles Third Child and Cara) we see a transmutation of unhappiness into magic that reaffirms the importance of the fantastic and, as always in Ryman, provides a clear-sighted sympathy for the real victims who are found under the fantasized images of the questing hero.

—Kim Newman

S

SABERHAGEN, Fred (Thomas)

Nationality: American. **Born:** Chicago, Illinois, 18 May 1930. **Education:** Wright Junior College, Chicago, 1956-57. **Military Service:** United States Air Force, 1951-55. **Family:** Married Joan Dorothy Spicci in 1968; one daughter and two sons. **Career:** Electronics technician, Motorola Inc., Chicago, 1956-62; assistant editor, *Encyclopaedia Britannica,* 1967-73. Freelance writer, 1962-67, and since 1973. **Agent:** Eleanor Wood, Spectrum Literary Agency, 111 Eighth Avenue, Suite 1502, New York, New York 10011, USA.

FANTASY PUBLICATIONS

Novels (series: Empire of the East; Lost Swords; Swords)

The Broken Lands (Empire of the East). New York, Ace, 1968.
The Black Mountains (Empire of the East). New York, Ace, 1971.
Changeling Earth (Empire of the East). New York, DAW, 1973; as *Ardneh's World,* New York, Baen, 1988.
The Empire of the East (omnibus; includes *The Broken Lands, The Black Mountains, Changeling Earth*). New York, Ace, 1979; London, Macdonald, 1984.
The First Book of Swords. New York, Tor, 1983; London, Futura, 1985.
The Second Book of Swords. New York, Tor, 1983; London, Futura, 1985.
The Third Book of Swords. New York, Tor, 1984; London, Futura, 1986.
The Complete Book of Swords (omnibus; includes *The First Book of Swords, The Second Book of Swords, The Third Book of Swords*). New York, Nelson Doubleday, 1985.
The First Book of Lost Swords: Woundhealer's Story. New York, Tor, 1986; London, Orbit, 1988.
The Second Book of Lost Swords: Sightblinder's Story. New York, Tor, 1987; London, Orbit, 1989.
The Third Book of Lost Swords: Stonecutter's Story. New York, Tor, 1988; London, Orbit, 1989.
The Lost Swords: The First Triad (omnibus; includes *The First Book of Lost Swords, The Second Book of Lost Swords, The Third Book of Lost Swords*). New York, Nelson Doubleday, 1988.
The Fourth Book of Lost Swords: Farslayer's Story. New York, Tor, 1989; London, Orbit, 1991.
The Fifth Book of Lost Swords: Coinspinner's Story. New York, Tor, 1989.
The Sixth Book of Lost Swords: Mindsword's Story. New York, Tor, 1990.
The Lost Swords: The Second Triad (omnibus; includes *The Fourth Book of Lost Swords, The Fifth Book of Lost Swords, The Sixth Book of Lost Swords*). New York, Guild America, 1991.
The Seventh Book of Lost Swords: Wayfinder's Story. New York, Tor, 1992.
The Last Book of Swords: Shieldbreaker's Story. New York, Tor, 1994.
Merlin's Bones. New York, Tor, 1995.

Other

Editor, *An Armory of Swords.* New York, Tor, 1995.

OTHER PUBLICATIONS

Novels

The Golden People. New York, Ace, 1964.
The Water of Thought. New York, Ace, 1965; complete edition, Los Angeles, Pinnacle, 1981.
Brother Assassin. New York, Ballantine, 1969; as *Brother Berserker,* London, Macdonald, 1969.
Berserker's Planet. New York, DAW, and London, Futura, 1975.
The Dracula Tape. New York, Warner, 1975.
Specimens. New York, Popular Library, 1976.
The Holmes-Dracula File. New York, Ace, 1978.
The Veils of Azlaroc. New York, Ace, 1978.
Love Conquers All. New York, Ace, 1979.
The Mask of the Sun. New York, Ace, 1979.
Berserker Man. New York, Ace, 1979; London, Gollancz, 1988.
An Old Friend of the Family. New York, Ace, 1979.
Coils, with Roger Zelazny. New York, Tor, 1980; London, Penguin, 1984.
Thorn. New York, Ace, 1980.
Octagon. New York, Ace, 1981; London, Sinclair Browne, 1984.
Dominion. New York, Tor, 1982.
A Century of Progress. New York, Tor, 1983.
The Berserker Throne. New York, Simon and Schuster, 1985.
Berserker Blue Death. New York, Tor, 1985; London, Gollancz, 1990.
The Frankenstein Papers. New York, Baen, 1986.
Pyramids. New York, Baen, 1987.
The Berserker Attack. New York, Waldenbooks, 1987.
After the Fact. New York, Baen, 1988.
The White Bull. New York, Baen, 1988.
The Black Throne, with Roger Zelazny. New York, Baen, 1990.
A Matter of Taste. New York, Tor, 1990.
Bram Stoker's Dracula, with James V. Hart (novelization of screenplay). New York, Signet, and London, Pan, 1992.
A Question of Time. New York, Tor, 1992.
Berserker Kill. New York, Tor, 1993.
Seance for a Vampire. New York, Tor, 1994.

Short Stories

Berserker. New York, Ballantine, 1967; London, Penguin, 1970.
The Book of Saberhagen. New York, DAW, 1975.
The Ultimate Enemy. New York, Ace, 1979; London, Gollancz, 1990.
The Berserker Wars. New York, Tor, 1981.
Earth Descended. New York, Tor, 1982.
Saberhagen: My Best. New York, Baen, 1987.
Berserker Lies. New York, Tor, 1991.

Other

Editor, *A Spadeful of Spacetime.* New York, Ace, 1981.

Editor, with Joan Saberhagen, *Pawn to Infinity*. New York, Ace, 1982.
Editor, with Martin H. Greenberg, *Machines that Kill*. New York, Ace, 1984.
Editor, *Berserker Base*. New York, Tor, 1985; London, Gollancz, 1990.

*

Bibliography: *Fred Saberhagen, Berserker Man: A Working Bibliography* by Phil Stephensen-Payne, Leeds, West Yorkshire, Galactic Central Publications, 1991.

*   *   *

Fred Saberhagen's best-known fantastic creations are the Berserkers, the implacable, spacefaring death machines of his hard science fiction, coldly unliving and forever inimical to life. Their legend is stronger and more influential than any of the actual stories in which it develops. (Some of these pay homage to fantasy: "Starsong" retells the Orpheus myth in a berserker Hades, and Poe's most unwanted guest is echoed in "Masque of the Red Shift.")

The exhilarating Empire of the East sequence may be Saberhagen's best actual fantasy—or science fantasy. Here magic is rationalized in a future world after nuclear war was halted by a quasi-mystical transformation of Earth, with energy sources reorganized into magical, often sentient entities. The crippled god Ardneh who inspires the virtuous West is the former U.S. defence system; the nastiest of all the East's demons was, before the change, a nuclear fireball.

The Broken Lands makes entertaining play with an Indian legend turning on a contractual quibble. The stormgod Indra, rider of elephants, promised not to slay a particular demon by day or by night, using a wet weapon or a dry, etc; and killed him in the morning twilight with sea-foam. This prophecy is quoted in chapter one, and quietly works out after various adventures centring on Western guerillas' discovery and use of an ancient nuclear tank (called Elephant) against the local satrapy of the East. When the satrap himself steals this behemoth, another functional relic is applied to its air vents: a foaming fire extinguisher. Explicitly magical devices also appear, like the Thunderstone—another nod to Indra—which attracts a devastating lightning bolt whenever it changes hands.

The Black Mountains shows the West on the offensive against the Eastern citadel run by Som the Dead, who has a permanent corpse-reek since making a deal with death that leaves him immune to any weapon, and the Demon Zapranoth, whose life is well hidden. Also present is the Beast-Lord Draffut (revealed to be a dog evolved by millennia of exposure to techno-magical life elixir), compelled to heal men of East and West alike. The climax sees Zapranoth's life traced and destroyed in the nick of time, while Som is neatly annihilated by a well-meant act of healing. Interesting extras include a technological djinn who builds whatever he's instructed to, and sniggers when a wizard orders an airship using huge, evacuated iron spheres—without regard for atmospheric pressure. . . .

Finally, *Changeling Earth* (also known as *Ardneh's World*) reveals the nature of Ardneh and introduces the top brass of the East: the all-devouring but deeply banal Emperor John Ominor, the wizard Wood and the caged Demon Orcus. Earth's transformation is explained (puzzlingly implying that the nuclear dreadnought of book one could not have worked). At the height of battle, with Ardneh ringed by Ominor's army and succumbing to the raging onslaught of Orcus . . . Ardneh releases the transformation and allows Orcus to re-assume its true nature as a thermonuclear blast. Not high fantasy, but clever and satisfying.

The many subsequent books in the Swords and Lost Swords series are linked to this first trilogy by legends of Ardneh and by certain long-lived characters (Draffut and later Wood). Two thousand years later, our mythological gods have re-emerged from human belief to play a game with humanity: Vulcan forges twelve magic swords to be scattered through the world, his little joke being that these swords can kill the gods. The game's rules are obscure. Apparently the series was devised as the basis of a computer game, perhaps accounting for its jerky and episodic nature, the plethora of loose ends, the general lack of that rounded satisfaction expected from a Saberhagen plot. (*The Second Book of Swords* consists largely of a find-the-guarded-treasure sequence that reeks of "Dungeons and Dragons" cliché.) There are several good ideas, but these are poorly organized, and there's a sense of auctorial laziness in the arbitrary way the swords move about the gameboard, often by divine intervention.

The swords themselves are plot devices of such power as to dominate the action and marginalize the characters. Dire mnemonic doggerel details their names, properties and restrictions, devised with considerable comic-book ingenuity. Shieldbreaker, for example, is invincible against all weapons including the other swords, the loophole being that its blade won't touch unarmed opponents. Farslayer flies irresistibly to kill a specified enemy anywhere on earth . . . but remains in the heart of the victim, whose friends may then return the favour.

With the gods eliminated by book three, the series straggles on with a new villain (Wood) forever manifesting and disappearing like the insidious Dr. Fu-Manchu, while the swords are relentlessly swapped, stolen, shuffled, lost, pursued . . . one, the luck-giving Coinspinner, even tends to sneak away of its own volition. *The Third Book of Lost Swords: Stonecutter's Story* seems one of the better books precisely because it shelves the endless skirmishing with Wood and his demonic allies to become a kind of detective caper about various factions' plans for this sword that cuts rock like butter—complete with a Holmes figure making plausible deductions.

The "real" Holmes appears more than once in Saberhagen's Dracula sequence of vampire thrillers, which presents undead Vlad Tepes/Drakulya as less black than Bram Stoker painted him. Scrupulously honest (he claims), occasionally sucking people dry for vengeance but perfectly able and willing to live on rats' blood, he's an old-style gentleman who under various names tends to battle, or even defend mortals from, worse things than himself—like the plague carried by the Giant Rat of Sumatra in *The Holmes-Dracula File*. Settling in America, he even gives occasional help to the vampire-beset Homicide squad of Chicago, where his police contact Joe Keogh learns like Holmes before him to use wooden bullets as high-tech stakes.

Saberhagen handles fantasy devices with the inventiveness and precision of a practised science-fiction writer, but can let his series run on too long.

—David Langford

SALMONSON, Jessica Amanda

Nationality: American. **Born:** Jesse Amos Salmonson in Seattle, Washington, 6 January 1950. **Career:** Editor of *Windhaven* magazine, 1977-79, and *Fantasy and Terror,* since 1973. **Awards:** World

Fantasy award, for anthology, 1980; Lambda award, for anthology, 1990. **Agent:** Susan Lee Cohen, Riverside Agency, 2673 Broadway, Number 132, New York, NY 10025, USA. **Address:** P.O. Box 20610, Seattle, WA 98102, USA.

Fantasy Publications

Novels (series: Tomoe Gozen)

Tomoe Gozen. New York, Ace, 1981.
The Golden Naginata (Tomoe Gozen). New York, Ace, 1982.
The Swordswoman. New York, Tor, 1982.
Thousand Shrine Warrior (Tomoe Gozen). New York, Ace, 1984.
Ou Lu Khen and the Beautiful Madwoman. New York, Ace, 1985.
Anthony Shriek; or, Lovers of Another Realm. New York, Dell Abyss, 1992.

Short Stories

Tragedy of the Moisty Morning. Seattle, Washington, Angst World Library, 1978.
Young Tyrone: A Melodrama. Seattle, Washington, Duck's-Foot Tree, 1983.
Hag's Tapestry. Runcorn, Cheshire, Haunted Library, 1984.
Innocent of Evil. Madison, Wisconsin, Dream House, 1984.
Fantasies in Black and White. Seattle, Washington, Duck's-Foot Tree, 1985.
A Silver Thread of Madness. New York, Ace, 1989.
John Collier and Fredric Brown Went Quarrelling Through My Head. Buffalo, New York, Ganley, 1989.
Harmless Ghosts. Hoole, Cheshire, Haunted Library, 1990.
A Celestial Occurrence. Seattle, Washington, Street of Crocodiles, 1991.
Mystic Women: Their Ancient Tales and Legends. Seattle, Washington, Street of Crocodiles, 1991.
The Goddess Under Siege. Seattle, Washington, Street of Crocodiles, 1992.
The Mysterious Doom and Other Ghost Stories of the Pacific Northwest. Seattle, Washington, Sasquatch Press, 1993.

Poetry

The Black Crusader and Other Poems of Horror. Springfield, Missouri, Firestone Press, 1979.
Moonstill Tulip Wine and Others (giftbook). Seattle, Washington, Duck's-Foot Tree, 1979.
Cheap Present (giftbook). Seattle, Washington, Duck's-Foot Tree, 1980.
On the Shores of Eternity. Seattle, Washington, Duck's-Foot Tree, 1981.
Feigned Death and Other Sorceries. Seattle, Washington, Duck's-Foot Tree, 1983.
Slide Show. Seattle, Washington, Duck's-Foot Tree, 1983.
In This Vent. Seattle, Washington, Duck's-Foot Tree, 1983.
The Patient Child. Seattle, Washington, Duck's-Foot Tree, 1985.
The Ghost Garden. Liverpool, Dark Dreams Press, 1988.
Sorceries and Sorrows (Early Poems). Polk City, Iowa, Drumm, 1992.
Songs of the Maenads. Seattle, Washington, Street of Crocodiles, 1993.

Mister Monkey and Other Sumerian Fables. Seattle, Washington, Tabula Rasa, 1994.

Other

Editor, *Amazons!* New York, DAW, 1979.
Editor, *Amazons II.* New York, DAW, 1982.
Editor, *Heroic Visions.* New York, Ace, 1983.
Editor, *Tales by Moonlight.* Chicago, Garcia, 1983.
Editor, *The Haunted Wherry and Other Rare Ghost Stories.* Madison, Wisconsin, Strange Company, 1985.
Editor, *The Faded Garden: The Collected Ghost Stories of Hildegarde Hawthorne.* Madison, Wisconsin, Strange Company, 1985.
Editor, *Heroic Visions II.* New York, Ace, 1985.
Editor, *The Supernatural Tales of Fitz-James O'Brien.* New York, Doubleday, 2 vols., 1988.
Editor, *Tales by Moonlight II.* New York, Tor, 1989.
Editor, *What Did Miss Darrington See? An Anthology of Feminist Supernatural Fiction.* New York, Feminist Press, 1989.
Editor, with Isabelle D. Waugh and Charles G. Waugh, *Wife or Spinster: Stories by 19th Century Women.* Camden, Maine, Yankee Books, 1991.
Editor, *From Out of the Past; The Indiana Ghost Stories of Anna Nicholas.* Liverpool, Ghost Story Society, 1991.
Editor, *Master of Fallen Years: Complete Supernatural Stories of Vincent O'Sullivan.* N.p., Ghost Story Press, 1994.

Other Publications

Other

The Encyclopedia of Amazons: Women Warriors from Antiquity to the Present Era. New York, Paragon House, 1991.
Wisewomen and Boggy-Boos: a Dictionary of Lesbian Fairy-Lore. Austin, Texas, Banned Books, 1992.
Miniature Vegetables. Seattle, Washington, Tabula Rasa, 1994.

*

Manuscript Collection: University of Oregon, Eugene.

Bibliography: In *Sorceries and Sorrows (Early Poems),* Polk City, Iowa, Drumm, 1992.

Jessica Amanda Salmonson comments:

Enamoured as I am of Victorian, Parisian, and Yellow Nineties Decadence; of folklore and medieval epics; of Kabbalah and ancient mythologies . . . much of my work is rather backward-looking, and I am as an individual adrift and out-of-place in our increasingly mechanized, unheroic age. I write with a sad nostalgia of worlds that probably never did exist, save in noble hearts, and consider myself a latter-day Romanticist. If there are odd, outcast, aesthetic readers at the end of the 21st century, I like to think they'll be hunting down rare old books of mine.

*   *   *

Salmonson came to fantasy fiction via the amateur press in which she still plays an active part. Her early *Literary Magazine of Fan-*

tasy and Terror (1973-1975; revived as Fantasy and Terror, 1984) together with later magazines Windhaven and Fantasy Macabre have been useful vehicles for her to display her wide range of interests, from feminist and gay issues to more esoteric matters of native myths, orientalism, decadence and death. All of these surface in her fiction, but it was her role as an editor that first established her name in the professional ranks.

This came with Amazons! an anthology of heroic fantasy that turned the image of mighty-thewed male heroes around and presented female warriors and adventurers. Female warriors weren't new: C. L. Moore had created Jirel of Joiry in Weird Tales in the mid-1930s, but the upsurge of interest in the late 1960s of sword-and-sorcery in imitation of Robert E. Howard's Conan had made the genre not only male-dominated but overly stereotyped. Salmonson's anthology redressed the imbalance. It received the World Fantasy Award as that year's best collection. Salmonson's authoritative introduction also aroused much interest and over the next few years was developed into a detailed reference work, The Encyclopedia of Amazons, revealing a subject hitherto ignored, or more often patronized, by historians. Salmonson produced a follow-up volume, Amazons II, as well as two other volumes of heroic fantasy (not restricted to female warriors), Heroic Visions and Heroic Visions II. Her other editing work has included two volumes of Tales By Moonlight, packaging horror and fantasy from the small press or by small-press writers, two excellent volumes of rare ghost stories by American writers (mostly female) over the last century, and several volumes of rare or complete stories by American fantasists. Salmonson's research into obscure literary passages is thorough and painstaking. Almost single-handedly she has restored some pedigree to the development of spectral fiction by women writers over the last century and a half. Many more projects are complete or in progress and await only interested publishers.

In Amazons! Salmonson referred to Tomoe Gozen, one of the most formidable of women amongst the samurai warrior elite of 13th-century Japan. Salmonson recreated this period in a fantastic alternate world called Naipon, and retold the story of Tomoe in a series of three novels: Tomoe Gozen, The Golden Naginata and Thousand Shrine Warrior. Salmonson's strengths are most evident here in her creation of strong, believable characters who are creatures of their culture, but controlled by their own code of ethics which Salmonson firmly establishes. The books are violent, particularly the first two, though no more violent than their earthly historical parallel, with a marked distinction between male and female character traits. Tomoe is strong and resourceful, and the series contains many vivid and original episodes. At times, though, Salmonson goes beyond establishing a point about the equivalent strength of women in power, to such an extent that some of the writing may be suspected as therapeutic in its working through of some of Salmonson's own neuroses. It is perhaps pertinent that the third novel in the series, written some time after the first two, is more reflective and philosophical, with even greater consideration of character, which shows the author's maturing skills. In all the trilogy is very satisfying.

Less satisfying is a non-series novel published at the same time, The Swordswoman, which is more formulaic. A woman accidentally kills a man during a martial-arts demonstration and while confined to a sanatorium is transported to Endsworld, a post-techno-logical primitive society. The novel explores how the protagonist is perceived by the Endsworlders, where a rigid caste system operates. The novel is Wellsian in vision, but has at its centre an explo-

ration of people and cultures. It is however not as vibrant or three-dimensional as Naipon.

Salmonson stayed in the orient for her next novel, though the locale moved to ancient south-east Asia. Ou Lu Khen and the Beautiful Madwoman is not a warrior fantasy, but a romantic novel filled with fascination. Ou Lu Khen, a peasant, has fallen in love with a mad, strongly religious woman, Mai Su. Law only permits that they marry if he becomes similarly afflicted, which leads to a quest in which the couple and other assorted characters seek out the reality of madness. Salmonson again draws a convincing culture and believable characters, even though the book is poles apart from the Tomoe Gozen series. It is more akin to recent works by E. Hoffmann Price and Barry Hughart.

Salmonson's only commercially published story collection continues the oriental slant, although it broadens to other countries' fables and legends, ancient and modern, including America's. A Silver Thread of Madness includes possibly Salmonson's two best stories, "Lincoy's Journey" and "A Child of Earth and Hell." The former, which tells of a child's post-death experience and return to life, is based on a story told to Salmonson by her stepmother about her childhood in Thailand.

Salmonson's short fiction is usually far more experimental and idiosyncratic and is unlikely to be commercially popular, though it is artistically exciting. Her most conventional stories are those in Harmless Ghosts, featuring a female psychic detective, although even these seek to challenge traditional views. Her other stories, particularly those in John Collier and Fredric Brown Went Quarrelling Through My Head, can sometimes be inconsequential and moody, at other times sharp and disturbing. They demonstrate the dichotomy between Salmonson's appreciation of traditional quality fiction, especially elder ghost stories, and her inner desire for more biting, challenging and above all non-traditional approaches to fiction. It is this ambivalence that prevents her stories being commercially accepted though they are always refreshing to explore.

This same approach has affected her novel-length work. Commercially typecast for her feminist and oriental fantasies, it was not easy to create a newly marketable persona, but there were darker visions Salmonson wanted to explore, and it required much to convince publishers. It was six years before Anthony Shriek, her next novel, was published. This volume shows the darker more decadent side of Salmonson's visions but, as with all her work, has a considerable depth of emotion and belief.

—Mike Ashley

SALVATORE, R(obert) A(nthony)

Nationality: American. Born: 1959. Lives in Massachusetts. Address: c/o TSR Inc., P.O. Box 756, Lake Geneva, WI 53147, USA.

FANTASY PUBLICATIONS

Novels (series: Forgotten Realms; Spearwielder's Tale)

The Crystal Shard (Forgotten Realms). Lake Geneva, Wisconsin, TSR, and London, Penguin, 1988.
Streams of Silver (Forgotten Realms). Lake Geneva, Wisconsin, TSR, and London, Penguin, 1989.

Echoes of the Fourth Magic. New York, Roc, 1990; London, Roc, 1991.

The Halfling's Gem (Forgotten Realms). Lake Geneva, Wisconsin, TSR, and London, Penguin, 1990.

Homeland (Forgotten Realms). Lake Geneva, Wisconsin, TSR, and London, Penguin, 1990.

Exile (Forgotten Realms). Lake Geneva, Wisconsin, TSR, and London, Penguin, 1990.

Sojourn (Forgotten Realms). Lake Geneva, Wisconsin, TSR, and London, Penguin, 1991.

Canticle (Forgotten Realms). Lake Geneva, Wisconsin, TSR, 1991.

The Witch's Daughter. New York, Roc, 1991.

In Sylvan Shadows (Forgotten Realms). Lake Geneva, Wisconsin, TSR, 1992.

The Legacy (Forgotten Realms). Lake Geneva, Wisconsin, TSR, 1992.

Night Masks (Forgotten Realms). Lake Geneva, Wisconsin, TSR, 1992.

The Fallen Fortress (Forgotten Realms). Lake Geneva, Wisconsin, TSR, 1993.

Starless Night (Forgotten Realms). Lake Geneva, Wisconsin, TSR, 1993.

The Woods Out Back (Spearwielder). New York, Ace, 1993.

The Chaos Curse (Forgotten Realms). Lake Geneva, Wisconsin, TSR, 1994.

The Dragon's Dagger (Spearwielder). New York, Ace, 1994.

Siege of Darkness (Forgotten Realms). Lake Geneva, Wisconsin, TSR, 1994.

The Sword of Bedwyr. New York, Warner, 1995.

Dragonslayer's Return (Spearwielder). New York, Ace, 1995.

*   *   *

R. A. Salvatore is best known for creating the character Drizzt Do'Urden. Many of his books have been published by TSR in the Forgotten Realms series and so are designed to fit in with the campaign background for their Advanced Dungeons and Dragons role-playing game. However, the popularity of the novels reaches far beyond games enthusiasts. Drizzt is an angst-ridden hero, in the style of Moorcock's Elric, who is fighting against his drow heritage. The drow are a race of black-skinned elves who are feared and hated for their cruelty. Drizzt comes from a subterranean city, Menzoberranzan, which is a matriarchy ruled by priestesses of the Demon Queen of Spiders, Loth. Noble houses vie for power using intrigue, bribery, blackmail, and murder as a matter of course. Drizzt rejects this in the hope of finding a more amicable way of life among the elves, dwarfs and humans of the surface world.

Drizzt is a brilliant swordsman but struggles against using his instinctive and deadly fighting abilities, fearing that by killing he will become as evil as the others of his race. His search for acceptance is made difficult as he is constantly judged by his appearance. Added to that his family, House Do'Urden, give him little respite in their attempts to track him down and kill him for the dishonour he has brought them.

Drizzt appeared in Salvatore's first published novel, *The Crystal Shard,* and gave the otherwise hackneyed story a degree of originality. His character was developed further in *Streams of Silver* and *The Halfling's Gem* (which together make up the Icewind Dale sub-trilogy of Forgotten Realms novels), along with his fellow-adventurers, whose archetypes can be found in numerous second-rate fantasy books—a grumpy dwarf, chubby halfling, muscle-bound barbarian, and beautiful female archer. Salvatore then went on to explore Drizzt's background in the Dark Elf sub-trilogy of Forgotten Realms books.

Homeland, first in the second trilogy, is a convincing portrayal of the totally corrupt society of Menzoberranzan. It begins as House Do'Urden plot the overthrow of a rival house. While their soldiers attack, Matron Malice, the matriarch of House Do'Urden, gives birth to her third son—Drizzt. She intends to sacrifice the baby to Loth to ensure victory, but the second son of the house, Dinin, murders his elder brother during the battle to gain rank. When Malice learns of this she decides to spare the baby's life in the opinion that a sacrifice has already been made.

Drizzt grows up and, despite being trained by his sisters to know his place as an inferior male, shows prodigious abilities and a strength of character which is supposedly uncharacteristic of drow males. After Drizzt's 16th birthday his mother allows the boy's father, the highly skilled weapon master Zaknafein, to train him in fighting. Zaknafein is an uncharacteristic drow in that he dislikes their evil and corrupt way of life. Drizzt is also upset by the drow cruelty he witnesses. His mother and sisters notice his reaction and try to rid Drizzt of his innocence and naivety by indoctrinating him in the ways of treachery and murder. They disguise a goblin as a drow and force Drizzt into mortal combat with him. Drizzt of course wins, but manages to retain his scruples even though he realizes that he must keep his opinions quiet or face a horrible death at the hands of Loth's priestesses.

All drow are taught to hate other races, especially the elves who live above ground, but when Drizzt's patrol is sent on a rare foray to the surface world to attack elves, he is shocked to learn that the elves are peace-loving and harmless. He cannot bring himself to take part in the slaughter and merely pretends to kill an elf child by covering her in blood and telling her to lie low. His deception remains secret; even his father is convinced that Drizzt has succumbed to his race's evil and decides it would be better if he was dead. Ironically, Drizzt also plans to kill Zaknafein for the same reason.

Although House Do'Urden are unaware that Drizzt has displeased Loth by his failure, another house discovers it and decide to strike while Do'Urden are in disfavor. Zaknafein and Drizzt fight a tense battle, but when Drizzt tells Zaknafein that he did not kill the elf child they regain each other's friendship. Unfortunately, Malice was spying on them and also learns of the deception. She decides to sacrifice Zaknafein, believing that he inspired Drizzt's attitude. Malice is delighted when Drizzt defeats two attacking sorcerers from a rival house, thinking that he will now take Zaknafein's place as weapon master. Drizzt refuses in his outrage at discovering his father's death. He flees the house and leaves Menzoberranzan.

Exile and *Sojourn* cover the events which take Drizzt from Menzoberranzan to the frozen valley of Icewind Dale, and lead up to the events of his earlier books. *The Legacy* adds to the two preceding trilogies, as House Do'Urden take their vendetta against Drizzt and his friends to the surface world. However, none of these later books has quite the same tension and horror that Salvatore managed to achieve in *Homeland.* That story of political intrigue in a supremely machiavellian society makes a welcome change from the standard battles between good and evil that make up the plots of most TSR novels—including Salvatore's next Forgotten Realms subseries, the Cleric Quintet.

The Cleric Quintet consists of *Canticle, In Sylvan Shadows, Night Masks, The Fallen Fortress,* and *The Chaos Curse*; and despite its setting at a conservatory for priests it is not a *Name of the Rose-*

style historical mystery. It follows the career of the young priest Cadderly and his cheerleader-look-alike martial-artist girlfriend as they foil the plots of a group of evil priests. Alas, the readers most likely to enjoy this subseries are adolescent males with a crush on *Streetfighter II*'s Chun Li. But Salvatore has been an extremely prolific writer in recent years and has branched out into non-TSR/Forgotten Realms areas, notably with his entertaining Bermuda Triangle mystery/fantasy *Echoes of the Fourth Magic* and with his later Spearwielder's Tale series. No doubt there are considerable riches still to come from his word processor.

—Lucya Szachnowski

SAMPSON, Fay (Elizabeth)

Nationality: British. **Born:** Devonport, Devon, 1935. **Family:** Married; two children. **Career:** Has taught adult education classes. **Address:** c/o Hodder Headline PLC, 338 Euston Road, London NW1 3BH.

FANTASY PUBLICATIONS

Novels (series: Daughter of Tintagel; Pangur Bán)

The Chains of Sleep. London, Dobson, 1981.
Pangur Bán: The White Cat. Tring, Hertfordshire, Lion, 1983.
Finnglas of the Horses (Pangur Bán). Tring, Hertfordshire, Lion, 1985.
Finnglas and the Stones of Choosing (Pangur Bán). Tring, Hertfordshire, Lion, 1986.
Shape-Shifter: The Naming of Pangur Bán. Tring, Hertfordshire, Lion, 1988.
The Serpent of Senargad (Pangur Bán). Oxford, Lion, 1989.
Wise Woman's Telling (Daughter of Tintagel). London, Headline, 1989.
White Nun's Telling (Daughter of Tintagel). London, Headline, 1989.
Black Smith's Telling (Daughter of Tintagel). London, Headline, 1990.
The White Horse is Running (Pangur Bán). Oxford, Lion, 1990.
Taliesin's Telling (Daughter of Tintagel). London, Headline, 1991.
Herself (Daughter of Tintagel). London, Headline, 1992.
Daughter of Tintagel (omnibus; includes *Wise Woman's Telling, White Nun's Telling, Black Smith's Telling, Taliesin's Telling, Herself*). London, Headline, 1992.
Star Dancer. London, Headline, 1993.

OTHER PUBLICATIONS

Fiction for Children

F.67. London, Hamish Hamilton, 1975.
Half a Welcome. London, Dobson, 1977.
The Watch on Patterick Fell. London, Dobson, 1978; New York, Greenwillow, 1980.
The Empty House. London, Dobson, 1979.

The Hungry Snow. London, Dobson, 1980.
Landfall on Innis Michael. London, Dobson, 1980.
Sus. London, Dobson, 1982.
Jenny and the Wreckers. London, Hamish Hamilton, 1984.
Chris and the Dragon. London, Gollancz, 1985.
Josh's Panther. London, Gollancz, 1986.
A Free Man on Sunday. London, Gollancz, 1987.
The Christmas Blizzard. Oxford, Lion, 1991.

Other

May Day. N.p., RMEP, 1985.
Ascensiontide and Pentecost. N.p., RMEP, 1986.

*   *   *

Fay Sampson has written, to date, over 25 novels, more than half of them fantasy. Her early books were all for children or teenagers, but in recent years she has turned to adult fiction. She is best known for two series, the six Pangur Bán books and the five Daughter of Tintagel books about Morgan le Fay. (*Daughter of Tintagel* itself is an omnibus volume containing all five books.) These eleven titles show Sampson at her best, in the world she knows best: Celtic Dark Age Britain.

The Pangur Bán books—children's fantasy, but quite readable by adults—are set at the time when the new religion of Christianity is beginning to make inroads against the native religion of Britain and Ireland. The main characters are Niall, a young monk; Finnglas, daughter of King Kernac of the Summer Land; and Pangur Bán, a white cat. Although published by Lion, an evangelical Christian publishing house, the books are not overtly preachy; rather, very much in the tradition of C. S. Lewis's Narnia books, they carry strong moral messages about love, courage, sacrifice, forgiveness and redemption. The animals, particularly Pangur Bán himself, talk; the characters visit fantastical places; there is real magic all around them; yet all of them, including the young monk, accept the reality of it all.

In the first in order of writing, *Pangur Bán: The White Cat,* the cat accidentally causes Niall to kill another young monk, Kernac's son. When Kernac comes to avenge the death, Niall and Pangur Bán escape; they are followed by Finnglas, who is determined to kill them. In a series of adventures they are captured by mermaids, and rescue each other with the help of the dolphin Arthmael, who eventually gives his own life to save Pangur Bán (cf. Aslan's sacrifice in the Narnia books).

Arthmael, although clearly a Christ-type, is portrayed more as the joyful holy fool. As the series progresses the main characters believe in Arthmael as a divine figure, and call on him in time of need; in this respect, he is a far more reliable god than most! No attempt is made to rationalize the monk Niall's belief in Arthmael with his continuing belief in Christ; if anything, they are seen simply as different names and manifestations of the same divine principle.

In *Finnglas of the Horses,* Finnglas learns the lesson of compassion for an island of starving horses, none of which is her own lost horse. She narrowly escapes being forcibly married to King Jarlath, and eventually returns to the Summer Land. Her father Kernac dies, naming her as his successor. *Finnglas and the Stones of Choosing* is an account of the seven trials she has to undertake, and the lessons she learns both from her friends and from within herself, before becoming queen.

Shape-Shifter: The Naming of Pangur Bán, although the fourth to be written, is (again cf. C. S. Lewis) chronologically the first, a flashback to how the monk Niall first met Pangur Bán, and how the cat got his name. It is the most "Christian versus pagan" of the series, and is the weaker for it, though it does have an excellent retelling of the old folk story of the two magicians, with Pangur Bán being turned into a hare and chased by a hound, then into a trout chased by an otter, and so on.

Unusually, the fifth book, *The Serpent of Senargad,* picks up the story mid-way through the second book, partly from the viewpoint of a very minor character in that book, King Jarlath's daughter Kara. In *The White Horse is Running,* the bards and military leaders of the Summer Land disobey Finnglas's instructions while she is away adventuring, and provoke a territorial war with the nearby kingdom of Erin, which Finnglas returns in time to stop.

The Daughter of Tintagel series sets out to explore the familiar Arthur mythos from his half-sister Morgan le Fay's point of view—or rather, to tell Morgan's own story through the eyes of several people around her. *Wise Woman's Telling* is narrated by Morgan's childhood nurse, a follower of the old religion. *White Nun's Telling* is by a nun at the convent on Tintagel, where Morgan spent her early teens. *Black Smith's Telling* is by a smith who is forced to dress and behave as a woman servant of Morgan, while *Taliesin's Telling* is by the poet. Each tells those parts of Morgan's life which she or he witnesses, in his or her own individual style.

The final book, *Herself,* is Morgan's own story as she remembers back through her life while waiting for the dying Arthur to cross the lake to her. Interwoven with Morgan's present and past are the myths of Morgan; she herself comments on Geoffrey of Monmouth, on Wace and Layamon, on Malory and Tennyson:

> I am dependable when all other help has failed. My plans are wise and effective. I am benevolent to those who trust me. Geoffrey puts this first description of me into the mouth of Taliesin, who says he took Arthur to Avalon himself. Geoffrey of Monmouth is notoriously unreliable.

She also comments on modern reinterpreters of the Morgan mythos, including T. H. White, Mary Stewart, Rosemary Sutcliff, Nikolai Tolstoy, Stephen Lawhead, Marion Bradley . . . and finally:

> Well, you may do with me what you will. I am the shape-shifter. I can assume whatever form you wish me to take. Each author alters my myth to serve their particular purpose. No doubt Fay Sampson is using me here for her own ends. This will not be the last you hear of me.

In both series of books Sampson's knowledge of Dark Age history and myth shines through. Unlike many Celtic fantasies, when it rains you get wet, and in winter the cold wind works through the chinks in your hut. Moreover, particularly in the Pangur Bán books, the new faith is Celtic Christianity, which in its love of and respect for nature and the turning of the seasons was far closer to British paganism than to the Christianity of Rome. At the time of writing (summer 1994), Sampson is working on a novel about the Synod of Whitby (664 AD), when for largely political reasons Celtic Christianity was defeated by Roman Christianity; one can guess where her sympathies lie.

With her most recent published book Sampson moves away from Celtic history, myth and legend. *Star Dancer* is a retelling of the Sumerian myth of Inanna journeying into the Underworld to find Erishkegal. A massive undertaking, it unfortunately gives the impression that the author has immersed herself in the mythology, and has not wanted to miss a single detail in her retelling. While both scholarly and imaginative, as a novel it's hard work to plough through. Sampson is more at home with the Matter of Britain, where she ranks alongside Mary Stewart and way above Stephen Lawhead; as for comparison with Marion Bradley, Sampson's Daughter of Tintagel series shows just how badly flawed *The Mists of Avalon* is.

—David V. Barrett

SAUNDERS, Charles R(obert)

Nationality: American (emigrated to Canada in 1971). **Born:** Elizabeth, Pennsylvania, 1946. **Education:** High school in Norristown, Pennsylvania; Lincoln University, graduated 1968. **Career:** Teacher of social sciences and creative writing, Algonquin College, Ottawa. **Awards:** Small Press Writers and Artists Organization Award for fantasy, 1980.

FANTASY PUBLICATIONS

Novels (series: Imaro in all books)

Imaro. New York, DAW, 1981.
The Quest for Cush. New York, DAW, 1984.
The Trail of Bohu. New York, DAW, 1985.

OTHER PUBLICATIONS

Other

Robert E. Howard: Adventure Unlimited. Gananoque, Ontario, Shadow Press, 1976.

*

Charles R. Saunders comments:

All cultures have mythical heroes who possess "powers above and beyond those of mortal men". Sounds familiar? That's a description of Superman, the modern North American heroic archetype. This cultural tradition can be traced back to the Sumerian Gilgamesh, the Hebrew Samson, the Greek Hercules, the Saxon Beowulf. In Ugandan legend there was a hero named Kimera who was so strong he could throw a spear all the way through the body of an elephant. . . . The tradition of the super-warrior is certainly a major element in my conception of Imaro.

There are also elements of contemporary black hero-figures in Imaro . . . Most of all, Imaro is the man I always wished would come busting out of the Hollywood jungle to beat the hell out of Tarzan! When I was a kid I watched Tarzan movies in the hope that Jim Brown or Sonny Liston would jump up and kick Johnny Weissmuller's ass off the screen. . . .

Although my stories feature black characters in an African-derived setting, I've gotten good feedback from white readers as well as black ones. I want anyone who reads my stuff to be entertained, and to come away with the realization that the same elements they enjoy in European-based fantasy may be found in African-based stories. (From an interview conducted by Jeffrey M. Elliot, *Fantasy Review* no. 74, December 1984.)

*   *   *

A major figure in the small-press fantasy movement that grew up in the middle 1970s in the absence of any satisfactory professional market, Charles Saunders was a prolific contributor to such little magazines as *Fantasy Crossroads, Beyond the Fields We Know, Black Lite, Dark Fantasy, Weirdbook, Night Voyages, The Diversifier, Space & Time,* and the like. Several of his stories from such sources were reprinted in Lin Carter's *The Year's Best Fantasy* anthologies. His novels are fix-ups of material from the small press. Late in his career, he had one story in *Twilight Zone,* which may be his only appearance in a professional magazine. He held office in the Small Press Writers and Artists Organization in the late 1970s. He seems to have fallen silent, and unfortunately his work is now little known. Although he has been living in Canada for well over 20 years, there is only a tiny passing mention of him in David Ketterer's otherwise thorough study *Canadian Science Fiction and Fantasy* (1992)—and there his name is mis-cited as "Clark R. Saunders."

Saunders' vigorous, sometimes crude story-telling amply reflects his fascination with Robert E. Howard, but, being black, he naturally took exception to some of Howard's racial attitudes. He published several articles about racial stereotyping in pulp fiction, one of which was entitled "Die, Black Dog!" (in *Toadstool Wine,* 1975). Ultimately he did for prehistoric Africa what Howard did for prehistoric Europe, creating his own equivalent of Howard's "Hyborean Age" (the milieu of Conan the Barbarian's adventures) in an "alternate" Africa called Nyumbani, across which swaggered the stalwart hero Imaro, who so resembled the pulp heroes of yore that DAW got itself into hot water with the Edgar Rice Burroughs estate by blurbing Saunders's *Imaro* as "the epic novel of a black Tarzan" (immediately recalled and changed to "a jungle hero," creating a second state of the first edition, also labelled as a first printing). Nyumbani is filled with pastoral tribesmen, proud warriors, vile wizards, assorted monsters, and fabulous lost cities as may be expected, but the environments, cultures, and mythologies involved resemble the real Africa far more than anything in the Tarzan books.

Saunders was a natural story-teller, skilled at thrilling action, but he seldom approached subtle characterization or thematic complexity, which may have limited his appeal. His fiction was showing signs of growth when he ceased publishing in the mid-1980s. Most of his work is lightweight adventure, significant for being the first attempt to create a black sword-and-sorcery hero, and the first serious attempt since Robert E. Howard himself (particularly in his Solomon Kane series) to use African settings for such fiction.

—Darrell Schweitzer

SCARBOROUGH, Elizabeth Ann

Nationality: American. **Born:** Kansas City, Missouri, 23 March 1947. **Education:** Bethany Hospital School of Nursing, R.N., 1968; University of Alaska, Fairbanks, B.A. in history, 1987. **Military**

Service: served as a nurse during the Vietnam War; United States Army, Nurse Corps, 1968-72: Captain. **Family:** Married Richard G. Kacsur in 1975 (divorced 1981). **Career:** Surgical nurse, St. David's Hospital, Austin, Texas; freelance writer from 1979. Lives in Port Townsend, Washington. **Awards:** Nebula award, 1989. **Agent:** Merrilee Heifetz, 21 West 26th Street, New York, NY 10010, USA. **Address:** c/o Ace Books, 200 Madison Avenue, New York, NY 10033, USA.

FANTASY PUBLICATIONS

Novels (series: Argonia; Songkiller)

Song of Sorcery (Argonia). New York, Bantam, 1982; London, Bantam, 1987.
The Unicorn Creed (Argonia). New York, Bantam, 1983; London, Bantam, 1987.
Bronwyn's Bane (Argonia). New York, Bantam, 1983; London, Bantam, 1987.
The Harem of Aman Akbar; or, The Djinn Decanted. New York, Bantam, 1984.
The Christening Quest (Argonia). New York, Bantam, 1985.
The Drastic Dragon of Draco, Texas. New York, Bantam, 1986.
The Goldcamp Vampire; or, The Sanguinary Sourdough. New York, Bantam, 1987.
Songs from the Seashell Archives (omnibus; includes *Song of Sorcery, The Unicorn Creed, Bronwyn's Bane, The Christening Quest*). New York, Bantam, 2 vols., 1987-88.
The Healer's War. New York, Doubleday, 1989.
Nothing Sacred. New York, Doubleday, 1991.
Phantom Banjo (Songkiller). New York, Bantam, 1991.
Picking the Ballad's Bones (Songkiller). New York, Bantam, 1991.
Strum Again? (Songkiller). New York, Bantam, 1992.
Last Refuge. New York, Bantam, 1992.
The Godmother. New York, Ace, 1994.

OTHER PUBLICATIONS

Novels

Powers That Be, with Anne McCaffrey. New York, Del Rey, and London, Bantam Press, 1993.
Power Lines, with Anne McCaffrey. New York, Del Rey, and London, Bantam Press, 1994.
Power Play, with Anne McCaffrey. New York, Del Rey, and London, Bantam Press, 1995.

Other

An Interview with a Vietnam Nurse. New York, Bantam, 1989.

*

Elizabeth Ann Scarborough comments:

I started out writing humorous fantasy—at first traditional and then historical western and Arabian Nights, which interested me after I studied Middle Eastern dance. Since *Healer's War,* I've also written some serious, fairly political, futuristic stuff in *Last Refuge* and *Nothing sacred.* Lately, I've been trying to blend some serious content with humour in *The Godmother* and to some extent in the books I've been writing in Ireland with Anne McCaffrey set in our new world. My experience living in Fairbanks, Alaska, for 15 years, and in the military, helped me make my contributions to Petaybee, the world Anne and I created together. My many friendships with concerned and caring social workers and other non-cynical types inspired *The Godmother* (set in Seattle) and my current book in progress *The Godmother Too* (set in Ireland).

*   *   *

Elizabeth Ann Scarborough is a popular writer of humorous fantasy and more recently of science-fiction fantasy. Her early stories are in the spirit of Piers Anthony's Xanth tales, but she developed her own witty style with later books, peaking with the Phantom Banjo or Songkiller series. With her Nebula Award-winning novel *The Healer's War,* Scarborough's leave-them-laughing approach became different, with only occasional touches of wryness and the exploration of Eastern religions very evident in that title and the two following.

In her first four books, republished as *Songs from the Seashell Archives,* Scarborough employs the usual trappings for her magical world of Argonia: unicorns, dwarfs, dragons, magic, witches, sorcerers, and a wonderful enchanted bear as well as a very chatty cat. The books are full of very human protagonists on various quests. In the first, *Song of Sorcery,* the heroine, Maggie Brown, is a hearthwitch, not an old hag but a pleasant, personable young woman who must save her half-sister of fairy blood, Amberwine, from a lovespell cast by Davey the gypsy. Maggie has only her housewifery magic and a callow, bumbling young minstrel to help her, but she gains the mystical protection of a unicorn and ultimately wins over the sceptics and outwits the wrongdoers. The four books of the Argonia series are related tales of Maggie and her mother, Bronwyn, yet the titles stand alone. There is playfulness and cheerfulness throughout the stories, with puns and comic situations to create humour as fast-paced as the action. As such, they belong in the "wacky" sub-genre of fantasy.

Scarborough's next two novels, *The Drastic Dragon of Draco, Texas* and *The Goldcamp Vampire,* bear a resemblance to Elizabeth Peters' mysteries set Victorian times featuring the irritating Amelia Peabody. The arch tone wears thin very quickly, although there are flashes of genuine wit. The settings of the frontier, both the Texas plains and the Yukon goldfields, provide the journalist heroine, Valentine Lovelace, with colourful milieus in which to pursue mystery, magic and the supernatural. Scarborough's originality is evident in the fact that she sets her vampire story in a land where night goes on for months, wonderful for recruiting vampires but not so great for unwilling recruits. Another title from this period, *The Harem of Aman Akbar,* is based on Arabian legends, but lacks the quirky charm of the Argonia books with almost forced humour and lacklustre characters.

The Songkiller series is the culmination of Scarborough's early humorous writing phase. The three novels, beginning with *The Phantom Banjo,* are filled with rollicking humour and just plain fun. They are based on the simple premise that the demons down below decide on a new bedevilment for the human race: they will eliminate music, particularly targeting folk songs. Their primary agent for the project is a female with a long history; she was once the Faerie Queen but the Tam Lin episode has put her in thrall to the devils. Since Tam Lin, she has served as Lady Luck, but her role in 20th-century permissive society has given her decreasing

importance and power. Usually seen by humans as a voluptuous redhead, she often goes by the name of Torchy. Things get under way with the destruction of written and recorded folk music, including a fire at the Library of Congress archives and contrived memory loss for performers and fans. Folk instruments are destroyed and fall into misuse, and little music is allowed, or even desired. As a result, the airwaves consist almost primarily of all-news stations.

A small disparate group of humans remember folk music and decide to save it. The courageous band includes performers, a cowboy poet, and lovers of the songs. Willie comes into the possession of a magic banjo which communicates, and he and the others go on their quest to save folk music, including a trip to Great Britain. The second volume of the series, *Picking the Ballad's Bones,* focuses on the saviours' deal with Torchy: she will help them if they agree to spend seven years living out the old ballads of the past. They agree, but Torchy is up to her usual tricks and neglects to tell the group that they will be cast as characters of the opposite sex for their servitude. Willie the womanizer finds it especially galling to be the betrayed maiden, over and over again. In the final book, *Strum Again?,* the courageous band triumphs with the quirky assistance of Torchy.

In 1989 Scarborough won the Nebula Award for *The Healer's War,* published before the Songkiller books. The novel is in amazing contrast to the author's earlier output. Scarborough had been an army nurse during the Vietnam conflict and readers might suppose that *The Healer's War* was written as a catharsis. But this title marked a major change in her writing style. As she explains in an long author's note in the paperback edition, "I chose to write the book as fiction because, as somebody is frequently misquoted as saying, fiction is supposed to make sense out of real life. And if there was ever an episode in my life that needed sense made out of it, it was Vietnam. In a nonfiction account, I could talk only about myself, what I saw and felt. I wasn't very clear about that when I started writing."

The heroine of *The Healer's War* is an army nurse, Kitty McCulley, probably very similar to Elizabeth Scarborough herself as a nurse in Vietnam. Much of the book is devoted to experiences common to many nurses in wartime, featuring irregular hours and nursing crises, combined with frantic love affairs with combat military personnel. Kitty nurses Vietnamese civilians as well as wounded Americans, and she becomes emotionally attached to a young Vietnamese amputee boy, and a dying old holy man. The holy man gives her an amulet that warns its owner of danger as well as helping diagnose illness. Kitty is sceptical at first, but learns to believe in its powers. The climax of the novel comes when Kitty is shot down over enemy territory and confronts evil in the form of a ferocious colonel with the power she now has with the amulet. Rescue by Americans does not bring automatic relief, for Kitty is treated with great suspicion by her countrymen. The scene then changes with the last section (really a chapter), which finds Kitty back in America, drifting as many Vietnam veterans were, seeking to find some meaning and purpose to her life.

The next two books by Scarborough are futuristic tales that also deal with Eastern mysticism. The first, *Nothing Sacred,* was based on a particularly vivid dream Scarborough had before completing *The Healer's War.* A middle-aged female soldier is taken captive in Tibet where strange dreams occur as she helps to organize a ruined and ancient library. Vivaca and the others in the camp in Shambala, prisoners and guards, have trouble keeping track of time. The prison camp becomes a hard and austere version of Shangri-

La, yet Vivaca becomes reconciled and almost happy with her existence. A nuclear explosion then destroys the world, except for the hidden valley. Scarborough comments that she introduces the book at author readings with, "There's bad news and good news about this book. The bad news is, I end the world. The good news is, there's a sequel." In that sequel, *Last Refuge,* Viveca's granddaughter, Chime Cincinnati, must leave the untouched valley of Shambala to find a cure for a mysterious illness. Her quest takes her into the aftermath of nuclear disaster, a world unlike anything Chime could imagine. Yet she perseveres in her task, finding hints of resurrection and hope as well as the immediately evident desolation and cruelty of a newly evolving civilization.

The Powers That Be, co-authored with Anne McCaffrey, is best described as fantastic science fiction. In a militaristic future time, Major Yanaba Maddock, is given a medical discharge and sent to a distant frontier planet. She has been ordered to spy and discovers a plot by native settlers to rebel against the corporation which controls the planet. Yanaba has become sympathetic to the settlers, not only because they have repaired her injured lungs and a romance with a local geneticist, and throws in her lot with the rebels. The basic goodness of the ecologically sensitive and nurturing settlers prevails over the cold bureaucratic corporation for the time being. The sequel, *Power Lines,* describes the continuing struggle between the corporation and planet's rebels.

Scarborough's output to date gives proof of her importance in the contemporary fantasy-genre scene. It is probable that she has influenced some newer writers, who also create humorous fantasy with down-to-earth heroines and delightful animal companions. Scarborough's own development as a writer appears to be leading her into a spare and lean phase with more emphasis on stories of the future rather than on the popular alternative worlds of high fantasy.

—Cosette Kies

SCHWEITZER, Darrell (Charles)

Nationality: American. **Born:** Woodbury, New Jersey, 1952. **Education:** Villanova University, 1970-76; B.S. in geography, 1974; M.A. in English, 1976. **Career:** Editorial assistant, *Isaac Asimov's SF Magazine,* Philadelphia, Pennsylvania, 1977-82; assistant, *Amazing Stories,* Philadelphia, 1982-86; co-editor, *Weird Tales,* Philadelphia, 1987-91; editor, *Weird Tales* (retitled *Worlds of Fantasy and Horror,* 1994), Philadelphia, from 1991. Part-time literary agent, Owlswick Agency, Philadelphia. **Awards:** World Fantasy Award, 1992. **Agent:** (foreign rights) Dorothy Lumley, Dorian Literary Agency, Upper Thornehill, 27 Church Road, St. Marychurch, Torquay, Devon TQ1 4QY, England. **Address:** 113 Deepdale Road, Strafford, PA 19087, USA.

FANTASY PUBLICATIONS

Novels

The Shattered Goddess. Virginia Beach, Virginia, Donning, 1982.
The White Isle. Philadelphia, Pennsylvania, Owlswick Press, 1989.
The Mask of the Sorcerer. London, New English Library, 1995.

Short Stories

We Are All Legends. Virginia Beach, Virginia, Donning, 1981.
Tom O'Bedlam's Night Out and Other Strange Excursions. Buffalo, New York, Ganley, 1985.
The Meaning of Life and Other Awesome Cosmic Revelations. Polk City, Iowa, Drumm, 1988.
Transients and Other Disquieting Stories. Buffalo, New York, Ganley, 1993.

OTHER PUBLICATIONS

Other

Lovecraft in the Cinema. Baltimore, Maryland, TK Graphics, 1975.
The Dream Quest of H. P. Lovecraft. San Bernardino, California, Borgo Press, 1978.
Conan's World and Robert E. Howard. San Bernardino, California, Borgo Press, 1979.
On Writing Science Fiction: The Editors Strike Back!, with George H. Scithers and John M. Ford. Philadelphia, Pennsylvania, Owlswick Press, 1981.
Pathways to Elfland: The Writings of Lord Dunsany. Philadelphia, Pennsylvania, Owlswick Press, 1989.
Lord Dunsany: A Bibliography, with S. T. Joshi. Metuchen, New Jersey, Scarecrow Press, 1993.

Editor, *Essays Lovecraftian.* Baltimore, Maryland, TK Graphics, 1976; revised as *Discovering H. P. Lovecraft,* Mercer Island, Washington, Starmont House, 1987.
Editor, *SF Voices.* Baltimore, Maryland, TK Graphics, 1976.
Editor, *Science Fiction Voices #1: Interviews with Science Fiction Writers.* San Bernardino, California, Borgo Press, 1979.
Editor, *The Ghosts of the Heaviside Layer and Other Fantasms,* by Lord Dunsany. Philadelphia, Pennsylvania, Owlswick Press, 1980.
Editor, *Science Fiction Voices #5: Interviews with American Science Fiction Writers of the Golden Age.* San Bernardino, California, Borgo Press, 1981.
Editor, *Discovering Modern Horror Fiction.* Mercer Island, Washington, Starmont House, 2 vols., 1985-89.
Editor, *Discovering Stephen King.* Mercer Island, Washington, Starmont House, 1985.
Editor, *Exploring Fantasy Worlds: Essays on Fantastic Literature.* San Bernardino, California, Borgo Press, 1985.
Editor, with George H. Scithers, *Tales from the Spaceport Bar.* New York, Avon, 1987; London, New English Library, 1988.
Editor, with George H. Scithers, *Another Round at the Spaceport Bar.* New York, Avon, 1989; London, New English Library, 1992.
Editor, *Discovering Classic Horror Fiction.* Mercer Island, Washington, Starmont House, 1992.

*

Darrell Schweitzer comments:
Beyond the occasional broad comedy, the bulk of my fiction falls into two categories: 1) *Far.* Stories set in remote or imaginary times and places, which attempt to address mythic materials directly, producing magic, gods, apparitions, etc., as needed. There are several descents into the underworld or the land of the dead: a distinct

Orphic strain, most obvious in *The White Isle*. These stories tend to cluster on the fantasy/horror border, but can often assume a tone of romantic melancholy, or heroic/romantic melancholy rather than outright horror. 2) *Near.* Stories set in the present day, dealing with intimate terrors and unrealities, particularly the unrealities, as in "Transients," the title story in the collection of the same name, which is about a man discovering that he no longer fits in the consensual universe around him. These stories, for commercial reasons, are usually published in the horror field. So far, all my novels have been in the *Far* mode.

*　　*　　*

Darrell Schweitzer's roots are in the twilight world of semi-professional science fiction, where he made an early name for himself as a reviewer and columnist, while today he's probably best known as a major magazine editor (*Weird Tales, Amazing Stories*). Although he has been writing since the early 1970s, Schweitzer has yet to receive an equally wide recognition for his imaginative fictions. His output is varied, but the best work belongs squarely to the tradition of high-end invented-world fantasy, as practised in this century by the likes of Lord Dunsany, Clark Ashton Smith, C. L. Moore and Gene Wolfe. He shares with Dunsany and Smith a penchant for exoticism, moody settings and epic quests; with Moore, an emphasis on the emotional landscape of his characters, dreamlike imagery and a air of all-pervading mystery; with Wolfe, a prose-style that's lucid, unobtrusive, involving and full of miracles related in first-person.

Schweitzer's best and best-known work is the Goddess sequence, a group of ten or so stories (several collected in *Tom O'Bedlam's Night Out*), culminating in his over-the-top novel *The Shattered Goddess*. The setting is the faded world of the far future, a millennium or two following the death of the Goddess of Earth. Fragments of Her divine power still flit across the world, lighting from time to time upon some unlucky mortal, while Her gargantuan corpse is hoarded as a relic below the holy city of Ai Hanlo.

The capstone *Shattered Goddess* does a good job of showing off Schweitzer's skills and inclinations as a fantasist. A dying witch of Ai Hanlo creates a baby out of mud and reeds, and uses it as a temporary vessel for her spirit. She has arranged that this child be placed within the palace, and she moves on to possess the infant ruler, Kaemon. Kaemon grows up to be a tyrant, while the other child, Ginna, is kept around as a palace stable-boy. Years pass. Things get bad in Ai Hanlo as Kaemon's cruelties become more sophisticated, and Ginna and his girlfriend Amaedig quit the town. As they travel, a curtain of darkness descends on the world. This is Kaemon's doing: the witch inside him is enacting a plan to re-flesh the titan Bones of the Goddess, possess the corpse, and attain the Godhead herself.

Their wanderings across the lightless earth are episodic, harrowing, and reminiscent of William Hope Hodgson's writing. During this period Ginna also notices certain supernatural abilities awakening within himself. In time they come to be transported to the centre of holiness in the world, "a great rose, half of fire, half of darkness . . . turning at the world's core," where it's made clear to Ginna that he must confront Kaemon. He is transported—clueless and unprepared—back to lightless Ai Hanlo, which has become a petting zoo of unseen horrors; the pages that follow are one-hundred-percent grade-A nightmare.

But Ginna is basically a loser, and his confrontation with Kaemon is no exception. He's forced to descend to the crypt of the God-dess, where the animated corpse eats him in one bite. But we're not done yet. Ginna awakens within the skull of the Goddess. Summoning his last strength, Ginna plays a trick he learned in his travels, making a ball of light appear between his hands. It balloons in all directions: Ginna has unknowingly created a template for a new Earth, which overlays and supplants the old, and extinguishes the evils of Kaemon and the witch.

In a sombre coda, Ginna awakens to find that centuries have passed. In Ai Hanlo he meets a wizened Amaedig, 500 years old. Her time with Ginna has given her a dose of holiness, and she has become the nearly immortal mother of a new human race. He grants her a peaceful death and wanders off, and is seen to vanish in the wind, having become the God of this cycle of Earth.

The novel's core concerns are with transcendence and sacrifice, and Schweitzer shows no reluctance at presenting us with a world suffused with holiness and sanctity. He defends his inclination towards the spiritual ("In fantasy fiction you can use such matter in an aesthetic fashion without doctrine or belief getting in the way"), and argues it's a more natural concern for fantasy writers "than capture and escape adventures or the politics of imaginary countries". His view of holiness as a blind force, no more sentient than cancer or the tides, is compelling.

Schweitzer also likes to point out that transcendence is a mixed bag: in the end Ginna attains divinity at the price of his humanity, and can never return to his simple life with Amaedig. In addition to this loss, Ginna suffers a lot of major-league physical torment, seemingly to no purpose. Schweitzer habitually subjects his poor, unwitting characters to this kind of sacrifice and suffering. His protagonists are buffeted through their adventures as bewildered pawns of the gods, succeeding only by a combination of perseverance and blind faith. This comes close to defining Schweitzer's idea of courage and heroism, the old idea of just taking the next step forward; and in fictional universes as numinous as Schweitzer's, where Fate is a real force to be reckoned with, this kind of passive behaviour can pay off. Predictably, children are Schweitzer's natural vehicles (being innocent, credulous, and preferring intuition over rationality), and make up the bulk of his main characters.

The epic quality of *The Shattered Goddess*—not to mention a child protagonist and another world bathed in holiness—reappears in the World Fantasy Award-nominated "To Become a Sorcerer" (1991; recently expanded as the novel *The Mask of the Sorcerer*). This novella belongs to the new Great River series, set at a time when the Gods are first awakening and have lots of truck with Mankind. The child Sekenre lives by the City of Reeds. His father Vashtem is a sorcerer, whose deeds have brought on the death of his wife and the disappearance of their daughter, Hamakina. Vashtem grows strange and inhuman—here again, Schweitzer makes his point about the cost of transcendence—and vanishes himself. Sekenre sets off for Tashe, land of the dead, to find Hamakina and to commit parricide. After many adventures (all very imaginative, Schweitzer is in excellent form here) we learn that Hamakina was created by Vashtem as a vessel to carry his spirit after death, and has no soul of her own. Sekenre confronts and kills Vashtem, but finds that the soul of a murdered sorcerer is taken up by the murderer. At the end, Sekenre is a sorcerer, struggling to retain his humanity.

It's worth noting that "To Become a Sorcerer" reworks the thematic material from Schweitzer's first novel, *The White Isle* (written in 1976, though not published until much later). This is probably his most traditional effort in fantasy, and tells of a prince's quest to retrieve his wife from death, its tragic failure, and his descent into madness. The linked stories of *We Are All Legends* depict the early medieval world, with the fallen knight Julian wandering about having supernatural adventures. The quality of these stories varies, but the best, like "The Island of Faces," are as good as anything Schweitzer's written. Modern horror stories comprise most of *Transients,* but one notable fantasy is "The Throwing Suit" (written with artist Jason Van Hollander), a strange story about a restraining garment, a sort of hooded strait-jacket, all hooks and straps, that somehow allows the wearer a glimpse of a bleak and thin world, a metaphysical desert (the wearer first has to jump out of a window with it on; but never mind). A lovely fantasy not yet collected is "Climbing," which begins on the campus of Villanova University, Schweitzer's *alma mater.* A student starts up a beautiful blue beech tree . . . and the climb never ends. In this endless tree he comes across another climber, a girl, and they live out their life together in the branches.

—Steve Behrends

———

SCOT, Michael. *See* SCOTT, Allan (James Julius).

———

SCOTT, Allan (James Julius)

Pseudonym: Michael Scot. **Nationality:** British. **Born:** 1952. **Education:** Oxford University. **Address:** c/o Orbit Books, Brettenham House, Lancaster Place, London WC2E 7EN, England.

FANTASY PUBLICATIONS

Novels

The Ice King, with Michael Scott Rohan (as Michael Scot). London, New English Library, 1986.
The Dragon in the Stone. London, Orbit, 1991.
A Spell of Empire: The Horns of Tartarus, with Michael Scott Rohan. London, Orbit, 1992.

OTHER PUBLICATIONS

Other

The Hammer and the Cross, with Michael Scott Rohan. Oxford, Alder Publishing, 1980.

*   *   *

Allan Scott's fantasy output has not been huge, and two of the three novels discussed here are collaborations with Michael Scott Rohan. A possible source of confusion to bibliographers is the fact that they wrote their first book together as "Michael Scot" (one

"t"); this pseudonym should not be mistaken for the byline of the Irish author Michael Scott (two "t"s), born 1959, who also has written fantasy, but whose work latterly falls into the horror-fiction area. Nor should either name be confused with that of British writer Alan Scott (one "l"), born 1947, who wrote a science-fiction novel called *Project Dracula* (1971).

The Ice King, written with Rohan, is a contemporary fantasy-horror thriller with an archaeological background—both authors had worked in archaeology—and effective use of the blacker byways of Norse myth, all set on the Yorkshire (Danelaw) coast. It soon emerges that the sealed chests found in the remains of a sunken Viking ship contained something still alive after a millennium, an authentic horror: *draugar,* the undead of Icelandic legend, irresistibly strong corpses who can recruit fellows from their kills. Meanwhile, a traditional local folk-dance connects fatally with the sacrificial rite of Odin. . . .

Much bloodshed ensues, with some interestingly and unusually choreographed fight scenes. Worldwide computer-net collation of myth databases reveals something of the true situation to an appalled professor of archaeology, who goes on an involuntary research trip to the Corpse Strand and Yggdrasil while in the real world the eternal Fimbulwinter is closing in. Hela and Odin both take a hand, and modern technology is ingeniously if unwisely turned against the ancient horror. In the end the chief *draug,* Raven the Ice King, is shown as not wholly unsympathetic and at last receives his due Viking funeral in fire and water.

The Ice King reads well enough despite a profusion of spelt-out dialect and that frequent horror-novel sense that numerous characters are there solely to be nastily killed.

Scott's one non-collaborative novel is *The Dragon in the Stone,* an original and distinguished treatment of Norse mythic themes which expands through time from a modern Danish setting to encompass the clear, icy despair of that Ragnarok where all must die and the only important choices remaining are how one falls and in what company.

A tight knot of connections is gradually established. The liosalfar and svartalfar, light and dark elves, are here stripped of any vestigial sentimentality to show as creatures of pure ice, fire, and darkness. The man who passes through the standing stone into magical time and returns prematurely old has more of a past and more of a future than convention dictates. The "Watcher," guardian of the stone gateways, is a fearful, detestable monster, and a cognate of Grendel whom (when the crosstime action shifts to the legendary and cursed mead-hall of Rolf Kraki) a cognate of Beowulf will maim and later kill (part of the emerging tangle of relationships clarifies why just this one man can do so)—while the monster is also our world's only protection from the destroying svartalfar.

Amid this complexity hard decisions must be made, notably when a modern-day farmhouse is besieged by various outer terrors culminating with real children temporarily possessed by svartalfar: can one humanly save oneself by killing attackers who at dawn will be ordinary Danish kids again? History bends on itself, old weapons and men may be reforged, and the moving finale shows time-loops made complete like Odin's symbol of the endless knot, implied prophecies fulfilled and much saved from ruin at a high cost in pain.

After an opening made just a trifle uninviting by confusing narrative cuts, human cross-purposes, and gestures of disbelief (in "fairies"), *The Dragon in the Stone* develops into a fine and hard-gripping novel.

Lastly . . . *A Spell of Empire: The Horns of Tartarus,* again written with Rohan, had an odd genesis. Originally plotted for the

Warhammer fantasy game-world, it was rejigged in haste when its prospective publisher severed the game connection; the slightly ramshackle result is a light-hearted swashbuckler studded with Warhammer-style mutant chaos abominations. It's set in an alternate world where the Germanic and Scandinavian "barbarians" allied themselves with Attila the Hun to create the Nibelung Empire, while over the Alps is "the Southern Empire, vast and decadent, last heir of vanished Rome . . . gangrenous and crumbling, yet still seething with malign life."

Little actually depends on the interesting pseudo-historical background. Our half-elf hero with his amusingly motley companions must transport one of two eponymous and powerfully magical wind instruments from Nurnberg to Syracuse in the far south, threatened by the usual gameworld succession of encounters with varied foes and horrors. The humorous touches are generally better than in the off-key prologue—where Emperor Constans demonstrates his Italianness with "So, whats-a da matter this-a time?" etc—but contrast oddly with desperate battling against slimy menaces, as though the whole mixture needed to be cooked a little more. Occasionally a light-hearted notion does successfully enter into the heavy action, as when a menacing sentient cavern whose voice is a waterfall is choked by the hero's alchemical conversion of the water to *aqua vitae* or schnapps. The apocalyptic resolution is exciting enough, and its aftermath leaves us smiling . . . but the book as a whole seems over-long and uneven.

Scott's knowledge of Old Norse (in which he has an Oxford degree) and the whole "Northern thing" brings a bleakly persuasive erudition to these aspects of the books. His solo novel is genuinely impressive.

—David Langford

SELDEN, George

Pseudonym for George Selden Thompson. **Nationality:** American. **Born:** Hartford, Connecticut, 14 May 1929. **Education:** Loomis School, 1943-47; Yale University, New Haven, Connecticut, B.A. 1951; University of Rome (Fulbright Fellow), 1951. **Awards:** Christopher Award, 1970. **Died:** 1989.

FANTASY PUBLICATIONS

Novels (series: Chester, Harry and Tucker)

The Garden Under the Sea, illustrated by Garry MacKenzie. New York, Viking Press, 1957; as *Oscar Lobster's Fair Exchange,* New York, Harper, 1966.
The Cricket in Times Square, illustrated by Garth Williams (Chester, Harry and Tucker). New York, Farrar Straus, 1960; London, Dent, 1961.
Tucker's Countryside, illustrated by Garth Williams (Chester Cricket). New York, Farrar Straus, 1969; London, Dent, 1971.
The Genie of Sutton Place. New York, Farrar Straus, 1973.
Harry Cat's Pet Puppy, illustrated by Garth Williams (Chester Cricket). New York, Farrar Straus, 1974; London, Dent, 1978.
Chester Cricket's Pigeon Ride, illustrated by Garth Williams. New York, Farrar Straus, 1981.

Chester Cricket's New Home, illustrated by Garth Williams. New York, Farrar Straus, and London, Dent, 1983.
Harry Kitten and Tucker Mouse, illustrated by Garth Williams. New York, Farrar Straus, 1986.

OTHER PUBLICATIONS

Fiction for Children

The Dog That Could Swim Under Water, illustrated by Morgan Dennis. New York, Viking Press, 1956.
I See What I See!, illustrated by Robert Galster. New York, Farrar Straus, 1962.
The Mice, The Monks, and the Christmas Tree, illustrated by Jan Balet. New York, Macmillan, and London, Collier Macmillan, 1963.
Sparrow Socks, illustrated by Peter Lippman. New York, Harper, 1965.
The Dunkard, illustrated by Peter Lippman. New York, Harper, 1968.
Irma and Jerry, illustrated by Leslie Morrill. New York, Avon, 1982.
The Old Meadow, illustrated by Garth Williams. New York, Farrar Straus, 1987.

Plays

The Children's Story, adaptation of the work by James Clavell. New York, Dramatists Play Service, 1966.

Television Play: *The Genie of Sutton Place.*

Other

Heinrich Schliemann, Discoverer of Buried Treasure, illustrated by Lorence Bjorklund. New York, Macmillan, and London, Collier Macmillan, 1964.
Sir Arthur Evans, Discoverer of Knossos, illustrated by Lee Ames. New York, Macmillan, and London, Collier Macmillan, 1964.

*   *   *

It may come as a surprise to many who love George Selden's *The Cricket in Times Square* to discover that Selden wrote several other books concerning the adventures of Chester Cricket, Tucker Mouse, Harry Cat and their friends in New York and Connecticut. On the other hand, it is doubtful that any of these tales quite reaches the heights achieved by Selden's first novel in the series. (He also wrote some non-series children's fantasies, of which the most notable is *The Genie of Sutton Place,* about a boy, a genie and a dog that is transformed into a human being.)

In *The Cricket in Times Square,* Chester finds himself in New York after crawling into a picnic basket to eat a piece of liverwurst and then falling asleep. As luck would have it, he is rescued by young Mario, whose parents keep a struggling newspaper stand in the subway station at Times Square; there Chester also meets Tucker Mouse and Harry Cat, the best of friends and one of the most delightful odd couples in children's fiction.

Once Mario has adopted Chester, he sets out on a series of adventures which provide the reader with a boy- and cricket-sized view of New York, a city Selden clearly feels great affection for. With them we explore Chinatown where Mario goes to find a house for Chester, and with Tucker and Harry we see the gaudy glory of Times Square and the hustle and bustle of the subways. New York scurries past, cynically viewed by many small eyes.

At the heart of the novel, though, is Chester's attempt to win Mama Bellini's heart. She has made many attempts to banish him from the newsstand, but when the newsstand catches fire she blames Chester, and it is only by chance, when he chirps a few bars from her favourite Italian song, that he is saved. For a week, he provides concerts at the news-stand until, eager to get back to the quiet life in his meadow, he begs Harry and Tucker to put him on the train and he slips quietly back to Connecticut.

Other stories in the series see Harry and Tucker travelling to Connecticut to help Chester save his meadow when it is under threat; see Chester in search of a new home when two over-weight picnickers crush his stump; and give Tucker and Harry a rapidly growing problem when they adopt a stray Old English sheepdog puppy. Although Chester was hero of the first story, there can be little doubt that the heart of the series is the relationship between Harry and Tucker: Harry gentle and resourceful, teasing his little friend; Tucker, voluble, excitable, streetwise but with a heart of gold and a passion for hoarding exotic and curious articles found in the gutters. Indeed, *Chester Cricket's New Home,* in which Chester alone figures, is very dull by comparison with, say, *Harry Cat's Pet Puppy,* in which the cricket does not appear.

Selden has a sharp eye for character, frequently indulging in gentle satire of the foibles of both animals and people, but at the same time knows how to create a heart-warming story without, on the whole, descending into sentiment. He also has a keen awareness of the need for magic in the most ordinary of lives, and it is difficult, for example, to shake the memory of the cricket singing to huge audiences in the subway station; Selden so wonderfully conveys the unspoken need of all those people for a little wonder and beauty in their lives. There are moments too when one is reminded of his fellow American, Peter Beagle's *A Fine and Private Place,* similarly invested with that particular sense of humour shown by Selden, a savvy street humour.

Of the Chester books, *The Cricket in Times Square* is undoubtedly the most successful; none of the other novels quite touches the reader in the same way, although *Harry Cat's Pet Puppy* comes close with its heart-warming concern for the fate of the hapless puppy. Mention should also be made of Garth Williams, the artist who illustrated all the books and whose evocative portraits of the animals surely contributed to the series' popularity.

—Maureen Speller

SEVERANCE, Carol (Ann Wilcox)

Nationality: American. **Born:** 1944. **Address:** c/o Ballantine/Del Rey, 201 East 50th Street, New York, NY 10022, USA.

FANTASY PUBLICATIONS

Novels (series: Island Warrior in all books)

Demon Drums. New York, Del Rey, 1992.
Storm Caller. New York, Del Rey, 1993.
Sorcerous Sea. New York, Del Rey, 1993.

OTHER PUBLICATIONS

Novel

Reefsong. New York, Del Rey, 1991.

*   *   *

Although Carol Severance's first novel was overtly science fiction, it nevertheless displayed many similar characteristics to those of her Island Warrior series, the fascination with water dwellers in particular, and the interest in Oceanic cultures; Severance herself now lives in Hawaii.

These interests blossomed with the Island Warrior series which eschewed science-fiction tropes for something altogether more fantastical and challenging. The three novels of the series centre on Iuti Mano; once feared as a warrior but now sickened by death and destruction she has retreated from war and lives on an isolated island, searching for healing. As proof of her peaceful intentions, she has even killed Mano Niuhi, the shark, severing her link with the creatures of the sea, with whom for centuries her family had shared a magical bond. Thus, as the first novel opens we see Iuti adrift spiritually and physically, but also becoming uneasily aware of mysteries on the small atoll, Fanape, where she had come to heal her wounds. Pahulu, the local sorceress, seems to be far more powerful than she ought to be, and Iuti swiftly discovers that she has the capability to drain magic from other users. But more worryingly, the Teronin war she sought to escape seems to have come to her own doorstep, for Pahulu is in league with the Teronin, supplying them with zombie warriors.

Forced to act against the Teronin, Iuti flees after the witch is mysteriously killed, accompanied by Tarawe, a girl who would be both witch and warrior, whose magical storm takes them into Teronin territory and into the hands of the Demon Drummers, who make drums from human skin. Iuti's skin, they believe, will make them a fine Mother drum. Escaping once again, Iuti seeks sanctuary, and also a cure for Tarawe, damaged by her unskilled use of magic, with Ola, a healer; and gradually she gathers around her the band of friends who will feature in the series—Ola, Ma'eva from the sea people, able to mimic many different creatures; the milimili, a pair of prostitutes who also wield magical powers—and who together defeat the Teronin.

The second book, *Storm Caller,* resolves Tarawe's struggle to combine her skills as warrior and as witch, and also sees the birth of Iuti and Ma'eva's son, Kanaka. They also adopt the mysterious Huluhulu, a girl disfigured by neglect, who is swathed in hair which has matted itself into her skin; yet her hair has magical abilities of its own, as is revealed in the third volume of the series, *Sorcerous Sea.*

Here, Kanaka and Huluhulu are captured by the mysterious Pala, a man who claims to be a magician and to have a Teronin army poised awaiting his command. He has gathered a band of children around him whom he is using as the source of his magical powers. Kanaka, the son of Iuti Mano and Ma'eva, is a source of great power and Pala hopes to exploit this power. While Iuti searches for her son, Kana and Hulu gradually win the confidence of the other children, who have been living a "Lord-of-the-Flies"-like existence, jockeying for power among themselves, exploiting one another's weaknesses. Among them is the mysterious Vatu, a female child of the Demon Drummers, who has herself learned to drum, although this is forbidden to the women. The discovery of her skill has caused her to be cast out, with her hands crushed to stop her drumming any more. Much as their parents did, Kana and Hulu marshal their resources and do what they can to defeat Pala, while their parents and the milimili bring help from outside.

Throughout the stories, Severance draws heavily on her knowledge of Oceanic myths and cultures in order to create a rich, colourful fantasy series which is very much out of the ordinary. She doesn't balk from looking at the darker side of magic, or from what might seem, at first sight, to be an unacceptable savagery in the world she has created. However, the reader quickly comes to perceive an inherent balance in her world. Wrongs are always righted, but it is recognized that sometimes blood must necessarily be shed in order to achieve this. Severance's world is a harsh one but nevertheless fair.

Her main characters are a delight, particularly the milimili; one wonders how many writers would be willing to include a pair of extremely camp prostitutes, male and female, as regular characters in their novels. This is simply one more example of Severance's splendidly robust approach to her work. And yet, her characters have their share of troubles. Kanaka may lead an idyllic, carefree life but his parents are touched by personal tragedies, as are the children Iuti adopts. Kinship and the need to help one another are both strong themes in the book.

Most prominent though is Severance's use of magic in her stories. This is not the intellectual magic of the West but a rough vibrant earth and water magic based on artefacts and using the elements. People are possessed, held captive by the beat of a drum or by a strand of hair, tracked by the taste they leave in the water. And the magic is a real and definite part of people's existence, recognized, used and accepted.

Carol Severance offers readers a new and remarkable kind of fantasy; although, as many writers do, she draws upon a mythology familiar in our own world, she has chosen one which is, in many ways, entirely alien to many people, and has used it to spin a series of novels which are colourful, believable and satisfying, an achievement too few other writers can match.

—Maureen Speller

SHEA, Michael

Nationality: American. **Born:** Los Angeles, 1946. **Education:** University of California. **Awards:** World Fantasy award, 1983.

FANTASY PUBLICATIONS

Novels

A Quest for Simbilis. New York, DAW, 1974; London, Grafton, 1985.
Nifft the Lean. New York, DAW, 1982; London, Granada, 1985.
Color Out of Time. New York, DAW, 1984; as *The Colour Out of Time,* London, Grafton, 1986.
In Yana, the Touch of Undying. New York, DAW, 1985; London, Grafton, 1987.

Short Stories

Fat Face. Seattle, Washington, Axolotl Press, 1987.

Polyphemus. Sauk City, Wisconsin, Arkham House, 1987; London, Grafton, 1990.

*   *   *

In his introduction to *Polyphemus* Algis Budrys regrets that Michael Shea has received less recognition than his talents would seem to merit. One can see his point: Shea has a racy line in grue and writes with energy, imagination, and precision; his visions of Hell capture Hieronymus Bosch in prose; but his is not yet a big name. There could be many reasons why, but the most likely is that for a writer of modest output he has cast his nets very wide.

His first book, *A Quest for Simbilis,* was a licensed sequel to Jack Vance's *The Eyes of the Overworld,* and while Shea captured the landscape of the Dying Earth and Vance's episodic style of development well enough, he tacked on an unconvincingly moralistic ending at odds with Vance's philosophy and urbanity alike. Even so, the book contains some very fine touches, including a game of strip poker where the winner gets eaten and a form of horticultural cannibalism. It must also be admitted that Vance himself undermined Shea by publishing his own continuation, *Cugel's Saga,* in 1983. *A Quest for Simbilis* inevitably suffered by comparison, since whatever its intrinsic virtues, it was not the real thing.

The short novel *The Color Out of Time* is also a sequel, on this occasion to H. P. Lovecraft's "The Color out of Space". Set many years after the flooding of the Blasted Heath, it recounts how a couple of middle-aged academics, on holiday by the reservoir thus formed, find that the remnant of the alien aerolite that sank back into Nahum Gardner's well is alive, active, and polluting the drinking-water. Fortified with prodigious amounts of hard liquor, they set about frustrating its evil intentions. As the alien presents rather an abstract enemy, the principal opposition comes from those already infected—sundry plebeian holiday-makers whose inherent loathsomeness (described with great gusto) has been exacerbated by drinking and swimming in the water. The tale reads like an allegory of the deracination of the American working class, and would doubtless have won Lovecraft's approval, though Shea may have lost favor with his admirers by making no attempt to pastiche Lovecraft's style.

Paradoxically, a factor in Shea's lack of recognition to date may be his exceptionally fine ear for prose rhythms. Most of his work is written in the first person, and he adopts an authentic-sounding grammar, vocabulary, and sentence-construction for each persona. Thus "Uncle Tuggs" is written in the voice of a jobbing handyman in rural North America, "The Horror on the #33" is pure *New Yorker,* and the incidents which make up the first-person adventures of *Nifft the Lean* are each introduced by "Shag Margold," an elderly archivist whose tone, mood, and preoccupations are very unlike those of his highly tuned protagonist. This is delightful for the connoisseur, but has the disadvantage that not everyone will like all the voices equally; one man's eclectic virtuoso is another man's uneven writer, and because Shea's superficial tics are his most stable qualities, they are the more likely to be noted.

The most obvious is a preoccupation with gigantism. Creatures of abnormal size throng his books, with both *A Quest for Simbilis* and *Nifft the Lean* featuring recumbent giants large enough to be classed in the topography rather than the fauna—two, in the latter case, which is a high incidence for a volume of four novelettes. Such excessive scale tends to be counter-productive, as it often vitiates Shea's mastery of grotesquerie in detail. Shea's other major weakness lies in his moral tone and is most evident in *Nifft the Lean.* Sword and sorcery is not noted for its moral delicacy. Deaths of prolonged excruciation, such as few would be prepared to condone if they were administered under a judicial code, are meted out to villains, traitors, and cowards as a matter of routine; it's quite acceptable, for instance, for a serial killer to be eaten alive by giant spiders, as happens in "The Angel of Death." Nor are the protagonists required to be overscrupulous in their regard for the truth, the rights of property, marriage vows to which they have not themselves been party, the justice of causes which they espouse for hire, nor any local laws, manners, customs or religious traditions which might stand between themselves and their pagan enjoyment of the good life.

Even so there are limits, and Shea sometimes flouts them. In "The Pearls of the Vampire Queen", Nifft and his friend Barnar, fresh from a pearl-poaching foray and bent on plunder, enter a city against which they hold no grudge. There they murder (with no pretensce of fair fight) an innocent guardsman, attack and wound a conscious but paralyzed man and, by an exercise in pure extortion, wring a great fortune from the local ruler. This they subsequently lay out on two years of riotous living. Now, Nifft and Barnar bear such a strong resemblance to Fritz Leiber's the Gray Mouser and Fafhrd that comparisons are unavoidable. Having compared, one feels that Leiber's disreputable heroes would certainly have poached the pearls and spent the proceeds the same way, and might have committed the extortion; but they would have held back from the wounding and murder.

The problem lies not in the actions, which Moorcock's Elric of Melniboné and Moonglum would surely have committed as well, but in Shea's apparent failure to recognize their nature, for Shag Margold (speaking unquestionably for the author) states that "If Nifft was not entirely honest, he was entirely honourable." We expect honor from the Gray Mouser, just as we expect treachery from Elric, which is why the two should not be confused. As when he pastiched Vance, so when he pastiches Leiber; the difference between the real thing and the imitation tells the more heavily against Shea because the imitation is apparent.

One cannot seriously quarrel with Budrys's contention that Shea deserves a higher rating; but if he is to obtain a stable following he needs to decide which of his many voices is to become his principal voice and deploy the others for variation and ornamentation rather than letting them compete for supremacy. He needs also to be a little more fastidious about who is on the side of the angels. Above all, he needs to write a lot more. Meanwhile, those seeking an introduction to his work will do best to approach him through the showcase collection *Polyphemus*.

—Chris Gilmore

SHERMAN, Delia

Nationality: American. **Born:** Cordelia Caroline Sherman, 1951.

FANTASY PUBLICATIONS

Novels

Through a Brazen Mirror. New York, Ace, 1989.
The Porcelain Dove. New York, Dutton, 1993.

*   *   *

Delia Sherman is a very clever historical fantasist. She weaves her modern political agenda so skilfully into the tapestry of traditional fantasy themes that it only gradually dawns on the reader that the lovers holding hands in the tableaux are both of the same sex.

With Sherman's first novel, *Through a Brazen Mirror,* she takes the conventional folk tale of Elinor Flower (known as "The Famous Flower of Serving Men"), and reworks it into a story about a strong woman and an "unnatural" man. Elinor was married to a Knight and bore him a son. Then her wicked sorceress mother, Margaret, had both the husband and son killed, fearing they would be her bane. After the massacre, Elinor dresses in men's clothing, calls herself William, and becomes a servant to the King. He falls in love with her and destroys the sorceress.

In the traditional tale the King then marries Elinor. Bending this conventional telling Sherman, has the King suffer "unnatural urges" for William, and feel nothing for the womanly Elinor. For her part Elinor now wants naught but to be a free woman, and at novel's end she has resumed wandering the world clad in masculine garb. This is an interestingly wrought tale, told from a time-shifting three-point perspective which covers William's rise from undercook to chamberlain, the sorceress' magical shenanigans, and Elinor's life before the massacre. Both Margaret and Elinor are portrayed as exceptionally determined women and the King's homo-erotic longings seem touchingly poignant (even if he is painted as a rather self-absorbed dolt.) The period detail is fascinating and not overdone—though the book is likely to disturb more traditional fantasists. Not only does *Through a Brazen Mirror* contain explicit homosexual overtones, but the ending is surprisingly bittersweet: the heroine walks off alone into the sunrise, and the King enters into a loveless political marriage wondering if his epithet will be "The Sodomite".

In Sherman's next novel, *The Porcelain Dove,* she gives herself freer reign, not binding the story directly to a traditional tale but instead unfurling the magical elements against the backdrop of the French Revolution. The story is narrated in the first person by Berthe Duvet, *femme de chambre* (ladies' maid) to the aristocrat Adele. Berthe spends her adolescence protecting and succouring her mistress, and remains with Adele when she marries the Duc de Malvoeux. The Duke is a nasty man who loves birds far more than his sweet but rather dim-witted wife. Adele and Berthe leave Paris and spend most of their time at the country estate Beauxprès, which could be an idyllically enchanted kingdom except for "some stink of old blood" about the place.

The family lives in the wastefully opulent splendour that was an aristocrat's right, until the Duke denies a beggar three times. The beggar then brings down an ancient curse upon the Duke claiming that "the family of Maindur will wither and die" unless they succeed in capturing the elusive (and perhaps mythical) "porcelain dove". Since the oldest son is a sadist, and the middle boy wants nothing other than to revere God, it is up to the youngest daughter, Linotte, to use magic to win the avian prize.

After Linotte goes on her quest Berthe struggles to keep the mad Duke and his raving wife fed and clothed while the Revolution ravages the country-side. Though Adele picks up the wrong magical implement and is turned into a bird, Berthe loves her too much to leave her. Things continue in this fashion for several years until a troupe of strolling players appear at Beauxprès. The play they perform is astonishing, both for its wonderful manipulation of period theatrical idiom and for the brilliance of its conceit. Sherman uses the play to dramatize Linotte's sorcerous trials allowing Berthe to magically view the scenes leading up to the successful acquisition of the porcelain dove. The climax of both the play and the quest comes during the rape scene.

This is the point in the novel where Sherman's agenda becomes clear. Though *The Porcelain Dove* is laden with violent and sadistic sexual acts they all performed by men. The brutal rape of Linotte is used to contrast Adele's sensual acceptance of her true nature. To leave the bird form (which her mad husband found so appealing) Adele must first sprawl naked in Berthe's arms, and then be returned to humanity by her female lover's kisses.

There is something very sweet about Berthe's constant attachment to Adele. What might, in some heavier hand, have become a tract on the joys of lesbianism is noticeably downplayed, even as the homosexual longings in *Through a Brazen Mirror* are finally subsumed into a hidden ideal of courtly love.

Berthe, herself, is a wonderful narrator. Though when she states that the reader need not fear "an endless catalogue of gowns and balls and small domestic occurrences," she is not completely accurate, since the book is so awash in detail that the reader is practically swamped with information on corsets, chemises, ribbons, fabrics, tisanes and the best ways to whiten lace. Yet this is exactly the sort of tale one would expect from a ladies' maid, and for sheer sass no one can cut a corset like Berthe. When the duc de Malvoeux's manservant tells her that she should be sure to know her place when they arrive at Beauxprès because, "Tis unbecoming to think oneself the equal of those who have served the ducs de Malvoeux for twenty generations." Berthe responds, "And here was I thinking your wrinkles and pustules were just ugliness, or too free a hand with the white-lead in your youth. Now I know you to be upwards of four hundred years old, I'll vow you're tolerable handsome."

Yet even such a lovely, plucky narrator is saddled with only a modified happy ending. Though Berthe has her beloved Adele as a companion she is still trapped in a timeless limbo (the implication being that this is the only place these two women of different classes can exist as lovers and equals) with several sadistic madmen.

Sherman's world-view is often disturbing, but her subversions of the conventional make for intriguing reading. While her themes may not be to everyone's taste, these novels (and hopefully others from her in the future) serve to remind us that the words "happily ever after" must, of necessity, means different things to different people.

—Shira Daemon

SHETTERLY, Will(iam Howard)

Nationality: American. **Born:** 1955. **Family:** Married fantasy writer Emma Bull, q.v.

FANTASY PUBLICATIONS

Novels (series: Borderlands)

Cats Have No Lord. New York, Ace, 1985.
Witch Blood. New York, Ace, 1986.
The Tangled Lands. New York, Ace, 1989.

Elsewhere (Borderlands). New York, Harcourt Brace Jovanovich, 1991.
Nevernever (Borderlands). New York, Harcourt Brace, 1993.

Short Stories

Double Feature, with Emma Bull. Framingham, Massachusetts, NESFA Press, 1994.

Other (series: Liavek in all books)

Editor, with Emma Bull, *Liavek.* New York, Ace, 1985.
Editor, with Emma Bull, *The Players of Luck.* New York, Ace, 1986.
Editor, with Emma Bull, *Wizard's Row.* New York, Ace, 1987.
Editor, with Emma Bull, *Spells of Binding.* New York, Ace, 1988.
Editor, with Emma Bull, *Festival Week.* New York, Ace, 1990.

*   *   *

One of the most rewarding things for a reader to discover is a new writer who seems to progress steadily from book to book, developing the skill to make each just a little bit better than the last. Will Shetterly is one such writer, who has moved from competent but middle-of-the-road fantasy adventure to the point where we can no longer anticipate which direction his work will take next. And even his early work has its moments of genuine originality.

When the Lady Lizelle is unjustly accused of theft in the early pages of *Cats Have No Order,* it's just the beginning of a series of adventures which will turn her life upside down. She next encounters Catseye Yellow, a rogue of sorts with an unusual eye, who asks her why it is that cats have no lord to rule their lives, even though all other animals do. In due course, and after finding additional companions, they are off on a quest to discover the reason for this oddity of nature, but their journey serves a deeper, secret and menacing purpose as well. Before she learns the truth about the cat lord, Lizelle will discover much about herself, travel between worlds, learn to use a mystical power, and find herself opposed to a demon and perhaps even a god. Shetterly's gift for characterization helps make an otherwise lacklustre plot seem more than it is, an ability which became more evident in subsequent books.

Witch Blood chronicles the adventures of Rifkin, a wanderer who finds himself bound to an overbearing woman living in a loosely defended castle in the fringes of what was once the Witches' Empire. Naiji and her brother Talivane, both with witch blood in their veins, are menaced by an acquisitive noble who is trying to take advantage of the uncertain times that surround a new king's early reign. Although Rifkin chafes at the necessity to remain with them, the obligations of his pledge are imperative. And despite the fact that Rifkin was raised in a faith that has long thought of itself as the last guardian of freedom from the tyranny of witches, Rifkin is himself tainted, or perhaps blessed, with their heritage, although in a stranger fashion than he could ever imagine.

Witch Blood is a considerable step forward from the entertaining but slight *Cats Have No Lords.* The interplay among the main characters is pivotal, although the fantastic elements remain a major part of the story. But with his third novel, *The Tangled Lands,* Shetterly began to demonstrate that he was more than just another interesting fantasy writer weaving new combinations of old themes. A pair of computer programmers are working to develop an interactive virtual-reality fantasy-role-playing game. To check on their work, they frequently log-in to the partially created universe as characters, locating the inconsistencies and paradoxes so that they can be fixed back in the real world. They've gone to great lengths to put part of themselves into their work, perhaps too great a part because along with their conscious projections, they have introduced into the program contradictions and fears which begin to reshape the created universe. *The Tangled Lands* features the most likeable characters yet from Shetterly, a nice twist in the ending, and demonstrates his sensitivity to the convolutions of the human mind and its tendency to turn upon itself.

Shetterly's fourth novel, *Elsewhere,* is set in the shared universe of the Borderlands anthology series. (Shetterly and Emma Bull were themselves the editors of the short-lived but highly acclaimed Liavek shared-world anthologies and clearly enjoy the form despite its limitations.) Shetterly contributed two stories set in the Borderlands, a twilight world that bridges the gap between contemporary America and the world of Faerie, a place where magic and technology intermingle, and where people who don't quite fit in the modern world can find refuge.

The novel details the adventures of Ron, a runaway searching for a new sense of family after the disruption of the one he once knew but has now lost. In the Borderlands he encounters elvish bikers and human outcasts, and more importantly a place where he once again can feel as though he belongs, although his newfound home is abruptly menaced by a plague of catastrophes that seem to have a magical origin. Ostensibly for young adults, *Elsewhere* is a powerful and mature work, sure evidence that Shetterly is destined to emerge as one of the major voices in modern fantasy fiction.

His other Borderlands-related work includes the novel *Nevernever,* and two shorter pieces. "Danceland," written in collaboration with Emma Bull, is a first-rate story of murder and friendship, love and anger, all set against a magical but somehow familiar background. Shetterly's solo story, "Nevernever," basis for the full length work of the same name, continues the adventures of Wolfboy and a companion as each seeks something in the wilderness surrounding Bordertown, he, his human shape, and she, the return of her magic.

In addition to editing the Liavek series, Shetterly contributed three short pieces, the best of which is "Six Days Outside the Year". Other tales of note include the macabre and convoluted "Time Travel, the Artifact, and a Famous Historical Personage," a very bizarre twist on the Jack the Ripper theme, and "Oldthings," a short but very wicked piece about what happens when science doesn't work and the old things of legend return, sometimes to a very unusual welcome. Shetterly's career has been too short and unpredictable to guess where it is headed next, but he is clearly one of the more significant new voices in the genre, and likely to have a major hand in shaping its future.

—Don D'Ammassa

SHWARTZ, Susan (Martha)

Pseudonym: Gordon Kendall. **Nationality:** American. **Born:** Youngstown, Ohio, 31 December 1949. **Education:** Mount Holyoke College, Massachusetts, 1968-72, B.A. in English; Harvard University, Cambridge, Massachusetts, 1972-73, M.A. in English 1973, Ph.D. in English 1977. **Career:** Summer study, Trinity College, Oxford, 1970, 1971; postdoctoral fellow, Dartmouth College, New Hampshire, 1978; teaching fellow, Harvard University, 1974-77; assistant professor of English, Ithaca College, New York, 1977-80; senior writer/researcher, Deutsch, Shea and Evans, New York, 1981-82; information coordinator, BEA Associates, New York, 1983-87; financial editor, Donaldson, Lufkin and Jenrette, New York, 1987-88; financial writer/editor and assistant vice-president, Prudential Securities, New York, since 1988. **Awards:** National Endowment for the Humanities grant, 1978. **Agent:** Richard Curtis Associates, 171 East 74th Street, New York, NY 10022, USA. **Address:** One Station Square, Number 306, Forest Hills, NY 11375, USA.

FANTASY PUBLICATIONS

Novels (series: Heirs to Byzantium)

Byzantium's Crown. New York, Warner, 1987; London, Pan, 1987.
The Woman of Flowers (Byzantium). New York, Warner, 1987; London, Pan, 1987.
Queensblade (Byzantium). New York, Warner, 1988; London, Pan, 1988.
Silk Roads and Shadows. New York, Tor, 1988; London, Pan, 1989.
Imperial Lady: A Fantasy of Han China, with Andre Norton. New York, Tor, 1989.
The Grail of Hearts. New York, Tor, 1992.
Empire of the Eagle, with Andre Norton. New York, Tor, 1993.

Other

Editor, *Hecate's Cauldron.* New York, DAW, 1982.
Editor, *Moonsinger's Friends: An Anthology in Honor of Andre Norton.* New York, Bluejay, 1985; London, Severn House, 1986.
Editor, *Arabesques: More Tales of the Arabian Nights.* New York, Avon, 1988; London, Pan, 1988.
Editor, *Arabesques II.* New York, Avon, 1989.

OTHER PUBLICATIONS

Novels

White Wing (as Gordon Kendall), with Shariann N. Lewitt. New York, Tor, 1985; London, Sphere, 1986.
Heritage of Flight. New York, Tor, 1989.

Other

Editor, *Habitats.* New York, DAW, 1984.

*   *   *

Before she ever wrote a novel, Susan Shwartz edited fantasy anthologies; and before that she was a classical scholar, with a bachelor's degree from Mount Holyoke College and an M.A. and Ph.D from Harvard. A classical education may have provided Shwartz with the tools to be a better editor than she is a fantasy novelist, however, and it is in her story anthologies that she excels (the exception to this is her trilogy, the Heirs to Byzantium, which thus far she has never equalled). The first anthology was *Hecate's Cauldron,* but the second, *Moonsinger's Friends,* was the best of her collections and one of the finest anthologies I've ever read. This volume has an unusual premise for a fantasy anthology: rather than adhering to a set theme, all the stories are written in the manner of Andre Norton, the "Moonsinger" of the title. Norton has acted as Shwartz's mentor in general, and as co-author of her novels *Imperial Lady* and *Empire of the Eagle.* Shwartz's other anthologies, *Arabesques, Arabesques II* and the science-fiction volume *Habitats,* are also fine.

The premise of the Heirs to Byzantium trilogy involves an alternative time-line: what would have happened to western civilization if Antony and Cleopatra had been successful in their war against Octavian, and the Roman Empire had become a joint Egyptian/Roman dynasty? If England was never conquered by Rome, its history would, of course, have been quite different. *Byzantium's Crown* introduces Alexa and her brother Marric, destined to rule the Empire jointly as consorts, "Isis and Osiris" on earth. That plan is disrupted by their stepmother Irene, an evil sorceress who takes over the kingdom, forces Alexa to flee into exile and sells Marric into slavery. In *The Woman of Flowers,* Marric eventually wins back the throne, but not until Alexa has made her way to Prydein (England), become apprenticed to the Druids, married an British prince and had his baby. Marric has a surprise destiny in store for himself when he tries to retrieve Alexa to rule with him, in the form of Olwen, Queen of Prydein.

In the final volume, *Queensblade,* Alexa, Marric, Olwen and Alexa's husband Gerient are middle-aged. Alexa's daughter Elen, and Olwen and Marric's children Mor and Gwenlliant, are just reaching adulthood. Marric thinks Gwenlliant will marry her brother Mor in the old tradition; but Gwenlliant and Mor have different ideas. By the end of the trilogy, Marric has renounced the throne of Byzantium in favour of Mor and his bride, Elen, to become a priest/adept, Olwen has died by her own hand in a traditional fertility ritual, and Gwenlliant has become the queen of Prydein.

The two historical fantasies Shwartz has written with Andre Norton are her second-best work in the fantasy field, surpassed only by the Heirs to Byzantium series. They both take place during the first century B.C.—the first, *Imperial Lady,* in China and the Mongolian plains, and the second, *Empire of the Eagle,* involving a hero named Quintus, a tribune in the Roman army. The fantasy elements in both books are secondary to the historical, but one involves the power of an eagle standard that proves to be a supernatural weapon, and the other the conflicting sorceries of a shape-shifter and an evil shaman. Of the two *Imperial Lady* is the best, because the characters and plot are more carefully developed and succeed in holding the reader's attention admirably.

The heroine of the book (which is based on an historical account of a woman named Chao Chun) is Silver Snow, daughter of a once-powerful Chinese general. Snow has grown up in exile, living on the very border of the Empire, because her father was disgraced by a corrupt government. She hunts and rides like a man and has known little of the ridiculous lives Chinese women led at the time. When an envoy arrives from the court of the Emperor, Snow leaves her home and journeys to the capital, to be one of a thousand maidens from whom the Emperor will choose a new Empress. He doesn't particularly want to do this, being a self-absorbed and weak young man who has devoted his life to mourning his first wife, now dead. When Silver Snow arrives at the court, she doesn't know anything about protocol or court intrigues. She immediately falls out of favor with the Chief Eunuch, who will paint the portraits that will help the Emperor choose his bride. Her resulting portrait is so ugly she is confined to the "cold palace" in

isolation, accompanied only by her maid, Willow—a shape-changer who becomes a red fox at will. Her other companion is an old man who was once a great general but who, like her father, has fallen out of favour. Eventually, however, an alliance is made between the Emperor and the nomad tribes called Hsiung-Nu. One of the court ladies will be adopted by the Emperor and sent to be the wife of the Hsiung-Nu chieftain. The Emperor decides it would be a good joke to send Silver Snow, the ugliest lady. When he actually sees her, however, he is stunned when she looks exactly like his dead wife. He would now retract his vow and offer another lady, but the Hsiung-Nu prince won't allow it. Finally it is left to Silver Snow to decide, and she goes with the Hsiung-Nu only to discover her "husband" is being poisoned by his first wife, a great sorceress. How Silver Snow saves her new people from a terrible fate and finds true love herself is the stuff of high fantasy.

Empire of the Eagle is also based on historical fact, about a Roman legion captured by the Chinese after losing a battle. In the earlier part of the narrative there is far too much about the long, tedious journey through the desert once the legion is captured and is on its way to be displayed as a trophy before the Emperor. But somewhere in the desert they pass through into a fantasy world, where they meet with two people who are thousands of years old. These people, great sorcerers, lead them on a quest to save the world from the powers of darkness that threaten to engulf it. Quintus is a good hero; it turns out he is the reincarnation of a supposedly mythical hero from the continent of Atlantis. He needs a "power" object to channel through, and this turns out to be the eagle standard of his legion. After some early longueurs, it develops into a fascinating story.

Shwartz herself considers her most ambitious solo work to be *The Grail of Hearts.* It is a loose retelling of the Parsival legend, and concerns a man named Amfortas who is the keeper of the Holy Grail, and a woman/sorceress named Kundry who is cursed to live forever because she laughed at the crucifixion of Christ. For some readers, there may be a perceived conflict in Shwartz's attempt to write a fantasy/romance in which she expects the reader to accept elements of Christianity as the basis of the story. The problem is that Christianity does not condone any kind of magical power except the religious, and anyone who has power that is not based on miracles or faith must therefore be of the Devil's party. The reader is, in this instance, asked for much too much of a suspension of disbelief.

Shwartz admits there may never have been a Grail, but feels it doesn't matter where the idea came from—even that it may have been based on the Cauldron of Cerridwen—because what is important is that is it became an undying symbol of religion. It is not a symbol that mixes well with classical fantasy, however, and this is where *The Grail of Hearts* fails. The characters are struggling with a premise that doesn't make sense; the whole thing becomes a sort of dysfunctional exercise that seems like a Master's thesis gone awry. Christian fantasy is difficult at the best of times, and most authors deal with the matter (Teresa Edgerton and Lisa Goldstein are good examples) by viewing the religious element as a problem that must be overcome in order for the hero or heroine to complete his or her training, job or quest. Unfortunately Shwartz has done just the opposite: all the good magic in the book actually comes from the religion itself, a religion that has spent nearly two thousand years persecuting anyone with supposedly magical power that doesn't come from God.

—Debora Hill

SILKE, James R.

Nationality: American.

FANTASY PUBLICATIONS

Novels (series: Frank Frazetta's Death Dealer in all books)

Prisoner of the Horned Helmet. New York, Tor, and London, Grafton, 1988.
Lords of Destruction. New York, Tor, 1989; London, Grafton, 1990.
Tooth and Claw. New York, Tor, 1989; London, Grafton, 1991.
Plague of Knives. New York, Tor, 1990.

*   *   *

In the grand but unliterary tradition of Robin Hood, Clint Eastwood's Man With No Name and The Equalizer, comes the Death Dealer: a protector of the innocent and vanquisher of evil who is not wholly good. This routine and undistinguished heroic fantasy series owes much to a 1973 picture by the top US fantasy artist, Frank Frazetta. Titled "The Death Dealer," that picture shows a fearsome warrior on horseback. The horse is black and breathing hard. The warrior, clad in chain mail, carries a long shield and a large single-bladed axe, its edge covered in blood. On the warrior's head is a helmet with downward-curving horns; the eye-holes of the helmet glow red. Overhead, vultures fly. This wonderfully seductive and atmospheric image has been novelized, for the most part disappointingly, by James Silke.

The Death Dealer is Gath of Baal, a big and hugely-muscled barbarian who uses his own mighty strength and the magic of that horned helmet to overcome the massed hordes of demon spawn, servants of the Master of Darkness. The helmet is, in fact, an artefact of black magic, having been stolen from the enemy, and it is this helmet which provides an entertaining (though not wholly original) twist by gradually taking over Gath's mind and reducing him to an inhuman killing-machine.

Gath's fight against the helmet is one of the plot-lines which runs through these books. Connected closely is his relationship with Robin Lakehair, a wonderfully beautiful young woman, whose purity allows her to help Gath by removing the helmet (from time to time) and saving him from a life as its slave. It is a relationship never resolved, since she never has sex with Gath; indeed, she marries another at the end of the second volume, does not feature at all in the third volume, and even her widowhood at the end of the fourth volume leads to no particular conclusion.

Another unresolved element is that Gath is seeking his roots—the place of his birth. Although the jungle sequences in the third volume suggest that he was born in such a lush, tropical region—he possesses the innate experience to be able to do a passable Tarzan impression, swinging from tree to tree by liana and killing various oversized animals needlessly with his bare hands—he fails to remain there, or to return there at the end.

A fascinating aspect of these books is their treatment of sex. Throughout there is a facade of sexual promise. Silke provides lingering descriptions of attractive, scantily-clad young women. In particular, he returns often to Tiyy, Nymph Queen of Pyram, picturing her in a whole wardrobe of g-strings. She (300 years old, but looking just 17) is Gath's principal adversary and is allowed to fornicate occasionally with a subordinate. Gath, on the other hand, refuses sex most of the time, and in the four books he only makes it with Cobra the snake-woman and Noon the jungle queen—both times in the manner of animals rutting. Hence the myths of sex as something evil and of muscle-building as a compensation for absent sex-drive are perpetuated.

The plots of all four volumes are short on credibility. In *Prisoner of the Horned Helmet,* Gath reluctantly leads a barbarian army to victory over the invading, oriental Kitzakk horde. *Lords of Destruction* sees him saving Robin from the murderous attentions of Tiyy, then eventually invading Tiyy's own castle, Pyram, and stealing the magical jewels which transform Robin into a kind of goddess. In *Tooth and Claw,* Gath joins an expedition to a far-off jungle, just so that he can have the opportunity of killing Chyak, an enormous sabre-toothed tiger. Gath is absent from half of *Plague of Knives,* though he returns in time to save Robin (and others) from a castle besieged by Tiyy's demon-spawn army.

It must be said that Gath survives and triumphs as often through the crass stupidity of his opponents as through his own strength. Silke's imagination fails to come up with sufficiently worthy opponents; he has Gath defeating snake-men, a shark-man, a giant bat and even mole-men. Too much of the action consists of familiar, recycled plot elements rather than anything new or surprising. Reader boredom is staved off as much by the brief chapters (up to 73 per book) as anything else. The settings cover a wide variety of terrains in prehistoric Europe and Africa, including forest, desert, savannah and jungle, at a time when the Mediterranean Sea was little more than a lake.

Silke's writing style is consistently over-the-top. This is no bad thing, since it complements the whole exaggerated ethos of heroic fantasy and fits in well with Frazetta's artwork. *Prisoner of the Horned Helmet* is the most polished; the other three volumes contain a higher proportion of clumsy passages. On the whole this is an undemanding series of predictable but relatively entertaining adventures.

—Chris Morgan

SINCLAIR, Andrew (Annandale)

Nationality: British. **Born:** Oxford, 21 January 1935. **Education:** Dragon School, Oxford; Eton College, Berkshire (King's Scholar), 1848-53; Trinity College, Cambridge, 1955-58, B.A. (double 1st) in history, 1958; Churchill College, Cambridge, Ph.D. in American history, 1963. **Military Service:** Coldstream Guards, British Army, 1953-55: lieutenant. **Family:** Married Marianne Alexandre in 1960 (divorced), one son; married Miranda Seymour in 1972 (divorced), one son; married Sonia, Lady Melchett in 1984. **Career:** Fellow and director of historical studies, Churchill College, Cambridge, 1961-63; lecturer in American history, University College, London, 1965-67; managing director, Lorrimer Publishing, London, 1967-89, and Timon Films, 1969-91; novelist, historian, screenwriter and film director. **Awards:** Harkness fellowship, Harvard University, Cambridge, Massachusetts, and Columbia University, New York, 1959-61; American Council of Learned Societies fellowship, 1963-65; Somerset Maugham Literary prize, 1967; Venice Film Festival award, 1971; Cannes Film Festival prize, 1972. Fellow, Royal Society of Literature; fellow, Society of American Historians. **Agent:** Aitken, Stone and Wylie Ltd., 29 Fernshaw Road, London SW10 0TG, England.

FANTASY PUBLICATIONS

Novels (series: The Albion Triptych)

Gog (Albion). London, Weidenfeld and Nicolson, and New York, Macmillan, 1967.
Magog (Albion). London, Weidenfeld and Nicolson, and New York, Harper, 1972.
King Ludd (Albion). London, Hodder and Stoughton, 1988.

OTHER PUBLICATIONS

Novels

The Breaking of Bumbo. London, Faber, and New York, Simon and Schuster, 1959.
My Friend Judas. London, Faber, 1959; New York, Simon and Schuster, 1961.
The Project. London, Faber, and New York, Simon and Schuster, 1960.
The Hallelujah Bum. London, Faber, 1963; as *The Paradise Bum,* New York, Atheneum, 1963.
The Raker. London, Cape, and New York, Atheneum, 1964.
The Surrey Cat. London, Joseph, 1976; as *Cat,* London, Sphere, 1977.
A Patriot for Hire. London, Joseph, 1978; as *Sea of the Dead,* London, Sphere, 1981.
The Facts in the Case of E. A. Poe. London, Weidenfeld and Nicolson, 1979; New York, Holt Rinehart, 1980.
Beau Bumbo. London, Weidenfeld and Nicolson, 1985.
The Far Corners of the Earth. London, Hodder and Stoughton, 1991.
The Strength of the Hills. London, Hodder and Stoughton, 1992.

Plays

My Friend Judas, adaptation of his own novel (produced London, 1959).
Adventures in the Skin Trade, adaptation of the work by Dylan Thomas (produced London, 1966). London, Dent, 1967; New York, New Directions, 1968.
Under Milk Wood (screenplay), adaptation of the radio play by Dylan Thomas. London, Lorrimer, and New York, Simon and Schuster, 1972.
The Blue Angel, adaptation of the screenplay by Josef von Sternberg, music by Jeremy Sams (produced Liverpool, 1983).

Screenplays: *Before Winter Comes,* 1969; *The Breaking of Bumbo,* from his own novel, 1970; *Under Milk Wood,* 1972; *Blue Blood,* 1974; *Malachi's Cove,* 1977.

Television Plays: *The Chocolate Tree,* 1963; *Old Soldiers,* 1964; *The Voyage of the Beagle,* 1970; *Martin Eden,* from the novel by Jack London, 1981.

Other

Prohibition: The Era of Excess. London, Faber, and Boston, Little Brown, 1962; as *Era of Excess: A Social History of Prohibition,* New York, Harper, 1964.

The Available Man: The Life Behind the Masks of Warren Gamaliel Harding. New York, Macmillan, 1965.
The Better Half: The Emancipation of the American Woman. New York, Harper, 1965; London, Cape, 1966.
A Concise History of the United States. London, Thames and Hudson, and New York, Viking Press, 1967; revised edition, Thames and Hudson, 1970; London, Lorrimer, 1984.
The Last of the Best: The Aristocracy of Europe in the Twentieth Century. London, Weidenfeld and Nicolson, and New York, Macmillan, 1969.
Guevara. London, Fontana, 1970; as *Che Guevara,* New York, Viking Press, 1970.
Dylan Thomas: Poet of His People. London, Joseph, 1975; as *Dylan Thomas: No Man More Magical,* New York, Holt Rinehart, 1975.
Inkydoo, the Wild Boy (for children). London, Abelard Schuman, 1976; as *Carina and the Wild Boy,* London, Beaver, 1977.
The Savage: A History of Misunderstanding. London, Weidenfeld and Nicolson, 1977.
Jack: A Biography of Jack London. New York, Harper, 1977; London, Weidenfeld and Nicolson, 1978.
John Ford: A Biography. London, Allen and Unwin, and New York, Dial Press, 1979.
Corsair: The Life of J. Pierpont Morgan. London, Weidenfeld and Nicolson, and Boston, Little Brown, 1981.
The Other Victoria: The Princess Royal and the Great Game of Europe. London, Weidenfeld and Nicolson, 1981; as *Royal Web: The Story of Princess Victoria and Frederick of Prussia,* New York, McGraw Hill, 1982.
Sir Walter Raleigh and the Age of Discovery. London, Penguin, 1984.
The Red and the Blue: Intelligence, Treason and the Universities. London, Weidenfeld and Nicolson, 1986; as *The Red and the Blue: Cambridge, Treason and Intelligence,* Boston, Little Brown, 1987. *Spiegel: The Man Behind the Pictures.* London, Weidenfeld and Nicolson, 1987; as *S. P. Eagle: A Biography of Sam Spiegel,* Boston, Little Brown, 1988.
War Like a Wasp: The Lost Decade of the Forties. London, Hamish Hamilton, 1989; New York, Viking Hamilton, 1990.
The Need to Give: The Patrons and the Arts. London, Sinclair Stevenson, 1990.
The Naked Savage. London, Sinclair Stevenson, 1991.
The Sword and the Grail. New York, Crown, 1992; London, Century, 1993.
In Love and Anger: A View of the Sixties. London, Sinclair Stevenson, 1994.

Editor, *GWTW: The Screenplay,* by Sidney Howard. London, Lorrimer, 1979.
Editor, *The Call of the Wild, White Fang and Other Stories* by Jack London. London, Penguin, 1981.
Editor, *The Sea Wolf and Other Stories* by Jack London. London, Penguin, 1989.
Editor, *The War Decade: An Anthology of the 1940s.* London, Hamish Hamilton, 1989.

Translator, *Selections from the Greek Anthology.* London, Weidenfeld and Nicolson, 1967; New York, Macmillan, 1968.
Translator, with Carlos P. Hansen, *Bolivian Diary: Ernesto "Che" Guevara.* London, Lorrimer, 1968.

Translator, with Marianne Alexandre. *La Grande Illusion,* by Jean Renoir. London, Lorrimer, 1968.

Translator, *Masterworks of the French Cinema.* London, Lorrimer, 1974.

*

Film Adaptations: *The Breaking of Bumbo,* 1970.

Theatrical Activities:
Director: **Films**—*The Breaking of Bumbo,* 1970; *Under Milk Wood,* 1972; *Blue Blood,* 1974.

* * *

To use fantasy at the behest of satire is as old as Aristophanes and Dean Swift, but few works of this nature have been as large and as spirited as Andrew Sinclair's monumental Albion Triptych. Each volume, *Gog, Magog* and *King Ludd,* takes us on a journey, through space or time, which represents a "people's history" of Britain, illuminated by sudden flashes of myth, magic and mayhem. Each journey is mapped out, as he says in *King Ludd,* to show "the way of the people as one British people, as they were and are not and shall be despite history and money, class and machine".

The first volume, *Gog,* sets the pace and tone of the trilogy and provides many of the images and set pieces which recur throughout. It takes place in that brief summer of 1945 between Victory in Europe and Victory over Japan, between the election of a Labour government and the assembly of parliament. The central character, Gog, is a seven-foot giant washed ashore near Edinburgh with no visible wounds and no memory. He is, we might assume, the last injury of the war, the only means of identification the words "Gog" and "Magog" tattooed on either hand. He sets out to walk from Edinburgh to London, and his journey takes him through a series of fantastic encounters. Some of these help to establish his identity: he is a historian, George Griffin, who comes from a wealthy family and has, since being a student at Cambridge, pursued a mad and romantic notion about the might and movement of the common people. His half-brother, whom he calls "Magog," is a government functionary and epitome of everything that Gog holds as evil; and his wife, Maire, might be trying to kill him. Other encounters, more bizarre, reflect and often undermine Gog's notions. In films, in stories, in dreams, in extracts from his own papers, Gog is granted kaleidoscopic glimpses of his notion of the tragic history of the people of England, a history in which he, his ancestors or his legendary namesake play a leading if ineffectual part. Characters such as Wayland Merlin Blake Smith, who sees himself as the fourth in a line of great visionaries with a mystical destiny to seize the means of broadcasting, and Maurice, the sly profiteer, reflect the dichotomy that lies at the heart of this book. The symbolic figures of Gog and Magog, the visionary and the profiteer, the common man and the ruler, the deluded and the powerful, echo throughout the trilogy and go to the core of Sinclair's profound, angry, panoramic vision of England, her people and her history.

It is not easy to disentangle the object of Sinclair's satire, for everything is a target. If his greatest wrath is reserved for industry and capital, for machines and for those who rule—collectively characterized as Moloch—he is quite as ready to castigate the working man, socialism, or failure to come to grips with

progress. At times the book reads as if he regrets the loss of a mythical golden age in which men worked the land free of machines and cities; at other times he dismisses such notions as fantasy.

The second volume, *Magog,* takes the story on from 1945 to 1970. The least fantastical of the three books, it is a chronicle of Magog's corruption as a civil servant ready to lie on oath, as head of the British film industry ready to destroy that industry for his own profit, as a Rachman-esque landlord, as a university chancellor ready to corrupt others to claim a spurious scholarship. At the same time his illicit relationship with the scheming Maire, and with his growing family, reveal the limits of what his corruption can achieve and the poverty of his emotional life. Here the satire is more tightly focused, though amid this biting attack on Britain in decline Sinclair manages to lash out at a number of other targets along the way, and many of the familiar oddballs from the first book, notably the greedy and unprincipled Maurice, reappear to telling effect.

But it is the third volume, *King Ludd,* which really ties the trilogy together in the most audacious and inventive way. The book begins in Cambridge in 1937, where Gog's imaginative account of the origins of the Luddites is rejected by his tutor as too fanciful, where his recreation of the runic alphabet inspires a mathematician, and where he finds himself on the fringes of fascist and communist groups. The novel then tells the story of Gog's life, his runic alphabet providing a key for wartime code makers and breakers, while his political associations find him drawn into the morally shady world of espionage with fatal consequences. This is counterpointed with the story of Luddism as imagined by Gog, in which Ned Ludd is identified with Gog's forefather who becomes a near-mythic figure stalking through episodes of popular revolt and discontent from 1811 to the General Strike of 1926 and beyond. Always the medieval giants, Gog and Magog, stand symbolically in the background and wild, often erotic or farcical moments of fantasy are counterpointed with historic tragedy or a wild, often farcical moment in Gog's history. But however monumental the fantasy, however bizarre the comedy, the overall tone of the satire is one of tragedy rather than farce, until at the end the book moves forward to take the story of Gog's son forward into the age of the computers.

Two elements which run consistently throughout these three books—which together add up to one of the most dazzling and fantastical accounts of Britain's history in literature—are the themes of family and of myth. The two are intimately connected: however dysfunctional Gog's family is (in any generation) it echoes or at times replays moments of myth which represent national identity. The popular history which is the subject of the Albion Triptych is also the history of any family. And these themes, without again amounting to such a grand design, have cropped up significantly in Sinclair's other works. In his non-fiction book *The Sword and the Grail,* for instance, which purports to examine such deeply mythic subjects as "the story of the Grail, the Templars and the true discovery of America," his investigations begin with a presumed ancestor, Sir William de St. Clair; while his most recent series of novels have used the story of his own family as the subject for a family saga which reflects the history the British Empire over the last century or so. It is as if his family has become entangled in the myth he is creating of his own Albion.

—Paul Kincaid

SKALDASPILLIR, Sigfridur. *See* **BROXON, Mildred Downey.**

SMITH, Clark Ashton

Nationality: American. **Born:** Long Valley, California, 13 January 1893. **Education:** Auburn, California; left school at 14 and largely self-educated. **Family:** Married Carolyn Jones Dorman in 1954. **Career:** Farmer and general labourer; poet, short-story writer (from 1910), artist and sculptor: regular contributor to *Weird Tales* in the early 1930s; ceased writing commercially in 1936. **Died:** 14 August 1961.

FANTASY PUBLICATIONS

Short Stories

The Double Shadow and Other Fantasies. Auburn, California, privately printed, 1933.
The White Sybil. Everett, Pennsylvania, Fantasy, 1935(?).
Out of Space and Time (includes verse). Sauk City, Wisconsin, Arkham House, 1942; London, Spearman, 1971.
Lost Worlds. Sauk City, Wisconsin, Arkham House, 1944; London, Spearman, 1971.
Genius Loci. Sauk City, Wisconsin, Arkham House, 1948; London, Spearman, 1972.
The Abominations of Yondo. Sauk City, Wisconsin, Arkham House, 1960; London, Spearman, 1972.
Tales of Science and Sorcery. Sauk City, Wisconsin, Arkham House, 1964; London, Panther, 1976.
Zothique, Hyperborea, Xiccarph, Poseidonis (selections), edited by Lin Carter. New York, Ballantine, 4 vols., 1970-73.
Other Dimensions. Sauk City, Wisconsin, Arkham House, 1970; London, Panther, 2 vols., 1977.
The Mortuary. Glendale, California, Squires, 1971.
Prince Alcouz and the Magician. Glendale, California, Squires, 1977.
The City of the Singing Flame, edited by Donald Sidney-Fryer. New York, Pocket, 1981.
The Last Incantation, edited by Donald Sidney-Fryer. New York, Pocket, 1982.
The Monster of the Prophecy, edited by Donald Sidney-Fryer. New York, Pocket, 1983.
Untold Tales. Bloomfield, New York, Cryptic, 1984.
The Unexpurgated Clark Ashton Smith, edited by Steve Behrends. West Warwick, Rhode Island, Necronomicon Press, 6 vols., 1987-88.
A Rendezvous in Averoigne: Best Fantastic Tales of Clark Ashton Smith. Sauk City, Wisconsin, Arkham House, 1988.
Strange Shadows: The Uncollected Fiction and Essays of Clark Ashton Smith, edited by Steve Behrends, Donald Sidney-Fryer, and Rah Hoffman. New York, and London, Greenwood, 1989.

Poetry

The Star-Treader and Other Poems. San Francisco, Robertson, 1912.

Odes and Sonnets. San Francisco, Book Club of California, 1918.
Ebony and Crystal: Poems in Verse and Prose. Privately printed, 1923.
Sandalwood. Privately printed, 1925.
Nero and Other Poems. Lakeport, California, Futile Press, 1937.
The Dark Chateau and Other Poems. Sauk City, Wisconsin, Arkham House, 1951.
Spells and Philtres. Sauk City, Wisconsin, Arkham House, 1958.
Poems in Prose. Sauk City, Wisconsin, Arkham House, 1964.
Fugitive Poems. Privately printed, 4 vols., 1974-75.
Nostalgia of the Unknown: The Complete Prose Poetry, edited by Marc and Susan Michaud. West Warwick, Rhode Island, Necronomicon Press, 1988.
The Hashish-Eater; or, The Apocalypse of Evil. West Warwick, Rhode Island, Necronomicon Press, 1989.

OTHER PUBLICATIONS

Short Stories

The Immortals of Mercury. New York, Stellar, 1932.

Other

Grotesques and Fantastiques (drawings), edited by Gerry de la Ree. Saddle River, New Jersey, de la Ree, 1973.
Planets and Dimensions: Collected Essays, edited by Charles K. Wolfe. Baltimore, Mirage Press, 1973.
Klarkash-ton and Monstro Ligriv, with Virgil Finlay (letters), edited by Gerry de la Ree. Saddle River, New Jersey, de la Ree, 1974.
The Black Book of Clark Ashton Smith, edited by Donald Sidney-Fryer and Rah Hoffman. Sauk City, Wisconsin, Arkham House, 1979.
Clark Ashton Smith: Letters to H. P. Lovecraft, edited by Steve Behrends. West Warwick, Rhode Island, Necronomicon Press, 1987.
The Devil's Notebook: Collected Epigrams and Pensées of Clark Ashton Smith, edited by Don Herron. Mercer Island, Washington, Starmont House, 1990.

*

Bibliography: *The Tales of Clark Ashton Smith: A Bibliography* by G. L. Cockcroft, Melling, New Zealand, Cockcroft, 1952; *Emperor of Dreams: A Clark Ashton Smith Bibliography* by Donald Sidney-Fryer and others, West Kingston, Rhode Island, Grant, 1978.

Critical Studies: *In Memoriam Clark Ashton Smith* edited by Jack L. Chalker, Baltimore, Anthem, 1963; *The Last of the Great Romantic Poets* by Donald Sidney-Fryer, Albuquerque, Silver Scarab Press, 1973; *The Fantastic Art of Clark Ashton Smith* by Dennis Rickard, Baltimore, Mirage Press, 1973; *Clark Ashton Smith* by Steve Behrends, Mercer Island, Washington, Starmont House, 1990.

*   *   *

The stories that Clark Ashton Smith produced during his one brief phase of hectic productivity, which extended from 1929 to 1934, constitute one of the most remarkable *oeuvres* in imaginative literature. His highly ornamented prose was directed to the purpose of building phantasmagoric dreamworlds stranger than any that had ever been described before. It was not enough for his fantastic narratives to escape the mundane world; Smith wanted to outdo in imaginative reach all the established mythologies of past and present. This ambition is summarized and made explicit in the prose-poem "To the Daemon," and in a letter to *Amazing Stories* (October 1932) where Smith proposed that "one of [literature's] most glorious prerogatives is the exercise of imagination on things that lie beyond human experience . . . into the awful, sublime and infinite cosmos outside the human aquarium . . . [offering] a welcome and salutary release from the somewhat oppressive tyranny of the homocentric, and [helping] to correct the deeply introverted, ingrowing values that are fostered by present-day 'humanism' and . . . unhealthy materialism." Despite its fervent escapist thrust, however, there is nothing comfortable or consolatory about Smith's fiction: his characters are almost invariably led by the irresistible allure of the exotic to disappointment, damnation and doom.

The most immediate influence on Smith's work was that of the California poet George Sterling, one of a group of West Coast "Bohemians" centred on Ambrose Bierce, but the real roots of his work are to be found in the French Decadent Movement which inspired the American Bohemians. Smith taught himself French so that he could read such work in the original, and produced many translations of work by Baudelaire and poets of a similar stripe. His early poetry shows these influences very clearly, especially the 29 poems in prose in *Ebony and Crystal*. Several of his later stories elaborate images from these prose-poems and it was here that he first cultivated the unique tone and worldview of his fiction. Although he shares with the French Decadents a desperate ennui and an intemperate spleen Smith's work differs from theirs by virtue of his adoption of a worldview similar to that of his friend H. P. Lovecraft, which drew extensively—if somewhat eccentrically—upon the imagery of science, involving both the awesomeness of the modern cosmic perspective and the detachment and clinicality of the scientific outlook.

Smith had some difficulty finding an appropriate milieu for his fiction. The imaginary French province of Averoigne allowed him scope for pastiches of French fantasy—"The End of the Story" (1930) echoes the theme of Théophile Gautier's "Clarimonde," while "The Disinterment of Venus" (1934) replays Prosper Merimée's "The Venus of Ille"—but not for the produce of his wilder imaginings. Atlantis, first featured in the extended prose-poem "The Last Incantation" (1930), was more promising, the exoticism of Atlantean sorcery being displayed to its fullest advantage in "The Double Shadow" (1933) and "The Death of Malygris" (1934), but also too narrow in scope.

Hyperborea, first used in "The Tale of Satampra Zeiros" (1931), features in a number of tales which Smith called "Hyperborean Grotesques" because of their heavy irony. "The Door to Saturn" (1932) is one of the least violent and most sardonic of all Smith's stories, but "The Weird of Avoosl Wuthoqquan" (1932), follows a typical pattern of reckless greed leading to macabre extinction, as do "The Ice-Demon" (1933), "Ubbo-Sathla" (1933) and the magnificently bizarre "The Coming of the White Worm" (1941). The most savagely sarcastic of all the Hyperborean tales is "The Testament of Athammaus" (1932)—in which a hapless headsman is called upon to execute a demonic bandit but finds his victim miraculously capable of rising from the dead, becoming more loathsome every time—but the best is "The Seven Geases" (1934), in which a vainglorious magistrate goes hunting for extraordinary prey but falls

prey himself to the wrath of a sorcerer and is condemned to descend through a series of Tartarean realms to "the ultimate source of all miscreation and abomination."

The most dramatically appropriate of all Smith's imaginary milieux was far-future Zothique, "the world's last continent." Because Hyperborea existed in Earth's past, the viewpoint of stories set there had to accept the implication that Order would ultimately oust Chaos, but in Zothique the implied future is empty; science and civilization are gone and utterly forgotten, and all that happens there is but a prelude to final annihilation. The first Zothique story was "The Empire of the Necromancers" (1932), a nightmarish extravaganza in which two magicians conjure themselves an empire out of the dust of the ages and the corpses of the ancient dead, but then reap a just reward after the rebellion of their subjects. Some stories set there—like "The Voyage of King Euvoran" (1933)—are as ironic as the Hyperborean grotesques, but the best of them are possessed of an unparalleled dramatic surge which carries them helter-skelter through a mass of bizarre detail to devastating conclusions. They frequently contain erotic elements, but the seductive sorceresses who feature in "The Witchcraft of Ulua" (1934) and "The Death of Ilalotha" (1937) are not treated with the same sentimental affection as the sorceresses and lamias of the tales of Averoigne. This somewhat necrophilic eroticism exists side-by-side with savage cruelty; torture is a commonplace in Zothique and sadism is the norm.

These quasi-pornographic features are not evidences of any depravity on the part of the author, but rather represent a determined effort to confront and make manageable the most nightmarish products of the imagination. The characters in the Zothique stories move in quasi-ritual step toward their predestined dooms, sometimes taking entire cities with them—as in "The Dark Eidolon" (1935), which features a literal feast of horrors. Such is the inversion of values permitted by the setting that it is the echoes of affection and success which resound in the tales which seem in the end to be the most awful things of all; this can be clearly seen in the horrible denouements of finest tales of Zothique, "Xeethra" (1934) and "Necromancy in Naat" (1936). Both these stories are among the numerous Smith tales known to have been censored; where the original texts could still be restored they were done so in the 1987-88 series of booklets published by the Necronomicon Press, but the true ending of "Necromancy in Naat" is unfortunately lost.

Fully to appreciate the work of Clark Ashton Smith requires more than a broad vocabulary and a sympathy for stylistic ornamentation; it requires the reader to identify with the curious world-view enshrined in that work: a determination to get as far away from mundanity as language and the imagination can take one, there to discover a universe utterly alien and inhumane and to find in that revelation a sense of propriety which outweighs in value any mere comfort or pleasure. This may make Smith a difficult writer to enjoy, but it should not detract at all from the great respect to which he is entitled.

—Brian Stableford

SMITH, Julie Dean

Nationality: American. **Born:** Lafayette, Indiana, 6 December 1960. **Education:** University of Michigan, 1978-82, B.A. in English and economics; Western Michigan University, 1983-84, M.A. in English. **Career:** Technical writer, Nastec Corporation, Southfield, Michigan, 1984-89; senior technical writer, Knowledge Ware, Novi, Michigan, 1989-93; senior creative writer, Imagine Multimedia, Ann Arbor, Michigan, from 1993. **Agent:** Joshua Bilmes, Scott Meredith Literary Agency, 845 Third Avenue, New York, NY 10022, USA. **Address:** 1308 Colgate Circle, Ann Arbor, MI 48103, USA.

FANTASY PUBLICATIONS

Novels (series: Caithan Crusade in all books)

Call of Madness. New York, Del Rey, 1990.
Mission of Magic. New York, Del Rey, 1991.
The Sage of Sare. New York, Del Rey, 1992.
The Wizard King. New York, Del Rey, 1994.

*

Julie Dean Smith comments:

I've always been intrigued by the idea of magic being a powerful force that can completely take over someone—whether they want to be taken over or not. I'm also fascinated by the differences—and similarities—between magic and religion, and enjoy exploring the moral/ethical consequences of using magic. I also have a fondness for good, old-fashioned story-telling, so I try to balance some of these "heavier" ideas with an exciting story and well-drawn, likable characters.

*   *   *

Julie Dean Smith's books show an originality that lifts them above the ranks of generic fantasy to which they might appear at first to belong. Her approaches to magic, to religion, and to people reveal depth and maturity. If her series of novels is not a major artistic achievement, it is a respectable one which shows promise for the future.

Her four novels to date make up a sequence called A Caithan Crusade. They are set in the kingdom of Caithe, where magic power is regarded as a curse, with good reason, since those who develop it inevitably descend into destructive, homicidal madness. It turns out, though, that this results only if those with magic—here called the Lorngeld—do not receive proper training, which they have been unable to do in Caithe since a long-ago crusade killed all the trained Lorngeld, outlawed the teaching of magic, and declared magic powers a gift of the Devil and their possessors damned. As soon as someone displays signs of magic, which usually occurs at about age 20, he or she is ritually slaughtered by the Church in a rite called "absolution."

A Caithan Crusade tells the story of Athaya Trelane, Princess of Caithe, who in the first book, *Call of Madness,* must come to terms with her own developing magic power, unlearning all she has believed about its evil. After she accidentally kills her father, the King, in a burst of untrained power, she is outlawed and flees to neighbouring Reyka, where magic is practised and respected. In the next book, *Mission of Magic,* Athaya begins the crusade of the series title, secretly training newborn Lorngeld, saving them from absolution, and trying to convince her obdurate brother Durek, who now holds the throne, that magic is not evil but is in fact a gift of God. In the third and fourth books of the series, Athaya confronts

an enemy even more dangerous than Durek or the Church, in the person of the Sage of Sare, an extraordinarily powerful wizard who believes that the Lorngeld, blessed by God, are destined to rule, and who plans to conquer Caithe and assume its throne. In the end, only Athaya can defeat the Sage, with some help from unexpected quarters, and at a high cost to herself and others.

The cost of magic is an important issue. Every power, every gift, has its cost, and Athaya must confront those costs with each step she takes, whether it be as grand as launching a crusade to liberate the Caithan Lorngeld or as personal as accepting the marriage proposal of the wizard she loves, but for whose safety she fears.

Athaya grows remarkably and convincingly throughout the books. She begins as spoiled, impulsive, hot-tempered, often annoying. The first book serves as her rite of passage, launching her into the world of adult responsibility. Even after Athaya's magic has begun to mature her, she remains impulsive, often doing things that better judgment would have advised against. These actions are also necessary to propel the plot, but the depiction of Athaya's character makes them convincing.

The period of madness preceding the arrival of a wizard's power is called the *mekahn,* and with its moodiness, its flares of temper, its uncertainty, and its uncontrollable impulses, it is adolescence writ large. It is no wonder that the reader, particularly the young reader, can identify with Athaya. The outcome is reassuring, as she develops into a capable, powerful woman and wizard.

Athaya's brother Durek is a fascinating character. Little better than a cartoon villain in the first book, his portrayal matures as the series progresses. He is filled with hatred and fear for the Lorngeld, convinced they are damned, unwilling to listen to anything said by anyone that does not accord with his preconceptions. Athaya and the reader gradually realize how much his hostility is hiding insecurity at his ability to fill his father's shoes, as well as reflecting long-term problems in his relationship with Athaya. As the two siblings ally in *The Wizard King* to defeat the Sage, their relationship warms in a convincing manner, until Durek's final self-sacrifice to save Athaya is believable and tragic.

One aspect of the novels that Smith does not handle as well as she might is the ethics of magic. One wonders why someone like the Sage has not taken over long ago, and how the ethics that prevent most Lorngeld from aspiring to power developed, but the issue does not come up. Some of Athaya's ethical decisions, in particular her decision not to use the power she develops to see who will become a wizard before the onset of the *mekahn,* are not well argued. There is also an ambiguity over her choice of tactics. Many argue with her that her strategy of peaceful civil disobedience while Lorngeld are being killed by a powerful inquisition will not accomplish her goal of freeing the Lorngeld to practice magic, and in the absence of the Sage's intervention, it is not clear that her Gandhi-like tactics would have worked. They seem to be making little or no progress against an entrenched, vicious hatred and a powerful Church.

Smith's characters are occasionally too obtuse, missing something that has been obvious to the reader for chapters. They also miss a major contradiction in Smith's world. The crystals called corbal are deadly to wizards, causing intense pain and an inability to do magic. Though we learn eventually that some wizards can overcome the pain and continue to function in a corbal's presence, that functioning is not perfect and magic remains unavailable. Yet Faltil, the wizard-king who, jealous of anyone else with power, launched the crusade that killed all the other Lorngeld in Caithe, wore a crown studded with enormous corbals, used as a weapon in this series. The perceptive reader keeps waiting for some explanation to be made, for some wizard to realize the contradiction; neither happens.

Smith's writing is generally good, though she is occasionally careless. It can be vivid, particularly in her descriptions of magic, but her depiction of the environment in which the characters operate is less memorable.

Smith's books are no vast departure from what has gone before, but neither are they cookie-cutter fantasy. She shows originality and a gift for creating character, along with occasional writing that rises above the ordinary. The Caithan Crusade novels are worth reading, and her future work is likely to be more so.

—Janice M. Eisen

SMITH, Thorne

Nationality: American. **Born:** Annapolis, Maryland, 1893; son of a naval officer. **Education:** Locust Dale Academy, Virginia; St. Luke's School, Wayne, Pennyslvania; Dartmouth College. **Military Service:** U.S. Navy during World War I (editor, service paper *Broadside*). **Family:** Married Celia Sullivan; two daughters. **Career:** In advertising, then freelance author; Hollywood screenwriter, 1933-34. **Died:** 21 June 1934.

Fantasy Publications

Novels (series: Topper)

Topper: An Improbable Adventure. New York, McBride, and London, Holden, 1926; as *The Jovial Ghosts: The Misadventures of Topper.* London, Barker, 1933.
The Stray Lamb. New York, Cosmopolitan, 1929; London, Heinemann, 1930.
The Night Life of the Gods. New York, Doubleday Doran, 1931; London, Barker, 1934.
Turnabout. New York, Doubleday Doran, 1931; London, Barker, 1933.
Topper Takes a Trip. New York, Doubleday Doran, 1932; London, Barker, 1935.
Skin and Bones. New York, Doubleday Doran, 1933; London, Barker, 1936.
Rain in the Doorway. New York, Doubleday Doran, 1933; London, Barker, 1936.
The Glorious Pool. New York, Doubleday Doran, 1934; London, Barker, 1935.
The Passionate Witch (completed by Norman Matson). New York, Doubleday Doran, 1941; London, Barker, 1942.

Other Publications

Novels

Dream's End. New York, McBride, 1927; London, Jarrolds, 1928.
Did She Fall? New York, Cosmopolitan, 1930; London, Barker, 1936.

The Bishop's Jaegers. New York, Doubleday Doran, 1932; London, Barker, 1934.

Poetry

Haunts and By-Paths. New York, Stokes, 1919.

Other

Biltmore Oswald. New York, Stokes, 1918.
Out o' Luck. New York, Stokes, 1919.
Lazy Bear Lane (for children). New York, Doubleday Doran, 1931.
Thorne Smith: His Life and Times, with Roland Young and others. New York, Doubleday Doran, 1934.

*

Film Adaptations: *Topper,* 1937, 1979 (TV movie); *Topper Takes a Trip,* 1939; *Turnabout,* 1940; *Topper Returns,* 1941, based on Smith's characters; *I Married a Witch,* 1942, from his novel *The Passionate Witch.*

*   *   *

If one were to attempt to fabricate a writer from bits and pieces of Charles Bukowski, S. J. Perelman, Damon Runyon, Lewis Carroll and Mark Twain, one might possibly come close to creating a figure like Thorne Smith. But such a chimera would still surely not possess the original's high-spirited elan, sense of utter irresponsibility and fine disdain for all forms of convention—traits which found their perfect embodiment in a series of "ribald" screwball novels where the fantastic plays a pivotal part in disrupting society, unleashing repressed individuals and shattering unnatural strictures.

Born to a career-navy father, Commodore James Thorne Smith, the younger Smith was caught up in the First World War—an experience that apparently led to a lifelong pacifism and repugnance for war (but not, paradoxically, for literary expression of individual acts of sometimes sadistic mischief). While enlisted, he helped edit a navy publication, *Broadside*. Upon being discharged, he wrote an autobiographical volume about his wartime experiences: *Biltmore Oswald.* This was a success, selling 70,000 copies, and he followed it with a sequel, *Out o' Luck.* He took up residence in New York's Greenwich Village, then a literary hotspot, and associated with writers such as Sinclair Lewis. Publishing poetry in various magazines such as *Smart Set* and *The Liberator,* he eventually compiled enough for a volume of verse, *Haunts and Bypaths.*

A marriage entailed greater expenses, and Smith found himself firmly ensconced in an advertising firm—an industry which was to come in for its share of derision in his novels. Then, in 1926, Smith unleashed *Topper.* This novel, a fully formed, unique and self-assured encapsulation of practically all of Smith's concerns and tropes, was to serve as a template for nearly all of his future books.

Mr. Cosmo Topper is a bored, civic-minded, rule-following commuter, a placid resident of suburbia (a sociological phenomenon which was just gaining steam during Smith's time). Henpecked by a woman who is no longer the one he fell in love with and married (wives who let themselves deteriorate and become unadventurous and unloving come in for a lot of flak in Smith's books, opening him up to charges of misogyny which fortunately evaporate when one considers that his scorn was equally withering when directed against similar members of his own gender), Topper goes about his daily routines feeling vaguely dissatisfied. This unease finds an outlet in the purchase of a car—a car haunted by the ghosts of its former owners, George and Marion Kerby, "the fastest young couple in town," who died in a spectacular crash.

Soon the ghosts—"low-plane spirits," explains Marion, still interested in sex, liquor, gambling and juvenile gags—attach themselves to Topper and, without much trouble, quickly seduce him into a life of heavy drinking (Prohibition loomed large in Smith's books as the ultimate icon of stupidity), ectoplasmic smooching and petting, and minor transgressions against the limbs, propriety and property of the stolid citizens and institutions of the surrounding countryside. One hilarious cataclysmic event follows another with a dream logic bordering on sheer randomness (Smith on his method of composition: "Like life itself my stories have no point and get absolutely nowhere . . . Quite casually, I wander into my plot, poke around with my characters for a while, then amble off, leaving no moral proved and no reader improved"). As society's nose is thoroughly and amusingly tweaked, Topper learns how to enjoy himself and what matters in life. The book's action is brought to a close by a second car crash, and the disappearance of the ghostly couple (who would later appear for similar hijinks in a French Riviera setting in *Topper Takes a Trip*).

To summarize: a Smith book is almost invariably told from the point of view of a middle-aged, stuck-in-a-rut protagonist whose life opens up upon the advent of a supernatural agent or miraculous invention without which no action could occur. Authority is mocked and seen as blind and misguided; life is revealed as a precarious mystery trip, exploding the false sense of security striven for by the majority of citizens; hedonism and a pagan libertine existence are experimented with and generally endorsed, even if eventually abandoned in favour of a less strenuous, yet open-eyed and newly catholic lifestyle.

During this ride, the reader will certainly encounter many of Smith's leitmotifs: uninhibited young women prone to cavort in their underwear; stern judges whose courtrooms soon become shambles; false beards and detached limbs; goofy dogs and wilful animals; flustered French maids and sputtering Irish cops (Smith's work is remarkably free of the ethnic stereotypes common to his era, and, unlike much older fiction, can be read without wincing); and pompous bosses and macho men who are easily reduced to tears by a good dose of Smith's illogic. (Smith was unsurpassed in the creation of meandering, stoned conversations calculated to force language close to the breaking point.)

In *The Stray Lamb*, Mr. T. Lawrence Lamb, whose ungainly lanky build is another Smith talisman, finds himself—due to attention from "a little russet man" demigod—changing form from one animal to another. Aided by an understanding daughter who's intent on fixing him up with her best girlfriend (despite the inconvenient presence of Lamb's wife) the protagonist has a generally marvellous time. The minor persecution Lamb suffers at the end of the book echoes the more serious, even Christ-like suffering experienced by the skeleton-exhibiting Quintus Bland of *Skin and Bones*: rare instances of Smith attempting to impose symbolic roles on his generally non-emblematic characters. *Turnabout* deals unabashedly and surprisingly candidly with a husband and wife who involuntarily swap bodies and are forced to step into each other's routines and roles. Sex between them inevitably follows the switch, the "husband" becomes pregnant, delivers a child, and, by the time their natural forms are restored, the couple have learned a valuable lesson in empathy.

The same year saw the publication of one of Smith's masterpieces, *The Night Life of the Gods*. From its deft opening chapter, "Criticizing an Explosion" (Smith was fond of bizarrely intriguing chapter titles), in which the cast is expertly introduced, to its final elegiac and surprisingly affecting ending, the book astonishingly conflates eccentric inventor Hunter Hawk and his petrification ray with elves and Greek gods, as they wreak havoc on Manhattan. *Did She Fall?* (which had seen magazine serialization in *Cosmopolitan,* 1930) is perhaps Smith's weakest book, and also his most rigorously plotted. A murder mystery without fantasy content, its characters exhibit the very same conventional attitudes mocked elsewhere.

Rain in the Doorway is Smith's other masterwork. Snatched into an adjacent dimension where all the women are willing, work is a joke, and booze flows like water, Mr. Hector Owen finds himself partner in a firm reminiscent of the establishment run by the Marx Brothers in *The Big Store* (1941). Accidentally forced to return to our own sorrowful, rain-drenched world, Mr. Owen manages to retain the company of his new girlfriend, who promises to brighten even this vale of tears. Continuing the Utopian theme of *Rain, The Bishop's Jaegers* finds Peter Van Dyck captive in an experimental nudist colony run by an authoritarian ideologist, at the mercy of his pursuing secretary, who eventually lands her man. A strong and enjoyable entry, despite lack of a fantasy motivator. Also missing from this book is any drunkenness, and a reader is tempted to see an actual turn to sobriety in Smith's real life.

The Glorious Pool, while full of fine moments—not the least of which is the resonant central notion of youth magically restored—suffers from a sense of distraction and ennui, and an unsatisfying, even bewildering climax. Published in the year of Smith's untimely death, it can be seen as a work in need of one more revision which death foreclosed. *The Passionate Witch* (published posthumously upon completion by Norman Matson), whose basic gimmick is identical to that of Fritz Leiber's later *Conjure Wife* (1943), is even less satisfying. Monitory and unsubtle, endorsing a good-evil dichotomy elsewhere nonexistent in Smith's novels, it includes the only onstage death of Smith's work, which, while undeniably underpinned and fuelled by a sense of mortality, always chose to concentrate upon the joys of life, however short and ragged.

From the blatant Smithian mouths and morals of Robert Heinlein's female characters, through the quintessential Smith pastiche by John D. MacDonald (*The Girl, the Gold Watch, & Everything,* 1962), and onward to the goofy and whimsical fantasies of James P. Blaylock, and the "freestyle" writing of Rudy Rucker, the organically zany, life-affirming fiction of Thorne Smith continues to make its influence felt.

—Paul Di Filippo

SNYDER, Midori

Nationality: American. **Address:** c/o Tor Books, 175 Fifth Avenue, New York, NY 10010, USA.

FANTASY PUBLICATIONS

Novels (series: The Queen's Quarter)

Soulstring. New York, Ace, 1987.

New Moon (Queen's Quarter). New York, Tor, and London, Unwin, 1989.
Sadar's Keep (Queen's Quarter). London, Unwin, 1990; New York, Tor, 1991.
Beldan's Fire (Queen's Quarter). New York, Tor, 1993.
The Flight of Michael McBride. New York, Tor, 1994.

* * *

Midori Snyder has developed strongly as a writer of high fantasy, from the relatively straightforward *Soulstring* to the much more complex Queen's Quarter trilogy, with its deeply entangled web of plots. *Soulstring,* written in the first person, concerns Magda de'Stain Moravia, who through the accident of being the firstborn child of a sorcerer father inherits his gift for enchantment, to his intense disgust; the de'Stains have for 13 generations produced sons as firstborn and heirs. Although her father, Gregor, binds her magic when she is young so she is unable to use it, he cannot take it from her; horrified at the prospect of providing any neighboring kingdom with a wife capable of producing a sorceress heir, Gregor invents a series of tests for Magda's potential suitors to ensure none can win her, torturing them to death when they fail the tests.

The story develops along fairly conventional lines, with the advent of a suitor gifted himself with magic and who passes the tests to win Magda, who duly falls in love with him. However, Snyder inserts a new twist to the plot with the invention of the eponymous soulstring, a physical bond between the lovers which protects Severin, the suitor, from the wrath of Gregor when the pair flee the castle to return to Severin's homeland. In the process of their flight Severin is transformed into a stag, and Magda must make the journey essentially alone, and only at the end may her love prove sufficient to bring Severin back to his human form. The development of Magda's character in the process of her flight is well done as she changes from the self-absorbed, self-centered girl of Moravia Castle to become the loving, generous woman who restores her husband's true form.

The Queen's Quarter trilogy, in contrast, is neither conventional nor simple. Snyder has created the world of Oran, held together only by the force and balance of elemental magic, without which it will cease to exist. Four women, each representing one of the powers of nature—air, water, earth, and fire—guarded the land until Zorah, the beautiful fire queen, destroyed the other three (Huld and her own two sisters) and made time stop for herself, terrified of ageing and death. She imposes her own oppressive rule on Oran, bringing in the Sileans from overseas to control her country, ordering the death of all Oran children who have the gift of magic so that no power may rise against her rule and form a new Queen's Quarter Knot to depose her. Of the old Knot, only Huld survives, but her power is being drained from her, and Oran is slowly being destroyed as it becomes unbalanced.

Yet Zorah has failed to destroy magic in Oran, and the New Moon—the rebel forces—have a plan to defeat her. Into the world, 200 years after her seizure of power, are born four children, each with one of the four elemental gifts. As the many plots of the trilogy develop, the quartet are drawn together in the New Moon to become a force to rival the queen herself. The various conflicts in the novels are far more complex than this simple summary. The four girls are not Queen Zorah's only nemesis, for there is also the part-Oran Re Desturo, the evil Silean nobleman who drinks the magic from Oran children; he has his own ambition to become King of Oran by stealing the elemental magic for himself. Nor are the

quartet a unity, since there is a strong antipathy implanted between Jobber, the urchin with the gift of fire, and Shedwyn, the peasant girl who possesses earth magic. Lirrel, whose element is air, is a Ghazali and opposed to fighting, and Shedwyn has chosen a renegade Silean as her mate, to the disgust of many. The Sileans themselves are dissatisfied with their position in Oran, and in the city of Beldan there is a constant battle between native Orans and the Silean guards. The action in the novels leaps from place to place, from character to character, but without losing the train of the narrative despite the wide scope of the plot. Snyder manages to incorporate an immense amount of detailed description of her world and its customs through her extensive variety of characters, which include such oddities as Shefek, the Kirian bird/man, renegade Sileans, a host of Beldan street urchins, and Zorah herself. The only criticism it might be fair to offer is that the constant skipping from place to place tends to reduce empathy with the leading players in the trilogy, since although they develop as characters they are only observed at brief moments; however, given the complexity of the novels it is hard to see how they might otherwise have been constructed.

There are many points of strong originality in the magic invention in Queen's Quarter; Snyder has avoided a great many obvious choices, electing some really unusual concepts such as the Oran Zein and his few companions who became trees with the deposed Queen Huld in order to slow the passage of time and reduce the flow of magic from Huld to Zorah. The elemental gifts in their lesser forms, as extant in some Oran children, also provide intriguing possibilities—such as the street-child Neive, whose earth-element guides him through tunnels of stone as he helps to rescue the rebel Kai and her fellow prisoners from a Silean prison in Beldan. There is a satisfying logic and consistency to Snyder's power-structure which nonetheless succeeds in not constraining the action of her characters.

The Queen's Quarter novels reveal how strongly Snyder's plotting, imaginative, and descriptive skills have developed and represent an impressive achievement. It will be intriguing to see where next her talents will lead her.

—Mary Corran

SPEDDING, (Alison Louise)

Nationality: British. **Born:** Belper, Derbyshire, 22 January 1962. **Education:** Abbey School, Reading, Berkshire, 1972-79; King's College, Cambridge, 1979-82, B.A., and 1984-85, M. Phil; London School of Economics, 1985-89, Ph.D. in social anthropology. **Career:** Lecturer in anthropology, Universidad Mayor de San Andres, La Paz, Bolivia, from 1992. **Address:** Casilla 3988, La Paz, Bolivia.

FANTASY PUBLICATIONS

Novels (series: A Walk in the Dark in all books)

The Road and the Hills. London, Allen and Unwin, 1986.
A Cloud Over Water. London, Unwin Hyman, 1988.
The Streets of the City. London, Unwin Hyman, 1988.

*

Spedding comments:

I have travelled in Jamaica, Peru, Columbia, the People's Republic of China and elsewhere. Since 1989 I have been resident in Bolivia, and apart from English I speak and write in Spanish and Aymara (a native American language spoken mainly in Bolivia and Peru). "Spedding" is the name I use, *tout court,* for my fictional publications; "Alison Spedding" publishes anthropological articles.

The Walk in the Dark series is historical fantasy, based on the career of Alexander the Great and the wars of his successors, with doses of anthropological speculation such as the matrilineal society of S'Thurrulass. It reads more like a historical novel than "conventional" fantasy (no elves, dwarfs or dragons here) and its main interest lies in its lively central character.

I now work mainly in Spanish; my forthcoming short-story collection, *El Tiempo, La Distancia, Otres Amantes* (Time, Distance, Other Lovers) includes only one fantasy story, "Mama Huaca in the First Circle," which combines Inca origin mythology with Dante. I have just completed a historical novel, about the coca trade and the extirpation of idolatry in the 17th-century Andes, to be followed by a thriller set in 1984 Bolivia (hyper-inflation and the cocaine trade) and a science-fiction novel (Aymara computer programmers travelling the galaxy). All three are parallel texts in Spanish and English, linked by always having a character called Satuka Mamani who deals in coca leaf—the principal subject of my anthropological work.

*   *   *

Alison Spedding, who prefers to be known by her last name alone, has to date published only one work of fantasy, the substantial three-volume novel *A Walk in the Dark,* issued in three separately-titled parts. It is set on the world of Sard, in a standard sort of heroic framework, wherein "Lord Ailixond of Safi" pursues a career strikingly similar to that of his analogue or avatar, Alexander the Great. A specialist in the life of Alexander will certainly be in a position to get more out of the book than any general reader, by sorting out the analogues of Ptolemy, Parmenion, etc., among Ailixond's entourage (for obvious reasons, there is no analogue to Hephaistion, nor to the Persian Boy). The many incidents, such as the crossing of the Surani (Issus) and the lung-wound that he sustains, which are obviously based on the accounts of Plutarch and Arrian, point up the notable dissimilarities, most conspicuously the activities of the principal character.

Aleizon Ailix Ayndra is a woman of mysterious antecedents and bi-sexual proclivities who disguises herself as a man in order to join Ailixond's army. Once there she brings herself to his attention by the ploy (not unprecedented in fantasy) of introducing gunpowder. From there it's but a short step to his bed, for though Ayndra is pushing 30, her looks are only so-so and her most usual expression is one of embittered melancholy, her combination of well-kept body, manic courage and salty conversation is guaranteed to attract the discerning. It's also guaranteed to attract censure; Ayndra is visible, vulnerable, and to the hidebound abominable. They have much more to complain about than her tastes for masculine clothing, hashish and over-spiced food. Ayndra resents the subservient role expected of women, and behaves with cultivated uncouthness to emphasize her disdain, but she is too much the individualist to adopt the agenda of a suffragette—or any other which would adequately account for the furrow she chooses to plough. Despite superficial resemblances, the tale of a woman whose appetite for glorious war is such that she cozens an entire army (which has had enough and

wants to quit while it's ahead) into yet another campaign, cannot be called a feminist chronicle in any conventional sense.

The distaste she arouses in her more priggish contemporaries is expressed in tones less of the Hellenistic age than that of John Knox; quite apart from the many whose noses she puts out of joint, plenty more are keen to bring her down on general principles. To deepen the sense of impending doom, Spedding adopts the rhythms and syntax of 17th-century melodrama for much of the dialogue, heightening the air of anachronism established by the level of technology (which has aspects of the classical and the medieval) with quotations from sources as diverse as Donne's "Go and Catch a Falling Star" and "The Ball at Kerrymuir."

Regardless of Spedding's intention, many will be most comfortable with Ayndra if they regard her as an anti-heroine, in which connection it's noteworthy that apart from the battle scenes very little is written from Ayndra's viewpoint; she is much more the observed than the observer, and the reader is hardly ever made privy to her thoughts, though when she tells the dying Ailixond her story one presumes that she's telling the truth.

As a psychological study of a woman of great capacity whose conflicts of emotion and values lead to a monstrous inferiority complex, *The Road and the Hills* works well enough, for all that Spedding makes heavy and not always justified demands on the reader. The books are written in single chunks, without parts or chapters, and Spedding makes the pointless experiment of using "O" for "Oh" throughout, and rendering it in lower case. This distracts attention from the far more interesting experiment (in the context of what is fundamentally a love story) of showing entirely from the outside how she takes it when Ailixond becomes enamoured of a local beauty, marries and rapidly impregnates her (Ayndra knows herself to be barren).

Spedding also scores with her well-visualized descriptions of battles, siegecraft and logistical problems, and the creation of an interesting imaginary society, but by the end of the first book it is becoming apparent that she has no more idea than her heroine of where the novel is heading. Its overarching weakness is a lack of shape, which begins to tell very seriously when Ailixond dies, leaving Ayndra to soldier on without him. This she does for over 600 more pages, with many fine scenes but never any clear end in view. Though her death is movingly described, it is from wounds taken in an otherwise nondescript engagement, and for no more pressing reason than that the book is by now over 1100 pages long, and to die in bed would be out of character.

But with all its faults, *A Walk in the Dark* is a notable debut, and it is to be regretted that Spedding has shown no sign of following it up with further fantasies—preferably under her full name.

—Chris Gilmore

SPRINGER, Nancy (Connor)

Nationality: American. **Born:** Montclair, New Jersey, 5 July 1948. **Education:** Gettysburg College, Pennsylvania, 1966-1970, B.A. **Family:** Married Joel Springer in 1969; one daughter and one son. **Career:** Library clerk, St. Joseph's College, Emmitsburg, Maryland, 1969; teacher, Delone Catholic High School, McSherrytown, Pennsylvania, 1970-71; teacher's aide, Hoffman Home for Children, Littlestown, Pennsylvania, 1972-73; communications instructor, Bradley Academy for the Visual Arts, since 1990. Since 1972, writer. **Awards:** Joan Fassler Memorial Award, 1992; James Tiptree Award, 1995. **Agent:** Jean V. Naggar Literary Agency, 216 East 75th Street, New York, NY 10021, USA. **Address:** 360 West Main Street, Dallastown, PA 17313, USA.

FANTASY PUBLICATIONS

Novels (series: Isle; Sea King)

The Book of Suns (Isle). New York, Pocket Books, 1977; revised edition, as *The Silver Sun,* New York, Pocket Books, 1980; Glasgow, Drew, 1984.
The White Hart (Isle). New York, Pocket Books, 1979; Glasgow, Drew, 1984.
The Sable Moon (Isle). New York, Pocket Books, 1981; Glasgow, Drew, 1985.
The Black Beast (Isle). New York, Pocket Books, 1982; Glasgow, Drew, 1985.
The Golden Swan (Isle). New York, Timescape, 1983; Glasgow, Drew, 1985.
The Book of Vale (omnibus; includes *The Black Beast* and *The Golden Swan*). New York, Nelson Doubleday, 1984.
Wings of Flame. New York, Tor, 1985; London, Arrow, 1986.
Chains of Gold. New York, Arbor House, 1986; London, Macdonald, 1987.
Madbond (Sea King). New York, Tor, 1987; London, Futura, 1988.
Mindbond (Sea King). New York, Tor, 1987; London, Futura, 1989.
Godbond (Sea King). New York, Tor, 1988; London, Futura, 1990.
The Hex Witch of Seldom. New York, Baen, 1988.
Apocalypse. Novato, California, Underwood Miller, 1989.
Red Wizard (for children). New York, Atheneum, 1990.
The Friendship Song (for children). New York, Atheneum, 1992.
Larque on the Wing. New York, AvonNova, 1994.
Metal Angel. New York, Roc, 1994.

Short Stories

Chance: And Other Gestures of the Hand of Fate (includes poetry). New York, Baen, 1987.
Damnbanna. Eugene, Oregon, Pulphouse, 1992.

OTHER PUBLICATIONS

Novels for children

A Horse to Love. New York, Harper and Row, 1987.
Not on a White Horse. New York, Atheneum, 1988.
They're All Named Wildfire. New York, Atheneum, 1989.
Colt. New York, Dial, 1991.
The Great Pony Hassle. New York, Dial, 1993.
The Boy on a Black Horse. New York, Atheneum, 1994.
Toughing It. New York, Harcourt Brace, 1994.
Looking for Jamie Bridger. New York, Dial, 1995.

Poetry

Stardark Songs. Buffalo, New York, Ganley, 1993.
Music of Their Hooves: Poems About Horses. Honesdale, Pennsylvania, Boyds Mills Press, 1994.

Other

Mythic Realism in Fantasy. Eugene, Oregon, Pulphouse, 1991.

*

Manuscript Collection: Gettysburg College Library, Gettysburg, Pennsylvania.

Nancy Springer comments:

From having been a writer of rather standard mythic fantasy, I have become very much a writer of magical realism, dealing with "themes usually reserved for mainstream fiction: middle age, child/parent relationships, comfortable marriage vs. the urge to cut loose, sexuality (both straight and gay), and the multiple levels of the mind" (from a review of *Larque on the Wing,* in *Locus,* April 1994). Though I still consider myself a fantasy writer, I am no longer able to create "long ago and far away" stories with any enthusiasm; I am much too interested in "here and now," and in exploring what is magical (or often, surreal) in everyday life. I am fascinated by popular culture, modern mythologies, "urban legends," whatever is tacky, archetypically American or hopelessly human, eccentric, quixotic, weird. My goal as a writer is to push against the self-imposed limits of the fantasy genre, using the insights of fantasy in order to illuminate contemporary reality as the bizarre and wonderful manifestation it is.

*   *   *

Comic fantasy, even from the subtlest of writers, has tended to take fantasy as its target, poking fun at the very witches and warlords, demons and dragons which make it fantasy. Nancy Springer writes fantasy which also happens to have a sense of irony, of the comedy of character; the fantasy and comedy are incidental to each other, yet the one enhances the other.

However, for most of her career, comic fantasy would hardly have been the most obvious description of Nancy Springer's work. Her first novels, *The Book of Suns* and *The White Hart,* were conventional quest narratives so steeped in Celtic mythology and the usual paraphernalia of heroic fantasy that there could have seemed nothing about them that might break the fantasy mould. Nor did the unnatural, heightened language help; it was as if in taking the reader to her world of Isle she wished to do nothing but evoke echoes of every other fantasy which followed slavishly in the footsteps of Tolkien. But this is to miss an underlying irony, a sense that the familiar elements are being knowingly and ever so slightly misused. So that when Bevan, the god-turned-man who is the non-heroic hero of *The White Hart,* battles the dragon, he does so with words, turning it round so that it fights against the enemy host opposing Bevan. In the same novel, the sharpness of the relationship between Ellid and Bevan, and particularly between Ellid and Cuin, her would-be fiance, presage the quality of the characterization and the feminism which would develop in Springer's later books.

As the series of novels about Isle was written Springer gradually dropped the arcane language and built up the gritty realism so that by *The Golden Swan* casual rape was on the menu for any traveller set upon by brigands. Nevertheless, she continued to see fantasy as primarily world-creation, as if only a medieval landscape with overtones of Celtic mythology is a fitting setting for magic. Both *Wings of Flame* and *Chains of Gold* feature strong female characters, but though the protagonists in *Chains of Gold* reject their ritual fate, they are still trapped within the conventions of fantasy. The Sea King trilogy, *Madbond, Mindbond* and *Godbond,* featured some of her best writing to date, but it was bound up in a fantasy setting which had little beyond the conventional to offer.

It was time for a change of pace, which came with her first exercise in contemporary fantasy, *The Hex Witch of Seldom,* which incorporated the folklore of her home state of Pennsylvania. All her fantasy novels since then have been set in the contemporary world—usually in Pennsylvania—and the vividness and familiarity of these settings have proved more conducive to the realistic writing style, strong yet subtle characterization, feminism and humour which had all been growing features of her work. Away from lands of the imagination she was able to abandon the traditional moral certainties of heroic fantasy and introduce stories filled with moral doubt and ambiguous characters.

In *Larque on the Wing,* for instance, the best of her recent books, she presents a 40-something heroine haunted by the ghost of her ten-year-old self. The certainties of the child highlight the compromises, the abandoned principles that come with living a normal life in the modern world. But in her attempts to come face to face with that old black and white view of the world, Larque finds herself transformed (literally by a sort of body-sculpture in a curious hidden street of her depressed Pennsylvania home town) into a homosexual man. In this way Springer uses fantasy to confront some of the darker aspects of modern life: prejudice, middle age, the abandonment of principle; yet she does so with a natural grace and humour that makes this an unusually affecting and effective novel.

There is a similar concern with the underside of society in *Apocalypse.* Set in a depressed Pennsylvanian mining town, its cast of characters includes a deformed and isolated girl who turns to magic, a simple-minded boy, and the "Four Horsewomen of the Apocalypse." The magic struggle that occurs in the book appears to follow the simple verities of a clash between good and evil, but away from the broad strokes and bold colours of a fantasy landscape it becomes a much more subtle and less clear-cut thing, questioning our notions of beauty and ugliness, strength and weakness. In *Metal Angel* also, in which an angel takes on human form and finds that his beauty equips him only for a role as rock star, Nancy Springer undermines traditional notions of beauty and goodness. It is as if, freed from the need to create neatly delineated worlds, she is able to use the tools of fantasy more pointedly and more effectively.

—Maureen Speller

STANTON, Mary

Nationality: American. **Born:** 1947.

FANTASY PUBLICATIONS

Novels

The Heavenly Horse from the Outermost West. New York, Baen, and London, New English Library, 1988.
Piper at the Gate. New York, Baen, 1989; as *Piper at the Gates of Dawn,* London, New English Library, 1989.

*   *   *

The two novels which are the current sum of Mary Stanton's output are examples of the talking animal sub-genre. When originally published there was no attempt to differentiate them from the rest of the fantasy novels available. They would have had a greater impact if they had been aimed at the juvenile market and, more specifically, the ten-year-old horse lover.

Both novels are narrated totally from a horse's perspective. The first, *The Heavenly Horse from the Outermost West,* begins with the arrival of Duchess at Bishop Farm. She has been badly treated by her last owner and distrusts people. The other horses try to welcome her. A little later, Dancer arrives at the farm. He is actually the Breedmaster of Appaloosa breed and normally lives in the Courts of the Outermost West. He has been sent to mate with Duchess and save the breed from extinction. However, instead of staying at the farm as he is supposed to, he runs off with Duchess and a Paint mare called Susie. Dancer adds a Shetland Pony to his herd and the collie, Cory, who has followed them from the farm. During the winter, Susie succumbs to the harsh weather and Dancer is offered her life in exchange for his own if he goes to the Black Barns, the horse equivalent of Hell. There he faces and fights Anor, the executioner of the Dark Horse who rules the underworld.

Piper at the Gate is a sequel. It is set about nine years later and begins with the death of Duchess and the disappearance of Dancer. Cory, the collie, brings the news to Piper, their first foal and now herd stallion at Sweetwater ranch. Normally, when horses die they follow the Green Road to Summer where they are judged. Duchess, however, has been lured off the Road and unless she can be rescued the Appaloosa breed will disappear. So Piper, taking with him four of the geldings from the ranch, has first to visit the Namer of Names in order to find the true Name of the Dark Horse and then breech the Gates of the underworld before Duchess can be released.

If read from the point of view of a child, these books have some interesting ideas. The horses have a hierarchy within a herd and each herd has a storyteller who will relate the myths of their kind. Both books are punctuated at intervals by such. Some herds also have a dreamspeaker and there are rituals that form a kind of religion. In *The Heavenly Horse of the Outermost West* the dreamspeaker is El Arat, the mare who, by the end of the book, has become the Soul Taker, the Dark Horse's mate and Duchess's deadly enemy. Frosty is the reluctant dreamspeaker in Piper's herd of brood mares. Part of her reticence is self-doubt and a feeling of unworthiness because when the moon is full and the dreamspeaker stands in a still pond they may be able to walk the Path of the Moon and talk to the Goddess Mare. This is actually quite a neat device as it allows the horses to find out what is going on elsewhere without having to leave their fields.

As well as religion, ritual and ranking, the horses also have a very distinct sense of right and wrong. In the early days of the species they made a Bargain with man and so must obey the Law of Fences, which is why the majority of horses are well behaved and do not try to escape from fields. However, they can be punished after death and sent to the Black Barns if they infringe the rules. And, because in both volumes there is a battle between good and evil and good triumphs, they make acceptable moral reading for any child. It is perhaps a bit too black and white for the more worldly-wise reader.

The adult fantasy reader will have to suspend a much greater weight of disbelief as the degree of naivety on the part of the author tends to irritate. An Appaloosa can be a very pretty horse, either spotted all over or just within a blanket covering the hind quarters. Because it is a colour breed (i.e. the markings make it Appaloosa, not height, shape, etc), the variation between one Appaloosa and the next can be wide. Not only are there six recognised variants of the breed but it ranks among the half dozen biggest breeds in the United States. Thus the premise that Duchess is the last Appaloosa mare on Earth stretches credibility a little thin. It is a nice idea and allows for the ramifications of her plot, but Stanton would have been wiser to choose either a much rarer breed or invent one of her own, especially as there is no hint that the setting is other than present day America.

There is also an assumption that the animals, whether horses, dogs, cats, deer or foxes, but not humans, can all understand each other perfectly. Imagine the mouse pleading with the cat not to eat it, or hearing the fleas as they discuss which part of you to bite? But probably most irritating of all is the over-anthropomorphization of the characters. Human emotions and motives are freely ascribed to both horses and dogs, especially grief, so that they become very much like people dressed up. Another factor that points the books in the direction of younger readers is the black and white drawings of the characters that are scattered throughout both volumes.

—Pauline Morgan

STASHEFF, Christopher

Nationality: American. **Born:** Mount Vernon, New York, January 1944. **Education:** University of Michigan, Ann Arbor, B.A. 1965, M.A. 1966; University of Nebraska, Lincoln, Ph.D. in theatre 1972. **Family:** Married Mary Miller in 1973; three daughters and one son. **Career:** Instructor, 1972-77, and since 1977, Assistant Professor of Speech and Theatre, Montclair State College, New Jersey. **Agent:** Blassingame-Spectrum Corporation, 111 Eighth Avenue, Suite 1501, New York, NY 10011, USA.

FANTASY PUBLICATIONS

Novels (series: Warlock; Wizard in Rhyme)

The Warlock in Spite of Himself. New York, Ace, 1969; London, Mayflower, 197?.
King Kobold (Warlock). New York, Ace, 1971; London, Mayflower, 197?; revised edition, as *King Kobold Revived,* Ace, 1984.
A Wizard in Bedlam. New York, Doubleday, 1979; London, Mayflower, 1982.
The Warlock Unlocked. New York, Ace, 1982; London, Panther, 1984. *Escape Velocity* (Warlock). New York, Ace, 1983.
The Warlock Enraged. New York, Ace, 1985.
To the Magic Born (omnibus; includes *Escape Velocity, The Warlock in Spite of Himself*). New York, Nelson Doubleday, 1986.
The Warlock Enlarged (omnibus; includes *King Kobold Revived, The Warlock Unlocked, The Warlock Enraged*). New York, Nelson Doubleday, 1986.
The Warlock Wandering. New York, Ace, 1986.
The Warlock Is Missing. New York, Ace, 1986.
Her Majesty's Wizard (Wizard in Rhyme). New York, Ballantine, 1986.
The Warlock Heretical. New York, Ace, 1987.

The Warlock's Companion. New York, Ace, 1988.
The Warlock's Night Out (omnibus; includes *The Warlock Wandering, The Warlock is Missing*). New York, Guild America, 1989.
The Warlock Insane. New York, Ace, 1989.
Odd Warlock Out (omnibus; includes *The Warlock Heretical, The Warlock's Companion, The Warlock Insane*). New York, Guild America, 1989.
Warlock: To the Magic Born (omnibus; includes *Escape Velocity, The Warlock in Spite of Himself, King Kobold Revived*). London, Pan, 1990.
The Warlock Rock. New York, Ace, 1990.
The Warlock Enlarged (omnibus; includes *The Warlock Unlocked, The Warlock Enraged*). London, Pan, 1991.
The Warlock's Night Out (omnibus; includes *The Warlock Wandering, The Warlock is Missing, The Warlock Heretical*). London, Pan, 1991.
Warlock and Son. New York, Ace, 1991.
A Wizard in Absentia. New York, Ace, 1993.
The Oathbound Wizard (Wizard in Rhyme). New York, Del Rey, 1993.
The Witch Doctor (Wizard in Rhyme). New York, Del Rey, 1994.
The Secular Wizard (Wizard in Rhyme). New York, Del Rey, 1995.

Short Story

Sir Harold and the Monkey King. N.p., Wildside, 1993.

Other

Editor, with Bill Fawcett, *The Crafters.* New York, Ace, 1991.
Editor, with Bill Fawcett, *The Crafters 2: Blessings and Curses.* New York, Ace, 1992.
Editor, with L. Sprague de Camp, *The Enchanter Reborn.* New York, Baen, 1992.
Editor, *The Gods of War.* New York, Ace, 1992.

OTHER PUBLICATIONS

Novels

A Company of Stars. New York, Del Rey, 1991.
We Open on Venus. New York, Del Rey, 1994.

Plays

The Three-Legged Man (produced Lincoln, Nebraska, 1970). *Cotton-Eye Joe* (produced Lincoln, Nebraska, 1970).
Joey Win (produced Lincoln, Nebraska, 1971).

*   *   *

If Christopher Stasheff had stopped writing in 1971, he would be remembered for two of the most original, charming, sensual, and liberal-minded "science-fantasy" novels ever published. *The Warlock in Spite of Himself* begins as Rodney d'Armand, and his robot horse Fess, land on the planet Gramarye. They find a medieval society of royalty, aristocracy, and peasants; barely altered since its creation by Earth colonists some centuries before, it is suddenly in the first throes of revolution. D'Armand, assuming the name

Rod Gallowglass, is drawn into the struggle, a struggle complicated by an unforeseen factor—magic. After the colonization of Gramarye, many human myths somehow became real: there are actual elves, dwarfs, ghosts, banshee, werewolves, and leprechauns. Some humans have also changed: female witches who move things by telekinesis—including the broomsticks they ride; male warlocks, who fly and teleport objects. All of them are telepathic. These witch-folk had been routinely brutalized and killed, until the new Queen, Catherine, championed their cause.

D'Armand's high-technology devices and scientific knowledge convince ordinary Gramaryans that he must be a warlock; even the witch-folk—who cannot read his mind, know he commands an iron horse, and find him blithely consorting with ghosts and time-machines—believe he has supernatural powers; the more Rod denies it, the more events seem to prove it; finally, even d'Armand begins to wonder.

This frothy, often hilarious surface plot is laid on a superb, if complex, rationale: Gramarye was settled by malcontents fleeing a repressive regime on Earth. When that tyranny was finally defeated, the new Earth government was determined to aid democracy on all the lost colonies. They use a network of secret agents to sabotage and undermine totalitarian states, and guide them towards freedom. Yet democracy depends on communication, and as the number of democratic worlds increases, the time delays in communication between them may lead the democratic alliance itself towards tyranny. Telepathy acts instantly across space. If the witches of Gramarye are allowed to multiply and spread to other worlds, they will form the core of a true democracy; in fact, many years in the future, they *have* won, but anarchists and totalitarians have by then gained access to time machines, and they are making forays into the past, to destroy the witch-folk before they can leave Gramarye.

The book has great charm; intelligent and committed, it strikes targets with incisive wit, and (though quickly written, with holes in logic that would be exploited in later books) it develops seamlessly from a light, hilarious start to a dark and powerful resolution that has the reader cheering—when d'Armand must make a stark choice on his responsibility for Gramarye and its future.

The sequel, *King Kobold,* is set a few years later; Gramarye is being raided by mysterious beastmen who slaughter all opposition; even the witches—still feared by many of the population—find them impossible to fight. The new king and queen ask their High Warlock, d'Armand, to lead the war against the beastmen. By the end of this wildly coincidental but coherent and smooth novel, Rod and family have uncovered a massive conspiracy spread across time: another attempt by the time-travelling villains to change their own past.

Then Stasheff went silent for eight years. When he came back, it was with an entirely different agenda. *A Wizard in Bedlam* was an abortive new start: harsh, flat, and unmemorable, it was a slim and predictable tale of a man trained in high technology, who landed on a planet with a repressive feudal system and helped to foment a revolution. The meagre differences from the d'Armand books were that the hero was actually a native of the planet who had been taken off, trained, then returned; and that he fell in love with only one woman. This led to heartbreak, since a pattern of the Stasheff books is the hero falling for a powerful and beautiful woman, who uses him for her own purposes; he later meets a more reticent but loyal woman who pursues him for love. With no second woman, *A Wizard in Bedlam* has a bleak ending.

The Warlock Unlocked brought back Rod and family, but on a radically altered Gramarye. The novel opens with the Roman Catholic Church on Earth learning of Gramarye; they send a priest to re-establish religious control of the planet; the priest succeeds. The book's surface plot pits royalty against the rights of the church, a crisis impelled by the villainous SPITE organization, who neutralize Rod and his family by kidnapping them to a parallel universe. Looking back from future books—which repeat variations on it—this surface plot is not so important to Stasheff as the reintroduction of the Catholic faith, the story of Saint Vidicon (patron saint of technology), and the idea that Rod's growing power—catalyzed by fear for his children—is not just dangerous (Power Corrupts), but verges on blasphemy.

Stasheff's problem had been that the first Gramarye novels pictured a future democracy of absolute and open communication; it had no reason for God. Its perfect communication would perfect humanity. Freedom had not become licence, despite Original Sin. Stasheff had to do two things: to ensure Gramarye was founded under the auspices of the Catholic Church; and to remove what seemed a blasphemous idea in *King Kobold*—a soul that conspired in its own creation, beyond the influence of God. Stasheff's light touch and romantic themes were subdued, the libertarian freedom was gone; here he attacked premarital sex, religious diversity, and the sanity of his hero. In later books, the attacks would grow wider and more sustained. Where magic had been charming and fun, it now had a bitter and dark aspect because "real" magic would be a true heresy, and such power must inevitably create great evil.

Having secured the present of Gramarye, Stasheff moved to its past. The turgid and colorless *Escape Velocity* tells of the first d'Armand: as the LORDS party increases its power over Earth and its colonies, Dar Mantra becomes involved with an ambitious, beautiful woman, and the Society for Creative Anachronism, medievalists who are about to flee from Earth. The ambitious, beautiful woman turns out to be a powerful telepath, who falls for an older man (who will become a ghost on Gramarye). Dar, now calling himself Dar d'Armand, settles for a hard-headed and practical woman who agrees to flee with him to a distant asteroid. The Romantic Emigres blast off to an unplanned destination, ready to have their minds wiped of all memory when they finally land (as they did, on Gramarye). They take a priest with them.

Stasheff had explained most logical holes in the first books, had rescued Gramarye for Rome; he only needed to repair the blasphemy in *King Kobold* by revising the book as *King Kobold Revived*. He removed a lot of the original characters, rationalized the "lost soul" into one from a parallel universe, eliminated all the extra-marital sex, and didn't even bother with the temporal paradox that was a surprise ending to the original. The revised version is smoother, less wild, and totally without charm.

The books began to appear at about one per year, and they soon fell into a pattern: Rod and his family would be kidnapped, or Rod would battle his inner demons. The Gallowglass family had just become too powerful, and their opponents less worthy; even the children could defeat whole armies, and after a time, their easy victories became embarrassing. Stasheff began to make the conflicts internal—concentrating on family temptation and tribulation, on growing pains, and the responsibilities of power. Rod went mad on several occasions, and his first-born son, Magnus, finally left the planet because he realized he and his father would have a huge battle for control.

The Warlock Enraged had Rod undergoing periodic explosions of fury; in *The Warlock Insane* an ingestion of witch-moss had him hallucinating dangerously until he was taken into the care of nuns. Rod and Gwen were kidnapped in *The Warlock Wandering,* and the children came under attack in *The Warlock is Missing* and *The Warlock Rock*. This last was the low point in the series: rock-and-roll rhythms and lyrics are proved to be sexually enticing, compelling, and dangerous. There are many puns and attacks on groups (Beatles, Rolling Stones, Judas Priest, Grateful Dead), and Rod even worries about the poem "Come live with me and be my love." Painfully narrow-minded, the massive warnings against premarital sex reach a peak in this book, and the subsequent neutering of Rod's eldest son, Magnus, is just the culmination of the attack.

That neutering comes in *Warlock and Son* parts of which are derived from ballads (including "La Belle Dame Sans Merci"); at the end, Magnus is deliberately left with a massive distrust of women, and no interest in sex. Stasheff was about to take the step of leaving Rod behind totally, and may not have wanted a hero who beds women on his travels; *A Wizard in Absentia* did find Magnus propositioned by several women (all wanting to use him for their own purposes), but he celibately evaded all their clutches, and moved on.

Through all these novels, plus *Warlock Heretical* (corruption in the Gramarye Church when an evil Bishop declares it is separate from Rome) and *Warlock's Companion* (where Fess relates his own history, including the later life of Dar Mantra and the early romantic failures of Rodney) Stasheff built a bewilderingly complex background to the saga. Acronyms and organizations proliferated: villainous LORDS, PEST, SPITE and VETO; their opponents SCA, DDT, SCENT, and the Guardians of the Rights of Individuals, Patentholders Especially [GRIPE] founded by Angus McAran. This inventor of the time machine actually undermined the entire series by declaring the fight for democracy was not to promote freedom but merely to ensure that patent rights were safeguarded! Indeed, McAran's control of time suggested that true free will didn't really exist at all.

The series has come to condemn the liberal, generous and bawdy sensuality of the first books; its courageous and open approach has gone. Yet for all their thoroughly science-fictional artifacts and principles, the books retain a ghost of the impact and appeal of their prime fantasy elements.

Stasheff wrote almost nothing but "Warlock" novels until *Her Majesty's Wizard*, wherein student Matthew Mantrall uses poetry to travel to a parallel Earth on which his verses can work magic. He is soon involved with an intelligent dragon and an imprisoned princess, who neatly shames him into helping her to regain her throne. Mantrall is a muddler, quick-witted yet innocent of the laws of magic and the Machiavellian stratagems of diplomacy; in the best traditions of fantasy, his honorable intentions bring success. This Wizard in Rhyme series lay fallow until *The Oathbound Wizard* and *The Witch Doctor*, well into Stasheff's most productive period.

That period opened with *A Company of Stars*, first in the Starship Troupers series of science-fiction novels: a group of actors flee a despotic Earth when their profession is about to be banned. It is the same Earth as in the Gramarye books but there is (so far) no other connection. The sequel, *We Open on Venus*, appeared three years later. Stasheff also co-edited and wrote the opening stories in the shared world of *The Crafters* and *The Crafters 2: Blessings and Curses*. These are stories of the Crafter family—the opening narrative, by Stasheff, has a 17th-century protoscientist pursued by, and finally marrying, a witch; in the subsequent tales, their psychic descendants meet magical perils and moral dilemmas; the stories, by a number of authors, are generally stylish but inconsequential. Stasheff also created the harsher and even more restricted *The Gods of War*. He had given technology a saint in *The Warlock Un-*

locked, now he donated Tek, the god of technological warfare. In stories again written by other authors, this newest god of war views the violent actions of past war gods. The book is fragmented and repetitive, and its presumed moral message is questionable.

There is a repeated pattern in much of Stasheff's work: an intelligent, eager, yet emotionally repressed male academic-cum-scientist meets a witch; object—confusion, fun, adventure, and romance, with the scientist uncovering and learning to use the logical rules behind magic. Most obvious in *Her Majesty's Wizard*—which captured the form but neither the heart nor sentiment of its model—Stasheff finally acknowledged his debt to the Harold Shea sequence of L. Sprague de Camp and Fletcher Pratt; Stasheff even suggested—when he co edited *The Enchanter Reborn* with de Camp—that his entire career had been spent rewriting *The Incompleat Enchanter.*

Stasheff's own contributions to *The Enchanter Reborn*, "Sir Harold and the Trustees" and "Sir Harold and the Monkey King" (the latter also separately published as a booklet) are much more than trivial pastiches: they seamlessly and superbly mimic the style, character, and plot of their originals, and—by lacking the increased moralizing of his own solo work—return part-way to the quality his pre-1971 novels. There is no doubt that Stasheff's work is intelligent and carefully crafted; the question is whether Stasheff is writing to entertain and impart moral conundra or if he is writing morality lessons glossed over with the patina of faery.

—Ian Covell

STEPHENS, James

Also wrote as James Esse. **Nationality:** Irish. **Born:** Dublin, either 9 February 1880 or 2 February 1882 (date of birth not firmly established). **Education:** Meath Protestant Industrial School for Boys, 1888-1896. **Family:** Married Millicent Josephine Kavanagh, 1919; one son, one stepdaughter. **Career:** Clerical and secretarial work in various Dublin legal firms, 1896-1908; Dublin stage actor, 1909-1911; co-founder and co-editor, with David Houston, Thomas MacDonagh and Padraic Colum, *Irish Review*, 1911-14. Unestablished Registrar of the National Gallery of Ireland, 1916-25. BBC radio lecturer on various topics, 1937-50. **Awards:** Edmond de Polignac Prize, 1913; Tailltean Gold Medal, 1923. Litt.D. honoris causa, Trinity College, Dublin, 1947. **Died:** 6 December 1950.

Fantasy Publications

Novels (series: the Great Tain)

The Crock of Gold. London, Macmillan, 1912; New York, Macmillan, 1913.
The Demi-Gods. London and New York, Macmillan, 1914.
Deirdre (Great Tain). London and New York, Macmillan, 1923.
In the Land of Youth (Great Tain). London and New York, Macmillan, 1924.

Short Stories

Irish Fairy Tales. London and New York, Macmillan, 1920.
How St. Patrick Saves the Irish. Privately printed, 1931.

OTHER PUBLICATIONS

Novels

The Charwoman's Daughter. London, Macmillan, 1912; as *Mary, Mary,* Boston, Small Maynard, 1912.

Short Stories

Here Are Ladies. London and New York, Macmillan, 1913.
Hunger: A Dublin Story (as James Esse). Dublin, Candle Press, 1918.
Etched in Moonlight. London and New York, Macmillan, 1928.

Play

Julia Elizabeth: A Comedy in One Act. New York, Crosby Gaige, 1929.

Poetry

Where the Demons Grin: A Broadside. Dundrum, Cuala Press, 1908.
Why Tomas Cam Was Grumpy. Dundrum, Cuala Press, 1909.
Insurrections. Dublin, Maunsel, 1909.
The Lonely God and Other Poems. New York, Macmillan, 1909.
The Adventures of Scumas Beg: The Visit from Abroad, A Broadside. Dundrum, Cuala Press, 1910.
The Adventures of Scumas Beg: In the Orchard, A Broadside. Dundrum, Cuala Press, 1910.
The Adventures of Scumas Beg: Treasure Trove. Dundrum, Cuala Press, 1910.
The Spy: A Broadside. Dundrum, Cuala Press, 1910.
The Hill of Vision. Dublin, Maunsel, 1912.
Five New Poems. Westminster, T. A. Stevens, 1913.
Songs from the Clay. London and New York, Macmillan, 1915.
The Adventures of Scumas Beg: The Rocky Road to Dublin. London, Macmillan, 1915; as *The Rocky Road to Dublin: The Adventures of Scumas Beg,* New York, Macmillan, 1915.
Green Branches. Dublin and London, Maunsel, 1916.
Reincarnations. London and New York, Macmillan, 1918.
Little Things and Other Poems. Chicago, W. M. Hill, 1924.
Christmas in Freelands. Chicago, W. M. Hill, 1925.
A Poetry Recital. London and New York, Macmillan, 1925.
Collected Poems. London and New York, Macmillan, 1926; second edition, 1954.
The Optimist. Gaylordsville, Slide Mountain Press, 1929.
The Outcast. London, Faber and Faber, 1929.
The Symbol Song. New York, Fountain Press, 1929.
Themes and Variation. New York, Fountain Press, 1930.
Strict Joy. London and New York, Macmillan, 1931.
The Fifteen Acres: A Broadside. Dublin, Cuala Press, 1935.
The Main-Deep: A Broadside. Dublin, Cuala Press, 1937.
The Rivals: A Broadside. Dublin, Cuala Press, 1937.
Kings and the Moon. London and New York, Macmillan, 1938.
A Singing Wind: Selected Poems. New York, Macmillan, 1968.

Other

The Insurrection in Dublin. Dublin and London, Maunsel, and New York, Macmillan, 1916.

Arthur Griffith: Journalist and Statesman. Dublin, Wilson Hartnell, 1924(?).
Dublin Letters. Gaylordsville, Connecticut, Slide Mountain Press, 1928.
On Prose and Verse. New York, Bowling Green Press, 1928.
Stars Do Not Make a Noise. Los Angeles, Deux Magots Press, 1931.
James Stephens: A Selection, edited by Lloyd Frankenberg. London, Macmillan, 1962.
James, Seumas and Jacques: Unpublished Writings by James Stephens, edited by Lloyd Frankenberg. London and New York, Macmillan, 1964.
Letters of James Stephens, edited by Richard Finneran. London and New York, Macmillan, 1974.

Editor, with Edwin L. Beck and Royall H. Snow, *English Romantic Poets.* New York, American Book Company, 1933.
Editor, with Edwin L. Beck and Royall H. Snow, *Victorian and Later English Poets.* New York, American Book Company, 1934.

*

Bibliography: *James Stephens: A Literary and Bibliographical Study* by Birgit Bramsbäck, Uppsala, Sweden, Lundequistska Bokhandeln, 1959.

Critical Studies: *James Stephens* by Padraic Colum and others, New York, Macmillan, 1928; *James Stephens: His Work and an Account of His Life* by Hilary Pyle, London, Routledge and Kegan Paul, 1965; *James Stephens: A Critical Study* by Augustine Martin, Dublin, Gill and Macmillan, 1977; *The Olympian and the Leprechaun: W. B. Yeats and James Stephens* by Richard J. Finneran, Dublin, Dolmen Press, 1978; *The Writings of James Stephens: Variations on a Theme of Love* by Patricia McFate, New York, St. Martin's Press, 1979.

James Stephens commented:

As to my life—It is to a greater extent than appears distilled into my books, not in the way of direct narrative, but in revolts, and angers and enthusiasms and vain imaginings. I am Mary in the *Charwoman's Daughter,* and I am her mother and the Policeman—I am the Philosopher in the *Crock of Gold,* and I am the children, the leprechauns and the goat: so, in the *Demi-Gods,* I am the gods, and Patsy McCann and Eileen Ni Cooley, and whoever else goes through those pages. So in the rest of my books, and I could give a reason, if I was drove to it, or bribed to it, for such and such a sunset, or fight, or feasting, or whatnot. There are two approaches to the same kind of knowledge: one is to study other people, the other is to study yourself: the result is inevitably the same thing—consciousness. My approach to humanity or life is through myself, and I try to cultivate the blessed cosmos inside my own head. (From a letter to Lewis Chase, 10 January 1917, in *Letters of James Stephens,* page 204.)

*   *   *

Although James Stephens can be read and appreciated as a fantasy writer in the modern sense, there are three alternative contexts which may better account for some aspects of his work. First, Stephens is one distinguished practitioner in the briefly flourishing sub-genre known as the adult fairy tale; this explains the jarring combination of childlike innocence and mature realism sometimes found in his stories. Second, Stephens was part of the extraordinary Irish Literary Renaissance of the early 20th century, when a number of writers struggled in various ways to escape the domination of English and European culture to forge a uniquely Irish literary tradition; this explains Stephens's frequent recourse to Irish mythology and folklore. Finally, Stephens always thought of himself primarily as a poet; this explains why his novels may read like anthologies of poems, with bright moments of beauty and wisdom but little sense of the unity and logical connectedness associated with novels.

In Stephens's first and most famous novel, *The Crock of Gold,* one subplot shows a young Irish maiden, Caitilin, who is first seduced by the Greek god Pan, but later abandons him to be the paramour of the Irish god Angus Og—a clear allegory about the Irish people, first awakened to a new maturity by foreign influences but ultimately obliged and destined to return to their own native traditions. Other aspects of this haunting and elusive novel, however, resist easy interpretation. The protagonists are two Philosophers—whose speeches are an apparently aimless jumble of observations that abruptly veer into relevant insights—and their wives, who live in an isolated collage. When a man takes away a leprechaun's pot of gold and hides it where they cannot retrieve it, the leprechauns kidnap two children in retaliation, until a Philosopher intervenes to have the children returned. Then, because one Philosopher has committed suicide, explaining that he has absorbed enough knowledge, policemen come to the cottage to arrest the other Philosopher for murder; his wife must then seek the help of Angus Og, who triumphantly leads a pageant through the countryside to effect his rescue, gathering support along the way. In these ways, Stephens seems to argue for some grand reconciliation—of the ancient and the modern, perhaps, or the intellect and the emotion—but even literary critics find it difficult to explain all aspects of the story; Stephens himself said that, "In this book there is only one character—Man—Pan is his sensual nature, Caitilin, his emotional nature, the Philosopher his intellect at play, Angus Og his intellect spiritualized, the policemen his conventions and logics, the leprechauns his elemental side, the children his innocence," but added that "the idea is not too rigidly carried out." Indeed.

Equally elusive is Stephens's second novel, *The Demi-Gods,* about three guardian angels who decide to accompany an Irish vagabond named Patsy Mac Cann and his daughter Mary because, they announce, they wish to learn something about life—though exactly why they chose these companions, and exactly what they learn, remain uncertain. Their adventures also involve Eileen Ni Cooley, a free-spirited woman whom Patsy both loves and hates, and Billy the Music, a formerly rich man who tells the story of Brien O'Brien and the hero Cuchulain, who are thrown out of Heaven for failing to return a missing coin. In the end, the angels prepare to return, but one decides to stay on Earth to be with Mary. Here, Stephens clearly offers commentary on the evils of private property and the folly of greed, and the angels' refusal to criticize Patsy's larcenous lifestyle may be read as a message: just as the Irish have learned from Christianity, so might Christianity learn something from the Irish. But some aspects of the book remain puzzling; while Stephens praised its style of writing, he also claimed that, "It is not as good as *The Crock,* but then I had the subject there and I hadn't here." More charitably, one could say *The Demi-Gods* is a book with an underdeveloped subject, or with several subjects.

As if discomfited by the challenge of creating meaningful fantasies in modern settings, Stephens later devoted his talents to retelling Irish legends and stories. His first book of this type, *Irish Fairy Tales,* is unfortunately titled; while each story can be read separately, almost all of them involve the hero Finn (Stephens spells the name Fionn), so the book could be read as an episodic novel about his exploits. Of the stories, "The Boyhood of Fionn" is the most charming, "The Carl of the Drab Coat" the most amusing, and "Mongan's Frenzy" the most involving.

Having dealt with one great tradition of Irish mythology, the Finn Cycle, in *Irish Fairy Tales,* Stephens then planned a five-volume series, called the Tain Bo Cuailigne or the Great Tain, drawn from the other great tradition, the Ulster Cycle; but only two volumes were completed. The first, *Deirdre,* is the story of an older king, Conachur, who orders the beautiful young woman Deirdre to marry him; instead, she flees to Scotland to marry her lover and live with him and his brothers. Through a series of stratagems, Conachur lures Deirdre and the band back to his estate, where he violates all dictates of honour and custom to launch an attack on his guests to recover Deirdre. After the men are captured and killed, Deirdre falls and dies on her husband's body. Certainly, this is Stephens's best novel, focused on telling its story with unusual conviction and single-mindedness, and offering Stephens's most fully developed characters. And, while undoubtedly lacking the mystery and profundity of *The Crock of Gold, Deirdre* may be the Stephens fantasy that would most appeal to modern readers.

The second Tain volume, *In the Land of Youth,* features two extended stories involving or told by Conachur's comrade Fergus mac Roy and his wife Maeve. First, a man in Fergus's company is mystically transported to the realm of Faery, where he meets a beautiful woman; when he returns to Ireland to claim a prize, Maeve tells him the story of how she once invaded the land of Faery to recapture a mortal woman chosen to be the wife of Angus Og. Second, Maeve relates how a god with two wives, Midir, lost the one he truly loved, Etain, when she was killed by his other wife, jealous because Angus Og had fallen in love with Etain, not her; but Etain's spirit is transported into a woman's womb where she is reborn, to be eventually reclaimed by Midir after she has grown to adulthood. Neither as energetic nor as involving as *Deirdre, In the Land of Youth* nevertheless has its own special appeal as the most relaxed and charming of Stephens's fantasies.

The last decades of Stephens's life were marked by poor health, depression, and little writing. Perhaps fortunately, because his friend James Joyce survived until 1941, Stephens was spared what would have been his most daunting assignment as a fantasy writer: completing Joyce's *Finnegans Wake.*

—Gary Westfahl

STEVENS, Francis

Pseudonym for Gertrude Barrows Bennett. **Nationality:** American. **Born:** Minneapolis, Minnesota, 18 September 1884. **Family:** Married Stewart Bennett in 1909 (died); one daughter. **Career:** Worked as a secretary after the death of her husband, then as a freelance writer, 1917-20. **Died** (disappeared in September 1939).

FANTASY PUBLICATIONS

Novels

The Heads of Cerberus. Reading, Pennsylvania, Polaris Press, 1952.

Claimed! New York, Avalon, 1966.
The Citadel of Fear. New York, Paperback Library, 1970.

* * *

The work of Francis Stevens (Gertrude Bennett) appeared in pulp magazines such as *The Argosy, All-Story Weekly* and *Weird Tales* up until the early 1920s and has rarely seen book form, although a small-press edition of *The Heads of Cerberus* appeared in the 1950s and her much-praised *The Citadel of Fear* was published in 1970 as part of the then-new "adult fantasy" boom. She was, however, enthusiastically praised by fellow writers such as H. P. Lovecraft and A. Merritt, and her stories were well received when reprinted in the 1940s in *Famous Fantastic Mysteries* magazine.

Sam Moskowitz, introducing the paperback edition of *The Citadel of Fear,* called Stevens "the most gifted woman writer of science fiction and science-fantasy between Mary Wollstonecraft Shelley and C. L. Moore". This perhaps reflects the masculine domination of the field as much as, if not more than, Stevens's intrinsic gifts as a writer, but her ability to write excellent adventure fiction with a touch of humour and a great deal of colour justified her status with her peers and later commentators. Everett Bleiler, in *Science Fiction: The Early Years,* describes the apocalyptic reality-shifts of her novel *The Heads of Cerberus* as "a fine anticipation of the work of Philip K. Dick". "Friend Island" (reprinted most recently in Sam Moskowitz's *Under the Moons of Mars,* 1970) is an amusing tall tale of a shipwreck on a desert island told by a stern old sea-captain (a female sea-captain) in a future where women have won and more than won the battle for equality. Its mockery of gender-stereotypes (on both sides) also serves gently to subvert the literary conventions of the yarn prised out of a salty dog by liberal offers of rum.

Claimed! (first published in *The Argosy,* 1920) features a conflict between human and supernatural stubbornness as a mysteriously-inscribed green lava box comes into the possession of a cantankerous millionaire. A young doctor and the tycoon's beautiful niece try to discover the casket's origins, and the reason for their shared hallucinations of tidal waters. The tension is well handled, with injections of wry humour: a self-possessed and determined medium assures Vanamon and Leilah that there is nothing to fear from the spirit world, only to collapse in terror when she attempts to psychometrically ascertain the box's history.

A short novel, "Serapion" (*Argosy,* 1920), also deals with spiritualism and is a markedly effective tale of identity. The narrator, Clayton S. Barbour, after attending a seance which he only half believes in, falls under the influence of one of the medium's "voices" called Serapion: an identity which not only seems to become part of Barbour's past and present life but which manipulates his will. Interestingly, the evil which Barbour is swamped by is no slavering demon but merely the paralysis of his will when it comes to moral choices. By the end, Barbour has lived what would outwardly be counted a successful life, but at the cost of his best friend and fiancee.

The Citadel of Fear begins with two exhausted prospectors in Mexico discovering a lost city ruled by a mysterious priesthood about which Biornson, the white man who rescues them, is fearfully reticent. "Boots," the happy-go-lucky, stalwart Irishman, manages to escape, but the avaricious Kennedy, after an encounter with a black idol in front of which he witnesses a terrifying sacrifice,

remains behind. Fifteen years later, our hero, now referred to by his baptismal name of Colin O'Hara, is visiting his newly-married sister when some monstrous beast breaks into her home. The connection with the Mexican adventure becomes clearer when the visitation is traced to a nearby farm whose owner, Reed, lives with a repulsive servant, Marco, and a beautiful daughter who is claimed to be insane. Rescuing the daughter from Marco's attentions, Colin discovers that "Reed" is in fact Kennedy, who has encompassed the destruction of the city of Tlapallan but is now engaged in experiments which will spread the power of its evil god worldwide.

Unholy secrets in South/Central American cities are stock issue for pulp melodrama (used more than once by Stevens herself), and fighting Irishmen who laugh lightly at danger come out of a similar drawer. Stevens does, however, convince the reader that the 15 years between "Boots" and "Colin" are more than a dramatic pause (for one thing, Colin's stage-Irish speech is less intrusive), and the liberal use of coincidence necessary to keep such stories running without stopping for breath is employed to positively beneficial effect when the white-haired "journalist," whom O'Hara brushes aside several times as he proceeds towards the climax of the story, turns out to be Biornson. He can then relate to O'Hara's sister and brother-in-law (and thus the reader) the necessary background information at a dramatically effective point in the action. The lightness of touch Stevens gives her melodrama is beautifully shown when the young "Boots" is dreadfully embarrassed by being dressed in kilt and feathers, or when the older "Colin" gives as good as he gets in the traditional explanation scene where Kennedy, now an equally traditional "mad scientist," recounts what he has been doing in the technical polysyllables designed to intimidate his audience ("'I understand all those words,' said Colin meekly"). The climax itself, touching all bases for its readership in its mixture of supernaturalism and unrestrained science (and which interestingly reflects current worries about bioengineering) is neatly forecast by Colin's speculations about its imminent nature: "O'Hara had been reading *The Island of Dr. Moreau,* and its vivisectionary horrors had been stirring his imagination." What Stevens comes up with is worthy of her source. The half-understood images of the novel's first half, which have maintained suspense throughout, are revealed as if to chords of relentless crescendo.

Given the long-lived popularity of pulp plots in exotic settings which resulted in the recent "Indiana Jones" series of films, it is surprising that stories like *The Citadel of Fear* were never taken up by Hollywood in any of its periodic revival of fantasy adventures or popular horror. From what little is known of Stevens's life she wrote, as did so many pulp authors, for money: widowed early with a mother and young daughter to support, she needed to supplement her job as a secretary. Her fading from the scene in the early 1920s may have been due to the death of her mother, which relieved at least one financial pressure. Nevertheless, while she wrote for a highly specific market she was remarkably good at what she did. Her fiction still has the capacity to thrill and amuse. Her stories are imaginative and speculative. Within the boundaries of the pulp format, they feature strong characters, while her ability to twist conventions show that she went somewhat beyond the pulp boundaries. The praise she received is largely deserved, and like certain other writers of her era, she merits far more attention than she receives today.

—Andy Sawyer

STEVERMER, Caroline (J.)

Nationality: American. **Address:** c/o Tor Books, 175 Fifth Avenue, New York, NY 10010, USA.

FANTASY PUBLICATIONS

Novels

The Serpent's Egg. New York, Ace, 1988.
Sorcery and Cecelia: An Epistolary Fantasy, with Patricia C. Wrede. New York, Ace, 1988.
A College of Magics. New York, Tor, 1994.

OTHER PUBLICATIONS

Novels

The Alchemist: Death of a Borgia (as C. J. Stevermer). New York, Charter, 1981.
The Duke and the Veil (as C. J. Stevermer). New York, Charter, 1981.
River Rats. New York, Harcourt Brace Jovanovich, 1992.

*   *   *

To date the course of Caroline Stevermer's uneven, by no means extensive, but fascinating *oeuvre* has largely been dictated by her clear admiration for the literary swashbucklers of the past: Rafael Sabatini (a primary influence to whom a number of modern fantasy writers—Tim Powers, *et al.*—owe a debt), Anthony Hope, George Barr McCutcheon (at any rate in his "Graustark" mode), and other purveyors of high romance and higher adventure. And not only writers: her first outright fantasy novel, *The Serpent's Egg,* was dedicated to the British actor Basil Rathbone, whose screen persona was suitably flamboyant as well as, perhaps significantly, attractively villainous (on occasion, even when playing Sherlock Holmes); certainly far more sleek and feline, at times positively pantherish, than those of other great silver-screen derring-doers such as Errol Flynn or the Fairbanks *pere et fils.*

Her first novels are unacknowledged by her later publishers, although it is hardly to be supposed that Stevermer herself has rejected them (although who knows?; authors are queer cattle). They are notable in that they point strongly to the direction in which Stevermer, even as a tyro writer, was heading. Though set in the *cinquecento,* firmly at the court of the great Valentinois and at the height of the Italian Renaissance (all Sabatini territory, with a vengeance), neither *Death of a Borgia* nor *The Duke and the Veil* are historical novels *per se,* but hugely entertaining mysteries featuring an English alchemist with the appetizing name of Coffin (Nicholas of that ilk) in thrall as a kind of tame court private eye to a languidly homicidal Cesare Borgia. Both novels feature perplexing problems with skilful solutions: *Death of a Borgia* an ingenious method of poisoning (toxins leaching out of a dish's ceramic glaze into hot food) which isn't quite a full-blown "impossible crime"; *The Duke and the Veil* murder, again by poisoning, in a room that is observed from the outside but is otherwise a sealed box, which is.

Both books were issued under the mildly cloaking byline "C. J. Stevermer" and feature even milder fantasy elements. While moonlighting as a post-medieval sleuth, Coffin, as alchemist, is serious in his esoteric quests, mainly to discover the "Philosopher's Stone" which can transform base metals into gold—largely fruitless in his case since his alchemical furnace keeps blowing up (Stevermer has a keenly developed sense of farce). One of the characters, Flamel, Coffin's mentor and possibly a genuine wizard, is a man of indeterminate, perhaps enormous—perhaps even fantastic—age.

Still, enjoyable as they are, the books are mystery- rather than fantasy-oriented. *The Serpent's Egg,* though it has a mystery—a murder even—at its heart, is solidly a fantasy, set in a not-quite Elizabethan world, in a not-quite Tudor England that yet has nudging echoes of our reality (names, especially, that ring recollective bells: Sir Robert *Edghill* . . . the Lady *Jehane* of Domremy . . . the villainous, and very Rathbone-ish, Duke of *Tilbury*), as well as echoes of other writers, other books, firm favourites, one imagines, of the author, now subtly and intelligently transmuted for her own purposes (a tense barge journey, entrapments at an inn, much eatings and drinkings, swordplay and jocosity all smack of a cross between the British writer who called himself Dornford Yates, and his fantasy masterpiece *The Stolen March,* and the elder Dumas).

The mystery—who killed the head of Queen Andred's victorious army—is swiftly settled: the courtier closest to the Queen, and thus inviolable. The Queen's son, Bertram, accused of plotting against her, is thrown into durance vile. The fair Lady Margaret Yewesley, champion of justice and the right, is dismissed ignominiously from the Queen's service. The dashing Sir Christopher Carrington is trapped in an alehouse cellar for much of the book then arrested for high treason (a trumped-up charge). Though it can lead to the unhinging of the user's mind, the "serpent's egg"— a fabulous crystal through which can be understood not only earthly matters and movements but the arcane shapings and shiftings of the magical universe—is sought by both sides in this engrossing and actionful struggle.

By comparison *Sorcery and Cecelia,* an epistolary novel written with Patricia Wrede and set in an alternative world of the Regency (1817) where magic works, is a romp, and very nearly flawless as a work of entertainment (the odd anachronism aside). Although dedicated to a couple of the usual suspects in this kind of genre—Tolkien and Jane Austen—*Sorcery and Cecelia* can in fact be far more justly summed up as Georgette Heyer-meets-magic. Both writers give immensely spirited performances, Wrede as Cecelia, a conventional Regency rich-miss whose brother has untapped magical resources lusted after by the villains, Stevermer as Kate, Cecy's cousin, hoydenish, feisty, and with much to put up with (including a tract-reading aunt). The plot, though good and complicated—with one or two splendidly chilling confrontations, is of little consequence; the book's chief delight, especially in the Stevermer sections, is the joyous, hilarious Heyer pastiche.

Stevermer is by no means a prolific writer of fantasy (her 1992 novel, *River Rats,* is science fiction for young adults). Her latest fantasy title is *A College of Magics,* a "break-out" novel whose publicity perhaps promises more than the book itself delivers, and whose dust-jacket champions appear to have been reading quite another work. This time—or this alternative—we are in a not-quite Edwardian era in which Edward himself has a mort of daughters instead of sons, both Graustark *and* Ruritania are realities, and (of course) magic works. In this world young Faris Nallaneen, Duchess of Galazon (the Balkans, sort of), is sent to Greenlaw College on the Normandy coast to learn magic; there she also makes an enemy of Menary of Aravill. Faris then discovers that she is in fact "Warden of the North," one of four magical guardians of the world, whose task is to seal a vast and sorcerous rift. After a certain amount of to-ing and fro-ing, this she does.

Alas, *A College of Magics,* for all the old-pals' praise heaped upon it, has a strong whiff not only of the machine-shop about it but those most dreary of American institutions: the writers' circle and the creative-writing course. Correct in all its attitudes, it yet lacks all the qualities one found so admirable in Stevermer's previous work: focus, purpose, acuity. There is no tension. The secondary-lead Jane Brailsford is a far more persuasive, and up-at-'em, character than the caponed males and lacklustre villains, and especially the moping heroine, who drearily drifts through the plot, so baffled and debilitated by events that one can only cheer the villainess in her efforts to destroy her (and despair when she in turn is disposed of by Faris in the most perfunctory manner possible). Perhaps, nestling in the warm womb of over-fulsome peer-praise, Stevermer has forgotten her swashbuckling roots. Instead of Captain Blood, in *A College of Magics* at any rate, she appears to be drawing inspiration from Nancy Drew.

In her "not-quite" worlds Caroline Stevermer has never demonstrated the immense research infrastructure of a Melissa Scott, say, or a Tim Powers, but she has movement and pace and drama and bite, and, crucially, that most intelligent and un-American of writing weapons, irony. She also has a wonderful sense of farce and (when on form) impeccable timing. It seems a pity to waste these not inconsiderable talents on writing books for the Camp-Fire Movement.

—Jack Adrian

STEWART, Mary (Florence Elinor)

Nationality: British. **Born:** Mary Rainbow, Sunderland, County Durham, 17 September 1916. **Education:** Eden Hall, Penrith, Cumberland; Skellfield School, Ripon, Yorkshire; St. Hilda's College, University of Durham, B.A. (honours) 1938, M.A. 1941. **Military Service:** Royal Observer Corps during World War II. **Family:** Married Sir Frederick Henry Stewart in 1945. **Career:** Lecturer in English, Durham University, 1941-45. **Awards:** Crime Writers Association Silver Dagger, 1961; Frederick Niven award, 1971; Scottish Arts Council award, 1975. Fellow, Royal Society of Arts, 1968; Fellow, Newnham College, Cambridge, 1986. Lives in Edinburgh. **Address:** c/o Hodder Headline PLC, 338 Euston Road, London NW1 3BH, England.

FANTASY PUBLICATIONS

Novels (series: Merlin in all books)

The Crystal Cave. London, Hodder and Stoughton, and New York, Morrow, 1970.
The Hollow Hills. London, Hodder and Stoughton, and New York, Morrow, 1973.
The Last Enchantment. London, Hodder and Stoughton, and New York, Morrow, 1979.
Merlin Trilogy (omnibus; includes *The Crystal Cave, The Hollow Hills, The Last Enchantment*). New York, Morrow, 1980.
The Wicked Day. London, Hodder and Stoughton, and New York, Morrow, 1983.

OTHER PUBLICATIONS

Novels

Madam, Will You Talk? London, Hodder and Stoughton, 1955; New York, Mill, 1956.
Wildfire at Midnight. London, Hodder and Stoughton, and New York, Appleton Century Crofts, 1956.
Thunder on the Right. London, Hodder and Stoughton, 1957; New York, Mill, 1958.
Nine Coaches Waiting. London, Hodder and Stoughton, 1958; New York, Mill, 1959.
My Brother Michael. London, Hodder and Stoughton, and New York, Mill, 1960.
The Ivy Tree. London, Hodder and Stoughton, 1961; New York, Mill, 1962.
The Moon Spinners. London, Hodder and Stoughton, 1962; New York, Mill, 1963.
This Rough Magic. London, Hodder and Stoughton, and New York, Mill, 1964.
Airs above the Ground. London, Hodder and Stoughton, and New York, Mill, 1965.
The Gabriel Hounds. London, Hodder and Stoughton, and New York, Mill, 1967.
The Wind Off the Small Isles. London, Hodder and Stoughton, 1968.
Touch Not the Cat. London, Hodder and Stoughton, and New York, Morrow, 1976.
Thornyhold. London, Hodder and Stoughton, and New York, Morrow, 1988.
Stormy Petrel. London, Hodder and Stoughton, and New York, Morrow, 1991.

Poetry

Frost on the Window and Other Poems. London, Hodder and Stoughton, 1990.

Plays

Radio Plays: *Lift from a Stranger, Call Me at Ten-Thirty, The Crime of Mr. Merry,* and *The Lord of Langdale,* 1957-58.

Other (for children)

The Little Broomstick. Leicester, Brockhampton Press, 1971; New York, Morrow, 1972.
Ludo and the Star Horse. Leicester, Brockhampton Press, 1974; New York, Morrow, 1975.
A Walk in Wolf Wood. London, Hodder and Stoughton, and New York, Morrow, 1980.

*

Film Adaptation: *The Moon-Spinners,* 1964.

Manuscript Collection: National Library of Scotland, Edinburgh.

*   *   *

Mary Stewart is a prolific writer of popular fiction. Her works of fantasy are her four Arthurian novels. The first three of these, which form the Merlin Trilogy, tell the life story of Merlin, Arthur's wizard. They are loosely based on *The History of the Kings of Britain* and *The Life of Merlin,* wholly spurious accounts by the 12th-century writer Geoffrey of Monmouth, and on the 15th-century *Le Morte D'Arthur* by Thomas Malory.

The first book, *The Crystal Cave,* tells of Merlin's early life. In Stewart's version of the legend, he is himself a prince—the illegitimate son of a Welsh princess and Aurelius Ambrosius, a Roman commander waiting in exile to retake Britain. The narrative tracks Merlin's progress as he avoids the murderous intentions of his maternal uncle, runs away from home and makes a place for himself with his father. Along the way, he has many of the adventures ascribed to him by Geoffrey of Monmouth.

In this first book, Stewart sets up the approach she will take to her material throughout the series. The story is told in the first person, from Merlin's point of view. He is an intriguing mixture of pragmatist and fey, believer and agnostic. He has visions, true dreams in which he sees what is and what is to come. These, he believes, come from the god: but he refuses to identify this god as being Christian, Mithraditic or of the Druidic, goddess-worshipping Old Faith. At the same time he is portrayed as a polymath, dedicated to understanding the world through scholarship in the fields of science, mathematics and engineering. These themes are encapsulated in the episode where is captured by Vortigern, who has been seeking a "fatherless boy" to sacrifice to make the walls of his castle stand. Merlin has a vision of red and white dragons (the Welsh and Saxons) fighting; this saves his life, but it is his knowledge of engineering that allows him to explain how to drain the water beneath the castle and make the walls stand.

In *The Hollow Hills,* which is based more on Malory, Merlin creates the tool he needs to unite Britain, by engineering the birth of Arthur. He sees to Arthur's education, protects him from those who would benefit from his death, and forces the local chieftains to accept him as High King. What he cannot do is stop Arthur from sleeping with his half-sister, the witch Morgause. Mordred, the child she has by him, will be his downfall. In this version, Morgause is clearly the knowing instigator of the incest, and her attempts to seduce Merlin—knowing that his power is linked to his virginity—are a recurrent theme. This foreshadows—and inverts—later events between Merlin and Nimue.

In this book, Stewart makes clear that, as she says in her afterword, Merlin is "the link between the worlds; the instrument by which, as he says 'all the kings become one King, all the gods one God.'" The crystal cave of the first book, where he is tutored by his first teacher, Galapas, now becomes an example of the hollow hills where, in myth, the faery-folk live; this in turn becomes a metaphor for all the secret knowledge that Merlin possesses—not only his human scholarship, nor even the special knowledge he is vouchsafed during his fits, but the wisdom of his heart, which will not tie the God that grants him visions to one religion, and which allows him to understand the politics of his time and the psychology of those around him so that he can achieve his ends (or, in his terms, those of the God).

The Last Enchantment relates the story of Merlin's old age, and his involvement with Nimue, a girl who first disguises herself as a boy in order to become his apprentice. When Merlin becomes old and infirm, she replaces him as Arthur's adviser. Merlin ends his days in his crystal cave, and the book concludes on note of elegiac acceptance of his fate.

The novel also deals with the love triangle between Arthur, his queen, Guinevere, and Bedwyr (the prototype for the Lancelot of Malory and the later romances). Something of Stewart's eclectic approach to her material can be seen in her use of Bedwyr rather than Lancelot as Guinevere's lover. Lancelot is a rather late addition to the Arthurian legend, while Bedwyr appears much earlier. Yet in other places, such as the abduction of Guinevere by Melwas, Stewart has used much of the later material.

Her real efforts seem to have been directed towards constructing plausible characters out of the stuff of the early legends, in which characterization in the modern sense was of little importance. For instance, according to legend Nimue was an enchantress who sealed Merlin in a cave (or otherwise led him to his doom) yet later went on to help Arthur and be trusted by him. In Stewart's version, Nimue is a trusted acolyte of Merlin; he becomes ill and she, with his full co-operation, takes his power; then, when he seems to have died, she buries him in his cave. This has the additional advantage of balancing some of the anti-female bias in the legends, where women of (magical) power, such as Morgause, are almost inevitably evil.

Stewart's approach works admirably for the most part, though some may feel that she is making Arthur too noble—and perhaps too modern—when he calmly accepts Guinevere's adultery with Bedwyr, on the grounds that if he is to be cuckolded, he would rather it were by his best friend.

In these books, Mordred is portrayed as nothing more than a villain, whom Merlin repeatedly warns Arthur about. This creates problems in the last of Stewart's Arthurian books, *The Wicked Day.* This is set after Merlin's death, and is told from the point of view of Mordred, though in the third person.

This novel was written some time after the others, and presented Stewart with some difficulties. The source material is full of improbabilities (for example Arthur leaves his kingdom in Mordred's care even though he knows his son to be treacherous; and Mordred tries to usurp his father's throne even though he has already been declared the heir). In her afterword, Stewart says she was tempted to ignore all of this, and make Mordred a worthy heir to his father's throne. However, this would have been inconsistent with her earlier work. In the light of this, telling the tale from Mordred's point of view works splendidly. It allows his character to emerge as much more complex and sympathetic than it might otherwise have done. Here, Mordred is clearly as much a victim of Morgause's machinations as Arthur ever was, and his attempts to overcome the weakness of character that leads him to his final clash with his father make him an engaging, if not wholly likeable, character.

—Liz Holliday

———

STOCKBRIDGE, Grant. *See* **PAGE, Norvell W(ooten).**

———

STRICKLAND, (William) Brad(ley)

Pseudonym: Will Bradley. **Nationality:** American. **Born:** New Holland, Georgia, 27 October 1947. **Education:** University of Georgia, A.B. 1969; M.A. 1971; Ph.D. in English Literature, 1976. **Family:** Married Barbara Justus; one son, one daughter. **Career:**

Teacher, Truett-McConnell College, Cleveland, Georgia, 1976-85; Lakeview Academy, Gainesville, Georgia, 1985-87; associate professor of English, Gainesville College, from 1987. **Address:** 5044 Valley Court, Oakwood, GA 30566, USA.

FANTASY PUBLICATIONS

Novels (series: Jeremy Moon)

Moon Dreams. New York, Signet, 1988; London, Headline, 1988.
Nul's Quest (Moon). New York, Signet, 1989; London, Headline, 1990.
Wizard's Mole (Moon). New York, Roc, 1991.
Dragon's Plunder. New York, Atheneum, 1992.
The Ghost in the Mirror, with John Bellairs. New York, Dial, 1993.
The Vengeance of the Witch-Finder, with John Bellairs. New York, Dial, 1993.
The Drum, the Doll, and the Zombie, with John Bellairs. New York, Dial, 1994.

OTHER PUBLICATIONS

Novels

To Stand Beneath the Sun. New York, Signet, 1986.
ShadowShow. New York, Onyx, 1988.
Children of the Knife. New York, Onyx, 1990.
Ark Liberty (as Will Bradley). New York, Roc, 1992.
The Star Ghost. New York, Pocket, 1994.
Stowaways. New York, Pocket, 1994.

Plays

The Tale of the Rooster, with Ed Cabell and Roy Forrester (produced Georgia, 1990).
C.O.'s D-Day (produced Georgia, 1991).
Farewell to Joe and Jackie, with Ed Cabell and Roy Forrester (produced Georgia, 1991).
The Great Air Monopoly, with Thomas E. Fuller, adaptation of a story by L. Ron Hubbard (produced Georgia, 1993).

Radio Plays: *The House on Nowhere Road,* 1990; *The Rats in the Walls,* with Thomas E. Fuller, adaptation of a story by H. P. Lovecraft, 1990.

*   *   *

Brad Strickland's fantasy fiction to date consists in the main of the adult trilogy *Moon Dreams, Nul's Quest* and *Wizard's Mole,* and the young adult novel *Dragon's Plunder* (although he has also completed several juvenile fantasy-mysteries by the late John Bellairs). These novels are adventure fantasies leavened with varying degrees of humour.

When you learn that the Jeremy Moon trilogy is about an advertising copywriter thrust into the fantasy world of Thaumia, where words have magical power, you might expect a madcap humorous fantasy *a la* Terry Pratchett. Instead, the Moon books are straightforward—and sometimes cliched—heroic adventure with redeeming touches of wit and irony.

In *Moon Dreams,* Jeremy's Thaumian double, the exiled wizard Sebastian Magister, trades places with him through Jeremy's nightmares. Once Jeremy has convinced the hostile wizardly establishment that he is not Sebastian, he finds himself learning magic and involved in the battle against the Hidden Hag of Illsmere, an ally of the Great Dark One, an evil wizard from the south bent on world domination. In *Nul's Quest,* Jeremy accompanies Nul, a short, furry creature called a pika, to the Twilight Valley, where magic does not work, to find and liberate Nul's people, enslaved by the hobs, former soldiers of the Great Dark One. In *Wizard's Mole,* Jeremy retrieves Sebastian from Earth and pressures him into helping with the final battle against the Great Dark One and his demon helpers, the Shadow Guard.

Strickland gives Thaumian magic a pseudo-scientific basis. As in our universe everything is a form of energy, so in Thaumia everything is a form of magic. As our universe tends toward entropy, when no work can be done, Thaumia tends toward mundanity, when no magic can be done. Thaumian magic is even governed by the "laws of thaumadynamics," which closely parallel our laws of thermodynamics. More important, Thaumian magic is verbal. Once the proper result has been visualized, one has merely to speak it in order to realize it. However, a verbal formula, once used, is no longer effective, so wizards must devote much time to new formulations of magical spells. Jeremy has great potential power because he speaks English, in which no spells have previously been done in Thaumia. Amusement comes from his couching of his spells in advertising terminology. The moment in *Moon Dreams* when, vastly outnumbered and with a broken weapon, Jeremy desperately shouts, "My sword is NEW and IMPROVED!" making it a powerful magical sword, is a high point.

There are not enough such high points in the first book, which too often plods along familiar, well-trodden paths. Some imagery stays with the reader, particularly the dead kingdom of the hag and her amphibian soldiers; the vilorgs, and the touches of wit help, but in general there is little to lift *Moon Dreams* above the myriad other fantasy adventure novels.

Nul's Quest has more points of interest, although the plot is, unfortunately, resolved by a *deus ex machina.* The plight of the enslaved pikas is moving, and the difficulties faced by wizards in the hostile Twilight Valley sustain the reader's attention. Moon is also facing an ethical dilemma: his translations of Shakespeare's plays into the Thaumian tongue are a great success, but the acclaim he receives for another man's work leaves him feeling guilty and hollow. At the end of the book, he resolves this problem by writing an original play. (However, in *Wizard's Mole* Moon is back translating Shakespeare, and all of his ethical difficulties seem to have vanished.)

Wizard's Mole is the best of the three books, its success resting on the interaction between Thaumia and our world. Sebastian, ironically, is more of a success on Earth than Jeremy ever was, having become an extremely successful advertising executive and conducting a run for public office. He provides a more cynical perspective on events in Thaumia. His attempts to convince Jeremy that the Great Dark One (evil) and Chief Mage Tremien (good) are just two sides of the same coin, with Tremien as dedicated as the Great Dark One to running people's lives and with little to choose between them, are unfortunately not followed through or resolved; Sebastian would seem to be proved wrong by Tremien's resignation as Chief Mage after the defeat of the Great Dark One, but the argument has long since been dropped. The theme of the books may be put into Sebastian's mouth when he says, "Maybe your world needs heroes every once in a long while. . . . Somebody to be so idiotically good that everyone else sees the measure of what people can be."

The humour in the Moon books is not intrusive and is generally successful, although the running joke of Nul the pika's literalism becomes tiresome. Much of it springs from the collision of Thaumia with Earth, as in, most prominently, Jeremy's ad-language spells. Some of it grows out of the Thaumian situations themselves; an example is the adventures of Fred and Busby, two enormous living stone gargoyles, when, in *Nul's Quest,* they are shrunk and disguised as cats.

There is a different sort of humour in *Dragon's Plunder,* Strickland's young adult novel, which is an enjoyable tribute to pirate novels. Some of the dialogue in this book has the absurd feel of a Monty Python routine. It is the story of Jamie Falconer, a 15-year-old boy who joins the crew of the privateer *Betty* because of his magical talent for whistling up the wind. It turns out that the captain of the *Betty,* Octavius Deadmon, is indeed a dead man, and has been for 20 years. Many years ago he swore an oath not to rest until he had stolen a dragon's hoard, an oath difficult to fulfil, as dragons are rare, and even death has not released him, or his crew, from the vow. The only dragon the privateers know of is on Windrose Island, which is protected by magical winds; only Jamie's talent can get them there. Along the way the crew fights vicious pirates and rescues a princess, albeit one from an extremely small kingdom.

Unfortunately, when they get to the dragon, they discover it is studious and has spent all its hoard on books. Nevertheless, Deadmon's vow is finally fulfilled when he takes a pirate ship named *The Golden Dragon*; this is a cheat, but the fulfilments of vows and curses often are. In a rather unbelievable turn of events, Jamie is made captain of the *Betty,* an ending presumably designed to please the book's teenage audience. A ship commanded by a dead man could easily be a horrific vision, but there is little or no horror to Deadmon as Strickland paints him: he is kind, and rather pathetic. The same might be said of the crew, which gives the *Betty* a cosy feeling. Even the enemy pirates have more of an air of moustache-twirling villainy than of true evil. Strickland is aiming for rousing adventure and humour, both of which are present in abundance. Though much simpler, *Dragon's Plunder* is more successfully constructed and more satisfying than the Moon books.

Strickland has a fine sense of humour and good storytelling abilities, both of which talents he is employing with increasing success in his fantasy novels. The Moon books, though flawed, are worth reading; his next work of adult fantasy should be much more so.

—Janice M. Eisen

SWANN, Thomas Burnett

Nationality: American. **Born:** Tampa, Florida, 12 October 1928. **Education:** Duke University, B.A. (Phi Beta Kappa) 1950; University of Tennessee, M.A. 1955; University of Florida, Ph.D. 1960. **Military Service:** United States Navy. **Career:** Taught English at Florida Southern College, Wesleyan College (Macon, Georgia), and Florida Atlantic University. **Died:** 5 May 1976.

FANTASY PUBLICATIONS

Novels (series: Minotaur; Rome)

Day of the Minotaur. New York, Ace 1966; London, Mayflower, 1975.
The Weirwoods. New York, Ace, 1967.
Moondust. New York, Ace, 1968.
The Forest of Forever (Minotaur). New York, Ace, 1971; London, Mayflower, 1975.
The Goat Without Horns. New York, Ballantine, 1971.
Wolfwinter. New York, Ballantine, 1972.
Green Phoenix (Rome). New York, DAW, 1972.
How Are the Mighty Fallen. New York, DAW, 1974.
The Not-World. New York, DAW, 1975.
The Tournament of Thorns. New York, Ace, 1976.
Lady of the Bees (Rome). New York, Ace, 1976.
Will-o-the-Wisp. London, Corgi, 1976.
The Gods Abide. New York, DAW, 1976.
The Minikins of Yam. New York, DAW, 1976.
Cry Silver Bells (Minotaur). New York, DAW, 1977.
Queens Walk in the Dusk (Rome). Forest Park, Georgia, Heritage Press, 1977.

Short Stories

The Dolphin and the Deep. New York, Ace, 1968.
Where Is the Bird of Fire? New York, Ace, 1970.

OTHER PUBLICATIONS

Other

Wonder and Whimsy: The Fantastic World of Christina Rossetti. Francestown, New Hampshire, M. Joes, 1960.
Ernest Dawson. New York, Twayne, 1965.
A. A. Milne. New York, Twayne, 1971.
The Heroine or the Horse: Leading Ladies in Republic's Films. South Brunswick, New Jersey, Barnes, 1977.

*

Bibliography: *Thomas Burnett Swann: A Brief Critical Biography and Annotated Bibliography* by Robert A. Collins, Boca Raton, Florida Atlantic University, 1979.

*   *   *

Thomas Burnett Swann's modest output of short novels and novellas lies on the cusp between historical fiction and heroic fantasy. His most favoured milieu was the pre-classical Mediterranean, but he ventured forward as far as 17th-century England. The flavour of his work is gentle and sensuous but elegiac—this last almost of necessity, since many of his characters are the semi-humans of classical myth. As the dryads, tritons, centaurs, fauns etc., are no longer with us, it must follow that they have been killed or dispossessed; Swann was writing allegories of habitat-destruction well before Green politics was invented. Yet his message, in so far as he has one, is hardly political—only that those who offer kindness and appreciate beauty will never lack the favour of the gods, however much they may incur the disfavour of sadistic and/or puritanical Man; and that though such favour may not save them from passing away, it will surely ease their passing. At worst, this can lead to sentimentality, but Swann at his best can be likened to Jack Vance viewed through gauze. In "The Dolphin and the Deep" Arnth, a young gentleman of Etruria, contemplates his own appearance:

> In the polished bronze of the mirror, the eyes which met my stare were dark and slanted, like those of my ancestors, the Lydians, and old with accumulated sorrows, with the weight of dead cities, buried and mouldering, of battles and tortures and beautiful shameless queens who smiled and shook poison from rings like golden spiders.

Arnth is innocent without being simple. Aged 25, he is too idealistic for casual sex and too serious-minded for light love. He dreams of some vaguely defined beauty who waits "patient and dreaming at the end of my furthest voyage". Meanwhile, there are chaste masculine friendships and the pleasures of exploration and adventure. And yes, he is tested by guile and misfortune; and yes, he finds love, in a manner which grows logically from the tale and is far less abstract than his imaginings. Swann avoids the sordid, and if he also avoids explicit sex scenes it is more from fastidiousness than prissiness. Indeed, he performs a deft double when a Myrmidon captures an Amazon:

> "I might, I suppose, keep you to wait on me. Milk the aphids and cook my mushrooms. And of course," he added wickedly, "perform the other functions of a woman." He looked like a small boy who has whispered a naughty word to his sister.

At the same time, it must be admitted that Swann is at his most characteristic when describing beauty, and he pretties-up his settings, beyond what his historical scholarship (considerable, but lightly worn) can really justify. Yet his range extends to the horror of a nest of harpies or a mandrake hunt, and to the pathos of a dryad, ravished and murdered beside her tree. His are tales of adventure, from which not all his principals emerge alive or whole in heart, and behind them all is the knowledge that those who disdain honour and scruple are always at an advantage vis-a-vis those who respond, however imperfectly, to the prick of conscience. They may well have the advantages of weight, numbers and surprise also— and it is then that they are most likely to take the offensive, against (of course) the unoffending. Swann more than anyone celebrates the desperate (and usually ineffective) valour of the weak.

The early tale, "Where is the Bird of Fire?," tells the story of the founding of Rome from the viewpoint of a faun who is a friend of Remus. Romulus is the villain of the piece, cheating Remus and then murdering him. There's a sense that though Remus was the better man, Romulus was the man the time required—for Rome was very much the creation of the new race of modern Man; and modern Man was destined to sweep aside the beauties of the Ancient World.

Although American, Swann found his first acceptance in Britain: his debut novel, *Day of the Minotaur,* was originally serialized in 1964 in the English magazine *Science Fantasy* (as "The Blue Monkeys"). Its setting is Crete, around 1500 B.C., when the rough Achaeans of mainland Greece are beginning to harry the island's Minoan civilization. The central characters are two teenaged children, Thea and Icarus—and their seven-foot friend, Eunostos the Minotaur. As the Achaeans attack, the prince and princess escape from their father's mansion, just south of Knossos, aboard one of the gliders built by the artificer Daedalus. They crash-land in the fabled Country of the Beasts, a little-known wooded area on the south of the island. They hope to find protection in the forest, for these young people are themselves "half-beast," with violet eyes and pointed ears and hair of a greenish hue (their mother was a Dryad). Sure enough, they are welcomed into the enchanted realm of the forest by its motley inhabitants—Centaurs, Dryads, Telchines, Panisci, blue monkeys and others. The benign leader of these woodland folk is the Minotaur, who also turns out to be the narrator of the story. This is Arcadia with a cosy, Walt Disney touch, but the novel's over-sweet, children's-story qualities are offset by a playful sexiness (young Icarus dallies with Zoe the Dryad among others), and by the underlying sombreness of the theme, which is the war between cruel men and the unfallen Beasts. *The Forest of Forever* and *Cry Silver Bells* are related novels.

The best introduction to Swann is probably the collection of three novelettes *The Dolphin and the Deep,* which includes "The Manor of Roses" and "The Murex" as well as the title story. They represent his range well enough, two settings being pre-classical (one of them featuring those rarest of mythological creatures, the Myrmidons), the other being medieval English. They also illustrate his limitations, as "The Manor of Roses" carries both flower imagery and cultivated sensitivity beyond the bounds of all but the lushest taste. It features a twelve-year-old boy whose favourite poem is "The Owl and the Nightingale"—a creation far more unlikely than any faun, siren, minotaur or mandrake. Yet it's also a tale of hard choices faced and made without flinching, and without the false comfort of self-induced hysteria. With Chesterton, Swann turns away

> From all that terror teaches;
> From lies of tongue and pen;
> From all the easy speeches
> That comfort cruel men,
> From shame and profanation
> Of honour and the sword . . .

and whatever his faults of taste or credibility, Swann never cheats.

—Chris Gilmore

SWITHIN, Antony

Nationality: Canadian. **Born:** In Britain.

FANTASY PUBLICATIONS

Novels (series: Perilous Quest for Lyonesse)

Princes of Sandastre. London, Fontana, 1990.
The Lords of the Stoney Mountains. London, Fontana, 1991.
The Winds of the Wastelands. London, Fontana, 1992.
The Nine Gods of Safaddne. London, Fontana, 1993.

*   *   *

Antony Swithin's fantasy series is called the Perilous Quest for Lyonesse, but despite the title it has little to do with Arthurian themes and more in common with those fantasies that take as their starting-point the hero's translation into a foreign realm and the marvels of flora and fauna he finds there. Simon Branthwaite's quest offers no contact with hobbits, dwarfs and elves, yet it is closer to the spirit of Tolkien than most fantasy explicitly written with *The Lord of the Rings* as a touchstone, simply because the author (like Tolkien) has allowed the reader entrance into a lovingly created world which is itself the focus of interest. The adventures are secondary.

The germ of the epic appears to have been a fascination with the lonely, windswept Atlantic island of Rockall, which Swithin has transformed into a country with its own geography and natural history: he introduces *Princes of Sandastre* as a medieval manuscript from its archives, presenting it with a context of its own. This conceit is not original, and indeed seems rather old-fashioned, as do many of the author's narrative devices. Yet it is precisely the somewhat archaic storytelling, evoking the heroic romances of Victorian and Edwardian times, which gives the epic its interest.

The young hero (whose slightly stilted air of self-deprecation as he relates his own actions is faintly reminiscent of Alan Quatermain in H. Rider Haggard's novels) is Simon Branthwaite, whose father and elder brother fought on the losing side in Henry Hotspur's revolt against the King of England in 1403. Simon, whose slight build and distaste for cruelty have mistakenly persuaded his father that he has no calling for adventure and wars, is left behind for a possible career in the Church when the others march off to battle. After the Battle of Shrewsbury, Simon receives a message that his father and brother have fled to the newly-founded realm of Lyonesse, carved out somewhere on the island of Rockall by the adventurer Arthur Thurlstone, steeped in the legends of his namesake who saw in Rockall the original of the Isle of Avalon. Knowing nothing of Lyonesse other than a few travellers' tales, Simon is determined to prove his valour and join his father. Escaping from Yorkshire to Bristol, he is instrumental in saving the life of Avran, a prince from the South-Rockallian realm of Sandastre, and joins him on his voyage home. There, he finds that the location of Lyonesse is more of a mystery than it was in England. Meanwhile, however, his bravery and ingenuity are put to the test in further conspiracies against his friend Avran and his people. The first volume ends with him leaving his new home, in company with Avran, heading northwards into strange lands to find his family.

Simon's quest is full of adventure and suspense, but is essentially a travelogue, in which the author is quite prepared to leave the adventuring to expand more upon the land of Rockall. We see Rockall through Simon's eyes, a land of marvellous beasts such as the semi-telepathic horned *sevdreyen* or *veludain* used as mounts instead of horses, populated by different nations and descendants of adventurers from Europe such as the crusader Sir Robert Randwulf. The author is careful not to allow Simon or his informants to know too much (one of the drawbacks of this kind of fiction is the amount of predigested history which is fed to the reader), but it is clear from what is revealed about Rockall's past that it is a remnant of Atlantis, and indeed references are made to islands to the south of Rockall where the descendants of the long-overthrown Atlantean empire are exiled. What is less clear is why the flora and fauna of the land should be so distinct from that of the rest of the world, but they seem to be those of previous geological ages: the "glagrang" or carnivorous river-turtle and the sabre-toothed "branath" are but two of the threats which Simon faces.

Eventually his journey takes him through central and northern Rockall to the mysterious land of Safaddne where his party is joined by the enigmatic Essa who is hailed by the Safaddnese as a lost princess of legend. There, the location of Lyonesse is eventually revealed and Simon is reunited with his relatives in time to avert full-scale war between the domains of North Rockall and to impress his brother Richard with his courage, coolness and ingenuity.

Essentially, the "Perilous Quest" is a historical adventure of the middle ages, with little introduction of the fantastic apart from the invented setting and the occasional hint that the "nine gods of Safaddne" have a more active part in the world than Simon, as an orthodox Christian, would approve of. It is exactly the kind of historical fantasy, in fact, which can be accused of being nothing but dramatized escape-clauses from both genres: apart from the first few chapters and occasional background reminders we do not really need to be in the 15th century of our own historical time-line. Nevertheless, it is a vivid creation. Simon is exactly the kind of hero this storyline requires; a youth who will develop into maturity, brave and competent if not over-gifted (he is a skilful knife-thrower and archer, but no swordsman) and reliant on luck, intelligence, and his companions. By creating an imaginary "other country," the author avoids the second besetting sin of his particular sub-genre: the anachronistic nature of having a hero too "progressively" at odds with many of the prevailing ethics of his time. Simon's 20th-century liberalism—he is sympathetic to the idea of having the Bible available in the vernacular and prefers observing animals to hunting them—finds echoes in Rockallian attitudes. "Now I was delighted to learn of a land where my personal prejudices were not considered freakish, but universally held."

Swithin's imagined world is detailed enough to feel real within the context of his story, with sufficient gaps left to suggest that there is more to be explored—indeed the ending of volume four, while technically the conclusion of Simon's quest, by no means precludes further chapters of this particular epic. Perhaps the most fascinating glimpse into his world, though, is the two-page introduction to the first volume which summarizes "Rockall" as a nation in our own world. One suspects that the 500 years between Simon Branthwaite's time and our own would have much to offer as a source for further fiction.

—Andy Sawyer

T

TARR, Judith

Nationality: American. **Born:** Augusta, Maine, 30 January 1955.
Education: Mount Holyoke College, 1972-76, A.B.; Cambridge
University, 1976-78, B.A. in classics, 1978; M.A. in classics, 1983;
Yale University, 1978-79, M.A. in medieval studies, 1979; Yale
University, 1981-88, Ph.D. in medieval studies, 1988. **Career:**
Teacher of Latin, Edward Little High School, Auburn, Maine, 1979-
81. Visiting lecturer in liberal studies and visiting writer, Wesleyan
University, Middletown, Connecticut, since 1989. Visiting Assis-
tant Professor of classics, Wesleyan University, since 1990.
Awards: Crawford Memorial award, 1987; Mary Lyon award, Mt.
Holyoke College, 1989. **Agent:** Jane Butler, 212 Third Street,
Milford, PA 18337, USA. **Address:** 94 Foster Street, Number 3,
New Haven, CT 06511, USA.

FANTASY PUBLICATIONS

Novels (series: Avaryan Rising; The Hound and the Falcon)

The Isle of Glass (Hound and the Falcon). New York, Bluejay,
1985; London, Bantam, 1986.
The Golden Horn (Hound and the Falcon). New York, Bluejay,
1985; London, Bantam, 1986.
The Hounds of God (Hound and the Falcon). New York, Bluejay,
1986; London, Bantam, 1987.
The Hound and the Falcon (omnibus; includes *The Isle of Glass,
The Golden Horn, A Hounds of God*). New York, Nelson
Doubleday, 1986.
The Hall of the Mountain King (Avaryan). New York, Tor, 1986;
London, Pan, 1988.
The Lady of Han-Gilen (Avaryan). New York, Tor, 1987; London,
Pan, 1989.
A Fall of Princes (Avaryan). New York, Tor, 1988; London, Pan,
1989.
Avaryan Rising (omnibus; includes *The Hall of the Mountain King,
The Lady of Han-Gilen, A Fall of Princes*). New York, Nelson
Doubleday, 1988.
A Wind in Cairo. New York, Bantam, 1989; London, Bantam, 1990.
Ars Magica. New York, Bantam, 1989.
Alamut. New York, Doubleday, 1989.
The Dagger and the Cross: A Novel of the Crusades. New York,
Doubleday, 1991.
Lord of the Two Lands. New York, Tor, 1993.
Arrows of the Sun (Avaryan). New York, Tor, 1993.
Throne of Isis. New York, Tor, 1994.
Spear of Heaven (Avaryan). New York, Tor, 1994.

*   *   *

Judith Tarr's background as a medieval historian was apparent
in her first trilogy, the Hound and the Falcon, set in a 12th-century
world identical to ours except that rarely but randomly children are
born who are known as changelings, elf-folk, Kindred of the Jann,
witches—people of great beauty and power. One such is Alf, whom
we first meet in *The Isle of Glass*. Named after his probable origins as a foundling left at St. Ruan's abbey Alf, "Brother Alfred"
is uncannily youthful; while his boyhood friend the Abbot is an
old man, Alf has the appearance of a lad in his teens. A scholar and
theologian, he is nevertheless forced into the outside world when a
wounded elf-lord from the kingdom of Rhiyana seeks sanctuary,
having been tortured by a baron who intends to raise fire and sword
along the borderlands. Taking his place as emissary to Richard the
Lionheart's court, Alf is forced into conflict between his nature and
his religion. Is he a true monk or does his vocation mask his own
wish-fulfilment? Is his longevity and beauty a cover for elvish soul-
lessness? Has he and his kind a place with God? Despite the loyalty of his pupil Jehan (and perhaps spurred by the love of the
shape-changing Thea, another of his kind), Alf is racked with
doubts. He gains Richard's friendship, but not to the extent of
changing his readiness for a war which would ravage three kingdoms. Eventually, he can only place himself in the hands of the
inquisitorial Hounds of God to be tried for sorcery in an attempt to
delay Richard's war-making. While this plan fails, Alf does eventually settle Baron Rhydderch's intrigues but at great cost to his
own self-image. With so many others attempting to define him as
priest, or elven-knight, Alf clings instead to what he can grasp of
his own being and departs for Jerusalem on a pilgrimage.

The Golden Horn sees him in Byzantium, adopted by a Greek
family whose deaf-mute son Nikki he teaches to communicate by
his own power of mind-speech. The time is just before the siege of
Constantinople, 1203-04. Jehan is with the crusaders, outside the
City, and Thea spends part of her time in the guise of a member of
the Varangian guard. Once more, Alf finds himself caught up in
powerful secular and ecclesiastical politics, but is unable to prevent the bloody sack of the city by the Fourth Crusade, nor his
own willing acceptance of Thea as a lover.

The Hounds of God shows us Alf and Thea, and their children,
back in the kingdom of Rhiyana, whose king is one of the changeling elf-folk (whom we would call mutations) and which is their
sanctuary on earth. With Pope Innocent's death, the Order of St.
Paul, dubbed the Hounds of God—Alf's old enemies from the first
book—are unleashed to preach a crusade against the "sorcery" of
Rhiyana's witchfolk. Another adversary reappears: Thea and her
newborn twins are abducted by a powerful enemy, a member of
the Folk who is in turn controlled by (we discover) the malevolent
Joscelin, a former squire of the Lionheart. Alf, Jehan, and Nikki
follow the trail to Rome, to combat the insane elf-monk and his
master and to persuade the Pope to call off the Hounds. The compromise lies with the Elven withdrawing from the world, but this
provides a dilemma for Nikki which counterpoints Alf's earlier conflict of loyalties between Church and kin. Does Nikki, a human
who can share some of the Folk's powers, belong with them, or
with his new lover Stefania, with whom he can only speak via the
telepathic gifts instilled into him by Alf?

The trilogy is an almost seamless mixture of fantasy and historical modes. The central novel with its Byzantine setting is perhaps
closest to "history," although this period and place would probably
be in any case less familiar to Tarr's readers. Tarr is (perhaps deliberately) unclear at first whether Alf and his people are a distinct
race or a mutation which appears throughout humanity. This is soon
resolved with references to African, Greek and Chinese "elven,"

and Alf's dilemma about which world he owes allegiance to is reflected in sub-plots which focus on the way Orthodox and Roman Catholicism are intertwined or opposed, or (though this may strike a suspiciously "modern" false note) Stefania's desire to transcend her own social conditioning by founding a school for female philosophers.

The sense of place and time in the Hound and the Falcon trilogy is lacking in Tarr's next major sequence, Avaryan Rising, which employs a more conventional fantasy setting in a world where the sun-god and shadow-goddess combat through human substitutes. It begins with *The Hall of the Mountain King,* in which young Mirain arrives in the Kingdom of Ianon to declare himself son of its king's missing daughter and the Sun-God Avaryan. Despite the golden brand of the Sun-God burning in Mirain's right hand, the king's bastard son Moranden is, not unnaturally, suspicious.

While Tarr's setting is not as interesting as her alternative-medieval Europe, the strength of her characters saves the Avaryan Rising books. We can feel for Moranden, by no means a villain. His natural hatred for his usurping nephew is tempered by his ethical opposition to the means by which his priestess-mother would help him. Moreover, Tarr leaves us unsure about whether we are meant to like Mirain (his squire Vidan falls in love with him, but that is different). The second volume is yet more conventional: Elian, Mirain's foster-sister who swore on his departure that she would fight for him, runs away to join his army, becoming (in the guise of a boy) his squire. Pulled between her bond with Mirain and her attraction to Ziad-Ilarios, heir to the Golden Empire of Asanian, she chooses Mirain, though here the sense is stronger that the destiny Mirain is marching towards is one which will tear the world apart. The third volume, *A Fall of Princes,* is an object lesson in the value of reading until the end of a fantasy trilogy, because the conventional structures of the previous volumes become the background to a long and complex web of political and sexual conspiracies and treasons at the centre of which is Hirel, son of Ziad-Ilarios (now Emperor), whom we meet fleeing from his treacherous usurping brothers and Sarevan, the son of Mirain and Elian. Natural enemies passionately attracted, Hirel and Sarevan are only partly in control of their fates, and the solution offered to the prospect of raging chaos if the forces of Light and Darkness have their way is astonishing. While the philosophy behind the conclusion (one step beyond that of most similarly-structured fantasy epics) is perhaps predictable, and the sexual tensions are overblown, it is not Tarr's aim simply to show a moral revelation but to lead the reader to it by a process of hints and reversals which make more of her story than is to be expected in the well-charted pathways of fantasy writing. This is trilogy-as-unfolding-vision rather than as serial story, and while its physical maps are generic its interplay of plot and character confirm Tarr as a writer capable of ignoring such limitations.

The historical era of the Hound and the Falcon trilogy is returned to tangentially in *A Wind in Cairo,* an "Arabian Nights" fantasy involving a spoiled brat of an emir's son who is transformed into the shape of a horse as penance for his reckless behaviour. It is returned to more specifically in *Alamut,* about a passionate love-affair between two characters briefly glimpsed in Alf and Thea's story—Prince Aidan and Morgiana, an Assassin who slays his kinsman. Set some years before the earlier novels, the story mixes magic and conventional history in similar manner to almost equal effect. Tarr's use of historical background is again vivid and gripping: she enables the reader to believe in the concrete detail of her descriptions as much as her magic. While the story echoes motifs previously used (down to the pointed development of a large measure of independence within the confines of their cultures in several of the major female characters), these are not motifs which militate against a strong story. A more pertinent criticism might be that this is the wish-fulfilment confirmation of fairy tale rather than the inspiration of subversion, and this might also be levelled at its sequel *The Dagger and the Cross,* more a historical love-story of rival causes than a metaphysical quest. The Avaryan Rising trilogy and its pendant novels prove that Judith Tarr can work to different rhythms when necessary, but her true strength may lie in the fusion of fantasy and Middle-Eastern history to which she returns in *Lord of the Two Lands,* about Alexander the Great, and in *Throne of Isis,* which retells the story of Anthony and Cleopatra.

—Andy Sawyer

TAYLOR, Roger

Nationality: British. **Born:** Heywood, Lancashire. **Family:** Married, two daughters. **Career:** Qualified as a civil and structural engineer.

FANTASY PUBLICATIONS

Novels (series: Chronicles of Hawklan; Nightfall)

The Call of the Sword (Hawklan). London, Headline, 1988.
The Fall of Fyorlund (Hawklan). London, Headline, 1989.
The Waking of Orthlund (Hawklan). London, Headline, 1989.
Into Narsindal (Hawklan). London, Headline, 1990.
Dream Finder. London, Headline, 1991.
Farnor (Nightfall). London, Headline, 1992.
Valderen (Nightfall). London, Headline, 1993.
Whistler. London, Headline, 1994.

* * *

Heroic fantasy has long since crystallized into a genre where precisely the expected is what the reader wants. Roger Taylor's first series is uninventively standard, with a Dark Lord, a magic sword, a hero waiting to define his role, orc-like "mandrocs" and a cod-medieval setting like dozens of other such fantasies. It is, though, professionally fluent in pacing and telling, with a nagging mystery—how and why the injured man discovered by the memory-maimed Hawklan in a blizzard in the prologue becomes for the rest of the four-book sequence the one-legged raven Gavor, whose sardonic foppishness makes him the series' most intriguing character.

It is clear half-way through the first book, *The Call of the Sword,* that the healer Hawklan is the reincarnation of the hero Ethriss, who defeated the dark power Sumeral in legendary times, but the dramatic power inherent in the oft-used device of a hero who doesn't know the nature of his identity is thrown away not so much by too early a revelation but by Hawklan's apparent passive acceptance of this role without understanding what is going on. Some interesting secondary characters, however, fill some of the gaps left by the absence of a fully-defined hero, in particular Dilrap, the ineffectual, cowardly Secretary to the King of Fyorlund, who himself takes on a heroic role by appearing to be so intimidated by the usurping Dan-Tor that he can continue in his function and work against Dan-Tor at the same time as the tool of Sumeral believes him to be too weak to oppose him. The series is also enlivened by the author's capacity to imagine, if not at this stage fully articulate, some sublime concepts such as the cloud-cities briefly glimpsed in *The Fall of Fyorlund.*

This potential for the grand sweep is seen in Taylor's best novel to date, the remarkable *Dream Finder.* Set in a world which may, from hints dropped towards the end of the story, be a distant part of Hawklan's world some years afterwards, *Dream Finder* also contains a reluctant hero and talking beasts, but is a much more assured piece of imagination and plotting. "Dream-finding" is a kind of literalization of psychoanalysis in which certain individuals, guided by an animal companion, can visit the territories of another's dreams. It is normally used for healing or interpretative purposes. Antyr, the talented but wastrel son of an adept in the art of dream-finding, is one night called to interpret the dreams of both Ibris, Duke of Serenstad, and the Duke's son Menedrion whose nightmare has caused him to viciously injure the woman with whom he was sleeping. Discovering in both dreams the signs of a terrifying but mysterious power, Antyr and his wolf-companion Tarrian find clues in a creation-myth which speaks of the Great Dream and how it was corrupted by an evil force itself defeated by Dream Finders. Aided by old Pendra and his companion, a cantankerous rabbit, Antyr finds further clues in the dreams of an envoy from Serenstad's traditional enemy, Bethlar. The Bethlarii, the Spartans to Serenstad's Athens (although the tone of the culture is closer to the civilized but ruthless Dukedoms of Renaissance Italy) are apparently beginning another religious war, and Antyr is recruited along with Menedrion and his illegitimate brother Arwain and the mysterious band of mercenaries called the Mantynnai, to combat them and whatever power is influencing them. Meanwhile, unknown to everyone else, a vast horde of barbarians from the north, whose charismatic but vicious leader is under the influence of a blind mage with supernatural powers, is set to sweep down upon the warring city-states.

Here, Taylor has allowed the genre fashion for embodying mystical conflicts between Light and Darkness to slip into the background, and what results is a well-crafted and exciting adventure story of war, political intrigue and a samurai-like moral about knowing one's true self. Antyr, whose defeat of the "Dark Mynedarion" is largely a matter of accepting his own potential for weakness, "laid no claim to understanding what he had truly done"—and this particularly human form of heroism counterpoints the wider geographical and metaphysical realms which are hinted at to add a sense of space to the narration. Here too, the interplay between Hawklan and Gavor becomes the exasperated commentary by the wolf Tarrian upon his partner's frailties and Antyr's perception that there are areas of lupine experience which are closed to him; an altogether richer ingredient of a novel which successfully undertakes one of post-Tolkienian fantasy's major tasks: to fuse moral and physical conflict and allow one to illuminate the other.

Dream Finder's successor, the two-part Nightfall series, *Farnor* and *Valderen,* seems to take one step backwards into familiar territory. The characters are those we know of through so many other examples in the standard fantasy library: the adolescent who will mature through tragedy and defeat evil, the feisty young girl, the wise old man. The scenario, a remote valley in a medieval-culture world whose villagers are so cut off from the world around them that even the tax-gatherers don't call, is also known to regular fan-

tasy readers. Yet Taylor manages to reach the end of a 500-page first book without other than the vaguest hints as to the nature of the threat which is disrupting the villagers' idyll, and still to carry the reader with him. At first, it is an unseen beast which is killing sheep. We see Rannick, the village layabout (whom Taylor manages to create some sympathy for even while blazoning "corruption" all over him), developing a power over inanimate and animate objects. We see Farnor, the hero, somehow connected with Rannick's activities. and when a group of ragged soldiers appear from the south, at first mistaken for the tax-gatherers but fleeing from who knows what, and adopt Rannick as their Lord, the suspense only deepens. As events unfold, we receive the impression that we are witnessing a chapter (even a brief footnote) in a much longer and more complex book. Something titanic has happened in the south and the forces of evil are apparently regrouping in the north, but most of the human characters are pawns in a greater plan.

This aspect at least is genuinely Tolkienian, and it is this authenticity of feeling which raises Taylor over the limitations of his backgrounds. While at the moment he is writing largely within the melodramatic confines of a sub-branch of fantasy which does not call very loudly for originality, he is in touch with the demand for something larger and grander which was at the root of that sub-genre's establishment. He has created at least one novel which puts him in the same league as many more fashionable names and if he can develop his particular ability to absorb and astonish, there may be many more.

—Andy Sawyer

TEPPER, Sheri S(tewart)

Pseudonyms: E. E. Horlak, B. J. Oliphant, A. J. Orde. **Nationality:** American. **Born:** Colorado, 1929. **Family:** Married Gene Eberhart; one son, one daughter. **Career:** Administrative posts in various non-profit organizations, including CARE and Planned Parenthood; poet and children's story writer from the early 1960s (initially as Sheri S. Eberhart); full-time novelist from the early 1980s. **Address:** c/o Bantam Books, 1540 Broadway, New York, NY 10036, USA.

FANTASY PUBLICATIONS

Novels (series: Jinian; Marianne; Mavin Manyshaped; True Game)

King's Blood Four (True Game). New York, Ace, 1983.
Necromancer Nine (True Game). New York, Ace, 1983.
The Revenants. New York, Ace, 1984; London, Corgi, 1986.
Wizard's Eleven (True Game). New York, Ace, 1984.
The True Game (omnibus; includes *King's Blood Four, Necromancer Nine, Wizard's Eleven*). London, Corgi, 1985.
The Song of Mavin Manyshaped. New York, Ace, 1985.
The Flight of Mavin Manyshaped. New York, Ace, 1985.
The Search of Mavin Manyshaped. New York, Ace, 1985.
Jinian Footseer. New York, Tor, 1985; London, Corgi, 1988.
Marianne, the Magus, and the Manticore. New York, Ace, 1985.
Dervish Daughter (Jinian). New York, Tor, 1986; London, Corgi, 1988.

Jinian Star-Eye. New York, Tor, 1986; London, Corgi, 1988.

The Chronicles of Mavin Manyshaped (omnibus; includes *The Song of Mavin Manyshaped, The Flight of Mavin Manyshaped, The Search of Mavin Manyshaped*). London, Corgi, 1986.

The End of the Game (omnibus; includes *Jinian Footseer, Dervish Daughter, Jinian Star-Eye*). New York, Nelson Doubleday, 1987.

Marianne, the Madame, and the Momentary Gods. New York, Ace, 1988.

Marianne, the Matchbox, and the Malachite Mouse. New York, Ace, 1989.

The Marianne Trilogy (omnibus; includes *Marianne, the Magus, and the Manticore* (1985), *Marianne, the Madame, and the Momentary Gods* (1988) and *Marianne, the Matchbox, and the Malachite Mouse*). London, Corgi, 1990.

Beauty: A Novel. New York, Doubleday, 1991; London, HarperCollins, 1992.

OTHER PUBLICATIONS

Novels

Blood Heritage. New York, Tor, 1986; London, Corgi, 1987.

After Long Silence. New York, Bantam, 1987; as *The Enigma Score,* London, Corgi, 1989.

Northshore. New York, Tor, 1987.

Southshore. New York, Tor, 1987.

The Awakeners (omnibus; includes *Northshore, Southshore*). New York, Nelson Doubleday, 1987; London, Bantam Press, 1988.

The Bones. New York, Tor, 1987; London, Corgi, 1988.

The Gate to Women's Country. New York, Doubleday, 1988; London, Bantam Press, 1989.

Grass. New York, Doubleday, and London, Bantam Press, 1989.

Still Life (as E. E. Horlak). New York, Bantam, 1989; as Sheri S. Tepper, London, Corgi, 1989.

Raising the Stones. New York, Doubleday, 1990; London, Grafton, 1991.

Sideshow. New York, Bantam, 1992; London, HarperCollins, 1993.

A Plague of Angels. New York, Bantam, 1993; London, HarperCollins, 1994.

Shadow's End. New York, Bantam, and London, HarperCollins, 1994.

Novels as A. J. Orde

A Little Neighborhood Murder. New York, Doubleday, 1989.

Death and the Dogwalker. New York, Doubleday, 1990.

Death For Old Time's Sake. New York, Doubleday, 1992.

Looking for the Aardvark. New York, Doubleday, 1993.

Novels as B. J. Oliphant

Dead in the Scrub. New York, Gold Medal, 1990.

The Unexpected Corpse. New York, Gold Medal, 1990.

Deservedly Dead. New York, Gold Medal, 1992

Death and the Delinquent. New York, Gold Medal, 1993

Death Served Up Cold. New York, Gold Medal, 1994.

*   *   *

When she began to write fantasy novels, in the early 1980s, Tepper was already in her fifties. Her fantasy has generally concerned young females using magical powers or inherited talents in worlds other than our own; it has often been fast moving and undemanding, and thus popular with many readers. Tepper's great talent is for the creation of ideas and settings. Her character development is sometimes limited and her plotting is often weak and unconvincing. It is worth noting that she is an awkward subject for an essay such as this because she has written science fiction and horror novels which will not be considered here despite their fantasy ingredients and because she tends to include science fiction elements in most of her fantasy novels, so some of the categorization is arbitrary.

The Revenants was Tepper's first-written novel. As with many first novels, it contains far too many ingredients and would have been better if developed into a trilogy. Fundamentally it is concerned with multiple quests and with the ongoing battle between the forces of good and evil for control of the Known World. Jaer is chief amongst the group of five protagonists, being a teenager who shifts overnight from male to female and back again. These shifts occur irregularly, perhaps once every week or two, and Jaer is not always the same person, even when the same sex. Such a fascinating concept deserves much more space for development. It is never even clear what Jaer feels about such an arrangement. The other protagonists are Medlo, a gay prince, Leona, an umpteenth daughter with no marriage prospects, Thewson, a big black Conan-type hero, and Jasmine, a courtesan and dancer. All have been forced to set off on quests, and it is eventually made clear that the wonderful artefacts each seeks are carried, unknowingly, by another of the group. At the end, good triumphs, and everything is tied up happily and neatly: just the sort of contrived and coincidental plotting which is rife in Tepper's books. On the other hand, there is a "separation" culture described early on in the book in which the members of different villages or towns are forbidden from coming face to face, but must go to extraordinary lengths to cover themselves in such a way that body size and shape are hidden—a terrific idea which could have been the central theme of a novel.

The True Game is Tepper's best known concept and has been explored in three linked trilogies. The first, *The True Game,* deals with the early life of Peter, *The Chronicles of Mavin Manyshaped* cover early and later adventures of Mavin, who is Peter's mother, and the three Jinian novels deal with the teenage years of the young woman who becomes Peter's chosen partner. In the land of the True Game, a small number of people possess great inherited talents, enabling them to fly or heal or raise the dead or teleport (move instantaneously from place to place), etc. Peter and Mavin are both shapeshifters and Jinian can communicate with animals. The Gamesmen habitually fight each other, singly or in groups, just for fun, an activity which consumes the resources of the whole land. Non-Gamesmen are just pawns, who are forced to suffer this, often getting caught up and killed.

The plots are extremely complex, though much space is devoted to the teenage doubts and hardships of the three protagonists. Each book contains ridiculously coincidental circumstances, and for a protagonist to overhear some of the antagonists discussing their evil plans is common. It is gradually revealed that this world contains not only talents and magic but also a good deal of ancient technology, still workable, from a starship that landed on the planet a thousand years earlier. In each book there is evil to be defeated by some combination of Peter, Mavin and Jinian (together with friends and allies). At the end of *Jinian Star-Eye* (the final volume of the sequence) the planet itself (a kind of Gaia figure called Lom, pronounced loam, i.e. earth) removes the talents of all Gamesmen. Individual volumes of this sequence cannot be read in isolation, since there are so many references to previous events and characters.

While the characters of Peter and Jinian are well developed and sympathetic, Mavin remains remote throughout. Other characters are, on the whole, rudimentary, with good characters being wholly good and evil ones wholly evil. Some episodes and social groups are strikingly described, especially the humans living up and down the roots of a gigantic tree in *The Flight of Mavin Manyshaped* and the dervishes in *Dervish Daughter* (Jinian's mother is a dervish). In too many cases Tepper's use of silly names for people and animals makes her work seem too light-hearted and jokey. For example, in *The Song of Mavin Manyshaped,* names such as Danderbat, Haribald Halfmad, Plandybast Ogbone and Wurstery Wimpole sit uneasily alongside the institutionalized serial rape of young female members of Mavin's family by older males.

The Marianne books are very different, being contemporary surreal fantasies. There is much more credibility and sophistication to the writing, yet they are spoilt by some of the same flaws as before. Marianne is a student in her early twenties, living quietly in an unnamed American city. Her parents are dead and her unpleasant half-brother, Harvey, keeps her poor by controlling her allowance (from a large inheritance). Then a distant cousin arrives on a lecture tour and everything changes. He is Makr Avehl Zahman, Prime Minister of Alphenlicht, a tiny country adjacent to Turkey and Iraq. He looks much like Harvey, and he falls in love with Marianne at once, wining and dining her. She is impressed but wary, due to her problems with Harvey. But if Makr Avehl is the good influence on her life, the evil influence comes from Madame Delubovoska, another distant relative, this time from Lubovosk, the northern portion of Alphenlicht, hived off under Russian control.

Despite Makr Avehl's prowess as a magician (the magus of the title), a malign spell is placed on Marianne, who finds herself in a strange fantasy world, where she is menaced by a manticore and is eventually rescued by Makr Avehl in the guise of a chimera. The fantasy worlds in the first Marianne novel are surreal and owe much to the art of Paul Delvaux. In the second book she is trapped in a fairy-tale world. In the third book Marianne, now married and pregnant, gets into a very odd board game. It is these wonderfully peculiar alternative realities which show Tepper at her most inventive and make the novels worth reading. The plots are as contrived as ever, and the villains as two-dimensional, though these can be ignored and the settings enjoyed.

If The Marianne Trilogy was a step up for Tepper from her previous fantasy, then *Beauty* was a much larger step up again. It is a clever, multifaceted novel, full of surprises. The book is presented as the autobiography of Beauty, a half-fairy, half-human noblewoman born in England in 1332. It is also a romance, a study of dystopias, a retelling of several familiar fairy tales and a chance for Tepper to preach on the subject of saving the environment.

At the age of 16, Beauty narrowly escapes becoming Sleeping Beauty; it is her look-alike and half-sister Beloved who pricks her finger and goes to sleep (along with all the rest of the inhabitants of Westfaire Castle) within a fast-growing rose hedge. So Beauty goes off in search of her missing fairy mother, Elladine, conveniently aided by a cloak of invisibility and magic boots which transport her wherever she commands, and watched over by Puck the Bogle and by Carabosse a fairy aunt. Kidnapped by 21st-century filmmakers, she visits their drab world before escaping to our own 1990s, being raped and returning to the mid-13th century to marry a lord so as to legitimize her baby. Then she leaves to seek her mother again. She travels through the dream world of Chinanga—vast, changeless and extraordinarily odd. She is transported on the boat of Captain Karon (= Charon) and visits such delightful places as the Cathedral of Helpful Amphibians before finding her mother. Chinanga is extinguished, and Beauty and Elladine stay in Faery (where everybody appears to be beautiful but is, in fact, dirty, emotionless and scheming) for quite a while—subjective weeks but objective years.

Aging quickly due to her travelling through time (accomplished by the magic boots), Beauty makes repeated trips between Faery and Westfaire, between the 13th and 14th centuries and the 20th. Mostly she is trying to help others, particularly her descendants. *En route* she encounters the original events that become the fairy tales of Cinderella, Thomas the Rhymer, Snow White, Rapunzel and the frog prince. Somewhere in her chest she carries an artefact, revealed at the end as genetic material sufficient to re-create all the world's creatures, threatened with extinction by the acts of our own and future generations.

Entertaining as the plot is, it is the settings and themes which make this a very good fantasy novel. With the exception of the brief 21st-century scenes (too cliched) and the 20th-century scenes (too full of propaganda), the backgrounds are inventive and entertaining. Chinanga is a joy to read about. The medieval settings are often too idyllic, yet this adds to the fairy-tale quality of the whole book.

Beauty is a first-rate character, believable and poignant. But she is, of course, used symbolically: the beauty of life diminishes from the 14th century to the 21st, just as the power of magic does. To misquote Keats, only Beauty is true to herself, and the only truth is Beauty. It would be churlish indeed to make much of the shortcomings of *Beauty*. There are occasional plot contrivances (some of the fairy tales seem to have been thumbtacked into place), too many shallow characters and a rape to which Beauty does not react in any kind of normal way, but none of these really spoil the novel. It has provided Tepper with critical as well as popular acclaim; after an uncertain start she must now be regarded as one of the better fantasy writers of the present day.

—Chris Morgan

THURBER, James (Grover)

Nationality: American. **Born:** Columbus, Ohio, 8 December 1894. **Education:** Ohio State University, Columbus, 1913-14, 1915-18. **Family:** Married 1) Althea Adams in 1922 (divorced 1935), one daughter; 2) Helen Wismer in 1935. **Career:** Code clerk, American Embassy, Paris, 1918-20; reporter, Columbus *Dispatch,* 1920-24, Paris edition of Chicago *Tribune,* 1925-26, and New York *Evening Post,* 1926-27; editor, 1927, writer, 1927-38, then freelance contributor, *New Yorker*; also an illustrator from 1929: several individual shows. **Awards:** Litt.D.: Kenyon College, Gambier, Ohio, 1950; Yale University, New Haven, Connecticut, 1953; L.H.D.: Williams College, Williamstown, Massachusetts, 1951. **Died:** 2 November 1961.

Fantasy Publications

Novels

The White Deer, illustrated by the author and Don Freeman. New York, Harcourt Brace, 1945; London, Hamish Hamilton, 1946.

The 13 Clocks, illustrated by Marc Simont. New York, Simon and Schuster, 1950; London, Hamish Hamilton, 1951.

The Wonderful O, illustrated by Marc Simont. New York, Simon and Schuster, and London, Hamish Hamilton, 1955.

Short Stories and Sketches (illustrated by the author)

Fables for Our Time and Famous Poems Illustrated. New York, Harper, and London, Hamish Hamilton, 1940.

My World—and Welcome to It. New York, Harcourt Brace, and London, Hamish Hamilton, 1942.

Many Moons, illustrated by Louis Slobodkin. New York, Harcourt Brace, 1943; London, Hamish Hamilton, 1945.

The Great Quillow, illustrated by Doris Lee. New York, Harcourt Brace, 1944.

Further Fables for Our Time. New York, Simon and Schuster, and London, Hamish Hamilton, 1956.

Other Publications

Short Stories and Sketches (illustrated by the author)

The Owl in the Attic and Other Perplexities. New York, Harper, 1931.

The Seal in the Bedroom and Other Predicaments. New York, Harper, 1932.

My Life and Hard Times. New York, Harper, 1933.

The Middle-Aged Man on the Flying Trapeze: A Collection of Short Pieces. New York, Harper, and London, Hamish Hamilton, 1935.

Let Your Mind Alone! and Other More or Less Inspirational Pieces. New York, Harper, and London, Hamish Hamilton, 1937.

Cream of Thurber. London, Hamish Hamilton, 1939.

The Last Flower: A Parable in Pictures. New York, Harper, and London, Hamish Hamilton, 1939.

Men, Women, and Dogs: A Book of Drawings. New York, Harcourt Brace, 1943; London, Hamish Hamilton, 1945.

The Thurber Carnival. New York, Harper, and London, Hamish Hamilton, 1945.

The Beast in Me, and Other Animals: A New Collection of Pieces and Drawings about Human Beings and Less Alarming Creatures. New York, Harcourt Brace, 1948; London, Hamish Hamilton, 1949.

The Thurber Album: A New Collection of Pieces about People. New York, Simon and Schuster, and London, Hamish Hamilton, 1952.

Thurber Country: A New Collection of Pieces about Males and Females, Mainly of Our Own Species. New York, Simon and Schuster, and London, Hamish Hamilton, 1953.

Thurber's Dogs: A Collection of the Master's Dogs, Written and Drawn, Real and Imaginary, Living and Long Ago. New York, Simon and Schuster, and London, Hamish Hamilton, 1955.

A Thurber Garland. London, Hamish Hamilton, 1955.

Alarms and Diversions. New York, Harper, and London, Hamish Hamilton, 1957.

Lanterns and Lances. New York, Harper, and London, Hamish Hamilton, 1961.

Credos and Curios. New York, Harper, and London, Hamish Hamilton, 1962.

Vintage Thurber: A Collection of the Best Writings and Drawings of James Thurber. London, Hamish Hamilton, 2 vols., 1963.

Thurber and Company. New York, Harper, 1966; London, Hamish Hamilton, 1967.

92 Stories. New York, Avenel, 1985.

The Works of James Thurber (selected stories). New York, Longmeadow Press, 1986.

Plays

The Male Animal, with Elliott Nugent (produced New York, 1940; London, 1949). New York, Random House, 1940; London, Hamish Hamilton, 1950.

A Thurber Carnival, adaptation of his own stories (produced Columbus and New York, 1960). New York, French, 1962.

Wrote the books for the following college musical comedies: *Oh My! Omar,* with Hayward M. Anderson, 1921; *Psychomania,* 1922; *Many Moons,* 1922; *A Twin Fix,* with Hayward M. Anderson, 1923; *The Cat and the Riddle,* 1924; *Nightingale,* 1924; *Tell Me Not,* 1924.

Other

Is Sex Necessary? or, Why You Feel the Way You Do, with E. B. White. New York, Harper, 1929; London, Heinemann, 1930.

Thurber on Humor. Columbus, Martha Kinney Cooper Ohioana Library Association, 1953.

The Years with Ross. Boston, Little Brown, and London, Hamish Hamilton, 1959.

Selected Letters, edited by Helen Thurber and Edward Weeks. Boston, Little Brown, 1981; London, Hamish Hamilton, 1982.

Illustrator: *No Nice Girl Swears* by Alice Leone Moates, 1933; *Her Foot Is on the Brass Rail* by Don Marquis, 1935; *How to Raise a Dog* by James R. Kinney and Ann Honeycutt, 1938; *Men Can Take It* by Elizabeth Hawes, 1939; *In a Word* by Margaret Samuels, 1939.

*

Film Adaptations: *The Male Animal,* 1942; *The Secret Life of Walter Mitty,* 1947.

Bibliographies: *James Thurber: A Bibliography* by Edwin T. Bowden, Columbus, Ohio State University Press, 1968; *James Thurber: An Annotated Bibliography of Criticism* by Sarah Eleanora Toombs, New York, Garland, 1987.

Manuscript Collection: Ohio State University Library, Columbus.

Critical Studies: *James Thurber* by Robert E. Morsberger, New York, Twayne, 1964; *The Art of James Thurber* by Richard C. Tobias, Athens, Ohio University Press, 1969; *James Thurber, His Masquerades: A Critical Study* by Stephen A. Black, The Hague, Mouton, 1970; *The Clocks of Columbus: The Literary Career of James Thurber* by Charles S. Holmes, New York, Atheneum, and London, Secker and Warburg, 1973, and *Thurber: A Collection of Critical Essays* edited by Holmes, Englewood Cliffs, New Jersey, Prentice Hall, 1974; *Thurber: A Biography* by Burton Bernstein,

New York, Dodd Mead, and London, Gollancz, 1975; *Thurber's Anatomy of Confusion* by Catherine McGehee Kenney, Hamden, Connecticut, Shoe String Press, 1984; *James Thurber* by Robert Emmet Long, New York, Ungar, 1988.

*   *   *

James Thurber became famous as a cartoonist and writer of humorous essays; his early ventures into fiction were a form of spin-off, taking the form of brief "fables," each with an explicit moral dutifully attached. The morals in question ranged, of course, from the piquantly quirky (often couched as rhyming couplets) to the bitterly sarcastic. Thus, for instance, the moral of "The Fairly Intelligent Fly" is that "There is no safety in numbers, or in anything else," and the moral of "The Owl Who Was God" is that "You can fool too many of the people too much of the time". There is a natural progression from such whimsies through the "parable in pictures," *The Last Flower,* to the fairy tales which were Thurber's most elaborate constructions in prose. These stories work on two levels: they are as deftly subversive in their moral lessons as the *Fables for Our Time,* and they exhibit a wholly genuine delight in fantastic fabrication. Thurber presumably would not have felt comfortable in such fabrication had he not had the excuse of entertaining children—his ambivalence to the business of fantasizing is made abundantly clear in his sentimental and sarcastic account of "The Secret Life of Walter Mitty," which is justly famous as a painfully accurate analysis of the absurdity of daydreaming—but he took full advantage of the excuse.

In *Many Moons* a princess falls ill, and all the wise men in the kingdom cannot find the cause—but the court jester does, because he has the common sense to ask her. *The Great Quillow* is a toymaker who cleverly succeeds where others fail in persuading a marauding giant to let his town alone. Such tales of the triumph of the humble after the mighty have failed are, of course, central to the fairy-tale tradition because they serve a consolatory function with respect to the least powerful members of all societies. Thurber took one of the standard formats long laid down for such tales as his template in *The White Deer,* in which the three sons of a king must compete to win the princess who has been magically transformed into the eponymous creature. Here, for the first time, Thurber indulged himself unstintingly in decorating the tale with wit and wordplay, neatly combining simplicity of theme and sophistication of language. Some critics prefer this to the two extended tales which followed it because it is the most traditional—and hence the lightest—of the three.

Thurber took the process of linguistic embellishment a stage further in *The Thirteen Clocks,* in which coruscating wordplay transforms the straightforward tale of a hero who must deliver the imprisoned heroine from the custody of her wicked uncle into a baroque extravaganza. The Duke of Coffin Castle, who is so cold that time itself has frozen around him, is a wonderful villain, and the paradoxical Golux who enables the hero to overcome him is an ingenious invention. Here, the imaginative force of the tale puts such a strain on the borrowed formula that the conventional happy ending is questioned and undermined, striking a distinctive bittersweet note similar to that of the best Thurberesque fables. *The Wonderful O* continues this evolutionary process, making the wordplay central to the plot. A pirate who loathes the letter O because of its unfortunate associations with the death of his mother bans all words containing it from an island he has conquered, but the islanders cannot and will not tolerate the resultant conceptual depletion (which

would, of course, involve the loss of humour as well as love). Their rebellion is successful, and they raise the inevitable statue to commemorate their victory—although there is one little girl sufficiently sceptical to question its meaning in wondering whether it is, after all, anything more than "a monument to zero".

Thurber's comedy has its darker side, as all comedy has, and he harboured real anxieties about the power of fantasy to disturb and spoil real life. Such anxieties are displayed in two other stories which sit side-by-side with "The Secret Life of Walter Mitty"—"A Friend to Alexander" and "The Whip-Poor-Will"—both published in *My World—And Welcome to It.* The melancholy edge which darkens both *The Thirteen Clocks* and *The Wonderful O* really serves, however, to frame the bright light at their heart. In his autobiography Thurber denied that humorous writing was a joyous experience, preferring to characterize it as "the manifestation of a twitchiness at once cosmic and mundane," but the three long fairy tales are far too extensive in their languorous extension to be dismissed as products of any mere "twitchiness"; they are well-wrought works of art.

The bleakest of all the tales in *My World—and Welcome To It* is "Interview with a Lemming," in which a man and a lemming who fall into conversation unexpectedly find that they have a great deal in common; as their dialogue ends the man confesses that the one thing he still can't understand is why lemmings periodically self-destruct by leaping off cliffs—and the lemming counters by confessing that the one thing he can't understand is why humans don't. Thurber's later work tacitly provides the answer that this story leaves achingly void. Humans don't commit mass suicide because, when all's said and done, the little girl was wrong: what she momentarily mistook for a monument to zero was instead a wholly justified celebration of the spectacular wonderfulness of the letter O, and all the words that can and do contain it.

—Brian Stableford

TIMLETT, Peter Valentine

Nationality: British. **Born:** London, 14 February 1933. **Education:** Pelham Grammar School, 1946-49. **Military Service:** Royal Air Force, 1951-53. **Family:** Married in 1972; two children. **Career:** Reservations clerk, Qantas, Sydney, Australia, 1959-60; booking clerk, Royal Interocean Lines, Sydney, 1960-64; shipping clerk, Heinemann Group of Publishers, Kingswood, Surrey, 1965-68; general manager, DMS, Kingswood, 1968-70; Book Department manager, Gordon and Gotch, London, 1970-72; export sales, Granada Publications, London, 1972-75; sales director, Wyndham Publications, London, 1975-78; administration and procedures executive, DMS (later Exel Logistics), from 1979. **Address:** Capri Villa, Littlebourne Road, Canterbury, Kent CT3 4AE, England.

FANTASY PUBLICATIONS

Novels (series: Seedbearers)

The Seedbearers. London, Quartet, 1974; New York, Bantam, 1976.
The Power of the Serpent (Seedbearers). London, Corgi, and New York, Bantam, 1976.

The Twilight of the Serpent (Seedbearers). London, Corgi, and New York, Bantam, 1977.

*

Peter Valentine Timlett comments:

Having been a student and practitioner of the moral and benign aspects of the western esoteric tradition (known popularly as "the occult"), I wrote the Seedbearers trilogy to present certain concepts/ ideas to a wider readership. The irony is that the novels are presented as fantasy, whereas to me they are not fantasy but serious occult philosophy presented in fictional and (I hope) entertaining form. Through those novels, and through the British Fantasy Society, I met such horror writers as Ramsey Campbell (UK) and Karl Edward Wagner (USA), and so wrote a horror short story just to see whether I could do it. I have written and published the occasional short story ever since.

*   *   *

Although Peter Valentine Timlett has been associated with the fantasy field for over 20 years he has published only one trilogy and a handful of short stories. The novels, known as the Seedbearers trilogy are, nevertheless, unique and worthy of greater consideration. Much has been written about Atlantis over the years but, with the possible exception of Ignatius Donnelly in *Atlantis: The Antediluvian World* (1882), few have taken the original legend seriously and built a novel based upon "fact".

As a student of the occult since his teens, and an initiate for many years, Timlett has a detailed knowledge of occult teachings, including the original western mystery legends of Atlantis. These have been passed down over the centuries and are accepted as fact by students of the occult. It is on that basis that Timlett's Seedbearers trilogy is developed, which brought him some rancour from fellow initiates at the time for revealing mystery traditions.

In Timlett's history, Atlantis is part of the Toltec world of Central America, based on the islands of Ruta and Daiteya, which were all that was left of a vast Atlantean continent destroyed ten millennia before. The first volume looks at how the Priesthood has become so corrupt over the years that the Army can openly defy its power and how this leads to a conflict that destroys the islands, ending in a cataclysmic eruption of the long-dormant island volcano. Atlantis and its people are totally destroyed except for Helios, the new High-Priest, and a handful of survivors.

The second novel, *The Power of the Serpent,* moves to Druid Britain centuries before the Roman invasion. The Druids are visited by the Priest of Ra from Egypt, who is himself descended from Atlanteans who fled at the time of the second destruction, 10,000 years earlier. These encounter Helios, who is directed to Britain to continue the Atlantean tradition. History now repeats itself. The existing High Priest of the Druids has become corrupt and seeks to raise a Dark Lord to lead his warrior-priests to evil. The novel features the building of Stonehenge.

The final book, *The Twilight of the Serpent,* is the most fascinating. Events have moved on 10,000 years to the first century A.D., when Joseph of Arimathaea comes to Britain to found the first Christian church in advance of the Roman invasion. The Druids must face either survival or death.

Each novel stands alone and can be read separately, but together they cover a 10,000-year history, tracing the passage of ancient teachings from Lemuria through Atlantis and Egypt to ancient Britain

and on into the Christian era. The novels are highly readable, though the repetition of plot throughout the sequence begins to pall by the third. But because of its closer association with our history, and because it provides a synopsis of the first two books, the final volume is on the whole the most satisfying.

Timlett has completed two other major novels, neither of which has been published—an Arthurian book, *Merlin and the Sword of Avalon,* and another based on a witchcraft trial, *Nor All Thy Tears,* both featuring much of the author's occult knowledge.

Timlett's few short stories are more horror than fantasy. He once planned a series of stories based on nursery rhymes, but only two of these have emerged: "Without Rhyme or Reason" (*New Terrors,* 1980), which intrudes the concept of missing children into "Mary, Mary, quite contrary . . . ," and the more obvious "Little Miss Muffet" (*Scare Care,* 1989) with its association with spiders.

—Mike Ashley

TOLKIEN, J(ohn) R(onald) R(euel)

Nationality: British. **Born:** Bloemfontein, Orange Free State, South Africa, 3 January 1892; came to England, 1895. **Education:** King Edward VI's School, Birmingham, 1900-02, 1903-11; St. Philip's School, Birmingham, 1902-03; Exeter College, Oxford (open classical exhibitioner; Skeat prize, 1914), 1911-15, B.A. (honours), 1915, M.A. 1919. **Military Service:** Lancashire Fusiliers, 1915-18: lieutenant. **Family:** Married Edith Mary Bratt in 1916 (died 1971); three sons and one daughter. **Career:** Assistant, *Oxford English Dictionary,* 1919-20; Reader in English, 1920-23, and Professor of the English language, 1924-25, University of Leeds, Yorkshire; at Oxford University: Rawlinson and Bosworth Professor of Anglo-Saxon, 1925-45; fellow, Pembroke College, 1926-45; Leverhulme research fellow, 1934-36; Merton Professor of English language and literature, 1945-59; honorary fellow, Exeter College, 1963, and Merton College, 1973. Andrew Lang lecturer, University of St. Andrews, Fife, 1939; W. P. Ker lecturer, University of Glasgow, 1953; lived in Bournemouth, Dorset, 1968-71, and Oxford, 1971-73. Artist: one-man show: Ashmolean Museum, Oxford, 1977. **Awards:** International Fantasy award, 1957; Royal Society of Literature Benson medal, 1966; Foreign Book prize (France), 1973; World Science Fiction Convention Gandalf award, 1974; Hugo award, 1978. D.Litt.: University College, Dublin, 1954; University of Nottingham, 1970; Oxford University, 1972; Dr. en Phil et Lettres: Liège, 1954; honorary degree: University of Edinburgh, 1973. Fellow, Royal Society of Literature, 1957. C.B.E. (Commander, Order of the British Empire), 1972. **Died:** 2 September 1973.

FANTASY PUBLICATIONS

Novels

The Hobbit; or, There and Back Again, illustrated by the author. London, Allen and Unwin, 1937; Boston, Houghton Mifflin, 1938; revised edition, 1951; revised edition, 1966; *The Annotated Hobbit,* edited by Douglas A. Anderson, London, Unwin Hyman, and Boston, Houghton Mifflin, 1989.

The Lord of the Rings:
The Fellowship of the Ring. London, Allen and Unwin, and Boston, Houghton Mifflin, 1954; revised edition, Allen and Unwin, 1966; Houghton Mifflin, 1967.
The Two Towers. London, Allen and Unwin, 1954; Boston, Houghton Mifflin, 1955; revised edition, Allen and Unwin, 1966; Houghton Mifflin, 1967.
The Return of the King. London, Allen and Unwin, 1955; Boston, Houghton Mifflin, 1956; revised edition, Allen and Unwin, 1966; Houghton Mifflin, 1967.
The Silmarillion, edited by Christopher Tolkien. London, Allen and Unwin, and Boston, Houghton Mifflin, 1977.

Short Stories

Farmer Giles of Ham, illustrated by Pauline Baynes. London, Allen and Unwin, 1949; Boston, Houghton Mifflin, 1950.
Tree and Leaf (includes story "Leaf by Niggle" and essay "On Fairy-Stories"). London, Allen and Unwin, 1964; Boston, Houghton Mifflin, 1965; revised edition (including poem "Mythopoeia" and preface by Christopher Tolkien), London, Unwin Hyman, 1988.
Smith of Wootton Major, illustrated by Pauline Baynes. London, Allen and Unwin, and Boston, Houghton Mifflin, 1967.
Tree and Leaf, Smith of Wootton Major, The Homecoming of Beorhtnoth Beorhthelm's Son. London, Allen and Unwin, 1975.
The Father Christmas Letters, edited by Baillie Tolkien, illustrated by the author. London, Allen and Unwin, and Boston, Houghton Mifflin, 1976.
Unfinished Tales of Númenór and Middle-Earth, edited by Christopher Tolkien. London, Allen and Unwin, and Boston, Houghton Mifflin, 1980.
Mr. Bliss, illustrated by the author. London, Allen and Unwin, 1982.
The History of Middle-Earth, edited by Christopher Tolkien:
The Book of Lost Tales 1-2. London, Allen and Unwin, 2 vols., 1983-84; Boston, Houghton Mifflin, 2 vols., 1984.
The Lays of Beleriand. London, Allen and Unwin, and Boston, Houghton Mifflin, 1985.
The Shaping of Middle-Earth. London, Allen and Unwin, and Boston, Houghton Mifflin, 1986.
The Lost Road and Other Writings. London, Unwin Hyman, and Boston, Houghton Mifflin, 1987.
The Return of the Shadow. London, Unwin Hyman, 1988; Boston, Houghton Mifflin, 1989.
The Treason of Isengard. London, Unwin Hyman, and Boston, Houghton Mifflin, 1989.
The War of the Ring. London, Unwin Hyman, and Boston, Houghton Mifflin, 1990.
Sauron Defeated. London, HarperCollins, and Boston, Houghton Mifflin, 1992.
Morgoth's Ring. London, HarperCollins, and Boston, Houghton Mifflin, 1993.
The War of the Jewels. London, HarperCollins, and Boston, Houghton Mifflin, 1994.

Poetry

The Adventures of Tom Bombadil and Other Verses from the Red Book, illustrated by Pauline Baynes. London, Allen and Unwin, 1962; Boston, Houghton Mifflin, 1963.

The Road Goes Ever On: A Song Cycle, music by Donald Swann. Boston, Houghton Mifflin, 1967; London, Allen and Unwin, 1968; revised edition, Houghton Mifflin, 1978.
Bilbo's Last Song, illustrated by Pauline Baynes. London, Allen and Unwin, and Boston, Houghton Mifflin, 1974.
Poems and Stories. London, Allen and Unwin, 1980; Boston, Houghton Mifflin, 1994.
Poems from The Lord of the Rings, illustrated by Alan Lee. London, HarperCollins, 1994.

OTHER PUBLICATIONS

Plays

Radio Play: *The Homecoming of Beorhtnoth Beorhthelm's Son* (broadcast, 1954). Included in *The Tolkien Reader,* 1966; in *Tree and Leaf, Smith of Wootton Major, The Homecoming of Beorhtnoth Beorhthelm's Son,* 1975.

Poetry

Songs for the Philologists, with others. Privately printed, 1936.

Other

A Middle English Vocabulary. Oxford, Clarendon Press, and New York, Oxford University Press, 1922.
Beowulf: The Monsters and the Critics. London, Oxford University Press, 1937.
The Tolkien Reader. New York, Ballantine, 1966.
Pictures by J. R. R. Tolkien. London, Allen and Unwin, and Boston, Houghton Mifflin, 1979.
Letters of J. R. R. Tolkien: A Selection, edited by Humphrey Carpenter. London, Allen and Unwin, and Boston, Houghton Mifflin, 1981.
Finn and Hengest: The Fragment and the Episode, edited by Alan Bliss. London, Allen and Unwin, and Boston, Houghton Mifflin, 1983.
The Monsters and the Critics and Other Essays, edited by Christopher Tolkien. London, Allen and Unwin, 1983; Boston, Houghton Mifflin, 1984.

Editor, with E. V. Gordon, *Sir Gawain and the Green Knight.* Oxford, Clarendon Press, and New York, Oxford University Press, 1925.
Editor, *Ancrene Wisse.* London, Oxford University Press, 1962; New York, Oxford University Press, 1963.

Translator, *Sir Gawain and the Green Knight, Pearl, and Sir Orfeo,* edited by Christopher Tolkien. London, Allen and Unwin, and Boston, Houghton Mifflin, 1975.
Translator, *The Old English Exodus,* edited by Joan Turville-Petre. Oxford, Clarendon Press, 1981.

*

Film Adaptations: *The Hobbit,* 1977 (television movie); *The Lord of the Rings,* 1978.

Bibliography: *Tolkien Criticism: An Annotated Checklist* by Richard C. West, Kent, Ohio, Kent State University Press, 1970; revised edition, 1981.

Manuscript Collections: Marion E. Wade Collection, Wheaton College, Illinois; Marquette University, Milwaukee.

Critical Studies (selection): *Tolkien and the Critics* edited by Neil D. Harvey and Rose A. Zimbardo, Notre Dame, Indiana, University of Notre Dame Press, 1968; *Tolkien: A Look Behind The Lord of the Rings* by Lin Carter, New York, Ballantine, 1969; *Master of Middle-Earth: The Fiction of J. R. R. Tolkien* by Paul Kocher, Boston, Houghton Mifflin, 1972, London, Thames and Hudson, 1973; *Tolkien's World,* London, Thames and Hudson, and Boston, Houghton Mifflin, 1974, and *Tolkien and the Silmarils,* Thames and Hudson, 1981, both by Randel Helms; *J. R. R. Tolkien: A Biography* by Humphrey Carpenter, London, Allen and Unwin, and Boston, Houghton Mifflin, 1977; *Lightning from a Clear Sky: J. R. R. Tolkien* by Richard Mathews, San Bernardino, California, Borgo Press, 1978; *The Mythology of Middle-Earth* by Ruth S. Noel, London, Thames and Hudson, and Boston, Houghton Mifflin, 1977; *The Complete Guide to Middle-Earth* by Robert Foster, London, Allen and Unwin, and New York, Ballantine, 1978; *Tolkien's Art: A Mythology for England* by Jane C. Nitzche, London, Macmillan, 1979; *The Individuated Hobbit* by Timothy R. O'Neill, Boston, Houghton Mifflin, 1979; *J. R. R. Tolkien* by Deborah and Ivor Rogers, Boston, Twayne, 1980; *J. R. R. Tolkien* by Katharyn F. Crabbe, New York, Ungar, 1981; *Tolkien: New Critical Perspectives* edited by Neil D. Isaacs and Rose A. Zimbardo, Lexington, University Press of Kentucky, 1981; *The Road to Middle-Earth* by T. A. Shippey, London, Allen and Unwin, 1982, Boston, Houghton Mifflin, 1983; *J. R. R. Tolkien: This Far Land* edited by Robert Giddings, London, Vision, 1983; *The Song of Middle-Earth: J. R. R. Tolkien's Themes, Symbols, and Myths* by David Harvey, London, Allen and Unwin, 1985; *J. R. R. Tolkien: Myth, Morality, and Religion* by Richard L. Purtill, New York, Harper & Row, 1985; *J. R. R. Tolkien: Six Decades of Criticism* edited by Judith A. Johnson, Westport, Connecticut, Greenwood Press, 1986; *The Magical World of the Inklings: J. R. R. Tolkien, C. S. Lewis, Charles Williams, Owen Barfield* by Gareth Knight, Shaftesbury, Dorset, Element, 1990; *A Tolkien Thesaurus* by Richard E. Blackwelder, New York, Garland, 1990; *Tolkien's Ring* by David Day, illustrated by Alan Lee, London, HarperCollins, 1994.

*   *   *

Tolkien's *The Lord of the Rings* is undoubtedly the most important and influential of all 20th-century fantasies. Eight million copies of this three-volume work had been sold by 1980; it has been translated into most of the world's major languages; it became a cult which inspired American hippies in the late 1960s, and Russian idealists in the 1990s (a group of Moscow fans set up a barricade at the time of the abortive coup against Gorbachev in 1991 under the banner "Frodo is with us"). Most important of all, *The Lord of the Rings* was very largely responsible for the fantasy boom which began in the 1960s, preparing an audience and inspiring (often depressingly directly) a large number of new writers of fantasy. Some of Tolkien's followers may have produced fantasies whose style was more in accord with modern literary taste and dealt with issues which Tolkien ignored (such as sexuality); but none have had the depth and impact of Tolkien's own work.

The impact of Tolkien's fantasy (like that, much more obscurely, of Austin Tappan Wright's *Islandia*) is indeed to a large extent a result of its depth. *The Lord of the Rings* rests on 40 years of creative activity, involving the invention of a mythology, a history, lan-

guages and alphabets. It therefore has a cultural realism which can be compared to that of Tolkien's own favourite work of literature, the Old English poem *Beowulf* (on which he wrote the classic academic essay): there are constant unexplained references to past history, to stories, legends, and literature. The reader is gradually led to believe in and (partly because of its length) to live in this imaginary world. There are signs that Tolkien himself took it just as seriously. Humphrey Carpenter (in *J. R. R. Tolkien: A Biography*) witnessed Tolkien dealing with an apparent contradiction in *The Lord of the Rings*: "He seems to see himself not as an author who has made a slight error that must now be corrected or explained away, but as an historian who must cast light on an obscurity in an historical document": "I always had the sense of recording what was already 'there', somewhere," Tolkien said, "not of 'inventing'" (*Biography*). In the process of "recording" he wrote millions of words between World War I and his death in 1973. He would produce different drafts of sections of his mythology; he would make two copies of a draft, and then make different amendments on each copy. The impossibility of deciding between different versions meant that his created mythology and early history of Middle-Earth, *The Silmarillion,* although basically complete by 1937, did not see publication until 1977, four years after his death.

Christopher Tolkien is still engaged in publishing his father's manuscripts. These variant versions and additional tales, now in twelve volumes, provide an extraordinarily detailed insight into Tolkien's creative processes (even though only a real enthusiast would want this much detail). The first to be published was *Unfinished Tales of Númenór and Middle-Earth*: subsequently they have appeared as numbered volumes in a series entitled "The History of Middle-Earth". Volumes 1 to 5 (*The Book of Lost Tales I, The Book of Lost Tales 2, The Lays of Beleriand, The Shaping of Middle-Earth* and *The Lost Road and Other Writings*) deal largely with early variant versions of *The Silmarillion*; volumes 10 and 11 (*Morgoth's Ring* and *The War of the Jewels*) are new versions of *The Silmarillion* story written after *The Lord of the Rings* had been finished; volumes 6 to 9 constitute volumes 1 to 4 of the sub-series "The History of *The Lord of the Rings*" (*The Return of the Shadow, The Treason of Isengard, The War of the Ring* and *Sauron Defeated*).

At the heart of Tolkien's fantasy-universe is language, as Tom Shippey has shown so well in his study of Tolkien, *The Road to Middle Earth*. As a young boy Tolkien had invented several languages; while still at school he became fascinated by the beauty of both Welsh and Finnish, neither of which he could then understand. When he went to Oxford he began by studying Latin and Greek, but took Comparative Philology as a special subject, and then moved from Classics to English, so that he could study Germanic philology. He began to develop his own private language based on Finnish, which was to become the elvish language Quenya; not long afterwards he began to work on Sindarin, another future elvish language, this time based on Welsh. In the summer of 1914 the 22-year-old undergraduate, fascinated by the Anglo-Saxon poem by Cynewulf which spoke of an angel called "Earendel," wrote a poem about a star-mariner, "The Voyage of Earendel the Evening Star". It was the beginning of his mythology of Middle-Earth. Throughout his time in the trenches and during his distinguished academic career he continued to develop his invented languages and his mythology.

Although he would read sections of his work to friends (notably that group known as the "Inklings," who included fantasists C. S. Lewis and Charles Williams), Tolkien's first published fantasy was an extension of the stories he devised specifically for his own children. *The Hobbit, Or There and Back Again* was an immediate success, and the publisher Stanley Unwin urged him to produce a sequel. The "sequel" was in the making all through the war years, and when it appeared, as *The Lord of the Rings* in the mid-1950s, it was very different from its predecessor. *The Hobbit,* the story of Bilbo Baggins and his adventures with a band of dwarves, is told in avuncular style, with somewhat patronising asides from the author to his childish readers. Tolkien himself found the tone jarring, and removed some of the offending passages in subsequent revised editions, in 1951 and 1966. What he wanted was to create what he called a Secondary World, which had no authorial interventions or direct connections with our own world to burst the bubble of imaginary realism. By the second volume of *The Lord of the Rings* he had found the right tone, far removed from the cosiness of *The Hobbit*: a grim, serious style, suited to the epic events of the War of the Rings, gaining its distance from our world by its use of archaic constructions and an elevated vocabulary.

What Tolkien had created in the hobbit, a small being with a large appetite and furry feet, was a way to bridge the gap between the heroic, distant world of the *Silmarillion* and the everyday world of the 20th century. "I am in fact a hobbit, in all but size," Tolkien wrote (*Biography*): he liked gardens, plain food, and home, and he had a simple sense of humour. The hobbits' homeland, the Shire, was the West Midlands in which Tolkien had grown up, threatened by the creeping industrialization and despoiling of the countryside that Tolkien so hated. Hobbits were not only like himself, but like those ordinary Englishmen whom Tolkien met in the trenches of the First World War, brought out of their ordinary lives against their will, yet responding to danger with decency and unexpected courage. In *The Hobbit* the reluctant traveller Bilbo Baggins shows himself to be even braver and more resourceful than his twelve companions, all warrior dwarfs. In *The Lord of the Rings* Frodo Baggins and Sam Gamgee (the officer and his batman), together with two younger hobbits, are brought out of the Shire and thrust into the world of wizards, near-immortal elves and evil orcs: it is Sam whose action eventually saves Middle-Earth from the evil power of Sauron.

In *The Lord of the Rings* we see epic events through the eyes of hobbits: strangers, like ourselves, to the heroic and magical world around them. Hobbits are not Tolkien's only creation: there are also the ents, near-immortal and sentient trees. But most of the inhabitants of Middle-Earth are derived from English folklore and mythology, including the elves (tall, powerful beings, not the tiny fairies of later tradition) and the dwarfs. There are various groups of men too, notably the Riders of Rohan, whose heroic lifestyle Tolkien derived from an idealized Anglo-Saxon past: they call their land the Mark, which would have been Latinized as Mercia (the Midland kingdom where Tolkien grew up), and Tolkien gives them Anglo-Saxon names in the long-lost Mercian form, which Tolkien himself recreated. Very few readers would appreciate what Tolkien had done, but it added to that sense of conviction that makes *The Lord of the Rings* so powerful. Names, for Tolkien, were all-important, and the philological correctness of his names adds to the solidity of Tolkien's world, in a way that anyone can appreciate by comparison with the linguistic ragbags confected by most of his imitators.

Tolkien always denied that *The Lord of the Rings* was allegorical, but there are certainly many resonances and applications to the modern age. Tolkien wanted his readers, ordinary hobbits like himself, to learn about the ancient Old English values of courage and

honour; he wanted them to appreciate a world in which poetry, tradition and history still meant something; he wanted them to share his love of the countryside and his horror at the way in which the evil wizard Saruman and his machines destroyed the forest and desecrated the landscape. Tolkien's Catholicism does not appear overtly in the book, but his desire to display the mystery of the world and the power of love and of evil makes his book profoundly religious. It was also the work of a man deeply out of sympathy with the world of the later 20th century; that as much as anything else explains the continued ability of *The Lord of the Rings* to attract devoted readers.

—Edward James

TOLSTOY, Nikolai

Nationality: British. **Born:** Maidstone, Kent, 23 June 1935. **Education:** Wellington College, Berkshire, 1949-53; Trinity College, Dublin, 1956-61, M.A. **Family:** Married in 1971; four children. Fellow of the Royal Society of Literature. **Agent:** Sheil Land Associates Ltd., 43 Doughty Street, London WC1N 2LF. **Address:** Court Close, Southmoor, Abingdon, Berkshire OX13 5HS, England.

FANTASY PUBLICATIONS

Novels

The Founding of Evil Hold School. London, Allen, 1968.
The Coming of the King. London, Bantam, 1988; New York, Bantam, 1989.

OTHER PUBLICATIONS

Other

Night of the Long Knives. New York, Ballantine, 1972.
Victims of Yalta. London, Hodder and Stoughton, and New York, Scribner, 1978.
The Half-Mad Lord. London, Cape, 1978; New York, Holt Rinehart, 1979.
Stalin's Secret War. London, Cape, 1981; New York, Holt Rinehart, 1982.
The Tolstoys. London, Hamilton, and New York, Morrow, 1983.
The Quest for Merlin. London, Hamilton, and Boston, Little Brown, Morrow, 1985.
The Minister and the Massacres. London, Century, 1986.

*

Nikolai Tolstoy comments:

My interests are primarily historical, and have been since I read the Waverley Novels at the age of 12. Two aspects fascinate me: 1) the imaginative exercise of recreating another world and mode of thought; 2) the detective work involved in discovering and analysing sources. Unfortunately, England is not a very healthy country for people like me to pursue such an interest. The absence of a Freedom of Information Act or written constitution, and the use of libel law for political ends, obliges British writers to exercise unusual caution. Of regret to me and many literary friends is the general lack of concern with this among British writers and academics. However, I believe belated changes are on the way.

*   *   *

Count Nikolai Tolstoy is perhaps better known as a controversial historian than as a fantasy writer. He is a direct descendant of the great Russian novelist Count Leo Tolstoy, but although his ancestry is one he could scarcely ignore, and while he has in fact written a group biography of his family, he has also immersed himself in British, especially Celtic, history. He has at times expressed this interest via fantasy.

Tolstoy's first novel, *The Founding of Evil Hold School,* was written while he was working as a teacher in a private preparatory school. One hopes its depiction of incompetent, venial and sadistic teachers is not taken too closely from life, though no doubt it does not spring entirely from the imagination. The main fantasy element appears early on. The central character, a born headmaster, is abandoned as a child in the African jungles, and raised, not by apes or even wolves, but by snakes. Eventually, he exhausts the tolerance of even this adoptive family, and makes his way to England in search of schoolboys to torment.

Luckily for him, there are a number of middle-class children in London whose parents are abroad. These realize he is endeavouring to get them into his power, and try to sabotage his plan. After a series of comic adventures, the children are all enroled in Evil Hold School. The head recruits a number of teachers as uninspiring as himself: they have names like Dr. Grimly-Fiendish. The school is in a remote country location, and it seems the children are helpless. However, the youngsters are predictably more resourceful than their oppressors, and succeed in turning the tables. *The Founding* reads as though a series of novels based at Evil Hold School was planned, but no more were published. Possibly the targeting was inexact. It is an enjoyable read for an adult, but the viewpoints and tone suggest a juvenile audience was intended. Despite this, there are some passages more likely to be appreciated by an older audience.

For two decades, Tolstoy's publications were all serious history. He attracted controversy by fiercely advocating the view that British ministers, some later very eminent, should share the blame for atrocities committed in the then Soviet Union and Yugoslavia at the end of World War II. This relates to the decision of the British authorities to return to those countries large numbers of former prisoners of the Axis, who were regarded as collaborators, sometimes wrongly, by the Communist regimes awaiting them at home. Tolstoy subsequently lost a well-publicized libel action resulting from these allegations.

During the 1980s Tolstoy found time to work on his other area of interest, Celtic history and mythology. His non-fiction *The Quest for Merlin* went a step further than the majority of researchers into the Dark Ages can manage. By then these were moving toward a tentative consensus that Arthur had probably existed, even if he didn't have the title of King, but that his encounters with Merlin were best classed among the barnacles of myth which had attached themselves to the original story. Tolstoy re-examined and tried to rehabilitate the work of Geoffrey of Monmouth, a 12th-century historian who is regarded as little more than a practical joker by orthodox academics. Tolstoy takes the view that there was a Merlin,

though he was not an exact contemporary of Arthur. If the lives of the two overlapped at all, Merlin was the younger man. Probably he acted as a kind of Shaman to the Selgovae, inhabitants of the area near modern Selkirk, apparently the last British tribe to hold out against Christianity.

In 1988 he published a novel, *The Coming of the King,* seemingly intended as the first book of a Merlin cycle. Though this might sound like familiar territory to the historical fantasy fan, it would be quite wrong to assume that Tolstoy was churning out yet more formulaic additions to a well-worked field. Much of the novel reads like a lyrical but unadapted straight translation from an early Welsh original. No doubt this was the intention, but it is likely to have narrowed interest in the proposed series to readers who had already gone beyond the recent glut of period fantasies, and familiarized themselves with the *Mabinogion* and other sources. Readers who have done this are likely to find nuggets of excellent prose and vivid descriptions of Dark Age life and thought. On the other hand, there are rapid changes of pace, theme and viewpoint. The lack of a glossary combined with an uncompromising view of the likely spelling of Welsh names and place-names at that period (no contemporary manuscripts survive) means that effort has to be invested in order to follow the plot and fix it in its historical context. This is, as implied above, the post-Arthurian period, one which has received less attention from novelists than one might suppose. Realistic and mythic elements are woven into the tapestry in almost equal measure: we see life in a Celtic warlord's hall as it is likely to have been; the extravagant, superstitious boasting and storytelling of the inhabitants; then the actual incursion of such mythical figures as Gwynn map Nudd.

Despite the novel's commercial success, no sequels to *The Coming of the King* have yet appeared. During this period, Tolstoy has been heavily involved in litigation. He remains in the public eye, and has become a prominent figure in international monarchist circles. Perhaps it is symbolic of his recent lack of luck that he took the role of King Harold in a live-action reconstruction of the Battle of Hastings.

—Peter T. Garratt

TURTLEDOVE, Harry (Norman)

Pseudonym: Eric Iverson. **Nationality:** American. **Born:** 1949. **Education:** University of California, Los Angeles, Ph.D. in history. **Family:** Married Laura Frankos; three daughters. **Address:** c/o Del Rey Books, 201 East 50th Street, New York, NY 10022, USA.

Fantasy Publications

Novels (series: Gerin the Fox; Videssos)

Wereblood (Gerin; as Eric Iverson). New York, Belmont, 1979.
Werenight (Gerin; as Eric Iverson). New York, Belmont, 1979.
The Misplaced Legion (Videssos). New York, Del Rey, 1987; London, Legend, 1988.
An Emperor for the Legion (Videssos). New York, Del Rey, 1987; London, Legend, 1988.

The Legion of Videssos. New York, Del Rey, 1987; London, Legend, 1988.

Swords of the Legion (Videssos). New York, Del Rey, 1987; London, Legend, 1988.

Krispos Rising (Videssos). New York, Del Rey, 1991.

Krispos of Videssos. New York, Del Rey, 1991.

The Case of the Toxic Spell Dump. New York, Baen, 1993

Krispos the Emperor (Videssos). New York, Del Rey, 1994.

Prince of the North (Gerin). New York, Baen, 1994.

Werenight (omnibus; includes revised versions of *Wereblood* and *Werenight*). New York: Baen, 1994.

OTHER PUBLICATIONS

Novels

Agent of Byzantium. New York, Congdon and Weed, 1987; London, New English Library, 1988; expanded edition, New York, Baen, 1994.

Noninterference. New York, Del Rey, 1988.

A Different Flesh. New York, Congdon and Weed, 1988.

The Pugnacious Peacekeeper, with *The Wheels of If* by L. Sprague de Camp. New York, Tor, 1990.

A World of Difference. New York, Del Rey, 1990.

Earthgrip. New York, Del Rey, 1991.

The Guns of the South: A Novel of the Civil War. New York, Del Rey, 1992.

Worldwar: In the Balance. New York, Del Rey, and London, Hodder and Stoughton, 1994.

Worldwar: Tilting the Balance. New York, Del Rey, and London, Hodder and Stoughton, 1995.

Short Stories

Kaleidoscope. New York, Del Rey, 1990.

Departures. New York, Del Rey, 1993.

Other

Translator, *The Chronicle of Theophanes: An English Translation of Anni Mundi 6095-6305 (A.D. 602-813).* Philadelphia, University of Pennsylvania Press, 1982.

*   *   *

The prolific Harry Turtledove started his career as a student of Byzantine history, which is reflected in a lot of his fantasy work. He also writes science fiction, with a distinct bent toward parallel-universe material, and the two themes appear together in many of his books. His early Gerin the Fox novels were published under the name Eric Iverson, and are now available as one volume under his own name as *Werenight.* These and their sequel *Prince of the North* deal with a situation in which an empire is in decline. It resembles a cross between Rome and medieval Europe. The hero is baron of a border province which pays no taxes, but in return receives little help when menaced by barbarians led by a powerful wizard.

In the more famous Videssos cycle, the hero, Marcus Scaurus, is an educated Roman officer of the late republic period. At the start of the first volume, *The Misplaced Legion,* he is campaigning in Gaul and is given a mysterious sword. Soon after, he comes into conflict with an enemy chieftain who has an identical sword. As soon as the two enchanted weapons touch each other, both men and all the Roman soldiers are transported to another world. At first it all goes rather easily. The planet is rather like Earth—indeed very like the Byzantine Empire of the 1060s. The Gaul decides to throw in his lot with the Romans, and they make contact with the local population. Luckily, they are in the Empire of Videssos, a civilized realm which has lost a lot of territory in the past but is now wealthy enough to have won some of it back, largely with the aid of hired mercenaries. They march to the capital and sign up.

Things continue to go well. Marcus Scaurus gets away with a republican refusal to prostrate himself before the Emperor and is invited to a party where he meets two beautiful women. Unfortunately, one of them, Helvis, is the wife of a powerful mercenary captain, and the other, Alypia, the daughter of the Emperor. Before Scaurus can decide if he stands any chance with either, his luck gets a lot worse. He mortally offends Avshar, the ambassador of the Yezda, a hostile nation dominated by evil magicians. (It's probably best not to speculate which enemy of the real Byzantium inspired it.) Avshar is a powerful sorcerer but a lousy diplomat, for he at once challenges Scaurus to a duel to the death. Naturally, our hero survives, but so does his opponent. The situation rapidly deteriorates. War breaks out, and Helvis's husband is killed. The first volume builds to a climax which will perhaps be more satisfying to readers who don't know the history, as the Empire reels to a Manzikert-like disaster.

The next two volumes, *An Emperor for the Legion* and *The Legion of Videssos,* are among the best things Turtledove has written. The Empire is in chaos, the Videssians fighting each other with as much enthusiasm as the Yezda. The portrait of the world, its disputes, customs, and theologies, gets deeper and livelier. Marcus is living with Helvis, who is devoted to him and bears him a child. This brings as many problems as it solves, for Helvis's people are mercenaries resembling the Normans. They are less corrupt than the Videssians and he rather prefers them, but they are out to make trouble on their own behalf. They are also heavily committed to one faction in a religious dispute which obsesses the Videssians, but is ignored by the more rational Romans. Marcus, desperate to bring the civil wars to an end and concentrate on defence against the Yezda, is forced to arrest some of Helvis's relatives. Torn between her lover and the code of her own country, Helvis escapes with them, taking with her Marcus's son.

These scenes of divided loyalty are the high point of the cycle. Scaurus helps to restore the Imperial family, and they take on the Yezda. He finds that Alypia, the scholarly princess clearly based on Alexia Comnena, is in love with him. Helvis does not reappear, and the fourth volume, *Swords of the Legion,* ends happily but with a slight sense of anticlimax. At the same time Turtledove was working on a more clear-cut derivative of his original studies, *Agent of Byzantium.* Here, the eponymous empire still dominates Europe in the medieval period, apparently because a religious leader who damaged it in the real world, in this one became a Christian. There is little fantasy here, most of the action dealing with the alternative discovery of a number of real-world scientific devices.

He later returned to Videssos with several further novels, which are prequels by several centuries to the main cycle. In the first two of these, *Krispos Rising* and *Krispos of Videssos,* the hero is born to the life of a farmer. Rather improbably, it is predicted that he is destined for great things, and oddly enough he eventually becomes Emperor of Videssos.

Turtledove's work is wide-ranging, and involves a number of alternative universes. He has changed the outcome of the second world war in a story in which the Nazis confront Mahatma Ghandi, sent South African agents through time to tinker with the outcome of the American Civil War, and even had aliens arrive on Earth during World War Two. In his story in the Susan Caspar/Gardner Dozois-edited *Jack the Ripper* anthology, Jack is a rogue vampire, whose publicity-seeking exploits deeply worry a group of gentleman undead who have survived quietly for centuries by deliberately keeping out of the public eye.

A later novel, *The Case of Toxic Spell Dump*, involves a new direction. The setting is Angels' City, a version of Los Angeles in which "mechanical" science is rudimentary and derided, but magical and spiritual technologies of all denominations are effective. Telephones and radios work through the communication of cloned imps. Micro-imps process information in computers. The freeways are clogged with flying carpets. All of this produces undesired side effects. The hero works for the Environmental Perfection Agency, and his job includes checking on the eponymous dump for the toxic residue of spells, which appears to be leaking. In many ways the book resembles an LA detective novel in the style of the Kellermans, with that mega-city's sweeping landscape of freeways, canyons, and squalid urban clutter realized with a similar vividness, enlivened by Turtledove's hitherto underdisplayed gift for the amusingly appalling pun. (CIA spooks here are actual immaterial beings. A spellchecker is a device for finding evidence of unauthorized magical activity in the environment.) It's a very welcome development in Turtledove's repertoire.

—Peter T. Garratt

TWAIN, Mark

Pseudonym for Samuel Langhorne Clemens. **Nationality:** American. **Born:** Florida, Missouri, 30 November 1835. **Family:** Married Olivia Langdon in 1870 (died 1904); one son and three daughters. **Career:** Printer's apprentice, 1837-50; helped brother with Hannibal newspapers, 1850-52; miscellaneous work in St. Louis, New York, Philadelphia, Keokuk, Iowa and Cincinnati, 1853-57; river pilot's apprentice on the Mississippi, 1857-59; licensed as a pilot, 1859; went to Nevada as secretary to his brother, then in the service of the governor, and worked as gold miner, 1861; staff member, *Territorial Enterprise*, Virginia City, Nevada, 1862-64; writer from 1867, lecturer from 1868; editor, *Buffalo Express*, New York, 1868-71; moved to Hartford, Connecticut, and became associated with Charles L. Webster Publishing Company, 1884-88: went bankrupt, 1888. **Awards:** M.A., Yale University, New Haven, Connecticut, 1888; Litt.D., Yale University, 1901; L.L.D., University of Missouri, Columbia, 1902; Litt.D., Oxford University, 1907. **Died:** 21 April 1910.

FANTASY PUBLICATIONS

Novels

The Prince and the Pauper. London, Chatto and Windus, 1881; Boston, Osgood, 1882.

A Connecticut Yankee in King Arthur's Court. New York, Webster, and London, Chatto and Windus, 1889.
Personal Recollections of Joan of Arc. New York, Harper, and London, Chatto and Windus, 1896.

Short Stories

Extracts from Adam's Diary Translated from the Original MS. New York and London, Harper, 1904.
A Dog's Tale. London, National Anti-Vivisection Society, and New York, Harper, 1904.
Eve's Diary Translated from the Original MS. New York and London, Harper, 1906.
A Horse's Tale. New York and London, Harper, 1907.
Extract from Captain Stormfield's Visit to Heaven. New York and London, Harper, 1909; revised edition adding "Letter to the Earth," as *Report from Paradise,* edited by Dixon Wecter, New York, Harper, 1952.
The Mysterious Stranger: A Romance. New York, Harper, 1916; London, Harper, 1917.
The Curious Republic of Gondour and Other Whimsical Stories. New York, Boni and Liveright, 1919.
The Mysterious Stranger and Other Stories. New York and London, Harper, 1922.
Concerning Cats: Two Tales by Mark Twain, edited by Frederick Anderson. San Francisco, Book Club of California, 1959.
Letters From the Earth, edited by Bernard de Voto. New York, Harper, 1962.
Mark Twain's Satires and Burlesques, edited by Franklin R. Rogers. Berkeley, University of California Press, 1967.
Which Was the Dream? and Other Symbolic Writings of the Later Years, edited by John S. Tuckey. Berkeley, University of California Press, 1967.
Mark Twain's Mysterious Stranger Manuscripts, edited by William M. Gibson. Berkeley, University of California Press, 1969.
Mark Twain's Quarrel with Heaven: Captain Stormfield's Visit to Heaven and Other Sketches, edited by Roy B. Browne. New Haven, Connecticut, College and University Press, 1970.
Mark Twain's Fables of Man, edited by John S. Tuckey. Berkeley, University of California Press, 1972.
The Devil's Race Track: Mark Twain's Great Dark Writings: The Best from "Which Was the Dream?" and "Fables of Man," edited by John S. Tuckey. Berkeley, University of California Press, 1980.
The Science Fiction of Mark Twain, edited by David Ketterer. Hamden, Connecticut, Shoe String Press, 1984.

OTHER PUBLICATIONS

Novels

The Gilded Age: A Tale of Today, with Charles Dudley Warner. Hartford, Connecticut, American Publishing Company, 1873; London, Routledge, 3 vols., 1874; partial version as *The Adventures of Captain Sellers, Being Twain's Share of "The Gilded Age,"* edited by Charles Neider, New York, Doubleday, 1965; London, Chatto and Windus, 1966.
The Adventures of Tom Sawyer. London, Chatto and Windus, and Hartford, Connecticut, American Publishing Company, 1876.
The Adventures of Huckleberry Finn (Tom Sawyer's Comrade). London, Chatto and Windus, 1884; New York, Webster, 1885.

The American Claimant. New York, Webster, and London, Chatto and Windus, 1892.

Pudd'nhead Wilson: A Tale. London, Chatto and Windus, 1894; as *The Tragedy of Pudd'nhead Wilson and the Comedy of Those Extraordinary Twins,* Hartford, Connecticut, American Publishing Company, 1894.

Simon Wheeler, Detective, edited by Charles Neider. New York, Doubleday, 2 vols., 1964.

The Complete Novels, edited by Charles Neider. New York, Doubleday, 2 vols., 1964.

Short Stories

The Celebrated Jumping Frog of Calaveras County and Other Sketches, edited by Charles Henry Webb (as John Paul). New York, Webb, 1867.

Screamers: A Gathering of Scraps of Humour, Delicious Bits, and Short Stories. London, Hotten, 1872.

A Curious Dream and Other Sketches. London, Routledge, 1872; revised, as *Information Wanted and Other Sketches,* London, Routledge, 1876.

Mark Twain's Sketches. New York, American News Company, 1874.

Mark Twain's Sketches, New and Old. Hartford, Connecticut, American Publishing Company, 1875.

The Stolen White Elephant Etc. London, Chatto and Windus, and Boston, Osgood, 1882.

Merry Tales. New York, Webster, 1892.

The £1,000,000 Bank-Note and Other New Stories. New York, Webster, and London, Chatto and Windus, 1893.

Tom Sawyer Abroad by Huck Finn Edited by Mark Twain. New York, Webster, 1894; as *Tom Sawyer Abroad,* London, Chatto and Windus, 1894.

Tom Sawyer Abroad, Tom Sawyer, Detective, and Other Stories. New York, Harper, 1896; as *Tom Sawyer, Detective, as Told by Huck Finn, and Other Tales,* London, Chatto and Windus, 1897.

The Man Who Corrupted Hadleyburg and Other Stories and Essays. New York, Harper, and London, Chatto and Windus, 1900.

A Double Barreled Detective Story. New York, Harper, and London, Chatto and Windus, 1902.

My Debut as a Literary Person, with Other Essays and Stories. Hartford, Connecticut, American Publishing Company, 1903.

The Jumping Frog in English, Then in French, Then Clawed Back into a Civilized Language Once More by Patient Unremunerated Toil. New York and London, Harper, 1903.

The $30,000 Bequest and Other Stories. New York and London, Harper, 1906.

Death-Disk. New York, Werner, 1913.

Who Was Sarah Findlay? with a Suggested Solution to the Mystery by J. M. Barrie. London, privately printed, 1917.

Humorous Fables. Girard, Kansas, Haldeman Julius, 1924.

The Adventures of Thomas Jefferson Snodgrass, edited by Charles Honce. Chicago, Covici, 1928.

A Boy's Adventure. Privately printed, 1928.

Jim Smiley and His Jumping Frog, edited by Albert Bigelow Paine. Chicago, Pocahontas Press, 1940.

A Murder, a Mystery, and a Marriage. New York, Manuscript House, 1945.

Mark Twain's First Story. Iowa City, Iowa, Prairie Press, 1952.

The Complete Short Stories, edited by Charles Neider. New York, Hanover House, 1957.

The Complete Humorous Sketches and Tales, edited by Charles Neider. New York, Doubleday, 1961.

Mark Twain's Best: Eight Short Stories by America's Master Humorist. New York, Scholastic, 1962.

Short Stories of Mark Twain. New York, Funk and Wagnalls, 1967.

Great Short Works of Mark Twain, edited by Justin Kaplan. New York, Harper, 1967.

Mark Twain's Hannibal, Huck and Tom, edited by Walter Blair. Berkeley, University of California Press, 1969.

Wapping Alice. Berkeley, California, Friends of the Bancroft Library, 1981.

Huck Finn and Tom Sawyer Among the Indians and Other Unfinished Stories, edited by Dahlia Armon and Walter Blair. Berkeley, University of California Press, 1989.

Goldminers and Guttersnipes: Tales of California, edited by Ken Chowder. San Francisco, Chronicle Books, 1991.

Plays

The Quaker City Holy Land Excursion: An Unfinished Play. New York, privately printed, 1927.

A Champagne Cocktail and a Catastrophe: Two Acting Charades. New York, privately printed, 1930.

Colonel Sellers as a Scientist, with William Dean Howells, adaptation of the novel *The Gilded Age* by Twain and Charles Dudley Warner (produced New Brunswick, New Jersey, and New York, 1887). Published in *The Complete Plays of William Dean Howells,* edited by Walter J. Meserve, New York, New York University Press, 1960.

Ah Sin, with Bret Harte, edited by Frederick Anderson (produced Washington, D.C., 1877). San Francisco, Book Club of California, 1961.

Poetry

Three Aces, Jim Todd's Episode in Social Euchre: A Poem and a Denial. Westport, Connecticut, privately printed, 1929.

Be Good, Be Good: A Poem. New York, privately printed, 1931.

Slovenly Peter (Der Struwwelpeter), Freely Translated into English Jingles by Mark Twain. New York and London, Harper, 1935.

On the Poetry of Mark Twain, with Selections from His Verse, edited by Arthur L. Scott. Urbana, University of Illinois Press, 1966.

Other

The Innocents Abroad; or, The New Pilgrims' Progress. Hartford, Connecticut, American Publishing Company, 1869; London, Routledge, 2 vols., 1872.

Mark Twain's (Burlesque) Autobiography and First Romance. New York, Sheldon, 1871.

Memoranda: From the Galaxy. Toronto, Canadian News and Publishing Company, 1871.

Roughing It. London, Routledge, and Hartford, Connecticut, American Publishing Company, 1872.

The Innocents at Home. London, Routledge, 1872.

Old Times on the Mississippi. Toronto, Belford, 1876.

A True Story of the Recent Carnival of Crime. Boston, Osgood, 1877.

An Idle Excursion. Toronto, Belford, 1878.

Punch, Brothers, Punch! and Other Sketches. New York, Slote Woodman, 1878.

A Tramp Abroad. Hartford, Connecticut, American Publishing Company, and London, Chatto and Windus, 1880.

Date 1601: Conversation as It Was by the Social Fireside in the Time of the Tudors. Privately printed, 1880; as *"1601" or Conversation at the Social Fireside as It Was in the Time of the Tudors,* San Francisco, Grabhorn Press, 1925.

A Curious Experience. Toronto, Gibson, 1881.

Life on the Mississippi. London, Chatto and Windus, and Boston, Osgood, 1883.

Mark Twain's Library of Humor, anonymously edited by William Dean Howells. New York, Webster, 1887.

Facts for Mark Twain's Memory Builder. New York, Webster, 1891.

How to Tell a Story and Other Essays. New York, Harper, 1897; revised edition, 1900.

Following the Equator: A Journey Around the World. Hartford, Connecticut, American Publishing Company, 1897; as *More Tramps Abroad,* London, Chatto and Windus, 1897.

The Writings of Mark Twain. Hartford, Connecticut, American Publishing Company, and London, Chatto and Windus, 25 vols., 1899-1907.

The Pains of Lowly Life. London, London Anti-Vivisectionist Society, 1900.

English as She Is Taught. Boston, Mutual, 1900; revised edition, New York, Century, 1901.

To the Person Sitting in Darkness. New York, Anti-Imperialist League, 1901.

Edmund Burke on Croker, and Tammany. New York, Economist Press, 1901.

An Unexpected Acquaintance (excerpt from *A Tramp Abroad*). New York and London, Harper, 1904.

Mark Twain on Vivisection. New York, New York Anti-Vivisection Society, 1905 (?).

King Leopold's Soliloquy: A Defense of His Congo Rule. Boston, Warren, 1905; revised edition, 1906; London, Unwin, 1907.

Editorial Wild Oats. New York and London, Harper, 1905.

What Is Man? (published anonymously). New York, DeVinne Press, 1906; as by Mark Twain, London, Watts, 1910.

Mark Twain on Spelling. New York, Simplified Spelling Board, 1906.

The Writings of Mark Twain, Hillcrest Edition. New York and London, Harper, 25 vols., 1906-07.

Christian Science with Notes Containing Corrections to Date. New York and London, Harper, 1907.

Is Shakespeare Dead? From My Autobiography. New York and London, Harper, 1909.

Mark Twain's Speeches, edited by F. A. Nast. New York and London, Harper, 1910; revised edition, 1923.

Queen Victoria's Jubilee. Privately printed, 1910.

Travels at Home. New York and London, Harper, 1910.

Mark Twain's Letter to the California Pioneers. Oakland, California, Dewitt and Snelling, 1911.

The Suppressed Chapter of "Life on the Mississippi". New York, privately printed, 1913.

What Is Man? and Other Essays. New York, Harper, 1917; London, Chatto and Windus, 1919.

Mark Twain's Letters, Arranged with Comment, edited by Albert Bigelow Paine. New York, Harper, 2 vols., 1917; shortened version, as *Letters,* London, Chatto and Windus, 1920.

Saint Joan of Arc. New York and London, Harper, 1919.

Moments with Mark Twain, edited by Albert Bigelow Paine. New York, Harper, 1920.

Mark Twain Able Yachtsman Interviews Himself on Why Lipton Failed to Lift the Cup. New York, privately printed, 1920.

"Coming Out": A Letter to a Rosebud of Two Generations Ago Inscribed to a Bud of Today from the Same Shoot. New York, privately printed, 1921.

The Writings of Mark Twain, Definitive Edition, edited by Albert Bigelow Paine. New York, Gabriel Wells, 37 vols., 1922-25.

Europe and Elsewhere. New York and London, Harper, 1923.

Mark Twain's Autobiography, edited by Albert Bigelow Paine. New York and London, Harper, 2 vols., 1924; as *The Autobiography of Mark Twain,* edited by Charles Neider, New York, Doubleday, 1959.

Humorous Sketches. Girard, Kansas, Haldeman Julius, 1924.

Amusing Answers to Correspondence and Other Pieces. Girard, Kansas, Haldeman Julius, 1924.

Journalism in Tennessee and Other Humorous Sketches. Girard, Kansas, Haldeman Julius, 1924.

A Curious Experience and Other Amusing Pieces. Girard, Kansas, Haldeman Julius, 1925.

Sketches of the Sixties by Bret Harte and Mark Twain, Being *Forgotten Material Now Collected for the First Time from "The Californian" 1864-67.* San Francisco, John Howell, 1926; as *California Sketches,* New York, Dover, 1991.

More Maxims of Mark. New York, privately printed, 1927.

The Suppressed Chapter of "Following the Equator." Privately printed, 1928.

A Letter From Mark Twain to His Publisher, Chatto and Windus. San Francisco, Penguin Press, 1929.

Mark Twain's Early Writings in Hannibal Missouri Papers, compiled by Willard Morse. Santa Monica, California, Morse, 1931.

Mark Twain, the Letter Writer, edited by Cyril Clemens. Boston, Meador, 1932.

Mark Twain's Works. New York, Harper, 23 vols., 1933.

Mark Twain: Wit and Wisdom, edited by Cyril Clemens. New York, Stokes, 1935.

The Family Mark Twain. New York and London, Harper, 1935; edited version, as *The Favorite Works of Mark Twain,* New York, Garden City Publishing Company, 1939.

The Mark Twain Omnibus, edited by Max J. Herzberg. New York, Harper, 1935.

Representative Selections, edited by Fred L. Patee. New York, American Book Company, 1935.

Mark Twain's Notebook, edited by Albert Bigelow Paine. New York and London, Harper, 1935.

Letters From the Sandwich Islands, Written for the "Sacramento Union," edited by G. Ezra Dane. San Francisco, Grabhorn Press, 1937; London, Oxford University Press, 1938.

The Washoe Giant in San Francisco, Being Heretofore Uncollected Sketches Published in "The Golden Era" in the Sixties, edited by Franklin Walker. San Francisco, Fields, 1938.

Mark Twain's Letter to William Bowen. San Francisco, Book Club of California, 1938.

Mark Twain's Western Years, Together with Hitherto Unreprinted Clemens Western Items, by Ivar Benson. Stanford, California, Stanford University, 1938.

Letters From Honolulu Written for the "Sacramento Union," edited by Thomas Nickerson. Honolulu, Nickerson, 1939.

The Complete Short Stories and Famous Essays. New York, Collier, 1940.

Mark Twain's Travels with Mr. Brown, Being Heretofore Uncollected Sketches Written for the San Francisco "Alta California" in 1866 and 1867, edited by Franklin Walker and G. Ezra Dane. New York, Knopf, 1940.

Mark Twain in Eruption: Hitherto Unpublished Pages about Men and Events, edited by Bernard De Voto. New York, Harper, 1940.

Republican Letters, edited by Cyril Clemens. Webster Groves, Missouri, International Mark Twain Society, 1941.

Letters to Will Brown, edited by Theodore Hornberger. Austin, University of Texas, 1941.

Mark Twain's Letters in the "Muscatine Journal," edited by Edgar M. Branch. Chicago, Mark Twain Association of America, 1942.

Washington in 1868, edited by Cyril Clemens. Webster Groves, Missouri, International Mark Twain Society, 1943.

Mark Twain, Business Man, edited by Samuel Charles Webster. Boston, Little Brown, 1946.

The Portable Mark Twain, edited by Bernard De Voto. New York, Viking Press, 1946; London, Penguin, 1947.

The Letters of Quintus Curtius Snodgrass, edited by Ernest E. Leisy. Dallas, Southern Methodist University Press, 1946.

Mark Twain in Three Moods: Three New Items of Twainiana, edited by Dixon Wecter. San Marino, California, Friends of the Huntington Library, 1948.

Mark Twain at Your Fingertips, edited by Caroline Thomas Harnsberger. New York, Beechhurst Press, 1948.

Mark Twain. New York, Bigger Press, 1948.

Mark Twain to Mrs. Fairbanks, edited by Dixon Wecter. San Marino, California, Huntington Library, 1949.

The Love Letters of Mark Twain, edited by Dixon Wecter. New York, Harper, 1949.

Some Thoughts on the Science of Onanism. Privately printed, 1952; as *Some Thoughts on the Science of Onanism or Mark Twain in Erection with Apologies to Bernard De Voto,* privately printed, 1964.

Mark Twain for Young People, compiled by Cyril Clemens. New York, Whittier, 1953.

Mark Twain to Uncle Remus 1881-1885, edited by Thomas H. English. Atlanta, Emory University Library, 1953.

Twins of Genius (letters to George Washington Cable), edited by Guy A. Cardwell. East Lansing, Michigan State College Press, 1953.

Mark Twain's Letters From Hawaii, edited by A. Grove Day. New York, Appleton Century, 1956; London, Chatto and Windus, 1967.

Mark Twain of the "Enterprise," edited by Henry Nash Smith and Frederick Anderson. Berkeley, University of California Press, 1957; abridged edition, as *Mark Twain: San Francisco Virginia City Territorial Enterprise Correspondent,* San Francisco, Book Club of California, 1957.

Mark Twain's Jest Book, edited by Cyril Clemens. Kirkwood, Missouri, Mark Twain Journal, 1957.

Traveling with Innocents Abroad: Mark Twain's Original Reports from Europe and the Holy Land, edited by Daniel Morley McKeithan. Norman, University of Oklahoma Press, 1958.

The Art, Humor, and Humanity of Mark Twain, edited by Minnie M. Bashear and Robert M. Rodney. Norman, University of Oklahoma Press, 1959.

Mark Twain: A Laurel Reader, edited by Edmund Fuller. New York, Dell, 1960.

Mark Twain and the Government, edited by Svend Petersen. Caldwell, Idaho, Caxton Printers, 1960.

Mark Twain-Howells Letters: The Correspondence of Samuel L. Clemens and William Dean Howells 1872-1910, edited by Henry Nash Smith, William M. Gibson, and Frederick Anderson. Cambridge, Harvard University Press, 2 vols., 1960; abridged edition, as *Selected Mark Twain-Howells Letters,* 1967.

Your Personal Mark Twain. New York, International Publishers, 1960.

Mark Twain: Wit and Wisecracks, edited by Doris Benardete. Mount Vernon and New York, Peter Pauper Press, 1961.

Letters to Mary, edited by Lewis Leary. New York, Columbia University Press, 1961.

Mark Twain: Life as I Find It, edited by Charles Neider. Garden City, Doubleday, 1961.

The Travels of Mark Twain, edited by Charles Neider. New York, Doubleday, 1961.

Contributions to "The Galaxy," 1868-1871, edited by Bruce R. McElderry. Gainesville, Florida, Scholars Facsimiles and Reprints, 1961.

Mark Twain on the Art of Writing, edited by Martin B. Fried. Buffalo, Salisbury Club, 1961.

The Pattern for Mark Twain's "Roughing It": Letters From Nevada by Samuel and Orion Clemens, 1861-1862, edited by Franklin R. Rogers. Berkeley, University of California Press, 1961.

Mark Twain on the Damned Human Race, edited by Janet Smith. New York, Hill and Wang, 1962.

Selected Shorter Writings of Mark Twain, edited by Walter Blair. Boston, Houghton Mifflin, 1962.

The Complete Essays of Mark Twain, edited by Charles Neider. New York, Doubleday, 1963.

Mark Twain's San Francisco, edited by Bernard Taper. New York and London, McGraw Hill, 1963.

The Forgotten Writings of Mark Twain, edited by Henry Duskus. New York, Citadel Press, 1963.

Mark Twain: A Cure for the Blues. Rutland, Vermont, Tuttle, 1964.

Susy and Mark Twain: Family Dialogues, edited by Edith Colgate Salisbury. New York, Harper, 1965.

General Grant by Matthew Arnold, with a Rejoinder by Mark Twain, edited by John Y. Simon. Carbondale, Southern Illinois University Press, 1966.

A Treasury of Mark Twain, edited by Edward Lewis and Robert Myers. Kansas City, Missouri, Hallmark Editions, 1967.

A Curious Lecture Concerning Skating; and Mrs. Mark Twain's Shoe. Denver, Colorado, Ralph Baldwin, 1967.

The Complete Travel Books, edited by Charles Neider. New York, Doubleday, 1967.

Mark Twain's Letters to His Publishers, 1876-1894, edited by Hamlin Hill. Berkeley, University of California Press, 1967.

Clemens of the "Call": Mark Twain in California, edited by Edgar M. Branch. Berkeley, University of California Press, 1969.

Mark Twain's Correspondence with Henry Huttleston Rogers, 1893-1909, edited by Lewis Leary. Berkeley, University of California Press, 1969.

Man Is the Only Animal That Blushes—Or Needs To: The Wisdom of Mark Twain, edited by Michael Joseph. Los Angeles, Random House, 1970.

Mark Twain's Letters to the Rogers Family, edited by Earl J. Dias. New Bedford, Massachusetts, Reynolds DeWalt, 1970.

The War Prayer. New York, Harper, 1970.

Mark Twain on Man and Beast, edited by Janet Smith. New York and Westport, Connecticut, Laurence Hill, 1972.

A Mark Twain Turnover: Advice for Good Little Girls; Mark Twain and the Devil. New Britain, Connecticut, Massman, 1972.

Everybody's Mark Twain, edited by Caroline Thomas Harnsberger. South Brunswick, New Jersey, Barnes, and London, Yoseloff, 1972.

A Pen Warmed Up in Hell: Mark Twain in Protest, edited by Frederick Anderson. New York, Harper, 1972.

Mark Twain and the Three R's: Race, Religion, Revolution and Related Matters, edited by Maxwell Geismar. Indianapolis and New York, Bobbs Merrill, 1973.

The Choice Humorous Works of Mark Twain. London, Chatto and Windus, 1973.

Mark Twain's Notebooks and Journals, edited by Frederick Anderson, Michael B. Frank, and Kenneth M. Sanderson. Berkeley, University of California Press, 3 vols., 1975-79.

Letters From the Sandwich Islands, edited by Joan Abramson. Norfolk Island, Australia, Island Heritage, 1975.

The Higher Animals: A Mark Twain Bestiary, edited by Maxwell Geismar. New York, Crowell, 1976.

Mark Twain and Fairhaven. Fairhaven, Massachusetts, Millicent Library, 1976.

The Unabridged Mark Twain, edited by Lawrence Teacher. Philadelphia, Running Press, 1976.

The Mammoth Cod and Address to the Stomach Club. Milwaukee, Maledicta, 1976.

The Comic Mark Twain Reader, edited by Charles Neider. New York, Doubleday, 1977.

Mark Twain Speaking, edited by Paul Fatout. Iowa City, University of Iowa Press, 1976.

Mark Twain Speaks for Himself, edited by Paul Fatout. West Lafayette, Indiana, Purdue University Press, 1978.

Early Tales and Sketches, edited by Edgar M. Branch and Robert H. Hirst. Berkeley, University of California Press, 2 vols., 1979-81.

Jim Wolf and the Cats. Buffalo, New York, Hillside Press, 1979.

Mark Twain: Social Critic for the 80s, edited by William L. McLinn and Stuart W. White. San Francisco, AT Press, 1980.

The Selected Letters of Mark Twain, edited by Charles Neider. New York, Harper, 1982.

Mississippi Writings (Library of America). New York, Literary Classics of the United States, and London, Cambridge University Press, 1982.

Mark Twain's Letters, edited by Edgar M. Branch, Michael B. Frank, and Kenneth M. Sanderson. Berkeley, University of California Press, 1987.

The Outrageous Mark Twain, edited by Charles Neider. New York, Doubleday, 1987.

Mark Twain's Aquarium: The Samuel Clemens Angelfish Correspondence. Athens, University of Georgia Press, 1991.

*

Film Adaptations: *The Prince and the Pauper,* 1915, 1937, 1961, 1977; *The Adventures of Tom Sawyer,* 1917, 1930, 1938, 1973, 1973 (TV movie); *The Adventures of Huckleberry Finn,* 1920, 1931, 1939, 1960, 1974, 1975 (TV movie), 1981 (TV movie), 1986 (TV mini-series); *A Connecticut Yankee at King Arthur's Court,* 1921, 1931, 1948, 1989 (TV movie); *Tom Sawyer, Detective,* 1938; *The Million Pound Note,* 1954.

Bibliographies: *A Bibliography of the Works of Mark Twain, Samuel Langhorne Clemens* by Merle Johnson, New York, Harper, revised edition, 1935; *Plots and Characters in the Works of Mark Twain* by Robert Gale, foreword by Frederick Anderson, Hamden, Connecticut, Shoe String Press, 2 vols., 1973; *Mark Twain, a Reference Guide* by Thomas Asa Teeney, Boston, Hall, 1977; *Mark*

Twain International: A Bibliography and Interpretation of His World-Wide Popularity edited by Robert H. Rodney, Westport, Connecticut, Greenwood Press, 1982; *Mark Twain: A Bibliography of the Collections of the Mark Twain Memorial and the Stowe-Day Foundation* compiled by William S. McBride, Hartford, Connecticut, McBridge/Publisher, 1984.

Critical Studies (selection): *Mark Twain: A Biography* by Albert Bigelow Paine, New York, Harper, 3 vols., 1912, abridged edition, as *A Short Life of Mark Twain,* 1920; *Mark Twain: The Man and His Work* by Edward Wagenknecht, New Haven, Connecticut, Yale University Press, 1935, revised edition, Norman, University of Oklahoma Press, 1961, 1967; *Mark Twain: Man and Legend* by De Lancey Ferguson, Indianapolis, Bobbs Merrill, 1943; *A Casebook on Mark Twain's Wound* edited by Lewis Leary, New York, Crowell, 1962; *Discussions of Mark Twain* edited by Guy A. Cardwell, Boston, Heath, 1963; *Mr. Clemens and Mark Twain: A Biography* by Justin Kaplan, New York, Simon and Schuster, 1966, London, Cape, 1967; *Mark Twain: The Fate of Humor* by James M. Cox, Princeton, New Jersey, Princeton University Press, 1966; *The Art of Mark Twain* by William M. Gibson, New York, Oxford University Press, 1976; *Mark Twain: A Collection of Criticism* edited by Dean Morgan Schmitter, New York, McGraw Hill, 1976; *Mark Twain* by Robert Keith Miller, New York, Ungar, 1983; *The Authentic Mark Twain: A Literary Biography of Samuel L. Clemens* by Everett Emerson, Philadelphia, University of Pennsylvania Press, 1984; *The Making of Mark Twain: A Biography* by John Lauber, Boston, Houghton Mifflin, 1985; *Mark Twain and Science* by Sherwood Cummings, Baton Rouge, Louisiana State University Press, 1989; *Mark Twain: The Bachelor Years* by Margaret Sanborn, New York, Doubleday, 1990; *The Inventions of Mark Twain* by John Lauber, New York, Hill and Wang, 1990.

*   *   *

A vigorous campaign has been mounted to claim Mark Twain as an early science-fiction writer, with the time-travel story *A Connecticut Yankee in King Arthur's Court* as its centrepiece. But a story about a man who gets hit on the head and wakes up in Arthurian England seems more like fantasy than science fiction; moreover, while the approach and theme of *A Connecticut Yankee* do not reverberate throughout later science fiction, it can be plausibly cast as precursor to a long and vibrant tradition of fantasies that juxtapose a mythological or legendary world with a modern observer. *A Connecticut Yankee* brilliantly demonstrates the two functions of the device: first, when Hank Morgan brings American common sense to highfalutin' Camelot, he gently punctures the pretensions of traditional fantasy worlds; later, when his social and technological innovations bring Camelot to a bloody war, he represents a savage attack on the values of modern civilization. (Critics of Twain as a science-fiction writer must see that conclusion only as an attack on modern technology, severely understating the extent of his concerns.) When Glen Cook's private eye Garrett interrogates a recalcitrant dwarf, or Stephen R. Donaldson's Thomas Covenant rapes a fair maiden, they are only two of fantasy's many successors to Hank Morgan.

Then, after discussing *A Connecticut Yankee,* proponents of Twain as a science-fiction writer must dubiously claim fantastic stories like "Sold to Satan" or focus on inconsequential efforts like "From the London Times of 1904". Those who would see Twain as a fantasy writer have richer fields to plough. One work to consider is *The Prince and the Pauper,* which despite being set in 16th-century England could be called an anticipation of one form of borderline fantasy, the Ruritanian romance, and surely influenced the novel that defined the sub-genre—Anthony Hope's *The Prisoner of Zenda.* (Both works describe a noble and a commoner who discover they are identical and trade places, but Twain characteristically emphasizes social commentary more than adventure.) Also related to Ruritania are "The Curious Republic of Gondour"—though Twain only discusses the country's system of granting additional votes to wealthy or well-educated citizens—and "A Medieval Romance"—the story of a noblewoman who pretends to be a man to inherit a throne and becomes entangled in a sticky situation that Twain announces he cannot resolve.

Next, many Twain writings could be called theological fantasies. While one might include *Personal Recollections of Joan of Arc,* a respectful if dull novel about the famous saint, Twain's other theological works present a revisionist and cynical view of Christian teachings and doctrines. Prominent among these are discordant fragments from what was planned as a narrative of history from the creation of Adam to the Flood, told by Adam, Eve, Methuselah and other canonical and invented characters; its completed parts are "Extracts from Adam's Diary," "Eve's Diary," and manuscripts gathered as "Papers of the Adam Family" in *Letters From the Earth.* In Twain's version of Genesis, early humans develop rapidly, experiment with democracy but revert to tyranny, experience scientific progress and population growth, and grow decadent as Noah builds his Ark—a framework designed to allow Twain to take a jaundiced look at the Bible and comment on modern events paralleling his Biblical events. In their diaries Adam and Eve gradually discover their world and learn to love each other; while these works find Twain in a charming and mellow mood, other materials suggest the project was wisely abandoned.

Twain's religious stories also include "Captain Stormfield's Visit to Heaven," where he constructs a Heaven to accord with modern knowledge about the extent of the universe and human history: Stormfield finds Heaven divided into numerous sections for various intelligent races, and Americans dislike the American section of Heaven because most residents are Indians. And while American newcomers want to wear wings and sing hymns, they soon realize this is an absurd way to spend eternity and abandon these affectations. In "Letter to the Earth," an angel writes to a man granting his selfish prayers and conveys by effusive praise of his minimal charity his true lack of virtue. In "Sold to Satan," Twain reverses the standard tale of a man selling his soul to the Devil; discovering the Devil is made of radium, the prospective soul-seller offers to purchase the Devil. Two other works about the Devil demand more attention. In the wickedly humorous "Letters From the Earth" Satan, temporarily exiled to Earth, writes letters to Heaven about people's ridiculous religious beliefs, devoting much time to an account of the Flood story, which he sees as devastating evidence of the evil and twisted personality of the God worshiped by humans. "The Mysterious Stranger" describes how three boys in 16th-century Austria befriend a strange boy who introduces himself as the angel Satan, unfallen nephew of his fallen namesake.

Satan performs tricks, takes the boys on several journeys and intervenes in villagers' affairs, though the boys are appalled by his idea of helpful intervention; Satan believes it a favour to kill people instead of letting them live predicted lives of misery. What makes Twain's devil sinister is not his malevolence towards humans but his utter indifference: he explains that beings like him can have no more regard for people than an elephant has for a spider. Denounced by scholars as an illegitimate mixture of three manuscripts, "The Mysterious Stranger" does powerfully convey the later Twain's pessimism and combines its elements in a manner one imagines Twain would have approved. Overall, "Letters From the Earth" and "The Mysterious Stranger" are the two Twain works published after his death that might be regarded as masterpieces.

Twain also produced several fables, the best probably being "A Dog's Tale," the story of a loyal dog who saves his master's baby from fire then watches the man kill his puppy in a scientific experiment—a strong if unsubtle argument against vivisection. Less successful is the longer and unfocused "A Horse's Tale," about Buffalo Bill's faithful horse who helps a charming young girl but is finally stolen and abused. Other fables include "Some Learned Fables for Good Old Boys and Girls," where some animal scientists venture into the human world to reach ludicrous conclusions about its artefacts—Twain's comment on the limitations of archaeologists and paleontologists; "A Fable," where a cat sees a beautiful picture in a mirror while the other animals stand in front to see only themselves—the moral being "You can find in a text whatever you bring"; and "The Five Boons of Life," where a man successively accepts four of the five gifts offered by a fairy—Pleasure, Love, Fame, and Riches—until finally realizing that the only truly valuable gift is the fifth one, Death. Twain also wrote ghost stories like "A Curious Dream," where Twain meets a skeleton in a shroud who is moving with other ghosts to new homes because their graveyard has not been properly cared for—a tale better written than its simple message about maintaining graveyards deserves—and "A Ghost Story," where the ghost of the Cardiff Giant mistakenly haunts a statue of his body. Finally, Twain was fascinated by dreams and produced dream visions like "The Great Dark," a dream journey in a miniature boat across a drop of water that becomes not so much a scientific description of microscopic worlds as a meditation on the problematic line between dreams and reality.

If it is stimulating to take Twain out of the box of science fiction and place him in the box of fantasy, one must also acknowledge that he is not a writer who fits comfortably into boxes. During his life, Twain disliked being cast as a regional humorist; were he alive today, he would no doubt dislike being cast as a pioneering science-fiction or fantasy writer. In truth, Twain was a man who wanted to be many things, including a serious novelist, celebrity, political spokesman and businessman; and his amazingly diverse and innumerable writings, still being sorted out by scholars, appropriately reflect the magnificent incoherence of his singular career.

—Gary Westfahl

V

VANCE, Jack

Pseudonyms: Peter Held; Ellery Queen, Alan Wade. **Nationality:** American. **Born:** John Holbrook Vance, San Francisco, 28 August 1916. **Education:** University of California, Berkeley, B.A. 1942. **Family:** Married Norma Ingold in 1946; one son. **Career:** Self-employed writer. **Awards:** Mystery Writers of America Edgar Allan Poe award, 1960; Hugo award, 1963, 1967; Nebula award, 1966; Jupiter award, 1974; World Fantasy Convention Life Achievement award, 1984; World Fantasy award, 1990. **Agent:** Ralph Vicinanza Ltd., 432 Park Avenue South, Suite 1205, New York, NY 10016, USA. **Address:** 6383 Valley View Road, Oakland, CA 94611, USA.

FANTASY PUBLICATIONS

Novels (series: Dying Earth; Lyonesse)

The Dying Earth. New York, Hillman, 1950; London, Mayflower, 1972.

The Eyes of the Overworld (Dying Earth). New York, Ace, 1966; London, Mayflower, 1972.

Cugel's Saga (Dying Earth). Columbia, Pennsylvania, Underwood Miller, 1983; London, Granada, 1985.

Suldrun's Garden (Lyonesse). New York, Berkley, 1983; London, Granada, 1984.

Rhialto the Marvellous (Dying Earth). Columbia, Pennsylvania, Underwood Miller, 1984; London, Grafton, 1985.

The Green Pearl (Lyonesse). Columbia, Pennsylvania, Underwood Miller, 1985; London, Grafton, 1986.

Madouc (Lyonesse). Lancaster, Pennsylvania, Underwood Miller, 1989; London, Grafton, 1990.

Short Stories

Eight Fantasms and Magics. New York, Macmillan, 1969; as *Fantasms and Magics,* London, Mayflower, 1978.

Green Magic: The Fantasy Realms of Jack Vance. Columbia, Pennsylvania, Underwood Miller, 1979.

The Bagful of Dreams (Dying Earth). Columbia, Pennsylvania, Underwood Miller, 1979.

Morreion: A Tale of Dying Earth. Columbia, Pennsylvania, Underwood Miller, 1979.

The Seventeen Virgins (Dying Earth). Columbia, Pennsylvania, Underwood Miller, 1979.

OTHER PUBLICATIONS

Novels

The Space Pirate. New York, Toby Press, 1953; abridged edition as *The Five Gold Bands,* New York, Ace, 1962; London, Granada, 1980.

Vandals of the Void (for children). Philadelphia, Winston, 1953.

To Live Forever. New York, Ballantine, 1956; London, Sphere, 1976.

Big Planet. New York, Avalon, 1957; London, Coronet, 1977; expanded edition, Columbia, Pennsylvania, Underwood Miller, 1978.

Isle of Peril (as Alan Wade). New York, Mystery House, 1957; as *Bird Isle,* Columbia, Pennsylvania, Underwood Miller, 1988.

Take My Face (as Peter Held). New York, Mystery House, 1957; as Jack Vance, Columbia, Pennsylvania, Underwood Miller, 1988.

The Languages of Pao. New York, Avalon, 1958; London, Mayflower, 1974.

Slaves of the Klau. New York, Ace, 1958; London, Coronet, 1980; expanded as *Gold and Iron,* Columbia, Pennsylvania, Underwood Miller, 1982.

The Dragon Masters. New York, Ace, 1963; London, Dobson, 1965.

The Four Johns (as Ellery Queen). New York, Pocket, 1964; as *Four Men Called John,* London, Gollancz, 1976.

The Houses of Iszm, Son of the Tree. New York, Ace, 1964; in 2 vols., as *The Houses of Iszm* and *Son of the Tree,* London, Mayflower, 1974.

The Star King. New York, Berkley, 1964; London, Dobson, 1966.

The Killing Machine. New York, Berkley, 1964; London, Dobson, 1967.

Monsters in Orbit. New York, Ace, 1965; London, Dobson, 1977.

A Room to Die In (as Ellery Queen). New York, Pocket, 1965; London, Kinnell, 1987.

Space Opera. New York, Pyramid, 1965; London, Coronet, 1982.

The Blue World. New York, Ballantine, 1966; London, Mayflower, 1976.

The Brains of Earth. New York, Ace, 1966; London, Dobson, 1975.

The Madman Theory (as Ellery Queen). New York, Pocket, 1966; London, Kinnell, 1988.

The Last Castle. New York, Ace, 1967.

The Palace of Love. New York, Berkley, 1967; London, Dobson, 1968.

City of the Chasch. New York, Ace, 1968; London, Mayflower, 1974; as *Chasch,* New York, Bluejay, 1986.

Emphyrio. New York, Doubleday, 1969; London, Coronet, 1980.

Servants of the Wankh. New York, Ace, 1969; London, Dobson, 1975; as *Wankh,* New York, Bluejay, 1986.

The Dirdir. New York, Ace, 1969; London, Dobson, 1975.

The Pnume. New York, Ace, 1970; London, Dobson, 1975.

The Anome. New York, Dell, 1973; London, Coronet, 1975; as *The Faceless Man,* New York, Ace, 1978; London, Gollancz, 1987.

The Brave Free Men. New York, Dell, 1973; London, Coronet, 1975.

Trullion: Alastor 2262. New York, Ballantine, 1973; London, Mayflower, 1978.

The Asutra. New York, Dell, 1974; London, Coronet, 1975.

The Gray Prince. Indianapolis, Bobbs Merrill, 1975; London, Coronet, 1976.

Marune: Alastor 933. New York, Ballantine, 1975; London, Coronet, 1978.

Showboat World. New York, Pyramid, 1975; London, Coronet, 1977.

Maske: Thaery. New York, Berkley, 1976; London, Fontana, 1977.

Wyst: Alastor 1716. New York, DAW, 1978; London, Coronet, 1980.

The Face. New York, DAW, 1979; London, Dobson, 1980.

Nopalgarth (omnibus; includes *The Brains of Earth, The Houses of Iszm, Son of the Tree*). New York, DAW, 1980.

The Book of Dreams. New York, DAW, 1981; London, Coronet, 1982.

The Dark Ocean. Columbia, Pennsylvania, Underwood Miller, 1985.

Strange Notions. Columbia, Pennsylvania, Underwood Miller, 1985.

Planet of Adventure (omnibus; includes *City of the Chasch, Servants of the Wankh, The Dirdir, The Pnume*). London, Grafton, 1985; New York, Tor, 1993.

Araminta Station. Columbia, Pennsylvania, Underwood Miller, 1987; London, New English Library, 1988.

Durdane (omnibus; includes *The Faceless Man, The Brave Free Men, The Asutra*). London, Gollancz, 1989.

Ecce and Old Earth. Lancaster, Pennsylvania, Underwood Miller, 1991; London, New English Library, 1992.

Throy. Lancaster, Pennsylvania, Underwood Miller, 1992; London, New English Library, 1993.

Novels as John Holbrook Vance

The Man in the Cage. New York, Random House, 1960; London, Boardman, 1961.

The Fox Valley Murders. Indianapolis, Bobbs Merrill, 1966; London, Hale, 1967.

The Pleasant Grove Murders. Indianapolis, Bobbs Merrill, 1967; London, Hale, 1968.

The Deadly Isles. Indianapolis, Bobbs Merrill, 1969; London, Hale, 1970.

Bad Ronald. New York, Ballantine, 1973.

The House on Lily Street. Columbia, Pennsylvania, Underwood Miller, 1979.

The View from Chickweed's Window. Columbia, Pennsylvania, Underwood Miller, 1979.

Short Stories

Future Tense. New York, Ballantine, 1964; as *Dust of Far Suns,* New York, DAW, 1981.

The World Between and Other Stories. New York, Ace, 1965; as *The Moon Moth and Other Stories,* London, Dobson, 1976.

The Many Worlds of Magnus Ridolph. New York, Ace, 1966; London, Dobson, 1977; expanded as *The Complete Magnus Ridolph,* Columbia, Pennsylvania, Underwood Miller, 1985.

The Worlds of Jack Vance. New York, Ace, 1973.

The Best of Jack Vance. New York, Pocket, 1976.

Galactic Effectuator. Columbia, Pennsylvania, Underwood Miller, 1980; London, Coronet, 1983.

The Narrow Land. New York, DAW, 1982; London, Coronet, 1984.

Lost Moons. Columbia, Pennsylvania, Underwood Miller, 1982.

Light from a Lone Star (includes essays). Cambridge, Massachusetts, NESFA Press, 1985.

The Augmented Agent and Other Stories, edited by Steven Owen Godersky. Columbia, Pennsylvania, Underwood Miller, 1986; London, New English Library, 1989.

The Dark Side of the Moon. Columbia, Pennsylvania, Underwood Miller, 1986; London, New English Library, 1989.

Chateau d'If and Other Stories. Lancaster, Pennsylvania, Underwood Miller, 1990.

When the Five Moons Rise. Lancaster, Pennsylvania, Underwood Miller, 1992.

Plays

Television Plays: *Captain Video* (6 episodes), 1952-53.

*

Bibliography: *Fantasms: A Bibliography of the Literature of Jack Vance* by Daniel J. H. Levack and Tim Underwood, Columbia, Pennsylvania, Underwood Miller, 1978; *Jack Vance: A Working Bibliography* by Phil Stephensen-Payne and Gordon Benson, Jr., Leeds, West Yorkshire, Galactic Central, 1988.

Manuscript Collection: Mugar Memorial Library, Boston University.

Critical Studies: *Jack Vance* edited by Tim Underwood and Chuck Miller, New York, Taplinger, 1980; *Demon Prince: The Dissonant Worlds of Jack Vance* by Jack Rawlins, San Bernardino, Borgo Press, 1986.

*   *   *

In this century, writers of good English have almost all used the plain style. Among the minority who have dared commit themselves to the baroque, most have performed lamentably, though even some of the worst (such as E. R. Eddison and Baron Corvo) have achieved cult status. Jack Vance is possibly the most accomplished practitioner surviving, for whatever the overt setting, the true *mise en scene* is always Vance's style, which is an ongoing and very sensuous love affair with the English language.

He deploys a huge vocabulary, not merely to show off, but to take maximum advantage of contrasting word-texture. He also playfully redefines words: the "deodands" of *The Dying Earth* are a species of cannibal monster. Vance constantly strives that every sentence, whether of narrative, dialogue or description, should be perfectly balanced, every image perfectly focused and serving to highlight the characters of the people involved, so that their depth is perceived as if for the first time. Best of all, every line is permeated with Vance's love of irony, which ranges from the airiest banter to the blackest and most venomous. Of his short fiction two fairy stories, "Noise" and "Green Magic," are among the finest ever produced. They vary greatly in form, "Noise" being told within a frame which allows it to masquerade as science fiction (for which Vance is best known) while "Green Magic" uses a "scientific" approach to magical operations: a golem raised from graveyard mould has for one eye an upturned beer bottle, for the other a television camera through which the controlling magician can monitor its experiences.

But it was in fantasy that Vance first made his reputation, with the six stories published in the form of the "fix-up" novel *The Dying Earth.* The Earth is here dying through the imminence of the moment when the bloated red sun will flicker one last time and grow dark forever, a circumstance to which many characters refer, but which seems to concern them little; they are far too busy with their day-to-day concerns of intrigue, magic, and the hedonistic enjoyment of carnivals, displays and the physical pleasures. The stories all feature people who set out on quests of various kinds, but within that framework they are highly inventive, and tend to feature the confrontation of mutually exclusive and incomprehensible systems of value and belief. But the reader is left in no doubt as to where Vance stands; he favours courtesy, gallantry, natural justice, heterosexuality and scepticism against uncouthness in men, boorishness towards women, legalism, pederasty and revealed religion. Priests enjoy little good fortune in Vance's worlds.

Two other Dying Earth story-cycles, *The Eyes of the Overworld* and *Cugel's Saga,* feature the adventures of an anti-hero, Cugel the Clever (soi-disant—he is actually rather naive), who is unwise enough to attempt to burgle the manse of a powerful magician. He is caught, and as punishment forced to go on a dangerous quest. Such a character is ideally suited to fall victim to the folly, venality and occasional brutality of Vance's heavies, and to furnish an unwilling audience to their pomposity, and Vance carefully sustains a minimal level of sympathy for him, less by having him come by virtue than by ensuring that he is generally more sinned against than sinning—though he sins plentifully when he can.

By the time of the latest set of Dying Earth stories, gathered in the "novel" *Rhialto the Marvellous,* the milieu has undergone a subtle change. The tone is if anything lighter than before, but the magicians are less competent in the deployment of spells, depending more on the services of Sandestins, time-travelling, shape-shifting immortal servitors magically bound to them. The Sandestins resent their servitude, and are wholly without sympathy for their despised masters, whom they constantly seek to overthrow by adhering to the letter of their instructions while violating the spirit as far as they can. To a Sandestin the pleasure which a tribe of cannibals will derive from cooking and eating a young girl is intellectually comparable with the pleasure she will feel at being rescued from them; morally, neither has the least significance. They thus recall the Yips of Vance's science fiction novels in the Chronicles of Cadwal series.

Sandestins also feature in the Lyonesse trilogy, *Suldrun's Garden, The Green Pearl* and *Madouc* (a huge three-decker novel, really), another fairy story of magnificent scope and complexity. The setting is loosely defined as the Elder Isles, of which the Scillies are the only modern remnant. The principal story concerns the rivalry between Aillas of Troicinet and Casmir of Lyonesse for hegemony over the islands, reinforced by the great wrong done by Casmir to his daughter Suldrun (Aillas's first wife), and counterpointed with the struggles of the magicians Murgan and Shimrod to fend off the islands' watery doom. These afford ample opportunity for scenes of bloodshed, magic, courtship and diplomacy, but the books are long enough to include plenty of vignettes. Vance keeps a great variety of subplots in the air, not only without losing sight of any of them, but without letting them proliferate beyond the range of the main plot to which they are all subordinate; the magic is always used in a controlled fashion, so that one comes to believe in it as a hazardous craft based on the paradigms of a developed science, with a rigorous internal logic.

This internal logic allows Vance to present episodes in violent meta-dimensions without bombast, and in the fairy kingdom without becoming twee. Almost casually he dashes off one of the most moving sets of wedding vows in any literature and a glorious passage from a cod book of court etiquette. There is a price to pay, of course. Because Vance's overriding concern is to write beautifully as only he can, the dialogue is invariably and not always appropriately stylized. A child bargaining for her life with an ogre will employ much the same cadences and analogies as a leathery old states-

man negotiating an armistice with a rival who has a temporary advantage.

Vance's writing has a certain raciness, though he disdains "explicit" sex scenes; he affords adult reading in other ways. In particular, he is capable of going to considerable lengths building up a sympathetic character, and still bring him (or her) to a sad and untimely end if the plot requires it. The knowledge that he is capable of this adds an element of suspense to the civilized pleasure he affords.

—Chris Gilmore

VARDEMAN, Robert E(dward)

Pseudonyms: Victor Appleton; Nick Carter; Edward George; Daniel Moran. **Nationality:** American. **Born:** 1947.

FANTASY PUBLICATIONS

Novels (series: Cenotaph Road; Demon Crown; Jade Demons; The Keys to Paradise; Swords of Raemllyn; The War of Powers)

The Sundered Realm, with Victor Milan (War of Powers). New York, Playboy, 1980.
The City in the Glacier, with Victor Milan (War of Powers). New York, Playboy, 1980.
The Destiny Stone, with Victor Milan (War of Powers). New York, Playboy, 1980.
The Fallen Ones, with Victor Milan (War of Powers). New York, Playboy, 1982.
In the Shadow of Omizantrim, with Victor Milan (War of Powers). New York, Playboy, 1982.
Demon of the Dark Ones, with Victor Milan (War of Powers). New York, Playboy, 1982.
Cenotaph Road. New York, Ace, 1983.
The Sorcerer's Skull (Cenotaph Road). New York, Ace, 1983.
World of Mazes (Cenotaph Road). New York, Ace, 1983.
Iron Tongue (Cenotaph Road). New York, Ace, 1984.
Fire and Fog (Cenotaph Road). New York, Ace, 1984.
Pillar of Night (Cenotaph Road). New York, Ace, 1984.
The War of Powers, with Victor Milan (omnibus; includes *The Sundered Realm, The City in the Glacier, The Destiny Stone*). London, New English Library, 1984.
To Demons Bound, with George W. Proctor (Swords of Raemllyn). New York, Ace, 1985.
A Yoke of Magic, with George W. Proctor (Swords of Raemllyn). New York, Ace, 1985.
Blood Fountain, with George W. Proctor (Swords of Raemllyn). New York, Ace, 1985.
The Quaking Lands (Jade Demons). New York, Avon, 1985.
The Frozen Waves (Jade Demons). New York, Avon, 1985.
The Crystal Clouds (Jade Demons). New York, Avon, 1985.
The War of Powers II: Istu Awakened, with Victor Milan (omnibus; includes *The Fallen Ones, In the Shadow of Omizantrim, Demon of the Dark Ones*). London, New English Library, 1985.
The White Fire (Jade Demons). Avon, 1986.

Death's Acolyte, with George W. Proctor (Swords of Raemllyn). New York, Ace, 1986.

The Beasts of the Mist, with George W. Proctor (Swords of Raemllyn). New York, Ace, 1986.

The Keys to Paradise (omnibus; includes *The Flame Key, The Skeleton Lord's Key, The Key of Ice and Steel*). London, New English Library, 1986.

For Crown and Kingdom, with George W. Proctor (Swords of Raemllyn). New York, Ace, 1987.

The Flame Key (as Daniel Moran; Keys to Paradise). New York, Tor, 1987.

The Jade Demons Quartet (omnibus; includes *The Quaking Lands, The Frozen Waves, The Crystal Clouds, The White Fire*). London, New English Library, 1987.

The Skeleton Lord's Key (as Daniel Moran; Keys to Paradise). New York, Tor, 1987.

The Key of Ice and Steel (as Daniel Moran; Keys to Paradise). New York, Tor, 1988.

The Glass Warrior (Demon Crown). New York, Tor, 1989.

Phantoms of the Wind (Demon Crown). New York, Tor, 1989.

A Symphony of Storms (Demon Crown). New York, Tor, 1990.

The Demon Crown Trilogy (omnibus; includes *The Glass Warrior, Phantoms on the Wind, A Symphony of Storms*). London, New English Library, 1990.

Swords of Raemllyn: Book 1, with George W. Proctor (omnibus; includes *To Demons Bound, A Yoke of Magic, Blood Fountain*). London, New English Library, 1992.

Swords of Raemllyn: Book 2, with George W. Proctor (omnibus; includes *Death's Acolyte, The Beasts of the Mist, For Crown and Kingdom*). London, New English Library, 1992.

Swords of Raemllyn: Book 3, with George W. Proctor (omnibus; includes *Blade of the Conqueror, The Tombs of A'bre, The Jewels of Life*). London, New English Library, 1995.

OTHER PUBLICATIONS

Novels

Pleasure Planet (with George W. Proctor, as Edward George). New York, Orpheus, 1974.

The Sandcats of Rhyl. Canoga Park, California, Major, 1978.

The Klingon Gambit. New York, Pocket, 1981.

The Solar Menace (as Nick Carter). New York, Charter, 1981.

Doctor DNA (as Nick Carter). New York, Charter, 1982.

Mutiny on the Enterprise. New York, Pocket, 1983.

Tom Swift: Gateway to Doom (as Victor Appleton). New York, Wanderer, 1983.

Echoes of Chaos. New York, Berkley, 1986.

Equations of Chaos. New York, Ace, 1987.

The Stellar Death Plan. New York, Avon, 1987.

The Alien Web. New York, Avon, 1987.

A Plague in Paradise. New York, Avon, 1987.

Colors of Chaos. New York, Ace, 1988.

Road to the Stars. New York, Harper and Row, 1988.

Ancient Heavens. New York, Avon, 1989.

The Infinity Plague. New York, Ace, 1989.

Weapons of Chaos (omnibus; includes *Echoes of Chaos, Equations of Chaos, Colors of Chaos*). London, New English Library, 1989.

Masters of Space (omnibus; includes *The Stellar Death Plan, The Alien Web, A Plague in Paradise*). London, New English Library, 1990.

Crisis at Starlight. New York, Ace, 1990.

The Screaming Knife. New York, Avon, 1990.

Space Vectors. New York, Ace, 1990.

Deathfall. New York, Onyx, 1991.

A Resonance of Blood. New York, Avon, 1992.

Death Channels. New York, Avon, 1992.

The Accursed. London, New English Library, 1994.

*   *   *

Robert Vardeman is a prolific writer who has worked in the science-fiction and mystery genres as well as fantasy, although the bulk of his published fiction falls into the last category. His first venture was the six-volume series, The War of Powers, written in collaboration with Victor Milan. The setting is a familiar one, a fantastic world torn by opposing forces of magic, and the protagonist is a fairly two-dimensional inadvertent hero who is dragged into dangerous situations almost against his wishes. But even with its limitations, the series is worth noting. There's enthusiasm and a sense of excitement in these early books, the prose is crisp, the plot straightforward and engrossing, and between the two of them the authors introduced some interesting new devices into their creation.

Fost Longstrider visits a city in the sky, then another under a glacier in his quest to find the power to avert a war. He dies, is reborn, finds himself in the company of genies, loses a war, discovers a race of reptilian creatures intent upon killing all humans, and disturbs the sleep of a long-slumbering monster. Filled with violence, mild humour, implied sex, and flashing swords, the series is appealing despite or perhaps even because of its flaws.

To Demons Bound started a new sequence, Swords of Raemllyn, this time with George W. Proctor as collaborator. The mood is more serious, the settings more traditional, and although the writing is considerably smoother and more controlled, some of the energy of the earlier books seems missing. Davin Anane must rescue a kidnapped girl in order to secure the release of a friend from the torture chamber. A major obstacle is the fact that the kidnapper is a demon who has possessed the girl's body, and is using her as the means by which it can search for a skilled sorcerer with the ability to free a host of demonic powers.

Eventually freed from her demonic master, Lijena languishes in a prison, while Davin continues to search for her. Lijena takes over the central role in the fourth book, *Death's Acolyte,* having escaped and returned home with an enchanted sword, only to discover that her father has been murdered, his place usurped by an evil magician. Meanwhile, Davin is sold into slavery, then menaced by mysterious creatures on an island beyond the edge of the known world. Ultimately the two are reunited and cooperate in their quest to overthrow a cruel dictator. There is lots of action in the predictable plot, and no real effort to develop the characters credibly until late in the series. (A belated third trilogy of Raemllyn novels has appeared as one volume in Britain in 1995, apparently preceding any American editions.)

Cenotaph Road was the opening volume of the first multi-book fantasy project Vardeman authored on his own, one that incorporates many of the devices of science fiction as well as fantasy. Lan Martak, an unjustly accused man, resorts to a legendary bit of magic to transport himself to another reality, only to find himself in worse trouble than ever. With a giant spider as his only friend, he is alternately pursued by and pursuing a malevolent magician whose body has been disassembled and scattered throughout the worlds.

Martak rescues a female warrior who becomes his ally in the fourth instalment, *Iron Tongue,* and the threesome chase after

Claybore, the evil magician, hoping to prevent him from reassembling his body and regaining his sorcerous powers. By securing the villain's tongue, Martak acquires the key to many of his spells, but can he learn to use them in time to stop his adversary? Vardeman didn't break any new ground with this series either, but he covered the old in a competent and entertaining fashion, and the spider character, Krek, adds an interesting element to the plot.

The Jade Demons series began to appear simultaneously with the later Cenotaph Road novels. This time Vardeman's protagonist is female, the beautiful Kesira, priestess of a dying faith, who assembles a group of companions to confront the evil Jade Demons in their lair. Although *The Quaking Lands* was not a particularly promising start, the series picked up considerably in quality with *The Frozen Waves* and maintained that higher level afterwards. Although Kesira and company enjoy initial success, they have caused one of the Jade Demons to inflict a new ice age on the world. No sooner is that danger averted than Kesira discovers the existence of a magical child whose destiny, whether for good or for evil, remains unknown. And finally she must confront and defeat the most powerful of the Jade Demons and end their reign of terror forever.

The Keys to Paradise trilogy, originally published in Britain in one volume under Vardeman's name, is a darker version of the Cenotaph Road sequence, similarly containing science-fiction elements along with magic and monsters. This time the quest is to find five keys that together supposedly provide entrance to paradise. The first volume was published in the United States as by Daniel Moran, but it so happens there is another American science-fiction author called Daniel Keys Moran (born 1962), who began publishing around that time, which is probably the reason why the following two books were presented as by "Robert E. Vardeman writing as Daniel Moran." The desert setting of the second volume, *The Skeleton Lord's Key,* is well realized and supports the best instalment of the trilogy, which follows Vardeman's usual pattern of chase and escape.

The Glass Warrior and its two sequels in the Demon Crown sequence are to date the best fantasy novels Vardeman has written. A civil war's ultimate resolution depends upon which side possesses a crown fashioned by demons, and perhaps by the fate of the twin sons of a dead king. One of the twins is found and installed on the throne, but it appears that he is mad and his misuse of the demon crown may bring supernatural retribution down upon the land. A pair of reluctant heroes sets out to find the mad king's twin sister and bring her to power, hoping to do so before an army of storm creatures descends from the nearby mountains to destroy the kingdom.

None of Vardeman's fantasies makes any pretence towards ambitious literary heights. They are clearly meant as entertainments, and with minor lapses, they deliver exactly what they promise. Perhaps their strongest asset is the sense that the author actually enjoys his own work, that the book was fun to write as well read.

—Don D'Ammassa

VIERECK, George Sylvester

Pseudonyms: Stuart Benton; George F. Corners. **Nationality:** American. **Born:** Munich, Germany, 31 December 1884; emigrated to the USA in 1895. **Family:** Married Margaret Hein; two sons (Peter Viereck, born 1916, became a leading academic historian and a Pulitzer prize-winning poet). **Career:** Poet; associate editor, *Current Literature*; editor, *The International*; editor, *The Fatherland,* from 1914 (retitled *American Monthly* in 1917); expelled from the Poetry Society of America and the Author's League for pro-German sympathies; later was rehabilitated and became a contributor to the *Saturday Evening Post, Liberty* and other magazines; interviewed many leading figures, including Freud, Einstein, Kaiser Wilhelm II, Henry Ford, Mussolini, Hitler. Imprisoned, 1942-47. **Died:** 18 March 1962.

FANTASY PUBLICATIONS

Novels

The House of the Vampire. New York, Moffat Yard, 1907.
My First Two Thousand Years: The Autobiography of the Wandering Jew, with Paul Eldridge. New York, Macaulay, 1928; London, Duckworth, 1929.
Salome, The Wandering Jewess, with Paul Eldridge. New York, Liveright, and London, Duckworth, 1930.
The Invincible Adam, with Paul Eldridge. New York, Liveright, and London, Duckworth, 1932.
Gloria: A Novel. London, Duckworth, 1952; as *The Nude in the Mirror,* New York, Woodford Press, 1953.

OTHER PUBLICATIONS

Novels

Prince Pax, with Paul Eldridge. London, Duckworth, 1933.
All Things Human (as Stuart Benton). New York, Sheridan House, 1949; as George Sylvester Viereck, London, Duckworth, 1951.

Plays

A Game at Love and Other Plays. New York, Brentano, 1906.

Poetry

Gedichte. New York, Progressive Printing, 1904.
Nineveh and Other Poems. New York, Moffatt Yard, and London, Brown Langham, 1907.
The Candle and the Flame: Poems. New York, Moffatt Yard, 1912.
Songs of Armageddon and Other Poems. New York, Kennerley, 1916.
The Haunted House and Other Poems. Girard, Kansas, Haldeman Julius, 1924.
The Three Sphinxes and Other Poems. Girard, Kansas, Haldeman Julius, 1924.
The Bankrupt. New York, Pyramid, 1955.

Other

Confessions of a Barbarian. New York, Moffatt Yard, and London, Lane, 1910.
Debate Between George Sylvester Viereck . . . and Cecil Chesterton . . . on "Whether the Cause of Germany or That of the Allied Powers is Just". New York, Fatherland Corporation, 1915.

Roosevelt: A Study in Ambivalence. New York, Jackson Press, 1919.

Rejuvenation: How Steinach Makes People Young (as George F. Corners). New York, Seltzer, 1923.

Glimpses of the Great. New York, Macaulay, and London, Duckworth, 1930.

Spreading Germs of Hate. New York, Liveright, 1930; London, Duckworth, 1931.

My Flesh and Blood: A Lyric Autobiography, with Indiscreet Annotations. New York, Liveright, 1931; London, Jarrolds, 1932.

The Strangest Friendship in History: Woodrow Wilson and Colonel House. New York, Liveright, 1932; London, Duckworth, 1933.

The Kaiser on Trial. New York, Greystone Press, 1937; London, Duckworth, 1938.

The Temptation of Jonathan. Boston, Christopher Publishing House, 1938.

The Seven Against Man. Scotch Plains, New Jersey, Flanders Hall, 1941.

Men Into Beasts. New York, Fawcett, 1952.

Editor, *The House of Life,* by Dante Gabriel Rossetti. Girard, Kansas, Haldeman Julius, 1925.

Editor, *Panthea, and Other Poems,* by Oscar Wilde. Girard, Kansas, Haldeman Julius, 1925.

Editor, *Perkin Warbeck, and Other Poems,* by Lord Alfred Douglas. Girard, Kansas, Haldeman Julius, 1925.

Editor, *The City of the Soul, and Other Sonnets,* by Lord Alfred Douglas. Girard, Kansas, Haldeman Julius, 1925.

Editor, *The Triumph of Time, and Other Poems,* by Algernon Swinburne. Girard, Kansas, Haldeman Julius, 1925.

Editor, with A. Paul Maerker-Branden. *As They Saw Us: Foch, Ludendorff and Other Leaders Write Our War History.* New York, Doubleday Doran, 1929.

*

Manuscript Collection: University of Iowa Library.

Critical Studies: *George Sylvester Viereck, German-American Propagandist* by Neil M. Johnson, Urbana, Chicago, University of Illinois Press, 1972; *Odyssey of a Barbarian: The Biography of George Sylvester Viereck* by Elmer Gertz, Buffalo, New York, Prometheus, 1978.

*   *   *

George Viereck was one of the literary "Bohemians" who attempted to import into America some of the ideals espoused by the Decadent movements of Europe. *The House of the Vampire* is a homoerotic tale of psychic vampirism seemingly inspired by Oscar Wilde's *The Picture of Dorian Gray,* in which the genius—and eventually the consciousness—of a young writer is leeched away by an older and ominously versatile artist. It followed hard on the heels of a volume of poetry and a collection of plays, but Viereck's fledgling literary career failed to take off, and he subsequently diverted his main efforts into journalism until his fortunes were spectacularly revived by *My First Two Thousand Years,* which rapidly achieved a *succès de scandale.* The book, written in collaboration with Paul Eldridge (1888-1982), marked something of a watershed in the history of American fantasy, parading a flagrant eroticism which would not have been tolerated a few years earlier.

The window of opportunity through which *My First Two Thousand Years* passed had already been pried open by other writers, but only very recently. In 1926 Thorne Smith began his series of assaults upon the blindness of those who hated sex and strong liquor with *Topper;* in 1927 James Branch Cabell—still pained by the prosecution of *Jurgen* in 1919—produced the deftly cutting *Something About Eve,* and John Erskine published *Adam and Eve,* which trod controversial ground in preferring the free-loving Lilith to the hectoring and hypocritical Eve; it was, however, *My First Two Thousand Years* which comprehensively shattered the barrier of primness which American publishers had erected in the wake of the moral crusade whose greatest triumph had been the passing of the Volstead Act.

The traditional image of the Wandering Jew is a miserable figure whose guilt-laden immortality is horribly burdensome, but Viereck and Eldridge's Cartaphilus is far more resilient. He is in the prime of life and fully appreciates the wonderful opportunity which has been afforded him by Jesus' curse. The problem of finding a purpose to guide him through a potentially limitless existence causes him some slight anxiety, but he is in no mood to submit to "the Great God Ennui," and he embarks zestfully upon a twofold quest in search of wisdom and sexual fulfilment—specifically, for the secret of "unendurable pleasure indefinitely prolonged." In pursuit of this end he frequently meets an immortal woman who seems to be his destined partner in life: Salome, similarly condemned to immortality by John the Baptist.

Cartaphilus tells his tale while under hypnosis in 1917. The psychoanalysts who hear it cannot agree as to whether the story is to be taken literally or figuratively, but they wholeheartedly endorse its significance as a record of the underlying meaning of humanity's progress to modern civilization. The final, rather surreal passages of Cartaphilus' tale describe his final rendezvous with Salome is a new Garden of Eden where she is attempting to create an artificial human being capable of becoming the mother of a new and better race. Meanwhile, Cartaphilus sets out to unleash the combined forces of a "Red King" (Lenin) and a "Black King" (Mussolini) upon the tottering "White King" which is Europe and Christendom, in order to clear the way for a Millennium very different from that imagined by the dutiful and misguided followers of Jesus.

Salome is more overtly erotic than its predecessor; although John the Baptist declares that its sexy heroine is "too vile for the grave" the authors clearly do not agree. The parallel quest which gives her life meaning is the liberation of women from the curse under which the entire sex labours. While Cartaphilus attempts to inspire an endless series of Antichrists, Salome cleaves to those women fortunate enough to reach positions of political power, hoping to use them to advance the cause of feminism—but in every case she is disappointed. Perhaps inevitably, in an overtly Freudian fantasy, it is accepted at the axiomatic level that the exercise of power is essentially masculine. Salome discovers that powerful women can remain effective only while the process of their physical and psychological development is arrested; in the end, all of them become incompetent when they are weakened by the delayed onset of their "bloody sacrifice to the moon." She looks forward avidly to the advent of a new species in which male and female attributes will be combined.

The Invincible Adam is the story of Kotikokura, the servant and sometime worshipper of Cartaphilus, who began life as a proto-human but has evolved into a handsome person of culture and intelligence. It begins with an account of his childhood in prehistoric Africa, when he was condemned to be sacrificed to his tribe's deity, the Great Ape, by virtue of possessing what the Great Ape has taken away from other men as a punishment: a penile bone, euphemistically described as a "rib." By virtue of his permanent erection Kotikokura is perennially popular with women, even though he retains a crucial immaturity, having been made immortal when not yet fully grown. *The Invincible Adam* concludes with a "personal note" which explains the supposed allegorical significance of the trilogy and serves to emphasize the fact that the authors' intention to offend against the taboos of the censorious American tribe was supported by a genuine conviction that such taboos must and ought to be broken in the name of Progress as well as that of Liberty.

Viereck's peculiar combination of prurience and eccentric feminism was given freer rein in his solo novel *Gloria,* in which a woman who might or might not be the Goddess of Love insists that all the great lovers of history and legend were, in fact, woefully inadequate to the task of satisfying their female companions. According to her, Casanova—with the aid of a cunning technological device akin to Kotikokura's "rib"—was the only man who ever managed to overcome the limitations of male physique, and even he remained prey to the dismal faults of male psychology. The other work which Viereck wrote in collaboration with Eldridge was a conventional scientific romance, *Prince Pax,* in which the Ultimate Weapon is used to put an end to war.

In addition to being a bestselling novelist and a remarkably successful journalist, Viereck was a not inconsiderable poet, hailed by some critics as one of the best in America in the pre-1914 period. He managed to wreck his public career twice as a result of his proGerman sympathies (although he always claimed to be an American patriot). His late "prison poems," published in a special edition of *Wisconsin Poetry Magazine,* July 1958, also have their admirers. His prison memoir, *Men Into Beasts* sold half a million copies in paperback during the 1950s. One son, George Sylvester Viereck, Jr., died fighting for the Allies against Germany in World War II; the other, Peter Viereck, estranged from his father for political reasons (but eventually reconciled), became a major poet in his own right.

—Brian Stableford

VIVIAN, E. Charles

Pseudonym for Charles Henry Cannell. **Other Pseudonyms:** Barry Lynd; Jack Mann; Evelyn C. H. Vivian. **Nationality:** British. **Born:** Lodden, Norfolk, 19 October 1882. **Military Service:** British army, South Africa, during Boer War, 1899-1902. **Family:** Married Marion Christmas Harvie in 1913; one daughter. **Career:** Journalist, *Daily Telegraph* and other newspapers, London; editor, *Flying,* 1917-18, *The Novel Magazine,* 1918-22, *Hutchinson's Adventure-Story Magazine,* 1922-25, *Hutchinson's Mystery-Story Magazine,* 1923-25. **Died:** 21 May 1947.

FANTASY PUBLICATIONS

Novels (series: Coulson; Drinkwater; Gees)

City of Wonder. London, Hutchinson, and New York, Moffatt, 1923.
Fields of Sleep. London, Hutchinson, 1923; Rhode Island, Grant, 1980.

People of the Darkness. London, Hutchinson, 1924.
Star Dust. London, Hutchinson, 1925.
The Lady of the Terraces. London, Hodder and Stoughton, 1925.
A King There Was. London, Hodder and Stoughton, 1926.
The Forbidden Door (Drinkwater). London, Ward Lock, 1927.
The Tale of Fleur (Drinkwater). London, Ward Lock, 1929.
Woman Dominant (Drinkwater). London, Ward Lock, 1929.

Novels as Jack Mann

Coulson Goes South. London, Wright and Brown, 1933.
The Dead Man's Chest (Coulson). London, Wright and Brown, 1934; New York, Godwin, 1935.
Grey Shapes (Gees). London, Wright and Brown, 1937; New York, Bookfinger, 1970.
Nightmare Farm (Gees). London, Wright and Brown, 1937; New York, Bookfinger, 1975.
Maker of Shadows (Gees). London, Wright and Brown, 1938; New York, Bookfinger, 1977.
The Ninth Life (Gees). London, Wright and Brown, 1939; New York, Bookfinger, 1970.
The Glass Too Many (Gees). London, Wright and Brown, 1940; New York, Bookfinger, 1973.
Her Ways Are Death (Gees). London, Wright and Brown, 1941; New York, Bookfinger, 1981.

OTHER PUBLICATIONS

Novels

The Shadow of Christine (as Evelyn C. H. Vivian). London, Gay and Bird, 1907; New York, Fenno, 1910.
The Woman Tempted Me. London, Melrose, 1909.
Wandering of Desire. London, Melrose, 1910.
Following Feet. London, Melrose, 1911.
Passion Fruit. London, Heinemann, 1912.
Divided Ways. London, Holden and Hardingham, 1914.
The Young Man Absalom. London, Chapman and Hall, and New York, Dutton, 1915.
The Yellow Streak. Toronto, Warwick and Rutter, 1921.
A Scout of the '45 (for children). London, Religious Tract Society, 1923.
Robin Hood and His Merry Men (for children). London, Ward Lock, 1927.
Man Alone. London, Ward Lock, 1928.
Nine Days. London, Ward Lock, 1928.
Shooting Stars (novelization of screenplay) London, Hurst and Blackett, 1928.
Double or Quit. London, Ward Lock, 1930.
One Tropic Night. London, Ward Lock, 1930.
Delicate Fiend. London, Ward Lock, 1930.
Unwashed Gods. London, Ward Lock, 1931.
Innocent Guilt. London, Ward Lock, 1931.
Infamous Fame. London, Ward Lock, 1932.
Lone Isle. London, Ward Lock, 1932.
False Truth. London, Ward Lock, 1932.
The Keys of the Flat. London, Ward Lock, 1933.
Ladies in the Case. London, Ward Lock, 1933.
Girl in the Dark. London, Ward Lock, 1933.
Shadow on the House. London, Ward Lock, 1934.

Jewels Go Back. London, Ward Lock, 1934.
Accessory After. London, Ward Lock, 1934.
House for Sale. London, Amalgamated Press, 1934; expanded as
    With Intent to Kill, London, Ward Lock, 1936.
Seventeen Cards. London, Ward Lock, 1935.
The Capsule Mystery. London, Ward Lock, 1935.
Cigar for Inspector Head. London, Ward Lock, 1935.
Who Killed Gatton? London, Ward Lock, 1936.
The Black Prince (for children). London, Ward Lock, 1936.
Tramp's Evidence. London, Ward Lock, 1937; as *The Barking Dog
    Mystery,* New York, Hillman Curl, 1937.
.38 Automatic. London, Ward Lock, 1937.
Evidence in Blue. London, Ward Lock, 1938; as *The Man in Gray,*
    New York, Hillman Curl, 1938.
The Rainbow Puzzle. London, Ward Lock, 1938.
Problem by Rail. London, Ward Lock, 1939.
Touch and Go. London, Ward Lock, 1939.
The Impossible Crime. London, Ward Lock, 1940.
Man With a Scar. London, Ward Lock, 1940.
And Then There Was One. London, Ward Lock, 1941.
Curses Come Home. London, Hale, 1942.
Dangerous Guide. London, Hale, 1943.
Samson. London, Hale, 1944.
She Who Will Not. London, Hale, 1945.
Other Gods. London, Hale, 1945.
Arrested. London, Hale, 1949.
Vain Escape. London, Hale, 1952.

Novels as Charles Cannell

The Guarded Woman. London, Hutchinson, 1923.
Broken Couplings. London, Hutchinson, 1923.
Barker's Drift. London, Hutchinson, 1924.
Ash. London, Hutchinson, 1925.
The Guardian of the Cup. London, Hodder and Stoughton, 1925.
The Passionless Quest. London, Hodder and Stoughton, 1925.
The Moon and Chelsea. London, Ward Lock, 1928.
And the Devil . . . London, Bodley Head, 1931.

Novels as Jack Mann

Reckless Coulson. London, Wright and Brown, 1933.
Egyptian Nights. London, Wright and Brown, 1934.
Detective Coulson. London, Wright and Brown, 1935.
Coulson Alone. London, Wright and Brown, 1936.
Gees' First Case. London, Wright and Brown, 1936.
The Kleinert Case. London, Wright and Brown, 1938.

Novels as Barry Lynd

Trailed Down. London, Ward Lock, 1938.
Dude Ranch. London, Ward Lock, 1938.
Ghost Canyon. London, Ward Lock, 1939.
Riders to Bald Butte. London, Ward Lock, 1939.
The Ten-Buck Trail. London, Ward Lock, 1941.
George on the Trail. London, Ward Lock, 1942.

Other

Peru. London, Pitman, 1914.

The British Army from Within. London, Hodder and Stoughton,
    and New York, Doran, 1914.
With the Royal Army Medical Corps at the Front. London, Hodder
    and Stoughton, 1914.
With the Scottish Regiments at the Front. London, Hodder and
    Stoughton, 1915.
The Way of the Red Cross, with J. E. Hodder Williams. London,
    Hodder and Stoughton, and New York, Doran, 1915.
A History of Aeronautics. London, Collins, and New York,
    Harcourt, 1921.

Editor, *Heard This One?: A Book of Funny Stories.* London,
    Pearson, 1922.

*

Critical Study: "Master of Mystery" by Peter Berresford Ellis,
Million no. 6, November-December 1991.

*   *   *

E. Charles Vivian was a man of multiple personalities and sundry aliases, a good many of which will never now be identified. It
is of course natural for a busy and prolific writer of popular fiction
to divide up his life, his time and, perhaps more importantly, his
psyche: here writing a thriller, there a story of the soccer field, here
an historical yarn, there a tale of terror. Not, perhaps, quite so natural so to order events that those who were looking after his affairs
had no idea that their efforts were being duplicated (perhaps tripli-
cated; perhaps even—who knows?—quadruplicated). His supposedly sole agent John Farquharson, who had taken Vivian on in the
1920s and was responsible for the crucial career shift from relatively poor-paying fantasy-adventure into the far more lucrative and
popular crime and mystery field, had no idea that his client was in
fact pouring out high-seas actioners and occult thrillers for quite
another agent during the 1930s under the name "Jack Mann." One
wonders: did Farquharson know that Vivian wasn't really Vivian?
    Charles Henry Cannell became E. C. Vivian (originally "Evelyn
C. H. Vivian" on his first published novel *The Shadow of Christine*) to escape his background. He never did (can one ever?), even
though he spent 40 or more years trying. It is an axiom that critics
should never read into an author's works his or her life. This, of
course, is absurd: even in the direst trash there is something of the
creator—never more so than with Cannell (who was certainly no
trash-merchant), who in his mainstream novels and stories not only
used names of friends, incidents from his past, transplanted memories, and places associated with his childhood as well as adulthood,
but in the novel *Ash* set out his life and the lives of his immediate
family in so thinly veiled a fashion that it is almost as though he
were writing straight autobiography. All this as a continuing, and
largely unsuccessful, exorcism of his childhood and youth—or, in
the words of the title of his posthumously published last novel, a
"vain escape."
    In a sense this "fleeing" of his roots is demonstrated rather more
tangibly in his fantasy fiction, much of which concerns adventurers leaving unsatisfactory normality (civilization) in pursuit of an
ideal (a Utopia, perhaps, hinted at in some old and musty document, or simply a lost treasure). Yet whether the locale is the impenetrable jungles of South America, the unknown parts of the Pacific, or the vast desert wastes of both North Africa and Asia, the
ideal is rarely discovered. What is found, invariably, is danger and

terror and death. And Vivian (as it seems easiest to call him) was certainly no sentimentalist: if the plot demanded a hero's death—or at any rate that of a main character—the hero, or main character, died. Many of his mainstream novels (he wrote over 20, from 1907 through to the early 1930s) end in despair, and much of his pure detective-fiction output carries lingering feelings of doom and despondency. Yet grim as even his fantasies often are, they are also bursting with ideas and colour and pace.

Vivian's fantasy career can be divided up surprisingly neatly. During the Great War he wrote weird and fantastic short fiction principally for *Colour* (a glossy fine-arts magazine) and *Flying* (the aviation weekly he launched under the auspices of the proprietors of the political weekly *Land and Water*). His stories were, even at this early stage, distinctly quirky, by no means the usual hackneyed fare of haunted houses and vengeful revenants. "A Fragment" (*Colour,* December 1916) is in fact made up of a number of fragments from the diary (possibly) of a man who has been incarcerated by unknown beings. These fragments are disjointed and not necessarily in order. Is the diarist to be executed? Has he been saved? Are his captors mad? Is he? It is a disturbing tale, all the more unsettling for the sly obliqueness of the author's approach.

Although unenticingly titled, "Laughter and Smell" (*Colour,* August 1916) is another, and superb, exercise in the indirect. A cottage in Norfolk is plagued by a smell—wild roses? hyacinth?: the occupants disagree—and something "grey . . . oval and fat," and laughter that can't be laughter. By the end of the story all the participants are dead. Of explanation there is none—only a sense of lurking unease.

The start of *Flying* in 1917 slowed the rate of Vivian's fantasy production: for the moment he was far too busy constructing a 14-part "Pioneers of Flying," later incorporated into his *History of Aeronautics.* But when the series finished he immediately published in the paper a bizarre short story which had nothing whatever to do with flying, unless of the inter-dimensional variety. "The Multiple Cube" (*Flying,* 13 June 1917) posits a kind of philosophical approach to travel in the fourth dimension, though initially by physical means (a cube that is not—or, perhaps more precisely, rather more than—a cube). At the end of the tale, the main protagonist fails to return from whatever strange journey he embarked upon, in much the same way that Wells's Time Traveller disappeared from the ken of his companions. The influence of H. G. Wells, more than most other writers, was crucial to Vivian, and permeates his work. Wells's immense breadth of vision and imagination appealed strongly to him, and perfectly chimed in with his own views. Vivian (in typically oblique fashion) acknowledged his debt by featuring an adventurer called Hubert Wells in certain of his later short stories.

The space allowed for fiction in *Flying* was meagre (partly due to the paper shortage); Vivian's tales were thus at times mere sketches. Nevertheless, he managed to get across a number of themes and plotlines he was later imaginatively to expand upon. "In the Desert" (*Flying,* 2 October 1918, as by A. K. Walton) is the eerily atmospheric story of a flyer who crash-lands in the North African desert and discovers among the dunes a lost temple dedicated to the elder gods; "Other World" (*Flying,* 10 October 1917) is the singular tale of aviators encountering in the upper atmosphere a kind of hurtling "black hole" with tentacled life in it. Even stranger, in its own way, is "Shepherded Out" (*Flying,* 29 January 1918) which, on the surface, is a description of an unknown plane being pursued but never caught, as it journeys relentlessly onwards, through the night and out of the dawn, ever south, ever just out of

gun-range, until it disappears into the blue. The unknown—the utterly unexplained—is what lifts the story into the realms of the eerie.

Vivian's writing career is still by no means fully charted. Around 1920 he certainly edited the *Novel Magazine* for a while, without, oddly (or so it appears), contributing to the *Novel*'s regular, and quite famous, "uncanny-story" slot. In 1922 he was poached by Walter Hutchinson to launch a new line of fiction magazines at Hutchinson's. Amongst others Vivian created and edited for over two years *Adventure-Story Magazine* and *Mystery-Story Magazine.* On a tight budget (Walter Hutchinson's stinginess was legendary) he used a good deal of second-rights material from the U.S. (principally from *Adventure* and *Weird Tales*), but also filled much editorial space with his own work, under a variety of pseudonyms including Vivian, A. K. Walton (mainly weirds), Galbraith Nicholson (historical and adventure yarns), and Sydney Barrie Lynd (cowboy stories and South Seas tales: he was later to write a number of westerns for the publisher Ward Lock as Barry Lynd).

In this two-year period, Vivian's supernatural and fantasy fiction for the Hutchinson group as a whole was immensely varied. Some of the stories published as by Vivian had originally been sketches by A. K. Walton half a decade before; some by Walton had been sketches by Vivian. "The Multiple Cube" was expanded into "Why Not?" (*Mystery-Story,* May 1924, as by Walton) which was not entirely a success since Vivian piled on facetiousness at the expense of the story's original strangeness. By comparison the expansion of Walton's "In the Desert" into "Ancient Evil" by Vivian (*Mystery-Story,* November 1923) was superbly handled: now a "Hubert Wells" story, the tension was screwed up even further, the atmosphere of horrible agelessness in the temple magnified to an extraordinary degree. Other ideas were dealt with excellently: in "The Abnormal Power" (*Mystery-Story,* April 1924) a girl can see emotions as coloured auras around the head; an "annihilation machine" was featured in "The House Among the Pines" (*Sovereign Magazine,* October 1924); in "The Man With the Box" (*Mystery-Story,* June 1924, as by Walton) the eponymous "hero" seems to have discovered how to harness the atom; "A Builder of Mind" (*Adventure-Story,* November 1924) has echoes of *The Island of Dr. Moreau,* though Vivian's concept—a 50-foot cross between a seal, a plesiosaurus and a brontosaurus, with a howling human voice and unimaginable ferocity—has a starker sophistication.

But initially Vivian used the magazines as vehicles for his own novels. All three of the celebrated high-adventure stories which first brought his name to the forefront of the Lost-Race fantasy subgenre appeared in *Hutchinson's Adventure-Story,* 1922 through 1924, and were each then issued in book form shortly after serialization. The story of *City of Wonder* features a potent mélange of lost-race themes, symbols and adjuncts: a quest sparked off by ancestral claims; a band of British adventurers battling savages with poisoned arrows; a wonderful aeons-old paved road discovered deep in the heart of the Borneo jungle; a host of gigantic primates, commanded by a beautiful woman, guarding a lost city, Kir-Asa, ruled by a mad king; the city the last outpost of Atlantis; internecine warfare; the overthrow of a ruling caste. The plot of *Fields of Sleep* is scarcely less enticing, the quest this time for a man who has disappeared into the wilds of Asia, where is found a fabulous valley inhabited by descendants of the Chaldeans. This might appear routine fare, except that Vivian creates an ingenious twist—indeed trap: a narcotic flower whose fragrance causes not only ecstatic visions but speechlessness and a paralysing dependence. Thus all those whose contact with the drug is a lengthy one can never leave the valley, but exist as (almost literally) lotus-eaters. When flooding destroys the "fields of sleep" the valley's inhabitants perish. Somewhat cheekily Vivian wrote a short story called "Atahuallpa's Emeralds" (*Chambers's Journal,* 1 March 1924), which was published long after the serialization and book-publication of *Fields of Sleep,* in which the narcotic fields and most of the rest of the plot were transported wholesale to a lost valley in South America: there a massive earthquake destroys both plants and drugged prisoners of the valley.

If Vivian's first two lost-race tales owed a good deal (as they did) to Rider Haggard, the third in his splendid triumvirate, *People of the Darkness* (a sequel to *Fields of Sleep*) owed something to Wells, particularly the latter's classic short story "The Country of the Blind". Vivian's version featured a trogloditish race of sightless men. *Star Dust,* by comparison, seems to have a rather more banal plotline, with its misanthropic hero, Leonard Ferrers, aiming to destabilize world governments by flooding the markets with synthetic gold. Mixing genres, however, Vivian throws in a machine that controls the weather, Ferrers, at one stage, devastating Surrey with a storm he has raised. With the last of his early fantasies, Vivian returned to the lost-race theme in *The Lady of the Terraces,* based on the short story "The Terraced Valley" (*Adventure-Story,* June 1924), and its sequel *A King There Was.* Both novels are set in a vast valley deep in the South American jungle, and although noble Haggardian tragedy (the death of the hero Colvin Barr, "a wanderer on the earth-face," in hand-to-hand struggle with the principal villain) climaxes the earlier novel, both books owe more to that fine, but now sadly neglected, novelist, adventure writer and mainstay of the superb American pulp *Adventure,* Arthur O. Friel (especially Friel's classic *Tiger River* and *The King of No Man's Land*).

Vivian shifted to the Far East again for a trio of slightly interrelated and mild fantasy-adventure yarns. *The Forbidden Door* introduces the cruel and treacherous Fleur Delage, a woman who has a mystic's knowledge and power. *The Tale of Fleur* continues then abruptly ends her story, with the lightest of fantastic props: an exotic poison, with which Fleur destroys herself. Josiah Drinkwater, a character who appears in both books, takes centre stage in the rather more relevant *Woman Dominant,* a full-blown lost-land novel with Odyssean echoes (Circe and the swine) in which men are the drug-stupefied slaves of their womenfolk.

Although his lost-race novels gave Vivian a measure of fame—are, indeed, for the most part superb examples of a fascinating breed—it is the supernatural thrillers from the third stage of his career that contain his most highly-regarded work. As Jack Mann he wrote 14 novels for Wright and Brown, a publisher who specialized in providing genre fiction fodder for the smaller rental libraries (it is virtually certain that Vivian wrote far more for this publisher, under names that in all probability will never now be uncovered). The early Manns have as their main protagonist a tough adventurer called Rex Coulson: two of his exploits, *Coulson Goes South* and *The Dead Man's Chest,* qualify as minor fantasies, the first a re-run of *Woman Dominant,* the second set on a South Pacific isle ruled by an enlightened leader.

The final eight Manns concern Gregory George Gordon Green—or "Gees"—on the surface something of a silly-ass detective who, in the general course of events, falls into the most bizarre adventures. His debut, *Gees's First Case,* is a Soviet-plot-to-sabotage-Britain piece of 1930s froth with no fantasy elements whatever (the later *The Kleinert Case* is similarly non-fantastic), but the rest are full-blooded weirds, distinguished by certain recurrent themes and concepts, principally: the endurance of superior beings, or "gods"

(both good and evil) through belief; the power of human thought to influence people or events; the power of real magic; the idea that those practising magic can live far beyond (not just by a few years, but a few thousand years) their natural span; reincarnation; the central idea that the earliest people, the "flint people," worshipped "fierce gods, made human sacrifices to them, and" (a crucial point) "were fierce themselves."

Many of the ideas Vivian utilized in the Mann books were based on contemporary anthropological knowledge, much of which is now recognized as hopelessly inaccurate. Further ideas were taken from Wells (especially his short "caveman" tale "The Grisly Folk," now viewed as somewhat risible) and Arthur Machen; thrown in for good measure, since Vivian was nothing if not catholic in his tastes, were concepts from J. G. Fraser's *The Golden Bough* (a favourite book), the mildly unhinged pseudo-scientist James Churchward (*The Lost Continent of Mu*) and Madame Blavatsky.

Nevertheless out of this splendid smorgasbord of bizarrerie Vivian created some notable weird thrillers. *Grey Shapes* features lycanthropy; *Nightmare Farm* elementals, madness, suicide and murder, as well as evidence of Vivian's dry wit (Mann at one point quotes approvingly an un-named book written some years before about the lost city of Kir-Asa—*City of Wonder,* of course, by E. Charles Vivian); *Maker of Shadows* split personality, the Eleusinian Mysteries, race memory, vampiric soul-sucking; *The Ninth Life* a beautiful, modern, but in fact 5,000-year-old, woman in thrall to an ancient Egyptian lion-god; *The Glass Too Many* murder by an ultra-rare Dyak poison, an ages-old underground labyrinth, voices from the dead; *Her Ways Are Death* witchcraft, the Fourth Dimension, a relic from Atlantis, and the god Thor, enraged and murderous, in a fitting climax to a breathtaking series of adventures and an extraordinary sequence of books.

A volume of Vivian's uncollected weird, supernatural and fantasy-oriented short stories is in preparation.

—Jack Adrian

VOLSKY, Paula

Nationality: American. **Born:** Fanwood, New Jersey. **Education:** Vassar, B.A. in English; University of Birmingham (England), M.A. in Shakespearean studies. **Career:** Worked for the US Department of Housing and Urban Development; now a freelance author, living near Washington DC.

FANTASY PUBLICATIONS

Novels (series: Sorcerer)

The Curse of the Witch-Queen. New York, Del Rey, 1982.
The Sorcerer's Lady. New York, Ace, 1986; London, Legend, 1988.
The Luck of Relian Kru. New York, Ace, 1987; London, Legend, 1989.
The Sorcerer's Heir. New York, Ace, 1988.
The Sorcerer's Curse. New York, Ace, 1989.
Illusion. London, Gollancz, 1991; New York, Bantam, 1992.
The Wolf of Winter. New York, Bantam, 1993; London, Bantam, 1994.

*   *   *

Paula Volsky's fantasies began with the minor *The Curse of the Witch-Queen,* a recomplicated romp about one Zargal, a duke's son afflicted with overeating and gigantism owing to the curse of an insulted king whose whole house lies under the curse of the eponymous witch-queen, who herself suffers from a curse.

Volsky attracted more attention with her Sorcerer trilogy, set in a kind of fantasy 17th-century Venice and couched in tones reminiscent of Jack Vance. In hope of retrieving the fortunes of her merchant father and family, the heroine is married off to the eponymous Sorcerer who runs the local magicians' guild. He is cold, proud and aloof; they predictably fall in love. One finds oneself on the Sorcerer's side despite his incredible arrogance, which along with intra-guild rivalries, conflicts with the city ruler and the hysteria of the populace eventually gets him killed. Continuing the trilogy, she finds sanctuary with their son amid the Sorcerer's non-human subterranean allies; the son becomes obsessed with revenge on the city and manipulates the cave-dwellers' culture to this end. Our heroine tends to dither in an ineffectually liberal way through books two and three, while more ruthless relatives and their allies finally save the city from the son's revenge.

Much more fun, the genial *The Luck of Relian Kru* is an entertaining exercise in quietly humorous fantasy which again owes something to Vance, and makes no secret of the debt: the luckless Relian Kru gives offence in refined foreign society by unknowingly wearing clothes whose colours convey the "Taunt Doubly Contemptuous of Matriarchal Liaison with Diseased Goat." Pursued for this by a charming though implacable assassin, he finds dodgy sanctuary with an exploitative wizard who forces him into various dangerous quests, such as stealing a (heavily guarded) magical disembodied hand which is not only good at evasive scuttling but makes extremely rude gestures at its pursuer. After several ingenious complications, Kru manages to get a grip on his own magical abilities—here magic involves complex finger exercises, training one to see and feel through a spare dimension called Forn—and goes off happily with a lady co-prisoner. Notably, there are no utter villains: the assassin is merely dutiful, the wizard a monster of self-centred egotism who nevertheless has endearing flaws, and even the dimwitted magico-mechanical snake that constrains the hero (around his neck) has a soft spot for its female counterpart.

Cynics have dismissed Volsky's fattest work, *Illusion,* as written to cash in on the bicentennial of the French Revolution. Certainly it feels like a worthy but familiar historical melodrama novel "fantasied up" to permit its sale in the genre where the author is established: we have the "Exalted" aristos with their incomprehension of growing popular wrath, the increasingly vituperative pamphleteers, the numbered city districts, the storming of something very like the Bastille, actual characters who can be matched with the movers of the Revolution, etc. Few other-world fantasies can be praised as "well researched."

The magical aspects of *Illusion* are of interest. Magic's great days are past and the ability to work it is an aristocratic thing. Three major "Sentient" relics remain and are pressed into the revolutionary cause, each a metaphor for part of the historical Terror. There is ZaZa the two-headed, flame-belching metal snake, useful in crowd control: terror on the streets. NuNu is a giant mechanical bee whose roving workers gather titbits of news from all over this alternative Paris: the terror of informers and anonymous denunciation. Kokotte, a fearsome, self-acting Iron Maiden that kills bloodily and in public, is of course the guillotine. The initially young and foolish Exalted heroine eventually escapes all three, with a good deal of help from her unworldly but illusion-adept Uncle Quinz. All in all, it's a pleasantly sugar-coated pill for readers who like fantasy and think they dislike historical romance.

The Wolf of Winter is ambitious in a different way: an expansive story of kings, usurpers, power and necromancy. In the icy country of Rhazaulle the king or Ulor takes his title from the legendary winged wolf of winter. His youngest brother Varis, the intending usurper, is initially a sympathetic if weak viewpoint character who is relentlessly bullied by the middle brother. In a classic "ineffectual man makes bad" development he discovers both that he has a talent for necromancy, command of the spirits of the dead, and that the addictive potions that enhance necromantic power will also bolster his poor health and eyesight. One thing leads to another: by inventive murders and magic he carves a path through his own relatives to the throne, heedless of the apparent fact that a necromancer will always eventually go too far and burn out his mind, thus becoming (in a term unfortunate to British ears at least, with its echo of children's comics) "spifflicated."

The viewpoint shifts to his niece Shalindra, whose brother Cerrov is the rightful Ulor: both are temporarily safe in exile, and she is further hidden in a dry-as-dust research library on an isolated island. Thanks to the librarians' secret plan to do away with necromancy by using its power to free the earthbound dead, Shalindra acquires a supply of magic-enhancing drug and is able to intervene slightly when Cerrov's loyalist army has been demoralized through necromancy and she herself captured by Varis. After dangling a romantic red herring (could Shalindra marry Varis, as for political reasons he wishes, and reform him?), Volsky offers a different and quite moving conclusion. The story reads well.

This author's knack for offbeat variants of fantasy magic, and engaging portrayals of even the nastiest characters, promises interesting books to come.

—David Langford

WAGNER, Karl Edward

Pseudonym: Kent Allard. **Nationality:** American. **Born:** Knoxville, Tennessee, 12 December 1945. **Education:** Kenyon College, 1963-67, A.B. *cum laude* in history; University of North Carolina School of Medicine, 1967-74, M.D. **Family:** Married Barbara Ruth Mott in 1974 (divorced 1986). **Career:** Resident psychiatrist, John Umstead Hospital, Buttner, North Carolina, 1974-75; freelance writer from 1975. **Awards:** British Fantasy award, 1975, 1976, 1982, 1983; World Fantasy award, 1976, 1983. **Died:** 15 October 1994.

FANTASY PUBLICATIONS

Novels (series: Kane)

Darkness Weaves With Many Shades (Kane). Reseda, California, Powell, 1970; revised and restored as *Darkness Weaves,* New York, Warner, 1978; London, Coronet, 1978.
Bloodstone (Kane). New York, Warner, 1975; London, Coronet, 1977.
The Sign of the Salamander. Columbus, Ohio, Hoppenstand, 1975.
Dark Crusade (Kane). New York, Warner, 1976; London, Coronet, 1981.
Legion From the Shadows. New York, Zebra, 1976.
Conan: The Road of Kings. New York, Bantam, 1979; London, Sphere, 1981.

Short Stories

Death Angel's Shadow (Kane). New York, Warner, 1973; London, Coronet, 1980.
Night Winds (Kane). New York, Warner, 1978; London, Coronet, 1979.
In a Lonely Place. New York, Warner, 1983; expanded edition, New York, Scribner, 1983.
The Book of Kane. West Kingston, Rhode Island, Donald M. Grant, 1985.

Other

Editor, *Echoes of Valor.* New York, Tor, 1987.
Editor, *Echoes of Valor II.* New York, Tor, 1989.
Editor, *Echoes of Valor III.* New York, Tor, 1991.

OTHER PUBLICATIONS

Novels

The Other Woman, as Kent Allard. New York, Carlyle, 1973.
Killer, with David Drake. New York, Baen, 1985.

Short Stories

Why Not You and I? New York, Tor, 1987; expanded edition, Arlington Heights, Illinois, Dark Harvest, 1987.

Unthreatened By the Morning Light. Eugene, Oregon, Pulphouse, 1989.
Where the Summer Ends. Eugene, Oregon, Pulphouse, 1991.

Poetry

Songs of the Damned. Knoxville, Tennessee, Silver Eel, 1981.

Other

Editor, *Worse Things Waiting,* by Manly Wade Wellman. Chapel Hill, North Carolina, Carcosa, 1973.
Editor, *Far Lands, Other Days,* by E. Hoffmann Price. Chapel Hill, North Carolina, Carcosa, 1975.
Editor, *Murgunstrumm and Others,* by Hugh B. Cave. Chapel Hill, North Carolina, Carcosa, 1977.
Editor, *The Year's Best Horror Stories, Series VIII-XXII.* New York, DAW, 15 vols., 1980-94.
Editor, *Lonely Vigils,* by Manly Wade Wellman. Chapel Hill, North Carolina, Carcosa, 1981.
Editor, *The Valley So Low,* by Manly Wade Wellman. Garden City, New York, Doubleday, 1987.
Editor, *Intensive Scare.* New York, DAW, 1990.

*

Critical Studies: "Interview" by Jeffrey M. Elliot, two parts, *Fantasy Newsletter,* July-August 1981.

Karl Edward Wagner commented:

I was raised in the American Southeast, educated in the Midwest, returned to live in the Southeast, but spend much of my time in London. My accent confuses everyone. I collect and read horror, fantasy, science fiction—have done so since learning to read, from pre-Code horror comics in the early 1950s. I'm fond of rock music, fast Fords, vintage motorcycles, guns, T-shirts, and I'm not politically correct.

I work primarily in two fields—as writer and as editor. I find both creative and exciting. As an editor, I have been able to preserve the work of older writers and present them to new readers, and, with *The Year's Best Horror Stories,* I have been able to discover and to introduce to a wider readership many new writers whose work might otherwise have perished in small-press obscurity.

I see myself primarily as a horror writer, but probably in a looser interpretation than many readers recognize. I originated the now in-vogue term "dark fantasy" to describe my Kane stories, which are more oriented toward atmospheric horror than swords-and-sorcery adventure. Earlier attempts to describe my work as "acid gothic" or "gothic fantasy" did not catch on.

My view of life is variously nihilistic, anarchistic and absurdist. This is reflected in my writing. There is no distinction between Good and Evil, other than in the eye of the beholder. Kane is based upon the legend of the Biblical Cain, and is my presentation of an amoral hero-villain who can survive through the eternal battle of Bad versus Evil. Kane is bad to the bone. Betrayal is a major underlying theme to my work. Friends use you, turn their backs on you, then turn against you. I worship Sam Peckinpah's movie *The Wild Bunch*.

*   *   *

In later years, before his untimely death at the age of 48, Karl Edward Wagner's writing consisted mainly of horror fiction, in which field he was also noted as an editor. His approach to fiction was such that often the borders between horror and fantasy blurred, and although his series of books about the sword-and-sorcery hero Kane are most easily categorized as fantasy, they sometimes may be taken as tales of brooding horror.

Wagner began the Kane stories around 1960 and the character developed and matured between then and the first book publication in 1970. Few characters in fantasy have had such an intense period of development, running alongside Wagner's own maturing of character and imagination. When Kane finally emerged in print he had become a dark synthesis of influences drawn from movies, books and comics, plus the student/hippie/Vietnam War milieu of the late 1960s.

The basic character of Kane is the Biblical Cain, an outcast, doomed to wander for eternity. Wagner wanted to distance the character from the Biblical imagery whilst retaining that sense of timelessness and awe in recognition of history's first murderer, and this he did by developing gothic imagery, drawn particularly from the influence of Charles Maturin's *Melmoth the Wanderer*. Although many see Kane as a literary descendant of Robert E. Howard's Conan (and the novels read very like Howard's work) he may be likened more to Howard's Solomon Kane and Michael Moorcock's Elric—both fated wanderers. Wagner's style is more controlled than Howard's, and though it lacks the brash exuberance of Howard's most exciting work this is more than compensated for by the relentlessness of Kane. For dark and brooding despair, heroic fantasy has no better example. Kane is no hero: he is depicted as an intelligent but determined villain, out to seek his own form of justice. He is first introduced to us as a man who looks to be in his 30s or 50s, but strangely ageless, with a mightily muscled body, thick neck and short red hair. But most striking of all are his eyes, "two blue-burning crystals of ice" suggesting "the eyes of a maddened killer".

The first Kane book that Wagner completed was *Bloodstone*, though it remained long unpublished and was revised several times. The first to appear in print, *Darkness Weaves With Many Shades*, was butchered by the publisher and reduced to half its text, which was restored in later editions. The first complete book to appear was a volume of three novellas dressed up as a novel, *Death Angel's Shadow*. As if that is not complicated enough, none of the books follows a particular order, and indeed some of the stories, like "Undertow," deliberately shift time out of sequence. Because of Kane's immortality the adventures are played out against a much larger tapestry, making some of his actions seem strange to mortals unaware of a grander scheme. All of this contributes to the mystique of the Kane character. In addition, Wagner deliberately tries to avoid the usual trappings of sword-and-sorcery, a label he disliked. In the Kane books nothing is quite what it seems. They are amongst the more intelligent works of heroic fantasy.

Wagner also continued two of Robert E. Howard's own creations: Conan and Bran Mak Morn. Here Wagner was restricted by the original settings and characters, but he had a respect for Howard's work which enabled him to look again at what that writer had been attempting to do—which was create a true barbarian—and to explore the consequences of that. Wagner was criticized for his interpretation of Conan in *The Road of Kings* because it was a departure from the way the character had developed under L. Sprague de Camp and Lin Carter, but Wagner was seeking to be honest to the original intent of the character, and his Conan has a close relationship to the Conan of Howard's best-developed stories. He also worked on the script for the never-filmed third Conan movie.

His only non-fantasy novel is *Killer*, written with David Drake, where a monstrous alien arrives in ancient Rome and is captured to fight in the arena. It is a clever blend of science fiction and ancient history.

Wagner wrote no full-length horror novels, but he did produce some of the most respected and trenchant short horror fiction of the last two decades. Apart from the Kane short stories, most of his short fiction falls into the horror field. His early short stories do have elements of fantasy, unlike his later horror stories which were more intense and visceral. "Sticks" (*Whispers,* 1974) merged local legends and Lovecraftian imagery to create a story regarded as a modern masterpiece by many. It received the British Fantasy Award for that year's best short story (the first of many awards Wagner received). Some of his quieter but no less potent ghost stories include "The River of Night's Dreaming" (*Whispers III,* 1981) and "Blue Lady, Come Back" (*Night Visions 2,* 1985). The latter is to some extent a spoof on all haunted-house and psychic-detective stories, though it is a powerful ghost story in its own right with a very surprising conclusion. It features Curtiss Stryker, a one-time pulp writer who created the character of John Chance, whom Wagner had written about in the incomplete novel *Sign of the Salamander*. Wagner's passion for the old pulps was no secret and was the basis for him establishing the small-press publishing imprint Carcosa to resurrect the best work by neglected pulp writers, particularly E. Hoffmann Price, Manly Wade Wellman and Hugh B. Cave. Wagner's interest not only went some way toward reviving those writers' careers, but also demonstrated that there was good, readable, enjoyable fiction—outside the generally recognized genre pulps like *Weird Tales*—that was being ignored by most devotees of fantasy. His commercially published three-volume *Echoes of Valor* anthology series was particularly valuable in that it made available to a wide audience rarely-reprinted stories from the lesser fantasy pulps of yesteryear, by authors such as Henry Kuttner and Nictzin Dyalhis among many others. Wagner received a special World Fantasy Award for his work with Carcosa in 1976, and two of the imprint's collections won their own awards in 1975 and 1978.

All of these aspects of his career reveal Wagner as an author with a strong knowledge of the past and a regard for tradition from which he was able to distil and update the essence of story and character, which is what makes his work so strong and durable.

—Mike Ashley

———

WAGS, Two. *See* **BANGS, John Kendrick.**

———

WALL, Mervyn

Nationality: Irish. **Born:** Dublin, 1908. **Education:** Belvedere College, Dublin; two years residence in Bonn, Germany (educational institution unspecified); University College, Dublin; B.A. from the National University of Ireland, 1928. **Career:** Irish civil service, 1934-1948; programme officer for Radio Eireann, 1948-1957; chief executive of Irish Arts Council, 1957-1975. Ten years honorary secretary and treasurer, two years president, of Irish Academy of Letters.

FANTASY PUBLICATIONS

Novels

The Unfortunate Fursey. London, Pilot Press, 1946.
The Return of Fursey. London, Pilot Press, 1948.
The Complete Fursey (omnibus). Dublin, Wolfhound Press, 1985.
The Garden of Echoes (novella). Dublin, Fingal Books, 1988.

Short Stories

A Flutter of Wings. Dublin, Talbot Press, 1974.

OTHER PUBLICATIONS

Novels

Leaves for the Burning. 1952.

*   *   *

Easily and with some accuracy described as the Irish T. H. White, Mervyn Wall is one of the finest comic fantasists ever, but also one of the most neglected. His career is an object lesson in the drawbacks and benefits of genre publishing. He is well respected by critics, a significant figure in Irish literature, primarily know for such realistic novels as *Leaves for the Burning,* but because his two fantastic novels have never been published as category fantasy, in the Ballantine Adult Fantasy Series or some equivalent, Wall has never reached a mass audience, and remains the enthusiasm of the fortunate few who have managed to obtain copies of his books.

The Unfortunate Fursey and *The Return of Fursey* are, in the words of Parke Godwin, "pure gold". E. F. Bleiler, writing in *The Guide to Supernatural Fiction,* calls the first "a landmark book in the history of fantasy," perhaps an exaggeration in terms of its impact and subsequent prominence, but not in terms of merit. Landmarks have to be noticed. It is a great loss to the field that these books were not. Both are treasures of the highest order, waiting to be rediscovered.

The Unfortunate Fursey tells the story of a lay brother at the Irish monastery of Clonmacnoise, circa 800 A.D. The monastery has been free from demonic invasion since its founding, secure in the sanctity of its monks, but, one night, having been thoroughly pummelled by the prayers of the virtuous brethren, a band of imps takes refuge in Brother Fursey's cell. Alas, he is too slow of speech and wit to utter the proper exorcisms in time, and Clonmacnoise

has been breached. For Fursey, the trouble is just beginning as he is soon cast out into the world, where he finds himself under the same roof for a single night with a supposedly virtuous crone who is actually a witch. For propriety's sake, Fursey must then marry her. (Was the marriage consummated? the Devil later asks. "Of course not! We're good Irish Catholics and we didn't know how.") When she is killed in a magical duel (fully the equal of the celebrated combat between Merlin and Madame Mim in *The Sword in the Stone*), Fursey accidentally swallows her spirit and becomes, through no fault of his own, not merely a consorter with demons, but an actual sorcerer, albeit an incompetent one whose sole trick consists of tossing a rope over a rafter to magically produce a mug of beer or a loaf of bread. He woefully neglects Albert, his blood-drinking familiar, and wants, more than anything else, to be readmitted to the monastery and put back to work in the kitchen.

Throughout the first book, Fursey is pursued by the authorities, yet tries to be reconciled with the Church. In the second, he turns on his tormentors, despairing of ever being a good Christian again, and attempts to become whole-heartedly wicked. But this course is no more successful than the first. Albert (who hasn't had a single drop of blood all this time) disgraces Fursey at the sabbat. When Fursey's lady-love marries a soldier, Fursey can't even work up enough malice to murder the fellow. He is, in the end, a tragic figure, too large for his old life in the monastery kitchen, but too small for the world.

Mere synopsis cannot even hint at the richness, pathos or barbed wit of these magnificent black comedies. There are moments of broad satire, as when, at the conclusion of the first book, the Irish Church shockingly sells out to the Devil, so that Satan promises not to tempt Irishmen with sex, in return for which the Church agrees to overlook robbery and murder. Wall has a great talent for comic invention. Both Fursey novels abound in hilarious circumstances and absurd—but still convincingly human—characters. For sheer delight, the encounters with George the vampire and with the cross-eyed basilisk are as good as anything in the entire canon of fantasy literature.

However, the truly remarkable thing about these books is that, like *The Once and Future King,* they become deeply moving as they unfold toward a tragic conclusion. Scenes of merriment give way to tears. Wall's technique is one of using comedy to approach subject matter so bleak that it would be unbearably depressing if handled any other way. Life is so painful, these books tell us, so terribly futile, that all one can do is laugh at it while one can. It is a difficult balancing act. The two novels seem all the more robust and emotionally wrenching for their slapstick. On the surface, they sparkle, but they are dark at heart.

"I would consider myself a very limited writer if I were only interested in fantasy," Wall once remarked. He was never a genre writer, having read James Branch Cabell, James Stephens, and J. R. R. Tolkien at various points in his life, but never developing any sense of being part of a specialist field or movement. He has always been, merely, a writer.

After *The Return of Fursey,* he published no fantasy for many years, turning to plays, mainstream novels and radio scripts. He wrote a few short stories of fantastic interest, if not always outright fantastic content, some of which are collected in *A Flutter of Wings.* Two of them, "Cloonaturk" and "The Demon Angler," are among the best ghost stories ever written that don't quite have ghosts in them. "The Man Who Could Outstare Cobras" is about a duel between two hypnotists. They freeze each other in place, and are eventually displayed in a museum.

The Garden of Echoes was written in the 1950s to amuse the author's children, but not published until its appearance in the Mervyn Wall number of *The Journal of Irish Literature* in 1982. Publishers rejected it because the author refused to make commercial compromises, and also, one suspects, because it simply too depressing for the children's market.

Wall describes this novella as a satire on adults from a child's point of view. It might also be imagined as a fairy tale by Ambrose Bierce at his bitterest. The plot is a venerable one for children's fantasy. Two little girls, at home alone with a babysitter, go through an enchanted bookcase into a fantastic land, where they have adventures. But the babysitter, a dreadfully empirically-minded science student, follows them, intending to shoot Santa Claus and put an end to this fantasy nonsense.

The writing is as fine as ever and Wall's invention never flags, but somewhere the laughter which made the Fursey books so special has gone sour. The satire is shrill, the allegory obvious, with only a few moments rising to the level of the author's earlier work. Probably the best occurs as the children encounter a king whose castle is overrun with rats. He can't get rid of them, he explains, because "they're the government."

At last report Wall was at work on another attack on contemporary society to be called *The Odious Generation,* "a satire on the present-day world of threatened nuclear destruction, destruction of the environment, the selfishness of youth and all the horrors we live with." While it could turn out to be a masterpiece, and Wall might have somewhere along the way regained his laughter, one suspects that for fantasy readers at least, he will always be a two-book author, admired for his timeless, wonderful *The Unfortunate Fursey* and *The Return of Fursey* as long as fantastic literature is read.

—Darrell Schweitzer

WALTON, Evangeline

Pseudonym for Evangeline Ensley. **Nationality:** American. **Born:** Indianapolis, Indiana, 24 November 1907.

FANTASY PUBLICATIONS

Novels (series: Four Branches of the Mabinogion)

The Virgin and the Swine (Mabinogion). Chicago, Willett Clark, 1936; as *The Island of the Mighty,* New York, Ballantine, 1970; London, Pan Ballantine, 1972.
Witch House. Sauk City, Wisconsin, Arkham House, 1945; revised edition, London, Skeffington, 1950.
The Children of Llyr (Mabinogion). New York, Ballantine, 1971.
The Song of Rhiannon (Mabinogion). New York, Ballantine, 1972.
Prince of Annwn (Mabinogion). New York, Ballantine, 1974.
The Sword is Forged. New York, Timescape, 1983.

OTHER PUBLICATIONS

Novel

Cross and the Sword. New York, Bouregy and Curl, 1956; as *Son of Darkness,* London, Hutchinson, 1957.

*

Bibliography: *Lloyd Alexander, Evangeline Walton Ensley, Kenneth Morris: A Primary and Secondary Bibliography* by Kenneth J. Zahorski and Robert H. Boyer, Boston, Hall, 1981.

Critical Studies: Evangeline Walton issue, *Fantasy Review* no. 77, March 1985.

Evangeline Walton comments:

"James Stephens' two mythological novels, *Deirdre* and *In the Land of Youth,* were practically my Bible for years. And I was also influenced by Lord Dunsany and Algernon Blackwood . . . I didn't discover *The Mabinogion* until I had read all the Irish stuff I could find, and was still looking hungrily for anything that might be Celtic. I then became fascinated with the scene in which Gwydion finds the eagle in the tree. I still think it is unique: the older man's deep emotion, and the struggle (merely implied in the Welsh original, of course) in the younger one's consciousness, as his human self and memories gradually begin to rise up through the sick eagle's dumb misery. I thought how wonderfully James Stephens could have written it—and ended by writing my own book . . . *The Island of the Mighty*—then called *The Virgin and the Swine*—got little attention from the general public, although it did get warm endorsement from writers as different as John Cowper Powys and Faith Baldwin. Perhaps it was just that the tides were flowing, and the other books had already started to well up in me. My memory is dim there . . . but I expect that whatever was welling up never would have got to the surface if it hadn't been for the encouragement—we corresponded for years—of Mr. Powys." (From an interview by Paul Spencer, *Fantasy Review,* 1985.)

*   *   *

Best known for her four-volume retelling of the ancient Welsh legends that comprise the Mabinogion cycle, Evangeline Walton also delved into other periods of history for two free-standing books, *Witch House,* a story of dark fantasy, *Cross and the Sword,* an historical novel about the struggle between Saxons and Vikings. Her last published work, *The Sword is Forged,* was to have been the first of a proposed trilogy dealing with ancient Greek legends.

It would seem that Walton was something of a feminist long before the current wave of feminist activism began, since her fictions pay tribute to the importance of women in the past. In the Mabinogion books she describes the matriarchal society of the ancient Welsh, while still telling the stories with chiefly male figures of heroism. She has pulled together many fragments to compose a cohesive saga, not a literal translation by any means, but her own version. As she explains in her notes for *Song of Rhiannon,* she tried not to change anything, but rather to add details and interpretation. It has been suggested that Walton was not a true feminist intent on revisionist history, but her appreciation for women is very evident, particularly in the Welsh books and *The Sword is Forged.*

She openly adheres to the principle that the earth then and now is feminine, and that with the coming of the Industrial Age men have polluted mother earth. As she states in the endnotes of *Prince of Annwn,* "Pollution has dimmed that last glory a little; I hope I will not be accused of sex bias for saying so; I like penicillin, electric toasters, jet travel, etc., as well as anybody. But when we were superstitious enough to hold the earth sacred and worship her, we did nothing to endanger our future upon her, as we do now."

Space does not permit a detailed synopsis of Walton's version of the Mabinogion. The first branch, *Prince of Annwn,* tells of

Pwyll, Prince of Dyfed, who pursues a quest in the shadowy world of death, Annwn. The second part of the book describes Pwyll's further adventures and search for a wife, who turns out to be the complex character of Rhiannon, goddess, mother and bride. The second branch, *The Children of Llyr,* is a dark and brooding story. It focuses, as the title suggests, on the five children of Llyr, called Bran the Blessed, ruler of Britain. A great war erupts between Britain and Ireland. In the war and its aftermath, four of the five children are slain. *The Song of Rhiannon,* the third branch, tells of the love between Rhiannon and Manawyddan, the father of her child, Pryderi. (Pwyll cannot sire an heir, so he sends his friend Manawyddan to mate with Rhiannon in secrecy.)

The final, fourth, branch was originally published as *The Virgin and the Swine* (later title, *The Island of the Mighty*) and was the first branch by Walton to be published. It is based on the best-known portion of the Mabinogion. The three parts of the novel describe the adventures of the children of the goddess Don. The first part is the story of Gwydion, who is punished by his uncle, Math, for the theft of pigs. The punishment is a test and a bit of character-building for the youthful wizard. In the second part, Gwydion's sorceress sister, Arianrhod, employs trickery in an attempt to gain power, like Morgan le Fay in the Arthurian legends. She is thwarted by Math. One of her children, Lleu, is raised by Gwydion who even creates a wife, Blodeuwedd, for Lleu through magic. Lleu is betrayed by Blodeuwedd, and his soul enters an eagle. The book's third part is about Blodeuwedd, the subhuman created from flowers for Lleu. It also describes the final end of Lleu's mother, Arianrhod.

As a work of fantasy, Walton's Mabinogion is superior to most other novels in a similar vein. It was never meant to be a literal translation of the old legends, and although many works of adult fantasy draw upon these tales, they do not compare with Walton's four volumes. One set of children's books by Lloyd Alexander, the "Prydain" series, comes closer in scope than others, but they do not contain the rich details and subplots of Walton's retelling.

Walton's second published work, *Witch House,* is sometimes described as a horror novel, although it is definitely in the dark fantasy tradition, reminiscent of later works such as Shirley Jackson's more successful *The Haunting of Hill House.* The plot revolves around the efforts of a psychic detective to exorcise the vindictive spirits of an old mansion. Evangeline Walton's final book publication, *The Sword is Forged,* is a retelling of the Greek myth of Theseus and the Amazon queen, Antiope. Their love-hate relationship forms the basis of the plot, and Walton's fantasy details make this title more than just another fictionalized account of classical myths. It is similar to the books of Mary Renault: both consciously tried to recreate the ancient world of Greece, placing emphasis on archaeological facts and literary texts and translations. Both authors developed their works separately. Renault was the first to publish her fictionalized account of Theseus, in *The King Must Die* (1958), and Walton held her novel back until later. In *The Sword is Forged* Walton admits to more embroidery on the original tales than was the case with the Mabinogion. However, she never deviates from what might have been: for example, she suggests that Crete used Delphi to dominate the Greek mainland during this period. This may not be the case, but it cannot be shown that it is false, either.

Walton is a skilled writer who employs appropriate styles for her various works. The Mabinogion books are told simply, yet in the spirit of the original legends. They are almost biblical in tone, certainly giving the flavour of medieval tales. Walton achieves this by using plain English in an almost poetic approach, as this passage from Prince of Annwn illustrates: "The bole of one enormous old tree hid it; for a breath's space Pwyll could not see it, and then a Grey Man on a Grey Horse rode out into the glade. And Pwyll's hand, that had leapt to his sword-hilt, froze there, and his eyes stared as if frozen in his head." In *Witch House* Walton employs straightforward prose with a Gothic touch, and in *The Sword is Forged,* she adopts a simple short-sentenced narrative approach that seems exactly right to describe events in classical Greece.

Walton's work has received critical success and respect, but has not been widely popular. Ironically, *Witch House,* her weakest fantasy work, is the one title to be occasionally reissued in the United States, riding on the coat-tails of the horror and Gothic enthusiasm of the past two decades.

—Cosette Kies

WANGERIN, Walter, Jr.

Nationality: American. **Born:** Portland, Oregon, 13 February 1944. **Education:** Concordia Senior College, Fort Wayne, Indiana, B.A. 1966; Miami University, Oxford, Ohio, M.A. 1968; Christ Seminary, Seminex, M.Div. 1976. **Family:** Married Ruthanne Bohlmann in 1968; two sons and two daughters. **Career:** Worked in a variety of jobs, including migrant peapicker, lifeguard and ghetto youth worker; producer, announcer, KFUO-Radiocomments, St. Louis, Montana, 1969-70; instructor in English literature, University of Evansville, Indiana, 1970-74; ordained Lutheran minister, 1976; assistant pastor, Lutheran Church of Our Redeemer, Evansville, from 1974; assistant pastor, 1974-77, and senior pastor, 1977-85, Grace Lutheran Church, Evansville; Jockum Professor in English and Theology, Valparaiso University, Valparaiso, Indiana, from 1991. Lives in Evansville, Indiana. **Awards:** Best Children's Book of the Year, *School Library Journal* and *New York Times,* both 1978; National Religious Book award, 1980; American Book award for paperback, 1981; Best Book of the Year, *School Library Journal,* 1983; Best Fiction, Association of Logos Bookstores, 1986.

FANTASY PUBLICATIONS

Novels (series: Chauntecleer)

The Book of the Dun Cow (Chauntecleer). New York, Harper and Row, 1978.
The Book of Sorrows (Chauntecleer). New York, Harper and Row, 1985.
The Crying for a Vision. New York, Simon and Schuster, 1995.

OTHER PUBLICATIONS

Fiction for Children

The Glory Story. Fort Wayne, Indiana, Concordia, 1974.
God, I've Gotta Talk to You. Fort Wayne, Indiana, Concordia, 1974.
A Penny is Everything, with A. Jennings. Fort Wayne, Indiana, Concordia, 1974.
The Baby God Promised. Fort Wayne, Indiana, Concordia, 1974.

The Bible for Children. Skokie, Illinois, Rand McNally, 1981.

O Happy Day! Fort Wayne, Indiana, Concordia, 1981.

My First Bible Book About Jesus, illustrated by Jim Cummins. Skokie, Illinois, Rand McNally, 1983.

Thistle, illustrated by Marcia Sewall. New York, Harper and Row, 1983.

Potter, Come Fly to the First of the Earth, illustrated by Daniel San Souci. N.p., Cook, 1985.

In the Beginning There Was No Sky. London(?), Nelson, 1986.

The Bible for Children. New York, Macmillan, 1987.

Elisabeth and the Water Troll. New York, Harper and Row, 1991.

Branta and the Golden Stone, illustrated by Deborah Healey. New York, Simon and Schuster, 1993.

Poetry

A Miniature Cathedral and Other Poems. New York, Harper and Row, 1986.

Other

Ragman and Other Cries of Faith. New York, Harper and Row, 1984.

The Orphean Passages: The Drama of Faith. New York, Harper and Row, 1986.

As for Me and My House: Crafting Your Marriage to Last. London, Nelson, 1987.

Miz Lil and the Chronicles of Grace. New York, Harper and Row, 1988.

The Manger is Empty. New York, Harper and Row, 1989.

Mourning into Dancing. Grand Rapids, Michigan, Zondervan, 1992.

Reliving the Passion: Meditations on the Suffering, Death, and Resurrection of Jesus as Recorded in Mark. Grand Rapids, Michigan, Zondervan, 1992.

*   *   *

The Book of the Dun Cow and its sequel *The Book of Sorrows* form one continuous story, with the setting and most characters in common, yet there are significant differences between the two novels. What we are dealing with here is a talking-animal fantasy which is largely allegorical and has very little contact with reality, despite the fact that almost all of the animals involved are common North American species.

The setting is a fantasy Earth, fixed at the centre of the Universe, with the Sun and stars revolving around it. Its population consists of animals of all kinds, living a Garden-of-Eden existence, with each geographical group of animals ruled over by a rooster (or, as Wangerin puts it throughout, since he capitalizes all his Animals, a Rooster). They live close to both a river and the shore of a salt-water lake.

Chauntecleer the Rooster lives an idyllic life with his thirty Hens, talking to and maintaining perfectly friendly relations with the Fox, the Weasel, Mice, Ants and sundry other species. (Note that although the names Chauntecleer for a cockerel and Pertelote for a hen are taken from "The Nun's Priest's Tale" in Chaucer's *Canterbury Tales,* Wangerin borrows nothing else from Chaucer.) A newly arrived Dog, Mundo Cani, proves to be an irritant (though a loveable one), due to his midnight howling and his perpetual state of depression.

Meanwhile, in another land upstream, the Rooster Senex lays an egg from which a Cockatrice—with scales and a tail, something like a small flying dragon—hatches, and he mates with the Hens, who produce eggs from which Basilisks hatch. These are serpents with a poisonous bite. They kill all the other Animals in that land and go looking for more lands to conquer and despoil.

The first that Chauntecleer knows of anything amiss upstream is when he has to rescue first a family of Mice and then a most beautiful Hen from the river, which is in flood. The Hen, whose name is Pertelote, brings the first news of the Cockatrice, for she has come from that other land where he reigns. She quickly becomes Chauntecleer's wife and they have a family of three Chicks.

It is clear from the early stages of the novel that it is concerned with the struggle between good and evil. Good is personified as the Dun Cow, who appears occasionally to Chauntecleer, offering comfort or aid. Evil is personified as Wyrm, a gigantic Ouroboros serpent who lives in caverns beneath the Earth's crust and is long enough to circle the world; he is not seen though his influence is felt.

The first attack of Basilisks upon Chauntecleer's land kills his three Chicks. He makes preparations for war which include a council of all the Animals and the building of a defensive rampart (by the Ants). In the great battle, many Animals fight heroically. John Wesley Weasel, who is impervious to the Basilisk venom, kills many of them, though a lot of Animals also die. In single combat, Chauntecleer (wearing Gaff and the Slasher, a pair of metal spikes) kills the Cockatrice, and Mundo Cani, using one of the Dun Cow's horns as a weapon, leaps into a deep gorge where Wyrm can be seen and stabs him in his single great eye. So the novel ends on a note of success and optimism.

By contrast, *The Book of Sorrows* lives up to its name by being a succession of depressing events. The first is the death of Russel the Fox, from wounds received during the great battle—a death spread over six of the first seven chapters. Throughout the book, Chauntecleer is tortured by grief and guilt and self-doubt. (In fact, Chauntecleer frequently overdoes his anguished breast-beating, sometimes with little cause, plunging into bathos.) An over-long plotting device, containing a Bird and a family of Coyotes, leads to Chauntecleer entering the caverns beneath the Earth with the intention of finishing off Wyrm. But Wyrm is already dead, his body decaying. Even so, he has engineered Chauntecleer's visit so as to infect him with emotional doubt, "entering at the heart" as Wangerin puts it.

In the end, feeling that he has become estranged from his beloved Pertelote, and with many of his Animals deserting him, Chauntecleer fights and kills three Wolves. Guilt, though, makes him kill himself, and the novel's finale is extremely sad. So, triumph and hope at the end of *The Book of the Dun Cow* become sadness and loss at the end of *The Book of Sorrows.* A second great difference is that, although the first novel was published for adults, it was hailed (as well) as an outstanding children's book. The second novel could not be termed a children's book. This is not due solely to its sadness and grimness, but also to its slowness of pace. While *The Book of the Dun Cow* is full of incident and is handled with an enchanting lightness of touch, its sequel is an overstuffed parody, full of superfluous descriptive passages and an excess of moral agonizing.

Both books are guilty of sentimentality. It is a quality which can touch the reader's heart if offered in small quantities, as (for the most part) in *The Book of the Dun Cow,* but which tends to spoil the sequel. Wangerin dwells far too much upon the supposedly loveable aspects of Chicks, a Faun, baby Mice, baby Coyotes and so on (especially when they have been orphaned), and he goes right over the top in his maudlin treatment of the death of any Animal, baby or adult.

It seems clear that the ending of *The Book of Sorrows* is meant to demonstrate the end of the Garden-of-Eden perfection of Chauntecleer's land. The end of Chauntecleer's innocence and the beginning of his fall from grace can be traced back to his decision (made and voiced, in fact, on the final page of *The Book of the Dun Cow*) to have his revenge on Wyrm by entering the subterranean caverns if he ever can. Instead, he should have turned the other cheek and forgiven Wyrm, as Coyote does to Chauntecleer near the end of *The Book of Sorrows,* precipitating Chauntecleer's suicide.

The religiosity of the books is pointed up by Wangerin's use of church-service names for Chauntecleer's crows (terce, sext, nones, etc) and by the Latin phrases he brings in on occasion.

—Chris Morgan

WARNER, Sylvia Townsend

Nationality: British. **Born:** Harrow, Middlesex, 6 December 1893. **Education:** Private. **Career:** Worked in a munitions factory, 1916; member of the editorial board, *Tudor Church Music,* Oxford University Press, London, 1917-26; joined Communist Party, 1935; Red Cross volunteer, Barcelona, 1935; contributor to the *New Yorker* from 1936. **Awards:** Katherine Mansfield-Menton prize, 1968. Fellow, Royal Society of Literature, 1967; honorary member, American Academy, 1972. **Died:** 1 May 1978.

FANTASY PUBLICATIONS

Novels

Lolly Willowes; or, The Loving Huntsman. London, Chatto and Windus, and New York, Viking Press, 1926.

Short Stories

The Cat's Cradle Book. New York, Viking Press, 1940; London, Chatto and Windus, 1960.
The Museum of Cheats. London, Chatto and Windus, and New York, Viking Press, 1947.
The Kingdoms of Elfin. London, Chatto and Windus, and New York, Viking Press, 1977.

OTHER PUBLICATIONS

Novels

Mr. Fortune's Maggot. London, Chatto and Windus, and New York, Viking Press, 1927.
The True Heart. London, Chatto and Windus, and New York, Viking Press, 1929.

Summer Will Show. London, Chatto and Windus, and New York, Viking Press, 1936.
After the Death of Don Juan. London, Chatto and Windus, 1938; New York, Viking Press, 1939.
The Corner That Held Them. London, Chatto and Windus, and New York, Viking Press, 1948.
The Flint Anchor. London, Chatto and Windus, and New York, Viking Press, 1954; as *The Barnards of Loseby,* New York, Popular Library, 1974.

Short Stories

The Maze: A Story to Be Read Aloud. London, The Fleuron, 1928.
Some World Far from Ours; and Stay, Corydon, Thou Swain. London, Mathews and Marrot, 1929.
Elinor Barley. London, Cresset Press, and Chicago, Argus, 1930.
A Moral Ending and Other Stories. London, Joiner and Steele, 1931.
The Salutation. London, Chatto and Windus, and New York, Viking Press, 1932.
More Joy in Heaven and Other Stories. London, Cresset Press, 1935.
24 Short Stories, with Graham Greene and James Laver. London, Cresset Press, 1939.
A Garland of Straw and Other Stories. London, Chatto and Windus, and New York, Viking Press, 1943.
Winter in the Air and Other Stories. London, Chatto and Windus, 1955; New York, Viking Press, 1956.
A Spirit Rises. London, Chatto and Windus, and New York, Viking Press, 1962.
A Stranger with a Bag and Other Stories. London, Chatto and Windus, 1966; as *Swans on an Autumn River,* New York, Viking Press, 1966.
The Innocent and the Guilty. London, Chatto and Windus, and New York, Viking Press, 1971.
Scenes of Childhood. London, Chatto and Windus, 1981; New York, Viking Press, 1982.
One Thing Leading to Another and Other Stories, edited by Susanna Pinney. London, Chatto and Windus, and New York, Viking, 1984.
Selected Stories, edited by Susanna Pinney and William Maxwell. London, Chatto and Windus, 1988.

Poetry

The Espalier. London, Chatto and Windus, and New York, Dial Press, 1925.
Time Importuned. London, Chatto and Windus, and New York, Viking Press, 1928.
Opus 7: A Poem. London, Chatto and Windus, and New York, Viking Press, 1931.
Rainbow. New York, Knopf, 1932.
Whether a Dove or a Seagull, with Valentine Ackland. New York, Viking Press, 1933; London, Chatto and Windus, 1934.
Two Poems. Privately printed, 1945.
Twenty-eight Poems, with Valentine Ackland. Privately printed, 1957.
Boxwood: Sixteen Engravings by Reynolds Stone Illustrated in Verse. Privately printed, 1957; revised edition, as *Boxwood: Twenty-one Engravings,* London, Chatto and Windus-Cape, 1960.
King Duffus and Other Poems. Privately printed, 1968.

Azrael and Other Poems. Privately printed, 1978; as *Twelve Poems,* London, Chatto and Windus, 1980.

Collected Poems, edited by Claire Harman. Manchester, Carcanet, and New York, Viking Press, 1982.

Selected Poems. Manchester, Carcanet, and New York, Viking, 1985.

Other

Somerset. London, Elek, 1949.

Jane Austen 1775-1817. London, Longman, 1951; revised edition, 1957.

Sketches from Nature (reminiscences). Privately printed, 1963.

T. H. White: A Biography. London, Cape-Chatto and Windus, 1967; New York, Viking Press, 1968.

Letters, edited by William Maxwell. London, Chatto and Windus, 1982; New York, Viking Press, 1983.

The Diaries of Sylvia Townsend Warner, edited by Claire Harman. London, Chatto and Windus, 1994.

Editor, *The Week-end Dickens.* London, Maclehose, 1932; New York, Loring and Mussey, c.1932.

Editor, *The Portrait of a Tortoise: Extracted from the Journals and Letters of Gilbert White.* London, Chatto and Windus, 1946.

Translator, *By Way of Saint-Beuve,* by Marcel Proust. London, Chatto and Windus, 1958; as *On Art and Literature 1896-1917,* New York, Meridian, 1958.

Translator, *A Place of Shipwreck,* by Jean Rene Huguenin. London, Chatto and Windus, 1963.

Published Music: *Alleluia: Anthem for Five Voices,* London, Oxford University Press, 1925.

*

Critical Studies: *This Narrow Place: Sylvia Townsend Warner and Valentine Ackland: Life, Letters and Politics 1930-1951* by Wendy Mulford, London, Pandora Press, 1988; *Sylvia Townsend Warner: A Biography* by Claire Harman, London, Chatto and Windus, 1989.

*   *   *

Primarily a mainstream writer, best known for delicately ironic short stories published in *The New Yorker,* and for such novels as *The Corner That Held Them* (about life in a medieval nunnery), Warner ventured into fantasy occasionally, and made significant contributions early in her career and again at the end. Her successful first novel, *Lolly Willowes, or, The Loving Huntsman,* is a wryly ironic account of a country spinster who revolts against traditional women's roles and achieves fulfilment as a witch. The Loving Huntsman of the title is the Devil, with whom the heroine has charming intellectual conversations. Satan, not too surprisingly, isn't really wicked, merely the victim of bad press, and offers individual freedom. This book—one of the few ever to explore why a woman becomes a witch—has since been rediscovered by feminist critics.

The Kingdoms of Elfin collects stories written in the classical, polished *New Yorker* manner, but dissecting the social mores of Elfland, with much of the inside information drawn from the 17th-century Scottish clergyman Robert Kirk's "non-fiction" treatise, *The Secret Commonwealth.* (Kirk, but for an inopportune abduction while wandering among fairy hills, could have become the Whitley

Strieber of his day. He turns up in one of the Elfin stories.) Warner's vignettes of irony, cruelty and sometimes strange beauty, are sometimes too condensed for full impact, but offer numerous memorable flashes: the many-centuried queen of Elfhame on her deathbed, remembering her love for Thomas the Rhymer; Welsh fairies with a talent for (literally) moving mountains having a harder time getting rid of a pesky lady bicyclist, the vicious coincidence of a changeling (turned vivisectionist) performing a fatal experiment on a tramp who was the very human child for whom the fairies once substituted the changeling. Warner's Elfin stories are deliberately artificial, and often self-mocking, but they have sharp edges. They reveal new complexities upon rereading. An uncollected Elfin episode, "The Duke of Orkney's Leonardo," appeared in *The New Yorker* after the book came out and has been collected in Windling and Arnold's anthology *Elsewhere III* (1984).

Warner's importance as a fantasist rests almost entirely on *Lolly Willowes* and *The Kingdoms of Elfin,* but other volumes are of at least secondary interest: *The Cat's Cradle Book* consists of fairy tales and beast-fables handed down through generations of cats, and told with Warner's characteristic wit and stylistic economy; and *The Museum of Cheats,* another collection, touches on the fantastic. Her *T. H. White* is the standard biography of that great fantasy author. Warner was also a poet of note, not particularly in any fantastic vein, but it is intriguing to note that her *Opus 7* is dedicated to Arthur Machen.

—Darrell Schweitzer

WARRINGTON, Freda

Nationality: British. **Born:** Leicester, 22 June 1956. **Education:** Loughborough High School, 1963-73; Loughborough College of Art and Design, 1973-76, diploma in graphic design. **Career:** Medical artist, Leicester Royal Infirmary, 1977-80; graphic designer, Author Graphics and Hunting Gate Ltd, Hitchin, Hertfordshire, 1980-84; freelance graphic designer and writer, Leicester, 1984-89; freelance novelist from 1989. **Agent:** John R. Parker, MBA Literary Agents Ltd, 45 Fitzroy Street, London W1P 5HR. **Address:** Blackbird Cottage, 49 Station Street, Castle Gresley, Swadlincote, Derbyshire DE11 9JU, England.

FANTASY PUBLICATIONS

Novels (series: Blackbird; Blood)

A Blackbird in Silver. London, New English Library, 1986.

A Blackbird in Darkness. London, New English Library, 1986.

A Blackbird in Amber. London, New English Library, 1987.

A Blackbird in Twilight. London, New English Library, 1988.

The Rainbow Gate. London, New English Library, 1989.

Darker Than the Storm. London, New English Library, 1992.

A Taste of Blood Wine. London, Pan, 1992.

Sorrow's Light. London, Pan, 1993.

A Dance in Blood Velvet. London, Pan, 1994.

*

Freda Warrington comments:

I was brought up in the beautiful Charnwood area of Leicestershire, which helped to inspire me to write. I've been writing since the age of five, and I try to write the sort of fantasy I would like to read: colourful, vivid, weird and wonderful, but with strong characters, the plot evolving as much from the interaction of the protagonists as from outside circumstances. The battles between good and evil are not simplistic but ambiguous and complex. The effect is (I hope) not just entertaining but emotionally involving. *A Blackbird in Silver* and its sequel *A Blackbird in Darkness* arose from a basic premise: if your world was in peril, to what lengths would you go to save it? How do the main characters react to the impossible situation in which they've been placed? This theme continues in the second pair, *A Blackbird in Amber* and *A Blackbird in Twilight* (and in the connected novel *Darker Than the Storm*). The adversaries are prepared to do anything to achieve their opposing ambitions, while the innocent people caught in their wake are powerless to warn or stop them. *The Rainbow Gate* sees a change of style, being set in the present: when the heroine's mysterious friend re-enters her life, she's drawn into another world and discovers unwelcome truths about life, death and reincarnation. *Sorrow's Light* is also a voyage of discovery, though a very different one: the heroine struggles to find a cure for her husband's madness, and discovers a whole lost history in the process.

I'm currently working on the vampire series begun with *A Taste of Blood Wine* and continuing with *A Dance in Blood Velvet*. From a lifelong fascination with vampires as figures of mystery and romance, I've tried to create a gothic romance with vampire (and human) characters of depth and complexity. The third book is in progress and will be called *The Dark Blood of Poppies,* and I'm planning a fourth.

* * *

Freda Warrington began her career as a professional author with the Blackbird sequence of fantasy novels, comprising *A Blackbird in Silver, A Blackbird in Darkness, A Blackbird in Amber* and *A Blackbird in Twilight.*

The first book Warrington actually completed, following a number of false starts, *A Blackbird in Silver* was written while she was at college between 1973 and 1976. It was intended as a stand-alone novel, but underwent a number of re-writes and had become the opener of a series by the time it was published a decade later. Arguably, the plots of the four Blackbird titles, while perfectly decent and well-structured, are their most stock element. The extended narrative of high sorcery and quest adventure is more notable for its competence of expression, sound characterization and zestful pace. It also unveiled a preoccupation with several themes—the blurred borderline between good and evil; guilt; acceptance of personal responsibilities; the power of religion—that have remained central to her work.

The fantasy in which (as this is written) these concerns have come together most coherently, and best demonstrates her growing confidence as a writer, is *Sorrow's Light.* It begins with Princess Antrid and her entourage on their way to the city of Torbyrgi, where she is to join its ruler, Prince Tykavn, for an arranged marriage. Crossing a barren waste called the Stolen Land, the princess is killed by its demonic inhabitants, the Unseen. We then meet the novel's 16 year-old narrator, Iolithie, a minor member of the royal dynasty who has arrived in Torbyrgi for the doomed wedding. In common with all the humans of this world, Iolithie is a follower of Ama, a deity associated with the sun, light and goodness. The hellish Unseen, who are steadily usurping Humanity and pushing it into isolated enclaves, worship Sudema, god of the moon, darkness and evil.

Tykavn chooses Iolithie as his replacement bride. Any reservations she has are tempered by knowing that marriage in this culture lasts only until any resulting children reach majority, after which the parents become "Perfects," assuming celibacy and totally dedicating themselves to Ama. But the Prince turns out to be religiously devout to the point where it's a debilitating obsession. Nevertheless, she falls in love with him, despite his neglect and occasional outbursts of violence. Eventually she decides to appeal to Tykavn's father, the King, for help. However, to reach his realm she has to cross the Stolen Land.

Sorrow's Light presents a strongly realized, internally consistent setting and a cast of real substance. There is an interesting cultural, religious and political set-up at work in this world and characters that look at home in it. On the theological level, the Prince's obsessive-compulsive disorder acts as a vehicle for Warrington's belief that organized religion, at least in its fundamentalist form, can foster destructive intolerance. This ties in with the part religion has played in promoting the notion of women's inferiority, as personified by Iolithie's feeling of powerlessness in the face of her man's instability (he is head of both State and Church). A subtext is the dichotomy, lifted from Christian doctrine and tailored to suit Warrington's fictional world, that women are to be likened to either Eve or Lilith. The former is what patriarchal religion expects women to be—submissive, "good," her husband's helper and the mother of his children; the latter represents everything they shouldn't be—disobedient, "bad" and anarchic. In this, and her other fictions, Warrington attempts to question such assumptions. The Lilith "persona" is not evil. It just *is.*

Also of note is the author's dark fantasy trilogy comprising (at this point) *A Taste of Blood Wine* and *A Dance in Blood Velvet,* both because she sees no real distinction between them and her pure fantasies—asserting they exist on the same imaginative scale—and because they employ many of the same themes and elements. The Blood sequence, essentially gothic romances, are superior vampire tales that draw heavily on her characterization skills. Warrington's vampires are complex creatures, far from the black-hearted villains of tradition, and many of them are riven by guilt over the dilemma of having to kill in order to live. At the same time, those opposed to the vampires aren't necessarily driven by entirely honest motives, which relates to the idea of misguided idealism as explored in *Sorrow's Light.* Characters fixated on false ideas figure large in this author's universe.

A writer of increasingly mature assurance, Freda Warrington conveys her philosophies without sacrificing foreground entertainment values in the process.

—Stan Nicholls

WATT-EVANS, Lawrence

Nationality: American. **Born:** Arlington, Massachusetts, 26 July 1954. **Education:** Bedford High School, Massachusetts, 1968-72; Princeton University, 1972-77 (no degree). **Family:** Married Julie F. McKenna in 1977; one son, one daughter. **Career:** Various jobs, including sacker, labourer, counterman-cook and bottlewasher; freelance writer from 1977. **Awards:** Hugo Award for short story, 1988. **Agent:** Russell Galen, Scovil-Chichak-Galen Literary Agency, 381 Park Avenue South, New York, NY 10016, USA. **Address:** 5 Solitaire Court, Gaithersburg, MD 20878, USA.

FANTASY PUBLICATIONS

Novels (series: Legend of Ethshar; Lords of Dus; Three Worlds)

The Lure of the Basilisk (Dus). New York, Del Rey, 1980; London, Grafton, 1987.
The Seven Altars of Dusarra (Dus). New York, Del Rey, 1981; London, Grafton, 1987.
The Sword of Bheleu (Dus). New York, Del Rey, 1983; London, Grafton, 1987.
The Book of Silence (Dus). New York, Del Rey, 1984; London, Grafton, 1987.
The Misenchanted Sword (Ethshar). New York, Del Rey, 1985; London, Grafton, 1988.
With a Single Spell (Ethshar). New York, Del Rey, 1987; London, Grafton, 1988.
The Unwilling Warlord (Ethshar). New York, Del Rey, 1989; London, Grafton, 1991.
The Blood of a Dragon (Ethshar). New York, Del Rey, 1991.
The Rebirth of Wonder. Newark, New Jersey, Wildside Press, 1992.
Taking Flight (Ethshar). New York, Del Rey, 1993.
The Spell of the Black Dagger (Ethshar). New York, Del Rey, 1993.
Split Heirs, with Esther Friesner. New York, Tor, 1993.
Out of This World (Three Worlds). New York, Del Rey, 1994.
In the Empire of Shadow (Three Worlds). New York, Del Rey, 1995.

Short Stories

Crosstime Traffic. New York, Del Rey, 1992.

OTHER PUBLICATIONS

Novels

The Cyborg and the Sorcerers. New York, Del Rey, 1982; London, Grafton, 1990.
The Chromosomal Code. New York, Avon, 1984.
Shining Steel. New York, Avon, 1986.
Denner's Wreck. New York, Avon, 1988.
Nightside City. New York, Del Rey, 1989.
The Nightmare People. New York, Onyx, 1990.

Other

Editor, *Newer York: Stories of Science Fiction and Fantasy About the World's Greatest City.* New York, Roc, 1991.

*

Lawrence Watt-Evans comments:

Like most writers, I write the stuff I want to read. Where fantasy is concerned, that means stories of ordinary people in extraor-

dinary situations; the traditional high-born hero on a grand quest bores me silly. Beyond that, I should probably just quote Watt-Evans's Laws of Fantasy, from an article I wrote for *Starlog*:

First law: stories are about *people*. Second law: real people are never wholly good or wholly evil, and therefore characters shouldn't be wholly good or wholly evil. Third law: the basic human motivations are universal. Fourth law: everything other than the basic human motivations will vary, depending on cultural setting. Fifth law: magic, like everything else, has rules. Sixth law: if a story can be written without a fantasy element, don't bother making it fantasy. I try to abide by those, and to have fun doing it.

*　　*　　*

Lawrence Watt-Evans has written several notable science-fiction novels and one exceptional horror novel, but he is best known for his fantasy, primarily the Lords of Dus series and his more recent and far better Ethshar stories. The Lords of Dus sequence opened with his earliest fantasy novel, *The Lure of the Basilisk,* and continued through a total of four volumes.

The protagonist of the Dus series is Garth, an overman, stronger than normal humans, part of a race of supermen created by human sorcery some time in the murky past. Although a prince of his own people, Garth is determined to ensure that his name becomes immortal, so he travels to Skelleth, a dying city, and meets the Forgotten King, an apparent beggar who promises that Garth's name will become immortal if he accomplishes a number of tasks.

What ensues is a variation of the Labours of Hercules. In the first book Garth travels to an abandoned city and captures a gigantic basilisk whose very gaze turns men to stone, employing a clever device the consequences of which are the heart of an amusing adventure tale. He is compelled to steal seven sacred items from seven temples in *The Seven Altars of Dusarra,* a magical sword in *The Sword of Bheleu,* and retrieves an arcane book of magic in *The Book of Silence.* Although superficially similar to many another fantasy adventure, the series is enlivened by the author's inventiveness and cleverly contrived plots. The series has remained popular even though the setting has been abandoned in favour of the Ethshar series.

In 1985, Watt-Evans gave up Dus and created Ethshar in *The Misenchanted Sword.* Ethshar is a kingdom locked in a war with the Northern Empire that has gone on so long no one can envision what life would be if it ended. And end it does, when the Northerners resort to demonic intervention and the Gods themselves intercede on the side of Ethshar. The enormous army is no longer necessary and even more unsettling is the revelation that the government of Ethshar has long since vanished, that the army has been holding things together for ages, and that the old seat of government is now broken up into dozens of tiny, squabbling states.

The first three Ethshar novels all involve an innocent who finds himself forced into a role of prominence. In the first, a self-deprecating scout stumbles across a hermit wizard who provides him with an enchanted sword. It will keep Valder alive against all enemies, but there's a catch. Each time it is drawn, it must take the life of a human male; until it has done so, Valder can neither set it down or sheathe it. And on the hundredth drawing, it will kill Valder himself. He becomes an involuntary hero, slaying countless enemies as a soldier and later as an assassin, before finding a way to reach a compromise with his fate and avoid the death promised him.

This pattern is followed in *With a Single Spell* and *The Unwilling Warlord*. In the first case, an apprenticed wizard finds himself pitted against a dragon with a single bit of magic, the ability to start fires. Before long he is involved with a flying castle that has crashed in a remote mountainous area and a tapestry which transports him to a tiny universe inhabited by a witch and her ghostly companions. The third novel follows the career of an itinerant gambler who discovers he is the heir to the post of Warlord of the diminutive kingdom of Semma, which is about to be overwhelmed by two much larger armies, and whose own army isn't fit to take to the field. Sterren would prefer to decline the honour, but the Semmans are determined to execute him for treason if he fails to serve. Not surprisingly, he saves the day by enlisting a Warlock and some other magical talents, but to his dismay the Warlock decides to establish a new empire, with himself as the head of state. As with the Dus books, the plots consist of familiar genre devices, but once again their appeal is in the way they are portrayed. The flying castle, the battle to save Semma, and other scenes are all vividly depicted, and the self-deprecating protagonists are all appealingly likable.

The next set of three Ethshar novels changed direction slightly. Although the main characters still find themselves propelled into roles they didn't expect, they are no longer totally innocent. Dumery of *The Blood of a Dragon* is a frustrated young man who discovers he has no magical abilities whatsoever, and sets out to kill a dragon in order to make his fortune selling its blood. Killing a dragon isn't quite as easy as he expected; in fact, even finding one presents certain difficulties.

Taking Flight uses a similar device. Kelder is a farmer who sets out on the road to see the world, and falls in with Irith, a winged girl who accompanies him on his journey. But there's something mysterious about Irith, the most interesting character in any of the Ethshar novels. They continually meet people who seem to know her, even though she is clearly too young to have travelled widely. And her attitude toward Kelder is perplexing at times, as though in anticipation of some unpleasantness to come. This is in many ways the best of the series, which handles even its action sequences in a restrained, quiet fashion, and which pays the most attention to its characters as people.

Tabaea the Thief is the focus of *The Spell of the Black Dagger*. She attempts to mimic a magic spell but, rather than acquire a simple magic dagger, she has created an enchanted object which will take possession of her personality and propel her to greatness. But there's a dark side to the magic, and an equally tragic fall is waiting for her first mis-step. The mood is darker here than in the previous works, even though horrible events take place in all of them. Perhaps to balance this mood, Watt-Evans' other recent fantasies are decidedly lighthearted.

Split Heirs, written in collaboration with Esther Friesner, is a marvellous send-up of a number of fantasy themes—the switched twins, the prince deprived of his throne. It features a cow turned into a dragon, the strangest sex-education training you ever read, and in general is designed to raise a smile on the dourest of faces. A sequel is planned. *Out of This World* is also the opening volume of a series, and one of the strangest things the author has attempted. The ultimate war between good and evil is being fought across several universes, our own, an intergalactic civilization out of early space opera, and a traditional fantasy world. Rebels from the last invade the other worlds in order to recruit help in their battle. It's an odd mix that works most of the time, although the constant switching of moods is rather disconcerting.

Watt-Evans has also written several shorter fantasy stories of note, the best of which are "The Frog Wizard," "Unicornutopia," "Visions," and "Portrait of a Hero."

—Don D'Ammassa

WEBBER, Collin

Nationality: British. **Address:** c/o Gollancz, Cassell Group, Wellington House, 125 Strand, London WC2R 0BB, England.

FANTASY PUBLICATIONS

Novels

Merlin and the Last Trump. London, Gollancz, 1993.
Ribwash. London, Gollancz, 1994.

*   *   *

Collin Webber's first novel, *Merlin and the Last Trump,* is a rather odd hybrid: its basic idea is that of C. S. Lewis's *That Hideous Strength,* and although the style and treatment are much more reminiscent of Terry Pratchett, the fundamental seriousness of the theme keeps showing through.

The magician Merlin, having foreseen a terrible doom poised to overwhelm a future universe, uses a dangerous magic to place himself in suspended animation until the late 20th century, there to seek out the one man whose innate gifts may be harnessed to stave it off. To supply muscle (and by speedier means) he also brings forward Sir Griswold des Arbres, greatest of Arthur's knights and the man who had done for Sir Lancelot, but whose name was subsequently (for reasons not immediately apparent) expunged from history.

As in *That Hideous Strength,* Merlin must contend not only with the malevolence of the opposition and his own frailty but with the human weaknesses of his allies; and as in the Lewis novel, the principal 20th-century viewpoint is a nerd. It is here that the approaches diverge most dramatically, for unlike the smug Mark Shaddock, James Dimmot is a computer-nerd and an enthusiast for trad jazz, now entering middle age, who perceives his own life as a wretched sequence of failures. In the act of throwing himself off a bridge he is rescued by Griswold, who has been jerked there from the midst of a passage of love with the nymphomaniac Queen Guinevere. Dimmot therefore finds himself lugged through the chilly waters of the wintry Thames by what he takes for a huge hairy demon with a monstrous erection.

It's a good way of introducing the characters to each other, and a good introduction to one aspect of the humour of the book, which is earthy and at times crude but (unlike much humorous fantasy) based on a surer foundation than the mere assertion that the physical passions, together with the physical appendages that serve them, do actually exist. On a slightly higher plane we have the mutual incomprehension of Griswold and Dimmot, as they attempt to accommodate each other to their irreconcilable intellectual universes, a task made harder rather than easier as they find in each other qualities to value.

On another level still we have the viewpoint of Merlin, which he needs to impress upon Dimmot and does so in terms which

Lewis would have found entirely familiar: "Even now the fight for supreme control over the Mind of Man has begun, and that Mind is the goal, the prize . . . and the battleground." The combination of broad and bawdy farce with an elevated metaphysic and serious characterization grates less often than one might have expected, mainly because Webber generally avoids the bad comics' standby of afflicting his characters with stupidity; bemused by concepts alien to their upbringing, abashed by responsibilities beyond their wildest anxiety-dreams, and scared rigid by the most direct of threats, they display a dogged kind of heroism as they set out to do battle with principalities and powers. To balance it, in the epilogue they also display a human perversity calculated to remind Merlin that some impulses are beyond even his manipulation. It rounds out a rough-hewn and unpretentious but often ingenious little romp and provides the opening for its sequel, *Ribwash*.

Once again Merlin sees fearful evil threatening the future of mankind, and once again he needs Griswold and Dimmot to help avert it, but as a side effect of his attempts to get the universe back on course both have lost their memories of how they helped to save it last time, which would be more confusing all round if Webber didn't get them restored pretty quick. As before, the plotting is fairly chaotic and made more so because thanks to time-travel the participants are anything from two days to 300 years older since the end of the last book, and a fair proportion of the most physically active are ghosts. In the circumstances, why should anyone worry about getting killed? On this occasion Hell is due to break loose (literally) in A.D. 4097, but the interested parties massing there (under Archeous, sometime banker, now Lucifer's deputy and designated heir) and Gnomedon (planet of the Gnomes, where the evil magician Grandeane is brewing the traditional four flavors of nastiness) are really no closer to the center of things than Merlin and Griswold (from A.D. 570) and Dimmot (from 1994). Apart from Grandeane, only Merlin has a complete vision of what's going on, which is no less than an assertion of the Manichaean Heresy; Grandeane plans to control the Four Horsemen for creative purposes.

This is no small theme, but its underlying seriousness is less prone to surface and torpedo all the slapstick and bawdry than was the case in the previous book; much of the very considerable violence (including the destruction of all Four) is on a par with Bugs Bunny. It makes for a mixture which many will find uneasy or distasteful; others will feel that this seam has already been worked sufficiently in *Good Omens* by Terry Pratchett and Neil Gaiman and in Robert Rankin's Armageddon books; yet others who find charm in the tension between manner and matter will find unfunny Webber's habitual misuse of the second person singular.

Despite these caveats, the books have a certain crude vigor and sufficient coherence to offer an undemanding read. It is also reasonable to expect at least one more in the series, as *Ribwash* ends very abruptly, in a cloud of loose ends. How Webber will conclude the series—short of Armageddon, which Robert Rankin has already played for laughs—is another question.

—Chris Gilmore

WEIS, Margaret (Edith)

Pseudonyms: Margaret Baldwin; Susan Lawson. **Nationality:** American. **Born:** Independence, Missouri, 16 March 1948. **Education:** University of Missouri, Columbia, B.A. in creative writing and literature 1970. **Family:** Married Mr. Baldwin (divorced); one son, one daughter. **Career:** Advertising director, Herald Publishing House, Independence, Missouri, 1972-83, and division director, Independence Press, 1981-83; editor, TSR Inc., Lake Geneva, Wisconsin, 1983-86; freelance author from 1986. **Agent:** Lazear Agency, Inc., 430 First Avenue North, Suite 416, Minneapolis, MN 55401, USA.

FANTASY PUBLICATIONS

Novels with Tracy Hickman (series: Darksword; Death Gate Cycle; DragonLance Chronicles; DragonLance Legends; Rose of the Prophet)

Dragons of Autumn Twilight (DragonLance Chronicles). Lake Geneva, Wisconsin, TSR, 1984; London, Penguin, 1986.
Dragons of Winter Night (DragonLance Chronicles). Lake Geneva, Wisconsin, TSR, 1985; London, Penguin, 1986.
Dragons of Spring Dawning (DragonLance Chronicles). Lake Geneva, Wisconsin, TSR, 1985; London, Penguin, 1986.
Time of the Twins (DragonLance Legends). Lake Geneva, Wisconsin, TSR, 1986; London, Penguin, 1987.
War of the Twins (DragonLance Legends). Lake Geneva, Wisconsin, TSR, 1986; London, Penguin, 1987.
Test of the Twins (DragonLance Legends). Lake Geneva, Wisconsin, TSR, 1986; London, Penguin, 1987.
Forging the Darksword. New York and London, Bantam, 1988.
Doom of the Darksword. New York, Bantam, 1988; London, Bantam, 1989.
DragonLance Chronicles (omnibus; includes *Dragons of Autumn Twilight, Dragons of Winter Night, Dragons of Spring Dawning*). Lake Geneva, Wisconsin, TSR, and London, Penguin, 1988.
DragonLance Legends (omnibus; includes *Time of the Twins, War of the Twins, Test of the Twins*). Lake Geneva, Wisconsin, TSR, 1988; London, Penguin, 1989.
Triumph of the Darksword. New York, Bantam, 1988; London, Bantam, 1989.
The Will of the Wanderer (Rose of the Prophet). New York, Bantam, 1989; London, Bantam, 1990.
The Paladin of the Night (Rose of the Prophet). New York, Bantam, 1989; London, Bantam, 1990.
The Prophet of Akhran (Rose of the Prophet). New York, Bantam, 1989; London, Bantam, 1990.
Dragon Wing (Death Gate). New York, Bantam, and London, Bantam Press, 1990.
Elven Star (Death Gate). New York, Bantam, 1990; London, Bantam Press, 1991.
Fire Sea (Death Gate). New York, Bantam, and London, Bantam Press, 1991.
Serpent Mage (Death Gate). New York, Bantam, and London, Bantam Press, 1992.
The Hand of Chaos (Death Gate). New York, Bantam, and London, Bantam Press, 1993.
Into the Labyrinth (Death Gate). New York, Bantam, 1993; London, Bantam Press, 1994.
The Seventh Gate (Death Gate). New York, Bantam, and London, Bantam Press, 1994.

Novels without Tracy Hickman

Endless Catacombs (as Margaret Baldwin Weis). Lake Geneva, Wisconsin, TSR, 1984.
The Tower of Midnight Dreams. Lake Geneva, Wisconsin, TSR, 198?.
Riddle of the Griffin (as Susan Lawson, with Roger E. Moore). Lake Geneva, Wisconsin, TSR, 1985.

Short Stories with Tracy Hickman

DragonLance Adventures. Lake Geneva, Wisconsin, 1987.
Darksword Adventures. New York, Bantam, 1988; London, Bantam, 1989.
DragonLance: The Second Generation. Lake Geneva, Wisconsin, TSR, 1994.

Other with Tracy Hickman

Editors, *The Magic of Krynn.* Lake Geneva, Wisconsin, 1987; London, Penguin, 1988.
Editors, *Kender, Gully Dwarves, and Gnomes.* Lake Geneva, Wisconsin, 1987; London, Penguin, 1988.
Editors, *Love and War.* Lake Geneva, Wisconsin, 1987; London, Penguin, 1988.
Editors, *DragonLance Tales* (omnibus; includes *The Magic of Krynn, Kender, Gully Dwarves, and Gnomes* and *Love and War*). London, Penguin, 1991.
Editors, *The Reign of Istar.* Lake Geneva, Wisconsin, TSR, 1992.
Editors, *The Cataclysm.* Lake Geneva, Wisconsin, TSR, 1992.
Editors, *The War of the Lance.* Lake Geneva, Wisconsin, TSR, 1992.
Editors, *The Dragons of Krynn.* Lake Geneva, Wisconsin, TSR, 1994.
Editor, *A Dragon Lover's Treasury of the Fantastic.* New York, Warner, 1994.

OTHER PUBLICATIONS

Novels

The Lost King. New York, Bantam, 1990; London, Bantam, 1991.
King's Test. New York and London, Bantam, 1991.
King's Sacrifice. New York, Bantam, 1991; London, Bantam, 1992.
Ghost Legion. New York, Bantam, 1993.
The Knights of the Black Earth, with Don Perrin. New York, Roc, and London, Gollancz, 1995.

Other (as Margaret Baldwin)

Wanted: Frank and Jesse James, the Real Story. New York, Simon and Schuster, 1981.
The Boys Who Saved the Children. New York, Simon and Schuster, 1981.
Kisses of Death. New York, Simon and Schuster, 1983.
Thanksgiving. New York, Franklin Watts, 1983.
Computer Graphics, with Gary Pack. New York, Franklin Watts, 1984.
Robots and Robotics, with Gary Pack. New York, Franklin Watts, 1984.

Fortune Telling. New York, Simon and Schuster, 1984.
Lost Childhood, with Janet Pack. New York, Simon and Schuster, 198?.
The Art of Dungeons & Dragons (as Margaret Baldwin Weis). Lake Geneva, Wisconsin, TSR, 1985.
Leaves from the Inn of the Last Home: The Complete Krynn Source Book (as Margaret Weis, with Tracy Hickman and Mary L. Kirchoff). Lake Geneva, Wisconsin, TSR, 1987.

*

Critical Studies: *The Atlas of the DragonLance World* by Karen Wynn Fonstad, Lake Geneva, Wisconsin, TSR, 1987; London, Penguin, 1988.

*   *   *

Most of Margaret Weis's novels have been written in collaboration with role-playing games-designer Tracy Hickman (born 1955). She is said to be the principal writer, Hickman's task being to provide plot ideas and those elements of background continuity which will most appeal to game-players. Their partnership has proved to be a commercial success, with their titles regularly entering the bestseller lists. All of their books are sword and sorcery, and most are conceived as trilogies which fit together as a continuous narrative (although it is possible to pick up many of the threads in the final volumes, to make an understandable story). The exception is the Death Gate series, which not only runs to seven volumes but must be pursued from the beginning if any sense is to be made of the events.

The first two Weis-and-Hickman trilogies have their genesis in Hickman's DragonLance role-playing games for the TSR company. The fantasy world in which they are set had therefore been extensively designed geographically, historically, and culturally, prior to chapter one of the first book, *Dragons of Autumn Twilight*. The principal characters meet, as they have arranged five years previously, in an inn in the tree-top township of Solace. Although coming from various races, they have roots here and form a cross-section of the population of this world—half-elf, kender (hobbit-like kleptomaniacs), knight, dwarf, warrior, and wizard. Evil has been awakened, and the draconian (vicious, scaly biped) hordes are marching south, destroying everything in their path. Along with the barmaid and two plains-people, our heroes embark on a series of adventures which ultimately lead to the defeat of the dark forces, but not until two volumes later.

The second trilogy, the DragonLance Legends, involves the survivors from the first trilogy and is set two years later. This time, some of the characters are sent back in time to a period just prior to the Cataclysm, a God-given catastrophe which changed the shape of the world, literally and figuratively. The set of books begins awkwardly, with information being repeated—a problem that can afflict any collaborative work—but also with a lot unsaid. The problem of setting the tale in such a highly designed setting is what do you leave out? In general, there are too many characters, and as a result there is little depth to them. In many respects they are stereotypes of the kind expected in books of this genre. There is, however, plenty of action, even if the writing is uneven. Some of the events are described in great detail and seem almost to be padding, as if the authors were worried about having enough material to fill the volumes (particularly noticeable in *Time of the Twins*), but in other places adventures are dismissed in a few lines although they subsequently prove important elements in the plot. Other, intriguing elements are introduced and then seem to get lost within the morass of characters and events. The DragonLance series has also spawned a series of "shared-world" anthologies edited by Weis and Hickman which include the occasional story written by Weis.

The Darksword Trilogy has an interesting premise. Everyone is born with magic—called Life. This can be enhanced by catalysts who channel the earth's magic into the people. Someone born without magic is declared Dead, and normally such a child is left to truly die. Joram is such a child but he is brought up secretly and taught sleight-of-hand to cover up his inability to perform real magic. When his handicap is finally disclosed, he flees into the Outlands and joins with a group of Technologists. Technology is the ninth mystery and is banned from the rest of the world. Here he forges the Darksword which has the property of being able to nullify magic. The excellent idea is marred by the predictability of the plot. A prophecy has stated that a member of the Royal House will be born Dead, yet live. It doesn't take much guess-work to predict that Joram will turn out to be that baby. While the first two volumes stick to and develop the setting, the third changes direction. Joram has vanished from sight but when he returns he brings non-magical forces from our Earth including firearms, marines and aircraft. The pendant volume *Darksword Adventures,* although initially taking the appearance of a travel guide to Thimhallen, where all these events are set, is basically a set of specifications for role-playing scenarios.

The Rose of the Prophet trilogy also has interesting aspects. The world is ruled by 20 gods, each of which has their followers and each of which has different qualities. Some are good, some are evil, some hold the middle ground. At the time of the book, the god Quar has decided that he will be the one and only god. Therefore he must wipe out the followers of all the other gods, but the only way he can do this is by getting his adherents to declare a jihad on everyone else. Akhran, the Wandering god, and the god of the nomadic desert people, is determined that Quar will not succeed. The gods cannot interfere directly in events on earth but only through their immortals. Promenthas's immortals are angels who only have contact with the upper echelons of the church hierarchy—although Mathew has a guardian angel. Akhran's immortals are djinn who live in close proximity with Akhran's adherents, acting as servants. The setting is mainly an "Arabian desert" scenario. To counteract Quar's plans, Akhran has decreed that Khardan and Zorha will marry and that their tribes will remain camped in the vicinity of the hill on which grows the cactus known as the Rose of the Prophet until that plant blooms. Unfortunately, Khardan and Zorha hate each other, and even when the spring comes the plant does not flower. The romance is predictable. Eventually they will come to love each other, their tribes will be united against the threat of Quar's minions, and the cactus will bloom. On another level are the schemes of the djinn to help things along. Mathew, the sole survivor after a shipwreck, is thrown into the middle of the conflict to act as a catalyst to the events.

The Death Gate series is an attempt to get away from the more usual kind of fantasy novel. The world has been Sundered into four realms—earth, air, fire, and water—each being very different and highly improbable. The first four books set out to introduce the four parts of this universe which is populated by *mensch*—humans, dwarves, and elves—and Patryn, magic workers who derive their power from the sigla tattooed on their bodies. Not much is said about the Sartan, who sundered the realms and built the gates that connect them. By the time we reach *Into the Labyrinth,*

Xar, a Patryn, has mastered the Death Gate and intends to conquer all the worlds. The Labyrinth can be reached only through the Death Gate, and it is a prison in which the Patryns were imprisoned by the Sartan and from which all the inhabitants wish to escape. Xar is also looking for the Seventh Gate, the place from where the realms were sundered and, presumably, where they can be reassembled. The relationship between the many parts of this world is difficult to visualize, and it is hard, particularly in later volumes, to understand what is going on. There is no plot summary at the beginning of each succeeding volume, just footnotes referring to earlier volumes to help the reader through the morass.

In all these novels, good ideas have been swamped by poor, predictable plots and weak characterization. Also in common, each series has a character introduced for light relief but who ends up doing something heroic.

Weis has written a number of books on her own, often under pseudonyms and for children, but her Star of the Guardian series is space-opera science fiction. Hickman has not written any novels on his own but has designed other role-playing scenarios.

—Pauline Morgan

WELLMAN, Manly Wade

Pseudonym: Gans T. Field. **Nationality:** American. **Born:** Kamundongo, Angola, 21 May 1903; brother of the writer Paul I. Wellman. **Education:** prep school in Utah; Wichita State University, Kansas, A.B. 1926; Columbia University, New York, B. Litt. 1927. **Family:** Married Frances Obrist in 1930; one son. **Career:** Reporter and feature writer, Wichita *Beacon,* 1927-30, and *Eagle,* 1930-34; freelance writer from 1934; assistant project supervisor, Works Projects Administration Writers Project, New York, 1936-1938; instructor in creative writing, Elon College, North Carolina, 1962-1970, and University of North Carolina evening college, Chapel Hill, 1963-1973. **Awards:** Ellery Queen Award, 1946; Mystery Writers of America Edgar Award, 1955; American Association of Local Historians Award of Merit, 1973; World Fantasy Award, 1975; British Fantasy Award, 1984; World Fantasy Award for lifetime achievement, 1980. **Died:** 8 April 1986.

<small>FANTASY PUBLICATIONS</small>

Novels (series: John the Balladeer; John Thunstone)

Romance in Black (as Gans T. Field). London, Utopian, 1946.
The Beasts from Beyond. Manchester, World, 1950.
The Beyonders. New York, Warner, 1977.
The Old Gods Waken (John the Balladeer). New York, Doubleday, 1979.
After Dark (John the Balladeer). New York, Doubleday, 1980.
The Lost and the Lurking (John the Balladeer). New York, Doubleday, 1981.
The Hanging Stones (John the Balladeer). New York, Doubleday, 1982.
What Dreams May Come (John Thunstone). New York, Doubleday, 1983.
The Voice from the Mountain (John the Balladeer). New York, Doubleday, 1984.

The School of Darkness (John Thunstone). New York, Doubleday, 1985.

Cahena: A Dream of the Past. New York, Doubleday, 1986.

Short Stories

Who Fears the Devil? Sauk City, Wisconsin, Arkham House, 1963; expanded as *John the Balladeer,* New York, Baen, 1988.

Worse Things Waiting. Chapel Hill, North Carolina, Carcosa House, 1973.

Lonely Vigils (John Thunstone). Chapel Hill, North Carolina, Carcosa House, 1981.

Valley So Low: Southern Mountain Stories. New York, Doubleday, 1987.

OTHER PUBLICATIONS

Novels

The Invading Asteroid. New York, Stellar, 1932.

A Double Life (novelization of screenplay). Chicago, Century, 1947.

Find My Killer. New York, Farrar Straus, 1947; London, Sampson Low, 1948.

Sojarr of Titan. New York, Crestwood, 1949.

Devil's Planet. Manchester, World, 1951.

Fort Sun Dance. New York, Dell, and London, Corgi, 1955.

Twice in Time. New York, Avalon, 1957; restored edition, New York, Baen, 1988.

Giants from Eternity. New York, Avalon, 1959.

The Dark Destroyers. New York, Avalon, 1959.

Candle of the Wicked. New York, Putnam, 1960.

Island in the Sky. New York, Avalon, 1961.

The Solar Invasion. New York, Popular Library, 1968.

Sherlock Holmes's War of the Worlds, with Wade Wellman. New York, Warner, 1975.

Novels for Children

The Sleuth Patrol. New York, Nelson, 1947.

The Mystery of Lost Valley. New York, Nelson, 1948.

The Raiders of Beaver Lake. New York, Nelson, 1950.

The Haunts of Drowning Creek. New York, Holiday House, 1951.

Wild Dogs of Drowning Creek. New York, Holiday House, 1952.

The Last Mammoth. New York, Holiday House, 1953.

Gray Riders: Jeb Stuart and His Men. New York, Aladdin, 1954.

Rebel Mail Runner. New York, Holiday House, 1954.

Flag on the Levee. New York, Washburn, 1955.

To Unknown lands. New York, Holiday House, 1956.

Young Squire Morgan. New York, Washburn, 1956.

Lights Over Skeleton Ridge. New York, Washburn, 1957.

The Ghost Battalion. New York, Washburn, 1958.

Ride, Rebels! New York, Washburn, 1959.

Appomattox Road. New York, Washburn, 1960.

Third String Center. New York, Washburn, 1960.

Rifles at Ramsour's Mill. New York, Washburn, 1961.

Battle for King's Mountain. New York, Washburn, 1962.

Clash on the Catawba. New York, Washburn, 1962.

The River Pirates. New York, Washburn, 1963.

Settlement on Shocco. Winston-Salem, North Carolina, Blair, 1963.

The South Fork Rangers. New York, Washburn, 1963.

The Master of Scare Hollow. New York, Washburn, 1964.

The Great Riverboat Race. New York, Washburn, 1965.

Mystery at Bear Paw Gap. New York, Washburn, 1965.

Battle at Bear Paw Gap. New York, Washburn, 1966.

The Specter of Bear Paw Gap. New York, Washburn, 1966.

Jamestown Adventure. New York, Washburn, 1967.

Brave Horse: The Story of Janus. Williamsburg, Virginia, Colonial Williamsburg, 1968.

Carolina Pirate. New York, Washburn, 1968.

Frontier Reporter. New York, Washburn, 1969.

Mountain Feud. New York, Washburn, 1969.

Napoleon of the West: A Story of the Aaron Burr Conspiracy. New York, Washburn, 1970.

Fast Break Five. New York, Washburn, 1971.

Short Story

A True Story of the Revolting and Bloody Crimes of Sergeant Stanlas, U.S.A. Wichita, Kansas, Four Ducks Press, 1964.

Play

Many Are the Hearts. Raleigh, North Carolina Confederate Centennial Commission, 1961.

Other

Giant in Gray: A Biography of Wade Hampton of South Carolina. New York, Scribner, 1949.

Dead and Gone: Classic Crimes of North Carolina. Chapel Hill, University of North Carolina Press, 1954.

Rebel Boast: First at Bethel—Last at Appomattox. New York, Holt, 1956.

Fastest on the River. New York, Holt, 1957.

The Life and Times of Sir Archie, with Elizabeth Amis Blanchard. Chapel Hill, University of North Carolina Press, 1958.

The County of Warren, North Carolina, 1586-1917. Chapel Hill, University of North Carolina Press, 1959.

They Took Their Stand: The Founders of the Confederacy. New York, Putnam, 1959.

The Rebel Songster, with Frances Wellman. New York, Heritage House, 1959.

Harpers Ferry, Prize of War. Charlotte, North Carolina, McNally and Loftin, 1960.

The County of Gaston, with Robert F. Cope. Gastonia, North Carolina, Gaston County Historical Society, 1961.

The County of Moore, 1847-1947. Southern Pines, North Carolina, Moore County Historical Association, 1962.

Winston-Salem in History: The Founders. Winston-Salem, North Carolina, Blair, 1966.

The Kingdom of Madison: A Southern Mountain Fastness and Its People. Chapel Hill, University of North Carolina Press, 1973.

The Story of Moore County. Southern Pines, North Carolina, Moore County Historical Association, 1974.

*

Film Adaptation: *The Legend of Hillbilly John,* 1972, from his collection *Who Fears the Devil?*

*   *   *

Though born in what was then Portuguese West Africa of missionary parents, Wellman was culturally an American, who identified most strongly with the people of the Appalachian Mountains. Later in life he would stay for long periods in a cabin in the North Carolina hills visiting the local people, listening to stories, and learning folk songs. This identity and experience gave a special flavour to his best fiction. Wellman was the first important fantasist since Stephen Vincent Benét to make creative use of American folk materials.

By training, Wellman was a pulp writer, who began his career in *Weird Tales* in 1927, sold science fiction to Hugo Gernsback, and went on to supply many colourful action novels to *Startling Stories* from the late 1930s to the mid-40s. He even wrote a novel of Captain Future, the space-hero invented by Edmond Hamilton in a series of formulaic, juvenile adventures which seemed to typify pulp hack work but which filled a magazine of their own in the early 40s. (Wellman's Captain Future novel, however, appeared in *Startling Stories*.) His contributions to the "Golden Age" of *Astounding* were minimal. He apparently did not get along with editor John W. Campbell, Jr. He drifted away from science fiction in the later 40s, as science-fiction writing was apparently more of a way of making a living for Wellman than a genuine enthusiasm. He also wrote large numbers of comic-book scripts in the same decade.

Wellman remained a stalwart of *Weird Tales,* particularly noted in the 40s for his John Thunstone series which made such convincing use of both genuine and imagined supernatural lore that many readers assumed the demonic "Shonokins" (which Wellman had invented) were real, either as authentic folklore, or genuinely extant. This was, however, the era of the Shaver Mystery in *Amazing Stories*—an elaborate paranoid mythos evolving evil little men in caves with ray machines, presented as fact—so clearly many readers didn't have a strong sense of reality to begin with, and Wellman can hardly be faulted.

Wellman's pulp fiction is well above average in many cases, but not the stuff on which a lasting reputation is built, although one cannot deny that much of his *Weird Tales* fiction and such works as *Twice in Time* (originally in *Startling Stories,* 1940), a time-travel novel about a man who goes back to the Italian Renaissance and becomes Leonardo da Vinci, remain readable and entertaining today. The breakthrough came in the pages of *The Magazine of Fantasy and Science Fiction* in the 1950s, when Wellman began publishing the first stories of John the Balladeer, a wandering minstrel of the Southern mountains, who confronts and defeats assorted supernatural menaces, often with the aid of appropriate verses from rural ballads or even the silver in his guitar strings. The earliest ones are the best, collected in the Arkham House edition of *Who Fears the Devil?*. These are stories of exceptional charm, drawing on material not otherwise familiar to most fantasy readers.

The weakness of much of Wellman's supernatural fiction is a reliance on a single formula, rather like that of Seabury Quinn's Jules de Grandin series in *Weird Tales* or the *Kolchak: The Night Stalker* TV show. In every episode the hero encounters yet another ghostly menace. There is some development of its background, but only a minimal plot before the foregone conclusion. After a while it becomes implausible that say John should encounter so many spooks. At least some of Wellman's other series characters, particularly John Thunstone, make a career out of deliberately seeking out such menaces, but the heavies continue to be dealt with far too quickly and easily in most cases. The interest therefore lies in the author's use of folklore, the incidental regional details, and Wellman's ability to build and maintain atmosphere.

John the Balladeer and John Thunstone were revived in a series of capable, but never outstanding, novels published late in Wellman's career. The John the Balladeer series was somewhat weakened at this point by too many intrusions of the contemporary world. The superstition-soaked milieu of the characters is far more convincing if closed-off and somehow timeless.

Other individual stories stand out: "The Devil is Not Mocked" (in *Unknown,* 1940) is about Nazi occupiers of Rumania encountering Count Dracula. "The Valley Was Still" (*Weird Tales,* 1939) is a superb short story, the best of several Wellman wrote about the American Civil War from a Southern viewpoint. Both were dramatized on television, far more effectively than the travesty Hollywood made out of *Who Fears the Devil?* as *The Legend of Hillbilly John* (1972), a title and film which met with Wellman's strong disapproval.

Wellman's final fantasy, *Cahena: A Dream of the Past,* is unconnected to his other work; set in North Africa in historical times, it was not a success. Wellman was a much-loved figure in the fantasy scene, whose best pulp work was collected by his friend and admirer Karl Edward Wagner in the two Carcosa omnibus volumes. A fair evaluation of his work is that he always maintained a basic standard of decent story-telling and sometimes rose well above it. A small but discernible fraction of his work, particularly the stories in *Who Fears the Devil?*, has genuinely enriched the field, because of its unique subject matter and Wellman's heartfelt enthusiasm for it.

—Darrell Schweitzer

WELLS, Angus

Pseudonyms: William S. Brady; J. B. Dancer; Ian Evans; Charles C. Garrett; Matthew Kirk; Richard Kirk; James A. Muir; Charles R. Pike; J. D. Sandon. **Nationality:** British. **Born:** 29 March 1943. **Education:** Bromley Grammar School, Kent. **Career:** Advertising executive, Roles and Parker, Pearl Publications and Design, Harris and Hunter, and Hunter and Barney; publicity manager, then fiction editor, Sphere Books, London; freelance writer from 1975.

FANTASY PUBLICATIONS

Novels (series: The Books of the Kingdoms; The Godwars; Raven)

Raven: Swordsmistress of Chaos (as Richard Kirk). London, Corgi, 1978.
The Frozen God (as Richard Kirk; Raven). London, Corgi, 1978.
A Time of Dying (as Richard Kirk; Raven). London, Corgi, 1979.
Wrath of Ashar (Kingdoms). London, Sphere, 1988; New York, Bantam, 1990.
The Usurper (Kingdoms). London, Sphere, 1989; New York, Bantam, 1990.
The Way Beneath (Kingdoms). London, Orbit, 1990; New York, Bantam, 1991.
Forbidden Magic (Godwars). London, Orbit, 1991; New York, Bantam, 1992.
Dark Magic (Godwars). New York, Bantam, 1992
Wild Magic (Godwars). New York, Bantam, 1993

Lords of the Sky. New York, Bantam, and London, Millennium, 1994.

OTHER PUBLICATIONS

Novels

Return of a Man Called Horse (novelization of screenplay). London, Star, 1976.
Starmaidens (as Ian Evans; novelization of TV script). London, Corgi, 1977.
The Brothers Macgregor (novelization of TV script). London, Granada, 1984.
Big Deal (novelization of TV script). London, Futura, 1984.
Roll Over Beethoven (novelization of TV script). London, Granada, 1985.

Novels as Charles R. Pike

Killer Silver. London, Mayflower, 1975.
Vengeance Hunt. London, Mayflower, 1976.
The Burning Man. London, Mayflower, 1976.
The Golden Dead. London, Mayflower, 1976.
Death Wears Grey. London, Mayflower, 1976.
Days of Blood. London, Mayflower, 1977.
The Killing Ground. London, Mayflower, 1977.
Brand of Vengeance. London, Mayflower, 1978.
Bounty Road. London, Mayflower, 1978.
Ashes and Blood. London, Mayflower, 1979.
The Death Pit. London, Mayflower, 1980.
Angel of Death. London, Mayflower, 1980.
Mourning is Red. London, Granada, 1981.
Bloody Christmas. London, Granada, 1981.
Time of the Damned. London, Granada, 1982.
The Waiting Game. London, Granada, 1982.
Spoils of War. London, Granada, 1982.
The Violent Land. London, Granada, 1983.
Gallows Bait. London, Granada, 1983.

Novels as James A. Muir

The Lonely Hunt. London, Sphere, 1976.
The Silent Kill. London, Sphere, 1977.
Cry for Vengeance. London, Sphere, 1977.
Death Stage. London, Sphere, 1977.
Death Stage. London, Sphere, 1977.
The Gallows Tree. London, Sphere, 1978.
The Judas Goat. London, Sphere, 1978.
Time of the Wolf. London, Sphere, 1978.
Blood Debt. London, Sphere, 1979.
Blood Stock. London, Sphere, 1979.
Outlaw Road. London, Sphere, 1979.
The Dying and the Damned. London, Sphere, 1980.
Killer's Moon. London, Sphere, 1980.
Bounty Hunter. London, Sphere, 1980.
Spanish Gold. London, Sphere, 1981.
Slaughter Time. London, Sphere, 1981.
Bad Habits. London, Sphere, 1981.
The Day of the Gun. London, Sphere, 1982.
The Colour of Death. London, Sphere, 1982.

Blood Valley. London, Sphere, 1983.
Gundown. London, Sphere, 1983.
Blood Hunt. London, Sphere, 1984.
Apache Blood. London, Sphere, 1985.

Novels as J. B. Dancer

Kansas, Bloody Kansas. London, Coronet, 1977.
Vengeance Trail. London, Coronet, 1978.
One Way to Die. London, Coronet, 1980.

Novels as Charles C. Garrett

Golden Gun. London, Sphere, 1978.
Fifty Calibre Kill. London, Sphere, 1978.
Rebel Vengeance. London, Sphere, 1979.
Peacemaker. London, Sphere, 1980.
The Russian Lode. London, Sphere, 1980.

Novels as William S. Brady

The Sudden Guns. London, Fontana, 1979.
Death's Bounty. London, Fontana, 1979.
Fool's Gold. London, Fontana, 1980.
Fool's Gold. London, Fontana, 1980.
The Gates of Death. London, Fontana, 1980.
The Widowmaker. London, Fontana, 1981.
Killer's Breed. London, Fontana, 1982.
Border War. London, Fontana, 1983.

Novels as J. D. Sandon

Guns Across the River. London, Granada, 1979.
Fire in the Wind. London, Granada, 1979.
Easy Money. London, Granada, 1980.
One Too Many Mornings. London, Granada, 1981.
Survivors. London, Granada, 1982.

Novels as William S. Brady

Comanche! London, Fontana, 1981.
Outlaws. London, Fontana, 1981.
Lynch Law. London, Fontana, 1981.
Blood Run. London, Fontana, 1982.
$1,000 Death. London, Fontana, 1984.
The Lost. London, Fontana, 1984.
Shootout! London, Fontana, 1984.

Novels as Matthew Kirk

Day of Fury. London, Granada, 1983.
Vengeance Road. London, Granada, 1983.
Yellow Stripe. London, Granada, 1983.
The Wild Hunt. London, Granada, 1983.
Blood for Blood. London, Granada, 1983.
Death in Red. London, Granada, 1984.

Other

Editor, *The Best of Arthur C. Clarke.* London, Sidgwick and Jackson, 1973.

Editor, *The Best of Isaac Asimov.* London, Sidgwick and Jackson, 1973.

Editor, *The Best of Robert Heinlein.* London, Sidgwick and Jackson, 1973.

Editor, *The Best of John Wyndham.* London, Sphere, 1973.

Editor, *The Best of A. E. van Vogt.* London, Sphere, 1974.

Editor, *The Best of Fritz Leiber.* London, Sphere, 1974.

Editor, *The Best of Frank Herbert.* London, Sidgwick and Jackson, 1975.

Editor, *The Best of Clifford D. Simak.* London, Sidgwick and Jackson, 1975.

*

Angus Wells comments:

My first venture into fantasy was with Rob Holdstock, when we shared the writing of the Raven series. Then it was mostly pseudonymously westerns (which are almost fantastical) until the mid-1980s, when I began work on the Books of the Kingdoms. That trilogy was followed by the three Godwars novels, only one of which got published in the UK when Macdonald publishers sank with Robert Maxwell. Bantam, however, went on publishing (and selling) in America, and kept me afloat. They, and Millennium (my new UK publisher), produced the fantasy *Lords of the Sky*—a long, single novel—in 1994.

*   *   *

Angus Wells's apprenticeship was in the writing of Westerns, a very large number over a short period of time. Inevitably, some of the qualities necessary for that genre spill over into his fantasy writing: all his fantasy novels are quest-driven sword-and-sorcery stories.

His first foray into the field was as Richard Kirk. Under this name he wrote numbers one, three and five in the Raven series, the others in the series being the work of Robert Holdstock. Each book is a separate adventure though the first, *Raven: Swordsmistress of Chaos,* also details Raven's background and how she changed from slave-girl to swordsmistress. In all books she travels with Spellbinder, a sorcerer-mage, and is permanently engaged in a sequence of journeys, fights, sex and baths. They are all short and action-packed with an element of good versus evil.

The Books of the Kingdoms series is Wells's first serious venture into high fantasy and has many of the hallmarks expected of this form of fantasy. The god Ashar is intent on ruling the world but Kyrie, worshipped as the Lady, opposes him. Ashar works by direct methods, sending his messenger to raise the forest tribes in the north and to sweep down as a horde obliterating the kingdoms. Kyrie works in more subtle ways. She has given advice and prophecies well in advance to her servants, but in such a way that it is difficult to interpret them. Everyone holds their breath, hoping they have got it right and that Prince Kedryn is the Chosen One who will thwart Ashar's designs. In *Wrath of Ashar,* Kedryn's prowess with a sword helps him defeat Ashar's schemes but at the end of the volume he is blinded. *The Usurper* follows Kedryn and Wynett (one of the Sisters of the Lady) into the underworld seeking the shade of Borsus, the warrior who wielded the magic sword which robbed him of his sight. Meanwhile, Ashar's messenger is busy fomenting rebellion and treachery in the Three Kingdoms. With the help of the Lady's talisman, of which Kedryn and Wynett hold half each, Ashar is again beaten. In the third volume, Ashar is allowed one more try at world-domination. Kedryn (his sight restored) and Wynett are now married and Kedryn is crowned High King. Ashar sends a leviathan to snatch Wynett, and Kedryn follows her to the underworld to get her back.

The plot in this trilogy owes a lot not only to earlier books in the genre but also to traditional myth and folk tale, thus much of it seems familiar and the outcomes and events predictable—so much so that if the first hundred pages of *The Way Beneath* had been omitted, nothing essential would have been lost.

The Godwars trilogy begins with a more carefully thought-out plot with all the elements introduced having some relevance to the plot even if not evident at first sight. The Godwars of the series title refer to events far in the past when brother gods, one mad, fought and were finally both forced into eternal sleep by their parents. This is a theme that Wells first explored in two of his Raven novels. It always seems ludicrous that an evil wizard should do his utmost to prevent the agents of a good wizard fetching the one thing he desires most instead of waiting for others to brave the hazards before stealing it from them. Yet this is what Calandryll, the hero of this series, believes to be true. Calandryll, told by his father that he must enter the priesthood, and spurned by the woman he loves, flees the city. His friend and fellow scholar, the ambassador Varant, tells him that an evil wizard intends awakening the mad god, thus causing the destruction of the world. So Calandryll sets out to find the *Arcanum,* a book from the legendary city of Tezindar, so that it might be destroyed and thwart the evil wizard. He is accompanied by Bracht, a mercenary, and is joined by Katya. During the journey, Calandryll changes from a naive and spoiled youth into a capable adventurer. Most of the first volume, *Forbidden Magic,* is taken up with the journey and, to break up something intrinsically boring, Wells adds increasing amounts of magic and convincing natural hazards. As in his earlier books he indulges in his habit of using clever words where a simple phrase would be more effective.

At the end of the first volume, Calandryll discovers he has been duped. The book has been acquired but Varent is on the wrong side, relieves him of the book and sets off to wake the mad god, leaving Calandryll and his companions to pursue him into the next volume. This series is a continuing story, unlike the earlier trilogy where each book could be read as an adventure on its own.

Wells's most recent fantasy is a single-volume epic. *Lords of the Sky* has elements familiar from other books but is also an attempt to be different. Unlike his other novels, this is mostly written in the first person. Passages with a third-person narrative can give an added perspective but do not quite work. The narrator is Daviot, who we meet as a 12-year-old seeing for the first time the airships that carry his people's enemies from over the sea to invade. It is this event that alerts the mage of the nearest town to the fact that Daviot is a likely candidate for the College of Mnemonikos, due to his remarkable memory. When he comes of age he is sent there to train as a storyteller—this is a world that despite having writing relies more on the specially trained Rememberers to recall history. Messages are sent mind-to-mind via the mages. Daviot gets into trouble through falling in love with a trainee mage, but as he matures the raids from overseas are increasing. Daviot gets to thinking, "what if dragons still existed and could be persuaded to fight our enemies?" He is also unusual in that he makes friends with the Changed: originally these were magically changed animals who have the appearance of men but are used as slaves. Daviot sees them as people.

This is a much more ambitious book than any of Wells's others, with much more attention given to detail. The society is carefully worked out but the pace is slow. The characters are much given to introspection and will go over and over something in their minds. While this is realistic it does not make for urgent story-telling. There is still a noticeable fascination with journeys, and in places the book takes on the aura of a travelogue. And everyone is scrupulously clean—the first thing anyone does on arriving is to ask for the bath house. The book also raises some ethical problems. The four main characters, each from a different race, all want peace for their peoples but they obtain it with a lot of bloodshed—by loosing the dragons on the armies. Is it right to advocate ending bloodshed with bloodshed? And is it right to hold peace by the threat of terror? Some of the arguments Wells solves by the constraints he sets into his plot, but others are open for discussion.

In Wells's fantasy writing he has shown an improvement in the complexity of his plots and has attempted to produce more realistic characters rather than cyphers. As a result, his books have less pace but are considerably longer. Particularly in *Lords of the Sky*, he has tried to move away from the standard elements of sword-and-sorcery quest novels and to introduce more original themes. One big problem he has yet to overcome is his lack of time sense. Some simultaneous events seem widely separated while distant ones appear too close, and the time taken to journey from various parts of his worlds seems to vary.

—Pauline Morgan

WELLS, Martha

Nationality: American. **Born:** 1 September, 1964 in Fort Worth, Texas. **Education:** Texas A&M University, B.A., 1986. **Career:** Texas A&M University, College Station, Texas, system operator and research assistant for Ocean Drilling Program, 1989—. **Agent:** Matt Bialer, William Morris Agency, 1350 Avenue of the Americas, New York, New York 10019, USA. **Address:** College Station, Texas.

FANTASY PUBLICATIONS

Novels

The Element of Fire. New York, Tor, 1993.
City of Bones. New York, Tor, 1995.

*   *   *

The problem with newcomer Martha Wells's fast-paced first novel, *The Element of Fire,* is that it is too good to ignore and yet it lacks the subtlety (or depth) of a more mature work; it relies on the flashy clichés of swashbuckling, and the fast-paced patter of witty repartee, to propel the plot along. That said, Wells has produced a really fine first work and the style and the patter and the action make it an original and entertaining, if not intellectually taxing, read.

Thomas Boniface, the Captain of the Queen's Guard, is having a rough life. In the overly politicized world of Ile-Rien he has great power, since he is the former lover and the current protector of the iron-willed Dowager Queen Ravenna. Yet there are so many ills besetting the Kingdom that it is hard to know which he should tackle first. The evil sorcerer Urban Grandier is causing mischief. The weak King Roland (Ravenna's son) is being led astray by his power-mad cousin Denzil, and the wards in the palace are failing.

To top off these difficulties Roland's older half-sister Kade Carrion has reappeared. Kade was fathered by the late King Fulstan, who was seduced by the Queen of Air and Darkness, Moire. Moire is currently stuck in Hell, so Kade is at loose ends and can spare some time to look in on her human relations and settle some old scores.

When the wards around the palace wander off, it is up to the brave Thomas and the sorcerous Kade to fix things. Meanwhile, the other royal personages are hustled out of town, supposedly to keep them from harm. Unfortunately for our heroes they all get into trouble as the intrigues of the nobility (and the fey) cause mayhem at almost every turn of the page. Ravenna ends up making the ultimate sacrifice for kingdom and kinder, while Kade and Thomas endear themselves to their readers by cutting a swath through both bogles and courtiers.

The panache Kade and Thomas exhibit is the very keynote of Wells' book, and their amusing banter helps spice her light-hearted confection:

> "I suppose I should be flattered that you find it necessary to have your pet witch here to deal with me," Dontane sneered.
>
> "'Pet witch.' I like that," Kade said, apparently addressing the blue faience vase sitting next to her on the sideboard. "I'm going to put a curse on him."
>
> "If you can't be quiet you'll have to leave, pet," Thomas said.

The character of Kade is a lovely achievement. She is bloodthirsty, intelligent and flawed—a fine fantastic heroine. To add a touch of modernity, she is also forced to fight back against that most prevalent of current villains—the domineering, sexually leering father. The scene in which she faces down Fulstan's sneering ghost is ultimately touching. In a literary landscape overpopulated by sexually abused women this is a nice riff on the popular theme.

Thomas' character is less flawed, but just as much fun. There is a lot to be said for the old swashbuckling cliché where "a man's gotta do what a man's gotta do" (and not agonize about it for pages on end). Plus this cliché is interested in Kade because it is her temperament (and not her looks) which make her his equal. There is something very cheering about Thomas and Kade's affair. Their ability (in a very politically correct non-sexist manner) to save each other time and again results in a more adult bonding then is usual in a fantasy novel.

Though the book lacks grounding in a specific period, stealing bits and pieces from a sort of generalized Magickal Middle Ages, it does nice things with those pieces: the Dowager Queen holds control by land-law, the sorcerers use gascoign powder to see through fayre illusion, the wards are personalized and have names, the religious knights wear sackcloths over their armour, etc. Unfortunately, the politics are so complicated (five sets of private guards, several priestly orders, dozens of named secondary characters) that it is a good thing the language is fairly simple or the reader would surely lose track of just who was doing what to whom.

Wells covers a lot of ground with this book. People bounce so quickly between different palaces, holding pens, villages and fayre domains that when Thomas states the first time he has a chance to breathe is in fayre the reader is grateful to stop and smell the ever-blooming flowers along with him. Yet Wells' Kingdoms are worth visiting. She makes good (if brief) use of Queen Titania and her cohorts by having Kade visit the Seelie Court and state that she is willing to trade something she deeply cares about "for the sake of love." Unlike many of her contemporaries Wells gets Titania exactly right. The Queen shows her soulless state by having no idea how to take Kade's pronouncement, since the cold-blooded fey are only capable of playing at love.

Though the upbeat ending is a foregone conclusion the novel has so many sacrifices and reversals that it is impossible to grudge the main characters' happiness. This leads to a sense of satisfaction that is often lacking in lesser works. Adding to the perception that this novel is attempting to be "adult" is the lack of that namby-pamby "maybe the bad guys will change for the better, and shouldn't we give all our enemies a chance?" feeling that so many adolescent novels are gooey with. When Thomas is duelling with the evil Denzil he assures Kade that if he dies and Denzil wins: "I want you to hurt him very badly before you kill him." As bloodthirsty as her beau, Kade responds, "I will. Very badly."

While this is not the most philosophically involved (or theme-driven) of first novels, it completely avoids the trap of fluff-and-blunder sameness so prevalent among the current batch of made-to-be-serialized epic maunderings. This is a warm, witty book with spitfire characters, a good ear for dialogue and a strong sense of fun. There is promise here, and the hope that as Wells matures, so will her writing. Her second novel, *City of Bones,* unavailable in time for this essay, is described by her publishers as "Scheherazade meets Dumas, a wondrous Arabian Nights fantasy."

—Shira Daemon

WESTALL, Robert (Atkinson)

Nationality: British. **Born:** Tynemouth, Northumberland, 7 October 1929. **Education:** Tynemouth High School, 1941-48; Durham University, 1948-53, B.A. in fine art; Slade School, University of London, 1955-57, D.F.A. **Military Service:** Royal Signals, 1953-55:Lance-Corporal. **Family:** Married Jean Underhill in 1958; one son (deceased). **Career:** Art master, Erdington Hall Secondary Modern School, Birmingham, 1957-58, and Keighley Boys' Grammar School, Yorkshire, 1958-60; Head of Art, 1960-85, and Head of Careers, 1970-85, Sir John Deane's College, Northwich, Cheshire; antiques dealer, Davenham, Cheshire, 1985-86. Art critic, *Chester Chronicle,* 1962-73; director, Telephone Samaritans of Mid-Cheshire, 1966-75; writer, Whitehorn Press, Manchester, 1968-71; Northern art critic, *Guardian,* London, 1970, 1980. **Awards:** Library Association Carnegie Medal, 1976, 1982; Senior Smarties Prize, 1989; *Guardian* Award, 1991. **Died:** 22 April 1993.

FANTASY PUBLICATIONS

Novels

The Wind Eye. London, Macmillan, 1976; New York, Greenwillow, 1977.

The Watch House. London, Macmillan, 1977; New York, Greenwillow, 1978.
The Devil on the Road. London, Macmillan, 1978; New York, Greenwillow, 1979.
The Scarecrows. London, Chatto and Windus, and New York, Greenwillow, 1981.
The Cats of Seroster. London, Macmillan, and New York, Greenwillow, 1984.
Rosalie. London, Macmillan, 1987.
The Creature in the Dark, illustrated by Liz Roberts. London, Blackie, 1988.
Ghost Abbey. London, Macmillan, 1988; New York, Scholastic, 1989.
Blitzcat. London, Macmillan, 1989; New York, Scholastic, 1990.
Old Man on a Horse. London, Blackie, 1989.
If Cats Could Fly . . . ? London, Methuen, 1990.
The Promise. London, Macmillan, 1990; New York, Scholastic, 1991.
Yaxley's Cat. London, Macmillan, 1991; New York, Scholastic, 1992.
Gulf. London, Methuen, and New York, Scholastic, 1992.
The Wheatstone Pond. London, Penguin, 1993.

Short Stories

Break of Dark. London, Chatto and Windus, and New York, Greenwillow, 1982.
The Haunting of Chas McGill and Other Stories. London, Macmillan, and New York, Greenwillow, 1983.
The Other: A Christmas Story. London, Macmillan, 1985.
Rachel and the Angel and Other Stories. London, Macmillan, 1986; New York, Greenwillow, 1987.
Ghosts and Journeys. London, Macmillan, 1988.
Antique Dust: Ghost Stories. London, Viking Kestrel, and New York, Viking, 1989.
The Call and Other Stories. London, Viking Kestrel, 1989.
Echoes of War. London, Viking Kestrel, 1989; New York, Farrar Straus, 1991.
A Walk on the Wild Side: Cat Stories. London, Methuen, 1989.
The Christmas Cat. London, Methuen, 1991.
The Stones of Muncaster Cathedral: Two Stories of the Supernatural. London, Viking Kestrel, and New York, Farrar Straus, 1991.
The Christmas Ghost. London, Methuen, 1992.
The Fearful Lovers. London, Macmillan, 1992; as *In Camera and Other Stories,* New York, Scholastic, 1993.
Demons and Shadows. New York, Farrar Straus, 1993.
Blitz. London, HarperCollins, 1994.
Christmas Spirit (omnibus; includes *The Christmas Cat, The Christmas Ghost*). New York, Farrar Straus, 1994.
Shades of Darkness. New York, Farrar Straus, 1994.

Other

Editor, *Ghost Stories.* London, Kingfisher, 1988.

OTHER PUBLICATIONS

Novels

The Machine-Gunners. London, Macmillan, 1975; New York, Greenwillow, 1976.

Fathom Five. London, Macmillan, 1979; New York, Greenwillow, 1980.

Futuretrack 5. London, Kestrel, 1983; New York, Greenwillow, 1984.

The Witness. London, Macmillan, 1985.

Urn Burial. London, Viking Kestrel, 1987; New York, Greenwillow, 1988.

Cat! London, Methuen, 1989.

Stormsearch. London, Blackie, 1990; New York, Farrar Straus, 1992.

The Kingdom by the Sea. London, Methuen, 1990; New York, Farrar Straus, 1991.

Size Twelve. London, Heinemann, 1992.

Falling Into Glory. London, Heinemann, 1993.

A Place for Me. London, Macmillan, 1993.

Time of Fire. London, Macmillan, 1994.

Play

The Machine-Gunners (adapted from his own novel). London, Macmillan, 1986.

Other

Editor, *Children of the Blitz: Memories of Wartime Childhood.* London, Viking, 1985.

*   *   *

Robert Westall made a unique contribution to the development of the teenage or young-adult novel in the 1970s and 1980s. Typically a young-adult novel on the American model deals with a young person's awakening sexuality and/or antagonism towards parents and society, and was pioneered by J. D. Salinger and Paul Zindel in the realistic mode. Westall added supernatural elements, confidently moving between or combining the genres of science fiction, fantasy, ghost story and horror, as well as writing realistic, non-magical fictions. He wrote with passionate commitment: faced with an anthology of anonymous short stories, one would always be able to pick out the Westall story.

Westall first qualified as an art teacher, later dabbled in journalism, and only began to write fiction professionally when his 12-year-old son asked him about his childhood on Tyneside in the northeast of England during World War II. The resulting novel, *The Machine-Gunners,* a dramatic tale of German bombing and souvenir-collecting, won the Carnegie Medal. Noteworthy for its violence and strong language, there was one supernatural touch: a boy dreams of his dead father calling him, and on waking, escapes from his house seconds before a bomb hits it.

From his second novel *The Wind Eye* onwards, Westall produced a series of literary fantasies for teenagers, his taboo-breaking scenes often causing publishers anxiety and bringing letters of complaint from parents and teachers. Well-read, he acknowledged few literary influences, but instead compiled a palette of idiosyncratic motifs which he deployed and varied for each novel and the short stories he began publishing in the 1980s, motifs such as: the genius of cats, woman as temptress, motor-bikes, Good versus Evil, vengeful ghosts, antiques, craftsman's skills, World War II, the waste of youth unemployment and the fallibility of adults. He favoured the settings of his native Tyneside, East Anglia, and Cheshire.

The Wind Eye displays a family at war with a new, aggressive stepmother. The father inherits a cottage with a nearby boat-house, where the teenage stepchildren find an old boat. They find that sailing it takes them back to the time of St. Cuthbert and the Vikings, and in fact it was Cuthbert's funeral boat. Encounters with the saint heal the family's wounds, and the miracle of healing his little daughter's burned hand, which doctors pronounced incurable, shakes the father's dogmatic atheism. *The Watch House,* also set on the northeast coast and featuring a real lifeboat museum, is Westall's first essay in horror, as three teenagers are caught by the curse of two feuding ghosts which haunt the museum.

The Devil on the Road is about a college student who travels back in time to the 17th century to save a witch from being hanged by the Witchfinder General. Featuring the motifs of motor-cycle and temptress, it was the last book Westall wrote for his son while still alive, as he died in a motor-cycle accident in 1978.

The 1980s showed Westall sublimating his grief in a more diversified body of work, including shorter fiction for younger readers; he refined his approach to genre by writing pure science fiction, fantasy and horror. In the latter genre, *The Scarecrows* won him his second Carnegie Medal, and his first three horror stories appeared in *Break of Dark,* including "Blackham's Wimpey," a characteristic male-bonding tale of a bomber-plane haunted by its last kill, a German pilot burning endlessly to death, and "St. Austin Friars," a vampire story set in Westall's imaginary city of Muncaster.

His first science-fiction short story was "Hitch-Hiker," in *Break of Dark.* A young man stranded in the countryside is accosted by a naked young woman with uncanny powers. When she produces triplets after a three-months pregnancy, he realizes she is an alien out to breed a super race. "Sergeant Nice," also in *Break of Dark,* describes how a commonsense policeman foils an alien plot to collect human artefacts, animals and children from a trap disguised as a horse trough. "The Vacancy," in *The Haunting of Chas McGill,* shows how a future society eliminates talented youngsters by sending then to the moon without oxygen. He also wrote two excellent science-fiction novels. *Futuretrack 5* is set in the near future when all youngsters are tested. The bright minority run Britain and everyone else is thrown on the scrapheap to live in urban squalor with breeding strictly controlled. *Urn Burial* is about a shepherd who stumbles on the coffin of a cat-headed, human-sized alien, and brings down on his countryside home the wrath of the alien dog-people who carry on a space war with the cats. We, the ape-people, are held in great contempt by the morally superior cats for our aggressive and polluting behaviour.

Westall had long had the ambition to write a fictional critique of Tolkien by describing the seamy side of medieval warfare and portraying characters who were neither pure Good nor totally Evil. A description of the walled city of Les Baux, Provence, "peopled" by cats, provided the setting of *The Cats of Seroster,* a brilliant heroic fantasy and a landmark in sword-and-sorcery fiction. In a fantasy version of 16th-century France, the Duke of a cliff-top city is murdered, and his young son is hidden away by the Miw, the tribe of large telepathic cats descended from the cats of Ancient Egypt, who are the luck of the city. They cast their traditional spell to bring back the legendary Seroster to restore legitimate rule. Cam, a travelling student, is tricked into accepting an ancient dagger, and finds he is compelled to go to the city and take up the Seroster's magic sword, to become an inexorable fighting machine. After vain attempts to get rid of his magic weapons, he accepts his destiny and leads the revolt against the tyrants. Westall's portrayal of the cats' language, culture and religion is fascinating, and the book is among his best, finding its natural audience among fans of adult fantasy.

Westall's only fiction published for adults was *Antique Dust,* dedicated to M. R. James, a sequence of ghost stories about the adventures of an antique dealer. His mastery of the James tradition is brilliantly displayed in the long short story "The Stones of Muncaster Cathedral," about a steeplejack who tracks down the evil spirit who has put a jinx on his work; and in *The Wheatstone Pond,* a superb horror novel which recalls *The Watch House* in its exorcism finale.

Westall's hatred of modern warfare is shown in two late fantasy novels. *Blitzcat,* set during World War II, is about a cat whose homing ability finally reunites her with her master in the air force, and who acts as a mascot to save many lives throughout her adventures. The other, *Gulf,* is about a sensitive British boy whose mind becomes twinned with that of an Iraqi soldier in the Gulf War, and he must endure the youth's agonies until he is killed. Westall himself died prematurely of pneumonia, at the height of his writing powers, leaving several posthumous novels to witness to his genius.

—Jessica Yates

WHITBOURN, John

Nationality: British. **Born:** Godalming, Surrey, 23 March 1958. **Education:** Broadwater County Secondary school, Farncombe, Surrey, 1969-74; Godalming Sixth-Form College, 1974-76; University College, Cardiff, B.A. in archaeology 1981. **Family:** Married Elizabeth Caroline Gale in 1982; one son, two daughters. **Awards:** BBC/Gollancz First Fantasy Novel Prize, 1991. **Agent:** Colin Smythe Ltd., PO Box 6, Gerrards Cross, Buckinghamshire SL9 8XA, England.

FANTASY PUBLICATIONS

Novels

A Dangerous Energy. London, Gollancz, 1992.
Popes and Phantoms. London, Gollancz, 1993.
To Build Jerusalem. London, Gollancz, 1994.

Short Stories

Binscombe Tales. Privately published, 1989.
Rollover Night. Privately published, 1990.

*

John Whitbourn comments:

I am particularly intrigued by the "what-ifs" (and "should-have-beens") of history; the literary consequence of which is the projected series of novels, commenced by *A Dangerous Energy,* set in a time-stream where the powers of the mind (or "magic") have been codified and harnessed, and where the Reformation failed. It could also be said that my writing (and especially the *Binscombe Tales* short-story series) strives towards the re-mythologizing of England (and Britain). However, it is equally true that I write because it comes as naturally as breathing and helps pay the bills.

*   *   *

John Whitbourn's debut novel, *A Dangerous Energy,* won first prize in a BBC Radio 4/Gollancz fantasy novel competition in 1991, and was published the following year. Although Whitbourn had previously published only occasional pieces in the small press, the maturity of this first novel is remarkable. In essence, it tells the story of Tobias Oakley from the day he is first enchanted by fairies as a child to the day he dies (and beyond). In the unfurling of Oakley's life, we are also vouchsafed a view of an alternative modern-day Britain where the Reformation did not happen, where Roman Catholicism is still the established English Church and the main pillar of the State, and where magic had been codified, regularized, and absorbed into the Church in the middle ages so that, in the book's parallel now, it largely supplants our "science"—steam engines and railways have been invented, but electricity has not been discovered. The resulting melange bears more than a passing resemblance to the works of Keith Roberts for his believable parallel England, John Crowley for his magic both in and of prose, and Gene Wolfe for his religious view and sheer complexity. It is both a wonderful first novel and a very difficult act to follow.

Which makes Whitbourn's next novel all the more extraordinary. *Popes and Phantoms* appeared less than a year later, but it is hard to say whether it is the similarities to, or the differences from, the previous book that mark it out. The setting is wildly different. This time, Whitbourn tells us the story of Admiral Slovo, a soldier of the Mediterranean in the late 16th century. I know much less of this period than I do of late 20th-century England, so it is difficult to say whether this story is parallel history or simply fiction set in an historical context. However, it does display the same sureness of story-telling and copious attention to detail that the first novel displays, and leaves the reader wondering what Whitbourn might manage next.

The answer is *To Build Jerusalem.* The story is set in the same parallel England as the first novel, but although the sequence of events broadly follow on from the previous book, this could in no way be considered either a sequel or the second book of a multipart fantasy blockbuster. Here, we follow the story of Adam, a man who was taken from England as a boy and turned into a janissary-like fanatic soldier-agent of the Vatican, and who is now returned to England to resolve certain extraordinary turns of events. The story centres on both Adam's skill as a soldier and his faith, and finally depicts his reward for both.

While each of these books is a novel in its own right, certain themes begin to emerge, and they have extraordinary range. There is the profound: each book contains an unswerving affirmation of faith in God. Then there is the standard novelistic: each tells the story of a strong man living through extraordinary times, and reveals by stages the layers of a complex and not very pleasant character. Then, there are the irrelevant: Whitbourn mines his own life extensively for settings, so that his native Guildford, and Pevensey Bay, where his wife's parents live, feature large in the stories; he also introduces real historical characters in minor or wildly different-from-history roles as a sideshow—anyone from his own brother, Yeoman Whitbourn in *To Build Jerusalem,* to a minor actress called Redgrave who works part time as a spy, to Oliver Cromwell, a mercenary in Rome.

Finally, though, Whitbourn's writing is notable for the apparent simplicity with which he breaks fundamental rules. There is no really sympathetic character in any book; nevertheless each central character is fascinating to the point of mesmerism. And, most glorious of all, each story culminates with what appears to be a *deus ex machina* that, on reflection, in fact perfectly resolves the plot without adding extraneous material—God does truly appear from the machinery of the story.

One minor point to note is that it is only on this fantastic level that flaws in the story-telling appear. Magic is codified as a quasi-science and strictly controlled by the church, but there are fantastic creatures not accounted for by this magic throughout the books—the fairy that tempts Oakley in *A Dangerous Energy,* the drowned sailor that follows Slovo's ship around the Mediterranean, and the elemental she-devil of *To Build Jerusalem* are all examples. In spite of this, the impression of the careful rigour of the story-telling in these books remains long after these problems are forgotten. Whitbourn is a history buff, and he uses history in his fiction as if it were a science and he a scientist, so that these books, although solid fantasy, carry all the hallmarks of good science fiction. They piqued my curiosity, reminded me of things I had forgotten I was fascinated by, and made me want to know more. It is some comfort to know that several more books have already been written and await publication.

—Paul Brazier

WHITE, E(lwyn) B(rooks)

Nationality: American. **Born:** Mount Vernon, New York, 11 July 1899. **Education:** Mount Vernon High School, graduated 1917; Cornell University, Ithaca, New York (editor, *Cornell Daily Sun,* 1920-21), 1917-21, A.B. 1921. **Military Service:** United States Army, 1918: Private. **Family:** Married Katharine Sergeant Angell in 1929 (died 1977); one son. **Career:** Worked for United Press and the American Legion News Service, 1921; reporter, Seattle *Times,* 1922-23; advertising copywriter and production assistant, Frank Seaman Inc. and Newmark Inc., New York, 1924-25; contributing editor, *New Yorker,* from 1926; columnist (*One Man's Meat*), *Harper's* magazine, New York, 1938-43. **Awards:** National Association of Independent Schools award, 1955; American Academy Gold Medal, for essays, 1960; Presidential Medal of Freedom, 1963; American Library Association Laura Ingalls Wilder award, 1970; George G. Stone Center for Children's Books award, 1970; National Medal for Literature, 1971; Pulitzer Special citation, 1978. Litt.D.: Dartmouth College, Hanover, New Hampshire, 1948; University of Maine, Orono, 1948; Yale University, New Haven, Connecticut, 1948; Bowdoin College, Brunswick, Maine, 1950; Hamilton College, Clinton, New York, 1952; Harvard University, Cambridge, Massachusetts, 1954; L.H.D.: Colby College, Waterville, Maine, 1954. Fellow, American Academy of Arts and Sciences, 1973; member, American Academy. **Died:** 1 October 1985.

FANTASY PUBLICATIONS

Novels

Stuart Little, illustrated by Garth Williams. New York, Harper, 1945; London, Hamish Hamilton, 1946.
Charlotte's Web, illustrated by Garth Williams. New York, Harper, and London, Hamish Hamilton, 1952.
The Trumpet of the Swan, illustrated by Edward Frascino. New York, Harper, and London, Hamish Hamilton, 1970.

OTHER PUBLICATIONS

Poetry

The Lady Is Cold. New York, Harper, 1929.
The Fox of Peapack and Other Poems. New York, Harper, 1938.
Poems and Sketches. New York, Harper, 1981.

Other

Is Sex Necessary? or, Why You Feel the Way You Do, with James Thurber. New York, Harper, 1929; London, Heinemann, 1930.
Alice Through the Cellophane. New York, Day, 1933.
Every Day Is Saturday. New York, Harper, 1934.
Farewell to Model T. New York, Putnam, 1936.
Quo Vadimus? or, The Case for the Bicycle. New York, Harper, 1939.
One Man's Meat. New York, Harper, 1942; London, Gollancz, 1943; augmented edition, Harper, 1944.
World Government and Peace: Selected Notes and Comment 1943-1945. New York, F. R. Publishing, 1945.
The Wild Flag: Editorials from the New Yorker on Federal World Government and Other Matters. Boston, Houghton Mifflin, 1946.
Here Is New York. New York, Harper, 1949.
The Second Tree from the Corner. New York, Harper, and London, Hamish Hamilton, 1954.
The Elements of Style, by William Strunk, Jr., revised by White. New York, Macmillan, 1959; London, Collier Macmillan, 1972; revised edition, New York, Macmillan, 1979.
The Points of My Compass: Letters from the East, The West, The North, The South. New York, Harper, 1962; London, Hamish Hamilton, 1963.
An E. B. White Reader, edited by William W. Watt and Robert W. Bradford. New York, Harper, 1966.
Letters of E. B. White, edited by Dorothy Lobrano Guth. New York, Harper, 1976.
Essays of E. B. White. New York, Harper, 1977.

Editor, *Ho Hum: Newsbreaks from the New Yorker.* New York, Farrar and Rinehart, 1931.
Editor, *Another Ho Hum: More Newsbreaks from the New Yorker.* New York, Farrar and Rinehart, 1932.
Editor, with Katharine S. White, *A Subtreasury of American Humor.* New York, Coward McCann, 1941.
Editor, *Onward and Upward in the Garden,* by Katharine S. White. New York, Farrar Straus, 1979.

*

Film Adaptation: *Charlotte's Web,* 1973.

Bibliography: *E. B. White: A Bibliography* by A. J. Anderson, Metuchen, New Jersey, Scarecrow Press, 1978; *E. B. White: A Bibliographic Catalogue of Printed Materials in the Department of Rare Books, Cornell University Library* by Katherine R. Hall, New York, Garland, 1979.

Manuscript Collection: Olin Library, Cornell University, Ithaca, New York.

Critical Studies: *E. B. White* by Edward C. Sampson, New York, Twayne, 1974; *E. B. White: A Biography* by Scott Elledge, New York, Norton, 1984; *Katharine and E. B. White: An Affectionate Memoir* by Isabel Russell, New York, Norton, 1988.

*   *   *

E. B. White has been greatly admired as a poet, essayist, journalist, grammarian, editor, and most of all, as the author of three books of children's fantasy. Of the three novels *Charlotte's Web* is the most revered and will probably account for White's continuing reputation in the years to come. White's fantasies are set in the real world, America of the mid-20th century. In all three, however, human characters are mixed with animals which have been humanized to various degrees. The animals may be unique, such as Stuart Little, a mouse, who is born into a human family, or they may be animals born and living with other animals, such as Wilbur the pig and Louis the swan. In all settings, however, there is interaction with humans, and although there is communication between animals and humans, the animals do not think of themselves as people. They are different, and they know it.

The first children's fantasy by White was *Stuart Little*. Stuart is mouse-sized and is described as looking like a mouse. Much of the charm in the early pages of the story comes from the ingenious ways the Little family cope with Stuart's size. As Stuart matures he finds ways to help his family, but he is increasingly bothered by his difference from humans. After a number of amusing adventures in New York City and narrowly escaping death from a cat, Stuart heads north into the countryside to find his friend, the bird Margola who had saved his life. This surface quest is underlaid by a more important meaning, for Stuart must seek his destiny. He meets and is enchanted by a lovely mouse maiden, but true love does not evolve. Stuart continues his trip to find the meaning of his life. In the end he is still on the road heading north. "As he peered ahead into the great land that stretched before him, the way seemed long. But the sky was bright, and he somehow felt he was headed in the right direction."

There is something admirable, yet wistful, in Stuart's story. One cannot help but wonder if White is projecting some of his own thoughts and dreams into the brave little protagonist. Stuart's personality is amazingly complex for a short children's book and although mouselike in appearance, Stuart is very human in his thoughts and actions.

The second of White's children's fantasies is *Charlotte's Web*. The bucolic midwestern farm scene is pure Americana, and the multiple animals in the story provide new dimensions to somewhat stereotypical expectations of humanized animals. All have distinct personalities, but unlike the animals in Orwell's *Animal Farm,* the assorted creatures do not engage in power struggles, nor do they project a Disney superficiality. Wilbur, the hero pig, is a bit simple and quick to panic. Templeton, the bad-tempered rat, is selfish, untrustworthy and mean spirited. But the real heroine, Charlotte the spider, is a masterpiece of creation. White presents his readers with a marvellous being who is kind, firm, and even inspired when it is necessary to save Wilbur's life. In many ways, Charlotte is a mother figure.

Wilbur is a pig who always seems to be in need of rescue. When he is born, he is declared the runt of the litter. Fern, the farmer's daughter, begs for a chance to help Wilbur survive. Fern is a nice child, but she tends to be passive and increasingly slips into a traditional female role as the tale evolves. True, Fern has the spunk to

ask her father for Wilbur, but the farmer doesn't really put up much of a fight. Charlotte, on the other hand, must save the older, plumper Wilbur from slaughter with fierce determination, cleverness, and leadership.

White's story of life and death in the barnyard is not idealized. Animals on farms are usually not reared to be pets, and pigs are raised to become food. They have little other purpose in the world of humans. Spiders are tolerated, at best, and rats are viewed as vermin. The fantasy elements of White's tale, however, shows drama beyond the ordinary pigsty. White's fantasies are always firmly based in the real world, and the laws of the real world are usually much in evidence. The only thing that can save Wilbur is magic; Charlotte's ability to weave testimonials about the hapless pig in her web. Charlotte makes Wilbur seem special to humans and that saves Wilbur's life. Ironically, it is not Wilbur who is outstanding at all, it is Charlotte who is extraordinary. It is only another female, Mrs. Zuckerman, who sees that it's Charlotte who is unusual, not the pig.

The third fantasy White wrote for children was *The Trumpet of the Swan,* and it contains some the elements of both *Stuart Little* and *Charlotte's Web.* White tells the story of a trumpeter swan who is born mute. Sam, a human boy, befriends the swan family, particularly Louis who cannot trumpet as he should. In fact, Louis cannot communicate well at all until Sam takes him to school where the brilliant cygnet quickly learns to read and write. Louis's father, a somewhat pompous bird, is concerned about his son, and flies to a distance city where he steals a trumpet for the young swan. Now Louis can communicate with humans and also swans. Louis is bothered by his father's theft of the trumpet and decides to earn enough money to repay the music store owner. Louis learns not only swan calls on his trumpet; he learns human songs as well and easily finds employment in the human world. Unlike Stuart, Louis is faithful to the young female swan he adores and they mate. The ending ties everything up neatly on a happy note. In an odd way, the happy ending makes *The Trumpet of the Swan* less successful than *Stuart Little* and *Charlotte's Web.* It all seems too pat, unlike the real world. For most people, more parallels can be made with Stuart Little's quest which may never be fulfilled, and with how Wilbur must deal emotionally with Charlotte's death. Louis ends up with it all, and although Louis is a fine fellow of a swan who has worked hard to achieve his goals, the reader may well wonder why White has made him the most deserving of his three animal heroes.

Overall, White's three fantasy books are memorable. One, however, is outstanding. *Charlotte's Web* is White's most lasting contribution to children's and fantasy literature. It is a book that bears the test of many re-readings. It has inspired generations of children to look upon spiders as friendly. It explains the concept of loyalty, and the importance of acting to reverse a bad situation. Its simple message of death and renewal is effectively presented for readers of all ages.

Although using animals with human characteristics is hardly original in fantasy literature, White has blended the real world and its problems into his fantasy stories successfully. His books work on different levels for both children and adults, partly because of his humour. White's characterizations are well rounded for such brief stories, most happily in *Charlotte's Web*. It may be that *Charlotte* works better because there is more emphasis on the animal characters. There is more communication between animals in *Charlotte's Web,* then between animals and humans. Part of the magic in the novel is its seeming ordinary quality: a spider is able to weave actual words into a web and a little girl can talk with animals. This may in part account for *Charlotte*'s greater success, for more fantasy does not guarantee a better story. In some cases, less is better.

—Cosette Kies

WHITE, T(erence) H(anbury)

Pseudonym: James Aston. **Nationality:** British. **Born:** Bombay, India, 29 May 1906; brought to England, 1911. **Education:** Cheltenham College, 1920-24; Queens' College, Cambridge (exhibitioner), 1925-27, 1928-29, B.A. 1929. **Career:** Taught at a preparatory school, 1930-32; head of the English department, Stowe School, Buckinghamshire, 1932-36; lived in Ireland, 1939-46, and in Jersey, 1946-47, and Alderney, 1947-64, Channel Islands. **Died:** 17 January 1964.

FANTASY PUBLICATIONS

Novels (series: Once and Future King)

The Sword in the Stone. London, Collins, 1938; New York, Putnam, 1939; revised edition in *The Once and Future King,* 1958.
The Witch in the Wood. New York, Putnam, 1939; London, Collins, 1940; revised edition, as *The Queen of Air and Darkness,* in *The Once and Future King,* 1958.
The Ill-Made Knight. New York, Putnam, 1940; London, Collins, 1941; revised edition in *The Once and Future King,* 1958.
Mistress Masham's Repose. New York, Putnam, 1946; London, Cape, 1947.
The Once and Future King (omnibus; includes *The Candle in the Wind* plus revised versions of the three earlier novels in the series). London, Collins, and New York, Putnam, 1958.
The Book of Merlyn: The Unpublished Conclusion to The Once and Future King. Austin, University of Texas Press, 1977; London, Collins, 1978.

OTHER PUBLICATIONS

Novels

Dead Mr. Nixon, with R. McNair Scott. London, Cassell, 1931.
Darkness at Pemberley. London, Gollancz, 1932; New York, Century, 1933.
They Winter Abroad (as James Aston). London, Chatto and Windus, and New York, Viking Press, 1932.
First Lesson (as James Aston). London, Chatto and Windus, 1932; New York, Knopf, 1933.
Farewell Victoria. London, Collins, 1933; New York, Smith and Haas, 1934.
The Elephant and the Kangaroo. New York, Putnam, 1947; London, Cape, 1948.
The Master: An Adventure Story (for children). London, Cape, and New York, Putnam, 1958.

Short Stories

Earth Stopped; or, Mr. Marx's Sporting Tour. London, Collins, 1934; New York, Putnam, 1935.
Gone to Ground. London, Collins, and New York, Putnam, 1935.
The Maharajah and Other Stories, edited by Kurth Sprague. London, Macdonald, and New York, Putnam, 1981.

Poetry

Loved Helen and Other Poems. London, Chatto and Windus, and New York, Viking Press, 1929.
The Green Bay Tree; or, The Wicked Man Touches Wood. Cambridge, Heffer, 1929.
Verses. Privately printed, 1962.
A Joy Proposed. London, Rota, 1980; Athens, University of Georgia Press, 1983.

Other

England Have My Bones. London, Collins, and New York, Macmillan, 1936.
Burke's Steerage; or, The Amateur Gentleman's Introduction to Noble Sports and Pastimes. London, Collins, 1938; New York, Putnam, 1939.
The Age of Scandal: An Excursion Through a Minor Period. London, Cape, and New York, Putnam, 1950.
The Goshawk (on falconry). London, Cape, 1951; New York, Putnam, 1952.
The Scandalmonger (on English scandals). London, Cape, and New York, Putnam, 1952.
The Godstone and the Blackymor (on Ireland). London, Cape, and New York, Putnam, 1959.
America at Last: The American Journal of T. H. White. New York, Putnam, 1965.
The White/Garnett Letters, edited by David Garnett. London, Cape, and New York, Viking Press, 1968.
Letters to a Friend: The Correspondence Between T. H. White and L. J. Potts, edited by Francois Gallix. New York, Putnam, 1982; Gloucester, Sutton, 1984.

Editor and Translator, *The Book of Beasts, Being a Translation from a Latin Bestiary of the Twelfth Century.* London, Cape, 1954; New York, Putnam, 1955.

*

Film Adaptations: *The Sword in the Stone,* 1963; *The Master,* 1966 (television serial); *Camelot,* 1967, from the stage musical based on *The Once and Future King.*

Bibliography: *T. H. White: An Annotated Bibliography* by Francois Gallix, New York, Garland, 1986.

Critical Studies: *T. H. White: A Biography* by Sylvia Townsend Warner, London, Cape-Chatto and Windus, 1967, New York, Viking Press, 1968; *T. H. White* by John K. Crane, New York, Twayne, 1974.

* * *

"On Mondays, Wednesdays, and Fridays it was Court Hand and Summulae Logicales, while the rest of the week it was Organon, Repetition and Astrology." This is a strikingly appropriate opening sentence for a fantasy novel whose subject is the education of a prince. *The Sword in the Stone* tells the hitherto untold story of the boyhood and education of Arthur prior to his drawing of the mysterious stone from the anvil outside a church and his acclamation as King of England. This was a part of Arthur's life that Sir Thomas Malory had neglected in his 15th-century romance *Le Morte D'Arthur*. Nevertheless, in *The Sword in the Stone* and in the volumes which followed it, White played all sorts of ingenious intertextual games with Malory's chivalric masterpiece, rewriting it in the light of his 1930s pacifist convictions and his strongly developed sense of humour. Young Arthur (called "Wart" by everybody) is reared in ignorance of his true origins by Sir Ector in a castle located in the heart of a fantasy medieval England which White calls "Grammarye." As a result of an adventure early on in the novel, Wart acquires Merlyn as a tutor. Merlyn, who (like White) was educated at Cambridge in the early 20th century, but who has been living backwards ever since, has eccentric notions about education and his favoured method of education is to transform Arthur into a series of birds, animals and insects. White as a writer brilliantly exploited his extensive practical knowledge of natural history and of the arts of the hunt in these episodes of magical transformation. White's artistic use of anachronism is also noteworthy. Some anachronisms are merely comic, but some are inserted in order (paradoxically) to make the middle ages seem more real to the reader.

In *The Queen of Air and Darkness* and in the volumes which follow the tone darkens and the treatment of Arthurian legend becomes more adult. Nevertheless, there is still plenty of comedy (in this volume much of it centring round the whisky-drinking, lapsed saint, Toirdealbhach and King Pellinore's absurd relationship with the Questing Beast). But two more serious themes predominate. White's account of the growing-up of Gareth and his brothers on the Orkneys shows much damage can be done to boys by a lustful and capricious mother who is by turns neglectful and possessive of the boys. The other theme very much to the fore in the chapters in which Arthur and his old tutor feature is war. Can it ever be justified? Can it be prevented? How can Might be subordinated to Right? Towards the end of the volume, Morgause and Arthur come together with evil consequences for the kingdom in the years to come.

The "Ill-Made Knight" of the title of the third volume is Lancelot, who, though ugly, is the best knight and jouster of his age. (White, making typical use of anachronism, compares him to the cricketer, Don Bradman.) At the centre of this volume is the story of Lancelot's adulterous, yet still somehow noble love for Arthur's queen, Guenever. Not only does Lancelot hate betraying his king, he is prey to superstitious fears that his adultery will somehow sap his prowess as champion knight, as well as preventing him from ever performing a miracle. In this volume, the Quest of the Grail, though important, takes place offstage (like a battle in a Shakespeare history play). Although Lancelot is denied the ultimate miracle which is the full vision of the Grail, he is finally accorded the power to work a miracle of healing. Together with *The Sword in the Stone*, this is the most successful of White's novels, much of the narrative's strength deriving from White's only partial success in presenting a sympathetic portrait of Guenever. While he cannot quite persuade himself to like her, his account of her love for Lancelot is still very moving.

The Candle in the Wind deals with the strife which destroyed Arthur's England. Crook-backed Mordred, son of Arthur and Morgause, exploits the adultery of the ageing Lancelot and Guenever to create suspicion between his kinsmen, the Orkney clan, and the King and to drive Lancelot into exile. Then, while Arthur is in France, Mordred stages a kind of proto-fascist revolt. Themes of might versus right are once again very much to the fore. Taken as a whole, *The Once and Future King* is a work of genius in which White beautifully evokes Merrie England, not as it was, but as it jolly well should have been. His is undoubtedly the most successful of modern retellings of the Arthurian legend.

In *The Book of Merlyn* (which was published posthumously), Arthur on the eve of the last battle is visited by his old tutor, is reunited with the some of the animals he loved as a boy and is transformed into yet more creatures in order to gain a clearer understanding of the roots of violence. As a work of fiction the book is not entirely successful, as it turns into a rather preachy symposium about man's aggressive instincts and how they can be controlled. However, the episode in which Arthur is transformed into a white-fronted goose and courts the gander Lyo-Lyok is very fine.

Mistress Masham's Repose is a fantasy novel written for children, about descendants of Gulliver's Lilliputians. Maria, a ten-year-old orphan, discovers the little people living (somewhat in the manner of Mary Norton's "Borrowers") in Mistress Masham's Repose, an old folly on a secluded island on the ducal estate of Malplaquet. Although Maria is heiress to Malplaquet, her governess and the vicar, Mr. Hater, plot to cheat her out of it. When they learn of the existence of the Lilliputians, they are determined to capture the mannikins, so that they can exhibit them at a profit. Maria and the Lilliputians combine forces to thwart the evil pair. They are helped in this by the absent-minded Professor, a pedagogic figure with more than a passing resemblance to Merlyn and indeed to White himself. It is possible to detect the strong influence of the structure and tone of John Masefield's classic fantasy novel for children, *The Midnight Folk*, on White's novel. However, much of the fun of the book arises from White's witty deployment of his extensive knowledge of 18th-century mores and diction, presenting the Lilliputians as preserving, as if in amber, 18th-century manners.

The Master, a less successful work, is a juvenile science fiction novel, in which a 157-year-old reclusive Master plots on the island of Rockall to take over the world, but is thwarted by two children and their dog.

—Robert Irwin

WILDE, Oscar (Fingall O'Flahertie Wills)

Nationality: British. **Born:** Dublin, 10 October 1854. **Education:** Trinity College, Dublin; Magdalen College, Oxford. **Family:** Married Constance Lloyd in 1884 (died 1898); two sons. **Career:** In London from 1879, poet, aesthete, raconteur, man-about-town; lecturer in the USA, 1882; editor, *Woman's World*, London, 1887-89; reviewer, playwright, short-story writer, novelist. Imprisoned, 1895-97; spent last three years of his life in exile in France. **Died:** 30 November 1900.

Fantasy Publications

Novels

The Picture of Dorian Gray. London, Ward Lock, 1891.

Short Stories

The Happy Prince and Other Tales. London, David Nutt, 1888.
Lord Arthur Savile's Crime and Other Stories. London, Osgood McIlvaine, 1891.
A House of Pomegranates. London, Osgood McIlvaine, 1891.
Poems in Prose. Paris, privately printed, 1905.
Complete Shorter Fiction (omnibus), edited by Isobel Murray. Oxford, Oxford University Press, 1979.

Other Publications

Plays

Vera. London, Ranken, 1880.
The Duchess of Padua. New York, privately printed, 1883; London, Methuen, 1907.
Salomé (in French). London, Matthews and Lane, 1893; English-language edition, Matthews and Lane, 1894.
Lady Windermere's Fan (produced 1892). London, Matthews and Lane, 1893.
A Woman of No Importance (produced 1893). London, Lane, 1894.
An Ideal Husband (produced 1895). London, Smithers, 1899.
The Importance of Being Earnest (produced 1895). London, Smithers, 1899.
For Love of the King: A Burmese Masque. Methuen, 1922.

Poetry

Poems. N.p., David Bogue, 1881.
The Sphinx. London, Matthews and Lane, 1894.
The Ballad of Reading Gaol. London, Smithers, 1898.
The Harlot's House. London, Smithers, 1904.
Pan, a Double Villanelle, and Desespoir, a Sonnet. J.W. Luce & Co., 1909.
Remorse: A Study in Saffron. William Andrews Clark Memorial Library, 1961.

Other

Intentions. London, Osgood McIlvaine, 1891.
Oscariana. London, privately printed, 1895.
The Soul of Man Under Socialism. London, Humphreys, 1895.
The Portrait of Mr. W.H. T.B. Mosher, 1901.
Phrases and Philosophies for the Use of the Young. privately printed, 1902.
De Profundis. London, Methuen, 1905.
The Rise and Fall of Historical Criticism. Sherwood Press, 1905.
Four Letters Which Were Not Included in the English Edition of De Profundis. privately printed, 1906.
Impressions of America. Keystone Press, 1906.
Decorative Art in America. Brentano's, 1906.
The Works of Oscar Wilde. London, Methuen, 1908.

The Suppressed Portion of "De Profundis," by Oscar Wilde, Now for the First Time Published by His Literary Executor. P.R. Reynolds, 1913.
A Critic in Pall Mall: Being Extracts From Reviews and Miscellanies. Methuen, 1919.
The Critic as Artist: A Dialogue. De Roos, 1957.
The Letters of Oscar Wilde. London, Hart Davis, 1962.

*

Film Adaptations: *Lady Windermere's Fan,* 1916, 1925, *The Fan,* 1949, all from his play *Lady Windermere's Fan*; *The Picture of Dorian Gray,* 1916, 1945, *Dorian Gray,* 1970, 1973 (TV movie), 1976 (TV movie), *The Sins of Dorian Gray,* 1983 (TV movie), all from his novel *The Picture of Dorian Gray*; *Salome,* 1923, 1987, *Salome's Last Dance,* 1988, all from his play *Salomé*; *The Canterville Ghost,* 1943, 1986 (TV movie); *Flesh and Fantasy,* 1943, from his short story "Lord Arthur Savile's Crime"; *An Ideal Husband,* 1948; *The Importance of Being Earnest,* 1952.

Critical Studies: *The Life of Oscar Wilde* by Hesketh Pearson, Greenwood Press, 1978; *Oscar Wilde* by Peter Raby, Cambridge University Press, 1988; *Oscar Wilde* by Richard Ellman, Knopf, 1988; *Oscar Wilde's "The Importance of Being Earnest,"* (edited by Harold Bloom), Chelsea House, 1988; *Critical Essays on Oscar Wilde,* (edited by Regenia Gagnier), G.K. Hall, 1991;

* * *

In 1887, the year that he became editor of *Woman's World,* Oscar Wilde began an intense period of literary activity which lasted until March 1895, when he launched the libel action against the Marquess of Queensberry that was to lead the way to his destruction. His two comic fantasies, "The Canterville Ghost" and "Lord Arthur Savile's Crime," both appeared in *The Court and Society Review* in 1887. The latter employs the sparkling wit for which he was to become famous, casting a heavily ironic gloss on Savile's increasingly desperate attempts to commit the murder (which a medium has detected in his destiny) in the manner least harmful to his fortunes. The former is much the better by virtue of its melancholy undercurrent, which (prophetically) laments the Americanization of English culture while acknowledging the irresistible force of American pragmaticism. The poor tradition-bound ghost has no chance against the positive thinking of his mansion's new tenants, but the manner of his eventual release introduces a note of earnest sentimentality to leaven the comedy. Such heartfelt notes were to become increasingly manifest in the series of fantasies featured in Wilde's two books of children's stories.

The contents of *The Happy Prince and Other Stories* are cast in a conventional mode, but a certain cynicism is already evident in the conclusions of all except the self-consciously sickly "The Selfish Giant," whose moral is wryly overturned in "A Devoted Friend." "The Happy Prince" gladly donates his coat of gold leaf to the poor, but when winter comes the swallow who has been his envoy freezes to death and the now-shabby statue is scrapped, only its immutably broken heart refusing to melt. This refusal to recapitulate traditional "happy endings" and the morality they endorse is taken further in "The Nightingale and the Rose"; the bird who sacrifices her life in order that a student may have the red rose demanded of him by the girl he loves turns out to have shed her life-blood for nothing when both parties to the bargain prove to be fickle and unworthy.

The stories in *A House of Pomegranates* abandon all pretence of lightness in their allegorical pursuit of a more profound moral consciousness. "The Young King" (1888), enthroned by self-seeking murderers, refuses the regalia of his office upon discovering the hardships which his people must endure to pay for his coronation; alas, only Heaven respects his decision. In the harrowing tale of "The Birthday of the Infanta" (1889) a similarly ostentatious display of wealth forms the background to the tale of a dwarf brought from the forest to amuse the infanta. The dwarf, at first overjoyed by the attention paid to him, has his illusions brutally shattered when he looks into a mirror for the first time, but his death leaves the celebrants totally unaffected. In the two stories original to the collection the dark mood is further intensified. "The Fisherman and His Soul"—perhaps the finest fantasy written in English in the 19th century—inverts the key images of Hans Christian Andersen's "The Little Mermaid". Andersen's mermaid tries desperately to acquire a soul so as to wed the fisherman she loves, but Wilde's fisherman casually drives his away. The rejected soul constantly return to tempt the fisherman away from cosy domesticity with visions of a world full of exotic promise and the fisherman eventually takes it back, but he finds it irredeemably tainted. During the meeting described in Laurence Housman's *Echo de Paris* Wilde, long since broken by his ordeals, recounts a brief and exceedingly bitter parable which uses the same central motif, reinforcing the suspicion that this story can be read as a transfiguration of Wilde's view of his own situation. "The Star-Child" may invite interpretation in the same way, but only retrospectively; it tracks the tribulations of an infant betrayed by delusions of grandeur who has to learn to be virtuous the hard way, and even then finds the rewards of his hard-won goodness blighted by the erosions of evil.

These tales clearly show the influence of the rich French tradition of sophisticated and morally subversive *contes,* which Wilde embraced as enthusiastically as he embraced all the theories and mannerisms of the French Decadent Movement—theories which he elaborated rather coyly in his essay "The Decay of Lying" and mannerisms which he extrapolated with great verve and style in *The Picture of Dorian Gray.* Wilde's only novel is, in spite of its prefatory declaration as to the irrelevance of such judgments, a highly moral book, although not everyone saw it that way. Dorian's attempts to make his life a work of art while his portrait suffers the ugly legacy of his sins is, in the end, doomed to failure because he cannot overcome the force of his guilty self-hatred. Unable to resist the force of his own genius, Wilde hurried like Arthur Savile to fulfil the terms of the doom-laden prophecy.

The further influence of the French Decadents is, of course, seen in the play *Salomé,* which Wilde published in French—Marcel Schwob and Pierre Louys helped him to fine-tune the language—after the Lord Chamberlain refused to allow such apparent blasphemy upon the English stage. The blasphemy is only apparent, for Wilde, like Baudelaire before him, could never shake off his faith in the Christian God, nor even—in spite of all the evidence offered by the state of the world—in His goodness. Wilde was also one of the very few English writers to dabble in prose-poetry (which chimerical genre Joris-Karl Huysmans' Jean Des Esseintes considered to be the most appropriate art-form of the Decadent Movement). The cycle of six published in the *Fortnightly Review* in 1894 includes two which had first appeared the previous year: "The House of Judgment," a sceptical account of the disputed weighing of a man's soul, and "The Disciple," which reveals that the pool into which Narcissus stared never knew whether he was handsome or not, because it was too busy admiring its own reflection in his eyes.

Wilde, as a writer and as a man, was far ahead of his time. His crucifixion by the malevolence of the Marquess of Queensberry (whose chief delight was to watch members of the lower classes beat one another senseless) put a viciously cruel end to his career, so we can only speculate as to what he might have produced given a free rein. The best of his fantasies are bitter parables in which human folly, vanity and infidelity cause untold misery—as, of course, they still do and probably always will.

—Brian Stableford

WILDER, Cherry

Pseudonym for Cherry Barbara Grimm. **Nationality:** New Zealander. **Born:** Cherry Barbara Lockett, Auckland, 3 September 1930. **Education:** Nelson Girls' College, 1943-48; Canterbury University College, Christchurch, 1949-52, B.A. 1952. **Family:** Married 1) A. J. Anderson in 1952; 2) H. K. F. Grimm in 1963 (died), two daughters. **Career:** Lived in Australia, 1954-76: high school teacher, editorial assistant, theatre director; regular reviewer for Sydney *Morning Herald* and *The Australian,* 1964-74; moved to Germany. **Awards:** Australia Council Grant, 1973, 1975. **Agent:** James Frenkel, 414 S. Randall Ave., Madison, WI 53715, USA. **Address:** Kurt-Schumacher-Strasse 36, 63225 Langen/Hessen, Germany.

FANTASY PUBLICATIONS

Novels (series: The Rulers of Hylor in all books)

A Princess of the Chameln. New York, Atheneum, 1984; London, Unwin, 1985.
Yorath the Wolf. New York, Atheneum, 1984; London, Unwin, 1986.
The Summer's King. New York, Atheneum, 1985; London, Unwin, 1987.

OTHER PUBLICATIONS

Novels

The Luck of Brin's Five. New York, Atheneum, 1977; London, Angus and Robertson, 1979.
The Nearest Fire. New York, Atheneum, 1980.
Second Nature. New York, Pocket Books, 1982; London, Allen and Unwin, 1986.
The Tapestry Warriors. New York, Atheneum, 1983.
Cruel Designs. London, Piatkus, 1988.

Short Stories

Dealers in Light and Darkness. Cambridge, Massachusetts, Edgewood Press, 1995.

*

Manuscript Collection: de Grummond Collection, University of Southern Mississippi, Hattiesburg.

*   *   *

Though she has produced several well-received works of science fiction and a horror novel, *Cruel Designs,* Cherry Wilder has also written a fantasy series, the Rulers of Hylor trilogy. These novels take a somewhat off-centre approach to a common fantasy theme: the young ruler of a peaceful land, threatened by an external arch-enemy of overweening power, ambition and ruthlessness. Chameln is one of a number of lands of the continent of Hylor. It is ruled over by the Daindru, co-sovereigns who unite its two races—the Firn and the Zor—not in marriage but in mutual respect and co-operation.

The first book, *A Princess of the Chameln,* follows the progress of Aidris am Firn. When first her parents, and then the remaining Daindru ruler, are assassinated and the Chameln lands invaded by the neighbouring Mel'nir, she goes into hiding as a kedran—a female cavalry soldier—in the land of Athron. Typically for this kind of story, along the way she learns to use the magic she possesses, and finds out who her real enemies—and friends—are.

Most importantly, she discovers that the real enemy of the Chameln is not Gol of Melnir, but his vizier, Rosmer. But she also befriends a tribe of "little people"—the ancient Firn from whom her people sprang; and she dispels a magical enchantment accidentally laid upon a tower. This aside, there is little magic in the story: Aidris has a magic stone, given to her by her dying mother. In this, she sees snatches of the future, and a mysterious Lady who is apparently an ally. This, however, amounts to little. For instance, the Lady in the mirror offers her a choice of gifts. She chooses a book; later she has it, though we are not shown how it arrived; but it is an ordinary book of poems, written by one Robillan Hazard, and it is only referred to again when her knowledge of the author allows her to start a friendship with a pretender to the throne. Its other major function is to let Aidris—and the reader—know that her cousin Yorath, whom she was told was born deformed and killed at birth, actually survived.

Aidris is an engaging heroine, which is just as well since the bulk of the narrative is taken up with her growth to maturity. Eventually, though, she is found by loyalists. Invaders and pretenders are ousted, and Aidris shows that she has not only the bravery and intelligence, but also the compassion and wisdom, to rule wisely.

Wilder peoples her story with real, complex characters—neither heroes nor villains, but human beings with virtues and vices. However, the language she chooses is quite formal. The dialogue, particularly, often seems quite stilted. This, coupled with the extremely complex names, genealogy and geography, makes the story quite difficult to follow. It also has the effect of distancing the reader from the story, and from Aidris's experiences. Another problem is that, though Aidris takes action first to save herself and then to secure her future, and though some of the adventures she has along the way are intrinsically interesting, essentially she simply waits for rescue.

In the second volume, *Yorath the Wolf,* Wilder explores the fate of Yorath, the deformed son of Gol, ruler of Mel'nir. As Aidris saw in her mirror in the first book, he was not killed at birth. Instead, he is taken to a cottage deep in the Nightwood and raised there. He grows to be a skilled soldier, with a twisted shoulder the only legacy of his bad birth. As with *A Princess of the Chameln,* the real story here is the one of how Yorath comes into his power—

by way of an encounter with Gundril Chawn, the Owlwife—and how he learns to deal with it.

Finally there is *The Summer King.* Wilder returns to the Chameln Lands to tell the story of Sharn Am Zor, Aidris's co-ruler in the Daindru. He has grown into a man readers will recognize from the child he was in the first book—likeable but a bit arrogant and headstrong—and, disastrously, inclined to trust the wrong people. When the time comes to take a wife, he will have none but Princess Moinagh of the Eildon, the magical kingdom. He courts her, but her people demand much tribute and many demeaning rituals. During one of these, he realizes she is not the right woman to be his queen. He returns home and weds another. The experience matures him, and he becomes a good king. But it also sows the seeds of his destruction, for he alienates his old, but untrustworthy, friend Tazlo. Tazlo betrays him to the Inchevin, a neighbouring people. They execute him, but he uses his death curse to kill the still dangerous Rosmer.

Though Wilder successfully ties up many of the plot threads from the earlier books (for instance, Hazard, the writer of Aidris's book appears as a major character), in some ways *The Summer King* is the least successful part of the trilogy. In it, she dwells at length on the rituals of the Zor court, particularly at the beginning. She also slips from viewpoint character to viewpoint character, and from past to present tense, apparently at whim. This is a shame, because Sharn Am Zor is an engaging character, and these devices distance the reader so much from him, and at times make his story so difficult to follow, that his death lacks the pathos and tragedy it should really attain. But, despite shortcomings, these novels add up to one of the most intelligent fantasy trilogies of the 1980s.

Cherry Wilder is also a fine, stylish short-story writer—alas, somewhat under-collected. Although most of her stories may be classified as science fiction, some of the pieces in *Dealers in Light and Darkness,* her one collection to date, do brush the edges of fantasy.

—Liz Holliday

WILKINS, Vaughan (William)

Nationality: British. **Born:** London, 6 March 1890. **Family:** Married Mary Powell in 1930; two sons. **Career:** Journalist; editor, London *Daily Call;* assistant editor, London *Daily Express.* **Died:** 1959.

FANTASY PUBLICATIONS

Novels

After Bath; or, The Remarkable Case of the Flying Hat. London, Cape, 1945.
The City of Frozen Fire. London, Cape, 1950.
Fanfare for a Witch. London, Cape, 1954.
Valley Beyond Time. London, Cape, 1955.

OTHER PUBLICATIONS

Novels

And So—Victoria. London, Cape, 1937.

Being Met Together. London, Cape, 1944.
Once Upon a Time. New York, Macmillan, 1949.
Crown Without Sceptre. London, Cape, 1952.
A King Reluctant. London, Cape, 1952.
Lady of Paris. London, Cape, 1956.
Dangerous Exile. London, Cape, 1956.
Husband for Victoria. London, Cape, 1958.

Other

Endless Prelude (editor). London, Routledge, 1937.
Seven Tempest. New York, Macmillan, 1942.

*   *   *

Vaughan Wilkins, who turned to literary work rather late in life, is best-known for his historical novels, and the fantasy element in his work appears to be a natural extrapolation of his sense of the past. His fantasy for younger children, *After Bath,* is a rather uneasy work loosely strung together by the haphazard movements of a windblown hat, but *The City of Frozen Fire*—which Wilkins always listed among his adult novels although it was marketed as a juvenile and was very obviously formulated as a "boys' book" set solidly in the tradition of Stevenson's *Treasure Island*—is a much more robust effort.

The City of Frozen Fire is set in 19th-century Wales. The story commences with the arrival in the Standish household of a wounded stranger who speaks only Latin and archaic Welsh. Much to his distress, his sole possession—a ruby crown by means of which he had hoped to claim the aid of modern Wales for the Welsh-descended inhabitants of his homeland—is mysteriously stolen. The Standishes' response is to assemble an expedition to recover it. The homeland in question is the lost land of Quivera, where descendants of the 12th-century adventurer Prince Madoc—whose heir and namesake the stranger is—have already been devastated by new diseases imported from the outside world, and are now further menaced by the evil pirate Captain Darkness.

The heroes of *The City of Frozen Fire* set forth on their mission in the *Volcano,* an experimental steamship somewhat ahead of the time of the story (Wilkins was fond of such devices; *Being Met Together* echoes Théophile Gautier's *The Belle-Jenny* in describing an attempt to rescue Napoleon from exile by means of a submarine). The invocation of such an ultra-modern device serves to highlight the fact that their destination is identified with the mythical Earthly Paradise, in search of which the original Madoc had set forth. The city of Cibola which is the new Madoc's heritage has indeed been a near-paradise, albeit one that had to be constructed rather than simply found, but when the ravages of influenza are supplemented by the eruption of a nearby volcano its legacy is lost forever. The name of the ship emphasizes the symbolic significance of this unfortunate obliteration.

In view of the evident strength of the feelings latent within the plot of *The City of Frozen Fire* it is by no means surprising that in his final work Wilkins turned again, with heavy nostalgia, to similar subject-matter. *Valley Beyond Time* offers a different but no less heartfelt account of the relationship between mythical Cibola and modern Wales. *Valley Beyond Time* places Cibola—here presumed to be identical to the legendary Fortunate Isles—in a parallel world which is occasionally reachable from the British Isles through a dimensional doorway. Emigrants from earth and their descendants

co-exist there with the superhuman natives of the Valley of the Ever-Young. The novel juxtaposes the exploits of a group of people associated with an American senator, who once glimpsed the other world in his youth and is hopeful of finding it again, with the experiences of a boy who returns to earth after a sojourn there, accompanied by a girl from the magical valley. There is no way, of course, that any of these dreams can come to full fruition—the boy and the girl cannot adapt themselves to a world ruled by time and the people who belong to the modern world are ill-fitted to a life unregulated by it—but the downbeat tendency of the story is, in the end, ameliorated by sense as well as sentimentality.

Valley Beyond Time is a self-conscious swan song, undertaken with grace and dignity; it did not find favour with Wilkins' regular readers and some critics found its dispirited elegiac mood uncongenial, but it is an interesting late addition to the partially submerged tradition of 20th-century British fantasy—which was, of course, to be swamped a decade later by mass-produced American pastiches of Tolkien's exactly contemporary *The Lord of the Rings.* Now that "Celtic fantasy" is a thriving but wholly synthetic sub-genre of American fiction it is worth recalling that it was not so very long ago that living Welsh writers could and did feel a certain authentic attachment to the relevant cultural and mythical materials.

—Brian Stableford

WILLARD, Nancy (Margaret)

Nationality: American. **Born:** Ann Arbor, Michigan, 26 June 1936. **Education:** University of Michigan, Ann Arbor (five Hopwood awards), B.A. 1958, Ph.D. in English 1963; Stanford University, California (Woodrow Wilson fellow), M.A. 1960. **Family:** Married Eric Lindbloom in 1964; one son. **Career:** Since 1965 Lecturer in English, Vassar College, Poughkeepsie, New York; since 1975 Instructor, Bread Loaf Writers Conference. **Awards:** Devins Memorial Award, for poetry, 1967; O. Henry Award, for short story, 1970; National Endowment for the Arts Grant, 1976, 1987; Creative Artists Public Service Award, 1977; American Library Association Newbery Medal, 1982. **Agent:** Jean V. Naggar, 336 East 73rd Street, New York, NY 10021, USA. **Address:** 133 College Avenue, Poughkeepsie, NY 12603, USA.

Fantasy Publications

Novels

Things Invisible to See. New York, Knopf, 1984.
Sister Water. New York, Knopf, 1993.

Short Stories

The Lively Anatomy of God. New York, Eakins Press, 1968.
Childhood of the Magician. New York, Liveright, 1973.
Angel in the Parlor: Five Stories and Eight Essays. New York, Harcourt Brace, 1983.

OTHER PUBLICATIONS

Fiction for Children

Sailing to Cythera and Other Anatole Stories, illustrated by David McPhail. New York, Harcourt Brace, 1974.

The Snow Rabbit, illustrated by Laura Lydecker. New York, Putnam, 1975.

Shoes Without Leather, illustrated by Laura Lydecker. New York, Putnam, 1976.

The Well-Mannered Balloon, illustrated by Haig and Regina Shekerjian. New York, Harcourt Brace, 1976.

Strangers' Bread, illustrated by David McPhail. New York, Harcourt Brace, 1977.

Simple Pictures Are Best, illustrated by Tomie de Paola. New York, Harcourt Brace, 1977; London, Collins, 1978.

The Highest Hit, illustrated by Emily McCully. New York, Harcourt Brace, 1978.

Papa's Panda, illustrated by Lillian Hoban. New York, Harcourt Brace, 1979.

The Island of the Grass King: The Further Adventures of Anatole, illustrated by David McPhail. New York, Harcourt Brace, 1979.

The Marzipan Moon, illustrated by Marcia Sewall. New York, Harcourt Brace, 1981.

Uncle Terrible: More Adventures of Anatole, illustrated by David McPhail. New York, Harcourt Brace, 1982.

The Nightgown of the Sullen Moon, illustrated by David McPhail. New York, Harcourt Brace, 1983.

The Mountains of Quilt, illustrated by Tomie de Paola. San Diego, Harcourt Brace, 1987.

Firebrat, illustrated by David Wiesner. New York, Knopf, 1988.

The High Rise Glorious Skittle Skat Roarious Sky Pie Angel Food Cake. N.p., 1990.

Pish, Posh, Said Hieronymous Bosch, illustrated by Leo, Diane and Lee Dillon. New York, Harcourt Brace, 1991.

Beauty and the Beast (retelling). New York, Harcourt Brace, 1992.

Play

East of the Sun and West of the Moon, illustrated by Bruce Moser. San Diego, Harcourt Brace, 1989.

Poetry

In His Country. Ann Arbor, Michigan, Generation, 1966.

Skin of Grace. Columbia, University of Missouri Press, 1967.

A New Herball. Baltimore, Ferdinand Roten Galleries, 1968.

19 Masks for the Naked Poet. Santa Cruz, California, Kayak, 1971.

Carpenter of the Sun. New York, Liveright, 1974.

The Merry History of a Christmas Pie, With a Delicious Description of a Christmas Soup, illustrated by Haig and Regina Shekerjian. New York, Putnam, 1974.

All on a May Morning, illustrated by Haig and Regina Shekerjian. New York, Putnam, 1975.

A Visit to William Blake's Inn: Poems for Innocent and Experienced Travelers, illustrated by Alice and Martin Provensen. New York, Harcourt Brace, 1981; London, Methuen, 1982.

Household Tales of Moon and Water. New York, Harcourt Brace, 1982.

Night Story, illustrated by Ilse Plume. San Diego, Harcourt Brace, and London, Methuen, 1986.

The Voyage of the Ludgate Hill: Travels with Robert Louis Stevenson, illustrated by Alice and Martin Provensen. San Diego, Harcourt Brace, 1987.

Water Walker. New York, Knopf, 1989.

The Sorcerer's Apprentice, illustrated by Leo and Diane Dillon. New York, Blue Sky Press, 1993.

Other

Testimony of the Invisible Man: William Carlos Williams, Francis Ponge, Rainer Maria Rilke, Pablo Neruda. Columbia, University of Missouri Press, 1970.

Telling Time: Angels, Ancestors and Stories. New York, Harcourt Brace, 1993.

*

Manuscript Collection: Kerlan Collection, University of Minnesota, Minneapolis.

Illustrator: *The Letter of John to James,* 1981, and *Another Letter of John to James about Church and the Eucharist,* 1982, both by John Kater.

*　　*　　*

In her essay "The Well-Tempered Falsehood: The Art of Storytelling" (in *The Angel in the Parlor*) Nancy Willard observes that of the various problems facing storytellers "the most unsettling and, at the same time, most exhilarating" is that "without knowing how or why, you cross over easily from the natural to the supernatural as if you felt absolutely no difference between them." All her essays on writing—many more are collected in *Telling Time: Angels, Ancestors and Stories*—insist on the necessity of writing from experience, but she points out that the supernatural plays a vital and perfectly normal role in that precious part of our experience which consists of dreams, daydreams and the stories we routinely tell one another. The element of fantasy in her work is, in consequence, thoroughly domesticated; it is manifest not as a threatening and disturbing disruption of normality but something which can fit into everyday life quite seamlessly, and which almost always has a constructive or healing effect. Active evil—whether human or supernatural—does not play a considerable part in her works, but active good does, often in the shape of literally- or metaphorically-ghostly ancestors and sometimes in the form of fully-fledged angels.

The absence of any robust boundary between the natural and the supernatural in Willard's work is mirrored in her conscientious disrespect for other kinds of conventional boundaries. She writes for children and for adults with precisely the same delicacy and suppleness, often with both audiences seemingly in mind; her Newbery Medal-winning collection *A Visit to William Blake's Inn* is subtitled "Poems for Innocent and Experienced Travelers." Her essays frequently make use of the same narrative techniques as her stories; her discourse on parables, "Danny Weinstein's Magic Book," mostly consists of parables, and her fine account of "How Poetry Came into the World and Why God Doesn't Write It" is part allegory and part anthology. In the general context of these endeavours it seems entirely appropriate that a story as phantasmagoric as "The Doctrine of the Leather-Stocking Jesus" (in *The Angel in the Par-*

lor) seems utterly realistic in her telling, and that *The High Rise Glorious Skittle Skat Roarious Sky Pie Angel Food Cake* convincingly involves angels in the prosaic business of cake-making. To bring off such effects casually requires an exceptionally good ear for the mannerisms of oral storytelling—a talent further extended in the neat fusion of ancient and contemporary modes and values contrived by her Americanized version of *Beauty and the Beast*.

Things Invisible to See is the story of the romance which develops between a boy growing up in the shadow of World War II and a girl who is tragically paralysed by a baseball which he carelessly hits into the night. The ripples of causality associated with this accident spread out to affect both families, and it is the resilience of family ties and family loyalties—extended and symbolized by the girl's phantom Ancestress—which provides the safety net that prevents the disaster becoming total. The hero is eventually cast adrift in a life-raft while on active service in the Pacific, but is able to make a bargain with Death which ties his fate to a baseball game in which his team of high school friends is nominated to play Death's own team of all-time greats. When the boys are injured on their way to the game the odds seem stacked in favour of Death's team, but while the Lord of the Universe—who seems to spend the greater part of His time as pitcher to the archangels—looks on with kindly but inactive interest the healthy persuasions of love and loyalty save the day. The story is unrepentantly sentimental but not in the least sickly, perhaps because it is not so much a tale of salvation as a tale of salvage (the title of the chapter which informs the stricken girl's little brother of the existence of the amazing "rude doctor" Cold Friday, who can and does cure her, is "Salvage for Victory").

Sister Water is also a tale of salvage, which similarly deploys its small and subtle miracles to the purpose of patching up the shattered lives of its main characters: a woman widowed by a car accident and a young man hired to look after her aging and ailing mother. Here, though, it is the "angel"—the young man, whose wings are humbly literal as well as metaphorical—who finally requires deliverance, when circumstantial evidence leads to his being charged with a homicide foolishly committed and fearfully covered up by his would-be rival for the widow's affections. The sentimentality of the story is as carefully understated as the supernatural element, but is no less powerful for its modesty. The many-layered symbolism which, among other things, likens the life-giving but sometimes misfortunate permeation of the natural environment by rivers, rivulets and pools to the permeation of the human community by relationships and moral obligations, is similarly unobtrusive and similarly effective.

A marked preference for angels over demons is rare in modern fiction; few writers are willing and able to deploy the mythical apparatus of Heaven, partly because it is intrinsically far less melodramatic than the apparatus of Hell and partly because miracles are generally the cheapest and most debased method of resolving plots. It is a tribute to Nancy Willard's great but quiet artistry that she is entirely at ease with such materials; there is nothing in any way false or excessively convenient about the manner in which she deploys her miraculous instruments. When she invokes a *deus ex machina* she does so with authentic reverence and careful scrupulousness. In her use of angels and other benign magical devices she may appear to be unashamedly rushing in where others sensibly fear to tread, but her narratives move with an authoritative grace and dexterity which could not possibly be thought foolish.

—Brian Stableford

WILLEY, Elizabeth

Nationality: American. **Address:** Lives in San Francisco, California.

FANTASY PUBLICATIONS

Novels

The Well-Favored Man. New York, Tor, 1993.
A Sorcerer and a Gentleman. New York, Tor, 1995.

*   *   *

Elizabeth Willey has a good thing going with her debut novel *The Well-Favored Man.* Unfortunately, it's much the same thing that Roger Zelazny made a killing on with his Amber series. Yet, for all the reminiscences invoked by reading a book about "walking the road" and "playing with patterns," Willey attempts to make this landscape her own. She's mostly successful, since her philosophically-minded dragons, Shakespearean essences, intermingling of high-tech genetics with low-tech sorcerers, and sexually ambiguous flirtations, all make this novel a multi-faceted gem of mannerist world-building.

Prince Gwydion is governing the land of Argylle, a task he has taken more seriously in his mother, Freia's, absence. About 20 years ago Freia got consumed by the family's primal energy "Spring," but the intelligent reader doesn't buy the permanence of her transubstantiation for one swift whirl of an energetic eddy. Meanwhile, a huge intelligent magic-using dragon has flown into the neighbourhood. Gwydion rounds up the more bellicose members of his family, and they gird their loins and go a-hunting. Unfortunately, during the initial encounter the dragon succeeds in (almost literally) blowing the family away.

The plot meanders amiably forward from this point on. It is propelled by Gwydion's battles with the dragon, and the search for a method to resurrect Freia. Gwydion's sister, Ulrike, is shoved through a "Way" by their father, Gaston. The girl arrives, confused and frightened, near the hearthstone of Argylle's palace. Intrigue surrounds her, since her looks are very like those of her lost mother. Gwydion suspects that by sacrificing this mousy creature they could retrieve their beloved Freia. Yet nothing much comes of this despicable, (but highly entertaining) notion.

Instead, the reader is treated to a kaleidoscopic whirl of lighthearted revelries, assorted masques, and fancy balls. Nice clothing is worn and admired. Horse breeding and wine making are intelligently discussed, and ways of diverting the fruits of these labours into the cellars and stables of family intimates are planned. These intrigues and entertainments take up the bulk of the book, and Gwydion (and Willey) both appear at their most charming during these diversions. Watching Gwydion follow his mother's advice of giving the townsfolk just a bit more than they bargained for has a certain charm to anyone who is sick of dealing with committee compromises. Although, even if he is a sorcerer, the ruling Prince is a much less interesting character than most of his exotic relations.

Such as Prospero, the Grandfather of Them All. Prospero created the Argyllian portion of the world by shaping the essence of the Primal Spring, but now he's basically retired. He spends most of his time wenching, trying to keep his family honest, and having vinicultural discussions. Clues to his literary origins include his once having had the spritely Ariel as a sidekick, and the digressions his speech patterns make when he becomes, well, *tempestuous*. Case in point: after he recovers from a cardiac arrest brought about by an attempt to wrest Freia from the Spring he says: "What devils' work this? Who hath dammed my world into such dead neap-tide? 'Tis unnatural, the Spring's denatured. . . ." When assured that his offspring expected no harm to come from the experiment he cries, "Twould not affect me! Why, am I sawdust and wood? Not affect me, and 'twas I opened the very Spring which sustains and bathes thee in its essence! What hast thou done, thou cold-blooded water-witted profligate thieving viper's son?"

The Freia portion of the plot quite successfully removes the novel from its non-technological realm, and contrasts the world of thud-and-blunder with that of group-minds and cloning. When Gwydion's father is faced with his beloved wife being trapped in a sanitized electrified room, he behaves in a straightforward, sorcerously barbaric manner: he blockades the door, sets a fire, and uses the flames to escape through a "Way." This has the added attraction of checking Freia out of the hospital without having to fill out any of those tedious insurance forms.

Then there are Gwydion's cousins, who both battled a far more interesting dragon than his. Their beast was attempting to live a vegetarian existence, so as to rise above his own base nature and eventually reach Nirvana. Unfortunately, the dragon broke his vows by eating a beefy tax collector. The discussions it has are quite lively, if difficult to survive without becoming an *hors d'oeuvre*.

In a more typical fantasy piece Gwydion would gain maturity by learning how to battle his own dragon (and thus metaphorically accept more responsibility). Though in the end Gwydion annihilates the monster (after twice being saved by more powerful relations) there seems little progression to his character. Willey appears afraid to play with the dark forces in her creations, so Gwydion is at his least constrained when the stakes are low, like when he is chasing bed partners from boudoir to bordello to beer-hall. (Although, even during his flirtations, his mother occasionally manages to intercede.)

Gwydion's solution to the dragon can either be seen as "cheating," since he uses his magic to create a situation he had earlier considered "unthinkable," or as his final initiation into his family. After all, his older relations created entire worlds using only the force of their personalities, so what's a blasted heath or two?

Yet what this book suffers in original magic or plot-by-numbers action it makes up for in charm. Ellen Kushner-like, it is laced with flirtations and hints of bisexual liaisons. Its sorceries, while familiar, are well-done and its witticisms are slick and layered enough to amuse the fantastic *intelligentsia*. If there are irritating loose ends left at the novel's conclusion (Why is Ulrike supposed to avoid the company of her cousins? Just what sex is the "superb" Hulda anyway? How did they form that Spring and what will happen once Freia leaves it?) it is both a factor of first novel-itis and partially intentional, since there's a prequel, *A Sorcerer and a Gentleman*, already in the works at the time of this writing.

Though it may be hard to read *The Well-Favored Man* and not hear footsteps ringing on the Patterns' flagstones, Zelazny need not yet leap to get out of Willey's way. Yet, considering the talent shown in this premiere novel, he might just want to brush up on his Shakespeare.

—Shira Daemon

WILLIAMS, Charles (Walter Stansby)

Nationality: British. **Born:** London, 20 September 1886. **Education:** St. Albans School, Hertfordshire; University College, University of London. **Family:** Married Florence Conway in 1917; one son. **Career:** Joined Oxford University Press as a reader, 1908, and remained a member of staff until his death; writer from 1908. M.A.: Oxford University, 1943. **Died:** 15 May 1945.

FANTASY PUBLICATIONS

Novels

War in Heaven. London, Gollancz, 1930.
The Place of the Lion. London, Gollancz, 1931.
Many Dimensions. London, Gollancz, 1931.
The Greater Trumps. London, Gollancz, 1932.
Shadows of Ecstasy. London, Gollancz, 1933.
Descent Into Hell. London, Faber, 1937.
All Hallows' Eve. London, Faber, 1945.

Poetry

Taliessin Through Logres. Oxford, Oxford University Press, 1938.
The Region of the Summer Stars. London, Poetry (London) Editions, 1944.

OTHER PUBLICATIONS

Plays

The Moon: A Cantata, music by William G. Whittaker. 1923.
The Masque of the Manuscript, music by Hubert Foss. 1927.
A Myth of Shakespeare. 1928.
The Masque of Perusal, music by Hubert Foss. 1929.
Three Plays (includes *The Witch, The Chaste Woman, The Rite of Passion*). 1931.
Thomas Cranmer of Canterbury (produced 1936). 1939.
The House of the Octopus. 1945.
Seed of Adam and Other Plays (includes *The Death of Good Fortune, The House by the Stable, Grab and Grace*). 1948.
Collected Plays. 1963.

Poetry

The Silver Stair. 1912.
Poems of Conformity. 1917.
Divorce. 1920.
Windows of Night. 1924.
An Urbanity. 1927(?).
Heroes and Kings. 1930.
Arthurian Torso, Containing the Posthumous Fragment of "The Figure of Arthur," edited by C. S. Lewis. London, and New York, Oxford University Press, 1948.

Other

Poetry at Present. 1930.

The English Poetic Mind. 1932.

Bacon. 1933.

Reason and Beauty in the Poetic Mind. 1933.

James I. 1934.

The Ring and the Book, Retold, by Robert Browning. 1934.

Rochester. 1935.

Queen Elizabeth. 1936.

The Story of the Aeneid, Retold, by Virgil. 1936.

Stories of Great Names. 1937.

Henry VII. 1937.

He Came Down from Heaven. 1938.

The Descent of the Dove: A Short History of the Holy Spirit in the Church. 1939.

The Way of Exchange. 1941.

Religion and Love in Dante: The Theology of Romantic Love. 1941.

Witchcraft. London, Faber and Faber, 1941.

The Forgiveness of Sins. 1942.

The Figure of Beatrice: A Study of Dante. 1943.

Flecker of Dean Close. 1946.

The Image of the City and Other Essays, edited by Anne Ridler. 1958.

Selected Writings, edited by Anne Ridler. 1961.

Editor, with V. H. Collins, *Poems of Home and Overseas.* 1921.

Editor, *A Book of Victorian Narrative Verse.* 1927.

Editor, with H. S. Milford, *The Oxford Book of Regency Verse.* 1928.

Editor, *Poems of G. M. Hopkins,* revised edition. 1930.

Editor, *A Short Life of Shakespeare,* by Edmund Chambers. 1933.

Editor, *The New Book of English Verse.* 1935.

Editor, *The Passion of Christ.* 1935.

Editor, *The New Christian Year.* 1941.

Editor, *The Letters of Evelyn Underhill.* 1943.

Editor, *Solway Ford and Other Poems,* by Wilfred Gibson. 1945.

*

Bibliography: *Williams: A Checklist* by Lois Glenn, 1975.

Critical Studies (selection): *Charles Williams* by John Heath-Stubbs, 1955; *The Theology of Romantic Love: A Study of the Writings of Charles Williams,* 1962, and *Charles Williams: A Critical Essay,* 1966, both by Mary M. Shideler; *Shadows of the Imagination: The Fantasies of C. S. Lewis, J. R. R. Tolkien and C. S. Lewis* edited by Mark R. Hillegas, 1969; *Shadows of Heaven: Religion and Fantasy in the Writing of C. S. Lewis, Charles Williams and J. R. R. Tolkien* by Gunar Urang, London, SCM Press, 1971; *The Inklings: C. S. Lewis, J. R. R. Tolkien, Charles Williams, and Their Friends* by Humphrey Carpenter, London, Allen and Unwin, 1978, Boston, Houghton Mifflin, 1979; *Charles Williams: Poet of Theology* by Glen Cavaliero, London, Macmillan, 1983; *Charles Williams: An Exploration of His Life and Works* by Alice Mary Hadfield, Oxford, Oxford University Press, 1983; *The Novels of Charles Williams* by Thomas T. Howard, Oxford, Oxford University Press, 1983; *Charles Williams* by Kathleen Spencer, Mercer Island, Washington, Starmont House, 1987; *The Magical World of the Inklings: J. R. R. Tolkien,* C. S. Lewis, Charles Williams, Owen Barfield by Gareth Knight, Shaftesbury, Element, 1990.

*   *   *

Charles Williams is best known for his weird and quirkily personal novels, all theological thrillers. Despite contemporary English settings, they tend to feature oddly-named characters, unlikely or stilted conversations and farewells ("Under the Mercy") and a view of women which seems odd to modern eyes. The young, nubile female who reverences and platonically obeys a much older man is a recurring figure. For more on the author's fascination with magic and power see his non-fiction *Witchcraft,* a brief history of ritual magic.

Despite its publication date, *Shadows of Ecstasy* is the first-written (1928) and weakest of the novels. Like the rest it involves a breaking-through of spiritual power into the world, this time via the charismatic leader Nigel Considine's Western adaptation of yogic discipline. One is a little unconvinced by the resulting war of a Considine-dominated Africa against the old colonial powers, and by the book's kitchen-sink jumble of magical themes and notions.

War in Heaven, the first published, nods frequently and sometimes wittily to the detective story: opening with a corpse, it continues with theft and police investigation where the coveted "McGuffin" is the Graal, the Holy Grail. "What an infernally religious case this is getting!" complains an Assistant Commissioner. Notable set-pieces include a spiritual assault which threatens to dissolve the Graal by remote control, and an occult booby-trap whose effect on the setter (let alone the victim) is graphically horrible. Overall, the book is a trifle confused: car chases and police work sit oddly with the metaphysical struggle and transcendent finale.

The next three novels are better integrated, each with a clear focus of magical power that informs the action. *The Place of the Lion* sees Earth invaded by Platonic archetypes, the ultimate pure forms of beasts real and mythical: lion, eagle, serpent, phoenix. One striking scene has all the merely physical butterflies of the world absorbed into the single, huge Ideal Butterfly. Characters become linked with archetypes, like the spiteful woman who finds her counterpart in the serpent and progresses through poison-pen letters to disconcerting habits of hissing and coiling herself around people. Meanwhile the nominal heroine Damaris Tighe is haunted by an archetypal pterodactyl stinking of carrion: Williams explains with relish that this is her come-uppance for academically studying ancient philosophies without believing in them. So much for uppity intellectual women. It is left to her boy-friend to accept and dispel the blazing idealizations by naming them (the parallel with Adam's naming of the beasts is explicit).

Many Dimensions revolves around the Stone of Solomon, whose attributes of teleportation, healing and even time travel are worked out with science-fictional cleverness but a non-sf sense of divine morality. The initial conflict is between those, notably the amoral Sir Giles Tumulty from *War in Heaven,* who regard the Stone's commercial exploitation as entirely sensible, and those who feel instinctively that it's holy—that dividing it (when split it yields two Stones identical to the original) is blasphemous. Some unusual and disquieting implications of travel into one's past or future are explored. Ultimately, through a strange act of submission, one of Williams's reverent young ladies is transfigured, re-unites the now countless Stones, removes them from the world—and dies.

The magic focus in *The Greater Trumps* is the "original" pack of Tarot cards (of special interest to Williams owing to his links with A. E. Waite, designer of a revisionist Tarot, and the Order of the Golden Dawn). Additionally there's a set of golden images, one for each card, forever in motion except for the central still figure of the Fool—though to the eyes of one enlightened woman (subtly named Sybil) the Fool moves fastest of all and is everywhere in the dance, an image that influenced T. S. Eliot's *Four Quartets*: "the still point of the turning world," "we must be still and still moving." The gipsy "hero" and his grandfather have the images and covet the cards . . . so eagerly unleash the cards' powers of air and water to kill their legal owner, the hero's prospective father-in-law, in a violent storm. Thanks to his daughter's and sister Sybil's intervention, he's saved; but the now uncontrolled storm promises to wreck the world. A typically mystical and surreal finale restores order, with both cards and images destroyed.

Descent into Hell was a new and ambitious venture. Supernatural strands intertwine, with the crucial action happening in what Lewis Carroll called "eerie" states of perception—landscapes of hypnagogic imagery. A woman goes in fear of meeting her doppelganger . . . until, by a curious pact, an older and wiser man offers to take on the agony himself (such "Substitution" or "Substituted Love" was an important notion to Williams and his circle), a solace which she is subsequently able to pass on to a martyr burned centuries earlier. A workman commits suicide and wanders the desolate construction site of houses which in "real life" are complete. Another woman's progress to death is described in hallucinatory detail. A historian dreams of ominous descent by rope, and later (by yielding to a petty jealousy) crosses some spiritual boundary into a pseudo-paradise which brings him the perverse, increasingly sickening love of a succubus. Lilith is present. Graves open. There is a scarifying closing scene of damnation. Following a slow start, *Descent* contains some of Williams's most powerful passages but diffuses its effect through the sheer quantity of unearthly happenings.

Lastly, the simpler *All Hallows' Eve* returns in part to *Shadows of Ecstasy* territory, tracing the downfall of the black magician Simon Leclerc (Simon Magus) who preaches Love but has no scruples about sacrificing his own daughter to the Art. Those against him include a recently dead woman who at one point saves the daughter through Substitution, and an artist who can't help painting this "Prophet" as an imbecile with a congregation of mindless insect-humans (the grotesquerie heightened when Simon *likes* the portrayal: "No one has painted me so well for a hundred years"). The left-hand path is treacherous: with each misjudgement Simon slips further back from pure mental mastery to crude ritual, confining the astral opposition in a grubby dwarf golem and finally resorting to sticking pins in images. He fails; his daughter triumphs. Character depiction has improved, with dead Lester Furnival the strongest personality—though slightly patronized for former uninterest in spiritual matters, she is at last a likeable, wilful, and credible ordinary woman. Her coming to terms with death in the eeriness of a subjectively depopulated London strikes a deeper note than the almost conventional doings of the black magus.

Williams's Arthurian poems in *Taliessin Through Logres* and *The Region of the Summer Stars* contain much fantasy interest (evil is represented by the un-Arthurian "headless Emperor" of P'o-lu on the far side of the world, with his bodyguard of tentacled abominations), but are knotty and problematic for outsiders. Even his friend and literary interpreter C. S. Lewis couldn't always unravel the poems' highly personal theological symbolism.

Charles Williams specialized in descriptions of piercingly strange or numinous experiences, and is still read for these scenes even when other material (like certain chunks of discursive exposition or unbelievable dialogue) may be skipped.

—David Langford

WILLIAMS, Michael (Leon)

Nationality: American. **Born:** Louisville, Kentucky, 17 December 1952. **Education:** Middlebury College, 1970-74, B.A. 1974; University of Rochester, 1974-78, M.A. 1978. **Family:** Married Teri Patterson in 1987. **Career:** Lecturer, University of Louisville, 1978-82; editor, TSR, Inc., Lake Geneva, Wisconsin, 1982-84; editor and staff writer, Pacesetter, Ltd, Delavan, Wisconsin, 1984-86; lecturer, University of Louisville, from 1986. **Agent:** Shawna McCarthy, c/o Scovil-Chichak-Galen Literary Agency, 381 Park Avenue South, New York, NY 10016, USA.

FANTASY PUBLICATIONS

Novels (series: DragonLance; From Thief to King)

Weasel's Luck (DragonLance). Lake Geneva, Wisconsin, TSR, 1988; London, Penguin, 1989.
Galen Beknighted (DragonLance). Lake Geneva, Wisconsin, TSR, 1990; London, Roc, 1991.
Sorcerer's Apprentice (From Thief to King). New York, Warner, 1990.
The Oath and the Measure (DragonLance). Lake Geneva, Wisconsin, TSR, 1991.
A Forest Lord (From Thief to King). New York, Warner, 1991.
The Balance of Power (From Thief to King). New York, Warner, 1992.
Before the Mask, with Teri Williams (DragonLance). Lake Geneva, Wisconsin, TSR, 1993.
Storm of Prophecy, with Teri Williams (DragonLance). Lake Geneva, Wisconsin, TSR, 1995(?).
Arcady. New York, Roc, 1995(?).

*

Michael Williams comments:

My first fantasy publications were the poetry and songs for Margaret Weis's and Tracy Hickman's highly successful DragonLance trilogies (Chronicles and Legends). My poetry has continued to appear in various fantasy anthologies, and my fiction concerns itself largely with what might be considered a "poet's subject"—the powers and limitations of language.

Most of my novels to date are set in heroic, medieval fantasy worlds in which words and belief are the primary shapers of reality. Action in these books is fierce, fabulous and frequently comic, but magic is a more interior matter, largely a question of faith, enabled by the character's choosing to believe in its transforming powers; the world is indeed changed by what is in the character's heart and in his words as well.

All my heroes partake of this central adventure of faith: from Galen Pathwarden, the sceptical, cynical hero of the parodic *Weasel's Luck* and *Galen Beknighted,* through the education into magic and spiritual kingship of Brennart of Maraven in the Thief to King trilogy, to the darker, more fragmentary landscapes of the more recent *The Oath and the Measure, Before the Mask* and *Arcady,* where both the price and the prize of believing is everything. The force of faith is the most powerful magic in my work, rising out of my central Christian vision.

*   *   *

Fantasy writer Michael Williams (not to be confused with sci-ence-fiction novelist Michael Lindsay Williams, born 1940) is best known for his poetry, stories and novels set against TSR's DragonLance background. Almost all TSR fantasy fiction has to be compatible with the company's Advanced Dungeons & Drag-ons role-playing system, but Williams manages to describe charac-ters and events in a way that avoids the usual stereotypes. Three of his novels concern the Solamnic Knights—upholders of justice with a stern code of honour who are nevertheless mistrusted by the peas-antry of Krynn (the world of the DragonLance stories).

Weasel's Luck follows the misfortunes of Galen Pathwarden, nick-named "Weasel." He is the youngest of three sons, none of whom show promise that they will live up to their father's expectations by following family tradition and becoming Solamnic knights. The eldest son, Alfric, is a bully of few wits, the middle son, Brithelm, seems set to become a hermit, while Weasel spends most of his time either committing delinquent acts himself or being blamed for those perpetrated by Alfric.

Weasel is also a coward. When a mysterious stranger in black, who calls himself the Scorpion, bribes him with opals and threat-ens to "dance in his skin" if Weasel doesn't help him steal the armour of Sir Bayard Brightblade, a Solamnic guest, Weasel readily acquiesces. The thief's demands do not end there and, when Galen is enlisted as Sir Bayard's squire, Weasel is expected to commit further treacherous deeds. These are designed to prevent Sir Bayard travelling to a tournament for the hand of Enid di Caela.

The di Caelas are haunted by a recurrent family curse which an old legend says will only be lifted by a "Bright Blade." However, Sir Bayard of that name arrives at the tournament too late, for an evil black knight has won Enid's hand in his absence. Of course, the mysterious stranger and the black knight are same person—an incarnation of an ancient di Caela accused of fratricide who died at the treacherous hand of his younger sibling. The parallel between that and the violence and hatred between Weasel and Alfric is obvi-ous, but not overstated.

Galen is the only one who realizes that the black knight is the Scorpion but finally, on the eve of the marriage between Enid and her family's nemesis, decides to tell his brother Brithelm. The black knight vanishes when accused, but later abducts Enid and takes her to his mountain stronghold. Galen slowly redeems himself as a party of knights attempt to rescue her. The final lines of the di Caela curse state that "generations from the grass" shall "rise up and lay the curse aside." The Scorpion intends to do this by raising an army of undead from the corpses of ancient Solamnic knights. But even in death the Knights are loyal to their order and turn on the Scor-pion instead.

Williams began his career as a writer of humour and poetry, and he intersperses his fiction with both. The poetry appears as short fortune-telling rhymes, song lyrics and the di Caela legend which is used to impart a sense of foreboding. Most of the humour in-volves the rather juvenile-delinquent acts of vandalism and violence perpetrated by the Pathwarden brothers and their attempts to get each other blamed for them. This contrasts with the epic nature of the Sir Brightblade quest and brings the story down to earth. The narrative is written in the first person, as seen through Galen's eyes, and as his character develops and he realizes the implications of his actions it becomes more serious in tone.

Galen Beknighted takes place several years later. Sir Brightblade has called in every favour he was ever owed by the Solamnic or-der to have Galen the Weasel knighted. Williams gets as much mile-age as he can out of Galen's lack of aptitude at knightly pursuits,

but Weasel is not really such an amusing character as in the first book. The story involves Galen's attempt to rescue his brother Brithelm who has been captured by plainsmen. It turns out that the opals which the Scorpion had given Galen were magical scrying devices revered by the plainsmen who want them back.

Williams's third book about the Solamnic Knights is *The Oath and the Measure*. This concerns the young Sturm Brightblade, great grandson of Sir Bayard, and is set some time before the DragonLance saga. The story starts out as a variation of "Sir Gawain and the Green Knight." A green man, who calls himself Virtumnus and can magically control the growth of plants, appears at a Solamnic Yuletide banquet and begins to make fun of the Knights. Sturm challenges him and is in turn challenged to meet Virtumnus on the first day of spring in the Southern Darkwoods. Although *The Oath and the Measure* is a tale about reaching adult-hood, it has a different message from the traditional story. Through his journey and encounter with Virtumnus, Sturm learns that the world is not always the way people are brought up to believe it is and that everyone has the right to choose what they want from their future without automatically accepting the role parents expect.

Short stories by Michael Williams have also appeared in various DragonLance anthologies, edited by Margaret Weis and Tracy Hickman, including *The Magic of Krynn, Kender, Gully Dwarves and Gnomes* and *Love and War* (all 1987). His verse has appeared in magazines and in the six original DragonLance novels by Weis and Hickman (1984-86). All of Williams's fantasy writings are en-joyable, thanks to their humour and characterization.

—Lucya Szachnowski

WILLIAMS, Roswell. *See* **OWEN, Frank.**

WILLIAMS, Tad

Nationality: American. **Born:** Robert Paul Williams in 1957. **Fam-ily:** Married 1) name not known (divorced); 2) Deborah Beale in 1994. **Career:** Miscellaneous occupations, including singer and songwriter for a rock and roll band; worked for Apple Computers. **Address:** c/o DAW Books, 375 Hudson Street, 3rd Floor, New York, NY 10014-3658, USA.

FANTASY PUBLICATIONS

Novels (series: Memory, Sorrow and Thorn)

Tailchaser's Song. New York, DAW, 1985; London, Futura, 1986.
The Dragonbone Chair (Memory, Sorrow and Thorn). New York, DAW, 1988; London, Legend, 1989.
Stone of Farewell (Memory, Sorrow and Thorn). New York, DAW, and London, Legend, 1990.

Child of an Ancient City, with Nina Kiriki Hoffman. New York, Atheneum, and London, Legend, 1992.

To Green Angel Tower (Memory, Sorrow and Thorn). New York, DAW, and London, Legend, 1993; in 2 vols., as *Siege: To Green Angel Tower, Part 1* and *Storm: To Green Angel Tower, Part II,* London, Legend, 1994.

Caliban's Song. London, Legend, 1994.

*   *   *

Tad Williams's reputation rests principally on his most substantial work to date, a lengthy trilogy which goes under the title "Memory, Sorrow and Thorn." In contrast, his first novel was a piece of very popular cat-whimsy, *Tailchaser's Song,* and he has produced two other slim volumes. Together with Nina Kiriki Hoffman he wrote *Child of an Ancient City,* a mood piece mixing vampirism and *The Arabian Nights* in which a group of benighted Baghdad travellers fends off a vampyr with a storytelling contest. Although well written and evocative there is little of depth here. Similarly *Caliban's Song,* an interesting but again slight piece, which tells the story of Shakespeare's *The Tempest* from Caliban's viewpoint, does not compare well with its source material. It ends at the interesting point when Caliban carries off Miranda's daughter—a daughter so stultified by the respectable, ordered life she leads that she is perfectly willing to go with him—but this is the moment at which the reader expects the narrative to get going and to prove its worth as an addition to, rather than a retelling of, the Shakespearean story. Regrettably Williams chooses not to oblige, and his book becomes little more than a *Lamb's Tales from Shakespeare* for the modern reader. Each of these three lesser books has interesting features but is not a substantial work.

No such complaint can be made about Memory, Sorrow and Thorn, which weighs in at well over 3,000 pages and was compared by *Locus* magazine to *War and Peace* (presumably on the grounds of length rather than content). But even though the trilogy has a number of astonishing and arresting set-piece moments it also has a remarkable number of longueurs, pages of motion without action, so that the whole work comes to seem baggy and shapeless rather than rich and lavish. It does, however, begin superbly, before slowing down to a virtual dead stop in volume two, and finally succeeds in coming to a teeth-gnashingly frustrating ending in the final pages of volume three.

The Dragonbone Chair introduces us to the hero, Simon, an orphan raised to adolescence in the kitchens of a great castle where a dying king rules. He becomes involved in affairs of state and of magic after the king's death—still very early in the novel—when he discovers the king's younger son, Josua, imprisoned in a dungeon by his now reigning brother and the brother's mentor magician who plan to sacrifice him in an arcane ritual. This discovery is one of several moments of genuine richness and strangeness in the novel, and Williams seems to have a particular talent for the arresting moment when something utterly surprising is revealed.

Later on in the same volume there is a particularly fine scene when Simon, fleeing the castle to join the escaped Prince Josua's rebellion, finds an elf (of a kind here called Sithi), helpless but feral, caught in a trap. The shock of meeting with an alien being has rarely been better described, but this is all of 300 pages into the novel and Simon has made so little progress he has yet to meet the other characters who will loom large in the story. Aside from Josua and the Sithi Jiriki, the most important characters are the troll Binabik and of course the princess Miriamele, each of whom lasts

the course to the end of volume three. However, after some painfully slow passages, volume one works up to a cliff-hanger ending—which no doubt built the author a ready audience for volume two.

Stone of Farewell, the second volume, has Simon making sure Binabik gets out of the bind he was in at the end of the previous volume, doing his best to deliver the magic sword to Josua and once more trading rescue-from-certain-death with Jiriki. This is a book not shaped to stand alone; it begins with the characters left scattered from the events of the first novel and then slowly brings them together ready for the climax promised in the third. At times there are sections where the only overwhelming emotion evoked in the reader is the desire for the passage to end: not because the material is badly written or fails to interest but simply because Williams underestimates the motivating force of the desire to know what happens next. There are characters who had minor roles in *The Dragonbone Chair* who have lives and histories and stories of their own to tell in *The Stone of Farewell,* and the sheer size of the novel, the sweep of character and setting, becomes almost too much to take in when set against the passionate longing to know how it all turns out.

Finally there is *To Green Angel Tower,* so immensely long that it needed to be split into two sizeable parts for paperback despite its forming the third volume of a larger trilogy. By the time we reach *To Green Angel Tower* our desire to piece together the overall shape of the story becomes irresistible but is frustrated by the failure of the final volume to live up to the promise of the beginning, and so as a coherent whole the work is disappointing. After three epic volumes, averaging about 1,000 pages, some of it very slow but some of it absorbing and engaging and with lead characters who are both vivid and likeable, there is a natural desire in the reader to see loose ends tied up and a credible state of happy-ever-after achieved. However at the end of the tale it is Princess Miriamele who strikes the symbolic blow that saves the universe, while the heroic Simon stands around in the throes of an enchantment. Nevertheless she is considered disqualified from inheriting the throne for the happy-ever-after section, and so the leftover characters offer the throne to Simon. It is not rampaging feminism but elementary common sense that finds it psychologically unlikely that the ending would work, and that the gifting of practical power away from the woman on the grounds she is a woman would lead to her settling for domestic subordination, particularly in a plot where Simon's "mooncalf" impracticality has been stressed from the beginning.

Given the length of time that the reader has had to devote to immersion in Williams's world in order to reach this stage, it is particularly disappointing to find a conclusion which does not fit the previous pattern of character development and so twists what has gone before out of shape. There is a certain satisfaction, however, in reaching the end of something so substantial and self-contained, and on balance there can be little doubt that the work is one of the more successful sub-Tolkien sagas of recent years.

—Wendy Bradley

WILLIAMSON, Philip G.

Pseudonym: Philip First. **Nationality:** British. **Born:** Worcestershire, 4 November 1955. **Education:** Worcester Royal

Grammar School; Torquay Boys' Grammar School; Goldsmith's College, London, postgraduate diploma in communications. **Family:** Married in 1987; one daughter. **Career:** Numerous short-term jobs in cosmetics industry, music industry, etc.; played in rock bands; travelled extensively, and wrote short stories and articles for various magazines. **Agent:** Charles Walker, Peters Fraser and Dunlop Ltd, 503-504 The Chambers, Chelsea Harbour, London SW10 0XF, England. **Address:** Flat 7, 30 South Villas, Camden, London NW1 9BT, England.

FANTASY PUBLICATIONS

Novels (series: Firstworld Chronicles in all books)

Dinbig of Khimmur. London, Grafton, 1991.
The Legend of Shadd's Torment. London, HarperCollins, 1993.
From Enchantery. London, HarperCollins, 1993.
Moonblood. London, Legend, 1994.
Heart of Shadows. London, Legend, 1994.
Citadel. London, Legend, 1995.

OTHER PUBLICATIONS

Novels (as Philip First)

The Great Pervader. London, Panther, 1985.
Dark Night. London, Paladin, 1989.

Short Stories (as Philip First)

Paper Thin and Other Stories. London, Paladin, 1987.

*

Philip G. Williamson comments:

Quests are agents of personal, often painful transformation. The world is rarely quite what it seems. Characters, acting for what they believe to be the good, may find themselves unwittingly the instruments of the very forces they thought to oppose. To continue, they are forced to look upon the world anew, at no little cost, and discard the assumptions and convictions of a lifetime. By such means the perceived courses of wars are altered; aspirations and ambitions modified; friendships and enmities re-evaluated; past and present understood in a new light. Nothing can ever be the same again.

I aim to create spellbinding adventure and exhilarating entertainment, but the Firstworld books can equally be read as a cultural, historical, mythological and anthropological study of an imaginary, evolving world, a world ostensibly unlike and yet in many ways accurately and often disturbingly mirroring our own.

While stretching the imagination and taking the reader afar, fantasy is always, for me, a means of examining our own existence in the fullest possible sense. Fantasy deals with eternal truths, internal struggles, rites of passage. Strangenesses and wonders abound, but the problems, dilemmas, quandaries, however coded, are in their essence familiar. Ultimately, fantasy is limitless imaginative inquiry, exploring our place in a perplexing universe and the immense mystery of our existence.

*   *   *

All this author's fantasy novels can be described as sword and sorcery; indeed they are all set in the same imaginary world. It is called Firstworld because the characters physically inhabit the first level of consciousness and have corporeality. Denizens of higher realms are spiritual in nature though not necessarily in philosophy.

The action of the original trilogy of Firstworld Chronicles occurs in a period of history characterized by bloodshed and warmongering as the armies of the country of Khimmur over-run all their neighbours under the leadership of the Beast of Rull. The stories are narrated principally by Ronbas Dinbig, a merchant-adventurer, womanizer, spy and Zan-Chassin sorcerer. The first book, *Dinbig of Khimmur,* is a dense, cumbersome volume that contains practically everything except a kitchen sink. It begins with a largely unnecessary history of Rull, a region of the world of which Khimmur is one country. Although it shows that the author has done a thorough job of developing a real world in all its aspects, it fails to grab the attention as it is written in pedantic, academic language. The style lightens a little once the narrative proper begins but still contains long passages providing the reader with very detailed descriptions of the geography, religious cultures and dangerous fauna of the region, as well as relating the personal histories of many of the lesser characters who appear.

Dinbig, the first-person narrator, doesn't become much more than a cypher, partly because everything is very matter-of-fact, lacking in passion. Even the sex romps, of which Dinbig tells us he has many, are coyly described. It seems that he, because he has travelled a lot during his business as merchant, has developed a network of spies which is invaluable to King Oshalan with whom he has a very close friendship. Even so, when Khimmur is apparently under threat from surrounding countries he fails to recognize that the threat actually comes from within, the king having been taken over by a demon from the Higher Realms called the Vulpasmage. The book ends with Dinbig's apparent death.

In *The Legend of Shadd's Torment,* we find that Dinbig's spirit is occupying the body of a *vhazz*—a semi-intelligent creature that runs in packs, on all fours or two legs, and can wield a sword. His original body did survive, minus part of an arm, and is in the custody of Yo. Yo is an entity from the Higher Realms bound to Dinbig's service and whose main function is to provide a little light relief. Dinbig, as a vhazz, accompanies Shadd (King Oshalan's half-brother) on a quest to find the means of restoring the Wonasina of Kemahamek to life. Not only is Shadd desperately in love with the Wonasina but he is accused of causing her death. Betrayed by some of her own people who have been corrupted by the Beast of Rull, she lies in a Semblance of Death for which there is no known cure. Shadd travels to Qotolr, the land of the Enchanters, looking for one.

The third volume, *From Enchantery,* sees Dinbig back in his own body and Shadd on his way back from Qotolr with an untranslatable item which may hold the formula for reviving the Wonasina. To some extent this is a collection of episodes happening during the journey. Also, so that the reader is aware of what is going on, some passages are written as a third-person narrative since there is no way that Dinbig would be likely to have access to the information and the author deems it necessary for understanding of the plot. There is also a very heavy use of coincidence to further the plot. This is by no means the intended end to this series, particularly as Williamson himself refers to a volume four in one of his footnotes (he likes footnotes) in *Moonblood,* and the introductory pre-history to *Dinbig of Khimmur* makes a passing reference to nine volumes.

Whereas these three books comprise a continuing story, Williamson's next two fantasy novels are complete stories, though set in the same world and both involving Dinbig. They are set some time before the original Firstworld Chronicles. *Moonblood* has a faster pace than the Chronicles, is less cluttered and easier to read. Dinbig is in Ravenscrag for the birth of Lord Flarefist's son who, according to the prophecy, will change the city's fortunes. But on the evening of his birth, the child is substituted for a monster and then Moonblood, Flarefist's daughter disappears. Dinbig is told to find them or die. The plot creaks and the denouement is too easy.

Heart of Shadows sees Dinbig at the other end of Rull. This volume, unlike any of the others, is entirely a third-person narrative and Dinbig plays only a peripheral role. The main characters are the twins Silemund and Meglan whose father finds an unusual stone hidden in a cave. Skalatin, an incredibly ancient and evil being who eats hearts to live, is seeking the stone as it is his heart. There is insufficient tension and the gory bits are played down so much so that the characters never become real. Dinbig always seems to have the right knowledge at the right time and the plot is that of a standard fantasy, again with quests, prophecies and god-like beings.

—Pauline Morgan

WILLIS, Connie

Nationality: American. **Born:** Constance Elaine Trimmer, in Denver, Colorado, 31 December 1945. **Education:** University of Northern Colorado, Greeley, B.A. in English and elementary education 1967. **Family:** Married Courtney W. Willis in 1967; one daughter. **Career:** Teacher in elementary and junior high schools, Branford, Connecticut, 1967-69; substitute teacher, Woodland Park, Colorado, 1974-81. Since 1982, full-time writer. **Awards:** National Endowment for the Arts Grant, 1982; Nebula Award, 1982 (twice), 1988, 1989, 1993; Hugo Award, 1982, 1988, 1993; John W. Campbell Memorial Award, 1988. **Agent:** Ralph Vicinanza, 111 8th Avenue, Suite 1501, New York, NY 10011, USA. **Address:** 1716 13th Avenue, Greeley, CO 80631, USA.

Fantasy Publications

Novel

Lincoln's Dreams. New York, Bantam, 1987; London, Grafton, 1988.

Short Stories

Impossible Things. New York, Bantam, 1994.

Other Publications

Novels

Water Witch, with Cynthia Felice. New York, Ace, 1982.
Light Raid, with Cynthia Felice. New York, Ace, 1989.

Doomsday Book. New York, Bantam, and London, New English Library, 1992.
Uncharted Territory. New York, Bantam, 1994; expanded edition (adds two short stories), London, New English Library, 1994.
Remake. Shingletown, California, Ziesing, 1994.

Short Stories

Fire Watch. New York, Bluejay, 1985.

Other

Editor, with Martin H. Greenberg. *The New Hugo Winners: Volume III.* New York, Baen, 1994.

*   *   *

Connie Willis has gained a formidable reputation as a fluent and often startling writer of science fiction. She is clearly comfortable with the rational underpinning of science fiction, even when, as in a number of stories such as "At the Rialto" and "The Schwarzschild Radius" (both collected in *Impossible Things*), her work follows a pattern of reflecting a scientific principle in the behaviour and psychology of characters in a non-science fictional situation. Where her work tends towards fantasy, however, she is much more ambivalent. She is not so comfortable with the irrational underpinning of fantasy, so that when she attempts to impose the same pattern on a story such as "Death on the Nile" (*Asimov's Science Fiction,* 1993) the result is much less satisfactory. Here the story of modern American tourists finding themselves drawn into an ancient Egyptian underworld is presented as a reflection of what one of the characters is reading about Egyptian religion. But his pattern imposes a rationality which undermines the horror of what is happening.

Her fantasy is better in those stories where she simply accepts the magic without question. "Cibola" (*Asimov's,* 1990), for example, is one of her simplest but most effective pieces. It tells of a journalist in Denver, Colorado, assigned to a human-interest story about the descendant of a conquistador. Although the narrator does not believe the old woman's claim to be able to lead her to Cibola, the legendary Seven Cities of Gold, and her research shows that the woman's claims about the conquistador and his Indian guide don't tally with recorded history, she is nevertheless drawn to her, accepting that there is something appealing in this unlikely tale. And it is this acceptance which allows her to see Cibola in the way the light of dawn is reflected in the glass towers of Denver.

"Cibola" is perhaps Willis's finest story, though it is closely matched by the much darker "Jack" (*Impossible Things*), which tells of a vampire working with the fire-fighters and rescue service in London of the Blitz. (The English setting occurs again and again in her work, though Willis has a tendency to get the detail of the setting so wildly wrong that it becomes almost a never-never land.) In "Jack" it is impossible to tell whether it is Willis or the English characters who do not know that Newcastle is not in Yorkshire; in *Doomsday Book* the lights of London are visible from Oxford, while we are asked to suppose that in the next century England will again have pound notes and wear mufflers; in "Adaptation" (*Asimov's,* 1994) a part of Surrey is served by only two trains a day from London and the journey is scheduled to take some three hours.)

Fantasies such as "Cibola," "Jack," and the understated but sharply observed ghost story "Service for the Burial of the Dead" (*Fire Watch*), however well or ill-imagined the setting, are as precise and unsentimental in their characterization as the best of her science fiction. It is hard to imagine, for example, any historical fantasy as bleakly or convincingly portrayed as the England of the Black Death visited by the time traveller in *Doomsday Book*. Yet the Connie Willis who achieved these heights is also capable of the bathetic depths of fantasies where the guiding spirit is not acceptance of magic but surrender to sentiment. Usually associated with Christmas these stories, such as "Miracle" (*Asimov's*, 1991), "Inn" (*Asimov's*, 1993) and "Adaptation," owe much of their structure and plot to earlier works (respectively the films *Miracle on 34th Street* and *It's a Wonderful Life*, the story of the nativity, and Dickens's *A Christmas Carol*) which are thinly reworked and updated and transparently manipulated to provide a neat but unsatisfying happy-ever-after. It can be difficult to remember that such saccarine confections come from the same author as the intense, vivid and convincing "Jack" or "Cibola."

Time travel is one of the most persistent themes in her science fiction, appearing regularly in novels (*Doomsday Book*) and stories ("Fire Watch"), and it provides the hook also for *Lincoln's Dreams*, a novel occupying the hinterland between science fiction and fantasy, although perhaps veering more towards the latter. Here the means of time travel is no physical machine but a psychical link: Annie is sharing the dreams of General Robert E. Lee (her dreams circling round his bloodiest defeats), while her companion, Civil War researcher Jeff Johnston, seems to be linked with Lee's horse, Traveller. At the same time, Johnston's employer, the novelist Thomas Braun, is becoming obsessed with Abraham Lincoln's prophetic dreams. Although the action of the novel stays firmly within the contemporary world, the Civil War haunts the book and creates resonances which have a devastating psychological effect. As with *Doomsday Book*, Willis displays an ability to portray the darker corners of the past with a harsh and uncompromising realism and an eye for the exact telling detail, which makes these unsentimental works profoundly moving.

—Paul Kincaid

WILSON, David Henry

Nationality: British. **Born:** London, 26 February 1937. **Education:** Dulwich College, 1948-55; Pembroke College, Cambridge, 1955-58. **Family:** Married Elizabeth Ayo Amaworo in 1965; two sons and one daughter. **Career:** Teacher, Lycee Hoche, Versailles, France, 1958-59, Lycee Thiers, Marseille, France, 1959-60, Fijai Secondary School, Sekondi, Ghana, 1960-64; lecturer, Universitat Koln, Germany, 1964-67, Universitat Konstanz, Germany, 1967-72; part-time lecturer, Bristol University, from 1972. **Agent:** Herta Ryder, Toby Eady Associates, 108 Park Walk, London SW10 0AQ, England. **Address:** 3 Beech Close, Hope Corner Lane, Taunton, Somerset TA2 7NZ, England.

FANTASY PUBLICATIONS

Novels

Ashmadi. Frankfurt, Fischer, 1985; as *The Coachman Rat*, London, Robinson, and New York, Carroll and Graf, 1989.
Der Fluch der Achten Fee. Frankfurt, Fischer, 1989.

Fiction for Children

Elephants Don't Sit on Cars. London, Chatto and Windus, 1977.
The Fastest Gun Alive. London, Chatto and Windus, 1978.
Getting Rich with Jeremy James. London, Chatto and Windus, 1979.
Beside the Sea with Jeremy James. London, Chatto and Windus, 1980.
How to Stop a Train with One Finger. London, Dent, 1984.
Superdog. London, Hodder and Stoughton, 1984.
Do Goldfish Play the Violin? London, Dent, 1985.
There's a Wolf in My Pudding. London, Dent, 1986.
Superdog the Hero. London, Hodder and Stoughton, 1986.
Yucky Ducky. London, Dent, 1988.
Superdog in Trouble. London, Hodder and Stoughton, 1988.
Gander of the Yard. London, Dent, 1989.
Little Billy and the Wump. London, Hodder and Stoughton, 1990.
Gideon Gander Solves the World's Greatest Mysteries. London, Pan Macmillan, 1993.
Please Keep Off the Dinosaur. London, Pan Macmillan, 1993.

Plays

All the World's a Stage (produced Ghana, 1961). London, French, 1968.
The Make-Up Artist (produced Konstanz, 1973). Chicago, Dramatic Publishing, 1973.
On Stage, Mr. Smith (produced Konstanz, 1975). Chicago, Dramatic Publishing, 1975.
Jones v. Jones (produced Sheffield, 1975). Privately printed, 1983.
Gas and Candles (produced Leicester, 1979). Chicago, Dramatic Publishing, 1985.
Shylock's Revenge (produced Hamburg, 1989). Privately printed, 1986.
We're Looking for Mary Pickford (produced London, 1971). Privately printed, 1987.
Him a-Layin' Bare (produced London, 1971). Privately printed, 1987.
The Dawn (produced London, 1975). Privately printed, 1987.
Are You Normal, Mr. Norman? (produced London, 1966). New York, French, 1988.
If Yer Take a Short Cut Yer Might Lose the Way (produced London, 1966). New York, French, 1988.
Wendlebury Day (produced Edinburgh, 1977). New York, French, 1988.
Iago, the Villain of Venice. Privately printed, 1992.
Lear's Fool and the Tragedy of Lady Macbeth. Privately printed, 1993.
Death of a Giant (produced London, 1993).

Other

Translator, *The Implied Reader*, by Wolfgang Iser. Baltimore, Johns Hopkins University Press, 1974.
Translator, *The Act of Reading*, by Wolfgang Iser. Baltimore, Johns Hopkins University Press, 1978.
Translator, *New Perspectives in Literary Criticism*, edited by Amacher and Lange. Princeton, New Jersey, Princeton University Press, 1979.
Translator, *Walter Pater: The Aesthetic Movement*, by Wolfgang Iser. Cambridge, Cambridge University Press, 1987.

Translator, *Sterne's Tristram Shandy,* by Wolfgang Iser. Cambridge, Cambridge University Press, 1988.

Translator, *Oscar Wilde: The Works of a Conformist Rebel,* by Norbert Kohl. Cambridge, Cambridge University Press, 1989.

Translator, *Prospecting,* by Wolfgang Iser. Baltimore, Johns Hopkins University Press, 1989.

Translator, *The Eighteenth-Century Mock-Heroic Poem,* by Ulrich Broich. Cambridge, Cambridge University Press, 1990.

Translator, *Wales,* by Peter Sager. London, Pallas Athene, 1991.

Translator, *The Fictive and the Imaginary,* by Wolfgang Iser. Baltimore, Johns Hopkins University Press, 1993.

Translator, *Staging Politics: The Lasting Impact of Shakespeare's Histories,* by Wolfgang Iser. New York, Columbia University Press, 1993.

*

David Henry Wilson comments:

The Coachman Rat comes from the darkest recesses of my imagination. The hero is caught between two worlds, as I suppose most of us are at different periods of our lives, but he is an extreme case. Not many of us have switched from four legs to two in our lifetime. If you want a laugh, though, you had better turn to my children's books, which vary from the absurdities of family life (the Jeremy James and Superdog books) to the gruesome delights of twisted fairy tales and nursery rhymes (*There's a Wolf in My Pudding, Yucky Ducky* and the Gideon Gander books). My plays also range from the real to the surreal, and from the light to the dark. The short plays in the collection *Are You Normal, Mr. Norman?* offer plenty of black humour in strange settings, as do the full-length plays *We're Looking for Mary Pickford, Him a-Layin' Bare* and *The Dawn.* For a more instantly recognizable world, try *Gas and Candles, Jones v. Jones* and *Death of a Giant.* Of my Shakespearean sequels and spin-offs, *Shylock's Revenge* is the only one so far to have been produced, but the "tender leaves of hope" have not yet fallen.

*   *   *

A small but distinct sub-genre in fantasy and science fiction is the reworking of fairy tales, the telling of a well-loved story from an unfamiliar viewpoint. At its most post-modern, the characters themselves are aware of being part of a tale which is ripe for subversion and take great delight in pointing out where this will occur. Angela Carter and Tanith Lee, in particular, have been great exponents of this, and also David Henry Wilson, with his remarkable novel, *The Coachman Rat.* Otherwise known as a playwright and a writer of stories for small children, Wilson published, initially in German, a novel which proceeded to set on its head, not only the story of Cinderella, but also Robert Browning's "Pied Piper of Hamelin," to the point where the tale entirely transcended the conventional genre and became *sui generis.*

The story, a first-person narrative, centres on a rat, whom we will later call Robert, who is convinced that a greater destiny awaits him in the outside world. The enemy, his father explains, is Man. "No animal can destroy as man can. He'll slaughter his own kind mercilessly so expect no mercy for yourself. He'll hunt you, trap you, poison you—but if you're clever you can out-think him and feed off him." Fired by his father's stories, Robert decides that his destiny lies with man and sets himself to observe man, waiting for something to happen.

What happens is that he blunders into Cinderella's story and finds himself turned into the coachman who will drive Amadea in a pumpkin coach to the ball. Although, when midnight strikes, he becomes once again a rat, he retains the power of human speech; alienated from his own family, he begins a quest through the world of men, looking for the mysterious woman of light who first turned him into a coachman.

First, he is exhibited as a curiosity, then taken into the care of Dr. Richter, a scientist who refuses to accept his story, seeking instead a rational explanation for the remarkable phenomenon. Frustrated that Robert himself argues against Richter's theories, Richter passes him on to Jenkins, a more open-minded researcher, who attempts to educate Robert in human culture, but still he is driven by the need to reach Amadea, now married to the Prince, convinced she will help him.

When he finally meets her, although she is compassionate and sympathetic, she cannot summon the mysterious woman of light, who comes and goes at her own will. In the meantime, Robert is coming to see that there is much amiss in the prince's kingdom. Devlin, a friend of Jenkins's, and a radical agitator, leads a rebellion in which the Prince is executed and Amadea burned at the stake. As she dies, the woman of light appears once again and Robert is restored to human shape.

Devlin, inevitably, proves himself to be less concerned with the welfare of the people, more concerned with his own safety, instituting harsh laws and taxes, and now Robert methodically sets about gaining his revenge. Summoning the rats from the sewers, he leads the battle against Devlin's soldiers, but in triumph realizes too late that he has destroyed the natural balance between men and rats, for now the people begin to die of the plague. Finally, Robert, now Amadeus, leads the rats out of the town, but himself contracts the plague.

Quite apart from his successful reworking of two familiar, almost over-familiar, classics, Wilson also infuses this story with an almost science-fictional awareness of the consequences which ensue when the natural balance is meddled with. One is indeed reminded of Mary Shelley's Creature in *Frankenstein* who sets about his revenge against Frankenstein with similar method and exactitude once he has learned to read and write and become aware of his plight. Robert eventually realizes that although he may seem human, may have wanted to be human, he is nevertheless still a rat and sees things with a rat's understanding, or rather, he has become aware of man's shortcomings and regards the rats' way as more acceptable. His tragedy, of course, is not to realize until it is far too late that there is no single right or wrong way. All in all, Wilson's novel is a singular piece of work, and it is to be regretted that he has not published other novels for adults in English.

—Maureen Speller

WINTERSON, Jeanette

Nationality: British. **Born:** Lancashire, 1959. **Education:** St. Catherine's College, Oxford. **Career:** Variety of jobs including ice-cream van driver, make-up artist in a funeral parlour, and domestic assistant in a mental hospital. **Awards:** Whitbread Prize, 1985; John Llewellyn Rhys prize, 1987; E. M. Forster award, American Academy of Arts and Letters, 1989. **Address:** c/o Jonathan Cape, Random House, 20 Vauxhall Bridge Road, London SW1V 2SA, England.

FANTASY PUBLICATIONS

Novels

Boating for Beginners. London, Methuen, 1985.
The Passion. London, Bloomsbury, 1987; New York, Atlantic Monthly Press, 1988.
Sexing the Cherry. London, Bloomsbury, 1989.

OTHER PUBLICATIONS

Novels

Oranges Are Not the Only Fruit. London, Pandora, 1985; New York, Atlantic Monthly Press, 1987.
Written on the Body. London, Cape, and New York, Knopf, 1992.
Art & Lies: A Piece for Three Voices and a Bawd. London, Cape, 1994.

Plays

Great Moments in Aviation; Oranges Are Not the Only Fruit (screenplays). London, Vintage, 1994.

Other

Fit for the Future: The Guide for Women Who Want to Live Well. London, Pandora Press, 1986.
Art Object: Essays on Ecstasy and Effrontery. London, Cape, 1995.

Editor, *Passion Fruit: Romantic Fiction With a Twist.* London, Pandora Press, 1986.

*

Film Adaptation: *Oranges Are Not the Only Fruit,* 1989 (television serial).

*   *   *

"I'm telling you stories. Trust me." This postmodern appeal to the reader recurs throughout Jeanette Winterson's third novel, *The Passion.* It draws deliberate attention to the fictionality of her work, but is not meant ironically; we need to trust the story-teller as our guide through these fantastical mental and sexual landscapes, and the journey is both revealing and rewarding.

Winterson's books are full of stories. In her first novel, *Oranges Are Not the Only Fruit,* she tells what is essentially a grim story of growing up in a repressed and repressive religious family in a small Northern town. But she lightens the story with religious imagery (a star comes to rest over the orphanage, the sections are named for books of the Old Testament) and interpolated tales of "a brilliant and beautiful princess, so sensitive that the death of a moth could distress her for weeks." Fantasy is, clearly, escape, both for the character and for the reader; but it is escape into another truth, the way the narrator sees herself, the way she would be, the way

she is. This imprecision of the boundaries between real and imaginary owes a lot to magic realism, though when Winterson turns to outright fantasy, as she does in *The Passion* and *Sexing the Cherry,* her work owes more to Calvino than it does to Marquez.

Her second novel, *Boating for Beginners,* later rather unfairly dismissed as "comedy," is actually a *jeu d'esprit* which exorcises oppressive religiosity by making the Bible ludicrous. It retells the story of Noah's Ark as if Noah were a TV evangelist in a world full of modern consumer indulgences: cat suits, film crews, health farms and an oppressively sweet romantic novelist called Bunny Mix. In among the jokes, however, are knowing references to the critic Northrop Frye which give an ironic, distanced perspective on the whole thing, and a feminist argument, expressed through the growing common purpose of the three main female characters, which is as strong as any in her other books.

If *The Passion* seemed like another dramatic change of pace in Winterson's work, it was actually a continuation in terms of theme and manner of the two previous novels. Like *Oranges Are Not the Only Fruit,* it concerns the growing independence of a woman marked out, by nature or by her own will, as being different. In this case, as the daughter of a Venetian boatman she has webbed feet and can walk on water, attributes which, the local folklore says, only men can possess. Like *Boating for Beginners,* it distorts our normal perspective of history for both comic and serious effect. It is set at the time of Napoleon's invasion of Russia. Henri is Napoleon's cook, serving him an endless diet of chicken and mixing with the strange hangers-on around the court, Domino the midget who is the Emperor's groom and Patrick, the defrocked Irish priest with the ability to see huge distances. One strand of the novel tells how Henri's hero-worship of Napoleon is replaced by disillusion; the other strand is the story of Villanelle who makes a living in the casinos of Venice, taking on a variety of disguises and suitors. Her real love is a woman of mystery, but their strange affair ends when Villanelle is forced to flee a disgruntled suitor. Disguised, she joins Napoleon's army, and with Henri escapes the Russian winter. Back in Venice their love fails to blossom amid the secret turnings and hidden rooms of an unreal city, until figures from their past precipitate a tragic ending. Throughout the novel elements of the fantastic occur without comment, as much part of the world as they are in magic realism, while Venice proves to be as shifting and ever-varied a setting for romance and magic as it is in Calvino's *Invisible Cities.*

Echoes of Calvino sound also in *Sexing the Cherry,* perhaps the most audacious of her fantasies. Set in the mid-17th century (again playing with our notions of history), it is also split into two narrative strands. One is told by the Dog Woman who is literally larger than life, a huge woman as extravagant in her pronouncements and her actions as she is in her bulk. She lives in a ramshackle hut by the Thames, raising dogs and engaged in a perpetual battle with her neighbours. Here she finds and raises a boy, Jordan, who is later taken up by John Tradescant and leaves with him on plant-collecting expeditions. But for Jordan, these expeditions take him into a world as strange as anything in *Gulliver's Travels.* Principal among these is a land where houses have no floors, and all the inhabitants occupy furniture suspended from the ceiling and move about on tightropes. Here he falls in love, and pursues the woman through a dreamscape of fairy-tale landscapes and bizarre adventures. Along the way he encounters the twelve dancing princesses whose tales of marriage, variations on a theme, all end with the woman victorious and independent. Heedless, he continues his pursuit of his love until, re-united with the Dog Woman, there is a final trick with time which casts the whole novel in a fresh and disturbing light.

Jeanette Winterson creates worlds with an abandon, a profligacy, that few other writers can match. In each novel the main tale is frequently interrupted to tell some other tale, to send the imagination off after some other scent, and always these imaginative worlds are signs not of escape but of a true engagement with reality. You can understand the characters only by knowing their dreams, their aspirations, their perceptions. The books, always beautifully written in a crisp, clear prose which adds to the magic of the fantasy a sense of matter-of-fact reality, tell stories which we have to trust, for they hold a distorted mirror to our most fundamental notions of identity, of sex roles and of religion.

—Paul Kincaid

WOLFE, Gene (Rodman)

Nationality: American. **Born:** Brooklyn, New York, 7 May 1931. **Education:** Texas A&M University, College Station, 1949, 1952; University of Houston, B.S. 1956; Miami University. **Military Service:** United States Army, 1952-54. **Family:** Married Rosemary Frances Dietsch in 1956; two sons and two daughters. **Career:** Project engineer, Procter and Gamble, 1956-72; senior editor, *Plant Engineering,* Barrington, Illinois, 1972-84. **Awards:** Nebula award, 1973, 1982; Rhysling award, for verse, 1978; *Locus* award, 1982, 1987; World Fantasy award, 1982, 1989; British Science Fiction Association award, 1982; British Fantasy award, 1983; John W. Campbell Memorial award, 1984. **Agent:** Virginia Kidd, Box 278, Milford, PA 18337, USA. **Address:** P.O. Box 69, Barrington, IL 60011, USA.

FANTASY PUBLICATIONS

Novels (series: Latro)

Peace. New York, Harper, 1975; London, Chatto and Windus, 1985.
The Devil in a Forest (for children). Chicago, Follett, 1976; London, Panther, 1985.
Free Live Free. New York, Tor, and London, Gollancz, 1985.
Soldier of the Mist (Latro). New York, Tor, and London, Gollancz, 1986.
There Are Doors. New York, Tor, 1988; London, Gollancz, 1989.
Soldier of Arete (Latro). New York, Tor, 1989; London, New English Library, 1990.
Castleview. New York, Tor, 1990; London, New English Library, 1991.

Short Stories

The Island of Doctor Death and Other Stories and Other Stories. New York, Pocket Books, 1980.
Gene Wolfe's Book of Days. New York, Doubleday, 1981; London, Arrow, 1985.
Storeys from the Old Hotel. Worcester Park, Surrey, Kerosina, 1988; New York, Tor, 1992.
Endangered Species. New York, Tor, 1989; London, Orbit, 1990.

Castle of Days. New York, Tor, 1992.

OTHER PUBLICATIONS

Novels

Operation ARES. New York, Berkley, 1970; London, Dobson, 1977.
The Shadow of the Torturer. New York, Simon and Schuster, 1980; London, Sidgwick and Jackson, 1981.
The Claw of the Conciliator. New York, Simon and Schuster, and London, Sidgwick and Jackson, 1981.
The Sword of the Lictor. New York, Simon and Schuster, and London, Sidgwick and Jackson, 1982.
The Citadel of the Autarch. New York, Simon and Schuster, and London, Sidgwick and Jackson, 1983.
The Urth of the New Sun. New York, Tor, and London, Gollancz, 1987.
Pandora by Holly Hollander. New York, Tor, 1990; London, New English Library, 1991.
Nightside the Long Sun. New York, Tor, and London, Hodder and Stoughton, 1993.
Lake of the Long Sun. New York, Tor, and London, Hodder and Stoughton, 1994.
Calde of the Long Sun. New York, Tor, and London, Hodder and Stoughton, 1994.

Short Stories

The Fifth Head of Cerberus. New York, Scribner, 1972; London, Gollancz, 1973.
The Castle of the Otter (includes essays). Willimantic, Connecticut, Ziesing, 1982.
The Wolfe Archipelago. Willimantic, Connecticut, Ziesing, 1983.
Bibliomen: Twenty Characters Waiting for a Book. New Castle, Virginia, Cheap Street, 1984.
Plan(e)t Engineering. Cambridge, Massachusetts, NESFA Press, 1984.
The Boy Who Hooked the Sun. New Castle, Virginia, Cheap Street, 1985.
Empires of Foliage and Flower. New Castle, Virginia, Cheap Street, 1987.
Slow Children at Play. New Castle, Virginia, Cheap Street, 1989.
The Hero as Werwolf. Eugene, Oregon, Pulphouse, 1991.
The Old Woman Whose Rolling Pin is the Sun. New Castle, Virginia, Cheap Street, 1991.
Young Wolfe: A Collection of Early Stories. Weston, Ontario, U.M. Press, 1992.

Poetry

For Rosemary. Worcester Park, Surrey, Kerosina, 1988.

Other

Letters Home. Weston, Ontario, U.M. Press, 1991.

*

Bibliography: In *The Castle of the Otter,* 1982; *Gene Wolfe: Urth-Man Extraordinary—A Working Bibliography* by Phil Stephensen-

Payne and Gordon Benson, Jr., Leeds, West Yorkshire, Galactic Central, 1991.

Manuscript Collection: Merril Collection, Toronto Public Library, Canada.

Critical Study: *Gene Wolfe* by Joan Gordon, Mercer Island, Washington, Starmont House, 1986.

Gene Wolfe comments:

In a recent letter, my classicist friend Todd Compton wrote: "There have been bad reviews of *Lake of the Long Sun?* De gustibus and all that, but I can't imagine what books they are reading that are better. I've read two reviews, and they were both reasonably good. One, in *SF Review,* I think, said that this book was uncommonly straightforward, for you. The other, I think in *Locus,* said that it was as dense and enigmatic as ever." That would seem to sum it up, though I would like to add that the late Clare Boothe Luce asked me to sign her copies of my books; I am immensely proud of that.

*   *   *

Despite the claims of some critics (based on the rule that any fiction in which the hero carries a sword must be fantasy, and the fact that one volume won the World Fantasy Award), Wolfe's best and most famous work, the tetralogy consisting of *The Shadow of the Torturer, The Claw of the Conciliator, The Sword of the Lictor* and *The Citadel of the Autarch* (known collectively as "The Book of the New Sun"), is definitely science fiction. The sword carried by its hero, Severian, is just that and no more, and while his trek across the landscape of a dying far-future Earth is crammed with elements drawn from fantasy as well as science fiction, all are explicable in terms of science and far-future or alien technology.

But Wolfe has also written a fantasy series, so far including *Soldier of the Mist* and *Soldier of Arete,* which has a mirror-image correspondence with The Book of the New Sun. While Severian is cursed with the ability to forget nothing, the wounded hero of the Soldier series, Latro, can remember only the past 24 hours, and the two novels are set in the beginning of history, Greece of 480 B.C., rather than the deep future. Severian is an orphan who knew nothing about his parents and voyages out from the place of his birth; Latro remembers his parents but little of his present, and seeks to return home.

A Roman mercenary enlisted in the huge army of Xerxes, Latro receives his injury at the battle of the Thermopylae (in which he may have killed the Spartan King, Leonidas). His subsequent adventures take him through the sea battle of Salamis, in which Xerxes is defeated, a rambling adventure in Thrace, in which it becomes clear that he is a true Hero, and finally to Sparta, where he is made a citizen but steals a ship and sets sail for Sicily and, presumably, his home. As is Severian's in The Book of the New Sun, Latro's story is told as a confessional, the account he keeps to remind him of what he has done. It is perhaps the only fiction in which the narrator knows no more than the reader; gaps in the account are also gaps in Latro's memory. All is a wonder to Latro, including his ability to see Gods and ghosts; it is this wonder, rather than Latro's tattered personality, which illuminates these extraordinary but difficult novels. The reader is further estranged by Latro's literal translations of place names (although the places and events through which Latro travels are familiar enough from the history of Ancient Greece), by the gaps in the narrative that only become

clear by careful reading, and by Latro's deepening depression in the second volume. Nevertheless, Wolfe fully rises to the challenge he has set himself; while the narrative is not straightforward, Wolfe is scrupulous in providing the reader (including Latro) with the clues necessary to parse it. It is not clear whether further volumes are to come, but even these two novels stand together as a major achievement.

Wolfe's other fantasy works stand by themselves. *Devil in a Forest* is a juvenile with not much fantasy in it, being at heart a murder mystery and a riddle of identity set in a little village by a medieval shrine, the St. Agnes Fountain of King Wenceslas's Christmas Carol. *Free Live Free* appears to be a fantasy, drawing heavily on *The Wizard of Oz,* but turns out to be a complex time-travel story, in which four desperate and disparate characters deploy surprising resources after they answer an ad to live free in the house of Ben Free, who disappears when demolition of his property begins. They hunt for him and discover, in a huge balsa-wood plane which never lands, that he is the secret ruler of America. Despite their failures to resist temptations offered by various incarnations of Free, they are rewarded by the revelation that their own redemption lies within themselves. Transfigured, they are sent back in time to transform and redeem their early lives.

There Are Doors is an alternate history in which Green, a depressive living in a time-stream that is not quite ours, falls in love with the goddess of another time-stream where men die after mating. He follows her, and after various adventures, which concatenate into each other like the geography of a dream, which this might be, he sets off for the Overwood where the goddess dwells and where he might love her without dying. It is more successful in the traps of its plot than in its depiction of a matriarchal society, in which predatory women stalk men who assuage their lust with tiny dolls which are the image of Green's goddess. *Castleview* is a hectic mystery story in which the land of faerie intersects rural Illinois, the whole of the Arthurian tragedy is replayed in a night and a day and a night, and a new hero is chosen to sustain the legend.

Wolfe's fictions are at their strongest when he is engaged in defining the way in which memory affects personality, just as stories which are a kind of shared memory (history) affect a culture. This theme has already been noted in both The Book of the New Sun and the Soldier series. It is dealt with most affectingly in an earlier work, *Peace,* which is cast in the form of a posthumous confession. An old man, Denis Alden Weer, haunts a mansion of many rooms which recreate the chambers of his past and which may be his own skull. He weaves his own past and personality from the stories he has heard, principally those of his aunt's three suitors, incidentally recreating 1920s America which itself, he claims, was made from stories, being formless before it was discovered. The novel is touching and funny, yet bears within it a dark irony, an acerbic cold touch found in most of Wolfe's fictions, and in his sardonic self-searching heroes. For the age of innocence Weer describes was entered into after he killed one of his playmates, and beneath the wide-eyed child's observations lurks the adult Weer's understanding of the manoeuvring and dissembling of adult behaviour. His own tale of adulthood is one in which a young woman betrays him for treasure they search for but never find. The diary they use as a clue is a forgery, and it is revealed that perhaps most books are forgeries—perhaps even this one.

Wolfe is one of the most important writers in science fiction and fantasy today, not because of his invention but because of his wide knowledge and masterful use of genre material. His works are powerful syntheses which irradiate and revitalize exhausted tropes. They demand, and reward, our attention.

—Paul J. McAuley

WOOD, Bridget

Pseudonym: Frances Gordon. **Nationality:** British. **Born:** Bridget Duggan, 4 December 1947; daughter of Irish actor Francis Douglas, sister of writer Tony Duggan. **Education:** Educated at a convent school. **Family:** Married Malcolm Wood (died 1970). **Career:** Estate agent, 1975-91. **Agent:** Jane Conway-Gordon, 1 Old Compton Street, London W1V 5PH, England.

FANTASY PUBLICATIONS

Novels

Wolfking. London, Headline, 1991; New York, Del Rey, 1992.
The Lost Prince. London, Headline, 1992; New York, Del Rey, 1993.
Rebel Angel. London, Headline, 1993.
Sorceress. London, Headline, 1994.

OTHER PUBLICATIONS

Novels

Mask of the Fox. London, Hale, 1982.
The Chessmen. London, Hale, 1983.
The Devil in Amber. London, Hale, 1984.
The Rose Window. London, Hale, 1985.
The Minstrel's Lute. London, Hale, 1987.
Satanic Lute. London, Hale, 1987.
Blood Ritual, as Frances Gordon. London, Headline, 1994.

*

Bridget Wood comments:

I have never intended or wanted my work to be regarded as anything other than entertainment for those who read it. My books are not soap-boxes; there are no explorations of, or comments on, the *mores* of this world, or any other world, concealed beneath plots or characters.

The fantasy novels, written under my own name of Bridget Wood, have been described by my publisher and my reviewers as "dark fantasy"—the classic tradition of "fairy stories for grown-ups." They have been compared to adult versions of the Brothers Grimm and C. S. Lewis. If they are sometimes blood-drenched and if they sometimes depict the darker sides of nature, they also have a vein of humour. To laugh is as important as to be frightened, but to enjoy being frightened by what we read or watch, has to many an inverted appeal. Perhaps this is because to be frightened—either by the printed word or the celluloid strip—reinforces our own sense of security. If we can get up from our armchair to check that the door really is locked midway through Stephen King or James Herbert's newest *tour de force*; if we can blink in the

bright lights of the theatre or cinema foyer and leave Hannibal Lecter or Vincent Price safely behind in the auditorium, we know ourselves to be in control. We have reaffirmed our own safety.

*   *   *

Bridget Wood's fantasy novels *Wolfking, The Lost Prince* and *Rebel Angel* all have to do with the adventures and amours of travellers from an era somewhat later than our present with members of the dynasty of Cormac mac Airt, High King of Bright Tara in Dark-Age Ireland. The means whereby transition through time is effected vary from book to book, but all can be classed as agreeable hokum. In all the novels suitably obnoxious Forces of Evil have usurped Tara from whoever is its rightful Lord in the current generation, and whom the future people are pleased to help restore.

Wood's plotlines are rather carelessly compiled, and rely heavily on the old standby of arranging for the principals to be separated so that suspense can be sustained as the author intercuts between them. It is skilfully done in the main, but becomes predictable with familiarity, so that one comes to suspect that she knows no other way of advancing the plot while avoiding longueurs.

The same carelessness sometimes threatens the internal logic of the tales. If the plot requires that a character should take on a new, inconsistent dimension, take it on he does; and no attempt will be made to account for the change. In much the same spirit, a one-eyed giant may "open his eyes," and a major character, having left his body in stasis while his soul goes adventuring in meta-dimensions, comes by a second body with neither comment nor explanation from the author, leaving the original unaccounted for. She is also capable of mixing fantasy with allegory in a manner which threatens the integrity of both, most notably when an attempt is made to stop the "clock of time" in order to avert the Apocalypse—a manoeuvre which requires the characters to inhabit two mutually incompatible universes at once. (All these examples are taken from *The Lost Prince,* incidentally; but any of these three would have served as well.)

So far, so conventional; but Wood brings a unique flavour to what would otherwise be standard sword and sorcery. The Lords of Tara are known as the Wolfkings, for the good reason that they are partly wolf; in common with the other noble families, who have equally intimate links with the brute creation, every three or four generations they require an admixture of animal blood in their gene-pool, which they obtain by traditional sexual means. This behaviour is not without its critics even among their contemporaries, and invariably comes as something of a shock to the future people, but when needs must . . . might as well enjoy it.

And enjoy it they do. As well as the unnatural couplings, *Wolfking* features group sex among monstrous mutants, a giant eaten alive by rats and a prolonged scene of lesbian rape. Torture, murder and dismemberment abate as the cycle proceeds. This is also conventional enough, but Wood's approach is unique in that everything is approached in a spirit of girlish high jinks, emphasized by vertiginous alternations of style between standard sword-and-sorcery (for the scenes of carnage and bestiality) and (for everything else) a surreal archness, reminiscent of Wilde at best, and Enid Blyton at worst. A verse like the following (from *Rebel Angel*)

Kill the babies, eat their eyes
Shred their skins and drink their slime.
Rip the wombs, deny them life.
Slit the birthsacs, wield the knife.

which is a literal programme of action, sits oddly in the context of a court where the demonic queen goes in mortal but unacknowledged fear of the bailiffs on account of the debts which she, in her prodigality, has run up in the cause of extravagant entertainment and with her dressmaker.

Anachronisms are blithely scattered, familiar quotations are gaily mangled, and the suspicion that the author is playing out a complex series of private jokes grows with every volume. The acknowledgement to *Rebel Angel* reads, "I am indebted to my brother, Tony, for his technical knowledge and insight and for his help with the Renascian background." This looks well enough until one starts reading. Renascia turns out to be a polity somewhere mid-way in character and credibility between Browning's Hamelin and Toytown, situated on an asteroid (though apparently with normal gravity) and menaced by something almost wholly unlike a black hole which nonetheless threatens to overwhelm the place.

Up until *Rebel Angel* the tendency was for these features to evolve from innate eccentricity to cultivated vice, but in *Sorceress* Wood shows a will to transcend them. All her most prominent stylistic features, good and bad, remain: the plot is even more complex than usual, with three major strands; agonizing deaths, disfigurements, tortures and rapes are described with girlish gusto; the allegorical characters might as well be ordinary people with appropriate nicknames. Yet she has dispensed with time-travellers, taking for her theme the conflict between representatives of the fading pagan and advancing Christian eras of Ireland; the jokes are fewer and better; the plot mechanisms creak less obtrusively; and there's much more of a sense that the evil beings of Dark Ireland have needs and ambitions of their own which are legitimate in their own eyes, and which therefore have some claim to sympathy, if not to approval.

Sorceress has all the hallmarks of a transitional piece, but only hindsight will disclose what Bridget Wood is in transition towards. The fact that her publishers have described the recent horror novel *Blood Ritual* (under her Frances Gordon pseudonym) as being "in the great tradition of Anne Rice" may or may not serve as an indication.

—Chris Gilmore

WREDE, Patricia C(ollins)

Nationality: American. **Born:** Chicago, Illinois, 27 March 1953. **Education:** Carleton College, Northfield, Minnesota, A.B. 1974; University of Minnesota, Minneapolis, M.B.A. 1977. **Family:** Married James M. Wrede in 1976 (divorced 1992). **Career:** Rate review analyst, Minnesota Hospital Association, Minneapolis, 1977-78; financial analyst, B. Dalton bookseller, Minneapolis, 1978-80; financial analyst, 1980-81, senior financial analyst, 1981-83, senior accountant, 1983-85, Dayton-Hudson Corporation, Minneapolis; full-time writer since 1985. **Awards:** Minnesota Book Award for Fantasy and Science Fiction, 1991. **Agent:** Valerie Smith, Route 44-55, RR Box 160, Modena, NY 12548, USA. **Address:** 4900 West 60th Street, Edina, MN 55424-1709, USA.

Fantasy Publications

Novels (series: Enchanted Forest Chronicles; Lyra)

Shadow Magic (Lyra). New York, Ace, 1982; London, Orbit, 1990.

Daughter of Witches (Lyra). New York, Ace, 1983; London, Orbit, 1990.
The Seven Towers. New York, Ace, 1984.
The Harp of Imach Thyssel (Lyra). New York, Ace, 1985.
Talking to Dragons (Enchanted Forest). New York, Tempo, 1985; revised edition, San Diego, Harcourt Brace, 1993.
Caught in Crystal (Lyra). New York, Ace, 1987; London, Orbit, 1989.
Sorcery and Cecelia: An Epistolary Fantasy, with Caroline Stevermer. New York, Ace, 1988.
Snow White and Rose Red. New York, Tor, 1989
Dealing with Dragons (Enchanted Forest). San Diego, Harcourt Brace, 1990.
Mairelon the Magician. New York, Tor, 1991.
Searching for Dragons (Enchanted Forest). San Diego, Harcourt Brace, 1991.
Calling on Dragons (Enchanted Forest). San Diego, Harcourt Brace, 1993.
The Raven Ring (Lyra). New York, Tor, 1994.

*

Patricia C. Wrede comments:

I started my first novel when I was in seventh grade—I wrote it during class and brought the pages home to my mother. Mom must have known when I'd written it, but she never said anything about it; she just typed my handwritten pages out on the yellow pages she used at the office. I thought it looked too professional for words.

Even so, I never planned to be "a writer." Oh, I expected to write, perhaps even publish a few things someday because I couldn't imagine not writing. But I never expected to make a living writing. I took biology in college and then went on to business school. In my spare time, I wrote short stories and even started on a novel, but it was a hobby, not something I ever expected anyone else to take seriously.

Then one of my friends found out I had half a novel in the bottom drawer of my desk. "Way cool,' he said (or words to that effect). "I want to read it." "It's not finished, but you can see what there is," I told him. "No, I don't read unfinished novels," he said. "You have to finish it so I can read it."

Pretty soon it became easier to finish the book than to keep thinking up excuses. And once that book was finished, I realized that I really could do this and immediately started on the next one. It took another six years and five more books before I could stop being an accountant and write full time, but when I finished that first book I became "a writer" in my own mind.

*   *   *

Much of Patricia Wrede's work is set in a world she calls Lyra, a mystical place with two moons, and shared by humans, the fairy folk who call themselves the Shee, the forest peoples known as the Wyrd, and the evil Shadow Born. Veteran readers of high fantasy will already recognize a certain Tolkienesque familiarity about the peoples of this world, but it would be fair to say that Wrede's creation is much softer, much warmer than Tolkien's, and for many readers this is undoubtedly its attraction. Bad things may happen but one can be sure that sooner or later everything will be comfortably resolved; rarely does anyone other than a bad character die, and loose ends are always neatly tucked into the fabric of the story.

This is a style which might not have much interest for those who like even their fantasy with a raw and gritty taste but there is no doubt that Wrede's romantic and magical fantasy appeals to many, particularly to teenagers and those who prefer a gentler style of writing.

But underneath it all, there are signs that if Wrede were to give her imagination full rein, she might even now create a more robust kind of fantasy. Her stories almost invariably focus on female characters, though it would overstate the case to call them "strong." As it is, they have the capability to be strong and resourceful as often as is required, but an equally regrettable tendency to sink back to being sweet and vulnerable as the occasion demands. Some may consider this to be further evidence of their ability to manipulate the men around them, but it is surely significant that Vandaris in *The Seven Towers,* the one immensely competent female figure, subject to no one's law but her own, and one of the few women not to be tidily married off by the end of the book, is presented almost as a figure of fun, as indeed is the vague witch, Amberglas, in the same book.

Wrede's plots also travel familiar paths. In *Shadow Magic,* Alethia, who once enjoyed stories of Alkyra's mythical past, finds as she grows older that the stories have taken on a reality and that childhood fairy tales will offer her allies as her country is torn apart by war between the ruling families. *Daughter of Witches* gives us Ranira, whose parents were burned as witches, and who has been forced to hide her skills for many years. When she meets Mist, a sorceress drawn by the scent of magic gone bad, she is obliged to reveal her powers, but fortunately quickly acquires allies.

The Seven Towers features Eltiron, Prince of Sevairn, enmeshed in his father's dangerous plans, but aided by outlaws, desert riders and able to counter the misguided plots of Carachel the Wizard-King. *The Harp of Imach Thyssel,* one of the darker stories in the series, nevertheless gives us a familiar story of a magical harp and a man destined to wield it. Similarly, we have stories of witches who have renounced their powers, only to be called back to right a wrong committed long ago (*Caught in Crystal*) and a magical ring which must be reclaimed (*The Raven Ring*).

Wrede delivers her stories never less than competently, but one frequently senses that for all the apparent feminist trappings of free and competent women, the emphasis is more on inept men being in need of good women to keep them out of trouble rather than women enjoying a free and independent existence. And it must be said that Wrede's plots rarely if ever stray from the conventional paths of fantasy writing.

Yet it is also clear that when Wrede wishes, she can turn her hand to something more remarkable. Her reworking of the story of *Snow White and Rose Red* for Terri Windling's Fairy Tale series, set this well-loved fairy-tale classic in Elizabethan England, weaving the story of John Dee the Elizabethan magician into her tale. Her tale of Regency magic, *Mairelon the Magician,* again set in England, also shows considerable skill and invention. Although we have the classic rags-to-riches story of a beggar girl living in the streets of London disguised as a boy, taken on by the travelling magician who is much more than he seems, Wrede seems positively to revel in the twists and turns of the Regency genre, an enthusiasm earlier demonstrated in *Sorcery and Cecelia,* co-written with Caroline Stevermer, and set in a similar quasi-historical era.

There is no doubt that Patricia C. Wrede is a popular writer, her very popularity almost certainly lying in the fact that she sticks to the main thoroughfare of fantasy writing, telling stories which are, for the most part, familiar but reliable. Her strength lies perhaps in the cast of vivid characters she creates for each book. Again, the types are familiar—the wizard, the unrecognized witch, the princess, the outlaw, the mercenary or thief with a heart of gold—but Wrede endows them with warm and endearing personalities so that, for the duration of the novel at least, one does care about their individual fates. And yet there is this nagging doubt that if she were to move beyond the familiar territory of the fantasy novel, she might produce something much more unusual. The signs are there but, for whatever reason, she chooses to remain as a generic fantasy writer.

—Maureen Speller

WRIGHTSON, (Alice) Patricia

Nationality: Australian. **Born:** Alice Patricia Furlonger, Lismore, New South Wales, 21 June 1921. **Education:** State Correspondence School; St. Catherine's College, Stanthorpe, Queensland. **Family:** Married in 1943 (divorced 1953); one daughter and one son. **Career:** Secretary and administrator, Bonalbo District Hospital, 1946-60, and Sydney District Nursing Association, 1960-64; assistant editor, 1964-70, and editor, 1970-75, *School Magazine,* Sydney. **Awards:** Australian Children's Book Council Book of the Year Award, 1956, 1974, 1978, 1984; *Boston Globe-Horn Book* award, 1984; Young *Observer* Prize, 1984; Dromkeen Children's Literature Foundation Medal, 1984; Golden Cat Award (Sweden), 1986; Hans Christian Andersen Medal, 1986; Lady Cutler Award, 1986; New South Wales Premier's Special Occasional Award, 1988. O.B.E. (Officer, Order of the British Empire), 1978. **Address:** P.O. Box 91, Maclean, New South Wales 2463, Australia.

FANTASY PUBLICATIONS

Novels (series: Wirrun)

An Older Kind of Magic, illustrated by Noela Young. London, Hutchinson, and New York, Harcourt Brace, 1972.
The Nargun and the Stars. London, Hutchinson, 1973; New York, Atheneum, 1974.
The Ice Is Coming (Wirrun). Richmond, Victoria, and London, Hutchinson, and New York, Atheneum, 1977.
The Dark Bright Water (Wirrun). Richmond, Victoria, and London, Hutchinson, and New York, Atheneum, 1979.
Night Outside, illustrated by Beth Peck. Melbourne, Rigby, 1979; New York, Atheneum, 1985.
Behind the Wind (Wirrun). Richmond, Victoria, and London, Hutchinson, 1981; as *Journey Behind the Wind,* New York, Atheneum, 1981.
A Little Fear. Richmond, Victoria, and London, Hutchinson, and New York, McElderry, 1983.
Moon-Dark, illustrated by Noela Young. Richmond, Victoria, Hutchinson, 1987; New York, McElderry, 1988.
The Song of Wirrun (omnibus; includes *The Ice Is Coming, The Dark Bright Water, Behind the Wind*). Richmond, Victoria, Century Hutchinson, 1987.

Balyet. Richmond, Victoria, and London, Hutchinson, and New York, McElderry, 1989.

The Sugar-Gum Tree, illustrated by David Cox. Ringwood, Victoria, and New York, Viking, 1991.

OTHER PUBLICATIONS

Novels

The Crooked Snake, illustrated by Margaret Horder. Sydney and London, Angus and Robertson, 1955.

The Bunyip Hole, illustrated by Margaret Horder. Sydney and London, Angus and Robertson, 1958.

The Rocks of Honey, illustrated by Margaret Horder. Sydney, Angus and Robertson, 1960; London, Angus and Robertson, 1961.

The Feather Star, illustrated by Noela Young. London, Hutchinson, 1962; New York, Harcourt Brace, 1963.

Down to Earth, illustrated by Margaret Horder. New York, Harcourt Brace, and London, Hutchinson, 1965.

I Own the Racecourse!, illustrated by Margaret Horder. London, Hutchinson, 1968; as *A Racecourse for Andy,* New York, Harcourt Brace, 1968.

Other

The Haunted Rivers. Maclean, New South Wales, Eighth State Press, 1983.

Editor, *Beneath the Sun: An Australian Collection for Children.* Sydney, Collins, 1972; London, Collins, 1973.

Editor, *Emu Stew: An Illustrated Collection of Stories and Poems for Children.* Melbourne and London, Kestrel, 1976.

*

Film Adaptations: *The Nargun and the Stars,* 1977 (TV serial); *I Own the Racecourse,* 1985.

Manuscript Collections: Lu Rees Archives, Canberra College of Advanced Education Library, Australia; Kerlan Collection, University of Minnesota.

*   *   *

There is a scene in Patricia Wrightson's first book for children, *The Crooked Snake,* where *The Wind in the Willows* is read to a school class; and here we could be reading any conventional British school story, down to the conventional plot regarding a children's club defeating some local vandals transposed to a rural Australian setting.

Wrightson soon began to incorporate fantastic elements into her stories (although the eponymous creature in *The Bunyip Hole* exists only in imagination). While *The Rocks of Honey* is only marginally fantasy, with the lore of the old Aboriginal tribes taking symbolic shape in a tribesman's stone axe buried to save his son from the results of a taboo he has unwittingly broken, it shows several of Wrightson's later concerns. Possession of the axe means different things to Barney, the white viewpoint character, the Aboriginal boy Eustace whom he befriends but takes some time to understand, and Winnie, the girl whom both boys treat as invisible. It is most important to Eustace, making him confront his own

heritage and becoming at once a symbol of the past he would prefer not to acknowledge and, as his uncle says, a link with "good people; kind and good and a little bit proud." Wrightson's picture of Eustace and his place in white society is sensitive: his nickname "Useless" could have been given to any boy of his name and soon becomes affectionate, but the unspoken commentary when Barney and he discuss plans for adulthood shows the gulf between them. Both boys have a certain future mapped for them: one involves possession of a farm, the other has a cousin with a pick-up truck.

While at first her characters were the "white" Australians like Barney in *The Rocks of Honey* and the "Collinses" of *The Bunyip Hole,* it became clear to Wrightson that she could not bring their own folkloric traditions into a land already had its own rich culture. The science-fictional *Down To Earth* could perhaps be a another version of the culture-clash of *The Rocks of Honey,* but its questioning of whether we can ever know if an alien speaking our language is expressing the same concepts we understand touches existential bleakness. Subsequent books appeal to a sense of place and "Australianness." *An Older Kind of Magic,* for instance, juxtaposes the return of a comet after a thousand years with a night in Sydney when the comet's light revives the old spirit-folk of Australia. The plot is a fairly thin and certainly standard one about three children overhearing plans to develop part of the Botanical Gardens, but the magic on the edge of their vision, which seeps into their activities, offers a possibility for a fantasy literature which is more firmly rooted in the land her readers have come to inhabit and which acknowledges the stories of the people who were there long before. "It is time," she writes, "we stopped trying to see elves and dragons and unicorns in Australia. They have never belonged here, and no ingenuity can make them real. We need to look for another kind of magic, a kind that must have been shaped by the land itself at the edge of Australian vision."

The Nargun and the Stars triumphantly expresses Wrightson's concern to develop an Australian fantasy. A Nargun is an elemental being of rock, a living memory of eras when the earth was filled with the newness of lava and fire. Driven by need and the slow swings of earth and moon it arrives in Wongadilla, farmed by Edie and Charlie who have adopted Simon, recently orphaned. Simon discovers the spirits of water and tree, the trickster Potkoorok and the Turongs, and then the Nargun, a Great Power too old and powerful to be allowed to stay where it is, but too dangerous to be overcome by ephemeral humans and almost-as-ephemeral nature-spirits. The story opens up a picture of the relationship between the Australian land and those who have taken it over from its original inhabitants, making them custodians (Charlie, to the Potkoorok, is "The Man in Charge," not the "Owner" and his position is necessarily temporary). The pain and need of the Nargun can be seen as that of the land itself, as Simon, dimly, realizes: troubled by humankind but eventually outlasting it.

Wrightson's masterpiece, however, is the trilogy comprising *The Ice is Coming, The Dark Bright Water* and *Behind the Wind* which develops the legends of various groups of Aboriginal peoples into a single story which it is not unfair to call at least the template for a kind of national saga. The trilogy's protagonist is Wirrun, a young Aboriginal whose adventures among the spiritfolk of the land that shared its dreams with those of his people form part of his own progression from Boy to Man to Hero, as well as possibly suggesting a return of the stories to their original owners (most of her central characters until then being white Australians). The Aboriginals are the People, from whose viewpoint the spirit-folk are simply part of the natural world, representing their own intensely personal and particular ties to their land. The urban white Australians are the "Happy Folk," who, in Wrightson's ironic words, "know that they are the land's true people and everything in it belongs to them" but who live "with their faces to the sea." From the same stock, but almost a separate race, are the Inlanders, who have felt the pull of the land but between whom and the People lies a deep bitterness.

The first volume tells how Wirrun is brought to combat the Ninya, the ice-folk from underground, and how he must find the Eldest Nargun before they do. In *The Dark Bright Water* a Yunggamurra (a kind of siren) is swept from her river by a storm to be trapped underground. Called to save the land from parched springs and watercourses, Wirrun is haunted by the Yunggamurra's song and has to face her dangerous love in the course of his own delving in the subterranean spirit-world. He wins the river-girl, but not before his friend Ularra has died to save him. Finally, *Behind the Wind* brings Wirrun's most dangerous quest, against a spirit of death which has taken upon itself the task of judgement which is not, in Aboriginal lore, a province of the spirit-realm.

Wrightson shows Wirrun (whose "other" name among the Happy Folk is never mentioned) within part of the political economy of modern Australia, working in low-status jobs, an occasional object of suspicion, but wisely does not attempt to write a protest on behalf of his people, preferring to allow the richness of their cultures to speak for itself. Indeed, she has adapted much of her source-material (already filtered through the viewpoints of folklore collectors and anthropologists who have "interpreted" from a Western standpoint), bringing together legends from many parts of Australia. For those unfamiliar with her sources—which would be most of her readers—she offers a refreshingly different combination of fantasy motifs which are certainly, when set against the Classical/Celtic roots of most generic fantasy, exotic, but which offer far more than even a simple attempt to replace unicorns with bunyips. She does not spell out everything for the reader, who must follow her hero's confusion and lack of understanding at some of the events: the crux of *Behind the Wind* is precisely that many of the spirits Wirrun encounters are not from his "own" culture. The writing is simple but dramatically poetic, with a wry irony. It is in keeping with the concerns just described that the Inlander who helps Wirrun and his friends right the ice-folk in *The Ice is Coming* (the only white Australian described at any length in the series) does so by turning away curious visitors to their fires by pretending to be an anthropologist studying a rarely-performed rite or a ticket-collector for the "experimental theatre group." Wirrun's human anguish at his role of "hero" and his love for his spirit-girl Murra, and his roughness and tenderness as he tries, somewhat guiltily, to introduce her to human customs, is remarkably touching.

In 1978, Wrightson was awarded the O.B.E. for her services to children's literature. She is, despite this, not as well-known as she should be in the adult fantasy world, despite the maturity and imaginative quality of the books written once she had firmly established her voice as a specifically Australian writer. The Wirrun trilogy is one of the most remarkable and original works of modern fantasy, and has been republished in the United States as part of Del Rey's paperback fantasy imprint. Its relative neglect by adult fantasy readers, usually attracted by "exotic" settings, is hard to understand, unless it is to do with her avoidance of the comforts of genre and stylistic padding. She is a writer whose economy of style is matched only by her richness of characterization and ability to evoke deeper and richer levels of meaning from an image.

—Andy Sawyer

WURTS, Janny

Nationality: American. **Born:** 1953. **Family:** Married to artist Don Maitz. Lives in Florida.

FANTASY PUBLICATIONS

Novels (series: Cycle of Fire; Empire; Wars of Light and Shadows)

Sorcerer's Legacy. New York, Ace, 1982; revised edition, New York, Bantam, and London, Grafton, 1989.
Stormwarden (Cycle of Fire). New York, Ace, 1984; London, Grafton, 1989.
Daughter of the Empire, with Raymond E. Feist. New York, Doubleday, and London, Grafton, 1987.
Keeper of the Keys (Cycle of Fire). New York, Ace, 1988; London, Grafton, 1989.
Shadowfane (Cycle of Fire). New York, Ace, 1988; London, Grafton, 1990.
Servant of the Empire, with Raymond E. Feist. New York, Doubleday, and London, Grafton, 1990.
The Master of Whitestorm. London, HarperCollins, and New York, Roc, 1992.
Mistress of the Empire, with Raymond E. Feist. New York, Doubleday, and London, HarperCollins, 1992.
The Curse of the Mistwraith (Wars of Light and Shadows). London, HarperCollins, 1993.
The Ships of Merior (Wars of Light and Shadows). London, HarperCollins, 1994.
Warhost of Vastmark (Wars of Light and Shadows). London, HarperCollins, 1995.

Short Stories

That Way Lies Camelot. London, HarperCollins, 1994.

*   *   *

All of Janny Wurts's longer fiction is high fantasy. Her first novel, *Sorcerer's Legacy,* although revised for the 1989 reprint, still shows a number of the awkwardnesses common in debut novels. Whereas the majority of fantasy novels involve a lengthy quest with a little magic to ease the way, this has a bias towards politics and brings magic to the fore, making it a very potent force. The heroine, Elienne, is sharp-tongued and newly widowed. The conqueror of her husband's lands has plenty of nasty things in store for her until she is snatched away by the sorcerer, Ielond. In a different time, she becomes a pawn in the power struggle at the court of Pendaire, knowing that her only chance of survival is to pass off her unborn child as that of the heir to the throne. If she fails, Prince Darion, her new husband, will die too. It is also a romance. The novel begins in an awkward style that uses cumbersome metaphors and overwritten descriptions, but as the author gets into the flow of the narrative many of the stylistic problems seem to dwindle. Her irritating habit of constantly changing point of view is however present throughout.

The Cycle of Fire trilogy which opens with *Stormwarden,* is really one novel divided into three parts. It starts with Anskiere, the stormwarden of the title, being arrested for the murder of thousands. The sorceress, Tathagres, offers him freedom of a sort, if he releases some rather nasty demons. Anskiere is a powerful sorcerer with dominion over wind and water who has a conscience. In desperation he summons Jaric, the son of Ivian, the sorcerer who helped him bind the demons then betrayed him in madness. He also contrives to send Taen, a crippled fisher-girl, to the Isle of the Vaere to develop her powers. The opening novel is complex, setting up situations to be explored in the later volumes. Although the setting appears to be a world with a low level of technology there are a number of surprises. The magic is not inherent on this world. It has been introduced by aliens who crash-landed on the planet many eons ago. The sorcerous powers are conveyed by sathid crystals which become symbiotically linked with their host. Not everyone survives the process, which often results in death or madness. The Vaere, who provide the training to potential sorcerers, are also guardians, keeping a race of demons from exploding across the universe and exterminating mankind. This trilogy has elements of science fiction, but the main thrust of the story can be regarded as fantasy, both in setting and approach.

The Master of Whitestorm is pure fantasy and has a different approach, being written almost as a series of shorter stories involving the same characters. It can be regarded as a novel because of the continuing theme and goal of the main character. Korendir is determined to build a fortress on the impregnable cliffs at Whitestorm. Not satisfied with the place, he also desires to make the fortress inaccessible to sorcery as well as any physical assault. To do this he sells his services for more and more money. He gains a reputation as a ruthless man and often leaves vast numbers of dead as a result of his actions. He also becomes a legend. Throughout, the characters, Korendir and his friend, Haldeth the smith, age and develop.

Janny Wurts's most recent fantasy series, the Wars of Light and Shadows, is a disappointment in comparison. It is overlong and full of the faults extant in her first novel, *Sorcerer's Legacy,* but magnified. It concerns two half-brothers, one of whom controls the power of light, the other of shadow. They begin as mortal enemies but after they have been exiled through a one-way gate into another world they work together to rid their new world of the mistwraith that has blanketed the skies for centuries. But in the final conquest of the wraith, Lysaer is tainted and they revert to their bitter and destructive enmity. In the first volume, *The Curse of the Mistwraith,* there are a number of standard elements such as a conclave of wizards, prophecies, lost princes returning from exile and a lot of travelling from one place to another. Apart from the unnecessary length, due largely to introspection by the characters—leaving little for readers to observe for themselves (a fault in common with *Daughter of the Empire* written in collaboration with Raymond E. Feist) what should be fast-moving action is slowed down almost to the point of tedium. This is exaggerated by the problem that occurs in all of Wurts's books to a greater or lesser extent—that of constantly switching point of view. In this book it is so marked that it detracts further from the story. The overall impression is that although her characters develop as human beings, Janny Wurts has not developed significantly as a writer.

The trilogy of novels that she has written with Raymond E. Feist are set in a fantasy Byzantine Empire and show a mixture of influences, including that of the Far East, but display some of the faults exhibited by Wurts's solo novels. The collection, *That Way Lies Camelot,* contains both science-fiction and fantasy stories. Although many of them were written in the first instance for shared-world anthologies (the *Fleet* series edited by Bill Fawcett, and the *Blood of Ten Chiefs* series), they demonstrate that at the shorter length Wurts is able to write cleverly and concisely.

Janny Wurts is also a talented artist and has produced excellent covers and interiors for most of the New York publishers and for a number of her own books.

—Pauline Morgan

WYLIE, Jonathan

Joint pseudonym for Mark and Julia Smith. **SMITH, Mark: Nationality:** British. **Born:** Ongar, Essex, 5 March 1952. **Education:** Farnborough Grammar School; Birmingham University, degree in mathematics. **Family:** Married Julia Smith in 1987. **Career:** Sales, administration and editorial work, Transworld Publishers, London, 1974-91. **SMITH, Julia: Nationality:** British. **Born:** Darlington, County Durham, 7 October 1955. **Education:** High school in Sleaford, Lincolnshire; secretarial college, Lincoln. **Family:** Married Mark Smith in 1987. **Career:** Secretary, Ministry of Defence, London, 1975-77; personnel assistant, R. M. Parsons, London, 1977-80; secretarial and editorial work, Transworld Publishers, London, 1980-91. **Agent:** Meg Davis, MBA Literary Agents Ltd, 45 Fitzroy Street, London W1P 5HR, England. **Address:** Field View, Melton Road, Hindolveston, Norfolk NR20 5DB, England.

FANTASY PUBLICATIONS

Novels (series: Island and Empire; Servants of Ark; The Unbalanced Earth)

The First Named (Servants of Ark). London, Corgi, and New York, Bantam, 1987.
The Centre of the Circle (Servants of Ark). London, Corgi, 1987; New York, Bantam, 1988.
The Mage-born Child (Servants of Ark). London, Corgi, and New York, Bantam, 1988.
Dreams of Stone (Unbalanced Earth). London, Corgi, and New York, Bantam, 1989.
The Lightless Kingdom (Unbalanced Earth). London, Corgi, and New York, Bantam, 1989.
The Age of Chaos (Unbalanced Earth). London, Corgi, 1989; New York, Bantam, 1990.
Dream-Weaver. London, Corgi, 1991.
Shadow-Maze. London, Corgi, 1992; as by Mark and Julia Smith, New York, Warner, 1994.
Dark Fire (Island and Empire). London, Corgi, 1993.
Echoes of Flame (Island and Empire). London, Corgi, 1994.
The Last Augury (Island and Empire). London, Corgi, 1994.
Other Lands. London, Orbit, 1995.

OTHER PUBLICATIONS

Other (by Julia Smith)

Editor, with Rog Peyton. *The People Collection,* by Zenna Henderson. London, Corgi, 1991.

*

Mark and Julia Smith comment:

We met at work (Transworld Publishers). Although we had both previously harboured ambitions to write, we produced nothing worthwhile until we got together. We began to write *The First Named* after we'd been living together for a few months. Initially the writing was done for our own amusement and confined to our spare time outside office hours, but in 1991 we gave up our day jobs to write full time, and moved from London to Norfolk.

Fantasy was a natural choice for us, both because of our own preferences and our joint editorial experience which led us to believe that we could create something original and worthwhile, while retaining some traditional elements of the genre. We began with two trilogies, Servants of the Ark and The Unbalanced Earth, which are linked by two characters but can be read separately. Two stand-alone novels, *Dream-Weaver* and *Shadow-Maze,* followed, and then we returned to the trilogy format for Island and Empire, which is darker and less humorous than our earlier writing. All our published works to date are set in entirely imaginary worlds, but we recently finished the first of two modern-day fantasies (*Other Lands*).

Writing together is an entirely natural process for us, a fact which many people find hard to understand. For us, the advantages are obvious: bouncing ideas off each other—and usually ending up with something vastly more complex and interesting than the original concept; avoiding getting stuck because the other person is there to rescue you; the ability to view things from both male and female perspectives; and so on. These far outweigh the disadvantages of occasional, minor disagreements over the text.

Our basic intention in writing is to tell a good story, to involve and entertain the reader, but within that the most important elements are always the characters. We grow to care deeply for them and, we hope, the reader will too.

*　　*　　*

Jonathan Wylie is the pseudonym for the collaborative partnership of Mark and Julia Smith. They began writing fantasy novels while they were still editors at Corgi but their success has been such that they are now able to concentrate on the writing full time.

Their first trilogy, Servants of Ark, was very much a learning process. Undoubtedly, they began with the advantage of knowing what elements make a successful fantasy novel but it is always more difficult to put theory into practice. In the first volume, *The First Named,* the story plunges into action from almost the first page. The king and queen of Ark are dead, having been assassinated by Amarino and her husband Parokkan. The three princes, however, have escaped along with their mentor, the wizard Ferragamo. Naturally, this is a mistake on Amarino's part as the youngest of the brothers, Mark, after adventures, romance and the discovery that he too is a wizard, finds the way to defeat her and regain the sovereignty of the kingdom. Between the end of this book and the beginning of the next, *The Centre of the Circle,* are 16 years during which Mark's son Luke has a chance to grow to maturity and the evil that beset Ark in *The First Named* has time to recover its strength. At first, the strange events that begin to occur around the edges of the archipelago of which Ark is the centre are ignored as freaks of nature. Only Ferragamo sees anything sinister in them but he is unable to convince his fellow wizards of this until it is too late. Much of the book concerns itself with Luke's development, and with Julia who has been brought up in strange circumstances on the isolated island of Strock. The third volume,

The Mage-Born Child, has its beginnings before the end of the previous volume, and the initial chapters chronicle the story of Yve who is the first female wizard. On her journey from the outlying island of Lugg in place of her Master, she finally meets her familiar, a dragon from another dimension which few beside herself can see. It is she who will have to play a principal role in the eventual defeat of Alzedo, the evil sorcerer who has been behind the previous attempts to subjugate the archipelago and here is trying for the third time.

There are many familiar elements in this trilogy—wizards, romance, prophecy, talking animals—and to begin with the characterization is clumsy and awkward, like a child taking its first steps. By the time *The Mage-Born Child* is reached, the authors have a much firmer understanding of their craft and are able to shape events with more confidence.

The provenance of the second trilogy, the Unbalanced Earth, is firmly rooted in the first. At the end of the Servants of Ark trilogy, the world has been effectively reshaped and magic is dead. Gemma, only a child in the first series and now a grown woman, turns her back on her royal heritage to follow a compulsion which draws her south to a new continent. This in itself is a puzzle as it only appeared above the surface of the ocean 14 years previously yet the cities, societies and ruins she finds there have obviously existed for centuries. Having got herself lost in the desert, her life is saved by a tribe of semi-intelligent meyrcats, and she is rescued by Arden, a young man seeking to save a magical valley from drought. By the end of this volume they have succeeded but have become separated and each believes that the other is dead. The second book, *The Lightless Kingdom,* follows Gemma and Arden separately. Arden has been swept under the mountains by the river and encounters a race of people who live entirely underground. They, however, are being driven out by pollution. Gemma returns to the city of Great Newport, joining a different kind of underground which hopes to overthrow the Guild that controls the region and represses the ordinary citizen. So far the original pull that has brought Gemma to this world has been set aside but towards the end of this volume it reasserts itself, setting up the framework for the final volume, *The Age of Chaos.*

During the trilogy Gemma is discovering a new form of magic. Power derives from groups or circles, like the meyrcats or the people of the Valley, who can co-operate. There is also an emphasis on the environment and the message of the final volume is anti-technology as it is this which is poisoning the land.

The majority of Wylie's protagonists are young and inexperienced and much of the plot revolves around these characters discovering aspects of life and themselves that they were unaware of. *Dream-Weaver* is a novel complete in itself and has a group of young people in the forefront of the action. Principal among these is Rebecca who lives on the edge of a vast sea of salt crystals. Her world is shaken apart when she objects to the man her father tries to marry her to, and her attempts to get out of it lead to unforseen events. As with the Servants of Ark, prophecy plays a large part in this plot, as do riddles that Rebecca has to solve to resolve the situation. The other freestanding novel, *Shadow-Maze,* again introduces its main characters at an early age—Varo and Brostek become friends when the rest of their village are all kidnapped or killed by the mysterious Knifemen. Seeking revenge for their loss they find allies and a riddle to solve.

Wylie's more recent work, the Island and Empire trilogy, again shares common themes with the earlier books. The principal characters are again youthful—one as young as three. There is evil to combat, this time in the shape of Verkho the Emperor's chancellor who, in an attempt to rule the empire seeks to wake a dead god. There are riddles—Verkho has to solve some to release the god's power and the ghosts that wander openly across the stage offer advice in riddles to Gaye, the blind girl who can hear them. Also circles again have their part to play. Some are the circles used to make magic, some are the circles formed by the walls in the Emperor's city of Xantium, others are more elusive like that in the riddle given to Gaye that the circles begin and end on Zalys, her home island.

In general, Wylie's writing has developed to such an extent that you can expect a good entertaining story. The strengths of all the books are the imaginative landscapes, from the underground Lightless Kingdoms, and the city buried beneath the salt in *Dream-Weaver,* to the intricacies of the valley that holds the *Shadow-Maze* in the book of that title.

—Pauline Morgan

Y-Z

YEOVIL, Jack

Pseudonym for Kim Newman. **Nationality:** British. **Born:** Bridgwater, Somerset, 31 July 1959. **Education:** Dr. Morgan's Grammar School, Bridgwater, 1970-75; Bridgwater College, 1975-77; University of Sussex, Brighton, 1977-80, B.A. in English. **Career:** Stage performer, film critic, broadcaster and writer; contributor, *Monthly Film Bulletin, Interzone, Empire, Sight and Sound* and many other magazines. **Awards:** Horror Writers of America Bram Stoker award for non-fiction, 1989; British Science Fiction Association award for short story, 1991; Dracula Society Children of the Night award for novel, 1993; Lord Ruthven Assembly fiction award, 1994; International Horror Critics' Guild award, 1995. **Agent:** Antony Harwood, Aitken, Stone and Wylie Ltd., 29 Fernshaw Road, London SW10 0TG, England.

FANTASY PUBLICATIONS

Novels (series: Dark Future; Warhammer)

Drachenfels (Warhammer). Brighton, East Sussex, Games Workshop, 1989.
Demon Download (Dark Future). Brighton, East Sussex, Games Workshop, 1990.
Krokodil Tears (Dark Future). Brighton, East Sussex, Games Workshop, 1991.
Beasts in Velvet (Warhammer). Brighton, East Sussex, Games Workshop, 1991.
Comeback Tour: The Sky Belongs to the Stars (Dark Future). Brighton, East Sussex, Games Workshop, 1991.
Genevieve Undead (Warhammer). London, Boxtree, 1993.
Route 666 (Dark Future). London, Boxtree, 1994.

Short Stories (as Kim Newman)

The Original Dr. Shade and Other Stories. London, Pocket, 1994.
Famous Monsters. London, Pocket, 1995.

OTHER PUBLICATIONS

Novel

Orgy of the Blood Parasites. London, Pocket, 1994.

Novels (as Kim Newman)

The Night Mayor. London, Simon and Schuster, 1989; New York, Carroll and Graf, 1991.
Bad Dreams. London, Simon and Schuster, 1990; New York, Carroll and Graf, 1991.
Jago. London, Simon and Schuster, 1991; New York, Carroll and Graf, 1993.
Anno Dracula. London, Simon and Schuster, 1992; New York, Carroll and Graf, 1993.

The Quorum. London, Simon and Schuster, and New York, Carroll and Graf, 1994.

Plays (as Kim Newman)

Another England (produced, Bridgwater, Somerset, 1980).
My One Little Murder Can't Do Any Harm (produced, Bridgwater, 1981).
The Gold-Diggers of 1981 (produced, Bridgwater, 1981).
Deep South (produced, Bridgwater, 1981).
The Roaring Eighties (produced, Bridgwater, 1982).
Rock Rock Rock Rock Rock, with Eugene Byrne, Neil Gaiman and Brian Smedley (produced, Bridgwater, 1987).

Other (as Kim Newman)

Nightmare Movies. London and New York, Proteus, 1984; revised edition, London, Bloomsbury, and New York, Harmony, 1989.
Wild West Movies. London, Bloomsbury, 1990.

Editor, with Neil Gaiman. *Ghastly Beyond Belief.* London, Arrow, 1985.
Editor, with Stephen Jones. *Horror: 100 Best Books.* London, Xanadu, 1988; New York, Carroll & Graf, 1989; revised edition, London, New English Library, 1992.
Editor, with Paul J. McAuley. *In Dreams.* London, Gollancz, 1992.

*   *   *

"Jack Yeovil" was one of the main critical successes of the series of roleplaying game-related novels produced by GW Books (the fiction publishing arm of leading games manufacturers and retailers Games Workshop) in the late 1980s and early 1990s. GW had appointed David Pringle of *Interzone* magazine to recruit the writers, and some of the fine qualities of that magazine were infused into the field of shared-world game-spinoff novels with a success which surprised the group of sceptics who doubted this sub-genre was worth devoting much effort to.

Yeovil had already had books and stories published under his real name, Kim Newman. Most of these featured a mix of elements that were starting to become his trademark: science fiction with a tinge of horror, leavened with humour and a postmodern cannibalization of themes from 20th-century culture and media. Most often, as in his award-winning *Anno Dracula,* Newman utilizes alternative worlds which feature characters drawn both from history and from fiction, in situations both amusing and horrifying.

Yeovil's *Drachenfels* was the first novel published by GW Books. It was part of their Warhammer Fantasy series, in which a semi-medieval world is crowded with races, creatures, settings and deities derived from a variety of real and imagined sources, as well as original elements. While Warhammer is too comprehensive to be an off-the-peg fantasy game-world, Yeovil surprised everyone with his ability to apply his own special style to it.

Drachenfels starts conventionally enough with a raid by a mixed group of adventurers on the grim castle of the evil magician of the title. Each has a different motive: revenge, gain, pure adventure. Some are traitors. It seems that the expedition is a great success:

Drachenfels is vanquished, though only the leader of the group, Oswald von Konigswald, is present and conscious when this happens. Twenty-five years later, Oswald decides to re-visit the castle, and commissions a play to be performed there to commemorate his success. Oswald is now heir to one of the Empire's greatest dukedoms, and a friend of the Emperor, so all the leading lights of Imperial society will attend. Predictably, the influence of Drachenfels is still active in the fortress, so things do not go according to plan.

The two central characters are the playwright Detlef Sierck and the vampire Genevieve Dieudonne, a survivor of the original expedition. Yeovil is not the first writer to experiment with vampires who are not wholly evil: it is typical of his innovative daring, however, that the shades of grey in Genevieve's character are rather nominal, and she functions as an essentially benevolent heroine. Her main fault is merely that, being over 600 years old, she is somewhat jaded and finds much human activity uninvolving. She is a type of benign vampire invented by Yeovil who feeds mainly on volunteers, usually her lovers, and never destroys them. Unfortunately, this restraint condemns her to a life of serial monogamy, as she inevitably outlives the lovers, being unwilling to turn them into fellow vampires. The unified theatrical theme means that this is a lot more than a hack-and-sack adventure, though there is plenty of excitement. Yeovil indulges his cinematic obsessions to the full: Detlef's career is loosely based on that of Orson Welles, and the names of many of the characters are taken from the early German cinema.

The cinematic theme continued in Yeovil's Warhammer novellas. *Drachenfels* came out in tandem with two anthologies edited by David Pringle, each including a Yeovil story. In *Wolf Riders* (1989), "No Gold in the Grey Mountains" uses another vampire character from *Drachenfels* and one of the settings; but in *Ignorant Armies* (1989), "The Ignorant Armies" deals with other characters against the same general background. The latter story is based loosely based on John Ford's film *The Searchers* (1956). In it, Johan von Mecklenberg searches for his brother, who has been kidnapped by deformed marauders known as Chaos Knights. He is assisted by a warrior named Vukotich, who is also in the title story of the next anthology: *Red Thirst* (1990). This last resembles an 1930s chain-gang movie. Vukotich and Genevieve find themselves chained together among the captives of a fanatically moral religious cult. Of course they escape, still chained and not liking each other, and of course the cult isn't what it seems . . . .

Many of the same characters appear in Yeovil's next novel, *Beasts in Velvet*. This is a re-telling of the Jack the Ripper story against a Warhammer Fantasy background. The hero is Filthy Harald, a watchman whose harsh methods are the only ones that are effective against the killer. *Beasts* is an excellent mystery as well as a fantasy: some scenes are from the murderer's viewpoint, but his identity doesn't become clear until the end. Nor are the victims merely ciphers, as they so often are in this type of book. The grim life of the poor and desperate in this sort of society is very clearly shown.

Genevieve Undead was published after the other books, under the Boxtree imprint which has been reissuing GW material. It is a "novel" comprised of three linked novellas. The first continues the story of Genevieve's relationship with Detlef. The playwright is working on a version of the Jekyll and Hyde story; unfortunately the theatre has a phantom, and a phantom which only Yeovil would have introduced . . . At the end of that story, Genevieve leaves Detlef, convinced she is having a bad effect on him, and the other stories deal with her further adventures.

It was never intended that Newman's involvement with GW would be a secret. Jack Yeovil was simply meant to be a name to distinguish his more commercial work, most of it written at much greater speed than his other (Kim Newman) material. The symbiotic nature of the writer's two personae is confirmed by the fact that Genevieve has now crossed over and appears in universes Newman has developed under his own name. She appears in "The Big Fish," a story in *Famous Monsters,* in which a hard-boiled private eye encounters a Lovecraftian cult; and more substantially in *Anno Dracula,* a novel published at the height of the recent vampire boom. Here, the Count has taken over the British Empire by marrying Queen Victoria, and Genevieve is one of the more cautious and moderate vampires who oppose him.

As Yeovil, Newman has produced a lot of material on the margins of the fantasy genre. He is the mainstay of the GW Dark Future series. This was based on a game which dealt with conflict on the roads of an ecologically devastated near-future America. Beginning with *Demon Download,* Yeovil simply took the world over, converting it into an alternative timeline with its own recent history, and adding a fantasy element which integrates it better into the GW *oeuvre* as a whole. He introduces a Mormon-like cult that is very far from what it seems, and a demon which is downloaded into a computer where it causes a great deal of mayhem with immense gusto, singing "Woolly Bully" as it takes over an armoured car and goes into battle against a gang of bikers.

Some Yeovil material has appeared that is quite unconnected with Games Workshop. The novelette "Pitbull Brittan" in the first *Temps* anthology (edited by Alex Stewart *et al,* 1991; reprinted by Newman in *Famous Monsters*) is an updated, fantasticated parody of the adventures and attitudes of 1920s thriller-hero Bulldog Drummond, set against the background of the Falklands War, Margaret Thatcher's premiership and the British miners' strike of 1984. Recently Yeovil has brought out *Orgy of the Blood Parasites,* a schlock-horror comedy, which is a way-over-the-top tribute to the novels of "Harry Adam Knight" (John Brosnan) and other paperback-original sleaze merchants—good fun, for those who are so minded.

Yeovil/Newman is at times disappointed that some of his fans are just as happy with a Yeovil novel as with a Newman. This reflects the fact that as Yeovil he is the last of the great hack writers—and possibly the finest of them all. Give him an idea for a story, and it will appear in double-quick time with embellishments no one else would have thought of. The extra care lavished on the Newman pieces doesn't necessarily make for a proportionate increase in quality. His one major fault, in some readers' eyes, is his tendency to base his alternative worlds on Hollywood's versions of history. (Possibly this is excusable in a novelist who is also a well-known film critic.) But there is no doubt that all of his fiction, whether as by Yeovil or Newman, is unfailingly stylish and supremely competent entertainment.

—Peter T. Garratt

YEP, Laurence (Michael)

Nationality: American. **Born:** San Francisco, California, 14 June 1948. **Education:** Marquette University, Milwaukee (Dretzka award, 1968), 1966-68; University of California, Santa Cruz, B.A. in English 1970; State University of New York, Buffalo, 1970-75,

Ph.D. in English 1975. **Family:** Married Joanne Ryder. **Career:** Part-time English teacher, Foothill College, Mountain View, California, 1975, and San Jose City College, California, 1975-76; professor, University of California, Berkeley, 1987-89; writer in residence, University of California, Santa Barbara, 1990. **Awards:** Book-of-the-Month Club Writing Fellowship, 1970; Newbery Honor Book award, 1976; American Library Association, Children's Book Award, 1976; International Reading Association Award, 1976; National Council for Social Studies, Carter A. Woodson Award, 1976; *Boston Globe-Horn Book* Award, 1977, 1989; Women's International League for Peace and Freedom, Jane Addams Award, 1978; Commonwealth Club of California Silver Medal, 1979; National Endowment for the Arts, Literature Fellow, 1990. **Agent:** Maureen Walters, Curtis Brown, 10 Astor Place, New York, NY 10003, USA. **Address:** 921 Populus Place, Sunnyvale, CA 94086, USA.

FANTASY PUBLICATIONS

Novels (series: Shimmer and Thorn)

Dragon of the Lost Sea (Shimmer and Thorn). New York, Harper, 1982.
Dragon Steel (Shimmer and Thorn). New York, Harper, 1985.
The Curse of the Squirrel, illustrated by Dirk Zimmer. New York, Random House, 1987.
Dragon Cauldron (Shimmer and Thorn). New York, HarperCollins, 1991.
Dragon War (Shimmer and Thorn). New York, HarperCollins, 1992.

Short Stories

The Rainbow People (retellings), illustrated by David Wiesner. New York, Harper, 1989.
Tongues of Jade (retellings), illustrated by David Wiesner. New York, HarperCollins, 1991.
The Shell Woman and the King: A Chinese Folktale, illustrated by Yang Ming-Yi. New York, Dial, 1993.
The Junior Thunder Lord. New York, Bridgewater, 1993.
Butterfly Boy, illustrated by Jeanne M. Lee. New York, Farrar Straus Giroux, 1993.
The Man Who Tricked a Ghost, illustrated by Isadore Seltzer. New York, Bridgewater, 1993.
Tiger Woman. New York, Bridgewater, 1994.
The Boy Who Swallowed Snakes, with others. New York, Scholastic, 1994.
The Ghost Fox. New York, Scholastic, 1994.

OTHER PUBLICATIONS

Novels

Sweetwater. New York, Harper, 1973; London, Faber, 1976.
Dragonwings. New York, Harper, 1975.
Child of the Owl. New York, Harper, 1977.
Seademons. New York, Harper, 1977.
Sea Glass. New York, Harper, 1979.
The Mark Twain Murders. New York, Four Winds Press, 1982.

Kind Hearts and Gentle Monsters. New York, Harper, 1982.
Liar, Liar. New York, Morrow, 1983.
The Serpent's Children. New York, Harper, 1984.
The Tom Sawyer Fires. New York, Morrow, 1984.
Mountain Light. New York, Harper, 1985.
The Shadow Lord. New York, Pocket Books, 1985; Bath, Chivers, 1987.
Monster Makers, Inc. New York, Arbor House, 1986.
The Star Fisher. New York, Morrow, 1991.
Dragon's Gate. New York, HarperCollins, 1993.

Plays

Pay the Chinaman, and Fairy Bones (produced San Francisco, 1987).
Dragonwings (adapted from the novel; produced Berkeley, 1991). New York, Dramatists Play Service, 1993.

Other

A Lesson Plan Book for Dragonwings. Jefferson City, Missouri, 1990.
When the Bomb Dropped: The Story of Hiroshima. New York, Random House, 1990.
The Lost Garden (autobiography). Englewood Cliffs, New Jersey, Messner, 1991.

Editor, *American Dragons: Twenty-Five Asian American Voices.* New York, HarperCollins, 1993.

* * *

Today, while children's writers strive to rediscover and present modern versions of myth and folklore from all the world's peoples and cultures, adult fantasy writers, as if smitten by the example of J. R. R. Tolkien, remain stubbornly parochial, with their stories, characters and motifs drawn almost exclusively from European traditions. It is only to be expected, then, that the foremost author of fantasies drawn from Chinese mythology, Laurence Yep, has found children's literature his most congenial medium. But his works deserve adult attention as well, if only as stimulating harbingers of the non-European adult fantasy that other writers—or Yep himself—might someday produce.

Yep's major contribution to fantasy is a four-volume series suggested by—but not derived from—Chinese legends. In its first and best novel, *Dragon of the Lost Sea,* the exiled dragon Shimmer, disguised as a poor woman, befriends the abused orphan Thorn and sets out to battle the witch who long ago stole away the sea that was home to her dragon clan; with the inept help of a monkey wizard, they confront and defeat the witch, though the sea is released in the wrong location. This imaginative and engaging story is enlivened by the cantankerous camaraderie that develops between the haughty dragon and the impetuous boy. In *Dragon Steel,* Shimmer and Thorn return to her dragon kingdom to get a magical cauldron that could move her sea to its proper place; almost as good as the first novel, the story does begin to seem cluttered with new characters—Monkey, the reformed witch, and a feisty servant girl rescued from the dragon palace. In *Dragon Cauldron* and *Dragon War,* the adventurers accidentally release a magically imprisoned wizard who takes over a human kingdom and wages war against the dragons before he is defeated and Shimmer's sea is restored.

These novels are weakened by two unfortunate decisions: first, while Shimmer narrated the first two novels, the others are narrated by Monkey, effectively making that less interesting character, not the dragon, the centre of attention. Second, at the end of *Dragon Cauldron,* Thorn merges with the retrieved cauldron so the damaged device can work again, entirely removing Yep's most involving character from the last book and lessening the impact of its conclusion, when Thorn is restored to life and revealed as a missing king.

Despite what might be termed technical flaws, the series remains a noteworthy achievement. Yep can develop his laws of magic with amazing logic and creativity: in *Dragon Cauldron,* Shimmer and her friends reach an underground island where a spell makes all objects placed in the surrounding river drift back to the island, apparently trapping them forever. But Thorn cleverly reasons that the spell must make an exception for dirt, since dirt drifting to the island would otherwise block the river; and, since pottery is made of hardened clay—a form of dirt—he concludes that a raft made of pots tied together will allow them to leave the island. Also, due to the freedom of children's literature and the expansiveness of Yep's sources, the novels display an imaginative audacity that makes some adult fantasy seem pallid by comparison: a witch steals an entire sea; Monkey turns hairs from his tail into tiny monkey helpers; the evil wizard, the Boneless King, is discovered as a mass of human skin slithering along the ground looking for a new body to inhabit; and two gods come to help Shimmer and the others by literally materializing their mountain home in front of them.

Yep's other fantasy works include two impressive collections of Chinese-American folk tales, *The Rainbow People* and *Tongues of Jade.* The stories are retold with graceful charm and effective undercurrents of bitterness; surprisingly, the second volume is better than the first, as if Yep gradually grew more confident about expanding the original versions and speaking in his own voice. The only problems in these collections are the intrusive introductions, where Yep strains to connect each story to the sad experiences of Chinese immigrants in 19th-century America. Since trickster stories occur in all cultures, for example, it hardly seems appropriate to assert that immigrants valued such stories as ways to provide "more confidence in themselves when it came to dealing with employers, labour contractors, storekeepers, and so on"; and when Yep states that "any of the new immigrants in America might have felt lost in this strange new country—just as the young man did in the marshlands in 'Snake-Spoke,'" the inanity of the claimed connection is obvious. Yep has realistically described the lives of Chinese immigrants in justly praised novels like *Mountain Light* and *Dragon's Gate*; he does a disservice to these folk tales by attempting to contort them into another way to describe their experiences.

Some of Yep's fantasies for smaller children might be briefly noted. *The Curse of the Squirrel* finds Yep far from his usual territory in describing an American farmer's hunting dog who is bitten by a gigantic squirrel and transformed into a "were-squirrel," destined to become a squirrel during a full moon. A possum cures the dog but also makes him a vegetarian, so he loses interest in hunting; gradually, the other dogs and the farmer follow his example. The argument against hunting is strengthened by its understatement. *The Shell Woman and the King* and *The Man Who Tricked a Ghost* are retold Chinese folktales similar in length and content to stories in *The Rainbow People* and *Tongues of Jade,* accompanied by lavish illustrations. *Butterfly Boy,* inspired by the work of "Butterfly Philosopher" Chuang Tzu, concerns a young Chinese boy who sometimes turns into a butterfly; when a general's invading army arrives, he publicly laughs because "the marching legs reminded

him of a centipede." When the army leaves, he is hailed as a hero for his show of defiance, though the praise means nothing to him. A beautifully told parable about the value of seeing things from different perspectives, *Butterfly Boy* could also be read as an evocative self-portrait: as someone who has both American and Chinese backgrounds, and someone who writes both children's fiction and adult fiction, Yep must often feel like a man who alternately looks at the world from different perspectives.

—Gary Westfahl

YOLEN, Jane (Hyatt)

Nationality: American. **Born:** New York City, 11 February 1939. **Education:** Staples High School, Westport, Connecticut, graduated 1956; Smith College, Northampton, Massachusetts, B.A. 1960; New School for Social Research, New York; University of Massachusetts, Amherst, 1975-76, M.Ed. 1976. **Family:** Married David W. Stemple in 1962; one daughter and two sons. **Career:** Staff member, *This Week* magazine and *Saturday Review,* New York, 1960-61; assistant editor, Gold Medal Books, New York, 1961-62; associate editor, Rutledge Books, New York, 1962-63; assistant editor, Alfred A. Knopf Juvenile Books, New York, 1963-65; lecturer in education, Smith College, 1979-84. Columnist ("Children's Bookfare"), *Daily Hampshire Gazette,* Northampton, Massachusetts, 1972-80. Massachusetts delegate, Democratic National Convention, Miami, 1972. Member of the Board of Directors, Society of Children's Book Writers since 1974, and Children's Literature Association, 1977-79; president, Science-Fiction Writers of America, 1986-88; editor in chief, Jane Yolen Books, imprint of Harcourt Brace, from 1989. **Awards:** Society of Children's Book Writers Golden Kite Award, 1974; Christopher Award, 1978; University of Minnesota Kerlan Award, 1988; New England SF Association Skylark Award, 1990; Smith College Medal, 1990; Catholic Library Association Regina Medal, 1992. LL.D.: College of Our Lady of the Elms, Chicopee, Massachusetts, 1980. **Agent:** Marilyn Marlow, Curtis Brown, 10 Astor Place, New York, NY 10003, USA. **Address:** Box 27, Hatfield, MA 01038, USA.

FANTASY PUBLICATIONS

Novels (series: Great Alta)

The Magic Three of Solatia. New York, Crowell, 1974.
The Mermaid's Three Wisdoms. New York, Collins World, 1978.
Sister Light, Sister Dark (Great Alta). New York, Tor, 1988; London, Futura, 1989.
White Jenna (Great Alta). New York, Tor, 1989; London, Futura, 1990.
The Book of Great Alta (omnibus; includes *Sister Light, Sister Dark, White Jenna*). New York, Guild America, 1990.
Briar Rose. New York, Tor, 1992; London, Pan, 1994.
The Wild Hunt. New York, Harcourt Brace, 1995.

Short Stories

The Girl Who Cried Flowers and Other Tales. New York, Crowell, 1974.

The Moon Ribbon and Other Tales. New York, Crowell, 1976; London, Dent, 1977.

The Hundredth Dove and Other Tales. New York, Crowell, 1977; London, Dent, 1979.

The Lady and the Merman: A Tale. Easthampton, Massachusetts, Pennyroyal Press, 1977.

Dream Weaver. New York, Collins, 1979.

Neptune Rising: Songs and Tales of the Undersea Folk. New York, Philomel, 1982.

Tales of Wonder. New York, Schocken, 1983; London, Futura, 1987.

The Whitethorn Wood and Other Magicks. Ottawa, Ontario, Triskell Press, 1984.

Dragonfield and Other Stories. New York, Ace, 1985.

Merlin's Booke: Thirteen Stories and Poems About the Arch-Mage. New York, Steeldragon Press, 1986.

The Faery Flag. New York, Orchard, 1989.

The Sword and the Stone. Eugene, Oregon, Pulphouse, 1991.

Storyteller. Boston, NESFA Press, 1992.

Here There Be Dragons. New York, Harcourt Brace, 1993.

Other

Editor, *Zoo 2000: Twelve Stories of Science Fiction and Fantasy Beasts.* New York, Seabury Press, 1973; London, Gollancz, 1975.

Editor, *Shape Shifters: Fantasy and Science Fiction Tales about Humans Who Can Change Their Shapes.* New York, Seabury Press, 1978.

Editor, with Martin H. Greenberg and Charles G. Waugh, *Dragons and Dreams: A Collection of New Fantasy and Science Fiction Stories.* New York, Harper, 1986.

Editor, *Favorite Folktales from Around the World.* New York, Pantheon, 1986.

Editor, with Martin H. Greenberg and Charles G. Waugh, *Spaceships and Spells.* New York, Harper, 1987.

Editor, with Martin H. Greenberg, *Werewolves.* New York, Harper, 1988.

Editor, with Martin H. Greenberg, *Things That Go Bump in the Night.* New York, Harper, 1989.

Editor, with Martin H. Greenberg, *Vampires.* New York, Harper Collins, 1991.

Editor, with Martin H. Greenberg. *Xanadu.* New York, Tor, 1993.

Editor, with Martin H. Greenberg. *Xanadu 2.* New York, Tor, 1994.

Editor, with Martin H. Greenberg. *Xanadu 3.* New York, Tor, 1995.

OTHER PUBLICATIONS

Novel

Cards of Grief. New York, Ace, 1984; London, Futura, 1986.

Fiction for Children

The Witch Who Wasn't. New York, Macmillan, and London, Collier Macmillan, 1964.

Gwinellen, The Princess Who Could Not Sleep. New York, Macmillan, 1965.

Trust a City Kid, with Anne Huston. New York, Lothrop, 1966; London, Dent, 1967.

Isabel's Noel. New York, Funk and Wagnalls, 1967.

The Emperor and the Kite. Cleveland, World, 1967; London, Macdonald, 1969.

The Minstrel and the Mountain. Cleveland, World, and Edinburgh, Oliver and Boyd, 1968.

Greyling. Cleveland, World, 1968; London, Bodley Head, 1969.

The Longest Name on the Block. New York, Funk and Wagnalls, 1968.

The Wizard of Washington Square. New York, World, 1969.

The Inway Investigators; or, The Mystery at McCracken's Place. New York, Seabury Press, 1969.

The Seventh Mandarin. New York, Seabury Press, and London, Macmillan, 1970.

Hobo Toad and the Motorcycle Gang. New York, World, 1970.

The Bird of Time. New York, Crowell, 1971.

The Girl Who Loved the Wind. New York, Crowell, 1972; London, Collins, 1973.

Rainbow Rider. New York, Crowell, 1974; London, Collins, 1975.

The Adventures of Eeka Mouse. Middletown, Connecticut, Xerox, 1974.

The Boy Who Had Wings. New York, Crowell, 1974.

The Little Spotted Fish. New York, Seabury Press, 1975.

The Transfigured Hart. New York, Crowell, 1975.

Milkweed Days. New York, Crowell, 1976.

The Sultan's Perfect Tree. New York, Parents' Magazine Press, 1977.

The Seeing Stick. New York, Crowell, 1977.

The Giants' Farm. New York, Seabury Press, 1977.

Hannah Dreaming. Springfield, Massachusetts, Springfield Museum of Fine Arts, 1977.

No Bath Tonight. New York, Crowell, 1978.

The Simple Prince. New York, Parents' Magazine Press, 1978.

Spider Jane. New York, Coward McCann, 1978.

The Giants Go Camping. New York, Seabury Press, 1979.

Spider Jane on the Move. New York, Coward McCann, 1980.

Mice on Ice. New York, Dutton, 1980.

Commander Toad in Space. New York, Coward McCann, 1980.

The Robot and Rebecca. New York, Random House, 1980.

Shirlick Holmes and the Case of the Wandering Wardrobe. New York, Coward McCann, 1981.

Uncle Lemon's Spring. New York, Dutton, 1981.

The Boy Who Spoke Chimp. New York, Knopf, 1981.

Brothers of the Wind. New York, Philomel, 1981.

The Gift of Sarah Barker. New York, Viking Press, 1981.

The Acorn Quest. New York, Crowell, 1981.

The Robot and Rebecca and the Missing Owser. New York, Knopf, 1981.

Sleeping Ugly. New York, Coward McCann, 1981.

Dragon's Blood. New York, Delacorte Press, 1982; London, MacRae, 1983.

Commander Toad and the Planet of the Grapes. New York, Coward McCann, 1982.

Commander Toad and the Big Black Hole. New York, Coward McCann, 1983.

Heart's Blood. New York, Delacorte Press, and London, MacRae, 1984.

Children of the Wolf. New York, Viking Kestrel, 1984.

The Stone Silenus. New York, Philomel, 1984.

Commander Toad and the Dis-Asteroid. New York, Coward McCann, 1985.

Commander Toad and the Intergalactic Spy. New York, Coward McCann, 1986.

A Sending of Dragons. New York, Delacorte Press, and London, MacRae, 1987.

Piggins. San Diego, Harcourt Brace, 1987; London, Piccadilly Press, 1988.

Owl Moon. New York, Philomel, 1987.

Commander Toad and the Space Pirates. New York, Putnam, 1987.

Picnic with Piggins. San Diego, Harcourt Brace, 1988.

The Devil's Arithmetic. New York, Viking Kestrel, 1988.

Piggins and the Royal Wedding. San Diego, Harcourt Brace, 1989.

Dove Isabeau. San Diego, Harcourt Brace, 1989.

Baby Bear's Bedtime Book. San Diego, Harcourt Brace, 1990.

Dinosaur Dances. New York, Putnam, 1990.

The Dragon's Boy. New York, Harper and Row, 1990.

Elfabet: An ABC of Elves. Boston, Little Brown, 1990.

Sky Dogs. San Diego, Harcourt Brace, 1990.

All Those Secrets of the World. Boston, Little Brown, 1991.

Grandad Bill's Song. New York, Philomel, 1991.

Greyling. New York, Philomel, 1991.

Letting Swift River Go. Boston, Little Brown, 1991.

Wings. San Diego, Harcourt Brace, 1991.

Wizard's Hall. San Diego, Harcourt Brace, 1991.

Play

Robin Hood, music by Barbara Green (produced Boston, 1967).

Poetry

See This Little Line? New York, McKay, 1963.

It All Depends. New York, Funk and Wagnalls, 1969.

An Invitation to the Butterfly Ball: A Counting Rhyme. New York, Parents' Magazine Press, 1976; Kingswood, Surrey, World's Work, 1978.

All in the Woodland Early: An ABC Book, music by the author. Cleveland, Collins, 1979.

How Beastly! A Menagerie of Nonsense Poems. New York, Collins, 1980.

Dragon Night and Other Lullabies. New York, Methuen, 1980; London, Methuen, 1981.

Ring of Earth: A Child's Book of Seasons. San Diego, Harcourt Brace, 1986.

The Three Bear Rhyme Book. San Diego, Harcourt Brace, 1987.

Best Witches: Poems for Halloween. New York, Putnam, 1989.

Bird Watch. New York, Philomel, 1990.

Other

Pirates in Petticoats. New York, McKay, 1963.

World on a String: The Story of Kites. Cleveland, World, 1968.

Friend: The Story of George Fox and the Quakers. New York, Seabury Press, 1972.

The Wizard Islands. New York, Crowell, 1973.

Writing Books for Children. Boston, The Writer, 1973; revised edition, 1983.

Ring Out! A Book of Bells. New York, Seabury Press, 1974; London, Evans, 1978.

Simple Gifts: The Story of the Shakers. New York, Viking Press, 1976.

Touch Magic: Fantasy, Faerie, and Folklore in the Literature of Childhood. New York, Philomel, 1981.

The Sleeping Beauty (retelling). New York, Knopf, 1986.

Guide to Writing for Children. Boston, The Writer, 1989.

Tam Lin: An Old Ballad (retelling). San Diego, Harcourt Brace, 1990.

Hark! A Christmas Sampler. New York, Putnam, 1991.

Editor, *The Fireside Song Book of Birds and Beasts,* music by Barbara Green. New York, Simon and Schuster, 1972.

Editor, *Rounds About Rounds,* music by Barbara Green, illustrated by Gail Gibbons. New York, Watts, 1977; London, Watts, 1978.

Editor, *The Lullaby Songbook,* music arranged by Adam Stemple, illustrated by Charles Mikolaycak. San Diego, Harcourt Brace, 1986.

Editor, *The Lap-Time Song and Play Book.* San Diego, Harcourt Brace, 1989.

Editor, *2041 A.D.: Twelve Stories about the Future by Today's Top Science Fiction Writers.* New York, Delacorte Press, 1991.

*

Manuscript Collection: Kerlan Collection, University of Minnesota, Minneapolis.

*   *   *

Jane Yolen, best-known as a much-anthologized writer of modern-day fairy tales, is the author of over 120 volumes, very many of them brief picture-books for young children or novels for adolescents. A few of them, such as the juvenile Pit Dragon series and the adult *Cards of Grief,* are ostensibly science fiction; however, even in these Yolen employs a voice that is much closer to fantasy. She has also been a significant editor in the field, notably with her recent series of original fantasy anthologies, *Xanadu,* and with her work on the young-adult "Jane Yolen Books" imprint for publisher Harcourt Brace. With such a wide range of work, it is possible only to talk in detail about a few outstanding examples of her adult fantasy writing.

Merlin's Booke is a collection of Arthurian tales which tell the story of Merlin from before his birth to his death and after. However, they are not all set in the same version of the Arthurian mythos. Each story characterizes Merlin differently, and is optimistic in a different degree about the Matter of Britain. For instance, "The Wild Child" is an essentially optimistic tale that takes its lead from the myth of Merlin as a "wild man of the woods" legend; "Dream Reader" is closer to genre fantasy, with its tale of Merlin finding his father, yet puts a pessimistic gloss on the story quite at odds with its genre form; and "The Gwynhfar" links Guinevere, Arthur and the whole idea of myth-making in a tale that plays off notions of goddess-worship without ever pandering to them. What does link the stories is a slightly detached writing style which gives the feeling that one is reading a folk tale or legend. This, together with the constantly changing settings, serves to distance the reader from the stories.

Yolen achieves much the same effect in the pair of novels *Sister Light, Sister Dark* and *White Jenna.* Here, what might have been a generic fantasy tale, in which a child discovers she is the Messiah and fulfils the prophecy of her coming to power, is transformed in the telling. Each section of the story is told in several different ways—as a song, as a folk tale or legend, as the scholarly notes made about it by different academics, complete with dissenting views—and as a traditional, plainly told narrative. Yolen also provides songs and children's rhymes based on the story. This stops readers immersing themselves in the narrative, and forces them to be constantly judging the story and the protagonists. Yet Yolen also maintains one of the central mysteries of the books—the nature of the Dark Sisters—and forces her readers to construct theory after theory about what they may be.

For instance, at the start of the tale, Jenna's mother dies in chilbirth, and her father rejects her. The midwife takes her to live with the warrior women in the mountains; but along the way the woman is killed. Jenna is found by the women, and is fostered by them. She is raised as a follower of Great Alta, the Goddess. But her foster-mother becomes obsessive and strange, and harms her Dark Sister. She is driven out of the Hame, and is killed by a man from the town. Thus, Jenna is the daughter of three mothers, as a prophecy predicts: but instead of leaving it at that, Yolen also tells the folk-tale that grows out of the story. In this way, readers experience something of the uncertainty faced by the high priestess of the Hame. Like her, they have the opportunity to decide whether Jenna is, in fact, the one spoken of in prophecy or just an unusual child surrounded by an unlikely set of coincidences. That the unfolding narrative makes the latter more and more implausible is irrelevant: readers have already been given an insight into what drives a potentially dislikeable character.

In the hands of a less skilled writer, the narrative would have become unwieldy, or the various layers woven around the story would have distanced readers so far from Jenna and her comrades that readers would have cared nothing for them. In fact, this does not happen. If anything, the contrast between Jenna in the story and the mythologized Jenna, serves only to make her seem more human.

Following this, *Briar Rose* appears a very simple tale simply told. However, the appearance is deceptive, for Yolen once again examines the connections between reality and story, mythology and the personal, artifice and naturalism. As the book opens, Becca Berlin's grandmother, Gemma, has died, leaving behind an inheritance of a wooden box filled with photos and documents from the Second World War. But her true legacy is the story she used to tell Becca and her sisters—her version of Sleeping Beauty, which she based on the older tale of Briar Rose. The novel follows Becca as she unravels her grandmother's story, starting with the secret of her very name, which is not as Becca always believed, Gemma; or even, as Becca's mother believed, Genevieve, with Dawn as a nickname. Her real name is Gitl, and she came to the America as a refugee. The story that Yolen tells is the one of how Becca traces back her history, almost inevitably, to the concentration camps of Germany and Poland—to Chelmno, most feared and most secret of them all.

Gemma—or rather, Gitl—was gassed. She was found almost dead, in a communal grave, and bought back to life by the freedom fighter who gave her the kiss of life. Traumatized, she used the tale of Sleeping Beauty as a defence and an explanation of what happened to her. Yolen does not make the mistake of letting Potocki—or Becca, or her readers—know too much of Gemma's story. What happened to her before she came to Chelmno is lost in the clouds of the poison gas. Potocki knows she joined his group of partisans, married one of their comrades, and was left a pregnant widow when her husband was killed in a fire fight. Potocki helped her leave Poland, but after that he knows nothing of her story. Thus, readers have to fill in the gaps.

If this was all Yolen had done, *Briar Rose* would be a good book. But it is not. Rather, it is one of a number of stories that she layers together. There is also the story of Becca's relationship with her sisters; there is the one of her journey to Poland and her friendship with Magda, her translator; and the one of how her friendship with Stan, who helps her, blossoms into love. Most of all, there is the story of Josef Potocki, the gay German who saved Gemma's life. He was educated in England and returned to Germany just before the War began; he refused to leave, despite his active sex life, because he simply could not believe anything bad could happen to him. It did—he was sent to Sachenhausen, a labour camp. He escaped and joined the resistance movement, and eventually came to the moment where he saved Gemma.

Finally, the whole narrative is bedded in keen observation of everyday life: the little rituals that take over to get one through a period of mourning, the taste of coffee gone lukewarm while one works, the defining moment when a friend's smile becomes the special one of a lover. These anchor the story, making Josef Potocki's terrible tale even more dreadful, and the fantastical elements seem almost naturalistic. This, finally, is Yolen's great achievement: to marry the realistic with the fantastic in such a way as to provide a comment on both, while at the same time leaving—or perhaps forcing—her readers to make their own evaluation.

—Liz Holliday

ZELAZNY, Roger (Joseph)

Nationality: American. **Born:** Cleveland, Ohio, 13 May 1937. **Education:** Noble School, 1943-49, Shore Junior High School, 1949-52, and Euclid Senior High School, 1952-55, all Euclid, Ohio; Western Reserve University, Cleveland (Foster Poetry award, 1957, 1959), 1955-59, B.A. in English 1959; Columbia University, New York, 1959-60, M.A. 1962. **Military Service:** Ohio National Guard, 1960-63, and the United States Army Reserve, 1963-66. **Family:** Married 1) Sharon Steberl in 1964 (divorced 1966); 2) Judith Callahan in 1966, two sons and one daughter. **Career:** Claims representative, Cleveland, 1963-65, and claims specialist, Baltimore, 1965-69, Social Security Administration. Since 1969, freelance writer and lecturer. Secretary-Treasurer, Science Fiction Writers of America, 1967-68. **Awards:** Nebula award, 1965 (twice), 1975; Hugo award, for novel, 1966, 1968, for story, 1976, 1982; Prix Apollo, 1972; American Library Association award, 1976; Locus award, 1984, 1986; United Nations Society of Writers award, 1989; Creative Achievement award, Case Western Reserve University, 1990. Guest of Honor, 32nd World Science Fiction Convention, 1974; Australian National Science Fiction Convention, 1978; European Science Fiction Convention, 1984; and World Fantasy Convention, 1993. **Agent:** Pimlico Agency, Box 20447, 1539 First Avenue, New York, NY 10028, USA.

FANTASY PUBLICATIONS

Novels (series: Amber; Azzie Elbub; Dilvish; Changeling)

Creatures of Light and Darkness. New York, Doubleday, 1969; London, Faber, 1970.
Nine Princes in Amber. New York, Doubleday, 1970; London, Faber, 1972.
Jack of Shadows. New York, Walker, 1971; London, Faber, 1973.

The Guns of Avalon (Amber). New York, Doubleday, 1972; London, Faber, 1974.
Sign of the Unicorn (Amber). New York, Doubleday, 1975; London, Faber, 1977.
The Hand of Oberon (Amber). New York, Doubleday, 1976; London, Faber, 1978.
The Courts of Chaos (Amber). New York, Doubleday, 1978; London, Faber, 1980.
The Chronicles of Amber (omnibus). New York, Doubleday, 2 vols., 1979.
Changeling. New York, Ace, 1980.
The Changing Land (Dilvish). New York, Ballantine, 1981.
Madwand (Changeling). Huntington Woods, Michigan, Phantasia Press, 1981.
Trumps of Doom (Amber). New York, Arbor House, 1985; London, Sphere, 1986.
Blood of Amber. New York, Arbor House, 1986; London, Sphere, 1987.
A Dark Traveling (for children). New York, Walker, 1987; London, Hutchinson, 1989.
Sign of Chaos (Amber). New York, Arbor House, 1987; London, Sphere, 1988.
Knight of Shadows (Amber). New York, Morrow, 1989; London, Orbit, 1991.
Wizard World (omnibus; includes *Changeling, Madwand*). New York, Baen, 1989.
Bring Me the Head of Prince Charming, with Robert Sheckley (Azzie Elbub). New York, Bantam, 1991; London, Pan, 1994.
Prince of Chaos (Amber). New York, Morrow, 1991; London, Orbit, 1993.
If at Faust You Don't Succeed, with Robert Sheckley (Azzie Elbub). New York, Bantam, 1993.
A Night in the Lonesome October. New York, Avon, 1993; London, Orbit, 1994.
A Farce to be Reckoned With, with Robert Sheckley (Azzie Elbub). New York, Bantam, 1995.

Short Stories

The Bells of Shoredan (Dilvish). Columbia, Pennsylvania, Underwood Miller, 1979.
A Rhapsody in Amber (includes verse). New Castle, Virginia, Cheap Street, 1981.
Dilvish, the Damned. New York, Del Rey, 1982.
Here There Be Dragons, illustrated by Vaughn Bode. Hampton Falls, New Hampshire, Grant, 1992.
Way Up High, illustrated by Vaughn Bode. Hampton Falls, New Hampshire, Grant, 1992.

OTHER PUBLICATIONS

Novels

This Immortal. New York, Ace, 1966; London, Hart Davis, 1967.
The Dream Master. New York, Ace, 1966; London, Hart Davis, 1968.
Lord of Light. New York, Doubleday, 1967; London, Faber, 1968.
Isle of the Dead. New York, Ace, 1969; London, Rapp and Whiting, 1970.
Damnation Alley. New York, Putnam, 1969; London, Faber, 1971.

Today We Choose Faces. New York, New American Library, 1973; London, Millington, 1974.
To Die in Italbar. New York, Doubleday, 1973; London, Faber, 1975.
Doorways in the Sand. New York, Harper, 1976; London, W. H. Allen, 1977.
Bridge of Ashes. New York, New American Library, 1976.
Deus Irae, with Philip K. Dick. New York, Doubleday, 1976; London, Gollancz, 1977.
Roadmarks. New York, Ballantine, 1979; London, Futura, 1981.
Coils, with Fred Saberhagen. New York, Tor, 1980; London, Penguin, 1984.
Eye of Cat. New York, Pocket Books, 1982; London, Sphere, 1984.
The Black Throne, with Fred Saberhagen. New York, Baen, 1990.
The Mask of Loki, with Thomas T. Thomas. New York, Baen, 1990.
Flare, with Thomas T. Thomas. New York, Baen, 1992.
Wilderness, with Gerald Hausman. New York: Tor, 1994.

Short Stories

Four for Tomorrow. New York, Ace, 1967; as *A Rose for Ecclesiastes,* London, Hart Davis, 1969.
The Doors of His Face, the Lamps of His Mouth, and Other Stories. New York, Doubleday, 1971; London, Faber, 1973.
My Name Is Legion. New York, Ballantine, 1976; London, Faber, 1979.
The Last Defender of Camelot. New York, Pocket Books, 1980; London, Sphere, 1986.
Unicorn Variations. New York, Pocket Books, 1983; London, Sphere, 1985.
Frost and Fire. New York, Morrow, 1989.

Poetry

Poems. N.p., Discon, 1974.
When Pussywillows Lost in the Catyard Bloomed. Carlton, Australia, Norstrilia Press, 1980.
To Spin Is Miracle Cat. Columbia, Pennsylvania, Underwood Miller, 1982.

Other

The Authorized Illustrated Book of Roger Zelazny, illustrated by Gray Morrow. New York, Baronet, 1978.
Roger Zelazny's Visual Guide to Castle Amber, with Neil Randall. New York, Avon, 1988.

Editor, *Nebula Award Stories 3.* New York, Doubleday, and London, Gollancz, 1968.

*

Film Adaptation: *Damnation Alley,* 1977.

Bibliography: *Roger Zelazny: A Primary and Secondary Bibliography* by Joseph L. Sanders, Boston, Hall, 1980; *Amber Dreams: A Roger Zelazny Bibliography* by Daniel J. H. Levack, Columbia, Pennsylvania, Underwood Miller, 1983; *Roger Zelazny: Master of Amber—A Working Bibliography* by Phil Stephensen-Payne, Leeds, West Yorkshire, Galactic Central, 1991.

Manuscript Collections: George Arendts Research Library, Syracuse University, New York; Special Collections, University of Maryland, Baltimore.

Critical Studies: *A Reader's Guide to Roger Zelazny* by Carl B. Yoke, West Linn, Oregon, Starmont House, 1979; *Roger Zelazny* by Theodore Krulik, New York, Ungar, 1986; *Roger Zelazny* by Jane M. Lindskold, Boston, Twayne, 1993.

Roger Zelazny comments:

Sometimes I write fantasy and sometimes I write science fiction. I like them both. My novels tend to be derived from characters, rather than plot ideas. Apart from books in a series, which necessarily bear each other a certain resemblance, I like to vary the things I write about quite a bit. Among my novels, my own favourites are *This Immortal, Lord of Light, Doorways in the Sand, Eye of Cat* and *A Night in the Lonesome October.* My favourite shorter pieces are "For a Breath I Tarry" and "24 Views of Mt. Fuji, by Hokusai."

*   *   *

Zelazny's best-known fantasy work is his Amber series, which has currently reached ten volumes: the original set of five books and five in the more recent sequence. The first volume, *Nine Princes in Amber,* opens when the protagonist wakes in a hospital bed, minus his memory, and a prisoner. He escapes and bluffs his way past strange and formidable people and somehow out of our world entirely. As the book progresses, his memory gradually comes back: he is Corwin, long-lost Prince of Amber, son of Oberon, the lord of that realm. Earth, it transpires, is but one of countless Shadows of the one true world—Amber. The only ones who can traverse Shadow are those of the royal blood of Amber—Oberon and his offspring, Corwin and his siblings, several sisters and eight surviving brothers. These can and do forge their own Shadow empires, and raise armies to attack their kin in medieval fashion. They are an envious lot, slow to forgive a slight, and ever ready to kill each other, often over the succession to the throne, which they almost all want to inherit; the succession itself is a sufficiently murky affair that most of them are able to find some justification for their claim. One of the siblings was responsible for Corwin losing his memory and spending several hundred years on our Earth, while another's much more recent attempt to kill Corwin accidentally started his memory returning. To complicate matters for Corwin, Oberon is currently missing and his brother and arch-rival, Eric, is about to take the throne. Corwin decides to oppose him, is defeated, imprisoned, escapes, and vows to succeed the second time around. Thus begins the first five-part saga and a major work of fantasy.

Although the opening book, *Nine Princes in Amber,* can stand comfortably on its own, thereafter the sequels become so increasingly interlocked it is probably best to regard them as one long work. After his unsuccessful bid for the throne, Corwin wanders Shadow, scheming to bring gunpowder to Amber; acquires a sidekick, his one-time enemy, Ganelon; encounters a major threat to Amber from the mysterious realm of Chaos, seemingly the antithesis of the order that Amber represents; has a romance that is to have important consequences; discovers profound secrets about Amber itself, its nature and its origin; forges new relationships with his siblings, for better or worse; and, eventually, finds Oberon. He also discovers just how much his long exile on our Shadow Earth has changed him. In the first half of the final volume, *The Courts of Chaos,* Corwin is forced to hellride his way across Shadow (ar-

guably the most disappointing segment of the series), duel the sibling who is the moving force behind events, and still bring the Jewel of Judgement to Oberon who is besieging Chaos in time for the climactic battle between the two forces.

Corwin is a memorable character, but he is also fairly typical of the favourite Zelazny protagonist in several ways. First there are his basic character traits: he is tough, stubborn, and a rugged individualist who keeps a sense of nobility buried beneath an amoral and cynical veneer. Then there is his potential immortality—he has already lived considerably more than the normal human lifespan and has every chance, barring accident or foul play, of going on doing so. Immortality is a theme Zelazny has returned to many times, and which has enriched several of his earliest and most memorable works. Finally, Corwin, the immortal, although all too human, is also effectively operating at the level of godhood—and gods and their associated mythology have also had great fascination for Zelazny throughout his career.

Many of the particular strengths of the first Amber series are the strengths of Zelazny's work in general. There is his distinctive and captivating prose, which is stylish, lyrical and vivid, particularly so in those works dating from the early phase of his career. In fact it is his prose that makes the repeated descriptions of journeys through Shadow seem fresh and engaging each time, making them into virtual prose-poems. Another feature of his work is the long and intriguing conversations his characters engage in between bouts of action: his dialogue is individualistic and highly effective, mixing formal speech with street slang.

Zelazny exhibited the peak of his inventiveness and literary energy during the early years of his novelistic career. Thereafter, despite occasional returns to something like his best form, his books have tended to become more routine and the Amber novels bear this out. While the first series is a work of originality and charm as well as an absorbing and satisfying read, the follow-up series is considerably inferior. Corwin is missing in action and the narrative centres on his son, Merlin, who is caught up in various plots by relatives and other rivals. Although the books are readable enough, they lack the zest, colour and conviction of the original series.

One of Zelazny's earliest free-standing fantasy novels is the baroque and enjoyable *Jack of Shadows,* set on a world that has one hemisphere where, much like our own, science rules and another where magic holds sway—which is where the thief, Shadowjack, comes from. Venturing into the interface, he is put to death. Magically reincarnated in the Dung Pits of Glyve, he sets out to have his revenge on those responsible for his execution, most particularly, the Lord of Bats. But although Jack lacks a soul, revenge eventually proves hollow.

Dilvish, the Damned shows early Zelazny side by side with the later. A set of short stories, set together to form a continuous narrative, parts of the work date from the mid-1960s and parts from 1979 to 1981. Dilvish is a warrior who rides a great metal horse called Black. His enemy, the sorcerer Jelerak, bespelled him for two hundred years. Now he has escaped and wants revenge, but first he has to save the city of Dilfar from siege, and then there are further adventures for him to have. It's colourful writing, if rather episodic, and interesting in its juxtaposition of the early and later-phase Zelaznys.

From middle-period Zelazny, we have *Changeling* and its sequel *Madwand.* The opening shows us a pure fantasy world where magic works and a sorcerer's stronghold is under siege. His baby son is then switched with a baby from our own Earth. Years pass; and the two young men, neither of them knowing their true origin or of the other's existence, find themselves misplaced in their adopted world and at odds with its basic nature. One is a natural sorcerer in a rational scientific world—our own—while the other is an born engineer, self-taught and supremely talented and rejected in his magic-dominant home. Eventually, the sorcerer's son finds a way home, to meet a girl that his changeling-brother is also attracted to: conflict between the two not-quite-brothers is inevitable. The story is continued in *Madwand*.

Zelazny has also collaborated with various other writers, including Fred Saberhagen for *The Black Throne,* with its Edgar Allan Poe relations, and, more recently, a tongue-in-cheek series with Robert Sheckley, beginning with *Bring Me the Head of Prince Charming.* A recent solo book, *A Night in the Lonesome October,* is a fantasy and something of a return to his better form. The narrator-protagonist is Snuff, an intelligent dog, whose master is called Jack and has a mysterious mission involving knives and night and London fogs. Besides Jack, there are a number of immediately recognizable characters, such as a vampire count, a great detective, a werewolf, a witch, and a mad scientist given to stitching used body-parts together. But they remain on the periphery of the narrative; centre-stage, at least as seen from Snuff's viewpoint, are their familiars: the witch's cat, Graymalk; a snake; an owl; a squirrel who has lost his shadow; an albino raven; and a rat. Their various masters are all players in a mysterious and sinister game, and are on one of two sides. The game runs for the entire month of October: there's a countdown of sorts as the month progresses—and an uneasy truce in operation as final preparations are made—until allegiances are gradually revealed and the finale occurs on the last day of October. If you imagine combining a whole string of Hammer horror films and then telling the story from a dog's point-of-view, you'll have the general idea. It's smoothly handled and charming.

Zelazny has also written a great deal of science fiction and much of his work in this field might be of interest from a fantasy point of view, particularly those that come from his earliest and most creative period, where he played, fairly freely, with various world mythologies. Most notable of these is the Hugo award-winning *Lord of Light,* in which he drew heavily on Indian mythology, although the framework has a science fiction rationale. After many centuries, the Hindu passengers of a long-lost starship have populated their new homeworld, building in the process a civilization akin to medieval India. The crew, however, retained access to high technology, including machines which allow them to reincarnate themselves—and others if they so wish—in vat-grown bodies, human or otherwise. They now rule the world and have taken on the names, and the powers, of the pantheon of Hindu gods. Eventually, one of the crew, Sam, decides the time has come to oppose them. He does this in various ways—releasing the energy-beings called demons that he once bound, and even setting himself up as the Buddha. Zelazny weaves a rich and colourful tapestry out of these story elements to produce his finest novel.

—Neil Jones

ZIMMER, Paul Edwin

Nationality: American. **Born:** Albany, New York, 16 October 1943; brother of writer Marion Zimmer Bradley (*q.v.*). **Education:** Averill Park High School, Regents Diploma 1963. **Family:** Married Tracy Elizabeth Blackstone; one child. **Agent:** Sharon Jarvis, c/o Toad Hall, Inc., RR2, Box 16B, Laceyville, PA 18623, USA. **Address:** Greyhaven, 90 El Camino Real, Berkeley, CA 94705, USA.

FANTASY PUBLICATIONS

Novels (series: The Dark Border)

The Lost Prince (Dark Border). New York, Playboy, 1982.
King Chondos' Ride (Dark Border). New York, Playboy, 1982.
A Gathering of Heroes (Dark Border). New York, Ace, 1987.
Blood of the Colyn Muir, with Jon DeCles. New York, Ace, 1988.
Ingulf the Mad (Dark Border). New York, Ace, 1989.

Short Story

Woman of the Elfmounds. Ottawa, Triskell Press, 1980.

OTHER PUBLICATIONS

Novels

Hunters of the Red Moon, with Marion Zimmer Bradley. New York, DAW, 1973; London, Arrow, 1979.
The Survivors, with Marion Zimmer Bradley. New York, DAW, 1979; London, Arrow, 1985.

*

Paul Edwin Zimmer comments:

A world invented for a single book will rarely have any great depth or consistency. A world that does have real depth cannot be explored within the limits of a single book. A mythic world must be *more* real than the primary world; "manured and watered," as Fritz Leiber used to say.

All but a few of my works are set in a world derived from the "Carcosa" tradition worked on by Bierce, Chambers and Lovecraft, as well as my sister, Marion Zimmer Bradley. None of us have done exactly the same thing, or even the same kind of thing. But the shared names and images set up certain resonances which add mythic depth to the background. I also draw on Celtic mythology and a thorough study of history. In order to research possible techniques of swordsmanship I helped to found the Society for Creative Anachronism, and later studied both Japanese and Chinese sword styles.

Each book must be a spell, to enchant the reader in a shining net that renews wonder.

*   *   *

Paul Edwin Zimmer's Dark Border series opens with a familiar setting and situation. Tarencia is a frontier kingdom that protects the civilized world from the infringement of the Shadow, a land of dark and evil forces which are constantly probing for a weakness in the shield of magic and soldiery that holds them at bay. But the king of Tarencia is failing after living far longer than anyone expected, and one of his twin sons must assume the throne. Prince Jodos is a sinister figure who has already been corrupted by a mysterious master who spirited him away into the dark lands and now commands his slavish obedience. Prince Chondos is of nobler stock, but there's a problem here as well, because Chondos has no desire whatsoever to assume the responsibilities of rule and is sorely lacking in the political sense required to forge a consensus. And some of the nobility, chafing under what they consider excessive taxes and other burdens, may not be willing to support Chondos' accession to the throne, regardless of the ultimate consequences.

Aided by magic that enables him to control minds, even those of the dead, Jodos arranges for his brother's abduction, takes the throne in his name, and immediately precipitates a rebellion in order to fragment resistance to the Shadow. As armies prepare to clash, Chondos finally escapes from his imprisonment, although he does not leave the empire of darkness until the sequel, *King Chondos' Ride.* His journey back to the border is fraught with danger, as every evil creature you can imagine—vampires, shape-changers, the walking dead—all attempt to destroy him before he can reach safety.

Zimmer's first two fantasies owe much to Tolkien and perhaps E. R. Eddison as well, and are essentially a single novel despite their packaging. The characters are for the most part larger than life, whether they be hero or villain, glorious warriors, with intelligent if sometimes twisted minds, and their battles take on a disproportionate significance. Fantasy is one of the few places that one can make clear distinctions between good and evil without sounding artificial, and Zimmer makes good use of that fact.

Although the second book ends with the suppression of the rebellion and defeat of the forces of the Dark Things, the latter aren't truly vanquished and there were clearly meant to be additional titles. A reshuffling and reconsolidation of the publishing industry eliminated the Playboy paperback line, however, and perhaps because of that there was a gap of several years before the third in the series, *A Gathering of Heroes,* finally appeared. Although the story continues with the same setting and some of the same characters, there is a noticeable change in the tone of the series, most visibly the switch to predominantly Scottish and Scandinavian names and imagery.

Y'Gora is an island kingdom where Istvan DiVega, the mercenary leader who helped defend Tarencia, is hired to avert another invasion by the Dark Things. Once again an army of humans and elves is assembled but this time, despite their mighty striving, it appears that evil is about to triumph. Fortunately, the evil forces themselves are divided, and a small group of heroes is able to take advantage of dissension among their enemies to cause a schism.

On the surface, the novel shares the scope and grandeur of the earlier novels. Zimmer is particularly skilful at describing battle scenes, whether between two individuals or two armies, but the scale is smaller and the plot seems less focused at times.

One of the heroes of *A Gathering of Heroes* has further adventures in *Ingulf the Mad,* which appeared two years later. Ingulf accidentally wounds a sea woman, who uses a love spell to bind him to her, then regrets it when she realizes she has strong feelings of her own for the man, and cannot now earn his love honestly. Abandoned, Ingulf takes a magic sword and travels to a city forbidden to humans, hoping to be reunited with the only woman he ever loved. There he leads a slave rebellion, is imprisoned, and eventually wins free with the aid of some of those whom he has befriended. Once again the mood of the series has changed drastically, particularly in the early chapters which read much more like a traditional fairy tale than a contemporary fantasy, and which contain some of the best writing Zimmer has done to date. The ending is rather abrupt, perhaps because of a planned sequel which has not yet appeared.

Zimmer's only other fantasy novel is *Blood of the Colyn Muir,* written in collaboration with Jon DeCles (a novelette, *Woman of the Elfmounds,* also appeared in Canada, but has not been generally available). Here a minor but underlying theme in Zimmer's work is most evident, that the cost of heroism is pain. Darith is another hero, heir to magical powers but also the bearer of a curse. Heroism is an obligation to Darith rather than an attribute, and in order to save his people from the ravages of a pirate fleet, he sets off to retrieve an ensorcelled sword, even as he is deserted by those who fear to be caught up in his death curse. Darith has a double mission then; not only must he overcome his enemies and secure a throne, but he must also find a way to escape the backlash of the very forces that will preserve him.

Zimmer's comprehensive knowledge of swordsmanship gives his work an air of authenticity that is missing from that of most of his contemporaries. He takes considerable care in the construction of his fantasy worlds to make them internally consistent, and his use of larger-than-life characters is never over-emphasized to the point where the reader loses sympathy for the protagonist. In all likelihood he'd be one of the leading fantasy writers of today if he were more productive and thereby built his readership.

—Don D'Ammassa

FOREIGN-LANGUAGE AUTHORS

ANDERSEN, Hans Christian (1805-1875)

Nationality: Danish. **Selected Publications:** *Eventyr, fortalte for Börn* (1835; second volume, 1836; third volume, 1842); *Nye Eventyr* (1845; second volume, 1846; third volume, 1847; fourth volume, 1848); *Historier* (1852; second volume, 1853; third volume, 1855); *Nye Eventyr og Historier* (1857; second volume, 1858; third and fourth volumes, 1859); *Nye Eventyr og Historier, Second Series* (1861; second volume, 1861; third volume, 1865; fourth volume, 1866); *The Wood Nymph* (1868); *Three New Tales* (1870); *Nye Eventyr og Historier, Third Series* (1871; second volume, 1872).

* * *

Hans Christian Andersen was the first great *creator* of fairy tales. Unlike Perrault or the Brothers Grimm, who adapted or transcribed folk tales with varying degrees of embellishment, Andersen, for the most part, invented his own. Of his 156 fairy tales and stories, only 12 are directly based on folk tales. Some others include elements of tales or legends he had heard, but for the most part are original. Moreover, most of Andersen's stories involve the supernatural or fantastic to some degree, and very few are set in the real world with totally mundane events. Finally, and most importantly, although Anderson started out writing the stories specially for children, he soon realized that adults could appreciate them at a secondary level, and his later stories are intended for all ages.

Andersen had not started his writing career with fairy tales in mind. His love was originally for the theatre. He was born into a poor family, the son of a shoemaker. He was 11 when his father died, which forced him to leave school and work in the factory, but he managed to obtain work at a local theatre. He soon earned a reputation for his singing and dancing, until his voice broke. By this time, however, he had earned the patronage of Jonas Collin, governor of the Royal Theatre, and Collin secured Andersen's further education. Although now 17, Andersen had much education to recover and he was placed in a class of 12-year-olds who mocked and bullied him. Being of a sensitive nature, Andersen looked for love, but because he was rather ungainly and unattractive he tended to receive more sympathy than affection. He turned back to the theatre and writing as an outlet for his passion and travelled throughout Europe. During this time he completed his first novel, *Improvisatoren* (1835), a thinly disguised autobiographical tale about a poor but gifted Italian boy who works his way into society. The novel was a great success and established Andersen's name.

It was that same year that a booklet of four short tales appeared: *Eventyr, fortalte for Börn* (*Tales Told for Children*), written as no more than a sideline, but about to take on a great significance. Andersen soon realized that he could convey much more powerful messages through the medium of the fairy story and also realized that this would appeal as much to parents as to children. After his first series of booklets he left out the reference to children, so that his stories would find a wider audience. Andersen began to produce a small booklet containing a handful of stories on a roughly annual basis, and these rapidly became a tradition. Individual booklets would later be reprinted in omnibus compilations, and this process continued throughout Andersen's life. Although Andersen would continue to write novels, plays and travel books, it was his fairy tales that attracted his main audience, and by 1845 they had become the talk of Europe. In 1846 no less than three different translations of Andersen's stories appeared in England. His work was greatly championed by Charles Dickens, who also furthered the cause of the fairy tale, which led to the great explosion of children's fantasies in the mid-1800s with works by Thackeray, Kingsley, Carroll, Ingelow and Macdonald.

Andersen's strength lay in his own background. Essentially he never grew up. He was always play-acting and on that level could relate directly to the imagination of children. But he was also sensitive and easily hurt, and his childhood, school life, and ill-matched love affairs caused him to bring a secondary level of passion and emotion into his work that could be appreciated by adults. Few would regard "The Little Match-Girl," "The Story of a Mother" or "The Dead Child" as fairy tales, but their power and poignancy appeal to all ages.

The fantastic is prevalent in most of Andersen's stories. His early ones are based more on folk tales and legends, and were clearly written for children, such as "The Tinderbox," "Little Claus and Big Claus," and even "The Emperor's New Clothes" (which is based on a 14th-century Spanish story). Of special interest is Andersen's "The Garden of Eden" which is his own version of Madame d'Aulnoy's "The Isle of Happiness," the first of all literary fairy tales.

Rapidly Andersen made the stories all his own invention, but he continued to imbue them with the fantastic. These include many of his best: "The Little Mermaid," "The Snow Queen," "The Elf Hill," "The Marsh King's Daughter," "The Ice Maiden" and "The Shadow." Many of these stories contain images that may have existed previously in folklore or legend but which Andersen made specially his own. The motifs in his work have proved a strong influence on later fantasy fiction, not solely on his immediate contemporaries, especially Dickens and Macdonald, and later writers like James Branch Cabell, Oscar Wilde, and James Thurber, but also in the recent works of Nicholas Stuart Gray, Joan D. Vinge, Ursula Synge, Jane Yolen and Patricia McKillip. While the works of Perrault and the Grimm Brothers have lent themselves to being twisted into dark fantasies by modern writers, Andersen's tales have inspired more tender, homespun fantasies.

Andersen was strongest in his portrayal of the outcast, drawing upon his own rough childhood. Here there are no better stories than "The Ugly Duckling," "The Steadfast Tin Soldier," "The Snowman," and "The Daisy."

At times Andersen was something of a visionary. He was only too aware of the scientific marvels developing in the world and sought to convey this sense of wonder through such stories as "The Wood Nymph," "The Millennium," and the remarkable "Muse of the Twentieth Century." This last story was criticized as being rather too philosophical for fantasy, but Andersen regarded this vision of the next century as being "a natural outgrowth of the fairy tale," which rather forecast the development of science fiction.

As Andersen grew old his stories became more sinister, their meanings deeper and more allegorical, as in "The World's Most Beautiful Rose," "Psyche," "On the Last Day," and "The Snowdrop." His last completed story, "Auntie Toothache," includes a frightening scene where Madame Toothache, the physical incarnation of pain, materializes to a young child.

Andersen's visions made the fabricated fairy tale respectable, and his work was the most significant contribution toward the development of children's fantasy in the 19th century. His spirit has continued to live on in the work of many modern fantasists. The best modern version of his stories is *The Complete Fairy Tales and Stories* translated by Erik Haugaard (1974).

—Mike Ashley

BORGES, Jorge Luis (1899-1986)

Nationality: Argentine. **Selected Publications:** *A Universal History of Infamy*, Buenos Aires, Emecé Editores, 1954 (as *Historia universal de la infamia*), New York, E.P.Dutton, 1972; London, Allen Lane, 1973. *Ficciones*, Buenos Aires, Emecé Editores, 1956; New York, Grove Press, 1962. *A Personal Anthology*, Buenos Aires, Editorial Sur, 1961 (as *Antología Personal*); New York, Grove Press, 1967. *Labyrinths*, New York, New Directions, 1964; Harmondsworth, Penguin, 1970. *Dreamtigers*, Austin, University of Texas Press, 1964. *The Aleph and Other Stories 1933-1969*, New York, E.P.Dutton, 1978; London, Jonathan Cape. *The Book of Sand*, Buenos Aires, Emecé Editores, 1975; New York, E.P.Dutton, 1977; London, Allen Lane, 1979. *Chronicles of Bustos Domecq*, with Adolfo Bioy-Casares, Buenos Aires, Editorial Losada, 1967 (as *Crónicas de Bostos Domecq*); New York, E.P.Dutton, 1979. *Extraordinary Tales*, with Adolfo Bioy-Casares, Buenos Aires, Editorial Santiago Rueda, 1967; New York, Herder & Herder, 1971; London, Souvenir Press, 1973. *The Book of Fantasy*, with Adolfo Bioy-Casares and Silvina Ocampo, Buenos Aires, Editorial Sudamericana, 1940 (as *Antología de la Literatura Fantástica*); revised edition, New York, Viking Penguin, 1988; London, Xanadu, 1988. *The Book of Imaginary Beings*, with Margarita Guerrero, Buenos Aires, Editorial Losada, 1967 (as *El libro de los seres imaginarios*); New York, E.P.Dutton, 1969; London, Jonathan Cape, 1970. Non-fiction: *Other Inquisitions 1937-52*, Austin, University of Texas Press, 1964; London, Souvenir Press, 1973. *Borges on Writing*, New York, E.P.Dutton, 1973; London, Allen Lane, 1974. Book about Borges: *Jorge Luis Borges: A Literary Biography* by Emir Rodriguez Monegal, New York, Paragon House, 1978.

*   *   *

In the dedication to his collection of stories and poems *Dreamtigers*, Borges writes: "Leaving behind the babble of the plaza, I enter the Library. I feel, almost physically, the gravitation of the books, the enveloping serenity of order, time magically desiccated and preserved." It is an image which almost perfectly encapsulates his work.

After a few early stories about mythic Argentine figures, the gaucho, the knife fighter, his work has consisted almost exclusively of serene intellectual speculations that are about as far as it is possible to get from the "babble of the plaza." Usually these speculations turn upon the ability of words to contain and create worlds. Time and again the book is seen as a symbol for infinity. In "The Book of Sand," for instance, the narrator (Borges himself, as it usually is) is a collector of Bibles. One day a stranger offers him a strange volume marked upon the spine: "Holy Writ." The book is in a script which the narrator cannot read (again a common device), and though he searches he can never find the same page twice, nor can he discover the first or last pages. In the same way, in "The Library of Babel," the universe is equated with the Library where men spend their entire life amid books whose meaning is impenetrable.

Yet these books, mysterious as they may be, must be treated with caution for they have the power to transform our world. A power Borges demonstrated in what is perhaps his most famous story, "Tlön, Uqbar, Orbis Tertius," which begins when an article on the unknown land of Uqbar is discovered in one errant copy of the *Anglo-American Cyclopaedia* of 1917. (Borges is always scrupulous in his bibliographical references; real or fictional, they are found throughout his work to provide a literal authority for his fantasies—another demonstration of the power of words.) The fiction of Uqbar is said to take place in the world of Tlön, yet shortly afterwards volume 11 of *A First Encyclopaedia of Tlön* is discovered. This gives fascinating, if incomplete, glimpses of a world of idealists where objects can be whatever anyone wants. Eventually Tlön, and the Encyclopaedia, are revealed to be the creation of a secret society, but in a final twist the fictional world is starting to take over our real world. The words have won.

In another sense also the world of Tlön is taking over our world, for it reflects the fantasies of Borges himself. The literature of this invented world, for instance, is described thus: "It has been established that all works are the creation of one author, who is atemporal and anonymous. The critics often invent authors." This is a practice that Borges also follows, not only in his elegant reviews of non-existent books which offer intriguing glimpses of other fictional worlds, but also in stories such as "Pierre Menard, Author of the Quixote." This pseudo-essay, a form which Borges made his own, tells of a Symbolist writer of the 1930s who sets out to recreate Cervantes's novel. The different milieux of the two writers allows for revealingly different interpretations of exactly the same words.

Throughout his life, Borges collected examples of marvels created with words, traditional tales and modern inventions which he gathered together in *The Book of Fantasy*, *Extraordinary Tales,* and *The Book of Imaginary Beings*, but the creatures of familiar fairy stories rarely featured in his own work. Though there were frequent references to the *Arabian Nights*, it was only really the golem who moved from traditional stories into his work. The golem is there in his poem, "The Golem," and, more significantly, in his story "The Circular Ruins." Here a stranger appears in a remote village and, in the circular ruins of an old temple, sets out to dream another man into existence. But when the child of his dreams has been born and died, he realizes that he himself has been dreamed into life. It is this circularity which attracted Borges, for his stories are full of such echoes and repetitions, the "illusory depths" of mirrors, labyrinths which constantly turn back upon themselves.

The doppelganger, for instance, is a literary golem dreamed into life in "Borges and I," which destroys any division between fantasy and reality with its conclusion: "I do not know which of us two is writing this page." And it is repeated, mirrored, in "The Other" in which an elderly Borges in Cambridge, Massachusetts, in 1969 sits down on a bench beside a young Borges who is in Geneva in 1914. This story also echoes "The Circular Ruins" in its conclusion: "The other man dreamed me, but he did not dream me exactly." The labyrinth of Borges's fiction always leads back to the same point.

And that point is the library of Borges's imagination. Whether he was turning the detective story into a formal metaphysical dance in "Death and the Compass" or rewriting history in "The Disinterested Killer Bill Harrigan," which so evades the facts in the life of Billy the Kid that it even changes the gunman's name, Borges's stories grew out of books and memory. But though his knowledge of world literature was immense, Borges could not simply repeat those stories, as Pierre Menard had done. In "Funes the Memorious" he tells of a man whose memory is so prodigious that he could not actually experience anything. In an analogous way, writing which attempted to recreate our reality or echo other writers would prevent him experiencing the world-creating power of words. Self-deprecatingly he talked of himself "falsifying and distorting....the tales of others," though he was in fact exercising the fantasy which was a necessary part of his writing and which gave his stories their inimitable impact.

—Paul Kincaid

CALVINO, Italo (1923-1985)

Nationality: Italian. **Selected Publications:** *The Cloven Viscount* (*Il visconte dimezzato*), Turin, Einaudi, 1951, London, Collins, 1962, New York, Random House, 1962. *Italian Folktales* (*Fiabe italiane*), Turin, Einaudi, 1956, New York, Harcourt Brace Jovanovich, 1980, Harmondsworth, Penguin, 1982. *Baron in the Trees* (*Il barone rampante*), Turin, Einaudi, 1957, London, Collins, 1959. *The Non-Existent Knight* (*Il cavaliere inesistente*), Turin, Einaudi, 1959, London, Collins, 1962, New York, Random House, 1962. *Cosmicomics*, Turin, Einaudi, 1965, London, Cape, 1968, New York, Harcourt Brace & World, 1968. *t zero* (*Ti con zero*), Turin, Einaudi, 1967, London, Cape, 1969, New York, Harcourt Brace Jovanovich, 1969. *Invisible Cities* (*Le citte invisibili*), Turin, Einaudi, 1972, London, Secker & Warburg, 1974, New York, Harcourt Brace Jovanovich, 1974. *If on a Winter's Night a Traveller* (*Se una notte d'inverno un viaggiatore*), Turin, Einaudi, 1979, London, Secker & Warburg, 1981, New York, Harcourt Brace Jovanovich, 1981. Nonfiction: *The Literature Machine*, Turin, Einaudi, 1982, New York, Harcourt Brace Jovanovich, 1982, London, Secker & Warburg, 1987.

* * *

In an essay appropriately entitled "Cybernetics and Ghosts" Italo Calvino described the story-telling process thus: "The storyteller began to put forth words...to test the extent to which words could fit with one another, could give birth to one another, in order to extract an explanation of the world from the thread of every possible spoken narrative, and from the arabesque that nouns and verbs, subjects and predicates performed as they unfolded from one another." It is a description which neatly encapsulates both the imaginative world-building of fabulists and mythologizers and the word-play of postmodernists. It is precisely this interplay of traditional fantastic tales (Calvino collected and retold a massive selection of *Italian Folktales*) and complex literary experimentation which best describes his own work.

Calvino's early work was firmly in the realist tradition of Italian literature and film in the immediate postwar years (his first novel, *The Path to the Nest of Spiders*, was based on his experiences as a partisan in northern Italy during the Second World War). But in 1951, in a radical change of direction, he brought out the first of his allegorical fantasies, *The Cloven Viscount*. The viscount, who rules a small Italian town, returns from a war against the Turks literally blown in half—he has one leg, one arm, half a face. He is the evil half, and for the people of the area there begins a time of ill-fortune. But things don't improve when, some time later, the good half turns up, for the cloven viscount's simple-minded attempts to do good end up making things worse for the local people. Only when the two halves are magically fused at the end of the novel do things improve. But along the way, Calvino has shown that the community itself is divided in many other ways: the lepers isolated in their own little village, the Huguenots who have lost touch with their own religious roots, and the mother and father of the heroine who are divided in their plans for her, neither of which take any regard of her wishes.

The Baron in the Trees has a similar allegorical role in its tale of 12-year-old Cosimo, who takes to the trees after a quarrel with his parents and ends up spending the rest of his life there. Less fantastical than the other two novels which make up the Our Ancestors trilogy, this is still a far from realist novel. Cosimo, able to get wherever he wants from treetop to treetop, developing curious philosophical theories, communicating with the leading figures of the Enlightenment, is shown to have his feet much more firmly on the ground than his father, who dreams of reviving lost aristocratic splendours, his mother, who dreams of military glory, his sister, with a curious penchant for cooking snails and insects, and all the others he comes into contact with.

The trilogy was completed by *The Non-Existent Knight*, set in the age of Charlemagne when one of the leading paladins is a suit of armour with no one inside. Agilulf is a martinet, dreaming of achieving humanity by a rigid adherence to the rules. Yet his servant is a fool who believes himself to be whatever he comes into contact with, so as he eats he believes he is the bowl of soup he holds. Agilulf's leading disciple is a woman disguised as a knight, escaping the rigid roles dictated for her. And in the central character of Raimbaud we have a youth who believes in the heroic and chivalric principles of the age, but who loses those beliefs as he comes into contact with the hilarious bureaucracy of Charlemagne's army (a revenge committee works out whether two captains are equal to one major) or the other-worldly brutality of the Knights of the Grail. So the fable becomes a moral debate about what it is to be human.

This loose trilogy still concerned itself with plot and character, but Calvino's subsequent work drifted away into exercises in seeing what words can create. Most of his best work is in short stories, or novels in which various tales are linked by theme and intent more than by character development or plot. In *Invisible Cities*, for instance, the linking device of Marco Polo telling Kublai Khan about the wonderful places he has visited provides a very loose format within which Calvino can place a series of vignettes describing aspects of cities that are curious or magical, yet which all, in some way, reflect Polo's home in Venice. The tales have no narrative drive, often they have no characters whatsoever, but they do capture a sense of place and of mystery which seems to fall part way between the short stories of Borges and the poetry of C. P. Cavafy.

Similarly, in *Cosmicomics* and *t zero*, he used scientific theories or speculations to launch a series of very curious fabulations. The tales seem to be linked by the character of Qfwfq, but this is a protean figure who will be a dinosaur in one tale, a human in another, an atom of primordial matter or intergalactic dust in yet others. Qfwfq is a continuing consciousness, but in no way a developing character. The tales are absurdities in which Qfwfq and his fellows can reach the Moon by ladder to gather cheese before gravity causes it to move away, or in which Qfwfq spends eternity betting with Dean (k)yK, starting with the bet that there will be a universe, or in which as one of the first land animals he introduces his fiancee to his uncle who is still a fish.

As well as the stories of Qfwfq, *t zero* also contains a group of stories which illustrate another aspect of Calvino's fascination with ideas. In "The Chase," for example, an assassin and his victim are in two cars trapped in the same traffic jam, and the story concerns the victim's speculations about the logical possibilities offered by the situation, leading to the conclusion that he is in turn an assassin also chasing yet another victim. While in one of Calvino's most intellectually challenging stories, "The Count of Monte Cristo," Edmond Dantes is in his cell in the Chateau d'If. While the Abb Faria digs endless tunnels in a fruitless quest to escape, Dantes stays in his cell planning in his mind the shape of the fortress (and also, incidentally, the shape of Dumas's novel) until he arrives at a logical but fantastical means of escape.

But Calvino's word-play and world-building is shown at its best in his finest novel, *If on a Winter's Night a Traveller*. This is a novel about reading the novel *If on a Winter's Night a Traveller* by Italo Calvino, but each novel that you, the reader, begin is somehow cut-off before the end and a new novel takes its place. Somehow the novels and the story of reading the novels interweave, until, at the end, the titles of the various novels themselves combine into yet another tale. In Calvino's work the arabesque of nouns and verbs does not explain the world, but they do recreate it endlessly until it becomes impossible to distinguish the world we live in from the world we imagine. And maybe, as one word fits with another, there is no distinction.

—Paul Kincaid

D'AULNOY, MADAME (c.1650-1705)

Nationality: French. **Selected Publications:** *Les Contes des fées* (4 vols., 1696-1698). *Contes nouveaux; ou, Les fées à la mode* (4 vols., 1698).

*   *   *

Madame d'Aulnoy (or D'Anois as sometimes rendered) was one of the leading figures in the creation of the literary fairy tale in France at the close of the 17th century. It had become traditional by the 1690s for the women of the French establishment, excluded from male society, to meet in their own salon at home for the discussion of art, science, and politics. Madame d'Aulnoy's salon was one of the most noted, and it was fashionable for those attending (who increasingly included men) to recount stories, usually satirizing events at the court of Louis XIV. Frequently the most cutting satires were told in the form of fantastic tales drawn from the oral folk tradition but embellished to explore current news and gossip. Among the most popular of these tales were those by Madame d'Aulnoy, and when the first volume of these stories was published in 1696 she not only began the vogue for fairy tales, which continues to this day, but in the direct translation of her book's title, she also gave the genre its name.

Madame d'Aulnoy's life prior to 1696 almost resembles a fairy tale itself, and certainly gave her enough material to incorporate in her recitations. Born Marie-Catherine Le Jumel, in Barneville, Normandy, she was descended from an aristocratic Norman family. Sometime around 1665 she married François de la Motte, Baron d'Aulnoy, who was in his mid-forties, and a man of questionable character. Although she had three children by him (and three others of uncertain paternity) she rapidly came to detest him, and in 1669, along with her mother (now widowed) and their respective lovers, Madame d'Aulnoy plotted to have her husband arrested on the grounds of high treason. The plan went wrong, and instead the two lovers were executed. Madame d'Aulnoy was imprisoned whilst her mother fled to England. Madame d'Aulnoy escaped, however, and hid in a convent. For the next 15 years the exact twists and turns of her life are uncertain, although if her own account is to be believed she travelled throughout Europe serving, for a period, as a secret agent for France. She later wrote three books purporting to be about her travels, *Mémoires de la cour d'Espagne* (1690), *Relation du voyage l'Espagne* (1691), and *Mémoires de la cour d'Angeleterre* (1695).

In 1685 Madame d'Aulnoy returned to Paris and established her literary salon. In 1690 she published a novel, *L'Histoire d'Hippolyte, comte de Douglas*, which incorporates the story "L'île de la Félicité" ("The Isle of Happiness"). This is the first-ever specially composed literary fairy tale. It tells of a Russian prince who is lost in a forest and finds his way to the cave of the winds. From there he is taken to the island of happiness where, enchanted by his love for a princess, he stays for three centuries, though he thinks it is only three months. Realizing with horror that the world has passed him by, he intends to return to his homeland, but then Father Time catches up with him and he dies. Like all good fairy tales, it even has a moral, in fact two: there is no such thing as perfect happiness, and no one can turn back the clock.

Madame d'Aulnoy continued to recount her stories at salon, and their popularity led to their publication in eight volumes from 1696 to 1698, under the titles *Les Contes des fées* (1696-1698) and *Contes nouveaux; ou, Les fées à la mode* (1698). In all, Madame d'Aulnoy composed 25 fairy stories of which the best known are "The Blue Bird" (which introduces us to the character of Prince Charming), "The White Cat," "The Green Serpent" and "The Yellow Dwarf." All the stock motifs and characters of fairy tales are present in these stories, including wicked stepmothers, cloaks of invisibility, enchanted transformations (Prince Charming into the blue bird; a beautiful queen into the white cat), and quests for the perfect treasure.

"The Yellow Dwarf" has, over the years, proved the most popular, though it is most notable for its sad ending. It tells of a dwarf who tricks a princess into becoming his betrothed. The princess, known as All-Fair, agrees, though in her heart she wishes to marry the King of the Golden Mines. The King, with the aid of a magic sword, comes to rescue the Princess. He succeeds but, at the last moment, drops his sword and the dwarf seizes it and kills him. The princess thereupon dies of grief. The moral of this tragic tale is not to make a promise in haste that you cannot later keep.

In "La Belle aux cheveux d'or" we are first introduced to the name of Goldilocks (though this is not the story of "Goldilocks and the Three Bears," which was written by Robert Southey) while in "Finette Cendron" we encounter the story better known in Perrault's version as "Cinderella."

Madame d'Aulnoy's stories are noted for their action and violence. It needs to be remembered that they were not written for children but were disguised parodies of court intrigue, much of which is now forgotten after three centuries. Not all of the sources for her stories are known, though she drew heavily upon Norman folk tales told to her in her infancy by an aunt, and from stories picked up in her travels. "The Blue Bird" was the first to appear in translation in English, in 1699, with others following until a complete translation appeared as *A Collection of Novels and Tales* (three volumes, 1721-22), which included the first translations of "The White Cat" and "The Yellow Dwarf." No single standard English translation of her fairy tales is in print today. The standard (though incomplete) work was *Countess D'Aulnoy's Fairy Tales*, translated by John R. Planché (1885). Andrew Lang included many scattered throughout his series of *Fairy Books*, and Jack Zipes has newly translated 15 of them in *Beauties, Beasts and Enchantments* (1989).

Madame d'Aulnoy continued to write other works, and was even involved in further intrigue when she helped a friend assassinate her husband. She was lucky to escape execution or imprisonment. Her own husband died in 1700 and disinherited her, but her reputation sustained her for her final years.

The nature of Madame d'Aulnoy's tales is such that they are not usually considered suitable for children other than in highly edited and revised versions, usually adapted from pantomime. As a consequence, her role in the development of the fairy tale is often overlooked in favour of Charles Perrault or the brothers Grimm, yet she remains the first popularizer and creator of the medium.

—Mike Ashley

ENDE, Michael (1929-1995)

Nationality: German. **Selected Publications:** *The Grey Gentlemen,* Burke Books, 1974; as *Momo* (Penguin, 1984). *The Neverending Story* (1983). *Mirror in the Mirror,* Viking, 1986. *The Night of Wishes,* New York, Farrar Straus and Giroux, 1992.

*   *   *

Michael Ende was the son of the Surrealist painter Edgar Ende, and his written fantasy owes as much if not more to the Surrealist tradition of images standing for psychological drives as to fantasy as a purely literary genre. Indeed, *Mirror in the Mirror* takes drawings by his father as cues for a series of stories/fables/images which have the complex structure of dream, while the differently-coloured inks and mirror-structure of *The Neverending Story*—Ende's most celebrated novel, thanks to the power of the cinema—are part of an artist's repertoire.

Momo is an allegory of the alienation of modern urban life, which although published as a children's story may be too bleak for many children. Momo, a ragged urchin who lives in a ruined amphitheatre, is friend and confidante to both children and adults who welcome her ability simply to listen to their problems in such a way as they can articulate their own solutions. Then the "men in grey" arrive: sinister bodies who suck time from people's lives by persuading them that efficiency and organization are so much better than the unplanned, frivolous ways in which they sacrifice materialism for happiness. It is the children, whose parents are too busy working that they have no time for them, who notice the problem first, but they have no power to act effectively. Neither do Momo's adult

friends, the storyteller Guido and the eccentric road-sweeper Beppo, who stand for the power of the imagination and the painstaking craftsmanship which makes even the most mundane task worthwhile. They are corrupted or neutralized, and it is Momo, with the advice of Professor Hora and his tortoise Cassiopeia, who defeats the men in grey and enables the people of the city once more to take as much time as they need or want for both work and social relationships. As a satire of bureaucracy, *Momo* falls uneasily between fable for adults and semi-realistic fantasy for children, but is also strongly reminiscent of Franz Kafka.

Readers who come to *The Neverending Story* with memories of the cinematic version, which took from the book much of its "soft" element—fantasy as dressing for metaphysical comfort-objects— and highlighted it over its cautionary-tale second half, may be in for a surprise. Although it was a bestseller and critically acclaimed, much of the praise, as can be seen from the comparisons used on the King Penguin edition of 1984, misses the mark. *The Neverending Story* cannot be more different from *The Lord of the Rings* or *Watership Down*.

It is a strongly visual book, both in the way it describes creatures and scenes and in the emblematic, surreal way in which Ende creates the inhabitants of Fantastica from the longings and fears of his young protagonist. Fat, unpopular Bastian Balthazar Bux steals a book and escapes from his unhappiness into it—literally, for the story takes him over to the point that he discovers that he is reading about himself in the land of Fantastica and is its potential saviour from the "Nothing" against which even the Childlike Empress is helpless. The book he is reading—which is called *The Neverending Story*—is the book we ourselves are reading and appears also in the story which Bastian "lives." This structure—like a pair of facing mirrors reflecting each other into infinity—is partly buttressed by the different colours of the type in the "here" and "fantastica" sections in the original editions of the book, but the story itself is even more complex. Bastian travels into and out of fantasy, touched by both its therapeutic nature and its perilous glamour. While the film adaptation of the first part stops with Bastian saving Fantastica and healing himself, the book shows that to achieve the integration of his imaginative and mundane lives he must, perforce, first lose himself. After he saves the Childlike Empress, Bastian revels in his status as a hero, loses his memory of his past life as a lonely boy, and each time he exercises his power of wish-fulfilment forgets more of his past. To the dismay of his new-found friends, he becomes the dupe of a sorceress and loses memory, even his name, before he gives up his ego and learns to love.

This makes the book more than the exercise in fashionable feel-good sentimentality it might have been—and, for a time, was marketed as. In context, the conclusion with Bastian's reunion with his father shows how the Fantastic is a rich part of everyday life but is the very opposite of escapism. Ende shows himself inventive in both whimsical and darker, allegorical fantasy. The land of Fantastica is deeply rooted in both folk tale and psychological archetype but, precisely unlike the worlds of Tolkien and Adams, its appeal is that it is overtly a mental map.

The surreal vein in Ende's fantasy is presented in more "adult" form in *Mirror in the Mirror*, a linked series of 30 stories and vignettes by Ende himself and 18 drawings by his father Edgar Ende. Here, Ende forsakes linear narrative for imagistic theme, and the reflective structuring of *The Neverending Story* is extended in both the organization (and title) of *Mirror in the Mirror* and the way a character or image in one episode is echoed or extended in others. This development becomes labyrinthine; most of the episodes are set against the background of states of flux and change: doors, bridges, transit stations. A man "with eyes like a fish" boards a streetcar on his usual journey home to be taken through ever-changing, ever-stranger landscapes. A ragged bridegroom is escorted by a faceless guide through a room which is also a desert, towards his bride. High in a ship's rigging, a sailor and a tight-rope-walker find their ways blocked each by the other. We encounter situations which are contrapuntal versions of earlier or later ones: characters (a fireman, a man in an astronaut suit, a one-legged beggar, an angel) are sometimes central, sometimes peripheral. Dictators and totalitarian societies come to the fore. The structure of the labyrinth becomes emphasized in events and characters who are clearly from the myth of Theseus and the Minotaur.

The Borgesian nature of this kind of fantasy is perhaps underlined in one story where the narrator makes reference to the "blind scholar in the library of Buenos Aires." In another, a "magician and an illusionist," one of whose names is "Ende" adopts a boy whom he calls "Michael" and they set off, apparently after having imagined each other onto existence, to look for a new world. While Ende, however, is exploring dream and reality he is doing so by emphasizing the connections between these states which can be seen in the surreal object: hence the use of his father's illustrations and the highly descriptive, visual nature of his writings. Despite the different sub-genres he appears to be writing in, this approach is constant. Even the ruined amphitheatre which is so visually a part of the scenery in Momo is a crystallization of the story's theme of "time." Taken individually, Ende's work may be flawed by the generic patterns of the structure within which he is working: the way, for instance, in which he forces Momo into the mould of a children's book, or the whimsy in The Neverending Story. But taken together, precisely as a series of different viewpoints, it is the work of one of the great fantasists of the century.

—Andy Sawyer

FOUQUÉ, Friedrich (Heinrich Karl), (Baron) de la Motte (1777-1843)

Nationality: German. **Selected Publications:** *Der Held des Nordens* (1810); *Undine* (1811); *Der Zauberring* (1813); *Sintram* (1815).

*   *   *

Fouqué was one of the leading writers of the Berlin Romantic school of fiction. Although not as accomplished as Ludwig Tieck, or as respected as E. T. A. Hoffmann, he was for a period (1810-1820) the most popular German writer, though he later fell out of fashion and died in poverty.

Of Huguenot descent, Fouqué served in the Prussian cavalry from 1794 to 1803 and again from 1813 to 1815. Always a highly imaginative child, Fouqué rapidly took the opportunity, after first resigning his commission, to devote himself to literature, particularly that inspired by tales of medieval legend and heroic deeds. His first sketches and poems began to appear in magazines in 1803.

His first success came with the play *Sigurd* (1808), drawn from the *Edda* and telling the legend of Siegfried. Fouqué was the first

to adapt this legend into prose. His retelling of Sigurd's battle with Fafnir the dragon, his awakening of the ensorcelled Brynhildur, his later quests and memory-loss, and his death from Brynhildur's own hand, proved instantly popular. The story enthralled the young Richard Wagner, who would return to it in the latter part of his Ring Cycle, with *Siegfried* (1871) and *Gotterdämmerung* (1874). Fouqué later added two further plays, *Sigurd's Rache* and *Aslaugas Ritter*, all three forming the drama trilogy *Der Held des Nordens* (*The Hero of the North*), completed in 1810. The third part, about the adventures of Sigurd's daughter, has been adapted and reprinted separately as *Aslauga's Knights* (the most faithful rendition being by Thomas Carlyle in his collection *German Romance*, 1827).

After a failed first marriage, Fouqué married the older Karoline von Briest, also a writer, and settled down on her estate at Nennhausen, near Brandenburg. The relationship gave Fouqué stability in his life and allowed his literary indulgences. He later founded his own magazine, *Die Jahreszeiten*, which published much of his and his wife's work. As most of this was anonymous, it is probable that some of the work attributed to Fouqué was that of his wife. That is certainly true of "The Cypress Crown" (also known as "Wolf") about a doomed soldier, and may also be the case with "The Magic Dollar."

In 1811 Fouqué produced his masterpiece, *Undine*. This quietly charming and understated fantasy tells of an old fisherman and his wife whose daughter is believed drowned. Soon, though, they discover and adopt another little girl, Undine, who is really a water elemental. She grows into a sprightly elfin girl and falls in love with the knight Sir Huldbrand, thereupon acquiring a soul. They wed, but the knight soon loses interest. He banishes Undine, but when he seeks to wed another, Undine returns and kills him with a kiss. The story is beautifully written, blending a genuine love story with a haunting and eerie legend. It remains the most enduring of Fouqué's works. It is perhaps too easy to read into the narrative Fouqué's own troubled first marriage and the freedom of the second, here reversed in the story. Its first English translation appeared in 1818, and was seldom out of print throughout the 19th century. George Macdonald regarded it as the most perfect of all fairy tales.

The success of *Undine* caused Fouqué to mine the vein further. He produced a long allegorical novel, *Der Zauberring* (1813, translated as *The Magic Ring*, 1825), which contains all the standard motifs of heroic fantasy and may be regarded as the first significant novel in the field. A complex work, it deals primarily with the exploits of Otto von Trautwanger, a knight who at the outset regains a stolen magical ring and uses its power in his subsequent quests against evil forces (natural and supernatural).

At this time Fouqué was producing a number of short stories, some of which have remained popular with anthologists over the years. The best known is "The Bottle-Imp" (1810), about an entrapped demon that grants wishes but which brings eternal damnation to the owner unless he can dispose of it more cheaply than he acquired it. The story, which has on occasions been wrongly attributed to Johann-Karl Musäus, was fondly remembered by Robert Louis Stevenson, who wrote his own version adapted to a Polynesian setting. Some of his fantasies, like "The Victor's Wreath" (1812), "The Field of Terror" (1814), "The Collier's Family" (1814) and "Rosaura" (1817) have a darker, more gothic atmosphere, but Fouqué continued to popularize the German and Teutonic myths as in *Adler und Loewe* (1816), set in medieval Norway, about a minstrel's attempts to marry a magical maiden, and of the various tasks he is set to win her hand. Few good collections of Fouqué's short fantasies exist in English, the most complete being the now very rare *Romantic Fiction* (1845), volume two of James Burns's six-volume *Fouqué's Works*. Fouqué assembled his own 12-volume collected works, *Ausgabe letzter Hand* (1841), completed just before his death.

Fouqué's final major work of fantasy was *Sintram* (1815, translated as *Sintram and His Companions*, 1820), which rivalled *Undine* for popularity in the 19th century, particularly because of its strong moral message. It was inspired by Dürer's engraving *The Knight, Death and the Devil*, death and temptation being the eponymous companions of Sintram in his travels. The supernatural is less overt than in *The Magic Ring*, but forms part of the background of Sintram's world of chivalry and conquest. *Sintram* had a magnetic influence over many who read it during the Victorian age. Charlotte M. Yonge referred to its remarkable power. It strongly moulded Cardinal Newman's character when he read it in his youth, and it served as a model for the early writings of William Morris. Its essence is still evident today in the more recent works of Michael Moorcock.

The success of Fouqué's novels had much to do with their ability, through the portrayal of heroic knights and good versus evil, to inspire and encourage national pride and valour during the Napoleonic wars. As such, their popularity faded after the defeat of Napoleon, and only *Undine* and *Sintram* have lived on, both because they are good stories and have a strong moral value. Goethe, while admiring *Undine*, believed that Fouqué had drawn only the superficial values of knightly chivalry and adventure from the legends and not interpreted or developed the characters or culture of the age. Nevertheless, his stories were highly influential upon Victorian writers and arguably formed the basis of modern heroic fantasy.

—Mike Ashley

FRANCE, Anatole (1844-1924)

Nationality: French. **Selected Publications:** Novels: *Thaïs*. Paris: Calmann-Lévy, 1890; tr. as *Thaïs*. London: Carrington, 1901. *Sur le pierre blanche*. Paris: Calmann-Lévy, 1905; tr. as *The White Stone*. London: John Lane, 1909. *L'île des pingouins*. Paris, Calmann-Lévy, 1908; tr. as *Penguin Island*. London: John Lane, 1909. *La révolte des anges*. Paris: Calmann-Lévy, 1914; tr. as *The Revolt of the Angels*. London: John Lane, 1914. Short stories: *Balthazar*. Paris: Calmann-Lévy, 1889; tr. as *Balthasar*. London: John Lane, 1909. Includes "The Honey-Bee," tr. as Honey-Bee. London: John Lane, 1911. *L'étui de nacre*. Paris: Calmann-Lévy, 1892; tr. as *Tales from a Mother of Pearl Casket*. New York: G. H. Richmond, 1896 and as *Mother of Pearl*. London: John Lane, 1908. *Le puits de Sainte Clare*. Paris. Calmann-Lévy, 1895; tr. as *The Well of Santa Clara*. Paris: Carrington, 1903. Includes L'humaine tragédie, tr. as *The Human Tragedy*. London: John Lane, 1917. *Les sept femmes de le Barbe-Bleu et autres contes merveilleux*. Paris: Calmann-Lévy, 1909. tr. as *The Seven Wives of Bluebeard and Other Marvellous Tales* London: John Lane, 1920.

* * *

Anatole-François Thibault was the son of a political conservative and devout Catholic whose rebellion against these ideals, although unfailingly polite, took him by degrees to opposite extremes.

His *nom de plume* mapped out this process of intellectual development in a remarkable series of essays and fictions, in which several excursions into the fantastic included the most spectacular products of the French tradition of "literary Satanism." France's contributions to this tradition influenced many later writers, but none of those who carried forward that tradition ever surpassed him in elegance, wit or philosophical acumen.

France's first work of fantasy, reprinted in the collection *Balthasar*, was an extended *conte* variously known in English as "Honey-Bee," "Bee" and (in Lin Carter's anthology *Great Short Novels of Adult Fantasy*, 1972) "The Kingdom of the Dwarfs." The eponymous princess and her foster-brother George visit a forbidden lake, where George is imprisoned by pixies and Honey-Bee abducted by dwarfs. The king of the dwarfs, Loc, falls in love with Honey-Bee, but her love for George is adamant. The power of Loc's love is initially expressed as jealousy but is ultimately transformed into an altruistic determination to rescue George and reunite him with Honey-Bee. As with so many other tales in this vein—its most celebrated predecessor was Charles Nodier's *Trilby* (1822)—it embeds its moral lesson in a fervently sentimental literary matrix, but France's tale is distinguished by a particularly dignified elegance.

The novel *Thaïs* is closely related to Flaubert's *The Temptation of St Anthony* (1874). The story follows the exploits of Anthony's disciple Paphnuce (Paphnutius in later translations), who is inspired by a vision to undertake a quest for the salvation of the eponymous actress. His ideological battle against the Epicureans of Alexandria seems to be won when he persuades Thaïs to enter a nunnery, but it turns out to be no victory at all when he is forced to realize—after being harassed by the devil and seduced by the sorceress Helen—that his desire to "save" her was really a sublimation of his sexual passion for her. He sets out to make good his error, but God has no intention of surrendering the hard-won prize. This attack on the pietistic perversity of ascetic Christianity is complemented by some of the short stories in *Mother of Pearl*, including "Amycus and Celestine," in which an Epicurean softening of Christian intolerance in allegorized in the warm relationship between a hermit and a faun, "The Legend of Saints Oliveria and Liberetta," in which a unicorn guides two differently-inclined sisters to faith in God, and "Leslie Wood," about a man who practises stern chastity while his wife is alive receives a chance to repent this folly once she is dead. A much lighter irony in exhibited in the Rabelaisian novel *La rôtisserie de la reine Pédauque* (1893; tr. as *At the Sign of the Reine Pédauque*), which deals in a conscientiously sceptical fashion with the follies of the would-be occultists of the 18th century.

The theme of "Amycus and Celestine" is taken to its logical extreme in the fine opening story of *The Well of St Clare*, known in English as "San Satiro" or "Saint Satyr," while later stories in the same collection broke new ground in Literary Satanism. In the trivial "Lucifer" a handsome black Satan calls to account a Florentine artist who has misrepresented him, while the brilliant novella separately issued as *The Human Tragedy* tells the story of an honest holy man imprisoned by corrupt churchmen who is reluctantly forced to recognise that Satan is his one true friend rather than his enemy.

The White Stone is a philosophical novel about the possibility (or rather the impossibility) of accurate foresight and takes the form of a Classical dialogue with two interpolated visions. The second of these is a futuristic fantasy which remains the best literary model of a Marxist Utopia. The central philosophical argument of the book—which suggests that it is the narrowness of our moral horizons rather than our inability to anticipate technological changes which dooms imaginative explorations of the future to failure—offers a challenge to the whole genre of science fiction which writers in that genre have yet to meet or properly acknowledge.

From conventional philosophical discourse France quickly moved on to more extravagant Voltairean *contes philosophiques*. His one novel-length exercise in that kind of scathing sarcasm is *Penguin Island*, a satire on human religious and political affairs which traces the history of a colony of penguins mistakenly baptized by a myopic saint. It caused a sensation because of the long section parodying the Dreyfus affair, although this section makes it somewhat less interesting to English readers who cannot identify with the extraordinary passions stirred up by that *cause célèbre* in France. *The Seven Wives of Bluebeard*, whose shorter pieces purport to reveal the "truth" behind certain well-known myths, is in similar black comedic vein; it concludes with the brilliant novella "The Shirt," a cautionary tale in which the courtiers of an unhappy king are sent forth to fetch him the shirt of a happy man in order that he might magically absorb its virtue.

The various strands evident in France's fantastic fiction came to a climax in the classic work of Literary Satanism, *The Revolt of the Angels*. The story's hero is the neglectful guardian angel Arcade, who reads Lucretius' classic summary of Epicurean philosophy *De rerum natura* and realizes that God is a petty tyrant unworthy of respect, let alone of worship. He sets out to organize a new revolution of the fallen angels, most of whom are living quietly on earth as teachers and artists, but when he finally locates Satan—now a humble gardener—and offers him a Napoleonic role in the coming crusade, that great friend of mankind explains to him that the good fight must be won in the hearts and minds of men, not on the bloody and ruinous field of battle. The book was, of course, published on the eve of the Great War; it remains, arguably, the great masterpiece of literary fantasy and amply justifies the Nobel Prize which Anatole France was awarded in 1921.

—Brian Stableford

GERMAIN, Sylvie

Nationality: French. **Selected Publications:** Novels: *The Book of Nights* (*Le Livre des Nuits*). Editions Gallimard, Paris, 1985; Sawtry, Cambs., Dedalus, 1992. *Night of Amber* (*Nuit d'Ambre*). Editions Gallimard, Paris, 1987; Sawtry, Cambs., Dedalus, 1994. *Days of Anger* (*Jours de Colere*). Editions Gallimard, Paris, 1989; Sawtry, Cambs., Dedalus, 1993. *The Medusa Child* (*L'Enfant Méduse*). Editions Gallimard, Paris, 1991; Sawtry, Cambs., Dedalus, 1994. *The Weeping Woman on the Streets of Prague* (*La Pleurante des Rues de Prague*). Editions Gallimard, Paris, 1992; Sawtry, Cambs., Dedalus, 1993. *L'Immensités*. Editions Gallimard, Paris, 1994.

*   *   *

> "She entered the book. She entered the pages of the book as a vagrant steals into an empty house, or a deserted garden."

The opening words of *The Weeping Woman on the Streets of Prague* emphasize the fictionality of Sylvie Germain's world. It is

a world created by words, and apprehended by them, a world in which the father at the start of *The Book of Nights* can cry at the birth of his child and find he has no words left to say, while later in the same book the Catholic image of the rose can invoke a virtual glossolalia. In everything, what matters is the words that are used, the names that are given; they are where the power lies. It is notable, for instance, that throughout the 12 short passages that make up the novella *The Weeping Woman in the Streets of Prague* not a single character is named, not a single line of dialogue is spoken. The ghostly figure, tall and limping, who becomes a symbol of universal sorrow and redemption can also smell of ink: she comes from an outside world into the book and from the book into an outside world. The crimes we commit upon this world are shaped by the way we shape the world in language.

There is, in other words, a very strong symbolic power in the books of Sylvie Germain: she comes as close as any European to the magic realism of Latin America. But where the Latin American magic realists imbue their books with a language of symbols drawn from sources as variant as native animism and Catholic liberation theology, Germain draws on European belief systems, traditional Catholicism and ancient folklore. Werewolves and other monsters of the night prowl around the edges of her fiction, but they can be tamed as Victor-Flandrin tames the wolf he sleeps with in *The Book of Nights*; what cannot be tamed are the monsters we make of ourselves. Thus Theodore-Faustin receives a sabre slash in the Franco-Prussian war and is split in two by the diagonal slice across his face.

Wars are very important to Germain. Her first book was to have been *Night of Amber*, but in tracing the background of her cynical, immoral anti-hero, giving shape to a life defined by his damaged ancestry, she created *The Book of Nights*, a novel as rich in scope and imagery as Gabriel Garcia Marquez's *One Hundred Years of Solitude*. *The Book of Nights* tells the story of the Peniel family, first on the canals then on a small farm in that part of France stormed over successively by the Franco-Prussian War, the First World War and the Second World War. Victor-Flandrin, the central character, fathers 15 children—all twins or triplets—by four different wives, and each of the children is distinguished by a fleck of gold in the eye. But this sign of grace is no protection from the vicissitudes of life: his wives die, two of his children turn their backs on the family and fight on the side of the Germans. By the end of the book we are left facing the eternal question of the survivor: why do those I love die? Grief fills the book, often taking symbolic physical form: milky tears that taste of quince and vanilla, for instance.

Out of this emerges Charles-Victor Peniel, the last of the line, whose crimes and transgressions are chronicled in *Nights of Amber*. But here death is no answer, and when he provokes the death of a good person he is tormented by remorse, leading to a climax which echoes the Biblical story of Jacob wrestling with the angel, a symbol which hangs over both books but which is only made explicit here.

Crime and grief are again central to *Days of Anger*, which tells of the murder of Catherine Corvol, who is killed out of love. The murder becomes central to the dream-like, magical images which haunt the novel, spreading a web of guilt among the peasant families in this remote corner of rural France.

The harm we do each other is again the key to *The Medusa Child*, as is the way Germain uses folklore to supply images which capture a very modern sensation of threat and horror. In this case Lucie is the eight-year-old child whose innocence is ended when she becomes the victim of sexual abuse. But this subject matter is transformed by the way the abuser is made into the ogre out of a fairy story, and the way Lucie must turn herself into a monster in response.

All of which paves the way for the fable of universal grief, the weight of torment generated by the 20th century, which is *The Weeping Woman on the Streets of Prague*. As in all her books, Germain creates a very solid sense of place: you could take a map of Prague and trace upon it the pattern of the various incarnations of the ghost woman. Yet this very solidity has a distancing effect, highlighting the rootlessness of the narrator and the magic of what she experiences. In prose that is rich, allusive, full of vivid, startling images, Germain has made one of the most magical and affecting contributions to European literature of the last decade or so.

—Paul Kincaid

GRIMM, Jakob (1785-1863) and
GRIMM, Wilhelm (1786-1859)

Nationality: German. **Selected Publications:** *Kinder- und Hausmärchen* (1812; with six further editions revised and extended to 1857).

*   *   *

The Brothers Grimm probably rival Hans Christian Andersen as the best-known tellers of fairy tales, even though they came over a century after Madame d'Aulnoy and Charles Perrault, who between them first created and popularized the literary fairy tale. In fact the Grimms' *Fairy Tales* are not really fairy tales at all: they are much closer to genuine folk tales. The brothers were keen folklorists, collecting tales from friends, family, and locals, all originally intended as material for their planned history of German literature. In the end, at the urging of friends, they published the tales for their own sake, and they rapidly became popular. Among the best-known are "Rapunzel," "Hansel and Gretel," "Snow White and the Seven Dwarfs," "Rumpelstiltskin," and "The Golden Goose."

They weren't the first to render folk tales into print, although earlier stories by Ludwig Tieck and Johann-Karl Musaeus were heavily retold and relied more on the gothic tradition than folklore. Also, unlike Perrault, who rewove his tales to suit his own purpose, the Grimms were more intent on capturing the genuine oral tradition, and they transcribed and related the stories as heard. Recent research has suggested that they did develop the stories rather more than originally believed, and certainly if one compares the texts over a series of editions, it is clear that the tales were increasingly embellished. Much of this was the work of Wilhelm, who was the more imaginative and literary of the two, while Jakob was more interested in language and philology.

Both brothers had been very close since childhood. Wilhelm always suffered from poor health, which made regular work difficult. Jakob spent several years in the German civil service, while Wilhelm spent six years as a librarian before they began teaching at Göttingen University in 1829. They were dismissed in 1837 because of their refusal to agree to constitutional changes and spent the rest of their lives continuing to research their folk tales and preparing the first ever German dictionary (though they never progressed beyond the letter F).

When the final edition of *Kinder- und Hausmärchen* was published in 1857 it contained 211 tales, and a further 28 had been dropped from earlier editions, making 239 in total. Most of these are no more than they were intended to be, anecdotes and local reportage of half-remembered tales. They were not the highly embellished stories that had been developed by constant relatings in the French literary salons. Some, like "The Fox and the Geese," "Knoist and His Three Sons," and "The Girl from Brakel," are less than a page long and resemble more the *Fables* of Aesop. Others, such as "Mary's Child," "The Fires of Youth," "The Lord's Animals and the Devil's," and "Eve's Unequal Children," have little relation to German folklore and are based on religious themes.

The real core of the Grimms' *märchen* were the genuine folk tales which had been told generation after generation from parent to child, and which best reflected their German heritage. The best example of this is "Snow White and the Seven Dwarfs." Snow White's mother dies in childbirth, and her stepmother is jealous of her beauty. She learns through her magic mirror that Snow White is "a thousand times more fair." She orders that Snow White be taken to the wood and killed and her liver and lungs brought back to be eaten. The huntsman cannot kill the girl and substitutes a boar's vitals. Snow White chances upon the home of the seven dwarfs who mine silver in the hills. She looks after the house for them. The wicked queen learns that Snow White still lives and tries various ways to kill her, succeeding at last with a poisoned apple. Snow White is encased in a glass coffin but is not buried. Years pass and she remains as pure as ever. Then a prince discovers her and, moving the coffin, causes Snow White to cough up the poisoned apple, and she returns to life. She marries the prince and the wicked Queen comes to the wedding where she is forced to put on red-hot iron slippers and dance till she dies. This story has all the trappings of the perfect fairy tale (which of course does not require the presence of fairies). Wicked stepmothers, magical devices, creatures of legend, and innocence triumphant over evil. The setting and characterization of the story is essentially German, though the plot is timeless.

The violence in the tale was removed by later editors, but the Grimms tended to retain violence where it was important to the story, although occasionally this may seem extreme as in the rather grotesque ending to "Rumpelstiltskin" where the gnome is so angry when his name is guessed that he tears himself in two.

Perhaps the most violent and frightening of all the Grimms' tales is "Hansel and Gretel." The brother and sister are abandoned in the forest by their parents who cannot afford to feed them. Although Hansel finds the way home they are abandoned again, and this time they find a house made out of food. They start eating it but the old lady who lives there invites them in. She is soon revealed as a witch who plans to eat them. Gretel, however, manages to fool her, and the witch ends up in the oven and is baked alive. The whole imagery is violent, but it successfully achieves its purpose in frightening children into not trusting strangers and being easily deceived. It is also a salutory lesson to parents about looking after children. The violence is an intrinsic part of the lesson intended in these long-lived folk tales and it is what has made them so memorable.

Because the Grimms had made a serious attempt at the scholarly study of folk tales, when the stories were first translated into English by Edgar Taylor in 1823 as *German Popular Stories*, they attracted the attention of antiquarians as well as romantics, and this gave the tales the stamp of approval. For a while they were arguably more popular in Britain than Germany, and their style and approach was immensely influential in the development of fantastic fiction at that time, particular among the Scottish writers Hogg, Scott, and Cunningham, and the Irish folklorist Thomas Croker. In fact, the Grimms picked up some stories from Croker for their later editions.

Stories by the Grimms have been utilized by many modern fantasists, including Tanith Lee, Robin McKinley, and Patricia Wrede, and their motifs used in many fantasy novels (the magic mirror, for example, receiving the humorous treatment in Piers Anthony's Xanth series). The original fairy tales have never been out of print, although most editions contain only a selection of the more popular stories, and these are usually specially edited and revised for young children. One of the more faithful of recent editions, containing 210 stories, is *Grimms' Tales for Young and Old* translated by Ralph Manheim (1977).

The Grimms' stories, like Perrault's, were popular because they avoided all pretension and presented a basic story for its own value. Through their efforts some of the best oral folk legends were saved for posterity.

—Mike Ashley

MÁRQUEZ, Gabriel García (1928—)

Nationality: Colombian. **Selected Publications:** *No One Writes to the Colonel and Other Stories* (1968). *One Hundred Years of Solitude*, Buenos Aires, Editorial Sudamericana (as *Cien Anos de Soledad*), 1967, New York, Harper & Row, 1970, London, Jonathan Cape, 1970. *The Autumn of the Patriarch* (1976). *Innocent Erendira and Other Stories* (1978). *In Evil Hour* (1979). *Leaf Storm and Other Stories* (1979). *Chronicle of a Death Foretold* (1982). *The Story of a Shipwrecked Sailor* (1986). *Clandestine in Chile: The Adventures of Miguel Littin* (1987). *Love in the Time of Cholera*, Bogota, Editorial Oveja Negra (as *El Amor en los Tiempos del Colera*), 1985, New York, Knopf, 1988, London, Penguin, 1989. *The General in his Labyrinth*, Madrid, Mondadori Espana (as *El General en Su Laberinto*), 1989, New York, Knopf, 1990. *Strange Pilgrims*, Madrid, Mondadori Espana (as *Doce Cuentos Peregrinos*), 1992, London, Jonathan Cape, 1993.

*   *   *

Gabriel García Márquez did not invent magic realism. It was already there in the fiction of Latin American and Spanish writers as varied as Jorge Luis Borges, Carlos Fuentes, Adolfo Bioy Casares and Julio Cortazar before Marquez gave it its most recognizable form in his first novel, *One Hundred Years of Solitude*. But it was Márquez who turned magic realism into an internationally recognized form of fantasy, influencing such writers as Isabel Allende, Peter Carey, and Jeanette Winterson among others.

In essence, magic realism describes illogical events with intense realism, heightening the symbolism of certain occurrences so that they are seen to move plot and character development along exactly as more familiar events would in a realist novel. Thus, in *One Hundred Years of Solitude*, the shooting of one character can be marked by a trickle of blood which flows unerringly but unseen

through the village of Macondo to the feet of his mother. Or a room can seem magically clean and ordered to one person yet filthy and littered to another. Such unreal events are invariably treated as if they are part of the normal course of things, while what might otherwise seem "real" events, the encounter with ice or some of the other wonders brought to Macondo by the gypsies, are heightened as if they are the fantastical intrusion from some other world. Even in what is otherwise his most realist novel, *Love in the Time of Cholera*, when Fermina Daza and Florentino Ariza renew their love after 50 years, they do so on a river journey which is magically extended so that every stage of the journey seems to take it further from the quondam world.

Márquez is an experimental writer (*The Autumn of the Patriarch* is told in long passages which are unbroken by paragraphs), and his books have ranged from journalism (*Clandestine in Chile*) to fictionalized accounts of real incidents (*The Story of a Shipwrecked Sailor*) to fictionalized biography (*The General in His Labyrinth*), but certain preoccupations underlie most of his work. Emerging from a political situation that is at best uncertain (the same unending civil war is in the background of both *One Hundred Years of Solitude* and *Love in the Time of Cholera*), his books revolve endlessly about figures of power and authority. This authority may prove to be illusory or insubstantial (*The Autumn of the Patriarch*), be based on fraud (Fermina Daza's wealthy father is eventually unmasked in *Love in the Time of Cholera* and flees into exile), or to slip away from those who desire it (*The General in his Labyrinth*). In fact, military power, authority that is imposed from without, never achieves genuine security in his books. From Colonel Aureliano Buendia in *One Hundred Years of Solitude* to the President in the late story "Bon Voyage, Mr President," power separates his characters from the magic of ordinary life. Only in those intervals when he gives up his role as a rebel leader in the civil war does Aureliano Buendia experience the symbolic richness of the life the rest of his family knows.

Unlike other forms of fantasy, magic realism does not involve an intrusion into, or from, another world. The stories are set firmly within everyday reality but, rather like a stage-lighting effect, some aspect of that reality is suddenly shown afresh, old beliefs are taken as true, peculiarities of character change the world to the way it is seen. Thus the sex-life of farmers can affect the fecundity of their livestock, an aged doctor who is the pillar of respectable society can die in ludicrous circumstances chasing a talking parrot, and, in the story "The Trail of Your Blood in the Snow," the geography of an unfamiliar city, Paris, can change bewilderingly into a labyrinth that traps a smug materialist husband while his new wife is dying in hospital.

Without being tragedies, the novels and stories of Márquez deal repeatedly with old age and death: the hero Bolivar on his final journey in *The General in His Labyrinth*; the aged lovers reunited after a lifetime in *Love in the Time of Cholera*; *Autumn of the Patriarch* opens with the patriarch's death; *One Hundred Years of Solitude* opens with Colonel Aureliano Buendia facing a firing squad; *Chronicle of a Death Foretold* makes death the central thread that binds the whole story together. Always, death or its approach is a time for reflection, and it is in such mists that magic and reality become confused. Timescales are often irregular, moving backwards and forwards in a way that is difficult to follow. Different characters can share the same name. We become dependent on the memories of old age, which brings with it no special wisdom, the magic of recall grants no dispensation. But what we do see is that life carries meanings above and beyond the mundane, magic is not something outside us but resides purely in how we perceive the world. And our perceptions change the way the world is and the way we behave in it. That is how the magic of Gabriel García Márquez becomes realism.

—Paul Kincaid

PERRAULT, Charles (1628-1703)

Nationality: French. **Selected Publications:** *Griselidis, Nouvelle, avec le conte de Peau d'Ane et celui des Souhaits ridicules* (1694); *Histoires ou contes du temps passé* (1697).

*   *   *

Although Madame d'Aulnoy created the medium of the literary fairy tale, it was Charles Perrault who produced the first popular book, *Histoires ou contes du temps passé*, which became an instant bestseller. It contains eight stories, all of which are well known, though four in particular are among the most popular of all fairy tales—"Sleeping Beauty," "Little Red Ridinghood," "Puss-in-Boots," and "Cinderella." The others are "Bluebeard," "The Fairies" (also known as "Diamonds and Toads"), "Riquet With the Tuft," and "Hop o' my Thumb." The stories have remained in print to this day, including recent translations by Angela Carter in England and Jack Zipes in the United States. These translations include two of Perrault's earlier fairy tales originally written in verse, "The Foolish Wishes" and "Donkey Skin." Along with "Griselidis," also written in verse, this brings the number of Perrault's fairy stories to eleven, a far smaller *oeuvre* than one might expect considering its influence.

Perrault was in his late sixties when he penned his fairy tales. He was a retired civil servant. He had been born in Paris into a wealthy family. His father was a barrister, and although young Charles trained and served as a lawyer for some years he tired of the practice and in 1654 switched to work as secretary to his brother, the head of the Parisian Revenue Service. During this period he began writing light poetry which brought him public notice. He gradually rose through the ranks in the civil service becoming, in 1671, the Controller-General of the Royal Buildings, in the same year that he was elected to the French Academy. He married in 1672 and had three sons, though his wife died in childbirth in 1678. He retired in 1683 and settled down to his literary pursuits.

His poem "Griselidis" (1691), is a fable in the style of La Fontaine, and a precursor to "Les Souhaits ridicules" (*Le Mercure Galant*, November 1693), a poem more in the style of a fairy tale. It considers the stupidity of those who are granted three wishes. A third poem, "Peau d'ane" ("Donkey-Skin") appeared in 1694. It is a different version of Cinderella and concerns a king whose wife dies. Her last wish was that he marry someone even more beautiful than she. The only woman who is more beautiful is the king's daughter, but she will only agree to marry him if he provides her with the most beautiful dresses in the world. This only delays the king for so long, at which stage the daughter disguises herself in a donkey's skin and escapes. She now works as a drudge, keeping her disguise, but occasionally dressing in her finery. A prince sees her one day, but is unable to find her. However she drops a ring and the prince declares he will marry whomever the ring fits.

Perrault was a frequent visitor to the literary salons in Paris and

shared in the vogue for fairy tales. But it was still a significant shift when he moved from verse to prose for his next story, "La Belle au bois dormant" (*Le Mercure Galant*, February 1696). This has now become the standard text for the story "Sleeping Beauty." The story of the newly-born princess who is cursed to fall asleep for a hundred years when she pricks her finger on a spindle is too well known to be related here. Although the story had been around in one form or another for at least 300 years, it was Perrault who shaped it into the current version and stamped it with immortality. The only variation added since is how the prince wakes the sleeping princess. In Perrault's tale he merely kneels by her bed. The kiss that woke her was added by Mrs Craik when she incorporated the story in her own *Fairy Book* (1863).

"Little Red Ridinghood" is believed to have been developed by Perrault from a narrative game. His version ends with the wolf eating the girl. The version recounted by the Grimm Brothers has two hunters rescue the girl and her grandmother from the belly of the wolf.

"Cinderella" is almost certainly the best known and probably the most popular of all fairy tales. It exists in scores of earlier traditional tales, but Perrault made the story quintessentially his own, introducing the memorable motifs of the Fairy Godmother, the pumpkin and mice transformed to a coach and horses, and very specifically the glass slipper which was thus a precise fit for only one pair of feet.

When *Histoires ou contes du temps passé* was published the dedication was signed P. Darmancour, the name adopted by Perrault's youngest son, Pierre. This gave rise to the belief that Pierre may have authored the tales, even though he was only 16 at the time. Pirated editions printed in Holland perpetuated this belief. Authorities are, however, convinced that the stories are the work of the father, though it was not until 1721 that a Dutch edition gave the true attribution. This Dutch edition was then translated into English by Robert Samber as *Histories, or Tales of Past Times* in 1729, and introduced these popular stories to English children. As an interesting aside, the original French edition had a frontispiece depicting an old lady telling stories by the fireside with a plaque saying "Contes de ma Mère L'oye," which later became the title of the collection in France. In English this was translated as "Mother Goose's Tales." In the original French the phrase was synonymous with "old wives' tales," but in English the character of Mother Goose took on an existence of her own. Thus, although she has nothing to do with Perrault's stories, it is true to say that Perrault inadvertently also created the character of Mother Goose.

Perrault's stories are simpler and more easily recounted than Madame d'Aulnoy's, and this almost certainly led to their rapid acceptance and popularity. They are also strongly moralistic—Perrault added one or two moral verses at the end of each story—and so lent themselves more readily as children's stories. They also lacked the more obvious satire of the French establishment which had inspired Madame d'Aulnoy's work and are thus more easily appreciated on a single level. By this same token they are less sophisticated than Madame d'Aulnoy's and less well developed, but they are no less violent. In "Hop o' My Thumb," the ogre's daughters suck the blood of little children, and the ogre ends up slitting his daughters' throats and their bodies are found swimming in blood.

Perrault's chief talent was that he accepted fairy tales at face value and presented them simply and concisely, emphasizing their moral value. After 300 years they are still among the most popular stories in the world.

—Mike Ashley

READING LIST

Apter, T. E. *Fantasy Literature: An Approach to Reality.* Bloomington, Indiana University Press, 1982.

Ashley, Mike. *Who's Who in Horror and Fantasy Fiction.* London, Elm Tree, 1977.

Attebery, Brian. *The Fantasy Tradition in American Literature: From Irving to Le Guin.* Bloomington, Indiana University Press, 1980.

Attebery, Brian. *Strategies of Fantasy.* Bloomington, Indiana University Press, 1992.

Barron, Neil, ed. *Fantasy Literature: A Reader's Guide.* New York, Garland, 1990.

Becker, Allienne R. *The Lost Worlds Romance: From Dawn to Dusk.* Westport, Connecticut, Greenwood Press, 1992.

Bettelheim, Bruno. *The Uses of Enchantment: The Meaning and Importance of Fairy Tales.* New York, Knopf, 1976.

Bleiler, Everett F. *The Checklist of Fantastic Literature: A Bibliography of Fantasy, Weird and Science Fiction Books Published in the English Language.* Chicago, Shasta, 1948; revised edition, as *The Checklist of Science Fiction and Supernatural Fiction,* Firebell, 1978.

Bleiler, Everett F., ed. *The Guide to Supernatural Fiction.* Kent, Ohio, Kent State University Press, 1983.

Bleiler, Everett F., ed. *Supernatural Fiction Writers: Fantasy and Horror.* New York, Scribner, 2 vols., 1985.

Blount, Margaret. *Animal Land: The Creatures of Children's Fiction.* New York, Morrow, 1974.

Boyer, Robert H., and Kenneth J. Zahorski, eds. *Fantasists on Fantasy: A Collection of Critical Reflections.* New York, Avon, 1984.

Brooke-Rose, Christine. *A Rhetoric of the Unreal: Studies in Narrative Structure, Especially of the Fantastic.* Cambridge, Cambridge University Press, 1981.

Burgin, Victor, James Donald and Cora Kaplan, eds. *Formations of Fantasy.* London, Methuen, 1986.

Carpenter, Humphrey. *The Inklings: C. S. Lewis, J. R. R. Tolkien, Charles Williams, and Their Friends.* London, Allen and Unwin, 1978.

Carter, Lin. *Imaginary Worlds: The Art of Fantasy.* New York, Ballantine, 1973.

Cawthorn, James, and Michael Moorcock. *Fantasy: The 100 Best Books.* London, Xanadu, 1988.

Collings, Michael R., ed. *Reflections on the Fantastic: Selected Essays from the Fourth International Conference on the Fantastic in the Arts.* Westport, Connecticut, Greenwood Press, 1986.

Collins, Robert A., and Howard D. Pearce, eds. *The Scope of the Fantastic.* I: *Theory, Technique, Major Authors.* II: *Culture, Biography, Themes, Children's Literature.* Westport, Connecticut, Greenwood Press, 1985.

Coyle, Willliam, ed. *Aspects of Fantasy: Selected Essays from the Second International Conference on the Fantastic.* Westport, Connecticut, Greenwood Press, 1986.

De Camp, L. Sprague. *The Conan Reader.* Baltimore, Mirage Press, 1968.

De Camp, L. Sprague. *Literary Swordsmen and Sorcerers: The Makers of Heroic Fantasy.* Sauk City, Wisconsin, Arkham House, 1976.

Duffy, Maureen. *The Erotic World of Faery.* London, Hodder and Stoughton, 1972.

Dziemianowicz, Stefan R. *The Annotated Guide to Known and Unknown Worlds.* Mercer Island, Washington, Starmont House, 1990.

Edwards, Malcolm, and Robert Holdstock. *Realms of Fantasy.* London, Dragon's World, 1983.

Elgin, Don D. *The Comedy of the Fantastic: Ecological Perspectives on the Fantasy Novel.* Westport, Connecticut, Greenwood Press, 1985.

Filmer, Kath, ed. *The Victorian Fantasists: Essays on Culture, Society and Belief in the Mythopoeic Literature of the Victorian Age.* London, Macmillan, 1991.

Fredericks, Casey. *The Future of Eternity: Mythologies of Science Fiction and Fantasy.* Bloomington, Indiana University Press, 1982.

Frye, Northrop. *The Secular Scripture: A Study in the Structure of Romance.* Cambridge, Massachusetts, Harvard Unversity Press, 1976.

Gove, Philip Babcock. *The Imaginary Voyage in Prose Fiction.* New York, Columbia University Press, 1941; London, Holland Press, 1961.

Hassler, Donald M., ed. *Patterns of the Fantastic.* Mercer Island, Washington, Starmont House, 1983.

Hearne, Betsy. *Beauty and the Beast: Visions and Revisions of an Old Tale.* Chicago, Illinois, University of Chicago Press, 1990.

Hokenson, Jan, and Howard Pearce, eds. *Forms of the Fantastic: Selected Essays from the Third International Conference on the Fantastic in Literature and Film.* Westport, Connecticut, Greenwood Press, 1986.

Hume, Kathryn. *Fantasy and Mimesis: Responses to Reality in Western Literature.* London, Methuen, 1984.

Irwin, Robert. *The Arabian Nights: A Companion.* London, Allen Lane, 1994.

Irwin, W. R. *The Game of the Impossible: A Rhetoric of Fantasy.* Urbana, Illinois, University of Illinois Press, 1976.

Jackson, Rosemary. *Fantasy: The Literature of Subversion.* London, Methuen, 1981.

Joshi, S. T. *The Weird Tale.* Austin, Texas, University of Texas Press, 1990.

Ketterer, David. *Canadian Science Fiction and Fantasy.* Bloomington, Indiana University Press, 1992.

Kroeber, Karl. *Romantic Fantasy and Science Fiction.* New Haven, Connecticut, Yale University Press, 1988.

Langford, Michelle K., ed. *Contours of the Fantastic: Selected Essays from the Eighth International Conference on the Fantastic in the Arts.* Westport, Connecticut, Greenwood Press, 1990.

Lea, Sydney L.W. *Gothic to Fantastic: Readings in Supernatural Fiction.* New York, Arno Press, 1980.

Le Guin, Ursula K. *The Language of the Night: Essays on Fantasy and Science Fiction,* edited by Susan Wood, New York, Putnam, 1979; revised edition, London, Women's Press, 1989.

Lochhead, Marion. *Renaissance of Wonder: The Fantasy Worlds of J. R. R. Tolkien, C. S. Lewis, George MacDonald, E. Nesbit, and Others.* New York, Harper and Row, 1980.

Luthi, Max. *The Fairytale as Art Form and Portrait of Man.* Bloomington, Indiana Unversity Press, 1985.

Lynn, Ruth Nadelman. *Fantasy for Children and Young Adults: An Annotated Bibliography.* New York, Bowker, 1979; 2nd edition, 1983; 3rd edition, 1989.

Magill, Frank N, ed. *Survey of Modern Fantasy Literature.* Englewood Cliffs, New Jersey, Salem Press, 5 vols., 1984.

Manlove, C. N. *The Impulse of Fantasy Literature.* Kent, Ohio, Kent State University Press, 1983.

Manlove, C. N. *Modern Fantasy: Five Studies.* Cambridge, Cambridge University Press, 1975.

Manlove, Colin. *Scottish Fantasy Literature: A Critical Survey.* Edinburgh, Canongate, 1994.

Michalson, Karen. *Victorian Fantasy Literature: Literary Battles with Church and Empire*. Lewiston, New York, Edwin Mellen Press, 1990.

Moorcock, Michael. *Wizardry and Wild Romance: A Study of Epic Fantasy*. London, Gollancz, 1987.

Morse, Donald E., and Csilla Bertha, eds. *More Real Than Reality: The Fantastic in Irish Literature and the Arts*. Westport, Connecticut, Greenwood Press, 1992.

Nadaff, Sandra. *Arabesque: Narrative Structure and the Aesthetics of Repetition in the 1001 Nights*. Evanston, Ilinois, Northwestern University Press, 1991.

Nicholls, Peter. *Fantastic Cinema*. London, Ebury Press, 1984.

Nicholls, Stan. *Wordsmiths of Wonder: Fifty Interviews with Writers of the Fantastic*. London, Orbit, 1993.

Palumbo, Donald, ed. *Erotic Universe: Sexuality and Fantastic Literature*. Westport, Connecticut, Greenwood Press, 1986.

Palumbo, Donald, ed. *Eros in the Mind's Eye: Sexuality and the Fantastic in Art and Film*. Westport, Connecticut, Greenwood Press, 1986.

Parish, James Robert. *Ghosts and Angels in Hollywood Films: Plots, Critiques, Casts and Credits for 264 Theatrical and Made-for-Television Releases*. Jefferson, North Carolina, McFarland, 1994.

Pflieger, Pat. *A Reference Guide to Modern Fantasy for Children*. Westport, Connecticut, Greenwood Press, 1984.

Post, J. B. *An Atlas of Fantasy*. Baltimore, Mirage Press, 1973.

Prickett, Stephen. *Victorian Fantasy*. Bloomington, Indiana University Press, and Brighton, Sussex, Harvester Press, 1979.

Pringle, David. *Modern Fantasy: The Hundred Best Novels*. London, Grafton, 1988; New York, Bedrick, 1989.

Rabkin, Eric S. *The Fantastic in Literature*. Princeton, New Jersey, Princeton University Press, 1976.

Reilly, Robert, ed. *The Transcendent Adventure: Studies of Religion in Science Fiction/Fantasy*. Westport, Connecticut, Greenwood Press, 1985.

Rottensteiner, Franz. *The Fantasy Book: An Illustrated History from Dracula to Tolkien*. London, Thames and Hudson, 1978.

Rovin, Jeff. *The Fabulous Fantasy Films*. South Brunswick, New Jersey, A. S. Barnes, and London, Yoseloff, 1979.

Rovin, Jeff. *The Fantasy Almanac*. New York, Dutton, 1979.

Ruddick, Nicholas, ed. *State of the Fantastic: Studies in the Theory and Practice of Fantastic Literature and Film*. Westport, Connecticut, Greenwood Press, 1992.

Saciuk, Olena H., ed. *The Shape of the Fantastic: Selected Essays from the Seventh International Conference on the Fantastic in the Arts*. Westport, Connecticut, Greenwood Press, 1990.

Sale, Roger. *Fairy Tales and After: From Snow White to E. B. White*. Cambridge, Massachusetts, Harvard University Press, 1978.

Schlobin, Roger C., ed. *The Aesthetics of Fantasy Literature and Art*. Indiana, Notre Dame University Press, 1982.

Schlobin, Roger C. *The Literature of Fantasy: An Annotated Bibliography of Modern Fantasy Fiction*. New York, Garland, 1979.

Scholes, Robert. *Fabulation and Metafiction*. Urbana, University of Illinois Press, 1979.

Scholes, Robert. *The Fabulators*. New York, Oxford University Press, 1967.

Schweitzer, Darrell, ed. *Exploring Fantasy Worlds: Essays on Fantastic Literature*. San Bernardino, California, Borgo Press, 1985.

Searles, Baird, Beth Meacham and Michael Franklin. *A Reader's Guide to Fantasy*. New York, Avon, 1982.

Shinn, Thelma J. *Worlds Within Women: Myth and Mythmaking in Fantastic Literature by Women*. Westport, Connecticut, Greenwood Press, 1986.

Slusser, George E., and Eric S. Rabkin, eds. *Intersections: Fantasy and Science Fiction*. Carbondale, Illinois, Southern Illinois University Press, 1987.

Slusser, George E., and Eric S. Rabkin, eds. *Shadows of the Magic Lamp: Fantasy and Science Fiction in Film*. Carbondale, Illinois, Southern Illinois University Press, 1985.

Slusser, George E., Eric S. Rabkin and Robert Scholes, eds. *Bridges to Fantasy*. Carbondale, Illinois, Southern Illinois University Press, 1982.

Smith, Karen Patricia. *The Fabulous Realm: A Literary-Historical Approach to British Fantasy, 1780-1990*. Metuchen, New Jersey, Scarecrow Press, 1993.

Spivack, Charlotte. *Merlin's Daughters: Contemporary Women Writers of Fantasy*. Westport, Connecticut, Greenwood Press, 1987.

Spivack, Charlotte, and Roberta Lynne Staples. *The Company of Camelot: Arthurian Characters in Romance and Fantasy*. Westport, Connecticut, Greenwood Press, 1994.

Swinfen, Ann. *In Defence of Fantasy: A Study of the Genre in English and American Literature Since 1945*. London, Routledge and Kegan Paul, 1984.

Thompson, Raymond H. *The Return from Avalon: A Study of the Arthurian Legend in Modern Fiction*. Westport, Connecticut, Greenwood Press, 1985.

Todorov, Tzvetan. *The Fantastic: A Structural Approach to a Literary Genre*. Cleveland, Case Western Reserve University Press, 1973.

Tymn, Marshall B., ed. *American Fantasy and Science Fiction: Towards a Bibliography of Works Published in the United States, 1948-1973*. West Linn, Oregon, Fax, 1979.

Tymn, Marshall B., and Mike Ashley, eds. *Science Fiction, Fantasy, and Weird Fiction Magazines*. Westport, Connecticut, Greenwood Press, 1985.

Tymn, Marshall B., K. J. Zahorski and R. H. Boyer. *Fantasy Literature: A Core Collection and Reference Guide*. New York, Bowker, 1979.

Urang, Gunar. *Shadows of Heaven: Religion and Fantasy in the Writing of C. S. Lewis, Charles Williams and J. R. R. Tolkien*. Philadelphia, Pilgrim Press, and London, SCM Press, 1971.

Veldman, Meredith. *Fantasy, the Bomb, and the Greening of Britain: Romantic Protest, 1945-80*. Cambridge, Cambridge University Press, 1994.

Waggoner, Diana. *The Hills of Faraway: A Guide to Fantasy*. New York, Atheneum, 1978.

Weinberg, Robert. *The Weird Tales Story*. West Linn, Oregon, Fax, 1977.

Zipes, Jack. *Breaking the Magic Spell, Radical Theories of Folk and Fairy Tales*. London, Heinemann, 1979.

NATIONALITY INDEX

Below is the list of entrants divided by nationality. The nationalities were chosen largely from information supplied by the entrants. A small number of poets submitted two nationalities (e.g., American and British) and thus are listed under both. It should be noted that "British" was used for all English entrants and for any other British entrant who chose that designation over a more specific one, such as "Scottish."

AMERICAN

Donald Aamodt
Dafydd ab Hugh
Lynn Abbey
Patrick H. Adkins
Lloyd Alexander
Poul Anderson
Piers Anthony
Eleanor Arnason
Constance Ash
Robert Asprin
Richard Bach
Robin W. Bailey
John Kendrick Bangs
John Barth
Donald Barthelme
Gael Baudino
L. Frank Baum
Peter S. Beagle
H. Bedford-Jones
Clare Bell
John Bellairs
Nancy Varian Berberick
Thomas Berger
Terry Bisson
James P. Blaylock
Hannes Bok
Elizabeth H. Boyer
Steven R. Boyett
Marion Zimmer Bradley
Gillian Bradshaw
Richard Brautigan
Mayer Alan Brenner
Terry Brooks
Mildred Downey Broxon
Steven Brust
Emma Bull
Edgar Rice Burroughs
Linda E. Bushyager
James Branch Cabell
Orson Scott Card
Jonathan Carroll
Lin Carter
Robert N. Charrette
C. J. Cherryh
M. Lucie Chin
Molly Cochran
Allan Cole and Chris Bunch
Glen Cook
Juanita Coulson
John Crowley
Kara Dalkey
Avram Davidson
Grania Davis
L Sprague de Camp
Tom De Haven
Pamela Dean

John DeChancie
Tom Deitz
Samuel R. Delany
Susan Dexter
Graham Diamond
Gordon R. Dickson
Stephen R. Donaldson
Carole Nelson Douglas
Diane Duane
Edward Eager
M. Coleman Easton
David Eddings
Teresa Edgerton
Claudia J. Edwards
Phyllis Eisenstein
Ru Emerson
Carol Emshwiller
John Erskine
Lloyd Arthur Eshbach
Rose Estes
Raymond E. Feist
Bruce Fergusson
Charles G. Finney
Jack Finney
Kenneth C. Flint
John M. Ford
Alan Dean Foster
Gardner F. Fox
Esther M. Friesner
Paul Gallico
R. Garcia y Robertson
Craig Shaw Gardner
John Gardner
Randall Garrett
Patricia Geary
Alexis A. Gilliland
Sheila Gilluly
Parke Godwin
William Goldman
Lisa Goldstein
Terry Goodkind
Roland J. Green
Sharon Green
Joyce Ballou Gregorian
Ken Grimwood
Stephan Grundy
Gary Gygax
Barbara Hambly
Niel Hancock
Lyndon Hardy
MacDonald Harris
Simon Hawke
Paul Hazel
Ben Hecht
Mark Helprin
Russell Hoban
P. C. Hodgell

Robert E. Howard
L. Ron Hubbard
Barry Hughart
John Jakes
Robert Jordan
Norton Juster
Phyllis Ann Karr
Patricia Kennealy-Morrison
Katharine Kerr
Richard A. Knaak
William Kotzwinkle
Katherine Kurtz
Ellen Kushner
Henry Kuttner
Mercedes Lackey
Stephen R. Lawhead
Ursula K. Le Guin
John Lee
Fritz Leiber
Megan Lindholm
Holly Lisle
Hugh Lofting
Eric Lustbader
Elizabeth A. Lynn
R. A. MacAvoy
Laurie J. Marks
Norman H. Matson
Julian May
Dan McGirt
Patricia A. McKillip
Robin McKinley
A. Merritt
Faren Miller
Steven Millhauser
L. E. Modesitt, Jr.
Richard Monaco
Elizabeth Moon
C. L. Moore
John Morressy
Janet E. Morris
James Morrow
Talbot Mundy
H. Warner Munn
Pat Murphy
Shirley Rousseau Murphy
John Myers Myers
Robert Nathan
Douglas Niles
John Norman
Andre Norton
Andrew J. Offutt
Frank Owen
Norvell W. Page
Diana L. Paxson
Steve Perry
Meredith Ann Pierce
Daniel Manus Pinkwater
Rachel Pollack
Tim Powers
Fletcher Pratt
E. Hoffmann Price

Alis A. Rasmussen
Melanie Rawn
Michael Reaves
Mickey Zucker Reichert
Jennifer Roberson
John Maddox Roberts
Michaela Roessner
Kristine Kathryn Rusch
Fred Saberhagen
Jessica Amanda Salmonson
R. A. Salvatore
Charles R. Saunders
Elizabeth Ann Scarborough
Darrell Schweitzer
George Selden
Carol Severance
Michael Shea
Delia Sherman
Will Shetterly
Susan Shwartz
James R. Silke
Clark Ashton Smith
Julie Dean Smith
Thorne Smith
Midori Snyder
Nancy Springer
Mary Stanton
Christopher Stasheff
Francis Stevens
Caroline Stevermer
Brad Strickland
Thomas Burnett Swann
Judith Tarr
Sheri S. Tepper
James Thurber
Harry Turtledove
Mark Twain
Jack Vance
Robert E. Vardeman
George Sylvester Viereck
Paula Volsky
Karl Edward Wagner
Evangeline Walton
Walter Wangerin, Jr.
Lawrence Watt-Evans
Margaret Weis
Manly Wade Wellman
Martha Wells
E. B. White
Nancy Willard
Elizabeth Willey
Michael Williams
Tad Williams
Connie Willis
Gene Wolfe
Patricia C. Wrede
Janny Wurts
Laurence Yep
Jane Yolen
Roger Zelazny
Paul Edwin Zimmer

ARGENTINE
Jorge Luis Borges

AUSTRALIAN
James Francis Dwyer
Patricia Wrightson

BRITISH
Achmed Abdullah
Gilbert Adair
Richard Adams
Joan Aiken
F. Anstey
Edwin L. Arnold
David Arscot and David J. Marl
Frank Baker
J. M. Barrie
Helen Beauclerk
Max Beerbohm
Stella Benson
L. M. Boston
Ernest Bramah
K. M. Briggs
Mary Brown
Gerald Bullett
Richard Burns
Moyra Caldecott
Lewis Carroll
Angela Carter
Joy Chant
Vera Chapman
G. K. Chesterton
Grace Chetwin
Adrian Cole
John Collier
Louise Cooper
Susan Cooper
W. J. Corbett
Marie Corelli
Mary Corran
Annie Dalton
W. A. Darlington
E. R. Eddison
Graham Edwards
Penelope Farmer
Pauline Fisk
Ronald Fraser
Michael Frayn
Nigel Frith
Maggie Furey
Alan Garner
David Garnett
Richard Garnett
Jane Gaskell
David A. Gemmell
Mary Gentle
Keren Gilfoyle
Deborah Grabien
Kenneth Grahame
Joan Grant
John Grant

Simon R. Green
Colin Greenland
Neil M. Gunn
H. Rider Haggard
Ann Halam
Andrew Harman
Geraldine Harris
M. John Harrison
Michael Harrison
James Hilton
Martin Hocke
Robert Holdstock
Tom Holt
William Horwood
Laurence Housman
Jean Ingelow
Margaret Irwin
Robert Irwin
Brian Jacques
John James
Mike Jefferies
Diana Wynne Jones
Jenny Jones
Paul Kearney
Susan Alice Kerby
Garry Kilworth
Bernard King
Charles Kingsley
Rudyard Kipling
Andrew Lang
Noel Langley
Tanith Lee
C. S. Lewis
Wyndham Lewis
David Lindsay
Penelope Lively
A. R. Lloyd
Nicholas Luard
George Macdonald
Stephen Marley
Graham Dunstan Martin
John Masefield
William Mayne
A. A. Milne
Hope Mirrlees
Michael Moorcock
Jean Morris
Kenneth Morris
William Morris
Peter Morwood
E. Nesbit
Jenny Nimmo
Mary Norton
Alfred Noyes
Robert Nye
Barry Pain
Mervyn Peake
Philippa Pearce
Eden Phillpotts
John Cowper Powys
T. F. Powys

Terry Pratchett
Michael Scott Rohan
Salman Rushdie
Geoff Ryman
Fay Sampson
Allan Scott
Andrew Sinclair
Spedding
Mary Stewart
Roger Taylor
Peter Valentine Timlett
J. R. R. Tolkien
Nikolai Tolstoy
E. Charles Vivian
Sylvia Townsend Warner
Freda Warrington
Collin Webber
Angus Wells
Robert Westall
John Whitbourn
T. H. White
Oscar Wilde
Vaughan Wilkins
Charles Williams
Philip G. Williamson
David Henry Wilson
Jeanette Winterson
Bridget Wood
Jonathan Wylie
Jack Yeovil

CANADIAN
Charles de Lint
Ian Dennis
Wayland Drew
Dave Duncan
Timothy Findley
Tanya Huff
Guy Gavriel Kay

W. P. Kinsella
Brian Moore
Ruth Nichols
Antony Swithin

COLOMBIAN
Gabriel García Márquez

DANISH
Hans Christian Andersen

FRENCH
Madame D'Aulnoy
Anatole France
Sylvie Germain
Charles Perrault

GERMAN
Michael Ende
Friedrich de la Motte Fouqué
Jakob and Wilhelm Grimm

IRISH
Lord Dunsany
Morgan Llywelyn
Dwina Murphy-Gibb
Flann O'Brien
Pat O'Shea
James Stephens
Mervyn Wall

ITALIAN
Italo Calvino

NEW ZEALANDER
Marc Alexander
Hugh Cook
Margaret Mahy
Cherry Wilder

TITLE INDEX

The following list includes the titles of all novels and short stories (designated "s") cited as fantasy publications. The name in parenthesis is meant to direct the user to the appropriate entry, where full publication information is given. The term "series" indicates a recurring distinctive word or phrase (or name) in the titles of the entrant's books; series characters are also listed here, even if their names do not appear in specific titles of works.

101 Damnations (Harman), 1995
13 Clocks (Thurber), 1950

Abandoned (Gallico), 1950
Abominations of Yondo (s S. Smith), 1960
Abortion (Brautigan), 1971
About Time (s J. Finney), 1986
Across the Far Mountain (Hancock), 1982
Adam and Eve (Erskine), 1927
Adela Cathcart (MacDonald), 1864
Adept series (Kurtz), from 1991
Adventures by Leaflight (s Caldecott), 1978
Adventures of Dr. Eszterhazy (s Davidson), 1991
Aegypt (Crowley), 1987
Aegypt series (Crowley), from 1987
Aeriel series (Pierce), from 1982
Affair of the Cuckolded Warlock (s Munn), 1975
After Bath (Wilkins), 1945
After Dark (Wellman), 1980
After Silence (J. Carroll), 1992
Afterdark Princess (Dalton), 1990
Against the Horde (Gemmell), 1988
Age of Chaos (Wylie), 1989
Agyar (Brust), 1993
Ahead of Time (s Kuttner), 1953
Aisling (L. Cooper), 1993
Alamut (Tarr), 1989
Alaric the Minstrel series (Eisenstein), from 1978
Albion (John Grant), 1991
Albion Triptych series (Sinclair), from 1967
Alcyone (Phillpotts), 1930
Alder Tree (Halam), 1982
Aleph (Borges, appendix), 1978
Alf series (Darlington), from 1919
Alfar series (Boyer), from 1980
Alice in Blunderland (Bangs), 1907
Alice Through the Needle's Eye (Adair), 1984
Alice's Adventures in Wonderland (L. Carroll), 1865
Alice's Adventures Underground (L. Carroll), 1886
Alien Souls (s Abdullah), 1922
Aliens in the Family (Mahy), 1986
All and More (s Aiken), 1971
All But a Few (s Aiken), 1974
All Darkness Met (G. Cook), 1980
All Hallows' Eve (C. Williams), 1945
All Ill Fate Marshalling (G. Cook), 1988
All or Nothing (J. Powys), 1960
All the King's Men (s Mayne), 1982
All the Mowgli Stories (s Kipling), 1933
All You've Ever Wanted (s Aiken), 1953

All-Fellows (s Housman), 1896
All-Fellows and The Cloak of Friendship (s Housman), 1923
Allan and the Ice Gods (Haggard), 1927
Allan's Wife (s Haggard), 1889
Ally, Ally Aster (Halam), 1981
Almuric (Howard), 1964
Alpha Box (Dalton), 1991
Alvin Maker series (Card), from 1987
Amateurs (s Barthelme), 1976
Amazon Slaughter (Anthony), 1976
Amber series (Zelazny), from 1970
American Fairy Tales (s Baum), 1901
American Ghosts and Old World Wonders (s A. Carter), 1993
Anackire (T. Lee), 1983
Ancient Allan (Haggard), 1920
Ancient Dreams (M. Alexander), 1988
Ancient Egypt series (Caldecott), from 1986
Ancient Solitary Reign (Hocke), 1989
And Don't Forget the One Red Rose (s Davidson), 1986
And Eternity (Anthony), 1990
And Then Put Out the Light (Grabien), 1993
Angel in the Parlor (s Willard), 1983
Animal Castle (T. Lee), 1972
Animal Fairy Tales (s Baum), 1969
Animal Library (s Mayne), 1986-87
Annals of the Black Company (G. Cook), 1986
Antar and the Eagles (Mayne), 1989
Anthony Shriek (Salmonson), 1992
Antique Dust (s Westall), 1989
Antiquities (s Crowley), 1993
Anubis Gates (Powers), 1983
Anubis Murders (Gygax), 1992
Anvil of Ice (Rohan), 1986
Apes (Phillpotts), 1929
Apocalypse (Springer), 1989
Apprentice Adept series (Anthony), from 1980
Arabian Nightmare (R. Irwin), 1983
Arabian Nights series (C. Gardner), from 1991
Arachne (Phillpotts), 1927
Ara's Field (Marks), 1991
Arcadia series (Hardy), from 1980
Arcady (M. Williams), 1995(?)
Archer's Goon (D. Jones), 1984
Architect of Sleep (Boyett), 1986
Architecture of Desire (Gentle), 1991
Ardath (Corelli), 1889
Ardneh's World (Saberhagen), 1988
Are All the Giants Dead? (M. Norton), 1975
Argonia series (Scarborough), from 1982
Ariel (Boyett), 1983

Birthgrave series (T. Lee), from 1975
Birthplace (John Grant), 1992
Bishop's Heir (Kurtz), 1984
Bishop's Wife (Nathan), 1928
Bitter Gold Hearts (G. Cook), 1988
Black Beast (Springer), 1982
Black Canaan (s Howard), 1978
Black Cauldron (L. Alexander), 1965
Black Cocktail (J. Carroll), 1990
Black Colossus (s Howard), 1979
Black Company series (G. Cook), from 1984
Black Dragon series (MacAvoy), from 1983
Black Flame (Abbey), 1980
Black God's Shadow (s C.L. Moore), 1977
Black Gryphon (Lackey), 1994
Black Heart and White Heart (s Haggard), 1900
Black Hearts in Battersea (Aiken), 1964
Black Legion of Callisto (L. Carter), 1972
Black Light (Mundy), 1930
Black Lynx (Boyer), 1993
Black Maria (D. Jones), 1991
Black Mountains (Saberhagen), 1971
Black Poodle (s Anstey), 1884
Black Shields (Roberts), 1991
Black Smith's Telling (Sampson), 1990
Black Sorcerer of the Black Castle (Offutt), 1976
Black Star (L. Carter), 1973
Black Trillium (Bradley, May, A. Norton), 1990
Black Unicorn (Brooks), 1987
Black Unicorn (T. Lee), 1991
Black Venus's Tale (s A. Carter), 1980
Black Wheel (Bok, Merritt), 1947
Black Wizards (Niles), 1988
Blackbird series (Warrington), from 1986
Blade, Richard series (R. Green), from 1974
Blaedud the Birdman (Chapman), 1978
Blemyahs (s Mayne), 1987
Blessed Are They (s Baker), 1953
Blessings of Pan (Dunsany), 1926
Blitz (s Westall), 1994
Blitzcat (Westall), 1989
Blood and Dreams (Monaco), 1985
Blood and Honour (Simon Green), 1992
Blood and Thunder Adventure on Hurricane Peak (Mahy), 1989
Blood Fountain (Vardeman), 1985
Blood Lines (Huff), 1993
Blood of a Dragon (Watt-Evans), 1991
Blood of Amber (Zelazny), 1986
Blood of Roses (T. Lee), 1990
Blood of the Colyn Muir (Zimmer), 1988
Blood of the Tiger (Estes), 1987
Blood Opera series (T. Lee), from 1992
Blood Pact (Huff), 1993
Blood Price (Huff), 1991
Blood Red Angel (Adrian Cole), 1993
Blood series (Warrington), from 1992
Blood Trail (Huff), 1992
Blood Trillium (Bradley, May, A. Norton), 1992
Bloodsongs (Bailey), 1986
Bloodstone (Gemmell), 1994
Bloodstone (Wagner), 1975

Bloody Chamber (s A. Carter), 1979
Blue Adept (Anthony), 1981
Blue Boat (s Mayne), 1957
Blue Manor (J. Jones), 1995
Blue Moon (s Housman), 1904
Blue Moon Rising series (Simon Green), from 1991
Blue Star (Pratt), 1969
Blue Sword (McKinley), 1982
Blue-Eyed Manchu (Abdullah), 1917
Boating for Beginners (Winterson), 1985
Boggart (S. Cooper), 1993
Bone Forest (s Holdstock), 1991
Bones (s Hodgell), 1993
Bones of Haven (Simon Green), 1992
Bones of the Moon (J. Carroll), 1987
Bones of the Past (Lisle), 1993
Bonfires and Broomsticks (M. Norton), 1947
Book of Dragons (s Nesbit), 1900
Book of Fantasy (Borges, appendix), 1988
Book of Imaginary Beings (Borges, appendix), 1969
Book of Kane (s Wagner), 1985
Book of Kells (MacAvoy), 1985
Book of Merlyn (T.H. White), 1977
Book of Miracles (s Hecht), 1939
Book of Nights (Germain, appendix), 1992
Book of Paradox (L. Cooper), 1973
Book of Robert E. Howard (s Howard), 1976
Book of Sand (Borges, appendix), 1977
Book of Silence (Watt-Evans), 1984
Book of Sorrows (Wangerin), 1985
Book of Suns (Springer), 1977
Book of the Beast (T. Lee), 1988
Book of the Damned (s T. Lee), 1988
Book of the Dead (T. Lee), 1991
Book of the Dun Cow (Wangerin), 1978
Book of the Mad (T. Lee), 1993
Book of the Magnakai (John Grant), 1992
Book of the Painter series (Gilluly), from 1990
Book of the Three Dragons (K. Morris), 1930
Book of Three (L. Alexander), 1964
Book of Vale (Springer), 1984
Book of Wonder (s Dunsany), 1912
Books of the Kingdoms series (A. Wells), from 1988
Borderlands series (Shetterly), from 1991
Born to Exile (Eisenstein), 1978
Born to Run (Lackey), 1992
Borrowers series (M. Norton), from 1952
Box of Delights (Masefield), 1935
Boxen (s C.S. Lewis), 1985
Boy from the Burren (Gilluly), 1990
Boy in Darkness (s Peake), 1976
Boy Who Swallowed Snakes (s Yep), 1994
Boy Who Was Followed Home (Mahy), 1975
Boy with Two Shadows (Mahy), 1971
Brain (Michael Harrison), 1953
Brak the Barbarian series (Jakes), from 1968
Bran Mak Morn (s Howard), 1969
Brass Bottle (Anstey), 1900
Brazen Head (J. Powys), 1956
Breach in the Watershed (Niles), 1995
Break of Dark (s Westall), 1982

Breath of the Jungle (s Dwyer), 1915
Brewster, Marvin series (Hawke), from 1992
Briar Rose (Yolen), 1992
Bride of Frankenstein (Michael Harrison, as Egremont), 1936
Bride of the Rat God (Hambly), 1994
Bride of the Slime Monster (C. Gardner), 1990
Bridge Across Forever (Bach), 1984
Bridge of Birds (Hughart), 1984
Bridge of Dawn (Hancock), 1991
Bridge of Lost Desire (Delany), 1987
Bright and Shining Tiger (C. Edwards), 1988
Bring Me the Head of Prince Charming (Zelazny), 1991
Brisingamen (Paxson), 1984
Bristling Wood (Kerr), 1989
Brokedown Palace (Brust), 1986
Broken Citadel (Gregorian), 1975
Broken Lands (Saberhagen), 1968
Broken Stone (Monaco), 1985
Broken Sword (Anderson), 1954
Bronwyn's Bane (Scarborough), 1983
Bronze of Eddarta (Garrett), 1983
Brother to the Lion (Estes), 1988
Brothers of the Dragon (Bailey), 1992
Buffalo Gals and Other Animal Presences (s Le Guin), 1987
Builder of the Black Empire (Page, as Stockbridge), 1980
Bull and the Spear (Moorcock), 1973
Bull Chief (Holdstock, as Carlsen), 1979
Bundle of Nerves (s Aiken), 1976
Bureaucats (s Adams), 1985
Burial Rites (Rohan), 1987
Burning Realm (Reaves), 1988
Burning Water (Lackey), 1989
Bus Under the Leaves (Mahy), 1975
But Gently Day (Nathan), 1943
Butterfly Boy (s Yep), 1993
By Chaos Cursed (Reichert), 1991
By the Light of the Green Star (L. Carter), 1974
By the Sword (Lackey), 1991
Bypass to Otherness (s Kuttner), 1961
Byzantium's Crown (Shwartz), 1987

Cafe Purgatorium (s de Lint), 1991
Cahena (Wellman), 1986
Caithan Crusade series (J. Smith), from 1990
Calendar of the Trees (s de Lint), 1984
Caliban's Song (T. Williams), 1994
Calix Stay (Hancock), 1977
Call (s Westall), 1989
Call of Madness (J. Smith), 1990
Call of the Sword (Taylor), 1988
Callanish (Horwood), 1984
Calling of the Three (Emerson), 1990
Calling on Dragons (Wrede), 1993
Callipygia (L. Carter), 1988
Callisto series (L. Carter), from 1972
Camber of Culdi (Kurtz), 1976
Camber the Heretic (Kurtz), 1981
Canticle (Salvatore), 1991
Captain Sinbad (Diamond), 1980
Carmen Dog (Emshwiller), 1988
Carnelian Cube (de Camp, Pratt), 1948

Carpet People (Pratchett), 1971
Cart & Cwidder (D. Jones), 1975
Case of the Dancing Dinosaur (Estes), 1985
Case of the Friendly Corpse (Hubbard), 1991
Case of the Toxic Spell Dump (Turtledove), 1993
Cast of Corbies (Lackey), 1994
Casting Fortune (s Ford), 1989
Castle Dreams (DeChancie), 1992
Castle for Rent (DeChancie), 1989
Castle in the Air (D. Jones), 1990
Castle Kidnapped (DeChancie), 1989
Castle Murders (DeChancie), 1991
Castle of Bone (Farmer), 1972
Castle of Dark (T. Lee), 1978
Castle of Days (s Wolfe), 1992
Castle of Deception (Lackey), 1992
Castle of Hape (S. Murphy), 1980
Castle of Iron (de Camp, Pratt), 1950
Castle of Llyr (L. Alexander), 1966
Castle of the Silver Wheel (Edgerton), 1993
Castle of Wizardry (Eddings), 1984
Castle of Yew (Boston), 1965
Castle Perilous series (DeChancie), from 1988
Castle Roogna (Anthony), 1979
Castle Spellbound (DeChancie), 1992
Castle War! (DeChancie), 1990
Castledown (Gregorian), 1977
Castleview (Wolfe), 1990
Cat Who Wished to Be a Man (L. Alexander), 1973
Catalogue of the Universe (Mahy), 1985
Catastrophe's Spell (Brenner), 1989
Catchfire (Martin), 1981
Cathedral Wednesday (s Mayne), 1960
Cat's Cradle Book (s Warner), 1940
Cats Have No Lord (Shetterly), 1985
Cats of Seroster (Westall), 1984
Catswold Portal (S. Murphy), 1992
Catwoman (Abbey, Asprin), 1992
Caught in Crystal (Wrede), 1987
Cave Girl (Burroughs), 1925
Caves of Fire and Ice (S. Murphy), 1980
Caves of Terror (Mundy), 1924
Celestial Occurrence (s Salmonson), 1991
Cenotaph Road series (Vardeman), from 1983
Centaur Aisle (Anthony), 1982
Centre of the Circle (Wylie), 1987
Chains of Gold (Springer), 1986
Chains of Sleep (Sampson), 1981
Chair Person (s D. Jones), 1989
Chalchiuhite Dragon (K. Morris), 1992
Challenge of the Clans (Flint), 1986
Champion of Garathorm (Moorcock), 1973
Champion of the Gods (R. Green, as Lord), 1976
Champions of the Sidhe (Flint), 1984
Chance (s Springer), 1987
Changeling (s Mayne), 1961
Changeling Earth (Saberhagen), 1973
Changeling Sea (McKillip), 1988
Changeling series (Zelazny), from 1980
Changeover (Mahy), 1984
Changing Land (Zelazny), 1981

Changing the Past (Berger), 1989
Chaos Curse (Salvatore), 1994
Chaos Gate series (L. Cooper), from 1991
Chaos Mode (Anthony), 1994
Charlotte Sometimes (Farmer), 1969
Charlotte's Web (E.B. White), 1952
Charmed Life (D. Jones), 1977
Charwoman's Shadow (Dunsany), 1924
Chase the Morning (Rohan), 1990
Chauntecleer series (Wangerin), from 1978
Chernevog (Cherryh), 1990
Chessboard Planet (s Kuttner, C.L. Moore), 1983
Chessmen of Doom (Bellairs), 1989
Chester Cricket's New Home (Selden), 1983
Chester Cricket's Pigeon Ride (Selden), 1981
Chester, Harry and Tucker series (Selden), from 1960
Chestnut Soldier (Nimmo), 1989
Cheysuli series (Roberson), from 1984
Chia Black Dragon series (Marley), from 1988
Child Across the Sky (J. Carroll), 1989
Child Christopher and Goldilind the Fair (W. Morris), 1895
Child of an Ancient City (T. Williams), 1992
Child of Darkness (s Hodgell), 1993
Child of Elvish (Berberick), 1992
Child of Saturn (Edgerton), 1989
Child of Storm (Haggard), 1913
Child of the Air (Chetwin), 1991
Child of the Dark Star (Caldecott), 1984
Child of the Grove (Huff), 1988
Child of Thunder (Reichert), 1993
Childermass (W. Lewis), 1928
Childhood of the Magician (s Willard), 1973
Children of Llyr (Walton), 1971
Children of the Dragon (Estes), 1985
Children of the Drake (Knaak), 1991
Children of the Flame (Jefferies), 1994
Children of the Night (Lackey), 1990
Children of the Wind (G. Harris), 1982
Children of Triad series (Marks), from 1989
Children of Ynell (S. Murphy), series from 1977
Chimaera's Copper (Anthony), 1990
Chimera (s Barth), 1972
Chimes of Alyafaleyn (Chetwin), 1993
Choose Your Enemies Carefully (Charrette), 1991
Choristers' Cake (s Mayne), 1956
Chorus Skating (Foster), 1994
Chosen of Mida (Sharon Green), 1984
Chrestomanci series (D. Jones), from 1977
Christening Quest (Scarborough), 1985
Christmas Cat (s Westall), 1991
Christmas Formula (s Benson), 1932
Christmas Garland (s Beerbohm), 1912
Christmas Ghost (s Westall), 1992
Christmas Spirit (s Westall), 1994
Chronicle of a Death Foretold (Marquez, appendix), 1982
Chronicles of Amber (Zelazny), 1979
Chronicles of an Age of Darkness series (H. Cook), from 1986
Chronicles of Bustos Domecq (Borges, appendix), 1979
Chronicles of Castle Brass (Moorcock), 1985
Chronicles of Celydonn series (Edgerton), from 1993
Chronicles of Hawklan series (Taylor), from 1988

Chronicles of Morgon series (McKillip), from 1981
Chronicles of Pantouflia (Lang), 1943
Chronicles of Rodriguez (Dunsany), 1922
Chronicles of the Keeper series (King), from 1987
Chronicles of the King's Tramp series (De Haven), from 1990
Chronicles of the Twelve Kingdoms series (Friesner), from 1985
Chronicles of Tornor series (Lynn), from 1979
Chronicles of Westria series (Paxson), from 1982
Cinderella's Daughter (s Erskine), 1930
Cineverse series (C. Gardner), from 1989
Cinnabar (Diamond), 1985
Circe's Island, and The Girl and the Faun (Phillpotts), 1926
Circle of Light series (Hancock), from 1977
Circus of Dr. Lao (C. Finney), 1935
Circus of Fear (Estes), 1983
Citadel (Williamson), 1995
Citadel of Fear (Stevens), 1970
Citadel of Hell (Page, as Stockbridge), 1983
City (Gaskell), 1966
City at the Edge of Time (Janet Morris), 1988
City Condemned to Hell (Page, as Craig), 1975
City Destroyer (Page, as Stockbridge), 1975
City in the Autumn Stars (Moorcock), 1986
City in the Glacier (Vardeman), 1980
City Life (s Barthelme), 1970
City of Bones (M. Wells), 1995
City of Cobras (Dwyer), 1938
City of Flaming Shadows (Page, as Stockbridge), 1969
City of Frozen Fire (Wilkins), 1950
City of Hawks (Gygax), 1987
City of the Living Dead (R. Green, as Lord), 1978
City of the Singing Flame (s S. Smith), 1981
City of the Sun (Fraser), 1961
City of Wonder (Vivian), 1923
Claimed! (Stevens), 1966
Clan Ground (Bell), 1984
Clan of the Warlord (Boyer), 1992
Clan Wars series (Morwood), from 1993
Clancy's Cabin (Mahy), 1974
Clandestine in Chile (Marquez, appendix), 1987
Clash by Night (s Kuttner, C.L. Moore), 1980
Clash of the Titans (Foster), 1981
Claws of Helgedad (John Grant), 1991
Cleopatra (Haggard), 1889
Cloak of Friendship (s Housman), 1905
Clock of Time (s J. Finney), 1958
Clocks of Iraz (de Camp), 1971
Cloud Castles (Rohan), 1993
Cloud Over Water (Spedding), 1988
Cloven Hooves (Lindholm), 1991
Cloven Viscount (Calvino, appendix), 1962
Coachman Rat (Wilson), 1989
Cold Blue Light (Godwin), 1983
Cold Copper Tears (G. Cook), 1988
Cold Heaven (B. Moore), 1983
Coll and His White Pig (L. Alexander), 1965
College of Magics (Stevermer), 1994
Color Out of Time (Shea), 1984
Colour of Her Panties (Anthony), 1992
Colour of Magic (Pratchett), 1983
Coloured Lands (s Chesterton), 1938

Darkangel (Pierce), 1982
Darker Than the Storm (Warrington), 1992
Darkest Road (Kay), 1986
Darkmage (Hambly), 1988
Darkness at Sethanon (Feist), 1986
Darkness, I (T. Lee), 1994
Darkness Weaves With Many Shades (Wagner), 1970
Darkspell (Kerr), 1987
Darksword series (Weis), from 1988
Darkthunder's Way (Deitz), 1989
Darkwalker on Moonshae (Niles), 1987
Darkwell (Niles), 1989
Darkworld Detective (s Reaves), 1982
Darwath series (Hambly), from 1982
Darya of the Bronze Age (L. Carter), 1981
Daughter of Amun (Caldecott), 1989
Daughter of Ra (Caldecott), 1990
Daughter of Regals (Donaldson), 1984
Daughter of the Bear King (Arnason), 1987
Daughter of the Bright Moon (Abbey), 1979
Daughter of the Empire (Feist, Wurts), 1987
Daughter of the Lion (Roberson), 1989
Daughter of Tintagel series (Sampson), from 1989
Daughter of Witches (Wrede), 1983
David's Witch Doctor (Mahy), 1976
Dawn of Fear (S. Cooper), 1970
Dawn Song (Sharon Green), 1990
Dawnspell (Kerr), 1989
Day by Night (T. Lee), 1980
Day of the Dissonance (Foster), 1984
Day of the Minotaur (Swann), 1966
Day without Wind (s Mayne), 1964
Daybreak on a Different Mountain (Greenland), 1984
Daylight and Nightmare (s Chesterton), 1986
Daymaker (Halam), 1987
Days of Air and Darkness (Kerr), 1994
Days of Anger (Germain, appendix), 1993
Days of Blood and Fire (Kerr), 1993
Dead Father (Barthelme), 1975
Dead Kingdom (G. Harris), 1983
Dead Man's Chest (Vivian, as Mann), 1934
Deadly Quicksilver Lies (G. Cook), 1993
Deal with the Devil (Phillpotts), 1895
Dealing with Dragons (Wrede), 1990
Dealings with the Fairies (s MacDonald), 1867
Dear Hill (Halam, as Jones), 1980
Death and the Spider (Page, as Stockbridge), 1975
Death Angel's Shadow (s Wagner), 1973
Death Gate Cycle series (Weis), from 1990
Death God's Citadel (Coulson), 1980
Death in Delhi (Gygax), 1993
Death of Chaos (Modesitt), 1995
Death of the Author (Adair), 1992
Death Reign of the Vampire King (Page, as Stockbridge), 1975
Death-Blinder (King), 1988
Deathknight (Offutt), 1990
Death's Acolyte (Vardeman), 1986
Death's Deputy (Hubbard), 1948
Death's Master (T. Lee), 1979
Deceiver (L. Cooper), 1991
Deep Wizardry (Duane), 1985

Deerskin (McKinley), 1993
Defy the Foul Fiend (Collier), 1934
Deirdre (Stephens), 1923
Del Eden series (Paxson), from 1984
Delan the Mislaid (Marks), 1989
Delirium's Mistress (T. Lee), 1986
Della-Wu, Chinese Courtesan (s Owen), 1931
Delusion's Master (T. Lee), 1981
Demi-Gods (Stephens), 1914
Demon Blues (Friesner), 1989
Demon Crown series (Vardeman), from 1989
Demon Download (Yeovil), 1990
Demon Drums (Severance), 1992
Demon Hand (Estes), 1988
Demon in the Mirror (Offutt), 1977
Demon Lord (Morwood), 1984
Demon Lord of Karanda (Eddings), 1988
Demon of Scattery (Anderson, Broxon), 1979
Demon of the Dark Ones (Vardeman), 1982
Demons and Shadows (s Westall), 1993
Demons Don't Dream (Anthony), 1993
Demons series (Friesner), from 1988
Demon-Spawn (Dalton), 1991
Dervish Daughter (Tepper), 1986
Deryni series (Kurtz), from 1970
Descent Into Hell (C. Williams), 1937
Desmond, Tim series (Friesner), from 1991
Destiny of the Sword (Duncan), 1988
Destiny Stone (Vardeman), 1980
Destroying Angel (King), 1987
Deverry series (Kerr), from 1986
Devil and All (s Collier), 1934
Devil in a Forest (Wolfe), 1976
Devil in Iron (s Howard), 1976
Devil on the Road (Westall), 1978
Devil Take the Hindmost (Simon Green), 1991
Devil Takes a Holiday (Noyes), 1955
Devil With Love (Nathan), 1963
Devil Wives of Li Fong (Price), 1979
Devil's Guard (Mundy), 1926
Devil's Own Dear Son (Cabell), 1949
Devil's Race Track (s Twain), 1980
Devil's Tor (Lindsay), 1932
Diamond Throne (Eddings), 1989
Diary of a Baby (Pain), 1907
Dido and Pa (Aiken), 1986
Different Kingdom (Kearney), 1993
Difficulty with Dwarves (C. Gardner), 1987
Digging Leviathan (Blaylock), 1984
Dilvish series (Zelazny), from 1981
Dimension of Dreams (R. Green, as Lord), 1974
Dinbig of Khimmur (Williamson), 1991
Dinner at Deviant's Palace (Powers), 1985
Dinosaur Junction (Halam), 1992
Dirge for Sabis (Cherryh), 1989
Dirty Work (McGirt), 1993
Disagreement with Death (C. Gardner), 1989
Disappearing Dwarf (Blaylock), 1983
Discworld series (Pratchett), from 1983
Divided Allegiance (Moon), 1988
Dixon, Johnny series (Bellairs), from 1983

Dr. Cyclops (s Kuttner), 1967
Dr. Dolittle series (Lofting), from 1920
Doctor Fogg (Matson), 1929
Doctor Rat (Kotzwinkle), 1976
Dr. Skull series (Page), from 1975
Dog and the Wolf (Anderson), 1988
Dog Wizard (Hambly), 1993
Dog's Tale (s Twain), 1904
Dogsbody (D. Jones), 1975
Dolphin and the Deep (s Swann), 1968
Domes of Fire (Eddings), 1992
Domnei (Cabell), 1920
Don Rodriguez (Dunsany), 1922
Donkey's Crusade (Jean Morris), 1983
Doom of the Darksword (Weis), 1988
Door in the Air (s Mahy), 1988
Door in the Hedge (s McKinley), 1981
Door into Fire (Duane), 1979
Door into Shadow (Duane), 1984
Door into Sunset (Duane), 1992
Doorway in Fairyland (s Housman), 1922
Dormouse Tales (s Mayne, as Molin), 1966
Dorothy and the Wizard in Oz (Baum), 1908
Dot and Tot of Merryland (Baum), 1901
Double Feature (s Bull, Shetterly), 1994
Double Shadow (s S. Smith), 1933
Doughnuts (s Blaylock), 1994
Dove of the East (s Helprin), 1975
Down Among the Dead Men (Simon Green), 1993
Down the Long Wind (Bradshaw), 1988
Downhill Crocodile Whizz (s Mahy), 1986
Downs So Free (Baker), 1948
Drachenfels (Yeovil), 1989
Drackenberg Adventure (L. Alexander), 1988
Dragon (Frith), 1987
Dragon (Gaskell), 1977
Dragon and the George (Dickson), 1976
Dragon and the Thief (Bradshaw), 1991
Dragon at War (Dickson), 1993
Dragon Cauldron (Yep), 1991
Dragon Circle series (C. Gardner), from 1994
Dragon Crown (Knaak), 1994
Dragon Death (Baudino), 1992
Dragon, Dragon (s J. Gardner), 1975
Dragon Hoard (T. Lee), 1971
Dragon in the Stone (Scott), 1991
Dragon in the Sword (Moorcock), 1986
Dragon King series (Lawhead), from 1982
Dragon Knight (Dickson), 1990
Dragon Lord (Morwood), 1986
Dragon Magic (A. Norton), 1972
Dragon of an Ordinary Family (Mahy), 1969
Dragon of Doom (Estes), 1983
Dragon of the Lost Sea (Yep), 1982
Dragon on a Pedestal (Anthony), 1983
Dragon on the Border (Dickson), 1992
Dragon Path (s K. Morris), 1995
Dragon Prince series (Rawn), from 1988
Dragon Reborn (Jordan), 1991
Dragon Revenant (Kerr), 1990
Dragon series (Bailey), from 1992

Dragon Sleeping (C. Gardner), 1994
Dragon Star series (Rawn), from 1990
Dragon Steel (Yep), 1985
Dragon, the Earl, and the Troll (Dickson), 1994
Dragon Token (Rawn), 1992
Dragon Tome (Knaak), 1992
Dragon Waiting (Ford), 1983
Dragon Waking (C. Gardner), 1995
Dragon War (Yep), 1992
Dragon Wing (Weis), 1990
Dragon Winter (Hancock), 1978
Dragonbards series (S. Murphy), from 1985
Dragonbone Chair (T. Williams), 1988
Dragoncharm (G. Edwards), 1995
Dragonfield (s Yolen), 1985
DragonLance Chronicles series (Weis), from 1984
DragonLance Heroes series (Knaak), from 1988
DragonLance Legends series (Weis), from 1986
DragonLance series (Niles), from 1986
DragonLance series (M. Williams), from 1988
Dragonpond (Lloyd), 1990
Dragonrank Master (Reichert), 1989
Dragonrealm series (Knaak), from 1989
Dragonrouge (L. Carter), 1984
Dragon's Carbuncle (Boyer), 1990
Dragon's Dagger (Salvatore), 1994
Dragon's Gold (Anthony), 1987
Dragons of Autumn Twilight (Weis), 1984
Dragons of Englor (R. Green, as Lord), 1977
Dragons of Spring Dawning (Weis), 1985
Dragons of Winter Night (Weis), 1985
Dragon's Plunder (Strickland), 1992
Dragonsbane (Hambly), 1986
Dragonslayer (Drew), 1981
Dragonslayer's Return (Salvatore), 1995
Dragonspell (Kerr), 1990
Dragonsword series (Baudino), from 1988
Dragonworld (Reaves), 1979
Drastic Dragon of Draco, Texas (Scarborough), 1986
Drawing of the Dark (Powers), 1979
Dread Brass Shadows (G. Cook), 1990
Dread Companion (A. Norton), 1970
Dread Empire series (G. Cook), from 1979
Dreadful Dragon of Hay Hill (s Beerbohm), 1928
Dream Days (s Grahame), 1898
Dream Finder (Taylor), 1991
Dream Lords series (Adrian Cole), from 1975
Dream Weaver (s Yolen), 1979
Dream Years (Goldstein), 1985
Dreambuilder (Deitz), 1992
Dreamer's Tales (s Dunsany), 1910
Dreaming City (Moorcock), 1972
Dreaming of Babylon (Brautigan), 1977
Dreaming Place (de Lint), 1990
Dreams of Dark and Light (s T. Lee), 1986
Dreams of Steel (G. Cook), 1990
Dreams of Stone (Wylie), 1989
Dreams Underfoot (s de Lint), 1993
Dreamstone (Cherryh), 1983
Dreamtigers (Borges, appendix), 1964
Dream-Weaver (Wylie), 1991

Drenai series (Gemmell), from 1984
Drift (s Mayne), 1985
Driftway (Lively), 1972
Drink Down the Moon (de Lint), 1990
Drinkwater series (Vivian), from 1927
Drowned Ammet (D. Jones), 1977
Drowned Man's Reel (s de Lint), 1988
Druid of Shannara (Brooks), 1991
Druid Queen (Niles), 1993
Druid Stone (Fox, as Majors), 1965
Druids (Llywelyn), 1991
Druid's Blood (Friesner), 1988
Drum, the Doll, and the Zombie (Bellairs, Strickland), 1994
Dubious Hills (Dean), 1994
Duel of Dragons (Baudino), 1991
Duncton Chronicles (Horwood), from 1980
Dungeon of Dread (Estes), 1982
Dungeon series (de Lint), from 1989
Dungeons of Kuba (Diamond), 1979
Dus series (Watt-Evans), from 1980
Dwellers in the Mirage (Merritt), 1932
Dying Earth series (Vance), from 1950

Ealdwood series (Cherryh), from 1983
Earl Aubec (Moorcock), 1993
Earthfasts (Mayne), 1966
Earthly Crown (Rasmussen, as Elliott), 1993
Earthsea series (Le Guin), from 1968
Earthstone (Paxson), 1987
East of Midnight (T. Lee), 1977
East, West (s Rushdie), 1994
Ebenezum series (C. Gardner), from 1986
Ecce Hominid (s Friesner), 1991
Echoes of Flame (Wylie), 1994
Echoes of the Fourth Magic (Salvatore), 1990
Echoes of War (s Westall), 1989
Eckert, Jim series (Dickson), from 1976
Eclipse (L. Cooper), 1994
Eclipse of the Kai (John Grant), 1989
Edge of Vengeance (J. Jones), 1991
Egbert (Darlington), 1924
Eight Days of Luke (D. Jones), 1975
Eight Fantasms and Magics (s Vance), 1969
Eight Skilled Gentlemen (Hughart), 1991
El Dorado Adventure (L. Alexander), 1987
Elak of Atlantis (s Kuttner), 1985
Eldrie the Healer (C. Edwards), 1989
Element of Fire (M. Wells), 1993
Elementals (Llywelyn), 1993
Elenium series (Eddings), from 1989
Elephantasm (T. Lee), 1993
Elf Defense (Friesner), 1988
Elfin Lights (s Eshbach), 1934
Elfin Ship series (Blaylock), from 1982
Elf-Queen of Shannara (Brooks), 1992
Elfstones of Shannara (Brooks), 1982
Elfwood (Estes), 1992
Elidor (Garner), 1965
Elissa (s Haggard), 1900
Elixir (Nathan), 1971
Ellis Island (s Helprin), 1981

Elric series (Moorcock), from 1965
Elsewhere (Shetterly), 1991
Elven Star (Weis), 1990
Elvenbane (Lackey, A. Norton), 1991
Elvenblood (Lackey), 1995
Elves and the Otterskin (Boyer), 1981
Elvish series (Berberick), from 1989
Embers (Baker), 1946
Emerald City of Oz (Baum), 1910
Emlyn's Moon (Nimmo), 1987
Emma in Winter (Farmer), 1966
Emperor and Clown (Duncan), 1992
Emperor for the Legion (Turtledove), 1987
Emperor of Earth-Above (Gilluly), 1993
Empire of Blood (R. Green, as Lord), 1977
Empire of the Eagle (A. Norton, Shwartz), 1993
Empire of the East series (Saberhagen), from 1968
Empire series (Feist, Wurts), from 1987
Enchanted Beggar (Matson), 1959
Enchanted Castle (Nesbit), 1907
Enchanted Forest Chronicles (Wrede), from 1983
Enchanted Island of Yew (Baum), 1903
Enchanted Isles (Flint, as Flynn), 1991
Enchanted Type-writer (Bangs), 1899
Enchanter (Bailey), 1989
Enchanter series (de Camp, Pratt), from 1941
Enchanter's Endgame (Eddings), 1984
Enchantment's End (M. Alexander), 1992
Enchantress of World's End (L. Carter), 1975
End of the Game (Tepper), 1987
End of the Road (Barth), 1958
Endangered Species (s Wolfe), 1989
Endless Catacombs (Weis), 1984
Endless Knot (Lawhead), 1993
Endless Quest series (Estes), from 1982
Endless Quest series (Niles), from 1985
Enquiries of Dr. Eszterhazy (s Davidson), 1975
Equal Rites (Pratchett), 1987
Erekosë series (Moorcock), from 1970
Eric (Pratchett), 1990
Eric Brighteyes (Haggard), 1891
Eric Brighteyes No. 2 (Broxon, as Skaldaspillir), 1979
Eric of Zanthodon (L. Carter), 1982
Erl King's Daughter (Aiken), 1988
Escape from Castle Quarras (Niles), 1985
Escape Velocity (Stasheff), 1983
Eternal Champion (Moorcock), 1970
Eternal Lover (Burroughs), 1925
Eternal Savage (Burroughs), 1963
Ethshar series (Watt-Evans), from 1985
Euryale (Dalkey), 1988
Evander (Phillpotts), 1919
Eve (Farmer), 1985
Evelyn (Dwyer), 1929
Evenor (s MacDonald), 1972
Eve's Diary (s Twain), 1906
Excess of Enchantments (C. Gardner), 1988
Exchange of Souls (Pain), 1911
Exile (Kotzwinkle), 1987
Exile (Salvatore), 1990
Exile's Gate (Cherryh), 1988

Exiles of the Rynth (Douglas), 1984
Exiles of the Stars (A. Norton), 1971
Expecting Someone Taller (Holt), 1987
Expiration Date (Powers), 1995
Exploits of Ebenezum (C. Gardner), 1987
Explorers in Hell (Janet Morris), 1989
Extract from Captain Stormfield's Visit to Heaven (s Twain), 1909
Extracts from Adam's Diary (s Twain), 1904
Extraordinary Tales (Borges, appendix), 1971
Eye of the World (Jordan), 1990
Eyes Have It (Estes), 1989
Eyes in the Fire (Grabien), 1989
Eyes of Horus (Joan Grant), 1942
Eyes of Sarsis (Offutt), 1980
Eyes of the Killer Robot (Bellairs), 1986
Eyes of the Overworld (Vance), 1966

Face in the Abyss (Merritt), 1931
Face in the Frost (Bellairs), 1969
Faerie Tale (Feist), 1988
Faerielands series (de Lint), from 1994
Faery Flag (s Yolen), 1989
Faery in Shadow (Cherryh), 1993
Faery Lands Forlorn (Duncan), 1991
Fafhrd and the Gray Mouser series (Leiber), from 1968
Fahrenheit 666 (Harman), 1995
Fair (Nathan), 1964
Fair in Emain Macha (de Lint), 1990
Fairy of Ku-She (Chin), 1988
Fairy Tales of Gold (s Garner), 1979
Faithless Lollybird (s Aiken), 1977
Falcons of Eden (Diamond), 1980
Fall of Fyorlund (Taylor), 1989
Fall of Princes (Tarr), 1988
Fallen Fortress (Salvatore), 1993
Fallen Idol (Anstey), 1886
Fallen Ones (Vardeman), 1982
Fallible Fiend (de Camp), 1973
Falling Woman (P. Murphy), 1986
Famous Monsters (s Yeovil, as Newman), 1995
Fancies and Goodnights (s Collier), 1951
Fancy Free (s Phillpotts), 1901
Fanfare for a Witch (Wilkins), 1954
Fantasies in Black and White (s Salmonson), 1985
Fantasms and Magics (s Vance), 1978
Fantasy (s Anderson), 1981
Fantasy Worlds of Peter S. Beagle (Beagle), 1978
Fantazius Mallare (Hecht), 1922
Far Forests (s Aiken), 1977
Far Kingdoms (Cole and Bunch), 1994
Far Lands, Other Days (s Price), 1975
Far Side of Forever series (Sharon Green), from 1987
Faragon Fairingay (Hancock), 1977
Farce to be Reckoned With (Zelazny), 1995
Farewell Miss Julie Logan (Barrie), 1932
Farm in Fairyland (s Housman), 1894
Farm that Ran Out of Names (s Mayne), 1989
Farmer Giles of Ham (s Tolkien), 1949
Farnor (Taylor), 1992
Farseer 1 (Lindholm, as Hobb), 1995
Farthest Shore (Le Guin), 1972

Fat Face (s Shea), 1987
Fata Morgana (Kotzwinkle), 1977
Fate (Corran), 1995
Fates of the Princes of Dyfed (K. Morris, as Morus), 1914
Father Christmas Letters (s Tolkien), 1976
Faust (Nye), 1980
Faust Among Equals (Holt), 1994
Fear, and The Ultimate Adventure (Hubbard), 1970
Fear, and Typewriter in the Sky (Hubbard), 1951
Fearful Lovers (s Westall), 1992
Feathered Dragon (Niles), 1991
Fellowship of the Ring (Tolkien), 1954
Fergus (B. Moore), 1970
Ficciones (Borges, appendix), 1962
Field of Clover (s Housman), 1898
Fields of Sleep (Vivian), 1923
Fiery Gate (Fraser), 1943
Fifth Quarter (Huff), 1995
Figure in the Shadows (Bellairs), 1975
Figures of Earth (Cabell), 1921
Final Quest (Monaco), 1980
Find Your Fate series (Estes), from 1984
Find Your Own Truth (Charrette), 1991
Finder (Bull), 1994
Fine and Private Place (Beagle), 1960
Finished (Haggard), 1916
Finn MacCool and the Small Men of Deeds (O'Shea), 1987
Finn MacCumhal series (Flint), from 1986
Finnbranch series (Hazel), from 1980
Finnglas and the Stones of Choosing (Sampson), 1986
Finnglas of the Horses (Sampson), 1985
Fionavar Tapestry series (Kay), from 1984
Fire and Fog (Vardeman), 1984
Fire and Hemlock (D. Jones), 1984
Fire Demon (Gygax), 1986
Fire in His Hands (G. Cook), 1984
Fire in the Mist (Lisle), 1992
Fire Queen (Grabien), 1990
Fire Sea (Weis), 1991
Fire When It Comes (s Godwin), 1984
Firebird (Morwood), 1992
Firebrand (Bradley), 1987
Firebringer series (Pierce), from 1985
Firedrake (Knaak), 1989
Firelord (Godwin), 1980
Fires of Azeroth (Cherryh), 1979
Fires of Heaven (Jordan), 1993
Fires of Windameir (Hancock), 1985
Fire's Stone (Huff), 1990
Fireshaper's Doom (Deitz), 1987
Fireworks (s A. Carter), 1974
First Chronicles of Druss the Legend (s Gemmell), 1993
First Named (Wylie), 1987
First Quest (Niles), 1995
First Two Lives of Lukas-Kasha (L. Alexander), 1978
First Whisper of The Wind in the Willows (s Grahame), 1944
Firstworld Chronicles (Williamson), from 1991
Fish Dinner in Memison (Eddison), 1941
Fisherman of the Inland Sea (s Le Guin), 1994
Fisherman's Curse (Easton), 1987
Fishing Party (s Mayne), 1960

Fit of Shivers (s Aiken), 1990
Five Children and It (Nesbit), 1902
Five Hundred Years After (Brust), 1994
Flame Key (Vardeman, as Moran), 1987
Flame Winds (Page), 1969
Flames of the Dragon (Bailey), 1994
Flat Earth series (T. Lee), from 1978
Flecker's Magic (Matson), 1926
Flight in Yiktor (A. Norton), 1986
Flight of Bright Birds (Arscott and Marl), 1985
Flight of Michael McBride (Snyder), 1994
Flight of the Raven (Roberson), 1990
Flight of the Shadow (MacDonald), 1891
Flight Over Fire series (J. Jones), from 1990
Flint Heart (Phillpotts), 1910
Flint, the King (Niles), 1990
Floating Gods (M. John Harrison), 1983
Floating Opera (Barth), 1956
Flower of the Gods (Abdullah), 1936
Flower Phantoms (Fraser), 1926
Flutter of Wings (s Wall), 1974
Fly by Night (J. Jones), 1990
Flying Draper (Fraser), 1924
Flying Dutch (Holt), 1991
Folk of the Air (Beagle), 1986
Follow the Footprints (s Mayne), 1953
Food of Death (s Dunsany), 1974
Foot in the Grave (s Aiken), 1989
For Crown and Kingdom (Vardeman), 1987
For Love of Evil (Anthony), 1988
Forbidden Door (Vivian), 1927
Forbidden Magic (A. Wells), 1991
Forerunner Foray (A. Norton), 1973
Forest House (Bradley), 1993
Forest King series (C. Edwards), from 1986
Forest Lord (M. Williams), 1991
Forest of Forever (Swann), 1971
Forest Wars (Diamond), 1994
Forests of Gleor (R. Green, as Lord), 1977
Forests of the Night (s T. Lee), 1989
Forever King (Cochran), 1992
Forge in the Forest (Rohan), 1987
Forge of Virtue (Abbey), 1991
Forging the Darksword (Weis), 1988
Forgotten Beasts of Eld (McKillip), 1974
Forgotten News (s J. Finney), 1983
Forgotten Realms series (Niles), from 1987
Forgotten Realms series (Salvatore), from 1988
Fortress of Frost and Fire (Emerson, Lackey), 1993
Fortress of the Pearl (Moorcock), 1989
Fossil Snake (Boston), 1975
Found Wanting (L. Carter), 1985
Founding of Evil Hold School (Tolstoy), 1968
Foundling (s L. Alexander), 1973
Four Grannies (s D. Jones), 1980
Fox Woman, and The Blue Pagoda (s Bok, Merritt), 1946
Fractal Mode (Anthony), 1992
Frank Frazetta's Death Dealer series (Silke), from 1988
Freddy's Book (J. Gardner), 1980
Free Live Free (Wolfe), 1985
Friends in Time (Chetwin), 1992

Friendship Song (Springer), 1992
Frogs of War (Harman), 1994
From Death to the Stars (Hubbard), 1953
From Enchantery (Williamson), 1993
From the Realm of Morpheus (Millhauser), 1986
From the Teeth of Angels (J. Carroll), 1994
From Thief to King series (M. Williams), from 1990
From Time to Time (J. Finney), 1995
Frost (Bailey), 1983
Frost Dancers (Kilworth), 1992
Frost series (Bailey), from 1983
Frostflower series (Karr), from 1980
Frostwing (Knaak), 1995
Frozen City (Arscott and Marl), 1984
Frozen God (A. Wells, as Kirk), 1978
Frozen Waves (Vardeman), 1985
Full Moon (Mundy), 1935
Funny Papers (De Haven), 1985
Fur Magic (A. Norton), 1968
Further Adventures of Slugger McBatt (s Kinsella), 1988
Further Fables for Our Time (s Thurber), 1956

Galahad (Erskine), 1926
Galen Beknighted (M. Williams), 1990
Gallery of Children (Milne), 1925
Gallicenae (Anderson), 1987
Game of Dark (Mayne), 1971
Gandalara series (Garrett), from 1981
Garan the Eternal (s A. Norton), 1972
Garden of Echoes (Wall), 1988
Garden Under the Sea (Selden), 1957
Garrett series (G. Cook), from 1987
Garroc series (Berberick), from 1991
Gate of Darkness, Circle of Light (Huff), 1989
Gate of Ivrel (Cherryh), 1976
Gate of the Cat (A. Norton), 1987
Gates of Hell (Cherryh, Janet Morris), 1986
Gates of Lucifer series (Eshbach), from 1984
Gates of Noon (Rohan), 1992
Gathering of Gargoyles (Pierce), 1984
Gathering of Heroes (Zimmer), 1987
Gavin Black series (Jakes), from 1970
Gees series (Vivian, as Mann), 1937
Geis of the Gargoyle (Anthony), 1995
Gene Wolfe's Book of Days (s Wolfe), 1981
General in His Labyrinth (Marquez, appendix), 1990
Genevieve Undead (Yeovil), 1993
Genie of Sutton Place (Selden), 1973
Genius Loci (s S. Smith), 1948
Gerin the Fox series (Turtledove), from 1979
Ghost Abbey (Westall), 1988
Ghost Dance (Norman), 1970
Ghost Fox (s Yep), 1994
Ghost in the Mirror (Bellairs), 1993
Ghost King (Gemmell), 1988
Ghost Kings (Haggard), 1908
Ghost Light (s Leiber), 1984
Ghost of Thomas Kempe (Lively), 1973
Ghosts and Journeys (s Westall), 1988
Ghosts I Have Met (s Bangs), 1898
Ghosts of Manacle (s C. Finney), 1964

Ghosts of the Heaviside Layer (s Dunsany), 1980
Ghosts of Wind and Shadow (s de Lint), 1990
Ghostwood (de Lint), 1990
Giant of Inishkerry (Gilluly), 1992
Giant of World's End (L. Carter), 1969
Gideon Ahoy (Mayne), 1987
Gift of Wings (s Bach), 1974
Gifts of the Child Christ (s MacDonald), 1882
Giftwish (Martin), 1980
Gilden-Fire (Donaldson), 1981
Giles Goat-Boy (Barth), 1966
Ginger-Bread Man (s Baum), 1917
Girl and the Faun (s Phillpotts), 1916
Girl in a Swing (Adams), 1980
Girl Who Cried Flowers (s Yolen), 1974
Give Yourself a Fright (s Aiken), 1989
Gladiators of Hapanu (R. Green, as Lord), 1979
Glass Ball (Mayne), 1961
Glass Eyes and Cotton Strings (s de Lint), 1982
Glass of Dyskornis (Garrett), 1982
Glass Too Many (Vivian, as Mann), 1940
Glass Warrior (Vardeman), 1989
Glastonbury Romance (J. Powys), 1932
Glinda of Oz (Baum), 1920
Glitterspike Hall (Jefferies), 1989
Gloria (Viereck), 1952
Gloriana (Moorcock), 1978
Glorious Pool (T. Smith), 1934
Gnole (Boyett), 1991
Gnome Man's Land (Friesner), 1991
Gnome There Was (s Kuttner and C.L. Moore, as Padgett), 1950
Gnome's Engine (Edgerton), 1991
Goat Without Horns (Swann), 1971
Gobbling Billy (s Mayne, as James), 1959
Goblin Mirror (Cherryh), 1992
Goblin series (Edgerton), from 1991
Goblin Tower (de Camp), 1968
God Killer (Simon Green), 1991
God of the Invincibly Strong Arms series (Abdullah), from 1915
God Stalk (Hodgell), 1982
Godbond (Springer), 1988
Goddess Under Siege (s Salmonson), 1992
Godmother (Scarborough), 1994
Gods Abide (Swann), 1976
Gods and Their Makers (Housman), 1897
Gods in Anger (Adrian Cole), 1988
Gods, Men, and Ghosts (s Dunsany), 1972
Gods of Bel-Sagoth (s Howard), 1979
Gods of Ireland series (Flint), from 1991
Gods of Pegana (s Dunsany), 1905
Godslayer (Reichert), 1987
Godwars series (A. Wells), from 1991
Gog (Sinclair), 1967
Going Home (Pain), 1921
Gold of Fairnilee (Lang), 1888
Gold Unicorn (T. Lee), 1994
Goldcamp Vampire (Scarborough), 1987
Golden Age (s Grahame), 1895
Golden Barge (Moorcock), 1979
Golden Horn (Tarr), 1985

Golden Island (Phillpotts), 1938
Golden Naginata (Salmonson), 1982
Golden Steed (R. Green, as Lord), 1975
Golden Swan (Springer), 1983
Golden Trillium (A. Norton), 1993
Golden Wings (s W. Morris), 1976
Golem in the Gears (Anthony), 1986
Gom series (Chetwin), from 1986
Gondar (Luard), 1988
Good Omens (Pratchett), 1990
Goose on Your Grave (s Aiken), 1987
Gor series (Norman), from 1966
Gord the Rogue series (Gygax), from 1987
Gorgon (s T. Lee), 1985
Gormenghast (Peake), 1950
Gossamer Axe (Baudino), 1990
Grail and the Ring (Edgerton), 1994
Grail of Hearts (Shwartz), 1992
Grail War (Monaco), 1979
Grailblazers (Holt), 1994
Grandmaster (Cochran), 1984
Grass Rope (Mayne), 1957
Grass Tower (S. Murphy), 1976
Gray Magic (A. Norton), 1967
Graymantle (Morressy), 1981
Great Alta series (Yolen), from 1988
Great Chewing-Gum Rescue (s Mahy), 1982
Great Days (s Barthelme), 1979
Great Divorce (C.S. Lewis), 1946
Great Hunt (Jordan), 1990
Great Millionaire Kidnap (Mahy), 1975
Great Piratical Rumbustification (Mahy), 1978
Great Quillow (s Thurber), 1944
Great Tain series (Stephens), from 1923
Great Victorian Collection (B. Moore), 1975
Great Wheel (Gregorian), 1987
Greater Trumps (C. Williams), 1932
Green Flash (s Aiken), 1971
Green Hydra (Gygax), 1985
Green Isle of the Great Deep (Gunn), 1944
Green Knight (Chapman), 1975
Green Knowe series (Boston), from 1954
Green Lacquer Pavilion (Beauclerk), 1926
Green Lion series (Edgerton), from 1989
Green Magic (s Vance), 1979
Green Man (Abbey), 1989
Green Pearl (Vance), 1985
Green Phoenix (Swann), 1972
Green Star series (L. Carter), from 1972
Green Thoughts (s Collier), 1932
Greenbriar Queen series (Gilluly), from 1988
Greenmantle (de Lint), 1988
Greenwitch (S. Cooper), 1974
Grendel (J. Gardner), 1971
Grey Gentlemen (Ende, appendix), 1974
Grey God Passes (s Howard), 1975
Grey Horse (MacAvoy), 1987
Grey King (S. Cooper), 1975
Grey Mane of Morning (Chant), 1977
Grey Shapes (Vivian, as Mann), 1937
Greyfax Grimwald (Hancock), 1977

Greyhawk Adventures series (Gygax), from 1985
Greyhawk series (Estes), from 1987
Greylady (Morwood), 1993
Grim Land (s Howard), 1976
Grimus (Rushdie), 1975
Grunts! (Gentle), 1992
Gryphon in Glory (A. Norton), 1981
Gryphon King (Deitz), 1989
Gryphon's Eyrie (A. Norton), 1984
Guard Against Dishonor (Simon Green), 1991
Guardians (Abbey), 1982
Guardians of the Coral Throne (R. Green, as Lord), 1976
Guardians of the House (Boston), 1974
Guardians of the Tall Stones (Caldecott), 1986
Guardians of the West (Eddings), 1987
Guards! Guards! (Pratchett), 1989
Gub Gub's Book (s Lofting), 1932
Gudgekin the Thistle Girl (s J. Gardner), 1976
Gulf (Westall), 1992
Gulliver of Mars (Arnold), 1964
Guns of Avalon (Zelazny), 1972
Gwalchmai series (Munn), from 1966
Gypsy (Brust, Lindholm), 1992

Hag's Tapestry (s Salmonson), 1984
Half a Glass of Moonshine (Martin), 1988
Half Magic series (Eager), from 1954
Halfblood Chronicles (Lackey), from 1991
Halfling's Gem (Salvatore), 1990
Hall of the Mountain King (Tarr), 1986
Hall of Whispers (Jefferies), 1990
Hamlet Had an Uncle (Cabell), 1940
Hammer of the Sun (Rohan), 1988
Hand of Chaos (Weis), 1993
Hand of Lazarus (Cochran), 1988
Hand of Mary Constable (Gallico), 1964
Hand of Oberon (Zelazny), 1976
Handful of Men series (Duncan), from 1992
Hands of Llyr (A. Norton), 1994
Hanging Stones (Wellman), 1982
Happy Hypocrite (s Beerbohm), 1897
Happy Prince (s Wilde), 1888
Harding's Luck (Nesbit), 1909
Harem of Aman Akbar (Scarborough), 1984
Harker, Kay series (Masefield), from 1927
Harlot's Ruse (Friesner), 1986
Harmless Ghosts (s Salmonson), 1990
Harm's Way (Greenland), 1993
Haroun and the Sea of Stories (Rushdie), 1990
Harp and the Blade (Myers), 1941
Harp of Fishbones (s Aiken), 1972
Harp of Imach Thyssel (Wrede), 1985
Harp of the Grey Rose (de Lint), 1985
Harp of Winds (Furey), 1994
Harpist in the Wind (McKillip), 1979
Harpy High (Friesner), 1991
Harpy Thyme (Anthony), 1994
Harpy's Flight (Lindholm), 1983
Harrowing of Gwynedd (Kurtz), 1989

Harry Cat's Pet Puppy (Selden), 1974
Harry Kitten and Tucker Mouse (Selden), 1986
Hart's Hope (Card), 1983
Hasan (Anthony), 1977
Hatrack River (Card), 1989
Haunted Woman (Lindsay), 1922
Haunting (Mahy), 1982
Haunting of Chas McGill (s Westall), 1983
Haunting of Jessica Raven (Halam), 1994
Haunting of Lamb House (Aiken), 1991
Haven (Diamond), 1977
Haven series (Diamond), from 1977
Hawk and Fisher series (Simon Green), from 1990
Hawk in Silver (Gentle), 1977
Hawk of May (Bradshaw), 1980
Hawkline Monster (Brautigan), 1974
Hawkmoon series (Moorcock), from 1967
Hawk's Grey Feather (Kennealy-Morrison), 1990
Hawks of Outremer (s Howard), 1979
He (Lang), 1887
Headhunter (Findley), 1993
Heads of Cerberus (Stevens), 1952
Headswoman (s Grahame), 1898
Healer's War (Scarborough), 1989
Heart of Shadows (Williamson), 1994
Heart of the World (Haggard), 1895
Heart Readers (Rusch), 1993
Heart-Beast (T. Lee), 1992
Hearts of Wood (s Kotzwinkle), 1986
Heaven and Hell and the Megas Factor (Nathan), 1975
Heaven Cent (Anthony), 1988
Heavenly Horse from the Outermost West (Stanton), 1988
Hedgework and Guessery (s de Lint), 1991
Heir of Rengarth (Douglas), 1988
Heir of Sea and Fire (McKillip), 1977
Heirs of Saint Camber series (Kurtz), from 1989
Heirs to Byzantium series (Shwartz), from 1987
Heirs to Gnarlsmyre series (Jefferies), from 1989
Helene (Mundy), 1967
Helen's Lovers (s Bullett), 1932
Hell series (Cherryh, Janet Morris), from 1986
Hellhound Magic (Sharon Green), 1989
Helma (Mundy), 1967
Her Majesty's Wizard (Stasheff), 1986
Her Ways Are Death (Vivian, as Mann), 1941
Heralds of Valdemar series (Lackey), from 1987
Here Abide Monsters (A. Norton), 1973
Here Be Demons (Friesner), 1988
Here Comes the Sun (Holt), 1993
Here There Be Dragons (s Zelazny), 1992
Here There Be Dragons (s Yolen), 1993
Herma (M. Harris), 1981
Hero and the Crown (McKinley), 1985
Hero of Washington Square (Estes), 1983
Heroes and Villains (A. Carter), 1969
Heroes, or Greek Fairy Tales for My Children (s Kingsley), 1856
Heroine of the World (T. Lee), 1989
Heroing (ab Hugh), 1987
Herr Nightingale and the Satin Woman (Kotzwinkle), 1978
Herself (Sampson), 1992
Heu-Heu (Haggard), 1924

Hex Witch of Seldom (Springer), 1988
Hexwood (D. Jones), 1993
Hidden City (de Lint), 1990
Hidden City (Eddings), 1994
Hidden Doors (s Gunn), 1929
Hidden Echoes (Jefferies), 1992
Hidden Land (Dean), 1986
Hidden Ones (Halam), 1988
Hidden Player (s Noyes), 1924
Hidden Realms (Sharon Green), 1993
High King (L. Alexander), 1968
High Place (Cabell), 1923
High Priest (Cochran), 1987
High Sorcery (s A. Norton), 1970
High Wizardry (Duane), 1990
Higher Things (Michael Harrison), 1945
Highroad series (Rasmussen), from 1990
Hill Road (Mayne), 1969
Hills of the Dead (s Howard), 1979
Himalaya (Luard), 1992
His Conquering Sword (Rasmussen, as Elliott), 1993
His Monkey Wife (Collier), 1930
Histories of King Kelson series (Kurtz), from 1984
History of Middle-Earth (s Tolkien), 1983-84
History of the Runestaff (Moorcock), 1979
Hobberdy Dick (Briggs), 1955
Hobbit (Tolkien), 1937
Hoboken Chicken Emergency (Pinkwater), 1977
Hogfoot Right and Bird-Hands (s Kilworth), 1993
Holger Danske series (Anderson), from 1961
Hollow Hills (Stewart), 1973
Hollow Land (s W. Morris), 1903
Hollowing (Holdstock), 1993
Holy Flower (Haggard), 1915
Homeland (Salvatore), 1990
Homeward Bounders (D. Jones), 1981
Homunculus (Blaylock), 1986
Honorable Barbarian (de Camp), 1989
Hook (Brooks), 1992
Hooray for Hellywood (Friesner), 1990
Hordes of the Red Butcher (Page, as Stockbridge), 1975
Horn Crown (A. Norton), 1981
Horned Warrior (Holdstock, as Carlsen), 1979
Horrible Story (s Mahy), 1987
Horse and His Boy (C.S. Lewis), 1954
Horse Goddess (Llywelyn), 1982
Horse Lords series (Morwood), from 1983
Horsegirl (Ash), 1988
Horses of Heaven (Bradshaw), 1991
Horse's Tale (s Twain), 1907
Horsewoman in Godsland (C. Edwards), 1987
Hot Jazz Trio (s Kotzwinkle), 1989
Hound and the Falcon series (Tarr), from 1985
Hound of Culain (Flint), 1986
Hounds of God (Tarr), 1986
Hounds of the Morrigan (O'Shea), 1985
Hour of the Gate (Foster), 1984
Hour of the Thin Ox (Greenland), 1987
House at Pooh Corner (Milne), 1928
House in Norham Gardens (Lively), 1974
House Inside Out (Lively), 1987

House Mother (Owen), 1929
House of Arden (Nesbit), 1908
House of Joy (s Housman), 1895
House of Pomegranates (s Wilde), 1891
House of Shadows (A. Norton), 1984
House of the Vampire (Viereck), 1907
House on Fairmont (s Mayne), 1968
House that Grew (Boston), 1969
House That Wouldn't Go Away (Gallico), 1979
House With a Clock in Its Walls (Bellairs), 1973
House-boat on the Styx series (Bangs), from 1895
How Are the Mighty Fallen (Swann), 1974
How St. Patrick Saves the Irish (s Stephens), 1931
Howl series (D. Jones), from 1986
Hrolf Kraki's Saga (Anderson), 1973
Human Age series (W. Lewis), from 1928
Human Tragedy (s France, appendix), 1917
Humorous Stories (Pain), 1930
Humour and Fantasy (Anstey), 1931
Hundredth Dove (s Yolen), 1977
Hunter series (Estes), from 1990
Hunter Victorious (Estes), 1992
Hunter's Haunt (Duncan), 1995
Hunter's Moon (Kilworth), 1989
Hunting Wolf (John Grant), 1990
Huon of the Horn (A. Norton), 1951
Hurok of the Stone Age (L. Carter), 1981
Husband for Kutani (s Owen), 1938

I Love Galesburg in the Springtime (s J. Finney), 1963
Ice Dragon (Gygax), 1985
Ice Dragon (R. Green, as Lord), 1974
Ice Is Coming (Wrightson), 1977
Ice King (Rohan; Scott, as Scot), 1986
Ice Monkey (s M. John Harrison), 1983
Icedragon (Knaak), 1989
Idylls of the Queen (Karr), 1982
If at Faust You Don't Succeed (Zelazny), 1993
If Cats Could Fly . . . ? (Westall), 1990
If on a Winter's Night a Traveller (Calvino, appendix), 1981
Ill Met in Lankhmar (Leiber), 1990
Ill-Made Knight (T.H. White), 1940
Illearth War (Donaldson), 1977
Illusion (Volsky), 1991
Illusionists (Miller), 1991
Illusions (Bach), 1977
Illustrated Gods of the North (s Howard), 1977
Illyrian Adventure (L. Alexander), 1986
Imaro series (Saunders), from 1981
Immortal Blood (Hambly), 1988
Immortal of World's End (L. Carter), 1976
Imperial Lady (A. Norton, Shwartz), 1989
Imperial Light (Corran), 1994
Impossible Things (s Willis), 1994
In a Lonely Place (s Wagner), 1983
In Brief Authority (Anstey), 1915
In Camera (s Westall), 1993
In Evil Hour (Marquez, appendix), 1979
In Mask and Motley (s de Lint), 1983
In Regard to the Opening of Doors (s Munn), 1979
In Sylvan Shadows (Salvatore), 1992

Jovial Ghosts (T. Smith), 1933
Joy in Our Cause (s Emshwiller), 1974
Jungle Book (s Kipling), 1894
Jungle Girl (Burroughs), 1932
Junior Thunder Lord (s Yep), 1993
Jupiter in the Chair (Fraser), 1958
Jurgen (Cabell), 1919
Just So Stories for Little Children (s Kipling), 1902
Juxtaposition (Anthony), 1982

Kai Lung series (Bramah), from 1922
Kala (Luard), 1990
Kane series (Wagner), from 1970
Kate Crackernuts (Briggs), 1963
Kaz the Minotaur (Knaak), 1990
Kedrigern series (Morressy), from 1986
Keeper of Cats (Boyer), 1995
Keeper of the City (Duane, Morwood), 1989
Keeper of the Keys (Wurts), 1988
Keepers of Edanvant (Douglas), 1987
Kellory the Warlock (L. Carter), 1984
Kelpie (s Mayne), 1987
Kelvin Rud series (Anthony), from 1987
Kencyrath series (Hodgell), from 1982
Kesrick (L. Carter), 1982
Kestrel (L. Alexander), 1982
Key of Ice and Steel (Vardeman, as Moran), 1988
Key of the Field (s T.F. Powys), 1930
Keys to Paradise series (Vardeman), from 1986
Khalindaine (Burns), 1986
Kiai! (Anthony), 1974
Kidnapped Santa Claus (Baum), 1969
Kill the Dead (T. Lee), 1980
Killer Plants of Binaark (R. Green, as Lord), 1980
Kind and the Foolish (s Housman), 1952
Kine series (Lloyd), from 1982
King (Barthelme), 1990
King and the Mangoes (s Davis), 1975
King Arthur's Daughter (Chapman), 1976
King Beneath the Mountain (Charrette), 1995
King Beyond the Gate (Gemmell), 1985
King Chondos' Ride (Zimmer), 1982
King Death's Garden (Halam, as Jones), 1986
King Javan's Year (Kurtz), 1992
King Kobold (Stasheff), 1971
King Kull (s L. Carter, Howard), 1967
King Ludd (Sinclair), 1988
King of Elfland's Daughter (Dunsany), 1924
King of Light and Shadows (Adrian Cole), 1988
King of the Dead (MacAvoy), 1991
King of the Grey (Knaak), 1993
King of the Hummingbirds (s J. Gardner), 1977
King of the Murgos (Eddings), 1988
King of the Swords (Moorcock), 1971
King of the Wood (Roberts), 1983
King of the World's Edge (Munn), 1966
King of Ys series (Anderson), from 1986
King of Zunga (R. Green, as Lord), 1975
King Solomon's Mines (Haggard), 1885
King There Was (Vivian), 1926
King/Yasmini series (Mundy), from 1924

Kingdom and the Cave (Aiken), 1960
Kingdom of Evil (Hecht), 1924
Kingdom of Royth (R. Green, as Lord), 1974
Kingdom of Summer (Bradshaw), 1981
Kingdom under the Sea (s Aiken), 1971
Kingdoms of Elfin (s Warner), 1977
Kingdoms of the Night (Cole and Bunch), 1995
King's Blood Four (Tepper), 1983
King's Buccaneer (Feist), 1992
King's Damosel (Chapman), 1976
King's Daughter (Gaskell), 1958
Kings in Hell (Cherryh, Janet Morris), 1987
King's Indian (s J. Gardner), 1974
King's Justice (Kurtz), 1985
Kingsbane (Morressy), 1982
Kingslayer (Hubbard), 1949
Kinslayer Wars (Niles), 1991
Kipling's Fantasy (s Kipling), 1992
Kleinzeit (Hoban), 1974
Knight and Knave of Swords (s Leiber), 1988
Knight of Ghosts and Shadows (Lackey), 1990
Knight of Shadows (Zelazny), 1989
Knight of the Swords (Moorcock), 1971
Knight's Castle (Eager), 1956
Knights of Dark Renown (Gemmell), 1989
Knot in the Grain (s McKinley), 1994
Kothar series (Fox), from 1969
Krishna (Frith), 1985
Krispos series (Turtledove), from 1991
Krokodil Tears (Yeovil), 1991
Krull (Foster), 1983
Kull series (Howard), from 1967
Kyala series (Easton), from 1985
Kylix series (L. Carter), from 1971
Kyrik series (Fox), from 1875

Labyrinth Gate (Rasmussen), 1988
Labyrinth of Worlds (Adrian Cole), 1990
Labyrinths (Borges, appendix), 1964
Lad and the Lion (Burroughs), 1938
Ladies of Mandrigyn (Hambly), 1984
Lady and the Merman (s Yolen), 1977
Lady Blade, Lord Fighter (Sharon Green), 1987
Lady into Fox (D. Garnett), 1922
Lady of Darkness (Paxson), 1983
Lady of Han-Gilen (Tarr), 1987
Lady of Darkness (Paxson), 1990
Lady of Light (Paxson), 1982
Lady of the Bees (Swann), 1976
Lady of the Haven (Diamond), 1978
Lady of the Heavens (Haggard), 1908
Lady of the Mansion (MacDonald), 1983
Lady of the Snowmist (Offutt), 1983
Lady of the Terraces (Vivian), 1925
Lady with Feet of Gold (Dwyer), 1937
Laird and the Lady (Joan Grant), 1949
Lake of Fire (Bailey), 1989
Lammas Night (Kurtz), 1983
Lamp from the Warlock's Tomb (Bellairs), 1988.
Land Beyond the Gate (Eshbach), 1984
Land of Dreams (Blaylock), 1987

Lord of Chaos (Jordan), 1994
Lord of Middle Air (Rohan), 1994
Lord of Nightmares (Adrian Cole), 1975
Lord of No Time (L. Cooper), 1977
Lord of the Crooked Paths (Adkins), 1987
Lord of the Dead (s Howard), 1981
Lord of the Horizon (Joan Grant), 1943
Lord of the Rings series (Tolkien), from 1954
Lord of the Troll-Bats (Gilliland), 1992
Lord of the Two Lands (Tarr), 1993
Lords and Ladies (Pratchett), 1992
Lords of Destruction (Silke), 1989
Lords of Doom (Niles), 1986
Lords of the Crimson River (R. Green, as Lord), 1981
Lords of the Shadows (Holdstock, as Kirk), 1979
Lords of the Sky (A. Wells), 1994
Lords of the Stoney Mountains (Swithin), 1991
Lords of the Sword (H. Cook), 1991
Lore of the Witch World (s A. Norton), 1980
Loremasters of Elundium series (Jefferies), from 1986
Lorestone of Varetta (John Grant), 1993
Loser's Night (s Anderson), 1991
Lost and the Lurking (Wellman), 1981
Lost City of Zork (Bailey), 1991
Lost Crown (Gemmell), 1989
Lost Domain (Hocke), 1993
Lost Horizon (Hilton), 1933
Lost in the Funhouse (s Barth), 1968
Lost Prince (Wood), 1992
Lost Prince (Zimmer), 1982
Lost Princess of Oz (Baum), 1917
Lost Road (s Tolkien), 1987
Lost Swords series (Saberhagen), from 1986
Lost Valley of Iskander (s Howard), 1974
Lost World of Time (L. Carter), 1969
Lost Worlds (s L. Carter), 1980
Lost Worlds (s S. Smith), 1944
Love & Sleep (Crowley), 1994
Love Eternal (Haggard), 1918
Love in the Time of Cholera (Marquez, appendix), 1988
Love of the Foolish Angel (Beauclerk), 1929
Loves of Lo-Foh (Owen, as Williams), 1936
Low Tide (s Mayne), 1993
Luana (Foster), 1974
Luck in the Head (s M. John Harrison), 1993
Luck of Relian Kru (Volsky), 1987
Luck of the Wheels (Lindholm), 1989
Lud of Lunden (Mundy), 1976
Lud-in-the-Mist (Mirrlees), 1926
Lure of the Basilisk (Watt-Evans), 1980
Lycanthia, or The Children of Wolves (T. Lee), 1981
Lyonesse series (Vance), from 1983
Lyra series (Wrede), from 1982
Lythande (s Bradley), 1986

Mace of Souls (Fergusson), 1989
Macedon series (Gemmell), from 1991
Mad Empress of Callisto (L. Carter), 1975
Mad God's Amulet (Moorcock), 1969
Madame Fears the Dark (s M. Irwin), 1935
Madame Two Swords (T. Lee), 1988

Madbond (Springer), 1987
Madouc (Vance), 1989
Madwand (Zelazny), 1981
Mage Storms series (Lackey), from 1994
Mage Wars series (Lackey), from 1994
Mage Winds series (Lackey), from 1992
Mage-born Child (Wylie), 1988
Magic Bed-Knob (M. Norton), 1943
Magic by the Lake (Eager), 1957
Magic Camera (Pinkwater), 1974
Magic Casement (Duncan), 1990
Magic Casements (M. Alexander), 1989
Magic City (Nesbit), 1910
Magic Cloak (s Baum), 1916
Magic Engineer (Modesitt), 1994
Magic Kingdom For Sale/Sold! (Brooks), 1986
Magic Kingdom of Landover series (Brooks), from 1986
Magic of Oz (Baum), 1919
Magic of Recluce (Modesitt), 1991
Magic or Not? (Eager), 1959
Magic series (A. Norton), from 1965
Magic Spectacles (Blaylock), 1991
Magic Stone (Farmer), 1964
Magic Three of Solatia (Yolen), 1974
Magician (Feist), 1982
Magician Out of Manchuria (C. Finney), 1968
Magician's Gambit (Eddings), 1983
Magician's Nephew (C.S. Lewis), 1955
Magicians of Caprona (D. Jones), 1980
Magicians of the Night (Hambly), 1992
Magicnet (DeChancie), 1994
Magic's Pawn (Lackey), 1989
Magic's Price (Lackey), 1990
Magic's Promise (Lackey), 1990
Magog (Sinclair), 1972
Mahatma and the Hare (Haggard), 1911
Mahy Magic (s Mahy), 1986
Maia (Adams), 1984
Mairelon the Magician (Wrede), 1991
Maiwa's Revenge (Haggard), 1888
Majyk series (Friesner), from 1993
Maker of Shadows (Vivian, as Mann), 1938
Malady of Magicks (C. Gardner), 1986
Malafrena (Le Guin), 1979
Malloreon series (Eddings), from 1987
Man from Mundania (Anthony), 1989
Man from the North Pole (s Mayne), 1963
Man in the Zoo (D. Garnett), 1924
Man of His Word series (Duncan), from 1990
Man Rides Through (Donaldson), 1987
Man Who Ate the Phoenix (s Dunsany), 1949
Man Who Missed the 'Bus (s Benson), 1928
Man Who Tricked a Ghost (s Yep), 1993
Man Who Was Magic (Gallico), 1966
Man Who Was Thursday (Chesterton), 1908
Man Whose Mother Was a Pirate (Mahy), 1972
Manalive (Chesterton), 1912
Mandricardo (L. Carter), 1987
Mansion in the Mist (Bellairs), 1992
Manxmouse (Gallico), 1968
Many Dimensions (C. Williams), 1931

Many Moons (s Thurber), 1943
Marchers of Valhalla (s Howard), 1972
Marco Polo and the Sleeping Beauty (Davidson, Davis), 1988
Marden Fee (Bullett), 1931
Marianne series (Tepper), from 1985
Marie (Haggard), 1912
Mariel of Redwall (Jacques), 1991
Marion's Wall (J. Finney), 1973
Mark of the Cat (A. Norton), 1992
Marrakesh series (Diamond), from 1981
Marrow of the World (Nichols), 1972
Marshworld (Lloyd), 1990
Martin the Warrior (Jacques), 1993
Marvelous Land of Oz (Baum), 1904
Marvelous Misadventures of Sebastian (L. Alexander), 1970
Mask for the General (Goldstein), 1987
Mask of Circe (Kuttner, C.L. Moore), 1971
Mask of the Sorcerer (Schweitzer), 1995
Master (L. Cooper), 1987
Master Key (Baum), 1901
Master Li and Number Ten Ox series (Hughart), from 1984
Master of Earth and Water (Paxson), 1993
Master of Hawks (Bushyager), 1979
Master of the Death Madness (Page, as Stockbridge), 1980
Master of the Fearful Depths (Adkins), 1989
Master of the Five Magics (Hardy), 1980
Master of the Hashomi (R. Green, as Lord), 1978
Master of the Sidhe (Flint), 1985
Master of Whitestorm (Wurts), 1992
Master Wolf (Estes), 1987
Masters of Glass (Easton), 1985
Masters of the Dark Gate (Jakes), 1970
Mating of the Blades (Abdullah), 1920
Matthew's Dragon (S. Cooper), 1991
Mattimeo (Jacques), 1989
Mavin Manyshaped series (Tepper), from 1985
Max's Dream (s Mayne), 1977
Maze of Moonlight (Baudino), 1993
Meaning of Life (s Schweitzer), 1988
Medallion of the Black Hound (S. Murphy), 1989
Medusa Child (Germain, appendix), 1994
Medusa Frequency (Hoban), 1987
Member of the Marsh (s Mayne), 1956
Memory (Mahy), 1987
Memory and Dream (de Lint), 1994
Memory, Sorrow and Thorn series (T. Williams), from 1988
Men at Arms (Pratchett), 1993
Mention My Name in Atlantis (Jakes), 1972
Mephistopheles (Bangs), 1889
Merlin (Lawhead), 1988
Merlin (Nye), 1978
Merlin and the Last Trump (Webber), 1993
Merlin Dreams in the Moondream Wood (s de Lint), 1992
Merlin series (Stewart), from 1970
Merlin's Bones (Saberhagen), 1995
Merlin's Booke (s Yolen), 1986
Merlin's Godson (Munn), 1976
Merlin's Ring (Munn), 1974
Merlin's Wood (Holdstock), 1994
Mermaid's Three Wisdoms (Yolen), 1978
Merman's Children (Anderson), 1979

Metal Angel (Springer), 1994
Metal Monster (Merritt), 1946
Mezentian Gate (Eddison), 1958
Mia (Nathan), 1970
Mickelsson's Ghosts (J. Gardner), 1982
Midnight Blue (Fisk), 1990
Midnight Folk (Masefield), 1927
Midnight Is a Place (Aiken), 1974
Midnight's Children (Rushdie), 1981
Midnight's Sun (Kilworth), 1990
Midsummer Tempest (Anderson), 1974
Mind Wizards of Callisto (L. Carter), 1975
Mindbond (Springer), 1987
Minerva Wakes (Lisle), 1994
Miniature (Phillpotts), 1926
Minikins of Yam (Swann), 1976
Minotaur series (Swann), from 1966
Miracle in the Rain (Hecht), 1943
Mirage (L. Cooper), 1987
Mirror in the Mirror (Ende, appendix), 1986
Mirror of Her Dreams (Donaldson), 1986
Misenchanted Sword (Watt-Evans), 1985
Misplaced Legion (Turtledove), 1987
Miss Carter and the Ifrit (Kerby), 1945
Miss Hargreaves (Baker), 1940
Miss Lucifer (Fraser), 1939
Mission of Magic (J. Smith), 1991
Mrs. Discombobulous (Mahy), 1969
Mr. Allenby Loses the Way (Baker), 1945
Mr. Bliss (s Tolkien), 1982
Mr. Bonaparte of Corsica (Bangs), 1895
Mr. Godly Beside Himself (Bullett), 1924
Mr. Kronion (Kerby), 1949
Mr. Munchausen (s Bangs), 1901
Mr. Pye (Peake), 1953
Mr. Weston's Good Wine (T.F. Powys), 1927
Mistress Masham's Repose (T.H. White), 1946
Mistress of Death (Anthony), 1974
Mistress of Jewels (Paxson), 1991
Mistress of Mistresses (Eddison), 1935
Mistress of the Empire (Feist, Wurts), 1992
Mists of Avalon (Bradley), 1982
Mists of Doom (Offutt), 1977
Mists of the Ages (Sharon Green), 1988
Mockery Gap (T.F. Powys), 1925
Mode series (Anthony), from 1991
Moment of the Magician (Foster), 1984
Moment Under the Moment (s Hoban), 1992
Momo (Ende, appendix), 1984
Monday, Anthony series (Bellairs), from 1978
Monster of the Prophecy (s S. Smith), 1983
Monstre Gai, Malign Fiesta (W. Lewis), 1955
Montezuma's Daughter (Haggard), 1893
Moon Called (A. Norton), 1982
Moon Dreams (Strickland), 1988
Moon in Hiding (Edgerton), 1989
Moon Is a Meadow (s de Lint), 1980
Moon, Jeremy series (Strickland), from 1988
Moon Magic series (A. Norton), from 1966
Moon Mirror (s A. Norton), 1988
Moon of Gomrath (Garner), 1963

Moon of Much Gladness (Bramah), 1932
Moon of Three Rings (A. Norton), 1966
Moon Pool (Merritt), 1919
Moon Ribbon (s Yolen), 1976
Moonbane Mage (Marks), 1990
Moonbird (Davis), 1986.
Moonblood (Williamson), 1994
Moon-Dark (Wrightson), 1987
Moondust (Swann), 1968
Moonheart series (de Lint), from 1984
Moon's Fire-Eating Daughter (Myers), 1981
Moon's Revenge (Aiken), 1987
Moonset (L. Cooper), 1995
Moonshine & Clover (s Housman), 1922
Moor's Last Sigh (Rushdie), 1995
Moorstones (Adrian Cole), 1982.
Mopsa the Fairy (Ingelow), 1869
Mordant's Need series (Donaldson), from 1986
More Than You Bargained For (s Aiken), 1955
Morgaine series (Cherryh), from 1976
Morgoth's Ring (s Tolkien), 1993
Morning Star (Haggard), 1910
Morningstar (Gemmell), 1992
Morreion (s Vance), 1979
Mort (Pratchett), 1987
Mortal Mask (Marley), 1991
Mortuary (s S. Smith), 1971
Morwyn (J. Powys), 1937
Mossflower (Jacques), 1988
Most Ancient Song (Flint, as Flynn), 1991
Mother Goose in Prose (s Baum), 1897
Mother of Pearl (s France, appendix), 1908
Mother of Storms (Adrian Cole), 1989
Mouldy (s Mayne), 1983
Mountain of Mirrors (Estes), 1982
Mountains and Madness (Estes), 1993
Mountains of Brega (R. Green, as Lord), 1976
Mountains of Channadran (Dexter), 1986
Mouse and His Child (Hoban), 1967
Mouse and the Egg (s Mayne), 1980
Mouvar's Magic (Anthony), 1992
Moving Pictures (Pratchett), 1990
Mulengro (de Lint), 1985
Multitude of Monsters (C. Gardner), 1986
Mummy, the Will, and the Crypt (Bellairs), 1983
Murder and Magic (s Garrett), 1979
Museum of Cheats (s Warner), 1947
Music from Behind the Moon (s Cabell), 1926
Mustapha and His Wise Dog (Friesner), 1985
My First Two Thousand Years (Viereck), 1928
My Lord Barbarian (Offutt), 1977
My Own Fairy Book (s Lang), 1895
My World—and Welcome to It (s Thurber), 1942
Mysteries of Asia (s Abdullah), 1935
Mysterious Doom (s Salmonson), 1993
Mysterious Stranger (s Twain), 1916
Mystery of Khufu's Tomb (Mundy), 1933
Mystic Women (s Salmonson), 1991
Myth series (Asprin), from 1978
Mythago series (Holdstock), from 1984

Myths of the Sacred Tree (s Caldecott), 1993

Nada the Lily (Haggard), 1892
Name of the Game (Estes), 1988
Name to Conjure With (Aamodt), 1989
Naming the Dark (Dalton), 1992
Nargun and the Stars (Wrightson), 1973
Narnia series (C.S. Lewis), from 1950
Nazhuret of Sordaling series (MacAvoy), from 1990
Necklace of Raindrops (s Aiken), 1968
Necromancer Nine (Tepper), 1983
Nedao series (Emerson), from 1987
Nemesis (L. Cooper), 1988
Neptune Rising (s Yolen), 1982
Never Deal With a Dragon (Charrette), 1990
Never Trust an Elf (Charrette), 1992
Neverending Story (Ende, appendix), 1983
Nevèryon series (Delany), from 1979
Nevernever (Shetterly), 1993
New Calling (Jean Morris), 1992
New Gulliver (s Pain), 1913
New Magic (Jean Morris), 1990
New Moon (Snyder), 1989
New Waggings of Old Tales (s Bangs, as Two Wags), 1888
New Wonderland (Baum), 1900
New York by Knight (Friesner), 1986
Nifft the Lean (Shea), 1982
Night Arrant (s Gygax), 1987
Night in the Lonesome October (Zelazny), 1993
Night in the Netherhells (C. Gardner), 1987
Night Life of the Gods (T. Smith), 1931
Night Mare (Anthony), 1983
Night Masks (Salvatore), 1992
Night Maze (Dalton), 1989
Night Moves (s Powers), 1986
Night of Amber (Germain, appendix), 1994
Night of Wishes (Ende, appendix), 1992
Night Outside (Wrightson), 1979
Night Relics (Blaylock), 1994
Night Winds (s Wagner), 1978
Nightbirds on Nantucket (Aiken), 1966
Nightfall series (Taylor), from 1992
Nightingale (Dalkey), 1988
Nightmare Farm (Vivian, as Mann), 1937
Nightmare Has Triplets series (Cabell), from 1934
Nightpool (S. Murphy), 1985
Nights at the Circus (A. Carter), 1984
Night's Black Agents (s Leiber), 1947
Night's Daughter (Bradley), 1985
Night's Master (T. Lee), 1978
Night's Sorceries (s T. Lee), 1987
Nightshades (s T. Lee), 1993
Night-Threads series (Emerson), from 1990
Nightwatch (Bailey), 1990
Nine Gods of Safaddne (Swithin), 1993
Nine Lives (L. Alexander), 1963
Nine Lives of Catseye Gomez (Hawke), 1991
Nine Princes in Amber (Zelazny), 1970
Nine Unknown (Mundy), 1924
Ninja's Revenge (Anthony), 1975
Ninth Life (Vivian, as Mann), 1939

No Boundaries (s Kuttner, C.L. Moore), 1955
No Haven for the Guilty (Simon Green), 1990
No One Writes to the Colonel (Marquez, appendix), 1968
No Painted Plumage (s T.F. Powys), 1934
Nocturne (L. Cooper), 1989
Non-Existent Knight (Calvino, appendix), 1962
Nonstop Nonsense (Mahy), 1977
Northern Girl (Lynn), 1980
Northwest of Earth (s C.L. Moore), 1954
Northwest Smith (s C.L. Moore), 1982
Not After Midnight (s M. Alexander), 1985
Not For All the Gold in Ireland (James), 1968
Not Wanted on the Voyage (Findley), 1984
Not What You Expected (s Aiken), 1974
Nothing Sacred (Scarborough), 1991
Nothing Said (Boston), 1971
Notorious Abbess (s Chapman), 1993
Not-World (Swann), 1975
Novels of Crystal series (Huff), from 1988
Novelty (s Crowley), 1989
Nowhere (Berger), 1985
Nude in the Mirror (Viereck), 1953
Nul's Quest (Strickland), 1989

Oak Above the Kings (Kennealy-Morrison), 1994
Oak and the Ram (Moorcock), 1973
Oak King's Daughter (s de Lint), 1979
Oath and the Measure (M. Williams), 1991
Oath of Gold (Moon), 1989
Oath to Mida (Sharon Green), 1983
Oathbound (Lackey), 1988
Oathbound Wizard (Stasheff), 1993
Oathbreakers (Lackey), 1989
Octagon Magic (A. Norton), 1967
October's Baby (G. Cook), 1980
Of Demons and Darkness (s Collier), 1965
Of Other Worlds (s C.S. Lewis), 1966
Ogre Downstairs (D. Jones), 1974
Ogre, Ogre (Anthony), 1982
Old Gods Waken (Wellman), 1979
Old Man on a Horse (Westall), 1989
Old Tin Sorrows (G. Cook), 1989
Old Ugly Face (Mundy), 1940
Old Zion (s Mayne), 1966
Older Kind of Magic (Wrightson), 1972
Olympiad (Frith), 1988
Olympian Nights (Bangs), 1902
Om: The Secret of Ahbor Valley (Mundy), 1924
Omara series (Adrian Cole), from 1986
Ommony series (Mundy), from 1924
On a Pale Horse (Anthony), 1984
On All Hallows' Eve (Chetwin), 1984
On Raven's Wing (Llywelyn), 1990
On Stranger Tides (Powers), 1987
On the Boundaries of Darkness (Hancock), 1982
On the Seas of Destiny (Emerson), 1989
On the Stepping Stones (s Mayne), 1963
Once and Future King series (T.H. White), from 1958
Once on a Time (Milne), 1917
Once Upon a Time (Barth), 1994
Once Upon a Time (s Baum), 1916

One (Bach), 1988
One Before (Pain), 1902
One Hundred Years of Solitude (Marquez, appendix), 1967
One Land, One Duke (Emerson), 1992
One Tree (Donaldson), 1982
Only Begotten Daughter (Morrow), 1990
Only Penitent (s T.F. Powys), 1931
Only Toys! (Anstey), 1903
Only You Can Save Mankind (Pratchett), 1992
Operation Chaos (Anderson), 1971
Or All the Seas with Oysters (s Davidson), 1962
Oracle (H. Cook), 1989
Orchard of the Crescent Moon (Nimmo), 1989
Orc's Opal (Anthony), 1990
Order War (Modesitt), 1995
Original Dr. Shade (s Yeovil, as Newman), 1994
Orsinia series (Le Guin), from 1976
Oscar Lobster's Fair Exchange (Selden), 1966
Other (s Westall), 1985
Other Dimensions (s S. Smith), 1970
Other Inquisitions 1937-52 (Borges, appendix), 1964
Other Lands (Wylie), 1995
Other Sinbad (C. Gardner), 1991
Other Voices (Greenland), 1988
Otherworld (Flint), 1992
Ou Lu Khen and the Beautiful Madwoman (Salmonson), 1985
Our Lady of the Harbour (de Lint), 1991
Out of Phaze (Anthony), 1987
Out of Space and Time (s S. Smith), 1942
Out of the Dark World (Chetwin), 1985
Out of the Ordinary (Dalton), 1988
Out of the Silent Planet (C.S. Lewis), 1938
Out of This World (Watt-Evans), 1994
Outcast (L. Cooper), 1986
Outlaws of Sherwood (McKinley), 1988
Outside the Dog Museum (J. Carroll), 1991
Over Sea, Under Stone (S. Cooper), 1965
Over the Hills and Far Away (s Dunsany), 1974
Over the Hills and Far Away (Mayne), 1968
Over the Plum-pudding (s Bangs), 1901
Overlord of the Damned (Page, as Stockbridge), 1980
Overnight to Many Distant Cities (s Barthelme), 1983
Overtime (Holt), 1993
Owl of Athene (Phillpotts), 1936
Owl Service (Garner), 1967
Owl, The Duck (s J. Powys), 1930
Oz series (Baum), from 1900

Pagan Passions (Garrett), 1959
Paksenarrion series (Moon), from 1988
Palace of Kings (Jefferies), 1987
Paladin (Cherryh), 1988
Paladin of the Night (Weis), 1989
Pale Rider (Foster), 1985
Paleface and Redskin (s Anstey), 1898
Pan and the Twins (Phillpotts), 1922
Pangur Bán series (Sampson), from 1983
Panic Hand (s J. Carroll), 1995
Panther's Hoard (Berberick), 1994
Paper Canoe (Jean Morris), 1988
Paper Dragons (s Blaylock), 1986

Paper Grail (Blaylock), 1991
Paperjack (s de Lint), 1991
Paradise Tree (Paxson), 1987
Paradise War (Lawhead), 1991
Paradys series (T. Lee), from 1988
Parcel of Trees (s Mayne), 1963
Parsival series (Monaco), from 1977
Party Pants (s Mayne), 1977
Passage of Stars (Rasmussen), 1990
Passion (Winterson), 1987
Passion of New Eve (A. Carter), 1977
Passionate Witch (Matson, T. Smith), 1941
Past Eight O'Clock (s Aiken), 1986
Pastel City (M. John Harrison), 1971
Patchwork Cat (s Mayne), 1981
Patchwork Girl of Oz (Baum), 1913
Path of the Dragons (Jean Morris), 1980
Paths of the Perambulator (Foster), 1985
Pattern of Silver Strings (s de Lint), 1981
Pawn of Prophecy (Eddings), 1982
Peace (Wolfe), 1975
Peake's Progress (s Peake), 1978
Pearl of the Soul of the World (Pierce), 1990
Pedant and the Shuffly (Bellairs), 1968
Pellucidar series (Burroughs), from 1922
Pendragon Cycle (Lawhead), from 1987
Penelope's Man (Erskine), 1928
Penguin Island (France, appendix), 1909
Pentecost series (Corbett), from 1982
People of the Black Circle (s Howard), 1974
People of the Darkness (Vivian), 1924
People of the Mist (Haggard), 1894
Peregrine series (Davidson), from 1971
Perelandra (C.S. Lewis), 1943
Perilous Seas (Duncan), 1991
Personal Anthology (Borges, appendix), 1967
Personal Darkness (T. Lee), 1993
Personal Recollections of Joan of Arc (Twain), 1896
Peter and Wendy (Barrie), 1911
Peter Pan and the Only Children (Adair), 1987
Peter Pan and Wendy (Barrie), 1921
Phantastes (MacDonald), 1858
Phantom Banjo (Scarborough), 1991
Phantom Tollbooth (Juster), 1961
Phantoms and Fantasies (s Kipling), 1965
Phantoms of the Wind (Vardeman), 1989
Phaze Doubt (Anthony), 1990
Philadelphia Adventure (L. Alexander), 1990
Phoenix (Brust), 1990
Phoenix and the Carpet (Nesbit), 1904
Phoenix and the Mirror (Davidson), 1969
Phoenix Guards series (Brust), from 1991
Phoenix in Obsidian (Moorcock), 1970
Picking the Ballad's Bones (Scarborough), 1991
Picture of Dorian Gray (Wilde), 1891
Pictures in the Fire (s Collier), 1958
Pig in the Middle (s Mayne), 1965
Pigeons from Hell (s Howard), 1976
Pigs Don't Fly (Brown), 1994
Pilgermann (Hoban), 1983
Pilgrim's Regress (C.S. Lewis), 1933

Pillar of Night (Vardeman), 1984
Pillars of Pentegarn (Estes), 1982
Pillycock's Shop (Mahy), 1969
Pink of Fading Neon (s Blaylock), 1986
Piper at the Gate (Stanton), 1989
Pirate of World's End (L. Carter), 1978
Pirate Uncle (Mahy), 1977
Pirates' Mixed-Up Voyage (Mahy), 1983
Pirates of Gohar (R. Green, as Lord), 1979
Pixilated Peeress (de Camp), 1991
Place Among the Fallen (Adrian Cole), 1986
Place of the Lion (C. Williams), 1931
Plague Dogs (Adams), 1977
Plague of Knives (Silke), 1990
Plague of Nightmares (Adrian Cole), 1975
Plains of the Sea (Hancock), 1982
Plainsong (Grabien), 1990
Plot Night (s Mayne), 1963
Poems in Prose (s Wilde), 1905
Points of Departure (s P. Murphy), 1990
Poisoned Lands (Roberts), 1992
Policeman Bluejay (Baum, as Bancroft), 1907
Polly Charms the Sleeping Woman (s Davidson), 1977
Polyphemus (s Shea), 1987
Pool of Swallows (s Mayne), 1974
Pool of the Black One (s Howard), 1986
Poor Stainless (s M. Norton), 1971
Popes and Phantoms (Whitbourn), 1993
Porcelain Dove (Sherman), 1993
Porcelain Magician (s Owen), 1948
Porius (J. Powys), 1951
Pornucopia (Anthony), 1989
Portent (MacDonald), 1864
Portrait of Jennie (Nathan), 1940
Power of the Serpent (Timlett), 1976
Power of Three (D. Jones), 1976
Power That Preserves (Donaldson), 1977
Praetor's Dungeon (Mundy), 1976
Prentice Alvin (Card), 1989
Presenting Moonshine (s Collier), 1941
Prester John series (Page), from 1969
Pretender (Anthony), 1979
Pretender (L. Cooper), 1991
Price of Power (Estes), 1987
Price of Ransom (Rasmussen), 1990
Pride of Princes (Roberson), 1988
Prince Alcouz and the Magician (s S. Smith), 1977
Prince Among Men (Charrette), 1994
Prince and the Pauper (Twain), 1881
Prince Caspian (C.S. Lewis), 1951
Prince Ivan series (Morwood), from 1990
Prince of Annwn (Walton), 1974
Prince of Chaos (Zelazny), 1991
Prince of Evil (Page, as Stockbridge), 1985
Prince of Ill Luck (Dexter), 1994
Prince of Stars (Dennis), 1987
Prince of the Blood (Feist), 1989
Prince of the Godborn (G. Harris), 1982
Prince of the North (Turtledove), 1994
Prince on a White Horse (T. Lee), 1982
Prince Prigio (Lang), 1889

Prince Rabbit, and the Princess Who Could Not Laugh (Milne), 1966
Prince Raynor (s Kuttner), 1987
Prince Ricardo of Pantouflia (Lang), 1893
Prince, the Fox, and the Dragon (Briggs), 1938
Princes of Sandastre (Swithin), 1990
Princess and Curdie (MacDonald), 1882
Princess and the Clown (Mahy), 1971
Princess and the Goblin (MacDonald), 1871
Princess and the Lord of Night (Bull), 1994
Princess Bride (Goldman), 1973
Princess Hynchatti and Some Other Surprises (s T. Lee), 1972
Princess Nobody (s Lang), 1884
Princess of Flames (Emerson), 1986
Princess of the Chameln (Wilder), 1984
Princess Ozma of Oz (Baum), 1942
Prison of Souls (Lackey), 1993
Prisoner of the Horned Helmet (Silke), 1988
Private Life of Helen of Troy (Erskine), 1925
Procession (Mahy), 1969
Promise (Westall), 1990
Prophet of Akhran (Weis), 1989
Prophet of Moonshae (Niles), 1992
Proud Peacock and the Mallard (s Davis), 1976
Prydain series (L. Alexander), from 1964
Puck of Pook's Hill (s Kipling), 1906
Purple Dragon (s Baum), 1976
Purple Pirate (Mundy), 1935
Purple Pterodactyls (s de Camp), 1979
Purple Sea (s Owen), 1929
Pursuit of the House-boat (Bangs), 1897
Pyramids (Pratchett), 1989

Quag Keep (A. Norton), 1978
Quaking Lands (Vardeman), 1985
Quatermain, Allan series (Haggard), from 1885
Queen Cleopatra (Mundy), 1929
Queen of Air and Darkness (T.H. White), 1958
Queen of Sorcery (Eddings), 1982
Queen of the Black Coast (s Howard), 1978
Queen of the Dawn (Haggard), 1925
Queen of the Swords (Moorcock), 1971
Queen Sheba's Ring (Haggard), 1910
Queen Zixi of Ix (Baum), 1905
Queens of Land and Sea (Roberts), 1994
Queen's Quarter series (Snyder), from 1989
Queens Walk in the Dusk (Swann), 1977
Queensblade (Shwartz), 1988
Quest for Cush (Saunders), 1984
Quest for Lost Heroes (Gemmell), 1990
Quest for Saint Camber (Kurtz), 1986
Quest for Simbilis (Shea), 1974
Quest for Tanelorn (Moorcock), 1975
Quest for the White Witch (T. Lee), 1978
Quest of Kadji (L. Carter), 1971
Questing Hero, and The Hero's Return (H. Cook), 1987-88
Questing of Kedrigern (Morressy), 1987
Question Quest (Anthony), 1991

Rachel and the Angel (s Westall), 1986
Rafters Were Ringing (s de Lint), 1986

Raging Robots and Unruly Uncles (Mahy), 1981
Railway Engine and the Hairy Brigands (Mahy), 1973
Rain in the Doorway (T. Smith), 1933
Rainbow Abyss (Hambly), 1991
Rainbow and Mr. Zed (Nimmo), 1992
Rainbow Annals (Davis), 1980
Rainbow Gate (Warrington), 1989
Rainbow People (s Yep), 1989
Ramsden (Mundy), 1926
Raphael (MacAvoy), 1984
Rare Earth (Owen), 1931
Rare Spotted Birthday Party (Mahy), 1974
Ratha series (Bell), from 1983
Rats and Gargoyles (Gentle), 1990
Raven Ring (Wrede), 1994
Raven series (Holdstock and A. Wells, as Kirk), 1978
Raven Walking (C. Gardner), 1994
Ravensgill (s Mayne), 1970
Real Tilly Beany (Dalton), 1993
Real Wraiths (s J. Powys), 1974
Reap the East Wind (G. Cook), 1987
Reap the Whirlwind (Cherryh, Lackey), 1989
Reaper Man (Pratchett), 1991
Reaver Road (Duncan), 1992
Rebel Angel (Wood), 1993
Rebel Prince (Sharon Green), 1987
Rebellious Heroine (Bangs), 1896
Rebirth of Wonder (Watt-Evans), 1992
Recluce series (Modesitt), from 1991
Red as Blood (s T. Lee), 1983
Red Blades of Black Cathay (s Howard), 1971
Red Branch (Llywelyn), 1989
Red Eve (Haggard), 1911
Red Hart Magic (A. Norton), 1976
Red Hawk (s Lynn), 1983
Red Iron Nights (G. Cook), 1991
Red Magician (Goldstein), 1982
Red Moon and Black Mountain (Chant), 1970
Red Nails (s Howard), 1975
Red Prophet (Card), 1988
Red Shadows (s Howard), 1968
Red Shift (Garner), 1973
Red Stain (Abdullah), 1915
Red Wizard (Springer), 1990
Red Wolf, Red Wolf (s Kinsella), 1987
Redskin Morning (s Joan Grant), 1944
Redwall series (Jacques), from 1986
Redward Edward Papers (s Davidson), 1978
Refiner's Fire (Helprin), 1977
Regiment of Women (Berger), 1973
Reigning Cats and Dogs (T. Lee), 1995
Reindeer People series (Lindholm), from 1988
Reluctant King (de Camp), 1985
Reluctant Sorcerer (Hawke), 1992
Reluctant Swordsman (Duncan), 1988
Remarkable Journey of Prince Jen (L. Alexander), 1991
Remember Tomorrow (s Kuttner), 1954
Remembrance for Kedrigern (Morressy), 1990
Rendezvous in Averoigne (s S. Smith), 1988
Renegade of Callisto (L. Carter), 1978

Renshai series (Reichert), from 1992
Replay (Grimwood), 1986
Report from Paradise (s Twain), 1952
Return of Fursey (Wall), 1948
Return of Skull-Face (Howard), 1977
Return of the King (Tolkien), 1955
Return of the Shadow (s Tolkien), 1988
Return to Brookmere (Estes), 1982
Return to Eddarta (Garrett), 1985
Return to Elysium (Joan Grant), 1947
Return to Harken House (Aiken), 1988
Return to Kaldac (R. Green, as Lord), 1983
Return to Otherness (s Kuttner), 1962
Revenant (L. Cooper), 1992
Revenants (Tepper), 1984
Revenge of Samuel Stokes (Lively), 1981
Revenge of the Fluffy Bunnies (C. Gardner), 1990
Revenge of the Rainbow Dragons (Estes), 1983
Revenge of the Rose (Moorcock), 1991
Revenge of the Wizard's Ghost (Bellairs), 1985
Revolt of the Angels (France, appendix), 1914
Revolt of the Dwarves (Estes), 1983
Revolution's Shore (Rasmussen), 1990
Rewards and Fairies (s Kipling), 1910
Rhapsody in Amber (s Zelazny), 1981
Rhialto the Marvellous (Vance), 1984
Rhinegold (Grundy), 1994
Ribwash (Webber), 1994
Riddle and the Rune (Chetwin), 1987
Riddle of Stars (McKillip), 1979
Riddle of the Griffin (Weis, as Lawson), 1985
Riddle of the Seven Realms (Hardy), 1988
Riddle of the Wren (de Lint), 1984
Riddle-Master of Hed (McKillip), 1976
Ride the Green Dragon (A. Norton), 1985
Riders of the Sidhe (Flint), 1984
Riding the Unicorn (Kearney), 1994
Rifkind Saga series (Abbey), from 1979
Riftwar series (Feist), from 1982
Rime Isle (Leiber), 1977
Ring of Allaire (Dexter), 1981
Ring of Fire (S. Murphy), 1977
Rinkitink in Oz (Baum), 1916
Ritnym's Daughter (Gilluly), 1989
River Journey (Nathan), 1949
River Wall (Garrett), 1986
Road and the Hills (Spedding), 1986
Road of Azrael (s Howard), 1979
Road to Oz (Baum), 1909
Road to the Middle Islands (Hancock), 1983
Road to Underfall (Jefferies), 1986
Robin and the Kestrel (Lackey), 1993
Robin and the King (Godwin), 1993
Robin Hood series (Godwin), from 1991
Robinson Crusoe's Return (Pain), 1906
Robot Adept (Anthony), 1988
Roger Camerden (Bangs), 1887
Rogue Reynard (A. Norton), 1947
Rogues in the House (s Howard), 1976
Rolling Season (s Mayne), 1960
Rollover Night (s Whitbourn), 1990

Roma Mater (Anderson), 1986
Roman Britain series (Godwin), from 1980
Romance in Black (Wellman, as Field), 1946
Romance of Two Worlds (Corelli), 1886
Rome series (Swann), from 1972
Rooftops (s Mayne), 1966
Rooms for Rent (Mahy), 1974
Rooms to Let (Mahy), 1975
Roots of the Mountains (W. Morris), 1890
Rosalie (Westall), 1987
Rose of the Prophet series (Weis), from 1989
Rose-Red City (Duncan), 1987
Rotting Land (John Grant), 1994
Route 666 (Yeovil), 1994
Royal Chaos (McGirt), 1990
Royal Harry (s Mayne), 1971
Ruby Knight (Eddings), 1990
Ruins of Ambrai (Rawn), 1994
Ruins of Kaldac (R. Green, as Lord), 1981
Rulers of Hylor series (Wilder), from 1984
Runes (Monaco), 1984
Runestaff (Moorcock), 1969
Rusalka series (Cherryh), from 1989

Sabbatical (Barth), 1982
Sabella (T. Lee), 1980
Sable Moon (Springer), 1981
Sacred Ground (Lackey), 1994
Sacrifice of Ruanon (John Grant), 1991
Sadar's Keep (Snyder), 1990
Sadness (s Barthelme), 1972
Saga of Eric Brighteyes (Haggard), 1974
Saga of Lost Lands series (Estes), from
Saga of Old City (Gygax), 1985
Sagamore series (Dalkey), from 1986
Sagard the Barbarian series (Gygax), from 1985
Sage of Sare (J. Smith), 1992
Sailor Jack and the 20 Orphans (Mahy), 1970
Sailor on the Seas of Fate (Moorcock), 1976
Saint Camber (Kurtz), 1978
St. Nicholas and the Valley Beyond (Kushner), 1994
Saints and Strangers (s A. Carter), 1986
Salamandastron (Jacques), 1992
Salome, The Wandering Jewess (Viereck), 1930
Salt River Times (s Mayne), 1980
Samarkand series (Diamond), from 1980
Samarkand Solution (Gygax), 1993
Samurai Wizard (Hawke), 1991
Sanctuary (Luard), 1994
Sand (s Mayne), 1964
Sapphire Rose (Eddings), 1991
Satanic Verses (Rushdie), 1988
Satan's Death Blast (Page, as Stockbridge), 1984
Satan's Incubators (Page, as Craig), 1975
Sauron Defeated (s Tolkien), 1992
Scarecrow of Oz (Baum), 1915
Scarecrows (Westall), 1981
Scarlet Dream (s C.L. Moore), 1981
Scarlet Feather (Joan Grant), 1945
Scarlet Fish (s Joan Grant), 1942
Scheherazade's Night Out (C. Gardner), 1992

Sidhe series (Flint), from 1981
Siege (T. Williams), 1994
Siege of Darkness (Salvatore), 1994
Sign of Chaos (Zelazny), 1987
Sign of the Moonbow (Offutt), 1977
Sign of the Salamander (Wagner), 1975
Sign of the Unicorn (Zelazny), 1975
Silent Gondoliers (Goldman), 1984
Silent Tower (Hambly), 1986
Silicon Mage (Hambly), 1988
Silk Roads and Shadows (Shwartz), 1988
Silmarillion (Tolkien), 1977
Silver Branch (Kennealy-Morrison), 1988
Silver Chair (C.S. Lewis), 1953
Silver Cow (S. Cooper), 1983
Silver Hand (Lawhead), 1992
Silver Horse (Lynn), 1984
Silver Lady and the Fortyish Man (s Lindholm), 1994
Silver Mountain (Friesner), 1986
Silver on the Tree (S. Cooper), 1977
Silver Princess, Golden Knight (Sharon Green), 1992
Silver Spike (G. Cook), 1989
Silver Stallion (Cabell), 1926
Silver Sun (Springer), 1980
Silver Thread of Madness (s Salmonson), 1989
Silver Vortex (Caldecott), 1987
Silver Warriors (Moorcock), 1973
Silver Woven in My Hair (S. Murphy), 1977
Silverhair the Wanderer (Paxson), 1986
Silverlock (Myers), 1949
Silverthorn (Feist), 1985
Sinful Ones (Leiber), 1953
Sing the Four Quarters (Huff), 1994
Singing Citadel (s Moorcock), 1970
Sipstrassi series (Gemmell), from 1987
Sir Harold and the Gnome King (de Camp), 1991
Sir Harold and the Monkey King (s Stasheff), 1993
Sister Light, Sister Dark (Yolen), 1988
Sister Water (Willard), 1993
Six Kingdoms series (Fergusson), from 1987
Six of Swords (Douglas), 1982
Sixty Stories (s Barthelme), 1981
Skallagrigg (Horwood), 1987
Skeleton Lord's Key (Vardeman, as Moran), 1987
Skiffy (s Mayne), 1972
Skiffy and the Twin Planets (s Mayne), 1982
Skin and Bones (T. Smith), 1933
Skryling's Blade (Estes), 1990
Skull Gate (Bailey), 1985
Skull-Face (s Howard), 1946
Skulls in the Stars (s Howard), 1978
Sky Island (Baum), 1912
Sky Pirates of Callisto (L. Carter), 1973
Skybowl (Rawn), 1993
Skybreaker (Halam), 1990
Skyfire (King), 1988
Slaves of Sleep (Hubbard), 1948
Slaves of the Volcano God (C. Gardner), 1989
Sleep of Giants (Adrian Cole), 1983.
Sleep of Stone (L. Cooper), 1991
Sleeping in Flame (J. Carroll), 1988

Sleeping Sorceress (Moorcock), 1971
Slightly Irregular Fire Engine (Barthelme), 1971
Small Gods (Pratchett), 1992
Small Miracle (s Gallico), 1951
Small Pinch of Weather (s Aiken), 1969
Small Pudding for Wee Gowrie (s Mayne), 1983
Smire: An Acceptance in the Third Person (Cabell), 1937
Smirt (Cabell), 1934
Smith: A Sylvan Interlude (Cabell), 1935
Smith and the Pharaohs (s Haggard), 1920
Smith of Wootton Major (s Tolkien), 1967
Smoke from Cromwell's Time (s Aiken), 1970
Snarkout Boys series (Pinkwater), from 1982
Snow (Frith), 1993
Snow Spider (Nimmo), 1986
Snow White (Barthelme), 1967
Snow White and Rose Red (Wrede), 1989
So Love Returns (Nathan), 1958
So Moses Was Born (Joan Grant), 1952.
So You Want to Be a Wizard? (Duane), 1983
Sojan (s Moorcock), 1977
Sojourn (Salvatore), 1991
Soldier of Arete (Wolfe), 1989
Soldier of the Mist (Wolfe), 1986
Solomon, John series (Bedford-Jones, as Hawkwood), 1924
Solomon Kane series (Howard), from 1968
Sombrero Fallout (Brautigan), 1976
Some Summer Lands (Gaskell), 1977
Something about Eve (Cabell), 1927
Something Rich and Strange (McKillip), 1994
Sometimes, After Sunset (T. Lee), 1981
Son of Ammitai (Nathan), 1925
Son of the Sun (Caldecott), 1986
Son of the White Wolf (s Howard), 1977
Song For Arbonne (Kay), 1992
Song of Albion series (Lawhead), from 1991
Song of Homana (Roberson), 1985
Song of Pentecost (Corbett), 1982
Song of Rhiannon (Walton), 1972
Song of Sorcery (Scarborough), 1982
Song of the Pearl (Nichols), 1976
Song of Wirrun (Wrightson), 1987
Song under the Water (Jean Morris), 1985
Songbirds of Pain (s Kilworth), 1984
Songkiller series (Scarborough), from 1991
Songs from the Seashell Archives (Scarborough), 1987-88
Songsmith (A. Norton), 1992
Sons of the Bear-God (Page), 1969
Sons of the Titans (Adkins), 1990
Soonie and the Dragon (S. Murphy), 1979
Sorcerer and a Gentleman (Willey), 1995
Sorcerer series (Volsky), from 1986
Sorcerer's Amulet (Moorcock), 1968
Sorcerer's Appendix (Harman), 1993
Sorcerer's Apprentice (M. Williams), 1990
Sorcerer's Legacy (Wurts), 1982
Sorcerer's Ship (Bok), 1969
Sorcerer's Skull (Vardeman), 1983
Sorcerer's Son (Eisenstein), 1979
Sorcerer's Ward (Hambly), 1994
Sorceress (Wood), 1994

Sorceress and the Cygnet (McKillip), 1991
Sorceress of Darshiva (Eddings), 1989
Sorceress of Seath (Eshbach), 1988
Sorceress of the Witch World (A. Norton), 1968
Sorcerous Sea (Severance), 1993
Sorcery and Cecelia (Stevermer, Wrede), 1988
Sorrow's Light (Warrington), 1993
Sorrows of Satan (Corelli), 1895
Sot-Weed Factor (Barth), 1960
Soul Master (Martin), 1984
Soul Music (Pratchett), 1994
Soul of Lilith (Corelli), 1892
Soul of Melicent (Cabell), 1913
Soul of the City (s Cherryh), 1986
Soulsmith series (Deitz), from 1991
Soulstring (Snyder), 1987
Source of Magic (Anthony), 1979
Sourcery (Pratchett), 1988
Sowers of the Thunder (s Howard), 1973
Space Trilogy (C.S. Lewis), 1986
Spear of Heaven (Tarr), 1994
Spear of Mistletoe (Frith), 1977
Spearwielder's Tale series (Salvatore), from 1993
Spell Bound (Emerson), 1990
Spell for Chameleon (Anthony), 1977
Spell of Apocalypse (Brenner), 1994
Spell of Empire (Rohan, Scott), 1992
Spell of Fate (Brenner), 1992
Spell of Intrigue (Brenner), 1990
Spell of the Black Dagger (Watt-Evans), 1993
Spell of the Sorcerer's Skull (Bellairs), 1984
Spell of the Witch World (s A. Norton), 1972
Spellcoats (D. Jones), 1979
Spells of Mortal Weaving (Friesner), 1986
Spellsinger series (Foster), from 1983
Spellstone of Shaltus (Bushyager), 1980
Sphinx (Lindsay), 1923
Sphynxes Wild (Friesner), 1989
Spider series (Page), from 1969
Spillane series (Dwyer), from 1937
Spiral Dance (Garcia y Robertson), 1991
Spiral series (Rohan), from 1990
Spiral Winds (Kilworth), 1987
Spirit Mirror (Marley), 1988
Spirit of Bambatse (Haggard), 1906
Spirit of the Hawk (Estes), 1988
Spirits of Cavern and Hearth (Easton), 1988
Spiritwalk (de Lint), 1992
Split Heirs (Friesner, Watt-Evans), 1993
Split Infinity (Anthony), 1980
Spotted Panther (Dwyer), 1913
Squaring the Circle (Hancock), 1977
Stalking Horse (Ash), 1990
Stallion Queen (Ash), 1992
Star Ascendant (L. Cooper), 1994
Star Dancer (Sampson), 1993
Star Dust (Vivian), 1925
Star Requiem series (Adrian Cole), from 1989
Star Scroll (Rawn), 1989
Star Shadow series (L. Cooper), from 1994
Star Wars: The Heart of the Jedi (Flint), 1993

Star Woman (Bedford-Jones), 1924
Starkadder series (King), from 1985
Starless Night (Salvatore), 1993
Starstone (Chetwin), 1989
Start of the End of It All (s Emshwiller), 1990
Stealer of Souls (s Moorcock), 1963
Steel Kings (Roberts), 1994
Steel Magic (A. Norton), 1965
Steel of Raithskar (Garrett), 1981
Stella Fregelius (Haggard), 1904
Stephen Archer (s MacDonald), 1883
Stepmother (Mahy), 1974
Still She Wished for Company (M. Irwin), 1924
Stitch in Time (Lively), 1976
Stolen Lake (Aiken), 1981
Stone Angels (Jefferies), 1993
Stone Croc (Farmer), 1991
Stone Drum (s de Lint), 1989
Stone Giant (Blaylock), 1989
Stone of Farewell (T. Williams), 1990
Stone of Tears (Goodkind), 1995
Stone of Time (Estes), 1992
Stones of Muncaster Cathedral (s Westall), 1991
Stoneskin's Revenge (Deitz), 1991
Stonor Eagles (Horwood), 1982
Storeys from the Old Hotel (s Wolfe), 1988
Stories in the Dark (s Pain), 1901
Stories of the Strange and Sinister (s Baker), 1983
Storm (T. Williams), 1994
Storm Caller (Severance), 1993
Storm Lord (T. Lee), 1976
Storm of Prophecy (M. Williams), 1995(?)
Storm of Wings (M. John Harrison), 1980
Storm Rising (Lackey), 1995
Storm Seed (Janet Morris), 1990
Storm Shield (Flint), 1986
Storm Upon Ulster (Flint), 1981
Storm Warning (Lackey), 1994
Stormblade (Berberick), 1988
Stormbringer (Moorcock), 1965
Stormlands series (Roberts), from 1990
Storms of Victory (A. Norton), 1991
Stormwarden (Wurts), 1984
Story of a Shipwrecked Sailor (Marquez, appendix), 1986
Story of the Amulet (Nesbit), 1906
Story of the Glittering Plain (W. Morris), 1891
Story of the Stone (Hughart), 1988
Story of Ulla (s Arnold), 1895
Story of Wan and the Remarkable Shrub (s Bramah), 1927
Storyteller (s Yolen), 1992
Straight on Till Mourning (Bailey), 1993
Strands of Starlight series (Baudino), from 1989
Strange Devices of the Sun and Moon (Goldstein), 1993
Strange Ends and Discoveries (s Housman), 1948
Strange Evil (Gaskell), 1957
Strange Gateways (s Price), 1967
Strange Journeys of Colonel Polders (Dunsany), 1950
Strange Pilgrims (Marquez, appendix), 1993
Strange Seas and Shores (s Davidson), 1971
Strange Shadows (s S. Smith), 1989
Strange Toys (Geary), 1987

Strange Visitation of Josiah McNason (Corelli), 1904
Stranger at the Wedding (Hambly), 1994
Stray Lamb (T. Smith), 1929
Streams of Silver (Salvatore), 1989
Street Magic (Reaves), 1991
Street of the Eye (s Bullett), 1923
Streets of the City (Spedding), 1988
Stress of Her Regard (Powers), 1989
Stricken Field (Duncan), 1993
Striker, Jason series (Anthony), from 1974
Stronghold (Rawn), 1990
Strum Again? (Scarborough), 1992
Stuart Little (E.B. White), 1945
Sudden Wild Magic (D. Jones), 1992
Sugar-Gum Tree (Wrightson), 1991
Suldrun's Garden (Vance), 1983
Sullivan, David series (Deitz), from 1986
Summer Birds (Farmer), 1962
Summer King, Winter Fool (Goldstein), 1994
Summer Meadows (Nathan), 1973
Summer Tree (Kay), 1984
Summer Visitors (s Mayne), 1961
Summer's King (Wilder), 1985
Summoned to Tourney (Lackey), 1992
Sun in Scorpio (Fraser), 1949
Sun, the Moon, and the Stars (Brust), 1987
Sun Wolf and Starhawk series (Hambly), from 1984
Sunburn Lake (s De Haven), 1988
Sun-Cross series (Hambly), from 1991
Sundered Realm (Vardeman), 1980
Sundering Flood (W. Morris), 1897
Sung in Shadow (T. Lee), 1983
Sunrunner's Fire (Rawn), 1990
Sunset Warrior series (Lustbader), from 1977
Sunshaker's War (Deitz), 1990
Support Your Local Wizard (Duane), 1990
Surprising Adventures of The Magical Monarch of Mo (Baum), 1903
Surrender None (Moon), 1990
Swallows (s Mayne, as Cobalt), 1972
Swan Lake (Helprin), 1989
Swan Sister (Dalton), 1992
Swarm in May (s Mayne), 1955
Swatting at the Cosmos (s Morrow), 1990
Sweet Chariot (Baker), 1942
Sweet Dreams (Frayn), 1973
Sweet Silver Blues (G. Cook), 1987
Sweet, Sweet Summer (Gaskell), 1969
Sword & Circlet series (Douglas), from 1982
Sword and the Flame (Lawhead), 1984
Sword and the Lion (Emerson, as Cray), 1993
Sword and the Satchel (Boyer), 1980
Sword and the Stallion (Moorcock), 1974
Sword and the Stone (s Yolen), 1991
Sword in the Stone (T.H. White), 1938
Sword is Forged (Walton), 1983
Sword of Bedwyr (Salvatore), 1995
Sword of Bheleu (Watt-Evans), 1983
Sword of Calandra (Dexter), 1985
Sword of Flame (Furey), 1995
Sword of Heaven series (Rasmussen, as Elliott), 1993

Sword of Knowledge series (Cherryh), from 1989
Sword of Sagamore (Dalkey), 1989
Sword of Shannara (Brooks), 1977
Sword of the Dawn (Moorcock), 1968
Sword of the Gael (Offutt), 1975
Sword of the Sun (John Grant), 1989
Sword of Truth series (Goodkind), from 1994
Sword of Welleran (s Dunsany), 1908
Sword Smith (Arnason), 1978
Sword Woman (s Howard), 1977
Swordbearer (G. Cook), 1982
Sword-Dancer series (Roberson), from 1987
Swords Against Death (s Leiber), 1970
Swords Against Wizardry (s Leiber), 1968
Swords and Deviltry (s Leiber), 1970
Swords and Ice Magic (s Leiber), 1977
Swords in the Mist (s Leiber), 1968
Swords' Masters (s Leiber), 1990
Swords of Heaven, the Flowers of Hell (s Moorcock), 1979
Swords of Lankhmar (Leiber), 1968
Swords of Raemllyn series (Vardeman), from 1985
Swords of Shahrazar (s Howard), 1976
Swords of the Legion (Turtledove), 1987
Swords series (Saberhagen), from 1983
Swords Trilogy (Moorcock), 1986
Swordsmistress of Chaos (Holdstock, as Kirk), 1978
Swordspoint (Kushner), 1987
Swordswoman (Salmonson), 1982
Sylvie and Bruno (L. Carroll), 1889
Sylvie and Bruno Concluded (L. Carroll), 1893
Symphony of Storms (Vardeman), 1990

t zero (Calvino, appendix), 1969
Tailchaser's Song (T. Williams), 1985
Takeoff Too (s Garrett), 1987
Takeoff! (s Garrett), 1979
Taking Flight (Watt-Evans), 1993
Tale of a One-Way Street (s Aiken), 1978
Tale of Fleur (Vivian), 1929
Tale of the Five series (Duane), from 1979
Tale of the House of the Wolfings (W. Morris), 1889
Tale of the Land of Green Ginger (Langley), 1937
Tale of Three Lions, and On Going Back (s Haggard), 1887
Tales from a Mother of Pearl Casket (s France, appendix), 1896
Tales from a Vanished Country (s Lynn), 1990
Tales from Gavagan's Bar (s de Camp, Pratt), 1953
Tales of a Fairy Court (s Tales for the Children no. 1), 1907
Tales of Mystery and Revenge (s Langley), 1950
Tales of Science and Sorcery (s S. Smith), 1964
Tales of the Werewolf Clan series (s Munn), from 1979
Tales of Three Hemispheres (s Dunsany), 1919
Tales of Wonder (s Dunsany), 1916
Tales of Wonder (s Yolen), 1983
Tales Told for Children series (Andersen, appendix), from 1835
Taliesin (Lawhead), 1987
Taliesin's Telling (Sampson), 1991
Talismans of Shannara (Brooks), 1993
Taliswoman series (Douglas), from 1991
Talk of the Devil (Baker), 1956
Talking Horse (s Anstey), 1892
Talking Man (Bisson), 1986

Talking to Dragons (Wrede), 1985
Tall Stones series (Caldecott), from 1977
Taltos, Vlad series (Brust), from 1983
Tam Lin (S. Cooper, Dean), 1991
Tamastara (s T. Lee), 1984
Taming the Forest King (C. Edwards), 1986
Tamuli series (Eddings), from 1992
Tangle Box (Brooks), 1994
Tangled Lands (Shetterly), 1989
Tapestry of Lions (Roberson), 1992
Tara of the Twilight (L. Carter), 1979
Taran Wanderer (L. Alexander), 1967
Tarnsman of Gor (Norman), 1966
Tarzan and the Well of Slaves (Niles), 1985
Tarzan series (Burroughs), from 1914
Taste of Blood Wine (Warrington), 1992
Tatham Mound (Anthony), 1991
Tea with the Black Dragon (MacAvoy), 1983
Teckla (Brust), 1987
Tehanu (Le Guin), 1990
Tellings (s John Grant), 1993
Telnarian Histories (Norman), 1991
Temper of Wisdom (Abbey), 1992
Templar Treasure (Kurtz), 1993
Temple of Elemental Evil (Gygax), 1985
Temple of the Sun (Caldecott), 1977
Temple of the Ten (Bedford-Jones), 1973
Temples of Ayocan (R. Green, as Lord), 1975
Temporary Agency (Pollack), 1994
Tempus (Janet Morris), 1987
Tempus Unbound (Janet Morris), 1989
Ten-Minute Tales (s Bullett), 1959
Terra Magica series (L. Carter), from 1982
Terrilian series (Sharon Green), from 1982
Test of the Twins (Weis), 1986
Thaïs (France, appendix), 1901
That Hideous Strength (C.S. Lewis), 1945
That Very Mab (Lang), 1885
That Way Lies Camelot (s Wurts), 1994
The Lost Princess (MacDonald), 1876
The Unbroken Web (s Adams), 1980
The-End-of-Everything-Man (De Haven), 1991
There Are Doors (Wolfe), 1988
There is Another Heaven (Nathan), 1929
There Was a Door (Mundy), 1935
There Were Two Pirates (Cabell), 1946
There's No Such Place as Far Away (Bach), 1979
These Mortals (M. Irwin), 1925
Thicker Than Water (Farmer), 1989
Thief of Bagdad (Abdullah), 1924
Thief of Dreams (Adrian Cole), 1989
Thief of Kalimar (Diamond), 1979
Thieves' World series (Janet Morris), from 1985
Thieves' World series (Offutt), from 1987
Things Invisible to See (Willard), 1984
Third Level (s J. Finney), 1957
Third Policeman (O'Brien), 1967
Thirteen O'Clock (s Mayne), 1960
This Is the Way the World Ends (Morrow), 1986
Thomas the Rhymer (Kushner), 1990
Thomasina (Gallico), 1957

Thongor series (L. Carter), from 1966
Thorn Key (L. Cooper), 1988
Those Who Hunt the Night (Hambly), 1988
Thousand Shrine Warrior (Salmonson), 1984
Thrall and the Dragon's Heart (Boyer), 1982
Three Against the Witch World (A. Norton), 1965
Three Damosels series (Chapman), from 1975
Three Fantasies (s J. Powys), 1985
Three Hearts and Three Lions (Anderson), 1961
Three Lines of Old French (s Merritt), 1939
Three of Swords (s Leiber), 1989
Three Plushketeers and the Garden Slugs (s de Lint), 1985
Three Worlds series (Watt-Evans), from 1994
Threshold (Le Guin), 1980
Thrill of the Grass (s Kinsella), 1984
Throne of Fools (Adrian Cole), 1987
Throne of Isis (Tarr), 1994
Throne of Scone (Kennealy-Morrison), 1986
Throne of Sherran (R. Green), 1985
Through a Brazen Mirror (Sherman), 1989
Through Dragon Eyes (s K. Morris), 1980
Through the Looking-Glass (L. Carroll), 1871
Thru the Dragon Glass (s Merritt), 1932
Thumbstick (s Mayne), 1959
Thunder Dragon Gate (Mundy), 1937
Thunstone, John series (Wellman), from 1983
Thy Servant a Dog, Told by Boots (s Kipling), 1930
Tides of Treachery (John Grant), 1990
Tidewater Tales (s Barth), 1987
Tigana (Kay), 1990
Tiger Woman (s Yep), 1994
Tiger's Railway (s Mayne), 1987
Tik-Tok of Oz (Baum), 1914
Till We Have Faces (C.S. Lewis), 1956
Tilly Beany and the Best Friend Machine (Dalton), 1993
Time and Again (J. Finney), 1970
Time and the Gods (s Dunsany), 1906
Time Cat (L. Alexander), 1963
Time Garden (Eager), 1958
Time Master series (L. Cooper), from 1985
Time of Dying (A. Wells, as Kirk), 1979
Time of Exile (Kerr), 1991
Time of Ghosts (Holdstock, as Kirk), 1978
Time of Justice (Kerr), 1994
Time of Omens (Kerr), 1992
Time of the Annihilator (Morressy), 1985
Time of the Dark (Hambly), 1982
Time of the Ghost (D. Jones), 1981
Time of the Transference (Foster), 1986
Time of the Twins (Weis), 1986
Time of War (Kerr), 1993
Time Slave (Norman), 1975
Time-Fighters (King), 1987
Tin Woodman of Oz (Baum), 1918
Tinted Venus (Anstey), 1885
Titans series (Adkins), from 1987
Titus series (Peake), from 1946
To Battle the Gods (Sharon Green), 1986
To Build Jerusalem (Whitbourn), 1994
To Demons Bound (Vardeman), 1985
To Green Angel Tower (T. Williams), 1993

To Reign in Hell (Brust), 1984
To the Haunted Mountains (Emerson), 1987
To the Magic Born (Stasheff), 1986
Toffee Join (s Mayne), 1968
Tokyo-Montana Express (Brautigan), 1980
Tom O'Bedlam's Night Out (s Schweitzer), 1985
Tombs of Atuan (Le Guin), 1971
Tome Tunnel (Harman), 1994
Tomoe Gozen series (Salmonson), from 1981
Tom's Midnight Garden (Pearce), 1958
Tongues of Jade (s Yep), 1991
Too Long a Sacrifice (Broxon), 1981
Too Many Ghosts (Gallico), 1959
Too Many Magicians (Garrett), 1967
Tooth and Claw (Silke), 1989
Topper series (T. Smith), from 1926
Toppleton's Client (Bangs), 1893
Torian Pearls (R. Green, as Lord), 1977
Tortured Planet (C.S. Lewis), 1958
Touch of Chill (s Aiken), 1979
Touch of Nutmeg (s Collier), 1943
Tourists (Goldstein), 1989
Tourmalin's Time Cheques (Anstey), 1891
Tournament of Thorns (Swann), 1976
Tower and the Emerald (Caldecott), 1985
Tower of Death (Offutt), 1982
Tower of Fear (G. Cook), 1989
Tower of Midnight Dreams (Weis), 198?
Tower of the Elephant (s Howard), 1975
Towers of Melnon (R. Green, as Lord), 1975
Towers of the Sunset (Modesitt), 1992
Towing Jehovah (Morrow), 1994
Town Cats (s L. Alexander), 1977
Track of the White Wolf (Roberson), 1987
Tragedy of the Moisty Morning (s Salmonson), 1978
Trail of Bohu (Saunders), 1985
Trail of Death (Estes), 1985
Train in the Meadow (Nathan), 1953
Traitors (Rusch), 1993
Transformations (Halam), 1988
Transient (s Munn), 1979
Transients (s Schweitzer), 1993
Transit of Venus (s Michael Harrison), 1936
Travelers in Magic (s Goldstein), 1994
Traveller (Adams), 1988
Travelling with the Dead (Hambly), 1995
Treason of Isengard (s Tolkien), 1989
Treasure of Alpheus Winterborn (Bellairs), 1978
Treasure of the Lake (Haggard), 1926
Treasure of the Stars (R. Green, as Lord), 1978
Treasure of Tranicos (de Camp, Howard), 1980
Treasures of Typhon (Phillpotts), 1924
Tredana series (Gregorian), from 1975
Tree and Leaf (s Tolkien), 1964
Tree of Swords and Jewels (Cherryh), 1983
Tregarde, Diana series (Lackey), from 1989
Trey of Swords (s A. Norton), 1977
Tricksters (Mahy), 1986
Trillium series (Bradley, May, A. Norton), from 1990
Trio for Lute (MacAvoy), 1985
Tristan and Isolde (Erskine), 1932

Triton, and Battle of Wizards (Hubbard), 1949
Tritonian Ring (s de Camp), 1953
Triumph of the Darksword (Weis), 1988
Triumph of the Dragon (Bailey), 1994
Troika (L. Cooper), 1991
Troll series (Estes), from 1993
Trolley to Yesterday (Bellairs), 1989
Troll's Grindstone (Boyer), 1986
Tros series (Mundy), from 1929
Trot and Cap'n Bill series (Baum), from 1911
Troubadour (Burns), 1988
Troubling Along the Border (Aamodt), 1991
Trout's Testament (Fraser), 1960
Troy Game (Jean Morris), 1987
Truce With Time (Godwin), 1988
True Game series (Tepper), from 1983
Trumpet of the Swan (E.B. White), 1970
Trumps of Doom (Zelazny), 1985
Truthful Harp (L. Alexander), 1967
Tucker's Countryside (Selden), 1969
Turn Again Tales (s Housman), 1930
Turnabout (T. Smith), 1931
Twelve Dancers (s Mayne), 1962
Twilight of Magic (Lofting), 1930
Twilight of the Gods (s R. Garnett), 1888
Twilight of the Serpent (Timlett), 1977
Twinkle and Chubbins (s Baum, as Bancroft), 1911
Twist of Eight (s Jean Morris), 1981
Twisted Tree (Baker), 1935
Twisting the Rope (MacAvoy), 1986
Two and Two (s J. Powys), 1974
Two by Two (D. Garnett), 1963
Two in Hiding (Emerson), 1991
Two Kings in Haven (Simon Green), 1992
Two Sought Adventure (s Leiber), 1957
Two Thieves (s T.F. Powys), 1932
Two Towers (Tolkien), 1954
Two Views of a Cave Painting (s Blaylock), 1987
Tyrant of Time (s Eshbach), 1955

Ultima Saga series (Abbey), from 1991
Ultramarine (Nimmo), 1991
Ultra-Violet Catastrophe! (Mahy), 1975
Unbalanced Earth series (Wylie), from 1989
Unbeheaded King (de Camp), 1983
Unclay (T.F. Powys), 1931
Uncle Dobbin's Parrot Fair (s de Lint), 1991
Unconquered Country (Ryman), 1986
Under the Green Star (L. Carter), 1972
Underground Alley (s Mayne), 1958
Underground Creatures (s Mayne), 1983
Undersea (Hazel), 1982
Undesired Princess (de Camp), 1951
Undying Wizard (Offutt), 1976
Unexpurgated Clark Ashton Smith (s S. Smith), 1987-88
Unfinished Tales of Númenór and Middle-Earth (s Tolkien), 1980
Unfortunate Fursey (Wall), 1946
Unholy City (C. Finney), 1937
Unicorn & Dragon (Abbey), 1987
Unicorn Creed (Scarborough), 1983
Unicorn Point (Anthony), 1989

Unicorn Saga series (Abbey), from 1987
Unicorn series (J. Lee), from 1986
Unicorn series (T. Lee), from 1991
Unicorn Trade (s Anderson), 1984
Unicorn U (Friesner), 1992
Uninvited Ghosts (s Lively), 1984
Universal History of Infamy (Borges, appendix), 1972
Unlikely Ones (Brown), 1986
Unquenchable Fire (Pollack), 1988
Unschooled Wizard (Hambly), 1987
Unsilent Night (s T. Lee), 1981
Unspeakable Practices, Unnatural Acts (s Barthelme), 1968
Untold Tales (s S. Smith), 1984
Unwilling Warlord (Watt-Evans), 1989
Up and Out (s J. Powys), 1957
Up the Chimney Down (s Aiken), 1984
Upland Outlaws (Duncan), 1993
Urban Faerie series (de Lint), from 1987
Ursus of Ultima Thule (Davidson), 1973
Usurper (A. Wells), 1989

Valderen (Taylor), 1993
Vale of the Vole (Anthony), 1987
Valentine for a Dragon (S. Murphy), 1984
Valley Beyond Time (Wilkins), 1955
Valley of the Flame (Kuttner, C.L. Moore), 1964
Valley of the Lost (s Howard), 1975
Valley of the Worms (s Howard), 1976
Valley of Thunder (de Lint), 1989
Valley So Low (s Wellman), 1987
Vandarei series (Chant), from 1970
Vanishing Tower (Moorcock), 1977
Vargr-Moon (King), 1986
Variation on a Theme (s Collier), 1935
Vazkor, Son of Vazkor (T. Lee), 1978
Vengeance for a Lonely Man (Simon Green), 1992
Vengeance of the Witch-Finder (Bellairs, Strickland), 1993
Venus Rising (s Emshwiller), 1992
Venus series (Fraser), from 1958
Venus, The Lonely Goddess (Erskine), 1949
Vergil Magus series (Davidson), from 1969
Verging on the Pertinent (s Emshwiller), 1989
Vesper Holly series (L. Alexander), from 1986
Vice Versa, or A Lesson to Fathers (Anstey), 1882
Victory Nelson series (Huff), from 1991
Videssos series (Turtledove), from 1987
Violet Apple, and The Witch (Lindsay), 1976
Viperhand (Niles), 1990
Virgin and the Swine (Walton), 1936
Virgin of the Sun (Haggard), 1922
Viriconium series (M. John Harrison), from 1971
Virtual Mode (Anthony), 1991
Visionary Novels (MacDonald), 1954
Visit from Venus (Fraser), 1958
Visitors from Oz (Baum), 1960
Vivia (T. Lee), 1995
Vlemk the Box-Painter (J. Gardner), 1980
Voice for Princess (Morressy), 1986
Voice from the Mountain (Wellman), 1984
Voice of Our Shadow (J. Carroll), 1983
Voices (Aiken), 1988

Volkhavaar (T. Lee), 1977
Von Bek series (Moorcock), from 1981
Votan (James), 1966
Vows and Honor series (Lackey), from 1988
Voyage of QV66 (Lively), 1978
Voyage of the "Dawn Treader" (C.S. Lewis), 1952
Voyage to Arcturus (Lindsay), 1920
Voyage to Venus (C.S. Lewis), 1953

Waking of Orthlund (Taylor), 1989
Walk in the Dark series (Spedding), from 1986
Walk on the Wild Side (s Westall), 1989
Walk Out of the World (Nichols), 1969
Walkabout Woman (Roessner), 1988
Walker of Worlds (De Haven), 1990
Walking Shadows (s Noyes), 1918
Wall of Serpents (de Camp, Pratt), 1960
Walls of Air (Hambly), 1983
Walrus and the Warwolf (H. Cook), 1988
Wanderer's Necklace (Haggard), 1914
Wanderer's Return (Hancock), 1988
Wandering Fire (Kay), 1986
Wanderings of Wuntvor (C. Gardner), 1989
Wandor series (R. Green), from 1975
War for the Oaks (Bull), 1987
War Hound and the World's Pain (Moorcock), 1981
War in Heaven (C. Williams), 1930
War of Dreams (A. Carter), 1974
War of Powers series (Vardeman), from 1980
War of the Gods on Earth series (Offutt), from 1979
War of the Jewels (s Tolkien), 1994
War of the Ring (s Tolkien), 1990
War of the Twins (Weis), 1986
War of the Wizards series (Offutt), from 1977
'Ware Hawk (A. Norton), 1983
Warhammer series (Yeovil), from 1989
Warhorse of Esdragon series (Dexter), from 1994
Warhost of Vastmark (Wurts), 1995
Warlock at the Wheel (s D. Jones), 1984
Warlock of the Witch World (A. Norton), 1967
Warlock series (Stasheff), from 1969
Warlord of Heaven (Adrian Cole), 1990
Warlord's Domain (Morwood), 1989
Warlords of Gaikon (R. Green, as Lord), 1976
Warlords of Nin (Lawhead), 1983
Warrior Challenged (Sharon Green), 1986
Warrior Enchained (Sharon Green), 1983
Warrior of World's End (L. Carter), 1974
Warrior Rearmed (Sharon Green), 1984
Warrior Victorious (Sharon Green), 1988
Warrior Who Carried Life (Ryman), 1985
Warrior Within (Sharon Green), 1982
Warriors of Latan (R. Green, as Lord), 1984
Warrior's Tale (Cole and Bunch), 1994
Warriorwards (ab Hugh), 1990
Wars of Light and Shadows series (Wurts), from 1993
Wars of Vis series (T. Lee), from 1976
"Was . . ." (Ryman), 1992
Watch House (Westall), 1977
Watchmaker's Mask (Marks), 1992
Watchtower (Lynn), 1979

Water Boatman (s Mayne), 1964
Water Ghost (s Bangs), 1894
Water in the Air (Halam, as Jones), 1977
Water King's Laughter (Friesner), 1989
Water of the Wondrous Isles (W. Morris), 1897
Water-Babies (Kingsley), 1863
Watership Down (Adams), 1972
Way Beneath (A. Wells), 1990
Way Down the Hill (s Powers), 1986
Way of Ecben (Cabell), 1929
Way of the Gods (s Kuttner), 1954
Way to Babylon (Kearney), 1992
Way Up High (s Zelazny), 1992
Waylander (Gemmell), 1986
Waylander II (Gemmell), 1992
Wazir and the Witch (H. Cook), 1990
We Are All Legends (s Schweitzer), 1981
Wealdwife's Tale (Hazel), 1993
Weasel's Luck (M. Williams), 1988
Web of Darkness (Bradley), 1983
Web of Light (Bradley), 1983
Web of the Spider (Offutt), 1981
Web of the Witch World (A. Norton), 1964
Web of Wizardry (Coulson), 1978
Webbed Hand (J. Jones), 1994
Weeping Woman on the Streets of Prague (Germain, appendix), 1993
Weird of the White Wolf (s Moorcock), 1977
Weirdstone of Brisingamen (Garner), 1960
Weirwoods (Swann), 1967
Well at the World's End (W. Morris), 1896
Well of Darkness (Garrett), 1983
Well of Santa Clara (s France, appendix), 1903
Well of Shiuan (Cherryh), 1978
Well of the Unicorn (Pratt, as Fletcher), 1948
Well of the Worlds (Kuttner and C.L. Moore, as Padgett), 1953
Well-Favored Man (Willey), 1993
Wells of Ythan series (M. Alexander), from 1988
Well-Wishers (Eager), 1960
Were-Wrath (A. Norton), 1984
Wereblood (Turtledove, as Iverson), 1979
Werenight (Turtledove, as Iverson), 1979
Werewolf and the Wormlord (H. Cook), 1991
Werewolf of Ponkert (s Munn), 1958
Western Wizard (Reichert), 1992
Westlin Wind (de Lint), 1989
Westmark series (L. Alexander), from 1981
Wet Magic (Nesbit), 1913
What Dreams May Come (s Munn), 1978
What Dreams May Come (Wellman), 1983
What Next? (s Housman), 1938
What Strange Stars and Skies (s Davidson), 1965
Wheatstone Pond (Westall), 1993
Wheel of Stars (A. Norton), 1983
Wheel of Time series (Jordan), from 1990
Wheels of Fire (Lackey), 1992
When Death Birds Fly (Offutt), 1980
When the Bough Breaks (Lackey, Lisle), 1993
When the Green Star Calls (L. Carter), 1973
When the World Shook (Haggard), 1919
When Voiha Wakes (Chant), 1983

Where Is the Bird of Fire? (s Swann), 1970
Where the Wild Geese Go (Pierce), 1988
Which Was the Dream? (s Twain), 1967
While the Bells Ring (s Mayne), 1979
Whim of the Dragon (Dean), 1989
Whisper in the Night (s Aiken), 1982
Whispering Knights (Lively), 1971
Whispering Mountain (Aiken), 1968
Whistler (Taylor), 1994
Whistling Rufus (s Mayne), 1964
White Cranes Castle (G. Harris), 1979
White Crow series (Gentle), from 1990
White Deer (Thurber), 1945
White Fire (Vardeman), 1986
White Gold Wielder (Donaldson), 1983
White Gryphon (Lackey), 1995
White Hart (Springer), 1979
White Horse Is Running (Sampson), 1990
White Isle (Schweitzer), 1989
White Jenna (Yolen), 1989
White Mare, Red Stallion (Paxson), 1986
White Mists of Power (Rusch), 1991
White Nun's Telling (Sampson), 1989
White Raven (Paxson), 1988
White Robe (s Cabell), 1928
White Rose (G. Cook), 1985
White Serpent (T. Lee), 1988
White Stone (France, appendix), 1909
White Sybil (s S. Smith), 1935(?)
White Waterfall (Dwyer), 1912
Whitethorn Wood and Other Magicks (s Yolen), 1984
Who Fears the Devil? (s Wellman), 1963
Who Got Rid of Angus Flint? (s D. Jones), 1978
Who's Afraid (s Pearce), 1986
Who's Afraid of Beowulf? (Holt), 1988
Wicked and the Witless (H. Cook), 1989
Wicked Day (Stewart), 1983
Widowmaker (Morwood), 1994
Wielding a Red Sword (Anthony), 1986
Wife of Bath (Chapman), 1978
Wild Hunt (Yolen), 1995
Wild Hunt of Hagworthy (Lively), 1971
Wild Hunt of the Ghost Hounds (Lively), 1972
Wild Magic (A. Wells), 1993
Wild Robert (s D. Jones), 1989
Wild Wood (de Lint), 1994
Wilderness of Four series (Hancock), from 1982
Wilderness-Stone (Nathan), 1961
Wildraith's Last Battle (Karr), 1982
Wilkins' Tooth (D. Jones), 1973
Will of the Gods (Sharon Green), 1985
Will of the Wanderer (Weis), 1989
Will-o'-the-Wisp (Swann), 1976
Willard and His Bowling Trophies (Brautigan), 1976
William and Mary (Farmer), 1974
Willow (Drew), 1988
Willows in Winter (Horwood), 1993
Wind Between the Stars (Mahy), 1976
Wind Crystal (Paxson), 1990
Wind Eye (Westall), 1976
Wind in Cairo (Tarr), 1989

Wind in the Willows (Grahame), 1908
Wind That Tramps the World (s Owen), 1929
Windameir Circle series (Hancock), from 1985
Windmaster's Bane (Deitz), 1986
Windrose series (Hambly), from 1986
Winds of Change (Lackey), 1992
Winds of Fate (Lackey), 1992
Winds of Fury (Lackey), 1993
Winds of the Wastelands (Swithin), 1992
Wind's Twelve Quarters (s Le Guin), 1975
Windscreen Weepers (s Aiken), 1969
Windsingers series (Lindholm), from 1983
Wind-Witch (Dexter), 1994
Winged Man (Caldecott), 1993
Winged Pharaoh (Joan Grant), 1937
Wings (s Abdullah), 1920
Wings of Flame (Springer), 1985
Wings of the Black Death (Page, as Stockbridge), 1969
Winner Takes All (Simon Green), 1991
Winnie-the-Pooh (Milne), 1926
Winter King's War series (Dexter), from 1981
Winter of the Wolf (MacAvoy), 1993
Winter of the World series (Rohan), from 1986
Winter Players (T. Lee), 1976
Winter Quarters (s Mayne), 1982
Winter Sleepwalker (Aiken), 1994
Winterking (Hazel), 1985
Winter's Tale (Helprin), 1983
Wirrun series (Wrightson), from 1977
Wisdom's Daughter (Haggard), 1923
Wise Woman (MacDonald), 1875
Wise Woman's Telling (Sampson), 1989
Wishbringer (C. Gardner), 1988
Wishes Limited (Darlington), 1922
Wishing Season (Friesner), 1993
Wishing Well (s de Lint), 1993
Wishsong of Shannara (Brooks), 1985
Wishstone and the Wonderworkers (H. Cook), 1990
Witch Blood (Shetterly), 1986
Witch Doctor (Stasheff), 1994
Witch House (Walton), 1945
Witch in the Cherry Tree (Mahy), 1974
Witch in the Wood (T.H. White), 1939
Witch of the Dark Gate (Jakes), 1972
Witch Rose (Dalton), 1990
Witch Shall Be Born (s Howard), 1975
Witch Week (D. Jones), 1982
Witch World series (A. Norton), from 1963
Witches Abroad (Pratchett), 1991
Witches of Wenshar (Hambly), 1987
Witches' Ride (Briggs), 1937
Witchlord and the Weaponmaster (H. Cook), 1992
Witch's Business (D. Jones), 1974
Witch's Daughter (Salvatore), 1991
Witch's Money (s Collier), 1940
Witch-Woman (s Cabell), 1948
Witchwood (Lloyd), 1989
Witchwood Cradle (Friesner), 1987
With a Single Spell (Watt-Evans), 1987
With a Tangled Skein (Anthony), 1985
With Mercy Toward None (G. Cook), 1985

Wizard Abroad (Duane), 1993
Wizard and the Warlord (Boyer), 1983
Wizard at Large (Brooks), 1988
Wizard Crystal (Pinkwater), 1973
Wizard in Rhyme series (Stasheff), from 1979
Wizard in the Tree (L. Alexander), 1975
Wizard King (J. Smith), 1994
Wizard of Earthsea (Le Guin), 1968
Wizard of Lemuria (L. Carter), 1967
Wizard of Rentoro (R. Green, as Lord), 1978
Wizard of the Atlas (Bedford-Jones, as Hawkwood), 1928
Wizard of the Pigeons (Lindholm), 1986
Wizard of Zao (L. Carter), 1978
Wizard series (Hawke), from 1987
Wizard Spawn (Cherryh), 1989
Wizard War (H. Cook), 1987
Wizard World (Zelazny), 1989
Wizardry series (Duane), from 1983
Wizards and the Warriors (H. Cook), 1986
Wizard's Eleven (Tepper), 1984
Wizard's First Rule (Goodkind), 1994
Wizard's Mole (Strickland), 1991
Wizard's Shadow (Dexter), 1993
Wizards' Worlds (s A. Norton), 1989
Wizenbeak series (Gilliland), from 1986
Woggle-Bug Book (Baum), 1905
Wolf and the Raven (Paxson), 1993
Wolf Bell (S. Murphy), 1979
Wolf in Shadow (Gemmell), 1987
Wolf in the Fold (Simon Green), 1991
Wolf Moon (de Lint), 1988
Wolf of Winter (Volsky), 1993
Wolfhelm (Knaak), 1990
Wolfking (Wood), 1991
Wolf's Brother (Lindholm), 1988
Wolfshead (s Howard), 1968
Wolfwinter (Swann), 1972
Wolves of Willoughby Chase (Aiken), 1962
Woman Dominant (Vivian), 1929
Woman of Fire (Grabien), 1988
Woman of Flowers (Shwartz), 1987
Woman of the Elfmounds (s Zimmer), 1980
Woman Who Loved Reindeer (Pierce), 1985
Woman Who Loved the Moon (s Lynn), 1981
Women and the Warlords (H. Cook), 1987
Women as Demons (s T. Lee), 1989
Women in Celtic Myth (s Caldecott), 1988
Wonderful Adventures of Phra the Phoenician (Arnold), 1890
Wonderful Garden (Nesbit), 1911
Wonderful O (Thurber), 1955
Wonderful Wizard of Oz (Baum), 1900
Wood Beyond the World (W. Morris), 1894
Wood Nymph (Andersen, appendix), 1868
Wooden Sword (Abbey), 1991
Woodrow Wilson Dime (J. Finney), 1968
Woods Out Back (Salvatore), 1993
Words and Music (s Mayne), 1963
Wordsmiths and the Warguild (H. Cook), 1987
Wordwright (Deitz), 1993
Work of the Imagination (Fraser), 1973
Work of the Sun (Edgerton), 1990

Works of Fancy and Imagination (s MacDonald), 1871
World (John Grant), 1992
World in Bud (s Bullett), 1928
World of Mazes (Vardeman), 1983
World Upside Down (s Mayne), 1954
World's Desire (Haggard, Lang), 1890
World's End series (L. Carter), from 1969
Worm Ouroboros (Eddison), 1922
Worms of Kukumlima (Pinkwater), 1981
Worms of the Earth (s Howard), 1974
Worse Things Waiting (s Wellman), 1973
Worshippers and the Way (H. Cook), 1992
Wounded Land (Donaldson), 1980
Wraiths of Time (A. Norton), 1976
Wrath of Ashar (A. Wells), 1988
Wuntvor series (C. Gardner), from 1987
Wyrd Sisters (Pratchett), 1988
Wyrldmaker (Bisson), 1981

Xanth series (Anthony), from 1977

Yarrow (de Lint), 1986
Yaxley's Cat (Westall), 1991
Ye Gods! (Holt), 1992
Year and a Day (Mayne), 1976
Year King (Farmer), 1977

Year of the Unicorn (A. Norton), 1965
Yearwood (Hazel), 1980
Yellow Aeroplane (s Mayne), 1968
Yellow God (Haggard), 1908
Yellow Hen (s Baum), 1916
Yendi (Brust), 1984
Yes, Dear (s D. Jones), 1993
Yesterday We Saw Mermaids (Friesner), 1992
Ylana of Callisto (L. Carter), 1977
Yobgorble (Pinkwater), 1979
Yoke of Magic (Vardeman), 1985
Yorath the Wolf (Wilder), 1984
You and Me (s J. Powys), 1975
You're All Alone (s Leiber), 1972
Young Diana (Corelli), 1918
Young Tyrone (s Salmonson), 1983
Yurth Burden (A. Norton), 1978
Yvgenie (Cherryh), 1991

Zanthodon series (L. Carter), from 1979
Zarsthor's Bane (A. Norton), 1978
Zimiamvia series (Eddison), from 1935
Ziska (Corelli), 1897
Zothique, Hyperborea, Xiccarph, Poseidonis (s S. Smith), 1970-73
Zuleika Dobson (Beerbohm), 1911

NOTES ON
ADVISERS AND CONTRIBUTORS

ADRIAN, Jack. Freelance writer. Editor of many anthologies for Oxford University Press, J. M. Dent and other publishers, and widely recognized as one of Britain's foremost experts on popular fiction. **Essays:** Kenneth Grahame; L. Ron Hubbard; Caroline Stevermer; E. Charles Vivian.

ANDREWS, Graham. Northern Irish writer, resident in Belgium. Author of short stories and a novel, plus essays in *Million, Book and Magazine Collector* and other journals. **Essays:** Frank Baker; Juanita Coulson; Graham Diamond; Gardner F. Fox.

ASHLEY, Mike. Editor, bibliographer and critic. Author or editor of numerous books, including *The History of the Science Fiction Magazine* (4 vols.), 1974-78, *Souls in Metal,* 1977, *Who's Who in Horror and Fantasy Fiction,* 1977, *The Illustrated Book of Science Fiction Lists,* 1982, *Science Fiction, Fantasy and Weird Fiction Magazines* (with Marshall B. Tymn), 1985, *The Mammoth Book of Short Horror Novels,* 1988, *The Pendragon Chronicles,* 1990, *The Camelot Chronicles,* 1992, and *The Merlin Chronicles,* 1995. **Essays:** Achmed Abdullah; Hans Christian Andersen; John Kendrick Bangs; H. Bedford-Jones; Vera Chapman; Madame D'Aulnoy; James F. Dwyer; Phyllis Eisenstein; Lloyd Arthur Eshbach; Fouque, De La Motte; R. Garcia y Robertson; Randall Garratt; Parke Godwin; Jakob & Wilhelm Grimm; Jean Ingelow; Phyllis Ann Karr; Talbot Mundy; H. Warner Munn; Norvell W. Page; Charles Perrault; Tim Powers; E. Hoffman Price; Michael Reaves; Jessica Amanda Salmonson; Keith Taylor; Peter Valentine Timlett; Karl Edward Wagner.

BAILEY, K.V. Retired employee of the British Broadcasting Corporation. Poet and critic. Author of several chapbooks of verse; frequent contributor to *Foundation: The Review of Science Fiction* and other journals. **Essays:** Alan Garner; Mary Gentle; Charles Kingsley; Julian May.

BARRETT, David V. Freelance writer. Past editor of *Vector.* Book reviewer for *The New Scientist* and other magazines. Editor of *Digital Dreams,* 1990. **Essays:** Ian Dennis; John James; Graham Dunstan Martin; Rachel Pollack; Fay Sampson.

BEHRENDS, Steve. Writer. Author of *Clark Ashton Smith,* 1990. **Essay:** Darrell Schweitzer.

BRADLEY, Wendy. Civil servant. Book reviewer for *Interzone* and *Locus.* **Essays:** Louise Cooper; Robert Jordan; L.E. Modesitt, Jr.; Tad Williams.

BRANDENBURG, Sandra. Writer and interviewer. **Essays:** Clare Bell; Carole Nelson Douglas; Mickey Zucker Reichert.

BRAZIER, Paul. Typesetter and graphic designer; ersthwile editor and publisher of the magazine *Science Fiction Nexus.* **Essays:** Simon R. Green; Paul Kearney; Kristine Kathryn Rusch; John Whitbourn.

CORRAN, Mary. See her own entry. **Essays:** Lynn Abbey; Susan Cooper; Paul Gallico; Mercedes Lackey; Margaret Mahy; Meredith Ann Pierce; Midori Snyder.

COVELL, Ian. Bibliographer. **Essays:** Marc Alexander; Lin Carter; Seamus Cullen; Gordon R. Dickson; Roland Green; Chris-

topher Stasheff.

COWARD, Mat. Critic and short-story writer. Columnist for various newspapers and magazines, principally on the subject of crime fiction. **Essay:** Robert Rankin.

CROWTHER, Peter. Anthologist. Regular book reviewer for *Interzone* magazine. **Essay:** Charles De Lint.

DAEMON, Shira. Actress and writer. **Essays:** Delia Sherman; Martha Wells; Elizabeth Willey.

D'AMMASSA, Don. Writer and critic. Regular book reviewer for *Science Fiction Chronicle.* **Essays:** Donald Aamodt; Patrick H. Adkins; Nancy Varian Berberick; Elizabeth H. Boyer; Mayer Alan Brenner; Emma Bull; Linda E. Bushyager; Don Callander; Catherine Cooke; Kara Dalkey; Pamela Dean; John DeChancie; Wayland Drew; Lyndon Hardy; Paul Hazel; John Lee; Holly Lisle; Laurie J. Marks; Steve Perry; Will Shetterly; Robert E. Vardeman; Lawrence Watt-Evans; Paul Edwin Zimmer.

EISEN, Janice M. Regular book reviewer for *Aboriginal SF.* **Essays:** Dafydd Ab Hugh,; Gael Baudino; Bruce Fergusson; Alexis A. Gilliland; P.C. Hodgell; Faren Miller; Michaela Roessner; Julie Dean Smith; Brad Strickland.

DI FILIPPO, Paul. Novelist and short-story writer. Author of *The Steampunk Trilogy,* 1994. Regular book reviewer for *Asimov's Science Fiction.* **Essays:** John Barth; Donald Barthelme; John Crowley; Mark Helprin; George MacDonald; A.A. Milne; Thorne Smith.

GARRATT, Peter. Clinical psychologist and short-story writer. **Essays:** Sharon Green; Stephen Lawhead; Nikolai Tolstoy; Harry Turtledove; Jack Yeovil.

GILMORE, Chris. Freelance editor, critic and short-story writer. Regular book reviewer for *Interzone* magazine. **Essays:** Richard Adams; Steven Brust; Allan Cole and Chris Bunch; John Collier; Mary Corran; Maggie Furey; Stephan Grundy; Barry Hughart; Jenny Jones; David Lindsay; John Morressy; Michael Shea; Spedding; Thomas Burnett Swann; Jack Vance; Bridget Wood.

GRANT, John. See his own entry. **Essays:** Craig Shaw Gardner; Jane Gaskell; Colin Greenland; Bernard King.

HILL, Debora. Writer and interviewer. **Essays:** Constance Ash; Molly Cochran; Hugh Cook; Susan Dexter; Teresa Edgerton; Tanya Huff; Janet E. Morris; Jennifer Roberson; Susan Shwartz.

HOLLIDAY, Liz. Writer and interviewer. **Essays:** Robin W. Bailey; Robert M. Charrette; M. Lucie Chin; Carol Emshwiller; William Goldman; Geraldine Harris; Megan Lindholm; Elizabeth A. Lynn; Mary Stewart; Cherry Wilder; Jane Yolen.

IRWIN, Robert. See his own entry. **Essays:** Russell Hoban; Flann O'Brien; Mervyn Peake; T.H. White.

JAMES, Edward. Professor of Medieval History, University of Reading. Author of *Science Fiction in the Twentieth Century,* 1994. Editor of *Foundation: The Review of Science Fiction.* **Essays:** Joan Aiken; Marion Zimmer Bradley; Orson Scott Card; Diana Wynne

Jones; Katherine Kurtz; William Morris; Andre Norton; J.R.R. Tolkien.

JEAPES, Ben. Short-story writer. **Essay:** Terry Brooks.

JONES, Neil. Language teacher and short-story writer. Former editor, Games Workshop Books. Regular book reviewer for *Interzone* magazine. **Essays:** C.J. Cherryh; Roger Zelazny.

JOSHI, S.T. Editor, critic and bibliographer. Author of The *Weird Tale,* 1990, *Lord Dunsany: A Bibliography* (with Darrell Schweitzer), 1993, and numerous other books. **Essay:** Lord Dunsany.

KIES, Cosette. Teacher. Author of *Presenting Young Adult Horror Fiction,* 1992. **Essays:** John Bellairs; Grace Chetwin; Edward Eager; Rose Estes; Patricia Geary; Richard Monaco; Shirley Rousseau Murphy; Daniel Manus Pinkwater; Elizabeth Ann Scarborough; Evangeline Walton; E.B. White.

KINCAID, Paul. Writer and critic. Book reviewer for *The Times Literary Supplement, Foundation, Vector* and other journals. **Essays:** Gilbert Adair; Terry Bisson; Jorge Luis Borges; Richard Brautigan; Richard Burns; Italo Calvino; Lisa Goldstein; Gabriel Garcia Marquez; Robert Nye; Andrew Sinclair; Jeanette Winterson.

LANGFORD, David. Freelance writer and computer software writer; winner of eleven Hugo awards as best science fiction fanwriter and for best fanzine (*Ansible*). Author of the novels *The Space Eater,* 1982, *The Leaky Establishment,* 1984, and *Earthdoom!* (with John Grant), 1987. Book reviewer and columnist for numerous magazines. **Essays:** Lloyd Alexander; David Arscott and David Marl; Max Beerbohm; Ernest Bramah; G.K. Chesterton; Michael Frayn; Barbara Hambly; Tom Holt; Rudyard Kipling; C.S. Lewis; Dan McGirt; William Mayne; Hope Mirrlees; Michael Moorcock; Pat O'Shea; Terry Pratchett; Mike Scott Rohan; Fred Saberhagen; Allan Scott; Paula Volsky; Charles Williams.

LATHAM, Rob. Critic. **Essays:** Stephen R. Boyett; Grania Davis; Steven Millhauser.

MCCAULEY, Paul J. Novelist and short-story writer; former lecturer in botany at St Andrews University. Author of the novels *Four Hundred Billion Stars,* 1988, *Secret Harmonies,* 1989, *Eternal Light,* 1991, *Red Dust,* 1993, *Pasquale's Angel,* 1994, and *Fairyland,* 1995. Regular book reviewer for *Interzone* magazine. **Essays:** James P. Blaylock; Samuel R. Delany; M. John Harrison; Gene Wolfe.

MELIA, Sally-Ann. Writer and interviewer. **Essays:** Alan Dean Foster; Gary Gygax; Nicholas Luard; Melanie Rawn.

MORGAN, Chris. Writer. Author of *The Shape of Futures Past,* 1980, *Future Man,* 1980, *Facts and Fallacies* (with David Langford), 1981; editor of *Dark Fantasies,* 1989. Frequent contributor to *Science Fiction and Fantasy Book Review Annual.* **Essays:** Mary Brown; Mildred Downey Broxon; Tom Deitz; M. Coleman Easton; Graham Edwards; Sheila Gilluly; Joyce Ballou Gregorian; Andrew Harman; Martin Hocke; William Horwood; Mike Jefferies; Katharine Kerr; William Kotzwinkle; Megan Lindholm; Eric (Van) Lustbader; Patricia McKillip; Dwina Murphy-Gibb; James Silke; Sheri S. Tepper; Walter Wangerin.

MORGAN, Pauline. Writer. Frequent contributor to *Science Fiction and Fantasy Book Review Annual.* **Essays:** Adrian Cole; Diane Duane; Ru Emerson; Kenneth C. Flint; John M. Ford; Nigel Frith; Keren Gilfoyle; Simon Hawke; A.R. Lloyd; Morgan Llewelyn; R.A. MacAvoy; Stephen Marley; Peter Morwood; Diana L. Paxson; Mary Stanton; Margaret Weis; Angus Wells; Philip G. Williamson; Janny Wurts; Jonathan Wylie.

NEWMAN, Kim. See his own entry (under YEOVIL, Jack). **Essays:** Jonathan Carroll; Jack Finney; Robert Holdstock; Geoff Ryman.

NICHOLLS, Stan. Freelance journalist, interviewer and novelist. Author of *Wordsmiths of Wonder,* 1993. **Essays:** Robert L. Asprin; David A. Gemmell; John Norman; Freda Warrington.

SAWYER, Andy. Administrator, Science Fiction Foundation Library, University of Liverpool. Book reviwer for *Vector, Foundation* and other journals. **Essays:** Piers Anthony; W.J. Corbett; Annie Dalton; Tom De Haven; E.R. Eddison; Michael Ende; Pauline Fisk; Joan Grant; Brian Jacques; Garry Kilworth; Ellen Kushner; Robin McKinley; John Masefield; Mary Norton; Francis Stevens; Antony Swithin; Judith Tarr; Roger Taylor; Patricia Wrightson.

SCHWEITZER, Darrell. See his own entry. **Essays:** Peter S. Beagle; Hannes Bok; James Branch Cabell; Avram Davidson; Charles G. Finney; John Gardner; Ken Grimwood; Robert E. Howard; Ursula Le Guin; C.L. Moore; Kenneth Morris; James Morrow; Frank Owen; Salman Rushdie; Charles R. Saunders; Mervyn Wall; Sylvia Townsend Warner; Manly Wade Wellman.

SZACHNOWSKI, Lucya. Writer. **Essays:** Richard A. Knaak; Douglas Niles; R.A. Salvatore; Michael Williams.

SPELLER, Maureen (formerly Maureen Porter). Administrator of the British Science Fiction Association. Book reviewer for *Vector* and other journals. **Essays:** Eleanor Arnason; Gillian Bradshaw; Moyra Caldecott; David Eddings; Claudia J. Edwards; Timothy Findley; Sylvie Germain; John Grant; Ann Halam (Gwyneth Jones); Niel Hancock; Norton Juster; Guy Gavriel Kay; Noel Langley; Tanith Lee; Hugh Lofting; Patricia Kennealy-Morrison; Ruth Nichols; Jenny Nimmo; George Selden; Carol Severance; Nancy Springer; Connie Willis; David Henry Wilson; Patricia C. Wrede.

STABLEFORD, Brian. Freelance novelist and critic. Former lecturer in sociology at the University of Reading. Author or editor of many books, including *The Mysteries of Modern Science,* 1977, *A Clash of Symbols: The Triumph of James Blish,* 1979, *Masters of Science Fiction,* 1981, *Future Man: Brave New World or Genetic Nightmare?,* 1984, *Scientific Romance in Britain 1890-1950,* 1985, *The Sociology of Science Fiction,* 1987, *The Way to Write Science Fiction,* 1989, *The Dedalus Book of Decadence,* 1990, *Tales of the Wandering Jew,* 1991, *The Dedalus Book of British Fantasy,* 1991, *The Dedalus Book of Femmes Fatales,* 1992, *Algebraic Fantasies and Realistic Romances,* 1995, and some 40 novels. **Essays:** F. Anstey; Edwin Lester Arnold; J.M. Barrie; Helen Beauclerk; Stella Benson; Thomas Berger; Gerald Bullett; Lewis Carroll; Angela Carter; Marie Corelli; W.A. Darlington; L. Sprague De Camp; Stephen R. Donaldson; John Erskine; Raymond E. Feist; Anatole

France; Ronald Fraser; David Garnett; Richard Garnett; Neil M. Gunn; Michael Harrison; Ben Hecht; James Hilton; Laurence Housman; Margaret Irwin; Robert Irwin; Susan Alice Kerby; Andrew Lang; Fritz Leiber; Wyndham Lewis; Norman H. Matson; A. Merritt; Robert Nathan; Alfred Noyes; Barry Pain; Eden Phillpotts; John Cowper Powys; T.F. Powys; Fletcher Pratt; Clark Ashton Smith; James Thurber; George Sylvester Viereck; Vaughan Wilkins; Oscar Wilde; Nancy Willard.

TUTTLE, Lisa. Freelance novelist and short-story writer. Author of *Familiar Spirit,* 1983, *A Nest of Nightmares,* 1986, *Gabriel,* 1987, *A Spaceship Built of Stone,* 1987, *Lost Futures,* 1992, *Memories of the Body,* 1992, and other works of fiction. Editor of *Encyclopedia of Feminism,* 1986. **Essays:** Lucy M. Boston; Penelope Farmer; Penelope Lively; Philippa Pearce; E. Nesbit.

WESTFAHL, Gary. Lecturer at the University of California, Riverside: prolific contributor to *Foundation, Science-Fiction Studies* and other journals. **Essays:** Richard Bach; L. Frank Baum; Glen Cook; Dave Duncan; Esther M. Friesner; H. Rider Haggard; John Jakes; W.P. Kinsella; Henry Kuttner; Elizabeth Moon; Pat Murphy; John Myers Myers; Andrew J. Offutt; James Stephens; Mark Twain; Laurence Yep.

WOOSTER, Martin Morse. Washington editor, *Reason.* Author of articles and reviews in numerous newspapers and magazines. **Essays:** Macdonald Harris; John Maddox Roberts.

YATES, Jessica. Freelance writer; former school librarian. Reviewer for *School Librarian, The Times Educational Supplemment* and other journals. **Essays:** K.M. Briggs; Joy Chant; Jean Morris; Robert Westall.